The Good Pub Guide 1998

Edited by Alisdair Aird

Deputy Editor: Fiona Stapley

Editorial Research: Karen Fick
Additional Research: Robert Unsworth
Editorial Assistance: Fiona Wright

EBURY PRESS
LONDON

Please send reports on pubs to

The Good Pub Guide
FREEPOST TN1569
WADHURST
East Sussex
TN5 7BR

This edition first published in 1997 by Ebury Press,
Random House, 20 Vauxhall Bridge Road,
London SW1V 2SA

1 3 5 7 9 10 8 6 4 2

A CIP catalogue record for this book is available from the British Library.

ISBN 0 09 181475 8

Typeset from author's disks by Clive Dorman & Co.
Printed and bound in Great Britain by Cox & Wyman Ltd, Reading, Berkshire

Contents

Introduction

Our unique annual price survey, comparing the price of beer now in 1198 pubs with what each of those pubs was charging for it a year ago, shows that beer prices have increased by 3¾% over this last year – about 1% more than the underlying rate of inflation. Though we deplore any increase above the basic inflation rate, this margin is very much smaller than we had to tolerate before the breakup of the big breweries' monopoly started taking effect. There can be no doubt that the reforms following the Monopolies & Mergers Commission 1989 report have gone a very long way towards keeping down the cost of beer, through limiting the big brewers' tied estates, allowing the growth of powerfully competitive independent pub chains, and allowing even tied pubs to shop around for an alternative beer.

Nowadays, independently owned pubs getting beers from the big national breweries are generally selling it at 11p a pint more cheaply than pubs tied to those breweries – this difference is partly a sign of the new purchasing power of the independent chains, partly a sign of how vigorously the big brewers now have to compete on price, now that they can no longer rely on captive sales to huge tied estates. However, the big national breweries are generally still a high-cost option. Bass is the only one whose beers cost close to the national average, with Whitbreads a little more expensive, and Tetleys-Carlsberg and particularly Scottish Courage markedly more expensive.

It's the smaller local and regional brewers which give drinkers the real bargains. They generally charge far lower prices in their pubs than other pubs in the same area. We list the breweries which came out of our price survey best for this below, showing how much cheaper beer in their pubs is than typical pub prices in their areas:

brewery	savings per pint
Holts	41p
Donnington	30p
Clarks	29p
Fullers	27p
Bathams	24p
Banks's/Hansons/Camerons	20p
Hook Norton	17p
Smiles	15p

Pubs brewing their own beers also save their customers about 20p a pint, compared with the local average. Another brewer, Sam Smiths, can also be counted as cheap: though its beers are not so very much cheaper than the (low) local average in Yorkshire, its home territory, they are also sold at similar prices in Sam Smiths pubs further south, where they do stand out as bargains.

Sparklers or super-sparklers have prompted a sudden surge of complaints from readers this year – over three times as many as last year. These are devices linked to beer handpumps which increase the force of the stream of beer, sucking air into it, so that it froths up to make a head in the glass. They have been used for many years in the North, and it's often held that the taste of Northern beers is suited by this. However, the main reason brewers and publicans like them is that the air they pump into the glass in place of the beer costs them nothing. It's generally accepted (for example by the Brewers & Licensed Retailers Association) that the frothy head takes up 5% of a pint, and in practice it may approach 10%. This means that a Yorkshireman paying a typical £1.48 or £1.49 for a pint "with a good head on it" is spending up to 15p on thin air – which in turn is simply inflating the pub's and/or the brewer's profit. And, with people spending £20 million a day on beer in pubs, that adds up to a massive volume of air-powered profiteering.

For years, this undersized pint has been a much-argued-over fact of Northern drinking life. And on balance it's seemed that Northern drinkers are reasonably happy with the status quo – one can even make the case that the lower price of a pint in the North has reflected the fact that a Northern pint contains less beer (and more air) than the traditionally flatter Southern one. To put it another way, if you allow for the space taken up by the froth the true price of that Yorkshire pint is actually £1.65 – no longer cheap, but closely in line with the national average.

What's new is that sparklers are now cropping up very widely indeed throughout the Midlands and South, putting their frothy head on Southern beers. But Southern beers are still being sold at high Southern prices. Pumping 10% air into a pint is equivalent to increasing the cost of the remaining smaller amount of beer by 11%. So grabby brewers and pub chains, suddenly putting sparklers into their pubs, are inflicting a massive price increase on customers.

What makes it worse is that this violent injection of air is held by many beer lovers to ruin the more finely balanced taste of beers which have traditionally been served flat – as one reader put it, turning the beers into a "tasteless shadow" of themselves; another – himself a former publican – finds them "totally flavourless" after one or two gulps, leaving him with a dry mouth after a pint. No wonder he fears that the spread of the practice makes him contemplate the terrible fate of turning into a coffee and wine drinker.

Many pubs will remove the sparkler if you ask them to; always worth asking. Also, it is standard practice for pubs to give a top-up on request (to make a full pint) if they've served beer with a head on it. Again, always make sure you get your top-up – you're entitled to it.

But individual customers should not be forced to fight their corner like this. We now believe that the sparkler invasion – far outside the territory where they've been traditional, and where there's been a well understood status quo – has made a change in the law necessary. Pubs serving beer through sparklers, though not other pubs, should by law have to serve it in lined glasses, which accept a full pint of liquid up to the line, with the froth extra on top.

Programmed tills are the latest threat to considerate individual service. When you order a drink or a meal, the operator doesn't need to look up the price. They just hit the Boddingtons button, say, or the lasagne button, and the correct price comes up; fully fledged versions of the system can then transmit the food order direct to the kitchen, and even run the stock control system – triggering a re-order request when (by deducting the number of orders it's put through from the number of units held in stock) it calculates that the lasagne freezer-packs are running low. It's easy to see the snag for customers in this Big Brother device. To work, it needs standard orders. As readers have found, this means that a simple request for a piece of cheese at the end of their meal is turned down – on the grounds that the computerised till can accept orders only for a full ploughman's. So the customers' verdict on programmed pub tills has to be a big No – until pubs using them make clear that they are happy to accept non-standard orders.

Smoky pubs now bring us far more complaints from readers than there were when no smoking areas were less common. Many people now find smoky pubs unacceptable – especially if they want to eat there. A survey of pubs listed in a previous edition of this Guide as having no smoking areas showed that three-quarters had increased food sales, and two-thirds had increased their overall turnover. So it seems folly for pubs to serve food in clouds of smoke – and yet they do, as a few of the hundred complaints we've had this year about smoky pubs show: "Our otherwise excellent meal was ruined by chain smokers at the next table." "Good food thoroughly spoilt by numerous smokers." "The dining room was so thick with smoke that one would have to eat by feel, not by sight."

A few pubs are now entirely no smoking, and many more are largely so. As most people now don't smoke, it makes sense for pubs which sell food – and seems essential for those which admit children – to set aside designated areas for smokers, rather than the other way round.

Pies are great favourites with readers – classic pub food. All too often, though, what's called a pie on the menu turns out to be bogus – only a casserole, with a puff of pastry floated on top. These floaters are anathema to pie-lovers. A pie should have a proper crust of shortcrust or flaky pastry, and it should be baked in one piece. So our message to pub cooks is: Ditch your floaters, give us proper pies.

Unsuitable piped music infuriates many readers more than anything else. Sometimes there's a good reason to have piped music: a pub that's known for its choice of jazz or blues music, for instance, well reproduced, with the music forming part of the pub's character, and even a reason for people choosing that pub to visit. In other pubs, sensitively chosen music played at an appropriate volume on good equipment is unlikely to upset even people who would prefer silence – or rather the sound of people enjoying themselves, chatting and laughing. The trouble is that there's usually no sign of any thought being given to the type of music; it's often intrusively loud; and (ridiculous in these CD days) the sound quality is often awful. Frequently, it seems that the only people in the pub who like it are the staff – surely a sign that they are in the wrong job.

With so many readers telling us how much they dislike piped music, we're coming to believe that licensees must simply misunderstand the public mood. They surely wouldn't be inflicting this noise on their customers if they realised how disliked it was. There's a simple remedy: if you'd rather not have the music, tell the landlord or landlady. The more people that speak up, the more quickly licensees will realise that unsuitable piped music is wrecking their pubs' atmosphere.

Pub accommodation is now very widely available. Outside London, 40% of the main entry pubs in this book have bedrooms. Pubs can be delightful places to stay in, and many of these have our Place to Stay Award bed symbol – a sign that, given the price, they are good at least for an overnight stop. However, pub accommodation standards are all too often pretty dire. Many pub bedrooms give the impression that they have been thrown together on a DIY basis, using the cheapest warehouse furniture, with little thought given to comfort, warmth or even appearance, and no thought whatsoever to reflecting or emphasising the pub's own individuality. Staying in country pubs with good bedrooms could be a magical discovery for foreign visitors, and excellent value even with the high price of the £. But as things are, we wince at the thought of how many a British pub bedroom must strike anyone from abroad – and that's before they've come down to breakfast in a smoky uncleaned bar. It's time publicans stopped treating their bedrooms as an afterthought; instead, they should be right at the top of their priority list.

The top pubs

We no longer have to struggle to find pubs that cook well, using carefully chosen fresh ingredients. Nowadays you can take it for granted that a meal in any of the better dining pubs will be based on the best fresh produce available locally – with more pubs growing their own herbs and vegetables, baking their own bread, making their own pickles and chutneys.

Throughout the Guide, our Food Awards show the pubs where you can be sure of rewarding, interesting food. And we have chosen three dozen which – combining good food with a most enjoyable atmosphere – deserve the title of County Dining Pubs of the Year. This tends to mask the exceptional concentration of outstanding dining pubs in Yorkshire, where the Crab & Lobster at Asenby, Foresters Arms at Carlton, Blue Lion at East Witton and Angel at Hetton are all among the country's very finest food pubs. This top group also includes the Knife & Cleaver at Houghton Conquest (Beds), the Punch Bowl at Crosthwaite (Cumbria), the Kings Head at Bledington and Gumstool near Tetbury (Gloucs), the Saracens Head near Erpingham (Norfolk), the Froize at Chillesford (Suffolk) and the Walnut Tree at Llandewi Skirrid (Wales). All these are admirable – mouth-wateringly so. The dining pub which is making the most memorable impression of all these days is the Blue Lion at East Witton: it is our **Dining Pub of the Year**.

One of the best results of the way pubs have turned to fresh produce is that so many now serve fish, at least as a dish of the day, and in some cases as their main speciality. This has great appeal to customers: even people who think of themselves as good home cooks tend not to cook fish very often, so it is a special treat to find it now in so many pubs. Ones which any fish lover should seek out are the Fish in Bray (Berks), the Red Lion at Great Kingshill (Bucks), the Trinity Foot at Swavesey (Cambs – they have their own fish shop next door), the Drewe Arms at

Broadhembury, Anchor at Cockwood and Start Bay at Torcross (Devon), the Smugglers at Osmington Mills (Dorset), the Dering Arms at Pluckley, Sankeys in Tunbridge Wells and Pearsons in Whitstable (Kent), the Oddfellows Arms in Mellor (Lancs chapter), the Froize at Chillesford (Suffolk), the Half Moon at Kirdford (Sussex), the Bulls Head at Wootton Wawen (Warwicks), the Foresters Arms at Carlton, Angel at Hetton and Sportsmans Arms at Wath in Nidderdale (Yorks), the Ferry Inn at Pembroke Ferry (Wales) and the Tayvallich Inn at Tayvallich and Morefield Motel in Ullapool (Scotland). For its astonishing range of fish and seafood, and really interesting preparation and cooking, we choose the Froize at Chillesford as **Fish Pub of the Year**.

Most pubs that do good food now offer at least one or two interesting vegetarian dishes (a fundamental change from say five years ago). And vegetarians have certainly benefited from the trend to Mediterranean cooking which has touched many pubs' menus this year. Really good vegetarian food can also be found in unlikely places – a glance through the door of the Snowdrop in Lewes (Sussex), for instance, would scarcely prepare you for the interest and quality of its offerings. It is another pub whose decor is decidedly idiosyncratic which carries off our award of **Vegetarian Pub of the Year**: the King William IV at Heydon (Cambs).

Italian food has always been popular in pubs. For authentic Italian dishes, we'd particularly recommend the White Hart at Hamstead Marshall (Berks), the Sun at Bassenthwaite (Cumbria), the Avon Inn at Avonwick (Devon), the Kings Head at Great Bircham (Norfolk), the Fox at Westcott Barton (Oxon); all these have Italian licensees. And the Cross Keys at Great Missenden (Bucks) serves nothing but Italian food.

Good food usually comes at a price. But you can still eat well in a pub on a strict budget. At least 30 of the pubs in this book offer proper main dishes, simple but enjoyable, for under £4. The Old Ale House in Truro (Cornwall), the Half Moon at Sheepwash (Devon – lunchtime), the Romany at Bampton (Oxon), the Lion of Morfe at Upper Farmcote (Shrops – lunchtime), the Fat Cat in Sheffield (Yorks) and Bannermans (Edinburgh) all serve particularly good value food; and the Horseshoe in Glasgow does a perfectly respectable three-course lunch for only £2.40. It's the Fat Cat in Sheffield which stands out for the sheer interest of its low-priced food (and its good drinks are cheap, too): it is our **Bargain Pub of the Year**.

There's something lacking in a pub if it won't make a sandwich. Certainly, it's nothing to do with smartness. Of course it's in the more traditional pub that one thinks of the humble sandwich or filled roll as a staple: two classic examples are the Bell at Aldworth (Berks) and Hobnails at Little Washbourne (Gloucs). But some of the classiest dining pubs also make superb lunchtime sandwiches: most notably, the Kings Head at Bledington and Crown at Blockley (Gloucs) and the Bingley Arms in Bardsey and Three Acres in Shelley (Yorks). For its really inventive fillings and excellent breads, we name the Kings Head at Bledington as **Sandwich Pub of the Year**.

Pubs which stand out for the quality and variety of the beers they sell are the Aston at Bhurtpore (Cheshire), Quayside in Falmouth and Old Ale House in Truro (Cornwall), Watermill at Ings and Masons Arms on Cartmel Fell (Cumbria), Alexandra and Brunswick in Derby and Derby Tup at Whittington Moor (Derbys), Fat Cat in Norwich and Fur & Feather at Woodbastwick (Norfolk), Victoria in Beeston (Notts), New Barracks in Sheffield and St Vincent Arms at Sutton upon Derwent (Yorks), and Bon Accord in Glasgow (Scotland). The phenomenal changing choice of well kept ales at the Fat Cat in Norwich – two dozen or more at a time – makes it our **Beer Pub of the Year**.

Each year the list at the back of the book showing main entry pubs brewing their own beer grows longer – good in two ways, as these own-brew beers usually show great individuality and are almost always cheaper than beers of comparable strength sold in other pubs in the same area. Taking quality into account, a top shortlist might consist of the Brunswick in Derby, Flower Pots at Cheriton (Hants), Old Brewery at Somerby (Leics), reopened Three Tuns in Bishops Castle (Shrops), Burton Bridge in Burton on Trent (Staffs), Victoria at Earl Soham (Suffolk), Sair in Linthwaite and Fat Cat in Sheffield (Yorks). Our choice as **Own Brew Pub of the Year** is the tidied-up Sair in Linthwaite.

Many pubs sell a traditional farm cider, particularly in the summer. But very few offer a choice – particularly outside the main cider areas, which are the West Country, Hereford and Worcester, and Kent. Pubs which will please any cider lover are the Monkey House at Defford (Herefs & Worcs), Rose & Crown at Huish Episcopi (Somerset), Ram at Farncombe (Surrey) – and, with its remarkable choice and effervescent enthusiasm for the drink, our **Cider Pub of the Year**, the Cider Centre at Brandy Wharf (Lincs).

This year we have had far fewer complaints about wine quality in pubs than in previous years. Many pubs now offer a fine choice by the glass. Those which stand out – for quality as well as choice are the Nobody at Doddicombsleigh (Devon), Three Horseshoes at Madingley (Cambs), Trengilly Wartha near Constantine (Cornwall), Cott at Dartington (Devon), Hare at Langton Green (Kent), Red Lion at Steeple Aston (Oxon), Crown in Southwold (Suffolk) and George & Dragon at Kirkby Moorside (Yorks). With the finest pub cellar in the country and a great choice by the glass, the Nobody at Doddiscombsleigh is **Wine Pub of the Year**.

Most pubs have a fair choice of malt whiskies. Some licensees, though, put real effort into tracking down unusual malts. We have tracked down superb collections in unexpected places: the Quayside in Falmouth (Cornwall), King George IV at Eskdale Green (Cumbria), Nobody at Doddiscombsleigh (Devon), George at St Briavels (Gloucs), Bulls Head at Clipston (Northants), Victoria in Beeston (Notts), White Horse at Pulverbatch (Shrops), Pack Horse at Widdop and – epic collection – Cragg Lodge at Wormald Green (Yorks), and Dinorben Arms at Bodfari (Wales). Many Scottish pubs and inns have an excellent choice; because the surroundings seem so perfectly appropriate for browsing through some of its 250 malts, the Crown at Portpatrick is our **Whisky Pub of the Year**.

Readers keep asking us for a list of favourite unspoilt pubs. Here it is. The Cock at Broom (Beds), Bell at Aldworth, Pot Kiln at Frilsham (Berks), Old Ship at Cadmore End, Prince Albert at Frieth, Chequers at Wheeler End (Bucks), Free Press in Cambridge and Queens Head at Newton (Cambs), White Lion at Barthomley (Cheshire), Hole in t' Wall at Bowness (Cumbria), Olde Gate at Brassington and Barley Mow at Kirk Ireton (Derbys), Masons Arms at Knowstone, Stag at Rackenford, Rugglestone at Widecombe and Northmore Arms at Wonson (Devon), Fox at Corfe Castle and Square & Compass at Worth Matravers (Dorset), Flitch of Bacon at Little Dunmow (Essex), Boat at Ashleworth Quay and Bakers Arms at Broad Campden (Gloucs), White Horse near Petersfield (Hants), Monkey House at Defford and Carpenters Arms at Walterstone (Herefs & Worcs), Gate at Boyden Gate, Woolpack at Brookland, Shipwrights Arms at Oare and Fox & Hounds at Toys Hill (Kent), Station Buffet in Stalybridge (Lancs), Lord Nelson at Burnham Thorpe (Norfolk), Black Horse at Checkendon (Oxon), Horseshoe at Llanyblodwel (Shrops), King William at Calcott, Tuckers Grave at Faulkland, George at Norton St Philip and Pack Horse at South Stoke (Somerset), Jolly Sailor in Orford (Suffolk), Cricketers Arms at Berwick and Blue Ship near Billingshurst (Sussex), Birch Hall at Beck Hole, Olde White Harte in Hull and Whitelocks in Leeds (Yorks), Owl at Little Cheverell (Wilts), Olde Mitre and Nags Head (London), Pendre at Cilgerran and Prince of Wales at Kenfig (Wales). From this satisfying list, the Queens Head at Newton (Cambs) emerges as **Unspoilt Country Pub of the Year**. The Olde White Harte in Hull is **Unspoilt Town Pub of the Year**.

Two other memorable pubs don't quite fit into this category, but have a similar appeal. The Fleece at Bretforton (Herefs & Worcs) is a marvellous old farmhouse-pub, full of antiques, carefully preserved – most recently by the National Trust, and before that by the same family for centuries. And then there's Alan East's idiosyncratic Yew Tree at Cauldon (Staffs), a very unpretentious country tavern that's filled with remarkable paraphernalia, including amazing collections of longcase clocks, pianolas, polyphons and symphonions (man-sized musical boxes). One reader suggests it should be declared a National Treasure; we content outselves with naming it **Britain's Most Fascinating Pub**.

This year we have added nearly 140 new main entries to the Guide. They run from simple country taverns to palatial conversions of remarkable buildings, from places that do good honest simple snacks to sophisticated dining pubs. Our favourite discoveries have been the Edgecumbe Arms at Cremyll (Cornwall), Fish in Bray and

Chequers at Wheeler End (Bucks), Old Bridge in Huntingdon (Cambs), Red Hart at Blaisdon and Gumstool near Tetbury (Gloucs), Carpenters Arms at Walterstone (Herefs & Worcs), Fat Cat in Norwich (Norfolk), Red Lion at Chalgrove (Oxon), Burlton Inn at Burlton, Cholmondeley Riverside at Cressage and Armoury in Shrewsbury (Shrops), Seven Stars near Woodborough (Wilts), Jerusalem Tavern, Lord Moon of the Mall and Moon Under Water (London), and Counting House in Glasgow (Scotland). The Cholmondeley Riverside at Cressage (Shrops) is our **Newcomer of the Year** – so good that we expect it may even surpass the huge popularity of its older sister the Cholmondeley Arms near Bickley Moss.

Four pub chains have stood out this year. One is very small and very new – traditional, civilised old-fashioned taverns tied to the little St Peters Brewery in Suffolk; we describe two in the main entries – the De La Pole Arms at Wingfield, and Jerusalem Tavern in London. Pubs Ltd is rather larger and older, but still family-run: interesting furnishings, decent food, good wines and well kept beers. Wetherspoons is now a very substantial chain indeed: excellent value pricing, decent wines as well as a good choice of beers, exemplary house-keeping, good solid and spacious furnishings in interesting conversions of often striking buildings, good no smoking areas, no piped music, children rarely admitted. Finally, there's Huntsbridge – another small family-run chain of stylish dining pubs with very imaginative food, first-class wines by the glass, well kept beers. Each of its pubs is run by a chef/patron who is completely responsible for it, and a profit-sharing partner in the main business. And all are now main entries: the Old Bridge at Huntingdon, Pheasant at Keyston and Three Horseshoes at Madingley (Cambs), and White Hart at Great Yeldham (Essex). With this 100% record, Huntsbridge is our **Pub Chain of the Year**.

In all the years that we have been producing this Guide, we have never before come across so many pubs which are this year giving such exceptional pleasure to so many of our readers. In each county introduction we draw attention to these top pubs. Here, we list the twelve which stand out as winning the very warmest praise for all the virtues which should distinguish a truly excellent pub: licensees and staff who really seem to care about your enjoyment, good food and drink, thriving atmosphere, and genuine individuality. These exceptional places are the Grosvenor Arms at Aldford (Cheshire), the Trengilly Wartha near Constantine (Cornwall), the Royal Oak in Appleby (Cumbria), the Cott at Dartington, the Nobody at Doddiscombsleigh and the Castle at Lydford (Devon), the Loders Arms at Loders (Dorset), the Kings Head at Bledington (Gloucs), the Wykeham Arms in Winchester (Hants), the Three Horseshoes at Warham (Norfolk), the Angel in Lavenham (Suffolk), and the Angel at Hetton (Yorks). All these are much loved, but the pub which brings out the superlatives in readers' comments these days is the Wykeham Arms in Winchester: it is our **Pub of the Year**.

All these have outstanding licensees – especially Colin and Hilary Cheyne of the Royal Oak, David and Susan Grey of the Cott and Graeme and Anne Jameson of the Wykeham Arms. Other superb licensees are John Pitchford of the Springer Spaniel at Treburley (Cornwall), Alan and Brian Coulthwaite of the Watermill at Ings (Cumbria), Don and Jackie Roderick of the Spyway at Askerswell and Ian and Anne Barrett of the Marquis of Lorne at Nettlecombe (Dorset), Johnny and Hilary Johnston of the Butchers Arms at Sheepscombe (Gloucs), Marina Atkinson of the Feathers at Hedley on the Hill (Northumberland), Trevor and Ann Cooper of the Five Bells at Broadwell, Colin Mead of the Red Lion at Steeple Aston and Tony and Amanda Fay of the Kings Head at Wootton (Oxon), Kevin and Rose Draper of the Royal Oak at Luxborough (Somerset), Tweazle Jones and Barry Horton of the Elsted Inn at Elsted (Sussex), and Michael and Margaret Fox of the Buck at Thorton Watlass (Yorks). Every single reader who has commented on the Kings Head at Wootton has underlined our own judgement – that the service here stands out as particularly welcoming and helpful. So Tony and Amanda Fay of the Kings Head at Wootton are our **Licensees of the Year**.

What is a Good Pub?

The main entries in this book have been through a two-stage sifting process. First of all, some 2,000 regular correspondents keep in touch with us about the pubs they visit, and nearly double that number report occasionally. The present edition has used a total of around 40,000 reports from readers, and from users of the electronic version of the book which is available on the Internet, on Compuserve. This keeps us up-to-date about pubs included in previous editions – it's their alarm signals that warn us when a pub's standards have dropped (after a change of management, say), and it's their continuing approval that reassures us about keeping a pub as a main entry for another year. Very important, though, are the reports they send us on pubs we don't know at all. It's from these new discoveries that we make up a shortlist, to be considered for possible inclusion as new main entries. The more people that report favourably on a new pub, the more likely it is to win a place on this shortlist – especially if some of the reporters belong to our hard core of about five hundred trusted correspondents whose judgement we have learned to rely on. These are people who have each given us detailed comments on dozens of pubs, and shown that (when we ourselves know some of those pubs too) their judgement is closely in line with our own.

This brings us to the acid test. Each pub, before inclusion as a main entry, is inspected anonymously by the Editor, the Deputy Editor, or both. They have to find some special quality that would make strangers enjoy visiting it. What often marks the pub out for special attention is good value food (and that might mean anything from a well made sandwich, with good fresh ingredients at a low price, to imaginative cooking outclassing most restaurants in the area). Maybe the drinks are out of the ordinary (pubs with several hundred whiskies, with remarkable wine lists, with home-made country wines or good beer or cider made on the premises, with a wide range of well kept real ales or bottled beers from all over the world). Perhaps there's a special appeal about it as a place to stay, with good bedrooms and obliging service. Maybe it's the building itself (from centuries-old parts of monasteries to extravagant Victorian gin-palaces), or its surroundings (lovely countryside, attractive waterside, extensive well kept garden), or what's in it (charming furnishings, extraordinary collections of bric-a-brac).

Above all, though, what makes the good pub is its atmosphere – you should be able to feel at home there, and feel not just that *you're* glad you've come but that *they're* glad you've come.

It follows from this that a great many ordinary locals, perfectly good in their own right, don't earn a place in the book. What makes them attractive to their regular customers (an almost clubby chumminess) may even make strangers feel rather out-of-place.

Another important point is that there's not necessarily any link between charm and luxury – though we like our creature comforts as much as anyone. A basic unspoilt village tavern, with hard seats and a flagstone floor, may be worth travelling miles to find, while a deluxe pub-restaurant may not be worth crossing the street for. Landlords can't buy the Good Pub accolade by spending thousands on thickly padded banquettes, soft music and luxuriously shrimpy sauces for their steaks – they can only win it, by having a genuinely personal concern for both their customers and their pub.

Using the *Guide*

THE COUNTIES

England has been split alphabetically into counties, mainly to make it easier for people scanning through the book to find pubs near them. Each chapter starts by picking out the pubs that are currently doing best in the area, or specially attractive for one reason or another.

Occasionally, counties have been grouped together into a single chapter, and metropolitan areas have been included in the counties around them – for example, Merseyside in Lancashire. When there's any risk of confusion, we have put a note about where to find a county at the place in the book where you'd probably look for it. But if in doubt, check the Contents.

Scotland and Wales have each been covered in single chapters, and London appears immediately before them at the end of England. Except in London (which is split into Central, North, South, West and East), pubs are listed alphabetically under the name of the town or village where they are. If the village is so small that you probably wouldn't find it on a road map, we've listed it under the name of the nearest sizeable village or town instead. The maps use the same town and village names, and additionally include a few big cities that don't have any listed pubs – for orientation.

We always list pubs in their true locations – so if a village is actually in Buckinghamshire that's where we list it, even if its postal address is via some town in Oxfordshire. Just once or twice, while the village itself is in one county the pub is just over the border in the next-door county. We then use the village county, not the pub one.

STARS ★

Specially good pubs are picked out with a star after their name. In a few cases, pubs have two stars: these are the aristocrats among pubs, really worth going out of your way to find. The stars do NOT signify extra luxury or specially good food – in fact some of the pubs which appeal most distinctively and strongly of all are decidedly basic in terms of food and surroundings. The detailed description of each pub shows what its special appeal is, and it's that that the stars refer to.

FOOD AND STAY AWARDS: 🍴 🛏

The knife-and-fork rosette shows those pubs where food is quite outstanding. The bed symbol shows pubs which we know to be good as places to stay in – bearing in mind the price of the rooms (obviously you can't expect the same level of luxury at £30 a head as you'd get for £60 a head). Pubs with bedrooms are now mapped and are marked on the maps as a square.

♀

This wine glass symbol marks out those pubs where wines are a cut above the usual run. This should mean that a glass of house wine will be at least palatable. The text of the entry will show whether you can expect much more than this.

🍺

The beer tankard symbol shows pubs where the quality of the beer is quite exceptional, or pubs which keep a particularly interesting range of beers in good condition.

£

This symbol picks out pubs where we have found decent snacks at £1.80 or less, or worthwhile main dishes at £4 or less.

RECOMMENDERS

At the end of each main entry we include the names of readers who have recently recommended that pub (unless they've asked us not to). Important note: the description of the pub and the comments on it are our own and *not* the recommenders'; they are based on our own personal inspections and on later verification of facts with each pub. As some recommenders' names appear quite often, you can get an extra idea of what a pub is like by seeing which other pubs those recommenders have approved.

LUCKY DIPS

We've continued to raise the standard for entry to the Lucky Dip section at the end of each county chapter. This includes brief descriptions of pubs that have been recommended by readers, with the readers' names in brackets. As the flood of reports from readers has given so much solid information about so many pubs, we have been able to include only those which seem really worth trying. Where only one single reader has recommended a pub, we have now not included that pub in the list unless the reader's description makes the nature of the pub quite clear, and gives us good grounds for trusting that other readers would be glad to know of the pub. So with most, the descriptions reflect the balanced judgement of a number of different readers, increasingly backed up by similar reports on the same pubs from different readers in previous years (we do not name these readers). Many have been inspected by us. In these cases, LYM means the pub was in a previous edition of the *Guide*. The usual reason that it's no longer a main entry is that, although we've heard nothing really condemnatory about it, we've not had enough favourable reports to be sure that it's still ahead of the local competition. BB means that, although the pub has never been a main entry, we have inspected it, and found nothing against it. In both these cases, the description is our own; in others, it's based on the readers' reports.

Lucky Dip pubs marked with a ✩ are ones where the information we have (either from our own inspections or from trusted reader/reporters) suggests a firm recommendation. Roughly speaking, we'd say that these pubs are as much worth considering, at least for the virtues described for them, as many of the main entries themselves. Note that in the Dips we always commend food if we have information supporting a positive recommendation. So a bare mention that food is served shouldn't be taken to imply a recommendation of the food. The same is true of accommodation and so forth.

The Lucky Dips (particularly, of course, the starred ones) are under consideration for inspection for a future edition – so please let us have any comments you can make on them. You can use the report forms at the end of the book, the report card which should be included in it, or just write direct (no stamp needed if posted in the UK). Our address is *The Good Pub Guide*, FREEPOST TN1569, WADHURST, East Sussex TN5 7BR.

MAP REFERENCES

All pubs are given four-figure map references. On the main entries, it looks like this: SX5678 Map 1. Map 1 means that it's on the first map at the end of the book. SX means it's in the square labelled SX on that map. The first figure, 5, tells you to look along the grid at the top and bottom of the SX square for the figure 5. The *third* figure, 7, tells you to look down he grid at the side of the square to find the figure 7. Imaginary lines drawn down and across the square from these figures should intersect near the pub itself.

The second and fourth figures, the 6 and the 8, are for more precise pinpointing, and are really for use with larger-scale maps such as road atlases or the Ordnance Survey 1:50,000 maps, which use exactly the same map reference system. On the relevant Ordnance Survey map, instead of finding the 5 marker on the top grid you'd find the 56 one; instead of the 7 on the side grid you'd look for the 78 marker. This makes it very easy to locate even the smallest village.

Where a pub is exceptionally difficult to find, we include a six-figure reference in the directions, such as OS Sheet 102 reference 654783. This refers to Sheet 102 of the Ordnance Survey 1:50,000 maps, which explain how to use the six-figure references to pin-point a pub to the nearest 100 metres.

MOTORWAY PUBS
If a pub is within four or five miles of a motorway junction, and reaching it doesn't involve much slow traffic, we give special directions for finding it from the motorway. And the Special Interest Lists at the end of the book include a list of these pubs, motorway by motorway.

PRICES AND OTHER FACTUAL DETAILS
The *Guide* went to press during the summer of 1997. As late as possible, each pub was sent a checking sheet to get up-to-date food, drink and bedroom prices and other factual information. By the summer of 1998 prices are bound to have increased a little – to be prudent, you should probably allow around 5% extra by then. But if you find a significantly different price *please let us know*.

Breweries to which pubs are "tied" are named at the beginning of the italic-print rubric after each main entry. That means the pub has to get most if not all of its drinks from that brewery. If the brewery is not an independent one but just part of a combine, we name the combine in brackets. Where a brewery no longer brews its own beers but gets them under contract from a different brewer, we name that brewer too. When the pub is tied, we have spelled out whether the landlord is a tenant, has the pub on a lease, or is a manager; tenants and leaseholders generally have considerably greater freedom to do things their own way, and in particular are allowed to buy drinks including a beer from sources other than their tied brewery.

Free houses are pubs not tied to a brewery, so in theory they can shop around to get the drinks their customers want, at the best prices they can find. But in practice many free houses have loans from the big brewers, on terms that bind them to sell those breweries' beers – indeed, about half of all the beer sold in free houses is supplied by the big national brewery combines to free houses that have these loan ties. So don't be too surprised to find that so-called free houses may be stocking a range of beers restricted to those from a single brewery.

Real ale is used by us to mean beer that has been maturing naturally in its cask. We do not count as real ale beer which has been pasteurised or filtered to remove its natural yeasts. If it is kept under a blanket of carbon dioxide to preserve it, we still generally mention it – as long as the pressure is too light for you to notice any extra fizz, it's hard to tell the difference. (For brevity, we use the expression "under light blanket pressure" to cover such pubs; we do not include among them pubs where the blanket pressure is high enough to force the beer up from the cellar, as this does make it unnaturally fizzy.) If we say a pub has, for example, "Whitbreads-related real ales", these may include not just beers brewed by the national company and its subsidiaries but also beers produced by independent breweries which the national company buys in bulk and distributes alongside its own.

Other drinks: we've also looked out particularly for pubs doing enterprising non-alcoholic drinks (including good tea or coffee), interesting spirits (especially malt whiskies), country wines (elderflower and the like) and good farm ciders. So many pubs now stock one of the main brands of draught cider that we normally mention cider only if the pub keeps quite a range, or one of the less common farm-made ciders.

Meals refers to what is sold in the bar, not in any separate restaurant. It means that pub sells food in its bar substantial enough to do as a proper meal – something you'd sit down to with knife and fork. It doesn't necessarily mean you can get three separate courses.

Snacks means sandwiches, ploughman's, pies and so forth, rather than pork scratchings or packets of crisps. We always mention sandwiches in the text if we know that a pub does them – if you don't see them mentioned, assume you can't get them.

The food listed in the description of each pub is an example of the sort of thing you'd find served in the bar on a normal day, and generally includes the dishes which are currently finding most favour with readers. We try to indicate any difference we know of between lunchtime and evening, and between summer and winter (on the whole stressing summer food more). In winter, many pubs tend to have a more restricted range, particularly of salads, and tend then to do more in the way of filled baked potatoes, casseroles and hot pies. We always mention barbecues if we know a pub does them. Food quality and variety may be affected by holidays – particularly in a small pub, where the licensees do the cooking themselves (May and early June seems to be a popular time for licensees to take their holidays).

Any separate *restaurant* is mentioned. But in general all comments on the type of food served, and in particular all the other details about meals and snacks at the end of each entry, relate to the pub food and not to the restaurant food.

Children's Certificates exist but in practice *Children* are allowed into at least some part of almost all the pubs included in this *Guide* (there is no legal restriction on the movement of children over 14 in any pub, though only people over 18 may get alcohol). As we went to press, we asked the main-entry pubs a series of detailed questions about their rules. *Children welcome* means the pub has told us that it simply lets them come in, with no special restrictions. In other cases we report exactly what arrangements pubs say they make for children. However, we have to note that in readers' experience some pubs make restrictions which they haven't told us about (children only if eating, for example), and very occasionally pubs which have previously allowed children change their policy altogether, virtually excluding them. If you come across this, please let us know, so that we can clarify the information for the pub concerned in the next edition. Beware that if children are confined to the restaurant, they may occasionally be expected to have a full restaurant meal. Also, please note that a welcome for children does not necessarily mean a welcome for breast-feeding in public. Even if we don't mention children at all, it is worth asking: one or two pubs told us frankly that they do welcome children but don't want to advertise the fact, for fear of being penalised. All but one or two pubs (we mention these in the text) allow children in their garden or on their terrace, if they have one. Note that in Scotland the law allows children more freely into pubs so long as they are eating (and with an adult). In the Lucky Dip entries we mention children only if readers have found either that they are allowed or that they are not allowed – the absence of any reference to children in a Dip entry means we don't know either way.

Dogs, cats and other animals are mentioned in the text if we know either that they are likely to be present or that they are specifically excluded – we depend chiefly on readers and partly on our own inspections for this information.

Parking is not mentioned if you should normally be able to park outside the pub, or in a private car park, without difficulty. But if we know that parking space is limited or metered, we say so.

Telephone numbers are given for all pubs that are not ex-directory.

Opening hours are for summer; we say if we know of differences in winter, or on particular days of the week. In the country, many pubs may open rather later and close earlier than their details show unless there are plenty of customers around (if you come across this, please let us know – with details). Pubs are allowed to stay open all day Mondays to Saturdays from 11am (earlier, if the area's licensing magistrates have permitted) till 11pm. However, outside cities most English and Welsh pubs close during the afternoon. Scottish pubs are allowed to stay open until later at night, and the Government has said that it may introduce legislation to allow later opening in England and Wales too. We'd be very grateful to hear of any differences from the hours we quote. You are allowed 20 minutes' drinking-up time after the quoted hours – half an hour if you've been having a meal in the pub.

Bedroom prices normally include full English breakfasts (if these are available, which they usually are), VAT and any automatic service charge that we know about. If we give just one price, it is the total price for two people sharing a double or twin-bedded room for one night. Otherwise, prices before the / are for single occupancy, prices after it for double. A capital B against the price means that it includes a private bathroom, a capital S a private shower. As all this coding packs in quite a lot of information, some examples may help to explain it:

£50 on its own means that's the total bill for two people sharing a twin or double room without private bath; the pub has no rooms with private bath, and a single person might have to pay that full price

£50B means exactly the same – but all the rooms have private bath

£50(£55B) means rooms with private baths cost £5 extra

£28/£50(£55B) means the same as the last example, but also shows that there are single rooms for £28, none of which have private bathrooms

If there's a choice of rooms at different prices, we normally give the cheapest. If there are seasonal price variations, we give the summer price (the highest). This winter – 1997-98 – many inns, particularly in the country, will have special cheaper rates. And at other times, especially in holiday areas, you will often find prices cheaper if you stay for several nights. On weekends, inns that aren't in obvious weekending areas often have bargain rates for two- or three-night stays.

MEAL TIMES
Bar food is commonly served from 12-2 and 7-9, at least from Monday to Saturday (food service often stops a bit earlier on Sundays). If we don't give a time against the Meals and snacks note at the bottom of a main entry, that means that you should be able to get bar food at those times. However, we do spell out the times if we know that bar food service starts after 12.15 or after 7.15; if it stops before 2 or before 8.45; or if food is served for significantly longer than usual (say, till 2.30 or 9.45).

Though we note days when pubs have told us they don't do food, experience suggests that you should play safe on Sundays and check first with any pub before planning an expedition that depends on getting a meal there. Also, out-of-the-way pubs often cut down on cooking during the week, especially the early part of the week, if they're quiet – as they tend to be, except at holiday times. Please let us know if you find anything different from what we say!

NO SMOKING
We say in the text of each entry what if any provision a pub makes for non-smokers. Pubs setting aside at least some sort of no smoking area are also listed county by county in the Special Interest Lists at the back of the book.

CHANGES DURING THE YEAR – PLEASE TELL US
Changes are inevitable, during the course of the year. Landlords change, and so do their policies. And, as we've said, not all returned our fact-checking sheets. We very much hope that you will find everything just as we say. But if you find anything different, please let us know, using the tear-out card in the middle of the book (which doesn't need an envelope), the report forms here, or just a letter. You don't need a stamp: the address is *The Good Pub Guide*, FREEPOST TN1569, WADHURST, East Sussex TN5 7BR.

Author's Acknowledgements

This book would not be possible without the enormous volume of help we get from several thousand readers, who send us reports on pubs they visit: thanks to you all. Many have now been reporting to us for a good few years, often in marvellously helpful detail, and in a number of cases have now sent us several hundred reports – even, in one or two cases, over a thousand. We rely heavily on this hugely generous help, all of it unpaid, to keep us up to date with existing entries, to warn us when standards start slipping, to build up a record of reports on the most promising Lucky Dip entries, and to uncover for us new gems that we'd otherwise never hear of.

For the exceptional help they've given us, I'm specially grateful to Ian Phillips, Richard Lewis, CMW, JJW, Gwen and Peter Andrews, Andy and Jill Kassube, Eddy and Emma Gibson, Ann and Colin Hunt, George Atkinson, Gordon, Stephen and Julie Brown, Roger and Jenny Huggins, Ewan McCall, Dave Irving, Tom McLean, Jenny and Michael Back, Thomas and Audrey Nott, Peter and Audrey Dowsett, James Nunns, Chris Raisin, Richard Houghton, David Carr, Joan and Michel Hooper-Immins, DWAJ, Eric Larkham, Jenny and Brian Seller, TBB, Phyl and Jack Street, Susan and John Douglas, Graham and Liz Bell, Joy and Peter Heatherley, Rona Murdoch, Charles Bardswell, John P Bowdler, David Hanley, John Evans, Lynn Sharpless and Bob Eardley, Tony and Louise Clarke, Comus Elliott, Marjorie and David Lamb, Sue Holland and Dave Webster, Ted George, John C Baker, John Fahy, Margaret and Nigel Dennis, Martin and Karen Wake, Tim Barrow and Sue Demont, Reverend John Morison, J F M West, Eric J Locker, Dave Braisted, John Wooll, Susan and Nigel Wilson, Ms S Watkin, Mr P Taylor, Andrew and Ruth Triggs, Pat and Tony Martin, Peter Baker, Tony and Wendy Hobden, Jo and Gary Charlton, Karen and Graham Oddey, Alan Risdon, HNJ, PEJ, David Wallington, Alan Risdon, Derek and Sylvia Stephenson, Arthur and Margaret Dickinson, Bruce Bird, Tony Scott, Sue and Bob Ward, Kevin Thorpe, Paul and Ursula Randall, Malcolm Taylor, Mr M Joyner, R J Walden, Iain Robertson, Mike Gorton, Jack and Gemima Valiant, Alan and Paula McCully, LM, H K Dyson, Mrs Pamela Goodwyn, Barry and Anne, Simon Collett-Jones, Lynda Paynton, Sam Samuells, Basil Minson, Mr and Mrs C H Stride, R T and J C Moggridge, Mrs K Clapp.

A word of special gratitude to Steve and Carolyn Harvey, our Channel Islands Inspectors.

Finally, heartfelt gratitude to the thousands of publicans and their staff who work so unstintingly and so warm-heartedly to give us so very many Good Pubs.

Alisdair Aird

The Good Pub Guide main entries are also available, with *The Good Guide to Britain* material, on **Personal Navigator**, a CD-ROM map and route-planning programme for computers using Ordnance Survey maps (with optional satellite position finding). It is sold by main software stores. More details from Softwair Ltd, Standbrook House, 2-5 Old Bond Street, London W1X 3TB, tel (0) 7000 784 662; email pnav@softwair.co.uk

England

Bedfordshire

For the third year running, the Knife & Cleaver at Houghton Conquest carries off our award as Bedfordshire Dining Pub of the Year – an outstanding record for this civilised place with its delicious modern food and a choice of wines by the glass that's almost unrivalled in this area. The quaint Olde Plough at Bolnhurst also has a tremendous choice by the glass, which this year gains it one of our Wine Awards – only the second in the county. If steaks are what you fancy, you can't do better than the cheerful Fox & Hounds at Riseley. And there's good straightforward food at the Three Tuns at Biddenham, Chequers at Keysoe and Bell at Odell. The Cock at Broom makes a reappearance in these pages after an absence: its current licensees have scored a hit with readers for the really old-fashioned atmosphere they've generated here. Among the Lucky Dips, current front-runners are the Black Horse at Ireland, Globe at Linslade, Hare & Hounds at Old Warden, Rose & Crown at Ridgmont, White Horse at Southill and Bell at Studham. Drinks prices in the county are just a shade higher than the national average; our cheapest pub for beer was the Three Cranes at Turvey (which has now been taken over by the Old English Pub Co.)

BIDDENHAM TL0249 Map 5
Three Tuns

57 Main Road; village signposted from A428 just W of Bedford

At lunchtime especially, this attractively placed thatched village pub is popular for its good, reasonably priced bar food from a fairly short straightforward menu. There are sandwiches (from £1.45), home-made soup (£1.65 – or with a choice of any sandwich £2.55), pâté (£2.20), ploughman's (£2.75), salads (£3.85), quiche, lasagne or chilli con carne (£4.95), seafood platter, home-made steak and kidney pie or chicken casserole (£5.70), and 8oz sirloin steak (£8.80); usual children's menu (£1.75) and puddings (£2.20). The bustling lounge has low beams and country paintings, and there are darts, table skittles, dominoes and a fruit machine in the public bar; piped music. Well kept Greene King IPA and Abbot, and cheerful prompt service. On warm summer days there are seats in the attractively sheltered spacious garden, and a big terrace has lots of picnic tables and white doves in a dovecote; the very good children's play area has swings for all ages and a big wooden climbing frame. *(Recommended by Maysie Thompson, Gordon Theaker, Ian Phillips, Margaret and Nigel Dennis, Arnold and Maureen East)*

Greene King ~ Tenant Alan Wilkins ~ Real ale ~ Meals and snacks (not Sun or Mon evenings) ~ (01234) 354847 ~ Children in small dining room ~ Open 11.30-2.30, 6-11; 12-2.30, 7-10.30 Sun; cl evening 25 Dec

BOLNHURST TL0859 Map 5
Olde Plough ♀

B660 Bedford—Kimbolton

The friendly and entertaining landlady of this pretty 500-year-old black-beamed cottage is a faith-healer who throws in free healing with your pint or pie, hosts clairvoyant sessions every couple of months in the restaurant, and organises yoga classes on the pub floor in winter and on the lawn in summer on a Wednesday morning; her cheerful poems and philosophy appear on the pub walls alongside enlarged naughty postcards and watercolours by a local artist. The relaxed and spacious carpeted lounge bar has little armchairs around low tables (where there are fresh flowers), a leather sofa and armchair and a log fire in the big stone fireplace. There's a big woodburning stove and a couple of refectory tables and settles in the flagstoned public bar – as well as darts, pool, hood skittles, cribbage, and dominoes. The dining room has seats around tables ingeniously made from salvaged barn oak and a wooden ceiling made with boards from a Bedford church. Upstairs, the restaurant (minimum charge £10 a person) has old beams and polished tables. Good bar food from a changing menu includes home-made soup (£2.50), mozzarella tartlets with fresh tomato sauce or smoked fish pâté (£3.95), vegetarian brazil nut and apricot loaf or enjoyable vegetable goulash (£4.95), home-cooked ham and chips or steak and kidney pie with herby dumplings (£5.95), thai prawn curry (£6.25), salmon and broccoli pancake, steaks, and puddings like home-made treacle tart or crème brûlée (£2.95). Well kept Courage Directors, Hook Norton Best, and Ruddles Best on handpump, and 18 wines by the glass, with mulled wine in winter. In summer there may be Morris men or country dancing, with bell ringers or carol singers at Christmas. The lovely tree-shaded garden has rustic seats and tables, and a long crazy-paved terrace looks on to the pond where you can still see the remains of a moat that used to surround the pub; free plant cuttings. The cats are called Blacky and Titch, the doberman Zeus, and the other dog Lica. *(Recommended by John Fahy, Ian Phillips, George Atkinson, Roger Danes, John Saul)*

Free house ~ Licensee Michael Horridge ~ Real ale ~ Meals and snacks (till 10 if busy) ~ Restaurant (not always open) ~ (01234) 376274 ~ Well behaved children welcome till 9pm ~ Open 12-2.30, 7-11; 12-3, 7-10.30 Sun; cl 25 and 26 Dec

BROOM TL1743 Map 5
Cock

23 High Street; from A1 opposite northernmost Biggleswade turn-off follow Old Warden 3, Aerodrome 2 signpost, and take first left signposted Broom

Readers enjoy this friendly and delightfully unspoilt 17th-c village inn with its attractively old-fashioned lay-out. The four cosy rooms have simple latch doors, low ochre ceilings, stripped panelling and farmhouse-style tables and chairs on the antique tile floors; winter log fires. There's no counter, and the very well kept Greene King IPA, Abbot, and Rayments are tapped straight from the cask. A central corridor runs down the middle of the building, with the sink for washing glasses on one side (pewter mugs hang over it) and on the other steps down to the cellar. Good bar food includes sandwiches (from £1.75), home-made soup (£2.50), ploughman's (from £3.45), proper gammon and egg or liver and bacon (£5.95), cajun chicken or mushroom stroganoff (£6.95), and puddings (from £2.50). There are picnic tables on the terrace by the back lawn, and a fenced off children's play area. *(Recommended by DAV, Tim Heywood, Sophie Wilne, R J Bland, Roger Danes, Colin McGaughley)*

Greene King ~ Tenants Gerry and Jean Lant ~ Real ale ~ Meals and snacks (not Sun evening) ~ (01767) 314411 ~ Children welcome ~ Open 12-3(4 Sat), 6-11; 12-4, 7-10.30 Sun

HOUGHTON CONQUEST TL0441 Map 5
Knife & Cleaver ⑪ ♀

Between B530 (old A418) and A6, S of Bedford
Bedfordshire Dining Pub of the Year

It's the delicious food that draws people to this civilised 17th-c brick-built dining pub – indeed, they were chosen to cater for the Queen and Prince Philip on their Bedfordshire visit. As well as regular sandwiches (from £2.50), they offer grilled ciabatta bread with smoked salmon, poached salmon and salad leaves with lime and pickled ginger (£5.50), focaccia bread with corn-fed chicken (£5.95), and french bread with fillet steak, smoked Applewood cheese and onions (£6.25).

From a menu that changes every three weeks, there might be home-made soup like roasted tomato with pesto croutons (£2.50), a small mixed hors d'oeuvre (£4.75; large £8.50), a dish of the day like braised beef in red wine with cheese cobbler or venison pasty with redcurrant gravy (£5.25), garlicky toulouse sausages with herb mash, lamb and leek pot or vegetarian burgers of aubergine, parmesan cheese and herbs with a mint leaf crème fraîche dip (£5.50), fresh fish such as seared squid with a spicy thai dressed salad (£4.95) or whiting fillets with a chive curry crust and hazelnut butter sauce (£7.95), home-made puddings such as sticky banana pudding with cinnamon custard, chocolate roulade or home-made ice creams (£2.75), and 10 good British cheeses (£2.95; you can enjoy these as a ploughman's £3.75). Well kept Adnams Extra and Batemans Best and XB on handpump, 24 good wines by the glass, and a fine choice of up to 20 well aged malt whiskies; good, attentive service and maybe unobtrusive piped classical music. The relaxed, comfortable bar has maps, drawings and old documents on the walls, and blazing fire in winter; the airy conservatory no-smoking restaurant has rugs on the tiled floor, swagged curtains, cane furniture and lots of hanging plants. There are tables out in the neatly kept garden. *(Recommended by Stephen, Julie and Hayley Brown, Dr B E Monk, Gordon Tong, Maysie Thompson, Rita Horridge, David Shillitoe, David and Mary Webb, Mr and Mrs T F Marshall, Colin McGaughley, Thomas Nott)*

Free house ~ Licensees David and Pauline Loom ~ Real ale ~ Meals and snacks (not Sun evening) ~ Restaurant (not Sun evening) ~ (01234) 740387 ~ Children in eating area of bar and in restaurant ~ Open 11.30-2.30(2 Sat), 7-10.30(11 Sat); 12-3 Sun (closed Sun evening); closed 27-30 Dec ~ Bedrooms: £45B/£59B

KEYSOE TL0762 Map 5
Chequers
B660 N of Bedford

This friendly and unpretentious village local has two neatly simple beamed rooms with an unusual stone-pillared fireplace dividing them, and leatherette seats that are a bit reminiscent of the 1960s; one bar is no smoking. Good bar food includes sandwiches (£1.75), home-made soup (£2), home-made chicken liver pâté (£3.25), ploughman's (£3.75), tagliatelle in a creamy mushroom and white wine sauce (£4.75), home-made steak pie (£5.50), glazed lamb cutlets (£7.50), steaks (from £8.75), puddings like bread and butter pudding with cointreau raisins, fresh fish on Friday and Saturday, and Sunday roast (£4.75); children's dishes (£2.75). Well kept Fullers London Pride and Hook Norton Best on handpumps on the stone bar counter; some malts. The terrace at the back looks over the garden which has a wendy house, play tree, swings and a sand-pit. *(Recommended by Jenny and Michael Back, Maysie Thompson, Arnold and Maureen East)*

Free house ~ Licensee Jeffrey Kearns ~ Real ale ~ Meals and snacks (not Tues) ~ (01234) 708678 ~ Children allowed away from main bar ~ Open 11.30-2.30, 6.30-11; 12-2.30, 7-10.30 Sun; closed Tuesdays, and may close 3 days in late summer

ODELL SP9658 Map 4
Bell
Horsefair Lane; off A6 S of Rushden, via Sharnbrook

Five small homely low-ceilinged rooms – some with shiny black beams – loop around a central servery of this friendly and pretty thatched stone village pub, and are furnished with quite a few handsome old oak settles, bentwood chairs and neat modern furniture; there's a log fire in one big stone fireplace and two coal fires elsewhere. Fairly priced bar food includes sandwiches (from £1.95), ploughman's (from £3.15), omelettes (from £3.65) savoury pancakes or home-made vegetable pie (£4.55), home-made lasagne (£4.70), steak and kidney pie or turkey, leek and mushroom pie (£5.65) and daily specials from the board such as seafood pasta or fish pie (£4.70), and beef, bacon and cider casserole or pork slices with bacon, mushroom and vermouth and cream sauce (£6.55); usual children's dishes (from

£1.95) and home-made puddings like boozy chocolate mousse or orange cheesecake shortbread (£2). Well kept Greene King Abbot, IPA, Rayments, and their seasonal ales on handpump. There are picnic tables on the flower-filled terrace overlooking the wooded garden that runs attractively down through a wild area to a bridge over the Great Ouse. The garden is full of golden pheasants, cockatiels, canaries, and a goose called Lucy. Further along the road is a very pretty church; handy for the local country park. *(Recommended by Stephen G Brown, Maysie Thompson, Martin and Karen Wake, Mr and Mrs A W Chapman, R A Buckler, Margaret and Howard Buchanan, Meg and Colin Hamilton, Bob and Maggie Atherton)*

Greene King ~ Tenant Derek Scott ~ Real ale ~ Meals and snacks (not Sun evening Sept-May) ~ (01234) 720254 ~ Children in eating area of bar only ~ Open 11-2.30, 6-11; 12-2.30, 7-10.30 Sun; all day Sat and Sun May-Sept

RISELEY TL0362 Map 5
Fox & Hounds

High St; village signposted off A6 and B660 N of Bedford

For lovers of good British steaks, this cheerful pub is the place to come to – it's their long-standing speciality. You choose which piece of meat you want from the cabinet at one end of the bar counter, say how much you want and how you want it cooked, and you're then charged by weight – £8.96 for 8oz rump, £9.60 for 8oz of sirloin and £11.60 for fillet. Other food includes home-made soups like stilton and broccoli and leek and potato (£1.95), king prawns in filo pastry (£3.25), moules marinières (£5.95), steak and kidney pie (£6.95), and a couple of vegetarian dishes. There are plenty of tables spreading around among timber uprights under the heavy low beams, with two candlelit side dining rooms; they plan to extend the grill room and build a terrace leading off. Well kept Charles Wells Eagle and Bombardier with regularly changing guests like Morlands Old Speckled Hen, Shepherd Neame Spitfire, and Theakstons XB on handpump, a decent collection of other drinks including several malts and a good range of cognacs; unobtrusive piped Glen Miller or light classics, very friendly, helpful service. There are picnic tables in the huge garden. The landlord is great fun – a real personality. *(Recommended by E J Etheridge, JJW, CMW, Keith and Cheryl Roe, Mr and Mrs A W Chapman)*

Charles Wells ~ Managers Jan and Lynne Zielinski ~ Real ale ~ Meals and snacks (12-1.45, 7-10) ~ Restaurant ~ (01234) 708240 ~ Children welcome ~ Open 11.30-2.30, 6.30-11; 12-3, 7-10.30 Sun

TURVEY SP9452 Map 4
Three Cranes 🍺

Just off A428 W of Bedford

Now owned by the growing Old English Pub Company and with new managers, this stone-built 17th-c inn has a striking portico and upper-storey jettied gable added in Victorian times. The airy and spacious two-level bar has lots of pictures, a quiet decor majoring on stuffed owls and other birds, and a solid fuel stove. Bar food now includes lunchtime sandwiches, soup (£2.25), beef in ale pie (£5.95), lasagne (£6.25), trout (£7.95), and steaks (from £9.95); there are plenty of sensible tables with upright seats. Well kept Courage Directors, Fullers London Pride, Smiles Golden Brew, John Smiths, Theakstons XB, and guest beers like Bass, Black Sheep, Fullers ESB, Shepherd Neame Spitfire, and Wadworths 6X on handpump. There are picnic tables in a neatly kept garden with a climbing frame; in summer, the pub's front has been a mass of colour from carefully tended hanging baskets and window boxes. *(Recommended by George Atkinson, Stephen Brown, L Eadon, Simon Walker, Mike Sheehan, John Saul, Maysie Thompson; more reports on the new regime, please)*

Old English Pub Co ~ Managers Paul and Sheila Linehan ~ Real ale ~ Meals and snacks ~ Restaurant ~ (01234) 881305 ~ Children in eating area of bar and in restaurant ~ Open 11-2.30, 6-11; 12-3, 7-10.30 Sun ~ Bedrooms: £35S/£48S

Lucky Dip

Besides the fully inspected pubs, you might like to try these Lucky Dips recommended to us and described by readers (if you do, please send us reports):

Aspley Guise [The Square; SP9335], *Bell*: Old Italian-run dining pub with bistro feel, carpeted bar, beautifully decorated conservatory dining area, tasty home-made food inc vegetarian choice and good pasta, Flowers Original and Fullers London Pride, espresso machine, good atmosphere, welcoming efficient service, pleasant piped music; tables in dog-free garden with play area, picturesque village *(George Atkinson)*

☆ **Astwick** [Taylors Rd, signed off A1 northbound; TL2138], *Tudor Oaks*: Open-plan, partly Tudor, with old beams and timbers, exposed brickwork, real fires and woodburner, barometer and lots of brass, banquettes and chesterfields, fresh flowers, friendly service and cat – no dogs allowed; good value generous fresh food inc OAP lunches, seven real ales from independent brewers, two local farm ciders, upstairs restaurant; tables in courtyard, small play area; bedrooms *(JJW, CMW)*

Bedford [Park Ave/Kimbolton Rd; TL0449], *Park*: Welcoming attractively refurbished Charles Wells pub, welcoming new licensees doing good food *(Rev Matthew Lawson)*

Bromham [Bridge End; nr A428, 2 miles W of Bedford; TL0050], *Swan*: Comfortable and welcoming beamed village pub with welcoming atmosphere, quick service, lots of pictures, well kept Greene King IPA and Abbot, decent coffee, popular food, provision for children; public bar with darts and fruit machine, pleasant garden *(Ian Phillips)*

Cardington [The Green; off A603 E of Bedford; TL0847], *Kings Arms*: Useful Brewers Fayre pub, quiet and pleasant, with food all day, three well kept ales, yards of elderly books and encyclopaedias, lawn with picnic tables *(JJW, CMW)*

☆ **Dunstable** [A5183 S, 4 miles N of M1 junction 9; TL0221], *Horse & Jockey*: Well done Chef & Brewer, huge interior divided up into many smaller areas, light pine furnishings, well kept ales, friendly staff, good promptly served food; children very welcome, play areas inside and out (huge garden), maybe bouncy castle *(the Sandy family, LYM)*

☆ **Eaton Bray** [SP9620], *White Horse*: Wide choice of good fresh food and welcoming licensees in well run and relaxing old low-beamed and timbered dining pub, suit of armour in one room, real ales; ranks of tables on back lawn, good walking nearby *(David Regan)*

Eggington [SP9525], *Horseshoes*: Efficient service, well kept ales inc regular guest, cosy atmosphere, good evening meals and lunchtime snacks, solid wooden tables; pub games *(Gavin Horner)*

Felmersham [Grange Rd; off A6 Bedford—Wellingboro; SP9857], *Six Ringers*: Attractive thatched Tudor stone-built pub, two small rooms and no-smoking dining room, pub food inc real puddings, real ales, no piped music, cards, cribbage, shove-ha'penny; garden with swing and play house, pleasant Ouse valley countryside *(JJW, CMW)*

Harrold [High St; SP9456], *Magpie*: Good evening meals (and even cookery classes in smartly equipped but friendly pub, efficient service *(JS)*

☆ **Ireland** [off A600 Shefford—Bedford – OS Sheet 153 map ref 135414; TL1341], *Black Horse*: Welcoming staff and good value food (not Sun evening) inc proper veg in pleasant pub's extensive dining area, well kept Bass, good coffee, tables in garden – attractive rural setting; cl Mon *(Mr and Mrs A Martin, Maysie Thompson, Scott Rumery)*

☆ **Kensworth** [B4540, Whipsnade end; TL0318], *Farmers Boy*: Fine village pub with good value generous food inc vegetarian, well kept Fullers, good lounge bar, good old-fashioned dining room (more restauranty evenings and Sun); play area and rabbit hutches in fenced-off garden by fields with horses; children very welcome *(the Sandy family, Mel Smith, Shirley Cannings)*

☆ **Linslade** [Globe Lane, off A4146 by bridge; SP9225], *Globe*: Interesting early 19th-c whitewashed pub in unusual location by Grand Union Canal, good enterprising food, particularly well kept ales such as Brains, Marstons Pedigree and local Tring Ridgeway, welcoming service, lots of rooms, beams and flagstones, cosy charm, wing armchair by open fire, canalia, mottoes and couplets; restaurant must be booked; waterside garden, children's play area; pleasant walks nearby *(Marianne and Andrew Bainbridge, Andrew Scarr, Graham and Karen Oddey, Tony O'Reilly, Ian Phillips, Mel Smith, Shirley Cannings, Lynda Payton, Sam Samuells)*

Luton [Tea Green; N of Luton Airport main runway; TL1323], *White Horse*: Tiny but immensely popular, cosy and very friendly; good range of food *(Ian Phillips)*

☆ **Odell** [Little Odell; SP9657], *Mad Dog*: Cosy and welcoming old beamed and thatched pub with wide choice of reasonably priced food, well kept Greene King ales, open fire in inglenook, quiet piped music and pleasant garden; handy for Harrold-Odell Country Park *(Tom Saul, John Saul)*

☆ **Old Warden** [High St; TL1343], *Hare & Hounds*: Small friendly beamed dining pub, neat as a new pin, with wide choice of good and generous if not cheap food, well kept Charles Wells Eagle and Bombardier and a guest such as Adnams or Badger, simple but comfortable decor, open fire; big sloping back garden with scramble net and tyre swings; beautiful thatched village, handy for local walks and Shuttleworth collection *(Cynthia Archer, Ian Phillips, Christopher Gallop, M*

Carey, Colin Lee, Dr B E Monk)

☆ **Potton** [TL2449], *Royal Oak*: Large comfortable bar, spacious dining area opening into restaurant, above-average straightforward bar food (served evenings too) inc bargain lunchtime roasts, very friendly service, well kept Greene King IPA, Abbot and seasonal ales *(P Stallard, Sidney and Erna Wells, Martyn Carey)*

Pulloxhill [off A6 N of Barton le Clay – OS Sheet 153 map ref 063341; TL0633], *Cross Keys*: Modernised early 17th-c, lots of timbering and flower baskets, roomy front bars, very friendly licensee and family, good value bar food, children in big back dining room, Charles Wells ales; garden with play area, pretty part of village in nice countryside *(Mr and Mrs A Budden)*

☆ **Radwell** [TL0057], *Swan*: Roomy and attractive beamed and thatched pub, two rooms joined by narrow passage, woodburner, lots of prints, unobtrusive piped music, friendly service, wide choice of good food, Charles Wells Eagle, decent coffee, popular evening restaurant; pleasant garden, small quiet village *(John Saul, Maysie Thompson)*

☆ **Ridgmont** [handy for M1 junction 13; SP9736], *Rose & Crown*: Consistently good sensible pub food served quickly even when busy, warm welcome, choice of well kept real ales, good coffee, interesting collection of *Rupert Annual* covers in well laid out lounge; low-ceilinged traditional public bar with open fire, games inc darts and pool; piped music, stables restaurant (not Mon or Tues evenings); long and attractive suntrap sheltered back garden; children allowed in bar eating area; easy parking, good wheelchair access *(F M Bunbury, Nick Holmes, LYM)*

☆ **Sandy** [Old London Rd; TL1649], *Kings Arms*: Attractive two-bar pub with friendly helpful staff, comfortable banquettes, lots of beams, open fire, wide choice of good reasonably priced food (veg charged separately), no-smoking eating area up steps, relaxed atmosphere, Greene King IPA, Abbot and Rayments, decent wines, restaurant; bedrooms in well built chalets *(Phil and Heidi Cook, Scott Rumery)*

☆ **nr Sandy** [Deepdale; B1042 towards Potton and Cambridge], *Locomotive*: Reliable pub nr RSPB HQ, packed with railway memorabilia; reasonably priced food nicely prepared and presented, friendly staff, well kept Charles Wells ales, no-smoking area, attractive and sizeable garden with views; piped radio, good service; can be busy weekends; children allowed in eating area *(Scott Rumery, LYM)*

☆ **Sharpenhoe** [Harlington Rd; TL0630], *Lynmore*: Much more attractive inside than you'd guess, spacious and comfortable, with friendly beamy family lounge and back dining area (good views), huge helpings of quick good value food inc children's dishes, good range of well kept ales, good garden for children, big wendy house; popular with walkers *(Eric Locker, Sidney and Erna Wells)*

Shefford [2 North Bridge St; Clifton Rd; TL1439], *White Hart*: Genuine-feeling old coaching inn, friendly rather than smart, with well kept Greene King Abbot, nicely cooked food, friendly service, pleasant lounge, dining room, basic public bar; four bedrooms, tables in garden *(Ian Phillips, Scott Rumery, BB)*

☆ **Southill** [off B658 SW of Biggleswade; TL1542], *White Horse*: Well decorated and comfortable lounge, dining room with spotlit well, small public bar with prints, harness and big woodburner; good value food (not Sun evening) inc wide choice of sandwiches and snacks, Whitbreads-related ales; children in eating areas; delightful big garden maybe with children's rides on diesel-engine miniature train, separate sheltered lawn with bird feeders, garden shop and good play area *(Roger Danes, Maysie Thompson, the Sandy family, Scott Rumery, Kay Neville-Rolfe, LYM)*

Stanbridge [pub signed off A5 N of Dunstable; SP9623], *Five Bells*: Attractive old coaching inn, well run, with tasty bar food and popular restaurant *(David Regan)*

Stotfold [A507; TL2136], *Fox & Duck*: Interestingly varied reasonably priced food in generous helpings, well kept beers, friendly obliging staff *(Jean and David Lewis)*

☆ **Studham** [Dunstable Rd; TL0215], *Bell*: Friendly and softly lit two-bar village pub dating from 16th c, beams, brasses, prints and plates, big helpings of consistently good home-cooked food (may be a wait), Tetleys-related ales; booking advised Sat, Sun lunch very popular; handy for Whipsnade and the Tree Cathedral *(Kay Neville-Rolfe, John Hawkins, Phil and Heidi Cook, Norma and Keith Bloomfield)*

Studham, *Red Lion*: Open-plan pub in attractive setting below grassy common, well kept Adnams and Greene King Abbot, decent food in back dining room, pleasant waitress service, bright and cheerful modernish decor, quiet piped music; tables outside, handy for Whipsnade *(Gwen and Peter Andrews, BB)*

Toddington [19 Church Sq; handy for M1 junction 12; main street from junction into village; TL0028], *Sow & Pigs*: 19th-c pub named after carving on church opp, with assorted furnishings inc pews, two armchairs and a retired chesterfield, bare boards, lots of old books and nick-nacks inc armless mannequin and amusing pig motifs, well kept Greene King ales, good coffee, wide choice of food (not Sun; back Victorian-style dining room can be booked for parties), two real fires, children allowed; picnic tables in small garden, attractive village *(CMW, JJW, Ian Phillips, Richard Hedges)*

Upper Dean [TL0467], *Three Compasses*: 350-year-old beamed and thatched Charles Wells pub with authentic beams, welcoming service, good choice of attractively priced food inc children's dishes (Sun lunch bookings only); shame about the piped music *(E Robinson)*

Wingfield [Tebworth Rd; off A600; SP9926],

Plough: Attractive recently rethatched old pub, low-beamed and largely unspoilt but spacious, with good atmosphere, friendly staff, six well kept ales inc Adnams and unusual guests, farm cider, good coffee, small no-smoking area, back conservatory; good value home-cooked food (not Sun evening) from sandwiches up inc good fresh chips, picnic tables and play area in back garden – dogs allowed out in front *(CMW, JJW, John Baker)*

Woburn [Bedford St; SP9433], *Bell*: Pleasant hotel with reliably good interesting food in small dining area and evening restaurant, well kept Greene King Abbot, friendly service, comfortable seating, lots of Spy cartoons,

piped music, tables outside; bedrooms *(Brian Horner, Brenda Arthur)*

Wootton [Hall End; TL0045], *Chequers*: Warm and cosy 15th-c Charles Wells local with friendly licensees and cat, masses of brightly polished brass, woodburning stove, real ales inc a guest, good food in bar and restaurant; nice quiet garden *(Ian Phillips, Colin McGaughley)*

Yielden [TL0166], *Chequers*: Welcoming village local, genuine home cooking by landlady in naval-theme dining room, Bass and Flowers IPA and Original, lots of WW2 relics fom nearby Chelveston USAF base, pool room *(Jenny and Michael Back)*

Post Office address codings confusingly give the impression that some pubs are in Berkshire, when they're really in Oxfordshire or Hampshire (which is where we list them).

Berkshire

New licensees at the Harrow at West Ilsley are doing well, with a warm response from readers to their new menus – a gentle move up market. But it's an entirely new entry, the Fish in Bray, which gains our award as Berkshire Dining Pub of the Year, appropriately enough specialising in fish and seafood. Other interesting new entries here are the quaintly rambling Stag & Hounds in Binfield (fresh modern cooking), and the civilised Bell at Boxford, a pleasant mock-Tudor village inn. Other Berkshire pubs which have a particularly warm place in readers' affections these days are the wonderfully unspoilt old Bell at Aldworth, the friendly Blue Boar at Chieveley, the enjoyably bustly Crown & Horns at East Ilsley, the rustic Pot Kiln at Frilsham (brewing its own ale), the Swan at Great Shefford (planned extension shouldn't change it much), the Queen Victoria at Hare Hatch (rather interesting food for what's essentially a friendly local), the homely Belgian Arms in Holyport and the warmly welcoming Fox & Hounds up on the downs at Peasemore. At the moment there's a lot of interest in the Lucky Dip section here, with attention attracted particularly by the Crown in Bray, Pineapple at Brimpton, Jolly Farmer and Inn on the Green in Cookham Dean, Bunk at Curridge, Pheasant at Great Shefford, Tally Ho at Hungerford Newtown (both these very handy for the motorway), Dundas Arms at Kintbury, Water Rat at Marsh Benham (too restauranty now for the main entries), both Old Windsor entries, Old Boot at Stanford Dingley (Andrew Lloyd Webber sparking off a flurry of interest in the Sunday papers), Winterbourne Arms at Winterbourne and Crooked Billet just outside Wokingham. We have inspected the great majority of these, and can firmly vouch for their quality. Reading has quite a few worthwhile pubs now, too. Berkshire pub prices are high, with beer costing about 15p a pint more than the national average, and prices rising rather more quickly than elsewhere; the Bell at Aldworth stands out as relatively very cheap for both food and drink, with the Pot Kiln at Frilsham and Fox & Hounds at Peasemore both good value too.

ALDWORTH SU5579 Map 2
Bell ★ £ ♀ ◗

A329 Reading—Wallingford; left on to B4009 at Streatley

'A gem' is how several readers describe this marvellously unspoilt 14th-c country pub, run by the same family for over 200 years. There's always a warm welcome from the friendly licensees – no matter how busy the pub is – and a good mix of customers in the cosy bar with its beams in the shiny ochre ceiling, benches around the panelled walls, woodburning stove, ancient one-handed clock, and glass-panelled hatch rather than a bar counter for service. Incredibly good value food is confined to hot crusty rolls (apart from winter home-made soup), filled with cheddar (£1), ham, brie, stilton or pâté (£1.10), smoked salmon, salt beef or ox tongue (£1.60), and particularly good Devon crab in season (£2); salad basket and garlic dressing (£1.70). Very well kept and very cheap Arkells BBB and Kingsdown, Morrells Bitter and Mild, and from the local West Berkshire Brewery, Old Tyler on handpump (they won't stock draught lager); particularly good house wines. Darts, shove-ha'penny, dominoes, cribbage, chess, and Aunt Sally. The quiet, old-fashioned garden is lovely in summer, and the pub is handy for the Ridgeway, so popular with walkers on Sundays. Occasional Morris dancing; Christmas mummers. *(Recommended by Maureen Hobbs, Liz and Ian Phillips, Sidney and Erna Wells, John Hayter, C P R Baxter, TRS, PHS, TBB, Sandra Kench, Steven Norman, Prof J R Leigh, Andy Jones, Bob and Maggie Atherton, Paul Chaundy, Mark Brock)*

Free house ~ Licensee H E Macaulay ~ Real ale ~ Snacks (11-2.50, 6-10.45; not Mon) ~ (01635) 578272 ~ Well behaved children in tap room ~ Open 11-3, 6-11; closed Mon (open bank holidays), 25 Dec

BINFIELD SU8571 Map 2
Stag & Hounds 🍺
Forest Rd (B3034 towards Windsor)

A real surprise for the area: lots of little rooms with extremely low black beams, soft lighting, snugly intimate corners, log fires, interesting furnishings and pictures – the sort of place where it's easy to believe the tale that Queen Elizabeth I once watched Morris men dancing on the green outside. There are attractive sporting and other prints, including a fine group relating to 19th-c Royal Ascot (these are in an airier end room on the right where claustrophobes would feel more at home – as they would in the plusher high-ceilinged lounge on the left). Despite unnecessary piped pop music there's a good buzzy atmosphere, and during the week the pub quickly fills with suits and neatly dressed young women from midday onwards. Bar food includes lunchtime sandwiches, hot filled ciabatta bread and filled olive rolls, lots of changing daily specials such as grilled goat's cheese and roasted red pepper salad (£5.95), chicken dupiazza with nan bread, chutney and pickles (£6.25), wild boar and apple sausages with creamy leek mash and gravy (£6.75), and roast breast of barbary duck with redcurrant, port and ginger and supreme of pheasant in a rich red wine sauce (£7.95); they always have fresh fish like baby dover soles, swordfish or king prawns, vegetarian dishes, evening steaks and grills, and roast Sunday lunch. Best to book for Friday and Saturday evenings and Sunday lunch. Well kept Courage Best and Directors, Eldridge Popes Traditional and Wadworths 6X on handpump, decent wines, daily papers; tables outside on front terrace and in back garden. *(Recommended by Gordon, G W A Pearce, A E Brace)*

Courage ~ Manageress Zoe Rugg ~ Real ale ~ Meals and snacks (till 10pm) ~ (01344) 483553 ~ Children welcome ~ Open 11-3, 5.30-11; 12-3, 7-10.30 Sun

BOXFORD SU4271 Map 2
Bell 🍷
Back road Newbury—Lambourn; village also signposted off B4000 between Speen and M4 junction 14

This civilised and neatly kept mock-Tudor village inn is notable for its thoughtful modern cooking: a changing choice of food from snacks such as wild mushroom tortelli (£3.95), susumi, crab and whitefish with oyster sauce, or carrot and parsnip rosti with cumin and sesame seeds (£4.95), to lamb done with honey and pink peppercorn sauce, salmon or good steaks perked up with interesting sauces (£12.95); they also do soup (£2.35; with a sandwich £3.95), croque monsieur (£3.45), filled french bread (£3.85), pork and leek sausage with onion gravy and mash (£4.25), home-cooked ham and eggs (£5.25), steak and Guinness pie (£6.25), and a roast of the day (£6.95). The most serious eating takes place in the rather smart restaurant area on the left; round to the right, the bar is quite long and snug, with a coal-effect fire at one end, a nice mix of racing pictures and smaller old advertisements (especially for Mercier champagne), red plush cushions for the mates' chairs, and some interesting bric-a-brac. Well kept Boddingtons, Courage Best and Flowers Original on handpump, decent wines and whiskies; fruit and Cluedo machine and juke box. A side courtyard had white cast-iron garden furniture; the lane is quiet enough for the main sound to be the nearby rookery. We have not yet heard from readers who have stayed here, but would expect it to be a very pleasant overnight stop. *(Recommended by HNJ, PEJ)*

Free house ~ Licensees Paul and Helen Lavis ~ Real ale ~ Meals and snacks ~ Restaurant ~ (01488) 608721 ~ Children in eating area of bar and in restaurant ~ Open 11-3, 6-11; 12-3, 7-10.30 Sun ~ Bedrooms: £56B/£68B

BRAY SU9079 Map 2
Fish 🍴 ♀

1¾ miles from M4 junction 8: A308(M), A308 towards Windsor, then first left into B3028 towards Bray; bear right into Old Mill Lane

Berkshire Dining Pub of the Year

Mrs Thaxter scored a palpable hit with readers at her former pub (the Angel in Burford, Oxon), though in her first year here few of them seem yet to have tracked her down to this tucked-away conversion of a former Georgian local. When they do, they are in for a treat. Scoring highly for its informal but committed and thoughtful service, it's now a handsome but relaxed dining pub, particularly strong on fresh fish – a choice that changes daily, but might typically include chargrilled swordfish with a caper and lime mayonnaise, steamed fillet of seabass with pernod and fennel, fresh cornish crab salad or medallions of monkfish with lobster sauce (£8.50-£11.95). Cooking is deft and adventurous, with fashionably eclectic but by no means overbearing accompaniments (onion and fennel confit for white fish, for example, or a small very fresh tapenade of olive and sun-dried tomato to balance seared tuna). Other dishes might include grilled goat's cheese salad with thyme, honey and pine nuts (£5.95), open ravioli of ratatouille with a basil and tomato vinaigrette (£7.95), calf liver with fresh sage (£9.50), and breast of maize-fed chicken with spinach and tarragon cream (£10.50); both bread and puddings like gooseberry fool, lovely steamed chocolate pudding with dark chocolate sauce or sharp lemon tart (£4.25) are most enjoyable. The bar servery is very much part of the scenery, helping the unstuffy feel of the bar, its two rooms linked by a broad row of arches. Above the venetian red dado, reproduction Old Master drawings and details of paintings decorate the subtly off-white walls. Caucasian rugs on the parquet floor are most attractive (though they don't do much to damp the cheerfully bright acoustics). Well spaced tables have little sprays of fresh flowers, candles at night, and a mix of continental-style rush-seat stained-wood dining chairs and country kitchen chairs; there are more tables in a no-smoking conservatory (with plenty of blinds) opening out beyond. They keep Brakspears Bitter, with Adnams in summer, on handpump, but the emphasis is on a fine range of mainly New World wines. *(Recommended by TBB)*

Free house ~ Licensee Jean Thaxter ~ Real ale ~ Meals and snacks (not Sun evening) ~ Restaurant (not Sun evening) ~ (01628) 781111 ~ Children in restaurant at lunchtime, but must be over 12 in evening ~ Open 11-3, 6-11; 12-3 Sun; closed Sun evening

BURCHETTS GREEN SU8381 Map 2
Crown

Side road between A4 and A404, W of Maidenhead

Although there is still a very small plain bar with two or three tables for casual customers, this busy little country pub places much emphasis on its generous helpings of very good, interesting food. The civilised main bar is clean, warm and comfortable with a restaurauty layout and unobtrusive piped music – but the licensees continue to preserve an informal and very welcoming atmosphere. From a changing menu there might be home-made soup, sandwiches (from £2.95; open chicken and avocado with cheese £4.95), a melt-in-the-mouth chicken liver parfait with home-made chutney (£3.95), cheese omelette (£4.45), mignons of pork fillet with a brandy, cream and mushroom sauce (£8.95), calf liver with bubble and squeak, crispy bacon and onion gravy (£9.55), roulade of lemon sole fillets filled with smoked salmon and spinach in a white wine sauce (£10.25), and twin fillets of Scottish beef in two sauces (£13.25). Presentation is careful and appetising and service is friendly and attentive. Well kept Morlands Original and Charles Wells Bombardier on handpump, kept under light blanket pressure, and a good range of wines by the glass; piped music. There are tables out in a pleasant quiet garden. *(Recommended by Mr and Mrs B Hobden, Peter Saville, MA,*

Mr and Mrs T A Bryan, TBB, Ron and Val Broom, P A Baxter; more reports please)

Morlands ~ Lease: Ian Price and Alex Turner ~ Real ale ~ Meals and snacks (till 10pm) ~ Restaurant ~ (01628) 822844 ~ Children in restaurant ~ Open 12-2.30, 6-11

CHEAPSIDE SU9469 Map 2
Thatched Tavern

Cheapside Road; off B383, which is itself off A332 and A329

Food is very much the attraction to this smartly civilised dining pub, though there is an area for drinkers (which fills up quickly at busy times, so best to get there early). It's not actually thatched but does have polished flagstones, very low gnarled and nibbled beams, small windows with cheerful cottagey curtains, and an old cast-iron range in a big inglenook with built-in wall benches snugly around it. Pretty red gingham tablecloths brighten up the longish carpeted back dining area, and a vast blackboard choice covering such dishes as sandwiches (from £2.50), home-made soup (£3.75), a plate of saucisson (£6.75), fresh anchovy, tomato, basil and garlic oil (£7.75), smoked haddock crumble (£8.50), cumberland sausages, mash and onion gravy (£8.75), home-made steak and kidney pudding or slow-roasted half shoulder of lamb (£10.50), local game such as venison, quail, hare, pigeon and so forth (from £11), fresh fish that's delivered daily like grilled cod or wild Tay salmon (from around £11.50), and lots of puddings such as fruit crumbles and bread and butter pudding (£3.75); limited bar snacks on Sunday as they do proper Sunday roasts. Well kept Greene King IPA, Abbot and Sorcerer on handpump, polite, friendly staff, spotless housekeeping, and no games or piped music. Rustic seats and tables are grouped on the sheltered back lawn, around a big old apple tree. Handy for walks around Virginia Water, with the Blacknest car park a mile or so down the road. *(Recommended by Susan and John Douglas, Margaret and Nigel Dennis, Martin and Karen Wake, Ian Phillips, Jerry Hughes, Simon Collett-Jones, Julian Bower, Chris Westmoreland, Mayur Shah)*

Greene King ~ Licensees Robert King, Jonathan Michael Mee ~ Real ale ~ Bar meals and snacks lunchtime only ~ Restaurant ~ (01344) 20874 ~ Well behaved children welcome away from bar ~ Open 11.30-3, 6-11

CHIEVELEY SU4774 Map 2
Blue Boar

2 miles from M4 junction 13: A34 N towards Oxford, 200 yds left for Chieveley, then left at Wheatsheaf pub and straight on until T-junction with B4494; turn right to Wantage and pub is 500 yds on right; heading S on A34, don't take first sign to Chieveley

Doing well at the moment, this thatched inn with its historic links to Cromwell and the Civil War is popular with both locals and visitors. There's a warm welcome from the licensees, and a good atmosphere in the beamed bar with its three rambling rooms furnished with high-backed settles, windsor chairs and polished tables, and decked out with a variety of heavy harness (including a massive collar); the left-hand room has a log fire and a seat built into the sunny bow window. A lot of space is given over to eating the well liked bar food, which includes soup (£1.95), sandwiches (from £2.10), ploughman's (£4.30), a good cheeseburger, speciality sausages (£5.40), half chargrilled chicken (£7), pies like beef in Guinness (£7.50), and puddings; there's a wider range in the civilised oak-panelled restaurant. Well kept Fullers London Pride and Wadworths 6X on handpump; several malt whiskies; soft piped music. There are tables among tubs and flowerbeds on the rough front cobbles outside. *(Recommended by John and Chris Simpson, Stephen and Julie Brown, John and Elisabeth Cox, HNJ, PEJ, M Hasslacher, Gordon, TBB, Tom McLean, Pauline Langley, Julie Peters, Colin Blinkhorn, Nigel Norman)*

Free house ~ Licensees Ann and Peter Ebsworth ~ Real ale ~ Meals and snacks ~ Restaurant (closed Sun) ~ (01635) 248236 ~ Children welcome ~ Open 11-3, 6-11; 12-3, 7-10.30 Sun ~ Bedrooms: £49B/£59B

Soup prices usually include a roll and butter.

COOKHAM SU8884 Map 2
Bel & the Dragon
High Street; B4447 N of Maidenhead

Civilised and smart, this restful old place has three rooms with old oak settles, deep leather chairs, pewter tankards hanging from heavy Tudor beams, and open fires; one room is no smoking. From the low zinc-topped bar counter well kept Brakspears PA is tapped from the cask, there's a good choice of wines, decent ports and champagne, and freshly squeezed orange juice; prompt, professional service. They do sandwiches as well as hot bar food; the restaurant is not cheap. The inn has no car park and street parking can be very difficult. The Stanley Spencer Gallery is almost opposite. *(Recommended by Lynda Payton, Sam Samuells, D Voller, David Carr, John and Patricia White, Mayur Shah)*

Free house ~ Licensee Malcolm Tall ~ Real ale ~ Meals and snacks (served throughout opening hours) ~ Restaurant (closed Sun and Mon evenings) ~ (01628) 521263 ~ Children welcome ~ Open 11.30(12 Sat)-2.30, 5.30-11; 12-3, 7-11 Sun

COOKHAM DEAN SU8785 Map 2
Uncle Toms Cabin
Hills Lane, Harding Green; village signposted off A308 Maidenhead—Marlow – keep on down past Post Office and village hall towards Cookham Rise and Cookham

The friendly series of 1930s-feeling mainly carpeted little rooms in this pretty cream-washed cottage offers a degree of intimacy when it's crowded (which it can be at weekends and in summer) but still give a feeling of being part of everything. The front rooms have low beams and joists, lots of shiny dark brown woodwork, and old-fashioned plush-cushioned wall seats, stools and so forth; quite a lot of breweryana, and some interesting golden discs. Bar food includes home-made soup (£2.75), french bread or granary rolls with a wide choice of good fillings (from £2.95), filled baked potatoes (from £3.75), home-made burgers (from £4), various pasta and crêpe dishes (from £5.75), and rump steak (£9.25). Well kept Benskins Best and a regularly changing guest such as Badger Tanglefoot, Fullers London Pride, Greene King Abbot or Hop Back Summer Lightning on handpump; sensibly placed darts, shove-ha'penny, cribbage, and dominoes. Piped music, if on, is well chosen and well reproduced. The two cats Jess (black and white) and Wilma (black) enjoy the winter coal fire and Oggie the busy black-and-white dog welcomes other dogs (who get a dog biscuit on arrival). There are picnic tables and a climbing frame in an attractive and sheltered back garden. *(Recommended by L F Vohryzek, Martin and Karen Wake, J and B Cressey, George Atkinson, Nigel Norman)*

Carlsberg Tetleys ~ Lease: Nick and Karen Ashman ~ Real ale ~ Meals and snacks ~ (01628) 483339 ~ Children welcome until 8pm if quiet ~ Open 11-3, 5.30-11; 12-3, 7-10.30 Sun

CRAZIES HILL SU7980 Map 2
Horns
From A4, take Warren Row Road at Cockpole Green signpost just E of Knowl Hill, then past Warren Row follow Crazies Hill signposts; from Wargrave, take A321 towards Henley, then follow Crazies Hill signposts right at Shell garage, then left

Surrounded by a three-acre garden, this little tiled whitewashed cottage continues to have no juke box, fruit machine or piped music. The bars have rugby mementoes on the walls, exposed beams, open fires and stripped wooden tables and chairs; the barn room is opened up to the roof like a medieval hall. Good bar food includes lunchtime french bread and ploughman's, home-made soup (£3.25), four-cheese terrine with apricot chutney (£4.50), warm salad with bacon, stilton and avocado (£4.95), vegetarian cassoulet or seafood pasta (£6.95), chicken breast with parma ham in a white wine and marsala sauce (£8.75), calf liver and bacon with black pudding, mashed potato and onion gravy (£9.95), and Aberdeen Angus steaks (from £11.95). Well kept Brakspears PA, Mild, SB, Old and OBJ on handpump, a thoughtful wine list, and several malt whiskies. *(Recommended by D Voller, L F Vohryzek, Dr G W Barnett, TBB, Chris Westmoreland)*

Brakspears ~ Tenant 'A J Hearn ~ Real ale ~ Meals and snacks (not Sun evening) ~ Restaurant (not Sun evening) ~ (01734) 401416 ~ Children in restaurant lunchtimes only ~ Open 11-2.30, 6-11; 12-3, 7-10.30 Sun; closed 25 and 26 Dec

EAST ILSLEY SU4981 Map 2
Crown & Horns 🏨 🍴

Just off A34, about 5 miles N of M4 junction 13

This is a reliably enjoyable pub with an unchanging friendly atmosphere. The walls of the four interesting beamed rooms are hung with racing prints and photographs, emphasising the fact that this is very much horse-training country; and the side bar may have locals watching the latest races on TV. The wide range of regularly changing real ales, all reasonably priced, and typically including Fullers London Pride, Mansfield Old Baily, Morlands Original and Old Speckled Hen, Theakstons Old Peculier and XB, and Wadworths 6X on handpump. There is also an impressive collection of 160 whiskies from all over the world – Morocco, Korea, Japan, China, Spain and New Zealand. Good, interesting bar food includes sandwiches (from £1.90), home-made soup (£3), filled baked potatoes (from £3.50), ploughman's (from £4.60), vegetable lasagne or steak and mushroom pie (£5.20), chicken breast with stilton and mushroom sauce or duck in a port and black cherry sauce (£7.95), steaks (from £8.75), and puddings (£3.50); quick, cheerful staff – even when busy. Skittle alley, darts, pool, bar billiards, pinball, dominoes, cribbage, fruit machine, juke box and piped music. The pretty paved stable yard has tables under two chestnut trees. We regret to say that the management failed to respond to our repeated requests for up-to-date prices, etc, so details included here are our estimates. *(Recommended by Tom McLean, Simon Penny, HNJ, PEJ, C P Baxter, Nick and Meriel Cox, Martin and Karen Wake, BJP Edwards, Nigel Norman, Percy and Cathy Paine)*

Free house ~ Licensees Chris and Jane Bexx ~ Real ale ~ Meals and snacks (till 10pm) ~ (01635) 281205 ~ Children in eating area, restaurant and TV room ~ Open 11-11; closed evening 25 Dec ~ Bedrooms: £32.50B/£45B

FRILSHAM SU5473 Map 2
Pot Kiln 🍴

From Yattendon take turning S, opposite church, follow first Frilsham signpost, but just after crossing motorway go straight on towards Bucklebury ignoring Frilsham signposted right; pub on right after about half a mile

This unpretentious country pub entirely lives up to expectations raised as you approach it – an old-fashioned cottagey building down a peaceful byway. The unchanging bar is not unsmart, with wooden floorboards and bare benches and pews, and there's a good winter log fire, too. Well kept Brick Kiln Bitter (from a micro brewery behind the pub) is served from a hatch in the panelled entrance lobby – which has room for just one bar stool – along with well kept Arkells BBB, and Morlands Original and Old Speckled Hen on handpump. Enjoyable, fairly simple food includes good filled hot rolls, home-made soup (£2.35), a decent ploughman's (from £3.65), vegetable gratin or vegetable and cheese suet pudding (£5.65), excellent salmon and broccoli fishcake or steak and kidney pudding (£5.95), and daily specials like pork or beef casserole (£6.50), fresh salmon fillets (£6.85), and sirloin steaks (£8.50); no chips, and vegetables are fresh. Rolls only on Sundays. The public bar has darts, dominoes, shove-ha'penny and cribbage. The back room/dining room is no smoking. There are picnic tables in the big suntrap garden with good views of the woods and countryside. It's a good dog-walking area and they are allowed in the public bar on a lead. *(Recommended by Gordon, TBB, C P R Baxter, Andy Jones, Mark Brock, Jamie Pratt, PHS, Mark and Diane Grist, Bob and Maggie Atherton, Thomas Neate)*

Own brew ~ Licensee Philip Gent ~ Real ale ~ Meals and snacks (not Tues) ~ (01635) 201366 ~ Well behaved children in back room and public bar ~ Irish music most Sun evenings ~ Open 12-2.30, 6.30-11; 12-3, 7-10.30 Sun; closed Tues lunchtime

GREAT SHEFFORD SU3875 Map 2

Swan

2 miles from M4 junction 14; on A338 towards Wantage

By the time this book is published, the licensees hope to have extended and carefully refurbished this neatly kept and friendly village pub. The low-ceilinged rooms of the spacious bow-windowed lounge bar are attractively and comfortably furnished and have old photographs of the village and horse and jockey pictures on the walls; the public side has darts, shove-ha'penny, cribbage, dominoes, pool, a fruit machine, and CD juke box. Good food includes sandwiches and home-made soup, and daily specials such as beef and Guinness pie (£6.95), lamb steak with redcurrant and rosemary (£7.95), vegetarian and children's meals, and Scotch steaks. Well kept Courage Best and guests like Butts Ale (from a microbrewery in the village), Eldridge Pope Dorchester, and Wadworths 6X on handpump; attentive service. There are tables on the terrace by big willows overhanging the River Lambourn; the restaurant shares the same view. *(Recommended by Paul and Ursula Randall, N and A Chesher, Hugh Spottiswoode, Gordon, Mrs S Wright, Mark Percy, Lesley Mayoh, Peter and Audrey Dowsett, Mark Brock)*

Courage ~ Managers Kevin Maul, Sue Jacobs ~ Real ale ~ Meals and snacks ~ Children in eating area of bar ~ Restaurant ~ (01488) 648271 ~ Open 11-3, 6-11; 12-3, 7-10.30 Sun

HAMSTEAD MARSHALL SU4165 Map 2

White Hart 🛏️

Village signposted from A4 W of Newbury

This is very much a dining pub with quite an emphasis on good (if pricey) Italian meals. The daily specials are popular and might include a warm salad of marinated crispy fried lamb strips with pine nuts or wild rabbit in a mustard and herb sauce with fettucine (£9.50), monkfish fillets in a spicy tomato and brandy sauce (£12.50) or beef meatballs stuffed with mozzarella and braised in wine sauce; also, home-made soup (£3.20), home-made liver pâté with ciabatta toast (£4.50), goat's cheese grilled with garlic and yoghurt (£5.50), various pasta dishes (£7.50) such as quadroni (mushroom and herb-stuffed ravioli with wild mushroom and cream sauce £7.50) or crespelle (pancakes filled with ricotta and spinach baked with cheese and tomato lasagne), dover sole poached in white wine with prawns and cream (£14.50), and puddings like Italian-style bread and butter pudding with chocolate, tiramisu or almond and black cherry tart (£4.50); the food boards are attractively illustrated with Mrs Aromando's drawings, they grow many of their own herbs and some vegetables, and their beef is from a local organic farm. The restaurant is partly no smoking. Ringwood Best and Wadworths 6X on handpump and decent Italian wines. The L-shaped bar has red plush seats built into the bow windows, cushioned chairs around oak and other tables, a copper-topped bar counter, and a log fire open on both sides. Their newfoundland cross dog is called Sophie, and Solo the pony is still with them. The interesting walled garden is lovely in summer, and the quiet and comfortable beamed newly refurbished bedrooms are in a converted barn across the courtyard. *(Recommended by Simon Morton, Glen and Nola Armstrong, Linda and Brian Davis, June and Tony Baldwin, Stephen Barney, Lynn Sharpless, Bob Eardley, Verity Kemp, Richard Mills)*

Free house ~ Licensee Mr Nicola Aromando ~ Real ale ~ Meals and snacks (not Sun) ~ Restaurant (not Sun) ~ (01488) 658201 ~ Children in eating area of bar ~ Open 12-2.30, 6-11; closed Sun, 25-26 Dec, 1 Jan, 2 wks summer ~ Bedrooms: £45B/£65B

HARE HATCH SU8077 Map 2

Queen Victoria

Blakes Lane, The Holt; just N of A4 Reading—Maidenhead, 3 miles W of exit roundabout from A404(M) – keep your eyes skinned for the turning

The two low-beamed rooms in this friendly local have a chatty atmosphere, strong spindleback chairs, wall benches and window seats, flowers on the tables, and decorations such as a stuffed sparrowhawk and a delft shelf lined with beaujolais bottles; the tables on the right are no smoking. Popular bar food might include sandwiches, port and stilton pâté (£2.95), prawns (£3.35), Chinese chicken kebab with a mild chilli dip (£5.50), teriyaki turkey (£5.75), lamb steak with rosemary and garlic (£7.95), and puddings like home-baked fruit pies and crumbles; vegetables are fresh. Well kept Brakspears PA, SB, and Old on handpump, a fair choice of wines by the glass, and obliging service. Dominoes, cribbage, fruit machine, video game, and three dimensional noughts and crosses. There's a flower-filled covered terrace with tables and chairs, and a robust table or two in front by the car park. *(Recommended by J and B Cressey, Mr and Mrs C J Ward, Mark Hydes, P J Caunt, Dr G W Barnett, James Nunns, TBB, Mark and Diane Grist, Mary Bowen Rees)*

Brakspears ~ Tenant Ronald Rossington ~ Real ale ~ Meals and snacks (11.30-2.30, 6.30-10.30; all day Sun) ~ (01734) 402477 ~ Children welcome ~ Open 11-3, 5.30-11; 12-10.30 Sun

HOLYPORT SU8977 Map 2
Belgian Arms

1½ miles from M4 junction 8/9; take A308(M) then at terminal roundabout follow Holyport signpost along A330 towards Bracknell; in village turn left on to big green, then left again at War Memorial shelter

Readers are fond of this bustling, homely pub, both in winter when there's a roaring log fire and in summer when you can sit in the charming garden looking over the pond towards the village green. The L-shaped, low-ceilinged bar has interesting framed postcards of Belgian military uniform and other good military prints on the walls, a china cupboard in one corner, and a variety of chairs around a few small tables. Bar food includes sandwiches (the toasted 'special' is very well liked), a good ploughman's, pizzas with different toppings (from £4.95), home-cooked ham and eggs, lasagne or chicken curry (£5.95), and duck in port or poached salmon fillet (£8.95); good Sunday lunch. You can also eat in the conservatory area. Well kept Brakspears PA, SB and in winter Old on handpump, and one or two good malts; friendly service. There is a pen with a goat and hens. *(Recommended by E J Gibson, Sue and Pete Robbins, J and B Cressey, Simon Collett-Jones, Jim Reid, Dr G W Barnett, Ian Phillips, Graham Tayar, Mrs S Wright)*

Brakspears ~ Tenant Alfred Morgan ~ Real ale ~ Meals and snacks (not Sun evening) ~ (01628) 34468 ~ Children in dining conservatory ~ Open 11-3, 5.30(6 Sat)-11; 12-3, 7-10.30 Sun

PEASEMORE SU4577 Map 2
Fox & Hounds ♀

Village signposted from B4494 Newbury—Wantage

It definitely is worth tracking down this pub so pleasantly tucked away in horse-training country – it's an attractive drive anyway, and once there you can be sure of a really welcoming atmosphere. The two bars have brocaded stripped wall settles, chairs and stools around shiny wooden tables, a log-effect gas fire (open to both rooms), and piped music. One wall has a full set of Somerville's entertaining *Slipper's ABC of Fox-Hunting* prints, and on a stripped-brick wall there's a row of flat-capped fox masks. Enjoyable bar food includes sandwiches, home-made soup (£1.95), a home-made pie of the day (£5.50), good chilli lamb and coconut curry or a parcel of potato and rabbit (£6.50), charcoal-grilled spicy chicken (£7.50), steaks (from £8.95), vegetarian dishes (£5.50), and daily specials. Well kept Fullers London Pride and Greene King IPA and Abbot on handpump, a good few malt whiskies, and a wide range of reasonably priced good wines. Pool, dominoes, cribbage, fruit machine, discreet juke box, and piped music. From the picnic tables outside, there are views of rolling fields – and on a clear day you can look right across to the high hills which form the Berkshire/Hampshire border about 20 miles southward. *(Recommended by Jenny and Roger Huggins, Julie Peters, Colin Blinkhorn)*

Free house ~ Licensees David and Loretta Smith ~ Real ale ~ Meals and snacks (till 10pm; not Mon) ~ Restaurant ~ (01635) 248252 ~ Children welcome ~ Live Irish music monthly ~ Open 11.30-3, 6.30-11; 12-3, 7-10.30 Sun; closed Mon

STANFORD DINGLEY SU5771 Map 2
Bull

From M4 junction 12, W on A4, then right at roundabout on to A340 towards Pangbourne; first left to Bradfield, where left, then Stanford Dingley signposted on right

Two standing timbers hung with horsebrasses divide the beamed tap room of this brick 15th-c pub firmly into two parts. The main part has red-cushioned seats carved out of barrels, a window settle, wheelback chairs on the red quarry tiles, an old brick fireplace, and an old station clock; the other is similarly furnished but carpeted. There's also a half-panelled lounge bar with refectory-type tables, and a smaller room leading off with quite a few musical instruments. Bar food includes sandwiches, filled baked potatoes (from £2.25), soups like carrot and orange or stilton (from £2.50), garlic bacon and mushrooms on toast (£3.25), ploughman's (from £3.35), cottage pie (£5.95), tagliatelle with bacon, mushroom and wine sauce (£6.25), trout with almonds (£7.95), steaks (from £6.95), and daily specials including two vegetarian dishes. Well kept (and cheap for the area) Bass, Brakspears, and West Berkshire Brewery Good Old Boy on handpump; friendly, helpful staff. Ring-the-bull, occasional classical or easy listening music. In front of the building are some big rustic tables and benches, and to the side is a small garden with a few more seats. *(Recommended by Tom Evans, Mr and Mrs W Welsh, TBB, PHS, Susan and John Douglas)*

Free house ~ Licensees Patrick and Trudi Langdon ~ Real ale ~ Meals and snacks (till 10pm; not Mon lunchtime) ~ (01734) 744409 ~ Children in saloon bar until 8.30pm; not Sat evening ~ Open 12-3, 7-11; 12-3, 7-10.30 Sun; closed Mon lunchtime – except bank holidays

WALTHAM ST LAWRENCE SU8276 Map 2
Bell

In village centre

The lounge bar in this attractive timbered black and white pub has finely carved oak panelling, a log fire, and a pleasant atmosphere, and the public bar has heavy beams, an attractive seat in the deep window recess, and well kept Bass, Brakspears PA, Wadworths 6X and other guest beers on handpump; the small front room is no smoking. Bar food includes sandwiches (from £2), bacon and cheese turnover or ploughman's (£3.50), pork and apple sausages (£4), vegetarian dishes or steak and kidney pie (£4.50), evening extras such as venison in red wine or tarragon chicken (£6), and duck in orange sauce (£6.50), daily specials, and puddings. In summer, the hanging baskets in front of the building are very pretty, and there are tables and a play area out behind – very popular with families in summer. *(Recommended by Linda Milbank, Ron and Val Broom, TBB, Chris Westmoreland; more reports please)*

Free house ~ Licensee Mrs Denise Slater ~ Real ale ~ Meals and snacks (not Sun or Mon evenings) ~ (0118) 934 1788 ~ Children in eating area of bar and in dining room ~ Open 11-3, 6-11; 12-3, 7-10.30 Sun

WEST ILSLEY SU4782 Map 2
Harrow 🍲 🍷

Signposted at East Ilsley slip road off A34 Newbury—Abingdon

New licensees have taken over this white tiled village pub and Mr Hunter also does the cooking – all dishes are home-made and they only use fresh produce. Early reports from readers have been most favourable but it's best to get there early as by 12.30 it may be hard to find a seat. Constantly changing, the very good food might include granary rolls filled with hot sausage and home-made chutney or stilton, celery and apple (£3.50), twice-baked goat's cheese soufflé on a walnut salad (£4.50), ploughman's with British farmhouse cheeses (from £5), lamb liver and bacon, oven-roasted salmon and deep-fried leeks, chicken in a Dijon and tarragon sauce or monkfish and mussels in white wine (all £8.70), shank of lamb on mashed roast potatoes (£10.95), and puddings like treacle tart and home-made ice creams; perfectly cooked vegetables. The dining room is no smoking. Well kept Morlands Original and Old Speckled Hen, and a guest like Flowers Original on handpump, and 8 good house wines including French regional ones. The open-plan bar has dark terracotta walls hung with many mainly Victorian prints and other ornaments, big turkey rugs on the floor, and a mix of antique oak tables, unpretentious old chairs, and a couple of more stately long settles; there's also an unusual stripped twin-seated high-backed settle between the log fire and the bow window. Fruit machine. This is a lovely spot with lots of nearby walks – the Ridgeway is just a mile away – and the big garden has picnic tables and other tables under cocktail parasols looking out over the duck pond and cricket green. *(Recommended by David Peakall, Simon Walker, HNJ, PEJ, R T and J C Moggridge; more reports on the new regime please)*

Morlands ~ Tenants Emily Hawes, Scott Hunter ~ Real ale ~ Meals and snacks (not winter Sun evenings) ~ (01635) 281260 ~ Children welcome ~ Open 11-3(3.30 Sat), 6-11; 12-11 summer Sun; 12-3.30, 7-10.30 winter Sun

YATTENDON SU5574 Map 2
Royal Oak 🛏 ♀

The Square; B4009 NE from Newbury; turn right at Hampstead Norreys, village signposted on left

This elegantly handsome inn is hardly a straightforward pub – but it does keep locally brewed West Berkshire Brewery's Good Old Boy, plus Banks's Bitter and Fullers London Pride on handpump in good condition, and there's a relaxed, comfortable atmosphere in the prettily decorated and panelled brasserie/bar with its lovely flowers and marvellous winter log fire; the restaurant is no smoking. Most people, of course, come to enjoy the bar food which, under the new managers, might include home-made soup (£3), vegetable terrine with pistou sauce (£5), cod and chips (£7.75), home-made tagliatelle with various sauces (£8.75), calf liver and bacon with onion gravy (£9.75), fresh chargrilled tuna (£11), sirloin steak (£11.50), and puddings such as rhubarb crumble, chocolate sponge pudding or home-made sorbets and ice creams (from £4); fresh vegetables are extra. Best to book. There's a good wine list. In summer, you can eat at tables in the pleasant walled garden – and there are more in front on the village square. The attractive village is one of the few still owned privately. *(Recommended by Mr and Mrs C R Little, Stephen Brown, C P R Baxter, TBB, PHS, Christine and Geoff Butler, Nigel Norman, Percy and Cathy Paine, Bob and Maggie Atherton)*

Free house ~ Managers Corinne and Robbie Macrae ~ Real ale ~ Meals and snacks (till 10pm Fri and Sat) ~ Restaurant (not Sun evenings) ~ (01635) 201325 ~ Children welcome ~ Open 11-3, 6-11; 12-3, 7-10.30 Sun ~ Bedrooms: £80B/£90B

Bedroom prices normally include full English breakfast, VAT and any inclusive service charge that we know of. Prices before the '/' are for single rooms, after for two people in double or twin (B includes a private bath, S a private shower). If there is no '/', the prices are only for twin or double rooms (as far as we know there are no singles). If there is no B or S, as far as we know no rooms have private facilities.

Lucky Dip

Besides the fully inspected pubs, you might like to try these Lucky Dips recommended to us and described by readers (if you do, please send us reports):

☆ **Aldermaston** [SU5965], *Hinds Head*: Interesting partly 16th-c village inn, refurbished but homely and comfortable, with good home-cooked food, good service, well kept ales such as Courage Best, Fullers London Pride and a guest; children welcome (separate dining room with high chairs), superb enclosed garden; bedrooms – a good place to stay *(Gordon, David Peakall)*

Aldworth [Haw Lane; B4009 towards Hampstead Norreys; SU5579], *Four Points*: Good range of freshly cooked food in recently refurbished thatched family pub, beams, horsebrasses, big log fire, lots of tables in dining area off small bar, well kept Morlands, friendly young landlord; neat garden with play area over road *(Stan Edwards, LYM)*

Ascot [SU9268], *Royal Foresters*: Large pleasantly decorated and comfortable family dining pub, genuine friendly welcome, relaxed atmosphere, four real ales well kept Courage Directors, good service *(Chris Westmoreland, Mr and Mrs T A Bryan)*

Ashmore Green [Stoney Lane; SU5069], *Sun in the Wood*: Surprisingly rural setting, pleasant flagstoned bar with adjoining restaurant area and imaginative well cooked food, Morlands beers, friendly welcome; big garden with play area *(S J Edwards)*

Aston [Ferry Lane; signed off A4130 Henley—Maidenhead; SU7884], *Flower Pot*: Big unspoilt pub with great garden – views over meadows to cottages and far side of Thames; well kept Brakspears, reasonably priced food, friendly young staff, bare-boards public bar with lots of fish in glass cases, darts, unobtrusive piped music; popular Sun lunchtimes, handy for riverside strolls *(Simon Collett-Jones)*

☆ **Bagnor** [SU4569], *Blackbird*: Homely and peaceful country pub in pretty hamlet nr Watermill Theatre and River Lambourn, low ceilings, leaded lights, good value straightforward lunches, separate evening menu, chatty friendly service, well kept ales such as Fullers London Pride, Marstons Pedigree, Ushers and Websters Yorkshire, sometimes quiet piped music; tables in biggish side garden *(TBB, HNJ, PEJ)*

Beech Hill [Beech Hill Rd; SU6964], *Old Elm Tree*: Good views from friendly family-run pub with pleasant bar and adjoining restaurant, attentive service, good value food, well kept Brakspears *(J and B Cressey, J S M Sheldon)*

☆ **Binfield** [Terrace Rd North; SU8471], *Victoria Arms*: Neat no-frills Fullers pub with good choice of seating areas, well kept real ales inc Chiswick, good reasonably priced bar food, children's room, summer barbecues in quiet garden *(Mr Bowler, LYM)*

Binfield [Forest Rd; B4034 Wokingham—Bracknell], *Warren*: Beams, log fire, extensive range of wines and good reasonably priced food in Stables bar, good homely atmosphere, five real ales inc a guest; play area in big garden *(Emma Peek)*

☆ **Bracknell** [Church Rd; SU8769], *Old Manor*: Big open-plan Wetherspoons pub, one of their few that welcome children, with usual good value food, sensibly priced real ales, big no-smoking area, good solid decor inc original oak beams, twice-yearly beer festival with up to 30 different beers, three pleasant outside areas; very useful for the M4/M25 short cut via M3 *(Chris Westmoreland, Jane Armstrong)*

☆ **Bray** [High St; handy for M4 junction 9; SU9079], *Crown*: 14th-c pub with lots of atmosphere, low beams, timbers and panelling, leather seats, popular food in bar and restaurant, Courage Best and Wadworths 6X, decent wines, friendly helpful service, log fires; well behaved children allowed, plenty of seating outside inc flagstoned vine arbour *(TBB, Martin and Karen Wake, Susan and John Douglas, A C Morrison, LYM)*

Bray, *Hinds Head*: New owners concentrating more on the food side in handsome building dating from 16th c *(TBB)*

☆ **Brimpton** [Brimpton Common; B3051, W of Heath End; SU5564], *Pineapple*: Friendly thatched and low-beamed country pub with stripped brick and timbering, tiled floor, heavy elm furnishings, open fire, snug and cosy atmosphere; friendly and obliging service, seven well kept Whitbreads-related ales, usual food noon-9, side games area, maybe piped pop music; lots of tables on sheltered lawn, play area; open all day; children in eating area, folk music first Sun of month *(Bill Scott, Gordon, LYM)*

☆ **Bucklebury** [Chapel Row; SU5570], *Blade Bone*: Warm, friendly and clean, with plush seats and dark tables, tasteful pictures and plates on pastel walls, matching carpets, small dining room with no-smoking conservatory overlooking neat garden, wide choice of food from sandwiches up inc good value specials cooked to order – so may be a wait; tables outside, play area *(F J and A Parmenter, HNJ, PEJ)*

Chaddleworth [off A338 Hungerford—Wantage; SU4177], *Ibex*: Under new management, with similar layout (but without the horse racing connections) and same chef (no food Sun evenings), Morlands Original and Old Speckled Hen, cheerful landlord; traditional games in public bar, maybe piped pop music; tables out on sheltered lawn and floodlit terrace *(Julie Peters, Colin Blinkhorn, LYM)*

Charvil [Lands End Lane; SU7776], *Lands End*: Warm welcome, several friendly bar cats, fire in winter, Brakspears and Boddingtons, good generous food; nice garden, summer barbecues *(Lynne Fowler, Richard Hanson)*

☆ **Chieveley** [East Lane – handy for M4 junction 13 via A34 N-bound; SU4774], *Olde Red Lion*: Handier for M4 and A34 than the main entry here, roomy and welcoming inside, with low beams, china, horsebrasses, framed cigarette cards, big pictures, farm tools, roaring log fire, good range of home-made food and fresh veg, Arkells ales, attentive quick service, pool, darts; piped music *(HNJ, PEJ, John and Chris Simpson)*

Cookham [Sutton Rd; SU8884], *Ferry*: Splendid riverside position for modernised pub with upstairs Harvester restaurant, nice choice of bar food; big terrace with views of the Thames *(David Carr, LYM)*; [High St], *Royal Exchange*: Pleasantly cosy and welcoming 15th-c Benskins pub with low ceiling, dark panelling, real ale; useful back garden *(Lynda Payton, Sam Samuells)*

☆ **Cookham Dean** [Church Lane, off Hills Lane; SU8785], *Jolly Farmer*: Traditional small rooms, open fires, well kept Courage Best and two guest beers, attractive dining room, good bar food, relaxed service, traditional games, no music or machines, good quiet garden with play area; well behaved children welcome away from bar *(Chris and Martin Taylor, Phoebe Thomas, Heather Martin, Sandra Kench, Steven Norman, Ellie Weld, LYM)*

☆ **Cookham Dean**, *Inn on the Green*: Inviting atmosphere, good solid furniture with attractive tables, unspoilt rambling layout, stripped beams, two-sided log fires, good genuine food, well kept ales inc Fullers London Pride, attractive restaurant; maybe piped music *(Martin and Karen Wake, Ron Leigh)*

Cookham Dean [Dean Lane], *Chequers*: Small very pubby-feeling dining bar with beams, flagstones, old fireplace, country furniture and decorations, imaginative reasonably priced food, well kept real ale, very helpful service, tiny garden, and seats out among hanging baskets *(Susan and John Douglas)*

Cookham Rise [The Pound; B4447 Cookham—Maidenhead; SU8984], *Swan Uppers*: Flagstones, low beams, log fire, friendly management, good range of real ales, bar food, restaurant, unobtrusive piped music; bedrooms *(J and B Cressey, LYM)*

☆ **Curridge** [3 miles from M4 junction 13: A34 towards Newbury, then first left to Curridge, Hermitage, and left into Curridge at Village Only sign – OS Sheet 174 map ref 492723; SU4871], *Bunk*: Stylish dining pub with good adventurous food (not Sun evening), smart stripped-wood tiled-floor bar on left, elegant stable-theme bistro on right with wooded-meadow views and conservatory; four well kept ales, good choice of wines, cheerful efficient service, tables in neat garden *(D C and J V Whitman, Roger Bourne, PHS, BB)*

☆ **East Ilsley** [SU4981], *Swan*: Spacious, neat and well decorated in a slightly hotelish way, with interesting things to look at; wide range

of bar food inc vegetarian, well kept Morlands Original and Charles Wells Bombardier, efficient service, daily papers; no-smoking restaurant, children allowed, tables in courtyard and walled garden with play area; good bedrooms, some in house down road *(Nigel Norman, Bruce Bird, LYM)*

☆ **Eton Wick** [32 Eton Wick Rd; SU9478], *Pickwick*: Welcoming and well kept, with good value food (inc authentic Malay Weds and Sat evenings), pleasant landlord, Youngs ales; maybe piped music *(Dr G W Barnett)*

☆ **Great Shefford** [Shefford Woodland; less than ½ mile N of M4 junction 14, by junction B4000/A338; SU3875], *Pheasant*: Good relaxing motorway break, friendly helpful service in four neat rooms, very wide choice of good generous food inc Sun lunches, well kept Brakspears & Wadworths IPA and 6X, decent wines and coffee, log fires; public bar with games inc ring-the-bull; children welcome, attractive views from garden *(Paul Hilditch, HNJ, PEJ, Roger and Pauline Pearce, Lynda Payton, Sam Samuells, LYM)*

☆ **Hampstead Norreys** [SU5276], *White Hart*: Friendly and spotless low-beamed Morlands pub with wide range of reasonably priced food inc good sandwiches and take-aways, real ales, decent coffee, children welcome; darts, pool and fruit machine in public bar, soft piped music; back terrace and garden *(Joan Olivier)*

Holyport [The Green; 1½ miles from M4 junction 8/9, via A308(M)/A330; SU8977], *George*: Generous helpings of reasonably priced real home cooking in busily pubby low-ceilinged open-plan bar with nice old fireplace, friendly efficient service, Courage real ales; maybe piped pop music; picnic tables outside, lovely village green *(TBB, Mr and Mrs T A Bryan)*

☆ **Hungerford Newtown** [A338 ½ mile S of M4 junction 14; SU3571], *Tally Ho*: Quiet, roomy and well appointed, with good well presented home-made food from sandwiches to steaks (popular with older people at lunchtime), small no-smoking area, well kept ales such as Boddingtons and Wadworths 6X, decent house wines, friendly efficient service, subdued piped music; children if eating *(HNJ, PEJ, J S Green, Mr and Mrs Peter Smith, John and Wendy Trentham)*

☆ **Hurley** [just W, off A4130 up Honey Lane then right at T], *Dew Drop*: Unchanging country pub in very rustic setting, very popular with weekend walkers; fine old inglenook, log fires, good simple bar food (not Sun evening or Mon), well kept Brakspears PA and Old, some good malt whiskies, darts; attractive informal sloping garden *(Mr and Mrs J Liversidge, Ian Phillips, Chris Westmoreland, Mark and Diane Grist, LYM)*

Hurley, *Olde Bell*: Handsome and unusual old-fashioned timbered inn with some remarkable ancient features inc Norman doorway and window; small but comfortable bar with decent bar food, fine gardens, very civilised gents', tolerable piped music; restaurant, bedrooms *(Gordon, TBB, LYM)*

☆ **Hurst** [Hinton Rd/Church Hill; SU7972], *Green Man*: Old-fashioned low-ceilinged local, freshly decorated, with wooden seats and tables and cosy little areas, well kept Brakspears, bar food (not Mon evening), pub games, piped music; pleasant sunny back garden *(D J and P M Taylor, LYM)*

☆ **Inkpen** [Lower Inkpen], *Swan*: Rambling beamed pub, beautifully kept and neat inside if rather sparse, pleasant service, well kept ales such as Adnams, Arkells Kingsdown, Ballards, Brakspears XXX Mild, local Butts, and farm ciders; bar food – also has organic food shop *(HNJ, PEJ, Gordon, LYM)*

☆ **Kintbury** [SU3866], *Dundas Arms*: Clean, tidy and welcoming, with comfortably upmarket feel, bar food (not Mon evening or Sun) from sandwiches to good fresh home-produced dishes, well kept real ales from smaller breweries, good coffee and wines by the glass, no piped music, remarkable range of clarets and burgundies in evening restaurant; pleasant walks by Kennet & Avon Canal, children welcome; comfortable bedrooms opening on to secluded waterside terrace *(Nigel Wilkinson, HNJ, PEJ, TBB, LYM)*

☆ **Knowl Hill** [A4 Reading—Maidenhead; SU8279], *Bird in Hand*: Relaxed civilised atmosphere and good home-made food from sandwiches up in spacious and attractive beamed main bar and restaurant; splendid log fire, cosy alcoves, much older side bar; well kept Brakspears and Fullers London Pride, wide choice of wines and other drinks, friendly helpful staff, good side garden; no-smoking buffet area – where children allowed; clean and tidy modern bedrooms *(R P Daniel, TBB, LYM)*

☆ **Knowl Hill** [A4], *Seven Stars*: Simple old-fashioned relaxing place with good honest bar food from sandwiches to steaks at sensible prices, well kept Brakspears (full range), good choice of wines, a lot of panelling, roaring log fire, sleepy dog and cat; helpful professional service, fruit machine, flowers, big garden with summer barbecue *(J and B Cressey, TBB, Nigel Norman, BB)*

Leckhampstead [SU4376], *Stag*: Very welcoming, with good choice of good value food from sandwiches up, choice of ales, restaurant; quiet village *(Mr and Mrs R Brown)*

☆ **Littlewick Green** [3¾ miles from M4 junction 9; A404(M) then left on to A4, from which village signposted on left; SU8379], *Cricketers*: Charming spot opp cricket green, decent food inc good lunch snacks, friendly service, well kept Brakspears and Boddingtons, neat housekeeping, lots of cricketing pictures *(TBB, Gordon, LYM)*

Maidenhead [High St; SU8783], *Bear*: Large rambling pub in pedestrian area, tables and flowers outside; food inc good soup and fresh bread, no piped music *(TBB, J and B Cressey)*; [Queen St], *Hand & Flowers*: Small,

basic, old-fashioned town pub, no piped music; basic but good food, well kept Brakspears *(TBB)*; [Pinkneys Green, just off A308 N], *Wagon & Horses*: Clean and friendly Morlands pub overlooking green, good value food, pleasant garden, pubby front bar, separate entrance to quiet back lounge *(Chris Westmoreland, TBB)*

☆ **Marsh Benham** [off A4 W of Newbury; SU4267], *Water Rat*: Attractive thatched country dining pub (all tablecloths and napkins, not really a place just for a drink), with good interesting if rather pricey food inc unusual vegetarian dishes, welcoming service; well kept ales such as Brakspears and Wadworths 6X, good choice of other drinks, cheerful Wind in the Willows murals, attractive furnishings, seats on terrace or in charming garden with play area *(Daniela Sieff, Mr and Mrs R A Bryan, Julie and Mike Taylor, Fiona Maclean, AEB, June S Bray, Ian Hepburn, Sue Everett, LYM)*

Newbury [towpath, nr main st; SU4666], *Lock Stock & Barrel*: Long wood-floored curved bar with tables out on canalside terrace, friendly helpful service, well kept Fullers ales, good value bar food, coffee shop open all afternoon; very popular lunchtime, handy for canal walks *(D J and P M Taylor, Phyl and Jack Street)*; [Market Pl], *Old Waggon & Horses*: Sunny flower-filled riverside terrace, big bright and friendly upstairs family dining bar above it, separate traditional front bar; very friendly staff *(Jon Roberts, LYM)*

☆ **Old Windsor** [17 Crimp Hill; off B3021 – itself off A308/A328; SU9874], *Union*: Tidy L-shaped bar with interesting collection of nostalgic show-business photographs, well kept ales such as Fullers London Pride, good bar food from sandwiches up, consistently good friendly service, woodburner in big fireplace, fruit machine; good value attractive copper-decorated restaurant, white plastic tables under cocktail parasols on sunny front terrace, country views; comfortable bedrooms *(Dave Rickell, Ian Phillips, PLB, Piotr Chodzko-Zajko, Mr and Mrs T A Bond, BB)*

☆ **Old Windsor** [Crimp Hill], *Oxford Blue*: Useful family pub, very welcoming, with lots of aeroplane memorabilia inc squadrons of model aeroplanes hanging from ceiling, big conservatory, new extension other end, good food, well kept beer inc Adnams, nice old benches built into front verandah, tables outside, children's play area *(Ian Phillips, Piotr Chodzko-Zajko, Mr and Mrs Cox, John and Elisabeth Cox)*

Pangbourne [Shooters Hill; SU6376], *Swan*: Attractive riverside pub dating from 1642, good range of bar food all day 7 days a week, good wine list, tea and coffee, Morlands ales, unobtrusive piped music; picnic tables and moorings; balcony and conservatory reserved for diners *(Roberto Villa, Paul C McPherson)*

☆ **Reading** [10 Castle St, next to PO; SU7272], *Sweeney & Todd*: Exceptional value home-made pies, adventurous and generously served, such as hare and cherry, peach and pigeon, in warren of small cosy rooms, restaurant with cubby holes in cellar area, four well kept real ales upstairs; access via front pie shop; very busy lunchtime, maybe cl bank hols *(Paul Bispham, D J and P M Taylor, Andy Cunningham, Yvonne Hannaford)*

☆ Reading [Kennet Side – easiest to walk from Orts Rd, off Kings Rd], *Fishermans Cottage*: Welcoming pub by canal lock and towpath, lovely big back garden, relaxed atmosphere, modern furnishings of character, pleasant stone snug behind woodburning range, light and airy conservatory; good value pub lunches (very popular then), evening food inc Mexican, well kept Fullers ales, small choice of wines, small darts room, SkyTV *(TBB, D J and P M Taylor, Mark and Diane Grist, C Scott-Malden)*

Reading [2 Broad St], *Hobgoblin*: Small real ale local with panelling, cubicles, basic seating, separate back room, four well kept Wychwood ales, three rapidly changing guests from small breweries (well over 1,000 so far), two farm ciders, unusual lunchtime filled rolls; piped music, occasional live; open all day *(Paul Bispham, Richard Lewis, DW)*; [Southampton St], *Hop Leaf*: Friendly local refurbished with a modern look by the Hop Back brewery, nice atmosphere, full range of well kept Hop Back beers and some brewed on the premises – maybe even an interesting stout; parking close by difficult *(Mark and Diane Grist, Graham Edwards, Allen Parker)*; [120 Castle Hill], *Horse & Jockey*: Comfortable and friendly, with half a dozen consistently well kept unusual real ales from changing small breweries (two you tap yourself down in the cellar), farm cider, good staff, wide choice of good value food; TV; open all day *(Richard Lewis)*; [Rly Stn, Platform 4], *Three Guineas*: Huge pub with lots of interest, well kept real ale, reasonable value food, good bustle at rush hour, American-style central bar *(Dr and Mrs A K Clarke, Mr and Mrs S G Turner)*

☆ Remenham [A4130, just over bridge E of Henley; SU7683], *Little Angel*: Good atmosphere, tasty bar meals from sandwiches up, more expensive restaurant food and friendly efficient service in low-beamed dining pub with panelling and darkly bistroish decor; splendid range of wines by the glass, well kept Brakspears, floodlit terrace *(Jenny Garrett, James Nunns)*

Riseley [SU7263], *Bull*: Good welcoming atmosphere, good range of well kept real ales, decent choice of good bar food inc huge vegetarian dishes *(Dr M Owton)*

Shinfield [Shinfield Rd; SU7368], *Black Boy*: Beamed local with old-world decor, stripped brickwork, good choice of good value food inc plenty of proper veg, friendly licensees *(E G Drain)*

Shurlock Row [SU8374], *White Hart*: Friendly staff in attractive panelled pub, warm, comfortable and relaxing, with

inglenook fireplace dividing bar from other rooms; flying memorabilia inc squadron badges, old pictures and brasses, Whitbreads-related ales, decent lunchtime food *(Chris and Martin Taylor, J and B Cressey)*

Slough [Albert St, Upton; SU9779], *Red Cow*: Friendly locals, good filled brown rolls, reasonably priced meals *(Mary Walters)*

☆ Sonning [High St – signed off A4 E of Reading; SU7575], *Bull*: Attractive old-fashioned inn in pretty setting nr Thames, low heavy beams, cosy alcoves, cushioned antique settles and low-slung chairs, inglenook fireplaces, no-smoking back dining area (children allowed); well kept Gales Best, HSB and BBB and a guest beer, lots of country wines, bar lunches from filled french sticks to seafood and steaks, charming courtyard; bedrooms *(Mr and Mrs J R Morris, I E Folkard-Evans, GWB, Gordon, Sandra Kench, Steven Norman, D and D Savidge, Christine and Geoff Butler, LYM)*

☆ Stanford Dingley [SU5771], *Old Boot*: Clean and stylishly comfortable 18th-c beamed pub in lovely village setting, simple country furniture and settles, inglenook fire, copper warming pans and prints, friendly chatty licensees, lively atmosphere, four real ales such as Archers and Brakspears, wide choice of generous reasonably priced bar food inc some really creative dishes, unpretentiously upmarket restaurant area, big suntrap back garden *(Susan and John Douglas, Roger Byrne, Gordon, LYM)*

☆ Swallowfield [S of Reading on Farley Hill lane – OS Sheet 175 map ref 735647; SU7364], *George & Dragon*: Old country pub attractively and comfortably modernised, good value food inc imaginative dishes, well kept Wadworths 6X and other ales (staff bring drinks to table), good choice of wines, welcoming young staff, broad appeal; can get very busy, best to book *(Nigel Norman, Louise Harrison)*

☆ Theale [Church St; SU6371], *Volunteer*: Open-plan, with flagstones in public bar, comfortable carpeted lounge with historical military prints, nice wooden furniture, well kept Fullers, good generous bar food (not Sun evening), friendly considerate staff, quiet piped music, free Sun nibbles; children at reasonable times, tables in small garden *(Bruce Bird, Chris and Andy Crow)*

☆ Waltham St Lawrence [Broadmoor Lane (B3024) – OS Sheet 175 map ref 833765; SU8376], *Star*: Interesting old pub, immaculately clean and tidy, with good enterprising restaurant meals (a couple of tables straying into bar area, some no-smoking), beams, brasses, newspapers on hangers, open fire, full range of Wadworths beers *(Dr and Mrs R Denning and friends, TRS)*

White Waltham [Waltham Rd; SU8577], *Beehive*: Friendly local by cricket field, smallish front bar and larger back saloon, Whitbreads-related beers, unpretentious food *(Chris Westmoreland, Mr and Mrs T A Bryan)*

Wickham [3 miles from M4 junction 14, via A338, B4000; SU3971], *Five Bells*: Neatly kept local in racehorse-training country, big log fire, tasty food, tables tucked into low eaves, well kept ales inc Ringwood, friendly landlord, garden with good play area; children in eating area, good value bedrooms *(Jeff Davies, Mark Brock, Gordon, LYM)*

Windsor [St Leonards Rd; SU9575], *Trooper*: Thriving small one-bar pub with pool table discreetly tucked away at back, Scottish Courage beers, cheap and cheerful lunchtime food, friendly faultless service; barbecues on terrace which seems much bigger than pub itself; bedrooms *(Ben Hanna)*; [Park St, off High St next to Mews], *Two Brewers*: Snug bars, good interesting home-made lunchtime food, relaxed and pleasant atmosphere, tables out on pavement of Georgian street; has been open all day summer *(I E Folkard-Evans)*

Winkfield [Lovel Rd; SU9171], *Winkfield*: Log fire, helpful friendly staff, great atmosphere, good food in bar and evening restaurant *(Deborah Peters)*

Winterbourne [not far from M4 junction 13; SU4572], *Winterbourne Arms*: Nice old building carefully refurbished to point up its interesting features, pleasantly old-fashioned decor, tables in attractive front garden and on green over quiet village lane; good rather restauranty food, friendly and obliging service, good choice of real ales, play area, nearby walks *(Jerry Hughes, Julie and Mike Taylor, Julie Peters, Colin Blinkhorn, LYM)*

Wokingham [Gardeners Green, Honey Hill – OS Sheet 175 map ref 826668; SU8266], *Crooked Billet*: Homely country pub with pews, tiles, brick serving counter, crooked black joists, big helpings of good value genuinely home-cooked lunchtime food, well kept Brakspears, friendly service, small no-smoking restaurant area where children allowed, cosy local atmosphere; nice outside

in summer, very busy weekends *(Mark and Diane Grist, J W Joseph, Andy Cunningham, Yvonne Hannaford, LYM)*

Wokingham [Denmark St], *Dukes Head*: Well kept Brakspears beers, wide range of lunchtime food, good atmosphere *(D J and P M Taylor)*; [Peach St], *Ship*: Popular lunchtime for food inc good doorstep sandwiches, well kept Fullers ESB *(Andy Cunningham, Yvonne Hannaford)*

Woodside [SU9270], *Rose & Crown*: New licensee doing well, good bar and service, lovely setting; bedrooms (not Sun) *(Nicholas Holmes)*

☆ **Woolhampton** [A4; SU5767], *Rising Sun*: Unpretentious pub which has had half a dozen or more well kept and interesting real ales, good welcoming service, plentiful home-made food inc huge reasonably priced sandwiches. Good choice of real ales and popular bar food in small friendly pub with games in public bar; restaurant *(Tony and Wendy Hobden, MG, DG, LYM)*

☆ **Woolhampton** [Station Rd (off A4 opp Angel)], *Rowbarge*: Big canalside family dining place, smartly done up with pheasants, blowlamps and so on, candlelit tables, beamed bar, panelled side room, small snug, no-smoking back conservatory, tables in big garden with fishpond, well kept Courage Best, Brakspears SB, Fullers London Pride, Greene King Abbot and Wadworths 6X; prices high, lots of children, service can lack personal touch *(Mr and Mrs J Hall, C P R Baxter, D E Twitchett, Sandra Kench, Steven Norman, Wilson Carlisle, Susan and John Douglas, Nigel and Lindsay Chapman, Dave Braisted, Mark and Diane Grist, LYM)*

Wraysbury [High St; TQ0174], *Perseverance*: Friendly staff, comfortably worn-in bar areas, small but decent restaurant (can have bar meals in there too), Courage ales, back garden with aviary *(Guy Charrison)* -

---

Post Office address codings confusingly give the impression that some pubs are in Berkshire, when they're really in Oxfordshire or Hampshire (which is where we list them).

Buckinghamshire

A good crop of new main entries here consists of the Russell Arms at Butlers Cross (exceptional food in what at first seems a very ordinary roadside pub), the Green Dragon in Haddenham (very good food here too, in rather upmarket surroundings), the Polecat at Prestwood (interesting and bustling – a popular lunch place), and the Chequers at Wheeler End (a delightfully unpretentious traditional pub of the very best sort). Other Buckinghamshire pubs currently doing really well include the Mole & Chicken at Easington (the new licensee of this very individual dining pub has worked there for years, so no need for crossed fingers), the Royal Standard of England at Forty Green (tremendous atmosphere), the civilised Hampden Arms at Great Hampden, the Stag & Huntsman at Hambleden (good all round), and the totally no smoking Old Crown at Skirmett. New licensees at the Angel in Long Crendon are doing very good modern cooking. Among the Lucky Dips at the end of the chapter, pubs of special note at the moment are the Old Thatched Inn at Adstock, Bull & Butcher at Akeley, Bottle & Glass near Aylesbury, Blue Flag at Cadmore End, Bell at Chearsley, Swan at Denham, Chequers at Fingest, Pink & Lily at Lacey Green, Two Brewers in Marlow (which has several other worthy pubs, too), Hit or Miss at Penn Street, White Hart at Preston Bisset and Old Swan at The Lee; we have inspected almost all of these, and can give them a clear thumbs-up. Pub prices here are among the highest in Britain, with a pint of beer typically costing about 15p more than the national average. In other areas local breweries often do a lot to hold prices down, with lower prices than the big national chains. Brakspears however, the main local brewer here, has prices which closely match the national brewers'; the pub which we did find was much the cheapest here was the Cross Keys in Great Missenden, tied to Fullers of London.

---

nr AMERSHAM SU9495 Map 4
Queens Head 🐷

Whielden Gate; pub in sight just off A404, 1½ miles towards High Wycombe at Winchmore Hill turn-off; OS Sheet 165 map reference 941957

The low-beamed, friendly bar in this unpretentious old brick and tile pub has traditional furnishings, horsebrasses, and lots of brass spigots; flagstones surround the big inglenook fireplace (which still has the old-fashioned wooden built-in wall seat curving around right in beside the woodburning stove – with plenty of space under the seat for logs), and there's also a stuffed albino pheasant, old guns, and a good cigarette card collection. The family room is no smoking. Home-made bar food – using home-grown vegetables from the garden – includes sandwiches, soup (£2.25), sweet pickled trout (£3.50), omelettes (£4), spinach and walnut pancakes with cheese sauce (£5), pizzas (from £5; you can take them away as well), and chicken supreme with stilton sauce (£5.75). Well kept Adnams, Greene King IPA, Marlow Rebellion and Smuggler, and Youngs Special on handpump, and several malt whiskies; darts, shove-ha'penny, dominoes, cribbage, fruit machine, and piped music. The garden is quite a busy place with bantams running around, an aviary with barns owls, a rabbit in a large run,

swings, a climbing frame and slide, and maybe Monty the elderly dalmatian.
(Recommended by Ian Phillips, Dr G W Barnett, SR, PM, Piotr Chodzko-Zajko; more reports please)

Free house ~ Licensees Les and Mary Anne Robbins ~ Real ale ~ Meals and snacks (till 10pm; not Sun evening) ~ (01494) 725240 ~ Children in family room ~ Open 11-3, 5.30(6 Sat)-11; 12-3, 7-10.30 Sun

BEACONSFIELD SU9490 Map 2
Greyhound

A mile from M40 junction 2, via A40; Windsor End, Old Town

You can be sure of a warm welcome from the entertaining landlord and his staff in this neatly kept and cosy two-bar former coaching inn. And the wide choice of good home-made food is quite a draw too: filled french bread or granary sandwiches (from £2.95), home-made burgers (from £4.95), interesting pies such as chicken and leek in stilton sauce, delicious pork, apple and cider, a vegetarian garlic mushroom one or seafood (from £4.75), popular bubble and squeak with sausage or ham, cheese or beef (from £5.45), and lots of daily specials (5 starters, 5 pastas, 5 main courses and 5 puddings) like crispy duck and spring onion salad or fresh sardines (around £3.45), pasta with all sorts of sauces (£5.95), fresh fish, steaks, and good traditional puddings like treacle tart, bread and butter pudding or summer pavlovas (from £2.75); there's also a partly no smoking back bistro-like restaurant. Well kept Courage Best, Fullers London Pride and Wadworths 6X, with two guest beers on handpump; no piped music and no children. *(Recommended by Kevin Thomas, Janet and Colin Roe, TBB, John Curry, GWB, DJW)*

Free house ~ Licensees Jamie and Wendy Godrich ~ Real ale ~ Meals and snacks (till 10pm; not Sun evening) ~ Restaurant ~ (01494) 673823 ~ Open 11-3, 5.30-11; 12-3, 7-10.30 Sun

BLEDLOW SP7702 Map 4
Lions of Bledlow

From B4009 from Chinnor towards Princes Risborough, the first right turn about 1 mile outside Chinnor goes straight to the pub; from the second, wider right turn, turn right through village

Set in the heart of the Chilterns – and with lots of surrounding walks – this 16th-c pub has marvellous views from its bay windows over a small quiet green to the plain stretched out below. There are seats on the sheltered crazy-paved terrace and more on the series of neatly kept small sloping lawns. Inside, the attractive low-beamed rooms are full of character. The inglenook bar has attractive oak stalls built into one partly panelled wall, more seats in a good bay window, and an antique settle resting on the deeply polished ancient tiles; log fires and a woodburning stove. Bar food includes big filled french bread (from £3.25), ploughman's (£4), vegetarian pancakes (£4.75), steak and Guinness pie (£5.50), chicken tikka masala (£6.25), Scotch rump steak (£8.95), and daily specials like salmon in dill sauce or fillet of pork in a cream and mushroom sauce; the restaurant is no smoking. Well kept Courage Best, Marstons Pedigree, Rebellion Mutiny, John Smiths, and Wadworths 6X on handpump. One of the two cottagey side rooms has a video game, as well as darts, shove-ha'penny, dominoes, cribbage, fruit machine, and trivia. *(Recommended by K Leist, Dr G W Barnett, Jan and Colin Roe, Paul Kitchener)*

Free house ~ Licensee Mark McKeown ~ Real ale ~ Meals and snacks (not winter Sun evening) ~ Restaurant ~ (01844) 343345 ~ Well behaved children welcome ~ Open 11.30-3(3.30 Sat), 6-11; 12-3.30, 7-10.30 Sun (may open longer hours in summer); closed 25 Dec

---

Food details, prices, timing etc refer to bar food – not to a separate restaurant if there is one.

BOLTER END SU7992 Map 4
Peacock

Just over 4 miles from M40 junction 5; A40 to Stokenchurch, then B482

After nearly 19 years here, the enthusiastic licensees tell us they are still enjoying themselves. The brightly modernised bar has a rambling series of alcoves, a good log fire, and a cheerful atmosphere; the Old Darts bar is no smoking. Good home-made bar food includes lunchtime sandwiches and ploughman's three changing hot specials, and cheesy mushroom pancakes (£5.25), local butcher sausages (£5.50), steak and kidney pie (£6.25), stir-fry lime and ginger sliced chicken breast (£6.95), stincotto (a big lean gammon hock with beans, £7.25 or £9.95), fillet of fresh salmon with herby mayonnaise (£7.50), half a roast shoulder of lamb (£8.95), Aberdeen Angus steaks (from £8.50), and puddings like fruit crumble, sponge pudding or orange and brandy crêpes (£2.75); roast topside of Aberdeen Angus beef (£6.50). Well kept Bass, Brakspears Bitter, and Tetleys Bitter on handpump, decent wines, and freshly squeezed orange juice; cribbage and dominoes. In summer there are seats around a low stone table and picnic tables in the neatly kept garden. The 'no children' is strictly enforced here and there is no piped music. *(Recommended by Mr and Mrs T A Bond, Mark Hydes, Dr G W Barnett, Mr and Mrs R A Bryan, John Waller)*

Carlsberg Tetley ~ Lease: Peter and Janet Hodges ~ Real ale ~ Meals and snacks (not Sun evening) ~ (01494) 881417 ~ Open 11.45-2.30, 6-11; 11.45-3 Sun (closed Sun evening)

BRILL SP6513 Map 4
Pheasant ♀

Windmill St; village signposted from B4011 Bicester—Long Crendon

Readers very much like the warm, friendly and unpretentious atmosphere here. The quietly modernised and neatly kept beamed bar has refectory tables and windsor chairs, a woodburning stove, and a step up to a dining area which is decorated with attractively framed Alken hunting prints. The views from both rooms are marvellous. Bar food includes Greek salad with feta cheese and olives (£3.95), home-cooked ham and eggs or king tiger prawns in garlic (£4.95), chicken breasts with five different types of sauces (£6.95), and rump steaks with six different sauces (£9.50). Well kept Marstons Pedigree and Tetleys on handpump, and at least six good wines by the glass; piped music. No dogs (they have two golden retrievers themselves). The verandah overlooks the windmill opposite – one of the oldest post windmills still in working order. There are also some picnic tables in the small, sheltered back garden. Roald Dahl used to drink here, and some of the tales the locals told him were worked into his short stories. *(Recommended by Andy and Jill Kassube, Steve de Mellow, E J Gibson, Mr and Mrs T Bryan, D and J McMillan, Howard Gregory, K H Frostick, Paul Kitchener, M Sargent)*

Free house ~ Licensee Mike Carr ~ Real ale ~ Meals and snacks ~ Restaurant ~ (01844) 237104 ~ Children welcome ~ Open 11-3, 6-11; 12-11 Sun; closed 25 Dec

BUTLERS CROSS SP8406 Map 4
Russell Arms ⊗

Chalkshire Rd; off A4010 S of Aylesbury, at Nash Lee roundabout; or off A413 in Wendover, passing station

A classic insider's pub, this: as you pass, it looks so ordinary that you'd never guess the food is so special. The small bar is also entirely straightforward, with standard pub furnishings, but here you get the first hints of a treat to come, in the fresh and subtle aromas that sometimes waft intriguingly through from the kitchen. The bar food is very good, and good value, with a wide standard choice and changing dishes of the day such as beef casseroled in red wine (£5.25), venison casserole or liver and bacon (£5.75), duck done with cherries and star anise (£6.25) or the day's fresh fish (£6.95), all served with vegetables done just so. But it's the main menu that has the gems, especially fish and seafood. On our inspection visit they were doing dressed crab (£5.25), giant prawns (£5.75), skate poached in cider with a cream and chive sauce (£9.95), tilapia done with rosemary and lemon (£10.35), bass with cucumber relish (£10.95), huge succulent scallops, their creamy richness cut with fennel and dill (£11.35) and lobster done with spinach and mushrooms in a brandy sauce (£12.95). Other dishes are equally inventive (rack of lamb done with red pepper, mango and coriander, for instance, at £11.35), and puddings excellent. You can eat any of this in the bar, but to do such cooking justice you'd probably choose the small but light and airy dining room opening off it – charmingly set tables. ABC Best and Flowers Original on handpump; decent wines; good friendly service, pleasantly relaxed atmosphere; darts, cribbage, dominoes, video game, and piped nostalgic pop music. Out in front are picnic tables, with more in a garden screened from the road by tall hedges. The pub is well placed for Chilterns walks. *(Recommended by B Hillyard, Mrs Y Goodwin)*

Pubmaster ~ Tenant Ron Redding ~ Real ale ~ Meals and snacks (not Sun evening, not Mon) ~ (01296) 622618 ~ Children allowed in lounge bar ~ Open 11-3, 6-11; 12-3, 7-10.30 Sun; closed Mon lunchtime

CADMORE END SU7892 Map 4
Old Ship 🍺

B482 Stokenchurch—Marlow

The same friendly family have run this genuinely unspoilt country pub since 1919. The furnishings in the tiny low-beamed two-room bar (unchanged for decades) are pretty basic – leatherette wall benches and stools in the carpeted room on the right, and on the left scrubbed country tables, bench seating (one still has a hole for a game called five-farthings) bare boards and darts, shove-ha'penny, cribbage, dominoes, and shut-the-box. But what matters is the warmth of the landlady's cheerful welcome, the fine quality of the Brakspears PA, SB and Old tapped directly from casks down in the cellar, and the unhurried atmosphere. Food is simple but decent and carefully prepared: filled french bread (from £1.80; bacon, lettuce and tomato £2.50, steak £3.25), soup (£2.15), chilli con carne (£4.95), and daily specials such as good local speciality sausages (£3.95), pork stew with sour cream (£5.25), and beef stroganoff (£5.95). There are seats on the terrace (with more in the sheltered garden), a large pergola with picnic tables, and an enclosed play area for children (who may not be allowed inside). Parking is on the other side of the road. *(Recommended by Mark Hydes, Mayur Shah, Gordon, Pete Baker, Ian Phillips)*

Brakspears ~ Tenants Thomas and Julie Chapman ~ Real ale ~ Meals and snacks (not Sun, Mon or Tues evenings) ~ (01494) 883496 ~ Open 12-2.30(3 Sat), 6-11; 12-3, 7-10.30 Sun; closed 26 Dec, 1 Jan

CHEDDINGTON SP9217 Map 4
Old Swan

58 High St

The quietly civilised bar rooms on the right in this mainly thatched old pub have quite a few horsebrasses and little hunting prints on the walls, old-fashioned plush dining chairs, a built-in wall bench, a few tables with nice country-style chairs on the bare boards, and a big inglenook with brass in glass cabinets on either side of it. On the other side of the main door is a room with housekeeper's chairs on the rugs and quarry tiles and country plates on the walls, and a step up to a carpeted part with stripey wallpaper and pine furniture. Bar food includes sandwiches (from £2), filled baked potatoes (from £2.75), vegetable lasagne or liver and bacon (£4.95), gammon and egg (£5.25), home-made steak and mushroom pie (£6.25), daily specials, children's dishes (£2.50), and puddings; the restaurant is partly no smoking. Well kept ABC Best, Adnams Bitter, Ridgeway Bitter (from Tring), and weekly changing guest beers on handpump, quite a few malt whiskies, and decent wines; pleasant staff. Fruit machine and piped music. In summer, the pub is attractively decorated with colourful hanging baskets and tubs, and there's a children's play area in the garden. *(Recommended by Monica Shelley, Laura Darlington, Ian Phillips, Peter and Liz Wilkins, Mel Smith, Shirley Cannings, George Atkinson, Gordon Tong)*

Carlsberg Tetleys ~ *Lease: Maurice and Joyce Cook ~ Real ale ~ Meals and snacks (12-2.30, 7-9 weekdays, 12-4, 7-9 weekends) ~ Restaurant ~ (01296) 668226 ~ Children welcome ~ Live music/quiz night Weds ~ Open 11-11; 11-3, 5-11 on winter Mon, Tues Weds; 12-10.30 Sun*

CHENIES TQ0198 Map 2
Red Lion

2 miles from M25 junction 18; A404 towards Amersham, then village signposted on right; Chesham Rd

There's usually quite a queue of cars outside this pub at lunchtime – which says quite a lot for the food here. The unpretentious L-shaped bar has original photographs of the village and of traction engines, beige or plum-coloured cushions on the built-in wall benches by the front windows, and traditional seats and tables; there's also a small back snug and a dining room. Bar food includes filled french bread and baps (from £3.50; the bacon and Mars Bar is new this year), baked potatoes with fillings such as tuna niçoise or chicken with watercress and grain mustard dressing (from £3.50), pasta with smoked salmon and courgettes in a pesto sauce and crumb topping or aubergine stuffed with lamb and sweet potato (£5.95), pies such as their much liked lamb pie or chicken and lemon (£6.75), escalope of pork stuffed with peanut and mushroom with a rum sauce (£9.95), steaks (from £10.50), daily specials, and puddings (from £2.50). Well kept Benskins Best, Rebellion Lion Pride (brewed for the pub), Vale Notley, and Wadworths 6X on handpump. The hanging baskets and window boxes are pretty in summer. No children, games machines or piped music. *(Recommended by Ian Phillips, Peter Saville, Ken and Jenny Simmonds, Thomas Nott, Gordon, Christopher Turner)*

Free house ~ Licensees Heather and Mike Norris ~ Real ale ~ Meals and snacks (till 10pm) ~ (01923) 282722 ~ Open 11-2.30, 5.30-11; 12-3, 6.30-10.30 Sun; closed 25 Dec

DINTON SP7611 Map 4
Seven Stars

Stars Lane; follow Dinton signpost into New Road off A418 Aylesbury—Thame, near Gibraltar turn-off

Readers enjoy coming to this pretty old village pub as they know they will be warmly welcomed and cared for by the attentive licensees. The characterful public bar (known as the Snug here) is notable for the two highly varnished ancient built-in settles facing each other across a table in front of the vast stone inglenook fireplace. The spotlessly kept lounge bar, with its beams, joists and growing numbers of old tools on the walls, is comfortably and simply modernised – and although these rooms are not large, there is a spacious and comfortable restaurant area. Popular, good value bar food includes sandwiches (from £1.80; toasties 25p extra), soup (£2.25), filled baked potatoes (from £2.90), ploughman's, vegetable lasagne or ham and egg (£4), good beef bourguignon (£5), steaks (from £9.25), daily specials (the liver and bacon and the chicken and leek pie are liked), and puddings (from £2.15). Well kept ABC, Ind Coope Burton, and Vale Wychert Ale on handpump; dominoes and piped music. There are tables under cocktail parasols on the terrace, with more on the lawn of the pleasant sheltered garden. *(Recommended by Marjorie and David Lamb, Douglas Miller, Ian Phillips, Duncan Satterly, Mark Hydes, M Sargent, Mick and Mel Smith, Graham and Karen Oddey, D P and J A Sweeney, Mrs J Oakes)*

Free house ~ Licensees Rainer and Sue Eccard ~ Real ale ~ Meals and snacks (not Sun or Tues evenings) ~ Restaurant ~ Children in eating area of bar and in restaurant ~ (01296) 748241 ~ Open 12-3, 6-11; 12-3, 7-10.30 Sun; closed Tues evening

---

All *Guide* inspections are anonymous. Anyone claiming to be a *Good Pub Guide* inspector is a fraud, and should be reported to us with name and description.

EASINGTON SP6810 Map 4
Mole & Chicken ⓜ ♀

From B4011 in Long Crendon follow Chearsley, Waddesdon signpost into Carters Lane opposite the Chandos Arms, then turn left into Chilton Road

It's the popular food that draws people to this bustling country dining pub – though there is quite a bit of standing space to enjoy the well kept Fullers London Pride, Morlands Old Speckled Hen and Tetleys on handpump. As well as daily specials, the menu includes home-made soup (£3.50), home-made duck liver pâté or chicken satay (£4.95), herring fillets in madeira (£5.50), steak and kidney pie (£6.95), pasta with various sauces, vegetarian dishes (from £6.95), chicken curry (£7.50), barbecued spare ribs (£7.95), chicken piri piri (£8.95), half shoulder of lamb with honey, garlic and rosemary sauce (£10.95), and steaks (from £11.95); it's essential to book. Decent French house wines (and a good choice by the bottle), and 79 malt whiskies; friendly staff. It's open-plan but very well done, so that all the different parts seem quite snug and self-contained without being cut off from what's going on, and the atmosphere is chatty and relaxed. The beamed bar curves around the serving counter in a sort of S-shape – unusual, as is the decor of designed-and-painted floor, pink walls with lots of big antique prints, and even at lunchtime lit candles on the medley of tables to go with the nice mix of old chairs; good winter log fires. There's a smallish garden with picnic tables under cocktail parasols, with an outside summer bar and maybe lunchtime summer barbecues. No dogs. *(Recommended by Graham and Karen Oddey, Peter Saville, Abigail Dombey, Kate Nash, Jim and Maggie Cowell, Alison Haines, D and J McMillan, Mark Gillis)*

Free house ~ Licensee Tracey Gardner ~ Real ale ~ Meals and snacks (till 10pm; all day Sun) ~ (01844) 208387 ~ Children welcome ~ Open 12-3, 6-11; all day Sun; closed 25 Dec

FAWLEY SU7586 Map 2
Walnut Tree 🛏 ♀

Village signposted off A4155 (then right at T-junction) and off B480, N of Henley

In a lovely Chilterns spot, this popular dining pub is not somewhere to come for a quick drink. You can choose to eat in the bar with its stripey red wallpaper and red carpet (and where the food is cheaper) or the no smoking conservatory or the restaurant. The bar menu offers ploughman's (£3.95), baked stuffed aubergine (£4.95), curry of the day or chicken oriental (£6.25), home-made burger or salmon and lemon sole goujons (£6.50), and daily specials like roast breast of barbary duck, braised rabbit or lemon sole with caper butter; potatoes are £1 extra and vegetables £1.50. Well kept Brakspears PA and Special on handpump, and a good range of wines. The big lawn around the front car park has some well spaced tables made from elm trees, with some seats in a covered terrace extension – and a hitching rail for riders. *(Recommended by Gwen and Peter Andrews, Mary and Des Kemp, Mayur Shah, Mark Hydes, June S Bray, GWB, Peter Saville, Cyril Brown, RJH)*

Brakspears ~ Tenants Ben and Diane Godbolt ~ Real ale ~ Meals and snacks ~ Restaurant ~ (01491) 638360 ~ Children in conservatory and in restaurant ~ Open 12-3, 6-11; 12-3, 7-10.30 Sun; closed Sun evenings Jan/Feb ~ Bedrooms: £40S/£50S

FORD SP7709 Map 4
Dinton Hermit

Village signposted between A418 and B4009, SW of Aylesbury

Relaxed and friendly, this tucked away stone cottage has an attractively traditional partly tiled public bar on the left with scrubbed tables, a woodburning stove in its huge inglenook, and prints of a lady out hunting. The lounge on the right, with a log fire, has red plush banquettes along the cream walls and red leatherette chairs around polished tables, and red leatherette seats built into the stripped stone walls of a small room leading off. Mrs Tompkins cooks the good bar food, and at lunchtime, when they don't take reservations, this might include sandwiches (from £1.50), soup

(£2.25), ploughman's (from £3.50), smoked haddock in mushroom and cheese sauce (£5.25), a vegetarian hotpot or home-made lasagne (£5.25), chicken curry or stilton and asparagus pancake (£5.95), and puddings such as home-made fruit pie or bread pudding (£2.75); in the evening (when you must book), dishes are slightly more expensive and include more grills and fish. Well kept ABC Best, Adnams, and Wadworths 6X on handpump; darts, shove-ha'penny, cribbage and dominoes. The sheltered and well planted garden opposite (they don't serve food out there in the evenings) has swings, a slide and a seesaw. *(Recommended by Quentin Williamson, Mary and Des Kemp, M Sargent, Karen and Graham Oddey, Gordon, John Fahy)*

Free house ~ Licensees John and Jane Tompkins ~ Real ale ~ Meals and snacks (not Sun or Mon) ~ (01296) 748379 ~ Well behaved children welcome ~ Open 11-2.30, 6-11; 12-2, 7-10.30 Sun; closed Mon lunchtimes

FORTY GREEN SU9292 Map 2
Royal Standard of England
3½ miles from M40 junction 2, via A40 to Beaconsfield, then follow sign to Forty Green, off B474 ¾ mile N of New Beaconsfield

A favourite with quite a few readers, this marvellously atmospheric old pub has rambling rooms with finely carved old oak panelling, roaring winter fires with handsomely decorated iron firebacks, huge black ship's timbers, and a massive settle apparently built to fit the curved transom of an Elizabethan ship; also, ancient pewter and pottery tankards, rifles, powder-flasks and bugles, lots of brass and copper, needlework samplers, and stained glass. Two areas are no smoking. Bar food includes home-made soup, locally-made sausages, various pies, properly made curries, several vegetarian dishes, steaks, and daily specials such as pork escalope with cider or poached salmon with herbed watercress sauce (£7.95), and mediterranean lamb brochettes with fragrant rice (£8.95). Well kept Adnams Best, Brakspears PA, and Vale Notley on handpump, and several malt whiskies. There are seats outside in a neatly hedged front rose garden, or in the shade of a tree. *(Recommended by Susan and John Douglas, Lawrence Pearse, Mayur Shah, DFL, Dr G W Barnett, Chris and Martin Taylor, Chris and Andy Crow, John and Phyllis Maloney)*

Free house ~ Licensees Cyril and Carol Cain, Georgina Henry ~ Real ale ~ Meals and snacks ~ (01494) 673382 ~ Children welcome ~ Open 11-3, 5.30-11; 12-3, 7-10.30 Sun

FRIETH SU7990 Map 2
Prince Albert 🍺 ♀
Village signposted off B482 in Lane End; turn right towards Fingest just before village

Warmly welcoming staff and locals will make you feel quickly at home in this cosy and pretty little tiled cottage with its quiet buzz of conversation – no noisy machines or piped music. On the left there are brocaded cushions on high-backed settles (one with its back panelled in neat squares), a big black stove in a brick inglenook with a bison's head looking out beside it, copper pots on top, and earthenware flagons in front, hop bines on the mantelbeam and on the low black beams and joists, a leaded-light built-in wall cabinet of miniature bottles. The slightly larger area on the right has more of a medley of chairs and a big log fire; magazines, books and local guides to read. Well kept Brakspears Bitter, Special, Mild, Old and OBJ on handpump; Georges Duboeuf house wines, decent whiskies on optic include Smiths Glenlivet and Jamesons, and elderflower pressé. Bar food includes good home-made soup (£2.85), an excellent assortment of generous fillings for hot granary bread rolls with salad (around £3.45), such as cheese and onion, giant sausage, black pudding and bacon or pastrami and cucumber, with a handful of robust hot dishes such as ham and eggs, special sausages or boiled bacon with parsley sauce (around £5.50). Cribbage and dominoes. The lovely dog is called Leo. A nicely planted informal side garden has views of woods and fields, and there are plenty of nearby walks. Please note, children are not allowed inside. *(Recommended by Anthony Longden, Mark Hydes, DJW, Mayur Shah, TBB, Pete Baker, Simon Collett-Jones, Lynda Payton, Sam Samuells, Pete Baker)*

Brakspears ~ Tenant Frank Reynolds ~ Real ale ~ Meals and snacks (lunchtime only; not Sun) ~ (01494) 881683 ~ Open 11-3, 5.30-11; 12-3, 7-10.30 Sun

GREAT HAMPDEN SP8401 Map 4
Hampden Arms ⑨

Village signposted off A4010 S of Princes Risborough; OS Sheet 165 map reference 845015

Don't be taken in by the slightly plain looking exterior here – this is a civilised dining pub offering some fine cooking. At lunchtime there's an additional brunch menu: filled baked potatoes, lemon sole with baby prawns in a robust cheese and lobster sauce or good cottage pie (£4.95), seafood pancake (£5.95) or 4oz sirloin steak (£7.95); also, home-made soup (£2.95), home-made chicken and brandy pâté (£4.95), vegetable lasagne (£5.95), enjoyable chicken curry (£6.95), steak and mushroom pie (£7.25), home-cooked ham (£7.95), trout with herbs (£9.95), steaks (from £16.95), and puddings like treacle pudding or Tia Maria torte (£3.50). A small corner bar has well kept Greene King Abbot, Tetleys, and Wadworths 6X on handpump; service is quietly obliging. The cream-walled front room has broad dark tables, with a few aeroplane pictures and country prints; the back room has a slightly more rustic feel, with its pink-cushioned wall benches and big woodburning stove. There are tables out in the tree-sheltered garden; on the edge of Hampden Common, the pub has good walks nearby. *(Recommended by George Atkinson, Francis and Deidre Gevers, Gordon Tong, Dr G W Barnett, Andrew and Joan Life, Peter Saville, Graham and Karen Oddey)*

Free house ~ Licensees Terry and Barbara Matthews ~ Real ale ~ Meals and snacks (all day summer Sun) ~ (01494) 488255 ~ Children welcome ~ Open 12-2.30, 7-11; 12-3, 7-10.30 Sun; closed Sun evenings Jan/Feb

GREAT KINGSHILL SU8798 Map 4
Red Lion ⑨ ♀

A4128 N of High Wycombe

Although the furnishings in this neatly kept little brick and flint dining cottage are unpretentious and pubby, the cooking is of an altogether higher order, and all the tables are set for dining. The friendly Spanish landlord is the chef, and there's a tremendous choice all fresh from Billingsgate, and very sensibly priced. Favourite examples include oysters (80p each), fresh calamares or moules marinières (£4.50), haddock (£7.50), skate (£8), brill (£10), dover soles (£14), lobsters (£18), and much more; the chips are freshly cut and good, and there's a bargain Sunday lunch; service charge is added automatically. Tetleys on handpump, good house wines, and freshly squeezed orange juice; excellent service. *(Recommended by TBB, Bob and Maggie Atherton, John and Hazel Waller, Tony Dickinson, Paul Coleman, Dr G W Barnett, H Kroll, Peter Saville, Ronald Buckler, R Brisbourne)*

Pubmaster ~ Tenant Jose Rivero-Cabrera ~ Real ale ~ Meals and snacks ~ Restaurant ~ (01494) 711262 ~ Children welcome ~ Open 12-3, 6-11; closed Sun evening, Mon

GREAT MISSENDEN SP8900 Map 4
Cross Keys

High St

It's unusual to find a pub that serves only Italian food, but this very friendly and old-fashioned little town pub does just that. The pasta dishes can be served as starters or main courses and include home-made minestrone soup (£3.60), pennette with a garlicky and chilli tomato sauce (£4.50) or lumachine with broccoli, herbs and chilli (£4.90); also, pork with olives, capers, peppers and tomatoes (£6.50), squid with tomatoes, garlic and wine (£7.50), and daily specials. Wooden standing timbers divide the bar – one half of which has old sewing machines on the window sill, collectors' postcards, various brewery mirrors, lots of photographs, and horse bits and spigots and pewter mugs on the beams by the bar counter. The other half has a bay window with a built-in seat overlooking the street, a couple of housekeeper's chairs in front of the big open fire, and a high-backed settle. Well kept Fullers Chiswick, London Pride, ESB on handpump, very cheap for the area. Cribbage, dominoes, fruit machine, and piped music. The terrace at the back of the building has picnic tables with umbrellas – and you can eat out here, too. (*Recommended by Dave Braisted, Ian Phillips; more reports please*)

Fullers ~ Tenant Martin Ridler ~ Real ale ~ Lunchtime meals and snacks (not Sun) ~ Restaurant (not Sun) ~ Well behaved children in restaurant ~ (01494) 865373 ~ Open 11-3, 5-11; 12-3, 7-10.30 Sun; closed 25 Dec

George

94 High St

Built in 1483, this friendly inn has attractively moulded heavy beams in the cosy two-roomed bar, timbered walls decorated with prints, little alcoves (including one with an attractively carved box settle – just room for two – under a fine carved early 17th-c oak panel), and Staffordshire and other figurines over the big log fire. A snug inner room has a sofa, little settles and a smaller coal fire; shove-ha'penny and dominoes. Enjoyable bar food includes sandwiches (from £1.95), home-made soup (£2.25), filled baked potatoes (from £2.75), fresh salmon fishcakes (£4.25), home-cooked ham with two eggs or roquefort crêpes (£4.75), fresh grilled herrings (£4.90), chicken balti (£5.75), and steak and kidney pie (£6.80); huge Sunday roast, and if you are staying, breakfasts are served until 10am. The restaurant is no smoking. Well kept Adnams Bitter, Bass, Greene King Abbot, and Wadworths 6X on handpump kept under light blanket pressure, mulled wine in winter, and several malt whiskies; prompt and cheerful service. Plenty of seats in the terrace and garden area. (*Recommended by Gill and Keith Croxton, Simon Penny, Mrs Jean Dundas, Ian Phillips, Nigel Norman*)

Greenalls ~ Tenants Guy and Sally Smith ~ Real ale ~ Snacks (served all day) and meals; not Sun or evenings 25-26 Dec ~ Restaurant ~ (01494) 862084 ~ Children welcome ~ Open 11-11; 12-3.30, 7-10.30 Sun; closed evenings 25-26 Dec ~ Bedrooms: £65.75B/£72.75B

HADDENHAM SP7408 Map 4

Green Dragon 🍴 ♀

Village signposted off A418 and A4129, E/NE of Thame; then follow Church End signs

Buckinghamshire Dining Pub of the Year

This very civilised dining pub has kept a respectable corner for people wanting just a drink, with a few blond cast-iron-framed tables, some bar stools and well kept Boddingtons, Marstons Pedigree and Vale Notley on handpump. But the main emphasis is certainly on food, with lunchtime dishes such as home-made soup (£3), home-made crab and fresh ginger tortellini with a spicy thai and fresh coriander sauce (starter £4.95, main course £6.95), terrine of smoked duck breasts and confied duck legs with a warm shallot and red wine marmalade (£5.45), good English cheeses with celery, a walnut salad, french bread, butter and biscuits (£3.75), omelettes (from £6.25), a vegetarian dish of the day (£7.50), fillet of lemon sole (£8.95), and English lamb with glazed spring vegetables and a light tarragon jus (£12.75), with evening extras such as provençale salad with fresh tuna (£5.25), poussin with a wild morrel mushroom, shallot and cream sauce (£12.95), scallops on a bed of home-made ink noodles with a 'Jacqueline' sauce (£13.95), and puddings like warm pear and almond tart with a dark rum sauce, mandarin orange crème brûlée or bread and butter pudding (from £2.95); daily specials such as grilled sardines (£4.55), skewers of rabbit mignons wrapped in smoked bacon (£4.85), and roast monkfish on a bed of home-made tomato noodles with a light saffron sauce (£12.45). The wines, mainly French and New World, are well chosen and sensibly priced, with a good choice by the glass. The main area, two high-ceilinged communicating rooms, has been thoughtfully decorated – walls midnight blue, or part stripped stone and part terracotta pink, attractive still lifes and country pictures, fruit-pattern tablecloths, a log fire on cool days. With the floor partly tiled and these big square rooms the acoustics are quite bright – reminiscent of a French brasserie, with a conversational buzz and the odd clatter of cutlery submerging a faint off-stage drone of piped pop music. There are white tables and picnic tables under cocktail parasols on a big sheltered gravel terrace behind, with more on the grass; this part of the village is very pretty, with a duckpond unusually close to the church. *(Recommended by B Andrews, Brian Atkin, C H Speakman, Jan and Colin Roe)*

Whitbreads ~ Lease: Julian Ehlers and Catherine Durgeil ~ Real ale ~ Meals and snacks (food service may stop early after a busy lunch) ~ (01844) 291403 ~ Children in restaurant ~ Open 11.30-2.30, 6-11; 12-2.30 Sun (closed Sun evening)

HAMBLEDEN SU7886 Map 2
Stag & Huntsman 🍺

Turn off A4155 (Henley—Marlow Rd) at Mill End, signposted to Hambleden; in a mile turn right into village centre

This is an especially pretty village and the peaceful brick and flint pub is set opposite the church. There's a bustling atmosphere in the half-panelled, L-shaped lounge bar, as well as low ceilings, a large fireplace, and upholstered seating and wooden chairs on the carpet. The attractively simple public bar has darts, shove-ha'penny, dominoes, cribbage, and trivia, and there's a cosy snug at the front, too; piped music. Good home-made bar food includes soup (£2.75), ploughman's (from £3.85), liver and bacon (£5.10), vegetable lasagne (£5.50), home-cooked ham and egg or very good yorkshire pudding filled with stew (£5.95), fresh salmon fishcakes (£6.35), spare ribs (£6.95), steaks (from £10.95), and puddings like fresh fruit crumble (£2.75). Well kept Burtonwood Top Hat, Brakspears Bitter and Special, and Wadworths 6X on handpump, farm ciders, and good wines. The spacious and neatly kept country garden is where they hold their popular big barbecues – cajun salmon, pork and apple burgers, pork and leek sausages, and various kebabs. *(Recommended by Graham and Karen Oddey, P J and J E F Caunt, Christine and Geoff Butler, D Voller, TBB, Chris and Ann Garnett, RJH, Dr G W Barnett, Helen Pickering, James Owen)*

Free house ~ Licensees Hon Henry Smith and Andrew Fry ~ Real ale ~ Meals and snacks ~ Restaurant ~ (01491) 571227 ~ Children in eating area of bar and in restaurant ~ Open 11-2.30(3 Sat), 6-11; 12-3, 7-10.30 Sun; closed bank hol Mon evenings ~ Bedrooms: £38.50S/£48.50S

IBSTONE SU7593 Map 4
Fox

1¾ miles from M40 junction 5: unclassified lane leading S from motorway exit roundabout; pub is on Ibstone Common

From the neat rose garden of this 17th-c country inn you can overlook the common, with rolling fields and the Chilterns oak and beech woods beyond; the village cricket ground is close by. Inside, the comfortable low-beamed lounge bar has high-backed settles and country seats, old village photographs on the walls, and log fires. In the public bar – which has darts, dominoes, and fruit machine – the pine settles and tables match the woodblock floor; piped music. Good bar food includes sandwiches, ploughman's, and changing hot meals like crispy duck salad with raspberry dressing (£3.95 starter, £5.95 main course), beef and Guinness pie (£6.50), baked cod with a courgette and thyme sauce (£6.95), and lamb steak on ratatouille with a rosemary and red wine sauce (£8.50). The small dining area is no smoking; there's also a smart restaurant. Well kept Brakspears PA and Fullers London Pride on handpump, with guests like Exmoor Gold and Everards Tiger. *(Recommended by M J Dowdy, Nigel Norman, George Atkinson, Alec Hamilton, GWB, Robert Gomme; more reports please)*

Free house ~ Licensee Ann Banks ~ Real ale ~ Meals and snacks (till 10pm) ~ Restaurant ~ (01491) 638722 ~ Open 11-3, 6-11; 12-3, 7-10.30 Sun ~ Bedrooms: £45B/£58B

Planning a day in the country? We list pubs in really attractive scenery at the back of the book.

LITTLE HAMPDEN SP8503 Map 4
Rising Sun 🍽

Village signposted from back road (ie W of A413) Great Missenden—Stoke Mandeville; pub at end of village lane; OS Sheet 165 map reference 856040

The imaginative food is the reason most people come to this smart dining pub – though the secluded setting with tracks leading through the woods in different directions is delightful; walkers are welcome as long as they leave their muddy boots outside and there are some tables on the terrace by the sloping front grass. From a constantly changing menu, the food might include a chicken tikka filo parcel, crispy duck wings with barbecue sauce or tagliatelle pasta with artichoke, mussels and prawns in a saffron cream sauce (all £4.95), chargrilled escalope of pork with a prune and brandy sauce (£8.45), breast of corn-fed chicken filled with feta cheese, coated with cous-cous and served with a tomato, red pepper and olive sauce (£8.75), chargrilled tuna steak marinated with lime leaf, garlic and oils with a mushroom and caper piquant sauce (£8.95), a vegetarian dish, and puddings like mango, banana and almond crumble or chocolate and chestnut tiramisu (£3.25). Well kept Adnams, Brakspears PA, Marstons Pedigree, and Morlands Old Speckled Hen on handpump, with home-made mulled wine and spiced cider in winter, and a short but decent wine list; efficient service. One part of the interlinked bar rooms is no smoking, and there's also a separate no-smoking dining room (which enjoys the same food as the bar). No noisy games machines or piped music. *(Recommended by Miss G Hume, P Saville, Dr G W Barnett, Mr and Mrs T F Marshall, Andrew and Joan Life, Dave Carter, M A and C R Starling, Graham and Karen Oddey, Mr and Mrs A J Murdoch, Nigel Norman)*

Free house ~ Licensee Rory Dawson ~ Real ale ~ Meals and snacks (not Sun evening, not Mon) ~ (01494) 488393 ~ Children welcome ~ Open 11.30-2.30, 6.30-11; 12-3 Sun; closed Sun evenings and Mon – except for bank holidays ~ Bedrooms planned

LITTLE HORWOOD SP7930 Map 4
Shoulder of Mutton

Church St; back road 1 mile S of A421 Buckingham—Bletchley

Set next to the quiet churchyard, this partly thatched and half-timbered old pub is a friendly place, popular with locals. The rambling T-shaped bar is attractively but simply furnished with sturdy seats around chunky rustic tables on the quarry-tiles, has a huge fireplace at one end with a woodburning stove, and a showcase of china swans; the black labrador-cross (who loves children) is called Billy, and the black cat, Trouble. Well kept ABC Best and Marstons Pedigree on handpump; shove-ha'penny, cribbage, dominoes, and fruit machine in the games area. Decent bar food includes sandwiches (from £1.80), filled baked potatoes (from £2.30), home-made dishes like steak and kidney pie, curry or chilli con carne (£5.20), diced lamb in ale (£7.90), and steaks. French windows look out on the pleasant back garden where there are plenty of tables. From the north, the car park entrance is tricky. *(Recommended by Graham and Karen Oddey, Gill and Keith Croxton, Ian Phillips, Marjorie and David Lamb, GO, KO, S Palmer)*

Pubmaster (Allied) ~ Tenant June Fessey ~ Real ale ~ Meals and snacks (not Sun evening, not Mon) ~ Restaurant ~ (01296) 712514 ~ Children in eating area of bar and in restaurant until 9pm ~ Open 11-2.30(3 Sat), 6-11; 12-3, 7-10.30 Sun; closed Mon lunchtime

LITTLE MISSENDEN SU9298 Map 4
Crown ◀

Crown Lane, SE end of village, which is signposted off A413 W of Amersham

The friendly licensees of this bustling small brick cottage are the third generation – it has been in the same family for over 90 years. The atmosphere is very chatty and relaxed, there's a good mix of customers, and the bars are thoroughly traditional and sparkling clean. There are old red flooring tiles on the left, oak parquet on the right, built-in wall seats, studded red leatherette chairs, a few small tables, and a complete absence of music and machines. The Adnams Broadside, Hook Norton Best, and a guest such as Shepherd Neame Spitfire on handpump are kept particularly well; they also have farm ciders and decent malt whiskies. Bar food is simple but all home-made, majoring on a wide choice of generous very reasonably priced sandwiches (from £2), as well as ploughman's (£3.50), pasties and Buck's bite (a special home-made pizza-like dish £3.75); darts, shove-ha'penny, cribbage, dominoes. There are picnic tables and other tables in an attractive sheltered garden behind. The village is pretty, with an interesting church. *(Recommended by John and Hazel Waller, M J Dowdy, Paul Kitchener, Ian Phillips)*

Free house ~ Licensees Trevor and Carolyn How ~ Real ale ~ Lunchtime snacks (not Sun) ~ (01494) 862571 ~ Open 11-2.30, 6-11; closed 25-26 Dec

LONG CRENDON SP6808 Map 4
Angel
Bicester Rd (B4011)

New licensees have taken over this carefully restored partly 17th-c civilised pub. It is perhaps more restaurant than pub in outlook, but has well kept Boddingtons Bitter, Jennings Bitter, and Ruddles on handpump, capacious sofas in a comfortable and pleasantly decorated lounge, and sturdy tables and chairs in another area. One menu serves both the restaurant and bar and the very good food might include sandwiches, roast sardines in chilli butter (£3.75), parfait of chicken livers with red onion confit and toasted brioche (£4.25), moules marinières (£5.25), chargrilled Oxford sausages with mashed potato and onion gravy (£7.25), salad of chargrilled vegetables and polenta dressed with olive tapenade (£8.75), baked cod with a provençal crust and spring onion mash (£9.75), roast best end of new season lamb on cassoulet of beans in a tomato and tarragon jus (£15.50) and puddings such as hot sticky toffee pudding in a caramel sauce, raspberry and vanilla crème brûlée or chocolate fallen angel (£4.50). There's a no-smoking conservatory dining room at the back looking out on the garden, and a terrace for summer eating out; piped music. *(Recommended by Tim Heywood, Sophie Wilne, Mark Hydes, Paul and Maggie Baker, M Sargent, Deborah Jackson; more reports on the new regime, please)*

Free house ~ Licensees Trevor Bosch, Angela Good ~ Real ale ~ Meals and snacks (till 10pm) ~ Restaurant ~ (01844) 208268 ~ Children in restaurant ~ Open 11-11; 12-3 Sun (closed Sun evening) ~ Bedrooms: £45B/£55B

NORTHEND SU7392 Map 4
White Hart
On back road up escarpment from Watlington, past Christmas Common; or valley road off A4155 Henley—Marlow at Mill End, past Hambleden, Skirmett and Turville, then sharp left in Northend itself

Run by friendly people, this little 16th-c pub has a quiet bar with very low handsomely carved oak beams, good log fires (one in a vast fireplace), some panelling, and comfortable window seats. A small choice of food includes sandwiches, good home-made soup with fresh baked bread (£2.50), home-made pâté (£3.95), cumberland sausage with mash and onion gravy (£4.95), warm salad with stilton, bacon and avocado (£5.75), various home-made pies, fresh salmon fillet with lime butter or king prawns (£7.50), and two Sunday roasts (and a home-made nut roast; £5.50); fresh vegetables. Well kept Brakspears PA and SB on handpump; shove-ha'penny; no piped music. There's a charming summer garden full of flowers and fruit trees. *(Recommended by Dr G W Barnett, Cicely Taylor; more reports please)*

Brakspears ~ Tenants Derek and Susie Passey ~ Real ale ~ Meals and snacks (not Sun or Mon evenings) ~ (01491) 638353 ~ Children in dining area ~ Open 11-2.30, 6-11; 12-3, 7-10.30 Sun; may open all day summer Sat and Sun

By law pubs must show a price list of their drinks. Let us know if you are inconvenienced by any breach of this law.

PRESTWOOD SP8700 Map 4
Polecat

170 Wycombe Rd (A4128 N of High Wycombe)

The attractive prices, unfailingly good service and pleasantly individual layout keep this extended pub busy – happy crowds of middle-aged lunchers, a broader mix of ages in the evening. Several smallish rooms open off the low-ceilinged bar, with a good medley of tables and chairs, all sorts of stuffed birds as well as the stuffed white polecats in one big cabinet, small country pictures, rugs on bare boards or red tiles, a couple of antique housekeeper's chairs by a good open fire in another; the Galley room is no smoking. Bar food includes daily specials such as mushroom bisque with sour cream (£2.50), pork and cider casserole with cheese and herb dumplings (£6.20), wild mushroom and lentil bolognese with home-made pasta and olive bread (£6.40), grilled dover sole with smoked salmon butter (£6.80), and quenelles of pike florentine (£8.20); also, sandwiches (from £2.10), hot dogs (£2.75), filled baked potatoes (from £3.75), ploughman's (£4), courgette and mushroom rissoles (£5.90), lasagne (£6.20), smoked cod fishcakes with parsley sauce (£7.50), steak and kidney pie (£7.60), and puddings like sherry trifle, raspberry shortcake or rhubarb and ginger crumble (£3.25). Well kept Marstons Pedigree, Morlands Old Speckled Hen, and Ruddles Best and County on handpump at the flint bar counter, a list on a board of wines by the glass, and at least 20 malt whiskies; quick friendly service, good relaxed chatty atmosphere. There are picnic tables on neat grass out in front beneath a big fairy-lit apple tree, with more on a big well kept lawn behind. *(Recommended by Nigel Norman, Mark Hydes, Gerald Barnett, Simon Collett-Jones, J Ramage)*

Free house ~ Licensee John Gamble ~ Real ale ~ Meals and snacks (12-2, 6.30-9) ~ (01494) 862253 ~ Children in eating area of bar ~ Open 11.30-2.30, 6-11; 12-3 Sun (closed Sun evening)

nr PRINCES RISBOROUGH SP8003 Map 4
Red Lion

Upper Icknield Way, Whiteleaf; village signposted off A4010 towards Aylesbury; OS Sheet 165 map reference 817040

The pleasantly old-fashioned bar in this friendly 17th-c pub has a good log fire, a growing collection of antique nautical items such as a ship's binnacle that came originally from an old warship, lots of propellers, navigation lamps, and pullies (there's a big ship's steering wheel in the restaurant), antique winged settles, various sporting and coaching prints and pictures, and a chatty local atmosphere. Good home-made bar food includes sandwiches, good soup, hot, spicy mushrooms, sausage with beans (£3.95), omelettes (from £3.95), pasta with mussels and prawns (£4.25), shepherd's pie (£4.50), lasagne (£4.95), steak and Guinness pie (£5.95), good steaks, and Sunday lunch. Well kept Brakspears PA, Hook Norton Best, Morlands Old Speckled Hen, and a guest beer on handpump; dominoes, cribbage, several hand-crafted puzzles, and piped music. Outside there are tables on a small front lawn surrounded by colourful window boxes and hanging baskets, with more in a most attractive large back garden; good nearby walks (the pub is set at the foot of the Chilterns), and handy for Whiteleaf Fields (National Trust). *(Recommended by Graham and Karen Oddey, Helen Hazzard, T R and J C Moggridge, M J Dowdy, Simon Penny, Joan and Andrew Life, Nigel Norman, Gladys Protheroe, Ian Phillips, Gwen and Peter Andrews)*

Free house ~ Licensee Richard Howard ~ Real ale ~ Meals and snacks ~ Resaurant ~ (01844) 344476 ~ Children in restaurant ~ Open 11.30-3, 5.30(6 Sat)-11; 12-3, 7-10.30 Sun ~ Bedrooms: £29.50B/£39.50B

Children welcome means the pub says it lets children inside without any special restriction. If it allows them in, but to restricted areas such as an eating area or family room, we specify this. Some pubs may impose an evening time limit.

SKIRMETT SU7790 Map 2
Old Crown 🍴

High St; from A4155 NE of Henley take Hambleden turn and keep on; or from B482 Stokenchurch—Marlow take Turville turn and keep on

In a pleasant Chilterns valley, this pretty 18th-c no-smoking dining pub is a relaxed and enjoyable place for a meal out (not somewhere for a quick drink). The three beamed rooms have open fires (two are inglenooks) and over 700 bric-a-brac items, paintings, antiques, bottles and tools; the small central room and larger one leading off have tankards hanging from the beams and windsor chairs, and the little white-painted tap room has trestle tables and an old-fashioned settle. Well presented and very good (if not cheap), the home-made food might include soup (£3.50), stilton and walnut pâté (£4.60), ploughman's (£5), smoked fish terrine (£5.55), filled baked potatoes (from £5.55), lasagne (£8.30), steak, kidney and mushroom pie (£8.65), pot-roasted guinea fowl with shallots and caramelised apples cooked in cider and calvados (£11.70), half a roast crispy barbary duck with a port and orange sauce (£13.90), scallops in garlic, butter and basil (£15), and Scotch fillet steak (£15.75); good service. Well kept Brakspears PA and SB are tapped from casks in a still room, and served though a hatch. A sheltered front terrace has flower tubs, and old oak casks as seats, and the pretty garden has picnic tables under cocktail parasols, and a fishpond. There are two pub alsatians. No children under 10. *(Recommended by Mr and Mrs C Moncreiffe, Graham and Karen Oddey, J and B Cressey, Mayur Shah, Christine and Geoff Butler, Gregor Macdonald, Dr G W Barnett, John Barker, Mary and Des Kemp, Ian and Liz Phillips, Jack and Philip Paxton, Nigel Norman, Dan Hayter)*

Brakspears ~ Tenants Peter and Liz Mumby ~ Real ale ~ Meals and snacks (not Sun evening and not Mon except bank holidays) ~ Restaurant ~ (01491) 638435 ~ Open 11-2.30, 6-11; 12-3 Sun (closed evening); closed Mon except bank holidays

TURVILLE SU7690 Map 2
Bull & Butcher

Valley road off A4155 Henley—Marlow at Mill End, past Hambleden and Skirmett

The friendly, characterful landord has exposed an inglenook fireplace and more oak beams in this pretty black-and-white timbered pub. The comfortable and atmospheric low-ceilinged bar – partly divided into two areas – has beams from ships seized in the Spanish Armada, cushioned wall settles, and an old-fashioned high-backed settle by one log fire. Generous helpings of good, enjoyable bar food include soup (£3.50), sandwiches like hot home-smoked pastrami on rye bread (£4.50), ploughman's (£4.95), stilton soufflé on pears poached in red wine and spices (£5.50), sausage of the day or vegetable hotch potch pudding (£6.95), steak and ale pie (£7.45), balti curries (£8.45), and chicken dijon in a brandy and cream sauce (£9.95). Well kept Brakspears Bitter, Mild, Special, Old, OBJ and Hop Demon on handpump, and good house wines; efficient service. Shove-ha'penny, dominoes, cribbage, and piped music. This is a fine place to finish a walk, and the attractive garden has tables on the lawn by fruit trees and a neatly umbrella-shaped hawthorn; good summer barbecues. Once a month (Tuesday evenings) the MG car club meet here. It does get crowded at weekends. *(Recommended by Graham and Karen Oddey, Gordon, TBB, Peter Saville, T G Brierly, A L Ingram, P Goodchild, S Fazackerley, Dr G W Barnett, Cyril Brown)*

Brakspears ~ Tenant Nicholas Abbott ~ Real ale ~ Meals and snacks ~ (01491) 638283 ~ Open 11-3, 6-11; 12-3, 7-10.30 Sun

WADDESDON SP7417 Map 4
Five Arrows 🛏 ♀ 🍷

A41 NW of Aylesbury

Originally built as lodgings for the architects and craftsmen while building Waddesdon Manor, this is a rather grand small hotel owned by Lord Rothschild. The informally pubby bar is an open-plan series of light and airy high-ceilinged rooms with a relaxed but civilised atmosphere, family portrait engravings and lots of old estate-worker photographs on the leafy green wallpaper, heavy dark green velvet curtains on wooden rails, mainly sturdy cushioned settles and good solid tables on on parquet flooring (though one room has comfortably worn-in armchairs and settees), and newspapers and copies of *Country Life* in an antique magazine rack. The bar counter is a handsome affair, carved with the five arrows of the Rothschild crest which symbolise the dispersal of the five founding sons of the international banking business. The regular bar menu includes staples such as sandwiches (from £3.20), and salads like home-cooked ham or grilled goat's cheese (from £5.20), but the highlights tend to be found among the wide choice of daily-changing specials: brandied chicken liver parfait with an orange confit (£5.15), Greek chargrilled chicken breast with a yoghurt, cucumber and garlic relish (£8.75), cajun blackened salmon with a remoulade sauce (£9), baked cod with a herb crust (£9.30), fillet steak with red shallot butter (£15.40), and good home-made puddings (£4). The country-house style restaurant is no smoking; must book at busy times. The formidable wine list naturally runs to Rothschild first-growth clarets as well as less well known Rothschild estate wines such as Los Vascos Chilean cabernet sauvignon. Well kept Chiltern Beechwood, and Fullers London Pride and ESB on handpump; other drinks including many malt whiskies are exemplary; efficient service, unobtrusive piped music. The sheltered back garden has attractively grouped wood and metal furnishings. *(Recommended by Graham and Karen Oddey, Susan and John Douglas, Michael Long, Comus Elliott, Michael and Lorna Bourdeaux, Gwen and Peter Andrews, Ian Phillips, D and J McMillan)*

Free house ~ Licensees Julian Alexander-Worster, Fabia Bromovsky ~ Real ale ~ Meals and snacks ~ Restaurant ~ (01296) 651727 ~ Children welcome ~ Open 11-3, 6-11; 12-3, 7-10.30 Sun ~ Bedrooms: £55B/£70B

WEST WYCOMBE SU8394 Map 4
George & Dragon
High St; A40 W of High Wycombe

This handsome Tudor inn has a comfortable and colourfully decorated rambling main bar with massive beams, sloping walls, and a big log fire; the magnificent oak staircase is said to be haunted by a wronged girl; one bar (the children's area) is no smoking. Good, fairly priced home-made bar food includes lunchtime sandwiches, home-made soup (£1.95), potted stilton (£4.25), brazil nut roast with tomato sauce (£5.45), minced lamb cooked with fruit and spices in beer and rum (£5.95), sweet and sour chicken on egg noodles (£6.25), lovely game pie (£6.45), salmon in pastry with soured cream (£7.75), 12oz Scotch sirloin steak (£11.95), daily specials such as wild mushroom and bean goulash (£5.35), venison and juniper pudding (£6.25), Malaysian fish curry (£6.95), and puddings like fresh fruit crumble, sticky toffee pudding and lovely bread and butter pudding (from £2.25). Well kept Courage Best and Directors and guests like Gales HSB, Ushers Founders or Youngs Special on handpump, and quite a few malt whiskies; dominoes and cribbage. The arched and cobbled coach entry leads to a spacious, peaceful garden with picnic tables, and a fenced in play area with a new climbing frame. The inn does get crowded at weekends, so it's best to get there early then. Nearby you can visit West Wycombe Park with its fine furnishings and classical landscaped grounds (it is closed on winter Saturdays). *(Recommended by Kevin Thomas, Susan and John Douglas, Alan Morton, TBB, Dave Braisted, Dr G W Barnett, Nigel Norman, Neville and Sarah Hargreaves, Wayne Brindle, Simon Collett-Jones)*

Courage ~ Lease: Philip Todd ~ Real ale ~ Meals and snacks (not 25 Dec) ~ (01494) 464414 ~ Children in room set aside for them ~ Open 12-2.30, 5.30-11; 11-11 Sat; 12-10.30 summer Sun (12-3, 7-10.30 winter Sun) ~ Bedrooms: £52B/£62B

WHEELER END SU8093 Map 4
Chequers 🏮
Village signposted off B482 in Lane End NW of Marlow, then first left also signposted Wheeler End; or can be reached by very narrow Bullocks Farm Lane (sign may be defaced) from A40 layby just W of W Wycombe

We get a real kick out of finding this sort of pub these days. So many of today's top licensees are targeting the dining market and setting their sights on one of our Food Awards that people like the Robinsons come as a mightily refreshing change. They are intent on preserving traditional pub values – a really welcoming atmosphere, good conversation, a fine range of real ales and other drinks, and good straightforward pub food; many readers will remember the way they transformed their previous pubs, the Prince Albert at Frieth and Horns at Crazies Hill. Under its low ochre ceiling the bar has what might be called an inherently friendly layout: it's so small, and shaped in such a way, that even a stranger quickly feels part of the general conversation. It angles back past a good inglenook log fire, and a little roomlet with a fruit machine, to a bigger back room with a couple of dart boards. Furniture is mainly scrubbed country-kitchen with a few board-backed wall benches, and the ochre walls have a liberal sprinkling of local notices alongside small hunting prints, cartoons and so forth; darts, shove-ha'penny, cribbage, dominoes, and fruit machine. There are good malt whiskies and excellent coffee, and well kept Bass, Brakspears PA, Fullers London Pride and Greene King IPA and Abbot on handpump, with a guest such as Brains Dark Mild tapped from the cask. Food includes good soups such as jerusalem artichoke or leek and potato with thyme (£2.95), excellent hot and cold filled rolls (the 'small' bacon and black pudding roll at £2.40 will set you up nicely for a stroll on the nearby common), ploughman's (from £4.95), pasta (£4.75), chilli con carne or vegetarian (£4.95), late breakfast (£4.95) and liver and bacon or bangers and mash (choice of cumberland or Abbot Ale sausage – £5). There are a few tables outside; no car park to speak of, but plenty of parking nearby. *(Recommended by Anthony Longden, TBB)*

Free house ~ Licensees David and Patsy Robinson ~ Real ale ~ Snacks and lunchtime meals (not Mon) ~ (01494) 883070 ~ Children in eating area of bar lunchtime only ~ Live blues Tues evening ~ Open 11-2.30, 5.30-11; 11-11 Sat; 12-10.30 Sun; closed Mon lunchtime

WOOBURN COMMON SU9187 Map 2

Chequers 🛏

2 miles from M40 junction 2; A355 towards Slough, first right, then right again; Kiln Lane, Widmoor – OS Sheet 175 map reference 910870

With a cheerful traditional atmosphere, the low-beamed partly stripped-brick bar here has standing timbers and alcoves to break it up, lived-in sofas on its bare boards, a bright log-effect gas fire, and various pictures, plates and tankards; it undoubtedly gets a lot of its custom from the flourishing hotel and restaurant side, but is none the worse for that. There's a tasteful dining room on the left, with bar food sandwiches (from £3.25), ploughman's (£4.25), home-made burger (£6.50), strips of chicken with a thai sauce (£7.25), home-made steak and kidney pie (£7.50), and poached salmon (£8.50). Well kept Fullers London Pride, Marstons Bitter and Pedigree, and Timothy Taylors Landlord on handpump, and a sizeable wine list; spacious garden away from the road, with cast-iron tables. The attractive stripped-pine bedrooms are in a 20th-c mock-Tudor wing; breakfasts are good. *(Recommended by Kevin Thomas, Ian and Liz Phillips, Mark Percy, Stephen N Whiteley, Wayne Brindle; more reports please)*

Free house ~ Licensee Peter Roehrig ~ Real ale ~ Meals and snacks ~ Restaurant ~ (01628) 529575 ~ Children welcome ~ Open 11-11; 12-10.30 Sun ~ Bedrooms: £82.50B/£87.50B

Lucky Dip

Besides the fully inspected pubs, you might like to try these Lucky Dips recommended to us and described by readers (if you do, please send us reports):

☆ **Adstock** [Main St (off A413); SP7330], *Old Thatched Inn*: Interesting beamed and flagstoned pub/restaurant comfortably done up with cosy corners and open fires; generous bar meals, well kept mainly Scottish Courage and guest ales (at a price), decent wines, friendly attentive staff; piped music; seats out in pleasant back arbour, children in restaurant and eating area *(Chris Raisin, K Frostick, Dr and Mrs A K Clarke, Graham and Karen Oddey, B J P Edwards, Nigel Norman, LYM)*

☆ **nr Adstock** [Verney Junction, Addington – OS Sheet 165 map ref 737274], *Verney Arms*:

Tucked-away country pub, recently reopened, with bright farmhouse feel, two eating areas, pleasant decor strong on chicken pictures, open fire, well kept Greene King IPA and a seasonal ale, and some emphasis on fine choice of good freshly cooked food (fantastic rose and cardamom ice cream); good friendly service *(Stuart Archer)*

☆ Akeley [The Square, just off A413; SP7037], *Bull & Butcher*: Genuine village pub, individualistic landlord, acupuncturist landlady, two friendly dogs, good value lunchtime buffet (maybe only cold food; not Sun) inc wide range of help-yourself salads, several puddings, also evening steak bar (not Sun or Mon); three good fires in long open-plan beamed bar with red plush banquettes, well kept Fullers London Pride, Marstons Pedigree, Morlands Original and a guest beer, decent house wines, winter spiced wine, traditional games; children allowed in eating area, tables in attractive garden, occasional live entertainment; handy for Stowe Gardens *(M Sargent, Graham and Karen Oddey, Ann Griffiths, Ian Phillips, LYM)*

☆ Amersham [High St, Old Town (A413); SU9597], *Kings Arms*: Picture-postcard timbered building in charming street, lots of heavy beams and snug alcoves, big inglenook, high-backed antique settles and other quaint old furnishings among more standard stuff; low-priced bar food inc vegetarian, restaurant, pleasant service, well kept Tetleys-related and other ales, children in eating area; open all day, rather a young person's pub evening; nice garden *(SR, PM, LYM)*
Amersham [High St], *Eagle*: Friendly low-beamed old town pub, wide choice of good straightforward lunchtime food (not Sun) inc good fresh fish, friendly efficient service, Tetleys-related and guest ales, log fire, maybe soft piped music, fruit machine; more lively young person's pub evenings *(GWB, Ken and Jenny Simmonds)*; [High St], *Elephant & Castle*: Low beams, china, velvet and brasses in popular food pub with fine U-shaped bar counter, several Whitbreads-related and guest ales; maybe piped music *(James Nunns, LYM)*
Ashley Green [A416 Chesham—Berkhamsted; SP9705], *Golden Eagle*: Friendly 17th-c beamed and timbered village pub with five real ales, good value generous home-cooked food (lunch Mon-Sat, evening Mon-Thurs), flame-effect fires, fresh flowers, darts, dominoes, fruit machine, TV; tables in back garden and out in front *(CMW, JJW)*
Aston Clinton [SP8712], *Bell*: More restaurant than pub, comfortable and smart with nice atmosphere, short choice of good interesting food (very good choice of English farmhouse cheeses), well chosen wines; a comfortable place to stay *(C and M Starling, M J Dowdy)*; *Oak*: Cosy and attractively refurbished Fullers pub, good if not cheap home cooking, decent wine list, real fire, no music or machines, obliging friendly service *(Helen Hazzard)*

☆ Astwood [off A422; SP9547], *Old Swan*: Attractive, clean, airy and spacious, with well kept Scottish Courage and guest ales, wine or port by the jug, good bar food, not cheap but generous, cosy old-fashioned atmosphere; side garden bar *(Sidney and Erna Wells, LYM)*
Aylesbury [1 Temple Sq; SP8213], *Queens Head*: Nice old corner pub on quiet square, main and back bar and dining area all with waitress service, very friendly welcome, simple but good bar food at very decent prices *(Klaus and Elizabeth Leist)*

☆ nr Aylesbury [Gibraltar; A418 some miles towards Thame, beyond Stone – OS Sheet 165 map ref 758108; SP7510], *Bottle & Glass*: Welcoming low-beamed thatched pub, tiled floor, rambling layout, wide choice of good imaginative food from sandwiches to good seafood up, lively atmosphere, helpful service, well kept Morrells Oxford and Varsity, good choice of wines, neat garden *(George Atkinson, Mial Pagan, Tim and Ann Newell, Tim Heywood, Sophie Wilne, LYM)*
Beachampton [Main St; SP7737], *Bell*: Large pub with modern extension, terrace and play area in big garden, wide choice of food inc good sandwiches, ales such as Frog Island Shoemaker and Wadworths 6X, piped classical music; nice little village with stream along street *(George Atkinson)*
Beaconsfield [41 Aylesbury End, a mile from M40 junction 2; SU9490], *Old Hare*: Relaxed and civilised dim-lit pub with old-fashioned touches, well kept Tetleys-related and guest ales, lots of malt whiskies, decent house wines, good strong coffee, cheerful staff (service can slow when busy), usual bar food (not Sun evening), no machines or music; children in eating area, big sunny back garden; open all day *(TBB, LYM)*; [High St], *Old Swan*: Friendly town pub with reasonably priced bar food, Boddingtons, Brakspears, Courage, Flowers, Fullers and Wadworths 6X, bare floors, wooden tables and pews for rustic feel; pool in separate room *(Nick and Meriel Cox)*
Bishopstone [Marsh Rd; SP8010], *Harrow*: Well run and welcoming country local with wide range of good food in bar and restaurant, Bass, Boddingtons and Flowers IPA, good choice of malt whiskies, plenty of pub games, big well kept garden with barbecues *(Michael Long, Tim Heywood, Sophie Wilne)*

☆ Botley [Tylers Hill Rd; narrow lane opp Hen & Chickens; SP9702], *Five Bells*: Friendly, quiet and cosy country local, well off the beaten track and popular with walkers, with inglenook fireplaces, good range of well kept Brakspears and other ales, generous heartening home-made food (not Mon evening, not Sun), good service, tables outside; well behaved children welcome *(Jan and Colin Roe, Gordon, LYM)*
Bourne End [Coldmoorholme Rd; lane towards Thames off A4155; SU8888], *Spade Oak*: Useful Brewers Fayre, three well kept

Whitbreads ales and Brakspears, pictures and books, piped music, a few benches outside; no dogs *(CMW, JJW)*

☆ **Bryants Bottom** [4 miles N of High Wycombe, via Hughenden Valley off A4128; SU8599], *Gate*: Country pub with rather formal beamed plush-seated lounge spreading back from traditional little tiled front bar, very well prepared inexpensive food, well kept ales such as Bass, Greene King Abbot, Morlands Old Speckled Hen and Wadworths 6X, deep fireplace, no piped music, tables in safely fenced garden with cockatiels and play area; popular with walkers and cyclists *(Nigel Norman, Mark Hydes, BB)*

☆ **Cadmore End** [B482 towards Stokenchurch; SU7892], *Blue Flag*: Wide choice of good value interesting generous food inc fresh fish in old-fashioned beamed pub attached to small modern hotel, lots of proper big dining tables; good range of well kept ales, decent wines, good atmosphere, expert unobtrusive service, fascinating vintage MG pictures in side room; attractive little restaurant; bedrooms *(Peter Saville, GWB, Nigel Bruce, Cyril S Brown, BB)*

Calverton [just S of Stony Stratford; SP7939], *Shoulder of Mutton*: Friendly old open-plan pub on edge of pretty village, big garden, good value food from sandwiches up in bar and restaurant, six well kept Scottish Courage and other ales, attractive garden with pleasant view and play area; piped music, games machines; well equipped bedrooms *(Simon Walker, Robert France)*

Chalfont St Giles [London Rd; SU9893], *Ivy House*: Attractive pub with big restaurant extension, tables in pretty little courtyard, Fullers London Pride and Gales Best, good range of popular food *(P J Keen, Ian Phillips)*; [Three Households, Deanway], *White Hart*: Good very friendly service, wide range of good generous food inc lots of fish and lovely puddings, cricketing decor, big garden; children welcome; bedrooms in barn at the back *(Wendy and Jim Shaw, Abigail Ingram, Paul Goodchild, Emma Pegler)*

☆ **Chearsley** [SP7110], *Bell*: Charming cottagey thatched pub on village green, long bar with lots of tankards and decorative plates, inviting settle by woodburner, very friendly licensees, wide choice of good value home-made food (not Mon lunchtime) from sandwiches up, well kept Fullers Chiswick and London Pride, good coffee, summer weekend barbecues in sizeable garden; children and dogs welcome *(Heather Couper, Mark Gillis, Mr and Mrs D Johnson, John Waller)*

☆ **Cheddington** [Station Rd; by stn, about a mile from village; SP9218], *Rosebery Arms*: Comfortable sofas by roaring log fire, pubbier seats by servery, old photographs on panelled walls, smart restaurant with no-smoking area; good food from sandwiches to imaginative main courses, Charles Wells and guest ales, friendly service; maybe piped music; well spaced picnic tables on back lawn with play equipment and wendy house *(Mel*

Smith, Shirley Cannings)

☆ **Chesham** [Church St/Wey Lane; SP9501], *Queens Head*: Generous well cooked good value food (good fish and chips Thurs/Fri) and well kept Brakspears PA, SB and Old and Fullers London Pride in small, cosy and friendly pub with tidy locals' back bar, sparkling brass, interesting pictures and paraphernalia, two coal fires, scrubbed tables; tables in small courtyard; next to River Chess, can be very busy *(DJW)*

☆ **nr Chesham** [Chesham Vale – back rd to Hawridge, Berkhamsted and Tring, off A416 as you leave centre], *Black Horse*: Big helpings of long-popular food inc lots of unusual home-made pies in quietly set and neatly extended country pub with black beams and joists, book-lined converted barn; well kept Tetleys-related and guest ales, decent wines, very professional service, lots of well spaced tables out on back grass *(Paul Coleman, Ronald Buckler, LYM)*

☆ **Chicheley** [A422, quite handy for M1 junction 14; SP9045], *Chester Arms*: Wide choice of generous tasty home-made bar food from sandwiches up inc vegetarian dishes and children's helpings in cosy and pretty two-bar beamed pub with log fire, comfortable settles and chairs, friendly service, Greene King Abbot, darts, fruit machine, quiet piped music; sizeable evening restaurant, picnic tables in garden *(Arnold and Maureen East, David Tonnison)*

Clifton Reynes [no through road; off back rd Emberton—Newton Blossomville; SP9051], *Robin Hood*: Small friendly local with two attractive bars, nice conservatory and very big garden leading to riverside walk to Olney; old dark beams, brasses, horns, inglenook, newspapers in lounge; open fire, table skittles and juke box in public bar; well kept Greene King and Charles Wells ales, varied food (not Mon evening) from good filled rolls up; no children inside *(George Atkinson, Simon Walker)*

Coleshill [A355; SU9495], *Magpies*: Brewers Fayre, modern interior, Whitbreads-related beers, wide choice of reasonably priced food, play area; piped music *(Peter Saville)*

Colnbrook [1¼ miles from M4 junction 5 via A4/B3378, then 'village only' rd; TQ0277], *Ostrich*: Striking Elizabethan pub, modernised but still giving feel of its long and entertaining history; good open fire, real ale and friendly service, though emphasis primarily on food side *(Doug Gault, LYM)*

Cublington [High St; SP8322], *Unicorn*: 16th-c beamed pub, supposedly haunted, with rickshaw, pictures and pine furniture, five changing real ales, very good value food (not Sun evening) inc vegetarian and vegan, friendly attentive service, picnic tables in garden behind with chickens and ducks *(Mary Walters, CMW, JJW)*

☆ **Denham** [¾ mile from M40 junction 1; follow Denham Village signs; TQ0486], *Swan*: Pretty pub in lovely village, now owned by Eldridge Pope and completely refitted – bright and tidy, with prints on timbered walls, picture windows overlooking splendid floodlit back garden with play area; comfortable seats, open fires, decent food and wines, well kept ales *(Mayur Shah, Stan Edwards, LYM)*

Denham [Village Rd], *Green Man*: Very warm and welcoming 18th-c pub, beams and flagstones in original part, dining area in raised extension, well kept beers *(R Houghton)*

Dorney [Lake End Rd; off A4 Maidenhead—Cippenham by Sainsburys; SU9278], *Pineapple*: Old-fashioned beamery and panelling, gleaming bar, simple furniture, good value usual food from sandwiches up, well kept Tetleys-related ales, decent house wine, friendly staff, verandah, small pleasant garden; handy for Bressingham Gardens plant centre *(John Waller, R A Buckler)*

Downley [Downley Common – OS Sheet 165 map ref 849959; SU8495], *Le De Spencer*: Unpretentious 18th-c Fullers pub hidden away on common, fairy-lit loggia overlooking lawn, friendly landlord, bar snacks; woodland walks to nearby Hughenden Manor *(Mark Percy, Lesley Mayoh, LYM)*

Farnham Common [The Broadway (A355); SU9684], *Foresters Arms*: Welcoming landlord and locals in relaxed and civilised two-room dining pub, rugs on woodblock floor, panelling, good food inc Sun roasts, Bass, Fullers and Greene King IPA, two log fires; soft piped music *(Simon Collett-Jones, Dave Uhrich, TBB)*; [Collinswood Rd (A355 a mile S of M40 junction 2)], *Yew Tree*: Well kept ales inc Morlands Old Speckled Hen, good choice of whiskies, friendly atmosphere, darts; really good traditional cooking by landlord (steak and kidney pie, game etc), excellent value breakfast from 8am (not Sun), separate dining room, reasonable prices, log fire in each small room; Burnham Beeches within an easy walk *(Nigel Quilter, Peter Burnstone, Dave Uhrich)*

☆ Farnham Royal [Blackpond Lane; SU9583], *Emperor of India*: Small vine-covered open-plan dining pub, buoyant atmosphere, wide range of interesting food from good choice of sandwiches and baguettes to excellent fish, six or seven Whitbreads-related and guest ales, interesting licensees and super dog, well kept garden and barn for summer eating *(K L Parsons, Ian Phillips, Mr and Mrs P Hertel)*

☆ Fingest [signed off B482 Marlow—Stokenchurch; SU7791], *Chequers*: Civilised and old-fashioned Tudor pub, interesting furniture, several rooms, sunny lounge by good-sized charming country garden, small no-smoking room, Brakspears PA, SB and Old, chatty licensees, dominoes, cribbage, backgammon, attractive restaurant; children in eating area, no food Sun evening; interesting church opp, good walks *(TBB, Nigel Norman, Maysie Thompson, Dr G W Barnett, Gordon, LYM)*

☆ Flackwell Heath [3½ miles from M40 junction 4; A404 towards High Wycombe, 1st right to Flackwell Heath, right into

Sheepridge Lane; SU8988], *Crooked Billet*: Cosy and comfortable old-fashioned 16th-c pub in lovely country setting, low beams, good choice of lunchtime food (not Sun), separate eating area, friendly prompt service, well kept Brakspears and Whitbreads-related ales; juke box; delightful little front garden with quiet views *(J and B Cressey, Ian Phillips, Simon Collett-Jones, BB)*

☆ Frieth [signed off B482 in Lane End; SU7990], *Yew Tree*: Short but interesting if not cheap choice of well cooked food in civilised candlelit dining pub, well kept ales such as Brakspears PA, Fullers London Pride and Gibbs Mew Bishops Tipple, prompt pleasant service; unobtrusive piped music; walkers with dogs welcome *(Simon Collett-Jones, Nigel Peterson, TBB, Cyril S Brown, GWB, Peter Saville, LYM)*

Fulmer [Windmill Rd; SU9985], *Black Horse*: Friendly and unpretentious local, very popular, with real ales, bar food, small garden *(M J Dowdy)*

☆ Great Brickhill [Ivy Lane; SP9030], *Old Red Lion*: The star is for the fabulous view over Buckinghamshire and beyond from the back lawn; decent straightforward food, friendly efficient service, well kept Whitbreads-related ales, lots of magazines; maybe unobtrusive piped music *(KC, LYM)*

☆ Great Horwood [The Green, off B4033 N of Winslow; SP7731], *Crown*: Attractive two-room Georgian pub with small but frequently changing choice of good value fresh home-made food, well kept Flowers IPA, Wadworths 6X and Whitbreads Fuggles, friendly landlady and spaniel called Toby, inglenook log fire, attractive front garden and back courtyard; quiz nights *(Graham and Karen Oddey, George Atkinson)*

Great Horwood [B4033], *Swan*: Friendly front lounge with inglenook fires and dining area, small back bar with pool and darts, very wide choice of well prepared straightforward food using good ingredients, well kept Bass, Greene King IPA and Websters Yorkshire; nice side garden; may cl some weekday lunchtimes *(B and K Hypher, Marjorie and David Lamb, Graham and Karen Oddey)*

☆ Great Kimble [Risborough Rd (A4010); SP8206], *Bernard Arms*: Plush and popular upmarket pub with some nice prints, daily papers, good imaginative bar food, four changing Tetleys-related and other ales, decent wines, good range of malt whiskies and bottled beer, good coffee, games room, well kept gardens, interesting food in restaurant; well equipped bedrooms *(Dave Braisted, P Saville)*

☆ Great Linford [4½ miles from M1, junction 14; from Newport Pagnell take Wolverton Rd towards Stony Stratford; SP8542], *Black Horse*: Large rambling pub with good range of good value food, well kept Tetleys-related and guest beers, Addlestone's cider, friendly staff, open fire, upstairs restaurant, fresh flowers; just below Grand Union Canal – drinks can be taken out on the towpath (good walks along here), and sizeable lawn with well spaced picnic tables and biggish play area; children allowed away from bar; evenings piped music, games machines and exuberant local youth may be more prominent *(JJW, CMW, Joe Hill, LYM)*

☆ **Great Missenden** [London Rd; old London rd, E – beyond Abbey; SP8901], *Nags Head*: Emphasis on quick straightforward food from sandwiches to good steaks in cosy creeper-covered small pub with well kept Tetleys-related and guest beers, big log fire, no piped music, picnic tables on back lawn *(M J Dowdy)*

Haversham [2 High St; SP8343], *Greyhound*: Pleasant 17th-c village pub in attractive countryside, some stripped stone and beams, Greene King IPA and Abbot, good choice of food inc doorstep sandwiches, friendly chatty staff; small garden with picnic tables and swing *(George Atkinson)*

☆ **Hawridge** [The Vale; signed from A416 N of Chesham – OS Sheet 165 map ref 960050; SP9505], *Rose & Crown*: Spaciously refurbished open-plan pub, comfortable and welcoming, with good value bar food, well kept Brakspears, helpful staff, big log fire, peaceful country views from restaurant area, broad terrace with lawn dropping down beyond, play area; children allowed *(Jan and Colin Roe, Ian Phillips, LYM)*

☆ **Hawridge Common** [off A416 N of Chesham, then towards Cholesbury; SP9505], *Full Moon*: Welcoming little country local with snugly comfortable low-beamed rambling bar and spacious common-edge lawn, good friendly service by cheerful young staff, small range of reasonably priced well presented food, wide choice of changing well kept real ales; children and dogs welcome *(Peter Saville, LYM)*

☆ **Hedgerley** [SE of M40 junction 2; SU9686], *White Horse*: Bustling country local with particularly well kept Charles Wells Eagle, Greene King IPA and six unusual changing ales tapped from the cask, friendly service; relaxed atmosphere in charming small public bar, jugs, ball cocks and other bric-a-brac, log fire, larger lounge with rather intrusive food display unit (usual decent food inc good lunchtime sandwiches and Sun lunch), occasional barbecues in big pleasant back garden, lovely window boxes, occasional beer festivals; no dogs, can be very busy; old attractive village, good walks nearby *(CMW, JJW, Simon Collett-Jones)*

Hedgerley [Village Lane, SE of M40 junction 2 – OS Sheet 175 map ref 968863], *One Pin*: Unchanging family-run local with warm friendly atmosphere, Scottish Courage beers, log fires, decent straightforward food and well kept garden *(Colin Draper, GWB, M J Dowdy)*

Hedsor [SU9187], *Garibaldi*: Good village pub with friendly staff, well kept beer, garden *(Christopher Glasson)*

High Wycombe [Amersham Rd, Terriers; SU8792], *Beech Tree*: Cosy little red brick local, vastly expanded conservatory eating area at the back, reasonably priced bar food, good value for families, well kept Courage Best and Directors and Wadworths 6X, cheerful staff even when busy; big well equipped play area, lots of picnic tables on grassy area, pleasant semi-rural setting *(Tony Dickinson, GWB)*; [Totteridge Lane, Totteridge], *Dolphin*: Doing well under current management, chintzy decor, well kept Greene King, friendly service, unusual reasonably priced food inc good Sun lunch *(Tony Dickinson)*

☆ **Ickford** [E of Thame; SP6407], *Rising Sun*: Cosy low-beamed bar in pretty thatched local, good value lunchtime buffet (over-55s and under-10s discount, admirable starters), separate dining room with German evening dishes (welcoming German landlady); well kept Bass ales, decent wine, fresh flowers, woodburner *(A Pantin)*

☆ **Iver** [TQ0381], *Gurkha*: Gurkha paintings and trophies in pleasant bar, spacious yet cosy and individual; good choice of plain well presented home cooking, wide choice in big restaurant, good service, nice staff *(Nick Holmes)*

Ivinghoe [Vicarage Lane; off B489 opp church; SP9416], *Rose & Crown*: Limited choice of reasonably priced fresh food, four well kept ales, quiet piped music, friendly service, L-shaped bar with second room up a few steps; children welcome, no muddy boots – nr one end of Ridgeway long-distance path; pleasant village *(CMW, JJW)*

Kingswood [A41; SP6919], *Crooked Billet*: Rambling white weatherboarded dining pub, interesting well cooked food, Tetleys-related ales, pleasant efficient service, piped classical music; can be busy; tables outside – attractive surroundings, handy for Waddesdon Manor *(Marjorie and David Lamb, George Atkinson, Hugh Spottiswoode, Tim and Ann Newell, M A and C R Starling)*

☆ **Lacey Green** [Parslows Hillock; from A4010 High Wycombe—Princes Risborough follow Loosley signpost, then Gt Hampden, Gt Missenden signpost; OS Sheet 165 map ref 826019; SP8201], *Pink & Lily*: Charming old-fashioned taproom (apostrophised sillily by Rupert Brooke – poem framed here) in much-extended Chilterns pub with airy and plush main bar, open fire, cheapish food (not Sun evening) from sandwiches up, well kept ales such as Batemans Valiant, Boddingtons, Brakspears PA, Courage Best and Glenny Hobgoblin, good wines, friendly efficient service, dominoes, cribbage, ring-the-bull; piped music, children over 5 if eating; conservatory, big garden *(R Morgan, Nigel Norman, Joan and Andrew Life, Ted George, M J Dowdy, LYM)*

Lacey Green [Pink Rd; SP8100], *Whip*: Cheery pubby local just below windmill, mix of simple traditional furnishings, reliable food from good lunchtime sandwiches to Sun lunches, well kept beer, friendly service; fruit machine, TV; tables in sheltered garden

(Alison Haines, Margaret Dyke, GWB, Nigel Pritchard, BB)

☆ **Little Kingshill** [Hare La; SU8999], *Full Moon*: Picturesque hidden-away pub with big helpings of well served food, changing real ales, friendly landlord, buoyant atmosphere, new restaurant area, no piped music; neat attractive garden *(Dave Carter, TBB)*

☆ **Little Marlow** [Church Rd; off A4155 about two miles E of Marlow, pub signed off main rd], *Kings Head*: Flower-covered old free house, immaculate open-plan interior, popular reasonably priced bar food from good toasties up, ales such as Bass, Fullers London Pride and Wadworths 6X, prompt pleasant service *(Don Mather, Simon Collett-Jones, TBB, Jenny Garrett, GWB)*
Little Marlow [cul de sac reached by turning off A4155 nr Kings Head], *Queens Head*: Very peaceful and attractive spot *(TBB)*

☆ **Little Missenden** [SU9298], *Red Lion*: Pleasant and popular 15th-c village local with Tetleys-related and other real ales, decent wines, good value traditional food from sandwiches to robust main courses, sunny garden with pets' corner for children – trout and ducks in the river to feed too *(Paul Kitchener, Peter Watts, Cyril S Brown)*

☆ **Little Tingewick** [Mere Lane – off A421/B4031 SW of Buckingham; SP6432], *Red Lion*: 16th-c thatched pub with big divided bar and small dining area, well kept Fullers beers, wide choice of good home-made bar food inc vegetarian, jovial Irish landlord and hospitable staff, pleasant piped music; no-smoking area, family garden *(Jeff Davies)*

☆ **Littleworth Common** [Common Lane; 3 miles from M40 junction 2, off A355 towards village then left after Jolly Woodman; SU9487], *Blackwood Arms*: Lively and friendly family atmosphere, well kept real ales, good value simple food, quick service, a roaring log fire, tables outside; good walks all around *(Alan Vere, David Lamb, LYM)*
Littleworth Common [Littleworth rd; 2 miles from M40 junction 2; off A355], *Jolly Woodman*: Big busy Whitbreads pub by Burnham Beeches, beamed and cottagey, wide range of food, usual Whitbreads-related beers, quick pleasant service, bar billiards, useful tourist leaflets *(Mr and Mrs R A Bryan, LYM)*

☆ **Lower Hartwell** [Oxford Rd (A418); SP7913], *Bugle Horn*: Rambling 17th-c pub, civilised and comfortable yet unspoilt, with polite friendly service, wide choice of food, good range of real ales, restaurant; big garden *(Dr and Mrs A K Clarke)*

☆ **Ludgershall** [The Green; off A41 Aylesbury—Bicester; SP6617], *Bull & Butcher*: Quiet little beamed country pub with good range of attractively presented meals, well kept Fullers London Pride and Tetleys, good friendly service, unobtrusive piped music; children allowed in back dining room, tables in nice front garden *(Marjorie and David Lamb, D and J McMillan, Paul Kitchener)*

☆ **Maids Moreton** [SP7035], *Wheatsheaf*: Little cosy rooms in small hidden-away thatched

local with cosy beamed original part, good food inc interesting specials and superb steaks cooked by landlord and served mainly in quaint home-built conservatory with woodburner, Whitbreads-related and other ales, friendly service, pleasant enclosed garden; piped music, opens noon *(Keith and Gill Croxton, Graham and Karen Oddey)*

☆ **Marlow** [St Peter St; first right off Station Rd from double roundabout; SU8586], *Two Brewers*: Bustling low-beamed bar with shiny black woodwork, nautical pictures, gleaming brassware, food all day (from 9.30 breakfast), well kept Brakspears, local Rebellion IPA and Wadworths 6X, good wines, considerate service, tables in sheltered back courtyard, front seats with glimpse of the Thames; children in eating area (no prams), very busy Sun lunchtime *(Christine and Geoff Butler, David Regan, Nigel Bruce, Arnold and Maureen East, I E Folkard-Evans, GWB, LYM)*

☆ **Marlow** [Henley Rd (A4155 W)], *Hare & Hounds*: Pretty and neatly kept ivy-clad cottage, cosy corners, inglenook log fire, comfortable armchairs, decent food, well kept Brakspears, Rebellion Smuggler and a guest beer, good house wines, darts, cribbage, dominoes; piped music; no-smoking restaurant, children welcome; small garden *(GWB, J and B Cressey, Susan and John Douglas, LYM)*
Marlow [High St], *Hogshead*: Vast interior with dozens of tables, about ten real ales *(J S Green)*; [West St (A4155 towards Henley)], *Ship*: Lots of interesting warship photographs and nautical equipment in low-beamed town local's small side-by-side bars, straightfoward bar lunches from sandwiches up, well kept Whitbreads-related ales, friendly service, piped music, tables on pleasant little back terrace, evening restaurant (children allowed here) *(TBB, LYM)*

☆ **Marsh Gibbon** [back rd about 4 miles E of Bicester, pub SW of village; SP6423], *Greyhound*: Unusual combination of traditional furnishings (stripped beams and stonework) with good Thai food, half-price for children (no under-6s), in bar and two-room restaurant with oriental statuary; Fullers London Pride, Greene King Abbot and IPA, Hook Norton Best, and McEwans 80/-, handsome woodburner, dominoes, cribbage, and classical piped music, tables outside with play area *(Ken and Jenny Simmonds, M A and C R Starling, Ian Phillips, Gordon, D and J McMillan, JJW, CMW, LYM)*
Marsh Gibbon [opp church], *Plough*: Old stone-built village pub with comfortable banquettes in bays, welcoming young landlord, good bar food inc fresh sandwiches, Morrells ales, decent house wine *(D and E Frewer)*

☆ **Marsworth** [Vicarage Rd; signed off B489 Dunstable—Aylesbury; SP9214], *Red Lion*: Friendly low-beamed partly thatched village pub with well kept ales such as Bass, Hook Norton Best and Wadworths 6X, decent wines, interesting good value food inc good vegetarian dishes, quiet lounge with two open fires, steps up to snug parlour and lively games area; sheltered garden, provision for children; not far from impressive flight of canal locks *(Lynda Payton, Sam Samuells, Sidney and Erna Wells, LYM)*

Marsworth [Startops End (B489)], *White Lion*: Comfortably plush modernised pub notable for position by Grand Union Canal (pleasant walk from Red Lion), nicely planted garden with lily pond, terrace with picnic tables; dining bar, small restaurant, well kept Greene King and local brewery, efficient polite service, good-sized children's room, unobtrusive piped music *(Mel Smith, Shirley Cannings)*

☆ **Medmenham** [A4155 Henley—Marlow; SU8084], *Dog & Badger*: Comfortably modernised low-beamed bar with open fire, brasses and soft lighting, usual food (not Sun evening) inc Fri fish and chips and proper old-fashioned puddings, well kept Brakspears PA and SB, Flowers Original and local Rebellion IPA, restaurant; children in eating area *(Val Stevenson, Rob Holmes, LYM)*

☆ **Milton Keynes** [Broughton Rd, Old Village; SP8938], *Swan*: Handsome and spacious dark-beamed thatched pub with big back dining extension, no-smoking area; Boddingtons, Courage Best and Wadworths 6X, vast choice of quite good food inc vegetarian, friendly attentive service, attractive furnishings, log-effect gas fire in inglenook; maybe piped pop music; popular with businesspeople lunchtime, very busy Sun; picnic tables in back garden, footpaths to nearby lakes *(Graham and Karen Oddey, Judi, Ian Phillips)*

☆ **Moulsoe** [Cranfield Rd; about a mile N of M1 junction 14; SP9041], *Carrington Arms*: Welcoming newly refurbished pub/restaurant with good food, esp steaks and fish chosen or cut to your size and barbecued indoors to order; good service, well kept Theakstons Old Peculier and other ales, children welcome, big garden *(Mark Hydes, Ian and Christina Allen, Stephen, Julie and Hayley Brown, Colin Pettit)*

☆ **Newport Pagnell** [Tickford St (B526), 2 miles from M1 junction 14; SP8743], *Bull*: Very welcoming traditional 17th-c coaching inn, eight well kept changing real ales inc rarities for the area, generous well priced straightforward food (not Sun evening), daily papers, friendly staff, softly lit low-ceilinged lounge decorated with front pages on famous events, bar with darts, juke box and pool; tables in pleasant courtyard; next to Aston Martin works, cars on show weekdays; bedrooms *(George Atkinson, Simon Walker, CMW, JJW, Darrell Kirsop, Ian Phillips, Richard Houghton)*

Newport Pagnell [High St], *Frog & Nightgown*: Small pub in stableyard of Swan Revisited hotel, well kept Ruddles and Theakstons, bar food, good sandwiches; bedrooms *(KC)*

Newton Longville [2 Westbrook End; off A421 S of Milton Keynes; SP8430], *Crooked Billet*: Good food and well kept beer in converted 17th-c thatched barn on edge of council estate, immaculate stylish decor, lounge and no-smoking dining room divided by log fires, four real ales, reasonably priced food inc children's helpings, nice garden; maybe piped local radio *(CMW, JJW, Ian Phillips)*

☆ **Olney** [12 High St (A509), S Olney; SP8851], *Swan*: Cosy mix of pub and bistro, good variety of generous home-cooked food, well kept beers inc Hook Norton, Jennings and Morrells ales, good competitively priced wine list, keen chatty landlord, friendly helpful staff, beams, open fires and soft lighting *(Ian and Christina Allen, Mark and Liz Slater, David and Mary Webb, Penny and Ron Westwood)*; [34 High St], *Two Brewers*: Very wide choice of generous popular food inc good home-made pies and Sun lunches, big dining area with plenty of different-sized tables, well stocked bar with well kept beer, good coffee, friendly prompt service, attractive courtyard decorated to show its brewery past, tables in garden too *(Meg and Colin Hamilton, George Atkinson, Stephen Brown)*

☆ **Oving** [Church Lane; off A413 Winslow rd out of Whitchurch; SP7821], *Black Boy*: Friendly and interesting old pub nr church, magnificent collection of jugs, well kept Whitbreads-related beer, good generous food inc Sun lunch, jovial landlord, superb views over terrace and big sloping garden; TV in small bar *(George Atkinson, Ann Griffiths, Dr and Mrs A K Clarke)*

Penn [SU9193], *Horse & Jockey*: Friendly and reliable, with good range of promptly served daily changing bar food, most home-made, well kept beers *(Gerald Barnett, Michael Tucker)*

☆ **Penn Street** [SU9295], *Hit or Miss*: Wide range of good generous food from ploughman's to wide range of seafood inc lobster and friendly bustling atmosphere in comfortably modernised low-beamed three-room pub with own cricket ground, good cricket and chair-making memorabilia, welcoming landlord, quick pleasant service, well kept ales such as Brakspears, Fullers and Hook Norton, log fire, no piped music or machines, occasional live music; pleasant setting *(Chris and Andy Crow, Michael Tucker, N Bushby, W Atkins, LYM)*

☆ **Penn Street**, *Squirrel*: Friendly and pubby, with good choice of home-cooked food at attractive prices, well kept Adnams, Bass and other ales, children's room, big garden; handy for lovely walks (and watching cricket) *(N Bushby, W Atkins)*

☆ **Preston Bisset** [Pound Lane, signed from A421; SP6529], *White Hart*: Attractive unspoilt 18th-c thatched and timbered pub with low beams, old pictures, good fresh home-made food inc fish and some unusual dishes, cosy atmosphere, well kept real ales inc Marstons Pedigree, farm cider, good house wines, good strong Irish coffee, friendly licensees, small dining room; hood skittles, tables in back garden; cl Tues lunchtime *(Graham and Karen Oddey, D and J McMillan, Mr and Mrs G Ricketts, Mr and Mrs Grimes, R Thompson, Marjorie and David Lamb)*

Preston Bisset, *Old Hat*: Has been quaint and homely village pub with quiet and relaxed cottage-parlour atmosphere, very traditional layout and considerable character; recently reopened after a year's closure *(News please)*

Saunderton [Wycombe Rd; SU8198], *Rose & Crown*: Nice log fires, big winged leather chairs, good restaurant food, comfortable coffee lounge, friendly staff; bedrooms comfortable *(Nigel Norman, GWB)*

☆ **Shabbington** [off A418 Oxford—Thame; SP6607], *Old Fisherman*: Attractive small riverside pub with Morrells ales and a guest such as Clarks Burglar Bill, good range of food inc good fish choice and enjoyable steaks, friendly spaniel; garden with play area, small camp site *(Tim and Ann Newell, Andy and Jill Kassube)*

☆ **Skirmett** [SU7790], *Frog*: Enjoyable country pub with good range of good value home-cooked food and of drinks inc local real ales, helpful cheerful service; children welcome; a pleasant place to stay, in attractive valley *(Mary and Des Kemp, Dave Carter)*

Slapton [Horton Rd; SP9320], *Carpenters Arms*: Small pub which doubles as an antique/book shop, inside divided into four, inc a dining room; very friendly staff, ales inc Morlands Old Speckled Hen, attractively served good food (not cheap – and may stop serving Sun) *(George Atkinson, D Billingham)*

Soulbury [SP8827], *Boot*: Good range of beers, wide choice of bar food *(J I Davies)*

☆ **Speen** [Flowers Bottom Lane; road from village towards Lacey Green and Saunderton Stn – OS Sheet 165 map ref 835995; SU8399], *Old Plow*: Restaurant not pub (they won't serve drinks unless you're eating, the bar's tiny compared with the dining room, and atmosphere's rather formal), but relaxing and charmingly cottagey, with good open fires, well kept Adnams and Brakspears, good food and wines (you can have just one course), fine service, log fires, children in eating area, pretty lawns, lovely countryside; cl Sun evening and Mon *(Cyril Brown, Francis and Deirdre Gevers, LYM)*

☆ **Stewkley** [High St N; SP8526], *Swan*: Old pub with tiled front public bar, comfortable lounge, nice dining area with huge log fire; well kept Scottish Courage ales, good value food, maybe piped pop music; children's room, extensive gardens inc good big enclosed children's play lawn *(Mel Smith, Shirley Cannings)*

Stoke Goldington [B526 NW of Newport Pagnell; SP8348], *White Hart*: Smartly modernised thatched and beamed pub with two bars and restaurant, good value food, well kept Charles Wells and guests such as Brains and Shepherd Neame Spitfire, cheerful attentive landlord; maybe local radio; picnic tables on sheltered back lawn *(George Atkinson, LYM)*

☆ **Stoke Green** [a mile S of Stoke Poges; off B416 signposted Wexham and George Green – OS Sheet 175 map ref 986824; SU9882], *Red Lion*: Recently totally refurbished, rambling and roomy with lots of little separate areas, pleasant atmosphere, basic range of well presented good value food, just a couple of beers (inc Fullers London Pride) but good choice of decent wines, log fires, no-smoking room, children welcome; tables outside, summer barbecues; has been open all day Fri/Sat *(Mr and Mrs P Hertel, David Regan, LYM)*

Stoke Poges [Hollybush Hill; SU9983], *Rose & Crown*: Good value food, pleasant decor, good service *(Mary Wood)*

☆ **Stony Stratford** [72 High St; SP7840], *Cock*: Quiet and comfortable old-fashioned hotel with leather settles and library chairs on bare floorboards, good bar food served piping hot, very friendly service, six well kept ales such as Fullers London Pride, Jennings, Morlands Old Speckled Hen and Theakstons; bedrooms *(George Atkinson, LYM)*

Stony Stratford [High St], *Bull*: Flagstoned bar with wooden benches and pine tables and chairs, lots of farm tools and country hardware, well kept Gales, food, friendly service; helpful cheerful staff in rather old-fashioned main hotel lounge too, with pleasant atmosphere; bedrooms *(Graham and Karen Oddey, LYM)*; [High St], *Old George*: Attractive, lively and friendly half-timbered inn, upstairs restaurant; bedrooms *(Graham and Karen Oddey)*

☆ **The Lee** [Swan Bottom; back rd ¾ mile N of The Lee – OS Sheet 165 map ref 902055; SP8904], *Old Swan*: Four attractively furnished interconnecting rooms, low beams and flagstones, cooking-range log fire in inglenook, relaxed civilised atmosphere, particularly well kept Brakspears and interesting guest beers, decent wines, welcoming long-serving landlord, friendly efficient service, fresh home-cooked food from sandwiches up (vegetarian on request); spacious prettily planted back lawns with play area, good walks *(John and Phyllis Maloney, John and Carol Rees, Jan and Colin Roe, Peter Saville, J Waller, Mr and Mrs A Hoyle, LYM)*

The Lee [back roads 2½ miles N of Great Missenden, E of A413], *Cock & Rabbit*: Stylish and comfortable panelled dining pub with strong Italian influence esp in attractively served home-made food (not Sun or Mon evening), well kept Boddingtons, Fullers and Morlands Speckled Hen, decent wines, good lively staff, big garden with tables on verandah, terraces and lawn; children in eating area and cafe-restaurant *(Keith Croxton, LYM)*

☆ **Thornborough** [just off A421 4 miles E of Buckingham, outside village – pub name on OS165; SP7433], *Lone Tree*: Six interesting quickly changing well kept beers from small breweries, good choice of wines and good coffee in friendly and spotless long stripped-brick bar with old-fashioned tables and chairs, magazines and books in alcove, real fire in inglenook; wide choice of ambitious food inc lots of vegetarian, quiet piped music; garden with play area (road noise) *(Keith Croxton, Dave Irving, John and Phyllis Maloney)*

Twyford [E of village; Calvert—Gawcott rd, just N of Twyford—Steeple Claydon one – OS Sheet 165 map ref 676268; SP6726], *Seven Stars*: Rambling low-beamed country pub popular for varied imaginative food in lounge bar and separate dining area (not Sun evening; fish and meat from London markets daily), friendly service, well kept Hook Norton Best and Old Hookey with two weekly changing guests, open fires, pictures and old farm tools; pool in games room, tables on pleasant lawn with animals for children, entertainment Sun evening; handy for Claydon House *(Marjorie and David Lamb, Gordon)*

Tylers Green [Hammersley Lane; two miles from M40, junction 3; SU9093], *Old Queens Head*: 17th-c, with flagstones and old beams; wide range of good value food in bar and restaurant area (up in former barn eaves), several well kept ales, pleasant atmosphere and service; children in eating area, open all day *(Steve Hickey, Richard Houghton, Jan and Colin Roe)*

Wavendon [not far from M1 junctions 13 and 14; SP9137], *Plough*: Pretty village pub reopened under new management, picturesque and comfortable, with promising food; good garden *(Monica Shelley, Laura Darlington, Lucy Spencer)*

Wendover [High St; SP8607], *Red Lion*: Wide choice of good value changing food, generous and imaginative, inc fish specialities and Sun lunch in pleasant bustling refurbished oak-beamed bar and adjacent good value restaurant, ales such as Brakspears, Courage Directors and Hancocks HB, good wines, friendly efficient staff; walker-friendly – on Ridgeway Long Distance Path; comfortable bedrooms *(Kathy Berry, Joan and Andrew Life)*

West Wycombe [London Rd (A40); SU8394], *Old Plough*: 17th-c National Trust pub with ever-burning log fire, reasonably priced food and real ales; old furniture and quiet piped music in welcoming snug low-beamed downstairs bar, more modern upstairs lounge, restaurant, darts, winter pool table; barbecue in pretty little garden up behind; interesting village *(Ian Phillips, CMW, JJW)*

Weston Turville [Church Lane; SP8510], *Chequers*: Concentration on good interesting

food (not Mon) from sandwiches up in low-beamed flagstoned two-level bar and attractive restaurant, good range of wines and malt whiskies, well kept Tetleys-related and other ales, open fire, stylish solid wooden furniture; tucked away in attractive part of village, some tables outside *(Tim Heywood, Sophie Wilne, M Sargent, Nuala Mahoney, Jan and Colin Roe)*

☆ **Weston Underwood** [off A509 at Olney; SP8650], *Cowpers Oak*: Charming old creeper-clad beamed pub with friendly service (can slow on busy days), Hook Norton Best and Marstons Pedigree, good value food in back restaurant area, tropical fish tank, games area with skittles and darts, unobtrusive piped music; tables in attractive garden, nearby zoo *(Mrs P J Pearce, Maysie Thompson, G R Braithwaite)*

☆ **Whitchurch** [10 High St; A413 Aylesbury—Buckingham], *White Swan*: Homely and pubby two-bar Fullers local with well kept beer, well prepared food, picnic tables in rambling garden behind *(Gill and Keith Croxton, Ian Phillips, Francis and Deirdre Gevers, John and Phyllis Maloney, LYM)*

Wing [9 High St; SP8822], *Queens Head*: Open fire in pleasant bar, good fairly priced home-cooked bar food, generous helpings, decent house wine, courteous service; has been cl Sun/Mon *(John and Margaret Whitehead)*

Winslow [Market Sq; SP7627], *Bell*: Unpretentious former coaching inn with comfortable modernised lounge, efficient landlord, friendly obliging staff, real ales, good bar food, popular good value carvery; bedrooms good value too, dogs allowed *(A Nunnerley, LYM)*

☆ **Wooburn Common** [Wooburn Common Rd, about 3½ miles from M40; SU9387], *Royal Standard*: Busy Whitbreads Wayside Inn with wide choice of enjoyable good value bar food, good friendly service, well chosen wines, well kept beers, mix of old and brighter new decor with popular restaurant area; tables outside, boules pitch behind *(Chris and Martin Taylor, Peter Saville, Cyril Brown, LYM)*

☆ **Worminghall** [Clifden La, not far from M40 junction 8; SP6308], *Clifden Arms*: Very picturesque 16th-c beamed and timbered thatched pub in pretty gardens, old-fashioned seats and rustic memorabilia in lounge bar with roaring log fire, another in public bar, well kept Adnams Broadside, Boddingtons, Fullers ESB and London Pride, Hook Norton and changing guest beers, traditional games, food (not Sun evening) from sandwiches to steaks (with newish restaurant); good play area, Aunt Sally, some live music; attractive village *(R Buckler, Sandria Parker, Paul Kitchener, Ted George, LM, LYM)*

Pubs with particularly interesting histories, or in unusually interesting buildings, are listed at the back of the book.

Cambridgeshire

One of this year's new entries here is actually a floating converted barge – Charters in Peterborough, with its own fine real ales. In the others, there's more emphasis on food: the attractively refurbished old George & Dragon at Elsworth, the King William IV at Heydon (extraordinary collections of rural and other bric-a-brac), and the Old Bridge in Huntingdon – food (and wine) so good that it also wins our award as Cambridgeshire Dining Pub of the Year. Other pubs currently doing particularly well in this favoured area include the Eagle in Cambridge (lots of character), the Pheasant at Keyston (excellent food), the splendidly unpretentious Queens Head at Newton, and the charming Anchor at Sutton Gault (another good dining pub). We'd like to draw particular attention to some of the Lucky Dip entries at the end of the chapter: the Royal Oak at Barrington, White Swan at Conington, Kings Head at Dullingham, Oliver Twist at Guyhirn, Pear Tree at Hildersham, Bell at Kennett, Red Lion at Stretham, White Horse at Swavesey and that idiosyncratic one-of-a-kind the Tickell Arms at Whittlesford. We have inspected virtually all of these and can vouch for their wide appeal. Local drinks prices are rather higher than the national average: the cheapest beer we found was on Charters in Peterborough (their own Oakham brews), in the Black Bull at Godmanchester (brewed for them locally, though they are tied to Whitbreads), and in the cheery Live & Let Live in Cambridge.

BARNACK TF0704 Map 5
Millstone ◀

Millstone Lane; off B1443 SE Stamford; turn off School Lane near the Fox

It's worth arriving at this friendly village inn early as the good reliable food is very popular and seats fill up quickly. The atmospheric and comfortable timbered bar with high beams weighed down with lots of heavy harness is split into imtimate areas with cushioned wall benches on the patterned carpet. The little snug is decorated with the memorabilia of a former regular, including his medals from both World Wars. The snug and dining room are no smoking; piped music. Served by pleasant, attentive staff, bar food includes sandwiches (the french bread with hot sausage and mushrooms is well liked), soup (£2), home-made chicken liver pâté (£3.45), ploughman's (£4.75), home-cooked ham and eggs (£5.25), lasagne or leek and mushroom bake (£6.95), cajun chicken or seafood crêpe (£7.45), sirloin steak (£8.95), and puddings like nice white chocolate and rum mousse; smaller helpings for OAPs; usual children's menu. Very well kept Adnams, Everards Old Original and Tiger and two guest beers on handpump; country wines and Scrumpy Jack cider; darts, pool, pinball, and dominoes. (Recommended by Jenny and Michael Back, Simon Collett-Jones, F J Robinson, Eric Locker, Tom Evans, John Fahy, Tony Gayfer)

Post Office address codings confusingly give the impression that some pubs are in Cambridgeshire, when they're really in the Leicestershire or Midlands groups of counties (which is where we list them).

Everards ~ Tenant Aubrey Sinclair-Ball ~ Real ale ~ Meals and snacks (not Sun evening) ~ Restaurant (not Sun evening) ~ (01780) 740296 ~ Children in eating area of bar ~ Open 11-2.30, 5.30(6 Sat)-11; 12-4, 7-10.30 Sun

BYTHORN TL0575 Map 5
White Hart ⓜ ⛉

Village signposted just off A14 Kettering—Cambridge

From the front, this looks simple – but once inside, you realise that this is a well run, restauranty pub with an emphasis on good, adventurous cooking. Changing daily, there may be starters like home-made chicken soup (£3.50), king prawns in garlic butter, spicy fish gumbo or roquefort quiche (£4.50), ploughman's with three cheeses (£4.95), braised barbury duck leg with cherry sauce, game and Guinness casserole, oriental chicken salad, seafood pasta, fresh tomato and pine nut pasta or toasted goat's cheese with garlic (all £6.50), and puddings like chocolate chestnut bombe, prune and brandy posset or toasted pineapple with ginger syrup (£4). There's an unpretentious mix of furnishings in the homely main bar and several linked smallish rooms such as a big leather chesterfield, lots of silver teapots and so forth on a carved dresser and in a built-in cabinet, and wing armchairs and attractive tables. One area with rugs on stripped boards has soft pale leather studded chairs and stools, and a cosy log fire in a huge brick fireplace; cookery books and plenty of magazines for reading. Well kept Greene King IPA and Abbot on handpump, and a good, no-nonsense, well chosen wine list; pleasant staff and very hospitable professional licensees. The restaurant is no smoking. *(Recommended by Maysie Thompson, John C Baker, M Sargent, John Fahy, R C Wiles, Mr Brooks, John Saul; more reports please)*

Free house ~ Licensees Bill and Pam Bennett ~ Real ale ~ Meals and snacks (till 10; no bar meals Saturday evening or Sunday lunchtime) ~ Restaurant ~ (01832) 710226 ~ Children welcome ~ Open 11-3, 6-11; 12-3 Sun (closed Sun evening); closed Monday and 26 Dec

CAMBRIDGE TL4658 Map 5
Anchor £ ◀

Silver St

This is a lively, young-feeling place popular with students – especially in the evening. It's set on four levels with two bars, and the area around the entrance is sectioned off to create a cosy atmosphere with lots of bric-a-brac and church pews, and a brick fireplace at each end. The no-smoking upstairs bar is pubby, with pews and wooden chairs and good riverside views. Downstairs the cafe-bar (open all day) has enamel signs on the walls and a mix of interesting tables, settles, farmhouse chairs, and hefty stools on the bare boards. Steps take you down to a simpler flagstoned room, and french windows lead out to the suntrap terrace – marvellously set right by the River Cam. You can hire punts here, and in summer they hold occasional events on the river. Good value bar food includes home-made soup (£1.95), filled baked potatoes (from £2.95), ploughman's (£3.50), four home-made daily specials such as aubergine and pasta bake, barbecue chicken casserole, sweet and sour pork, or lamb and apple pie (all £3.95), and puddings like sticky toffee fudge cake (from £1.95); Sunday roasts (£4.75). Lots of well kept real ales such as Boddingtons Bitter, Brains Early Bird, Flowers Original, Fremlins, Fullers London Pride, Marstons Pedigree, Wadworths 6X, and Whitbread Castle Eden tapped from the cask, and there's a good range of foreign bottled beers; cheerful young service, and various trivia and fruit machines, and a juke box. *(Recommended by David Carr, JJB, John Fahy, RWD, Amanda Dauncey, John Rudolf; more reports please)*

Whitbreads ~ Manager Alastair Langton ~ Real ale ~ Meals and snacks (12-8, till 5 Fri and Sat, 12-2.30 Sun) ~ (01223) 353554 ~ Children in eating area of bar ~ Open 11-11; 12-10.30 Sun

Eagle ♀

Bene't Street

This is our most popular Cambridge pub. It's an old stone-fronted 16th-c building with many of the original architectural features in its five rambling and relaxed bars still intact: worn wooden floors and plenty of original pine panelling, two fireplaces dating back to around 1600, two medieval mullioned windows, and the remains of two possibly medieval wall paintings. The high dark red ceiling has been left unpainted since the war to preserve the signatures of British and American airmen worked in with Zippo lighters, candle smoke and lipstick. The furniture is nicely old and creaky. Hidden behind sturdy wooden gates is an attractive cobbled and galleried courtyard with heavy wooden seats and tables and pretty hanging baskets. Straightforward but good value food is served from a display counter in a small room at the back. At lunchtime, there might be pâté (£2.50), ploughman's, quiche or cauliflower and broccoli au gratin (£4.25), chilli or roast chicken (£4.50), and gammon and egg (£4.95), with evening burgers (from £3.95), barbecue chicken (£4.75), and plaice (£4.95); daily specials, too. A neat little booklet lists up to 20 fresh wines, sparkling wines and champagne by the glass. Well kept Greene King IPA, Abbot, and Rayments and seasonal ales on handpump. This was the local of Nobel Prize winning scientists Crick and Watson, who discovered the structure of DNA. No noisy fruit machines or juke box, and no smoking in one area; friendly service from well dressed staff. *(Recommended by Jeff Davies, Norman and Valerie Housley, J F M West, Scott Rumery, John Wooll, Keith and Janet Morris, G W Stephenson, Andy and Jill Kassube, Michael and Lynne Gittins, Stephen and Julie Brown)*

Greene King ~ Licensees Peter and Carol Hill ~ Real ale ~ Meals and snacks (12-2.30, 5.30-9; not Fri, Sat, Sun evenings) ~ (01223) 505020 ~ Children in eating area of bar only ~ Open 11-11; 12-10.30 Sun

Free Press

Prospect Row

As a registered boat club, this completely no-smoking distinctive old pub can display its collection of oars and rowing photographs with more legitimacy than most Cambridge pubs. It has been run by the same friendly licensee for 20 years, and the civilised and unspoilt rooms are full of character and popular with locals; best to get there early for a seat. Good wholesome home-made bar food served in generous well priced helpings from a fairly short menu includes soup (a choice of two vegetarian soups daily; £2.25), chilli con carne (£4.25), at least two meat and two vegetarian specials like pork and cider casserole, beef in beer, bombay vegetables or leek croustade (£4.25), nut roast or game pie (£4.75), and puddings like apple crumble, lemon torte or sticky toffee pudding (£1.95). Well kept Greene King IPA, Abbot and Mild on handpump, with a good selection of malt whiskies and freshly squeezed orange juice; cribbage and dominoes behind the bar. The sheltered paved garden at the back is quite a suntrap; friendly cat. *(Recommended by David Carr, Jeff Davies, Hazel and Michael Duncombe, John Fahy, Keith and Janet Morris, J F M West, T L Rees, Frank Gadbois, Amanda Dauncey, John Rudolf, Steve and Angela Maycock, Mike Beiley, Brian Horner, Brenda Arthur)*

Greene King ~ Lease: Christopher Lloyd ~ Real ale ~ Meals and snacks (12-2, 6-8.30) ~ (01223) 368337 ~ Well behaved children welcome ~ Open 12-2.30(3 Sat and Sun), 6-11; 12-3, 7-10.30 Sun; cl 25 Dec after 2pm, 26 Dec

Live & Let Live £ ◖

40 Mawson Road; off Mill Road SE of centre

The heavily timbered brickwork rooms in this unpretentious pub are furnished with sturdy varnished pine tables with pale wood chairs on bare boards, alongside lots of interesting old country bric-a-brac and posters about local forthcoming events; piped music. The eating area is no-smoking, and basic but generous bar food includes big sandwiches (from £1.40), home-made soup (£1.75), and daily specials like bangers and mash (£3.50), and beef and Guinness pie, chicken curry or vegetable lasagne (£3.75). Well kept Adnams Southwold, Banks & Taylor SOS, Boddingtons Mild, and Everards Beacon and Tiger on handpump, and local cider; friendly service. On Sunday evenings they serve free garlic bread and potato wedges and dips with the live music. There is now a small terrace. *(Recommended by Tessa Stone, P and D Carpenter, David Carr, Susan and Nigel Wilson)*

Free house ~ Peter Gray ~ Real ale ~ Meals and snacks ~ (01223) 460261 ~ Children in eating area till 8.30 ~ Folk group Sun evening ~ Open 11(12 Sat)-2.30, 5.30(6 Sat)-11; 12-2.30, 7-10.30 Sun

ELSWORTH TL3163 Map 5
George & Dragon
Off A604 NW of Cambridge, via Boxworth

Set back from the quiet village street, this brick-built pub has been transformed inside, the traditional but very civilised panelled main bar opening on the left to a slightly elevated no-smoking dining area with comfortable tables and a good woodburning stove. From here are steps down to a another quiet no-smoking section behind, with more tables overlooking the back garden. From the wide choice of carefully prepared fresh food, we or readers have particularly enjoyed the good home-made soups (£3), gammon (£5.50), chicken breasts with a well balanced mushroom sauce (£6.80) and a tender mixed grill (£9.50), with plenty of fresh vegetables and proper potatoes; good puddings (from £2). Well kept Greene King IPA, Nethergate, Ruddles County and Tetleys on handpump, decent wines, friendly waitress service. Despite the emphasis on food, there's a good deal of character, with appealing lighting, plenty of pictures, and sparkling brass and copper on the beams; everything is spotless. On the right is a more formal restaurant. There are attractive terraces and so forth in the back garden, with a play area. *(Recommended by Maysie Thompson, Jenny and Michael Back, E A George)*

Free house ~ Licensees Barry and Marion Ashworth ~ Real ale ~ Meals and snacks (not Sun evening) ~ Restaurant ~ (01954) 267236 ~ Children in eating area of bar and in restaurant ~ Open 11-2.30, 6-11; 12-2.30 Sun (closed Sun evening)

ETTON TF1406 Map 5
Golden Pheasant 🍺
Village just off B1443, just E of Helpston level crossing; and will no doubt be signposted from near N end of new A15 Peterborough bypass

Bustling and cheerful, this stone-built pub is popular for its seven or eight well kept real ales on handpump: Adnams Broadside and Southwold, Badger Tanglefoot, Bass, Batemans XXXB, Greene King IPA, Kelham Island Pale Rider, and Woodfordes Wherry. Quite a few malt whiskies, too. The comfortable homely bar has an open fire, high-backed maroon plush settles built against the walls and around the corners, and prints on the walls. In the airy, glass-walled, no-smoking side room are some Lloyd Loom chairs around glass-topped cane tables. Tasty bar food includes home-made soup (£2.75), garlic mushrooms (£3.50), stir-fry vegetables (£6.85), chicken curry or steak and ale pie (£6.95), good minted lamb bake (£7.75), steaks (from £9.95), and specials like glazed giant ribs, venison steak with pepper sauce or trout with parsley butter (£8.95). Pool, dominoes, fruit machine, and piped music. The stone-walled garden looks out across flat countryside, and has boules, an adventure playground, an aviary with about 70 golden pheasants, quail, cockatiels, rosella parakeets and budgerigars, and a big paddock. The golden labrador is called Bonnie. *(Recommended by M J Morgan, John Fahy, John Baker; more reports please)*

Free house ~ Licensee Dennis Wilson ~ Real ale ~ Meals and snacks (till 10pm) ~ Restaurant ~ (01733) 252387 ~ Children in eating area of bar, in restaurant and pool room ~ Open 11.30-11; 12-10.30 Sun ~ Bedrooms: £20/£40

FEN DRAYTON TL3368 Map 5
Three Tuns
High Street; village signposted off A14 NW of Cambridge

This pretty thatched country pub has two inglenook fireplaces in its unpretentious and cosy bar, as well as heavy-set moulded Tudor beams and timbers, and comfortable cushioned settles and an interesting variety of chairs. It's decorated with old local photographs, old song-sheets of local folk songs, big portraits, brass plates, fresh flowers, and old crockery in a corner dresser. There's plenty of drinking space, and helpful staff serve very well kept Greene King IPA, Abbot, Rayments and seasonal ales on handpump as well as a range of malt whiskies. Generous helpings of good value bar food (the licensee tells us prices are unchanged from last year) include sandwiches (from £1.25), home-made soup (£1.80), chicken liver and bacon pâté (£2.50), ploughman's (£3), meaty or vegetable lasagne (£4.25), chicken curry (£4.50), and 8oz rump steak (£8); daily specials like good stuffed lamb heart, a pie of the day, and babotie, and puddings such as home-made apple pie and good treacle tart. Sensibly placed darts, shove-ha'penny, dominoes, cribbage and fruit machine. A well tended lawn at the back has tables under cocktail parasols, apple and flowering cherry trees, and some children's play equipment. The pub can get very crowded, so it's best to arrive early if you want to eat. *(Recommended by Maysie Thompson, Rona Murdoch, Barry and Anne, B N F and M Parkin, Dr and Mrs B Baker, F J Robinson, Gordon Theaker, Colin McGaughey, Andrew and Joan Life)*

Greene King ~ Tenant Michael Nugent ~ Real ale ~ Meals and snacks (not evenings of 24/25 Dec) ~ (01954) 230242 ~ Children in eating area of bar until 8pm ~ Open 11(12 Sun)-2.30, 6.30-11(7-10.30 Sun); cl evening 25 Dec

FOWLMERE TL4245 Map 5
Chequers 🍽 ♀
B1368

Rather smart and attractive, this 16th-c country pub is very much somewhere to come for an imaginative meal. Served by black-and-white-dressed waiters there might be cauliflower, stilton and celery soup with chervil cream and croûtons (£2.80), grilled Greek halloumi cheese with aubergine dip and pitta bread (£4.10), brochette of king prawns with sun-dried tomato and aioli mayonnaise dips or tomato and spinach risotto with chargrilled Mediterranean vegetables (£6.90), chicken breast in a cream, champagne and wild mushroom sauce (£7.60), beef and Guinness casserole with dumplings (£8.20), steamed plaice and green lipped mussels on a yellow pepper sauce with sweet potatoes and broccoli (£8.80), grilled venison steak on a compote of red cabbage (£11), puddings such as hot date sponge with a sticky toffee sauce or rich chocolate truffle cake with dark chocolate sauce (from £3.80), Irish farmhouse cheeses (£3.60), and Sunday roast sirloin of English beef (£9.80). There's an excellent choice of very well priced fine wines by the glass (including vintage and late-bottled ports), quite a few malt whiskies, well kept Adnams Broadside on handpump, freshly squeezed orange juice, and a good choice of brandies. There are two warm and cosy comfortably furnished communicating rooms downstairs with an open log fire – look out for the priest's hole above the bar. Upstairs there are beams, wall timbering and some interesting moulded plasterwork above the fireplace. The pub sign honours British and American pilots who'd made this their second home, with the blue and white chequers of No 19 Sqdn RAF on one side, and the red and white chequers of USAF 339th Fighter Group on the other; there are some interesting black and white photographs in the bar showing the local WW1 and WW2 airfields. The airy no-smoking conservatory overlooks white tables under cocktail parasols among flowers and shrub roses in a pleasant well tended garden. *(Recommended by F C Johnston, Nick and Meriel Cox, TRS, Derek Patey, Ian Phillips, Mayur Shah, Conor McGaughey, Howard Gregory, Susan and Nigel Wilson, Paul McPherson, Neil and Angela Huxter)*

Free house ~ Licensee Norman Rushton ~ Real ale ~ Meals and snacks (till 10pm) ~ Restaurant ~ (01763) 208369 ~ Well behaved children welcome ~ Open 12-2.30, 6-11; 12-2.30, 7-10.30 Sun; cl 25 Dec

GODMANCHESTER TL 2740 Map 5
Black Bull

Post St; follow village signposts off A14 (was A604) just E of Huntingdon

Readers enjoy their visits to this heavy-beamed old pub by the church. The main bar has seats built into the inglenook of the enormous fireplace, settles forming booths by leaded-light windows, quite a bit of glinting brassware, and a good winter log fire; a side room up a step is hung with lots of black agricultural and other rustic ironwork; all three bar areas are to be refurbished. Courteous staff serve good, straightforward bar food such as home-made soup (£1.75), ploughman's (£3.75), ham and egg (£4.95), turkey curry, home-made steak and ale pie or a vegetarian dish (£6.25), spicy chicken (£7.25), mixed grill (£9.25), daily specials, and puddings like apple crumble with toffee and pecans (£2.25). Well kept Black Bull (made locally for them), Boddingtons, Flowers Original and Whitbreads Castle Eden kept under light blanket pressure; unobtrusive piped pop music and fruit machine. There's a big courtyard and pretty garden behind the car park. *(Recommended by J R Morris, Ian and Jane Irving, D Byng, Dr and Mrs B Baker, CMW, JJW, Stephen Brown, George Atkinson)*

Whitbreads ~ Lease: Colin Dryer ~ Real ale ~ Meals and snacks (till 10pm; all day Sun) ~ Restaurant ~ (01480) 453310 ~ Children welcome ~ Open 11-2.30(3 Sat), 6-11; 12-10.30 Sun; closed 25 Dec ~ Bedrooms: £19/£35

GOREFIELD TF4111 Map 5
Woodmans Cottage 🍽

Main St; off B1169 W of Wisbech

There may be a staggering choice of up to 60 puddings at weekends made by the buoyantly cheerful landlady and her staff in this thriving village inn. Other food is popular too: toasties (from £1.25), omelettes or ploughman's (£4), steak and kidney pie, mushroom stroganoff or gammon and pineapple (all £6), cajun chicken (£6.75), mixed grill (£7), daily specials like good pork vindaloo or seafood platter, and children's dishes (from £1.25); roast Sunday lunch (£6; children £4). The spacious modernised bar, with leatherette stools and brocaded banquettes around the tables on its carpet, rambles back around the bar counter. A comfortable side eating area has a big collection of china plates, as well as 1920s prints on its stripped brick walls. There's a space for non-smoking diners called the Cellar, with a display of Lucille's paintings. Beyond is an attractive pitched-ceiling restaurant – best to book some time ahead. At the other end of the pub, a games area has darts, pool and CD juke box; Monday bridge nights, and piped music. Well kept Bass and Greene King IPA on handpump and quite a lot of Australian wines. There are tables out on a sheltered back terrace, with a few more on a front verandah. *(Recommended by Jenny and Michael Back, Bernard and Marjorie Parkin, Stephen Brown, R C Wiles, Terry and Eileen Stott, Mrs Pat Crabb, Anthony Barnes)*

Free house ~ Licensees Lucille and Barry Carter ~ Real ale ~ Meals and snacks (till 10pm) ~ Restaurant (cl Sun evening) ~ (01945) 870669 ~ Supervised children welcome away from the bar counter ~ Open 11-3, 7-11; 12-3, 7-10.30 Sun; closed evenings 25 and 26 Dec

GREAT CHISHILL TL4239 Map 5
Pheasant

Follow Heydon signpost from B1039 in village

The Old English Pub Company has taken over this little pub and installed new managers. The attractive split-level bar has some elaborately carved though modern seats and settles, a few plates on timbered walls, and a stuffed pheasant on the mantelpiece. There are bar stools with decent backs and, and at one end, dining chairs around the tables. Bar food now includes sandwiches, home-made soup (£3.25), queen scallops with garlic butter and parmesan cheese (£3.95), chargrilled cumberland sausage with onion gravy and mash (£5.25), smoked haddock and salmon fishcakes (£5.50), thai chicken (£6.25), steaks (from £10.95), honey-glazed duck breast on ginger flavoured vegetables (£11.25), fresh fish dishes, and daily specials; two-course Sunday roast (£6.50). Well kept Adnams, Ruddles Best, Shepherd Neame Spitfire, and Theakstons on handpump, and a decent wine list; darts, cribbage, dominoes, and piped music. A rising lawn behind the pub has seats among flowering cherries and a weeping willow, and there's a small children's play area. There is quiet farmland beyond the back rose hedge. *(Recommended by John Fahy, Stephen Brown, P and D Carpenter, Susan and Nigel Wilson; more reports on the new regime please)*

Old English Pub Company ~ Managers Mandy and Malcolm Drewery ~ Real ale ~ Meals and snacks ~ Restaurant ~ (01763) 838535 ~ Children in eating area of bar ~ Open 12-2.30(3 Sat), 6-11; 12-3, 7-10.30 Sun

HEYDON TL4340 Map 5
King William IV
Village signposted from A505 W of M11 junction 10; bear right in village

Mrs Nicholls who made the Royal Oak in Barrington such a success while she was there, has now moved to this village pub, and has brought her very enjoyable cooking with her. The rambling rooms have quite a few nooks and crannies and an overwhelming number of spotlessly clean agricultural implements on the standing props, wall timbers and dark oak beams – ploughshares, yokes, iron tools, cowbells, beer steins, samovars, cut-glass brass or black wrought-iron lamps, copper-bound casks and milk ewers, harness, horsebrasses, smith's bellows, and decorative plates and china ornaments; warm log fire. Very good bar food includes lunchtime snacks such as sandwiches (from £2.15), filled baked potatoes (from £3.50), and filled french bread (from £3.95; sirloin steak with chicken and orange pâté £4.95), as well as soup (£3.25), cream cheese and herb pâté (£4.40), devilled mushrooms with a hot mustard, garlic and horseradish sauce (£4.45), steak and kidney pie (£6.95), interesting vegetarian dishes such as cashew and pine kernel stir-fry with noodles and crackers or wild mushroom and apricot tagliatelle, sun-dried tomatoes and split almonds in a creamy sauce (from £6.95), creamy seafood crumble (£7.45), beef and mushrooms in stout with herb dumplings (£7.95), loin of pork coated with an oatmeal and cheese crunch with a cider, apple and sage sauce (£8.25), chargrilled steaks (from £10.95), and puddings (from £3.95). Well kept Adnams, Greene King IPA, Abbot, Rayments, and Kings Champion, and Ruddles County on handpump; friendly, efficient staff. There are seats in the pretty garden. *(Recommended by B N F and M Parkin, Stephen Horsley, Keith and Janet Morris)*

Free house ~ Licensees Elizabeth and Edward Nicholls ~ Real ale ~ Meals and snacks ~ Restaurant ~ (01763) 838773 ~ Children in eating area of bar ~ Open 12-3, 7-11(10.30 Sun)

HINXTON TL4945 Map 5
Red Lion
2 miles from M11 junction 9, 3½ miles from junction 10; just off A1301 S of Great Shelford

There's quite a collection of interesting ornaments and so forth in this carefully extended 16th-c local. The mainly open-plan bustling bar is filled with clocks, mirrors and pictures, grandfather and grandmother clocks, a barometer, some big prints and quite a few smaller rustic pictures on the walls, shelves of china in one corner, horsebrasses on the beams and timbers, and a stuffed tarantula, egret and guillemot – George the chatty Amazon parrot is very much alive. Good, reasonably priced bar food includes home-made soup (£2.50), ploughman's (£4.25), vegetable curry (£4.95), home-baked ham (£5.25), steak and ale pie

(£6.50), tandoori chicken (£6.95), Scotch salmon steak with fresh tarragon, white wine and cream (£7.95), steaks (from £8.75), and puddings like toffee crunch pie or lemon meringue pie (£2.50). Part of the restaurant is no smoking. Well kept Adnams, Boddingtons, Greene King IPA, Nethergate Bitter on handpump at the central bar counter, and trivia and unobtrusive piped classical music. The neatly kept garden has picnic tables, there's a new terrace, and a paddock with a small pony and goat; handy for Duxford Aeroplane Museum. *(Recommended by Bill and Sheila McCardy, Luke Worthington, Keith and Janet Morris, D R Eberlin, Quentin Williamson, Ian Phillips, A W, B W)*

Free house ~ Licensees James and Lynda Crawford ~ Real ale ~ Meals and snacks (till 10pm; 9.30pm Sun and Mon) ~ Restaurant ~ (01799) 530601 ~ Children in eating area of bar and restaurant ~ Open 11-2.30, 6.30-11; 12-3, 7-10.30 Sun

HOLYWELL TL3370 Map 5
Old Ferry Boat

Village and pub both signposted (keep your eyes skinned, it's easy to go wrong!) from Needingworth, which is just off the A1123

Sadly, this thatched old pub suffered a serious fire in March 1997 and had to close for some months. But by the time this book is published, things will be up and running again. Most of the damage was to the first floor which had to be rebuilt, and the bedrooms have been completely refurbished – but the fine old wisteria was lost. Luckily, the six characterful open-plan bar areas only suffered smoke damage and the very low beams and timbered and panelled walls were saved. There are window seats overlooking the river, one of the four open fires has a fish and an eel among rushes moulded on its chimney beam, and a stone in the bar marks the ancient grave of the resident ghost Juliette, said to return every year on 17 March; most of the pub is now no smoking. Good bar food includes home-made soup (£2.95), filled granary bread (from £3.25), chicken liver pâté (£3.75), ploughman's (£4.75), tagliatelle with mushrooms and a blue cheese sauce (£6.50), big fish and chips (£6.95), honey chilli chicken (£7.95), pork in a barbecue sauce (£8.25), sirloin steak (£10.95), and puddings (£2.95); children's dishes (£3.95). Well kept Bass, Nethergate IPA and Old Growler, Websters Yorkshire, and three guests on handpump; friendly, attentive, efficient service even when it gets very busy in summer and at weekends. Fruit machine and piped music. The pub is charmingly set in a remote part of the fens, with lazy tables and cocktail parasols on a manicured rose lawn (more on a front terrace) by the Great Ouse – where there's mooring for boats. *(Recommended by David Carr, E Robinson, Mr Gibson Warner, Charles and Pauline Stride, Ian Phillips, John Fahy, Jenny and Michael Back, Julian Holland, Nick and Meriel Cox, George Atkinson, Rita Horridge, Dr and Mrs S Jones; more reports on the refurbishments please)*

Free house ~ Licensees Richard and Shelley Jeffrey ~ Real ale ~ Meals and snacks ~ (01480) 463227 ~ Well behaved children welcome ~ Open 11.30-3, 6-11; 12-10.30 Sun (12-3, 7-11 winter Sun)~ Bedrooms: £44.50B/£55B

HORNINGSEA TL4962 Map 5
Plough & Fleece ★

Just NE of Cambridge: first slip-road off A45 heading E after A10, then left at T; or take B1047 Fen Ditton road off A1303

Bustling and friendly, this small but rambling country pub is quite handy for Cambridge. The homely low black-beamed public bar has comfortably worn high-backed settles and plain seats on the red tiled floor, a stuffed parrot and a fox by the log fire, and plain wooden tables including an unusually long pine one with an equally elongated pew to match. Enjoyable bar food includes lunchtime sandwiches (from £1.60; toasties £1.90), home-made soup (£2), home-made pâté (£3.25), stilton and broccoli flan (£3.50), home-cooked ham and egg (£4.25), delicious ham hotpot (£5.25), steak, kidney and mushroom pie (£6.50), rabbit with bacon (£7.50), barbary duck breast with hot, spicy sauce (£9.50), sirloin steak (£10.50), and puddings such as cherry cobbler or treacle tart (£2.50); prices are higher in the evening; friendly service. There's a good no-smoking dining room with lots of wood and old bricks and tiles, linked by a terrace to the garden, and a conservatory at the back. Well kept Greene King IPA and Abbot on handpump; dominoes and cribbage. The mix of wild and cultivated flowers in the garden is a nice touch; picnic tables beyond the car park. *(Recommended by P and D Carpenter, Chris and Ann Garnett, Malcolm Taylor, Stephen Brown, Nigel Clifton, Dr I Crichton, J F M West, TBB, Sue Rowland, Paul Mallett, Dr and Mrs S Jones)*

Greene King ~ Tenant Kenneth Grimes ~ Real ale ~ Meals and snacks (not Sun or Mon evenings) ~ Restaurant ~ (01223) 860795 ~ Children over 5 in restaurant only ~ Open 11.30-2.30, 7-11; 12-2, 7-10.30 Sun; closed evenings 25 and 26 Dec

HUNTINGDON TL2371 Map 5
Old Bridge 🍴 🛏 🍷

1 High St; just off B1043 entering town from the easternmost A604 sliproad
Cambridgeshire Dining Pub of the Year

Civilised and not too big, this attractive hotel is tucked away in a good spot by the River Great Ouse, with its own landing stage, and tables on the well kept garden's waterside terraces. With a spacious and comfortable dining area, the main emphasis is on the wide choice of good imaginative if not cheap food, including soups such as fennel, leek and onion broth (£3.75), pressed rabbit terrine with rabbit jelly and green bean salad (£4.95), dressed crab salad with apple, avocado, spring onion, samphire and tomato vinaigrette (£6.50), seafood risotto (£8.95), chargrilled salmon with fennel and spinach salad, asparagus, herb dressing and new potatoes (£11.95), roast monkfish (£13.50), roast saddle of hare with spinach and fresh pasta in black olive butter (£13.95), and puddings like passion fruit soufflé or treacle and pecan tart (from £3.95); they do small helpings for children. Perhaps the best value for people with big appetites is the unlimited-choice lunchtime cold table (£10.50); Sunday roasts lunch (£11.95); good waitress service. The charming bar, panelling and plush with a good log fire, has a good friendly atmosphere and well kept Adnams Best, Banks & Taylors and a guest beer on handpump, but it's the wines that are outstanding – a fascinating list, with an excellent choice of wines by the glass; good coffee, too. The lavatories are down steepish steps, but there are some ground-floor bedrooms. In the same small family chain as the Pheasant at Keyston and Three Horseshoes at Madingley. *(Recommended by D H Tew, E Robinson, John Fahy, J F M West)*

Free house ~ Licensee Nick Steiger ~ Real ale ~ Meals and snacks ~ Restaurant ~ (01480) 452681 ~ Well behaved children welcome ~ Live music first Fri of month Feb-Nov ~ Open 11-11; 12-10.30 Sun; closed 25 Dec ~ Bedrooms: £79.50B/£89.50B- £139.50B

KEYSTON TL0475 Map 5
Pheasant 🍴 🍷

Village loop road; from A604 SE of Thrapston, right on to B663

This is a thoroughly enjoyable and civilised place to come for a delicious meal. It's very well run and friendly, service is courteous and efficient – and the Adnams Bitter and changing guests like Adnams Broadside, Boddingtons or Fullers London Pride are well kept. The same menu is on offer throughout the building, with linen napkins and bigger tables in the no-smoking Red Room. From a changing menu, the imaginative dishes might include spicy fish soup with rouille and garlic croutons (£3.95), terrine of confit of duck leg with a piccalilli of peas (£4.50), chargrilled baby squid with stir-fried vegetables and ginger (£4.95), good wild boar sausages and mash with mustard sauce (£7.25), fresh tagliatelle with sun-dried tomatoes, black olives and pesto (£8.95), corn-fed chicken stuffed with tarragon, with risotto, morel mushrooms and cream (£11.75), chargrilled tuna with mediterranean vegetables (£12.50), roast rack of spring lamb with couscous and green vegetable broth with garlic and thyme (£13.95), and puddings such as sticky toffee pudding with toffee sauce and cream (£3.50) or poached peach with an apricot purée and cardamon ice cream (£4.25); Sunday roast sirloin of beef with yorkshire pudding (£10.75), and smaller helpings for children. The wine list has a good interesting choice of reasonably priced bottles (though to make the most of their list you need quite a deep pocket), with around 14 by the glass plus sweet wines and ports; freshly squeezed juices like carrot, orange and ginger. A friendly low-beamed room has old photographs, leather slung stools and a heavily carved wooden armchair; another room, with high rafters, used to be the village smithy – hence the heavy-horse harness and old horse-drawn harrow there. Wooden tables are set in front of the pub. *(Recommended by J F M West and Dr M West, Deborah Weston, John Fahy, Stephen Brown, M J Morgan, Paul and Maggie Baker, R K Sledge, Geoffrey and Irene Lindley, Dr and Mrs S Jones, Jane Kingsbury, Bob and Maggie Atherton, D Goodger, Thomas Nott, Simon Cottrell, M Sargent)*

Free house ~ Licensees Martin Lee and John Hoskins ~ Real ale ~ Meals and snacks (12-2, 6-10) ~ Restaurant ~ (01832) 710241 ~ Children welcome ~ Occasional music events ~ Open 12-3, 6-11; Sun evening opening 7; closed evening 25 Dec

MADINGLEY TL3960 Map 5
Three Horseshoes 🍴 ♀

Off A1303 W of Cambridge

Perhaps this is the most restaurGrasy of this little chain of pubs, yet it still has a pleasantly relaxed if civilised atmosphere – most so of course by the bar. From a stylish menu, the very good imaginative food might include toasted bread with olives and new season's Tuscan olive oil (£2.75), cannellini bean soup with poached egg and crème fraîche (£3.75), oxtail terrine with celeriac remoulade (£4.50), crab, saffron and chive tart with red pepper relish (£5.75), roast cod with mushroom ragout and baby leeks (£9.75), calf liver with pea purée and grilled raddichio with balsamic vinegar (£12.50), fillet of spring lamb with kidney and liver, girolle mushrooms, tomato, basil and asparagus with truffle oil (£14.50), and puddings like chocolate panetone bread and butter pudding, caramelised lemon tart or sticky toffee pudding with hot caramel sauce and rum and raisin ice cream (from £4). Four well kept real ales on handpump such as Adnams Southwold, Batemans XXXB, Everards Tiger, Fullers London Pride, Morlands Old Speckled Hen, Shepherd Neame Spitfire, and Wadworths 6X on handpump, and a wine list that is interesting in all price ranges with around 17 by the glass plus champagne, dessert wines and port. The charming traditional bar is comfortably furnished and has an open fire, and service is efficient and attentive. In summer it's nice to sit out on the lawn, surrounded by flowering shrubs, roses and trees. *(Recommended by Derek and Sylvia Stephenson, Sebastian Leach, J F M West, Maysie Thompson, Gwen and Peter Andrews, Charles Bardswell, Nick and Meriel Cox, Patrick Milner, Dr and Mrs S Jones, Paul and Janet Waring, Stephen and Julie Brown, Frank Gadbois, R C Wiles, J Sanderson, Patrick Milner, Paul McPherson, M Sargent, Amanda Dauncey, John Saul)*

Free house ~ Licensee Richard Stokes ~ Real ale ~ Meals and snacks ~ Children welcome ~ Restaurant ~ (01954) 210221 ~ Open 11.30-2.30, 6-11; 12-2.30, 7-10.30 Sun

NEWTON TL4349 Map 5
Queens Head ★ 🍺

2½ miles from M11 junction 11; A10 towards Royston, then left on to B1368

This is a smashing little pub – traditional and unpretentious and run by the same licensee for 25 years (he took it over from his father, now a nonagenarian living next door). The well worn friendly main bar has a low ceiling and crooked beams, bare wooden benches and seats built into the walls and bow windows, a curved high-backed settle on the yellow tiled floor, a loudly ticking clock, paintings on the cream walls, and a lovely big log fire. The little carpeted saloon is similar but cosier. Don't expect anything elaborate to eat – food is limited to a good choice of

exceptionally good value doorstep sandwiches (from £1.60) including banana and smoked salmon and very good roast beef ones, excellent beef dripping on toast (£1.60), and mugs of superb home-made soup (£1.90), or maybe filled baked potatoes (£1.90); in the evening and on Sunday lunchtime they serve plates of excellent cold meat, smoked salmon, cheeses and pâté (from £2.80). Adnams Bitter, Broadside and Extra are tapped straight from the barrel, with Old Ale in winter and Tally Ho at Christmas; country wines and Crone's and Cassells ciders. Darts in a no-smoking side room, with shove-ha'penny, table skittles, dominoes, cribbage, and nine men's morris. There are seats in front of the pub, with its vine trellis and unusually tall chimney, or you can sit on the village green. Belinda the goose who used to patrol the car park now sits stuffed in a glass case, but lives on in the pub sign, painted by the licensee's father and son; no-smoking games room.
(Recommended by Owen and Rosemary Warnock, Tony Beaulah, Charles Bardswell, Gregor Macdonald, Ian Phillips, Nick and Meriel Cox, Susan and Nigel Wilson, Conor McGaughey, Gervas Douglas, Graham and Karen Oddey)

Free house ~ Licensee David Short ~ Real ale ~ Snacks ~ (01223) 870436 ~ Well behaved children in games room ~ Open 11.30-2.30, 6-11; 12-2.30, 7-10.30 Sun; closed 25 Dec

PETERBOROUGH TL1999 Map 5
Charters 🏴

Town Bridge, S side

Just a short walk from the city centre, this is a sturdy 1907 Dutch barge, with a sizeable bar below decks – all the timbering and so on that you'd expect, with a friendly bustle, and an excellent choice of interesting well kept real ales on handpump. These include Bishops Farewell, Jeffrey Hudson Bitter, and Mompressons Gold from the owner's recently established Oakham microbrewery (he's hoping eventually to move it to a new brewpub he plans to set up here in Westgate), as well as Bass, Everards Tiger, Fullers London Pride and quickly changing interesting guest beers, usually from unfamiliar small breweries. On the upper deck is an informal restaurant, with enjoyable food such as doorstep sandwiches (from £1.50), nachos (vegetarian £1.75, meaty £2.25), steak in ale pie (£1.75), sausage and egg (£2.25); the restaurant is no smoking; piped music. Landlubbers can opt for tables in the bankside garden. No children. *(Recommended by Reg Nelson, Dagmar Junghanns, Colin Keane, John C Baker)*

Own brew ~ Licensee Paul Hook ~ Real ale ~ Lunchtime bar meals and snacks ~ Evening restaurant ~ (01733) 315700 ~ Open 12-11; 12-10.30 Sun; closed 25-26 Dec

STILTON TL1689 Map 5
Bell 🛏 🍷

High Street; village signposted from A1 S of Peterborough

A fine lunchtime stop if travelling on the A1, this rather elegant old stone coaching inn is most friendly and relaxed. The two spacious, attractive bars have sturdy upright wooden seats, plush-cushioned button-back banquettes built around the walls and bow windows, big prints of sailing and winter coaching scenes on the partly stripped walls, and a large warm log fire in the fine stone fireplace. Good bar food might include stilton and celery soup (£1.95), stilton pâté with pickle (£3.95), grilled garlicky oyster mushrooms on toasted brioche (£4.25), tagliatelle with smoked bacon, mushrooms, sage and cream (£5.75), vegetable chilli (£6.75), king prawn and monkfish brochette with a spicy thai sauce (£7.75), steak, mushroom and ale pie (£7.95), 10oz rib-eye steak on a cracked pepper sauce (£9.25), and puddings such as glazed lemon tart or bread and butter pudding (£2.75); part of the restaurant is no smoking. You can eat outside at tables in a lovely sheltered cobbled and flagstoned courtyard which has the distances to various cities carved on the walls – and a well which is believed to date back to Roman times. Well kept Marstons Pedigree and Tetleys and guest beers on handpump, and a broad choice of wines by the glass; good friendly service; dominoes, backgammon, and Scrabble.

Chintzy bedrooms make an elegent stay. *(Recommended by Andy Cunningham, Simon Collett-Jones, Yvonne Hannaford, Lady M H Moir, Nick and Meriel Cox, F J Robinson, Dr B and Mrs P B Baker, Mr Miller, P Rome, Barry and Anne, June and Malcolm Farmer, Christopher Turner, David Peakall, Richard Siebert, John Fahy, Geoffrey and Irene Lindley, Tony Dickinson, N B Thompson, Gill and Andy Plumb)*

Free house ~ Licensees John and Liam McGivern ~ Real ale ~ Meals and snacks ~ Restaurant ~ (01733) 241066 ~ Children in eating area of bar till 8pm ~ Open 12-2.30, 6-11; 11-3, 6-11 Sat; 12-3, 7-10.30 Sun; closed evenings 25 and 26 Dec ~ Bedrooms: £45B/£59B

SUTTON GAULT TL4279 Map 5
Anchor ★ ⑪ 🍴 ♀

Village signed off B1381 in Sutton

Deservedly popular, this is a well run pub with friendly licensees and staff, extremely good food, and a cosy intimate atmosphere in the four heavily timbered stylishly simple rooms. There are three log fires, lighting by gas and candles, antique settles and well spaced scrubbed pine tables on the gently undulating old floors, and good lithographs and big prints on the walls; three-quarters of the pub is now no smoking. Imaginative food might include home-made spicy ham and chick pea soup (£3.75), home-made fresh herring fillets in a madeira marinade (£4.75), tagliatelle with cream, mushrooms and blue cheese (£8.50), seafood crumble with fresh salmon, cod and prawns (£9.95), steak, kidney and Guinness pie (£10.50), calf liver and bacon (£12.95), Scotch sirloin steak with cream and coarse grain mustard sauce (£13.50), puddings such as a rich sharp lemon tart, chocolate and nut roulade with raspberry sauce and hot sticky toffee pudding (£4.25), and a good cheeseboard; very sensibly, children can have most of their dishes in half-helpings. There's a thoughtful wine list (including a wine of the week and 10 by the glass), winter mulled wine, a local cider and freshly squeezed orange and grapefruit juice. Well kept Adnams Best, Elgoods Cambridge Bitter, Nethergate IPA, and Wolf Bitter tapped from the cask; a fine choice of teas and coffees. In summer you can sit outside at the tables or on the bank of the Old Bedford River watching the swans and house martins; the river bank walks are lovely. No dogs. *(Recommended by Gordon Theaker, P and D Carpenter, P A Devitt, M Brooks, M C and S Jeanes, Luke Worthington, Julian Holland, Gwen and Peter Andrews, Rita Horridge, Jane Kingsbury, Stephen and Julie Brown, Andrew and Jo Litten, Ken and Jenny Simmonds, John Fahy, Mr Brooks, Karin and Steve Flintoff)*

Free house ~ Licensee Robin Moore ~ Real ale ~ Meals and snacks (till 9.30 on Sat) ~ (01353) 778537 ~ Well behaved children in no-smoking rooms (over 5 after 8pm) ~ Open 12-3, 7(6.30 Sat)-11; 12-3, 7-10.30 Sun; closed 25 and 26 Dec ~ Bedrooms: £45B/£57.50B

SWAVESEY TL3668 Map 5
Trinity Foot ♀

A14; to reach it from the westbound carriageway, take Swavesey, Fen Drayton turn-off

As good as ever, this bustling pub remains popular for its fresh fish delivered here daily direct from the East Coast ports and sold both in the pub and in their fish shop next door (open Tuesday-Saturday 11-2.30, 6-7.30). The popular menu includes spiced herring fillets or soft herring roe on toast (£3.75), 6 oysters (£5), grilled butterfish, haddock or cod (all £7.50), grilled skate wings (£8.25), monkfish with wine and cream or grilled tuna steak (£9.75), and fresh lobster (£17.50; also, sandwiches (from £1.25), soup (£2.50), ploughman's (£3.75), omelettes (£6), mixed grill (£9.95), and daily specials like courgettes stuffed with cream cheese, ginger and sunflower seeds (£6.25), liver and bacon (£7) and steak and kidney pie (£7.50). Well kept Boddingtons and Flowers on handpump, decent wines, and freshly squeezed orange juice. Service is cheerfully efficient, and there are well spaced tables, fresh flowers, and a light and airy flower-filled conservatory; no-smoking dining room. There are shrubs and trees in the big enclosed garden.

(Recommended by Ian Phillips, P and D Carpenter, David Surridge, N B Thompson, Pauline Langley)

Whitbreads ~ Lease: H J Mole ~ Real ale ~ Meals and snacks (till 10 Fri and Sat) ~ (01954) 230315 ~ Children welcome ~ Open 12-2.30, 6-11; 12-3 Sun (cl Sun evenings)

WANSFORD TL0799 Map 5
Haycock ★ 🍽 🛏 ♀
Village clearly signposted from A1 W of Peterborough

This well run civilised golden stone inn continues to offer the best of a traditional pub in its chatty main bar in tandem with the facilities of a comfortable hotel. The fine flagstoned main entry hall has antique hunting prints, seats and a longcase clock, and leads into the panelled main bar with its dark terracotta walls, sturdy dado rail above a mulberry dado, and old settles. Through two handsome stone arches is another attractive area, while the comfortable front sitting room has some squared oak panelling by the bar counter, a nice wall clock, and a big log fire. There's an airy stripped brick eating bar by the garden with dark blue and light blue basketweave chairs around glass-topped basket tables, pretty flowery curtains and nice modern prints; doors open on to a big terrace with lots of tables. Friendly, courteous staff serve the good bar food which may include sandwiches, home-made soup with ciabatta bread (£3.50), chicken liver pâté (£4.95), spinach and gruyère fritters (starter £5.95, main course £8.50), antipasto (£6.95, main course £9.95), open sandwiches (£7.25), vegetable chinese stir-fry (£7.50), tortellini with a bolognese sauce (£7.95), steak and kidney pie or lamb liver and bacon with bubble and squeak and onion gravy (£8.95), thai chicken curry (£9.50), 10oz rib eye steak (£11.95), and puddings like old-fashioned chocolate pudding with toffee and pecan nuts or crème brûlée with griddled toffee bananas; lunchtime cold buffet (£9.95). Well kept Adnams Broadside and Southwold, Bass, Ruddles Best, and a beer named after the inn on handpump, a good range of around 11 good house wines by the glass from an exceptional list, and properly mature vintage ports by the glass. The sheltered outdoor eating area with its big cream Italian umbrellas is very popular, and the spacious walled formal garden has boules and fishing as well as cricket (they have their own field). The restaurant is no smoking. *(Recommended by Gordon Neighbour, Tony Dickinson, Julian Holland, O K Smyth, Hanns P Golez, Susan and Nigel Wilson, Tony Gayfer)*

Free house ~ Licensee Andrew Underwood ~ Real ale ~ Meals and snacks (12-10.30; not 25 Dec) ~ Restaurant ~ (01780) 782223 ~ Children welcome ~ Open 11-11 ~ Bedrooms: £85B/£115B

WOODDITTON TL6659 Map 5
Three Blackbirds
Village signposted off B1063 at Cheveley

This rather smart thatched pub is set in stud country just outside Newmarket. The comfortable bar rooms have high winged settles or dining chairs around fairly closely spaced neat tables, cigarette cards, Derby-Day photographs, little country prints, and winter fires – the room on the left has the pubbier atmosphere; piped music. Bar food includes sandwiches (not Sunday), home-made soup (£2.70), smoked chicken salad (£3.85), roulade of spring chicken filled with smoked chicken mousse with an oyster mushroom sauce (£9.85), rack of English lamb with rosemary and honey sauce (£12), fresh fish dishes (from £9.35), a vegetarian dish like Mediterranean vegetable terrine (£9.80), and home-made puddings such as treacle tart, summer fruit crème brûlée or bakewell tart (£2.70); the restaurant is no smoking. Two changing real ales like Bass, Greene King IPA, Flowers Original or Whitbreads Castle Eden well kept on handpump, and a very good wine list. The attractive front lawn, sheltered by an ivy-covered flint wall, has flowers, roses, and a flowering cherry. *(Recommended by Mark Hydes, John and Elizabeth Cox, Stephen Brown; more reports please)*

Whitbread/Carlsberg Tetleys ~ Tenant Mark Roberts ~ Real ale ~ Meals and snacks ~
Restaurant ~ (01638) 730811 ~ Well behaved children welcome ~ Open 11.30-3,
6.30-11; 12-3.30, 7-10.30 Sun

Lucky Dip

Besides the fully inspected pubs, you might like to try these Lucky Dips recommended to us
and described by readers (if you do, please send us reports):

☆ **Alconbury** [Vinegar Hill, Alconbury Weston –
handy for A1, nr A14/M11 turn-offs;
TL1875], *White Hart*: Friendly and
comfortable pub in charming village, good
value generous food inc home-made chips,
eating areas left and right, back bar with
darts, Scottish Courage ales and an interesting
guest beer, very helpful licensees *(Norma and
Keith Bloomfield, Jenny and Michael Back,
Irene and Geoffrey Lindley)*

☆ **Barrington** [from M11 junction 11 take A10
to Newton, turn right; TL3949], *Royal Oak*:
Rambling thatched Tudor pub now run by
Old English Pub Co, heavy low beams and
timbers, lots of character, pleasant no-
smoking dining conservatory, tables out
overlooking charming green; well kept Greene
King IPA and Abbot, prompt service, food inc
wide vegetarian range; maybe piped music,
children in one area *(Howard Gregory, TRS,
M Sargent, Jeff Davies, D Horsman, Keith
and Janet Morris, Dr and Mrs S Jones, Nigel
and Amanda Thorp, P and D Carpenter,
Nigel Norman, Malcolm Taylor, LYM)*

☆ **Bourn** [signed off B1046 and A1198 W of
Cambridge; at N end of village; TL3256],
Duke of Wellington: Consistently good range
of generous imaginative food inc good home-
made puddings in quiet and civilised relaxing
bar divided by arches and so forth – where
the locals come to dine out; well spaced
tables, pleasant attentive staff, well kept
Greene King; cl Mon *(Mr and Mrs A J
Martin, John Fahy, Maysie Thompson, BB)*

Boxworth [TL3463], *Golden Ball*: Popular
dining pub, attractively refurbished, with
helpful staff, good value food, well kept
Greene King and Nethergate, separate
restaurant/family room (no children in main
bar), seats and play area in big well kept
garden; nice setting *(K and J Morris)*

☆ **Brampton** [Bromholme Lane; off A141
Huntingdon Rd opp Hinchingbrooke House;
TL2170], *Olde Mill*: Popular riverside
Beefeater, idyllic summer setting – converted
mill with working waterwheel and mill race
rushing under lounge's glass 'tables', usual
good value bar food inc nicely garnished
sandwiches, upper restaurant, Whitbreads-
related ales, quick pleasant service, tables out
by water *(Mrs P J Pearce)*

☆ **Cambridge** [85 Gwydir St], *Cambridge Blue*:
Comfortable, small and interestingly
decorated with university sports photographs
and local paintings; well kept Nethergate and
frequently changed guest beers, good value
food (not Sun evening) inc home-made pies

and vegetarian, one room no smoking, simple
furnishings, welcoming knowledgeable staff,
sheltered terrace with children's climbing
frame and entertaining model train *(Sandy
McIlwain, Susan and Nigel Wilson, Andy and
Jill Kassube, LYM)*

☆ **Cambridge** [Mill Lane], *Mill*: Fine spot by
main punt station on River Cam, summer
crowds out on the waterside grass; simple
bars with chunky furnishings on bare boards
and ancient quarry tiles, collections of clay
pipes, brewery taps and slings, college team
photographs etc, changing ales such as
Adnams, Black Sheep Bitter and Special,
Daleside Bitter and Monkey Wrench,
Marstons Pedigree, and Nethergate Bitter and
Growler, farm ciders, country wines, simple
lunchtime bar food from sandwiches up, fruit
machine, piped pop; children in eating area,
open all day *(David Carr, Andy and Jill
Kassube, Susan and Nigel Wilson, JJB, E A
Thwaite)*

☆ **Cambridge** [Ferry Path; car park on
Chesterton Rd], *Old Spring*: Good individual
atmosphere, cosy old-fashioned furnishings
and decor, bare boards, gas lighting, lots of
old pictures, decent straightforward bar food
inc Sun roasts, well kept Greene King IPA and
Abbot, two log fires, long back conservatory,
summer barbecues; children till 8, has been
open all day Sat *(Ian Phillips, David Carr,
Keith and Janet Morris, LYM)*

☆ **Cambridge** [Castle St], *Castle*: Properly
pubby, with full Adnams range kept well and
guests such as Fullers London Pride, good
value food inc vegetarian, friendly staff; large,
airy and well appointed, with easy chairs
upstairs, wood grain tables on bare boards in
bright, clean and cheerful downstairs tap
room, no-smoking area; maybe piped pop
music; picnic tables in good garden *(Terry
Barlow, P and D Carpenter, Keith and Janet
Morris)*

☆ **Cambridge** [Midsummer Common], *Fort St
George*: Picturesque, and very popular for its
charming waterside position on Midsummer
Common, overlooking ducks, swans, punts
and boathouses; extended around old-
fashioned Tudor core, interesting bar food
and traditional Sun lunches, well kept Greene
King ales, decent wines, games in public bar,
historic boating photographs, tables outside
(Clare Wilson, J F M West, LYM)

☆ **Cambridge** [14 Chesterton Rd], *Boathouse*:
Carpeted extension with verandah
overlooking river (wonderful playground on
opp bank), unspoilt relaxed atmosphere, L-

shaped main room with varnished wood tables, framed prints and rowing memorabilia inc suspended eights boat, eight or so beers such as Brakspears and Boddingtons, good choice of ciders, decent coffee, generous food; juke box; children welcome, pretty garden with hungry ducks, open all day; no dogs *(KM, JM, Sue Grossey, Mr Brooks, David Carr, LYM)*

☆ Cambridge [129 King St], *St Radegund*: Smallest pub in town, unusual decor with interesting former-student memorabilia, friendly landlord, well kept ales such as Fullers London Pride, Hook Norton Best and Nethergate, good malt whisky collection *(Keith and Janet Morris, FWG)*

Cambridge [Napier St, next to Grafton Centre], *Ancient Druids*: Big bright air-conditioned modern pub notable for Kite, Merlin and Druids Special ales brewed on premises; popular lunchtime food inc good chilli, daily papers *(E A Thwaite, J F M and M West)*; [Clarendon St], *Clarendon Arms*: Popular unpretentious local with well kept Greene King and Rayments, friendly staff, wide choice of cheap but adventurous bar lunches inc giant crusty sandwiches; open all day; bedrooms clean and comfortable *(E A Thwaite, Jeff Davies)*; [16 Chesterton Rd], *Fresher & Firkin*: Brews its own good beers, good value food, friendly helpful service; back windows overlook river *(R Houghton)*; [Granta Pl], *Garden House*: Hotel not pub, but good informal eating in lounge bar by River Cam, and easy parking; bedrooms comfortable *(J F M West)*; [335 Milton Rd], *Golden Hind*: Recently spaciously refurbished as a southern outpost of John Barras pub chain, cheap substantial food – good value; well kept Scottish Courage ales *(J F M West)*; [Newnham Rd], *Granta*: Balcony and terrace take full advantage of view over mill pond and attractive adjoining open area; punt hire *(Keith and Janet Morris)*; [Water St, Chesterton; TL4660], *Green Dragon*: Attractive timber-framed building in quiet street by the Cam, good value substantial food lunchtime and late evening (not Sat), friendly and comfortable with beams, inglenooks and so forth, and well kept Greene King Mild; waterside tables *(Keith and Janet Morris)*; [17 Bridge St, opp St Johns Coll], *Mitre*: Friendly attentive service, half a dozen real ales, well priced wines inc some New World ones, attractively priced food from fine sandwiches and hot beef baps up, no-smoking area, log-effect fire, back-to-basics alehouse decor *(Susan and Nigel Wilson, Kevin and Pam Withers)*; [Dover St (off East Rd)], *Tram Depot*: Unusual former tram stables with bare bricks, flagstones, old furniture, unconventional layout; reasonably priced bar food (not Sat evening), well kept Everards and wide range of other changing ales, seats out in courtyard; can be crowded with students *(E A Thwaite, David Carr)*

Castor [off A47 W of Peterborough; TL1298], *Fitzwilliam Arms*: Long low

thatched pub, low beams, bays of plush wall banquettes, further no-smoking lounge (children allowed here), games machines at one end, Morlands Old Speckled Hen and Tetleys, friendly helpful service, sensibly priced food from filled baps and baked potatoes to steaks, tables out on back grass; attractive village *(Jenny and Michael Back)*; [24 Peterborough Rd], *Royal Oak*: Another part-thatched inn, partly 16th-c, with good value freshly prepared bar snacks, well kept Bass, Tetleys and a guest, chatty licensees, beams, open fires and several small traditional bar areas; tables outside *(JJW, CMW, LYM)*

Chatteris [Pickle Fen; B1050 towards St Ives; TL3986], *Crafty Fox*: Unpretentious but distinctive roadside pub with small bar area, adjacent country-kitchen lounge, big back glass-covered summer-only eating area with fountain, fishpond and mature vines; well kept ales, interesting food *(Julian Holland, LYM)*; [16 Market Hill], *Cross Keys*: Attractive 16th-c coaching inn opp church in sleepy fenland town, long bar part public and part comfortable armchairs, pleasant back courtyard, good value food in bar and restaurant, friendly service, Greene King beers, inexpensive wine, tea and coffee; comfortable bedrooms *(John Wooll, R Garside)*

Cherry Hinton [TL4856], *Unicorn*: Wide evening choice of proper Thai food, cooked by someone from Bangkok, with more orthodox lunchtime dishes inc OAP lunches in spacious restaurant area; pleasant service, no piped music *(P and D Carpenter)*

☆ Conington [Boxworth Rd; signed off A14 (was A604) Cambridge—Huntingdon; TL3266], *White Swan*: Attractive and unpretentious country local with children welcome in several eating areas on right of cheerful traditional bar, games inc bar billiards and juke box on left, good big front garden with play area; good range of popular bar food inc fidgit pie and decent steaks, quick friendly service, well kept Greene King IPA and Abbot tapped from the cask, snuffs; tables outside, play house *(Jenny and Michael Back, BB)*

☆ Croydon [TL3149], *Queen Adelaide*: Friendly and comfortable beamed dining bar with standing timbers dividing off separate eating area, sofas, banquettes and stools, good value enjoyable home-made food, well kept ales such as Boddingtons and Greene King *(Derek Patey, Brian Dorer, Simon Watkins)*

☆ Downham [Main St; sometimes known as Little Downham – the one near Ely; TL5283], *Plough*: Charming neat but unspoilt fenland village local with short changing choice of good value home cooking, friendly staff, lots of old photographs and bric-a-brac, Greene King ales under light top pressure, good choice of malt whiskies, decent house wines, tables outside; bustling atmosphere; the friendly well behaved golden retrievers are called Abbot and Indi *(Richard Balls, Basil Minson, Roy Bromell)*

☆ **Dry Drayton** [Park St, opp church; signed off A428 W of Cambridge; TL3862], *Black Horse*: Unpretentiously straightforward village local with good generous food inc wide vegetarian choice, well kept Greene King and other ales inc weekly changing guests, friendly prompt service, welcoming fire in central fireplace, games area, tables on pretty back terrace and neat lawn; camping/caravanning in meadow behind, maybe geese at end of car park *(Ian and Nita Cooper, E Robinson, Keith and Janet Morris, P and D Carpenter, BB)*

☆ **Dullingham** [50 Station Rd; TL6357], *Kings Head*: Cosy dining pub, popular for a wide range of food from sandwiches to interesting main dishes (inc German specialities and plenty of vegetarian) and lots of puddings at very reasonable prices; coal fires, well kept ABC Bitter and Flowers IPA, good choice of fairly priced wines, friendly attentive staff, no-smoking room; fairy-lit seats out above the broad village green, adventure playground, no dogs; children in restaurant, and separate family room *(B and K Hypher, Mark Hydes, Gwen and Peter Andrews, John Fahy, LYM)*

☆ **Duxford** [village signed off A1301, pub at far end; TL4745], *John Barleycorn*: Thatched and shuttered early 17th-c cottage, tables out among flowers, softly lit relaxed bar with old prints, decorative plates and so forth, generous well cooked food from open sandwiches to jugged hare (worth booking, evening), Greene King IPA, Abbot and seasonal ales under light blanket pressure, decent wines, generous food; prices on the high side, service can slow *(TRS, D E Twitchett, Susan and Nigel Wilson, Comus Elliott, Brian and Jill Bond, LYM)*

☆ **Eaton Socon** [nr A1/A428 interchange; TL1658], *Crown*: Welcoming bustle in old inn, refurbished but keeping the low beams and separate areas, good choice of moderately priced food (not Sun) from sandwiches up, generous choice of changing ales kept well but served on sparkler, friendly service, two coal-effect gas fires, restaurant (good steaks); piped music may be loud, no T-shirts; garden *(Ian Phillips, FWG, Bob and Maggie Atherton, Scott Rumery)*

Eaton Socon [Gt North Rd], *Waggon & Horses*: Popular and busy old open-plan pub with lots of low beams and brasses, Bass and Tetleys-related ales, good value quick generous food inc copious fresh veg, delicious home-made puddings, good Sun lunches; restaurant *(D A Tinley)*

☆ **Eltisley** [signed off A428; TL2659], *Leeds Arms*: Comfortable knocked-through beamed bar overlooking peaceful village green, huge log fire, plenty of dining tables, nicely presented sometimes unusual bar food from sandwiches up, Greene King IPA and Hook Norton Best or Charles Wells Bombardier under light blanket pressure, restaurant; children in eating area, pleasant garden with play area; simple comfortable bedrooms in separate block *(E Robinson, LYM)*

☆ **Ely** [Annesdale, off A10 on outskirts; TL5380], *Cutter*: Lovely riverside setting, with plenty of tables outside and a genuine welcome for children; friendly series of unpretentious bars, generous decent food inc good home-made pies, real ales, good house wines; best to book Fri/Sat in boating season *(Mark and Heather Williamson, Neil and Angela Huxter, LYM)*

☆ **Ely** [62 Silver St], *Prince Albert*: Cheerfully traditional unpretentious town pub with full range of Greene King ales in peak condition, good welcome, tasty snacks, no juke box, attractive garden *(John C Baker, Charles and Pauline Stride, Ian Phillips)*

Ely [Barton Sq/Silver St], *Fountain*: Transformed by careful refurbishment, quiet and friendly, with perfectly kept Adnams and a guest beer such as Youngs Special, interesting wines, chatty landlord, promising food *(John Baker, D H Taillat)*; [2 Brook St], *Lamb*: Pleasant hotel nr cathedral, comfortable panelled and carpeted lounge bar with armchairs and settee, friendly attentive staff, good bar snacks inc warm smoked eel (local delicacy), well kept real ales; popular restaurant; decent bedrooms *(George Atkinson, W H and E Thomas)*

☆ **Fen Ditton** [High St; TL4860], *Ancient Shepherds*: Well cooked generous bar food inc imaginative dishes in comfortable and immaculate old-world lounge with settees and no music or fruit machines; friendly helpful staff, cosy restaurant (not Sun) *(David Lee)*

Fenstanton [High St (off A604 nr St Ives); TL3168], *King William IV*: Civilised but friendly low-beamed pub with wide choice of above-average food, cosy bar with adjoining restaurant; well kept Greene King ales, good range of spirits, pretty outside *(Mark Hydes, Gordon Theaker)*

Fordham [TL6270], *White Pheasant*: Well converted promising dining pub under same ownership as Red Lion at Icklingham, good food, nice friendly service *(Wayne Brindle)*

☆ **Fowlmere** [High St; TL4245], *Swan House*: Friendly and comfortable local with enormous log fire, good interesting reasonably priced bar food, good choice of well kept ales, attentive landlord, piano *(TRS, John Fahy)*

Friday Bridge [TF4604], *Chequers*: Beams, red plush seats, brassware and sporting trophies, reasonably priced bar food inc bargain early suppers Mon-Thurs, Elgoods ales; neat garden *(Jenny and Michael Back)*

Glatton [Sawtry Rd; off A1 S of Peterborough via B660; TL1585], *Addison Arms*: Comfortable and friendly atmosphere in spotless and popular two-bar local with good home-cooked food esp steak pie, well kept Ruddles County; piped music can be a touch loud; attractive village *(Tom McLean, PGP)*

Glinton [B1443 opp church; TF1505], *Blue Bell*: Big rambling free house, lots of nooks and crannies, log fire; welcoming new licensees, wide choice of beers and of very fairly priced bar food; piped music *(PGP)*; [Lincoln Rd], *Crown*: Good choice of competitively priced food inc vegetarian, relaxed atmosphere, restaurant *(Brian and Jill Bond)*

Grantchester [TL4455], *Red Lion*: Big food pub with sheltered terrace and good-sized lawn (with animals to entertain the many children); comfortable and spacious, busy food counter, restaurant *(Mike Beiley, LYM)*; [junction Coton rd with Cambridge—Trumpington rd], *Rupert Brooke*: Friendly and cosy renovated beamed pub with Whitbreads-related ales, wide choice of bar food inc vegetarian, discreet piped music *(Margaret and Roy Randle, Julian Holland)*

☆ **Guyhirn** [off B1187 nr A47/A141 junction S of Wisbech; TF3903], *Oliver Twist*: Comfortable open-plan lounge with well kept sturdy furnishings, good range of good value generous food from sandwiches to steaks, Everards Beacon and Tiger with a weekly guest beer, big open fire; restaurant, very popular at lunchtime business meeting place; opp River Nene embankment *(Jenny and Michael Back, E Robinson, Anthony Barnes, BB)*

☆ **Hardwick** [signed off A428 (was A45) W of Cambridge; TL1968], *Blue Lion*: Enjoyably friendly local with fairly priced good food inc quite a lot of fresh fish, well kept beer, very extensive restaurant area, conservatory, Greene King IPA and Abbot, log fires, old farm tools; piped music, unobtrusive ginger tom; pretty roadside front garden *(Jane Kingsbury, BB)*

☆ **Hildersham** [off A604 N of Linton; TL5448], *Pear Tree*: Busy straightforward village local with odd crazy-paved floor, huge woodburner, generous genuine home cooking inc some unusual dishes and good vegetarian ones as well as usual cheery pub food, children's helpings and special dishes cooked to order, home-made bread and ice creams; well kept Greene King IPA and Abbot, decent wines, welcoming staff, daily papers, board games, tables in back garden with aviary; children welcome *(D A and A M Blackadder, Jenny and Michael Back, Keith and Janet Morris, BB)*

Holme [Station Rd; TL1987], *Admiral Wells*: Well refurbished, with cheerful atmosphere, well kept ales esp Oakham JHB and Bishops Farewell, good friendly service, interesting food such as smoked eel salad and lavish balti dishes, and railway paintings; restaurant; Inter-City trains hurtling by *(John C Baker, Richard Balls)*

☆ **Horningsea** [TL4962], *Crown & Punchbowl*: Three particularly well kept ales inc Adnams, but main emphasis is on good food inc wonderful puddings; friendly if not always speedy service, pool, piped music (can be rather loud); bedrooms *(Comus Elliott, Amanda Dauncey, John Rudolf)*

Houghton [Sawtry Way; TL2872], *Three Horseshoes*: Good cosy village local with low black beams, inglenook and darts in public

bar, french windows into garden from comfortable lounge, well kept Scottish Courage ales, bar food (not Sun evening) inc good Sun roasts; nr watermill *(Quentin Williamson, Eddie Winter, LYM)*

☆ **Kennett** [Bury Rd; TL7066], *Bell*: Delightful 16th-c heavy-beamed and timbered inn, neatly and plushly refurbished, with wide choice of well cooked and presented generous food inc some creative dishes, well kept Greene King and guest ales such as Bass, Marstons and Nethergate, friendly efficient staff; very busy weekends; bedrooms *(FWG, John Baker, Gordon Theaker, LYM)*

☆ **Kimbolton** [20 High St; TL0968], *New Sun*: Character old Charles Wells pub doing well under new licensees, good variety of often imaginative food from chunky sandwiches to ostrich or swordfish, attractive beamed restaurant, conservatory leading to terrace, pleasant service, well kept Bombardier and Eagle and Morlands Old Speckled Hen *(Mr and Mrs A W Chapman)*

☆ **Leighton Bromswold** [signed off A604 Huntingdon—Kettering; TL1175], *Green Man*: Neatly modernised open-plan village pub with hundreds of good horsebrasses on heavy low beams, inglenook fireplace, original skittle alley; real ales such as Timothy Taylors Landlord, good food and service *(Alan and Heather Jacques, LYM)*

March [Acre Rd; turn off B1101 opp Royal Exchange pub; TL4195], *Acre*: Separated by a narrow stretch of meadow from the River Nene, with airy main bar, smaller side bar, tables out on verandah and terrace; good value food, friendly licensees; very limited parking, may be best to walk from Mkt Sq *(Miss J Sanderson, BB)*; [Norwood Rd], *Great Northern*: Sociable pub, well refurbished with added dining room, well kept Elgoods, cheap food *(E Robinson)*; [61 Dartford Rd], *Hammer & Anvil*: Extensively refurbished by new licensees, new lounge bar and dining area, real ales inc Courage Directors, Marstons Pedigree and Woodfordes Great Eastern *(E Robinson)*; [High St], *King William IV*: Extended by welcoming new licensees, generous freshly prepared food, Courage beers with a guest such as Marstons Pedigree; restaurant *(M Brooks, E Robinson)*

☆ **Needingworth** [Overcote Lane; pub signed from A1123; TL3472], *Pike & Eel*: Marvellous peaceful riverside location, with spacious lawns and marina; two separate eating areas, one a carvery, in extensively glass-walled block overlooking water, boats and swans; easy chairs, settees and big open fire in room off separate rather hotelish plush bar, well kept Adnams, Bass, and Greene King Abbot, good coffee, friendly and helpful staff, provision for children; clean simple bedrooms, good breakfasts *(Julian Holland, George Atkinson, D E Twitchett, Dr and Mrs S Jones, LYM)*

Needingworth [High St (A1123)], *Queens Head*: Friendly little village pub, six real ales, Inch's cider, good value food (not Sun or

Mon evening) inc special offers, small dining room (which doubles as pool room), real fire; piped music, no dogs; small attractive garden behind *(CMW, JJW)*

Old Weston [SP7560], *Swan*: Friendly low-beamed old pub with big inglenook, brass and pictures, eight real ales, good value straightforward food from sandwiches up (not Mon/Tues), flowers and encyclopedia in no-smoking dining room, no piped music, picnic tables outside *(CMW, JJW, LYM)*

Pampisford [1 Town Lane; TL4948], *Chequers*: Picturesque pub with lovely window boxes and hanging baskets, pleasant atmosphere despite rather obtrusive games machine, Greene King ales, good standard food inc fresh fish; handy for M11 *(D Regan)*

☆ **Peakirk** [12 St Pegas Rd; TF1606], *Ruddy Duck*: Low beams, plush seats and copper-topped tables, unusually wide range of generous food inc sandwiches, fresh fish and vegetarian (and late lunches), Adnams Broadside, Bass, Ruddles Best and County and John Smiths, friendly helpful service, restaurant, terrace; children in end dining room by prior arrangement, piped music may obtrude; handy for Wildfowl Trust, open all day *(Jenny and Michael Back, Brian and Jill Bond, M J Brooks, Keith and Janet Morris)*

Peterborough [17 North St; TL1999], *Bogarts*: At least six well kept ales such as Adnams and Bass, good simple food, fine mix of customers in basic but genuine pub handy for the Westgate shopping centre; friendly staff, open all day *(Reg Nelson)*; [10 Queen St], *HGs*: Theme pub with open cooking counter, good choice of good food, attractive prices; interesting cocktails, huge range of flavoured vodkas *(Hayley Fulcher)*; [Queensgate/Arcade], *Old Still*: Newly refurbished, with small welcoming wood-furnished rooms, tables in small courtyard, good varied food inc several vegetarian dishes, Greene King ales, good value wines and good teas, friendly efficient staff *(John Wooll)*

Reach [off B1102 NE of Cambridge; TL5666], *Kings*: Friendly unpretentious local overlooking village green at N end of Devil's Dyke, landlord's German wife expertly cooks local produce, Elgoods Cambridge, local pictures for sale, seats outside *(John Fahy)*

☆ **Sawston** [High St (Cambridge Rd); TL4849], *Greyhound*: Smart grey banquettes in cosy L-shaped bar, light and airy high glass-roofed dining room overlooking good big garden, generous prompt food inc vegetarian, Flowers IPA and Oakham ales, pleasant and obliging staff, big open fires, games room down steps, good facilities for children; discreet games machines, maybe piped pop music; resident pyrenean mountain dog *(Ian Phillips)*

☆ **Shepreth** [12 High St; just off A10 S of Cambridge; TL3947], *Plough*: Neatly kept bright and airy local with popular well presented home-cooked food from sandwiches and good home-made soup up, changing well kept ales such as Adnams,

Boddingtons, Tetleys and Wadworths 6X, decent wines, modern furnishings, bow-tied staff, side dining room, piped music; well tended back garden with fairy-lit arbour and pond, summer barbecues and play area *(Susan and Nigel Wilson, BB)*

Somersham [St Ives Rd (B1086 SW); TL3477], *Windmill*: Panelled bar with windmill pictures, attractive two-part lounge/dining area with stripped bricks and beams, helpful friendly staff, decent food inc good puddings, Greene King IPA and Abbot, garden with play area *(Jenny and Michael Back)*

☆ **Spaldwick** [just off A14; TL1372], *George*: Recently refurbished 16th-c village inn with very friendly and helpful landlord, good value well presented food esp fish, well kept Charles Wells ales, decent wines, lots of pictures, brasses and dried flowers, three interconnecting restaurant rooms, darts and pool in public bar; very busy – booking needed Fri/Sat *(Mrs E Buckman, Roy and Margaret Randle, Mary and David Webb)*

Stapleford [Church St; TL4651], *Longbow*: Country atmosphere in clean and popular pub with good choice of well kept beers, friendly service and nicely served good value food; well chosen reasonably priced wines, good jazz every other Thurs *(E A George, Mr and Mrs N Thorp)*

Stibbington [off A1 northbound; TL0898], *Sibson*: Neatly kept beamed bars, well kept Scottish Courage and guest ales, friendly staff, tempting if not cheap food, attractive garden – handy stop from A1 northbound; bedrooms *(James Nunns, Comus Elliott)*

☆ **Stretham** [Elford Closes; off A10 S of Stretham roundabout; TL5072], *Lazy Otter*: Big family pub in fine spot on the Great Ouse, with waterside conservatory and neat terrace tables; generous food inc children's, warm fire in bar, Greene King, Marstons Pedigree and a guest ale, matey service; piped music, can get busy weekends; open all day *(R C Wiles, LYM)*

☆ **Stretham** [High St (off A10); TL5374], *Red Lion*: Very neat village pub with wide choice of good generous food inc some unusual dishes, vegetarian and children's food and Sun lunch, solid pine furniture and old village photographs in lounge, marble-topped tables in pleasant no-smoking dining conservatory, five well kept real ales such as Ansells Mild, Greene King, Marstons Pedigree and Morlands Old Speckled Hen, attractive upstairs games room, friendly attentive service; children welcome, picnic tables in garden *(Mike Turner, Quentin Williamson)*

Sutton [the one nr Ely; TL4478], *Chequers*: Good atmosphere in bright and attractive bar with good genuine home cooking inc tempting puddings, well kept Greene King and other ales, friendly licensees *(Julian Holland)*

☆ **Swaffham Prior** [B1102 NE of Cambridge; TL5764], *Red Lion*: Welcoming and attractive local in pleasant village, well kept

Greene King ales, wide range of generous fresh food from sandwiches and baked potatoes to steaks, comfortably divided dining area, quick cheerful service; unusually plush gents' *(Maysie Thompson, M J Brooks)*

☆ Swavesey [High St/Market Pl; signed off A14 (ex A604) NW of Cambridge; TL3668], *White Horse*: Good fresh home-cooked food from sandwiches to steaks inc vegetarian dishes and notable steak and kidney pie and curries (not Sun evening or Mon lunch) in welcoming village local with attractive traditional furnishings in public bar, more straightforward spacious lounge and no-smoking eating room; three Whitbreads-related ales, enterprising wines and spirits, winter Gluhwein, friendly service, children allowed; maybe discreet piped music *(P and D Carpenter, Ian Phillips, S Durrant, Pauline Langley, Mr and Mrs David J C Frost, BB)*

☆ The Turves [signed off A605 W of March; TL3396], *Three Horseshoes*: Friendly beamed Fenland local, extended with family conservatory, good original food esp fish, well kept ales, usually one interesting guest and two nationals *(John Baker)*

☆ Thorney [A47/B1040; TF2804], *Rose & Crown*: Welcoming pub with wide range of freshly made food (so may be a wait), real ales inc guests, real fire, pleasant lounge, restaurant, pool in public bar; piped music, no dogs, charge for credit cards; children welcome, garden with play area *(CMW, JJW, E Robinson)*

Upwood [High St; SW of Ramsey, off B1040; TL2586], *Cross Keys*: Fairly spacious, with some character, pleasant staff, food inc popular good value Sun lunch, Courage, Chestnut Mild and Bitter, and Theakstons XB, tables in garden, no piped music *(Keith and Janet Morris)*

Wansford [Wansford Stn; TL0799], *Britannia Bar*: Actually the vintage buffet car on Nene Valley Railway, interesting range of bottled beers; when not in motion stands at platform *(Dave Braisted)*

☆ Whittlesey [North Side; B1040 towards Thorney; TL2799], *Dog in a Doublet*: Comfortable riverside pub with bric-a-brac, old prints, well spaced solid seating; open fire, cheerful prompt service even when crowded with family lunch parties, reasonably priced bar food inc cheap children's dishes, well kept

ales such as Adnams Broadside and Theakstons Best, decent wines; small games room with pool; handy for Hereward Way walks, restaurant has been open all day Sun *(Anthony Barnes, PR, UR, Jenny and Michael Back)*

☆ Whittlesford [off B1379 S of Cambridge; handy for M10 junction 10, via A505; TL4748], *Tickell Arms*: A long-time favourite, great character and atmosphere, ornate heavy furnishings, dim lighting, lovely log fires, attractive flower-filled Victorian-style conservatory and formal garden, wide range of imaginative bar food, friendly if occasionally erratic service, well reproduced classical music, decent wines, well kept Adnams; cl Mon (exc bank hols), no credit cards *(Kevin Thorpe, Richard Siebert, Conor McGaughey, Wilma and Ian Smith, John Fahy, L W Guthrie, LYM)*

Whittlesford [handy for M11 junction 10], *Red Lion*: Atmospheric bar opening off hotel reception, friendly staff, Charles Wells Bombardier, decent food; bedrooms *(Andrew and Ruth Triggs)*

Wicken [High St; TL5670], *Maids Head*: Neatly kept dining pub overlooking village green, well kept Bass, Greene King IPA and guest beers, appetising bar food inc good value starters and puddings, fair-priced wines, evening restaurant, quiet piped music; tables outside, handy for Wicken Fen nature reserve (NT) *(R C Morgan, J Morgan)*

Wiggenhall St Germans [TF5913], *Crown & Anchor*: Good food using fine fresh ingredients *(John Selwyn)*

☆ Wisbech [North Brink; TF4609], *Red Lion*: Hospitable and civilised long front bar in lovely Georgian terrace on River Nene, nr centre and NT Peckover House; very popular lunchtime for good range of good value home-cooked food inc several vegetarian and fish, Fri bargain salad bar, well kept local Elgoods beer, decent wines *(M Morgan, John Wooll)*

☆ Wisbech [53 North Brink], *Rose*: Cosy, friendly and popular little local in same splendid riverside spot, knowledgeable and enthusiastic landlord will guide you through his notable choice of changing well kept real ales from small breweries; good value filled rolls and sandwiches, quick service *(Geoff Tomlinson)*

We mention bottled beers and spirits only if there is something unusual about them – imported Belgian real ales, say, or dozens of malt whiskies; so do please let us know about them in your reports.

Cheshire

A front-runner here is the Grosvenor Arms at Aldford – giving so much pleasure to such a wide variety of readers that it gains a star award this year, and being such a good place for a meal out that for the second year running it is our Cheshire Dining Pub of the Year. Other places which are on top form at the moment include the Bhurtpore at Aston (great for beer lovers, but good wines and food too), the fine old White Lion at Barthomley, the Cholmondeley Arms near Bickley Moss (this good friendly dining pub has just opened a 'branch' over the Shropshire border – the Cholmondeley Riverside at Cressage), the Old Harkers Arms overlooking the canal in Chester, the handsome Bells of Peover at Lower Peover (thriving under new managers), and the friendly Smoker at Plumley. The new landlord of the canalside Dusty Miller at Wrenbury did extremely well in his previous pubs, so we have high hopes here. There's a new man too at the pleasantly tucked-away Boot & Slipper at Wettenhall. Another change to mention is that the long-serving landlord of the Leathers Smithy up at Langley has now bought the freehold of his pub from Tetleys; we've found in the past that this change of status is normally excellent news for customers. Perhaps the most important change is the promotion of two pubs to the main entries: the inviting old Calveley Arms at Handley (good inventive cooking) and the excellently run Plough at Whitegate (good all round). In the Lucky Dip at the end of the chapter, pubs to note include the Maypole at Acton Bridge, White Lion at Alvanley, Alvanley Arms at Cotebrook, Thatch at Faddiley, Harrington Arms at Gawsworth, George & Dragon at Great Budworth (unbeatable on its usual form), Bird in Hand at Mobberley, Olde Park Gate at Over Peover, Highwayman at Rainow, Legs of Man at Smallwood, Swan at Tarporley and Swan at Wybunbury; we have inspected and can vouch for all of these. There's a fine choice in Chester, and the Dysart Arms at Bunbury, a new venture of that excellent small chain Pubs Ltd, should turn out well. Cheshire drinks prices are well below the national average, with the Blue Bell at Bell o th Hill particularly cheap.

ALDFORD SJ4159 Map 7

Grosvenor Arms ★ 🍽 🍷 🍺

B5130 S of Chester

Cheshire Dining Pub of the Year

For a big pub – moreover one that is part of a small chain – this has a great deal of character, and an unusually friendly and individual atmosphere. But then, those are the features that Pubs Limited have been aiming at. Here in the HQ they have succeeded so well that this year we have awarded them a star. They've cleverly combined traditional decor with a spacious open-plan layout, with the best room probably the huge panelled library with floor-to-ceiling book shelves along one wall. Buzzing with conversation, this also has long wooden floor boards, lots of well spaced substantial tables, and quite a cosmopolitan feel. Several quieter rooms are well furnished with good individual pieces including a very comfortable parliamentary type leather settle. Throughout there are plenty of interesting pictures, and the lighting's exemplary. The airy terracotta-floored conservatory has lots of huge low-hanging flowering baskets and chunky pale wood garden furniture, and opens on to a large elegant suntrap terrace and neat lawn with picnic tables, young trees and a tractor. Bar food is very good indeed – and even though you'll have to get there early to be sure of a table (they only take bookings on some tables), it's not at all the kind of place where eating dominates to the exclusion of all else – indeed the range of drinks at the good solid bar counter is excellent. Boddingtons, Buckleys, Flowers IPA and two or three guest beers well kept on handpump, 35 malt whiskies, and each of the remarkable collection of wines – largely New World – is served by the glass. The menu changes every day, but might include home-made soup or sandwiches (£2.95), venison liver and chilli pâté with cumberland sauce or ploughman's (£4.95), cumberland sausage with bubble and squeak and rich gravy (£5.25), salmon and haddock fishcakes with a tomato and onion salad and lemon mayonnaise or pancake filled with rich ratatouille and a cheese sauce (£5.95), 8oz steak burger topped with an egg (£6.45), steak and venison casserole (£8.25), chicken supreme with an orange mousse wrapped in bacon with a ginger and orange sauce (£8.95), roast half shoulder of lamb with a lemon and thyme sauce (£10.45), marinated duck breast with noodles and mange-tout with a plum and five spice sauce (£10.95), steaks (from £11.45), and puddings (£3.45); good service, even when busy (which it usually is). Two log fires, shove-ha'penny and dominoes. *(Recommended by Joan Yew, SLC, Olive and Ray Hebson, Brian and Anna Marsden, David and July Walmsley, Rosemary Johnston, Richard Lewis, Paul and Maggie Baker, S Williamson, Olive and Ray Hebson, Paul Boot, Peter Neate, Rita and Keith Pollard, KB, DH, Sue Holland, Dave Webster, S L Clemens)*

Free house ~ Licensees Gary Kidd and Jeremy Brunning ~ Real ale ~ Meals and snacks (till 10pm) ~ (01244) 620228 ~ Children in eating area of bar lunchtime only ~ Open 11.30-3, 5-11; 11.30-11 Sat and Sun

ASTON SJ6147 Map 7
Bhurtpore 🍺

Off A530 SW of Nantwich; in village follow Wrenbury signpost

'A real ale enthusiast's dream' is how one reader describes this warmly friendly and relaxed bustling pub. In 1997, they had over 700 real ales and now have 10 handpumps serving a rotating choice of well kept beers like All Nations PA, Blewitts Wages, Church End RIP, Enville High Gravity Mild, Hanbys Drawwell Bitter, Hilden Special Reserve, Sam Truemans Best, Six Bells Little Jem, Stanway Oatmeal Stout, and Three Tuns XXX Bitter; a beer festival is held in March with at least 60 real ales. They have dozens of good bottled beers, too, including Belgian Liefmans Cherry Ale and Rodenbach fruit beers (and fruit-flavoured gins new this year), keep a changing farm cider or perry, and try to encourage people to try malt whiskies they've not had before (there's a choice of around 70; they've added Irish whiskies this year, too). The wine list is interesting and attractively priced, and they now keep country wines. The pub's unusual name comes from a town in India where local landowner Lord Combermere won a battle, and there's a slightly Indian theme to the decor and the menu. The carpeted lounge bar has a growing collection of Indian artefacts (one statue behind the bar proudly sports a pair of Ray-Bans), as well as good local period photographs, and some attractive furniture. As well as very good home-made curries and baltis (from £5.75), enjoyable bar food includes home-made soup (£1.75), sandwiches (from £1.75; toasties £2.25), Shropshire sausages and egg (£2.95), ploughman's (from £2.95), steak, kidney and ale pie (£5.25), mushroom stroganoff (£5.50), haddock fillets with lemon and parsley butter (£5.95), 10oz gammon with egg (£5.95), pork fillet with a cream, apple and mustard sauce (£6.95), steaks (from £7.95), daily specials including fresh fish and game, and puddings like lemon brûlée or sticky toffee pudding (from £2.75); children's menu. It can get packed at weekends, but earlyish on a weekday evening or at lunchtime the atmosphere is cosy and civilised. Tables in the comfortable public bar are reserved for people not eating; darts, dominoes, pool, fruit machine, pool, and piped folk, jazz or blues; friendly landlord and staff; tables in garden. *(Recommended by Sue Holland, Dave Webster, Andy Chetwood, Andy Lace, Howard Harrison, Richard Lewis, SLC, Sue and Bob Ward, Sue and Cliff Wise, N E Turner, Norman Huntbach, Nigel Woolliscroft, S L Clemens, Mairi McArthur)*

Free house ~ Licensee Simon George ~ Real ale ~ Meals and snacks ~ Restaurant ~ (01270) 780917 ~ Well behaved children welcome till 8.30 ~ Folk night third Tues of month ~ Open 12-2.30, 6.30-11; 12-3, 7-10.30 Sun

BARTHOMLEY SJ7752 Map 7
White Lion ★ £

A mile from M6 junction 16; take Alsager rd and is signposted at roundabout

A good mix of people come to this delightfully unpretentious black and white timbered pub to enjoy the friendly, relaxed and timeless atmosphere. The simply furnished main bar has a lovely open fire, heavy oak beams dating back to Stuart times (one big enough to house quite a collection of plates), attractively moulded black panelling, wobbly old tables, Cheshire watercolours and prints on the walls, and latticed windows. Up some steps, a second room has another open fire, more oak panelling, a high-backed winged settle, a paraffin lamp hinged to the wall, and shove-ha'penny, cribbage and dominoes; a third room is very well liked by local societies. The remarkably cheap lunchtime bar food fits in splendidly with the overall style of the place: cheese and onion oatcakes with beans and tomato (£1.50), pie, peas and gravy (£1.70), hot beef sandwich or hot lamb with redcurrant jelly and mint sauce (£1.80), a particularly good home-made hotpot or ploughman's (£2.50); only pies and rolls are available at weekends (when they can get very busy). Very well kept Buccaneer, Burtonwood Bitter, Forshaws, and Top Hat on handpump; no noisy games machines or music. The cats are friendly. They provide hostel-type accommodation in a converted grain store for walkers and cyclists (£3.50 per night). There's a barbecue area in the improved back terrace. The early 15th-c red sandstone church of St Bertiline across the road is worth a visit. *(Recommended by Sue Holland, Dave Webster, Howard Harrison, Richard Lewis, Liz and Graham Bell, Andy and Jill Kassube, John Honnor, Dr and Mrs A K Clarke, Esther and John Sprinkle, Nigel Norman, George and Chris Miller, D R Shillitoe, Nigel Woolliscroft, Ian Williams, Linda Mar)*

Burtonwood ~ Tenant Terence Cartwright ~ Real ale ~ Lunchtime meals and snacks (not Thurs) ~ (01270) 882242 ~ Children welcome except in main bar – must be gone by 9pm ~ Spontaneous folk music first Sun lunchtime of month ~ Open 11.30-11; 12-10.30 Sun; closed Thurs lunchtime

BELL O TH HILL SJ5245 Map 7
Blue Bell ▰

Signed just off A41 N of Whitchurch

The friendly licensees in this characterful black and white timbered pub see themselves very much as a country pub in the old tradition with no noisy games machines, piped music or pool, but with proper home-made food, newspapers to read in front of warm coal fires, and well kept real ales; they will also let walkers park in their car park and offer big mugs of coffee or tea (50p) on their return. The entrance to the building – with its massive central chimney – is through a great oak door by a mounting-block; you then find yourself in a small quarry-tiled hallway, with stairs up, and another formidable oak door on your right. This leads into three very heavily beamed communicating rooms, two served by hatch; the main bar is in an inglenook with an attractively moulded black oak mantelbeam. Comfortably plush wall seats among the cheerful mix of furnishings, and lots of brass ornaments; the back dining room is no smoking. Very well kept Hanby Drawwell, All Seasons and Treacleminer plus ales from Batemans, Cains, Coach House, and Hadrian Brewery on handpump. Generous helpings of home-made bar food include hearty soup (£1.35), sandwiches (from £1.50), smoked mussels (£2.25), 14 or 16oz gammon and egg or steak and kidney pie (£4.95), various curries (£5.50), big local trout (£6.50), and steaks (from £7.50); children's helpings (and they will do egg and chips for them if that is what they want); Sunday roast (£4.95); dominoes. Toby the poodle and Dina the great dane are very sociable, and bowls of water and biscuits are offered to other canine visitors. Picnic tables among flowers on the front grass, and maybe cows and a donkey or two in the adjoining field. *(Recommended by Richard Lewis, Phil Putwain, A Croall, KB, DH; more reports please)*

Free house ~ Licensees Patrick and Lydia Gage ~ Real ale ~ Meals and snacks ~ (01948) 662172 ~ Children welcome ~ Open 12-3, 6-11; 12-3, 7-11 Sun

BICKLEY MOSS SJ5549 Map 7
Cholmondeley Arms ★ ⑪ ⇐ ♀

Cholmondeley; A49 5½ miles N of Whitchurch; the owners would like us to list them under Cholmondeley Village, but as this is rarely located on maps we have mentioned the nearest village which appears more often

The emphasis in this friendly converted Victorian schoolhouse is very much on the imaginative, popular food, though the atmosphere is much more relaxed than you'd expect from the style of cooking. And there's plenty to look at in the cross-shaped and high-ceilinged bar such as old school desks above the bar on a gantry, masses of Victorian pictures (especially portraits and military subjects), and a great stag's head over one of the side arches; seats from cane and bentwood to pews and carved oak settles, patterned paper on the shutters to match the curtains, and well kept Boddingtons, Greene King Abbot, and Marstons Best and Pedigree on handpump. From a daily changing menu there might be carrot or celery soup, hot baked prawns in sour cream and garlic (£3.95), terrine of sweetbreads with bacon and garlic or goat's cheese soufflé with devilled tomato sauce (£4.50), farfalle with porcini and oyster mushrooms and parmesan cheese (£7.25), rabbit braised with wine, mustard and lemon thyme (£7.50), steak and kidney pie, fillet of Whitby cod with butter and herbs (£7.75), kashmiri lamb curry (£8.65), rare lightly peppered rib-eye steak (£10.95), and puddings like rhubarb and ginger crumble or strawberry pavlova; children's dishes. Unless you can spare the time to wait booking ahead is a good idea, especially on a Saturday. An old blackboard lists ten or so interesting and often uncommon wines by the glass; big (4 cup) pot of cafetière coffee, teas, and hot chocolate; good service. There are seats out on a sizeable lawn, and Cholmondeley Castle and gardens are close by. *(Recommended by Mike and Karen England, Prof B L Underwood, Andrew Shore, Lorna and Howard Lambert, B J P Edwards, Dr Jim Mackay, Arthur and Margaret Dickinson, Wendy Arnold, David and Judy Walmsley, SLC, Wayne Brindle, Liz and Graham Bell, Gwen and Peter Andrews, J and B Gibson, T and G Alderman, W C M Jones, Clare Wilson, Carl Travis, W F M West, KB, DH, Martin and Penny Fletcher, Basil Minson, Martin Bromfield, Bernadette Garner, Nigel Woolliscroft, Mr and Mrs C Cole, Phil Putwain, Mike and Wendy Proctor, Carolyn Renier, David and Fiona Pemberton, Mr and Mrs E J Rogers, Andrew Shore, M Turner, D Maplethorpe, B Helliwell, David Shillitoe)*

Free house ~ Licensees Guy and Carolyn Ross-Lowe ~ Real ale ~ Meals and snacks (till 10 Sat; not 25 Dec) ~ (01829) 720300 ~ Well behaved children welcome ~ Open 11-3, 7(6.30 Sat)-11; 11-3, 7-11 Sun ~ Bedrooms: £43S/£55S

BRERETON GREEN SJ7864 Map 7
Bears Head ⇐

1¾ miles from M6, junction 17; fork left from Congleton road almost immediately, then left on to A50; also from junction 18, via Holmes Chapel

This civilised timber-framed old pub is relaxed and quietly friendly and popular with locals coming for a drink and a chat – as well as those wanting to enjoy a bar snack or smarter restaurant meal. The rambling open-plan rooms have masses of heavy black beams and timbers, a section of wall (under glass for protection) with the plaster removed to show the construction of timber underneath, some traditional oak panel-back settles, and a corner cupboard full of Venetian glass. Only one of the two serving bars is normally in use. Served by smartly dressed staff, popular bar food includes home-made soup, sandwiches (from £2.30), home-made pâté, home-made lasagne (£5.95), roast chicken with home-made stuffing (£6.95), and mixed grill (£8.95); also daily specials and a roast of the day, good chips and home-made puddings. Bass, Burtonwood Bitter, and Theakstons on handpump, kept in fine deep cellars, a good range of blend and malt whiskies, brandies and liqueurs and decent wines (especially Italian); piped music. Outside a pretty side terrace has white cast-iron tables and chairs under cocktail parasols, big black cast-iron lamp clusters and a central fountain; barbecues are held outside on the terrace in the summer. The pub is handy for the M6. *(Recommended by P R and S A White, Ian Phillips, Mrs R Scholes, Suzanne and Steve Griffiths, June and Tony Baldwin, Joy and Peter Heatherley, Peter and Maris Brigginshaw, David Braisted, M L and G Clarke)*

Free house ~ Licensee Roberto Tarquini ~ Real ale ~ Meals and snacks (till 10pm) ~ Restaurant ~ (01477) 535251 ~ Children welcome ~ Open 12-3, 6-11; 12-3, 7-11 Sun ~ Bedrooms: £42B/£56.50B

BROXTON SJ4754 Map 7
Egerton Arms
A41/A534 S of Chester

After a good walk in the surrounding sandstone country, you can relax at the tables under cocktail parasols on the balcony terrace here and enjoy the lovely Cheshire views, as far as the River Dee. Inside, the roomy and attractive dark-panelled bar has well polished old furniture, brasses, antique plates and prints; maybe unobtrusive piped music. The neatly kept dining area opens off here; half the inn is no smoking. A good choice of bar food includes soup (£1.65), sandwiches (from £1.95), chilli con carne (£3.75), steak and ale pie or vegetable karahi (£4.95), gammon and egg (£5.25), lasagne (£5.65), creole prawns (£6.25), steaks (from £6.95), and puddings (from £2.25); children's menu and Sunday lunch. Well kept Burtonwood Bitter, James Forshaws, Tom Thumper and Top Hat, and a guest beer on handpump, decent wines by the glass; service is consistently welcoming and efficient. Children may be given colouring materials, and the garden, with picnic tables, has a play area with a wendy house; piped music, fruit machine. We still have not yet had reports on the bedrooms here. *(Recommended by Paul and Maggie Baker, SLC, E G Parish)*

Burtonwood ~ Manager Jim Monaghan ~ Real ale ~ Meals and snacks (12-9.30) ~ Restaurant ~ (01829) 782241 ~ Children in eating area of bar and in indoor play area till 9 ~ Open 11-11; 12-10.30 Sun ~ Bedrooms: £39S/£43.50S

CHESTER SJ4166 Map 7
Old Harkers Arms ♀ ◼
1 Russell St, down steps off City Rd where it crosses canal – under Mike Melody antiques

You can watch canal and cruise boats from the windows of this attractive and comfortable conversion of an early Victorian canal warehouse. The lofty ceiling and tall windows give a feeling of space and light, yet the seats and tables are carefully arranged to allow a sense of privacy too. It's comfortably busy at lunchtime, but evenings can be lively – when the friendly service remains impressively efficient. There's a good variety of things to look at, without too much clutter; attractive lamps, sepia nudes, accordion, various books. The bar counter, apparently constructed from salvaged doors, dispenses well kept Boddingtons, Cheriton Diggers Gold, Fullers London Pride, Timothy Taylors Landlord and a guest like Hop Back Summer Lightning on handpump; there are 27 malt whiskies, 13 flavoured Polish vodkas, and decent well described wines (many from the New World); dominoes and cribbage (but no pool, piped music or noisy games machines). A good changing choice of well presented food might include sandwiches, soups like cream of broccoli and stilton (£2.95), smoked mackerel mousse with horseradish mayonnaise (£4.15), cajun chicken in pitta with a caesar salad dressing (£4.50), salmon and smoked haddock fishcakes with lemon mayonnaise (£5.95), mediterranean vegetable gratin (£6.45), braised sausage casserole in a big yorkshire pudding with cheddar mash and onion gravy (£6.75), gammon and egg (£7.55), rump steak (£9.95), and puddings like sticky banana pudding with toffee sauce (£3.25). Helpings are generous; and high marks for housekeeping – often what lets city pubs down. *(Recommended by SLC, Liz and Graham Bell, Jason Wilding, Simon and Pie Barker)*

Free house ~ David Harding ~ Real ale ~ Meals and snacks (12-2.30, 5-9.30; not Fri or Sat evenings) ~ (01244) 344525 ~ Open 11.30-3, 5-11; 11.30-11 Sat; 12-3, 7-10.30 Sun; cl 25 and 26 Dec

DELAMERE SJ5669 Map 7
Fishpool
A54/B5152

The four comfortable small room areas in this attractive and well liked pub have neatly polished tables and upholstered stools and wall settles, and are bright with polished brasses and china. Well kept Greenalls Bitter, Mild and Original on handpump. Good value bar food includes sandwiches, and hot dishes such as chicken tikka or cumberland sausage in mustard sauce (£5.50), and braised steak with mushroom and onions (£5.95). No games or music; picnic tables outside on the lawn. The pub is so well placed near the pike-haunted lake and Delamere Forest it can be particularly busy at weekends – best to go early, then. Please note, they no longer do bedrooms. *(Recommended by Sue Holland, Dave Webster, Olive and Ray Hebson, Martin Bromfield, Bernadette Garner, Bill and Irene Morley)*

Greenalls (Allied) ~ Tenants Richard and Maureen Lamb ~ Real ale ~ Meals and snacks (12-2, 6-9) ~ (01606) 883277 ~ Children welcome ~ Open 11.30-3, 6-11; 12-3, 7-10.30 Sun

HANDLEY SJ4758 Map 7
Calveley Arms
Village loop road, just off A41 Chester—Whitchurch

Behind its flower-decked forecourt, this black and white country pub lures you invitingly into a well furnished roomy beamed lounge, with leaded windows, an open fire at one end, and some cosy alcove seating. The menus have their own lure, too: they come in the covers of old children's annuals (and indeed include children's helpings). The cooking is interesting and original, with some unusual sandwiches, and a wide choice of hot dishes often showing real flair. Things we or readers have recently enjoyed include sandwiches (from £1.95), steak and kidney pie (£4.95), ploughman's (£5.50), shark steak in whisky butter (£7.50), breton chicken, spinach and cream cheese tortillas spiked with pine nuts, pheasant (£6.95), and tender steaks (£7.95); there's usually a good choice of fresh fish like sardines in olive oil (£3.50), plaice with a prawn sauce (£6.95) or medallions of monkfish with bacon, cream and garlic (£9.95). These are people who clearly enjoy probing and stimulating customers' tastes, organising popular themed evenings – and their last New Year's Day Hangover Breakfast is still fondly remembered. It might be wise to book on Friday or Saturday night. Service is good and friendly, and they have well kept Boddingtons and Burtonwood, and guest beers like Flowers Original or Whitbreads Castle Eden on handpump; dominoes, cribbage, bar skittles, and boules. There are tables out in a secluded garden. *(Recommended by David and Judy Walmsley, R S Fidler, SLC, Sarah Evans, E G Parish)*

Paramount (part tie to several big brewers) ~ Managers Grant Wilson and Chris Manley ~ Real ale ~ Meals and snacks ~ Children in eating area of bar till 8.30 ~ (01829) 770619 ~ Open 12-3, 5.30-11; 12-3, 7-10.30 Sun; closed evening 25 Dec

---

All main entries have been inspected anonymously by the Editor or Deputy Editor. We accept no payment for inclusion, no advertising, and no sponsorship from the drinks industry – or from anyone else.

HIGHER BURWARDSLEY SJ5256 Map 7
Pheasant 🏠

Burwardsley signposted from Tattenhall (which itself is signposted off A41 S of Chester) and from Harthill (reached by turning off A534 Nantwich—Holt at the Copper Mine); follow pub's signpost on up hill from Post Office; OS Sheet 117 map reference 523566

Two new bedrooms have been opened in this well placed 17th-c inn – one would be ideal for a family, the other for anyone with a dog (it has a private terrace). The bedrooms are in an attractively and very comfortably converted sandstone-built barn, and all have views. And for those staying over the weekend, the helpful licensees will drive walkers out to their start point. The walls of the beamed and timbered bar are covered with pictures and rosettes of the licensees' own Highland cattle from shows they've won prizes in, and there are plenty of reminders of the landlord's previous career as a ship's pilot, such as his Merchant Navy apprenticeship papers, some ship photographs, and a brass ship's barometer. Even the parrot – who enjoys the splendid view of the Cheshire Plain towards the Wirral and beyond – is called Sailor. Other decorations include a stuffed pheasant, a set of whimsical little cock-fighting pictures done in real feathers, and big colour engravings of Victorian officials of the North Cheshire Hunt. There are some plates above the high stone mantelpiece of the see-through fireplace (said to house the biggest log fire in the county), and around the fire is a tall leather-cushioned fender. Other seats range from red leatherette or plush wall seats to one or two antique oak settles; there's a pleasant conservatory. Bar food includes sandwiches (from £2), soup (£2.25), ploughman's or home-made vegetarian quiche (£3.75), mushroom stroganoff (£5.95), home-made pie or curry (£6), steak (£9.50), fresh fish dishes, and home-made puddings (£2.25); three course Sunday lunch (£10.50); they charge 50p for cheques or cards. Well kept Bass and a guest beer on handpump, and a choice of over 40 malts; friendly staff. Dominoes, cribbage, and piped music. Picnic tables on a big side lawn. The pub is well placed for walks along the Peckforton Hills, and the nearby Candle Workshops are quite a draw in summer. *(Recommended by Sue Holland, Dave Webster, Andrew Hodges, SLC, JCW, David and Judy Walmsley, J C Brittain-Long, Mr and Mrs E J W Rogers, David Gittins, Geoffrey and Irene Lindley, M Turner)*

Free house ~ Licensee David Greenhaugh ~ Real ale ~ Meals and snacks ~ Restaurant ~ (01829) 770434 ~ Children in conservatory ~ Horses welcomed, and horse-and-trap rides can be arranged ~ Open 11-3, 7-11; 11-11 summer Sat; 12-3, 7-10.30 Sun ~ Bedrooms: £45B/£70B

nr LANGLEY SJ9471 Map 7
Hanging Gate

Meg Lane, Higher Sutton; follow Langley signpost from A54 beside Fourways Motel, and that road passes the pub; from Macclesfield, heading S from centre on A523 turn left into Byrons Lane at Langley, Wincle signpost; in Sutton (half-mile after going under canal bridge, ie before Langley) fork right at Church House Inn, following Wildboarclough signpost, then two miles later turning sharp right at steep hairpin bend; OS Sheet 118 map ref 952696

First licensed nearly 300 years ago but actually built much earlier, this cosy old drovers' pub has three low-beamed rooms that are simply and traditionally furnished, and have big coal fires, a stuffed otter, and some attractive old photographs of Cheshire towns around the walls. Down some stone steps is an airier garden room. Bar food includes sandwiches, and a changing range of hot dishes such as steak and kidney pie, chicken balti, mexican pancakes or chicken in tarragon (all £5.75). Well kept Courage Directors, Ruddles County and Theakstons Best on handpump, and quite a few malt whiskies; friendly service. The blue room is no smoking. Seats outside on a crazy-paved terrace have lovely views looking out beyond a patchwork of valley pastures to distant moors (and the tall Sutton Common transmitter above them). *(Recommended by Philip and Ann Falkner, Mike and Wendy Proctor, Andy Hazeldine, J Muir, Jack Morley; more reports please)*

Free house ~ Licensees John and Lyn Vernon ~ Real ale ~ Meals and snacks (not Thurs) ~ (01260) 252238 ~ Children in two family rooms ~ Open 12-3, 7-11; 12-3, 7-10.30 Sun; closed Thurs

LANGLEY SJ9471 Map 7
Leathers Smithy ◧

From Macclesfield, heading S from centre on A523 turn left into Byrons Lane at Langley, Wincle signpost; in Langley follow main road forking left at church into Clarke Lane – keep on towards the moors; OS Sheet 118 map reference 952715

Mr Hadfield who has been here for 18 years has now bought this pub from Tetleys and is able to offer a greater choice of real ales on handpump: Banks's Bitter and Mild, Camerons Strongarm, Marstons Pedigree, and Morrells Graduate and Varsity; also, Scrumpy Jack cider, Gluhwein in winter from a copper salamander, and a decent collection of spirits, including around 80 malt whiskies and 10 Irish. The room with perhaps the most character is the lively, partly flagstoned right-hand bar with its bow window seats or wheelback chairs, and roughcast cream walls hung with gin traps, farrier's pincers, a hay basket and other ironwork. On the left, there are more wheelback chairs around cast-iron-framed tables on a turkey carpet, little country pictures and drawings of Cheshire buildings, Wills steam engine cigarette cards and a locomotive name-plate curving over one of the two open fires; faint piped music. The family room is no smoking; dominoes. Bar food (with prices unchanged since last year) includes sandwiches (from £2), black pudding and mushy peas (£3.95), ploughman's, vegetarian dishes such as spinach and walnut pancake (£4.95), lasagne (£5.20), home-made steak pie (£5.50), halibut or gammon and egg (£6.75), steaks (from £8.95), and puddings. The pub is a popular stop for walkers, being close to Macclesfield Forest. *(Recommended by David and Judy Walmsley, Michael Butler, Philip and Ann Falkner, Mike Howes)*

Free house ~ Licensee Paul Hadfield ~ Real ale ~ Meals and snacks (limited Mon lunchtime, not Mon evening; till 8.30 other evenings, though Fri and Sat till 9.30) ~ (01260) 252313 ~ Children in family room Sat and Sun lunchtime only ~ Occasional pianola music ~ Open 12-3, 7(5.30 Fri)-11; all day Sat and summer Sun

LOWER PEOVER SJ7474 Map 7
Bells of Peover ★

The Cobbles; from B5081 take short cobbled lane signposted to church

The setting for this wisteria-covered pub is delightful – a spacious lawn beyond the old coachyard at the side spreads down through trees and rose pergolas to a little stream, while the sheltered crazy-paved terrace in front faces a lovely black and white timbered church. Inside is very neatly kept, and the little tiled bar has side hatches for its serving counter, toby jugs, and comic Victorian prints, and the original lounge has antique settles, high-backed windsor armchairs and a spacious window seat, antique china in the dresser, pictures above the panelling, and two small coal fires. There's a second similar lounge. Under the new managers, good bar food now includes soup (£1.95), sandwiches (from £2.50), vegetarian dishes (from £5.50), home-made steak and kidney pie (£6.25), chicken in a cream sauce (£6.85), monkfish with white wine and mushrooms (£7.95), bass in a tomato and basil sauce (£8.25), steaks (from £9.95), and puddings (£2.50); enjoyable Sunday lunch. Most people wear a jacket and tie in the restaurant. Well kept Greenalls Bitter and Original with a guest like Boddingtons on handpump or tapped from the cask; dominoes. *(Recommended by Liz and Graham Bell, James Nunns, David and Judy Walmsley, Basil Minson, G McGrath, P R and S A White, Mrs E E Sanders, Martin Bromfield, Bernadette Garner, Jack and Philip Paxton, RJH, J F M West, Paul and Lyn Benny, John Waller)*

Greenalls (Allied) ~ Managers Ken and Wendy Brown ~ Real ale ~ Meals and snacks ~ Restaurant (closed Sat lunchtime, Sun evening, Mon) ~ (01565) 722269 ~ Children in restaurant ~ Open 11-3, 5.30-11; 12-3, 6.30-10.30 Sun

MACCLESFIELD SJ9271 Map 7

Sutton Hall Hotel ★ 🛏

Leaving Macclesfield southwards on A523, turn left into Byrons Lane signposted Langley, Wincle, then just before canal viaduct fork right into Bullocks Lane; OS Sheet 118 map reference 925715

Although this is a civilised 16th-c baronial hall, readers are consistently pleased at the friendly welcome and relaxed atmosphere. The bar (divided into separate areas by tall black timbers) has some antique squared oak panelling, lightly patterned art nouveau stained-glass windows, broad flagstones around the bar counter (carpet elsewhere), and a raised open fire. It is furnished mainly with straightforward ladderback chairs around sturdy thick-topped cast-iron-framed tables, though there are a few unusual touches such as an enormous bronze bell for calling time, a brass cigar-lighting gas taper on the bar counter itself, a suit of armour by another big stone fireplace, and a longcase clock. Served by friendly waitresses, the reasonably priced home-made bar food includes soup (£1.45), pâté (£3.25), lasagne (£4.95), steak and kidney pie or spinach pancakes filled with ratatouille with a sour cream dressing (£5.25), daily specials such as grilled smoked quail wrapped in bacon with warm redcurrant jelly (£3.95), beef in ale (£5.75), and lamb liver and bacon (£5.95), and puddings like apple and blackberry crumble or sticky toffee pudding (£2). Well kept Bass, Marstons Best, Stones Best and a guest beer on handpump, 40 malt whiskies, decent wines, and a proper Pimms; piped music. It's set in lovely grounds with tables on a tree-sheltered lawn; they can arrange clay shooting, golf or local fishing for residents. *(Recommended by Kate and Robert Hodkinson, James Nunns, David and Ruth Hollands, G R Roberts, Jack Morley, J F M West, J C T Tan, Clare Wilson, C H and P Stride, Thomas Nott)*

Free house ~ Licensee Robert Bradshaw ~ Real ale ~ Meals and snacks ~ Restaurant ~ (01260) 253211 ~ Children allowed weekend and bank hol lunchtimes only ~ Open 11-11; 12-4, 7-10.30 Sun ~ Four-poster bedrooms: £75B/£90B

MARBURY SJ5645 Map 7

Swan

NNE of Whitchurch; OS Sheet 117 map reference 562457

The long-standing licensees of this creeper-covered white pub extend a warm welcome to both locals and visitors – which perhaps accounts for the buoyantly cheerful atmosphere. The neatly kept, partly panelled no-smoking lounge has upholstered easy chairs and other country furniture, a grandfather clock, a copper-canopied fireplace with a good winter fire (masses of greenery in summer), and discreet lighting. Good, enjoyable bar food might include daily specials such as parsnip and apple soup (£1.95), deep-fried feta cheese with cranberry sauce (£2.50), mushrooms and pasta in stilton sauce (£5.50), home-made fresh salmon fishcakes (£5.85), minted lamb casserole (£5.95), chicken breast with apricots and brandy or wild rabbit casserole (£6.50), braised steak with green peppercorn sauce (£7.50), and puddings like chocolate and almond torte or coffee and Tia Maria cheesecake; chips are home-made and they also have a standard snack menu with sandwiches, scampi and so forth. Well kept Greenalls Original and Tetleys Bitter on handpump, 40 malt whiskies, decent wines, and friendly service. Darts and dominoes; no machines or piped music. Rebuilt in 1884, the pub is in a quiet and attractive village, a half-mile's country walk from the Llangollen Canal, Bridges 23 and 24. The nearby church is worth a visit. *(Recommended by David and Judy Walmsley, Lorna and Howard Lambert, John Cockell, Sue and Bob Ward, George Jonas, Jean and Richard Phillips)*

Greenalls (Allied) ~ Lease: George, Ann and Mark Sumner ~ Real ale ~ Meals and snacks (not Mon lunchtime) ~ Restaurant ~ (01948) 663715 ~ Children welcome ~ Open 12-3, 7-11; 12-3, 7-10.30 Sun; closed Mon lunchtime (except bank holidays)

There are report forms at the back of the book.

OVERTON SJ5277 Map 7
Ring o' Bells   £

Just over 2 miles from M56, junction 12; 2 Bellemonte Road – from A56 in Frodsham take
B5152 and turn right (uphill) at Parish Church signpost

This early 17th-c pub is friendly and old-fashioned with plenty of chatty locals and
a couple of nicely old-fashioned little rambling rooms with windows giving a view
past the stone church to the Mersey far below; one at the back has some antique
settles, brass-and-leather fender seats by the log fire, and old hunting prints on its
butter-coloured walls. A beamed room with antique dark oak panelling and stained
glass leads through to a darts room (there's also dominoes and cribbage, but no
noisy games machines or music). Good value waitress-served bar food is served at
lunchtime only, and includes popular sandwiches and toasties, home-made beef
and Guinness pie or chilli (£3.45), cumberland sausage with mash and onion gravy,
tuna and pasta bake or chicken tikka masala (£3.95), and scrambled eggs with
smoked salmon (£4.45). Well kept Greenalls Bitter and Original on handpump,
and around 80 different malt whiskies served from the old-fashioned hatch-like
central servery; cheerful service. The tabby twins are called Shula and Tilly, and
there's another cat, Lottie. The prize-winning hanging baskets in front are quite a
sight in summer, and at the back is a secluded garden with tables and chairs, a
pond, and lots of trees. *(Recommended by David and Judy Walmsley, D A Goult, Don
Kellaway, Angie Coles, Dr M Owton, Comus Elliott, Dave Thompson, Margaret Mason)*

*Greenalls (Allied) ~ Tenant Shirley Wroughton-Craig ~ Real ale ~ Lunchtime meals
and snacks ~ Children welcome away from bar area ~ (01928) 732068 ~ Open 11.30-
3(3.30 Sat), 5.30(6 Sat)-11; 12-3, 7-10.30 Sun*

PEOVER HEATH SJ7973 Map 7
Dog

Off A50 N of Holmes Chapel at the Whippings Stocks, keep on past Parkgate into Wellbank
Lane; OS Sheet 118 map reference 794735; note that this village is called Peover Heath on
the OS map and shown under that name on many road maps, but the pub is often listed
under Over Peover instead

An engaging series of small areas rambles around the main bar in this civilised inn.
Logs burn in one old-fashioned black grate, a coal fire opposite is flanked by two
wood-backed built-in fireside seats, and there are seats ranging from a comfortable
easy chair, through wall seats (one built into a snug alcove around an oak table), to
the handsome ribbed banquettes in the quiet and spacious dining room on the left;
the main eating area is no smoking. Well liked bar food includes sandwiches (from
£2.60), home-made soup (£2.75), mushrooms in beer batter with garlic dip
(£4.30), ploughman's (from £4.85), rack of lamb with apricots and ginger, a huge
deep-fried cod, fish and vegetarian dishes (around £8.20), and puddings such as
home-made fruit crumble or sticky toffee pudding (£2.75); dishes are more
expensive in the evening. Well kept Boddingtons, Flowers IPA, Greenalls Original
and a guest on handpump, Addlestones cider, over 50 malt whiskies, decent wine
list, freshly squeezed orange juice and espresso and cappuccino coffee; darts, pool,
dominoes, video game, juke box, and piped music. Friendly service. Quiz nights on
Thursdays and Sundays. There are picnic tables out on the quiet lane, underneath
the pub's pretty hanging baskets, and an attractive beer garden, nicely lit in the
evenings. The licensees also run the Swettenham Arms, Swettenham. *(Recommended
by Dr Jim Mackay, Dr Phil Putwain, G McGrath, Ray Cuckow, Harold Harris, R Davies, Jack
Morley)*

*Free house ~ Licensee Frances Cunningham ~ Real ale ~ Meals and snacks ~ (01625)
861421 ~ Children welcome ~ Pianist Tues, solo artist Weds ~ Open 12-3(4 summer
Sat), 6-11; 12-4; 7-10.30 Sun; closed evening 25 Dec ~ Bedrooms: £47.50B/£67.50B*

The details at the end of each main entry start by saying whether the pub is a
free house, or if it's tied to a brewery (which we name).

PLUMLEY SJ7175 Map 7
Smoker

2½ miles from M6 junction 19: A556 towards Northwich and Chester

The friendly licensees of this well run thatched pub have introduced a menu to cover both the bar and brasserie (though they will reserve tables and give full waitress service in the brasserie). This has created a more relaxed atmosphere, with the brasserie becoming even more part of the pub. The three well decorated connecting rooms have dark panelling, open fires in impressive period fireplaces, some military prints, a collection of copper kettles, and an Edwardian print on the wall capturing a hunt meeting outside (which shows how little the appearance of the pub has changed over the centuries); also, comfortable deep sofas, cushioned settles, windsor chairs, and some rush-seat dining chairs; one area is no-smoking. A glass case contains an interesting remnant from the Houses of Parliament salvaged after it was hit by a bomb in World War II. Really enjoyable bar food includes home-made soup (£2), sandwiches (from £2.30; the bacon and egg batch is well liked), black pudding with a mustard and white wine sauce (£3.85), home-made savoury pancake (£3.95), fresh cod in a home-made beer batter with chips (£6.35), vegetarian tagliatelle (£6.35), hock of ham with mustard sauce (£6.95), steaks (from £8.95), and daily specials such as hot chicken and bacon batch with melted cheese (£3.75), cold chicken tikka in a poppadom (£5.95), braised steak in a white wine, tomato and herb sauce (£6.65), and thai-style pork in a lime and orange sauce on a bed of noodles (£6.75); children's helpings and own menu. Well kept Robinsons Best, Hatters Mild, Frederics, and Old Stockport on handpump, 30 malt whiskies and a good choice of wines; friendly service. Outside there's a sizeable side lawn with roses and flower beds, and a children's play area in the extended garden. *(Recommended by Dr Jim Mackay, Peter Walker, Derek and Sylvia Stephenson, W C M Jones, John Stanfield, Keith and Judith Ashcroft, Liz and Graham Bell, SLC, Mr and Mrs J A Phipps, George Jonas, A R and B E Sayer, Charlotte Wrigley, FMH, Mr and Mrs C Cole, S L Clemens, Jack Morley)*

Robinsons ~ Tenants John and Diana Bailey ~ Real ale ~ Meals and snacks (12-2.30, 6-10; all day Sun) ~ Restaurant ~ (01565) 722338 ~ Children in eating area of bar and in restaurant ~ Open 11-3, 5.30-11; 12-10.30 Sun

POTT SHRIGLEY SJ9479 Map 7
Cheshire Hunt

At end of B5091 in Bollington, where main road bends left at Turners Arms, fork straight ahead off it into Ingersley Road to follow Rainow signpost, then up hill take left turn signposted Pott Shrigley; OS Sheet 118 map reference 945782

Quite a lot of emphasis is placed on the popular food in this isolated former farmhouse. As well as daily specials, there might be sandwiches, home-made soup (£1.95), white stilton cheese spiced with nutmeg and peppercorns, breaded, deep fried and set on a fresh apple and cinnamon purée (£3.95), Portuguese sardines with home-made garlic mayonnaise (£4.75), home-cooked ham on toast with two eggs (£4.95), omelettes (£5.50), lasagne (£5.95), pork loin on spiced mushrooms with white wine and cream sauce (£6.95), beef bourguignon (£7.70), steaks (from £8.95), grilled halibut (£9.50), and puddings like home-made bilberry pie or cheesecake (from £2.20); Sunday lunch carvery (£6.25 main course, £9.50 for 3 courses; best to book); children's dishes (from £1.95). There are several small rooms that ramble up and down steps with spindleback and wheelback chairs, beams and black joists, and roaring log fires; one room is no smoking. Well kept Bass, Boddingtons, Marstons Pedigree and Morlands Old Speckled Hen on handpump; good efficient service. No games machines or piped music. Outside, there are seats on three terraces, gardens, and views over pastures. *(Recommended by Philip and Ann Falkner, Stephen, Julie and Hayley Brown, Wendy and Ian Phillips, Mrs E E Sanders, Mrs E Dakin, FMH, Jack Morley, Gill and Maurice McMahon, Brian and Anna Marsden)*

Free house ~ Licensee Alan Harvey ~ Real ale ~ Meals and snacks (till 10pm; not Mon

lunchtime) ~ Restaurant ~ (01625) 573185 ~ Children in eating area of bar and in restaurant ~ Open 12-3, 5.30-11; 12-3, 7-11 Sun; closed Mon lunchtime

SWETTENHAM SJ8067 Map 7
Swettenham Arms

Village signed off A535 just S of Jodrell Bank or just N of Holmes Chapel – keep following sign; pub behind brick-towered church

Said to be as old as the church, which partly dates from the 13th c, this bustling spacious country pub has three communicating room areas in the heavily beamed bar that are linked by a sweep of fitted turkey carpet. There's some interesting and individual furnishings, several winter log fires, and a variety of old prints – military, hunting, old ships, reproduction Old Masters and so forth. Wherever you eat, you order food from a separate counter in the end no-smoking dining room (where there's a huge inglenook). The range of food really is enormous: around 20 starters and just as many main courses, with favourite dishes including baked rack of chicken with cheese, bacon and mushrooms, medallions of pork with bacon and stilton sauce, and casserole of venison (all £7.95); popular puddings (£2.75). The main dining area is no smoking. Well kept Greenalls Original and Tetleys Bitter on handpump, Addlestones cider, freshly squeezed orange juice, and a range of malt whiskies; piped music. You can sit outside at picnic tables on the quiet neat side lawn surrounded by shrubs and trees; the hanging baskets at the front are pretty. Quiz night on Tuesdays. The pub is run by the same people as the Dog at Peover Heath. *(Recommended by Dr Jim Mackay, JFMW, Ray Cuckow, Geoff Kay, R D Kelso, Ena and Rodney Wood)*

Free house ~ Licensee Barry Orai ~ Real ale ~ Meals and snacks ~ (01477) 571284 ~ Children welcome ~ Live music Weds ~ Open 12-3(4 summer Sat), 6-11; 12-4(3 in winter), 7-10.30 Sun; closed evening 25 Dec

TARPORLEY SJ5563 Map 7
Rising Sun

High St; village signposted off A51 Nantwich—Chester

Bustling and friendly, this cheery village pub is enjoyed by locals and visitors alike. The well chosen tables are surrounded by character seats including creaky 19th-c mahogany and oak settles, and there's also an attractively blacked iron kitchen range (and three open fires), sporting and other old-fashioned prints on the walls, and a big oriental rug in the back room. Generously served lunchtime bar food includes sandwiches (from £1.80), filled baked potatoes (from £2.40), home-made cottage pie (£2.95), home-made steak and kidney pie (£5.25), gammon and egg (£5.60), pork and apple in cider (£5.75), and beef in ale (£5.75); more elaborate dishes in the evening from the restaurant menu. Well kept Robinsons Best and Mild on handpump; fruit machine, maybe piped music (usually drowned by conversation). The pub is pretty in summer with its mass of hanging baskets and flowering tubs. *(Recommended by Alan and Paula McCully, Philip and Ann Falkner, David and Judy Walmsley, Brian Wainwright, Sue Holland, Dave Webster, George Jonas, Iain Robertson, A R and B E Sayer)*

Robinsons ~ Tenant Alec Robertson ~ Real ale ~ Meals and snacks (11.30-2, 5.30-9.30) ~ Restaurant ~ (01829) 732423 ~ Open 11.30-3, 5.30-11; 11.30-11 Sat; 12-10.30 Sun

WESTON SJ7352 Map 7
White Lion 🍺

3½ miles from M6 junction 16; A500 towards Crewe, then village signposted on right

Originally a Tudor farmhouse, this pretty black and white timbered inn has a busy low-beamed main room divided up into smaller areas by very gnarled black oak standing timbers. There's a varied mix of seats from cushioned modern settles to ancient oak ones, plenty of smaller chairs, and a friendly, relaxing atmosphere. In a smaller room on the left are three fine settles, well carved in 18th-c style. Served by smartly dressed staff, the bar food includes home-made soup (£1.50), sandwiches (£1.75), filled baguettes (from £2.25) or batch cakes (£2.50), smoked salmon pâté (£3), vegetarian quiche (£3.95), ploughman's or a daily roast (£4.50), poached local Dee salmon (£6.50), steak (£8.25), and home-made puddings (£1.90). Get there early at lunchtime as it can fill up quickly then. Well kept Bass, Boddingtons, and Worthington on handpump, and a sizeable wine list; dominoes, trivia, and piped music. Two side rooms and the restaurant are no smoking. Picnic tables shelter on neat grass behind, by the pub's own bowling green. The hotel part is discreetly hidden away at the back. *(Recommended by Neville Kenyon, Kate and Robert Hodkinson, D A Goult, S Williamson, George Jonas, Ian and Villy White, Graham and Karen Oddey, Alan and Paula McCully, Sue Holland, Dave Webster)*

Free house ~ Licensee Alison Davies ~ Real ale ~ Meals and snacks (12-2, 5.30-9.30 during the week; not 25 Dec) ~ Restaurant ~ (01270) 500303 ~ Children in eating area of bar ~ Open 11-3, 5(6.30 Sat)-11; 12-3, 7-11 Sun; closed evening 25 Dec ~ Bedrooms: £49B/£59B

WETTENHALL SJ6261 Map 7
Boot & Slipper 🍺

From B5074 on S edge of Winsford, turn into Darnhall School Lane, then right at Wettenhall signpost: keep on for 2 or 3 miles

The knocked-through beamed main bar here has a chatty and relaxed atmosphere as well as three shiny old dark settles and more straightforward chairs, and a fishing rod above the deep low fireplace with its big log fire. The modern bar counter also serves the left-hand communicating beamed room with its shiny pale brown tiled floor, cast-iron-framed long table, panelled settle and bar stools; darts, dominoes, and piped music. An unusual trio of back-lit arched pseudo-fireplaces form one stripped-brick wall and there are two further areas on the right, as well as a back restaurant with big country pictures. Under the new licensee, good bar food includes home-made soup (£1.60), sandwiches (from £2.35; steak batch £2.75), steak and Guinness pie (£4.80), seafood pancake or vegetarian dishes (£4.95), gammon steak (£5.95), peppered salmon (£8.95), pheasant (£10.95), and children's meals (from £2.30); they hold themed food evenings every two months. Well kept Marstons Pedigree and Tetleys on handpump, and a decent wine list. Outside a few picnic tables sit on the cobbled front terrace by the big car park, and there's a children's play area. *(Recommended by S Williamson, Ann Griffiths, Thomas Nott; more reports on the new regime please)*

Free house ~ Licensee Joan Jones ~ Real ale ~ Meals and snacks ~ Restaurant ~ (01270) 528238 ~ Children welcome ~ Open 12-3, 5.30-11; 12-11 Sat; 12-10.30 Sun ~ Bedrooms: £30S/£44S

WHITEGATE SJ6268 Map 7
Plough

Foxwist Green; along Beauty Bank, opp Methodist chapel – OS Sheet 118 map reference 624684; from A556 at W end roundabout of Northwich bypass take Whitegate road, bear right in village and then take Foxwist Green turn left; or from A54 W of Winsford turn off at Salterswell roundabout, then first left

This very welcoming old building has comfortably straightforward furnishings in its several bright and cheerful rooms – including an intimate little dining room with just half a dozen tables. People who knew Mr and Mrs Hughes at the Spinner & Bergamot over at Comberbach have been quick to track them down here, and they already look like making this enjoyable place just as successful. They are doing a wide range of good home-made food using fresh produce, such as soup (£1.95), sandwiches (from £2.25), ploughman's (£4.50), steak pie (£4.95), and daily specials like liver and bacon (£5), lamb and apricot casserole (£5.25), and fresh fish dishes such as red snapper (£5.25), cod (£5.75) or halibut and haddock (£6.25).

There are two sittings for Sunday lunch. Well kept Robinsons Best, Mild and Old Tom, good considerate service. The Whitegate Way – a former railway track – is one of several popular walks nearby. No children. *(Recommended by Ray and Liz Monk, N Revell, John Broughton)*

Robinsons ~ Tenants Doug and Mavis Hughes ~ Real ale ~ Meals and snacks ~ (01606) 889455 ~ Open 11.30-4, 5.30-11; 11-11 Sat; 12-4, 7-10.30 Sun

WINCLE SJ9666 Map
Ship 🍺

Village signposted off A54 Congleton—Buxton

The old-fashioned and simple little rooms in this quaint but friendly 16th-c pub have a nice atmosphere, very thick stone walls, a coal fire and consistently well kept Boddingtons Bitter and a weekly changing guest beer on handpump; decent wines. Good bar food includes soup, filled french bread with chips (lunchtime only), fresh fish on Wednesday such as haddock in crispy batter or local trout (£5.25), well liked gammon and eggs (£5.95), puddings like orange steamed sponge (£2.50), and children's meals (£2.50); fondue bourguignon is the house speciality and includes a bottle of house red wine. There are good walks in the surrounding scenic countryside. Please note, they no longer do bedrooms. *(Recommended by John and Christine Lowe, Philip and Ann Falkner, J F West, Peter and Joy Heatherley, Jack Morley, Nigel Woolliscroft, Mike and Wendy Proctor, Iain Robertson)*

Free house ~ Licensees Andrew Harmer and Penelope Hinchliffe ~ Real ale ~ Meals and snacks (not winter Mon) ~ (01260) 227217 ~ Well behaved children in family room ~ Open 12-3ish (maybe longer if busy), 7-11 (10.30 Sun); closed Monday Nov-Mar

WRENBURY SJ5948 Map 7
Dusty Miller

Village signposted from A530 Nantwich—Whitchurch

This imaginatively converted mill has now been taken over by Mr Sumner – for years we have known of him as someone who knows how to run a really good pub. The position is lovely, set right by the Llangollen branch of the Shropshire Union Canal and next to a striking counter-weighted drawbridge, and picnic tables are set on a gravel terrace among rose bushes by the water; they're reached either by the towpath or by a high wooden catwalk above the River Weaver. Inside, the main area is comfortably modern, with a series of tall glazed arches facing the water, and has had long low hunting prints on the white walls, and tapestried banquettes and wheelback chairs flanking rustic tables. Further in, there's a quarry-tiled standing-only part by the bar counter, which has well kept Robinsons Best, Frederics, Hartleys XB, Hatters Mild and Old Stockport with winter Old Tom on handpump. As well as lunchtime snacks such as home-made soup (£2.50), stotties (soft floury rolls filled with things like bacon and black pudding or grilled cumberland sausage with egg, from £2.95), freshly baked ciabatta-style loaves filled with avocado and prawn mousse, cheese or hot bacon and tomato relish (£3.95), and ploughman's (£4.95), the good bar food includes home-made soup (£2.50), chicken liver and cognac parfait (£3.75), roast mediterranean vegetables finished with melted goat's cheese and pesto dressed salad leaves or beef in ale cobbler with a cheese dumpling (£5.95), fresh cod in beer batter (£6.95), steaks (from £8.95), puddings like sticky toffee pudding with fudge and walnut sauce, chocolate truffle torte or raspberry pavlova (£3.25), and children's meals (£3.50); the upstairs dining area is no smoking. Dominoes and piped music. *(Recommended by David and Judy Walmsley, Paul and Maggie Baker, Mike and Wendy Proctor, Andrew Rogers, Amanda Milsom; more reports on the new regime please)*

Robinsons ~ Tenant Mark Sumner ~ Real ale ~ Meals and snacks ~ Upstairs restaurant ~ (01270) 780537 ~ Children in eating area of bar ~ Open 11-3, 6.30-11; 11-11 Sat (11-3, 6.30-11 winter Sat); 12-3, 7-10.30 Sun; closed 25 Dec

Lucky Dip

Besides the fully inspected pubs, you might like to try these Lucky Dips recommended to us and described by readers (if you do, please send us reports):

☆ **Acton Bridge** [Hilltop Rd; B5153 off A49 in Weaverham, then right towards Acton Cliff; SJ5975], *Maypole*: Wide choice of good varied generous food in spacious and civilised beamed dining pub, pleasant dining room with lots of brass, copper and china, some antique settles as well as more modern furnishings, two coal fires, friendly staff, well kept Greenalls Bitter and Mild, gentle piped music; attractive outside with hanging baskets and tubs, seats in well kept garden with orchard behind *(Mr and Mrs E J W Rogers, John Mallen, Graham and Lynn Mason, LYM)*

Acton Bridge [A49], *Horns*: Cosy country pub atmosphere, good range of good value family food (all day Sun), well kept Greenalls Bitter and Original, horns and horse memorabilia, restaurant, big garden with play area; occasional folk music; bedrooms *(Brian Capper, SLC)*

☆ **Adlington** [Wood Lane North, by Middlewood Way – OS Sheet 109 map ref 936818; SJ9381], *Miners Arms*: Extended Greenalls Millers Kitchen family dining pub in good setting beside Macclesfield Canal, efficient service even when packed, generous standardised sensible food choice from sandwiches to steaks inc vegetarian and smaller helpings, plenty of quiet corners, no-smoking area, well kept Whitbreads-related ales; picnic tables and play area outside *(R Davies, Pete Yearsley, Philip and Ann Falkner, Malcolm and Pat Rudlin)*

Alpraham [A51 Nantwich—Chester; SJ5959], *Travellers Rest*: Unchanging four-room country local, 1950s decor, leatherette, wicker and Formica, some flock wallpaper, well kept Tetleys Bitter and Mild and McEwans 70/-, darts, back bowling green; no food, cl weekday lunchtimes *(Richard Lewis)*

Alsager [Crewe Rd; SJ8048], *Plough*: Elaborately refurbished and spaciously extended Big Steak pub, low beams and country decor, good facilities for children (inside and out) and disabled, good service, well kept Tetleys-related ales; open all day *(Richard Lewis, Sue Holland, Dave Webster)*; [Crewe Rd], *Poachers Pocket*: Another useful family chain pub, former Old Mill; beams and country bygones, indoor adventure play area, well kept Banks's, Camerons Strongarm and Marstons Pedigree and Banks Bitter, tables out by millpond; open all day, bedrooms *(Richard Lewis)*

☆ **Alvanley** [Manley Rd – OS Sheet 117 map ref 496740; SJ4974], *White Lion*: Remarkably wide changing choice of generous food from sandwiches up inc vegetarian and children's dishes in comfortable, civilised yet homely extended dining pub, friendly service, plush seats in low-ceilinged lounge, games in smaller public bar, Greenalls Mild, Bitter and

Original, tables and play area outside with some small farm animals; very popular – must book evenings and Sun lunchtime *(Graham and Lynn Mason, Mr and Mrs E J W Rogers, LYM)*

Astbury [off A34 S of Congleton; SJ8461], *Egerton Arms*: Big village local dating from 14th c, in nice spot on green opp interesting old church in pretty village (though busy main rd), wide choice of usual food with OAP bargains, well kept Robinsons ales, log fires, no-smoking lounge and part of restaurant, tables in back garden with play area; children welcome; bedrooms *(Richard Lewis)*

☆ **Audlem** [Audlem Wharf – OS Sheet 118 map ref 658436; SJ6543], *Shroppie Fly*: Beautifully placed canal pub, one bar shaped like a barge, good canal photographs, collection of brightly painted bargees' china and bric-a-brac, seats on waterside terrace; usual food, well kept Boddingtons, friendly staff, mainly modern furnishings, children in room off bar and restaurant; open almost all day summer, closed winter lunchtimes *(SLC, LYM)*

Audlem [A525, Audlem Wharf], *Bridge*: Particularly well kept Marstons and guest ales and good food from sandwiches up in friendly unspoilt pub with coal fire, tiled floor, darts, pool, juke box and games machines; dogs allowed, seats out by canal *(Sue Holland, Dave Webster, SLC)*

☆ **Barbridge** [just off A51 N of Nantwich; SJ6156], *Barbridge Inn*: Friendly and well run open-plan Greenalls Millers Kitchen family dining pub in pretty setting at junction of Shropshire Union and Middlewich canals, with busy riverside garden, conservatory, no-smoking area, decent food, well kept Boddingtons, Cains and weekend guest beers, games room, quiet piped music; good disabled facilities, open all day, quiz Tues, jazz Thurs, barbecue *(Richard and Anne Lewis, GT, Mike and Wendy Proctor, W C M Jones, William Cissna, LYM)*

☆ **Beeston** [Bunbury Heath, A49 S of Tarporley; SJ5459], *Beeston Castle*: Good value interesting generous food from huge open sandwiches up inc mouth-watering puddings, in clean, comfortable and well restored pub, good friendly service even when busy, short but well chosen wine list, well kept beers; children until 8 *(Mr and Mrs E J W Rogers)*

Bickerton [Bulkeley; A534 E of junction with A41; SJ5052], *Bickerton Poacher*: Rambling old poacher-theme pub with well kept Greenalls Bitter and Original, good choice of food, open fires, friendly staff, copper-mining memorabilia, attractive barbecue extension around sheltered courtyard; children welcome *(Richard Lewis, LYM)*

☆ **Bollington** [Church St; SJ9377], *Church House*: Wide choice of good value quickly served lunchtime food esp steaks in corner terrace pub, small and friendly; well kept Marstons and Tetleys, furnishings inc pews and working sewing-machine treadle tables, roaring fire, separate dining room, friendly prompt staff; can book tables for busy lunchtimes *(Pat and Tony Young, Joanne Morris, Bill Sykes)*

Bollington [Ingersley Rd], *Poachers*: Friendly old stone-built village local, good choice of well kept ales, decent wines, generous value for money home cooking; attractive garden and terrace behind, pretty setting, handy for walkers *(Philip and Ann Falkner, Mrs E E Sanders)*

Bollington Cross [SJ9277], *Cock & Pheasant*: Comfortable beamed family lounge bar with log fire, dark wood, old prints, promptly served interesting food inc children's dishes in attractive little dining room, well kept ales inc Boddingtons and Wadworths 6X, affable landlord, conservatory, plenty of tables in garden, back playground *(R F Grieve)*

☆ **Bottom of the Oven** [A537 Buxton— Macclesfield, 1st left past Cat & Fiddle – OS Sheet 118 map ref 980723; SJ9872], *Stanley Arms*: Isolated moorland pub with cosy rooms, lots of shiny black woodwork, plush seats, dimpled copper tables, open winter fires, dining room (children allowed here), generous reasonably priced food, well kept Marstons Burton and Pedigree, piped music, picnic tables on grass behind; may close Mon in winter if weather bad *(Geoffrey and Irene Lindley, John and Barbara Gibson, Ray Cuckow, LYM)*

☆ **Broomedge** [A56 E of Lymm; SJ7085], *Jolly Thresher*: Spacious open-plan pub with country chairs and tables on stripped boards, two open fires, attractively priced bar food (not Sun evening or Mon) from lunchtime sandwiches up, well kept Hydes, pub games; piped music, occasional folk nights *(M A Robinson, Paul Boot, LYM)*

☆ **Brownlow** [off A34 S of Congleton; SJ8260], *Brownlow Inn*: Spick-and-span extended Whitbreads dining pub, exposed timbers and several alcoves, good range of food from good ploughman's up (busy lunchtime), Boddingtons and Flowers, choice of wines by the glass, reasonable prices, good service; handy for Little Moreton Hall *(Janet Pickles, Ann and Colin Hunt, Sue Holland, Dave Webster, Ian Phillips)*

☆ **Bunbury** [Bows Gate Rd; SJ5758], *Dysart Arms*: Immaculate former farmhouse beautifully placed by village church, now same small chain as Grosvenor Arms at Aldford (see main entries), with civilised old-fashioned atmosphere, lots of antique furnishiture, cosy alcoves, interesting food, well kept ales and good changing house wines, tables in lovely elevated big garden; cl winter weekday lunchtimes *(Sue Holland, Dave Webster, George Jonas)*

☆ **Burleydam** [A525 Whitchurch—Audlem; SJ6143], *Combermere Arms*: 16th-c beamed pub with Bass, Worthington and guest beers from unusual circular bar, traditional decor,

bar food from sandwiches up, jovial landlord, pub games and big indoor adventure play area, restaurant; lighting a bit bright, piped music; open all day *(Sue and Bob Ward, LYM)*

☆ **Chester** [Upper Northgate St], *Pied Bull*: Attractive and comfortable beamed and panelled Jacobean pub behind late 18th-c façade, well kept Greenalls and unusual guest beers, warm welcome, staff attentive even when busy, wide choice of generous reasonably priced interesting food even Sun evening, afternoon teas too, no-smoking area; bedrooms *(Sidney and Erna Wells, William Cissna, SLC, Gordon Theaker, E G Parish)*

☆ **Chester** [Watergate St], *Watergates*: Wide range of quickly served good food from ploughman's up in lovely medieval crypt – a wine bar, with candlelit tables and good wine choice, but also real ales such as Boddingtons and Cains; can get packed Sat evening and race days *(Simon and Pie Barker, SLC, Mr and Mrs E J W Rogers, Andrew Hodges)*

☆ **Chester** [Park St; by Roman Walls, off Albion St], *Albion*: Just below city wall, idiosyncratic but very welcoming, with three carefully refurbished Victorian rooms, masses of WWI, 40s and 50s memorabilia, big helpings of low-priced home-cooked chip-free food all sessions inc unusual things such as haggis or Staffordshire oatcakes, Cains and Greenalls beers, quick friendly service, no piped music *(Sue Holland, Dave Webster, Brian Wainwright, Bill Sykes, Tony and Wendy Hobden)*

☆ **Chester** [Eastgate Row N], *Boot*: Fine position on The Rows, heavy beams, lots of old woodwork, oak flooring and flagstones, even some exposed Tudor wattle and daub, black-leaded kitchen range in lounge beyond food servery, no-smoking oak-panelled upper room, good atmosphere, friendly new licensee, cheap well kept Sam Smiths; children allowed *(Martin Hickes, Sue Holland, Dave Webster, SLC, LYM)*

☆ **Chester** [Lower Bridge St], *Falcon*: Good bustling atmosphere in striking building with beams, handsome stripped brickwork, well kept Sam Smiths OB and Museum, decent basic bar meals (not Sun), fruit machine, piped music; children allowed lunchtime (not Sat) in airy upstairs room; jazz Sat lunchtime, open all day Sat, interesting tours of the vaults; can get packed *(E G Parish, SLC, JH, Sue Holland, Dave Webster, Simon and Pie Barker, Brian and Anna Marsden, LYM)*

☆ **Chester** [Tower Wharf, Raymond St; behind Northgate St, nr rly], *Telfords Warehouse*: Interesting pub in former warehouse designed by Thomas Telford, full-sized derrick in original position, great views over canal basin, well kept ales such as Theakstons and changing guest beers, good unusual food in pub, cellar wine bar and upper restaurant; blond furniture, nightly live music; children welcome *(M Phillips, WS)*

☆ **Chester** [Watergate St], *Old Custom House*: Quiet and civilised old pub with lots of good pottery and brass in three character rooms, good value straightforward food, good range of Marstons ales inc Mild, prompt service, good evening atmosphere, fruit machine in lounge *(Brian Wainwright, SLC)*

Chester [Northgate St], *Coach & Horses*: Lots of woodwork, bric-a-brac and prints, massive range of sandwiches, also baked potatoes, baguettes and fry-ups, two monthly guest ales; piped music, fruit machine *(SLC)*; [City Rd], *Jones's*: More wine bar than pub, but does have Belgian Leffe ale as well as Theakstons, splendid food from bangers and mash to gumbo and game pie, huge cheap puddings; bare brick and boards, roaring fire, small window alcoves, mezzanine, upstairs restaurant, more formal downstairs dining area; children welcome *(Anon)*; [Milton St], *Mill*: Popular real ale bar in ex-mill hotel, spacious and comfortable, friendly efficient staff, decent bar food till late evening, good value Sun lunch, restaurant overlooking canal, well kept house beer from Coach House in Warrington, interesting guest and bottled beers, good view of cask stillage, well chosen piped music – some live; good with children, waterside tables, boat trips; bedrooms *(Richard Lewis)*[Bridge St], *Olde Vaults*: Panelling and leaded lights, well kept Greenalls, upstairs lounge *(Sue Holland, Dave Webster, SLC)*

☆ **Comberbach** [off A553 and A559 NW of Northwich, pub towards Great Budworth; SJ6477], *Spinner & Bergamot*: Neat plush beamed bar with log fire, hunting prints and toby jugs, softly lit back dining room with country-kitchen furniture and big inglenook, red-tiled public bar, usual bar food, well kept Greenalls Bitter, Original and Mild; piped music; picnic tables on sloping lawn, lots of flowers, bowling green *(Keith and Judith Ashcroft, John Broughton, Martin Bromfield, Bernadette Garner, LYM)*

☆ **Cotebrook** [junction A49/B5152 N of Tarporley; SJ5765], *Alvanley Arms*: Two rooms (one no smoking) off chintzy hall, big open fire, neat high beams, interesting sporting and other prints, plenty of tables, well kept Robinsons Mild and Best, decent house wines, several malt whiskies, good value waitress-served food from sandwiches to duck or monkfish (may be a wait unless you arrive early), attractive fairy-lit garden by pond with geese; children in restaurant; good value bedrooms *(Comus Elliott, KB, DH, David and Judy Walmsley, Paul Barnett, Paul Bailey, SH, DW, Mr and Mrs R Allan, S Williamson, LYM)*

☆ **Crewe** [Nantwich Rd (A534) opp rly stn; SJ7056], *Crewe Arms*: Good value attractive bar meals in comfortable and spacious lounge which one reader has been visiting now for 50 years, Victorian pictures, marble-topped tables, alabaster figurines, curtained alcoves, ornate ceiling; good pubby public bar; Tetleys well kept when it's on, civilised bar food, friendly staff, open all day; bedrooms *(E G Parish)*

Crewe [1 Pedley St], *Albion*: Popular local with comfortable lounge and bar, friendly staff, ever-changing well kept interesting beers, lots of railway prints and pump clips, darts, dominoes, pool and quiz nights; piped music, cl weekday lunchtimes *(Richard Lewis, Sue Holland, Dave Webster)*; [58 Nantwich Rd], *British Lion*: Known locally as the Pig, with comfortable partly panelled bar, back snug, well kept Tetleys-related ales and a good guest beer, friendly staff; can get smoky when the locals crowd in *(Richard Lewis, Sue Holland, Dave Webster)*; [Weston Lane], *Brocklebank*: Roomy new open-plan Brewers Fayre with lots of room, bric-a-brac, railway-theme prints, comfortable seating, big conservatory, Lego play room, lots of high chairs, baby changing room, adventure playground; wide choice of food inc lots of specials, Whitbreads-related ales, friendly efficient staff; open all day *(Richard Lewis)*; [332 Crewe Rd, Shavington (B5071); SJ7053], *Cheshire Cheese*: Recently well refurbished as Greenalls Millers Kitchen family dining pub, plenty of friendly efficient staff, well kept Boddingtons, Greenalls Original, Tetleys and a guest such as Burtonwood Top Hat, good choice of food inc OAPs' menu, good wheelchair facilities, high chairs, babychanging; tables outside, play area *(Richard Lewis)*; [25 Earle St], *Crown*: Original fittings, old-fashioned furnishings and wallpaper; busy main front bar, back games room with pool and juke box, two quietly chatty lounges and drinking corridor; welcoming landlady and locals, well kept Robinsons; handy for Railway Heritage Centre *(PB, SH, DW)*; [Nantwich Rd], *Earl of Crewe*: Big mock-Tudor pub with lots of railway prints and beer memorabilia, panelling, copper cauldrons; cosy atmosphere, good choice of ever-changing real ales kept well, reasonably priced food *(Sue Holland, Dave Webster)*; [56 Earle St], *Kings Arms*: Several friendly rooms recently redecorated (keeping nice tiling), well kept Whitbreads-related ales esp Mild, pool, darts, dominoes and cribbage; very busy lunchtime, no food *(Richard Lewis, Sue Holland, Dave Webster)*; [Victoria St], *New Burton*: Lots of snooker tables, friendly staff and locals, pleasant furnishings, bar food, well kept Tetleys *(Richard Lewis)*; [Middlewich Rd (A530), Wolstanwood; SJ6755], *Rising Sun*: Well refurbished, with panelling, prints and comfortable seating in lots of separate areas, raised eating area, disabled lift, children's facilities; friendly staff, good range of generous food, well kept Greenalls, Tetleys and a good guest beer; tables and play area outside, open all day, good disabled access (inc lift), bedrooms *(Richard Lewis)*; [Earle St], *Three Lamps*: Smartly refurbished, with lots of woodwork and attractive prints, comfortable seats, back food area, relaxed atmosphere, friendly staff; well kept Banks's ales inc Mild, good choice of bottled drinks; piped music, games machines, live music some nights; open all day, handy for Lyceum Theatre *(Richard Lewis, Sue Holland, Dave Webster)*

Crowton [Station Rd; SJ5875], *Hare & Hounds*: Good varied reasonably priced meals freshly prepared by landlord/chef, warmly welcoming staff and landlady, beautifully appointed restaurant – booking needed Sun lunch *(Norman Revell, Mr and Mrs J Nicholson)*

Daresbury [Old Chester Rd; SJ5983], *Ring o' Bells*: Well refurbished, with roaring log fire, good choice of reasonably priced good food inc vegetarian, well kept Greenalls Bitter, Original and Mild and a weekly guest beer, friendly efficient service, big garden and play area; short walk from canal; village church has window showing all the characters in *Alice in Wonderland*; bedrooms *(Sue Kelly)*

Disley [up side road by Rams Head Hotel; SJ9784], *White Horse*: Clean and civilised, popular esp on pensioner lunch days, efficiently served good food using fresh ingredients, well kept Robinsons *(R Davies)*

☆ **Eaton** [School Lane (A536 Congleton—Macclesfield); SJ8765], *Plough*: Smart and pretty 17th-c beamed inn, cosy fires, friendly landlord, imaginative reasonably priced French-influence food, carvery all day Sun, well kept Banks's, Marstons and a guest such as Morrells Graduate; piped music; attractive newly built bedrooms in renovated barn annexe with own bathrooms *(James Nunns, John and Janet Warren)*

Eaton [Beech Lane; the one nr Tarporley, at SJ5763], *Red Lion*: Nicely decorated comfortable country pub, wide choice of good generous food inc vegetarian, lots of sandwiches and OAP bargains, efficient service, no-smoking areas, separate bar with pool and darts, floodlit bowling green, barbecues and play area; well kept Greenalls and Stones, unobjectionable piped music; children welcome, open all day *(Richard Lewis, N Revell)*

Ellesmere Port [Old Chester Rd; SJ4077], *White Swan*: Comfortable two-roomed local with good value food, keen landlord and friendly staff, half a dozen interesting well kept real ales, pub games *(Richard Lewis)*

Ettiley Heath [Elton Rd; SJ7460], *Rookery*: Welcoming two-bar pub with well kept Marstons Pedigree and Tetleys, simple meals, tables outside *(Joan and Michel Hooper-Immins)*

☆ **Faddiley** [A534 Wrexham—Nantwich; SJ5753], *Thatch*: Attractively cottagey thatched, beamed and timbered dining pub with classy food, proper napkins, good home-made bread, good friendly service, cosy open fire, well kept ales such as McEwans 70/-, Morlands Old Speckled Hen and Theakstons Old Peculier; children welcome *(Nigel Woolliscroft, SH, DW, Clive Gilbert, Basil Minson, Sue Holland, Dave Webster, LYM)*

Farndon [SJ4254], *Farndon Arms*: Nicely decorated timbered pub in pretty village; very friendly staff, good interesting reasonably

priced food, smart upstairs restaurant area, seven well kept largely Whitbreads-related beers; dogs welcome *(Jenny and Neil Spink, Mike Ridgway, Sarah Miles)*

☆ **Frodsham** [Church St; SJ5278], *Rowlands*: Friendly single-roomed pub with several well kept quickly changing real ales (well over 1,000 in last five years), as well as bottled wheat beers and good choice of wines by the glass; sensibly short choice of good simple bar food, upstairs bistro, children welcome, open all day *(Sue and Glenn Crooks, Richard Lewis, Derek and Syvlia Stephenson)*

☆ **Fullers Moor** [A534 – OS Sheet 117 map ref 500542; SJ5054], *Copper Mine*: Comfortable dining pub, light and airy, with pine furnishings, interesting copper-mining memorabilia, pretty nooks and crannies, well presented tasty food from big lunchtime sandwiches up to good Sun lunches, well kept Bass and Burtonwood Best, friendly staff, children welcome; spacious garden with barbecues and lovely views; handy for Sandstone Trail *(Jenny and Neil Spink, Arthur and Margaret Dickinson, Paul Robinshaw, LYM)*

☆ **Gawsworth** [nr Macclesfield; SJ8969], *Harrington Arms*: Farm pub's two small rooms with bare wooden floorboards, fine carved bar counter, well kept Robinsons Best and Hatters Mild served in big old enamelled jugs, friendly service, benches on small front cobbled terrace *(Richard Lewis)*

Goostrey [111 Main Rd; off A50 and A535; SJ7870], *Crown*: Extended Marstons dining pub with lots of beams and pictures, cosy and friendly atmosphere, popular landlord, well kept ale; bedrooms *(Tony Young, LYM)*; [Station Rd, towards A535], *Red Lion*: Friendly modernised open-plan bar and back family restaurant with enjoyable food, well kept Boddingtons, Tetleys and a guest beer, friendly efficient service, restaurant, nice garden with play area; piped music, fruit machines, quiz night, videos; children welcome *(Joan Edwards, LYM)*

☆ **Great Budworth** [signed off A559 NE of Northwich; SJ6778], *George & Dragon*: Attractive 17th-c building in delightful village, rambling panelled lounge, beams hung with copper jugs, red plush button-back banquettes and older settles, no-smoking area, games in public bar, upstairs restaurant, sensibly priced bar food, well kept Tetleys and two weekly changing guest beers, farm cider; children welcome, open all day Sat/Sun *(Alan and Paula McCully, S J Barber, Martin Bromfield, Bernadette Garner, Derek and Sylvia Stephenson, David and Judy Walmsley, John and Phyllis Maloney, Bill and Sheila McLardy, S P Watkin, P A Taylor, LYM)*

☆ **Hatchmere** [B5152, off A556 at Abbey Arms; SJ5572], *Carriers*: Clean comfortable split-level lounge with bare brickwork, draught horse prints, old brewery photographs and pictures of pike caught nearby, friendly service, reasonably priced food from good sandwiches up inc children's helpings, well kept Burtonwood Bitter, Mild and Top Hat; attractive garden leading down to lake, handy for Delamere Forest *(Jenny and Michael Back)*

☆ **Hatton** [Warrington Rd (B5356, handy for M56 junction 10); SJ6082], *Hatton Arms*: Cosy and friendly 18th-c bar with open fire, two plainer rooms off; bar lunches inc good value soup and sandwiches, real ales, good service, popular evening restaurant (not Sun); cobbled pavement outside, local Lewis Carroll connections; now has bedrooms *(Chris Walling)*

Haughton Moss [Long Lane; off A49 S of Tarporley; SJ5856], *Nags Head*: Warm friendly atmosphere, good value food and beer; children welcome *(SH, DW)*

☆ **Higher Whitley** [1¼ miles from M56 junction 10; A559 towards Northwich; SJ6280], *Birch & Bottle*: Good value food inc OAP lunches in civilised and attractively decorated pub with well kept Greenalls Mild, Bitter and Original, decent wines, good log fires, attractive conservatory; children allowed if eating *(R H Sawyer, LYM)*

Holmes Chapel [Station Rd; A54 not far from M6 junction 18; SJ7667], *Swan*: Welcoming, bright and clean, with plush banquettes, decorative china, old prints and photographs; well kept Sam Smiths, good range of lunches, big TV in one area; bedrooms *(Joan and Michel Hooper-Immins)*

☆ **Kelsall** [Chester Rd (A54); SJ5268], *Morris Dancer*: Cosy yet roomy, two bars, wine bar area and restaurant, wide choice of generous tasty food (Italian chef) inc good fresh veg and game in season, efficient genuinely friendly staff, good cross-section of customers, pleasant and relaxing atmosphere; well kept Greenalls, decent wines, sensible prices *(W D Hollins, Derek and Margaret Underwood, John Honnor)*

☆ **Kerridge** [Redway Lane – OS Sheet 118 map ref 937773; SJ9377], *Redway*: Extended stone pub with large family area inc indoor playroom, very generous good food (beware service charge), well kept Boddingtons and Courage Directors, attentive staff, warm conservatory; big barbecue area, adventure play area, sheep and ducks in pets corner; open all day Sun *(Dave and Doreen Irving, Brian and Anna Marsden, James Nunns)*

Knutsford [King St; SJ7578], *Angel*: Former open-plan pub refurbished to give civilised and comfortable two-room panelled front lounge, long side bar with air of baronial hall; well kept cheap Holts Bitter and Mild from central servery, good choice of no-nonsense food, friendly landlady and staff; bedrooms planned *(Richard Lewis)*; [King St], *Cross Keys*: Ancient building, well kept ale inc guests, good bar menu inc well served steaks, very pleasant service *(R T and J C Moggridge)*

☆ **Little Bollington** [the one nr Altrincham, 2 miles from M56 junction 7: A56 towards Lymm, then first right at Stamford Arms into Park Lane – use A556 to get back on to M56 westbound; SJ7286], *Swan With Two Nicks*:

Extended and refurbished beamed village pub full of brass, copper and bric-a-brac, cheerful atmosphere, snug alcoves, some antique settles, log fire, emphasis on popular generous food served quickly, well kept Whitbreads-related ales, tables outside; attractive hamlet by Dunham Hall deer park *(R Davies, LYM)*

Little Leigh [A49, just S of A533; not far from M56 junction 10; SJ6276], *Holly Bush*: Cosy reasonably priced no-smoking restaurant with busy young waitresses, pleasant friendly landlady, well kept Burtonwood and guest beers, traditional old-fashioned public bar *(Brian Wainwright, Chris Walling, LYM)*

☆ **Lower Whitley** [SJ6179], *Chetwode Arms*: Very popular and relaxing Millers Kitchen family dining pub with traditional layout, solid furnishings all clean and polished, warm coal fires, Greenalls Mild and Bitter, good food and service; immaculate bowling green, play area, open all day Sat *(P H Sawyer, LYM)*

Lymm [Agden Wharf; Warrington Lane; SJ6787], *Admiral Benbow*: Small comfortable newish pub in picturesque setting by Bridgewater Canal, *Treasure Island* theme, well kept Bass-family ales, good range of bottled beers, good value food, jovial friendly atmosphere; live music Sat, organ music Sun pm, canal trips *(Alan Gough, A R Walton)*; *Old Number Three*: Interesting choice of good food *(Pat and Robert Watt)*

Macclesfield [27 Churchwallgate; SJ9273], *Castle*: Timeless feel in deceptively big pub with small public bar, two lounges and end sitting area up steps with glass roof giving conservatory feel; well kept Scottish Courage ales, friendly staff, simple lunchtime food *(Richard Lewis)*; [Steeple St], *Franklin*: Good example of unchanging basic three-room town pub, well kept Robinsons Bitter and Hatters Mild, darts and pool *(Richard Lewis)*

Marston [Ollershaw Lane; SJ6775], *Salt Barge*: Smart, bright and spotless pub by Trent & Mersey Canal, new extension, Burtonwood Bitter and Buccaneer, decent food *(Joan and Michel Hooper-Immins)*

☆ **Middlewich** [22 Lewin St (A533); SJ7066], *Narrowboat*: Friendly pub not far from Trent & Mersey Canal, with appropriate memorabilia, old timbers, good value food running to kangaroo and ostrich with restaurant seating in balcony-like upper no-smoking area, well kept Burtonwood Bitter, Flowers Original and a guest such as Ridleys Rumpus; darts and games machines, piped music can be obtrusive *(William Cissna, Kate and Robert Hodkinson, Brian and Anna Marsden)*

Middlewich [Webbs Lane], *Big Lock*: 19th-c canalside pub with Scottish Courage ales, good food range in bar and restaurant inc well cooked steaks; open all day summer *(Joan and Michel Hooper-Immins)*

☆ **Mobberley** [Knolls Green (B5085 towards Alderley); SJ7879], *Bird in Hand*: Cosy low-ceilinged rooms with comfortably cushioned heavy wooden seats, warm coal fires, small pictures on Victorian wallpaper, little panelled snug, no-smoking top dining area, promptly served home-made bar food from sandwiches up, summer afternoon teas, helpful staff, well kept Sam Smiths OB and Museum, lots of malt whiskies, pub games; occasional piped music; children allowed, open all day *(Dave and Doreen Irving, Philip and Ann Falkner, Malcolm Taylor, Dr Jim Mackay, Martin Bromfield, Bernadette Garner, Clare Wilson, Dr and Mrs J H Hills, LYM)*

☆ **Mobberley** [opp church], *Church*: Smart but friendly and comfortable, with wide choice of good generous food, great log fire, well kept Greenalls, cheerful service; tables in courtyard, big garden with play area, own bowling green; children welcome *(Martin Bromfield, Bernadette Garner)*

Mobberley [Paddock Hill; small sign off B5085 Knutsford—Wilmslow], *Plough & Flail*: Small comfortable three-roomed pub with big helpings of good food inc fish, good toasties, welcoming log fire and dog, well kept Boddingtons and Marstons Pedigree; restaurant *(J F M West, Mr and Mrs C Roberts)*

☆ **Nantwich** [Hospital St – by side passage to central church; SJ6552], *Lamb*: Civilised hotel bar with leather chesterfields and other comfortable seats, well kept Burtonwood Forshaws, decent malt whiskies, good value nicely served generous home-cooked food inc outstanding fish and chips in bar and traditional upstairs dining room, attentive staff, unobtrusive piped music; bedrooms *(W C M Jones, SH, DW, Olive and Ray Hebson, Martin Bromfield, Bernadette Garner, BB)*

☆ **Nantwich** [51 Beam St], *Red Cow*: Well renovated former Tudor farmhouse, good relaxed atmosphere, smallish lounge and bar, no-smoking dining area, good range of good value food esp vegetarian, well kept Robinsons Best, Mild, Old Tom, Frederics and Hartleys XB, back pool table *(Mrs P J Elfick, Sue Holland, Dave Webster, SLC)*

Nantwich [Churchyard Side], *Bowling Green*: Well set in pedestrian area, beams and panelling, good choice of reasonably pricd food, well kept Scottish Courage ales, friendly staff, back garden with lots of tables; piped music, games machines *(Richard Lewis)*; [High St – centre almost opp W end of church], *Crown*: Striking Elizabethan inn with rambling comfortably modernised beamed and timbered bar (packed weekend evenings), real ales, bar food, good value attached Italian restaurant, helpful service; comfortable bedrooms *(Pamela and Merlyn Horswell, BB)*

Neston [19 Quayside; SW of Little Neston – OS Sheet 117 map ref 290760; SJ2976], *Harp*: Charming tiny old pub in marvellous spot by ruined quay on the Burton Marshes looking out over the River Dee to Wales; one cosy and friendly beamed room with real fire, the other workingman's-club-style; well kept Cains, Timothy Taylors Landlord and

Jennings Sneck Lifter, basic cheese or ham sandwiches, friendly staff, cheery locals, no piped music *(Richard Lewis)*

No Mans Heath [A41 N of Whitchurch; SJ5148], *Wheatsheaf*: Low beams, lots of pictures, brasses, wrought iron, comfortable seats, cosy fires, friendly staff, well kept Bass, Ruddles County, Theakstons Best and Worthington Best, usual decent food, relaxing atmosphere; piped music; play area in garden *(Sue and Bob Ward, SLC)*

☆ **Ollerton** [A537 – OS Sheet 118 map ref 775769; SJ7877], *Dun Cow*: Pretty country pub, small-roomed and friendly, with attractive and individual furnishings, two fine log fires, well kept Greenalls Bitter and Original, drinkable wine, dominoes, shove-ha'penny and darts in small tap room, interesting bar food from sandwiches up inc vegetarian; open all day (inc restaurant in summer), children in snug and restaurant *(Douglas Miller, LYM)*

☆ **Over Peover** [off A50 S of Knutsford; SJ7674], *Olde Park Gate*: Pleasant quiet atmosphere in three small black-beamed rooms with some attractive furnishings inc fine Macclesfield oak chairs and lots of pictures, well kept Sam Smiths Best, Mild and Stout, good value food, good welcoming service, new lounge with dining area, keen darts team; family room, tables outside *(Richard Lewis, Leo and Barbara Lionet, BB)*

☆ **Parkgate** [The Parade, Parkgate Rd; SJ2878], *Red Lion*: Comfortable and welcoming Victorian-feel pub on attractive waterfront with great view to Welsh hills, good value sandwiches and home-cooked main dishes, well kept Tetleys-related ales, 19th-c paintings and beer-mug collection, open fire, good service, darts and pool; the chatty parrot's called Nelson *(Richard Lewis)*

Parkgate [The Parade], *Old Quay*: Roomy modern single-storey Brewers Fayre family dining pub in conservation area among parkland, facing Dee and Welsh hills, comfortable banquettes, sensible tables, old prints, big picture windows, food all day, helpful staff, Whitbreads Castle Eden; indoor play area *(Richard Lewis, E G Parish)*

Pickmere [Park Lane; B5391 NE of Northwich; SJ6977], *Red Lion*: 18th-c beamed pub with roaring fire, lovely hanging baskets etc, tables in attractive garden, well kept Tetleys Bitter and Mild and a guest beer, good value home-made food (not Sun evening), helpful staff; the billiards corner can get lively Sat *(Jean Bernard Brisset)*

☆ **Prestbury** [SJ9077], *Legh Arms*: Striking long heavy-beamed 16th-c building with lots of woodwork, gallery, smart atmosphere, tables laid with cloths and cutlery in main dining bar, good choice of good value inventive food inc vegetarian, cosy comfortable separate lounge bar, well kept Robinsons Best and Frederics, friendly largely Italian service; open all day, children welcome *(Richard Lewis)*

Prestbury [opp St Peter's church], *Admiral Rodney*: Comfortable old-world pub, friendly staff, well kept Robinsons Best and Hatters Mild, limited lunchtime menu, real fire *(Richard Lewis)*

☆ **Rainow** [NE of village on A5002 Whalley Bridge—Macclesfield; SJ9576], *Highwayman*: Timeless unchanging moorside pub with small rooms, low 17th-c beams, good winter fires (electric other times), plenty of atmosphere, lovely views; Thwaites real ales, bar food inc good sandwiches, rather late opening *(Philip and Ann Falkner, Jack and Philip Paxton, Gwen and Peter Andrews, LYM)*

Sandbach [High St; SJ7661], *Black Bear*: Busy black and white thatched pub, beams and panelling, well kept Marstons Pedigree and Tetleys, Addlestone's cider, alcove area, lots of tables in side room, games machines and juke box; friendly staff *(Richard Lewis)*; [Crown Banks, The Square], *Lower Chequer*: Refurbished 16th-c pub just off cobbled square; island bar, eight well kept ales inc some from small breweries, generous helpings of good value home-made food, friendly staff, coal-effect gas fire; TV now in original small bar *(A Croall, Richard Lewis, Sue Holland, Dave Webster)*

☆ **Scholar Green** [off A34 N of Kidsgrove; SJ8356], *Rising Sun*: Good country-pub atmosphere, welcoming service, good choice of well kept ales inc Marstons (inc special brews) and Tetleys, wide range of generous interesting home-cooked food, family room, pleasantly refurbished no-smoking dining room; separate games room, unobtrusive piped music *(Bill Sykes, Kate and Robert Hodkinson)*

Scholar Green [Congleton Rd N], *Travellers Rest*: Busy, comfortable and cosy, lots of panelling, brass and prints, leather seats, well kept Banks's, Cottage Normans Conquest, Marstons Best and current Brewers Choice, wide choice of good value bar food inc skillet cooking, friendly staff; tables and swings outside *(Richard Lewis)*

☆ **Smallwood** [Knutsford Rd (A50 N of Alsager); SJ8160], *Legs of Man*: Comfortable roadside Robinsons pub with carefully matched chairs, banquettes, carpet, curtains and wallpaper, fin de siècle tall white nymphs on columns, lush potted plants, big helpings of good home-cooked food inc some imaginative dishes (and they try to suit special diets), well kept Best, Frederics and Hatters Mild, staff friendly and effective even when very busy; restaurant, children truly welcome; well spaced tables on side lawn with play area *(Richard Lewis, Mr and Mrs Wroe, BB)*

☆ **Smallwood** [Newcastle Rd (A50)], *Bulls Head*: Attractive interestingly decorated dining pub with lots of space and particularly good garden with play area; well kept Burtonwood and Tetleys, decent house wines, imaginative range of well presented generous food inc interesting salads and good puddings, good service; piped pop music, children welcome; quite handy for Biddulph Grange (NT) *(K Plant, LYM)*

☆ **Styal** [Altrincham Rd (B5166 nr Ringway

Airport); SJ8383], *Ship*: Friendly service, well kept Scottish Courage ales, wide choice of reasonably priced food (long lunch Sat/Sun), children allowed, open all day; seats out in front, attractive NT village, walks in riverside woods *(Geoffrey and Brenda Wilson)*

☆ **Sutton** [Higher Sutton, off A54 Congleton—Buxton, 2¾ miles E of A523 – OS Sheet 118 map ref 942694; SJ9469], *Ryles Arms*: Large popular dining pub in fine countryside, wide choice of food from sandwiches to game in season, no-smoking dining area and family room, some attractively individual furnishings, french windows to terrace, well kept Coach House Best, Marstons Pedigree, and Ruddles Best and County, good choice of whiskies, friendly Irish landlord, no music or games *(Mike and Wendy Proctor, Andy Hazeldine, J Muir, LYM)*

☆ **Tarporley** [50 High St (off A49); SJ5563], *Swan*: Tastefully modernised Georgian inn with cosy little spaces, well kept Ruddles and three guests such as Adnams, Charles Wells Bombardier and Jennings, bottled Belgian beers, lots of malt whiskies, bistro bar with rather smart food inc superb goat cheeses (also lunchtime sandwiches and snacks), restaurant, tables outside, provision for children; comfortable well equipped bedrooms *(Sue and Bob Ward, M Joyner, Derek and Sylvia Stephenson, Sue Holland, Dave Webster, LYM)*

☆ nr **Tiverton** [Wharton's Lock, Bates Mill Lane – OS Sheet 117 map ref 532603; SJ5660], *Shady Oak*: Canalside country pub with plenty of seats and good play area in waterside garden and terrace, fine views of Beeston Castle, airy lounge, small carpeted conservatory, pleasant young licensee, well kept Scottish Courage ales, decent Chef & Brewer food, summer barbecues, moorings *(William Cissna, LYM)*

Walgherton [London Rd; A51 between Bridgemere Gdn Centre and Stapeley Water Gdns; SJ6949], *Boars Head*: Large main road Greenalls pub with local farming-theme decor, lots of corners in lounge, games, prints and boars' heads in bar, nice dining conservatory, good quick food all day from sandwiches up, very friendly uniformed staff, big garden with children's play area *(Sue and Bob Ward, SLC)*

☆ **Walker Barn** [A537 Macclesfield—Buxton; SJ9573], *Setter Dog*: Warm, clean and civilised extended dining pub with windswept moors view, well kept real ales such as Fullers London Pride, good food inc good value roasts in small bar and restaurant, good friendly service, roaring fire; handy for Teggs Nose Country Park *(Gill and Maurice McMahon)*

☆ **Warmingham** [School Lane; SJ7161], *Bears Paw*: Good food inc lots of specials and enormous filled baguettes in small plush bar and restaurant, well kept Bass, Boddingtons, Flowers IPA and Marstons Pedigree, relaxed atmosphere, friendly staff, pool room, children very welcome; good spot by river and ancient church in small hamlet, seats in front garden *(Richard Lewis)*

☆ nr **Warrington** [Fiddlers Ferry; leave A562 in Penketh – park in Station rd off Tannery Lane – OS Sheet 108 map ref 560863; SJ5686], *Ferry:* Picturesquely isolated between St Helens Canal and Mersey, four well kept real ales inc very quickly changing guest beers, over 100 whiskies, good home-cooked food in nice upstairs dining room (not Sun evening), cosy and friendly low-beamed bar, log fires, provision for children; tables outside with play area, pets corner, pony paddock *(B D Craig, LYM)*

☆ **Waverton** [A41 S of Chester; SJ4663], *Black Dog:* Clean and inviting old Greenalls dining pub done out in modern pine and light oak style, good choice of popular food, real ales inc guests, cordial licensees, big tasteful lounge, small garden; occasional jazz evenings, piped music *(Gill and Keith Croxton, SLC)*

Wheelock [466 Crewe Rd (A534); SJ7559], *Cheshire Cheese:* Canalside local in quiet suburb of Sandbach, Banks's Mild and Bitter and Marstons Pedigree, good range of generous food inc three home-made soups, friendly service; popular with boaters *(Joan and Michel Hooper-Immins)*

☆ **Whiteley Green** [OS Sheet 118 map ref 924789; SJ9278], *Windmill:* Roomy modernised lounge and dining area, good mid-priced bar food from lunchtime sandwiches up inc good vegetarian dishes and very popular themed food nights, Tetleys-related ales, friendly service; provision for children; spacious and attractive garden with summer bar and barbecues, nice countryside with canal and other walks *(Rev John Hibberd, Mr and Mrs C Roberts, Philip and Ann Falkner, BB)*

Willaston [Newcastle Rd, Blakelow – OS Sheet 118 map ref 680517; SJ6851], *Horseshoe:* Panelled lounge with fire, dining room and no-smoking restaurant extension, public bar, decent food, Robinsons Best, Old Stockport and Old Tom, new young licensee; garden with swings *(Sue Holland, Dave Webster)*

Willaston [Wistaston Rd – OS Sheet 117 map ref 329777; SJ3378], *Pollards:* Striking partly 14th-c building with cheerily comfortable beamed and flagstoned bar, unusual cushioned wall seats with some stone armrests, fruit machines, wide choice of good value food inc early supper bargains,

Greenalls ales, dining conservatory overlooking sizeable pleasant garden, separate restaurant; bedrooms *(Graham and Lynn Mason)*

☆ **Willington Corner** [Boothsdale; off A54 at Kelsall; SJ5367], *Boot:* Warmly welcoming, with Greenalls and guest ales, good food from sandwiches, vegetarian and children's dishes to pheasant casserole, fresh veg, charming restaurant with log fire, pleasant service, very acceptable prices; handy for the picturesque area known locally as Little Switzerland *(Mrs K Forber, J Honnor, W C M Jones)*

Wilmslow [Alderley rd; SJ8481], *New Inn:* Comfortable and spacious, two or three softly lit areas off big central bar with well kept Hydes ales, reasonably priced food from separate servery, quiet piped music *(Ian Phillips)*

Winnington [off A533 NW of Northwich; SJ6474], *Winnington Hall:* Good fresh well chosen modestly priced food in bar, also restaurant Thurs-Sat evening and Sun lunch; good low-priced wine list; a club, but open to public; cl Sun evening *(S Williamson)*

☆ **Wistaston** [Nantwich Rd; SJ6853], *Old Manor:* Old manor house recently refurbished by Bass, olde-worlde feel, lots of wood, plenty of comfortable seating, friendly staff, extensive range of food, Bass, Stones and Worthington; fully supervised Deep Sea Den for children *(Richard Lewis)*

Withington [Trap St, Lower Withington, a mile S of B5392 – OS Sheet 118 map ref 820682; SJ8268], *Black Swan:* Extended and refurbished more as restaurant with bar, beautifully presented good original food, well kept ales such as Marstons Pedigree and Timothy Taylors Landlord *(W D Christian, June and Malcolm Farmer)*; [Trap St], *Red Lion:* Friendly and relaxing two-bar country pub with good varied bar food from huge sandwiches up, well kept Robinsons ales inc the rare Dark Mild, good service, restaurant, children welcome; tables outside, handy for Jodrell Bank *(Richard Lewis)*

☆ **Wybunbury** [Main Rd (B5071); SJ6950], *Swan:* Well run pub with nooks and crannies in rambling lounge, pleasant public bar, well kept beer inc good choice of guests, reasonably priced genuine home cooking inc interesting dishes, warmly welcoming staff, tasteful furnishings inc some antiques – shop at the back; seats in garden by beautiful churchyard *(Sue Holland, Dave Webster, BB)*

Post Office address codings confusingly give the impression that some pubs are in Cheshire, when they're really in Derbyshire (and therefore included in this book under that chapter) or in Greater Manchester (see the Lancashire chapter).

Cornwall

Quite a few changes here this year. Newcomers to the main entries are the charming waterside Edgcumbe Arms at Cremyll, the rather unusual Quarryman at Edmonton, the friendly Lugger at Polruan (most of its customers seem to arrive by boat) and the White Hart at St Keverne, overhauled by keen new licensees, with lots of good fresh fish. Other Cornish pubs doing particularly well at the moment include the Trengilly Wartha at Constantine (doing so well all round – as a local, as a restaurant and as a hotel – that this year it earns one of our coveted star awards), the well run Halzephron in a lovely position at Gunwalloe near Helston (good food), the Crown at Lanlivery, the Royal Oak in Lostwithiel (both of these are fine all-rounders), the friendly and interesting old White Hart at Ludgvan, the Roseland at Philleigh (one of our favourite West Country locals), the Ship in its wonderful position above Porthleven harbour, the Fox & Hounds at Scorrier (but they don't allow children), the Turks Head out in its enviable spot on the shores of St Agnes, the friendly St Kew Inn (which now has letting bedrooms), the Springer Spaniel at Treburley (friendly, with fine food), and the outstanding Eliot Arms at Tregadillett. The Old Ale House in Truro's new manager is doing very well, and there are new people at the nice little Victory at St Mawes, the Quayside in Falmouth and at the Railway in St Agnes (the fascinating shoe collection has stayed behind). The Blue Anchor in Helston, long famous for its own ancient small brewery, has done some smartening up – more women seem to be dropping in these days. The Lucky Dip section at the end of this chapter is particularly choice: if there were no constraints on the sheer size of the book we could very happily more than double the length of the Cornwall chapter. Pubs to note specially there are the Napoleon at Boscastle, Ship at Lerryn, Ferryboat at Helford Passage (for its position), Top House at Lizard (rather the reverse), Heron at Malpas, Red Lion at Mawnan Smith, Bush at Morwenstow, Old Inn at Mullion, London Inn in Padstow, Victoria at Perranuthnoe, Royal Oak at Perranwell, Blue Peter in Polperro, Port Gaverne just outside Port Isaac, Rising Sun on Portmellon Cove, Preston Gate at Poughill, Sloop in St Ives, Mill House at Trebarwith and Tinners Arms at Zennor; we have inspected each of these and give them all the thumbs-up. The drinks scene here has been rather dominated by the recent widespread adoption of sparklers for real ale service. These gadgets increase handpump pressure to give a foaming head – which seems to suit Northern beers, but can quickly dissipate the taste of most others. So traditionalist readers greatly regret the way that down here even the local St Austell ales now seem to be succumbing to this trend. However, a bright spot is that St Austell ales are generally much cheaper than those supplied by the big national brewers, typically saving you around 20p a pint – more than 40p in the cheapest pubs we found, the Lugger at Polruan and Ship in Mousehole.

BOSCASTLE SX0990 Map 1
Cobweb

B3263, just E of harbour

Handy for the harbour and witchcraft museum, this popular old pub has plenty of atmosphere in the lively public bar where hundreds of old bottles hang from the heavy beams, there's a cosy log fire, two or three curved high-backed winged settles against the dark stone walls, and a few leatherette dining chairs. Well kept Bass, Greene King Abbot, St Austell Tinners, HSD, and guest beers on handpump, and several malt whiskies. Quickly served, good value bar food includes sandwiches (from £1.50), ploughman's (from £3.25), vegetarian dishes or a daily roast (£4.50), steaks (from £7), and mixed grill (£9.75); the restaurant is no smoking. Darts, pool, dominoes, cribbage, video game, fruit machine, and juke box; the big communicating family room has an enormous armchair carved out of a tree trunk as well as its more conventional windsor armchairs, and another winter fire. Opening off this is a good-sized children's room and more machines. *(Recommended by Jo and Gary Charlton, Val Stevenson, Rob Holmes, Ann and Colin Hunt, Wayne Wheeler, Barry Perfect, K Flack, Clare Wilson, Linda and Mike Proctor, Dr S Savvas, M Martin, Craig and Gillian Brown, R Walden)*

Free house ~ Licensees Ivor and Adrian Bright ~ Real ale ~ Meals and snacks (till 10pm) ~ Restaurant ~ (01840) 250278 ~ Children in own room and eating area of bar ~ Live entertainment Sat evening ~ Open 11-11 in summer and on winter Fri and Sat; closed winter weekday afternoons

CHAPEL AMBLE SW9975 Map 1
Maltsters Arms ♀

Village signposted from A39 NE of Wadebridge; and from B3314

An extension to the bar area has now been completed here and is hung with ship pictures and the beginnings of a collection of seafaring memorabilia. The other attractively knocked-together rooms have black oak joists in the white ceiling, partly panelled stripped stone walls, heavy wooden tables on the partly carpeted big flagstones, a large stone fireplace, and a relaxed atmosphere; there's also a side room with windsor chairs and an upstairs family room. Popular bar food includes lunchtime sandwiches (from £1.50), filled baked potatoes and ploughman's (from £3.50), as well as home-made soup (£2.25), cheesy garlic mushrooms (£3.25), home-cooked ham and egg (£4.25), steak in ale pie (£6.50), sirloin steak (£8.95), daily specials like avocado pear with local crab (£4.95), chicken and mushroom pie (£6.50) or T-bone steak (£14.50), and fresh fish such as very good sardines in garlic butter (starter £3.95, main course £7.95), scallops with bacon (starter £5.25, main course £10.50), and big bass stuffed with herbs (£14.95); friendly service. Well kept Courage Directors, Fullers London Pride, Greene King Abbot, Sharps Cornish and a beer brewed for the pub by Sharps (who are a local brewery) on handpump kept under light blanket pressure; up to 20 wines by the glass, several malt whiskies, and a few brandies. Winter darts, cribbage, dominoes, and piped music. Benches outside in a sheltered sunny corner and pretty hanging baskets and tubs. *(Recommended by P H Boot, M A Borthwick, Mr and Mrs M N Greenwood, Mr and Mrs B Hobden, Pamela and Merlyn Horswell, Mr and Mrs A C Curry, Andy and Jill Kassube, Iain Robertson, Rita Horridge, Ian Wilson, Mr and Mrs G McNeill, Jenny and Brian Seller, R and S Bentley, Val Stevenson, Rob Holmes, Brian Skelcher, D Horsman, David and Julie Glover, Paul and Lynn Benny, John Ledbury, Sharon Handock, Pete and Rosie Flower, Dr S Savvas, M Martin, Howard Clutterbuck)*

Free house ~ Licensees David and Marie Gray and David Coles ~ Real ale ~ Meals and snacks ~ Restaurant ~ (01208) 812473 ~ Children in family room and in restaurant (must be over 8) ~ Open 10.30-2.30, 5.30(6 in winter)-11(10.30 in winter); 12-2.30, 4-10.30 Sun; closed evening 25 Dec

We say if we or readers have seen dogs or cats in a pub.

CONSTANTINE SW7229 Map 1
Trengilly Wartha ★ 🛏 ♀ 🍴

Constantine signposted from Penryn—Gweek rd (former B3291); in village turn right just before Minimarket (towards Gweek); in nearly a mile pub signposted left; at Nancenoy, OS sheet 204, map reference 731282

We've decided to award this extremely well run, tucked away inn a star this year. Unusually, it's not really helped towards this top ranking by anything inherent in the building itself; it owes everything to the remarkable skill the owners have shown in blending a local, a restaurant, and a comfortable hotel successfully into one distinctive place, with a really enjoyable atmosphere. The low-beamed main bar has a wood burning stove and modern high-backed settles boxing in polished heavy wooden tables, and the lounge has cushioned wall benches, a log fire and some harness. Up a step from the bar is an eating area with tables and winged settles, and there's also a bright no-smoking conservatory family room. Most enjoyable bar food includes daily specials like home-made smoked chicken and lentil soup (£2.30), mixed fried fish (£3.50), half-a-dozen Helford oysters (£6), a mild lamb curry (£6.40), crab cakes with a white wine sauce (£7.80), stir-fried smoked duck with mangetout and ginger (£10.20), and puddings such as steamed ginger pudding, pear, chocolate and almond tart or passion fruit parfait; from the menu there might be grilled local goat's cheese with olives on ciabatta bread (£3.80), spicy sausage (£3.60), king prawns in saffron butter (£4.20), lunchtime ploughman's (from £4.20), leek and cheese soufflé (£5.20), tagliatelle and smoked trout (£5.30), thai pork with noodles (£6.80), steaks (£9.80), and a children's menu (from £2); on winter Wednesday evenings they do a bargain home-made steak and kidney pudding and a pint of Dartmoor Best offer (£5.70); good breakfasts with home-made jam and marmalade. They keep an unusually wide choice of drinks for the area, such as well kept Dartmoor Best, St Austell HSD and XXXX Mild, Sharps Cornish (a local brewery) on handpump with regularly changing ales from smaller brewers tapped from the cask such as Cotleigh Tawny, Exmoor Gold, Gibbs Mew Bishops Tipple, Hook Norton, Otter Bright, Smiles, and so forth. Also, over 40 malt whiskies (including several extinct ones), and lots of interesting wines (up to 20 by the glass). Darts, pool, cribbage, shove-ha'penny, dominoes, fruit machine, and video and trivia machines. The pretty landscaped garden has some new tables with large parasols, an international sized piste for boules, and a lake; lots of walks. *(Recommended by R and S Bentley, Anthony Barnes, J and B Cressey, Bryan Taylor, RB, John and Christine Lowe, S E Dark, Nick Wikeley, P and M Rudlin, Iain Robertson, John and Joan Calvert, Philip Orbell, David and Jane Russell, Nigel Flook, Betsy Brown, Brian Skelcher, Gwen and Peter Andrews, Colin Draper, David Carr, Wendy Arnold, E A Thwaite, P Eberlin, Martin and Penny Fletcher, Richard Hearn, Dr D A Spencer, E D Bailey, Dr G W Barnett, Molly and Robin Taylor, Ron Shelton)*

Free house ~ Licensees Nigel Logan, Michael Maguire ~ Real ale ~ Meals and snacks (not 25 Dec) ~ Restaurant ~ (01326) 340332 ~ Children welcome ~ Open 11-3(2.30 winter), 6(6.30 winter)-11 ~ Bedrooms: £39(£42B)/£52(£62B)

CREMYLL SX4553 Map 1
Edgcumbe Arms

End of B3247, off A374 at Crafthole (coming from A38) or Antony (from Torpoint car ferry)

In a super setting by the foot ferry from Plymouth, with good Tamar views from its bow-window seats and from waterside tables outside, this has been completely rebuilt after a fire at the end of 1995. The results are very good: lots of old-fashioned small rooms with panelling, beam-and-plank ceilings, slate flagstones and bare boards, and furnishings to match – big stripped high-backed settles, pews, fireside sofa, housekeeper's chairs, pretty cushions and the like, with candles on tables and plenty of decorative china, copper, brass and old pictures. Good value food at lunchtime includes soup (£2.95), filled french bread (£3.95), ploughman's (£4.95), four cheese and spinach lasagne or home-made pies (£5.95), and moussaka (£6.50), with evening dishes such as prawns in filo pastry with a dip (£3.95), chicken breast in stilton sauce (£5.95), fresh cod fillet with mustard sauce (£9.95), and steaks (from £10.50). Well kept Courage Best and St Austell Tinners, HSD, and Trelawny's Pride on handpump, decent house wines, quick friendly service, nostalgic piped pop music; darts. We've not yet had reports on the bedrooms, but would expect this to be a nice place to stay in. There are splendid walks in nearby waterfront parkland. *(Recommended by George Atkinson, S Parr, P Birch, Mike Woodhead, James Cartwright)*

St Austell ~ Tenants Nigel and Mary Trubody ~ Real ale ~ Meals and snacks ~ (01752) 822294 ~ Children welcome ~ Open 11-3, 6-11; 11-11 during school holidays and at weekends; 12-10.30 Sun (in deep winter they may close between 5 and 7) ~ Bedrooms: £25S/£50S

CROWS NEST SX2669 Map 1
Crows Nest £

Signposted off B3264 N of Liskeard; or pleasant drive from A30 by Siblyback/St Cleer rd from Bolventor, turning left at Common Moor, Siblyback signpost, then forking right to Darite; OS Sheet 201 map reference 263692

Handy for Caradon copper mine (and indeed this used to be the pay office/company store where tin and copper miners were paid), this is a friendly old pub popular with locals and tourists. There are lots of stirrups, bits and spurs hanging from the bowed dark oak beams, an interesting table converted from a huge blacksmith's bellows (which still works), and an unusually long black wall settle by the big log fire as well as other more orthodox seats. On the right, and divided by a balustered partition, is a similar area with old local photographs. Cheap bar food includes lunchtime filled soft rolls (from £1.30), lunchtime ploughman's (£3), home-cooked ham and egg (£3.75), vegetable lasagne (£4), puddings like spotted dick and custard, and children's dishes (£2), with evening grills (from £6); Sunday roast lunch (£3.95; no other food is served then). Well kept St Austell Tinners and HSD on handpump kept under light blanket pressure; shove-ha'penny, euchre, and juke box. On the terrace by the quiet lane there are picnic tables. *(Recommended by Dr and Mrs B D Smith, James Macrae, Mr and Mrs D E Powell, Andrew and Joan Life, A E and J Toogood, Stephen and Susan Breen, Peter Cornall, Philip and Trisha Ferris, J K W, John Ledbury, R Turnham; more reports please)*

St Austell ~ Tenant C R Sargeant ~ Real ale ~ Meals and snacks (not Sun evenings) ~ (01579) 345930 ~ Children welcome ~ Open 11-3, 6-11; 12-3, 7-10.30 Sun

EDMONTON SW9672 Map 1
Quarryman

Village signposted off A39 just W of Wadebridge bypass

This interesting pub forms part of an attractively understated small health and holiday complex, around a carefully reconstructed slate-built courtyard of former quarrymen's quarters. The three beamed rooms (one is no smoking) have an excellent relaxed atmosphere, simple pleasant furnishings, fresh flowers on tables, a woodburner, and a couple of bow windows (one with a charming stained-glass quarryman panel) looking out to a distant wind farm. Gravel-voiced Mr Kuun was a Springboks rugby international, and there's some interesting sporting memorabilia – particularly the Roy Ullyett menu cartoons for British Sportsman's Club Savoy lunches for visiting cricket and rugby international teams. Good bar food includes sandwiches (from £2.50; a bumper bacon one £2.50), chicken and walnut pâté (£2.50), filled baked potatoes or ploughman's (£3.90), deep-fried brie with thai chutney (£3.95), chargrilled sardines (£5.50), spare ribs (£5.25) outstanding Aberdeen Angus sizzle steaks (£10.90) and fresh locally caught fish; very tempting puddings (£2.50). Well kept Bass, Ind Coope Burton, Sharps Doom Bar, and guest beers on handpump; decent house wines and some interesting good value bottles, good malt whiskies; pool, darts, fruit machine. The dog's called Floyd. Virtue rewarded: on a tight inspection schedule we arrived at 11.30, only to find the pub didn't open till noon. But just as we were deciding we'd have to move on (and give the pub's chances of promotion to the main entries a miss for this year), the landlord – of course not knowing who we were – welcomed us in half an hour early. There's a cosy bistro on the other side of the courtyard. We have not yet had reports from people staying here, but it's a pleasant spot, a good brisk walk from the sandy Camel estuary. *(Recommended by Bill Hendry, Jenny and Brian Seller, J R Harbottle, Mr and Mrs R Searston, Andy and Jill Kassube)*

Free house ~ Licensee Terry De Villiers Kuun ~ Real ale ~ Meals and snacks ~ Restaurant ~ (01208) 816444 ~ Children in eating area of bar and in restaurant ~ Open 12-11; 12-10.30 Sun

EGLOSHAYLE SX0172 Map 1
Earl of St Vincent

Just outside Wadebridge, on A389 Bodmin road

In summer, there are picnic tables in the lovely garden here and marvellous flowering baskets and tubs. Inside, it is comfortable and civilised with a combination of rich furnishings and a fascinating collection of antique clocks, golfing memorabilia and art deco ornaments – and although there is some emphasis on the food side, there's still a welcome for people who want a quiet pint of their well kept St Austell Tinners, HSD or Trelawneys Pride. Enjoyable food includes sandwiches, soup (£1.90), pâté (£2.30), mushroom and broccoli au gratin (£4.50), scallops in white wine (£4.75), good liver and bacon, chicken in leek and stilton sauce (£8.50), steaks (from £8.75), salmon poached in cream (£9), roast duckling (£9.50), beef stroganoff (£11), and three-course Sunday lunch (£6.50); friendly service; piped music. *(Recommended by Jenny and Brian Seller, Andy and Jill Kassube, Val Stevenson, Rob Holmes, Rita Horridge, Mr and Mrs B Hobden, D and B Taylor, Graham Tayar, Ian Smith, R E Jones, M C F Lloyd)*

St Austell ~ Tenants Edward and Anne Connolly ~ Real ale ~ Meals and snacks (not Sun) ~ (01208) 814807 ~ Well behaved children in eating area of bar ~ Open 11-3, 6.30-11; 12-3, 7-10.30 Sun

FALMOUTH SW8032 Map 1
Chain Locker

With Marine Restaurant, on Custom House Quay off Church Street – the main shopping street, parallel to waterfront

Many people working with boats use this friendly local and there's a strong nautical atmosphere in the bar. The plank ceiling is hung with ships' pennants and wheels, there are marine photographs and a collection of ship models, strip-panelled walls, and seats in the big corner windows with a fine view of fishing boats a few feet away in Falmouth's small central harbour. A bigger communicating inner room has a good separate darts alley. Well kept Bass, Flowers Original, and Worthington Best on handpump; bar food includes sandwiches (crab £3.95) and snacks as well as local scallops (£5.25), local monkfish cooked with prawns and mushrooms (£6.25), whole lemon sole (£6.95), daily specials (from £3.95), and puddings; fruit machine and piped music. The dog is called William. They have self-catering accommodation. *(Recommended by Reg Nelson, E A Thwaite, David Carr; more reports please)*

Greenalls ~ Managers Trevor and Liz Jones ~ Real ale ~ Meals and snacks ~ (01326) 311085 ~ Well behaved children welcome ~ Parking may be difficult ~ Open 11-11; 12-10.30 Sun

Quayside ◀

ArwenackSt/Fore St

Another change of management here sees the same fine range of real ales: Bass, Courage Directors, Flowers Original, Fullers London Pride, Ruddles County, Sharps Doom Bar, John Smiths, and Tetleys on handpump, with up to 14 tapped from the cask such as Archers Golden, Belhaven 80/-, Black Sheep, Cotleigh Old Buzzard, Exmoor Stag, Gibbs Mew Bishops Tipple, Orkney Raven and Skullsplitter, and Shepherd Neame; they hold beer fesitvals during the Spring and Autumn half-terms; Scrumpy Jack cider and country wines. There are lots of beer mats on the panelled walls, book matches on the black ceiling, malt sacks tacked into the counter, a big white ensign, a mix of ordinary pub chairs on the bare boards, and a log-effect gas fire in the stripped stone fireplace; piped music. Upstairs is the lounge bar (which you enter from the attractively bustling street) with comfortable armchairs and sofas at one end, more straightforward tables and chairs at the other, picture windows overlooking the harbour, and huge range of over 219 whiskies (179 are single malts). Bar food includes home-made doorstep sandwiches, bangers and mash (£3.79), meaty or vegetarian chilli (£4.30), beef in ale pie (£5), and scallops in white wine sauce (£5.45). There are picnic tables on the tarmac by the Custom House Dock and next to the handsome Georgian harbourmasters' office. *(Recommended by Eamonn and Natasha Skyrme, Andy and Jill Kassube, J and B Cressey, Ted George, Dr S P Willavoys, John Wooll, P and M Rudlin, David Carr, Reg Nelson, George Atkinson, Peter and Gwyneth Eastwood, Steve Felstead; more reports on the new regime please)*

Greenalls ~ Managers Ray and Jean Gascoigne ~ Real ale ~ Meals and snacks ~ (01326) 312113 ~ Children welcome ~ Live music Fri and Sat evenings ~ Open 11-11; 11-3, 6-11 in winter; 12-10.30 Sun

HELFORD SW7526 Map 1
Shipwrights Arms
Off B3293 SE of Helston, via Mawgan

The lovely position is this thatched pub's main draw in summer – it's set above a beautiful wooded creek, and you can sit on the terraces, the top part of which is roofed over with Perspex. Inside there's quite a nautical theme with navigation lamps, models of ships, sea pictures, drawings of lifeboat coxwains and shark fishing photographs – as well as a collection of foreign banknotes behind the bar counter. A dining area has oak settles and tables; winter open fire. Well kept Flowers IPA and Whitbreads Castle Eden on handpump, and bar food such as a summer buffet with various ploughman's (from £4.20) and salads with crab, salmon and cold meats (from £5.95), as well as steak and kidney pie (£6.90), chargrilled tuna (£8.25), steaks (from £8.25), monkfish, scallop and bacon kebab (£9.25), and home-made puddings (£3.40); summer barbecues. It does get crowded at peak times. *(Recommended by Carol Fellowes, J and B Cressey, S P Watkin, P A Taylor, P and S White, John and June Freeman, Ted George, Nigel Flook, Betsy Brown, Brian Skelcher, David Carr, Mr and Mrs Claude Bemis, David Hillcox, Christopher Wright, E A Thwaite, D and B Taylor)*

Greenalls ~ Lease: Charles Herbert ~ Real ale ~ Meals and snacks (not winter Sun evenings) ~ (01326) 231235 ~ Children in eating area of bar ~ Parking only right outside the village in summer ~ Open 10.30-2.30, 6-11; 12-2.30, 7-10.30 Sun; closed winter Sun evenings

HELSTON SW6527 Map 1
Blue Anchor £ 🍺
50 Coinagehall Street

There's been some refurbishment to this old thatched town pub, plans to expand the garden are going ahead, and the brewery is to be upgraded. But it remains the sort of basic place that some people enjoy very much – though it's not to everyone's taste. A series of small, low-ceilinged rooms opens off the central corridor, with simple old-fashioned furniture on the flagstones, interesting old prints, some bared stone walls, and in one room a fine inglenook fireplace. A family room has darts. They still produce their very cheap Middle, Best, 'Spingo' Special (the name comes from the Victorian word for strong beer) and Extra Special ales in what is probably the oldest brewing house in the country. At lunchtimes you can usually go and look round the brewery and the cellar; they also sell farm cider. Bar food includes rolls and sandwiches (from £1.20), ploughman's (from £2.75), liver and bacon hotpot or home-cooked ham with two eggs (£2.95), fish pie (£3.50), steak and kidney pie (£3.75), and daily specials. Past an old stone bench in the sheltered little terrace area is a skittle alley which you can hire – £15 for three hours. *(Recommended by Jeanne Cross, Paul Silvestri, Brian Skelcher, James Nunns, Jim Reid, Sue Holland, Dave Webster, Colin Draper, David Carr)*

Own brew ~ Licensee Kim Corbett ~ Real ale ~ Snacks (12-4; not Sun except in July and Aug for trad Sun lunch) ~ (01326) 562821 ~ Children in family room ~ Jazz 1st Mon of month ~ Parking sometimes difficult ~ Open 11-11; 12-10.30 Sun

Halzephron ♀ ⇌

Gunwalloe, village about 4 miles S but not marked on many road maps; signposted off A3083 Lizard rd by RNAS *Culdrose*

This is a lovely spot with Gunwalloe fishing cove just 300 yards away, a sandy beach one mile away at Gunwalloe Church Cove, and lots of unspoilt coastal walks with fine views of Mount's Bay. Inside this well run old smugglers' haunt, the quietly welcoming pleasant bar is spotlessly clean and has a warm fire in the big hearth, comfortable seating, copper on the walls and mantelpiece, and maybe the two cats (Humphrey the gentle black one and a lively marmalade one called Mr Chivers); there's also a family room with toys, games and puzzles. Good, popular bar food includes good sandwiches (lunchtimes from £2.20), home-made soup (£2.80), fresh pâté (£3.50), grilled goat's cheese on garlic bread (£3.50), ploughman's (from £3.80), daily pasta and vegetarian dishes (£6.20), several delicious platters (from £8.60; crab £9.80), enjoyable daily specials such as prawn fritters (£4.30), cheese and herb soufflé (£7.60), lamb tagine (£8.60), and duck casserole (£9.50), chargrilled sirloin steak (£9.60), and puddings (£3); the restaurant amd the snug are no smoking. Well kept Dartmoor Best and Sharps Own and Doom Bar on handpump, a good wine list, 40 malt whiskies, and around 50 liqueurs; darts, dominoes and cribbage. Small but comfortable and well equipped bedrooms – and huge breakfasts. *(Recommended by Brian Skelcher, J and B Cressey, John and Sally Clarke, Bryan Taylor, Paul and Pam Penrose, Cliff Blaemore, RB, Peter and Gwyneth Eastwood, Gwen and Peter Andrews, Mr and Mrs J Barrett, Michele Gunning, Ron Shelton, C and D Pike, Sybille Weber, Margaret Dyke, Barry and Anne)*

Free house ~ Licensees Harry and Angela Thomas ~ Real ale ~ Meals and snacks (not 25 Dec) ~ Restaurant ~ (01326) 240406 ~ Children in family room ~ Open 11-3(2.30 winter), 6.30-11; 12-3, 7-10.30 Sun; closed 25 Dec ~ Bedrooms: £35B/£60B

KINGSAND SX4350 Map 1
Halfway House ⇌

Fore St, towards Cawsand

To reach this attractive old inn, it might be most enjoyable to park and walk through the narrow hilly streets down towards the sea and harbour. The simply furnished but quite smart neat bar is cosy and softly lit and rambles around a huge central fireplace. It's low-ceilinged, and mildly Victorian in style, popular with locals but with a warm welcome for the many summer visitors. As well as lots of fresh fish dishes like grilled sardines, scallops with bacon, hake with leeks, onions and wild mushrooms, roast garlic monkfish, bass with an orange butter sauce, and grilled dover sole, the bar menu offers filled french bread (from £1.95), soup (£2.20), garlic mushrooms with a bacon and cheese topping (£3.85), filled baked potatoes (from £3.85), ploughman's (from £4.80), a good breakfast (£5.20), local home-cooked ham and egg (£5.40), cashew nut paella (£7.65), and steaks (from £8.95); also, daily specials and puddings; vegetables are fresh and carefully cooked. There are often attractive fresh flowers on the tables. Well kept Bass, Boddingtons, Flowers Original and a guest beer on handpump, and decent wines. Service is quick and friendly, and the bar staff add a lot to the enjoyable atmosphere; the landlord himself is a man of strong opinions, not shy of stating them – though always courteous. The piped music is generally unobtrusive; cribbage, backgammon, and fruit machine. The village is well placed for marvellous cliff walks on Rame Head, or for visiting Mount Edgcumbe. *(Recommended by Roy and Judy Tudor Hughes, Ted George, Jacquie and Jim Jones, Nicholas Regan, Mr and Mrs M Fletcher, Andrew and Joan Life, R Turnham, Jacky Darville, C E Taylor, Mr and Mrs W J Soames)*

Free house ~ Licensees Sarah and David Riggs ~ Real ale ~ Meals and snacks ~ Restaurant ~ (01752) 822279 ~ Children welcome ~ Choir Weds evenings, quiz winter Thurs evenings ~ Open 11-4, 6-11; 12-3, 7-11 in winter; 12-4, 7-10.30 Sun ~ Bedrooms: £22S/£44S

LANLIVERY SX0759 Map 1
Crown ◖

Signed off A390 Lostwithiel—St Austell

Genuinely friendly licensees run this pretty 12th-c pub and readers have enjoyed their recent visits very much. Some refurbishment has taken place this year but the character of the rambling series of rooms remains unchanged. The small, dimly-lit public bar has heavy beams, a slate floor, and built-in wall settles and attractive alcove of seats in the dark former chimney; darts. A much lighter room leads off here with beams in the white boarded ceiling, some comfortable plush sofas in one corner, cushioned black settles, a small cabinet with wood turnings for sale, owl and badger pictures, and a little fireplace with an old-fashioned fire; there's another similar small room. No noisy games machines, music or pool tables. The slate-floored no-smoking porch room has lots of succulents and a few cacti, and wood-and-stone seats. Good bar food includes sandwiches, nice home-made soup, ploughman's, mussels or cumberland sausages with red onion relish (£3.95), home-made curries and home-made steak and kidney pie, vegetarian dishes, fresh battered haddock (£5.25), and rack of lamb with herb crust (£8.95); puddings with clotted cream, and a children's menu. Well kept Bass, Sharps Own and Coasters, and Worthington on handpump; dominoes, cribbage, and shove-ha'penny. In the garden are some new granite faced seats as well as white cast-iron furniture and sheltered picnic tables. *(Recommended by Ian Phillips, Anthony Barnes, D B Kenkin, Peter and Audrey Dowsett, John Woodward, Joan and Michael Johnstone, P and M Rudlin, Lawrence Bacon, Jean Scott, P and S White, R J Walden, Sean McCarthy, Mr and Mrs J M Lefeaux)*

Free house ~ Licensees Ros and Dave Williams ~ Real ale ~ Meals and snacks ~ Restaurant ~ (01208) 872707 ~ Children in eating area of bar ~ Open 11-3, 6-11; 12-3, 7-10.30 Sun ~ Bedrooms: £25S/£40S

LOSTWITHIEL SX1059 Map 1
Royal Oak ◖

Duke St; pub just visible from A390 in centre

Even when this old town-centre pub is really busy, you can be sure of a friendly welcome from the helpful staff. They keep a fine range of real ales on handpump such as Bass, Fullers London Pride, Marstons Pedigree, Sharps Own, and two guests such as Greene King Sorcerer or Springhead Cromwell's Hat – as well as lots of bottled beers from around the world. Popular bar food includes lunchtime sandwiches (from £1.35) and ploughman's (from £3.10), soup (£1.95), good stuffed mushrooms (£3.25), vegetarian crêpes (£5.95), scallops in white wine sauce (£8.25), steaks (from £8.35), daily specials such as a curry (£5.95), steak and kidney pie (£6.25) or fresh whole plaice (£8.50), and puddings like home-made cherry pie or treacle tart (£1.85); children's menu (from £1.80). The neat lounge is spacious and comfortable, with captain's chairs and high-backed wall benches on its patterned carpet, and a couple of wooden armchairs by the log-effect gas fire; there's also a delft shelf, with a small dresser in one inner alcove. The flagstoned and beamed back public bar has darts, dominoes, cribbage, fruit machine and juke box, and is popular with younger customers. On a raised terrace by the car park are some picnic tables. *(Recommended by P and S White, P H Boot, Charles Gysin, Graham Tayar, Barry and Anne)*

Free house ~ Licensees Malcolm and Eileen Hine ~ Real ale ~ Meals and snacks ~ Restaurant ~ (01208) 872552 ~ Children welcome ~ Open 11-11; 12-10.30 Sun ~ Bedrooms: £33B/£55B

LUDGVAN SW5033 Map 1
White Hart

Churchtown; off A30 Penzance—Hayle at Crowlas ~ OS Sheet 203 map reference 505330

Well worth a visit at any time of year, this 14th-c local is genuinely welcoming to both regulars and visitors. The small, cosy and unspoilt beamed rooms have masses of mugs and jugs glinting in cottagey corners, bric-a-brac, pictures and photographs (including some good ones of Exmoor), soft oil-lamp-style lighting, stripped boards with attractive rugs on them, and a fascinating mix of interesting old seats and tables; the two big woodburning stoves run radiators too. Highly enjoyable simple bar food includes sandwiches (from £1.30), village-made pasties (£1.60), ploughman's (from £2.75), omelettes (£3.95), home-made vegetable or meaty lasagne or ham and egg (£4.20), steaks (from £8), puddings such as home-made crumble or treacle tart (£1.75), and daily specials such as lovely fresh mackerel (£3.25), toad-in-the-hole (£4.25) or green lipped mussels (£7); part of the dining area is no smoking. Well kept Flowers IPA, Marstons Pedigree and a summer guest beer tapped from the cask, and several whiskies; cribbage, dominoes. *(Recommended by John and Christine Lowe, James Nunns, P Williams, P and M Rudlin, Mr and Mrs G McNeill, Molly and Robin Taylor, R and S Bentley, DAV, Chris and Sally Blackler, Jill and Patrick Sawdon, S Beele, D Eberlin, Pat and Roger Fereday, DWAJ, George Atkinson)*

Devenish (Greenalls) ~ Tenant Dennis Churchill ~ Real ale ~ Meals and snacks (not Mon evening Oct-Apr) ~ (01736) 740574 ~ Children in eating area of bar ~ Open 11-2.30, 6-11; 12-3, 7-10.30 Sun

MITHIAN SW7450 Map 1
Miners Arms

Just off B3285 E of St Agnes

Winter open fires warm the several cosy little rooms and passages in this 16th-c pub. The atmospheric small back bar has an irregular beam and plank ceiling, a wood block floor, and bulging squint walls (one with a fine old wall painting of Elizabeth I), and another small room has a decorative low ceiling, lots of books and quite a few interesting ornaments. Bar food includes sandwiches, good crab bake, pasta bake or chilli (£5.75), nice steak and kidney pie or fish on a bed of spinach with a creamy sauce and cheese crumble topping (£6), chicken breast in a garlic and cream sauce, and sirloin steak (£10.95). The dining room is no smoking. Bass and Marstons Pedigree on handpump kept under light blanket pressure, and decent wines. There are seats on the back terrace, with more on the sheltered front cobbled forecourt. *(Recommended by Brian Skelcher, David and Jane Russell, Mr and Mrs J D Marsh, James Nunns, John and Moira Hawkes, R Turnham, Mick Hitchman, George Atkinson)*

Greenalls ~ Lease: David Charnock ~ Real ale ~ Meals and snacks ~ (01872) 552375 ~ Children welcome ~ Open 12-3, 6-11; 12-2.30, 7-11 in winter and on Sun

MOUSEHOLE SW4726 Map 1
Ship

Follow Newlyn coast rd out of Penzance; also signposted off B3315

Even when it's packed with tourists this fisherman's local, at the heart of a lovely village, still has real character. While the regulars are in, the opened-up main bar has a bustling, cheerful atmosphere as well as black beams and panelling, built-in wooden wall benches and stools around the low tables, photographs of local events, sailors' fancy ropework, granite flagstones, and a cosy open fire. Bar food includes sandwiches (crab £4.20), local mussels (£4.20), and local fish dishes

(£6.50) and steaks (£8.70). On 23 December they bake Starry Gazy pie (£6) to celebrate Tom Bawcock's Eve, a tradition that recalls Tom's brave expedition out to sea in a fierce storm 200 years ago. He caught seven types of fish, which were then cooked in a pie with their heads and tails sticking out. Well kept St Austell BB, Tinners, HSD and Trelawney's Pride on handpump, and several malt whiskies; friendly staff. The elaborate harbour lights at Christmas are worth a visit; best to park at the top of the village and walk down. *(Recommended by David Warrellow, Gwen and Peter Andrews, P R White, D and B Taylor, John Ledbury, TBB, Sue Holland, Dave Webster, Bronwen and Steve Wrigley, C P Scott-Malden, Steve Felstead)*

St Austell ~ Tenants Michael and Tracey Maddern ~ Meals and snacks ~ Restaurant ~ (01736) 731234 ~ Children welcome if kept away from bar ~ Summer parking can be difficult ~ Open 10.30am-11pm; 12-10.30 Sun ~ Bedrooms: /£40B

nr MYLOR BRIDGE SW8036 Map 1
Pandora ★ ★ ♀

Restronguet Passage: from A39 in Penryn, take turning signposted Mylor Church, Mylor Bridge, Flushing and go straight through Mylor Bridge following Restronguet Passage signs; or from A39 further N, at or near Perranarworthal, take turning signposted Mylor, Restronguet, then follow Restronguet Weir signs, but turn left down hill at Restronguet Passage sign

On a quiet day at high tide, it would be hard to beat this medieval thatched pub's sheltered waterfront position – best enjoyed from the picnic tables in front or on the long floating jetty. Quite a few people arrive by boat and there are showers for visiting yachtsmen. The several rambling, interconnecting rooms are marvellously atmospheric and have low wooden ceilings (mind your head on some of the beams), beautifully polished big flagstones, cosy alcoves with leatherette benches built into the walls, a kitchen range, and a log fire in a high hearth (to protect it against tidal floods); three areas are no smoking (as is the restaurant). Bar food includes home-made soup (from £2.45), sandwiches (from £2.75, local crab £6.25), local sausages in onion gravy (£4.50), fish pie (£5.75), daily specials, puddings like home-made treacle tart (£2.50), Sunday roast (£5.25), and children's dishes (from £1.50). Bass, St Austell Tinners, HSD, BB, and Trelawney's Pride on handpump from a temperature controlled cellar, several malt whiskies, 20 good wines by the glass, and farm cider; dominoes, winter pool, and cribbage. It does get very crowded in summer, and parking is difficult at peak times. *(Recommended by Catherine Lloyd, Gethin Lewis, George Atkinson, Nigel Flook, Betsy Brown, Louise Lyons, Peter Elliot, J H Bell, Sybille Weber, RB, Dr B and Mrs B B Baker, P P and J Salmon, Brian Skelcher, David Carr, D and B Taylor, Canon Michael Bordeaux, M J How, Cliff Blakemore, E A Thwaite, D Alexander, Ian and Gayle Woodhead, Nick Wikeley, E D Bailey, Pete and Rosie Flower, Mick Hitchman, James Nunns, Steve Felstead, DWAJ, S Beele, J C Aldridge, R J Doe)*

St Austell ~ Tenant Helen Hough ~ Real ale ~ Meals and snacks (till 10pm in summer) ~ Evening restaurant ~ (01326) 372678 ~ Children in eating area of bar ~ Open 11-11; 12-2.30, 7-11 winter weekdays; winter weekend opening 12; 12-10.30 Sun; closed evening 25 Dec

PELYNT SX2055 Map 1
Jubilee ⌂

B3359 NW of Looe

One couple were delighted to find this neatly kept 16th-c inn was much as it was 24 years ago when they stayed here on their honeymoon. The relaxed, beamed lounge bar has mementoes of Queen Victoria, such as a tapestry portrait, old prints, and Staffordshire figurines of the Queen and her consort, an early 18th-c derbyshire oak armchair, cushioned wall and window seats, windsor armchairs around oak tables, and a good winter log fire in the stone fireplace; the Victorian bar has some carved settles and more mementoes. The flagstoned entry is separated from the bar by an attractively old-fangled glass-paned partition. Bar food includes

home-made soup (£2.40), ploughman's (from £3.10), chicken curry (£4.90), thai-style stir-fry vegetables (£5.50), fresh cod (£5.90), gammon and egg (£7.50), sirloin steak (£10.50), and puddings (from £2.20). Well kept Bass and St Austell Trelawney's Pride on handpump, and several malt whiskies. The quite separate public bar has sensibly placed darts, pool, fruit machine, and piped music. A crazy-paved central courtyard has picnic tables with red and white striped umbrellas and pretty tubs of flowers, and there's a well equipped children's play area.
(Recommended by Terry and Eileen Stott, Edward Froggatt, Janet and Colin Roe, Eamonn and Natasha Skyrme, Paul and Pam Penrose, Peter and Audrey Dowsett, The Sandy Family, R A Cullingham, W F C Phillips, R S A Suddaby, A N Ellis, Dr G W Barnett, M J How, Ian Phillips, Mr and Mrs D E Powell)

Free House ~ Licensee Frank Williams ~ Real ale ~ Meals and snacks ~ Restaurant ~ (01503) 220312 ~ Children welcome ~ Open 11-3, 6-11; 11-11 Sat; 12-10.30 Sun ~ Bedrooms: £36B/£59B

PENZANCE SW4730 Map 1
Turks Head

At top of main street, by big domed building (Lloyds Bank), turn left down Chapel Street

This friendly little pub has remained consistently reliable over the years, and the atmosphere is at its best when the chatty main bar is full of both locals and visitors. There are old flat irons, jugs and so forth hanging from the beams, pottery above the wood-effect panelling, wall seats and tables, and a couple of elbow rests around central pillars. The menu has quite an emphasis on seafood, with crab soup (£1.70), fish pie (£5.50), crab salad (mixed meat £6.95, white meat £7.80), and cold seafood platter (£9.20), as well as sandwiches (from £1.45), filled baked potatoes (from £1.95), ham and egg (£3.50), ratatouille topped with cheese (£3.40), meaty or vegetarian lasagne (£4.55), steak and mushroom pie (£4.75), good steaks (from £6.50), and daily specials like two stuffed quail with apricot and brandy sauce or grilled venison steak with brandy sauce (£7.50). Bass, Boddingtons, and Ringwood Bitter on handpump, and helpful service; piped music. The suntrap back garden has big urns of flowers. There has been a Turks Head here for over 700 years – though most of the original building was destroyed by a Spanish raiding party in the 16th c. *(Recommended by S P Watkin, P A Taylor, D J Priestley, P and M Rudlin, SH, DW, S Beele, Phil Putwain, David Carr, P R White, John Ledbury, George Atkinson)*

Greenalls ~ Tenant William Morris ~ Real ale ~ Meals and snacks (11-2.30, 6-10) ~ Restaurant ~ (01736) 363093 ~ Children in cellar dining room ~ Open 11-3, 5.30-11; 12-3, 5.30-10.30 Sun; closed 25 Dec

PHILLEIGH SW8639 Map 1
Roseland ★

Between A3078 and B3289, just E of King Harry ferry

Handy for the King Harry ferry and Trelissick Gardens, this is an enjoyable and warmly friendly little 17th-c pub. The low beamed bar has a good chatty atmosphere, a nice oak settle and antique seats around the sturdy tables on the flagstones, an old wall clock, a good winter fire, and lots of rugby and rowing prints (the landlord's sports); several friendly cats. Good, popular home-made bar food includes soup, sandwiches (from £2.60), chicken liver and bacon pâté (£3.95), ploughman's (from £3.95), filled baked potatoes (from £4.25), smoked haddock bake (£5.95), crab salad (£7.50), evening extras such as root vegetable croustade (£7.25), barnsley lamb chop (£9.30), and local skate wing (£9.65). Well kept Bass, Greenalls Bitter, Marstons Pedigree, Morlands Old Speckled Hen, and Sharps Doom Bar on handpump, farm cider in summer, and quite a few malt whiskies; darts, cribbage, shove-ha'penny, and table skittles. The pretty paved front courtyard is a lovely place to sit in the lunchtime sunshine beneath the cherry blossom, and the back garden has been converted into a small outdoor children's play area. *(Recommended by James and Ruth Morrell, Iain Robertson, D B Kenkin, P and M*

Rudlin, R A Cullingham, Mrs M Furness, N Lawless, John and Joan Calvert, John and Christine Lowe, Nick Wikeley, P and S White, Peter Baggott, Brian Skelcher, Christopher Wright, M E Wellington, A N Ellis, James Nunns, Penny and Martin Fletcher, George Atkinson, David Luke, DJW, Karen Eliot, John Waller, R Walden)

Greenalls ~ Licensee Graham Hill ~ Real ale ~ Meals and snacks ~ Restaurant ~ (01872) 580254 ~ Children welcome ~ Open 11.30-3, 6(6.30 winter)-11; 12-3, 7-10.30 Sun

POLKERRIS SX0952 Map 1
Rashleigh

Signposted off A3082 Fowey—St Austell

In summer, you can sit on the stone terrace here and enjoy the views towards the far side of St Austell and Mevagissey bays or wander down to the isolated beach with its restored jetty. Inside, the front part of the bar has comfortably cushioned seats, with local photographs on the brown panelling of a more simply furnished back area; winter log fire and piped classical music. Bar food includes soup (£2.25), sandwiches (from £1.85; open ones from £4.50), ploughman's (from £4), home-cooked ham (£4.75), pasta and mushroom bake (£5.25), fish pie (£6.50), a lunchtime cold buffet (£6.50), daily specials such as fresh cod or deep-fried brie (£4.95), lemon sole (£9.50) or dover sole (£15), and puddings (£2.50). Bass, Dartmoor Best, Ind Coope Burton, St Austell HSD and a weekly guest beer on handpump or tapped from the cask, decent wine list and several malt whiskies. Though parking space next to the pub is limited, there's a large village car park, and there are safe moorings for small yachts in the cove. This whole section of the Cornish coast path is renowned for its striking scenery. *(Recommended by Pamela and Merlyn Horswell, Christopher Turner, C and E M Watson, Luke Worthington, Brian Skelcher, John and Moira Hawkes, Mayur Shah, Piotr Chodzko-Zajko, Romey Heaton, John Ledbury)*

Free house ~ Licensees Bernard and Carole Smith ~ Real ale ~ Meals and snacks (11-2, 6-10) ~ Restaurant ~ (01726) 813991 ~ Well behaved children welcome until 8.30 ~ Pianist Fri and Sat evenings ~ Open 11-3, 6-11; 12-3, 6-10.30 Sun

POLRUAN SX1251 Map 1
Lugger

Reached from A390 in Lostwithiel; nearby parking expensive and limited, or steep walk down from village-edge car park; passenger/bicycle ferry from Fowey

You can get to this friendly local by taking the boat from Fowey. From the quay there's a flight of steep stone steps, and once there, you can enjoy fine views of the little harbour and across to Fowey. The two knocked-together bars have beams, high-backed wall settles, wheelback chairs, and a slightly nautical theme with big model boats and local boat photographs. Good bar food includes sandwiches (from £1.40), ploughman's (£3.10), scampi (£4.35), steak and kidney pie (£4.45), rump steak topped with prawns (£10.95), and fresh fish when available; the restaurant is no smoking. St Austell BB, Tinners, Trelawneys Pride, HSD and XXXX Mild on handpump; pool (winter only), fruit machine, and piped music. Good surrounding walks. Self-catering cottage available. *(Recommended by Peter and Audrey Dowsett, Janet and Colin Roe, P and M Rudlin, D and J Tapper, R A Cullingham, Dr and Mrs B D Smith, C Moncreiffe, Martin Bromfield, Bernadette Garner)*

St Austell ~ Managers Dick and Judy Bear ~ Real ale ~ Meals and snacks (not Sun evening) ~ Summer restaurant ~ Children in restaurant ~ (01726) 870007 ~ Open 11-11; 11-3, 6.30-11 winter Tues and Weds; 11-10.30 Sun; 12-3, 7-10.30 winter Sun

---

Stars after the name of a pub show exceptional quality. One star means most people (after reading the report to see just why the star has been won) would think a special trip worth while. Two stars mean that the pub is really outstanding – many that for their particular qualities cannot be bettered.

PORT ISAAC SW9980 Map 1
Golden Lion

Fore Street

You can sit at the windows of the cosy rooms in this bustling, friendly pub (or on the small back terrace) and look down on the rocky harbour and lifeboat slip far below. The bar has a fine antique settle among other comfortable seats, decorative ceiling plasterwork, perhaps the pub dog Hollie, and a relaxed, friendly atmosphere – despite the summer crowds. Good home-made food includes sandwiches (lunchtime only; lovely crab £4.25), ploughman's, good fish pie (£6.25), and steak in ale pie (£6.50); during the summer, evening meals are served in the bistro. Well kept St Austell Tinners, HSD and Trelawney's Pride on handpump and several malt whiskies. Darts, shove-ha'penny, dominoes, cribbage, a fruit machine in the public bar, and piped music. You can park at the top of the village unless you are lucky enough to park on the beach at low tide. The very steep narrow lanes of this working fishing village are most attractive. *(Recommended by Jenny and Brian Seller, Andy and Jill Kassube, Nigel Flook, Betsy Brown, D and J Tapper, Alan and Paula McCully, Jo and Gary Charlton, K Flack, Sharon Hancock, R Turnham, Margaret Mason, David Thompson, Ronnie and Joan Fisher, John and Joy Winterbottom, Graham Tayar, David Jones, Ted George, Nigel Clifton)*

St Austell ~ Tenants Mike and Nikki Edkins ~ Real ale ~ Meals and snacks ~ Evening restaurant ~ (01208) 880336 ~ Children in eating area of bar ~ No parking nearby ~ Open 11.30-11; 12-3, 6.30-11 winter Mon-Thurs; 12-10.30 Sun

PORTHALLOW SW7923 Map 1
Five Pilchards

SE of Helston; B3293 to St Keverne, then village signposted

Set just off the beach, this robustly stone-built pub has been run by the same licensees for 33 years. The walls and ceilings of the bars are hung with an abundance of salvaged nautical gear, lamps made from puffer fish, and interesting photographs and clippings about local shipwrecks. Well kept Greene King Abbot and weekly guest beers like Brakspears, Fullers, Smiles or Charles Wells Eagle on handpump, and lunchtime food such as home-made soup or pasties (£1.75), ploughman's (from £3.25), local crab sandwich (£3.95), daily specials (from £3.95), and prawn platter (£6.95); darts in winter, shove-ha'penny, dominoes, and piped music. The attractive cove is largely protected against unsightly development by being owned by its residents. Tides and winds allowing, you can park on the foreshore. Please note that children are not welcome. *(Recommended by P and J Shapley, John and Sally Clarke, S P Watkin, P A Taylor, Debbie Tunstall, Mark Sullivan, David Carr)*

Free house ~ Licensee David Tripp ~ Real ale ~ Lunchtime snacks ~ (01326) 280256 ~ Open 12-2.30(3 Sat), 7-11; 12-2, 7.30-11 in winter; 12-3, 7-10.30 Sun; closed Mon from Jan-Whitsun ~ Self-contained flat sleeps 6

PORTHLEVEN SW6225 Map 1
Ship ★

From seats inside this friendly old fisherman's pub – it is actually built into the steep cliffs – you can watch the sea only yards away from the window as it pounds the harbour wall; the view from the terraced garden is just as good, especially in the evening when the harbour is interestingly floodlit. The knocked-through bar has log fires in big stone fireplaces and some genuine character, and there's a warmly chatty atmosphere and happy mix of locals and visitors; the family room is a conversion of an old smithy and has logs burning in the huge open fireplace. Nicely presented, popular bar food (with prices unchanged since last year) is served by friendly staff and includes sandwiches (from £1.80; fine toasties; excellent crusty loaf from £3.75), filled oven-baked potatoes (from £2.10), ploughman's (from £4.65), pot meals like vegetable curry, steak and kidney pudding or fish pie (from

£5.50), interesting daily specials like fish and tomato bake or chicken tikka, sirloin steak (£8.75), puddings like home-made apple torte, evening extras, and children's meals; the candlelit dining room also enjoys the good view. Well kept Greene King Abbot, Fullers London Pride, and Sharps Doom Bar and Coaster on handpump, and several malt whiskies; dominoes, fruit machine and piped music. *(Recommended by John and Christine Lowe, John and Sally Clarke, James Nunns, Paul and Pam Penrose, Ewan and Moira McCall, P and J Shapley, Pete and Rosie Flower, RB, CB, James and Ruth Morrell, Brian Skelcher, Chris and Sally Blackler, Victoria Regan, Cliff Blakemore, Bronwen and Steve Wrigley, Ian Fraser, Hanns P Golez, David Carr, Steve Felstead, Barry and Anne, Chris and Margaret Southon, Martin Bromfield, Bernadette Garner, Colin Draper, Mr and Mrs Bemis)*

Free house ~ Licensee Colin Oakden ~ Real ale ~ Meals and snacks ~ (01326) 572841 ~ Children in family room ~ Parking can be difficult in summer ~ Open 11.30-11; 11.30-3, 7-11 in winter; 12-10.30 Sun

RUAN LANIHORNE SW8942 Map 1
Kings Head

Village signposted off A3078 St Mawes road

Set in the heart of the Roseland Peninsula, this attractive and neatly kept pub with its welcoming local atmosphere looks down over the pretty convolutions of the River Fal's tidal estuary – a lovely view, especially from some of the seats outside. The beamed bar is decorated with hanging china and framed cigarette cards, and there's an attractive no-smoking family room with lots of mirrors next door. Besides good open sandwiches (from £3.95), well presented home-made bar food includes soups such as courgette and tomato (£2.25), ploughman's or potted shrimps (£3.95), moussaka, fish gratin with pasta and leeks in a mustardy cheese sauce or chicken pasta bake in provençale sauce (all £4.95), lots of salads (from £4.95), trout meunière (£6.95), grilled salmon fillet marinated in sun-dried tomatoes and yoghurt (£7.95), very good fillet steak (£10.95), super puddings like fruit and nut torte, various cheesecakes and popular tiramisu (£2.50), daily specials, good Sunday roasts (£4.95), and excellent steaks. Well kept Eldridge Pope Royal Oak and Hardy, Sharps Coaster on handpump, with Worthington Best kept under light blanket pressure, quick service, a welcoming local atmosphere, and piped music. The sunken garden is a real suntrap in summer. The pub is opposite the fine old church in this pleasant out-of-the-way village. *(Recommended by Peter and Gwyneth Eastwood, DJW, Ian and Deborah Carrington, John and Joan Calvert, Julia Constable, Dr B and Mrs B Baker, C and E M Watson, Brian Skelcher, Mr and Mrs J A Goodall, Christopher Wright, Peter Cornall, Nick Wikeley, Mr and Mrs R Head)*

Free house ~ Licensees Peter and Shirley Trenoweth-Farley ~ Real ale ~ Meals and snacks ~ (01872) 501263 ~ Children in eating area of bar ~ Open 12-2.30, 7-11(10.30 Sun); closed winter Mon, closed Mon lunchtime in summer (except bank holidays)

SCORRIER SW7244 Map 1
Fox & Hounds

Village signposted from A30; B3298 Falmouth road

It's always a pleasure to visit this neatly kept and well run white cottage. As well as the friendly licensees and their quick, efficient staff, a particular reason for coming here is the fine range of good, interesting food. Served by uniformed waitresses, this might include lunchtime sandwiches or filled baked potatoes (from £3.10), and ploughman's (from £3.70), home-made soup (£2.15), omelettes (from £4.20), Lebanese kofta (£4.90), nut roast (£5.65), cold meat platter with home-cooked ham (£5.70), home-made curry of the day (£5.75), salmon and broccoli bake (£6.95), sirloin steak (£8.55), half-a-dozen daily specials like hot atlantic avocado (£6.95), salmon en croûte (£8.25), and pork grilled with mustard and brown sugar (£9.35), and up to 16 home-made puddings such as sherry trifle, fresh plum and apple pie or lovely sticky toffee pudding (£2.25). Well kept Boddingtons and

Flowers IPA and Original on handpump; piped music. The long bar is divided into sections by a partition wall and low screens and has big log fires, comfortable furnishings, stripped stonework, creaky joists, vertical panelling, and hunting prints, as well as a stuffed fox and fox mask; there's also more seating in a front extension, formerly a verandah. Half the premises is no smoking. The long building is prettily decorated outside with hanging baskets and window boxes, and has picnic tables under cocktail parasols in front. *(Recommended by Mr and Mrs C R Little, Mrs H Murphy, Mr and Mrs B Hobden, Chris and Margaret Southon, Jim Reid, George Atkinson, R J Herd, Mr and Mrs Jack Pitts, Colin Draper)*

Greenalls ~ Tenants David and Linda Halfpenny ~ Real ale ~ Meals and snacks (see below) ~ (01209) 820205 ~ Well behaved children over 7 may be allowed in eating area of bar, subject to landlord's approval ~ Open 11.30-2.30, 6-11; 12-2.30, 7-10.30 Sun; closed 25-26 Dec and Mon evenings 2 Jan-end Mar

ST AGNES SW7250 Map 1
Railway

10 Vicarage Rd; from centre follow B3277 signs for Porthtowan and Truro

A new licensee has taken over this busy little local and although she plans to freshen things up a bit, the character of the various nooks and crannies will remain the same. There is still the remarkable collection of shoes in the older part – minute or giant, made of strange skins, fur, leather, wood, mother-of-pearl, or embroidered with gold and silver, from Turkey, Persia, China or Japan, and worn by ordinary people or famous men; also, some splendid brasswork that includes one of the finest original horsebrass collections in the country – and a notable collection of naval memorabilia from model sailing ships and rope fancywork to the texts of Admiralty messages at important historical moments, such as the announcement of the ceasefire at the end of the First World War. Bar food now includes sandwiches (from £2.25), ploughman's (from £4.50), and home-made daily specials like steak and kidney pie (£4.75) and seafood lasagne (£4.95). Well kept Boddingtons and Flowers Original and IPA on handpump; darts, juke box, and piped music. *(Recommended by Mrs M Furness, Chris and Margaret Southon, David Hillcox, George Atkinson; more reports on the new regime, please)*

Greenalls ~ Tenant Patsy Davey ~ Real ale ~ Meals and snacks ~ (01872) 552310 ~ Children in family room ~ Open 11-11; 11-3, 6-11 in winter; closed lunchtime 25 Dec

ST AGNES (Isles of Scilly) SV8807 Map 1
Turks Head 🍺

The Quay

There are wonderful sea views from this little slate-roofed white cottage set in a lovely position just above a sweeping bay. You can enjoy this from the few tables on a patch of lawn across the sleepy lane from the pub, and there are steps down to the slipway so you can walk down with your drinks and food and sit right on the shore. Inside, the simply furnished but cosy and very friendly pine-panelled bar has quite a collection of flags, helmets and headwear and banknotes, as well as maritime photographs and model ships; the dining extension is no smoking, the cats are called Taggart and Lacey, and the collie, Tina. Decent bar food includes legendary huge locally made pasties (though they do sell out; £3.25), open rolls (from £1.95; local crab £3.75), ploughman's (from £3.95), salads (from £4.75), cold roast beef with chips (£4.85), cajun vegetable casserole (£4.95), and puddings (from £2.35), with evening gammon in port wine sauce (£5.95), fresh fish of the day, and sirloin steak (£8.75); children's meals (from £1.95). Ice cream and cakes are sold through the afternoon, and in good weather they do good evening barbecues (£3-7 Tuesday, Thursday and Sunday, July/August only), arranging special boats from St Mary's – as most tripper boats leave by 5-ish. Remarkably, they also have real ale which arrives in St Agnes via a beer supplier in St Austell and two boat trips: Bass, Dartmoor Best, Flowers Original and IPA, and Ind Coope Burton well kept on handpump, besides decent house wines, a good range of malt whiskies, and hot chocolate with brandy. Darts and piped music. In spring and autumn hours may be shorter, and winter opening is sporadic, given that only some 70 people live on the island; they do then try to open if people ask, and otherwise tend to open on Saturday night, Sunday lunchtime (bookings only, roast lunch), over Christmas and the New Year, and for a Wednesday quiz night. *(Recommended by Pete and Rosie Flower, John and June Freeman, D J Priestley, David Mead, Steve and Carolyn Harvey, Robin and Molly Taylor, A Noad, V H and J M Vanstone)*

Free house ~ Licensees John and Pauline Dart ~ Real ale ~ Meals and snacks ~ (01720) 422434 ~ Well behaved children welcome ~ Open 11-11; 12-10.30 Sun (see text for winter) ~ Bedroom: /£44B

ST BREWARD SX0977 Map 1
Old Inn

Old Town; village signposted off B3266 S of Camelford, also signed off A30 Bolventor — Bodmin

The church, whose tower is a landmark for miles around, shares its hilltop with this genuinely friendly little country pub. The two roomed bar has a lot of character, fine broad slate flagstones, banknotes and horsebrasses hanging from the low oak joists that support the ochre upstairs floorboards, and plates on the stripped stonework. The outer room has fewer tables (old ones, of character), an open log fire in a big granite fireplace, a piano and sensibly placed darts. The inner room has cushioned wall benches and chairs around its tables, naïf paintings on slate by a local artist (for sale cheaply), a good log fire, and a glass panel showing a separate games room with darts, pool, juke box, video game and fruit machine, where children are allowed; cribbage. Big helpings of popular home-made bar food include sandwiches (the large bacon bap is praised) and ploughman's, chicken curry (£5.50), home-made steak and kidney pie (£5.75), and a huge mixed grill (£8.50); the restaurant is no smoking. Well kept Bass, Ruddles County, and Sharps Doom Bar and Special on handpump; the landlord is from the West Highlands and his range of 100 malt whiskies reflects this – only coming from the Highlands and Islands; fast, efficient service. Picnic tables outside are protected by low stone walls. There's plenty of open moorland behind, and cattle and sheep wander freely into the village. In front of the building is a very worn carved stone; no one knows exactly what it is but it may be part of a Saxon cross. *(Recommended by Jeff Davies, Andy and Jill Kassube, Jo and Gary Charlton, Kate and Kevin Gamm, Paul and Judith Booth, A N Ellis, Margaret Mason, David Thompson)*

Free house ~ Licensees Iain and Ann Cameron ~ Real ale ~ Meals and snacks (not 25 Dec) ~ Restaurant ~ (01208) 850711 ~ Children in eating areas and games room ~ Open 12-3, 6-11; 12-3, 7-10.30 Sun

ST EWE SW9746 Map 1
Crown

Village signposted from B3287; easy to find from Mevagissey

Handy for the Lost Gardens of Heligan, this popular unspoilt cottage has been run by the same friendly licensees for nearly 40 years. The traditional bar has 16th-c flagstones, a very high-backed curved old settle with flowery cushions, long shiny wooden tables, an ancient weight-driven working spit, and a relaxed atmosphere; the fireside shelves hold plates, and a brass teapot and jug. The eating area has cushioned old church pews and velvet curtains. Bar food includes good, fresh pasties, sandwiches (from £1.95, local crab in season £4.25, open sandwiches from £4.25), soup (£2), ploughman's or filled baked potatoes (from £3.95), gammon and egg or fresh seasonal crab salad (£7.50), tasty steaks (from £8.50), grilled lemon sole (£9.95; evenings only), daily specials, and puddings like home-made fruit or very good mincemeat and brandy pies (from £2.10). Well kept St Austell Tinners and HSD on handpump, several malt whiskies, and local wine; fruit machine and piped music. Several picnic tables on a raised back lawn. *(Recommended by Christopher Wright, David and Jane Russell, DJW, A Cowell, Mr and Mrs*

A C Curry, Wayne Wheeler, John and June Freeman, Rita Horridge, Brian Skelcher, Mrs C M Elkington, Howard Clutterbuck, Karen Eliot, N J Lawless, Gwen and Peter Andrews, A N Ellis, Michael Sargent, Martin and Penny Fletcher)

St Austell ~ Tenant Norman Jeffery ~ Real ale ~ Meals and snacks ~ Restaurant ~ (01726) 843322 ~ Children in eating area of bar and in restaurant ~ Open 11-3, 6-11; 12-3, 7-10.30 Sun; closed 25 Dec ~ Bedrooms: /£36; s/c cottage next door

ST JUST IN PENWITH SW3631 Map 1
Star 🛏

Fore Street

Little has changed over the years in this very relaxed and informal old place with its bearded, characterful regulars. The dimly lit L-shaped bar has appropriately old-fashioned furnishings, tankards hanging over the serving counter, some stripped masonry, and a good many mining samples and mementoes; there's also a small separate snug. Good value bar food includes home-made soup or pasties (£2), cheese melties (£3.20), local crab sandwich (£3.90), boiled ham with fried herb potatoes (£3.90), home-made pies, crab averock (£4.90); no chips. Well kept St Austell Tinners, HSD, XXXX Mild, and Trelawnys Pride on handpump or tapped from the cask, with farm cider in summer, mulled wine in winter, and old-fashioned drinks like mead, lovage and brandy or shrub with rum; shove-ha'penny, cribbage, dominoes, table skittles, fruit machine, shut-the-box, euchre, and juke box. Attractive back yard with roses, a gunnera, and tables. The bedrooms are simple but comfortably furnished in period style, with notable breakfasts; the pub's not far from the coast path. *(Recommended by Wayne Wheeler, Val Stevenson, Rob Holmes, Mick Hitchman, Graham and Lynn Mason, Hanns P Golez, Clare O'Connor, S Beele, Pat and Roger Fereday, Colin Draper; more reports please)*

St Austell ~ Tenants Rosie and Peter Angwin ~ Real ale ~ Meals and snacks ~ (01736) 788767 ~ Children in snug ~ Live music Mon and Sat and impromptu entertainment any time ~ Open 11-11; 12-10.30 Sun; 11-3, 6-11 Mon-Thurs in winter ~ Bedrooms: £15/£30(£40B)

ST KEVERNE SW7921 Map 1
White Hart

The Square; at the end of B3293 SE of Helston – the village is well signposted

The welcoming licensees here have made quite a few changes since this well liked inn was last in our book. They have decorated inside and outside, uncovered old floorboards and opened up one of the fireplaces to house an open fire, and created a new entrance to the restaurant, which saves the squeeze through the pub. And during the winter, there are now steak and pint nights, live music, quiz nights and a bi-monthly newsletter to keep people up to date with events. Being close to the sea, they specialise in really fresh fish which is listed on the specials board and might include hot baked crab (£4.50), half-a-dozen Helford oysters (£7), grilled mackerel with chilli oil (£7.50), monkfish and pepper kebab (£9.95), dover sole with citrus butter (£10.50), and bass with a prawn and cream sauce (£10.95); other specials such as spicy bean and tomato soup (£2.50), pasta with mushrooms, pesto and goat's cheese (£6.25), cajun chicken (£6.75), and beef and mushroom stroganoff (£7.95). From the bar menu there might be lunchtime filled baked potatoes (from £2.75) or sandwiches or french bread (from £3.25), home-made lasagne (£4.95), rump steak (£7.75), barbecue spare ribs with home-made chips (£7.95), puddings like sherry trifle or twice-baked chocolate soufflé (from £2.95), and children's menu (£3); you can eat from the restaurant menu in the bar, too. Well kept Flowers Original, Morlands Old Speckled Hen, Wadworths 6X, and a guest beer on handpump, a decent wine list, and country wines. The black beams are hung with horsebrasses, and there's a mix of wall seats, mate's chairs and some heavy rustic small wooden seats around sturdy tables, and a relaxed, chatty atmosphere; pool, cribbage, dominoes, fruit machine, euchre, backgammon, and colouring books for children. Outside are some picnic tables on a narrow front terrace, with more on a side lawn – the garden has been restocked. Dogs welcome – their own black labrador bitch is called Inky. *(Recommended by A Evans, Sylvia Sutherland, P Boultwood, R Moon, Mr and Mrs D T Deas, Vicki Berry, Alex Roberts, David and Rachael Padfield)*

Greenalls ~ Tenants Nick Botting, Pippa Woodland ~ Real ale ~ Meals and snacks ~ Restaurant ~ (01326) 280325 ~ Children welcome ~ Open 11-2.30, 6-11 ~ Bedrooms: /£40B

ST KEW SX0276 Map 1
St Kew Inn
Village signposted from A39 NE of Wadebridge

This rather grand-looking old stone building is in a peaceful hamlet surrounded by pretty countryside. The neatly kept and friendly bar has winged high-backed settles and varnished rustic tables on the lovely dark Delabol flagstones, black wrought-iron rings for lamps or hams hanging from the high ceiling, a handsome window seat, pretty fresh flowers, and an open kitchen range under a high mantelpiece decorated with earthenware flagons. At lunchtime, bar food includes sandwiches, home-made soup (£1.95), filled baked potatoes (£3.75), ploughman's (£3.95), leeks and bacon in a cheese sauce (£4.50), a pie of the day (£5.50), vegetable chilli (£5.95), and sirloin steak (£9.50), with evening extras like mussels in wine and cream (£3.25), cold cured mackerel (£3.50), seafood provençale (£6.50), fresh fish (from £6.95), king prawns in garlic (£7.25), and roast duck (£9.50); children's menu (from £3.25) and Sunday lunch (£4.25; children £3.50). Well kept St Austell Tinners and HSD tapped from wooden casks behind the counter (lots of tankards hang from the beams above it). The big garden has seats on the grass (one built specifically for children – and there's plenty of space for them to play), and a friendly goat called Aneka; there are also picnic tables on the front cobbles. Parking is in what must have been a really imposing stable yard. The church next door is lovely. *(Recommended by D Marsh, Andy and Jill Kassube, Jo and Gary Charlton, Pamela and Merlyn Horswell, Jacquie and Jim Jones, Brian and Bett Cox, Jenny and Brian Seller, Iain Robertson, James and Ruth Morrell, Rita Horridge, P Eberlin, Howard Clutterbuck, Don Kellaway, Angie Coles, Graham Tayar, Margaret and Roy Randle, Mr and Mrs J Jones, Sharon Hancock, Giles Quick, Pete and Rosie Flower, Richard Cole, Paul and Judith Booth, Piotr Chodzko-Zajko)*

St Austell ~ Tenant Steve Anderson ~ Real ale ~ Meals and snacks ~ Restaurant ~ (01208) 841259 ~ Well behaved children in eating area of bar and in restaurant ~ Open 11-2.30, 6-11; 12-2.30, 7-10.30 Sun ~ Bedrooms: £17.50/£35

ST MAWES SW8433 Map 1
Victory
New licensees have taken over this little fisherman's local, tucked away up a steep lane just up from the harbour and Falmouth ferry. Popular with regulars, the simple bar is full of sailing and other sea photographs, and there's a carpeted back part with comfortable seats, an antique settle and old prints of Cornish scenes. Bar food includes sandwiches (from £2.75; crab £4.95), ploughman's, daily specials of fresh fish like salmon (£6.50), fillet of plaice (£6.95), steaks, and puddings. Well kept Bass and Greenalls Original on handpump; piped music. Benches outside on the cobbles give glimpses of the sea; dogs welcome. *(Recommended by A Ball, DJW, G W Stephenson, John Waller, Gwen and Peter Andrews, John and Joan Calvert, George Atkinson, Jim Reid)*

Greenalls ~ Lease: Phillip and Bridget Savage ~ Real ale ~ Meals and snacks (not Sun evening) ~ Restaurant ~ (01326) 270324 ~ Children welcome ~ Parking in public car park ~ Open 11-11; 12-10.30 Sun ~ Bedrooms: £20B/£40B

Ideas for a country day out? We list pubs in really attractive scenery at the back of the book – and there are separate lists for waterside pubs, ones with really good garden, and ones with lovely views.

ST MAWGAN SW8765 Map 1
Falcon
NE of Newquay, off B3276 or A3059

To get away from the seaside crowds, it's worth travelling inland a bit to find this wisteria-covered old pub in a quiet village. The big friendly bar has a log fire, small modern settles and large antique coaching prints on the walls, and plenty of space for eating the well presented food, which might include lunchtime sandwiches, garlic mushrooms and bacon in white wine and cream (£3.65), vegetable and hazelnut crumble (£4.75), fresh cod in herb butter (£4.95), lamb and cranberry casserole (£5.25), chicken and lemon casserole (£5.65), sirloin steak (from £8.95), and puddings like home-made apple pie (£1.95). The restaurant is no smoking. Well kept St Austell Tinners, HSD and Trelawnys Pride on handpump; efficient service even when busy. Darts, dominoes, and trivia. As well as being quite a summer suntrap, the peaceful, pretty garden has plenty of seats, a wishing well, play equipment for children, and good views of the village; also, stone tables in a cobbled courtyard. A handsome church is nearby. *(Recommended by Neil and Anita Christopher, Mrs M Furness, Edward Frogatt, Andy and Jill Kassube, Pamela and Merlyn Horswell, Iain Robertson, Gareth and Toni Edwards, Piotr Chodzko-Zajko, R Turnham, John and Moira Hawkes, P Eberlin, John and Joan Calvert)*

St Austell ~ Tenant Andy Banks ~ Real ale ~ Meals and snacks (not 25 Dec) ~ Restaurant ~ Children in restaurant ~ (01637) 860225 ~ Open 11-3, 6-11; 12-3, 7-10.30 Sun ~ Bedrooms: £15(£30B)/£42(£50S)

ST TEATH SX0680 Map 1
White Hart
B3267; signposted off A39 SW of Camelford

The main bar and lounge are the rooms to head for in this friendly village pub. There are sailor hat-ribands and ship's pennants from all over the world, swords and a cutlass, and a coin collection embedded in the ceiling over the serving counter in the main bar – which also has a fine Delabole flagstone floor. Between the counter and the coal fire is a snug little high-backed settle, and leading off is a carpeted room, mainly for eating, with modern chairs around neat tables, and brass and copper jugs on its stone mantelpiece; piped music. Straightforward popular bar food includes sandwiches (good bacon and cheese rolls), ham ploughman's, home-made steak and onion pie or curries (£5.95), spicy chicken (£6.95), sirloin steak (£9.95), and Sunday roasts (£4.50); the restaurant is no smoking. Well kept Bass, Ruddles County and Ushers Best on handpump. The games bar has darts, two pool tables, dominoes, and fruit machine. Bedrooms were being refurbished as we went to press. *(Recommended by Mrs Jill Silversides, Barry Brown, Rita Horridge, Graham Tayar; more reports please)*

Free house ~ Licensees Barry and Rob Burton ~ Real ale ~ Meals and snacks (all day) ~ Restaurant ~ (01208) 850281 ~ Children welcome ~ Open 11-11

TREBARWITH SX0585 Map 1
Port William
Trebarwith Strand

A new conservatory has been added to this converted old harbourmaster's house, and the licensees have refurbished the inn itself. The setting is lovely with waves crashing on rocks only yards from the main door, and glorious views over the beach and out to sea from the picnic tables on the terrace. Inside, there's quite a nautical theme with fishing nets and maritime memorabilia decorating the walls, a separate gallery area with work by local artists, and the no-smoking 'captain's cabin' which has a full-size fishing dinghy mounted on the wall. Bar food includes home-made soup (£2.45), granary or jumbo rolls (from £2.75, local crab or steak £3.95), pasties (£2.50), platters (from £5.25), steaks (from £9.45), daily specials such as mussels in cream and cider (£4.50), vegetable and lentil bake (£5.95), steak and kidney pie (£6.45), halibut with mustard, cream and cheese sauce (£8.75), and local crab salad (£7.25), and puddings like treacle tart (£2.35); children's meals (from £2.35). Bass, Boddingtons, Flowers, and St Austell Tinners on handpump, kept under light blanket pressure. Darts, pool, cribbage, dominoes, fruit machine, video game and piped music. *(Recommended by Andy and Jill Kassube, Barry Perfect, Jeff Davies, Anna Ralph, K Flack, Jenny and Brian Seller, Margaret Mason, David Thompson, Dr S Savvas, M Martin, Margaret and Roy Randle, Hanns P Golez)*

Free house ~ Licensee Peter Hale ~ Real ale ~ Meals and snacks ~ Restaurant ~ (01840) 770230 ~ Children welcome away from main bar ~ Folk music Fri evening ~ Open 11-11; 12-10.30 Sun ~ Bedrooms: £43.50£67B

TREBURLEY SX3477 Map 1
Springer Spaniel 🍺
A388 Callington—Launceston

Readers continue to enthuse about this well run pub – not just for the particularly good food, but for the friendly welcome and good atmosphere, too. As well as planning a garden, the licensees aim to grow more of their own soft fruits, vegetables and unusual salad leaves, and work hard at changing the menus to reflect the use of local produce. There might be sandwiches, freshly made soup (£2.50; seafood chowder £2.95), terrine of duck livers with a gooseberry and elderflower chutney (£3.95), chicken breast with white wine, cream and mushroom sauce (£5.95), vegetables and cheese en croûte (£6.25), lamb kidneys in meaux mustard or grilled lamb chops with crabapple and sloe jelly (£8.50), beef stroganoff (£9.25), breast of duck with a rich blackberry sauce (£10.50), and puddings such as lemon mousse with blackcurrant compote, treacle tart or mixed fruit savarin with clotted cream (from £2.95). Well kept Dartmoor Best, St Austell HSD, and occasional guest beers on handpump, freshly squeezed fruit juice, and farm ciders; very good service. The bar has a lovely, very high-backed settle by the woodburning stove in the big fireplace, high-backed farmhouse chairs and other seats, and pictures of olde-worlde stage-coach arrivals at inns, and this leads into a room with chinzy-cushioned armchairs and sofa in one corner, and a big solid teak table. Up some steps from the main bar is the beamed, attractively furnished, partly no-smoking restaurant; friendly black cat. *(Recommended by R J Walden, Mrs H Murphy, R A Cullingham, Jacquie and Jim Jones, Bett and Brian Cox, Mrs R Pearson, Patrick Freeman, Sarah Jones, Gay Richardson, James Macrae, Graham Tayar, E Robinson, D J Underhill, Mr and Mrs Jack Pitts, Mr and Mrs J Jones)*

Free house ~ Licensee John Pitchford ~ Real ale ~ Meals and snacks ~ Restaurant ~ (01579) 370424 ~ Children in eating area of bar, in restaurant or snug ~ Open 11-3, 5.30-11; 12-3, 7-10.30 Sun

TREEN SW3824 Map 1
Logan Rock
Just off B3315 – the back rd Penzance—Land's End

After a walk along the wild cliffs and a look at the Logan Rock (an 80-ton boulder after which the pub is named), you can enjoy a pint of well kept St Austell Tinners, HSD or Trelawnys Pride on handpump in this friendly, genuine local. The low-beamed main bar has a good atmosphere, a mix of visitors and regulars, a series of old prints telling the story of the rock, high-backed modern oak settles, wall seats, and a really warm coal fire. Popular bar food includes sandwiches (from £1.60, local crab when available £4.50), good pasties (£1.50), home-made soup (£2.10), ploughman's (from £3.95), fish and vegetable pasta bake (£4.25), lasagne (£4.75), good steaks (from £7.75), daily specials, and puddings like home-made fruit pie or crumble (£2.25); children's dishes (from £1.50) and afternoon cream teas. Lots of games such as darts, dominoes, cribbage, fruit machine, video games, winter pool and another fruit machine in the family room across the way; juke box, piped music. Dogs are allowed in if on a lead. There are some tables in a small wall-sheltered garden, looking over fields, with more in the front court. *(Recommended by Brian Smart, P and S White, Val Stevenson, Rob Holmes, Susan and Nigel Wilson, Peter and*

Gwyneth Eastwood, Kevin Thorpe, Gwen and Peter Andrews, Brian Skelcher, Bronwen and Steve Wrigley, George Atkinson, Cliff Blakemore, Mr and Mrs Peter Smith, John Ledbury, Colin Draper, Pat and Roger Fereday, Steve Felstead)

St Austell ~ Tenants Peter and Anita George ~ Real ale ~ Meals and snacks (from June-Sept all day, otherwise 12-2, 7-9) ~ Restaurant ~ (01736) 810495 ~ Well behaved children in family room only ~ Open 10.30am-11pm; 12-10.30 Sun; 10.30-3, 5-11 in winter

TREGADILLETT SX2984 Map 1

Eliot Arms ★ ★ ♀

Village signposted off A30 at junction with A395, W end of Launceston bypass

For a great many of our readers, this is one of their favourite pubs. It has a marvellous atmosphere and the welcoming licensees have filled the charming series of little softly lit rooms with some fascinating collections: 72 antique clocks including 7 grandfathers, nearly 400 snuffs, hundreds of horsebrasses, old prints, old postcards or cigarette cards grouped in frames on the walls, and shelves of books and china. Also, a fine old mix of furniture, from high-backed built-in curved settles, through plush Victorian dining chairs, armed seats, chaise longues and mahogany housekeeper's chairs, to more modern seats, open fires, flowers on most tables, and a lovely ginger cat called Peewee; inoffensive piped music. The good home-made food comes in very big helpings, and might include open sandwiches (from £4.25), chargrilled burgers and basket meals (from £3.50), lots of ploughman's (from £3.95), vegetable pasta bake with nuts (£4.95), steak, kidney and mushroom pie (£5.50), fisherman's crunch (£5.75), cajun chicken (£7.25), steaks (from £8.75), an oriental platter (£9.25), and daily specials such as pork crunch in sherry (£5.50), beef and stilton casserole (£5.75), scallops poached in cream and prawns (£7.95), and home-made puddings; enjoyable Sunday lunch. Well kept Flowers Original, Marstons Pedigree, Morlands Old Speckled Hen, and Wadworths 6X on handpump, a fine choice of wines, several malt whiskies, and friendly service; darts, shove-ha'penny, dominoes, and fruit machine. A garden beyond the car park has picnic tables, a good climbing frame, swing and playhouse. *(Recommended by David and Edwyna Prior-Beaumont, Christopher Turner, James Nunns, Philip Orbell, Nick Lawless, Dr and Mrs A Whiteway, P and J Shapley, Ian Phillips, S P Watkin, P A Taylor, P P and J Salmon, James and Ruth Morrell, Val Stevenson, Rob Holmes, Mrs M Furness, Jo and Gary Charlton, Brian and Bett Cox, Jeff Davies, Edward Froggatt, Brian Skelcher, Ron Shelton, Basil J S Minson, Graham Tayar, Pete and Rosie Flower, M and P Rudlin, Heather March, Moira and John Cole, M D Davies)*

Free House ~ Licensees John Cook and Lesley Elliott ~ Real ale ~ Meals and snacks (not 25 Dec) ~ (01566) 772051 ~ Children in eating area of bar ~ Open 11-2.30(3 Sat), 6-11; 12-3, 7-10.30 Sun; closed 25 Dec ~ Bedrooms: £24/£40

TRESCO (Isles of Scilly) SV8915 Map 1

New Inn ⇐ ♀

New Grimsby

This inn, once a row of fishermen's cottages, has light and airy bars refurbished with lots of washed-up wood from a ship's cargo, a nice pubby atmosphere, and friendly locals. Good bar food includes sandwiches, and lots of changing daily specials such as fresh fish, pasta, and grills including good steaks (from £6). The well regarded no-smoking restaurant also has a separate children's menu. Flowers IPA, St Austell Trelawney Pride, Wadworths 6X, and Whitbreads Castle Eden on handpump, interesting wines, and 25 malt whiskies. Pool, juke box, cribbage, dominoes and piped music. There are wooden tables and chairs in the garden. Many of the people staying here are regular return visitors. *(Recommended by Nigel Abbott, Cliff Blakemore, Steve and Carolyn Harvey, R J Herd, V H and J M Vanstone)*

Free house ~ Licensee Graham Shone ~ Real ale ~ Meals and snacks ~ Restaurant ~ (01720) 422844 ~ Children welcome in eating area of bar until 9.30 ~ Open 11-11; 12-2, 7-11 in winter; 12-10.30 Sun ~ Bedrooms: /£138B – this includes dinner

TRURO SW8244 Map 1
Old Ale House ★ ◖ £
7 Quay St/Princes St

Readers are very fond of the friendly and bustling atmosphere and good mix of customers in this old-fashioned, back-to-basics pub. They keep up to 24 constantly changing real ales on handpump or tapped from the cask such as Boddingtons, Bass, Cotleigh Old Buzzard and Tawny, Courage Best and Directors, Exmoor Gold, Ale and Beast, Fullers London Pride, Kings Head Golden Goose, Morlands Old Speckled Hen, RCH East St Cream, Sharps Own, John Smiths Bitter, Shepherd Neame Spitfire, Smiles Heritage, Theakstons Old Peculier, and Wadworths 6X; also country wines. The bar has an engagingly old-fashioned diversity of furnishings, newspapers and magazines to read, some interesting 1920s bric-a-brac, and a barrel full of monkey nuts whose crunchy discarded shells mix affably with the fresh sawdust on the floor; piped music. Enjoyable bar food, freshly prepared in a spotless kitchen in full view of the bar, includes doorstep sandwiches (from £2.65; delicious hot baked garlic bread with melted cheese from £1.95), filled oven baked potatoes (from £3.10), ploughman's (from £3.65), hot meals served in a skillet pan like oriental chicken, sizzling beef or vegetable stir-fry (small helpings from £3.50, big helpings from £3.95), lasagne or steak in ale pie (£4.55), daily specials, and puddings (£2.25). *(Recommended by Andy and Jill Kassube, Catherine Lloyd, Philip Orbell, Peter Baggott, Keith and Janet Morris, P and M Rudline, Ted George, Mr and Mrs A C Curry, Jeff Davies, Jacquie and Jim Jones, N J Lawless, Chris and Margaret Southon, Karen Eliot, Colin Draper, M E Wellington, Linda and Brian Davis, KM, JM, DAV, David Carr, David Luke, Canon Bourdeaux)*

Greenalls ~ Manager Howard Grave ~ Real ale ~ Meals and snacks (not Sat or Sun evening) ~ (01872) 71122 ~ Children in eating area of bar at lunchtime ~ Live bands Mon/Thurs evenings, solo or duo Sat evening ~ Open 11-11; 12-3, 7-11 Sun

---

Lucky Dip

Besides the fully inspected pubs, you might like to try these Lucky Dips recommended to us and described by readers (if you do, please send us reports):

Altarnun [N of village, OS Sheet 201 map ref 215825; SX2182], *Rising Sun*: Basic old local, not smart but friendly, with very traditional flagstoned bar, six well kept ales inc some rare for the area, good value simple food, restaurant *(Richard Houghton)*
Angarrack [SW5838], *Angarrack*: Friendly and comfortable village local in secluded valley, well kept St Austell beer inc HSD and Tinners, good food, no fruit machines or music – just local chat *(D Cheesbrough)*
☆ **Bodinnick** [across the water from Fowey; SX1352], *Old Ferry*: Simple inn with character back flagstoned public bar partly cut into rock, lots of boating pictures, bar food, well kept real ales, lively games room where children allowed; hotel part looking over water, with summer evening restaurant, most bedrooms comfortable and roomy; lovely walk from Polruan *(Mr and Mrs J M Lefeaux, LYM)*
☆ **Bodmin** [Dunmere (A389 NW); SX0467], *Borough Arms*: Neat and friendly, with stripped stone, open fire, lots of railway photographs and posters, well kept Bass, Boddingtons and Whitbreads, decent wines, friendly atmosphere, speedy service and plenty of room even when busy, big helpings

of good value straightforward food (no sandwiches), unobtrusive piped music, fruit machine; children in side room, picnic tables out among shady apple trees *(P and M Rudlin, Christopher Warner, BB)*
☆ **Bolventor** [signed just off A30 on Bodmin Moor; SX1876], *Jamaica Inn*: All sorts of tourist attractions and trunk-road catering, but welcoming, with lots of character in clean, comfortable and cosy oak-beamed bar, log fire, well kept Whitbreads ales, and pretty secluded garden with play area; bleak moorland setting *(Ted George)*
☆ **Boscastle** [upper village, stiff climb from harbour; SX0990], *Napoleon*: Charming 16th-c pub, comfortable and welcoming little low-beamed rooms, interesting Napoleon prints, basic good value food inc vegetarian, well kept Bass and St Austell tapped from the cask, decent wines, good coffee, friendly staff and locals, polished slate floor, big open fire, pool room, children allowed; piped music, maybe folk music; suntrap terrace, second garden too; may close early if quiet *(Stuart Williams, Richard Houghton, Ann and Colin Hunt, Jeff Davies, LYM)*
Boscastle [The Harbour], *Wellington*: Long low-beamed bar, Bass and Whitbreads-related

ales, log fire, cats and dogs, food in bar and restaurant, very popular Mon folk night; comfortable bedrooms, big secluded garden, children welcome *(Clare Wilson, Alan Wilcock, Christine Davidson, Richard Cole, BB)*

Botusfleming [off A388; SX4061], *Rising Sun*: Unspoilt local in same family for many years, rather spartan but cosy, with good fire, well kept ales such as Bass, Moles Barley Brew and Morlands Old Speckled Hen; cl weekday lunchtimes *(Andy and Jill Kassube, James Macrae)*

Breage [3 miles W of Helston; SW6128], *Queens Arms*: Popular local with open fire in long narrow plate-festooned bar with open fire, no-smoking dining room, decent choice of food worth waiting for inc mammoth grill, vegetarian and children's dishes, Whitbreads-related ales, enthusiastic young landlord; tables and children's games room outside, another play area and garden over the lane; quiz night Weds; bedrooms *(P and M Rudlin)*

☆ **Bude** [Falcon Terrace; SS2005], *Falcon*: Comfortable locals' bar overlooking canal in impressive 19th-c hotel, lots of quick good value generous food inc daily roast, local fish and home-made puddings, well kept Bass and St Austell Tinners and HSD, pleasant efficient staff, big family room with two pool tables, very efficient and reliable service; bedrooms *(Mrs R Horridge, Tony McLaughlin, Clare Wilson, Malcolm and Pat Rudlin)*

☆ **Cadgwith** [SW7214], *Cadgwith Cove*: Friendly local open all day at least in summer, roomy and clean, snacks in lounge inc sandwiches, ploughman's and lots of well priced plain food with chips, lively local sing-song Fri; big front terrace overlooking fish sheds and bay; separate restaurant *(Paul and Pam Penrose, Molly and Robin Taylor, Ian Fraser)*

☆ **Callington** [Newport Sq (A388 towards Launceston); SX3669], *Coachmakers Arms*: Old inn with banquettes in modernised beamed and timbered bar, reliable bar food from sandwiches up, well kept Bass and Greene King Abbot, decent wines, friendly efficient service; children in eating area and restaurant; bedrooms *(Tony and Wendy Hobden, Gwen and Peter Andrews, LYM)*

☆ **Camborne** [Treswithian, W end of Church St, or follow Camborne W sign off A30; SW6340], *Cornish Choughs*: Good interesting well cooked food with particularly carefully prepared fish and seafood, fresh veg, welcoming regulars and staff, Bass and Flowers, good value wines; bedrooms *(Murray J Daffern, Dennis Heatley)*

☆ **Camborne** [B3303 out towards Helston; SW6440], *Old Shire*: Homely family pub with reasonably priced food in bar and restaurant, young efficient staff, Bass and Dartmoor Best, decent wines, lots of chintzy chairs and sofas, pictures for sale and great coal fire; garden with summer barbecues, five bedrooms *(Malcolm and Pat Rudlin, Eamonn and Natasha Skyrme, Gwen and Peter Andrews)*

Camborne, *Tyacks*: Atmospheric 18th-c coaching inn with good bar food, well kept St Austell ales, restaurant; bedrooms well equipped *(Andy and Jill Kassube)*

Camelford [Main St (A39); SX1083], *Masons Arms*: Unpretentious heavy-beamed stonebuilt pub with St Austell ales, decent value bar food inc children's dishes and good steak and kidney pudding, local photographs, advertising mirrors, houseplants; pool and juke box in one bar; children allowed *(Mike Beiley)*

Cargreen [the Quay; off A388 Callington—Saltash; SX4362], *Crooked Spaniard*: Extensively refurbished to give big river-view dining area, but keeping small panelled bar and huge fireplace in another smallish room; well kept ales, lovely spot, with waterside tables on terrace by Tamar – always some river activity, esp at high tide *(A N Ellis, M Joyner, Ted George)*

Cawsand [SX4350], *Old Ship*: Welcoming, with very fresh fish and particularly good veg – the landlady cook is vegetarian, potatoes for chips come from local allotment *(Roy and Judy Tudor Hughes)*

Chacewater [SW7544], *Kings Head*: Spotless and comfortable, with obliging licensees, good value food, cheap beer *(Chris and Margaret Southon)*

Charlestown [SX0351], *Rashleigh Arms*: Large pub with good generous quick straightforward food inc fresh fish and popular puddings, seats out by picturesque little harbour in interesting conservation village, shipwreck museum nearby; good range of local ales inc Sharps, friendly service, good canalside family room; piped music; big restaurant; good value bedrooms *(N Lawless, John and Jill Woodfield)*

Coverack [SW7818], *Paris*: Friendly old-fashioned pub with spectacular views over sea and harbour, well kept ale, food inc good Sun lunch and teas, interesting wooden moulds from Falmouth churchyard; restaurant *(Eamonn and Natasha Skyrme)*

☆ **Crackington Haven** [SX1396], *Coombe Barton*: Huge clean open-plan pub in tiny village, spectacular sea view from roomy lounge/dining area, friendly service, good usual bar food inc local fish, well kept local and other ales, good coffee, back family room, tables on terrace, games room with pool tables; bedrooms *(Nigel Clifton, D and B Taylor)*

☆ **Crafthole** [SX3654], *Finnygook*: Under new management, with clean and comfortable much-modernised lounge bar, good range of cheap bar food, Bass and Worthington, pleasant restaurant, good sea views from residents' lounge; low-priced bedrooms *(Dr B Hamilton, BB)*

Cubert [Trebellan; off A3075 S of Newquay; SW7858], *Smugglers Den*: 16th-c thatched granite pub in isolated spot down narrow winding lane, recently considerably improved; pool table, armchairs and settee on one side, small barrel seats and tables in centre, dining tables and huge woodburner in enormous inglenook, a few steps down to big family room; attentive efficient staff, generous quickly served fresh food, well kept ales inc Morlands Old Speckled Hen, Whitbreads Fuggles Imperial and one or two tapped from the cask; tables outside *(P M Rudlin)*

Delabole [B3314; SX0683], *Bettle & Chisel*: Attractive interior, open fire, two St Austells ales, good promptly served reasonably priced home-cooked food, helpful staff; open all day, handy for nearby Slate Mines (pictures on walls) and Wind Farm *(Barry Perfect, Graham Leigh)*

Downderry [SX3153], *Inn on the Shore*: Generous good value food, helpful friendly staff, well kept beers, restaurant with views over Whitsand Bay and boats, good garden *(David Watters)*

☆ Duloe [B3254 N of Looe; SX2358], *Olde Plough House*: Good value interesting food inc fresh seafood in spacious pub comfortably full with diners, quick friendly service, two log fires, cushioned settles, polished sewing-machine treadle tables, good wine; locals' area with pool and darts *(Mr and Mrs R F E Smith, Keith Archer)*

☆ Falmouth [The Moor; SW8032], *Seven Stars*: Unchanging local with wonderfully entertaining vicar-landlord, tatty furnishings, warm welcome, well kept Bass, Flowers Original and St Austell HSD tapped from the cask, minimal food, tables on roadside courtyard *(Reg Nelson, David Carr, BB)*

Falmouth [Prinslow Lane, Swanvale], *Boslowick*: Good value straightforward food and well kept ale in spacious suburban black and white beamed and panelled pub, friendly staff, plenty of seats inc plush sofas, log-effect gas fires, family room with games machines; children's play area *(John Wooll, David Carr)*; [Dracaena Ave/Grenville Rd], *Four Winds*: Spotless room, bright plants in conservatory, consistently good generous food inc particularly good value puddings, friendly staff, pleasant garden *(Mr and Mrs B Hobden, D B Kenkin)*; [Wodehouse Terr], *Seaview*: Convivial maritime local above 111-step Jacob's Ladder, lots of appropriate bric-a-brac, stunning harbour view from picture windows and tables outside, good range of well kept ales; bedrooms *(Reg Nelson)*

☆ Fowey [Fore St; SX1252], *Ship*: Pubby local, good choice of good value generous food from sandwiches through good local fish and chips to steak, comfortably worn-in cloth-banquette main bar with coal fire, pool/darts room, family dining room with big stained-glass window; well kept St Austell Tinners and HSD, juke box or piped music (may obtrude), dogs allowed; bedrooms old-fashioned, some oak-panelled *(AW, BW, Dr S P Willavoys, Christopher Turner, Catherine Lloyd, Steve Felstead, R W A Suddaby, BB)*

☆ Fowey [Town Quay; from centre follow Car Ferry signs], *Galleon*: Well refurbished with solid pine, terrace overlooking harbour and estuary, generous fresh good value food, well kept and priced Bass, Flowers IPA and Sharps, fast friendly service, tables out on extended terrace *(P and M Rudlin, BB)*

☆ Fowey [Town Quay], *King of Prussia*: Upstairs bay windows looking over harbour to Polruan, well kept St Austell ales, good welcoming service, piped pop music (may obtrude), side family food bar with wide choice of fish and seafood, seats outside; bedrooms *(Steve Felstead, M Jeanes, W F C Phillips, Ian and Gayle Woodhead, LYM)*

Fowey, *Lugger*: Unpretentious locals' bar, comfortable small dining area popular with older people for good inexpensive food, tables outside; bedrooms *(Janet and Colin Roe, BB)*

☆ Golant [off B3269; SX1155], *Fishermans Arms*: Plain but charming waterside local, nice garden, lovely views from terrace and window; warm welcome, good generous straightforward home-made food, well kept Ushers, log fire, interesting pictures, tropical fish *(Dr and Mrs B D Smith)*

Goldsithney [B3280; SW5430], *Crown*: Straightforward pub with bargain lunches, St Austell ales, decent house wines, friendly service; pretty suntrap glass-roofed front loggia, masses of flowers outside *(J and B Cressey, G G Young)*

☆ Gorran Haven [33 Chute Lane; SX0141], *Llawnroc*: Friendly local adjoining hotel overlooking harbour and fishing village; generous fresh home cooking, well kept Whitbreads-related and other ales such as Sharps, prompt service, very sunny tables out in front, barbecues; family/games room; bedrooms, handy for Lost Gardens of Heligan *(Nick Wikeley, R W A Suddaby, Nick Lawless)*

☆ Grampound [Fore St; A390 St Austell—Truro; SW9348], *Dolphin*: Small village inn with very friendly helpful staff, good value generous straightforward food inc OAP lunches Weds and home-made pasties, well kept St Austell ales, decent house wines, comfortable chintzy settees and easy chairs, interesting prints; children allowed, pool, fruit machine; handy for Trewithen Gardens; bedrooms *(Gwen and Peter Andrews, D B Kenkin, Margaret Dyke, Andy and Jill Kassube)*

☆ Gunnislake [lower Calstock rd; SX4371], *Rising Sun*: Comfortable 17th-c dining pub with particularly good serious if not cheap food using seasonal produce, pleasant furniture, lots of pictures and bric-a-brac (almost too much china), friendly service, stunning Tamar valley views from pretty garden with play area; live music Mon *(Dr and Mrs B D Smith)*

Gunnislake, *Tavistock Arms*: Good interesting bar food inc very popular Sun lunch *(Jacquie and Jim Jones)*

☆ Gurnards Head [B3306 Zennor—St Just; SW4338], *Gurnards Head*: Unspoilt flagstoned pubby bar surrounded by wonderful NT scenery, inland and along the cliffy coast; real ales such as Bass, Flowers Original and Fullers London Pride, friendly service, substantial home-made food (not Mon evening), real fires each end; piped music may sometimes obtrude, some live music; family room, bedrooms *(Lawrence Bacon, Jean Scott, Jeanne Cross, Paul Silvestri, D and B Taylor, Bronwen and Steve Wrigley)*

Gweek [SW7027], *Gweek Inn*: Large low-ceilinged bar with open fire, good home-made food here and in new restaurant, good service, moderate prices; lots of motoring trophies (enthusiast licensees); short walk from seal sanctuary *(John and Wendy Allin)*

Halsetown [B3311 SW of St Ives; TL8130], *Halsetown*: Old-fashioned pub with pleasant licensees, good reasonably priced food, well kept beers; bedrooms *(Lesley Anning, Jim McKee)*

Hayle [Bird Paradise Park; SW5536], *Bird in Hand*: Busy and friendly barn-like former coach house geared to families visiting the Bird Park, with food to match, good choice of ales sometimes including ones brewed here, four-table upstairs pool room, play area in garden *(Martin McGowan)*

☆ **Helford Passage** [signed from B3291; SW7627], *Ferryboat*: Extensive bar in great summer spot by sandy beach with swimming, small boat hire, fishing trips and summer ferry to Helford, full well kept St Austell range, wide choice of bar food, no-smoking restaurant; piped music, games area with juke box and SkyTV; suntrap waterside terrace, barbecues, usually open all day summer (with cream teas and frequent live entertainment); about a mile's walk from gate at bottom of Glendurgan Garden (NT); children allowed; can seem a bit brash and loud in summer, glass-clearing can sometimes seem a bit too enthusiastic, and parking can be difficult *(David Carr, John and Joan Calvert, James Nunns, Carol Fellowes, George Atkinson, Sybille Weber, Ewan and Moira McCall, Steve Felstead, Guy Consterdine, S P Watkin, P A Taylor, R J Bland, LYM)*

Kingsand [village green; SX4350], *Rising Sun*: Good atmosphere in welcoming unpretentious local, generous food from sandwiches, pasties and burgers up, well kept ales such as Bass, Brains and local Sharps, open fire; can get packed *(Andrew and Joan Life, Roy and Judy Tudor Hughes, BDS, M Joyner)*

☆ **Lamorna** [off B3315 SW of Penzance; SW4424], *Lamorna Wink*: Unspoilt no-frills country local, hardly needs to put itself out given charming surroundings – short walk from pretty cove with good coast walks; cheap food (pasties, baked potatoes, plenty of fish etc) served briskly from hatch, Whitbreads-related ales, maybe under blanket pressure; interesting naval memorabilia and pictures *(Chris and Margaret Southon, Brian Smart, Kevin Thorpe, Sue Holland, Dave Webster, LYM)*

Langdon [B3254 N of Launceston; SX3089], *Countryman*: Well kept beer, bar food inc good snacks, friendly staff; very busy Sun lunchtime *(D B Kenkin)*

☆ **Lanner** [Comford (A393/B3298); SW7240], *Fox & Hounds*: Relaxed rambling bar with black beams, stripped stone, dark panelling, high-backed settles and cottagey chairs, warm fires, food from sandwiches up inc plenty of vegetarian, well kept Bass and St Austell Tinners, HSD and Winter Warmer tapped from the cask, friendly service, partly no-smoking restaurant, children in dining area; pub games, piped music (may be loud); great floral displays in front, neat back garden with pond and play area; open all day weekends *(Colin Draper, Mr and Mrs J D Marsh, P and S White, LYM)*

Launceston [15 Broad St; SX3384], *White Hart*: Civilised and popular old-fashioned dining room with home-made food from good sandwiches up inc good value help-yourself fresh salad bar, low prices; bar with Courage Best and Directors, button-back banquettes, flame-effect fire, darts, fruit machine and TV (shame about the piped pop music); bedrooms *(Brian Websdale, Guy Consterdine, M Joyner, BB)*

☆ **Lerryn** [signed from A390 in Lostwithiel; SX1457], *Ship*: Busy local, partly no smoking, with popular bar food from sandwiches up, well kept ales such as Bass, Courage Best, Morlands Old Speckled Hen and Sharps Doom Bar, local farm cider, fruit wines and malt whiskies, huge woodburner, games room with pool, children welcome; service – normally speedy – can slow, landlord taciturn; picnic tables outside, play area; famous stepping-stones and three well signposted waterside walks nearby; nice bedrooms in adjoining building, wonderful breakfasts, self-catering flat *(W F C Phillips, D and B Taylor, Iain Robertson, MS, Peter and Audrey Dowsett, P and M Rudlin, Mr and Mrs D E Powell, Dr and Mrs B D Smith, Stephen Horsley, Catherine Lloyd, Patrick Freeman, Edward Froggatt, LYM)*

Linkinhorne [off B3257 NW of Callington; SX3173], *Church House*: Reopened under new landlord, good traditional atmosphere, good food in cosy bar, well kept Bass, family room, restaurant; opp church, cl Mon *(R A Cullingham, M E Pountney)*

☆ **Lizard** [SW7012], *Top House*: Spotless well run pub particularly popular with older people; in same family for 40 years, lots of interesting local sea fixtures, fine shipwreck relics and serpentine craftwork in neat bar with generous good value bar food inc good local fish and seafood specials, interesting vegetarian dishes, well kept Bass, Marstons Pedigree, Flowers IPA and Sharps, decent wines, sincere friendly staff, roaring log fire, big no-smoking area, no piped music (occasional live); fruit machine, darts, pool; tables on terrace, interesting nearby serpentine shop *(Jim Reid, Paul and Pam Penrose, Ian Fraser, Colin and Pat Bristow, Gwen and Peter Andrews, Jeanne Cross, Paul Silvestri, Malcolm and Pat Rudlin, John and Joan Calvert, Margaret Dyke, Paul and Maggie Baker, BB)*

☆ **Longrock** [old coast rd Penzance—Marazion; SW5031], *Mexico*: Interesting – even adventurous – choice of generous good value food from substantial sandwiches up, no-smoking dining extension, cheerful local atmosphere, comfortable surroundings; former office of Mexico Mine Company, with massive stone walls (*P and M Rudlin, Brian Skelcher, Brenda and Derek Savage*)

☆ **Looe** [Fore St, E Looe; SX2553], *Olde Salutation*: Small pub with ancient heavy beams and timbers, sloping floors, shark-fishing photographs, busy with locals and fishermen; consistently good simple food (not Sat evening) esp crab sandwiches and Sun roasts, also vegetarian dishes, fast friendly service, well kept Ushers Best; piped music not too loud, handy for coast path (*Dr and Mrs B D Smith, Ted George, M E Williamson, M Joyner*)

☆ **Malpas** [off A39 S of Truro; SW8442], *Heron*: Genuine and friendly, in stunning setting above wooded creek; thriving atmosphere, big helpings of decent quick but fresh food inc good crab sandwiches, St Austell Tinners and HSD, log fire, lots of local photographs; pool, machines, piped music; suntrap slate-paved terrace; children welcome, can be very busy (*George Atkinson, Mr and Mrs J O Hicks, G W Stevenson, P R White, LYM*)

☆ **Manaccan** [down hill signed to Gillan and St Keverne; SW7625], *New*: New licensees again in attractive old thatched local (long-serving barman still there), friendly landlady, wide choice of decent bar food, well kept Flowers IPA and Wadworths 6X tapped from the cask, traditional games – but modern tables and chairs; children and dogs welcome, big garden with swing, pretty waterside village (*John and Sally Clarke, Gwen and Peter Andrews, Brian Skelcher, LYM*)

Marazion [The Square; SW5231], *Cutty Sark*: More hotel than pub, not far from beach, public bar with well kept Whitbreads-related ale, decent food, open fire, some stripped stone and nautical bric-a-brac, pleasant separate hotel bar, restaurant; bedrooms large and comfortable, with shower and lovely view of St Michaels Mount (*DAV, Iain Robertson*)

☆ **Marhamchurch** [off A39 just S of Bude; SS2203], *Bullers Arms*: Big rambling L-shaped bar, wide choice of generous low-priced food inc some unusual dishes, friendly staff, well kept Bass and Morlands Old Speckled Hen, decent wine by the glass, good CD juke box, darts in flagstoned back part, restaurant; children welcome; tables and play area in sizeable garden, a mile's walk to the sea; bedrooms (*Jeanne Cross, Paul Silvestri, R J Walden, LYM*)

Mawgan [St Martin; SW7323], *Old Courthouse*: Prettily placed and welcoming open-plan split-level pub, spacious, clean and comfortable, with good choice of food, well kept Whitbreads-related ales, three cats, pool, maybe piped music, pleasant garden; bistro Thurs-Sat evenings and Sun lunchtime;

children welcome (*Gwen and Peter Andrews*)

☆ **Mawnan Smith** [W of Falmouth, off Penryn—Gweek rd – old B3291; SW7728], *Red Lion*: Generous helpings of good attractively presented food esp seafood (not cheap but restaurant quality) from open-view kitchens in pleasantly furnished thatched pub, lots of pictures and bric-a-brac in cosy softly lit interconnected beamed rooms inc no-smoking room behind restaurant, lots of wines by the glass, well kept Bass, Greenalls, Worthington and a guest beer, friendly efficient service; piped music, booking needed in high summer; children allowed, handy for Glendurgan and Trebah Gardens (*Cliff Blakemore, Sybille Weber, R J Bland, Nick Wikeley, Pam Honour, Gwen and Peter Andrews, Chris and Margaret Southon, Brian Skelcher, LYM*)

☆ **Menheniot** [off A38; SX2862], *White Hart*: Stripped stone, red leatherette button-back seats and lots of brass in friendly relaxing bar with well kept Bass and Boddingtons, wide choice of generous good food (can be taken away); bedrooms well equipped and neatly modernised (*Ted George*)

☆ **Metherell** [Lower Metherell; follow Honicombe sign from St Anns Chapel just W of Gunnislake on A390; SX4069], *Carpenters Arms*: Heavily black-beamed inn with huge polished flagstones and massive stone walls, latest licensees (another change) leaning restaurant style but still a wide choice of decent bar food and well kept ales; handy for Cotehele; children welcome, bedrooms (*Tony and Wendy Hobden, Paul and Heather Bettesworth, LYM*)

☆ **Mevagissey** [off Fore St by Post Office; SX0145], *Fountain*: Welcoming unpretentious local with good simple food inc fresh fish, well kept St Austell ales, obliging service, plenty of atmosphere, lots of old local prints and photographs; piano sing-songs some evenings, popular upstairs restaurant (*John and June Gale, Iain Robertson, Christopher Wright, N J Lawless, Eric and Margarette Sibbit*)

Mevagissey [Fore St, nr harbour], *Ship*: 16th-c pub with generous reasonably priced food inc good fish and chips, full range of well kept St Austell beers, welcoming landlord; big comfortable room divided into small interesting areas, ships' memorabilia, open fire, friendly cat; fruit machines, piped music can be loud; bedrooms (*Jim Reid, Christopher Wright, Edward Froggatt, Keith and Janet Morris*)

Mitchell [off A30 Bodmin—Redruth; SW8654], *Plume of Feathers*: Rambling bar with lots of bric-a-brac, Whitbreads-related ales, food from open-plan back kitchen, flame-effect gas fire; piped music, darts and winter pool; tables outside, with play area and farm animals; children welcome, has been found cl winter (*Brian Skelcher, LYM*)

Morval [SX2556], *Snooty Fox*: Busy local atmosphere, popular food; bedrooms (*Brian and Jill Bond*)

☆ **Morwenstow** [signed off A39 N of

Kilkhampton; *SS2015*], *Bush*: One of Britain's oldest pubs, part Saxon, with serpentine Celtic piscina in one wall, ancient built-in settles, flagstones, and big stone fireplace, upper bar with interesting bric-a-brac, well kept St Austell HSD and Worthington BB tapped from the cask, Inch's cider, cheap malt whisky, basic lunchtime food (not Sun), darts; run in a take-us-as-you-find-us old-fashioned way, no piped music, children or dogs, seats out in yard; lovely setting, interesting village church with good nearby teashop, great cliff walks; cl Mon in winter *(Mr and Mrs J D Marsh, Jo and Gary Charlton, Colin Draper, Bruce Bird, Basil Minson, Hanns P Golez, Jeanne Cross, LYM)*

☆ **Mousehole** [*SW4726*], *Old Coastguard*: Spacious yet cosy and relaxed, with board floor, pine and cane furniture, interesting prints and superb views; friendly attentive staff, good interesting food inc lots of fish, rich puddings, ales such as Bass, Sharps Doom Bar, St Austell Trelawnys Pride; no restrictions on families, piped music, lots of musical events; pleasant terrace and sizeable gardens leading down to rocky beach; comfortable bedrooms, good breakfast *(Sue Holland, Dave Webster, Molly and Robin Taylor, George Atkinson)*

☆ **Mullion** [*SW6719*], *Old Inn*: Thatched and beamed village inn with interesting warren of nooks and crannies, lots of brasses, nautical items and old wreck pictures, big inglenook fireplace, no-smoking room, usual Greenalls bar food (all day Jul/Aug) from sandwiches to evening steaks, well kept Bass and guests such as Flowers IPA and Wadworths 6X; children welcome, open all day Sat/Sun and Aug; wandering cat, can be very busy, darts, fruit machine, duo most Fri evenings; picnic tables in pretty garden *(Gwen and Peter Andrews, George Atkinson, Jo and Gary Charlton, M Wellington, Barry and Anne, Edward Froggatt, Pam Honour, LYM)*

Newquay [Fore St; *SW8061*], *Fort*: Former master mariner's house, now hotel with brass and comfortable seating in roomy front bar, two further bars inc one for back conservatory, garden behind, good food all day, Bass, St Austell HSD and Wadworths 6X; good bedrooms *(Tony Scott)*

☆ **Notter** [Notter Bridge; just off A38 Saltash—Liskeard; *SX3861*], *Notter Bridge*: Attractive spot in wooded valley, knocked-through bar/lounge, dining conservatory (can get hot) overlooking river, wide choice of good cheap generous food inc curry evenings, happy bustling atmosphere, friendly service, well kept beer, tables on terrace *(Ted George, Jacquie and Jim Jones, Bronwen and Steve Wrigley)*

☆ **Padstow** [Lanadwell St; *SW9175*], *London*: Friendly and unpretentious fishermen's local with lots of pictures and nautical memorabilia, good atmosphere (busy evenings), well kept St Austell ales, decent choice of malt whiskies, good value food in small back dining area, great real fire; games

machines but no piped music; open all day; bedrooms good value too – made to feel one of the family; bedrooms *(Val Stevenson, Rob Holmes, Graham and Lynn Mason, Catherine Lloyd, Neil Franklin, George Atkinson, Mike Beiley, LYM)*

☆ **Padstow** [Lanadwell St], *Golden Lion*: Friendly and cosy backstreet local with pleasant black-beamed front bar, high-raftered back lounge with plush banquettes against ancient white stone walls; reasonably priced simple lunches, evening steaks and fresh seafood; well kept Cornish Original, piped music, juke box, fruit machines; bedrooms *(Ted George, Brian Skelcher, BB)*

☆ **Padstow** [South Quay], *Old Custom House*: Airy and spacious open-plan quayside bar with conservatory and big family area, good reasonably priced unpretentious food inc fresh fish and vegetarian from adjoining restaurant, comfortable chesterfields around open fire, lots of prints of old harbour, big beams and timbers; efficient friendly staff, well kept St Austell ales, restaurant; good spot by harbour, with conservatory; attractive sea-view bedrooms *(Mr and Mrs Pitt, Andy and Jill Kassube, Sandra Kench, Steven Norman, George Atkinson, BB)*

☆ **Penelewey** [Feock Downs, B3289; *SW8240*], *Punch Bowl & Ladle*: Much extended thatched pub in picturesque setting, bar done out with rustic artefacts, and strong emphasis on the plush and spreading dining side, with US-style hostess allocating seating and taking orders for the wide choice of good fresh food; Bass and Flowers original, friendly staff, unobtrusive piped music, children welcome in restaurant; handy for Trelissick Gardens; open all day summer, live music winter Fri *(Ian and Nita Cooper, Howard Clutterbuck, Nick Wikeley, A Ball, M D Davies, Mrs M Furness, David Luke, Brian Skelcher, LYM)*

Penhallow [*SW7651*], *Plume of Feathers*: Cosy 18th-c beamed pub full of pictures, jugs and bric-a-brac collected by newish licensees from Russia and beyond; animals inc pot bellied pig for children in back paddock; good value bar food *(Roger Smith)*

☆ **Penzance** [Barbican; Newlyn rd, opp harbour after swing-bridge; *SW4730*], *Dolphin*: Welcoming and attractive nautical pub with good harbour views, quick bar food inc good pasties, well kept St Austell ales, great fireplace, big pool room with juke box etc; children in room off main bar; no obvious nearby parking *(Colin Draper, LYM)*

Penzance [Chapel St], *Admiral Benbow*: Elaborately nautical decor, friendly staff, decent food inc good curries, Scottish Courage ales, children allowed, downstairs restaurant, pleasant view from top back room; open all day summer *(Ted George, David Carr, LYM)*

☆ **Perranuthnoe** [signed off A394 Penzance—Helston; *SW5329*], *Victoria*: Sociable new landlord and good atmosphere in comfortable L-shaped bar with coastal and wreck photographs, some stripped stonework, well kept Ushers Best, Founders and Summer, good value bar food inc good value crab sandwich, neat coal fire, booth seating in family area, games area; handy for Mounts Bay; bedrooms *(Cliff Blakemore, Jeremy and Kate Honeybun, LYM)*

☆ **Perranwell** [off A393 Redruth—Falmouth and A39 Falmouth—Truro; SW7839], *Royal Oak*: Unpretentious welcoming black-beamed village pub, friendly staff and locals, cosy seats, buoyant atmosphere, good value bar food inc sandwiches and attractive lunchtime cold table, well kept Whitbreads-related ales and decent wines, good winter fire, provision for children, garden with picnic tables *(Gwen and Peter Andrews, James and Ruth Morrell, LYM)*

☆ **Pillaton** [off Callington—Landrake back rd; SX3664], *Weary Friar*: Pretty tucked-away 12th-c pub with four tidy but interesting knocked-together rooms (one no smoking), comfortable seats around sturdy tables, easy chairs one end, well kept Bass, Courage Directors, Morlands Old Speckled Hen and Wadworths 6X, farm cider, country wines, bar food inc lunchtime sandwiches (service stops on the dot); restaurant (cl Mon), children in eating area; piped music; tables outside; comfortable bedrooms *(R A Cullingham, James Macrae, Mayur Shah, Ted George, John Kirk, Iain Robertson, Mr and Mrs J Jones, R Walden, LYM)*

☆ **Polperro** [The Quay; SX2051], *Blue Peter*: Cosy and unpretentious little low-beamed wood-floored local up narrow steps from harbour, nautical memorabilia, well kept St Austell and guest beers such as Sharps Doom Bar, farm cider, log fire, traditional games, some seats outside, family area upstairs with video game; open all day – can get crowded, and piped music can be loudish; no food (but maybe a Bonio for dogs) *(Michael Sandy, M J How, Tony Scott, David Carr, Ted George, Kerry Law, Annemarie Firstbrook, Emma Kingdon, LYM)*

☆ **Polperro** [Quay], *Three Pilchards*: Low-beamed dim-lit fishermen's local high over harbour, generous good value food inc lots of seafood, open fire, neat helpful and chatty staff, Ushers Best and Founders, tables on terrace up 30 steep steps; piped music can be fairly loud, open all day *(Michael Sandy, David Carr, AW, BW, Ted George, Dr and Mrs B D Smith, M Joyner)*

☆ **Polperro** [top of village nr main car park], *Crumplehorn Mill*: Friendly service and good value generous food inc local fish in converted mill, separate cosily dark areas inc upper gallery, beams, stripped stone, flagstones, log fire, comfortable seats, well kept Bass and St Austell HSD and XXXX, farm cider; pool area, piped music (can be fairly loud); families welcome, good value bedrooms *(Terry and Eileen Stott, BB)*

Polperro, *Manor*: Friendly little wood and stone inn tucked away in back street, stuffed cat in one window, nice back eating room, well kept beers, tasty reasonably priced bar food *(Ted George)*; [Mill Hill], *Mill House*:

Civilised hotel with woody old bar, separate pool room, back evening bistro, attractive children's room, surprisingly big garden by stream; Bass and Exmoor Gold, draught cider, decent children's menu; bedrooms *(Michael Sandy)*; [Llansallos St – bear right approaching harbour], *Noughts & Crosses*: Cheerful riverside bar down steps, soft lighting, comfortable banquettes, beams, stripped stone and panelling; good value food inc cheap children's dishes, prompt friendly service, Courage Best, upper family areas, pool, fruit machine, unobtrusive piped music; pretty street *(Michael Sandy, Dr and Mrs A Whiteway)*; [Fore St], *Ship*: Very welcoming service in big comfortable bar, well kept Ushers, generous good value fresh food, steps down to well furnished family room, small back terrace *(Ted George, Mr and Mrs B Hobden)*

Port Isaac [The Terrace; SX0080], *Shipwright*: Great clifftop views from small hotel's restaurant, snooker table brings young people to lively public bar, friendly staff, good home-cooked food esp seafood, real ale, warm solid fuel stove; bedrooms *(Graham Tayar, F E Jarman)*

☆ nr **Port Isaac** [Port Gaverne signed from Port Isaac, and from B3314 E of Pendoggett], *Port Gaverne*: In lovely spot with splendid cliff walks all around; early 17th-c, big log fires, low beams some flagstones and stripped stone, interesting pictures (inc local art society's spring exhibition); bar food from sandwiches to steaks, no-smoking restaurant, well kept Bass, Flowers IPA and Sharps Doom Bar, good bin-end wine list, fine choice of whiskies and other spirits; open all day summer, but cl early Jan to mid-Feb; provision for children, bedrooms in attached cottages with beautiful views *(Sue and Bob Ward, Jim Reid, Nigel Flook, Betsy Brown, Graham Tayar, Edward Froggatt, John and Jackie Chalcraft, Sharon Hancock, D Marsh, Brian and Jill Bond, Jenny and Brian Seller, Dr H V Hughes, LYM)*

Porthleven [SW6225], *Harbour*: Panelled inn close to beach, good choice of food in bar and restaurant, informal local atmosphere, good service, St Austell ales, comprehensive wine list; comfortable bedrooms overlooking working harbour *(B and M Beesley, Andy and Jill Kassube)*

☆ **Portloe** [SW9339], *Lugger*: Not really pubby, and its restaurant licence means you can't go just for a drink, but has well presented bar lunches inc children's, simple easy chairs, two fires, good evening restaurant, decent wines, tables on terrace, delightful setting in unspoilt almost souvenir-free village above cove; bedrooms (not all with sea view) *(R W Suddaby, G W Stevenson, LYM)*

Portloe, *Ship*: Recently refurbished by newish licensees, pleasantly unfussy atmosphere, decent food, sheltered streamside garden – useful alternative to Lugger for people on coast path; well kept St Austell *(DJW, Christopher Wright)*

☆ **Portmellon Cove** [SX0144], *Rising Sun*: Fine spot overlooking sandy cove nr Mevagissey, flagstoned nautical bar with unusual open fire, big upper family/games room and dining room, decent generous food inc children's, vegetarian and good value Sun roast, well kept Boddingtons, Marstons Pedigree and Wadworths 6X, good coffee and hot chocolate, friendly landlord, seats outside; comfortable beamed bedrooms, most with sea view *(N Lawless, Dr M Robson, DJW, BB)*

☆ **Poughill** [SS2207], *Preston Gate*: Welcoming local with pews and long mahogany tables on flagstones, log fires, well kept Tetleys-related ales, simple tasty food (evenings get there early or book), darts, some seats outside; children welcome, dogs looked after well *(Richard Cole, James Flory, Tony McLaughlin, LYM)*

Redruth [SW6842], *Rose Cottage*: Promptly served good value food, children welcome if eating; piped music can be a little loud *(A R Harris)*

☆ nr **Redruth** [Tolgus Mount; SW6842], *Tricky Dickies*: Well converted isolated former tin-mine smithy, dark inside, with interesting industrial relics, good value food esp pizzas, changing well kept beers, decent wines, efficient service, partly covered terrace with barbecues *(Don and Shirley Parrish, Malcolm and Pat Rudlin)*

☆ **Sennen Cove** [SW3526], *Old Success*: Old but radically modernised – the setting's the best part, by clean beach with glorious view along Whitesand Bay; big bustling nautical-theme bar, perhaps best out of season, lots of old photographs, well kept Bass, St Austell, Tetleys and Worthington, piped music, bar food, carvery restaurant; gents' past car park; children welcome, attractive bedrooms, good breakfasts *(Gwen and Peter Andrews, Sue Holland, David Webster, C P Scott-Malden, James Nunns)*

Sladesbridge [A389 SE of Wadebridge; SX0171], *Slades House*: Friendly welcome, beautifully clean, nice atmosphere, good service, well kept Bass, usual food; children welcome *(Jenny and Brian Seller)*

☆ **St Dominick** [Saltash; a mile E of A388, S of Callington – OS Sheet 201 map ref 406674; SX3967], *Who'd Have Thought It*: Spick and span, with flock wallpaper, tasselled plush seats, Gothick tables, gleaming pottery and copper; well kept Bass and Whitbreads-related ales, decent wines, friendly staff, generous food inc fresh fish, impeccable lavatories, superb Tamar views from attractively furnished family conservatory; quiet countryside nr Cotehele *(Ted George, Peter Massocchi, Jacquie and Jim Jones, LYM)*

☆ **St Issey** [SW9271], *Ring o' Bells*: Neatly modernised cheerful village inn with consistently good food inc fresh local crab, children's helpings and good value Sun roasts, well kept Courage, pleasant staff, open fire; darts, pool, some seats outside; can get packed in summer; bedrooms *(Howard Clutterbuck, Mr and Mrs B Hobden, J R T Powys-Smith, LYM)*

St Issey [Burgois; SW9272], *Pickwick*: Spacious and comfortable lounge and bar, restaurant, family room, cheerful staff, good reasonably priced food inc vegetarian and fine steaks, decent wines, good play area inc tractors; bedrooms *(Mr and Mrs R Searston, Bett and Brian Cox)*

☆ **St Ives** [The Wharf; SW5441], *Sloop*: Simple but charming 14th-c seafront inn, snug pews, slate floor and beams in cosy right-hand front bar, interesting pictures (some for sale), wide range of bar food inc lots of fish, Ruddles and Theakstons Old Peculier, decent wines, benches out in front; open all day, very busy in summer, handy for Tate Gallery; bedrooms *(Liz and John Soden, George Atkinson, John Wooll, Jim Reid, Martin Bromfield, Bernadette Garner, Alan and Heather Jacques, Jenny and Brian Seller, Brian Skelcher, Ted George)*

St Ives [Fore St], *Queens*: Biggish comfortable dining pub with wide choice of well prepared food, St Austell HSD, Princes and Tinners, good friendly service, family area, pool table; bedrooms *(Steve Jennings)*; [Fore St], *Union*: Friendly cosy local, Courage ales; can get very crowded *(Steve Jennings)*

☆ **St Just in Penwith** [Mkt Sq; SW3631], *Wellington*: Well kept St Austell beers, generous food inc local fish, good ploughman's, fine steaks, polite cheerful service, decent wines; bedrooms, good breakfast *(Graham and Lynn Mason, Stephen Horsley, Mr and Mrs D T Deas, Dr B and Mrs P B Baker)*

☆ **St Keverne** [The Square; SW7921], *Three Tuns*: Relaxing local by church, pleasantly refurbished, with generous well presented food, well kept Whitbreads-related ales, quick friendly service, picnic tables out by square; bedrooms *(Gwen and Peter Andrews, Ted George, LYM)*

☆ **St Mabyn** [SX0473], *St Mabyn Inn*: Good interesting food in sympathetically refurbished pub/restaurant, all cooked freshly so may be a wait *(A N Ellis)*

☆ **St Mawes** [SW8433], *Rising Sun*: Waterside hotel recently refurbished to give big comfortable open-plan bar; attractive conservatory, slate-topped tables on sunny terrace just across lane from harbour wall, decent food, well kept St Austell ales and wines, excellent coffee, good service; open all day summer; pretty bedrooms *(DJW, LYM)*

☆ **St Merryn** [Church Town (B3276 towards Padstow); SW8873], *Cornish Arms*: Well kept St Austell ales and usual bar food at reasonable prices in firmly run and spotless local with fine slate floor and some 12th-c stonework; good games room, picnic tables outside; children over 6 may be allowed in eating area *(Bett and Brian Cox, LYM)*

☆ **St Merryn**, *Farmers Arms*: Big busy family dining pub with bright and spacious no-smoking dining area, St Austell ales, good value house wine, attentive helpful landlady, quick service, floodlit well, children's games room with videos and so forth, tables on back terrace; bedrooms – handy for Trevose Head and superb walks *(Jenny and Brian Seller)*

☆ **St Neot** [N of A38 Liskeard—Bodmin; SX1867], *London*: Nice range of home-made food, well kept Boddingtons and John Smiths, cheerful service, beams and two open fires, pleasant local atmosphere, restaurant, unobtrusive piped music; attractive village in wooded valley; bedrooms *(Janet and Colin Roe, R A Cullingham)*

☆ **Stratton** [A3072; SS2406], *Kings Arms*: Fine old well kept three-room 17th-c free house, six or more well kept mainly local ales, attentive helpful staff, varied good value food; children welcome *(Malcolm and Pat Rudlin, James Flory, Richard Houghton)*

☆ **Stratton**, *Tree*: Rambling and interesting pub with seats alongside unusual old dovecot in attractive ancient coachyard, very friendly bar rooms, well kept Bass, St Austell Tinners and a guest ale, farm ciders, good range of well priced bar food, great log fires, character evening restaurant; children welcome in back bar, cheap bedrooms with huge breakfasts *(Alan and Heather Jacques, P and D Carpenter, BB)*

☆ **Trebarwith** [signed off B3263 and B3314 SE of Tintagel – OS Sheet 200 map ref 058865; SX0585], *Mill House*: Marvellously placed in steep streamside woods above sea, darkish bar with fine Delabole flagstones and interesting local pictures, games room with pool table and children's play area, food inc children's dishes, real ales, decent coffee, friendly owners (and Millie the spaniel), evening restaurant (not Mon-Weds in winter); dogs welcome, tables out on terrace and by stream; five comfortable bedrooms *(Alan and Paula McCully, SED, LYM)*

Tregony [B3287; SW9245], *Kings Arms*: Relaxed and welcoming old coaching inn, two chatty bars, dining area, usual food at reasonable prices, well kept Boddingtons and Wadworths 6X *(Christopher Wright, DJW)*

☆ **Trelights** [signed off B3314 Wadebridge—Delabole; SW9979], *Long Cross*: Coastal hotel with fine restored Victorian garden, modern bar with plush-and-varnish furnishings, stained-glass panels, unusual heptagonal bench around small central fountain; family room, further dining bar, good play area; well kept St Austell ales, good value bar food, good afternoon teas, lively folk nights; bedrooms comfortable and well furnished, many with good views *(Pete and Rosie Flower, BB)*

Trematon [Stoketon Cross; SX3959], *Crooked Inn*: Wide choice of good value generous home-cooked food, good range of Whitbreads-related ales and cider; comfortable bedrooms *(John Kirk, Joy Pearson, Mr and Mrs T A Bryan)*

Tresillian [A39 Truro—St Austell; SW8646], *Wheel*: Neatly thatched and friendly, pleasant mix of plush seating with timbering, stripped stone and low ceiling joists, steps between two cosy main areas, generous usual food from large filled rolls to steaks inc children's dishes, well kept Whitbreads-related ales; piped music may obtrude; play area in neat garden stretching down to tidal inlet *(Brian Skelcher, John Ledbury, Susan and Nigel Wilson, LYM)*

Tresparrett [SX1491], *Horseshoe*: Welcoming traditional village local, well kept beers, food inc some unusual things *(Richard Houghton)*

☆ **Trevarrian** [B3276 NE of Newquay; SW8566], *Travellers Rest*: Good plentiful food, well kept St Austell beers, good friendly service; can get crowded in summer *(R G Bywaters)*

☆ **Truro** [Frances St; SW8244], *Globe*: Comfortable and welcoming, with good choice of reliable generous home-made food inc good value self-help salad bar, well kept Whitbreads-related ales, good service, mix of furnishings inc leather armchairs and sofas, several rooms off central serving area; old panelling and beamery, fine antique prints, bottle-glass screens, taxidermy *(Reg Nelson, P and M Rudlin)*

☆ **Truro** [Frances St/Castle St], *Wig & Pen*: Good generous reasonably priced bar food with interesting specials in big neatly kept L-shaped pub, well spaced comfortable chairs and tables, newspapers to read, unobtrusive piped music, pleasant service, well kept St Austell ales, decent house wines in big glasses; tables out on busy street *(M Wellington, David Carr)*

☆ **Truro** [Kenwyn St], *William IV*: Busy dark-panelled bar with slightly secluded raised areas and lots of bric-a-brac, well kept St Austell beers, decent wine, good value buffet food inc hot dishes in elegantly tiled airy two-level conservatory dining room opening into small flowery garden *(David Carr)*

Truro [Pydar St], *City*: Superior local with genuine character, cosy atmosphere, attractive bric-a-brac, particularly well kept Courage, hot roast cashews *(Reg Nelson, Simon Walker)*

Upton Cross [B3254 N of Liskeard; SX2872], *Caradon*: Friendly and attractive 17th-c local on edge of Bodmin Moor with good value home cooking, well kept Flowers Original, St Austell HSD and guests like Sharps Doom Bar; good advice on local attractions *(Andy and Jill Kassube)*

☆ **Veryan** [SW9139], *New Inn*: Interesting choice of good value nicely done bar food with fresh veg in neat, welcoming and homely one-bar pub, popular with locals and visitors; quick cheerful service, chilled St Austell ales tapped from the cask, good value house wine, good coffee, dachshund called Boris, quiet seats out behind; bedrooms, lovely village *(Chris and Margaret Southon, Christopher Wright, G J Newman, DJW, Nick Wikeley)*

☆ **Zennor** [SW4538], *Tinners Arms*: Gently extended country local in lovely windswept setting by church nr coast path, limited but good value food (all day in summer), normally welcoming, with well kept ales such as Wadworths 6X from casks behind bar, Lane's farm cider, decent coffee, rather spartan feel with flagstones, lots of granite and stripped pine; real fires each end, child-free upstairs bar, back pool room, friendly dogs and lots of cats, no music, tables on small attractive front terrace *(Pat and Roger Fereday, David Warrellow, Richard and Anne Ansell, Jeanne Cross, Paul Silvestri, Sue Holland, Dave Webster, Brian Skelcher, S Beele, Gwen and Peter Andrews, Lawrence Bacon, Jean Scott, Stephen Horsley, Jacquie and Jim Jones)*

Isles of Scilly

St Mary's – Hugh Town [The Strand; SV9010], *Atlantic*: Big low-beamed L-shaped bar full of interesting nautical bric-a-brac, wreck salvage and photographs, wonderful harbour views from all tables, good cheery atmosphere (esp on live music nights), wide choice of simple reliable generous bar food inc sandwiches and local fish, well kept St Austell Tinners and HSD, great assortment of customers; piped music (may be obtrusive); family room, no-smoking restaurant; good views, esp from small back terrace over harbour; bedrooms in adjacent hotel *(A Noad, David Mead, V H and J M Vanstone, BB)*

☆ **St Mary's – Hugh Town** [Silver St (A3110)], *Bishop & Wolf*: Very wide choice of good value well presented generous food esp fish, helpful lively staff, St Austell Tinners and HSD, good local atmosphere, interesting sea/boating decor with gallery above rd, nets, maritime bric-a-brac, lifeboat photographs, attractive upstairs restaurant, popular summer live music *(A Noad, Peter and Gwyneth Eastwood, Steve and Carolyn Harvey)*

St Mary's – Hugh Town [The Quay], *Mermaid*: Fine harbour view from picture-window main bar full of nautical relics, rough wood, stone floor, large winter stove and dim lighting; cellar bar with boat counter, pool table and music for young people (live at weekends); well kept Boddingtons, bar food, restaurant *(Steve and Carolyn Harvey)*

Tresco [SV8915], *Island*: Friendly upmarket hotel in beautiful spot, very comfortable bar, excellent reasonably priced food, good atmosphere; fine grounds, tables out on terrace by grass (with badminton); right by shore with superb sea and island views; bedrooms *(V H and J M Vanstone, BB)*

Bedroom prices normally include full English breakfast, VAT and any inclusive service charge that we know of. Prices before the '/' are for single rooms, after for two people in double or twin (B includes a private bath, S a private shower). If there is no '/', the prices are only for twin or double rooms (as far as we know there are no singles).

Cumbria

*This county has a rewarding mix of warmly welcoming simple walkers' pubs
with more civilised foody places – these also often in wonderful countryside.
The places that stand out as being on top form these days are the Royal Oak
in Appleby (a formidable all-rounder), the friendly Dukes Head at
Armathwaite, the Cavendish Arms in Cartmel (another all-rounder), the
Masons Arms on Cartmel Fell (fine beers, lovely position), the Punch Bowl at
Crosthwaite (first-class food, and friendly with it), the Britannia in its lovely
spot at Elterwater (marvellous service even when it's packed), the well run
Travellers Rest at Grasmere, the very friendly Watermill at Ings (massive
choice of beers), the Abbey Bridge tucked away by Lanercost Priory, the
Shepherds at Melmerby (irresistible to many readers), and the Salutation at
Threlkeld (much enjoyed by walkers, with appetising food). We should also
mention three very enjoyable new entries: the unpretentious Blacksmiths Arms
near Broughton in Furness, with newish licensees doing good food; the
excellently refurbished Bitter End in Cockermouth, brewing its own good
beers; and the big bustling Black Bull at Coniston, just right for this popular
village. There's a friendly and hard-working new couple at the Queens Head
at Tirril, and the popular Drunken Duck up above Hawkshead has started
brewing its own beer. The Bay Horse outside Ulverston is now making a point
of calling itself a Hotel and Restaurant, which does underline its upmarket
character – but the food's really excellent. It's one place to consider for a
special meal out, as is the Royal Oak in Appleby, but the pub that stands out
as Cumbria Dining Pub of the Year is the Punch Bowl at Crosthwaite. In the
Lucky Dip section at the end of the chapter, pubs on which we have had
uniformly good reports recently are the Queens Head at Askham, Barbon Inn
at Barbon, Engine at Cark in Cartmel, Kings Arms in Cartmel, Sun at Crook,
Old Posting House at Deanscales, Sawrey Hotel at Far Sawrey, Old Crown at
Hesket Newmarket, Howtown Hotel at Howtown, Farmers Arms at Lowick
Green, Herdwick at Penruddock and Wasdale Head Inn at Wasdale Head; we
have already inspected and approved almost all of these. This is still a
relatively cheap area, with drinks costing significantly less than the national
average, but this last year we have seen Cumbrian beer prices rising
significantly more quickly than elsewhere. The Blue Bell at Heversham, tied to
Sam Smiths of Yorkshire, stood out as the cheapest pub in our survey, and
generally pubs tied to the smaller local and regional breweries here are holding
their prices down better than free houses or pubs tied to the big national
chains.*

Bedroom prices are for high summer. Even then you may get reductions
for more than one night, or (outside tourist areas) weekends. Winter special
rates are common, and many inns cut bedroom prices if you have a
full evening meal.

AMBLESIDE NY3804 Map 9
Golden Rule

Smithy Brow; follow Kirkstone Pass signpost from A591 on N side of town

This is very much an honest Lakeland local, and though it's popular with regulars, visitors can be sure of a friendly welcome, too. There are lots of local country pictures and a few fox masks decorating the butter-coloured walls, horsebrasses on the black beams, built-in leatherette wall seats, and cast-iron-framed tables; dominoes and cribbage. The room on the left has darts and a fruit machine, and the one down a few steps on the right is a quieter sitting room. Well kept Hartleys XB and Robinsons Best, Old Stockport, and Hatters Mild on handpump; local pork pies (40p), filled rolls (£1.50), and winter soup (£1.75). There's a back yard with tables, a small pretty summer garden, and wonderfully colourful window boxes. The golden rule referred to in its name is a brass measuring yard mounted over the bar counter. *(Recommended by Mr and Mrs Richard Osborne, Tim Heywood, Sophie Wilne, David Carr, H K Dyson, Andy and Jill Kassube, Pete and Sue Wells, Jeanne Cross, Paul Silvestri, SLC, H Dyson)*

Hartleys (Robinsons) ~ Tenant John Lockley ~ Real ale ~ Limited snacks ~ (015394) 32257 ~ Children welcome ~ Nearby parking virtually out of the question ~ Open 11-11; 12-10.30 Sun

APPLEBY NY6921 Map 10
Royal Oak ★ 🍽 🛏 ♀ 🍷

Bongate; B6542 on S edge of town

As one reader commented, it would be hard to see how this very popular old-fashioned coaching inn could be improved. There's a particularly enjoyable atmosphere, a fine range of beers in top condition, imaginative food, and a warm welcome from the thoughtful, friendly licensees. It's a long low partly 14th-c building, and the beamed lounge has old pictures on the timbered walls, some armchairs and a carved settle, and a panelling-and-glass snug enclosing the bar counter; there's a good open fire in the smaller, oak-panelled public bar; darts. Good food from fresh ingredients includes daily specials like baked mushrooms stuffed with green salsa (£6.95), Black Isle mussels (£6.95), tuna steak with roast red peppers or seared bass with baby vine tomatoes (£10.95), braised knuckle of local lamb with chicory (they use top quality meat from a local butcher who has his own stock), and home-made puddings (around £3) and interesting, properly kept cheeses; also, lunchtime sandwiches, soup like roast tomato and fennel (£1.90), home-made pâté such as chicken liver, pork and apple or stilton, port and smoked bacon (from £3), ploughman's with home-made bread (£3.25), little brown shrimps (£4), glazed cumberland sausage with apple sauce or lentil, red pepper and mushroom lasagne (£5.45), Whitby scampi (£6), and pork fillet with mushrooms, madeira and cream (£9.85). One of the dining rooms is no smoking. There are usually eight real ales on handpump: Bongate Special Pale Ale (their own beer made locally) and Theakstons Best, with regular visitors such as Black Sheep Bitter, Special and Rigwelter, Fraoch Heather Ale (they say it is superb), Yates Bitter, and Youngers Scotch; several malt whiskies, and a carefully chosen wine list with around 8 by the glass and quite a few half bottles; darts. In summer the outside is very colourful, with seats on the front terrace among masses of flowers in tubs, troughs and hanging baskets. You can get here on the scenic Leeds/Settle/Carlisle railway (best to check times and any possible delays to avoid missing lunch). *(Recommended by Richard Fallon, Keith Wright, Richard Houghton, V W Prime, Wm Van Laaten, Susan and John Douglas, Tom McLean, Roger Huggins, Mr and Mrs D Wilson, Derek and Sylvia Stephenson, Malcolm Taylor, David and Margaret Bloomfield, D Knott, Mark Fennell, Walter and Susan Rimaldi-Butcher, Paul Boot, Martin Hickes, Paul Cornock, H Webb, Chris and Andy Crow, John Fazakerley, Angus Lyon, Andrew and Kerstin Lewis, Richard Holloway, John and Jackie Chalcruft, John Fazakerley)*

Free house ~ Licensees Colin and Hilary Cheyne ~ Real ale ~ Meals and snacks (12-2, 6-9) ~ Restaurant ~ (017683) 51463 ~ Well behaved children welcome ~ Open 11-3, 6-11 ~ bedrooms: £29.50B/£42.25(£62.50B)

See also entry under nearby BRAMPTON

ARMATHWAITE NY5146 Map 10
Dukes Head 🛏

Off A6 a few miles S of Carlisle

Run by particularly helpful, friendly people, this is a most enjoyable inn to visit. The civilised lounge bar has oak settles and little armchairs among more upright seats, oak and mahogany tables, antique hunting and other prints, and some brass and copper powder-flasks above its coal fire. Good bar food includes sandwiches and ploughman's, nice soup, delicious roast duck (£9.90), daily specials like pheasant with a redcurrant sauce (£6.50), monkfish in herby batter (£7.20), and fresh crab salad (£7.50), and super home-made puddings like chewy meringues with toffee sauce and ice cream, and fine trifles. Out of season, they do themed food evenings and offer three-course set meals (from £7.75); the breakfasts are huge. Well kept Boddingtons and guests such as Ind Coope Burton, Marstons Pedigree, and Tetleys on handpump; piped music, and dominoes; separate public bar with darts, pool, and a fruit machine. There are tables out on the lawn behind. *(Recommended by Douglas Miller, Jackie Moffat, Malcolm Taylor, N Sarbutts, Joy and Peter Heatherley, Enid and Henry Stephens, Richard Holloway, David and Margaret Bloomfield, Chris Rounthwaite, Simon and Amanda Southwell, Bob Ellis)*

Pubmaster ~ Licensee Peter Lynch ~ Real ale ~ Meals and snacks ~ Restaurant ~ (016974) 72226 ~ Children welcome ~ Open 12-3, 5.30-11; 12-3, 6-10.30 Sun ~ Bedrooms: £26.50B/£46.50B

ASKHAM NY5123 Map 9
Punch Bowl

Village signposted on right from A6 4 miles S of Penrith

Locals are fond of this friendly pub in its attractive village green setting – but there's a warm welcome for visitors as well. The rambling bar has an antique settle by an open log fire, interesting furnishings such as Chippendale dining chairs and rushwork ladder-back seats around sturdy wooden tables, well cushioned window seats in the white-painted thick stone walls, coins stuck into the cracks of the dark wooden beams (periodically taken out and sent to charity), and local photographs and prints of Askham. The old-fashioned woodburning stove, with its gleaming stainless chimney in the big main fireplace, is largely decorative. Generous helpings of bar food include home-made soup (£2.45), lunchtime sandwiches (£2.75), shrimp pot (£3.10), mushroom and tomato lasagne (£6.55), and specials such as ginger and garlic chicken (£5.70), baked local trout (£6.35), venison in a red wine sauce (£6.70), and steaks (from £10.45); children's dishes (£3.30). Marstons Pedigree, Morlands Old Speckled Hen, Ruddles Best, and Whitbreads Castle Eden on handpump; dominoes and piped pop music, and in the separate public bar darts, pool, juke box and fruit machine. There are tables out on a flower-filled terrace. *(Recommended by Sheila and John French, Eric Locker, Richard Lewis, RJH, A Preston, H Dyson, Angus Lyon)* ·

Whitbreads ~ Lease: David and Frances Riley ~ Real ale ~ Snacks (lunchtime) and meals ~ (01931) 712443 ~ Children welcome until 9pm ~ Open 11.30-3, 6-11; 12-3, 6.30-11 in winter ~ Bedrooms: £19.50/£39

BASSENTHWAITE LAKE NY1930 Map 9
Pheasant ★ 🛏

Follow Wythop Mill signpost at N end of dual carriageway stretch of A66 by Bassenthwaite Lake

It's quite a surprise to find the little bars in this rather smart and civilised hotel are so pleasantly old-fashioned and pubby. Well kept Bass, Morlands Old Speckled Hen, and Theakstons Best on handpump and quite a few malt whiskies are served from a low serving counter, and there are persian rugs on the parquet floor, rush-seat chairs, library seats, and cushioned settles, and hunting prints and photographs on the fine ochre walls. Under the new licensee, good lunchtime bar food includes home-made soup (£2.45), ploughman's (£4.75), stilton, leek and walnut cheesecake with an apple and cinnamon sauce (£5.20), potted Silloth shrimps (£5.25), smoked local trout with cucumber and dill vinaigrette (£5.50), smoked Herdwick lamb with a honey, mint and pear dressing (£5.75), tagliatelle with tuna, sweet peppers and fennel with a dill vinaigrette (£5.95), and home-made puddings (£2.95); the elegant restaurant is no smoking. If the bars are full, you might want to move to the large and airy beamed lounge at the back, which has easy chairs on its polished parquet floor and a big log fire on cool days; there are also some chintzy sitting rooms with antique furniture (one is no smoking). The hotel is surrounded by very attractive woodlands, with beeches, larches and douglas firs, and you can walk into them from the garden. This is a fine walking area. *(Recommended by Neville Kenyon, William Cunliffe, Alan Risdon, SLC, Mr and Mrs D Wilson, RWD, Jason Caulkin, Paul Bailey, Val Stevenson, Rob Holmes, C A Hall, Nigel Wooliscroft, Gwen and Steve Walker, H K Dyson)*

Free house ~ Licensee R Wolff-Vorbeck ~ Real ale ~ Lunchtime bar meals and snacks ~ Restaurant ~ (017687) 76234 ~ Children in restaurant only ~ Open 11-3, 5.30-10.30(11 Sat); 12-3, 7-10.30 Sun; closed 25 Dec ~ bedrooms: £64B/£100B

BASSENTHWAITE NY2332 Map 9
Sun

Village itself, signposted off A591 a few miles NW of Keswick

The enjoyable bar food here draws on both the licensees' backgrounds – the landlady is from the Lakes, while her husband is Italian: minestrone soup (£1.50), spicy prawns in breadcrumbs (£3), lunchtime ploughman's (£4), lancashire hotpot (£5), home-made steak pie or home-made lasagne (£5.50), pork steaks in mushroom sauce (£6.50), sirloin steak (£8.50), and puddings such as syrup sponge or sticky toffee pudding (£2.25). Well kept Jennings Bitter on handpump. The rambling bar has low 17th-c black oak beams, two good stone fireplaces with big logs burning in winter, lots of brasses, built-in wall seats and plush stools around heavy wooden tables, and areas that stretch usefully back on both sides of the servery. A huddle of white houses looks up to Skiddaw and other high fells, and you can enjoy the view from the tables in the pub's front yard by the rose bushes and honeysuckle; no dogs. *(Recommended by D and N Towle, Ewan and Moira McCall, William Cunliffe, David and July Walmsley, H K Dyson, Mayur Shah, Vann and Terry Prime, Richard Holloway, Chris and Andy Crow, C A Hall, Tina and David Woods-Taylor)*

Jennings ~ Tenants Giuseppe and Josephine Scopelliti ~ Real ale ~ Meals and snacks (12-1.30, 6.30-8.30ish; not Sun evening) ~ (017687) 76439 ~ Children in side rooms whenever possible ~ Open 12-2.30, 6-11; may close earlier winter lunchtimes if very quiet; closed Mon and Weds lunchtimes Nov-Mar

BEETHAM SD5079 Map 7
Wheatsheaf 🍺

Village (and inn) signposted just off A6 S of Milnthorpe

The timbered cornerpiece of this fine 17th-c coaching inn is very striking – a two storey set of gabled oriel windows jettied out from the corner into the quiet village street. Inside, the relaxed lounge bar has lots of exposed beams and joists, attractive built-in wall settles, tapestry-cushioned chairs, a massive antique carved oak armchair, and a cabinet filled with foreign costume dolls. Beyond a little central snug is a tiled-floor bar with darts and dominoes. Good, reasonably priced bar food includes soup (£1.70), sandwiches (from £2), home-made cheese, steak and kidney or cottage pies (from £3.60), sausage, liver and bacon (£3.85), steaks (from £7.40), daily specials, and puddings (£2.20); courteous, friendly staff. If the bar is too crowded, you can eat in the upstairs no-smoking dining room for the same price. Well kept Boddingtons and Tetleys on handpump, and quite a few malt whiskies; darts and dominoes. *(Recommended by R D Knight, Alan Risdon, IHR, Michael and Alison Leyland, Angus Lyon, Gill and Keith Croxton)*

Free house ~ Licensee Mrs Margaret Shaw ~ Real ale ~ Meals and snacks ~ Restaurant ~ (015395) 62123 ~ Children welcome till 8.30pm ~ Open 11-3, 6-11; 12-3, 7-10.30 Sun; closed evenings 25-26 Dec ~ Bedrooms: £30B/£40B

BOOT NY1801 Map 9

Burnmoor

Village signposted just off the Wrynose/Hardknott Pass road, OS Sheet 89 map reference 175010

Even in summer, the surroundings here are more peaceful than much of the Lakeland. It's a popular place to stay with peaceful fells all round, lots of attractive tracks to walk along, and is close to Dalegarth Station (the top terminus of the Ravenglass and Eskdale light steam railway), and to a restored watermill, said to be the oldest in the country. The beamed and carpeted white-painted bar has an open fire, red leatherette seats and settles, and small copper-topped tables. Mrs Foster is Austrian and there are always some speciality dishes on the menu: sandwiches, delicious soup (£1.50), lunchtime ploughman's (£3.60), several flans such as cheese and onion or Austrian smoked ham and cheese (from £3.80), home-cooked cold meats (£4.20), Cumberland game pie (£5.80), wienerschnitzel (£6.40), sirloin steak (£8.20), and daily specials such as cauliflower and broccoli crumble (£4) and gammon steak (£5.80); children's helpings. They grow a lot of the vegetables themselves, and keep hens and pigs. Well kept Jennings Bitter, Cumberland and Snecklifter on handpump, Austrian wines, and gluhwein in winter; pool, dominoes, cribbage, and juke box. There are seats outside on the sheltered front lawn. *(Recommended by Simon Watkins, David and Judy Walmsley, H K Dyson, Tony Young, Romey Heaton)*

Free house ~ Licensees Tony and Heidi Foster ~ Real ale ~ Meals and snacks (12-2, 6-9) ~ Restaurant ~ (019467) 23224 ~ Children welcome till 9pm ~ Open 11-2.45, 4.30-11(10.30 Sun) ~ Bedrooms: £26(£30B)/£52(£56B)

BOUTH SD3386 Map 9

White Hart

Village signposted off A590 near Haverthwaite

Run by a friendly and energetic landlord, this small village inn has a very relaxed atmosphere. Sloping ceilings and floors show its age, there are lots of old local photographs and bric-a-brac – farm tools, stuffed animals, a collection of long-stemmed clay pipes – and two log fires, one in a fine old kitchen range; no noisy games machines except in the games room (where there are darts, pool, pinball, football, video, and juke box). A fair choice of home-made food includes good value sandwiches (from £1.65), ploughman's (from £3.85), tuna and pasta bake (£5.45), vegetable lasagne (£5.50), 1lb gammon and egg (£6.55), daily specials like venison or wild boar steaks, lancashire hotpot, pork and pineapple curry or local trout (from around £5.45), steaks (from £9.80), and puddings like blackberry and apple crumble or sticky toffee pudding (£2.75). Well kept Black Sheep, Boddingtons, Highgate Mild, and Tetleys on handpump, and quite a few malt whiskies; tables out in the attractively planted and well kept garden, with occasional summer barbecues. The inn is well placed in good walking country. *(Recommended by JDM, KM, Andy and Jill Kassube, Dr J Morley, Stan and Hazel Allen, David Carr)*

Free house ~ Licensee Dave Trotter ~ Real ale ~ Meals and snacks (not Mon lunchtime) ~ Restaurant ~ (01229) 861229 ~ Children welcome until 8.30pm in bar and in family room ~ Open 12-2(3 Sat), 6-11; closed Mon lunchtime (exc bank holidays) ~ Bedrooms: /£30

Children welcome means the pub says it lets children inside without any special restriction. If it allows them in, but to restricted areas such as an eating area or family room, we specify this. Some pubs may impose an evening time limit.

BOWLAND BRIDGE SD4289 Map 9
Hare & Hounds 🍴

Village signposted from A5074; OS Sheet 97 map reference 417895

What sets this attractive white-painted inn above many others is the genuinely warm welcome and concern shown by the licensee, ex-international soccer player Peter Thompson. The comfortably modernised bar, divided into smaller areas by stone walls, has Liverpool and England team photographs and caps, oak beams, ladder-back chairs around dark wood tables on the spread of turkey carpet, reproduction hunting prints, a stuffed pheasant, and open fires. Bar food includes soup (£1.70), sandwiches (from £2.25), pizzas (from £4.25), ploughman's (£4.95), mushroom and vegetable stroganoff (£5.75), giant yorkshire pudding filled with cumberland sausage and onion gravy (£5.95), chicken in creamy white wine and tarragon sauce with asparagus tips and strips of ham (£6.50), poached swordfish steak with prawn sauce (£6.95), steaks (from £10.50), daily specials, 4-course Sunday roast lunch, and children's menu (£3.25); very good, prompt service. Well kept Tetleys and a weekly guest beer on handpump, and several malt whiskies from a long bar counter with a cushioned red leatherette elbow rest for people using the sensible backrest-type bar stools. Dominoes, video game, and piped music. The climbing roses, window boxes and hanging baskets are pretty in summer, and there are picnic tables in the spacious garden at one side, with more by the road. The pub is set by the bridge itself. *(Recommended by John Honnor, Mr and Dr J Harrop, Malcolm Taylor, P A Legon, A Lock, Mark Fennell, R D Knight, Chris Walling, Mrs R D Knight, Julie Peters, Colin Blinkhorn, Bill and Irene Morley, Beryl and Bill Farmer)*

Free house ~ Licensees Peter and Debbie Thompson ~ Real ale ~ Meals and snacks ~ Restaurant (residents only) ~ (015395) 68333 ~ Children welcome ~ Open 11-11; 11-10.30 Sun ~ bedrooms: £35B/£50B

BOWNESS ON WINDERMERE SD4097 Map 9
Hole in t' Wall 🍺

Lowside

Full of character and interest, this bustling pub, tucked away in a back street, is the sort of place where both locals and visitors mingle quite happily. The bar has lots to look at such as giant smith's bellows, old farm implements and ploughshares, and jugs hanging from the ceiling, and a room upstairs has handsome plasterwork in its coffered ceiling. On cool days a splendid log fire burns under a vast slate mantelbeam. The tiny flagstoned front courtyard (where there are sheltered seats) has an ancient outside flight of stone steps to the upper floor. Mrs Mitton decides what to cook each day once she gets into her kitchen. There might be sandwiches (from £2), vegetarian chilli or broccoli and cauliflower bake (£5.25), whisky chicken (£5.50), fish pie (£5.75), sirloin steak (£7.50), popular whole roast pheasant with red wine sauce (£7.65), and puddings like lemon meringue pie or fruit cake and cheese (£2). Hartleys XB and Robinsons Frederics, Best, Old Stockport, and Old Tom on handpump in excellent condition, home-made lemonade and very good mulled winter wine; darts, pool, fruit machine and juke box upstairs. If you'd rather catch it on a quiet day, it's better to visit out of season. *(Recommended by H K Dyson, SLC, Richard Lewis, Dr and Mrs A K Clarke, Alan Risdon, A Lock, Mike and Wendy Proctor, Mayur Shah, Ian and Gayle Woodhead, Miss K Law, K M Timmins, M Joyner, A R and B E Sayer, Val Stevenson, Rob Holmes, Joy and Peter Heatherley)*

Hartleys (Robinsons) ~ Tenants: Andrew and Audrey Mitton ~ Real ale ~ Meals and snacks (not Sun evening) ~ (015394) 43488 ~ Children in family room off taproom until 9pm ~ Live music Sun lunchtime and evening ~ Parking nearby can be difficult ~ Open 11-11; 12-10.30 Sun

---

Anyone claiming to arrange or prevent inclusion of a pub in the *Guide* is a fraud. Pubs are included only if recommended by genuine readers and if our own anonymous inspection confirms that they are suitable.

BRAITHWAITE NY2324 Map 9
Coledale Inn
Village signposted off A66 W of Keswick; pub then signed left off B5292

Walkers can start their hike straight from the door of this popular inn as it is perfectly placed at the foot of Whinlatter Pass. The left-hand bar has fine views of Skiddaw and the much closer bracken-covered hills from the window seats, a winter coal fire, and little 19th-c Lakeland engravings; the green-toned bar on the right, with a bigger bay window, is more of a dining bar. Bar food includes home-made soup (£1.65), lunchtime sandwiches (from £1.80), filled baked potatoes (from £3.30), platters (from £3.80), vegetarian chilli (£5.50), cumberland sausage (£5.85), gammon and egg (£6.30), sirloin steak (£8.90), and puddings with custard or cream (from £2.30); daily specials, and several children's dishes (£2). Well kept Jennings Bitter, Theakstons XB, Yates Bitter, and Youngers on handpump; darts, cribbage, dominoes, and piped music. The dining room is no smoking. The garden has tables and chairs on the slate terrace beyond the sheltered lawn, and a popular play area for children. *(Recommended by D and N Towle, Colin Draper, SLC, David Yandle, Maurice Thompson, IHR, Jason Caulkin, Ian and Gayle Woodhead, Roger Davey, SLC, Mike Beiley, P and M Rudlin)*

Free house ~ Licensees Geoffrey and Michael Mawdsley ~ Real ale ~ Meals and snacks ~ (017687) 78272 ~ Children welcome ~ Open 11-11; 12-10.30 Sun; closed Mon-Thurs winter weekdays until 6.30 ~ Bedrooms: £21.50S/£53S

BRAMPTON NY6723 Map 10
New Inn
Note: this is the small Brampton near Appleby, not the bigger one up by Carlisle. Off A66 N of Appleby – follow Long Marton 1 signpost then turn right at church; village also signposted off B6542 at N end of Appleby

In June, the Appleby Horse Fair tends to use this attractively traditional inn as its base, so things tend to get crowded then. It's popular at other times, too, and the two cosy little rooms have nice stripped and polished old pine benches with upholstered cushions and old pine tables, and are decorated with a good range of local pictures (mainly sheep and wildlife), a stuffed fox curled on top of the corner TV, and a red squirrel poking out of a little hole in the dividing wall. The particularly interesting flagstoned dining room has horsebrasses on its low black beams, well spaced tables, and a splendid original black cooking range at one end, separated from the door by an immensely sturdy old oak built-in settle. Good bar food includes lunchtime sandwiches (from £1.25; steak £2.95), home-made soup (£1.95), smoked fish hotpot (£3.20), pizzas (from £3.50), ploughman's (£3.75), home-made nut roast (£4.95), steak and kidney pie (£5.20), chicken and cheese crunch (£5.75), gammon and egg (£7.25), seafood gratinée (£6.95), sirloin steak (£8.30), and puddings (£2.20); 3-course Sunday lunch (£6.50; children £3). Well kept Boddingtons, Theakstons Best, and Youngers Scotch on handpump, and a good choice of whiskies with some eminent malts; friendly service, darts, dominoes and piped music. There are seats on the lawn and a barbecue area. Incidentally another Brampton near Chesterfield has a pub of the same name. *(Recommended by Maureen and Bryan Cully, Judith Hirst, Mr and Mrs R Ray, Richard Fallon, Val Stevenson, Rob Holmes, Richard Holloway, Roger Davey, David and Margaret Bloomfield, Beryl and Bill Farmer, Malcolm Taylor)*

Free house ~ Licensees Roger and Anne Cranswick ~ Real ale ~ Meals and snacks ~ Restaurant ~ (017683) 51231 ~ Children in eating area of bar until 9pm ~ Open 12-3, 6-11; 12-11 Sat and Sun (12-3, 6-11 winter Sat and Sun); closed 25 Dec ~ Bedrooms: £20/£40

Most of the big breweries now work through regional operating companies, with different names. If a pub is tied to one of these regional companies, we put the parent company's name in brackets – in the details at the end of each main entry.

nr BROUGHTON IN FURNESS SD2290 Map 9
Blacksmiths Arms
Broughton Mills; off A593 N

Tucked away in a charming hamlet in pretty countryside that's never too overrun with summer visitors, this small friendly pub dating from 1748 has been sensitively refurbished by hard-working new young licensees. They've retained and added to the attractively plain furnishings that go well with its ancient slate floors, and there are good log fires in both bars. Simple but enjoyable lunchtime food includes open sandwiches (from £2.25), ploughman's (from £3.25), steak and ale pie or lasagne (£4.95) and trout (£5.25). Evening dishes are more elaborate: devilled mushrooms (£2.95), pineapple prawns (£3.75), pork provençal (£4.95), Italian baked fish (£5.75), good steak diane, steak au poivre or steak with stilton and cream sauce (£8.25); puddings like apple or rhubarb crumble (£2.25) and ice cream sundaes (£2.75) are traditional; there are two smallish dining rooms. Well kept Theakstons Best and two guests like Gales HSB and Greene King IPA on handpump. We have not yet heard from people staying here, but would expect it to be a pleasant base for walkers. *(Recommended by Jack and Philip Paxton, Derek Harvey-Piper, RJH)*

Free house ~ Licensee Philip Blackburn ~ Real ale ~ Meals and snacks ~ (01229) 716824 ~ Children welcome ~ Open 12-11 (12 Sat); 12-10.30 Sun; cl 25 Dec

CARTMEL SD3879 Map 7
Cavendish Arms 🛏 🍺
Off main sq

Five more bedrooms have been added to this warmly welcoming and much enjoyed inn, and for those here on a walking break, the landlord will give advice and maps about the area. There's a happy, relaxed atmosphere, good popular bar food, and well kept real ales such as Bass, excellent Cartmel Lakeland Gold, Thoroughbred and Pride (brewed by Mr Murray's son), and various guest beers on handpump; a fair choice of malt whiskies. As well as sandwiches (from £3.25), light lunches include soup (£2.25), pasta with smoked salmon and prawns in a herb and cream sauce (£4.50), liver, bacon and onions or cumberland sausage with spicy apple sauce and onion gravy (£5.95), a hotpot topped with local black pudding (£6), steak in ale pie (£6.50), sirloin steak (£11.95), daily specials like vegetable stir-fry with sweet and sour sauce (£6.95), halibut with lemon butter (£11.50), and pheasant coated with blue cheese with a port wine sauce (£11.95); they still do Sunday roasts on the spit in the no-smoking restaurant; very helpful staff. There are tables in front of the pub, with more at the back by the stream, and their flower displays tend to win awards. *(Recommended by Peter Richards, JDM, KM, Jack and Gemima Valiant, E A George, SLC, Alan Risdon, David and Judy Walmsley, Mark Fennell, Phill and Elaine Wylie, Duncan Small, Jane Taylor, David Dutton, S P Watkin, P A Taylor, Stan and Hazel Allen, Marianne Jones, Ann Collins, Jack Morley, Mr and Mrs Gardner, Mike and Sue Walton, Ian and Nita Cooper, Ian Coburn, Joy and Peter Heatherley, Jim and Maggie Cowell, C Reed, Colin Partington, Karen Connolly, Chris and Andy Crow, G Davidson, J Gilbert)*

Free house ~ Tom and Howard Murray ~ Real ale ~ Meals and snacks (11-2.15, 6-9.30; all day Sun) ~ Restaurant ~ (015395) 36240 ~ Children welcome until 8.30pm ~ Open 11-11; 12-10.30 Sun ~ Bedrooms: £25B/£46B

CARTMEL FELL SD4288 Map 9
Masons Arms ★ 🍺
Strawberry Bank, a few miles S of Windermere between A592 and A5074; perhaps the simplest way of finding the pub is to go uphill W from Bowland Bridge (which is signposted off A5074) towards Newby Bridge and keep right then left at the staggered crossroads – it's then on your right, below Gummer's How; OS Sheet 97 map ref 413895

It's quite a feat that a pub that has been so popular for as long as this has, continues to draw such warmly enthusiastic reports from readers. The setting is lovely and the choice of beers quite extraordinary – as well as their own Strawberry Bank Brewery Neds Tipple, Blackbeck, Rulbuts and Damson Ale, they keep two guest beers, and several Belgian real ales on handpump, and a booklet clearly describes hundreds of bottled beers, most stocked and some even imported, which is now in its 17th edition and, considering its scale, is unique. You can be sure of finding some beers here that simply don't exist anywhere else in the country, and many of the beers have their own particular-shaped glasses. Carefully chosen mainly New World wines, too. Wholesome food (lots of vegetarian choices) includes soup (£2.75), sandwiches (from £3.75), hazelnut and lentil pâté or Morecambe Bay potted shrimps (£4.75), spicy vegetable burritos (£6.95), cumberland sausage casserole or fish pie (£7.95), home-made puddings like fruit cheesecake or toffee banoffi, and daily specials such as coronation chicken (£7), and thai green lamb curry or roast aubergine, sundried tomato and black olive quiche (£7.25). The main bar has low black beams in the bowed ceiling, country chairs and plain wooden tables on polished flagstones, and a grandly Gothick seat with snarling dogs as its arms. A small lounge has oak tables and settles to match its fine Jacobean panelling, and a plain little room beyond the serving counter has pictures and a fire in an open range; the family room has an old-parlourish atmosphere, and there's also an upstairs room which helps at peak times. From the terrace with rustic benches and tables is an unrivalled view overlooking the Winster Valley to the woods below Whitbarrow Scar. They sell leaflets outlining local walks of varying lengths and difficulty. As it's such a favourite with so many people, don't be surprised if the bar is extremely crowded; it's often much quieter mid-week. *(Recommended by Richard May, Arthur and Margaret Dickinson, Tina and David Woods-Taylor, JDM, KM, Alan Risdon, Andy and Jill Kassube, Phil and Heidi Cook, Richard Houghton, Malcolm Taylor, LM, John and Barbara Burns, Martin Hickes, David and Judy Walmsley, V W Prime, Wm Van Laaten, Hugh Roberts, Mark Fennell, S P Watkin, P A Taylor, Jack and Gemma Valiant, Jane Taylor, David Dutton, Mr and Mrs C Cole, Jim and Maggie Cowell, Nigel Woolliscroft, Ian and Gayle Woodhead, John Zeffertt, Paul McPherson, Mike Whitehouse, M J Morgan, Julie Peters, Colin Blinkhorn, Kim and Anne Schofield, John Andrew, Brian Wainwright, Mick Hitchman, N K Lawless, Jason Caulkin, Joy and Peter Heatherley, Bill and Irene Morley, Howard Gregory, John Allsopp, Carl Travis, R D Greatorex and family, H Dyson)*

Own brew ~ Licensee Helen Stevenson ~ Real ale ~ Meals and snacks (12-2, 6-8.45) ~ (015395) 68486 ~ Children welcome till 9 ~ Open 11.30-11; 12-10.30 Sun; 11.30-3, 6-11 winter Mon-Thurs; closed 25 Dec ~ Four s/c flats and two s/c cottages available

CHAPEL STILE NY3205 Map 9
Wainwrights

B5343

This white-rendered pub is now a free house. It is in a lovely spot for walkers, and there are picnic tables on the terrace with fine views. Inside, there's a relaxed and friendly atmosphere and plenty of room in the characterful slate-floored bar with its old kitchen range and cushioned settles. Good food includes home-made soup (£1.95), sandwiches (from £2.05), filled baked potatoes (£3.50), ploughman's or quiche (£5.20), cannelloni filled with spinach and ricotta cheese (£6.25), lamb shoulder with honey and mint (£7.25), children's dishes (£2.65), and daily specials; good, prompt service. The dining area is no smoking. Well kept Cartmel Lakeland Gold, and Jennings Bitter, Cumberland Ale, and Sneck Lifter on handpump; darts, dominoes, fruit machine, video game, trivia, and piped music. *(Recommended by Colin Draper, Suzanne and Steve Griffiths, Phil and Heidi Cook, Joy and Peter Heatherley, Mayur Shah, Howard Gregory; more reports please)*

Free house ~ Licensee Alan Hurst ~ Real ale ~ Meals and snacks ~ (015394) 38088 ~ Children welcome until 9.30 ~ Quiz night Tues evening ~ Open 11-11; 11-3, 6-11 winter weekdays; 12-10.30 Sun

---

If you see cars parked in the lane outside a country pub have left their lights on at night, leave yours on too: it's a sign that the police check up there.

COCKERMOUTH NY1231 Map 9
Bitter End ◀

15 Kirkgate

Standing derelict until recently, this has been transformed into an interestingly refurbished pub, attractive and lively. As in all the best town pubs, there's a different atmosphere in each of its three main rooms from quietly chatty to sporty, with the decor reflecting this – from unusual pictures of a Cockermouth that even Wordsworth might have recognised to more up-to-date sporting memorabilia. What now sets this apart from most pubs is the tiny Victorian style shop window view of the little brewery room behind the back room where the landlord brews Cockersnoot and Skinners Old Strong – you can see the equipment without even getting up from your seat and on the days when he's brewing the landlord leaves the door open and you can wander in for a chat. He also keeps Ind Coope Burton, Derwent Bitter and Mutineers Jennings and two guests like Maclays Heather ale or Yates Bitter on handpump, in good condition. A limited choice of decent generous bar food includes sandwiches (from £1.65), cumberland sausage (£3.95), chicken rogan josh (£4.25), chicken and leek pie or steak and mushroom pie (£4.50) and a daily special like sweet and sour chicken (£3.95). Service is very welcoming; piped music; the public car park round the back is free after 6. *(Recommended by A and R Lees, Richard Houghton, Ian and Gayle Woodhead, Mike Woodhead)*

Own brew ~ Licensee Mike Askey ~ Real ale ~ Meals and snacks (12-2, 5.30-8.30; 7-8.30 Sun) ~ (01900) 826626 ~ Children welcome at meal times ~ Open 11.30-2.30(3 Sat), 5.30-11; 12-3, 7-10.30 Sun

Trout ⇌

Crown St

A new front lobby and reception area and more bedrooms have been added to this solid 17th-c hotel. It's very much somewhere to come if you are interested in fishing and it's worth knowing that they have fishing rights on the River Derwent behind, holding fishing weekends for beginners from February to June. The comfortable and friendly bar has an open fire in the stone fireplace, low pink plush sofas and captain's chairs around dark polished tables, some patterned plates on the walls, and several pot plants; the coffee lounge (at lunchtime) and the restaurant are both no smoking. Well kept Jennings Cumberland, Marstons Pedigree, and Theakstons Best on handpump, over 50 malt whiskies, wines of the month, and freshly squeezed orange or grapefruit juices; piped music. Bar food includes home-made soup (£1.65), good sandwiches (from £2.35; hot beef butty £4.25), chicken liver and bacon terrine flavoured with brandy, pernod and spices (£3.15), a vegetarian dish (£5.50), cumberland sausage with apple sauce (£5.75), chicken madras (£6.55), beef in ale pie (£6.75), and sirloin steak (£9.25); courteous staff. In summer you can eat in the pretty gardens next to the river, and William Wordsworth's birthplace is next door. *(Recommended by IHR, RWD, Ann Bartlett; more reports please)*

Free house ~ Licensee Gill Blackah ~ Real ale ~ Meals and snacks (not 25 Dec) ~ Restaurant ~ (01900) 823591 ~ Children welcome ~ Open 10.30-3, 5.30-11; 11.30-3, 7-10.30 Sun ~ Bedrooms: £59.95B/£79.95B

CONISTON SD3098 Map 9
Black Bull ⇌ ◀

Yewdale Rd (A593)

Very popular with summer visitors, this former coaching inn has a good extensive layout to cope. The beamed and carpeted front part has cast-iron-framed tables, comfortable red banquettes and stools, and a relatively 'dressed up' style and atmosphere, while the cheerful back area has slate flagstones – so walkers (and dogs) are welcome here. There's quite a lot of Donald Campbell memorabilia, and they brew a beer on the premises named for his Bluebird. They also brew the stronger Coniston Old Man, and will happily give tours of their back brewhouse (they also keep Theakstons Old Peculier and a guest like locally brewed Peter Yeates Premium on handpump). Filling bar food, good if not cheap, includes sandwiches (from £2.50), filled baked potatoes (from £3.50), ploughman's (£5.50), cumberland sausage (£5.75), a spicy chilli con carne (£6.50), beef in red wine, steak and mushroom or chicken and mushroom pies, and half a dozen vegetarian or vegan dishes like vegetable moussaka (£6.95) and mixed grill (£9.95). Service is prompt and friendly even under pressure; unobtrusive piped music, often classical. There are tables out in the former coachyard, and the inn is well placed at the foot of the Old Man of Coniston. Parking may not be easy at peak times. *(Recommended by Mayur Shah, Alan Risdon, P J S Goward, Richard Lewis, JCW, SLC, V W Prime, Wm Van Laaten, Richard Houghton, Pamela and Merlyn Horswell)*

Own Brew ~ Licensee Mr Bradley ~ Real ale ~ Meals and snacks (all day) ~ Restaurant ~ (0153 94) 41335 ~ Children welcome in eating area of bar ~ Open 11-11; 12-10.30 Sun ~ Bedrooms: £37.50/£65B

CROSTHWAITE SD4491 Map 9
Punch Bowl 🍽 🍷

Village signposted off A5074 SE of Windermere

Cumbria Dining Pub of the Year

This idyllically placed 16th-c inn really is worth a special journey not just for the scrumptious food, but for the warm welcome from both the licensee and his friendly staff, the well kept real ales, and thoughtful wine list. There are several separate areas carefully reworked to give a lot of space, and a high-raftered central area by the serving counter with an upper minstrels' gallery on either side; several no-smoking areas. Steps lead down into a couple of small dimly lit rooms on the right, and there's a doorway through into two more airy rooms on the left. It's all spick and span, with lots of tables and chairs, beams, pictures, and an open fire. Given the fine quality, the food is very fairly priced, and might include tomato and basil soup with croutons (£2.25), pork terrine with pickle and chutney (£3.75), an interesting hors d'oeuvre plate (£5), seared tuna steak club sandwich with a spicy ginger Asian slaw (lunchtime, £6), courgette, red onion and aubergine tortino (£6.75), baked cod fillet on creamed spinach topped with a cheese sauce (£7.50), roasted fillet of lamb with a creamy thai curry sauce (£8.50), sirloin steak with a spicy herb butter (£8.95), and puddings like lemon tart, white chocolate truffle cake or orange and Grand Marnier crème brûlée (from £2.75); local and British cheeses (£3.50), and super Sunday lunch (two-course £9.25, three-course £11.25). Well kept Jennings Snecklifter, and Theakstons Best and Old Peculier on handpump. If they are very busy, all the eating areas are no smoking, otherwise there is one smoking area above the bar. There are some tables on a terrace stepped into the hillside. *(Recommended by Mr and Mrs A C Chapman, Malcolm Taylor, Peter Walker, Tina and David Woods-Taylor, John and Barbara Burns, Dr J Morley, Dr Stewart Rae, JDM, KM, Tim and Sue Halstead, RJH, Tony Hall, Melanie Jackson, Joan Yew, Revd and Mrs McFie, Brian and Ursula Kirby, Dr J R Norman, Margaret Dyke, A Preston)*

Free house ~ Licensee Steven Doherty ~ Real ale ~ Meals and snacks (12-2, 6-9) ~ (015395) 68237 ~ Children welcome ~ Open 12-3, 6-11; 12-3, 6-10.30 Sun; closed 25 Dec, evenings 26 Dec, 1 Jan ~ Bedrooms: £35B/£50B

DENT SD7187 Map 10
Sun ◖

Village signposted from Sedbergh; and from Barbon, off A683

The Dent Brewery, just a few miles up in the dale, supplies this pretty pub with its own real ales – and indeed, supplies other pubs all over the country with them: Bitter, T'Owd Tup, and Kamikazee Strong Ale on handpump. There's a pleasant, traditional atmosphere in the bar and fine old oak timbers and beams studded with coins, as well as dark armed chairs, brown leatherette wall benches, lots of local snapshots and old Schweppes advertisements on the walls, and a coal fire; one of the areas is no smoking. Through the arch to the left are banquettes upholstered to match the carpet (as do the curtains). Good value, straightforward bar food includes home-made soup (£1.70), sandwiches (£1.80), ploughman's (£3.95), home-made steak and kidney pie, cumberland sausage or vegetarian lasagne (£4.65), gammon and egg (£5.95), rump steak (£6.25), puddings (£1.90), children's helpings (£2.60), and nice breakfasts; prompt service. Darts, pool, bar billiards, dominoes, cribbage, fruit machine, video game, and juke box (in the pool room). There are rustic seats and tables outside and the surrounding fells are popular with walkers. *(Recommended by Derek and Sylvia Stephenson, Alan J Morton, Denis and Margaret Kilner, R H Rowley, Andy and Jill Kassube, David and Judy Walmsley, Alan Risdon, Dagmar Junghanns, Colin Keane, John Fazakerley, Paul McPherson, Angus Lyon)*

Own brew ~ Licensee Martin Stafford ~ Real ale ~ Meals and snacks ~ (015396) 25208 ~ Children in eating area of bar until 9pm ~ Open 11-11; 11-2, 7-11 in winter; 12-10.30 Sun; closed 25 Dec ~ Bedrooms: £19.50/£35

DOCKRAY NY3921 Map 9
Royal 🏨 ♀ 🍺
A5091, off A66 W of Penrith

William and Dorothy Wordsworth stayed in this carefully renovated and friendly little white inn and enjoyed the walks among the lovely surrounding low hills. The unusually spacious open-plan bar is comfortably plush with built-in bays of olive-green herringbone button-back banquettes, a spread of flowery pink and green carpet, and a woodburning stove. For walkers, an area of more traditional seating has stripped settles on flagstones, with darts, cribbage, and dominoes, and there are unusual leatherette-topped sewing-machine tables throughout. Two dining areas (one no smoking) spread beyond the bar, and good food includes nice daily specials such as fish pie (£6.50), roast local Herdwick mutton with garlic and rosemary (£6.75), medallions of venison with a blackcurrant sauce (£8.75), and monkfish in a coriander and vermouth sauce (£9.50); also, home-made soup (£2), lunchtime filled rolls (from £2.60), filled baked potatoes (from £2.85) or ploughman's (£4.75), omelettes (£5.50), home-made steak, kidney and mushroom pie (£6), grilled barnsley chop (£7.75), 8oz sirloin steak (£8.50), and puddings (£2.90); children's helpings (£3.25). Well kept Black Sheep, Boddingtons Bitter, Jennings Cumberland, Marstons Pedigree, Timothy Taylors Landlord, and Whitbreads Castle Eden on handpump, a decent range of malt whiskies, and good wines by the glass for this area; piped music and TV (which perhaps could be moved out of sight of the bar staff). As well as picnic tables on a tree-sheltered lawn, there is a landscaped garden and field areas with a pond. *(Recommended by T Loft, Timothy Galligan, Mark Fennell, Mr and Mrs W B Barnes, Mike Stokes, Kim and Anne Schofield, John Gay, F J and A Parmenter, Ewan and Aileen McEwan, Mike and Wendy Proctor, R and B Davies)*

Free house ~ Licensees James and Sarah Johnson ~ Real ale ~ Meals and snacks (12-2.30, 6-9.30) ~ Restaurant ~ (017684) 82356 ~ Children in eating area of bar and in restaurant ~ Open 11-11; 12-10.30 Sun ~ Bedrooms: £27B/£55B

ELTERWATER NY3305 Map 9
Britannia Inn ★ 🏨 🍺
Off B5343

No matter how busy this very friendly and unpretentious little pub is (and it does get packed at peak times), the staff always cope cheerfully and competently. The view over the village green from the chairs and slate-topped tables on the front terrace is much loved by readers, and the inn is obviously popular with walkers with so many tracks over the surrounding fells; walking boots are not barred. At the back is a small and traditionally furnished bar, while the front bar has winter coal fires and settles, oak benches, windsor chairs, a big old rocking chair, and a couple of window seats looking across to Elterwater itself through the trees on the far side; there's also a comfortable no-smoking lounge. Well kept Cartmel Lakeland Gold and Coniston Bluebird Bitter (both local micro breweries), Jennings Bitter, and two guest beers on handpump, quite a few malt whiskies, a well chosen, good value wine list, and country wines. Sturdy bar food includes filled rolls, home-made soup (£1.40), ploughman's, vegetable tikka masala or local trout (£6), home-made steak and mushroom pie (£6.50), evening extras like carrot and mushroom bake with tomato and basil coulis (£6), roast pork with crackling (£6.50) or sirloin steak (£8.50), and puddings such as home-made sticky toffee pudding or raspberry brûlée (£2.50); children's meals (£3.25), super breakfasts, and home-baked fruit scones for afternoon cream teas. The restaurant is no smoking; dominoes. In summer, people flock to watch Morris and Step and Garland Dancers. *(Recommended by V W Prime, Wm Van Laaten, Andy and Jill Kassube, Tina and David Woods-Taylor, Mr and Mrs Richard Osborne, David Carr, H K Dyson, Alan Risdon, Ewan and Moira McCall, Colin and Sue Graham, David Hoult, Sue and Bob Ward,   R and B Davies, Joy and Peter Heatherley, Graham and Karen Oddey, Jack Morley, Howard Gregory, Ian and Gayle Woodhead, Jason Caulkin, Michael and Alison Leyland, Vann and Terry Prime)*

Free house ~ Judith Fry and Julie Carmichael ~ Real ale ~ Meals and snacks (snacks are sold all afternoon) ~ Restaurant ~ (015394) 37210 ~ Children welcome until 9 ~ Summer parking may be difficult ~ Open 11-11; 12-10.30 Sun; closed 25 Dec and evening 26 Dec ~ Bedrooms: £24/£48(£62B)

ESKDALE GREEN NY1300 Map 9
Bower House 🛏

½ mile W of village towards Santon Bridge

The nicely tended sheltered garden here is a pleasant place to relax and on summer Sundays you can watch the cricket on the field alongside the pub. Inside, the lounge bar has a good winter log fire, cushioned settles and windsor chairs that blend in well with the original beamed and alcoved nucleus around the serving counter, and a quietly relaxed atmosphere – no noisy machines or piped music; also, a separate lounge with easy chairs and sofas. Decent bar food includes soup (£2), sandwiches (from £2), ploughman's (from £3.50), spicy bean casserole or cumberland sausage (£5.50), steak and kidney pie (£6.50), Aberdeen Angus sirloin steak (£9.95), daily specials, and home-made puddings (£2.50). Well kept Hartleys XB, Theakstons Best, and three changing real ales on handpump, a reasonably priced wine list, and summer Pimms and long cocktails; friendly staff; dominoes, shove-ha'penny, and table skittles. The restaurant and residents' lounge are no smoking. Some of the comfortable bedrooms are in the annexe across the garden. *(Recommended by Martin, Patricia and Hilary Forrest, Tina and David Woods-Taylor, Rob Holt, B J P Edwards, H K Dyson, R and S Bentley, Mayur Shah, Romey Heaton, B Eastwood, John Allsopp, Robert and Ann Lees, Dave Braisted)*

Free house ~ Licensees Derek and Beryl Connor ~ Real ale ~ Meals and snacks (12-2, 6.30-9.30) ~ Restaurant ~ (019467) 23244 ~ Children in eating area of bar ~ Open 11-11 ~ Bedrooms: £49B/£64B

GARRIGILL NY7441 Map 9
George & Dragon 🍺

Village signposted off B6277 S of Alston

Walkers have long known of this stonebuilt inn, part of a largely 17th-c terrace in a pretty village, as the Pennine Way passes the door. Inside on the right, the bar has a relaxed and cosy atmosphere, solid traditional furnishings on the very broad polished flagstones, and lovely stone fireplace with a really good log fire; there's a separate tartan-carpeted games room with sensibly placed darts, pool and dominoes; piped music. The friendly landlord's wife prepares the good value straightforward bar food, such as soup (£1.40), sandwiches (from £1.45), filled yorkshire pudding (from £1.75), filled baked potatoes (from £2.10), cumberland sausage and egg (£4.30), home-made steak pie (£4.60), broccoli and cream cheese bake (£4.75), and sirloin steak (£7.75); daily specials, and children's dishes (from £1.75). The dining room is no smoking. Well kept Boddingtons, Marstons Pedigree, and Whitbreads Castle Eden and Trophy on handpump. *(Recommended by John Fazakerley, GSB; more reports please)*

Free house ~ Licensees Brian and Jean Holmes ~ Real ale ~ Meals and snacks ~ Restaurant ~ (01434) 381293 ~ Children welcome ~ Open 12-4(3 in winter), 6.30(7 in winter)-11; 12-4, 7-10.30 Sun ~ Bedrooms: £15/£30(£37B), also very cheap small bunkhouse

GRASMERE NY3406 Map 9
Travellers Rest

Just N of Grasmere on A591 Ambleside—Keswick rd; OS sheet 90, map ref 335089

The refurbishments to this welcoming and deservedly popular little 16th-c pub have been praised by readers who are pleased that they have not spoilt its considerable character. It is in a lovely spot, surrounded by wonderful scenery and good walks, and from the picnic tables in the side garden, you can admire the marvellous views. The comfortable, beamed lounge bar has a relaxed atmosphere, a warming log fire, banquettes and cushioned wooden chairs around varnished wooden tables, and local watercolours and suggested walks and coast-to-coast information on the walls; piped classical music. The games room is popular with families: darts, pool, bar billiards, dominoes, fruit machine, and juke box. Bar food includes home-made soup (£1.95), sandwiches (from £2.45; open ones from £5.25), burger (£5.35), fish and chips with mushy peas (£5.75), ploughman's or steak and kidney pie (£5.95), pine nut and vegetable parcels (£6.25), cajun chicken (£6.95), chargrilled steaks (from £10.45), puddings (from £2.75), and a good children's menu (from 75p); the restaurant is no smoking. Well kept Jennings Bitter, Cumberland, Mild and Snecklifter, and Marstons Pedigree on handpump, and at least a dozen malt whiskies; friendly, efficient service. *(Recommended by David Carr, Dr A C Williams, Dr F M Ellard, V W Prime, Wm Van Laaten, SLC, Andy and Jill Kassube, Norman and Angela Harries, Mark Fennell, N J Lawless, Judith Erlandsen, Tim and Ann Newell, Tony Kemp, Rachel Weston, Phil and Heidi Cook, Sue Holland, David Webster, Dave Thompson, Margaret Mason, Roger and Pauline Pearce, R H Rowley, Helen Pickering, James Owen, Mr and Mrs J Watson, Graham and Karen Oddey, Jack Morley, Euan and Aileen McEwan, Tina and David Woods-Taylor, H K Dyson)*

Free house ~ Licensees Lynne, Derek and Graham Sweeney ~ Real ale ~ Meals and snacks (12-9.30 in summer; 12-3, 6-9.30) ~ (015394) 35604 ~ Children welcome ~ Open 11-11; 12-10.30 Sun ~ Bedrooms: £24.95(£27.95B)/£49.90(£54.90B)

nr HAWKSHEAD NY3501 Map 9
Drunken Duck ★ 🍺

Barngates; the hamlet is signposted from B5286 Hawkshead—Ambleside, opposite the Outgate Inn; or it may be quicker to take the first right from B5286, after the wooded caravan site; OS Sheet 90 map reference 350013

Barngates Brewery has just opened in the cellar of this friendly and very popular pub, and as we went to press they had just brewed their first beer, Cracker Ale (after the characterful Jack Russell who lived here for 17 years). They also keep Jennings Bitter and Cumberland, Mitchells Lancaster Bomber, Theakstons Old Peculier, and Yates Bitter on handpump; 60 malt whiskies. There are several cosy and traditionally pubby beamed rooms (one is no smoking) with good winter fires, tub chairs, cushioned old settles, blond pews, ladderback country chairs, and wheelbacks on the fitted turkey carpet, and maybe the multi-coloured cat. Around the walls are pictures, cartoons, cards, fox masks, and cases of fishing flies and lures; darts, dominoes, and cribbage. Good, interesting bar food includes lunchtime rolls (£2.50), ploughman's (£4.25), spicy bean nachos or mediterranean vegetable casserole (£5.50), pork casserole or chinese chicken (£6.50), chicken and mushroom pie (£6.95), and evening extras such as marinated chicken stir fry (£9.50), grilled fillet of salmon on niçoise salad (£9.75), and lamb rack on a herb potato cake with chasseur sauce and turned vegetables (£12.75). The no-smoking restaurant is now open to non residents. Seats on the front verandah look across to Lake Windermere in the distance; to the side there are quite a few rustic wooden chairs and tables, sheltered by a stone wall with alpine plants along its top, and the pub has fishing in a private tarn behind. *(Recommended by P H Roberts, Alastair Campbell, Tina and David Woods-*

Taylor, Jerry and Alison Oakes, Alan Risdon, V W Prime, Wm Van Laaten, Walter and Susan Rinaldi-Butcher, John Honnor, Dr J Morley, JDM, KM, Richard Houghton, SLC, Andy and Jill Kassube, JCW, Phil and Heidi Cook, Kim and Anne Schofield, Alan and Louise Duggan, Ian and Gayle Woodhead, Howard Gregory, Joy and Peter Heatherley, R and S Bentley, Mrs P Hare, Jack and Phillip Paxton)

Free house ~ Licensee Stephanie Barton ~ Real ale ~ Meals and snacks ~ (015394) 36347 ~ Children welcome ~ Occasional jazz or folk ~ Open 11.30-3, 6-11; 12-3, 7-10.30 Sun; closed evening 25 Dec ~ Bedrooms: £55B/£75B

HAWKSHEAD SD3598 Map 9
Kings Arms ⇐ ◀

This pretty old inn is a relaxed and chatty local with a traditional low-ceilinged bar, comfortable red-cushioned wall and window seats and red plush stools on the turkey carpet, and an open fire. Bar food includes sandwiches, and hot dishes like steak and mushroom pie, home-made lasagne and seafood fettucine (around £6); the restaurant is no smoking. Well kept Coniston Bluebird Bitter (from a local microbrewery), Greenalls Original, Tetleys, Theakstons XB and guest beers on handpump, and a fair choice of malt whiskies; summer cider. Darts, dominoes, cribbage, fruit machine, and piped pop music. Some of the bedrooms have coins embedded in the old oak beams. You can sit outside on the terrace and look over the central square of this lovely Elizabethan village. The village car park is some way away, but if you're staying at the inn, you'll get a free permit. *(Recommended by Colin Draper, SLC, Mark Fennell, M J Morgan, Val Stevenson, Rob Holmes, John Allsopp, Michael and Alison Leyland)*

Free house ~ Lease: Rosalie Johnson ~ Real ale ~ Meals and snacks (12-2.30, 6-9.30) ~ Restaurant ~ (015394) 36372 ~ Well behaved children welcome ~ Occasional live folk music/country & western ~ Open 11-11; 12-10.30 Sun; closed 25 Dec ~ Bedrooms: £30(£35B)/£50(£60B)

Queens Head

In the heart of the village is this lovely black and white timbered pub with its pretty summer window boxes. Inside, the bustling low-ceilinged bar has heavy bowed black beams, red plush wall seats and plush stools around heavy traditional tables, lots of decorative plates on the panelled walls, and an open fire; a snug little room leads off. Lunchtime bar food includes sandwiches (from £1.75), soup (£2.25), filled baked potatoes (from £2.75), home-made chicken liver pâté (£3.75), ploughman's (£5), game pie (£6.25), beef and mushroom pie in Guinness or cashew nut korma (£6.75), gammon with two eggs or baked cod in a parsley cream sauce (£7.75), and sirloin steak (£10.75); evening extras such as pot-roast pheasant (£9.25), saddle of lamb (£10.75), and half a Lunsdale duck with a sloe gin and berry sauce (£12.50); helpful staff. The restaurant is no smoking. Well kept Hartleys XB and Robinsons Bitter, Frederics, and Mild on handpump, and quite a few whiskies; dominoes, cribbage, and piped music. Walkers must take their boots off. *(Recommended by SLC, Alan Risdon, D Stokes, Val Stevenson, Rob Holmes, Kim and Anne Schofield, Vann and Terry Prime, John Waller, M J Morgan, Chris and Andy Crow, Mike and Heather Watson, Richard Lewis)*

Robinsons ~ Tenant Tony Merrick ~ Real ale ~ Meals and snacks (12-2.30, 6.15-9.30) ~ Restaurant ~ (015394) 36271 ~ Children in eating area of bar, restaurant, and snug ~ Open 11-11; 11-10.30 Sun ~ Bedrooms: £35(£45)/£56.50(£63B)

HEVERSHAM SD4983 Map 9
Blue Bell

A6 (now a relatively very quiet road here)

As this former vicarage is on a slight hill, it dominates the surrounding modest fields. It's civilised and comfortable and the lounge bar has bay windows, warm winter fires, pewter platters hanging from the beams, an antique carved settle, cushioned windsor armchairs and upholstered stools on the flowery carpet, and small antique sporting prints and a display cabinet with two stuffed fighting cocks on the partly panelled walls. One big bay-windowed area has been divided off as a children's room, and the long, tiled-floor public bar has darts, pool, cribbage, dominoes, fruit machine, and piped music. Good bar food based on fresh local produce includes sandwiches, home-made soup, lovely Morecambe Bay potted shrimps, filled giant yorkshire puddings (£5.95), local game casserole, roast breast of duck (£7.95), sirloin steak (£8.95), and puddings like sticky toffee pudding (£2.45). The restaurant is no smoking. Well kept Sam Smiths OB on handpump, several malt whiskies, a decent wine list, and their own cider; helpful staff. Crossing over the A6 into the village itself, you come to a picturesque church with a rambling little graveyard; if you walk through this and on to the hills beyond, there's a fine view across to the estuary of the River Kent. The estuary itself is a short walk from the pub down the country road that runs by its side. Pets welcome by arrangement. *(Recommended by Alan Risdon, S M Denbigh, SLC, Christopher Tobitt, Vann and Terry Prime, Enid and Henry Stephens, Mr and Mrs Greenhalgh, S L Clemens)*

Sam Smiths ~ Manager Richard Cowie ~ Real ale ~ Meals and snacks (11-9.30) ~ Restaurant ~ (015395) 62018 ~ Children welcome ~ Open 11-11 ~ Bedrooms: £39B/£64B

INGS SD4599 Map 9
Watermill 🛏 🍺
Just off A591 E of Windermere

An incredible range of 14 real ales are perfectly kept on handpump in this splendid pub – many from small local breweries: Black Sheep Special, Coniston Bluebird Bitter, Jennings Cumberland, Lees Moonraker, and Theakstons Best, Old Peculier and XB, with changing guests like Black Sheep Bitter, Cartmel Lakeland Gold, Dent Bitter, Hop Back Summer Lightning, Ind Coope Burton, Jennings Bitter, Marstons Pedigree, Moorhouses Black Cat Mild and Pendle Witches Brew, and Old Cottage Red Pyke; Old Rosie cider, bottled beers, and up to 50 malt whiskies; thirsty dogs are kindly catered for, too, with a biscuit and bowl of water. There's a friendly welcome from the chatty landlord and his staff and a bustling atmosphere – no noisy machines or juke box. The bars have a happy mix of chairs, padded benches and solid oak tables, bar counters made from old church wood, open fires, and amusing cartoons by a local artist on the wall; one room is no smoking as are some tables in the extension. The spacious lounge bar, in much the same traditional style as the other rooms, has rocking chairs and a big open fire. Bar food includes home-made soup (£1.75), lunchtime sandwiches (from £2), lunchtime ploughman's (£3.75; a huge one with soup £5.25), cumberland sausage (£4.75), lasagne (£5.20), various curries (£5.50), beef in ale or chicken, leek and bacon pie (£5.70), local grilled gammon (£6), lamb cutlets (£7.95), and steak (from £9.10). Darts, table skittles, dominoes, Jenga, and card games. There are seats in the front garden. Lots of climbing, fell-walking, fishing, boating of all kinds, swimming and pony-trekking within easy reach. *(Recommended by M Thompson, JDM, KM, Mark Fennell, SLC, Ian and Villy White, Dr J Morley, Andy and Jill Kassube, Colin Draper, R J Bland, Alan Risdon, V W Prime, Wm Van Laaten, John Scarisbrick, Richard Houghton, Jim and Maggie Cowell, Dick Brown, M Joyner, Paul Boot, William Harper, Julie Peters, Colin Blinkhorn, D R Shillitoe, Karen Eliot, Howard Gregory, David and Helen Wilkins, Jim and Maggie Cowell, Jack Morley)*

Free House ~ Licensees Alan and Brian Coulthwaite ~ Real ale ~ Meals and snacks (not 25 Dec) ~ (01539) 821309 ~ Children in lounge until 9pm ~ Story telling first Tues of month ~ Open 12-2.30, 6-11; 12-3, 6-10.30 Sun; closed 25 Dec ~ Bedrooms: /£45S

People don't usually tip bar staff (different in a really smart hotel, say). If you want to thank them – for dealing with a really large party say, or special friendliness – offer them a drink.

KIRKBY LONSDALE SD6278 Map 7

Snooty Fox

Main Street (B6254)

The food here is very good indeed, but that in no way detracts from this rambling inn's relaxed pubby atmosphere. At lunchtime there are plenty of shoppers and tourists, while the evening customers are aiming for a more restful meal. The various rooms are full of interest: mugs hanging from beams, eye-catching coloured engravings, stuffed wildfowl and falcons, mounted badger and fox masks, guns and a powder-flask, stage gladiator costumes, and horse-collars and stirrups. The bar counters are made from English oak, as is some panelling, and there are also country kitchen chairs, pews, one or two high-backed settles and marble-topped sewing-trestle tables on the flagstones, and two coal fires. Much liked home-made food includes soup with freshly baked walnut and apricot bread (£2), filled french bread (from £2.45), filled baked potatoes (from £2.25), warm mussel and bacon salad with anchovy dressing or caramelised onion and capsicum tart with home-made onion marmalade (£3.95), cumberland sausage with onion gravy (£5.50), steak and kidney pudding (£5.95), pasta with broccoli, sun-dried tomatoes, smoked bacon, mushrooms and clotted cream or thai-style chicken (£6.95), Loch Fyne salmon on a fresh ginger and spring onion butter sauce (£8.25), and Scottish sirloin steak with oyster mushrooms and cognac cream (£11.95); traditional Sunday lunch. The dining annexe is no smoking. Well kept Hartleys XB, Theakstons Best, and Timothy Taylors Landlord on handpump, several malt whiskies, and country wines; fruit machine and good juke box in back bar only; dominoes. There are tables out on a small terrace beside the biggish back cobbled stableyard, with more in a pretty garden; small play area for children. *(Recommended by Mrs J Kemp, Barnie, John Fazakerley, Jackie Laister, Paul Robinshaw, Roger and Lynda Goldstone, Paul and Sue Merrick, Richard Holloway, Ian and Gayle Woodhead, Neil Townend, R Hatton-Evans, Sue Holland, Dave Webster, Mr and Mrs French, Angus Lyon)*

Free house ~ Licensee Jack Shone ~ Real ale ~ Meals and snacks (till 10pm) ~ Restaurant ~ (015242) 71308 ~ Children in eating area of bar and in restaurant ~ Open 11-11; 12-10.30 Sun; closed evening 25 Dec ~ Bedrooms: £30B/£45B

Sun 🛏 🍺

Market St (B6254)

In quite a touristy town, it's a pleasure to find an enjoyable local atmosphere in this bustling and warmly friendly little pub. The rambling rooms have low beams, window seats, cosy pews, and good winter fires, and are filled with a collection of some 500 banknotes, maps, old engravings, and other interesting antiques on the walls – some of which are stripped to bare stone or have panelled dados. Very well kept Black Sheep Bitter, Boddingtons, Dent Bitter, and Youngers No 3 on handpump, and 50 malt whiskies; dominoes and piped music. Generous helpings of tasty bar food include home-made soup (£1.90), filled french bread (£3.85), devilled lamb kidneys (£4.65), feta cheese and spinach strudel (£5.40), pizzas with choose-your-own topping (from £5.45; take-away also), home-made steak and kidney or chicken, leek and cheese pies (£5.75), mixed grill (£7.60), and Aberdeen Angus rump steak (£8.70). Good personal service and super breakfasts. There's an unusual pillared porch; the steep cobbled alley is also attractive. Some of the bedrooms are in a stone barn with lovely views across the Barbon Fells. *(Recommended by Andy and Jill Kassube, Alan Risdon, Noel and Roni Flatley, John and Beryl Knight, Graham Prodger, Paul and Sue Merrick, Steve Calvert, Mr and Mrs R P Begg, Angus Lyon, Walter Oston, Sue Holland, Dave Webster)*

Free house ~ Licensee Andrew Wilkinson ~ Real ale ~ Meals and snacks (11-2, 6-10) ~ Restaurant ~ (015242) 71965 ~ Children welcome ~ Open 11-11; 12-10.30 Sun ~ Bedrooms: £22.50(£27.50B)/£44(£48B)

It's against the law for bar staff to smoke while handling food or drink.

LANERCOST NY5664 Map 9
Abbey Bridge Inn 🛏 🍴

Follow brown Lanercost Priory signs from A69 or in Brampton

After a visit to the great 12th-c priory just down the lane, it's well worth visiting this popular inn. The pub part is in a side building (formerly a smithy) with high pitched rafters and knobby whited stone walls, an understated rustic decor that includes charming Ashley Boon prints as well as a large woodburning stove, and a relaxed but rather stylish atmosphere. Enjoyable food includes sandwiches, good soup (£1.99), onion rings in beer batter with a dip (£2.95), potted brown shrimps (£3.75), home-made vegetable pie (£7.50), cajun chicken (£8.99), roast beef with yorkshire pudding (£9.99), Scottish salmon fillet with a prawn and cream sauce or rack of lamb (£10.99), and puddings like chocolate rumpots, home-made apple pie or ginger and lemon steamed pudding (from £2.45); it's normally served restaurant-style in a no-smoking gallery up spiral stairs. Well kept and well chosen real ales on handpump change every few days: Burton Bridge, Fullers Chiswick, Shepherd Neame and Yates, and other good drinks, such as the excellent Fentimans ginger beer and quite a few malt whiskies; welcoming service. Very faint piped pop music, chess, cribbage, and dominoes. There are a few seats outside, and the pub is set in lovely quiet off-the-beaten-track countryside. *(Recommended by David and Margaret Bloomfield, Bob and Marg Griffiths, Vann and Terry Prime, June and Tony Baldwin, Dave Thompson, Margaret Mason, D and J Tapper, Wayne A Wheeler; more reports please)*

Free house ~ Licensee Philip Sayers ~ Real ale ~ Meals and snacks ~ Evening restaurant ~ (016977) 2224 ~ Children welcome ~ Open 12-2.30, 7-11 (10.30 Sun); closed 25 Dec ~ Bedrooms: £22(£35B)/£50(£60B)

LANGDALE NY2906 Map 9
Old Dungeon Ghyll 🛏

B5343

This is the place to call after a day on the fells and it's always full of walkers and climbers who fit in well with the basic interior. It's at the heart of the Great Langdale Valley and surrounded by fells including the Langdale Pikes flanking the Dungeon Ghyll Force waterfall and there are grand views of the Pike of Blisco rising behind Kettle Crag from the window seats cut into the thick stone walls of the bar. Furnishings are very simple, and straightforward food includes lunchtime sandwiches (£2), filled baked potatoes (£3.25), home-made pizzas (£4.20), cumberland sausage (£5.25), chilli con carne (£5.75), puddings (£2.25), and children's meals (£3.25); if you are not a resident and want to eat in the restaurant you must book ahead. Well kept Jennings Cumberland and Mild, Theakstons XB and Old Peculier, Yates Bitter, and guest ales on handpump, and farm cider; darts, cribbage and dominoes. It can get really lively on a Saturday night (there's a popular National Trust campsite opposite). *(Recommended by R J Bland, H K Dyson, Tim Heywood, Sophie Wilne, G Oglanby, Ian and Gayle Woodhead, M Joyner, Michael and Alison Leyland, LM, Nigel Woolliscroft)*

Free house ~ Licensee Neil Walmsley ~ Real ale ~ Meals and snacks (12-2, 6-9) ~ Evening restaurant ~ (015394) 37272 ~ Children welcome ~ Open 11-11; 12-10.30 Sun; closed 23-26 Dec ~ Bedrooms: £31(£34.50B)/£62(£68B)

LEVENS SD4886 Map 7
Hare & Hounds

From A6 South, take A590 for Barrow, turn immediately right into village; from M6 junction 36 take A590 for Barrow and after 1½ miles turn right into village

Handy for Sizergh Castle, this attractive little village pub has a low-beamed lounge bar with antique settles and a wicker-backed Jacobean-style armchair on its sloping floor, and old-fashioned brown leatherette dining seats and red-cushioned seats built into the partly panelled walls. There's also a brief history of the pub and its licensees dating back to 1714. The snug front taproom has an open coal fire and darts, cribbage and dominoes; the juke box and fruit machine are in the separate pool room, down some steps. Bar food includes home-made soup (£1.70), lunchtime sandwiches (from £1.90; toasties from £2.10), filled baked potatoes (from £3.20), cumberland sausage or home-made steak and kidney pie (£5.25), gammon and egg (£6.95), sirloin steak (£8.95), daily specials, a vegetarian dish, and puddings (from £2.20); part of the lounge is no smoking during meal times. Well kept Vaux Samson and Wards Thorne on handpump, and several malt whiskies; friendly service. Outside there is a terrace with nice views of the local fells and Kent estuary. *(Recommended by IHR, Andy and Jill Kassube, Howard Gregory)*

Vaux ~ Tenants Colin and Sheila Burrow ~ Real ale ~ Meals and snacks ~ Restaurant ~ (015395) 60408 ~ Children in eating area of bar if eating and must be gone by 9 ~ Open 11-3, 6-11; 12-3, 6-10.30 Sun

LITTLE LANGDALE NY3204 Map 9
Three Shires 🛏

From A593 3 miles W of Ambleside take small road signposted The Langdales, Wrynose Pass; then bear left at first fork

You can relax after a long walk at seats on the terrace here and there are more on a well kept lawn behind the car park, backed by a small oak wood; the views over the valley to the partly wooded hills below Tilberthwaite Fells are lovely. Inside, the comfortably extended back bar has antique oak carved settles, country kitchen chairs and stools on its big dark slate flagstones, stripped timbers and a beam-and-joist stripped ceiling, Lakeland photographs lining the walls, and a warm winter fire in the modern stone fireplace with a couple of recesses for ornaments; an arch leads through to a small, additional area. Tasty bar food includes soup (£2), lunchtime sandwiches (from £2.25), filled baked potatoes (£3.75), chicken liver pâté (£3.50), ploughman's (£4.75), good cumberland sausage (£5.75), pie of the day (£6), evening dishes such as salmon with steamed leek and ginger and an orange butter sauce (£7.50), pork steaks with a cider, apple and mustard sauce (£7.25), and confit of duck (£9); home-made puddings (£2.75) and children's meals (£3). The restaurant and snug are no smoking. Well kept Black Sheep Bitter, Coniston Old Man, Marstons Pedigree, Morlands Old Speckled Hen, Ruddles County, and Websters Yorkshire on handpump, and quite a few malt whiskies and wines; darts, cribbage and dominoes. The three shires are Cumberland, Westmorland and Lancashire, which used to meet at the top of the nearby Wrynose Pass. *(Recommended by David Carr, JDM, KM, Philip and Ann Falkner, Julie Peters, Malcolm Taylor, Tina and David Woods-Taylor, Colin Blinkhorn, Michael and Alison Leyland, Phil and Heidi Cook, Chris and Andy Crow, Anthony Barnes, Jack Morley, Steve Playle, H K Dyson)*

Free house ~ Licensee Ian Stephenson ~ Real ale ~ Meals and snacks (no evening food Dec/Jan) ~ Evening restaurant ~ (015394) 37215 ~ Children welcome until 9pm ~ Open 11-11; 11-3, 8-10.30 Dec/Jan; 12-10.30 Sun; closed 25 Dec ~ Bedrooms: £35B/£64B

LOWESWATER NY1222 Map 9
Kirkstile

From B5289 follow signs to Loweswater Lake; OS Sheet 89, map reference 140210

Between Loweswater and Crummock Water, this friendly little pub is a haven for walkers and there's plenty of room for wet boots and gear – and a roaring log fire to dry in front of. From the picnic tables on the lawn and from the very attractive covered verandah, there are views of the spectacular surrounding peaks and soaring fells. The bar is low-beamed and carpeted, with comfortably cushioned small settles and pews, and partly stripped stone walls; from the bow windows in one of the rooms off the bar are more lovely views. Decent bar food includes sandwiches or rolls (from £2.25), filled baked potatoes (from £3.25), ploughman's (£4.95), fruit and vegetable curry (£5.25), mixed omelette (£5.50), cumberland sausage (£5.95), sirloin steak (£9.75), daily specials like steak and kidney pie or barbecue chicken (£5.95), and giant yorkshire pudding with beef stew (£6.50), puddings like jam roly poly or banoffi pie (£2.60), children's menu (from £2.80), and afternoon tea with home-made scones and cakes (from 95p); big breakfasts. Well kept Jennings Bitter and Cocker Hoop on handpump, and several malt whiskies; darts, cribbage, dominoes, and a slate shove-ha'penny board; a side games room called the Little Barn has pool, fruit machine, video game and juke box. *(Recommended by John Honnor, William Cunliffe, Peter Walker, Nick and Meriel Cox, N J Lawless, Andy and Jill Kassube, John and Christine Lowe, Simon Watkins, David Hoult, H K Dyson, Jack Morley, John Allsopp, A Preston, Enid and Henry Stephens, Chris Rounthwaite, Michael and Alison Leyland)*

Free house ~ Licensees Ken and Shirley Gorley ~ Real ale ~ Meals and snacks (12-9) ~ Restaurant ~ (01900) 85219 ~ Children welcome ~ Open 11-11; 12-10.30 Sun ~ Bedrooms: £35(£45B)/£45(£55B)

MELMERBY NY6237 Map 10
Shepherds ★ ⓎⒾ ♀
About half way along A686 Penrith—Alston

It's always heartening to come across a pub that remains consistently popular – as this bustling place does. For many people, this is their favourite Lakeland pub and the hard-working and friendly staff continue to provide most enjoyable food and well kept beer. Using fresh local produce, there is now a menu of the week: soups like spicy tomato or lamb and vegetable (£1.80), stilton and mushroom macaroni (£3.20), chicken and ham cobbler (£5.80), catfish with cajun spices (£6), lamb and apricot lattice pie (£6.20), pork with a mushroom and ginger sauce (£7.20), half a roast duckling with kumquat sauce (£8.80), and steaks (from £10.50); they still have their fine range of cheeses – 11 North Country and 6 other English cheeses (£4.80 with home-made granary and white rolls and locally made pickles, chutneys and mustards), and favourites such as cumberland sausage hotpot (£5.50), lovely barbecued spare ribs (£6.90), chicken leoni (£7.20), very good venison and roquefort crumble (£7.90), and puddings (£2.40); half helpings for children. Much of the main eating area is no smoking. Well kept Badger Tanglefoot, Black Sheep Bitter, Holts Bitter, Jennings Cumberland, and Shepherd Neame Spitfire on handpump, as well as 56 malt whiskies, a good wine list, country wines, and quite a few bottled continental beers. The bar is divided up into several areas; the heavy beamed no-smoking room to the left of the door is carpeted and comfortable with bottles on the mantelbeam over the warm open fire, sunny window seats, and sensible tables and chairs, and to the right is a stone-floored drinking part with a few plush bar stools and chairs. At the end is a spacious room with a high-raftered ceiling and pine tables and farmhouse chairs, a woodburning stove, and big wrought-iron candelabra, and steps up to a games area with pool and darts; shove-ha'penny, dominoes, fruit machine and juke box. Hartside Nursery Garden, a noted alpine and primula plant specialist, is just over the Hartside Pass, and there are fine views across the green to the Pennines. *(Recommended by Andy and Jill Kassube, Richard Holloway, Malcolm Taylor, Jerry and Alison Oakes, Mr Miller, David Carr, Nick and Meriel Cox, F J Robinson, Peter Richards, Bob and Marg Griffiths, June and Tony Baldwin, William Wright and family, William and Edward Stapley, Graham and Karen Oddey, Dick Brown, SS, John Prescott, Paul Cornock)*

Free house ~ Licensees Martin and Christine Baucutt ~ Real ale ~ Meals and snacks (11-2.30, 6-9.45) ~ (01768) 881217 ~ Children welcome away from bar until 9 ~ Folk music every 2 weeks, Fri evenings ~ Open 10.30-11; 10.30-3, 6-11 in winter; 12-3, 7-10.30 Sun; closed 25 Dec ~ Several holiday cottages

NEAR SAWREY SD3796 Map 9
Tower Bank Arms ◖
B5285 towards the Windermere ferry

At peak times, this bustling pub does get very busy as it backs on to Beatrix Potter's Hill Top Farm (owned by the National Trust). The low-beamed main bar has a fine log fire in the big cooking range, high-backed settles on the rough slate floor, local hunting photographs and signed photographs of celebrities on the walls, a grandfather clock, and good traditional atmosphere. Lunchtime bar food includes home-made soup (£1.95), filled rolls (from £2.40), ploughman's (from £3.95), home-made cheese and onion flan (£4.95), and a home-made pie of the day or stilton and pork sausage (£5.25); more substantial evening main meals such as local trout (£6.90), grilled gammon and eggs (£7), duckling (£7.25), and puddings. Well kept Theakstons Best and Old Peculier and weekly changing guest beers on handpump, as well as 28 malt whiskies, and Belgian fruit beers and other foreign beers; darts, shove-ha'penny, cribbage, dominoes, backgammon, and shut-the-box. Seats outside have pleasant views of the wooded Claife Heights. This is a good area for golf, sailing, birdwatching, fishing (they have a license for two rods a day on selected waters in the area), and walking, but if you want to stay at the pub, you'll have to book well in advance. *(Recommended by JDM, KM, Jacquie Kirk, Dr J Morley, Colin Draper, R and S Bentley, R Hatton-Evans, Brian and Anna Marsden, Vann and Terry Prime)*

Free house ~ Licensee Philip Broadley ~ Real ale ~ Meals and lunchtime snacks (not 25 Dec) ~ Restaurant ~ (015394) 36334 ~ Children in eating area of bar at lunchtime, in restaurant in evening ~ Open 11-3, 5.30(6 in winter)-11; 12-3, 5.30-11 Sun; closed evening 25 Dec ~ Bedrooms: £33B/£45B

SCALES NY3427 Map 9
White Horse

A66 1½ miles NE of Threlkeld: keep your eyes skinned – it looks like a farmhouse up on a slope

In a lovely dramatic setting under Blencathra, this isolated old farmhouse is neatly kept and cosy, and the little no-smoking snug and no-smoking old kitchen have all sorts of farming implements such as a marmalade slicer, butter churns, kettles, and a black range. The comfortable beamed bar has warm winter fires, hunting pictures and local hunting cartoons on the walls. Good, carefully presented bar food at lunchtime includes home-made soup (£1.95), chicken liver pâté (£3.95), cheese omelette or ploughman's (£4.50), ratatouille with melted cheese (£4.95), Waberthwaite sausage with pickled red cabbage (£5.50), daily specials, and sticky toffee pudding or chocolate terrine (from £2.25); evening dishes such as grilled black pudding with whisky and mustard sauce (£2.75), cured Waberthwaite ham (£3.85), chicken with sherry, peppers, cream and almonds (£7.70), roast duckling (£8.50), and sirloin steak (£9.90). Well kept Hesket Newmarket Blencathra Bitter and Skiddaw Special Bitter, Jennings Bitter, and Yates Bitter on handpump; no noisy games machines though they may have piped music. From the cluster of pub and farm buildings, tracks lead up into the splendidly daunting and rocky fells with names like Foule Crag and Sharp Edge. *(Recommended by David and Judy Walmsley, Elizabeth Barraclough, Dorothy Hind, Ann and Frank Bowman, N H White, L Dixon, Tina and David Woods-Taylor, C A Hall, R J and A Parmenter, Paul Bailey, H K Dyson)*

Free house ~ Licensee Bruce Jackson ~ Real ale ~ Meals and snacks (not Mon) ~ (017687) 79241 ~ Well behaved children over 5 welcome ~ Open 12-2.30, 6.45-11; closed Mon Nov-Easter

SEATHWAITE SD2396 Map 9
Newfield

Duddon Valley, nr Ulpha (ie not Seathwaite in Borrowdale)

The slate-floored bar still manages to keep a relaxed and genuinely local atmosphere, even when this cottagey 16th-c inn is full of walkers and climbers; there's a comfortable side room and a games room with pool, darts, and dominoes. Good value bar food (they tell us prices have not changed since last year) includes filled granary french bread or proper home-made soup (£1.75), big cumberland sausages (£4.95), home-made steak pie or a vegetarian dish (from £4.95), huge gammon steaks with local farm eggs (£6.50), and good steaks; the restaurant is no smoking. Well kept Theakstons Best, XB and Old Peculier and a guest such as Marstons

Pedigree or Morlands Old Speckled Hen on handpump, and several Polish vodkas and malt whiskies; good service. Tables out in the nice garden have good hill views. The pub owns and lets the next-door cottages. *(Recommended by Derek Harvey-Piper, J Hibberd, Romey Heaton, LM, H K Dyson, Jack Morley)*

Free house ~ Licensee Chris Burgess ~ Real ale ~ Meals and snacks ~ Restaurant ~ (01229) 716208 ~ Well behaved children welcome ~ Open 11-3, 6-11; 11-11 Sat; 12-10.30 Sun ~ S/c flats available

SEDBERGH SD6692 Map 10
Dalesman 🛏

Main St

There's quite a mix of decorations and styles in this nicely modernised old pub. Lots of stripped stone and beams, cushioned farmhouse chairs and stools around dimpled copper tables, and a raised stone hearth with a log-effect gas fire; also, horsebrasses and spigots, Vernon Stokes gundog pictures, various stuffed animals including a badger and a greater spotted woodpecker, tropical fish, and a blunderbuss. Through stone arches on the right a no-smoking buttery area serves good value lunchtime food such as home-made soup (£1), filled rolls (from £1.20; grilled bacon and egg £1.70, steak and onions £3.95), lots of filled baked potatoes (from £2.50), breakfast (£2.95), and lasagne (£4); a more substantial menu offers spare ribs (£3.50), ploughman's (£4.50), home-made cumberland sausage with two eggs (£4.95), vegetable lasagne (£5.25), three-egg omelettes (£5.50), local trout (£6.95), local venison casserole (£6.75), Aberdeen Angus sirloin steak (£9.25), daily specials, puddings, Sunday lunch (£4.95), and children's menu (from £2.50); friendly, helpful service. Well kept Tetleys Bitter and Theakstons Best on handpump; dominoes, fruit machine, and piped music. There are some picnic tables out in front; small car park. *(Recommended by David Warrellow, John Fazakerley, Paul McPherson, Addie and Irene Henry; more reports please)*

Free house ~ Licensee Michael Garnett ~ Real ale ~ Meals and snacks (12-2.30, 5.30-9.30) ~ Restaurant ~ (015396) 21183 ~ Children in eating area of bar ~ Open 11-11; 11-3, 6-11 in winter ~ Bedrooms: £25S/£50B

STAINTON NY4928 Map 10
Kings Arms

1¾ miles from M6 junction 40: village signposted from A66 towards Keswick, though quickest to fork left at A592 roundabout then turn first right

Although the open-plan bar in this pleasant, modernised old pub is quite roomy, it still has rather a cosy feel. There are leatherette wall banquettes, stools and armchairs, wood-effect tables, brasses on the black beams, and prints and paintings of the Lake District on the swirly cream walls. Enjoyable traditional bar food (with prices unchanged since last year) includes home-made soup (£1.35), sandwiches (from £1.80; toasties from £1.95), filled baked potatoes (from £3.30), cumberland sausage with egg (£4.20), home-made steak and kidney pie (£4.70), breast of chicken with sage and onion stuffing (£5.10), vegetable lasagne (£5.80), sirloin steak (£9.45), puddings (from £1.70), children's dishes (£2.50), and daily specials (from £3.75). Well kept Whitbreads Castle Eden and summer guest beers on handpump, and friendly service. Sensibly placed darts, dominoes, and fruit machine, and general knowledge quiz every second Friday (May-end September). There are tables outside on the side terrace and a small lawn. *(Recommended by IHR, Jenny and Roger Huggins, B J P Edwards, Colin Draper, Alan Risdon, Roger Bellingham, Anthony Barnes, Roger and Pauline Pearce, Mike and Wendy Proctor)*

Whitbreads ~ Tenants James and Anne Downie ~ Real ale ~ Meals and snacks (not 24-25 Dec, not 1 Jan) ~ (01768) 862778 ~ Children in eating area of bar until 9pm ~ Open 11.30-3, 6.30(6 Sat)-11.30; 11.30-3, 7-11 in winter; 11.30-3, 6.30-10.30 Sun; closed winter Mon lunchtime

THRELKELD NY3325 Map 9
Salutation

Old main rd, bypassed by A66 W of Penrith

Walkers are fond of this friendly and unpretentious little village local and the tiled floor is used to muddy boots. There's a good atmosphere, a roaring log fire and simple furnishings in the low-beamed connecting rooms, and Courage Directors, Marstons Pedigree and Theakstons Best and XB on handpump. Appetising home-made bar food includes sandwiches (from £2), soup (£2.25), basket meals (from £3.50), large ploughman's (from £4.75), meaty or vegetarian lasagne, steak and mushroom pie, local trout or hungarian goulash (all £5.45), steaks (from £10.85), daily specials, and puddings like rum and raisin sponge with cream rum sauce or sticky toffee pudding (£2.65). The spacious upstairs children's room has a pool table and juke box (oldies); also, cribbage, dominoes, video game and piped music. The owners let a couple of holiday cottages in the village. *(Recommended by David and Margaret Bloomfield, Bob and Marg Griffiths, T M Dobby, Maurice Thompson, IHR, J W Jones, H K Dyson, Mike and Wendy Proctor, S L Clemens)*

S & N ~ Tenants Ken and Rose Burchill ~ Real ale ~ Meals and snacks (not 25 Dec) ~ (017687) 79614 ~ Children welcome ~ Open 11-3, 5.30-11; 12-2, 6-11 in winter; 12-3, 6.30-10.30 Sun

TIRRIL NY5126 Map 10
Queens Head 🍴 🛏

3½ miles from M6 junction 40; take A66 towards Brough, A6 towards Shap, then B5320 towards Ullswater

New licensees have taken over this popular inn and tell us they are trying to change the focus back to that of a local pub rather than a more tourist-oriented restaurant. They will expose the original flagstones and floorboards in the bar (and the parquet floor in the restaurant), have done some redecorating and tidied up the back bar, and aim to upgrade the bedrooms. The oldest parts of the bar have low bare beams, black panelling, high-backed settles, and a roomy inglenook fireplace (once a cupboard for smoking hams); piped music. At lunchtime they now offer snacks and OAP specials: sandwiches (from £2.25; not Sunday lunchtime), garlic mushrooms and pâté (around £2.75), filled baked potatoes (from £2.95), OAP lunches (£3.50), ploughman's (from £4.25), and lasagne, cumberland sausage, curries and chilli (from £4.95). Also, home-made soup (£2.25), pasta dishes like thai noodles or spaghetti carbonara (starter £3, main course £5.95), smoked salmon mousse (£3.25), home-made pie (£5.95), mixed nut loaf (£7.25), swordfish in a cream and dijon mustard sauce (£8.75), steaks (from £9.95), fillet of ostrich in a creamy pepper sauce (£14.95), daily specials, and puddings like home-made apple pie or sticky toffee pudding (£2.50); most of the restaurant is no smoking. Well kept Theakstons Best and XB and guests like Black Sheep Bitter, Bushy's Best Bitter, Greene King Sorcerer, Hesket Newmarket Doris's 90th Birthday Ale on handpump, and quite a few malt whiskies; darts, pool, and dominoes in the back bar. The pub is very close to a number of interesting places, such as Dalemain House at Dacre. *(Recommended by June and Tony Baldwin, Malcolm Taylor, Peter and Ann Mumford, D Knott, Ewan and Moira McCall, Neville Kenyon, Kevin Thorpe, Alan Risdon, Bob and Marg Griffiths, Keith Kelly, John Waller, Tina and David Woods-Taylor, David Heath, Mike and Wendy Proctor, H K Dyson, John and Phyllis Maloney)*

Free house ~ Licensees Chris and Jo Tomlinson ~ Real ale ~ Meals and snacks ~ Restaurant ~ (01768) 863219 ~ Children welcome ~ Open 11-3, 6-11; 11-11 Sat; 12-10.30 Sun ~ Bedrooms: £32B/£42B

> Though we don't usually mention it in the text, most pubs will now make coffee – always worth asking. And many – particularly in the North – will do tea.

TROUBECK NY4103 Map 9

Mortal Man

Upper Rd, nr High Green – OS Sheet 90, map ref 411035

Surrounded by marvellous scenery, this spotlessly kept inn has a partly-panelled bar with a big roaring fire, a nice medley of seats including a cushioned settle and some farmhouse chairs around copper-topped tables, horsebrasses on its dark beams, and no piped music; there's also a small, cosy lounge. Good bar food includes lunchtime sandwiches, home-made soup (£2.25), chicken liver pâté (£3.50), vegetable sausages with tomato and basil sauce (£5.50), baked cumberland sausage with red onion gravy or local trout (£6), beef in ale pie (£6.50), roast rack of lamb with rosemary gravy (£8), Aberdeen Angus fillet steak (£12), and puddings (£2.75). The restaurant, with its big picture windows, is no smoking. Well kept Theakstons Best and S & N related guest beers on handpump; darts and dominoes. Walkers' boots must be left outside. *(Recommended by Pat Bruce, Alan Risdon, RJH, JDM, KM, Kim and Anne Schofield, A Preston, H K Dyson)*

Free house ~ Licensee Christopher Poulsom ~ Real ale ~ Meals and snacks (not Mon evening) ~ Restaurant ~ (015394) 33193 ~ Children in eating area of bar if over 5 ~ Open 12-2.30, 5.30-11; 12-2.30, 7-10.30 Sun; closed Jan/Feb ~ Bedrooms: £39B/£74B

Queens Head ★ ⊕ ⇌

A592 N of Windermere

A massive Elizabethan four-poster bed is the basis of the serving counter in this very popular 17th-c coaching inn, and there's also some other fine antique carving, cushioned antique settles among more orthodox furniture, and two roaring log fires in imposing fireplaces. The bar rambles through some half-dozen attractively decorated rooms, including an unusual lower gallery, a comfortable dining area and lots of alcoves and heavy beams; two areas are no smoking. Beautifully presented, imaginative bar food includes lunchtime filled french bread (from £2.75) and a light lunch special such as scallops of beef liver with an onion ragout (£4.95), and home-made carrot and coriander soup with home-made bread (£1.95), home-made muffins with honey and topped with seared chicken livers edged with raspberry dressing (£4.95), broccoli roulade with cream cheese and peppers on a saffron sauce (£6.95), fillet of salmon marinated in ginger, orange juice and soya sauce (£8.95), medallions of pork with black pudding on a compote of apples with a grain mustard sauce (£10.25), and puddings such as pineapple fritter in a cinnamon batter with honey ice cream (£2.95); there will be a wait at busy times. Well kept Boddingtons, Cartmel Lakeland Gold, Coniston Old Man, Jennings Bitter, Mitchells Lancaster Bomber, and Tetleys on handpump. Darts, dominoes, and piped music. Plenty of seats outside have a fine view over the Trout valley to Applethwaite moors. The bedrooms over the bar can be a bit noisy. *(Recommended by Brian and Anna Marsden, Mr and Mrs A G Leece, JDM, KM, David Carr, Andrew Shore, S P Watkin, P A Taylor, John and Christine Lowe, Mark Fennell, Tina and David Woods-Taylor, Phil and Heidi Cook, Mr and Mrs R Osborne, G Oglanby, Mr and Mrs D Wilson, Mike Woodhead, H K Dyson, David and Judy Walmsley, Ewan and Moira McCall, Vann and Terry Prime, John Waller, A Preston, Paul Boot, Mick Hitchman, LM, Roger and Pauline Pearce, Darrell and Frances Kemp, R and B Davies, Carl Travis, Walker and Debra Lapthorne, C and G Fraser, Ian Morley, Dene Caton, Gwen and Steve Walker, Mike Beiley)*

Free house ~ Licensees Mark Stewardson and Joanne Sherratt ~ Real ale ~ Meals and snacks ~ Restaurant ~ (015394) 32174 ~ Children welcome ~ Open 11-11; 12-10.30 Sun; closed 25 Dec ~ Bedrooms: £40B/£60B

ULVERSTON SD2978 Map 7

Bay Horse ⊕ ♀

Canal Foot signposted off A590 and then you wend your way past the huge Glaxo factory

The imaginative and beautifully presented food continues to draw people to this very well run and civilised hotel, once a staging post for coaches crossing the sands of Morecambe Bay to Lancaster. In the bar, food is served at lunchtime only and might include sandwiches (£1.75), home-made soup (£2.50), home-made herb and cheese pâté or savoury terrine with cranberry and ginger purée (£5.50), slices of aubergine, courgette, tomato and basil in a savoury egg custard with emmenthal cheese (£7.75), baked haggis, black pudding and apple rings on a grain mustard cream sauce (£7.95), flakes of smoked haddock in a rich cheddar cheese and mustard sauce with a savoury breadcrumb topping, strips of chicken, leeks and button mushrooms on savoury rice with a sweet and sour sauce or braised lamb, apricot and ginger pie (£8.25), and puddings like tipsy trifle or chocolate shortbread tartlet (£3.95). There's also the grill with well hung Scotch steaks, and a no-smoking conservatory restaurant (with exceptional views across to Morecambe Bay, and where bookings are essential). Well kept Boddingtons, Mitchells Lancaster Bomber, and Morlands Old Speckled Hen on handpump, a decent choice of spirits, and a carefully chosen and interesting wine list. The bar has a relaxed atmosphere and a huge stone horse's head, as well as attractive wooden armchairs, some pale green plush built-in wall banquettes, glossy hardwood traditional tables, blue plates on a delft shelf, and black beams and props with lots of horsebrasses. Magazines are dotted about, there's a handsomely marbled green granite fireplace, and decently reproduced piped music; darts, bar billiards, shove-ha'penny, cribbage and dominoes. Out on the terrace are some picnic tables. They hold friendly and informal day cookery demonstrations in March. The owners also run a very good restaurant at their Miller Howe hotel on Windermere. The fact that they now call themselves the Bay Horse Hotel and Restaurant underlines how far they've moved upmarket. *(Recommended by David Carr, R Gorick, Dr B Williams, Derek Harvey-Piper, JDM, KM, Mick Hitchman, Neville Kenyon, Robert and Ann Lees, Jack Morley, Kim Maidment, Philip Vernon)*

Free house ~ Licensee Robert Lyons ~ Real ale ~ Lunchtime bar meals and snacks (not Mon) ~ Separate lunchtime and evening restaurant (not Mon lunchtimes) ~ (01229) 583972 ~ Children in eating area of bar only ~ Open 11-11; 12-10.30 Sun ~ Bedrooms: £60B/£130B inc dinner

YANWATH NY5128 Map 9
Gate 🍴

2¼ miles from M6 junction 40; A66 towards Brough, then right on A6, right on B5320, then follow village signpost

This is a quiet old side-tracked hamlet, so it's a surprise to find this unpretentious village local serving particularly good inventive food. This might include sandwiches, home-made soup (£2.25), good 'black devils' (sliced black pudding in a thin mildly peppery cream sauce – an excellent starter or very light snack at £2.95), stilton and port pâté with cumberland sauce (£3.25), smoked fish pie, cumberland sausage casserole, chicken, ham and egg pie or bean cobbler (all £5.80), sirloin steak (£9.75), excellent gin and lime duck (£10.50), and puddings such as orange and brandy pudding with mandarin coulis, fresh fruit crumble or black forest roulade (£2.50). The simple turkey-carpeted bar, full of chatting regulars, has a log fire in an attractive stone inglenook and one or two nice pieces of furniture and middle-eastern brassware among more orthodox seats; or you can go through to eat in a more staid back two-level no-smoking restaurant. Well kept Theakstons Best and a local beer brewed for them called Creaking Gate Bitter on handpump, and obliging service; darts, dominoes, a quiz night on the last Sunday of the month, and unobtrusive piped music; the friendly border collie is called Domino and is good with children. There are a few picnic tables outside. *(Recommended by Mike and Maggie Betton, Mr and Mrs D Wilson, Bob and Marg Griffiths, Richard Holloway, John Prescott, Paul McPherson, Steve and Carolyn, H K Dyson, Mike and Wendy Proctor)*

Free house ~ Licensees Ian and Sue Rhind ~ Real ale ~ Meals and snacks ~ Restaurant ~ (01768) 862386 ~ Children welcome ~ Folk music 1st Sun of month ~ Open 12-3, 6.30(7 Sun)-11; 12-2.30, 7-11 in winter

Lucky Dip

Besides the fully inspected pubs, you might like to try these Lucky Dips recommended to us and described by readers (if you do, please send us reports):

☆ **Alston** [Front St (A689); NY7246], *Angel*: Friendly 17th-c pub on steep cobbled street of charming Pennine village, beams, timbers, big log fire, traditional furnishings, good value quickly served food (not Tues evening) from sandwiches to steaks, well kept Whitbreads-related ales; children welcome in eating area, tables in sheltered back garden; cheap bedrooms; well worth a main entry, but too few reports to keep its place *(R Davies, L Dixon, LYM)*

☆ **Alston** [Main St], *Turks Head*: Convivial local with good value food, pleasant landlord, well kept Boddingtons and Theakstons, spotless housekeeping; bar counter dividing big front room into two areas, back lounge with cosy coal fire and small tables; at top of steep cobbled street *(L Dixon, Kevin Thorpe)*

Alston [Townfoot, A686], *Blue Bell*: Cosy and appealing, two bars (one with juke box), stripped stone, decent food in bar and restaurant, Theakstons beers; can be very busy; bedrooms *(Kevin Thorpe, L Dixon)*

☆ **Ambleside** [Market Sq; NY3804], *Queens*: Neatly comfortable hotel bar, good value food inc vegetarian, generous puddings and good children's menu, prompt friendly service, well kept Jennings, Tetleys, Theakstons XB and guest, separate cellar bar with pool room; shame about the piped music; well equipped bedrooms *(Ron Gentry, Alan Risdon, H K Dyson)*

Ambleside [Lake Rd], *Churchill*: Bustling comfortable hotel bar and separate cosy dining area, varied generous home-made food from sandwiches and baked potatoes up, Boddingtons (happy hour 8-9 Thurs); bedrooms *(S P Watkin, P A Taylor, A Lock)*; [A592 N of Troutbeck; NY4007], *Kirkstone Pass*: Lakeland's highest inn, best out of season, with fine surrounding scenery, not smart but cheery, with lots of old photographs and bric-a-brac, good coffee, well kept Tetleys, friendly staff, open fire, lively amusements, simple food, maybe piped Classic FM *(H K Dyson, LYM)*

☆ **Askham** [lower green; NY5123], *Queens Head*: Comfortably pubby two-room lounge, open fire, lots of beams, copper and brass, generous good home-made food from sandwiches to steaks and fresh fish, well kept Wards Sheffield Best, wide choice of wines, friendly young local licensees; children welcome, pleasant garden; bedrooms comfortable with creaking floorboards, splendid breakfast *(Angus Lyon, Bob Ellis, A N Ellis, H Dyson, Chris Brown, J V Dadswell, LYM)*

☆ **Bampton** [NY5118], *St Patricks Well*: Pretty little village local, friendly landlord, well kept Jennings Bitter and Mild, bar food inc good shepherd's pie and steaks, big open fire, pool room, darts, juke box; a couple of seats outside; bedrooms good value, huge breakfasts *(Dr B and Mrs P Baker, H K Dyson, BB)*

☆ **Barbon** [off A683 Kirkby Lonsdale—Sedbergh; SD6383], *Barbon Inn*: Charming village setting below fells, with sheltered garden, some individual furnishings in small somewhat hotelish rooms off plain little bar with big blacked range, well kept Theakstons Best and Old Peculier, decent well served food from sandwiches up inc vegetarian dishes, no-smoking restaurant with log fire, pleasant service; children welcome, attractive recently upgraded bedrooms *(Sue Holland, Dave Webster, John and Joan Nash, Mrs Hilarie Taylor, Paul Robinshaw, Paul and Sue Merrick, Denis and Margaret Kilner, R Davies, LYM)*

Barrow in Furness [Central Dr, Walney Is; SD2069], *George*: Good food, friendly staff, two bars – one with good entertainment; nr beach *(AR)*

Baycliff [A5087 Barrow—Ulverston; SD2972], *Fishermans Arms*: Well presented tasty food popular with older people midweek lunchtime, efficient service; garden with play area, bedrooms *(Arthur and Margaret Dickinson)*

Blackbeck [A595 S of Egremont; NY0307], *Blackbeck Bridge*: Comfortable hotel lounge, Scottish Courage ales, bar food; bedrooms *(SLC)*

Bowness on Windermere [Rayrigg Rd; SD4097], *Olde John Peel*: Attractively refurbished lounge, panelled bar and upstairs family room, country artefacts, good value family bar food inc vegetarian, Theakstons ales, friendly staff; darts, games machines, juke box, quiz and karaoke nights; handy for World of Beatrix Potter *(Richard Lewis, SLC)*; [Brantfell Rd], *Royal Oak*: Whitbreads pub with guest like Morlands Old Speckled Hen, dining area, slightly raised games area, front garden; children welcome *(SLC)*

Brampton [High Cross St, just off A69 E of Carlisle; NY5361], *White Lion*: Warm and friendly old-world Victorian hotel, real ales inc Whitbreads Castle Eden, good generous home-cooked food, two comfortable well decorated rooms with coal fires, obliging service; bedrooms *(David and Margaret Bloomfield)*

Branthwaite [NY0625], *Riverside*: Soft furnishings, stone fireplace and Venetian pictures in nice bar area, Jennings and Tetleys, emphasis on food inc good range of pastas and grills (Italian chef), efficient service, river-view restaurant *(William Cunliffe)*

☆ **Broughton in Furness** [The Square; SD2187], *Manor Arms*: From outside scarcely looks like a pub, but has wide range of well kept ales such as Bass, Butterknowle Banner, Courage

Best, Hopback wheat beer, Timothy Taylors Landlord, Ushers Spring Fever, Worthington BB and Yates; good snacks, comfortable relaxed atmosphere; well appointed good value bedrooms, big breakfast *(Camille Walsh, Derek Harvey-Piper, H K Dyson, Bill and Pam Baker)*

☆ **Buttermere** [NY1817], *Bridge*: Very popular for its position, with flagstoned bar suitable for walkers, comfortable lounge bar, food from lunchtime baked potatoes to steaks, no-smoking evening restaurant, well kept Tetleys-related ales, quite a few malt whiskies, Addlestone's cider; sheltered flagstoned terrace, marvellous views from bedrooms; children welcome, open all day (from 9am summer) *(Chris and Andy Crow, Jack Morley, K and F Giles, RWD, SLC, Colin Draper, H Dyson, Michael and Alison Leyland, Mark Percy, Richard Holloway, AW, BW, Christine Bartley, Ian and Gayle Woodhead, Vicky and David Sarti, LYM)*

☆ **Buttermere** [NY1817], *Fish*: Spacious and smartly refurbished former coaching inn on NT property between Buttermere and Crummock Water, wide range of good value bar food from fresh sandwiches to trout, good range of well kept Jennings and Theakstons and guests such as Charles Wells Bombardier and Morlands Old Speckled Hen; can get crowded; bedrooms *(E A George, SLC, Janet Stephenson, Christopher Warner, BB)*

☆ **Caldbeck** [B5299; NY3239], *Oddfellows Arms*: Comfortably extended village pub with wide choice of good generous food, well kept Jennings ales, friendly staff, pleasant dining room, careful housekeeping *(David and Margaret Bloomfield, Ian and Lynn Brown, Margaret Davis)*

Cark in Cartmel [B5278; follow Holker Hall signs; SD3776], *Engine*: Comfortably refurbished, with good home-made food from lunchtime sandwiches up, Theakstons Best and Mild, Tetleys and Wadworths 6X, quick friendly service, good fire, games room, restaurant; tables out by little stream, has been open all day; self-contained holiday flats *(D J Cooke, SLC, LYM)*

Carlisle [17 Botchergate; NY4056], *Caledonian Cask House*: Large open-plan pub with lots of seating, prints, railway memorabilia, flagstones and panelling, wide choice of good value home-cooked lunchtime bar food, Whitbreads-related ales and a couple of interesting guests, Weston's farm cider, busy friendly staff; pool, fruit machine, TV *(Richard Lewis, M Walker, SLC)*; [John St, Caldewgate – A595 W], *Maltsters Arms*: Welcoming down-to-earth little local, well kept Jennings, good value food (not Sun evening), darts; cl lunchtime Mon-Fri *(PB)*; [Mary St], *Marys Chambers*: Comfortable open-plan stripped-pine bar, dining area with reasonably priced food all day, well kept Marstons Pedigree, Morlands Old Speckled Hen, Theakstons Best and (on electric pump) Youngers Scotch, friendly staff, games machines, piped music; open all day, handy

for stn; bedrooms (hotel is on main rd) *(Richard Lewis)*

☆ **Cartmel** [The Square; SD3879], *Kings Arms*: Picturesque pub nicely placed at the head of the attractive town square – rambling heavy-beamed bar, mix of furnishings from traditional settles to banquettes, usual bar food and no-smoking restaurant all day, well kept Wards Darleys Thorne, children welcome, seats outside *(Alan Risdon, M J Morgan, Julie Peters, Colin Blinkhorn, LYM)*

☆ **Casterton** [A683, just NE of Kirkby Lonsdale; SD6279], *Pheasant*: Neat and plushly modernised in a low-key way, with log fire, newspapers and magazines to read, second room which is no smoking during meal times, Charles Wells Bombardier, Marstons Pedigree, Morlands Old Speckled Hen, Theakstons Bitter and XB under light blanket pressure, small but good wine list, lots of malt whiskies, generally good food, not cheap, from home-made soup and sandwiches to crispy duck, darts, dominoes, winter quiz night, piped music, no-smoking restaurant, tables outside; children welcome, comfortable bedrooms, good breakfast *(A T Rhone, Dr W S M Hood, R A Cook, David and Judy Walmsley, David and Margaret Bloomfield, Richard Holloway, Peter and Hazel Fawthrop, Karen Eliot, Paul and Sue Merrick, Luke Worthington, Graham Mair, J H and S A Harrop, T J Bagley, Stan and Hazel Allen, LYM)*

☆ **Cockermouth** [Main St; NY1231], *Bush*: Four welcoming and cosy communicating areas, two with carpets and banquettes, two with bare boards, beams and old tables, attractive decor, well kept Jennings (full range) and guest beers, very friendly bar staff, open fires; cheap and cheerful generous lunchtime food, fairly unobtrusive piped music; children allowed *(Margaret Mason, Dave Thompson, A and R Lees)*

Cockermouth [14 Crown St], *Kingfisher*: Good generous carefully served food with good fresh veg (no vegetarian dishes), very hard-working licensees, cosy atmosphere, decent house wines, stupendous ladies'; bedrooms *(Monica Shelley)*

☆ **Coniston** [signed from centre; SD3098], *Sun*: Attractively placed below mountains (doubling as rescue post), with interesting Donald Campbell and other Lakeland photographs in basic back bar, friendly atmosphere, good log fire, bar food, well kept Jennings, Tetleys and perhaps local Coniston Old Man from the deep granite cellar; children in carpeted no-smoking eating area and restaurant, darts, dominoes, piped music; open all day; comfortable bedrooms *(Tina and David Woods-Taylor, David Carr, S P Watkin, P A Taylor, Jeanne Cross, Paul Silvestri, Alan Risdon, H K Dyson, LYM)*

☆ **Crook** [B5284 Kendal—Bowness; SD4795], *Sun*: Extensive range of inventive fresh food and good value wines, a surprise find in this otherwise straightforward more or less open-plan village local; well kept Jennings and

Theakstons, happy efficient staff, welcoming fire *(A Preston, Cyril E Higgs, RJH, David Dolman, LYM)*

Dacre [between A66 and A592 SW of Penrith; NY4626], *Horse & Farrier*: Quaint 18th-c inn with friendly helpful staff, varied well prepared food *(Patrick Herratt)*

Dean [just off A5086 S of Cockermouth; NY0825], *Royal Yew*: Busy modernised village local, good range of good value food, efficient service, well kept Jennings, Stones and Theakstons *(William Cunliffe)*

☆ Deanscales [A5086 S of Cockermouth; NY0927], *Old Posting House*: Homely and friendly comfortable split-level dining pub, very popular for good value generous well presented home-made food from sandwiches to steaks, interesting old fittings surviving from posting and coaching days, lots of brass and copper, Lakeland and heavy-horse prints; well kept Jennings Bitter and Cumberland, no-smoking restaurant *(R Davies, William Cunliffe, Jackie Moffat, BB)*

☆ Dent [Main St; SD7187], *George & Dragon*: Clean, comfortable and quiet pub/hotel, local Dent Bitter, Ramsbottom and T'Owd Tup, also Scottish Courage ales, good generously served bar food, bargain Sun lunch, reasonably priced evening restaurant, no piped music; pleasant staff, pool, darts; bedrooms comfortable *(D Gardner, J Turner, Paul S McPherson)*

☆ Durdar [NY4051], *Black Lion*: Generous well presented home-made food, well kept Theakstons Best, pleasant staff, no-smoking room, all extremely clean; handy for Carlisle racecourse, not far from M6 junction 42 *(Mr and Mrs J H Cookson)*

Eamont Bridge [handy for M6 junction 40; NY5328], *Beehive*: Pleasant roadside pub, seats out under hanging baskets, cosy bar with good straightforward food, open fire, Whitbreads-related ales; big back play area, attractive village *(Angus Lyon, David and Margaret Bloomfield)*

Ennerdale Bridge [NY0716], *Fox & Hounds*: Attractive and cosy ancient beamed local, clean and tidy, with reasonably priced bar food, well kept Jennings and Theakstons Best, good range of wines, pews; popular with walkers, quiet village *(Brian Seller, Mr and Mrs M F Norton)*

☆ Eskdale Green [E of village; NY1400], *King George IV*: Traditional beamed and flagstoned bar, comfortable lounge, back games room, wide choice of generously served good bar food from sandwiches to steaks, Bass, Jennings Cumberland and Theakstons Best, XB and Old Peculier, excellent collection of malt whiskies, restaurant; friendly staff, log fire, fine views from garden – idyllic spot, lots of good walks; children welcome, open all day summer; good value bedrooms *(H K Dyson, Paul M Harris, J Hibberd, John Abbott, Neil Townend, Dave Thompson, Margaret Mason, Robert and Ann Lees, LYM)*

Far Sawrey [B5285 across from Bowness ferry; SD3893], *Sawrey*: Simple but comfortable and welcoming stable bar with tables in wooden stalls, harness on rough white walls, big helpings of good simple lunchtime bar food, well kept Black Sheep Bitter and Special and Jennings, pleasant staff, attractive prices; separate hotel bar, evening restaurant; seats on nice lawn, beautiful setting, walkers, children and dogs welcome; bedrooms comfortable and well equipped *(M Joyner, N J Lawless, LM, Gordon Smith, Ron Gentry, LYM)*

☆ Grange over Sands [Grange Fell Rd, off B5277; SD4077], *Hardcrag Hall*: Friendly former 16th-c farmhouse, two character panelled rooms and dining rooms, good choice of bar meals with children's helpings, well kept Thwaites and a weekend guest beer, reasonable prices; bedrooms *(P A Legon, R Gorick)*

Grasmere [NY3406], *Red Lion*: Friendly staff, tasty bar food in plush lounge bar and cane-chair conservatory, well priced restaurant meals, well kept beers, good range of malt whiskies, lovely views; good bedrooms and breakfast, though bar can be noisy *(D Stokes, A Preston)*; *Tweedies*: Rather functional big bar and separate dining room, useful for families, with food inc vegetarian choice, well kept Jennings Bitter and Cumberland with a guest beer, friendly staff, pleasant hotel garden *(Tim and Ann Newell, Alan Risdon)*; *Wordsworth*: Well kept and stylish hotel with cheerful separate Dove & Olive Branch bar for good cheap bar food, log fire and well kept Tetleys, Mitchells Lancaster Bomber and a summer guest; good light lunches in conservatory, nice garden, comfortable bedrooms *(Alan Risdon, LYM)*

Great Corby [NY4854], *Queen*: Cosy and friendly, with well kept ales, open fires *(Alan Risdon)*

Grizebeck [SD2485], *Greyhound*: Very warm welcome, well kept John Smiths, Morlands Old Speckled Hen and Theakstons XB, interesting well priced food, part stone floor, woodburners, friendly staff; bedrooms good value *(Joe Shone)*

Hallbankgate [A689 E of Brampton – OS Sheet 86 map ref 579596; NY5759], *Belted Will*: Cosy cheerful local with good value generous food, well kept Bass and Worthington BB, friendly ex-pat Geordie licensees, log fire, dining room, amiable sheepdog called Rob *(David and Margaret Bloomfield)*

☆ Haverigg [Main St; SD1678], *Harbour*: Sandwiches fit for a king and some seriously good simple home cooking with well kept Boddingtons and Theakstons Best in unpretentious atmospheric pub handy for this unsmart but enjoyable resort's beautiful beaches, interesting nature dunes and lagoon *(David and Margaret Bloomfield, JDM, KM)*

☆ Haverthwaite [A590 Barrow rd; SD3284], *Dicksons Arms*: Good rather classy if not cheap food inc delicious puddings and well kept Jennings and Marstons Pedigree in pleasant low-beamed bar with woodburner and hunting prints; prompt friendly service, restaurant *(Dr J Norman, Alan Risdon, JDM, KM)*

☆ **Haverthwaite** [OS Sheet 97 map ref 328842], *Anglers Arms*: Busy and friendly refurbished local with generous fresh food inc excellent gammon and salads, attractive prices, Theakstons Best and Whitbreads Castle Eden, overflow upstairs dining room – must book Fri/Sat night *(JDM, KM, Diane and Maurice Flint, Alan Risdon)*

Haweswater [NY4914], *Haweswater*: On reservoir, smartened up by newish owner, with well kept Jennings – handy for walks in spectacular scenery; bedrooms *(H K Dyson)*

Hawkshead [SD3598], *Red Lion*: Friendly modernised local with some old-fashioned touches, good log fire, well kept Courage-related ales with guests such as Jennings, good range of usual food, piped music; bedrooms *(SLC, Lisa Roberts, Richard Lewis)*

☆ **Hesket Newmarket** [signed from B5299 in Caldbeck; NY3438], *Old Crown*: Relaxed and homely traditional local in attractive village, decent food inc good curries and tapas, friendly new landlord, good unusual real ales brewed here; cl weekday lunchtimes exc school hols; bedrooms *(Patrick Rivett, Ian and Gayle Woodhead, Alan Risdon, Richard Houghton, LYM)*

☆ **Howtown** [NY4519], *Howtown Hotel*: Stunning setting nr Ullswater, small cosy hotel lounge bar, separate public bar with good lunchtime sandwiches for hungry walkers, restaurant, morning coffee or afternoon tea; book for good Sun lunch; welcoming very long-serving owners, keg Theakstons Best but decent wines by the glass, pleasant garden; charming old-fashioned bedrooms, early morning tea ladies *(Christine and Geoff Butler, AR, Chris Rounthwaite, Enid and Henry Stephens)*

Hutton Roof [SD5778], *Horseshoe*: Quiet and well placed, with lovely views, friendly welcome, good range of home-made food inc old-fashioned puddings and children's dishes, Jennings ales; children welcome, garden; bedrooms *(Dr and Mrs I May)*

Ireby [NY2439], *Paddys Bar*: Friendly pub in small village below Caldbeck Fells, wide range of beers; back post office and shop *(Alan Risdon)*

Kendal [Crook Rd (B5284 NW); SD5293], *Gateway*: Newish pub/restaurant with good food and service, well kept Thwaites; tables out on terrace, play area; bedrooms *(SLC, Mike and Carole Dixon)*

☆ **Keswick** [Lake Rd, off top end Mkt Sq; NY2624], *Dog & Gun*: Lively and unpretentious town local with some high settles, low beams, partly slate floor (rest carpeted or boards), fine Abrahams mountain photographs, coins in beams and timbers by fireplace, log fire; well kept Theakstons Best and Old Peculier and a guest such as Black Sheep, open fires, unchanging choice of generous bar food from sandwiches up,

friendly efficient staff; piped music may be loud; children if eating, no dogs while food served, no credit cards, open all day Sat in summer *(Kevin Thorpe, Jason Caulkin, SLC, F J and A Parmenter, Alan Risdon, LYM)*

☆ **Keswick** [St Johns St], *George*: Attractive traditional black-panelled side room with interesting Wordsworth connection (and good log fire), more straightforward open-plan main bar with old-fashioned settles and modern banquettes under Elizabethan beams, usual bar food inc children's, well kept Theakstons and Yates, smartish restaurant; bedrooms comfortable *(H Dyson, Kevin Thorpe, Neil and Anita Christopher, P and M Rudlin, LYM)*

Keswick [Lake Rd], *Four in Hand*: Cosy and inviting back lounge, stage-coach bric-a-brac, decent-sized tables in dining room, full Jennings range; very busy in summer *(Jason Caulkin, Vann and Terry Prime)*; [Main St], *Keswick Lodge*: Hotel lounge bar with comfortable pubby feel, well kept Theakstons and a guest such as Timothy Taylors Landlord, wide choice of reasonably priced bar food, pleasant service; bedrooms *(SLC, Alan Risdon)*; [Market Sq], *Kings Arms*: Comfortable and relaxing hotel front bar, bar food, Scottish Courage beers, open all day; bedrooms *(SLC)*; [off Market Sq], *Lake Road*: Old town pub with Victorian fireplace, panelling and prints in two communicating rooms, well kept Jennings and guests such as Black Sheep Special and Greene King Abbot, keen young landlord, generous food; tables on small terrace *(Neil and Anita Christopher, P and M Rudlin)*; [Main St], *Oddfellows Arms*: Popular, cosy and comfortable panelled pub, well kept Jennings, quick service, lots of horse-racing photographs; back family room with TV and fruit machines *(SLC, Lesley Macklin, Richard Lewis)*; [Pack Horse Ct – off Market Sq, behind Lloyds Bank], *Pack Horse*: Lushly refurbished low-beamed pub in attractive alley courtyard, well kept Jennings (full range) and interesting guest beers, reasonably priced food, friendly service, cheery locals – upstairs is an oasis of calm *(Richard Lewis, R V G Brown, LYM)*

☆ nr **Keswick** [Crosthwaite Rd; by A66, a mile out], *Pheasant*: Small friendly beamed pub with lots of local cartoons, big helpings of good value tasty food, no-smoking dining room, full Jennings range kept well, friendly prompt service; children if eating; bedrooms *(P and M Rudlin, SLC, H K Dyson, P and M Rudlin)*

☆ nr **Keswick** [Newlands Valley – OS Sheet 90 map ref 242217], *Swinside*: Welcoming newish family doing well in clean and friendly modernised pub in peaceful valley below marvellous crags and fells, full Jennings range kept well, decent wines, good fires, good value bar food, restaurant, dogs allowed, tables outside with best view, open all day Sat and summer; bedrooms *(David Yandle, Mrs M Grimwood, SLC, LYM)*

Kirkby Stephen [NY7808], *Crogrin Arms*:

Ordinary pub with fine bar food inc tender tasty steaks, Theakstons Best *(Brian Seller)*

Kirkoswald [NY5641], *Crown*: Friendly local, good generous home-cooked food inc fresh fish *(Anne Crowley, John Plumridge)*; *Fetherston Arms*: Good value food with fine salads and real chips, pleasant landlord; good reasonably priced bedrooms *(Arthur and Margaret Dickinson)*

Langdale [by car park for Stickle Ghyll; NY2906], *Stickle Barn*: In lovely setting, suiting walkers and mountaineers well, good choice of food inc packed lunches, well kept Scottish Courage beers; fruit machines, maybe loud piped music; big pleasant terrace, open all day; bunkhouse accommodation, live music in loft *(Alan Risdon)*

☆ **Lazonby** [NY5539], *Joiners Arms*: Small spotless pub furnished brewery-style, roaring fire, brasses and china, beautifully presented food from sandwiches to oriental dishes, well kept Bass and Stones (friendly landlord was a head brewer there) with a guest such as Batemans, pool table in lower bar; clean comfortable bedrooms, good breakfasts *(DJW, Jack and Heather Coyle)*

☆ **Levens** [Sedgwick Rd, by Sizergh Castle gates – OS Sheet 97 map ref 500872; SD5087], *Strickland Arms*: Wide choice of generous imaginative well cooked food, friendly prompt service even when very busy, well kept Scottish Courage ales with a guest such as Marstons Pedigree, log fire; piped music, pool table; no-smoking upstairs restaurant, children allowed, good garden *(R Davies, Alan Risdon)*

Lindale [B5277 N of Grange-over-Sands – OS Sheet 97 map ref 419805; SD4280], *Lindale*: Good generous reasonably priced food from sandwiches to huge steaks in nice big oak-beamed dining area (children welcome here), well kept Whitbreads-related ales and a guest such as Lakeland Cartmel Pride; fruit machine, pool and TV in bar area up a few steps, open all day Fri and Sat in summer, good friendly service; bedrooms *(SLC)*

Lorton [Low Lorton; B5289 Buttermere–Cockermouth; NY1525], *Wheat Sheaf*: Bar and dining lounge, good food inc huge filled Yorkshire puddings and big helpings of other traditional dishes, well kept Jennings, fast service; caravan park behind *(Tim Heywood, Sophie Wilne, SLC)*

☆ **Lowick Bridge** [just off A5084; SD2986], *Red Lion*: Busy family food pub, warm, comfortable and clean, with two spacious and attractive areas, well kept Hartleys XB and Robinsons, good choice of generous tasty bar food inc vegetarian and Sun roasts, half helpings if you want, pleasant helpful service, open fire; tables outside, charming spot, open all day Sun and summer Sat, quiz night Thurs *(Mr and Mrs M F Norton, Alan Risdon, SLC, David Heath, Julie Peters, Colin Blinkhorn)*

☆ **Lowick Green** [A5092 SE of village; SD2985], *Farmers Arms*: Charming cosy public bar with heavy beams, huge slate flagstones, big open fire, cosy corners and pub games (also

piped music, TV; this part may be cl winter), some interesting furniture and pictures in plusher hotel lounge bar across yard, tasty well presented food in bar and restaurant inc two-person bargains, well kept Theakstons XB, friendly attentive staff; children welcome, open all day Sat/Sun; piped music; comfortable bedrooms *(JCW, K H Frostick, David Carr, SLC, B J P Edwards, Alan Risdon, LYM)*

Metal Bridge [off A74 Carlisle—Gretna, nr Rockcliffe; NY3565], *Metal Bridge*: Friendly staff, decent bar food, good choice of Scottish Courage related beers, nice river view from sun lounge *(Steve Jennings)*

☆ **Middleton** [A683 Kirkby Lonsdale—Sedbergh; SD6288], *Head*: Comfortably plush open-plan oak-beamed bar, formerly the Middleton Fells, with lots of brasswork, three good fires, good value straightforward food, well kept ales, attractive garden, fine scenery; children welcome *(Arthur and Margaret Dickinson, BB)*

☆ **Mungrisdale** [village signed off A66 Penrith—Keswick, a bit over a mile W of A5091 Ullswater rd – OS Sheet 90 map ref 363302; NY3731], *Mill Inn*: Simple but hospitable pub in lovely valley hamlet, quickly served food, Jennings Bitter, lots of malt whiskies, plain games room, separate restaurant; children and walkers welcome, tables on gravel forecourt and neat lawn sloping to little river; warm pleasant bedrooms (note that there's a quite separate Mill Hotel here) *(Monica Shelley, Laura Darlington, A Preston, H Dyson, LYM)*

☆ **Nether Wasdale** [NY1204], *Strands*: Warm and friendly hotel in lovely spot below the remote high fells around Wastwater, spacious bar with big open fires, local pictures and lots of horse brasses, good range of generous bar food, well kept Hartleys XB and Robinsons Best, friendly helpful service; bedrooms

Newby Bridge [just off A590; SD3786], *Swan*: Fine setting next to river with waterside picnic tables by old stone bridge, hotelish atmosphere even when very busy, decent food inc Sun roasts, Boddingtons ale; bedrooms *(LM, Ron Gentry)*

☆ **Newton Reigny** [off B5305 just W of M6 junction 41], *Sun*: Open-plan village inn with plush seats and velvet curtains, stripped stone and wrought iron, central open fire, well kept Boddingtons, good coffee, no-smoking restaurant; darts, dominoes and pool off at one end, children away from bar, open all day Sat; piped music *(Mike and Wendy Proctor, David and Margaret Bloomfield, MM, DT, Richard Holloway, LYM)*

☆ **Outgate** [B5286 Ambleside—Hawkshead; SD3699], *Outgate Inn*: Attractively placed country pub with three comfortably modernised rooms, banjoes, trumpets and tuba hanging from beams, decent food from sandwiches up, well kept Hartleys XB and Robinsons Bitter and Frederics, friendly staff, popular jazz Fri; open all day, bedrooms *(Kim and Anne Schofield, Mark Percy, SLC, Dr J*

Morley, H Dyson, David Carr, LYM)

Penny Bridge [just off A5092 N of Ulverston; SD3183], *Britannia*: Pleasant landlord, well kept Robinsons, bar meals in dining area, open all day summer *(SLC)*

☆ **Penrith** [NY5130], *George*: Decorous beamed and oak-panelled lounge hall with fine plasterwork, oak settles and easy chairs around good open fire, big bow windows; short choice of reasonably priced lunchtime bar food, well kept Marstons Pedigree, friendly and lively back bar with good juke box, restaurant; comfortable bedrooms *(E Howbrook, Kevin Thorpe, LYM)*

Penrith [Bowscar (A6 N) – OS Sheet 90 map ref 505341], *Stoneybeck*: Big comfortable pub, cheap and cheerful, generous food, well kept Theakstons and Youngers Scotch *(David and Margaret Bloomfield)*; [Great Dockray], *Two Lions*: Unpretentious and friendly, with pleasant front bar, big back room, good basic food inc vegetarian, quiet piped music, good wheelchair access *(L Dixon)*

☆ **Penruddock** [NY4327], *Herdwick*: Carefully refurbished old pub with consistently good well priced food esp Sun roast, good atmosphere, efficient friendly service, attractive restaurant – worth booking evenings; bedrooms *(Mr and Mrs D Wilson, Malcolm Taylor, Mike and Wendy Proctor)*

Pooley Bridge [NY4724], *Sun*: Warm and cosy lounge bar with plush settee by fire, steps past servery to second interesting room, well kept Jennings ales, good value generous simple bar food inc sandwiches, restaurant; tables in garden *(A Preston, Mike and Wendy Proctor)*

Ravenglass [SD0996], *Ratty Arms*: Ex-railway bar (terminus for England's oldest narrow-gauge steam railway) with well kept beer, good service, good value restaurant, pool table in busy public bar *(P A Legon, LYM)*

☆ **Ravenstonedale** [signed off A685 Kirkby Stephen—M6; NY7204], *Black Swan*: Good bar food with interesting specials in genteel bar with open fire and some stripped stone, well kept Hartleys XB, Robinsons, Theakstons, Worthington, Youngers and a changing guest, lots of country wines, good service; dogs welcome, tables in pretty tree-sheltered streamside garden over road; comfortable bedrooms inc some for disabled, very good breakfasts, peaceful setting *(Michael Tucker, Kim and Anne Schofield, Arthur and Margaret Dickinson, SS, H Dyson, BB)*

Ravenstonedale, *Kings Head*: Friendly two-room beamed bar with log fires, button-back banquettes and dining chairs, good range of generous food, well kept Jennings and other ales, games room; bedrooms *(H Dyson, D Varney, LYM)*

☆ *nr* **Ravenstonedale** [Crossbank; A683 Sedbergh—Kirkby Stephen; SD6996], *Fat Lamb*: Remote friendly inn with pews in brightly modernised bar, log fire in traditional black kitchen range, good local photographs; cheerful service, usual bar food, well kept

Mitchells, maybe piped classical music, restaurant, seats out by sheep pastures; facilities for disabled, children really welcome; comfortable bedrooms with own bathrooms, good walks from inn *(David Varney, BB)*

☆ **Rosthwaite** [NY2615], *Scafell*: Lots of walkers and locals in extended slate-floored bar, lunchtime food from sandwiches to steak and salmon, children's helpings of most dishes, full range of Theakstons ales kept well, afternoon teas, log fire, enthusiastic licensee, quick friendly service; glassed-in verandah overlooking river, picnic tables outside; piped music; hotel has cosy sun-lounge bar and dining room; bedrooms not big but good *(H Dyson)*

☆ **Sandside** [B5282 Milnthorpe—Arnside; SD4781], *Ship*: Spacious modernised pub with glorious view of estuary and mountains beyond; friendly staff, good generous varied bar food inc unusual fresh veg, well kept Scottish Courage ales, decent wines, summer barbecues, tables out on grass by good children's play area; children allowed in eating area *(Annette and Stephen Marsden, LYM)*

Sandwith [off A595 or B5345; NX9715], *Lowther Arms*: Good home cooking, friendly atmosphere; bedrooms clean, homely and cheap, handy for coast-to-coast walkers *(D G Hughes)*

☆ **Satterthwaite** [SD3492], *Eagles Head*: Small and unpretentious but friendly, with good value generous home-cooked lunchtime food esp soup, sandwiches and home-made pies (also Fri/Sat summer evenings), big log fire, helpful landlord, well kept Thwaites, pool, darts; papers and guidebooks for sale; handy for Grizedale Forest; bedrooms comfortable and clean, shared bathroom; maybe some closures winter esp Mon, but usually open all day at least Thurs-Sat in summer *(LM)*

☆ **Seatoller** [NY2414], *Yew Tree*: Restaurant rather than pub, with well presented imaginative food inc local specialities in good low-ceilinged restaurant at foot of Honister Pass, good choice of whiskies and wines in cosy back bar with wonderful collections from old police hats through cameras to antique scales, garden behind; can get crowded, but efficient friendly staff *(Richard Holloway, CLS, RMB, Paul McKeever)*

Skelwith Bridge [part of Skelwith Bridge Hotel; A593 W of Ambleside; NY3503], *Talbot*: 17th-c lakeland hotel nr River Brathay, smart cheerful staff in oak-panelled bar, Theakstons on handpump, good daily changing lunchtime bar food inc good big ploughman's (choice of cheeses); bedrooms *(S P Watkin, P A Taylor, Ewan and Moira McCall)*

Spark Bridge [off A5092 N of Ulverston; SD3185], *Royal Oak*: Large riverside food pub with raftered upper dining area, relaxed informal atmosphere, friendly service, well kept Boddingtons, Flowers Original and Wadworths 6X, good value food (all day Sun) inc wonderful steaks and fresh seafood, good children's menu, open fire; large pool room *(Camille Walsh, SLC)*

St Bees [NX9712], *Albion*: Wainwright bar with lots of pictures and memorabilia (village is one end of this walkers' guru's coast-to-coast walk), huge bar meals, reasonable prices, friendly staff, Theakstons Best *(Brian Seller)*; [Main St], *Queens*: Simple three-room bar, well kept Scottish Courage ales, lots of whiskies, friendly locals, big helpings of good home-made bar food in dining area with big tables, conservatory, garden behind; bedrooms *(SLC)*

☆ **Staveley** [SD4798], *Eagle & Child*: Simple good value home-cooked bar food with fresh veg, well kept Newcastle Exhibition, Tetleys and Theakstons Best, friendly service, bright but comfortable little modern front lounge and more spacious carpeted bar; well kept, with small neat garden; recently redecorated good value bedrooms, good breakfast. Local village inn (free house), six bedrooms, one with private bath, all with hot and cold water and tea making facilities, satellite television in all rooms *(Dr and Mrs B Baker, BB)*

☆ **Stonethwaite** [Borrowdale; NY2613], *Langstrath*: Friendly, neat and clean, more restaurant than pub but good fresh bar food, plenty of walkers and locals, good choice of ales inc Black Sheep, lots of malt whiskies, good service; delightful peaceful village, pleasant bedrooms *(Mr and Mrs Woods, Nigel Woolliscroft, H Dyson, S O'Connor, Brian Seller)*

☆ **Talkin** [village signed off B6413 S of Brampton; NY5557], *Blacksmiths Arms*: Good generous food in bar or dining room inc popular cheap Sun lunch (booking advisable), quick polite waitress service, Black Sheep and Theakstons, open fire, local pictures; unobtrusive piped music, fruit machine; five well appointed bedrooms, prettily set village nr good walks *(David and Margaret Bloomfield, L Dixon)*

☆ **Thirlspot** [A591 Grasmere—Keswick; NY3217], *Kings Head*: Attractively placed and well refurbished beamed bar, long and low, with inglenook fires, wide choice of usual food inc good puddings, well kept Jennings, Theakstons Best, XB and Mild, Yates and a guest ale, tables in garden, games room with pool; piped music; children welcome, with toy box; good value bedrooms (the hotel part and restaurant are quite separate) *(Judith Erlandsen, H Dyson, LYM)*

☆ **Torver** [A593 S of Coniston; SD2894], *Church House*: Decent varied food in tidy and civilised low-beamed bar, pleasant service, splendid hill views, good fire, particularly well kept Whitbreads Castle Eden, big garden; children welcome, attractive evening restaurant; open all day at least in summer; bedrooms *(LM)*

Torver, *Wilson Arms*: Comfortable, with friendly helpful staff, good log fires, plentiful well presented food inc good vegetarian

choice, well kept beer, discreet piped music, polished brass, some antiques; dog who asks you to play with beer mats; bedrooms *(Dr and Mrs B D Smith)*

Troutbeck [the one nr Penrith; NY3926], *Sportsman*: Big improvements under welcoming new licensee, tasty food inc good choice of specials *(Maureen Cully)*

Uldale [NY2537], *Snooty Fox*: Unpretentious but comfortable two-bar village local, friendly helpful landlord, well kept Theakstons and a beer brewed for them in Hesket Newmarket, good generous food; reasonably priced bedrooms, tiny village *(David Heath, Richard Houghton)*

Ulverston [Market St; SD2978], *Piel Castle*: Lofty-ceilinged town pub, medieval theme, real ales, good value food beautifully prepared by French chef; some live jazz; bedrooms *(Arthur and Margaret Dickinson)*; [King St], *Rose & Crown*: Open-plan traditional local with decent food all day, well kept Hartleys XB, Robinsons Best Mild and Bitter, quick service even when busy on Sat market day, pleasant garden and pavement tables *(M J Morgan, David Carr)*

☆ **Wasdale Head** [NY1808], *Wasdale Head Inn*: Mountain hotel in marvellous fellside setting, spacious panelled main bar with cushioned settles on slate floor and great mountain photographs, adjoining pool room, no-smoking snug and children's room; good value food in bar and restaurant, well kept Jennings, Theakstons Best and Old Peculier and Yates, decent choice of wines and malt whiskies, lively helpful staff; open all day, cl much of winter; comfortable bedrooms, well equipped self-catering accommodation *(Mick Hitchman, P and M Rudlin, John Abbott, David Honeyman, A and R Lees, H K Dyson, Nigel Woolliscroft, LYM)*

☆ **Winster** [A5074; SD4293], *Brown Horse*: Restauranty dining place, open-plan, smart, light and comfortable, with well spaced tables and good log fire, popular especially among older people for very good attractively priced food, prompt friendly service, well kept Jennings Bitter and Cumberland and Marstons Pedigree, decent wines, children welcome; booking essential in season *(Tina and David Woods-Taylor, Philip and Ann Falkner, Diane and Maurice Flint, T Large, Miss V Smith, John Logan, Rachel Thomas, IHR, SLC, Dr J R Norman, Mike and Sue Walton, A D Robson, Dave Braisted, LYM)*

☆ **Winton** [just off A685 N of Kirkby Stephen; NY7810], *Bay Horse*: Two low-key and low-ceilinged rooms with Pennine photographs and local fly-tying, generous reasonably priced home-cooked food inc fresh veg, well kept Theakstons Best, Jennings Bitter and Cumberland and Youngers Scotch, summer guest beers, pool in games room; cl Mon/Tues lunchtimes in winter; comfortable modestly priced bedrooms, good breakfasts; peaceful moorland hamlet *(Alan Risdon, LYM)*

Derbyshire

New entries here (or pubs back in these pages after a longish break) are the handsome Devonshire Arms at Beeley, doing well under its current management, with a wide choice of food; the cheerful and appealingly furnished Navigation at Buxworth (a pleasant place to stay), and the snug little Cheshire Cheese at Hope (good food under its present friendly owners). Other changes here include some refurbishment at Smiths in Ashbourne, a cheerful new landlord at the fascinating partly medieval Bull i' th' Thorn south of Buxton, and new people at the rather individual Chequers perched on Froggatt Edge (readers enjoy staying here). Pubs which have been doing particularly well in recent months include the attractive Olde Gate in Brassington, the Brunswick in Derby (no less than 17 handpumps – lots for beers they brew themselves), the John Thompson near Melbourne (also brews its own, with a new brewmaster this year, but good all round), and the bustling White Horse at Woolley Moor. The White Horse stands out for a particularly enjoyable meal out, as does the civilised Waltzing Weasel at Birch Vale, and the restauranty Druid at Birchover (huge interesing choice); of these three, it's the White Horse at Woolley Moor which we select as Derbyshire Dining Pub of the Year. Some Lucky Dip entries at the end of the chapter are showing particularly well these days: the Black Bull at Ashford in the Water, Derwent at Bamford, Castle in Castleton, Quiet Woman at Earl Sterndale, Bentley Brook near Fenny Bentley, Red Lion at Litton (pleasantly pubby atmosphere though it's really a restaurant) and George at Tideswell. We've inspected almost all of these and vouch for the merits we describe for them – as we do for the Barrel near Foolow and Lathkil at Over Haddon. Drinks prices here are considerably lower than the national average, with the high proportion of free houses benefiting from keen price competition among the various big Burton breweries almost on their doorsteps, as well as shopping around enthusiastically among smaller breweries. By far the cheapest beer we found was that brewed on the premises by the Brunswick in Derby; the quaint old Barley Mow at Kirk Ireton has exemplary pricing too, especially considering its interesting range.

ASHBOURNE SK1846 Map 7
Smiths Tavern

St Johns St; bottom of market place

As well as the replacing of some furnishings and furniture, this nicely old-fashioned town tavern has got rid of the fruit machine and piped music and now provides five daily newspapers for customers to enjoy in a relaxed, chatty atmosphere. The attractive bar has horsebrasses and tankards hanging from heavy black beams, a delft shelf of antique blue and white china, old cigarette and drinks advertisements, and a plush wall seat facing the bar counter. Steps take you up to a middle room with more plush seating around solid tables, a log-effect gas fire and piano; beyond that a light and airy end dining room has three nice antique settles among more ordinary seats around simple cloth-covered dining tables. Well kept Marstons Best and Pedigree and a guest on handpump, around 36 malt whiskies, and a range of vodkas. Popular and generously served bar food includes soup (£2), sandwiches, ploughman's, home-made pies such as steak and kidney (£5.20), a couple of vegetarian meals, and fish dishes such as local trout (£5.45); good fresh vegetables, and a three-course Sunday lunch. Very friendly service, and dominoes. *(Recommended by Stephen, Julie and Hayley Brown, Graham and Karen Oddey, George Atkinson, Sue Holland, Dave Webster, Ann and Colin Hunt, T and G Alderman)*

Marstons ~ Tenants John and Elaine Bishop ~ Real ale ~ Meals and snacks ~ Restaurant ~ (01335) 342264 ~ Children in middle room and restaurant ~ Open 11-11; 12-10.30 Sun

ASHFORD IN THE WATER SK1969 Map 7
Ashford Hotel 🛏 ♀

Church Street; village signposted just off A6 Bakewell—Buxton

This is a popular eating place in a particularly pretty village. The cosy refurbished bar has a relaxed, pleasant atmosphere, lots of gleaming brass and copper on the stripped brick of the broad stone inglenook fireplace, plush seats and stools around its traditional cast-iron-framed tables on the patterned carpet, and an imposing bar counter. Bar food includes soup (£1.95), sandwiches (from £2.25), filled baked potatoes (from £2.75), ploughman's (£4.75), chicken, ham and leek pie (£5.75), a casserole and a roast of the day (£6.25), daily specials like vegetable curry (£5.25), chicken sherry casserole (£6.25), and evening dishes like salmon poached in vermouth wrapped in smoked salmon (£3.50), crab thermidor (£4.25), and goose breasts with brandy and apricot (£8.95); part of the restaurant is no smoking. Friendly neatly dressed staff serve well kept Mansfield Best, Ridings and seasonal brews, and a guest like Shepherd Neame Spitfire on handpump; quite a few malt whiskies; winter darts, cribbage, dominoes, fruit machine and piped music. There are tables out in the garden. *(Recommended by Walter and Susan Rinaldi-Butcher, Paul Robinshaw, Dr and Mrs I H Maine, Eddy and Emma Gibson, Hugh and Sarah McShane, H Bramwell, Derek and Sylvia Stephenson, Peter and Maris Brigginshaw, David Carr, M Mason, D Thompson, Mike and Wendy Proctor, Ann and Colin Hunt, Brian and Margaret Beesley)*

Free house ~ Licensees John and Sue Dawson ~ Real ale ~ Meals and snacks (bar meals 12-5, restaurant 5-9) ~ Restaurant ~ Children in eating area of bar and restaurant ~ (01629) 812725 ~ Open 11-11; 12-10.30 Sun ~ Bedrooms: £50B/£85B

BEELEY SK2667 Map 7
Devonshire Arms

B6012, off A6 Matlock—Bakewell

Handy for Chatsworth, this handsome old stone pub is in an attractive spot in a pretty village – which summer seats outside make the most of. It was originally three cottages built in 1726 and was converted into an inn in 1741. The black-beamed rooms have comfortably cushioned stone seats along their stripped walls, antique settles, simpler wooden chairs, flagstones, and big log fires; one area is no smoking. Good food from an extensive menu includes home-made soup (£2.10), sandwiches (from £2.40), grilled radicchio and goat's cheese (£3.95), ploughman's (£4.75), black pudding with wholegrain mustard (£4.95), steak and ale pie or leek and mushroom crumble (£5.75), chicken breast with stilton sauce (£6.75), steaks (from £9.50), and puddings (from £2.25). Friday night is fish night with butterfly king prawns (£4.50), cod with a lemon parsley crust (£6.50), sole or seafood platter (£6.95), scallops mornay (£7.95), and salmon and prawns in a seafood cream sauce (£8.95); on Sundays they do a special breakfast with a glass of bucks fizz and the Sunday newspapers (£9.50, booking essential). Well kept Black Sheep Special and Best, Boddingtons, Theakstons XB and Old Peculier, and guest beers on handpump, a decent choice of malt whiskies, and mulled wine and cider in winter. *(Recommended by Jeanne Cross, Paul Silvestri, Martin and Catherine Snelling, John and Annette Derbyshire, John and Mary Holderness, Derek and Sylvia Stephenson, Allan Preston)*

Free house ~ Licensee John Grosvenor ~ Real ale ~ Meals and snacks (12-9.30 in summer; not 25 Dec) ~ Restaurant ~ (01629) 733259 ~ Children welcome ~ Open 11-11; 11-3, 7-11 in winter; 12-10.30 Sun; 12-3, 7-10.30 winter Sun

BIRCH VALE SK0286 Map 7
Waltzing Weasel ♀ 🛏
A6015 E of New Mills

The friendly licensees here have worked hard to cater for those wanting just a drink, a full meal, or a civilised place to stay, with a great deal of success. The U-shaped bar has comfortably chatty corners, some handsome oak settles and tables among more usual furniture (Mr and Mrs Atkinson used to deal in antiques), houseplants on corner tables, lots of nicely-framed mainly sporting Victorian prints, a good longcase clock, and a cheerful fire; there are daily papers on sticks, and a friendly dog, Sam. Well kept Marstons Best and Pedigree with occasional guests like Adnams, Churchills and Hartingtons on handpump, and a good choice of decent wines and malt whiskies; no games but maybe classical piped music. Though not cheap, the food is a strong point, with a lunchtime spread taking in sandwiches, soup (£2.50), ploughman's (£6.75), smoked tuna (£4), crayfish tails in garlic mayonnaise (£5.50), vegetable tart (£6.75), lamb and walnut pie (£7.75), and seafood tart (£8.75), plus shrimps on toast (£4), ham and eggs or chicken curry (£6.75), steak and kidney pie (£8.50), grilled lemon sole (£10.50), and puddings such as bread and butter pudding or treacle tart; fine cheeses. The charming back restaurant has picture-window views of Kinder Scout and the moors, and these are shared by a pretty garden and terrace. Service is obliging and attentive. *(Recommended by Stephen Brown, Peter Marshall, Joan and Tony Walker, Julie Peters, Colin Blinkhorn, Martin and Karen Wake, Brian and Anna Marsden, Peter Marshall, G V Price, David Hoult, Tony Young, K and B Forman, J F M West, Tony Young; also in Good Hotel Guide)*

Free house ~ Licensee Mike Atkinson ~ Real ale ~ Meals and snacks ~ Restaurant ~ (01663) 743402 ~ Children welcome (must be over 5 in evening restaurant) ~ Open 12-3, 5.30-11; 12-3, 6-10.30 Sun ~ Bedrooms: £45.75B/£65.95B

BIRCHOVER SK2462 Map 7
Druid
Village signposted from B5056

Even on a Monday before opening time, there's usually quite a few people waiting for this creeper-covered dining pub to open. The vast choice of food is written up on the blackboards that line the long fairly narrow bar (at busy times it can be hard to get close enough to read it let alone make up your mind), and favourite dishes amongst the 100 or so listed currently include very good vegetable wellington with gooseberry and ginger sauce on one side and spicy tomato and herb on the other (£6.90), soochow crispy vegetables with szechuan sauce (£7.40), medieval chicken or ribs, prawns, chicken and vegetables in a palm sugar and chilli broth (£8.90), halibut in orange, ginger and garlic with black olives and water chestnuts (£10.50), and saddle of lamb (£11.90); readers have also particularly enjoyed jugged steak with sausage dumplings, delicious steak and kidney pie, and venison casserole with bitter chocolate sauce. Half-price helpings for children. It's extremely popular so bookings are advisable for evenings and weekends – you probably won't be able to sit down at all if you're not eating. The bustling bar is small and plain, with plush-upholstered wooden wall benches around straightforward tables, and a big coal fire; the Garden Room is reserved for non-smokers. The spacious and airy two-storey dining extension, candlelit at night, is really the heart of the place, with pink plush seats on olive-green carpet, and pepper-grinders and sea salt on all the tables. Well kept Leatherbritches Ashbourne Ale and Belt 'n' Braces, Mansfield Bitter, Morlands Old Speckled Hen, and Charles Wells Bombardier on handpump, and a good collection of malt whiskies; welcoming service. A small public bar has dominoes; well reproduced classical music. There are picnic tables in front. *(Recommended by John and June Freeman, Wilma and Ian Smith, Miss S Watkin, P Taylor, Victoria Herriott, John and*

Christine Lowe, Sue and Geoff Price, JDM, KM, J Gibbs, J F Knutton, Rona Murdoch, Paul Robinshaw, Simon Walker, C Dyson, Ann and Colin Hunt, Neville Kenyon, Kath Wetherill, Margaret and Nigel Dennis, FMH, Mr and Mrs B Langrish, Mike and Wendy Proctor, J E Rycroft)

Free house ~ Licensee Brian Bunce ~ Real ale ~ Meals and snacks ~ Restaurant ~ (01629) 650302 ~ Children in dining area if eating but must be gone by 8.15 ~ Open 12-3(2.30 in winter), 7-11(10.30 in winter); closed 25-26 Dec

BRASSINGTON SK2354 Map 7
Olde Gate
Village signposted off B5056 and B5035 NE of Ashbourne

There are no noisy games machines or piped music to spoil the relaxed, convivial atmosphere in this traditional country pub. The peaceful public bar has gleaming copper pots on the lovely old kitchen range, pewter mugs hanging from a beam, embossed Doulton stoneware flagons on a side shelf, an ancient wall clock, and rush-seated old chairs and antique settles (one ancient, partly reframed, black oak solid one). Stone-mullioned windows look across lots of garden tables to small silvery-walled pastures. On the left of a small hatch-served lobby, another cosy beamed room has stripped panelled settles, tables with scrubbed tops, and a roaring fire under a huge mantelbeam. Bar food includes big open sandwiches, steak and ale pie (£7.30), balti dishes (from £8.50) and a popular summer barbecue, with lamb steaks, cajun chicken, swordfish and tuna (from £8.95); good puddings. No chips. The dining room is no smoking. Well kept Marstons Pedigree and a guest on handpump, and a good selection of malt whiskies; cribbage and dominoes. The small front yard has a couple of benches – a nice spot in summer to listen to the village bell-ringers practising on Friday evenings. Five minutes' drive away is Carsington reservoir, ideal for water sports and so forth. Children must be over 10 to be allowed in. *(Recommended by Andy and Jill Kassube, JDM, KM, Gillian Russell, Dr R F Fletcher, John and June Freeman, Paul Robinshaw, Jerry and Alison Oakes, J K Knutton, John and Christine Lowe, Phil and Sally Gorton, Jack and Philip Paxton, Mike and Wendy Proctor, Peter Marshall)*

Marstons ~ Tenant Paul Burlinson ~ Real ale ~ Meals and snacks (not Mon, not Sun evenings in winter) ~ (01629) 540448 ~ Open 12-2.30(3 Sat), 6-11; 12-3, 7-10.30 Sun; closed Mon lunchtimes in winter

nr BUXTON SK0673 Map 7
Bull i' th' Thorn
Ashbourne Road (A515) six miles S of Buxton, nr Hurdlow; OS Sheet 119 map reference 128665

New licensees have taken over this solid old place and offer a warm welcome to children, dogs, and walkers (who don't need to remove their boots) – early reports from readers are most favourable. The main bar is a fascinating medieval hall that's survived since 1472. A massive central beam runs parallel with a forest of smaller ones, there are panelled window seats in the embrasures of the thick stone walls, handsome panelling, and old flagstones stepping gently down to a big open fire. It's furnished with fine long settles, an ornately carved hunting chair, a longcase clock, a powder-horn, and armour that includes 17th-c German helmets, swords, and blunderbusses and so forth. Despite all this, the atmosphere is that of any straightforward roadside pub. No-frills bar food includes sandwiches, pork chops or gammon and egg (£4.50), barnsley chops (£5), daily specials (from £4.50), and children's menu (£1.85). An adjoining room has darts, pool, dominoes, cribbage, and juke box; piped music. Robinsons Best on handpump. The simple family room opens on to a terrace and big lawn, with swings, and there are more tables in a sheltered angle in front. Look out for the lively old carvings at the main entrance: one shows a bull caught in a thornbush, and others an eagle with a freshly caught hare, and some spaniels chasing a rabbit. The pub is handy for the High Peak Trail. *(Recommended by D O Savidge, Eddy and Emma Gibson, David Hoult, Paul S McPherson, James Nunns, Mike and Wendy Proctor)*

Robinsons ~ Tenant Mrs Annette Maltby-Baker ~ Real ale ~ Meals and snacks (9.30-
9pm) ~ Restaurant ~ (01298) 83348 ~ Children welcome ~ Live bands Sat evening ~
Open 9.30-11(10.30 Sun); may close in the afternoon in winter ~ Two bedrooms:
£18/£36

BUXWORTH SK0282 Map 7
Navigation 🛏

Silkhill, off B6062, which itself leads off the A6 just NW of Whaley Bridge roundabout – OS
Sheet 110 map ref 022821

Very welcoming indeed, this bustling extended pub is tucked down by a former
canal basin, interesting as the earliest to have its own waterside railway; an
ambitious restoration project is nearing completion. The linked low-ceilinged rooms
do have some canalia, but bring the bargees' days back to life more vividly in their
bright clutter of brassware, china and lacy curtains, all neat and shiny as a new pin.
It's a smashing place to wander around at quiet times (some of the prints are
particularly interesting), and when it's busy there are plenty of snug corners to tuck
yourself into, with good coal and log fires and flagstone floors. Good value generous
food includes soup (£1.90), sandwiches (from £2), ploughman's (£4.50), dishes
called 'golden oldies' such as ham hock with parsley sauce, bubble and squeak,
chicken, leek and stilton pie or cumberland sausage (all £5), a huge grilled meat
platter (£14), and puddings such as apple pie or bread and butter pudding (£2.25),
with vegetarian and children's dishes. Well kept Marstons Pedigree, Timothy Taylors
Landlord, Websters Yorkshire and one or two guest beers on handpump, and
changing farm ciders; cheery staff. A games room has pinball, pool, darts, dominoes,
and TV; quiet piped music. There are tables out on a sunken flagstoned terrace, with
a side play area and pets corner. (Recommended by David Carr, J F M West, Tony Young,
G Coates, C H and P Stride, Jack Morley, Ann and Colin Hunt, Sue Demont, Tim Barrow)

Free house ~ Licensees Alan and Lynda Hall ~ Real ale ~ Meals and snacks (all day) ~
(01663) 732072 ~ Children welcome away from bar ~ Occasional live entertainment
~ Open 11-11; 12-10.30 Sun ~ Bedrooms: £25/£38B

DERBY SK3435 Map 7
Alexandra 🍺 £

Siddals Rd, just up from station

Only two minutes from Derby station, this solid Victorian town pub has lots of
railway prints and memorabilia about Derby railway history on the walls of the
lively bar. There's an attractive 1920s feel, good heavy traditional furnishings on
dark-stained floorboards, shelves of bottles, and a fine choice of real ales. As well as
Batemans XB and Mild, Marstons Pedigree, and Shepherd Neame Masterbrew,
there are six ever-changing guest beers on handpump – often from little known
breweries. Also, traditional cider, country wines, around two dozen malt whiskies, a
good range of Belgian bottled beers, and changing continental beers on draught.
Though this is perhaps a pub more for drinking than for eating, the bar food is so
remarkably priced it's an ideal place for an informal snack: popular filled rolls, hot
cobs and toasties (from £1), various pies (£2.50), ploughman's and cold meat salads,
various pies (£2.50), and liver and bacon (£3); friendly service and locals; dominoes,
fruit machine and piped music. (Recommended by Richard Lewis, JDM, KM, Andy and Jill
Kassube, Chris Raisin, Mrs A Haswell, D Eberlin, Jack and Philip Paxton, Richard Houghton,
Dr and Mrs B Baker, Mr and Mrs P Byatt)

Free house ~ Licensee Mark Robins ~ Real ale ~ Lunchtime meals and snacks (not
Sun) ~ (01332) 293993 ~ Open 11-11; 12-3, 7-10.30 Sun ~ Bedrooms: £25B/£35B

Brunswick £ 🍺

1 Railway Terrace; close to Derby Midland railway station

An incredible 17 handpumps are kept in constant use in this traditional old railway
pub. Seven are from their own Brunswick Brewery (the workings of which are visible

from a viewing area), including Recession Ale, First Brew, Second Brew, the highly-praised Railway Porter, Triple Hop, Festival Ale, and Old Accidental; prices are well below the average beer price for the area. Guest beers include Bass (straight from the cask), Batemans Mild, Burton Bridge Bitter, Kelham Island Pale Rider, Marstons Pedigree, Theakstons Old Peculier (tapped from the cask), and Timothy Taylors Landlord. They have beer festivals in February and the first week in October; draught farm cider. The very welcoming high-ceilinged serving bar has heavy, well padded leather seats, whisky-water jugs above the dado, and a dark blue ceiling and upper wall, with squared dark panelling below. The no-smoking room is decorated with little old-fashioned prints and swan's neck lamps, and has a high-backed wall settle and a coal fire; behind a curved glazed partition wall is a quietly chatty family parlour narrowing to the apex of the triangular building. Darts, cribbage, dominoes, fruit machine; good friendly service. Daily changing home-made bar food includes filled salad rolls with turkey, beef, ham, cheese and tuna and sweetcorn (£1.10), hot beef, hot turkey, cheese and bacon or hot traditional sausage beef cobs (£1.60), home-made celery and stilton soup (£1.95), ploughman's (£2.95), home-made chicken, leek, mushroom and celery pie (£3); note they do only rolls on Sunday. There are seats in the terrace area behind. (*Recommended by Richard Lewis, Chris Raisin, JDM, KM, Andy and Jill Kassube, Mrs A Haswell, Dr David Webster, Sue Holland, Mr and Mrs P Byatt, Jack and Philip Paxton*)

Own brew ~ Licensee Trevor Harris ~ Real ale ~ Lunchtime meals and snacks (11.30-2.30; evening meals by arrangemnt) ~ Restaurant ~ (01332) 290677 ~ Children in family room and no-smoking room ~ Jazz Thurs evenings ~ Open 11-11; 12-10.30 Sun

Olde Dolphin £

6 Queen St; nearest car park King St/St Michaels Lane

The cathedral and main pedestrianised area are very close, so this friendly and civilised pub is a useful resting place. The four cosy rooms, two with their own separate street doors, are traditional and old-fashioned – from the varnished wall benches of the tiled-floor public bar to the little carpeted snug with its brocaded seat; there are big bowed black beams, shiny panelling, cast-iron-framed tables, a coal fire, lantern lights and opaque leaded windows; the atmosphere is friendly and quietly chatty, and they have the daily papers and board games (no piped music). Well kept Bass, Marstons Pedigree, Ruddles and Worthington BB on handpump, with a couple of interesting guest beers each week; very cheap food includes sandwiches (from £1.35; toasties £1.75), filled baked potatoes (from £2), omelettes (from £2.80), all-day breakfast (£2.95), gammon and egg and a generous mixed grill (£3.99), with dishes of the day such as liver and onion or braised steak. There is a no-smoking upstairs tearoom. (*Recommended by JDM, KM, Alan and Charlotte Sykes, Chris Raisin, David Carr; more reports please*)

Bass ~ Manager Paul Needham ~ Real ale ~ Meals and snacks (10.30-10 – till 7 Fri/Sat; 12-5 Sun) ~ (01332) 349115 ~ Children allowed in tearoom ~ Live music Sun and Tues evenings ~ Open 10.30am-11pm; Sun 12-10.30

EYAM SK2276 Map 7
Miners Arms 🛏

Signposted off A263 Chesterfield—Chapel en le Frith

Careful refurbishments have taken place here – the licensees have aimed these to be in keeping with the traditional feel of the place. It's well organised and friendly and very popular at lunchtime for the good fresh food, though as the evening draws on you'll find the locals arriving to drink; they don't do bar meals then. Well served by attentive staff, the choice of dishes includes soups such as carrot and lentil (£1.95), crispy filled french bread (from £2.10), ploughman's with the area's traditional fruitcake (from £3.75), cumberland sausage with onion gravy (£3.95), daily quiche such as salmon and broccoli (£4.60), beef braised in stout (£5.50), chicken breast in cream and prawn sauce (£5.75), crispy roast duck or a fish of the day like smoked haddock florentine (£5.95), and home-made bakewell tart, sherry trifle or apple crumble (£2.20). There's a pleasant restful atmosphere in the three little plush beamed rooms, each of which has its own stone fireplace. Well kept Stones and Tetleys on handpump. Decent walks nearby, especially below Froggatt Edge. *(Recommended by Peter Marshall, Pat and Tony Young, Norma and Keith Bloomfield, David Carr, Pat and Tony Martin, C Smith, B, M and P Kendall, Barry and Anne, Peter and Jan Humphreys, Alan and Heather Jacques, R D Kelso, M Mason, D Thompson)*

Free house ~ Licensees Nicholas and Ruth Cook ~ Real ales ~ Lunchtime meals and snacks (not Sun, not Mon evening) ~ Evening restaurant (they do Sun lunch, too) ~ (01433) 630853 ~ Children welcome ~ Open 12-3, 7-11; closed Sun evening, Mon lunchtime and first 2 weeks Jan ~ Bedrooms: £25B/£50B

FENNY BENTLEY SK1750 Map 7
Coach & Horses
A515 N of Ashbourne

After a walk (muddy boots must be left outside), the two log fires in this comfortable coaching inn are most welcoming. The little no-smoking back room has ribbed green built-in wall banquettes and old prints and engravings on its dark green leafy Victorian wallpaper. There are more old prints in the friendly front bar, which has flowery-cushioned wall settles and library chairs around the dark tables on its turkey carpet, waggonwheels hanging from the black beams, horsebrasses and pewter mugs, and a huge mirror. Popular bar meals include soup (£1.75), baps and sandwiches (from £2, toasties from £2.95), filled baked potatoes (from £3.95), grilled trout or filled yorkshire puddings (£5.50), chicken balti (£5.55), steak and kidney pie (£5.65), lamb liver and onions or well-praised vegetarian meals like mushroom and stilton bake (£5.95), and steaks (from £9.45); Sunday roasts (£5.95), and children's meals (£2.50). The dining room is no smoking. Well kept Bass on handpump, along with Black Bull and Dovedale brewed a couple of fields away; darts, dominoes and piped music. Picnic tables on the back grass by an elder tree, with rustic benches and white tables and chairs under cocktail parasols on the terrace in front of this pretty rendered stone house. *(Recommended by Derek and Sylvia Stephenson, Colin Fisher, Eric Locker, Dorothee and Dennis Glover, John Scarisbrick, Mike and Wendy Proctor, Joy and Peter Heatherley, Norma and Keith Bloomfield, Richard Houghton, Pat and Roger Fereday, Jack and Philip Paxton)*

Free house ~ Licensee Edward Anderson ~ Real ale ~ Meals and snacks ~ Restaurant ~ (01335) 350246 ~ Children in family room ~ Open 11.30-2.30, 6.30-11; closed 25 Dec

FROGGATT EDGE SK2477 Map 7
Chequers 🍺
B6054, off A623 N of Bakewell; Ordnance Survey Sheet 119, map reference 247761

The fairly smart bar in this beautifully placed country inn has library chairs or small high-backed winged settles on the well waxed floorboards, an attractive, richly varnished beam-and-board ceiling, antique prints on the white walls, partly stripped back to big dark stone blocks, and a big solid-fuel stove; one corner has a nicely carved oak cupboard. Under the new licensees, bar food includes soup (£1.40), courgette and carrot roulade (£2.25), sandwiches (from £2.25; egg and bacon £3.95), mushroom and pine nut tart (£4.95), crispy garlic cod (£5.50), steak and kidney pie or chicken casserole with dumplings (£5.95), grilled lamb cutlets with a herb crust (£6.96), sirloin steak (£7.95), and puddings such as sticky toffee pudding or walnut and honey tart (from £1.95). Well kept Wards Best and a guest like Vaux Waggle Dance on handpump, about 25 malt whiskies and a good wine list. The restaurant is no smoking; piped music. There are seats in the peaceful back garden. Froggatt Edge itself is just up through the woods behind the inn. *(Recommended by John Fahy, Paul Barnett, IHR, Richard Fallon, JDM, KM, John Davis, Margaret and Nigel Dennis, Mike and Karen England, R H Rowley, Barry and Anne, DC, John and Christine Simpson, Mike Gorton, G P Kernan, Mike and Wendy Proctor)*

Wards ~ Lease: Miss M Wheelden, Mr R Graham ~ Real ale ~ Meals and snacks ~ Restaurant ~ (01433) 630231 ~ Children welcome ~ Open 11-3, 5.30-11; 11-11 Sat; 12-10.30 Sun ~ Bedrooms: £44B/£55B

GRINDLEFORD SK2478 Map 7
Maynard Arms 🛏

B6521 N of village

The neatly kept gardens here have a new water feature this year and there has been some further refurbishment to the hotel side. It's a civilised and comfortable place, and the smart and spacious high-ceilinged main bar has some dark wood panelling, silver tankards above the bar, and local and cricketing photographs on the walls. Bar food includes soup (£1.75), sandwiches (from £2.25; open ones from £3.35), vegetable and nut crumble (£4.45), mussels in a leek and mushroom sauce (£4.75), all-day breakfast or prawn linguini (£5.25), spicy beef (£6.15), steaks (from £7.95), and puddings like home-made strawberry cheesecake (from £2.55). The restaurant is no smoking, and overlooks the neatly kept gardens. Well kept Boddingtons and Whitbreads Castle Eden on handpump; piped music. *(Recommended by Derek and Sylvia Stephenson, Alan and Heather Jacques, Margaret and Nigel Dennis, IHR, Mike and Wendy Proctor, FMH, I P G Derwent, Sue Holland, Dave Webster)*

Free house ~ Licensees Jonathan and Joanne Tindall ~ Real ale ~ Meals and snacks ~ Restaurant ~ (01433) 630321 ~ Children in restaurant and eating area of bar ~ Open 11-3, 6-11; 12-10.30 Sun ~ Bedrooms: £49B/£65B

HARDWICK HALL SK4663 Map 7
Hardwick Inn

2¾ miles from M1 junction 29: at roundabout A6175 towards Clay Cross; after ½ mile turn left signed Stainsby and Hardwick Hall (ignore any further sign for Hardwick Hall); at Stainsby follow rd to left; a fter 2½ miles staggered rd junction, turn left

The National Trust owns this 17th-c golden stone house – it was built around 1600 as the lodge for the lovely Elizabethan hall. The separate rooms have a relaxed old-fashioned atmosphere and stone-mullioned latticed windows, though perhaps the most comfortable is the carpeted lounge with its upholstered wall settles, tub chairs and stools around varnished wooden tables; one room has an attractive 18th-c carved settle. Generous helpings of popular bar food include soup (£1.35), sandwiches (from £2.20), ploughman's (from £3.60), lincolnshire sausage with egg (£3.95), home-made steak and kidney pie (£4.75), a daily vegetarian dish (£5), grilled trout (£5.25), daily specials such as liver, bacon and sausage casserole (£4.75), rabbit pie (£5.25) or kangaroo steak (£7.85), and steaks (from £8.25); puddings (£2.20), children's menu (from £2.25), and afternoon teas (from £2.50). The restaurant is no smoking. Well kept Marstons Pedigree, Morlands Old Speckled Hen, Theakstons XB and Old Peculier and Youngers Scotch on handpump, and 70 malt whiskies; prompt, friendly service, even when busy. Tables outside offer a very nice view. The pub can get crowded, especially at weekends. There's a charge for entry to the park, which you can no longer get into from the inn. *(Recommended by C Booth, DC, R H Rowley, Andy and Jill Kassube, Peter and Audrey Dowsett, H E and E A Simpson)*

Free house ~ Lease: Peter and Pauline Batty ~ Real ale ~ Meals and snacks (11.30-9.30; 12-9 Sun) ~ Carvery restaurant (not Mon, not Sun evening) ~ (01246) 850245 ~ Children in restaurant and three family rooms ~ Open 11.30-11; 12-10.30 Sun

HAYFIELD SK0388 Map 7
Lantern Pike 🛏

Little Hayfield; A624 towards Glossop

It's the warmly friendly service from the landlady and her staff that makes this neatly kept pub special. The bar is unpretentious but cosy with a warm fire, plush seats, flowers on the tables, and lots of brass platters, china and toby jugs. Well kept Boddingtons, Flowers IPA, and Timothy Taylors Landlord on handpump, and a good selection of malt whiskies. Tasty home-made bar food (with prices the same as last year) includes soup (£1.95), sandwiches from (£2.35), breaded plaice (£4.80), lasagne, curry, chilli or vegetarian dishes like leek and mushroom crumble (£5.15), and several daily specials such as steak and stout pie (£5.50); children's menu (£2.25), Sunday roast (£5.25); OAPs' two-course lunch (weekday lunchtimes only, £3.90). Darts, dominoes, and sometimes piped nostalgic music. The back dining room is no smoking. Tables on a two-level stonewalled back terrace, served from a window, look over a big-windowed weaver's house to the Lantern Pike itself, and the pub's very well placed for walkers. *(Recommended by Stephen Brown, Amanda and Simon Southwell, Eddie Edwards, Mr and Mrs N Thorp, Stephen Holman, Philip and Ann Falkner, Helen and Keith Bowers and friends, Mike and Wendy Proctor, J E Rycroft, Wallis Taylor, Dorothy and Leslie Pilson, E J Hawkes)*

Free house ~ Licensee Geraldine McDonald ~ Real ale ~ Meals and snacks ~ Restaurant ~ (01663) 747590 ~ Children welcome ~ Open 11.30-3, 6-11; 11.30-11 Sat; 11.30-10.30 Sun ~ Bedrooms: £25B/£40B

HOLMESFIELD SK3277 Map 7
Robin Hood
Lydgate; just through Holmesfield on B6054

After a walk along the footpaths opposite this friendly moorland inn, there are lovely open fires to relax in front of. The neat extended lounge area has exposed beams, chintz and paisley curtains, plush button-back wall banquettes around wood-effect tables, and partly carpeted flagstone floors. Promptly served by smart and pleasant staff, generous helpings of bar food might include home-made soup (£2.25), sandwiches (from £2.25; hot roast beef in french bread £4.75), filled baked potatoes (from £2.95), ploughman's (£4.95), lasagne (£5.75), home-made steak, ale and mushroom pie or stilton and walnut quiche (£5.95), steaks (from £10.95), daily specials like barbecue spare ribs (£2.50), vegetable stroganoff (£5.95) or chicken in a prawn and chive sauce (£8.95), and puddings like home-made cheesecake (from £2.35); they offer half helpings to children and OAPs. It's best to book at weekends. Charles Wells Bombardier on handpump, and several malt whiskies; piped music. There are stone tables outside on the cobbled front courtyard. *(Recommended by G P Kernan, Michael Butler, K Frostick, Mr and Mrs B Langrish, FMH; more reports please)*

Free house ~ Licensees Chris and Jackie Hughes ~ Real ale ~ Meals and snacks (11.30-2.30, 6-9.30; all day Sat and Sun) ~ (0114) 289 0360 ~ Children in eating area of bar and in restaurant ~ Open 11.30-3, 6-11; 11.30-11 Sat; 12-10.30 Sun

HOPE SK1783 Map 7
Cheshire Cheese
Edale Road

Inside, this 16th-c village pub has three snug oak-beamed rooms, divided by thick stone walls and up and down steps – particularly cosy in cool weather, as each has its own coal fire. Though this is a genuine pub (walkers can keep their boots on), the food is so good these days that in the evenings the emphasis turns to dining. Rabbit pie (£6.95) and other game often comes courtesy of the chef's own marksmanship, and there's plenty of fish in summer (cod and chips £4.95, halibut, dover sole, lemon sole and halibut from £8.95). Other dishes include good soups such as cauliflower and stilton, sandwiches (from £2.50), cumberland sausage (£3.95), steak and kidney pie, and steaks; children's menu. The nicely presented main dishes come with lots of fresh vegetables, and puddings are particularly tempting. The two small dining rooms (one on the same level as the serving bar) are no smoking. Decoration includes lots of old local photographs and prints (besides some horsebrasses). Service is very obliging; well kept Wards Sheffield Best and Darleys Thorne with a guest such as Caledonian 80/- on handpump, a good choice of house wines; darts, dominoes, cribbage, unobtrusive piped music. Parking can be a problem at busy times. We have not yet heard from people staying here, but it's an attractive village in a fine walking area. *(Recommended by Alan Thwaite, Sam Samuells, Lynda Payton, Simon and Ann Ward, Malcolm and Pat Rudlin, Simon Watkins, Jeanne Cross, Paul Silvestri, David Carr)*

Free house ~ Licensees Mandy and Peter Eustace ~ Real ale ~ Meals and snacks (not Sun evening) ~ (01433) 620381 ~ Children in eating area ~ Open 12-3, 6-11; closed winter Sun evening and winter Mon lunchtime ~ Two bedrooms: /£45B

KINGS NEWTON SK3826 Map 7
Hardinge Arms

5 miles from M1 junction 23A; follow signs to E Midlands airport; A453, in 3 miles (Isley) turn right signed Melbourne, Wilson; right turn in 2 miles to Kings Newton; pub is on left at end of village

The rambling front bar in this civilised and friendly place has open fires, beams, a fine panelled and carved bar counter, and blue plush cushioned seats and stools – some in a pleasantly big bow window. At the back is a stately and spacious lounge. As well as a carvery (popular at lunchtimes with older people and businessmen), bar food includes home-made soup (£1.90), open sandwiches (from £3.35; not Sunday), cod and chips (£4.25), lentil crumble (£5.50), chicken curry (£5.95), pork in a mustard, dry vermouth and cream sauce (£6.50), steaks (from £6.95), and puddings (£2.50). Well kept Boddingtons and Flowers IPA on handpump, and several malt whiskies. *(Recommended by Theo, Anne and Jane Gaskin, A and R Cooper, Mr and Mrs E M Clarke, Derek and Leslie Martin, Eric Locker, C H and P Stride; more reports please)*

Free house ~ Licensee Mel Stevens ~ Real ale ~ Meals and snacks (12-2, 6-10; till 9 Sun) ~ (01332) 863808 ~ Children in eating area of bar ~ Open 11.30-2.30, 6-11; 12-3, 7-10.30 Sun ~ Bedrooms: £25B/£40B

KIRK IRETON SK2650 Map 7
Barley Mow 🛏 🍺

Signposted off B5023 S of Wirksworth

This handsome Jacobean stone house can hardly have changed inside or out since it was built. The simple sign outside is almost obscured by a tree branch, time is measured by a 17th-c sundial, and the only games you'll find in the unspoilt little rooms are dominoes and cards. The timeless and quietly pubby small main bar has antique settles on the tiled floor or built into the panelling, a coal fire, old prints, shuttered mullioned windows – and a modest wooden counter behind which are the casks of Cottage Southern Bitter, Hartington IPA, Hook Norton Bitter and Old Hookey, Marstons Pedigree, and Whim Old Izaak, all costing a bit less than you'd usually pay for a pint in this area. Another room has cushioned pews built in, oak parquet flooring and a small woodburner, and a third has more pews, tiled floor, beams and joists, and big landscape prints. One room is no smoking. Popular filled lunchtime rolls; good value evening meals for residents only. Civilised old-fashioned service, a couple of friendly pugs and a somnolent newfoundland. There's a good-sized garden, as well as a couple of benches out in front. The charming village is in good walking country. *(Recommended by J F Knutton, J Roy Smylie, Pete Baker, JDM, KM, Jo and Gary Charlton, Neil Ferguson-Lee, Jack and Philip Paxton, David Carr, John Beeken, Phil and Sally Gorton, Wayne Brindle)*

Free house ~ Licensee Mary Short ~ Real ale ~ Lunchtime sandwiches ~ (01335) 370306 ~ Children at lunchtime, not in bar ~ Open 12-2, 7-11(10.30 Sun); closed 25 Dec, 1 Jan ~ Bedrooms: £25B/£42B

Most pubs in this book sell wine by the glass. We mention wines only if they are a cut above the – generally low – average. Please let us know of any good pubs for wine.

LADYBOWER RESERVOIR SK1986 Map 7
Yorkshire Bridge
A6013 N of Bamford

Below rather than beside the reservoir, this substantial late Victorian roadside hotel is very busy in summer as the countryside around is good for walking; service remains invariably pleasant and efficient, however. One area has sturdy cushioned wall settles, staffordshire dogs and toby jugs on a big stone fireplace with a warm coal-effect gas fire, china on delft shelves, a panelled dado and so forth. A second extensive area, with another fire, is lighter and more airy, with floral wallpaper, pale wooden furniture, good big black and white photographs and lots of plates on the walls, and a small no-smoking conservatory with wicker chairs. Bar food, served generously, includes soup (£1.80), ploughman's (£4.10), cod fillet or chicken and mushroom pie (£5.60), steak and kidney pie or lasagne (£5.75), scampi (£6.50) and puddings (from £2.50). Well kept Bass, John Smiths Magnet and Stones on handpump, and good coffee with real cream; darts, cribbage, dominoes, fruit machine, and piped music. *(Recommended by Gwen and Peter Andrews, Victoria Regan, Harold Bramhall)*

Free house ~ Licensee Molly Herling ~ Real ale ~ Meals and snacks (all day Sun) ~ (01433) 651361 ~ Children welcome ~ Open 11-11; 12-10.30 Sun ~ Bedrooms: £38B/£49.50B

LITTLE HUCKLOW SK1678 Map 7
Old Bulls Head
Pub signposted from B6049

Upland sheep pastures surround this atmospheric and friendly little country pub in its quiet and pleasant village setting. The two neatly kept main rooms have old oak beams, thickly cushioned built-in settles, antique brass and iron household tools, local photographs, and a coal fire in a neatly restored stone hearth. One room is served from a hatch, the other over a polished bar counter; there's also an unusual little 'cave' room at the back. Tasty bar food includes home-made soup (£2.25), sandwiches or filled baked potatoes (from £3.25), cheesy vegetable bake or home-made steak and kidney pie (£6.25), chicken with leek and stilton (£7.85), popular gammon with egg (£7.95), and steaks (from £9.25). Well kept Tetleys and Wards guest from carved handpumps, and several malt whiskies; darts, dominoes. There are tables in the neatly tended garden, which is full of an unusual collection of well restored and attractively painted old farm machinery. *(Recommended by Michael Butler, Peter Marshall, John Fahy and others)*

Free house ~ Licensee Julie Denton ~ Real ale ~ Meals and snacks ~ (01298) 871097 ~ Children welcome ~ Open 12-3, 6(6.30 Sat)-11; 12-3, 6.30-10.30 Sun

nr MELBOURNE SK3825 Map 7
John Thompson 🍺
Ingleby; village signposted from A514 at Swarkestone

This is a tremendously enjoyable pub, run with enthusiasm by Mr Thompson and his warmly friendly staff. Their own-brewed real ale – JTS, Summer Gold and winter Porter are very good indeed – as is the popular food. The big, pleasantly modernised lounge has ceiling joists, some old oak settles, button-back leather seats, sturdy oak tables, antique prints and paintings, and a log-effect gas fire; a couple of smaller cosier rooms open off, with pool, a fruit machine, video game, and a juke box in the children's room, and a no-smoking area in the lounge; piped music. Straightforward but good and well-priced bar food consists of sandwiches or rolls (from £1, nothing else on Sundays; the beef is excellent), home-made soup (£1.50), salads with cold ham or beef (£4), excellent roast beef with yorkshire puddings (£5, not Mondays) and well liked puddings (£1.50). The pub is in a lovely setting above the River Trent, with lots of tables on the well kept lawns by flowerbeds, and on a partly covered outside terrace with its own serving bar. *(Recommended by Michael Marlow, Colin Fisher,*

Jean Bernard Brisset, Pamela and Merlyn Horswell, Jean and Richard James, Peter and Audrey Dowsett, JDM, KM, Andy and Jill Kassube, Peter and Patricia Burton, CW, JW, Richard Houghton, R & A, Beryl and Bill Farmer)

Own brew ~ Licensee John Thompson ~ Real ale ~ Lunchtime meals and snacks (sandwiches only Sun; cold buffet only, Mon) ~ (01332) 862469 ~ Children in separate room ~ Open 10.30-2.30, 7-11; 12-2.30, 7-10.30 Sun

MONSAL HEAD SK1871 Map 7
Monsal Head Hotel 🛏
B6465

The best places to admire the dramatic views down over the valley are from the terrace in front of this extended Victorian hotel or from big windows in the upstairs lounge. The cosy side stable bar (which once housed the unfortunate horses that lugged people and their luggage up from the station deep down at the end of the valley viaduct) still has a bit of a horsey theme, with stripped timber horse-stalls, harness and brassware, as well as flagstones, a big warming woodburning stove in an inglenook, cushioned oak pews around flowery-clothed tables, farm tools, and railway signs and lamps from the local disused station; steps lead up into a crafts gallery. Well kept Hartington Bitter, Marstons Pedigree, Monsal Best Bitter, John Smiths, Theakstons Best, Old Peculier, and XB, and Charles Wells Bombardier on handpump; polite, helpful service. Bar food includes sandwiches, lasagne (£4.65), scampi and a vegetarian dish (£4.95), home-made leek and mushroom au gratin (£5.20), home-made steak and kidney pie (£6.30), pheasant braised in madeira (£10.45) and mixed grill (£11.55); Sunday roast (£6.50). The back garden has a play area. The spacious high-ceilinged no-smoking front bar is set out like a wine bar, with dining chairs around big tables; it's partitioned off from a no-smoking restaurant area. *(Recommended by A Bradbury, Mrs A Haswell, Jo and Gary Charlton, Jack and Philip Paxton, Mike and Wendy Proctor, Dennis Stevens, David Carr, Ann and Colin Hunt)*

Free house ~ Licensees Alan Smith, Martin Ward ~ Real ale ~ Meals and snacks (12-9.30) ~ Restaurant ~ (01629) 640250 ~ Children welcome until 7pm ~ Folk music winter Fri evenings ~ Open 11-11; 12-11 Sun; closed 25 Dec ~ Bedrooms: £40B/£54B

SHARDLOW SK4330 Map 7
Old Crown ♟
Cavendish Bridge

Although this thriving 17th-c coaching inn is often very busy, the friendly staff seem to cope with cheerful efficiency. They keep a good range of real ales on handpump: Bass, Batemans XXXB, Fullers London Pride, Golden Newt, Greene King Abbot, Marstons Pedigree, Thwaites Best, Timothy Taylors Landlord, and Wide Eyed and Crownless (from Leicestershire); a nice choice of malt whiskies. The daily specials are the meals to go for, with a good choice of dishes like meatballs in a rich onion gravy (£5.25), beef with ox kidneys in ale pudding (£5.95), fresh cod pie (£6.75), grilled bacon steak topped with melted cheese (£6.95), chicken with ginger and mustard in a sherry and cream sauce (£7.25), and roast shank of lamb (£8.25). The bar is packed with bric-a-brac, including hundreds of jugs and mugs hanging from the beamed ceiling, brewery and railway memorabilia, and lots of pictures. The pub is next to the River Trent and was once the deportation point for convicts bound for the colonies. *(Recommended by Susan and John Douglas, Andy and Jill Kassube, Jo and Gary Charlton, JDM, KM, Stephen Brown, Sue Holland, Dave Webster, Roger Bellingham, GSB, Jack and Philip Paxton, Wayne Brindle, A and R Cooper, Chris Raisin, Martin and Penny Fletcher, Rona Murdoch)*

Free house ~ Licensees Peter and Gillian Morton-Harrison ~ Real ale ~ Lunchtime meals and snacks ~ (01332) 792392 ~ Children in eating area of bar only ~ Open 11-3, 5-11; 12-4, 7-10.30 Sun; cl evenings 25/26 Dec

---

If we know a pub does summer barbecues, we say so.

WARDLOW SK1875 Map 7
Three Stags Heads ◖

Wardlow Mires; A623 by junction with B6465

A really old-fashioned place this, and certainly not in any twee sense: this is where you might find several dogs taking a hopeful interest in your meal, let alone hogging the fire, and where the furnishings look elderly rather than antique – though there are antiques. In short, it appeals hugely to those who really dislike the sterilised and hygienic comfort of today's efficient chain pubs. The tiny unassuming parlour bar has old leathercloth seats, a couple of antique settles with flowery cushions, two high-backed windsor armchairs and simple oak tables on the flagstones, and a cast-iron kitchen range which is kept alight in winter; one curiosity is the petrified cat in a glass case. Tables in the small no-smoking dining parlour – where there's an open fire – are bookable. They try to vary the seasonal menu to suit the weather so dishes served on their hardy home-made plates (the barn is a pottery workshop) might include a leek and stilton hotpot or vegetable curry (£5.50), lamb and spinach curry (£6.50), steak and kidney pie (£7), seasonal game (£8.50), and fillet steak (£12.50). Abbeydale Brewery Matins, Absolution, and Black Lurcher (brewed for them only), and Springhead Bitter on handpump, and lots of continental and British bottled beers. Cribbage and dominoes, nine men's morris, backgammon, and chess. Walkers, their boots and dogs are welcome; they have some cats. The front terrace outside looks across the main road to the distant hills. The car park is across the road by the petrol station. *(Recommended by John Plumridge, Victoria Herriott, Richard Fallon, Nigel Woolliscroft, Barbara Wensworth, Addie and Irene Henry, David Carr, Ian and Trish Avis, Esther and John Sprinkle, Mike and Wendy Proctor, Fiona and David Pemberton)*

Free house ~ Licensees Geoff and Pat Fuller ~ Real ale ~ Meals and snacks (12-3, 7-10) ~ Restaurant ~ (01298) 872268 ~ Children welcome away from bar room until 8.30 ~ Live folk/Irish music Sat evening ~ Open 7-11 weekdays; 12-11 Sat; 12-10.30 Sun; closed Mon except bank holidays

WHITTINGTON MOOR SK3873 Map 7
Derby Tup ◖ £

387 Sheffield Rd; B6057 just S of A61 roundabout

Eleven real ales are kept on handpump at this straightforward corner pub, with regulars like Batemans XXXB, Kelham Island Golden Eagle, Greene King Abbot, Marstons Pedigree, Tetleys, Theakstons Old Peculier, and Timothy Taylors Landlord, and five quickly changing guest beers such as Ash Vine Casablanca, Gibbs Mew Bishops Tipple, Woodfordes Wherry, and Youngs Special. They also have lots of continental and bottle-conditioned beers, changing ciders, and decent malt whiskies. The unspoiled plain rectangular bar with frosted street windows and old dark brown linoleum has simple furniture arranged around the walls – there's a tremendously long red plastic banquette – leaving lots of standing room; two more small unpretentious rooms. Besides good sandwiches, the daily changing bar food, home-made with fresh ingredients, might include mushroom soup (£1.95), spaghetti bolognese or cauliflower cheese (£3.50), chilli con carne or chicken casserole (£3.95), and beef in ale or thai minted lamb (£4.50); cheerful relaxed atmosphere, piped rock and blues, and trivia machine. The dining area is no smoking. Despite the remote-sounding name, Whittington Moor is on the northern edge of Chesterfield. *(Recommended by JJW, CMW, Colin Bournes, Tony Sheppard, David Atkinson, Jack and Philip Paxton)*

Free house ~ Licensee Peter Hayes ~ Real ale ~ Meals and snacks (12-2.30, 5-7.30; not Sun evening) ~ (01246) 454316 ~ Children in eating area of bar ~ Irish folk/blues every 2nd Tues or Thurs ~ Open 11-11; 12-4, 7-10.30 Sun

If you enjoy your visit to a pub, please tell the publican. They work extraordinarily long hours, and when people show their appreciation it makes it all seem worth while.

WOOLLEY MOOR SK3661 Map 7
White Horse 🍺
White Horse Lane, off B6014 Matlock—Clay Cross
Derbyshire Dining Pub of the Year

A firm favourite with several readers, this attractive, bustling old pub is run by friendly enthusiastic licensees who keep a good balance between the popular food served in the cottagey beamed dining lounge, and the original tap room where the cheerful locals gather to organise their various teams – darts, dominoes, and two each for football and boules (they have their own pitch and piste); cribbage. They plan to add a no-smoking conservatory. Enjoyable, popular bar food, made with fresh local produce, includes quite a few daily specials like warming spicy bean and beef soup, excellent feta cheese, cashew nut and grape slice, Italian beef pasta (£3.75), seafood quiche (£3.95), game pie (£4.25), venison sausage bake (£5.50), chilli lamb (£6.50), fresh salmon florentine (£6.75), good pork and wild mushroom stroganoff, and puddings (£2.25); sandwiches (from £2.40); children's meals come with a puzzle sheet and crayons. Well kept Bass and four weekly changing guests on handpump, and a decent wine list; piped music in the lounge. The restaurant is no smoking. Picnic tables in the garden have lovely views across the Amber Valley, and there's a very good children's play area with wooden play train, climbing frame and swings. A booklet describes eight walks from the pub, and the landlord is a keen walker; the pub is handy for Ogston Reservoir. *(Recommended by Neil Porter, Norma and Keith Bloomfield, Pat and Roger Fereday, Peter and Audrey Dowsett, M Buchanan, J Warren, Peter Marshall, David Carr, Andrew Pashley, Luke Worthington, Mike and Sue Walton, John and Christine Lowe, Derek and Sylvia Stephenson, Sue and Geoff Price, JDM, KM, G P Kernan, Jack and Philip Paxton, Tony Young, David and Fiona Pemberton, Joy and Peter Heatherley, David and June Harwood, John Saul, Miss P Poole, Vicky and David Sarti)*

Free house ~ Licensees Bill and Jill Taylor ~ Real ale ~ Meals and snacks ~ Restaurant (not Sun evening) ~ (01246) 590319 ~ Children in restaurant ~ Open 11.30-2.30(3 Sat), 6-11; 12-2.30, 5-10.30 Sun

---

Lucky Dip

Besides the fully inspected pubs, you might like to try these Lucky Dips recommended to us and described by readers (if you do, please send us reports):

☆ **Ashbourne** [Ashbourne Green (A515 towards Matlock); SK1846], *Bowling Green*: Well kept Bass, Worthington and two other changing ales, wide choice of good value home-cooked food inc vegetarian, friendly atmosphere, straightforward comfort; good bedrooms (Colin Sims)
Ashbourne [central], *Green Man*: Well kept Mansfield beers, friendly welcoming landlord, good reasonably priced pub food; good value recently refurbished bedrooms *(Bill and Pam Baker)*; [Market Sq], *White Lion*: Well kept Vaux Samson and Waggle Dance, good choice of food inc interesting fish, good steaks and vegetarian dishes; friendly and welcoming; bedrooms *(Bill and Pam Baker)*
☆ **Ashford in the Water** [SK1969], *Black Bull*: Cosy and homely comfortable lounge with a more pubby atmosphere than our main entry here, well kept Robinsons ales, nicely presented home-cooked food from good soup and sandwiches up, reasonable prices, quick friendly service, no piped music; tables out in front *(Ann and Colin Hunt, John Waller, Dorothy and Leslie Pilson, IHR, David Carr,*

Sue and Geoff Price)
Aston upon Trent [off A6 SE of Derby; SK4129], *Malt Shovel*: Comfortable Victorian pub with separate games bar, cheap lunchtime sandwiches, Marstons Pedigree, Tetleys and a guest beer, back terrace; open all day Sat *(Anon)*
☆ **Bamford** [A6013; SK2083], *Derwent*: Interestingly varied separate rooms off central hall-servery, big pictures and windows, welcoming helpful service, bar food inc vegetarian, well kept Marstons Best and Pedigree and Stones Best, RAF Dambuster photographs, good value restaurant; children welcome, quiz nights, seats in garden; comfortable reasonably priced bedrooms, open all day *(Derek Patey, K Flack, Pat and Tony Young, LYM)*
Baslow [Church Lane; SK2572], *Cavendish*: An upmarket hotel, but delightful, with very good bar food, drinks and informal dining in Garden Room with magnificent views over Chatsworth estate; bedrooms *(J F M West)*; [Nether End], *Devonshire Arms*: Small straightforward hotel in pleasant

surroundings, usual food inc decent sandwiches, evening restaurant, real ales inc Marstons Pedigree and Tetleys, quiet piped music, footpath to Chatsworth; bedrooms *(JDM, KM)*

☆ Biggin [W of A515; SK1559], *Waterloo*: Wide choice of good value generous food inc help-yourself salads and children's dishes, Bass, welcoming service; dales views *(D and D Savidge, Paul Robinshaw)*

☆ Birch Vale [via Station Rd towards Thornsett off A6015; SK0287], *Sycamore*: Good reasonably priced food inc children's dishes and rich puddings in thriving four-roomed dining pub; well kept ales, friendly helpful service, piped music, fountain in downstairs drinking bar; spacious streamside gardens with good play area, pets' corner and summer bar; restaurant open all day Sun, children welcome, handy for Sett Valley trail; bedrooms comfortable, good breakfast *(David Hoult, LYM)*

Birch Vale [Hayfield Rd (A6015)], *Vine*: Sensibly renovated, clean, warm and welcoming, efficient service, well kept beer, ample food inc OAP lunches *(R Davies)*

Bonsall [SK2858], *Barley Mow*: Friendly pub of character, with particularly well kept beer, good food *(Paul Robinshaw)*

☆ Brassington [SK2354], *Miners Arms*: Very welcoming and pubby, with good food from hot pork rolls up, well kept Marstons Pedigree and fortnightly guest beers, hard-working landlord, tables out among flower tubs; open all day, children welcome, live music some nights; bedrooms *(Miss S Watkin, P Taylor, JDM, KM, Paul Robinshaw)*

Bullbridge [off A610 W of Ripley; SK3652], *Lord Nelson*: Popular mid 19th-c pub with beamed lounge, good value lunchtime food, three or four Mansfield real ales; piped music; picnic tables in small garden *(JJW, CMW)*

Buxton [Water St; SK0673], *Clubhouse*: Spacious comfortable lounge on several levels, polished floorboards, armchairs, good decoration, cheerful long-serving staff, nice atmosphere, decent food, Ind Coope Burton and Tetleys; opp Opera House *(G Curtis)*; [Bridge St], *Railway*: Large welcoming railway-theme food pub under viaduct, huge helpings of varied well cooked food, well kept Hardys & Hansons, prompt service *(Richard Houghton)*

Calver [off A623 N of Baslow; SK2474], *Bridge*: Unspoilt but comfortable and roomy, with well kept Hardys & Hansons, quick good value food, pleasant landlord, old brass and local prints; tables in nice big garden by River Derwent *(Alan and Heather Jacques, IHR)*

☆ Castleton [High St/Castle St; SK1583], *Castle*: Plush hotel bars with handsome flagstones, beams, stripped stonework, roaring fires, good choice of food, good friendly service and attention to detail; keg beers; open all day summer, tables outside; good bedrooms *(Martin Bromfield, Bernadette Garner, Mike and Wendy Proctor, Peter Blake, Mrs S Miller, Dr F M Halle, LYM)*

☆ Castleton [Cross St], *Olde Nags Head*: Small but solid hotel dating from 17th c, civilised turkey-carpeted main bar with interesting antique furnishings, coal fire, faint piped music, friendly staff, well kept ales, good coffee, decent bar food from sandwiches up inc vegetarian dishes, cosy Victorian restaurant; open all day, comfortable bedrooms *(Simon Watkins, Mrs B Sugarman, LYM)*

☆ Castleton [How Lane], *Peak*: Roomy airy bar, dining room with high ceiling and picture window view of Peak hills, wide choice of above-average generous reasonably priced food inc vegetarian, Tetleys and other ales, friendly service *(DC, Dr F M Halle)*

☆ Castleton, *George*: Good atmosphere and good value simple food in roomy bars with friendly helpful staff, well kept Bass; tables on wide forecourt; popular with young people – nr YHA; dogs welcome *(DC)*

Castleton, *Olde Cheshire Cheese*: Two communicating bar areas, cheery and cosy, with well kept Wards tapped from the cask, friendly staff, wide choice of reasonably priced food, open fire, sensibly placed darts; bedrooms *(Dr F M Halle, Philip and Ann Falkner, BB)*

Chellaston [High St; SK3730], *Lawns*: Attractive hotel, comfortable oak-beamed main lounge popular lunchtime with older people for food inc good value thatched lunchtime carvery, friendly efficient service, Bass, Marstons Pedigree and a changing guest beer; bedrooms *(Andrew and Ruth Triggs)*; [Derby Rd], *Rose & Crown*: Well upgraded, good outside drinking area, well kept Marstons Pedigree *(Dr and Mrs A K Clarke)*

☆ Chesterfield [43 Chatsworth Rd; SK3871], *Royal Oak*: Friendly pub doing very well under young landlord, fine choice of well kept beers and good atmosphere *(Richard Houghton, David Carr)*

☆ Chinley [off A624 towards Hayfield; SK0482], *Lamb*: Profusely decorated three-room stone-built roadside pub with friendly atmosphere, good value quick bar food inc notable fish pie, well kept Bass and other ales; children till 8.30; lots of tables out in front *(Mike and Wendy Proctor, Michael Graubart, BB)*

☆ Chunal [A624 a mile S of Glossop; SK0391], *Grouse*: Pleasant open-plan but cosy moorland pub, good bar food inc enjoyable home-made pies, good chips and interesting specials, friendly service, well kept Thwaites; spectacular views of Glossop, real fires, old photographs of surrounding countryside, traditional furnishings and candlelit tables, unobtrusive piped music; children allowed in upstairs restaurant *(J F M West, David Hoult)*

☆ Church Broughton [High St; SK2033], *Holly Bush*: Neat and attractive village pub, popular for good cheap simple home cooking inc Sun lunch; well kept Marstons Pedigree, friendly labradors *(Chris Raisin)*

Coxbench [Alfreton Rd; off B6179 N of Derby; SK3743], *Fox & Hounds*: Extensive choice of interesting reasonably priced food, good range of beers inc guests *(J F Knutton)*

☆ Cromford [Scarthin – one-way st behind mkt pl; SK2956], *Boat*: Long narrow bar with bric-a-brac and books, very welcoming staff, well priced food from black pudding to wild boar inc good Sun lunch, log fire, Bass and Mansfield ales; TV may be on for sports; children welcome, garden *(Dave Irving, David and Helen Wilkins, David Carr, Pete Yearsley)*

☆ Cutthorpe [NW of Chesterfield; B6050 well W of village; SK3273], *Gate*: Picture-window views over eastern Peak District from chatty area around bar, neat dining lounge down steps, decent fair-priced food in bargain lunches popular with older people, well kept ales such as Bass, Boddingtons, Flowers Original and Mansfield Riding, friendly efficient staff, lots of biggish pictures *(Dr F M Halle, BB)*

☆ Dale [Main St, Dale Abbey; off A6096 NE of Derby; SK4339], *Carpenters Arms*: Recently refurbished picturesque pub, small and friendly, with good value food in bar, lounge (no dogs here) and restaurant, well kept Ind Coope Burton and a guest beer, real fire, darts, fruit machine; garden with play area, camping and caravan park behind, pleasant village with Abbey ruins and unusual church attached to house *(JJW, CMW, Peter Clarke, Jack and Philip Paxton)*

☆ Derby [25 King St], *Flower Pot*: Extended and improving real ale pub with choice of ten or more kept well, some behind glass and feeding gravity taps, friendly staff, good value food, comfortable back bar with lots of books and old Derby photographs, three other simply furnished rooms, good live bands Sat, pleasant garden *(Richard Houghton, Michael Cox, Chris Raisin, Joan and Michel Hooper-Immins)*

☆ Derby [Irongate], *Standing Order*: Vast Wetherspoons conversion of imposing bank, central bar, booths down each side, elaborately painted plasterwork, pseudo-classical torsos, high portraits of mainly local notables; usual popular food all day, good range of well kept ales, reasonable prices, neat efficient young staff, no-smoking area; rather daunting acoustics *(Chris Raisin, BB)*
Derby [13 Exeter Pl], *Exeter Arms*: Super little snug with leaded and polished brass range, black and white tiled floor and two built-in curved settles, rest of pub refurbished in keeping; friendly staff, well kept Marstons, HMS *Exeter* memorabilia *(Chris Raisin)*; [King St], *Seven Stars*: 17th-c heavily beamed front bar, refurbished back bar with glass-topped well *(Chris Raisin)*; [Meadows Rd], *Smithfield*: Attractive curved brick frontage, high-ceilinged bar and three cosy rooms, seven changing well kept ales, wholesome plain lunchtime food, friendly helpful staff, garden by River Derwent; can get crowded *(Chris Raisin, G Coates)*

Dronfield [SK3378], *Old Sidings*: Interestingly designed railway memorabilia

pub with wide choice of reasonably priced good bar food inc special offers, well kept beer, restaurant *(Mr and Mrs Smith)*
Duffield [SK3443], *Bridge*: Mansfield family pub in lovely setting by River Derwent, good play area, riverside terrace, children's room – but large part of open-plan bar set aside for adults; usual food, well kept ales, shelves of nick-nacks *(Rona Murdoch)*

☆ Earl Sterndale [signed off B4053 S of Buxton; SK0967], *Quiet Woman*: Friendly little stonebuilt village pub, low-beamed and softly lit, lots of china ornaments, real fires, good sandwiches and pork pies, maybe a winter hotpot, maybe free-range bantam and goose eggs and local cheese for sale; well kept Marstons Pedigree and Best and a guest such as Banks's Mild; picnic tables out in front, lots of small animals *(M Mason, D Thompson, David Carr, Derek and Sylvia Stephenson, Paul Robinshaw, BB)*

☆ Edale [SK1285], *Old Nags Head*: Useful walkers' pub at start of Pennine Way, substantial basic cheap food, open fire, S&N and other ales; can be very busy, piped music sometimes loud; children in airy back family room, tables on front terrace and in garden – short path down to pretty streamside cottages *(Victoria Regan, Simon Watkins, David Carr, David Hoult, BB)*
Edale, *Rambler*: Another useful pub in this walkers' village, several rooms inc no-smoking and pool rooms, usual food, keg beer, friendly service *(Simon Watkins)*

☆ Elton [SK2261], *Duke of York*: Unspoilt old-fashioned local, like stepping back in time, lovely little quarry-tiled back tap room with massive fireplace, glazed bar and hatch to corridor, two front rooms – one like private parlour with dining table (no food, just crisps); darts, cl lunchtime, open 8-11 *(Richard Lewis, D and D Savidge)*

☆ Farnah Green [follow Hazelwood sign off A517 in Blackbrook, W edge of Belper; SK3346], *Bluebell*: Plush smartly run dining pub, good prompt food in relaxing small rooms; sturdy tables out on terrace and in quiet gently sloping spacious side garden, restaurant with inventive cooking, well kept Bass *(JDM, KM, BB)*

☆ Fenny Bentley [A515 N of Ashbourne; SK1750], *Bentley Brook*: Big open-plan bar/dining room with bare boards, mix of set tables and cushioned settles, bow windows, log fire, communicating airy carpeted restaurant; one or two changing own-brewed Leatherbritches ales and guest beers such as Brains SA, Mansfield Riding, Marstons Pedigree, Morlands Old Speckled Hen and Shepherd Neame Spitfire, usual food (maybe free meals for children eating with adults early evening), well reproduced piped music, games machines; picnic tables on terrace with proper barbecue area, skittles; open all day, handy for Dovedale; bedrooms *(Richard Lewis, David and Shelia, John Scarisbrick, Derek and Sylvia Stephenson, BB)*

Flagg [off A515 Buxton—Ashbourne, five miles from Buxton; SK1368], *Duke of York*: Popular low-ceilinged dining pub with very well kept Robinsons ales, friendly staff, wide choice of food, traditional decor, open fires, restaurant with sofas in plush ante-room; piped music *(Richard Lewis, SLC)*

☆ **Foolow** [signed off A623 just E of B6465 junction; SK1976], *Bulls Head*: Attractive moorland village pub, good helpings of interesting and well served if not cheap food in good no-smoking restaurant area, also cheaper bar snacks; Wards and Vaux beers and one or two guests, good welcoming service; bedrooms, fine views *(Miss A G Drake, David Carr, LYM)*

☆ nr **Foolow** [Bretton, signed from Foolow ; SK2077], *Barrel*: Splendid site on ridge edge, seats on breezy front terrace, five-county views and good walks; cosy beamed bar with snug areas and log fire, generous cheap food from sandwiches up with new owners promising more elaborate dishes (and restaurant section), real ales *(JDM, KM, IHR, Dr F M Halle, Eddy and Emma Gibson, LYM)*

Ford [off B6054 S of Sheffield; SK4080], *Bridge*: Nice setting in pretty village, good service, pleasant beer, good sandwiches *(J S Rutter, Dr F M Halle)*

Froggatt Edge [B6054 – OS Sheet 119 map ref 247761; SK2477], *Grouse*: Useful friendly walkers' pub, big back dining room *(David Carr)*

☆ **Great Hucklow** [SK1878], *Queen Anne*: Comfortable beamed bar with good range of home-cooked food inc fresh veg, well kept beer, friendly staff, open fire, walkers' bar, small terrace and pleasant garden with lovely views; children welcome, handy for walks *(Jeanne Cross, Paul Silvestri, Alex and Betty McAllan, Mike and Wendy Proctor, David Carr, Neville Kenyon)*

Grindleford [B6001; SK2478], *Sir William*: Comfortable and friendly, with wide choice of good value food, good coffee, pool table in spacious room; splendid view from new terrace, walking nearby *(Alex and Betty McAllan, Dr F M Halle, IHR, David Carr)*

Hartington [SK1360], *Charles Cotton*: Scottish Courage ales, good value food, roaring coal fires; bedrooms *(Monica Shelley, Laura Darlington)*; [The Square], *Devonshire Arms*: Good choice of tasty food at sensible prices, well kept beer, friendly efficient service; bedrooms comfortable *(D and D Savidge)*

☆ **Hassop** [B6001 N of Bakewell; SK2272], *Eyre Arms*: Cosy 17th-c manorial pub with grandfather clock in beamed lounge, good adventurous food in small dining area, ales such as Adnams, Black Sheep, Marstons Pedigree, John Smiths, cheerful helpful staff, piped classical music; Peak views from garden tables, good walks nearby *(John Beeken, Mike and Wendy Proctor, J Gibbs)*

☆ **Hathersage** [Leadmill Bridge; A622 (ex B6001) towards Bakewell; SK2380], *Plough*: More seating in beautifully placed ex-farm with Derwent-side garden, good helpings of good fresh food in bar and two dining areas, charming prompt service even when very busy; well kept ales such as Wadworths 6X, decent wines *(IHR, James Waller, Dr F M Halle, Rose, Richard and Sally Melvin, Janet and Peter Race)*

☆ **Hathersage** [Church Lane], *Scotsmans Pack*: Big welcoming open-plan local, good choice of generous nicely presented interesting food (best to book Sun lunch), reasonable prices, well kept Burtonwood Bitter and Forshaws, decent wines; some seats on pleasant side terrace by trout stream; good bedrooms, huge breakfast *(Jeanne Cross, Paul Silvestri, James Waller, Derek and Sylvia Stephenson)*

Hathersage [Main Rd], *Hathersage*: Comfortable and friendly, modernised with restraint, good value food in spacious hotelish bar and lounge, well kept Courage-related ales, log fires; bedrooms good value *(John and Joan Calvert)*

Hatton [A50, by Tutbury rly stn; SK2130], *Castle*: Hotel in converted mill with river and castle views, good choice of generous good value food from sandwiches up, well kept Banks's and guests such as Bass and Marstons Pedigree, friendly helpful staff; four good value well equipped bedrooms *(Mrs A Haswell, P S Compton)*

☆ **Hayfield** [Market St; SK0387], *Royal*: Spacious and well run 18th-c former vicarage, oak panelling, six well kept ales and occasional beer festivals, relaxed cheerful atmosphere, friendly efficient service, local papers, good sensibly priced food; pleasantly decorated bedrooms *(David Hoult, Mike and Wendy Proctor)*

Hayfield [Kinder Rd], *Sportsman*: Traditional, friendly, roomy pub, two coal fires, well kept Thwaites beers, lots of malt whiskies, wide choice of food inc exotic dishes; handy for Kinder Scout walks *(Richard and Ruth Dean)*

Higham [Old Higham (B6013); SK3959], *Crown*: Ancient pub with blazing log fire, imaginative menu, good range of real ales such as Charles Wells Bombardier; pity about the piped pop music; bedrooms *(Peter and Audrey Dowsett)*

☆ **Hognaston** [Main St; SK2350], *Red Lion*: Well renovated cross between pub and bistro, with old flagstones, oak beams and three fires in open-plan bar, candles on antique tables, well kept real ales such as Marstons Pedigree and Morlands Old Speckled Hen, good well presented food (booking advised), good relaxed atmosphere *(Clare Jones, Jonathon Smith, M R Bennett, John and Christine Lowe)*

Holbrook [14 Chapel St; SK3644], *Wheel*: Friendly local with well kept ales inc guests, wide choice of food, good log fire, cheerful helpful staff, snug and dining room, tables on terrace and in pleasant secluded garden *(Anon)*

Hope [A625 towards Castleton; SK1783], *Poachers Arms*: Pleasant relaxed atmosphere in modern but traditionally furnished interconnected rooms, friendly staff, wide choice of popular food from sandwiches up (may be a wait), well kept Scottish Courage ales, children welcome, back conservatory; darts, dominoes, maybe piped music; the two dogs are Barney and Tina; comfortable bedrooms *(Dr F M Halle, LYM)*; [1 Castleton Rd], *Woodroffe Arms*: Several friendly rooms inc conservatory, wide choice of good value food inc children's dishes and Sun lunch, Whitbreads-related ales and Addlestone's cider, real fire, polite service; Sun quiz night, garden with swings; bedrooms *(Dave Braisted, Dr F M Halle)*

Idridgehay [Main St; SK2848], *Black Swan*: Warm welcome, well kept beers inc guests, attractive building; pool table, cl lunchtime *(G Curtis)*

Ilkeston [Station Rd, Ilkeston Junction], *Dewdrop*: Large three-room local by rly in old industrial area, friendly staff, good value bar snacks inc huge cheap sandwiches, Ind Coope Burton, Hook Norton Old Hookey, Kelham Island Pale Rider, Wards Kirby and guests, two coal fires, barbecue; good value bedrooms *(RMT)*

Knockerdown [1½ miles S of Brassington on B5035; SK2352], *Knockerdown*: Firmly run pub with teacups on beams, pictures and bric-a-brac, extensive reasonably priced menu, good value food Sun lunch, well kept Banks's Mild and Marstons Pedigree, no piped music; good views from garden, nr Carsington reservoir; well behaved children may be allowed *(A Preston, Mike and Wendy Proctor)*

☆ **Ladybower Reservoir** [A57 Sheffield—Glossop, at junction with A6013; SK1986], *Ladybower*: Fine views of attractive reservoir from unpretentious open-plan stone pub, clean and spacious; reasonably priced popular food, Tetleys-related ales, red plush seats, discreet piped music; children welcome, stone seats outside, good walks *(David Carr)*

☆ **Little Longstone** [off A6 NW of Bakewell via Monsal Dale; SK1971], *Packhorse*: Snug 16th-c cottage with old-fashioned country furnishings in two cosy beamed rooms, well kept Marstons Best or Pedigree, basic if not cheap food, pub games, terrace in steep little garden; new tenants 1997 *(Barry and Anne, LYM)*

☆ **Litton** [off A623; SK1675], *Red Lion*: Pretty village pub/restaurant (you can't just have a drink), above-average generous food esp game in cosy low-ceilinged partly panelled front rooms or bigger back room with stripped stone and antique prints; welcoming log fires, candles and tablecloths, obliging service, well kept Boddingtons, decent wine, quiet piped classical music; dogs allowed; cl weekday lunchtimes, Sun/Mon evenings *(Bill and Brenda Lemon, David Carr, B, M and P Kendall, LYM)*

☆ **Lullington** [SK2513], *Colvile Arms*: 18th-c village pub with basic panelled bar, plush lounge, pleasant atmosphere, friendly staff, piped music, well kept Bass and Marstons Pedigree, good value snacks (no cooking), tables on small sheltered back lawn

overlooking bowling green; cl weekday lunchtimes *(Graham Richardson, LYM)*

☆ **Makeney** [Holly Bush Lane; A6 N, cross river Derwent, before Milford turn right, then left; SK3544], *Holly Bush*: Unspoilt two-bar village pub, cosy and friendly, with five well kept ales brought from cellar in jugs, besides Ruddles County and one named for the pub on handpump – also annual beer festival; three roaring open fires (one by curved settle in snug's old-fashioned range), flagstones, beams, tiled floors, good value basic meals inc lunchtime snacks, Thurs steak night, dining area; games machines in lobby, can be smoky; children allowed in back conservatory, dogs welcome, aviary on small terrace *(JJW, CMW, Richard Houghton, David Lloyd-Jones, Chris Raisin)*

Mapleton [back rd just NW of Ashbourne; SK1648], *Okeover Arms*: Small and comfortable, well kept Tetleys-related ales, decent bar food inc sandwiches, willing friendly service, restaurant; pleasant village with interesting domed church, good riverside walks *(D W Atkinson)*

Marshlane [B6056 S of Sheffield; SK4079], *Fox & Hounds*: Cosy dark-beamed pub with pictures, plates and brass, fresh flowers, open fire, separate tap room with darts, four well kept Burtonwood ales, good coffee, good value food inc children's, quiet piped music, friendly landlord and dogs; big garden with picnic tables, good play area, good views *(JJW, CMW, Dr F M Halle)*

Matlock [48 Jackson Rd; SK2959], *Thorn Tree*: Superb views over the Wye Valley and town from the garden; well kept beers usually include one from Whim brewery *(Richard Houghton, David Carr)*

☆ **Melbourne** [Castle Sq; SK3825], *White Swan*: Welcoming and interestingly restored 15th-c pub with good value imaginative food, friendly service, well kept Marstons Pedigree, comfortable wing armchairs, separate rather austere dining room; can get quite smoky nr bar; pleasant narrow garden; children welcome *(Mr and Mrs B H James, LYM)*

Middle Handley [off B6052 NE of Chesterfield; SK4078], *Devonshire Arms*: Friendly three-roomed village local with Stones and weekly changing guest beer, sporting prints, darts, dominoes, cards etc, weekly quiz, no food *(Anon)*

☆ **Millthorpe** [Cordwell Lane; SK3276], *Royal Oak*: Stripped stone, oak beams, relaxed welcome for all inc walkers, cosy snug, real fires, inexpensive simple but interesting home-made lunchtime food, well kept Wards, good helpful service, no piped music; no children inside, tables out on pleasant terrace; good walks nearby, cl Mon lunchtime exc bank hols *(R E Kay, David Carr, LYM)*

Milltown [SK3561], *Miners Arms*: Good value home-cooked food (need to book lunchtime), well kept Mansfield beers, good friendly service; peaceful rural setting *(Mr and Mrs Smith)*

Milton [just E of Repton; SK3126], *Coach*

House: Imaginative range of home-made food, well kept guest beers, pleasant surroundings, occasional entertainment, attractive garden *(Patricia and Peter Burton, Allan Randall)*

☆ **Monyash** [SK1566], *Bulls Head*: Attractive furnishings in homely and relaxed high-ceilinged two-room bar inc oak wall seats and panelled settle, horse pictures, shelf of china, roaring log fire, mullioned windows, good generous low-priced home-cooked food inc sandwiches, vegetarian and good salads, Black Sheep and Tetleys Mild and Bitter, efficient staff; nicely set tables in plush two-room dining room, pool in small back bar, maybe quiet piped music; long pews outside facing small green, friendly ginger cat, children and muddy dogs welcome; simple bedrooms *(Nick and Meriel Cox, M G Hart, Mrs B Sugarman, Paul Robinshaw, BB)*
Nether Padley [OS Sheet 119 map ref 258779; SK2577], *Grouse*: Friendly and comfortable back bar welcoming walkers and children, plusher front lounge, well cooked basic food, real ale, nice atmosphere *(IHR)*
New Mills [Brookbottom – OS Sheet 109 map ref 985864; SJ9886], *Fox*: Friendly well cared-for unspoilt country pub in splendid tucked-away hamlet down single track lane, characterful old building, open fire, well kept Robinsons, good range of basic food inc sandwiches, darts, pool; children welcome, handy for walkers *(David Hoult)*; [Mellor Rd], *Pack Horse*: Popular and friendly unpretentious pub with plentiful good value food, lovely views across broad valley, well kept Tetleys; open all day; bedrooms *(Michael Graubart, Stephen, Julie and Hayley Brown)*; [Wirksmoor Rd], *Rock*: Good food cooked by Italian landlord, OAP bargains all day Mon and lunchtime Sat, friendly atmosphere, Theakstons Best and Old Peculier, five-star lavatories *(Tony Young)*
Osmaston [off A52 SE of Ashbourne; SK1944], *Shoulder of Mutton*: Snug and inviting down-to-earth pub in attractive peaceful village with thatched cottages and good walks; varied generous home-made food, well kept Bass, Jennings Mild and Marstons Pedigree, pleasant garden *(David W Atkinson, D and D Savidge)*
☆ **Over Haddon** [signed from B5055 just SW of Bakewell; SK2066], *Lathkil*: Comfortable inn with stupendous views over Lathkil Dale (fine walks), airy beamed bar with good fire and old-fashioned settles, spacious sunny family dining area – partly no-smoking – doubling as evening restaurant, somewhat formal or functional atmosphere; bar food inc lunchtime buffet, some elaborate dishes (esp Fri/Sat evenings), Wards Best, Mild and Thorne Best, decent wines, piped classical music or jazz, shove-ha'penny, dominoes, cribbage; children in dining area if eating, good bedrooms; as the long list of supporters shows this can be excellent and is still a firm recommendation, but there have been some disappointments recently *(Gwen and Peter*

Andrews, Andy and Jill Kassube, Dennis Stevens, M Mason, D Thompson, Christopher Warner, JDM, KM, Mike and Wendy Proctor, Michael Graubart, PGP, David Carr, Paul Robinshaw, Richard Houghton, J E Rycroft, Charley and Ann Hardwick, Roy Y Bromell, Mrs A Haswell, Esther and John Sprinkle, Dr F M Halle, S Palmer, Eddy and Emma Gibson, IHR, Joy and Peter Heatherley, LYM)

☆ **Pilsley** [off A619 Bakewell—Baslow; SK2471], *Devonshire Arms*: Cosy and welcoming local with limited good value homely food using fresh Chatsworth and other ingredients lunchtime and early evening, well kept Mansfield Riding and Old Baily and other ales; lovely village handy for Chatsworth Farm and Craft Shops *(Peter Marshall, IHR)*
☆ **Ripley** [Buckland Hollow; A610 towards Ambergate, junction B6013 – OS Sheet 119 map ref 380510; SK3851], *Excavator*: Welcoming open-plan Marstons Tavern Table with family dining area and no-smoking area, wide choice of good value food (all day Sun) inc vegetarian and good children's menu, friendly efficient staff, reasonable prices, particularly well kept Pedigree and other ales *(Mike and Penny Sanders, Andrew Bush)*
☆ **Rowarth** [off A626 in Marple Bridge at Mellor sign, sharp left at Rowarth sign, then follow Little Mill sign; OS Sheet 110 map ref 011889 – but need Sheet 109 too; SK0189], *Little Mill*: Beautiful tucked-away setting, unusual features inc working waterwheel, vintage Pullman-carriage bedrooms; cheap plentiful bar food all day (may be a wait), big open-plan bar with lots of little settees, armchairs and small tables, Banks's, Hansons, Robinsons Best Mild and Bitter and a guest beer, hospitable landlord, busy upstairs restaurant; can be smoky, pub games, juke box; children welcome, pretty garden dell across stream with good play area; bedrooms *(Martin and Karen Wake, Eddie Edwards, LYM)*
☆ **Rowsley** [A6; SK2566], *Grouse & Claret*: Spacious and comfortable Mansfield Landlords Table family dining pub in well refurbished old stone building, good reasonably priced food (all day weekends) from carvery counter with appetising salad bar, friendly helpful efficient service, no-smoking area, decent wines, open fires; tap room popular with walkers, tables outside; good value bedrooms, caravan and camping site behind *(A Preston, David Carr, David and Mary Webb, Richard Lewis)*
☆ **Shardlow** [3½ miles from M1 junction 24, via A6 towards Derby; The Wharf; SK4330], *Malt Shovel*: Friendly and genuine old pub in 18th-c former maltings attractively set by canal, good cheap changing lunchtime food, well kept Marstons and guest ales; odd-angled walls, good open fire heating two rooms, welcoming quick service; no small children, seats out by water *(P R White, JDM, KM, Roger Bellingham, LYM)*
Shardlow, *Clock Warehouse*: Handsome

18th-c brick-built warehouse in attractive spot with picture windows overlooking canal basin, a pub for some time and now converted into family dining pub, with well kept Mansfield real ales, play areas indoors and out, tables outside too; bedrooms *(GSB, LYM)*

Shottle [A517 Belper—Ashbourne; SK3149], *Hanging Gate*: Charming new pub, cosy relaxing atmosphere, big back restaurant, reasonably priced good generous food inc interesting vegetarian, polite helpful staff, garden *(Louise Medcalf, Jo and Gary Charlton)*

Smisby [off B5006; SK3419], *Nelson*: Cosy low-ceilinged lounge bar with Marstons real ales, good value varied food (bookable tables), open fire in area off; pretty village *(Dorsan Baker)*

☆ **Sparrowpit** [A623/B6061 nr Chapel en le Frith; SK0980], *Wanted Inn*: Attractive easy-going 16th-c stonebuilt inn, two rooms each with real fire, good value home cooking inc good Sun lunch, friendly service, well kept Robinsons Bitter and Mild, lots of copper; piped music; picnic tables by car park, beautiful countryside *(David Carr, David Hoult, Derek and Sylvia Stephenson)*

☆ **Stanton by Dale** [3 miles from M1 junction 25; SK4638], *Stanhope Arms*: Cosy and attractive unpretentious rambling local, friendly staff, well kept Tetleys-related ales, good value generous fresh food, upstairs dining room converted from adjoining cottage; unspoilt village *(Dr and Mrs J H Hills)*

Swarkestone [A514/A5132; SK3628], *Crewe & Harpur Arms*: Marstons family dining pub, welcoming staff, wide choice of popular food served noon till 9, separate bar area, Marstons ales, adequate wines, outside play area; handy for Calke Abbey *(M Joyner, Gordon Theaker)*

Taddington [SK1472], *Queens Arms*: Attractively furnished and decorated, particularly welcoming landlord, varied generous nicely presented food inc good children's dishes, Mitchells and Tetleys; quiet village in good walking country *(R Davies)*

Tansley [A615 Matlock—Mansfield; SK3259], *Tavern*: Very wide choice of good reasonably priced food inc nice unusual puddings and home-made ice cream, friendly and relaxed atmosphere, well kept beer *(Eddy and Emma Gibson)*

Ticknall [B5006 towards Ashby de la Zouch], *Chequers*: Small, friendly and full of atmosphere, with vast 16th-c inglenook fireplace, bright brass, old prints, well kept Marstons Pedigree and Ruddles, very welcoming licensees, no machines, seats in sizeable garden; no food *(Allan Randall, LYM)*; [7 High St], *Staff of Life*: Neat and friendly local with a dozen or so well kept ales on handpump or tapped from the cask inc ones from distant breweries, popular inexpensive bar food, open fire, restaurant *(Pete Yearsley, Janet Box, Joan and Michel Hooper-Immins)*

☆ **Tideswell** [SK1575], *George*: Spacious and comfortably refurbished, with simple traditional decor and furnishings, separate room areas with nice balance between eating and drinking, wide choice of good value simple but generous home cooking, well kept Hardys & Hansons, open fires, welcoming staff; tables in front overlooking pretty village, sheltered back garden; children welcome; 60s music Fri, good value bedrooms, pleasant walks *(A F and J Gifford, Norma and Keith Bloomfield, Derek and Sylvia Stephenson, Mike and Wendy Proctor, Kay Neville-Rolfe, BB)*

Tunstead Milton [SK0380], *Rose & Crown*: Doing well since refurbishment, with consistently satisfying food inc huge mixed grill *(Philip and Ann Falkner)*

☆ **Wardlow** [B6465; SK1874], *Bulls Head*: Plushly comfortable country dining pub with short menu of decent food, good specials and steaks, Wards ale, helpful landlord and welcoming staff, provision for children; no dogs or walking boots; simple bedrooms *(A Preston, Geoffrey and Irene Lindley, LYM)*

Whaley Bridge [Old Rd; SK0181], *Shepherds Arms*: Unspoilt country pub with low-ceilinged lounge, flagstones, wall benches and scrubbed pine tables in public bar, coal fires, well kept Marstons Bitter and Pedigree and Banks's Mild, welcoming service, traditional games *(J W Jones, Phil and Sally Gorton)*

Whatstandwell [A6/Crich rd; SK3354], *Derwent*: Pleasant atmosphere, good bar food inc sandwiches, quick friendly service even when busy, well kept Hardys & Hansons, sensible prices *(Derek Patey, PGP)*

Whitwell [Chesterfield Rd (A619); SK5376], *Half Moon*: Large modern split-level Tom Cobleigh family dining pub, plenty of tables, generous food, helpful quick service even when busy, well kept John Smiths, Stones and Theakstons *(William Cunliffe, SLC)*

☆ **Youlgreave** [Church St; SK2164], *George*: Handsome yet unpretentious stonebuilt local opp church, quick friendly service, good range of reasonably priced home-cooked food, comfortable banquettes, well kept S&N ales; flagstoned locals' snug, games room, juke box; attractive village, roadside tables outside; handy for Lathkill Dale and Haddon Hall, walkers welcome *(Jeanne Cross, Paul Silvestri, David Carr)*

☆ **Youlgreave** [High St], *Farmyard*: Welcoming local with low ceilings, fire in impressive stone fireplace, old farm tools, friendly landlady, well kept Mansfield Mild, Riding and a guest beer, good cheap food, comfortable banquettes, big upstairs restaurant; children and walkers welcome, tables in garden *(Gwen and Peter Andrews, Paul Robinshaw, Mike and Wendy Proctor, David Carr)*

Youlgreave, *Bulls Head*: Comfortable old village inn, several cosy cavernous rooms, decent bar food, well kept Marstons ales inc changing Head Brewers Choice *(Sue Holland, Dave Webster, David Carr)*

Devon

A fine clutch of new entries here includes the buoyant Royal Oak tucked away in the attractive village of Dunsford, the imposing Imperial in Exeter (a grand conversion by the independent Wetherspoons chain), the intriguingly ancient Stag at Rackenford, the civilised Tradesmans Arms at Stokenham (good food), the charmingly set Maltsters Arms at Tuckenhay (ex-Floyd, back to its original name), the remarkably unspoilt little Rugglestone at Widecombe, and the spacious and comfortable Rising Sun at Woodland (good food here). Other pubs currently doing particularly well in this favoured county, increasingly notable for its very generous food servings, are the Sloop not far from the sea at Bantham, the attractive and prettily placed Masons Arms in Branscombe, the Rockford Inn at Brendon (very friendly, another pub in a fine spot), the Drewe Arms at Broadhembury (delicious fish), the Coach & Horses at Buckland Brewer (but we've heard that the very popular landlord may be starting to think of retiring), the friendly Five Bells at Clyst Hydon (earning its Food Award this year), the Tuckers Arms at Dalwood, the Cott at Dartington (outstanding all round, and recently they've been making special efforts with the food), the unchanging Nobody Inn at Doddiscombsleigh (massive choice of wines and malt whiskies), the Turf by the end of the ship canal at Exminster, the relaxing Rock at Haytor Vale, the Old Rydon at Kingsteignton (rewarding for a meal out), the very enjoyable Tally Ho! at Littlehempston, the Cleave in the idyllic village of Lustleigh, the Castle at Lydford (one of the county's very best pubs), the civilised little Half Moon at Sheepwash, the cheery Blue Ball at Sidford, the grand old Oxenham Arms at South Zeal, the Start Bay at Torcross (for its fresh fish), and the Otter at Weston (a marvellous A30 break, especially for families). A pub we have not mentioned yet is the New Inn at Coleford – very good imaginative food, and a good bet for a special meal out. But our choice as Devon Dining Pub of the Year is the Cott at Dartington, for its combination of really enjoyable food with quite special surroundings and atmosphere. The new people at the Old Thatch at Cheriton Bishop now allow children in, and those at the George in Hatherleigh have opened up another bar, among other changes there. Enthusiastic new people at the Royal at Horsebridge are doing home-made food (and still brewing their own beer), and the new team in the Duke of York at Iddesleigh are also doing good value food. The Lucky Dip section at the end of the chapter shows a fine choice in both Exeter and Topsham, and other pubs standing out are the Fishermans Cot at Bickleigh, Poltimore Arms at Brayford, Pilchard at Burgh Island, George at Chardstock, Linny at Coffinswell, Kingfisher at Colyton, Union at Denbury, Anglers Rest near Drewsteignton, Sir Walter Raleigh at East Budleigh, Pyne Arms at East Down, Stags Head at Filleigh, Rock at Georgeham, Church House at Holne, Hoops at Horns Cross, Boat House at Instow, Ley Arms at Kenn, New Inn at Moreleigh, White Hart at Moretonhampstead, Two Mile Oak near Newton Abbot, Sandy Park at Sandy Park, Devonshire at Sticklepath, Olde Inne at Widecombe and Kings Arms at Winkleigh. We have inspected and can vouch for almost all of these. Devon drinks prices are perhaps a shade higher than the national average, but have been holding quite steady recently. The Imperial in Exeter stood out for its low beer prices, and the Fountain Head at Branscombe, brewing its own, was also cheap.

ABBOTSKERSWELL SX8569 Map 1
Court Farm

Wilton Way; look for the church tower

In a pleasant spot, this attractive old farmhouse has a long bar with a mix of seats on the polished crazy flagstones, a nice big round table by an angled black oak screen, a turkey rug in one alcove formed by a low granite wall with timbers above, a long rough-boarded bar counter, and a woodburning stove in a stripped red granite fireplace; a further small room is broadly similar with stripped kitchen tables and more spindleback chairs; piped music. On the right of the entrance is the two-roomed public bar with a woodburning stove, and fruit machine, and a simple end room with darts, cribbage and dominoes. Bar food includes home-made soup (£1.75), doorstep sandwiches (from £2.25), ploughman's (from £3.55), home-cooked ham and egg or mushroom and stilton tagliatelle (£4.75), home-made steak and kidney pie (£5.85), whole grilled fresh local plaice (£6.55), steaks (from £7.95), roast rack of lamb with rich madeira sauce (£9.45), and puddings (£2.35). Well kept Bass, Boddingtons, and Wadworths 6X on handpump, and helpful staff. The garden is pretty, and they have their own cricket team. *(Recommended by Chris Reeve, M Joyner, David and Brenda Begg, Andrew Hodges, H James, Ian Phillips)*

Heavitree (who no longer brew) ~ Tenant Robin Huggins ~ Real ale ~ Meals and snacks (till 10pm) ~ (01626) 61866 ~ Children in eating area of bar ~ Open 11-3, 5-11; 11-11 Sat, 12-10.30 Sun; closed evening 25 Dec

ASHBURTON SX7569 Map 1
London Hotel ◀

11 West St

Behind this substantial coaching house is the Thompson's Brewery where they brew their own Best, Figurehead, Man o' War, Black Velvet Stout, Celebration Porter, and IPA on handpump. The spacious turkey-carpeted lounge has little brocaded or red leatherette armchairs and other seats around the copper-topped casks they use as tables, stripped stone walls, and roaring log fires, and the room spreads back into a softly lit dining area. Decent bar food includes sandwiches, ploughman's, chicken and ham pie or steak in ale (£4.75), grilled trout, steaks, daily specials, and puddings; local farm ciders. There is some connection here to Conan Doyle's *Hound of the Baskervilles*. *(Recommended by P Rome, Dr B and Mrs P B Baker, D B Kenkin, June and Malcolm Farmer, Hanns P Golez, John and Christine Vittoe)*

Own brew ~ Manager David Reese ~ Real ale ~ Meals and snacks (not winter Sun evening) ~ Restaurant ~ (01364) 652478 ~ Children welcome ~ Open 11-11; 11-3, 5.30-11 in winter; 12-10.30 Sun; 12-3, 7-10.30 winter Sun ~ Bedrooms: £27.50S/£40S

ASHPRINGTON SX8156 Map 1
Durant Arms

Village signposted off A381 S of Totnes; OS Sheet 202 map reference 819571

Apart from some freshening up, this neatly kept and friendly gable-ended dining inn remains much the same. The open-plan bar has beams, several open fires, lamps and horsebrasses, fresh flowers, and a mix of seats and tables on the red turkey carpet; there's a lower no-smoking carpeted lounge too, with another open fire; best to book (as most people do). Good bar food includes sandwiches (from £3.25), liver and bacon or ham and egg (£5.25), seafood bake (£5.45), chicken curry (£5.50), plaice fillets (£5.95), and puddings (£2.85). Well kept Flowers Original and IPA, and Wadworths 6X on handpump; no games machines or piped music. Tables in the sheltered back garden. The church is opposite and this is a pretty village. *(Recommended by Andrew Hodges, J S Evans, Iain Robertson, B J Harding, David Carr, Dr A J and Mrs P G Newton, Peter Haines, David and June Harwood, S Demont, T Barrow, Roger and Lin Lawrence, Viv Middlebrook)*

Free house ~ Licensees Graham and Eileen Ellis ~ Real ale ~ Meals and snacks ~ Restaurant ~ (01803) 732240 ~ Children in eating area of bar and in restaurant ~ Open 11.30-2.30, 6(6.30 in winter)-11; closed evenings 25/26 Dec ~ Bedrooms: £25S/£40S

AVONWICK SX7157 Map 1
Avon Inn 🍴

B3210, off A38 E of Plymouth, at South Brent

With an Italian chef/patron at the helm of this busy dining pub, it's not surprising that many of the dishes have an Italian mood. Listed on boards in the small back bar, the robust food might include sandwiches (on Mondays, they serve nothing else), aubergine and mozzarella roll-ups (£3.25), lots of pasta dishes such as penne with gorgonzola and artichokes, tortelloni with wild mushrooms or seafood spaghetti (from £4.75), pork with stilton and cider (£9.50), Italian beef roll (£11.50), bass thai-style (£12), and puddings like white chocolate torte or raspberry and apple crumble (£2.95), and interestingly flavoured ice creams; authentic espresso coffee. Decent Italian wines alongside the well kept Badger Best and Bass on handpump; fruit machine and piped music. It's in the big front restaurant, with very good friendly service from neat efficient waitresses, that his cooking really comes into its own, and here it's best to book on Friday or Saturday night. Decor and furnishings are comfortable and pleasant in a fairly modern style. There are tables out in a pleasant garden by the River Avon. *(Recommended by John Evans, Stan Edwards, Walker and Debra Lapthorne, DJW; more reports please)*

Free house ~ Licensees Mario and Marilyn Velotti ~ Real ale ~ Meals and snacks (not winter Sun evenings) ~ Restaurant (01364) 73475 ~ Children in restaurant ~ Open 11.30-2.30, 6-11; 12-3, 7-10.30 Sun

AXMOUTH SY2591 Map 1
Harbour

B3172 Seaton—Axminster

Even on a weekday in winter, this thatched stone pub fills up quickly. The Harbour Bar has a friendly atmosphere, black oak beams and joists, fat pots hanging from pot-irons in the huge inglenook fireplace, brass-bound cask seats, a high-backed oak settle, and an antique wall clock. A central lounge has more cask seats and settles, and over on the left another room is divided from the no-smoking dining room by a two-way log fireplace. At the back, a big flagstoned lobby with sturdy seats leads on to a very spacious and simply furnished family bar. Well kept Flowers IPA and Original, Otter Ale, and Wadworths 6X on handpump; darts, pool, and winter skittle alley. Good bar food includes sandwiches (from £1.45), ploughman's (from £3.50), vegetarian dishes (from £4.75), fresh fish (from £5.25), puddings (from £1.85), and children's menu (£2.25); cheerful service even when busy. They have a lavatory for disabled people, and general access is good. There are tables in the neat flower garden behind. The handsome church has some fine stone gargoyles. *(Recommended by Galen Strawson, Peter and Audrey Dowsett, P and S White, David Holloway, Pat and John Charles)*

Free house ~ Licensees Dave and Pat Squire ~ Real ale ~ Meals and snacks (not winter Sun evenings) ~ (01297) 20371 ~ Children in eating area of bar and in family room ~ Open 11-11; 12-10.30 Sun; 11-2.30, 6-11 in winter

BANTHAM SX6643 Map 1

Sloop 🛏 ♀

Off A379/B3197 NW of Kingsbridge

It's not surprising that this 16th-c inn gets so busy in summer as there are good surrounding walks (the pub is on the South West Coastal Path), and a lovely sandy beach with rock pools and surfing is just 300 yards over the dunes. Even at its busiest, the licensee and his staff manage to remain efficient and friendly, and the very good bar food is promptly served: sandwiches, ploughman's and basket meals, home-made soups (£2.20), hot potted shrimps (£3.65), scallop mornay (£4.95), braised liver and onions (£4.60), vegetable lasagne (£5.45), smoked haddock with a creamy spinach sauce (£6.80), roast pheasant on a bed of lentils or Devon lamb steak (£7.95), skate wing (£8.15), crab or prawn salad (£8.95), and steaks (from £8.95); hearty breakfasts. Well kept Bass, Blackawton Bitter, Ushers Best and a guest beer on handpump, Churchward's cider from Paignton, 16 malt whiskies, and a carefully chosen wine list (including some local ones). The black-beamed bar has country chairs around wooden tables, stripped stone walls and flagstones, and easy chairs in a quieter side area with a nautical theme. Darts, dominoes, cribbage, and table skittles. There are some seats at the back. The bedrooms in the pub itself have the most character. *(Recommended by A M Stephenson, J L Hall, Andrew Woodgate, Jeanne Cross, Paul Silvestri, Andrew Hodges, Jo and Gary Charlton, Michael Marlow, David Carr, Liz Bell, G W Stephenson, Bryan Taylor, Verity Kemp, Richard Mills, Marianne Lantree, Steve Webb, John and Vivienne Rice, G L Brown, Chris and Martin Taylor, Mr and Mrs J Jones, M Clifford)*

Free house ~ Licensee Neil Girling ~ Real ale ~ Meals and snacks (till 10pm) ~ Restaurant ~ (01548) 560489/560215 ~ Children welcome ~ Open 11-2.30, 6-11; Nov-Mar evening opening 6.30; 12-2.30, 7-10.30 Sun ~ Bedrooms: £29.50B/£59B; s/c cottages also

BERRYNARBOR SS5646 Map 1

Olde Globe ★

Village signposted from A399 E of Ilfracombe

Bigger than it appears at first, this rambling and atmospheric 13th-c pub has a series of dimly lit homely rooms with low ceilings, curved deep-ochre walls, and floors of flagstones or of ancient lime-ash (with silver coins embedded in them). There are old high-backed oak settles (some carved) and plush cushioned cask seats around antique tables, and lots of cutlasses, swords, shields and fine powder flasks, a profusion of genuinely old pictures, priests (fish-coshes), thatcher's knives, sheep shears, gin traps, pitchforks, antlers, and copper warming pans. Well kept Courage Directors and Ushers Best and a guest beer on handpump, and several country wines; sensibly placed darts, pool, skittle alley, dominoes, cribbage, fruit machine, and piped music. Bar food includes sandwiches (from £1.30), home-made soup (£1.60), ploughman's (£2.60), pasties (£2.65), vegetarian sausages (£2.70), steak and kidney pie or chilli con carne (£4.20), steaks (from £6.95), puddings (from £1.90), children's dishes (£1.95), and popular main course Sunday lunch (£3.95, children £2); quick, friendly service. In high season, the restaurant is used as a no smoking room for bar rather than restaurant meals. There's a children's activity house in the garden (and a play frame and ball pool indoors), and the crazy-paved front terrace has some old-fashioned garden seats. *(Recommended by Ian Phillips, Tony Dickinson, Rita Horridge, R J Walden, Tony Gayfer, Philip and Jude Simmons, Dr A J and Mrs P G Newton, Lynne Sharpless, Bob Eardley, Dave Irving, Dr G W Barnett)*

Courage ~ Lease: Phil and Lynne Bridle ~ Real ale ~ Meals and snacks ~ Gaslit restaurant ~ (01271) 882465 ~ Children in family/function room with toys ~ Open 11.30-2.30, 6-11; 12-2.30, 7-11 Sun; winter evening opening 7pm

---

If we know a pub has an outdoor play area for children, we mention it.

BISHOPS TAWTON SS5630 Map 1
Chichester Arms
Pub signposted off A377 outside Barnstaple

Though busy Barnstaple is so close, the village of Bishops Tawton and this thatched pub are pleasantly peaceful. The rather smart bar has low heavy beams and stout supporting timbers, plush wall banquettes and cushioned wheelback chairs on its patterned carpet, a solid old bar counter, uneven sloping floors, and an open fire. The family room has its own bar: darts, skittle alley, cribbage, dominoes, fruit machine, video game, piped music, and doors out to barbecue area. Bar food includes home-made soup (£1.75), sandwiches (from £1.75; soup and sandwich £3.25), filled baked potatoes (from £2.75), beef and Guinness casserole (£3.95), vegetable curry or big cod and chips (£4.25), big meat platter with salad (£4.95), a daily special, puddings (£1.95), and children's menu (from £1.95); the restaurant has a no-smoking area. Well kept Dartmoor Best, Ind Coope Burton, and Tetleys on handpump. There are picnic tables on a flagstoned front terrace, with more in a sheltered back area. *(Recommended by Sheila and John French, Alan and Heather Jacques, R J Walden, Sue and Bob Ward, Dr A J and Mrs P G Newton, Colin Draper, Rita Horridge, Alan and Charlotte Sykes, Joan and Andrew Life)*

Free house ~ Lease: Hugh Johnston ~ Real ale ~ Meals and snacks ~ Restaurant ~ (01271) 43945 ~ Children in eating area of bar and in restaurant ~ Occasional live entertainment Sun evening ~ Open 11.30-11; 12-10.30 Sun

BLACKAWTON SX8050 Map 1
Normandy Arms ⇌
Signposted off A3122 W of Dartmouth; OS Sheet 202 map reference 807509

This is a most pleasant place to stay with a warm welcome from both staff and other customers. The quaint main bar has an interesting display of World War II battle gear, a good log fire, and well kept Bass, Blackawton Bitter Shepherd's Delight, and Marstons Pedigree on handpump. Good bar food includes home-made soup (£1.95), sandwiches (from £1.80), ploughman's (£3.95), home-made chicken liver pâté (£4.50), home-made steak and kidney pie or vegetable lasagne (£4.95), whole lemon sole or pork in cider (£8.95), steaks (from £8.95), and home-made puddings like tipsy cake or chocolate mousse (from £2.75). Sensibly placed darts, pool, shove-ha'penny, cribbage, euchre, and dominoes. Some tables out in the garden. *(Recommended by A M Stephenson, J D Cloud, C Sinclair, Sheila and John French, Elven Money, John and June Freeman, D B Kenkin, Dr S Willavoys, Paul and Janet Waring)*

Free house ~ Licensees Jonathan and Mark Gibson ~ Real ale ~ Meals and snacks (not Sun evenings Nov-Mar) ~ Restaurant ~ (01803) 712316 ~ Children in restaurant ~ Open 12-2.30(5 Sat), 6.30(7 in winter)-11; 12-2.30, 7-10.30 Sun; closed 25 Dec ~ Bedrooms: £30/£48B

BRANSCOMBE SY1988 Map1
Fountain Head ◀
Upper village, above the robust old church; village signposted off A3052 Sidmouth—Seaton

The midsummer weekend beer festival held at this old tiled stone house goes from strength to strength – three days of spitroasts, barbecues, live music, Morris men, and over 30 real ales – as well as their own-brewed beers, Branoc, Jolly Geff (named after Mrs Luxton's father, the ex-licensee), summer Summa'that, winter Olde Stoker, and Christmas Yo Ho Ho. The room on the left – formerly a smithy – has forge tools and horseshoes on the high oak beams, a log fire in the original raised firebed with its tall central chimney, and cushioned pews and mate's chairs. On the right, an irregularly shaped, more orthodox snug room has a another log fire, white-painted plank ceiling with an unusual carved ceiling-rose, brown-varnished panelled walls, and rugs on its flagstone-and-lime-ash floor; the children's room is no smoking, the airedale is called Max, and the black and white cat, Casey Jones. Bar food includes cockles or mussels (£1.75), sandwiches (from £1.75; fresh crab when available

£2.95), ploughman's (£3.95), home-made meat or vegetable lasagne (£4.25), home-made steak and kidney pie or home-cooked ham and egg (£4.95), evening steaks (from £8.50), daily specials like moussaka (£4.95), fresh battered cod (Friday evening, £4.95), and pork steak in mustard sauce (£5.95), and children's dishes (from £1.50). Darts, cribbage, dominoes. There are seats out on the front loggia and terrace, and a little stream rustling under the flagstoned path. *(Recommended by R J Walden, David Holloway, Sue Demont, Tim Barrow, Jane Warren, A Preston, Howard Clutterbuck, Jack and Philip Paxton)*

Free house ~ Licensee Mrs Catherine Luxton ~ Real ale ~ Meals and snacks ~ (01297) 680359 ~ Children in own small room; must be over 10 in Forge in evening ~ Solo/duo guitar last Sun lunchtime of month ~ Open 11-3, 6-11; 11.30-2.30, 7-11 in winter; 12-3, 6-10.30 Sun ~ S/c available

Masons Arms ♀ 🍴

Main St; signed off A3052 Sidmouth—Seaton

The long-planned new no-smoking bar here has now been built, and extends into the top room of the restaurant. This gives much more room during the day, and in the evening, the chatty conversation in the bar can be heard by diners, giving a relaxed, informal atmosphere. The rambling low-beamed bar has a massive central hearth in front of the roaring log fire (spit roasts most days), windsor chairs and settles, and a good atmosphere. Popular bar food includes two soups like carrot and orange or bouillabaisse (from £2.25), lunchtime sandwiches, moules marinères (£3.50), vegetarian pease pudding (£5.95), steak and kidney pudding or braised silverside with a madeira sauce (£6.25), crab cakes (they only use crab caught from Branscombe Mouth and supply is limited, £6.50), smoked haddock gougere (£6.75), braised oxtail (£6.95), and half duckling with orange sauce (£7.25); the pub does get very busy in summer, but service remains friendly and helpful. Well kept Bass, and Otter Bitter and Ale, and two guests like Eldridge Pope Royal Oak, Greene King Abbott, Morlands Old Speckled Hen, Wadworths 6X, and Youngs Special on handpump. They hold a summer beer festival with over 36 real ales, keep a fine choice of malt whiskies, and offer 14 wines by the glass. Darts and skittle alley. Outside, the quiet flower-filled front terrace has tables with little thatched roofs, extending into a side garden. *(Recommended by L W King, Alan and Barbara Mence, George Atkinson, MCG, P Williams, Gordon, R Boyd, Peter and Audrey Dowsett, Sue Demont, Tim Barrow, James Nunns, Jane Warren, J A Snell, Ann and Colin Hunt)*

Free house ~ Licensee Murray Inglis ~ Real ale ~ Meals and snacks ~ Restaurant ~ (01297) 680300 ~ Children welcome ~ Occasional live bands ~ Open 11-11; 11-3, 6-11 in winter; 12-10.30 Sun ~ Bedrooms (some in cottage across road): £22/£44(£60B)

BRENDON SS7748 Map 1
Rockford

Lynton—Simonsbath rd, off B3223

Much enjoyed by readers, this is a homely little inn with a really friendly welcome from the helpful licensee, and there's a strong local following as well as lots of visitors – always a good sign. The original stables and hay loft have been converted into bars and there are lots of old photographs on the walls (which the landlord is happy to describe to you). Good lunchtime bar food (with prices unchanged since last year) includes home-made cottage pie (£2.95), smoked trout (£3.95), or home-made chicken and mushroom pie (£4.50), and evening dishes such as gammon home-braised in ale with honey glaze, salmon with hollandaise sauce or lamb in redcurrant and port (all £6.95); they now serve snacks and cream teas during the afternoon in summer. Well kept Cotleigh Barn Owl, Courage Best, and a guest beer every other month on handpump, and decent wines. Darts, pool, shove-ha'penny, cribbage, dominoes, and piped music. The pub is handy for walkers from Lynmouth and Watersmeet, and is set by East Lyn river with its good salmon, brown trout and sea trout fishing. *(Recommended by Mark Matthewman, Victoria Herriott, M G Hart, Jerry Hughes, Roger and Jenny Huggins, John A Barker, Dave Irving, Bruce Bird, R and S Bentley, Nigel Clifton)*

Free house ~ Licensees D W Sturmer and S J Tasker ~ Real ale ~ Meals and snacks ~ Restaurant ~ (01598) 741214 ~ Children in eating area of bar and in restaurant ~ Local folk every 3rd Sat evening of month ~ Open 11-11; 12-2, 7-11 in winter; 12-10.30 Sun ~ Bedrooms: £18/£36

BROADCLYST SX9897 Map 1
Red Lion

B3121, by church

With thatched houses behind and an interesting church next door, this tiled and wisteria-clad old pub looks most attractive. The long red-carpeted bar has heavy beams, cushioned window seats, some nice chairs around a mix of oak and other tables, and a collection of carpenters' planes; a flagstoned area has cushioned pews and low tables by the fireplace, and at the end of the L-shaped room are big hunting prints and lots of team photographs. Reasonably priced food includes home-made soup (£1.70), sandwiches (from £1.90), home-made chicken liver pâté (£3.20), lamb kidneys in sherry (£3.80), ploughman's (from £3.90), vegetable lasagne (£4.80), steak and kidney pie or pork and apple in cider casserole (£5.20), rump steak (£7.90), daily specials, children's meals (from £2.40), and roast Sunday lunch (£4.95). Well kept Bass, Eldridge Pope Royal Oak, Worthington Best, and a guest like Greene King Abbot on handpump. Darts and a beamed skittle alley – but no piped music or games machines. There are picnic tables on the front cobbles and more seats in a small enclosed garden across the quiet lane. *(Recommended by Wayne Wheeler, Lynn Sharpless, Bob Eardley, Alan Kitchener, E V M Whiteway, James Flory, Anthony Barnes)*

Free house ~ Licensees Stephen and Susan Smith ~ Real ale ~ Meals and snacks (till 10pm) ~ Restaurant ~ (01392) 461271 ~ Children welcome if quiet ~ Open 11-3, 5.30-11; 12-3, 7-10.30 Sun

BROADHEMBURY ST1004 Map 1
Drewe Arms ★ ⊕ ⏚

Signposted off A373 Cullompton—Honiton

Of course much of the emphasis in this charming 15th-c inn is on the particularly good fresh fish dishes, but the landlord has worked hard to ensure that locals continue to feel able to drop in for just a chat and a drink. If you are eating (and most visitors are doing just that), it's almost essential to book to be sure of a table, and you can eat bar food or a three-course meal anywhere in the pub – or in the flower-filled garden: open sandwiches such as crab, marinated herring, prawns, gravadlax, sirloin steak with stilton, and rare beef (from £4.95), lovely scallops in hollandaise, delicious mussels, lovely cod with roasted anchovies (£8.25), sea bream and herb butter (£8.80), excellent salmon fishcakes, delicious monkfish with whole grain mustard sauce (£10.45), half lobster salad (£11.55), fresh langoustines (£13.75), and puddings such as hot lemon pudding or sticky toffee, chocolate and banana pudding; three courses for around £21. Well kept Otter Bitter, Ale, Bright and Head tapped from the cask, and a very good wine list laid out extremely helpfully – including 10 by the glass. The chatty bar has neatly carved beams in its high ceiling, and handsome stone-mullioned windows (one with a small carved roundabout horse). On the left, a high-backed stripped settle separates off a little room with three tables, a mix of chairs, flowers on sturdy country tables, plank-panelled walls painted brown below and yellow above with attractive engravings and prints, and a big black-painted fireplace with bric-a-brac on a high mantelpiece; some wood carvings and walking sticks for sale. The flagstoned entry has a narrow corridor of a room by the servery with a couple of tables, and the cellar bar has simple pews on the stone floor. There are picnic tables in the lovely garden which has a lawn stretching back under the shadow of chestnut trees towards a church with its singularly melodious hour-bell. The village with its thatched cottages is most attractive. *Recommended by Galen Strawson, Jacquie and Jim Jones, T L Rees, Alan and Paula McCully, Basil Minson, S Rolt, Philip Vernon, Kim Maidment, James Flory, Helen*

Morton, Liz Bell, R J Walden, Mavis and Robert Harford, Howard and Margaret Buchanan, A N Ellis, M R Gorton, Mr and Mrs J Jones, Gethin Lewis, George Jonas, Malcolm Smith, C Hardacre, John Fahy)

Free house ~ Licensees Kerstin and Nigel Burge ~ Real ale ~ Meals and snacks (till 10pm; not Sun evening) ~ Restaurant (not Sun evening) ~ (01404) 841267 ~ Children in eating area of bar and in restaurant ~ Open 11-3, 6-11

BUCKLAND BREWER SS4220 Map 1
Coach & Horses ★ 🛏

Village signposted off A388 S of Bideford; OS Sheet 190 map reference 423206

The landlord of this delightful pub is such a warmly welcoming character that his talk of retirement is keeping our fingers firmly crossed. There's an easy going mix of chatty locals and visitors in the attractively furnished bar with its heavy oak beams, comfortable seats (including a handsome antique settle), and woodburning stove in the inglenook; a good log fire also burns in the big stone inglenook of the cosy lounge. A small back room serves as a children's room; three very friendly cats. Tasty bar food includes hearty home-made soup (£1.80), filled baked potatoes (from £2.35), good home-made pasties (£2.65), ploughman's (from £3.55), home-made Irish stew (£4.85), home-cooked ham and egg, vegetable lasagne or tasty liver and bacon (£5.10), good home-made steak and kidney pie (£5.60), lamb, chicken or beef curries (£6), steaks (£9.15), daily specials like venison casserole, sole in white wine, mustard and prawn sauce or beef bourguignon, and puddings like sticky toffee pudding with butterscotch sauce or treacle tart with lemon and ginger (£2.55); children's menu (from £1.55), and Sunday roast (£5). Well kept Flowers Original, Fullers London Pride, and Wadworths 6X on handpump; friendly and efficient service. Pool, shove-ha'penny, dominoes, cribbage, fruit machine, video game, and piped music. There are tables on a terrace in front, and in the side garden.

Recommended by Patrick Renouf, Mr and Mrs G McNeill, Desmond and Pat Morris, Mr and Mrs J Marsh, Rita Horridge, Mr and Mrs D Ross, Wayne Wheeler, Mrs M Furness, Ann and Colin Hunt, R J Walden, Ben and Sheila Walker, Roger and Jenny Huggins, D B Kenkin, Joan and Andrew Life, Simon Collett-Jones, Nick Lawless, Graham Tayar, Gerard O'Hanlon, Chris Westmoreland, George Atkinson, Martin Bromfield, Bernadette Garner, Colin Draper, Basil Minson, R Walden, Nigel and Lindsay Chapman, Mr and Mrs Greenhalgh)

Free house ~ Licensees Kenneth and Oliver Wolfe ~ Real ales ~ Meals and snacks ~ Restaurant ~ (01237) 451395 ~ Well behaved children welcome until 9pm ~ Open 11.30-3, 6-11; 12-3, 7-11 Sun; closed evening 25 Dec ~ Bedrooms: £20B/£40B

BUDLEIGH SALTERTON SY0682 Map 1
Salterton Arms

Chapel Street

The licensee of this tucked away town pub is a jazz enthusiast and there are plenty of prints of jazz musicians and so forth, piped jazz music, and live jazz on winter Sunday evenings. The L-shaped bar has small open fires, and dark green plush wall seats, red plush stools and solid chairs around plain pub tables on the dark red carpet, and a very comfortable upper gallery serves as restaurant. Good bar food at lunchtime includes sandwiches and baked potatoes (from £2.25), fresh battered cod (£3.25), liver and bacon (£3.75), roast lamb cutlets with cranberry gravy (£4.25), and daily specials, with evening dishes such as sizzling chinese stir-fry or italian sausage in spicy tomato sauce with pasta (£4.95), scallops with white wine and fennel (£9.50), monkfish and king prawns in a thai green curry sauce (£10.50), and half a crispy roast duck glazed with orange and honey (£11.50); vegetarian and children's meals. Well kept Bass, John Smiths, and Theakstons Old Peculier on handpump, a good few Irish whiskies, and neatly uniformed staff. In summer, the flowering tubs and hanging baskets are very pretty. *(Recommended by Basil Minson, Mark and Heather Williamson, Peter and Audrey Dowsett, David Holloway)*

Free house ~ Licensees Steve and Jennifer Stevens ~ Real ale ~ Meals and snacks (till 10pm) ~ Restaurant ~ (01395) 445048 ~ Children welcome ~ Jazz winter Sun evenings ~ Open 11-3, 5.30-11; 11-11 Sat; 12-3, 7-10.30 Sun

BUTTERLEIGH SS9708 Map 1
Butterleigh Inn

Village signposted off A396 in Bickleigh; or in Cullompton take turning by Manor House Hotel – it's the old Tiverton road, with the village eventually signposted off on the left

There's a good local atmosphere in the little rooms of this unpretentious village pub, and interesting decorations such as pictures of birds and dogs, topographical prints and watercolours, a fine embroidery of the Devonshire Regiment's coat-of-arms, and plates hanging by one big fireplace. One room has a mix of Edwardian and Victorian dining chairs around country kitchen tables, another has an attractive elm trestle table and sensibly placed darts, and there are prettily upholstered settles around the three tables that just fit into the cosy back snug. Bar food includes filled rolls (lunchtimes, £1.75), home-made soup (£2.25; always vegetarian), ploughman's (£3.75), good home-made burgers (£4.95), salmon and asparagus pancakes (£5.95), pork chops with a spicy pepper and coconut cajun sauce (£7.95), rump steak (£8.95), mixed grill (£11.95), daily specials, and puddings. Well kept Cotleigh Tawny and Barn Owl on handpump; darts, shove-ha'penny, cribbage, dominoes, and piped music; jars of snuff on the bar. Outside are tables on a sheltered terrace and neat small lawn, with a log cabin for children. *(Recommended by Gordon, James Flory, Val and Rob Farrant, R T and J C Moggridge, Jenny and Roger Huggins, P and J Shapley, John and Vivienne Rice, Margaret Dyke, John Fahy)*

Free house ~ Licensees Mike and Penny Wolter ~ Real ale ~ Meals and snacks ~ (01884) 855407 ~ Children may be allowed lunchtimes only ~ Open 12-2.30(3 Sat), 6-11; 12-3, 7-10.30 Sun ~ Bedrooms: £20/£34

CHAGFORD SX7087 Map 1
Ring o' Bells

Off A348 Moretonhampstead—Whiddon Down

The oak-panelled bar in this big friendly old pub has black and white photographs of the village and local characters past and present on the walls, comfortable seats, a big fireplace full of copper and brass, and a log-effect gas fire; there's a small candlelit dining room with a fireplace; the new cat is called Coriander. They now open at 8.30 in the morning for non-resident breakfasts and serve coffee and snacks and afternoon tea, as well as good bar food like nice prawn and crab sandwiches, home-made soup (from £2.20; with a pudding £4), home-cooked ham (£4), fresh fish and chips (from £4.95), vegetarian dishes, and home-made puddings such as fruit crumbles or treacle tart (£2.25); Sunday roasts (from £5). Well kept Bass, Butcombe Bitter, and Worthington Best on handpump, Addlestones cider, and quite a few malt whiskies. Darts, shove-ha'penny, dominoes, and piped music. The sunny walled garden behind the pub has seats on the lawn. Good moorland walks nearby. *(Recommended by Mike Gorton, Basil Minson, John and Vivienne Rice, G W Stevenson, I Maw, Alan and Paula McCully, John and Christine Vittoe, P and J Shapley)*

Free house ~ Licensee Mrs Judith Pool ~ Real ale ~ Meals and snacks (all day) ~ Restaurant ~ (01647) 432466 ~ Well behaved children in eating area of bar and in restaurant ~ Open 11-11; 12-10.30 Sun ~ Bedrooms: £20/£40(£45B)

CHERITON BISHOP SX7793 Map 1
Old Thatch

Village signposted from A30

Friendly new licensees have taken over this popular old pub and are opening up (and landscaping) the garden, changing the menu, and now allow children onto the premises. The rambling, beamed bar is separated from the lounge by a large open stone fireplace (lit in the cooler months), and serves Badger Tanglefoot, Cotleigh Tawny, and Otter Ale on handpump. Bar food now includes the home-made soup (£1.75), sandwiches and toasties (from £2.40), ploughman's (£3), stuffed lamb hearts (£6.75), pork fillet in a mushroom, sherry and cream sauce (£7.95), steaks (from £8.25), chicken with fried banana, sweetcorn fritter and bacon roll (£8.95), and daily specials like fish terrine, mushrooms in a creamy stilton and green peppercorn sauce, fishcakes, grilled plaice, pasta with ham, mushrooms and cream, and red mullet with lemon grass and chilli. Darts, dominoes, cribbage, and piped music. *(Recommended by Ewan and Moira McCall, John and Sally Clarke, Andy and Jill Kassube, Lyn and Geoff Hallchurch, Ian Phillips, R J Walden, Dr A J and Mrs P G Newton, Mr and Mrs D E Powell, Jenny and Brian Seller; more reports on the new regime, please)*

Free house ~ Licensee Stephen Horn ~ Real ale ~ Meals and snacks ~ (01647) 24204 ~ Children in eating area of bar ~ Open 11.30-3, 6-11; 12-3, 7-10.30 Sun ~ Bedrooms: £34.50B/£46B

CHITTLEHAMHOLT SS6521 Map 1
Exeter Inn 🛏

Village signposted from A377 Barnstaple—Crediton and from B3226 SW of South Molton

Set on the edge of Exmoor National Park, this pleasant thatched 16th-c inn has an interesting collection of matchboxes, bottles and foreign banknotes, an open woodburning stove in the huge stone fireplace, and cushioned mate's chairs, settles and a couple of big cushioned cask armchairs. In the side area there are seats set out as booths around the tables under the sloping ceiling. Good bar food served by attentive staff includes home-made soup (£1.95), sandwiches (from £1.85; filled french bread from £2.40), filled baked potatoes (from £2.45), home-made chicken liver pâté (£2.75), ploughman's and salads (from £3.95), vegetarian cheese and nut croquettes or hog (haggis-like) pudding (£4.95), local trout (£6.25), good local steaks (£9.95), daily specials, children's meals (from £2.75), and home-made puddings with clotted cream (£2.30); Sunday roast (£5.25; children £4.25). Well kept Dartmoor Best, Marstons Pedigree, and Tetleys Bitter on handpump or tapped from the cask; freshly squeezed orange juice and farm ciders; darts, shove-ha'penny, dominoes, cribbage, fruit machine, trivia, and piped music. The dog is called Alice and the cat, Clyde. The terrace has benches and flower baskets. The pub's cricket team play on Sundays. *(Recommended by R J Walden, Dr A J and Mrs P G Newton, Alan Pursell, Ian and Deborah Carrington)*

Free house ~ Licensees Norman and Margaret Glenister ~ Real ale ~ Meals and snacks ~ Restaurant ~ (01769) 540281 ~ Children in eating area of bar and in restaurant ~ Open 11.30-2.30, 6-11; 12-3, 7-10.30 Sun ~ Bedrooms: £20S/£40S; s/c cottages available

CHURCHSTOW SX7145 Map 1
Church House

A379 NW of Kingsbridge

The carvery here (Wednesday-Saturday evenings and Sunday lunchtimes; two courses £8.65) is very popular, and the place is positively bustling by 7pm. They also offer home-made soup (£2), sandwiches (from £2), ploughman's (£3.45), battered fresh haddock (from £4.25), sweet and sour pork or fresh pasta with home-made sauces (£4.50), steak and kidney pie or devilled chicken (£4.75), gammon and egg (£7.50), steak (£8.25), children's menu (from £1.45), and home-made puddings with clotted cream; the carvery area is no smoking. Well kept Bass and Hancocks HB on handpump. A great stone fireplace has a side bread oven and the long and cosy characterful bar also has low and heavy black oak beams, cushioned seats cut into the deep window embrasures of the stripped stone walls, an antique curved high-backed settle as well as lots of smaller red-cushioned ones, and a line of stools – each with its own brass coathook – along the long glossy black serving counter. Cribbage, dominoes, euchre, and fruit machine. Just inside the back entrance there's a conservatory area with a floodlit well in the centre, and there are seats outside.

(Recommended by Michael Marlow, C Sinclair, David Carr, Verity Kemp, Richard Mills, TBB, Nick Wikeley)

Free house ~ Licensee H Nicholson ~ Real ale ~ Meals and snacks (12-1.30, 6.30-9) ~ (01548) 852237 ~ Children welcome ~ Open 11-2.30, 6-11; 12-3, 7-10.30 Sun

CLYST HYDON ST0301 Map 1
Five Bells 🍺

Off B3181 S of Cullompton, via Westcott and Langford

Readers have so much enjoyed the good food in this charming and warmly friendly white-painted thatched pub (with its reed pheasants on top), that we have decided this year to give it a Food Award. The home-made daily specials are the thing to go for and might include marinated pigeon breasts (£4.25), fresh scallops with bacon and coriander (£4.95), home-made pasta with sun-dried tomatoes and wild mushrooms or chicken curry with chutneys and poppadums (£5.95), cod fillet topped with tomato, onion and mint, venison and apricot pie or steak and kidney pudding (£6.95), and puddings such as treacle tart, peach and honey sponge or raspberry and sloe gin mousse (£2.95); also, sandwiches (from £2), home-made soup (£2.25), ploughman's (from £4), smoked prawns with garlic mayonnaise (£4.25), courgette provençale (£4.50), home-made curry or cold rare roast beef with chips (£5.95), sirloin steak (from £8.95), and children's menu (from £2.25). The long bar is spotlessly kept and very attractive, and divided at one end into different seating areas by brick and timber pillars; china jugs hang from big beams that are studded with horsebrasses, many plates line the delft shelves, there's lots of sparkling copper and brass, and a nice mix of dining chairs around small tables (fresh flowers and evening candles in bottles), with some comfortable pink plush banquettes on a little raised area; the pretty restaurant is up some steps to the left. Past the inglenook fireplace is another big (but narrower) room they call the Long Barn with a pine dresser at one end and similar furnishings. Well kept Cotleigh Tawny, Dartmoor Best, and Wadworths 6X on handpump, a thoughtful wine list, and several malt whiskies; unobtrusive piped music. The cottagey front garden is filled both in spring and summer with thousands of flowers, the big window boxes and hanging baskets are very pretty, too, and up some steps is a sizeable flat lawn with picnic tables, a waggon filled with flowers, a slide, and pleasant country views. *(Recommended by Dr M Owton, James Flory, Alan McQuillian, John Franklin, Evelyn and Derek Walter, Stan Edwards, Alan Kitchener, Mike and Maggie Betton, Mrs J E Hilditch, Jacquie and Jim Jones, Anna Ralph, Heather March, G Shove, Mr and Mrs Greenhalgh, Catherine Pocock, Mr and Mrs G Ricketts, Mr and Mrs J Jones)*

Free house ~ Licensees Robin Bean and Charles Hume Smith ~ Real ale ~ Meals and snacks (till 10pm) ~ Restaurant ~ (01884) 277288 ~ Well behaved children in eating area to right of the front door and in the Long Barn ~ Open 11.30-2.30, 6.30(7 in winter)-11; 12-3, 7-10.30 Sun

COCKWOOD SX9780 Map 1
Anchor 🍴

Off, but visible from, A379 Exeter—Torbay

The wide choice of good fresh fish is what draws so many customers to this friendly pub. There are 30 different ways of serving mussels (£5.95 normal size helping, £9.95 for a large one), 12 ways of serving scallops (from £5.25 for a starter, from £12.95 for a main course), and 10 ways of serving oysters (from £5.95 for starter, from £12.95 for main course); other fresh fish dishes might include fried shark steak (£5.50), locally caught cod (£5.95), whole grilled plaice (£6.50), local crab platter (£6.95), and maybe red snapper, bream, grouper and parrot fish. Non-fishy dishes feature as well, such as sandwiches (from £2.65), home-made chicken liver pâté (£3.85), ratatouille (£3.95), home-made steak and kidney pudding (£4.95), 8oz rump steak (£8.95), and children's dishes (£2.10). The restaurant is no smoking. The small, low-ceilinged, rambling rooms have black panelling, good-sized tables in various alcoves, and a cheerful winter coal fire in the snug. Well kept Bass,

Boddingtons, Eldridge Pope Royal Oak, Flowers IPA, Whitbreads Fuggles, Marstons Pedigree, and two guests on handpump (under light blanket pressure) or tapped from the cask, with rather a good wine list (10 by the glass; they do monthly wine tasting evenings September-June), a good choice of brandies, 50 malt whiskies, and West Country cider; darts, dominoes, cribbage, fruit machine, and piped music. From the tables on the sheltered verandah here you can look across the road to the bobbing yachts and crabbing boats in the landlocked harbour. Nearby parking is difficult when the pub is busy – which it usually is. *(Recommended by John Beeken, Jean and Douglas Troup, Basil Minson, R J Walden, Peter and Rosie Flower, Peter and Jenny Quine, James Nunns, Wendy Arnold, Bob Medland, Rip and Pauline Kirby, John and Vivienne Rice, JWC, MC, George Jonas, Rita Horridge)*

Heavitree (who no longer brew) ~ Tenants T Morgan, Miss A L Sanders, Mrs J Wetton ~ Real ale ~ Meals and snacks (sandwiches and platters all day; meals till 10pm) ~ Restaurant ~ (01626) 890203 ~ Children in eating area of bar ~ Open 11-11; 12-10.30 Sun

COLEFORD SS7701 Map 1
New Inn ⓘ 🛏 ♟
Just off A377 Crediton—Barnstaple

It's hard in our limited space to give an idea of how well the licensees of this 600-year-old inn are succeeding in combining honest pub food with interesting restaurant-oriented dishes, using locally caught fish, locally made cheeses, clotted cream, and local meats and vegetables: cream of Devon crab soup (£3.50), grilled goat's cheese with walnuts and walnut oil salad (£3.95), Brixham fish pie (£5.95), venison sausages with cumberland sauce (£6.25), cider and lentil loaf with a tomato and herb sauce (£6.95), seafood provençal (£8.25), fillet of pork in a cider and cream sauce or lamb fillet and mushroom concassé with a madeira sauce (£9.25), fillet of brill with a cream, lemon and butter sauce (£9.50), and puddings such as chocolate cups filled with chocolate rum mousse with orange sauce or steamed ginger or lemon pudding (£2.75). Well kept Badger Best, Otter Ale, Wadworths 6X, and a guest beer on handpump, an extensive wine list (some from a local vineyard), quite a range of malt whiskies, and ports and cognacs. Four interestingly furnished areas spiral around the central servery with ancient and modern settles, spindleback chairs, plush-cushioned stone wall seats, some character tables – a pheasant worked into the grain of one – and carved dressers and chests, as well as paraffin lamps, antique prints and old guns on the white walls, and landscape plates on one of the beams and pewter tankards on another; the resident parrot is chatty and entertaining. The servery itself has settles forming stalls around tables on the russet carpet, and there's a winter log fire; fruit machine (out of the way up by the door), darts, and piped music. Big car park. There are some benches and seats outside by the stream. *(Recommended by Dr A J and Mrs P G Newton, D B Kenkin, M Fynes-Clinton, T Pascall, David and Mandy Allen, Neil and Anita Christopher, R J Walden, Pat and Tony Martin, Peter Burton, Rita Horridge, Dr and Mrs Brian Hamilton)*

Free house ~ Licensees Paul and Irene Butt ~ Real ale ~ Meals and snacks (till 10pm) ~ Restaurant ~ (01363) 84242 ~ Children in eating area of bar ~ Open 12-2.30, 6-11; 12-2.30, 7-10.30 Sun; closed 25-26 Dec ~ Bedrooms: £40B/£54B

CORNWORTHY SX8255 Map 1
Hunters Lodge
Off A381 Totnes—Kingsbridge ½ mile S of Harbertonford, turning left at Washbourne; can also be reached direct from Totnes, on the Ashprington—Dittisham road

The chatty, helpful licensees here make both locals and tourists feel welcome. It is extremely popular with those wanting to eat and is well worth booking ahead. From an extensive menu there might be sandwiches (from £1.95), home-made soup (£2.50), ploughman's (from £3.95), grilled sardines (£5.25), home-cooked honey roast ham (£5.50), home-made steak and kidney pie (£5.95), chicken maryland (£6.25), guinea fowl (£9.50), seafood grill (£9.75), and puddings (£2.50); three-course Sunday roast (£7.50). Well kept Blackawton Special and Forty-four, John Smiths and Ushers Best on handpump and local Pig Squeal cider. The two rooms of the little low-ceilinged bar have only around half-a-dozen red plush wall seats and captain's chairs around heavy elm tables, and there's also a small and pretty cottagey dining room with a good log fire in its big 17th-c stone fireplace. Darts, dominoes, shove-ha'penny, children's games, puzzles and colouring place-mats, and piped music. In summer, there is plenty of room to sit outside – either at the picnic tables on a big lawn stretching up behind the car park or on the flower-filled terrace closer to the pub; several walks start from here. They have three dogs (only let loose after closing time). *(Recommended by Jo and Gary Charlton, Liz Bell, Dr S P Willavoys, D I Baddeley, John Fahy, C and E M Watson)*

Free house ~ Licensee Robin Thorns ~ Real ale ~ Meals and snacks (till 10pm) ~ Cottagey restaurant ~ (01803) 732204 ~ Children in eating area of bar ~ Open 11-3, 6.30-11; 12-3, 7-11 Sun; closed evening 25 Dec

DALWOOD ST2400 Map 1
Tuckers Arms
Village signposted off A35 Axminster—Honiton

Particularly in summer when all the flowering tubs, window boxes and hanging baskets are in full bloom, this cream-washed thatched medieval longhouse is a lovely sight. The fine flagstoned bar has lots of beams, a log fire in the inglenook fireplace, a woodburning stove, and a random mixture of dining chairs, window-seats, and wall settles – including a high-backed winged black one. A side lounge has shiny black woodwork and a couple of cushioned oak armchairs and other comfortable but unpretentious seats, and the back bar has an enormous collection of miniature bottles. As well as lunchtime things such as home-made soup (£1.95), filled french bread (from £3.25), potato skins with interesting dips (from £3.50), ploughman's, and daily specials like fresh fish in beer batter or cumberland sausage (£5.95), the very good food is listed on a menu where you can choose between a main course (£9.55), two courses (£12.95), and three courses (£15.55): crêpe with spinach, tomato and cheese, grilled goat's cheese with strawberries, spinach and mint dressing, queen scallops grilled with bacon and worcester sauce, whole fresh lemon sole, roasted skate wings with prawns in garlic butter, rack of lamb with rosemary, shallots and garlic, chicken with wild mushrooms, ostrich fillet with cheese, tomato and pine nuts, and rump steak with brandy, cream and peppercorn sauce. The main dining room is no smoking. Well kept Flowers Original, Otter Ale and Bitter, and Wadworths 6X on handpump, and quite a few malt whiskies; skittle alley and piped music. *(Recommended by John and Elspeth Howell, James Nunns, Anthony Barnes, Martin Pritchard, R Walden, David Wallington, K S Pike, George Atkinson)*

Free house ~ Licensees David and Kate Beck ~ Real ale ~ Meals and snacks (till 10pm; not evenings 25-26 Dec) ~ Restaurant ~ (01404) 881342 ~ Children in restaurant and skittle alley ~ Open 12-3, 6.30-11 ~ Bedrooms: £27S/£45S

DARTINGTON SX7762 Map 1
Cott ★ ⑪ ⇌ ♁
In hamlet with the same name, signposted off A385 W of Totnes opposite A384 turn-off
Devon Dining Pub of the Year

One couple arriving at this lovely thatched 14th-c inn on a Saturday night to enjoy the very good food, had not booked a table. Undeterred, they ordered their meal and their wine and sat at a table in the garden to enjoy it – in mid February! Whilst many might not be quite so dedicated, this is one of the most popular pubs in our book, not just because of the marvellous atmosphere, but particularly for the genuinely warm and friendly welcome given to all by the caring licensees. The communicating rooms of the traditional, heavy-beamed bar have big open fires, flagstones, and polished brass and horse-harnesses on the whitewashed walls; one area is no smoking. Food now changes daily and may include soups such as mushroom and goat's cheese or tomato, basil and watercress (£3), smoked haddock and gruyère tart with mustard and dill sauce (£3.95), mussels in cream, lemon and dill (£4.75), vegetable goulash or wild mushroom risotto (£6.95), steak and kidney pie (£7.25), braised half shoulder of English lamb in crabapple and blackberry sauce (£9.95), fillet of brill with lemon, cucumber and baby clams (£12.25), gurnard fillets with Cornish scallops and a lemon and chive beurre blanc (£12.50), and suprême of duck with port, lemon and raspberries (£13.50); it is essential to book; ample breakfasts. The restaurant is no smoking. Well kept Bass, Butcombe Bitter and Otter Bitter on handpump, Inch's cider, 11 interesting wines by the glass from a very good wine list, and a good selection of malt whiskies. There's a pub cricket team – they'd welcome enquiries from visiting teams. Harvey the cat still likes to creep into bedroom windows in the middle of the night (despite advancing age), and Minnie and Digger the jack russells have been joined by Molly the black labrador and remain keen to greet visitors. There are picnic tables in the garden with more eating on the terrace amidst the attractive tubs of flowers. Good walks through the grounds of nearby Dartington Hall, and it's pleasant touring country – particularly for the popular Dartington craft centre, the Totnes-Buckfastleigh steam railway, and one of the prettiest towns in the West Country, Totnes. *(Recommended by Mr and Mrs D Wilson, Chris Nelson, DWJ, Andrew Hodges, DAV, Mr and Mrs W Welsh, Ian Phillips, S C Nelson, D H and M C Watkinson, Ian and Jane Irving, David and Nina Pugsley, Brian and Bett Cox, Catherine Lloyd, Ted George, Michelle Matel, Liz Bell, P Rome, J D Cloud, Alan McQuillian, Verity Combes, S Demont, T Barrow, R J Isaac, Walker and Debra Lapthorne, Paul and Janet Waring, R Morgan, Bryan Taylor, John Waller, Anne Davenport, Ed Southall, Mr and Mrs J Jones, Miss R Thomas, Dr G Blackwell, Mr and Mrs A O Meakin, Pam and Tim Moorey, M V and J Melling, Moira and John Cole, John Evans, Revd A Nunnerley)*

Free house ~ Licensees David and Susan Grey ~ Real ale ~ Meals and snacks (12-2.15, 6.30-9.30; not 25 Dec) ~ Restaurant ~ (01803) 863777 ~ Children in restaurant ~ Live entertainment Sun evenings ~ Open 11-2.30, 5.30-11; 12-3, 7-10.30 Sun; closed evening 25 Dec ~ Bedrooms: £45B/£55B

DARTMOUTH SX8751 Map 1
Cherub
Higher St

When Francis Drake used this lovely, friendly little inn, it was already 300 years old. It's Dartmouth's oldest building and is Grade II* listed, with each of the two heavily timbered upper floors jutting further out than the one below. Inside, the bustling bar has tapestried seats under creaky heavy beams, red-curtained leaded-light windows, an open stove in the big stone fireplace, and is popular with locals; visitors tend to head upstairs to the little dining room. Well kept Exmoor Gold, Morlands Old Speckled Hen, Wadworths 6X and a guest beer on handpump, quite a few malt whiskies, and farm cider; piped music. Bar food (they tell us prices have not changed) includes soup (£2.25), filled baked potatoes (from £3.50), ploughman's (from £3.95), smoked haddock in white wine and cheese sauce (£3.95), chilli con carne or beef in ale stew (£4.95), and seafood pasta (£6.55). In summer (when it does get packed), the flower baskets are very pretty. *(Recommended by Ted George, J D Cloud, Alan McQuillian, Mr and Mrs I Buckmaster, Luke Worthington, David Carr, Peter and Rosie Flower, K and J Brooks, Mary Woods, Catherine Lloyd, Ian and Jane Irving, TBB, M Joyner, Simon Penny, Simon Walker, Alan and Paula McCully, Jo and Gary Charlton, Christopher Turner, Bryan Taylor, Miss K Law, K M Timmins, John Fahy, Rip and Pauline Kirby)*

Free house ~ Licensee Alan Jones ~ Real ale ~ Meals and snacks (till 10pm) ~ Restaurant ~ (01803) 832571 ~ Children in restaurant lunchtime only ~ Open 11-11; 11-3, 6-11 in winter; 12-10.30 Sun

---

Please keep sending us reports. We rely on readers for news of new discoveries, and particularly for news of changes – however slight – at the fully described pubs. No stamp needed: *The Good Pub Guide*, FREEPOST TN1569, Wadhurst, E Sussex TN5 7BR.

Royal Castle 🛏

11 The Quay

The bustling left-hand local bar in this 350-year-old hotel has a chatty, relaxed atmosphere and a balanced mix of locals and visitors (depending on the time of year). There are navigation lanterns, glass net-floats and old local ship photographs, and a mix of furnishings from stripped pine kitchen chairs to some interesting old settles and mahogany tables; one wall is stripped to the original stonework and there's a big log fire. On the right in the more sedate, partly no-smoking carpeted bar, they may do winter spit-roast joints on some lunchtimes; there's also a Tudor fireplace with copper jugs and kettles (beside which are the remains of a spiral staircase), and plush furnishings, including some Jacobean-style chairs. One alcove has swords and heraldic shields on the wall. Well kept Boddingtons, Blackawton Bitter, Courage Directors, and Flowers Original on handpump, 50 malt whiskies, and local farm cider; welcoming staff. Dominoes, fruit machine, and piped music. Generous helpings of tasty bar food include home-made soup (£2), sandwiches (from £2.15; crab £3.15; not evenings), baked potatoes (from £3), deep fried brie with gooseberry sauce (£3.65), ploughman's (from £3.75), vegetable curry or tagliatelle with smoked salmon in a cream sauce (£4.75), home-made steak and kidney pie (£4.95), gammon with egg (£5.25), a daily curry (£5.45), fish casserole (£5.75), steaks (from £10.25), daily specials, and puddings (£2.60). *(Recommended by M Joyner, B A Gunary, Mike Gorton, Mary Woods, Alan and Paula McCully, Simon Penny, David Carr, Dave and Doreen Irving, Mr and Mrs R Head, John Fahy, Colin and Marjorie Roberts)*

Free house ~ Licensees Nigel and Anne Way ~ Real ale ~ Meals and snacks (all day) ~ Restaurant ~ (01803) 833033 ~ Children in first-floor library lunchtimes only ~ Jazz Sun lunchtime, country rock 2 nights a week ~ Open 11-11; 12-10.30 Sun ~ Bedrooms: £55.50B/£91B

DODDISCOMBSLEIGH SX8586 Map 1
Nobody Inn ★ ★ 🛏 ♀ ◗

Village signposted off B3193, opposite northernmost Christow turn-off

Luckily for the huge numbers of people who enjoy this atmospheric inn so much, little changes. There's still a warm welcome from the very friendly staff, interesting, popular food, and a marvellous choice of drinks. They keep perhaps the best pub wine cellar in the country – 800 well cellared wines by the bottle and 20 by the glass kept oxidation-free; there's also properly mulled wine and twice-monthly tutored tastings (they also sell wine retail, and the good tasting-notes in their detailed list are worth the £3 it costs – anyway refunded if you buy more than £30-worth); also, a choice of 250 whiskies, Gray's and Luscombe's ciders, and well kept Bass, Elgoods Cambridge Bitter or RCH PG Steam, and a guest beer on handpump or tapped straight from the cask. Tasty bar food includes home-made soup (£2), hot wholemeal pitta bread filled with cheese, tomato, onion and herbs (£2.75), sausages and mash with onion gravy (£3.50), coarse home-made duck liver pâté with port (£3.10), daily specials like broccoli and almond quiche, sweet and sour spare ribs, salmon fishcake, Arabian lamb, and spinach and peanut loaf, and puddings such as hot chocolate pudding with fudge sauce, summer pudding or apple and lovage strudel. There's a marvellous choice of around 50 West Country cheeses (half-a-dozen £4.20; you can buy them to take away as well). The restaurant is no smoking. The two rooms of the lounge bar have a relaxed, friendly atmosphere, handsomely carved antique settles, windsor and wheelback chairs, benches, carriage lanterns hanging from the beams, and guns and hunting prints in a snug area by one of the big inglenook fireplaces. There are picnic tables on the terrace, with views of the surrounding wooded hill pastures. The medieval stained glass in the local church is some of the best in the West Country. *(Recommended by Mr and Mrs J B Bishop, Helen Morton, Lynn Sharpless, Bob Eardley, Jo and Gary Charlton, Mr and Mrs D T Deas, Susan and Nigel Wilson, Nigel Flook, Betsy Brown, M and J Madley, John Mackeonis, D H and M C Mackeonis, D H and M C Watkinson, J Mustoe, E V Whiteway, Mrs F A Ricketts, Catherine*

Lloyd, David and Nina Pugsley, M Fynes-Clinton, Comus Elliott, R J Walden, Christopher Turner, Hanns P Golez, Bryan Taylor, John Fahy, John Waller, Mr and Mrs D E Powell, Jim and Maggie Cowell, John and Christine Vittoe)

Free house ~ Licensee Nicholas Borst-Smith ~ Real ale ~ Meals and snacks (till 10pm) ~ Evening restaurant (not Sun) ~ (01647) 252394 ~ Children allowed in restaurant (when open; best to check beforehand) ~ Open 12-2.30, 6-11; 12-3, 6-10.30 Sun; closed evenings 25-26 Dec ~ Bedrooms (some in distinguished eigteenth-c house 150yds away): £23(£35B)/£59B

DREWSTEIGNTON SX7390 Map 1
Drewe Arms
Signposted off A30 NW of Moretonhampstead

A few changes to this old thatched pub include the opening up of bedrooms and a restaurant, and the modernisation of the kitchen. It still remains a basic village tavern with no serving counter and well kept Flowers IPA, Marstons Pedigree, Morlands Old Speckled Hen and Wadworths 6X and Grays cider kept on racks in the tap room at the back. Bar food includes sandwiches, good ploughman's (£3.95), duck liver parfait (£3.95), fresh scallops in filo pastry with lime butter (£4.95), pork in cider and cream (£9), steaks (from £9), half a roast duck (£10), and venison and beef with a cream and green peppercorn sauce (£12). Darts, and skittle alley. Castle Drogo nearby (open for visits) looks medieval, though it was actually built earlier this c. *(Recommended by Neil and Anita Christopher, John and Sally Clarke, Catherine Lloyd, Kerry Law, Annemarie Firstbrook, John Franklin, Gordon, Jonathan Williams, John Fahy, Jeanne Cross, Wendy and Ray Bryn Davies, Jack and Philip Paxton, John Hazel)*

Whitbreads ~ Lease Janice and Colin Sparks ~ Real ale ~ Meals and snacks ~ Restaurant ~ (01647) 281224 ~ Children in eating area of bar ~ Jazz Fri evening in barn behind pub ~ Open 11-2.30, 6-11; 12-3, 7-10.30 Sun ~ Bedrooms: £35/£50

DUNSFORD SX8189 Map 1
Royal Oak
Village signposted from B3212

Hard-working new owners have brought this Victorian pub back up to standard again. There's a friendly village atmosphere in the light and airy bar with windows looking out over the thatched white cottages of this small hill village, and beyond to the fringes of Dartmoor. The central bar, flanked by two dining areas (one is no smoking), dispenses the well kept Badgers Tanglefoot, Flowers IPA, Fullers London Pride, Greene King Abbot, and Wadworths 6X on handpump. Good, well presented home-made bar food includes soup (£1.65), sandwiches (from £1.95), always three vegetarian dishes like a nut roast or curry (£3.95), a meaty curry (£4.50), pies like beef and stilton or fish (£5.50), gammon and egg (£5.95), and rump steak (£9.95); prompt service. Darts, pool, cribbage, dominoes, video game, and piped music; dogs welcome. *(Recommended by Ian Wilson, MRSM, Mike Gorton, Val and Rob Farrant, C and E M Watson)*

Free house ~ Licensees Mark and Judy Harrison ~ Real ale ~ Meals and snacks ~ Restaurant ~ (01657) 252256 ~ Children in eating area of bar ~ Live entertainment Fri evening ~ Open 12-2.30, 6.30-11; 12-2.30, 7-10.30 Sun ~ Bedrooms: £22.50(£27.50)/£40(£45B)

If a service charge is mentioned prominently on a menu or accommodation terms, you must pay it if service was satisfactory. If service is really bad you are legally entitled to refuse to pay some or all of the service charge as compensation for not getting the service you might reasonably have expected.

EXETER SX9292 Map 1

Double Locks ★ 🍺

Canal Banks, Alphington; from A30 take main Exeter turn-off (A377/396) then next right into Marsh Barton Industrial Estate and follow Refuse Incinerator signs; when road bends round in front of the factory-like incinerator, take narrow dead end track over humpy bridge, cross narrow canal swing bridge and follow track along canal; much quicker than it sounds, and a very worthwhile diversion from the final M5 junction

Lively students are fond of this busy and remote old lockhouse – particularly in summer when there are picnic tables outside and they can enjoy the cycle paths along the ship canal. A fine range of beers on handpump or tapped from the cask might include Smiles Bitter, Best and Exhibition with guests like Adnams Broadside, Courage Directors, Everards Old Original, Greene King Abbot, and Wadworths 6X; Grays farm cider. Bar food includes sandwiches, soup (£2), feta cheese and spinach pie (£4.20), liver and onions (£4.50), and chicken kebab (£5.20). There's quite a nautical theme in the bar – with ship's lamps and model ships – and friendly service; there have been a few comments from readers about housekeeping this year. Darts, shove-ha'penny, cribbage, dominoes, trivia, and piped music. *(Recommended by Mike Gorton, R J Walden, Andy and Jill Kassube, John and Vivienne Rice, Barry and Anne, Catherine Lloyd, Andrew Hodges, Simon Walker, PM, AM, David Carr, Steve Felstead, Henry Paulinski)*

Smiles ~ Manager Tony Stearman ~ Real ale ~ Meals and snacks (all day) ~ (01392) 56947 ~ Children welcome ~ Folk Weds evening, Jazz Thurs evening ~ Open 11-11; 12-10.30 Sun

Imperial 🍺

New North Road; just off A377 nr St Davids Station

One of Wetherspoons' grandest conversions, this sumptuous new place standing in a 6-acre hillside park (with its own lodge and sweeping drive) has had £2 million spent on the refurbishments. Built in 1801 as a private mansion, and latterly a hotel, it has a glorious ex-ballroom filled with elaborate plasterwork and gilding brought here in the 1920s from Haldon House (a Robert Adam stately home that was falling on hard times). All sorts of other areas include a couple of little clubby side bars and a great island bar looking into a light and airy former orangery – the huge glassy fan of its end wall lightly mirrored to give an intriguing shifting fusion of the reflected customers with the trees outside. The furnishings give Wetherspoons' usual solid well spaced comfort, and there are plenty of interesting pictures and other things to look at. On our St George's Day inspection visit there was a massive choice of esoteric real ales, but the usual choice, kept well on handpump, runs to Butcombe, Courage Directors, Theakstons Best, Youngers Scotch and three or four guest beers; prices are low enough to have prompted something of a price war with some other Exeter pubs. Good value bar food includes filled french bread (from £1.75), soup (£1.95; soup and a sandwich £2.50), fish and chips (£3.50), steak in ale pie (£3.95), and between four and seven o'clock two people can eat for £5; evening grills. The two fruit machines are silenced and there's no piped music. Besides elegant metal garden furniture in an attractive cobbled courtyard, there are plenty of picnic tables in the grounds. No under-18s. *(Recommended by Mike Gorton, Andrew Hodges, E V M Whiteway)*

Free house ~ Licensees Jonathon Randall and Wendy Gardner ~ Real ale ~ Meals and snacks (11-10) ~ (01392) 434050 ~ Open 11-11; 12-10.30 Sun

White Hart ★ 🛏 🍷

66 South St; 4 rather slow miles from M5 junction 30; follow City Centre signs via A379, B3182; straight towards centre if you're coming from A377 Topsham Road

The rambling atmospheric bar of this nicely old-fashioned 14th-c inn is the sort of place, one feels, where people have congregated for centuries. The heavy bowed beams in the dark terracotta ceiling are hung with big copper jugs, there are windsor armchairs and built-in winged settles with latticed glass tops to their high backs, oak tables on the bare oak floorboards (carpet in the quieter lower area), and a log fire in one great fireplace with long-barrelled rifles above it. In one of the bay windows is a set of fine old brass beer engines, the walls are decorated with pictorial plates, old copper and brass platters (on which the antique lantern lights glisten), and a wall cabinet holds some silver and copper. From the latticed windows, with their stained-glass coats-of-arms, one can look out on the cobbled courtyard – lovely when the wisteria is flowering in May. The Tap Bar, across the yard, with flagstones, candles in bottles and a more wine-barish feel, serves soup (£2.25), sandwiches (from £2.30), steak and kidney pudding or chicken and chestnut pies (£5.95), chargrilled pure beefburger (£4.55), duck breast (£8.75) or steaks (from £9.50), and daily specials like pot roast lamb shank or marinated loin of pork with sesame and ginger (£7.95). There is yet another bar, called Bottlescreu Bill's, even more dimly candlelit, with bare stone walls and sawdust on the floor. It serves much the same food, as well as a respectable range of Davy's wines and pint jugs of vintage port from the wood or tankards of bucks fizz, and in summer does lunchtime barbecue grills in a second, sheltered courtyard. On Sundays both these bars are closed. Bass, Davy's Old Wallop (served in pewter tankards in Bottlescreu Bill's) and John Smiths on handpump. Bedrooms are in a separate modern block. *(Recommended by E V Whiteway, Barry and Anne, Comus Elliott, Brian and Bett Cox, R J Walden, R T and J C Moggridge, Mrs H Murphy, Anthony Barnes, Andrew Hodges, Jim and Maggie Cowell, David Carr, JWC, MC, M E Wellington)*

Free house ~ Licensee Graham Stone ~ Real ale ~ Meals and snacks (till 10pm) ~ Restaurant ~ (01392) 279897 ~ Children in eating area of bar and in lounges ~ Open 11.30-3, 5-11; 11.30-11 Sat; 12-3, 7-10.30 Sun ~ Bedrooms: £57B/£84B – not 24-26 Dec

EXMINSTER SX9487 Map 1
Turf ★

Follow sign to Swans Nest, signposted from A739 S of village, then continue to end of track, by gates; park, and walk right along canal towpath – nearly a mile

You can't reach this attractively isolated, very friendly pub by car. It's set by the last lock of the Exeter Canal before the estuary of the River Exe and you can either walk (which takes about 20 minutes along the ship canal) or take a 40-minute ride from Countess Wear in their own boat, the *Water Mongoose* (bar on board; £4 adult, £2.50 child return, charter for up to 56 people £140). They also operate a 12-seater and an 8-seater boat which bring people down the Exe estuary from Topsham quay (15 minute trip, adults £2.50, child £2). For those arriving in their own boat there is a large pontoon as well as several moorings. From the bay windows of the pleasantly airy bar there are views out to the mudflats – which are full of gulls and waders at low tide – and mahogany decking and caulking tables on the polished bare floorboards, church pews, wooden chairs and alcove seats, and big bright shorebird prints by John Tennent and pictures and old photographs of the pub and its characters over the years on the walls; woodburning stove and antique gas fire. Home-made bar food includes sandwiches, garlic bread with melted cheese (£2.95), homity pie (£3.75), fresh Exe salmon sandwich or smoked salmon and gruyère toastie (£3.95), cumberland sausage hotpot (£5.25), aubergine and lentil moussaka (£5.50), beef, mushroom and Guinness casserole (£6.50), and puddings like apple and rhubarb crumble or treacle pudding (£2.50); maybe summer barbecues. The dining room is no smoking. Well kept Dartmoor Best, Morlands Old Speckled Hen, Oakhill Yeoman, and guests like Greene King Abbot and Marstons Pedigree on handpump, Green Valley farm cider, and lemongrass and elderflower cordials; shove-ha'penny, cribbage, dominoes, trivia, and evening/weekend piped music; friendly, efficient service. The garden has a children's play area. *(Recommended by Mike Gorton, Mrs F A Ricketts, Catherine Lloyd, EML, Jeanne Cross, Paul Silvestri, Chris Westmoreland)*

Free house ~ Licensees Clive and Ginny Redfern ~ Real ale ~ Meals and snacks (not Sun evening) ~ (01392) 833128 ~ Children welcome ~ Open 11-11; 12-10.30 Sun; closed Nov-March ~ Bedrooms: £25/£50

HARBERTON SX7758 Map 1

Church House

Village signposted from A381 just S of Totnes

This ancient pub is in a steep little twisting village, pretty and surrounded by hills. It was probably used as a chantry-house for monks connected with the church, and parts of it may, in fact, be Norman. Furnishings include attractive 17th- and 18th-c pews and settles, candles, and a large inglenook fireplace with a woodburning stove; one half of the room is set out for eating. The family room is no smoking. Daily specials are the most popular dishes and might include deep-fried brie wrapped in bacon with a spicy redcurrant jelly (£3.95), steak picado (£7.50), seafood piri-piri (£7.95), mussel and clam casserole or lamb kleftico (£15.90 for two people), and sticky toffee pudding with clotted cream (£2.95); the standard menu includes sandwiches (from £2.25), home-made soup (£2.95), ploughman's (from £3.75), three locally made sausages with chips (£4.50), a fry-up (£5.75), prawn curry (£7.30), grilled whole plaice (£7.95), and steaks (from £7.95). Well kept Bass and Courage Best and two weekly-changing guest beers such as Shepherd Neame Spitfire and Charles Wells Bombardier on handpump, Churchward's cider, and several malt whiskies; darts, dominoes and cribbage. Anyone interested in ancient buildings will get a kick out of looking for the magnificent medieval oak panelling and the latticed glass on the back wall of the open-plan bar, which is almost 700 years old and one of the earliest examples of non-ecclesiastical glass in the country (it had been walled off until Victorian times). *(Recommended by Jo and Gary Charlton, Richard May, Mr and Mrs D Wilson, Patrick Freeman, Dr and Mrs A Whiteway, DWJ, Dr A J and Mrs P G Newton, Viv Middlebrook, M G Hart, Colin and Marjorie Roberts, Mr and Mrs R Head)*

Free house ~ Licensees David and Jennifer Wright ~ Real ale ~ Meals and snacks (12-1.45, 7-9.30) ~ (01803) 863707 ~ Children in family room ~ Occasional Morris men and folk bands in summer ~ Open 12(11.30 Sat)-3, 6-11; 12-3, 7-10.30 Sun; closed evenings 25-26 Dec and 1 Jan ~ Bedrooms: £14/£30 (ensuite available Spring 1988)

HATHERLEIGH SS5404 Map 1

George ♀

A386 N of Okehampton

New licensees have made some changes to this friendly inn. They've re-opened the right-hand bar and geared it towards younger customers and installed the pool table, juke box, fruit machine, and darts there. The extension to the main bar has been refurbished which has increased the eating area, much of the roof has been re-thatched, and the swimming pool has been overhauled. The little front bar in the original part of the building has huge oak beams, stone walls two or three feet thick, an enormous fireplace, and easy chairs, sofas and antique cushioned settles. The spacious L-shaped main bar was built from the wreck of the inn's old brewhouse and coachmen's loft, and has more beams, a woodburning stove, and antique settles around sewing-machine treadle tables; dominoes, piped music. Well kept Bass, Boddingtons, and Wadworths 6X with guests like Greene King Abbot, Jollyboat Plunder, and Shepherd Neame Spitfire on handpump, and an extensive wine list. Bar food now includes sandwiches, soup (£2.20), filled baked potatoes (from £2.75), fried halloumi with lime vinaigrette (£2.95), vegetarian stuffed peppers (£3.75), spaghetti carbonara (£4.25), chilli con carne (£4.50), all-day breakfast, steak in ale pie with mushrooms or gammon and egg (£4.95), steaks (from £8.50), daily specials, and puddings (£2.50); children's menus. In summer, the courtyard is very pretty with hanging baskets and window boxes on the black and white timbering, and rustic wooden seats and tables on its cobblestones; there's also a walled cobbled garden. *(Recommended by Rita Horridge, Richard and Rosemary Hoare, R J Walden, Rob Cope, Mrs B Sugarman, Mr and Mrs J D Marsh, Catherine Lloyd, Mrs H Murphy, Dr A J and Mrs P G Newton, Colin Draper, Mr and Mrs Jack Pitts)*

Free house ~ Licensees David and Christine Jeffries ~ Real ale ~ Meals and snacks (11.30-2.30, 6.30-9.30) ~ Restaurant ~ (01837) 810454 ~ Children welcome ~ Open 11-3(3.30 Sat), 6-11; 12-3, 7-11 Sun ~ Bedrooms: £28.50(£48B)/£49.50(£69B)

Tally Ho 🍺 🍴

Market St (A386)

Through a big window in one building of the former back coach yard here you can see the spotless copper equipment where they brew their own Potboiler, Jollop (winter only), Tarka Tipple, Thurgia, Nutters, and Master Jack's Mild (spring only). The opened-together rooms of the bar have heavy beams, sturdy old oak and elm tables on the partly carpeted wooden floor, decorative plates between the wall timbers, shelves of old bottles and pottery, and two woodburning stoves; the two cockatiels are called Squeaky and Squashy. Bar food includes lunchtime sandwiches and fillings on a fresh bagel or croissant or warm french bread (from £2), omelettes (from £3.25), and ploughman's (from £3.75), as well as soup, home-made game pâté (£3.90), trout (£8.75), steaks (from £9.50), daily specials like pasta with smoked salmon, white wine and vodka, thai green curry or cod fillet with beer batter; pizzas on Wednesdays (from £3.95) and a Swiss fondue on Thursdays (£20 per couple; not summer). Darts, shove-ha'penny, dominoes, cribbage, trivia, and piped music. There are tables and an aviary in the sheltered garden. *(Recommended by Phil and Anne Smithson, Lynn Sharpless, Bob Eardley, Rob Cope, Catherine Lloyd, Andy and Jill Kassube, Mr and Mrs J D Marsh, John Perry, Moira and John Cole, Mr and Mrs Jack Pitts)*

Own brew ~ Licensee Miss M J Leonard ~ Real ale ~ Meals and snacks ~ Restaurant ~ (01837) 810306 ~ Well behaved children in eating area of bar ~ Open 11-3(2 in winter), 6-11; 12-2.30, 7-10.30 Sun ~ Bedrooms: £30B/£60B

HAYTOR VALE SX7677 Map 1
Rock ★ 🛏

Haytor signposted off B3387 just W of Bovey Tracey, on good moorland road to Widecombe

Much enjoyed by readers, this is a rather civilised inn with courteous, friendly service and a restful, chatty atmosphere – no noisy games machines or piped music. The two communicating, partly panelled bar rooms have easy chairs, oak windsor armchairs and high-backed settles, candlelit, polished antique tables, old-fashioned prints and decorative plates on the walls, and good winter log fires (the main fireplace has a fine Stuart fireback); two lounges are no smoking. A wide choice of very good bar food includes home-made soup (£2.50), sandwiches (from £2.95), duck and port pâté (£4.95), ploughman's and platters (from £5.25), local rabbit in a grain mustard sauce (£5.75), steak and kidney pie (£5.95), warm scallops with a roasted red pepper and saffron dressing (£6.25), spinach and mushroom pie (£6.55), whole grilled plaice with pink peppercorn butter (£7.95), chicken filled with devon stilton wrapped in bacon with a leek sauce (£8.95), steaks (from £11.95), and puddings like lemon crème brûlée and treacle and walnut tart (from £3.25). Well kept Bass, Dartmoor Best, and Eldridge Pope Hardy on handpump, and several malt whiskies. In summer, the pretty, well kept large garden opposite the inn is a popular place to sit and there are some tables and chairs on a small terrace next to the pub itself. The village is just inside the National Park, and golf, horse riding and fishing (and walking, of course) are nearby. *(Recommended by Andy and Jill Kassube, Dr a J and Mrs P G Newton, P D Kudelka, Comus Elliott, Mr and Mrs C R Little, Ted George, Liz Bell, Marc and Yvonne Weller, Alan and Paula McCully, G W Stevenson, Sue Demont, Tim Barrow, Mr and Mrs C Roberts)*

Free house ~ Licensee Christopher Graves ~ Real ale ~ Snacks (not Sun or bank hols) ~ Restaurant ~ (01364) 661305 ~ Children in restaurant ~ Open 11-3, 6(6.30 winter)-11(10.30 winter); 12-3, 6.30-10.30 Sun ~ Bedrooms: £45.95B/£59B

HOLBETON SX6150 Map 1
Mildmay Colours 🍴

Signposted off A379 W of A3121 junction

A new licensee has taken over this off-the-beaten-track pub – but they are still brewing their own real ales: Colours Best, SP, 50/1, Old Horse Whip, and Tipster on handpump; local farm cider, too. The bar has plenty of bar stools as well as cushioned wall seats and wheelback chairs on the turkey carpet, various horse and racing pictures on the partly stripped stone and partly white walls, and a tile-sided woodburning stove; an arch leads to a smaller, similarly decorated family area. One area is no smoking. The separate plain back bar has pool, sensible darts, dominoes, fruit machine, and juke box; piped music. Bar food includes home-made soup (£2.50), sandwiches (from £2.50), home-made chicken liver and hazelnut pâté (£2.95), sliced pork or beef with pickle (£3.50), home-cooked ham and egg (£3.95), ploughman's (£4.95), Mexican chicken enchilada (£5.95), rump steak (£8.95), daily specials, puddings (£2.75), and children's meals (£2.50); they hold a curry night on Wednesdays, a steak night on Fridays, and a carvery on Saturday night and Sunday lunchtime; helpful service. The well kept back garden has picnic tables, a swing, and a bird cage, and there's a small front terrace. *(Recommended by Elven Money, Mrs M Rolfe, Andy and Jill Kassube, Hugh Roberts, Nick Lawless, Mr and Mrs C R Little, Mr and Mrs N Spink; more reports on the new regime, please)*

Own brew ~ Licensee Louise Price ~ Real ale ~ Meals and snacks (served throughout opening hours) ~ Upstairs restaurant ~ 01752 830248 ~ Children in eating area of bar and in restaurant ~ Open 11-3, 6-11; occasional all day opening in summer; 12-3, 7-10.30 Sun ~ Bedrooms in two cottages opposite: £20B/£40B

HORNDON SX5280 Map 1
Elephants Nest ★ ◀

If coming from Okehampton on A386 turn left at Mary Tavy Inn, then left after about ½ mile; pub signposted beside Mary Tavy Inn, then Horndon signposted; on the Ordnance Survey Outdoor Leisure Map it's named as the New Inn

Wooden benches and tables on the spacious, flower-bordered lawn in front of this old pub look over the walls to the pastures of Dartmoor's lower slopes. Inside, there's a good log fire, large rugs and flagstones, a beams-and-board ceiling, and cushioned stone seats built into the windows, with captain's chairs around the tables; the name of the pub is written up on the beams in 60 languages. Another room – created from the old beer cellar and with views over the garden and beyond to the moors – acts as a dining or function room or an overspill from the bar on busy nights. Good home-made bar food at lunchtime includes soup (£1.50), good filled granary rolls (£1.60), home-made pâté (£3.20), ploughman's (from £3.50; the elephant's lunch £3.80 is good), steak and kidney pie (£5.40), and daily specials such as lamb vindaloo, kidney and bacon casserole or tuna and tomato lasagne (£5), with evening dishes like garlic prawns or stilton and walnut pâté (£3.20), gammon with pineapple (£5.45), local game pie (£6.90), steaks (from £9.90), and puddings like sherry trifle, apple crumble or steamed plum pudding (£2.20). Well kept Boddingtons Bitter, Palmers IPA, St Austells HSD, and a local and another guest on handpump; Inch's cider. Sensibly placed darts, cribbage, dominoes, and piped music. You can walk from here straight onto the moor or Black Down, though a better start (army exercises permitting) might be to drive past Wapsworthy to the end of the lane, at OS Sheet 191 map reference 546805. They have four dogs, one cat, ducks, chickens, rabbits, and horses; customers' dogs are allowed in on a lead. *(Recommended by John and Vivienne Rice, Paul and Heather Bettesworth, Andy and Jill Kassube, R A Cullingham, Alan and Heather Jacques, Tom McLean, R Huggins, E McCall, Kerry Law, Annemarie Firstbrook, Emma Kingdon, R J Walden)*

Free house ~ Licensee Nick Hamer ~ Real ale ~ Meals and snacks (11.30-2, 6.30-10) ~ (01822) 810273 ~ Children welcome away from bar ~ Open 11.30-2.30, 6.30-11; 12-2.30, 7-10.30 Sun

HORSEBRIDGE SX3975 Map 1
Royal ◀

Village signposted off A384 Tavistock—Launceston

Enthusiastic new licensees have taken over this prettily-set pub and reports from readers are most favourable. The brewer has stayed on and continues to brew the popular beers: Horsebridge Right Royal, Tamar and the more powerful Heller – plus

Bass, Sharps Own, and Wadworths 6X on handpump, and country wines. The two bar rooms are simple and old-fashioned and there's another small room (no smoking), called the Drip Tray, for the overflow at busy times; darts, bar billiards, cribbage, and dominoes. Home-made bar food includes soup (£2), filled french bread (£3), filled baked potatoes or ploughman's (£3.50), home-cooked ham and egg (£3.75), a choice of three curries (£4.95), sirloin steak (£7.50), and home-made daily specials such as stir-fried vegetables in black bean sauce, pigeon breast in red wine with bacon and mushrooms or smoked haddock, poached egg and new potatoes (£3.50-£6; Sunday roast with five fresh vegetables £4.25; Oct-Whitsun). The big garden is gradually being done up and there is a new terrace at the back. The pub was originally called the Packhorse, and got its present name for services rendered to Charles I (whose seal is carved in the doorstep). Children must be over six. *(Recommended by John and Vivienne Rice, Jacquie and Jim Jones, Paul and Heather Bettesworth, Patrick Freeman, R J Walden, T Pascall, J R Hawkes, James Macrae, R and S Bentley)*

Own brew ~ Licensees Paul Eaton, Catherine Bromidge ~ Real ale ~ Meals and snacks ~ (01822) 870214 ~ Children in eating area of bar lunchtime only ~ Open 12-3, 7-11

IDDESLEIGH SS5708 Map 1
Duke of York
B3217 Exbourne—Dolton

Though the licensees are new, the atmosphere in this old thatched pub remains relaxed and friendly, the beer well kept, and the food good and reasonably priced. The bar has rocking chairs by the roaring log fire, cushioned wall benches built into the wall's black-painted wooden dado, stripped tables, and other homely country furnishings, and well kept Adnams Broadside, Cotleigh Tawny, Sharps Doom Bar, Smiles Golden and guest beers tapped from the cask; farm cider, Irish whiskies, and freshly squeezed orange and grapefruit juices. Bar food now includes sandwiches, home-made soup (£2), home-made pâté (£2.20), liver and bacon (£4.75), steak and kidney pudding or home-baked ham with two eggs (£5), a fresh fish of the day, vegetarian dishes, steaks (from £8.25), and Sunday roast; three-course menu in the dining room (£12.50). Darts, shove-ha'penny, cribbage, dominoes, and chess. Through a small coach arch is a little back garden with some picnic tables under cocktail parasols. Good fishing nearby. *(Recommended by Mr and Mrs J D Marsh, David Wallington, Ron and Sheila Corbett, Brian Skelcher, R J Walden, Dr A J and Mrs P G Newton, Douglas Dwyer)*

Free house ~ Licensees Jamie Stuart, Pippa Hutchinson ~ Real ale ~ Meals and snacks (11am-10pm) ~ Restaurant ~ (01837) 810253 ~ Children in eating area of bar and in restaurant ~ Open 11-11; 12-10.30 Sun ~ Bedrooms: £25(£25B)/£50(£50B)

KINGSKERSWELL SX8767 Map 1
Barn Owl 🏠
Aller Mills; just off A380 Newton Abbot—Torquay – inn-sign on main road opposite RAC post

Friendly licensees run this 16th-c inn, originally a substantial farmhouse. The large bar has an elaborate ornamental plaster ceiling, antique dark oak panelling, some grand furnishings such as a couple of carved oak settles and old-fashioned dining chairs around the handsome polished tables on its flowery carpet, and a decorative wooden chimney piece; lots of pictures and artefacts, and old lamps and fresh flowers on the tables. The other rooms have low black oak beams, with polished flagstones and a kitchen range in one, and an inglenook fireplace in the other; Good popular bar food includes home-made soup (£2.25), sandwiches with side salad (from £3.20), filled baked potatoes (from £3.50), a salad of tomato and crab (£3.95), ploughman's (from £4), quite a few cold platters (from £5.95; fresh local crab £7.25), home-made steak and kidney pie (£6.95), fresh fillet of lemon sole (£7.25), gammon with egg (£7.95), steaks (from £8.25), puddings (£3), and daily specials like poached hake on a bed of leeks with beurre blanc sauce (£8.95), fillet of pork stuffed with prunes in a rich armagnac and cream sauce (£10.75), and quail stuffed with pâté in a red wine sauce (£12.25). Well kept Dartmoor Best, Ind Coope Burton, and Marstons Pedigree on handpump, 15 malt whiskies, and 18 wines by the glass. There are picnic tables in a small sheltered garden. No children. *(Recommended by Brian and Bett Cox, Andrew Hodges, P Rome, Jean and Douglas Troup, Ian and Jane Irving, Ian Phillips, Alan and Paula McCully, Joan and Michel Hooper-Immins, R T Moggridge)*

Free house ~ Licensees Derek and Margaret Warner ~ Real ale ~ Meals and snacks (till 10pm) ~ Restaurant ~ (01803) 872130 ~ Open 11.30-2.30, 6(6.30 in winter)-11; 12-2.30, 6-10.30 Sun; closed evening 25 Dec, closed 26-27 Dec ~ Bedrooms: £47.50B/£60B

KINGSTEIGNTON SX8773 Map 1
Old Rydon ★ ⑪

Rydon Rd; from A381/A380 junction follow signs to Kingsteignton (B3193), taking first right turn (Longford Lane), go straight on to the bottom of the hill, then next right turn into Rydon Rd following Council Office signpost; pub is just past the school, OS Sheet 192 map reference 872739

It's a surprise to find this very popular old pub in the middle of a residential area. The nice biggish sheltered garden has seats under parasols, with more on the terrace – but what readers like very much is the conservatory with its prolific shrubbery: two different sorts of bougainvillea, a vine with bunches of purple grapes, and lots of pretty geraniums and busy lizzies. The small, cosy bar has a big winter log fire in a raised fireplace, cask seats and upholstered seats built against the white-painted stone walls, and lots of beer mugs hanging from the heavy beam-and-plank ceiling. There are a few more seats in an upper former cider loft facing the antlers and antelope horns on one high white wall; piped music. From a varied menu, the very good food includes sandwiches (from £2.50), filled baked potatoes (from £2.95), and ploughman's (from £3.75), and daily specials such as home-made bacon, vegetable and herb soup (£2.25), grilled mussels, butter clams and flat cap mushrooms in garlic butter (£3.40), homity pie with leeks, potato, spinach, parsley and cheese with a red pepper sauce (£4.95), grilled chicken breast with a ginger, honey and mustard dressed salad topped with deep-fried crisp egg noodles or venison, pigeon and hare pie (£6.25), cantonese style seafood chow mein in a rich lemon, ginger and dill sauce (£6.50), puddings like apricot and raspberry trifle with mascarpone and amaretti topping or steamed chocolate and pecan pudding with hot chocolate sauce (£2.75), and children's meals. The restaurant is no smoking. Well kept Bass, Wadworths 6X, and a changing guest ale such as Fullers London Pride, Smiles Bitter, Summerskills Bitter or Teignworthy Reel Ale on handpump, and helpful, friendly service. *(Recommended by Stan Edwards, Liz Bell, Andrew Hodges, B Ferris Harms, Chris Reeve, D I Baddeley, Dr A J and Mrs P G Newton, James Cowell, John Waller, Simon and Hayley Marks, R T Moggridge, Alan and Paula McCully, Don and Shirley Parrish, M G Hart)*

Free house ~ Licensees Hermann and Miranda Hruby ~ Real ale ~ Meals and snacks ~ Restaurant ~ (01626) 54626 ~ Children in eating area of bar, but no under 8s after 8pm ~ Open 11-2.30, 6-11; 12-3, 7-10.30 Sun; closed 25 Dec

KNOWSTONE SS8223 Map 1
Masons Arms ★ ♀

Village signposted off A361 Bampton—South Molton

Set opposite the quiet village church, this is an unspoilt thatched 13th-c inn with a great deal of character and atmosphere. The casually personal way it's run doesn't of course appeal to everyone, but most really like the difference from more standardised places. The unspoilt small main bar has heavy medieval black beams hung with ancient bottles of all shapes and sizes, farm tools on the walls, substantial rustic furniture on the stone floor, and a fine open fireplace with a big log fire and side bread oven. A small lower sitting room has pinkish plush chairs around a low table in front of the fire, and bar billiards. Bar food can be very good indeed: widely praised home-made soup (£1.95) and home-made pâté like cheese and walnut or smoked mackerel (£2.75), ploughman's with proper local cheese and butter in a pot or Greek salad (£3.75), fried plaice (£4.25), home-made pies, varying from day to day, like venison, cheese and leek or rabbit (£4.75), and home-made puddings like pear and strawberry crunch (£2.25); daily specials such as courgette and mushroom stroganoff (£4.25), liver and bacon casserole (£4.50), lamb and aubergine or prawn and spinach curries (£5.75), and local lamb chops (£7.25); Sunday lunch (£4.25 one course, £7.75 three courses), and occasional themed food nights with appropriate music. The restaurant is no smoking. They often sell home-made marmalades, fruit breads or hot gooseberry chutney over the counter. Well kept Badger Best and Cotleigh Tawny tapped from the cask (and an occasional guest beer like Bass or Fullers London Pride), farm cider, a small but well chosen wine list, and a fair choice of malt whiskies; several snuffs on the counter; darts, shove-ha'penny, bar billiards, dominoes, cribbage, and board games. *(Recommended by Philip and Jude Simmons, Neil and Anita Christopher, Mr and Mrs G R Turner, Jo and Gary Charlton, Mr and Mrs G McNeill, M and M Carter, R J Walden, Dr and Mrs I H Maine, A and G Evans, Sheila and John French, Dr A J and Mrs P G Newton, Sue Demont, Tim Barrow, Joyce McKimm, Tony and Wendy Hobden, Paul Boot, Ian and Nita Cooper, Anna Bramhill, Simon Clarke, Linda and Mike Proctor, James Nunns)*

Free house ~ Licensees David and Elizabeth Todd ~ Real ale ~ Meals and snacks ~ Restaurant ~ (01398) 341231/341582 ~ Children in eating area of bar and in restaurant ~ Open 11-3, 6(7 in winter)-11; 12-4, 7-10.30 Sun; closed evenings 25-26 Dec ~ Bedrooms: £27.50B/£55B; dogs £1.50

LITTLEHEMPSTON SX8162 Map 1
Tally Ho!
Signposted off A381 NE of Totnes

This is a smashing little pub – bustling and very friendly and spotlessly kept. The cosy low-beamed rooms have fresh flowers and candles on the tables, panelling, and bare stone walls covered with lots of porcelain, brass, copperware, mounted butterflies, stuffed wildlife, old swords, and shields and hunting horns and so forth; there's also an interesting mix of chairs and settles (many antique and with comfortable cushions), and two coal-effect gas fires; no noisy machines or piped music. Very good bar food includes home-made soup (£2.95), sandwiches (from £2.75), mussels in cream and white wine (£3.50), ploughman's (£4.45), rabbit casserole (£6.50), steak and kidney pie or whole local plaice (£7.25), pork with a cider, almond, apple and cream sauce (£7.95), Brixham fish pie (£9.50), steaks (from £9.25), fresh roast duckling (£11.95), home-made puddings with clotted cream, and daily specials; Sunday lunchtime roast beef. Well kept Dartmoor Best, Palmers Tally Ho!, and Teignworthy Reel Ale on handpump from a temperature controlled cellar, and several whiskies. The friendly dog is called Marty and there's a nice ginger cat. The terraces is a mass of flowers in summer. *(Recommended by Andrew Hodges, Ian and Jane Irving, Jean and Douglas Troup, Bill and Brenda Lemon, DWAJ, Alan and Paula McCully, Dennis Glover, David and June Harwood)*

Free house ~ Licensees Alan and Dale Hitchman ~ Real ale ~ Meals and snacks (till 10pm) ~ (01803) 862316 ~ Children in eating area of bar ~ Open 12-2.30, 6-11; 12-3, 7-10.30 Sun; closed 25 Dec

LOWER ASHTON SX8484 Map 1
Manor 🍺
Ashton signposted off B3193 N of Chudleigh

Set in a charming valley, this creeper-covered, unspoilt pub is run by friendly, hard-working licensees. The left-hand room is more for locals enjoying the well kept Wadworths 6X tapped from the cask and RCH Pitchfork, Teignworthy Reel Ale, Theakstons XB and a changing guest ale such as Burton Bridge on handpump, or perhaps the local Grays farm cider; its walls are covered in beer mats and brewery advertisements. On the right, two rather more discreet rooms have a wider appeal, bolstered by tasty home-made food including sandwiches (from £1.70), soup (£1.70), ploughman's (from £3.75), filled baked potatoes (from £2.75), vegetable bake (£4.45), steak and kidney pie (£5.20) and steaks (from £8.50), with a good choice of changing specials (many topped with melted cheese and served with very garlicky garlic bread) such as mixed bean chilli or vegetable and nut curry (£4.50), beef casserole (£5.50), lamb goulash (£5.65), tuna and prawn bake (£5.95), and grilled lemon sole, trout and salmon (£6.95), and puddings (£2.25); service is quick. Shove-ha'penny, spoof. The garden has lots of picnic tables under cocktail parasols (and a fine tall Scots pine). No children. *(Recommended by N Wills, Mike Gorton; more reports please)*

Free house ~ Licensees Geoff and Clare Mann ~ Real ale ~ Meals and snacks (12-1.30, 7-9.30; not Mon) ~ (01647) 252304 ~ Open 12-2.30, 6(7 Sat)-11(10.30 Sun); closed Mon exc bank holidays

LUSTLEIGH SX7881 Map 1
Cleave

Village signposted off A382 Bovey Tracey—Moretonhampstead

This friendly old thatched pub is lovely to visit at any time of year in summer when the hanging baskets are pretty and the neat and very pretty sheltered garden is full of cottagey flowers, and in winter when you can sit in the low-ceilinged lounge bar in front of a roaring log fire. There are attractive antique high-backed settles, pale leatherette bucket chairs, red-cushioned wall seats, and wheelback chairs around the tables on its patterned carpet. A second bar has similar furnishings, a large dresser, harmonium, an HMV gramophone, and prints, and the no-smoking family room has crayons, books and toys for children. Generously served, the enjoyable bar food includes home-made soup (£2.50), sandwiches (£2.95), ploughman's (from £3.50), home-made chicken liver pâté (£3.95), very good local sausages (£5.50), home-made steak, kidney and Guinness pie (£6.50), good roast pork with apple sauce or home-made nut roast with spicy tomato sauce (£6.95), daily specials like breast of chicken in a lemon and tarragon sauce (£7.95), whole fresh lemon sole (£11.25), and half a honey roast duckling with black cherry sauce (£12.45), puddings like treacle tart or blackcurrant cheesecake (£2.25), and children's dishes (from £2.95). Well kept Bass, Flowers Original and Wadworths 6X on handpump, several malt whiskies, and farm ciders; cribbage and pool. The village is most attractive. *(Recommended by Dr A J and Mrs P G Newton, Richard and Rosemary Hoare, R J Walden, Barry and Anne, John and Vivienne Rice, Comus Elliott, Margaret Dyke, Alan and Paula McCully, M G Hart, G and M Stewart, John and Christine Vittoe, Alan Newman, Mr and Mrs C Roberts, A Lock, Joan and Gordon Edwards, Sue Hobley, Werner Arend)*

Heavitree (who no longer brew) ~ Tenant Alison Perring ~ Real ale ~ Meals and snacks ~ (01647) 277223 ~ Children in eating area of bar ~ Parking may be difficult ~ Open 11-11; 11-3, 6.30-11 in winter; 12-10.30 Sun

LUTTON SX5959 Map 1
Mountain

Off Cornwood—Sparkwell road, though pub not signposted from it

From seats on the terrace (and from one room inside) there is a fine view over the lower slopes of Dartmoor. It's a friendly local and the bar has a high-backed settle by the log fire and some walls stripped back to the bare stone, with windsor chairs around old-fashioned polished tables in a larger connecting room. Well kept Summerskills Best Bitter, Suttons XSB, and two weekly guest beers on handpump, several malt whiskies, and farm cider; darts, cribbage, and dominoes. Generous helpings of good straightforward bar food (with prices unchanged since last year) include pasties (£1.20), sandwiches (from £1.60), soup (£1.70; with a hunk of cheese as well £3), sausage and chips (£2.60), cottage pie (£3.50), ploughman's or ham cooked in cider (£3.80), and chicken kiev (£4.50). *(Recommended by D Cheesebrough, John Poulter, Elven Money, Mervyn Jonas, John Poulter)*

Free house ~ Licensees Charles and Margaret Bullock ~ Real ale ~ Meals and snacks (till 10 evening) ~ (01752) 837247 ~ Children in eating area of bar ~ Open 11-3(2.30 winter), 6(7 winter Mon-Weds)-11; 12-3, 7-10.30 Sun

LYDFORD SX5184 Map 1

Castle ★ 🛏 🍴 🍺

Signposted off A386 Okehampton—Tavistock

The new lounge area for diners and residents in this very well run and warmly friendly pink-washed Tudor inn has now been completed and has been favourably received by customers. There are stylishly old-fashioned sofas on the slate flagstoned floor, a Stuart oak dresser, thoughtfully chosen table lamps, attractive antique tables, a high backed settle, lots of pictures and plates on the walls, local oak beams supporting the bowed ceiling, and an open fire in the granite fireplace. The twin-roomed bar has a relaxed atmosphere, and country kitchen chairs, high-backed winged settles and old captain's chairs around mahogany tripod tables on big slate flagstones. One of the rooms (where the bar food is served) has low lamp-lit beams, a sizeable open fire, masses of brightly decorated plates, some Hogarth prints, an attractive grandfather clock, and, near the serving-counter, seven Lydford pennies hammered out in the old Saxon mint in the reign of Ethelred the Unready, in the 11th c; the second room has an interesting collection of antique stallion posters; unusual stained-glass doors. From a daily changing menu, the good, enjoyable home-made bar food might include soups like asparagus, artichoke and herb or stilton, celery and sweet almond (£2.40), ploughman's (from £3.75), duck terrine with brandy and black cherries (£3.95), leek, cream cheese and sweetcorn roulade (£5.75), steak and kidney pie (£5.90), fresh salmon and trout fishcakes with a wine and prawn sauce (£6.15), Dartmoor venison and juniper berry pie (£6.35), lemon chicken with thai rice and stir-fried vegetables (£6.75), grilled fillet of bass on a bed of roasted red pepper (£8.25), and lovely puddings such as apple and blackberry crumble, sticky toffee pudding or fresh strawberry fool and clotted cream (from £2.75); Sunday roast (occasionally including wild boar, £5.70; always a vegetarian option). The partly no-smoking restaurant now has a fixed-price menu with supplemented dishes, and there are Indian and Thai evenings. Well kept Blackawton Bitter and Fullers London Pride with a winter guest and up to four summer ones such as Bass, Mildmay Old Horsewhip and Colours (a little brewery at Holbeton) on handpump or tapped from the cask, and around 17 wines by the glass from a carefully chosen wine list; sensibly placed darts, cribbage, and dominoes; trivia. The garden has been extended slightly and the terrace has a pets' corner for residents' children with ducks, chickens and goats. The pub is next to the village's daunting, ruined 12th-c castle and close to a beautiful river gorge (owned by the National Trust; closed Nov-Easter); the village itself was one of the four strongpoints developed by Alfred the Great as a defence against the Danes. *(Recommended by Andy and Jill Kassube, Joan and Tony Walker, Lynn Sharpless, Bob Eardley, Jacquie and Jim Jones, Neil Franklin, Nigel Wikeley, Liz Bell, Mrs M Rolfe, Elven Money, John and Vivienne Rice, R J Walden, David and Mandy Allen, Mike Gorton, Anthony Barnes, Michael and Lynne Steane, Paul and Lynn Benny, Geoff Dibble, Colin Draper, Jonathan Williams, Mr and Mrs A O Meakin, John and Christine Vittoe, V G and P A Nutt, Hanns P Golez, Clive Hall-Tomkin, B J Cox, Pete and Rosie Flower, Viv Middlebrook,)*

Free house ~ Licensees Clive and Mo Walker ~ Real ale ~ Meals and snacks (not 25 Dec) ~ Evening restaurant ~ (01822) 820241/820242 ~ Children in eating area of bar, in restaurant and in snug area; must be over 7 in evening restaurant ~ Open 11.30-3, 6-11; 12-3, 6(7 in winter)-10.30 Sun ~ Bedrooms: £30(£40B)/£46(£59B)

Real ale may be served from handpumps, electric pumps (not just the on-off switches used for keg beer) or – common in Scotland – tall taps called founts (pronounced 'fonts') where a separate pump pushes the beer up under air pressure. The landlord can adjust the force of the flow – a tight spigot gives the good creamy head that Yorkshire lads like.

LYNMOUTH SS7249 Map 1
Rising Sun 🛏

Mars Hill; down by harbour

This is a lovely place to stay with plenty of good surrounding walks (the steep walk up the Lyn valley to Watersmeet, National Trust, and Exmoor is particularly pleasant), and a delightful setting with views over the boats in the little harbour and out to sea; hearty breakfasts. The modernised panelled bar has a relaxed atmosphere, as well as cushioned built-in stall-seats on the uneven oak floors, black beams in the crooked ceiling, some stripped stone at the fireplace end, and latticed windows facing the harbour; piped music. Well kept Courage Best, Exmoor Gold, Ruddles County, and Theakstons XB on handpump, and decent bar food (only available at lunchtime) such as home-made soup (£2.75), filled rolls (from £3.25), two jumbo spicy sausages with egg (£5.50), generous ploughman's (£5.75), steak, mushroom and Guinness pie (£5.95), local trout (£5.75), and 6oz sirloin steak (£8.50); the attractive restaurant is no smoking. There's a charming terraced garden behind the inn, cut into the hillside. Shelley reputedly spent his honeymoon with his 16-year-old bride, Harriet, in one of the cottages here. *(Recommended by R J Walden, Paul Barnett, Jerry Hughes, James House, Neil and Anita Christopher, Sheila O'Donnell, M G Hart, Dr A J and Mrs P G Newton, Rip and Pauline Kirby, Simon Collett-Jones, PM, AM, S Demont, T Barrow, Tina and David Woods-Taylor, V Kavanagh)*

Free house ~ Licensee Hugo Jeune ~ Real ale ~ Lunchtime meals and snacks ~ Restaurant ~ (01598) 753223 ~ Children in eating area of the bar and restaurant ~ Open 11-2.30, 6.30-11; 12-3, 7-10.30 Sun ~ Bedrooms: £49.50B/£79B

MEAVY SX5467 Map 1
Royal Oak

Off B3212 E of Yelverton

In summer, particularly on Sunday lunchtime, this friendly traditional old pub is very busy – but you can sit at the picnic tables and benches outside or on the attractive village green. The carpeted L-shaped bar has pews from the next door church, red plush banquettes and old agricultural prints and church pictures on the walls, and there's a smaller bar – where the locals like to gather – with a big fireplace and side bread oven, and red-topped barrel seats. Bar food includes sandwiches (£1.80), soup (£1.90), ploughman's (£3.50), filled crêpes (£3.95), cold ham and sautéed potatoes (£4.50), fish pie or spinach and mushroom lasagne (£5.25), mussels and cockles and cheese with a garlic and white wine sauce (£5.50), steak and kidney pie (£5.75), daily specials like cheese and vegetable bake (£5.25), roast beef or turkey (£5.50), and salmon fillet with new potatoes (£6.50), and puddings (£2.25). Well kept Bass, Courage Best, Eldridge Pope Strong Ale, and Meavy Valley Bitter on handpump kept under light blanket pressure, and three draught ciders. Dominoes, euchre, and piped music. No children. *(Recommended by Barry and Anne, Emma Kingdon, A and G Evans, Jacquie and Jim Jones, R J Walden, R A Cunningham, James Macrae, G and M Stewart, Colin Draper, C A Hall, M J How, Joan and Michael Hooper-Immins)*

Free house ~ Licensees Roger and Susan Barber ~ Real ale ~ Meals and snacks (11.30-2.30, 6.30-9.30) ~ (01822) 852944 ~ Open 11.30-3, 6.30-11; 12-3, 7-10.30 Sun

MILTONCOMBE SX4865 Map 1
Who'd Have Thought It ★

On A386 ¾ mile S of Yelverton, turn W onto signposted country road for 2 miles

By the time this book is published, new licensees will probably have taken over this attractive 16th-c pub. The atmospheric, black-panelled bar has a woodburning stove in the big stone fireplace, cushioned barrel seats and high-backed winged settles around solid, polished wooden tables, colourful plates on a big black dresser, and rapiers, sabres and other weapons on its walls; two other rooms (one is no smoking) have seats made from barrels; fruit machine. Bar food has included sandwiches (from £2.25), ploughman's (from £3.25), home-made curries (£3.50), home-made pies like chicken and asparagus, pork and apple or steak and kidney (all £4.50), salmon salad or braised steak in red wine (£5.95), rabbit in honey and mustard (£6.25), lemon sole (£9.75), and puddings (£2.20); Sunday roasts. Well kept Blackawton Headstrong, Eldridge Pope Royal Oak, Exmoor Ale, and a monthly changing guest beer on handpump. There are picnic tables on a terrace with hanging baskets by the little stream. The pub is handy for Buckland Abbey or the lovely gardens of the Garden House at Buckland Monachorum. No children. *(Recommended by Andy and Jill Kassube, R J Walden, Jason Caulkin, T Pascall, A and G Evans, R Turnham, Philip and Trisha Ferris, Nigel Clifton, Dennis Glover, Peter Burton, Colin Draper, James Macrae)*

Free house ~ Licensees Keith Yeo and Gary Rager ~ Real ale ~ Meals and snacks ~ (01822) 853313 ~ Folk club Sun evening in lower bar ~ Open 11.30-2.30(3 Sat), 6.30-11; 12-3, 7-10.30 Sun

NEWTON ST CYRES SX8798 Map 1
Beer Engine 🐝

Sweetham; from Newton St Cyres on A377 follow St Cyres Station, Thorverton signpost

When this friendly old station hotel is full of locals, there's a good chatty atmosphere. Most come to enjoy the good own-brewed real ales on handpump: Rail Ale, Piston Bitter, Return Ticket (Mild), and the very strong Sleeper. The spacious main bar has partitioning alcoves, and windsor chairs and some cinnamon-coloured button-back banquettes around dark varnished tables on the brown carpet. Decent bar food includes chicken in barbecue sauce (£5.25), pork and garlic sausages, curries or home-made steak and kidney pie (all £5.50), and rump steak (£7.50); roast Sunday lunch (£5.25 one course, £6.95 two courses). Darts, shove-ha'penny, dominoes and cribbage; fruit machine and video game in the downstairs lobby. There's a large sunny garden on several interesting levels with lots of sheltered seating; you can eat out here, too. *(Recommended by R J Walden, Catherine Lloyd, A and G Evans, Ian Jones, Dr A J and Mrs P G Newton, Dr and Mrs J M Coles)*

Own brew ~ Licensee Peter Hawksley ~ Real ale ~ Meals and snacks (till 10pm) ~ (01392) 851282 ~ Children in eating area of bar ~ Open 11-11; 12-10.30 Sun

PETER TAVY SX5177 Map 1
Peter Tavy

Off A386 nr Mary Tavy, N of Tavistock

John and Gill Diprose who used to run a popular main entry the Durant Arms in Ashprington, have now taken over this 15th-c stone inn. The friendly bar has a lot of atmosphere, as well as low beams, high-backed settles on the black flagstones by the big stone fireplace (a good log fire on cold days), smaller settles in stone-mullioned windows, and a snug side dining area (which is no smoking at weekends). Bar food at lunchtime now includes home-made soups (£1.95), filled french bread (£3.20), ploughman's (£3.50), liver, bacon and onion casserole or cottage pie (£4.95), steak and kidney pie or pudding (£5.25), and baked cod (£5.95), with evening dishes like pork tenderloin in cider sauce or fresh scallops (£7.95), pheasant with a port sauce (£8.25), chicken with lemon and asparagus (£8.50), crab salad or rack of lamb (£8.95), and home-made puddings (£2.75); good service. Well kept Bass, Beer Engine Rail Ale (from our Newton St Cyres main entry), Cotleigh Tawny, Exmoor Gold, and Shepherd Neame Spitfire on handpump, and 30 malt whiskies; darts and piped music. Henry the labrador is friendly and welcomes other dogs (on a lead). From the picnic tables in the pretty garden there are peaceful views of the moor rising above nearby pastures. Please note, they no longer do bedrooms. *(Recommended by P and J Shapley, Lynn Sharpless, Bob Eardley, Iain Robertson, R J Walden, Barry and Anne, H Paulinski, James Bailey, Richard and Rosemary Hoare, R A Cullingham, Paul and Heather Bettesworth, John Evans, Elven Money, S E Dark, Dr A J and Mrs P G Newton, M J G Martin, C Hardacre; more reports on the new regime, please)*

Free house ~ Licensees John and Gill Diprose ~ Real ale ~ Meals and snacks ~ (01822) 810348 ~ Children in dining room ~ Open 11.30-2.30(3 Sat), 6(7 in winter)-11; 12-3, 7-10.30 Sun

PLYMOUTH SX4755 Map 1
China House ★

Marrowbone Slip, Sutton Harbour, via Sutton Road off Exeter Street (A374)

It's the marvellous position that customers particularly enjoy here. This is a carefully converted 17th-c warehouse (the oldest in Plymouth) with picnic tables and benches on the now heated verandah – which means you can sit out all year round – overlooking Sutton Harbour. Inside is lofty and very spacious but cleverly partitioned into smaller booth-like areas, with great beams and flagstone floors, bare slate and stone walls, and lots of nets, kegs and fishing gear; there's even a clinker-built boat. On the left is the main bar with plain wooden seats around dark tables in front of a good log fire – all very comfortable and relaxed. Bar food includes sandwiches, home-made soup (£2.95), seafood fritters with lemon mayonnaise (£3.95), chicken with mushrooms, capers and dijon mustard (£6.20), nut and broccoli rice cakes with a mustard and herb sauce or pasta with bacon and mushrooms (£7.95), grilled fish with sour cream and spicy dressing and caramelised pork fillet with a piquant orange sauce (£9.95), sirloin steak (£10.95); cold food is served all day. Well kept Dartmoor Best, Marstons Pedigree, and Tetleys on handpump; fruit machine, trivia and piped music. *(Recommended by Andrew Hodges, R A Cullingham, P and M Rudlin, Steve and Maggie Willey, David Carr, Anthony Barnes, Mr and Mrs P Byatt, Karen Eliot, Mrs P V Burdett, Ian and Gayle Woodhead, James Macrae, Mr and Mrs D S Price)*

Ansells (Allied) ~ Manageress Nicole Quinn ~ Real ale ~ Meals and snacks (all day; no hot food Sun evening) ~ Restaurant ~ (01752) 260930 ~ Children in eating area of bar ~ Jazz Sun lunchtime, live bands and DJ Fri/Sat evenings ~ Open 11-11 Mon-Thurs (till 12.30 Fri/Sat); 12-10.30 Sun

nr POSTBRIDGE SX6780 Map 1
Warren House

B3212 1¾ miles NE of Postbridge

In glorious solitude on a pleasant moorland road, this friendly place is a welcome oasis for walkers and birdwatchers and a popular meeting place for the scattered communities. The cosy bar has a fireplace at either end (one is said to have been kept almost continuously alight since 1845), and is simply furnished with easy chairs and settles under a beamed ochre ceiling, wild animal pictures on the partly panelled stone walls, and dim lighting (fuelled by the pub's own generator). Good no-nonsense home cooking includes locally made meaty or vegetable pasties (£1.60), home-made soup (£1.90), sandwiches (from £2.50), filled baked potatoes (from £2.75), good ploughman's with local cheeses (£4.50), mushroom and nut fettucine (£5.25), and home-made pies like rabbit (£6) or steak in ale pie (£6.50), with evening dishes such as spicy prawns, lemon sole with a home-made prawn and mushroom sauce (£7.50), and Scottish salmon (£8.50), and puddings such as toffee apple sponge pudding or lemon and lime parfait with a Crunchie base (£2.80). Well kept Badger Tanglefoot, Butcombe Bitter, Gibbs Mew Bishops Tipple, and St Austell HSD on handpump, farm cider, and local country wines. Darts, pool, cribbage, dominoes, and video game. *(Recommended by R J Walden, John Beeken, Barry and Anne, Mayur Shah, Mr and Mrs D E Powell, John and Vivienne Rice, M G Hart, A N Ellis, Hanns P Golez, Andrew Hodges)*

Free house ~ Licensee Peter Parsons ~ Real ale ~ Meals and snacks (noon-9.30 in summer) ~ (01822) 880208 ~ Children in family room ~ Open 11-11; 11-2.30, 5.30-11 winter weekdays; 12-10.30 Sun

---

The letters and figures after the name of each town are its Ordnance Survey map reference. *How to use the Guide* at the beginning of the book explains how it helps you find a pub, in road atlases or large-scale maps as well as in our own maps.

RACKENFORD SS8518 Map 1
Stag
Off A361 NW of Tiverton

Dating in part from 1237 and reopened under new owners a couple of years ago, this little thatched inn may be Devon's oldest. You go in through a wonderfully ancient cobbled entrance corridor between massive stone and cob walls, and the bar lives up to this first impression. The shiny dark ochre ceiling is very low, and a couple of very high-backed old settles face each other in front of the massive fireplace with its ancient bressumer beam (and good log fire). The bar counter is a grand piece of oak, and there are some other interesting old pieces of furniture as well as more modern seats; a narrow sloping side area has darts, and leading off is a cottagey dining room. Good bar food includes sandwiches (from £1.60), filled baked potatoes (from £2.40), ham and egg (£3.25), omelettes (£3.95), cauliflower cheese (£4.25), grilled salmon steak (£5.95), and 8oz rump steak (£7.50), and children's menu (from £1). Well kept Adnams Broadside, Cotleigh Tawny and Fullers ESB on handpump, good house wines, very friendly service – a nice relaxed atmosphere; pool, alley skittles, cribbage, dominoes, and piped music. The dog is called Spanner, and the cat, Mr Pudge. *(Recommended by Peter Churchill, Paul Boot, Paul and Heather Bettesworth)*

Free house ~ Licensees Norman and Jennie Foot ~ Real ale ~ Meals and snacks ~ (01884) 881369 ~ Evening restaurant ~ Local musicians weekends ~ Children welcome ~ Open 12-2,30, 6-11; 12-11 Sat; 12-10.30 Sun ~ Bedrooms: £16.50(£17.50B)/£33(£35B)

RATTERY SX7461 Map 1
Church House
Village signposted from A385 W of Totnes, and A38 S of Buckfastleigh

The craftsmen who built the Norman church were probably housed in the original building here – parts of it still survive, notably the spiral stone steps behind a little stone doorway on your left. There are massive oak beams and standing timbers in the homely open-plan bar, large fireplaces (one with a little cosy nook partitioned off around it), windsor armchairs, comfortable seats and window seats, and prints on the plain white walls; the dining room is separated from this room by heavy curtains; Shandy the golden labrador is very amiable. Good bar food includes filled rolls and ploughman's with local cheeses, and daily specials such as roast guinea fowl with apricots (£6.70), chicken with smoked sausage and prawns (£6.75), beef balti (£6.80), and poached salmon with a lemon grass and dill sauce (£6.95); children's meals. Well kept Dartmoor Best, Marstons Pedigree, and a weekly guest beer on handpump, around 40 malt whiskies, and a decent wine list. Outside, there are peaceful views of the partly wooded surrounding hills from picnic tables in a hedged courtyard by the churchyard. *(Recommended by Andrew Hodges, Andy and Jill Kassube, Mr and Mrs D Wilson, Jo and Gary Charlton, B J Harding, Mike Gorton, M Joyner, David and Nina Pugsley, Dr A J and Mrs P G Newton, Paul and Janet Waring, Hanns P Golez, John Evans, Mr and Mrs B Cox, Bryan Taylor)*

Free house ~ Licensees Brian and Jill Evans ~ Real ale ~ Meals and snacks ~ (01364) 642220 ~ Children in eating area of bar and in dining room ~ Open 11-2.30, 6-11; 12-2.30, 7-10.30 Sun

RINGMORE SX6545 Map 1
Journeys End 🛏 🍺
Off B3392 at Pickwick Inn, St Anns Chapel, nr Bigbury

The circular walks to the beach and cliffs (National Trust) are a must from this friendly partly 13th-c inn – and it's worth a wander around the pretty village, too. Inside, the tidy main bar has bare boards, flagstones and panelling, an unusual partly pitched ceiling, soft lighting from a nice mix of lamps, and a blazing log fire. Good bar food includes sandwiches (from £2; hot bacon and mushroom £3.50), ploughman's (from £3.50), lentil and split pea moussaka or mushroom stroganoff (£4.50), local trout or gammon and egg (£6.50), steaks (from £7.95), good daily specials, and puddings like treacle tart or home-made apple pie (£2.50); smashing breakfasts and monthly themed food evenings (3 courses £12.50) in the candlelit no-smoking restaurant; pleasant efficient staff. Well kept Adnams Broadside, Archers Golden, Exmoor Ale, Mildmay Colours, Otter Ale, and Shepherd Neame Spitfire on handpump or tapped from the cask, and they hold two beer festivals – usually April and September; Stancombe farm cider, and dominoes and fruit machine. The big, attractively planted garden has plenty of seats. *(Recommended by S P Goddard, B J Harding, Mike and Wena Stevenson, Mark Fennell, Mr and Mrs C R Little, T G Brierly, David Wallington, Dave Irving, Tom McLean, Ewan McCall, Marianne Lantree, Steve Webb, Tim Brierly, Jenny and Roger Huggins, Jeanne Cross, Paul Silvester, J Brunel Cohen)*

Free house ~ Licensee James Parkin ~ Real ale ~ Meals and snacks (not evening 25 Dec) ~ Conservatory restaurant ~ (01548) 810205 ~ Children in restaurant and conservatory bar ~ Open 11.30-3, 6-11; 12-10.30 Sun; closed evening 25 Dec ~ Bedrooms: £25B/£45B

SHEEPWASH SS4806 Map 1
Half Moon 🛏 🍷 £

Off A3072 Holsworthy—Hatherleigh at Highampton

The whole side of the village square with its thatched or slate-roofed cottages is taken up with this buff-painted, civilised inn. It's a most enjoyable place to visit and has lots of fishing pictures on the white walls of the neatly-kept and friendly carpeted main bar, solid old furniture under the beams, and a big log fire fronted by slate flagstones. Lunchtime bar food is attractively straightforward and good, including sandwiches (£1.50, toasties £2), super home-made vegetable soup (£1.75), home-made pasties (£2.50), ploughman's (£3.25), home-cooked ham salad (£3.75), and home-made puddings (from £2). Well kept Courage Best, Jollyboat Mainbrace Bitter (brewed locally), Marstons Pedigree, and an occasional guest on handpump (well kept in a temperature-controlled cellar), a fine choice of malt whiskies, and an extensive wine list; darts, fruit machine, and separate pool room. This is the place to stay if you love fishing as they have 10 miles of private fishing on the River Torridge (salmon, sea trout and brown trout) as well as a rod room, good drying facilities and a small shop stocking the basic things needed to catch fish. *(Recommended by R J Walden, Sheila and John French, George Barnwell, Mr and Mrs J D Marsh, Dr A J and Mrs P G Newton, Colin Draper)*

Free house ~ Licensees Benjamin Robert Inniss and Charles Inniss ~ Real ale ~ Snacks (lunchtime)~ Evening restaurant ~ (01409) 231376 ~ Children welcome lunchtime only ~ Open 11-2.30(3 Sat), 6-11 ~ Bedrooms: £36B/£70B

SIDFORD SY1390 Map 1
Blue Ball ★ 🛏 🍺

A3052 just N of Sidmouth

Since 1912 the same friendly family have been running this popular thatched inn, which probably accounts for its consistently relaxed and cheerful atmosphere. The low, partly-panelled and neatly kept lounge bar has a lovely winter log fire in the stone fireplace (there are two other open fires as well), heavy beams, upholstered wall benches and windsor chairs, and lots of bric-a-brac; the snug is no smoking. Quickly served bar food includes soup (£1.75), sandwiches with several choices of bread (from £1.80; crab £2.75), filled baked potatoes (£3.50), lots of ploughman's and salads (from £3.50), omelettes (£4.50), vegetable lasagne (£4.95), chicken balti (£6.25), steaks (from £8.75), daily specials, children's dishes (£1.99), and puddings (£2.25); they hold themed food evenings with appropriate music. Bass, Boddingtons, Flowers IPA, and Wadworths 6X on handpump, kept well in a temperature-controlled cellar; helpful staff. A plainer public bar has darts, dominoes, cribbage and a fruit machine; piped music. Tables on a terrace look out over a colourful front flower garden, and there are more seats on a bigger back lawn – as well as in a covered area next to the barbecue; safe swing, see saw and play house for children. *(Recommended by Arnold Day, Klaus and Elizabeth Leist, G G Lawrence, Peter and Audrey Dowsett, Basil Minson, Stan Edwards, R Boyd, Shirley Pielou, D Godden, M E Wellington, Clem Stephens, VG and P Nutt, John and Christine Vittoe, Graham and Lynn Mason, Rita Horridge, David Holloway, G J Newman, James Nunns, D Toulson)*

Greenalls ~ Tenant Roger Newton ~ Real ale ~ Meals and snacks (11-3, 6.30-9.30) ~ Well behaved children in eating area of bar ~ (01395) 514062 ~ Open 10.30-2.30(3 Sat), 5.30-11; 12-3, 6-10.30 Sun ~ Bedrooms: £24/£40

SOURTON SX5390 Map 1
Highwayman ★
A386 SW of Okehampton; a short detour from the A30

You will be amazed at the sheer eccentricity of this pub's design. It doesn't have a lot of the things that people expect from a pub – no real ale and virtually no food – but what it does have is a marvellously well executed fantasy decor that the friendly owners have over 36 years put great enthusiasm and masses of hard work into. The porch (a pastiche of a nobleman's carriage) leads into a warren of dimly lit stonework and flagstone-floored burrows and alcoves, richly fitted with red plush seats discreetly cut into the higgledy-piggledy walls, elaborately carved pews, a leather porter's chair, Jacobean-style wicker chairs, and seats in quaintly bulging small-paned bow windows; the ceiling in one part, where there's an array of stuffed animals, gives the impression of being underneath a tree, roots and all. The separate Rita Jones' Locker is a make-believe sailing galleon, full of intricate woodwork and splendid timber baulks, with white antique lace-clothed tables in the embrasures that might have held cannons. They only sell keg beer, but specialise in farm cider, and food is confined to a range of meaty and vegetarian pasties (£1.50); service is warmly welcoming and full of character; old-fashioned penny fruit machine, and 40s piped music; no smoking at the bar counters. Outside, there's a play area in similar style for children with little black and white roundabouts like a Victorian fairground, a fairy-tale pumpkin house and an old-lady-who-lived-in-the-shoe house. You can take children in to look around the pub but they can't stay inside. The period bedrooms are attractive. *(Recommended by James and Ruth Morrell, George Atkinson, Paul Boot, Graham Tayar, Jim and Judie McGettigan, Pete and Rosie Flower; more reports please)*

Free house ~ Licensees Buster and Rita Jones and Sally Thomson ~ Snacks (11-1.45, 6-10) ~ (01837) 861243 ~ Open 11-2, 6-10.30; 12-2, 7-10.30 Sun ~ Bedrooms: £36

SOUTH POOL SX7740 Map 1
Millbrook
Off A379 E of Kingsbridge

When high tide coincides with meal times, this tiny spotlessly kept pub (one of the smallest in the book) does get pretty packed with boating visitors; there are seats on the terrace by the stream with its Aylesbury ducks. Inside, the charming little back bar has handsome windsor chairs, a chintz easy chair, drawings and paintings (and a chart) on its cream walls, clay pipes on the beams, and fresh flowers; there's also a top bar. Home-made bar food includes sandwiches (from £2.20), home-made soup (£2.50), good ploughman's (from £4), cottage pie (£4.40), chilli con carne (£4.65), vegetarian dishes, daily specials such as beef in stout or barbecued ribs (£5.95), fresh pasta dishes, halibut au poivre (£6.95), Aberdeen Angus sirloin steak (£9.10), and puddings like pavlova with fresh fruit compote (£3). Bass, Ruddles Best, Wadworths 6X and a guest ale on handpump, and Churchwards farm ciders; good, friendly service even when busy. Darts and euchre in the public bar in winter. *(Recommended by Ann and Frank Bowman, TBB, DJW, Mr and Mrs W Welsh, Peter and Rosie Flower, Peter Lewis, Nick Wikeley)*

Free house ~ Licensees Jed Spedding and Liz Stirland ~ Real ale ~ Meals and snacks ~ (01548) 531581 ~ Children in top bar ~ Open 11(11.30 winter)-2.30, 5.30-11; 12-3, 7-10.30 Sun – these times depend on high tide

SOUTH ZEAL SX6593 Map 1
Oxenham Arms ★ 🛏 ♀

Village signposted from A30 at A382 roundabout and B3260 Okehampton turn-off

A lovely relaxed and friendly place to unwind after the busy A30, this fine old inn was first licensed in 1477 and has grown up around the remains of a Norman monastery, built here to combat the pagan power of the neolithic standing stone that still forms part of the wall in the family TV room behind the bar (there are actually twenty more feet of stone below the floor). It later became the Dower House of the Burgoynes, whose heiress carried it to the Oxenham family. The beamed and partly panelled front bar has elegant mullioned windows and Stuart fireplaces, and windsor armchairs around low oak tables and built-in wall seats. The small no-smoking family room has beams, wheelback chairs around polished tables, decorative plates, and another open fire. Popular bar food includes soup (£1.85), sandwiches (from £2.25), good ploughman's (£3.50), home-made steak, kidney, Guinness and mushroom pie (£5.45), fish and chips (£5.75), daily specials such as vegetable stroganoff (£4.25), chicken cacciatore or squab pie (lamb, apple, sultanas) or salmon and broccoli mornay (all £5.45), evening steaks (£9.25), and puddings (£2.45). Well kept Princetown IPA and Jail Ale (brewed locally) on handpump or tapped from the cask, and an extensive list of wines including good house claret; darts, shove-ha'penny, dominoes, and cribbage. Note the imposing curved stone steps leading up to the garden where there's a sloping spread of lawn. *(Recommended by Nigel Flook, Betsy Brown, John and Sally Clarke, Mrs H Murphy, Klaus and Elizabeth Leist, Jacquie and Jim Jones, George and Jeanne Barnwell, Jeff Davies, Alan and Paula McCully, Mrs M Rolfe, Jane and Adrian Tierney-Jones, Mr and Mrs G McNeill, IHR, Brian and Bett Cox, R J Walden, Mr and Mrs J Jones, A N Ellis, John and Christine Vittoe, Mr and Mrs M Peck, Ian Phillips, Nigel Clifton)*

Free house ~ Licensee James Henry ~ Real ale ~ Meals and snacks ~ Restaurant ~ (01837) 840244 ~ Children in family room ~ Open 11-2.30, 6-11; 12-2.30, 7-10.30 Sun ~ Bedrooms: £45B/£60B

STAVERTON SX7964 Map 1
Sea Trout 🛏

Village signposted from A384 NW of Totnes

A previous landlord renamed this reliably friendly old village inn after he caught a seatrout in the River Dart just 400 yards away – it had been known as the Church House for several hundred years. The neatly kept rambling beamed lounge bar has sea trout and salmon flies and stuffed fish on the walls, cushioned settles and stools, and a stag's head above the fireplace, and the main bar has low banquettes, soft lighting and an open fire. There's also a public bar with pool, darts, table skittles, shove-ha'penny, and juke box; the conservatory is no smoking. Good bar food includes home-made soup (£2.10), sandwiches (from £2.75; foccacia ones from £3.65), home-made pâté (£3.25), ploughman's (£3.95), pork and apple sausages (£4.25), vegetable hotpot (£4.50), home-cooked ham and egg (£4.95), smoked haddock and prawn crumble (£5.75), whole Brixham plaice (£6.95), lamb cutlets (£7.95), steaks (from £8.50), daily specials, puddings, children's meals (from £2.85), and good Sunday lunch. Well kept Bass, Dartmoor Best, Wadworths 6X, and guest beers like Blackawton Best, Mildmay Colours, and Palmers on handpump, and efficient, helpful staff. There are seats under parasols on the attractive paved back garden. A station for the Torbay Steam Railway is not far away. *(Recommended by Julie Peters, Colin Blinkhorn, J H Bell, Andrew Hodges, Dr A J and Mrs P G Newton, B J Cox, Chris Reeve, Peter and Wendy Arnold)*

Free house ~ Licensees Andrew and Pym Mogford ~ Real ale ~ Meals and snacks ~ Restaurant ~ (01803) 762274 ~ Children in eating area of bar ~ Occasional Spanish guitar Fri evenings ~ Open 11-3, 6-11; 12-3, 7-11 Sun; closed evenings 25-26 Dec ~ Bedrooms: £42.50B/£64B

STOCKLAND ST2404 Map 1
Kings Arms 🍴 🛏 ♟

Village signposted from A30 Honiton—Chard

The dark beamed, elegant dining lounge here is extremely popular with customers from miles around for its good, interesting food. There are solid refectory tables and settles, attractive landscapes, a medieval oak screen (which divides the room into two), and a great stone fireplace across almost the whole width of one end; the cosy restaurant with its huge inglenook fireplace and bread oven has the same menu as the bar. Booking is essential. Bar food includes lunchtime snacks and sandwiches, as well as soup (£2), smoked mackerel pâté (£3.50), vegetable pancake or mushroom thermidor (£6.50), pheasant braised with cointreau, apple and smoked bacon or lamb curry (£7.50), fillet of cod portugaise (£8.50), steaks (from £8.50), rack of lamb with dijon mustard and breadcrumbs and roasted with madeira, grilled king prawns or monkfish with pernod, dill and cream (£9.50), puddings like crème brûlée with raspberries, gooseberry crunch or apple and treacle crumble (£3), and a good choice of local cheeses (£3); hearty breakfasts. Well kept Exmoor Ale, Otter Ale, John Smiths, and Theakstons XB on handpump, over 40 malt whiskies (including island and west coast ones; large spirit measures), a good wine list with house wines and special offers by the bottle or glass chalked up on a board, and farm ciders. At the back, a flagstone bar has captain's-style tub chairs and cushioned stools around heavy wooden tables, and leads on to a carpeted darts room with two boards, another room with dark beige plush armchairs and settees (and a fruit machine), and a neat ten-pin skittle alley; table skittles, cribbage, dominoes, fruit machine, and quiet mainly classical piped music. There are tables under cocktail parasols on the terrace in front of the white-faced thatched pub and a lawn enclosed by trees and shrubs. *(Recommended by Mike Gorton, R J Walden, John Bowdler, Ann and Colin Hunt, R Morgan, James Nunns, Clifford Hall; more reports please)*

Free house ~ Licensees Heinz Kiefer, Paul Diviani, and John O'Leary ~ Real ale ~ Snacks (lunchtime) and meals ~ Restaurant ~ (01404) 881361 ~ Well behaved/supervised children welcome ~ Live music Sun evenings and bank hol Mon evenings ~ Open 12-3, 6.30-11; 12-3, 7-11 Sun ~ Bedrooms: £25B/£40B

STOKE FLEMING SX8648 Map 1
Green Dragon ♟

Church Rd

Some changes to this very relaxed and friendly pub in the last year include the laying of a slate flagstone floor in the beamed main bar, the discovery of a nice wooden floor under the old carpet in the snug, and the addition of old charts on the ceiling of the Mess Deck. There are two small settles, bay window seats, boat pictures, and maybe Electra or Maia the burmese cats or Rhea the relaxed german shepherd in the main part, while down on the right is an area with throws and cushions on battered sofas and armchairs, a few books (20p to RNLI), adult board games, a grandfather clock, a wringer, and cuttings about the landlord (who is a long-distance yachtsman – but sadly lost his boat in the mid Atlantic in 1996) and maps of his races on the walls. Down some steps is the Mess Deck decorated with lots of ensigns and flags, and there's a playbox of children's games; darts, shove-ha'penny, cribbage, and dominoes. Good home-made bar food includes soup (£1.90), sandwiches (from £2.20), ploughman's with three cheeses (£3.50), malaysian stuffed mushrooms, fish wellington, salmon en croûte, Wiltshire plait, and pepper pithivers (all £5.50), and puddings and children's menu. Well kept Bass, Eldridge Pope Royal Oak, Flowers Original, and Wadworths 6X on handpump (all except Bass kept under light blanket pressure), big glasses of six good house wines from Australia, California, France and Germany, Luscombe cider, and a good range of spirits; you can take the beer away with you. There's a back garden with swings, a climbing frame and picnic tables and a front terrace with some white plastic garden tables and chairs. The tall church tower opposite is interesting. *(Recommended by B J Harding, Elven Money, D G Clarke, A M Stephenson, Patricia Dodd, Pam and Tim Moorey, Alan and Paula McCully)*

*Heavitree (who no longer brew) ~ Tenants Peter and Alix Crowther ~ Real ale ~
Meals and snacks (not winter Sun evenings) ~ 01803 770238 ~ Children welcome ~
Open 11-3, 5.30-11;.12-3, 6-10.30 Sun*

STOKE GABRIEL SX8457 Map 1
Church House ★

Village signposted from A385 just W of junction with A3022, in Collaton St Mary; can also
be reached from nearer Totnes; nearby parking not easy

This early 14th-c pub is warm, comfortable and welcoming and much liked by a
wide mix of customers. The lounge bar has an exceptionally fine medieval beam-
and-plank ceiling, a black oak partition wall, window seats cut into the thick butter-
colour walls, decorative plates and vases of flowers on a dresser, and a huge fireplace
still used in winter to cook the stew. The mummified cat in a case, probably about
200 years old, was found during restoration of the roof space in the verger's cottage
three doors up the lane – one of a handful found in the West Country and believed
to have been a talisman against evil spirits. Home-made bar food includes soup
(£1.95), a huge choice of sandwiches and toasties (from £1.75; good cheese and
prawn toasties, lovely local river salmon and local crab), ploughman's (from £3.25),
daily specials like tuna and broccoli bake or home-made steak, kidney and ale pie
(£5.50), fresh Dart salmon (£7.25), and puddings (from £2.25); well kept Bass,
Worthington Best, and a weekly guest ale on handpump, and quite a few malt
whiskies. Cribbage in the little public locals' bar. There are picnic tables on the little
terrace in front of the building. No children. *(Recommended by David Carr, M Joyner,
Ian and Jane Irving, Mike Gorton, John and June Freeman, Julie and Tony Baldwin, Dr S
Willavoys, Peter and Penelope Gurowich, Andrew Hodges)*

*Free house ~ Lease: Glyn Patch ~ Real ale ~ Meals and snacks (till 10pm) ~ (01803)
782384 ~ Open 11-3, 6-11; 11-11 Sat; 11-3.30, 7-10.30 Sun*

STOKENHAM SX8042 Map 1
Tradesmans Arms

Just off A379 Dartmouth—Kingsbridge

Very individually run by Mr Henderson, this pretty thatched cottage is in a charming
village. The little beamed bar has plenty of nice antique tables and neat dining chairs –
with more up a step or two at the back, window seats looking across a field to the
village church, and a big fireplace. Good bar food includes fresh fish delivered daily
from Plymouth, such as lemon sole, scallops, plaice, haddock and Dart river salmon
(from £5.75), as well as a smashing french onion soup (£2.25), sandwiches (from
£2.50), home-made avocado and herb or chicken liver pâté (£3.50), ploughman's
(from £3.50), a vegetarian pasta dish (£5.25), daily specials such as stuffed gammon or
chicken in tarragon, and steaks (£11.50). Well kept Adnams Southwold and perhaps
Bass, Greene King Abbot or Hook Norton Best on handpump, and 50 good malt
whiskies. Dogs are welcome – their italian sheepdog is called The Blanket, and there
are four cats: Flotsam, Jetsam, Gregory and Harry. There are some seats outside in the
garden. *(Recommended by TBB, DJW, Mr and Mrs Welsh, Elven Money)*

*Free house ~ Licensee Peter Henderson ~ Real ale ~ Meals and snacks ~ (01548)
580313 ~ Children in dining room only ~ Open 12-3, 6-11; 12-3, 7-11 Fri/Sat
between Nov-March; closed Mon-Thurs and Sun evenings during that period (but
open lunchtimes)*

TIPTON ST JOHN SY0991 Map 1
Golden Lion 🛏

Pub signposted off B3176 Sidmouth—Ottery St Mary

For 27 years, Mr and Mrs Radford have been running this thriving village pub, and
although from outside it might look a bit unprepossessing, once inside there's a
friendly bustling atmosphere and a good mix of people. The bar has an attractive

gothick carved box settle, a carved dresser, a comfortable old settee, red leatherette built-in wall banquettes, fresh flowers, and a longcase clock, and an open fire. Decorations include lots of guns, little kegs, a brass cauldron and other brassware, and bottles and jars along a delft shelf. Generous helpings of bar food such as soup (£1.50), sandwiches (from £2.40), ploughman's (from £3.45), vegetarian curry (£4.25), home-made lasagne (£4.85), steak and kidney pie (£4.95 lunch, £6.25 evening), tipsy pork with mushrooms and cream sauce (£7.45), steaks (from £7.95), puddings like gooseberry and apple crumble with clotted cream (from £2.45), and daily specials at lunchtime like chicken livers with bacon (£3.25), wild rabbit pie (£5.50), and at least one roast (beef or pork), with evening specials such as fresh fish – whole lemon sole or brill or their popular seafood salad (£8.55), fillet of lamb with apricot sauce (£8.85), and duck breast with cumberland sauce (£9.75); three-course Sunday lunch (£6.95). The restaurant and children's area are no smoking. Well kept Bass, Boddingtons, Eldridge Pope Hardy and Wadworths 6X on handpump, farm cider, and decent wines; darts, shove-ha'penny, and dominoes. There are pretty summer hanging baskets, a few picnic tables on the side lawn, an attractive walled area, and a terrace. *(Recommended by P and S White, Desmond and Pat Morris, Ken and Janet Bracey, David Holloway, Peter and Audrey Dowsett)*

Heavitree (who no longer brew) ~ Tenants Colin and Carolyn Radford ~ Real ale ~ Meals and snacks ~ Small restaurant ~ (01404) 812881 ~ Children in eating area of bar and in own small area ~ Open 11-3, 6-11; 11-11 Sat; 12-3, 7-10.30 Sun ~ Two bedrooms: £20.56S/£41.10S

TOPSHAM SX9688 Map 1
Passage House

2 miles from M5 junction 30: Topsham signposted from exit roundabout; in Topsham, turn right into Follett Road just before centre, then turn left into Ferry Road

A bar has been built on the quiet shoreside terrace here where there are seats, and there are more benches and tables in the front courtyard. Inside, the traditional bar has wall pews and bar stools and is decorated with electrified oil lamps hanging from big black oak beams in the ochre ceiling, and the lower dining area still has its slate floor; best to book if you want to be sure of a table. Popuar fresh fish dishes include fresh mussels, pollock, grilled monkfish, lemon sole, dover sole, turbot, cod, halibut, crab and so forth (£6.50-£12); other food includes filled rolls (from £1.90), ploughman's (from £4), ham and eggs (£4.30), crab or prawn platters (£4.50), and steaks; the restaurant is no smoking. Well kept Bass, Boddingtons, Flowers IPA, and Wadworths 6X on handpump. As the car park is small, you can park on the quay and walk the 150 yards to the pub. No children. *(Recommended by Dr A J and Mrs P G Newton, John and Vivienne Rice, John and Sally Clarke, Klaus and Elizabeth Leist, Mrs F A W Ricketts, Basil Minson, John Fahy, Andrew Hodges, DMT, Chris Westmoreland)*

Heavitree (who no longer brew) ~ Tenant David Evans ~ Real ale ~ Meals and snacks (not winter Sun evening) ~ Restaurant ~ (01392) 873653 ~ Parking can be a problem ~ Open 11-11

TORBRYAN SX8266 Map 1
Old Church House

Most easily reached from A381 Newton Abbot—Totnes via Ipplepen

Henry VIII is said to have called at this atmospheric early 15th-c inn, quietly set next to the part-Saxon church with its battlemented Norman tower. The bar on the right of the door is particularly attractive, and has benches built into the fine old panelling as well as the cushioned high-backed settle and leather-backed small seats around its big log fire. On the left there are a series of comfortable and discreetly lit lounges, one with a splendid deep Tudor inglenook fireplace with a side bread oven. Bar food includes sandwiches, home-made soup, steak and mushroom pie (£6.95), salmon in cream and white wine (£7.45), and chicken breast with cherry sauce or trout (£7.95). Well kept Bass, Flowers IPA and Original, Marstons Pedigree, Wadworths 6X, and Worthington Best on handpump or tapped from the cask, around 25 malt whiskies, and decent wine list; piped music. *(Recommended by Dr A J and Mrs P G Newton, Andrew Woodgate, John and Vivienne Rice, John Robertson, Alan and Paula McCully, H Cazalet, Bryan Taylor)*

Free house ~ Licensee Eric Pimm ~ Real ale ~ Meals and snacks (till 10pm) ~ Restaurant ~ (01803) 812372 ~ Children welcome away from bar ~ Open 11-3, 6-11 ~ Bedrooms: £45B/£60B

TORCROSS SX8241 Map 1
Start Bay

A379 S of Dartmouth

The particularly good fresh fish continues to pull in the crowds at this immensely popular dining pub. It's in a fine spot by the beach, with some picnic tables on the terrace looking out over the three-mile pebble beach; in summer, especially, there may be queues before the doors open, so it really is worth getting there early. A local trawler catches the fish, a local crabber drops the crabs at the back door, and the landlord enjoys catching plaice, scallops, and bass. Whole lemon sole (from £3.75), cod and haddock (medium £3.95; large £4.95; jumbo £6.25 – truly enormous), whole dover sole (in four sizes from £4.50), skate (£5.10), bass (small £5.95; medium £8.95; large £9.95), local scallops (£7.75), and brill (from £8.50). Other food includes sandwiches (from £1.95), ploughman's (from £3), vegetable lasagne (£4.75), gammon and pineapple (£5.75), steaks (from £7.95), puddings (£2.60), and children's meals (from £1.95); the sachets of tomato sauce or tartar sauce are not to everyone's taste. Well kept Bass and Flowers Original on handpump, Luscombe cider and fresh apple juice, and local wine. The unassuming main bar is very much set out for eating with wheelback chairs around plenty of dark tables or (round a corner) back-to-back settles forming booths; there are some photographs of storms buffeting the pub and country pictures on its cream walls, and a winter coal fire; a small chatty drinking area by the counter has a brass ship's clock and barometer; one area is no smoking as is part of the family room. The good winter games room has pool, darts, shove-ha'penny, cribbage, dominoes, fruit machine, video game, and juke box; there's more booth seating in a family room with sailing boat pictures. Fruit machine in the lobby. The freshwater wildlife lagoon of Slapton Ley is just behind the pub. *(Recommended by TBB, B J Harding, Peter and Rosie Flower, Liz Bell, A M Stephenson, P and J Shapley, Mary Woods, Peter Haines, George Jonas, John Fahy, Viv Middlebrook, Bryan Taylor, J B Tuckey)*

Heavitree (who no longer brew; Whitbreads tie) ~ Tenant Paul Stubbs ~ Real ale ~ Meals and snacks (11.30-2, 6-10; not evening 25 Dec) ~ (01548) 580553 ~ Children in family room ~ Open 11.30-11; 11.30-2.30, 6-11 in winter; 12-10.30 Sun; 12-2.30, 6-10.30 winter Sun; closed evening 25 Dec

TORRINGTON SS4919 Map 1
Black Horse

High St

This is one of the oldest inns in North Devon: the overhanging upper storeys are dated 1616 but this pretty twin-gabled family-run inn actually goes back to the 15th c. General Fairfax's headquarters are reputed to have been here during the civil war. The bar on the left has an oak counter, a couple of fat black beams hung with stirrups, a comfortable seat running right along its full-width window, and chunky elm tables; on the right, a lounge has a striking ancient black oak partition wall, a couple of attractive oak seats, muted plush easy chairs and a settee. The restaurant is oak-panelled. Generously served and good value, the bar food might include sandwiches (from £1.55; triple deckers with chips £2.85), filled baked potatoes (from £1.85), ploughman's (from £3.25), roast chicken with gravy (£3.95), gammon steak (£4.20), hot and spicy prawns with a garlic dip (£4.70), steak and kidney pie (£4.75), lots of steaks (from £7.45; lots of sauces to go with them), daily specials, weekend fresh fish, and children's dishes; promptly served Sunday roast lunch and enjoyable breakfasts. Well kept Courage Best and Directors and John Smiths, with a daily guest beer on handpump; darts, shove-ha'penny, cribbage, dominoes, fruit machine, and well reproduced piped music; friendly cat and dogs. Handy for the RHS Rosemoor garden and Dartington Crystal. *(Recommended by Roger and Jenny Huggins, M R Austen, J P Lee, R J Walden, Dr A J and Mrs P G Newton, Graham and Lynn Mason, P and J Shapley, K R Harris, Colin Draper, Jeanne Cross, Joan and Andrew Life, K H Frostick)*

Ushers ~ Lease: David and Val Sawyer ~ Real ale ~ Meals and snacks (not Sun evening) ~ Restaurant (not winter Sun evening) ~ (01805) 622121 ~ Children in eating lounge and in restaurant ~ Open 11-3, 6-11; 11-11 Sat; 12-4, 7-10.30 Sun ~ Bedrooms: £16B/£28B

TRUSHAM SX8582 Map 1
Cridford Inn 🍴 ♀ 🛏

Village and pub signposted from B3193 NW of Chudleigh, just N of big ARC works; 1½ very narrow miles

The very early medieval window which is in the bar of this 14th-c longhouse is said to be the oldest domestic window in Britain and is Grade I listed. The bar has stout standing timbers, natural stone walls, flagstones, window-seats, pews and chapel chairs around kitchen and pub tables, and a big woodburning stove in the stone fireplace. Very good home-made bar food includes soup (£2.35), garlic mushrooms with cheese and a little chilli (£4.75), lunchtime ploughman's with good local cheeses (£5.95), pasta bake with tuna and prawns (£6.25), mushroom, chestnut and stilton pie or steak and kidney pie (£6.50), chicken provençale (£6.95), grilled lamb chops (£7.95), roast duckling with sage stuffing and orange sauce (£10.95), daily specials like local pork sausages with spicy red cabbage and mustard mash (£6.25), and tuna steak with teriyaki sauce or steamed Brixham hake with a prawn and mushroom sauce, and puddings (£3.50). The no-smoking restaurant has a mosaic date stone showing 1081 and the initials of the then Abbot of Buckfastleigh, and the top bar is also no smoking. Well kept Adnams Broadside, Bass, and a beer they call Trusham Bitter on handpump, 20 wines by the glass from an interesting wine list, and country wines. The cats are called Smudge and Sophie, and the jack russell, Jack; quiet piped music. You can sit on the suntrap front terrace. One party of readers felt they should have been treated more considerately when they pointed out that the wine they were served was not the year they had ordered and were very upset about this, but readers' reports generally show that this is not the norm here. *(Recommended by DAV, P and J Shapley, David and Jane Russell, Michael Kirby, Mrs M Rolfe, Andrew Woodgate, Dr and Mrs G K Blackwell, Gwen and Peter Andrews, John and Vivienne Rice, Ian and Deborah Carrington, S Demont, T Barrow, Don and Shirley Parrish, Hanns P Golez, Dr I Maine, David Saunders, Marion Nott, John Allsopp; more reports please)*

Free house ~ Licensees David and Sally Hesmondhalgh ~ Real ale ~ Meals and snacks (12.15-1.45, 6.45-8.45) ~ Evening restaurant ~ (01626) 853694 ~ Open 12-2.30, 6-11; 12-2.30, 6.30-10.30 in winter; closed 25 Dec ~ Bedrooms: £40B/£60B

TUCKENHAY SX8156 Map 1
Maltsters Arms

Take Ashprington road out of Totnes (signed left off A381 on outskirts), keeping on past Watermans Arms

Back to its original name and under friendly new licensees, this popular dining pub is in a lovely spot by a peaceful wooded creek; there are tables by the water, and you can arrive here by boat. There are plans for refurbishment and perhaps even the opening of a microbrewery in the old winery part of the building – they would also provide the Sea Trout at Staverton with ales, too (Mr Mogford is the licensee there as well). Very good food includes sandwiches (from £3.50; grilled chicken with avocado and tomato £3.95), pork and herb sausages (£4.25), roasted vegetables on toasted olive bread with melted mozzarella (£4.65), very good mixed meat antipasta (£4.95), fresh tagliatelle with olive and basil ratatouille, grilled gammon and egg or freshly breaded plaice (£5.95), pheasant, pigeon breast, venison and rabbit pie (£6.25), fish pie (£6.95), chargrilled lamb steak (£7.25), sirloin steak (£9.25), and puddings. Well kept Bass, Blackawton Bitter, Exmoor Ale, and Palmers IPA on handpump. The long, narrow bar links the two other rooms, and there are two open fires; darts. *(Recommended by David Wallington, C Sinclair, P Furse, Mr Barlow, Ms Goddard, Elven Money, Dr A J and and Mrs P G Newton, Mr and Mrs T A Towers, Andrew Hodges; more reports on the new regime, please)*

Free house ~ Licensees Andrew Mogford, Tony Williams ~ Real ale ~ Meals and snacks ~ Restaurant ~ (01803) 732350 ~ Children in eating area of bar ~ Live music every other Wednesday ~ Open 11-3, 6-11 (may open all day during high summer); 12-3, 7-10.30 Sun ~ Bedrooms: £55B/£70B

UGBOROUGH SX6755 Map 1
Anchor

Off A3121 – village signposted from A38 W of South Brent

As well as being in an attractive village, what customers enjoy so much about this friendly pub here is the wide choice of very good food. You can choose from either the bar or restaurant menus and sit anywhere in the pub (apart from Saturday night when there are no bar snacks in the restaurant): unusual choices such as ostrich, alligator, emu, bison, and wild boar, lots of fresh fish, delicious crispy quail with smoky bacon dip, and fantastic peppered steak, as well as home-made soup (£2.95), filled long crusty rolls (from £2.50; hot bacon and mushroom £4), ploughman's (from £3.50), omelettes (from £3.75), several pasta dishes (from £4.40), pizzas (from £4.25), vegetarian dishes (from £5.20), steak and kidney pie (£5.45), gammon and egg (£5.95), quite a few steaks (from £10.95), veal limona (£12.75), duck simmered in kirsch and served with black cherries (£12.85), and children's meals (from £2.50); courteous service. Well kept Bass tapped from the cask and Wadworths 6X and three local guest beers on handpump, and quite a few malt whiskies. The oak-beamed public bar has a log fire in its stone fireplace, wall settles and seats around wooden tables on the polished woodblock floor; there are windsor armchairs in the comfortable restaurant (the top area is no smoking). Darts, cribbage, fruit machine, and piped music. There's a small outside seating area. *(Recommended by Mike Gorton, P H Boot, Walker and Debra Lapthorne, J Burrage, Mr and Mrs J Brown, Stephen and Susan Breen)*

Free house ~ Licensees Sheelagh and Ken Jeffreys-Simmons ~ Real ale ~ Meals and snacks ~ Restaurant ~ (01752) 892283 ~ Children welcome ~ Live music most Mons and Fris ~ Open 11-3.30, 5-11; 11am-11.30pm Sat; 11-10.30 Sun ~ Bedrooms: £30B/£40B

WESTON ST1400 Map 1
Otter ★ ♀

Village signposted off A30 at W end of Honiton bypass

You can be sure of a warm welcome from the friendly licensees and their staff in this popular pub. It's a most useful break from the A30 and the very low-beamed main bar has comfortable chairs by the log fire (that stays alight right through from autumn to spring), an interesting mix of polished wooden antique tables, wooden chairs, and handsome chapel pews, candles in bottles, and chamber-pots and jugs hanging from beams; each day a page of the Bible on the lectern that ends one pew is turned, and attractive bric-a-brac includes some formidable arms and armour, horse collar and bits, quite a few pictures, and an old mangle; a veritable antique library leads off, with quite a few readable books and magazines, as well as board games, darts, shove-ha'penny, cribbage, dominoes, table skittles, pinball, bar billiards, pool, fruit machine, video game, trivia, juke box and piped music. Tasty bar food includes home-made soup (£2.55), sandwiches (from £2.75), filled baked potatoes (from £3.50), mussels with orange, ginger, saffron and cream (£4.55), ploughman's (£4.85), local butcher's sausages with onion gravy and mashed potato (£5.75), pasta with cheese and garlic in a basil and wine sauce (£5.85), steak and kidney pie (£6.85), steaks (£11.50), and daily specials like monkfish, sea bream and halibut on a banana and mustard sauce (£10.95), turbot with a fruit sauce (£11.65), and braised duck with an orange and black cherry sauce (£12.95); 3-course Sunday lunch (£9.95) and they do spit roasts (£5.75) on Thursday evenings from 8pm. Well kept Bass, Boddingtons, and Eldridge Pope Hardy on handpump, good inexpensive wines, farm cider, and freshly squeezed orange juice; good service. They are very kind to children, with high chairs (children sitting in them get a free meal), a children's menu (£1, with a picture to colour and free lollipop), a box of toys, rocking-horse, a bike, and a climbing frame and slide. The sizeable lawn (where there are often quacking ducks) runs down to the little River Otter, and has picnic tables, pretty climbing plants, hanging baskets and flowering tubs. *(Recommended by Richard Dolphin, R J Walden, Mary Woods, Alan and Paula McCully, Mavis and Robert Harford, Mark and Mary Fairman, G R Sunderland, Nigel Wikeley, Mrs M Furness, E V M Whiteway, R and S Bentley, Stephen Horsley, Mayur Shah, E M Clague, Jane and Adrian Tierney-Jones)*

Free house ~ Lease: Brian and Susan Wilkinson ~ Real ale ~ Meals and snacks (till 10pm; not 25 Dec) ~ (01404) 42594 ~ Children welcome ~ Live entertainment some winter Thurs evenings ~ Open 11-3, 6-11; 12-3, 7-10.30 Sun; only 11-1 on 25 Dec

WIDECOMBE SX7076 Map 1
Rugglestone

Village at end of B3387; pub just S – turn left at church and NT church house, OS Sheet 191 map reference 720765

For such a popular tourist area, the little bar here comes as a complete surprise, and for one reader conjured up vivid recollections of black and white silent films. It's very much an unspoilt local, with a cluster of regulars swapping sloe gin recipes by the rudimentary bar counter, just four small tables, a few window and wall seats, a one-person pew built into the corner by the nice old stone fireplace. The room on the right is a bit bigger and lighter-feeling, and shy strangers may feel more at home here: another stone fireplace, beam-and-plank ceiling, stripped deal tables, a built-in wall bench, darts; shove-ha'penny, cribbage, dominoes, and euchre. Well kept Bass, Flowers IPA, Butcombe and St Austell Tinners tapped from the cask, local farm cider, a decent clutch of malt whiskies; simple bar food includes pasties (from £1.60), home-made soup (£2.15), cottage rolls filled with a roast of the day (£2.75), cottage pie (£3.65), ploughman's (£3.75), steak and kidney pie (£4.15), and puddings like treacle and walnut tart (£2.75). The two cats are called Marbles and Elbi, there's a flat-coated retriever, Mogul, and two terriers, Tinker and Belle. Outside across the little medieval leat bringing moor water down to the village is a field with lots of picnic tables (and a couple of muscovy ducks); old-fashioned outside lavatories. No children. *(Recommended by Comus Elliott, Andy and Jill Kassube, Paul and Heather Bettesworth, Gwen and Peter Andrews, G and M Stewart)*

Free house ~ Licensees Lorrie and Moira Ensor ~ Real ale ~ Meals and snacks (not Sun evening, not Mon in winter) ~ (01364) 621327 ~ Open 11-2.30(3 Sat), 6(7 winter; 5 Sat)-11; 12-3, 7-10.30 Sun

WONSON SX6790 Map 1
Northmore Arms ♀ ◀

Off A388 2 miles from A30, at Murchington, Gidleigh signpost; then at junction where Murchington and Gidleigh are signposted left, keep straight on – eventually, round Throwleigh, Wonson itself is signposted; OS Sheet 191 map reference 674903

This remote country cottage is very casually run, which is what appeals so much to those who like it; but this does have obvious pitfalls for those who like things more cleanly organised. The two small connected beamed rooms are modest and informal but civilised, with wall settles, a few elderly chairs, three tables in one room and just one in the other. There are two open fires (only one may be lit), and some attractive photographs on the stripped stone walls; darts, cribbage, and dominoes. Besides well kept changing ales such as Adnams Broadside, Cotleigh Tawny and Exe Valley Dobs, they have good house wines, and food such as sandwiches, pâté (£2.45), home-made duck and orange pie (£3.95), steak and kidney pudding (£4.50), Sunday lunch (£4.95), and sticky toffee pudding (£1.95). Tables and chairs sit precariously in the steep little garden – all very peaceful and rustic; excellent walking from the pub (or to it, perhaps from Chagford or Gidleigh Park). *(Recommended by David and Jane Russell, Brian and Bett Cox, Helen Morton, Mike Gorton)*

Free house ~ Licensee Mo Miles ~ Real ale ~ Meals and snacks (12-9) ~ (01647) 231428 ~ Open 11-11(10.30 Sun) ~ Two bedrooms: £15/£25

WOODBURY SALTERTON SY0189 Map 1
Digger's Rest

3½ miles from M5 junction 30: A3052 towards Sidmouth, village signposted on right about ½ mile after Clyst St Mary; also signposted from B3179 SE of Exeter

This pleasant thatched village pub is particularly busy at lunchtime, so it's best to get there early then. The heavy beamed bar has a log fire at one end with an ornate solid fuel stove at the other, comfortable old-fashioned country chairs and settles around polished antique tables, a dark oak Jacobean screen, a grandfather clock, and plates decorating the walls of one alcove. The big skittles alley can be used for families, and there's a games room with darts and dominoes. Well kept Bass and Dartmoor Best on ancient handpumps, and local farm ciders; sensibly placed darts and dominoes in the small brick-walled public bar. Decent bar food includes home-made soup (£1.75), sandwiches with home-cooked meats (from £2.85; local crab £3.45), home-made pâté (£3.35), filled baked potatoes (from £3.55), ploughman's (from £3.75), vegetable or meaty curry (£4.65), steaks (from £8.85), daily specials, puddings (£2.65), and Sunday roasts (£5.25). The terrace garden has views of the countryside. *(Recommended by Elven Money, Basil Minson, Mr and Mrs C R Little, Dr A J and Mrs P G Newton, D Toulson, Alan and Paula McCully, John and Vivienne Rice)*

Free house ~ Licensee Sally Pratt ~ Real ale ~ Meals and snacks (12-1.45, 7-9.45) ~ (01395) 232375 ~ Children welcome ~ Open 11-2.30, 6.30-11; closed evenings 25-26 Dec

WOODLAND SX7968 Map 1
Rising Sun

Village signposted off A38 just NE of Ashburton – then keep eyes peeled for Rising Sun signposts

Virtually rebuilt after a fire in 1989, this is an unexpected place – a considerable expanse of softly lit red plush button-back banquettes and matching studded chairs, partly divided by wooded banister rails, masonry pillars and the odd high-backed settle. Given the isolated spot, there have been problems in the last decade finding enough customers to fill such a sizeable establishment. Its new landlady looks like being the solution. When she ran the Harrow at West Ilsley in Berkshire Heather Humphreys won our award as Berkshire Dining Pub of 1997, and here she is making the most of a large beautifully equipped kitchen. Her food, good country cooking using fresh largely local ingredients, varies with what's available; on our inspection visit the choice included broccoli soup (£2.95), stilton and pear bruschetta with mixed leaves (£3.95), mixed smoked meats with cumberland sauce (£4.25), sausages and mash with onion gravy (£4.95), ploughman's with good local cheeses (£5), broccoli, walnut and mushroom gratin topped with yarg cheese and a couple of other vegetarian dishes (£5.50), lamb and apricot casseroled with Newcastle Brown Ale (£5.95), free-range pork with caramelised apples (£6.95) and salmon in a chive cream sauce (£7.25). Her puddings, such as chocolate truffle torte, treacle tart, plum and almond tart, come with rich local cream (£2.95), and she does afternoon cream teas. Well kept Bass and Tetleys on handpump; very cheerful service; two family areas include one up a couple of steps with various toys (and a collection of cookery books). The dining area is no smoking. There are some picnic tables in the spacious garden, which has a play area including a redundant tractor. *(More reports please)*

Free house ~ Licensee Heather Humphreys ~ Real ale ~ Meals and snacks ~ (01364) 652544 ~ Children in family areas ~ Open 11-11; 11-3, 6-11 in winter; 12-10.30 Sun; closed Sun evenings and Mon Jan-Feb

Lucky Dip

Besides the fully inspected pubs, you might like to try these Lucky Dips recommended to us and described by readers (if you do, please send us reports):

Abbotskerswell [SX8569], *Butchers Arms*: Tucked-away little old pub, well kept Whitbreads-related ales, friendly staff, pleasant nooks and corners; garden with very good play area (*Chris Reeve, Andrew Hodges*)

☆ **Appledore** [Irsha St; SS4630], *Royal George*: Simple but good fresh food inc local fish in dining room with superb estuary views, cosy and unspoilt front bar (where dogs allowed), well kept ales such as Bass, Ind Coope Burton, Morlands Old Speckled Hen, good friendly service, attractive pictures, fresh flowers; picnic tables outside, picturesque street sloping to sea (*Mr and Mrs J D Marsh, PM, AM, Nigel and Lindsay Chapman, Chris Westmoreland, Rip and Pauline Kirby*)
Appledore [Irsha St], *Beaver*: Great estuary views from raised area in light airy pub, good value food (esp fish), friendly staff, well kept changing ales such as Bass, Butcombe, Flowers, pool in smaller games room, views from outdoor tables; children welcome (*Rip and Pauline Kirby, Philip and Jude Simmons, Dr A J and Mrs P G Newton, Nigel and Lindsay Chapman, Chris Westmoreland*)

☆ **Ashburton** [West St], *Exeter*: Good atmosphere in old-fashioned pub with welcoming Scottish licensees, well kept Badger, good value food (*Dr B and Mrs P B Baker*)

☆ **Ashprington** [Bow Bridge, towards Tuckenhay; SX8156], *Watermans Arms*: Pretty flower-filled garden, fun watching the ducks on the river (or the cars attempting the narrow bridge); interesting interior with heavy beams, tiles, stripped stone, log fires, some high-backed settles; wide choice of freshly cooked food from sandwiches to steaks, partly no-smoking restaurant, well kept Bass, Dartmoor Best, Palmers IPA, and Tetleys, farm cider, good quick service; children in side area, comfortable bedrooms with good breakfast (*P and J Shapley, S N Robieson, David Carr, Liz Bell, LYM; more reports on new regime please*)
Avonwick [B3210 1/2 mile from A38; SX7157], *Mill*: Good value bar food inc interesting specials in pretty converted mill with play area in big lakeside garden, friendly service, children's helpings (they have high chairs), Bass on handpump; generous lunchtime carvery, reasonable disabled access (*John Evans*)

☆ **Axmouth** [SY2591], *Ship*: Comfortable and civilised, good fresh local fish, well kept Whitbreads-related ales, good wine and coffee, friendly staff and samoyeds, lots of embroidered folk dolls; attractive garden with sanctuary for convalescent owls (*M E Wellington, LYM*)

☆ **Beer** [Fore St; ST2389], *Anchor*: Rows of tables in bustling restaurant and several

simply furnished bar rooms, good value generous food inc wide choice of good fresh fish, quick friendly service, well kept beer; spacious garden looking over delightful sheltered cove, charming village; can get crowded, public car park quite a long walk; bedrooms clean and comfortable (*D G Clarke, Peter and Audrey Dowsett, Don and Thelma Beeson, Mrs Greenwood*)
Beer, *Dolphin*: Friendly open-plan local with interesting artefacts, fresh tasty generous attractively priced food, restaurant; bedrooms (*Jeanne Cross, Paul Silvestri*)
Belstone [a mile off A30; SX6293], *Tors*: Imposing stone building, good choice of reasonably priced generous food, well kept Butcombe and Otter ales, decent wines, winter mulled wine and malt whiskies, lovely woodburner; bedrooms, attractive village well placed for N Dartmoor walks (*John and Vivienne Rice*)
Bere Ferrers [SX4563], *Old Plough*: Stripped stone, low plank ceilings, panelling, slate flagstones, old armchairs and other old-fashioned furniture, woodburner, steps down to cosy restaurant (plenty of fish); well kept beer, friendly atmosphere (*Ted George*)

☆ **Bickleigh** [SS9406; A396/A3072 N of Exeter], *Fishermans Cot*: Lots of tables on acres of turkey carpet in greatly extended thatched fishing inn, attractively broken up with pillars, plants and some panelled parts, charming view over shallow rocky race below 1640 Exe bridge, more tables out on terrace and waterside lawn; good well served food inc popular reasonably priced carvery, well kept Bass and Wadworths 6X, pleasant service; piped pop music; comfortable bedrooms looking over own terrace to river (*E Robinson, Mr and Mrs R Head, Alan Kitchener, BB*)

☆ **Bickleigh**, *Trout*: Thatched pub with comfortable easy chairs in huge bar and dining lounge, sizeable buffet counter with good choice of food from sandwiches up and tempting puddings cabinet, well kept ales such as Cotleigh Tawny, Bass, Boddingtons, Exmoor Gold, nice coffee, efficient friendly service; tables on pretty lawn, car park across rd; five well equipped bedrooms, good breakfast (*E Robinson, Basil Minson, Alan and Barbara Mence, LYM*)
Black Dog [off B3042 at Thelbridge – OS Sheet 191 map ref 805098; SS8009], *Black Dog*: Thatched village pub with lots of beams and horsebrasses, decent bar food (may not be served if restaurant fully booked), Wadworths 6X, friendly landlord; no dogs (*Anon*)

☆ **Blackawton** [SX8050], *George*: Friendly unspoilt local in interesting old building with open fires in two comfortable bars, hard-working new young licensees, good changing range of well kept ales from all over, also Belgian beers and occasional beer festival, wide choice of interesting food inc lots of vegetarian, friendly efficient service, beautiful views from lounge and garden; clean and comfortable cottagey bedrooms *(Elven Money, Mrs M Gaze, Mark Tabbron, Jim Cornish)*

☆ **Blackmoor Gate** [SS6443], *Old Station House*: Former station on redundant line interestingly converted into big dining pub; decent food inc popular carvery Sat night/Sun lunch, well kept ales, carved pews, plush dining chairs, soft red lighting, lots of bric-a-brac, character no-smoking area with grandfather clock; spacious games area with two well lit pool tables, darts and juke box; big garden with good views; skittle alley; children allowed (but under-5s in small family room only) *(Neil and Anita Christopher, PM, AM, Bruce Bird, BB)*

☆ **Bolberry** [Bolberry Down – OS Sheet 202 map ref 691392; SX6939], *Port Light*: Unlikely building (recently refurbished blocky ex-RAF radar station) alone on dramatic NT clifftop, amazing views; bright, spacious and popular if rather hotelish inside, with generous fresh food, well kept Dartmoor, friendly efficient service, restaurant, conservatory, tables in garden with play area; well behaved children allowed, play area outside; five bedrooms, nr fine beaches *(Nick Wikeley, A M Stephenson, Ian and Jane Irving)*

Bovey Tracey [SX8278], *Cromwell Arms*: Good basic reasonably priced food piled high in well run town local, friendly quick service, good range of well kept well priced beers, several areas with high-backed settles, no piped music *(Mr and Mrs M Cross, Paul and Heather Bettesworth)*

Braunton [South St; SS4836], *Mariners Arms*: Busy pleasantly untouristy local, friendly and comfortable, lots of nautical prints, cheerful service, dining area with good range of meals (not Mon), Courage Best and Directors, Exmoor and Morlands Old Speckled Hen, unobtrusive piped music, skittle alley *(Ian and Nita Cooper)*

☆ **Brayford** [Yarde Down; 3 miles from Brayford, on Simonsbath rd over Exmoor – OS Sheet 180 map ref 726356; SS6834], *Poltimore Arms*: Chatty and pubby old two-bar local with friendly newish licensees, attractive traditional decor inc inglenook, good value bar food, well kept Cotleigh Tawny and Wadworths 6X tapped from the cask; good service, maybe piped music, simple games room; children allowed in restaurant, picnic tables in side garden; no dogs inside *(R J Walden, D Rooke, Dr A J and Mrs P G Newton, LYM)*

Brixham [King St; SX9255], *Blue Anchor*: In harbour area, well kept Tetleys and guest beers, decent usual range of food inc local fish, nautical bar, two small dining rooms; open all day *(M Joyner)*

Broadclyst [Whimple Rd; SX9897], *New Inn*:

Warm and friendly former farmhouse with stripped bricks, boarded ceiling, low doorways, roaring log fires, country and horsey bygones, good range of reasonably priced food esp fish, well kept Whitbreads-related ales, decent wine; small restaurant, skittle alley *(E V M Whiteway, Mr and Mrs Bruce Watkin)*

☆ **Broadhempston** [off A381, signed from centre; SX8066], *Coppa Dolla*: Good ambitious food in comfortable and welcoming beamed bar divided by sturdy timber props, well kept ales such as Bass, Dartmoor Best, Palmers and Wadworths 6X, good cheery service, decent wines, log fires, pleasant upstairs restaurant; Sun quiz night; well spaced picnic tables in attractive garden with pleasant views; two apartments *(Andrew Woodgate, C A Hall, Andrew Hodges, Dennis Glover, BB)*

Broadhempston [The Square], *Monks Retreat*: Black beams, lots of copper, brass and china, log fire in huge stone fireplace, no-smoking dining area, very wide choice of straightforward food inc sizzler steaks, well kept Bass and Teignworthy Reel Ale, very cheerful service – can slow when busy; by arch to attractive churchyard, a few picnic tables out in front *(Andrew Hodges, C A Hall, Jeanne Cross, Paul Silvestri, BB)*

☆ **Buckfastleigh** [Totnes Rd; SX7366], *Dartbridge*: Picturesque inn, functional inside and well equipped for families, opp Dart Valley Rly – very popular in summer; good reasonably priced food, well kept beers and decent house wines, quick friendly service, reasonable disabled access, tables in neatly kept roadside garden, ten letting chalets *(John Evans, Mr and Mrs Buckmaster)*

☆ **Buckland Monachorum** [SX4868], *Drakes Manor*: Well kept Scottish Courage ales, good friendly service, good value food inc good Sun lunches, beams and oak panelling; public bar with games machines *(G W Stevenson)*

☆ **Burgh Island** [SX6443], *Pilchard*: The star's for the setting, high above sea on tidal island with great cliff walks; not at all smart, but atmospheric, with blazing fire; Scottish Courage ales, basic food (all day summer, lunchtime only winter), piped music, children in downstairs bistro *(Hanns P Golez, Richard Gibbs, Dave and Doreen Irving, Marianne Lantree, Steve Webb, LYM)*

California Cross [SX7052], *California*: Popular 18th-c beamed pub with nicely decorated old-fashioned lounge, well kept Dartmoor and Wadworths 6X, local Churchward's cider, decent wines, wide choice of good value food inc local fish, friendly staff (service can slow under pressure), children's room with toys, restaurant, games room with skittles and pool; craft shop, tables in garden *(BHT)*

Calverleigh [B3221 Tiverton—Rackenford; SS9214], *Rose & Crown*: Attractive, with good value food in decent-sized helpings, pleasant friendly atmosphere *(Helen Morton)*

☆ **Chagford** [Mill St; SX7087], *Bullers Arms*:

Welcoming panelled local with food servery doing very wide range inc vegetarian, Dartmoor Best and Ind Coope Burton, decent coffee, very friendly licensees, militaria, copper and brass, darts; can get smoky at night; summer barbecues *(Neil and Anita Christopher, John and Christine Vittoe, LYM)*

Chagford, *Three Crowns*: Ancient thatched building of great potential, but rather unsympathetic furnishings; popular food, friendly service, well kept Bass and Flowers Original, big fire, stripped-stone public bar with pool and darts; dogs welcome, tables on front cobbles and in back garden; good old-fashioned bedrooms *(Jeanne Cross, Paul Silvestri, Ted George, BB)*

☆ **Challacombe** [B3358 Blackmoor Gate—Simonsbath; SS6941], *Black Venus*: Good varied interesting home-cooked food reasonably priced, Scottish Courage ales, low 16th-c beams, pews, decent chairs, stuffed birds, woodburner and big open fire, separate games room, attractive big dining area (children over 5 allowed); seats in garden, attractive countryside; bedrooms *(D Rooke, D Alexander, M C and S Jeanes, Philip and Jude Simmons, BB)*

☆ **Chardstock** [off A358 Chard—Axminster; ST3004], *George*: Only a shortage of reports keeps this chatty and relaxing thatched 13th-c inn out of the main entries this year; massive beams, ancient oak partition walls, character furnishings, stone-mullioned windows, well converted old gas lamps, two good log fires, separate two-level back bar, generous good home-made food from sandwiches up inc lots of vegetarian, well kept Boddingtons, Otter and three rotating ales such as Adnams, Bass, or Cotleigh Tawny, traditional games; provision for children, tables out in back loggia and garden with play area; comfortable bedrooms in well converted stable block, good walks *(M E Wellington, LYM)*

Chawleigh [B3042 – formerly Chilcott Arms; SS7112], *Earl of Portsmouth*: Good value interesting food, comfortable surroundings, good service, Bass and Flowers ales; children welcome, skittle alley *(Dr A J and Mrs P G Newton)*

Chillington [SX7942], *Chillington Inn*: Friendly village local with old settles, benches and low tables in front bar, good individual chairs in back bar, good bar food often inc local seafood, well kept Bass, Palmers and guests, restaurant; parking can be difficult, may be cl winter lunchtimes Mon-Thurs; bedrooms *(TBB)*

Chittlehampton [The Square; signed off B3227 S Molton—Umberleigh; SS6425], *Bell*: Cheerful family-run village pub, plentiful varied inexpensive food, well kept Bass and two guests such as Greene King Abbot and Youngs; children and dogs welcome *(John and Maureen Watt, Philip Jewell)*

☆ **Christow** [signed off B3193 N of A38; SX8385], *Artichoke*: Pretty thatched local with open-plan rooms stepped down hill, low beams, some black panelling, flagstones,

straightforward food inc decent specials, vegetarian, fish and game, big log fire (2nd one in no-smoking end dining room), mainly Whitbreads-related ales; rather prominent games machine; tables on back terrace, pretty hillside village nr Canonteign Waterfalls and Country Park *(James Nunns, Michael and Lynne Steane, BB)*

Chulmleigh [SS6814], *Globe*: Attractive little pub by church, good home cooking, well kept Butcombe and Marstons Pedigree; good bedrooms *(R J Walden)*

☆ **Clayhidon** [off A38 via Culmstock, Hemyock; ST1615], *Half Moon*: Good well presented food in civilised pub with simple unfussy decor, well kept Bass and Cotleigh, good house wine, welcoming service; quiet views from picnic tables in garden over road; opens noon *(Shirley Pielou, BB)*

Clearbrook [off A386 Tavistock—Plymouth, edge of Dartmoor; SX5265], *Skylark*: Pronounced local feel though big and often busy with walkers, generous good value food, Bass and Courage Best and Directors, simple furnishings, log fire, children's room; good Dartmoor and Plymouth Sound views, big back garden *(Ted George, Val Biro)*

Clovelly [Steep St; SS3225], *New Inn*: Attractive old inn, recently well refurbished, halfway down the steep cobbled street; friendly efficient service even when busy, very calm; varied good snacks and bar meals, Dartmoor Best; bedrooms *(Paul and Maggie Baker)*; *Red Lion*: Lots of character in locals' back bar, bar food inc good pasties and crab sandwiches, good fresh fish in restaurant, friendly staff, Marstons Pedigree; simple attractive bedrooms, lovely spot on curving quay *(David Carr, Ann and Colin Hunt, DJW)*

Clyst St Mary [nr M5 junction 30; SX9790], *Half Moon*: Pleasant old pub next to multi-arched bridge over Clyst, well kept Bass tapped from the cask, decent food, reasonably priced if not gargantuan; bedrooms *(Chris Westmoreland, Ken and Janet Bracey)*

Cockington [SX8963], *Drum*: Olde-worlde pastiche thatched and beamed tavern in quaintly touristy Torquay-edge village by 500-acre park, spacious and well run, with Dartmoor Bitter and Legend, wide choice of reasonably priced food esp steaks in bar and two family eating areas, quick friendly service, Weds summer barbecues, winter skittle evenings and live music; juke box or piped music; seats on terrace and in attractive back garden *(Richard Houghton, Ian and Jane Irving, Andrew Hodges)*

☆ **Cockwood** [SX9780], *Ship*: Comfortable and welcoming 17th-c inn overlooking estuary and harbour, seafaring memorabilia, food from open crab sandwiches up inc good evening fish dishes (freshly made so takes time), Ushers BB and Founders, reasonable prices, keen new landlord, good steep-sided garden *(V H and J M Vanstone, DAV, John Beeken)*

☆ **Coffinswell** [off A380 N of Torquay;

SX8968], *Linny*: Very pretty partly 14th-c thatched country pub with big cheerful beamed bar, settles and other old seats, smaller areas off; some concentration on wide choice of good value bar food; well kept Bass, Ind Coope Burton and Morlands Old Speckled Hen, cosy log fires, lots of twinkling brass, chatty atmosphere, neat friendly service, children's room, upstairs restaurant extension, some tables outside; picturesque village *(Gordon, Andrew Hodges, Alan and Paula McCully, Jeanne Cross, Paul Silvestri, Paul and Janet Waring, BB)*

Colaton Raleigh [A376 Newton Poppleford—Budleigh Salterton; SY0787], *Otter*: Friendly new licensees making real effort, well cooked food, children's room, restaurant, long bar, lovely big garden *(Mark and Heather Williamson, Chris Westmoreland, Stan Edwards)*

Colyford [A3052 Exeter—Lyme Regis, by tramway stn; SY2492], *White Hart*: Good food inc wonderful Italian menu in bistro (authentic Caruso recipes and opera memorabilia – pub run by ex-tenor Craig Sullivan), wide choice of wine, very friendly, children's games room, skittle alley; garden, boules; trad jazz Sun night *(Brian Websdale)*

☆ **Colyton** [Dolphin St – village signed off A35 and A3052 E of Sidmouth; SY2493], *Kingfisher*: Homely beamed local with friendly staff, hearty popular food, stripped stone, plush seats and elm settles, big open fire, well kept Badger Best and Tanglefoot, Charles Wells Bombardier and changing guests, low-priced soft drinks, basic bar food from good sandwiches and baked potatoes up; pub games, upstairs family room, skittle alley, tables out on terrace, garden with water feature *(R T and J C Moggridge, Peter and Rosie Flower, Mark and Heather Williamson, R Boyd, Derek and Iris Martin, George Atkinson, LYM)*

☆ **Combeinteignhead** [SX9071], *Wild Goose*: Spacious 17th-c beamed pub, lots of hanging jugs and teapots, comfortably well worn furnishings, more formal big dining room with wide choice of good food, lots of well kept changing ales, cheerful service, big log fire; pool room, darts, weekly jazz *(Colin and Marjorie Roberts, John Wilson, Richard Houghton, Colin McKerrow)*

Combeinteignhead [signed off back rd Shaldon—Newton Abbot stn; SX9271], *Coombe Cellars*: Big bustling family Brewers Fayre with lots for children inc indoor play area, their own menu, baby-changing, fun days and parties with entertainment, outside play galleon and fenced-in playground; lovely estuary setting, tables on pontoons, jetties and big terraces, water-sports; roomy and comfortable bar with plenty of sporting and nautical bric-a-brac, usual food all day, well kept Whitbreads-related ales, lots of wines by the glass, friendly efficient staff, various events; good disabled facilities *(Alan and Paula McCully, Chris Reeve, Geoff Dibble, Basil Minson, John Wilson, LYM)*

☆ **Countisbury** [A39, E of Lynton – OS Sheet 180 map ref 747497; SS7449], *Exmoor Sandpiper*: Beautifully set rambling and friendly heavy-beamed pub with antique furniture, several log fires, good choice of usual food from sandwiches to steaks, well kept Bass, Exmoor Best and Eldridge Pope Royal Oak, restaurant with weekend smorgasbord and carvery; children in eating area, garden tables, open all day; comfortable bedrooms, good walks *(Meg and Colin Hamilton, Pat and Robert Watt, Richard Gibbs, LYM)*

Croyde [B3231 NW of Braunton; SS4439], *Thatch*: Popular rambling thatched pub nr great surfing beaches, with laid-back feel and customers to match; generous bar food, well kept Bass, St Austell HSD and Tetleys, informal smiling staff, tables outside; restaurant, children in eating area, open all day; piped music may be a bit loud, can be packed in summer; bedrooms *(Paul and Ursula Randall, Jo Rees, LYM)*

☆ **Dartmouth** [Smith St; SX8751], *Seven Stars*: Crowded beamed and panelled local, quick well priced popular food, real ales such as Wadworths 6X, coal fire, chummy service; maybe piped pop music, fruit machine; upstairs restaurant, children's room *(C A Hall, David Carr, June and Malcolm Farmer, John Evans, Dr S Willavoys, BB)*

Dartmouth [Bayards Cove], *Dartmouth Arms*: Friendly panelled local in lovely setting with benches by River Dart, good ploughman's and lots of pizzas all day (can be taken away), open fire, boating memorabilia; popular with naval students evening *(Andrew Hodges, I J and N K Buckmaster)*

Dawlish Warren [SX9979], *Mount Pleasant*: Marvellous view from garden and front window over the Warren, Exe estuary and sea, decent food, well kept Whitbreads-related ales, two pool tables, darts *(Susan and Nigel Wilson, Chris Westmoreland)*

☆ **Denbury** [The Green; SX8168], *Union*: Spotless well run low-beamed local, comfortable and friendly, on edge of old village green, good food from sandwiches to steaks inc vegetarian, fresh fish and lots of puddings, Whitbreads-related ales, good coffee; tables in garden by green, pretty sheltered village *(Clare and Roy Head, Mr and Mrs C Roberts, Jean and Douglas Troup, BB)*

☆ **Dittisham** [best to park in village and walk steeply down; SX8654], *Ferry Boat*: Big windows make the most of beautiful waterside spot, nr little foot-ferry you call by bell; good range of low-priced bar food, well kept Ushers, pleasant staff *(DJW, Liz Bell, Jo and Gary Charlton, Patricia Dodd, LYM)*

☆ **Dittisham** [The Level], *Red Lion*: Welcoming well run local with well kept Bass and good value wines, open fires, sleeping dogs, good value innovative food in restaurant, friendly licensees, family room; attractive village *(John and Wendy Trentham, Jo and Gary Charlton, JWC, MC, BHT, Andrew Hodges)*

Dog Village [B3185 S – 1/2 mile off A30 opp airport; SX9896], *Hungry Fox*: Roomy mock-Tudor dining pub, good value home cooking, Whitbreads-related ales, good service *(E V M Whiteway)*

☆ **Dolton** [SS5712], *Union*: Interesting and thoughtful well prepared food in small restaurant and comfortable lounge bar with handsome mahogany bar counter, log fire, welcoming service, well kept Dartmoor and Hicks HSD, public bar with games room; bedrooms comfortable and well equipped *(DJW)*

Dolton [The Square], *Royal Oak*: Attractive bar and restaurant, very extensive bar menu inc fresh fish, good range of beers inc some local, friendly professional staff; bedrooms *(Simon and Jane Williams)*

☆ **Down Thomas** [follow HMS Cambridge signs from Plymouth; SX5149], *Langdon Court*: Interesting old country-house hotel with good food in welcoming lounge bar and family room, reasonable prices, good fire, country views, well kept Bass from ornate servery, subdued piped music, picnic tables outside; dogs allowed; comfortable bedrooms *(D Batten, P Broughton)*

nr **Drewsteignton** [Fingle Bridge, off A38 at Crockernwell via Preston or Drewsteignton; OS Sheet 191 map ref 743899; SX7489], *Anglers Rest*: Idyllic wooded Teign valley spot by 16th-c pack-horse bridge, lovely walks, tourist souvenirs and airy cafe feel, but has well kept Cotleigh and Courage ales and reliable food inc children's meals (not Sun); friendly helpful service, waterside picnic tables; cl winter evenings *(Tony Dickinson, JWC, MC, John Franklin, BB)*

☆ **East Budleigh** [SY0684], *Sir Walter Raleigh*: Small neat village inn with faultless service, good range of nicely presented hot and cold food inc help-yourself salad bar and good Sun lunch, friendly staff and locals, cosy charming dining room, Flowers IPA and Marstons Pedigree; the village itself, and its church, are well worth a visit; bedrooms *(J T Bugby, Basil Minson, Marjorie and David Lamb, LYM)*

☆ **East Down** [off A39 Barnstaple—Lynton nr Arlington – OS Sheet 180 map ref 600415; SS5941], *Pyne Arms*: Low-beamed bar with very wide choice of generous food from sandwiches up (but they stop serving too early), lots of nooks and crannies, attractive furnishings inc high-backed curved settle, small no-smoking galleried loft (where children allowed), well kept Bass and Scottish Courage ales, decent house wines, flagstoned games area with unobtrusive juke box; handy for Arlington Court, good walks *(Mr and Mrs Greenhalgh, Dr A J and Mrs P G Newton, Joan and Andrew Life, Steve and Carolyn Harvey, Steve and Angela Maycock, LYM)*

East Prawle [SX7836], *Freebooters Arms*: Small friendly 18th-c inn recently tastefully refurbished under newish landlord, lovely old parquet floor, simple well chosen furnishings, some no-smoking tables, good value home cooking using organic produce, Dartmoor Best, Greene King Abbot, and local Salcombe cider, fresh flowers; nr superb coastal scenery and beaches *(Ann and Frank Bowman, Jeanne Cross, Paul Silvestri)*

Ermington [SX6353], *First & Last*: Beautiful setting, lots of ivy and hanging baskets, affable licensee, limited choice of good cheap food with ample veg, well kept Bass and local beers *(John Evans, B J Harding)*

☆ **Exeter** [Martins Lane – just off cathedral close], *Ship*: Pretty 14th-c pub with substantial comfortable furniture in heavy-beamed busy but atmospheric bar, well kept Bass and Boddingtons, good service, decent generous food, quieter upstairs restaurant *(Chris Westmoreland, Galen Strawson, David Carr, Dr A J and Mrs P G Newton, M E Wellington, LYM)*

☆ **Exeter** [The Close; bar of Royal Clarence Hotel], *Well House*: Big windows looking across to cathedral in open-plan bar divided by inner walls and partitions; lots of Victorian prints, well kept changing ales, popular bar lunches inc good salads, good service; Roman well beneath (can be viewed when pub not busy); piped music *(David Carr, Andrew Hodges, BB)*

☆ **Exeter** [223 High St (basement of C&A)], *Chaucers*: Large dim-lit modern pub/bistro/wine bar down lots of steps, candles in bottles, well kept Bass and Tetleys, good range of generous good value food inc adventurous dishes, quick friendly service, pleasant atmosphere *(Steve and Carolyn Harvey, H G Robertson)*

Exeter [Cowick Lane, between A377 and B3212], *Cowick Barton*: Friendly comfortable former 17th-c red sandstone farmhouse, wide choice of good generous food, Bass, Courage Best and Ruddles County, lots of country wines, good service, log fire, small back restaurant *(E V M Whiteway)*; [St Davids Hill], *Great Western*: Busy and comfortable, with pleasant lounge, locals' bar with SkyTV, reasonably priced bar food, well kept Bass, Greene King Abbot and Worthington *(E V M Whiteway)*; [Bonhay Rd (A377)], *Mill on the Exe*: Comfortably done out with old bricks and timbers, good helpings of reasonably priced food, well kept St Austell, quick friendly service; children welcome, riverside terrace *(Andy and Jill Kassube, E V M Whiteway, Dr A J and Mrs P G Newton, BB)*; [14 Exe St, off Bonhay Rd], *Papermakers*: Pub/wine bar/bistro with charming continental atmosphere, wide choice of good if not cheap unusual food, friendly efficient service, Wadworths 6X and well chosen guest beers, good choice of wines, reasonable prices *(H G Robertson, Steve and Carolyn Harvey)*; [The Quay], *Prospect*: Pleasant setting overlooking waterfront nr Maritime Museum, beams, panelling and settles, old safari pictures and local prints, wide range of good value fresh food inc good fish in big river-view dining area up a few steps, well kept Bass and Eldridge Pope Royal Oak, helpful staff; welcoming feel, but shame about the piped music and games machines *(P and J Shapley, David Carr, Alan and Heather Jacques)*; [2 Countess Wear Rd], *Tally Ho*: Long comfortable beamed bar with banquettes in bays, good value home-cooked food inc good fish and Italian dishes, good landlady, well kept Bass, Flowers IPA and Morlands Old Speckled Hen, decent wine; attractive high-walled garden, interesting spot on River Exe *(Mike Gorton, Robert J Green)*

☆ **Exminster** [just off A379; SX9487], *Swans Nest*: Huge choice of reasonably priced self-service food from sandwiches up in very popular high-throughput food pub, handy for M5, well arranged rambling dining bar; no-smoking areas, Bass and Dartmoor, long attractive carvery/buffet, salads and children's dishes, helpful staff; especially good for family groups with children *(V H and J M Vanstone, Alan and Barbara Mence, Mr and Mrs C R Little, LYM)*

Exmouth [Victoria Rd; SY0080], *Beach*: Nr harbour (now a yachting marina), one room covered with shipping and lifeboat photographs, real ales, food, welcoming service *(Peter and Audrey Dowsett)*

☆ **Filleigh** [off A361 N Devon link rd; SS6627], *Stags Head*: Good food, generous if not cheap, in friendly and attractive 16th-c thatched pub with lake, neat furnishings, well kept Bass and Cotleigh Barn Owl, reasonably priced wines, small locals' bar, dining room and restaurant; bedrooms comfortable and good value, good breakfasts *(Peter Churchill, Mr and Mrs Greenhalgh, Don and Thelma Beeson)*

Folly Gate [A386 Hatherleigh—Okehampton; SX5797], *Crossways*: Wide range of good interesting food inc fresh lobster and crab, well kept St Austell ales *(R J Walden)*

☆ **Fremington** [B3233 Barnstaple—Instow; SS5132], *New Inn*: Good choice of popular home-cooked food in bar and restaurant, well kept beer, pleasant service *(Dr A J and Mrs P G Newton)*

☆ **George Nympton** [SS7023], *Castle*: Homely yet comfortably stylish two-bar village inn with good range of generous above-average home cooking inc vegetarian, welcoming service, Flowers IPA and a guest beer; bedrooms comfortable too, fishing rights; handy for the attractive market town of South Molton; bedrooms *(Stuart Cook, Marion and John Hadfield)*

☆ **Georgeham** [Rock Hill, above village – OS Sheet 180 map ref 466399; SS4639], *Rock*: Convivial well restored oak-beamed pub, old red quarry tiles, open fire, pleasant mix of rustic furniture, lots of bric-a-brac; well kept Marstons Pedigree, Morlands Old Speckled Hen, Tetleys, Theakstons and Ushers Best, local farm cider, decent wines, good value food from huge baguettes up, good service; children in pleasant back room, piped music, darts, fruit machine, pool room; tables under cocktail parasols on front terrace, pretty hanging baskets *(K H Frostick, Dr A J and Mrs P G Newton, Alan and Heather Jacques,*

Richard and Ann Higgs, E A Moore, Richard and Ruth Dean, N and A Chesher, Philip and Jude Simmons, BB)

Georgeham [B3231 Croyde—Woolacombe, by church], *Kings Arms*: Enthusiastic licensees take real pride in frequently changing well kept ales, tapped from the cask *(DJW)*

Hartland Quay [down toll rd; SS2224], *Hartland Quay*: Outstanding cliff scenery, rugged coast walks, unpretentious maritime feel with fishing memorabilia and shipwreck pictures; good value generous basic food (dogs treat you as honoured guests if you're eating), St Austell Tinners, Inch's cider, quick pleasant service, small no-smoking bar, lots of tables outside – very popular with holidaymakers; good value bedrooms, seawater swimming pool *(David Surridge, Joan and Andrew Life)*

Hawkchurch [off B3165 E of Axminster – pub just over Dorset border – OS Sheet 193 map ref 340005; ST3400], *Old Inn*: Two log fires in long comfortably refurbished main bar, real ales such as Cotleigh Barn Owl, Flowers IPA and Original and Wadworths 6X, good choice of bar food, popular licensees, darts, fruit machines, maybe piped music, skittle alley; picnic tables and flowers in back courtyard *(R Shelton, John and Moira Hawkes)*

Hemborough Post [B3207 Dartmouth—Halwell; SX8352], *Sportsmans Arms*: Big pleasantly modernised pub, wide choice of good eclectic food, well kept beers, big fireplaces, family room, friendly service; good garden with play area *(Derek and Gillian Henshaw)*

☆ **Hexworthy** [signed off B3357 Tavistock—Ashburton, E of B3212; SX6572], *Forest*: Solid Dartmoor hotel in fine surroundings, comfortable and spacious open-plan bar and back walkers' bar, hospitable and efficient newish tenants, short choice of good bar food changing daily with perfect veg; good-sized bedrooms, bunkhouse *(Alan Heselden, Lyn and Geoff Hallchurch, BB)*

Heybrook Bay [off A379 SW of Plymouth – follow HMS Cambridge signs; SX4948], *Eddystone*: Modern dining pub with good views of sea, coast and shipping; friendly staff, short range of good value hot dishes, tables out on balcony *(Roy Bromell)*

☆ **Highampton** [A3072 W of Hatherleigh; SS4804], *Golden*: Attractive 16th-c thatched pub with Dartmoor views from garden behind, homely low-beamed alcovey lounge, brasses, watercolours, farm tools, stove in big stone fireplace; good value food, well kept Bass tapped from the cask, pool room; well behaved children allowed *(R J Walden)*

☆ **Holne** [signed off B3357 W of Ashburton; SX7069], *Church House*: Country inn well placed for attractive walks, open log fires, some fascinating signs of antiquity, log fires in both rooms, food from lunchtime sandwiches up, no-smoking restaurant, Dartmoor Bitter and Legend, Palmers IPA and 2000, and Wadworths 6X, Gray's farm cider, country wines, decent house wines, traditional games in public bar; well behaved children in eating area; good bedrooms *(Mr and Mrs M Matthews, Dr S P Willavoys, M G Hart, Abigail Dombey, Kate Naish, Mrs M Rolfe, Ian Dunkin, R and S Bentley, Catherine Lloyd, EHW, RFW, Mike Gorton, John and Vivienne Rice, Mark and Heather Williamson, R J Walden, LYM)*

☆ Honiton [43 High St; ST1500], *Red Cow*: Busy welcoming local, scrubbed tables, pleasant alcoves, log fires, good choice of Scottish Courage and local ales, decent wines and malt whiskies, wide choice of good value home-made food inc some enterprising dishes, friendly Welsh licensees, loads of chamber-pots and big mugs on beams, pavement tables; bedrooms *(June and Malcolm Farmer, Ron Wallwork, K R Harris, Pat and John Charles, Stan Edwards, Jim Reid, John and Pat Charles, BB)*

☆ Horns Cross [A39 Clovelly—Bideford – OS Sheet 190 map ref 385233; SS3823], *Hoops*: Attractive much modernised thatched dining pub with wide choice of Whitbreads-related ales and of tasty food, pleasant friendly service, big inglenook log fires, eating area in central courtyard as well as cosy restaurant and bar, decent wines, Easter beer festival, aircraft-minded landlord, provision for children and disabled; comfortable bedrooms *(R J Walden, Andy and Jill Kassube, Mr and Mrs P Fisk, David Carr, Rita Horridge, LYM)*

Horrabridge [SX5169], *Leaping Salmon*: Friendly atmosphere, wide choice of popular food (worth booking evening), good ciders, jovial Irish landlord; beautiful Dartmoor village *(Emma Kingdon)*

☆ Ilfracombe [Broad St; SS5147], *Royal Britannia*: Simple old-fashioned pub in attractive spot above harbour; low seats, armchairs, copper tables and lots of prints in series of connecting rooms; wide choice of good value bar food inc local fish, well kept Scottish Courage beers; bedrooms *(Martin Bromfield, Bernadette Garner, David Carr)*

Ilfracombe, *George & Dragon*: Lots of local and other bric-a-brac, well kept Courage, bar food inc good Sun lunch and lots for vegetarians, piped music *(Mr and Mrs E J W Rogers)*

☆ Instow [Marine Pde; SS4730], *Boat House*: Very long bar with picture-window views over beach, estuary and Appledore, very popular esp with families and older people for beautifully prepared generous good value food inc local fish and delicious puddings; good atmosphere and range of beers, meticulous all-female service, open fire at one end, model ships and boats, series of prints showing America's Cup yacht race incidents from 1899 on; well behaved dogs allowed *(Joan and Andrew Life, Mr and Mrs J Marsh)*

Ivybridge [Exeter Rd; SX6356], *Sportsmans*: Large open-plan bar with big dining area, lots of panelling, wide choice of food all day starting from breakfast, OAP and other bargains, children's menu, Boddingtons,

Wadworths 6X and Whitbreads, entertainment Fri, Sat and Sun; bedrooms *(Neil and Anita Christopher)*

☆ Kenn [signed off A380 just S of Exeter; SX9285], *Ley Arms*: Extended thatched pub in nice spot nr church, polished granite floor in attractive beamed public bar, plush black-panelled lounge with striking fireplace, good wines, Bass and Whitbreads-related ales, bar food, sizeable restaurant side; piped music, no-smoking family room, games area *(Don and Shirley Parrish, Catherine Lloyd, John Fahy, Miss A Donoghue, E V M Whiteway, LYM)*

☆ Kilmington [A35; SY2797], *Old Inn*: Thatched pub with character front bar (dogs allowed here), back lounge with leather armchairs by inglenook fire, good value bar food and good Sun lunch, well kept Bass and Worthington BB, traditional games, small no-smoking restaurant; maybe piped radio; children welcome, two gardens *(John and Elspeth Howell, J A Snell, LYM)*

Kings Nympton [SS6819], *Grove*: Friendly thatched and beamed family local, well-kept Ushers and farm cider, good value food (fish and chips Tues); lots of games, skittle alley, picturesque village *(Mr and Mrs J Marsh, LYM)*

☆ Kingsbridge [quayside, edge of town; SX7344], *Crabshell*: Lovely waterside position, charming when tide in, with big windows and tables out on the hard, wide choice of bar food inc lunchtime shrimp or crab sandwiches; hot food (ambitious, concentrating on local fish) may be confined to upstairs restaurant, with good views; quick friendly staff, well kept Bass and Charrington IPA, decent choice of wines, good farm cider, warm fire; maybe piped music *(Simon Barriskell, Tina Rossiter, JT, WT, George Jonas, D G Clarke, Liz Bell, BB)*

☆ Kingskerswell [towards N Whilborough – OS Sheet 202 map ref 864665; SX8666], *Bickley Mill*: Rambling converted out-of-the-way mill, comfortable seats, dark wood and brasses, carpet spreading into all the alcoves, popular generous interesting bar food inc vegetarian and good ploughman's, well kept ales such as Ansells, Bass, Wadworths 6X, speedy cheerful service; restaurant Weds-Sat evenings; bedrooms *(Andrew Hodges, Mr and Mrs D Wilson, Dr A J and Mrs P G Newton, Gordon)*

Kingskerswell [Torquay Rd (A386); SX8767], *Hare & Hounds*: Busy extended beamed and timbered food pub with good value food from open kitchen inc vegetarian, sizzling stir-fries, interesting salads, children's dishes; friendly helpful service, good wheelchair access, good play area *(Alison Townsend)*

☆ Kingston [off B3392 S of Modbury; SX6347], *Dolphin*: Relaxed knocked-through 16th-c village local with beams and stripped stone, log fire, rustic tables and cushioned seats and settles, small no-smoking area, home-made bar food from sandwiches to steaks inc children's meals, well kept Courage Best and

Ushers Founders, good coffee, tables and swings outside; comfortable bedrooms from lane, several tracks down to the sea (*H F C Barclay, Jeanne Cross, Paul Silvestri, Michael Marlow, Marianne Lantree, Steve Webb, J B Tuckey, LYM*)

Kingswear [Higher St; SX8851], *Ship*: Friendly unpretentious local, good basic quickly served food, well kept Bass, good service; one table with Dart views, a couple outside (*Dr S Willavoys, B A Gunary*)

☆ Knowle [just off A361 2 miles N of Braunton; SS4938], *Ebrington Arms*: Welcoming and friendly, good food inc vegetarian, well kept Bass and Wadworths 6X, lots of bric-a-brac in comfortable main bar, attractive candlelit dining area; pool room, piped music (*Steve and Carolyn Harvey, R J Walden, David Carr, LYM*)

Lamerton [A384 Launceston—Tavistock; SX4476], *Blacksmiths Arms*: Welcoming local with good value generous fresh food, friendly efficient service, well kept ales; children very welcome (*Paul and Heather Bettesworth*)

☆ Landscove [Woolston Green – OS Sheet 202 map ref 778662; SX7766], *Live & Let Live*: Friendly, homely and spotless open-plan bar with popular bar food, well kept ales inc one brewed for the pub at Plympton, woodburner, tables in small orchard facing over moors to Dart valley (*C A Hall, LYM*)

☆ Lee [SS4846], *Grampus*: Attractive 14th-c pub short stroll from sea, lots of seats in quiet sheltered garden, wide range of basic but good well presented home-made food, well kept Whitbreads-related ales, decent piped music; two bedrooms; superb coastal walks; bedrooms (*Philip and Jude Simmons, LYM*)

☆ Loddiswell [SX7148], *Loddiswell Inn*: Welcoming landlady, well kept Ushers, freshly cooked generous food using local ingredients, bargain specials, log fire, thriving local atmosphere (*Nigel and Elizabeth Holmes*)

☆ Lympstone [Exmouth Rd (A376); SX9984], *Nutwell Lodge*: Big modern-looking roadside dining pub, surprisingly attractive inside, with good value food inc generous carvery and early lunchtime bargains, well kept Bass and Dartmoor, decent wines, good service; children welcome; roadside garden (*Alan and Margaret Griffiths, Dr A J and Mrs P G Newton, LYM*)

Lympstone [The Strand], *Globe*: Simple easy-going two-room local, popular food esp seafood and salads, quick friendly service, Flowers IPA, small pleasant restaurant; pretty waterside village (*Stan Edwards, Chris Westmoreland, BB*); [Exmouth Rd], *Saddlers Arms*: Useful roadside Country Carvery, warm, friendly and spacious, with Scottish Courage ales (*Mark and Heather Williamson*); [The Strand – off A376 at Saddlers Arms], *Swan*: Done up in olde-worlde style, well priced food inc good fresh fish (booking advisable Thurs-Sun), mainly Whitbreads-related ales; pool and fruit machine in pleasant public bar, piped music can be rather intrusive; pretty flower troughs and hanging

baskets (*Malcolm Smith, Stan Edwards*)

Lynmouth [High St; SS7249], *Village Inn*: Well kept beer, quick welcoming service, reasonably priced food; piped pop music may be rather obtrusive, credit card surcharge (*Dave Irving, Meg and Colin Hamilton*)

☆ Lynton [North Walk, Lynbridge; B3234 just S – OS Sheet 180 map ref 720485; SS7248], *Olde Cottage*: Genuinely friendly relaxed local, good home-made bar food, well kept ales such as Butcombe, Greene King Abbot, Exmoor Gold, Flowers Original and a seasonal guest, good eclectic mix of customers, pleasant straightforward decor, churchy Victorian windows; right by West Lyn gorge, with glorious coast views from terrace, footbridge to wooded NT walks up to Watersmeet or even the Rockford Inn at Brendon – and there's a lovely short walk from Lynton centre, on the Lynway; bedrooms (*Mark Matthewman*)

Lynton [Castle Hill], *Royal Castle*: Comfortably cushioned chairs, floors an attractive combination of wood and tile, nice moulded-tin ceilings, subdued but interesting decor with things related to Lynton, several rooms, well kept ales such as Adnams Broadside, Badger Tanglefoot, Butcombe and Cotleigh Tawny, polite service, great views from back terrace and garden – at night you can see the lights on the Welsh coast; bedrooms (*David Carr, Mark Matthewman, Bruce Bird, Dr A J and Mrs P G Newton*)

nr Lynton [Martinhoe, Heddon's Gate – which is well signed down narrow hairpin rd off A39 W of Lynton – OS Sheet 180 map ref 654482; SS6548], *Hunters Inn*: Outstanding remote setting in lovely wooded NT valley, great walks; most of rambling bar set aside for food (beware, maybe no lunchtime sandwiches or rolls), well kept Exmoor Ale and Stag and St Austell HSD, good farm cider, unobtrusive piped music; attractive bedrooms (*Simon Collett-Jones, Bruce Bird, Dr A J and Mrs P G Newton*)

☆ Maidencombe [Steep Hill; SX9268], *Thatched Tavern*: Picturesque extended thatched pub, good range of food inc local fish, well kept Bass and Tetleys-related ales, quick friendly service, big family room, no-smoking areas, restaurant; attractive garden with small thatched huts (dogs allowed out here but not in pub); children allowed; attractive bedrooms in annexe, good breakfast; small attractive village (half-price parking if you go to the pub), lovely coastal views nearby (*Mr and Mrs H Lambert, Mr and Mrs T A Bryan, Andrew Hodges*)

☆ Malborough [SX7039], *Old Inn*: Plain and unpretentious country pub notable for straightforward but really good bar food (esp mussels and puddings); charming quick service, good house wine, pleasant children's room (*H F C Barclay, David Carr*)

Manaton [SX7581], *Kestor*: Useful modern Dartmoor-edge inn in splendid spot nr Becky Falls, wide range of food, well kept Boddingtons and Marstons Pedigree, farm cider, helpful service, open fire; piped music; attractive bedrooms *(John and Vivienne Rice, G and M Stewart)*

☆ **Marsh** [signed off A303 Ilminster—Honiton; ST2510], *Flintlock*: Comfortable 17th-c inn doing well under current welcoming management, wide choice of good bar food inc vegetarian, well kept beer and cider, armoury and horsebrasses *(Mr and Mrs W B Walker, Howard Clutterbuck)*

☆ **Mary Tavy** [Lane Head; A386 Tavistock—Okehampton; SX5079], *Mary Tavy*: Warmly welcoming unpretentious old pub, friendly locals, well kept Bass, St Austell HSD and Mild and two guest beers, woodburner, reasonably priced freshly cooked food inc vegetarian, weekend front carvery; good value bedrooms, big breakfast *(Joan and Michel Hooper-Immins, Tom McLean, R Huggins, E McCall, Mrs M Connor)*

☆ **Meeth** [A386 Hatherleigh—Torrington; SS5408], *Bull & Dragon*: 16th-c beamed and thatched village pub, Butcombe and Dartmoor ales, decent wines, good value freshly cooked food, friendly staff and locals, unobtrusive piped music; children and dogs welcome, exemplary lavatories *(Elaine Hawkins, R J Walden, A N Ellis)*

☆ **Merrivale** [B3357 4 miles E of Tavistock; SX5475], *Dartmoor*: Refurbished pub with high Dartmoor views, nr bronze-age hut circles, stone rows and pretty river; generous reasonably priced lunchtime food, well kept ales inc Bass, Stones and one labelled for the pub, water from their 120-ft well, good choice of country wines, open fire, tables outside – very popular summer evenings; good walks *(John and Vivienne Rice, Dr and Mrs A K Clarke, Gwen and Peter Andrews)*

☆ **Molland** [SS8028], *London*: Unspoilt dim-lit basic Exmoor-edge pub, well worth tackling the narrow country lanes to get there; Bass and Worthington BB tapped from casks behind bar, good farm cider, good value food inc children's meals in big dining room, log fire, welcoming landlord, upper-crust locals; next to wonderfully untouched church *(John and Elspeth Howell, S Beele, Dr A J and Mrs P G Newton)*

Morchard Bishop [signed off A377 Crediton—Barnstaple; SS7707], *London*: Done-up 16th-c coaching inn, big carpeted red plush bar with woodburner in big fireplace, good value food in bar or small dining room, real ales inc Fullers London Pride, pool, darts and skittles *(Neil and Anita Christopher)*

☆ **Moreleigh** [B3207; off Kingsbridge—Totnes in Stanborough, left in village; SX7652], *New Inn*: Busy country local with character old furniture, nice pictures, candles in bottles; limited choice of good wholesome home-cooked food served generously (book if you want a table nr the big inglenook log fire), low prices, well kept Palmers tapped from the cask; may be cl Sat lunchtime/race days *(DWJ, Andy and Jill Kassube, Dr and Mrs N Holmes, LYM)*

Moretonhampstead [A382 N of Bovey Tracey; SX7585], *White Hart*: Little change under new owners, wide choice of usual food from sandwiches up, well kept Bass, Dartmoor and Princetown Jail, farm cider, friendly service; attractive big lounge, lively traditional back public bar, log fires, cream teas, no-smoking restaurant, traditional games; children welcome, open all day; attractive bedrooms, well placed for Dartmoor, good walks *(Mike Gorton, Dr and Mrs A K Clarke, LYM)*

☆ **Mortehoe** [off A361 Ilfracombe—Braunton; SS4545], *Ship Aground*: Welcoming open-plan village pub with big family room, well kept Cotleigh ales, Hancock's cider in summer, decent wine, friendly staff, bar food inc good pizzas, two log fires; massive rustic furnishings, lots of nautical brassware, friendly cross-eyed cat, pool, skittles and other games, tables on sheltered sunny terrace with good views; piped music may be intrusive; by interesting church, wonderful walking on nearby coast footpath *(Ian and Nita Cooper, Sue Demont, Tim Barrow, Dr A J and Mrs P G Newton, Jill Grain, Jo Rees, Tony McLaughlin, LYM)*

Mortehoe, *Chichester Arms*: Warm and welcoming, with lots of old village prints in plush and leatherette panelled lounge and restaurant area, wide choice of good value usual bar food, Morlands Old Speckled Hen, Ruddles County and Ushers, good service, no piped music *(Lynn Sharpless, Bob Eardley, Rip and Pauline Kirby, Dr A J and Mrs P G Newton, Alec and Susan Hamilton)*

☆ **nr Newton Abbot** [A381 2 miles S, by turn to Abbotskerswell], *Two Mile Oak*: Atractively quiet and old-fashioned, with good log fire, black panelling, low beams, stripped stone, lots of brasses, comfortable candlelit alcoves, cushioned settles and chairs; wide choice of enjoyable generous food, cosy little dining room, well kept Bass, Flowers IPA, Eldridge Pope Royal Oak and guest beers, friendly if not speedy service, seats on back terrace, attractive garden *(Gordon, Mr and Mrs C Roberts, LYM)*

☆ **Newton Ferrers** [Riverside Rd E; SX5448], *Dolphin*: Friendly pub in lovely village overlooking yachting harbour, good value food *(Mr and Mrs Peter Smith)*

☆ **Newton Tracey** [5 miles S of Barnstaple on B3232 to Torrington; SS5226], *Hunters*: Friendly old pub with good value food inc vegetarian and children's, four real ales, log fire, evening restaurant, skittle alley/games room; juke box, fruit machines; tables outside, play area; provision for children *(Angela and Derek Wood)*

☆ **No Mans Land** [B3131 Tiverton—South Molton; SS8313], *Mount Pleasant*: Cosy traditional country pub with wide range of good inexpensive home-made food from huge sandwiches up, real ales such as Bass and Butcombe, decent wines, friendly service, open fires, ex-forge restaurant; children's room, tables outside *(Paul and Heather Bettesworth)*

☆ **North Bovey** [SX7483], *Ring of Bells*: Bulgy-walled 13th-c thatched inn, well kept Dartmoor, Ind Coope Burton, Marstons Pedigree and Wadworths 6X, Gray's farm cider, games etc, good log fire, friendly staff, decent bar food (little under £5), restaurant; children welcome; seats outside by lovely tree-covered village green below Dartmoor; big bedrooms with four-posters *(John and Vivienne Rice, Dr and Mrs A K Clarke, Tony Dickinson, LYM)*

☆ **Noss Mayo** [off A379 via B3186, E of Plymouth; SX5447], *Old Ship*: Delicious setting with tables on waterside terrace (watch the tide if you park on the slipway), two thick-walled friendly bars, bar food from sandwiches to steaks inc local fish, well kept Bass, Dartmoor and a changing guest beer, swift helpful service; darts, fruit machine, piped music; children welcome, no-smoking restaurant upstairs with Sun carvery *(Ian and Gayle Woodhead, Mr and Mrs Peter Smith, Ted George , Lyn and Geoff Hallchurch, Elven Money, LYM)*

☆ **Noss Mayo** [off Junket Corner], *Swan*: Small pub with charming waterside views, good range of bar food inc fresh fish, well kept Courage Best and Directors, old beams, open fire; can get crowded, with difficult parking; dogs on leads and children welcome, tables outside – picturesque village *(Elizabeth Jenner, M J How)*

Otterton [Fore St; SY0885], *Kings Arms*: Comfortably refurbished open-plan pub in charming village, with beautiful evening view from picnic tables in good-sized back garden, skittle alley doubling as family room; has had good choice of food inc fresh fish and well kept Bass, but no reports since much-praised landlady gave up licence early 1997 *(News please)*

Paignton [Totnes Rd; SX8960], *Ship*: Homely atmosphere in dimly lit bar, good service, consistently good food, restaurant *(N Phillips)*

nr Paignton [Totnes Rd, off A385 2 miles out; SX8561], *Blagdon Inn*: Comfortable thatched pub with spacious open-plan beamed bar, some stripped brickwork, family room, friendly staff, good food inc vegetarian in bar and restaurant; tables on terrace, play area *(P Rome)*

☆ **Parkham** [SS3821], *Bell*: Spacious and comfortable thatched village pub, good value fresh food, lots of nooks and crannies, log fire, old-fashioned furnishings, Bass and Charrington IPA, pleasant friendly staff *(Nigel and Lindsay Chapman, Mr and Mrs G McNeill, Mr and Mrs J Marsh, LYM)*

☆ **Plymouth** [Citadel Rd/Saltram Pl – back of Plymouth Hoe, behind Moat House], *Yard Arm*: In fine spot overlooking the Hoe, touristy but well done with attractive woodwork and some interesting nautical bric-a-brac, three levels and intimate snug feel, Scottish Courage ales and a guest such as Bass, generous straightforward food inc children's, cheerful service; subdued piped music, children allowed in bottom area, tables

in small yard behind *(the Sandy family, Andrew Hodges, Brian and Anna Marsden)*

☆ **Plymouth** [Old George St; Derrys Cross, behind Theatre Royal], *Bank*: Smart and busy three-level pub interestingly converted from former bank, dark wood balustrades, conservatory area upstairs (children allowed here), tables outside; cheerful service (quickest on the top level, which is quieter), good value food all day, Tetleys-related ales; music nights, lively young evening atmosphere *(Mayur Shah, John Barker)*

Plymouth [Barbican], *Dolphin*: Good lively unpretentious atmosphere, particularly well kept Bass tapped from the cask; Beryl Cook paintings (you may see her here) *(John Poulter, David Carr, James Macrae, John Barker)*; [6 Commercial Rd], *Fareham*: Small pleasantly refurbished pub by modern fish quay, friendly staff and regulars, St Austell HSD *(John Barker)*; [Looe St (nr Barbican)], *Minerva*: Lively backstreet pub dating from 1555, Scottish Courage ales; quite small so can get packed *(David Carr)*; *Notte*: Small so it can get crowded, but good service; good generous food inc sizzlers and seafood specials, well kept Bass and Wadworths 6X *(Keith Waters, Helen Osborne)*; [Buckwell St], *O'Neills*: Irish pub with bare boards, nooks and corners, and live music; good table service *(Paul Redgrave)*; [Southside St, Barbican], *Queens Arms*: Friendly and clean, with excellent fresh crab sandwiches *(NWN)*; [32 Commercial Rd], *Thistle Park*: Well kept Sutton ales, tasty well presented food, interesting decor, friendly landlady; children welcome *(John Barker)*

Plympton [Chaddlewood; SX5556], *Chaddlewood*: Lively new pub with big helpings of good value food, well kept Bass, family room *(Keith Waters)*

Portgate [Launceston Rd (old A30); SX4185], *Harris Arms*: Bright and friendly, comfortably furnished and generally peaceful, good choice of food (meat particularly well chosen), real ales inc two guests *(T Pascall)*

Postbridge [B3212; SX6579], *East Dart*: Central Dartmoor hotel by pretty river, cheerful open-plan bar largely given over to promptly served good value bar food, well kept Exmoor and other real ales, farm cider, good fire, pool room; children welcome; bedrooms, some 30 miles of fishing *(C and E Watson, BB)*

☆ **Poundsgate** [between Ashburton and B3357; SX7072], *Tavistock*: 13th-c Dartmoor-edge village local with narrow-stepped granite spiral staircase, original flagstones and ancient fireplaces, bar food inc good pasties, well kept Courage Best and Ushers Best and Founders, local farm cider, enterprising summer and winter special drinks, good welcoming service, pub games, family room, tables outside *(Mike Gorton, Lyn and Geoff Hallchurch, Jonathan Williams, Barry and Anne, Paul and Heather Bettesworth, LYM)*

☆ **Princetown** [SX5873], *Plume of Feathers*: Much-extended hikers' pub, good value food inc good pasties, service quick and friendly even with crowds, well kept Bass and St Austell HSD and Tinners, two log fires, solid slate tables, live music Fri night, Sun lunchtime – can be lively then; children welcome, play area outside; good value bedrooms, also bunkhouse and camping (M J How, J R Harris)

☆ **Pusehill** [SS4228], *Pig on the Hill*: Newish family dining pub on farm, pig decorations, bar, raised gallery and adjacent room through archways; decent food inc children's, well kept Ind Coope Burton, reasonable prices, children's TV room; big adventure playground, small swimming pool, boules (Chris Westmoreland)

Pyworthy [SW of Holsworthy; SS3102], *Molesworth Arms*: Popular country pub with attractively priced food inc good curries in bar or restaurant, well kept Bass and a guest beer, friendly staff (Mrs R Horridge, Mr and Mrs J D Marsh)

☆ **Roborough** [off B3217 N of Winkleigh; SS5717], *Olde Inn*: 16th-c thatched country pub, good value food from cheap sandwiches to salmon (must book Sun lunch), well kept beers inc Exmoor, Wadworths 6X and a weekly guest, good range of malt whiskies, decent house wine, friendly helpful staff, locals' bar, comfortable lounge leading to snug dining area – log fire in inglenook, lots of brass and old farm tools; small garden, cl weekday lunchtimes (Alan and Heather Jacques, BB)

☆ **Rockbeare** [SY0295], *Jack in the Green*: Good varied well priced food, local fish and game, delicious puddings, well kept Bass and Wadworths 6X, good reasonably priced wines, pleasant staff, back restaurant (Kim Dawson, Chris Jaworski, Mr and Mrs J B Bishop)

Salcombe [off Fore St nr Portlemouth Ferry; SX7338], *Ferry*: Fine spot overlooking water, bottom stripped-stone bar giving on to sheltered flagstoned waterside terrace, top lounge opening off street, and between them a popular dining bar; well kept Palmers ales; piped music may be intrusive, can get busy (June and Malcolm Farmer, David Carr, Chris and Martin Taylor, Hilarie Dobbie, LYM)

Salcombe [Union St], *Fortescue*: Busy local nr harbour, three bars, terrace, reliable food, well kept Courage Directors; can get busy in summer (David Carr, G W Stevenson); [Fore St], *Victoria*: Well placed and attractive, with comfortable lounge, copious good food cooked to order, pleasant eating area, jovial landlord, well kept Bass and Wadworths 6X; segregated children's room, bedrooms (David Carr)

Sampford Peverell [16 Lower Town; a mile from M5 junction 27, village signed from Tiverton turn-off; ST0214], *Globe*: Spacious and comfortably modernised bar, handy for decent waitress-served food from sandwiches to steaks inc children's dishes and popular Sun lunch, well kept Flowers IPA and Original, piped music, games in public bar, pool room, skittle alley, tables in front; open all day; children allowed in eating area and family room (Nick Wikeley, W H and E Thomas, LYM)

☆ **Sandy Park** [SX7189], *Sandy Park*: Interesting varied food inc home-grown salads under new owner in thatched country local with convivial old-fashioned small bar, stripped old tables, built-in high-backed wall seats, big black iron fireplace, well kept ales such as Cotleigh Tawny, Eldridge Pope Hardy and Wadworths 6X, decent wines and farm cider; children in eating area, cosy restaurant; simple clean bedrooms (James Macrae, Dr and Mrs G K Blackwell, John Mann, Maureen Jenkins, LYM)

Scorriton [SX7068], *Tradesmans Arms*: Good-sized Dartmoor-edge open-plan local in attractive countryside, unpretentious and clean, friendly licensees, good value basic home-cooked food inc children's, Bass and Dartmoor IPA, farm cider, open fire, snug one end, lots of board games, big children's room; bedrooms (Neil and Anita Christopher)

Shaldon [Fore St; SX9372], *Clifford Arms*: Friendly 18th-c pub in pleasant seaside village, good value home-cooked food inc fresh local fish, well kept Bass and Dartmoor Best, pub games, family room (Mr and Mrs W Welsh); [Ringmore Rd (B3195 to Newton Abbot)], *Shipwrights Arms*: Chatty village local of real character, pleasant river views from back garden, good value basic food, obliging service, well kept ales (Mr and Mrs W Welsh, LYM)

Shebbear [SS4409], *Devils Stone*: Friendly village pub with big oak-beamed bar, three other rooms inc restaurant, warm welcome (for children and dogs too), good range of beers, good food at very reasonable prices with bargain OAP helpings; handy for Tarka Trail; simple bedrooms (C P Scott-Malden, BB)

Shillingford [SS9823], *Barleycorn*: Handsomely decorated old beamed inn handy for Exmoor, good range of real ales, decent wines, reasonably priced fresh generous food inc vegetarian, welcoming family service, sheltered back garden; bedrooms comfortable and clean (M Lycett Green, Peter Woolls, M Carter)

☆ **Shiphay** [off A380/A3022, NW edge of Torquay; SX8865], *Devon Dumpling*: Popular for its country style, with good value straightforward food inc vegetarian, well kept Scottish Courage ales with a guest such as Bass, cheerful service, plenty of space inc upper barn loft; aquarium, occasional live music, no dogs inside (Mr and Mrs C Roberts)

☆ **Sidbury** [Putts Corner; A375 Sidbury—Honiton; SY1595], *Hare & Hounds*: Roomy lounge bar, wood-and-tiles tap room, two fine old chesterfields and more usual furnishings, stuffed birds, blazing log fire; four or five well kept changing ales, very friendly staff, wide choice of quick bar food, restaurant with Sun carvery, pool in side room, another with big TV; big garden, good views of valley below *(Howard Clutterbuck, Peter and Audrey Dowsett, C Kyprianou, V Jenner)*

☆ Sidmouth [Old Fore St; SY1287], *Old Ship*: Mellow black woodwork, ship pictures, wide choice of fair-priced food inc vegetarian and home-made specials, well kept ales such as Boddingtons, Marstons Pedigree, Wadworths 6X, friendly atmosphere, good service even when busy; close-set tables but roomier raftered upstairs bar with family room, dogs allowed; just moments from the sea *(Alan and Paula McCully, M E Wellington, A and R Cooper, Peter and Rosie Flower, Ann and Colin Hunt, E V M Whiteway, BB)*
Sidmouth [High St], *Tudor Rose*: Reopened after comfortable refurbishment, wide choice of reasonably priced bar food inc children's, Boddingtons, Fullers London Pride, Morlands Old Speckled Hen and Wadworths 6X, extensive wine list, relaxing atmosphere, quiet piped music; open all day in summer *(Brian Websdale)*

☆ nr Sidmouth [Bowd Cross; junction B3176/A3052; SY1089], *Bowd*: Big thatched family roadhouse with attractive garden, popular friendly service even when busy, well kept Bass and Flowers Original, indoor and outdoor play areas *(P and M Rudlin, Jack Barnwell, Mrs G Greenslade, L W King, BB)*
Slapton [SX8244], *Queens Arms*: Comfortable and snug old inn with good value food, well kept Bass, Exmoor and Palmers, lovely suntrap garden with plenty of tables *(Roger Wain-Heapy)*; *Tower*: Ancient low-ceilinged flagstoned pub with open fires, family room, usual bar food, real ales such as Badger Tanglefoot, Exmoor and Gibbs Mew Bishops Tipple, cosy family atmosphere, peaceful garden overhung by romantic ivy-covered ruined jackdaw tower; bedrooms *(Elven Money, M and J Madley, Roger Wain-Heapy, LYM)*
Sourton [A386 S; SX5390], *Bearslake*: Interesting stonebuilt 13th-c pub with pleasant bar, well kept Dartmoor, wide choice of food in restaurant *(John and Vivienne Rice)*
South Brent [Plymouth Rd; SX6960], *Pack Horse*: Relaxed, comfortable and characterful local; good choice of good food inc fine crab salad, well kept Flowers, good landlord; bedrooms *(Patrick Freeman)*

☆ South Tawton [off A30 at Whiddon Down or Okehampton, then signed from Sticklepath; SX6594], *Seven Stars*: Friendly and unpretentious local in attractive village, good range of well prepared good value food, well kept Bass, Boddingtons and a guest beer, decent wines; pool and other bar games, restaurant (cl Sun and Mon evenings winter); children welcome; bedrooms *(Matthew Baker, LYM)*
Starcross [SX9781], *Atmospheric Railway*: Named for Brunel's experimental 1830s railway here, Brunel and railway

memorabilia, prints and signs, Bass, Boddingtons, Eldridge Pope Royal Oak and Wadworths 6X, good value no-nonsense home cooking well prepared and presented, obliging efficient staff, family room, skittle alley; garden with tables and play area *(John Beeken, Colin Marsden, BB)*

☆ Sticklepath [off A30 at Whiddon Down or Okehampton; SX6494], *Devonshire*: Warm and cosy 16th-c thatched village inn with low-beamed slate-floored bar, big log fire, some nice old furniture, comfortable armchairs in room off, good filling low-priced snacks, bookable Sun lunches and evening meals, welcoming owners and locals, well kept St Austell Tinners and HSD tapped from the cask, farm cider, magazines to read; open all day Fri/Sat; bedrooms *(Ray and Wendy Bryn Davies, Andy and Jill Kassube, LYM)*
Stoke Gabriel [SX8457], *Victoria & Albert*: Friendly atmosphere, good food *(M Joyner)*

☆ Stokeinteignhead [SX9170], *Church House*: Civilised and friendly 13th-c thatched dining pub, character bar, dining lounge and restaurant area, delightful spiral staircase, well presented food, well kept Bass, Flowers IPA and Marstons Pedigree, farm cider, good coffee; nice back garden with little stream, lovely unspoilt village *(John Wilson, Andrew Hodges)*

☆ Stokeinteignhead, *Chasers Arms*: Good value often interesting food inc imaginative veg and unusual puddings in busy 16th-c thatched pub/restaurant (you can't go just for a drink, but they do bar snacks too and the style emulates a country pub); fine range of house wines, quick friendly service *(John Wilson, Mr and Mrs W Welsh, Geraldine Bristol)*

☆ Stokenham [opp church, N of A379 towards Torcross; SX8042], *Church House*: Comfortable firmly run open-plan family pub, good food inc fresh local seafood, well kept Bass, Eldridge Pope Hardy and Flowers Original, farm cider, decent wines, pleasant service, no-smoking dining room, unobtrusive piped music; children's room with writing/drawing materials, attractive garden with enjoyable play area, fishpond and chipmunks *(Paul and Janet Waring, Colin Draper, RCV, Dr A J and Mrs P G Newton, Hanns P Golez, Mary Woods, LYM)*
Teignmouth [Queen St; SX9473], *Ship*: Upper and lower decks like a ship, good atmosphere, nice mix of locals and tourists, good value food inc simply cooked local seafood, good service, well kept Bass, Flowers Original and Wadworths 6X, interesting wine list, fresh coffee, gallery restaurant; open all day, food served all day in summer; fine floral displays, lovely riverside setting, beautiful views *(A and R Cooper and others)*
Thelbridge Cross [off B3137 W of Tiverton – OS Sheet 180 map ref 790120; SS7912], *Thelbridge Cross*: Welcoming lounge bar with log fire and elderly plush settees, good generous food inc some unusual dishes in extensive dining area and separate restaurant, particularly well kept Bass and Butcombe;

bedrooms *(Alan Kitchener, Dr A J and Mrs P G Newton, J Anderson, John Evans, BB)*

Thorverton [SS9202], *Bell:* Friendly, with Flowers IPA, Fullers London Pride, good food *(E Robinson)*

Thurlestone [SX6743], *Village Inn:* Much refurbished but convivial pub emphasising food (cool cabinet, open kitchen behind servery, blackboards, etc) – wide choice, reasonable prices; well kept Bass, Dartmoor, Palmers and Wadworths 6X, comfortable new country-style furnishings, dividers forming alcoves, pleasant efficient service; children and dogs catered for, darts, quiz nights, live music, handy for coast path *(DJW, Marianne Lantree, Steve Webb)*

Tiverton [opp old Blundells School building; SS9512], *Prince Regent:* Good basic pub with good value food, real ales and cider *(Veronica Brown)*

☆ **Topsham** [Fore St; 2 miles from M5 junction 30; SX9688], *Globe:* Good solid traditional furnishings, log fire and plenty of character in heavy-beamed bow-windowed bar of friendly and relaxed 16th-c inn; low-priced straightforward home-cooked food, well kept Bass, Ushers Best and Worthington BB on handpump, decent reasonably priced wine, snug little bar-dining room, separate restaurant, new back extension blending in well; children in eating area, open all day; good value attractive bedrooms *(Chris Westmoreland, Andrew Hodges, LYM)*

☆ **Topsham** [from centre head towards Exmouth via Elmgrove Rd], *Bridge:* Unchanging and unspoilt 16th-c pub with fine old traditional furnishings in little no-smoking lounge partitioned off from inner corridor by high-backed settle, open fire, bigger lower room open at busy times, cosy regulars' inner sanctum with almost too wide a choice of real ales tapped from the cask; lunchtime pasties, sandwiches and ploughman's, children welcome *(JP, PP, Jo and Gary Charlton, LYM)*

☆ **Topsham**, *Lighter:* Spacious and comfortably refurbished family pub, panelling and tall windows looking out over tidal flats, more intimate side room, well kept Badger ales and a beer brewed for the pub, good friendly staff, good quickly served bar food inc local fish; games machines; tables out on old quay, good value bedrooms *(John Beeken, John Fahy, Ann and Colin Hunt, R J Walden, BB)*

☆ **Topsham** [High St], *Lord Nelson:* Good value generous food inc giant open sandwiches, pleasant atmosphere, attentive service *(Dr A J and Mrs P G Newton, Andrew Hodges)*

Topsham [Fore St], *Drakes:* Attractive beamed pub with Bass, Boddingtons, Devenish Royal Wessex, a beer named for the pub and guest beers, good choice of wines by the glass, tempting food, welcoming service, intimate restaurant upstairs *(Stan Edwards, Brian Websdale, Andrew Hodges)*; [68 Fore St], *Salutation:* Victorian pastiche complete with flagstoned period courtyard; clean and comfortable, happy obliging staff, well kept

Bass and Worthington BB, good value freshly cooked food esp local fish *(K R Harris, Andrew Hodges)*; [Monmouth Hill], *Steam Packet:* Cheap bar food, several well kept ales, dark flagstones, scrubbed boards, panelling, stripped masonry, a lighter dining room; on boat-builders' quay *(Andrew Hodges, Ann and Colin Hunt, LYM)*

☆ **Torquay** [Park Lane, opp clock tower; SX9264], *Hole in the Wall:* More emphasis on food under current management in small two-bar 16th-c local nr harbour, low beams and flagstones, well kept Courage, friendly service, lots of naval memorabilia, old local photographs, chamber-pots; open all day *(Jim and Maggie Cowell, JWC, MC)*

Torquay [Beach Rd, Babbacombe; SX9265], *Cary Arms:* Cheerful service, decent straightforward food inc lots of sandwiches, well kept beers, pleasant piped music, good sea and cliff views, tables on terrace; bedrooms *(Ian and Jane Irving)*; [Strand], *London:* Nicely furnished new Wetherspoons bank conversion on three levels with two bars, good reasonably priced food, no-smoking area *(Andrew Hodges)*

☆ **Totnes** [9 Leechwell St; SX8060], *Kingsbridge:* Low-beamed rambling bar with timbering and some stripped stone, plush seats, small no-smoking area, home-made bar food from interesting sandwiches to steaks and local fish, Badger Best, Bass, Courage Best, Dartmoor Best, and Theakstons Old Peculier, local farm cider, decent house wines; children in eating area, some live music *(Dr S P Willavoys, David Carr, Jo and Gary Charlton, LYM)*

☆ **Totnes** [Fore St, The Plains], *Royal Seven Stars:* Civilised old hotel, full of character, with late 1960s decor, impressive central hall below sunny skylight and stairs off, Bass and Courage Best, cheerful helpful service, cheap food, tables out in front – ideal on a Tues market day when the tradespeople wear Elizabethan dress; bedrooms, river on other side of busy main road *(JWC, MC, David Carr, Ian Phillips, Jim and Maggie Cowell)*

Totnes [32 Bridgetown], *Albert:* Dark-beamed red plush lounge bar with lots of nick-nacks, good generous reasonably priced food (not Sun), well kept Bass, Brakspears and Worthington BB, welcoming back snug locals' bar, handsome pub dog Henry, nice garden *(C J W Penrose, S Miles, Nigel Ash)*; [The Plains], *Steam Packet:* Good atmosphere, good home-cooked Italian food, well kept and served real ales, carefully chosen wines inc some English ones, new welcoming young licensees; bedrooms *(C H and J V Smith, B Langton)*

☆ **Two Bridges** [B3357/B3212; SX6175], *Two Bridges:* Friendly and gently refurbished old hotel in protected central Dartmoor hollow, nice log fire in cosy bar, another in spacious lounge, decent bar food inc useful buffet lunch from restaurant, afternoon tea, own-brewed beer; comfortable bedrooms, good walks – a romantic winter hideaway, but very busy with tourists and their children in summer *(John and Christine Vittoe, Janet and Colin Roe, Gordon Neighbour)*

Tytherleigh [A358 Chard—Axminster; ST3103], *Tytherleigh Arms*: Spacious and comfortable, with good range of usual food inc local fish, Eldridge Pope ales, small restaurant *(Howard Clutterbuck)*

☆ **Ugborough** [SX6755], *Ship*: Well run open-plan dining pub extended from cosy 16th-c flagstoned core, remarkably wide choice of good food inc lots of fresh fish, good fresh veg and farm ice cream, pleasant efficient waitresses, well kept Bass; tables outside *(M G Hart, BHT)*

Umberleigh [SS6023], *Rising Sun*: Welcoming neatly kept traditional inn by River Taw, bar food inc river trout and salmon, well kept Scottish Courage ales, good range of malt whiskies and of wines by the glass; comfortable bedrooms *(Mr and Mrs J McCurdy, Clive Skilton)*

☆ **Welcombe** [Darracott; village signed off A39 S of Hartland; SS2217], *Old Smithy*: Thatched pub in lovely setting by lane leading eventually to attractive rocky cove, open-plan bar with woodburners and button-back banquettes, restaurant in former forge, plenty of seats in pretty terraced garden, handy for nearby campsite; too few reports since closure winter 1996/7 to be sure of its status *(LYM; news please)*

☆ **Westleigh** [½ mile off A39 Bideford—Instow; SS4628], *Westleigh Inn*: Very welcoming village pub with old local pictures in single room split by serving bar, well kept Ruddles County and Ushers, farm cider, good straightforward home-cooked food, family atmosphere, gorgeous views down over the Torridge estuary from spacious neatly kept hillside garden, good play area *(David and Michelle James, Chris Westmoreland, LYM)*

Whiddon Down [Exeter Rd, off A30; SX6992], *Post*: Friendly local with enthusiastic newish landlady, good reasonably priced food, well kept Whitbreads-related ales, separate bar with darts, pool and skittles, small garden *(B J Cox, EC)*

Whimple [off A30 Exeter—Honiton; SY4097], *New Fountain*: Civilised and attractive village local with friendly landlord and good food *(MRSM, JS, LYM)*

☆ **Widecombe** [SX7176], *Olde Inne*: Friendly and comfortable, with stripped 14th-c

stonework, big log fires in both bars, some concentration on wide choice of good generous food cooked to order with fresh veg, prominent restaurant area, well kept Ushers and other beers, local farm cider, decent wines, good friendly service, family room; in pretty moorland village, very popular with tourists though perhaps at its best out of season; room to dance on music nights, good big garden; great walks – the one to or from Grimspound gives spectacular views *(John and June Gale, Comus Elliott, Paul and Janet Waring, Jeanne Cross, Paul Silvestri, LYM)*

☆ **Winkleigh** [off B3220 Crediton—Torrington; SS6308], *Kings Arms*: Beams, flagstones, scrubbed pine tables, woodburner and big log fire, big helpings of good food inc some outstanding dishes, also well kept Scottish Courage ales and local Inch's farm cider, friendly staff and locals, good efficient service, well reproduced piped music, no-smoking restaurant; small sheltered side courtyard with pool *(R J Walden, Mrs B Sugarman, Dr A J and Mrs P G Newton, LYM)*

Witheridge [SS8014], *Mitre*: In sleepy village on Two Moors Way, good welcome, well kept Exmoor, cheap tasty food; bedrooms *(G H H Vowles)*

☆ **Wrafton** [A361 just SE of Braunton; SS4935], *Williams Arms*: Friendly modernised thatched dining pub, two big bars divided into several cosy areas, interesting wall hangings, wide choice of good value bar food, unlimited self-service from good carvery, quick service, Bass; pool, darts, piped music, discreet TV; children welcome; picnic tables outside with play area and aviary *(Jane Basso, Roger and Pauline Pearce)*

Yarcombe [A30; ST2408], *Yarcombe*: Attractive and welcoming 14th-c thatched pub doing well under newish owners, wide range of good if not cheap food from tasty ploughman's up, separate dining room, nice little spotless front bar, several guest beers *(A M Pring, D B Jenkin)*

Yelverton [by roundabout on A386 Plymouth—Tavistock; SX5267], *Rock*: Spaciously extended pub with games room and good facilities for children, wide choice of food, friendly efficient waitress service, good range of ales and ciders, popular terrace, safe play area; open all day; bedrooms *(Paul Redgrave)*

Children welcome means the pubs says it lets children inside without any special restriction. If it allows them in, but to restricted areas such as an eating area or family room, we specify this. Places with separate restaurants usually let children use them, hotels usually let them into public areas such as lounges. Some pubs impose an evening time limit – let us know if you find this.

Dorset

This county now has an excellent choice of attractive pubs with real character, often of genuine antiquity, run carefully by nice people. Those which have been giving readers most pleasure recently are the Spyway at Askerswell (excellent choice of drinks, lovely views), the cheerful and very well run Anchor by the sea near Chideock, the relaxed Loders Arms at Loders (good interesting food and a properly pubby atmosphere), the superbly run Marquis of Lorne at Nettlecombe, and the pretty Brace of Pheasants at Plush (very enjoyable food). It's the Brace of Pheasants which gains our award as Dorset Dining Pub of the Year, with strong competition from two previous winners, both very individual places – the Fox at Corscombe and the Museum at Farnham. Enjoyable new entries are the extended 16th-c Barley Mow at Colehill (genuine and traditional, with good food), the charmingly laid out Cock & Bottle at East Morden (largely a dining pub, but with a proper public bar too), the Acorn at Evershot (very popular new chef, and a nice place to stay), and the ancient Halfway on Norden Heath (welcoming Greek landlord). Some other changes to note include the way the White Hart at Bishops Caundle is doing more for families; some gentle upgrading at the very popular Red Lion in Cerne Abbas; careful restoration of the well liked and cottagey New Inn at Church Knowle after last year's fire; and the takeover of the Scott Arms at Kingston by Greenalls – it's still a useful family pub. In the Lucky Dip at the end of the chapter, pubs currently attracting a lot of attention (almost all inspected and approved by us) are the Worlds End at Almer, Weld Arms at East Lulworth, Crown at Puncknowle, Crown at Uploders and Nothe Tavern in Weymouth; there's a good choice in Shaftesbury. Dorset pubs generally charge a few pence more for drinks than the national average – our survey found pubs supplied by Palmers of Bridport were generally a bit cheaper. The cheapest pub we found was the Greyhound in Corfe Castle, tied to Whitbreads but getting a cheaper beer from the small Poole brewery. Eldridge Pope the Dorchester brewers are changing to Hardy as their main brand name; we have kept the familiar Eldridge Pope name this year, but will probably be switching to the space-saving Hardy in future.

ABBOTSBURY SY5785 Map 2
Ilchester Arms 🍺
B3157

This handsome and rambling stone inn makes a good base for looking around the interesting old village as well as for exploring further afield – walking, pony trekking and so forth. The bustling main bar has over 1,000 prints on the walls, many depicting swans from the nearby abbey, as well as red plush button-back seats and spindleback chairs around cast-iron-framed and other tables on a turkey carpet, and comfortable armchairs in front of the open log fire. Hunting horns, stirrups and horsebrasses hang from the beams, there's a stag's head, and some stuffed fish. Bass, Flowers Orginal and Wadworths 6X under light blanket pressure, and winter pool, fruit machine, and piped music. Bar food (they tell us prices have not changed since last year) includes soup (£2), Dorset sausage baguette (£2.60), ploughman's (from £3.25), baked potato with cheese and bacon (£3.95), home-made steak and ale pie (£4.95), roast beef and yorkshire pudding (£6.25), daily specials like stir-fried pork with bean sprouts, seafood such as local lemon sole (£8.95) or red mullet with chive sauce (£9.25), and home-made puddings (all £2.25); children's menu (from £1.95), and big breakfasts. Service can be slow in the sizeable and attractive no-smoking conservatory restaurant; afternoon teas, too. *(Recommended by Jo and Gary Charlton, Galen Strawson, P and J Caunt, David Mead, Paul Seligman, Ken and Jenny Simmonds, Chris and Kate Lyons, Jenny and Brian Seller, J Sheldon, Neil Townend, Brian and Anna Marsden, Richard Gibbs, David Holloway, Cheryl and Keith Roe)*

Greenalls ~ Managers Mike and May Doyle ~ Real ale ~ Meals and snacks ~ Restaurant ~ (01305) 871243 ~ Children in eating area of bar ~ Open 11-11; 11-3, 6-11 winter Mon and Tues; 12-3, 7-10.30 Sun ~ Bedrooms: £23B/£46B

ASKERSWELL SY5292 Map 2
Spyway ★ ♀

Village signposted N of A35 Bridport—Dorchester; inn signposted locally; OS Sheet 194 map reference 529933

From the back terrace and gardens here (where you can eat on warm days), there are marvellous views across the valley. Inside, it's bustling and characterful and run by a particularly helpful, friendly licensee. The cosy little rooms have old-fashioned high-backed settles, cushioned wall and window seats, a vast collection of china teacups, harness and a milkmaid's yoke, and a longcase clock; there's also a no-smoking dining area decorated with blue and white china, old oak beams and timber uprights. Promptly served and reasonably priced, the good bar food includes a range of generous and tasty ploughman's such as hot sausages and tomato pickle or home-cooked ham (from £3.35), three-egg omelettes (£3.25), haddock or plaice (from £3.80), evening extras like gammon and egg (£6.75) or steak (£8.75), and daily specials such as home-made quiche or vegetarian dishes (£3.95), and home-made chicken and bacon, game or steak and onion pies (all £4.25). There's a fine choice of drinks: Adnams Best and Southwold, Ruddles County and Ushers Best on handpump, 24 reasonably priced decent wines by the glass, 20 country wines, around 40 whiskies and some unusual non-alcoholic drinks. Shove-ha'penny, table skittles, dominoes and cribbage. Plenty of pleasant nearby walks along the paths and bridleways. Eggardon Hill, which the pub's steep lane leads up, is one of the highest in the region, with lovely views of the downs and to the coast. No children. *(Recommended by George Atkinson, D B Jenkin, Peter and Audrey Dowsett, Dr and Mrs J H Hills, C A Hall, JM, SM, TBB, Simon and Jane Williams, James and Lynne House, Dr S Willavoys, E A George, Chris and Margaret Southon, Pete and Rosie Flower, Stephen and Julie Brown, Jack and Philip Paxton)*

Free house ~ Licensees Don and Jackie Roderick ~ Real ale ~ Meals and snacks ~ (01308) 485250 ~ Open 11-2.30(3 Sat), 6-11; 12-3, 7-10.30 Sun; cl Mon except bank holidays

BISHOPS CAUNDLE ST6913 Map 2
White Hart

A3030

Plans are afoot to enlarge the no-smoking family area and put in french windows to the garden area here, as well as a new entrance to the skittle alley – this would make the bar more accessible to both areas. They have also added volley ball, netball, badminton, junior basketball and short tennis (the big prettily floodlit garden already has a play area made up of trampolines, a playhouse with slides, and a sandpit); there's a covered area for sitting outside on those summer days when the weather isn't quite so perfect. The ancient panelled walls of the spacious, irregularly shaped bar are attractively decorated with brass trays and farming equipment, and furnishings include a good variety of seats and tables, dark red curtains, and nice lamps under the handsomely moulded low beams. Good bar food includes home-made soup (£1.95), sandwiches (from £2.50), ploughman's (£4.25), shepherd's pie (£4.95), vegetable crunch bake (£5.25), home-made steak, kidney and ale pie (£5.50), apricot glazed chicken or gammon and egg (£6.75), steaks (from £6.75), orange and basil pork or grilled salmon steak (£6.95), and puddings such as home-made profiteroles or syrup sponge pudding (from £2.75); they offer smaller helpings at cheaper prices; children's menu (£2.50), and Sunday roast lunch. Well kept Badger Best and Tanglefoot on handpump; friendly helpful service; darts, skittle alley, fruit machine and piped music. *(Recommended by Brian Chambers, James and Lynne House, Marjorie and David Lamb, Christopher Gallop, Cheryl and Keith Roe)*

Badger ~ Manager Gordon Pitman ~ Real ale ~ Meals and snacks ~ (01963) 23301 ~ Children in restaurant ~ Open 11-2.30, 6.30-11; 12-3, 7-10.30 Sun ~ Bedroom: £15/£30

BRIDPORT SY4692 Map 1
George
South St

They go in for long-standing staff at this good old-fashioned local – both the licensee and the characterful barman have now been here for 20 years. Divided by a coloured tiled hallway, the two sizeable bars – one is served by a hatch from the main lounge – are full of friendly old-fashioned charm and atmosphere. There are nicely spaced old dining tables and country seats and wheelback chairs, big rugs on tiled floors, a mahogany bar counter, fresh flowers, and a winter log fire, along with an interesting pre-fruit-machine ball game. Thursday night chess club – all welcome. Well kept Palmers Bitter, IPA, Tally Ho and Bicentenary on handpump, a spread of maltes and other spirits, decent wines, and hot toddies, proper Pimms, and frozen daiquiris. Bar food includes sandwiches (from £1.90; toasted bacon and mushroom £2.80), home-made soup (£2), home-made pâté or welsh rarebit (£3), home-made pies (from £3.75), ploughman's or omelettes (£3.95), daily vegetarian dishes, kedgeree, whole fresh plaice or lamb kidneys in madeira (£5), and puddings or English cheeses; vegetables are extra (£1.50); you can usually see the licensee at work preparing your meal. You can only have an evening meal out of season if you make a reservation; Radio 3 or maybe classical, jazz or opera tapes. *(Recommended by Michael Graubart, Jo and Gary Charlton, Simon and Jane Williams, Stephen and Julie Brown, Jack and Philip Paxton, Paul M Harris)*

Palmers ~ Tenant John Mander ~ Real ale ~ Meals and snacks (not Sun lunch or bank holidays – and see note above about evening meals) ~ (01308) 423187 ~ Children in side room only ~ Open 10am-11pm (8.30am for coffee every day); 12-3, 7-10.30 Sun; closed 25 Dec ~ Bedrooms: £20/£40

BURTON BRADSTOCK SY4889 Map 1
Three Horseshoes
Mill St

In a pretty village (well worth a stroll around), this friendly family-run thatched inn is full of chatty locals. The pleasant roomy bar has an enjoyable homely atmosphere, an open fire, comfortable seating, and Palmers 200, Bridport, IPA and Tally Ho kept under light blanket pressure. Nicely presented promptly served bar food from a menu full of groan-inducing jokes includes lunchtime sandwiches – there's a good crab one (from £2.10), several ploughman's (from £3.70), steak and kidney pie (£4.15), fish and chips (£4.45), lasagne or mushroom and nut fettucine (£4.95), puddings (from £2.30), and usual children's meals (£2.70); evening extras like cantonese prawns or cajun chicken (£6.20), and sirloin steak (£10.35). The dining room is no smoking; table football and pool in family room; sporadic piped music. There are tables on the lawn, and Chesil beach and cliff walks are only 400 yards away. *(Recommended by John and Vivienne Rice, C A Hall, David Mead, PM, AM, C and E M Watson, Eric Locker)*

Palmers ~ Tenant Bill Attrill ~ Real ale ~ Meals and snacks ~ Restaurant ~ (01308) 897259 ~ Children in restaurant ~ Open 11-2.30, 6-11; 12-3, 6.30-10.30 Sun ~ Bedrooms: £26B/£40B

CERNE ABBAS ST6601 Map 2
Red Lion ♀

Long St

The licensees of this genteel and neatly kept cottagey inn are carefully and gradually upgrading their furnishings and aim to improve their already good bar food – though not at the cost of becoming too restauranty. There's a relaxed, friendly welcome, and the bar has a handsome wooden counter, wheelback chairs on the green patterned carpet, a good deal of china, plants on tables and two more little areas leading off. Parts of the comfortable building are a lot older than the unassuming mid-Victorian frontage suggests – the fine fireplace in the bar for instance is 16th c. The friendly white terrier is called Gemma. Most of the popular meals are available in a reduced size for those with a smaller appetite: soup (£1.95), sandwiches (from £2.50), filled baked potatoes (from £3.75), good ploughman's (from £4.40), omelettes (from £4.40), pancakes (from £4.95), several vegetarian pasta dishes (£5.45), local trout (£7.60), grilled loin of pork (£8.25) and steaks (from £9.80), with puddings such as apricot strudel (from £1.75). Daily specials might include excellent duck in cider sauce, pheasant breasts in cream and sherry sauce, salmon and seafood lasagne, haunch of venison in red wine, and chicken fricassee in lemon and garlic sauce. Some of the vegetables come from local gardeners and allotments. Well kept Wadworths IPA and 6X and two interesting guests such as Exmoor Hart or Goldfinch's Flashmans Clout on handpump, a decent wine list, with several available by the glass, and a fair choice of malt whiskies. Darts, skittle alley, shove-ha'penny, cribbage, and piped music. There's a secluded flower-filled garden. *(Recommended by Andy and Jill Kassube, Jack and Gemima Valiant, Mrs T A Bizat, Joan and Michel Hooper-Immins, N J Lawless, Anthony Barnes, Cheryl and Keith Roe, Brian and Anna Marsden)*

Free house ~ Licensees Brian and Jane Cheeseman ~ Real ale ~ Meals and snacks ~ (01300) 341441 ~ Children in eating area of bar and in restaurant ~ Open 11-2.30, 6-11; 12-2.30, 7-10.30 Sun

Royal Oak ♀

Long Street

An incredible range of small ornaments covers the stone walls and ceilings of this Tudor pub – local photographs, antique china, brasses and farm tools. The three friendly flagstoned communicating rooms have sturdy oak beams, lots of shiny black panelling, warm winter log fires, and well kept Bass, Flowers Original, Mansfield Bitter, Morlands Old Speckled Hen, Otter Bitter, and Palmers IPA on handpump from the uncommonly long bar counter, 16 wines by the glass, and a decent range of malt whiskies. After a recent chimney fire, the licensees discovered that behind one of the three fireplaces there is an original inglenook with an oven. As well as daily specials such as vegetable lasagne (£4.95), venison casserole (£5.50), seafood au gratin or fresh Portland crab (£5.95), and chicken chasseur (£6.25), the menu might include sandwiches (from £1.75), home-made soup (£1.95), pâté (£2.50), omelettes or ploughman's (from £4.25), home-made lasagne (£5.25), home-cooked ham and egg (£5.50), steaks (from £6.95), and puddings (from £2.45). There are seats and tables in the enclosed back garden, and seats at the front where you can watch the world go by. *(Recommended by P A Legon, JCW, Dr and Mrs J H Hills, DAV, Jack and Gemima Valiant, N J Lawless, Joan and Michel Hooper-Immins, Simon and Jane Williams, Tim and Ann Meaden, Galen Strawson, Mr and Mrs J Boler, Jane Warren, David Holloway, Anthony Barnes)*

Free house ~ Licensees Brendan and Liz Malone ~ Real ale ~ Meals and snacks ~ Children in eating area of bar ~ (01300) 341797 ~ Open 11-3, 5-11; 12-3, 6-10.30 Sun

nr CHIDEOCK SY4292 Map 1
Anchor
Seatown; signposted off A35 from Chideock

It's always rewarding to come across a pub that doesn't just rely on its lovely position, but is run by licensees who work hard at making it an all round winner – this is just such a place. The setting is splendid as it is just a few steps from a nearly idyllic cove beach and nestles dramatically beneath the 617 foot Golden Cap pinnacle – it almost straddles the Dorset Coast path, too. New seats and tables on the spacious front terrace are ideally placed for lovely sea and cliff views, but you'll have to get there pretty early in summer to bag a spot. Our own preference is to visit out of season, when the crowds have gone and the cosy little bars seem especially snug. The two small rooms have warming winter fires, some sea pictures and lots of interesting local photographs, a few fossils and shells, simple but comfortable seats around neat tables, and low white-planked ceilings; the family room and a further corner of the bar are no smoking, and there are friendly animals (especially the cats). Service is charming and obliging whatever time of year you go. Good bar food includes quite a few fresh fish dishes as daily specials such as cod in parsley sauce (£5.75), monkfish kebabs or fish pie (£5.95), cod in thai sauce (£6.50), whole local plaice (£7.95), bass (£8.45), and half local lobster (£8.50); from the menu there might be home-made soup (£2.75), sandwiches (from £1.95, crab £3.75), filled baked potatoes (from £3.25), vegetable, chicken or meaty burgers (£3.75), ploughman's (£3.95), good ham and egg (£4.75), pizzas (from £4.95), steak and kidney pie (£5.45), hot spicy chicken breast (£5.95), evening steak (£8.75), and children's dishes (from £2.45). Well kept Palmers 200, Bridport, IPA and Tally Ho on handpump, under light blanket pressure in winter only; freshly squeezed orange juice, and a decent little wine list. Darts, shove-ha'penny, table skittles, cribbage, dominoes, fruit machine (summer only), a carom board, and piped, mainly classical, music. There are fridges and toasters in the bedrooms so you can make your own breakfast and eat it looking out over the sea. The licensees now also run the Ferry at Salcombe. *(Recommended by C A Hall, Jo and Gary Charlton, Jeff Davies, Peter and Audrey Dowsett, Lynn Sharpless, Bob Eardley, Eric Locker, George Atkinson, Trevor Swindells, JM, SM, Michael Graubart, John and Sally Clarke, Mark Matthewman, Jeremy Condliffe, E A George, M Carr, Niki and Terry Pursey, Giles Quick, Clem Stephens, Stephen and Julie Brown, P Gillbe, Marjorie and David Lamb, Ted George, D G Clarke, Mr and Mrs D Towle)*

Palmers ~ Tenants David and Sadie Miles ~ Real ale ~ Meals and snacks (12-9.30 during summer; not winter Sun evenings or 25 Dec) ~ (01297) 489215 ~ Well behaved children welcome ~ Folk, blues or jazz Sat evenings ~ Open 11-11; 11-2.30, 7-11 in winter; 12-10.30 Sun; closed evening 25 Dec ~ Bedrooms: £17.50/£35

nr CHRISTCHURCH SZ1696 Map 2
Fishermans Haunt
Winton: B3347 Ringwood road nearly 3 miles N of Christchurch

The quiet back garden of this creeper-covered hotel has tables among the shrubs, roses and other flowers, and is close to weirs on the river; the building looks especially good at night when the fairy lights are lit. The interconnecting rooms are filled with a variety of furnishings on a heavily patterned carpet and eye-catching adornments, from copper, brass and plates to stuffed fish and fishing pictures, and oryx and reindeer heads. At one end of the chain of rooms big windows look out on the neat front garden, and at the other there's a fruit machine and video game; the restaurant and one bar lounge are no smoking. Good value straightforward bar food includes soup (£2), sandwiches (from £2.25; toasties from £2.75), filled baked potatoes (from £3.25), salads (from £4.95), steak and kidney pie or mushroom and nut fettucine (£5.25), and children's dishes (£2.95). Well kept Bass, Gales HSB, and Ringwood Fortyniner on handpump, and lots of country wines; cheerful staff. *(Recommended by Mrs M A Newman, D P and J A Sweeney, P Gillbe, Wayne Brindle; more reports please)*

George Gale & Co Ltd ~ Manager Kevin A Crowley ~ Real ale ~ Meals and snacks (till 10) ~ Restaurant ~ Children welcome ~ (01202) 477283 ~ Open 10.30-2.30, 5-11; 10.30-11 Sat; 12-10.30 Sun ~ Bedrooms: £42B/£60B

CHURCH KNOWLE (Isle of Purbeck) SY9481 Map 2
New Inn ♀

Beautifully restored after a fire last year, this partly thatched 16th-c pub is run with great care by the helpful licensee. The two main bar areas are nicely furnished with farmhouse chairs and tables and lots of bric-a-brac on the walls, and there's a log fire at each end; the dining lounge has a good relaxed atmosphere. Fresh fish is delivered daily and dishes might include a hearty bouillabaisse, moules marinières (£5.50), fresh fillets of Cornish hake (£5.50), local trout (£6.65), Brixham plaice (£6.90), crab salad (£7.50), big haddock in beer batter (very popular, £7.75), whole lemon sole (£9.95), and dover sole (£12.95); also, sandwiches (from £2), much liked home-made blue vinney soup (£2.35; the crab with cream and brandy is popular, £3), ploughman's (from £4.25), very good Dorset roast lamb or home-made steak and kidney pie (£5.50), spinach and ricotta cheese cannelloni (£5.95), game pie (£7), chicken tikka masala (£7.25), and puddings such as spotted dick, blackberry and apple pie or treacle tart (£2.95). Well kept Flowers Original and Wadworths 6X and a changing guest beer on handpump, a dozen or so very reasonably priced wines all available in two sizes of glass, and around 20 malt whiskies and bourbons; skittle alley, darts, and piped music. When the local post office closed recently this became the first pub in the county to serve as local village post office and shop, and you can generally buy locally made cheese to take away. You can hire the skittle alley for functions. Plenty of tables in the good-sized garden, which has fine views of the Purbeck hills. No dogs; camping in two fields at the back but you need to book beforehand; good provision for the disabled. *(Recommended by E A George, Derek Patey, Eric Locker, Andrew Rogers, Amanda Milsom, Ian and Nita Cooper, DAV, M G Hart, David Holloway, Hanns P Golez)*

Greenalls ~ Tenant Maurice Estop ~ Meals and snacks ~ Restaurant ~ (01929) 480357 ~ Children in eating area of bar ~ Open 10-3, 6(7 in mid-winter)-11; 12-3, 6-11 Sun; closed Mon Jan-March

COLEHILL SU0302 Map 2
Barley Mow

From roundabout junction of A31 Ferndown bypass and B3073 Wimborne rd, follow Colehill signpost up Middlehill Rd, pass Post Office, and at church turn right into Colehill Lane; Ordnance Survey Sheet 195 map reference 032024

The original part of this pretty partly thatched and partly tiled pub dates back 400 years when it was built as a drover's cottage. The comfortable beamed main bar has a good fire in the huge brick fireplace, attractively moulded oak panelling, and is decorated with some Hogarth prints; the cat is called Misty. Good food, using home grown herbs, includes open sandwiches (from £2.95), filled baked potatoes (from £3.50), chicken tikka (£3.75), ploughman's (£4.25), broccoli, leek and stilton pie (£5.25), lasagne (£5.75), rabbit or steak in ale pies (£5.95), red mullet fillets with a lemon and caper butter or chicken in a creamy mushroom sauce (£6.95), and steaks (from £7.95); they also offer smaller appetite dishes like salmon fishcakes (£2.50), spaghetti bolognese (£3.50), and ham and egg or shepherd's pie (£3.75). The family dining area is no smoking. Well kept Badger Best and Tanglefoot, and Gribble Black Adder II on handpump; fruit machine and piped music. The pub is particularly attractive in summer, when there are colourful tubs of flowers in front, and more flowers in hanging baskets set off vividly against the whitewash. At the back is a pleasant and enclosed big lawn sheltered by oak trees; boules; good nearby walks. *(Recommended by M J Dowdy, Maurice Southon, A E Brace, B and K Hypher, John Davies)*

Badger ~ Managers Bruce and Sue Cichocki ~ Real ale ~ Meals and snacks ~ Children in family room ~ Singer/guitarist every other Wednesday ~ Open 11-3, 5.30-11; 12-3, 7-10.30 Sun

CORFE CASTLE (Isle of Purbeck) SY9681 Map 2
Fox ◖

West Street, off A351; from town centre, follow dead-end Car Park sign behind church

As parts of this characterful pub are made from the same stone as the little town's ruined castle (easily one of the most dramatic in the country) it must therefore be just as old. There's a pre-1300 stone fireplace, and another alcove has further ancient stonework and a number of fossils. An ancient well was discovered in the lounge bar during restoration and is now on display, under glass and effectively lit from within. The tiny front bar has small tables and chairs squeezed in, a painting of the castle in its prime among other pictures above the panelling, old-fashioned iron lamps, and hatch service. Bar food includes sandwiches (from £1.95), home-made soup (£1.90), filled baked potatoes (from £3.20), ploughman's (from £3.50), home-made steak and kidney pie, fresh cod or sweet and sour vegetable stir fry (£4.75), steaks (from £7.20), daily specials like lamb rogan josh or cajun chicken (£4.75) or turkey caribbean (£6.20), and puddings (from £2.05). Well kept Eldridge Pope Thomas Hardy and Royal Oak, Gibbs Mew Bishops Tipple, Greene King Abbot, Ind Coope Burton and Wadworths 6X tapped from the cask. Reached by a pretty flower-hung side entrance, the garden is divided into secluded areas by flowerbeds and a twisted apple tree, and really comes into its own in summer. The countryside surrounding this National Trust village is worth exploring, and there's a local museum opposite. No children. *(Recommended by Stephen Brown, D Eberlin, David Carr, Eric Locker, B and K Hypher, James and Lynne House, Howard England, David Holloway, Hanns P Golez, Chris Westmoreland, Ann and Colin Hunt, Richard Siebert)*

Free house ~ Licensees Miss A L Brown and G B White ~ Real ale ~ Meals and snacks ~ (01929) 480449 ~ Open 11-3, 6.30-11; 12-3, 7-10.30 Sun

Greyhound

A351

The garden of this bustling old pub, bordering the castle moat, is now finished and offers fine views of both the battlements and the surrounding Purbeck hills, and the courtyard (which opens onto the castle bridge) has lots of pretty climbing and flowering shrubs. The licensees have discovered that this was originally two cottages built before 1570, and a stable at the back has some 12th-c timbers and stone. The three small low-ceilinged areas of the main bar have mellowed oak panelling and lots of paintings, brasses, and old photographs of the town on the walls. Popular bar food includes filled rolls (from £1.50), filled baked potatoes (from £2.75; local crab £3.75), ploughman's (from £3.25), home-made pizzas (from £3.50), home-made chilli con carne (£4), home-made steak in ale pie (£5.95), daily specials such as home-made faggots in rich onion gravy (£4.75), Scotch salmon steaks in a hollandaise sauce (£5.50), Scotch rump steak (£7.95), and local bass (£8.50), puddings (£2.50), and children's meals; Sunday roast beef or pork (two courses £5.75), and afternoon teas. Well kept Boddingtons, Flowers Original, local Poole Best, and a guest beer on handpump. Sensibly placed darts, pool, cribbage, dominoes, Purbeck shove-ha'penny on a 5ft mahogany board, and piped music. *(Recommended by David Carr, Stephen Brown, Kath Wetherill, Hanns P Golez, Derek Patey, David Mead, James and Jojo Newman, Brian and Anna Marsden, Chris Westmoreland)*

Whitbreads ~ Lease: Mike and Louisa Barnard ~ Real ale ~ Meals and snacks ~ (01929) 480205 ~ Children in eating area of bar and in family room ~ Folk music Sun lunchtime and some Sats ~ Open 11-11; 12-10.30 Sun

CORSCOMBE ST5105 Map 2
Fox ⦿ � ◖

On outskirts, towards Halstock

Although the very good food in this cosy thatched pub does attract a great many people, it has retained a real pubby atmosphere where locals can comfortably drop in for just a drink. The daily specials are what people enjoy most: wild mushroom risotto (£4.50), grilled duck liver salad with onion marmalade (£4.75), lots of fish like flash-fried squid with garlic, chilli, lemon and basil (£5.25), whole cracked Lyme Bay crab (£7.95), cajun black-cooked fillet of brill (£9.75) or monkfish with roast red pepper salsa (£10.50), local wild rabbit braised with mustard, shallots, wine and cream (£8.75), roast rack of Dorset lamb with rosemary gravy (£12.75), and puddings such as caramelised apple and pear tart, dark chocolate mousse or crème caramel (£2.95); filled french bread, too. No chips or microwaves. Well kept Exmoor Ale, Fullers London Pride and Shepherd Neame Spitfire on handpump, a thoughtful wine list, local cider and home-made elderflower cordial, damson vodka, and sloe gin. The flagstoned room on the right has lots of beautifully polished copper pots, pans and teapots, harness hanging from the beams, small Leech hunting prints and Snaffles prints, Spy cartoons of fox-hunting gentlemen, a long scrubbed pine table (a highly polished smaller one is tucked behind the door), and an open fire. In the left-hand room there are built-in wall benches, candles in champagne bottles on the cloth-covered or barrel tables, an assortment of chairs, lots of horse prints, antlers on the beams, two glass cabinets with a couple of stuffed owls in each, and an L-shaped wall settle by the inglenook fireplace; darts, dominoes, bridge on Thursday, backgammon, and winter Sunday quiz. A flower-filled conservatory has a huge oak table. The labrador Bramble loves a bit of attention. There are seats across the quiet village lane, on a lawn by the little stream. This is a nice area for walks. *(Recommended by N Latham, James and Lynne House, Desmond and Pat Morris, Nigel Wilkinson, Tim and Ann Meaden, E A George, Jo and Gary Charlton, LM, Stephen and Julie Brown, Roger Price)*

Free house ~ Licensee Martyn Lee ~ Real ale ~ Meals and snacks (not 25 Dec) ~ (01935) 891330 ~ Well behaved children welcome ~ Occasional piano and saxophone player ~ Open 12-2.30, 7-11; 12-4, 7-11 Sat; 12-4, 7-10.30 Sun; closed 25 Dec

CRANBORNE SU0513 Map 2
Fleur-de-Lys 🛏

B3078 N of Wimborne Minster

The comfortable bedrooms in this consistently welcoming old inn (run by Mr Hancock for 20 years now) are much enjoyed by readers – indeed, this is where Thomas Hardy stayed while writing *Tess of the d'Urbervilles* – if you fork left past the church you can follow the pretty downland track that he must have visualised Tess taking home to 'Trentridge' (actually Pentridge), after dancing in what's now the garage. A Gothic arch and a pair of ancient stone pillars are said to have come from the ruins of a nearby monastery, while the walls are lined with historical documents and mementoes of some of the other people who have stayed here over the centuries, from Hanging Judge Jeffreys to Rupert Brooke, whose poem about the pub takes pride of place above the fireplace. The oak-panelled lounge bar is attractively modernised, and there's also a more simply furnished beamed public bar with well kept Badger Best and Tanglefoot on handpump, farm cider, and some good malt whiskies. Well liked bar food includes home-made soup (£1.95), sandwiches (from £2.25), ploughman's (£3.75), nutty mushroom layer (£4.95), home-made steak pie (£5.75), local trout (£6.95), steaks (from £8.25), daily specials such as chicken, gammon and mushroom pie (£5.45), minted lamb casserole or prawn and crab mornay (£6.95), and pork medallions with a port and stilton sauce (£8.95), puddings like treacle tart or banoffi pie (from £2.60), and children's dishes (£2.95); the 3-course set menu including a glass of wine (£12.95) is popular; best to arrive early for Sunday lunch. Darts, dominoes, cribbage, fruit machine, and piped music. There are swings and a slide on the lawn behind the car park. *(Recommended by Mike and Heather Watson, Tim and Ann Meaden, Colin Fisher, John and Mary Bartolf, P and M Rudlin, Joy and Peter Heatherley, Ian Jones, Dr and Mrs A H Young)*

Badger ~ Tenant Charles Hancock ~ Real ale ~ Meals and snacks ~ (01725) 517282 ~ Children in eating area of bar and in restaurant ~ Open 10.30-3, 6(7 winter)-11; 12-3, 7-10.30 Sun ~ Bedrooms: £24(£30B)/£40(£45B)

DORCHESTER SY6890 Map 2
Kings Arms 🛏️
High East St

This pleasantly old-fashioned Georgian coaching inn has close associations with Nelson, and Thomas Hardy's *Mayor of Casterbridge*. The spaciously comfortable bar has some interesting old maps and pictures, a capacious fireplace, and plenty of tables full of eaters enjoying the well presented fairly straightforward bar food: soup (£1.75), sandwiches (from £2.45), ploughman's or chilli (£5.45), lasagne (£5.75), fish and chips (£6), steak, kidney and mushroom pie (£6.50), grilled salmon (£7.60), and three vegetarian dishes; they also have evening grills and a coffee shop. Well kept Boddingtons, Courage Directors and Flowers Original on handpump, a range of malt whiskies and fruit wines from the long mahogany bar counter; consistently friendly service from neatly dressed staff. Fruit machine, piped music, and a quiz night every second Tuesday. *(Recommended by Simon Penny, J F M and M West, Miss R Kingsmill, JM, SM, Jack and Gemima Valiant, Janet and Colin Roe, David Carr, D B Jenkin, Brian and Anna Marsden, Mark Matthewman, Stephen and Julie Brown, Anthony Barnes)*

Greenalls ~ Manager Stephen Walmsley ~ Real ale ~ Meals and snacks ~ Restaurants ~ (01305) 265353 ~ Children welcome away from public bar ~ Live band Thurs evening ~ Open 11-2.30, 6-11; 11-11 Fri and Sat ~ Bedrooms: £49.20B/£54.15B

EAST CHALDON SY7983 Map 2
Sailors Return
Village signposted from A352 Wareham—Dorchester; from village green, follow Dorchester, Weymouth signpost; note that the village is also known as Chaldon Herring; Ordnance Survey sheet 194, map reference 790834

In a quiet spot close to Lulworth Cove, this popular long, low whitewashed pub has benches, picnic tables and log seats on the grass in front that look down over cow pastures to the village. From nearby West Chaldon a bridleway leads across to join the Dorset Coast Path by the National Trust cliffs above Ringstead Bay. The cheerfully welcoming bar still keeps much of its original character, and the newer part has open beams showing the roof above, uncompromisingly plain and unfussy furnishings, and old notices for decoration; the dining area has solid old tables in nooks and crannies. Even when busy, service remains as good as ever: sandwiches, filled baked potatoes, and popular daily specials such as fisherman's or game pie (£5.25), whole gammon hock (£6.75), whole local crab (£6.95), whole local plaice (£7.50), and half a shoulder of lamb (£8.95); best to get here early if you plan to eat, especially on Sunday, when the good value roast is popular. Half the restaurant is no smoking. Well kept Exmoor Gold, Fullers IPA and London Pride, and Wadworths 6X on handpump, country wines, and farm cider. Darts, dominoes, and piped music. *(Recommended by Tim and Ann Meaden, James and Lynne House, Alan and Barbara Mence, Pat and Robert Watt, JM, SM, Marjorie and David Lamb, David Carr, Sue Cutler, Chris and Margaret Southon, Sue and David Heaton, John and Joan Nash, Ian Phillips)*

Free house ~ Licensees Bob and Pat Hodson ~ Real ale ~ Meals and snacks ~ Restaurant ~ (01305) 853847 ~ Children in restaurant ~ Open 11-2.30, 6.30-11; 12-2.30, 6-10.30 Sun

EAST KNIGHTON SY8185 Map 2
Countryman 🛏️ 🍴
Just off A352 Dorchester—Wareham; OS Sheet 194 map reference 811857

Very well run by friendly, helpful people, this bustling pub is very popular. The neatly comfortable, long main bar has a mixture of tables, wheelback chairs and relaxing sofas, and a fire at either end. It opens into several other smaller areas, including a no-smoking family room, a games bar with pool and darts, and a carvery (£9.95 for a roast and pudding). Generous helpings of bar food include sandwiches or filled rolls (from £1.90), home-made soup (£2.10), omelettes (from £3.25), ploughman's (from £4.50), vegetable curry (£5.25), tomato and lentil lasagne (£5.50), sardines in garlic butter (£6.25), gammon and pineapple (£8.25), steaks (from £10), daily specials like chicken curry or steak and kidney pie (£5.75), home-made puddings (£2.50) and children's meals (from £2.45); nice breakfasts. Well kept Courage Best and Directors, Ringwood Best and Old Thumper, Wadworths 6X, and a rotating guest like Morlands Old Speckled Hen on handpump; farm cider, good choice of wines, and courteous well trained staff; piped music. There are tables and children's play equipment out in the garden as well as some toys inside; dogs welcome. *(Recommended by James and Lynne House, P and J Caunt, Bruce Bird, Tim and Ann Meaden, Mr and Mrs N A Spink, GDS, E H and R F Warner, Stephen, Julie and Hayley Brown, Marjorie and David Lamb, David Carr, John and Beryl Knight, Ann and Colin Hunt, Brian and Anna Marsden, Nigel Clifton, Andrea Carr)*

Free house ~ Licensees Jeremy and Nina Evans ~ Real ale ~ Meals and snacks ~ Restaurant ~ (01305) 852666 ~ Children welcome ~ Open 11-3, 6-11; 12-4, 6.30-10.30 Sun; closed 25 Dec ~ Bedrooms: £38B/£48B

EAST MORDEN SY9195 Map 2
Cock & Bottle 🍷 ◀
B3075 between A35 and A31 W of Poole

This popular dining pub is divided into several communicating areas, with a warmly rustic feel – heavy rough beams, some stripped ceiling boards, some squared panelling, a nice mix of old furnishings in various sizes and degrees of antiquity, small Victorian prints and some engaging bric-a-brac. There's a good log fire, intimate corners each with just a couple of tables, plenty of no-smoking space, and a separate proper public bar (with piped music, dominoes, a fruit machine and a sensibly placed darts alcove); this in turn leads on to yet another dining room, again with plenty of character. You have to order the food course by course from the bar: it's good, with plenty of fish, poultry and game in season, and might include sandwiches (from £1.75), home-made pâté (£4.25), faggots with onion gravy (£5.25), ploughman's (£5.25), home-made beefburger topped with smoked bacon and stilton (£5.75), leek and mushroom crumble (£6.50), Scotch sirloin steak (£9.95), and daily specials such as wild mushroom and ricotta cheese in filo pastry with a spicy plum sauce (£6.50), home-made curries (£6.75), steak and kidney pudding (£7.25), large whole plaice with parsley butter (£8.50), red bream with cajun spices and stir-fried vegetables with a light soy dressing (£9.25), roast partridge (£10.25), puddings like banana and toffee crumble or honey and walnut flan (£3.25), and children's dishes (from £2.50). Well kept Badger IPA, Best and Tanglefoot on handpump, a good choice of decent house wines, cordial service (though when it's busy food can take a time to come); spotless lavatories, facilities for the disabled. There are a few picnic tables outside, a garden area, and an adjoining field with a nice pastoral outlook. *(Recommended by E G Parish, Jack Triplett, John and Joan Nash, James and Lynne House, WHBM, Mr and Mrs D Johnson, Chris Westmoreland)*

Badger ~ Tenant Peter Meadley ~ Real ale ~ Meals and snacks ~ Restaurant ~ (01929) 459238 ~ Children in eating area of bar ~ Open 11-2.30(3 Sat), 6-11; 12-3, 7-10.30 Sun

EVERSHOT ST5704 Map 2
Acorn ⇌
Village signposted from A37 8 miles S of Yeovil

This friendly village inn was the model for Thomas Hardy's pub the Sow & Acorn in Evershead in *Tess of the d'Urbervilles*. It's a nice village to stay in and there are lots of good surrounding walks. The comfortable L-shaped lounge bar has tapestry covered wooden benches, two fine old fireplaces, and copies of the inn's deeds going back to the 17th c on the partly hessian-covered stone walls; another lounge has a woodburning stove and comfortable sofas and armchairs. Bar food includes soup (£1.95), sandwiches (from £2.25), ploughman's (from £4.50), a roast of the day (£5.95), thai dishes like sizzling prawns in ginger and garlic or bang-bang chicken with cashew nuts (around £7), steak in ale pie (£7.20), venison, rabbit and pigeon in madeira, vegetable wellington or noisettes of lamb (all £9.45), and puddings like popular Dorset apple cake (£3.25); children's meals (from £2.95); good breakfasts. Well kept Adnams Broadside, Bass, Butcombe Bitter, Oakhill Bitter, and Wadworths 6X on handpump; pool, darts, skittle alley, dominoes, cribbage and piped music. Outside, there's a terrace with dark oak furniture. There are lots of good walks around. *(Recommended by John and Joan Calvert, James and Lynne House, Michael and Hazel Lyons, Tim and Ann Meaden, Mike and Heather Watson, David Lamb, Gwyneth and Salvo Spadaro-Dutturi)*

Free house ~ Licensees Keith and Denise Morley ~ Real ale ~ Meals and snacks ~ Restaurant ~ (01935) 83228 ~ Children in family room and restaurant ~ Open 11-2.30, 6.30-11; 12-3, 7-10.30 Sun ~ Bedrooms: £55B/£80B

FARNHAM ST9515 Map 2
Museum 🍺 ♀ 🍴

Village signposted off A354 Blandford Forum—Salisbury

It would be easy to drive past this unassuming looking pub, which would be a great pity because you would miss out on some very good cooking by the ever-jovial landlord. As well as the usual bar meals there's a wide range of daily specials, which at lunchtime might include home-made minestrone or chilled tomato and basil soups (from £2.75), butterfly prawns with sweet and sour sauce (£4.95), scrambled eggs with smoked salmon (£5.25), roast vegetables with polenta (£6.25), home-made fish pie (£6.95), gammon steak with parsley sauce (£7.25); in the evening there may be grilled aubergine with parmesan and rocket or cassoulet of snails (£5.25), pork provençale (£10.95), osso bucco (£11.25), salmon fishcakes with crab sauce (£11.95), and breast of duck with olives and fresh mango (£12.25). The attractive Coopers Bar has green cloth-cushioned seats set into walls and windows, local pictures by Robin Davidson, an inglenook fireplace with bread oven, and piped classical music. Very well kept Wadworths 6X and changing guests such as Butcombe, Fullers London Pride, and Greene King IPA on handpump, around 20 malt whiskies, and a large wine list (the licensee may like to recommend one for you). There's a most attractive small brick-walled dining conservatory, leading out to a sheltered terrace with white tables under cocktail parasols, and beyond an arched wall is a garden with swings and a colourful tractor. The bedrooms are in converted former stables. *(Recommended by Gwen and Peter Andrews, Dave Braisted, Chris Elford, Phil and Heidi Cook, B and K Hypher, Ian Phillips, J Morris, Dr and Mrs M Beale, Joy and Peter Heatherley, John and Mary Bartolf)*

Free house ~ Licensee John Barnes ~ Real ale ~ Meals and snacks (service stops at 1.45 lunchtime) ~ Restaurant ~ (01725) 516261 ~ Children welcome ~ Live music 3rd Thurs of month ~ Open 11-3, 6-11; 12-3, 7-10.30 Sun; cl 25 Dec ~ Bedrooms: £45B/£65B

GODMANSTONE SY6697 Map 2
Smiths Arms

A352 N of Dorchester

Measuring just 12 by 4 metres, this 15th-c thatched building is absolutely tiny (and, not surprisingly, one of the smallest pubs in the country). There are only six tables inside, and they couldn't add any more even if they wanted to, though further seats and tables are set outside on a crazy-paved terrace or on the grassy mound by the narrow River Cerne. The little bar has some antique waxed and polished small pews hugging the walls (there's also one elegant little high-backed settle), long wooden stools and chunky tables, National Hunt racing pictures and some brass plates on the walls, and an open fire. Well kept Ringwood Best tapped from casks behind the bar; friendly, helpful staff (the landlord is quite a character); dominoes, trivia, cribbage and piped music. Simple but tasty home-made food typically includes sandwiches (from £1.70; the roast beef is lovely), giant sausage (£3.10), ploughman's (from £3.50), quiche or chilli con carne (£4.55), a range of salads (from £4.35), home-cooked ham (£5.45), daily specials such as curried prawn lasagne or topside of beef and steak and kidney pie (£5.45) and puddings (£2). A pleasant walk leads over Cowdon Hill to the River Piddle. No children. *(Recommended by Dr and Mrs A K Clarke, James and Lynne House, David Holloway, Jack and Philip Paxton, James Nunns, Mr and Mrs Bonner)*

Free house ~ Licensees John and Linda Foster ~ Real ale ~ Meals and snacks (till 9.45) ~ (01300) 341236 ~ Open 11-3, 6-11; 12-3, 7-10.30 Sun; closed Jan

KINGSTON (Isle of Purbeck) SY9579 Map 2
Scott Arms
B3069

A new licensee has taken over this busy pub and early reports are favourable. The main attraction has to be the views of Corfe Castle and the Purbeck hills from the well kept garden – they are quite magnificent. Inside, the rambling warren-like rooms are capable of absorbing more people than you might think. All have old panelling, stripped stone walls, some fine antique prints and a friendly, chatty feel; an attractive room overlooks the garden, and there's a decent extension well liked by families. Good home-made bar food includes lots of fresh fish from Brixham like lemon or dover sole, john dory or bass (all about £8.95), as well as home-made soup (£2.50), mushrooms in cream and garlic (£3.25), ploughman's (£4.25), steak in Guinness pie (£5.95), lamb and apricot casserole (£6.25), chicken and asparagus (£6.95), puddings (£2.95), and children's meals (£3.75); they do afternoon cream teas in summer. Well kept Greenalls Original, Ringwood Best and a guest like Worthington Best on handpump; darts, fruit machine, and piped music. *(Recommended by JM, SM, S J and C C Davidson, Stephen Brown, B and K Hypher, JDM, KM, Andy and Jill Kassube, Simon and Jane Williams, Stephen, Julie and Hayley Brown, J Boucher, Jeff Davies, DAV, Revd A Nunnerley, Jack and Philip Paxton, David Mead, E G Parish, James and Jojo Newman, Chris Westmoreland; more reports on the new regime please)*

Greenalls ~ Manager Hugh McGill ~ Real ale ~ Meals and snacks ~ (01929) 480270 ~ Children welcome except in one small bar ~ Live entertainment Weds and Thurs evenings ~ Open 11-11; 11-2.30, 6-11 in winter; 12-10.30 Sun ~ Bedrooms: /£40B

LANGTON HERRING SY6182 Map 2
Elm Tree 🐶
Village signposted off B3157

It's the interesting, well prepared daily specials that earn praise from customers in this slate-roofed cottage: creamed fennel and celery soup (£2.65), roasted red pepper and goat's cheese bruschetta (£4.95), pasta with fresh asparagus, leeks and pecorino cheese (£5.25), loin of pork with creamed shallot and rosemary sauce (£8.50), roasted red snapper fillet in Moroccan marinade (£9.25), sirloin steak in a creamed oyster mushroom sauce (£9.75), and puddings such as treacle tart with clotted cream or hot banana fudge biscuit (£2.95). More standard dishes from the bar menu include sandwiches (from £2), soup (£2.50), filled baked potatoes (from £2.50), ploughman's or ciabatta with goat's cheese and tomatoes (£3.75), hot garlic bread filled with hot roast beef (£3.45), lasagne (£6.50), steak and ale pie (£6.95), cider, pork and apple casserole (£7.50) and baked crab mornay (£7.95), puddings like butterscotch banana fritters (from £2.75) and the usual children's menu (from £2.25). There may be a bit of a wait for food when they get busy. The Portland spy ring is said to have met in the main beamed and carpeted rooms, which have walls festooned with copper, brass and bellows, cushioned window seats, red leatherette stools, windsor chairs, and lots of tables; one has some old-fashioned settles and an inglenook. The traditionally furnished extension gives more room for diners. Greenalls Original and a guest such as Wadworths 6X on handpump. Outside in the pretty flower-filled sunken garden are colourful hanging baskets, flower tubs, and tables; a track leads down to the Dorset Coast Path, which here skirts the eight-mile lagoon enclosed by Chesil Beach. *(Recommended by James and Lynne House, Mrs A Wiseman, Richard and Rosemary Hoare, Galen Strawson, David Mead, B and K Hypher, Kim Maidment, Philip Vernon, Jenny and Brian Seller, D Mead, Brian and Anna Marsden, D Eberlin, Dr S Willavoys)*

Greenalls ~ Tenants Roberto D'Agostino, L M Horlock ~ Real ale ~ Meals and snacks ~ (01305) 871257 ~ Children welcome in eating area of bar ~ Open 11-3, 6.30-11

LODERS SY4994 Map 1
Loders Arms 🛏

Off A3066 just N of Bridport; can also be reached off A35 E of Bridport, via Uploders

The good interesting food here is a large part of the reason that this is such a popular place. But it's kept a friendly and unspoilt atmosphere, with an unhurried and relaxed feel even when busy. The smallish long bar, still well used by local people, is welcoming and comfortable, with a log fire, maybe piped classical music, and amiable dogs; well kept Palmers Bridport, 200 and IPA, a good choice of wines, good service. The menu changes daily and might include huge fresh baked french bread (from £3, smoked salmon and cream cheese £3.95), devilled kidneys (£3.95), tiger prawns in garlic or fresh anchovies with tomato and basil salad (£4.25), sausage, mash and onion gravy (£4.95), mushroom and aubergine risotto or lemon and ginger chicken (£5.95), rabbit in cider (£6.95), pork tenderloin with a cream and horseradish sauce (£8.95), venison steak with gin and juniper berry sauce (£10.95), and puddings like chocolate and brandy mousse, fruit crumbles or apricot pudding (£3). There's a skittle alley; cribbage. This is a pretty stonebuilt village of largely thatched cottages tucked into a sheltered fold of these steep Dorset hills. *(Recommended by Jo and Gary Charlton, Galen Strawson, R C Morgan, Dr B and Mrs P B Baker, Brian and Bett Cox, Simon and Jane Williams, Brian Lister, Hugh Robertson, Roger Price, Frances Pennell, D and J Whitman)*

Palmers ~ Tenants Roger and Helen Flint ~ Real ale ~ Meals and snacks (not Sun evening Nov-end May) ~ Restaurant ~ (01308) 422431 ~ Children welcome until 9pm ~ Open 11.30(11 Sat), 6-11; 12-10.30 Sun ~ Bedrooms: £25S/£35S(£40B)

LYME REGIS SY3492 Map 1
Pilot Boat ♀

Bridge Street

This simple and airy pub has a character that suits the seaside, and is handy for a meal after a day on the beach. The bar is decorated with local pictures, navy and helicopter photographs, lobster-pot lamps, sharks' heads, an interesting collection of local fossils, a model of one of the last sailing ships to use the harbour, and a notable collection of sailors' hat ribands. At the back, there's a long and narrow lounge bar overlooking the little River Lym; skittle alley and piped music. Bar food includes home-made soup (£1.95), sandwiches (from £1.95, crab £2.95), ploughman's (£3.50), crab pâté or sausage and chips (£3.75), steak and kidney pie or nut and mushroom loaf (£5.95), pork and cider casserole (£6.75), whole grilled lemon sole (£9.50), steaks (from £9.50), grilled fish platter (£10.95), daily specials like lentil loaf with leek sauce (£5.25), chicken supreme in a cream and tarragon sauce (£6.95), and poached salmon in creamy lemon sauce (£7.25), and children's dishes (from £1.95, not just burgers and fish fingers). The dining area is no smoking. Well kept Palmers Bridport, IPA and 200 on handpump, and a decent wine. The licensees run another Lyme Regis pub, the Cobb Arms, which has bedrooms. There are seats on a terrace outside. *(Recommended by Stephen, Julie and Hayley Brown, JM, SM, Tim and Ann Meaden, David Gittins, Simon and Jane Williams, Niki and Terry Pursey, Don and Shirley Parrish, Jane Warren, Joan and Michel Hooper-Immins, Mrs Cynthia Archer, Marjorie and David Lamb, M E Wellington, Judith Reay, Chris and Kate Lyons, David Holloway)*

Palmers ~ Tenants Bill and Caroline Wiscombe ~ Real ale ~ Meals and snacks (till 10pm in summer) ~ Restaurant ~ Lyme Regis (01297) 443242 ~ Children welcome ~ Occasional live entertainment ~ Open 11-11; 12-10.30 Sun

MARNHULL ST7718 Map 2
Blackmore Vale
Burton Street; quiet side street

A good mix of people and age groups like to gather in this warmly welcoming old pub. One of the main draws is the enjoyable food, which might include sandwiches or soup (£2.25), prawn and egg mayonnaise (£3.95), ploughman's (£4.25), gammon and egg (£4.95), chilli con carne (£5.85), whole grilled plaice or game pie (£6.95), spicy vegetable salsa (£5.60), lamb and mango curry (£7.45), steaks (from £8.75), daily specials such as various stir fries – chicken in cajun spices, prawn in Chinese green curry sauce, cashew nuts in a sweet and sour sauce, and beef in black bean sauce (all £5.95), and lots of home-made puddings; Friday is fish night, and they offer six good roasts on Sundays (£3.95-£4.25). They will bring your food to the garden, where one of the tables is thatched. The comfortably modernised lounge bar is decorated with fourteen guns and rifles, keys, a few horsebrasses and old brass spigots on the beams, and there's a log fire; one bar is no smoking. Well kept Badger Best and Tanglefoot on handpump, farm cider and a good wine list. Cribbage, dominoes, shove-ha'penny, and a skittle alley. The pub was used by Thomas Hardy in Tess of the D'Urbervilles as the model for Rollivers. No children. *(Recommended by R J Walden, G G Lawrence, Mrs M L Carter, Gregor Macdonald, Lynn Sharpless, Bob Eardley, Joy and Peter Heatherley, C H and P Stride, Derek Wilson, Tony and Wendy Hobden, Anthony Barnes, Mr and Mrs D C Stevens)*

Badger ~ Tenants Roger and Marion Hiron ~ Real ale ~ Meals and snacks (till 10pm) ~ (01258) 820701 ~ Open 11.30-2.30, 6.30-11; 12-3, 7-11 Sun

MILTON ABBAS ST8001 Map 2
Hambro Arms 🍺
Village signposted from A354 SW of Blandford, in Winterborne Whitechurch and Milborne St Andrew

This pretty pub has a beamed front lounge bar with a bow window seat looking down over the attractive village houses, captain's chairs and round tables on the carpet, and in winter an excellent log fire. Well kept Bass and Boddingtons on handpump, and several malt whiskies; darts in the cosy back public bar. Big helpings of good bar food include sandwiches (£1.90), soup (£2.45), ploughman's (£4.30) and daily specials like fresh battered or grilled cod (£6.55), grilled whole plaice, fillet of sea bream, poached salmon or pheasant in mushroom and red wine (£7.65), halibut with white wine and mushroom sauce or venison steaks in a rich madeira sauce (£8.75); roast Sunday lunch (£12.65). The outside terrace has some tables and chairs. The lane which winds gently uphill through the village and between the surrounding woods is lined by lawns and cream-coloured thatched cottages – a 1770s exercise in landscape art. *(Recommended by G G Lawrence, James and Lynne House, Mr and Mrs M Budd, Stephen Brown, Andy and Jill Kassube, Paul Seligman, WHBM, M J Dowdy, J Sheldon, Ken and Jenny Simmonds, E G Parish)*

Greenalls ~ Tenants Ken and Brenda Baines ~ Real ale ~ Meals and snacks ~ Restaurant ~ (01258) 880233 ~ Children in restaurant ~ Open 11-3, 6-11; 12-3, 7-10.30 Sun ~ Bedrooms: £30B/£55B

NETTLECOMBE SY5195 Map 2
Marquis of Lorne 🍺 ▮
Turn E off A3066 Bridport—Beaminster Road 1½ miles N of Bridport. Pass Mangerton Mill and 1m after West Milton go straight across give-way junction. Pub is on left 300 yards up the hill.

The Barretts are exceptionally good licensees. They run a superb pub and make everybody feel like old friends, and their involvement in the local community means the pub remains a proper local even though part of their customers are outsiders. The bustling main bar has a log fire, mahogany panelling and old prints and photographs around its neatly matching chairs and tables; two dining areas lead off, the smaller of which has another log fire and is no smoking. Bar food is very good and popular and might include sandwiches and ploughman's, home-made soup such as curried parsnip or tomato and orange (£2.25), avocado and curried chicken (£3.95), deep-fried brie, mozzarella and camembert with a minted gooseberry dip (£4.25), fresh battered cod or minted lamb chops (£6.95), fresh crab salad (£7.25), peppered rib-eye steak (£9.25), four vegetarian dishes, and puddings such as treacle tart or sticky toffee pudding; good vegetables, and they may have home-made chutneys and marmalade for sale. Well kept Palmers Bridport and IPA on handpump with their 200 tapped straight from the cask, and good wine list with around eight by the glass. A wooden-floored snug has darts, cribbage and table skittles; the piped music is mainly classical. Outside, the summer hanging baskets are pretty, and the big garden has a rustic style play area among the picnic tables under its apple trees. It's quite a tortuous drive to get to the pub, but you couldn't hope for a more pleasant journey, through lovely peaceful countryside. The earth-fort of Eggardon Hill is close by. *(Recommended by Philip Cooper, C A Hall, Peter and Audrey Dowsett, Dr and Mrs J H Hills, J R Williams, Galen Strawson, Mick and Hillary Stiffin, Michael Graubart, Mrs M Rolfe, Brian Lister, Jo and Gary Charlton, Simon and Jane Williams, George Atkinson, Desmond and Pat Morris, Lynn Sharpless, Bob Eardley, Mrs G W Green, Mr and Mrs J Lyons, Avril Hanson, Niki and Terry Pursey, Adrian Wood)*

Palmers ~ Tenants Ian and Anne Barrett ~ Real ale ~ Meals and snacks ~ (01308) 485236 ~ Children in eating area of bar (must be over 10 if staying) ~ Open 11-2.30, 6(6.30 winter)-11; 12-3, 7-10.30 Sun ~ Bedrooms: £35S/£55S

NORDEN HEATH SY9483 Map 2
Halfway 🍺

Furzebrook – A351 Wareham—Corfe Castle

Set back from the road, this pretty mainly thatched 16th-c house has recently been extended, yet keeps a pleasantly homely feel – an excellent example of sensitive planning, combined with genuinely warm-hearted management. The convivial carpeted back bar, decorated with hops and hop sacks, has a narrow little room leading snugly off, and a hatch to serve a flagstoned front room with shiny tables and wheelback chairs, plates over its big fireplace (log fire in winter, flowers in summer), and a boarded ceiling. On the right as you go in, another pair of front rooms have a pleasant mix of tables and small dining chairs on their carpet, local pictures, bird prints and colourful plates on stripped stone walls, another log fire. The friendly and attentive landlord is a Greek Cypriot, and bar food includes a lot of Greek dishes, from snacky ones that go well with drinks or club together to make a meal (good lounza and loukanika, for instance), to proper home-made versions of moussaka (£6.25), afelia (£6.75), and a very slow-cooked kleftiko (£7.50) and so forth; or you can have a good selection of mezedes (£12.75 each, for two or more people). A wide choice of more orthodox food with light meals (from £3.75), and a dish of the day (£5). Well kept Flowers IPA, Poole Best and Wye Valley on handpump, with Ringwood Best and Wadworths 6X tapped from casks behind the bar, inexpensive wines, good coffee, piped Greek music; very pleasant service. Darts and cribbage. There are some tables out in a sheltered back courtyard, more out in front. *(Recommended by Chris Westmoreland, James and Lynne House, Derek Patey, G R Sunderland)*

Free house ~ Licensees George and Mary Evripides ~ Real ale ~ Meals and snacks ~ (01929) 480402 ~ Children in eating area of bar ~ Open 11-3, 6-11

OSMINGTON MILLS SY7341 Map 2
Smugglers 🍷

Village signposted off A353 NE of Weymouth

The sea is just a short stroll away from this partly thatched inn – it was Osmington Mills beach that Constable painted in the Weymouth Bay picture (hanging in National Gallery). There are stunning clifftop views to Weymouth and Portland from its car park. Inside, the pub is well run and spacious, with shiny black panelling and woodwork dividing the relaxing bar into cosy, friendly areas. Soft red lantern-lights give an atmospheric hue to the stormy sea pictures and big wooden blocks and tackle on the walls, and there are logs burning in an open stove. Some seats are tucked into alcoves and window embrasures, with one forming part of an upended boat. As well as a snack menu with home-made soup (£2), filled soft french sticks (from £3.25), ploughman's (£4.50), and home-made steak, kidney and mushroom pie (£6), the popular daily specials include tandoori chicken legs (£4), lovely spare ribs (£4.50), potted fresh lobster with a thermidor sauce (£6.50), and lots of fish like roast monkfish with bacon on a sweet pepper and vermouth cream sauce, local crab, grilled bass on fresh tomato pasta with a cider vinegar dressing, grilled grey mullet with a fresh mango and chilli salsa, whole lemon sole, and brill fillet with a tomato and basil cream sauce (between £10-£12). Service stays efficient and friendly even when they're busy. Over half the restaurant area is no smoking. Well kept Courage Best and Directors, Marstons Pedigree, Quay Bombshell Bitter, Ruddles County, Wadworths 6X, and guest beers on handpump, and about six wines by the glass. Darts, pool and fruit machine are kept sensibly out of the way; also cribbage and shut-the-box – and piped music. There are picnic tables out on crazy paving by a little stream, with a thatched summer bar and a good play area over on a steep lawn; barbecues out here in summer. It gets very busy in high season (there's a holiday settlement just up the lane). *(Recommended by J F M West, Kath Wetherill, Tony Scott, P Eberlin, M Rutherford, Andy and Jill Kassube, Simon and Jane Williams, Simon Penny, Dr and Mrs A H Young, Eddie Edwards, A Smith, Clive Gilbert, Ian Phillips, PM, AM, J Morris, Joan and Michel Hooper-Immins)*

Free house ~ Licensee Bill Bishop ~ Real ale ~ Meals and snacks ~ Restaurant ~ (01305) 833125 ~ Children in eating area of bar and in restaurant ~ Occasional Sunday lunchtime jazz or steel bands in summer ~ Open 11-11; 11-2.30, 6.30-11 in winter; 12-10.30 Sun ~ Bedrooms: £30B/£65B

PIDDLEHINTON SY7197 Map 1
Thimble

B3143

The setting for this pretty thatched pub, tucked away down winding lanes and approached by a little footbridge over the River Piddle, is charming. And the flower-filled garden (attractively floodlit at night) is a most restful place to enjoy lunch. Inside, the neatly kept and friendly low-beamed bar is simpler than the exterior suggests, although nicely spacious so that in spite of drawing quite a lot of people in the summer, it never feels too crowded. There's a handsome open stone fireplace, and a deep well. Tasty bar food includes sandwiches, fresh pasta and fresh fish dishes (from £5), chilli con carne (£5.10), various curries (£5.50), good game pie, cajun spiced chicken or lamb (£6.55), steak and oyster pudding (£7.95), steaks (from £9), and three Sunday roasts (£5.75). Well kept Badger Best and Hard Tackle, Eldridge Pope Hardy Country, and Ringwood Old Thumper on handpump, along with farm cider and quite a few malt whiskies; friendly service; darts, shove-ha'penny, dominoes, cribbage, trivia, and piped music. *(Recommended by Ian and Nita Cooper, Galen Strawson, Pat and Robert Watt, Mrs M Rolfe, Richard and Rosemary Hoare, Tim and Ann Meaden, Jack and Philip Paxton, Mr and Mrs M Cody, M L and G Clarke, R H Rowley, Nigel Clifton, Glen Mitton, K H Frostick, James Nunns, Joy and Peter Heatherley, H and E Simpson)*

Free house ~ Licensees N R White and V J Lanfear ~ Real ale ~ Meals and snacks ~ (01300) 348270 ~ Children in eating area of bar ~ Open 12-2.30, 7-11(10.30 Sun); closed 25 Dec

We mention bottled beers and spirits only if there is something unusual about them – imported Belgian real ales, say, or dozens of malt whiskies; so do please let us know about them in your reports.

PLUSH ST7102 Map 2
Brace of Pheasants ⊕
Village signposted from B3143 N of Dorchester at Piddletrenthide
Dorset Dining Pub of the Year

Carefully run by welcoming staff, this long, low 16th-c thatched pub is popular with lots of locals as well as visitors. The wide choice of good, enjoyable bar food might include soup (£2.25), crab savoury (£3.50), ploughman's (from £3.95), ham and egg (£5.25), venison sausages (£5.75), warm salad of scallops (£5.95), liver, bacon and onions or pies such as steak and kidney or delicious lamb and rosemary (£6.75), and perhaps some dishes borrowed from the restaurant such as grilled salmon with lime and ginger butter (£10.75) or roast monkfish with a dijon and prawn cream sauce (£11.75); good children's menu (from £1.50). The restaurant and family room are no smoking. The airy beamed bar has good solid tables, windsor chairs, fresh flowers, a heavy-beamed inglenook at one end with cosy seating inside, and a good log fire at the other. Well kept Fullers London Pride and Smiles Golden, and a summer guest; the friendly black labrador is called Bodger, and the gold retriever Molly; skittle alley. There's a decent-sized garden and terrace with an aviary, a rabbit cage and a lawn sloping up towards a rockery. Originally a row of cottages that included the village forge, the pub lies alongside Plush Brook, and an attractive bridleway behind goes to the left of the woods and over to Church Hill. *(Recommended by Tim and Ann Meaden, Sharon Hancock, Jack Triplett, R M Wickenden, Mike and Heather Watson, James and Lynne House, Louie Eze, R H Rowley, Miss B Oakeley, Mr and Mrs D C Stevens, Mr and Mrs J Boler, Stephen and Julie Brown, Dr and Mrs M Beale, M Carr, Christopher Gallop, John and Pat Smyth)*

Free house ~ Licensees Jane and Geoffrey Knights ~ Real ale ~ Meals and snacks (12-1.45, 7-9.45) ~ Restaurant ~ (01300) 348357 ~ Children in family room ~ Open 12-2.30, 7-11; 12-3, 7-10.30 Sun; closed evening 25 Dec

SHAVE CROSS SY4198 Map 1
Shave Cross Inn ★
On back lane Bridport—Marshwood, signposted locally; OS Sheet 193, map ref 415980

In summer, the pretty flower-filled sheltered garden of this charming partly 14th-c flint and thatch inn is a special place to enjoy their particularly good ploughman's and Bass, Badger Best and Eldridge Pope Royal Oak well kept on handpump; there's also a thatched wishing-well, a goldfish pool, and a children's play area. Inside, the original timbered bar is a lovely flagstoned room, surprisingly roomy and full of character, with one big table in the middle, a smaller one by the window seat, a row of chintz-cushioned windsor chairs, and an enormous inglenook fireplace with plates hanging from the chimney breast. The larger carpeted side lounge has a dresser at one end set with plates, and modern rustic light-coloured seats making booths around the tables, and is partly no smoking. Served by friendly staff, bar food includes daily specials such as lasagne (£4.25), mushroom and nut fettucine (£4.45), and chargrilled swordfish (£7.75) or rainbow trout stuffed with smoked trout (£8.45), as well as good sausages (£2.95), ploughman's (from £2.95), steak sandwich (£3.95), vegetable balti (£4.45), gammon (£7.25), sirloin steak (£8.45), children's meals (from £2.15), and puddings like redcurrant and blackcurrant crumble with vanilla sauce (£2.45); they keep local cider in summer. Darts, skittle alley, table skittles, dominoes and cribbage. There's a small secluded campsite for touring caravans and campers. Travelling monks once lodged here, when they might get their tonsures shaved in preparation for the last stage of their pilgrimage to the shrine of St Wita at Whitchurch – hence the pub's name. *(Recommended by E A George, Galen Strawson, Stephen, Julie and Hayley Brown, JM, SM, Dr and Mrs J H Hills, Michael Graubart, Marjorie and David Lamb, George Atkinson, Brian Lister, M E Wellington, Niki and Terry Pursey, Jack and Philip Paxton, B and K Hypher, M Carr, K S Pike, Dr S Willavoys)*

Free house ~ Licensees Bill and Ruth Slade ~ Real ale ~ Meals and snacks (not Mon, except bank holidays) ~ (01308) 868358 ~ Children in eating area of bar ~ Open 12-3(2.30 in winter), 7-11; closed Mon (except bank holidays)

SHERBORNE ST6316 Map 2
Digby Tap £ 🍺
Cooks Lane; park in Digby Road and walk round corner

With its simple uncluttered decor, this is a fine example of an old-fashioned town pub. The flagstone-floored main bar has plenty of character and traditional seating and seems to make for an easy mix of customers who enjoy the pleasant relaxed atmosphere. The openly friendly landlord keeps up to 24 different ales a week including Ash Vine Bitter, Exmoor Ale, Hook Norton Best, Ringwood Best, Shepherd Neame Spitfire, Teignworthy Reel Ale, and Wadworths 6X on handpump. Huge helpings of very reasonably priced bar food include soup (£1.50), good sandwiches (from £1.50), cheesy stuffed mushrooms (£2.25), ploughman's (from £3), sausages, beans, carbonara pasta or home-made pastie (£3.25), chilli with cheese topping (£3.50), omelettes or gammon and egg (£3.75), and daily specials (£3.50). Several small games rooms with pool, darts, fruit machine, and trivia; piped music; there are some seats outside. The pub is close to the glorious golden stone abbey. *(Recommended by Andy and Jill Kassube, Ian Mauger, Jo and Gary Charlton, Stephen Brown, Gregor Macdonald, Brian Chambers, W W Burke, Ron Shelton)*

Free house ~ Licensee Dennis Parker ~ Real ale ~ Meals and snacks (not evenings, not Sun, bank holiday Mons, 25-26 Dec, 1 Jan) ~ (01935) 813148 ~ Children in eating area of bar, lunchtime only ~ Open 11-2.30(3 Sat), 5.30(6 Sat)-11; 12-2.30, 7-10.30 Sun

TARRANT MONKTON ST9408 Map 2
Langton Arms
Village signposted from A354, then head for church

This friendly 17th-c thatched inn is attractively placed next to the church in a pretty village. The comfortable beamed main bar has settles that form a couple of secluded booths around tables at the carpeted end, window seats, and another table or two at the serving end where the floor's tiled. There's a big inglenook fireplace in the public bar, and an old stable is the no-smoking restaurant area. Generous helpings of popular bar food include filled french bread, chicken curry (£5.50), venison sausages or fillet of salmon (£5.95), minted lamb cutlets (£7.95), and puddings. Well kept Smiles Best (labelled as Langton Arms Best in the pub), and guests such as Exmoor Ale, Hook Norton Old Hookey and Ringwood Fortyniner on handpump; decent wines by the glass, and helpful staff; dominoes, cribbage, pool, fruit machine, juke box and piped music. The skittle alley doubles as a family room during the day, and there are children's play areas in here and in the garden. Tracks lead up to Crichel Down above the village, and Badbury Rings, a hill fort by the B3082 just south of here, is very striking. *(Recommended by Tim and Ann Meaden, K H Frostick, Martin and Karen Wake, Joy and Harold Dermott, Phil and Heidi Cook, EML, John and Fiona McDougal, Mr and Mrs D C Stevens, Joy and Peter Heatherley, John and Joan Nash)*

Free house ~ Licensees James Cossins and Michael Angell ~ Real ale ~ Meals and snacks (till 10pm) ~ Restaurant ~ (01258) 830225 ~ Children in family room only ~ Open 11.30-2.30, 6-11; 11.30-11 Sat; 12-10.30 Sun ~ Bedrooms: £35B/£54B

UPWEY SY6684 Map 2
Old Ship ♀
Ridgeway; turn left off A354 at bottom of Ridgeway Hill into old Roman Rd

This is a friendly and popular little pub, and the several attractive interconnected beamed rooms have a peaceful and welcoming atmosphere, as well as a mix of sturdy chairs, some built-in wooden wall settles, fresh flowers on the solid panelled wood bar counter and tables, china plates, copper pans and old clocks on the walls, a couple of comfortable armchairs, and an open fire with horsebrasses along the mantelbeam. Good bar food includes nice soup and sandwiches, creamy garlic mushrooms (£3.95), grilled liver and bacon (£6.50), chicken breast with a wine and onion sauce, venison steak with red wine and cranberry sauce (£10.50), and a big range of salads. Well kept Bass, Boddingtons, and Greenalls Original on handpump, and a good wine list that always includes a dozen or so by the glass; attentive service. There are colourful hanging baskets outside, and picnic tables and umbrellas in the garden. *(Recommended by JDM, KM, Joan and Michel Hooper-Immins, Michael Tucker, George Atkinson, Galen Strawson, Simon and Jane Williams, J F M and Dr M West, Desmond and Pat Morris, P Devitt, Peter Toms, Stephen and Julie Brown, D J and P M Taylor, Bill and Sheila McLardy)*

Greenalls ~ Tenant Paul Edmunds ~ Real ale ~ Meals and snacks (not 25-26 Dec) ~ (01305) 812522 ~ Children in eating area of bar ~ Open 11-2.30, 6-11; 12-3, 7-10.30 Sun

WEST BEXINGTON SY5387 Map 2
Manor Hotel 🏨

Village signposted off B3157 SE of Bridport, opposite the Bull in Swyre

As good as ever, this is a well run and very relaxing old stone hotel with a bustling downstairs cellar bar, actually on the same level as the south-sloping garden. Small country pictures and good leather-mounted horsebrasses decorate the walls, and there are red leatherette stools and low-backed chairs (with one fat seat carved from a beer cask) under the black beams and joists, as well as heavy harness over the log fire. A smart no-smoking Victorian-style conservatory has airy furnishings and lots of plants. Very good popular bar food includes sandwiches (from £2.45; crab £3.95), home-made soup (£2.95), ploughman's (£4.95), moules marinières or crab cakes (£5.95), aubergine crumble (£7.55), rabbit casserole or liver and bacon (£7.65), roast cod or pheasant with chestnuts (£9.45), steaks (from £10.95), monkfish tandoori (£11.95), puddings (£3.35), and children's meals (£3.55); good breakfasts. Well kept Dartmoor Best, Eldridge Pope Bitter, Palmers Bridport, Tetleys, and Wadworths 6X on handpump, quite a few malt whiskies and several wines by the glass. Helpful courteous service. It's a short stroll from the beach, and you can see the sea from the bedrooms and from the garden, where there are picnic tables on a small lawn with flowerbeds along the low sheltering walls; a much bigger side lawn has a children's play area. *(Recommended by Brian Lister, Joy and Harold Dermott, R M Wickenden, Brian and Jill Bond, Basil Minson, Galen Strawson, Mrs M L Carter, Nigel Wilkinson, Richard Gibbs, Jane Warren, Nigel Norman, Andrea Carr, Jason Good, M G Hart, Mr and Mrs D C Stevens)*

Free house ~ Licensee Richard Childs ~ Real ale ~ Meals and snacks (till 10pm) ~ Restaurant ~(01308) 897616 ~ Children in eating area of bar ~ Open 11-11; 12-10.30 Sun ~ Bedrooms: £51B/£82B

WORTH MATRAVERS SY9777 (Isle of Purbeck) Map 2
Square & Compass 🍺

At fork of both roads signposted to village from B3069

For well over 90 years, the various generations of the same family have remained determined that this basic little pub should stay just that – an unchanging place with a quite unique atmosphere. The old-fashioned main bar has simple wall benches around the elbow-polished old tables on the flagstones, interesting local pictures under its low ceilings, and well kept Badger Tanglefoot, Quay Old Rott, Ringwood Fortyniner, and Whitbreads Castle Eden tapped from a row of casks behind a couple of hatches in the flagstoned corridor (local fossils back here, and various curios inside the servery), which leads to a more conventional summer bar; farm cider. Bar food is limited to Cornish, cheese and onion or pork and chilli pasties (£1), served when they're open; cribbage, shove-ha'penny and dominoes. On a clear day the view from the peaceful hilltop setting is hard to beat, looking down over the village rooftops to the sea between the East Man and the West Man (the hills that guard the coastal approach), and on summer evenings the sun setting out beyond Portland Bill. There are benches in front of the pub to admire the view, and free-roaming hens, chickens and other birds may cluck happily around your feet. There are good walks from the pub. Perhaps best to park in the public car park 100 yards along the Corfe Castle road. *(Recommended by David Carr, Kath Wetherill, Stephen, Julie and Hayley Brown, Andy and Jill Kassube, Simon and Jane Williams, P A Legon, R C Morgan, Ann and Colin Hunt, David Holloway, Gabrielle Coyle, Ian Lock, Chris Westmoreland, Richard Siebert, Jack and Philip Paxton)*

Free house ~ Licensee Charlie Newman ~ Real ale ~ Snacks ~ (01929) 439229 ~ Children welcome ~ Occasional live music ~ Open 11-3, 6-11; 11-11 Sat; 12-3, 7-10.30 Sun

Lucky Dip

Besides the fully inspected pubs, you might like to try these Lucky Dips recommended to us and described by readers (if you do, please send us reports):

☆ nr **Almer** [B3075, just off A31 towards Wareham; SY9097], *Worlds End*: Outstanding play area outside comfortable and roomy open-plan thatched family dining pub, good decor with panelled alcoves, very wide choice of generous food, well kept Badger Best and Tanglefoot, good service; open all day, picnic tables out in front and behind *(the Sandy family, Mrs J Lockhart, Joy and Peter Heatherley, G G Lawrence, Bruce Bird, WHBM, BB)*
Bere Regis [High St; SY8494], *Drax Arms*: Open-plan village local with good home cooking (landlady will do her best to suit you if you want something not on menu), well kept Badger Best, IPA and Hard Tackle, friendly staff, newly opened-up fireplace, plenty of good walking nearby *(John and Joan Nash)*; [West St], *Royal Oak*: Lively open-plan modernised local, good value home-cooked food inc takeaways, well kept Whitbreads-related ales, woodburner, bar billiards, sensibly placed darts, cribbage, fruit machine; dining room; open all day Fri and Sat *(Chris de Wet, BB)*
Blandford Forum [Market Pl; ST8806], *Greyhound*: Generous sensibly priced home cooking, friendly staff, well kept Badger Best and Tanglefoot, coin and matchbox collections, stripped brick, carved wood, comfortable seats, popular restaurant *(Dennis and Jean Richards)*; [77 Salisbury St], *Nelsons*: Very old dim-lit bar, beams and sawdust, good value interesting food in big or small helpings, good Sun lunch, half a dozen well kept Whitbreads-related and other ales, hospitable landlord, newspapers *(I Phillips, Dr and Mrs A K Clarke)*
☆ **Bournemouth** [4 Exeter Rd; SZ0991], *Moon on the Square*: Spacious and well fitted Wetherspoons pub, no-smoking upstairs bar, well kept beers inc Ringwood Fortyniner and three guests, awesome helpings of bar food inc good baguettes and specials, friendly service, sensible prices, no piped music; can get crowded, tables on terrace *(Chris and Margaret Southon, P A Legon, JJB)*
Bournemouth [Firvale Rd], *Artful Dodger*: Pleasant pub with Badger beers; not too crowded at weekends *(Anon)*; [Durley Chine], *Durley*: Very enjoyable pub lunches *(Hugh Spottiswoode, Audrey and Peter Reeves)*; [Old Christchurch Rd], *Jug of Ale*: Well kept Whitbreads-related and other changing ales, reasonable prices, straightforward food inc good value Sun lunch; open all day, busy weekend evenings *(Dr and Mrs A K Clarke, JJB, P A Legon)*
Broadmayne [SY7286], *Black Dog*: Comfortably modernised village pub with good range of reasonably priced food inc good sandwiches, popular Sun lunch, pleasant staff *(Pat and Robert Watt, G G Lawrence)*
Buckhorn Weston [ST7524], *Stapleton Arms*: Friendly and spacious, wide choice of food inc fresh fish Weds, steaks Fri, good puddings, bargain Sun lunch, quick service, restaurant, games room, tables outside; pleasant countryside *(Brian Chambers)*
Burton Bradstock [Southover – off B3157 at E end of village; SY4889], *Dove*: Thatched local with two simple little bars, some stripped stone, inglenook fireplace, well kept Branscombe Vale ales, Thatcher's farm cider, darts, piped nostalgic pop music (may be loud), a few 1960ish theatrical photographs from Steve Berkoff to Frank Sinatra, rather smarter dining rooms; picnic tables on steeply terraced back grass, rabbits and fancy fowl *(George Atkinson, Dr S L Hurst, BB)*; [B3157], *Anchor*: Comfortable, clean and roomy, well kept Ushers Best and Founders, good choice of good value bar food till 10 inc some exotic specials, particularly friendly attentive service *(George Atkinson)*
☆ **Cattistock** [SY5999], *Fox & Hounds*: Hidden-away unspoilt village local, maybe Tudor in parts, with open fires, one local and one national beer kept well, bar food *(Gwyneth and Salvo Spadaro-Dutturi, LYM)*
☆ **Charlton Marshall** [A350 Poole—Blandford; ST9003], *Charlton Inn*: Good cheery welcoming oak-beamed local with massive helpings of wholesome food from sandwiches and lots of baked potatoes up, well kept Badger Best and Tanglefoot and well chosen wine list, quick friendly service, unobtrusive piped music, small garden *(K Watson, WHBM, James and Lynne House)*
Chesil [Big Ope; follow Chiswell signposts; SY6873], *Cove House*: Modest bare-boards pub listed for its superb position just above

the miles-long Chesil pebble beach, with three tables out by sea wall; friendly staff, Whitbreads-related ales, usual food; piped music may be obtrusive *(Tim and Ann Meaden, Clare Wilson, David Carr, John Fahy, LYM)*

Chideock [A35 Bridport—Lyme Regis; SY4292], *George*: Welcoming thatched 17th-c pub with neat rows of tables in simple front bar, big log fire in dark-beamed plush lounge, wide choice of bar food, well kept Palmers, efficient staff, restaurant, tables in back garden; bedrooms *(R Boyd, LYM)*

☆ **Child Okeford** [Gold Hill – village signed off A350 Blandford Forum—Shaftesbury and A357 Blandford—Sherborne; ST8313], *Saxon*: Cosy old village pub, quietly clubby bar with log fire and more spacious side room (where children allowed), well kept Bass, Butcombe and a guest beer, country wines, traditional games, simple food (not Tues evening, not winter Sun evening) inc sandwiches and children's dishes; piped music, dry dogs on leads welcome; quite a menagerie in attractive back garden, also friendly golden retrievers and cats; good walks on neolithic Hambledon Hill *(Joy and Harold Dermott, Mark Matthewman, A Homes, LYM)*

Christchurch [High St; SZ1593], *Ship*: Pleasingly dark and low-beamed Hogshead, with good choice of well kept ales and good honest bar food, reasonably priced *(Ian Baillie)*

☆ nr **Christchurch** [Ringwood Rd, Walkford; just off A35 by Hants border; SZ2294], *Amberwood Arms*: Imaginative food in spacious bar and comfortable restaurant (booking advised), friendly staff; some live music, weekly trivia night, picnic tables and play area; open all day, festooned with hanging baskets and flower tubs in summer; nice seafront walks, handy for Highcliffe Castle *(Phyl and Jack Street)*

☆ **Corfe Castle** [SY9681], *Bankes Arms*: Big and busy but welcoming, with flagstones and comfortable traditional decor, subtle lighting, Whitbreads-related ales, generous good value food, friendly service, tables on terrace and in long garden with big climbing frame, running down to newly opened tourist railway; children and dogs welcome; bedrooms, on attractive village square *(Miss T Browne, Mr and Mrs N A Spink, Chris Westmoreland)*

Corfe Mullen [A31 W of Wimborne Minster; SY9798], *Coventry Arms*: Nooks and crannies of reconstituted antiquity in two interconnecting bars separated by very open fire, Ringwood Best and three or four interesting guest ales tapped from the cask, good food from filled baked potatoes and baguettes up, tables out by small stream; quiet lunchtime but busy evenings. with weekly live music and lots of special events; decent clutch of malt whiskies *(WHBM)*

Cranborne [The Square; SU0513], *Sheaf of Arrows*: Very welcoming pub brewing its own Cranborne Quiver and Old Shafter (brewery visits encouraged); good range of other ales, bar food inc good roast beef lunch, somewhat old-fashioned decor, friendly dogs and cats; children welcome; bedrooms *(Mrs V Brown, Graham Moss)*

☆ **Dorchester** [40 Allington Ave; A352 towards Wareham, just off bypass; SY6890], *Trumpet Major*: Bright and airy big-windowed modern lounge bar, emphasis on food inc good help-yourself salad bar and speciality apple cake, well kept Eldridge Pope ales; handy for Max Gate (Thomas Hardy's house, now open to the public); conservatories, garden, children welcome, very busy lunchtime *(Joan and Michel Hooper-Immins, J F M West, Dr B and Mrs P B Baker)*

Dorchester [Church St], *Blue Raddle*: Compact cosy local reopened with new licensee, small menu of reasonably priced food, well kept ales such as Greene King Abbot; very quiet piped jazz *(M Vann)*; [High West St], *Old Ship*: Unmodernised low-ceilinged local with generous cheap food, well kept Eldridge Pope Dorchester, Hardy Country and Royal Oak, back dining room, friendly staff *(John and Wendy Trentham, Dr B and Mrs P B Baker)*; [20 High West St], *Royal Oak*: Well kept Eldridge Pope Dorchester, Hardy Country and Royal Oak, plentiful hot food, very friendly service; piped music may be loud, back games room; bedrooms *(Alan Newman, David Carr)*; [Weymouth Ave, by Dorchester Sth Stn – handy for bypass], *Station Masters House*: Spacious open-plan railway-theme pub with friendly service, notable for well kept Eldridge Pope ales straight from the handsome adjacent brewery; plush Victorian-style decor, courteous young staff, generous sensibly priced food; games area with darts, fruit machines and pool tables, piped music can be rather loud; open all day Weds-Sat, busy Weds (market opp) *(Brian Chambers, David Carr, Dr B and Mrs P B Baker)*; [47 High East St], *Tom Browns*: Two or three beers from the microbrewery you can see at the back, in basic but friendly well run local with simple good value food; juke box *(Gwyneth and Salvo Spadaro-Dutturi, Dr B and Mrs P B Baker)*

☆ **East Lulworth** [B3070; SY8581], *Weld Arms*: Very friendly and relaxed, with nice mix of individual furnishings, attractive little snug, good interesting food from well filled rolls up inc vegetarian and good puddings, tables out in big garden; good value bedrooms *(Richard Gibbs, Veronica Brown, R H Brown, Phil Putwain, LYM)*

☆ **Ferndown** [Wimborne Rd E; SZ0700], *Pure Drop*: Large Eldridge Pope pub with their beers kept well, sizeable restaurant with enterprising varied food, good wines *(S J Edwards, John and Vivienne Rice)*

☆ **Fiddleford** [A357 Sturminster Newton—Blandford Forum; ST8013], *Fiddleford Inn*: Comfortable and spacious refurbished pub keeping ancient flagstones and some other nice touches, well kept Scottish Courage ales, friendly service, unobtrusive piped music, quickly served food in lounge bar, restaurant area and back family area; big attractive garden with play area *(Dorothy and Leslie Pilson, Brian Chambers, Jenny and Michael Back, James Martin, LYM)*

Furzehill [SU0101], *Stocks*: Busy extended thatched dining pub, attractive interior with copper and brass, old prints and even a lobster pot and fishing net, wide range of food inc good value OAP lunch Thurs, friendly and attentive young staff; spacious back restaurant *(M Reading)*

☆ **Gillingham** [Peacemarsh; ST8026], *Dolphin*: Good choice of particularly good value food all freshly cooked to order, attentive friendly staff, partly no-smoking restaurant area, well kept Badger and guest ales *(Clifford Sharp, C and E Watson, Matthew Haig)*

☆ **Gussage All Saints** [signed off B3078 Wimborne—Cranborne; SU0010], *Drovers*: Sturdily furnished country dining pub with peaceful views, generous well presented food inc vegetarian, well kept Bass, Marstons Pedigree and Ruddles County, country wines, friendly service, tables out on terrace, good play area; children in eating area, in summer has been open all day Sat *(B and K Hypher, Tim and Ann Meaden, LYM)*

Hinton St Mary [just off B3092 a mile N of Sturminster; ST7816], *White Horse*: Village local with unusual inglenook fireplace in cheery tiled bar, nicely set dining tables in extended lounge, reasonably priced food (booking advised Sun lunch), well kept John Smiths, Tetleys and changing guest beers, good landlord, darts; tables in flower garden *(Jenny and Michael Back, S J and C C Davidson, Pat and Robert Watt, Brian Chambers)*

Holt [SU0304], *Old Inn*: Well appointed dining pub doing well under current very friendly management, good generous food inc fresh fish, two restaurants, winter fires, Badger beers *(J Morris)*

Horton [SU0207], *Drusillas*: Picturesque renovated and extended 17th-c pub, food inc good fish and OAP bargains, nice restaurant, real ales, wood fire under copper canopy in beamed bar; children welcome, adventure playground *(John and Vivienne Rice)*

Hurn [village signed off A338, then follow Avon, Sopley, Mutchams sign; SZ1397], *Avon Causeway*: Big rather touristy pub, but civilised and comfortable, with Wadworths and guest ales, good choice of wines and spirits, interesting railway decorations, pleasantly enlarged dining area; Pullman-coach restaurant by former 1870s station platform; piped music, open all day; bedrooms *(Chris and Martin Taylor, LYM)*

Leigh [the one nr Sherborne; ST6208], *Carpenters Arms*: Clean and tidy village pub with good service, good choice of food, good range of beers; skittle alley in side bar, restaurant extension planned, tables on sheltered terrace; new bedroom annexe *(Stephen G Brown)*

Litton Cheney [off A35 Dorchester—Bridport, OS Sheet 194 map ref 549900; SY5590], *White Horse*: Lovely spot on quiet lane into quaint village, picnic tables on pleasant streamside front lawn, pictures on stripped stone walls, country kitchen chairs in dining area, bar food inc reasonably priced Sun lunch, well kept Palmers BB and Tally Ho, table skittles, friendly helpful staff *(Malcolm Thomas)*

☆ **Lyme Regis** [25 Marine Parade, The Cobb; SY3492], *Royal Standard*: Lively but cosy local, open-plan but keeping three separate low-ceilinged areas, with well kept Palmers, good value food inc sensibly priced sandwiches, local crabs and good cream teas with home-made scones, good friendly service, pool table, suntrap terrace (floodlit at night) leading to beach; three bedrooms *(B R Shiner, JWC, MC, Dr and Mrs J H Hills)*

Lyme Regis [Marine Parade, Monmouth Beach], *Cobb Arms*: Spaciously refurbished, lots of interesting ship pictures, wide range of reasonably priced bar food, good value cream teas, well kept Palmers ales; next to harbour, beach and coastal walk; three bedrooms *(Joan and Michel Hooper-Immins, Tony Scott, Marjorie and David Lamb)*

Manston [B3091 Shaftesbury—Sturminster Newton, just N; ST8115], *Plough*: Richly decorated plasterwork, ceilings and bar front, quick helpful service, real ales such as Black Sheep, Butcombe and Websters Yorkshire, good choice of good value food from sandwiches up inc vegetarian dishes; tables in garden, cl Sun evening *(C and E Watson, Jenny and Michael Back)*

☆ **Marnhull** [B3092 N of Sturminster Newton; ST7718], *Crown*: Part-thatched 17th-c inn with oak beams, huge flagstones, old settles and elm tables, window seats cut into thick stone walls, and logs burning in a big stone hearth; small more modern lounge, friendly service, reasonably priced bar food, Badger Best and Tanglefoot, skittle alley and pub games, maybe piped music; restaurant, tables in peaceful enclosed garden, children welcome; bedrooms, good breakfast *(Nick Hawkins, Jacky Andrew, Tony and Wendy Hobden, Derek Wilson, LYM)*

☆ **Marshwood** [B3165 Lyme Regis—Crewkerne; SY3799], *Bottle*: 16th-c thatched country local, inglenook in low-ceilinged bar, Hook Norton and Wadworths 6X, cheap bar food, small games bar, skittle alley; good spacious garden, pretty walking country *(C A Hall, LYM)*

Morecombelake [A35 Bridport—Lyme Regis; SY4093], *Ship*: Welcoming atmosphere, good bar food inc generously filled baked potatoes, small helpings available, well kept Palmers, hospitable landlord; bedrooms *(Mrs Best)*

Mosterton [High St; ST4505], *Admiral Hood*: Civilised and popular dining pub with neatly furnished spacious L-shaped bar, well kept Courage-related ales, coal fire in handsome stone fireplace, quick welcoming service, simple skittle alley behind the thatched 18th-c stone building *(Pat and Robert Watt, BB)*

☆ **North Wootton** [A3030; ST6514], *Three Elms*: Lively and welcoming, with wide range of good food esp vegetarian, well served sandwiches, reasonable prices, half a dozen well kept ales such as Fullers London Pride, jovial barman, enormous number of Matchbox and other model cars; interesting gents', three bedrooms, good breakfasts, big garden *(Stephen G Brown, Pat and Robert Watt)*

☆ **Poole** [Pinewood Rd, Branksome Park; off A338 on edge of Poole, towards Branksome Chine – via The Avenue; SZ0590], *Inn in the Park*: Popular pleasantly redecorated small hotel bar, well kept Bass and Wadworths 6X, good value generous bar food (not Sun evening) inc fresh veg, attractive dining room (children allowed), log fire, tables on small sunny terrace; comfortable bedrooms, quiet pine-filled residential area above sea *(B and K Hypher, M J Dowdy, LYM)*

☆ **Poole** [The Quay], *Portsmouth Hoy*: Enjoyable nautical theme, lots of brass, bustling atmosphere, good choice of reasonably priced food inc good value fish and chips special, well kept Eldridge Pope and guest beers, smart bar service, nice back dining area, separate no-smoking area; on lively quay, handy for aquarium *(Howard and Margaret Buchanan, G R Sunderland, M E Wellington, Nigel Flook, Betsy Brown)*

Poole [The Quay], *Lord Nelson*: Good value food inc tasty sandwiches in handy quayside pub, lots of nautical memorabilia, good range of beers *(Hugh Spottiswoode, Dr and Mrs A K Clarke, David Carr)*; [Longfleet Rd/Fernside Rd], *Shah of Persia*: Recently refurbished, with pleasant atmosphere, good choice of good generous food, well kept Eldridge Pope ales, big no-smoking area; may be delays on busy evenings *(Audrey and Peter Reeves, Betty Davey)*

☆ **Portland Bill** [SY6870], *Pulpit*: Comfortable and particularly welcoming food pub in great spot nr Pulpit Rock, short stroll to lighthouse and cliffs; local shellfish and interesting puddings as well as good value usual bar and restaurant food inc vegetarian, four well kept Gibbs Mew ales, good service; piped music *(P Devitt, Tony Scott, M Hart, David Carr)*

☆ **Powerstock** [off A3066 Beaminster—Bridport via W Milton; SY5196], *Three Horseshoes*: Busy but now somewhat overpriced country pub, with perhaps rather the air of a Londoners' weekend retreat, and this year service has not had the plaudits it earned in the past – resting on its laurels? Delightful setting, food from filled baguettes to interesting choice of good fresh fish, no-smoking restaurant, small panelled L-shaped bar, warm fires, well kept Palmers Bridport and IPA, excellent choice of wines by the glass, freshly squeezed fruit juice; friendly retrievers and springer spaniel, lovely views from garden above sea with play area; bedrooms *(Mr and Mrs J Boler, Jerry and Alison Oakes, J W Hill, Anthony Barnes, Simon and Jane*

Williams, David and June Harwood, V H and J M Vanstone, Mrs C Jimenez, Ian Dunkin, Jo and Gary Charlton, Michael Graubart, Philip Cooper, LYM)

☆ **Puncknowle** [Church St; SY5388], *Crown*: 16th-c beamed and thatched flint inn with huge hearth in clean and comfortable lounge, good choice of reasonably priced home-cooked food inc wide vegetarian choice and tasty puddings, well kept Palmers, decent wines, Taunton Vale cider, lots of country wines, pictures for sale; two family rooms, locals' bar; dogs welcome by arrangement, fine views from attractive garden, pretty setting opp church; bedrooms clean and comfortable, filling breakfast *(George Atkinson, G G Lawrence, Mick and Hilary Stiffin, Jo and Gary Charlton, Richard Burton)*

☆ **Shaftesbury** [St James St; ST8622], *Two Brewers*: At bottom of steep famously photogenic Gold Hill (those Hovis ads), with good atmosphere in well divided open-plan turkey-carpeted bar, lots of decorative plates, very wide choice of reasonably priced popular bar food (children's helpings of any dish) freshly prepared inc vegetarian, good puddings and good Sun roasts, chatty landlord and good service, well kept Courage Best and Directors, Wadworths 6X and guests such as Batemans XB and Brains SA, quiet piped music in restaurant; picnic tables in garden with pretty views, masses of hanging baskets etc *(John and Jill Woodfield, Bruce Bird, DP, Tim and Ann Meaden, Alan and Paula McCully, Marjorie and David Lamb, BB)*

☆ **Shaftesbury** [The Commons], *Grosvenor*: Charming old-fashioned coaching hotel, warm and comfortable; good genuine fair-priced bar snacks, well kept beers inc Bass, stylish restaurant; ask Reception if you can see the magnificently carved oak 19th-c Chevy Chase sideboard in the first-floor residents' lounge; good bedrooms *(Veronica Brown)*

☆ **Shaftesbury** [Bleke St], *Ship*: Traditional 17th-c local with black panelling, oak woodwork, well kept Badger Best and Tanglefoot, farm cider, bar food, separate eating area, helpful friendly service, pool and other games in public bar (crowded with young people weekend evenings), tables on terrace *(Howard England, V G and P A Nutt, Brian Chambers, David Carr, LYM)*

Shaftesbury [Bleke St], *Kings Arms*: Wide choice of good quickly served food inc good pies in sizeable dining pub, cottagey decor with lots of china and other bric-a-brac, big inglenook, some stripped masonry, partly timbered divisions to give feel of series of separate rooms; charming three-legged cat, attentive friendly staff, well kept Badger Best and Tanglefoot, tables outside; open all day, good disabled facilities *(Howard England)*; [High St], *Mitre*: Cheerfully unpretentious, with quickly served good generous food from sandwiches up inc vegetarian, Blackmore Vale views from back dining room, well kept Eldridge Pope beers, good choice of malt whiskies and wines, daily papers, small suntrap garden; bedrooms *(Brian Chambers, BB)*

☆ **Sherborne** [Horsecastles; ST6316], *Skippers*: Pleasant local bustle, service welcoming and quick in spite of crowds, good range of reasonably priced food, well kept Bass and other ales; just outside centre *(C and E M Watson)*

Sherborne [88 Cheap St], *Cross Keys*: Comfortably refurbished with three distinct bars, extraordinarily wide choice of food, quick cheerful attentive service, well kept Eldridge Pope ales; interesting display of postal history, postbox in corridor *(Joan and Michel Hooper-Immins, Hugh MacLean)*; [Cheap St], *Swan*: Newly refurbished welcoming family pub, popular good value food, wide range of drinks *(Steve Clarke, Jill Bickerton)*

Shipton Gorge [off A35/B3157 E of Bridport; SY4991], *New Inn*: Friendly village pub, huge log fire, limited choice of good value food inc freshly caught local fish, well kept Palmers *(Desmond and Pat Morris)*

Shroton [off A350 N of Blandford; ST8512], *Cricketers*: Welcoming and popular with locals and visitors, home-made bar meals inc game and fish specials, ales such as Bass, Greene King IPA, Smiles and Wadworths 6X *(Deirdre Lambe)*

Sixpenny Handley [High St; ST9917], *Roebuck*: Plain village local well worth knowing for good fish, meat and game cooked by the landlord's French wife, with home-grown veg; Ringwood Porter, Hop Back Special and Tisbury Bitter, seats outside *(Margaret Owen, Joan and Michel Hooper-Immins)*

Southbourne [Overcliff Dr; SZ1391], *Spyglass & Kettle*: Good big newly refurbished hotel bar with no-smoking area, wide choice of good reasonably priced food, Flowers, Greenalls Original, Tetleys and Worthington, attentive staff *(Audrey and Peter Reeves, Betty Davey)*

☆ **Stoke Abbott** [off B3162 and B3163 2 m W of Beaminster; ST4500], *New Inn*: 17th-c thatched pub with beams, brasses, stripped stone alcoves on either side of one big log fireplace, another which has handsome panelling, well kept Palmers Bridport, IPA and 200, good choice of food, no-smoking dining room, well kept attractive garden with play area, nice setting in quiet village; children welcome, bedrooms, has been cl Mon lunchtime *(T A Bizat, Miss R Kingsmill, LYM; more reports please)*

☆ **Studland** [SZ0382], *Bankes Arms*: Wonderful peaceful spot above fine beach, outstanding country, sea and cliff views from huge pleasant garden; friendly and easy-going, substantial simple food, well kept Poole and Whitbreads-related ales, attractive log fire, pool table; children welcome, nr Coast Path; can get trippery in summer, parking can be complicated or expensive if you're not a NT member; big comfortable bedrooms, has been cl winter *(David Carr, Ian and Nita Cooper, M Joyner, Michael Dunn, A Ellis, Nigel Flook, Betsy Brown, David Holloway)*

Sturminster Marshall [High St, opp church; SY9499], *Red Lion*: Thriving open-plan pub, clean and pleasant, with consistently good varied food inc bargain OAP two-course meal lunchtime and evening (not w/e), Badger ales, log fire, skittle alley doubling as family room; shame they encourage you to tip, and booking needed Fri and w/e *(WHBM)*

☆ **Sturminster Newton** [Market Cross (B3092); ST7814], *White Hart*: Homely 18th-c thatched and black-beamed inn, warm cosy bar, well kept Badger Best and Tanglefoot with a guest such as Charles Wells, pleasant staff, jolly landlord, short choice of reasonably priced bar food, afternoon teas, garden beyond cobbled coach entry; bedrooms comfortable, though road not quiet *(Joan and Michel Hooper-Immins)*

☆ **Sutton Poyntz** [off A353 SE of Weymouth; SY7083], *Springhead*: Spacious but cosy, with comfortable furnishings, beams, well kept Eldridge Pope and Marstons Pedigree, decent reasonably priced wines, good range of malt whiskies, good choice of tempting freshly cooked food in bar and restaurant, log fires, welcoming attentive staff, newspapers, bar billiards, well chosen piped music – often jazz; lovely spot opp willow stream in quiet village, entertaining ducks, good play area in big garden, walks to White Horse Hill and Dorset Coastal Path *(S J Edwards, Don Nairn, Tony Scott)*

☆ **Swanage** [Shore Rd; SZ0278], *Mowlem*: First-floor theatre restaurant, not a pub, but good food inc bar lunches, well kept Badger Best and Tanglefoot from downstairs bar, good service, delightful sea views *(Joan and Michel Hooper-Immins, Hugh Spottiswoode, Derek Patey)*

Swanage [Bell St, Herston – just off 1st turn into town off A351], *Globe*: Small unspoilt local, quiet and relaxed, with well kept Whitbreads-related ales *(Derek Patey)*; *Red Lion*: Snug two-bar pub, beams densely hung with mugs and keys, lots of blow lamps, decent inexpensive food, well kept Ringwood and Whitbreads, friendly staff; children's annexe, partly covered back terrace *(Peter and Audrey Dowsett, Chris Westmoreland)*

☆ **Symondsbury** [signed from A35 just W of Bridport; SY4493], *Ilchester Arms*: Attractive old thatched inn in peaceful village, cosy and welcoming open-plan low-ceilinged bar with high-backed settle built in by big inglenook, cosy no-smoking area with candlelit evening dining tables and another fire, well kept Palmers Best, Bridport, Tally Ho and 200, friendly service and dog called Skip, food (not winter Mon) from big filled rolls to casseroles and cassoulet; pub games, skittle alley, piped music; tables by pretty brookside back garden; children welcome, bedrooms, good walks nearby *(Dr and Mrs A H Young, Ted*

*George, M R Austen, J P Lee, S J Edwards,
John and Vivienne Rice, C and E M Watson,
P and J Caunt, A and I Stewart, O and H
Steinmann, JM, SM, Jenny and Michael Back,
Romey Heaton, George Atkinson, LYM;
more reports please)*

Tarrant Keynston [ST9304], *True Lovers
Knot*: Simple village local with very
entertaining landlord, well kept Badger ales,
decent range of food, good atmosphere;
children in eating area, big garden *(Joy and
Harold Dermott)*

Tolpuddle [SY7994], *Martyrs*: Well kept
Badger beers, friendly staff, home-cooked
food in bar and busy restaurant, nice garden
with ducks, hens and rabbits *(R Shelton)*

Trent [ST5918], *Rose & Crown*: Attractively
sparse old-fashioned pub with log fire,
flagstones, oak settles, nice pictures, fresh
flowers, books, no piped music or machines;
friendly licensees, well kept ales and wide
choice of good food inc very popular Sun
lunch, but a black mark for their
encouragement of tipping (with service charge
for big parties) and for surcharge on puddings
if you just have ploughman's; dining
conservatory, children welcome, picnic tables
behind *(NT)*

Uploders [signed off A35 E of Bridport;
SY5093], *Crown*: Friendly and brightly
furnished village pub, mainly no smoking,
festooned with polished bric-a-brac; good
genuine food (not Sun evening) inc vegetarian
dishes and two bars off flagstoned corridor,
well kept Palmers BB and 200, good service, log
fires, tables in pleasant two-tier garden;
bedrooms *(Brian Lister, Richard and
Rosemary Hoare, Ian and Anne Barrett, P
Furse, Ian and Deborah Carrington, Galen
Strawson, BB)*

Wareham [41 North St; A351, N end of
town; SY9287], *Kings Arms*: Friendly and
lively traditional thatched town local, back
serving counter and two bars off flagstoned
central corridor, well kept Whitbreads-related
ales, reasonably priced bar food (not Fri—Sun
evenings), back garden *(Tim and Ann
Meaden, LYM)*

Wareham [South St], *Quay*: Comfortable,
light and airy stripped-stone bars, bar food
from soup and sandwiches up, open fire, well
kept Whitbreads-related and other ales,
friendly staff, children allowed away from
main bar; picnic tables out on the quay,
parking nearby can be difficult *(David Carr)*

Wareham [14 South St], *Black Bear*: Bow-
windowed 18th-c hotel with pleasant bar on
right of through corridor, well kept Eldridge
Pope Royal Oak and Hardy Country, good
choice of well priced bar food, decent coffee,
picnic tables in back yard; bedrooms *(Ann
and Colin Hunt, David Carr)*

Wareham Forest [Coldharbour; Wareham—
Bere Regis – OS Sheet 195 map ref 902897;
SY9089], *Silent Woman*: Wide choice of good
value standard food in busy lounge bar
extended into stripped-masonry dining area
with country bygones; well kept Badger ales,

more interesting books than usual on walls,
military insignia, access for wheelchairs;
children welcome, good play area, walks
nearby *(D Illing, Gordon Neighbour)*

Waytown [between B3162 and A3066 N of
Bridport; SY4697], *Hare & Hounds*:
Attractively refurbished 17th-c pub, helpful
and friendly licensees with growing reputation
for good value well presented food inc OAP
bargains, Palmers ales, simple garden with
good play area *(Ian and Anne Barrett,
Desmond and Pat Morris, Tim and Ann
Meaden, Galen Strawson)*

☆ **West Bay** [SY4590], *Bridport Arms*: Thatched
pub on beach of Bridport's holiday village,
good range of generous good value food esp
local fish, friendly staff, well kept Palmers BB,
big fireplace in flagstoned back bar, no music;
bedrooms, nr harbour and cliff walks *(David
Carr)*

West Bay [George St], *George*: Popular and
unassuming harbourside inn with well kept
Palmers ales, lots of ship prints, food inc fresh
local fish and seafood; freshly landed fish and
shellfish may be sold at the pub door;
comfortable bedrooms *(Joan and Michel
Hooper-Immins)*

☆ **West Knighton** [off A352 E of Dorchester;
SY7387], *New Inn*: Biggish neatly refurbished
pub, very busy in summer, with interesting
range of reasonably priced food, small
restaurant, quick friendly staff, real ales,
country wines, skittle alley, good provision
for children; big colourful garden, pleasant
setting in quiet village with wonderful views
*(Dr and Mrs S Jones, Tim and Ann Meaden,
G G Lawrence)*

☆ **West Lulworth** [B3070; SY8280], *Castle*:
Pretty thatched inn in lovely spot nr Lulworth
Cove, good walks; flagstoned bar bustling
with summer visitors, maze of booth seating,
usual food inc children's, well kept Devenish
Wessex, Flowers Original and Marstons
Pedigree, decent house wines, farm cider,
piped music (may be loud), video and board
games; cosy more modern-feeling lounge bar,
pleasant dining room, splendid ladies',
popular garden with giant chess boards,
boules, barbecues; recently redecorated
bedrooms, good breakfasts *(Mark Percy,
David Holloway, LE, Jenny and Brian Seller,
Andrew Rogers, Amanda Milsom, Mrs V
Brown, Ann and Colin Hunt, Hanns P Golez,
Anthony Barnes, Kath Wetherill, LYM)*

West Parley [SZ0897], *Manor*: Pleasant pub
associated with Avon Causeway at Hurn, lots
of armour, swords etc, no-smoking area, well
kept Wadworths 6X, food inc good value
baguettes *(John and Vivienne Rice)*

☆ **West Stafford** [signed off A352 Dorchester—
Wareham; SY7289], *Wise Man*: Comfortable
16th-c local nr Hardy's cottage, very busy in
summer; thatch, beams and toby jugs, with
wide choice of good value generous standard
food, charming staff, well kept Whitbreads-
related ales, decent wines and country wines,
public bar with darts; children not encouraged
(Howard Clutterbuck, R Walden, Brian and

Anna Marsden, Dr and Mrs S Jones)

☆ **Weymouth** [Barrack Rd; SY6778], *Nothe Tavern*: Roomy well run local with good atmosphere, good range of food inc local fresh fish specialities and children's dishes, friendly service, well kept Eldridge Pope Royal Oak, Hardy and Popes, decent wines; distant harbour glimpses from garden *(Joan and Michel Hooper-Immins, Peter and Audrey Dowsett, J F M West, Tony Scott, David Carr, BB)*

Weymouth [Hope Sq], *Dorset Brewers*: Bare boards and lots of nautical hardware, Badger Best, Bass, Eldridge Pope Dorchester and Ringwood Old Thumper, quickly served simple meals; tables outside; opp showpiece (but expensive) Brewers Quay in former Devenish brewery *(Joan and Michel Hooper-Immins)*; [harbour], *Kings Arms*: Comfortable and friendly, good choice of bar food, popular with locals in the evening *(David Carr)*; [Trinity Rd], *Old Rooms*: Interesting harbour views over part-pedestrianised street from recently extended terrace in front of bustling low-beamed pub, well priced straightforward food (some all day at least in summer), friendly staff, unpretentious restaurant; John Smiths and Worthington, piped music may be loud, no nearby parking *(Eric Locker, Tony Scott, Joan and Michel Hooper-Immins, David Carr)*

Wimborne Minster [Leigh Common (B3073 E); SZ0199], *Sir Winston Churchill*: Hardworking young licensees in new Badger pub with attractively furnished bar and spacious dining room, decent choice of food, covered eating area outside, lots of tables on big lawns, purpose-built barbecue, amusements for children *(Brian Chambers)*

Winterborne Kingston [SY8697], *Greyhound*: Good value home-made food inc popular carvery, well kept Wadworths 6X, staff friendly even when busy, good atmosphere *(R T and J C Moggridge)*

Post Office address codings confusingly give the impression that some pubs are in Dorset, when they're really in Somerset (which is where we list them).

Essex

New entries here this year are the civilised Square & Compasses at Fuller Street (good food), the Green Man at Toot Hill (excellent choice of wines), and the cheerful and relaxing Rainbow & Dove at Hastingwood (a fine motorway refuge). Other places doing particularly well here these days are the Bull at Blackmore End (this dining pub now gains our Food Award), the strikingly individual Bell at Castle Hedingham (its new fish barbecues are popular), the Green Man at Gosfield (good English cooking), the Bell at Horndon on the Hill (a popular all-rounder, its good restaurant food now available in the bar too), and the Hoop at Stock (good real ales at this welcoming local). There's a lot of good food to be had in this county, but for a special meal out it's the White Hart at Great Yeldham which stands out – and for the second year running carries off our award as Essex Dining Pub of the Year. In the Lucky Dip section at the end of the chapter, pubs which we'd now pick out as specially noteworthy (most of them already inspected and approved by us) are the Queens Head at Boreham, White Harte in Burnham on Crouch, Three Horseshoes at Duton Hill, White Hart at Great Saling, Cock at Hatfield Broad Oak, Wheatsheaf at High Ongar, Black Horse at Pilgrims Hatch, White Horse at Pleshey, Bell at Purleigh, both Wivenhoe entries and Bell at Woodham Walter. We'd also be glad of more reports on the Rose at Peldon and Cricketers Arms at Rickling Green – popular main entries in the past, but very few readers have mentioned them recently. Drinks prices here are usually a few pence more than the national average, but the Queens Head at Littlebury was outstandingly cheap (£1 a pint), and the Crooked Billet in Leigh on Sea, thriving under new licensees, was also very cheap.

ARKESDEN TL4834 Map 5
Axe & Compasses ★ ♀

Village signposted from B1038 – but B1039 from Wendens Ambo, then forking left, is prettier; OS Sheet 154 map reference 482344

Although pleasantly busy, there's a comfortably restful atmosphere at this rambling thatched country inn which is situated in a particularly lovely village. The carpeted lounge bar dating back to the 17th c is the oldest part with beautifully polished upholstered oak and elm seats, easy chairs and wooden tables, as well as a warm fire, lots of brasses on the walls, and a friendly cat called Spikey. The smaller uncarpeted characterful public bar, with cosy built-in settles, has darts, cribbage, shove-ha'penny and dominoes. Popular meals served with good vegetables can be eaten in the bar or the restaurant, and might include home-made soup (£2), grilled sardines (£3.50), deep-fried mushrooms with garlic dip (£3.95), lamb liver and bacon (£5.95), mushroom pancake with a creamy cheesy sauce, lasagne or loin of pork on a stilton and mushroom sauce (£7.25), grilled skate (£7.95), grilled lemon sole (£9.75) and monkfish cooked on roasted pepper sauce (£10.95) as well as daily specials such as sea bass steak on fettucine with red pepper coulis (£10.95); impressive pudding trolly; prompt, attentive and welcoming service. Well kept

Greene King IPA and Abbott on handpump under light blanket pressure, a very good wine list, and about two dozen malt whiskies. There are seats outside on a side terrace with pretty hanging baskets; parking at the back. *(Recommended by A Bradbury, DFL, Gwen and Peter Andrews, Ian and Liz Phillips, Peter Plumridge, Tina and David Woods-Taylor, Richard Siebert)*

Greene King ~ Lease: Themis and Diáne Christou ~ Real ale ~ Meals and snacks (till 9.30) ~ Restaurant (not winter Sun evening) ~ (01799) 550272 ~ Children in restaurant until 8.30 ~ Open 11-2.30, 6-11; 12-3, 7-10.30 Sun

BLACKMORE END TL7430 Map 5
Bull 🍴 ♀

Signposted via Beazley End from Bocking Church Street, itself signed off A131 just N of Braintree bypass; pub is on Wethersfield side of village

We're pleased to give this comfortable tucked away dining pub a food award this year as it's been a main entry in the Guide for the last couple of years for its very good carefully prepared food. There's a refreshingly good range of sandwiches (from £2.95, french sticks £3.50), and ploughman's (£4.50) but the real draw is the very well prepared specials menu neatly written up on blackboards every two weeks, possibly including beautifully presented fresh mushroom and thyme soup with wild mushrooms (£2.75), tiger prawns and wild mushrooms in garlic and parsley butter on a crouton (£5.50), pan-fried lamb liver topped with avocado and garlic butter or chicken collops with glazed shallots and thyme and white wine cream sauce (£7.50), breast of guinea fowl on parsnip and apple purée with cider cream sauce (£10.25), mignons of fillet steak with stilton and port sauce (£10.95), venison cutlet with pink peppercorns and red wine cherry sauce (£11.95) and ostrich fillet with green peppercorn brandy cream (£13.50), all served in generous helpings with fresh vegetables in separate dishes. There are lots of tempting home-made puddings such as bread pudding with rum, whipped cream and toasted nuts, meringue filled with kiwi and pineapple with kirsch cream, hot apple and apricot strudel or pear and ginger sponge (from £3.50). The flowery-carpeted dining bar has red plush built-in button-back banquettes, low black beams and lots of menu blackboards. Beyond a massive brick chimneypiece is a pretty cosy cottagey restaurant area (no cigars or pipes). Well kept Adnams, Greene King IPA, Mauldons Whiteadder and changing guest ales on handpump; ten wines by the glass from a wine list of about 70 which includes some enterprising bin-ends, vintage ports and dessert wines; picnic tables outside. *(Recommended by Gwen and Peter Andrews, Tony Beaulah, Richard Siebert, M W Bond, Roy and Margaret Jones)*

Free house ~ Licensees Christopher and Mary Bruce ~ Real ale ~ Meals and snacks (till 9.30 Tues-Sat; no sandwiches or snacks Sat evening) ~ Restaurant ~ (01371) 851037 ~ Children in restaurant ~ Open 12-3, 6.30-11(7-10.30 Sun); cl Mon (except bank holidays)

CASTLE HEDINGHAM TL7835 Map 5
Bell

B1058 E of Sible Hedingham, towards Sudbury

The cheerful smiling licensee Sandra Ferguson (with her lovely great dane Lucia) at this historic old coaching inn is particuarly well loved by readers, many paying tribute to the way her warm character lights up these historic rooms. The beamed and timbered saloon bar remains unchanged over the years, with Jacobean-style seats and windsor chairs around sturdy oak tables, and beyond the standing timbers left from a knocked-through wall, some steps lead up to a little gallery. Behind the traditionally furnished public bar a games room has dominoes, backgammon and cribbage; piped pop music. One bar is no smoking, and each of the rooms has a good welcoming log fire. Promptly served bar food from a fixed menu includes tomato soup (£2), lamb or beefburger (£3), ploughman's (£3.50), half pint smoked prawns (£4, pint £7.50), ham and broccoli bake, fisherman's pie, chicken kebabs, steak and Guinness pie, thai chicken curry, liver and bacon casserole or salmon steak (£5.50), sirloin steak (£7.50), and puddings like treacle tart, bread and butter pudding or banoffi pie (£2.20); fish barbecue Friday and Saturday evening and Sunday lunchtime (about £7). This year Sandra has increased the number of real ales on handpump to Greene King IPA and Abbot, Shepherd Neame Masterbrew and Spitfire and a guest beer like Ridleys Rumpus tapped from the cask. The big walled garden behind the pub – an acre or so, with grass, trees and shrubs – is a particular draw in summer; there are more seats on a small terrace. The nearby 12th-c castle keep is worth a visit. *(Recommended by Paul Edwards, Gwen and Peter Andrews, Ian Phillips, W W Burke, Richard Siebert)*

Grays (Greene King, Ridleys) ~ Tenant Mrs Sandra Ferguson ~ Real ale ~ Meals and snacks (limited menu Mon evening, except bank holidays; till 10pm Tues-Sat) ~ (01787) 460350 ~ Children except in public bar ~ Trad Jazz last Sun lunchtime of month, acoustic guitar group Fri evening ~ Open 11.30-3, 6-11; 12-3,7-10.30 Sun

CHAPPEL TL8927 Map 5
Swan

Wakes Colne; pub visible just off A604 Colchester—Halstead

In summer, the sheltered suntrap cobbled courtyard of this charming old pub has a rather continental feel with parasols, big tubs overflowing with flowers, and French street signs. The friendly spacious and low-beamed rambling bar has standing oak timbers dividing off side areas, banquettes around lots of dark tables, one or two swan pictures and plates on the white and partly panelled walls, and a few attractive tiles above the very big fireplace which is filled with lots of plants in summer; one bar is no smoking. Good value popular bar food includes filled french rolls or sandwiches (from £1.60, delicious rare roast beef £2.95), ploughman's (from £3.50), chicken curry, home-made chicken and mushroom pie or gammon with pineapple (£4.95), very good fried cod or rock eel (£5.45), scampi (£5.95) and sirloin steak (£9.95), fresh fish dishes, and good puddings (from £2.25). Well kept Greene King IPA and Abbot and Mauldons on handpump, a good selection of wines by the glass and just under two dozen malt whiskies served by cheery helpful staff; fruit machine, cribbage, dominoes, and faint piped music. The nearby Railway Centre (a must for train buffs) is just a few minutes' walk away. *(Recommended by Gwen and Peter Andrews, R A Buckler, DFL, B and M Parkin, C H and P Stride, Jill Bickerton, Mavis and John Wright, Paul Randall, Mrs P Goodwyn)*

Free house ~ Licensees Terence Martin and M A Hubbard ~ Real ale ~ Meals and snacks (till 10.30) ~ Restaurant ~ (01787) 222353 ~ Children over 5 in restaurant and eating area of bar ~ Open 11-3, 6-11; 12-3, 7-10.30 Sun

CLAVERING TL4731 Map 5
Cricketers

B1038 Newport—Buntingford, Newport end of village

The plushly comfortable interior of this spotlessly kept 16th-c dining pub accommodates a well heeled set drawn by its elaborate menu: starters like duck liver and pink peppercorn terrine, roasted red peppers with tomatoes, garlic, anchovies and olive oil with olive foccalia (£4.25), crabmeat and spring onion pasta parcels with crab bisque (£4.75) and main courses such as steak, mushroom, onion and ale puff pastry pie (£8.75), bream grilled with ginger butter sauce, cucumber and lemon (£9.50), pork loin stuffed with stilton cheese and apricots with armagnac sauce or grilled salmon with fresh dill and tomato (£9.75) and beef fillet on a crouton and pâté with red wine sauce. The roomy L-shaped beamed bar has standing timbers resting on new brickwork, and pale green plush button-backed banquettes, stools and windsor chairs around shiny wooden tables on a pale green carpet, with gleaming copper pans and horsebrasses and dried flowers in the big fireplace (open fire in colder weather), and fresh flowers; one area is no smoking; piped music. Well kept Adnams, Boddingtons, and Flowers IPA on handpump. The attractive front terrace has picnic tables and umbrellas and colourful flowering shrubs. Pretty new bedrooms. *(Recommended by Maysie*

Thompson, Quentin Williamson, Ian Phillips, Mr and Mrs N Chesher, Andrew and Joan Life, Michael Boniface; more reports please)

Free house ~ Licensees Trevor and Sally Oliver ~ Real ale ~ Meals and snacks (till 10pm) ~ Restaurant ~ (01799) 550442 ~ Children in eating area of bar and in restaurant ~ Open 10.30-3, 6-11; 12-3, 7-10.30 Sun; cl 25-26 December ~ Bedrooms: £58B/£76B

nr COGGESHALL TL8522 Map 5
Compasses

Pattiswick; signposted from A120 about 2 miles W of Coggeshall; OS Sheet 168 map reference 820247

Readers enjoy the very friendly welcome at this remote country pub with its neatly kept spaciously attractive comfortable beamed bars with tiled floors and lots of brass ornaments, Greene King IPA, Abbot and Rayments on handpump, and darts and piped music. Popular good value home-made bar food in generous helpings includes sandwiches and filled baguettes (from £3.65), filled baked potatoes (from £4.25), ploughman's (£5.50), turkey curry or battered cod (£6.95), liver and bacon suet pudding or toad in the hole (£7.95), fisherman's pie or steak and kidney pie (£8.50), poached hake fillet in lobster sauce or turkey (£10.95), pork fillet steak in cream cheese, leek and ham sauce (£11.95). Several interesting vegetarian dishes include thai cashew nut risotto or vegetables, cream cheese and mozzarella bake (£8.95). Puddings (£2.95). Outside there are seats on the lawns, and a new adventure playground. *(Recommended by Michael Hyde, Roger and Pauline Pearce, Evelyn and Derek Walter, Gordon Neighbour, Richard Siebert, John Fahy, Mrs P Goodwyn)*

Free house ~ Licensees Chris and Gilbert Heap ~ Real ale ~ Meals and sncaks ~ Restaurant ~ (01376) 561322 ~ Children in eating area of bar and restaurant ~ Open 11-3, 6.30(6 Sat)-11; 12-10.30 Sun (12-3, 7-10.30 Sun winter); cl 25-26 Dec evening

DEDHAM TM0533 Map 5
Marlborough Head 🍺

This nicely old-fashioned friendly pub is right in the heart of Constable's old town, directly opposite the artist's school, and the handsome flushwork church tower that features in a number of his paintings. The lovely old central lounge has lots of beams and pictures, a wealth of finely carved woodwork, and a couple of roaring log fires. The beamed and timbered bar is set out for eating with lots of tables (which have a numbered pebble for ordering food) in wooden alcoves around its plum-coloured carpet. Although the imaginative menu is very popular there's still a smartly relaxed pubby atmosphere; it's best to arrive early as it fills up quickly. Bar food includes sandwiches (from £1.95), soup (£2), pâté (£3.95), marinated herring fillets (£3.75), chestnut bake (£5.95), cod fillet or braised lamb hearts in gravy (£6.35), bacon, mushroom and tomato quiche (£4.60), hare casserole (£6.65), fried chicken breast with buttery asparagus sauce (£6.85) and puddings such as treacle tart (£2.75), carrot cake (£2.95) and baby almond meringues with butterscotch sauce and cream (£3.10); they also do morning coffee and afternoon teas. Ind Coope Burton and Greene King IPA on handpump or under light blanket pressure. Seats on the terrace or in the garden at the back; nice comfortable bedrooms. *(Recommended by B N F and M Parkin, John Kirk, Mark Baynham, Gordon Tong, Simon Penny, Ian Phillips, Melanie Bradshaw, Derek and Margaret Underwood)*

Ind Coope (Allied) ~ Lease: Brian and Jackie Wills and Linda Mower ~ Real ale ~ Meals and snacks (all day) ~ (01206) 323250/323124 ~ Children in restaurant ~ Open 10am-11pm; 11.30-10.30 Sun; cl Dec 25 ~ Bedrooms: £32.50S/£50S

It's very helpful if you let us know up-to-date food prices when you report on pubs.

FEERING TL8720 Map 5
Sun ◀

3 Feering Hill; before Feering proper, B1024 just NE of Kelvedon

There's a busy chatty atmosphere in the comfortably refurbished bar of this handsome 16th-c inn. Standing timbers break up the several areas of the friendly beamed bar which has plenty of neatly matching tables and chairs, and green-cushioned stools and banquettes around the walls. Carvings on the beams in the lounge are said to be linked with Catherine of Aragon, and there's a handsome canopy with a sun motif over the woodburning stove; newspapers to read, piped music, fruit machine, chess, cards, backgammon. Five very well kept real ales change virtually daily, with around 17 different brews passing through the handpumps each week, possibly Charles Wells Bombardier, Fullers London Pride, Jennings Cumberland, Wadworths 6X or Wolf Coyote. They also have a changing farm cider, and a good range of malt whiskies. Their Easter and August bank holiday beer festivals have a regional theme, when they'll stock ales from a particular county or area. The very big choice of bar meals is written up on blackboards over the fireplace and might include soup (£1.80), deep-fried cheddar with tikka dip (£2.80), smoked salmon and asparagus terrine (£3.30), rabbit in red wine and caper sauce (£5.20), pork and apple or vegetable pie (£4.95), lasagne or lamb steak in plum sauce (£5.95), venison steak in port and apple sauce (£6.30), and puddings such as spotted dick (£1.95) or white and dark chocolate mousse with cherries in sugared shell (£3.50). There are quite a few seats and tables on a partly-covered paved patio behind; there may be barbecues out here on sunny weekends. There are more tables in an attractive garden beyond the car park. *(Recommended by John Fahy, M A and C R Starling, Pat and Tony Martin, Peter Baggott, Chris Smith)*

Free house ~ Licensees Charles and Kim Scicluna ~ Real ale ~ Meals and snacks (not 25-26 Dec or 1 Jan) ~ (01376) 570442 ~ Well behaved children ~ Open 11-3, 6-11; 12-3, 6-10.30 Sun

FULLER STREET TL7416 Map 5
Square & Compasses

From A12 Chelmsford—Witham take Hatfield Peverel exit, and from B1137 there follow Terling singpost, keeping straight on past Terling towards Great Leighs; from A131 Chelmsford—Braintree turn off in Great Leighs towards Fairstead and Terling

Quiet and even a bit gentrified at lunchtime, this small civilised pub is in attractive countryside, and handy for the Essex Way long-distance footpath. The open-plan L-shaped beamed bar, comfortable and well lit, has a woodburner as well as a big log fire, and an understated rural decor – stuffed birds including an albino pheasant above the mantelpiece, traps, old country photographs, brasses. Tables outside have gentle country views. Good if not cheap food all cooked to order (so there may be a wait) includes sandwiches (from £2.25), a most enjoyable tomato soup, nourishing winter game soup (£2.50), deep-fried brie (£3.20); main courses come with lots of fresh vegetables, and puddings are good. A dish of chicken leg stuffed with chopped pork, ham, sage and onion has been much enjoyed recently, they do skate very well (£6.75), and the pheasant casserole (£7) is popular – there's usually game in season, as the landlord shoots; the pub is much used by shooting parties. Tables can be booked. Well kept Ridleys PA and ESX tapped from the cask, decent French regional wines, good coffee, attentive service, unobtrusive piped music, fruit machine. There's a warm rather more relaxed atmosphere in the evenings. *(Recommended by Gwen and Peter Andrews, Eddie Edwards, Paul and Ursula Randall)*

Ridleys ~ Licensees Howard and Jenny Potts ~ Real ale ~ Meals and snacks ~ (01245) 361477 ~ Chilren in eating area of bar ~ Open 11.30-3, 6.30(7 in winter)-11; 12-3, 7-10.30 Sun

Pubs brewing their own beers are listed at the back of the book.

FYFIELD TL5606 Map 5
Black Bull
B184, N end of village

This comfortably welcoming 15th-c vine covered pub is popular for its wide range of good value very tasty bar food such as soft roes (£3), green lip mussels with black bean sauce (£3.65), tiger prawns cooked with fresh chillies and garlic (£3.95), chilli (£4), home-made gravadlax (£4.75), steak and kidney pudding (£6.95), kleftiko (£7.20), pork fillet pan fried with fresh cranberries (£7.15), poached salmon fillet with dill sauce (£7.35), skate wing (£7.50), duck breast with plum and brandy sauce (£7.75) and a seafood selection in garlic butter (£8.75); puddings like chocolate trifle cake or bread pudding (from £2). Inside, the series of communicating rooms have low ceilings, big black beams, standing timbers, and cushioned wheelback chairs and modern settles on the muted maroon carpet; warm winter fire; no-smoking area. Well kept Courage Directors, Ruddles Best and Wadworths 6X on handpump; darts, cribbage, piped music, fruit machine. Outside there are lots of barrels for tables, or filled with flowers, and by the car park is an aviary with budgerigars and cockatiels. There are picnic tables on a nearby stretch of grass, as well as to the side of the building. *(Recommended by DFL, Gwen and Peter Andrews, S Palmer, Nigel and Lindsay Chapman, Paul Barstow, Karyn Taylor, Ian Phillips, Beryl and Bill Farmer, Mr and Mrs N Spink)*

Free house ~ Licensees Alan Smith and Nicola Eldridge ~ Real ale ~ Meals and snacks ~ Restaurant ~ (01277) 899225 ~ Open 11-2.30(3 Sat), 6.30-11; 12-3, 7-10.30 Sun

GOSFIELD TL7829 Map 5
Green Man 🍴 ♀
3 m N of Braintree

Even when this smart restauranty pub is very busy (you will need to book) service is always impeccable and the atmosphere cheerfully relaxed and conversational. One of the main attractions is the splendid lunchtime cold table which has a marvellous help-yourself choice of home-cooked ham, tongue, beef and turkey, dressed salmon or crab in season, game pie, salads and home-made pickles (£6.95). Well cooked English style menu includes soups like stilton and celery (£2.90), home-made duck and brandy pâté (£3.25), fresh battered cod (£6.50), home-made steak and kidney pudding (£6.95), sirloin of beef (£7), lamb chops in port and cranberry sauce (£7.75), venison in beer (£8.95) and half roast duck with orange sauce (£9.95). A fabulous range of puddings might include raspberry pavlova or steamed marmalade pudding (£3.20), vegetables are fresh and the chips home-made. The two little bars have a relaxed atmosphere, and the dining room is no smoking. Greene King IPA and Abbot on handpump, and decent nicely priced wines, many by the glass; darts, pool, fruit machine and juke box, dominoes, cribbage. *(Recommended by Gwen and Peter Andrews, Mike and Heather Watson, Evelyn and Derek Walter, DFL, R C Morgan, Thomas Nott)*

Greene King ~ Lease: John Arnold ~ Real ale ~ Meals and snacks (not Sun evening) ~ Restaurant ~ (01787) 472746 ~ Well behaved children in eating area lunchtime and early evening ~ Open 11-3, 6.30-11; 12-3, 7-10.30 Sun

GREAT YELDHAM TL7638 Map 5
White Hart 🍴 ♀
Poole Street; A604 Halstead—Haverhill
Essex Dining Pub of the Year

This attractive black and white timbered Tudor house really stands apart for its exceptionally good inventive menu, superbly prepared food and extensive wine list. You can make your meal as smart or informal as you choose as the same menu is available in the bar or restaurant. This year they've introduced a very good value set menu (two course £7.50, three course £10.50) which might include broccoli and blue cheese soup, goat and pepper stew with hazelnut dumplings and orange mousse with almond biscuits. Friendly informed and interested service. From the main menu starters might be spinach risotto with parmesan and roasted red peppers (£4.25), parma ham with chargrilled polenta and sun-dried tomato salsa (£4.95), fried scallops with stir-fried beansprouts and chilli relish (£6.50), with main courses such as ploughman's (£4.95), hot thai chicken curry with lemon rice and stir-fry vegetables (£7.75), baked aubergine with stir-fried vegetables and coriander pesto or fried breast of wood pigeon (£7.95), tenderloin of pork with apple and spinach tart (£9.75), chargrilled breast of chicken with gorgonzola polenta and mediterranean vegetables (£9.25), fried monkfish with courgette tagliatelle, aubergine purée, pancetta and tomato salsa (£12.95). Irresistible puddings might include sultana and apple pudding with blueberry custard (£3), treacle tart with crème fraîche and hazelnut ice cream (£3.75), warm rice pudding with exotic fruit brochette and coconut ice cream (£4.25), and unpasteurised cheeses (£5.25); smaller helpings for children; no-smoking restaurant. As well as an impressive list of about 100 well described wines there are about 17 wines by the glass including a good selection of pudding wines. Well kept Adnams Best, Charles Wells Bombardier, Shepherd Neame Spitfire and Wadworths 6X on handpump. The main areas have stone and wood floors with some dark oak panelling especially around the fireplace. The pretty well kept garden has seats among a variety of trees and shrubs on the lawns. *(Gwen and Peter Andrews, John Fahy, Gordon Neighbour, Richard Siebert, B and M Parkin, Paul Randall; more reports please)*

Free house ~ Licensees Roger Jones and John Hoskins ~ Real ale ~ Meals and snacks (12-2, 6.30-10) ~ Restaurant ~ (01787) 237250 ~ Well behaved seated children ~ Open 11-3, 6-11; 12-2, 7-10.30 Sun; cl 25-26 Dec and 1 Jan evenings

HASTINGWOOD TL4807 Map 5
Rainbow & Dove

¼ mile from M11, junction 7; Hastingwood signposted after Ongar signs at exit roundabout

This warmly welcoming 17th-c rose-covered cottage with its jovially charismatic landlord makes a cheerfully relaxing break away from the busy motorway nearby. There are cosy fires in the three homely little low-beamed rooms which open off the main bar area; the one on the left is particularly snug and beamy, with the lower part of its wall stripped back to bare brick and decorated with brass pistols and plates. Very much improved under the new licensees, bar food includes sandwiches (from £1.75), ploughman's (from £3.60), steak and kidney pie (£4.75) and lots of fresh fish like cod mornay, brill in lemon sauce, hake and skate on a specials board. They now serve real ales: well kept Ansells, Friary Meux and a guest like Flowers Original; piped music; picnic tables under cocktail parasols, on a stretch of grass hedged off from the car park. *(Recommended by Joy and Peter Heatherley, L Miall, Tony Beaulah, Mr and Mrs N Chesher, Wayne Brindle, Quentin Williamson)*

Carlsberg Tetleys ~ Tenants Jamie and Richard Keep ~ Real ale ~ Meals and snacks ~ (01279) 415419 ~ Children welcome ~ Open 11.30-3, 6-11; 12-4, 7-10.30 Sun

HORNDON ON THE HILL TQ6683 Map 3
Bell 🍴 ♀ 🛏

M25 junction 30 into A13, then left into B1007 after 7 miles, village signposted from here

For the last half century this lovely old flower bedecked medieval inn has been meticulously run by the same enthusiastic hard-working family. Recently the restaurant menu has proved so popular that they've started offering it throughout the pub and laying up tables at one side of the warmly welcoming open-plan bar for dining – they operate a book as you arrive system for these few tables. Imaginative carefully home-prepared bar food which tends towards English country style might include carrot and coriander soup (£2.85), venison and vegetable pasty (£4.95), lamb and vegetable hotpot (£6.25), home-made pork and leek sausages (£6.50), chicken leg stuffed with black pudding (£6.95), loin of pork with morel mushrooms (£7.50), chicken breast, mussels, saffron and pernod

(£9.95), venison cutlets, haggis and potato rosti (£10.80) and puddings like steamed orange pudding and chocolate ice cream and citrus sauce (£3.50). There's a wine list of over 100 well chosen wines from all over the world with about 13 by the glass listed on a blackboard with suggestions on what to drink with your food; you can also buy them off-sales; Bass and Fullers London Pride and three changing guests such as Adnams, Crouchvale, Mauldons or Ridleys on handpump. The heavily beamed bar has some antique high-backed settles and plush burgundy stools and benches, and rugs on the flagstones or highly polished oak floorboards. Seats in a bow window at the back give onto views over the fields. On the last weekend in June the High Road outside is closed (by Royal Charter) for period-costume festivities and a crafts fair; the pub holds a feast then. Very attractive beamed bedrooms; no-smoking area in restaurant. *(Recommended by DFL, Richard Siebert, Joy and Peter Heatherley, K Flack, Thomas Nott, Mrs S Miller, Quentin Williamson, Dr and Mrs Baker, James Nunns, M J How, Bob and Maggie Atherton, Mr and Mrs J R Morris, Kenneth and Muriel Holden, Mavis and John Wright, Stephen Brown, Ron Gentry, Dave Irving, Mark Newbould)*

Free house ~ Licensee John Vereker ~ Real ale ~ Meals and snacks (12-1.45, 6.30-9.45) ~ Restaurant ~ (01375) 673154/672451 ~ Children in eating area of bar and restaurant ~ Open 11-2.30(3 Sat), 6-11; 12-3, 7-10.30 Sun ~ Bedrooms: £46.25B/£52.50B

LAMARSH TL8835 Map 5
Lion

From Bures on B1508 Sudbury—Colchester take Station Road, passing station; Lamarsh then signposted

There are marvellous views over the fields and colour-washed houses of the Stour valley from tables and pews (in stalls with red velvet curtain dividers) in the charmingly atmospheric yellow-painted bar of this friendly isolated old hunting lodge. As well as abundant timbering there are attractive dried flowers and plants, local scenes on the walls, a roaring log fire, and unobtrusive piped music; no-smoking area. Hearty bar food might include soups such as carrot and orange (£2.25), huge filled rolls with a very flexible range of fillings (from £3.35), stilton and walnut bake or chicken, ham and broccoli pie (£5.25), well liked salads such as Greek-style tuna with feta cheese (£5.95), Greek lamb (£6.20), fresh fish on Thursday and Friday, and home-made puddings such as cherry pie (£2.95). Well kept Nethergate Suffolk and two guests like Fullers London Pride and Greene King IPA on handpump, a range of malt whiskies, and decent dry white wine by the glass; friendly staff. Pool, darts, cribbage, fruit machine, video game. Biggish sheltered sloping garden. *(Recommended by Gwen and Peter Andrews, Ian Phillips, MDN; more reports please)*

Free house ~ Licensees John and Jackie O'Sullivan ~ Real ale ~ Meals and snacks (till 10pm, not Sun evening) ~ Restaurant ~ (01787) 227918 ~ Children in eating area ~ Open 11-3, 6-11; 12-3, 7-10.30 Sun; cl evening 25 Dec

LANGHAM TM0233 Map 5
Shepherd & Dog ♀

Moor Rd/High St; village signposted off A12 N of Colchester

This good natured warmly friendly inn is notable for its cheerful well run atmosphere – we're sure you won't find a more happily dedicated team of hard working licensees and staff in the county. Virtually all their produce is bought in the village and the not over elaborate but reliably interesting daily changing menu of good very reasonably priced tasty food served in huge helpings might include tomato and basil soup (£1.95), home-made chicken liver and walnut pâté (£3.50), prawns in garlic mayonnaise (£3.90), chicken curry (£5.25), steak and suet pudding or cassoulet (£5.95), feta and spinach filo parcels (£4.95), a range of steaks (from £6.95), skate (£7.95). Well kept Greene King IPA, Abbot, Rayments and Sorcerer and Nethergate Bitter and Old Growler on handpump, and a short but decent wine list. An engaging hotchpotch of styles, the spick and span L-shaped bar has an interesting collection of continental bottled beers, and there's often a sale of books for charity. Tables outside. *(Recommended by Quentin Williamson, Gwen and Peter Andrews, Thomas Nott, A C Morrison, C H and P Stride, Cheryl and Keith Roe, J S Rutter)*

Free house ~ Licensees Paul Barnes and Jane Graham ~ Real ale ~ Meals and snacks (12-2.15, 6-9.30) ~ Restaurant ~ (01206) 272711 ~ Children till 9pm ~ Open 11-3, 5.30(6 Sat)-11; 12-3, 7-10.30 Sun; cl 26 Dec

LEIGH ON SEA TQ8385 Map 3
Crooked Billet ◗

51 High St; from A13 follow signpost to station, then cross bridge over railway towards waterside

New licensees have perked up this inviting old place braced right up against the sea wall with fresh paint and lots more characterful nautical bric-a-brac. There are good sea views from big bay windows in the traditional homely lounge bar which has seats built around the walls, a solid fuel stove, and photographs of local cockle smacks; on the left, the bare-floored public bar has a big coal effect gas fire and more photographs. Well kept Adnams, Benskins, Billet (brewed for the pub by Carlsberg Tetleys), Ind Coope Burton and Marstons Pedigree on handpump or tapped from the cask as well as upwards of three guests from a range of about 300. The spring and autumn beer festivals at this inviting old place are quite a novelty as you can go down to their cellar to choose from about 30 independent cask-conditioned ales; they're also planning to have a summer cider festival. Lunchtime home-made bar food includes soup and baguette (£2.50), sausage baguette (from £3.25), ploughman's, crab or salmon platter and vegetarian dishes (£4.25). Friendly service may be a bit stretched on busy sunny days. You can watch the shellfish boats in the old-fashioned working harbour from seats out on the big terrace, which has an outside servery used on fine afternoons, and there's a new garden and terrace at the side of the building. No children. *(Recommended by Tim Heywood, Sophie Wilne, Dawn Krendall, E G Parish, Nigel Norman, Tina and David Woods-Taylor, Thomas Nott; more reports please)*

Carlsberg Tetleys ~ Managers Wayne and Tracy Bowes ~ Real ale ~ Lunchtime meals and snacks (till 2.30; not Sunday) ~ (01702) 714854 ~ Live music Mon or Thurs evening ~ Open 11(12 winter)-11; Sun 12-10.30

LITTLE BRAXTED TL8314 Map 5
Green Man

Kelvedon Road; village signposted off B1389 by NE end of A12 Witham bypass – keep on patiently

The unpretentious rural character of this isolated brick house which is tucked away on a very quiet lane remains unchanging over the years. The cosy welcoming little lounge houses an interesting collection of bric-a-brac, including some 200 horsebrasses, some harness, mugs hanging from a beam, a lovely copper urn, and an open fire. The tiled public bar leads to a games room with darts, shove-ha'penny, dominoes, cribbage, and fruit machine. Well kept Ridleys IPA and Rumpus dispensed from handpumps in the form of 40mm brass cannon shells; several malt whiskies, home-made lemonade in summer and mulled wine in winter. Good, hearty home-made bar food includes sandwiches (from £1.80), filled french bread (£2.50), filled baked potatoes (from £2.55), and daily specials like liver and apple casserole (£4.25), tuna and sweetcorn pasta pot, mushroom stroganoff or chicken breast in mushroom sauce (£5.25) and lasagne or fidget pie (£5.50), steak and ale pie (£5.95) and puddings like chocolate mousse or blackberry and apple coconut crumble (£1.95). There are picnic tables and a pretty pond in the delightfully sheltered garden behind. No children. *(Recommended by Gwen and Peter Andrews, Jill Bickerton, Thomas Nott, Cheryl and Keith Roe, Tina and David Woods-Taylor)*

Ridleys ~ Tenants Tony and Andrea Wiley ~ Real ale ~ Meals and snacks ~ (01621) 891659 ~ Open 11.30-3, 6-11; 12-3, 7-10.30 Sun

LITTLE DUNMOW TL6521 Map 5
Flitch of Bacon 🛏

Village signposted off A120 E of Dunmow, then turn right on village loop road

There's a genuinely friendly atmosphere at this delightfully unspoilt rural tavern where country characters rub shoulders with visiting businessmen. The small timbered bar is simply but attractively furnished, mainly with flowery-cushioned pews, and has prettily arranged flowers on the tables, and ochre walls. Quietly relaxing at lunchtime during the week, the atmosphere can be vibrantly cheerful in the evenings – especially on one of the Saturdays they're singing through a musical around the piano at the back. A sensibly small range of unpretentious very tasty bar food all freshly cooked by the landlady might include generous sandwiches (£1.95) – including excellent home-carved ham (£1.95) – soup (£2.50), ploughman's (£3.25), anchovies on toast (£3.50), ham and eggs with a crusty roll (£4), Friday fish and chips (£4.50), smoked salmon and scrambled eggs (£5.50), and three or four changing hot dishes such as sausage hotpot (£4.50) game dishes, pork and apple or steak and kidney pie (£6.50), and a couple of puddings; good buffet lunch on Sunday. Fullers London Pride, Greene King IPA and Shepherd Neame Spitfire under light blanket pressure. Friendly and thoughtful service; cribbage, dominoes. The pub looks across the quiet lane to a broad expanse of green, and has a few picnic tables on the edge; the nearby church of St Mary is well worth a visit. *(Recommended by Gwen and Peter Andrews, Michael Gittins, Neville Kenyon, Tony Beaulah, Charles and Daniele Smith, John Fahy, Mike and Karen England, Nikki Moffat, C H and P Stride, N G Neate, S D Penn)*

Free house ~ Licensees Bernard and Barbara Walker ~ Real ale ~ Meals and snacks ~ (01371) 820323 ~ Children in restaurant ~ Open 12-3(3.30 Sat), 6-11; 12-6(5 winter) Sun ~ Bedrooms: £29.60S/£49.60S

LITTLEBURY TL5139 Map 5
Queens Head ♀ 🍺 🛏

B1383 NW of Saffron Walden; not far from M11 junction 9, but exit northbound only, access southbound only

This vibrant bustling old village inn is carefully refurbished to make the most of its unassuming appeal – flooring tiles, beams, simple but attractive wooden furniture, old local photographs, bunches of dried flowers and plants, and snug side areas leading off the bar; a small area in the restaurant is no smoking; darts, shove-ha'penny, cribbage, dominoes and piped music. A very good range of real ales described in helpful tasting notes is an attraction here (with one beer for just £1 a pint on Monday-Thursday), they have well kept Bass and Timothy Taylor Landlord and around five guests like Hancocks HB, Marstons Best, Mansfield Riding, and Mauldons Black Adder as well as interesting bottled beers. During their Easter real ale festival they might have over 70 different beers. Good value bar food might include baked avocado with stilton butter (£3.10), seared scallops on endive with lardons and lemon sauce (£4.50), vegetarian moussaka or fresh herb omelette (£5.80), scampi (£6.10), roast rock eel on mushroom butter sauce (£6.40), chicken supreme on red wine mushroom sauce, pork fillet on red onion confit or poached skate with caper sauce (£6.80), puddings like hot pear and chocolate cake with chocolate fudge sauce or bread and butter pudding (£2.50); decent wine list. There are tables out in a nicely planted walled garden, with swings, stepping stumps, a climbing frame and slide for children. *(Recommended by Evelyn and Derek Walter, Gwen and Peter Andrews, Richard Siebert, John Fahy, Joy and Peter Heatherley, Sarah and Ian Shannon, S Palmer, Wayne Brindle, AW, BW, Marjorie and Bernard Parkin)*

Free house ~ Licensees Deborah and Jeremy O'Gorman ~ Real ale ~ Meals and lunchtime snacks (not Sun evening) ~ Restaurant ~ (01799) 522251 ~ Children in eating area of bar till 9.30 ~ Open 12-11; 12-4.30, 6.30-10.30 Sun ~ Bedrooms: £32.95B/£49.95B

MILL GREEN TL6400 Map 5
Viper ◀

Mill Green Rd; from Fryerning (which is signposted off north-east bound A12 Ingatestone bypass) follow Writtle signposts; OS Sheet 167 map reference 640019

In summer this quaint little woodland pub is almost hidden by overflowing hanging baskets and window boxes, and the cottage garden is an enchanting mass of colour. Two timeless little lounge rooms have spindleback seats, armed country kitchen chairs, and tapestried wall seats around neat little old tables, and a warming log fire. The fairly basic parquet-floored tap room (where booted walkers are directed) is more simply furnished with shiny wooden traditional wall seats, and beyond there's another room with country kitchen chairs and sensibly placed darts; shove-ha'penny, dominoes, cribbage and a fruit machine. Three very well kept changing real ales such as Crouch Vale Best, Mansfield Bitter and Ridleys IPA on handpump are served from an oak-panelled counter. Simple bar snacks include soup (£1.60), good sandwiches (from £1.85), chilli (£3.25), and ploughman's (£3.60). No children. *(Recommended by Quentin Williamson, John Fahy, R H Rowley, Peter Baggott, R T and J L Moggridge, Pete Baker, James Nunns, Andrew Robson, Richard Siebert, Mr and Mrs J R Morris)*

Free house ~ Licensee Fred Beard ~ Real ale ~ Lunchtime snacks ~ (01277) 352010 ~ Open 11-2.30(3 Sat), 6-11; 12-3, 7-10.30 Sun

NAVESTOCK TQ5397 Map 5
Plough ◀

Sabines Rd, Navestock Heath (off main rd at Alma Arms)

This enjoyable friendly no-frills country pub is worth knowing for its very good range of around eight rotating well kept real ales such as Burntwood Bitter, Fullers London Pride, Flowers IPA, Nethergate IPA, Marstons Pedigree, Ridleys IPA on handpump. Several neatly kept interconnecting rooms have a mix of dark wood solid chairs with flowery-cushioned seats around polished wood tables, with horsebrasses and dried flowers on the beams, and an open fire. Straightforward good value bar food from a simple menu includes baguettes (from £2.45), filled baked potatoes (from £2.75), ploughman's (from £3.85), ham, egg and chips (£4.25), scampi (£4.65), roast chicken (£4.95), lasagne (£5.25), fish and chips or steak and mushroom pie (£5.45), as well as a couple of daily specials; puddings (£2.25); two course Sunday roast (£7.25). Darts, cribbage, dominoes, piped music; no-smoking dining area. *(Recommended by John Fahy, Derek Patey, Richard Siebert; more reports please)*

Free house ~ Managers Marlene Brown and Rita Titchner ~ Real ale ~ Meals and snacks (12-9; not Sun evening) ~ (01277) 372296 ~ Children welcome ~ Open 11-11; 12-10.30 Sun

NORTH FAMBRIDGE TQ8597 Map 5
Ferryboat £

The Quay; village signposted from B1012 E off S Woodham Ferrers; keep on past railway

The nearby River Crouch sometimes creeps up the lane towards the car park of this genuinely unpretentious 500-year-old weatherboarded pub, which is quietly tucked away with lovely marsh views and some good lonely walks. It's simply furnished with traditional wall benches, settles and chairs on its stone floor, nautical memorabilia, old-fashioned lamps, and a few historic boxing-gloves. There's a log fire at one end, and a woodburning stove at the other. Very good value straightforward bar food includes sandwiches (from £1.50), soup (£1.60), ploughman's (from £3), deep-fried cod or plaice (£3.50), roast chicken (£3.95), lemon sole (£6.50), venison in port and red wine or fried chicken stuffed with prawns and lobster (£7). Well kept Flowers IPA on handpump and guests like Morlands Old Speckled Hen or Wadworths 6X; friendly chatty landlord; shove ha'penny, table skittles, cribbage, dominoes, and piped music. There's a pond with ducks and carp, and seats in the garden. *(Recommended by Peter Baggott, Richard Siebert, George Atkinson, Mike and Karen England, Paul Mason, Gwen and Peter Andrews, Keith and Cheryl Roe)*

Free house ~ Licensee Roy Maltwood ~ Real ale ~ Meals and snacks (till 10pm) ~ Restaurant ~ (01621) 740208 ~ Children in family room or dining conservatory ~ Open 11-3, 6-11; 12-10.30 Sun; 12-3, 7-10.30 winter Sun

SAFFRON WALDEN TL5438 Map 5
Eight Bells
Bridge Street; B184 towards Cambridge

Fresh fish from Lowestoft or Billingsgate is one attraction at this handsomely timbered black and white Tudor inn. The bar menu includes home-made soup (£2.10), ploughman's (from £4.25), Cromer crab (£4.75), lasagne (£5.85), mushrooms thermidor (£5.95), skate with capers (£7.25), calf liver with smoked ham, mushroom and cream sauce (£8.60), and steaks (from £10.30), as well as daily specials. Well kept Adnams, Friary Meux, Ind Coope Burton, Tetleys, and a changing guest on handpump, and half a dozen decent wines by the glass (with a choice of glass size). The neatly kept friendly open-plan bar is divided by old timbers, with modern oak settles forming small booths around the tables. The bar leads into the old kitchen which is now a carpeted family room with an open fire. The partly no-smoking restaurant is in a splendidly timbered hall with high rafters, tapestries and flags. There are seats in the garden. Nearby Audley End makes a good family outing, and the pub is close to some good walks. *(Recommended by Maysie Thompson, Andy Cunningham, Yvonne Hannaford, M A Butler, M J How, John Fahy, Sarah and Ian Shannon, Stephen Brown)*

Ind Coope (Allied) ~ Manager David Gregory ~ Real ale ~ Meals and snacks (12-9.30) ~ Restaurant ~ (01799) 522790 ~ Children in restaurant and family room ~ Open 11-11; 12-10.30 Sun

STOCK TQ6998 Map 5
Hoop ♠
B1007; from A12 Chelsmford bypass take Galleywood, Billericay turn-off

There's a really friendly atmosphere in the classless and happily unsophisticated little bar of this well liked village local, as well as a fine range of about six changing real ales that might be from Adnams, Batemans, Crouch Vale, Everards, Fullers, Nethergate or Wolf, on handpump or tapped from the cask. During the May Day week they hold a beer festival when there might be around 150; farm ciders, summer country wines, and winter mulled wine. There are brocaded wall seats around dimpled copper tables on the left, a cluster of brocaded stools on the right, and a coal-effect gas fire in the big brick fireplace. Big helpings of good value bar food include soup (£1.50), ploughman's (from £3), steak and kidney pie or cod (£3.50), beef and ale pie (£4), chicken curry, fish pie or braised steak and dumpling (£4.50), skate (£5), lemon sole and lots of other fresh fish (£5.50); vegetables are charged in addition to these prices; puddings (£1.50). Sensibly placed darts (the heavy black beams are studded with hundreds of darts flights). Lots of picnic tables in the big sheltered back garden are prettily bordered with flowers. *(Recommended by Tina and David Woods-Taylor, D E Twitchett, Beryl and Bill Farmer, DFL, Derek Patey, Richard Byrne, Gwen and Peter Andrews, Mr and Mrs N Spink, Mr and Mrs J R Morris)*

Free house ~ Licensee Albert Kitchin ~ Real ale ~ Meals and snacks (11-10.30, 12-10 Sun) ~ (01277) 841137 ~ Children in restaurant ~ Open 11-11: 12-10.30 Sun

---

The ♠ symbol shows pubs which keep their beer unusually well or have a particularly good range.

STOW MARIES TQ8399 Map 5
Prince of Wales ◀

B1012 between S Woodham Ferrers and Cold Norton

Posters and certificates reflect the landlord's knowledge and enthusiasm for beer; he runs a beer wholesaling business (supplying rare ales for local beer festivals), and changes his five or six real ales weekly. As well as Fullers Chiswick, you might find Burton Bridge Bitter and Porter, Hop Back Summer Lightning, or the unusual honey-flavoured Mysicha; they also have draught Belpils lager, and a particularly unusual range of continental bottled beers, Belgian fruit beers, farm cider, and a good choice of malt whiskies and vintage ports. There's a friendly chatty atmosphere in the several cosy low-ceilinged rooms which although seemingly unchanged since the turn of the century are carefully restored in genuinely traditional style only a few years ago; few have space for more than one or two tables or wall benches on the tiled or bare-boards floors, though the room in the middle squeezes in quite a jumble of chairs and stools. One room used to be the village bakery, and in winter the oven there is still used to make bread and pizzas. Home-made bar food includes blackboard specials like fresh grilled sardines (£4.95), double lamb chops with herbs and wine (£5.45), swordfish steak or chicken breast with cheese and bacon (£5.75), and seafood pie (£7.55); the chef is Greek so expect a proper moussaka or kleftiko. In summer the gap between this simple country pub's white picket fence and the weatherboarded frontage is filled with beautiful dark red roses, with some scented pink ones at the side. There are seats and tables in a garden behind. *(Recommended by Ian Nicolson, Peter Baggott, Paul Mason, R E Baldwin)*

Free house ~ Licensee Rob Walster ~ Real ale ~ Meals and snacks ~ (01621) 828971 ~ Children in family room ~ Live music pm Sun in winter, occasionally summer too ~ . Open 11-11; 12-10.30 Sun; cl evening 25 Dec

TOOT HILL TL5103 Map 5
Green Man ♀

Village signposted from A113 in Stanford Rivers, S of Ongar; and from A414 W of Ongar

There's a very good wine list at this friendly family run country dining pub, with around 100 well chosen varieties, several half bottles and many by the glass; they also have free monthly tastings and talks by visiting merchants. The main emphasis is on the neatly looked after simply furnished long dining lounge, with its candlelit tables, fresh flowers, and attractively figured plates on a delft shelf. In the evenings they take bookings for tables in here, but only for 7.30; after that, when you turn up they put you on a queue for tables that come free. Bar food includes asparagus with herb dressing (£3.75), Scotch salmon on bed of sweet fennel (£7), lamb cutlets with mustard and herb crust (£7.50), chicken breast with wild mushroom wrapped in pastry (£8.50). A smallish and simply furnished area by the bar has mushroom plush chairs and pale mustard leatherette stools and settles, one or two hunting prints above the dark varnished wood dado, brass platters on a shelf just below the very dark grey-green ceiling, and an open fire; darts around the other side, shove-ha'penny, dominoes, cribbage and piped music; well kept Crouch Vale IPA and a weekly changing guest such as Fullers London Pride on handpump. In summer, there's a lovely mass of colourful hanging baskets, window boxes and flower tubs, prettily set off by the curlicued white iron tables and chairs – there may be Morris dancers out here then; more tables behind. A couple of miles through the attractive countryside at Greensted is St Andrews, the oldest wooden church in the world. *(Recommended by Mrs S Lamprecht, J H Gracey, Mr and Mrs N Chesher, Wayne Brindle, H O Dickinson, Lesley Zammit, JF)*

Free house ~ Licensee Peter Roads ~ Real ale ~ Meals and snacks ~ Restaurant ~ (01992) 522255 ~ Children over 10 only ~ Open 11-3, 6-11; 12-3, 7-11 Sun

It is illegal for bar staff to smoke while handling your drink.

WENDENS AMBO TL5136 Map 5
Bell 🍺

B1039 just W of village

The very extensive back garden of this jolly little beamed village pub is quite special with a big tree-sheltered lawn, lots of flower borders and unusual plant-holders. Children will be happily engaged by the wooden wendy house, a proper tree swing, a sort of mini nature-trail wandering off through the shrubs and Gertie the goat. Spotlessly kept small cottagey low ceilinged rooms ramble engagingly round to the back, with brasses on ancient timbers, wheelback chairs around neat tables, comfortably cushioned seats worked into snug alcoves, and quite a few pictures on the cream walls as well as friendly open fires. Hearty bar food includes filled rolls (from £1.90), particulary good ploughman's (£3.75), vegetarian dishes (£5.25), chillies and curries (£5.50), cajun chicken (£6.50), venison casserole (£6.75), mixed grill (£7) and puddings such as spotted dick or treacle tart (£2.20). Four well kept real ales which might be from Adnams, Everards, Fullers, Mauldons or Wadworths are well kept on handpump or tapped straight from the cask by the motherly barmaid; dominoes, cards, Monopoly and boules. The two dogs are called Kate and Samson and the friendly black cat is Thug. *(Recommended by Ian Phillips, Wayne Brindle, Maysie Thompson, B N F and M Parkin, Gwen and Peter Andrews, Stephen Brown, Mrs P J Pearce, Joe Platts)*

Free house ~ Licensees Geoff and Bernie Bates ~ Real ale ~ Meals and snacks (not Mon evening) ~ Restaurant ~ Children in dining room ~ (01799) 540382 ~ August bank hol Sat live music festival ~ Open 11.30-3(2.30 winter Mon-Fri), 6-11; 12-3, 7-10.30 Sun

WOODHAM WALTER TL8006 Map 5
Cats 🍺

Back road to Curling Tye and Maldon, from N end of village

We can't be too specific with factual information about this attractively timbered black and white country cottage as the pleasantly chatty landlord would rather we didn't include his pub in the Guide, so we can only tell you as much as we've been able to glean from readers' reports in the last year or so (in our defence we must say that letting licensees decide for us which pubs *not* to include would damage our independence almost as much as allowing other landlords to pay for their inclusion). There's a wonderfully relaxed atmosphere in the rambling low-ceilinged friendly bar which is full of interesting nooks and crannies, and traditionally decorated with low black beams and timbering set off well by neat white paintwork, as well as a warming open fire. Well kept Adnams Southwold and Broadside, Greene King IPA and Abbot and Rayments Special on handpump, and friendly service; no children or piped music. Prowling stone cats picket the roof and the feline theme is continued inside where there are shelves of china cats. *(Recommended by Sam Clark, R Morgan, Peter Baggott, Mike and Karen England; more reports please)*

Free house ~ Real ale ~ Lunchtime snacks (Thurs-Sat but see note above) ~ Open 11-2.30ish, 6.30ish-11; possibly closed Mon; may close if not busy in winter

YOUNGS END TL7319 Map 5
Green Dragon

A131 Braintree—Chelmsford, just N of Essex Showground

This well run dining pub is popular for its extensive range of very good bar food which includes quite a range of fresh fish, all served by courteous tidily dressed staff. The changing specials board might include soup (£2.25), prawn cocktail (£3.95), ploughman's (from £4), leek, mushroom and potato cakes or brown rice and hazelnut roast (£6.25), steak and kidney pie (£6.50), chicken stuffed with wild mushroom risotto with mushroom sauce (£7.25), kleftiko (£8.55), half roast duckling (£10.95), and fresh fish such as cod fishcakes with parsley sauce (£5.50), six rock oysters (£6), skate (£8.50), moules (£7.95) and bass baked with oranges and coriander (£9.95); fresh vegetables; good puddings like spotted dick or treacle sponge and a pudding trolley (£2.55). The bar part has normal pub furnishings in its two rooms, with a little extra low-ceilinged snug just beside the serving counter. Turkey carpet sweeps from the main bar room into the restaurant area, which has an understated barn theme – stripped brick walls, a manger at one end, and low beams supporting the floor of an upper 'hayloft' with steep pitched rafters. At lunchtime (not Sunday) you can have bar food down this end, where the tables are a better size than in the bar. Well kept Greene King IPA, Abbot and their seasonal beers; unobtrusive piped music (jazz on our inspection visit); fruit machine. The neat back garden has lots of picnic tables under cocktail parasols, a big green play dragon, climbing frame and budgerigar aviary. *(Recommended by Angela Copeland, Keith and Janet Morris, Paul and Ursula Randall)*

Greene King ~ Lease: Bob and Mandy Greybrook ~ Real ale ~ Meals and snacks ~ Restaurant ~ (01245) 361030 ~ Children in eating area ~ Open 11.30-3.30, 6(5.30 Sat)-11; 12-4, 6-10.30 Sun

---

Lucky Dip

Besides the fully inspected pubs, you might like to try these Lucky Dips recommended to us and described by readers (if you do, please send us reports):

Abridge [London Rd (A113); TQ4696], *Maltsters Arms*: Well kept Greene King IPA and Abbot in largely 18th-c two-bar beamed pub, open fires *(Mr and Mrs N Chesher)*

☆ **Ardleigh** [Harwich Rd; A137 – actually towards Colchester; TM0529], *Wooden Fender*: Good choice of home-cooked food inc Sun lunch and well kept Adnams, Fullers ESB, Greene King IPA and Morlands Old Speckled Hen in friendly beamed bar, open-plan but traditional; character landlord, log fires, restaurant allowing children, a pool in back garden; immaculate lavatories *(Virginia Jones, LYM)*

☆ **Barnston** [A130 SE of Dunmow; TL6419], *Bushel & Sack*: Cheerful attentive service in pleasant uncarpeted 19th-c bar with friendly atmosphere, big helpings of good value food, comfortable restaurant beyond sitting room, well kept guest beers such as Butterknowle Conciliation and Woodfordes Mother In Laws Tongue; no music *(Gwen and Peter Andrews, Cheryl and Keith Roe, Tony Beaulah)*

☆ **Battlesbridge** [Hawk Hill; TQ7894], *Barge*: Weatherboarded pub by art and craft centre in interesting village nr Crouch estuary, warren of refurbished rooms, dark beams, panelling, tucked-away corners, some flagstones, lantern lights, interesting pictures; good value bar meals, well kept Tetleys-related ales and guests such as Eldridge Pope and Marstons Pedigree, Addlestone's cider, quick friendly service; pervasive piped pop music, busy weekend lunchtimes; children's room, lots of tables in attractive front garden with barbecues *(P Barstow, K Taylor, D Brown, J Taylor, P Pearce)*

Battlesbridge [Hawk Hill], *Hawk*: Spacious refurbished beamed 17th-c pub now incorporating next-door cottage, with Bass and Worthington, enjoyable food, friendly landlord, lots of pictures, log fire, fruit machines, maybe local radio; big garden, also handy for craft centre *(George Atkinson)*

Billericay [Southend Rd, South Green; TQ6893], *Duke of York*: Pleasant beamed local with real fire, longcase clock, local photographs, upholstered settles and wheelback chairs, good value food in bar and modern restaurant, long-serving licensees, Greene King and occasional guest beers, maybe unobtrusive piped 60s pop music *(D E Twitchett)*

Bishops Green [S of Dunmow – OS Sheet 167 map ref 631179; TL6317], *Spotted Dog*: Pretty thatched pub, comfortable and welcoming, with good fire and lots of dalmatian pictures; tables in garden with dovecote of white doves – ramblers can picnic here if they buy their drinks *(Mrs P J Pearce)*

Blackmore [off A414 Chipping Ongar—Chelmsford; TL6001], *Bull*: Old partly timbered pub, extensively refurbished with concentration on dining side; well kept Flowers IPA, Ind Coope Burton and Wadworths 6X, bar food, brasses, quiet piped music; fruit machine in public bar; nr church in quietly attractive village with big antique and craft shop *(Paul Randall, Mr and Mrs N Chesher, Gwen and Peter Andrews)*

☆ **Boreham** [Church Rd; TL7509], *Queens Head*: Homely traditional pub with welcoming licensees, well kept Greene King IPA and Abbot, decent wines, good value generous straightforward food (not Sun evening) inc Weds roast and Sun lunch; small snug beamed saloon with stripped brickwork, more tables down one side of long public bar with darts at end; maybe piped music; small garden *(Gwen and Peter Andrews, George Atkinson)*

☆ **Boreham**, *Cock*: Two partly curtained-off no-smoking restaurant areas off pleasant beamed

central bar, cheerful young staff, good value food from sandwiches and ploughman's to generous fish fresh daily from Lowestoft, good puddings, well kept Ridleys, decent wines and coffee, pleasant young staff; piped music, some traffic/rail noise in family garden *(Gwen and Peter Andrews, Paul Randall)*
Bradwell on Sea [Waterside; TM0006], *Green Man*: Interestingly furnished traditional flagstoned 15th-c local close to Blackwater estuary, with real ale inc guests, good reasonably priced home cooking, lovely winter fire, games room and garden *(Roger Moore, LYM)*
Brentwood [Ongar Rd (A128); TQ5993], *Black Horse*: Well run family pub, former coaching inn with modern extensions and old furniture in character; good food all day, well kept beer inc guests; pleasant garden with play area *(DFL)*; [High St], *Swan*: Well kept local Burntwood Bitter in pleasant unspoilt pub, some simple lunchtime food, pleasant staff *(Derek Patey)*
Broxted [TL5726], *Prince of Wales*: Friendly and softly lit L-shaped dining pub, low beams, brick pillars, some settees, food from hearty sandwiches up, particularly good choice of wines by the glass, Tetleys-related ales with a guest such as Kelham Island Gatecrasher, smiling helpful service; piped music; conservatory, good garden with play area *(Gwen and Peter Andrews, John Fahy)*
☆ Burnham on Crouch [The Quay; TQ9596], *White Harte*: Two high-ceilinged panelled bars in old-fashioned Georgian yachting inn overlooking anchorage, very busy weekends with mix of sailors and locals inc retired captains; oak tables, polished parquet, attractive nautical memorabilia and sea pictures, panelling and stripped brickwork, log fire; good value food from sandwiches to local fish, restaurant, well kept Adnams and Tolly, welcoming staff, terrace above river; children allowed in eating area; simple bedrooms overlooking water, good breakfasts *(Paul Mason, Gwen and Peter Andrews, Colin Laffan, LYM)*
Canfield End [Little Canfield; A120 Bishops Stortford—Dunmow; TL5821], *Lion & Lamb*: Neat and comfortable, with wide choice of good value food inc children's in bar and spacious restaurant, well kept Ridleys, decent wines and coffee; piped music; back garden with barbecue and play area *(D Horsman, GA, PA)*
Chelmsford [TL7006], *County*: Smallish hotel bar, pubby but always civilised, well kept Adnams, Greene King IPA and Ridleys, good straightforward bar food inc sandwiches, friendly barman, no music; bedrooms *(Gwen and Peter Andrews)*
Chignall Smealy [TL6711], *Pig & Whistle*: Pleasantly refurbished country local, reasonably priced food inc good steak and kidney pie, well kept Adnams *(Tony Beaulah)*
Chignall St James [TL6609], *Three Elms*: Small open-plan country pub, off the beaten track; food cooked to order inc good local

ham and egg, real ale *(Paul and Ursula Randall)*
☆ Chigwell [High Rd (A113); TQ4693], *Kings Head*: Beautiful 17th-c building with interesting Dickens memorabilia, some antique furnishings; Chef & Brewer bar food, quick friendly service, well kept ales, upstairs restaurant; piped music, can get very crowded weekend evenings; attractive garden *(John Fahy, Mrs P J Pearce)*
Chipping Ongar [corner Greensted Rd, off A113; TL5502], *Two Brewers*: Good value generous food inc Sun roast, pleasant efficient service, Flowers and Friary Meux, unobtrusive piped music; family-oriented *(Sandra Iles)*
Clacton on Sea [211 London Rd; TM1715], *Robin Hood*: Recently well refurbished for eating rather than drinking, with good but not too extensive choice of good food inc interesting vegetarian specials and wonderful puddings, very friendly good service, good choice of sensibly priced wines, tables in nice garden; children welcome *(Judy Wayman, Bob Arnett)*
☆ Coggeshall [West St; TL8522], *Fleece*: Handsome Tudor pub with thriving local atmosphere, well kept Greene King IPA and Abbot, decent wines, reliable straightforward bar food (not Tues or Sun evenings), cheery service, children welcome, open all day; spacious sheltered garden with play area, next to Paycocke's *(Gordon Tong, Gwen and Peter Andrews, LYM)*
Coggeshall, *White Hart*: Lots of low Tudor beams, antique settles among other more usual seats, prints and fishing trophies on cream walls, wide choice of food, Adnams, decent wines and coffee; bedrooms comfortable; *(John Fahy, D E Twitchett, LYM)*
☆ Colchester [East St; TM0025], *Rose & Crown*: Carefully modernised handsome Tudor inn, timbered and jettied, parts of a former gaol preserved in its rambling beamed bar, usual bar food, pricey restaurant, well kept Adnams; comfortably functional bedrooms, many in modern extension, with good breakfast; handy for interesting museum and castle *(Paul Mason, Mrs B Sugarman, LYM)*
Colchester [High St], *George*: Large entrance lobby of civilised country-town hotel, drinks all day, locals pop in to read the paper; bedrooms comfortable and good value, with good evening meals and breakfast *(Chris and Ann Garnett)*; [Crouch St], *Kings Arms*: Whitbreads Hogshead pub with good choice of guest beers *(Richard Houghton)*; [28 Mersea Rd], *Odd One Out*: Basic unspoilt pub with several cosy if not exactly bright drinking areas, with well kept ales inc four interesting guests and a Mild; filled rolls etc *(Paul Mason, Mark Lowther)*; [St Johns St], *Playhouse*: Stupendous Wetherspoon conversion of an old Moss Empire theatre – tremendous atmosphere, real fun; all the usual virtues *(John Fahy)*

Coopersale Common [TL4702], *Garnon Bushes*: Welcoming beamed country pub, log fires, brasses, fresh flowers, WW2 memorabilia from nearby North Weald Airfield, well kept beer, reasonably priced good bar food, quiet piped music, tables on front terrace; small restaurant *(Mr and Mrs N Chesher)*; *Theydon Oak*: Welcoming beamed pub with lots of brasses, friendly service, well kept Bass and Hancocks HB, varied bar food, popular restaurant with interesting old maps, brass kettles, pots hanging from the ceiling; popular with all ages – even Rod Stewart; tables in garden with play area *(Eddie Edwards)*

Cressing [TL7920], *Three Ashes*: Unpretentious Greene King pub with well kept ales, usual food, darts in public bar, charming garden *(Gwen and Peter Andrews)*

Danbury [Penny Royal Rd; TL7805], *Cricketers Arms*: Cheerful pub by common, three beamed areas and restaurant, friendly bar staff, huge helpings of promising food, Ind Coope Burton and a guest beer; piped music *(George Atkinson, Gwen and Peter Andrews)*

☆ **Dedham** [TM0533], *Sun*: Roomy and comfortably refurbished Tudor pub, cosy panelled rooms with log fires in huge brick fireplaces, handsomely carved beams, well kept ales inc Charles Wells Bombardier, decent wines, good range of generous reasonably priced food, cheerful staff, good piped music; tables on back lawn, car park behind reached through medieval arch, wonderful wrought-iron inn sign; panelled bedrooms with four-posters, good walk to or from Flatford Mill *(Quentin Williamson, LYM)*

Dunmow [Churchend; B1057 to Finchingfield/Haverhill; TL6222], *Angel & Harp*: Well run local with friendly American landlord – Stars & Stripes draped over the piano; good ploughman's with mature cheddar or ham, real ales; open all day *(John Fahy, Thomas Nott)*

☆ **Duton Hill** [off B184 Dunmow—Thaxted, 3 miles N of Dunmow; TL6026], *Three Horseshoes*: Welcoming licensees in quiet country pub gently updated to keep traditional atmosphere, decent low-priced food inc good value big Lincs sausages with choice of mustards in wholemeal baps, well kept Flowers Original, Ridleys IPA and a guest such as Shepherd Neame Spitfire, aged armchairs by fireplace in homely left-hand parlour, interesting theatrical memorabilia and enamel advertising signs; pool in small public bar, fine views from garden where local drama groups perform in summer *(Gwen and Peter Andrews, John Fahy, BB)*

☆ **Fiddlers Hamlet** [Stewards Green Rd, a mile SE of Epping; TL4700], *Merry Fiddlers*: Long low-ceilinged 17th-c country pub, lots of chamber-pots, beer mugs, brasses and plates, Adnams, Greene King IPA and Morlands Old Speckled Hen, usual pub food, attentive friendly staff, unobtrusive piped music,

occasional live sessions; big garden with play area (can hear Mway) *(George Atkinson, Mr and Mrs N Chesher)*

Finchingfield [TL6832], *Fox*: Splendidly pargeted late 18th-c pub (older in parts) with clean and spacious bar, jug collection, lots of brass, Greene King IPA and Abbot with a guest such as Websters Yorkshire, pleasant service, good value food (not winter Sun evening); steps down to lavatories; open all day, tables in garden, very photogenic village *(Gwen and Peter Andrews)*

Fordham Heath [Spring Lane, off A12; TL9426], *Cricketers*: Spacious lounge, separate dining room, good value substantial food inc very popular Sun lunch from separate order area, brisk pleasant service; Greene King *(Charles and Pauline Stride)*

Fordstreet [A604 W of Colchester; TL9126], *Shoulder of Mutton*: Picturesque and welcoming old beamed riverside pub, log fire and country prints, well kept Flowers, bar food inc good ploughman's; piped music *(Clare and Roy Head)*

Fyfield [Church St (off B184); TL5606], *Queens Head*: Welcoming local, amusing landlord, well kept Adnams, Ridleys and other changing ales, good value generous food from sandwiches and giant filled baps to freshly cooked hot dishes (may be a wait when busy); low beams and local prints, high-backed upholstered settles forming cosy areas, tabby cat, scottie dog; can be a bit smoky *(Jean, Bill and Sandra Iles, Joy and Peter Heatherley)*

Goldhanger [B1026 E of Heybridge; TL9009], *Chequers*: Nice old village pub with good variety of food inc extremely fresh Friday fish, well kept Greene King and Tolly; good walks and birdwatching nearby *(Colin and Joyce Lassan, Mike Beiley)*

☆ **Great Baddow** [Galleywood Rd; or off B1007 at Galleywood Eagle; TL7204], *Seabrights Barn*: Fine Greene King family pub in rustic raftered barn conversion, lots for children though also a spacious child-free bar, good food (all day Sun), good friendly service, well kept ales, decent wines, summer barbecues *(Mr and Mrs N Chesher, LYM)*

Great Baddow [High St; TL7204], *White Horse*: Friendly beamed bar and restaurant (up steps; more steps down to lavatories), usual food, waitress service; no music, fruit machines *(Gwen and Peter Andrews)*

☆ **Great Bromley** [Harwich Rd (B1029 just off A120); TM0826], *Old Black Boy*: Friendly rambling 18th-c pub, attractively refurbished, with wide choice of good value homely food inc lots of fish, Greene King ales, decent wines, no-smoking area; big garden *(Quentin Williamson)*

☆ **Great Easton** [Mill End Green; pub signed 2 miles N of Dunmow, off B184 towards Lindsell; TL6126], *Green Man*: Dates from 15th c, smart but cosy beamed bar, conservatory, decent food inc good interesting specials, welcoming service, well kept ales such as Adnams, Greene King IPA, Ridleys

SX and St Peters Best, quiet piped music, attractive garden in pleasant rural setting *(Jean, Bill and Sandra Iles, Gwen and Peter Andrews, John Fahy)*

Great Hallingbury [Bedlars Green; handy for M11 junction 8; A120 towards Dunmow, 1st fork R – OS Sheet 167 map ref 524204; TL5119], *Hop Poles*: Small, clean and well kept village pub, good value bar food inc attractive puddings and good Sun roast, Tetleys-related ales *(DFL)*

☆ **nr Great Henny** [Henny Street; Sudbury—Lamarsh rd E; TL8738], *Swan*: Tables on lawn by quiet river opp cosy well furnished darkly timbered pub with partly no-smoking conservatory restaurant, generous good value bar food (not Sun evening), barbecues, well kept Greene King IPA and Abbot, decent wines, good coffee, friendly staff; children allowed, maybe unobtrusive piped music *(Gwen and Peter Andrews, Mrs P Goodwyn, LYM)*

☆ **Great Saling** [signed from A120; TL7025], *White Hart*: Friendly and distinctive Tudor pub with easy chairs in upper gallery, ancient timbering and flooring tiles, lots of plates, brass and copperware, good speciality giant filled baps inc hot roast beef and melted cheese and other snacks served till late, well kept Adnams and Ridleys, decent wines, good service, restaurant Tues-Sat evenings, well behaved children welcome; seats outside *(Nikki Moffat, John Fahy, LYM)*

Great Totham [B1022 N of Maldon; TL8511], *Bull*: Leisurely family dining pub with over-55 bargains Mon/Tues, attentive staff, well kept Mitchells, good coffee, tables in garden; tiled public bar with piped music *(Gwen and Peter Andrews)*

☆ **Great Waltham** [old A130; TL6913], *Beehive*: Neatly kept pub very popular with older people for lunch (freshly cooked, so there may be a wait), well kept Ridleys, welcoming service, good log fire; tables outside, opp attractive church – pleasant village, peaceful countryside *(Gwen and Peter Andrews, PGP, Paul and Ursula Randall)*

☆ **Great Warley Street** [TQ5890], *Thatchers Arms*: Pretty Chef and Brewer in attractive village, reliable food, well kept Scottish Courage ales, helpful service *(John Fahy)*

Hadleigh [London Rd (A13); TQ8087], *Waggon & Horses*: Extensively refurbished as good comfortable family restaurant rather than pub *(Klaus and Elizabeth Leist)*

☆ **Hatfield Broad Oak** [High St; TL5416], *Cock*: Character 15th-c beamed village pub with well kept Adnams Best, Nethergate IPA and guests such as Fullers London Pride and Shepherd Neame Spitfire, Easter beer festival, friendly service, recently renovated light sunny L-shaped bar with open fire, music hall song sheets and old advertisements, enjoyable food (not Sun evening) from sandwiches to interesting hot dishes, restaurant; bar billiards, juke box and darts; children in eating area. Friendly prompt service even when busy, several real ales, May beer

festival, good food, huge home-made burger, light sunny rooms *(Jackie Orme, John Fahy, S G Brown, Gwen and Peter Andrews, G Brooke-Williams, LYM)*

Hatfield Heath [A1005 towards Bishops Stortford], *Thatchers*: Sprucely refurbished beamed and thatched pub with woodburner, copper kettles and brasses, well kept Bass, Greene King IPA and Morlands Old Speckled Hen, decent house wines, wide choice of bar food, friendly licensees; piped music; tables out under cocktail parasols *(Gwen and Peter Andrews)*

Helions Bumpstead [Water Lane; TL6541], *Three Horseshoes*: Good two-bar local with friendly landlord, well kept Greene King ales, wide choice of good value food, restaurant up a step; tables in attractive garden, charming unspoilt village *(Gwen and Peter Andrews)*

Hempstead [B1054 E of Saffron Walden; TL6337], *Bluebell*: Comfortable bar with two small rooms off and restaurant, wide choice of food, Adnams, Greene King IPA and Ruddles County; piped radio; outside seating *(John Fahy)*

Henham [Chickney Rd; TL5428], *Cock*: Neat heavily timbered family pub/restaurant, Tetleys-related ales with a guest such as Adnams, wide range of food, local pictures and shelves of bric-a-brac; maybe piped music; relaxing views from nice tables outside, attractive village *(Gwen and Peter Andrews, Eddie Edwards)*

☆ **Herongate** [Billericay Rd; A128 Brentwood—Grays; TQ6391], *Green Man*: Good value food inc popular baked potatoes and children's dishes, big bright and welcoming beamed bar area with jug collection, cricket memorabilia, log fires each end, Adnams and Tetleys-related ales, decent wines, helpful staff; unobtrusive piped music, ginger cat called Tigger; children allowed in back rooms, side garden *(Paul Barstow, Karyn Taylor, DFL)*

Herongate [Billericay Rd, Ingrave, just off A128], *Boars Head*: Picturesque beamed Chef & Brewer with pleasant nooks and crannies, garden, seats by big attractive pond with ducks and moorhens, Courage Directors and John Smiths, reliable food all day; can get crowded at weekends *(George Atkinson, DFL)*; [off A128 at Boars Head sign], *Old Dog*: Friendly and relaxed, with good choice of well kept ales and of lunchtime bar food inc good sandwiches in long traditional dark-raftered bar, open fire, comfortable back lounge; front terrace and neat sheltered side garden *(Beryl and Bill Farmer, DFL, LYM)*

Heybridge [34 The Street; TL8508], *Heybridge Inn*: Clean bright happy local popular for lunch, friendly waitresses, quiet piped music *(Keith and Janet Morris)*

Heybridge Basin [Basin Rd; TL8707], *Jolly Sailor*: Doing well under new owners, good value food inc fresh fish, well kept real ale, friendly atmosphere *(Paul and Ursula Randall)*; [Lockhill], *Old Ship*: Clean and spruce pub by remote lock, well kept Adnams

Broadside and Tetleys, lots of nautical memorabilia, eating area one end with reasonably priced blond wooden furniture, unobtrusive piped music; well behaved dogs welcome but no children, can be very busy, esp in summer when parking nearby impossible (but public park five mins' walk); lovely views of the Blackwater saltings and across to Northey Island *(David Dimock)*

☆ **High Easter** [off A1060 or B184 nr Leaden Roding; TL6214], *Cock & Bell*: Friendly timbered Tudor pub with grand old beams, dining area up steps from lounge, log fire in cheery second bar, generous home-cooked straightforward food, well kept ales such as Batemans, Crouch Vale, Fullers London Pride, Morlands Old Speckled Hen; children welcome; piped radio may obtrude; comfortable bedrooms *(D Broughton, R Jupp, FWG, LYM)*

☆ **High Ongar** [King St, Nine Ashes – signed Blackmore, Ingatestone off A414 just E; TL5603], *Wheatsheaf*: Comfortable and very welcoming low-beamed country dining pub, some intimate tables in bay-window alcoves, two log fires, fresh flowers, wide choice of home-cooked food inc good veg, fish and steaks, well kept Flowers IPA and Original and Ridleys SX, attentive service, spacious attractive garden with play house *(Gwen and Peter Andrews, Peter Baggott, Sandra Iles, BB)*

☆ **High Roding** [The Street (B184); TL6017], *Black Lion*: Attractive low-beamed bar dating from 15th c, good food esp authentic Italian dishes, courteous long-serving landlord and cheerful staff, comfortable relaxed surroundings, well kept Ridleys; discreet piped music *(Mr and Mrs N Chesher)*

Howe Street [off A130 N of Chelmsford; TL6914], *Green Man*: Spacious timbered two-bar pub dating from 14th c, comfortably plush lounge, nice brass and prints, well kept Adnams Extra and Ridleys IPA, helpful welcoming service, bar food inc generous ploughman's and speciality fish, restaurant (very popular Sun lunch); unobtrusive piped music; garden with play area *(Sandra Iles)*

Kirby le Soken [B1034 Thorpe—Walton; TM2222], *Red Lion*: Attractive 14th-c pub, relaxing at lunchtime, with friendly helpful service, well kept beers, good range of food inc good vegetarian choice, well kept Scottish Courage and guest ales such as Marstons Pedigree and Morlands Old Speckled Hen; piped music can obtrude, predominantly young people in the evenings *(Rev J Hibberd, Thomas Nott)*

Knowl Green [TL7841], *Cherry Tree*: Step down to rustic split-level bar, 15th-c beams, guns, brass trays, cricket photographs and vases, simple reasonably priced bar food, Greene King IPA and Ridleys SX, back steps to pool and darts board, also further eating area *(Gwen and Peter Andrews)*

Layer de la Haye [B1026 towards Colchester; TL9619], *Donkey & Buskins*: Old-fashioned country pub with good range of reasonably priced food inc fish, pleasant service; handy for Abberton Reservoir *(Gordon Neighbour)*

Little Hallingbury [Hall Green; TL5017], *Sutton Arms*: Good interesting generous food in pleasant beamed and thatched pub with quick friendly service; close to M11, can get very busy *(Stephen and Jean Curtis, Mr and Mrs C J Pink)*

Little Oakley [B1414 Harwich—Clacton; TM2129], *Olde Cherry Tree*: Friendly and unpretentious, long bar divided by log fire, five real ales such as Adnams Broadside, Buckleys Rev James and Charles Wells Bombardier, simple cheap food from sandwiches up inc good vegetarian choice; piped music, quieter dining room *(Rev J Hibberd)*

Little Walden [B1052; TL5441], *Crown*: Neat L-shaped bar with big log fire, flowers on tables, Greene King IPA and Abbot and Worthington BB, decent wines, good range of home-cooked food (not Sun evening), unobtrusive piped music *(Gwen and Peter Andrews)*

☆ **Little Waltham** [TL7012], *Dog & Gun*: Comfortable banquettes and chairs in spacious timbered L-shaped bar, welcoming attentive staff, wide choice of generous interesting fresh-cooked food (so may be a wait), well kept Greene King IPA, Abbot and Rayments, good house wines; piped music usually off weekday lunchtimes; garden with elegant willow *(Gwen and Peter Andrews)*

☆ **Loughton** [103 York Hill, off A121 High Rd; TQ4296], *Gardeners Arms*: Country feel in (and outside) traditional low-ceilinged pub with Adnams and Scottish Courage ales, two open fires, friendly service, good straightforward lunchtime bar food (not Sun) from sandwiches up with hot dishes all fresh-cooked (so can be delays), children in restaurant *(Mr and Mrs N Chesher, Joy and Peter Heatherley, LYM)*

Loughton [153 High Rd (A121)], *Rat & Carrot*: Comfortable one-bar pub (formerly the Crown) with Toby on handpump; big screen TV sports *(Robert Lester)*

☆ **Maldon** [Silver St; TL8506], *Blue Boar*: Fine old ex-Forte coaching inn, pubby atmospheric bar in separate coach house on left, with beams, roaring log fire, Adnams tapped from the cask, keen and friendly young staff, good if not cheap lunchtime bar food; pleasant well equipped bedrooms, good breakfast *(Paul Mason)*

Maldon [Gate St], *Carpenters Arms*: Convivial and welcoming, with well kept beer, inexpensive well cooked food for the hungry, friendly staff *(Andrew Hayes)*

☆ **Manningtree** [Manningtree Stn, out towards Lawford; TM1031], *Station Buffet*: Nostalgic early 1950s long marble-topped bar, three little tables and a handful of unassuming seats, interesting well kept ales such as Adnams, Greene King, Mauldons and Summerskills, real cheese and ham baps etc, traditional hot dishes, cheerful service *(Thomas Nott)*

Margaretting [B1002 towards Mountnessing; TL6701], *Red Lion*: Foody pub with wide choice of dishes, well kept Ridleys *(Peter Baggott)*

☆ **Mashbury** [towards the Walthams; TL6411], *Fox*: Friendly beamed and flagstoned lounge, old-fashioned long tables, rewarding food, well kept Adnams and Ridleys tapped from the cask, decent wine; dominoes, cribbage, skittles; quiet countryside *(Paul and Ursula Randall)*

Matching Green [TL5311], *Chequers*: Truly rural atmosphere, nice spot overlooking pretty cricket green, good cheap food, well kept Adnams, Boddingtons and Greene King, good choice of decent wines, welcoming landlord, one bar opening on to garden, another with piped music, TV and lots of aircraft pictures *(Nikki Moffat, Gwen and Peter Andrews)*

☆ **Mill Green** [TL6401], *Cricketers Arms*: Country pub/restaurant in picturesque setting, comfortable and spruce, popular for wide choice of well prepared attractively presented food, good value though not cheap; no-smoking area, Greene King IPA and Abbot tapped from the cask, good wines, cheerful staff, lots of cricketing memorabilia, some farm tools, friendly jack russell called Bonney *(Peter and Gwen Andrews, John Fahy, Keith and Janet Morris)*

☆ **Moreton** [signed off B184 at Fyfield or opp Chipping Ongar school; TL5307], *White Hart*: Popular local with cosy rooms rambling through different levels, sloping floor and ceilings, well kept ales such as Adnams, Courage Best and Directors and Everards Tiger, lovely log fire, wide choice of generous briskly served home-cooked food inc good fish and veg (dining rooms may not be open at quiet times); bedrooms, pleasant circular walk from pub *(Joy and Peter Heatherley, H O Dickinson, M A Starling, Mr and Mrs N Chesher, Tony Gayfer, Quentin Williamson)*

☆ **Navestock** [Huntsmanside, off B175; TQ5397], *Alma Arms*: Concentration on generous good value well presented food (may be a wait) in spacious dining area, with good choice of wines, well kept ales such as Adnams, Greene King Abbot and Rayments; low beams, comfortable seats *(P Pearce, DFL, Joy and Peter Heatherley)*

☆ **Newney Green** [off A414 or A1060 W of Chelmsford; TL6507], *Duck*: Comfortable dining pub with engaging rambling bar full of beams, timbering and panelling; very friendly service, enjoyable food inc good value roasts, drinkers welcomed too – enjoyable range of ales; attractive garden *(George Atkinson, LYM)*

☆ **Norton Heath** [just off A414 Chelmsford—Ongar; TL6004], *White Horse*: Good bar food Tues-Sat lunchtimes in comfortably modernised somewhat formal long timbered bar, well kept Courage Directors and Sam Smiths; piped music usually unobtrusive, bar billiards; restaurant (Tues-Sat evening, Sun lunch); garden with play area; cl Mon *(John Davison, Richard Siebert, Peter Andrews, Paul Randall)*

Paglesham [TQ9293], *Plough & Sail*: Beautifully kept dining pub with wide and attractive menu from sandwiches to carvery, warm and friendly atmosphere, well kept Courage-related beers, quick helpful service even when busy, good flower arrangements; pleasant garden very popular on warm summer evenings, in pretty spot nr marshes *(Tim Heywood, Sophie Wilne)*; [East End], *Punchbowl*: Pretty and beautifully kept, with decent food *(Tim Heywood, Sophie Wilne)*

☆ **Peldon** [junction unclassified Maldon road with B1025 Peldon—Mersea; TL9916], *Rose*: Cosy low-beamed bar with creaky close-set tables, some antique mahogany, chintz curtains and leaded lights, brass and copper, wide range of bar food, well kept Flowers IPA and Marstons Pedigree, good service even when busy; children welcome away from bar, restaurant Fri/Sat evening, big no-smoking conservatory, spacious relaxing garden with geese, ducks and two ponds; bedrooms *(Gwen and Peter Andrews, B N F and M Parkin, Ian, Liz and James Phillips, Richard Seibert, Mayur Shah, LYM)*

☆ **Pilgrims Hatch** [Ongar Rd (A128); TQ5895], *Black Horse*: Busy olde-worlde low-beamed dining pub with bare boards and flooring tiles, timbers, lots of pictures and country bygones, small fireplace at either end, big eating areas off small attractive bar, very generous good value home cooking (all day Sun) inc fresh veg and vegetarian; well kept Bass and Charrington IPA, friendly service; piped music may obtrude a bit; good garden with play area *(Paul Barstow, Karyn Taylor, R C Morgan, Eddie Edwards, Robert Lester)*

Pilgrims Hatch [390 Ongar Rd], *Rose & Crown*: Good cheery atmosphere in traditional timbered pub, public bar, bar meals, Courage Best and Directors *(Robert Lester)*

☆ **Pleshey** [signed with Howe Street off A130 Dunmow—Chelmsford; TL6614], *White Horse*: Cheerful 15th-c pub with nooks and crannies, lots of bric-a-brac, comfortable sofa in snug room by servery, more orthodox tables and chairs in other rooms, big dining room with huge collection of miniatures, bar food from good big hot filled baps upwards, well kept Archers, Batemans, Crouch Vale, Elgoods, Jennings, and Nethergate, local cider, tables out on terrace and in garden with small safe play area; children welcome, fruit machine, cat called Tigger; pretty village with ruined castle *(Basil Minson, Peter Baggott, Tony Beaulah, Maysie Thompson, DFL, Thomas Nott, LYM)*

☆ **Purleigh** [TL8401], *Bell*: Cosy rambling beamed and timbered pub up by church, fine views over the marshes and Blackwater estuary; beams, nooks and crannies, big inglenook log fire, well kept Adnams, Benskins Best, Greene King IPA and Marstons Pedigree, decent house wines, good reasonably priced home-made lunchtime food, magazines to read, welcoming landlord, friendly dog; picnic tables on side grass *(Comus Elliott, Gwen and Peter Andrews, S Dominey, George Atkinson, LYM)*

☆ Radwinter [B1053 E of Saffron Walden – OS Sheet 154 map ref 612376; TL6137], *Plough*: Neatly kept red plush open-plan black-timbered beamed bar with central log fire and separate woodburner; good choice of popular bar food inc vegetarian, well kept Greene King IPA and guests such as Nethergate Garden Gate and Robinsons Best, decent wine, friendly staff; children and dogs welcome, very attractive terrace and garden, open countryside; bedrooms *(Gwen and Peter Andrews, John Fahy, BB)*

Ramsey [The Street; TM2130], *Castle*: Friendly landlord, good food from sandwiches to very popular Sun lunch, cheap well kept Tolly and other ales *(Rev J Hibberd)*

☆ Rickling Green [just off B1383 N of Stansted Mountfitchet; TL5029], *Cricketers Arms*: Lots of cricket cigarette cards and other memorabilia in softly lit comfortable saloon, standing timbers, log fire, good food from sandwiches to steaks inc fresh fish, plenty of vegetarian and sensible children's menu, well kept Flowers IPA tapped from the cask and a changing strong ale, very good choice of bottle-conditioned ales, good wines by the glass, friendly staff, games room with pool etc; open all day summer Sat/Sun, children welcome in restaurant, modern bedrooms handy for Stansted (courtesy car) *(Gwen and Peter Andrews, JR, CR, Lynne Gittins, Stephen and Jean Curtis, LYM)*

Rochford [1 Southend Rd; TQ8790], *Horse & Groom*: Pleasant one-bar pub, Tolly and Websters *(Robert Lester)*

Rowhedge [Quay; TM0021], *Anchor*: Cosy old-fashioned pub in wonderful spot overlooking River Colne with its swans, gulls and yachts; fishing bric-a-brac, good atmosphere, good reasonably priced food inc fresh bass, well kept Bass, restaurant; gets very busy *(A P Farley)*

Roydon [43 High St (B181); TL4109], *White Hart*: 15th-c, with good helpings of nicely cooked food – good value; four well kept ales inc Eldridge Pope Hardy, Greene King and Tetleys, friendly staff; charming village *(Gordon Neighbour)*

Saffron Walden [High St; TL5438], *Cross Keys*: A Big Steak pub, but with quite a lot of character inc interetsing jettied exterior and old carvings *(Mrs P J Pearce)*; *Old English Gentleman*: Good reasonably priced food in welcoming and busy town pub *(Geoff Meek)*; [10-18 High St], *Saffron*: Comfortably modernised former coaching inn, wide choice of waitress-served food in bar and restaurant, tables on terrace; bedrooms *(John Fahy)*

☆ Shalford [TL7229], *George*: Exposed brickwork, decorative plates and brassware, good solid tables and chairs, log fire in enormous fireplace, good home cooking (worth the wait), well kept Adnams Broadside, Greene King IPA and guests,

decent wines, friendly helpful staff, lots of children at weekends, no music; tables on terrace *(Gwen and Peter Andrews)*

South Weald [Weald Rd (off A1023); TQ5793], *Tower Arms*: Thoughtfully refurbished Chef & Brewer, several small high-ceilinged rooms, conservatory restaurant (not Sun-Tues evenings), well kept Scottish Courage ales, friendly staff; children allowed, extensive secluded garden with boules (you can hire the balls); opp church in picturesque village *(Gwen and Peter Andrews)*

Southend [53 Alexandra St; TQ8885], *Fish & Firkin*: Home-brewed beers, friendly helpful service, bars on two levels and picnic tables outside *(Richard Houghton)*

Southminster [2 High St; TQ9599], *Kings Head*: Clean, comfortable and friendly old pub, good range of good value food inc wide vegetarian choice, several real ales *(P Hunkin)*

☆ Stapleford Tawney [about 2 miles N on Tawney Common – OS Sheet 167 map ref 500013; TL5001], *Mole Trap*: Delightful little low-beamed country pub, friendly landlord, Hook Norton Best and Old Hookey, rustic artefacts and framed account of how the pub got its name, two long settles for the tables in its small bar, limited basic food, pleasant seats outside; popular with walkers and cyclists *(Robert Lester, Mr and Mrs N Chesher, J H Gracey)*

Stebbing [High St; TL6624], *Kings Head*: Cosy and comfortable 17th-c beamed local, cheap food, Adnams Southwold, Greene King IPA, Tetleys and Youngers Ram Rod, polite service, farm tools and copper pans, barbecues; beautiful walking trails in delightful village *(Gwen and Peter Andrews)*

☆ Stock [Common Rd; just off B1007 Chelmsford—Billericay; TQ6998], *Bakers Arms*: Open-plan beamed pub with smart banquettes, above-average home-cooked bar food inc vegetarian, attractive dining room with french windows, pleasant service, no piped music; charming well kept garden *(Tina and David Woods-Taylor, David J Brown, Phyl and Jack Street)*

Stock [The Square (just off main st)], *Bear*: Has been lovely comfortably unmodernised building with wise old men in front bar, stained glass and bric-a-brac, well kept Adnams, Greene King Abbot and a guest, cosy no-smoking restaurant with cases of maps and photographs, interesting well cooked and presented food inc OAP bargains Thurs/Fri, good staff; children's room, fine inn sign, nice back garden overlooking pond; was to have been a main entry, but taken back into management by Allied Domecq as we go to press, to become a themed Golden Oak Inn *(BB – news please)*

☆ Sturmer [The Street; A604 SE of Haverhill; TL6944], *Red Lion*: Warm and welcoming thatched and beamed dining pub, good choice of generous reasonably priced good food (not Sun evening); well kept Greene King ales, jovial landlord, helpful staff, plenty of tables with solid cushioned chairs, convenient layout if you don't like steps, big fireplace; unobtrusive piped music, children in dining room and conservatory, pleasant garden *(Gwen and Peter Andrews)*

Thaxted [Bullring; TL6130], *Swan*: Thriving and attractive Tudor pub with well kept ales inc Adnams and Greene King, warm atmosphere in big bar area, plenty of well spaced tables, restaurant; bedrooms *(John Fahy, PGP)*

Theydon Bois [Coppice Row (B172); TQ4599], *Queen Victoria*: Beautifully kept pub on green, discreetly enlarged but keeping character, with friendly staff, McMullens beers, well presented quick straightforward good value food, bright end dining area with interesting nick-nacks, older low-ceilinged front bar now no smoking, pleasant bustle; tables on terrace *(Quentin Williamson, Joy and Peter Heatherley)*

Thorpe le Soken [High St; TM1922], *Crown*: Satisfying food in largish bar, good friendly service, attractive restaurant *(Tony Beaulah)*

Tillingham [B1021 N of Southminster; TL9011], *Cap & Feathers*: Low-beamed and timbered 15th-c pub, attractive old-fashioned furniture, well kept Crouch Vale Best, IPA, Best Dark and a guest beer, traditional games, home-cooked bar food, no-smoking family room, picnic tables on side terrace; three bedrooms; has been a popular main entry, but too few reports since new tenant to be sure of current status *(LYM)*

Tolleshunt Major [TL9011], *Bell*: Pleasant long building, beams and studwork, comfortable banquettes and bay windows in L-shaped saloon with woodburner, welcoming licensees, decent food, well kept Greene King IPA and Abbot, decent wines, good coffee, no music, public bar with fruit machine; children welcome, verandah and barbecue area overlooking big rustic pond, immaculate lavatories, disabled facilities *(Colin Laffan, Gwen and Peter Andrews)*

☆ nr **Waltham Abbey** [very handy for M25 junction 26; A121 towards Waltham Abbey, then follow Epping, Loughton sign from exit roundabout; TL3800], *Volunteer*: Good genuine chow mein and big pancake rolls (unless Chinese landlady away Mar/Apr) and generous more usual food in big recently decorated open-plan McMullens pub; attractive conservatory, guest beer, some tables on side terrace, pretty hanging baskets; nice spot by Epping Forest, can get very busy weekends *(C H and P Stride, Joy and Peter Heatherley, BB)*

Weeley [Colchester Rd; TM1422], *Black Boy*: Very well run, with friendly service, wide range of competitively priced meals and sandwiches, pleasant dining room, well kept ales such as Charles Wells Bombardier, Ruddles Best, Wiltshire Old Devil and Wychwood *(Ian Phillips)*

Wethersfield [High St; TL7131], *Dog*: Fine Georgian building, good value fresh food inc home-made Italian ice creams in two spacious pleasantly furnished bars and restaurant, Greene King and other ales, welcoming service, good Italian house wines, muted piped music *(John Fahy, Gwen and Peter Andrews)*

White Roding [TL5613], *Black Horse*: Sprucely well kept plush Ridleys pub with generous home cooking (not Sun evening; fresh fish Thurs), well kept IPA and Best, decent house wines, welcoming attentive service, relaxing atmosphere, bar billiards, very quiet piped music *(Gwen and Peter Andrews)*

Wickham Bishops [TL8412], *Mitre*: Snugly refurbished bars and spacious family dining area, reasonably priced food cooked to order inc good Sun lunch, well kept Ridleys IPA and SX, decent wines, good fire *(Gwen and Peter Andrews, Colin Laffan)*

☆ **Wivenhoe** [Quayside, off A133; TM0321], *Rose & Crown*: Friendly unspoilt inn in delightful quayside position on River Colne, log fire, low beams, scrubbed floors, well kept reasonably priced Adnams, local and nautical books, no piped music, waterside seats (when the tide's in) *(Mick and Hilary Stiffin, John Fahy, Hazel Morgan)*

☆ **Wivenhoe** [Black Buoy Hill], *Black Buoy*: Well kept Greene King and weekly guest ale in 16th-c local's spacious open-plan bar, well separated dining area with wide choice of good food inc local fish and interesting vegetarian dishes, charming building, convivial atmosphere, open fires; may be obtrusive piped music; tucked away from water in conservation area, but has river views *(K B Bacon, Paul and Ursula Randall, Hazel Morgan, John Fahy, G and M Stewart)*

☆ **Woodham Walter** [signed off A414 E from Chelmsford; TL8006], *Bell*: Striking Elizabethan pub with beams and timbers, decorative plates and lots of brass, comfortable alcoves on various levels, log fire, wide choice of decent bar food (not Mon) from well priced sandwiches to steaks, pretty dining room in partly panelled upper gallery, Adnams, Friary Meux Best and a guest beer; children in eating area *(Thomas Nott, Beryl and Bill Farmer, R Morgan, Mike and Karen England, Ian and Nita Cooper, Nigel Norman, LYM)*

Writtle [TL6706], *New Inn on the Green*: Spacious pub with buoyant atmosphere, well kept ales such as Courage Best and Directors, Nethergate IPA and Old Growler, friendly well dressed staff, great choice of good bar food, games area one end with pool and fruit machines (popular with young people), old advertisements, sepia photographs *(Gwen and Peter Andrews, FWG)*

Post Office address codings confusingly give the impression that some pubs are in Suffolk, when they're really in Essex (which is where we list them).

Gloucestershire

Many of this county's pubs are among the most popular in Britain – lovely buildings, with a good mix of unspoilt taverns and very smart places, often with fine food. Currently shining brightest in this firmament are the utterly unspoilt Boat at Ashleworth Quay (but don't expect food), the Kings Head at Bledington (very good all round, an attractive new sitting room – and this year gains our Star Award), the lovely old Crown at Blockley, the attractive and bustling Wild Duck at Ewen, the Hobnails at Little Washbourne (in the same family for over 250 years, with legendary filled baps), the Anchor at Oldbury on Severn (another fine all-rounder, gaining our Beer Award this year), and the Butchers Arms at Sheepscombe (caring staff, enjoyable food, lovely views). New entries are the Red Hart at Blaisdon (very welcoming new young licensees), the carefully refurbished old Masons Arms at Meysey Hampton, the attractively tucked-away Daneway at Sapperton (bought by Wadworths since it was last in these pages, but the cheerful new tenants were previously managers here) and the stylish Gumstool near Tetbury. The Gumstool, very much a dining pub, has some outstanding food, and is our choice as Gloucestershire Dining Pub of the Year. The very high standards in this county mean that many of the Lucky Dip entries at the end of the chapter are sound main-entry material. We'd mention particularly the Craven Arms at Brockhampton, Lygon Arms in Chipping Campden, eccentric Tunnel House at Coates, Five Mile House at Duntisbourne Abbots (one of very few in this list not yet inspected and approved by us, but a most promising newcomer), Highwayman near Elkstone, Crown at Frampton Mansell, Farmers Boy at Longhope, Snowshill Arms at Snowshill, both the Bell and the Black Bear in Tewkesbury, Crown at Tolldown, Red Lion at Westbury on Severn, Hare & Hounds at Westonbirt and Ram at Woodchester. There's an enjoyable choice in Cirencester. Gloucestershire drinks prices tend to be below the national average, though pubs supplied by the big national brewers have higher prices than average. We found pubs tied to Donnington particularly cheap (but some are now keeping these nice local beers under a preservative blanket of carbon dioxide, which seems a shame for such generally unspoilt and traditional pubs). The Mill at Withington, tied to Sam Smiths of Yorkshire, and Greyhound at Siddington (tied to Wadworths) were also very cheap.

ALMONDSBURY ST6084 Map 2
Bowl 🛏 ♀

1¼ miles from M5, junction 16 (and therefore quite handy for M4, junction 20; from A38 towards Thornbury, turn first left signposted Lower Almondsbury, then first right down Sundays Hill, then at bottom right again into Church Road

On a sunny weekend this white cottage is very popular with customers enjoying the wide choice of bar food: sandwiches (from £2.25; toasties from £2.50; filled french bread £3.35), home-made soup (£2.45), spaghetti carbonara (£4.95), home-made vegetable and cashew nut balti or haddock provençale with parmesan and walnuts

(£5.95), gammon and egg (£6.45), steak, mushroom and ale pie (£7.45), moussaka (£7.65), and puddings (£2.95); service can slow down under pressure but remains pleasant. They charge extra if you eat bar meals in the restaurant. The long neatly kept beamed bar has blue plush-patterned modern settles, pink cushioned stools and mate's chairs around elm tables, quite a few horsebrasses, stripped bare stone walls, and a big winter log fire at one end, with a woodburning stove at the other. Well kept Courage Directors, Marstons Pedigree, Morlands Old Speckled Hen, Smiles Best, Wadworths 6X, and Websters on handpump, several malt whiskies, and freshly pressed fruit juices; fruit machine, piped music. The brown spaniel is called Charlie, another dog Corrie, and there's a black and white cat. The flowering tubs, hanging baskets and window boxes are pretty, a back terrace overlooks a field, and there are some picnic tables across the quiet road. *(Recommended by Peter Neate, Paul Barnett, Mr and Mrs R Maggs, Alan and Paula McCully, J and B Cressey, Daren Haines, Ian and Jane Irving, Amanda and Simon Southwell, Mr and Mrs M J Bastin, A and R Cooper, Virginia Jones, H F C Barclay)*

Courage ~ Lease: John Alley ~ Real ale ~ Meals and snacks (till 10pm; not 25 Dec, evening 26 Dec) ~ Restaurant ~ (01454) 612757 ~ Children welcome ~ Open 11-3, 5(6 Sat)-11; 12-3, 7-10.30 Sun; closed evening 25 Dec ~ Bedrooms: £29.50B/£47.50B

AMBERLEY SO8401 Map 4
Black Horse 🍺

Village signposted off A46 Stroud—Nailsworth; as you pass village name take first very sharp left turn (before Amberley Inn) then bear steeply right – pub on your left

In a nice spot on the edge of Minchinhampton Common (which has some prehistoric remains), this busy little pub has remarkable views of the surrounding hills. A back terrace has teak seats, picnic tables and a barbecue and spit roast area, and on the other side of the building, a lawn with pretty flowers and honeysuckle has more picnic tables. Inside, the dining bar has wheelback chairs, green-cushioned window seats, a few prints on the plain cream walls, and a fire in a small stone fireplace, and there's a conservatory, and a family bar on the left which is partly no smoking. Bar food includes sandwiches, soup (£1.95), tagliatelle with mushrooms, steak in ale pie or gammon and egg (£4.95), cajun chicken (£5.95), steaks (from £5.95), whole lemon sole (£7.50), and specials such as Friday fish and chips (£3.50), Saturday lunchtime brunch (£4.95), and Sunday lunchtime carvery (£4.95). A good range of well kept real ales on handpump such as Archers Village, Best and Golden, Dartmoor Best, Ind Coope Burton, Smiles Best, Tetleys, and Wadworths 6X. Darts, pool, shove-ha'penny, and cribbage. *(Recommended by D Irving, R Huggins, T McLean, E McCall, T L Rees, Andy and Jill Kassube, S Godsell, Craig Peck, Cherry Ann Knott, Pat and Roger Fereday)*

Free house ~ Licensee Patrick O'Flynn ~ Real ale ~ Meals and snacks ~ (01453) 872556 ~ Children welcome ~ Open 12-3, 6-11; 12-11 Sat (closed winter Sat afternoon); 12-10.30 Sun

AMPNEY CRUCIS SP0602 Map 4
Crown of Crucis 🛏️

A417 E of Cirencester

This is a most pleasant place to stay with some rooms looking over the stream with ducks and maybe swans; the back grass has lots of tables with the same view. It's the reliable food that most people come to enjoy, though. From the bar menu there might be home-made soup (£2.50), sandwiches (from £2.90), ploughman's (£4.45), herb crêpes (£4.95), tex-mex nachos (£5.20), devilled vegetables (£5.45), chicken, bacon and avocado salad (£5.75), grilled red snapper on a bed of roasted tomatoes (£6.45), king scallops with a soya dressing (£9.40), steaks (from £9.40), lunchtime home-made daily specials (£4), and home-made puddings (£2.60); children's menu (£2.40), two course Sunday lunch (£8.45), and themed food evenings. It's worth arriving early to be sure of a table; part of the restaurant is no smoking. The spacious and comfortably modernised bar has a relaxed atmosphere, well kept

Archers Village, Marstons Pedigree, and Wadworths 6X on handpump, and helpful, friendly service. *(Recommended by Dorsan Baker, Tony Dickinson, TRS, TBB, NWN, Steve Goodchild, Dick Brown, David Surridge)*

Free house ~ Licensee Ken Mills ~ Real ale ~ Meals and snacks (till 10pm) ~ Restaurant ~ (01285) 851806 ~ Children welcome ~ Open 11-11; 12-10.30 Sun; closed 25 Dec ~ Bedrooms: £54B/£78B

APPERLEY SO8628 Map 4
Farmers Arms 🍺

Nr Apperley on B4213, which is off A38 N of Gloucester

The modern little brick and thatch brewhouse in the grounds of this extended friendly local is where they brew their own Mayhems Oddas Light and Sundowner Heavy; also, guests such as Wadworths 6X and Henry's Original IPA on handpump. Guns line the beams of the bar, there are old prints, horseshoes and stuffed pheasants dotted about, coal-effect gas fires, and plenty of room – though you'll generally find most people in the comfortable and spacious dining lounge; piped music. Fresh fish is delivered daily, which leads to several interesting blackboard specials, and there's also open sandwiches, ploughman's (£3.95), lasagne (£5.25), lamb in rosemary and red wine or a vegetarian dish (£5.75), good pork in cider and sage or beef in ale pie (£5.95), several steaks, and quite a few puddings; friendly service. The neat garden has picnic tables by a thatched well, with a wendy house and play area. *(Recommended by Sue and Bob Ward, Mike and Mary Carter, Daren Haines, Andy and Jill Kassube, Nigel Clifton, Jeanne and George Barnwell, Dave Irving, Roger Huggins, Ewan McCall, Tom McLean, John and Vivienne Rice)*

Own brew/Wadworths ~ Manager Geoffrey Adams ~ Real ale ~ Meals and snacks (till 10pm) ~ Restaurant ~ (01452) 780307 ~ Children welcome ~ Open 10.30-3, 6-11; 12-3.30, 7-10.30 Sun

ASHLEWORTH QUAY SO8125 Map 4
Boat ★

Ashleworth signposted off A417 N of Gloucester; Quay signed from village

We think this gentle, unspoilt old cottage probably holds the record for continuous pub ownership – it has been run by the same family ever since it was first granted a licence by Charles II. It's very much the kind of place where strangers soon start talking with each other and the charming landladies work hard at preserving the unique character. Spotlessly kept, the little front parlour has a great built-in settle by a long scrubbed deal table that faces an old-fashioned open kitchen range with a side bread oven and a couple of elderly fireside chairs; there are rush mats on the scrubbed flagstones, houseplants in the window, fresh garden flowers, and old magazines to read; shove-ha'penny, dominoes and cribbage (the front room has darts and a game called Dobbers). A pair of flower-cushioned antique settles face each other in the back room where Arkells BBB, Oakhill Yeoman, and Smiles Best or March Hare and guests like Brandycask Whistling Joe, Exmoor Gold, RCH East Street Cream, and Wye Valley Bitter are tapped from the cask, along with a full range of Westons farm ciders. They usually do good lunchtime rolls (from £1.40) or ploughman's with home-made chutney (£3) during the week. This is a lovely spot on the banks of the River Severn and there's a front suntrap crazy-paved courtyard, bright with plant tubs in summer, with a couple of picnic tables under cocktail parasols; more seats and tables under cover at the sides. The medieval tithe barn nearby is striking; some readers prefer to park here and walk to the pub. *(Recommended by Dave Irving, Roger Huggins, Tom McLean, Ewan McCall, D H and M C Watkinson, Stephen Pine, Alfred Lawrence, Andy and Jill Kassube, Peter and Anne Cornall, Mike and Mary Carter, Daren Haines, Sandra Kench, Steven Norman, Alan and Paula McCully, Brian Wainwright, Derek and Sylvia Stephenson, Meg Bowell, David Campbell, Vicki McLean, AEB)*

Free house ~ Licensees Irene Jelf and Jacquie Nicholls ~ Real ale ~ Lunchtime snacks ~ (01452) 700272 ~ Children welcome till 8pm ~ Open 11-2.30(3 Sat), 6-11; 12-3, 7-10.30 Sun; winter evening opening 7pm

AUST ST5789 Map 2
Boars Head

½ mile from M4, junction 21; village signposted from A403

At lunchtime especially, this bustling village pub is full of people. The small rooms have an informal, friendly atmosphere and the neatly kept and comfortable main bar has well polished country kitchen tables and others made from old casks, old-fashioned high-backed winged settles in stripped pine, decorative plates hanging from one stout black beam, some walls stripped back to the dark stone, big rugs on dark lino, and a large log fire. In another room is a woodburning stove, while a third has dining tables with lace tablecloths, fresh flowers and candles. Popular bar food includes good soup, sandwiches and ploughman's, and daily specials like good tagliatelle, smoked haddock and eggs (£5.95), steak and kidney pie or smoked salmon and scrambled eggs (£6.95), fresh whole plaice or roast half pheasant (£7.95), and Sunday roast lunch (£6.50). Part of the eating area is no smoking; piped music. Well kept Bass, Courage Best and Directors, and John Smiths on handpump. There's a medieval stone well in the pretty sheltered garden, which has an aviary and rabbits. Also a touring caravan site. *(Recommended by James and Ruth Morrell, Philip and Jude Simmons, S H Godsell, Charles and Pauline Stride, Simon and Amanda Southwell, Jack and Gemima Valiant, Mrs B Sugarman, Meg and Colin Hamilton, Stan Edwards, Dennis Shirley, Heather and Trevor Shaw, Mayur Shah, Mr and Mrs J R Morris, Ken and Jenny Simmonds, A R and B E Sayer)*

Eldridge Pope ~ Manageress Mary May ~ Real ale ~ Meals and snacks (not Sun evening) ~ (01454) 632278 ~ Children in Pine Room only ~ Open 11-3, 6.30-11

AWRE SO7108 Map 4
Red Hart

Village signposted off A48 S of Newnham

Very neatly kept, the L-shaped main part of the bar in this friendly and surprisingly tall country pub has a deep glass-covered illuminated well, an upholstered wall settle, and wheelback chairs; there are plates on a delft shelf at the end, as well as a gun and a stuffed pheasant over the stone fireplace, and big prints on the walls. Decent bar food includes sandwiches, wholesome home-made soup (£2.50), home-made pâté (£3.75), ploughman's (£4.20), home-made lasagne (£5.60), broccoli and cream cheese bake or cold home-baked ham with egg (£6), home-made steak and kidney pie (£6.50), and steaks (from £10); service can slow down under pressure; the restaurant is no smoking. Well kept Bass, Wye Valley Bitter, and a changing guest beer on handpump, and several malt whiskies; darts, cribbage, fruit machine and piped music. In front of the building are some picnic tables. *(Recommended by Alan and Paula McCully, S H Godsell, Daren Haines, Paul and Heather Bettesworth, S P Watkin, P A Taylor, Mr and Mrs J T V Harris, K H Frostick, Tom McLean, Roger Huggins, Dave Irving, Ewan McCall)*

Free house ~ Licensee James Purtill ~ Real ale ~ Meals and snacks (not Sun evenings, not Mon) ~ Restaurant ~ (01594) 510220 ~ Children in eating area of the bar ~ Open 11-3, 7-11; 12-3, 7-10.30 Sun; closed Mon exc bank hol lunchtimes

BARNSLEY SP0705 Map 4
Village Pub

A433 Cirencester—Burford

Readers like this friendly, relaxing place, particularly for the good food served by helpful staff. This might include sandwiches (from £1.75), filled bagels or toasted muffins (from £2.75), grilled fresh sardines (£3), smoked trout and cream cheese pâté (£3.25), ploughman's (from £3.25), cold gammon and egg (£4.95), home-made steak and kidney pie (£5.50), chicken curry (£5.95), and daily specials such as quorn tikka masala (£5.25), beef in Guinness or lamb and apricot casserole (£6.75), with evening steaks (from £8.75); the dining area is no smoking. Well kept Oakhill Best Bitter and Wadworths 6X on handpump, and country wines. The walls of the comfortable low-ceilinged communicating rooms are decorated with country pictures, gin-traps, scythes and other farm tools, and there are several winter log fires, as well as plush chairs, stools and window settles around the polished tables (which have candles in the evening). Shove-ha'penny, cribbage, and dominoes. The sheltered back courtyard has plenty of tables, and its own outside servery. The pub is handy for Rosemary Verey's garden in the village. *(Recommended by D H and M C Watkinson, Maysie Thompson, N C Hinton, Richard and Stephanie Scholey, Derek Wilkinson, Dave Irving, Roger Huggins, Tom McLean, Ewan McCall, Dorsan Baker, Gordon, John and Joan Wyatt, Jean Minner, John Broughton, Dr and Mrs A Young, Paul and Sue Merrick, Don and Shirley Parrish, Steve Gilbert, Helen Cox, Andrew and Ruth Triggs, Sue Lee)*

Free house ~ Licensee Mrs Susan Wardrop ~ Real ale ~ Meals and snacks ~ Restaurant ~ (01285) 740421 ~ Children in eating area of bar ~ Open 11-3, 6-11; 12-3, 6-10.30 Sun; closed 25 Dec ~ Bedrooms: £30B/£45B

BIBURY SP1106 Map 4
Catherine Wheel 🍺
Arlington; B4425 NE of Cirencester

A friendly new licensee has taken over this bustling low-beamed pub set in a pretty Cotswold village. The main bar at the front dates back in part to the 15th c, and has lots of old-fashioned dark wood furniture, gleaming copper pots and pans around the fireplace, and a good log fire; there are also two smaller and quieter back rooms. Bar food now includes sandwiches, home-cooked ham with egg (£5.75), fidget pie, lamb and apricot casserole or steak and Guinness pie (all £5.95), and local trout (£7.25). Well kept Archers Village, Courage Best and Directors, and Eldridge Pope Hardy Country on handpump, and decent wines; shove-ha'penny, table skittles, dominoes, cribbage, fruit machine, and piped music. There's a good sized and well kept garden behind with picnic tables among fruit trees (and a play area), and some seats out in front. *(Recommended by Fiona Narman, Gordon, Charles and Vic Lund, Dave Irving, Tom McLean, Ewan McCall, Roger Huggins, Joan and Michel Hooper-Immins, Peter Woolls, Simon Collett-Jones, D G King, Andrew and Ruth Triggs, D I Williams, Richard J Raeon, Karen Barnes, Mrs K Neville-Rolfe)*

Free house ~ Licensee Paul Wood ~ Real ale ~ Meals and snacks (all day) ~ (01285) 740250 ~ Children welcome ~ Open 11-11; 12-2, 7-10.30 Sun ~ Bedrooms: /£50S

BISLEY SO9006 Map 4
Bear 🛏 🍺
Village signposted off A419 just E of Stroud

Readers have enjoyed staying at this elegant rather gothic little stone building – and the breakfasts are particularly good. The meandering L-shaped bar has a good relaxed atmosphere, a long shiny black built-in settle and a smaller but even sturdier oak settle by the front entrance, and an enormously wide low stone fireplace (not very high – the ochre ceiling's too low for that); a separate no-smoking stripped-stone area is used for families. The good bar food is all home-made using fresh local produce and includes daily specials such as pigeon breasts caramelised in a red wine and port sauce (£3.95), crab and coriander rosti cakes with chilli and lime mayonnaise (£4.45), baked aubergine with a garlic and chickpea stuffing with red onion marmalade (£4.95), seared tuna steak with a lemon and basil cream (£6.95), and venison steak in a brandy and orange sauce (£8.95); also, a huge choice of filled french bread (from £3.50 for venison sausages or tuna salad niçoise, £4 for smoked kipper and poached egg, stilton, hazelnut and onion pâté or 4oz lamb steak with redcurrant jelly), rabbit and vegetable stew with herb dumplings, excellent steak and kidney pie, vegetable pasty (fennel, mushrooms and pine kernels in white wine sauce) or fish crumble (from £5), and puddings (£2.25); they can serve most dishes in smaller helpings for children. Well kept Bass, Flowers Original, Tetleys, and Whitbread Castle Eden on handpump; helpful, attentive service. Darts, table skittles, cribbage, and dominoes. A small front colonnade supports the upper floor of the pub, and the sheltered little flagstoned courtyard made by this has a traditional bench; as well as the garden across the quiet road, there's quite a collection of stone mounting-blocks. The steep stone-built village is attractive. *(Recommended by Daren Haines, George Atkinson, CLS, RMB, P R and S A White, F J and A Parmenter, Mr and Mrs D Hack, Joan and Alex Timpson, Richard Gibbs, Nick and Meriel Cox, Mike Beiley, Roger Huggins, Ewan McCall, Tom McLean, Dave Irving, John and Phyllis Maloney, Don and Shirley Parrish)*

Pubmaster ~ Tenants Nick and Vanessa Evans ~ Real ale ~ Meals and snacks (till 10pm; not Sun evening or 25-26 Dec) ~ (01452) 770265 ~ Children in family room ~ Open 11-3(2.30 in winter), 6-11; 12-3, 7-10.30 Sun; open all day Sat and Sun if busy in summer; closed evenings 25-26 Dec ~ Bedrooms: £18/£36

BLAISDON SO7017 Map 4
Red Hart ⬤

Village signposted off A4136 just SW of junction with A40 W of Gloucester; OS Sheet 162 map reference 703169

The young couple who took this over towards the end of summer 1996 look set to make it one of the most welcoming places in the county. The flagstoned main bar has pink-cushioned wall and window seats, traditional pub tables, a big sailing-ship painting above the good log fire; the thoroughly relaxing atmosphere is helped along by sympathetic lighting, well reproduced piped bluesy music, and maybe Spotty the perky young jack russell. The previous landlord's tradition of interesting guest beers (unobtrusively immortalised in neat lettering on the beams) is maintained: on our visit we found well kept Hook Norton Best and Cottage Goldrush, alongside the regular Tetleys and Theakstons Best on handpump. Given that the newcomers have started a guest wines policy, alongside their regular house wines, we suspect they may be headed for a Wine Award too, and would welcome more reports on this aspect. On the right, an attractive two-room no-smoking dining area with some interesting prints has good home-cooked specials such as ham, egg and bubble and squeak (£3.75), scrambled egg and smoked salmon, liver and bacon, pork fillet with honey and apples (£7.50), rack of lamb with a port and cranberry sauce (£7.95), various vegetarian dishes and fish dishes like salmon and coriander fishcakes, and bar snacks (from £3); sandwiches. A comfortable little separate games room has a well lit pool table, darts, and table skittles. There are some picnic tables out beside flowerbeds by the quiet road, and more in a pretty garden up behind. Dogs welcome. *(Recommended by Ian Phillips; more reports please)*

Free house ~ Licensee Guy Wilkins ~ Real ale ~ Meals and snacks ~ Restaurant ~ (01452) 830477 ~ Well behaved children welcome ~ Open 12-3, 6-11; 12-3, 7-10.30 Sun

BLEDINGTON SP2422 Map 4
Kings Head ★ ⑪ 🛏 ♀ ⬤

B4450

A thoroughly enjoyable all-rounder is one way of describing this bustling pub in its pretty setting by the village green. There's a lot of character, a friendly welcome from both staff and locals, extremely good food, a thoughtful choice of both beers and wines, and comfortable accommodation. The spotlessly kept, smart main bar is full of ancient beams and other atmospheric furnishings, such as high-backed wooden settles, gateleg or pedestal tables, and there's a warming log fire in the stone inglenook (which has a big black kettle hanging in it); the lounge looks on to the garden, and this year they have converted a room to the left of the bar into a carpeted sitting room with comfortable new sofas, magazines to read, views of the village green from a small window, and some attractive antiques and old gilt-edged paintings on the walls. From the bar menu, the very good food might include home-made soup (£1.95), ploughman's or sandwiches on granary or ciabatta bread with interesting fillings like vodka-soused red mullet or chargrilled tuna with apple and horseradish or crispy bacon and banana (from £3.25, with straw potatoes), salads (from £3.50; hot kipper strips with dill and whisky £3.95, poached fillet of salmon with lemon mayonnaise £6.95), tartlet of mushrooms with watercress dressing (£3.95), aubergine and tomato gratinée (£4.95), and steak and mushroom pie (£5.95), with monthly changing specials such as fresh squid in chilli batter with soy dip or omelettes (£3.95), filo parcels of parma ham and baby ratatouille on stilton sauce (£4.95), interesting pasta dishes, bubble and squeak or stir-fried chinese leaves and scallops with a carrot and orange dressing (£5.25), local rabbit wrapped in spinach with a sherry and berry sauce (£6.95), good children's dishes (from £1.50), and puddings (£2); they also do a good value 3-course meal (£9.95). An antique bar counter dispenses well kept Adnams Broadside, Eccleshall Hi Duck, Hook Norton Best, Stanway Old Eccentric, Uley Old Spot, and Wadworths 6X, an excellent extensive wine list, with 10 by the glass and an encouragement to try lesser known growers like Greece, Israel, the Lebanon, Chile and so forth, and 50 or so malt whiskies; efficient, friendly service. Part of the restaurant area is no smoking; piped music. The public bar has darts, bar billiards, shove-ha'penny, table skittles, and dominoes. The back garden has tables that look over to a little stream with lots of ducks. *(Recommended by Pam Adsley, Dave Irving, Roger Huggins, Tom McLean, Ewan McCall, Liz Bell, Tony Hall, Melanie Jackson, Maysie Thompson, John Bowdler, Kevin Plant, Robert Whittle, Derek Hayman, John and Hazel Waller, Michael Kirby, Andrew Hudson, Mr and Mrs Peter Woods, M A and C R Starling, John C Baker, Julia Doust, M J Morgan, Andrew and Ruth Triggs, Sue Demont, Tim Barrow, Adam and Elizabeth Duff, Richard Baker, Arnold Day, D C T and E A Frewer, D J Harman, Paul Boot)*

Free house ~ Licensees Michael and Annette Royce ~ Real ale ~ Meals and snacks (12-2, 6.30-10) ~ Restaurant ~ (01608) 658365 ~ Children in restaurant ~ Open 11-2.30(3 Sat), 6-11; 12-2.30, 7-10.30 Sun; closed 25 Dec ~ Bedrooms: £45B/£60B

BLOCKLEY SP1634 Map 4
Crown ★ 🍴 🍷 🛏

High Street

In a pretty village surrounded by peaceful countryside, this civilised honey-coloured stone Elizabethan inn has a relaxed, welcoming atmosphere, especially in the split-level bustling bar. Food is highly regarded, and in the bar includes home-made soup (£3.25), sandwiches (from £3.25 for 1½ rounds; open toasties like roast spicy lamb or welsh rarebit with chips £6.25), spinach and feta cheese pie or chicken tikka with minty yoghurt (£5.95), home-made steak and kidney pie or very popular local cod in a beer and chive batter (£6.95), casserole of local pheasant or fresh salmon fishcakes with a parsley and lemon butter sauce (£7.95), and home-made puddings (£3.95); good Sunday lunch. Well kept Goff's Jouster, Hook Norton Best, and Shepherd Neame Spitfire on handpump, a large choice of wines, several malt whiskies, and freshly squeezed fruit juice; friendly staff. The two rooms of the bar have comfortable padded leather chairs and plush stools around pubby tables, padded window seats, various prints on the walls, and an open fire; there's a sitting room with newspapers to read, comfortable sofas and chairs, and another open fire, and a restaurant and grill room with its famous choice of fresh fish. The terraced coachyard is surrounded by beautiful trees and shrubs, and there's a hatch to hand drinks down to people sitting out in front, by the lane. The inn is handy for Batsford Park Arboretum. *(Recommended by Martin and Karen Wake, Rob Whittle, A Cowell, Roy Bromell, Kerry Law, Simon Smith, Liz Bell, D P Brown, Ted George, John and Hazel Waller, Bob and Maggie Atherton, M A and C R Starling, E V Walder, J Rankin, Mike and Maggie Betton, D H and M C Watkinson, R Davies, Richard Raeon, Karen Barnes, M J Dowdy, Hanns P Golez, Neville Kenyon, Jenny and Michael Back, Martin and Maren Wake, M A Robinson, Andrew and Ruth Triggs)*

Free house ~ Licensees John and Betty Champion ~ Real ale ~ Meals (not in bar Sat evening) and snacks ~ Restaurant ~ (01386) 700245 ~ Well behaved children welcome ~ Open 11-midnight; 12-3, 7-midnight Sun ~ Bedrooms: £64B/£89B

Most pubs in the *Guide* sell draught cider. We mention it specifically only if they have unusual farm-produced 'scrumpy' or even specialise in it.

BRIMPSFIELD SO9312 Map 4

Golden Heart ♀ ◀

Nettleton Bottom; A417 Birdlip—Cirencester

Friendly and relaxed, this extended partly 16th-c country pub has plenty to look at in its five rooms. The main low-ceilinged bar is divided into three cosily distinct areas, with a roaring log fire in the huge stone inglenook fireplace in one, traditional built-in settles and other old-fashioned furnishings throughout, and quite a few brass items, typewriters, exposed stone, and wood panelling. A comfortable parlour on the right has another decorative fireplace, and leads into a further room that opens onto the terrace; two rooms are no smoking. Well kept Bass, Marstons Pedigree, Timothy Taylors Landlord, and guest beers on handpump or tapped from the cask, and a good range of wines by the glass. Served by friendly staff, bar food might include sandwiches, generous ploughman's, good tortellini stuffed with spinach and cheese (£6.95), lamb and apricot pie (£7), hot bacon, chicken and avocado salad (£7.25), chicken breast stuffed with stilton and wrapped in bacon (£7.50), kangaroo casserole (£7.95), and wild boar with a date and cherry sauce (£8.75). There are pleasant views down over a valley from the rustic cask-supported tables on its suntrap gravel terrace; good nearby walks. *(Recommended by Dave Irving, Ewan McCall, Roger Huggins, Tom McLean, David Ling, D G King, Jo Rees, Neil and Anita Christopher, Tony Dickinson, Lynda Payton, Sam Samuells, Joan and Alex Timpson, Paula Massey, Mervyn Hall, Jeremy Brittain-Long, Dave Braisted)*

Free house ~ Licensee Catherine Stevens ~ Real ale ~ Meals and snacks (till 10pm) ~ (01242) 870261 ~ Children welcome ~ Open 11-2.30, 6-11; 12-3, 7-10.30 Sun ~ Bedrooms: £25B/£40B

BROAD CAMPDEN SP1637 Map 4

Bakers Arms ★ ◀

Village signposted from B4081 in Chipping Campden

Full of unpretentious character, this basic little pub keeps six changing real ales on handpump (maybe fewer in winter): Donnington BB, Hook Norton Best, Marstons Pedigree, Stanway Stanney Bitter, and Wickwar BOB. The tiny beamed bar has a pleasant mix of tables and seats around the walls (which are stripped back to bare stone), a log fire under a big black iron canopy at one end with a rocking chair beside it, and another at the other end; several friendly cats. The oak bar counter is attractive, and there's a big framed rugwork picture of the pub. Bar food includes lunchtime sandwiches (from £2.25) and ploughman's (from £1.50), as well as herby tomato soup (£2), cottage pie (£3.25), smoked haddock bake (£3.95), chilli con carne or vegetable lasagne (£4.25), chicken madras (£4.75), steak and kidney pie (£5.75), daily specials such as liver and onion casserole (£4.50), salmon and broccoli pasta (£4.95); smaller appetite dishes (from £2), Sunday roast lunch (£4.25), and afternoon teas. Darts, cribbage, dominoes. There are white tables under cocktail parasols by flower tubs on a side terrace and in the back garden, some seats under a fairy-lit arbour, and a play area. The lavatories are pretty primitive. The tranquil village is handy for the Barnfield cider mill. *(Recommended by Tom Evans, Stephen and Yvonne Agar, Ted George, Wilma and Ian Smith, Andrew and Ruth Triggs, H O Dickinson, Martin Jones, A Cowell, Terry and Vann W Prime, Jason Caulkin, M L and G Clarke, Martin and Karen Wake, Alain and Rose Foote, Jerry and Alison Oakes, Mr and Mrs C Moncreiffe, H O Dickinson, Hanns P Golez)*

Free house ~ Licensee Carolyn Perry ~ Real ale ~ Meals and snacks (till 10pm Fri and Sat) ~ (01386) 840515´ ~ Children welcome ~ Folk night 3rd Tues of month ~ Open 11.30-11; 11.30-2.30, 6-11 in winter; 12-3, 7-10.30 Sun; closed 25 Dec, evening 26 Dec

Looking for a pub with a really special garden, or in lovely countryside, or with an outstanding view, or right by the water? They are listed separately, at the back of the book.

BROCKWEIR SO5401 Map 4
Brockweir

Village signposted just off A466 Chepstow—Monmouth

A new licensee has taken over this 17th-c pub and has redecorated the bars and refurbished the bedrooms. The main bar has sturdy settles on quarry tiles in the front part, a winter open fire, beams and bare stone walls, and brocaded seats and copper-topped tables in a series of carpeted alcoves at the back; darts, pool, cribbage, dominoes, trivia, and piped music in the bare-floored and traditionally furnished public bar. Well kept Fullers London Pride, Greene King Abbot, Hook Norton Best, and Thwaites Bitter on handpump, and traditional ciders. Bar food includes sandwiches, ploughman's (£3.50), ham and egg, chilli con carne, pork in cider, vegetarian dishes, and chicken tikka (all under £5). A covered courtyard at the back opens into a sheltered terrace, and there are picnic tables in a garden behind. As the pub is not too far away from the steep sheep-pastures leading up to Offa's Dyke Path and the Devil's Pulpit, with views over the Wye and Tintern Abbey, it's understandably a popular stop with walkers (no muddy boots); canoeing, horse riding and salmon fishing are available locally. *(Recommended by Barry and Anne, Paul Barnett, Wayne Brindle, Daren Haines; more reports on the new regime, please)*

Free house ~ Licensee Jim Mills ~ Real ale ~ Meals and snacks (not Tues evening) ~ (01291) 689548 ~ Children in eating area of the bar ~ Open 12-3, 6-11; 12-11 Sat; 12-3, 7-10.30 Sun; closed 25 Dec ~ Bedrooms: £28/£40

CHEDWORTH SP0511 Map 4
Seven Tuns

Queen Street, Upper Chedworth; village signposted off A429 NE of Cirencester; then take second signposted right turn and bear left towards church

Depending on your mood or whether you have muddy walking boots, you can choose between the two completely different bars here. On the right, the smarter but cosily atmospheric little lounge has comfortable seats and decent tables, sizeable antique prints, tankards hanging from the beam over the serving bar, a partly boarded ceiling, a good winter log fire in the big stone fireplace, and a relaxed, quiet atmosphere; no muddy boots in here. The basic public bar on the left is more lively, and opens into a games room with darts, pool, dominoes, pinball, fruit machine, video game, and juke box; there's also a skittle alley (which can be hired). Enjoyable bar food includes daily specials such as stir-fried purple sprouting broccoli in garlic butter with freshly baked olive ciabatta (£4.95), grilled goat's cheese with a fresh orange and redcurrant sauce (£5.50), Gloucester Old Spot sausages with parsnip, potato, bacon, garlic and onion bubble and squeak and rich onion gravy (£5.95), fillet of fresh Scottish salmon with creamy parsley sauce (£7.50), and roast fillet of pork with pistachio nuts and apple and a brandy, cream and cider sauce (£8.50); from the standard menu there might be sandwiches, good ploughman's, home-made soup (£2.95), stilton and herb pâté (£3.95), home-made steak in ale pie (£6.95), and steaks (from £9.50); children's menu (£2.95). Well kept George's Traditional, Ruddles County and guest beers on handpump; friendly, helpful staff. Across the road is a little walled raised terrace with a stream running through it with a waterwheel, and there are plenty of tables both here and under cocktail parasols on a side terrace. The famous Roman villa is only a pleasant walk away, and there are other nice walks through the valley, too. *(Recommended by Neil and Anita Christopher, Alan and Barbara Mence, Liz Bell, John and Lynn Busenbark, Tom McLean, Roger Huggins, Ewan McCall, Dave Irving, Tony Dickinson, Sharon Hancock, Alan and Charlotte Sykes, John and Joan Wyatt, Lawrence Pearse, Mr and Mrs J Brown)*

Free house ~ Licensee Brian Eacott ~ Real ale ~ Meals and snacks (not Mon, or 25 Dec) ~ (01285) 720242 ~ Well-behaved children in eating area of the bar ~ Open 12(11.30 Sat)-3, 6.30-11; 12-3, 7-10.30 Sun

CHIPPING CAMPDEN SP1539 Map 4
Eight Bells 🏠 📷 ♀
Church Street

Popular with both locals and visitors, this handsome inn, dating from the 13th or 14th c, is busy at lunchtime and in the evening. There's a friendly, bustling atmosphere, cushioned pews and solid dark wood furniture on its broad flagstones, stripped stone walls (with caricatures of regulars and photographs of pub events), heavy oak beams with massive timber supports, fresh flowers on tables, and log fires in up to three restored stone fireplaces – one enormous one has a painting of the pub in summer. Good changing bar food might include a whole board's-worth of filled baguettes (from £3), as well as soups like tomato with orange (£2.95), baked brie with garlic toast or bacon and avocado salad (£4.95), paella (£5.95), rabbit casserole (£6.25), steak and kidney pie (£6.75), chicken supreme cooked with ginger and spring onions or sautéed pork fillet with apricot and cream sauce (£7.50), seasonal venison, and sirloin steak (£9.25); puddings such as a delicious crème brûlée (£2.95); obliging service. Well kept Greene King Abbot, Marstons Pedigree and Tetleys, and a changing guest such as Donnington SBA from handpumps on a striking oak bar counter, up to a dozen good wines by the glass, nice coffee, and daily papers; backgammon, dominoes. A fine old courtyard surrounded by roses and climbers has picnic tables. *(Recommended by David Shillitoe, Roger and Fiona Todd, IHR, R Davies, Nick Lawless, Martin Jones, H O Dickinson, Andrew and Ruth Triggs, John Bowdler, E V Walder, Martin and Sarah Constable, Martin and Karen Wake, MDN, George Atkinson, Owen Warnock, Ann and Bob Westbrook)*

Free house ~ Licensees Paul and Patrick Dare ~ Real ale ~ Meals and snacks ~ Restaurant ~ (01386) 840371 ~ Children welcome ~ Open 11-3, 6-11; cl evening 25 Dec ~ Bedrooms: £38B/£48B

Noel Arms 🏠 ♀

The sunny enclosed courtyard of this smart old inn is a most inviting place to sit in summer and enjoy a drink or meal surrounded by lots of pretty hanging baskets. Inside, there's a friendly welcome from the licensee and his helpful staff, and the relaxed, friendly bar has old oak settles, attractive old tables, seats and newer settles among the windsor chairs, and is decorated with casks hanging from its beams, farm tools, horseshoes and gin-traps on the bare stone walls, and armour; there's a winter coal fire, and a conservatory behind. The small lounge areas are comfortable and traditionally furnished with coach horns, lantern lighting, and some stripped stonework, and the reception area has its quota of pikes, halberds, swords, muskets, and breastplates. Well kept Bass and Hook Norton Best plus changing guest beers on handpump, and quite a few malt whiskies; piped music. Under the new licensees, good bar food includes sandwiches (from £2.40; ham with apricot and honey mayonnaise £2.80), grilled goat's cheese with bacon and an apple and ginger chutney (£3.95), moules marinières or liver and bacon (£5.95), chicken with a piquant creole sauce (£6.50), braised shoulder of lamb with mixed herbs (£7.75), rib eye steak (£8.75), and daily specials. *(Recommended by Andrew and Ruth Triggs, Neil and Angela Huxter, George Atkinson, SLC, M Joyner, Liz Bell, G V Price, John and Moira Cole, Martin Jones, Pam Adsley)*

Free house ~ Licensees Mark Cleaver, Paul Rees ~ Real ale ~ Lunchtime bar meals and snacks ~ Restaurant ~ (01386) 840317 ~ Children welcome ~ Open 11-3, 6-11; 12-3, 7-10.30 Sun ~ Bedrooms: £65B/£92B

CLEARWELL SO5708 Map 4
Wyndham Arms 🏠 ♀
B4231, signposted from A466 S of Monmouth towards Lydney

In six acres of lovely gardens, this 600-year-old family run inn has a relaxed, friendly atmosphere in its smart beamed bar. There are red plush seats and velvet curtains, a collection of flat-irons by the log-effect gas fire in its spacious stone fireplace, and two big unusual patchwork pictures on its bared stone walls. Well kept Bass on handpump, 25 malt whiskies, a very good range of generously served wines by the glass (12) or half bottle – and gherkins, onions and olives on the counter; good service from smartly turned-out staff. Good bar food includes home-made soup (£2.50), sandwiches (from £2.75; open ones from £3.25), ploughman's (£3.75), home-made pâtés like cheese and fresh herb or chicken liver (£3.95), smoked haddock with poached egg or a daily pasta dish (£4.95), a vegetarian dish of the day, deep-fried lemon sole with home-made tartare sauce or liver and bacon (all £8.25), steaks (from £11.50), and puddings (£2.50); some of the fruits, vegetables and herbs are grown in the garden; the restaurant is no smoking and they now also have a Grill Room. Cribbage and dominoes. There are seats out on the neat terraces; the friendly and characterful flat-coated retriever is called Theo and the huge black newfoundland is called Brian. This is a comfortable place to stay, with excellent breakfasts, and is well placed for exploring the area – and you can stay free on Sundays if you eat in the restaurant. *(Recommended by Alan and Barbara Mence, Dave Irving, Roger Huggins, Tom McLean, E McCall, E H and R F Warner, Wayne Brindle, G and T Edwards, LM, Mrs P Goodwyn, M J Morgan)*

Free house ~ Licensees John and Robert Stanford ~ Real ale ~ Meals and snacks ~ Restaurant ~ (01594) 833666 ~ Children welcome ~ Open 11-11; 12-10.30 Sun ~ Bedrooms: £52.50B/£65B

COLD ASTON SP1219 Map 4
Plough

Village signposted from A436 and A429 SW of Stow on the Wold; beware that on some maps the village is called Aston Blank, and the A436 called the B4068

Standing timbers divide the bar of this neatly kept and friendly 17th-c village pub into snug little areas, with low black beams, a built-in white-painted traditional settle facing the stone fireplace, simple old-fashioned seats on the flagstone and lime-ash floor, and a happy mix of customers. Bar food includes filled rolls and ploughman's, and chicken supreme stuffed with stilton, pork fillet with calvados sauce or half shoulder of lamb (£8.95); they've built a new restaurant – bookings only. Well kept Hook Norton Best, John Smiths, Theakstons Best, and Wadworths 6X on handpump; darts. The small side terraces have picnic tables under parasols, and there may be Morris dancers out here in summer. *(Recommended by Liz Bell, Ted George, DFL, Mr and Mrs M F Norton, Dorothy and Leslie Pilson, Martin and Karen Wake, I R Bell, Tim Brierly, Don and Shirley Parrish, Dave Irving, Ewan McCall, Roger Huggins, Tom McLean)*

Free house ~ Licensees Ernest and Christine Goodwin ~ Real ale ~ Meals and snacks ~ Restaurant ~ (01451) 821459 ~ Children over 5 welcome ~ Open 11-3, 6.30-11; 12-3, 7-10.30 Sun

nr COLEFORD SO5813 Map 4
Dog & Muffler

Joyford, best approached from Christchurch 5-ways junction B4432/B4428, by church – B4432 towards Broadwell, then follow signpost; also signposted from the Berry Hill post office cross-roads; beyond the hamlet itself, bear right and keep your eyes skinned for the pub sign, which may be obscured by the hedge; OS Sheet 162 map reference 580134

This looks from the outside like an idealised farmhouse and it's in an attractively rural setting. The turkey-carpeted lounge bar, open yet cosy-feeling, has neat tables and comfortably cushioned wall settles and wheelback chairs, under black beams hung with pewter and china. A separate beamed and flagstoned extension has a games area with darts, pool, juke box, and a nearby skittle alley. At the back, a pleasant carpeted sun-lounge dining room with raj ceiling fans looks out past more tables on a verandah. Bar food includes sandwiches, soup (£2.50), filled baked potatoes (from £3.75), cold ham and egg (£4.95), broccoli and cream cheese bake (£5.25), lasagne (£5.75), steak and kidney pie (£5.95), poached salmon with a white wine and tarragon sauce (£9.50), steaks (from £9.70), and puddings. Well kept Fullers London Pride and Sam Smiths on handpump, and very pleasant cheerful service; piped music. The lawn is well sheltered, with some shade from mature trees, and well spaced picnic tables – some under thatched conical roofs; it has swings and a climbing frame. There are nice walks nearby. *(Recommended by Pete Yearsley, Neil and Anita Christopher; more reports please)*

Free house ~ Licensee Dennis Brain ~ Real ale ~ Meals and snacks (till 10pm) ~ Restaurant ~ (01594) 832444 ~ Children welcome ~ Open 12-3, 7-11 ~ Bedrooms: £30B/£45B

COLN ST ALDWYNS SP1405 Map 4
New Inn ⊕ 🛏 ♀

On good back road between Bibury and Fairford

Most people come to this civilised ivy-covered inn to enjoy the good food – either in the relaxed bar or the smarter restaurant. From the bar menu, dishes might include soup (£2.95), coarse pâté of pork and wild mushrooms with toasted orange and parsley brioche (£5.50), crab and coriander cakes with a light curry sauce (£6.50), fish and chips (£7.25), gammon and egg or grilled lamb liver and bacon with mustard mash and an onion and ale gravy (£7.95), confit of duck with creamed potatoes and a sherry vinegar and lentil jus (£9.95), fillet of brill with a chive sauce (£12.75), and puddings such as steamed marmalade sponge pudding with vanilla egg custard, rhubarb, honey and saffron cream or rich chocolate tart with Baileys ice cream and an espresso sauce (£3.95); cheeses with home-made pear and saffron chutney and rosemary and olive bread (£4.50); vegetarian and children's dishes also. The restaurant is no smoking. The two main rooms are most attractively furnished and decorated, and divided by a central log fire in a neat stone fireplace with wooden mantelbeam and willow-pattern plates on the chimney breast; there are also low beams, some stripped stonework around the bar servery and hops above it, oriental rugs on the red tiles, and a mix of seating from library chairs to stripped pews. Down a slight slope, a further room has a log fire in an old kitchen range at one end, and a stuffed buzzard on the wall. Well kept Bass, Hook Norton Best, Morlands Original, and Wadworths 6X on handpump, up to 10 good wines by the glass, and several malt whiskies. Darts and dominoes. Lots of seats under umbrellas in the split-level terraced garden, and maybe sunny weekend barbecues. The peaceful Cotswold village is pretty, and the surrounding countryside is good for walking – readers say the riverside walk to Bibury is not to be missed. *(Recommended by G V Price, George and Jean Dundas, B J Cox, John Bowdler, Liz Bell, Karen Paginton, Pat and John Millward, John and Barbara Burns, Dr I Maine, Rob Pope, Dorothy and Leslie Pilson, John Waller, Adam and Elizabeth Duff, D G King, Robin and Laura Hillman, Esther and John Sprinkle, Nigel Norman, Jason Caulkin, Miss A Henry, Andrew and Ruth Triggs)*

Free house ~ Licensee Brian Evans ~ Real ale ~ Meals and snacks ~ Restaurant ~ (01285) 750651 ~ Children welcome ~ Open 11-11; 11-2.30, 5.30-11 winter weekdays; 12-10.30 Sun ~ Bedrooms: £59B/£87B

CRANHAM SO8912 Map 4
Black Horse 🍺

Village signposted off A46 and B4070 N of Stroud; up side turning

Tucked away down narrow lanes, this friendly and old-fashioned pub dates back to the 17th c. A cosy little lounge has just three or four tables, and the main bar is quarry-tiled, with cushioned high-backed wall settles and window seats, and a good log fire. Most people come to enjoy the good food which includes bar snacks such as soup (£1.50), sandwiches (from £1.50; toasties from £2), and ploughman's (from £3.25), as well as dishes like roast pheasant (in season, £6.50), fresh trout with garlic and herb butter, chicken breast in a wine, cream and mustard sauce, pork in a stilton sauce, or beef and Guinness pie (all £6.75), prawn mornay (£7.95), and kleftiko (half shoulder of lamb with wine and herbs £8.25); Sunday roast lunches (£5.95). You can eat the same menu in the upstairs dining rooms

(best to book at weekends). Very well kept Boddingtons, Flowers Original, Hook Norton Best, Marstons Pedigree, and Wickwar BOB on handpump, and country wines. Shove-ha'penny, cribbage, dominoes, fruit machine, and piped music; Truffle the brittany spaniel is quite a character. Tables in the sizeable garden behind have a good view out over the steep village and wooded valley.
(Recommended by IHR, Stephen Pine, Alfred Lawrence, Tony Dickinson, Mike and Mary Carter, Daren Haines, LM, Tom McLean, Roger Huggins, Dave Irving, Ewan McCall)

Free house ~ Licensees David and Julie Job ~ Real ale ~ Meals and snacks (not Sun evening) ~ (01452) 812217 ~ Children welcome ~ Occasional Irish music or Morris men ~ Open 11.30-2.30, 6.30-11; 12-3, 7-10.30 Sun

EBRINGTON SP1840 Map 4
Ebrington Arms

Signposted from B4035 E of Chipping Campden; and from A429 N of Moreton in Marsh

In this part of the world, it makes quite a change to come across an unspoilt, old-fashioned local with plenty of regulars enjoying a cheerful game of cards and a pint of Donnington SBA, Hook Norton Best or a changing guest on handpump or traditional cider; the licensees have just bought a pianola (absolutely no piped music or games machines). The little bar has some fine old low beams, stone walls, flagstoned floors and inglenook fireplaces – the one in the dining room still has the original iron work – sturdy traditional furnishings, with seats built into the airy bow window, and a slightly raised woodfloored area. A lower room, also beamed and flagstoned, has stripped country-kitchen furnishings. Enjoyable simple bar food (chalked up on the beams) might include sandwiches (£2.25; filled french bread £3.75), egg and chips (£2.50), omelettes (£3.75), ratatouille or ploughman's (£3.95), good local sausages (£4.95), steak, mushroom and Guinness pie or delicious fresh cod (£5.45), and steaks (from £8.50); decent breakfasts. Trophies bear witness to the success of the pub's dominoes team, and you can also play cribbage, darts and shove-ha'penny. An arched stone wall shelters a terrace with picnic tables under cocktail parasols. No dogs – at least at mealtimes, when even the licensees' friendly welsh springer is kept out. Handy for Hidcote and Kiftsgate.
(Recommended by David Heath, Martin Jones, Mr and Mrs C Roberts, Geoffrey and Penny Hughes, Peter and Anne Hollindale, E V Walder, Ted George, MDN, Jerry and Alison Oakes, Martin and Karen Wake, Don and Shirley Parrish)

Free house ~ Licensee Gareth Richards ~ Real ale ~ Meals and snacks (not Sun evening) ~ (01386) 593223 ~ Children in dining room ~ Open 11-2.30, 6-11; winter Mon-Thurs evening opening 7; 12-3, 7-10.30 Sun; closed 25 Dec ~ Bedrooms: £30/£35B

EDGE SO8509 Map 4
Edgemoor

A4173 N of Stroud

After a walk, the terrace here is a marvellous place to relax with its fine view looking down over the valley to Painswick – you get the same view from the big picture windows inside, too. And if you're here at dusk you'll see the lights in the little cluster of houses come on one by one, watched over by the serenely superior church spire towering above them. There's quite an emphasis on the wide choice of home-made bar food, which includes daily fresh fish dishes, vegetarian choices, and home-made specials, as well as sandwiches, soup (£2.25), smoked salmon pâté (£3.75), stir-fry vegetables and cashew nuts or fried fillet of plaice (£5.50), lamb liver and bacon (£6.50), garlic and herb chicken (£6.95), mixed grill (£9.50), steaks (from £9.95), and puddings; the two dining rooms are no smoking. Clean and tidy, the main bar is an orderly place, with West Country cloth upholstery and pale wood furniture on the patterned carpet, and neat bare stone walls. Well kept Butcombe Bitter, Smiles Best, Tetleys, and Uley Old Spot on handpump, kept under light top pressure in winter, good wines by the glass, and an interesting range of malt whiskies. An extension gives new lavatories (including a disabled one) and wheelchair access. *(Recommended by M W and I E Bayley, Kay Neville-Rolfe, M Joyner, Roger Huggins)*

Free house ~ Licensee Chris Bayes ~ Real ale ~ Meals and snacks (not Sun evening Oct-March) ~ Restaurant ~ (01452) 813576 ~ Children welcome ~ Open 11-3, 6-11; 12-3, 7-10.30 Sun; closed Sun evening Oct-Mar

EWEN SU0097 Map 4
Wild Duck ★ ⊕ ♀ ◧

Village signposted from A429 S of Cirencester

Quietly placed on the edge of a peaceful village, this civilised 16th-c inn is extremely popular with a very wide mix of customers – many who have come to enjoy the splendid food. The high-beamed main bar has a nice mix of comfortable armchairs and other seats, candles on the tables, paintings on the coral walls, crimson drapes, magazines to read, and an open winter fire; another bar has a handsome Elizabethan fireplace and antique furnishings, and looks over the garden. Bar food includes soup (£2.95), pineapple wedges with prawns and mayonnaise or ploughman's (£4.95), bacon and brie french bread (£5.50), tagliatelle with vegetables in a stilton sauce, chicken stir fry or fish and chips (£6.95), lamb and apricot pie (£7.50), thai-style chicken or duck bread with a ginger and garlic glaze (£9.95), steaks (£12.95), and daily changing fish dishes; there may be a wait when service is pushed. As well as Duckpond Bitter, brewed especially for the pub, well kept beers might include Courage Directors, Smiles Best, Theakstons Best and Old Peculier, and Wadworths 6X. Good wines, several malt whiskies, and freshly squeezed fruit juice; shove-ha'penny. There are attractive white painted cast-iron tables and seats in the neatly kept and sheltered garden. *(Recommended by Dave Irving, Roger Huggins, Tom McLean, Ewan McCall, J F Knutton, Simon Small, E V Walder, T Halstead, S H Godsell, Nick and Meriel Cox, Peter Neate, M A and C R Starling, G R Braithwaite, Dorsan Baker, Julie and James Horsley, Liz Bell, John Bowdler, D G King, Amanda and Simon Southwell, Brian and Bett Cox, Mark Percy, Lesley Mayoh, Mrs J Oakes, John and Alex Timpson, Dr J R Hilton, Miss A Henry, S H Godsell, Mr and Mrs G H Rutter, Dr I Maine, Mr and Mrs P Fisk, D G King)*

Free house ~ Licensees Brian and Tina Mussell ~ Real ale ~ Meals and snacks (till 10pm) ~ Restaurant ~ (01285) 770310 ~ Children in eating area of bar ~ Open 11-11; 12-10.30 Sun; closed evening 25 Dec ~ Bedrooms: £49.50B/£69.50B

FORD SP0829 Map 4
Plough

B4077

Even on a bleak January weekday this pretty stone pub tends to be bustling with customers, though there are several log fires (and a log-effect gas one) to keep you warm. The beamed and stripped-stone bar has racing prints and photos on the walls, log fires, old settles and benches around the big tables on its uneven flagstones, oak tables in a snug alcove, and a traditional, friendly feel. The gallops for local stables are opposite, so there's quite a racing feel – particularly on the days when the horse owned by a partnership of locals is running at Cheltenham. Dominoes, cribbage, shove-ha'penny, fruit machine, and piped music. Home-made bar food changes constantly but might include good sandwiches (the rare beef is recommended), home-made soup (£2.95), home-made pâté (£3.95), mixed cheese platter (£4.50), home-cooked ham and eggs (£5.95), lamb and apricot pie or steak, mushroom and Guinness casserole (£7.25), knuckle of lamb (£9.25), steaks, and fish and vegetarian options. They still have their traditional asparagus feasts every April-June, when the first asparagus spears to be sold at auction in the Vale of Evesham usually end up here. Well kept Donnington BB and SBA on handpump, Addlestones cider, a few malt whiskies, and decent wines. There are benches in front, with rustic tables and chairs on grass by white lilacs and fairy lights, and a play area at the back. Look out for the llama farm between here and Kineton. *(Recommended by BHP, Peter and Audrey Dowsett, Jackie Orme, RKP, Wayne Wheeler,*

Daren Haines, Pat and Roger Fereday, Guy Vowles, Dr and Mrs J Hills, Liz Bell, R Watkins, E Walder, Angus Lyon, Dave Irving, Roger Huggins, T McLean, Ewan McCall, John and Joan Wyatt, Dr and Mrs A K Clarke, Andrew and Ruth Triggs, V Kavanagh)

Donnington ~ Tenant W Skinner ~ Real ale ~ Meals and snacks (not Sun evenings) ~ (01386) 584215 ~ Children welcome ~ Open 11-11; 12-10.30 Sun; closed 25 Dec ~ Bedrooms: £35B/£50B

GREAT BARRINGTON SP2013 Map 4
Fox

Village signposted from A40 Burford—Northleach; pub between Little and Great Barrington

With its pretty setting beside a stone bridge over the Windrush, this simple inn is most popular in summer when you can sit on the riverside terrace or near the landscaped pond in the orchard. Inside, the low-ceilinged little bar has rustic wooden chairs, tables and window seats, stripped stone walls, and two roaring log fires; sensibly placed darts, pool, shove-ha'penny, dominoes, cribbage, fruit machine, and piped music. Donnington BB, SBA, XXX and summer Dark Mild on handpump, and Addlestones cider. The pub dog is called Bruiser (though he's only little). Bar food includes sandwiches (not Sundays), warm prawn and bacon salad (£4.25), thai chicken curry or home-made fresh salmon fishcakes (£6.50), and beef in ale pie or oriental pork and noodle stir-fry with oyster sauce (£6.95). There's a skittles alley out beyond the sheltered yard, and they have private fishing. *(Recommended by Geoffrey and Penny Hughes, Ted George, Liz Bell, John and Shirley Dyson, Stephen Pine, Alfred Lawrence, Daren Haines, Margaret Dyke, P and J Shapley, Dr A Drummond, Canon Michael Bordeaux, P R Ferris, Roger and Jenny Huggins, Andrew and Ruth Triggs, P G Topp)*

Donnington ~ Tenants Paul and Kate Porter ~ Real ale ~ Meals and snacks (all day on summer weekends; not winter Mon evenings) ~ (01451) 844385 ~ Children welcome ~ Open 11-11; 12-10.30 Sun; 12-3, 7-10.30 winter Sun ~ Bedrooms: £25/£42.50

GREAT RISSINGTON SP1917 Map 4
Lamb 🛏 ♀

Many of our readers come to this rather civilised partly 17th-c inn to spend a few nights – and enjoy themselves very much indeed. The cosy two-roomed bar has lots to look at including part of a propeller from the Wellington bomber that crashed in the garden in October 1943, an interesting collection of old cigarette and tobacco tins, photographs of the guide dogs the staff and customers have raised money to buy (over 20), a history of the village, and various plates and pictures. Wheelback and tub chairs with cushioned seats are grouped around polished tables on the light brown carpet, a table and settle are hidden in a nook under the stairs, and there's a log-effect gas fire in the stone fireplace. Bar food changes daily but might include home-made soup (£2.50), sandwiches (£3), potato wedges with a fiery dip (£3.95), pasta with salmon (£5.50), home-made pork and leek sausages (£5.65), steak and Guinness pie (£5.95), and 14oz rump steak (£12.50), and puddings (£2.95); the restaurant is no smoking. Well kept Smiles, Wadworths 6X and a guest beer on handpump, a good wine list, and several malt whiskies; helpful service. You can sit out in the sheltered hillside garden or really take advantage of the scenery and walk (via gravel pits now used as a habitat for water birds) to Bourton on the Water. Bedrooms do vary tremendously in quality and price – check when booking. *(Recommended by Ted George, Martin and Karen Wake, Ian and Jane Irving, M S Catling, Andrew and Ruth Triggs, Arnold Day, John and Shirley Dyson, Stephen and Yvonne Agar, John and Jackie Chalcraft, D J Hayman, Peter Neate, Simon Collett-Jones, V Kavanagh)*

Free house ~ Licensees Richard and Kate Cleverly ~ Real ale ~ Meals and snacks ~ Restaurant ~ (01451) 820388 ~ Children welcome ~ Open 11.30-2.30(3 Sat), 6.30-11; 12-2.30, 7-10.30 Sun; closed 25-26 Dec ~ Bedrooms: £35B-£65B/£50-£75B

GREET SP0230 Map 4

Harvest Home

B4078 just N of Winchcombe

This year, the licensees of this spotlessly kept pub have linked the lounge bar to the dining room by creating a new servery which gives a much less formal feel; they have added a bric-a-brac shelf, a big cartwheel centre light, and lots of hop bines to the exposed beams. The bar has a dozen or so well spaced tables, with seats built into the bay windows and other sturdy blue-cushioned seats; there are pretty flower prints and country scenes on the walls, and several dried-flower arrangements. But it is the wide choice of good food that is the main draw: home-made soup (£1.75), filled french sticks (from £2.50), garlic mushrooms (£3.25), ploughman's (from £4.25), omelettes (£4.50), three local spicy sausages (£4.75), ham and eggs (£5.75), chicken tikka (£5.95), tasty duck and bacon pie or fresh local trout (£6.25), steaks (from £6.75), pork schnitzel (£7.25), daily specials such as salmon wellington with puréed mushrooms (£6.95), vegetarian dishes, puddings like wonderful apple strudel with vanilla sauce or nice white chocolate pudding (£2.50), and children's menu (from £2.25). Boddingtons, Hook Norton Best, Wadworths 6X, and a guest beer on handpump, decent wines, and several malt whiskies; darts down at one end (the other, with a good open fire, is no smoking), cribbage, dominoes, and unobtrusive piped classical music; helpful and pleasant young staff. There's a big beamed pitched-roof side restaurant (same food, also no smoking). The sizeable garden has a play area and boules, a terrace with access to the restaurant, and a narrow-gauge GWR railway that passes it. The miniature schnauzers are called Oscar and Boris. The pub is not far from medieval Sudeley Castle. *(Recommended by Martin Jones, Norman and Angela Harries, John Bowdler, Mr and Mrs J Brown, R W Phillips, AH, S Richardson)*

Whitbreads ~ Lease: Heinz and Lisa Stolzenberg ~ Real ale ~ Meals and snacks ~ Restaurant ~ (01242) 602430 ~ Children welcome ~ Open 10.30-3, 6-11; 12-3, 6-10.30 Sun

GRETTON SP0131 Map 4

Royal Oak

Village signposted off what is now officially B4077 (still often mapped and even signed as A438), E of Tewkesbury; keep on through village

There's a friendly bustling atmosphere in the series of bare-boarded or flagstoned rooms here – the pub was once a pair of old stone-built cottages – all softly lit (including candles in bottles on the mix of stripped oak and pine tables), and with dark ochre walls, beams (some hung with tankards, hop bines and chamber-pots), old prints, and a medley of pews and various chairs; the friendly setter is called George and there are two cats. The no-smoking dining conservatory has stripped country furnishings, and a broad view over the countryside. Enjoyable bar food includes mushroom and three cheese lasagne or Gloucester sausages with cumberland sauce (£5.50), chicken wrapped in bacon in a dijon mustard sauce (£6.95), grilled salmon steak with sour cream and chives (£7.25), and puddings such as lemon tart or raspberry mousse. Well kept Goff's Jouster or White Knight, John Smiths, Marstons Pedigree, Ruddles County, Theakstons Best, and Wickwar BOB on handpump, and a decent wine list; shove-ha'penny, fruit machine, and piped music. From seats on the flower-filled terrace you can enjoy the wonderful views over the village and across the valley to Dumbleton Hills and the Malverns. There are more seats under a giant pear tree, a neatly kept big lawn running down past a small hen-run to a play area (with an old tractor and see-saw), and even a bookable tennis court. *(Recommended by E V Walder, G and M Stewart, Daren Haines, Ted George, Martin Jones, Andrew and Ruth Triggs, D G King, The Goldsons, Dave Braisted, Dr and Mrs M Beale)*

Free house ~ Licensees Bob and Kathy Willison ~ Real ale ~ Meals and snacks ~ Restaurant ~ (01242) 602477 ~ Well-behaved children welcome ~ Folk Weds evening ~ Open 11-3, 6-11; 12-3, 7-10.30 Sun; closed 25-26 Dec

GUITING POWER SP0924 Map 4
Farmers Arms 🍺

Village signposted off B4068 SW of Stow on the Wold (still called A436 on many maps)

The licensees of this pub and the Black Horse at Naunton have done a direct swap, and apart from the redecorating of the skittle alley, there have been few changes here so far. It's a busy, friendly creeper-covered village pub with a warm welcome for visitors, too. The long bar is partly flagstoned and partly carpeted, and has some bared stone walls, a good log fire, and (at the front part) a window seat and a high old settle; lots more seating further back. Well kept Donnington BB and SBA on handpump, and decent home-made bar food such as soup (£2), garlic mushrooms (£3.25), ploughman's (4.50), omelettes (from £3.75), sausage and egg with chips (£4.50), spaghetti bolognese (£4.75), quorn chilli or vegetable lasagne (£4.95), ham and two eggs (£5.25), steak in ale or chicken stroganoff (£5.75), steak (from £8.75), and puddings like treacle sponge (£2.50). Darts, pool, cribbage, dominoes, fruit machine, and piped music; friendly staff. There are seats (and quoits) in the garden, set attractively against the backdrop of the village. Good walks nearby. *(Recommended by Jo Rees, S G Bennett, Neil and Anita Christopher, Guy Consterdine, Tim Brierly, Diane Bassett, Dennis Murray, Angus Lyon, M Mason, D Thompson*

Donnington ~ Tenant Leo O'Callaghan ~ Real ale ~ Meals and snacks ~ (01451) 850358 ~ Children welcome ~ Occasional live music in skittle alley ~ Open 11-3, 6-11; 12-3, 7-10.30 Sun ~ Bedrooms: £25B/£38(£40B)

HYDE SO8801 Map 4
Ragged Cot 🛏️ 🍷 🍺

Burnt Ash; Hyde signposted with Minchinhampton from A419 E of Stroud; or (better road) follow Minchinhampton, Aston Down signposted from A419 at Aston Down airfield; OS Sheet 162 map reference 886012

The rambling bar in this relaxed old place has a log fire at each end (with a traditional dark wood settle by one of them), lots of stripped stone and black beams, cushioned wheelback chairs and bar stools, and cushioned window seats; off to the right is a no-smoking restaurant area. Good bar food includes daily specials such as half-a-dozen vegetarian dishes, a stir fry or pasta dish (all £4.95), pork and cider casserole or haddock mornay (£5.25), beef in Guinness (£5.50), and red mullet (£5.75); also, sandwiches and filled rolls (from £1.25), soup (£1.80), ploughman's (from £3.25), filled baked potatoes (£3.95), steak and kidney pie (£4.95), a roast (£5.25), salmon steak (£5.95), and sirloin steak (£8.95); home-made puddings (£2.50), and 3-course Sunday lunch (£7.95). Well kept Bass, Theakstons Best, Uley Old Spot, and Wadworths 6X on handpump, a thoughtful wine list, over 30 malt whiskies, Westons cider; shove-ha'penny, cribbage, dominoes, backgammon, Scrabble, and fruit machine. There are picnic tables (and an interesting pavilion) in the garden, and bedrooms in an adjacent converted barn. *(Recommended by Andy and Jill Kassube, John and Shirley Dyson, M J Morgan, Dave Irving, Roger Huggins, Tom McLean, Ewan McCall, Don and Shirley Parrish)*

Free house ~ Licensee Nicholas Winch ~ Real ale ~ Meals and snacks (not 25-26 Dec) ~ Restaurant ~ (01453) 884643 ~ Children in eating area of bar and in restaurant ~ Open 11-2.30, 6-11; 12-3, 7-10.30 Sun ~ Bedrooms: £35B/£50B

KILKENNY SP0018 Map 4
Kilkeney Inn 🍽️ 🍷

On A436, 1 mile W of Andoversford, nr Cheltenham – OS Sheet 163 map reference 007187

The efficient staff in this comfortable dining pub always manage to cope with large numbers of customers with a smile and welcome. The emphasis is very firmly on the good imaginative food that changes regularly but might include light lunches such as filled french sticks (from £2.75), ploughman's (£3.95), warm croissant filled with a tossed tuna salad with a mint and honey dressing (£4.25), local pork sausage with mash and onion gravy (£4.75), and fish pie (£5.95), as well as soup (£2.25), deep-fried filo-wrapped prawns with a black bean and ginger dip (£4.50), steak, mushroom and ale pie (£6.25), savoury lentil, herb and cheese frangipani tart with a fennel cream sauce (£6.95), pot-roasted shoulder of lamb with mint and garlic in a red wine and root vegetable gravy (£7.50), steaks (from £10.75), half crispy roast duck with a port wine and gooseberry sauce (£11.50), daily specials like chargrilled scallop of pork loin with a white onion sauce (£6.25), roast sirloin of beef with yorkshire pudding (£7.25) and baked fillet of salmon with lemon and parsley butter (£8.75), and puddings like apple and raspberry crumble or brandy and apricot bread and butter pudding (£2.95). Booking is recommended, especially at weekends. The extended and modernised bar, quite bright and airily spacious, has neatly alternated stripped Cotswold stone and white plasterwork, as well as gleaming dark wheelback chairs around the tables, and an open fire. Up at the other end of the same long bar is more of a drinking area, with well kept Ruddles Best on handpump, an excellent range of decent wines and lots of malt whiskies. It opens into a comfortable no-smoking conservatory. Attractive Cotswold views, and good parking. *(Recommended by Mr and Mrs J Brown, Gordon Tong, D H and M C Watkinson, NWN, Stephen Pine, Alfred Lawrence, Gwen and Peter Andrews, Sandra Kench, Steven Norman, C and M Starling, David Surridge, Joan and Alex Timpson, Pat and Roger Fereday)*

Free house ~ Licensees John and Judy Fennell ~ Real ale ~ Meals and lunchtime snacks ~ (01242) 820341 ~ Well behaved children in eating areas ~ Open 11.30-2.30, 6.30-11; 12-3, 7-10.30 Sun; closed 25-26 Dec, and Sun evenings Jan-March

KINETON SP0926 Map 4
Halfway House

Village signposted from B4068 and B4077 W of Stow on the Wold

The unpretentious bar in this pretty and friendly little stone house has a good mix of customers, a warm winter log fire, attractive plates and colourful posters on the walls, and some old ancient farm tools and pictures at one end, with beams at the other; one area of the dining room is no smoking. Well kept Donnington BB and SBA (fresh from the nearby brewery) on handpump, and bar food such as sandwiches (£2.95), liver, bacon and onions (£4.95), local trout (£5.95), and steak and stout pie (£6.95). Darts, cribbage, fruit machine, juke box, and piped music. A sheltered back lawn has some seats, and there are more on the narrow flagstoned front terrace (separated from the slow, quiet village lane by tubs of bright flowers on top of a low stone wall). The pub is handy for Sudeley Castle and Cotswold Farm Park. *(Recommended by Rob Whittle, Gwen and Peter Andrews, Peter Phillips; more reports please)*

Donnington ~ Tenant Paul Hamer ~ Real ale ~ Meals and snacks ~ (01451) 850344 ~ Children in eating area of bar ~ Open 11-2.30, 6.30-11; 12-2.30, 7-10.30 Sun ~ Bedrooms: £20/£30

KINGSCOTE ST8196 Map 4
Hunters Hall ★

A4135 Dursley—Tetbury

Now owned by the Old English Pub Company and with a new manageress, this civilised, creeper-covered old inn has a series of bar rooms and lounges with fine high Tudor beams and stone walls, a lovely old box settle, sofas and miscellaneous easy chairs, and sturdy settles and oak tables on the flagstones in the lower-ceilinged, cosy public bar. An airy end room serves the bar food which now includes sandwiches (not Sunday lunch), cold roast meats, quiches and salads from a buffet table (£5.75), good fish and chips (£5.95), and sausages with mustard sauce or steak and kidney pie (£6.50); there's more space to eat in the no-smoking Gallery upstairs. Well kept Bass, Courage Directors, Theakstons Best, and Uley Hogs Head on handpump. A back room – relatively untouched – is popular with local lads playing pool; darts, cribbage, and juke box. The garden has seats, and for children, a fortress of thatched whisky-kegs linked by timber catwalks, a climber, and some swings. *(Recommended by John and Barbara Burns, T L Rees, Tom McLean, Ewan McCall, Roger Huggins, Dave Irving, D H and M C Watkinson, Peter and Rosie Flower, P H Roberts, R Davies, Andy and Jill Kassube, Nick and Meriel Cox, Dr and Mrs A K Clarke, Mr and Mrs P Smith, V H and J M Vanstone)*

Free house ~ Manageress Stephanie Curwen-Reed ~ Real ale ~ Meals and snacks (till 10pm) ~ Restaurant ~ (01453) 860393 ~ Children welcome ~ Live music Sun evenings ~ Open 11-11; 12-10.30 Sun ~ Bedrooms: £45B/£60B

LITTLE BARRINGTON SP2012 Map 4
Inn For All Seasons 🛏 ♀

A40 3 miles W of Burford

If you want to explore the Cotswolds, then this handsome old inn is a good place to stay. The attractively decorated mellow lounge bar has a relaxed, friendly atmosphere, low beams, stripped stone, and flagstones, old prints, leather-upholstered wing armchairs and other comfortable seats, country magazines to read, and a big log fire (with a big piece of World War II shrapnel above it); maybe quiet piped classical music. The licensee has a fish business in Brixham, so their half-a-dozen fresh fish dishes are particularly good: light smoked fillet of Dart salmon with a chive and cucumber sauce (£9.75), fillet of grey mullet lightly grilled and served with fried fennel in a red wine sauce (£9.95), scallops and smoked bacon salad in a sweet and sour vinaigrette (£10.50), and whole bass stuffed with ginger and spring onion and cooked in a soy and fish sauce (£12.50). Other good generous bar food might include home-made soup (£3.25), ploughman's (£5.50), terrine of oak-smoked salmon and baby leeks with pickled shallots and a mustard dressing (£5.95), roasted vegetables on fresh noodles with a ginger and lemon flavoured olive oil dressing or chicken, ham and leek pie (£6.95), Scotch rump steak (£11.75), and puddings like mango and cointreau cheesecake on a mango coulis or caramelised oranges with clotted cream; good breakfasts. Well kept Bass, Glenny Wychwood Special, and Wadworths 6X on handpump, a good wine list, and over 60 malt whiskies; welcoming owners, friendly staff. Cribbage, dominoes and piped music. The pleasant garden has tables, and there are walks straight from the inn – if you're staying, you may be asked to take the owners' two well trained dogs along with you. It's very busy during Cheltenham Gold Cup Week – when the adjoining field is pressed into service as a helicopter pad. *(Recommended by Peter and Audrey Dowsett, Rob Whittle, Gordon, Jeremy Palmer, Simon Collett-Jones)*

Free house ~ Matthew Sharp ~ Real ale ~ Meals and snacks (11-2.30, 6-9.30) ~ Restaurant ~ (01451) 844324 ~ Children welcome ~ Open 11-2.30, 6-10.30; 12-2.30, 7-10.30 Sun; closed 25-26 Dec ~ Bedrooms: £42.50B/£78B

LITTLE WASHBOURNE SO9933 Map 4
Hobnails

B4077 (though often mapped still as the A438) Tewkesbury—Stow on the Wold; 7½ miles E of M5 junction 9

A particularly obliging landlord runs this friendly and characterful 15th-c pub – his family have been here since 1743. The snug and welcoming little front bar has low sway-backed beams hung with pewter tankards, lots of old prints and horsebrasses, and old wall benches by a couple of tables on its quarry-tiled floor; there's a more modern, carpeted back bar with comfortable button-back leatherette banquettes and newspaper cuttings about the pub and the family; open fire. Bar food includes their speciality baps (from £1.40; liver £3; steak in wine £4.95; you can build your bap with extras like fried banana, fried egg, and so forth), innovative soups like squash and apricot or asparagus and almond (£2.65), hazelnut, cashew nut and chestnut stuffed loaf, apricot lamb casserole or lasagne (£6.45), specials like roast rib of beef on a potato, leek and mustard cake with masala gravy (£5.75), a special fish pie (£6.55), and chicken, leek and gammon pie (£7.40), puddings such as home-made sherry trifle (£2.95), and their special cider cake with cheese (£2.55);

children's menu (from £1.95); fresh vegetables £2.55. One dining room is no smoking, as is half of a second. Well kept Boddingtons, Flowers Original, Hook Norton, and Wadworths 6X on handpump; shove-ha'penny, quiet piped music. A separate skittle alley (with tables) can be hired weekday evenings. Between the two buildings, and beside a small lawn and flowerbed, there's a terrace with tables, and children's playground. *(Recommended by Andrew and Ruth Triggs, Mr Miller, Hugh and Sarah McShane, Mrs Jeane Dundas, Ted George, John Barnwell, JCW, Lawrence Bacon, Jean Scott, Mrs J Oakes, Jack Barnwell, Bob Arnett, Judy Wayman)*

Whitbreads ~ Lease: Stephen Farbrother ~ Real ale ~ Meals and snacks (till 10) ~ Restaurant ~ (01242) 620237 ~ Children in eating area of bar and in restaurant ~ Open 11-2.30, 6-11; 12-2.30, 7-11 Sun; closed 25-26 Dec

LITTLETON UPON SEVERN ST5990 Map 2
White Hart ◀

3½ miles from M4 junction 21; B4461 towards Thornbury, then village signposted

A favourite locally, this carefully restored old farmhouse is slightly off the beaten track but is very popular in the evenings and at weekends. The three atmospheric main rooms have some fine furnishings that include long cushioned wooden settles, high-backed settles, oak and elm tables, a loveseat in the big low inglenook fireplace, flagstones in the front, huge tiles at the back, and smaller tiles on the left, some old pots and pans, and a lovely old White Hart Inn Simonds Ale sign. By the black wooden staircase are some nice little alcove seats, there's a black-panelled big fireplace in the front room, and hops on beams, fresh flowers, and candles in bottles. An excellent no-smoking family room, similarly furnished, has some sentimental engravings, plates on a delft shelf, and a couple of high chairs, and a back snug has pokerwork seats, table football and table skittles; darts, shove-ha'penny, cribbage, dominoes, trivia (not much used). Under the new managers, bar food includes soup (£2.25), filled baps (from £2.25), mushroom and cannellini stroganoff (£5.75), steak, kidney and ale pie (£6.25), lamb provençale (£6.75), thai green chicken curry (£6.95), daily specials, puddings (£2.70), children's meals (from £2.95), and Sunday lunch (£5.75). Well kept Smiles Best, Golden and Heritage, Greene King Abbot, John Smiths, and changing guest beers on handpump. Picnic tables sit on the neat front lawn, intersected by interesting cottagey flowerbeds, and by the good big back car park are some attractive shrubs and teak furniture on a small brick terrace. Several walks from the pub itself. *(Recommended by Ian and Villy White, Dr and Mrs A Whiteway, Andrew Shore, Tom McLean, Ewan McCall, Roger Huggins, Dave Irving, Simon and Amanda Southwell, S H Godsell, M G Hart, Steve and Carolyn Harvey)*

Smiles ~ Managers Anne and Steve Harbour ~ Real ale ~ Meals and snacks ~ (01454) 412275 ~ Children in family area ~ Open 11.30-2.30, 6-11; 12-3, 6-10.30 Sun ~ Bedrooms: £31.50B/£41.50B

LOWER ODDINGTON SP2325 Map 4
Fox ⑪ ♈

Nr Stow on the Wold

At lunchtime during the week, you can usually find a table at this well run, stylish dining pub; this is not so easy at weekends when you need to arrive pretty early. The simply and spotlessly furnished rooms have a relaxed but smart feel, fresh flowers, flagstones, and an open fire, and there's a lovely dining room; piped classical music. Served by courteous, knowledgeable staff, the good, interesting food might include a quad of Cotswold sausages with meaux mustard (£2), soup such as brie and broccoli (£2.50), french bread sandwiches (£2.95), spinach mousse with anchovy sauce (£3.95), chilli con carne (£5.95), spinach and mushroom lasagne with three cheese sauce (£6.50), smoked haddock fishcakes with parsley sauce (£6.95), warm chicken, bacon and avocado salad (£7.95), rack of English lamb with onion sauce (£8.95), rib eye steak (£9.95), puddings like apple and cinnamon pie, treacle tart or petit pot au chocolat (£2.95), and Sunday roast sirloin of beef with yorkshire pudding (£8.95). The wine list is excellent and shipped in conjunction with a highly regarded wine guru, they keep good Hook Norton Best, Marstons Pedigree and a guest such as Badger Tanglefoot, Shepherd Neame Bishops Finger or Smiles Best on handpump, and do a proper pimms. A good eight-mile walk starts from here (though a stroll around the pretty village might be less taxing after a fine meal). *(Recommended by Rob Whittle, Mike Gorton, Paul Barnett, Wilma and Ian Smith, J H Kane, Paula Williams, K J Jeavons, A Turner, Martin Jones, Liz Bell, John Bowdler, Dave Irving, Roger Huggins, Tom McLean, Ewan McCall, Peter Dubois, Sue Demont, Tim Barrow, Tom Evans, Mr and Mrs J R Morris, Tim and Pam Moorey, Mike and Maggie Betton, Pam Adsley, P H Boot, Mike and Heather Watson, C D and E A Frewer)*

Free house ~ Licensees Vicky Elliot and Luli Birch ~ Real ale ~ Meals and snacks (till 10pm) ~ (01451) 870555 ~ Children in restaurant ~ Open 12-3, 6.30-11; 12-3, 7-10.30 Sun; closed 25 Dec and evening 1 Jan

MEYSEY HAMPTON SU1199 Map 4
Masons Arms

High Street; just off A417 Cirencester—Lechlade

This 17th-c stonebuilt inn's extensive recent renovations have mellowed well now – good solid light wood furnishings on the parquet floor of the main room, a big inglenook log fire at one end, carefully stripped beams, a few steps up to the no-smoking dining room. It's kept a properly pubby atmosphere, with the bar counter a definite focus for the regulars: well kept Courage Directors, Marstons Pedigree, John Smiths, Wadworths 6X and a guest beer such as Adnams Broadside on handpump, decent wines including several ports. There are daily papers to read; dominoes, cribbage, maybe piped music. Bar food includes home-made soup (£2.35), good filled baguettes (£2.50, not Sun lunchtime), stilton and bacon mushrooms (£3.50), ham and egg (£4.75), vegetable chilli (£4.95), steak and kidney pie or lamb hotpot (£5.50), grilled salmon (£6.75), duck breast with a rich plum sauce (£8.50), steaks (from £8.50), and children's meals; commendable service. The well equipped but homely and cosy bedrooms probably deserve one of our stay awards (more reports please), and breakfasts are good. It's an attractive village with a charming green. *(Recommended by D G King, D Irving, E McCall, R Huggins, T McLean, TRS, George Atkinson, Miss R Booth, D H and M C Watkinson, David Campbell, Vicki McLean)*

Free house ~ Licensees Andrew and Jane O'Dell ~ Real ale ~ Meals and snacks (not Sun evening) ~ (01285) 850164 ~ Children welcome at lunchtime, in restaurant in evening till 9pm ~ Open 11.30-3, 6-11; 12-4, 7-10.30 Sun ~ Bedrooms: £32S/£48S

MINCHINHAMPTON SO8600 Map 4
Old Lodge

Minchinhampton Common; from centre of common take Box turn-off then fork right at pub's signpost

The common on which this former hunting lodge stands is a plateau raised well above the surrounding area by steep slopes on most sides, so you get quite a feel of separateness; there are tables on a neat lawn by an attractive herbaceous border that look over grey stone walls to the grazing cows and horses. Inside, the small and snug central bar has a relaxed, friendly atmosphere and substantial pine tables and chairs, and opens into a pleasant bare-brick-walled room and an airy stripped-stone dining area, both of which are no smoking; no noisy games or piped music. Very interesting bar food includes home-made soup (£2.25), pork strips cooked in soya sauce and ginger and topped with crispy seaweed and spring onions or scallops and prawns in a rich gorgonzolla cream sauce with tagliatelle and melted mozzarella (£3.75 starter, £5.75 main course), pithiviers of goat's cheese with warm sesame broccoli (£4.95), mezza of wild mushrooms on caramelised onions topped with a parmesan crouton fan (£6.75), breast of chicken stuffed with garlic mushrooms wrapped in filo pastry on a bed of tomato and red pepper salsa laced with cream (£8.25), roast fillet of monkfish with roasted garlic and rich red wine sauce (£9.95), 10oz porterhouse steak (£11.95), puddings like sticky toffee sponge with toffee sauce, a rich lemon and lime cheesecake topped with wild fruits or fresh pineapple, orange and drambuie trifle (from £2.75), and children's menu (£2.50). Well kept Marstons Pedigree and Thwaites Bitter with a guest like Fullers London Pride on handpump, a good range of wines including a wine of the month, country wines, and summer drinks like elderflower spritzer. Service is friendly and helpful. They share car parking with the adjoining golf club, so lots of cars outside doesn't necessarily mean the pub is full. *(Recommended by D Etheridge, D G King, M G Hart, Wendy, Liz and Ian Phillips, Roger Huggins, Tom McLean, Dave Irving, Ewan McCall, S Godsell, Tom Tees)*

Free house ~ Licensees David Barnett-Roberts and Eugene Halford ~ Real ale ~ Meals and snacks (till 10pm; not Mon) ~ (01453) 832047 ~ Children in eating area of bar ~ Open 11-3, 6.30(7 in winter)-11; 11-3, 7-10.30 Sun; closed Mon (except bank holidays)

NAILSWORTH ST8699 Map 4
Weighbridge
B4014 towards Tetbury

Happily, not much changes here. The friendly bar has three cosily old-fashioned rooms with antique settles and country chairs, stripped stone walls, and window seats; one even has a bell to ring for prompt service. The black beam-and-plank ceiling of the left-hand room is thickly festooned with black ironware – sheepshears, gin-traps, lamps, cauldrons and bellows – while up some steps a rafted loft has candles in bottles on an engaging mix of rustic tables, as well as unexpected decorations such as a butcher's block; no noisy games machines or piped music. Bar food (with prices unchanged since last year) includes filled rolls (from £1.60), ploughman's (from £3.40), meaty or vegetarian lasagne (£4.20), a two-in-one pie with cauliflower cheese in one half and steak and mushroom or chicken, ham and leek in the other (small £4.90, big £5.90; lovely pastry), and puddings like treacle tart or banoffi pie; helpful service. Well kept Marstons Pedigree, Smiles Best, Theakstons Best, and Wadworths 6X on handpump, and up to 10 wines by the glass. Behind is a sheltered garden with swings and picnic tables under cocktail parasols. Back in the days when the landlord used to run the bridge from which the pub takes its name, it would cost you 3d for each score of pigs you wanted to take along the turnpike. *(Recommended by Peter and Audrey Dowsett, Tony Dickinson, T L Rees, Gwen and Peter Andrews, Tom McLean, Roger Huggins, Don and Shirley Parrish)*

Free house ~ Licensee Richard Kulesza ~ Real ale ~ Meals and snacks ~ (01453) 832520 ~ Children welcome away from bar ~ Open 11-2.30, 7(6.30 Sat)-11; 12-3, 7-10.30 Sun

NAUNTON SP1123 Map 4
Black Horse ⏚ ♀
Village signposted from B4068 (shown as A436 on older maps) W of Stow on the Wold

The licensee here has come from the Farmers Arms at Guiting Power, nearby, and aims to offer the same friendly services. It is a bustling old inn, tucked away in an unspoilt little village, and the comfortable bar has black beams, stripped stonework, simple country-kitchen chairs, built-in oak pews, polished elm cast-iron-framed tables, and warming open fire. Good food now includes sandwiches, home-made soup (£2.50), lasagne (£5.75), steak and kidney pudding (£5.95), beef and mushroom in red wine (£6.30), gammon and egg, bass in a wine and mushroom sauce (£9.95), steaks, and a Sunday roast. Well kept and well priced Donnington BB and SBA on handpump, and sensibly placed darts, cribbage, shove-ha'penny, dominoes, and piped music. Some tables outside, popular with walkers. *(Recommended by Guy Consterdine, Graham and Karen Oddey, R Davies, Andy and Jill Kassube, Dr and Mrs J Hills, Margaret Dyke, Rob Whittle, Glen and Nola Armstrong, E V Walder, Mrs J Oakes, Dr I Maine, Peter Wade, Michael Monday, Simon Collett-Jones, MDN, John Waller)*

Donnington ~ Tenant Martin Macklin ~ Real ale ~ Meals and snacks ~ Restaurant ~ (01451) 850565 ~ Children in eating area of bar ~ Open 11.30-3, 6-11; 12-3, 7-10.30 Sun ~ One bedroom: /£50B

NEWLAND SO5509 Map 4
Ostrich ♀ ◀

B4231 Lydney—Monmouth, OS Sheet 162 map reference 555096

Bustling and full of atmosphere, this friendly partly 13th-c inn keeps a fine range of around eight real ales on handpump: Church End What the Fox's Hat and Coffin Stout, Freeminer Ostrich Ale, Hook Norton Best, Monmouth Rebellion, RCH Pitchfork, Shepherd Neame Spitfire, and Timothy Taylors Landlord; 30 malt whiskies, Westons Old Rose cider, fresh fruit juices, and 7 wines by the glass. The spacious but cosily traditional low-ceilinged bar has creaky floors, uneven walls, magazines to read, candles on the tables, and comfortable furnishings such as cushioned window seats, wall settles and rod-backed country-kitchen chairs, and a fine big fireplace decorated with a very capacious copper kettle and brass-bound bellows; quiet classical music. Listed on the blackboard are about 30 light lunch dishes served with salad and a home-baked roll (all £5), about 15 starter and light dishes (between £1.50 and £5), and over 30 main dishes (between £8 and £14); good vegetables, and they bake all their own bread. Tables out in the small garden, walkers are welcome if they leave their muddy boots at the door, and dogs are permitted on a lead. No children. *(Recommended by Phil and Heidi Cook, Paul Barnett, James Nunns, R V G Brown, Alan and Barbara Mence, Christine Timmon, Mrs P Goodwyn, Mr and Mrs C J S Pink, Terry and Vann Prime, Neil and Anita Christopher, Helen Pickering, James Owen)*

Free house ~ Licensees Richard and Veronica Dewe ~ Real ale ~ Meals and snacks ~ (01594) 833260 ~ Open 12-2.30(3 Sat), 6.30-11; 12-3, 6.30-11 Sun ~ Two bedrooms: £25/£40

NORTH CERNEY SP0208 Map 2
Bathurst Arms ♀

A435 Cirencester—Cheltenham

There's a relaxed, friendly atmosphere in this handsome old inn and the beamed and panelled bar has a fireplace at each end (one quite huge and housing an open woodburner), a good mix of old tables and nicely faded chairs, old-fashioned window seats, and some pewter plates. There are country tables in a little carpeted room off the bar, as well as winged high-backed settles forming booths around other tables; all is highly polished and obviously cared for. A good choice of bar food might include sandwiches (from £2.20), home-made pâté (£3.25), warm goat's cheese salad (£3.75), various pasta dishes (£5.50), home-made pies (£5.75), home-made salmon fishcakes (£6.75), steaks with good sauces, duck with a sweet and sour sauce (£9.25), monkfish in bacon and cream (£10.95), and ostrich with hunter sauce. Well kept Arkells BBB, Hook Norton Best, Wadworths 6X and three guest beers on handpump, good wines by the glass, and freshly squeezed fruit juice. The Stables Bar has darts, pool, cribbage, dominoes, and piped music. The attractive flower-filled front lawn runs down to the little River Churn, and there are picnic tables sheltered by small trees and shrubs; plenty of surrounding walks. *(Recommended by Oliver Hill, Lynn Sharpless, Bob Eardley, Mrs Jean Dundas, Tom McLean; more reports please)*

Free house ~ Licensee Mike Costley-White ~ Real ale ~ Meals and snacks ~ Restaurant ~ (01285) 831281 ~ Children in eating area of bar and in restaurant ~ Occasional live entertainment ~ Open 11-3, 6-11; 12-2, 7-10.30 Sun; closed 25 Dec ~ Bedrooms: £35B/£45B

Prices of main dishes usually include vegetables or a side salad.

NORTH NIBLEY ST7596 Map 4

New Inn 🍺 🍴

Waterley Bottom, which is quite well signposted from surrounding lanes; inn signposted from the Bottom itself; one route is from A4135 S of Dursley, via lane with red sign saying Steep Hill, 1 in 5 (just SE of Stinchcombe Golf Course turn-off), turning right when you get to the bottom; another is to follow Waterley Bottom signpost from previous main entry, keeping eyes skinned for small low signpost to inn; OS Sheet 162 map reference 758963; though this is the way we know best, one reader suggests the road is wider if you approach directly from North Nibley

During the summer months, they serve afternoon teas on the neatly kept terrace of this country inn, surrounded by attractive pastures and woods – and it's certainly a fine place to relax after a walk. At the far end of the garden is a small orchard with swings, slides and a timber tree-house. Inside, the carpeted lounge bar has cushioned windsor chairs and varnished high-backed settles against the partly stripped stone walls, and sensibly placed darts, dominoes, shove-ha'penny, cribbage, table skittles, and trivia in the simple public bar. Particularly well kept Cotleigh Tawny and WB (a beer brewed specially for the pub), Greene King Abbot, Smiles Best, and Theakstons Old Peculier; changing guests are either dispensed from Barmaid's Delight (the name of one of the antique beer engines) or tapped from the cask; the character landlady is quite a real ale expert; lots of malt whiskies, and Inch's cider. Bar food includes filled brown baps or toasties, curry or steak and onion pie (£4.15), lasagne (£4.40), and puddings like peach and banana crumble (£1.95); piped music. No children. *(Recommended by Malcolm Taylor, T L Rees, Stephen Brown, B A Hayward, D Godden, Richard Raeon, Karen Barnes, Vicky and David Sarti, Tom McLean, Roger Huggins, Dave Irving, Ewan McCall; more reports please)*

Free house ~ Licensee Ruby Sainty ~ Real ale ~ Meals and snacks ~ (01453) 543659 ~ Open 12-2.30, 7-11; 12-5(3 in winter), 6(7 in winter)-11 Sat; 12-5(3 in winter), 6(7 in winter)-10.30 Sun; closed evening 25 Dec ~ Two bedrooms: £20/£35

OAKRIDGE LYNCH SO9102 Map 4

Butchers Arms

Village signposted off Eastcombe—Bisley road, E of Stroud, which is the easiest approach; with a good map you could brave the steep lanes via Frampton Mansell, which is signposted off A419 Stroud—Cirencester

Although this neatly kept pub is popular for its enjoyable food, this is still very much a drinkers' pub, too. The spacious rambling bar has a few beams in its low ceiling, some walls stripped back to the bare stone, old photographs, three open fires, and comfortable, traditional furnishings like wheelback chairs around the neat tables on its patterned carpet. Bar food includes rolls, ploughman's, tasty hot french sticks filled with things like melted brie and salami (£3.75), garlic prawns (£4.75), haddock in celery sauce (£5.95), nice curries, rib-eye steak (£7.95), and daily specials (£4.95-£6.95); popular Sunday lunch (£7.95; 3 courses £11.95). Best to book at the weekend; the restaurant is no smoking. Well kept Archers Best, Goffs Jouster, Hook Norton Old Hookey, Tetleys Bitter, and Theakstons Best on handpump; a little room off the main bar has darts, fruit machine, and trivia, and there's a skittle alley. Picnic sets on a stretch of lawn look down over the valley, and you can really appreciate the village's rather odd remote setting; pretty hanging baskets in summer. There are good walks in the valley along the old Thames & Severn canal. Usefully, the pub's car park is up on the level top road, so you don't have to plunge into the tortuous network of village lanes. *(Recommended by P R and S A White, Neil and Anita Christopher, Nick and Meriel Cox, Dr M I Crichton, Peter and Audrey Dowsett, Dave Irving, Ewan McCall, Tom MacLean, Roger Huggins, Dr S Willavoys, Don and Shirley Parrish, Lawrence Pearse)*

Free house ~ Licensee Peter Coupe ~ Real ale ~ Meals and snacks (not Sun evening) ~ Restaurant (Weds-Sat evenings, Sun lunch) ~ (01285) 760371 ~ Children in small ante-room and in restaurant ~ Open 11-3, 6-11; 12-3.30, 7-10.30 Sun; closed 25 Dec

ODDINGTON SP2225 Map 4
Horse & Groom

Upper Oddington; signposted from A436 E of Stow on the Wold

For the third year running there has been a change of licensee here – the new people look more entrenched. They have made some changes in that a couple of bedrooms have been refurbished, the woodburning stove has been removed and an ingelnook fireplace has been opened up, and the fish tank now includes tropical fish. The bar has pale polished flagstones, a handsome antique oak box settle among other more modern seats, some horsebrasses on the dark 16th-c oak beams in the ochre ceiling, and stripped stone walls with some harness and a few brass platters. Bar food, changing with the season, might include sandwiches and filled baked potatoes, home-made soup (£2.50), home-made chicken liver pâté (£2.95), strips of oak smoked chicken in a mild curry and coriander mayonnaise (£4.25), broccoli and leek galette or liver and bacon (£5.95), quite a few fish dishes like fresh local trout glazed with honey and almonds (£6.95), lemon sole fillets on an asparagus cream sauce (£8.95) or baked turbot on a green peppercorn sauce (£9.95), guinea fowl served with a red wine jus (£8.50), steaks (from £8.75), and children's menu (£3); the candlelit dining room is pretty. Well kept Hook Norton Best and guests like Mansfield Bitter, Shepherd Neame Spitfire, Wadworths 6X and Wychwood Best on handpump, Bulmers cider, and a decent wine list. There's a little water-garden beyond a rose hedge, picnic tables on the neat lawn below the car park, apple trees, aunt sally, and a fine play area including an enormous log climber and pet rabbits and other animals. *(Recommended by Dr and Mrs J Hills, R Vincent, Ted George, Dr A Y Drummond, J H Kane, Liz Bell; more reports on the new regime, please)*

Free house ~ Licensees David and Jill South ~ Real ale ~ Meals and snacks (not 25 Dec) ~ Restaurant ~ (01451) 830584 ~ Children in eating area of bar and in restaurant ~ Open 11.30-2.30, 6-11; 12-2.30, 7-10.30 Sun; may open all afternoon on Sat or Sun in summer; closed evening 25 Dec ~ Bedrooms: £37.50S/£55S

OLD SODBURY ST7581 Map 2
Dog

Not far from M4 junction 18: A46 N, then A432 left towards Chipping Sodbury

This is a very popular place with most people coming to enjoy the wide choice of good value food. With prices unchanged since last year, there might be fresh fish dishes like plaice, red mullet, halibut, shark or tuna, whole fresh sole, Devon scallops or clam fries, several different ways of serving mussels (from £3.25), and squid (£4.95), as well as sandwiches (from £1.75), ploughman's (£3.95), cottage pie (£4.75), home-made steak and kidney pie or cheese and onion flan (£4.95), Mexican tamales with chilli sauce (£5.95), sweet and sour pork (£6.25), curries or Hawaiian chicken creole (£6.50), steaks (from £6.95), puddings (from £1.95), children's menu (from £1.50), and daily specials. The two-level bar and smaller no-smoking room both have areas of original bare stone walls, beams and timbering, low ceilings, wall benches and cushioned chairs, open fires, and a bustling atmosphere. Well kept Flowers Original, Marstons Pedigree, Wadworths 6X, and Wickwar BOB on handpump; good service. Darts, table skittles, dominoes, fruit machine, juke box, and skittle alley. Trophy, the border collie, likes playing football with customers. There's a large garden with lots of seating, a summer barbecue area, pets' corner with rabbits, guinea pigs and so forth, climbing frames, swings, slides, football net, see-saws and so forth, and bouncy castle most bank holidays. Lots of good walks nearby. *(Recommended by Neville Kenyon, Tom Evans, Hugh Roberts, Keith Waters, Miss Helen Osborne, M G Hart, Charles and Pauline Stride, Mr and Mrs R Maggs, Lyn and Geoff Hallchurch, M W Turner, V H and J M Vanstone, the Sandy family)*

Whitbreads ~ Lease: John and Joan Harris ~ Real ale ~ Meals and snacks noon-10pm) ~ (01454)·312006 ~ Children in eating area of bar, in skittle alley, and small area on the upper level (till 9pm) ~ Open 11-11; 12-3, 7-10.30 Sun ~ Bedrooms: £23.50/£37.50

OLDBURY ON SEVERN ST6292 Map 2

Anchor ◀

Village signposted from B4061

Although you can't see the River Severn from this comfortably furnished village pub, there is a nice walk down to it; there are also lots of paths over the meadows to the sea dyke which overlooks the tidal flats. Inside, the lounge has a mix of modern beams and stone, a mix of tables including an attractive oval oak gateleg one, cushioned window seats, winged seats against the wall, pictures in gilt frames, and a big winter log fire; no piped music or games machines. Diners can eat in the lounge or bar area or in the no-smoking dining room at the back of the building (good for larger groups) and the menu is the same in all rooms. Good and home-made, the food changes daily and uses fresh, local produce: leek and potato bake (£4.80), Painswick pork (£5.95), seafood pancake (£6.25), good steak, and puddings such as rhubarb and ginger tart, pecan and walnut flan, and lemon syllabub (from £2.60); no chips but they do offer dauphinois or don quizote (sliced and cooked with cheese and onion), new potatoes or baked ones. Well kept Bass, Black Sheep, Butcombe Best Bitter, Theakstons Best and Old Peculier, and Worthingtons Best on handpump or tapped from the cask, all well priced for the area. Also over 75 malts, a decent choice of good quality wines, and Inch's cider; darts, shove-ha'penny, dominoes and cribbage; they have wheelchair access and a disabled lavatory. There are seats in the pretty garden (where there is the largest boules pitch in the South West). St Arilda's church nearby is interesting, on its odd little knoll with wild flowers among the gravestones (the primroses and daffodils in spring are lovely). *(Recommended by Gwen and Peter Andrews, Andrew Shore, Ian Wagg, James and Ruth Morrell, Tom McLean, Roger Huggins, Ewan McCall, Dave Irving, Dr and Mrs A Whiteway, M G Hart, John and Joan Wyatt, S H Godsell, Helen Pickering, James Owen, V H and J M Vanstone, Peter Cornall, Dr and Mrs B Smith, Simon and Amanda Southwell)*

Free house ~ Licensees Michael Dowdeswell, Alex de la Torre ~ Real ale ~ Meals and snacks ~ Restaurant ~ (01454) 413331 ~ Children in restaurant only ~ Open 11.30-2.30(3 Sat), 6.30(6 Sat)-11; 12-4, 7-10.30 Sun; closed 25 Dec and evening 26 Dec

REDBROOK SO5410 Map 4

Boat ◀

Pub's car park is now signed in village on A466 Chepstow—Monmouth; from here 100-yard footbridge crosses Wye (pub actually in Penallt in Wales – but much easier to find this way); OS Sheet 162 map reference 534097

You can sit on the sturdy new home-built seats by the interestingly shaped tables in the garden here and listen to the waters of the River Wye spilling down the waterfall cliffs into the duck pond below – it's a popular spot with walkers. Inside, the unpretentious bar has been redecorated, though they still have lots of pictures of the pub during floods, landscapes, a wall settle, a grey-painted piano, and a woodburning stove on the tiled floor; the lavatories have been redecorated, too. They keep a fine choice of between 8 and 10 well kept beers, tapped straight from casks behind the bar counter that might include Adnams Broadside, Badger Best, Boddingtons Bitter, Butcombe Bitter, Freeminer Speculation, Fullers London Pride, Greene King Abbott, Hook Norton Best, Theakstons Old Peculier, and Wadworths 6X; a range of country wines, too. Decent bar food includes filled baked potatoes (from £1.65), soup (£1.75), ploughman's (£3.80), chicken and pistachio slice (£3.95), vegetable curry (£4.10), aubergine parmesan (£4.35), Moroccan honeyed lamb (£4.55), spicy beef (£4.95), and puddings (from £1.90). Darts, shove-ha'penny, table skittles, cribbage, and dominoes. They do get busy on sunny days. *(Recommended by JKW, Mark Percy, Lesley Mayoh, P Fowler, G and T Edwards, Daren Haines, Wayne Brindle, Ted George, Nick and Meriel Cox, Liz Bell, Pete and Rosie Flower, Piotr Chodzko-Zajko, Michel Hooper-Immins, Christopher Gallop, Joan and Alex Timpson)*

Free house ~ Licensees Steffan and Dawn Rowlands ~ Real ale ~ Meals and snacks ~ (01600) 712615 ~ Children welcome ~ Folk Tues evening, blues Thurs, occasional jazz Fri evenings ~ Open 11.30-3, 6-11; 11-11 Sat; 12-4, 6.30-10.30 Sun; all day during school summer holidays

SAPPERTON SO9403 Map 4
Daneway

Village signposted from A419 Stroud—Cirencester; from village centre follow Edgeworth, Bisley signpost; OS Sheet 163 map reference 939034

Now taken over by Wadworths, with the previous cheerful managers as tenants, this is a bustling and friendly old pub. The welcoming bar has a remarkably grand and dominating fireplace, elaborately carved oak from floor to ceiling, racing and hunting prints on the walls, and Polly the talking parrot. Bar food at lunchtime includes winter soup (£1.90), baps filled with things like Aberdeen Angus steak or good bacon and mushrooms (from £2.40), ploughman's (from £3.90), home-made chilli or lasagne (£4.75), and beef and Guinness pie (£5.50), with evening gammon and egg (£6.75) and steaks (from £7.50); afternoon teas in summer. Well kept Wadworths IPA, 6X, and seasonal beers, and Adnams Best on handpump, and local farm cider; darts, dominoes, shove-ha'penny, and ring-the-bull in the public bar, which has a big inglenook fireplace; quoits. The lovely sloping lawn is bright with flowerbeds and a rose trellis, and lots of seats look down over the canal and the valley of the little River Frome. There are good walks along the canal banks in either direction, and it's particularly worth the short stroll to the entrance of the Sapperton Tunnel, which was used at the end of the 18th-c by the 'leggers', men who lay on top of the canal boats and pushed them through the two-and-a-half-mile tunnel with their feet. They hold a vintage motor cycle club meeting twice a year. *(Recommended by Dave Irving, Roger Huggins, Tom McLean, Ewan McColl, Dr A Drummond, Barry and Anne, Kay Neville-Rolfe, Peter and Audrey Dowsett, Malcolm Taylor)*.

Wadworths ~ Tenants Richard and Liz Goodfellow ~ Real ale ~ Meals and snacks ~ (01285) 760297 ~ Children in small no-smoking family room off lounge ~ Open 11-2.30, 6.30-11; 11-5, 6.30-11 Sat; 12-5, 7-10.30 Sun; closed evening 25 Dec

SHEEPSCOMBE SO8910 Map 4
Butchers Arms ♀

Village signposted from B4070 NE of Stroud, and A46 N of Painswick (narrow lanes)

It really is well worth negotiating the narrow lanes to get to this smashing country pub – indeed, many people travel for miles to do just that. But even when they are really busy, the licensees and their staff remain attentive and friendly. There's a good smart chatty atmosphere (no noisy games machines or piped music), and the busy bar has seats in big bay windows, flowery-cushioned chairs and rustic benches, and log fires, and is decorated with lots of interesting oddments like assorted blow lamps, irons, and plates. Good lunchtime bar food includes soup (£2.25), filled rolls (from £2.75; hot crispy bacon £3.50), filled baked potatoes (from £3.50), lentil and mushroom cannelloni (£4.95), home-cooked honey roast ham with chips (£5.75), home-made steak and kidney pie (£5.95), and mixed grill (£8.50), with evening dishes like smoked tarragon chicken breast with tarragon mayonnaise (£3.95), tuna steak with watercress sauce (£6.50), breast of duck with raspberry sauce (£9.25), and steaks (from £9.25), and daily specials such as courgette and cheese bake topped with toasted breadcrumbs and nuts, spicy lamb in a sweet chilli sauce, fruit caribbean chicken curry or salmon and prawn en croûte with lobster sauce. The restaurant and a small area in the bar are no smoking. Well kept Archers Best Bitter, Hook Norton Best, Uley Old Spot, and guest beers on handpump, decent wines, traditional ciders, and country wines; darts, cribbage, dominoes. The views are marvellous and there are teak seats below the building, tables on the steep grass behind, and a cricket ground behind on such a steep slope that the boundary fielders at one end can scarcely see the bowler. *(Recommended by Pat and Roger Fereday, George Atkinson, Dr and Mrs J H Hills, James Nunns, Kay Neville-Rolfe, Dave Irving, Roger Huggins, Tom McLean, Ewan McColl, Stephen Pine, Alfred Lawrence, Daren*

Haines, Steve Goodchild, R and S Bentley, Graham Tayar, LM, Peter and Lynn Brueton, Howard Allen, S G N Bennett)

Free house ~ Licensees Johnny and Hilary Johnston ~ Real ale ~ Meals and snacks (till 10pm) ~ Restaurant ~ (01452) 812113 ~ Children welcome ~ Open 11-11; 11-2.30, 6.30-11 in winter; 12-10.30 Sun

SIDDINGTON SU0399 Map 4
Greyhound

Ashton Rd; village signposted from A419 roundabout at Tesco

A new passageway has been knocked between the bar and lounge in this bustling, friendly pub, the high-backed settles have now gone, and a skittle alley/function room is to be added. The biggish lounge bar has two big log fires, high dining chairs, chapel seats and so forth on the old herringbone brick floor, and good tables – mainly stripped pine, but one fine circular mahogany one. The beams and ochre walls are covered with lots of copper and brass, as well as a few hunting prints, some black-lacquered farm tools, and china and other bric-a-brac. Good, home-made bar food includes sandwiches or filled baked potatoes (from £2.95), chicken liver pâté (£3.15), ploughman's (from £4.25), chilli con carne or macaroni cheese (£4.95), steak and kidney pie (£6.15), gammon with honey and mustard (£6.95), lamb steak with garlic butter (£8.95), steaks (from £8.95), and salmon fillet with lemon butter (£9.25). Well kept Wadworths IPA and 6X, and Badger Tanglefoot on handpump, and decent wines; the public bar has darts. There are seats among lilacs, apple trees, flower borders and short stone walls behind the car park. *(Recommended by Dave Irving, Roger Huggins, Ewan McCall, Tom McLean, F J and A Parmenter, Peter and Audrey Dowsett, Pat Crabb, MRSM, Mark Matthewman, Esther and John Sprinkle)*

Wadworths ~ Managers Mike and Louise Grattan ~ Real ale ~ Meals and snacks (till 10pm) ~ (01285) 653573 ~ Children in eating area of bar ~ Open 11.30-3, 6.30-11; 12-3, 7-10.30 Sun

SOUTH CERNEY SU0497 Map 4
Eliot Arms

Village signposted off A419 SE of Cirencester; Clarks Hay

When the locals crowd in, this handsome 16th-c stone inn has a friendly, bustling atmosphere. On the right is the small solid pale wooden counter, and on the left is the main bar with sturdy plush-cushioned captain's chairs, built-in corner seats, plush round stools, and lots of shiny copper pots and jugs and some enamel water pots hanging from high beams – tastefully arranged. Lots of separate snug places to sit are linked by short passages lined with decorative plates, and the back room is packed with carpentry tools, stirrups, and horse bits hanging from the ceiling, hundreds of dug-up ancient bottles on the mantelpiece over the log fire (with little snug pews tucked in beside it), a housekeeper's chair, and some interesting racing-car pictures from Fangio and Moss to Mansell. Bar food includes sandwiches (from £2.25; french bread from £3.25), filled baked potatoes (from £2.95), home-made chicken liver pâté (£3.75), ploughman's (from £4.25), home-made lasagne (£5.50), lamb and apricot pie (£6.25), home-made salmon fishcakes (£6.95), steaks (from £8.95), and duck with an orange and cointreau sauce (£9.95). As well as the cosily attractive little dining room down a step or two, there's a smart separate no-smoking restaurant, and a coffee shop. Well kept Boddingtons, Flowers Original, and Wadworths 6X on handpump, 120 malt whiskies, a variety of foreign bottled beers, and helpful service; shove-ha'penny, cribbage, dominoes, a tucked-away fruit machine, and piped music; skittle alley. There are picnic tables and a swing in the neat back garden. *(Recommended by Malcolm Thomas, Roger Huggins, Tom McLean, Dave Irving, Ewan McCall, David Peakall, S P Bobeldijk, Mrs B Sugarman, Dr M I Crichton, Mr and Mrs P Smith, Esther and John Sprinkle, M L and G Clarke)*

Free house ~ Licensees Duncan and Linda Hickling ~ Real ale ~ Meals and snacks (till 10pm) ~ Restaurants ~ (01285) 860215 ~ Children welcome till 9pm ~ Open 10.30-11; 12-10.30 Sun ~ Bedrooms: £38B/£49B

ST BRIAVELS SO5605 Map 4
George 🛏

The oldest part of this friendly and attractive little white painted pub with its stripey window awnings, dates from medieval times and overlooks the 12th-c castle once used by King John as a hunting lodge (it is now a youth hostel). Inside, the three rambling rooms have old-fashioned built-in wall seats, some booth seating, green-cushioned small settles, toby jugs and antique bottles on black beams over the servery, and a large stone open fireplace; a Celtic coffin lid dating from 1070, discovered when a fireplace was removed, is now mounted next to the bar counter. Enjoyable home-made bar food includes lunchtime hot crusty baps or filled baked potatoes (£3.95), as well as soup (£2.50), chicken pâté (£3.95), moussaka (£5.95), steak and kidney pie, chilli or home-made crunchy nut loaf (£6.95), fresh tuna steak (£7.95), duck breast in madeira sauce (£8.95), steaks (from £7.95), and Sunday roast lunch (£6.95); friendly service. The dining room is no smoking. Well kept Boddingtons, Courage Directors, Marstons Pedigree, Shepherd Neame Spitfire, and Wadworths 6X on handpump, and lots of malt whiskies. There are tables on a flagstoned terrace at the back overlooking the grassy former castle moat with more among roses and shrubs, and an outdoor chess board. Lots of walks start nearby. If staying, you may not be able to get in until they open. *(Recommended by Paul Barnett, LM, Wayne Brindle, Peter and Gwyneth Eastwood, JKW, Brian and Liz Whitford, Mr and Mrs C J S Pink, Michael and Alison Leyland, M L Hughes, Geoffrey Lindley)*

Free house ~ Licensee Bruce Bennett ~ Real ale ~ Meals and snacks ~ Restaurant ~ (01594) 530228 ~ Children welcome ~ Open 11-3, 6.30-11; 12-3, 7-10.30 Sun ~ Bedrooms: /£40B

STANTON SO0634 Map 4
Mount

Village signposted off B4632 (the old A46) SW of Broadway; Old Snowshill Road – take no-through road up hill and bear left

Seats on the pretty terrace in front of this pub, set up a steep quiet lane, look back down over the lovely golden stone village – and on a good day you can see across to the Welsh mountains; boules on the lawn. Inside, the original simple but friendly bar has black beams, cask seats on big flagstones, heavy-horse harness and racing photographs, and a big fireplace. A spacious extension, with some big picture windows, has comfortable oak wall seats and cigarette cards of Derby and Grand National winners, and another extension (no smoking) is used in winter as a restaurant and in summer as a more informal eating bar. Donnington BB and SBA on handpump kept under light blanket pressure and served through sparklers, and farm cider; darts, shove-ha'penny, dominoes, cribbage, bar billiards, and piped music. Straightforward bar food includes sandwiches (£2.75), ploughman's (£4.25), and half a chicken, medallions of venison or steak (£7.50); at busy times a PA announces when your meal is ready. *(Recommended by Rob Whittle, Graham and Karen Oddey, Kay Neville-Rolfe, Martin Jones, Peter and Audrey Dowsett, Ted George, Andrew and Ruth Triggs, Liz Bell, Sally Shaw, Mrs Jean Dundas, MDN, Alan and Paula McCully)*

Donnington ~ Tenant Colin Johns ~ Real ale ~ Meals and snacks (not Sun evening) ~ (01386) 584316 ~ Well behaved children welcome until 9pm ~ Open 11-3, 6-11; 11-11 Sat; 12-10.30 Sun; closed 25 Dec

nr STOW ON THE WOLD SP1729 Map 4
Coach & Horses

Ganborough; A424 2½ miles N of Stow; OS Sheet 163 map reference 172292

New licensees have taken over this pleasant little Cotswold pub and have replaced the upholstery and cushioned some wooden seats, and the tables now have fresh flowers and evening candles; there are still the flagstones, coach horns on the ceiling joists, winter log fire in the central chimney-piece, and steps leading up to a carpeted part with high-backed settles. Bar food now includes stilton and whisky mushrooms (£3.50), moules marinières (£3.95), salmon, prawn and asparagus pancake (£4.95), vegetarian dishes, cajun chicken (£6.50), steak and kidney pie, monkfish wrapped in bacon on a cream and garlic sauce or Cornish crab in a dijon mustard sauce (£7.95), tuna steak (£8.50), and beef wellington (£11.95); home-made chips. Donnington BB and SBA on handpump, kept under light blanket pressure; this is the nearest pub to the brewery. Eight wines by the glass; darts, fruit machine and popular skittle alley. The garden has a waterfall and rockery, as well as seats on a terrace and a narrow lawn. *(Recommended by E V Walder, Peter and Anne Hollindale, Dr and Mrs A K Clarke, Peter Lloyd, JJW, CMW, Andrew and Ruth Triggs, Derek and Margaret Underwood)*

Donnington ~ Tenant Ben Sands ~ Real ale ~ Meals and snacks (all day summer Fri/Sat) ~ (01451) 830208 ~ Children welcome ~ Open 11.30-2.30, 6-11; 11-11 summer Sat; 12-10.30 Sun

TETBURY ST8394 Map 4
Gumstool 🍴 🛏 🍷

Part of Calcot Manor Hotel; A4135 W of town, just E of junction with A46
Gloucestershire Dining Pub of the Year

This civilised newish dining bar fills so quickly with happy people obviously looking forward to a spanking good meal that it would be wise to book a table if you can't be sure of arriving early. The changing menu has plenty of sensibly priced starters that for a little extra would do as a snack lunch – soups such as cream of broccoli (£2.75; generous £4), local English cheeses with celery, grapes and crusty bread (£3.95; generous £5.95), roasted red peppers with mediterranean vegetables, rocket and mozzarella (£4.75; generous £6.75), and slow roasted duck salad with pickled ginger and carrot and sweet and sour dressing (£6.50; generous £8.50); also, Gloucestershire Old Spot beer sausages with mash and onion gravy (£6.50), salmon with roast leeks and crispy bacon (£7.95), lovely liver and bacon, and beef casserole with herb dumplings (£8.50). You can splash out on double-figure daily specials such as beef fillet with peppercorn sauce (£11) or bass with chargrilled mediterranean vegetables (£12). Save space for excellent puddings such as banana and toffee crumble with coconut ice cream (from £3.50). A very wide choice of interesting wines by the glass spans a wide price range, Bass, Uley Old Spot and Wadworths 6X on handpump are kept well, and service is good. Materials are old-fashioned (lots of stripped pine, flagstones, gingham curtains, hop bines) but the style is neatly modern; the layout is well divided to give a feeling of intimacy without losing the overall sense of contented bustle, and the lighting is attractive. There are concessions to people just wanting a drink – a couple of marble-topped pub tables beyond one screen, leather armchair by the big log fire, daily papers – but this is really one of our more restauranty entries; dominoes, piped music. The neat side lawn has a couple of picnic tables; Westonbirt Arboretum is not far. *(Recommended by Peter Neate, D G King, Pat and John Millward, Trevor Marshall, John and Annette Derbyshire)*

Free house ~ Licensees Paul Sadler, Richard Ball ~ Real ale ~ Meals and snacks ~ Restaurant ~ (01666) 890391 ~ Children welcome ~ Occasional live jazz ~ Open 11.30-2.30, 6-11; 11.30-11 summer Sat and Sun ~ Bedrooms: £95B/£97-£150B

WITHINGTON SP0315 Map 4
Mill Inn

Village signposted from A436, and from A40; from village centre follow sign towards Roman villa (but don't be tempted astray by villa signs before you reach the village!)

This old stone inn stands virtually alone in a little valley surrounded by beech and chestnut trees and a rookery. It has a pretty garden with the River Coln running through it, which is bridged, and there are seats and tables on the small island and on the main lawn. Inside, the beamed and flagstoned bar and other wooden floored rooms have little nooks and corners with antique high-backed settles and large stone fireplaces; one room is no smoking. Good bar food includes cheese, a roll and pickle or ham, a roll and mustard (£2.95), ploughman's (£3.95), very good local goat's cheese wrapped in filo pastry with a tomato coulis (£3.95), pasta with mixed seafood in a creamy dill and cucumber sauce or nut roast with tomato provençale (£5.95), chicken in honey and mustard with chinese noodles (£6.50), gigot of lamb with cranberry and sage (£6.75), duck breast with apple and blackberry gloop (£8.95), and puddings like gooseberry crunch or apricot crumble (£2.65). Well kept Sam Smiths OB on handpump, a decent wine list, and quite a few malt whiskies; piped jazz and classical music. *(Recommended by Daren Haines, Mr and Mrs Scott, Tom McLean, Roger Huggins, E McCall, Dave Irving, John and Joan Wyatt, Mrs J Huntly; more reports please)*

Sam Smiths ~ Managers Peter Nielson and Robin Collyns ~ Real ale ~ Meals and snacks ~ (01242) 890204 ~ Children in two side rooms ~ Open 12-2.30, 7-11; 12-3, 7-10.30 Sun ~ Bedrooms: £25B/£49.50B

Lucky Dip

Besides the fully inspected pubs, you might like to try these Lucky Dips recommended to us and described by readers (if you do, please send us reports):

☆ **Alderton** [off B4077 Tewkesbury—Stow, Beckford Rd; SO9933], *Gardeners Arms*: Civilised old-fashioned thatched Tudor pub with well kept Hook Norton Best, Theakstons Best and XB and Wadworths 6X, reasonably priced lunchtime sandwiches, soup or ham and eggs, log fire, good antique prints, high-backed settles among more usual seats; interesting restaurant food (evenings not Sun, and weekend lunchtimes; worth booking), extension keeping bar sensibly separate; swift friendly service, tables on sheltered terrace, well kept garden; children welcome *(BHP, LYM)*

☆ **Aldsworth** [A433 Burford—Cirencester; SP1510], *Sherborne Arms*: Much-extended relaxing modernised dining pub with beams, bric-a-brac and spacious and attractive no-smoking conservatory dining area, wide choice of good fresh food esp fish, Whitbreads-related ales, log fire, service welcoming and attentive without being fussy, lovely garden; fills quickly weekends, lavatory for disabled *(Marjorie and David Lamb, Cherry Ann Knott)*

Ampney Crucis [SP0602], *Butchers Arms*: This popular and picturesque village pub closed in spring 1997; any hope of its reopening? *(News please)*

☆ **Ampney St Peter** [A417, 1/2 mile E of village; SP0801], *Red Lion*: Unspoilt traditional 17th-c country local, clean and polished, with old-fashioned benches facing open fire, informal counterless serving area (well kept Flowers IPA), welcoming landlord and chatty regulars, hatch to corridor; separate room with wall benches around single table, darts, cards and dominoes; cl weekday lunchtimes *(D Irving, R Huggins, E McCall, T McLean, TRS, Jack and Philip Paxton, Pete Baker, BB)*

☆ **Apperley** [village signed off B4213 S of Tewkesbury, go down lane beside PO opp Sawpit Lane; SO8628], *Coal House*: Airy bar notable for its splendid riverside position,

with Bass, Wadworths 6X and a guest ale, red plush seats; front terrace with Severn views, play area *(E McCall, R Huggins, T McLean, D Irving, BB)*

Arlingham [SO7111], *Old Passage*: Spacious and well furnished, reasonably priced bar food, good range of Marstons ales, small restaurant; games machines, service can be slow, live music Fri; big garden with play area, extending down to River Severn *(Dr A Drummond)*

☆ **Ashleworth** [signed off A417 at Hartpury; SO8125], *Queens Arms*: Comfortable and friendly, with good choice of bar food inc some unusual dishes, lovely fresh veg; well kept Donnington, attractive restaurant alongside; skittle alley *(David and Margaret Bloomfield)*

Avening [High St; ST8897], *Bell*: Thriving lively local with well kept Marstons, Wickwar BOB and guests such as Timothy Taylors Landlord, Aug bank hol beer festival, welcoming fire, simple well priced food inc vegetarian, cheery knowledgeable landlord, quiz night; sleepy valley village nestling below Gatcombe Park *(Dave Irving, R Huggins, T McLean, E McCall, Andy and Jill Kassube)*

Berkeley [Salter St; bottom of main rd through village; ST6899], *Mariners Arms*: Friendly beamed 15th-c pub with small range of good home-made food from sandwiches up, well kept Bass, tables outside *(Bob Tivey, Pete)*

Bibury [B4425; SP1106], *Swan*: Hotel in lovely spot on River Coln, very comfortable relaxing bar, nice brasserie (though not cheap), good service, tables out by pergola with masses of flowers; limited parking; comfortable bedrooms *(George Atkinson)*

Birdlip [A417/A436 roundabout; SO9316], *Air Balloon*: Useful Whitbreads Wayside Inn dining pub, sound value for family groups, with good service, nothing fancy *(A E Brace, E A George)*; [OS Sheet 163 map ref 926143],

Royal George: Pleasant and spacious, with variously furnished little room areas; Bass and Boddingtons, guest beer tapped from the cask, wide range of reasonably priced lunchtime bar food from sandwiches up, good service, restaurant; bedrooms *(D G King, John and Phyllis Maloney, Neil and Anita Christopher, Dr and Mrs A K Clarke)*

Bishops Cleeve [Cheltenham Rd; SO9527], *Crown & Harp*: Relaxed and friendly, good value food, wide choice of Whitbreads-related ales with a guest such as Bunces Old Smoky, big garden and play area, good location; quiz night Thurs *(Joshua Corbion, David Walker)*

☆ **Bisley** [SO9006], *Stirrup Cup*: Spacious well furnished local under new landlord, enjoyable modestly priced food from sandwiches up, well kept Flowers Original, Uley Hogs Back and Wadworths 6X, friendly bustle, no music *(Dorothy and Leslie Pilson, A Y Drummond)*

☆ **Blockley** [Station Rd; SP1634], *Great Western Arms*: Peaceful, comfortable and spacious modern-style lounge, wide choice of reasonably priced home-cooked food, well kept Flowers, Hook Norton and Marstons Pedigree, welcoming service, no piped music, busy public bar with games room; attractive village, lovely valley view *(H and B Bauer, F and E Lindemann, G W A Pearce)*

Bourton on the Water [Bridge End Walk; SP1620], *Old Manse*: Lovely setting with front garden overlooking River Windrush, wide range of beers inc well kept Morlands Old Speckled Hen, generous helpings of well cooked food, courteous service, staff helpful and efficient; bedrooms *(Mr and Mrs A G Bennett, Tony Scott, Derek and Margaret Underwood)*

☆ **Bourton on the Water** [SP1620], *Old New Inn*: Unchanging old hotel next to 1:9 scale model of village built here in 1930s by present landlord's father, comfortably worn and welcoming, with big painted panels and collection of beer bottles in interesting back bar, particularly well kept Bass and a weekly guest beer, good changing home-made food inc children's dishes, lovely dining room overlooking ford through River Windrush, unobtrusive piped classical music; bedrooms good *(Rob Whittle, Meg and Colin Hamilton)*

Bourton on the Water [Riverside], *Parrot & Alligator*: Attractive Cotswold stone ex-guest house in nice spot overlooking river, good friendly atmosphere in L-shaped bar, wide choice of unusual well cooked food inc good salads and puddings in dining area (children welcome), superb choice of well kept ales, wide choice of wines, obliging staff; big no-smoking area, plenty of space outside *(John and Joan Wyatt, Clare Jones, Jonathon Smith, Richard Lewis)*

Brimscombe [off A419 SE of Stroud; SO8602], *Ship*: Named for former shipping canal here (its trans-shipment port, England's biggest in 1700s, now an industrial estate); well laid out to combine roominess with feeling of snugness, varied good value food, well kept Bass and Boddingtons *(D Irving, R Huggins, T McLean, E McCall)*

Broadwell [off A429 2 miles N of Stow on the Wold; SP2027], *Fox*: Pleasant local opp attractive village's broad green, with well kept Donnington BB, SB and SBA, Addlestone's cider, cheerful service, stripped stone walls, flagstones, darts, dominoes and chess, pool room extension, piped music; big back garden with wooden tables and Aunt Sally, field behind for Caravan Club members; bedrooms *(Peter and Anne Hollindale)*

☆ **Brockhampton** [signed off A436 Andoversford—Naunton – OS Sheet 163 map ref 035223; SP0322], *Craven Arms*: Generous helpings of sensibly priced good food (wide choice) in cosy series of interlinked rooms inc restaurant, well kept Bass, Hook Norton Best and Wadworths 6X, low beams, sturdy stripped stone, pine furniture with some wall settles, tub chairs and a log fire, darts, shove-ha'penny, busy local atmosphere; children welcome, swings in sizeable garden, attractive gentrified hillside village with lovely views; out of the main entries this year as they didn't let us have up-to-date price and timing details etc *(FWG, Malcolm Taylor, Stephen Pine, Alfred Lawrence, Nick and Meriel Cox, Glen and Nola Armstrong, Tony Dickinson, David and Natalie Towle, John and Joan Wyatt, Julie Peters, Colin Blinkhorn, Mrs Burdett, Dr and Mrs J Hills, Daren Haines, E V Walder, LYM)*

Bussage [SO8804], *Ram*: Well kept Cotswold stone village pub sensitively extended by fairly new landlord, good valley view esp from terrace, good friendly atmosphere, generous helpings of good value wholesome food, several well kept ales, decent wines *(Derek Smith)*

Cambridge [3 miles from M5 junction 13 – A38 towards Bristol; SO7403], *George*: Busy and attractive, with two spacious dining extensions, good value bar food, well kept Hook Norton Best and Marstons Pedigree, welcoming service; restaurant, garden with barbecues and play area *(M Hasslacher)*

nr **Camp** [B4070 Birdlip—Stroud, junction with Calf Way; SO9111], *Fostons Ash*: Open-plan refurbished Cotswold pub with comfortable well spaced tables, woodburners each end, good value home-made food, well kept Greene King Abbot, Tetleys and local Stanway, friendly service; piped music can be obtrusive; children and walkers welcome, garden with play area *(John and Joan Wyatt, Kay Neville-Rolfe)*

☆ **Cerney Wick** [SU0796], *Crown*: Roomy modernised lounge bar, neat and clean, opening into comfortable semi-conservatory extension, public bar with pool, darts, fruit machine and log fire, popular straightforward food inc good Sun roasts, well kept Whitbreads-related ales, helpful service; children welcome, good-sized garden with swings, small motel-style bedroom extension *(G W A Pearce, BB)*

Charlton Kings [Cirencester Rd (A435); SO9620], *Clock Tower*: Useful Milestone

Tavern, with their standard menu done well, Banks's ales, decent wines (given a taste before buying), good service *(E A George)*; [A435], *Little Owl*: Much extended and smartened up, with good bar lunches (some things – even sandwiches – may not be available if restaurant busy), Whitbreads-related ales, decent wines, friendly licensees *(John and Joan Wyatt)*; [London Rd (A40)], *London*: Wide range of lunchtime food inc good salads and filled baked potatoes in plush lounge-restaurant, big public bar, real ales such as Fullers London Pride and Morlands Old Speckled Hen; bedrooms *(John and Joan Wyatt)*

Chedworth [SP0511], *Hare & Hounds*: Wide choice of good food from the basics to more interesting dishes, good value *(Lyn and Geoff Hallchurch)*

Cheltenham [Bath Rd; SO9422], *Bath*: Basic unspoilt 1920s two-bar layout and simple furnishings, friendly landlady, locals' smoke room, well kept Bass and Uley *(Jack and Philip Paxton, PB)*; [184 London Rd – A40 towards Charlton Kings, nr junction A435], *Beaufort Arms*: Friendly family-run local, well kept Wadworths and changing guest ales, good home-made food, evening bistro, pool room, obliging friendly service, tables out by road *(John and Joan Wyatt, M Mason, D Thompson)*; [1-3 Montpellier Villas], *Beehive*: Enjoyable rather raffish bare-boards atmosphere, coal fire, wide range of beers and spirits, good house wines, wide choice of good food inc imaginative baguette fillings and Sun lunch *(Mr and Mrs P Goldman)*; [Grosvenor/High St], *Restoration*: Very convenient for the two main shopping arcades, long open-plan pub, genuinely old though much restored, with lots of beams and dim-lit bric-a-brac, simple wooden furniture, good bustling atmosphere, well kept Marstons and other ales, good coffee, raised dining area with separate food servery, friendly staff *(George Atkinson, Meg and Colin Hamilton)*

Cheltenham [4 Cambray Pl; SO9422], *Tailors*: More wine bar/brasserie than pub, but useful for limited choice of good value interesting food, and does have well kept Wadworths 6X and guest ales; lots of dark wood and steps, split-level main bar and two rooms off (Garden Room is furthest from piped music, which can be loud), some tables outside; can get crowded and smoky lunchtime – best to go early or late *(John and Joan Wyatt)*

☆ Chipping Campden [High St; SP1539], *Lygon Arms*: Welcoming stripped-stone bar with lots of horse pictures, open fires, well kept Donnington SBA, Hook Norton Best, Wadworths 6X and interesting guest beers, helpful service, interesting range of plentiful food from well filled rolls and good ploughman's up, back dining area, raftered evening restaurant beyond shady courtyard with tables; children welcome, open all day exc winter weekdays; good bedrooms *(Andrew and Ruth Triggs, Nick Lawless, Terry and Vann W Prime, E V Walder, Jason Caulkin, Keith and Janet Morris, LYM)*

☆ Chipping Campden [Lower High St], *Volunteer*: Cosy little early 18th-c pub with two bars, friendly family staff, good range of food and of well kept beers such as Fullers London Pride and Wadworths 6X, log fire, traditional games, military memorabilia, books, lots of bric-a-brac; tiny attractive courtyard with beautiful garden running down to river *(Terry and Vann W Prime, Richard Lewis, Pam Adsley, Lawrence Pearse, R Davies, Nick Lawless)*

Chipping Campden [Sheep St], *Red Lion*: Upstairs dining room, attractive left-hand bar, separate locals' back bar, bedrooms; has been good value, with well kept Bass and accommodating service, but appears to be under new ownership 1996/7 *(News please)*

☆ Cirencester [Black Jack St; SP0201], *Golden Cross*: Backstreet 1920s local with longish comfortable bar, sensible tables, simple cheap generous food, three Arkells ales, good friendly service, good beer mug collection; piped music may obtrude; skittle alley, tables in back garden, nr wonderful church *(D Irving, R Huggins, T McLean, E McCall, Mr and Mrs C Roberts, FWG, Keith and Janet Morris)*

☆ Cirencester [W Market Pl], *Slug & Lettuce*: Civilised atmosphere, flagstones, bare boards, lots of woodwork, wooden benches and chairs, good big bars, no-smoking area, big log fires; well kept Scottish Courage ales and Marstons Pedigree, good coffee, wide choice of bar food inc good vegetarian, friendly helpful staff, children welcome; tables in inner courtyard; piped pop music, very popular with young people evenings *(Simon Collett-Jones, Rona Murdoch, Alan and Charlotte Sykes, LYM)*

☆ Cirencester [Lewis Lane], *Twelve Bells*: Lively backstreet pub with friendly simple but comfortable back rooms, coal fires, pictures for sale, clay pipe collection, particularly well kept Archers Best, Uley and two or three very quickly changing guests, good bar food; small garden with fountain *(D Irving, E McCall, R Huggins, T McLean, Nick Dowson)*

Cirencester [Castle St], *Black Horse*: Quietly welcoming refurbished pub with decent lunchtime food, Scottish Courage ales; bedrooms *(D Irving, E McCall, R Huggins, T McLean)*; [Dollar St/Gloucester St], *Corinium Court*: Smart but relaxed and cosy, with friendly landlord, well kept Hook Norton Old Hookey and Wadworths 6X, decent wine, reasonably priced food, big log fire, attractive restaurant, no piped music; entrance through charming courtyard with tables; bedrooms *(Peter and Audrey Dowsett)*; [10-14 Chester St], *Oddfellows Arms*: Cosy backstreet local with several well kept strong ales, changing reasonably priced food, friendly service, live music twice weekly *(D Irving, E McCall, R Huggins, T McLean)*

Clearwell [SO5708], *Butchers Arms*: Cosy

inside with subdued red upholstery, dark woodwork, big log fire; obliging staff, good choice of food from cheap filled rolls up, well kept beer; piped pop music may obtrude *(Mrs L M Jordan)*

Cliffords Mesne [out of Newent, past Falconry Centre – OS Sheet 162 map ref 699228; SO6922], *Yew Tree*: Good value straightforward food (not Mon) in very red-plush beamed country pub on slopes of May Hill (NT); well kept Scottish Courage ales and Wadworths 6X, friendly service; restaurant, children welcome, pool table in separate area, tables out on sunny terrace *(P G Topp, F J and A Parmenter)*

☆ **Coates** [follow Tarleton signs from village (right then left), pub up rough track on right after rly bridge, OS Sheet 163 map ref 965005; SO9600], *Tunnel House*: Idyllically placed idiosyncratic beamed country pub by interesting abandoned canal tunnel, very relaxed management style, mix of well worn armchairs, sofa, rustic benches, enamel advertising signs, stuffed mustelids, race tickets, real ales such as Archers Best, Morlands Old Speckled Hen, Wadworths 6X and Youngs, basic bar food, Sunday barbecues, log fires (not always lit), pub games, big juke box much appreciated by Royal Agricultural College students; children welcome (good safe play area), camping facilities *(Rick and Torti Friedberger, Dr and Mrs A K Clarke, Esther and John Sprinkle, Giles Francis, LYM)*

☆ **Codrington** [handy for M4 junction 18, via B4465; ST7579], *Codrington Arms*: Refurbished village pub with several comfortable rooms, wide choice of inexpensive food, quick friendly service, impressive housekeeping, good range of beers inc Eldridge Pope, good house wines, roaring log fire, big gardens with good views; piped music may be rather loud *(D G Clarke, Peter and Audrey Dowsett)*

☆ **Colesbourne** [A435; SO9913], *Colesbourne Inn*: Comfortable and friendly old-fashioned inn with panelling, flagstones and timber, imaginative generous home-made food, well kept Badger Tanglefoot and Wadworths 6X and seasonal brews, country wines, huge log fires, hunting prints, settles and oak tables, masses of mugs on beams; comfortable bedrooms *(Neil and Anita Christopher, Malcolm Taylor, D Irving, R Huggins, T McLean, E McCall, John and Joan Wyatt)*

Compton Abdale [A40 outside village; SP0616], *Cotswold Explorer*: Relaxing refurbished pub with ancient origins, cosy decor, two log fires, wide choice of good fresh home-cooked food inc delicious puddings, well kept ales and winter mulled wine; comfortable bedrooms *(A Halliday, Clare Turner, Judith Wilson, Steve Jones)*

☆ **Cowley** [Cockleford; off A435 S of Cheltenham at Elkstone signpost – OS Sheet 163 map ref 970142; SO9614], *Green Dragon*: Attractive old-fashioned country pub in nice spot, beams, flagstones, bare boards,

huge fireplace; has been a popular main entry, but reopened by new owner after refurbishment (intended to bring out the best points of its age) in late summer 1997, too late for reassessment – should be good *(LYM; news please)*

Cromhall [ST6990], *Royal Oak*: Lots of little rooms with covered well in centre bar, good value varied food in separate dining rooms, tables outside *(Meg and Colin Hamilton, Neville Kenyon)*

☆ **Didmarton** [A433 Tetbury rd; ST8187], *Kings Arms*: Three soberly decorated bars with a few nick-nacks, Bass, John Smiths and local beers, open fire, imaginative choice of good value food, candlelit restaurant with white linen and relaxed atmosphere; children and dogs welcome, tables out behind *(D G Clarke, Peter Robinson)*

☆ **Duntisbourne Abbots** [A417 5 miles N of Cirencester; SO9709], *Five Mile House*: Reopened spring 1997 after extensive renovations, keeping traditional feel of bay-windowed flagstoned bar, with snug formed from two huge and ancient high-backed settles, woodburner in carefully exposed old fireplace, new cellar bar, and back part converted to dining area – all very promising; well kept Bass, Marstons and Timothy Taylors Landlord *(Giles Francis, T McLean, E McCall, R Huggins, D Irving)*

☆ **Dursley** [May Lane/Hill Rd, by bus stn; ST7598], *Old Spot*: Simple, friendly pub with relaxing atmosphere, well kept Bass, Worthington, Uley Old Spot and Old Ric and two guest beers, lots of malt whiskies, friendly landlord, doorstep sandwiches and home-made pasties, pig paraphernalia; bar billiards, cribbage, dominoes and boules, no music or machines *(Matt Nicholson, Giles Francis)*

☆ **Eastleach Turville** [off A361 S of Burford; SP1905], *Victoria*: Charming unpretentious back lounge/dining extension, pool in big locals' bar, welcoming staff, well kept Arkells, nice views, good value home cooking; quiet midweek lunchtime, busy evenings; pleasant front garden overlooking picturesque buildings opposite, delightful village esp at daffodil time *(David Campbell, Vicki McLean, Gordon, D Irving, T McLean, E McCall, R Huggins, Peter and Audrey Dowsett, Dick Brown, Mr and Mrs J Brown)*

☆ nr **Elkstone** [Beechpike; A417 6 miles N of Cirencester – OS Sheet 163 map ref 966108; SO9610], *Highwayman*: Well kept Arkells ales, good house wines, big back eating area (wide choice inc vegetarian), good friendly staff, and considerable character in rambling 16th-c warren of low beams, stripped stone, alcoves, antique settles among more modern furnishings, log fires, rustic decorations; quiet piped music; disabled access, outside play area, good indoors provision for children *(G Coates, John and Joan Wyatt, LYM)*

Epney [off A38 S of Gloucester; SO7611], *Anchor*: Popular pub with good value basic bar food, decent beer, big lounge bar, lots of sporting prints and photographs, good-sized public bar; Severn-side lawns, skittle alley *(Neil and Anita Christopher)*

Fairford [Market Pl; SP1501], *Bull*: Friendly beamed hotel, no-smoking areas at mealtimes, very wide choice of reasonably priced good food, service efficient even when busy, Arkells 3B and Kingsdown; piped music; charming village, church has remarkable stained glass; bedrooms small but fresh, all different, with a bright decor *(Peter and Audrey Dowsett, Caroline Raphael)*

☆ **Frampton Mansell** [off A491 Cirencester—Stroud – OS Sheet 163 map ref 923027; SO9202], *Crown*: Welcoming stripped stone lounge bar with dark beam-and-plank ceiling, flagstones, well kept ales such as Archers Village, Oakhill Farmers, Wadworths 6X, public bar with darts, good food in bar and attractive restaurant; lovely views over village and steep wooded valley; children in eating area, teak seats outside *(D Irving, R Huggins, Tom McLean, E McCall, Don and Shirley Parrish, David Surridge, BB)*

☆ **Gloucester** [Llanthony Rd; off Merchants Rd, S end of Docks], *Waterfront*: Atmospheric bare-boards black-beamed waterside bar with wide range of ales tapped from the cask inc some special offers, scrubbed tables, tin helmets, barrels you can chalk on, free peanuts (shells go on the floor), beermat collection, other interesting bric-a-brac; bar billiards, table football, ninepins etc; generous cheap food, eating area up a step with back-to-back cubicle seating; piped music (live some nights), fruit machine, SkyTV *(T McLean, R Huggins, D Irving, E McCall, Tony Scott, M Joyner)*

Gloucester [Westgate St/Berkeley St], *Fountain*: Pleasant, comfortable and quiet 17th-c inn handy for cathedral, well kept Whitbreads-related ales, good value straightforward food *(D G King)*; [Worcester St], *Kingsholm*: Well kept beers, good filled rolls, friendly atmosphere, landlord a real rugby buff *(D G King)*; [73 Bristol Rd; A38 about 1½ miles S of centre, out past docks], *Linden Tree*: Lively and attractive local with beams and stripped stone, particularly well kept ales – three Wadworths, three interesting guests, on unusual gravity dispense through wall from cellar; varied straightforward lunchtime food, back skittle alley; bedrooms *(Joan and Michel Hooper-Immins)*; [Westgate St], *New Inn*: Chef & Brewer in lovely medieval building with courtyard, rather over-restored (wood shavings on bar floor to go with all the beams and woodwork), but still has atmosphere in its four separate areas, good value food, warm welcome and several well kept ales; piped pop music may be rather loud; bedrooms *(Steve Willey, George Atkinson)*

☆ **Guiting Power** [signed off B4068 SW of Stow on the Wold; SP0924], *Olde*: Beamed pub smartened up by new licensees with racing connections, well priced and presented food inc good local trout in main bar with log fire, flagstoned public bar with darts, cribbage and

dominoes, Bass, Boddingtons and Hook Norton Best, some tables out by back car park, good walks; restaurant *(Jo Rees, Glen and Nola Armstrong, Lawrence Pearse, LYM)*

Hanham [Hanham Mills; ST6472], *Chequers*: Smartly refurbished pub in lovely spot overlooking River Avon, nicely presented reasonably priced food inc good specials, spacious bar and separate dining area; overnight moorings *(Charles and Pauline Stride)*

Hartpury [Ledbury Rd (A417); SO7924], *Canning Arms*: Charmingly idiosyncratic, with lots of red bows and nick-nacks, horsebrasses on beams, country prints; log fire, Tetleys-related ales, pleasant licensees, decent genuine bar food in eating area; live jazz some nights *(D Irving, R Huggins, T McLean, E McCall)*

Hawkesbury Upton [ST7786], *Duke of Beaufort*: Friendly landlord, good choice of bar food, well kept local Wickwar ales, also John Smiths and Smiles, extended uncluttered lounge, darts in quite cosy stripped-brick bar *(J Lloyd Jones)*

Hinton Dyrham [nr M4 junction 18; A46 towards Bath, then 1st right; ST7376], *Bull*: Pretty 16th-c village pub, two unspoilt bars each with log fires, beams and stripped stone, good food (not Sun night), well kept Bass and Wadworths IPA, 6X and Old Timer, well equipped family room, oak and elm settles in public bar, big garden with picnic tables and play area; cl Mon *(T H Adams, Ian and Nita Cooper)*

☆ **Horsley** [B4058 just S of Stroud; ST8397], *Bell & Castle*: Friendly village pub flourishing under new landlady, whose earlier success at the Catherine Wheel in Bibury won it a place in the main entries; wide choice of reasonably priced food with some good vegetarian dishes, friendly service, pub games *(MD)*

Huntley [A40 Gloucester—Ross; SO7219], *Red Lion*: Comfortable lounge with open fire, good service, nice atmosphere, good range of food, Bass and Flowers beers, separate bar *(Daren Haines)*

Kempsford [SU1597], *George*: Pleasant interior, well kept Arkells BBB, friendly landlord; two bars, limited food *(Peter and Audrey Dowsett)*

Lechlade [The Square (A361); SU2199], *New Inn*: Good range of well kept ales and vast choice of food inc alligator, bison and kangaroo, big busy bar with huge log fire; friendly staff, back restaurant; piped music can be obtrusive; play area in big garden extending to Thames; bedrooms *(Peter and Audrey Dowsett); Red Lion*: Traditional village local with wide range of good value food inc good Sun lunches, friendly service, well kept Arkells, restaurant with log fire; gents' due for updating *(Michael and Hazel Duncombe)*

☆ nr **Lechlade** [St John's Bridge; A417 a mile E], *Trout*: Low-beamed three-room pub dating from 15th c, with some flagstones, stuffed fish and fishing prints, big Thameside garden with boules, Aunt Sally and a simple summer family bar; Courage Best and Directors and John Smiths, popular well presented food from ploughman's through pizzas to steaks, friendly staff, no-smoking dining room; children in eating areas, jazz Tues and Sun, fishing rights; very busy in summer – open all day Sat then, and not cheap *(David Carr, FWG, I Maw, LYM)*

☆ **Longhope** [Ross Rd (A40); SO6919], *Farmers Boy*: A relaxing respite from the trunk road – heavy beams, middle of the road music, warm fire, candles in attractive two-room country restaurant with curry specialities, good specials, OAP bargains Thurs; well kept ales such as Boddingtons, Marlow Rebellion, Smiles Best, Theakstons and Thwaites, separate public bar with big screen TV and electric organ; pleasant garden and terrace *(Dennis Shirley, F J and A Parmenter, S Godsell, Mike and Mary Carter, Neil and Anita Christopher, BB)*

Longhope [A4136 Gloucester—Monmouth; SO6818], *Yew Tree*: Locally popular for usual food from sandwiches up inc good roast of the day, good-sized helpings, friendly staff, Whitbreads-related ales, big log fire, beams and stripped stone, piped music; no dogs, play area outside *(Jenny and Michael Back, Dennis Shirley)*

Lower Lydbrook [SO5916], *Courtfield Arms*: Decent food inc good rabbit pie and vegetarian dishes, well kept Ruddles and other beers, lively happy hour *(R V G Brown)*

☆ **Lower Swell** [B4068 W of Stow on the Wold; SP1725], *Golden Ball*: Simple unspoilt local with log fire, Donnington BB and SBA from the pretty brewery just 20 mins' walk away, good range of ciders and perry, games area with fruit machine and juke box behind big chimneystack, bar food inc home-made dishes, small evening restaurant (no food Sun evening), small garden with occasional barbecues, Aunt Sally and quoits; no dogs or children, decent simple bedrooms; pretty village, good walks *(G and T Edwards, John and Joan Wyatt, Colin Fisher, LYM)*

☆ **Lower Wick** [off A38 Bristol—Gloucester just N of Newport; ST7196], *Pickwick*: Popular food in carpeted bar with woodburner and lots of wheelback chairs around shiny dark tables, brocaded small settles and more of the wheelbacks in second room, some stripped stone, well kept Smiles Best and Golden, traditional games inc antique table skittles, no music; picnic tables and play fort by back paddock – Mway noise out here; children welcome, cl 2.30 sharp weekdays *(D G Clarke, Charles and Pauline Stride)*

Maisemore [just NW of Gloucester; SO8121], *White Hart*: Cosy pub hung with chamber-pots, friendly staff, good value imaginative food *(Jo Rees)*

☆ **Marshfield** [signed off A420 Bristol—Chippenham; ST7773], *Catherine Wheel*: Interesting and attractive old pub with plates and prints on stripped stone walls, medley of settles, chairs and stripped tables, open fire in

impressive fireplace, cottagey back family bar, charming no-smoking Georgian dining room, flower-decked back yard; cheerful service, good food inc Thurs fresh fish, (not Sun), well kept Ruddles County and Wadworths IPA and 6X, farm cider, decent wines; golden labrador called Elmer, darts, dominoes; provision for children *(M G Hart, Rowan and Melanie Hardy, Mr and Mrs R Maggs, Peter Neate, LYM)*

☆ **Mickleton** [B4632 (ex A46); SP1543], *Kings Arms*: Comfortable, clean, relaxed and civilised, popular food inc notable ploughman's and Sun roasts, nice puddings, vegetarian dishes; considerate service, Whitbreads-related ales, farm cider, small log fire; some tables outside, handy for Kiftsgate and Hidcote *(Anita and Neil Christopher, P J Keen, Pat and Robert Watt, BB)*

☆ **Miserden** [OS Sheet 163 map ref 936089; SO9308], *Carpenters Arms*: Cheerful friendly local in pretty village, two open-plan bar areas, nice old wooden tables on bare boards, exposed stone, two big open fires, well kept ales such as Brakspears, Boddingtons and Greene King Abbot, good value food inc greedy puddings, small dining room with dark wood traditional furniture; tables in garden, idyllic quiet Cotswold village *(Margaret Dyke, Alec Hamilton, Giles Francis, John and Joan Wyatt, Peter and Audrey Dowsett, Neil and Anita Christopher, D G King)*

☆ **Mitcheldean** [SO6718], *Lamb*: Attractively presented fresh food, pleasant speedy service, two unspoilt bars, refurbished restaurant, well kept beer; bedrooms good – well placed for Forest of Dean *(Paul and Heather Bettesworth, Alan Meecham)*

☆ **Moreton in Marsh** [High St; SP2032], *White Hart Royal*: Busy and comfortable old-world inn, partly 15th-c, with interesting Civil War history, oak beams, stripped stone, big inglenook fire in lounge area just off main bar, particularly well kept Bass and Worthington BB, good value straightforward food changing daily in bar and simple but pleasant restaurant, inc good seafood and Sun lunch, efficient welcoming staff; a real welcome for children, can get crowded esp on Tues market day; good value bedrooms *(E V Walder, Andrew and Ruth Triggs, Pam Adsley)*

Moreton in Marsh [High St], *Bell*: Pleasant homely pub with Scottish Courage and other ales, good value food all day inc afternoon tea, efficient service; bar covered with banknotes and beermats, no-smoking family area, tables (some under cover) in attractive courtyard; bedrooms *(Dr and Mrs A K Clarke, SLC)*; [Market Pl], *Black Bear*: Two-bar pub with good value home-made food, local Donnington SBA, BB and XX, efficient service, back garden *(Mr and Mrs Carr, SLC, Joan and Michel Hooper-Immins, Don and Shirley Parrish)*; [High St], *Redesdale Arms*: Fine old coaching inn with prettily lit alcoves and big stone fireplace in solidly furnished comfortable panelled bar on right, well kept

Bass, Boddingtons and a guest beer, quickly served generous food inc vegetarian, restaurant, darts and fruit machine in flagstoned public bar, back conservatory; piped music, TV; tables in big back garden, comfortable well equipped bedrooms *(SLC, Pam Adsley)*

☆ **Nailsworth** [coming from Stroud on A46, left and left again at roundabout; ST8599], *Egypt Mill*: Attractively converted three-floor mill with working waterwheel in one room, static machinery in second area, lots of stripped beams, Ind Coope Burton and Wadworths 6X, wide choice of good generous bar food inc fresh fish, quick service, good value meals in civilised upstairs restaurant; can get crowded weekends; children welcome, no dogs; lovely gardens, neat comfortable bedrooms, good breakfast *(Andy and Jill Kassube)*

☆ **North Nibley** [B4060; ST7496], *Black Horse*: Straightforward village local with good atmosphere, wide range of generous good value fresh home-made food (service may slow when busy) well kept Whitbreads-related ales and an interesting guest beer, good log fire, maybe piped music; popular restaurant Tues-Sat evenings, Sun lunchtime, tables in pretty garden; good value cottagey bedrooms, good breakfasts *(Margaret Dyke, DAV, LYM)*

Northleach [Cheltenham Rd; SP1114], *Wheatsheaf*: Clean and smartly comfortable, almost more hotel than pub, with pleasantly upmarket atmosphere, quiet piped classical music, very polite friendly staff; good if not cheap lunchtime bar food, real ales inc Marstons Pedigree; restaurant, lovely terraced garden; well equipped modern bedrooms *(John and Wendy Trentham)*

Norton [Wainlode Hill; back rd N of village; SO8523], *Red Lion*: Cosy isolated fishermen's pub on River Severn, stuffed fish, good range of reasonably priced bar food, well kept local beers and ciders, log fires, friendly very long-serving licensees; children's room, plenty of seats outside, views to Malvern Hills, good walks, camp site *(M W and I E Bayley)*

☆ **Nympsfield** [signed off B4066 Stroud—Dursley; SO8000], *Rose & Crown*: Stone-built village inn, open all day, with well kept ales such as Bass, Boddingtons, Severn Boar, Smiles Best, Theakstons Old Peculier, Uley Old Spot, Wadworths 6X and Wickwar BOB, decent wines, food piled high, pink plush banquettes and lots of brass in pubby beamed bar with log fire and fruit machine, dark pews around tables in back saloon opening into dining room, picnic tables in side yard and on sheltered lawn with good play area; comfortable well equipped bedrooms, big breakfasts – handy for Cotswold walks *(M Joyner, T Dobby, Gill Cathles, Tom Evans, G L Jones, DAV, T L Rees, Ken Hull, Vanessa Mudge, Dorothy and Leslie Pilson, BB)*

Old Sodbury [junction of A46 with A432; 1½ miles from M4 junction 18; ST7581], *Cross Hands*: Popular and comfortably done-up

spacious pub/hotel, extremely obliging staff, subdued piped music, good reasonably priced bar menu (good coffee), log-effect gas fire, Bass, Wadworths 6X and Worthington BB; restaurant, comfortable bedrooms *(Peter and Audrey Dowsett, LYM)*

Olveston [ST6088], *White Hart*: Clean and carefully modernised old village pub with flagstones, stripped stone walls and exposed beams; particularly well kept Ushers Founders, bar food *(Dr and Mrs A K Clarke, BB)*

☆ **Painswick** [St Mary's St; SO8609], *Royal Oak*: Buoyant atmosphere in bustling old town local with interesting layout and furnishings inc some attractive old or antique seats, good value honest food (bar nibbles only, Sun) from sandwiches to changing hot dishes inc Thurs fresh fish, well kept Whitbreads-related ales, friendly family service, small sun lounge by suntrap pretty courtyard; children in eating area; can get crowded, nearby parking may be difficult *(R Michael Richards, LM, M J How, LYM)*

Painswick [New St], *Falcon*: Reopened after upmarket refurbishment, smart bistro-style atmosphere, high ceilings, chandeliers, oak panelling, high bookshelves on either side of one fire, variety of wooden tables inc one inlaid, good reasonably priced beers, separate dining area; bedrooms *(D Irving, E McCall, R Huggins, T McLean)*

☆ **Parkend** [Whitecroft, just off B4234 N of Lydney; SO6208], *Woodman*: Relaxing, spacious and comfortable without being plush, two open fires, heavy beams, stripped stone, forest and forestry decorations, mix of furnishings inc some modern seats, well presented food (not Sun or Mon evenings) inc children's meals and Sun lunch, well kept Bass and Boddingtons, decent wines, evening bistro (Thurs-Sat); picnic tables on front terrace, facing green, good walks into Forest of Dean; maybe darts, fruit machine, juke box; bedrooms *(Piotr Chodzko-Zajko, S P Watkin, P A Taylor, Dennis Shirley, LYM)*

Pennsylvania [4 miles from M4 junction 18 – A46 towards Bath; ST7373], *Swan*: Friendly and unspoilt local, well kept ales such as Archers and Bunces, good food, interesting fireplace depicting battle *(Roberto Villa, Luke Worthington, Giles Francis)*

☆ **Prestbury** [Mill St; SO9624], *Plough*: Good generous food in well preserved thatched village local's cosy and pleasant oak-panelled front lounge, friendly and comfortable; lots of regulars in basic but roomy flagstoned back taproom with grandfather clock and big log fire, good value homely food, well kept Whitbreads-related ales tapped from casks, pleasant back garden *(Lew Badger)*

Prestbury, *Royal Oak*: Welcoming and comfortable village local with well kept Fflowers Original, varied wholesome simple food *(D G King)*

☆ **Quenington** [SP1404], *Keepers Arms*: Cosy and comfortable stripped-stone pub, very friendly, with traditional settles, lots of mugs hanging from low beams, good coal fire, decent food in both bars and rtestaurant, Whitbreads-related ales, no piped music; bedrooms *(Don and Shirley Parrish)*

Randwick [Church St; SO8206], *Vine Tree*: Roomy hillside village pub, wonderful valley views esp from terrace and garden; well kept Whitbreads-related ales, good choice of food (not Tues), Spanish chef (gives Spanish lessons here Mon), beams, timbering, stripped stone, rush matting, copper-topped tables, plates and Lawson Wood prints on walls, warm welcome; children welcome, play area, good walks *(Sue and Pete Robbins)*

☆ **Sapperton** [signed off A419 Stroud—Cirencester; SO9403], *Bell*: Neat village pub with extending stripped stone lounge, good log fire, sturdy pine tables, well kept Flowers Original, Tetleys and Wadworths 6X, simple food from sandwiches to steaks, friendly service, traditional public bar with games, skittle alley, tables outside; children welcome *(Mrs J Turner, D Irving, E McCall, R Huggins, T McLean, Don and Shirley Parrish, W W Burke, LYM)*

Shurdington [Shurdington Rd; A46 just S of Cheltenham; SO8318], *Bell*: Friendly local with consistently well kept beer, decent wines, wide choice of home-cooked food; conservatory looking over playing field; children welcome, some live music *(A E Brace, Stephen Pine, Alfred Lawrence)*

Slad [B4070 Stroud—Birdlip; SO8707], *Woolpack*: Basic village local in splendid setting, lovely valley views, friendly landlord, cheap food, well kept Bass and Uley Old Spot *(Roger Huggins, D Irving, E McCall, T McLean)*

Slimbridge [Shepherds Patch – OS Sheet 162 map ref 728042; SO7303], *Tudor Arms*: Character not its strongest point, but very handy for Wildfowl Trust and canal, popular home-cooked food in bar and evening restaurant, three or four real ales, children's room; bedrooms in small annexe *(P A Haywood, Tom McLean, Roger Huggins, John Broughton)*

☆ **Snowshill** [SP0934], *Snowshill Arms*: Handy for Snowshill Manor (which closes lunchtime), with good popular sensibly priced food, well kept Donnington BB and SBA, efficient friendly service, spruce and airy bar with neat array of tables, log fire; charming village views from bow windows and from big back garden with little stream, friendly local feel midweek winter, can be very crowded other times – get there early; skittle alley, good play area; children welcome if eating, nearby parking may be difficult; beautiful village *(George Atkinson, SLC, Maysie Thompson, Roger and Jenny Huggins, RP, BP, Dorothee and Dennis Glover, A C Morrison, Ian and Liz Phillips, Lawrence Pearse, DFL, Peter and Audrey Dowsett, LYM)*

☆ **Somerford Keynes** [OS Sheet 163 map ref 018954; SU0195], *Bakers Arms*: Homely and traditional partly stripped-stone local in lovely Cotswold village, wide choice of enjoyable food inc good specials, vegetarian and Sun lunch, well kept Bass and other frequently changing ales, knowledgeable and very friendly barman; busy lunchtime (booking recommended), big garden *(M A and C R Starling, D G King)*

☆ **Southrop** [signed off A417 and A361, nr Lechlade; SP2003], *Swan*: Cottagey seats and log fire in low-ceilinged dining lounge with generally good and often interesting food, small no-smoking restaurant (not Sun evening); stripped stone skittle alley, public bar, Morlands Original and guests such as Archers Golden, good wines; children welcome; pretty village esp at daffodil time *(Peter and Audrey Dowsett, John Bowdler, Mary Walters, Pat Crabb, Peter Neate, FWG, Kay Neville-Rolfe, George Atkinson, D H and M C Watkinson)*

Staunton [A4136, Forest of Dean – OS Sheet 162 map ref 548126; SO5513], *White Horse*: Well kept Scottish Courage real ales, wide choice of quickly served food inc unusual dishes and Sun lunch, big garden with penned wildfowl and adventure play area, good walks *(S P Watkin, P A Taylor)*

Staverton [Haydon, W of Cheltenham; B4063 – OS Sheet 163 map ref 902248; SO9024], *House in the Tree*: Pleasantly busy spick-and-span pub with splendid choice of farm ciders, Bass and Flowers, good value food in big dining lounge, more traditional public bar, log fire; may get crowded at weekends, plenty of tables in garden with good play area and pets' corner *(John and Joan Wyatt, Mel Hadfield)*

☆ **Stow on the Wold** [The Square; SP1925], *Queens Head*: Chatty old local with heavily beamed and flagstoned traditional back bar, high-backed settles, big log fire, horse prints, piped classical or opera, usual games, nice dogs; lots of tables in civilised stripped stone front lounge, good value straightforward bar food (not Mon evening or Sun), well kept Donnington BB and SBA, mulled wine, quick helpful service; children welcome, tables outside, occasional jazz Sun lunchtime; for second year running failed to let us have up-to-date price details etc even after reminders, so no main entry *(John Baker, Liz Bell, Brian Wainwright, Rob Whittle, Andrew and Ruth Triggs, Neville Kenyon, Hugh MacLean, Wayne Wheeler, John Bowdler, D Irving, E McCall, R Huggins, T McLean, Peter Baggott, Joan and Michel Hooper-Immins, Albert and Margaret Horton, LYM)*

Stow on the Wold [The Square], *Talbot*: Popular local with quick friendly service even when busy, well kept Wadworths IPA and 6X and a guest beer, decent lunches; open all day inc Sun *(Pat and Robert Watt, Joan and Michel Hooper-Immins)*; [A429 edge of centre], *Unicorn*: Ex-Forte hotel with comfortable beamed bar used by locals, good food at a price, helpful staff; bedrooms *(Derek Allpass)*; [The Square], *White Hart*: Decent food and well kept beer in cheery and pleasant old front bar or plush back dining

lounge; bedrooms *(Eddie Edwards, BB)*
Stroud [1 Bath Rd; SO8504], *Clothiers Arms*:
Extended 18th-c pub with well kept Tetleys-
related ales in busy bar with old Stroud
brewery decorations, pleasant airy dining
room, garden *(D G King)*; [Bath Rd,
Rooksmoor – A46 a mile S; SO8403], *Old
Fleece*: Wide choice of good food, candlelit
tables; Benson the golden labrador a favourite
(D G King); [top end of High St], *Retreat*:
Pink walls, polished wooden floors and tables,
well kept Archers Best and Boddingtons,
imaginative lunchtime food, children welcome;
can get crowded evenings *(Dave Irving)*
☆ **Tetbury** [Gumstool Hill, Mkt Pl; ST8893],
Crown: 17th-c town pub popular with older
people for good bar lunches with upmarket
touches, well kept Hook Norton Best and
Whitbreads-related ales, long oak-beamed
front bar with big log fire and attractive
medley of tables, friendly service, unobtrusive
piped music; back family dining conservatory
with lots of plants, picnic tables on back
terrace; comfortable bedrooms, sharing
bathroom *(D G Clarke, Grahame McNulty,
Brian Kirby, Simon Penny)*
☆ **Tewkesbury** [52 Church St; SO8932], *Bell*:
Plush but interesting hotel bar with friendly
helpful service, black oak beams and timbers,
some neat 17th-c oak panelling, medieval
leaf-and-fruit frescoes, armchairs, settees and
tapestries; generally good bar food from
sandwiches up inc vegetarian and civilised
Sun buffet lunch, comfortable restaurant, well
kept Bass and Banks's, big log fire; garden
above Severnside walk, nr abbey; good
recently refurbished bedrooms *(Andrew and
Ruth Triggs, Mr and Mrs J Brown, Lawrence
Bacon, Jean Scott, BB)*
☆ **Tewkesbury** [High St], *Black Bear*: Extremely
picturesque timbered pub, said to be county's
oldest, with rambling heavy-beamed rooms
off black-timbered corridors, inviting yet not
too crowded, five or six ales such as Flowers,
Greenalls Original, Ruddles and Wadworths
6X, some tapped from the cask, good food
inc daily roast and good children's menu,
friendly service; open all day, pleasant
riverside terrace *(Andy and Jill Kassube,
Andrew and Ruth Triggs, LYM)*
Tewkesbury [9 Church St], *Berkeley Arms*:
Pleasant olde-worlde refurbishment in striking
medieval timbered pub, well kept Wadworths
6X, Farmers Glory and winter Old Timer
with a summer guest beer, friendly staff, open
fire, wide range of good value food inc
succulent real chips, separate front public bar
(can be smoky), raftered ancient back barn
restaurant; open all day summer, bedrooms
*(Andy and Jill Kassube, Michel Hooper-
Immins, Brian Wainwright)*; [Gloucester Rd
(A38)], *Gupshill Manor*: Much restored as
Whitbreads pub, with lovely flower garden,
good choice of freshly cooked hot meals and
salads, fresh veg *(Mrs P V Burdett)*
☆ **Thornbury** [Chapel St; ST6390], *Wheatsheaf*:
Good home cooking in straightforward 1930s
local (the evening specials may run out early),

obliging service, wide range of real ales,
children's helpings, minimal music *(K R
Harris, Meg Hamilton, Catherine Waite, D G
Clarke, Pat Woodward)*
☆ **Tockington** [ST6186], *Swan*: Spacious pub
with beams, standing timbers, bric-a-brac on
stripped stone walls, Bass and Boddingtons on
handpump, guests such as Smiles and
Theakstons Best tapped from the cask,
country wines, good range of reasonably
priced food (dragon pie tipped if you like hot
food), friendly staff; picnic tables in
tree-shaded garden, quiet village *(Meg and
Colin Hamilton, Simon and Amanda
Southwell)*
Toddington [A46 Broadway—Winchcombe,
junction with A438 and B4077; SP0432],
Pheasant: Recently refurbished and doing well
under current owners, with quickly served
good food and lots of veg, local real ale; very
easy parking *(Martin Jones, John and Joan
Wyatt)*
Todenham [between A34 and A429 N of
Moreton in Marsh; SP2436], *Farriers Arms*:
Cotswold pub by church in quiet village,
extensively refurbished under new landlord
(ex-Claridges chef), good home-made food inc
interesting evening dishes, Scottish Courage
ales with a guest such as Hook Norton,
friendly staff; bedrooms *(Steven Carter, J
Kane)*
☆ **Tolldown** [under a mile from M4 junction 18
– A46 towards Bath; ST7577], *Crown*: Tidy
but largely unspoilt, with usual food inc good
steaks and fresh veg in heavy-beamed stripped
stone bar, no-smoking area, well kept
Wadworths with a guest such as Morlands
Old Speckled Hen, woodburner or coal fire,
quick friendly service (and cat); dominoes,
darts and fruit machine, piped music, good
garden with play area; no dogs, children in
eating area and restaurant; comfortable
bedrooms *(Ian and Nita Cooper, Phil Lovell,
Andrew Shore, Alan Kilpatrick, Mark and
Heather Williamson, LYM)*
Tormarton [handy for M4 junction 18, signed
off A46 N; ST7678], *Compass*: Very extended
off-motorway hotel with choice of rooms inc
cosy local-feeling bar open all day for wide
choice of food, pleasant conservatory, well
kept ales inc Archers and Smiles, friendly
staff, rather pricy restaurant; children
welcome in eating areas, comfortable
bedrooms *(Ian and Nita Cooper, LYM)*;
Portcullis: Good atmosphere, beams and
stonework, generous interesting food from
filled baguettes up inc vegetarian, good range
of real ales, log fire (sometimes two),
attractive panelled dining room; piped music
may be rather loud; tables in garden, quiet
village *(Ian and Nita Cooper, Luke
Worthington, Dick Mattick)*
Tytherington [just off A38; ST6688], *Swan*:
Big well furnished family food pub with no-
smoking area (but log fire may sometimes
smoke); reasonable prices, very busy
weekends *(Andrew Shore)*
☆ **Uley** [The Street; ST7898], *Old Crown*:

Welcoming prettily placed village local with long narrow lounge, good value standard food inc children's, well kept Boddingtons, Hook Norton Best, Uley Bitter and Old Spot (the brewer is a regular) and guest beers, attractive garden; dogs welcome, service may slow when busy; darts and fruit machine, small pool room up spiral stairs, unobtrusive piped music; bedrooms good value with super breakfast, good base for walks *(Andrew Day, Joan and Michel Hooper-Immins, Pat and John Millward)*

☆ **Upton Cheyney** [Brewery Hill; signed off A431 at Bitton; ST6969], *Upton Inn*: Clean, plush and spacious, with wide choice of good generous reasonably priced home-cooked food inc vegetarian in bar or attractive red-decor crystal-chandelier restaurant with art deco pictures, well kept Bass, Smiles and Wadworths 6X, decent wine and coffee, prompt friendly service; delightful surroundings, lovely Avon Valley views *(Roy Storm, Meg and Colin Hamilton, Andrew Rogers, Amanda Milsom, Graham Fogelman)*

Wanswell Green [SO6901], *Salmon*: Good value food, well kept Whitbreads-related ales, decent wines and cider, two attractive candlelit back dining rooms, good friendly staff helpful with children; big front play area; nr Berkeley Castle and Severn walks *(Mr and Mrs J Brown)*

☆ **Westbury on Severn** [Bell Lane (A48 Gloucester—Chepstow); SO7114], *Red Lion*: Substantial half-timbered building on busy road but by quiet church-side lane to river, cosy carpeted bar with button-back wall seats and velvet curtains, cotton cap collection on beams, coal stove, well kept ales such as Fullers and Smiles, decent wine, very friendly service; good generous interesting food in big dining room with old pews; evening opening 7; handy for Westbury Court gardens (NT) *(Neil and Anita Christopher, Mr and Mrs D Towle, Dr and Mrs B Baker, S H Godsell, BB)*

Westbury on Severn [Grange Court – signed off A48 in Westbury], *Junction*: Straightforward house converted into two-bar pub, full of railway memorabilia – pictures, timetables, even an old telephone; authentic local feel, log fire, darts, skittle alley, SkyTV, nostalgic juke box; Bass and Boddingtons *(Daren Haines)*

☆ **Westonbirt** [A433 SW of Tetbury; ST8690], *Hare & Hounds*: Well run old-fashioned hotel bar, comfortable, relaxed and surprisingly pubby, with high-backed settles, decent reasonably priced lunches inc salad bar and enterprising open sandwiches, Smiles or John Smiths, Wadworths IPA and 6X (beware, they've been using a sparkler), friendly efficient staff, separate locals' bar, pleasant gardens; handy for Arboretum; limited space for families; bedrooms *(Kay Neville-Rolfe, Brian and Anna Marsden, Meg and Colin Hamilton)*

Whitminster [A38 1½ miles N of M5 junction 13; SO7708], *Old Forge*: Small beamed pub, not smart but handy for nearby nursery, with welcoming staff, good choice of beers and wines, small restaurant; children welcome *(Pamela and Merlyn Horswell, H F C Barclay)*

☆ **Willersey** [B4632 Cheltenham—Stratford, nr Broadway; SP1039], *Bell*: Civilised and spotless 14th-c golden stone dining pub, comfortable and welcoming, with good food from well presented sandwiches up; well kept Boddingtons, Tetleys and Wadworths 6X, friendly Yorkshire landlord; no dogs; overlooks delightful village's green and duck pond, lots of tables in big garden *(Albert and Margaret Horton, George Atkinson)*

☆ **Winchcombe** [High St; SP0228], *Old Corner Cupboard*: New licensees doing well in subtly modernised pub with beams, stripped stone and good inglenook log fire, good bar food, well kept ales, attractive small back garden; bedrooms in self-contained wing; at top of charming village with interesting pottery *(IHR, D G Clarke)*

☆ **Winchcombe** [Abbey Terr], *Plaisterers Arms*: Split-level 18th-c pub with stripped stonework, beams, good generous straightforward food inc vegetarian, children's and good puddings, prompt service, well kept Tetleys, Wadworths and local Goffs Jouster and White Knight, open fire, plenty of seating inc comfortably worn settles, copper, brass and old tools, dim-lit lower back area, dining area, lots of steps; good play area in attractive garden, long and narrow; comfortable bedrooms, handy for Sudeley Castle *(Neil and Anita Christopher, Dr P Lavender, Michael and Hazel Lyons, Lew Badger)*

Winterbourne Down [Down Rd, Kendleshire; just off A432 Bristol—Yate, towards Winterbourne; ST6679], *Golden Heart*: Well furnished old coaching inn, beams, open fires, inglenook, wide choice of well kept ales and of reasonably priced food, good welcoming service, country view from restaurant; fruit machines; children's room, huge lawns front and back, both with play equipment *(Dr and Mrs A K Clarke)*

☆ **Woodchester** [South Woodchester, signed off A46 Stroud—Nailsworth; SO8302], *Ram*: Fine choice of ales such as Archers Best, Boddingtons, John Smiths and Uley Old Spot with several interestng guest beers, in relaxed L-shaped beamed bar with nice mix of traditional furnishings, some stripped stonework and three open fires, darts, bar food from sandwiches to steaks, restaurant; children welcome, open all day Sat/Sun, spectacular views from terrace tables *(Stephen Pine, Alfred Lawrence, FWG, Joan and Michel Hooper-Immins, Stephen Brown, Cherry Ann Knott, Geoffrey and Penny Hughes, Roger Huggins, Alec Hamilton, Tom Rees, LYM)*

☆ **Woodmancote** [Stockwell Lane; SO9727], *Apple Tree*: Wide choice of good popular food in roomy local with cheerful courteous staff, Bass, Wadworths and Whitbreads-related ales, decent wines, restaurant; small children looked after well; garden – fine views, secluded setting at foot of hill *(Mr and Mrs J Brown)*

Hampshire

Quite a few new entries here (or pubs back in these pages after an absence)
include the Globe in its delightful spot in Alresford, the charming Star tucked
away at East Tytherley, the cheerful Hen & Chicken at Froyle, the Ship at
Owslebury (showing that there need be no contradiction between relaxing and
bustling!), the Plough at Sparsholt (hard-working new tenants), and the well
(and distinctively) run Hare & Hounds at Sway, an enjoyable New Forest
local. Against fairly stiff competition, our choice as Hampshire Dining Pub of
the Year is the Red Lion at Boldre. Other pubs on particularly fine form here
these days are the Jolly Sailor by the water at Bursledon, the Fox & Hounds at
Crawley, the Hawkley Inn at Hawkley, and – a tremendous favourite among
our readers – the Wykeham Arms in Winchester. This is such a favoured area
for good pubs that many of those in the Lucky Dip section at the end of the
chapter are well in the running for the main entries. We'd mention especially
the Furze Bush at Ball Hill, Bull at Bentley, Sir John Barleycorn in Cadnam,
Hampshire Bowman at Dundridge, George at East Meon, Osborne View at
Hill Head, Chequers in Lymington, Pilgrim at Marchwood, Royal Oak at
North Gorley, George in Odiham, Fish at Ringwood, George at Vernham
Dean and Cartwheel at Whitsbury; and the Old Horse & Jockey in Romsey –
entirely new to us, so not a pub we've been able to inspect yet ourselves –
sounds very promising. There's a good wide choice in Portsmouth and in
Winchester. Drinks prices in the area tend to be much higher than the national
average. The Flower Pots at Cheriton, brewing its own excellent ales, was the
cheapest pub we found in our price survey here.

ALRESFORD SU5832 Map 2
Globe ♀

The Soke, Broad Street (extreme lower end – B3046 towards Old Alresford); town signposted off A31 bypass

What makes this a favourite is the view from the back over the Alresford Ponds, a sizeable stretch of water created in the 12th c – for food then (fish and wildfowling), but now a lovely haven for ducks, swans and dragonflies; some of the birds hope for scraps in the attractive garden, and in summer offer endless amusement for small children. Inside, the pub has been comfortably refurbished, with big log fires at each end, a friendly busy atmosphere, and a clean and uncluttered decor – old local photographs, information about the ponds. Well presented good value food, which changes day by day, includes soup (£2.45), sandwiches (from £2.75), ploughman's (£3.75), chicken liver parfait or stilton and walnut pâté (£3.95), cod and chips, home-made fishcakes, steak and kidney pie or chicken leg stuffed with mushrooms and herbs (all £5.75), and deep-fried mussels, squid and prawns (£7.95). Readers have recently particularly enjoyed lamb meatballs on couscous (£4.95) and pigeon breast in a delicious sauce (£5.95); and while it's easy enough to make bangers and mash (£3.95) taste nice, this is one of the few places we know that makes it look alluring too. Part of the restaurant is no smoking. Well kept Courage Best with a guest such as Marstons Pedigree, John Smiths or Wadworths 6X on handpump, a wide choice of decent wines by the glass, winter mulled wine, maybe free Sunday bar nibbles, helpful staff;

unobtrusive piped music, board games. Nearby parking is rather limited; there's plenty about 100 metres away, at the bottom of truly named Broad St. *(Recommended by Patricia and Anthony Daley, John and Joan Nash, Jo and Gary Charlton, Christopher Warner, Ann and Colin Hunt, Howard Allen, Mr and Mrs R J Foreman)*

Scottish Courage ~ Lease: Lyn O'Callaghan and Terry McTurk ~ Real ale ~ Meals and snacks ~ Restaurant (Tues-Sat evenings) ~ (01962) 732294 ~ Children welcome ~ Open 11-3, 6-11; 12-3, 7-10.30 Sun

BATTRAMSLEY SZ3099 Map 2
Hobler

A337 a couple of miles S of Brockenhurst; OS Sheet 196 map reference 307990

A particular draw to this bustling pub is the enjoyable, popular food; meat is especially well looked after – the landlord is also the local butcher. From a changing menu, there might be ploughman's (£3.95), stuffed jalapeno chillies (£5.50), home-made pies (£5.95), peppers in pasta or half shoulder of lamb (£7.95), lamb kidneys in a thick bacon and wholegrain mustard sauce (£8.95), bass in a lemony butter sauce or their popular 'Hot Rocks', a hot stone on a plate upon which you cook your own sirloin steak or chicken breast (£9.95), and scallops (£10.95). They recommend booking in the evening, and even at lunchtime it's worth arriving early, as tables soon fill up. The black-beamed bar – divided by the massive stub of an ancient wall – has a very relaxed feel, and is furnished with pews, little dining chairs and a comfortable bow-window seat. Guns, china, New-Forest saws, the odd big engraving, and a growing collection of customer photographs decorate the walls, some of which are stripped back to timbered brick; the cosy area on the left is black-panelled and full of books. Well kept Flowers IPA, Wadworths 6X and guest beers like Bass, Greene King Abbot, Ringwood Best, and Ruddles on handpump, a good range of malt whiskies (over 75) and country wines. In summer, a spacious forest-edge lawn has a summer bar, a huge timber climbing fort in the very good play area, and picnic tables, as well as a paddock with ponies, pigs, donkeys, a peacock and hens. Note children aren't allowed inside. *(Recommended by Mr and Mrs A J Woolstone, Lynn Sharpless, Bob Eardley, D Marsh, Dr and Mrs A K Clarke, M Joyner, Brian Hall)*

Whitbreads ~ Licensee Pip Steven ~ Real ale ~ Meals and snacks (till 10) ~ (01590) 623291 ~ Jazz Tues evening, blues Thurs evening ~ Open 10.30-2.30(3 Sat), 6-11; 12-3, 7-10.30 Sun

BEAUWORTH SU5624 Map 2
Milbury's ◧

Turn off A272 Winchester—Petersfield at Beauworth ¼. Bishops Waltham 6 signpost, then continue straight on past village

The name of this pub was at first only a nickname, coming from the Millbarrow, a Bronze Age cemetery surrounding it, briefly famous back in 1833 when a Norman hoard of 6,000 silver coins was found here. There's a 600-year-old well in the bar with a massive 250-year-old treadmill – if you drop an ice cube into the spotlit shaft it takes five full seconds to reach the bottom, which apparently means it is 300 feet deep. Sturdy beams and panelling, stripped masonry, interesting old furnishings, and massive open fireplaces (with good winter log fires) offer other reminders of the building's age. Well kept Boddingtons, Hampshire Judge Bitter, King Alfred's, Arthur Pendragon, and a beer named for the pub on handpump, Addlestones cider, and country wines. Enjoyable bar food includes home-made soup (£2.50), filled french bread or baked potatoes (£4.20), stuffed vegetarian pancake (£5.25), chicken with lemon and ginger (£5.95), steak and kidney pie (£6.25), rack of lamb (£8.75), steaks (from £9.95), puddings (£2.45), children's dishes (from £2.50), and Sunday brunch (from £4.25); friendly service. There may be two fluffy cats and a big dog; darts, fruit machine, skittle alley. The pub has fine views from the garden and good walks nearby. *(Recommended by Mr and Mrs Jonathan Russell, Mrs F A W Ricketts, Michael Inskip, N E Bushby, W E Atkins, Jo and Gary Charlton, Ann and Colin Hunt, Joy and Harold Dermott, Susan and John Douglas, John Sanders, A R and B E Sayer, J Sheldon, Jane Warren, Andy Jones, Martin and Karen Wake, Dave Braisted, Margaret and Nigel Dennis, Lynn Sharpless, Bob Eardley, W George Preston, John and Fiona McDougal)*

Free house ~ Licensees Jan and Lenny Larden ~ Real ale ~ Meals and snacks (till 10pm) ~ Restaurant ~ (01962) 771248 ~ Children welcome ~ Open 11-2.30(3.30 Sat), 6-11; 12-3.30, 7-10.30 Sun ~ Bedrooms: £27.50/£38.50

BENTWORTH SU6740 Map 2
Sun 🍺

Sun Hill; from the A339 coming from Alton the first turning takes you there direct; or in village follow Shalden 2¼, Alton 4¼ signpost

A new licensee has taken over this unspoilt old cottage and has added a beer garden. Inside, the two tiny traditional communicating rooms have open fires in the big fireplaces, high-backed antique settles, pews and schoolroom chairs, olde-worlde prints and blacksmith's tools on the walls, and bare boards and scrubbed deal tables on the left. An arch leads to a brick-floored room with another open fire and hanging baskets. Bar food now includes sandwiches, home-made carrot and orange soup (£2.20), home-made chicken liver pâté (£2.95), ploughman's (£3.50), filled baked potatoes (from £4), cumberland sausage and mash (£4.50), creamy mushroom pasta (£5.50), home-made chicken and ham pie (£6.50), and puddings like lemon cream pie (£2.50). Well kept Badger Best, Ballards Best, Cheriton Pots Ale, Courage Best, Ringwood Best, Ruddles Best, and Timothy Taylors Landlord on handpump, and several malt whiskies. *(Recommended by Lynn Sharpless, Bob Eardley, Martin and Karen Wake, Christopher Wade, Howard Allen, Gordon Prince, Ann and Colin Hunt, Thomas Nott, Jo and Gary Charlton, Peter and Michele Rayment, Malcolm Taylor, Derek and Margaret Underwood)*

Free house ~ Licensee Mary Holmes ~ Real ale ~ Meals and snacks ~ (01420) 562338 ~ Children welcome ~ Occasional Morris dancers (26 Dec and odd Fri nights in summer) ~ Open 12-3, 6-11; 12-10.30 Sun

BOLDRE SZ3298 Map 2
Red Lion ★ 🍽 ♀

Village signposted from A337 N of Lymington

Hampshire Dining Pub of the Year

There's a really warm and thriving yet very civilised atmosphere here, thanks largely to friendly and efficient licensees. The four black-beamed rooms are filled with heavy urns, platters, handiwork, rural landscapes, and so forth, taking in farm tools, heavy-horse harness, needlework, gin traps and even ferocious-looking man traps along the way; the central room with its profusion of chamber-pots is no-smoking. An end room has pews, wheelback chairs and tapestried stools, and a dainty collection of old bottles and glasses in the window by the counter. Good, very popular bar food, changing weekly, includes home-made soup (£2.50), super triple decker sandwiches with chips (£4.90), well liked basket meals ranging from sausages to duck with wine-soaked orange slices (from £4.90; the duck is £8.90), quite a few ploughman's (£5.50), stuffed aubergine (£5.90), lamb liver with crispy bacon or home-made vegetable casserole (£6.50), mango chicken (£7.80), cold home-cooked gammon with poached eggs or medallions of pork with a mushroom, white wine and cream sauce (£8.20), daily specials such as dressed crab salad (£7.90), whole brill with citrus sauce (£8.20), and pheasant casserole (£8.90), and good puddings; get there early to be sure of a seat. Well kept Eldridge Pope Hardy Country and Royal Oak on handpump, a range of malt whiskies, and up to 20 wines by the glass; prompt and friendly service. In summer, the flowering tubs and hanging baskets are lovely and there's a cart festooned with colour near the car park. This is a fine area for walking, with 1,000 acres of Raydon Wood Nature Reserve. No children. *(Recommended by Jo and Gary Charlton, Phyl and Jack Street, M J Dowdy, Betsy Brown, Nigel Flook, D Marsh, P R and S A White, N E Bushby, W E Atkins, Lynn Sharpless, Bob Eardley, Pat and Roger Fereday, Mrs F A W Ricketts, Vann and Terry Prime, Derek and Margaret Underwood, Jenny and Michael Back, John and Phyllis Maloney, J and D Tapper)*

Eldridge Pope ~ Lease: John and Penny Bicknell ~ Real ale ~ Meals and snacks (11.30-2.30, 6.30-10) ~ (01590) 673177 ~ Open 11-3, 6-11; 11-11 Sat; 12-10.30 Sun

BRAMDEAN SU6128 Map 2
Fox

A272 Winchester—Petersfield

The bar in this white 17th-c weatherboarded dining pub has been redecorated this year and the furniture re-upholstered, too. It's open plan and carefully modernised with black beams, tall stools with proper backrests around the L-shaped counter, and comfortably cushioned wall pews and wheelback chairs; the fox motif shows in a big painting over the fireplace, and on much of the decorative china. At least one area is no smoking. Changing daily, the popular food includes sandwiches (from £2.50), soup (£2.95), brandied mushrooms with bacon on a crouton (£4.75), and ploughman's (from £4.95), with lunchtime dishes like fresh whole grilled plaice (£7.95), grilled lamb cutlets, fresh fillet of monkfish thermidor or gammon and egg (£8.95), and evening meals such as chicken breast with parma ham in boursin sauce (£10.95), roast rack of lamb with garlic and rosemary (£11.95), pork fillet with wild mushrooms in a cream and brandy sauce or steaks (£12.95), and grilled bass with a red pepper salsa (£13.95). Well kept Marstons Pedigree on handpump; piped music. At the back of the building is a walled-in terraced area, and a spacious lawn spreading among the fruit trees, with a really good play area – trampoline as well as swings and a seesaw. No children inside. *(Recommended by Iain Robertson, Phyl and Jack Street, Janet and Colin Roe, Mr and Mrs Cody, John Sanders, Dennis Stevens)*

Marstons ~ Tenants Jane and Ian Inder ~ Real ale ~ Meals and snacks ~ (01962) 771363 ~ Open 10.30-3, 6-11; 12-3, 7-10.30 Sun; closed 25 Dec

BURITON SU7420 Map 2
Five Bells 🍺

Village signposted off A3 S of Petersfield

There are lots of different interesting rooms in this friendly country pub. The low-beamed lounge on the left is dominated by a big log fire, and has period photographs on the partly stripped brick walls and a rather worn turkey carpet on oak parquet; the public side has some ancient stripped masonry, a woodburning stove, and old-fashioned tables. An end alcove with cushioned pews and old fishing prints has board games. A good choice of popular bar food includes lunchtime filled french bread (£2.75) and ploughman's or filled baked potatoes (£3.75), as well as baked brie with toast and preserve (£3.75), moules marinières (£4.75), nut roast with red wine and mushroom sauce or Indonesian pork (£5.95), steak and kidney pie or liver and bacon casserole (£6.95), grilled red snapper or swordfish in garlic butter (£7.95), seasonal game such as wild rabbit in prunes and calvados (£7.95) or partridge stuffed with bacon, walnut and stilton (£9.95), and home-made puddings (£2.75). Well kept Ballards Best, Friary Meux Best, Greene King IPA, Ind Coope Burton, and Ringwood Best and Old Thumper on handpump, and decent wines. Prompt, friendly service; darts, shove-ha'penny, cribbage, dominoes, trivia, piped music (in one bar only). There are a few tables on sheltered terraces just outside, with many more on an informal lawn stretching back above the pub. The converted stables are self-catering cottages, and the village with its duck pond is pretty. *(Recommended by A Cowell, Ian Phillips, Jo and Gary Charlton, Paula Williams, Roger and Fiona Todd, Lynn Sharpless, Bob Eardley, A E Green, Pete Yearsley, Dennis Stevens, Ann and Colin Hunt, Mrs S Peregrine)*

Free house ~ Licensee John Ligertwood ~ Real ale ~ Meals and snacks (till 10) ~ Restaurant (not Sun evening) ~ (01730) 263584 ~ Children in restaurant ~ Jazz last Mon in month, folk, blues or R&B Weds evening ~ Open 11-2.30(3 Fri/Sat) 5.30-11; 12-3, 7-11 Sun ~ Self-catering cottages: /£35S

By law pubs must show a price list of their drinks. Let us know if you are inconvenienced by any breach of this law.

BURSLEDON SU4809 Map 2
Jolly Sailor

2 miles from M27 junction 8; then A27 towards Salisbury, then just before going under railway bridge turn right towards Bursledon station; it's best to park round here and walk as the lane up from the station is now closed to cars

Although this charmingly unspoilt pub does get crowded in the summer, it rarely feels touristy. You can sit out at the tables under the big yew tree or on the wooden jetty, watching all the goings on in the rather pretty harbour, or enjoy the same view from the window seat inside. The airy front bar has ship pictures, nets and shells, as well as windsor chairs and settles on the floorboards. The atmospheric beamed and flagstoned back bar, with pews and settles by its huge fireplace, is a fair bit older. Bar food includes sandwiches, coronation chicken or moules marinières (£4.95), home-made mushroom, bacon and pasta crunch (£5.80), five home-made daily vegetarian dishes, steak and stilton (£11.70), and rack of lamb (£11.95); friendly efficient service. The dining area is no smoking. Well kept Badger Best, IPA, and Tanglefoot on handpump, and country wines; darts, fruit machine, and piped music. The path down to the pub (and of course back up again) from the lane is steep. *(Recommended by Ann and Colin Hunt, D Marsh, Martin and Karen Wake, James Flory, Stephen, Julie and Hayley Brown, Eric and June Heley, N S Smith, Lynn Sharpless, Bob Eardley, David Carr, Clive Gilbert, John Knighton)*

Badger ~ Managers Stephen and Kathryn Housley ~ Real ale ~ Meals and snacks (12-9.30) ~ Restaurant ~ (01703) 405557 ~ Children in dining area ~ Open 11-11; 12-10.30 Sun; closed 25 Dec

CADNAM SU2913 Map 2
White Hart

½ mile from M27 junction 1; A336 towards village, pub off village roundabout

This bustling pub is somewhere to come for a relaxing meal rather than just a quick snack. Attractively presented, the popular food might include soup (£3.25), open sandwiches (£4.50), ham and cheese platter or chicken and spring onion satay (£4.75), sausages with onion gravy or freshly battered cod (£6.25), a daily pasta dish or aubergine fritters with grilled vegetables and pesto (£7.50), gammon and egg (£8.25), duck breast with orange and green peppercorn sauce or lamb fillet with apricot and coriander (£10.75), and home-made puddings. The spacious multi-level dining lounge has good solid furnishings, soft lighting, country prints and appropriate New Forest pictures and mementoes; well kept Courage Best, Flowers Original, Morlands Old Speckled Hen, and Wadworths 6X on handpump, and decent wines; no games machines or piped music, and efficient service. There are picnic tables under cocktail parasols outside. *(Recommended by Lynn Sharpless, Bob Eardley, D Marsh, Phyl and Jack Street, Mark and Heather Williamson, D B Jenkin, Kim Maidment, Philip Vernon, Mrs J A Blanks, Lyn and Simon Gretton, Joan and Dudley Payne)*

Whitbreads ~ Lease: Nick and Sue Emberley ~ Real ale ~ Meals and snacks ~ (01703) 812277 ~ Children welcome ~ Open 11-3, 6-11; 12-3, 7-10.30 Sun

CHALTON SU7315 Map 2
Red Lion ♀

Village signposted E of A3 Petersfield—Horndean

Parts of this lovely thatched house date back to 1150 when a workshop here was site office for the rebuilding of the Norman church opposite. It's the oldest pub in Hampshire and was first licensed in 1503. The most characterful part is the heavy-beamed and panelled bar with high-backed traditional settles and elm tables and an ancient inglenook fireplace with a frieze of burnished threepenny bits set into its mantelbeam. Generous helpings of well liked bar food include sandwiches and snacks, and daily specials such as oak-smoked trout fillets or chicken breast in a thai cream sauce (£6.75), honey-roasted pheasant (in season) or grilled talapia with parsley butter (£6.95), and baked pigeon with redcurrants (£7.50). Families are usually directed to a modern no-smoking dining extension. Well kept Gales BBB, Best, HSB, Winter Brew, and a guest beer on handpump, a good choice of wines by the glass or bottle, country wines, and over 50 malt whiskies; efficient service; piped music. The garden is pretty in summer and the pub is popular with walkers and riders as it is fairly close to the extensive Queen Elizabeth Country Park and about half a mile down the lane from a growing Iron Age farm and settlement; it's only about 20 minutes to the car ferry, too. *(Recommended by N E Bushby, W E Atkins, Mike and Mary Carter, Ian Phillips, Tony and Wendy Hobden, P and S White, Drs R and M Woodford, Pete Yearsley, Phyl and Jack Street, Ann and Colin Hunt, D Maplethorpe, B Helliwell, Dennis Stevens, John Sanders)*

Gales ~ Managers Mick and Mary McGee ~ Real ale ~ Meals and snacks (not Sun evening) ~ (01705) 592246 ~ Children in family dining room ~ Open 11-3, 6-11; 12-3, 7-10.30 Sun; closed evenings 25-26 Dec

CHERITON SU5828 Map 2
Flower Pots ★ ◗

Pub just off B3046 (main village road) towards Beauworth and Winchester; OS Sheet 185 map reference 581282

The charming licensees of this bustling village local were delighted to win the Gold Award in the Strong Bitter Category and achieve the Silver Award in the Supreme Champion Beer of Britain at the Great British Beer Festival in London last year for their own Diggers Gold, produced in the little Cheriton Brewhouse here; they also brew Pots Ale and Cheriton Best Bitter, too. There's a friendly country atmosphere in the two little rooms and the one on the left feels almost like someone's front room, with pictures of hounds and ploughmen on its striped wallpaper, bunches of flowers, and a horse and foal and other ornaments on the mantelpiece over a small log fire; it can get smoky in here. Behind the servery there's disused copper filtering equipment, and lots of hanging gin-traps, drag-hooks, scaleyards and other ironwork. Good value straightforward bar food includes sandwiches (from £1.80, toasties or big baps from £2), ploughman's (from £3.30), and chilli con carne, lamb and apricot casserole or beef and ale stew (from £4.10); efficient service. Darts in the neat extended plain public bar (where there's a covered well), also cribbage, shove-ha'penny and dominoes; the family room has a TV, board games and colouring books. There are old-fashioned seats on the pretty front and back lawns – very useful in fine weather as it can quickly fill up inside; they sometimes have Morris dancers out here in summer. Near the site of one of the final battles of the Civil War, the pub once belonged to the retired head gardener of nearby Avington Park, which explains the unusual name. *(Recommended by Lynn Sharpless, Bob Eardley, Ron Gentry, Thomas Nott, Martin and Karen Wake, Stephen Harvey, Mrs F A W Ricketts, J S M Sheldon, Jo and Gary Charlton, Kevin and Katharine Cripps, Andy Jones, Joone Fairweather, James Macrae, M L and G Clarke, G S Stoney, Marjorie and David Lamb, John and Joy Winterbottom, Ron Shelton, Bruce Bird, Ann and Colin Hunt, A R and B E Sayer)*

Own Brew ~ Licensees Patricia and Joanna Bartlett ~ Real ale ~ Meals and snacks (not Sun evening) ~ (01962) 771318 ~ Children in small sitting room off lounge bar ~ Open 12-2.30, 6-11; 12-3, 7-10.30 Sun ~ Bedrooms: £27B/£45B

CRAWLEY SU4234 Map 2
Fox & Hounds ⇌

Village signposted from A272 Winchester—Stockbridge and B3420 Winchester—Andover

This solidly constructed mock Tudor building is one of the most striking in a village of fine old houses. Each timbered upper storey successively juts further out, with lots of pegged structural timbers in the neat brickwork (especially around the latticed windows), and elaborately carved steep gable-ends. The scrupulous workmanship continues inside, with oak parquet, latticed windows, and an elegant black timber arch in the small lounge, and neatly panelled upholstered wall benches around the tables of the beamed main bar. There are fires in both spotlessly maintained rooms – real logs in the lounge, log-effect gas in the other. Bar food is good and very popular and might include sandwiches (not Sunday), soup such as cauliflower and stilton, delicious feta cheese and olive salad (£3.75), home-made trout and mackerel pâté (£3.95), spicy cheese and lentil loaf or home-made steak and kidney pie (£6.75), fresh grilled fillets of Cornish plaice meunière (£6.95), gammon and egg or home-made fishcakes with a fresh tomato sauce (£6.95), rump steak (£8.95), and wild boar au poivre (£10.95). Well kept Gales BBB and Wadworths 6X on handpump. *(Recommended by Gordon, TRS, Nigel Wikeley, Michael Inskip, Peter and Gwen Andrews, Howard Allen, Phyl and Jack Street, Colin Laffan, DC, Prof A N Black, John and Phyllis Maloney, Mike and Heather Watson)*

Free house ~ Licensees Doreen and Luis Sanz-Diez ~ Real ale ~ Meals and snacks ~ Restaurant (not Sun evening) ~ (01962) 776285 ~ Children in eating area of bar and in restaurant ~ Open 11.45-2.30(3 Sat), 6.30-11; 12-3, 7-10.30 Sun ~ Bedrooms: £45B/£65B

DROXFORD SU6018 Map 2
White Horse 🍺 ⇐

4 miles along A32 from Wickham

A series of small cosy rooms makes up the atmospheric lounge bar here – low beams, bow windows, alcoves, and log fires, while the public bar is larger and more straightforward: pool, table football, shove-ha'penny, cribbage, dominoes, video game, and CD juke box. Reasonably priced bar food includes sandwiches (from £1.80; hot crusty french sticks from £2.75), home-made soup (£2), spicy cumberland sausage (£4.25), a daily roast (£4.50), tomato and vegetable tagliatelle (£4.95), a home-made pie of the day (from £5.25), gammon and egg (£5.65), a brace of locally smoked quail (£5.95), steaks (from £9.15), specials, and puddings such as home-made fruit crumbles (from £2); children's menu (from £2.10). The restaurant is no smoking. Well kept Morlands IPA and Old Speckled Hen and Flowers Original, and Ind Coope Burton on handpump, and country wines. One of the cubicles in the gents' overlooks an illuminated well. There are tables in a secluded flower-filled courtyard comfortably sheltered by the building's back wings. *(Recommended by Mrs F A Ricketts, David Heath, Gwen and Peter Andrews, T W Fleckney, Ann and Colin Hunt, Dave Braisted, Steven Tait, Susie Lonie, Lynn Sharpless, Bob Eardley, Phyl and Jack Street, Derek and Margaret Underwood, Mr and Mrs R J Foreman, Andrew Shore, John Sanders)*

Morlands ~ Tenant Paul Young ~ Real ale ~ Meals and snacks (till 9.45) ~ Restaurant ~ (01489) 877490 ~ Children in family room and restaurant ~ Open 11-3, 6-11; 12-3, 7-10.30 Sun in lounge bar – open all day in back bar ~ Bedrooms: £25(£40B)/£35(£50B)

DUMMER SU5846 Map 2
Queen

Half a mile from M3, junction 7; take Dummer slip road

Particularly at lunchtime, this tiled white cottage is full of customers enjoying the hearty food. There's a good choice of dishes like home-made soup (£2.50), sandwiches (from £3.25), filled baked potatoes (from £4.25), home-made vegetable lasagne (£5.95), cod in their own beer batter (£6.95 medium, £8.95 large), seven types of burger (from £6.50), lasagne (£6.95), steak and kidney pudding (£10.95), Scotch Angus steaks (from £12.95), daily specials, puddings, and roast Sunday lunch (from £6.95); friendly service. The bar is open-plan, but has a pleasantly alcovey feel, with a liberal use of timbered brick and plaster partition walls, as well as beams and joists and an open fire. There are built-in padded seats, cushioned spindleback chairs and stools around the tables on the dark blue patterned carpet, and pictures of queens, old photographs, small steeplechase prints and advertisements. Well kept Courage Best and Directors, Fullers London Pride, and Marstons Pedigree on handpump; fruit machine in one corner, cribbage, and well reproduced piped music. Picnic tables under cocktail parasols on the terrace and in a neat little sheltered back garden. *(Recommended by Mrs H Murphy, Nigel and Sue Foster, J and B Cressey, Susan and John Douglas, Ian Phillips, Mr and Mrs D S Price, Phyl and Jack Street, B N F and M Parkin)*

Courage ~ Managers David and Sally Greenhalgh ~ Real ale ~ Meals and snacks (till 10) ~ Restaurant ~ (01256) 397367 ~ Children in restaurant ~ Open 11-3, 5.30 (6 Sat)-11; 12-3, 7-10.30 Sun

EAST TYTHERLEY SU2929 Map 2
Star

Off B3084 N of Romsey, via Lockerleigh – turn off by railway crossing nr Mottisfont Abbey

This friendly country local by the village cricket field always seems to have something going on – maybe the Morris dancers performing, maybe a group of gleaming veteran motorcycles turning up, maybe just people tackling a game of giant chess or draughts on the forecourt, or a skittles team from a neighbouring village challenging the local champions. It's pleasantly informal inside, with an unassuming mix of comfortably homely furnishing, log fires in attractive fireplaces, a no-smoking lower lounge bar, and a cosy and pretty restaurant; despite the very relaxed feel of the place, staff are smart and efficient – an excellent balance. Enjoyable home-made food includes soup (£1.95), sandwiches (from £3.50), ploughman's (£4.25), steak and kidney pie, lasagne or chilli con carne (£5.95), daily specials such as lamb and vegetable bake, salmon in leek and ginger, guinea fowl in a raspberry sauce (£5.95-£7.95), three vegetarian dishes like mushroom stroganoff, and puddings such as apple and blackberry crumble, treacle sponge or spotted dick and custard (£2.95). The restaurant is no smoking. Well kept Courage Directors, Gales HSB and Ringwood Best on handpump, country wines, and good coffee. The garden has a play area, and there are picnic tables on the forecourt; full size chess and draughts; skittle alley. *(Recommended by Phyl and Jack Street, Howard Allen, Ann and Colin Hunt, Adrian and Mandy Bateman, D Marsh, L M Parsons, John Knighton)*

Free house ~ Licensee Carol Mitchell ~ Real ale ~ Meals and snacks ~ Restaurant ~ (01794) 340225 ~ Well behaved children welcome ~ Open 11-3, 6-11; 12-3, 7-10.30 Sun ~ Bedrooms: £50B/£50B

FROYLE SU7542 Map 2
Hen & Chicken

A31 Alton—Farnham

Though this welcoming coaching inn dates back some 400 years, it was rebuilt in 1760 after a bad fire and given a new frontage. The three interconnecting rooms have beams hung with hops, candles on the tables, chestnuts roasting on the fire in the inglenook fireplace, daily papers, soft piped music and a discreetly positioned fruit machine. Served by staff in neat waistcoats, the well presented good food includes home-made soup (£3.25), sandwiches (from £3.50), garlic mushrooms (£3.95), filled french bread (from £4.25), ploughman's (£5.50), basket meals (from £4.95), omelettes (from £5.50), tagliatelle with asparagus spears and oven baked cherry tomatoes (£7.50), Chinese beef stir-fry (£8.25), liver and bacon on a madeira sauce (£8.95), fillet of sea bream with a cabbage and bacon sauce (£9.75), steaks (from £10.95), and children's dishes (£2.95); part of the restaurant is no smoking. Well kept Badger Best, Courage Best, Flowers Original, Fullers London Pride, Hook Norton Old Hookey, and Timothy Taylors Landlord on handpump kept under light blanket pressure, several malt whiskies, and a good pimms; cheerful, friendly service. The big garden has rabbits and children's play equipment. *(Recommended by Thomas Nott, Jo and Gary Charlton, Simon Collett-Jones, V Harris, Chris and Ann Garnett, E G Parish, Victor Harris, Peter and Liz Wilkins)*

Free house ~ Licensee Bill Thompson ~ Real ale ~ Meals and snacks (11-2.30, 6-10; all day Sat/Sun) ~ Restaurant ~ (01420) 22115 ~ Children in eating area of bar and in restaurant ~ Jazz in the garden on summer Suns ~ Open 10.30-11; 12-10.30 Sun

HAWKLEY SU7429 Map 2
Hawkley Inn ◗

Pococks Lane; village signposted off B3006, first turning left after leaving its junction with A325 in Greatham; OS Sheet 186 map reference 746292

Readers are delighted with this unpretentious pub, tucked away in attractive countryside. The opened-up bar and back dining room have a friendly, relaxed atmosphere and simple, airy decor – big pine tables, a moose head, dried flowers, and prints on the mellowing walls; there's a good mixed bunch of customers. Parts of the bar can get a bit smoky when it's busy, but there is a no-smoking area to the left of the bar. Good, promptly served bar food includes various types of ploughman's (£4.85), baked potato with garlic mushrooms and stilton or goat's cheese or scallops in a tarragon sauce (£5.85), Tunisian fish tart, ham and leek pancakes or tarte provençale (£6.85), beef stew (£8.85), lamb tagine (£8.95), and puddings like fresh fruit crumble or nougat glace (£3.25). Helpings are generous, and service is friendly. Well kept ales from local brewers such as Ballard's, Cheriton Flower Pots or Worldham, as well as Arundel Best Bitter, Hop Back Summer Lightning, Rebellion IPA, Ringwood Buncer on handpump. There are tables and a climbing frame in the pleasant garden behind, and the pub is on the Hangers Way Path. *(Recommended by Derek Harvey-Piper, Ann and Colin Hunt, Lynn Sharpless, Bob Eardley, Philip and Trisha Ferris, Mr Sedgewick, Mr and Mrs Kirkwood, Sue Cubitt, Mike Fitzgerald, J O Jonkler, Martin and Karen Wake, Nigel Norman)*

Free house ~ E N Collins and A Stringer ~ Real ale ~ Meals and snacks (not Sun evening) ~ Restaurant ~ (01730) 827205 ~ Children welcome till 8pm ~ Blues, folk and 60s/70s music ~ Open 12-2.30(3 Sat), 6-11; 12-3, 7-10.30 Sun; closed evening 25 Dec

IBSLEY SU1509 Map 2
Old Beams 🏆

A338 Ringwood—Salisbury

This is very much somewhere to come for a meal, and at lunchtime particularly, the spacious rooms in this popular dining pub are full of customers enjoying the promptly served totally home-made food – they shout your order when it's ready. As well as an appetising cold buffet (from £6.50), there might be sandwiches (from £2.90), curries (£5.30), braised oxtail (£5.90), pork normandie (£7.20), venison in red wine (£7.85), duck with orange or pheasant in port wine (£8.20), and chargrilled Scotch steaks (from £9.50). Well kept Eldridge Pope Royal Oak, Gales HSB, Gibbs Mew Bishops Tipple, Ringwood Best and Old Thumper, Wadworths 6X, and maybe a guest beer on handpump, country wines, foreign bottled beers, and a decent wine list. The main room is divided by wooden panelling and a canopied log-effect gas fire, and there are lots of varnished wooden tables and country-kitchen chairs under the appropriately aged oak beams. The buffet area and conservatory are no smoking – as is half the restaurant. Fruit machine. *(Recommended by Lord Sandhurst, Dr D G Twyman, Richard and Rosemary Hoare, Colin Draper, P J and J E F Caunt, Simon Penny, Klaus and Elizabeth Leist, David N Ing, Chris and Margaret Southon, GWB, A Ellis)*

Free house ~ Licensees R Major and C Newell ~ Real ale ~ Meals and snacks (till 10pm in summer) ~ Restaurant (not Sun evening) ~ (01425) 473387 ~ Children welcome ~ Open 10.30-2.30, 6-11(10.30 in winter); 12-3, 7-10.30 Sun

LANGSTONE SU7105 Map 2
Royal Oak

High Street (marked as cul-de-sac – actually stops short of the pub itself); village is last turn left off A3023 (confusingly called A324 on some signs) before Hayling Island bridge

At high tide, you can reach this charmingly placed pub by boat – landlubbers may be marooned if they don't consult the tide tables. There are seats on the terrace where you can watch the goings-on in the adjacent harbour, and good coastal paths for walking nearby. Inside, the spacious and atmospheric flagstoned bar has windows from which you can see the ancient wadeway to Hayling Island, and simple furnishings like windsor chairs around old wooden tables on the wooden parquet and ancient flagstones, and two winter open fires. Under the new managers, changing bar food includes filled french bread (£2.85), mushroom stroganoff (£5.95), chicken curry (£6.25), beef in ale casserole (£6.95), lots of fresh fish such as good moules marinières (£5.25), fresh sole or crab salad (£7.50), tilapia in Singapore sauce (£9.95), and whole brill (£10.50), and home-made puddings like gooseberry crumble or banoffi pie (£2.85); friendly, obliging service. Well kept Boddingtons, Flowers Original, Gales HSB, Morlands Old Speckled Hen, and Whitbreads Castle Eden on handpump, Bulmer's cider, country wines, decent wines, and cappuccino machine; no noisy piped music or games machines. Morris dancers in summer. *(Recommended by Phyl and Jack Street, A E Brace, A G Drake, D Marsh, Martin and Karen Wake, Ann and Colin Hunt, Chris and Margaret Southon, Ian Jones, Ian Phillips, Lynn Sharpless, Bob Eardley, David Carr, John Sanders)*

Whitbreads ~ Managers Garry and Jan Treacher-Evans ~ Real ale ~ Meals and snacks (snacks available all day) ~ (01705) 483125 ~ Children welcome ~ Folk nights monthly Mon evenings in restaurant area ~ Parking at all close may be very difficult ~ Open 11-11; 12-10.30 Sun

LOCKS HEATH SU5006 Map 2
Jolly Farmer

2½ miles from M27 junction 9; A27 towards Bursledon, left into Locks Rd, at end T-junction right into Warsash Rd then left at hire shop into Fleet End Rd; OS Sheet 196 map reference 509062

Although there is a little drinking area, this thriving white-painted inn with its pretty hanging baskets, is very much a dining pub. The small bar on the right and extensive series of softly lit rooms on the left have nice old scrubbed tables, cushioned oak pews and smaller chairs; their ochre walls and beams are hung with a veritable forest of country bric-a-brac, racing prints, Victorian engravings and so on, making for a very cosy feeling that's amplified by the coal-effect gas fires. The wide choice of quickly served good value bar food includes filled baps (from £2.15, steak £4.65), soup (£3.25), ploughman's (from £3.55), spicy crisped vegetables (£4.60), home-baked ham and eggs or steak and kidney pie (£5.90) and specials such as moules marinières (£5.45), whole plaice or mixed meat salad (£6.55), and ribeye steak (£7.65); one restaurant is no smoking. Well kept Boddingtons, Brakspears Bitter, Flowers Original and Gales HSB on handpump, and country wines; silenced fruit machine, piped music. Neat friendly staff. There are tables under cocktail parasols on two sheltered terraces, one with a play area. *(Recommended by Ann and Colin Hunt, Michael Inskip, John and Chris Simpson, Stephen, Julie and Hayley Brown, C H and P Stride, Phyl and Jack Street, D Maplethorpe, B Helliwell)*

Whitbreads ~ Lease: Martin and Cilla O'Grady ~ Real ale ~ Meals and snacks (till 10pm) ~ Two restaurants ~ (01489) 572500 ~ Children in eating area of bar and in restaurant ~ Open 11-11; 12-10.30 Sun ~ Bedrooms: £36.50S/£48S

MATTINGLEY SU7357 Map 2
Leather Bottle

3 miles from M3, junction 5; in Hook, turn right-and-left on to B3349 Reading Road (former A32)

This brick and tiled pub is a pretty sight in summer with its flowering baskets and tubs, honeysuckle, and virginia creeper, and there are seats in the tree-sheltered garden. The beamed main bar is friendly and relaxed, and has brocaded built-in wall seats, little curved low backed wooden chairs, some sabres on the cream walls, and a ticking metal clock over one of the inglenook fireplaces (both have good winter log fires). At the back is the characterful cottagey second bar with lots of black beams, an antique clock, country pictures on the walls (some stripped to brick), lantern lighting, sturdy inlaid tables with seats, and a red carpet on bare floorboards. Tasty bar food includes sandwiches (from £2.20; toasted ham, mushroom and egg £3.80), soup (£2.50), ploughman's (£4.20), ham off the bone with eggs and chips (£6), vegetable chilli (£6.20), lasagne (£7.20), chicken korma or fish pie (£7.50), minted lamb cutlets (£9.95), steaks (from £12.50), and puddings (from £2.70). Well kept Courage Best and Directors and guest beers such as Brakspears Bitter, Gales HSB, Greene King Abbot, and Wychwood Dogs Bollocks on handpump or tapped from the cask. Prompt friendly service; fruit machine and piped music. *(Recommended by G and M Stewart, Chris and Ann Garnett, D Voller, Ian Phillips, Andy Cunningham, Yvonne Hannaford, Neville Kenyon, KC, Nigel Norman, Henry Winters, Gordon)*

Courage ~ Lease: Richard and Pauline Moore ~ Real ale ~ Meals and snacks (till 10pm) ~ (01734) 326371 ~ Children in eating area of bar ~ Open 11-2.30, 6-11; 12-3, 6.30-10.30 Sun

MICHELDEVER SU5142 Map 2
Dever Arms
Village signposted off A33 N of Winchester

Friendly new tenants have taken over this attractive country pub (now owned by Marstons). The simply decorated bar has beams, heavy tables and good solid seats – a nice cushioned panelled oak settle and a couple of long dark pews as well as wheelback chairs – and a woodburning stove at each end; a no-smoking area with lighter-coloured furniture opens off. As well as the usual bar meals such as sandwiches (from £1.50), home-made soup (£2.50), ploughman's (from £2.95), cottage pie, vegetable lasagne, curries or cod in batter (around £4.50), you can choose from the restaurant menu (and eat it anywhere in the pub): lots of fish such as Portuguese sardines, smoked haddock in cheese sauce, trout in almonds and lemon sole (from £6.95), as well as mushroom stroganoff or vegetable cannelloni (£4.95), supreme of chicken with garlic, cream and wine (£7.95), fillet of lamb with an apple and mint glaze, roast duck with a cranberry and orange sauce or pork medallions with cream and mushrooms (all £8.95), puddings (from £2.60), Sunday roast beef (£5.95), and children's menu (from £2.50); the restaurant is no smoking. Well kept Batemans Mild, Marstons Best, Smooth and Pedigree, and a monthly guest beer on handpump, quite a few malt whiskies, country wines, and decent wines. Darts, pool, cribbage, dominoes, fruit machine, and piped music. There are seats on a small sheltered back terrace, and some more widely spaced picnic tables and a play area on the edge of a big cricket green behind. This is a good starting point for exploring the Dever Valley (there are lots of good walks nearby). *(Recommended by C Sinclair, Ann and Colin Hunt, Mr and Mrs J Ramage, Stephen and Jean Curtis, J L Hall, G Freemantle, A J Stevens, John and Sherry Moate, Phyl and Jack Street; more reports on the new regime, please)*

Marstons ~ Tenants John and Joanne Campbell ~ Real ale ~ Meals and snacks (12-3, 6-10) ~ Restaurant ~ (01962) 774339 ~ Children in eating area of bar and in restaurant ~ Open 12-3, 6(7 Sun)-11

OVINGTON SU5531 Map 2
Bush
Village signposted from A31 on Winchester side of Alresford

Wadworths now own this charming little cottage and have installed friendly new managers. It's in a lovely spot with lots of seats in the garden behind running down to the River Itchen, and more on a tree-sheltered pergola dining terrace with a good-sized fountain pool. Inside, the low-ceilinged bar has a roaring fire on one side with an antique solid fuel stove opposite, as well as cushioned high-backed settles, elm tables with pews and kitchen chairs, and masses of old pictures in heavy gilt frames on the green walls. Bar food now includes sandwiches (from £2.25), home-made soup (£2.95), ploughman's (from £4.25), chilli bake, coriander chicken or spinach and ricotta cheese pancakes (£6.95), sirloin steak (£9.95), and home-made puddings like spotted dick or bread and butter pudding (£3.50). The full range of well kept Wadworths beers plus a guest on handpump. No games machines or piped music. The pub is handy for the A31, and there are nice walks nearby. *(Recommended by Jo and Gary Charlton, Stephen, Julie and Hayley Brown, P R and S A White, Mrs F A W Ricketts, Lady M H Moir; more reports on the new regime, please)*

Wadworths ~ Managers Les and Bunty Morgan ~ Real ale ~ Meals and snacks ~ (01962) 732764 ~ Nearby parking may be difficult ~ Children in eating area of bar, lunchtime only ~ Open 11-2.30, 6-11; closed 25 Dec

OWSLEBURY SU5124 Map 2
Ship
From both the garden areas here, there are fine views: one side looks right across the Solent to the Isle of Wight, the other gives a view down to Winchester; there's a summer marquee, a children's play area and pets corner, and a bouncy castle at weekends. The knocked-through bar has a friendly bustling atmosphere, varnished

black oak 17th-c ship's timbers as beams and wall props, a big central fireplace, and built-in cushioned wall seats with wheelback chairs around wooden tables. From a menu that changes every two weeks, the good food might include sandwiches (from £1.50; toasties from £2.85), soup (£2.50), filled baked potatoes (from £3.15), ploughman's (from £3.45), ham and egg (£4.95), home-made meatloaf (£5.95), vegetarian tagliatelle or lamb livers with red wine and juniper (£6.95), steaks (from £7.50), prawn and asparagus crêpes or poussin with bacon and sage (£8.95), children's meals (£1.95), and puddings. Well kept Batemans Mild, Marstons Best and Pedigree, and a guest beer on handpump, and country wines. There are seats in the garden. *(Recommended by P R White, Lyn Sharpless, Iain Robertson, Michael Inskip, Ann and Colin Hunt)*

Marstons ~ Lease: Clive Mansell ~ Real ale ~ Meals and snacks ~ Children welcome ~ Open 11-3, 6-11; 11-11 summer Sat; 12-10.30 Sun

nr PETERSFIELD SU7423 Map 2
White Horse ★ ◀

Priors Dean – but don't follow Priors Dean signposts: simplest route is from Petersfield, leaving centre on A272 towards Winchester, take right turn at roundabout after level crossing, towards Steep, and keep on for four miles or so, up on to the downs, passing another pub on your right (and not turning off into Steep there); at last, at crossroads signposted East Tisted/Privett, turn right towards East Tisted, then almost at once turn right on to second gravel track (the first just goes into a field); there's no inn sign; alternatively, from A32 5 miles S of Alton, take road by bus lay-by signposted Steep, then, after 1¾ miles, turn off as above – though obviously left this time – at East Tisted/Privett crossroads; OS Sheet 197 coming from Petersfield (Sheet 186 is better the other way), map reference 715290

New licensees moved into this marvellous old farmhouse just as we went to press, and the only firm change planned is the addition of a dining room to be done in the style of an old barn. It will be separate from the two charming and idiosyncratic parlour rooms, which will remain untouched: various old pictures, farm tools, drop-leaf tables, oak settles, rugs, stuffed antelope heads, a longcase clock, and a fireside rocking-chair, and so forth. A fine range of beers on handpump includes the very strong No Name Bitter and Strong, as well as Ballards Best, Bass, Fullers London Pride, Gales Best and HSB, Ringwood Fortyniner, Wadworths 6X and guest beers. Shove-ha'penny, dominoes, cribbage. Bar food now includes soup (£2.50), sandwiches (£2.75), ploughman's or ham and eggs (£4.95), liver and bacon or steak and kidney pie (£4.95), chicken in orange and ginger (£6.95), sirloin steak (£6.95), and puddings such as orange and ginger sponge or apple pie (£2.95). Rustic seats (which include chunks of tree-trunk) and a terrace outside; as this is one of the highest spots in the county it can be quite breezy. If trying to find it for the first time, keep your eyes skinned – not for nothing is this known as the Pub With No Name. Dogs are welcome.
(Recommended by John and Elizabeth Cox, Jo and Gary Charlton, Mrs F A W Ricketts, MCG, Tom Evans, John Beeken, Martin and Karen Wake, AH, CH, James Nunns, Mr and Mrs Vancourt Carlyle-Lyon, Shirley Mackenzie, J Sheldon; more reports on the new regime, please)

Gales ~ Managers Stephen and Lynn Tickner ~ Real ale ~ Meals and snacks (not Sun evening) ~ (01420) 588387 ~ Children in dining room ~ Open 11-2.30(3 Sat), 6-11; 12-3, 7-10.30 Sun

PILLEY SZ3298 Map 2
Fleur de Lys ⊕ ◀

Village signposted off A337 Brockenhurst—Lymington

Originally, this characterful old place was a pair of foresters' cottages, and was established as an inn in 1096 – not surprisingly, this makes it the oldest pub in the New Forest. The attractive lounge bar has heavy low beams, lots of bric-a-brac, a friendly country atmosphere, and a huge inglenook log fire, and in the entrance-way is a list of landlords that goes back to 1498. From a comprehensive menu, good bar food includes soup (£2.65), rich game pâté on a fruit coulis (£3.95), ploughman's (from £3.95), barbecue spare ribs (£4.15; main course £7.25), open sandwiches (£4.45), spinach pancakes or potato and nut cutlets (£6.95), a curry of the day (£6.99), medallions of lamb in rosemary, honey and ginger (£8.99), duck breast in an apricot and cream sauce (£9.95), and daily specials such as rabbit and mushroom steamed pudding (£6.99), baked cod on a light cream wine sauce (£7.25), venison steak in red wine (£9.25) or lobster thermidor (£14.99); in winter, they cook some dishes over the open log fire. The restaurant area is no smoking and there's a heated marquee restaurant which is used both in summer and winter. Well kept Boddingtons, Flowers Original, Marstons Pedigree, Morlands Old Speckled Hen, and Ringwood Old Thumper on handpump or tapped from the cask, good wines, and farm ciders; helpful, courteous service. Seats in the garden with its waterfall and dovecote, and maybe summer weekend barbecues; fine forest and heathland walks nearby. *(Recommended by Terry and Eileen Stott, Colin Fisher, Jack Triplett, J and B Cressey, John and Chris Simpson, John Corless, Phyl and Jack Street, Lyn Sharpless, Bob Eardley, Mrs F A W Ricketts, John and Vivienne Rice, Gwen and Peter Andrews, Meg and Colin Hamilton, Jerry and Alison Oakes, Mrs P McFarlane, Sheila and Norman Davies, M J How, Dr and Mrs A K Clarke, D G King)*

Whitbreads ~ Lease: Craig Smallwood ~ Real ale ~ Meals and snacks ~ Restaurant ~ (01590) 672158 ~ Children in eating area of bar and in restaurant ~ Open 11.30-3, 6-11; 11.30-11 summer Sat; 12-11 summer Sun

PORTSMOUTH SZ6501 Map 2
Still & West

Bath Square; follow A3 and Isle of Wight Ferry signs to Old Portsmouth water's edge

On a sunny day, most people sit outside on the terrace to enjoy the wonderful views as far as the Isle of Wight; but in poor weather you can get just as much enjoyment from the upstairs restaurant, watching the boats and ships fighting the strong tides in the very narrow mouth of Portsmouth harbour. It's a friendly, cheerful place, and the bar is comfortably decorated in nautical style, with ship models, old cable, and even a powder drum, and has very well kept Gales BBB and HSB tapped from the cask, and two guest beers on handpump, along with some aged whiskies and country wines; piped music, fruit machine. Chatty landlord and staff. Bar food (unchanged since last year) includes traditional fish and chips (wrapped in newspaper ready to take away if you want, £3.75), a proper ploughman's (£3.95) and 10 or 15 cheeses from around the world. There's a wider range of meals upstairs, with eight or so fresh fish dishes; part of the dining area is no smoking. The pub is quite near to HMS *Victory*, and can get busy on fine days; the floral displays are splendid. Nearby parking can be difficult. *(Recommended by Amanda and Simon Southwell, David Heath, J Warren, Ann and Colin Hunt, LM, PM, AM, John Fahy, June S Bray, Steve Felstead, Phyl and Jack Street, David Carr, Ann and Colin Hunt, JJB, Peter and Jenny Quine, Peter and Audrey Dowsett)*

Gales ~ Managers Mick and Lynn Finnerty ~ Real ale ~ Meals and snacks ~ Restaurant ~ (01705) 821567 ~ Children in eating area of bar ~ Open 11-11

ROCKBOURNE SU1118 Map 2
Rose & Thistle

Village signposted from B3078 Fordingbridge—Cranborne

This attractive thatched 17th-c pub with its smartly civilised atmosphere is popular for the very good food served in both the bar and restaurant. At lunchtime, this might include home-made soup (£2.60), ploughman's (£4.55), locally-made sausages with onion gravy (£4.65), tagliatelle carbonara (£6.25), steak and kidney pie (£6.45), and specials like broccoli and cheese pancake with almond topping (£3.95), liver and bacon (£6.25), pork and apple casserole with a sage scone (£6.45), and fillet of lemon sole (£7.95), with evening dishes such as smoked duck breast and nut salad (£4.45), veal escalope with a mushroom and marsala sauce or poached salmon with a chive sauce (£8.95), medallions of beef fillet with a stilton cheese and port sauce (£12.45), and grilled dover sole (£15.95); vegetarian dishes (£5.95), puddings like sticky toffee and date pudding (from £3.45), and Sunday lunch roast rare Scotch sirloin of beef (£8.95). Well kept Courage Best, Marstons Pedigree, Ushers seasonal brews,

Wadworths 6X, and Youngers Scotch on handpump, and a good range of wines; friendly service. The public bar has polished tables arranged like booths, carved benches, old engravings, sparkling brass and a good log fire; darts, shove-ha'penny, cribbage, and dominoes. One small area is no smoking. There are tables by a thatched dovecot in the neat front garden. The charming village has the excavated remains of a Roman villa. *(Recommended by M J Dowdy, P J and J E F Caunt, Dr and Mrs A K Clarke, Mark Matthewman, John Le Sage, Howard Allen, J O Jonkler)*

Free house ~ Licensee Tim Norfolk ~ Real ale ~ Meals and snacks ~ Restaurant ~ (01725) 518236 ~ Children welcome till 9pm ~ Open 11-3, 6-11; 12-3, 7-10.30 Sun

ROTHERWICK SU7156 Map 2
Coach & Horses ◀

4 miles from M3, junction 5; follow Newnham signpost from exit roundabout, then Rotherwick signpost, then turn right at Mattingley, Heckfield signpost; village also signposted from B3349 N of Hook

Since last year, this friendly creeper-covered pub has been spruced up inside and out, and a new garden at the back of the building has been opened up; the summer tubs and hanging baskets are pretty. The two small beamed front rooms (one is tiled, the other flagstoned, and one is no smoking) have oak chairs and other interesting furniture, attractive pictures, a stripped brick open fireplace, and a nice, relaxed atmosphere. Good bar food includes filled french bread, home-made soup (£2.50), mushrooms topped with stilton (£3.95), venison sausages (£5.25), tuna, cauliflower and broccoli bake (£6.95), seafood pancake (£7.25), steaks (£8.25), grilled halibut steak (£9.25), and puddings like home-baked apple, pear and cinnamon pie or trifle (from £2.25); three-course Sunday lunch (£9.95). Well kept real ales on handpump at the servery in the parquet-floored inner area include Badger Best, IPA, and Tanglefoot, Gribble Black Adder II and Reg's Tipple, and Wadworths 6X; darts, table skittles, cribbage, dominoes, fruit machine, board games, and piped music. *(Recommended by Francis Johnston, TBB, Mrs P J Pearce, Andy Cunningham, Yvonne Hannaford, Mr and Mrs A J Woolstone, Gordon, Neville Kenyon, KC)*

Badger ~ Manager Colin Sanderson ~ Real ale ~ Meals and snacks (served all day) ~ Restaurant ~ (01256) 762542 ~ Children welcome ~ Open 11-11; 12-10.30 Sun

SOBERTON SU6116 Map 2
White Lion

Village signposted off A32 S of Droxford

The rambling bar on the right in this 16th-c country pub is now more of a bistro with red and white check tablecloths and a no-smoking area, and is popular with customers. The irregularly shaped public bar remains unchanged, with built-in wooden wall seats, and well kept Gales HSB, Morlands Old Speckled Hen, Wadworths 6X, and a beer named after the pub brewed for them by Hampshire Brewery on handpump. Bar food includes filled french bread (£2.95), home-made soup (£2.95), liver and bacon in yorkshire pudding, home-made steak and kidney pie or six different sausages (£5.50), and curry of the day (£5.95). Darts, shove-ha'penny, table skittles, cribbage, dominoes, fruit machine, and piped music. The friendly welsh collie is called Spike and likes to retrieve beer mats. There are very pleasant views from the sheltered garden over the quiet green to the tall trees of the churchyard, and picnic tables and play equipment for children; more seats on a suntrap fairy-lit terrace. *(Recommended by Jo and Gary Charlton, Lynn Sharpless, Bob Eardley, Ann and Colin Hunt, Pete Yearsley)*

Whitbreads ~ Lease: Graham Acres ~ Real ale ~ Snacks (served all day) and meals ~ Restaurant ~ (01489) 877346 ~ Children in eating area of bar and in restaurant ~ Open 11-11; 12-10.30 Sun

---

Pubs in outstandingly attractive surroundings are listed at the back of the book.

SOPLEY SZ1597 Map 2
Woolpack

B3347 N of Christchurch; village signposted off A338 N of Bournemouth

The rambling open-plan bar here has low beams, red leatherette wall seats and simple wooden chairs around heavy rustic tables, a woodburning stove and a small black kitchen range, and a friendly, bustling atmosphere; there's also a conservatory. Good bar food includes lunchtime filled rolls (from £3.50) and ploughman's (£3.95), home-made soup (£2.95), vegetable lasagne (£5.95), steak and kidney pudding (£6.25), generous battered cod, sausage in ale casserole or vegetable bake (£7), chicken in a brandy, cream and shallot sauce (£7.40), baked gammon hock in honey, cider and apricot sauce (£8.70), pan-fried duck in orange and cointreau sauce (£12), and steaks (from £12). Well kept Flowers Original, Ringwood Best and Wadworths 6X on handpump; piped music. The garden has seats from which you can watch the ducks dabbling about on the little chalk stream under the weeping willows, by the little bridge. Please note, they no longer do bedrooms. *(Recommended by Annette and Stephen Marsden, Howard Allen, Andy and Jill Kassube, John Knighton, P A Legon, John and Vivienne Rice, John and Joan Nash, Lynn Sharpless, Bob Eardley, Martyn Carey, J Morris, Joy and Peter Heatherley, Jerry and Alison Oakes)*

Whitbreads ~ Lease: C L and C E Hankins ~ Real ale ~ Meals and snacks ~ (01425) 672252 ~ Children in eating area of bar ~ Pianist some evenings ~ Open 11-11; 12-10.30 Sun

SOUTHSEA SZ6498 Map 2
Wine Vaults ◀

Albert Rd, opp Kings Theatre

As well as their own brewed Spikes Impaled Ale and Stinger on handpump, guest beers here might include Bass, Fullers London Pride, Greene King IPA, Ruddles Best, and Theakstons Old Peculier; Monday evening sees two separate happy hours, and they hold beer festivals in May and November with up to 70 different ales. The simple bar, usually full of students, has wood-panelled walls, a wooden floor, Wild West saloon-type swing doors, and an easy-going, chatty feel; pool, and piped music. Bar food is good value and served in decent sized helpings, with vegetarian dishes like mediterranean vegetables in pitta bread (all priced at £4.25), and meat dishes such as pork in ginger and orange (all £4.95); they also have some Mexican meals (£4.95). Friendly staff. The one-eyed black labrador is called Ziggy; other dogs are welcome. *(Recommended by Tom Evans, Andy and Colin Hunt, J Warren, JJB, JWC, MC, Richard Houghton)*

Own brew ~ Licensees J Stevens and M Huges ~ Real ale ~ Meals and snacks (all day) ~ (01705) 864712 ~ Children in eating area of bar till 9.30pm ~ Open 12-11; 11-11 Sat; 12-10.30 Sun

SPARSHOLT SU4331 Map 2
Plough ♀

Village signposted off A272 a little W of Winchester

Under its friendly new licensee, this attractive, neatly kept and efficiently run pub is doing very well. At lunchtime, the main bar area has a good bustling atmosphere, and is furnished with an interesting mix of wooden tables and chairs, with farm tools, scythes and pitchforks attached to the ceiling; one area is no smoking. Good, popular bar food includes sandwiches, wild mushroom tagliatelle (£5.75), tasty bacon, potato and caramelised onion salad (£5.95), sauté of lamb liver and avocado with a herb crust (£7.25), good salmon and basil tagliatelle, and leg of lamb steak in juniper and gin (£9.25); it might be best to book a table. Well kept Wadworths IPA, 6X, and Summersault on handpump, and a good wine list; piped music. There are tables outside on the lawn. *(Recommended by Patrick Renouf, Gordon, Lynn Sharpless, Bob Eardley, Mrs J A Taylar, John and Joan Calvert)*

Wadworths ~ Tenants R C and K J Crawford ~ Real ale ~ Meals and snacks ~ (01962) 776353 ~ Children in restaurant ~ Open 11-3, 6-10.30(11 Sat); 12-3, 6-10.30 Sun

STEEP SU7425 Map 2
Harrow

Take Midhurst exit from Petersfield bypass, at exit roundabout first left towards Midhurst, then first turning on left opposite garage, and left again at Sheet church; follow over dual carriageway bridge to pub

As charming and unchanging as ever, this old-fashioned place has a lovely relaxed and friendly atmosphere. There are wild flowers on the scrubbed deal tables in the little public bar (and on the tables outside), hops and dried flowers hanging from the beams, built-in wall benches on the tiled floor, stripped pine wallboards, and a good log fire in the big inglenook; cribbage, dominoes. Enormous helpings of good simple home-cooked bar food include home-made scotch eggs (£1.60), sandwiches (from £2.20), excellent soups such as ham, split pea and vegetable (£2.80), huge ploughman's (from £4, some come with home-cooked meats), home-made quiches or ham lasagne (£5.25), and puddings such as delicious treacle tart or seasonal fruit pies (£2.60). Well kept Ballards, Flowers Original, Marstons Pedigree, Ringwood Best, and Wadworths 6X tapped from casks behind the counter, country wines, and Bulmers cider; polite and friendly staff, even when under pressure. The big garden is left free-flowering so that goldfinches can collect thistle seeds from the grass. The Petersfield bypass doesn't intrude on this idyll, though you will need to follow the directions above to find it. No children inside. *(Recommended by Derek Harvey-Piper, M J Hydes, Mrs D M Gray, Lynn Sharpless, Bob Eardley, Ann and Colin Hunt, James Nunns, M J P Martin, MCG, TBB, David Machinek-Tidd, David Carr, Prof A N Black, Wendy Arnold)*

Free house ~ Licensee Mrs McCutcheon ~ Real ale ~ Meals and snacks ~ (01730) 262685 ~ Open 12-2.30, 6-11; 11-3, 6-11 Sat; 12-3, 7-10.30 Sun; closed evening 25 Dec

SWAY SZ2898 Map 2
Hare & Hounds

Sway Rd, Durns Town (just off B3055 SW of Brockenhurst)

This airy and comfortable New Forest local is doing well under its fairly new management, with some nautical touches in the decor, and a casual but lively and bustling atmosphere, particularly in the evenings. However, for people eating its well spaced tables (and good solidly comfortable seats) ensure a relaxed time – and there is a separate restaurant area. The food is generous and home-made, and at lunchtime includes soup (£2.95), sandwiches (from £2.95), filled french bread (from £3.95), and hot dishes such as fish pie, smoked chicken salad, tagliatelle, and popular steak and kidney pie (£6.25); in the evening (when you can still choose from the lunchtime menu), there might be chicken with a wild mushroom sauce, haddock on a bed of spinach with cheese sauce, liver and bacon, and a poached egg or salmon in a cream and fennel bordelaise sauce (all £8.95), leg of duck in plum sauce (£9.95), steak with stilton sauce (£10.50), and puddings such as chocolate terrine, bread and butter pudding and fruit crumble (£3.50); part of the restaurant is no smoking. Well kept Flowers Original, Fullers London Pride, and Ringwood Best on handpump, a decent wine list, and quite a few malt whiskies; friendly helpful service. The friendly dog is called Timmy. There are picnic tables and a children's play frame out in a fairly sizeable neatly kept garden. *(Recommended by Andrew Scarr, Trevor Swindells, David Surridge, Simon Harcourt-Webster, Tim Palmer, David Craig, Dr and Mrs A K Clarke, Jeanne Cross, Paul Silvestri)*

Whitbreads ~ Lease: Liz and Andy Cottingham ~ Real ale ~ Meals and snacks ~ Restaurant ~ (01590) 682404 ~ Live Irish band/acoustic rock and so forth Weds evenings (not July-Sept) ~ Children welcome ~ Open 11-3, 6-11; 11-11 Sat; 12-3, 7-10.30 Sun; closed 25 Dec

TICHBORNE SU5630 Map 2
Tichborne Arms
Village signed off A31 just W of Alresford

When one reader turned up at this reliable country local with 30 friends for lunch during a day's walking, the cheerful landlord and his willing staff coped admirably. On the right, the comfortable, square-panelled room has a log fire in an attractive stone fireplace, pictures and documents on the walls recalling the bizarre Tichborne Case, when a mystery man from Australia claimed fraudulently to be the heir to this estate, wheelback chairs and settles (one very long), and latticed windows with flowery curtains. On the left, a larger and livelier room, partly panelled and also carpeted, has sensibly placed darts, shove-ha'penny, cribbage, dominoes and a fruit machine. Good bar food might include sandwiches (from £1.65; toasties from £2.20), home-made soup (£2.50), liver and bacon nibbles with a home-made dip (£2.75), lots of baked potatoes (from £3.50), ploughman's (from £3.70), daily specials such as paprika pork casserole (£5.50) or home-made fish pie (£5.95), and puddings like home-made raspberry jam sponge, lemon cheesecake or fudge and walnut flan (£2.50). Well kept Flowers IPA and Wadworths 6X tapped from the cask, and country wines; excellent friendly service. There are picnic tables outside in the big well kept garden. Dogs are welcome, but no children or credit cards. *(Recommended by Sheila and Robert Robinson, J S M Sheldon, Philip and Trisha Ferris, Lady M H Moir, Michael Inskip, TBB, Glen and Nola Armstrong, Lynn Sharpless, Bob Eardley, John and Joan Nash, A M Pickup, Mark Percy, Tony and Wendy Hobden, G R Sunderland)*

Free house ~ Licensees Chris and Peter Byron ~ Real ale ~ Meals and snacks (12-1.45, 6.30-9.45) ~ (01962) 733760 ~ Open 11.30-2.30, 6-11; 12-3, 7-10.30 Sun

TITCHFIELD SU5305 Map 2
Fishermans Rest ♀
Mill Lane, Segensworth; off A27 W of Fareham at Titchfield Abbey sign

Although many people come to this clean and comfortably extended dining pub to eat – it's particularly popular with older people at lunchtime – the friendly landlord and his cheerful staff are just as welcoming to those wanting only a drink. This is a fine spot by the River Meon, opposite Titchfield Abbey, and tables out behind overlook the river running along the back. Separate warm cosy rooms including a mellow eating area, and a no-smoking family room lead off the long bar; there are two log fires, light wood furnishings, daily papers, and a good deal of fishing memorabilia including stuffed fish. A wide choice of good food includes cob rolls with chips (from £2.70), filled baked potatoes (from £3.25), fish and chips (£4.95), lasagne (£5.45) and steak and kidney pudding (£6.20). The specials board might offer vegetable pie (£5.20), turkey fricassee or beef, celery and rosemary pie (£6.20), salmon steak with lemon and dill or creamy tarragon sauce (£7.90); puddings like sticky toffee pudding, apple pie or bannoffi pie (from £2.25). Well kept Boddingtons Bitter and Mild, Flowers IPA, Gales HSB, Wadworths 6X and a guest on handpump, and about a dozen decent wines by the glass; cribbage dominoes – no piped music. *(Recommended by Charles and Pauline Stride, Stephen, Julie and Hayley Brown, Ann and Colin Hunt, John and Chris Simpson, A E Green, Michael Inskip, Gwen and Peter Andrews, A N C Hunt)*

Whitbreads ~ Manager Harry Griffiths ~ Real ale ~ Meals and snacks (12-9.30) ~ (01329) 842848 ~ Children welcome in family area ~ Open 11-11; 12-10.30 Sun

UPHAM SU5320 Map 2
Brushmakers Arms
Shoe Lane; village signposted from Winchester—Bishops Waltham downs road, and from B2177 (former A333)

As soon as you enter this neatly attractive old pub you are aware of the notably welcoming and relaxed atmosphere, which makes visitors feel very much at home. The comfortable L-shaped bar, divided into two by a central brick chimney with a woodburning stove in the raised two-way fireplace, has comfortably cushioned wall settles and chairs, a variety of tables including some in country-style stripped wood, a few beams in the low ceiling, and quite a collection of ethnic-looking brushes. Well kept Bass, Fullers London Pride, Gales Best, and a weekly guest beer on handpump, and country wines. Good reasonably priced bar food includes sandwiches, salmon and cream cheese filo pastry parcel (£3.25), cajun spiced chicken breast (£5.95), lamb cutlets in redcurrant sauce (£6.50), and fillet steak in creamy stilton sauce (£9.75); Sunday roasts and occasional themed evenings. Sensibly placed darts, dominoes, and cribbage; the friendly dog is called Rosie. The big garden is well stocked with mature shrubs and trees, and there are picnic tables on a sheltered back terrace among lots of tubs of flowers, with more on the tidy tree-sheltered lawn; Morris dancers occasionally visit in summer. Good walks nearby – though not much parking. *(Recommended by John and Joan Nash, Luke Worthington, Ann and Colin Hunt, Mrs F A W Ricketts, P and S White, Lorraine Cornelius-Brown, Don and Carole Kane, Lynn Sharpless, Bob Eardley, Phyl and Jack Street, John and Chris Simpson, Stephen and Sophie Mazzier)*

Free house ~ Licensees Sue and Andy Cobb ~ Real ale ~ Meals and snacks ~ (01489) 860231 ~ Children welcome away from bar ~ Open 11.30-2.30, 6-11; 11-2.30, 6.30-11 Sat; 12-3, 7-10.30 Sun

WELL SU7646 Map 2
Chequers

5 miles W of Farnham; off A287 via Crondall, or A31 via Froyle and Lower Froyle (easier if longer than via Bentley); from A32 S of Odiham, go via Long Sutton; OS Sheet 186 map reference 761467

Although there's a new licensee and this comfortably civilised pub is now owned by Badger, little seems to have changed – happily. The low-beamed cosy rooms have lots of alcoves, wooden pews, old stools, and GWR carriage lamps, and the panelled walls are hung with 18th-c country-life prints and old sepia photographs of locals enjoying a drink. The original Australian chef is back and the food is very good indeed: home-made soup (£2.75), pumpkin ravioli with parmesan cheese sauce (£4.25), home-made burgers with bacon and brie or moules marinières (£5.25), poached smoked haddock with a poached egg (£5.75), whole cracked crab in blackbean stir-fry (£5.95), braised wild rabbit with tomato and olives or fresh wild boar sausages (£6.50), whole grilled lemon sole with a caper and tomato sauce (£8.95), and puddings like chocolate tart and strawberries, baked ricotta cheesecake or chilled rice pudding and honeyed pears (from £3). In the back garden are some chunky picnic tables, and at the front there's a vine-covered arbour. The pub can get busy at weekends. *(Recommended by TBB, Martin and Karen Wake, Lynn Sharpless, Bob Eardley, Jon and Julie Gibson, Brenda and Derek Savage, Susan and John Douglas, J Sheldon; more reports on the new regime, please)*

Badger ~ Manager T J Bew ~ Meals and snacks (till 10pm) ~ Restaurant (Fri/Sat evenings only) ~ (01256) 862605 ~ Children in eating area of bar only ~ Open 10-3, 6-11; 10-11 summer Sat; 12-10.30 summer Sun

nr WHERWELL SU3839 Map 2
Mayfly ♀

Testcombe (i.e. not in Wherwell itself); A3057 SE of Andover, between B3420 turn-off and Leckford where road crosses River Test; OS Sheet 185 map reference 382390

Delightfully placed beside the River Test with plenty of tables from which to watch the swans, ducks and, if you're lucky, plump trout, this busy place does draw the crowds – though staff seem able to handle huge numbers of people without any fuss. The spacious, beamed and carpeted bar has fishing pictures and bric-a-brac on the cream walls above its dark wood dado, windsor chairs around lots of tables, two woodburning stoves, and bow windows overlooking the water; there's also a conservatory. Bar food from a buffet-style servery (with prices unchanged since last year), includes a wide range of cheeses (around three dozen) or home-made quiche (£3.95), smoked trout (£3.95), chicken tandoori (£6), winter pies, casseroles and so forth, and a good choice of cold meats such as rare topside of beef (£4.20); salads are an extra 70p per spoonful, which can bump up the total cost. You'll usually find queues at busy periods. Well kept Boddingtons, Flowers Original, Wadworths 6X and Whitbreads Castle Eden on handpump, 14 wines by the glass, and country wines; fruit machine and piped music. *(Recommended by Ian Phillips, G C Brown, R Lake, Mrs P J Pearce, Dr D G Twyman, Michael Inskip, Derek Harvey-Piper, Mr and Mrs T A Bryan, Luke Worthington, Jane Warren, Ron Gentry, Lynn Sharpless, Cherry Ann Knott, A J Stevens, John Voos, Sue Demont, Tim Barrow, A R and B E Sayer, Mrs Cynthia Archer, K A Louden)*

Whitbreads ~ Managers Barry and Julie Lane ~ Real ale ~ Meals and snacks (11.30-10) ~ (01264) 860283 ~ Children welcome ~ Open 11-11; 12-10.30 Sun

White Lion

B3420, in village itself

The outside of this unpretentious 17th-c village pub is to be redecorated and new wooden tables and benches added to the courtyard garden. They also plan to open up the lounge and public bar to create a bigger no-smoking dining area, open up a new fireplace, and refurbish the fittings. The multi-level beamed bar will still be decorated with plates on delft shelves, and have fresh flowers and sparkling brass. Cheerfully served by chatty staff, the bar food includes lunchtime sandwiches (not Sunday or bank holidays), filled baked potatoes or ploughman's, and daily specials like chilli bean hotpot (£4.60), pork and peach crumble (£5), chicken supreme with leeks and stilton or lamb liver and bacon casserole (£5.20), steak and mushroom pie (£5.30), and seafood pie (£5.50), with good Sunday roasts (worth booking for these). They hold regular themed evenings, too. Well kept Boddingtons Bitter, Flowers Original, Tetleys, and Whitbreads Castle Eden on handpump; there's a good log fire, and darts, hexagonal pool table, shove-ha'penny, cribbage, dominoes, video game, and juke box. Two friendly dogs and cats. The village is well worth strolling through. *(Recommended by Ann and Colin Hunt, John and Joan Nash, Gordon, James Nunns, A J Stevens, Peter Neate)*

Greenalls ~ Tenants Adrian and Patsy Stent ~ Real ale ~ Meals and snacks (not Sun evening) ~ (01264) 860317 ~ Children in eating area of bar ~ Folk club Thurs evening in back barn ~ Open 10-2.30(3 Sat), 7(6 Weds-Sat)-11; 12-3, 7-10.30 Sun ~ Bedrooms: £22/£36

WINCHESTER SU4829 Map 2
Wykeham Arms ★ ★ 🍽 🛏 �

75 Kingsgate Street (Kingsgate Arch and College Street are now closed to traffic; there is access via Canon Street)

This year, the Saint George, a 16th-c annexe directly across the street (and overlooking Winchester College Chapel) has been added to this tremendously popular and very well run civilised place. There are 6 bedrooms, a sitting room with open fire, a post office/general stores, and a Burgundian wine store; you can enjoy the good breakfasts either in your room or here at the Wykeham Arms. There's always a warm welcome and a feeling that they are glad you came, and a series of busy and stylish rooms radiating from the central bar that are furnished with 19th-c oak desks retired from nearby Winchester College (the inkwells imaginatively filled with fresh flowers), a redundant pew from the same source, kitchen chairs and candlelit deal tables and big windows with swagged paisley curtains; all sorts of interesting collections are dotted around. A snug room at the back, known as the Watchmakers, is decorated with a set of Ronald Searle 'Winespeak' prints, a second one is panelled, and all of them have a log fire; several areas are no smoking. Particularly good food includes good lunchtime sandwiches such as blue cheese, grape and walnut or rare roast beef with horseradish cream (£2.55; toasties £2.95), delicious soups like chunky parsnip and bacon (£2.55), coarse country pork pâté with cumberland sauce (£4.50), continental mixed cheese platter with home-made pickle, ciabatta and multigrain bread (£4.95), daily specials like caramelised onion, red pepper and aubergine tart tatin, smoked haddock and chorizo dauphinoise or warm barbecue chicken salad (£5.25), steak and kidney pie (£5.95), beef in red wine casserole, and puddings such as white chocolate and kumquat bavarois or banana, rum and raisin bread and butter pudding (from £3.95), with evening dishes like steaks (from £10.75), noisettes of monkfish wrapped in bacon and filo pastry, served on a dijon mustard sauce (£11.75), and roast rack of Hampshire Down lamb with an aubergine, onion and sesame tart tatin with rosemary glaze (£12.30); courteous service. There's an excellent seasonally-changing list of wines including around 20 by the glass and quite a few half-bottles, and helpful tasting notes. Also well kept Bass and Eldridge Pope Bitter, Hardy and Royal Oak on handpump, and a number of cognacs and liqueurs. There are tables on a covered back terrace, with more on a small but sheltered lawn. The lovely bedrooms are thoughtfully equipped, and residents have the use of a sauna. No children. *(Recommended by Mike and Sally Serridge, John Beeken, Mrs F A W Ricketts, D H and M C Watkinson, Comus Elliott, A E Green, Ann and Colin Hunt, DJW, M J Dowdy, Francis Johnston, N Matthews, P R and S A White, Karen Eliot, Lynn Sharpless, Bob Eardley, Mrs E A Macdonald, Canon and Mrs M A Bourdeaux, Gregor Macdonald, Colin and Alma Gent, Jim and Maggie Cowell, J L Kelly, Jo and Gary Charlton, Martin and Karen Wake, H L Davis, Ian Phillips, Phyl and Jack Street, A N Hunt, Susan and John Douglas, Pat and Tony Martin, Mr and Mrs T Savage, John and Phyllis Maloney, D Horsman, Malcolm Taylor, Martin and Penny Fletcher, Bob and Maggie Atherton, Mr and Mrs R J Foreman, John and Joan Nash, David Carr; also in Good Hotel Guide)*

Eldridge Pope ~ Lease: Graeme and Anne Jameson ~ Real ale ~ Meals and snacks ~ Restaurant ~ (01962) 853834 ~ If the small car park is full local parking may be difficult – don't be tempted to block up Kingsgate Street itself ~ Open 11-11; 12-10.30 Sun; closed 25 Dec ~ Bedrooms: £69.50B/£79.50B

Lucky Dip

Besides the fully inspected pubs, you might like to try these Lucky Dips recommended to us and described by readers (if you do, please send us reports):

☆ **Alresford** [Broad St; SU5832], *Horse & Groom*: Open-plan bar with rambling nooks and crannies, beams, timbers and some stripped brickwork, nice bow window seats, half a dozen Whitbreads-related ales under light blanket pressure, bar food from sandwiches to steaks, coal-effect gas fire, unobtrusive piped music; children welcome, open all day at least in summer. Useful for a quick half of beer when shopping *(Ann and Colin Hunt, Thomas Nott, John and Joan Nash, Mrs H Murphy, Dr Ian Crichton, MCG, Mr and Mrs R J Foreman, John Sanders, Pete Yearsley, J Sheldon, LYM)*
Alresford [West St], *Bell*: Georgian coaching inn with extended relaxing bar, smallish dining room, quickly served good value food inc children's helpings, well kept Ringwood Best and Old Thumper, good coffee, friendly service, pleasant back courtyard; comfortable bedrooms *(Christopher Warner, P J and J E F Caunt, Ann and Colin Hunt)*

☆ **Alton** [The Butts; S of centre on old Basingstoke rd, by rly line; SU7138], *French Horn*: Welcoming dining pub refurbished in attractive traditional style with inglenook fireplace each end, good value generous-priced straightforward food, obliging prompt service, well kept Ushers, skittle alley; bedroom *(Chris Baldwin, Karen Arnett, Thomas Nott, Phyl and Jack Street)*
Alton [Church St], *Eight Bells*: Simple local with good choice of beers, helpful landlord; children welcome *(Richard Houghton, Ann and Colin Hunt)*

☆ **Ampfield** [off A31 Winchester—Romsey; SU3923], *White Horse*: Comfortably done-up extended open-plan Whitbreads dining pub with reliable reasonably priced food, period-effect furniture, log fire, well kept ales (but served through sparkler), decent wine, welcoming efficient service, Victorian prints and advertising posters in dining room; good play area, pub backs on to golf course and village cricket green; handy for Hillier arboretum *(Stephen Harvey, Andrew and Joan Life, B D Craig)*

Appleshaw [SU3148], *Walnut Tree*: Picturesque low-ceilinged local with attentive staff, comfortable bay-window bar, good affordable food in small green-panelled dining room, nice choice of wines; no piped music *(A J Stevens, Gordon, Mr and Mrs J M Colvill)*

Ashmansworth [SU4157], *Plough*: No-frills pub in attractive village, Hampshire's highest; two rooms knocked together, hard-working friendly landlord, simple home-cooked food with good attentive service, well kept Archers ales and changing guest tapped from the cask; seats outside, good walks *(Phyl and Jack Street, Ann and Colin Hunt)*

☆ **Avon** [B3347 N of Sopley; SZ1498], *New Queen*: Recently refurbished dining pub with different areas and levels, low pitched ceiling, good range of popular reasonably priced food, friendly feel, well kept Badger ales, helpful staff; tables out on spacious covered terrace and lawn; bedrooms *(the Sandy family, David Flagg)*

Axford [SU6043], *Crown*: Badger Best and other real ales, good range of pub food, separate dining area *(David Lamb)*

☆ **Ball Hill** [Hatt Common; leaving Newbury on A343 turn right towards East Woodhay; SU4263], *Furze Bush*: Clean and airy decor, pews and pine tables, wide choice of quickly served generous food, well kept Bass and Marstons Pedigree, seasonal beer festivals, decent wines by the bottle, log fire, pub cat, tables on terrace by good-sized sheltered lawn with fenced play area, restaurant; children welcome, no-smoking area in dining room *(Mrs J Ashdown, Belinda Cox, LYM)*

Bank [signed off A35 S of Lyndhurst; SU2807], *Royal Oak*: Cleanly refurbished New Forest pub, village attractive and untouristy though within outskirts of A35, good choice of food inc real doorstep sandwiches, chilled real ales tapped from the cask; piped music, very busy evenings; goats in garden, lovely spot for walks *(John and Joan Calvert, Frances Pennell, M Joyner, D Marsh, Dr and Mrs A K Clarke)*

Basing [Bartons Lane (attached to Bartons Mill Restaurant), Old Basing; SU6653], *Millstone*: Simply decorated converted mill in lovely spot by River Loddon, decent good value food, Wadworths and other well kept ales tapped from the cask; big garden, handy for ruins of Basing House *(Andy Jones, J S M Sheldon)*

☆ **Beaulieu** [almost opp Palace House; SU3802], *Montagu Arms*: Civilised comfortable hotel in attractive surroundings; separate more basic Wine Press bar, open all day, has simple lunchtime bar food, well kept Whitbreads-related ales, decent wines, lots of malt whiskies, quick friendly service, picnic tables out on front courtyard, piped pop music (maybe loud); children welcome; comfortable bedrooms *(Mr and Mrs R J Foreman, D H and M C Watkinson)*

☆ **Bentley** [A31 Alton—Farnham dual carriageway, a mile E; SU8044], *Bull*: Civilised low-beamed respite from the trunk road, welcoming service, traditional furnishings, lots of interesting pictures, soft lighting, log-effect gas fire, good well presented bar food from sandwiches to fresh fish and seafood, well kept Courage Best, Fullers London Pride and Gales HSB, darts, fruit machine, piped music; children in eating area and restaurant; open all day, tables on side terrace, play area, jazz Sun lunchtime *(James Macrae, HNJ, PEJ, Beryl and Bill Farmer, TBB, Pat Martin, J S M Sheldon, LYM)*

Bentley, *Star*: Small and unpretentious, cheerful and chatty, food prices below average *(HNJ, PEJ)*

☆ **Bighton** [off B3046 in Alresford just N of pond; or off A31 in Bishops Sutton – OS Sheet 185 map ref 615344; SU6134], *Three Horseshoes*: Good simple lunchtime food (not Mon, maybe just sandwiches in summer) in modest village local with open fire in small lounge, police memorabilia (ex-police landlord), well kept Gales HSB, BBB, winter 5X and Prize Old Ale, lots of country wines, friendly family service; children welcome,

geese in garden *(John H L Davis, Jo and Gary Charlton)*

☆ **Bishops Sutton** [former A31 Alresford—Alton; SU6031], *Ship*: Pleasantly relaxed local under good new management, cosy back eating area off main bar, good reasonably priced bar food, Boddingtons, Ruddles and Worthington, attentive staff, restaurant; tables in garden with a couple of thatched parasols, handy for Watercress Line *(Phyl and Jack Street, Ann and Colin Hunt, Christopher Warner, BB)*

Bishops Waltham [Basingwell St; SU5517], *Barleycorn*: Georgian or earlier, pleasant mix of dark oak and cream, Marstons beers, log fire, friendly people, good food inc home-made and children's dishes; garden *(A E Green)*; [Church St], *Bunch of Grapes*: Unspoilt simple two-room village local run by third family generation; well kept Ushers ales, plenty of character *(A and C Hunt, Stephen and Jean Curtis)*

Botley [Botley Rd, nr stn; SU5213], *Railway*: Popular good value generous food, fresh veg, quick cheerful service, well priced Marstons with a guest such as Banks's Mild; large comfortable railway-theme bar, extensive restaurant area *(Phyl and Jack Street, John Sanders)*

☆ **Braishfield** [Newport Lane; SU3725], *Newport*: Particularly well kept Gales HSB, Best and Butser in friendly and unpretentious unmodernised two-bar village local with simple good value food inc huge sandwiches and good value ploughman's, country wines, decent coffee, down-to-earth licensees, weekend singsongs; good summer garden with geese, ducks and chickens *(John and Phyllis Maloney, Lynn Sharpless, Bob Eardley, Ann and Colin Hunt, John and Chris Simpson)*

Braishfield, *Wheatsheaf*: Fine views over meadowland to distant woods from big garden with lots of amusements for children inc field for ball games, decent food, Boddingtons, Flowers and Ringwood Fortyniner, small pleasant dining area, small bar; pleasant walks *(Phyl and Jack Street)*

Bramshill [Heckfield Rd; SU7561], *Hatch Gate*: Recently refurbished, good varied food, pleasant attentive staff; big garden *(Mrs B Gibbons)*

☆ **Bransgore** [Ringwood Rd, off A35 N of Christchurch; SZ1897], *Three Tuns*: Pretty little thatched whitewashed pub, much restored inside with beamery etc; comfortable dining area popular with older people at lunchtime for wide range of food inc vegetarian, good friendly service, well kept Whitbreads-related ales and others such as Ringwood Fortyniner, tasteful bar, fresh flowers, small restaurant; pleasant back garden with play area and open country views, flower-decked front courtyard; bedrooms; *(Mr and Mrs J Jackson, D Marsh, Sue and Mike Todd, W W Burke, John and Vivienne Rice)*

☆ **Bransgore** [Ringwood Rd], *Crown*: Well kept

comfortable Brewers Fayre pub with quick friendly service, vast choice of good value generous food from sandwiches up inc children's and lots of puddings, Whitbreads-related ales, big garden with good play area *(J Hibberd, D Marsh, DWAJ)*

Bransgore [Burley Rd], *Carpenters Arms*: Well kept Eldridge Pope beers and interesting food inc children's and OAP specials, well spaced tables, some in alcoves; good garden with play area *(J Hibberd, D Marsh)*

Breamore [SU1518], *Bat & Ball*: Bustling village pub with locals' corner, two connecting bars, attractive restaurant, real ales, well prepared appetising food; pleasant side garden, Avon fishing and walks, inc lovely ones up by church and stately Breamore House to Breamore Woods and maze *(Phyl and Jack Street)*

Brockenhurst [Lyndhurst Rd; SU2902], *Snakecatcher*: Long narrow lounge bar with decent food from sandwiches to steaks inc good Sat fish specials and children's food, well kept Eldridge Pope ales, good choice of wines by the glass, good service, candles at night; function room doubling as restaurant; tables outside *(K Flack, Mrs J Cowley)*

Brook [SU2714], *Bell*: More hotel than pub, but friendly and comfortable, with well kept Wadworths 6X, good bar lunches, prompt pleasant service, several spacious rooms leading out into big garden; delightful village; bedrooms *(TBB)*

☆ Broughton [opp church; signed off A30 Stockbridge—Salisbury; SU3032], *Tally Ho*: Sympathetically renovated local, big plain modern flagstoned bar with darts (they don't mind walking boots), comfortable hunting-print lounge, unpretentious sensibly priced food inc good sandwiches, homely fires, welcoming landlord, well kept beers tapped from the cask inc those brewed at the Cheriton Flower Pots (it was in the same family as that main entry until summer 1997), decent wines in two glass sizes; tables in pretty garden behind, good walks *(Ann and Colin Hunt, J L Hall, Howard Allen, Phyl and Jack Street, BB)*

Bucklers Hard [SU4000], *Master Builders*: Original core with beams, flagstones and big log fire, attractive when not too crowded, Tetleys-related ales, food from filled baked potatoes up, tables in garden; part of a substantial hotel complex in charming carefully preserved waterside village, good bedrooms *(M Joyner, Peter Innes, Dr and Mrs A K Clarke, LYM)*

Bucks Horn Oak [A325 Farnham—Petersfield; SU8041], *Halfway House*: Good food, well kept beers, big cosy bar with separate restaurant area *(G C Hackemer)*

☆ Burghclere [Harts Lane, off A34 – OS Sheet 174 map ref 462608; SU4660], *Carpenters Arms*: Pleasantly furnished small pub with good country views from attractively laid-out dining conservatory, big helpings of bar food from well presented sandwiches up, well kept Arkells, unobtrusive piped music; garden;

handy for Sandham Memorial Chapel (NT) *(R T and J C Moggridge)*

☆ Burley [on back rd Ringwood—Lymington; SU2003], *Queens Head*: Done-up Tudor pub, some flagstones, beams, timbering and panelling, wide choice of good generous straightforward bar meals, well kept Whitbreads-related ales, maybe piped music; gift/souvenir shop in courtyard – pub and New Forest village can get packed in summer; children welcome *(K Flack, Andy and Jill Kassube, M Joyner, LYM)*

☆ Burley [Bisterne Close, ¾ mile E], *White Buck*: Plushly elegant high-ceilinged pub/restaurant in attractive quiet spot, polite service, good choice of reasonably priced food, friendly service, well kept Ringwood Best and Old Thumper and Wadworths 6X, separate dining room, children's room; dogs allowed, hitching posts, tables on spacious lawn; well equipped bedrooms, nice walks nearby *(Phyl and Jack Street, Sheila and Norman Davies, D Marsh, Jenny and Michael Back)*

☆ Bursledon [Hungerford Bottom; SU4809], *Fox & Hounds*: Chef & Brewer reopened 1997 after costly refurbishment, original pub linked by family conservatory area to ancient back barn with cheerful rustic atmosphere, immense refectory table, lantern-lit side stalls, lots of interesting and authentic farm equipment, wide choice from food bar, well kept Scottish Courage ales and Marstons Pedigree, country wines, roaring log fires; children allowed *(Gill and Mike Grout, LYM)*

Bursledon [Bridge Rd], *Yachtsman*: Good friendly service and wide-ranging choice of good well served food; children welcome *(Mr and Mrs D Price)*

☆ Cadnam [by M27, junction 1; SU2913], *Sir John Barleycorn*: Attractive low-slung long thatched pub dating from 12th c, dim lighting, low beams and timbers, traditional decor, Whitbreads-related ales, big helpings of good value standard food, smiling service, two log fires; can be very busy; suntrap benches in front, eye-catching flowers *(A Y Drummond, Dr and Mrs A Whiteway, Dr and Mrs A K Clarke, C Gilbert, K A Louden, Chris and Margaret Southon, John H L Davies, BB)*

☆ Canterton [Upper Canterton; off A31 W of Cadnam follow Rufus's Stone sign; SU2613], *Sir Walter Tyrell*: Pretty pub by lovely New Forest clearing often with ponies, ideal base for walks; restaurant, wide choice of bar food (could do with more simple snacks), well kept Scottish Courage ales, friendly atmosphere, roomy bar and restaurant; big play area, sheltered terrace *(Dr and Mrs A K Clarke, M Joyner, Eric and June Heley)*

Chawton [SU7037], *Greyfriar*: Good basic village local with low Tudor beams, standing timbers studded with foreign coins, decent reasonably priced food, real ales, good coffee, small garden behind with barbecue; opp Jane Austen's house, good walks *(Phyl and Jack Street)*

Chilbolton [off A3057 S of Andover; SU3939], *Abbots Mitre*: Busy recently refurbished Whitbreads pub with guest beers, big helpings of good food, friendly attentive staff, games room, pleasant terrace with baskets and tubs of flowers; attractive village *(P Gillbe, Mr and Mrs Peter Smith, Stephen Logan)*

Chilworth [A27 Romsey Rd; SU4118], *Clump*: Comfortably extended dining pub, clean and tasteful, with wide choice of good value efficiently served food (popular lunchtime with business people), Whitbreads-related ales served through sparkler, conservatory, tables in sizeable garden; open all day *(Phyl and Jack Street, Clive Gilbert, John and Chris Simpson, Stephen Harvey, D Marsh)*

Clanfield [SD6916], *Hogs Lodge*: Warm and friendly, with good value generous food in bar and restaurant *(Mr and Mrs Treagust, Mr and Mrs Soar)*

Colden Common [B3354; SU4822], *Fishers Pond*: Refurbished Brewers Fayre big enough for coach parties, open all day, smiling waitresses, attentive landlord, decent food inc children's menu; pretty setting by pond with ducks, handy for Marwell Zoo *(Phyl and Jack Street, Ann and Colin Hunt)*

☆ **Crondall** [The Borough; SU7948], *Plume of Feathers*: Interesting if not always freshly cooked food (so may be a wait) in cosy and attractive 17th-c local, well kept Marstons with guest beers such as Morlands Old Speckled Hen and Theakstons, entertaining Irish landlord; two red telephone boxes in garden, picturesque village *(Clive Gilbert, P J Caunt, Miss S E Barnes, J Sheldon)*

Crondall, *Hampshire Arms*: Unpretentious welcoming local, particularly good value food from sandwiches up, well kept Morlands, open fires, traditional games, boules *(KC, Iain Robertson)*

Crookham [The Street; SU7852], *Black Horse*: Friendly beamed village local with sturdy satisfying food, well kept beer, tables out on nice back and side areas with some amusements for children; pleasant Basingstoke Canal towpath walks *(Phyl and Jack Street, Chris and Ann Garnett)*

☆ **Curbridge** [Botley Rd (A3051); SU5211], *Horse & Jockey*: Beautiful setting by River Hamble tidal tributary at start of NT woodland trail, well refurbished with separate dining area; two spotless bars, well presented good value home-made food inc vegetarian and imaginative specials, Gales ales, country wines, cheerful licensees, prompt friendly service; lovely garden with trees and fenced play area *(Ann and Colin Hunt, John and Chris Simpson, John and Joy Winterbottom)*

Curdridge [Curdridge Lane (B3035); just off A334 Wickham—Botley; SU5313], *Cricketers*: Open-plan country pub popular for above-average food inc good specials, nice dining area, banquettes in refurbished lounge area, little-changed public part, welcoming licensee, Marstons ales; quiet piped music,

tables on front lawn *(John and Chris Simpson, Ann and Colin Hunt, Jo and Gary Charlton)*

☆ **Denmead** [Forest Rd, Worlds End; SU6211], *Chairmakers Arms*: Simple roomy country pub surrounded by paddocks and farmland, comfortable bar but most space given over to bays of tables for good value generous food, no-smoking area, well kept Gales BBB, HSB and XXXL, decent wine, quick polite service, log fires; no music, plenty of tables in garden with attractive pergola, nice walks *(HNJ, PEJ, Ann and Colin Hunt, Phyl and Jack Street, LYM)*

Denmead [School Lane, Anthill Common; SU6611], *Fox & Hounds*: Open-plan bar with restaurant off, friendly staff, well kept ales such as Bass, Boddingtons, Fullers London Pride and Marstons Pedigree, decent food *(Ann and Colin Hunt)*

☆ **Dogmersfield** [Pilcot Lane; SU7853], *Queens Head*: 17th-c coaching inn in attractive country setting, concentration on tasty well priced food inc interesting restauranty main dishes (booking advised evenings); friendly atmosphere, well kept ales, good choice of wines, courteous staff *(Andy Cunningham, Yvonne Hannaford, Adrian Greene, G W Stevenson, Mr and Mrs M J Bastin)*

☆ **Downton** [A337; SZ2793], *Royal Oak*: Wide choice of good home cooking inc some imaginative dishes in neat and quiet partly panelled family pub, half no smoking, with well kept Whitbreads-related ales, decent wines, friendly landlady, unobtrusive piped music; huge well kept garden with good play area *(Howard Clutterbuck, J F Cook, W W Burke)*

☆ **Droxford** [Station Rd; SU6018], *Hurdles*: Good generous home cooking, pleasant mature staff, well kept ales; not at all pubby, little room for drinkers; nice tables outside *(John Sanders, Ann and Colin Hunt, Jo and Gary Charlton)*

☆ **Dunbridge** [Barley Hill; SU3126], *Mill Arms*: Friendly and cosy after refurbishment, good well presented food inc fine Sunday beef, four real ales, open fire, conservatory, tables in garden *(Bernadette Williams)*

☆ **Dundridge** [Dundridge Lane; off B3035 towards Droxford, Swanmore, then right towards Bishops Waltham – OS Sheet 185 map ref 579185; SU5718], *Hampshire Bowman*: Good atmosphere, not too smart, in friendly and cosy downland pub with well kept Archers Golden, King & Barnes Festive and Ringwood Best and Fortyniner tapped from the cask, decent house wines, country wines, good straightforward home cooking inc vegetarian, sensible prices, efficient staff; children, dogs and walkers welcome, tables on spacious and attractive lawn, usually some classic cars or vintage motor cycles *(John and Joy Winterbottom, Ann and Colin Hunt, John and Joan Nash, Jo and Gary Charlton, BB)*

☆ **Durley** [Heathen St; Curdridge rd – OS Sheet 185 map ref 516160; SU5116], *Farmers Home*: Good value home-cooked food inc vegetarian, children's and interesting specials, well kept Bass, Boddingtons, Flowers Original and Ringwood Best, decent wine, log fire in small bar, big dining area, relaxed atmosphere, quick friendly service; children welcome, big garden with good play area and pets' corner; pleasant walks *(Brian Mills, Peter and Audrey Dowsett, Ann and Colin Hunt, Mr and Mrs A G Leece, Phyl and Jack Street)*

☆ **Durley** [Durley Street; just off B2177 Bishops Waltham—Winchester; SU5116], *Robin Hood*: Friendly and homely two-bar Marstons pub, log fire, impressive food running up to kangaroo and crocodile, cheerful waitresses; back terrace and pleasant garden with play area overlooking field *(Jo and Gary Charlton, Lynn Sharpless, Ann and Colin Hunt)*

☆ **East Boldre** [SU3700], *Turf Cutters Arms*: Roomy and relaxed dim-lit New Forest pub with good original atmosphere, lots of beams and pictures, elderly furnishings, two log fires, Flowers Original, Wadworths 6X and a guest such as Gales HSB, several dozen malt whiskies, character landlord, friendly service and very enjoyable food – worth waiting for a table; no children, unusual charity coin-collecting device in gents', live jazz first Sun lunchtime of month; tables in garden; three big old-fashioned bedrooms, huge breakfasts *(J V Dadswell, D Marsh, Howard West, M Joyner)*

East Dean [OS Sheet 184 map ref 269267; SU2626], *Old Brewers*: Unusual pavilion-like building with bright and tidy beamed lounge and restaurant, log-effect gas fire as well as central heating, good quickly served well presented home-cooked food, good range of real ales *(Geoffrey and Penny Hughes, Phyl and Jack Street)*

East End [off A343 S of Newbury; SU4161], *Axe & Compasses*: Village pub with welcoming landlord, log fire, Shepherd Neame Spitfire, home-cooked snacks and restaurant food; quiet piped music, pool, darts; pretty village, handy for Highclere Castle *(Peter and Audrey Dowsett)*

East End [the one on back rd Lymington—Beaulieu, parallel to B3054; SZ3697], *East End Arms*: Popular New Forest pub with Ringwood ales tapped from the cask, good value home cooking (may be a wait at busy times), log fire, curious tree trunk in lounge bar, tables in small garden *(Derek and Sylvia Stephenson, Paul Duell)*

☆ **East Meon** [Church St; signed off A272 W of Petersfield, and off A32 in West Meon; SU6822], *George*: Attractive rambling beamy country pub, cosy areas around central bar counter, scrubbed deal tables and horse tack; well kept Badger Tanglefoot, Ballards, Bass, Flowers and Gales HSB, decent wines, substantial straightforward food in bar and restaurant, obliging service, four log fires; children welcome, good outdoor seating arrangements, quiz night Sun; small but comfortable bedrooms, good breakfast; pretty village with fine church, good walks *(Phyl and Jack Street, Ann and Colin Hunt, Martin and Karen Wake, Jo and Gary Charlton, John Sanders, Pete Yearsley, LYM)*

East Meon [High St], *Izaak Walton*: Good fresh food inc vegetarian and children's, attractive prices, pleasant welcome, well kept beers inc an interesting guest, smartly decorated lounge, darts and pool in public bar; children welcome, tables in big garden with unusual rabbits, new side terrace; busy weekends, open all day Sun, quiz night most Weds *(Ann and Colin Hunt)*

East Stratton [SU5439], *Plough*: Simple two-bar pub in attractive village, reasonably priced bar meals, cosy little lounge with adjoining restaurant, basic public bar, friendly service, seats out on grass *(Ann and Colin Hunt)*

Easton [SU5132], *Chestnut Horse*: Comfortable rambling beamed dining pub in lovely sleepy village, wide choice of food, Bass, Charrington IPA, Courage Best, Fullers London Pride, quick friendly service, good log fire, smart prints and decorations; attractive garden behind, good Itchen valley walks *(Lynn Sharpless, Bob Eardley, Phyl and Jack Street)*

☆ **Ellisfield** [Fox Green Lane, Upper Common; SU6345], *Fox*: Comfortable and interesting two-bar village local with well priced food, good choice of beers such as Badger Tanglefoot, Fullers London Pride, Gales HSB, Theakstons Old Peculier and Wadworths 6X, decent wines and country wines, friendly attentive service; restaurant area, pleasant garden *(Jim Reid)*

☆ **Emery Down** [signed off A35 just W of Lyndhurst; SU2808], *New Forest*: Good position in one of the nicest parts of the Forest, with good walks nearby, tables out on three-level back lawn; attractive softly lit open-plan lounge with log fires, Whitbreads-related ales, wide choice of house wines, popular food; children allowed *(Mr and Mrs D J Nash, Dr and Mrs A K Clarke, G W Stevenson, David Holloway, M Joyner, Margaret and Geoffrey Tobin, Alan and Barbara Mence, Lynn Sharpless, Bob Eardley, LYM)*

Emsworth [Ships Quay, South St; SU7406], *Coal Exchange*: Compact Victorian local, cheerful bustle, welcoming young licensees, good lunchtime food, a real fire at each end, well kept Gales and a guest beer *(Steve de Mellow, Percy and Cathy Paine, Tony and Wendy Hobden)*; [High St], *Crown*: Good range of ales, good food and friendly service in bar and restaurant, competitive prices; bedrooms *(R B Gee, Ann and Colin Hunt)*; [Havant Rd], *Kings Arms*: Comfortable friendly local with good generous well priced food cooked by landlady, fresh veg, good choice of wines, good service, Gales and a guest ale; garden behind *(R B Gee, Ann and Colin Hunt, Brian Lock)*; [Queen St], *Lord Raglan*: Welcoming and relaxing little Gales pub with log fire, good range of food esp fish, restaurant (must book summer w/e), live music Sun; children welcome if eating, garden behind nr water *(Ann and Colin Hunt)*

Enborne [W, towards Hamstead Marshall; SU4264], *Craven Arms*: Good varied generous food, friendly atmosphere, well kept Wadworths and guest beers, spacious bars and grounds *(P Slater)*

☆ **Everton** [Old Christchurch Rd, 3 miles W of Lymington; SZ2994], *Crown*: Good cheap food in relaxing traditional bar with log fire (bookable tables), well kept Bass, Ringwood and Whitbreads-related ales, lots of jugs and china, second lively bar with pool, darts, table football, Sky TV and good juke box, welcoming chatty locals and ex-Navy landlord; picnic tables outside, quite handy for New Forest *(SLC)*

Ewshot [off A287; SU8149], *Windmill*: Friendly two-bar pub with well kept Ind Coope Burton and Ushers, popular food inc Sun roast, enormous garden with putting green and Sun lunchtime barbecues *(Chris and Ann Garnett, Tim and Chris Ford)*

☆ **Exton** [signed from A32; SU6120], *Shoe*: Smart facade and decor, brightly refurbished with red carpets and curtains; attractive food inc good vegetarian choice (may find all tables booked for Sun lunch – very popular with older people, and maybe a wait if busy), bar with panelled room off, log fire in cosy restaurant, friendly efficient service, well kept Bass, tables on lawn down to River Meon; pretty village, good walks *(Phyl and Jack Street, Dave Braisted, R Michael Richards, N Smith)*

Faccombe [SU3858], *Jack Russell*: Smart yet comfortably homely bar with lots of pictures, attractive dining conservatory with good interesting food (not cheap), helpful service, tables in lovely garden, nice setting opp village pond by flint church; piped music may be obtrusive; disabled facilities; bedrooms spotless and cheerful, good breakfast, good walks with rewarding views *(HNJ, PEJ, G Gallagher, Phyl and Jack Street, Philip and Trisha Ferris, Douglas Rough, Jayshree Joshi, Ann and Colin Hunt)*

☆ **Fair Oak** [Winchester Rd (A3051); SU4918], *Fox & Hounds*: Busy, comfortable and attractive open-plan family dining pub with exposed brickwork, beam-and-plank ceilings, soft lighting; wide choice of reasonably priced food (all day weekends) in old-world bar and separate modern family area, good polite service, Scottish Courage ales, decent wines; piped music may obtrude; children's play area by car park *(Lynn Sharpless, Bob Eardley, Ann and Colin Hunt)*

Fareham [Lower Quay, Old Gosport Rd; SU5706], *Castle in the Air*: Spacious refurbished open-plan bar with separate raised eating area, big fireplace, Flowers Original and Wadworths 6X, good value bar food inc vegetarian; tables outside, good views over Fareham Creek *(Ann and Colin Hunt)*; [Trinity St], *Cheese & Ale*: Friendly and cheerful, bottles and brass around the walls, sawdust on the floor, Whitbreads-related and good guest beers, cheese with most food, served until quite late; good service, piped music gets louder in evenings when mostly young people; open all day *(A E Green)*; [Porchester Rd (A27), Cams Hill], *Delme Arms*: Comfortable two-bar Victorian pub with well kept Archers Village and Bass, well priced standard bar meals, friendly service; opp splendidly restored Cams Hall *(Ann and Colin Hunt, A E Green)*

☆ **Farnborough** [Rectory Rd, nr Farnborough North stn; SU8753], *Prince of Wales*: Good choice of real ales and whiskies in lively and friendly local with three small connecting rooms, good service, lunchtime food; can get very crowded *(Steve Jones)*

Fleet [High St; SU8054], *Hogshead*: New pub with emphasis on decent range of real ales inc continental beers *(M Owton)*

☆ **Freefolk** [N of B3400; SU4848], *Watership Down*: Cheerful partly brick-floored bar, lounge with lots of tables for popular food with good specials, games area with plenty of old-fashioned slot machines and table football, five well kept ales such as Archers Best, Brakspears PA and Mild and even Bunny Hop, friendly landlord; piped music, Sun quiz night; attractive garden with play area and rabbit pen, pleasant walks *(Rick and Torti Friedberger, Ann and Colin Hunt, Andy Jones)*

☆ **Fritham** [village signed from exit roundabout, M27 junction 1; SU2314], *Royal Oak*: Thatched New Forest pub in same family for 80 years, no concessions to modernity (and you can get the feeling they don't need your custom); well kept Ringwood Best and Fortyniner tapped from the cask, maybe Wadworths 6X, odd assortment of furniture inc high-backed settles, pots and kettles hanging in wide old chimney, log fires – but there is a video game; tables in garden with climbing frame, all sorts of passing animals; no food beyond crisps, nuts, seafood in jars and occasional barbecues, bring your own sandwiches; children in back room *(David Holloway, Howard Allen, PB, Andy and Jill Kassube, LYM)*

Frogham [Abbotswell Rd – OS Sheet 195 map ref 172128; SU1712], *Foresters Arms*: Extensively refurbished New Forest pub under new management, flagstones and small woodburner, Wadworths ales, good food and service, pleasant garden and front verandah; children welcome, good walks *(Phyl and Jack Street, LYM)*

Gosport [Stokes Bay Rd, Alverstoke; SZ6099], *Alverbank House*: Nice setting with Solent and Isle of Wight views, more hotel than pub, but at lunchtime comfortable main bar gets busily pubby, with good choice of food, changing ales such as Banks & Taylors, Cheriton Diggers Gold and Ringwood Best, friendly staff; big garden with play area, bedrooms very well appointed *(Peter and Audrey Dowsett)*; [Queens Rd], *Queens*: Popular real ale pub with five well kept beers, basic food, nice atmosphere, cosy fire, family room, good service; parking may be difficult *(John and Chris Simpson, Ann and Colin Hunt)*

Grayshott [SU8735], *Fox & Pelican*: Large recently refurbished pub with reasonably priced decent food and Gales ales; lively in evening, popular with young people *(Mike Fitzgerald)*

☆ **Griggs Green** [Longmoor Rd; off A3 S of Hindhead – OS Sheet 186 map ref 825317; SU8231], *Deers Hut*: Pleasantly laid out L-shaped bar, welcoming licensees, nice atmosphere, Morlands ales; picnic tables in pretty front garden, attractive woodland setting; touring caravan site behind *(John Sanders, P R White)*

☆ **Hambledon** [West St; SU6414], *Vine*: Friendly beamed pub, traditional and unpretentious, in pretty downland village, good range of beers such as Charles Wells Bombardier, Fullers London Pride, Gales HSB and BBB, Hampshire Hare, country wines, good simple home cooking (not Tues evening) esp fish, welcoming attentive staff, open fire in lounge, old prints, china, ornaments, farm tools, high-backed settles, well in bar; shove-ha'penny, darts *(Ann and Colin Hunt, P R White, John Sanders, Jo and Gary Charlton, Pete Yearsley)*
Hambledon [Broadhalfpenny Down, about 2 miles E towards Clanfield; SU6716], *Bat & Ball*: Extended dining pub opp historic cricket pitch, lovely downs views; good reasonably priced food under new management, well kept Gales, big panelled dining area with lots of cricketing memorabilia, pleasant log fire *(David Heath, LYM)*; [West St], *New Inn*: Simple two-bar village local with Ringwood ales at low prices, pool room with darts, friendly landlord *(Ann and Colin Hunt)*

☆ **Hammer Vale** [Hammer Lane; between A3, A287 and B2131 W of Haslemere; SU8832], *Prince of Wales*: Open-plan country local with particularly well kept Gales ales (full range) and a guest such as Adnams Broadside tapped from the cask, friendly staff, wide choice of generous good value food inc good Sun roasts and some imaginative dishes, log fire; well behaved children allowed, heathland walks *(Mike Fitzgerald, Rev J Hibberd, LYM)*
Hatherden [SU3450], *Hamster*: Pretty thatched coaching inn in isolated spot, rambling and relaxing at lunchtime, with well kept Gales, decent standard food, attractive side restaurant, tables outside with play area in garden; tends to lose its village flavour in the evening, attracting people out from Andover with theme nights, loud piped music, maybe karaoke *(Gordon)*
Havant [South St; SU7106], *Old House At Home*: Fine Tudor two-bar pub, enlarged and much modernised, with low beams, two fireplaces in lounge, well kept Gales BBB and HSB, good choice of bar food inc vegetarian, welcoming licensees; piped music (live Sat), back garden *(Ann and Colin Hunt, LYM)*
Hazeley [B3011 N of H Wintney; SU7459], *Shoulder of Mutton*: Friendly dining pub with

home-cooked food from speciality burgers to good steaks, good vegetarian choice, efficient service, good fire in cosy lounge, no-smoking area, Scottish Courage ales, quiet piped music; attractive building, terrace and garden *(Francis Johnston)*
Headley [Newbury Rd (A339); SU5162], *Harrow*: Friendly little pub nr Greenham Common, good range of real ales *(Dr and Mrs A K Clarke)*

☆ **Heckfield** [B3349 Hook—Reading; SU7260], *New Inn*: Big well run rambling open-plan dining pub with good choice of reliable food, some traditional furniture in original core, two good log fires, well kept ales such as Badger Tanglefoot, Courage Directors, Fullers London Pride, decent wines, unobtrusive piped music; restaurant (not Sun); bedrooms in comfortable and well equipped extension *(Andy Cunningham, Yvonne Hannaford, John Walker, Chris and Ann Garnett, LYM)*

☆ **Highclere** [Hollington Cross, Andover Rd (A343 S); SU4358], *Yew Tree*: Relaxing comfortably plush small dining bar with sensible short choice of good value fresh food, good atmosphere, big inglenook log fire, low beams, friendly efficient service, well kept ales such as Brakspears, Ringwoods Fortyniner, Wadworths 6X, decent wines, some attractive decorations; restaurant; six comfortable bedrooms, good breakfasts *(Steve Hall, Robert and Kim Williams, LYM)*
Highclere [A343], *Red House*: Welcoming spotless lounge with pine furniture, friendly staff and dogs Czar and Murphy, good value food inc children's, Ushers Best and a seasonal ale, relaxing atmosphere, bar with pool; couple of tables out in front *(Jane Wright, Mandy Dancocks)*

☆ **Hill Head** [67 Hill Head Rd; SU5402], *Osborne View*: Modern clifftop pub by Titchfield Haven bird reserve, with good generous bar food inc Sun roasts, well kept Badger Best and Tanglefoot and guest ales, good service and exceptional picture-window Solent views (you need field-glasses to see Osborne House itself); spacious and roomy, though bays of banquette seating keep some privacy; evening restaurant; open all day, good walks *(Phyl and Jack Street, E Cowdray, Eric and June Heley, Ann and Colin Hunt, Michael Inskip, John Sanders)*

☆ **Hook** [London Rd – about a mile E; SU7254], *Crooked Billet*: Smartly refurbished, with lots of tables, wide choice of good attractively presented food all day, swift pleasant service, well kept Scottish Courage ales, homely open fires, good range of soft drinks, early-evening happy hour, soft piped music; attractive streamside garden with ducks; children welcome *(Alan Newman, Eric Locker)*
Horndean [London Rd; SU7013], *Ship & Bell*: Big pub/hotel adjoining Gales brewery, full range of their beers kept well, cosy relaxed local atmosphere in bar with deep well, comfortable snug lounge with steps up to dining room, good staff; bedrooms *(John Sanders, Comus Elliott)*

☆ **Horsebridge** [off A3057 Romsey—Andover, just SW of Kings Somborne; SU3430], *John o' Gaunt*: Friendly village local with simple L-shaped bar, well kept Adnams, Palmers IPA and Ringwood Fortyniner with a guest such as Butts Jester; picnic tables outside, by mill on River Test; very popular with walkers for cheap food (not Tues evening), dogs welcome, no piped music *(Thomas Nott, Ann and Colin Hunt, Sheila and Robert Robinson)*

Hursley [A3090 Winchester—Romsey; SU4225], *Kings Head*: Pleasant open-plan food pub with individual decor, well kept Bass, Charrington IPA and Wadworths 6X, good friendly service, good fresh food, well kept Bass, Charrington IPA and Wadworths 6X; bedrooms *(Thomas Nott, M J Dowdy)*

Hurstbourne Tarrant [A343; SU3853], *George & Dragon*: Low beams and inglenook, separate rooms and eating area, real ales inc Greene King IPA and Wadworths 6X, friendly welcome, good straightforward food; bedrooms, attractive village; *(Ann and Colin Hunt, Prof A N Black, LYM)*

☆ **Itchen Abbas** [4 miles from M3 junction 9; A34 towards Newbury, fork right on A33, first right on B3047; SU5333], *Trout*: Smallish country pub with discreet partly no-smoking lounge bar, chatty public bar with darts and bar billiards, well kept Marstons Bitter and Pedigree, decent wines, good value changing bar food inc some interesting hot dishes, friendly service, restaurant; pretty side garden with good play area; roomy comfortable bedrooms, good breakfast *(Michael Bird, Colin and Joyce Laffan, C and E M Watson, LYM)*

☆ **Keyhaven** [SZ3091], *Gun*: 17th-c nautical-theme beamed pub overlooking boatyard, popular at lunchtime particularly with older people for wide choice of generous bar food, well kept Whitbreads-related ales; garden with swings and fishpond; children welcome *(Graham and Karen Oddey, D Marsh)*

Kings Somborne [Romsey Rd; SU3631], *Crown*: Long low pub opp village church and school, several cosy rooms off, good value generous food, pleasant service; smallish back garden with play area, Test Way and Clarendon Way footpaths nearby *(Phyl and Jack Street)*

☆ **Kings Worthy** [A3090 E of Winchester, just off A33; SU4933], *Cart & Horses*: Well run Marstons Tavern Table family dining pub with softly lit alcoves, lots of well spaced tables, conservatory, home-cooked food from sandwiches up, well kept beer, sensible prices, good service, tables in pleasant garden with marvellous play houses *(Graham and Karen Oddey, P R and S A White, LYM)*

☆ **Langstone** [A3023; SU7105], *Ship*: Waterside pub with lovely view from roomy pleasantly decorated bar and upstairs restaurant, plenty of space, good generous food esp fish cooked within sight, fast friendly service, well kept Gales, country wines, log fire; children's room, seats out on quiet quay, long opening hours *(John Sanders, Alan Skull, John and Chris Simpson, Francis Bugg, D Marsh)*

☆ **Lasham** [SU6742], *Royal Oak*: Friendly and comfortable country pub, well kept Hampshire King Alfred and Ringwood Best with interesting guest beers, good generous home cooking inc vegetarian, log fire, quiet piped music, friendly cat; tables in pleasant garden, attractive village nr gliding centre *(H L Davis, Ann and Colin Hunt, Bruce Bird)*

Lee on the Solent [Crofton Ave/Sea Lane, off Stubbington Lane; SU5600], *Swordfish*: Big comfortable pub notable for outstanding position with Solent views; big family room, usual pub food, Scottish Courage ales *(A E Green)*

☆ **Linwood** [signed from A338 via Moyles Court, and from A31; keep on – OS Sheet 195 map ref 196107; SU1910], *High Corner*: Big rambling pub very popular for its splendid New Forest position, with extensive neatly kept lawn and sizeable play area; some character in original upper bar, lots of back extension for the summer crowds, food from sandwiches to steaks inc Sun carvery (nicely partitioned restaurant open all day Sun), Whitbreads-related and other ales such as Hampshire King Arthur, decent wine, no-smoking verandah lounge; children and dogs welcome in some parts, open all day Sat; bedrooms *(M Joyner, John and Vivienne Rice, K Flack, Margaret and Geoffrey Tobin, M J Dowdy, LYM)*

☆ **Linwood** [up on heath – OS Sheet 195 map ref 186094; SU1909], *Red Shoot*: Very touristy in summer (by big caravan park), with lots of room for families, some attractive old furniture and rugs on the floorboards, generous decent food inc good sandwiches, well kept Wadworths IPA, 6X and Morrells Varsity, friendly staff, nice New Forest setting, plenty of dogs *(Jo and Gary Charlton, John and Vivienne Rice)*

Liss [Farnham Rd (A325), West Liss; SU7728], *Blue Bell*: Major refurbishments under new licensee, good interesting food from bar snacks to genuinely French main dishes, good wine list *(C L Kauffmann)*

☆ **Longparish** [B3048 off A303 just E of Andover; SU4344], *Plough*: Huge range of food from sandwiches (they come with chips here) to fresh fish in open-plan dining bar divided by arches; Boddingtons, Flowers Original, Hampshire King Alfreds and Wadworths 6X, decent wines and country wines, efficient waitress service; children in eating area, restaurant, piped music, SkyTV, tables on side terrace, pleasant garden with occasional barbecues – pub on Test Way for lovely riverside walks; bedrooms *(Carol and Brian Perrin, Mr and Mrs D S Price, Jenny and Michael Bade, John Evans, Stephen Brown, Phyl and Jack Street, Lynn Sharpless, Bob Eardley, LYM)*

Longparish, *Cricketers*: Small two-bar village local with lots of games, well kept Marstons beers; good garden *(Dr and Mrs A K Clarke)*

☆ **Longstock** [SU3536], *Peat Spade*: Good new licensees – ex Plough at Sparsholt – in airy dining pub, good food inc some interesting dishes, decent wines; small pleasant garden, handy for Test Way long-distance path, and Danebury hill fort *(Views please)*

☆ **Lower Froyle** [signed off A31; SU7643], *Anchor*: Well run, warm and attractive brightly lit pub with wide range of good value food inc sandwiches and fish, cheerful informal service, well kept ales; well in one of the two connecting bars, restaurant; piped music; seats outside *(KC, G and M Stewart, R B Crail, GSS)*

Lower Upham [B2177 Winchester—Bishops Waltham; SU5219], *Woodman*: Busy little family-run two-bar pub, attractive in summer with hanging baskets; Marstons ales, play area *(Ann and Colin Hunt)*

☆ **Lower Wield** [SU6340], *Yew Tree*: Reliably good value dining pub opp cricket pitch, kept spotless, with good choice (not Sun) from soup to steaks, salmon and bass, can eat in dining room or bar; cheerful and friendly, with well kept Marstons Pedigree, fresh flowers; has been cl Mon *(A J Stevens, P and J Ferris)*

☆ **Lymington** [Ridgeway Lane, Lower Woodside, marked as dead end just S of A337 roundabout in Pennington W of Lymington, by White Hart; SZ3294], *Chequers*: Simple but stylish yachtsmen's local with polished boards and quarry-tiles, attractive pictures, plain chairs and wall pews; good range of good reasonably priced food from lunchtime filled french sticks to duck, steak and fresh fish, inc vegetarian, well kept Marstons Pedigree and Wadworths 6X, good wines, fine rums; friendly service, well if not quietly reproduced piped pop music, traditional games, tables in neat garden with terrace; well behaved children allowed *(G W Stevenson, Mr and Mrs A Marsh, James Flory, Mrs F A W Ricketts, VB, D Marsh, LYM)*

☆ **Lymington** [108 High St], *Angel*: Popular but roomy and peaceful dark-decor modernised bar with largely home-made bar food, three well kept Eldridge Pope ales, neat young staff, open all day; tables in attractive inner courtyard, bedrooms *(SLC, D Marsh, Dr and Mrs A K Clarke, LYM)*

Lymington [Station St], *Bosuns Chair*: Yachty pub recently refurbished in restrained current style, light and airy high-ceilinged rooms, food inc fish cooked plainly or with options, well kept Wadworths ales; bedrooms *(Thomas Nott)*; [Captains Row], *Captains*: Ushers pub nr centre and quay, very friendly dog, tasty good value food, quiet piped music *(Mrs V Brown)*; *Fishermens Rest*: New licensees doing well, wide choice of interesting reasonably priced food, well kept beers *(Mr and Mrs A Marsh)*; [The Quay], *Ship*: Waterfront Brewers Fayre family food pub, spacious and well decorated, with some flagstones, open all day from breakfast on, good value usual food, Whitbreads-related ales, some seating outside with boating views

(Audrey and Peter Reeves, SLC, Hugh Spottiswoode)

Lyndhurst [Clay Hill (A337 ½ mile S); SU3007], *Crown Stirrup*: 17th-c or older, extensive but cosy bar with two low-ceilinged rooms, nicely prepared food inc unusual dishes, well kept Boddingtons and Wadworths 6X, good friendly service, log fire; children welcome, covered back terrace, pleasant garden with play area and gate to Forest *(M Joyner, Phyl and Jack Street)*; [22 High St], *Fox & Hounds*: Big cheery much modernised dining pub with lots of exposed brickwork, standing timbers as divisions, family room beyond former coach entry, games room with pool, darts etc, welcoming staff, Whitbreads-related and local guest ales, usual food from good ploughman's and brunch to steaks *(B and K Hypher, Simon Penny)*

Mapledurwell [Tunworth Rd, off A30 Hook—Basingstoke; SU6851], *Gamekeepers*: Interesting old bar with well kept Badger Best, farm cider, good value wines, friendly smart staff, good value food from sandwiches to steak – opens into bigger upmarket restaurant; piped music; in lovely thatched village with duckpond *(Roger Byrne)*

☆ **Marchwood** [off A326; SU3810], *Pilgrim*: Immaculately sprightly decor in smart and attractive thatched pub with well kept Bass and Courage, wide choice of well prepared food, welcoming service, open fire; can be crowded, handy for Longdown Dairy Farm and Nature Quest; neat garden *(Dr and Mrs A K Clarke, Stephen Harvey, Phyl and Jack Street, Steve Colley, BB)*

Meonstoke [SU6119], *Bucks Head*: Dark red banquettes and good log fire in popular dining lounge, well kept Bass and Morlands Old Speckled Hen, country wines, good value substantial bar food, friendly service, comfortable public bar, log fire; pleasant walled garden, lovely village setting with ducks on pretty little River Meon, good walks *(Lynn Sharpless, Bob Eardley, Ann and Colin Hunt, Phyl and Jack Street)*

Milford on Sea [High St; SZ2891], *Smugglers*: Big cheery pub well geared for holiday crowds, good value well presented generous food, Whitbreads-related ales, children welcome; side play area with boat to play on *(P Gillbe, A E Brace)*; [Keyhaven Rd], *White Horse*: Eight consistently well kept real ales and wide choice of reasonably priced food in very well run village inn with sheltered garden; very popular midweek with older people *(Maurice Southon)*

☆ **Minstead** [just off A31 nr M21 junction 1; SU2811], *Trusty Servant*: In pretty New Forest village with wandering ponies; small bare-boards public bar, unsophisticated back lounge (also small), wide choice of good fresh fish and other bar food inc enormous sandwiches, well kept changing ales such as Hook Norton Best, Hop Back Summer Lightning, Smiles Best and Wadworths 6X, country wines; sizeable attractive restaurant, airy by day, candlelit by night; piped music may be loud, and rather a take-us-as-you-find-us feel; comfortable bedrooms *(W Wonham, Ann and Colin Hunt, K A Louden, D Marsh, BB)*

☆ **Mortimer West End** [Silchester turn off Mortimer—Aldermaston rd; SU6363], *Red Lion*: Welcoming country dining pub with lots of beams, stripped masonry, timbers and panelling, good range of Badger and other well kept ales, good log fire; quiet piped music; plenty of seats outside, inc small flower-filled front terrace *(Pat and Robert Watt, Gordon, LYM)*

Nether Wallop [signed off A30 or B2084 W of Stockbridge; SU3036], *Five Bells*: Simple village pub with long cushioned settles and good log fire in beamed bar (one end serving as local post office), cheap bar food, well kept Marstons, bar billiards and other traditional games in locals' bar, small restaurant, seats outside, provision for children *(Ann and Colin Hunt, LYM)*

Netley Marsh [A336; 2 miles from M27 junction 1; SU3313], *White Horse*: Attractive sympathetically refurbished village local on edge of New Forest, good range of real ales, standard choice of good reasonably priced bar food; interest in steam traction engines *(Dr and Mrs A K Clarke)*

☆ **North Gorley** [Ringwood Rd, just off A338; SU1611], *Royal Oak*: Recently refurbished 17th-c thatched pub, comfortable and welcoming, with beam and plank ceiling, flagstones, panelled dado, generous reasonably priced usual food from sandwiches to steaks inc children's dishes, well kept Fullers London Pride, Wadworths 6X and Whitbreads Best, open fire, friendly young staff; children in family room, big well kept garden with swings and climber, idyllic New Forest setting nr pond *(Chris and Margaret Southon, D Marsh, N B Thompson, John and Vivienne Rice, P Gillbe)*

☆ **North Warnborough** [nr M3 junction 5; SU7351], *Swan*: Friendly village pub with good choice of well priced good food, well kept Courage Best, Marstons Pedigree, Wadsworth 6X *(A E Brace)*

Oakhanger [off A325 Farnham—Petersfield; SU7635], *Red Lion*: Unpretentious and well worn in, with well kept Courage and a guest ale such as Worldham Old Dray, good food esp seafood, big log fire, friendly staff *(Mike Fitzgerald)*

☆ **Odiham** [High St (A287); SU7450], *George*: Civilised old-fashioned market-town hotel with well kept Scottish Courage ales, decent wines by the glass, good value bar food from rare beef sandwiches up, welcoming attentive staff, interesting old photographs, fish restaurant; comfortable little back locals' bar overlooking garden, soundproofed bedrooms, with some in annex *(Martin and Karen Wake, Francis Johnston, Christine and Geoff Butler, Mike Fothergill, J Sheldon, B J P Edwards, Clive Gilbert, BB)*

☆ **Petersfield** [College St; SU7423], *Good Intent*:

Friendly welcoming service, Gales IPA, BBB, HSB and Gold, good generous home-cooked food changing daily, reasonable prices, willingness to vary dishes for individual preferences; children in cosy former restaurant area *(A J Blacker, C A Stanbridge)*

☆ **nr Petersfield** [old coach rd NW past Steep – OS Sheet 186 map ref 726273], *Trooper*: Well kept Bass, Ringwood and guest beers such as Wadworths, interesting good value wines, decent straightforward bar food inc good evening steaks, friendly service, candlelight, scrubbed pine tables and bare boards, good views *(WA)*

Portchester [next to Portchester Castle; SU6204], *Cormorant*: Whitbreads pub in pleasant close handy for the castle and views over Portsmouth harbour, reasonably priced plentiful food all day, attentive courteous staff, children in dining area; seats outside, plenty of parking *(David Dimock, Phyl and Jack Street)*

☆ **Portsmouth** [Bath Sq, Old Town; SU6501], *Spice Island*: Roomy modernised waterside Whitbreads pub with seafaring theme, big windows and outside seats overlooking passing ships, well kept ales, food all day inc vegetarian, family room (one of the few in Portsmouth), bright upstairs restaurant; can be very crowded, and as with other pubs here nearby parking may be difficult *(Richie Berryman, David Carr)*

☆ **Portsmouth** [High St, Old Town], *Dolphin*: Spacious and genteel old timber-framed pub with ten or more Whitbreads-related and other ales, wide range of food, good log fire, cosy snug; video games; open all day Sat, children welcome in eating area, small terrace *(Chris and Ann Garnett, JJB, Andy and Jill Kassube)*

Portsmouth [opp Guildhall], *Fleet & Firkin*: Naval memorabilia in roomy two-floor pub with friendly staff, wide choice of real ales, simple bar food *(Ann and Colin Hunt)*; [Portsdown Hill Rd, Widley; SU6706], *George*: Unspoilt Georgian pub handy for Portsdown Hill nature reserve, wonderful views of Hayling Island, Portsmouth, Southsea and Isle of Wight from terrace; mainly a local, with home-cooked specials, Whitbreads-related and Marstons ales, friendly new tenants *(A E Green)*; [Queen St, nr dockyard entrance], *George*: Small, cosy and and restful, partly 18th-c, with beams, timbers, brass and copperware, well in bar, friendly staff and locals inc Marstons Pedigree, Theakstons, Wadworths 6X and Youngers No 3, good choice of wines, good reasonably priced food, pleasant new restaurant; children over 5 allowed in no-smoking lounge *(Chris and Ann Garnett, Ann and Colin Hunt)*; [Surrey St], *Hogshead & Bucket*: Roomy pub with 10 real ales, usual food, polite service, no-smoking area, comfortable lounge, nice mirrors, old prints and mixed furniture *(Ann and Colin Hunt)*; [Highland Rd, Eastney; SU6899], *Mayflower Beer Engine*: Fairly smart two-bar pub with old pictures and stone jars etc, well kept Tetleys and other ales, simple bar food, friendly new licensee, black cat; darts, juke box, garden *(Ann and Colin Hunt)*; [High St, Old Town], *Sally Port*: Spick-and-span, brightly modernised but still interesting, with reasonably priced bar food esp fish, well kept Marstons, upstairs restaurant; comfortable bedrooms *(David Carr, Robert and Gladys Flux)*; [London Rd, North End; SU6503], *Tap*: Free house with ten or more changing well kept ales, thriving atmosphere, genuine service, straightforward weekday bar food inc king-sized sandwiches *(Ann and Colin Hunt)*; [opp Guildhall], *Wetherspoons*: Roomy new pub with smart decor, simple bar food, good choice of ales, sensible prices *(Ann and Colin Hunt)*

☆ **Preston Candover** [Arlesford Rd; SU6041], *Purefoy Arms*: Straightforward village pub with good range of generous food inc speciality topped garlic breads, interesting salads, vegetarian dishes, friendly enthusiastic licensees, Ushers and Courage ales, games in public bar; get there early for live jazz Thurs and first Sun in month; big peaceful garden with play area overlooking fields, nearby snowdrop walks, open all day Sun *(Gill and Mike Grout, John Evans, Ann and Colin Hunt, Alasdair Pountain)*

☆ **Ringwood** [The Bridges, West St, just W of town; SU1505], *Fish*: Several quiet and cosy areas (some away from bar perhaps a bit dark), intriguing fishy decorations, well kept Boddingtons, Brakspears, Flowers and Fullers ales such as London Pride, coffee and tea, wide choice of good value generous food maybe inc bargains, log fire, friendly if not always speedy service, no-smoking eating area allowing children, no dogs; tables on riverside lawn with play area and budgerigar aviary, open all day *(Annette and Stephen Marsden, Nick Wikeley, DC, J Sheldon, A Pring, LYM)*

Ringwood [12 Meeting House Lane], *Inn on the Furlong*: Several rooms, flagstones, stripped brick and oak timbering, conservatory restaurant; full range of Ringwood beers kept well, good value lunchtime bar food; live music some nights, Easter beer festival *(Bruce Bird)*; [Mkt Sq], *White Hart*: Venerable pub, lots of panelling, big log fire, comfortable atmosphere, helpful friendly staff, food inc good home-made specials and Sun roasts, Bass and Eldridge Pope Thomas Hardy, lunchtime no-smoking area *(T A and B J Bryan, Bruce Bird)*

☆ **Rockford** [OS Sheet 195 map ref 160081; SU1608], *Alice Lisle*: Friendly and pleasant open-plan pub attractively placed on green by New Forest, generous helpings of good food inc sandwiches, some interesting dishes and sensible children's menu, big conservatory-style family eating area, well kept Gales and guest beers, country wines, helpful staff, baby-changing facilities; garden with extensive play area, peacock and other birds, ponies wander nearby; handy for Moyles Court *(Rev John Hibberd, BB)*

☆ **Romsey** [23 Mainstone; SU3521], *Old Horse & Jockey*: Recently opened but already very popular for the reasonably priced good food that is its main attraction; under same management as White Hart at Cadnam – see main entries *(J L Kelly)*

Romsey [Love Lane], *Old House At Home*: Nice-looking 16th-c thatched pub with long-serving licensee and basic old-fashioned decor; decent food inc good ploughman's *(Mr and Mrs R J Foreman, J Reay)*; [Middlebridge St], *Three Tuns*: Comfortable atmosphere, good reasonably priced generous food, pleasant landlord *(A R Nuttall, Shirley Pielou)*; [bypass, 300 yds from entrance to Broadlands], *Three Tuns*: Roomy but cosy, two bars with old beams and good log fires, well kept Bass, Flowers, Ringwood, Wadworths 6X, generous well presented reasonably priced home-made food from good baguettes up, friendly efficient service, afternoon teas, pleasant terrace *(Phyl and Jack Street, Mr and Mrs D J Ross)*

nr **Romsey** [Greatbridge (A3057 towards Stockbridge); SU3422], *Dukes Head*: Attractive dining pub festooned with flowering baskets in summer; smart efficient waitresses, Whitbreads-related ales, decent house wines, inglenook eating places, no piped music, charming back garden wth old tractor and rabbits *(Lynn Sharpless, Bob Eardley, Ian Phillips, Brian Mills)*

☆ **Rotherwick** [The Street; SU7156], *Falcon*: Welcoming and lively country local with well kept ales such as Brakspears PA, Marstons Pedigree, Morrells Varsity, Wadworths 6X and a couple of guests chosen after six-monthly tastings, good food inc Tex/Mex and Sun roasts, open fire, smartish public bar with darts, bar billiards, TV, smaller lounge; children welcome, big garden *(Simon Collett-Jones, Tracy Conway, John Rawlings)*

Rowlands Castle [Finchdean Rd; SU7310], *Castle*: Enjoyable village pub, good range of food, perfectly kept Gales beers, friendly efficient young staff; children and dogs welcome, garden *(Comus Elliott, Nigel and Diana Littler)*

Selborne [SU7433], *Queens*: Unpretentious village pub with interesting local memorabilia, well kept Ushers, good value standard food inc children's, open fires; children welcome, occasional jazz; bedrooms, very handy for Gilbert White's home *(Thomas Nott, J S M Sheldon, Jo and Gary Charlton, LYM)*

☆ **Setley** [A337 Brockenhurst—Lymington; SU3000], *Filly*: Relaxing and comfortable, with two contrasting attractive bars, interesting choice of generous well presented food inc vegetarian, well kept Bass, Ringwood Old Thumper and Wadworths 6X, decent wines, friendly landlord, quick service – very popular with older people (and children) lunchtime; piped music; some tables outside, New Forest walks *(Dr and Mrs A K Clarke, LYM)*

☆ **Sherfield on Loddon** [off A33 NE of

Basingstoke; SU6857], *White Hart*: Neatly refurbished, with thriving atmosphere, wide choice of generous fresh food from good bacon sandwiches up (can be a wait if busy), huge inglenook fireplace, friendly efficient service, well kept Courage and guest ales, good choice of wines, interesting coaching-era relics, tables outside; soft piped music; handy for The Vyne *(D Voller, LYM)*

Soberton Heath [Forester Rd; SU6014], *Bold Forester*: Friendly new licensees in country pub with well kept Adnams Broadside and Morlands, plentiful straightforward food; good outside seating area, fenced play area, field for camping behind, good walks nearby, dogs welcome *(Jo and Gary Charlton)*

Southampton [Bellemoor Rd (A35); SU4212], *Bellemoor*: Open-plan, with reasonably priced good food, friendly staff and well kept Theakstons Best and Old Peculier, log fire; boules *(Mike Fitzgerald)*; [Osborne Rd, opp St Denys Stn], *Dolphin*: Done out well in basic bare-boards style with three roaring coal fires, big tables, interesting photographs; six interesting changing ales, welcoming staff, enterprising reasonably priced food from hot sandwiches to Sun lunch inc vegetarian, no-smoking area; live mainly Irish music Weds, barbecues Mon *(Ian Phillips, J Warren)*; [36 Bugle St], *Duke of Wellington*: Ancient timber-framed building on 13th-c foundations, bare boards, log fire, relaxed atmosphere, good range of beers, decent standard food; very handy for Tudor House Museum *(B and K Hypher, S and J Curtis, Fiona Ricketts)*; [55 High St, off inner ring rd], *Red Lion*: Interesting for its lofty galleried hall, genuinely medieval, with armour and Tudor panelling; open all day, Scottish Courage ales, cheap snacks *(S and J Curtis, LYM)*; [38 Adelaide Rd, by St Denys stn], *South Western Arms*: A dozen or so real ales inc Badger and Gales, enthusiastic staff, basic food, bare board's exposed brickwork, toby jugs and stag's head on beams, lots of woodwork, beermats on ceiling, upper gallery where children allowed; popular with students, easy-going atmosphere; picnic tables on terrace, live jazz Sun afternoon *(M Owton, Jane Warren)*; [Above Bar], *Square Balloon*: Shoppers and business people lunchtime, young people later evening, in vast pub recently converted from ABC cinema, three different levels, good decor, wide range of drinks, interesting (though not extensive) choice of food, attractive range of coffees; enormous balloon over the circular bar, no trainers allowed *(Sarah Jones, Phyl and Jack Street)*; [20 High St], *Standing Order*: Reliable Wetherspoons pub with no-smoking area, good choice of well presented good value food, good range of beers inc changing guests, popular bargain Sun lunch *(John and Chris Simpson)*

☆ **Southsea** [15 Eldon St/Norfolk St; SZ6498], *Eldon Arms*: Big comfortable rambling bar with old pictures and advertisements, attractive mirrors, lots of nick-nacks; half a

dozen Eldridge Pope and other changing well kept ales, decent wines, good changing range of promptly served food, sensibly placed darts; pool and fruit machine, restaurant, tables in back garden *(Stephen and Judy Parish, Ann and Colin Hunt)*

Southsea [Victoria St], *Fuzz & Firkin*: Usual bare boards and solid furnishings, friendly staff, good beer brewed at the pub, nice atmosphere; loud music and lots of young people Sat night *(Richard Houghton, Ann and Colin Hunt)*; [Osborne Rd], *Osborne*: Reasonably priced food in L-shaped bare-bricks bar, real ales inc Courage Directors, Flowers Original and Gales HSB *(Ann and Colin Hunt)*

Southwick [just off B2177 on Portsdown Hill; SU6208], *Golden Lion*: Unspoilt two-bar local with well kept Charles Wells Eagle and Gales, friendly staff, good value homely food inc Sun lunch, pleasant restaurant; where Eisenhower and Montgomery came before D-Day, attractive village nr scenic walks *(Ann and Colin Hunt, Phyl and Jack Street)*

St Mary Bourne [B3048; SU4250], *George*: Comfortable plush refurbishment, well kept Courage Best and Wadworths 6X, good standard bar food, very welcoming landlord, restaurant; tables outside, attractive village *(Ann and Colin Hunt, M Hasslacher)*

☆ **Steep** [Church Rd; Petersfield—Alton, signed Steep off A325 and A272; SU7425], *Cricketers*: Spacious carpeted lounge, massively pine-oriented and almost urban-feeling, with lots of cricket prints, good generous food, well kept Gales ales, decent wines and malt whiskies; restaurant, picnic tables on back lawn with swings and play-house; comfortable good value bedrooms *(Colin Laffan, LYM)*

☆ **Stockbridge** [High St; SU3535], *Grosvenor*: Good atmosphere and quick cheerfully courteous service in pleasant and comfortable old country-town hotel's two smallish bars and dining room, decent food, Courage Directors and Whitbreads Best, log fire; big attractive garden behind; bedrooms good value *(W H E Thomas, John and Phyllis Maloney, BB)*

☆ **Stockbridge** [High St], *Vine*: Comfortable bustle, with interesting combination of woodwork, brickwork and purple papered walls, delft shelf of china and pewter, bright floral curtains, popular food from huge sandwiches up, half helpings for children, restaurant, well kept Boddingtons, Flowers Original, Ringwood Best and a guest, unobtrusive piped music; open all day, children welcome, tables in nice big garden, weekend barbecues *(DP, Phyl and Jack Street, P P and J Salmon, Mr and Mrs T Savage, J S M Sheldon, A R and B E Sayer, D Voller, Gordon, Tim and Ann Meaden, LYM)*

Stockbridge [High St], *Greyhound*: Spacious but cosy, with dark beams, log fires each end, guitars and prints on wall, carved high-backed settles among other seats, wide choice of good value food inc some imaginative dishes, Courage Best, Ushers Founders and a seasonal ale, decent wines, public bar with pool, friendly courteous service; children and dogs allowed *(Lynn Sharpless, Bob Eardley, John and Phyllis Maloney)*; [A272/A3057 roundabout, E end], *White Hart*: Cheerful and welcoming divided bar, oak pews and other seats, antique prints, shaving-mug collection, reasonably priced bar food, Sun lunches, Bass and Charrington IPA, country wines, courteous service; children allowed in comfortable beamed restaurant with blazing log fire; bedrooms *(Christopher Warner, LYM)*

☆ **Stratfield Turgis** [off A33 Reading—Basingstoke; SU6960], *Wellington Arms*: Elegant small country inn with individual furnishings in restful and attractively decorated tall-windowed two-room lounge bar, part with polished flagstones, part carpeted; well kept Badger Best, Tanglefoot and BXB, orange juice pressed to order, wide choice of good bar food, open fire, garden; comfortable well equipped bedrooms *(J O Jonkler)*

☆ **Swanmore** [Hill Pound Rd; SU5815], *Rising Sun*: Welcoming and comfortably pubby, good log fires, good choice of popular food (booking advised weekends), well kept Whitbreads-related ales, decent wines, log fire, good courteous service; pleasant garden with play area, good walks *(John and Chris Simpson, Ann and Colin Hunt, Phyl and Jack Street, Jo and Gary Charlton, P Harbut)*
Swanwick [Swanwick Lane (A3051), handy for M27 junction 9; SU5109], *Elm Tree*: Neat and comfortably refurbished, with two bars and dining room off, Courage, Gales HSB, Ruddles and Wadworths 6X, wide range of home-cooked food, quiet piped music; children welcome, tables in garden; handy for Hampshire Wildlife Reserve *(Alan Green)*

☆ **Tangley** [Tangley Bottom, towards the Chutes – OS Sheet 185 map ref 327529; SU3252], *Cricketers Arms*: Recently tastefully refurbished, tiled floor with massive inglenook and roaring log fire in small front bar with bar billiards and friendly labrador called Pots, bistroish back extension with green paint, woodwork, flagstones and a one-table alcove off, imaginative range of bar food inc fresh baguettes and mix-your-own evening pizzas, well kept Bass and Cheriton Pots, some good cricketing prints; tables on neat terrace *(Heather Couper, LYM)*

☆ **Tangley** [SU3252], *Fox*: Cosy but lively little pub with generous good value imaginative food inc good puddings, well kept Scottish Courage and guest ales, good choice of wines, two big log fires, friendly chatty landlord, prompt helpful service, pleasant restaurant *(G Freemantle, Clive Wilkinson, Mr and Mrs Johnson)*

☆ **Timsbury** [Michelmersh; A3057 towards Stockbridge; SU3424], *Bear & Ragged Staff*: Very busy Whitbreads beamed country dining pub, airy and comfortable, with wide choice of food all day from good value ploughman's

up, several well kept ales, lots of wines by the glass, country wines, tables out in garden, good play area; children in eating area *(P J Caunt, Thomas Nott, D Illing, Gordon, R Lake, LYM)*
Titchfield [High St; SU5305], *Bugle*: Roomy and comfortable old village pub, flagstones and blue carpet, Boddingtons, Flowers IPA, Gales HSB and Wadworths 6X, popular value bar food, restaurant in old barn behind, efficient friendly service; handy for Titchfield Haven nature reserve, fine walk by former canal to coast; bedrooms *(Ian Phillips, Ann and Colin Hunt, Phyl and Jack Street)*
Titchfield [High St], *Queens Head*: Sympathetically restored ancient pub in conservation area (traffic humps to slow cars), good food cooked by landlord (esp fish) in bar or restaurant, friendly atmosphere, regularly changing well kept ales such as Morlands Old Speckled Hen and Ringwood Fortyniner, 1930s ambience; bedrooms *(Eric and June Heley, Ann and Colin Hunt)*

☆ **Turgis Green** [A33 Reading—Basingstoke; SU6959], *Jekyll & Hyde*: Busy rambling black-beamed pub with wide range of good food from sandwiches up, all day inc breakfast; five changing real ales, some interesting furnishings and prints particularly in back room, prompt friendly service; lots of picnic tables in good sheltered garden (some traffic noise), play area and various games; piped music; lavatories for the disabled, children allowed *(Simon Collett-Jones, LYM)*
Twyford [High St; SU4724], *Phoenix*: Friendly open-plan local with sensibly priced straightforward food, well kept Marstons, decent wines, back room with skittle alley *(John Knighton, Ann and Colin Hunt, Lynn Sharpless, Bob Eardley, Stephen Harvey)*

☆ **Upton** [the one nr Hurstbourne Tarrant; SU3555], *Crown*: Classic comfortable country pub, neat and clean, with lots of panelling, friendly hard-working licensees, good bar food inc good value triple-decker sandwiches, well kept Bass, Marstons Best and Ringwood True Glory, good coffee, small garden and terrace *(George Atkinson, Rupert Cook, BB)*

☆ **Upton Grey** [SU6948], *Hoddington Arms*: Consistently good value interesting food inc good puddings in unpretentious two-bar local; well kept Morlands and other ales, Australian wines by glass, friendly service, family room, bar billiards; piped music; garden, attractive village *(G and M Stewart, Guy Consterdine)*

☆ **Vernham Dean** [off A343 via Upton, or off A338 S of Hungerford via Oxenwood; SU3456], *George*: Relaxed and neatly kept rambling open-plan beamed and timbered bar, carefully refurbished, with some easy chairs, inglenook log fire, good value bar food (not Sun evening) from toasties to steaks inc good home-made puddings, well kept Marstons Best and Pedigree, darts, shove-ha'penny, dominoes and cribbage; well behaved children allowed in no-smoking eating area, tables in pretty garden behind

(Marjorie and David Lamb, Glen and Nola Armstong, Mark Matthewman, E V Walder, Gordon, LYM)

Wallington [1 Wallington Shore Rd; nr M27 junction 11; SU5806], *Cob & Pen*: Wide choice of good value food, well kept Whitbreads-related ales; large garden *(Ann and Colin Hunt)*; [nr M27 junction 11], *White Horse*: Cosy and neat well furnished two-bar local with pictures of old Fareham, good value lunchtime food popular with executives from nearby industrial estate; friendly welcome, well kept Bass tapped from the cask and changing guest ales *(Terry and Eileen Stott, Ann and Colin Hunt)*

Warsash [Shire Rd; SU4906], *Rising Sun*: Revamped waterside pub open all day for well presented food inc seafood specialities, efficient service, Whitbreads-related ales, decent wines, long bar part tiled-floor and part boards, spiral stairs to evening restaurant with fine views over Hamble estuary and Solent; Solent Way walk passes pub, handy for Hook nature reserve *(Phyl and Jack Street, Michael Inskip, D Marsh, Ann and Colin Hunt)*

☆ **West Meon** [High St; SU6424], *Thomas Lord*: Attractive cricket-theme village pub settling down well under friendly newish management, well kept Whitbreads-related ales, good value generous food inc fish and some Caribbean-style dishes, collection of club ties in lounge; tables in garden *(T W Fleckney)*

West Wellow [nr M27 junction 2; A36 2 miles N of junction with A431; SU2919], *Red Rover*: Warm welcome, wide range of good value food, Whitbreads-related ales, roomy and comfortable partly no-smoking dining area, friendly staff *(Ann and Colin Hunt)*; [Canada Rd; off A36 Romsey—Ower at roundabout, signposted Canada], *Rockingham Arms*: Plush beamed 19th-c pub on Forest edge, good value food, well kept drinks, friendly atmosphere and service, open fire; children welcome, garden with play area *(Mr and Mrs A Marsh)*

☆ **Weyhill** [A342, signed off A303 bypass; SU3146], *Weyhill Fair*: Popular local with six well kept ales inc Gales HSB, Marstons, Morrells and good varied guests, wide choice of good value food from filling baps to enjoyable puddings; spacious solidly furnished lounge with easy chairs around woodburner, old advertisements, smaller family room, no-smoking area; children welcome, occasional live music, handy for Hawk Conservancy *(Peter and Lynn Brueton, Joe Walker, BB)*

Whitchurch [SU4648], *Red House*: Ancient flagstones under 14th-c beams by inglenook fireplace, good value food from home-made rolls to restaurant dishes, well kept ales *(BB)*

☆ **Whitsbury** [follow Rockbourne sign off A354 SW of Salisbury, turning left just before village; or head W off A338 at S end of Breamore, or in Upper Burgate; SU1219], *Cartwheel*: Smart low-beamed country pub with wide choice of well presented reasonably priced food inc good sandwiches, interesting main dishes and fresh veg, good range of changing real ales with Aug beer festival, horse-racing decorations, particularly good service, neat restaurant (children allowed here if it's not being used); dogs allowed, weekly barbecue in attractive secluded sloping garden with play area, pleasant walks *(Rev John Hibberd, Jerry and Alison Oakes, Dr and Mrs A K Clarke, Dr M Smith)*

☆ **Whitway** [Winchester Rd (old A34); SU4559], *Carnarvon Arms*: Locally very popular for extraordinarily wide choice of good well presented food – walls in main bar too small to cope with menu; well kept Ushers, friendly Northern licensees, open fire, OAP bargain lunches Tues-Thurs, fish and chips Fri; bedrooms *(R T and J C Moggridge, Colin Couper)*

Wickham [Botley Rd (A334); SU5711], *Wheatsheaf*: Busy little two-bar local, simple food and well kept Marstons Best and Pedigree, reasonable prices *(Ann and Colin Hunt)*

☆ **Winchester** [The Square, between High St and cathedral; SU4829], *Eclipse*: Picturesque little partly 14th-c pub with massive beams and timbers, oak settles, well kept Whitbreads-related ales, Hampshire Pendragon and Ringwood Old Thumper, well done lunchtime bar food inc good value toasties, welcoming service even when very busy; children in back room, seats outside, very handy for cathedral *(A and C Hunt, John and Joan Nash, LYM)*

☆ **Winchester** [Royal Oak Passage, off upper end of pedestrian part of High St], *Royal Oak*: Cheerful well kept town pub done out as Hogshead real ale tavern with ten or so kept well, little rooms (some raised) off main bar, beams and bare boards, scrubbed tables, no-smoking areas, well priced straightforward quick food, cheerful service; the cellar bar (not always open) has massive 12th-c beams and a Saxon wall which gives it some claim to be the country's oldest drinking spot *(Ann and Colin Hunt, DJW, Jim and Maggie Cowell, LYM)*

☆ **Winchester** [14 Durngate Terr], *Willow Tree*: Intimate and friendly nicely furnished pub in beautiful riverside setting, good value well presented generous food inc fresh veg and bargain daily special, well kept Marstons, decent wines *(A R Humphrys, M Rowe, A and C Hunt)*

Winchester [57 Hyde St (A333, beyond Jewry St)], *Hyde*: Unspoilt 15th-c local with hardly a true right-angle, friendly welcome, sensible prices, particularly well kept Marstons Pedigree; a country pub in a nice part of town *(Dr and Mrs A K Clarke, Ann and Colin Hunt, Tom Espley)*; [Kingsgate Rd], *Queen*: Comfortably refurbished roomy pub in attractive setting opp college cricket ground, dark dado, cricketing prints on cream walls, well kept Marstons, decent wines, good value standard food inc popular Sun lunch, disabled facilities; open all day Fri-Sun *(Lynn*

Sharpless, Bob Eardley); [57 Stockbridge Rd (A272 past stn)], *Roebuck*: Cosy Victorianised sitting-room atmosphere, clean, friendly and welcoming, Marstons and guest ales, good value simple generous food inc OAP bargains, attractive conservatory restaurant, disabled access *(Lynn Sharpless, Bob Eardley, C McAuliffe)*

☆ **Winchfield** [Winchfield Hurst; SU7753], *Barley Mow*: Two-bar local with light and airy dining extension, wide choice of good value generous home-cooked food from sandwiches up, well kept Ushers ales inc a seasonal beer, decent wine, unobtrusive piped music; dogs welcome, nr Basingstoke canal – lots of good walks *(Chris and Ann Garnett, J Sheldon, Ian Phillips, G W Stevenson)*

☆ **Woodgreen** [OS Sheet 184 map ref 171176; SU1717], *Horse & Groom*: Busy beamed New Forest local, good choice of home-cooked food inc lovely old-fashioned puddings and good value Sun roast; prompt welcoming service, real ale, log fire, eating area off bar, pleasant garden with aviary and rabbit *(Jim and Liz Meier, Lyn and Geoff Hallchurch, Phyl and Jack Street)*

People don't usually tip bar staff (different in a really smart hotel, say). If you want to thank a barman – dealing with a really large party say, or special friendliness – offer him a drink. Common expressions are: 'And what's yours?' or 'And won't you have something for yourself?'.

Hereford & Worcester

An interesting crop of new entries here this year includes the charmingly laid out (and appropriately named) Riverside at Aymestrey, the cheerful Walter de Cantelupe at Kempsey, the civilised old Stockton Cross Inn at Stockton Cross, the idiosyncratic Moody Cow at Upton Bishop, and the delightfully cottagey Carpenters Arms tucked away at Walterstone. The first four of these have decidedly above-average food, and this area does stand out as particularly good for pub food, with a very high proportion of the main entries offering really enjoyable meals. For a special meal out, the places which stand out here at the moment are the Feathers in Ledbury, the Hunters Inn at Longdon, and the Olde Salutation at Weobley (now open all day); of these, it's the Feathers in Ledbury which gains the accolade of Hereford & Worcester Dining Pub of the Year. Other pubs currently doing really well here are the Little Pack Horse in Bewdley (flourishing under new licensees), the Crown & Sandys Arms and the Kings Arms at Ombersley, the Bell at Pensax (a great place for quickly changing interesting real ales), and the Lough Pool at Sellack. In the Lucky Dip section at the end of the chapter, places currently on very good form include the Pandy at Dorstone, Firs at Dunhampstead, Queen Elizabeth at Elmley Castle, Boot at Flyford Flavell, Green Man at Fownhope, Little Tumbling Sailor in Kidderminster, New Inn at Pembridge and Peacock outside Tenbury Wells (we've inspected almost all of these, and give them a clear thumbs-up). Although there are quite a few decent pubs in Worcester, we're surprised that we've never heard of anything really outstanding in Hereford – a town that seems an ideal environment for producing good pubs. Drinks prices in the area are well below the national average. We found the Talbot at Knightwick the cheapest for beers, with the Crown and the Butchers Arms at Woolhope, Three Kings at Hanley Castle and Farmers Arms at Birtsmorton also very cheap indeed. This is of course an outstanding area for cider, and any true lover of that drink really ought to make the pilgrimage to the Monkey House at Defford.

Post Office address codings confusingly give the impression that some pubs are in Hereford and Worcestershire, when they're really in the Midlands, Shropshire, Gloucestershire or even Wales (which is where we list them).

AYMESTREY SO4265 Map 6

Riverside Inn ♀

A4110; N off A44 at Mortimers Cross, W of Leominster

Expectations soar at the entrance of this black and white timbered inn facing a low two-arched bridge: a handsome new oak door, then a civilised little hall with woodburner, fresh and dried flowers, lots of house plants, a little desk and a writing table. The rambling beamed bar, with several cosy areas and no shortage of log fires, has a pleasant mix of periods and styles: from fine antique oak tables and chair to stripped pine country kitchen tables, from flowers on the tables to hops strung from a ceiling waggon-wheel, from horse tack through a Librairie Romantique poster for Victor Hugo's poems to a cheerful modern print of a plump red toadstool. Food is a good eclectic mix, too: changing daily, it might include an excellent creamy fish soup as well as say roast tomato soup (£2.25), liver and bacon casserole, lasagne or fried squid with garlic and parsley (£4.95), fish bake or monkfish provençale (£5.95), pheasant breast with caramelised apples and chestnuts (£9.95), spiced duck breast with honey and soy (£10.95) and venison with damson compote (£11.95); they bake good bread. Besides well kept Marstons Pedigree, Otter Ale and Bitter and Timothy Taylor Landlord they have their own-brew beers, Woodhampton Dipper and Kingfisher Ale; local farm cider, decent house wines, good coffee, and friendly obliging service. There's a big restaurant area; table skittles but no machines, virtually imperceptible piped music – maybe classical. Outside are waterside picnic tables, and rustic tables and benches up above in a steep tree-sheltered garden; up beyond, also beautifully sheltered, is a former bowling green. We have not had recent reports on the bedrooms here, but would expect this to be a very nice place to stay, especially as they have fishing rights on a mile of the River Lugg; it does get busy at weekends, when booking would be wise; dominoes, shove-ha'penny, table skittles. *(Recommended by John and Joan Wyatt, Trevor Swindells, Mrs J Hailstone, Paddy and Marilyn Gibbon, C R Whitham, Basil Minson, J M Potter)*

Own Brew ~ Licensees Val and Steve Bowen ~ Real ale ~ Meals and snacks ~ Restaurant ~ (01568) 708440 ~ Children over five welcome in restaurant ~ Open 12-3, 6.30-11; 12-3, 7-10.30 Sun ~ Bedrooms: £25/£40(£45B)

BEWDLEY SO7875 Map 4

Little Pack Horse ◀

High Street; no nearby parking – best to park in main car park, cross A4117 Cleobury road, and keep walking on down narrowing High Street; can park 150 yds at bottom of Lax Lane

This ancient timber frame building, nestled in the quiet back streets of an historic riverside town, is the first and probably the best of Mr O'Rourke's eccentric chain of 'Little' pubs. The rough and ready but cosy pubby rooms, nicely warmed by a big woodburning stove and candlelit at night, are full of eccentricities and oddities like clocks, wood-working tools, Indian clubs, a fireman's helmet, an old car horn, lots of old photographs and advertisements, and even an incendiary bomb on its walls; a wall-mounted wooden pig's mask is used in the pub's idiosyncratic game of swinging a weighted string to knock a coin off its ear or snout. There are pews, red leatherette wall settles, a mixed bag of tables on the red-tiled floor, roughly plastered white walls, and low beams. Very good value bar food includes home-made soup (£1.95), very substantial lunchtime sandwiches (from £2.20), ploughman's (£4.15), fresh pasta with field and oyster mushrooms and pesto (£3.65), shepherd's pie (£3.80), sausage and mash (£3.90), vegetarian pie (£4.80), fillet of salmon on tomato and black olive salsa (£4.90), Desperate Dan pie: steak and kidney (£5.25), and sirloin steak (£6.30), with puddings such as treacle roly poly with custard (£1.95); good welcoming and friendly service. As well as their own Lumphammer on handpump, they keep Ind Coope Burton, Morlands Old Speckled Hen and a changing range of guest beers; dominoes, fruit machine, cribbage, piped music. *(Recommended by Peter and Audrey Dowsett, Daren Haines, Roger and Pauline Pearce, Dorothee and Dennis Glover, Teresa Boddy, Peter and Rosie Flower, Lucy James, Dean Foden, Tony Kemp, Rachel Weston)*

Free house ~ Licensee Michael Gaunt ~ Real ale ~ Meals and snacks (12.30-7.30 Sun) ~ (01299) 403762 ~ Children welcome in eating area of bar ~ Open 11-3, 6-11, 11-11 Sat; 12-10.30 Sun

BIRTSMORTON SO7935 Map 4
Farmers Arms 🍺

Birts Street, off B4208 W of Birtsmorton

There's a warmly welcoming old-fashioned country atmosphere at this attractively placed, neatly kept black and white timbered village local. On the right a big room rambles away under low dark beams, with some standing timbers, and flowery-panelled cushioned settles as well as spindleback chairs; on the left an even lower-beamed room seems even snugger, and in both the white walls have black timbering. Limited but good value home-made bar food includes sandwiches (from £1.20), ploughman's (from £2.30), cauliflower cheese (£3), chilli (£3.80), fish and chips (£3.90) and steak and kidney pie (£4.95), and puddings (from £1.60). Well kept Hook Norton Best and Old Hookey and a guest such as Hobsons or Woods on handpump; darts in a good tiled area, shove-ha'penny, cribbage, and dominoes. There are seats out on the grass and they have a self-catering cottage. *(Recommended by JKW, Stephen Pine, Alfred Lawrence, Alan and Paula McCully, Derek Hayman, Dorothy and Leslie Pilson, V Kavanagh)*

Free house ~ Licensees Jill and Julie Moore ~ Real ale ~ Meals and snacks (11-2, 6-10) ~ (01684) 833308 ~ Children welcome in eating area of bar ~ Open 11-2.30, 6-11; 12-3, 7-10.30 Sun; cl evening 25 Dec

BRANSFORD SO7852 Map 4
Bear & Ragged Staff ♀

Powick Rd; off A4103 SW of Worcester

There's quite an emphasis on dining at this stylish place with its proper tablecloths, linen napkins, and fresh flowers; it's best to book a table. The menu includes soup (£2.55), prawn cocktail (£3.80), scampi (£5.75), several vegetarian dishes such as mushroom and leek bake (£5.95) and quite a few sirloin steaks (£10.50) as well as daily specials such as faggots and gravy (£5.95), lamb and apricot cobbler (£6.95), thai style turkey breast (£7.25), chicken and mushroom stroganoff or pork tenderloin stir fried with green peppercorns, brandy and cream (£9.85). There are fine views over rolling country from the relaxed and cheerful interconnecting rooms (the restaurant is no smoking) as well as some seats by an open fire and well kept Boddingtons and Wadworths 6X on handpump kept under light blanket pressure; a good range of wines (mainly New World ones), lots of malt whiskies, and quite a few brandies and liqueurs; willing, helpful service; darts, cribbage, dominoes, and piped music. *(Recommended by Gwen and Peter Andrews, John and Christine Lowe, E A George, Denys Gueroult, Theo, Anne and Jane Gaskin, A Preston, T H G Lewis, Dave Braisted, Lucy James, Dean Foden, M V and J Melling, Joy and Peter Heatherley, Gethin Lewis)*

Free house ~ Licensee John Owen ~ Real ale ~ Meals and snacks (till 10pm; not Sun evening) ~ (01886) 833399 ~ Children welcome ~ Piano Fri and Sat evenings ~ Open 12-2.30, 6.30-11; 12-2.30, cl evening Sun

BREDON SO9236 Map 4
Fox & Hounds

4½ miles from M5 junction 9; A438 to Northway, left at B4079, then in Bredon follow To church and river signpost on right

This neatly thatched place – prettily set down a quiet lane leading to the river and next to the church – has gradually become more and more restaurary over the years and readers suggest that a visit is likely to include a full sit-down meal. The comfortable and well-modernised carpeted bar has a friendly atmosphere, dressed stone pillars and stripped timbers, a central woodburning stove, upholstered settles, wheelback, tub, and ktichen chairs around attractive mahogany and cast-iron-framed tables, dried grasses and flowers, a toy fox dressed in hunting scarlet, and elegant wall lamps. A smaller side bar has assorted wooden kitchen chairs, wheelbacks, and settles, and an open fire at each end; no-smoking area in lounge and restaurant. The very wide choice of popular food includes soup (£2.45), avocado, stilton and port pâté (£3.95), grilled tiger prawns on garlic crouton with garlic mayonnaise (£4.95), chilli (£5.95), several vegetarian dishes such as vegetable and cheese pie (£6.50), steak and kidney pie (£6.50), lamb shoulder roasted on rosemary with mint and honey glaze (£10.95), beef and bacon stroganoff (£11.50) as well as a seasonal daily specials board; Sunday roast; very pleasant service. Well kept Banks's Bitter, Boddingtons and Morlands Old Speckled Hen on handpump, freshly squeezed fruit juice, several malt whiskies and wines by the glass; dominoes, shove-ha'penny, cribbage, fruit machine and piped music. The pub is pretty in summer with its colourful hanging baskets, and some of the picnic tables are under Perspex; there's a thatched wendy house. *(Recommended by J F Knutton, Paul and Maggie Baker, M A Borthwick, C Moncreiffe, IHR, Derek and Sylvia Stephenson, M Joyner, Mrs K Neville-Rolfe, Mrs J Oakes, M L and G Clarke, Dorothee and Dennis Glover)*

Whitbreads ~ Lease: Michael Hardwick ~ Real ale ~ Meals and snacks (till 10pm) ~ Restaurant ~ (01684) 772377 ~ Children welcome ~ Open 11-2.30, 6-11; 12-3, 6-10.30 Sun

BRETFORTON SP0943 Map 4
Fleece ★ ★

B4035 E of Evesham: turn S off this road into village; pub is in centre square by church; there's a sizeable car park at one side of the church

When the last member of the family that had owned this marvellous old farm for around 500 years bequeathed it to the National Trust in 1977 she ensured that it would become a piece of living history. Its fine country rooms remain filled with original antique furnishings, many of them heirlooms: a great oak dresser holds a priceless 48-piece set of Stuart pewter, there's a fine grandfather clock, ancient kitchen chairs, curved high-backed settles, a rocking chair, and a rack of heavy pointed iron shafts, probably for spit roasting, in one of the huge inglenook fireplaces. There are massive beams and exposed timbers, worn and crazed flagstones (scored with marks to keep out demons), and plenty of oddities such as a great cheese-press and set of cheese moulds, and a rare dough-proving table; a leaflet details the more bizarre items, and there are three warming winter fires. The room with the pewter is no smoking. Well kept Brandy Cask Brandy Snapper, Chalk Hill CHB, M & B Brew XI and Uley Old Spot on handpump, over a dozen country wines. Simple generously served bar food (which may be a bit slow on busy days owing to limited kitchen facilities) includes sandwiches (from £1.50), ploughman's (from £3.40), lasagne or ratatouille lasagne (£4), steak and kidney pie (£4.50), locally cured gammon (£5.25), and steak (£6.25). Darts, cribbage, dominoes, shove-ha'penny. In summer, when it gets very busy, they make the most of the extensive orchard, with seats on the goat-cropped grass that spreads around the beautifully restored thatched and timbered barn, among the fruit trees, and at the front by the stone pump-trough. There's also an adventure playground, a display of farm engines, an aviary, and an enclosure with sheep, chicken, geese and a goat. They also hold the village fete and annual asparagus auctions at the end of May. *(Recommended by Nick and Meriel Cox, Denys Gueroult, Sheila and John French, Chris and Andy Crow, Alan Eames, Peter Baggott, Liz Bell, Chris Reeve, Tom Evans, Michael and Hazel Lyons, Bryan Taylor, B J Cox, Susan and John French, Martin and Penny Fletcher, Paul Boot, Dr P Jackson, Jerry and Alison Oakes, JJW, CMW, Medwin Bew, MDN, Miss K Law, K M Timmins, Terry and Vann W Prime)*

Free house ~ Licensee N J Griffiths ~ Real ale ~ Meals and snacks (not Mon evening) ~ (01386) 831173 ~ Children welcome ~ Morris men summer weekends ~ Open 11-2.30, 6-11; 12-2.30, 7-10.30 Sun

Please let us know of any pubs where the wine is particularly good.

BRIMFIELD SO5368 Map 4
Roebuck 🛏 ♀

Village signposted just off A49 Shrewsbury—Leominster

New licensees have brought a bit of gentle relaxed pubbishness back to this smart country dining pub, they've also improved food prices a bit without detracting from the previously established imaginative good quality hospitality and cooking. The stylish bar menu includes sandwiches made with home-made bread (from £2.95), ploughman's (£4.25), home-made dips with pitta bread (£3.25), three-salmon terrine, warm chicken liver and bacon salad or a selection of home-made pâtés (£4.25), and main courses like grilled mediterranean vegetables and goat's cheese (£4.75), trio of home-made sausages (£5.25), steak, mushroom and claret pie (£5.75), free range chicken breast stuffed with garlic and fresh herbs with wild mushroom sauce (£6.95), salmon fillet with saffron and chive sauce (£8.25) and buck fillet stuffed with shropshire blue cheese wrapped in bacon and grilled (£11.95). The interesting reasonably priced wine list is sourced from several merchants, also well kept Bass, Tetleys and a guest like Greene King Abbot on handpump. The quiet and old-fashioned locals' snug has an impressive inglenook fireplace, and two other quietly civilised bars have decorative plates mounted over dark ply panelling and a small open fire. Kind intelligent landlord and caring, pleasant staff; table skittles, backgammon, cribbage and shove-ha'penny. *(Reports on the new regime please)*

Free house ~ Licensees David and Sue Willson-Lloyd ~ Real ale ~ Meals and snacks ~ Restaurant ~ (01584) 711230 ~ Well behaved children welcome ~ Open 12-3, 6-11; 12-10.30 Sun; cl evening 25 Dec ~ Bedrooms: £40B/£55B

CAREY SO5631 Map 4
Cottage of Content 🛏 ♀

Village signposted from good road through Hoarwithy

What everybody agrees about is the charm of the setting for this very pretty and out-of-the-way medieval country cottage with picnic tables on the flower-filled front terrace and a couple more on a back terrace looking up a steep expanse of lawn, and just the little lane running past by a stream. Inside is more opened up than some readers remember, but there's still a nice mix of country furnishings – stripped pine, country kitchen chairs, long pews by one big table and a mix of other old-fashioned tables. One room has flagstones, another bare boards, and there are plenty of beams and prints. There's more emphasis on food than you might expect in a little county pub, with lots of daily specials (especially at weekends when they are very busy) such as soup (£1.95), chargrilled baby squid (£4.25), plaice or chicken (£4.95), broccoli, cheese and almond bake (£5.50), bison sausage casserole (£6.95), smoked duck (£10.50) and fresh fish and game in season. Well kept Hook Norton Best and Old Hookey on handpump. The two samoyed dogs are called Shadow and Storm. *(Recommended by Wayne Brindle, Dr M Smith, Chris Philip, David Peakall, Denys Gueroult, Dennis Shirley, Christopher Tobitt, Malcolm Taylor, Ted George, Simon Small)*

Free house ~ Licensee Mike Wainford ~ Real ale ~ Meals and snacks (till 10pm Sat) ~ (01432) 840242 ~ Children welcome ~ Open 12-2, 7-11(10.30 Sun); cl Mon and Tues lunchtime; cl 25 Dec ~ Bedrooms: £48B

DEFFORD SO9143 Map 4
Monkey House

Woodmancote; A4104 towards Upton – immediately after passing Oak public house on right, there's a small group of cottages, of which this is the last

This pretty black and white cottage – set back from the road behind a small garden with one or two fruit trees and with no inn-sign to give a clue to its role – is one of the few remaining absolutely traditional cider-houses. Very cheap Bulmer's Medium or Special Dry cider is tapped from barrels and poured by jug into pottery mugs and served from a hatch beside the door. Beer is sold in cans – a concession to modern tastes. They don't do food (except crisps and nuts), but allow you to bring your own.

In good weather, you can stand outside with Tess the bull terrier and Tapper the jack russell, and hens and cockerels that wander in from an adjacent collection of caravans and sheds; they have two horses called Murphy and Mandy. Or you can retreat to a small side outbuilding with a couple of plain tables, a settle and an open fire; darts and dominoes. The name came from a drunken customer some years ago who fell into bramble bushes and insisted he was attacked by monkeys. *(Recommended by Chris Raisin; more reports please)*

Free house ~ Licensee Graham Collins ~ (01386) 750234 ~ Children welcome in one room ~ Open 12-2.30, 6-11; closed Mon evening, all day Tues

HANLEY CASTLE SO8442 Map 4
Three Kings £ ◖

Pub signposted (not prominently) off B4211 opposite Manor House gates, N of Upton upon Severn, follow Church End signpost

Readers describe the way they feel part of the family circle at this genuinely unspoilt friendly country local that's been in the same family for around 85 years now. Although the decor is a bit dusty and well worn and the fires might be a little bit smoky if you're sitting too close you probably won't notice because of the warmth of the welcome, and if you do you'll just enjoy them as part of the characterful atmosphere. The little tiled-floor tap room on the right is separated off from the entrance corridor by the monumental built-in settle which faces its equally vast inglenook fireplace. A hatch here serves very well kept Butcombe Bitter, Thwaites and usually three guest beers from small independent breweries on handpump, 50 malt whiskies and farm cider. On the left, another room is decorated with lots of small locomotive pictures, and has darts, dominoes, shove-ha'penny and cribbage. A separate entrance leads to the comfortable timbered lounge with another inglenook fireplace and a neatly blacked kitchen range, little leatherette armchairs and spindleback chairs arounds its tables, and another antique winged and high-backed settle. Straightforward reasonably priced, homely bar food includes soup (£1), sandwiches (from £1), omelettes (from £2.25), sausage and chips (£2.75), ploughman's (from £2.75), scampi or trout (£4.50), salmon en croûte (£5.25) and daily specials. Readers almost unanimously concur that food service is very slow but in such a way that's quite appropriate to the relaxed and natural family atmosphere – so you will need to be in the right frame of mind for a leisurely wait. Bow windows in the three main rooms and old-fashioned wood-and-iron seats on the front terrace look across to the great cedar which shades the tiny green, and there are rickety benches in a somewhat overgrown garden. *(Recommended by Dr I Crichton, D Eberlin, Pat and Tony Martin, Alan and Paula McCully, M Joyner, Anne, J and P Maloney, Hugh MacLean, Mr and Mrs H M Mortimer)*

Free house ~ Licensee Mrs Sheila Roberts ~ Real ale ~ Meals and snacks (not Sun evening) ~ (01684) 592686 ~ Children welcome in family room ~ Singer/guitar Sun evening, sing-along alternate Sat evenings, folk club alternate Thurs evenings ~ Open 11-3, 7-11; 12-3, 7-10.30 Sun; cl evening Dec 25 ~ Bedroom: £27.50B/£45B

KEMPSEY SO8548 Map 4
Walter de Cantelupe ♀

Main Road; A38 S of Worcester

It's a surprise to find the kitchen at the front of this roadside pub - but perhaps it's symptomatic of the effort that goes into the food side: as much care goes into traditional standbys such as beef in ale pie (£5.45) as into more inventive dishes such as warm goat's cheese with red and green peppers and oatmeal biscuits (£3.65), lamb, date and mint pie (£5.45), chicken fillet on mediterranean sauce with fresh pasta (£6.45), poached breast of chicken with tarragon and green peppercorn sauce (£7.80) or pan-fried duck breast with minted peas (£10.90); they do a good value three course Sunday lunch (£7.90); no smoking in eating area until all diners have finished eating. The dining area is pleasantly furnished with a mix of plush or yellow leather dining chairs, an old settle, a sonorous clock and candles and flowers on the tables. The bar side is friendly and relaxed, with an informal mix of furniture, red tiles with a worn rug by the serving counter, a couple of steps up to a carpeted area, and a good big fireplace. Well kept Marstons Bitter, Timothy Taylors Landlord, Woods Shropshire Lad and frequently changing guest beers on handpump, good choice of wines by the glass (they import direct from Italy and have reguarly changing bin ends); hard-working young landlord – and no music or games machines. There are tables in a pretty walled garden at the back, and the friendly labrador Monti may show up. *(Recommended by Drs Ben and Caroline Maxwell, Mrs Sarah Blenkinsop; more reports please)*

Free house ~ Licensee Martin Lloyd-Morris ~ Real ale ~ Meals and snacks (till 10pm Fri and Sat) ~ Restaurant ~ (01905) 820572 ~ Children welcome till 8.30 in bar area ~ Open 11.30-2.30, 6(5.30 Fri)-11; 12-3, 7-10.30 Sun; cl Mon lunchtime except bank holidays

KIDDERMINSTER SO8376 Map 4
King & Castle
Railway Station, Comberton Hill

Although our primary interest in this cheery place is that it's a good welcoming pub, it also happens to be a fascinating recreation of a classic station refreshment room, set on the terminus of Britain's most lively private steam railway and perfectly conjuring up the feel of a better-class Edwardian establishment that has unbent a little to greet the more informal ways of the 1920s. The cheery good-humoured landlady and her friendly staff cope well with the bustle of bank holidays and railway gala days (when it can be very difficult to find a seat). Furnishings are solid and in character (even to the occasional obvious need for a touch of reupholstery), and there is the railway memorabilia that you would expect. The atmosphere is lively and sometimes noisily good-humoured (and again in character can sometimes be rather smoky). With steam trains right outside, some railway-buff readers are quite content to start and end their journeys right here; others have used a Rover ticket to shuttle happily between here and the Railwaymans Arms in Bridgnorth (see Shropshire chapter). They serve well kept Bathams and Marstons Pedigree and two guests such as Enville, Hook Norton or Wye Valley on handpump and a wide choice of straightforward good value bar food such as filled rolls (£1.50), filled baked potatoes (from £2.25), ploughman's (£3.95), lasagne (£4.25), beef and beer pie (£4.75) and chicken kiev (£4.95). *(Recommended by John C Baker, John Price, Andy and Jill Kassube)*

Free House ~ Licensee Rosemary Hyde ~ Real ale ~ Meals and snacks (not Mon-Wed evenings) ~ (01562) 747505 ~ Children welcome till 9pm ~ Open 11-3, 5-11; 11-11 Sat; 12-10.30 Sun

KNIGHTWICK SO7355 Map 4
Talbot 🍺 ♀
Knightsford Bridge; B4197 just off A44 Worcester—Bromyard

The enterprising licensees at this bustling attractively placed 14th-c coaching inn are offering produce from their own small farm as a sure way of controlling the quality of the meals they serve – they grow hops as well and are hoping to offer an own-brew beer soon. There's quite an emphasis on the almost completely home-made not cheap food which might include starters such as four cheese tagliatelle, scallops wrapped in seaweed and fried in beer batter with sweet and sour dip, pigeon breast salad, crab blinis or pork, orange and cognac pâté (£4.95) and main courses such as liver and bacon (£7.95), steak and kidney pie (£8.50), aubergine and goat's cheese (£9.50), chicken and mushroom pie or rabbit casserole (£9.95), chicken baked in turmeric and yoghurt, skate with fennel and mustard sauce or lobster (£11.95) and puddings such as sticky date and toffee pudding or pickled damson meringue (from £3); several varieties of home-baked bread, and good breakfasts. The heavily beamed lounge bar has entertaining and rather distinguished coaching and sporting prints and paintings on its butter-coloured walls, a variety of interesting seats from small carved or leatherette armchairs to the winged settles by the tall bow windows, and a vast stove which squats in the big central stone hearth; there's another log fire. Well kept Bass,

Hobsons Bitter and Worthingtons Best on handpump, and decent wines by the glass. The well furnished back public bar has pool on a raised side area, darts, fruit machine, video game and juke box; dominoes and cribbage. There are some old-fashioned seats outside, in front, with more on a good-sized lawn over the lane by the river (they serve out here too); boules. Some of the bedrooms are above the bar. *(Recommended by Mavis and Robert Harford, Ian Jones, Robert Whittle, John Bowdler, W C M Jones, James Nunns)*

Free house ~ Licensees Annie and Wiz Clift ~ Real ale ~ Meals and snacks ~ Restaurant ~ (01886) 821235 ~ Children welcome ~ Open 11-11(11.30 Sat); 12-10.30 Sun; cl evening 25 Dec ~ Bedrooms: £24.50(£31B)/£42(£56.50B)

LEDBURY SO7138 Map 4
Feathers 🍴 🛏 ♀

High Street, Ledbury, A417

Hereford & Worcester Dining Pub of the Year

Drinkers and diners indulge harmoniously in the atmospheric and rather civilised Fuggles Bar at this elegantly striking mainly 16th-c timbered inn, with locals gathered at one end of the room or at stools by the bar counter, uninhibited by those enjoying the imaginative food and fine wines. And if you do want to get away from drinkers there are some very snug and cosy tables with nicely upholstered seats with bays around them off to one side, as well as beams and timbers, hop bines, some country antiques, 19th-c caricatures and fowl prints on the stripped brick chimney breast (lovely winter fire), and fresh flowers on the tables. Very attractively presented good food includes home-made soup (£2.95), ragout of peppers on raw mushroom salad (£4.25), leek, bacon and stilton gratin (£4.95), fettucine with fresh salmon, chive and dill cream sauce (£5.25) and main courses such as hamburgers (£6.75), salmon and cumin fishcakes (£6.95), filo strudel with roasted mediterranean vegetables and ricotta (£9.25), breast of chicken and parma ham skewer with lemon and sun-dried tomatoes (£10.95), spiced coconut lamb cutlets (£12.95) and roast pork tenderloin with five-spice, spring onions and plum sauce (£12.50) and home-made puddings like steamed chocolate orange pudding with bitter chocolate sauce or plum and almond syllabub (all £4.25); friendly, attentive service. They do good afternoon teas in the more formal quiet lounge by the reception area with comfortable high-sided armchairs and sofas in front of a big log fire, and newspapers to read. Well kept Bass, Fullers London Pride, Shepherd Neame Spitfire and Worthington Best on handpump, a fine wine list, various malt whiskies, and farm cider. Abundant pots and hanging baskets adorn the new lawn at the back, and they have their own squash courts. *(Recommended by K J Jeavons, A Turner, G S and E M Dorey, Alan and Paula McCully, John and Christine Lowe, Helen Morton, Denys Gueroult, Chris Philip, Tim and Linda Collins, Mavis and Robert Harford, John Bowdler, Pamela and Merlyn Horswell, W A and S Rinaldi-Butcher, Andy and Jill Kassube, Joan and Tony Walker, JAH, Dave Braisted, V Kavanagh, Hugh MacLean, Chris Wheaton, Mrs J A Powell, Mr and Mrs T A Bryan)*

Free house ~ Licensee David Elliston ~ Real ale ~ Meals and snacks (till 10pm Fri/Sat) ~ Restaurant ~ (01531) 635266 ~ Children welcome in eating area of bar and in hotel lounge area ~ Jazz/blues/folk jazz Weds evening ~ Open 11-11; 12-10.30 Sun ~ Bedrooms: £65B/£85B

LONGDON SO8336 Map 4
Hunters Inn 🍴 ♀

B4211 S

The very well prepared imaginative bar food, cheerfully served in the relaxed and friendly bar rooms of this civilised pub, is deservedly popular: sandwiches (from £1.75; hot open ones from £4.25), home-made soup (£2.25), stilton pâté (£3.75), ploughman's (£3.95), steak and kidney pie (£6.50), mushroom, broccoli and stilton pancake (£6.75), thai green chicken curry (£7.75), salmon with prawns in lobster sauce (£9.25), stir fried duck breast with oriental vegetables, cashews and black bean sauce (£9.75), individual roasted loin of pork (£9.95) and medallions of beef sautéed with wild mushrooms in garlic butter, malt whisky and cream (£12.50). On the right as you go in there are two comfortable armchairs in a bay window, one-person pews and wheelbacks around a mix of tables, plates and dried flowers on a delft shelf, a warm open fire, and photographs of the licensees in racing cars, and so forth; on the left is a similarly furnished room with polished flagstones and a big woodburning stove – a small dining room leads off here, and there's a smart heavily beamed restaurant as well. Well kept Everards Beacon, Ruddles Best and Theakstons Best on handpump, and good wine by the glass; piped music. There's always a lot going on in their six acres of grounds, and the attractive back garden has some picnic tables on the crazy-paved terrace, with more on the big lawn; dogs, rabbits and ponies. *(Recommended by John and Moira Cole, S Holder, Alan and Paula McCully, V Kavanagh; more reports please)*

Free house ~ Licensees Howard and Polly Hill-Lines ~ Real ale ~ Meals and snacks (till 10pm) ~ Restaurant ~ (01684) 833388 ~ Children welcome away from immediate bar area ~ Open 11-3, 6-11; 11-10.30 Sun; 11-3, 7-10.30 Sun in winter

LUGWARDINE SO5541 Map 4
Crown & Anchor ♀
Cotts Lane; just off A438 E of Hereford

The several smallish characterful rooms (one suitable for families) at this attractive old black and white timbered inn are smartly comfortable, with an interesting mix of furnishings and a big log fire. There's well kept Bass, Hobsons Best, Worthington Best, and weekly guest beers such as Jennings Cumberland, Timothy Taylor Landlord and Woods Hopping Mad on handpump and decent wines including a clutch of usefully priced bin ends. Bar food includes soup (£2), herrings in mustard cream sauce (£2.60), ploughman's (£4), battered cod (£4.50), several vegetarian dishes such as lentil and aubergine curry or blackeye bean and seaweed casserole (from £5.25), grilled trout or seafood platter (£6), lemon chicken with sweet pepper sauce or baked loin of pork with spinach and mozzarella in tomato sauce (£6.75) and quite a few daily specials; small no-smoking area. *(Recommended by Peter J King, Lynn Sharpless, Bob Eardley, Chris Wheaton, Trevor Swindells)*

Free house ~ Licensees Nick and Julie Squire ~ Real ale ~ Meals and snacks (till 10pm) ~ (01432) 851303 ~ Children welcome ~ Jazz first Tues of month ~ Open 11.30-11; 12-10.30 Sun

MICHAELCHURCH ESCLEY SO3134 Map 6
Bridge
Off back rd SE of Hay on Wye, along Escley Brook valley; or can be reached off B4348 W of Hereford, via Vowchurch, then eventually left at Michaelchurch T-junction, and next left

In summer, you can sit outside this remote homely inn – delightfully tucked away down a steep lane in an attractive valley – and watch muscovy ducks and brown trout on the river. There's a relaxed homely atmosphere in the simple left-hand bar which has dark black beams, straightforward pine pews and dining chairs, brocaded bar stools, some paintings of the pub and detailed farm scenes, a TV in one corner, and a very big woodburning stove. The quarry-tiled public bar has sensible darts, two video games, board games, cribbage, dominoes, and darts. Very well kept Bass, Ruddles Best, Smiles Best and Wye Valley Bitter on handpump or air pressure, several farm ciders, country wines, and a good choice of fairly priced wines. Good value simple bar food includes sandwiches, home-made soups like cream of watercress or leek and potato (£2.20), bacon, egg and chips (£3.10), deep-fried camembert (£3.55), filled baked potatoes (£4.20), local sausages and onions (£4.65), salmon and broccoli flan or pasta with various sauces (£4.95), rump steak (£8.25), and puddings like fruit pies or trifle (£2.75); best to book Sunday lunch. There's a small riverside campsite with hot showers and changing room. *(Recommended by Victoria Herriott, Patrick Freeman, D Eberlin, Pete and Rosie Flower; more reports please)*

Free house ~ Licensee Jean Draper ~ Real ale ~ Meals and snacks ~ (not Mon) ~ Restaurant ~ (01981) 510646 ~ Children welcome till 9.30pm ~ Open 12-2.30, 6.30-11; 11.30-11 Sat; 12-3, 6-11 winter Sat; 12-10.30 Sun; cl Mon except bank holidays

MUCH MARCLE SO6633 Map 4
Slip Tavern ♀

Off A449 SW of Ledbury; take Woolhope turning at village stores, then right at pub sign

The landlord at this quiet country pub used to be a nurseryman and the gardens that stretch out behind the building are really lovely and full of interesting plants; the hanging baskets and big urns in front are very pretty too. The cosy chatty bar is popular with older people at lunchtime with a more villagey local atmosphere in the evening. There are ladderback, wheelback and leather chairs around the black tables and little country prints on neat white walls; well kept Hook Norton Best and Wadworths 6X on handpump or tapped straight from the cask and about ten wines by the glass; pleasant service, muted piped music. At lunchtime, bar food includes soup (£1.70), ploughman's (£3.85), tasty faggots and peas (£5), home-cooked ham and salad (£5.30) chilli (£5.45), steak pie (£5.30), with evening extras such as trout and almonds (£5.95), chicken tikka masala (£7.20), steaks (from £8.20). Quite a few daily specials might be pork and leek casserole (£5.95), coq au vin (£6.25), poached salmon with lobster sauce (£6.30), and puddings such as creamy lemon crunch or strawberry and apple crumble (£2.50). There's more space for eating in the attractively planted conservatory, though it's best to book. There's a well separated play area. *(Recommended by June and Malcolm Farmer, P G Topp, Denys Gueroult, Daren Haines, Stephen Pine, Alfred Lawrence, Brian and Barbara Matthews, Joy and Peter Heatherley, Mr and Mrs Blackbourn, R Michael Richards, Mrs B Sugarman)*

Free house ~ Licensee Gilbert E Jeanes ~ Real ale ~ Meals and snacks ~ Restaurant (not Sun) ~ (01531) 660246 ~ Children welcome ~ Fun folk night first Thurs of month ~ Open 11.30-2.30, 6.30-11; 12-2.30, 7-10.30 Sun

OMBERSLEY SO8463 Map 4
Crown & Sandys Arms 🛏 ♀

Coming into the village from the A4133, turn left at the roundabout in middle of village, and pub is on the left

Readers enjoy the friendly welcoming atmosphere and well prepared generously served food at this pretty, civilised Dutch-gabled white inn. The lounge bar has black beams and some flagstones, comfortable windsor armchairs, antique settles, a couple of easy chairs, old prints and maps on its timbered walls, log fires, and daily newspapers; half is no smoking. Bar snacks include soup or sandwiches (£1.95), smoked salmon terrine (£2.95), ploughman's (from £3.50), prawn cocktail (£3.75), curry, home-cooked ham or vegetarian quiche (£5.25), steak and kidney pie (£5.75), cajun chicken (£5.95) and steaks (from £9.50), as well as daily specials which include lots of fresh fish such as sole, hake, tuna, monkfish, and cod, vegetarian dishes, seasonal game, guinea fowl, and pot-roast lamb. Two to four well kept real ales rotate constantly and might include Bass, Fullers, Hobsons, Hook Norton, Shepherd Neame or Woods; four wines by the glass, litre or half-litre, and country wines. There are picnic tables in the garden behind the building; no dogs. *(Recommended by Alan Morton, Stephen Pine, Alfred Lawrence, Dr I Crichton, J Boucher, Chris Philip, Nigel Clifton, Denys Gueroult, G S and E M Dorey, John and Joan Nash, G Robinson, F J Robinson, Chris and Shirley Machin, C I Harvey, Paul and Maggie Baker, A G Drake, Colin Draper, Lucy James, Dean Foden, JAH, Bryan Taylor, A Lock, W H and E Thomas, Mr and Mrs Blackbourn)*

Free house ~ Licensee R E Ransome ~ Real ale ~ Meals and snacks (till 9.50) ~ Restaurant ~ (01905) 620252 ~ Well behaved children welcome until 7pm ~ Open 11-3, 5.30-11; 12-3, 7-11; closed 25 Dec and evening 26 Dec and 1 Jan ~ Bedrooms: £33B/£43B

Kings Arms

They've recently upgraded the now monthly changing seasonal menu at this big black-beamed and timbered Tudor pub, and it certainly seems to be drawing a satisfied crowd. Meals are very generously served and might include a soup like garlic, bean and tomato with pesto (£2.95), grilled goat's cheese (£3.95), stuffed squid in tomato salsa or prawn and crab pâté (£4.95), cajun chicken sandwich

(£5.75), steak and kidney pie (£6.50), vegetarian chilli pie, chicken casserole with cheese dumplings or smoked haddock with spinach (£6.75), grilled scallops with smoked salmon (£6.95), oxtail braised in stout (£7.50), pot roasted game (£7.95), baked salmon en croûte (£9.50) and herb crusted rack of lamb (£9.75), and puddings like apple and rhubarb crumble or bread and butter pudding (all £3.50). The comfortably informal atmospheric rambling rooms have a friendly, bustling feel, various cosy nooks and crannies, a collection of rustic bric-a-brac, and four open fires, and are full of stuffed animals and birds; one room has Charles II's coat of arms moulded into its decorated plaster ceiling – he's reputed to have been here in 1651. Well kept Bass, B & B Brew XI, Morlands Speckled Hen and Worthingtons Best on handpump, Old Rosie Scrumpy cider and several Irish malts; quick cheerful service, even when busy. A tree-sheltered courtyard has tables under cocktail parasols, and colourful hanging baskets and tubs in summer, and there's also a terrace.
(Recommended by Chris Philip, John Bowdler, John and Joan Nash, Mike and Mary Carter, Denys Gueroult, G S and E M Dorey, Theo, Anne and Jane Gaskin, J Barnwell Basil Minson, Alan and Paula McCully, Bryan Taylor)

Free house ~ Licensees Chris and Judy Blundell ~ Real ale ~ Meals and snacks (till 10pm) ~ (01905) 620142/620315 ~ No children under 8 and older ones must leave by 8.30pm ~ Open 11-2.45, 5.30-11; 12-10.30 Sun; cl 25/26 Dec

PENSAX SO7269 Map 4
Bell 🍺

B4202 Abberley—Clows Top, S of village

Four handpumps quickly rotate an incredible number of around 400 beers a year at this friendly country pub, although this is by no means exclusively a pub for real-ale fans. Readers also love the very warmly relaxed welcome proffered by the cheery licensees, as well as the generously served good value mostly home-made food such as soup (£1.95), garlic mushrooms (£2.75), sautéed mushrooms (£2.95), fisherman's platter or several vegetarian dishes like vegetable curry (£4.95), steak and kidney pie or minty lamb and apricot pie (£5.75), whisky spiced beef with walnuts or beef stroganoff (£6.95), 8oz peppered steaks (£8.95), and about ten specials like seafood tagliatelle (£5.75); home-made puddings like treacle tart (£1.90). The L-shaped main bar has a restrained traditional decor, with long cushioned pews on its bare boards, good solid pub tables, and a woodburning stove. Beyond a small carpeted area on the left with a couple more tables is a more airy dining room added in the late 1980s, with french windows opening on to a wooden deck that on hot days can give a slightly Californian feel; it has a log fire for our more usual weather; cribbage and piped music. Service is very friendly, There are decent reasonably priced wines and good coffee. In the back garden, picnic tables look out over rolling fields and copses to the Wyre Forest. *(Recommended by Kerry Law, Hilary Soms, Denise Harbord, Peter and Rosie Flower, Patrick Herratt, Lawrence Bacon, Jean Scott, Mrs Blenkinsop)*

Free house ~ Licensee Graham Titcombe ~ Real ale ~ Meals and snacks ~ Restaurant ~ (01299) 896677 ~ Children welcome in snug and restaurant ~ Open 11-2.30, 5-11; 12-10.30 Sun

RUCKHALL SO4539 Map 4
Ancient Camp 🛏 ♀

Ruckhall signposted off A465 W of Hereford at Belmont Abbey; from Ruckhall pub signed down private drive; can reach it too from Bridge Sollers, W of Hereford on A438 – cross Wye, then after a mile or so take first left, then left again to Eaton Bishop, and left to Ruckhall

If you do stay the night at this smart country restaurant ask for a room with a view over the river Wye to the Black Mountains beyond – seats on the terrace among the roses share the same magnificent view. The licensee owns a stretch of the river so you could combine your stay with some fishing. There's quite some emphasis on the stylish (not cheap) food which might include tomato and basil soup (£3.75), venison terrine with pistachio and redcurrant (£6), warm smoked chicken salad (£6.50), and main courses like salmon with saffron and ginger, duck breast with cherries and marsala, pheasant with spinach or cranberry and chestnut roast (£12.50) and medallions of beef with mushrooms and foie gras (£14.75). The very civilised central beamed and flagstoned bar is simply but thoughtfully furnished with comfortably solid green-upholstered settles and library chairs around nice old elm tables. On the left, a green-carpeted room has matching sofas around the walls and kitchen chairs around tripod tables. On the right, there are simple dining chairs around stripped kitchen tables on a brown carpet, and stripped stonework; nice log fire. Well kept Hook Norton Best and Woods Parish on handpump, and fine wines and vintage port; piped classical music. *(Recommended by Chris Philip, Bob Arnett, Judy Wayman, Victoria Herriott, James Andrew, Denys Gueroult, John Bowdler, JAH, Martin and Penny Fletcher, Joy and Peter Heatherley, Chris Wheaton, Greta and Christopher Wells, Jim and Maggie Cowell, Joan Olivier, Mrs S Wright)*

Free house ~ Licensees Pauline and Ewart McKie ~ Real ale ~ Meals and snacks ~ Restaurant (not Mon) ~ (01981) 250449 ~ Open 12-3, 7-11; cl Monday ~ Bedrooms: £40B/£50B

SELLACK SO5627 Map 4
Lough Pool Inn ★ ♀

Back road Hoarwithy—Ross on Wye; OS Sheet 162 map reference 558268

Readers report happily about their enjoyable visits to this attractive black and white timbered country pub with its good value tasty food, relaxing atmosphere and warmly welcoming licensees. The beamed central room has kitchen chairs and cushioned window seats around plain wooden tables on the mainly flagstoned floor, sporting prints and bunches of dried flowers, and a log fire at each end. Other rooms lead off, with attractive individual furnishings and nice touches like the dresser of patterned plates. Bar food includes soup like carrot and coriander (£2.30), stilton and port pâté (£3.40), ploughman's (£4.20), caribbean fruit curry or home-made steak and kidney pie (£6.50), chicken korma (£7.85), popular greek-style goat casserole (£9.50), local steaks (from £9.75), daily specials such as wild boar casserole or seafood bake, and puddings like chocolate rum pot or lemon syllabub (from £2.75); the restaurant is no smoking. Well kept Bass, John Smiths and Wye Valley Hereford on handpump, as well as a good range of malt whiskies, local farm ciders and a well chosen reasonably priced wine list; piped classical music. *(Recommended by Dr J A Harvey, Daren Haines, Ted George, Dr M Smith, June and Malcolm Farmer, Dorothy and Leslie Pilson, Pamela and Merlyn Horswell, S P Watkin, P A Taylor, JKW, Mark Percy, Lesley Mayoh, Wayne Brindle, D H and M C Watkinson, Robin Hillman, Mr and Mrs M J Matthews, Mrs J Crawford, Malcolm Taylor, JAH)*

Free house ~ Licensees Malcolm and Janet Hall ~ Real ale ~ Meals and snacks ~ Restaurant ~ (01989) 730236 ~ Well behaved children in restaurant and snug ~ Open 11.30-3, 6.30-11; 12-2.30, 7-10.30 Sun; cl 25 Dec, evening 26 Dec

ST OWENS CROSS SO5425 Map 4
New Inn

Harewood End

Both the characterful lounge bar and the restaurant at this old timbered split level coaching inn have huge inglenook fireplaces, intriguing nooks and crannies, settles, old pews, beams, and timbers. The bar menu includes soup (£2.45), sweet pickled herrings (£3.95), chicken liver pâté (£4.25), half roast chicken (£5.95), scampi or steak and kidney pie (£6.45), mushroom and asparagus pancake (£6.95), chicken breast in white wine and cream (£7.95) and lemon sole (£8.95), there is also a specials board and they do Sunday lunch. Well kept Bass, Fullers London Pride, Smiles Best, Tetleys Bitter, Wadworths 6X, and guest beers on handpump, and a fair choice of malt whiskies; darts, shove-ha'penny, cribbage, dominoes, and piped music. The three characterful dobermans are called Baileys and her two daughters Tia Maria and Ginnie. There are fine views over rolling countryside to the distant Black Mountains. *(Recommended by Mark Percy, Lesley Mayoh, Wayne Brindle, Patrick Freeman, JKW, David Gregory, S P Watkin, P A Taylor, Dr and Mrs R Booth, Mike Perks, F A Owens)*

Free house ~ Licensee Nigel Donovan ~ Real ale ~ Meals and snacks ~ Restaurant ~ (01989) 730274 ~ Children welcome ~ Open 12-2.30, 6-11; 12-3, 7-10.30 Sun ~ Bedrooms: £35S(£45B)/£60S(£80B)

STOCKTON CROSS SO5161 Map 4
Stockton Cross Inn
Kimbolton; A4112, off A49 just N of Leominster

The long heavily beamed bar's old-fashioned feel is perhaps at its best on a cold winter's day, when it's really snug at the top end: a handsome antique settle facing an old black kitchen range, and old leather chairs and brocaded stools by the huge log fire in the broad stone fireplace. There's a woodburning stove at the far end too, with heavy cast-iron-framed tables and sturdy dining chairs; there are more tables and chairs up a step in a small no-smoking side area. Old-time prints, a couple of épées on one beam and lots of copper and brass complete the picture. Blackboards cover a massive choice of enjoyable food including rabbit caught by Percy the local rabbit catcher which the landlady prepares in so many enterprising ways (rabbit casserole £8.50) that a local radio station has chosen to run a series on her recipes, also soup (£2.50), Portuguese sardines (£3.95), deep-fried camembert with gooseberry sauce (£4.25), black pudding with bacon and melted cheese (£4.50), steak and kidney pie or home-baked ham and eggs (£5.75), beef in red wine, lamb casserole or macaroni cheese done with leeks, mushrooms and onions (£5.95), Finnan haddock (£9.50), venison (£11) – and puddings like baked lemon cheesecake with lemon and lime sauce and chocolate cake with fudge sauce. Well kept Flowers Original and Whitbreads Castle Eden on handpump; good welcoming service; tables out in the garden, with maybe a fine summer show of sweet peas. It can get busy at weekends. *(Recommended by W C Jones, Basil Minson, Mike and Emma, Joy and Peter Heatherley)*

Free house ~ Licensee Mr R Wood ~ Real ale ~ Meals and snacks (no snacks Sat evening) ~ (01568) 612509 ~ Open 12-3, 7-11; cl Mon evening

ULLINGSWICK SO5949 Map 4
Three Crowns ♀
Village off A465 S of Bromyard (and just S of Stoke Lacy) and signposted off A417; pub at Bleak Acre, towards Little Cowarne

The carefully cooked and generously served food at this attractive old country pub – pretty in summer with its well tended hanging baskets – is well worth knowing about. They try to be flexible about the menu, so it's worth asking about a favourite omelette or salad. As well as a few lunchtime sandwiches and snacks the extensive seasonally changing menu might include bacon and haricot bean salad with poached egg and mustard mayonnaise or polenta with marinated mushrooms (£3.95), crab tart (£4.75), spinach and mushroom pancake gateaux (£6.95), pot roast neck of pork with ginger and spices, rack of lamb with bearnaise sauce and asparagus or fried lamb liver with balsamic sauce (£9.95), roast duck breast with lentils and glazed shallots or bouillaibaisse (£11.50). The charmingly cosy traditional interior has hops strung along the low beams of its smallish bar, a couple of traditional settles besides more usual seats, open fires and one or two gently sophisticated touches like candles on tables and napkins. Service is very welcoming; well kept Bass, Ind Coope Burton, Tetleys and a guest like Hobsons Best on handpump; good house wines; cribbage. There are tables out on the lawn, not large but attractively planted, with good summer views. *(Recommended by John Hackett, Mr and Mrs Paul Aynsley; more reports please)*

Free house ~ Licensees Derrick and Sue Horwood ~ Real ale ~ Meals and snacks ~ (01432) 820279 ~ Well behaved children welcome ~ Open 12-2.30, 7-11; 12-3, 7-10.30 Sun; cl Tues

---

The details at the end of each main entry start by saying whether the pub is a free house, or if it's tied to a brewery (which we name).

UPTON BISHOP SO6527 Map 4

Moody Cow

2 miles from M50 junction 3 westbound (or junction 4 eastbound), via B4221; continue on B4221 to rejoin at next junction

A merry place, with several snug separate areas angling in an L around the bar counter, a pleasant medley of stripped country furniture, stripped floorboards and stonework, a few cow ornaments and naive cow paintings, a big log fire. On the far right is a biggish no-smoking restaurant, rustic and candlelit, with hop-draped rafters and a fireside area with armchairs and sofas. The far left has a second smaller dining area, just five or six tables with rush seats, green-stained woodwork, shelves of country china. A good changing choice of well cooked food might include starters like soup (£3.15), tagliatelle with tomato, sweet pepper, cockles, mussels and prawns (£4.35), baked goat's cheese (£4.95), and main courses like battered cod and chips in newspaper (£6.45), an enormous helping of steak and kidney pie (£7.45), celery, apple, walnut, mushroom and stilton in filo pastry (£8.75), fried red snapper with prawns, capers, lemon and nut butter (£9.95) and noisettes of lamb with redcurrant and rosemary sauce (£10.95); puddings like steamed syrup sponge (£3.25); Flowers IPA, Smiles Best, Herefordshire Wye Valley and Wadworths 6X on handpump, local farm cider. *(Recommended by D H and M C Watkinson, Steve Marchant, David Ling)*

Free house ~ Licensee James Lloyd ~ Real ale ~ Meals and snacks (not Sun eve or Mon) ~ Restaurant ~ (01989) 780470 ~ Well behaved children welcome ~ Jazz Thurs evening ~ Open 12-2.30, 6.30-11; 12-2.30, 7-10.30 Sun; cl 25/26 Dec and 1 Jan evening

WALTERSTONE SO3425 Map 6

Carpenters Arms

Village signposted off A465 E of Abergavenny, beside Old Pandy Inn; follow village signs, and keep eyes skinned for sign to pub, off to right, by lane-side barn; OS Sheet 161, map reference 340250

Tucked away by a church on a small hill in very quiet and secluded countryside, this charming little stone cottage is the best sort of unspoilt homely country tavern. There are ancient settles against stripped stone walls, some pieces of carpet on broad polished flagstones, a roaring log fire in a gleaming black range (complete with pot-iron, hot water tap, bread oven and salt cupboard), pewter mugs hanging from beams, well kept Wadworths 6X and one of their seasonal ales tapped from the cask, farm cider, the slow tick of a clock, the promising aroma of stock simmering in the kitchen, a big vase of flowers on the dresser in the snug dining room with its mahogany tables and oak corner cupboards, and a friendly landlady (helped out by her family at weekends) with plenty of time for a chat. Food might include soup (£2.25), rolls and sandwiches (from £1.25), prawn cocktail (£2.80), ploughman's (£3), sausage (£3.50), vegetarian chilli or beef curry (£4.50), scampi (£4.90), lamb chop with redcurrant sauce (£8.50) and pepper fillet steak (£10); puddings (£2.50). There's a separate pool room with fruit machine and juke box; lavatories are in character. *(Recommended by Gordon, Gwyneth and Salvo Spadaro-Dutturi)*

Free house ~ Licensee Vera Watkins ~ Real ale ~ Meals and snacks (12-3, 7-10) ~ (01873) 890353 ~ Children welcome ~ Open 11-11; 12-10.30 Sun

WEOBLEY SO4052 Map 6

Olde Salutation 🍽 🛏 ♟

Village signposted from A4112 SW of Leominster; and from A44 NW of Hereford (there's also a good back road direct from Hereford – straight out past S side of racecourse)

Looking straight down the broad main street of a picture-book village, this beautifully kept 500-year-old hotel is popular for its lovely setting, atmospheric bedrooms and good bar food. The two areas of the quiet, comfortable lounge – separated by a few steps and standing timbers – have a relaxed, pubby feel, brocaded modern winged settles and smaller seats, a couple of big cut-away cask seats, wildlife decorations, a hop bine over the bar counter, and logs burning in a big stone fireplace; more standing timbers separate it from the neat no-smoking restaurant area, and there's a separate smaller parquet-floored public bar with sensibly placed darts, juke box, and a fruit machine; dominoes and cribbage. Bar food includes lentil and vegetable terrine, pasta and blue cheese bake or fried black pudding with mashed potato and red wine and onion gravy (£5.85), home-baked ham with orange sauce or roast beef (£6.10), grilled trout with white wine and herb sauce (£6.95), pheasant with red wine, mushrooms and herbs (£7.50) and sirloin steak with brandy and peppercorn sauce (£10.50); lovely breakfasts. Well kept Boddingtons and Hook Norton Best on handpump, an interesting extensive wine list and quite a good collection of whiskies. On a sheltered back terrace are tables and chairs with parasols. *(Recommended by Denys Gueroult, JKW, MRSM, Mrs Jill Jones, Chris Philip, Victoria Herriott, Nigel Clifton, Mrs J E Hilditch, Andrew Shore, Mr and Mrs D Jackson, Glenn and Gillian Miller, Mike and Wena Stevenson, Ian Jones, P P and J Salmon, Wayne Brindle, David Gregory, Dorothee and Dennis Glover, R C Hopton, O K Smyth, Robin and Laura Hillman, Sarah and Peter Gooderham, Chris Wheaton, Basil Minson, Mr and Mrs C Cole; also in Good Hotel Guide)*

Free house ~ Licensees Chris and Frances Anthony ~ Real ale ~ Meals and snacks ~ Restaurant ~ (01544) 318443 ~ Children welcome in eating area of bar ~ Open 11-11; 12-10.30 Sun ~ Bedrooms: £36B/£60B

WINFORTON SO2947 Map 6
Sun

The inventive bar food at this neatly kept little dining pub includes onion tart with wild mushroom dressing (£3.95), burgers with onion marmalade (£3.99), pork and leek sausages or pork and apple pie (£4.50), duck and apricot pie (£6.99), half a shoulder of lamb with mint and saffron sauce (£11.99), grilled ostrich steak with game and red wine sauce (£12.99) and puddings like rhubarb and elderflower fool (£3.50). The two friendly beamed areas on either side of the central servery have an individual assortment of comfortable country-kitchen chairs, high-backed settles and good solid wooden tables, heavy-horse harness, brasses and old farm tools on the mainly stripped stone walls, and two log-burning stoves; partly no-smoking area. Well kept Brains, Hook Horton, Jennings Cumberland and Woods Parish on handpump, several malt whiskies, and local cider; sensibly placed darts, cribbage, dominoes, maybe piped music. As well as sheltered tables and a good timbery play area the garden has an 18 hole pitch-and-putt/crazy golf course. *(Recommended by Mrs L Minchella, P Mapstone; more reports please)*

Free house ~ Licensees Brian and Wendy Hibbard ~ Real ale ~ Meals and snacks (not winter Tues) ~ (01544) 327677 ~ Children welcome in eating area of bar ~ Open 11(12 Sun)-3, 6.30-11; closed Tues ~ Bedrooms: £30B/£45B

WOOLHOPE SO6136 Map 4
Butchers Arms

Signposted from B4224 in Fownhope; carry straight on past Woolhope village

This relaxed and atmospheric place is popular with both locals and visitors. One of the spaciously welcoming bars has very low beams decorated with hops, old-fashioned well worn built-in seats with brocaded cushions, captain's chairs and stools around small tables and a brick fireplace filled with dried flowers. The other, broadly similar though with less beams, has a large built-in settle and another log fire; there are often fresh flowers. Good bar food includes lots of lunchtime sandwiches (from £2.50), soup or spicy potato wedges (£3.50), chicken liver pâté (£3.95) and main courses: wild rabbit and cider pie, chilli (£5.75), lasagne (£5.95), chicken curry (£6.50), beef and ale pie (£6.95), several vegetarian dishes including leek and potato bake (£5.50) and daily specials like pork in ginger beer, beef and walnut casserole, pork with apricot and brandy or lamb and cranberry casserole (£7.50) and puddings like choc hazelnut meringue (£3.95); very good, hearty breakfasts; the restaurant is no smoking. Well kept Hook Norton Best and Old Hookey and two or three guests like Plassey Bitter, RCH Pitchfork and Wood Shropshire Lad on handpump, local ciders, quite a few malt whiskies, and decent wines. Friendly cat – dogs not welcome. Sliding french windows lead from the bar to a little terrace with teak furniture, a few parasols and cheerful flowering tubs; there's also a tiny willow-lined brook. The countryside around is really lovely – to enjoy some of the best of it, turn left as you come out of the pub and take the tiny left-hand road at the end of the car park; this turns into a track and then into a path; the view from the top of the hill is quite something. *(Recommended by Daren Haines, John Bowdler, Chris Philip, Lynn Sharpless, Bob Eardley, Wayne Brindle, David Gittins, Jan and Nita Cooper, Luke Worthington, Denys Gueroult, Dr M Smith, JKW, Gwen and Peter Andrews, Graham and Lynn Mason, L T Lionet, Mr and Mrs H M Mortimer, Chris Wheaton, Iain Robertson, S G N Bennett, Ian Jones)*

Free house ~ Licensees Patrick Power and Lucinda Matthews ~ Real ale ~ Meals and snacks ~ Restaurant ~ (01432) 860281 ~ Well behaved children welcome ~ Open 11.30-3, 6(6.30 Fri/Sat, 7 Mon-Thurs in winter)-11; 12-3, 6-10.30 Sun; cl evening 25 Dec ~ Bedrooms: £30/£39

Crown ♀

In village centre

This year the attentive licensees at this carefully managed popular old place have smartened up the neatly kept lounge bar with new plush button-back built-in wall banquettes and new dark wood tables and chairs. There's also an open fire, a timbered divider strung with hop bines, good wildlife photographs and little country pictures on the cream walls, and lots of attention to details like flowers on tables and spotless housekeeping. Generous helpings of good value attractively served bar food include home-made soup (£2.25), broccoli and blue cheese or smoked salmon quiche (£3), prawn cocktail (£3.25), ploughman's (from £4.50), fried plaice (£4.75), chestnut, onion and apple pie with cumberland sauce or liver and onions (£5.25), faggots in onion gravy (£5.50), steak and kidney pie, sweet and sour chicken with rice or lamb and cranberry casserole (£5.95), fish pie (£6.25) and mixed grill (£9.95); Sunday roast (£5.75); the restaurant is no smoking. Well kept Hook Norton Best, Smiles Best, Tetleys Bitter and a guest beer on handpump, decent wine list, and farm cider. There are picnic tables under cocktail parasols on the neat front lawn; darts, summer quoits. *(Recommended by David Ling, Chris Philip, Wayne Brindle, Denys Gueroult, Daren Haines, S G N Bennett, DMT, Derek and Sylvia Stephenson)*

Free house ~ Licensees Neil and Sally Gordon ~ Real ale ~ Meals and snacks (till 10pm) ~ Restaurant ~ (01432) 860468 ~ Well behaved children welcome though customers are asked to check beforehand because of limited space ~ Open 12-2.30, 6.30(6 Sat)-11; 12-3, 6.30-10.30 Sun; winter evening opening 7; cl evening 25 Dec

WYRE PIDDLE SO9647 Map 4
Anchor

B4084 NW of Evesham

Quite a few customers arrive at this easy-going, marvellously positioned unpretentious pub by boat, as its spacious lawn runs down to the River Avon. There are views spreading out over the Vale of Evesham as far as the Cotswolds, the Malverns and Bredon Hill from tables on this lawn and also from the big airy back bar. The friendly and well kept little lounge has a good log fire in its attractively restored inglenook fireplace, comfortably upholstered chairs and settles, and two beams in the shiny ceiling. More than decent bar food (service can be a little slow when they are very busy in the summer months) includes soup (£2.45), filled baps (from £3), Indian savoury selection or ploughman's (£4.25), moules marinières (£5.25), lasagne (£5.75), scampi, steak and kidney pie or spinach cannelloni (£6.25) and blackboard specials like spiced chicken breast or green thai curry (£6.25), salmon fillet with hollandaise sauce (£7.25), venison casserole in brandy (£7.50) and grilled duck breast with orange and Grand Marnier (£9), puddings like treacle sponge or apricot crumble (£2.35); Sunday lunch (£11.75). Friendly, obliging service. Well kept Boddingtons, Brains Best, Flowers IPA and Original and Marstons Pedigree on handpump, a few whiskies, and country wines; darts and fruit machine. *(Recommended by Ian and Nita Cooper, J and P Daggett, S H Godsell, Brian and Anna Marsden, Mark Fennell, Mavis and Robert Harford, Nick*

Lawless, Sheila Keene, Andy Petersen, Dorothee and Dennis Glover, Paul Boot, Lucy James, Dean Foden, Mrs J Huntly)

Whitbreads ~ Lease: Michael Senior ~ Real ale ~ Meals and snacks (not Sun evening) ~ River-view lunchtime restaurant (not Sun evening) ~ (01386) 552799 ~ Children welcome ~ Open 11(12 Sat)-3, 6-11; 12-3, 7-10.30 Sun

---

Lucky Dip

Besides the fully inspected pubs, you might like to try these Lucky Dips recommended to us and described by readers (if you do, please send us reports):

Almeley [off A480, A4111 or A4112 S of Kington; SO3351], *Bell*: Roomy and welcoming, with particularly well kept Marstons Bitter and Pedigree, darts and hoopla; no piped music *(P A Reynolds)*

Alvechurch [Red Lion St; SP0272], *Red Lion*: Big beamed lounge with side snugs, big log fire, low lighting, good varied reasonably priced generous food all day, good service, Bass and other ales, quiet piped music; big back garden *(Dave and Sue Price, Mike and Emma)*

Astley [Astley Burf; E of B4196, S of Stourport; SO8167], *Hampstall*: Comfortable pub overlooking River Severn, food inc good home-made chilli con carne, tables on terrace with play area *(Paul and Pam Penrose)*

Astwood Bank [A441 towards Cook Hill; SP0462], *Why Not*: Useful Whitbreads pub, modern, clean and busy, with tasty good value bar meals *(Dave Braisted)*

☆ **Bastonford** [A449 Worcester—Malvern; SO8150], *Halfway House*: Plain roadside pub transformed by friendly and industrious landlord, generous good value honest food (not Tues evening; Sun lunch can be booked), well kept Fullers London Pride, Marstons Bitter and a guest such as Timothy Taylors Landlord, perhaps even home-made orange brandy; two spacious rather bright rooms with routine pub furnishings, some interesting aircraft pictures, shove-ha'penny, middle of the road piped music, fruit machine; tables and play tree in garden, open all day Sat in summer *(J H E Peters, BB)*

Baughton [A4104 Pershore—Upton; SO8741], *Jockey*: Real ales such as Adnams Broadside, Banks's, Woods Parish and Gibbs Mew Bishops Tipple, decent Australian wines, good bar and restaurant food inc good vegetarian choice and fine puddings (esp damson and sloe gin ice cream); friendly landlord *(Mrs A Oakley, Derek and Sylvia Stephenson)*

Beckford [A435; SO9835], *Beckford Inn*: Very wide choice of food esp grills, well kept Scottish Courage ales, old-fashioned yet pleasantly pubby atmosphere, quick service, big front lawn; bedrooms *(Chris Reeve)*

☆ **Belbroughton** [High St (off A491); SO9277], *Queens*: Bustling friendly local with good value food in enjoyable specials, interesting regulars, polite staff, well kept Marstons, comfortable alcove seating, bigger tables in family area, fresh flowers; picnic tables on small terrace, quiet village *(Andy Petersen, Pat Millward)*

Berrow [Ryecross; junction A438/B4208; SO7934], *Duke of York*: Two linked rooms, 15th-c beams, nooks and crannies, good log fire, enjoyable food inc good veg and good range of puddings (may be a wait at busy times), well kept Boddingtons, Fremlins and Ruddles Best, farm cider, friendly staff and locals, dominoes, cribbage; piped music; children welcome, extended back restaurant, part no smoking, picnic tables in big back garden; handy for Malvern Hills *(B Walton, P Lloyd, Dave Braisted, Don Ransom, DMT, V Kavanagh, LYM)*

Bournheath [Dodford Rd; handy for M5 junction 3; SO9474], *Gate*: Attractive country dining pub with wide choice of food inc vegetarian, Mexican and Asian dishes and lunchtime and early evening bargains, well kept Smiles Best and Exhibition and a weekly guest beer, restaurant; nice garden *(P H Boot)*

☆ **Bredenbury** [A44 Bromyard—Leominster; SO6056], *Barneby Arms*: Substantial hotel popular for wide range of generous well served food inc vegetarian in clean bright busy bar with ceiling joists, horse tack, lots of old woodworking tools; well kept Banks's and Marstons Pedigree, friendly staff, restaurant; children welcome, big garden *(Richard Gibbs, Bob and Audrey Meacock)*

Bredon [High St; SO9236], *Royal Oak*: Roomy and relaxed carpeted bar with open fire, Banks's and Marstons Pedigree, nice choice of well presented food in bar and dining room inc Fri fish and chips, friendly staff; pool, darts, skittle alley, barbecues *(Neil and Anita Christopher, Derek and Sylvia Stephenson)*

Bredwardine [SO3344], *Red Lion*: Interesting 17th-c inn with pleasant landlord and attractive restaurant; nice bedrooms *(Wendy Arnold)*

☆ **Broadway** [Church St; SP0937], *Crown & Trumpet*: Cosy unspoilt beamed and timbered local with dark high-backed settles, big log fire, well kept Boddingtons, Flowers IPA and Original, Morlands Old Speckled Hen, local Stanway and Wadworths 6X, seasonal made drinks, straightforward food, good range of pub games but also intrusive fruit machine and piped music; Thurs quiz night, Sat duo; children welcome, open all day Sat, seats on front terrace; bedrooms *(Angus Lyon, Norma and David Hardy, SLC, Nick Lawless, Terry* *and Vann W Prime, Pat and Roger Fereday, LYM)*

☆ **Broadway** [Collin Lane; follow Willersey sign off A44 NW – marked Gt Collin Farm on OS Sheet 150 map ref 076391], *Collin House*: Wide choice of good interesting freshly done bar food inc traditional puddings in lovely bar of small country hotel, very relaxed and civilised – good log fires, no machines or piped music (but no sandwiches or ploughman's either), very accommodating; nice restaurant not overpriced (wise to book), good wines, local beers, proper coffee, pleasant staff; tables outside; comfortable bedrooms *(W C M Jones)*

☆ **Castlemorton** [B4208, Castlemorton Common; SO7838], *Plume of Feathers*: Friendly country local notable for its well kept changing ales, such as Dorothy Goodbodys Autumn Ale, a couple of Hobsons, Hook Norton Best and Woods Shropshire Lad; heavy black beams (one studded with regulars' holiday PCs), big log fire snugged in by a corral of built-in settles, side room with darts and fruit machine; attractively priced home cooking, afternoon teas, tables and swings on side lawn; children welcome; small neat dining room *(A Y Drummond, BB)*

Castlemorton [B4208, 1¼ mile S of Welland crossroads; SO7937], *Robin Hood*: Charming old beamed country pub, relaxed atmosphere, medley of cushioned pews etc, big brick fireplace, lots of horsebrasses, hops, jugs, welcoming landlady, good generous interesting food, well kept Boddingtons, Flowers and Theakstons, local Weston's cider; area with fruit machine and darts, separate small dining room; big lawns and space for caravans behind *(Tom Evans, Colin Fisher)*

Catshill [nr Barleymow Lane, Satshill Estate; SO9573], *Royal Oak*: Popular for huge helpings of good value food; well kept Banks's Mild and Bitter and Marstons Pedigree *(Steve Jennings, Dave Braisted)*

Chaddesley Corbett [off A448 Bromsgrove—Kidderminster – OS Sheet 139 map ref 892736; SO8973], *Talbot*: Attractive timbered pub in quiet village street, welcoming landlord, Banks's Bitter, bar food inc good chunky sandwiches, attractive prices, good service *(Dr M I Crichton, Mike and Mary Carter)*

☆ **Claines** [3 miles from M5 junction 6; A449 towards Ombersley, then leave dual carriageway at second exit for Worcester; village signposted from here, and park in Cornmeadow Lane; SO8558], *Mug House*: Fine views from ancient basic country tavern in unique churchyard setting by fields below the Malvern Hills, low doorways, heavy oak beams, well kept cheap Banks's Bitter and Mild, minimal choice of basic but generous snacks (not Sun), children allowed in snug away from servery *(Gwen and Peter Andrews, LYM)*

☆ **Clent** [A491 Bromsgrove—Stourbridge; SO9279], *Holly Bush*: Pleasant country pub

very popular midweek lunchtime (they will book tables) for good range of freshly cooked bar food esp fish, Holt Plant & Deakins Bitter and Entire *(J Barnwell)*

☆ **Clows Top** [A456 Bewdley—Tenbury; SO7171], *Colliers Arms*: Good value dining pub, roomy and comfortable, with wide choice of generous food inc vegetarian and interesting filled rolls, spacious no-smoking back restaurant, efficient service, log fires, well kept Theakstons Best and XB, unobtrusive piped music; no dogs, nice countryside *(P and M Rudlin, Monica Shelley, Laura Darlington, Peter and Rosie Flower)*

☆ **Crowle** [SO9256], *Old Chequers*: Smart and busy, with more modern restaurant extension opening off old pubby core of some character, good generous food inc unusual dishes (no sandwiches etc, but good value light lunches), well kept Bass and other ales, prompt service *(G S and E M Dorey)*

☆ **Dorstone** [pub signed off B4348 E of Hay on Wye; SO3141], *Pandy*: County's oldest pub, in pretty countryside, heavy beams, stout timbers, broad worn flagstones, traditional furnishings, alcoves, vast log fireplace, generally good bar food from sandwiches to interesting main courses and themed food evenings, well kept Bass, Smiles, Wye Valley and guest ales, welcoming service, good choice of whiskies, traditional games; piped music; picnic tables and play area in neat garden; children welcome, cl winter Mon lunchtime, winter Tues *(Ian Williams, Linda Mar, C Park, Victoria Herriott, G Robinson, O K Smyth, Ian Jones, Richard and Jean Phillips, LYM)*

Drakes Broughton [A44 towards Pershore, off M5 junction 7; SO9248], *Plough & Harrow*: Attractive rambling lounge, well kept ales, friendly efficient service; tables nicely set behind, by old orchard *(Mrs Greenwood , Denis and Margaret Kilner)*

☆ **Dunhampstead** [just SE of Droitwich; pub towards Sale Green – OS Sheet 150 map ref 919600; SO9160], *Firs*: Civilised and relaxing, with concentration on food and good enthusiastic chef, but still works too as a country local, with well kept Banks's and Marstons, prompt welcoming service, friendly dogs, flowers on tables and comfortable conservatory; tables in garden – nice spot nr canal *(G S and E M Dorey, Pete Yearsley, Stephen Pine, Alfred Lawrence, LYM)*

Eardisland [A44; SO4258], *White Swan*: Interesting old pub in lovely black and white village, with armchairs and enormous fire in cosy inner core, two rooms furnished more suitably for eating, pleasant public bar with pool and fruit machine, good back garden with play house *(Lynn Sharpless, Bob Eardley, BB)*

Eckington [Church St (B4080); SO9241], *Bell*: Attractive and inviting village pub, central bar serves bar and dining areas, pleasantly cool dining conservatory, wide choice of good value food, quick helpful staff, real ales, pool table in bar, unobtrusive piped music; charge for credit cards *(Malcolm Thomas, Margaret and David Watson)*

Eldersfield [Lime St; signed from B4211; SO8031], *Greyhound*: Unspoilt two-bar country local with good inexpensive food, friendly young licensees, surprisingly modern lavatories with interesting mosaic in gents', pretty garden and room for children to play in *(Mrs A Oakley)*

☆ **Elmley Castle** [village signed off A44 and A435, not far from Evesham; SO9841], *Queen Elizabeth*: Very good genuine cooking using fresh local and more exotic ingredients in restaurant attached to ancient tavern in pretty village below Bredon Hill (no food Sun); pub part has cheap farm cider and well kept Marstons in attractive old-fashioned tap room, haphazard medley of periods in decoration and furnishings, friendly locals and landlord (here for over 30 years), maybe piped classical music *(Nick Lawless, LYM)*

Evesham [Vine St; SP0344], *Ducks Don't Float*: Spit 'n' sawdust refurbishment of former Maidens Head, well kept M&B Brew XI, attractive service, piped music *(Paul Rencher)*; [Oat St – off High St at Barclays, follow Library signs], *Green Dragon*: 16th-c coaching inn, formerly part of monastery, brewing own Asum and Gold (can arrange to see brewery); small dining lounge, big comfortable public bar, back pool room and skittle alley, old well in corridor, friendly staff, attractive prints, cheap food, quiet at lunchtime; evening piped music, maybe TV, karaoke, live music, bouncers; good value bedrooms, good breakfast *(G Coates, Pete Baker, Chris Reeve)*

Far Forest [A4117 Bewdley—Ludlow, just W of junction with A456; SO7374], *Plough*: Bright and cosy beamed dining area popular lunchtime with older people for nicely cooked food inc vegetarian, efficient friendly service, well kept Bass, Boddingtons and a guest beer on electric pump, woodburner, lots of brass and china; picnic tables on neat lawn, subdued piped pop music; children allowed if eating, tables out on grass; good walks *(P and M Rudlin)*

Felton [SO5848], *Crozen*: Dining pub with very good value food esp roast beef with help-yourself veg, good puddings *(Dorothy and Leslie Pilson)*

☆ **Flyford Flavell** [½ mile off A422 Worcester—Alcester; SO9754], *Boot*: Unpretentious beamed pub with 18th-c front but core dating from 13th c, plenty of character, wide range of good generous food (cooked to order so may be a short wait) inc popular Sun lunch, well kept Bass, Boddingtons, Marstons Pedigree and a couple of less common guest beers, good wine choice; dining room with open fire, no-smoking area, conservatory; children welcome to eat, garden with play area, lovely surroundings *(June and Mike Coleman, Andrew Cameron)*

☆ **Fownhope** [B4224; SO5834], *Green Man*: Striking 15th-c black and white inn, often very busy (so the friendly service can slow), with big log fire, wall settles, window seats and armchairs in one beamed bar, standing timbers dividing another, popular food from sandwiches to steak inc children's and Sun carvery (no-smoking main restaurant), well kept Courage Directors, Hook Norton Best, Marstons Pedigree, John Smiths and Sam Smiths OB, Weston's farm ciders, attractive prices; children welcome, quiet garden with play area; comfortable bedrooms *(Iain Robertson, Wayne Brindle, P J Keen, Stephen Pine, Alfred Lawrence, John Bowdler, Chris Wheaton, N C Hinton, LYM)*

☆ **Gorcott Hill** [off A435 3 miles S of M42 junction 3; SP0868], *Hollybush*: Quietly placed country pub with wide range of generous good value home-made food inc seafood, well kept Scottish Courage ales, good service; busy with office people weekday lunchtime *(Dave Braisted)*

☆ **Hadley** [Hadley Heath; A4133 Droitwich—Ombersley; SO8664], *Bowling Green*: Large but cosy beamed bar in attractively refurbished 16th-c inn, wide range of reasonably priced food inc enterprising filled baguettes, interesting hot dishes and good value Sun carvery; well kept Banks's Bitter and Mild, Marstons Pedigree and Hook Norton, good value wines, big log fire, attractive restaurant, comfortable bedrooms; children welcome, tables outside, has UK's oldest bowling green *(Martin and Karen Wake, Dorothee and Dennis Glover, Denys Gueroult, Dave Braisted, Chris Philip, Bryan Taylor)*

Hampton Bishop [SO5638], *Bunch of Carrots*: Busy spaciously refurbished beamed country pub with good value imaginative daily specials inc fish, popular Sun lunch, well kept ales inc Boddingtons, local farm cider, friendly efficient service; play area *(D H Gittins, Richard and Cathy Barker)*

Hanley Swan [B4209 Malvern—Upton; SO8142], *Swan*: Neatly run traditional pub by village green and duck pond, with good value small attractive restaurant, decent wine, well kept Theakstons, nice locals' bar, prompt friendly service, tables on lawn with play area *(S Holder, Bill and Brenda Lemon)*

☆ **Harewood End** [A49 Hereford—Ross; SO5327], *Harewood End*: Attractive panelled dining lounge with old candlelit tables, big log fire, old prints and antiques, good range of consistently enjoyable food inc children's and massive mixed grill, well kept beers, decent wines; good value bedrooms *(S Watkin, P Taylor, John and Joan Hilliard)*

☆ **Howle Hill** [coming from Ross fork left off B4228 on sharp right bend, first right, then left at crossroads after a mile – OS Sheet 162 map ref 603204; SO6020], *Crown*: Immaculate little hidden-away pub with good range of well priced tasty food inc exceptional value puddings (not Sun evening, Mon; no sandwiches), well kept Whitbreads-related ales, friendly landlord and labradors (no visiting dogs), padded pews; bar skittles, tables in garden; winter opening may be limited.

☆ Inkberrow [A422 Worcester—Alcester, set well back; SP0157], *Old Bull*: Photogenic Tudor pub with bulging walls, huge inglenooks, flagstones, oak beams and trusses, and some old-fashioned high-backed settles among more modern furnishings; lots of Archers memorabilia (it's the model for the Ambridge Bull), friendly service, simple home-made food inc vegetarian and Sun roast, Whitbreads-related and guest ales; children allowed in eating area, tables outside *(Angus Lyon, Alan and Barbara Mence, LYM)*
Inkberrow [High St], *Bulls Head*: Welcoming, with beams and flagstones, log fire, Banks's, Bass, Boddingtons and guest beers, food inc vegetarian *(Moira and John Culpan)*

☆ Kemerton [Bredon—Beckford; SO9437], *Crown*: Welcoming 18th-c local with bustling L-shaped lounge bar, panelled benches, well kept Whitbreads-related ales, enjoyable food inc popular family lunches *(David Campbell, Vicki McLean, Michael Herman)*

☆ Kidderminster [42 Mill Lane; signed off ring rd by A442 to Bridgnorth; fork rt opp General Hosp; SO8376], *Little Tumbling Sailor*: Lots of good naval photographs as well as nautical hardware from brass and model ships to saucy figurehead; several rooms around central servery, home-made food from sandwiches up, well kept Holt Plant & Deakins Entire, Marstons Tipenny, Morlands Old Speckled Hen, Little Lumphammer; piped pop music (live Mon and Fri); well behaved children welcome, small garden with trawler deckhouse and sandpit *(Jeanne Cross, Paul Silvestri, LYM)*
Kingsland [SO4561], *Angel*: Timbered former coaching inn with new licensees developing interesting food, relaxed beamed bar, big stove, fresh flowers, prompt friendly service, well kept ales, decent sensibly priced wines; attractive restaurant, some tables outside *(Alec Hamilton)*
Kington [Victoria Rd; note this is the Herefs Kington; SO3057], *Olde Tavern*: Wonderful time-warp old place, ornate exterior (without inn sign), small plain often enjoyably crowded parlour and public bar, dark brown woodwork, old settles and other antique furniture, china, pewter and curios; well kept Ansells, no music, machines or food; children welcome, though not a family pub *(Pete Baker)*; [Bridge St], *Queens Head*: Wide variety of farm ciders and real ales, inc its good own-brewed Solstice Golden Torc, Talisman and Capstone; good range of generous reasonably priced food inc imaginative dishes *(Geoffrey and Irene Lindley, Ronald and Ruth Locke)*

☆ Ledbury [New St; SO7138], *Olde Talbot*: Relaxed local atmosphere in 16th-c inn's black-beamed bar rambling around island servery, antique hunting prints, plush wall banquettes or more traditional seats, log fire in big stone fireplace, Hancocks HB, Highgate Saddlers and Marstons served through

sparkler, usual bar food, smart restaurant, tales of a friendly poltergeist; fruit machine, shame about the piped music; decent bedrooms sharing bath *(Peter Lloyd, Jim Lipton, J and P Maloney, BB)*
Ledbury [Homend], *Horse Shoe*: Welcoming timbered pub bright with hanging baskets etc, good choice of beers, good bar food, log fire *(Tracy Dawson)*; [Southend], *Royal Oak*: Brews its own Ledbury Best, Doghill and SB, good food inc Greek dishes; comfortable bedrooms *(Andy and Jill Kassube)*
Leintwardine [High St; SO4174], *Lion*: Nicely presented good value food in bar and popular restaurant, well kept Boddingtons and Morlands Old Speckled Hen, welcoming efficient staff *(Mr Kennedy, Robert Whittle)*

☆ Leintwardine [Rosemary Lane, just off A4113; SO4174], *Sun*: More private house than pub, three tables and benches in red-tiled room with faded blue wallpaper and roaring fire, also small settee and a couple of chairs in octogenarian landlady's own sitting room – she makes you feel very much at home; Pitfield PA and Mild drawn from casks in her kitchen *(Pete Baker, Wayne Brindle)*

☆ Leominster [West St; SO4959], *Talbot*: Comfortable and attractive old coaching inn with heavy beams and standing timbers, antique carved settles, log fires with 18th-c oak-panelled chimneybreasts, sporting prints; decent straightforward home-made bar food inc good sandwiches, well kept Scottish Courage ales, efficient cheerful service; piped music; bedrooms *(W H and E Thomas, BB)*
Leominster [74 South St], *Black Horse*: Comfortable town pub with interesting changing ales such as Burton Bridge, Hobsons Towncrier, Marches BHB and Woods Hopping Mad; food too *(Gwyneth and Salvo Spadaro-Dutturi)*; [Broad St], *Grape Vaults*: Welcoming and attractive old local with well kept Marstons Pedigree, Best and guests, wide range of simple freshly cooked food, open fire, no games machines or music *(Roger Thompson, Stephen Pine, Alfred Lawrence)*; [South St], *Royal Oak*: Generous cheap home-made food inc good sandwiches in handsome Georgian-fronted small hotel's bustling locals' bar, friendly service, big log fire, several well kept ales inc Hook Norton and Woods; unobtrusive piped music; spotless genuine Edwardian gents'; simple bedrooms *(Dr and Mrs A H Young, BB)*
Letton [off A438 NW of Hereford; SO3346], *Old Swan*: Friendly and accommodating, good value home-made food (served till late to suit the earnest Wye fishermen), well kept cheap beers inc one brewed locally for them, good games room *(S P Bobeldijk)*

☆ Little Cowarne [off A465 S of Bromyard, towards Ullingswick; SO6051], *Three Horseshoes*: Wide choice of good home cooking in quarry-tiled bar and spacious restaurant (lunchtime carvery), well kept Bass and other ales, decent wines, log fire, mix of solid tables and chairs, friendly obliging licensees, disabled access; juke box, pool, darts and fruit machine; lovely country views from terrace and charming simple garden, quite unspoilt village; comfortable bedrooms *(David Griffiths)*

Longtown [SO3229], *Crown*: Village pub distinguished by exceptionally friendly service *(Peter and Sarah Gooderham)*

Monnington on Wye [A438 Hereford—Hay; SO3744], *Portway*: Roomy 16th-c pub with elegant oak-beamed lounge, good atmosphere, wide range of good imaginative home-cooked bar food inc vegetarian, using local produce; restaurant *(Dr M Smith)*

Mordiford [just off B4224 SE of Hereford – OS Sheet 149 map ref 572374; SO5737], *Moon*: Lounge with roaring fire, good value food from filled baked potatoes to unusual dishes of the day, front restaurant, friendly relaxed service, Bass, Boddingtons, Flowers IPA and Wye Valley Bitter, local farm ciders; back bar popular with young locals *(Paul and Sue Merrick, M G Hart)*

Ombersley [SO8463], *Cross Keys*: Arches and rustic decor in four small comfortable beamed bars, good food, Marstons Bitter and Pedigree and Timothy Taylor Landlord *(James Nunns)*

☆ **Pembridge** [Mkt Sq (A44); SO3958], *New Inn*: Ancient inn overlooking small black and white town's church, comfortable and atmospheric three-room bar, antique settles, worn flagstones, substantial log fire, one room with sofas, pine furniture and books, good food from sandwiches up inc some interesting dishes, attentive friendly staff, well kept Ruddles Best and County, Theakstons and a guest beer, farm cider, traditional games; small carpeted family dining room (not Sun evening); outside lavatories, simple bedrooms *(Glenn and Gillian Miller, D Lorking, Brian Skelcher, N H E Lewis, LYM)*

☆ **Pershore** [Bridge St; SO9445], *Brandy Cask*: Own-brewed Brandysnapper and John Baker, guest beers, good freshly made food from sandwiches up in bar and brasserie, quick friendly service *(R O Goss, Pat and Tony Martin)*

Pound Green [B4194 NW of Bewdley; SO7678], *New Inn*: Old and attractive inn, with friendly staff, good food in bar and dining room, well kept beer with usually two guests *(Patrick Herratt)*

Priors Frome [SO5839], *Yew Tree*: Good imaginative generous food, with an attractive beer brewed for the pub *(Felicity Toube)*

Ross on Wye [Riverside; coming in from A40 W side, 1st left after bridge; SO6024], *Hope & Anchor*: Plain big-windowed family extension looking out on flower-lined lawns leading down to river, plenty of tables out here (and summer ice-cream bar and barbecues), boating theme in cheery main bar, cosy upstairs parlour bar and Victorian-style dining room, generous food inc good choice for children, well kept Banks's ales, farm cider; open all day, can be crowded weekends, summer boat trips *(IHR, LYM; more reports on new regime please)*; [High St], *Rosswyn*: Well kept Scottish Courage and other beers

and ciders, friendly staff and wide choice of good bar food in 15th-c inn with curious 17th-c carvings in back bar, open fire; fruit machines round corner, juke box; children welcome, restaurant, big well kept secluded garden behind; comfortable bedrooms *(M Churchill)*

☆ **Severn Stoke** [A38 S of Worcester; SO8544], *Rose & Crown*: Beautiful 16th-c black and white pub, well modernised keeping low beams, nick-nacks and good fire in character front bar, well kept Scottish Courage and other ales, good value generous food inc children's dishes and enormous granary rolls, welcoming atmosphere, back room where children allowed; lovely big garden with picnic tables, playhouse and play area *(Dorothy and Leslie Pilson)*

Shatterford [Bridgnorth Rd (A442); SO7782], *Red Lion*: Comfortable olde-worlde pub with gleaming copper and brass, lively coal fire, dining extension – food good if not cheap; real ales such as Banks's Mild, Bathams, Morrells Varsity, courteous service, fine views *(Ian Phillips)*

Shobdon [OS Sheet 149 map ref 405625; SO4062], *Bateman Arms*: Comfortable two-bar local with good food inc vegetarian choice, well kept ales, friendly father and son; restaurant; bedrooms *(Chris Walling)*

Staunton on Wye [SO3645], *New Inn*: Pleasantly relaxed 16th-c local, roomy but cosy alcoves, good value generous home-cooked food inc vegetarian, Scottish Courage ales, friendly helpful landlord; boules *(Richard and Stephanie Foskett, Dr M Smith)*

Stoke Lacy [A465 Bromyard—Hereford, just N of village; SO6249], *Plough*: Attractively modernised beamed pub by Symonds' cider plant, comfortable and clean, with good range of reasonably priced pleasantly served food in separate dining area, log fire, well kept Tetleys and Wethereds, choice of ciders; children welcome *(Nigel and Sue Foster, G and M Hollis)*

☆ **Stoke Prior** [Hanbury Rd (B4091); the one nr Bromsgrove, SO9468], *Country Girl*: Rustic brickwork, light oak beams, farm tools, soft lighting for Victorian feel, vast choice of good generous food inc huge sandwiches and enterprising specials, reasonable prices, efficient service, good choice of Whitbreads-related ales, unobtrusive piped music; handy for walks on Dodderhill Common *(Jean and Richard Phillips, Dave Braisted)*

Stoke Wharf [Hanbury Rd (B4091); SO9566], *Navigation*: Friendly Davenports pub nr Worcs & Birmingham Canal, popular for good food inc (by prior arrangement) fantastic seafood platter, also Thurs paella night (chef is Spanish) *(Emmanuel Clave, Dave Braisted)*

Stoke Works [SO9365], *Boat & Railway*: Popular and unpretentious canalside Banks's pub with good lunchtime snacks, pretty hanging baskets *(Dave Braisted, BB)*

Stourport on Severn [River Basin; SO8171], *Tontine*: Large Banks's pub converted from big Georgian building between Staffs & Worcs Canal and River Severn, usual food, well kept beer, big waterside garden *(Tony Hobden)*

☆ **Tenbury Wells** [A4112 S; SO5968], *Fountain*: Quaint low timbered pub with lots of black beams in open-plan lounge bar, red and gold flock wallpaper, big brass platters, delft shelf of bright china, masses of artificial flowers, coal-effect gas fire, big dining room beyond, side bar with pool; quickly served home-cooked food inc fine specials, well kept Ruddles and a guest beer, decent wines by the glass, friendly service, maybe unobtrusive piped music; picnic tables on side lawn with lots of play equipment *(Andrew Rogers, Amanda Milsom, Malcolm Taylor, BB)*

☆ **Tenbury Wells** [Worcester Rd (A456), Newnham, about 1½ miles E – so inn actually in Shrops; SO6168], *Peacock*: 14th-c roadside inn under newish ownership, concentrating on good attractively served reasonably priced food (four French chefs); several separate rooms, heavy black beams, cheerful log fires, comfortable kitchen chairs and ex-pew settles, good service, well kept ales, decent wines, back family room; picnic tables on terrace, lovely setting by River Teme *(C H Wood, LYM)*

☆ **Tenbury Wells** [Teme St], *Ship*: Snug old town pub with lots of dark wood inc fine Elizabethan beams, little hunting prints and other pictures, well kept changing ales such as Timothy Taylors Landlord, decent wines, good coffee, good imaginative bar food and Sun lunch in bright no-smoking dining room with fresh flowers, reasonable prices, friendly landlord and staff, good relaxed atmosphere; piped music; picnic tables in coach yard and on neat sheltered back lawn; comfortable bedrooms *(D Balmer, Luke Worthington, Ann Robbins, RP, BP)*

Uphampton [off A449 N of Ombersley; SO8364], *Fruiterers Arms*: Small country pub (looks like a private house with a porch) brewing its own Cannon Royall Arrowhead, Buckshot and good strong Mild, also has John Smiths and farm cider; Jacobean panelled bar serving lounge with beamery, log fire, lots of photographs and local memorabilia, comfortable armchairs; tasty lunchtime food, no music, plain pool room, garden *(G Coates)*

Upper Wyche [Chase Rd off Walwyn Rd; off B4218 Malvern—Colwall, 1st left after hilltop on bend going W; SO7643], *Chase*: Great views from attractive garden and refined and comfortable lounge of genteel rather clubby country two-bar pub on Malvern Hills, well kept Donnington BB, Wye Valley Bitter and HBA and guest ales, limited choice of good bar food – may stop well before 2 *(Ian and Nita Cooper, Peter and Anne Cornall)*

☆ **Upton Snodsbury** [A422 Worcester—Stratford; SO9454], *Coventry Arms*: Hunting prints, fox masks, horse tack and racing gossip in welcoming country inn with

cottagey armchairs among other seats, coal fire, well kept Bass, Boddingtons, Marstons Pedigree and Morlands Old Speckled Hen, lots of malt whiskies and ports, good friendly service, good choice of food – two comfortable dining rooms; well equipped play area; bedrooms attractively decorated *(Mr and Mrs Hammond, BB)*

☆ **Upton upon Severn** [High St; SO8540], *Olde Anchor*: Picturesque and rambling but neat and tidy 16th-c pub with helpful service, old-fashioned furnishings, black timbers propping its low beams, lots of copper, brass and pewter, good fire in unusual central fireplace; well kept Scottish Courage ales, straightforward low-priced food; has been open all day summer, can get crowded evenings then *(Mrs F A W Ricketts, LYM)*

Upton upon Severn, *Kings Head*: Good riverside setting, extended well furnished lounge bar area, Whitbreads-related ales, separate eating area, food popular at lunchtime *(Mrs F A W Ricketts)*; [Riverside], *Swan*: Straightforward low-beamed riverside bar, well kept Banks's and Marstons Pedigree, two open fires, boating memorabilia, fruit machine, games machines in anteroom; small smarter bar with sizeable dining room off, good value interesting food; garden with summer barbecues *(Mrs F A W Ricketts, JAH, LYM)*

☆ **Weatheroak Hill** [Icknield St – coming S on A435 from Wythall roundabout, filter right off dual carriageway a mile S, then in village turn left towards Alvechurch; not far from M42, junction 3; SP0674], *Coach & Horses*: Roomy country pub popular for its wide choice of interesting well kept ales, most from small breweries; plush-seated low-ceilinged two-level lounge bar, tiled-floor public bar, bar food, modern restaurant, plenty of seats out on lawns and upper terrace; piped music; children allowed in eating area *(Dave Braisted, LYM)*

Welland [SO7940], *Anchor*: Good if not cheap food, good range of ales *(Michael Tucker)*; *Pheasant*: Large modestly furnished dining pub useful for decent food inc early evening bargains Mon-Thurs; woodburner, machines, piped music, big garden with barbecue and play area *(Malcolm Thomas)*

Wellington Heath [The Common; off B4214 just N of Ledbury – pub signed right, at top of village; SO7141], *Farmers Arms*: Big much modernised pub, almost suburban-feeling, with plenty of comfortable plush banquettes, flame-effect gas fire, soft lighting from Tiffany-style lamps, a few big country prints, Marstons Bitter, Pedigree and Oatmeal Stout, popular good value food inc Sun lunch *(Joy and Peter Heatherley, Dr F M Halle, BB)*

☆ **Whitney on Wye** [A438 Hereford—Brecon; SO2747], *Rhydspence*: Very picturesque country inn with attractive old-fashioned furnishings, heavy beams and timbers in rambling spick-and-span rooms, good interesting food, pretty dining room, Bass,

Hook Norton Best and Robinsons Best, attentive service; children allowed, tables in attractive garden with fine views over Wye valley; comfortable bedrooms *(Pamela and Merlyn Horswell, LYM)*

Whitney on Wye, *Boat*: Spacious, quiet, friendly and neatly kept redbrick pub with lovely views of river and far beyond from big windows and pleasant garden; wide choice of food, good friendly service, comfortable furnishings; bedrooms *(Nicholas Holmes, BB)*

Whittington [nr M5 junction 7; SO8752], *Swan*: Brightly painted country-style bar with lots of seating, friendly staff, well kept Banks's, Marstons Pedigree and Morrells varsity, decent wine, some interesting food, log fire; happy hour 5-7pm, garden with play area *(Richard Lewis)*

Wigmore [SO4169], *Compasses*: Walker-friendly village pub – landlord has his own walks leaflet *(Peter and Sarah Gooderham)*

Worcester [Fish St; SO8555], *Farriers Arms*: Busy but relaxed city pub with pleasantly furnished lounge, basic public bar, interesting decorations, wide choice of reasonably priced food, cheerful service, well kept ales such as Glenny Hobgobling and Wychwood, good house wines; very handy for cathedral *(Geoffrey and Irene Lindley, SLC, LYM)*; [London Rd, about ½ mile from centre], *Little Worcester Sauce Factory*: Fun pub with tiled walls advertising sauces, tiled map of Britain

filling ceiling of largest room, lots of stripped pine and sawdust – and lots more sauce; good atmosphere, decent range of hearty good value food, friendly staff, Tetleys-related ales and their own Lumphammer *(SLC)*; [42 Severn St], *Potters Wheel*: Good choice of inexpensive food, Marstons Pedigree, decent house wine; handy for Royal Worcester pottery opp, and the cathedral *(Peter and Audrey Dowsett)*

Wychbold [Worcester Rd (A38); SO9265], *Crown*: Spotless Banks's Milestone Tavern dining pub with good friendly service, good value food, Marstons Pedigree *(W and E Thomas)*

☆ **Wythall** [Icknield St; SP0775], *Peacock*: Good food from baps to chargrilled steaks (just roasts, Sun) and well kept Banks's with a guest such as Morrells Graduate in reliable country pub with old tiled floors; no-smoking area, open all day *(Dave Braisted, Jack Barnwell)*

☆ **Yarpole** [just off B4361 N of Leominster; SO4765], *Bell*: Welcoming licensees and wide choice of food inc unusual oriental dishes and omelette specialities in comfortably smart picturesquely timbered ancient pub, extended into former cider mill; lots of brass and bric-a-brac, Whitbreads-related ales, former skittle alley prettily decked out as country dining area; tables in sunny flower-filled garden, very handy for Croft Castle *(Rebecca and Chris Stanners, Chris Walling)*

Hertfordshire

*Pubs doing particularly well here at the moment are the cheery Fox & Hounds
at Barley (lots of real ales, unusually wide choice of vegetarian dishes), the
cosy Bricklayers Arms at Flaunden, and (a new main entry) the civilised old
Three Tuns at Ashwell. It's the Bricklayers Arms at Flaunden which gains our
award as Hertfordshire Dining Pub of the Year; another place for a good meal
out is the George & Dragon in Watton at Stone. The Sword in Hand at
Westmill has been reopened after rebuilding following a bad fire: it has a good
new big dining room (and more exposed beams than before). Quite a few
other changes include new licensees at the Boat at Berkhamsted, the Green
Man at Great Offley, the Garibaldi in St Albans (extending the food side, and
the conservatory), and the Plume of Feathers at Tewin. The White Lion at
Walkern now has lots for children, including an exciting play area. A small
group of pubs in the Lucky Dip section at the end of the chapter has been
pleasing readers a lot recently: both Aldbury entries, the Green Dragon at
Flaunden, Silver Fox at Hertford Heath, Three Horseshoes at Letchmore
Heath, White Hart at Puckeridge and Cabinet at Reed. We have inspected and
can recommend all of these. There's a good choice too in St Albans. Drinks
prices in the county are rather higher than the national average, and in general
we found free houses decidedly more expensive than tied pubs; pubs tied to
Fullers of London tended to be particularly cheap – as was the Fox & Hounds
at Barley, brewing its own ale.*

ARDELEY TL3027 Map 5
Jolly Waggoner

Cromer Windmill is near this charming little pink-washed inn which is peacefully set
in a pretty tucked-away village. The sensitively refurbished comfortable bar has lots of
open woodwork and a relaxed and civilised atmosphere, while the restaurant
(extended into the cottage next door) is decorated with modern prints. Very carefully
cooked using good ingredients, the attractively presented bar food includes sandwiches
(from £2.20), cauliflower cheese soup (£3.25), fried goat's cheese and tomato salad
(£5), home-made burgers (from £4.75), vegetable and pasta bake (£5.95), omelette
filled with smoked haddock and topped with cheese (£6.50), calf liver with sage and
butter or roquefort cheese and horseradish (£11.50) and fillet steak (£13.50), and
delicious puddings; booking is essential for their Sunday lunch, and there's a £1
surcharge for credit cards. Friendly, flexible service. Well kept Greene King IPA and
Abbot on handpump, a good range of wines and freshly squeezed juice in summer;
darts, cribbage, dominoes, fruit machine and piped music. They may play boules in
the lovely garden on Monday evening. *(Recommended by Charles Bardswell, Andrew Scarr,
Bob and Maggie Atherton, K Archard, R S Reid)*

*Greene King ~ Tenant Darren Perkins ~ Real ale ~ Meals and snacks (not Mon) ~
Restaurant ~ (01438) 861350 ~ Children over seven welcome ~ Open 12-2.30(3 Sat),
6.30-11; 12-3, 7-10.30 Sun; cl Monday*

If we know a pub has a no-smoking area, we say so.

ASHWELL TL2639 Map 5
Bushel & Strike

Off A507 just E of A1(M) junction 10, N of Baldock, via Newnham; also signposted off A1 southbound; and off A505 Baldock—Royston; in village turn off High St into Gardiners Lane, pub is opposite the Church (car park can be reached down Swan Lane)

Leather chesterfields on polished floorboards in front of an open fire lend a civilised air to the bar of this cheerful old village pub. Through a passage the bar opens up into an enchanting trompe dl'oeil Edwardian conservatory restaurant – it's actually an old school hall – with abundant painted foliage, horses and rolling hills. The front part of the pub is devoted to eating, with a large salad bar and pudding display cabinet as well as neatly laid tables with fresh flowers, attractive hunting and coaching prints, and local colour photographs – this is a pretty village, with some ancient timbered houses. The wide choice of popular food includes a bowl of olives (£1.20), soup (£2.50), chicken liver pâté (£3.75), prawn salad or deep fried cheeses (£3.95), pork chop grilled with soy sauce, cloves and honey (£5.25), ratatouillle and brie lasagne (£6.75), lamb kleftiko (£6.95), fajitas or chicken on stilton cream and madeira sauce (£8.25) and 8oz sirloin steak (£8.50); the restaurant is completely no smoking till 9pm. Well kept Charles Wells Bombardier and Eagle and two guests such as Badger Tanglefoot or Morlands Old Speckled Hen on handpump, as well as cask cider, freshly squeezed fruit juice and half a dozen wines by the glass; very friendly staff. There are tables out on a small terrace and more spacious fenced lawn, under a big apple tree and flowering cherry. *(Recommended by Stephen, Julie and Hayley Brown, Wayne Brindle, Thomas Nott; more reports please)*

Charles Wells ~ Tenant Michael Mills-Roberts ~ Real ale ~ Meals and snacks (not Sun evening) Restaurant ~ (01462) 742394 ~ Children welcome in eating area of bar, restaurant and play area ~ Live music alternate Sunday nights ~ Open 11-3, 6-11; 11-. 11 Sat; 12-10.30 Sun ~ Bedrooms: £30

Three Tuns
High St

Quite different from our other entry here, this flower-decked 18th-c inn has elements of the atmosphere of a pleasantly old-fashioned but unstuffy hotel in its lounge bar. This is opulently Victorian, with lots of pictures, stuffed pheasants and antiques; there are comfortable chairs, and some big family tables. A wide choice of quickly served good food using seasonal vegetables includes sandwiches (from £2.25), pate or peppered smoked mackerel fillet (£2.95), whitebait (£3.95), ploughman's (from £3.95), particularly good steak and kidney pie (£6.50), several vegetarian dishes like thai vegetable schnitzel or vegetable pasta bake (£6.95), pork in cream and basil, liver and bacon (£6.95), lamb in red wine, herbs, garlic and black olives (£7.95), venison in orange sauce (£8.95) and 16oz rib eye steak (£11.95); generous Sunday roasts. Greene King IPA, Abbot and Rayments on handpump, a good choice of wines, good coffee; friendly staff. It can get very busy, especially on summer weekends. The simpler more modern public bar has pool, darts and a fruit machine; piped music, boules. We haven't yet had reports from readers on the bedrooms here, but would imagine that it would be a pleasant place to stay in. *(Recommended by Brian Horner, Brenda Arthur, T Loft, Sheila Samuels)*

Greene King ~ Tenant Claire Stanley ~ Real ale ~ Meals and snacks ~ Restaurant ~ (01462) 742107 ~ Children in eating area of bar and restaurant ~ Open 11-11; 12-10.30 Sun ~ Bedrooms: £25/£40

AYOT ST LAWRENCE TL1916 Map 5
Brocket Arms

B651 N of St Albans for about 6 miles; village signposted on right after Wheathampstead and Mid Herts golf course; or B653 NE of Luton, then right on to B651

The two very traditional low-ceilinged rooms of this peacefully set ancient pub have sturdy oak beams, a big inglenook fireplace (with a woodburning stove in the back room), old-fashioned furnishings and magazines to read; darts, dominoes, shove ha'penny, piped music. Real ales include Adnams Broadside, Everards Old Original, Greene King IPA and Morlands Old Speckled Hen; about 11 wines by the glass. Big helpings of straightforward lunchtime bar food include soup (£2.50), sandwiches or filled baked potatoes (from £2.50), ploughman's (£4.50), pies like cold pork and cranberry (£5), and 8oz sirloin steak (£9.50). The evening menu is a bit different with 4oz steak in french bread or scampi (£5), salads (from £5), chicken or halibut steak and lobster sauce (£11.50) and roast duck, pheasant or venison (£12.50); afternoon cream teas; no-smoking area in restaurant. It can get very crowded at weekends. The extensive south-facing suntrap walled garden has a summer bar and a children's play area; this is attractive countryside, near Shaw's Corner. Dogs on leads welcome away from eating areas. *(Recommended by BG, CH, Gwen and Peter Andrews, Gareth and Toni Edwards, Thomas Nott, Graham and Karen Oddey, Zach Hurst, James Nunns, Colin Steer, Howard Gregory, I P G Derwent, Michael Sandy, Ian Phillips)*

Free house ~ Lease: Toby Wingfield Digby ~ Real ale ~ Meals and snacks (reduced menu Sun and Mon evenings) ~ Restaurant ~ (01438) 820250 ~ Children in eating area of bar and restaurant ~ Open 11-11; 12-10.30 Sun ~ Bedrooms: £45B/£55(£60B)

BARLEY TL3938 Map 5
Fox & Hounds 🍺
Junction 10 of M11 then A505 towards Royston, then left on to B1368 after 4 miles

It's nearly always busy at this really friendly old rural pub, which is well liked for its range of beers, very tasty good value food (its best to get there early or book) and welcoming atmosphere. As well as more than a dozen vegetarian dishes (many vegan) such as pasta and mushrooms baked with stilton and mozzarella, beefsteak tomatoes stuffed with olives, pine nuts, onion, pimento and beans or cashew nut roast with wild berry and port sauce (from £4.95-£6.95), hearty English country style cooking includes tomato, orange and basil soup (£1.95), chestnut and port pâté (£3.45), spare ribs (£3.65), curries (from £5.95), steak and kidney pie (£5.95), rabbit with mustard and cider casserole (£6.45), beef stew with dumplings (£6.75), breast of chicken in apricot, brandy and cream sauce (£7.25), half honey roast duck (£7.95) and skate (£8.95). In addition to their own very well priced Flamethrower kept beers on handpump include Adnams Broadside as well as up to seven changing guests, with lots more during their real-ale festivals. Also farm cider, a good range of wines by the bottle or glass and several malt whiskies. There's a nicely furnished series of atmospheric candlelit low-ceilinged and alcovey rambling rooms (one no smoking), with substantial log fires on both sides of a massive central chimney. The dining area with its odd-shaped nooks and crannies was originally the kitchen and cellar; half of it is no smoking. Friendly staff, locals and cat, and a fine range of games, from darts, bar billiards and dominoes (two schools), to shove-ha'penny, cribbage, fruit machine, skittles and lots of board games; also a league cricket team, and pétanque. They have disabled lavatories and ramp access to the dining room at the back; children's play area in large garden; baby changing facilities. *(Recommended by T Loft, TRS, Luke Worthington, Mr and Mrs N Thorp, Robert Turnham, Ian Phillips, Amanda and Nigel Thorp, Susan and Nigel Wilson, R Turnham)*

Own brew ~ Licensee Rita Nicholson ~ Real ale ~ Meals and snacks (12-1.45, 7-9) ~ Restaurant ~ (01763) 848459 ~ Well behaved children welcome ~ Open 12-2.30, 6-11; 12-3, 7-10.30 Sun

BERKHAMSTED SP9807 Map 5
Boat ♀ 🍺
Gravel Path

This cheerily friendly little flower-decked pub is very prettily placed in a lovely canalside setting. As we went to press the new manager was serving tasty home-made food at lunchtime only but he does have plans to start doing evening food soon: sandwiches (from £2.50), ploughman's (from £4.75) and daily specials such as pie of the day (£6.50), chicken with coriander and lemon glaze and cream and mushroom sauce (£7.25), pork fillet with pink peppercorn sauce (£7.50) and roast duck with port and cranberry sauce or peppered steak (£8.25). Very helpful happy staff serve well kept and reasonably priced Fullers Chiswick, ESB, London Pride and Fullers seasonal ale on handpump. There's a good wine list with about twenty wines (and champagne) by the glass. Fruit machine and piped music. *(Recommended by Ian Phillips, David and Ruth Shillitoe, Simon Penny, Gwen and Peter Andrews, Jan and Colin Roe, Susan Stevens, Craig Turnbull, Thomas Nott, Peter and Maris Brigginshaw)*

Fullers ~ Manager Jonathon Curtis ~ Real ale ~ Meals and snacks (12-3, check for evening food) ~ (01442) 877152 ~ Children welcome at weekends ~ Open 11-11; 12-10.30 Sun; 11-3, 5.30-11 Mon-Thurs in winter

BURNHAM GREEN TL2516 Map 5
White Horse

Off B1000 N of Welwyn, just E of railway bridge by Welwyn Station

The nicest part of this smartly refurbished and extended beamed dining pub is the original black-beamed bit by the bar, with solid traditional furnishings, hunting prints, corner china cupboards and log-effect gas fire in two small communicating areas. There are many more tables in a two-floor extension with pitched rafters in its upper gallery, no smoking downstairs. Good value lunchtime bar food includes sandwiches (from £1.75), soup (£2.25), local sausages (£3.25), ploughman's (£3.50), scampi, omelettes, vegetable lasagne or broccoli and cream cheese bake (£4.60), fresh burger (£4.95), chilli (£5.95), chargrilled breast of chicken (£8.95), rack of lamb in mustard and herbs (£10.95) and beef wellington (£11.95). There's a more elaborate restaurant menu. A back brick terrace by a fountain, with a gentle country view, has neat green garden furniture, large umbrellas and outdoor heaters, so you can eat outside even on cooler evenings; there are rustic benches on grass by a pond beyond. Children under 16 are not allowed in this garden unless they stay seated as the pond is deep, but there is lots of room to play on the broad green in front. Well kept Adnams, Fullers London Pride, Greene King IPA and Abbot, Ind Coope Burton, Theakstons Old Peculier and Tetleys on handpump, quick friendly service; piped music. *(Recommended by K Leist; more reports please)*

Free house ~ Licensees Richard Blackett and Nicky Hill ~ Real ale ~ Meals and snacks (12.30-2, 6.30-8) ~ Restaurant ~ (01438) 798416 ~ Well behaved children welcome in restaurant ~ Open 11.30-3, 6-11; 12-4, 7-10.30 Sun

COTTERED TL3129 Map 5
Bull

A507 W of Buntingford

There's a pleasantly spacious feel at this neatly renovated old tree-surrounded inn, which is prettily placed opposite a row of thatched cottages. There are antiques on a stripped wood floor in the roomy and comfortable low-beamed front lounge as well as lots of horsebrasses, and a good fire. A second bar has darts, shove-ha'penny, cribbage, fruit machine, and trivia; unobtrusive piped music. Well kept Greene King IPA and Abbot on handpump, decent wines; quick pleasant service. Bar food includes ploughman's (from £4.95), calf liver, roast rack of lamb and garlic chicken (£10) and beef fillet (£12). There's a £1 surcharge for credit cards. The well reworked sizeable garden has boules and a play area. The village is very attractive and Cromer Windmill is nearby. *(Recommended by Gwen and Peter Andrews, Phil and Heidi Cook, Charles Bardswell, Ian Phillips, Enid and Henry Stephens, Michael Taylor)*

Greene King ~ Lease: Darren Perkins ~ Real ale ~ Meals and snacks ~ Restaurant ~ (01763) 281243 ~ Children over 7 welcome ~ Open 12-3, 6.30-11; 12-3, 7-10.30 Sun

---

Most pubs in the *Guide* sell draught cider. We mention it specifically only if they have unusual farm-produced 'scrumpy' or specialise in it. Do please let us know about any uncommon draught cider you find in a pub.

FLAUNDEN TL0100 Map 5
Bricklayers Arms

Village signposted from A41; Hogpits Bottom – from village centre follow Boxmoor, Bovingdon road and turn right at Belsize, Watford signpost

Hertfordshire Dining Pub of the Year

This low cottagey tiled pub with its roaring log fires and snug cottagey rooms is a cosily comfortable place to enjoy a well prepared evening meal and a very well kept pint from a range of half a dozen or so real ales. The warmly decorated low-beamed bar has dark brown painted traditional wooden wall seats and stubs of knocked-through oak-timbered walls that give a snug feeling to the three areas that used to be separate rooms. The life-size bronze dogs and model gorilla at the bar certainly catch the eye. Good value bar snacks include soup (£1.95), sandwiches (from £2.95), ploughman's (from £3.95), chilli, fish pie, chicken and mushroom pie, (£5.95) and steak and kidney pudding or fajitas (£6.95). More elaborate starters include fried lamb sweetbreads (£3.50), warm duck salad (£5.45) and main courses such as mushroom and three pepper stroganoff (£8.25), steamed chicken stuffed with crab meat with white wine, tarragon and cream (£9.95), fried duck breast with port and black cherry sauce (£11.95), blackened cajun sirloin steak (£12.75) and venison rolled and filled with haggis on juniper berry and rhubarb sauce (£13.95). Half a dozen well kept beers on handpump might include Fullers London Pride, Marstons Pedigree, Ringwood Old Thumper, Shepherd Neame Spitfire or Wadworths 6X, and there's a good range of wines; prompt professional service from welcoming staff; cribbage, dominoes. It gets very busy at the weekends, so arrive early for a table. In summer tables in the lovely old-fashioned garden are surrounded by foxgloves against sheltering hawthorn and ivy hedges. Just up the Belsize road there's a path on the left, through woods, to more Forestry Commission woods around Hollow Hedge. *(Recommended by Roger Bellingham, Cyril Brown, Wayne Brindle, David Shillitoe, Joan and Andrew Life, Howard Gregory, Keith and Cheryl Roe, Ian Phillips, Kath Wetherill)*

Free house ~ Licensees R C Mitchell and D J Winteridge ~ Real ale ~ Meals and snacks ~ Restaurant ~ (01442) 833322 ~ Children welcome in restaurant ~ Open 11-2.30(3 Sat), 6-11; 12-10.30 Sun; 12-3, 7-10.30 winter Sun

GREAT OFFLEY TL1427 Map 5
Green Man ♀

Village signposted off A505 Luton—Hitchin

The neat low beamed bars at this efficiently run carvery dining pub have lots of antique farm-tool illustrations, wheelback and spindleback chairs around simple country pine scrubbed tables, some stripped brick, an open fire and a woodburning stove. An airier right-hand room has countryside prints, cushioned built-in wall seats, and another big woodburner with a row of brass spigots decorating the chimneypiece. There's an impressive view from the spaciously elegant conservatory across the picturesque garden, pond and waterfall, and beyond to flatter land stretching for miles to the east The flagstoned terrace around three sides of the conservatory has chairs and tables and a profusion of flowers in hanging baskets and tubs. As we went to press the new licensee had made no changes to the carvery and bar menu which still includes generously served soup (£1.60), sandwiches and large filled rolls (from £2.40), ploughman's (from £3), hot salt beef sandwich (£3.95), yorkshire pudding filled with curry or chilli (£4.65), steak and kidney pie, cottage pie or chicken and mushroom pie (£5.15), vegetarian dishes like leek and potato bake (£5.25), salads from a buffet table (from £6), scampi or lamb chop (£6.40) and a carvery (£6.50). Courage Directors, John Smiths, Marstons Pedigree, Ruddles County, Theakston XB and Websters on handpump, and a decent choice of wines by the glass; piped-music. Children are encouraged to play in the front garden, where there are swings and a slide, rather than the back. *(Recommended by Gordon Neighbour, Ian Phillips, Klaus and Elizabeth Leist, James Nunns, Phil and Heidi Cook, R A Buckler, James Waller, David and Ruth Shillitoe, Bob and Maggie Atherton, the Sandy family, Barry O'Keefe, I P G Derwent)*

Free house ~ Licensee Peter Annibal ~ Real ale ~ Meals and snacks (cold food all day) ~ Restaurant ~ (01462) 768256 ~ Open 10.30-11; 12-10.30 Sun

KNEBWORTH TL2320 Map 5
Lytton Arms 🍺

Park Lane, Old Knebworth, 3 miles from A1(M) junction 7; A602 towards Stevenage, 2nd roundabout right on B191 towards Knebworth, then right into Old Knebworth Lane; at village T-junction, right towards Codicote

The friendly licensee at this unaffected Victorian pub is a real-ale enthusiast who has a fabulous range of about seven well kept guest ales, alongside a regular crew of Bass, Fullers London Pride, Nethergate Old Growler, Theakstons Best and Woodfordes Wherry. He also has Staropramen beer from Prague on draught, about 50 Belgian bottled beers, country wines, about 50 malt whiskies, Weston's Old Rosie farm cider, and hot chocolate and herb teas as well as coffee; in the winter, hot glühwein served by the log fire, with chestnuts roasting, and regular beer festivals. Several solidly furnished simple big-windowed carpeted rooms, some panelled and each with a slightly different decor (railway memorabilia here, old Knebworth estate photographs there), ramble around the big central servery, ending in a newish no-smoking conservatory with orderly pale tables on its shiny brown tiles; the dining area is also no smoking. Bar food includes soup (£2.40), sandwiches (from £2.60), dim sum (£3.40), chilli (£4.80), cauliflower and broccoli with stilton cheese sauce (£4.95), steak and kidney pie (£5.80), scampi (£6.20), mixed grill (£8) with children's dishes (from £2.30); there may be a delay at busy times. There are picnic tables on the front grass, and the back garden has a play area; summer barbecues. Dominoes, shove-ha'penny, table skittles and maybe piped music; friendly efficient service; Rimau the three-legged cat has now got used to being called Tripod. *(Recommended by John Fahy, Mayur Shah, Richard Houghton, Howard Gregory, Steve Gledhill)*

Free house ~ Licensee Stephen Nye ~ Real ale ~ Meals and snacks ~ Restaurant ~ (01438) 812312 ~ Well behaved children welcome in eating area of bar ~ Open 11-3, 5-11; 11-11 Fri/Sat; 12-10.30 Sun

RUSHDEN TL3031 Map 5
Moon & Stars

Village signposted from A507 Baldock—Buntingford, about 1 mile W of Cottered

There's even a friendly welcome from Fred and Lucy, the two pub dogs who inhabit the bar alongside the friendly easy-going locals and staff at this comfortably unassuming old-fashioned inn. There's a vast inglenook fireplace beneath the heavy-beamed low ceiling, and leading off is a table-filled no-smoking lounge bar. The straightforward but well liked bar menu includes sandwiches (from £1.95), soup (£2.95), ploughman's (from £4.50), ham and egg (£4.75), steak and kidney pie (£6.25), roast rack of lamb (£8) and 10oz steaks (from £9.95). Tuesday night is a home-made pie and pudding night (£6.95), Wednesday night is curry night (three courses £8.95), and on Friday and Saturday nights they substitute the menu with a full blackboard menu which includes starters like smoked salmon and scrambled eggs (£3.95) or Spanish vegetable salad (£3.95) and main courses like chicken breast in orange and horseradish or rabbit in mustard (£7.95). They're particularly proud of the home-made puddings (£3); and they do two course Sunday roasts (£7.95). Well kept Greene King IPA, Abbot and their seasonal ale on handpump, and a short, decent wine list; darts, dominoes, shove-ha'penny, cribbage, fruit machine, pétanque, piped music. There are good views from the tables on the rolling lawns that extend up the hillside and benches at the front. *(Recommended by Charles Bardswell, Gwen and Peter Andrews; more reports please)*

Greene King ~ Tenant Robbie Davidson ~ Real ale ~ Meals and snacks (not Mon, or evening Sun) ~ (01763) 288330 ~ Children over 5 in eating area lunchtime only ~ Open 12-2.30, 6(6.30 Sat)-11; 12-3, 7-10.30 Sun; cl Mon lunchtime

SARRATT TQ0499 Map 5
Cock

Church End: a very pretty approach is via North Hill, a lane N off A404, just under a mile W of A405

Benches in front of this cosy white 17th-c country pub look across a quiet lane towards the churchyard, and at the back there's an outside summer bar on a terrace, and tables under umbrellas on a small sheltered lawn with open country views. The latched door opens into a carpeted snug with a vaulted ceiling, original bread oven, bar stools and a television, plus well kept beers from Bass, Brakspears, Fullers, Scanlons, Shepherd Neame and Vale Brewery on handpump. Through an archway, the partly oak-panelled cream-walled lounge has a log fire in an inglenook, pretty Liberty-style curtains, pink plush chairs at dark oak tables, and lots of interesting artefacts. Well liked freshly cooked bar food in generous helpings includes sandwiches (from £3.10), ploughman's (from £4.65), seafood pasta (£6.25), steak and ale pie (£7.10), and a specials board with imaginative dishes like pork fillet with dijon mustard and cream sauce (£7.60), salmon with asparagus en croûte (£8.60) or grilled shark steak wth asparagus tips (£10.50); lovely puddings like brandy sponge with meringue topping (£3.55); pleasant young staff; darts, shove-ha'penny, table skittles, cribbage, dominoes and piped music. The restaurant is in a nicely restored thatched barn. *Recommended by James Nunns, Simon Walker, Neville Kenyon, David Shillitoe, Barbara Dickens, Bill Martin, Ian Phillips, A L Ingram, P Goodchild, David English, Keith Archer, Nick Chettle, Mr and Mrs T E Warr, K L Smart)*

Free house ~ Licensees Anthony Power and Julian Thompson ~ Real ale ~ Meals and snacks (till 10pm) ~ Restaurant ~ (01923) 282908 ~ Children welcome in eating area of bar and restaurant ~ Open 11-3, 5.30-11; 11-11 Sat; 12-10.30 Sun

ST ALBANS TL1507 Map 5
Garibaldi

61 Albert Street; off Holywell Hill below White Hart Hotel – some parking at end of street

There's a good friendly atmosphere and a nice mix of customers in the refurbished Victorian style bar, which angles round the central island servery at this bustling town pub. Up some steps is a little tiled-floor snug, while a separate food counter on a lower level opens out into a neat and cosy little no-smoking conservatory. Victorian and Edwardian theatrical prints decorate the walls. Bar food under the new licensee includes specials like steak in ale pie, chilli, lasagne, spinach and ricotta cannelloni (£4.95). Well kept Fullers Chiswick, London Pride, ESB and a seasonal ale on handpump; darts, cribbage, dominoes, fruit machine, piped pop music. The pub has its own cricket team. A terrace at the side has a few picnic tables. *(Recommended by Klaus and Elizabeth Leist, Ian Phillips, Michael Sandy; more reports please)*

Fullers ~ Manager Anne Rutter ~ Real ale ~ Meals and snacks (not Sun evening) ~ Restaurant ~ (01727) 855046 ~ Children in conservatory until 9 ~ Live blues music at least once a month ~ Open 11-11; 12-10.30 Sun

Rose & Crown

St Michaels Street; from town centre follow George Street down past the Abbey towards the Roman town

The Amerian-style gourmet sandwiches which were originated here by the friendly American landlord are a good reason for a lunchtime stop at this relaxed and civilised Victorian town pub. They range from straightforward cheese (£1.60), through Royalty sandwiches served with potato salad, crisps and pickled cucumber on a granary or white loaf or bap filled with for example beef, salami, swiss cheese, onion and English mustard (£3.95) to toasted double-deckers like roast beef, horseradish, mustard, tomato, American cheese and salad (£3.95). A few other dishes include soup (£1.95), chilli (£3.75) or lasagne (£4.65). The very traditional beamed public bars have unevenly timbered walls, old-fashioned wall benches, chintzy curtains and cushions and black cauldrons in a deep fireplace which houses a big fire in winter. Well kept

Adnams, Tetleys, Wadworths 6X and a guest on electric pump; a dozen or so malt whiskies; efficient service. Darts (placed sensibly to one side), dominoes, cribbage. Lots of tables and benches along the side and at the back of the pub with shrubs and roses, flowerbeds and hanging baskets. *(Recommended by Michael Hyde, JJB; more reports please)*

Greenalls ~ Tenant Neil Dekker ~ Real ale ~ Lunchtime meals and snacks (not Sun) ~ (01727) 851903 ~ Children welcome in eating area of bar ~ Live music Mon night ~ Open 11.30-3, 5.30(6 Sat)-11; 12-3, 7-10.30 Sun

TEWIN TL2714 Map 5
Plume of Feathers

Village signposted off B1000 NE of Welwyn Garden City; Upper Green Road, N end of village, OS Sheet 166 map reference 273153

We think the nicest part of this roomy but cosy dining pub is a snug clubby area up some steps at one side, where there's a big oriental rug, easy chairs and sofas, a low table and oak-panelled bookcases covering most of one wall. Decor is generally very low key, with just a few carefully chosen prints on the cream walls. Behind the bar is a pretty pink-tablecloth restaurant, and there are well spaced picnic tables in a pleasant back garden overlooking a golf course, with some more tables out in front. Good interesting bar food, all home-made from fresh ingredients, includes soup (£2.95), filled potato skins (from £4.25), salads (from £4.50), tagliatelle (£5.75), steak and kidney pudding (£6.95), with a few changing specials such as avocado and tomato bake (£4.95), liver and bacon, brill or braised cod (£6.95), they'll do a bowl of olives (£1.25), and sandwiches (from £3.25); good Sunday lunch. Half a dozen well kept real ales might include Adnams, Courage Best, Flowers Original, Morlands Old Speckled Hen, Ridleys ESX Best and Wadworths 6X. *(Recommended by Kim and Sara Tidy, Gordon Neighbour, Enid and Henry Stephens, A C Morrison)*

Free house ~ Licensees A E Dawson and Mrs R Mitchell ~ Real ale ~ Meals and snacks ~ Restaurant ~ (01438) 717265 ~ Children welcome in restaurant ~ Open 11-3, 6-11; 12-3, 7-10.30 Sun

WADESMILL TL3517 Map 5
Sow & Pigs

Thundridge (the village where it's actually situated – but not marked on many road maps, which is why we list it under nearby Wadesmill); A10 just S of Wadesmill, towards Ware

There are picnic tables under cocktail parasols, with their own service hatch, on a smallish fairy-lit grass area sheltered by tall oaks and chestnut trees behind this cheery little village pub. Inside, the plank-panelled central serving bar has a small ship's wheel and binnacle, a rustic table supported by two barrels in the bay of the cosy window seat, and, as the name of the pub suggests, quite a porcine theme. There are lots of little pigs in a glass cabinet and amusing pictures in this vein on the wall. More spacious rooms lead off on both sides – the dining room on the right has dark beams and massive rustic tables, while the area on the left has a timber part divider, and a couple of steps half way along, helping to break it up. A box of activities should keep children occupied. Well kept Adnams, Shipstones, Wadworths 6X and one or two guests on handpump. Very generously served bar food includes sandwiches (£2.95), ploughman's (£4.95), fish and chips (£5.75) and salads, scampi or lasagne (£5.95); access directly on to the A10 can be difficult; no dogs. *(Recommended by Nigel Wikeley, A C Morrison; more reports please)*

Greenalls ~ Tenant Meriel Riches ~ Real ale ~ Meals and snacks ~ Restaurant ~ (01920) 463281 ~ Children welcome in eating area of bar and restaurant ~ Open 11-11; 12-10.30 Sun

---

Bedroom prices normally include full English breakfast, VAT and any inclusive service charge that we know of. Prices before the '/' are for single rooms, after for two people in double or twin (B includes a private bath, S a private shower).

WALKERN TL2826 Map 5
White Lion
B1037

This sensitively restored 17th-c brick building is a good place to visit with children who will be happily occupied by the exciting wooden play area through conifers in the pleasant garden, a bouncy castle, football nets (the football-playing dog is called Mr Bobby), and the satellite cartoon channel on the terrace in summer. Inside, the comfortable open-plan bar (with very low beams where its separate rooms have been knocked together, making cosy little alcoves) has an inglenook fireplace with a good fire in winter. Well kept Greene King IPA and Abbot sometimes kept under light blanket pressure, jugs of pimms in summer. Generously served tasty bar food includes soup (£2.95), hot bacon and avocado salad (£3.25), garlic sardines (£3.45), moules marinières (£4.25), liver and bacon or steak and kidney pie (£5.95), fresh fish and chips (£6.95), chicken with mango and coconut (£7.95) and 8oz sirloin steak (£9.95); there is also a small separate no-smoking restaurant. (*Recommended by Charles Bardswell, Tony Spring, I P G Derwent, Kerry Samson, Jonathan Bridger, Mr and Mrs Peter Gregory, Sidney and Erna Wells*)

Greene King ~ Licensees Gerry Diaz and Helen Ward ~ Real ale ~ Meals and snacks (from 5pm; no food for 10 days in Jan and Oct) ~ Restaurant ~ (01438) 861251 ~ Children welcome ~ Open 11-3, 5-11; 11-11 Sat ; 12-5 Sun; cl Mon

WATTON AT STONE TL3019 Map 5
George & Dragon ★ ⑪
Village signposted off A602 about 5 miles S of Stevenage, on B1001; High St

There's a pleasantly sophisticated atmosphere at this civilised country dining pub which has kitchen armchairs around attractive old tables, dark blue cloth-upholstered seats in its bay windows, an interesting mix of antique and modern prints on the partly timbered ochre walls, and a big inglenook fireplace. A quieter room off the main bar has spindleback chairs and wall settles cushioned to match the green floral curtains, a hunting print and old photographs of the village above its panelled dado. Proper napkins, antiques and daily newspapers add to the smart feel. Very popular imaginative bar food (they do get busy so book or arrive early) includes sandwiches (from £1.50), soup (£1.85), pâté (£3.95), brie grilled on toast with apricot brandy sauce (£4.55), home-made burger (£3.95), pasta with spinach, mushrooms, garlic and smoked ham (£5.75), lamb liver with madeira sauce (£7.85), aubergine stuffed with vegetables and pulses in a spicy sauce or strips of chicken cooked with mushrooms in cream, vodka and fresh herb sauce (£6.85), salmon poached in white wine and shallots with a prawn and cream sauce (£8.95), as well as daily specials such as taramasalata with hot pitta bread or herring, apple and red onion salad (£3.85), salmon and broccoli quiche (£5.75) and turbot with white wine and cream sauce or roast duck breast with brandy and sage sauce (£11.85). The restaurant is partly no smoking. As well as a very good wine list they have Greene King Abbot, IPA and seasonal ales under light blanket pressure and several malt whiskies; fruit machine, summer quiz nights, and boules in the pretty extended shrub-screened garden. The pub is handy for Benington Lordship Gardens. (*Recommended by Miss J Reay, Charles Bardswell, Gordon Tong, Maysie Thompson, B M and P Kendall, Mayur Shah, Michael Gittins, R C Wiles, Steve Gledhill, Howard Gregory, Colin Steer, Peter Saville*)

Greene King ~ Lease: Kevin Dinnin ~ Real ale ~ Meals and snacks (till 10; not Sun evening) ~ Restaurant ~ (01920) 830285 ~ Children welcome in eating area of bar and restaurant until 9pm ~ Open 11-2.30, 6-11; 11-11 Sat; 12-3, 7-10.30 Sun

WESTMILL TL3626 Map 5
Sword in Hand
Village signposted W of A10, about 1 mile S of Buntingford

Following a fairly serious fire last year this pretty 14th-c colour-washed listed building has been quite heavily refurbished, but there's still lots of atmosphere with even more exposed beams than before, log fires and traditional style furniture. A new larger dining room (with no-smoking area) has unspoilt views over the church, garden and fields beyond. Starters include garlic mushrooms or chicken cajun style (£3.50), prawn cocktail with malt whisky (£3.95) and moules marinières (£4.50) with main courses such as ploughman's (£4.25), battered cod (£5.95), steak and kidney pie (£6.25), cod with tomato, basil and olive sauce (£6.50), lemon chicken (£7.95), halibut steak in parsley liquor (£8.95) and mixed grill (£9.50). They also do daily specials like dijon pork (£7.95) or bass (£9.50). Well kept Greene King IPA, Abbot and Rayments and Marstons Pedigree, and a changing range of wines; cribbage, piped music. There are seats on a terrace surrounded by climbing roses and clematis, and more in the partly crazy-paved side garden running down to the fields, where a play area has a log cabin, slide, and an old tractor to climb on; nice walks nearby. *(Andrew and Joan Life, Maysie Thompson, Pam and Mike Collett; more reports please)*

Free house ~ Licensees David and Heather Hopperton ~ Real ale ~ Meals and snacks ~ Restaurant ~ (01763) 271356 ~ Children welcome in eating area of bar till 9pm ~ Open 11.30-3, 5.30-11; 12-4, 7-10.30 Sun

---

Post Office address codings confusingly give the impression that some pubs are in Hertfordshire, when they're really in Bedfordshire or Cambridgeshire (which is where we list them).

Lucky Dip

Besides the fully inspected pubs, you might like to try these Lucky Dips recommended to us and described by readers (if you do, please send us reports):

☆ **Aldbury** [Stocks Rd; SP9612], *Greyhound*: Homely old Georgian-faced inn by village duckpond below Chilterns beechwoods, handy for walks (plastic bags in entrance for muddy boots); wide range of enjoyable good value food, plenty of tables in cosy eating areas with separate drinks and food serveries in passage between them, efficient welcoming service, three well kept ales inc local Tring, no piped music; children and dogs welcome, good value bedrooms *(JJW, CMW, R C Morgan, Francis Bugg, LYM)*

☆ **Aldbury** [Trooper Rd], *Valiant Trooper*: Lively beamed and tiled bar with woodburner in inglenook, some exposed brick in carpeted middle bar, far room (no smoking at lunchtime), well kept Bass, Fullers London Pride, John Smiths, Youngs Special and a guest beer, popular food (not Sun or Mon evenings; good Sun lunch in restaurant), good prices, good friendly service, traditional games, tables in pretty safely fenced garden – good walks nearby; children and dogs welcome (the pub's is called Alexander) *(Sue Grossey, Ted George, Jan and Colin Roe, R C Morgan, D and J McMillan, John and Patricia White, LYM)*

☆ **Amwell** [village signed SW from Wheathampstead; TL1613], *Elephant & Castle*: Secluded and spacious floodlit grass garden behind low-beamed ancient pub with inglenook fireplace, panelling, stripped brickwork, 200-ft well shaft in bar; bar food (not Sun), well kept Marstons, friendly locals, good service; restaurant, children in

eating area *(Richard Houghton)*
Ashwell [nr stn, just off A505; TL2639], *Jester*: Attractive and friendly, good varied reasonably priced food, ales such as Boddingtons, Morlands Old Speckled Hen and Wadworths 6X, pretty conservatory extension overlooking well kept garden; bedrooms comfortable *(Sidney and Erna Wells)*; [69 High St], *Rose & Crown*: Comfortable open-plan local, 16th-c beams, lovely log fire, usual bar food, candlelit restaurant, well kept Adnams, Greene King IPA, Abbot and Rayments, pleasant service, darts and machines at plainer public end of L-shaped bar; tables in big pretty country garden *(Phil and Heidi Cook, T Loft)*

☆ **Ayot Green** [Brickwall Cl; off B197 S of Welwyn, nr A1(M); TL2213], *Waggoners*: Friendly, good well presented bar food, three cosy well kept areas, lots of mugs hanging from low ceiling, separate eating area, six changing real ales, good service and atmosphere; quiet suntrap back garden with play area, wooded walks nearby *(Howard Gregory)*
Ballinger [Ballinger Common; off B485 NNE of Gt Missenden; SP9103], *Pheasant*: Good if not cheap food, first-class service, dining area recently extended into big conservatory area; can book *(Miss A Drake)*

☆ **Benington** [just past PO, towards Stevenage; TL3023], *Bell*: Generous food (not evenings Sun-Weds), good service, well kept Greene King Abbot and IPA in attractive part 14th-c pub, low beams, sloping walls, unusual stag-hunt mural over big fireplace with lots of brasses, dining room, games area, good coffee; walkers welcome, picnic tables in garden, interesting secluded village *(CMW, JJW, Charles Bardswell)*

Benington [42 Whempstead Rd], *Lordship Arms*: Welcoming well run pub with interest in real ales *(Richard Houghton)*

Bishops Stortford [North St; TL4820], *Tap & Spile*: Good changing choice of well kept beers, lots of country wines, staff friendly, knowledgeable and efficient without being intrusive *(Elaine Pugh, Steve Mitchell)*

☆ **Bourne End** [Winkwell; just off A41 Berkhamsted—Hemel, by Texaco at E end; TL0206], *Three Horseshoes*: 16th-c pub in charming canal setting by unusual swing bridge. tables out by water, three cosy and homely low-beamed rooms with inglenooks, one with an Aga, bay-windowed extension overlooking canal, good range of well kept Tetleys-related and guest ales, friendly staff, bar food (not Sun evening); children welcome, open all day *(Wayne Brindle, K Archard, R S Reid, Thomas Nott, LYM)*

☆ **Brickendon** [1 Brickendon Lane; S of Hertford – OS Sheet 166 map ref 323081; TL3208], *Farmers Boy*: Roomy refurbished village pub in attractive spot nr village green, friendly service, good range of Whitbreads-related and other ales and of wines, wide choice of good value food from sandwiches up, dining area; seats in back garden and over road *(Howard Gregory, B N F and M Parkin, Chris Mawson, R A Buckler)*

Bushey [25 Park Rd, off A411; TQ0395], *Swan*: Homely atmosphere in rare surviving example of single-room backstreet terraced pub, reminiscent of 1920s *(PB, LYM)*

Chandlers Cross [TQ0698], *Clarendon Arms*: Friendly traditional country pub with well kept Marstons Bitter, Pedigree and Pale Ale, attractive verandah, lots of tables and cocktail umbrellas; handy for woodland and canal walks, bar lunches (limited Sun) *(Jenny and Brian Seller)*

Chipperfield [Commonwood, just S; TL0400], *Cart & Horses*: Popular small pub with plenty of picnic tables, plentiful good value food, real ales *(Cyril Brown)*; [The Common], *Two Brewers*: Country hotel with relaxed and pubby dark-beamed main bar, cushioned antique settles, well kept Bass, Greene King IPA and Abbot, Marstons Pedigree and a guest beer, pleasant staff; popular lunchtime bar food in bow-windowed lounge with comfortable sofas and easy chairs, good restaurant; overlooks pretty tree-flanked cricket green; children allowed in lounge and restaurant, open all day Sat; darkly furnished bedrooms, comfortable but not cheap *(LYM)*

Chiswell Green [Watford Rd, just S of St Albans; TL1304], *Three Hammers*: Handsomely renovated in good solid style with several different areas; good choice of reasonably priced food in bar and restaurant, guest beers, friendly efficient service *(S J Edwards)*

Chorleywood [Dog Kennel Lane, the Common – signed The Swillet off A404 nr lights; TQ0295], *Black Horse*: Nice seating under low dark beams in attractively divided room with thick carpet, two massive log fires, wide choice of well prepared food from sandwiches up, real ales such as Adnams and Greenalls Original, friendly welcoming staff, no music; family area, dogs welcome (popular walking territory), biscuits on bar *(Ian Phillips)*

Dane End [Great Munden; from Dane End go two miles past the Boot – OS Sheet 166 map ref 352234; TL3321], *Plough*: Included for the unique full-size Compton theatre organ in the comfortable and lofty lounge extension that's been built specially to house it; otherwise, usual bar food, well kept Greene King IPA and Abbot and Rayments, local atmosphere, pleasant walks *(David and Daphne Carter, LYM)*

☆ **Datchworth** [Watton Rd; TL2718], *Tilbury*: Two-bar pub with pleasant atmosphere, friendly polite service, good range of up to ten changing well kept beers, good home-made bar food inc vegetarian and a pie of the day, bookable restaurant *(Richard Houghton, Robert Turnham, Norma and David Hardy)*

nr **Datchworth** [Bramfield Rd, Bulls Grn; TL2717], *Horns*: Pretty 15th-c country pub, beams and inglenook log fire, rugs on brick floor, china and pictures, well extended into roomy dining area with alcoves, lots of woodwork, writings painted on the beams; charming service, Whitbreads-related ales *(Charles Bardswell, LYM)*

Digswell [Digswell Hill; TL2314], *Red Lion*: Large and attractive, with wide choice of very promptly served good value food; very popular with business people from Welwyn *(Charles Bardswell)*

Epping Green [back rd Cuffley—Little Berkhamsted – OS Sheet 166 map ref 297068; TL2906], *Beehive*: Cosy and popular local with immense helpings of good food esp fish, friendly service, Greene King ales *(Gordon Neighbour)*

Flamstead [High St (just off A5); TL0714], *Three Blackbirds*: Cosy low-beamed pub under new management, partly Tudor, with old dark wood and brickwork, pictures, brass and copper, two real fires; well kept Scottish Courage ales from central bar, friendly service, usual food from sandwiches up, no-smoking area; pool, darts and fruit machine in games area, piped music; good walks nearby, children welcome *(Ian Phillips, George Atkinson)*

☆ **Flaunden** [TL0100], *Green Dragon*: Imaginative fresh food inc good puddings in attractive and comfortable Chilterns pub with well kept Greene King IPA and Abbot and Marstons Pedigree, partly panelled extended lounge with small back restaurant area, darts and shove-ha'penny in traditional 17th-c small tap bar; friendly service, fruit machine, quiet piped music; very popular Sun lunchtime; charming well kept garden with summer-house and aviaries, pretty village, only a short diversion from Chess Valley Walk *(Kath Wetherill, CMW, JJW, LYM)*

☆ **Frithsden** [from Berkhamsted take unmarked rd towards Potten End, pass Potten End turning on right then take next left towards Ashridge College; TL0110], *Alford Arms*: Secluded Whitbreads country local, pleasant old-world atmosphere, good plain bar food from filled rolls up (step down to nicely furnished eating area), quick friendly service, open all day Sat; darts, bar billiards, fruit machine; in attractive countryside, picnic tables out in front; may have ales brewed at the pub *(Peter and Maris Brigginshaw, LYM)*

Graveley [TL2327], *George & Dragon*: Well run old coaching inn, recently extended restaurant popular with business people from Stevenage *(Charles Bardswell)*; *Waggon & Horses*: Former coaching inn with reasonably priced straightforward food, comfortable beamed and timbered lounge, big open fire, locals' snug by door, Whitbreads-related ales; plenty of seats in secluded attractive garden with big terrace by village duckpond, summer lunchtime barbecues *(Mrs P Hare)*

Great Amwell [TL3712], *George IV*: Quiet spot by church and river, generous helpings of good value varied reasonably priced food inc fish, vegetarian and good puddings, friendly staff, Adnams ales *(Rev D F Perryman, R E and P Pearce, Mr and Mrs N Chesher)*

Great Offley [towards Kings Walden; TL1427], *Red Lion*: Cosy and friendly, with low ceiling, stripped brickwork and brick floor, wide range of ales such as Boddingtons Bitter and Gold, Hook Norton Old Hookey, Timothy Taylors Landlord, Wychwood Fiddlers Elbow, log fire, enjoyable foor from sandwiches up, restaurant; piped music; picnic tables in small back garden, bedrooms *(Ian Phillips)*

☆ **Halls Green** [NW of Stevenage; TL2728], *Rising Sun*: Well restored 18th-c beamed country pub with interesting food in bar or pleasant conservatory restaurant inc special evenings (booking recommended weekends), convivial atmosphere, well kept McMullens and a guest ale, big open fire in small lounge, good big garden with terrace, summer barbecues and play area *(Jeffery Smith, Charles Bardswell)*

☆ **Harpenden** [Luton Rd, Kinsbourne Green; 2¼ miles from M1 junction 10; A1081 towards town, on edge; TL1015], *Fox*: Beamed and panelled lounge with pews and plusher seats, lots of bric-a-brac and masses of prints, smaller tidied public bar; good value food, friendly efficient staff, Eldridge Pope and other well kept ales, good coffee, log fires, board games, daily paper, fresh flowers, no music; children welcome, garden

with lots of tables and play area *(Michael Sandy, Howard Gregory, JJW, CMW, BB)*

☆ **Harpenden** [Cravells Rd; TL1314], *Carpenters Arms*: Small and welcoming, with chatty landlord, friendly efficient staff, good cheap home cooking from sandwiches up, well kept Dartmoor and Ruddles, displays of overseas number-plates, miniature cars and special issue bottled beers; neat well planned terrace garden *(Howard Gregory, Steve and Sue Griffiths)*

☆ **Hatfield** [Park St, Old Hatfield; TL2308], *Eight Bells*: Quaint and attractive old beamed pub with well kept Tetleys-related and guest ales, decent bar food, couple of tables in back yard, piped music; open all day, occasional live music; best at quiet times, crowded Fri/Sat nights *(Anon)*

Hatfield [Old Hatfield], *Horse & Groom*: Pleasant pub with Scottish Courage ales, tables outside *(Anon)*

☆ nr **Hemel Hempstead** [Bridens Camp; leaving on A4146, right at Flamstead/Markyate signpost opp Red Lion – OS Sheet 166 map ref 044111; TL0411], *Crown & Sceptre*: Country pub keeping some character, with three rooms, roaring fire, well kept Greene King and Rayments BBA, friendly staff, reasonably priced food inc doorstep sandwiches, tables outside *(Ian Phillips, LYM)*

☆ **Hertford** [Fore St; TL3212], *Salisbury Arms*: Relaxing hotel lounge, lots of character, well kept McMullens inc AK Mild, efficient cheerful service, decent food (not Sun evening); splendid Jacobean staircase to bedrooms *(D E Twitchett)*

☆ **Hertford** [33 Castle St], *White Horse*: Unpretentious 17th-c pub with good range of ales inc good Dark Horse beers brewed by the landlord, guest beers, open fire between the two bars, interesting furniture in three beamed and timbered no-smoking rooms upstairs, wide range of country wines, simple wholesome weekday lunchtime food, friendly service; popular with younger people evenings, opp Castle grounds *(Dave Vokins)*

☆ **Hertford Heath** [B1197, signed off A414 S edge of Hertford; TL3510], *Silver Fox*: Bustling and friendly well kept rather suburban-feeling local, very popular lunchtime (busy most nights too) for good value food from sandwiches up inc good range of puddings, quick service, particularly well kept Adnams, Tetleys and Theakstons Best and Old Peculier; busy most evenings too; relaxing sheltered back terrace with fountain *(Chris Mawson, B N F and M Parkin, BB)*

☆ **Hexton** [signed off B656; TL1230], *Raven*: Friendly plush rambling pub with four bar areas inc long tidy public bar (open fire, pool one end), big no-smoking room, plenty of dining tables; good well presented food inc two children's menus, four well kept ales inc Boddingtons and Morlands Old Speckled Hen; children welcome, big garden with terrace, barbecue, well segregated play area (*Phil and Heidi Cook, the Sandy family, Brian Lock*)

High Wych [Hand Lane, just W of Sawbridgeworth; TL4614], *Hand & Crown*: Attractive bar and restaurant separated by open fire, wide choice of good value generous food inc well cooked fresh veg, Flowers IPA and Original, plenty of whiskies, quick friendly service; booking advised (*Mr and Mrs Chesher*)

☆ **Hinxworth** [High St, just off A1(M); TL2340], *Three Horseshoes*: Thatched; beamed and timbered 18th-c dining pub with friendly licensees, good value food (not Sun evening, Mon) inc children's, big brick inglenook, small dining extension, well kept Greene King IPA and Abbot, decent wines, lots of premium lagers, friendly licensees, no juke box or piped music; children welcome, big garden with play area (*S R Spokes*)

Hunsdon [OS Sheet 167 map ref 417143; TL4114], *Fox & Hounds*: Smart village pub, very popular weekends, with Greene King ales, wide good choice of good generous food, prompt service, friendly atmosphere; very popular weekends; big garden, pretty village (*Mrs P J Pearce*)

☆ **Langley** [off B656 S of Hitchin, edge of Knebworth Park; TL2122], *Farmers Boy*: Friendly well-beamed and timbered local, huge inglenook fire one end, woodburner at the other, small public bar behind; lots of brasses, old photographs and prints, well kept Greene King IPA and Abbot, wide-ranging bar food from toasties up; garden behind (*G W Stevenson*)

nr **Lemsford** [Cromer Hyde – B653 towards Wheathampstead; TL2112], *Crooked Chimney*: Roomy open-plan dining pub refurbished to emphasise age – stripped brickwork, woodwork, alcoves, central feature fireplace; real ales inc Morlands Old Speckled Hen (but served through sparkler), good if not cheap food; garden by fields (*K Flack, LYM*)

☆ **Letchmore Heath** [2 miles from M1 junction 5, first left off A41 towards Harrow; TQ0597], *Three Horseshoes*: Thriving atmosphere in cottagey little low-ceilinged local opp duck pond on serenely tree-shaded green, wide choice of straightforward honest home-made lunchtime food (not Sun), well kept Benskins Best and Wadworths 6X, maybe faint piped music; white tables outside the pretty flower-decked pub (*Colin Fisher, Comus Elliott, LYM*)

Letchworth [18 Leys Ave; TL2132], *Three Magnets*: New Wetherspoons pub with well kept reasonably priced beer inc good local guest beers, no music, friendly staff, enjoyable food (*Chris Southon*)

☆ **Little Berkhamsted** [1 Church Rd; TL2908], *Five Horseshoes*: 17th-c beams and stripped brickwork, two log fires, well kept Greene King and Tetleys-related ales, decent wines, wide range of good generous bar food inc sandwiches and vegetarian, quick friendly

service; good restaurant, and cosy little attic room for private dinners; garden with picnic tables, busy in summer; attractive countryside (*James and Ulrike Henderson*)

☆ **Little Hadham** [The Ford, just S of A120 W of Bishops Stortford; TL4322], *Nags Head*: Cosy and relaxed 16th-c dining pub, handy for Hopleys nursery, with good fresh changing food inc lots of fish and al dente veg (but they put a service charge on food bills); well kept Greene King IPA, Abbot, Rayments and a seasonal beer tapped from the cask, decent wines, freshly squeezed orange juice, efficient friendly staff; comfortable heavily black-beamed interconnecting rooms, old local photographs, guns, copper pans; restaurant; children welcome (*Joy and Peter Heatherley, Michael Gittins, BB*)

☆ **Much Hadham** [Widford Rd (B1004 S); TL4319], *Jolly Waggoners*: Mock-Tudor family dining pub with terrace, huge garden and friendly donkeys, horses and sheep, good home-cooked food inc children's dishes and popular Sun lunch, attentive service, McMullens AK and IPA, good range of malt whiskies, nice window seats; handy for Hopleys nursery, some live jazz (*John Wooll, George Atkinson*)

☆ **Nuthampstead** [TL4034], *Woodman*: Out-of-the-way but welcoming thatched and weatherboarded local, good range of well kept ales, generous home-cooked food, inglenook log fire, interesting USAF memorabilia (nearby WWII airfield); pleasant garden, lovely setting (*Stephen Horsley*)

☆ **Perry Green** [B1004 Widford—Much Hadham; TL4317], *Hoops*: Cosy and friendly, in small village opp the Henry Moore Foundation (can be visited by appt; good reasonably priced food from freshly baked baguettes up, real ales, children allowed in no-smoking dining area, tables in garden (*Elaine Pugh, Steve Mitchell, B and M Parkin*)

☆ **Potters Crouch** [off A4147; TL1105], *Holly Bush*: Clean and spacious, with highly varnished good-sized tables, particularly well kept Fullers Chiswick, London Pride and ESB, simple mainly snacky food (not Sun), efficient service, decent wines, lots of pictures, brasses and antlers, crockery on welsh dresser, old-fashioned lighting; busy weekends; no dogs, good big garden with picnic tables (*Jan and Colin Roe, CMW, JJW*)

☆ **Puckeridge** [just off A10 nr A120 junction; TL3823], *White Hart*: Quiet and cosy, with good new licensees, extensive good value food inc lots of fish in rambling bar and dining room, four well kept McMullens ales, log fire, lots of wooden armchairs as well as button-back banquettes, interesting collection of copper utensils hanging from ceiling; children welcome, tables outside (*Les and Pam Leeds, George Atkinson, LYM*)

☆ **Reed** [High St, just off A10 S of Royston;

TL3636], *Cabinet*: Friendly and relaxed tiled and weatherboarded local, a pub for centuries, with helpful welcoming service, log fire in little rustic parlourish public bar, pleasant lounge, five well kept ales, simple food, helpful staff, tables in charming big garden with pond and flowers; up for sale as we go to press *(Charles Bardswell, Amanda and Nigel Thorp, LYM)*

Rickmansworth [Church St; TQ0594], *Feathers*: Much remodelled, but still has low beams and flagstones alongside comfortable banquettes etc in several seating areas; attentive courteous service, reasonably priced food, good range of well kept ales *(S J Edwards)*; [Scots Hill Rd, off Park Rd (A412) towards Watford], *Scotsbridge Mill*: Beefeater chain pub, with well kept Whitbreads-related ales and pleasant willing staff in comfortable rambling former watermill with River Chess running through, well spaced waterside tables outside *(Chris and Ann Garnett)*

☆ Sarratt [The Green; TQ0499], *Boot*: Friendly and attractive early 18th-c tiled pub in pleasant spot facing green, cosy rambling rooms, nice inglenook fireplace, well kept Tetleys-related ales, good changing bar food; handy for Chess Valley walks *(Adele Fishleigh, J S M Sheldon, LYM)*
Sarratt [The Green], *Cricketers*: Busy pub in lovely village setting, well kept Courage Best and Directors, good choice of food esp seafood, friendly service; dining area, tables out by pond; open all day *(Adele Fishleigh, Ian and Colin Roe)*

☆ St Albans [off George St, through abbey gateway – you can drive down; TL1507], *Fighting Cocks*: Odd-shaped former abbey gatehouse, much modernised inside but still showing the sunken area which was a Stuart cockpit, some low and heavy beams, inglenook fires, and pleasant nooks, corners and window alcoves; eight well kept Tetleys-related and changing guest ales, farm cider, bar food (not Sun and Mon evenings) from filled baps up; piped music and machines may obtrude; children welcome, attractive public park beyond garden, open all day *(Ben Seale, Thomas Nott, David and Ruth Shillitoe, Ian Phillips, LYM)*

☆ St Albans [Sopwell Lane, off Holywell Hill], *Goat*: Surviving fragment of substantial 18th-c inn, old pews, lots of bric-a-brac, books and prints in rambling areas around central servery, open fire, cheery atmosphere, Adnams, Courage Directors, Greene King IPA, Marstons Pedigree and Worthington Best, good range of malt whiskies, cheapish home-made bar food (not Fri-Sun evenings) inc Sun lunch, games machines, piped music, tables in neat back garden; children in eating area, jazz Sun lunchtime, open all day *(Michael Sandy, Ian Phillips, LYM)*
St Albans [2 Keyfield Terr, off London Rd], *Beehive*: Friendly alehouse revival, with period photographs, well kept Whitbreads-

related ales, tempting cheap bar food (not Fri/Sat evenings); piped music may be loud (live Thurs and some other nights), quiz night Tues, very busy with young Fri/Sat *(Allan Engelhardt)*; [Sopwell Lane], *Hare & Hounds*: Plenty of seats outside, bar food lunchtime and evening, beers inc Boddingtons and Fullers London Pride *(Anon)*; [36 Fishpool St], *Lower Red Lion*: Old building with good choice of changing real ales in two friendly bars, log fire, red plush seats, home cooking, live music Weds; tables in pleasant good-sized back garden; pleasant bedrooms *(Neil Franklin, Richard Houghton)*; [St Michaels], *Six Bells*: Well kept low-beamed food pub on site of an old Roman bath house, well kept Tetleys-related ales and one named for the pub, cheerful helpful service, big helpings of good value freshly cooked food in quieter panelled eating area; children welcome, occasional barbecues behind *(Ian and Nita Cooper, LYM)*; [Holywell Hill], *White Hart*: Comfortable and civilised old hotel, two small bar areas opening into larger one with tables; antique panelling, handsome fireplaces and furnishings, relaxed atmosphere, helpful service, food all day Sat, Tetleys-related ales, good coffee; restaurant, bedrooms; limited back parking, access not easy *(George Atkinson, LYM)*

☆ Therfield [off A505 Baldock—Royston; TL3336], *Fox & Duck*: Pleasantly refurbished village pub currently doing well, with old tiled floor and solid furnishings, four real ales, good value bar food and more pricy dishes (pleasant dining room extension), good children's garden with climbing frames, swings and tree house *(Sidney and Erna Wells, Susan and Nigel Wilson)*

Tring [Tring Hill; A41 just N of bypass – just over Bucks border; SP9211], *Crows Nest*: Beefeater with decent standard food, well kept Whitbreads-related ales, friendly staff, big back garden with good play area and old boat, some barbecues; bedrooms in adjacent Travel Inn *(R C Vincent)*; [King St], *Kings Arms*: Unspoilt genuine backstreet local, nicely refurbished in green, with no juke box or video screens; tasty food, usually at least six well kept ales inc local Tring brews; friendly welcome *(Mr and Mrs S Groves)*

Walkern [B1036; TL2826], *Yew Tree*: Wide choice of well cooked good food in ancient pub with good unpretentious atmosphere; getting popular as word gets round *(Charles Bardswell)*

Ware [London Rd; TL3614], *John Gilpin*: Attractive layout with no-smoking eating area, food all home-made and good value, with a good choice of puddings, McMullens AK, Gladstone and a quarterly Reserve beer *(David Regan)*

Watford [Station Rd; TQ0196], *Pennant*: Friendly and comfortable, with plenty of room, decent food, well kept Tetleys-related

ales with a guest such as Greene King Kings Champion; tables outside *(Richard Lewis)*
Watton at Stone [High St (A602); TL3019], *Bull*: Picturesque coaching inn attractively refurbished after 1992 fire, beams, massive inglenook, varied food, friendly staff, Tetleys-related ales, public bar with darts and unobtrusive juke box; restaurant, pleasant flowered terrace overlooking big well kept back garden *(Sidney and Erna Wells)*
Wheathampstead [Ballslough Lane; off B651

at Gustard Wood 1½ miles N; TL1716], *Cross Keys*: Gently dated 17th-c pub attractively placed in rolling wooded countryside, with banquettes, pictures, plates and old clocks, good reasonably priced food from sandwiches to Sun lunch inc half helpings for children (not Sun/Mon evenings), beamed restaurant with more clocks, very friendly staff, four Tetleys-related and guest ales; big garden with very rustic furniture and play area *(JJW, CMW,*

Children welcome means the pubs says it lets children inside without any special restriction. If it allows them in, but to restricted areas such as an eating area or family room, we specify this. Places with separate restaurants usually let children use them, hotels usually let them into public areas such as lounges. Some pubs impose an evening time limit – let us know if you find this.

Isle of Wight

This year the civilised old Red Lion at Freshwater gains a Food Award for its interesting if not cheap food; it's also our choice as Isle of Wight Dining Pub of the Year. On the whole, food in the island's other pubs tends to be cheerfully straightforward rather than gourmet, but the Seaview Hotel at Seaview and Crown at Shorwell are also good places for a meal out. Almost all the island's pubs provide well for families; the Clarendon at Chale's pub part is outstandingly good with children. Although we have not found any new pubs on the island shouting out to join the main entries this year, three promising ones in the Lucky Dip section at the end of the chapter deserve more attention: the Chequers at Rookley, New Inn at Shalfleet and Bugle in Yarmouth. There's some indication that the big national breweries are being a little too greedy with their pricing on the island. They have quite a monopoly here, supplying a high proportion of the island's pubs, and our price survey this year shows that beer prices here are now nearly 15p a pint higher than the national average. Incomes on the island, however, are below the national average. Two or three popular pubs on the island have closed down in the last couple of years, perhaps partly because of this squeeze on customers' pockets. There are however two rays of sunshine on the drinks side. First, there's a much wider choice of mainland beers available on the island these days; and secondly, it now has three breweries of its own – Burts based now in Newport (and no longer connected with Hartridges), Goddards in Ryde, and the newer Ventnor Brewery, in part of the former Burts Brewery in Ventnor.

ARRETON SZ5486 Map 2
White Lion

A3056 Newport—Sandown

The pleasant beamed lounge bar at this white village pub has shining brass and horse-harness on the partly panelled walls, and cushioned wheelback chairs on the red carpet; piped music, fruit machine, shove ha'penny, table skittles and darts. Straightforward bar food includes sandwiches (from £1.95), soup (£1.95), ploughman's (from £2.95), filled baked potatoes (from £3.50), smoked haddock pasta (£3.95), chilli (£4.50), steak and kidney pie and curry of the day (£5.75) steaks and mixed grills (from £7.50) and home-made specials such as vegetarian lasagne or prawn stir fry (£4.95). The restaurant is no smoking until 9pm. Well kept Bass, Flowers IPA, Morlands Old Speckled Hen and Goddards Fuggle Dee Dum on handpump or tapped from casks behind the bar, with an interesting cask-levelling device. The pleasant garden has a children's play area and aviary, and you can also sit out in front by the tubs of flowers – you may need to as it does get very busy. *(Recommended by Martin and Julie Robinson, Andy and Jill Kassube, Alan Skull, Mary Aldersey-Williams, June and Malcolm Farmer, Derek and Sylvia Stephenson, D P and J A Sweeney, Dr and Mrs A K Clarke)*

Whitbreads ~ Lease: Mark and Rucky Griffith ~ Real ale ~ Meals and snacks (not Sun and Mon evening Jan 1-March 31) ~ (01983) 528479 ~ Children welcome in eating area of bar ~ Open 11-11; 12-10.30 Sun; 11-3, 7-11 winter; 12-3, 7-10.30 winter Sun

BONCHURCH SZ5778 Map 2
Bonchurch Inn

Bonchurch Shute; from A3055 E of Ventnor turn down to Old Bonchurch opposite Leconfield Hotel

It's quite a surprise when you turn into the courtyard of this curious little place to see the pub's separate bar, restaurant, rooms and kitchens spread around the courtyard, and all dwarfed below a steep rock slope. Locals cluster in the chatty furniture-packed Victorian bar, which conjures up an image of salvaged shipwrecks with its floor of narrow-planked ship's decking, and seats of the sort that old-fashioned steamers used to have. There's a separate entrance to the very simple no-smoking family room which is a bit separate from the welcoming atmosphere of the public bar, making this not the best place on the island for families. Courage Best and Directors and a guest like Morlands Old Speckled Hen tapped from the cask, Italian wines by the glass, a few bottled French wines, and coffee; darts, bar billiards, shove-ha'penny, table tennis, dominoes and cribbage; piped music. Bar food includes sandwiches (from £2.25), minestrone soup (£2), ploughman's (from £3.50), spaghetti bolognese, canelloni with spinach, seafood risotto or grilled plaice (£4.95) and duckling with orange sauce (£6.50), and puddings such as zabaglione (£3.50); they don't always open the homely continental little dining room across the courtyard; loos could probably do with a bit of smartening up. *(Recommended by Lynn Sharpless, Bob Eardley, HNJ, PEJ, Gifford and Annabelle Cox, James and Susie McQuhae, Meg and Colin Hamilton)*

Free house ~ Licensees Ulisse and Aline Besozzi ~ Real ale ~ Meals and snacks (11.30-2.15, 6-10.30) ~ Restaurant ~ (01983) 852611 ~ Children welcome in family room ~ Open 11-3, 6.30-11; 12-3, 7-10.30 Sun; cl 25 Dec ~ Bedrooms: £17.50/£35

CHALE SZ4877 Map 2
Clarendon / Wight Mouse ♀

In village, on B3399; also access road directly off A3055

This rambling extended family pub has always been terribly well geared up for children and this year the cheerfully enthusiastic licensees plan to improve the family facilities with a new toddler play area and a junior adventure challenge – so along with the pony rides on Sid and Arthur, the well liked Shetlands, a pets corner, and maybe even Punch and Judy shows in the spacious sheltered back garden, this might even be a better value place for an afternoon out than Blackgang Chine across the road. Its original core is quite pubby, with musical instruments, guns, pistols and so forth hanging over an open log fire. One end opens through sliding doors into a pool room with dark old pews, large antique tables, video game, juke box, dominoes, fruit machine, and pinball. At the other end there's a woody extension with more musical instruments, lots of china mice around a corner fireplace, decorative plates and other bric-a-brac, and even part of a rowing eight hanging from its high pitched ceiling. A very good range of drinks includes well kept Boddingtons, Gales HSB, Marstons Pedigree, Morlands Old Speckled Hen, Wadworths 6X, Whitbreads Fuggles Imperial on handpump and an occasional guest, an outstanding choice of around 365 whiskies, over 50 wines, and some uncommon brandies, madeiras and country wines. Popular bar food includes sandwiches (from £2.10), soup (£1.80), ploughman's (from £3.30), vegetarian pasta bake or vegetarian quiche (from £3.90), burgers (from £3.90), breaded plaice (£5.10), moules (£5.60) and fisherman's platter (£7.30). Daily specials might be sweet and sour pork, beef in red wine or liver and bacon. Despite serving hundreds of meals every day, service is always efficient and smiling; no-smoking dining area. Live music every evening is never too loud for conversation. More restful souls can soak up the lovely views out towards the Needles and Tennyson Downs. *(Recommended by Mike Starke, Andy and Jill Kassube, John and Joan Calvert, the Sandy family, Mr and Mrs T Savage)*

Free house ~ Licensees John and Jean Bradshaw ~ Real ale ~ Meals and snacks (12-10, till 9.30 Sun) ~ Restaurant ~ (01983) 730431 ~ Children welcome ~ Live music every night ~ Open 11am-12pm; 12-10.30 Sun ~ Bedrooms: £35B/£70B

nr COWES (EAST) SZ5092 Map 2
Folly

Folly Lane – which is signposted off A3021 just S of Whippingham

This shipshape old pub is prettily set on the bank of the estuary, with big windows, and seats on a waterside terrace offering bird's-eye views of the boats. Its maritime connections go back a long way, as the original building was based around a beached sea-going barge; the roof still includes part of the deck. These days it's a very handy and well known yachting stop, with moorings, a water taxi, long-term parking, and showers; they keep an eye on weather forecasts and warnings. The nautically themed opened-out bar has a wind speed indicator, barometer and a chronometer around the old timbered walls, as well as venerable wooden chairs and refectory-type tables, shelves of old books and plates, railway bric-a-brac and farm tools, old pictures, and brass lights. It gets very busy at weekends during the summer. Bar food includes liver and onion casserole (£4.95), steak and kidney pie (£5.95), half shoulder of lamb (£9.95), and fresh fish. Well kept Boddingtons, Flowers IPA and Original, Morlands Old Speckled Hen and Wadworths 6X on handpump; no-smoking area, pool, darts, fruit machine and sometimes fairly loud piped music. There's a bouncy castle in the landscaped garden in summer, and it's not far to Osborne House. If you're coming by land, watch out for the sleeping policemen along the lane. *(Recommended by Joy and Peter Heatherley, Andy Cunningham, Yvonne Hannaford, A E Bruce, D P and J A Sweeney, Andy and Jill Kassube, W F C Phillips)*

Whitbreads ~ Managers Andrew and Cheryl Greenwood and Jeannie Moffat ~ Real ale ~ Meals and snacks (from 9am for breakfast till 10pm) ~ (01983) 297171 ~ Children welcome in eating area of bar ~ Live entertainment evenings Thurs and Sat and summer Sun ~ Open 11-11(9 for breakfast); 12-10.30 Sun

FRESHWATER SZ3487 Map 2
Red Lion 🍴

Church Place; from A3055 at E end of village by Freshwater Garage mini-roundabout follow Yarmouth signpost, then take first real right turn signed to Parish Church

Isle of Wight Dining Pub of the Year

There are a couple of picnic tables in a quiet tucked away square with a church to one side, at the front of this carefully run civilised pub. The comfortably furnished open-plan bar has open fires, low grey sofas and sturdy country-kitchen style furnishings on mainly flagstoned floors with bare boards at one end, and lots of local pictures and photographs and china platters on the walls. Readers' reports about bar food – there's quite a big choice listed on a big blackboard behind the bar – are very complimentary this year: starters like leek and potato or fish soup (£2.50), crab sandwiches (£2.95), herring roes on toast or tomato, mozzarella and basil salad (£3.95), Turkish lamb sticks (£4.50), main courses such as shepherd's pie or steak and kidney pie (£6.50), honey marinaded pork steaks with spiced apple sauce (£8.25), duck breast with cranberry and orange sauce (£9.95) and baby leg of lamb for two (£12.50), and very tempting puddings like amaretto pavlova, chocolate sponge pudding and home-made ice creams (all £2.50). Well kept Flowers Original, Fullers London Pride, Goddards Best and Wadworths 6X on handpump; small but carefully selected wine list; fruit machine, darts, shove-ha'penny, piped classical music; tables on a grassy area at the back. There are good walks nearby, especially around the River Yar. *(Recommended by John Beeken, Joy and Peter Heatherley, A E Brace, Jeanne Cross, Paul Silvestri, E Baxter, Derek and Sylvia Stephenson, Mrs V Brown, D C T and E A Frewer, D P and J A Sweeney, A Kilpatrick, W F C Phillips, Mr and Mrs T Savage, Meg and Colin Hamilton)*

Whitbreads ~ Lease: Michael Mence ~ Real ale ~ Meals and snacks (not winter Sun evening) ~ (01983) 754925 ~ Children over 10 welcome ~ Open 11.30-3, 5.30-11; 11-4, 6-11 Sat; 12-3, 7-10.30 Sun

SEAVIEW SZ6291 Map 2
Seaview Hotel 🛏 ♀
High Street; off B3330 Ryde—Bembridge

Facing a quiet road on a steep hill down to the sea, this smartly bustling little hotel has white metal chairs on small continental-style terraces on either side of the path to its door. Its nautical back bar – along a corridor towards the back – is a lot pubbier than you might expect, with traditional wooden furnishings on the bare boards, and lots of seafaring paraphernlia around its softly lit ochre walls, and a log fire; it can be busy with young locals and merry yachtsmen. The civilised airier bay-windowed bar at the front has a splendid array of naval and merchant ship photographs, as well as Spy nautical cartoons for *Vanity Fair*, original receipts fom Cunard's shipyard payments for the *Queen Mary* and the *Queen Elizabeth*, and a line of close-set tables down each side on the turkey carpet. Freshly made bar food is very popular, starters include soup (£2.25), crab with cream and spices grilled with cheese, sautéed herring roes on toasted brioche with green leaves and capers, Greek salad or prawn cocktail with Pernod and fennel dressing (£3.95) and main courses such as warm roasted tomato and aubergine with basil dressing and melted mozzarella (£4.95), fried strips of smoked ham steak with whole grain mustard (£6.95), steak and kidney pie or roast salmon with tarragon butter (£7.95), roast lamb (£12.95) and fresh island lobster if available; no-smoking restaurant. We've been very surprised to read mixed reports from readers about the friendliness of the service, which in our own experience has always been irreproachable. Well kept Flowers IPA and Goddards on handpump, good wine list, local apple juice, and a choice of malt whiskies; darts, cribbage, dominoes and piped music. More tables in a sheltered inner courtyard. There are sea views from some of the bedrooms. (*Recommended by J Barnwell, Yvonne and Peter Griffiths, Joy and Peter Heatherley, A E Brace, Alan Skull, Andy and Jill Kassube, Glen and Gillian Miller*)

Free house ~ Licensees Nicholas and Nicola Hayward ~ Real ale ~ Meals and snacks ~ Restaurant ~ (01983) 612711 ~ Children welcome in eating area of bar ~ Open 11-3, 6-11; 12-3, 7-10.30 Sun ~ Bedrooms: £45B/£70B

SHANKLIN SZ5881 Map 2
Fishermans Cottage
Bottom of Shanklin Chine

Only a few minutes' walk from busy Shanklin's Esplanade, this simple thatched cottage, peacefully tucked into the cliffs on Appley beach, enjoys one of the nicest and most unusual settings of any pub we know, and it's a lovely walk to here along the zigzag path down the steep and sinuous chine, the beautiful gorge that was the area's original tourist attraction. Tables on the terrace soak up the sun by day and later moonlight romantically shimmers on the lapping waves. Inside, the clean low-beamed and flagstoned rooms have photographs, paintings and engravings on the stripped stone walls. Very simple bar food includes sandwiches (from £2.20), ploughman's (from £3.20), salads (from £3.80, crab or prawn £6.40), steak and kidney pie (£3.90), cottage pie (£4.20), scampi (£5.20), and a pint of prawns (£6.50). Courage Directors under light blanket pressure, coffee all day, and a range of local country wines; polite and friendly bar staff. Fruit machine, piped music; wheelchair access. Do remember before starting out that the pub is closed out of season. (*Recommended by D P and J A Sweeney, GWB, Mr and Mrs P C Clark; more reports please*)

Free house ~ Licensees Mrs A P P Springman and Mrs E Barsdell ~ Real ale ~ Meals and snacks (12-3, 6-9) ~ (01983) 863882 ~ Children welcome in eating area of bar ~ Live entertainment Mon, Wed, Fri and Sat evenings ~ Open 11-3, 7-11; 12-3, 7-10.30 Sun; cl Nov-Feb

---

Stars after the name of a pub show exceptional quality. One star means most people (after reading the report to see just why the star has been won) would think a special trip worth while. Two stars mean that the pub is really outstanding – many that for their particular qualities cannot be bettered.

SHORWELL SZ4582 Map 2
Crown

B3323 SW of Newport; OS Sheet 196 map reference 456829

You reach this delightfully set old place by crossing a little footbridge over a miniature stream which runs down one side of a peaceful tree-sheltered garden (with closely spaced picnic tables and white plastic chairs and tables) and then broadens into a wider trout filled pool. Inside, four friendly atmospheric rooms wander round a central bar. The characterful, warm and cosy beamed two-room lounge has blue and white china in an attractive carved dresser, old country prints on the stripped stone walls, other individual furnishings, a cabinet of model vintage cars, and a winter log fire with a fancy tilework surround; two areas are no smoking. Black pews form bays around tables in a stripped-stone room off to the left, with another log fire; the stone window ledges are full of houseplants. Tasty good value bar food includes steak and kidney pie (£3.95), local mackerel in mustard sauce (£5.50), beef casserole (£6.95), sea bream with crab sauce (£7.50) and duck breast with orange sauce (£9.50). Well kept Badger Tanglefoot, Boddingtons, Flowers Original and Wadworths 6X on handpump, local apple juice, cider and country wines. Efficient service from cheery staff and landlord; darts, fruit machine, trivia, boules, faint piped music. A decent children's play area blends in comfortably at the end of the garden. *(Recommended by Penny and Peter Keevil, D P J A Sweeney, Andy and Jill Kassube, Martin and Julie Robinson, L G Milligan, John Hayter, Meg and Colin Hamilton, John Evans, Ian Phillips, HNJ, PEJ, Sybille Weber)*

Whitbreads ~ Lease: Mike Grace ~ Real ale ~ Meals and snacks ~ (01983) 740293 ~ Children welcome ~ Open 10.30-11; 12-10.30 Sun; 10.30-3, 6-11 in winter

VENTNOR SZ5677 Map 2
Spyglass

Esplanade, SW end; road down is very steep and twisty, and parking can be difficult

The spacious sunny terrace at this splendidly placed pub is perched on top of the sea wall with wonderfully relaxing views out to sea and along the bay. Inside wrecked rudders, ships' wheels, old local advertisements, stuffed seagulls, an Admiral Benbow barometer and an old brass telescope are just part of the interesting jumble of memorabilia that fills the snug separate areas of the mostly quarry-tiled bar. Furnishings include pews around traditional pub tables, with a carpeted no-smoking room at one end and a family area (with piped pop music) at the other. Bar food includes sandwiches (from £2), ploughman's (from £3.50), burgers (from £3.95), a couple of vegetarian dishes like vegetable and cheese bake (£4.65), chilli (£4.95), lasagne (£5.30), lemon and pepper butterfly chicken (£5.95) and a couple of daily specials like crab and lobster bisque (£2.95), crab and smoked mackerel pâté (£4.50) and chicken in creamy asparagus and white wine sauce or beef braised in red wine (£6.25). Well kept Badger Dorset Best and Tanglefoot with a guest like Wadworths 6X on handpump or tapped from the cask; on special occasions such as a lifeboat support week there may be half a dozen or more. Also White Monk cask-conditioned cider. Fruit machine, and a boat rocker for children. They have no objection to dogs or muddy boots. *(Recommended by Andy and Jilly Kassube, Derek and Sylvia Stephenson, D P and J A Sweeney, John Kirk, David Heath, Alan Skull, Glen and Gillian Miller, Derek and Margaret Underwood, GWB)*

Free house ~ Licensees Neil and Stephanie Gibbs ~ Real ale ~ Meals and snacks; afternoon tea in summer ~ (01983) 855338 ~ Children in family room ~ Live traditional Irish, blues or jazz every night ~ Open 10.30-11(10.30 Sun); 10.30-3, 7-11 winter weekdays ~ Bedrooms: £40B

Real ale to us means beer which has matured naturally in its cask – not pressurised or filtered. We name all real ales stocked. We usually name ales preserved under a light blanket of carbon dioxide too, though purists – pointing out that this stops the natural yeasts developing – would disagree (most people, including us, can't tell the difference!).

YARMOUTH SZ3589 Map 2
Wheatsheaf

Bridge Rd

This pleasantly welcoming and unassuming place (it's the nearest pub to the ferry) is comfortably relaxed and spacious, with four eating areas including a light and airy conservatory. Reliable generously served bar meals include soup (£1.75), prawn cocktail (£3.45), trout with stilton, vegetarian kiev or home-cooked ham (£5.95), chicken tikka masala (£6.75), pasta with a sauce (£6.75), giant garlic and cheese crunch mussels (£7.50). Service is quick and friendly. Four well kept beers include Boddingtons, Flowers Original, Goddards Fuggle Dee Dum and Morlands Old Speckled Hen on handpump or under light blanket pressure; fruit machine, pool (winter only) and juke box (in public bar). *(Recommended by David Heath, Joy and Peter Heatherley, Thomas Nott, Andy Cunningham, Yvonne Hannaford, Andy and Jill Kassube, Dr and Mrs A K Clarke, Sheila and Robert Robinson)*

Whitbreads ~ Lease: Anthony David and Suzanne Keen ~ Real ale ~ Meals and snacks (11-10.30; 12-10 Sun; 11-2.15, 6-10.30 weekdays in winter; 12-2.15, 6-10 Sun in winter) ~ (01983) 760456 ~ Children welcome in harbour lounge and conservatory ~ Open 11-11; 12-10.30 Sun; 11-3, 6-11 weekdays in winter; 12-3, 6-10.30 Sun in winter; cl 25 Dec, 26 Dec evening

---

Lucky Dip

Besides the fully inspected pubs, you might like to try these Lucky Dips recommended to us and described by readers (if you do, please send us reports):

☆ **Bembridge** [via Foreland Fields Rd, off Howgate Lane; SZ6587], *Crab & Lobster*: Great views from attractive clifftop pub by coastguard stn, prettily refurbished in parlour style with small restaurant area and lots of old local photographs and yachting memorabilia; very good seafood inc huge local prawns, generous helpings, welcoming service, well kept ales; good beach walks below; bedrooms *(SLR, N Zurich)*

☆ **Bembridge** [Station Rd; SZ6487], *Row Barge*: Friendly landlord and staff, good home-made pizzas and wide range of well kept Whitbreads-related and other ales in open-plan pub with unpretentious nautical decor, farm cider; children welcome, bedrooms, nr harbour *(S Holder, Alan Skull, Keith Stevens)*

☆ **Carisbrooke** [Park Cross; Calbourne Rd, B3401 1½ miles W; SZ4687], *Blacksmiths Arms*: Quiet and spotless hillside pub with homely upper bar, panoramic views from dining extension and terraced back garden, welcoming Bavarian landlord, draught German beers as well as changing ales such as Archers, Batemans, Fullers London Pride and Ventnor Gold, reasonably priced food inc enjoyable German specialities; play area *(Derek and Sylvia Stephenson, John Beeken)*

☆ **Carisbrooke** [High St; SZ4888], *Eight Bells*: Clean and tidy refurbished dining pub, big and busy, well set at foot of castle, with Whitbreads-related and other beers such as the well priced local Goddards, reasonably priced generous straightforward food with sparkling fresh veg, polite prompt service, children welcome; charming garden behind running down to lovely lake with lots of waterfowl, also play area; car park *(HNJ, PEJ, Meg and Colin Hamilton, L G Milligan)*

Carisbrooke [Clatterford Shute, just off B3323; SZ4887], *Shute*: Unpretentious friendly pub with family and snooker room, usual food inc home-made soups (much liked by walkers), evening curries and fish and chips *(Penny and Peter Keevil)*

Colwell Bay [A3054 Yarmouth—Freshwater; SZ3387], *Colwell Bay*: Large old-fashioned plush main bar, pubby yet welcoming for families, with well spaced tables, real ales inc Bass, Boddingtons, Goddards, Greene King Abbot, cheap spirits, wide choice of good generous standard food with good veg, lots of ornaments, very cheery helpful staff; quiet piped music, pool room; open all day *(HNJ, PEJ)*

Cowes [Shooters Hill; SZ5092], *Anchor*: Good value food, well kept ale *(Andy Cunningham, Yvonne Hannaford)*; *Harbour Lights*: Welcoming good value pizza-pub with large windows overlooking harbour *(Michael Inskip)*; [Watchhouse Lane], *Union*: Small Gales local with good atmosphere, cosy side room, good choice of beers inc interesting guest beer, generous well cooked nicely presented food – good value; bedrooms *(Dr and Mrs A K Clarke, Ian Pickard)*

Culver Down [nr Yarborough Monument, seaward end; SZ6385], *Culver Haven*: Isolated clifftop pub with superb Channel views, modern, clean and very friendly, with good straightforward home cooking inc fresh veg, fair prices, quick service, real ales, good coffee; big restaurant, piped music, children and pets welcome, small terrace *(D P and J A Sweeney)*

Downend [A3056, at the crossroads; SZ5387], *Hare & Hounds*: Refurbished and extended thatched dining pub with lots of beams and stripped brickwork, separate areas, friendly waitress service, decent straightforward food, Whitbreads-related and other ales, good views from terrace, nice spot by Robin Hill Country Park which has good play area *(J Barnwell, BB)*

Godshill [Eden Dale; SZ5282], *Cask & Taverners*: Contrived interior, redeemed by well kept Scottish Courage ales, good service and good food in bar and restaurant; decent wines, tables in courtyard; no car park – public one 200 yds away *(Martyn and Mary Mullins, D P and J A Sweeney)*

Gurnard [1 Princes Esplanade; SZ4795], *Woodvale*: Recently refurbished 1930s Wayside Inn with picture windows overlooking Solent, glass-panelled ceilings, decent range of standard food inc bargain steaks, well kept Whitbreads-related ales and decent wines, obliging staff, smaller bar and billiards room; boules *(Jenny and Brian Seller, Dr and Mrs A K Clarke)*

Havenstreet [off A3054 Newport—Ryde; SZ5690], *White Hart*: Ancient building, tidy and comfortable, with two clean and pubby bars, well kept Badger ales, varied generous food esp pies with fresh veg and splendid salads, friendly staff; interesting beer-bottle collection *(A Kilpatrick, D P and J A Sweeney)*

☆ Hulverstone [B3399 – OS Sheet 196 map ref 398840; SZ3984], *Sun*: Picture-book thatched pub with charming flower-filled garden, even village stocks; friendly informal licensees, well kept Gales BB and HSB tapped from the cask, food inc good home-made steak and kidney pie; piped music; sea views, lovely garden *(J B and P N Bishop, Dr and Mrs A K Clarke)*

☆ Limerstone [B3399 towards Brighstone; SZ4382], *Countryman*: Large brightly lit high-ceilinged open-plan bars and restaurant area, mock dark beams, white paintwork, horse/farming equipment and pictures, usual food from filled rolls to steaks, prompt polite service, well kept Badger Best and Tanglefoot, Hampshire and guest ales; moderate piped music; front garden with sea view *(Derek and Sylvia Stephenson)*

☆ Newchurch [SZ5685], *Pointer*: Good generous straightforward home cooking, very fair prices, well kept Gales BBB and HSB, good range of country wines, taciturn new landlord; brightly lit plush lounge, flame-effect fires, old photographs, L-shaped games bar on right, pleasant back garden with floodlit boules area; piped music may obtrude *(HNJ, PEJ, Chris Brooker, BB)*

Newport [High St; SZ4988], *Cask & Crispin*: Small friendly local with well kept Ventnor VPA, good bar food, pleasant atmosphere, no piped music *(D P and J A Sweeney)*; [91 High St], *Castle*: Well kept Whitbreads-related ales, friendly service, good varied cheap lunchtime food, smiling service, plenty of local atmosphere, tables in back courtyard, open all day; maybe piped music; behind the dark beamery, lattice-effect windows, log-effect gas fire and reproduction furniture and brasses,

there's a genuinely ancient pub – as the flagstones and massive end stone wall show; was the last English pub to hold a cock-fighting licence *(HNJ, PEJ, Dr and Mrs A K Clarke)*; [centre], *George*: Friendly staff, nice atmosphere, good food, garden *(Laura Wendt, Scot Mario)*; [St Thomas Sq], *Wheatsheaf*: Dating from 17th c, in attractive old part by parish church; comfortable bare-bricks refurbishment, good atmosphere, friendly helpful staff, generous reasonably priced food, Whitbreads-related ales; piped music may be rather obtrusive; children welcome, comfortable bedrooms *(Ian Phillips)*

☆ Niton [off A3055 just S of village, towards St Catherines Point; SZ5075], *Buddle*: Extended former smugglers' haunt, heavy black beams, big flagstones, broad stone fireplace, no-smoking areas, good range of Whitbreads-related and guest ales, some tapped from the cask, local farm cider, bar food inc good seafood and griddled dishes (service can slow at busy times), family dining room/games annexe, friendly dogs; well cared for sloping garden and terraces, good walks; open all day, some live jazz *(HNJ, PEJ, Andy and Jill Kassube, Meg and Colin Hamilton, A E Brace, D P and J A Sweeney, Sybille Weber, June and Malcolm Farmer, LYM)*

☆ Northwood [85 Pallance Rd, off B3325 S of Cowes; SZ4983], *Travellers Joy*: Not the smartest pub, but this busy local is a boon to serious real-ale drinkers on the island, with interesting well kept mainland guest beers alongside the local ones; good range of generous reasonably priced simple bar food, friendly staff, old island prints; fruit machine, subdued piped music; family room, garden behind with swings and lots of rabbits; open all day *(Derek and Sylvia Stephenson, Andy and Jill Kassube)*

☆ Rookley [Niton Rd; pub signed off A3020; SZ5183], *Chequers*: Good straightforward food using fresh ingredients, plenty of veg served separately, attractive prices; clean and spacious plush refurbished dining lounge looking over road to rolling downland, good attentive service even when busy, well kept Scottish Courage ales, small log fire, partly flagstoned games area on left; Lego in family room, baby-changing, picnic tables out on grass, realistic play house in safely fenced play area; open all day, next to riding stables *(HNJ, PEJ, J Barnwell, BB)*

☆ Shalfleet [A3054 Newport—Yarmouth; SZ4189], *New Inn*: More restaurant than pub, with plenty of good seafood and short choice of other dishes, generous helpings, roaring log fire in traditional beamed and panelled bar, pleasantly redecorated carpeted dining lounge and restaurant, no-smoking family area; well kept Gales HSB and island beers, decent wines, country wines, cider and coffee, children in eating area, open all day summer *(HNJ, PEJ, Penny and Peter Keevil, W F C Phillips, D P and J A Sweeney, LYM)*

☆ Shanklin [Chine Hill; SZ5881], *Chine*: Tastefully refurbished, with beams and flagstones, separate bright family conservatory, wide choice of decent pub food (not Sun evening, Tues or Sat) inc good value specials, well kept real ales; lovely wooded setting with good sea views *(D P and J A Sweeney, Martyn and Mary Mullins)*

Shanklin [The Esplanade], *Longshoreman*: Comfortable low-beamed seafront pub with good Sandown Bay views, old Island photographs *(D P and J A Sweeney)*; [Old Village], *Village Pub*: Big helpings of good value food cooked to order (so can be a wait), upstairs dining room open if downstairs bar full, small pleasant back garden with wendy house; children allowed in family area if eating, piped music may obtrude *(M J Stow, A M Pring)*

Totland [Alum Bay Old Rd; SZ3185], *High Down*: Out-of-the-way refurbished local at foot of NT Tennyson Down, popular with walkers; well kept Ushers, freshly cooked bar food, smart little dining room, good service; piped music can be a little obtrusive; picnic tables out in raised paddock area; bedrooms *(HNJ, PEJ, L G Milligan)*

Ventnor [Botanic Garden; SZ5677], *Garden Tavern*: Superb setting in the formal rather subtropical garden, very friendly landlord, local Goddards beers, popular food *(Alan Skull)*

☆ **Whitwell** [High St; SZ5277], *White Horse*: Welcoming, with wide range of enjoyable food inc vegetarian, full range of Gales ales, well furnished big interconnected beamed bars with separate comfortable family areas; cheerful quick service, horsebrasses, log fire, muted piped music *(T Harman Smith, David Heath)*

☆ **Wootton Bridge** [A3054 Ryde—Newport; SZ5492], *Sloop*: Reliable Whitbreads Brewers Fayre pub, very popular, with good value generous food, lots of tables in huge spacious split-level bar, smart upmarket decor, friendly quick service, subdued piped music; nice setting, fine views over yacht moorings *(Andy and Jill Kassube)*

Wroxall [Clarence Rd (B3327); SZ5579], *Star*: This plush two-bar local, popular with readers for local ales, friendly atmosphere and decent food, has been closed this last year *(News please)*

☆ **Yarmouth** [St James' Sq; SZ3589], *Bugle*: Peaceful lounge, lively bar with counter like galleon stern, handsome dark panelling, usual food from well filled sandwiches up, friendly staff, well kept Whitbreads-related ales, children very welcome; piped music can be rather loud; restaurant, games room with pool, sizeable garden, summer barbecues; good big airy bedrooms – make sure you get one that's not over the bar *(L G Milligan, Dr and Mrs A K Clarke, LYM)*

Stars after the name of a pub show exceptional character and appeal. They don't mean extra comfort. And they are nothing to do with food quality, for which there's a separate knife-and-fork rosette. Even quite a basic pub can win stars, if it's individual enough.

Kent

*New entries here this year are the civilised old Chafford Arms at Fordcombe
(good seafood), the carefully run Green Man at Hodsoll Street (great choice of
puddings), the staunchly traditional Harrow at Ightham Common, and the
attractively placed Cock at Luddesdown (good fresh fish here, too). Other
changes to note here are the new bedrooms at the tucked-away Yew Tree at
Barfreston, new licensees doing rather more restauranty food at the Dove at
Dargate, a change of style at the George at Newnham (good new licensees),
and new people at the Bell at Smarden and the George & Dragon at
Speldhurst. Our selection as Kent Dining Pub of the Year is the very well run
Hare at Langton Green, and other pubs doing really well here these days
include the thoughtfully run Wheatsheaf at Bough Beech, the friendly Bottle
House above Penshurst, the cheerful Dering Arms at Pluckley (good fish), the
Ringlestone at Ringlestone (they've bought the farmhouse opposite – with
some land – and can now do B&B), the charming Rose & Crown near Selling,
and the Pepper Box at Ulcombe – a good-all-round country pub. Pubs to note
particularly in the Lucky Dip at the end of the chapter include the Hooden
Horse on the Hill in Ashford, White Hart at Brasted, Canterbury Tales in
Canterbury, Ship at Conyer Quay, Carpenters Arms at Eastling, Four Elms at
Four Elms, Artichoke at Hadlow, Oak & Ivy near Hawkhurst, Duke William
at Ickham, Plough at Ivy Hatch (too much of a restaurant for the main entries,
but a very good place), King William IV at Littlebourne, Red Lion at Snargate
and Tickled Trout in Wye. Kent pubs tend to charge quite a bit more for
drinks than the national average, though pubs tied to Shepherd Neame of
Faversham were generally cheaper; the cheapest pub we found was the
idiosyncratic Fox & Hounds on Toys Hill, tied to Greene King. It's always
worth looking out for farm ciders in Kent pubs – almost as good an area for
this as Hereford & Worcester or the west country.*

BARFRESTON TR2650 Map 3
Yew Tree

They have now opened two bedrooms in this friendly pub, tucked away in a little
hamlet and next to a very pretty Saxon church. The chatty main bar has a log fire,
upholstered pine chairs and wall seats around a mix of old pine tables on the bare
boards, candles in bottles, cream walls with old local photographs, lots of hops draped
over a large beam, and a delft shelf with an ancient wooden yoke and a few
horsebrasses; fresh flowers on the bar counter. There's a second, simply furnished little
bar, and a cosy dining room (which some readers wish was no smoking) with just four
tables, a piano, and an open fire in the stone fireplace – you can book this for a private
party. Enjoyable bar food includes doorstep sandwiches (£2.50), good soups such as
curried parsnip or celery (£2.65), home-made pâté (£2.95), tasty pies such as
mushroom, spinach and feta cheese or boozy beef or rabbit, ham and leek (£5.75),
evening fish and game dishes, and steaks. Winter Sunday roast lunch. They offer seven
real ales, well kept on handpump, such as Black Sheep Bitter, Fullers ESB, Greene
King IPA and Dark Mild, Timothy Taylors Landlord, and two guest beers, farm

ciders, several malt whiskies, and 7 different fresh coffees; cribbage, piped music and a table-top skittles game called daddlums. *(Recommended by Stephen G Brown, David and Margaret Bloomfield, Patricia Dodd)*

Free house ~ Licensee Angie McFadyen ~ Real ale ~ Snacks (all day) and meals ~ (01304) 831619 ~ Irish folk Sun evening, jazz Mon evening, a mixture Thurs evening ~ Open 11-11; 12-10.30 Sun ~ Bedrooms: £15/£30

nr BIDDENDEN TQ8538 Map 3
Three Chimneys ♀ ◖

A262, a mile W of village

It's the character of this old country pub that appeals to readers most. The rambling and low oak-beamed series of small, very traditional rooms have simple wooden furniture and old settles on flagstones and coir matting, some harness and sporting prints on the exposed brick walls, and good winter log fires. The simple public bar has darts, shove-ha'penny, dominoes and cribbage, and the good range of well kept real ales tapped from the cask might include Adnams Best, Brakspears, Fremlins, Harveys Best, Marstons Pedigree, Morlands Old Speckled Hen and Wadworths 6X, along with Biddenden local cider, a carefully chosen wine list with a range of half bottles (as well as local wine), and about twenty malt whiskies. Bar food is limited to four starters, four main courses, and four puddings each day: soup such as tomato and celeriac (from £2.50), duck and orange pâté (£3.85), stuffed green pepper (£6.30), lamb pie (£6.50), salmon and dill filo tart (£6.75), and date and walnut pudding or treacle tart (from £2.70). You can book tables in the Garden room. At the back the lusciously growing garden has nut trees at the end, and densely planted curving borders with flowering shrubs and shrub roses. Sissinghurst gardens are just down the road. *(Recommended by J Tross, Mrs J Burrows, Birgit Rohowsky, A Homes, Ian and Nita Cooper, Paul Williams, John Le Sage, K Flack, C Sinclair, Stephen Brown, Tina and David Woods-Taylor, Pam and Tim Moorey, AEB, James Nunns, Dr R Sparks, D Jardine, Thomas Nott, RWD, M Holdsworth, G Garvey, J O Jonkler)*

Free house ~ Licensees C F W Sayers and G A Sheepwash ~ Real ale ~ Meals and snacks (till 10pm) ~ (01580) 291472 ~ Children in garden room ~ Open 11-2.30, 6-11; 12-2.30, 7-10.30 Sun; closed 25-26 Dec

BOUGH BEECH TQ4846 Map 3
Wheatsheaf ◖

B2027, S of reservoir

Much liked by readers, this delightful old pub has some thoughtful touches like piles of smart magazines to read, nice nibbles, and garlands of local hops, and on the walls and above the massive stone fireplaces are quite a few horns and heads – as well as a sword from Fiji, crocodiles, stuffed birds, swordfish spears, and the only manatee in the south of England. The atmosphere is congenial and welcoming, as are the staff. The neat central bar and recently renovated long bar have unusually high-ceilings with lofty oak timbers, a screen of standing timbers and a newly revealed king post. Divided from the central bar by two more rows of standing timbers – one formerly an outside wall to the building – is the snug, and a new bar where the old kitchen formerly stood. Other similarly aged features include a piece of 1607 graffitto, 'Foxy Galumpy', thought to have been a whimsical local squire. The long bar has an attractive old settle carved with wheatsheaves, shove-ha'penny, dominoes, and board games. Bar food – served all day – includes home-baked ham with honey and mustard, home-made ham and potato pie in onion sauce, home-made curries, and fresh fish dishes (from £4.50); special deals for those over 55. Well kept Flowers Original, Fullers London Pride, Morlands Old Speckled Hen, Shepherd Neame Master Brew, and seasonal beers on handpump, decent wines including local wine, summer pimms, winter mulled wine, and several malt whiskies; piped music. There's a rustic cottage in the garden and swings for children to play on, and flowerbeds and fruit trees fill the sheltered side and back gardens. *(Recommended by Susan and John Douglas, Simon Small, D E Twitchett, Paul Hilditch, Timothy Galligan, Tim Barrow, Sue Demont, B J Harding, A M Pring,*

Mark Percy, RWD, Michael Grigg, J and P Maloney, Winifrede Morrison, G S B Dudley, Mr and Mrs C Starling, Mrs M Boulson)

Whitbreads ~ Lease: Elizabeth Currie ~ Real ale ~ Meals and snacks (noon-10pm) ~ (01732) 700254 ~ Folk music Weds evening ~ Open 11-11; 12-10.30 Sun

BOUGHTON ALUPH TR0247 Map 3
Flying Horse 🍺

Boughton Lees; just off A251 N of Ashford

This 15th-c pub is in a most attractive setting by the broad village green – at its best in summer when there are weekly cricket matches. Inside, the open-plan bar has fresh flowers, hop bines around the serving area, horsebrasses, stone animals on either side of the blazing log fire, lots of standing room (as well as comfortable upholstered modern wall benches), and a friendly atmosphere; two more open fireplaces. A few clues to the building's age still remain, mainly in the shiny old black panelling and the arched windows (though they are a later Gothic addition), and two ancient spring-water wells are illuminated and covered at ground level with walk-over glass. From the back room, big doors open out onto the spacious rose filled garden, where there are seats and tables; summer barbecues. Good bar food such as sandwiches, lamb and apricot or steak and kidney pies (£5.75), good Indonesian nasi goreng (£5.95), tagliatelle with salmon, prawns and cream (£6.50), breast of chicken in stilton (£6.95), and fillet of duck in morello cherry sauce or noisettes of lamb with rosemary (£7.95); good breakfasts. Well kept Courage Best and Directors, Morlands Old Speckled Hen, Ruddles County, Theakstons XB, and Wadworths 6X on handpump, and good wines. Shove-ha'penny, cribbage, dominoes, fruit machine, and piped music. The Shuttle is only 8 miles away. *(Recommended by Stephen Brown, Mr and Mrs Jonathan Russell, Gregor Macdonald, D and J Tapper, Thomas Nott, R T and J C Moggridge, Mayur Shah, Martin Hickes, Christopher Warner, Roger Davey, James House)*

Courage ~ Lease: Howard and Christine Smith ~ Real ale ~ Meals and snacks (11.45-2.15, 6-10; all day Sat and Sun) ~ Restaurant ~ (01233) 620914 ~ Children in restaurant ~ Occasional live music ~ Open 11-11; 11-3, 6-11 in winter; 12-10.30 Sun ~ Bedrooms: £25/£40

BOYDEN GATE TR2265 Map 3
Gate Inn ★ 🍺

Off A299 Herne Bay—Ramsgate – follow Chislet, Upstreet signpost opposite Roman Gallery; Chislet also signposted off A28 Canterbury—Margate at Upstreet – after turning right into Chislet main street keep right on to Boyden; the pub gives its address as Marshside, though Boyden Gate seems more usual on maps

Right on the edge of the marshes, this remains a splendid old-style, welcoming local. Mr Smith has now been here for 22 years and has kept the pub very much a focus for local activities. There's a good winter log fire (which serves both quarry-tiled rooms), flowery-cushioned pews around tables of considerable character, hop bines hanging from the beam, attractively etched windows, and photographs on the walls – some ancient sepia ones, others new. Tasty bar food includes sandwiches (from £1.40; fried egg, sausage and bacon £2.60), winter soup (£2), quite a few filled baked potatoes (from £2.25), generous ploughman's (£3.95), home-cooked spicy hotpots with toppings like grilled sausage chunks (£4.50), gammon and pineapple (£4.60), various pasta dishes (£4.75), and puddings; they use organically grown local produce where possible, and you can generally buy local honey and free-range eggs. The eating area is no smoking at lunchtime. Well kept Shepherd Neame Bitter, Spitfire, Mild, and Bishops Finger tapped from the cask, with country wines and local apple juice. Shove-ha'penny, dominoes, and cribbage. On a fine evening, it's marvellously relaxing to sit at the picnic tables on the sheltered side lawn listening to the contented quacking of what seems like a million happy ducks and geese (they sell duck food inside – 10p a bag). *(Recommended by Ian and Nita Cooper, Ian Phillips, Gregor Macdonald, David Gregory, Mr and Mrs A Budden, Sue Lee, James Nunns, Dave Braisted)*

Shepherd Neame ~ Tenant Christopher Smith ~ Real ale ~ Meals and snacks ~ (01227) 860498 ~ Children in eating area of bar and in family room ~ Open 11-2.30(3 Sat), 6-11; 12-3, 7-10.30 Sun

BROOKLAND TQ9926 Map 3
Woolpack

On A259 from Rye, as you approach Brookland, take the first right turn just after the expanse of Walland Marsh

Particularly welcoming and cosy on a cold day when it's swathed in the marsh mists, this crooked early 15th-c cottage has a good warming log fire in the massive inglenook fireplace and plenty of old-fashioned character. The tremendous age of the building is immediately apparent in the ancient entrance lobby with its uneven brick floor and black painted pine panelled walls. On the right, the simple but homely softly lit main bar has basic cushioned plank seats in the fireplace itself, a painted wood effect bar counter hung with lots of water jugs, and some ships' timbers in the low-beamed ceiling that may date from the 12th c. On the quarry-tiled floor is a long elm table with shove-ha'penny carved into one end, other old and new wall benches, chairs at mixed tables, and characterful photos of the locals (and perhaps their award winning sheep) on the walls. To the left of the lobby a sparsely-furnished tiny room leads to an open-plan games room with central chimney stack, modern bar counter, and young locals playing darts or pool; dominoes, fruit machine, piped music. Well kept Shepherd Neame Bitter, Bishops Finger and Spitfire on handpump. Generous helpings of good value, straightforward bar food include sandwiches (from £1.40), ploughman's (£3.50), steak pie (£3.75), meaty or vegetarian lasagne (£3.95), ham and egg (£4.25), trout (£6.25), and mixed grill (£7.65). Tables outside look down the garden to a stream where the pub has fishing rights. *(Recommended by Quentin Williamson, Paul Davis, Carl and Jackie Cranmer, Comus Elliott, Neil Hardwick, Kevin Thorpe, Thomas Nott, J and D Tapper, L M Miall, R and S Bentley, James Nunns, Stephen George Brown)*

Shepherd Neame ~ Tenants John and Pat Palmer ~ Real ale ~ Meals and snacks ~ (01797) 344321 ~ Children in family bar ~ Open 11-3, 6-11; 12-3, 7-10.30 Sun

CHIDDINGSTONE TQ4944 Map 3
Castle ♀

Village signposted from B2027 Tonbridge—Edenbridge

This rambling old place – run by Mr Lucas for 32 years now – has a handsome, carefully modernised beamed bar with well made settles forming booths around the tables, cushioned sturdy wall benches, an attractive mullioned window seat in one small alcove, and latticed windows; best to get here early in summer. Well kept Harveys Best, Larkins Traditional (brewed in the village), and Youngs Bitter on handpump, a good range of malt whiskies, and a very good wine list (the quality is reflected in the prices, though the house wines should suit all pockets) – some readers had hoped that more would be available by the glass. Darts, shove-ha'penny, dominoes and cribbage. Bar food includes home-made soup (£3.05), open sandwiches (from £3.75), home-made pâté (£3.75), filled baked potatoes (from £4.25), a daily pasta dish (£4.95), ploughman's (£5.75), very hot chilli con carne (£5.30), local sausages (£5.55), and puddings (from £4.25); children's dishes (from £2.70). The pretty back garden has a small pool and fountain set in a rockery and tables on a brick terrace (which can be covered in poor weather) and neat lawn where they are constructing a raised trellis area. There are more tables at the front opposite the church, and it's worth a walk around the village to look at the marvellously picturesque cluster of unspoilt Tudor houses; the countryside around here is lovely. *(Recommended by Paul Hilditch, Pat and Tony Martin, B and M Parkin, Mr and Mrs C G Fraser, Mrs M Furness, J S Evans, R and S B Bentley, A Homes, LM, J and P Maloney, June S Bray, Sue Lee)*

Free house ~ Licensee Nigel Lucas ~ Real ale ~ Meals and snacks (served all day) ~ Restaurant ~ (01892) 870247 ~ Children welcome (not in public bar) ~ Open 11-11; 12-10.30 Sun

DARGATE TR0761 Map 3
Dove

Village signposted from A299

New licensees had just taken over this attractive old pub as we went to press, and as they have spent some time in the restaurant trade, the food is now quite different. Changing daily, there might be french bread with prawns and spring onion (£3.75) or minute steak in ciabatta bread (£4.50), smoked haddock fishcakes or salad niçoise (£4.50), grilled fillet of salmon with provençale vegetables (£8.50), navarin of lamb (£9), loin of swordfish (£9.50), steak with shallot and bacon sauce (£10), and puddings such as iced grand marnier soufflé, baked chocolate pudding or orange and lemon crème brûlée (from £3.50). Well kept Shepherd Neame Bitter and Spitfire on handpump. The rambling rooms have photographs of the pub and its licensees throughout the century on the walls, a good winter log fire, and plenty of seats on the bare boards; piped music. The sheltered garden has roses, lilacs, paeonies and many other flowers, picnic tables under pear trees, a dovecot with white doves, a rockery and pool, and a swing. A bridlepath leads up from the pub (along the charmingly-named Plumpudding Lane) into Blean Wood. *(Recommended by Dave Braisted, Ian Phillips, David Gregory, D R Eberlin, M Miall, John Fahy)*

Shepherd Neame ~ Tenants Nigel and Bridget Morris ~ Real ale ~ Meals and snacks (not Sun evening) ~ (01227) 751360 ~ Well behaved children welcome ~ Open 11.30-3, 6-11; closed 25 Dec

FAVERSHAM TR0161 Map 3
Albion 🍷

Follow road through town and in centre turn left into Keyland Road; just before Shepherd Neame Brewery walkway over road turn right over bridge, bear right, first right into public car park

Set beside Faversham creek, this attractive weatherboarded cottage is just across the water from the Shepherd Neame Brewery: Bishops Finger, Bitter, and Spitfire on handpump kept under light blanket pressure; a decent French wine list, too. You can be sure of a warm welcome in the light and airy open-plan bar with its simple but solid mixed old pine furniture on wood and sisal flooring, and the big picture windows give lots of light (and nice views); the pale pea green walls have some nautical paraphernalia and old pine mirrors. Interesting food includes sandwiches or filled french bread (from £2.25), soup (£2.50), roquefort and nut terrine (£3.25), ploughman's (from £4.25), warm salad of chicken livers and wild mushrooms with raspberry vinegar dressing (£4.25), leek and goat's cheese wellington (£6.25), pork with a cider and coriander sauce (£7.30), whole grilled plaice (£7.95), stuffed breast of chicken wrapped in bacon with a cream, mushroom and wine sauce (£8.25), lamb rump with a blackcurrant and red wine sauce (£9.75), calf liver with a beetroot and wine sauce (£10.25), and puddings such as moist chocolate banana loaf or steamed date and apple pudding (from £3.15). There are picnic tables out on the walkway and you can stroll along the bank for about an hour. *(Recommended by Peter Smith, Mr and Mrs D Ross, Geoffrey Stephenson, David Gregory, Stephen Brown, A Cowell, Comus Elliott, Ian Phillips, Martyn Golesworthy, Andrew and Ruth Triggs, Stephen and Julie Brown, Belinda Price, Bryn Evans)*

Shepherd Neame ~ Tenants Patrick and Josephine Coevoet ~ Real ale ~ Meals and snacks ~ (01795) 591411 ~ Children in eating area of bar ~ Open 11-3, 6.30-11; 12-3, 6.30-10.30 Sun

FORDCOMBE TQ5240 Map 3
Chafford Arms

B2188, off A264 W of Langton Green

This tile-hung old pub is an absolute mass of flowers in summer, with cascading creepers and carefully tended shrubs and perennials – very inviting. Most of the flowers are in front; behind is a sheltered lawn, with plenty of shade from attractive shrubbery and arbours, and a fine big tree. It's been so carefully extended inside as to seem all of a piece, with plenty of room between the neat tables and comfortable seats, and the uncluttered decor includes some show-jumping pictures and memorabilia. Popular food includes sandwiches (from £2.15; fresh crab, too), sausage and chips (£3.45), ploughman's with good cheese (£4.45), steak and kidney pie (£5.95), rib-eye steak (£8.95), and a good range of fresh fish and seafood (picked up from Hastings by the landlord) such as moules marinières, skate (£9.45), crab (£9.95), dover sole (from £11.95), and seafood platter (£23.95 for two people). Tables can be booked. Unusually for a foody pub, it has a thriving local side, the pubby bar often getting busier towards the close of the evening while the dining side winds down. Well kept King & Barnes Sussex, Larkins, and Wadworths 6X on handpump, local farm cider, and decent house wines; friendly and very attentive long-serving licensees and staff; two amiable old labradors, their natural interest in the food kept politely in check. Darts, shove-ha'penny, and fruit machine. Just up the (steepish) lane is an archetypal village cricket green. *(Recommended by Mr and Mrs C Moncreiffe, Mr and Mrs R D Knight, John and Elspeth Howell, G G Lawrence, K H Frostick, Eddie Edwards)*

Whitbreads ~ Lease: Barrie Leppard ~ Real ale ~ Meals and snacks ~ Restaurant ~ (01892) 740267 ~ Children welcome ~ Open 11-3, 6-11; 12-4, 7-10.30 Sun

GROOMBRIDGE TQ5337 Map 3
Crown

B2110

This quaint Elizabethan inn is prettily set at the end of a row of comely cottages overlooking a steep village green. There are several beamed snug rooms, lots of old teapots, pewter tankards, and antique bottles, and large logs burning in the big brick inglenook; locals tend to crowd around the long copper-topped serving bar. The walls, mostly rough yellowing plaster with some squared panelling and some timbering, are decorated with small topographical, game and sporting prints, and a circular large-scale map with the pub at its centre; a little no-smoking dining area leads off the main bar. The end room, normally for eaters, has fairly close-spaced tables with a variety of good solid chairs, and a log-effect gas fire in a big fireplace. At lunchtime, tasty bar food includes home-made soup (£1.80), ploughman's (from £3), filled baked potatoes (from £3.20), vegetable lasagne (£4.50), good local sausages (£4.80), steak and mushroom pie (£5.50), prawn curry (£6), and puddings (£2.25); in the evening there might be grilled sardines (£6), roast whole poussin with garlic and rosemary (£6.80), steaks (from £7.80), and poached Scotch salmon (£8). Well kept Courage Directors, Harveys IPA and Marstons Pedigree on handpump. There are picnic tables on the sunny front brick terrace or on the green. Across the road is a public footpath beside the small chapel which leads, across a field, to moated Groombridge Place (the gardens of which are now open to the public) and fields beyond. *(Recommended by B J Harding, Tony and Wendy Hobden, Pat and Tony Martin, Graham and Lynn Mason, J S M Sheldon, K Flack, Quentin Williamson, Ian and Nita Cooper, David and Lynne Cure, M Holdsworth, Margaret and Nigel Dennis, Sue Lee, Colin and Joyce Laffan, Mr and Mrs C Starling, Richard Gibbs)*

Free house ~ Licensees Bill and Vivienne Rhodes ~ Real ale ~ Meals and snacks (not Sun evening) ~ Evening restaurant (not Sun) ~ (01892) 864742 ~ Children in eating area of bar and in restaurant ~ Open 11-2.30, 6-11; 11-11 summer Sat; 12-10.30 summer Sun ~ Bedrooms: £23/£38

HEVER TQ4744 Map 3
King Henry VIII

Comfortable seats by the big leaded-light windows here look across to the church where Anne Boleyn's father, the local landlord, is buried, and the pub's origins go back to the 14th c. There's some fine panelling and heavy beams, an inglenook fireplace, a good mix of tables and chairs on the carpet (woven with pictures of Henry VIII), and lots of Henry VIII decorations. Bar food includes home-baked rolls (from £2.20), and a wide choice of ploughman's, casseroles, curries, vegetarian dishes and so forth (from £4.50). Well kept Harveys Best, a beer named for the pub called Old Henry, and a guest beer on handpump, and several malt whiskies; piped music but no games. There are seats and umbrellas on the terrace with picnic tables on the grass by the big pond and a view of rolling fields and distant woods. No dogs. *(Recommended by R C Morgan, W Ruxton, Sue Lee, Quentin Williamson, Peter and Wendy Arnold, Michael Grigg; more reports please)*

Free house ~ Licensees Mike and Julie James ~ Real ale ~ Meals and snacks (not Sun or Mon evenings) ~ (01732) 862163 ~ Children in eating area of the bar only ~ Open 11-3, 6-11; 12-3, 7-10.30 Sun

HODSOLL STREET TQ6263 Map 3
Green Man

Hodsoll Street and pub signposted off A227 S of Meopham; turn right in village

This carefully run flower-decked pub is quietly set overlooking a tiny village green. Big airy carpeted rooms work their way round a hop-draped central bar, with a turkey rug in front of a log fire at one end. Neat tables are spaced tidily around the dark dado, with interesting old local photographs and antique plates on the creamy walls above. Popular dependable bar food from the menu or neatly listed on three boards in front of the bar might include filled rolls (from £2.50), ploughman's (£4), lamb and rosemary or steak and kidney pie (£5), liver and bacon, lasagne, spaghetti bolognese, curry platter (£7) and fish platter (£8.50). One of the main draws here is the incredible choice of puddings temptingly laid out in a big glass display cabinet (£2.50). Well kept Fremlins, Marstons Pedigree, Wadworths 6X and a guest such as Bass or Fullers London Pride on handpump; friendly staff; fruit machines and piped pop music; walkers are welcome but are asked to remove their boots. Behind the back car park are picnic tables under parasols on a well tended lawn, as well as a play area and aviary. *(Recommended by Ian Phillips, Gwen and Pip Piper, T Neate)*

Whitbreads ~ Lease: Mr and Mrs Colin McLeod ~ Real ale ~ Meals and snacks (till 6.45; not Sun or Mon evenings) ~ (01732) 823575 ~ Children welcome till 9pm ~ Open 11-2.30(3 Sat), 6.30-11; 12-3, 7-10.30 Sun; cl Mon evening Oct-May

IGHTHAM COMMON TQ5755 Map 3
Harrow

Signposted off A25 just W of Ightham; pub sign may be hard to spot

The friendly young landlord at this creeper-covered country pub is determined to keep a traditional local public bar and relaxed atmosphere as an alternative to the smarter dining pubs that tend to dominate this area, so there's a pleasant mix of customers from pensioners to pool players to well spoken young ladies. Mixed country furniture stands on old linoleum tiles (some missing) and brick flooring in two unpretentious rooms, one cheerfully painted a sunny yellow above the dark green dado, and although things are well worn there's good-hearted attention to detail with daily papers, and fresh flowers and candles on the tables. A short but useful wine list with plenty of good wines by the glass is reasonably priced; well kept Greene King Abbot, IPA and Marstons Pedigree on handpump. A couple of starters and main courses rather faintly listed on a blackboard might include lentil soup (£3.10), ploughman's (£4.40), moules marinières (£4.50), duck pâté (£4.95), beef goulash (£5.95) and pork dijon or paella (£7.95); puddings like bread and butter pudding or summer pudding (£3.25). A lush grapevine grows around the delightful little antiquated conservatory which leads off an elegantly jaded dining room (some might say a lick of paint wouldn't go amiss); piped rock music, pleasant young bar staff; picnic tables on a pretty little pergola-enclosed back lawn. *(Recommended by Derek Thomas, Catherine Kanter, Eddy and Emma Gibson)*

Free house ~ Licensees J Elton and M S O'Connor ~ Real ale ~ Meals and snacks ~ Restaurant ~ (01732) 885912 ~ Children welcome in one room ~ Open 11.30-3, 5.30-11; 12-3, 7-10.30 Sun; cl 1 Jan ~ Bedrooms: £27.50B/£46

LAMBERHURST TQ6635 Map 3
Brown Trout ♀

B2169, just off A21 S of village nearly opposite entrance to Scotney Castle

The nicest place to eat the popular fresh fish dishes here is in the smallish bar with its big central counter surrounded by small country prints, glowing copper and beams hung with lots of brass. There might be mediterranean prawns in garlic butter (£4.95), 8-10oz cod or fillet of plaice (£5.25), halibut steak (£6.75), dressed crab with prawns (£8.50), and whole lobster (£14.95); also non-fishy dishes like chicken kiev, steak and kidney pie or 10oz gammon steak (£5.25), and steaks (from £9.50), with good value three-course meals (£10.95; one menu is vegetarian); friendly service. You may have to book ahead, particularly on Saturday evenings. Most people tend to eat in the biggish extension dining room which has many closely set tables and a fish tank. Well kept Fullers London Pride and Marstons Pedigree on handpump, and a fair choice of wines; darts. Picnic tables under cocktail parasols on the sloping front grass to the road and a large, safe garden behind with swings, slides and trampolines. The hanging baskets are quite a sight in summer. (Recommended by David Gregory, Dave Braisted, Paula Williams, Dorothee and Dennis Glover, B and M Parkin, Kath Wetherill, M Holdsworth, Dr S Willavoys)

Whitbreads ~ Lease: Joseph Stringer ~ Real ale ~ Meals and snacks (till 10pm) ~ Restaurant ~ (01892) 890312 ~ Children in eating area of bar or in restaurant ~ Open 10.30-11; 10.30-3, 6-11 in winter; 12-10.30 Sun

LANGTON GREEN TQ5538 Map 3
Hare ⑪ ♀

A264 W of Tunbridge Wells

Kent Dining Pub of the Year

Well run, and with attentive knowledgeable staff, this spacious Victorian pub is very popular for its good, interesting food. As well as sandwiches (from £3.25) and ploughman's (£4.75), there might be home-made soup (£2.95), three cheese tartlet with pickle (£3.95), good tiger prawns in filo pastry with an oyster sauce (£5.95), spinach and wild mushroom pancake with cheese sauce and roasted pine kernels (£5.95), steak burger with smoked bacon, mozzarella and salsa (£7.95), gammon with a cauliflower cheese bake (£8.95), lovely roast shoulder of lamb with a garlic crumb topping and a ginger and redcurrant sauce (£11.25), and fillet of bass with a coriander and spring onion sauce (£12.95); they only take bookings in the back room, and your food is brought to you. The knocked-through ground floor is light and airy, with good-sized rooms, high ceilings and lots of big windows: dark-painted dados below light walls and dark ceilings, oak furniture and turkey carpets on stained wooden floors, and largely period romantic pastels and bric-a-brac (including a huge collection of chamber-pots). The chatty big room at the back has old books and pictures crowding its walls, two big mahogany mirror-backed display cabinets, and lots of large tables (one big enough for at least 12) on a light brown carpet; french windows open on to a terrace with picnic tables, looking out on to a tree-ringed green (you don't see the main road). Well kept Greene King IPA and Abbot and Rayments on handpump, 14 wines by the glass, and up to 50 malt whiskies; piped pop music in the front bar area, shove-ha'penny, cribbage, dominoes, and trivia. (Recommended by Margaret and Nigel Dennis, David and Lynne Cure, Hilarie Dobbie, Mr and Mrs G Turner)

Greene King ~ Tenant Brian Whiting ~ Real ale ~ Meals and snacks (served all day) ~ Restaurant ~ (01892) 862419 ~ Children in restaurant ~ Open 11.30-11; 12-10.30 Sun

---

We accept no free drinks or payment for inclusion. We take no advertising, and are not sponsored by the brewing industry – or by anyone else. So all reports are independent.

LUDDESDOWN TQ6667 Map 3
Cock

Henley Street, OS Sheet 177 map reference 664672; Luddesdown signposted with Cuxton off A227 in Meopham, and off A228 in Cuxton (first real turn-off S of M2 junction 2); Henley Street is off the N end of Luddesdown village

Light pours through a huge bay window into the calmly comfortable, neat and tidy little red-carpeted lounge at this tucked-away country pub. When we inspected, the few copper- or wood-topped tables were occupied by diners quietly enjoying the tasty bar food, with a couple of locals perched at the bar sampling one or two of the well kept ales such as Adnams Bitter and Broadside, Bridge Bitter, Harveys Best, Viking Island Mild and Youngs Special. They also keep Addlestone's, Biddenden and Gibbon Strangler farm ciders. One of the main draws here is the fresh fish and seafood collected by the licensees from Billingsgate market: pint of prawns (£2.20), prawn cocktail (£4.25), dressed crab (£4.80), and scallops, tempura of fish with spicy pickle and chargrilled bass. Other bar food includes sandwiches (from £2.60), pâté (£2.90), ploughman's (£5.40), lasagne, vegetarian lasagne or chilli con carne (£5.90), chicken madras (£7.40) and beef fillet (£12.90). The attractive quarry-tiled back bar has a pubbier atmosphere, with pews, bar billiards, darts, TV, sports photographs and a glass case of model cars. Some tables outside; boules. *(Recommended by Comus Elliott, Andy Stedman, Sue Lee, A R Turner)*

Free house ~ Licensee Andrew Turner ~ Real ale ~ Meals and snacks (not Sun or Mon evenings) ~ (01474) 814208 ~ Open 12-11

NEWNHAM TQ9557 Map 3
George

44 The Street; village signposted from A2 just W of Ospringe, outside Faversham

As we went to press, Mr and Mrs Richards (who came from another well liked main entry, the White Lion at Selling) took over this 16th-c village pub. The spreading series of atmospheric rooms have dressers with lots of teapots, prettily upholstered mahogany settles, dining chairs and leather carving chairs around candlelit tables, table lamps and gas-type ceiling chandeliers, and rugs on the waxed floorboards; hop bines hang from the beams and there are open fires and fresh flowers. The dining room has been completely redesigned. Bar food now includes sandwiches, fried goat's cheese on a raspberry coulis (£3.95), smoked salmon with rosemary-scented cream-cheese pin wheels (£4.95), fresh salmon, spinach and cream-cheese lasagne (£6.50), pork fillet in cider and apple (£8.25), calf liver and bacon with red wine gravy (£8.75), and puddings like home-made lemon meringue pie or banoffi pie (£2.95). Well kept Shepherd Neame Bitter, Bishops Finger, Porter, and Spitfire on handpump, and piped music. There are picnic tables in a spacious sheltered garden with a fine spreading cobnut tree, below the slopes of the sheep pastures. Dogs allowed (drinking bowl in lobby). Good walks nearby. *(Recommended by Tina and David Woods-Taylor, Geoffrey Stephenson, Michael Tucker, David Gregory, James Nunns, Frank Ashbee, D Hayman; more reports on the new regime, please)*

Shepherd Neame ~ Tenants Tony and Jackie Richards ~ Real ale ~ Meals and snacks ~ Restaurant ~ (01795) 890237 ~ Children welcome ~ Jazz and curry Mon evening, live 60s music last Tues of month ~ Open 11-3, 6.30-11; 12-3.30, 7-10.30 Sun

OARE TR0163 Map 3
Shipwrights Arms

Ham Road, Hollow Shore; from A2 just W of Faversham, follow Oare—Luddenham signpost; fork right at Oare—Harty Ferry signpost, drive straight through Oare (don't turn off to Harty Ferry), then left into Ham Street on the outskirts of Faversham, following pub signpost

'A delightful change' is how one reader described this marvellously unaltered 17th-c pub. The surrounding salt marshes are designated as areas of Special Scientifc Interest, and the nature reserve across the creek and the marshes are populated by rare birds.

Many people do still arrive by boat and on the notice board opposite the entrance are several interesting vessels for sale. There is no mains electricity (power is by generator) and no mains water – it's pumped from an artesian well. The three unspoilt little bars are dark and cosy, and separated by standing timbers and wood part-partitions or narrow door arches. There's a medley of seats from tapestry cushioned stools and chairs through some big windsor armchairs to black wood-panelled built-in settles forming little booths, hops and pewter tankards hanging over the bar counter, boating jumble and pictures, flags or boating pennants on the ceilings, several brick fireplaces, and a woodburning stove. Simple home-made bar food such as sandwiches (from £1.80), winter vegetable soup (£1.95), filled baked potatoes (from £1.95), pizzas (from £2.50), ploughman's (£3.95), liver and onions (£4.95), steak and kidney pie (£5.95), and puddings (£2); part of the eating area is no smoking. Well kept beers such as Adnams, Coachers Mild, and Sehpherd Neame Bitter and Spitfire tapped from the cask, and strong local farm cider; darts and fruit machine. The small front and back gardens outside the white weatherboarded and tiled building lead up a bank to the path above the creek where lots of boats are moored, and the Saxon Shore Way runs right past. *(Recommended by Paul Hilditch, Thomas Nott, Stephen Brown, Comus Elliott; more reports please)*

Free house ~ Landlord Rod Carroll ~ Real ale ~ Meals and snacks (12-3, 7-9.30) ~ (01795) 590088 ~ Children welcome ~ Live bands Thurs evenings, disco Fri evenings ~ Open 11-11; 12-10.30 Sun

PENSHURST TQ5243 Map 3

Bottle House ◖

Coldharbour Lane, Smarts Hill; leaving Penshurst SW on B2188 turn right at Smarts Hill signpost, then bear right towards Chiddingstone and Cowden; keep straight on

Whatever the weather, this bustling and notably welcoming 15th-c pub is full of customers enjoying the well kept Harveys Best, local Larkins or Ind Coope Burton, and good food from an extensive menu. The front bar is low beamed and neatly kept, and has an exposed brick floor, smoothed with age, that extends to behind the polished copper topped bar counter. Big windows look to a terrace with climbing plants and hanging baskets around picnic tables under cocktail parasols, and beyond to views of quiet fields and oak trees. Down a step, the unpretentious main red-carpeted bar has massive hop-covered supporting beams, two large stone pillars with a small brick fireplace (with a stuffed turtle to one side), and old paintings and photographs on mainly plastered walls. To the far right, an isolated extension forms a small pine panelled snug hung with part of an extensive collection of china pot lids; the rest are in the low ceilinged dining room. Changing daily, the bar food might include home-made soup (£2.95), pork and liver pâté with cumberland sauce (£4.25), local sausages (£5.95), honey and mustard cold roast gammon or home-battered cod (£6.95), vegetable and nut wellington with spicy tomato sauce (£7.95), cajun chicken (£8.95), grilled bass with ginger and spring onion sauce (£10.50), chargrilled lamb steak with green peppercorn sauce (£10.95), roast duck breasts with plum, orange and honey sauce (£12.95), and children's menu (£4.50 which includes an ice cream); cider from Chiddingstone, and local wine; unobtrusive piped music. Dogs welcome (they may offer them biscuits). *(Recommended by R and S Bentley, DFL, D H and M C Watkinson, Nigel Wikeley, Gwen and Peter Andrews, A Homes, B J Harding, B and M Parkin, Margaret and Nigel Dennis, Bob and Maggie Atherton, J and P Maloney)*

Free house ~ Licensees Gordon and Val Meer ~ Real ale ~ Meals and snacks (till 10pm) ~ Restaurant ~ (01892) 870306 ~ Children welcome till 9pm ~ Open 11-3, 6-11; 12-3, 7-10.30 Sun

---

Children welcome means the pubs says it lets children inside without any special restriction; readers have found that some may impose an evening time limit – please tell us if you find this.

PENSHURST TQ5243 Map 3

Spotted Dog

Smarts Hill; going S from village centre on B2188, fork right up hill at telephone box: in just under ½ mile the pub is on your left

One reader was delighted to find that after 18 years since her last visit, this quaint old tiled house was as good as ever. It is in a wonderful spot with twenty miles of untouched countryside stretching away from the tiered garden slopes (where there are plenty of picnic tables which not, surprisingly, fill up quickly on a fine day). The neatly kept and heavily beamed and timbered bar, down a few steps, has some antique settles as well as wheelback chairs on its rugs and tiles, a fine brick inglenook fireplace, and attractive moulded panelling in one alcove. It's quite small, so there may be an overflow into the restaurant at busy times. Enjoyable and imaginative food listed on several blackboards (with prices unchanged since last year) might include lovely celery and stilton soup, smoked chicken, avocado and wild mushroom bake or spinach, cream cheese and green peppercorn roulade (£6.25), good fresh fish dishes like tasty lemon sole, red snapper, red mullet or bass grilled with lime, ginger and coriander butter (£9.25), half a shoulder of lamb braised in red wine, garlic and rosemary (£9.45), and puddings such as cherry strudel or treacle tart; staff stay smiling amidst the cheery bustle. Well kept Adnams, Eldridge Pope Royal Oak and King & Barnes Sussex on handpump, along with Old Spotty – a Best Bitter brewed specially for them; decent wine list. Lots of room for children to play outside. *(Recommended by Paul Hilditch, Liz Bell, Tina and David Woods-Taylor, B and M Parkin, D P Brown, Dr Richard Crane, James House, DFL, R J Walden, Mrs M Furness, J and P Maloney, Peter and Wendy Arnold, Dr S Willavoys, Bob and Maggie Atherton, Sue Lee, Mr and Mrs J Jackson)*

Carlsberg-Tetley ~ Lease: Andy Tucker ~ Real ale ~ Meals and snacks (not Mon evening) ~ Restaurant ~ (01892) 870253 ~ Children in restaurant ~ Open 12-2.30(3 Sat), 6-11; 12-3.30, 7-10.30 Sun; closed 25-26 Dec

PLUCKLEY TQ9243 Map 3

Dering Arms 🍽 ♀ ⛽

Pluckley Station, which is signposted from B2077 in village

Although this striking old Dutch-gabled pub is much liked for its good food, it is also very popular locally, which means the atmosphere tends to be both jolly and friendly. The high ceilinged bar has a good pubby ambiance, stylishly simple decorations, a variety of good solid wooden furniture, wood and stone floors, and a log fire in the great fireplace. A smaller panelled bar has similar furnishings; dominoes and cribbage. There is quite some emphasis on very well cooked fresh fish such as mussels in cider and cream sauce (£3.95), crab newberg (£4.45), grilled plaice (£6.95), monkfish in creamy bacon and orange sauce, fillet of red bream meunière or fresh tuna baked with saffron onions (£9.65), and scallops with garlic butter or grilled lemon sole (£10.95); also, sandwiches (£1.70), home-made soup (£2.95), ploughman's (£3.50), ham and chips (£3.75), pasta with stilton and basil sauce (£6.95), a home-made pie (£7.45), rabbit in mustard and ale (£9.65), roast partridge (£10.65), and puddings like chocolate parfait or sherry trifle (£2.50). Well kept Goachers's Maidstone Dark Porter and Dering ale (a beer brewed specially for them) on handpump, a very good extensive wine list, home-made lemonade, local cider and quite a few malt whiskies. There's a vintage car rally once a month, and maybe summer garden parties with barbecues and music. *(Recommended by Mr and Mrs Jonathan Russell, Jennie Munro, Jim Wingate, J Tross, D H Gittins, C and M Starling, Thomas Nott, Lin Stephens, Hilarie Dobbie, Melanie Bradshaw, Mayhur Shah, Hilary Patrinos, John Fahy, Stephen Brown)*

Free house ~ Licensee James Buss ~ Real ale ~ Meals and snacks (not Sun evening) ~ Restaurant (not Sun evening) ~ (01233) 840371 ~ Children welcome ~ Open 11-3.30, 6-11; 12-3.30, 7-10.30 Sun; closed 26-27 Dec ~ Bedrooms: £28/£36

Pubs with outstanding views are listed at the back of the book.

RINGLESTONE TQ8755 Map 3

Ringlestone ★ ♀ ◀

M20 Junction 8 to Lenham/Leeds Castle; join B2163 neading N towards Sittingbourne via Hollingbourne; at water tower above Hollingbourne turn right towards Doddington (signposted), and straight ahead at next crossroads; OS Sheet 178 map reference 879558

The enterprising licensee here has now bought the farmhouse opposite in which they offer bedrooms, and plans to refurbish the barn complex for functions. The inn is now surrounded by eight acres of land, including two acres of beautifully landscaped lawns, with shrubs, trees and rockeries, a water garden with four pretty ponds and cascading waterfalls, a delightful fountain, and troughs of pretty flowers along the pub walls; plenty of seats. It's a characterful place with a happy, relaxed atmosphere, and a fine choice of good food and well kept real ales. The help-yourself hot and cold lunchtime buffet is well worth a short queue for meals like lamb, coconut and banana curry, liver and apple pâté salad, seafood pie or ham, leek, apples and cider pie (from £3.25; salads and vegetables are extra); also, a thick soup with sherry and croutons (£3.45), Kentish pork sausages (£5.35), macaroni with tuna and clams (£6.45), popular pies like vegetable and nut, fish in elderflower wine, duck in damson wine or beef in black beer and raisin wine (from £8.25; vegetables are £2.95 exra), and rump steak (£9.65). Puddings such as home-made cheesecake, treacle, orange and nut tart or fruit crumble (£3.75). Three or four changing well kept real ales tapped from casks behind the bar or on handpump, and chalked up on a board, might include Adnams, Cains Formidable, Fremlins, Fullers London Pride, Marstons Pedigree, Morlands Old Speckled Hen, Ringlestone Bitter (a beer brewed for them by Tolly), Shepherd Neame Spitfire or Wadworths 6X; two dozen country wines (including sparkling ones), local cider and fresh fruit cordials. The central room has farmhouse chairs, cushioned wall settles, and tables with candle lanterns (and bowls of shell-on peanuts) on its worn brick floor, and old-fashioned brass and glass lamps on the exposed brick and flint walls; there's a woodburning stove and small bread oven in an inglenook fireplace. An arch from here through a wall – rather like the outside of a house, windows and all – opens into a long, quieter room with cushioned wall benches, tiny farmhouse chairs, three old carved settles (one rather fine and dated 1620), similar tables, and etchings of country folk on its walls (bare brick too). Regulars tend to sit at the wood-panelled bar counter, or liven up a little wood-floored side room; dominoes, cribbage, and piped music. Hard-working, friendly staff. Well behaved dogs welcome. We have not heard from readers who've stayed here, but would expect the bedrooms to be good. *(Recommended by Thomas Nott, Ian Phillips, Tina and David Woods-Taylor, Mr Miller, Comus Elliott, Kay Neville-Rolfe, J Tross, Evelyn and Derek Walter, Lin Stephens, Melanie Bradshaw, D Hayman, AEB, Carole and Philip Bacon, Gill and Bryan Trueman, Julie Peters, Colin Blinkhorn, M J How, E D Bailey, Clive Gilbert)*

Free house ~ Licensees Michael Millington-Buck and Michelle Stanley ~ Real ale ~ Meals and snacks ~ Restaurant ~ (01622) 859900 ~ Children welcome ~ Open 12-3, 6(6.30 winter weekdays)-11; 12-11 Sat; 12-10.30 Sun ~ Bedrooms: £48.75B/£58.75B

SANDGATE TR2035 Map 3

Clarendon

Head W out of Sandgate on main road to Hythe; about 100m after you emerge onto the seafront park on the road across from a telephone box on the right; just back from the telephone box is an uphill track.

Run by a homely and friendly couple, this relaxing little local is set half way up a steep lane from the sea. Visitors will probably feel most comfortable in the big windowed lounge on the left – you can just see the sea through one window. Decor is unaffected, with copper topped or new pine tables on a light patterned carpet, a few impressions of the pub, and a coal-effect gas fire. There's a very simple chatty atmosphere and a winter open fire in the straightforward right hand bar (popular with locals), and the well kept real ales include Shepherd Neame Best and Bitter, Spitfire and seasonal ales from a rather nice Victorian mahogany bar and mirrored gantry, as well as a surprisingly good chardonnay by the glass; piped music. Good plain home cooking includes sandwiches (from £1.80), simple ploughman's (£3.50), chilli (£3.95), beef in beer pie (£5.50), and delicious, simply cooked lemon sole or plaice. The hanging baskets and boxes are lovely. *Recommended by Thomas Nott, Peter Chamberlain, Derek St Clair-Stannard; more reports please)*

Shepherd Neame ~ Tenants Dave and Judy Smith ~ Real ale ~ Meals and snacks (not Sun or Tues evenings) ~ (01303) 248684 ~ Children in eating area of bar ~ Open 11.30-3.30, 6(7 Sat)-11; 12-3, 7-10.30 Sun; they will open all day in summer if trade demands it

SELLING TR0455 Map 3
Rose & Crown

Selling signposted from exit roundabout of M2 junction 7: keep right on through village and follow Perry Wood signposts; or from A252 just W of junction with A28 at Chilham follow Shottenden signpost, then right turn signposted Selling, then right signposted Perry Wood

The award-winning, sizeable garden behind this little 16th-c country pub is lovely and full of flowers – there's a new children's wooden play frame to go with the rocking horse and swing, lots of picnic tables, bat and trap, and a small aviary; the outside of the pub has been redecorated and window boxes have been added to all the hanging baskets, tubs, and chimney pots with climbing roses. Inside, you can be sure of a warm welcome from the hard-working licensees and their staff, and there's lots to look at in the attractive bar; the Christmas decorations are said to be very special. The central servery has pretty fresh flowers by each of its sturdy corner timbers, and the beams are strung with hop bines, and decorated with an interesting variety of corn-dolly work – there's more of this in a wall cabinet in one cosy side alcove, and much more again down steps in the comfortably cottagey restaurant (which has been redecorated with stencils hand-made by Mrs Prebble of woodland animals). Apart from a couple of old-fashioned housekeeper's chairs by the huge log fire (replaced in summer by an enjoyably colourful mass of silk flowers interlaced with more corn dollies and so forth), the seats are very snugly cushioned. Good generously served bar food includes steak and kidney pie (£5.50), chicken tikka masala or China Town platter (£7), fisherman's platter (£9), daily specials such as prawn creole, beef in red wine, and Jamaican chicken (£7), and puddings (on show in a cold cabinet down steps in a small family room) like fresh nectarine bakewell, raspberry torte or lemon meringue pie (£2.70). Well kept changing ales such as Adnams Southwold, Goacher's Maidstone, Harveys Best, and guests such as Bass or Charles Wells Bombardier on handpump, decent wines in good measures; informal, helpful service. *(Recommended by Maria Edwards, Geoffrey Stephenson, Heidi Conroy, Stephen Brown, D J Roseveáre, Comus Elliott, Mr and Mrs S R White, Mr and Mrs C Neame, Chris Westmoreland, LM, K Smith)*

Free house ~ Licensees Richard and Jocelyn Prebble ~ Real ale ~ Meals and snacks (not Sun or Mon evenings) ~ Restaurant ~ (01227) 752214 ~ Children in snug area and in restaurant ~ Open 11-3, 6.30-11; 12-3, 7-10.30 Sun; closed evening 25 Dec

nr SMARDEN TQ8842 Map 3
Bell ★ ◀

From Smarden follow lane between church and The Chequers, then turn left at T-junction; or from A274 take unsignposted turn E a mile N of B2077 to Smarden

New licensees have taken over this pretty 16th-c pub and as we went to press, no major changes had been made. There's a good, jolly pubby atmosphere, and the snug dimly lit little back rooms have low beams, ancient walls of bare brick or rough ochre plaster, brick or flagstone floors, pews and the like around simple tables, and warm fires; one room is no smoking. The larger airy white painted and green matchboarded bar has a beamed ceiling and quarry tiled floor, a woodburning stove in the big fireplace, and a games area with darts, pool, cribbage, dominoes, fruit machine and juke box at one end. Straightforward bar food includes sandwiches, home-made steak and kidney pie (£5.75), poached salmon (£6.50), mixed grill (£10.50), and home-made apple pie (£2.75); Friday night curries, and Sunday roast (£6.50). Well kept Flowers Original, Fullers London Pride, Goachers Maidstone, Harveys Best, Marstons

Pedigree, Morlands Old Speckled Hen, Shepherd Neame Bitter, and guests on handpump, local cider, country wines, and winter mulled wine. In summer (when it does get crowded) it's very pleasant sitting in the garden amongst the mature fruit trees and shrubs, looking up at the attractive rose-covered building with its massive chimneys. *(Recommended by Colin Laffan, Janet and Colin Roe, Paula Williams, Serena Hebeler, Mrs M Furness, Graham and Lynn Mason, C Sinclair, Thomas Nott, Jeremy Palmer, Stephen Brown, Kath Wetherill, Christopher Warner, Sue Lee; more reports on the new regime, please)*

Free house ~ Licensees Mr and Mrs C J Smith ~ Real ale ~ Meals and snacks (till 10pm) ~ (01233) 770283 ~ Children in games room ~ Open 11.30-3, 6-11; 12-3, 7-10.30 Sun ~ Bedrooms: £30/£42

SPELDHURST TQ5541 Map 3
George & Dragon ♀
Village signposted from A264 W of Tunbridge Wells

The couple who were managing this fine half-timbered building, based around a 13th-c manorial hall, have now taken it over. The partly panelled bar has massive oak beams (that were added during 'modernisation' in 1589), and it's not hard to picture Kentish archers returning from their victory at Agincourt in 1415 resting on the enormous flagstones; there's a huge sandstone fireplace with a vast iron fireback that's over three hundred years old, and seating is on high backed wooden benches at several old wood topped cast iron tables. To the left is a partly enclosed panelled and carpeted bar with a comfortable sofa and padded banquettes, exposed beams and rough plaster walls, a grandfather clock that marks the half hour and a small fireplace. Well kept Bass, Fullers London Pride and Harveys Best on handpump, lots of malt whiskies and a large wine cellar; darts, cribbage, fruit machine, and piped music. Bar food now includes home-made soup (£2.50), terrine with walnut bread and cumberland sauce (£4.95), fried goat's cheese on a bed of salad with tomato and pine nuts (£4.95), grilled toulouse sausages with mustard mash and red wine sauce (£8.50), bass with lobster and chive sauce (£9.95), marinated venison steak with blueberry and redcurrant sauce (£10.95). The first-floor restaurant under burdensome roof timbers is striking. There are white tables and chairs on the neat little lawn, ringed with flowers, in front of the building. *(Recommended by Eddie Edwards, John and Elspeth Howell, LM, A Homes, Paul and Pam Penrose, David and Lynne Cure, Bruce Bird, Mavis and John Wright, Dr S Willavoys, James Nunns, Richard Gibbs)*

Free house ~ Licensees David and Louise Ferris ~ Real ale ~ Meals and snacks ~ Restaurant ~ (01892) 863125 ~ Children in one bar and in restaurant ~ Open 11-11; 12-10.30 Sun

TOYS HILL TQ4751 Map 3
Fox & Hounds
Off A25 in Brasted, via Brasted Chart and The Chart

Little changes over the years in this slightly eccentric remote country local, run by the fairly firm but kind Mrs Pelling who doesn't allow mobile phones, and has little notices by the open fires warning against 'unofficial stoking'. When your eyes have adjusted to the dim lighting you can sit comfortably on one of the homely and well worn old sofas or armchairs which are scattered with cushions and throws, and read the latest *Country Life*, *Hello* or *Private Eye*. Some of the aged local photographs, letters and pictures on the nicotine-stained walls don't look as if they've moved since they were put up in the 1960s, and it's unlikely that much in the two simple rooms, including the decor, has changed since then. Lunchtime bar food is at an absolute minimum with pre-wrapped filled rolls (from £1.40) and ploughman's, pastie or cauliflower cheese (£3.80); well stocked chocolate shelves. Well kept Greene King IPA and Abbot on handpump; occasional sing-songs around the piano; darts, shove-ha'penny, cribbage and dominoes. The garden is particulary lovely with picnic tables on a good area of flat lawn surrounded by mature shrubs. As you approach this peaceful retreat from the pretty village (one of the highest in the county) you will catch glimpses through the trees of one of the most magnificent views in Kent. There are good walks nearby, and it's handy for Chartwell and for Emmetts garden. *(Recommended by Jenny and Brian Seller, D E Twitchett, TBB, Ian Phillips)*

Greene King ~ Tenant Mrs R Pelling ~ Real ale ~ Lunchtime snacks ~ (01732) 750328 ~ Children away from bar lunchtime only ~ 12-2.30(3 Sat), 6-11; 12-3, 7-10.30 Sun; closed 25 Dec

TUNBRIDGE WELLS TQ5839 Map 3
Sankeys ❶ ♀

39 Mount Ephraim (A26 just N of junction with A267)

The downstairs bar of this popular seafood restaurant has a good bustling and relaxed atmosphere. It's furnished with lots of sturdy old pine tables on the york stone floor, and decorated with old mirrors, prints, enamel advertising signs, antique beer engines and other bric-a-brac (most of which has been salvaged from local pub closures); french windows lead to a small suntrap terrace with white tables and chairs under cocktail parasols. Good, enjoyable food includes cheeses with biscuits (£3.50), a plate of charcuterie (£4.50), moules and frites (£5), pork and leek sausages (£4.50), kentish lamb cutlets with mustard sauce (£10), and daily specials; you can also eat from the restaurant menu, too: warm salad of king scallops with wild mushrooms and tagliatelle or Loch Fyne langoustines tossed in garlic butter (£6.50), skate wing with black butter (£10), lovely Cornish cock crab (£14.50), roast monkfish with sweet pepper sauce, tuna steak griddled mediterranean style or halibut grilled with herbs (£15), and fruits de mer (£17.50). Adnams, Harveys Best or Larkins Chiddingstone from an antique beer engine, though most people seem to be taking advantage of the superb wine list; they also have quite a choice of unusual teas. You need to get there early for a table in the bar; the restaurant is no smoking. *(Recommended by D Hayman, Heather Martin; more reports please)*

Free house ~ Licensee Guy Sankey ~ Real ale ~ Meals and snacks (12-3, 7-10) ~ Restaurant (not Sun) ~ (01892) 511422 ~ Children welcome ~ Open 10am-11pm; 11-3, 6-11 Sat; cl Sun, cl 25-26 Dec

ULCOMBE TQ8550 Map 3
Pepper Box ◗

Fairbourne Heath (signposted from A20 in Harrietsham; or follow Ulcombe signpost from A20, then turn left at crossroads with sign to pub)

The two armchairs and sofa by the splendid inglenook with its warm log fire here are a favourite place with some readers. It's a cosy, traditional old country inn with a friendly, homely bar, standing timbers and low beams hung with hops, copper kettles and pans on window sills, and some very low-seated windsor chairs and wing armchairs. A side area is more functionally furnished for eating, and there's a very snug little no-smoking dining room. Enjoyable bar food includes crab pâté (£4.50), sizzling prawns in garlic and chilli butter (£5.50), sweet and sour chicken (£6.50), smoked salmon and mushroom tagliatelle (£7.50), calf liver with an apple and sage sauce (£8.50), lamb rumps with elderberry and rosemary sauce (£9.50), and sirloin steak with brandy and mushroom cream sauce (£10.50); they also do lunchtime sandwiches, good puddings, and a Sunday roast. Very well kept Shepherd Neame Bitter, Bishops Finger and Spitfire tapped from the cask, and country wines; efficient, courteous service. The pub is very nicely placed on high ground above the weald, looking out over a great plateau of rolling arable farmland, and if you're in the garden, with its small pond, swing and tables among trees, shrubs and flowerbeds, you may catch a glimpse of the deer that sometimes come up, but if not you're quite likely to meet Jones the tabby tom, the other two cats, or Boots the plump collie. The name of the pub refers to the pepperbox pistol – an early type of revolver with numerous barrels. No children inside. *(Recommended by Janet and Colin Roe, Carl and Jackie Cranmer, Mrs P J Pearce, Comus Elliott, Mrs M Furness, Quentin Williamson, D Hayman, G S B G Dudley)*

Shepherd Neame ~ Tenants Geoff and Sarah Pemble ~ Real ale ~ Meals and snacks (12-1.45, 7-9.45; not Sun or Mon evenings) ~ Restaurant (not Sun evening) ~ (01622) 842558 ~ Live music, Sun evening ~ Open 11-3, 6.30-11; 12-3, 7-11 Sun

WHITSTABLE TR1166 Map 3
Pearsons 🍴

Sea Wall; follow main road into centre as far as you can, turning L into Horsebridge Rd; pub opposite Royal Free Fishers & Dredgers; parking limited

This cheery, busy pub with its fine sea views is included because readers really love the delicious fresh seafood served in the upstairs restaurant: cockles (£1.75), mussels (£4.95), grilled king prawns (£5.95), six local oysters in season (£6), fresh battered cod, skate or plaice (from £6.95; not Sun lunchtime), vegetarian meals like spinach and mushroom lasagne (£8.50), seafood platter (£10.95), Pearson's paradise – a huge meal for two involving lobster, crab, prawns, oysters, mussels and more (£36), and changing fresh fish (excellent plaice) or shellfish specials; children's menu (from £3.25). There's a nicely relaxed atmosphere, with lots of tables close together, and fine sea views. They serve a few seaside lunchtime snacks in the bar downstairs such as rollmops (£2.25), smoked mackerel (£2.50) and platter of prawns (£2.95), as well as the usual reasonably priced bar food. Well kept Boddingtons, Flowers Original, and Fremlins and a changing guest on handpump; decent house wines; piped pop music, fruit machine. There are some picnic tables outside between the pub and the sea. *(Recommended by Shirley Pielou, Frank Ashbee, Mr and Mrs R A Broadbent, LM, D Bryan, David Shillitoe, Heather Martin, Claude and Bennie Bemis; more reports please)*

Whitbreads ~ Lease: Linda Wingrove ~ Real ale ~ Meals and snacks ~ Restaurant ~ (01227) 272005 ~ Children welcome ~ Open 11-3, 6-11; 11-11 summer Sat; 12-4, 7-10.30 Sun

---

Lucky Dip

Besides the fully inspected pubs, you might like to try these Lucky Dips recommended to us and described by readers (if you do, please send us reports):

☆ **Addington** [handy for M20 via junctions 2 and 4; TQ6559], *Angel*: 14th-c inn in classic village green setting, plenty of well spaced tables, usual food inc sandwiches and generous ploughman's, quick friendly service, reasonable prices; Scottish Courage ales *(C R Bridgeman)*

Alkham [between Folkestone and Dover on the Broad behind A20; TR2542], *Marquis of Granby*: White Georgian house with beautiful garden in attractive old village, modernised inside, warm and pleasant; good food esp fish in bar and restaurant, welcoming staff *(Gethin Lewis)*

Appledore [15 The Street – formerly Red Lion; TQ9529], *Black Lion*: Friendly pub with partitioned eating area, good value food esp local fish; comfortable bedrooms *(Max and Jan Logan, Janet and Colin Roe)*

☆ **Ashford** [Silverhill Rd, Willesborough; TR0241], *Hooden Horse on the Hill*: Rambling 19th-c cottage done up cheerfully with hopsacks and old advertisements, well kept ales served through sparkler inc Goachers and five guests, farm ciders, country wines, candlelight, good value food esp Mexican, good enthusiastic staff *(Richard Balls, John C Baker, Darren Palmer)*

Ashurst [High St (A264 by stn); TQ5038], *Bald Faced Stag*: Clean and bright, with well kept Harveys, informal atmosphere, good pub food inc good value Sun lunch and interesting snacks, well kept King & Barnes and Harveys, helpful landlord, daily papers, plain decor; pleasant garden with play area, country walks nearby *(Mr and Mrs J Jackson, Quentin Williamson, John Kimber)*

☆ **Barham** [The Street; TR2050], *Duke of Cumberland*: Pleasant open-plan country local with good value generous straightforward food, good curries Fri night, Whitbreads-related ales, friendly service, open fire, cat and dog; bedrooms, caravan site *(Sybille Weber)*

Bekesbourne [Bekesbourne Hill; TR1856], *Unicorn*: Clean and friendly country pub with good bar food and well kept Shepherd Neame *(D J Hayman)*

Beltring [A228/B2160; TQ6747], *Bluebell*: Whitbreads Wayside Inn dating from 17th c, opp their Hop Farm; cosy olde-worlde decor, Whitbreads-related and guest ales, blazing log fire, decent home cooking inc Sun lunch, tables in garden; open all day *(Jenny and Michael Back)*

Benenden [The Street (B2086); TQ8033], *King William IV*: Compact low-ceilinged village local with rustic furnishings, Shepherd Neame ales, food inc imaginative dishes, good log fire; games in public bar, small garden

(Janet and Colin Roe, Michael Grigg, LYM)

☆ **Benover** [Benover Rd (B2162); TQ7048], *Woolpack*: Pretty tile-hung pub with good value food inc vegetarian in panelled and beamed lounge, inglenook fire, quick friendly service, well kept ales, games bar; provision for children, summer barbecues on big lawn, not far from Whitbreads Hop Farm, attractive walks nearby *(A Budden, P Lenney, LYM)*

☆ **Biddenden** [High St; TQ8538], *Red Lion*: Plush but friendly Tudor inn in lovely village, good straightforward food and service, well kept Whitbreads-related ales *(Tim Masters, Mrs Kay Neville-Rolfe)*

Bodsham [Bodsham Green; TR1045], *Timber Batts*: Attractive and busy, with very wide range of tasty food inc lots of vegetarian dishes, good service, unspoilt country setting *(Pauline Langley)*

Botolphs Bridge [Lower Wall Rd, W of Hythe; TR1233], *Botolphs Bridge*: Handsome Edwardian local with airy and chatty open-plan bar, small dining room one end (children allowed here), pool table the other, Greene King IPA and Morlands Old Speckled Hen, big helpings of home-made food with real chips; occasional barbecues in small garden; children in restaurant *(Jenny and Michael Back)*

Boughton Street [¾ mile from M2 junction 7, off A2; TR0559], *White Horse*: Carefully restored dark-beamed bars and timbered dining room, well prepared food all day inc early breakfast and good value carvery Fri, Sat and Sun, well kept Shepherd Neame beers, decent wines, good tea and coffee; tables in garden, children allowed; good value bedrooms (back ones quieter), good breakfasts *(Steve Goodchild, Andrew and Ruth Triggs, LYM)*

Brabourne [Canterbury Rd, E Brabourne; TR1041], *Five Bells*: Big open-plan bar with comfortable banquettes, friendly staff, wide choice of good fresh food inc Austrian dishes (and good sandwiches), several well kept ales, continental beers, log fire; tables in garden with play area *(Cyril and Janet Morley, AT)*

Brabourne Lees [The Lees; TR0740], *Plough*: Lively beamed village local dating from 16th c, well kept Shepherd Neame ales, decent wines, wide choice of home-made food, woodburner in inglenook, traditional games, friendly licensees; fruit machine, piped music; garden with animal sanctuary and bat & trap, attractive countryside; open all day (exc Tues, when opens at 4) *(Mr and Mrs J Russell)*

☆ **Brasted** [A25, 3 miles from M25 junction 5; TQ4654], *White Hart*: Spacious relaxing lounge and extension sun lounge, interesting Battle of Britain bar with signatures and mementoes of Biggin Hill fighter pilots, Bass and Hancocks HB served through chiller; children welcome, big neatly kept garden with well spaced tables and play area; good food in bar and restaurant (homely table-numbering system using wooden spoons); bedrooms, pretty village with several antique shops *(Sue Lee, E G Parish, B J Harding, Jill Carey, John*

Sharp, Christopher Warner, Margaret and Nigel Dennis, LYM)

Brasted [High St (A25)], *Bull*: Friendly local with well kept Shepherd Neame, intimate dining lounge, separate public bar with darts and maybe skittles; tables in garden *(Mr and Mrs A Budden)*

Broadstairs [by quay; TR3967], *Tartar Frigate*: Comfortable in Victorian tile-and-plush style, decorated with fishing nick-nacks, overlooking bay; enjoyable upstairs fish restaurant, well kept beer, friendly landlord; quayside car park *(Howard Allen)*

Brook [not far from M20 junction 10, via Willesborough Lees; TR0644], *Honest Miller*: Friendly new landlord, Whitbreads-related ales and farm ciders, generous food inc interesting specials and vegetarian; handcrafted wooden tables, bar stools and so forth; play area *(Mr and Mrs Jonathan Russell)*

Brookland [village loop; TQ9825], *Royal Oak*: Dating from 16th c, with helpful staff, food from sandwiches to steaks, decent ales such as Batemans XB and Morlands Old Speckled Hen, unusual lamps *(Jenny and Michael Back)*

☆ **Canterbury** [12 The Friars, just off main St Peters St pedestrian area], *Canterbury Tales*: Clean airy pub, recently redecorated, with a lively winebar feel, but a good range of well kept ales such as Fullers London Pride and Shepherd Neame, good bar food inc Mexican specialities, books, games and chess table, more noise from conversation than the piped music (maybe jazz, Rolling Stones or Beatles), staff cheerily friendly and efficient even with extra crowds at Oct Festival time (opp Marlow Theatre); good mix from young students to business people, some live jazz *(Mr and Mrs D Ross, Mark Matthewman, R T and J C Moggridge, LMM, Tony and Wendy Hobden, Kevin and Sarah Foster)*

Canterbury [140 Blean Common; TR1557], *Royal Oak*: Good value food, good range of real ales, decent wine, friendly staff and dog, good housekeeping; games room, garden *(Shelagh Hutton, Evan Pritchard, Gordon Smith)* ; [21 Best Lane], *Thomas Becket*: Well decorated, with good food, real ales, cheerful Sat night *(D H Taillat)*; [Watling St; opp St Margaret St], *Three Tuns*: Scottish Courage ales, friendly atmosphere, above-average food, popular with tourists lunchtime; bedrooms *(G P Kernan)*

Challock [Church Lane; TR0050], *Chequers*: Cosy and pleasant 17th-c beamed pub with well kept Shepherd Neame Spitfire, good value food, friendly talkative landlord, some tables on front terrace opp village green, more in garden *(Eddie Edwards, Dr I Crichton)*

Chartham [Rottington St; TR1054], *Artichoke*: Well kept beer, good bar food, friendly landlord, log fire, well matched extension with old timbers; darts popular with locals *(Colin McKerrow)*

Chatham [Dock Rd; TQ7567], *Command House*: Superb location by the water, just below the churchyard of what is now the Medway Heritage Centre, with Victorian fort above; limited food *(B J Harding)*

☆ **Chiddingstone Causeway** [Charcott; off back rd to Weald; TQ5247], *Greyhound:* Unchanging country local, very unpretentious, with good value sandwiches, genuine home cooking (no food Tues), well kept Flowers, small sensible wine list, good coffee, helpful service, small restaurant; very welcoming to young children *(W Ruxton, Dagmar Junghanns, Colin Keane)*

☆ **Chiddingstone Causeway** [B2027; TQ5146], *Little Brown Jug:* Heavily refurbished in olde-brick-and-beam style, spacious, clean and comfortable even when busy, well kept Harveys and other ales such as local Larkins, decent wines, good friendly service, wide range of promptly served generous food (no sandwiches), restaurant, no-smoking area; children welcome if eating, attractive garden with play area; bedrooms *(Stephen Harvey, John C Baker)*

Chilham [off A28/A252; TR0753], *Woolpack:* Reasonably priced bar food inc vegetarian and good sandwiches, cheerful service, pews, sofa, little armchairs, inglenook fires, well kept Shepherd Neame ales; restaurant (children allowed till early evening); bedrooms, delightful village *(Thomas and Audrey Nott, Alan Thwaite, LYM)*

☆ **Chillenden** [TR2653], *Griffins Head:* Good-sized helpings of reliable if not cheap food in attractive beamed, timbered and flagstoned 14th-c pub with three comfortable rooms, good choice of house wines, big log fire, local regulars; pleasant garden surrounded by wild roses, attractive countryside *(D Hayman, Jacqui Murphy, Alan Thwaite)*

Chipstead [39 High St; nr M25 junction 5; TQ4956], *George & Dragon:* Dining pub with heavy black beams and standing timbers, very wide choice of good food inc vegetarian, good value wines, relaxed friendly service, children welcome in most areas; tables in pleasant garden *(James and Karen Davies, Ian and Colin Roe, LYM)*

Cliffe [Church St; TQ7376], *Black Bull:* Good genuine Malaysian bar food in friendly cosy village local with good choice of well kept ales, weekday evening basement restaurant, darts/pool room, quiet juke box; very welcoming to children *(Pam and Tim Moorey)*

☆ **Cobham** [B2009, handy for M2 junction 1; TQ6768], *Leather Bottle:* Beautifully laid-out extensive colourful garden with fishpond and play area, masses of interesting Dickens memorabilia, ancient beams and timbers (but extensive modernisation), real ales; quiet, pretty village; bedrooms *(Sue Lee, LYM)*

☆ **Conyer Quay** [from A2 Sittingbourne—Faversham take Deerton St turn, then at T-junction left towards Teynham, then follow Conyer signs; TQ9664], *Ship:* Rambling nooks and crannies in cheerily nautical creekside pub, well kept ales and good range of other drinks, good straightforward food from ploughman's up, friendly landlord, decent wines, restaurant; open all day, tables outside facing waterfront – road outside can flood at spring tides *(K Flack, Dr I Russell Eggitt, Richard Gibbs, Sue Lee, LYM)*

☆ **Cowden** [Cowden Pound; junction B2026 with Markbeech rd; TQ4642], *Queens Arms:* Unspoilt two-room country pub like something from the 1930s, with splendid landlady, well kept Whitbreads, darts; strangers quickly feel like regulars *(Pete Baker)*

Cranbrook [TQ7735], *White Horse:* Useful inn in attractive small town; good value bedrooms, good breakfast *(Dave Braisted)*

Darenth [Darenth Rd; TQ5671], *Chequers:* Friendly old traditional local with good choice of generous food (not Sun-Tues evenings) inc good value Sun roast, Courage Best and a guest beer, helpful interested staff, cheap drinks and crisps for children; can book tables in pleasant dining room, good view from garden *(T Neate, Sue Lee)*

Dartford [80 High St; TQ5373], *Wat Tyler:* Very long narrow local, recently much improved, with bar, lounge, raised second bar, Scottish Courage ales; open all day, no piped music *(Comus Elliott)*

Deal [Beach St; TR3752], *Kings Head:* Late 18th-c former smugglers' pub in lovely position overlooking sea, with good atmosphere, interesting marine architectural drawings and other maritime pictures, attentive staff, wide choice of good value standard food, five real ales; piped music, have to use municipal car park; bedrooms *(Mrs P Pearce, Thomas Nott, George Jonas)*

☆ **Detling** [TQ7958], *Cock Horse:* Pretty tiled and weatherboarded pub, well run, with friendly atmosphere, well kept Whitbreads-related and other ales, good value bar food, separate restaurant; tables in yard behind *(Neville Kenyon, Ian Phillips)*

☆ **Dunks Green** [Silver Hill; TQ6152], *Kentish Rifleman:* Cosy early 16th-c local, interesting freshly cooked bar food, friendly prompt service, well kept real ales such as Fullers and Marstons Pedigree, decent wine, plenty of character, no machines; dogs welcome; plenty of seats in unusually well designed garden behind *(A Quinsee, A Cowell, R C Watkins)*

East Farleigh [by church; TQ7353], *Bull:* Light and airy Whitbreads pub with decent traditional food and friendly atmosphere *(Thomas and Audrey Nott)*; [Dean St], *White Lion:* Friendly newish owners doing good reasonably priced food using local produce in cosy old pub, good choice of wines by the glass, log fire *(Pat Turvill, Mrs B Gibbons)*

East Malling [TQ7056], *King & Queen:* Boddingtons, Brakspears, Fullers London Pride, Wadworths 6X, good choice of enjoyable food *(James Nunns)*

East Stourmouth [B2046 N of Wingham; TR2662], *Rising Sun:* Attractive pub dating from 14th c, very attractive, generous food, attentive service in neat dining room, Greene

King IPA, Morlands Old Speckled Hen and Shepherd Neame; children allowed, games room *(Jenny and Michael Back)*

East Sutton [TQ8349], *Shant Hotel*: Good pub atmosphere in big bar/restaurant facing cricket green, vast choice of good value food, welcoming obliging staff, real ales; bedrooms *(Mrs M Furness)*

☆ **Eastling** [The Street; off A251 S of M2 junction 6, via Painters Forstal; TQ9656], *Carpenters Arms*: Pretty and cottagey oak-beamed pub with big fireplaces front and back, friendly service, decent food (not Sun evening), well kept Shepherd Neame, some seats outside; children allowed in restaurant; small but well equipped bedrooms in separate building, huge breakfast *(Joy Crowley, Wayne Brindle, E D Bailey, LYM)*

Egerton [The Street; TQ9047], *George*: Friendly two-bar village pub with welcoming licensee brothers, limited but good food, wide range of well kept ales, dining room; pretty setting *(Adam Robertson)*

☆ **Elham** [St Marys Rd; TR1743], *Kings Arms*: Good interesting reasonably priced food, relaxing attractive lounge bar, good open fire, unobtrusively attentive friendly service, steps down to big dining area (booking advised); pool table in public bar; opp church in square of charming village *(Sybille Weber)*

☆ **Eynsford** [TQ5365], *Malt Shovel*: Neatly kept spacious old-fashioned dining pub handy for castles and Roman villa, generous bar food inc lots of good value seafood (lobster tank), Pilgrims ales, quick friendly service, nice atmosphere; car park across busy road *(Jenny and Brian Seller, Margaret and Nigel Dennis)*

Eythorne [The Street; TR2849], *Crown*: Small and attractive Georgian pub with friendly staff, separate dining room, generous well presented food; good range of real ales inc guests *(Christopher Hatch)*

Faversham [Abbey St; TR0161], *Anchor*: Smallish friendly two-room Shepherd Neame local nr quay, pleasantly quaint atmosphere with bare boards and individual furniture, hall with bench seats, a couple of picnic tables outside *(Chris Westmoreland, Mrs M Hall)*; [31 the Mall, handy for M2 junction 6], *Elephant*: Very picturesque flower-decked terrace town pub with very good choice of well kept changing ales, prompt welcoming service, simple but attractive furnishings on stripped boards, food inc vegetarian and summer barbecues; can be smoky *(Frank Ashbee, Richard Houghton, Geoffrey Stephenson)*; [99 Abbey St], *Phoenix*: Good food inc imaginative daily specials, real ale, very pleasant ambiance *(Geoffrey Stephenson)*; [10 West St], *Sun*: Roomy and rambling old-world 15th-c weatherboarded town pub with good unpretentious atmosphere, reasonably priced lunchtime bar food inc unusual dishes, well kept Shepherd Neame, good service; tables in pleasant back courtyard, interesting street *(Mr and Mrs J Rudolf, Mrs L Surman, Geoffrey Stephenson)*

Folkestone [Cherry Green Lane; TR2336],

Brickfield: Big new Whitbreads pub, efficient and friendly, reasonably priced food, good range of real ales *(Ian Phillips)*

☆ **Fordwich** [off A28 in Sturry; TR1759], *Fordwich Arms*: Generous helpings of decent plain cooking inc fresh veg and vegetarian in civilised and handsome pub with open fire in attractive fireplace, welcoming atmosphere, Whitbreads-related ales, discreet piped music, dining room; spacious garden by River Stour; ancient town hall opp worth visiting *(David and Margaret Bloomfield, LYM)*

☆ **Four Elms** [B2027/B269 E of Edenbridge; TQ4648], *Four Elms*: Busy dining pub, welcoming and comfortable, wide choice of consistently good value generous food inc fresh fish and fine rabbit pie, well kept Courage Directors and Harveys, decent wine, friendly service, some interesting decorations in several rambling rooms inc huge boar's head, two big open fires, no music, pleasant restaurant; family room, tables outside; juke box, fruit machine; handy for Chartwell *(Colin Laffan, Margaret and Nigel Dennis, R Waters)*

Frittenden [TQ8141], *Bell & Jorrocks*: Traditional timber-framed village local doing well under new licensees, well kept Whitbreads-related ales, good home-cooked food, open fire, Battle of Britain memorabilia *(Cluny South)*

Goodnestone [the one off B2046 E of Canterbury; TR2554], *Fitzwalter Arms*: Really nice pub, with attractively priced good food *(Eirlys Roberts)*

☆ **Goudhurst** [TQ7238], *Star & Eagle*: Attractively timbered medieval inn with settles and Jacobean-style seats in relaxing heavily beamed open-plan bar, good bar food (separate servery) using local produce, well kept Whitbreads-related ales, decent wine, friendly helpful staff, restaurant; lovely views esp from tables out behind; children welcome, bedrooms comfortable *(Thomas Nott, Ken Frostick, David Newsome, Lesley Meagher, Hanns P Golez, Janet and Colin Roe, LYM)*

☆ nr **Goudhurst** [A262 W], *Green Cross*: Good value genuine home cooking inc Sat night carvery (winter cold cuts, summer roasts), well kept Harveys and other ales, bar with open fires and friendly staff, big beamed back restaurant with different evening menu; bedrooms light and airy, good value *(Mark Percy, Dr I Crichton, M Holdsworth)*

☆ **Hadlow** [Hamptons; 4 miles SE of Plaxtol – OS Sheet 188 map ref 627524; TQ6352], *Artichoke*: Dating from 13th c, with ancient low beams, high-backed wooden settles, some unusual wrought-iron glass-topped tables, huge inglenook log fire, gleaming brass, country pictures and bric-a-brac, bar food inc good home-made pies, no-smoking restaurant, well kept Adnams, Fullers London Pride, Greene King Abbot and Youngs Special, good range of spirits; children in eating area, seats outside inc pews in shower-proof arbour, quiet rural setting; cl winter Sun evenings *(Tim Barrow, Sue Demont, Ian*

Phillips, Tina and David Woods-Taylor, A Homes, Sue Lee, Dr S Willavoys, LMM, LYM)

Halstead [Otford Lane; TQ4861], *Rose & Crown*: Friendly flint village local, comfortable but not over-modernised, well kept Harveys and Larkins, enthusiastic landlord, limited but good bar food *(John C Baker)*

☆ **Hawkhurst** [Pipsden – A268 towards Rye; TQ7730], *Oak & Ivy*: Immaculately refurbished and extended, with well kept Whitbreads-related ales, friendly efficient staff, generous good value home cooking inc popular Sun roasts, heavy low beams and timbers, dark brown terracotta walls and ceilings, roaring log fires (one in massive inglenook), dark tables on quarry tiles; farm tools, piped music, fruit machine; tables outside, good play area *(G G Lawrence, Charles Gysin, Colin and Joyce Laffan, A M Pring, BB)*

☆ **Heaverham** [Watery Lane; TQ5758], *Chequers*: Wide choice of good food and friendly service in quietly attractive two-bar country pub with well kept range of beers; lots of birds in big garden *(LMM)*

☆ **Hernhill** [off A299 at Highstreet roundabout via Dargate, or off A2 via Boughton Street and Staplestreet; TR0660], *Red Lion*: Pretty Tudor inn by church, densely beamed and flagstoned, with generous good food in bar and upstairs restaurant, well kept ales, decent house wines, attentive staff, pine tables, log fires; children welcome, garden with boules and good play area, bedrooms *(David Gregory, A Homes, David and Doreen Gregory, LYM)*

☆ **Hollingbourne** [Eyhorne St (B2163, off A20); TQ8454], *Dirty Habit*: Dim-lit old pub with lots of different old kitchen and dining tables and chairs, nooks, crannies and uneven floors, interesting food, well kept ales, decent house wines, flame-effect gas fire in big fireplace; games area, unobtrusive juke box, maybe live music Sun lunchtime; on Pilgrims Way, handy for Leeds Castle *(Steve Goodchild)*
Hollingbourne [Eyhorne St (B2163)], *Windmill*: Interesting, comfortable and welcoming Whitbreads Wayside Inn, with various different levels and nooks around central servery, quick food inc good sandwiches, well kept Whitbreads-related ales, sunny garden with children's play area *(Thomas Nott)*

☆ **Horsmonden** [TQ7040], *Gun & Spitroast*: Pleasantly furnished clean and polished pub on village green, doing well under new licensees; wide choice of good value food inc spitroast in corner of pretty dining room, well kept Harveys and own Spitroast beer, good service, big new terrace with adjoining play area *(Colin Laffan)*
Horsmonden, *Highwayman*: Good value unpretentious food inc good filled rolls, side terrace overlooking village green *(Dr I Crichton)*
Hucking [off B2163 E of Maidstone;

TQ8458], *Hook & Hatchet*: Isolated old-fashioned country pub in idyllic countryside, nice little dining area, well kept local Swale Kentish Pride; good garden with goose, goat and chickens *(Comus Elliott)*

☆ **Ickham** [TR2257], *Duke William*: Very wide choice of good food inc original dishes in friendly and comfortable family-run pub, old-world front bar with big inglenook, brasses, copper, grandfather clock and gas lamp, long dining room and big well shaded conservatory, well kept beers such as Adnams, Fullers, McMullens and Shepherd Neame; smart garden *(D G Hayman, Alan Thwaite)*

☆ **Ide Hill** [off B2042 SW of Sevenoaks; TQ4851], *Cock*: Pretty village-green local with well kept Greene King, fine log fire, bar billiards, straightforward bar food (not Sun evening, only sandwiches Sun lunchtime), piped music, some seats out in front; handy for Chartwell and nearby walks – so gets busy, with nearby parking sometimes out of the question *(Sue Lee, Timothy Galligan, David Dimock, LYM)*

☆ **Iden Green** [the one between Benenden and the A268 E of Hawkhurst; Woodcock Lane – off Benenden Rd by bus stop, then pub signed; TQ8031], *Woodcock*: Small 17th-c country local, relaxed and homely, with beams and bare boards, big inglenook, single bar with cosy alcoves off, couple of steps up to eating area, ample reasonably priced food inc good filled baguettes, well kept Beards, Fremlins and John Smiths, friendly newish landlord; maybe piped pop music; hatch to pleasant garden with mistletoe in big tree *(B and M Parkin, Janet and Colin Roe, BB)*
Iden Green [Benenden Rd], *Royal Oak*: Stripped pine, newspapers, quiet corner with sofas, interesting well presented freshly cooked food; can get very busy *(Paula Williams)*
Ightham [The Street; TQ5956], *George & Dragon*: Attractive heavily timbered 17th-c or earlier coaching inn which blends well with surrounding old buildings, decent choice of food in bar and restaurant, well kept Shepherd Neame, attentive staff, spotless housekeeping; garden with play area *(K H Frostick)*

☆ **Ivy Hatch** [off A227 N of Tunbridge; TQ5854], *Plough*: More restaurant than pub now, by no means cheap, but it's good (and often fully booked), with fastidious French cooking, good wines (and decent real ales), attractive candlelit surroundings, solidly professional service, and delightful conservatory and garden *(Eddy and Emma Gibson, Mavis and John Wright, Nigel Wikeley, N B Thompson, W Ruxton, RWD, Mrs Olive Oxley, M Carr, G Kirkland, Sue Lee, LMM, LYM)*

☆ **Kingston** [TR1951], *Black Robin*: Good unusual food inc gorgeous puddings and enjoyable Sun lunch in friendly pub with Shepherd Neame beers, chatty staff, wooden floors, old pine tables, flowers, lots of hop bines around bar, low lighting – maybe candles *(June Goncalves, Tim Lancefield, David and Doreen Gregory, Roger Goodsell)*

Lamberhurst [School Hill; TQ6635], *Chequers*: Good home-cooked food in homely pub with friendly service, separate dining area; good value bedrooms, good breakfast *(Mrs J Lichfield, A M Pring, Paula Williams)*

☆ nr **Lamberhurst** [Hook Green (B2169 towards T Wells)], *Elephants Head*: Ancient rambling country pub with wide choice of food inc vegetarian, well kept Harveys, heavy beams, some timbering, brick or oak flooring, log fire and woodburner, plush-cushioned pews etc; darts and fruit machine in small side area, picnic tables on back terrace and grass with play area (peaceful view), and by front green; nr Bayham Abbey and Owl House, very popular with families weekends *(Michael Grigg, Dr S P Willavoys, TBB, LYM)*

Leeds [B2163 S of Castle entry; TQ8253], *Ten Bells*: Small, old pub with recently added conservatory dining area; usual food, Morlands beers, pleasant screened garden area *(Thomas Nott)*

☆ **Leigh** [Powder Mill Lane; TQ5646], *Plough*: Beams, timbers, roaring fire in enormous inglenook, well kept ales inc Harveys, King & Barnes and Youngs, decent wines, quick friendly service, nonchalant iguana called Arnie, good value Sun carvery in attached 16th-c barn decorated with farm tools and hop bines; wide choice of reasonably priced bar food, juke box; extensive well kept garden with old well and duck lake – children like the waterfowl *(Kate Leahy, Sue Lee, Dominic Green)*

Lenham [The Square; TQ8952], *Dog & Bear*: Friendly inn with decent choice of food from sandwiches up inc OAP bargains, Shepherd Neame ales, no-smoking bar, restaurant; authentic period coat of arms for Queen Anne, not many of which have survived; piped music may obtrude a bit; good value bedrooms, pretty village *(Thomas Nott, A Budden)*

☆ **Linton** [Linton Hill; A229 S of Maidstone; TQ7550], *Bull*: Friendly 17th-c heavily beamed pub with well kept Shepherd Neame, friendly staff, good if not cheap food esp fresh fish and shellfish, no-smoking area; restaurant; superb well kept garden with wonderful Weald views *(Lesley Zammit, D Twitchett, Comus Elliott)*

☆ **Littlebourne** [4 High St; TR2057], *King William IV*: Straightforward character and decor, but unusual range of good interesting freshly prepared food running up to ostrich and kangaroo, good friendly service, well kept ales, interesting wines inc New World ones; small dining area, good value bedrooms; handy for Howletts Zoo *(Desmond and Gillian Bellew, A Ellis, Martin Hickes, Christopher Warner, J Randall)*

☆ **Loose** [Old Loose Rd; TQ7552], *Chequers*: Attractive riverside pub with unusual range of good food, good choice of Whitbreads-related ales, warmly welcoming and efficient service

(Marie-Christine Bouilles, F Barwell, Mrs Allerston)

☆ **Lower Hardres** [TR1552], *Three Horseshoes*: Old-fashioned furnishings, beams and bare boards in country pub with character landlord, Papas prints of Canterbury, real ales such as Marstons Pedigree, Tomintoul and Youngs tapped from the cask, Inch's farm cider, bar food inc wide choice of cheeses for ploughman's, good piped music; tables in garden, Parisian bus in working order *(Mr and Mrs Jonathan Russell, BB)*

Lympne [Aldington Rd; marked on OS Sheet 189 map ref 118351; TR1135], *County Members*: Comfortable, with exceptionally wide choice of reasonably priced bar food, well kept Harveys *(Thomas Nott)*

☆ **Maidstone** [8 High St; TQ7656], *Muggleton*: Former grand colonnaded Victorian insurance HQ, beautifully converted by Wetherspoons in conjunction with English Heritage; lovely muted atmosphere, high ceilings, plenty of room; good value food all day, six real ales, attractive prices *(Comus Elliott, Mark Baynham, Rachael Ward)*

Maidstone [Market Buildings, between High St and Earl St], *Ashes*: Newly done in colourful light and airy continental style, interesting artwork, ash fittings, comfortable mix of seating; inexpensive snacks, Courage Directors, Theakstons, Youngs and a beer brewed for the pub *(Thomas and Audrey Nott)*; [Earl St], *Hogs Head*: Whitbreads town pub done up well as bare-boards tavern, lots of real ales, ciders and country wines, open fires, good snacks, friendly staff *(Comus Elliott)*

Marden Thorn [Pagehurst Lane; TQ7842], *Wild Duck*: Friendly and comfortable, with good well presented food in bar and dining room, real pub atmosphere, well kept ales inc Fullers London Pride and Harveys, good range of wines *(Frank Ashbee, R E Cripps)*

☆ **Martin** [off A258 Dover—Deal; TR3346], *Old Lantern*: Popular food, friendly service, beautiful setting, with sizeable play area and wendy house in sprawling pretty gardens *(Desmond and Gillian Bellew, Martin Hickes)*

☆ **Meopham** [Meopham Green; A227 Gravesend—Wrotham; TQ6466], *Cricketers*: Neatly kept 17th-c Big Steak pub with seats out overlooking green, more in back garden, cricket memorabilia, Tetleys-related ales with a guest such as Wild Boar, usual food, friendly service, log fire, tasteful modern restaurant extension; piped music *(Ian Phillips)*

☆ **Mersham** [Flood St; TR0438], *Farriers Arms*: Smart and attractive three-room local based on early 17th-c forge, wide choice of good value straightforward food, well kept Tetleys-related ales, good friendly service; tranquil well kept streamside garden behind, pleasant country views; bedrooms *(Mr and Mrs J Russell)*

Molash [A251; TR0251], *George*: Friendly low-beamed candlelit 16th-c village local up on the downs, helpful service, well kept

Boddingtons and a guest beer, old kitchen tables and chairs; pleasant garden, plenty of pets *(Chris Westmoreland, Eddie Edwards)*

Nettlestead [Nettlestead Green; B2015 Pembury—Maidstone; TQ6852], *Hop Pole*: Spacious carpeted bar with interesting prints, copper and brass, wide range of decent food inc good value Sun lunch, well kept ales such as Adnams and Fullers London Pride, decent wine, friendly service, central fire, fresh flowers; tables out in pleasant back area, hops and orchards around *(N B Thompson)*

New Romney [High St; TR0624], *Ship*: Attractive former 14th-c smugglers' pub, reopened after complete but understated refit; Shepherd Neame ales, reasonably priced food *(Thomas and Audrey Nott)*

Northbourne [TR3352], *Hare & Hounds*: Friendly country pub, log fire, good reasonably priced food, well kept Shepherd Neame ales; small garden *(Christopher Hatch)*

Oad Street [nr M2 junction 5; TQ8662], *Plough & Harrow*: Nice old village pub opp craft centre, friendly landlord, well kept Shepherd Neame and several changing ales, good value home cooking, one small bar, another much larger, light and airy at the back; children welcome; picnic tables in secluded back garden *(Chris Westmoreland)*

☆ **Otford** [High St; TQ5359], *Crown*: Pretty pub opp pond in delightful village with pleasant walks; airy bar with banknotes on beams, inglenook, secondhand book exchange, welcoming landlord, good value food (not Sun night or Mon) inc good sandwiches, fresh veg and bargain Mon-Thurs suppers for two, well kept Adnams, Friary Meux Best, Ind Coope Burton, Marstons Pedigree and Tetleys, decent house wines; games in public bar, jazz Sun, quiz night Mon; lovely garden behind with terrace, pergola and play area *(Hazel and Michael Duncombe, B J Harding, Sue Lee, James Nunns, Margaret and Nigel Dennis, Roger and Pauline Pearce, A M Pring, BB)*

☆ **Otford** [66 High St], *Horns*: Friendly and cosy pub with hops on dark 15th-c beams, standing timbers, big inglenook log fire, blue plush seats and wheelback chairs, neatly cottagey decorations, second room on left, attentive welcoming service, tables set for short choice of good well presented standard food from well filled sandwiches up, well kept Fullers London Pride and Harveys, cheerful service *(A Pring, David Friett, Ellis and Norma Myers, Janet and Colin Roe, BB)*

☆ **Painters Forstal** [signed off A2 at Ospringe; TQ9958], *Alma*: Friendly, neat and tidy weatherboarded village local, very popular, with wide choice of decent food, largeish dining lounge, small bare-boards public bar, well kept Shepherd Neame inc winter Porter, maybe piped classical music, picnic tables on lawn *(June and Tony Baldwin, Chris Westmoreland, G Bond)*

☆ **Penshurst** [centre; TQ5243], *Leicester Arms*: Busy pub in charming village by Penshurst Place, extended eating area (best bit is old dining room up steps, with country views), wide choice of reasonably priced bar food inc good steaks, well kept if very cool real ale, willing young staff; children welcome, economical bedrooms *(Colin Laffan, Pam and Tim Moorey)*

☆ **nr Penshurst** [Hoath Corner – OS Sheet 188 map ref 497431], *Rock*: Charmingly old-fashioned untouristy atmosphere in tiny beamed rooms, wonky brick floors, woodburner in inglenook, pleasant licensees, good value sandwiches and generous home cooking, well kept local Larkins and Shepherd Neame, ring the bull; children and dogs welcome (pub dog very shy); tables outside, beautiful countryside nearby *(Colin Laffan, LM, J and P Maloney)*

Petteridge [Petteridge Lane; TQ6740], *Hopbine*: Friendly village pub, tidied up without being spoilt, with good generous food (Texas toothpicks recommended), well kept King & Barnes, faultless service, occasional folk music *(John C Baker)*

Plaxtol [Sheet Hill; TQ6054], *Golding Hop*: Secluded country pub, good in summer with suntrap streamside lawn; small and simple inside, with real ales tapped from the cask, choice of ciders (sometimes even their own), limited bar food (not Mon evening), woodburner *(Sue Lee, LYM)*

Pluckley [TQ9245], *Black Horse*: Comfortable and spacious open-plan bar with roomy dark dining area in attractive old house, hops on beams, vast inglenook, usual furnishings and food, cheery atmosphere, Whitbreads-related and guest ales; piped music may seem rather loud, service can slow a bit when busy, fruit machine; children allowed if eating; picnic tables in spacious informal garden by tall sycamores, good walks *(Martin Hickes, CM, BB)*; [Munday Bois; TQ9144], *Rose & Crown*: Welcoming little pub with nicely furnished dining room, good varied food esp fresh fish, soups, puddings and Sun lunch, interesting wines and country wines, well kept ales, reasonable prices, good service; friendly dog *(Pat Turvill)*

☆ **Rochester** [10 St Margarets St; TQ7467], *Coopers Arms*: Quaint and interesting ancient local, good bustling atmosphere with fine mix of customers, friendly licensees, comfortable seating, generous low-priced bar lunches, well kept Scottish Courage ales; handy for castle and cathedral *(A W Lewis)*

Sandgate [High St; TR2035], *Ship*: Old-fashioned, not smart but welcoming, ten or so quickly changing real ales tapped from the cask, generous cheap food, good service, seafaring theme; seats outside *(Michael Mills, Kay Macara, John Havery, LMM, Peter Haines)*

Sandling [nestling under M20 just N of Maidstone – OS Sheet 188 map ref 756585; TQ7558], *Yew Tree*: Comfortable and peaceful old Shepherd Neame local, a relaxing break from junction 6; decent lunchtime food, pretty village with attractive church *(Comus Elliott)*

Sandwich [The Quay; TR3358], *Bell*: Comfortable carpeted hotel lounge bar, soft piped music, bar food inc good sandwiches, three real ales, restaurant; bedrooms; charming town *(Comus Elliott)*; [Fisher St], *George & Dragon*: Smart newly refurbished old building in centre of very pretty town, good if not cheap food inc pizzas from woodburning oven, four local ales *(Paul Stubbings)*; [Cattlemarket/Mote Sole], *Red Cow*: Carefully refurbished old pub, cosy, neat and clean, with welcoming staff, several Whitbreads-related and other ales, good value food, lovely log fire, old prints and photographs; guide dogs only, garden bar, hanging baskets *(Mr and Mrs N Spink, D and J Tapper)*

☆ **Sarre** [A28 Canterbury—Margate; TR2565], *Crown*: Carefully restored pub making much of its long history as the Cherry Brandy House, pleasant bars, quiet restaurant, good range of reasonably priced home-cooked food, several well kept Shepherd Neame real ales; comfortable bedrooms *(Jean Minner)*

☆ **Selling** [village signed from exit roundabout, M2 junction 7, also off A251 S of Faversham; TR0456], *White Lion*: 17th-c pub with colourful hanging baskets, comfortable bar with two big log fires (one with a spit), pews on stripped floorboards, unusual semi-circular bar counter, rustic picnic tables in attractive garden; has had good food (all day Sat/Sun), well kept Shepherd Neame Bitter and Spitfire and plenty of wines, with a welcome for children, but tenants have moved to the George at Newnham *(LYM; news please)*

☆ **Sevenoaks** [London Rd, nr stn; 2½ miles from M25 junction 5; TQ5355], *Halfway House*: Quiet and friendly partly 16th-c local with beams and brasses, well kept Greene King IPA, Abbot and Rayments, wide range of reasonably priced home-made food inc crisp fresh veg, good service, helpful licensees; parking may be difficult *(Sue and Mike Todd, Pam and Tim Moorey)*

Sevenoaks [Tonbridge Rd (A225 S, past Knole)], *White Hart*: Comfortably refurbished, with some old settles, two bars, good family lunches in secluded no-smoking back room with high chairs, fine array of prints inc several fascinating vintage posters, huge net on ceiling with bric-a-brac, enormous Welsh dresser, Tetleys-related ales; well appointed restaurant, baby-changing facilities, pleasant lawns with well established shrubs *(Eddy and Emma Gibson)*

☆ **nr Sevenoaks** [Godden Green, off B2019 just E; TQ5555], *Bucks Head*: Picturesque old village-green local in pretty spot by duckpond, surrounded by cherry blossom in spring; particularly well kept Scottish Courage and guest beers, friendly atmosphere, decent bar food, cosy furnishings; children really welcome; in attractive walking country nr Knole *(Mr and Mrs A Budden)*

Shatterling [TR2658], *Frog & Orange*: Very welcoming, newly refurbished with lots of stripped pine, exposed brick, dried hops and old photographs; good if not cheap food, good range of drinks inc honey beer *(Kevin and Sarah Foster)*

Shipbourne [Stumble Hill; TQ5952], *Chaser*: Bar food from ploughman's up, bistro-like end part with candles and stripped pine, cheerful public bar welcoming walkers, friendly efficient service, well kept Harveys, decent wines, high-vaulted restaurant, tables outside; comfortable bedrooms – lovely spot by village church and green *(Jenny and Brian Seller, Nigel Wikeley)*

Shoreham [High St; TQ5161], *Olde George*: Simply furnished old beamed pub with roaring open fire, well kept Courage Best and Tetleys, decent sandwiches, ploughman's, home-made soup, friendly service; children and dogs welcome *(Simon Pyle, A M Pring)*

Shorne [32 The Street; off A226; TQ6971], *Rose & Crown*: Attractive pub, good food; piped music may be a bit loud; terrace and garden *(Mr and Mrs A Budden)*

☆ **Sissinghurst** [TQ7937], *Bull*: New licensees doing well presented food in bar and big pleasant dark-beamed restaurant area; some armchairs, log fire, Harveys and Whitbreads-related ales, shelves of books and china, quiet piped music, fruit machine; neat quiet garden *(Janet and Colin Roe, C Sinclair)*

Sittingbourne [17 Crown Quay Lane; TQ9163], *Barge*: Well kept Swale and guest beer, welcoming service, fair-sized garden *(Richard Houghton)*

☆ **Smarden** [TQ8842], *Chequers*: Cosy and relaxed beamed local in lovely village, one small eating area with a good deal of rustic character off main turkey-carpeted bar, another at the back more orthodox; second parquet-floored bar largely laid for diners; good varied freshly made food from a fine filled baguette to quite exotic main dishes inc vegetarian, Bass, Morlands Old Speckled Hen, Ruddles County, Worthington and Youngs Special, decent wines and spirits, log fire, local-interest books, no music or machines; pleasant tables outside; bedrooms simple (and some within earshot of bar) but good value, with huge breakfast *(Hilary Dobbie, BB)*

☆ **Snargate** [Romney Marsh, B2080 Appledore—Brenzett; TQ9928], *Red Lion*: Delightfully old-fashioned and unspoilt 19th-c country pub, bare boards and old kitchen furniture, marble bar top, well kept Adnams and Batemans tapped from the cask or via antique handpumps, classic landlady, traditional games, sawdust on the floor, no music or food *(Comus Elliott, Kevin Thorpe, Thomas Nott)*

☆ **Sole Street** [the one nr Wye; TR0949], *Compasses*: Big neatly kept garden with rustic tables, play area and various pets, easy-going rambling bars with bare boards or flagstones, antique or reclaimed furnishings, massive brick bread oven, enamel advertisements, well kept Boddingtons, Fremlins, Fullers London

Pride and ESB and a guest like Timothy Taylors Landlord or Wadworths 6X, local farm cider, fruit wines, bar food from filled rolls to steak, children welcome in extended garden room; bar billiards, piped music; good walks *(Stephen Brown, James Nunns, Christopher Warner, LMM, LYM)*

☆ **Southfleet** [off A2 via A227 S towards Southfleet; or from B262 turn left at Ship in Southfleet then sharp right into Red St – pub about half-mile on right; TQ6171], *Black Lion*: Character two-room local, with good generous bar food from ploughman's up, well kept Scottish Courage beers, friendly helpful staff, handsome no-smoking restaurant; children in eating area; big shrub-sheltered garden *(Sue Lee, N B Thompson, LYM)*

☆ **Southfleet** [High Cross Rd, Westwood; from A2, keep straight on through Southfleet itself, past The Ship], *Wheatsheaf*: Unpretentious thatched and beamed Tudor country pub with ornamental pheasants and fowl on big lawn above car park, tables around sizeable softly floodlit carp pond, aviaries with parakeets and owls; heavy beams and partitions inside, padded barrel chairs, traditional high-backed settles, inglenook with big woodburner; well kept Boddingtons, Brains Dark Mild, Courage Best and Morlands Old Speckled Hen, good value food, resident african grey parrot *(Jenny and Michael Back, BB)*

St Margarets at Cliffe [High Street; TR3644], *Cliffe Tavern Hotel*: Attractive clapboard-and-brick inn opp church with well worn in bar and open-plan lounge, good log fire, well kept Greene King and Shepherd Neame ales, interesting filled baguettes and other food, secluded back walled garden, separate dining room; has been open all day Sat, allowing well behaved children; tenant said to be thinking of moving on in 1997; bedrooms, inc some in cottages across yard, good walks nearby *(John Fahy, C Elliott, Mrs H Dobbie, LYM)*

St Margarets at Cliffe, *Hope*: Friendly landlord and staff, good beer and bar food *(Colin McKerrow)*

☆ **St Margarets Bay** [on shore below Nat Trust cliffs; TR3844], *Coastguard*: Tremendous views to France on a clear day from cheery modernised seaside pub, open all day in summer; good range of food inc popular fish and chips, well kept sensibly priced real ales, friendly young staff; children welcome, lots of tables on balcony with wheelchair access (and summer cream teas), dramatic sense of isolation on a misty autumn evening *(F T Cardiff, Roger Goodsell, Howard Allen, Mrs M Hall, BB)*

St Mary in the Marsh [opp church; TR0627], *Star*: Relaxed remote pub, Tudor but very much modernised; friendly family service, well kept Shepherd Neame ale Mild tapped from the cask, good value competent food; bedrooms attractive, with views of Romney Marsh *(Thomas Nott, John C Baker)*

Stalisfield Green [off A252 in Charing; TQ9553], *Plough*: Good choice of well presented home-cooked food from filled baguettes up, friendly service, four real ales, Pawley farm cider, big but tasteful side extension, tables in big pleasant garden, attractive village green setting, good view and walks *(Comus Elliott)*

Staplehurst [Chart Hill Rd; TQ7847], *Lord Raglan*: Comfortable, dark and cool in summer with two log fires in winter, good-sized garden, reasonably priced food, well kept Goachers and guests such as Shepherd Neame Spitfire and Youngs Special, friendly staff and locals *(John C Baker)*

Stodmarsh [High St; TR2160], *Red Lion*: Hops on beams, flagstones, log fires, pine furniture, pictures and rustic bric-a-brac, good food in an unhurried atmosphere, friendly and intimate; well kept Greene King IPA, Abbot and a guest ale, farm cider, limited choice of decent wine, pub games; can get very busy, some live music; bedrooms, handy for bird sanctuary *(Alex Smith, K M Thorpe)*

Stone in Oxney [TQ9427], *Crown*: Pleasant old-fashioned country pub under new management, good sensibly priced bar food from sandwiches to imaginative hot dishes, reasonably priced local wine by the glass, Shepherd Neame and Otter Bitter, good coffee *(Janet and Colin Roe)*

☆ **Stone Street** [by-road Seal—Plaxtol – OS Sheet 188 map ref 573546; TQ5754], *Padwell Arms*: Small relaxed local with tables on front terrace overlooking orchards, more in back garden, good choice of genuinely home-cooked food using local produce, sensible prices, friendly staff, well kept Badger, Hook Norton Old Hookey and changing guest ales, farm ciders, open fires; occasional live music and other events; good walks *(Paul Brown, P H Roberts, Michael Dunn, Dave Robinson)*

☆ **Stowting** [off B2068 N of M20 junction 11; TR1242], *Tiger*: Character country pub, partly 17th-c, with attractive unpretentious furniture, candles on tables, faded rugs on bare boards, chatty hard-working licensees, three or more well kept real ales, Biddenden farm cider, good log fire, tables outside with occasional barbecues; well behaved children allowed, good jazz Mon *(Martin Hickes, Mr and Mrs R A Broadbent, LYM)*

Sundridge [A25; TQ4854], *Lamb*: Straightforward roomy bar with good value standard food, cheerful staff, Ind Coope Burton, King & Barnes and Tetleys; children welcome; big garden and field behind for camping or caravanning *(R M Macnaughton, A Budden)*

☆ **Tenterden** [High St; TQ8833], *Woolpack*: Striking 15th-c inn with several oak-beamed rooms inc family dining room, inglenook log fires, pleasant modest atmosphere, good generous home-cooked food, friendly service, well kept Whitbreads-related and other ales, decent coffee; open all day; comfortable bedrooms *(Thomas Nott)*

Thurnham [not far from M20 junction 7, off A249 at Detling; TQ8057], *Black Horse*: Friendly and attractively restored pub nr Pilgrims Way, six Whitbreads-related and other ales, good food in bar and restaurant, nice views; children welcome *(Dave Braisted)*

☆ **Tunbridge Wells** [Tea Garden Lane, Rusthall; TQ5639], *Beacon*: Comfortable sofas, stripped wood, relaxing atmosphere and imaginative food from filled french bread to Sun lunch, interesting wines; live music or theatre downstairs weekends; lovely views from terrace *(Hilary Dobbie, Janet and Colin Roe)*

Tunbridge Wells [Spa Hotel, Mt Ephraim], *Equestrian Bar*: Stylish and comfortable bar with unusual equestrian floor-tile painting and steeplechasing pictures, good polite helpful service, fine choice of bar food inc excellent bangers and mash, well kept real ales; hotel lounge takes overflow; bedrooms *(E G Parish, Mrs R D Knight, BB)*; [Chapel Pl/Castle Sq], *Grapevine*: Refurbished cellar restaurant handy for Pantiles, good food (booking essential Sat night), good range of wines by the glass *(Hilarie Dobbie, Pat and Tony Martin)*

Ulcombe [The Street; TQ8548], *Harrow*: Warm and friendly two-bar pub with good value freshly cooked food in dining area (Weds curry night), good range of real ale and malt whiskies *(D Crofts, Thomas Nott)*

Under River [SE of Sevenoaks, off B245; TQ5551], *White Rock*: Friendly old-fashioned two-bar pub with several real ales such as Adnams Broadside, good choice of well presented good value bar food, popular as restaurant, chatty landlord, interesting bar games as well as pool and bar billiards; good big garden, not far from Ightham Mote *(A E Brace, Sue Lee, Mr and Mrs A Budden)*

Warehorne [off B2067 nr Hamstreet; TQ9832], *Woolpack*: Recently reopened 16th-c beamed pub on edge of Romney Marsh, very wide choice of food inc good puddings, very friendly relaxed service, well kept Greene King ales, peaceful setting with tables out overlooking lane, church and fields *(C Elliott, A and A Dale)*

☆ **Warren Street** [just off A20 at top of North Downs – OS Sheet 189 map ref 926529; TQ9253], *Harrow*: Quiet and comfortable dining pub neatly extended around 16th-c low-beamed core, generous above-average food, well kept Shepherd Neame and a guest beer, flowers and candles, big woodburner, faint piped music; restaurant (not Sun evening) with attractive conservatory extension; good bedrooms, on Pilgrims Way *(Carl and Jackie Cranmer, Wayne Brindle, BB)*

Wateringbury [Livesey St, Red Hill; TQ6853], *North Pole*: Small country pub with unusual range of reasonably priced tasty food, friendly staff, well kept beers; beautiful garden *(F Barwell)*

☆ **West Farleigh** [B2010 off A26 Tonbridge—Maidstone; TQ7152], *Tickled Trout*: New licensee doing good food in pleasant bar and attractive dining room, decor gently toned down, well kept Whitbreads-related ales; Medway views (esp from garden), path down to river with good walks *(Thomas Nott, LYM)*

West Malling [High St; TQ6857], *Bear*: Wide range of food in bar and restaurant, immaculate housekeeping, well kept beer, friendly efficient service; plenty of room *(Thomas Nott)*

West Peckham [TQ6452], *Swan*: Good simple home cooking inc some original recipes, well kept Harveys, friendly staff, attractive pub on village green – popular on summer weekends *(Paul Hilditch)*

Wickhambreaux [TR2158], *Rose*: Old village-green pub with three smallish panelled rooms, log fire in big fireplace, good fish-oriented food (worth booking), Greene King and Whitbreads-related ales *(K M Thorpe)*

☆ **Wingham** [Canterbury Rd; TR2457], *Dog*: Medieval beams, lots of character, good range of Whitbreads-related ales, good-sized wine glasses, good food, friendly service, landlord in good voice; comfortable bedrooms *(Frank Ashbee)*

☆ **Wingham** [High St (A257)], *Red Lion*: Lovely jettied 14th-c inn, neatly modernised but cosy and old-fashioned, with good varied bar food, well kept Whitbreads-related ales, restaurant; bedrooms *(Quentin Williamson, LYM)*

Woodchurch [Front Rd; TQ9434], *Bonny Cravat*: Jovial efficient landlord, Shepherd Neame beers, standard bar food from tasty sandwiches up, plainly furnished bar, small restaurant, pool in games room, side garden *(Janet and Colin Roe, Jenny and Michael Back)*; [Front Rd], *Six Bells*: Attractive pub with tables out in front under huge wisteria, oak beams inside, pleasant helpful staff, Whitbreads-related ales, bar food *(Jenny and Michael Back)*

Wormshill [The Street, off B2163 SW of Sittingbourne; TQ8757], *Blacksmiths Arms*: Comfortably old-fashioned renovation of isolated low-beamed country cottage, two compact bars with a touch of style, dining area, open fire, friendly staff, well kept Shepherd Neame ales and changing guests, good varied food (not Tues evening) inc vegetarian and doorstep sandwiches; beautiful garden with country views *(Thomas Nott)*

☆ **Worth** [The Street; TR3356], *St Crispin*: Friendly and relaxed low-beamed refurbished pub lit by several genuine paraffin lamps (some might say this calls for more ventilation), well kept Boddingtons Mild, Marstons Pedigree, Gales HSB, Shepherd Neame and two changing guest beers, local farm cider, simple but interesting sensibly priced bar food, restaurant, cheerful service, central log fire, charming big garden with barbecue; lovely village position not far from beach; bedrooms *(Alan Thwaite, Richard Farmer, Howard Allen, Patricia Dodd)*

☆ **Wrotham** [signed 1¾ miles from M20, junction 2; TQ6159], *Bull*: Welcoming helpful service in attractive 14th-c inn with good food, log fires, well kept Whitbreads-related ales, decent wines; children welcome, separate restaurant; comfortable bedrooms, huge breakfasts, attractive village *(L T Lionet, LYM)*

☆ Wye [signed off A28 NE of Ashford; TR0546], *Tickled Trout*: Good summer family pub with lots of tables and occasional barbecues on pleasant riverside lawn, spacious conservatory/restaurant; clean tidy modernised rustic-style bar with usual bar food, Whitbreads-related ales, good open fire; open all day Weds-Sun in summer, children welcome *(Mr and Mrs Jonathan Russell, Stephen Brown, Howard Allen, Martin Hickes, Jackie Oliver, LYM)*

Wye [Upper Bridge St], *New Flying Horse*: Friendly and comfortably modernised 17th-c beamed inn, pleasantly light, wide choice of interesting bar food, well kept Shepherd Neame ales, bric-a-brac inc carousel horse, attractive garden; bedrooms pleasant, good breakfasts *(Mr and Mrs Jonathan Russell)*

If you have to cancel a reservation for a bedroom or restaurant, please telephone or write to warn them. A small place – and its customers – will suffer if you don't. And recently people who failed to cancel have been taken to court for breach of contract.

Lancashire

Quite a number of changes here this year include new licensees for the Black Horse at Croston (more home-made food, wider beer choice), and the prettily placed Parkers Arms at Newton. The Royal Oak at Didsbury in Manchester is getting a new licensee too, but it seems likely he'll keep on the cheese choice which has been its great draw. Burtonwood have taken the very individual Cavendish Arms at Brindle back into management; fortunately the previous tenant stays on as manager, and is a strongly moderating influence on their plans for expansion. The Assheton Arms at Downham have more seats outside now, to make the most of this idyllic spot. The Wheatsheaf at Raby, now doing very well under its newish licensees, has a new conservatory, with plans for a new bar, too. That unique institution the Stalybridge Station Buffet, whose final closure we mourned in last year's Guide, has been reopened and looks in safe hands – so is back among the main entries. Other new entries are the attractive decorated Forest at Fence and the nice old Oddfellows Arms at Mellor – both with good food. Existing main entries currently doing particularly well include the Taps in Lytham (eight constantly changing real ales), the stylish Dukes 92 in Manchester and its sister pub there the Mark Addy (great cheese choice), the Devonshire Arms in Mellor under its popular landlord/chef, and the fine old Inn at Whitewell – a great place for a meal out. Other outstanding pubs for good food include the Eagle & Child at Bispham Green, the Bushells Arms at Goosnargh, and the New Inn up towards the Lakes at Yealand Conyers; overall, it's the Inn at Whitewell which we choose as Lancashire Dining Pub of the Year. Apart from the fine choice in Manchester, some pubs to note particularly in the Lucky Dip section at the end of the chapter are the Fox & Hounds at Barnston, Red Pump at Bashall Eaves, Waggon & Horses in Brierfield, Lord Raglan up above Bury, Rams Head at Denshaw, Farmers Arms at Heskin Green, Irby Mill at Irby, Ship at Lathom, Robin Hood at Mawdesley and Cross Keys at Uppermill; we have inspected and can firmly vouch for most of these. And Preston seems to be becoming quite a place for lovers of real ale. Incidentally, we've noticed quite a few pubs in this area introducing middle eastern dishes recently: has Turkey become the holiday destination for Lancashire publicans? Both food and drinks prices are well below the national average here – lucky Lancashire drinkers saving 20p every time they pay for a pint. The local brewery Holts keeps prices particularly low, with the Black Dog at Belmont (tied to them) a fine example; we also found the Marble Arch in Manchester very cheap. Incidentally, please note that we include in this chapter those places around Stockport which have for the last couple of decades been absorbed into the Greater Manchester area – and those parts of the Wirral which were at the same time 'pinched' from Cheshire by Merseyside.

Post Office address codings confusingly give the impression that some pubs are in Lancashire when they're really in Yorkshire (which is where we list them).

nr BALDERSTONE (Lancs) SD6332 Map 7
Myerscough Hotel
Whalley Rd, Salmesbury; A59 Preston—Skipton, over 3 miles from M6 junction 31

This bustling 18th-c pub is a handy stop not far from the M6 which is popular during the day with families, businessmen or workers from the British Aerospace plant across the road. In the evening it takes on a more traditionally pubby feel, when the softly lit beamed bar has a pleasant relaxed and cottagey feel. There are well made and comfortable oak settles around dimpled copper or heavy cast-iron-framed tables, as well as nice pen and ink drawings of local scenes, a painting of the month by a local artist, and lots of brass and copper. The serving counter has a nice padded elbow rest, and dispenses well kept Robinsons Best and Mild and occasionally Hartleys XB on handpump, and several malt whiskies; darts, shove-ha'penny, dominoes, and fruit machine. Bar food includes sandwiches (£1.95), ploughman's (£3.25), stilton and mushroom bake (£3.95), steak and kidney pie (£4.25), chilli (£4.50) and lamb balti (£4.95). The front room is no smoking. There are picnic tables, bantams and their chicks, and rabbits in the garden. *(Recommended by Carl Travis, David Peakall, Mrs A L Stride)*

Robinsons ~ Tenant John Pedder ~ Real ale ~ Meals and snacks (12-2, 6.30-8.30) ~ (01254) 812222 ~ Well behaved children in front room at mealtimes ~ Weds quiz night ~ Open 11.30-2.30, 5.30-11; 12-3, 7-10.30 Sun ~ Bedrooms: £41.50S

BELMONT (Lancs) SD6716 Map 7
Black Dog £ 🛏
A675

Readers love the consistency of this friendly 18th-c farmhouse, not to mention the way food and drink prices barely increase (if at all) from one year to the next – one reader said it's such good value that it more than justifies his purchase of a Guide every year. The original cheery and traditional small rooms are packed with antiques and bric-a-brac, from railwaymen's lamps, bedpans and chamber-pots to landscape paintings, as well as service bells for the sturdy built-in curved seats, rush-seated mahogany chairs, and coal fires. The atmosphere is perhaps best on a winter evening, especially if you're tucked away in one of the various snug alcoves, one of which used to house the village court. Twice a year they have a small orchestral concert, and on New Year's Day at lunchtime a Viennese concert. Very popular, generously served bar food includes home-made soup (£1; they do a winter broth with dumplings, £1.50), sandwiches (from £1.70), steak barm cake £1.90), ploughman's (from £3.30), scampi, gammon or lamb cutlets (£3.90), steaks (from £5.90), well liked salads with various fruits like grape, banana and strawberry, and daily specials like deep-fried camembert or whitebait (£2.50), spinach and ricotta cheese lasagne (£4.50), swordfish steak in lemon and herb butter (£6), venison in red wine (£6.50) or goose breast in plum sauce (£7). We like the way they've kept it pubby by not taking bookings, but it does tend to fill up quickly so get there early for a table. An airy extension lounge with a picture window has more modern furnishings; morning coffee, darts, pool, shove-ha'penny, dominoes, cribbage, and fruit machine; softly piped classical music. From two long benches on the sheltered sunny side of the pub there are delightful views of the moors above the nearby trees and houses; there's a track from the village up Winter Hill and (from the lane to Rivington) on to Anglezarke Moor, and paths from the dam of the nearby Belmont Reservoir. *(Recommended by Brian Wainwright, Dr J Morley, Humphry and Angela Crum Ewing, Peter Haines, Gordon Tong, T M Tomkinson, Iain Robertson, E M Walton, Andy Hazeldine, Nick Wikeley)*

Holts ~ Tenant James Pilkington ~ Real ale ~ Meals and snacks (till 8pm Sun; not Mon or Tues evenings except for residents) ~ (01204) 811218 ~ Children welcome in eating area of bar ~ Open 12-4, 7-11 ~ Bedrooms: £29.50B/£38B

We say if we know a pub has piped music.

BILSBORROW (Lancs) SD5139 Map 7
Owd Nells 🍺

Guy's Thatched Hamlet, St Michaels Road; at S end of village (which is on A6 N of Preston) take Myerscough College turn

This busy purpose built canalside family pub is part of a thriving little complex called 'Guy's Thatched Hamlet', which, with its expanding hotel, craft and tea shops and so forth has transformed a previously neglected stretch of canal into quite a tourist attraction. The three or four spacious communicating rooms of the pub have an easy-going rustic feel, with their mix of brocaded button-back banquettes, stable-stall seating, library chairs and other seats, high pitched rafters at either end, and lower beams (and flagstones) by the bar counter in the middle; a couple of areas are no smoking. Children are made especially welcome; there may be free lollipops and bags of bread for feeding the ducks. Colourful seats out on the terrace, part of which is covered by a thatched roof; a small walled-in play area has a timber castle, and you can play cricket or boules. There may be Morris dancers out here on summer weekends. Generously served bar meals such as minestrone (£1.90), chicken wings in tangy sauce (£3.20), hot buttered shrimps on toast (£3.40), marinated herring (£3.55), lots of pizzas (from £5), pasta dishes (from £5.50), seafood pancake (£6.75), steak and kidney pie (£6.85), fillet of pork fried in cider and cream or rack of ribs (£9.50), salmon and prawns in white wine cream (£10.60) and entrecote steak (£10.95). Waitress service is prompt and professional even under pressure – it often gets busy, especially in school holidays. Around seven well kept real ales might include Owd Nells Bitter which is brewed for the pub by Whitbreads, with possibly Black Sheep, Boddingtons, Flowers, Mitchells, Marstons Pedigree, Timothy Taylors Landlord or Wadworths 6X on handpump, lots of fruit wines, about two dozen malts, tea and coffee; darts, dominoes, cribbage, shove ha'penny, fruit machine, Connect-Four, and unobtrusive piped pop music. *(Recommended by Emma Critchley, SLC, Carl Travis, JWC, MC, Bill and Steph Brownson, Emma Darlington, Mayur Shah)*

Free house ~ Licensee Roy Wilkinson ~ Real ale ~ Meals and snacks (all day) ~ Next-door restaurant (all day inc Sun) ~ (01995) 640010 ~ Children welcome ~ Live music Thurs and Fri evenings ~ Open 10.30-11; 12-10.30 Sun ~ Bedrooms: £23.50B/£41.50B

BISPHAM GREEN (Lancs) SD4914 Map 7
Eagle & Child 🍽️ 🍺

Maltkiln Lane (Parbold—Croston rd) off B5246

Refurbished in an attractively understated old-fashioned style, the civilised bar at this sriking three-storey dark brick pub is largely open-plan, but well divided by stubs of walls. There are fine old stone fireplaces, oriental rugs and some coir matting on flagstones, old hunting prints and engravings, and a mix of individual furnishings including small oak chairs around tables in corners, and several handsomely carved antique oak settles – the finest apparently made partly from a 16th-c wedding bed-head. House plants stand on a big oak coffer. One area is no smoking. The owner's family farm much of the land around Parbold, so there may be well hung meat from their various herds. Imaginative bar food might include soups like smoked chicken and almond soup (£1.80), coronation chicken salad and mango (£6), warm crispy duck salad with mortadella, lardons and croutons and walnut dressing (£7), beef bourguignon or sauté chicken fillet and mustard mascarpone (£8), fried pigeon breast with roquefort and pear dressing, roasted wild salmon with tomato and basil or seafood in a mild cream curry sauce (£9), grilled lamb neck fillet with cous-cous salad, grilled brill with lemon, fresh king scallops with garlic and cream or fillet steak with button onions, white wine and cream (£11). A particularly good range of well kept beers on handpump consists of Coach House Gunpowder Dark Mild, Theakstons Best, Thwaites, Timothy Taylor Landlord, with three or four changing guest ales one of which might be from their newly aquired own-brew pub, the Liverpool Brewing Co. in the centre of Liverpool. Also farm cider, decent wines, and a good collection of malt whiskies. Friendly and interested service; maybe piped pop radio. There is a neat if not entirely orthodox bowling green behind (with croquet in summer), and the pub garden has recently been restored and a new wild garden added. Harry the dog is not the most sober individual. *(Recommended by Comus Elliott, Keith and Judith Ashcroft, M Buchanan, Phil and Dilys Unsworth, Janet Pickles, Brian Kneale, Janet Lee, Tony Young, John and Diana Davies, Mrs J Anderton, Mike Meadley, James Cowell)*

Free house ~ Manager Monica Evans~ Real ale ~ Meals and snacks (12-2, 6-8.30) ~ (01257) 462297 ~ Children in eating area of bar ~ Jazz in the garden on summer Sun evenings ~ Open 12-3, 5.30-11; 12-11 Sat; 12-10.30 Sun; 12-3, 5.30-11 Sat in winter

BLACKSTONE EDGE (Gtr Manchester) SD9716 Map 7
White House
A58 Ripponden—Littleborough, just W of B6138

This imposing 17th-c pub is spectacularly set 1,300 feet above sea level on the Pennine Way, with panoramic views stretching far off into the distance. The busy, welcoming and cheery main bar has a turkey carpet in front of a blazing coal fire and a large-scale map of the area (windswept walkers hardly know whether to head for the map or the fire first). The snug Pennine Room opens off here, with brightly coloured antimacassars on its small soft settees, and there's a new extension. A spacious room on the left has a big horseshoe window looking over the moors, as well as comfortable seating. Good helpings of homely bar food include vegetable soup (£1.50), sandwiches (from £2.20), recommended cumberland sausage with egg (£3.90), steak and kidney pie, roast chicken breast or vegetarian quiche (£4.30), chilli, beef curry or lasagne (£5), daily specials and home-made apple pie (£1.40); children's meals (£1.65). Prompt friendly service. Two well kept beers on handpump such as Black Sheep, Moorhouses Pendle Witches Brew or Theakstons Best, farm cider, and malt whiskies; fruit machine. Muddy boots can be left in the long, enclosed porch. *(Recommended by David and Judy Walmsley, Alison Wills, M Buchanan, M L and G Clarke)*

Free house ~ Licensee Neville Marney ~ Real ale ~ Meals and snacks (11.30-2; 7-10) ~ (01706) 378456 ~ Children welcome till 9pm ~ Open 11.30-3, 7(6 Sat)-11

BRINDLE (Lancs) SD6024 Map 7
Cavendish Arms
3 miles from M6 junction 29; A6 towards Whittle le Woods then left on B5256

The friendly easy-going licensee at this snug old building was at something of a loss when it came to telling us about plans for the pub this year. It seems that the brewery can't quite make their mind up about extending the pub through to the three cottages next door (the brewery bought them back in the 1930s with just this intention). We think it's rather a good thing that the pub's several cosy and characterful little rooms which ramble round a central servery remain unaltered for as long as possible. You might expect the intricate carvings and fascinating stained glass to be amongst the oldest features, but in fact both were comparatively recent additions. The glasswork has many colourful depictions of medieval warriors and minstrels, with the liveliest scenes commemorating a nasty skirmish between the Vikings and Anglo-Saxons that took place nearby in the year 937. There are lots of pictorial plates and Devonshire heraldic devices in plaster on the walls, as well as comfortable seats and discreet flowery curtains. Two well kept Burtonwood beers on handpump, and a good choice of malt whiskies; darts and dominoes. Simple bar food (although the brewery has their eye on this as well) includes soup (£2), open sandwiches (£3.95), peppered prawns or home-made beef pie (£4.50), breaded haddock (£4.50), spinach and mushroom lasagne (£5), chicken balti (£6), and daily specials like broccoli and pasta bake (£4.50), fried fisherman's platter, garlic and ginger prawns or chicken goujons (£4.95). There are white metal and plastic tables and chairs on a terrace by a rockery with a small water cascade, with another table on a small lawn behind. It's nicely set in a tranquil little village, and there's a handsome stone church across the road. *(Recommended by Dave Braisted, Brian Kneale, F C Johnston, M Buchanan, Jim and Maggie Cowell)*

Burtonwood ~ Manager Peter Bowling ~ Real ale ~ Meals and snacks (12-2, 5.30-9; not Sun evening) ~ Restaurant ~ (01254) 852912 ~ Children in restaurant ~ Open 11-2.30, 5.30-11; 12-4, 7-10.30 Sun; cl 25 Dec

CHIPPING (Lancs) SD6243 Map 7
Dog & Partridge ♀

Hesketh Lane; crossroads Chipping—Longridge with Inglewhite—Clitheroe, OS Sheet 103 map reference 619413

This comfortably relaxed and spotlessly kept dining pub is popular for its good home-made food. The choice typically includes dishes like sandwiches (from £2.75), soup (£2), ploughman's (£6), three vegetarian dishes like leek and mushroom crumble (£5.50), steak and kidney pie (£6.50), halibut fillet with prawn sauce, honey roast wild duck or seasonal game (£7.50) and sirloin steak (£8); the home-made chips are particularly well liked and they do various fish and game specials. Parts of the building date back to 1515, though it's been much modernised since, with the eating space now spreading over into a nearby stable. The main lounge is comfortably furnished with small armchairs around fairly close-set low wood-effect tables on a blue patterned carpet, brown-painted beams, a good winter log fire, and multi-coloured lanterns; service is friendly and helpful. Tetleys and a weekly changing guest on handpump, over 40 wines, and a good range of malt whiskies; piped music. Jacket and tie are preferred in the restaurant; dining areas are no smoking. *(Recommended by Margaret and Peter Brierley, Arthur and Margaret Dickinson, Sue and Geoff Price, Brian and Sue Wharton, J Boucher, Carl Travis, RJH, K C and B Forman)*

Free house ~ Licensee Peter Barr ~ Real ale ~ Meals and snacks (12-1.45, 7-9.30; 3.30-9.45 Sun; not Sat evening) ~ Restaurant ~ (01995) 61201 ~ Children welcome ~ Open 11.45-3, 6.45-11; 11.45-10.30 Sun

CROSTON (Lancs) SD4818 Map 7
Black Horse ◖ £

Westhead Road; A581 Chorley—Southport

This friendly village free house is popular with locals for its range of half a dozen or more real ales, its very reasonably priced straightforward home-cooked food and its amiable local atmosphere. The neatly kept bar has a quietly comfortable Victorian-style appeal, with patterned carpets, attractive wallpaper, solid upholstered wall settles and cast-iron-framed pub tables, a fireplace tiled in the Victorian manner and reproduction prints of that period (also a couple of nice 1950s street-scene prints by M Grimshaw), as well as darts, pool, cribbage, dominoes, fruit machine, juke box, maybe TV, piped music. Reliable home cooking is popular with local pensioners and includes sandwiches (from £1.85), ploughman's (£2.50), pie of the day (savoury mince and onion £3, steak and kidney £3.75, chicken, ham and mushroom £3.95), chilli or curry (£3.25), braised steak (£3.75) and lamb marinated in red wine, mint and cranberries (£3.95). Beers might include Jennings Bitter or Sneck Lifter, Hancocks HB, Ruddles, Theakstons Bitter and Mild and others, all well kept on handpump. There are picnic tables outside, and a good solid safely railed-off play area; the pub has its own crown bowls green and boules pitch (boules available from the bar). *(Recommended by Richard Lewis, John Fazakerley; more reports please)*

Free house ~ Licensee Graeme Conroy ~ Real ale ~ Meals and snacks (12-2.30, 6-8; 12-6 Sun) ~ Restaurant ~ (01772) 600338 ~ Children in eating area of bar till 8pm ~ Open 11-11; 12-10.30 Sun

---

Though we don't usually mention it in the text, most pubs will now make coffee – always worth asking. And many – particularly in the North – will do tea.

nr DARWEN (Lancs) SD6922 Map 7
Old Rosins 🛏

Pickup Bank, Hoddlesden; from B6232 Haslingden—Belthorn, turn off towards Edgeworth opposite the Grey Mare – pub then signposted off to the right; OS Sheet 103 map reference 722227

Although there are lovely views over the moors and down into the wooded valley on clear days, this pub is arguably at its best on one of those foggy days when the moorland mists obscure everything except the welcoming lights of this particularly friendly place. There's a good pubby atmosphere in the open-plan bar which is comfortably furnished with red plush built-in button-back banquettes, and stools and small wooden chairs around dark cast-iron-framed tables. Lots of mugs, whisky-water jugs and so forth hang from the high joists, while the walls are decorated with small prints, plates and old farm tools; there's also a good log fire. Parts of the bar and restaurant are no smoking. Well kept Boddingtons, Flowers Original, Marstons Pedigree and Theakstons Old Peculier on handpump, plenty of malt whiskies, and coffee; fruit machine and maybe piped music. Served all day (right through till 10 o'clock), the good value bar food includes steak and chicken pie (£4.25), beef in Old Peculier (£4.45) and chicken tikka (£5.25). There are picnic tables on a spacious crazy-paved terrace. Readers have enjoyed their murder weekends and other themed evenings. *(Recommended by M Buchanan, Andy Hazeldine, Charlotte Wrigley, K and B Forman, Steven and Denise Waugh, Vicky and David Sarti, Carl Travis)*

Free house ~ Licensee Bryan Hankinson ~ Meals and snacks (all day) ~ Restaurant ~ (01254) 771264 ~ Children welcome ~ Open 11-11; 12-10.30 Sun ~ Bedrooms: £39.50B/£49.50B

DOWNHAM (Lancs) SD7844 Map 7
Assheton Arms

From A59 NE of Clitheroe turn off into Chatburn (signposted); in Chatburn follow Downham signpost; OS Sheet 103 map reference 785443

This pretty pub takes its name from the family of Lord Clitheroe, who have ensured that this charming stonebuilt village, spreading out along a duck-inhabited stream, has been preserved in traditional style ever since the family bought it in 1558. Picnic sets outside look across to the church, and inside the rambling, beamed and red-carpeted bar has olive plush-cushioned winged settles around attractive grainy oak tables, some cushioned window seats, and two grenadier busts on the mantelpiece over a massive stone fireplace that helps to divide the areas; part of the bar is no smoking. As well as seasonal fish specialities such as oysters, monkfish, crab and lobster, bar food includes ham and vegetable broth (£2.25), sandwiches (from £3.25 not Saturday evening or Sunday lunchtime), brie and lancashire cheese deep fried in batter with gooseberry sauce or ploughman's (£3.95), mushrooms and cream with pasta (£5.50), steak and kidney pie (£5.95), venison, bacon and cranberry casserole (£7.95), halibut steak with cream cheese sauce (£8.95), scampi (£10.25) and strips of beef fillet stir-fried with ginger and spring onion (£11.50). Well kept Boddingtons, Flowers Original and Whitbreads Castle Eden under light blanket pressure; decent wines by the glass or bottle; piped music. *(Recommended by Peter Miatee, Alan Griffiths; more reports please)*

Whitbreads ~ Tenants David and Wendy Busby ~ Real ale ~ Meals and snacks (till 10pm) ~ (01200) 441227 ~ Children welcome ~ Open 12-3, 7-11(10.30 Sun)

FENCE (Lancs) SD8237 Map 7
Forest

Cuckstool Lane; off A6088 opp B6248 to Brierfield

Recently refurbished with striking red ceilings, heavy panelling, lots of paintings, vases, plates and books, this comfortable place has a cosy feel, thanks to its big open fire and subdued lighting. The open-plan bar has two rooms opening off it, and a side restaurant. Good varied food uses fresh local produce where possible – salmon from the river instead of a fish farm, perhaps pork from a free-range Gloucester Old Spot instead of some modern genetic wonder. And the cooking is inventive: tasty sandwiches (from £2.45), smoked trout with lemon herb dressing (£4.25), crab claw salad with tarragon and mustard mayonnaise and endive and cucumber salad (£4.50), rump steak baguette (£4.65), filo parcel of crispy Chinese duck, spring onion and tomato or half a dozen queen scallops with gruyère and garlic (£4.95), Indonesian chicken satay (£8.50), pork medallions with madeira and mushrooms (£9.50), grilled loin of tuna with fricasee of wild mushrooms and courgettes provençale (£10.50), seabass with Chinese stir fry (£11.50); puddings and ice creams are home-made and come in combinations like fresh strawberrys with cinnamon ice cream and strawberry coulis or compote of fresh fruit with home-made vanilla ice cream with raspberry coulis (from £3.50); there is no children's menu but they will do small helpings of suitable dishes; no-smoking area in dining room; piped music. Ruddles and Theakstons Best on handpump as well as a couple of guests, that are chosen with the help of the customers, a good choice of wines, friendly helpful service. *(Recommended by Brian Kneale, D and E M Kershaw, F J Robinson)*

Free house ~ Licensee Jonathan Seedall ~ Real ale ~ Meals and snacks (12-2.30, 5.30-9.30) ~ Restaurant ~ (01282) 613641 ~ Children welcome ~ Open 12-11(10.30 Sun); cl 25 Dec evening

GARSTANG (Lancs) SD4845 Map 7
Th'Owd Tithebarn ★

Signposted off Church Street; turn left off one-way system at Farmers Arms

There are lots of new benches on the big flagstoned terrace that overlooks ducks and boats wending their way along the Lancaster Canal, beside this beautifully set creeper-covered barn. It's a fascinating and quite unique old building, in some ways a bit like an old-fashioned farmhouse kitchen parlour. There's an old kitchen range, prints of agricultural equipment on the walls, stuffed animals and birds, and pews and glossy tables spaced out on the flagstones under the high rafters, and we're told that only the York Museum has a bigger collection of antique farming equipment. Waitresses in period costume with mob-caps complete the vintage flavour. The site gets busy, and is something of a tourist attraction. Simple but well prepared bar food includes soup (£1.95), filled cottage loaves (from £3.25, lunchtime only), soused Scottish herrings (£2.85), spicy bean tortilla bake (£4.95), steak and kidney pudding (£5.75) and lamb cobbler (£5.95). They do afternoon teas in summer. Well kept Mitchells Original and Lancaster Bomber on handpump; lots of country wines, dominoes. *(Recommended by Ian Phillips, Vicky and David Sarti, Mike and Wendy Proctor; more reports please)*

Mitchells ~ Manager Gordon Hutchinson ~ Real ale ~ Meals and snacks (12-9.30(10 Sat); 12-2.30, 6-9.30(10 Sat) in winter) ~ Restaurant ~ (01995) 604486 ~ Children in restaurant ~ Open 11-11; 11-3, 6-11 in winter; 12-10.30 Sun

GOOSNARGH (Lancs) SD5537 Map 7
Bushells Arms 🍴 ♀

4 miles from M6 junction 32; A6 towards Garstang, turn right at Broughton traffic lights (the first ones you come to), then left at Goosnargh Village signpost (it's pretty insignificant – the turn's more or less opposite Whittingham Post Office)

The knowledgeable licensees at this bustling pub give tremendous care and attention to all aspects of their business. There's particular emphasis on their very well prepared bar food, a carefully constructed wine list, and considering the high standards, very competitive pricing. The menu tends towards Mediterranean and Middle Eastern food with daily specials determined by the availability of good fresh ingredients, often local; fresh fish is delivered daily from Fleetwood. As well as an unusual soup like Dutch pea with ham and garlic sausage, recent daily specials have included local black pudding (£2), cinnamon flavoured minced lamb layered with pasta and topped with savoury custard (£5), vegetable cobbler or pork, apple, prune and walnut meatballs braised in cider sauce (£5.50), Moroccan chicken, fresh salmon marinated in red wine, blackberries and mint and chicken fillet in mild spicy curry sauce with sliced peppers, sultanas and thyme (£6). The bar menu includes spring rolls, samosas or falafel (£2), steak and kidney pie (£5.50), and salmon and broccoli parcel, stifatho (a Greek beef stew), or chicken fillet filled with smoked bacon, asparagus, grated cheese in hollandaise sauce and wrapped in puff pastry (£6). Crisp and fresh vegetables include tasty potatoes done with garlic, cream, peppers and parmesan, and there's a good range of puddings like pecan pie and pecan ice cream or orange bread and butter pudding (£2). The spacious, modernised bar has lots of snug bays, each holding not more than two or three tables and often faced with big chunks of sandstone (plastic plants and spotlit bare boughs heighten the rockery effect); also soft red plush button-back banquettes, with flagstones by the bar; fruit machine. Two areas are no smoking. The well chosen and constantly developing wine list is excellent, with some New World ones and several half bottles, as well as changing wines of the month and helpful notes. Also well kept Boddingtons and Tetleys on handpump, and several malt whiskies. Tables in a little back garden, and hanging baskets at the front. The signal for opening the doors at lunchtime is the tolling of the church clock, and haunted Chingle Hall is not far away. *(Recommended by Michael Tucker, M Buchanan, John and Moira Cole, Arthur and Margaret Dickinson, Peter Miatee, Dave Braisted, Neil Townend, Carl Travis, RTM, JCM, P H Boot, Esther and John Sprinkle, David Shillitoe)*

Whitbreads ~ Lease: David Best ~ Meals and snacks ~ (01772) 865235 ~ Seated well behaved children in eating area of bar until 9pm ~ Open 12-3, 6-11(7-10.30 Sun); cl 25 Dec, occasional Mondays and the last Sat in May or first Sat in June

Horns ♀

Pub signed from village, about 2 miles towards Chipping below Beacon Fell

The friendly welcoming staff and licensees at this pleasantly positioned old coaching inn contribute in large measure to the enjoyably relaxed but attentive atmosphere. The polished but snug rooms haven't changed much since they were built, and all have log fires in winter. Dotted around are a number of colourful flower displays – a good indication of the care and effort the friendly licensees put into running the place. Beyond the lobby, the pleasant front bar opens into attractively decorated middle rooms with antique and other period furnishings. At lunchtime it's mostly popular with people enjoying the tasty bar food such as wholesome soups (£1.95), beautifully presented sandwiches (from £2.50), ploughman's (£3.75), steak and kidney pie (£5.75), plaice or roast pheasant (£5.95), a daily roast (the beef is well liked) and fresh fish of the day like halibut or scallops, and sirloin steak with mushrooms (£9.50), all nicely served with freshly cooked, piping hot chips; home-made puddings like sherry trifle or an excellent sticky toffee pudding (£2.75). A very good range of up to ten or so wines by the glass, an extensive wine list and a fine choice of malt whiskies; cheerful and helpful young staff, piped music. *(Recommended by John Fazakerley, Mike and Mary Carter, J A Boucher, K C and B Forman, Brian and Sue Wharton, Sarah Bradbury)*

Free house ~ Licensee Mark Woods ~ Meals and snacks (not Mon lunch) ~ Restaurant ~ (01772) 865230 ~ Children in eating area of bar and restaurant ~ Open 11.30-3, 6.30-11; 11-11 Sat; 12-3, 6-10.30 Sun; cl Mon lunchtime ~ Bedrooms: £45B/£70B

LIVERPOOL SJ4395 Map 7
Philharmonic ★ £ ◖

36 Hope Street; corner of Hardman Street

It's worth a visit to this Victorian gin palace – properly called the Philharmonic Dining Rooms – just for its historical interest; to enjoy the wonderful opulence of its original, exquisitely decorated rooms. But this is no fusty museum, a cheery bustle of theatre-goers, students, locals and tourists keeps the atmosphere alive and contemporary. The heart of the building is a mosaic-faced serving counter, from where heavily carved and polished mahogany partitions radiate under the intricate plasterwork high ceiling. The echoing main hall is decorated with stained glass including contemporary portraits of Boer War heroes such as Baden-Powell and Lord Roberts, rich panelling, a huge mosaic floor, and copper panels of musicians in an alcove above the fireplace. More stained glass in one of the little lounges declares *Music is the universal language of mankind* and backs this up with illustrations of musical instruments; there are two plushly comfortable sitting rooms. Lavatory devotees may be interested to know that the famous gents' are original 1890s Rouge Royale by Twyfords: all red marble and glinting mosaics, some readers have long felt these alone earn the pub its star. Well kept Ind Coope Burton, Marstons Pedigree and Tetleys Bitter on handpump, some malt whiskies and cask cider; fruit machine, video game, trivia and juke box. Good value home-made bar food includes soup (£1.25), filled baguettes (from £2.15, hot £2.35), and various well priced dishes like lasagne, steak and kidney pie or haddock (all £3.95), gammon, cajun chicken or cod and prawn pie (£4.95), mixed grill (£8.45) and puddings (£1.85); they do a very well-priced three-course Sunday lunch; no-smoking area in restaurant. Friendly service. (*Recommended by Brian Kneale, Chris Raisin, Richard Fallon, Sue and Bob Ward, Thomas Nott, Paul and Ursula Randall, Eric and Jackie Robinson*)

Walkers (Carlsberg Tetleys) ~ Manager Phil Ross ~ Real ale ~ Meals and snacks (11.30-2.30, 5.30-8.30) ~ Restaurant ~ (0151) 709 1163 ~ Children in eating area of bar ~ Weds quiz night, karaoke on Tues ~ Open 11.30-11; 12-3, 7-11 Sun

LYTHAM (Lancs) SD3627 Map 7
Taps ▪ £

A584 S of Blackpool; Henry Street – in centre, one street in from West Beach

The enthusiastic landlord at this cheery drinker's pub is forever hunting out new beers, and every time he changes a barrel it's to something different; so far he's had over 1,000. There are usually eight ales on at a time, with maybe Everards Chesters Mild, Flowers Original, Marstons Pedigree, Colonel Pepper's Lemon Ale, Timothy Taylors Landlord, and Wadworths IPA; Boddingtons is more or less a regular fixture, and they usually have some country wines. The Victorian-style bare-boarded bar has a really friendly and unassuming atmosphere, as well as plenty of stained-glass decoration in the windows, with depictions of fish and gulls reflecting the pub's proximity to the beach; also captain's chairs in bays around the sides, open fires, and a coal-effect gas fire between two built-in bookcases at one end. As well as a TV for special sporting events there's a bit of a rugby theme, with old photographs and portraits of rugby stars on the walls; piped music, shove-ha'penny, dominoes, fruit machine and juke box. Anyone who's taken sampling the beers a little too seriously will appreciate the seat belts on the bar stools, and the headrest in the gents'. The home-made bar food is simple but good value, with the most popular dishes including a good pea and ham soup (95p), hot roast beef sandwich (£2.35), beer sausages and mash or chilli (£2.95) and chicken curry or ploughman's (£3.25); the ham and beef are home cooked. There are no meals on Sunday, but instead they have free platters of food laid out, with tasty morsels like black pudding, chicken wings or minted lamb. There a few seats outside. (*Recommended by Kate and Robert Hodkinson, Michael and Alison Leyland, Paul Swan, Carl Travis, Andy Hazeldine*)

Whitbreads ~ Manager Ian Rigg ~ Real ale ~ Lunchtime meals and snacks (no menu on Sun, free snacks only then) ~ (01253) 736226 ~ Open 11-11; 12-10.30 Sun

MANCHESTER SJ8498 Map 7
Dukes 92 £

Castle Street, below the bottom end of Deansgate

In a superbly atmospheric setting by locks and under railway arches in the rejuvenated heart of old industrial Manchester, this spacious building has been stylishly converted from old canal-horse stables, with black wrought-iron work contrasting boldly with whitewashed bare plaster walls, a handsome marble-topped bar, and an elegant spiral staircase to an upper room and balcony. Up here are some modern director's chairs, but down in the main room the fine mix of furnishings is mainly rather Edwardian in mood, with one particularly massive table, elegantly comfortable chaises-longues and deep armchairs. It's under the same ownership as the well established Mark Addy (see entry below), and has a similar excellent choice of cheeses and pâtés – some quite unusual – served in huge helpings with granary bread (£3.20). They also serve a soup in winter (£1.95), toasted sandwiches (from £2.50), filled baked potatoes (from £2.75) and mozzarella and tomato platter or a dip with vegetables and pitta bread (£3). Well kept Boddingtons and a couple of rotated guests like Morlands Old Speckled Hen or Timothy Taylor Landlord on handpump, along with the Belgian wheat beer Hoegarden, and quite a few Belgian fruit beers; decent wines and a large selection of malts, friendly staff; piped music. There are tables out by the canal basin which opens into the bottom lock of the Rochdale Canal. On bank holiday weekends events in the forecourt may include jazz and children's theatre, and there's a permanent theatre in the function room. *(Recommended by Meg Hamilton, Ian Phillips, John Fazakerley, Stephen and Julie Brown, Dr M Bridge, Carl Travis, Brian Wainwright)*

Free house ~ Licensee Sara Louise Ratcliffe ~ Real ale ~ Snacks (all day) ~ (0161) 839 8646 ~ Children welcome away from bar till 7pm ~ Theatre in the function room, and on outside stage on bank holiday weekends ~ Open 11.30-11; 12-10.30 Sun; cl 25, 26 Dec and 1 Jan

Lass o' Gowrie ◗ £

36 Charles Street; off Oxford Street at BBC

The main point of this tiled Victorian pub is the malt-extract beers that are brewed here. Named for their original gravity (strength) – LOG35 is quite lightly flavoured and slips down very easily, while LOG42 is a little meatier. Seats around a sort of glass cage give a view of the brewing process in the microbrewery downstairs in the cellar. There's also well kept Batemans XXXB, Fullers London Pride, Whitbreads Castle Eden and several guest beers on handpump, and Old Hazy cider; it might take some while to get served at busy periods. The simple but characterful long bar has gas lighting and bare floorboards and lots of exposed brickwork. Hop sacks drape from the ceiling, and the bar has big windows in its richly tiled arched brown facade. As the pub is now part of Whitbread's Hogshead brand, the good value bar food is the same as you'll find at others in the chain: sandwiches (from £1.75), burger, steak and kidney pie or a choice of five types of sausage with mash (£2.85) and lasagne (£3.75); efficient cheery service. The volume of the piped pop music really depends on the youth of the customers at the time; fruit machine. At really busy periods (usually only Friday and Sarurday nights during term times), the bar may be so full of good-natured university students you'll have to drink your own-brew pint on the pavement outside in true city-centre pub style. *(Recommended by Richard Lewis, Wayne Brindle, Nigel and Amanda Thorp; more reports please)*

Own brew (Whitbreads) ~ Manager Joe Fylan ~ Real ale ~ Lunchtime meals and snacks ~ (0161) 273 6932 ~ Children over 2 in eating area of bar ~ Open 11.30-11; 12-10.30 Sun; cl 25 Dec

Marble Arch £ ◗

73 Rochdale Rd (A664), Ancoats; corner of Gould St, just E of Victoria Station

The original name of this late Victorian drinking house was the Elephant's Head. Its current name was a nickname inspired by its porphyry entrance pillars, its name was only formally changed in the 1970s. Inside there's a magnificently restored lightly barrel-vaulted high ceiling and extensive marble and tiling, amongst which the frieze advertising various spirits and the chimney breast above the carved wooden mantelpiece particularly stand out. A mosaic floor slopes down to the bar, and some of the walls are partly stripped back to the glazed brick. There are armchairs by a fire in the back bar. Well kept real ales include Hopwood Bitter (very reasonably priced at less than the regional average), Marstons Pedigree, Oak Wobbly Bob, and three changing guests like Goachers, Titanic Captain Smith and Youngs Special. They also keep a good choice of bottled beers (including Belgian Trappist beers), Biddenden cider, and a selection of country wines. Remarkably low-priced bar food, served in the lounge extension at the back, includes burgers, lamb and rosemary, pork with apple and ginger and pork chilli (£2.50), vegetarian lasagne (£2.50) and lasagne (£3); they have a monthly curry night when you can eat as much as you like for £3. Table skittles, chess, cards, pinball, fruit machine, juke box and lively background music. The Laurel and Hardy Preservation Society meet here on the third Wednesday of the month and show old films. *(Recommended by Peter Plumridge, Richard Lewis, PGP, Paul Carter)*

Free house ~ Manager Mark Dade ~ Real ale ~ Meal and snacks 11.30-4, after that snacks only ~ (0161) 832 5914 ~ Live music some evenings ~ Open 11.30(12 Sat)-11; 7-10.30 Sun (closed lunchtime)

Mark Addy ♀ £

Stanley Street, Salford, Manchester 3 (if it's not on your street map head for New Bailey St); look out not for a pub but for what looks like a smoked glass modernist subway entrance

They offer a quite incredible choice of almost 50 different cheeses, all carefully described on the menu, from all over Britain and Europe at this atmospheric cheese pub. Impossibly huge chunks (they automatically give you a doggy bag) are served with granary bread (£3.20), and there's also a range of pâtés including a vegetarian one (£3.20) and toasted sandwiches (£2.50). Well converted from waiting rooms for boat passengers, the pub has quite a civilised and trendy atmosphere, especially in the flower-filled waterside courtyard from where you can watch the home-bred ducks. Inside, the series of barrel-vaulted red sandstone bays is furnished with russet or dove plush seats and upholstered stalls, wide glassed-in brick arches, cast-iron pillars, and a flagstone floor; piped music. Well kept Bass, Boddingtons and a changing guests like Marstons Pedigree or Timothy Taylors Landlord on handpump; quite a few wines too, with a sign by the entrance recommending which go best with particular cheeses. They get very busy, so it is worth getting there early, and they prefer smart dress. Named after a 19th-c man who rescued over 50 people from drowning in the River Irwell outside, the pub is run by the same people as another Manchester main entry, Dukes 92 (see above); the two recently swapped licensees. *(Recommended by Ian Phillips, Meg and Colin Hamilton, Martin McGowan, Carl Travis, Tom McLean, Dr M Bridge)*

Free house ~ Licensee Thomas Joyce ~ Real ale ~ Snacks (all day) ~ (0161) 832 4080 ~ Children welcome ~ Open 11.30-11; 12-10.30 Sun

Royal Oak £

729 Wilmslow Road, Didsbury

Marstons tell us that there will be a new licensee at this bustling pub by the time this book reaches the shops; we're hoping that they will continue to serve the vast array of cheeses that the pub's become famous for – as it's such a well proved formula we can't see any reason why they wouldn't. Huge hunks of cheese are served with a substantial chunk of bread, salad and extras such as beetroot and pickled onions (about £3.30 for a choice of two cheeses). Up till now it's been unusual to be served with less than a pound of even the rarer ones, so take-away bags are provided; there may also be pâtés and winter soup. Well kept Batemans Mild, Marstons Bitter and Pedigree and a fortnightly changing guest beer on handpump, and some sherries and ports from the wood; efficient, friendly service. Antique theatre bills and so forth cover the walls of the busy bar which is very popular with drinkers. There are some seats outside (though the exterior is pretty ordinary). *(Reports on the new regime please)*

Marstons ~ Real ale ~ Lunchtime snacks (not weekends or bank holidays) ~ (0161) 434 4788 ~ Children over 14 allowed 12-2 ~ Open 11-11; 12-10.30 Sun; cl evening 25 Dec

MELLOR (Gtr Manchester) SJ9888 Map 7
Devonshire Arms

Longhurst Lane; follow Mellor signpost off A626 Marple—Glossop and keep on up hill; note that this is Mellor near Stockport, NOT the other one on the north side of Manchester

Readers enjoy the tasty lunchtime bar food, cooked by the landlord, at this friendly unpretentious well maintained local. Typical dishes might include pea and ham or leek and potato soup (£1.80), potted shrimps or hummus (£3.60), extremely popular mussel chowder (£3.90), steamed fresh mussels (£4.40), courgettes provençal or ploughman's (£4.80), smoked sausage, egg curry or tortellini (£5.50), seafood pasta, bean curry or spiced chick pea curry (£5.75), diced chicken and peppers in a spicy sherry sauce (£5.75), tarragon salmon, braised oxtail or beef in Guinness (£6), and a couple of puddings such as crêpes with orange and Grand Marnier (£3.55). The only evening they do food is Monday. There's a delightfully welcoming atmosphere in the cheerful little front bar which has a couple of old leather-seated settles among other seats, lots of old local and family photographs, and a sizeable Victorian fireplace with a deep-chiming clock above it. A couple of small back rooms, attractively papered and with something of a period flavour, both have their own Victorian fireplaces – the one on the right including an unusual lion couchant in place of a mantelpiece. Robinsons Best and Mild on electric pump, a decent collection of spirits including about 50 malt whiskies, several New World wines, and good coffee; cribbage, shove-ha'penny and dominoes; possibly background radio; one room is no smoking. There are picnic tables out in front, and behind, where an attractively planted terrace leads back to a small tree-sheltered lawn. Recent extensions and additions out here are the handiwork of Mrs Harrison, a keen gardener. Walkers are welcome if they take their boots off. *(Recommended by Stephen and Julie Brown, J F M and M West, David Hoult, S Williamson, Michael Graubart, J C T Tan, Allan Worsley, Jack Morley)*

Robinsons ~ Tenant Brian Harrison ~ Real ale ~ Meals and snacks every lunchtime and Mon evening ~ (0161) 427 2563 ~ Well behaved children in eating area ~ Open 11.30-3, 5.30(7 Sat)-11; 12-3, 8-10.30 Sun; cl 25 Dec evening

Oddfellows Arms

73 Moor End Road; follow Mellor signpost off A626 Marple—Glossop and keep further on up hill – this too is the Mellor near Stockport

In the last couple of years the keen young chef/landlord who has taken over this fine old building has won a lot of admirers for his wide-ranging interesting food. This might include three or four soups (£1.75), sandwiches (from £1.95), ploughman's (from £4.95), roast of the day (£5.75), chicken marinated in yoghurt and garlic (£7.95), cold smoked meat and fish platter or pork tenderloin fried with green peppercorns, mushrooms, brandy and cream (£8.95) and up to nine different types of fish like natural cured haddock poached in white wine (£7.25), monkfish fried with capers, prawns, vermouth and cream (£10.25) and steamed bass (£11.95). Puddings like cheesecake, bread and butter pudding or rhubarb and ginger pie (£2.50) are traditional; three course Sunday lunch (£7.95); no-smoking restaurant. With no piped music or games, there's a pleasantly civilised buzz of conversation in the bar – two flagstoned rooms, with low ceilings, open fires, and well kept Marstons Best and Pedigree and an interesting guest beer on handpump, such as Oak Double Dagger. There's a small restaurant upstairs, and a few tables out by the road. *(Recommended by Stephen and Julie Brown, Tony Young, David Hoult)*

Free house ~ Licensee Roger Cloughley ~ Real ale ~ Meals and snacks ~ Restaurant ~ (0161) 449 7826 ~ Children in eating area of bar and restaurant till 7.30 ~ Open 12-3, 5.30-11; 12-3, 7-10.30 Sun; cl Mon, cl 25, 26 Dec

NEWTON (Lancs) SD6950 Map 7
Parkers Arms

B6478 7 miles N of Clitheroe

Some of the joists in the spacious and welcoming bar of this delightfully set timbered pub are from the same oak used to repair the Blitz-damaged Houses of Parliament. There are plenty of stuffed animals and paintings on the walls in here, as well as red plush button-back banquettes, a mix of new chairs and tables, and an open fire. Beyond an arch is a similar area with sensibly placed darts, pool, dominoes, bar billiards, fruit machine, and discreet piped music. Well kept Boddingtons and Flowers IPA and guests like Theakstons and Whitbread Castle Eden on handpump, a good range of malt whiskies, and regularly changing wine list. Bar food under the new licensee might include soup (£2.50), very generous sandwiches (from £2.40), big ploughman's, and a wide choice of daily blackboard specials like liver and onions (£5.50), home-made beef and ale pie (£5.50), home-cooked ham salad (£5.95), fillet of plaice with prawns and cheese sauce (£6.95), fresh poached salmon salad (£6.95). They have two amiable black labradors (who have been known to bring customers a stick to throw) and a children's play area. Well spaced picnic tables on the big lawn look down towards the river, and beyond to the hills. *(Recommended by John and Joan Wyatt, Gary and Sarah Goldson, Julie and Steve Anderton, Sue and Geoff Price, Arthur and Margaret Dickinson, Helen Pickering, James Owen, Paul McPherson, J Honnor)*

Whitbreads ~ Lease: Barbara Clayton ~ Real ale ~ Meals and snacks (all day Sat, Sun) ~ Restaurant ~ (01200) 446236 ~ Children welcome in eating area of bar and restaurant ~ Open 11-11; 12-10.30 Sun; 11-2.30, 5-11 weekdays in winter ~ Bedrooms: £28/£40

RABY (Merseyside) SJ3180 Map 7
Wheatsheaf 🍺

The Green, Rabymere Road; off A540 S of Heswall

There's lots of character in the charming little low-ceilinged rooms of this half-timbered, thatched and whitewashed country cottage (known locally as the Thatch). Furnishing is simple and characterful, with an old wall clock and homely black kitchen shelves in the cosy central bar, and a nice snug formed by antique settles built in around its fine old fireplace. A second, more spacious room has upholstered wall seats around the tables, small hunting prints on the cream walls, and a smaller coal fire. There's a new conservatory and a stables bar this year. Filling up a good chunk of the menu is the enormous range of toasted sandwiches (from £2.05) – nearly 50 different varieties are listed (including such flavours as black pudding), and they're happy to put together any other combination that springs to mind. Other food includes soup (£1.50), burgers (£2.90), ploughman's (from £3.95), steak and kidney pie or fried cod (£4.80), scampi (£5.10) and gammon steak (£5.80). Well kept beers on handpump include Greene King Abbot, Tetleys, Theakstons Best, Old Peculier and XB, Thwaites and Youngers Scotch, and there's also a good choice of malt whiskies. The landlord (who used to farm the land next door) has added a patio area with picnic tables behind. *(Recommended by Liz and Graham Bell, Graham and Lynn Mason, Dr Jim Mackay, D Maplethorpe, B Helliwell)*

Free house ~ Licensee Thomas Charlesworth ~ Real ale ~ Lunchtime meals and snacks ~ (0151) 336 3416 ~ Well behaved children in lounge and conservatory till 8pm ~ Open 11.30-11; 12-10.30 Sun; 11.30-3.30, 5.30-11 Mon-Thurs in winter

RIBCHESTER (Lancs) SD6435 Map 7
White Bull

Church Street; turn off B6245 at sharp corner by Black Bull

This stately stone dining pub was built in 1707, but the Tuscan pillars that guard the entrance porch have been in the area for nearly 2,000 years. The spacious and attractively refurbished main bar has comfortable old settles, and is decorated with Victorian advertisements and various prints, as well as a stuffed fox in two halves that looks as if it's jumping through the wall; most areas are set out for eating during the day, and you can also eat out in the garden behind. Half the dining area is no smoking. Service is friendly and attentive, even during busy periods, and children are made particularly welcome. Good value bar meals include soup (£1.60), open sandwiches (from £2.60), prawn cocktail (£3.20), steak and kidney pie (£4.50), meat or vegetable lasagne (£5), ploughman's (£5.10), various steaks with a choice of toppings (from £7), braised shoulder of lamb (£8.50), and changing specials such as swordfish with garlic and prawns; children's menu. Well kept Boddingtons Bitter and Mild, Flowers IPA and a guest beer like Greene King Abbot or Whitbread Castle Eden on handpump, a good range of malt whiskies, and a blackboard list of several wines by the glass or bottle; they also do coffees, teas, and hot chocolate. It can get busy, so it's worth arriving early for a table. Darts, dominoes, fruit machine, piped music. Behind the pub are the remains of a Roman bath house, and there's a small Roman museum close by. *(Recommended by Peter Walker, M Buchanan, Sue and Geoff Price, Caroline Lloyd, Louise Miller, Richard Waddington; more reports please)*

Whitbreads ~ Lease: Marilyn Brooks ~ Real ale ~ Meals and snacks (not Mon evening) ~ (01254) 878303 ~ Children in eating area of bar till 9pm ~ Open 11.30-3, 6.30-11; 12-10.30 Sun

STALYBRIDGE (Gtr Manchester) SJ9698 Map 7
Stalybridge Station Buffet ◗ £

After last year's closure this charming place has been rescued by the licensees of the Station Hotel at Ashton under Lyne, and its future now (dare we say it?) seems secure. It's a classic Victorian platform bar, not smart but very nostalgic, with barge and sail pictures set into its marble-topped bar counter, roaring fire below an etched-glass mirror of Queen Victoria, newspapers and magazines to read, old photographs of the station in its heyday and other railway memorabilia, even a little conservatory. It's expanded along the platform into what was the ladies' waiting room and part of the station-master's quarters, with a second open fire, original ornate ceilings and a dining/function room with Victorian-style wallpaper; dominoes, cribbage. On a sunny day you can sit out on the platform. Well kept Flowers IPA, Wadworths 6X and up to six interesting changing guest beers on handpump, farm cider, Belgian and other foreign bottled beers, tea made freshly by the pot, friendly staff, cheap old-fashioned snacks such as sandwiches (from £1.30), ploughman's (£1.75), and three or four daily specials like lasagne, hotpot or curry (£1.75) – more substantial offerings planned as a new kitchen comes on stream. Readers who knew it before will welcome one innovation – neat inside lavatories. *(Recommended by Richard Lewis, David Hoult, Richard Fallon)*

Free house ~ Licensees Sylvia Wood and John Hesketh ~ Real ale ~ Snacks (11-9.30) ~ (0161) 303 0007 ~ Children welcome in eating area of bar and conservatory ~ Folk singers Sat evening ~ Open 11-11; 12-10.30 Sun; cl 25 Dec

WHARLES (Lancs) SD4435 Map 7
Eagle & Child

Church Road; from B5269 W of Broughton turn left into Higham Side Road at HMS Inskip sign; OS Sheet 102 map reference 448356

It's hard to understand why we don't get more reports about this delightfully timeless place. We're hoping it's not that our readers only want to go out for a lunchtime meal these days (they don't do bar food and it's closed on weekday lunchtimes). Dotted throughout the neatly kept rooms of this friendly thatched ale house is the landlord's marvellous collection of lovely antique furnishings. The most interesting are in the L-shaped bar, where a beamed area round the corner past the counter has a whole cluster of them. One of the highlights is a magnificent, elaborately carved Jacobean settle which originally came from Aston Hall in Birmingham, carrying the motto *exaltavit humiles*. There's also a carved oak chimneypiece, and a couple of fine longcase clocks, one from Chester, and another with a nicely painted face and an almost silent movement from Manchester. The plain cream walls are hung with modern advertising mirrors and some older mirrors, and there are a few exotic knives, carpentry tools and so forth on the plastered structural beams; even when it's not particularly cold, there should be a good fire burning in the intricate cast-iron stove. Well kept Boddingtons and three regularly changing guests such as Cains Traditional, Wadworths 6X or Wards on handpump; darts in a sensible side area, dominoes, friendly cat. One or two picnic tables outside. *(Recommended by Graham Bush; more reports please)*

Free house ~ Licensee Brian Tatham ~ Real ale ~ No food ~ (01772) 690312 ~ Open 7pm-11; 12-4, 7-10.30 Sun

WHITEWELL (Lancs) SD6546 Map 7
Inn at Whitewell ★ ★ ⊙ ♉ ⇌

Most easily reached by B6246 from Whalley; road through Dunsop Bridge from B6478 is also good

Lancashire Dining Pub of the Year

The civilised atmosphere and the individual furnishings at this lovely hotel lend it the air of a hospitable country house. It houses a wine merchant (hence the unusually wide range of around 180 wines available – the claret is recommended) and an art gallery, and owns several miles of trout, salmon and sea trout fishing on the Hodder; with notice they'll arrange shooting. Perhaps most dramatically approached from

Abbeystead, it's beautifully set deep in the Forest of Bowland and surrounded by well wooded rolling hills set off against higher moors. Although it gets very busy, it's very spacious inside and out, so usually stays peaceful and relaxing. The old-fashioned pubby bar has antique settles, oak gateleg tables, sonorous clocks, old cricketing and sporting prints, log fires (the lounge has a very attractive stone fireplace), and heavy curtains on sturdy wooden rails; one area has a selection of newspapers, dominoes, local maps and guide books. There's a piano for anyone who wants to play. Down a corridor with strange objects like a stuffed fox disappearing into the wall is the pleasant suntrap garden, with wonderful views down to the valley. The public bar is being extended, and will probably be closed for the next year or more. Highly praised bar food includes soup (£2.80), open sandwiches (from £3.70), haddock with welsh rarebit (£5.20), stuffed roast peppers (£5.70), warm salad of bacon and mushrooms (£6), beef bourguignon or braised oxtail (£7.50), fish pie (£7.80), bacon chop with whisky sauce (£8.50), home-made puddings like chocolate roulade (£3) and hand-made farmhouse cheeses (from £3.50); the evening menu is just slightly different; they serve coffee and cream teas all day; very civil service. Well kept Boddingtons and Marstons Pedigree on hand or electric pump. Some of the spacious and beautifully refurbished bedrooms even have their own CD players. *(Recommended by Kathleen Newton, Miller, J A Boucher, Sarah Bradbury, Richard Fallon, J S M Sheldon, D M Sayers, Peter Walker, John and Barbara Burns, Keith and Judith Ashcroft, Paul McPherson, T Large, V Smith, Malcolm Taylor, Nigel Hopkins, John and Diana Davies, James Nunns, Michael and Alison Leyland; also in Good Hotel Guide)*

Free house ~ Licensee Richard Bowman ~ Real ale ~ Meals and snacks ~ Restaurant (not Sun lunchtime) ~ (01200) 448222 ~ Children welcome ~ Open 11-3, 6-11; 12-3, 7-11 Sun ~ Bedrooms: from £52B/£73B

YEALAND CONYERS (Lancs) SD5074 Map 7
New Inn 🍺

3 miles from M6 junction 35; village signposted off A6 N

We think that the imaginative well prepared bar food at this simple ivy-covered stone pub is rather good value considering the high standard and popularity of the cooking. Starters include marinated kidneys cooked in red wine, onions and mushrooms on leeks and topped with crispy croutons (£3.95), smoked duck breast, bobotie, fillet of sole wrapped round banana baked in single cream and topped with parmesan and herb crumble (£4.50), baked goat's cheese with diced black pudding, bacon and parmesan dressing (£4.65), main courses like potato bake or cumberland sausage (£6.50), tagliatelle with wild mushrooms, garlic, parmesan and olives or courgette and hazelnut roulade (£6.95), chicken breast filled with onion and apricot stuffing with a mushroom marsala sauce (£7.45) and puddings like chocolate tart with crème fraîche and sugared almonds or sticky toffee pudding (from £2.95) as well as daily specials such as apple, celery and tomato soup (£2.25), pork marinated in white wine cooked in tomato sauce with pineapple and onion (£6.95); good value Sunday lunch. There is a good professional reception, with the emphasis very clearly on dining. On the left is a simply furnished little beamed bar with a log fire in the big stone fireplace, and on the right are two communicating cottagey dining rooms with black furniture to match the shiny beams, an attractive kitchen range and another winter fire. The dining room is no smoking, and they've won awards for their ladies' lavatory. Well kept Robinsons Best, Hartleys XB, Hatters Mild and Old Tom on handpump, a good choice of around 30 malt whiskies, home-made lemonade in summer and mulled wine in winter. Dominoes, cribbage, piped music. A sheltered lawn at the side has picnic tables among roses and flowering shrubs. *(Recommended by M Buchanan, P A Legon, E Locker, David and Judy Walmsley, A C Chapman, Chris Walling, Paul and Maggie Baker, C McKerrow, Malcolm Taylor, Sue and Bob Ward, Eric Locker, Peter Walker, Rob and Ann Horley, Mike and Wendy Proctor, Angus Lyon, Yvonne and Mike Meadley, Charlotte Wrigley, Margaret Dyke, Mrs J Anderton, Louise Miller, Richard Waddington)*

Hartleys (Robinsons) ~ Tenant Annette Dutton ~ Real ale ~ Meals and snacks (all day in summer) ~ Restaurant ~ (01524) 732938 ~ Children welcome ~ Open 11-11; 12-10.30 Sun; winter weekdays 11-3, 5.30-11

Lucky Dip

Besides the fully inspected pubs, you might like to try these Lucky Dips recommended to us and described by readers (if you do, please send us reports):

☆ **Altrincham** Gtr Man [Navigation Rd, Broadheath; junction with Manchester Rd (A56); SJ7689], *Old Packet House*: Pleasantly restored local with attractive Victorianised decor, shiny black woodwork, good solid furnishings, turkey carpet, well kept Boddingtons and Websters, open fires, good bar food inc lots of sandwiches and well presented salads, some fresh-cooked hot dishes, nice plush back dining room, prompt friendly service; fruit machines, juke box; under same ownership as Dog at Peover Heath (see Cheshire main entries); small sheltered back terrace, well equipped bedrooms, good breakfast *(Dr and Mrs S Taylor, Ian Phillips, Erik Williams, BB)*
Appley Bridge Gtr Man [Station Approach; SD5210], *Old Station House*: Attractively furnished interesting conversion of station buildings, appetising range of home-made bar food inc ten soups, beef and bamboo sizzles, lovely brasserie with generous Sun roasts (children welcome), well kept Holts and Jennings, decent coffee *(Dr and Mrs B Baker)*
Ashton under Lyne Gtr Man [Mossley Rd; SJ9399], *Junction*: Attractive early 19th-c stonebuilt pub with welcoming low-ceilinged bar, hatch service to basic vault with darts and TV, comfortable lounge with local pictures (some for sale), well kept Robinsons Bitter, Frederics and Hatters Mild, food, friendly staff and locals, pool room; tables out in front, handy for walk to Hartshead Pike; open all day Fri/Sat *(Richard Lewis)*; [2 Warrington St], *Station*: Lots of railway memorabilia, handsome collection of pump clips and old snuff and cigarette tins; side food servery, back conservatory, friendly staff, good choice of home-cooked food, good range of well kept beers *(Richard Lewis)*
☆ **Barnston** Mer [Barnston Rd (A551); SJ2883], *Fox & Hounds*: Partly flagstoned long lounge bar with blacked range, copper kettles, china on delft shelf, intriguing hat collection, plush wall banquettes, good value quickly served straightforward food from ploughman's up inc very popular Sun lunch, well kept Scottish Courage and guest ales, lots of malt whiskies, comfortable restaurant area; pretty summer courtyard and garden with outside bar; by farm and lovely wooded dell *(Liz and Graham Bell, Jack Morley, Paul Boot, Douglas and Jean Troup)*
☆ **Bashall Eaves** [SD6943], *Red Pump*: Tucked-away country pub with very relaxed unpretentious atmosphere, friendly service, good interesting food inc good value Sun lunch, Whitbreads-related ales, two roaring log fires, no piped music, restaurant; two bedrooms, good breakfast, own fishing on River Hodder *(Drs Philip and Jane Davis, KC, John and Paula Whybrow, J A Boucher, Arthur and Margaret Dickinson)*
Birkenhead Mer [Claughton Firs, Oxton;

SJ3087], *Shrewsbury Arms*: Particularly well kept Cains and Whitbreads-related ales in friendly and bustling pub, spacious tastefully refurbished lounge and matching extension, good bar food; tables on terrace *(Liz and Graham Bell)*
☆ **Blacko** [A682 towards Gisburn; SD8541], *Moorcock*: Beautifully placed moorland pub with spaciously comfortable bar, big picture windows for breathtaking views, tables set close for the popular and often enterprising food inc lamb using meat from their own flock and some German dishes, decent wine but nitrokeg beers, hillside garden with various animals; open all day Sun, children welcome, bedrooms *(David Shillitoe, Gwen and Peter Andrews, B A Hayward, Arthur and Margaret Dickinson, Sarah Bradbury, Brian Wainwright)*
Blackpool [204 Talbot Rd; opp Blackpool North stn; SD3035], *Ramsden Arms*: Attractive decor with masses of bric-a-brac and pictures, friendly helpful staff, no-smoking area, well kept cheap house beer, also Boddingtons, Jennings, Tetleys and guest ales, over 40 whiskies, CD juke box, games; good value bedrooms *(Andy Hazeldine)*
Blacksnape [Blacksnape Rd; Roman rd above Darwen – OS Sheet 103 map ref 712215; SD7121], *Red Lion*: Cosy bar, well kept Burtonwood and occasional guest beers, wide range of good food esp giant filled yorkshire puddings, good puddings, dining area; high moorland setting *(Mrs M Mcgurk, Dr K M Buchanan)*
Bolton Gtr Man [1 Higher Bridge St; SD7108], *Moat House*: Hotel, but worth knowing for good value bar snacks; bedrooms *(Gordon Tong)*
Bolton le Sands [Main Rd (A6); SD4868], *Royal*: Well furnished, flame-effect fires, well kept Mitchells, good value lunches, pool; car park across rd *(P A Legon)*
☆ **Brierfield** [Burnley Rd (A682), just off M65 junction 12; SD8436], *Waggon & Horses*: Prettily restored and cosy late Victorian small-roomed local, lots of interest, well kept Thwaites Bitter, Craftsman and Mild, good malt whiskies, warm fires; bar food (not evenings Sun-Weds), children allowed away from servery, open all day Fri/Sat *(Alan and Charlotte Sykes, LYM)*
☆ nr **Bury** [Nangreaves; off A56/A666 N under a mile E of M66 junction 1, down cobbled track; SD8115], *Lord Raglan*: Notable for its lonely moorside location, with great views; enjoyable varied food inc fresh veg, well kept mainly Scottish Courage ales, interesting foreign bottled beers, lots of bric-a-brac in traditional front bar, big open fire in back room, plainer blond-panelled dining room (where children allowed) *(RJH, P M Lane, LYM)*
Catforth [SD4736], *Running Pump*: Small

pub with real atmosphere, good home-made bar food, well kept Robinsons; separate restaurant *(Dr and Mrs D Awbery)*

Cheadle Hulme Gtr Man [Ladybridge Rd; SJ8787], *Old Mill*: Modern steakhouse-style building with high roof, lots of rustic timber and stonework, but quite a range of well kept ales such as Batemans XB, Everards Beacon, Ind Coope Burton, Jennings Snecklifter, Oak Thirsty Moon *(Richard Lewis)*

Churchtown [nr church off A586 Garstang—St Michaels on Wyre; SD4843], *Punchbowl*: Good choice of good food in attractive mock-Tudor beamed pub/restaurant with panelling, stained glass, lots of stuffed animals; friendly staff, well kept Tetleys and Dark Mild, good fires; lavatory for disabled people; lovely village *(J A Boucher)*

☆ **Conder Green** [Cockerham Rd (A588); not far from M6 junction 33; SD4556], *Stork*: Rambling and convivial 17th-c pub, isolated (but very popular) and unspoilt, with good views from outside seats; several cosy panelled rooms, Boddingtons and Tetleys, good coffee, good generous home cooking inc wide vegetarian choice in bar or separate dining room; good service even on crowded Sat night; bedrooms, nr Lune estuary and Glasson Dock *(Tony Hobden, Ann Franklin, Dr and Mrs D Awbery)*

☆ **Cowan Bridge** [Burrow by Burrow; A65 towards Kirkby Lonsdale; SD6277], *Whoop Hall*: Spacious, airy and comfortable open-plan bar with interesting quick food inc decent vegetarian choice all day from 8am from popular buttery, well kept Boddingtons and Theakstons Best and XB, decent wines, pleasant restaurant, friendly service; tables in garden well off road, with play area; children allowed in eating area; well appointed bedrooms *(John Davidson, LYM)*

Croston [by rly stn; SD4818], *De Trafford Arms*: Big comfortable local with well kept Whitbreads-related and guest ales, side pool/games room, bar snacks *(Richard Lewis)*

☆ **nr Darwen** [Roman Rd, Grimehills; SD7120], *Crown & Thistle*: Small and cosy two-room country dining pub with good if not cheap food (all tables set for diners, must book Fri/Sat), friendly accommodating staff, fresh flowers, moorland views, well kept Thwaites Bitter and Mild, lovely log fires *(Nigel and Amanda Thorp, Neville Kenyon)*

Delph Gtr Man [Huddersfield Rd (A62); SE0009], *Old Bell*: Good if not cheap restaurant food with emphasis on seafood, comfortable bar, good choice of beers such as Boddingtons and Timothy Taylors Landlord, friendly efficient service *(Ian and Karen Hargreaves)*

☆ **Denshaw** Gtr Man [Rippenden Rd; 2 miles from M62 junction 2; A672 towards Oldham, pub N of village; SD9710], *Rams Head*: Cosy and comfortable moorland farm/pub with several small rooms mainly for diners (good food), with well kept Theakstons, Timothy Taylors and maybe a guest beer, good range of wines by bottle and glass, bric-a-brac on

beams and panelling, log fires, traditional settles, unobtrusive piped music; on special days eg Mothering Sunday dining room may be fully booked with no bar snacks served, but otherwise popular with walkers – lovely scenery, good walking; has been cl weekday lunchtimes *(Nancy Cleave, Edward Leetham, LYM)*

☆ **Diggle** Gtr Man [Diglea Hamlet, Sam Rd; village signed off A670 just N of Dobcross; SE0008], *Diggle Hotel*: Modernised three-room hillside pub popular lunchtime and early evening for food from sandwiches up inc generous Sun roasts and children's dishes; well kept Oldham and Timothy Taylors Golden Best and Landlord, decent wines, good choice of malt whiskies, good coffee, prompt friendly service, soft piped music, rustic fairy-lit tables among the trees, quiet spot just below the moors; opens noon *(Chris Westmoreland, BB)*

Dolphinholme [back rds, a couple of miles from M6 junction 33; SD5153], *Fleece*: Friendly hotel with comfortably worn-in beamed lounge, bar with darts and table skittles, open fire, well kept Mitchells Best and Special, friendly atmosphere, tasty bar food, dining area (no hot food Mon lunchtime); bedrooms *(Gregg Davies, Tony Hobden)*

☆ **Dukinfield** Gtr Man [Globe Sq; SJ9497], *Globe*: Welcoming family-run pub with good value generous home cooking, well kept John Smiths and Tetleys, comfortable bustle, games room; children welcome, open all day weekdays, bedrooms clean and comfortable, attractive surroundings nr Lower Peak Forest Canal *(J F M West)*

Dunham Town Gtr Man [OS Sheet 109 map ref 740881; SJ7488], *Axe & Cleaver*: Big 19th-c country house knocked into spacious open-plan family dining pub, decent food inc particularly good veg, Scottish Courage ales, conservatory; piped music, garden with play area and maybe bouncy castle; handy for nearby Dunham Massey Hall *(Phil and Dilys Unsworth)*

Eccles Gtr Man [Liverpool Rd, Peel Grn; A57 ½ mile from M63 junction 2; SJ7798], *Grapes*: Magnificent Edwardian local, warmly welcoming, with fairly quiet lounge and smoke room, pool room, vault with Manchester darts (can get quite loud and smoky), drinking corridor; good value Holts, plenty of mahogany, finely etched glass and intricate tilework *(Pete Baker)*; [33 Regent St (A57 – handy for M602 junction 2)], *Lamb*: Untouched Edwardian Holts local with splendid etched windows, fine woodwork and furnishings; cheap well kept beer, full-size snooker table *(Jack and Philip Paxton)*; [133 Liverpool Rd, Patricroft], *White Lion*: Classic Edwardian Holts local with drinking corridor, games in lively vaults bar, separate smoke room (with weekend sing-songs) and quiet lounge *(JP, PP, PB)*

Eccleston [Towngate; B5250, off A581 Chorley—Southport; SD5117], *Farmers*

Arms: Big friendly low-beamed pub/restaurant, modernised but keeping character – black cottagey furniture, red plush wall seats, rough plaster covered with plates, pastoral prints, clocks and brasses; well kept largely Whitbreads-related ales, wide choice of popular if not cheap food all day, darts; parking can be a problem when busy; bedrooms *(Derek Stafford)*

Entwistle [Overshores Rd; village signed off Blackburn Rd N of Edgworth – OS Sheet 109 map ref 726177; SD7217], *Strawbury Duck*: Cosy dim-lit beamed and flagstoned country pub by isolated station – trains from Blackburn and Bolton; well kept Boddingtons, Moorhouses Pendle Witches Brew, Timothy Taylors Best and Landlord and a house beer, bar food (all day Sat and Sun) inc children's; games room, no-smoking lounge, restaurant, good unobtrusive piped music (live Thurs), tables outside; children till 8.30; cl Mon lunchtime; comfortable bedrooms, big sizzling breakfasts, good Pennine walks *(Dr and Mrs B Baker, LYM)*

Fleetwood [The Esplanade; nr tram terminus; SD3247], *North Euston*: Big comfortably refurbished bar in architecturally interesting Victorian hotel overlooking seafront, decent lunchtime food, well kept mainstream real ales, no-smoking family area (till 7), seats outside; bedrooms *(Brian Wainwright, Andy Hazeldine)*

Formby Mer [1 Massams Lane; SD2808], *Freshfield*: Friendly Hogshead real ale pub enjoyably refurbished in 'spit & sawdust' style, open all day, very popular esp weekends; good choice of well kept beers, viewing room showing casks and brewing process, good value food; quiz nights, darts *(Richard Lewis)*

Greasby Mer [Hillbark Rd/Montgomery Hill; SJ2587], *Farmers Arms*: Extended and refurbished two-bar country pub with welcoming enthusiastic service, well kept ales such as Boddingtons Mild and Bitter, Cains, Flowers IPA, Fullers London Pride, Jennings Cocker Hoop, Marstons Pedigree, Mitchells Best, summer bar food, plenty of tables outside – enclosed garden, play area, big lawn *(E G Parish, Richard Lewis)*

Great Mitton [Mitton Rd (B6246 NW of Whalley); SD7139], *Aspinall Arms*: Popular pub with big garden by River Ribble; well kept Timothy Taylors and Whitbreads Castle Eden, decent food inc good value sandwiches and good puddings, magazines to read; children welcome away from bar; bedrooms *(Arthur and Margaret Dickinson)*; [Mitton Hall, Mitton Rd], *Owd Neds*: Good value generous food all day inc vegetarian, well kept Boddingtons and Jennings, helpful staff, flagstoned bar, big conservatory, tables on terrace, plenty of space for children in informal grounds with stream and woodland; part of mansion which includes restaurant, frequent entertainment, bedrooms *(Arthur and Margaret Dickinson, Simon Woodhouse, Maria Dobson)*

Grindleton [off A69 via Chatburn; SD7545], *Duke of York*: Smart, cheery and bright old pub in attractive Ribble Valley countryside, personable landlady, various areas inc one with open fire, Tetleys and Whitbreads Castle Eden, good food from sandwiches up, homely attentive staff, separate dining room *(RJH)*

Haskayne [Rosemary Lane; just off A567 – OS Sheet 108 map ref 364082; SD3608], *Ship*: Useful canalside pub comfortably refurbished with navigation lights, ship models etc, two cosy rooms, two more airy, prompt courteous service, well cooked usual food *(Olive and Ray Hebson, Keith and Judith Ashcroft)*

☆ **Hawkshaw** Gtr Man [91 Ramsbottom Rd; SD7615], *Red Lion*: Attractively renovated, with good reasonably priced home cooking in bar and restaurant (popular with OAPs lunchtime), well kept Thwaites, Timothy Taylors and Charles Wells beers, friendly staff; comfortable bedrooms, quiet spot by River Irwell *(Mr and Mrs D C Stevens, Gordon Tong)*

☆ **Heskin Green** [Wood Lane; B5250, N of M6 junction 27; SD5214], *Farmers Arms*: Cheerful sparkling clean country pub, spacious but cosy (and does get packed weekends), with wide choice of well kept Whitbreads-related and good guest ales, heavy black beams, brasses and china, very wide choice of good value home cooking (even local ostrich) inc nicely cooked veg in two-level dining area, very friendly staff; picnic tables outside, good play area, pets' corner from pigs to peacocks; open 12-11 *(Pat Woodward, BB)*

☆ **Heswall** Mer [2 Telegraph Rd; SJ2781], *Devon Doorway*: Smart thatched and low-beamed country pub, inglenook log fire, pine tables on flagstones, carpeted restaurant area, interesting range of good well priced meals inc two vegetarian dishes, well kept real ales, very good choice of wines by the glass and bin ends, good coffee, extremely courteous staff, newspapers, no music or machines; back and front gardens *(Liz and Graham Bell, Mr and Mrs Gordon McConnell)*

☆ **Holden** [the one up by Bolton by Bowland – OS Sheet 103 map ref 777494; SD7749], *Copy Nook*: Spick-and-span roomy and well renovated roadside pub with efficient obliging staff, wide choice of good food, well kept Tetleys *(John and Joan Wyatt)*

Hoylake Mer [Stanley Rd, Kings Gap; SJ2289], *Green Lodge*: Famous old hotel associated with nearby Royal Liverpool golf links; recently refurbished, usual bar food and well kept Burtonwood; handy for the beautiful Hoylake beach and Red Rocks Nature Reserve; bedrooms *(Liz Bell)*

☆ **Hurst Green** [off B6243 Longridge—Clitheroe, towards Stoneyhurst Coll; SD6838], *Bayley Arms*: Sympathetically renovated carpeted bar with attractive mix of old furniture, sporting and music memorabilia, brasses, log fire; enjoyable good value bar food inc children's, several mainly

Whitbreads-related ales, more formal restaurant, friendly licensees, smart staff; comfortable bedrooms, attractive Ribble valley village *(RJH, Ann and Frank Bowman)*

☆ **Hurst Green** [Longridge Rd (B6243)], *Punch Bowl*: Very well run and welcoming, with good choice of food inc vegetarian, imaginative daily specials, Mon bargains, good value Sun high tea, nook-and-cranny eating areas off pleasant bar as well as big Jacobean dining room with minstrel gallery, heraldic shields on walls, tables out on spacious lawn; bedrooms *(Arthur and Margaret Dickinson, Chris Walling)*

Hurst Green [OS Sheet 103 map ref 685379], *Shireburn Arms*: Quiet comfortable 17th-c hotel in idyllic setting with panoramic Ribble valley views, good reasonably priced food, Thwaites and other ales; separate tea room, occasional pianist, lovely neatly kept back garden and terrace, safe low-key play area; bedrooms *(Arthur and Margaret Dickinson)*

☆ **Irby** Mer [Irby Mill Hill, off Greasby rd; SJ2684], *Irby Mill*: Well kept Bass, Boddingtons, Cains Bitter and Dark Mild, Jennings and two interesting weekly guest beers, good house wines and decent generous fresh-cooked lunchtime food (not Sun) in four low-beamed largely flagstoned rooms, comfortable pub furniture, coal-effect gas fire, relaxed local atmosphere, interesting old photographs and history of the former mill, a few tables outside *(Liz and Graham Bell, Mike Waring, Paul Boot, Graham and Lynn Mason, Robert Campbell, BB)*

☆ **Lathom** [Wheat Lane, off A5209; Parbold Rd after Ring o' Bells heading into Burscough; SD4511], *Ship*: Big busy well run pub tucked below canal embankment, several separate rooms with decor varying from interestingly cluttered canal memorabilia through naval pictures and crests to hunting prints, lots of copper and brass, cheap popular lunchtime food (not Sun) served promptly, friendly staff, ten well kept changing ales, often interesting; games room *(Mr and Mrs A Craig, Nancy Cleave, Edward Leetham, Julie and Steve Anderton, BB)*

Leigh Gtr Man [Twist Lane; SJ6699], *Waterside*: Converted 19th-c canalside warehouses handy for indoor and outdoor markets, plenty of tables by Leigh branch of Liverpool—Leeds Canal, lots of ducks and swans; wide choice of food popular at lunchtime with office workers and shoppers, Boddingtons and Robinsons Hatters Mild *(Colin and Sue Graham)*

Limbrick [off A6 at Adlington; SD6016], *Black Horse*: Tastefully restored old-world up and down low-ceilinged pub, the first recorded in Lancs (1577); good wholesome food, Scottish Courage ales, garden behind; open all day *(Dr J Morley)*

Little Eccleston [Cartford Lane; off A586 Garstang—Blackpool, by toll bridge; SD4139], *Cartford*: In scenic countryside by toll bridge on River Wyre (hosts fishing nights), very busy esp weekends; oak beams

and dried flowers, well kept changing guest beers alongside its Hart ales brewed here, two of its three floors set with tables for reasonably priced generous food inc vegetarian and children's; quiet juke box, pool, tables outside (not by water), play area; well equipped bedrooms *(Harry Gleave)*

☆ **Liverpool** [Grafton St], *Cains Brewery Tap*: Splendidly restored Victorian architecture with nicely understated decor, wooden floors, plush raised side snug, lots of old prints, wonderful bar, flame-effect gas fire, newspapers; cosy relaxing atmosphere, friendly staff, good well priced food, and above all well kept attractively priced Cains ales with guest beers from other small breweries; popular brewery tour ending here with buffet and singing; sports TV *(Richard Lewis)*

☆ **Liverpool** [Albert Dock Complex], *Pump House*: Relaxing multi-level conversion of dock building, good Mersey views, lots of polished dark wood, bare bricks, mezzanine and upper gallery with exposed roof trusses; marble counter with bulbous beer engines and brass rail supported by elephants' heads, tall chimney; wide choice of generous cheeses, some hot food, friendly efficient service; waterside tables, boat trips in season; keg beers, busy weekend evenings *(John Fazakerley, Brian Kneale)*

Liverpool [Wood St], *Beluga*: More wine bar than pub, in basement of refurbished warehouse; bare boards, spartan decoration, superb food *(Brian Kneale)*; [Berry St], *Brewery*: Open-plan bare-boards late Victorian pub brewing its own good ales – front window shows brewery, tours available; real fire, friendly staff, good value food, games machines, juke box *(Richard Lewis)*; [13 Rice St], *Cracke*: Attractively basic, bare boards, walls covered with posters for local events and pictures of local buildings, unusual Beatles diorama in largest room, juke box and TV, very cheap lunchtime food, well kept Marstons Pedigree; popular mainly with young people; sizeable garden *(Eric and Jackie Robinson, Simon Curran)*; [43 Lime St], *Florin & Firkin*: Lots of barrels, bare boards, brewery memorabilia, newspapers, carefully restored ceiling, copper panelled bar, good choice of food, Firkin beers, Addlestone's cider *(Richard Lewis)*; [Quarry Lane, Woolton], *Grapes*: Welcoming local, sympathetically restored to keep much of the original fabric; well kept Walkers *(Chris Raisin)*; [Albert Dock], *Harveys*: Spacious underground pub, comfortable and well designed *(Eric and Jackie Robinson)*; [Dale St], *Rigbys*: Beamed and panelled character bar in large preserved 18th-c former coaching inn, said to be Liverpool's oldest surviving pub; cheap lunchtime meals, well kept Tetleys *(Eric and Jackie Robinson)*; [Dale St], *Ship & Mitre*: Friendly local with very wide changing choice of well kept unusual beers served in over-sized lined glasses, good cheap basic food, pool, occasional beer festivals *(Richard*

Lewis)

☆ **Manchester** [Shambles Sq, Arndale Centre], *Sinclairs*: Timeless 18th-c pub with lots of snugs and dining areas, low ceilings, squared oak panelling, traditional furnishings, tall marble-topped eating bar, larger room upstairs with low wall settles, scrolly old leather settee, small no-smoking dining room; good cheap food (12-8 weekdays, 11-3 Sat, 12-5 Sun), well kept Sam Smiths OB, neat friendly service, dominoes, cribbage etc; children welcome till 7, open all day, picnic tables outside; may be moved (again) during the Arndale rebuilding *(John Fazakerley, Richard Lewis, Tom McLean, E M Walton, LYM)*

☆ **Manchester** [50 Great Bridgewater St; corner of Lower Mosley St], *Britons Protection*: Chatty, genuine and well run by long-serving licensees, with fine tilework, solid woodwork and elaborate plastering in rather plush front bar, attractive softly lit inner lounge with coal-effect gas fire, battle murals in passage leading to it; exceptional choice of whiskies, well kept Jennings, Robinsons and Tetleys, good wines, good home-cooked bar lunches, reasonable prices, no juke box or machines, tables outside behind; old-time music hall first Tues of month, otherwise quiet and relaxed evenings, handy for Bridgewater Hall and GMEX centre *(Richard Lewis, Ian Phillips, BB)*

☆ **Manchester** [127 Gt Bridgewater St (Oxford St side)], *Peveril of the Peak*: Three traditional rooms around central servery, busy lunchtime but welcoming and homely evenings, with cheap basic lunchtime food (not Sun), very welcoming family service, log fire, well kept Scottish Courage ales (but three Guinness pumps too now, and Irish music); lots of mahogany, mirrors and stained glass, sturdy furnishings, interesting pictures, pub games inc table football, juke box; splendidly lurid green external tilework, seats outside; children welcome, cl weekend lunchtimes *(Ian Phillips, Richard Lewis, BB)*

☆ **Manchester** [6 Angel St; off Rochdale Rd], *Beer House*: Lively basic real-ale pub with ten or so well kept changing ones (extra in summer), also three farm ciders, several Belgian beers on tap, good range of bottled foreign beers, country wines, cheap spirits doubles (wide choice); bare boards, lots of seating, friendly staff, old local prints, good CD juke box, bar billiards, darts, robust cheap lunchtime bar food inc vegetarian (bargains Mon, free chip butties Weds early evening, curries Thurs evening, cheap cheerful food Fri evening) *(John Hallam, Richard Lewis)*

☆ **Manchester** [Honey St, off Red Bank, nr Victoria Stn], *Queens Arms*: Well preserved Empress Brewery tiled facade for unusually welcoming extended pub with well kept Batemans Mild and XXXB, Federation Buchanans Mild and Special, Mitchells and Timothy Taylors Landlord and Best, several Belgian beers on tap, Weston's farm cider, simple but often unusual lunchtime and evening bar food, coal fire, bar billiards, backgammon, chess, good juke box; children welcome, open all day weekdays; unexpected views of Manchester across the Irk Valley and its railway lines from pleasant garden with good play area, worth penetrating the surrounding viaducts, scrapyards and industrial premises *(Richard Lewis)*

Manchester [1 York St], *Athenaeum*: Well restored with brass and mahogany fittings, ornate high ceilings, well kept Tetleys-related ales, quite a few wines, good food under separate franchise – big salad table with up to 50 help-yourself salads, 25 cheeses, 5 pâtés and 8 quiches, also next door restaurant; very busy Fri *(Roser Ward)*; [2 Audenshaw Rd (B6390), Guide Bridge; SJ8896], *Boundary*: Imposing pub extended over the years, two main rooms and traditional vault with games, long lounge with wide range of good honest generous pub food, well kept ales such as Cotleigh Harrier, Hadrian Gladiator, Phoenix Wobbly Bob, John Smiths *(Richard Lewis)*; [Church Lane, Prestwich; SD8103], *Church*: Classic Victorian pub, three unspoilt rooms with a villagey feel, well kept Holts and friendly staff; attractive location, shame about the piped music *(Alan Gough)*; [86 Portland St], *Circus*: Two tiny rooms, back one panelled with leatherette banquettes, very well kept Tetleys from minute corridor bar, friendly landlord, no music or machines; often looks closed but normally open all day weekdays (you have to knock) *(PGP, Richard Lewis, Ian Phillips)*; [48 Kennedy St], *City Arms*: Well kept Ind Coope Burton, Tetleys and interesting changing guest beers, Belgian bottled beers, occasional beer festivals, popular bar lunches, quiet evenings; bare boards, wheelchair access but steps down to back lounge, open all day (cl Sat afternoon, Sun) *(PGP, Richard Lewis)*; [14 Albion St, cnr Whitworth St], *City Road*: Impressive exterior, bare boards and panelling inside, well kept Boddingtons, Morlands Old Speckled Hen and a cheap beer brewed for the pub, games machines, pool, piped music, friendly staff, bar food; open all day *(Richard Lewis)*; [227 Belle Vue St (A57), Gorton; SJ8796], *Coach & Horses*: Warm, welcoming two-room local with fine tiled bar, well kept Robinsons Bitter and Hatters Mild, darts, cards, juke box in lounge, TV in vault; open all day weekends, cl weekday lunchtimes *(Richard Lewis)*; [192 Corporation St], *Crown & Cushion*: Comfortable open-plan local with cheap Holts Bitter and Mild, darts, friendly staff *(Richard Lewis)*; [Collier St, off Greengate, Salford], *Eagle*: Seems untouched since the 1950s, absolutely no frills, well kept Holts Bitter and Mild at old-fashioned prices, bar servery to tap and passage with comfortable snug, old Salford pictures, very friendly manager, cheap filled rolls *(Alan Gough)*; [137 Grosvenor St], *Footage & Firkin*: Cinema conversion, brewing memorabilia, reasonably priced food, well kept beers, SkyTV, balcony seating; open all day (to midnight Mon/Tues, 2am Weds-Sat) *(Richard Lewis)*; [High St, opp Arndale Centre], *Hogshead*: Bare-boards alehouse conversion with cask seats, good interesting range of real ales, lots of bottled beers, country wines, food all day; pool, friendly staff *(Richard Lewis)*; [47 Ducie St], *Jolly Angler*: Unpretentious backstreet local, small and friendly, with well kept Hydes, pool and darts, informal folk singing Mon, open all day Fri/Sat *(PB)*; [106 Princess St], *Joshua Brookes*: Brightly decorated American-style printworks conversion, well kept ales inc Flowers IPA and Tetleys, dozens of flavoured vodkas, decent wines, bar food, friendly staff; wheelchair access, open all day *(Richard Lewis)*; [40 Chorlton St], *Mash & Air*: Futuristic new bar reminiscent of set of Starship Enterprise, built around a microbrewery; good upmarket bistro food, value for money but not cheap, decent house wines, restaurant *(J F M West)*; [68 Deansgate], *Moon Under Water*: Impressive Wetherspoons cinema conversion, superb ceiling, lovely plasterwork, masses of room inc balcony, no-smoking area; good choice of food all day, friendly efficient staff, well kept beers, sensible prices *(Richard Lewis, Jennifer Nelhans)*; [520 Manchester Rd (A6), Wardley, W of Swinton; SD7602], *Morning Star*: Busy Holts local, well kept ales, good value basic food weekday lunchtime, lively games-oriented bar, usually some Sat entertainment in lounge *(PB)*; [33 Back Piccadilly], *Mother Macs*: Comfortably solid backstreet local, very welcoming to strangers, with tall etched glass windows, old local photographs, cheap weekday bar food inc huge baps and generous cheap hot dishes, Boddingtons, Chesters Best and Flowers IPA; piped music, TV; open all day (12-3 Sun) *(Alan Gough, PGP)*; [52 Cross St], *Mr Thomas Chop House*: Popular food from fresh hot beef sandwiches to steaks in busy oak-panelled bare-boards front bar and Victorian tiled back dining room with shellfish bar; well kept Boddingtons and Tetleys, decent wines, no-smoking area, open all day *(Richard Lewis, BB)*; [90 Portland St], *Old Monkey*: Two-floor traditional Holts pub, built 1993 but you'd never guess from the etched glass and mosaic tiling; interesting memorabilia, well kept cheap Bitter and Mild, low-priced food, warm hospitality, wide mix of customers *(Richard Lewis, P A Legon, Ian Phillips)*; [2 Adelphi St, Salford], *Old Pint Pot*: By River Irwell, brewing its own Bens Best and Old Pint Pot; bare boards, brewing memorabilia, views into brewery, big glass conservatory, friendly staff, food inc early evening bargains *(Richard Lewis)*; [Shambles Sq, behind Arndale off Market St in centre], *Old Wellington*: Genuinely ancient, with flagstones, gnarled oak timbers, oak panelling; well kept Bass and Stones, bar food (from noon, not Sun) esp hot beef sandwiches, small upstairs carvery; may have to be moved for Arndale rebuilding; open all

day, tables outside, often packed lunchtime *(Richard Lewis, BB)*; [by Metro Stn, Heaton Park; SD8103], *Ostrich*: Very old Holts pub, with their Bitter and Mild kept well *(Alan Gough)*; [36 New Mount St], *Pot of Beer*: Former Harp & Shamrock reopened after closure, attractively done out with exposed timber and brickwork, bare boards, open fire and well kept ales such as Cains Best, Cambrian Best, Robinsons Dark Mild, Ryburn Best and Titanic White Star tapped from visible casks mounted in temperature-controlled chamber; good piped music, plans for food and tables outside *(Richard Lewis)*; [43 Spring Gdns, top of King St], *Rothwells*: Converted 19th-c banking hall with granite columns and white Portland stone, superb ceiling, carved solid oak bar, tiled floor, lots of comfortable seating inc armchairs and raised front area overlooking street; good value food, good choice of well kept Marstons beers; open all day Mon-Sat, with early breakfasts *(Richard Lewis)*; [126 Grosvenor St], *Scruffy Murphys*: Huge pastiche of Irish pub, several levels, nooks and crannies, loud piped Irish folk music and Gaelic pipes, good value bar food, Tetleys and other real ales, decent house wine *(Ian Phillips, John Wooll)*; [50 New Wakefield St], *Thirsty Scholar*: Under Oxford Road station railway lines, bare boards, cask tables, lots of prints, newspapers, good juke box, sound basic food with good choice of filled rolls, friendly staff, well kept ales such as Boddingtons, Moorhouses Peter Yates and Timothy Taylors Landlord; SkyTV; open all day *(Richard Lewis)*; [12 Gore St], *Waldorf*: Modernised but not spoilt, central bar, alcove areas, busy friendly staff, wide choice of food, well kept Boddingtons and Chesters Mild; games machines, music nights *(Richard Lewis)*; [139 Barlow Moor Rd, Didsbury; SJ8591], *Woodstock*: Impressive conversion of roomy 1920s house hidden from road by trees, Bass and other real ales, drinks table service after 8pm, good value generous food all day from vegetarian to kangaroo, deep leather sofas and family portraits, friendly even when busy; picnic tables outside *(Clare Wilson, Wendy and Jan Phillips)*; [Bury Old Rd, Prestwich, by Heaton Pk main gate; SD8103], *Woodthorpe*: Huge Victorian pile, former home of Holts brewing family, extensively refurbished 1993 without altering character; main room still has original Gothick fireplace with log fires, exterior has lots of terracotta decoration; well kept cheap Holts and guest beers, friendly fast service, good bar food, good restaurant *(Dennis D'Vigne, Alan Gough)*

☆ **Marple**, Gtr Man [off A626 via Church Lane, following The Ridge signs – OS Sheet 109 map ref 963862; SJ9686], *Romper*: Beautifully placed country dining pub above Peak Forest Canal in Goyt Valley, four softly lit knocked-through oak-beamed rooms, reliable generous food (all day Sun) inc plenty of vegetarian, well kept Boddingtons,

Marstons Pedigree, Theakstons Old Peculier and Timothy Taylors Landlord, decent wines and malt whiskies, efficient friendly staff; tables outside, opens noon *(Meg and Colin Hamilton, Pat and Tony Martin, C H and P Stride, M Buchanan, Kathy and Steven Barker, LYM)*

Marple Bridge Gtr Man [SJ9689], *George*: Clean and well run, with good food at low prices, nice furnishings, Robinsons Bitter and Mild *(Derek Wood)*

☆ **Mawdesley** [Bluestone Lane; follow Eccleston sign from village which is signed off B5246 Parbold—Rufford; SD5016], *Robin Hood*: Busy, neat and comfortable open-plan dining pub with button-back wall banquettes, reproduction Victorian prints, decorative plates, stained-glass seat dividers, some stripped stone; good value generous straightforward home cooking with fresh veg and cheap children's helpings, small pretty upstairs restaurant (often booked well ahead), good friendly service, well kept Whitbreads-related and good guest ales, decent wines, children's room; piped nostalgic pop music, fruit machine; picnic tables on neat side terrace, good fenced play area *(Kevin Potts, BB)*

Morecambe [19 Bare Lane, Bare; SD4665], *Dog & Partridge*: Friendly traditional layout, ten real ales inc Boddingtons and Timothy Taylors, freshly cooked standardised food; can get crowded weekends *(P A Legon)*

☆ **Mottram** Gtr Man [off A57 M'ter—Barnsley; at central traffic lights turn opp B6174 into Broadbottom Rd; SJ9995], *Waggon*: Generous reliable food served very promptly all day in comfortable open-plan local, sensible prices, well kept Robinsons Best and Best Mild on electric pump, friendly waitresses, big central fire, good wheelchair access; picnic tables and good play area outside *(A Preston, LYM)*

☆ **Much Hoole** [Liverpool Old Rd; SD4723], *Rose & Crown*: Huge squarish pitched-roof family dining pub recently taken over by its chefs, welcoming service, good home-cooked food using fresh ingredients, Greenalls and Tetleys ales; bar food inc sandwiches lunchtime and early evening in plain locals' bar (refurbishment planned), piped pop music and games area; cl Mon exc bank hols *(Janet Lee, Jim and Maggie Cowell, Janet Robinson, BB)*

New Brighton Mer [Victoria Rd; SJ2994], *Old Mother Redcaps*: Recently refurbished seafront pub with well kept Vaux Samson and Waggle Dance and Wards Best, friendly staff and locals, bar food, raised side lounge *(Richard Lewis)*

Newburgh [SD4710], *Red Lion*: Extensively refurbished Burtonwood dining pub, useful food all day, piped music, cheerful service, bedrooms *(Comus Elliott, BB)*

nr **Oldham** Gtr Man [Grains Bar, A672/B6197; SD9608], *Bulls Head*: Snug two-room moorland pub with good home cooking inc real chips, open fire, Disney plates, fish pictures, live music some evenings,

pitch and putt, walks in nearby open country *(Pauline Crossland, Dave Cawley, LYM)*

Ormskirk [County Rd; SD4108], *Hayfield*: Relaxing refurbished pub with character American manager, friendly efficient staff, Scottish Courage ales and up to 10 guest beers, good range of food; promotional nights, occasional live music *(Julie and Steve Anderton)*

Orrell Gtr Man [A577 Wigan—Ormskirk, nr M6 junction 26; SD5203], *Priory Wood*: Beefeater in former 18th-c convent school, decor takes up school theme with notices, photographs etc; fair choice of ales, decent food and service; bedrooms in attached Travel Inn *(Thomas and Audrey Nott)*

Parbold [SD4911], *Windmill*: Convivial, old and cosy, with several small rooms, open fires, lots of brass and pewter hanging from beams and walls; well kept Greenalls, wide range of good value generous food, friendly rugby-enthusiast landlord; by Leeds—Liverpool Canal *(Comus Elliott, Brian Kneale)*

Paythorne [off A582 N of Gisburn; SD8351], *Buck*: Country pub doing well under newish owners, generous home-made food, real fire, real ales; outside seating *(Arthur and Margaret Dickinson)*

Pleasington [Pleasington Lane; SD6426], *Railway*: Good variety of wholesome plain food, friendly landlord *(Nancy Cleave, Edward Leetham)*

Preston [166 Friargate], *Black Horse*: Thriving friendly old-fashioned pub with full Robinsons ale range and Hartleys XB, lunchtime food, side rooms, upstairs 1920s-style bar, unusual curved and tiled Victorian main bar, panelling, stained glass, mosaic floor and small rooms off; pictures of old town, lots of artefacts, good juke box, open all day *(Andy Hazeldine, Richard Lewis)*; [Corn Exchange], *Flax & Firkin*: Impressive refurbishment of former Corn Exchange, tall brick building with bare boards, high ceilings, elaborate cornices, brewing memorabilia, plenty of seats, well kept Flax, Bobbin, Reel and of course Dogbolter from back microbrewery, daily papers, games machines, bar food, friendly efficient staff, working red telephone box; tables outside, some live music; open all day *(Richard Lewis)*; [15 Fox St], *Fox & Grapes*: Busy traditional pub with bare boards, basic fittings, old Preston prints, panelling, cheap lunchtime food, friendly staff, well kept Scottish Courage ales with guests such as Bushys Old Bushy Tail, Charles Wells Bombardier; juke box, pub games, can get smoky, open all day *(Richard Lewis)*; [99 Fylde Rd], *Hogshead*: Former millowner's house superbly restored by Whitbreads as one of the best in their bare-boards wood-and-bricks alehouse chain, a dozen or more changing well kept ales mainly from small breweries, big window into cellar where casks tilt automatically; no music or games, lots of old photographs, friendly staff, food served 11-7 (not Sun), chef happy to make things not on menu; open all day, lots of picnic tables outside *(Richard Lewis, Andrew Watt, Comus Elliot)*; [Friargate], *Lamb & Packet*: Well kept Thwaites ales in cosy two-level pub, pleasant decor, low-priced food, friendly staff, juke box *(Richard Lewis)*; [35 Friargate], *Old Black Bull*: Big open-plan Tudor-fronted alehouse now extended into next shop to give comfortable leather-seat snug as well as main lounge, side public bar with half a dozen well kept changing ales and Inch's farm cider, barrels racked behind servery, big back open fireplace, relaxing atmosphere, friendly staff and locals, wide choice of reasonably priced food, games room, darts *(Richard Lewis)*; [114 Church St], *Olde Blue Bell*: Large but cosy and chatty, oldest pub in town, run by Peter Sayer, former Welsh International footballer, with good lunchtime choice of sandwiches and cheap meals from back servery, cheap well kept Sam Smiths from long bar *(Richard Lewis)*; [24 Lancaster Rd, by Guildhall], *Stanley Arms*: Fine mirrors, bare boards, four areas, different levels; friendly staff, popular lunchtime food, half a dozen or more well kept changing ales, German and Belgian beers, Bulmer's cider; pool room, TV, open all day, can be packed evenings *(Richard Lewis)*

Ramsbottom Gtr Man [Bye Rd, Twine Valley; signed off A56 N of Bury at Shuttleworth; SD7916], *Fishermans Retreat*: Surrounded by well stocked trout lakes, good interesting well presented reasonably priced food with proper chips, generous helpings, good choice of changing beers (and of whiskies), busy restaurant, games room with two pool tables and games machines; open all day from 8am *(Nicholas Teague, Martyn Smith, V Bateson)*

☆ **Riley Green** [A6061/A675 Preston—Bolton; SD6225], *Royal Oak*: Cosy low-beamed three-room pub nr canal, decent reliable food, Thwaites Bitter and Mild, friendly efficient service; ancient stripped stone, open fires, seats from high-backed settles to red plush armchairs, turkey carpet, soft lighting, impressive woodwork, fresh flowers, interesting model steam engines; can be packed weekends *(Arthur and Margaret Dickinson, RJH, John Fazakerley, BB)*

Rimington [OS Sheet 103 map ref 806457; SD8045], *Black Bull*: Spotless popular dining pub, charming dining area (bar tables may be booked too), flower arrangements and other nice touches, comfortable furniture, real fire, lots of wildlife paintings, railway memorabilia, impressive model trains; good food from sandwiches with real chips through salmon, pheasant etc to three-course Sun lunch, well kept Theakstons, courteous well trained staff, well chosen piped music; cl Mon exc bank hols, no food Sun evening *(Arthur and Margaret Dickinson)*

Sale Gtr Man [Britannia Rd; SJ8092], *Kings Ransom*: New pub on Bridgewater Canal, roaring fires, antique oil paintings, candlelight, Ruddles, inviting food *(Pat and Robert Watt)*

Samlesbury [Nabs Head Lane; SD6229], *Nabs Head*: Simple and cosy pub in peaceful country hamlet, good value home-made food inc imaginative specials, welcoming efficient service, Thwaites ales, charming decor and curtains *(Dr and Mrs D Awbery, Arthur and Margaret Dickinson)*

Scarisbrick [B5242 SE; SD4011], *Heatons Bridge*: Unspoilt friendly pub by canal crossing, four smallish rooms and dining room, Tetleys-related ales, good friendly service, well priced home-cooked food esp pies and stews *(Andy and Jill Kassube, Chris Westmoreland)*

Seacombe Mer [3 Church Rd; SJ3291], *Prince Alfred*: Small, friendly and comfortable, handy for ferry terminal; well kept Cains Bitter and Brewers Droop, Fullers London Pride, Boddingtons Mild and Bitter, pub games, no food; tables outside *(Richard Lewis)*

☆ **Simonstone** [Trapp Lane, off School Lane – Simonstone—Sabden trans-Pendle rd, OS Sheet 103 map ref 776356; SD7735], *Higher Trapp*: Attractive refurbished bar with relaxing views, well kept Boddingtons and Theakstons, food in bar and restaurant (all day Sun), no-smoking areas, big conservatory; children welcome, comfortable bedrooms *(A and M Dickinson)*

☆ **Slaidburn** [B6478 N of Clitheroe; SD7152], *Hark to Bounty*: Relaxed country atmosphere, friendly service, decor a pleasant mix of old and new, open fire, brasses, new chef doing good value food (lots of tables), good range of S&N ales, decent wines; bedrooms – a nice place to stay in a charming Forest of Bowland village, pleasant garden behind, good walks *(John and Joan Wyatt, Alan Griffiths, LYM)*

Southport Mer [34 Upper Aughton Rd; SD3315], *Blundell Arms*: Tastefully refurbished in 1996, bar, lounge and dining extension, good choice of reasonably priced generous food, well kept ales, friendly staff, live music Sun, quiz nights, play area *(Richard Lewis)*

Stalmine [SD3745], *Seven Stars*: Comfortable, good pub atmosphere, good value food in bar and restaurant, Greenalls ales, friendly staff; bedrooms good *(Phil and Anne Smithson)*

Stalybridge Gtr Man [3 Market St; SJ9698], *Q*: Continental feel, upstairs cocktail bar and conservatory, lots of bare brick, friendly staff, good food, good range of well kept real ales, well reproduced piped music; the shortest pub name we've yet come across *(Richard Lewis)*; [7 Market St], *Rose & Crown*: Popular local with friendly staff, well kept Vaux Bitter, Mild and Samson, games room; open all day *(Richard Lewis)*; [Water St/Market St], *White House*: Traditional three-room pub with low beams, pews, lots of prints, red letterbox for weekly tote, friendly mix of customers, well kept Marstons Pedigree, Theakstons Best and XB, cheap meals; pool room, games machines, open all day weekdays *(Richard Lewis)*

Standish Gtr Man [A49/A5106 (Chorley Rd); SD5610], *Boars Head*: Heavy low beams, open fire, cosy bays of curved wall seats, high wooden stools, sofa, two quieter rooms off; helpful staff, Burtonwood and guest beers, occasional unusual guest wines; bowling green *(Brian Kneale)*; [Almond Brook; not far from M6 junction 27], *Charnley Arms*: Tidy modern Greenalls family dining pub, useful for its position; reasonable prices, open all day *(Mr and Mrs E J W Rogers, Ian and Villy White)*

Stockport Gtr Man [23 Millgate St, behind Asda; SJ8991], *Arden Arms*: Traditional and welcoming, with several room areas inc old-fashioned snug through servery, good value limited lunchtime bar food, well kept Robinsons, several grandfather clocks, Dinky toy collection *(PB, Brian Wainwright)*; [27 Bowden St, Edgeley; SJ8889], *Greyhound*: Well kept Boddingtons Mild and Bitter, Cains Formidable and a seasonal ale such as Ushers Spring Fever, no food; pub games, tables outside; open all day *(Richard Lewis)*; [Manchester Rd, Heaton Chapel; SJ9090], *Hinds Head*: Traditional recently built mock-Tudor pub with popular food in conservatory restaurant, well kept Whitbreads-related and guest ales, friendly staff, children welcome if eating; big garden *(Richard Lewis)*; [12 Little Underbank, steps from St Petersgate], *Queens Head*: Long narrow late Victorian pub with delightful separate snug and back dining area; good bustling atmosphere, reasonable bar food, well kept Sam Smiths, rare brass cordials fountain, daily papers, old posters and adverts; no-smoking area, some live jazz, open all day; famous narrow gents' *(Richard Lewis)*

☆ **Tockholes** [just N of village, which is signed off A666 S of Blackburn; SD6623], *Rock*: Welcoming comfortable two-room beamed moorland inn with great views (as far as coast), hard-working licensees, well kept Thwaites Bitter and Mild, unusual whiskies, decent wines by the glass, good generous food from sandwiches up; unobtrusive piped music, children welcome, tables on a small terrace; cl Mon lunchtime exc bank hols *(Andy Hazeldine, M Buchanan, Ann Bolton, Karen Eliot, LYM)*

Trawden [SD9138], *Sun*: Pleasant pub off the beaten track, with memorable freshly cooked food at very reasonable prices four days a week, generous helpings, cooked by local who rents kitchen from landlord *(Andrew Dewhurst)*

Two Mills Mer [Parkgate Rd (A540/A550); SJ3474], *Tudor Rose*: Extended and refurbished, bright, spacious and comfortable, yet pleasantly pubby bars, with four real ales, good bar meals, convivial atmosphere, good service, restaurant; reasonably priced good bedrooms *(E G Parish)*

☆ **Uppermill** Gtr Man [Runninghill Gate, off A670 via New St; SD9905], *Cross Keys*: Homely low-beamed moorland local up long steep lane, flagstones and original cooking range, big fires, local pictures for sale, good value basic well cooked food inc good Sun lunch (all day other days), well kept Lees Bitter and Mild, lots of malt whiskies, pub games, children in side rooms, tables out on terraces with adventure playground; lovely setting, lots of walks; clog dancing Mon, folk Weds *(Graham and Lynn Mason, Wallis Taylor, Richard Fallon, Pat Martin, LYM)*

☆ **Waddington** [SD7243], *Lower Buck*: Traditional busy local welcoming walkers, with Timothy Taylors Best, Ruddles County and other well kept ales, popular basic home cooking, hatch-service lobby, front bar with built-in dresser, plain back room, pool room; pretty village *(J A Boucher, Arthur and Margaret Dickinson, Chris Walling, BB)*

Waddington, *Higher Buck*: Welcoming service, good value good food, well kept beer, open all day Sun *(E E Starling)*; *Waddington Arms*: Prettily kept, with new dining extension, imaginative well prepared food (not Mon) using fresh local produce, two airy rooms with woodburners, well kept Morlands Old Speckled Hen, Theakstons Mild and Bitter and a beer brewed for the pub, well chosen piped music, no-smoking area; children welcome; bedrooms *(Arthur and Margaret Dickinson, J A Boucher)*

Whalley Gtr Man [55 King St; SD7336], *Dog*: Spotless well run local with warm welcome for visitors, relaxed regulars' bar, quiet areas for eating and coffee inc no-smoking family dining room, interesting bric-a-brac and Victorian prints, quiet classical piped music; good generous lunchtime food inc vegetarian, well kept Scottish Courage ales, nicely served wine, daily papers *(Mrs M Hughes, Mr and Mrs K Berkins, Arthur and Margaret Dickinson)*

Whitefield Gtr Man [61 Bury Old Rd, nr M62 junction 17; SD8104], *Welcome*: Baronial hall style interior with inglenook fireplace and superb panelling, friendly staff, well kept Holts Mild and Bitter, reasonably priced bar snacks; handy for Metro *(Alan Gough)*

Wigan Gtr Man [5 Mkt Pl; SD5805], *Moon Under Water*: Stylish new Wetherspoons conversion, bright and airy, with nice old Wigan prints (and nice young Wigan faces at the bar); lots of room, no music, friendly efficient service, good value food all day, well kept Scottish Courage and other ales *(Richard Lewis, Comus Elliott)*

☆ **Wiswell** [just NE of Whalley; SD7437], *Freemasons Arms*: Cosy country pub, wide choice of good value well presented interesting fresh food (must book restaurant Fri/Sat evening) in small bar and overflow upstairs dining room, friendly efficient service, good range of beers, lots of malt whiskies; lovely village below Pendle Hill; cl Mon/Tues evening *(Beatrice Clark, Yvonne and Mike Meadley)*

☆ **Woodford** Gtr Man [550 Chester Rd; A5149 SW of BAe entrance; SJ8882], *Davenport Arms*: Down-to-earth convivial country pub, simple but comfortable, with small rooms, coal fires, friendly staff (in same family for 60 years), well kept Robinsons Best and Best Mild, good reasonably priced home cooking lunchtime (toasted sandwiches evening), good games room; children allowed in back no-smoking snug, live music Tues/Sat; tables on front terrace and in attractive garden with play area *(Richard Lewis, Mr Cosgrove, Bob Cooke)*

☆ **Wrea Green** [Station Rd; SD3931], *Grapes*: Busy but roomy open-plan local with good value food inc imaginative dishes, pleasant clean dining area, well kept Boddingtons, Marstons Pedigree and Theakstons, open fire, good service; tables out overlooking village green, picturesque church *(RJH)*

Wrightington Bar [2 miles from junction 27 M6; SD5313], *Hinds Head*: Roomy modern pub with good varied menu in dining area, friendly service *(Dick Brown)*; [Whittle Lane, High Moor; off A5209 Parbold—Standish at Dangerous Corner opp B5375, then first left; SD5011], *Rigbye Arms*: Tasty good value bar food, nice relaxed atmosphere, pleasant country setting *(Brian Kneale)*

Please tell us if any Lucky Dips deserve to be upgraded to a main entry and why. No stamp needed: *The Good Pub Guide*, FREEPOST TN1569, Wadhurst, E Sussex TN5 7BR.

Leicestershire (with Rutland)

There are some exceptionally nice pubs, often with excellent food, in this part of the world. Ones on particularly fine form these days are the Old Plough at Braunston (friendly, with imaginative food), the bustling White Horse at Empingham, the Bell at East Langton (a new entry, nice staff, good chef), the Monckton Arms at Glaston (back in these pages after an absence, current licensees doing well – a nice place to stay), the delightful Old Barn at Glooston, the very traditional Cap & Stocking at Kegworth, and the restauranty Peacock at Redmile (a beautifully decorated new bedroom block). For a really enjoyable meal out the Peacock, the Old Barn, and the Crown at Old Dalby are hard to beat; it's the Peacock, space problems relieved by its new restaurant extension, which we choose as Leicestershire Dining Pub of the Year. Drinks prices here are a shade lower than the national average; the Old Brewery at Somerby, brewing its own fine Parish ales, was the cheapest place we found for beer, and the Peacock at Redmile and (with a splendid beer choice) the Swan in the Rushes in Loughborough were also very good value for drinks. In the Lucky Dip section at the end of the chapter the Barnsdale Lodge at Barnsdale, Wheatsheaf at Greetham, Ram Jam at Stretton, Noel Arms at Whitwell and Wheatsheaf at Woodhouse Eaves (all inspected and vouched for by us) are particularly recommended; and the stylish Welford Place now seems the pick of Leicester's pubs.

BRAUNSTON SK8306 Map 4
Blue Ball

Village signposted off A606 in Oakham

There's a very pleasant relaxed and informal atmosphere at this ancient thatched pub. The main area preserves its original form of separate rooms, while the furnishings and decorations – not too fussy – are individual and interesting. As well as sandwiches (from £2.50) and soup (£2.25), dishes might typically include a pâté of the day (£3.75), cheeses with salad and walnut oil dressing (£4.50), warm spinach timbale with pine kernels (£4.75), spicy fishcakes (£5.30), stir-fried vegetable curry (£6.50), tagliatelle with tomato, bacon, garlic and basil (£6.95), fresh salmon salad (£7.95), rack of lamb or duck breast (£12.50), and puddings such as strawberry bavarois or nougat flavoured with kirsch and mango (£3.75); children's helpings. Service is very good, even when busy. Well kept Bass, Courage Directors, John Smiths, Ruddles County and a guest on handpump. Dominoes, shove-ha'penny and piped music; no-smoking bar area and restaurant. *(Recommended by Sue and Bob Ward, George Atkinson, Howard and Margaret Buchanan, Peter Burton, Michael Coshall, Stephen Brown, J F Knutton, Gill and Bryan Trueman, Jane Kingsbury, Eric Locker, Keith and Margaret Kettell, David and Fiona Pemberton, Peter and Patricia Burton, Joan and Michel Hooper-Immins, Penny and Martin Fletcher, Mavis and John Wright, Brian and Jill Bond)*

Free house ~ Managers Linda Maxwell and Joe Webb ~ Real ale ~ Meals and snacks (till 10pm) ~ Restaurant ~ (01572) 722135 ~ Children welcome ~ Open 12-11; 12-10.30 Sun; 12-3, 6-11 Mon-Sat in winter

Old Plough ♀

Village signposted off A606 in Oakham

Although this well run pub does serve very good imaginative food it's not exclusively a dining pub. The atmosphere is still pubby and friendly, they hold lots of social and sporting events for locals, and the beers are carefully chosen. The menu changes every season, but might include attractively served dishes such as home-made soup (£2.25), really big filled rolls (from £3.15), sauté chicken livers in a filo basket with sherry cream sauce (£3.75), grilled sardines stuffed with lemon and anchovy on tomato vinaigrette (£4.25), lasagne (£5.95), steak and kidney pie or scampi (£6.95), seared salmon fillet with mango and coriander salsa (£8.75), pepper crusted chicken breast on sweet red pimento coulis (£8.95) and roast duck with port sauce (£11.25); very good service. The traditional bars have upholstered seats around cast-iron-framed tables under the heavy and irregular back beams, and plenty of brass ornaments on the mantelpiece. At the back is a stylish modern no-smoking conservatory dining room. The well kept real ales are generally all brewed locally: Ruddles Best and County, and brews from the Grainstore Brewery. Also a good, interesting well noted wine list, fruit punches in summer, Scrumpy Jack cider, and a choice of teas and coffees. The carpeted public bar has darts in winter; maybe piped music. Picnic tables shelter among fruit trees, and there's a boules pitch. The inn-sign is attractive. *(Recommended by Eric Locker, Mrs J Burrows, Brian Aitkin, J R Morris)*

Free house ~ Licensees Andrew and Amanda Reid ~ Real ale ~ Meals and snacks (till 10) ~ Restaurant ~ (01572) 722714 ~ Children welcome ~ Open 11-3, 6-11(12 Sat); 12-4, 6-10.30 Sun

EAST LANGTON SP7292 Map 4

Bell

The Langtons signposted from A6 N of Market Harborough; East Langton signposted from B6047

After a very restaurantly previous spell, this pretty white pub has been revitalised as a proper country pub by a new landlord. Its long stripped-stone beamed bar has a good log fire, simple solid stripped pine tables, country-kitchen chairs and settles, and a warm and inviting atmosphere. The good home-cooked food shows imaginative touches without being over-ambitious, and includes sandwiches (from £1.80), slices of smoked duck breast with salad and raspberry vinegar dressing (£3.95), ploughman's (£4), smoked salmon timbale (£4.25), turkey and asparagus pie or fruity chicken korma (£6.95), pork fillet stuffed with prunes and almonds with a honey and cider glaze (£8.65), tuna steak with tomato and pepper sauce topped with mozzarella (£8.70), chicken breast with boursin and filo pastry (£8.95), with good traditional home-made puddings like banoffi pie, bakewell tart and spotted dick (£2.85) and an interesting cheese of the month (£3.25). Well kept Greene King Abbot, Jennings Cumberland and Hook Norton Old Hookey on handpump and a guest beer tapped from the cask; cheerful and well trained young staff, no-smoking green-hued dining room. There are tables out in the garden; the attractive village is set in peaceful countryside. *(Recommended by O K Smyth, Mrs E Lorey, Owen and Rosemary Warnock)*

Free house ~ Licensee Alistair Chapman ~ Meals and snacks (till 10pm; 9.30 Sun) ~ Restaurant ~ (01858) 545278 ~ Children welcome till 8.30pm ~ Open 11.30-2.30, 7-11; 12-3, 7-10.30 Sun; cl 25 Dec ~ Bedrooms: £35S/£45S

EMPINGHAM SK9408 Map 4

White Horse ⑪ ⇌

Main Street; A606 Stamford—Oakham

We think this cheerfully bustling old inn is a particularly nice place to stay. Some of the bedrooms are in a delightfully converted stable block, and the breakfasts are very good. The open-plan carpeted lounge bar has a big log fire below an unusual free-standing chimney-funnel, lots of fresh flowers, and a very relaxed and comfortable atmosphere. Very popular well cooked bar food includes soup (£2.30), cream cheese pâté (£3.75), prawns in filo pastry (£4.25), chilli or pasta and nut bake (£5.95), lasagne (£6.25), seafood pie or a huge ploughman's (£6.45), and about ten well presented daily specials such as pork escalope with wild mushroom and cheese sauce (£6.75) and sauté of lamb liver with smoked bacon and onion in red wine sauce (£6.95); they also do morning coffee and afternoon tea. Helpings are big and vegetables are served separately in a little dish; the restaurant and the Orange Room are no smoking. Well kept Courage Directors, Grainstore Triple B, John Smiths and Ruddles County; fruit machine and piped music. Outside are some rustic tables among urns of flowers. *(Recommended by D W Atkinson, Michael and Lynne Gittins, Jenny and Michael Back, Jo and Gary Charlton, Melanie Bradshaw, RJH, R M Macnaughton, John Faby, Paul McPherson)*

S & N ~ Tenant Roger Bourne ~ Real ale ~ Meals and snacks (till 9.45) ~ Restaurant ~ (01780) 460221 ~ Children in eating area of bar and restaurant ~ Open 10-11 (10.30 Sun) ~ Bedrooms: £37(£45B)/£49(£58B)

EXTON SK9211 Map 8
Fox & Hounds

Signposed off A606 Stamford—Oakham

The striking grandeur of this building is a reminder of the days when the characterful village was part of the main coach route to Oakham. Drinkers feel welcome in the comfortable high-ceilinged lounge bar which has some dark red plush easy chairs as well as wheelback seats around lots of dark tables, maps and hunting and military prints on the walls, brass and copper ornaments, and a winter log fire in a large stone fireplace. Generously served bar food includes stilton and broccoli en croûte (£5), lasagne or liver, bacon and onions (£6.25), plaice and prawns (£6.75), sautéed chicken with sherry, cream and mushroom sauce or steak and kidney pie (£6.95) and honey roasted local trout. One well kept changing real ale such as Charles Wells Bombardier, Fullers London Pride or Morlands Old Speckled Hen on handpump might increase to up to three on busy weekends; piped music. The lively and quite separate public bar has darts, pool, cribbage, dominoes, juke box, fruit machine, and video game. There are seats among large rose beds on the well kept back lawn, overlooking paddocks. Rutland Water is only a couple of miles away and it's very handy for walkers on the Viking Way. *(Recommended by Eric Locker, Gordon Theaker, Bill and Sheila McLardy, John Faby, Jo and Gary Charlton, L Walker, J M Wright, H Bramwell, Chris Raisin, Jim Farmer, RWD)*

Free house ~ Licensees David and Jennifer Hillier ~ Real ale ~ Meals and snacks ~ Restaurant (not Sun evening) ~ (01572) 812403 ~ Children welcome ~ Open 11-3, 6-11; 12-3, 7-10.30 ~ Bedrooms: £22/£36

GLASTON SK8900 Map 4
Monckton Arms 🍺

A47 Leicester—Peterborough, E of Uppingham

Set in the heart of Rutland County, this stone roadside inn is popular with both locals and visitors, and readers particularly like it as a place to stay (they offer golf and fishing breaks). It was originally a 16th-c farmhouse, most of which now forms the bar and snug area, and there's a sizeable modern extension. The nicest seats are by a big woodburner in an inglenook fireplace. Bar food, which is cooked to order, includes sandwiches (from £2.45), filled baguettes (from £2.95), ploughman's (£4.75), liver and bacon (£4.95), cottage pie (£5.25), lasagne (£5.95), several vegetarian dishes such as pancake filled with tropical and dried fruit and topped with coconut sauce (£6.75), steak and ale pie (£6.95), seafood kebab with fish, garlic and soy sauce (£10.95) and fish platter (£11.25), also daily specials like pork chop topped with stilton, cod in cheese and chive sauce and braised beef. Well kept Bass, Courage Directors, John Smiths and Ruddles Best and County on handpump; dominoes, cribbage, piped music. There are picnic tables on a sheltered terrace; the popular black labrador puppy is called Scully – yes, the licensee is an *X-Files* fan. Rutland Water is ten minutes' drive away, its also handy for Burghley House and Rockingham Castle.

(Recommended by Duncan Cloud, Ash, Samantha and Josie Wright, J F Knutton, A Bradbury, R and A Cooper, M A Mees, Rona Murdoch, Janet Box)

Free house ~ Licensee Spencer Dainton ~ Real ale ~ Meals and snacks (till 10 Mon-Sat) ~ Restaurant ~ (01572) 822326 ~ Children welcome ~ Open 11(12 Sun)-11; 12-3, 7-11 in winter; cl 25 Dec evening ~ Bedrooms: £35B/£48B

GLOOSTON SP7595 Map 4
Old Barn ★ ⑪ 🛏 ♀ 🍺

From B6047 in Tur Langton follow Hallaton signpost, then fork left following Glooston signpost

Every dish on the very inventive monthly changing menus at this carefully restored 16th-c pub is so tempting that it's hard to limit ourselves to giving just three or four examples – we finally picked pigeon breast on warm salad with raspberry and port glaze (£3.95), aubergine roulade filled with ricotta, parmesan and basil with tomato and white wine sauce or goat's cheese and nectarine parcles encased in spinach leaves, grilled with tomato vinaigrette (£4.25), poached marrow filled with prawns and smoked salmon in yoghurt, green peppercorn and dill sauce (£4.50) and as main course examples, bread and cheese pudding baked with sun dried tomatoes, herbs and spices (£7.45), medallions of pork fillet marinated in elderflowers and honey with apple, elderflower and chive stuffing (£9.25), chicken fried in garlic, almonds and spices with yoghurt and cream sauce garnished with bananas and sultanas (£9.95), telapia fillet with lemon sorrel sauce (£10.95) and roast saddle of hare in plum and ginger sauce (£11.95). It's worth taking careful note of their opening times given below as they close on weekday lunchtimes, and they only serve snacks on Saturday lunchtime; the three-course lunch on Sunday is good value at £13.25. The lower beamed main bar has stripped kitchen tables and country chairs, pewter plates, Players cricketer cigarette cards, and an open fire. Four well kept real ales on handpump rotated from a wide choice of beers like Adnams Broadside, Batemans, Fullers London Pride, Morlands Old Speckled Hen; good wine list (with half a dozen by the glass). The dining area is no smoking. There are a few old-fashioned teak seats and picnic tables in front. Bedrooms are very nice with French-style shower-and-wash cabinets that please most readers, but might perhaps suit best those with at least a modest degree of mobility. Well behaved dogs welcome. *(Recommended by Stephen, Julie and Hayley Brown, Anthony Barnes, Mary Wood, Simon Walker, Alan Morton, Brian Atkin, Eric Locker, Stephen Brown, Mrs S F Front, Red and Mary Hepburn, V W Burgess, Jim Farmer, J D Cloud, Vicky and David Sarti)*

Free house ~ Licensees Charles Edmondson-Jones and Stewart Sturge ~ Real ale ~ Meals and snacks (not weekday lunchtimes or Sun evening, till 1.30 Sat) ~ Restaurant ~ (01858) 545215 ~ Children welcome ~ Open 7-11 only during the week; 12-2.30, 7-11 Sat; 12-3 Sun, cl Sun evening ~ Bedrooms: £37.50S/£49.50S

HALLATON SP7896 (Map 4)
Bewicke Arms ★

On good fast back road across open rolling countryside between Uppingham and Kibworth; village signposted from B6047 in Tur Langton and from B664 SW of Uppingham

There are delightful views of the characteful village from tables in the front room of this ancient thatched inn, which is prettily set on the edge of the village green. On Easter Monday after the famous pagan 'Hare Pie Scrambling' has taken place the 'bottle-kicking race' procession sets out from the green for Hare Hill, and in the summer there may be Morris dancing here. The unpretentious beamed main bar has two small oddly shaped rooms with farming implements and deer heads on the walls, pokerwork seats, old-fashioned settles (including some with high backs and wings), wall benches, and stripped oak tables, and four copper kettles gleaming over one of the log fires; the bottom room is no smoking during the week. Big helpings of popular bar food include sandwiches (from £1.50), ploughman's (£4.20), breaded plaice (£5.40), scampi (£5.95), 10oz rump steak (£9.20), as well as weekly changing specials such as deep fried brie and cranberry dip (£4.45), creamy seafood pancake, chilli or lasagne (£6.80), grilled salmon fillet with honey and mustard sauce (£7.20), chicken breast with herb and garlic cheese (£7.80) and grilled leg of lamb steak marinated in mint and yoghurt (£8.20); you can book a table most days, otherwise get there early. Readers have been particularly impressed by the warm welcome and friendly service, especially from the genial landlord. Well kept Marstons Pedigree, Ruddles Best and County and a guest beer on handpump, maybe kept under light blanket pressure; darts, fruit machine in the side corridor, and piped music. No dogs. They have a big self-catering apartment to rent. Picnic tables on a crazy-paved terrace behind the building look over the ex-stableyard car park to the hills behind. *(Recommended by Stephen, Julie and Hayley Brown, Eric Locker, John Wooll, Brian Atkin, Brian and Jill Bond, Howard and Margaret Buchanan, Ted George, Jim Farmer, Thomas Nott, Rona Murdoch)*

Free house ~ Licensee Neil Spiers ~ Real ale ~ Meals and snacks (till 9.45) ~ Restaurant ~ (01858) 555217 ~ Well behaved children welcome ~ Open 12-3, 7-11

HOSE SK7329 Map 7
Rose & Crown ♠
Bolton Lane

One of the eight very well kept real ales at this atmospheric old place is Carl's Tipple which is brewed exclusively for its namesake, the cheery landlord here, by Butterknowle. Other brews are likely to be ones you won't often find in this area, from smaller breweries in the west country or in the north such as Archers Golden, Bathams Best, Butterknowle High Force, Caledonian Deuchars IPA, Fullers ESB, Greene King Abbot, Hook Norton Old Hookey, Ruddles Best and County, Shepherd Neame Spitfire, and Youngs Special to name just a few. They also keep around a dozen malt whiskies. There's a relaxed lighthearted atmosphere in the more-or-less open-plan bar which has pool, darts, dominoes, a fruit machine, trivia and juke box; no-smoking areas in restaurant and lounge bar. Bar food includes filled rolls (from £1.60), soup (£2.25), prawn cocktail (£2.50), ploughman's (from £3.95), battered cod (£4.95), steak and ale pie (£5.50), chicken in red wine sauce (£5.95), lots of steaks (9oz sirloin £9.60) and a couple of blackboard specials like pork fillet in port and mustard, rack of lamb with mint gravy or chicken fillet in stilton and cream sauce (£7.95). There are tables on a fairy-lit sheltered terrace behind the building and a fenced family area at the rear of the car park. Campers and caravanners are welcome. *(Recommended by Dr and Mrs J H Hills, R M Taylor, D C Roberts, Rona Murdoch, Chris Raisin, Graham Doyle, D R Eberlin, Keith and Norma Bloomfield, June and Malcolm Farmer, D C Roberts, Jack and Philip Paxton)*

Free house ~ Licensee Carl Routh ~ Real ale ~ Meals and snacks (till 8.30 Sun) ~ Restaurant ~ (01949) 860424 ~ Children in eating area of bar and restaurant till 9 ~ Open 11.30-3, 7-11; 12-3, 7-10.30 Sun; cl 25 Dec

KEGWORTH SK4826 Map 7
Cap & Stocking ★ £ ♠
Under a mile from M1 junction 24: follow A6 towards Loughborough; in village, turn left at chemists' down one-way Dragwall opposite High Street, then left and left again, into Borough Street

Readers, along with a nicely mixed group of customers, love the unpretentious unspoilt atmosphere at this genuinely old-fashioned small town local. Each of the two determinedly simple but cosy front rooms has its own coal fire, and a friendly and easy-going feel; on the right there's lots of etched glass, big cases of stuffed birds and locally caught fish, fabric-covered wall benches and heavy cast-iron-framed tables, and a cast-iron range. Well kept beers on handpump include Bass, Hancocks HB and M & B Mild with a guest such as Fullers London Pride or Shepherd Neame Bishops Finger. Good value bar food includes filled rolls (from 90p; hot sausage and onion £1.10), soup (£1.50), ploughman's (from £3.75), pizzas (from £3.75), chilli or vegetable curry (£3.95), hungarian goulash (£4.75), beef stroganoff (£5.25), daily specials such as apricot pork, Sri Lankan chicken or Szechuan meatballs (from £4.50), and puddings like hot treacle sponge (£1.50). Dominoes, cribbage, trivia, and Monday evening quiz. The back room has french windows to the pleasant garden where there is floodlit boules. *(Recommended by K and J Brooks, Val Stevenson, Rob Holmes, Jack and Jemima Valiant, Peter and Anne Hollindale, K Fell, Jo and Gary Charlton, Pete Baker, P V Burdett, Adam and Joan Bunting, Lucy James, C H and P Stride, Michael Butler, RT and J C Moggridge, D Eberlin, James Nunns, Christopher Turner, David and Fiona Pemberton, PM, AM, Jack and Philip Paxton, Vicky and David Sarti)*

Bass ~ Lease: Graham and Mary Walsh ~ Real ale ~ Meals and snacks (till 8.45) ~ (01509) 674814 ~ Children in eating area of bar ~ Open 11.30-3(2.30 in winter), 6.30-11; 12-3, 7-10.30 Sun

KNIPTON SK8231 Map 7
Red House ♀ ⇔

Village signposted off A607 Grantham—Melton Mowbray

The roomy turkey-carpeted bar of this fine Georgian hunting lodge, which is divided by a central hearth with a woodburning stove, has sturdy old-fashioned furnishings, hunting pictures, a delft shelf of sporting or game bird decorative plates, and a relaxed, friendly atmosphere. There are lovely views of the garden and surrounding landscape from the neatly furnished no-smoking conservatory which opens off the airy restaurant. A good choice of very tasty and very good value bar food might include stilton and cream soup (from £1.95), cajun spiced whitebait (£3.50), filo bundles of smoked salmon and prawns on ratatouille (£3.95), ploughman's (£4.25), chicken, stilton and herb pie and several vegetarian dishes like aubergine fritters on sweet spiced vegetables, fruit, garlic and herb couscous (around £5.65), roast rack of lamb on ratatouille with onion and tarragon sauce, chicken breast with carbonara sauce and pasta or pork escalope griddled and served with baked avocado and stilton (£6.45). Well kept Marstons Pedigree, Tetleys and a guest on handpump, a good choice of about 120 bin-ends, 20 malt whiskies, and quite a few brandies and vintage ports; service is friendly and obliging – though can slow down when they're busy. The public bar area has darts, cribbage, dominoes and fruit machine; there may be unobtrusive piped music. *(Recommended by Canon and Mrs M Bourdeaux, Michael Marlow, Paul and Maggie Baker, P Stallard, R and A Cooper)*

Free house ~ Lease: Robin Newport ~ Real ale ~ Meals and snacks ~ Restaurant ~ (01476) 870352 ~ Children welcome ~ Occasional trad jazz Sun lunchtime ~ Open 11.30-3(4 Sat), 6-11; 12-4, 7-10.30 Sun; cl evening 25 Dec ~ Bedrooms: £21(£36B)/ £32.50(£48B)

LOUGHBOROUGH SK5319 Map 7
Swan in the Rushes ◀

The Rushes (A6)

The main draw at this homely no-frills town pub is the fine collection of beers – interesting German, Belgian and other bottled beers, and on handpump well kept Archers Golden, Batemans XB, Greene King Abbot, Marstons Pedigree, Springhead Roaring Meg alongside four regularly changing guests. Also two ciders, a good range of malt whiskies, and country wines. There are several neatly kept separate room areas, each with its own style – the most comfortable seats are in the left-hand bay-windowed bar (which has an open fire) and in the snug back dining room. It can get very crowded, but service is good. Very reasonably priced, the home-made bar food includes filled rolls, a choice of ploughman's (from £3.75), tagliatelle bolognese or chilli con carne (£4.25), broccoli and cauliflower mornay filled pancakes (£4.25), bobotie, beef in ale or chicken in apple wine (£5.25), 8oz rump steak (£5.75), and puddings like apple strudel (£1.50). Shove-ha'penny, cribbage, dominoes, juke box, and backgammon. The simple bedrooms are clean and cosy. There are tables in an outside drinking area. *(Recommended by Stephen and Julie Brown, JJW, CMW, Jack and Gemima Valiant, Joan and Michel Hooper-Immins, Jack and Philip Paxton, R M Taylor, James Nunns)*

Free house ~ Licensee Andrew Hambleton ~ Real ale ~ Meals and snacks (12-2, 6-8.30; not Sat/Sun evenings) ~ (01509) 217014 ~ Children in dining room ~ Blues or R&B Sat evening, folk every other Sun and occasional Fris ~ Open 11-11; 12-10.30 Sun ~ Bedrooms: £20(£25B)/£30(£35B)

LYDDINGTON SP8797 Map 4
Old White Hart
Village signposted off A6003 N of Corby

The cosy softly lit bar at this traditional 17th-c village inn has just three close-set tables in front of the warm log fire, with heavy bowed beams and lots of attractive dried flower arrangements. The bar opens into an attractive restaurant with corn dollies and a big oak dresser, and on the other side is a tiled-floor room with some stripped stone, cushioned wall seats and mate's chairs, a woodburning stove, darts and a thriving dominoes school. Well kept Greene King IPA and Abbot, Marstons Pedigree, Timothy Taylor Landlord and possibly a guest on handpump. Bar food under the new licensee includes filled baguettes (£3.95), ploughman's (£5.95), fried Whitby haddock (£6.25), steak and mushroom pie (£6.50), seafood pie (£7.25), saddle of rabbit (£8.85) and rack of lamb (£9.95), with daily specials like garlic mushrooms or salmon and dill fishcakes (£3.75), medallions of fillet steak (£7.95) or roast monkfish (£10.75); one of the restaurants is no smoking. There are picnic tables in the safe and pretty walled garden – on Thursday you can listen to the church bell ringers – which has twelve floodlit boules pitches. Good nearby walks; handy for the Bede House. *(Recommended by Anthony Barnes, Stephen Brown, George Atkinson, Grant Wicks, Rona Murdoch)*

Free house ~ Licensee Stuart East ~ Real ale ~ Meals and snacks (not Sun evening) ~ Restaurant ~ (01572) 821703 ~ Children welcome in eating area of bar and restaurant ~ Open 12-3, 6-11; 12-3, 7-10.30 Sun

MEDBOURNE SP7993 Map 4
Nevill Arms 🏠 🍺
B664 Market Harborough—Uppingham

A footbridge takes you over a duck-filled stream to this warmly welcoming village-centre pub, with its handsome stonework and latticed mullioned windows. The appealing main bar has an especially cheerful atmosphere, as well as two winter log fires, chairs and small wall settles around its tables, a lofty, dark-joisted ceiling and maybe a couple of dogs or a cat; piped music. A spacious back room by the former coachyard has pews around more tables (much needed at busy times), and there's a conservatory with newspapers – but in summer most people prefer eating at the tables outside on the grass by the dovecote. Well kept Adnams Southwold, Ruddles Best and County and two changing guests on handpump; about two dozen country wines. Good value bar food includes home-made soups like curried parsnip or cauliflower and stilton (£2.15), smoked haddock and spinach bake, chicken in orange and tarragon or pork in white wine and mushrooms (£4.95). Darts, shove-ha'penny, cribbage, table skittles, dominoes and other board games on request. The winter Tuesday evening Muddlemind quiz is popular with locals. Readers particularly enjoy staying here, and from this Easter rooms will be available in a neighbouring cottage as well as the pub itself. *(Recommended by Jo and Gary Charlton, A J Morton, Eric Locker, Mr and Mrs J T V Harris, M J Morgan, R Murdoch, Joan and Michel Hooper-Immins, Alan Morton, Dr Jim Mackay, Stephen and Julie Brown, Cliff Blakemore, Angus Lyon, Keith Wright, Jim Farmer, Robert P Anderson)*

Free house ~ Licensees E F Hall and partners ~ Real ale ~ Meals and snacks (till 9.45) ~ (01858) 565288 ~ Children welcome ~ Open 12-2.30, 6-11; 12-3, 7-10.30 Sun ~ Bedrooms: £40B/£50B

OLD DALBY SK6723 Map 7
Crown ★ 🍴 🍷
By school in village centre turn into Longcliff Hill then left into Debdale Hill

As well as a very stylish menu there's quite an impressive range of well kept real ales at this smart creeper-covered old farmhouse. Food isn't cheap here but then they do grow their own herbs and make their own bread, vinegars and ice creams, and the standard of cooking is very ambitious. The atmosphere is fairly formal with staff in black-and-white uniforms and bow ties. As well as soup or sandwiches (£2.95), the menu might include starters like caramelised goat's cheese with basil dressing (£5.95), warm salad of smoked chicken with bacon, pear and blue cheese dressing (£6.95), smoked salmon and avocado roulade (£7.95), and main courses like risotto of sun-dried tomatos and wild mushrooms or ploughman's (£7.95), venison sausage (£10.50), beef, venison and apricot casserole with stilton pastry lid (£11.95), marinated fillet of sea bass with Chinese noodles, lemon, lime and ginger (£12.95) and entrecôte of beef with glazed stilton and port sauce (£15.95); puddings like marinated banana in filo with chocolate sauce or caramelised thick lemon tart (£4.50). Their good range of beers might include Adnams, Batemans XB and XXB, Black Sheep, Greene King Abbot, Marstons Pedigree, Morlands Old Speckled Hen, Smiles and Timothy Taylors Landlord and guests; they also have an interesting wine list, quite a few malt whiskies, and several brandies and Italian liqueurs. Three or four intimate little rooms have black beams, one or two antique oak settles, William Morris style armchairs and easy chairs, hunting and other rustic prints, fresh flowers, and open fires; the snug is no smoking. One room has cribbage, cards and dominoes, and they also have table skittles. There are plenty of tables on a terrace, with a big, sheltered lawn sloping down among roses and fruit trees; you can play boules out here. No credit cards. The licensees run another main entry, the Martins Arms at Colston Bassett (see Notts chapter). *(Recommended by Tim Barrow, Sue Demont, D J and P M Taylor, M Buchanan, Steven Tait, Susie Lonie, John Poulter, Alan Hopkin, Thomas Nott, Eric Locker, Vicky and David Sarti, Chris Raisin, Mr McGrath, David and Helen Wilkins, R and A Cooper, SS)*

Free house ~ Licensees Lynne Strafford Bryan and Salvatore Inguanta ~ Real ale ~ Meals and snacks (till 10; not Sun evening) ~ Restaurant ~ (01664) 823134 ~ Children welcome away from bar ~ Open 12-3(2.30 in winter), 6-11; (7-10.30 Sun)

PEATLING MAGNA SP5992 Map 4
Cock

Village signposted off A50 S of Leicester

There's a cheery start to the evening at this chatty village pub with discounted beers and spirits and free cut-your-own sandwiches, from loaves of good crusty bread and hunks of excellent stilton or red leicester on the bar, and during the evening the friendly and energetic landlord likes the kitchen to send out little snacks like free baked potatoes. With that kind of hospitality it's not surprising that visitors feel so warmly welcomed into the lcoal village atmosphere. Courage Directors and John Smiths are well kept, and there are decent house wines. The narrow main bar has horsey pictures and plates above the coal-effect gas fire and on some beams, cushioned wall benches and plush stools; there's a neat country dining area in the right-hand room. Good bar food includes home-made soup (£1.95), sandwiches such as local ham and cheese with a salad garnish and chips (£2.75), steak and kidney pie or vegetarian lasagne (£5.95), chicken tikka masala (£7.95), steaks (from £7.95), honey roast duck or halibut steak (£8.95), puddings like hot chocolate fudgecake or sticky toffee pudding (£1.95), and about a dozen daily specials such as stuffed mackerel (£6.95), salmon steak or chicken à la crème (£7.95), rack of lamb (£8.95) and 16oz rib eye steak with stilton and mushrooms (£10.45). The very popular Sunday lunch has three bookable sittings. They organise lots of events – curry nights, quiz nights, treasure hunts, golf; maybe piped pop music. *(Recommended by Stephen and Julie Brown, Rona Murdoch, David W Atkinson)*

Free house ~ Licensee Max Brown ~ Real ale ~ Meals and snacks (not Sun, Mon evening or Sat lunchtime) ~ Restaurant ~ (0116) 247 8308 ~ Children welcome if seated ~ Open 5.30-11 (closed weekday lunchtimes); 10-2.30, 6-11 Sat; 12-4, 7-10.30 Sun

---

Children welcome means the pubs says it lets children inside without any special restriction; readers have found that some may impose an evening time limit – please tell us if you find this.

REDMILE SK7935 Map 7

Peacock 🍴 ♀ 🗝

Off A52 W of Grantham; at crossroads follow sign for Belvoir Castle, Harlby, and Melton

Leicestershire Dining Pub of the Year

This is one of those places that seems to be going from strength to strength. The completion of a new no-smoking restaurant and colour-washed garden room are testament to the tremendous popularity of the very good continental style cooking here, and readers who have stayed overnight all speak very highly of the beautifully decorated new bedrooms. The very imaginative freshly prepared bar food changes almost daily but might include soup (£2.35), very good lunchtime filled sandwiches (from £2.50), moules marinières (£4.20), antipasto (£4.95), tuna and salmon marinated in lime and fennel with aubergine and courgette caviars (£5.75), salad of fresh morels sautéed with asparagus with a shallot and balsamic dressing (£6.95), smoked salmon and fresh salmon tagliatelle with fresh herbs and julienne of leeks or tagliatelle with roasted pepper tomato coulis, basil and melted goat's cheese (£6.95), venison sausage and mash (£7.95), fried chicken breast stuffed with cheese with three different purées on asparagus sauce (£8.95), lamb medallion with sauté courgette on a tarragon and balsamic vinegar sauce (£9.50) and duck breast with spinach and passion fruit glaze (£10.95) and lots of delicious puddings such as caramelised apple tart or poached meringue and banana flambé; vegetables are very good. Service is friendly and helpful, but can slow down at busy times; they recommend booking at lunchtimes. The range of well kept beers on handpump includes Bass, Marstons Pedigree, Tetleys, nicely priced Theakstons Best, Timothy Taylors Landlord, and maybe a guest, and they have an interesting wine list including fairly priced bottles and some by the glass; occasional special events such as cookery demonstrations or wine tastings. The four spotless beamed pubby rooms have an easy-going feel, with open fires, pews, stripped country tables and chairs, the odd sofa and easy chair, some stripped golden stone, old prints, chintzy curtains for the small windows, and a variety of wall and table lamps; the snug and the Green Room are no smoking; cribbage, dominoes, maybe unobtrusive piped music, and tables outside. The pub is in an extremely pleasant tranquil setting near Belvoir Castle. *(Recommended by J F Knutton, June and Malcolm Farmer, RB, Dr and Mrs J Hills, R Clare, J A Hodgson, Mr and Mrs R Head, Roxanne Chamberlain, R and A Cooper, Simon Collett-Jones, Helen and Keith Bowers and friends, Simon Morton, Vicki and David Sarti, Paul and Janet Waring, Janet Pickles, Patsy Quick, J and P Maloney, Paul Boot, James Nunns, JAH, Wayne Brindle, C J Darwent)*

Free house ~ Licensees Celia and Colin Craword ~ Real ale ~ Meals and snacks (12-3, 7-10; afternoon teas) ~ Restaurant ~ (01949) 842554 ~ Children in eating area of bar and restaurant ~ Open 11-11; 12-10.30 Sun ~ Bedrooms: £65B/£75B

SIBSON SK3500 Map 4

Cock

A444 N of Nuneaton

This very charming thatched building dates back to the 13th c, and though it's changed a fair bit over the years, proof of its age can still be seen in the unusually low doorways, ancient wall timbers, heavy black beams, and genuine latticed windows. An atmospheric room on the right has comfortable seats around cast-iron tables, and more seats built in to what was once an immense fireplace. The room on the left has country kitchen chairs around wooden tables, and there's a no-smoking dining area. Generous helpings of good value bar food include home-made soup (£1.70), good sandwiches (from £2), home-made pâté (£2.20), steak and kidney pie or beef curry (£5.50), honey roast ham and egg (£6.25), steaks (from £8.25), and daily specials such as stuffed pork belly, sizzling chicken in black bean sauce or beef and Guinness pie (£6.25), game pie or bacon steak with parsley sauce (£6.50), halibut steak (£7.50) and beef wellington (£9.25); on Sunday the only food is roasts in the restaurant, and there are regular gourmet evenings. It can seem cramped at times but that just adds to the cosy atmosphere. Well kept Bass and M & B Brew XI on handpump, good service; fruit machine and piped music. A little garden and courtyard area has tables and maybe summer barbecues. The restaurant (in a former stable block) is popular, the summer hanging baskets are attractive, and they have a caravan field (certified with the Caravan Club). *(Recommended by Tony and Joan Walker, Jim Farmer, Graham Richardson, Paul and Janet Waring)*

Bass ~ Lease: Graham and Stephanie Lindsay ~ Real ale ~ Meals and snacks (till 9.45; not in bar Sun lunchtime) ~ Restaurant (not Sun evening) ~ (01827) 880357 ~ Children in eating area of bar and restaurant ~ Open 11.30-2.30, 6.30-11; 11.30-3, 6-11 Sat; 12-3, 7-10.30 Sun

SOMERBY SK7710 Map 4
Old Brewery 🍺

Off A606 Oakham—Melton Mowbray, via Cold Overton, or Leesthorpe and Pickwell; can also be reached direct from Oakham via Knossington

Baz's Bonce Blower – one of an interesting range of distinctive and award winning beers brewed here by the landlord – is listed in the Guiness Book of Records for its awesome strength. There's also Parish Mild, a Special, Poachers Ale, Somerby Premium and Farm Gold all very well kept on handpump. Groups can book tours of the little brewery in the former stables. The comfortable L-shaped main bar has red plush stools and banquettes and plush-cushioned captain's chairs, a sofa in one corner, and a good log fire in the big stone fireplace; another bar has bays of button-back red seating. There's a cheerful relaxed atmosphere, with a much broader mix of customers than you might expect, from children to grannies. Straightforward bar food includes soup (£1.95), pâté (£2.75), garlic mushrooms (£2.95), delicious local sausages (£4.50), ploughman's, lasagne, steak pie or vegetarian nuggets (£4.95), three minted lamb chops or breaded plaice (£5.95), breaded lemon sole (£6.95) and 8oz sirloin (£7.95); no-smoking area in lounge. Pool, dominoes, video game, fruit machine, maybe quiet piped pop music, no dogs. A fenced-off area by the car park has white plastic tables and a climbing frame; boules. *(Recommended by Rona Murdoch, Sue Brodrick, Joan and Michel Hooper-Immins, Mr and Mrs B H James)*

Own brew ~ Licensee Baz Parish~ Real ale ~ Meals and snacks (till 10) ~ (01664) 454866 ~ Children welcome ~ Open 11-3, 6-11; 12-10.30 Sun ~ Bedrooms: £15/£25

THORPE LANGTON SP7492 Map 4
Bakers Arms 🍽

Village signposted off B6047 N of Market Harborough

You'll probably need to book some time ahead for a table at this spacious thatched dining pub which is very popular in the evenings for its wide choice of regularly changing imaginative meals written up on the blackboards. Cooking is very good, with fresh ingredients and good presentation. Dishes might include parma ham rolls stuffed with stilton and mango or fried chicken livers with tarragon and cream (£3.75), crevettes in garlic butter (£3.95), fried calf liver with marsala cream sauce (£9.25), rack of lamb with redcurrant and rosemary sauce (£9.95) and scallops wrapped in bacon on a bed of spinach and fresh tomato (£11), with puddings like sticky toffee pudding or hazelnut meringue filled with raspberries and cream (£2.75); on Thursday evenings they have an extensive fish menu. Furnishing is simple, with straightforward seating and stripped pine tables – you'll probably find just about all the tables given over to eating – in lots of nooks and crannies. Well kept Ind Coope Burton and Tetleys on handpump, and an extensive wine list with five by the glass; good friendly service, and no games or piped music. The snug is no smoking. There are picnic tables in the garden – the only place where they allow children. *(Recommended by Brian Atkin, Henry Paulinski, George Atkinson, Angus Lyon, Eric Locker, Doug and June Miles, Jim Farmer, Mr and Mrs D J Nash, J D Cloud)*

Carlsberg Tetley ~ Lease: Kate Hubbard ~ Real ale ~ Meals and snacks (see opening times) ~ Restaurant ~ (01858) 545201 ~ Pianist Fri evenings ~ Open Mon-Fri 6.30-11; 12-2.30, 6.30-11 Sat; 12-3 Sun; cl weekday lunchtimes, Sun evening

WOODHOUSE EAVES SK5214 Map 7
Pear Tree

Church Hill; main street, off B591 W of Quorndon

This busy modern-looking pub is a well run and friendly place, with reliable food and a pleasantly chatty landlord. It's the upper flagstoned food area which is special, with pews forming booths around the walls, flagstone floor, and a pitched roof giving a pleasantly airy and open feel at lunchtime; at night, despite low lighting, the atmosphere is pleasantly lively. The end food servery looks straight through into the kitchen, which does generous helpings of good food such as sandwiches (from £2.25), soup (£2.50), deep-fried camembert with cranberry and orange sauce (£3.95), ploughman's (£4.95), burgers (from £5.95), chargrilled nut cutlets (£6.50), spit-roast chicken (£6.50), salmon and tuna fishcakes (£6.75), 8oz sirloin steak (£9.95), and puddings (£2.95). There's a log fire in an attractive Victorian fireplace (there may be a couple of labradors sitting in front of here), and decent wines. The lower part of the pub is a straightforward comfortable turkey-carpeted local, with well kept Ind Coope Burton, Marstons Pedigree and Tetleys on handpump, several malt whiskies, fruit machine, and an open fire. Outside there are a few picnic tables under cocktail parasols, with a summer bar by an arbour of climbing plants; good nearby walks. *(Recommended by Jenny and Michael Back, R and A Cooper)*

Allied ~ Lease: Richard Dimblebee ~ Real ale ~ Meals and snacks (till 3 Sat, till 10 Mon-Sat; all day bank holiday weekends) ~ (01509) 890243 ~ Children welcome ~ Open 11-3(5 Sat), 6-11; 12-5, 7-10.30 Sun

---

Lucky Dip

Besides the fully inspected pubs, you might like to try these Lucky Dips recommended to us and described by readers (if you do, please send us reports):

Acresford [A444 Burton—Nuneaton; SK3113], *Cricketts*: Busy refurbished open-plan Marstons Tavern Table dining pub, families welcome, tables in garden *(GR)*
Ashby de la Zouch [Mkt St; SK3516], *White Hart*: Friendly relaxed town pub, reasonably priced bar food (not Sun), Marstons Pedigree, some pub events; popular with Old Ashbeians RFC Sat *(Graham Richardson)*
Ashby Folville [SK7011], *Carington Arms*: Half a dozen well kept Everards and interesting guest ales and jovial welcoming landlord in attractively placed spacious and comfortable Tudor-style country pub, solid rural home cooking inc good chips; children welcome, nice garden, maybe calves or horses in back paddock *(O K Smyth)*
Barkby [35 Brookside; off A607 6 miles NE of Leicester; towards Beeby; SK6309], *Brookside*: Unpretentious pub in pretty village with a brook running past the front door, homely, welcoming and cosy, reasonably priced food, real ales inc Burtonwood Top Hat; lounge, bar and extended dining area, lots of toby jugs, brass and copper *(Rona Murdoch)*
☆ Barnsdale [just off A606 Oakham—Stamford; SK9008], *Barnsdale Lodge*: Extensive conservatory dining bar with attractively presented food, charming decor, comfortable sitting-roomish coffee lounge, real ales such as Morlands Old Speckled Hen, Ruddles County and Tetleys, cream teas, friendly attentive staff; bedrooms comfortable and attractive, with good breakfasts, adjacent antiques centre *(Gordon Theaker, George Atkinson, BB)*

Barrow upon Soar [87 Mill Lane; off South St (B5328); SK5717], *Navigation*: Extended split-level pub based on former barge-horse stabling, attractive and comfortable, with lovely canal view from small back terrace with moorings; good value home-made food (may be limited winter), interesting bar top made from old pennies, central open fire, friendly service; well kept Courage Directors, Marstons Pedigree and Shipstones, skittle alley; piped music, SkyTV *(Jim Farmer, R and A Cooper)*
Belton [off A512/A453 between junctions 23 and 24, M1; SK4420], *Queens Head*: Former coaching inn with well kept Bass, two pleasant bars, restaurant, pleasant staff, above-average food very popular with older people at lunchtime; bedrooms *(Anthony Barnes)*
Billesdon [Church St; SK7202], *Queens Head*: Beamed and partly thatched pub with wide range of good well priced food, Everards and guest ales, comfortable lounge bar with warm log fire, unspoilt public bar, small conservatory eating area and upstairs restaurant, friendly efficient staff; children welcome, pretty stone village *(John Wooll)*
☆ Breedon on the Hill [A453 Ashby—Castle Donington; SK4022], *Holly Bush*: Comfortably plush, with low black beams, lots of brass, sporting plates etc, well kept Marstons Pedigree and Tetleys, bar food (stops early lunchtime; not Sun), restaurant (may be fully booked Sat, cl Sun), no-smoking area, friendly efficient staff; piped music;

some tables outside, nice bedrooms; interesting village with Anglo-Saxon carvings in hilltop church above huge limestone face; bedrooms *(R and A Cooper, Theo, Anne and Jane Gaskin, BB)*

Carlton [Main St; SK3904], *Gate Hangs Well*: Friendly landlord and staff, well kept Marstons Best and Pedigree, cosy bar with winter fire *(Andrew Ward)*

Catthorpe [just off A5 S of Gibbet Island; SP5578], *Cherry Tree*: Welcoming and attractive country local, cosy, clean and warm, with good value food from heavily garnished sandwiches up, dark panelling, lots of plates and pictures, coal-effect fire, attentive service, well kept ales such as Ansells, Bass, Greene King Abbot and Hook Norton Best; no juke box, machines or pool table, but maybe piped radio; cl Mon/Tues lunchtimes *(P Tailyour, DAV)*

Church Langton [B6047 about 3 miles N of Mkt Harborough; just off A6; SP7293], *Langton Arms*: Extended village pub with good mix of customers, good service even when busy, well kept Marstons Pedigree and fortnightly guest beers, wide choice of food; piped music; garden with play area *(Rona Murdoch)*

Coleorton [The Moor; SK4017], *Angel*: Modernised old inn with attractive oak beams, coal fires and somewhat wonky floor; friendly, with well kept Marstons Pedigree, lots of Laurel and Hardy photographs, nostalgic piped pop music, food inc very cheap prawn sandwiches, coffee, hospitable attentive staff *(George Atkinson)*

☆ **Cossington** [Main St (B5328); SK6013], *Royal Oak*: Consistently good imaginative home cooking in recently refurbished pub/restaurant, pleasant atmosphere, well kept guest beers, moderately priced wines; has been cl Sun *(Joan Gregory, Brian Atkin)*

Foxton [Foxton Locks; off A6 NW of Market Harborough (park by bridge 60/62 and walk); SP6989], *Bridge 61*: In good setting by locks, spartan flagstones and pine furniture decor, quickly served chippy food, lots of canalia and boating relics, Everards and a guest ale, games and family room; gift and provision shop next door *(Dorsan Baker)*; [off A6 N of Market Harborough], *Shoulder of Mutton*: Friendly service, big log fire, lots of pine tables and chairs, well kept Ruddles and Tetleys, wide choice of food, well kept beers, small restaurant; pleasant big garden *(Rona Murdoch, Jim Farmer)*

☆ **Greetham** [B668 Stretton—Cottesmore; SK9214], *Wheatsheaf*: Extremely wide choice of good value generous food served till 11 inc lots of chargrills, Fri bargain steak suppers and fish take-aways, welcoming L-shaped communicating rooms, well kept Tetleys and Whitbreads-related ales, attentive staff, coal fire, soft piped music; pool and other games in end room, restaurant, tables on side grass; bedrooms in annexe *(Jenny and Michael Back, Jim Farmer, Bill and Sheila McLardy, BB)*

Hallaton [North End; SP7896], *Fox*: Welcoming comfortable local, Spanish landlord sticking to the same dependable good value menu, also vegetarian dishes and Sun carvery; well kept Marstons Pedigree and Tetleys, children welcome; tables out by village duckpond *(Rona Murdoch)*

Halstead [Oakham Rd; SK7405], *Salisbury Arms*: Village pub with lovely country views from restaurant conservatory, good varied food esp roast duck, good choice of beers inc local brew *(Mrs E Lambert)*

Heath End [follow coach signs from main rd, next to Staunton Harold Hall entry; SK3621], *Saracens Head*: Basic two-room farm pub by Staunton Harold Reservoir visitor centre, handy for Calke Abbey; well kept Bass served by jug from the cask, cosy coal fires, notable very cheap filled cobs, picnic tables on nice grass area *(Julia, Simon and Laura Plumbley, Chris Raisin, Graham Doyle)*

Hemington [21 Main St; SK4528], *Jolly Sailor*: Very welcoming village local with well kept Bass, Mansfield, Marstons Pedigree and two guest ales, farm cider, excellent range of malt whiskies and other spirits, good big fresh rolls; good open fire each end, big country pictures, brasses, blow-torches and bric-a-brac, table skittles; beautiful hanging baskets and tables outside *(Pete Storey, Pete Cherrett, Julia, Simon and Laura Plumbley)*

Hoby [SK6717], *Blue Bell*: Attractive thatched pub with friendly landlord, well kept Everards, three spacious rooms, attractive garden with play area; generous fried and other food (not Sun-Tues) *(Jim Farmer, R and A Cooper)*

Hose [Bolton Lane; SK7329], *Black Horse*: Friendly local with real ale, quarry tiles, darts, open fire *(Anon)*

Houghton on the Hill [36 Main St; SK6703], *Old Black Horse*: Recently extensively refurbished, now doing good varied nicely presented food inc vegetarian, with separate restaurant; Everards ales, friendly helpful staff, pleasant atmosphere, big garden *(Prof and Mrs H Prins, Mrs E Lambert)*

Husbands Bosworth [A427 Market Harborough—Lutterworth, junction A50; SP6484], *Bell*: Genuine and unpretentious two-bar local with enjoyable food inc good value steaks and interesting specials; Ansells and Tetleys real ales *(T Loft)*

☆ **Illston on the Hill** [off B6047 Mkt Harboro—Melton; SP7099], *Fox & Goose*: Welcoming and idiosyncratic unspoilt pub full of interesting decorations, well kept Everards Mild, Beacon, Old Original and Tiger, good coal fires; no food *(Jim Farmer, LYM)*

☆ **Kegworth** [towards West Leake – OS Sheet 129 map ref 501268; SK5026], *Station*: Attractively refurbished, with stripped brickwork and open fires, two rooms off small bar area, well kept Bass and Worthington, well served good food, upstairs dining room; tables on big back lawn; simple good bedrooms, sharing bathroom *(JP, PP, Trevor Millum)*

Kibworth Beauchamp [Leicester Rd; SP6893], *Coach & Horses*: Huge helpings of popular food in welcoming tastefully decorated pub with well kept Bass, log fires (*H Paulinski*); [5 High St], *Old Swan*: Friendly pub/restaurant with wide range of good value food inc popular Mon/Tues curry nights, well kept Marstons Pedigree (*I C Smith, Jim Farmer*)

Kilby Bridge [A50 S of Leicester; SP6097], *Navigation*: Fine canalside position with waterside garden, compact areas off central bar, big dining area, generous straightforward meaty food, well kept Tetleys-related ales and Marstons Pedigree, good coffee; piped music (may be loud), fruit machines, busy bookable restaurant; children welcome, no dogs (*C H and P Stride, Roger and Pauline Pearce*)

Kirby Muxloe [35 Main St; SK5104], *Royal Oak*: Unassuming 1960s exterior, nice atmosphere and comfortable interior, full range of Everards ales kept well, food inc good value early lunch and wide range of filled baguettes; piped music (*Andy and Jill Kassube*)

Langham [Bridge St; SK8411], *Noel Arms*: Comfortable and attractively furnished low-ceilinged lounge, smart covered terrace, well kept beers inc Ruddles from nearby brewery, usual bar food (*David and Helen Wilkins, LYM*)

☆ **Leicester** [9 Welford Pl, corner Newarke St/Welford Rd], *Welford Place*: Semicircular Victorian bar in spacious former Constitutional Club, up impressive flight of stone steps; quiet, comfortable and clubby but not stuffy by day, more lively some evenings; Ruddles Best and County, good choice of wines and other drinks, obliging management, friendly staff who seat you kindly even for just a drink, imaginative changing bar food, attractive dining room; same management as Wig & Mitre, Lincoln (*Duncan Cloud, O K Smyth, Mr and Mrs P Byatt*)

Leicester [90 High St], *Cafe Bruxelles*: Former bank with tall Victorian bar gantry, ornate domed ceiling with painted scenes between gold filigree plasterwork, back area done out as Belgian cafe with more plasterwork, check oilcloth tablecloths, old labels and coloured tiles on walls, short choice of well presented food inc Belgian snacks (Sun limited to roast, filled baguettes and ciabattas), lots of bottled beers and several continentals on draught, coffees, good budget wines, small downstairs bar; good service (*Joan and Michel Hooper-Immins, John Wooll*); [Loseby Lane], *Fourpence & Firkin*: Plain but pleasant, with wooden tables and settles, good value food; juke box loudish, but good choice (*John Wooll*); [The Ford, Glen Parva; SP5799], *Glen Parva Manor*: Pleasant pub with good facilities inside and out, food inc well filled baguettes and interesting specials, well kept Mansfield ales (*Andy and Jill Kassube*); [Silver St/Carts Lane], *Globe*: Old-fashioned three-room local with lots of woodwork, gas lighting, coal-effect gas fire, good value simple generous lunchtime food from sandwiches up,

more peaceful upstairs dining room with friendly service; well kept Everards and guest beers; juke box in sometimes noisy back room, can be smoky, children allowed in some parts (*Mr and Mrs P Byatt, John Wooll, Nigel and Sue Foster, Joan and Michel Hooper-Immins, BB*); [Market St S], *Mollie O'Gradys*: Despite the name this former Saracens Head has not been overly Irished; still welcoming, with Bass and other beers, usual food, good coffee (*Rona Murdoch*); [185 Charles St], *Rainbow & Dove*: Convivial open-plan bare-boards bar nr station with well kept Banks's Bitter, Hansons Mild, Camerons Strongarm, Marstons Pedigree and three guest ales, farm cider, limited weekday lunchtime food; students evening, professionals too lunchtime, regular beer festivals (*Mr and Mrs P Byatt, Michel Hooper-Immins*)

Little Bowden [SP7487], *Cherry Tree*: Attractive low-beamed and timbered pub with two sitting rooms, lots of pictures, well kept Everards Beacon, Tiger and Old Original with a guest beer, good value food (not Sun evening), no-smoking dining room, games room; piped pop music may obtrude a bit; children welcome, garden with picnic tables and play area; open all day Sat/Sun, nr 12th-c church (*CMW, JJW, Bryan and Betty Southwell*)

Littlethorpe [Station Rd (off B4114, not far from M1 junction 21); SP5496], *Plough*: Friendly 16th-c thatched local, local pictures and china in beamed lounge (a couple of bedlington terriers may hog the fire), smoke room with darts, copper tabletops and kettles, well kept Everards ales and a guest such as Fullers and Morlands Old Speckled Hen, usual bar food inc fish and chip suppers some nights, dining room (must book Sun lunch); piped local radio; children welcome, picnic tables outside (*Paul Read, Rona Murdoch*)

☆ **Loughborough** [The Rushes (A6); SK5319], *Black Lion*: Wide range of Hoskins and other beers, stripped pine and pews, bare boards and sawdust in front bar area, cosier back lounge; very helpful bar service, good value simple food, peaceful at lunchtime but noisy evenings; handy for canal basin (*PM, AM, R and A Cooper*)

Loughborough [Wards End], *Blacksmiths Arms*: Take-us-as-you-find-us pub with good range of well kept ales, modestly priced food esp pies; can get smoky (*Jack and Gemima Valiant*); [Canal Bank, Meadow Lane], *Boat*: Picturesque refurbished canalside pub with good atmosphere, very obliging service, good food at reasonable prices inc bargain Sun lunch, good range of beers, boating memorabilia; very popular with local office staff weekday lunchtimes (*R and A Cooper, C H and P Stride*)

☆ **Lyddington** [off A6003 N of Corby; SP8797], *Marquess of Exeter*: Comfortable series of well furnished decorous rooms, wing armchairs by big inglenook log fire, black beams, neat staff, good bar food, well kept

Ruddles, good coffee, restaurant (children allowed), good bedrooms *(Rona Murdoch, LYM)*

☆ **Market Bosworth** [Mkt Pl; SK4003], *Black Horse*: Several cosy beamed rooms, wide choice of good food, friendly attentive service, well kept Marstons Pedigree, John Smiths and Tetleys, good coffee; restaurant; bedrooms, nice setting next to alms houses in attractive village not far from Bosworth Field *(George Atkinson, Jim Farmer, Graham Richardson)*

☆ **Market Bosworth** [Mkt Pl], *Softleys*: Wine bar/restaurant (but it does have well kept Hook Norton Best and Adnams Broadside or Wadworths 6X, with a little space for drinkers by the bar) in fine old building with oak beams, brassware, hanging mugs, grand fireplace; good individually prepared food inc sandwiches and changing hot dishes, some interesting; very friendly service, decent wine, spotless housekeeping, attractive upstairs dining room; cl Mon; bedrooms *(Joan and Michel Hooper-Immins, Dorothee and Dennis Glover)*

Market Bosworth [1 Park St, towards Leicester and Hinckley], *Olde Red Lion*: Clean and tidy beamed pub, recently refurbished, with obliging staff, huge range of beers and ciders from Victorian tap room, fair-priced bar food; children welcome, tables and play area in sheltered courtyard; bedrooms *(Keith Day, Graham Richardson, LYM)*

☆ **Markfield** [A50 just under a mile from M1 junction 22; SK4810], *Field Head*: Huge beamed lounge/dining area around hotel's horseshoe bar, pictures and tasteful bric-a-brac, friendly nooks and corners; good value generous food in bar and restaurant, well kept Hoskins and others ales, decent house wine; bedrooms, big breakfasts *(O K Smyth, Ash Samanta, Josie Wright)*

Melton Mowbray [Burton St, by St Mary's Church; SK7518], *Anne of Cleaves*: Old stone-built pub recently fairly smartly refurbished, with exposed beams, nice fireplace, scrubbed tables and Tudor theme – even the piped music; daily papers *(Chris Raisin, Graham Doyle)*; [Leicester St], *Fox*: Several comfortable adjoining areas round big bar, banquettes and pub furniture, well kept beers and guests, darts, pool *(Chris Raisin, Graham Doyle)*

☆ **Mountsorrel** [Loughborough Rd, off A6; SK5714], *Swan*: Two plain but relaxing low-key whitewashed bars with warm log fires and red banquettes, good value home cooking inc vegetarian – all fresh cooked so can be slow, courteous staff, well kept Batemans XB, Theakstons XB and two guest ales, wide choice of good wines by the glass, unusual non-alcoholic drinks; small walled back garden leading down to canalised River Soar; bedrooms; not much nearby parking *(Rona Murdoch, J H Kane, Jim Farmer)*

Nether Broughton [A606 Nottingham—Mowbray; SK6925], *Red Lion*: Comfortable food pub, wide choice inc good value Sun

lunch, generous helpings *(Peter and Jenny Quine)*

☆ **Newton Burgoland** [Main St, off B586 W of Ibstock; SK3708], *Belper Arms*: Friendly and interesting pub said to date from 13th c, good reasonably priced food esp fish, also vegetarian, in roomy lounge and low-beamed areas off, masses of bric-a-brac, well kept Adnams, Marstons Pedigree and guests such as Archers, interesting farm cider, good choice of malt whiskies, restaurant; Aug bank hol beer festival; children and locals' dogs welcome, resident ghost, big garden with play area *(John Hancock, Rona Murdoch)*

Newtown Linford [Main St; SK5110], *Bradgate*: Large family pub with no-smoking conservatory, pictures and books, food inc carvery, Everards and three guest beers, family room with games machines; piped pop music; open all day Sun, garden with picnic tables and play area *(CMW, JJW)*

North Kilworth [A427, 4½ miles from M1 junction 20; SP6184], *Swan*: Pleasantly refurbished village pub, two rooms linked by arch, promising food under friendly new landlord, real ales *(Patrick Tailyour)*; *White Lion*: Clean and bright, with well kept Marstons Pedigree, welcoming staff, good home cooking, log fire, unobtrusive piped music; tables in garden *(Patrick Tailyour)*

☆ **Oadby** [Florence Wragg Way; SK6200], *Grange Farm*: Roomy and sympathetically converted attractive early 19th-c farmhouse, open fires, old local photographs, newspapers, wide range of imaginative generous food, no-smoking area, friendly staff, well kept Bass-related ales, good choice of wines and whiskies, good mix of customers *(Rona Murdoch, Christopher Evans, J D Cloud)*

Oadby [Stoughton Farm Pk, Stoughton Rd – follow Farmworld signs off A6], *Cow & Plough*: Pub in working farm open to the public 5-9 (and to farm patrons 12-2), up to seven real ales such as Belvoir Star, Fullers London Pride and Steamin' Billy, good choice of bottled beers of wines by the glass, Weston's cider, three rooms filled with brewing memorabilia, enamel signs, old church pews – no food; can start watching milking and so forth *(Andy and Jill Kassube)*

Oakham [Station Yard; SK8508], *Grainstore*: Bare brick and boards, ex-Ruddles brewer producing his own Cooking, Triple B, Tom Cribb Winter Ale and Ten Fifty here; filled rolls, good service *(Joan and Michel Hooper-Immins)*; [off A606 E, nr Empingham; SK9306], *Normanton Park*: Refreshingly informal waterside hotel's Sailing Bar with interestingly varied choice of good if pricy food inc 'healthy' menu, well kept Morlands Old Speckled Hen, Ruddles Best and County and Tetleys; bedrooms, fine views *(M J Morgan, Gwen and Peter Andrews)*; [2 Northgate], *Wheatsheaf*: Neat and friendly three-room 17th-c pub nr church, Everards and guest ales, decent usual food, open fire; back garden *(Angus Lyon, Julian Holland)*

Oakthorpe [Main St; SK3213], *Holly Bush*: Friendly recently renovated pub with bar food, well kept Marstons Pedigree, Mon folk night, annual weekend folk festival and charity events *(John Hancock)*

☆ **Preston** [Uppingham Rd; SK8602], *Kingfisher*: Attractive flower-decked pub with lots of exposed stone, beams, plates, jugs, etc, all immaculate; very friendly efficient service, good simple reasonably priced food, Marstons Pedigree, Tetleys and Worthington, comfortable chairs and sofas, no piped music; tables in garden, live entertainment Thurs *(Patrick Tailyour)*

Redmile [off A52 Grantham—Nottingham; SK8036], *Olde Windmill*: Welcoming and comfortable lounge and dining room, well kept Boddingtons and Ruddles, good range of reasonably priced bar food, tables outside *(Elizabeth and Anthony Watts, Norma and Keith Bloomfield)*

Ryhall [TF0310], *Green Dragon*: Interesting old pub with attractive pillared lounge, open fire in plush dining area, separate public bar and games room; good choice of well priced food, Ansells Mild, Bass, Boddingtons, Greene King IPA and Tetleys, helpful service *(Jenny and Michael Back)*

☆ **Saddington** [S of Leicester between A50 and A6 – OS Sheet 141 map ref 658918; SP6592], *Queens Head*: Welcoming and popular, with enterprising landlord, good food inc fresh mussels and good Sun lunch in recently built no-smoking dining room, separate smaller one for smokers, OAP bargain lunches, well kept Adnams, Everards Beacon and Tiger and Ruddles, long sloping garden with lovely reservoir view *(Elizabeth and Anthony Watts, Nick Clarke, R Murdoch)*

Shawell [not far from M6 junction 1; village signed off A5/A427 roundabout – turn right in village; SP5480], *White Swan*: Now rather more restaurant than pub, and some main dishes on the expensive side, but good choice of beers, friendly helpful service, good hot beef baguettes *(I Blackwell, DAV)*

☆ **Shearsby** [off A50 Leicester—Northampton; SP6290], *Chandlers Arms*: Comfortable village pub with brocaded wall seats, wheelback chairs, flowers on tables, house plants, swagged curtains, dog pictures for sale, popular straightforward food (helpings not too big), Marstons Bitter and Pedigree and Fullers London Pride, good service; piped pop music may be intrusive; tables in garden *(CMW, JJW, P Tailyour, Jim Farmer, BB)*

Sheepy Magna [Main St (B4116); SK3201], *Black Horse*: Neatly kept village pub with good value generous food from filled rolls up, friendly licensees, well kept Ansells Mild and Marstons Pedigree, games in lively public bar, family area, tables on pleasantly arranged back terrace *(Paul and Karen Cornock, BB)*

Shepshed [Iveshead Rd; handy for M1 junction 23; SK4719], *Jolly Farmers*: Character beamed pub, nicely carpeted, plates on wall, friendly obliging staff, spotless housekeeping; good range of beers such as Ansells Mild, Bass, Marstons Pedigree and Tetleys, usual bar food inc vegetarian and good salads (not Sun or Mon evenings); piped music *(Rona Murdoch)*

Sibson [A444 N; SK3500], *Millers*: Warm welcome in large hotel around converted bakery and watermill, mill wheel and stream nr entrance, even a small fountain in flagstoned corridor to low-beamed lounge bar with well kept Scottish Courage ales and good range of good value popular food, good service; restaurant, afternoon teas, handy for Twycross Zoo and Bosworth Field; bedrooms good *(Paul Sutton)*

☆ **Sileby** [Swan St; SK6015], *White Swan*: Small unspoilt sidestreet pub with comfortable and welcoming dining lounge, interesting good value generous home-cooked food (not Sun eve or Mon lunchtime), well kept Ansells and Marstons Pedigree, entertaining boxer dogs, small tasteful restaurant (booking needed); children's playroom in converted back bowling alley with closed-circuit TV *(Jim Farmer)*

Somerby [Main St; SK7710], *Stilton Cheese*: Comfortable and friendly 16th-c pub with good range of good value food in bar and upstairs restaurant, Marstons Pedigree, Ruddles County, Tetleys and a guest beer *(Joan and Michel Hooper-Immins)*

South Kilworth [Rugby Rd (B5414); SP6081], *White Hart*: Intimate and cosy old village pub with quaint snug dining room, larger bar with real fire, well kept Banks's, cheap freshly cooked bar food inc Sun lunch, welcoming family service; piped pop music, skittles, darts and fruit machine *(Eric Locker, Patrick Tailyour)*

Stapleton [A447 N of Hinckley; SP4398], *Nags Head*: Small, pubby atmosphere, friendly helpful service, fair range of moderately priced food from sandwiches up, wines by the glass; no music *(A C Morrison)*

Stathern [Red Lion St; SK7731], *Red Lion*: Lively extensively renovated pub with big warm homely carpeted lounge, smaller cosy flagstone bar with abundant old woodwork and bric-a-brac, open fires, candles in sconces, well kept Whitbreads-related ales, attentive staff, imaginative food in bar and restaurant, various equally imaginative events *(R M Taylor, the Gentlemen)*

☆ **Stretton** [just off A1; SK9416], *Ram Jam*: Not a pub, but a great many travel-worn readers have been glad to find this civilised and relaxing modern version of a Great North Road coaching stop: mix of sofas and neat contemporary seating in airy modern cafe-restaurant, open fire, good unusual food from light snacks up, friendly efficient service, good wines, freshly squeezed orange juice, fresh-ground coffee and so forth, daily papers; children welcome, comfortable bedrooms, open all day, food 7am-10pm *(John Fahy, F C Johnston, Sue Blackburn, Gill and Andy Plumb, Andrew and Ruth Triggs, R and S Bentley, Frank Davidson, Eddy and Emma Gibson, Mr and Mrs D Powell, Stephen and*

Julie Brown, Paul and Ursula Randall, Lesley Sones, Luke Worthington, LYM)

☆ **Stretton** [just off A1], *Jackson Stops*: Thatched pub in quiet village, well kept Ruddles and Theakstons, decent wines, good range of generous freshly cooked standard food inc good puddings, log fire, old farm tools, pleasant landlord, bar on left kept for drinkers; local for three-nation fighter squadron at RAF Cottesmore with lots of relevant memorabilia; may cl at 2 *(Dorothee and Dennis Glover, RB, Stephen and Julie Brown, M J Brooks, LYM)*

☆ **Sutton Cheney** [Main St – off A447 3 miles S of Mkt Bosworth; SK4100], *Royal Arms*: Dining pub with three small low-ceilinged front rooms, big back extension with upstairs restaurant, friendly local atmosphere, wide choice of good value food with good fresh veg, two open fires, well kept Marstons and changing guest beers, flagstone floors, regal bric-a-brac, piped music; upstairs restaurant, family conservatory with wishing well, lots of picnic tables in big garden with good children's play area; handy for Bosworth Field and Mallory Park, can get busy *(Julie Peters, Colin Blinkhorn, George Atkinson, Norma and Keith Bloomfield)*

Thrussington [37 The Green; SK6415], *Star*: 18th-c pub with heavily beamed front lounge, popular sensibly priced food, Ansells, Marstons Pedigree, Tetleys and a guest beer, more modern back area with games machines; children welcome *(Wendy and Jim Shaw, E A Roberts)*

Tur Langton [Shangton Rd; SP7194], *Bulls Head*: Very welcoming landlady, well kept Marstons Bitter and Pedigree and Timothy Taylors Landlord, eating area off lounge, unspoilt bar with open fire and darts, good choice of freshly made food from doorstep sandwiches up, unobtrusive piped music (classical lunchtime, pop evening) *(PGP, Phil Davies)*

Ullesthorpe [Main St; SP5087], *Chequers*: Big country inn popular with lunchtime businessmen, beamed and flagstoned bar and most of lounge areas with emphasis on very wide choice of reasonably priced food from large servery, real ales such as Batemans XXXB, Gales HSB and Theakstons Old Peculier, faint semi-classical music, no-smoking areas; normally prompt service; children welcome, family room and play area; comfortable bedrooms *(George Atkinson, Nigel Wilson)*

☆ **Upper Hambleton** [village signed from A606 on E edge of Oakham; SK9007], *Finches Arms*: Outstanding views of Rutland Water from tables on back gravel terrace and picture-window restaurant extension, built-in button-back leatherette banquettes and open fire in knocked-through front bar, friendly staff, well kept Grainstore Oakham and another ale such as Bass or Greene King Abbot; piped music, some enjoyable food *(M J Morgan, Jacqueline Orme, Bernard and Becky Robinson, Rona Murdoch, LYM)*

☆ **Uppingham** [High Street W; SP8699], *White Hart*: Wide choice of good value simple tasty food using local produce, inglenook fire in panelled front lounge, quite a warren of passages and rooms, two well kept Scottish Courage ales with a guest such as Morlands Speckled Hen, reasonably priced wines, good service, back restaurant; bedrooms *(Eric Locker)*

☆ **Walcote** [1½ miles from M1 junction 20, A427 towards Market Harboro; SP5683], *Black Horse*: Not a smart pub, but noted for authentic Thai food (not Mon or Tues lunchtime) cooked by the landlady, in good value big helpings, also well kept ales such as Hook Norton Best and Old Hookey, Timothy Taylors Landlord, Judges Old Growler, interesting bottled beers and country wines, no-smoking restaurant; no dogs *(David Peakall, Jim Farmer, LYM)*

☆ **Welham** [off B664 Mkt Harboro—Uppingham; SP7692], *Old Red Lion*: Popular dining pub (part of small local chain) with several beamed rooms and attractive if rather dark barrel-vaulted back area, limited choice of low-priced good food inc good steaks, Courage Best and Directors, decent wines, efficient hard-working staff, no-smoking areas, lovely fire; piped music may be loudish *(George Atkinson, Stephen Brown, Norman S Smith)*

☆ **Whitwell** [A606 Stamford—Oakham; SK9208], *Noel Arms*: Wide choice of good food (till 10) esp fish and delicious puddings, in spaciously extended plush dining lounge, smart customers; cheerful local atmosphere in original unpretentious little front rooms, well kept Marstons Pedigree and Timothy Taylors Landlord, friendly efficient staff, suntrap tables outside, occasional barbecues; piped music, can get busy; handy for Rutland Water, children welcome; bedrooms *(David Eberlin, P Stallard, LYM)*

☆ **Whitwick** [B587 towards Copt Oak; quite handy for M1 junction 22; SK4514], *Bulls Head*: Busy but welcoming L-shaped plush beamed bar with splendid views over Charnwood Forest – highest pub in Leics; well kept Tetleys-related ales, quickly served home-made food (lunchtime, not Sun) using good ingredients, friendly efficient service, back games room with piped music, big garden with menagerie of farm animals; children very welcome away from bar *(Mr and Mrs E M Clarke, R and A Cooper)*

Whitwick [off B587 NW, nr junction A447/A512; SK4117], *New Inn*: Masses of bric-a-brac and farming memorabilia in two main rooms and snug, particularly well kept ales, friendly licensees with interesting Irish background; food limited to rolls *(B Adams)*

☆ **Wing** [Top St, signed off A6003 S of Oakham; SK8903], *Kings Arms*: Recently renovated early 17th-c stone-built inn, small bar, big no-smoking restaurant, beams, log fires in two-way hearth, good helpings of good food, friendly attentive service, real ales inc unusual ones such as Salem Porter and one brewed for them by Batemans; seats in sheltered yard, good bedrooms with home-made marmalade at breakfast, pretty village, interesting medieval turf maze just up the road *(George Atkinson, Joe Besso, Pam and Mike Collett, Rona Murdoch, LYM)*

Wing [3 Top St], *Cuckoo*: Friendly thatched country pub, divided open-plan bar, friendly staff and locals, well kept Bass, Marstons Pedigree and an interesting guest beer, midsummer beer festival, cuckoo clock, darts and pool at one end, dining area with small fishtank the other, good value generous food (not Tues) inc Indian and even ostrich, weekend live music; tables in garden *(JJW, CMW)*

☆ **Woodhouse Eaves** [Brand Hill; beyond Main St, off B591 S of Loughborough – OS Sheet 129 map ref 533148; SK5314], *Wheatsheaf*: Plush and busy open-plan beamed country pub, smart customers, pleasant service, good home-cooked food inc sandwiches, good value ploughman's and vegetarian, Bass, Ruddles County, Timothy Taylors Landlord

and several well kept changing guest ales, decent wines, log fires, upstairs restaurant; floodlit tables outside, no motorcyclists *(Mr and Mrs E I Clark, Joan and Michel Hooper-Immins, Rona Murdoch, P J Caunt, John Broughton, LYM)*

Wymeswold [A6006; SK6023], *Hammer & Pincers*: Clean, bright and spaciously extended country dining pub with pine furniture in four or five rooms on several levels, good value generous home-cooked food inc vegetarian, well kept Bass, Ruddles County, Marstons Pedigree, Theakstons Best and XB and guest beers, friendly service; tables on terrace and in neat garden *(Jim Farmer, Roy Bromell)*

Wymondham [Edmonthorpe Rd; off B676 E of Melton Mowbray; SK8518], *Hunters Arms*: French chef/patron doing interesting dishes as well as more usual food in cosy and friendly two-bar pub with restaurant, well kept ales such as Bass, Batemans, Greene King IPA and Abbot; good pool room off bar *(Chris Raisin, Graham Doyle)*

If a service charge is mentioned prominently on a menu or accommodation terms, you must pay it if service was satisfactory. If service is really bad you are legally entitled to refuse to pay some or all of the service charge as compensation for not getting the service you might reasonably have expected.

Lincolnshire

Just one new entry here this year: the very well run Abbey Lodge at Woodhall Spa, a thoroughly reliable place for a meal out. Other pubs here that currently stand out for good food include the Tally Ho at Aswarby (excellent service, too), the Chequers at Gedney Dyke (imaginative cooking, lots of fresh fish), the Wig & Mitre in Lincoln (very unusual in serving food from 8am till 11pm), the Red Lion at Newton (impressive cold buffet), and the handsome and stylish old George in Stamford. For the second year running, it's the Chequers at Gedney Dyke which we choose as Lincolnshire Dining Pub of the Year, for its refreshingly successful mixture of honest village pub with informally elegant restaurant. The Cider Centre at Brandy Wharf is a very special place for anyone interested in farm ciders; the Wishing Well at Dyke gains our Beer Award this year for the quality and interest of its offerings; the chatty Beehive in Grantham stands out for the cheapness of its food (not to mention its extraordinary and historic living inn sign); and the Brewers Arms at Snaith is well worth a visit for the good interesting beers from its own brewery. It was one of the cheapest places we found for beer (another was the Black Horse at Donington on Bain); and in general drinks prices here are a bit lower than the national average. This is of course the home county of Batemans of Skegness, an excellent traditional family-run brewery whose equally traditional tied pubs are always worth stopping at. We'd also recommend four pubs from the Lucky Dip section at the end of the chapter, all inspected and approved by us: the Five Horseshoes at Barholm, Five Bells at Edenham, Bull in Market Deeping and Fox & Hounds at Old Somerby. The Victoria (not yet seen by us) seems a good bet in Lincoln itself.

ALLINGTON SK8540 Map 7
Welby Arms ◀

The Green; off A1 N of Grantham, or A52 W of Grantham

There's a warmly relaxing atmosphere at this pleasantly set friendly village local, and it's an excellent respite from the A1. A stone archway divides the two rooms of the bar. There are comfortable burgundy button-back wall banquettes and stools, some Lloyd Loom chairs, black beams and joists, red velvet curtains, a coal fire in one stone fireplace and logs burning in an attractive arched brick fireplace. One area has lots of signed celebrity photographs (Phil Collins, Gary Lineker etc); the dining lounge off to one side is no smoking. Straightforward but tasty home-cooked food might include home-cooked ham (£4.95), fish pie or recommended fresh Grimsby haddock in beer batter (£5.95) and pork schnitzel (£6.95), and home-made puddings like treacle sponge or bread and butter pudding; good value tasty Sunday roast; the restaurant is no smoking; one reader told us there was no bar food when he visited at the same time as a coach party. Particularly well kept Bass, John Smiths, Timothy Taylors Landlord and up to six guest beers such as Brains SA and Championship a week on handpump, decent wines and a good range of country wines; maybe piped nostalgic pop music; sheltered terrace. *(Recommended by John Baker, Derek and Sylvia Stephenson, Avis Spencer, Chris Mawson, Keith and Norma Bloomfield, Colin and Sue Graham, Keith Wright)*

Free house ~ Licensee R B Dyer ~ Real ale ~ Meals and snacks (not Sun evening) ~ Restaurant ~ (01400) 281361 ~ Children in restaurant ~ Open 12-2.30(3 Sat), 5.30(6.30 Sat)-11; 12-3, 7-10.30 Sun

ASWARBY TF0639 Map 8
Tally Ho 🛏️ ♀

Villaged signedposted off A15 S of Sleaford

There's a gently civilised atmosphere at this handsome stone-built 17th-c country inn. Inside, the friendly country-style bar has dark oak beams and cast-iron-framed tables, a big log fire, some stripped masonry and country prints. Great care and attention is taken over the imaginative daily specials like fennel, olive and tomato tartlet (£3.95), warm fillet of mackerel salad (£4.25) and main courses like chicken breast stuffed with cream cheese and spinach and fried in breadcrumbs or fried pork fillet with pimento pepper and white wine cream sauce (£7.95), game casserole (£8.25), strips of beef quickly fried with port and horseradish sauce (£11.50) with puddings like chocolate pecan pie or fresh fruit pavlova (£3.95). There are also the usual bar favourites like home-made soup (£2.50), Lincolnshire sausages (£3.25), filled freshly baked french bread or ploughman's (£3.50), home-made salmon and spinach fishcakes with a creamy parsley sauce (£6.25), 10oz rump steak (£8.50); vegetables are cooked to perfection; nothing is too much trouble for the attentive staff. Well kept Bass, Batemans XB and Greene King Abbot on handpump, good house wines; daily papers. It's wise to book for the attractive pine-furnished restaurant. There are tables out behind among fruit trees, and usually sheep in the meadow beyond. The bedrooms are in a neatly converted back block. Over the road, the pretty estate church, glimpsed through the stately oaks of the park, is worth a visit. (*Recommended by Bill and Brenda Lemon, Humphry and Angela Crum Ewing, Sue and Bob Ward, Julia and Peter Baker, M J Morgan, Stephen Brown, F and A Parmenter, M Morgan, June and Malcolm Farmer, D Maplethorpe, B Helliwell, Peter Coombs, Anthony Barnes*)

Free house ~ Licensee William Wood ~ Real ale ~ Meals and snacks (till 10pm) ~ Restaurant ~ (01529) 455205 ~ Children in eating area of bar and in restaurant ~ Open 12-3, 6(7 Sun)-11; cl 25-26 Dec ~ Bedrooms: £30B/£45B

BRANDY WHARF TF0197 Map 8
Cider Centre

B1205 SE of Scunthorpe (off A15 about 16 miles N of Lincoln)

This almost unique cider centre with tavern and museum is set in four acres of orchard and meadow beside the River Ancholme. The main bar is a simple room with wheelback chairs and brown plush wall banquettes, cheery customer photographs, a good little coal fire, and – the main point, of course – Addlestone's, Scrumpy Jack and Weston's Old Rosie on handpump, and some five dozen other farm ciders and perries – up to 8 tapped from casks, the rest from stacks of intriguing bottles and small plastic or earthenware kegs on shelves behind the bar; they also keep country wines and mead. The friendly landlord's very happy to talk cider, and will on request show you his extraordinary collection of hundreds of different cider flagons, jugs and bottles. A dim-lit lounge bar has all sorts of cider memorabilia and good-humoured sidelights on cider-making and drinking (not to mention the foot of 'Cyril the Plumber' poking down through the ceiling). Good value generous plain food includes sandwiches (£1.40), ploughman's (£2.90), pork and cider sausage (£3.90), home-made steak and vegetable pie (£4.90), and chicken curry (£4.90), with wonderful real chips; piped British folk music. A simple glazed verandah overlooks the river, and there's lots of space outside with an orchard, a caravan site, moorings and slipway; the landlord lays on quite a few appropriate jolly events. No children. (*Recommended by Pat and Tony Martin, Andy and Jill Kassube, CMW, JJW, Arnold and Maureen East*)

Free house ~ Licensee Ian Horsley ~ Meals and snacks (not Tues lunchtime or Mon in winter) ~ (01652) 678364 ~ Open 12-3(maybe 2 in winter), 7-11(10.30 Sun); cl Mon lunchtimes mid Oct-Easter; cl Fri before Christmas-early Jan

COLEBY SK9760 Map 8
Bell 🍺

Far Lane; village signposted off A607 S of Lincoln, turn right and right into Far Lane at church

Readers particularly enjoy the very friendly welcome at this comfortable dining pub. The three communicating carpeted rooms each have a roaring winter log fire and low black joists, and the lounge is decorated with horsebrasses, a variety of small prints, and lots of number plates from around the world. Generously served and nicely presented food includes spicy chicken wings, pâté or crispy mushrooms (£2.50), prawn cocktail (£3.50), mushroom stroganoff (£5.25), boeuf stroganoff (£7.95), salmon fillet (£8.25), chicken topped with smoked salmon and prawns en croûte with cream and mushroom sauce (£8.95), steaks (from £9.95), and specials like seafood crêpe (£2.95), chicken breast with apricot sauce (£7.95), bass with basil crust and white wine sauce or duck breast with black cherry and brandy sauce (£9.25), beef olives in mushroom and herb sauce (£9.75); Wednesday night is fish night with fresh fish delivered from Grimsby, and on Saturday and Sunday morning from 9.30-11.45 they serve a big breakfast with Sunday newspapers; no-smoking restaurant. Well kept Bass, Flowers Original, and Tetleys on handpump, and several malt whiskies. There's a quite separate pool room, darts, juke box, and board games. Several picnic tables outside, and walks along the Viking Way. *(Recommended by Ken and Jenny Simmonds, Brian Skelcher, M J Morgan, Stephen G Brown, Simon Collett-Jones, David and Ruth Hollands, Andy and Jill Kassube, Canon and Mrs M Bourdeaux, Brian Horner, P R Morley, D Maplethorpe, B Helliwell, H and C Ingham, F J and A Parmenter, Arnold and Maureen East)*

Pubmaster ~ Tenants Robert Pickles and Sara Roe ~ Real ale ~ Meals and snacks (served all day April-Dec) ~ Restaurant ~ (01522) 810240 ~ Children welcome ~ Live bands Fri evenings ~ Open 11.30-11(10.30 Sun); 11.30-3, 5.30-11 Jan-April ~ Bedrooms: £39.50B

DONINGTON ON BAIN TF2382 Map 8
Black Horse

Between A153 and A157, SW of Louth

Walkers tend to congregate at this bustling village pub, which is handily situated right on the Viking Way (muddy boots must be left in the hall). Inside, a softly lit little inner room has some unusual big murals of carousing Vikings, while the snug back bar, with cushioned seats by the log fire in the reconstructed brick inglenook, has very low black beams, and antlers around the wall lanterns. There's more room in the main bar area, popular with locals, with some heavy-horse prints and harness, a very twisty heavy low beam under its ceiling joists, and a big woodburning stove. Bar food, served in relaxed, cheerful surroundings, includes filled baked potatoes (from £2.65), ploughman's (£3.95), macaroni cheese or roast of the day (£4.75), fresh Grimsby cod or haddock (£5.25), rabbit pie or steaks (from £5.95), chicken curry (£6.95); puddings and children's dishes (£1.95); the restaurant is no smoking. Well kept Courage Directors, John Smiths, Ruddles Best, Theaksons Old Peculier and guests on handpump or tapped straight from the cask; friendly service. The public bar (another log fire) has a games room off, with darts, pool, dominoes, pinball, fruit machine, and juke box and piped music; picnic tables in the back garden. *(Recommended by Humphry and Angela Crum Ewing, Bill and Sheila McLardy, G G Lawrence, B D Craig, Elizabeth and Anthony Watts, F C Johnston, Paul and Janet Waring, Peter Coombs, Keith Wright, Arnold and Maureen East)*

Free house ~ Licensee Micheal Pogson ~ Real ale ~ Meals and snacks (till 10pm) ~ Restaurant ~ (01507) 343640 ~ Children in eating area of bar and in restaurant ~ Open 11.30-3, 6-11(10.30 Sun) ~ Bedrooms: £25S/£40S

If you have to cancel a reservation for a bedroom or restaurant, please telephone or write to warn them. A small place – and its customers – will suffer if you don't.

DYKE TF1022 Map 8

Wishing Well 🍺

21 Main Street; village signposted off A15 N of Bourne

The efficient welcoming landlord at this homely village inn is quite a beer buff, his well kept real ales change all the time and are sometimes quite unusual, there might be Batemans Jawbreaker, Everards Tiger, Greene King Abbot, Morlands Aunt Sally, Tetleys Bitter, Woodfordes Wherry and possibly one brewed for the pub by Enderby called Going Down Well, all on handpump. There is a wishing well at the dining end of the long, rambling bustling front bar – as well as lots of heavy beams, dark stone, brasswork, candlelight and a cavern of an open fireplace. The carpeted lounge area has green plush button-back low settles and wheelback chairs around individual wooden tables. The good solid reputation for tasty food continues, there might be home-made soup (£2.10), sandwiches (from £2.10), ploughman's (from £4.50), pork ribs in barbecue sauce (£5.50), several home-made pies (£5.95), vegetarian lasagne (£5.50), steak (£6.95), children's meals (from £2.25), several more imaginative daily specials like mixed grill (£4.95), rabbit casserole (£5.50) and lemon and tarragon chicken (£5.50) as well as vegetarian dishes and fresh fish; popular Sunday lunch (£8.50; children £5.50 – must book); both restaurants are no smoking. The quite separate public bar, smaller and plainer, has sensibly placed darts, pool, shove-ha'penny, dominoes, fruit machine and juke box. There's a play area by the garden. *(Recommended by Jenny and Michael Back, Jill Bickerton, M J Morgan, F J and A Parmenter)*

Free house ~ Licensee Barrie Creaser ~ Real ale ~ Meals and snacks (till 10pm) ~ Restaurant ~ (01778) 422970 ~ Children welcome ~ Open 11-3, 6-11 ~ Bedrooms: £21S/£42S

GEDNEY DYKE TF4125 Map 8

Chequers 🍴

Village signposted off A17 Holbeach—Kings Lynn

Lincolnshire Dining Pub of the Year

There is a comfortable mix of locals, drinkers and diners at this stylish but friendly and informal Fenland village pub which is particularly popular for its very good imaginative food. A speciality is the really fresh fish and seafood such as grilled plaice, lemon sole, monkfish with herb crust and tomato and chilli salsa, roast salmon with horseradish sauce, skate wing, Cromer crabs and Brancaster scallops. There's a wide choice of other good freshly cooked and attractively presented food, including home-made soup (£2.50), open sandwiches (from £3.95; Loch Fyne smoked salmon with rillette of Scottish salmon £4.95), ploughman's (£3.95), smoked eel fillets (£4.50), mushroom omelette (£4.50), spinach potato cake with cheese and mustard rarebit, beef and ale or ham and leek pie (£6.50), chicken breast stuffed with sun dried tomatoes with lemon sauce (£7.95), lamb with chervil and lemon crust (£9.50), beef fillet with smoked salmon and wild mushroom sauce (£9.95), duck breast with sage polenta and orange sauce (£10.95); children's helpings, and good home-made puddings; roast Sunday lunch; service is friendly and professional. Everything's kept spotless, with an open fire in the bar, a small rather old-fashioned no-smoking restaurant area at one end, and an elegantly done new dining conservatory at the other, overlooking a garden with picnic tables. Well kept Adnams Bitter, Bass, Elgood Pageant, Greene King Abbot, and Morlands Old Speckled Hen on handpump, about ten decent wines by the glass, elderflower pressé and apple juice; dominoes and chess. *(Recommended by Stephen G Brown, Derek and Sylvia Stephenson, Peter Burton, Mr and Mrs N Thorp, JDM, KM, Geoff Tomlinson, Chris and Shirley Machin, Anthony Barnes, F J and A Parmenter, John Wooll)*

Free house ~ Licensee Judith Marshall ~ Real ale ~ Meals and snacks (12-1.45, 7-9) ~ Restaurant ~ (01406) 362666 ~ Children welcome ~ Open 12-2, 7-11; 12-3, 7-10.30 Sun; cl 25-26 Dec

GRANTHAM SK9135 Map 7

Beehive £

Castlegate; from main street turn down Finkin Street opposite St Peter's Place

The old rhyme

> *Grantham, now two rarities are thine:*
> *A lofty steeple and a living sign,*

with the rejoinder

> *Grantham, Grantham don't you boast*
> *About your box upon a post*
> *Or about your lofty spire*
> *As Lincoln's got one six foot higher*

refers to this friendly town pub's unique inn-sign – a hive full of living bees, mounted high up in a lime tree outside. It's been here since at least 1830, and probably the 18th c, making this one of the oldest populations of bees in the world. The comfortably straightforward bar which is popular with students has a bustling, friendly atmosphere, and Batemans XB, and two guests like Shepherd Neame Spitfire, and South Yorkshire Barnsley Bitter on handpump. Very good value bar food includes sandwiches (from £1.35), filled baked potatoes and good value basic ploughman's (from £1.65), omelettes or sweet and sour chicken (£2.95), gammon and egg (£3.50) as well as three daily specials like steak, mushroom and ale pie, vegetarian pizza flan or pasta carbonara (all £3.25), and puddings like spotted dick (£1.55); cheerful service. Fruit machine, pinball, trivia, video game, good juke box and piped music. *(Recommended by Andy and Jill Kassube, Comus Elliott, C and G Fraser)*

Free house ~ Licensee S J Parkes ~ Real ale ~ Lunchtime meals and snacks (not Sun) ~ (01476) 567794 ~ Well behaved children welcome till 8pm ~ Open 11-11; 11-5, 7-11 Sat; 7-10.30 Sun

HECKINGTON TF1444 Map 8

Nags Head

High Street; village signposted from A17 Sleaford—Boston

Inside this low white-painted comfortably lived-in 17th-c village pub, the left-hand part of the snug two-roomed bar has a coal fire below a shiny black wooden chimney-piece in what must once have been a great inglenook, curving into the corner and taking up the whole of one end of the small room – it now houses three tables, one of them of beaten brass. On the right there are red plush button-back built-in wall banquettes, small spindleback chairs, and an attractive bronze statuette-lamp on the mantelpiece of its coal fire; also, a lively watercolour of a horse-race finish (the horses racing straight towards you), and a modern sporting print of a problematic gun dog. Homely changing bar food might include sandwiches or carrot and orange soup (£2.25), garlic mushrooms on a crouton or pâté (£3.25), pears and stilton grilled on toast (£3.50), hot beef or pork and stuffing sandwich (£4.25), ploughman's (£4.50), smoked salmon, salmon and prawn quiche (£5.25), potato, cheese and leek pie (£5.50), Lincolnshire sausage pie (£5.75) and warm salmon with cream, lemon and chives or grilled tuna steak with tomato and basil (£6.50) as well as puddings like rhubarb crumble (all £2.50). Well kept Wards Sheffield Best and Double Maxim, and a guest beer on handpump, and cheery, efficient service; darts, pool, shove-ha'penny, fruit machine, and juke box. The garden behind has picnic tables, and it's not far to an unusual eight-sailed windmill. *(Recommended by G G Lawrence, Andy and Jill Kassube, R E and P Pearce, K and J Brooks, Janet and Peter Race, B D Craig, Anthony Barnes, Sue Rowland, John Fahy)*

Wards ~ Lease: Bruce Pickworth ~ Real ale ~ Meals and snacks ~ (01529) 460218 ~ Well behaved children welcome ~ Open 11-3, 5-11; 12-3, 7-10.30 Sun ~ Bedrooms: £22/£32

Pubs close to motorway junctions are listed at the back of the book.

LINCOLN SK9872 Map 8
Wig & Mitre ★ ⑪ ♀
29 Steep Hill; just below cathedral

This welcoming old pub, on a steeply picturesque alley that runs down from the cathedral towards the town centre, still has many carefully preserved original 14th-c features. There's a section of the original lime-ash and reed floor, exposed oak rafters, and part of the medieval wattle-and-daub by the stairs. Downstairs, the cheerful, simpler bar has pews and other more straightforward furniture on its tiles, and a couple of window tables on either side of the entrance; the civilised upstairs dining room has settees, elegant small settles, Victorian armchairs, shelves of old books, and an open fire, and is decorated with antique prints and more modern caricatures of lawyers and clerics, with plenty of newspapers and periodicals lying about. There's an incredible range of very well prepared food from several different menus – including a full breakfast menu (English breakfast £5.95) – served non-stop from 8 o'clock in the morning to closing, and however rushed or busy they are service always stays cordial and efficient. The several menus vary in style and are not particularly cheap. Dishes might include sandwiches (from £2.95, warm fillet steak with tarragon mustard £6.75), asparagus and leek soup (£4), lentil and garlic or stilton, port and celery pâté (£4.75), asparagus, avocado and prawn salad with lemon and lime dressing (£6), lamb simmered in rosemary and garlic or braised beef with mushrooms and red wine (£7.50), layered sun-dried tomato polenta with mozzarella and vegetables on a tomato and herb sauce (£8.50), skate on crispy risotto and herb cake on saffron butter sauce (£13), roast breast of duck with soubise tartlet and honeyed sauce (£14.50), roast rack of lamb with minted pea purée (£14.95), puddings such as tiramisu or baked strawberry cheesecake (£3.50). There's an excellent and extensive, if somewhat pricy, selection of over 95 wines, many of them available by the glass. Sam Smiths OB on handpump, lots of liqueurs and spirits, and freshly squeezed orange juice.
(Recommended by David and Ruth Hollands, Canon and Mrs M Bourdeaux, J Oglanby, Walter and Susan Rinaldi-Butcher, Ian Phillips, Tony Dickinson, Chris Raisin, Graham Doyle, Nick Zotov, A Morton, Sue and Bob Ward, R C Wiles, A Preston, Mr and Mrs B Langrish, Alain and Rose Foote, B D Craig, F C Johnston, F J and A Parmenter, Arnold and Maureen East)

Sam Smiths ~ Tenants Michael Hope and Paul Vidic ~ Real ale ~ Meals and snacks (8-11; 10.30 Sun) ~ Restaurant ~ (01522) 535190 ~ Children in restaurant ~ Open 8-11(10.30 Sun); cl 25 Dec

NEWTON TF0436 Map 8
Red Lion ★ ⑪
Village signposted from A52 E of Grantham; pub itself also discreetly signed off A52

There is an impressive cold buffet with an splendid choice of meats, fish and salads at this impeccably kept civilised old place. You help yourself to as much as you like, a small helping is £8.50, normal £9.50, and large £12.50, with children's helpings £3.50. On Saturday evening and Sunday lunchtime there are also four roasts, and at other times there's a choice of dishes on the blackboard: steak pie or lasagne (£6.75), lamb, beef and ale stew or liver and onions (£6.95), fisherman's hotpot (£7.25) and lamb cutlets or breast of chicken with cider and tarragon sauce (£7.50). The licensee used to be a butcher, and it does show – the meat and fish could hardly taste better; no-smoking area in dining room. The welcoming communicating rooms have fresh flowers, old-fashioned oak and elm seats and cream-rendered or bare stone walls covered with farm tools, malters' wooden shovels, a stuffed fox, stag's head and green woodpecker, pictures made from pressed flowers, and hunting and coaching prints. Very well kept Bass and Batemans XXXB on handpump; friendly service, unobtrusive but well reproduced piped music, a fruit machine, and a nice dog. During the day and at weekends two squash courts run by the pub can be used by non-members. The neat, well sheltered back garden has some seats on the grass and on a terrace, and a good play area. The countryside nearby is ideal for walking, and acccording to local tradition this village is the highest point between Grantham and the Urals.
(Recommended by Andy and Jill Kassube, Brian and Jill Bond, M J Morgan, RB, James Nunns,

Stephen Brown, F J and A Parmenter, Keith Wright, Chris Walling, Peter and Gwyneth Eastwood)
*Free house ~ Licensee Graham Watkin ~ Real ale ~ Meals and snacks (till 10pm) ~
(01529) 497256 ~ Children welcome ~ Open 11.30-3, 6-11; 12-3, 7-10.30; cl 25 Dec*

ROTHWELL TF1599 Map 8
Nickerson Arms

Village signposted off B1225 S of Caistor, about a mile S of its junction with the A46

There is an enjoyably relaxed and civilised atmosphere at this long white-painted
building which is a refreshing oasis in this part of the world. The pleasant bar is
divided by a couple of arches with a warm central coal fire, a good balance between
standing room and comfortable chairs and tables (with little bunches of fresh flowers),
attractive wildlife prints, and heavy beams; there's a spacious dining area. Bar food
under the new licensees includes sandwiches (from £2), soup (£2.25), fried brie with
lemon and dill dressing (£3.85), fish and chips (£5.75), lasagne (£6), breast of chicken
in tomato, mushroom and white wine cream sauce (£6.95), steak, Guinness and
smoked mussel pie or aubergine filled with chilli rice and tomato and basil sauce
(£7.25), 10oz sirloin steak (£9.95), and specials: salmon wrapped in plaice on spinach
with prawn and cheese sauce (£12.95), monkfish with lemon and caper butter
(£13.75), king scallops topped with asparagus with mushroom and white wine
gratinée (£15.95). Well kept Batemans XB and XXXB, Courage Directors, Fullers
London Pride, Marstons Pedigree, a guest beer on handpump, and about three dozen
malt whiskies; piped music, darts and dominoes; tables outside. Take care coming out
of the car park: it's a blind bend. If you're up here, Potterton & Martin's plant nursery
on the B1205 on the far side of Nettleton is well worth a visit. *(Recommended by Andy
and Jill Kassube, Peter Toms, David and Michelle James, Peter Coombs)*

*Free house ~ Licensees Mr and Mrs V Schofield ~ Real ale ~ Meals and snacks ~
(01472) 371300 ~ Children welcome ~ Open 12-3(4 Sun), 7-11(10.30 Sun)*

SNAITH SE6422 Map 7
Brewers Arms 🍺

10 Pontefract Rd

Old Mill Traditional, Mild, Bullion, Old Curiosity, Black Jack, and Nellie Dean on
electric pump are all brewed just round the corner – you can arrange a tour – from
this attractively converted old mill. Unusually, they also do their own lager as well;
quite a few malt whiskies. There are old local photographs, exposed ceiling joists and
a neat brick and timber bar counter in the pleasantly comfortable clean and bright
open-plan rooms of the bar. Standard but popular good value bar food in generous
helpings includes steak pie or peppered pork (£4.50) and fresh crab salad (£4.95);
friendly, obliging staff. There are good value home-cooked restaurant meals too, with
green plush chairs and turkey carpet in a fresh and airy conservatory-style dining area
(no smoking) with a pine plank ceiling and lots of plants. Beware of joining the
skeleton at the bottom of the old well; fruit machine and piped music. *(Recommended
by H K Dyson, Mr and Mrs B Hobden, Michael Butler, Derek and Sylvia Stephenson, Comus
Elliott, CW, JW)*

*Own brew ~ Manager John McCue ~ Real ale ~ Meals and snacks ~ Restaurant ~
(01405) 862404 ~ Children in eating area of bar and in restaurant till 9pm ~
Singalong to organist Sun eve ~ Open 11-3, 6-11(7-10.30 Sun) ~ Bedrooms: £45/£57*

STAMFORD TF0207 Map 8
George ★ 🍺 🛏 ♀

71 High St, St Martins

This smartly bustling old coaching inn was built in 1597 for Lord Burghley, though
there are surviving parts of a much older Norman pilgrims' hospice – and a crypt
under the cocktail bar that may be 1000 years old. It's sited on what was the Great
North Road and in the 18th and 19th c, this historic building was the hub of 20 coach

trips a day each way from London and York (two of the front rooms are still named after these destinations). There's a medley of seats in its civilised, but relaxed rooms ranging from sturdy bar settles through leather, cane and antique wicker to soft settees and easy chairs, while the central lounge has sturdy timbers, broad flagstones, heavy beams, and massive stonework. The nicest place for lunch (if it's not a warm sunny day) is the indoor Garden Lounge, with well spaced white cast-iron furniture on herringbone glazed bricks around a central tropical grove. There's waiter drinks service in the cobbled courtyard at the back which is lovely in summer, with comfortable chairs and tables among attractive plant tubs and colourful hanging baskets. Not cheap but very good bar food includes soup of the day with Italian bread (£4.30), chicken liver pâté with orange and redcurrant sauce (£5.45), pasta and gnocchi dishes (£8.95), fresh haddock from Billingsgate or lamb liver and bacon (£9.95), tuna steak niçoise (£10.95), and 10oz sirloin steak or a splendidly tempting help-yourself buffet (from £14.50); in the York bar there are more snacky dishes such as sandwiches (from £3.85; french stick with sirloin steak, onions, tomato and mushroom £6.55), cheddar and stilton platter with french bread (£5.95), and puddings (£3.25). Adnams Broadside, Ruddles Best and a guest on handpump, but the best drinks are the Italian wines, many of which are good value and sold by the glass; also freshly squeezed orange juice, filter, espresso or cappuccino coffee. Professional friendly, helpful staff. Besides the courtyard, there's a neatly maintained walled garden, with a sunken lawn where croquet is often played. *(Recommended by Neville Kenyon, David and Ruth Hollands, Deborah Weston, Rona Murdoch, Stephen Holman, Sue Holland, Dave Webster, Joan and Tony Walker, Julian Holland, Angela Copeland, Mavis and John Wright, Vicky and David Sarti, D Maplethorpe, B Helliwell, R C Wiles, Andrew and Ruth Triggs, Cliff Blakemore, Jane Kingsbury; also in Good Hotel Guide)*

Free house ~ Licensees Ivo Vannocci and Chris Pitman ~ Real ale ~ Meals and snacks (all day) ~ Two restaurants ~ (01780) 755171 ~ Children welcome ~ Open 11-11; 12-10.30 Sun ~ Bedrooms: £78B/£105B

WOODHALL SPA TF1963 Map 8
Abbey Lodge

Tattersall Rd, Kirkstead (B1192 Woodhall Spa—Coningsby)

A reliable and popular place for a good meal, this solid discreetly decorated roadside pub has some Victorian or older furnishings, and pictures showing its World War II connections with RAF Coningsby – Squadron 627, based at the former airfield opposite, still holds reunion dinners here. The wide range of good generous bar food includes sandwiches (from £1.25), ploughman's or a very popular lamb lasagne (£4.50), steak and kidney pie (£5.25), chilli (£5.50), beef in beer (£5.95), rolled plaice fillet in wine and prawn sauce or coq au vin (£6.50), poached halibut with prawns (£6.75) and steaks (from £8.75); the restaurant has good Sunday roasts. Well kept Bass and Worthington Best on handpump; affable licensee; good welcoming service; piped music sometimes. *(Recommended by D Maplethorpe, B Helliwell, Bill and Sheila McLardy, Arnold and Maureen East, G W Stevenson, G G Lawrence)*

Free house ~ Licensee Mrs Inglis ~ Real ale ~ Meals and snacks (till 10pm Fri, Sat) ~ Restaurant ~ (01526) 352538 ~ Children over 5 in restaurant ~ Open 11-2.30, 6.30-11; 12-2.30, 6.30-10.30 Sun

---

Most of the big breweries now work through regional operating companies, with different names. If a pub is tied to one of these regional companies, we put the parent company's name in brackets – in the details at the end of each main entry.

Lucky Dip

Besides the fully inspected pubs, you might like to try these Lucky Dips recommended to us and described by readers (if you do, please send us reports):

Althorpe [SE8309], *Dolphin*: Friendly, clean and tidy, with comfortable banquettes in dining area, pictures, plates and bric-a-brac, wide choice of good value home cooking (not Sun/Mon evenings), three real ales; piped pop music; tables and play area outside *(JJW, CMW)*

☆ **Barholm** [TF0810], *Five Horseshoes*: Old-fashioned relaxed village local, clean, cosy and friendly, with well kept Adnams, Batemans and interesting guest beers, mini beer festivals, decent wines, comfortable seats, rustic bric-a-brac, maybe weekend food; tables out under shady arbour, weekend barbecues, paddocks behind *(M J Morgan, Alan and Heather Jacques, Steve Hughes, BB)*

☆ **Barnoldby le Beck** [SW of Grimsby; TA2303], *Ship*: Warm well furnished nautical-theme country pub with good sensibly priced food inc game, vegetarian, esp fresh Grimsby fish, attentive welcoming staff, good range of wines, comfortable dining room, pleasant village setting *(John Smith, Marie and Edwin Legard, Maggie Middleton)*

☆ **Bicker** [A52 NE of Donnington; TF2237], *Red Lion*: Simply modernised and relaxing 17th-c pub with masses of china hanging from bowed black beams, huge fireplace, well kept Batemans and other ales, wide choice of good generous food, staff friendly and efficient even when busy; tables on terrace and tree-shaded lawn *(Gary Carter, Bill and Sheila McLardy, BB)*

Billingborough [High St; TF1134], *Fortescue Arms*: Cosy traditional atmosphere, beams, big log fire, country bygones, good value food esp home-made pies and good veg, bar dining area and restaurant, well kept Ansells, Bass, Ind Coope Burton and a guest ale, decent wines, friendly attentive staff; tables under apple trees in big garden, attractive village *(D and M Elmer)*

☆ **Boston** [Wormgate; TF3244], *Goodbarns Yard*: Popular and comfortable, with old beams in original core (former riverside cottages looking up to Boston Stump), modern but matching back extension, plenty of alcoves, terrace overlooking river, well kept Scottish Courage and guest ales, wide choice of good value food from filled french bread and baked potatoes to steaks inc interesting snacks *(John Honnor, Ian Phillips)*

Boston [Horncastle Rd (B1183)], *Kings Arms*: Fine spot by canal opp tall five-sail working windpump, airy unpretentious front bar, plush little back bar, well kept Batemans Mild, XB and XXXB, friendly efficient service, low-priced usual bar food; cheery modern bedrooms *(Ian Phillips, BB)*

Burton upon Stather [N of Scunthorpe; SE8717], *Sheffield Arms*: Good choice of well kept ales and of generous food in attractively furnished old-fashioned stone pub, old photographs *(G G Lawrence)*

☆ **Castle Bytham** [High St; SK9818], *Castle*: Consistently good generous bar food (not Mon evening) with lots of veg, friendly efficient service, Ansells Mild, Boddingtons Bitter and Gold, Tetleys, Theakstons Best and Old Peculier and a guest such as Vaux Samson, roaring log fire, nicely laid out side dining room; piped music, no children at the bar; CCTV for parked cars *(Jenny and Michael Back, A W C Perry)*

Caythorpe [SK9348], *Red Lion*: Friendly 16th-c pub in pleasant surroundings, wide choice of fair-priced food from sandwiches to good fresh Grimsby fish, well kept ales inc Boddingtons, Greene King Abbot, Timothy Taylors Landlord and Youngs Special, no piped music, attentive service *(H and C Ingham, Peter Burton)*

Cleethorpes [High Cliff Rd; south promenade; TA3008], *Willys*: Modern bistro-style pub with cafe tables, tiled floor and painted brick walls; brews its own good beers, also well kept guest beers and well priced basic lunchtime food; quiet juke box, Humber estuary views; annual beer festival *(Michael Butler, R M Taylor)*

Coleby [Hill Rise; SK9760], *Tempest Arms*: Roomy, friendly and comfortable local, with well kept Batemans XB, good value food Thurs-Sat, friendly staff and spaniel, lots of hanging baskets, wonderful view from pretty garden; on Viking Way *(Mike and G Turner, M J Morgan)*

Coningsby [Boston Rd (B1192); 1/2 mile NW of village – OS Sheet 122 map ref 242588; TF2458], *Leagate*: Dark old heavy-beamed fenland local with three linked areas, ageing medley of furnishings inc great high-backed settles around the biggest of the three log fires; prompt attractively priced straightforward home-made food (service can deteriorate if very busy), several Scottish Courage and other ales; piped jazz or pop music, fruit machine; rustic garden with play area; children if eating *(M J Morgan, LYM)*

Cowbit [Barrier Bank; A1073 S of Spalding; TF2618], *Olde Dun Cow*: Welcoming 17th-c local with wide choice of generous good value bar food, well kept ales such as Crown Buckley Rev James, Batemans XXXB, Exmoor Gold and Theakstons Best and XB, pleasant black and white split-level bar with old oak beams, antique notices, restaurant one end, family games area at the other; fairly subdued piped pop music, satellite TV plans, maybe live music; tables in garden with play area, bedrooms *(E Robinson, Gwen and Peter Andrews)*

☆ **Edenham** [A151; TF0621], *Five Bells*: Welcoming family service, wide choice of reliable generous food in neat busy modernised dining lounge, well kept Bass and Tetleys, two log fires, dominoes, piped music, lots of foreign banknotes, soft lighting; back restaurant/function room, tables in garden with good play area; children and walkers welcome *(Mike and Penny Sanders, Nigel Sopp, Jenny and Michael Back, F J and A Parmenter, LYM)*

☆ **Gedney** [Chapelgate, just off A17 W of Long Sutton; TF4024], *Old Black Lion*: Good welcoming service, wide choice of good value quickly served food inc fresh veg, Whitbreads-related ales, good house wines *(John Wooll)*

☆ **Grantham** [High St; SK9135], *Angel & Royal*: Remarkable new medieval carved stone facade, ancient oriel window seat in upstairs plush bar on left, massive inglenook in friendly high-beamed main bar opp, well kept Bass and occasional guest beers, bar food; bedrooms in comfortable modern hotel block extending behind *(Comus Elliott, LYM)*

Grantham [Vine St], *Blue Pig*: Another of the few buildings here to survive the great fire of 1660, beams, character, well kept beer, welcoming service, simple lunchtime bar food, three rooms – one with machines *(RB)*

Grimsby [88 Freeman St; TA2609], *Corporation*: Well kept Bass and Worthington in traditional town pub with nice back lounge – original panelling, leather seats, old Grimsby photographs; second lounge, lively public bar with games and TV *(Pete Baker)*; [Victoria St], *Hope & Anchor*: Basic traditional chatty local with bar and lounge off central servery, friendly genuine staff, reasonably priced lunchtime food inc hot filled rolls, well kept real ales with ambitious two-week beer festival *(R M Taylor)*; [Alexandra Dock – follow Heritage Cente signs, behind Sainsburys], *Lincoln Castle*: Former Humber paddle-steamer now with friendly bar and lower deck restaurant, good value food inc Sun carvery, well kept Bass and Youngers No 3, engines preserved and on view, cabinet showing ship's history, seats out on upper deck; games machine, piped music; handy for National Fishing Heritage Centre *(Val Stevenson, Rob Holmes, JJW, CMW)*; [Garth Lane], *Tap & Spile*: Basic but very welcoming alehouse with spartan stone floors and heavy wooden chairs and tables; good choice of ales with tasting samples, unusual dishes on the light menu *(R M Taylor)*

Habrough [Station Rd (B1210); TA1413], *Station*: Friendly Victorian village pub, good value standard food, dining area and separate games room, up to half a dozen real ales; piped local radio, quiz Mon evening, sing-along Tues and Sat; bedrooms, open all day (not Sun afternoon) *(CMW, JJW)*

☆ **Halton Holegate** [B1195 E of Spilsby; TF4165], *Bell*: Pretty village local, simple but comfortable and consistently friendly, with wide choice of decent home-made food inc outstanding fish and chips, vegetarian dishes and Sun lunches, well kept Bass, Batemans and Mansfield Old Baily, aircraft pictures, pub games, maybe piped music; children in eating area and restaurant *(Derek and Sylvia Stephenson, BB)*

Hatton [A158 Wragby—Horncastle; TF1776], *Midge*: Good changing well presented fresh-cooked food (not Mon) in bar and restaurant, sensible prices, well kept Bass, Stones and a guest ale *(Arnold and Maureen East, R A Nuttall)*

Haxey [31 Church St (B1396); SK7699], *Loco*: Shop conversion full of railway memorabilia inc large chunk of a steam loco, lots more inc clocks and armour; reasonably priced bar food, Sun lunches, occasional gourmet evenings, Scottish Courage ales; children welcome, cl Mon-Weds lunchtimes, Sat/Sun evening *(CMW, JJW)*

☆ **Hough on the Hill** [SK9246], *Brownlow Arms*: Wide range of good value well cooked and presented food (not Sun evening or Mon lunchtime) in attractive dining pub's relaxing lounge, sofas and comfortable chairs, Marstons Pedigree and changing guest beers, decent wines, friendly efficient service; pubby separate bar, good restaurant; good value pretty bedrooms, good breakfasts, peaceful picturesque village handy for Belton House *(J and P Maloney, Sue and Bob Ward)*

Kirkby on Bain [TF2462], *Ebrington Arms*: Low beams and partitions, eating areas each side, copper-topped tables, wall banquettes, aircraft and racing car pictures, nicely set out restaurant; prompt welcoming service, five or more changing ales mainly from small breweries such as Crofters Backwoods, Oakham JHB, Old Mill Mild, Rudgates Thunderflash, good range of sensibly priced food *(Jenny and Michael Back)*

☆ **Langworth** [A158 Lincoln—Wragby; TF0676], *New Station*: Pleasant pub (station long gone, railway still there) with roomy conservatory, well kept Scottish Courage ales, reasonably priced wine, generous food esp fish and chips; Sunday carvery *(Arnold and Maureen East)*

Leadenham [A17 Newark—Sleaford; SK9552], *George*: Remarkable range of several hundred whiskies, a good choice of wines by the glass inc their own direct German imports, and well kept ales inc Boddingtons, fair-priced quickly served food from sandwiches to steaks in unassuming bar, side games room, piped music, restaurant; bedrooms plain but good value; good breakfasts, for non-residents too *(M J Gale, C H Daly, D Maplethorpe, B Helliwell, LYM)*

☆ **Lincoln** [6 Union Rd, behind Castle], *Victoria*: Well kept Batemans, Everards, Timothy Taylors Landlord and half a dozen or more interesting changing guest beers in classic quaint backstreet Victorian local behind castle, two cosy rooms, warm chatty atmosphere, country wines, basic cheap lunchtime food (Sun too), friendly staff; children allowed in back room, but not really a family pub – can get crowded lunchtime, lively late evening; impromptu Sun afternoon folk/rock jam sessions, June beer festival *(Gwyneth and Salvo Spadaro-Dutturi, Dr and Mrs A K Clarke, Jon Hale, Andrew Young)*

☆ **Lincoln** [Bunkers Hill], *Lincolnshire Poacher*:

Roomy and comfortable, with old chairs and books, Lincolnshire memorabilia inc interesting prints, big dining part with no-smoking areas, good range of food inc local dishes, Mansfield Riding and Old Baily ale, attentive considerate service; play areas inside and (with video surveillance) outside; open all day Sun *(M Morgan, Gordon Thornton)*

☆ **Lincoln** [Steep Hill], *Browns Pie Shop*: Wide choice of good food inc popular chunky pies; restaurant licence only, but does have Everards Tiger and Ruddles Best as well as decent wines, comfortable seats, friendly staff, pleasant traditional atmosphere *(M J Morgan, D Maplethorpe, B Helliwell)*

Lincoln [7 Langworthgate], *Bull & Chain*: Popular local with comfortable banquettes, decorative plates, cheap food (all day Sun) inc vegetarian, friendly staff, Bass and John Smiths ales, good darts team, dominoes, juke box, machines; children welcome, big garden overlooking tennis court, not far from cathedral *(Keith Wright, JJW, CMW, Geoffrey Lindley)*; [Exchange Arcade], *Corn Hill Vaults*: Popular bar with unusual sandwiches, well kept Sam Smiths, pool table in separate area, friendly staff; juke box after 3 *(Chris Raisin, Graham Doyle)*; [21 High St], *Golden Eagle*: Busy town pub with well kept changing ales such as Fullers London Pride, Timothy Taylors Landlord and Woodfordes Great Eastern served through sparklers, good choice of country wines, good value lunchtime food inc vegetarian *(John Baker)*

Little Reedness [Main St (off A161 SE of Goole); SE8023], *Ferry House*: 15th-c pub in delightful spot on River Ouse, open-plan bar with huge log fire, cheap filling food, well kept Mansfield Bitter and Riding, wines by the glass, pictures, piano, darts, piped music; children welcome, tables outside, cl Mon lunchtime; bedrooms planned, pleasant village with 14th-c church, river walks, not far from Blacktoft Sands RSPB reserve *(CMW, JJW)*

☆ **Long Bennington** [Main Rd; just off A1 N of Grantham; SK8344], *Reindeer*: Clean and welcoming local, nice bustly atmosphere, chatty staff, good choice of generous home-cooked food in bar and more formal dining lounge, well kept Scottish Courage ales, good wines *(Mrs F Stubbs, Mike and Karen England)*

Long Sutton [Main St; off bypass A17 Kings Lynn—Holbeach; TF4222], *Crown & Woolpack*: Good generous cheap home cooking (filled rolls only, Mon-Weds) in attractively redecorated lively local with panelled back dining room, good Sun lunch (must book), Bass and Worthington BB, roaring fire; dominoes, piped music (may be rather loud, bar may be smoky) *(Jenny and Michael Back)*; [89 London Rd], *Olde Ship*: Welcoming attractive 17th-c black and white inn, log fires; well kept Bass, Boddingtons, Greene King Abbot and sometimes a guest beer, good home-cooked bar food, cosy restaurant with good Sun roasts and some

unusual dishes *(R H Freeman, Mrs Viv Elce)*

Louth [Cornmarket; TF3387], *Masons Arms*: Edwardian pub with well restored woodwork and fancy glass, friendly landlord, several well kept ales, good vegetarian food, good upstairs dining room (remarkably decorated former masonic lodge meeting room); bedrooms *(Marcus Bates, David and Michelle James)*; [Westgate], *Wheatsheaf*: Well kept pub with decent food, good changing choice of ales, cheerful atmosphere; can be crowded *(David and Michelle James)*

Mareham le Fen [A115; TF2861], *Royal Oak*: Welcoming partly thatched 14th-c building with pleasant interior, well kept Batemans XB and guest ales, limited good value food *(M J Morgan)*

☆ **Market Deeping** [Market Pl; TF1310], *Bull*: Bustling local, warmly friendly, with cosy low-ceilinged alcoves, little corridors, interesting heavy-beamed medieval Dugout Bar; well kept Everards Tiger and Old Original and guest beers, amiable landlord, popular food (not Sun or Mon evening), attractive eating area, restaurant (booking now advised); no piped music lunchtime, seats in pretty coachyard; children in eating areas; open all day Fri, Sat *(Mr and Mrs N M Cook, M J Morgan, Sue and Bob Ward, LYM)*

Marston [2 miles E of A1 just N of Grantham; SK8943], *Thorold Arms*: Pleasantly refurbished, with good food and atmosphere, friendly service, well kept ales *(Peter Coombs)*

☆ **Navenby** [High St; SK9858], *Kings Head*: Small village pub with decent food inc good varied puddings in pleasant no-smoking area off bar, interesting knick-knacks, books, quick friendly service, well kept Bass, no piped music *(D Toulson)*

☆ **Nettleham** [A46 N of Lincoln; TF0075], *Brown Cow*: Comfortable civilised lounge bar, kept spotless, with wide range of good varied reasonably priced food, friendly service; Sun lunch very popular; pleasant village *(Gordon Thornton, G G Lawrence)*

Nettleton [off A46 just SW of Caistor; TF1100], *Salutation*: Useful pub for walkers, at foot of Castor Top, highest part of the Wolds; popular and hospitable *(David and Michelle James)*

North Kelsey [off B1434 S of Brigg; TA0401], *Butchers Arms*: Reopened again after long closure by local farmer who brews his own beer on the farm; tastefully refurbished, with good atmosphere, good wholesome sensibly priced food, no chips; no juke box *(E M Jones)*

North Thoresby [High St (A16/B1201); TF2998], *Granby*: Traditional two-bar pub with Bass, Worthington and weekly guest beers, good food inc Sun lunch in lounge bar and no-smoking restaurant, most attractive prices, good service; tables out on terrace *(David Lord, Mr and Mrs Ecob)*

☆ **Norton Disney** [off A46 Newark—Lincoln; SK8859], *St Vincent Arms*: Attractive and cheerful village pub with well kept Batemans

Mild and XXXB, Marstons Pedigree, three guest beers, open fire, good value generous plain food from sandwiches up inc beautifully cooked veg, pleasant landlord; tables and big adventure playground out behind *(H and C Ingham)*

☆ **Old Somerby** [B1176 E of Grantham; SK9633], *Fox & Hounds*: Enjoyable bar food from sandwiches to steaks inc good fish in spacious rambling pub with big no-smoking area, hunting-theme decor, well kept Marstons Pedigree, Ruddles Best and County and a guest beer, restaurant; piped music, darts, machines; children welcome, tables in big garden, jazz alternate Thurs; cl Mon exc bank hols *(RB, Andy and Jill Kassube, H and C Ingham, F J and A Parmenter, Peter Coombs, D Maplethorpe, B Helliwell, Simon Collett-Jones, M G Hart, F C Johnston, LYM)*

Ropsley [SK9934], *Green Man*: Genuine two-bar village local, good range of beers, friendly welcome, snacks, darts, dominoes *(RB)*

Saltfleetby all Saints [B1200; TF4590], *Prussian Queen*: Old pennies embedded in bar counter, chatty helpful licensees, Bass and Saddlers ale, good value basic bar food, books, TV, darts, piano, fruit machine, pool; ship's wheel in dining room *(CMW, JJW)*

☆ **Skegness** [Vine Rd, Seacroft (off Drummond Rd); TF5660], *Vine*: Handsome extended country house dating mainly from late 18th c, comfortable well run bar overlooking drive and own bowling green, imposing antique seats and grandfather clock in turkey-carpeted hall, juke box in inner oak-panelled room; three well kept Batemans ales, good value food in bar and restaurant, friendly staff, tables on big back sheltered lawn with swings; pleasant bedrooms, peaceful suburban setting not far from beach and birdwatching *(Christine and Geoff Butler, R and A Cooper, LYM)*

Spilsby [High St; TF4066], *White Hart*: Well kept Hardys & Hansons, very welcoming service, good home cooking, lace cloths on tables, fire in tiny original Victorian grate in lounge area *(David and Ruth Hollands)*

Springthorpe [SK8789], *Red Lion*: Bar, small lounge and little cosy dining room; good food inc fresh fish and four roasts of the day, very generous puddings *(Nigel Clifton)*

Stamford [All Saints Pl; TF0207], *Crown*: Good value food and well kept Ruddles County in large rambling stone-built pub's 60sish panelled bar and no-smoking dining room; dogs welcome; comfortable quiet bedrooms *(Michael Gittins, David Peakall)*; [East St], *Dolphin*: Small pub with good atmosphere, several rooms around bar set with dining tables, good range of generous food, well kept Badger Best and Charles Wells Eagle – may be packed Fri mkt day *(Rona Murdoch)*; [5 Cheyne Lane, between High St and St Marys St], *Hole in the Wall*: Cosy and busy old L-shaped room with old tables, chairs and settles, central servery, good lunchtime food (may be a wait), well kept Bass, Courage Directors, Boddingtons, Fullers London Pride and Marstons Pedigree, decent

reasonably priced wine *(Joan and Michel Hooper-Immins, Julian Holland)*; [Scotgate], *White Swan*: Civilised and comfortable with pine furniture and a cosy feel; good choice of Batemans beers *(Sue Holland, David Webster)*

Surfleet [A16 N of Spalding; TF2528], *Mermaid*: Welcoming food stop, with wide choice from sandwiches to good value Sun lunch, two dining areas, well kept ales such as Adnams, Buchanans, Robinsons and John Smiths, friendly family service; by river with footpaths, interesting church nearby with leaning tower; garden with play area; bedrooms *(PGP, Bill and Sheila McLardy)*

Surfleet Seas End [154 Reservoir Rd; off A16 N of Spalding; TF2728], *Ship*: Unspoilt 17th-c riverside pub, flagstone bar, open fires, well kept Marstons Bitter and Pedigree and guests such as Fullers London Pride, good home-cooked meals (delicious seafood platter needs 24 hrs' notice), no-smoking dining room; bedrooms *(Mr and Mrs Cocks, M J Morgan)*

Swayfield [off A151 NW of Bourne; SK9922], *Royal Oak*: Friendly family pub, lots of character, good value generous usual food from ploughman's to steaks inc good Sun lunch, well kept Bass, Tetleys and Oakham ales, efficient service *(J and P Maloney, F J and A Parmenter)*

Tealby [11 Kingsway, off B1203; TF1590], *Kings Head*: 14th-c thatched and beamed pub in quiet and attractive Wolds village, handy for Viking Way walk; food freshly prepared to order inc vegetarian, real ale, farm cider *(A R Moore)*; [Cow Lane], *Olde Barn*: Pleasant pub handy for Viking Way, cheerfully served straightforward food inc fresh fish, well kept Everards, big back garden with lawn *(David and Michelle James, Derek and Sylvia Stephenson)*

☆ **Tetford** [off A158 E of Horncastle; TF3374], *White Hart*: Early 16th-c pub with good atmosphere, fine mix of people, well kept Mansfield Riding and a guest beer, wide choice of food from good value sandwiches to popular Sun lunches; old-fashioned settles, slabby elm tables and red tiled floor in pleasant quiet inglenook bar, no-smoking snug, basic games room; seats and swings on sheltered back lawn, simple bedrooms *(Rita and Keith Pollard, Sue and Bob Ward, DJ, MJ, LYM)*

Threekingham [just off A52 12 miles E of Grantham; TF0836], *Three Kings*: Big entrance hall, two small bars and dining room; warm and comfortable, good service, wide choice of good value food, well kept Bass, M&B Brew XI and Stones; tables outside *(M J Morgan, R Vincent)*

Uffington [Bertie Lane; TF0607], *Old Bertie Arms*: Beautifully kept thatched pub with good food, excellent landlord *(Mr Gibson-Warner)*

☆ **Wellingore** [High St; off A607 Lincoln—Grantham; SK9856], *Marquis of Granby*: Cheerful, attractive and neatly kept old pub in tiny pretty village, concentration on good value bar food inc interesting specials in bar and restaurant, good filled rolls, welcoming service, well kept Theakstons Best and XB and changing guest ales, comfortable button-back banquettes, log fire; bedrooms *(H and C Ingham, D Toulson)*

West Deeping [King St; TF1109], *Red Lion*: Long low bar with plenty of tables, roaring coal fires each end, old stonework and beams, well kept Ansells Mild, Bass, Ind Coope Burton and Shepherd Neame Spitfire, wide choice of generous food from sandwiches up inc vegetarian, puddings from cold cabinet, prompt welcoming service; big pool room, open all day, tables out behind *(Jenny and Michael Back)*

Woolsthorpe [the one nr Belvoir; signed off A52 Grantham—Nottingham; SK8435],

Chequers: Attractively refurbished and extended village pub within sight of Belvoir Castle, with good food (French chef) in bar and restaurant, well kept ale, friendly service, lots of events esp Fri in big entertainments area, own cricket ground; tables outside, boules; bedrooms *(N J Stokes, Stuart Pear, BB)*; *Rutland Arms*: Comfortable and welcoming country pub with popular food in bars and restaurant, well kept Whitbreads-related ales, lounge with some high-backed settles, hunting prints, brasses and bric-a-brac, open fire, family extension; video juke box, two pool tables in annexe; big lawn with good play area, quiet spot nr restored canal *(Elizabeth and Anthony Watts, M J Morgan, F and A Parmenter)*

Norfolk

*After a monster crop of new entries here last year, we add another three this:
the distinctive and carefully furnished Hare Arms at Docking (good food), the
civilised new Wensum Lodge in Fakenham (a comfortable place to stay) and
the Fat Cat in Norwich (outstanding range of interesting real ales). Other pubs
currently on top form here include the White Horse near the harbour at
Blakeney, the upmarket Hoste Arms at Burnham Market, the Lord Nelson at
Burnham Thorpe (still delightfully unspoilt, but carefully tidied up by the
current licensees), the Crown at Colkirk (great to have any of their 50 wines
by the glass), the Saracens Head near Erpingham (interesting food, interesting
place), the charmingly placed Earle Arms at Heydon (now Norfolk's first fully
licensed pub/theatre), the striking and bustling old Adam & Eve in Norwich,
the very welcoming Hare Arms at Stow Bardolph (a proper country pub with
very long-serving licensees), Darbys at Swanton Morley (another reliable
country pub, lots of real ales), and the Three Horseshoes at Warham (a
sympathetic extension for this super country local). It's good news that the
licensees of that nice pub the Fishermans Return at Winterton on Sea, after 22
years as tenants, have now bought the freehold. Though so many Norfolk
pubs do enjoyable food, the Saracens Head near Erpingham stands out as such
a fine place for a meal out that it is our choice as Norfolk Dining Pub of the
Year, for the second year running. Some changes to mention here include an
extension with four new bedrooms for the Kings Arms in Blakeney, better
fresher food and quite a lot of refurbishment at the Rose & Crown at
Snettisham (including more bedrooms), and plans for a new conservatory at
the Manor Hotel at Titchwell. The Fur & Feather at Woodbastwick deserves
special mention as the tap for the excellent Woodfordes beers (and for an
own-brew pub is surprisingly food-oriented). Pubs in the Lucky Dip section at
the end of the chapter currently giving readers a lot of pleasure include the
Chequers at Binham, Jolly Sailors at Brancaster Staithe, Crown at Great
Ellingham, Kings Head at Hethersett, Marsham Arms at Hevingham, Victoria
at Holkham and Walpole Arms at Itteringham; and we have inspected and
approved almost all of these.*

BAWBURGH TG1508 Map 5
Kings Head

Pub signposted down Hats Lane off B1108, which leads off A47 just W of Norwich

There's a warm welcome from the friendly licensee and his staff in this bustling old
pub. The four linked rooms have low beams, some standing timbers, a log fire in a
large knocked-through canopied fireplace, a woodburner and dried flowers in the
attractive inglenook in the end room, and comfortable green or rust plush banquettes.
A huge choice of good food might include home-made soup (£1.95), sandwiches or
filled french bread (from £3), mushrooms with strips of bacon, cream and brandy
(£3.95), mushroom and nut pasta bake (£4), filled baked potatoes (from £4.45),
omelettes (from £4.70), ploughman's (from £5.75), honey and lime chicken or steak
and kidney pie (£6.95), curry of the day (£7.60), lots of daily specials, steaks (from

£12.95), and children's menu (£3.95). Helpings are generous; no-smoking restaurant. Well kept Adnams, Boddingtons, Flowers and Original, and two guest beers on handpump; good quick service. There are rustic tables and benches on the gravel outside. *(Recommended by Bill and Sheila McLardy, Anthony Barnes, Ian Phillips, David Gregory, Bob Arnett, Judy Wayman, MDN, John Whitehouse, Brian and Jean Hepworth; more reports please)*

Free house ~ Licensee A E Wimmer ~ Real ale ~ Meals and snacks (till 10pm) ~ Restaurant ~ (01603) 744977 ~ Children welcome ~ Open 11-11; 11-3, 6-11 in winter; 12-10.30 summer Sun

BLAKENEY TG0243 Map 8
Kings Arms 🏠

West Gate St

The airy extension here – used for dining and for families – is proving very popular, and on top of this are the four new ensuite bedrooms with views to Blakeney Point. It's a busy place (particularly in summer) but the little rooms keep a cheery pubby atmosphere, and service remains efficient and friendly. The three simply furnished, knocked-together rooms have some interesting photographs of the licensees' theatrical careers, other pictures including work by local artists, and what's said to be the smallest cartoon gallery in England in a former telephone kiosk; three rooms are no smoking. Decent bar food in generous helpings includes sandwiches (from £1.50, the crab are good), soup (£2), filled baked potatoes or ploughman's, whitebait or samphire (£3.95), and crab, fresh cod, haddock or plaice (£5.50); enjoyable breakfasts. Very well kept Marstons Pedigree, Morlands Old Speckled Hen, Websters Yorkshire and Woodfordes Wherry on handpump. The large garden has lots of tables and chairs and a separate, equipped children's area; there are baby-changing facilities, too. They can supply information on boat trips out to the seals and birds of Blakeney Point. Dogs welcome. *(Recommended by Peter Plumridge, Chris Rounthwaite, John Fahy, Dr Jim Mackay, R Suddaby, J F Knutton, Sue Holland, Dave Webster, Melanie Bradshaw, M Morgan, Charles Bardswell, Helen and Ian Cookson, Pam and Mike Collett, Anne Morris, M A Mees, Tony Dickinson)*

Free house ~ Licensees Howard and Marjorie Davies ~ Meals and snacks (all day in summer) ~ (01263) 740341 ~ Children welcome ~ Open 11-11; 12-10.30 Sun ~ Bedrooms: /£50S, and self-catering flats upstairs £50

White Horse 🍺 🛏

4 High Street

Nicely set near the harbour, this small hotel has a long main bar with an enjoyably chatty atmosphere, and a good mix of both visitors and locals. It's predominantly green (despite the venetian red ceiling), with a restrained but attractive decor (including two big reproductions of Audubon waterfowl prints up at the far end), and well kept Adnams, Bass, and Stones on handpump, and a good choice of reasonably priced wines; cribbage, dominoes, chess, Connect-4, backgammon. There's wheelchair access, though a short flight of steps to the back part of the bar. Good food served by swift, courteous staff includes sandwiches (from £1.95), home-made soup (£2.25; the cockle chowder is very good £3), scrambled eggs and smoked salmon (£3.95), smoked haddock and leek pie, lamb a la greque, aubergine, tomato and mozzarella or pork with cider, leeks and stilton (all £5.50), steak (£9.95), daily specials such as roast mediterranean vegetable flan (£5.50) or skate wings with brown butter (£6.25), and home-made puddings (£2.50); children's menu (£3); no-smoking area. There's a pleasant little dining room with nice pictures on its white-painted flint walls, and tables out in a suntrap courtyard. *(Recommended by Charles Bardswell, George and Shirley Campey, Norman and Valerie Housley, Dr B and Mrs P B Baker, Frank Davidson, Sue Holland, Dave Webster, P Gillbe, John Beeken, Ken and Jenny Simmonds, George Atkinson)*

Free house ~ Licensee Daniel Rees ~ Real ale ~ Meals and snacks ~ Restaurant ~ (01263) 740574 ~ Children in gallery room and eating area of bar ~ Open 11-3, 6-11; 12-3, 7-10.30 Sun ~ Bedrooms: £30B/£60B

BLICKLING TG1728 Map 8
Buckinghamshire Arms
Off B1354 N of Aylsham

Standing at the entrance to Blickling Hall, this handsome Jacobean inn has lots of tables on the big lawn, and they serve food from an out-building here in summer. The small front snug is simply furnished with fabric-cushioned banquettes, while the bigger lounge has neatly built-in pews, stripped deal tables, and Spy pictures. Lunchtime bar food includes home-made soup (£2.75), open sandwiches or filled french bread (from £2.75), filo king prawns with garlic mayonnaise or ploughman's (£4.50), home-made steak and kidney pie (£5.95), and smoked chicken and avocado salad with a blue cheese dressing (£6.50), with evening dishes such as home-made pâté with cumberland sauce (£3.50), aubergine and mushroom risotto with pepper salsa or thai-style chicken curry (£5.95), tagliatelle with chicken, mushrooms and garlic cream (£6.25), grilled fresh lemon sole (£8.25), and steaks (from £9.50); puddings such as treacle tart or banoffi pie (£2.75). Adnams Broadside and Best, and Reepham Granary Bitter on handpump, and a good range of wines; shove-ha'penny. Blickling Hall is open 1-4.30pm Tuesday-Sunday 1st July-14th September, and Thursday-Sunday 18th September-2nd November; the garden is open Wednesdays-Sundays. *(Recommended by J R Hughes-Lewis, John Fahy, Bob Arnett, Judy Wayman, Colin Barnes, John Wooll, Nigel Clifton, Howard Clutterbuck, R C Vincent, Melanie Bradshaw, Simon Penny, John Honnor)*

Free house ~ Licensee Pip Wilkinson ~ Real ale ~ Meals and snacks ~ Evening restaurant ~ (01263) 732133 ~ Open 11-3, 6-11; 12-3, 7-10.30 Sun ~ Bedrooms: /£60S

BURNHAM MARKET TF8342 Map 8
Hoste Arms 🛏
The Green (B1155)

In a lovely village of Georgian houses, this rather smart 17th-c hotel is doing very well at the moment. There's an informally civilised atmosphere in the boldly decorated bars, massive log fires, and a good mix of people, especially at the weekend. The panelled bar on the right has a series of watercolours showing scenes from local walks, there's a bow-windowed bar on the left, a nice sitting room, a little art gallery in the staircase area, and well kept Greene King Abbot and IPA, and Woodfordes Wherry on handpump, a good wine list, decent choice of malt whiskies, and freshly squeezed orange juice. Good, well presented bar food includes lunchtime sandwiches (from £3.50; toasted sirloin sandwich with caramelised onions £6.25), soup such as green pea or broccoli (£3.25), half-a-dozen local oysters (£5.25), seared king scallops with cucumber noodles and a white wine sauce (£6.50; main course £13), lovely braised ham hock with root vegetables and haricot beans (£6.95), beef bourguignon (£7.50), chilli chicken stir-fry with oriental vegetables and egg noodles (£8.95), and honey-roasted guinea fowl, bamboo shoots and water chestnuts or roasted brill with fettucine and roasted peppers and a red pepper vinaigrette (£9.95); efficient, friendly service. The conservatory and part of the restaurant are no smoking. At the back is a pleasant walled garden with tables on a terrace. *(Recommended by David Heath, J F Knutton, John Fahy, P and M Pumfrey, M J Morgan, David and Anne Culley, Robert and Anne Lees, Dennis and Barbara Cook, Minda and Stanley Alexander, Sebastian Leach, Sue Holland, Dave Webster, Chris Rounthwaite, Ian Phillips, Mark Hydes, Ken and Jenny Simmonds, M A and C R Starling, Howard and Margaret Buchanan, Charlie Ballantyne, John Wool, Anthony Barnes, MDN, D and J Tapper, F C Johnston, D Hayman, Jo and Den Reeve, Mr and Mrs M J Matthews, George Atkinson, DJW, Jack and Philip Paxton, Bill and Sheila McLardy, Paul Boot, Melanie Bradshaw; also in Good Hotel Guide)*

Free house ~ Licensees Paul Whittome, Mrs Jeanne Whittome, Miss Rebecca Mackenzie ~ Real ale ~ Meals and snacks ~ Restaurant ~ (01328) 738777 ~ Children welcome ~ Jazz Fri evenings ~ Open 11-11; 12-10.30 Sun ~ Bedrooms: £60B/£86B

BURNHAM THORPE TF8541 Map 8
Lord Nelson ◀

Village signposted from B1155 and B1355, near Burnham Market

Nelson was born in this village and held a party here (he knew this unspoilt pub as the Plough) before leaving to take command of his 64-gun ship the *Agamemnon* in 1793 – so it's no surprise to find lots of pictures and memorabilia of him lining the walls. The characterful little bar has well waxed antique settles on the worn red flooring tiles, smoke ovens in the original fireplace, and well kept Greene King IPA, Abbot and Mild and Woodfordes Nelsons Revenge tapped from the cask in a back stillroom (there's no bar counter); there's an unusual rum concoction called Nelson's Blood. A no-smoking eating room has flagstones, an open fire, and more pictures of the celebrated sailor. Bar food in generous helpings includes sandwiches (from £2), home-made soup (£2.20), English breakfast (£4.10), ploughman's (from £4.25), omelettes (from £4.15), a home-made pie of the day (£5.40), and daily specials like warm salad of salmon, onions and mushroom on a bed of winter leaves with croutons (£4), pancakes filled with spinach, leeks, mushrooms and sweetcorn with spicy tomato sauce (£5.40), roast loin of lamb with garlic and rosemary stuffing on a red wine and rosemary sauce (£8.15), and fried pork loin with apple and calvados sauce (£8.50); children's meals (from £2.75); hardworking, friendly staff. It can get busy so it may be necessary to book; shove-ha'penny, cribbage, dominoes. There's a play area with football, basketball and a climbing frame outside. *(Recommended by F G Drain, Dennis and Barbara Cook, Ian Phillips, John Wooll, D J Hayman, J F Knutton, Mrs S F Front, Quentin Williamson, Michael Switzer, D R Blake, MDN, M J Morgan, Paul Boot, Jack and Philip Paxton, D Hayman, Emily Heading, R D Greaves, H and C Ingham)*

Greene King ~ Lease: Lucy Stafford ~ Real ale ~ Meals and snacks ~ (01328) 738241 ~ Children in eating area of bar ~ Rhythm and blues monthly Fri evenings ~ Open 11-3, 6-11; 12-3, 7-10.30 Sun

COLKIRK TF9126 Map 8
Crown ♀

Village signposted off B1146 S of Fakenham; and off A1065

This is still very much a proper village pub – even though you'll find a good few people enjoying the interesting food. The calmly welcoming public bar and small lounge both have open fires, solid straightforward country furniture, rugs and flooring tiles, and sympathetic lighting; the no-smoking dining room leading off is pleasantly informal. Well kept Greene King IPA, Abbot, Mild, Rayments, and winter Dark Ale on handpump, several malt whiskies, and 50 wines (all are available by the glass). Promptly served bar food includes home-made soup (£2.15), lunchtime filled french bread (from £2.95), lunchtime ploughman's (£3.80), fried brunch (£5.35), gammon and egg (£6.75), steaks (£10.95), and daily specials such as fresh haddock or cod (£5.85), tomato and spinach nut roast (£5.75), steak and kidney pie (£5.95), and fillet of chicken in leek and stilton sauce (£6.75), and puddings; the dining room is no smoking. Darts, shove-ha'penny, cribbage, dominoes, and fruit machine. There's a garden and suntrap terrace with picnic tables. *(Recommended by Frank Davidson, Chris and Ann Garnett, Jeremy Gough, Dr B and Mrs P B Baker, Anthony Barnes, Brian and Jill Bond, Philip and Susan Philcox, Bill and Sheila McLardy, John Wooll)*

Greene King ~ Tenant Patrick Whitmore ~ Real ale ~ Meals and snacks (12-1.45, 7-9.30; not 25-26 Dec) ~ (01328) 862172 ~ Children welcome ~ Open 11-2.30, 6-11; 12-2.30, 7-10.30 Sun

DOCKING TF7637 Map 8
Hare Arms

Station Rd (B1153 towards Brancaster)

Attractively and individually decorated in unusual relaxing deep colours, with lots of entertaining bric-a-brac and Victorian pictures, this has two smallish main bar rooms and a cosy and pretty end dining room. The licensees' son (who specified the colour scheme) cooks enjoyable food, with crisp fresh vegetables. Changing day by day, it generally includes delicious soups (£2.75), and there might be lunchtime sandwiches (from £1.95), ploughman's (from £4.50), home-made steak and kidney pie (£5.95), daily fresh fish such as baked cod (£6.95) or shark steaks (£9.75), avocado and spinach bake with mediterranean vegetables or Moroccan pork casserole (£7.25), chicken stuffed with sun-dried tomatoes and ricotta cheese (£9), steaks (from £10.95), and puddings such as banana fritters with toffee sauce or apple or rhubarb pies (£2.50). Well kept Flowers Original, Ind Coope Burton, Tetleys, and a beer named after the pub on handpump, decent wines, good log fire, welcoming service, and piped music; the jack russell is called Jessie. There's a small site for touring caravans behind. *(Recommended by John Wooll, Meriel and John Beveridge, Charles Bardswell)*

Free house ~ Licensee Christine Milner ~ Real ale ~ Meals and snacks ~ Restaurant ~ (01485) 518402 ~ Children welcome away from bar ~ Live bands (60s/70s, cabaret) alternate Thurs and Fri evenings ~ Open 11-3, 6-11; 12-3, 7-10.30 Sun

ERPINGHAM TG1631 Map 8
Saracens Head 🍴 ♈ 🛏

Address is Wolterton – not shown on many maps; Erpingham signed off A140 N of Aylsham, keep on through Calthorpe, then where road bends right take the straight-ahead turn-off signposted Wolterton

Norfolk Dining Pub of the Year

This civilised inn continues to prove that orginality and quality need not be expensive. It's run by a friendly, relaxed licensee who warmly welcomes his customers, and clearly enjoys cooking the imaginative food. The regularly changing menu at lunchtime might include soup (£2.75), crispy fried brie with apricot sauce (£4.25), mussels with cider and cream (£4.75), dolmas of cabbage leaves stuffed with savoury rice and tomato sauce (£6.95), braised duo of wood pigeon masala (£7.75), and large grilled dover sole (£9.50), with evening dishes like rich home-made game and smoked ham pâté (£3.50), creamy wild mushroom pancakes (£4.75), crab and whitefish fishcakes with olive mayonnaise (£7.95), and fried julienne of veal with olive, basil and tomato (£8.50); puddings such as brown bread and butter pudding, chocolate pot with rich orange jus or banana fritters with maple syrup (£2.95); very good value two-course weekday lunch (£4.95), Sunday supper (£5.95), and three-course monthly feasts (£11.50); booking is almost essential. The two-room bar is simple and stylish, with high ceilings and tall windows giving a feeling of space, though it's not large, and around the terracotta walls are a mix of seats from built-in leather wall settles to wicker fireside chairs, solid-colour carpets and curtains, log fires and flowers on the mantelpieces. It looks out on a charming old-fashioned gravel stableyard with picnic tables. There's a pretty little four-table parlour on the right – cheerful nursery colours, and another big log fire. Very well kept Adnams and guest beers such as Adnams Broadside or Morlands Old Speckled Hen on handpump; decent malt whiskies. The wine list is really quite interesting, with some shipped direct from a French chateau. *(Recommended by Rita Horridge, Minda Alexander, Dr P Lavender, Bob Arnett, Judy Wayman, D E Twitchett, Charles Bardswell, Robert Turnham, Dr Jim Mackay, John Wooll, Frank Davidson, J F Knutton, Roger Danes, BHP, Wayne Brindle, Paul Boot, Ian Phillips, Mrs M Lewis, Simon Penny, David Culley, Mr and Mrs J R Morris, Jason Caulkin, Neil and Angela Huxter, Ken and Jenny Simmonds)*

Free house ~ Licensee Robert Dawson-Smith ~ Real ale ~ Meals and snacks ~ Restaurant ~ (01263) 768909 ~ Well behaved children welcome ~ Open 11-3, 6-11; 12-3, 7-10.30 Sun ~ Bedrooms: £35B/£50B

FAKENHAM TF9229 Map 8
Wensum Lodge 🛏

Bridge St (B1146 S of centre)

This careful new development is based on the brick-built former grain store for a huge watermill on the River Wensum, and the original structure is evident enough to make for an environment that's well out of the ordinary, without being overly quaint.

There's a very roomy and relaxing civilised bar with lots of pictures, mates' chairs grouped around polished tables, and Manchester Gold, Scotts Blues & Bloater, and Theakstons XB on handpump, kept under light blanket pressure; fruit machine and piped music. Two beamed dining areas (one is no smoking) lead off, with more dark tables and chairs, prints and houseplants. Interesting reasonably priced food includes bacon, lettuce and tomato french bread (£3.25), baked potato with ham, cheese and mushrooms and grilled crispy brown (£3.45), vegetarian pancake (£5.35), chicken, leek and asparagus pie (£6.55), home-made steak, mushroom and Guinness pie or giant vol-au-vent with wild mushrooms in a madeira sauce (£7.25), half a spring Norfolk chicken with barbecue sauce (£8.25), gammon topped with tomato and mozzarella cheese (£9.75), chargrilled steaks (from £10.75); they will do sandwiches or filled baked potatoes at any time during opening hours; attentive service. There are tables outside, with grass running down to the river, weeping willows along its banks. *(Recommended by Charles Bardswell, Mrs Dorothy Smith, George Atkinson)*

Free house ~ Licensees P and G Hobday ~ Real ale ~ Meals and snacks (11-3, 6.30-10) ~ Restaurant ~ (01328) 862100 ~ Children welcome ~ Open 11-11; 12-10.30 Sun ~ Bedrooms: £45B/£55B

GREAT BIRCHAM TF7632 Map 8
Kings Head ♀ 🛏

B1155, S end of village (which is called and signposted Bircham locally)

Handy for the very striking windmill, this rather grand looking place – used as a lunch place for Sandringham shooting parties – has a warmly welcoming Italian licensee. The unassuming lounge bar (two room areas) has a pleasantly quiet and relaxed atmosphere and a mix of high and low tables suiting both diners and drinkers, with a good hot fire in a third more homely bit round behind. Reliably good bar food includes lunchtime sandwiches (from £2.70), ploughman's (£4.90), smoked haddock mornay (£6.95), home-made fishcakes with crab sauce, moules or steak and kidney pudding (£7.50), and quite a few Italian specialities such as fresh spaghetti or tortellini (£5.90); tempting puddings; the dining area is no smoking. Besides well kept Bass, Charrington IPA and Hancocks Bitter, there's a good choice of malt whiskies, freshly squeezed juices and decent wines; maybe unobtrusive piped music, dominoes. The somnolent alsatian is called Brandy. The big side lawn, with a well kept herbaceous border, has picnic tables and play things. The attractive village has a decent art gallery, and Houghton Hall is not far off. *(Recommended by Charles Bardswell, John Wooll, R Vincent, A K Clemow)*

Free house ~ Licensees Isidoro and Iris Verrando ~ Real ale ~ Meals and snacks ~ Restaurant ~ (01485) 578265 ~ Children in eating area of bar and in restaurant ~ Open 11-3, 6.30-11; 12-3.30, 7-10.30 Sun; closed evenings 25-26 Dec ~ Bedrooms: £35B/£57B

HEYDON TG1127 Map 8
Earle Arms

Village signposted from B1149 about midway between Norwich and Holt

This is Norfolk's only fully licensed pub theatre and they are committed to the production of the new work of local writers and performers; they also have a gallery for local artists. Two carpeted rooms, one with hatch service, open off a small lobby with a handsomely carved longcase clock, and are individually furnished and decorated, with pretty rosehip wallpaper over a stripped dado, china on shelves, deep tiled-floor cupboards with interesting bric-a-brac, attractive prints and good log fires; dominoes, shove-ha'penny, cribbage and chess. There's a tiny homely dining room, and a simple but well heated conservatory beyond; booking is advised for weekends. Food is good fresh home cooking with lunchtime dishes such as sandwiches (£2.25), ploughman's (£4.95), East African vegetable and fruit curry or mushroom and seaweed lasagne (£5.25), pork stroganoff (£5.25), and fresh grilled mackerel with mustard sauce (£5.45), with evening dishes such as smoked cheese and broccoli kugel (£8.25), grilled salmon trout fillet with herb butter (£9.45), duck breast italienne

(£10.45), steak au poivre (£10.95), and home-made puddings (£3.25). Well kept Morlands Old Speckled Hen and Woodfordes Wherry, Great Eastern, and Norfolk Nog on handpump, a decent wine list, and several malt whiskies; a friendly and enthusiastic licensee, and good service. The well behaved dogs sometimes in evidence are called Barnaby and Bendoodle. There are picnic tables in a small and prettily cottagey back garden, and on the front wall above the colourful front flower borders is what looks like a figurehead from a ship wrecked in the Dutch Wars. The village, so cut off from the outside world that you might meet partridges wandering up the street, is very special. *(Recommended by David Gregory, Brian Horner, Brenda Arthur, D E Twitchett, John Wooll, Frank Davidson, Judy Wayman, Bob Arnett)*

Free house ~ Licensees Keith and Sara Holman-Howes ~ Real ale ~ Meals and snacks (not Sun evening, not Mon) ~ (01263) 587376 ~ Well behaved children accepted ~ Gaelic band first Thurs of month, 8pm ~ Open 12-3, 7-11; closed Mon (except bank holidays)

HORSEY TG4522 Map 8
Nelson Head

Signposted off B1159 (in series of S-bends) N of Gt Yarmouth

As well as the beach down the road, this small tiled brick house is also handy for interesting walks around Horsey Mill and the Mere – and thus popular with birdwatchers. It's a very genuine country pub, with two unpretentious rooms divided by a slung-back red velvet curtain, simple but comfortable seats (including four tractor-seat bar stools), lots of shiny bric-a-brac and small local pictures for sale, geraniums on the window sill and in all a relaxed cottagey feel. Besides usual dishes such as ploughman's (£3.95), ham and egg (£4), cod or vegetarian tagliatelle (£4.25), steaks (from £8.50), and children's dishes (£2.50), the Austrian managers do several good specialities such as znaimer goulash (£6.95), wiener schnitzel (£7.25), sachertorte and apple strudel (£2.75). Woodfordes Wherry and (of course) Nelsons Revenge on handpump, decent coffee, good fire; piped music. Dogs on leads are allowed, there's a homely family dining room, and the garden has picnic tables. *(Recommended by Maureen Hobbs, Eric Locker, David and Anne Culley, Dr Andrew Schuman, Anna Brewer, Norman and Keith Bloomfield)*

Free house ~ Licensee Reg Parsons ~ Real ale ~ Meals and snacks ~ (01493) 393378 ~ Children in eating area of bar and in dining room ~ Open 11-2.30, 6(7 in winter)-11; 12-3, 7-11 Sun

HUNWORTH TG0635 Map 8
Hunny Bell

Village signposted off B roads S of Holt

In summer, the garden of this cosy village local is very pleasant, and there's bar service to the tables on the lawn; children's play area. Inside, the pleasantly welcoming L-shaped bar has windsor chairs around dark wooden tables, comfortable settees (some of which are grouped around the log fire) and Norfolk watercolours and pictures for sale hanging above the panelling dado; one room is no smoking. Well kept Adnams Best and Broadside, and Greene King Abbot on handpump, quite a few malt whiskies, and decent wines. Bar food includes sandwiches (from £2.75), soup or home-made pâté (£2.95), ploughman's (£3.50), local sausages (£4.45), home-made steak and kidney pie or chicken and ham pie (£5.25), and sirloin steak (£9.50). Darts, dominoes, cribbage, and piped music. *(Recommended by Minda and Stanley Alexander, Mrs M Sloper, Mrs J Hale, Anthony Barnes, J H Bell, BHP)*

Free house ~ Licensees Sally and Thomas King ~ Real ale ~ Meals and snacks ~ Restaurant ~ (01263) 712300 ~ Children welcome ~ Open 11-3, 5-11; 11-11 Sat; 12-4, 6-10.30 Sun

If you know a pub's ever open all day, please tell us.

KINGS LYNN TF6220 Map 8

Tudor Rose 🛏 🍽 £

St Nicholas St (just off Tuesday Market Place – main square)

This bustling town pub with its attractive half-timbered facade is welcoming to both locals and tourists, young and old. The old-fashioned snug little front bar has high beams, reproduction squared panelling, a big wrought-iron wheel-rim chandelier, and newspapers to read. The quite separate back bar is more spacious, with sturdy wall benches, cribbage, fruit machine and juke box. Good food includes cheap home-made daily specials such as sandwiches (from £1.35), home-made soup (£1.95), cheesy topped mushrooms (£2.75), chilli con carne (£3.25), crispy vegetables in a sweet and sour sauce (£3.50), gammon and egg (£3.95), chicken curry or cod and chips (£4.50), and scampi (£5.50), with more elaborate dishes from the restaurant menu (available in the bar) like steak and kidney pie (£7.50), cajun chicken (£8.50), venison casserole with blackcurrant sauce (£8.75), and rump steak (£9.25); puddings such as sticky toffee pudding (£3.50). Well kept Bass, Batemans XB, Woodfordes Wherry, and a guest beer on handpump, a fine choice of whiskies, and decent wines. The upstairs raftered restaurant and a small area of the lounge are no smoking. There are seats in the garden. Bedrooms are simple and modern but comfortable, and some have a pretty view of St Nicholas's Chapel. *(Recommended by John Wooll, David and Ruth Hollands, Charles Gysin, R C Vincent, Mr and Mrs R Maggs, Mrs Pat Crabb, Simon Penny, Hanns P Golez, Terry and Eileen Stott, Peter and Pat Frogley, David Carr, Ian Phillips)*

Free house ~ Licensees John and Andrea Bull ~ Real ale ~ Meals and snacks (not Sun) ~ Restaurant ~ (01553) 762824 ~ Children welcome ~ Open 11-11; 12-3, 7-10.30 Sun (closed winter Sun lunchtimes) ~ Bedrooms: £30(£38.50B)/£50B

LARLING TL9889 Map 5

Angel 🍽

A11 S of Attleborough

The same family have run this neatly kept tiled, cream-washed building since 1913, and they still have the original visitors books with guests from 1897-1909. The comfortable 1930-style lounge on the right has cushioned wheelback chairs, a nice long cushioned panelled corner settle, some good solid tables for eating and some lower ones, squared panelling, a collection of whisky-water jugs on the delft shelf over the big brick fireplace which houses a big woodburner, a couple of copper kettles, and some hunting prints. Reliable bar food includes sandwiches (from £1.95; toasties such as bacon and banana £2.50), cheese and asparagus crêpe or ploughman's (£3.95), balti dishes, ham and egg or vegetarian moussaka (all £4.95), good home-made burgers (from £4.95), steaks (from £9.50), daily specials like home-made steak and kidney pie or fresh cod, haddock or plaice in beer batter (£5.95), and home-made puddings (£2.50). Well kept Adnams Best and beers from local brewers like Church End or Old Mill on handpump, and over 100 malt whiskies; friendly helpful service. The quarry-tiled black-beamed public bar has a good local atmosphere, with darts, dominoes, juke box and fruit machine; piped music. A neat grass area behind the car park has picnic tables around a big fairy-lit apple tree, and a safely fenced play area. Peter Beale's old-fashioned rose nursery is nearby. *(Recommended by Frank Davidson, John Baker, Anthony Barnes; more reports please)*

Free house ~ Licensee Brian Stammers ~ Real ale ~ Meals and snacks (12-2, 6.30-9.30, till 10pm Fri/Sat) ~ (01953) 717963 ~ Children welcome ~ Occasional live music ~ Open 10-11; 12-10.30 Sun ~ Bedrooms: £25B/£45B

MUNDFORD TL8093 Map 5

Crown 🛏 🍽

Crown Street; village signposted off A1065 Thetford—Swaffham

Set on the quiet village square, this attractive 17th-c posting inn has a relaxed and cosy beamed lounge bar with a huge open fireplace in a flint wall, captain's chairs around highly polished tables, and interesting local advertisements and other memorabilia. If the pub is full, a spiral iron staircase with Vanity Fair cartoons beside it leads up to the club room, an elegant restaurant and the garden. There are more heavy beams in the separate red-tiled locals' bar on the left, which has cast-iron-framed tables, another smaller brick fireplace with a copper hood, sensibly placed darts, cribbage, dominoes, fruit machine, a juke box and a screened-off pool table. Well kept Marstons Pedigree, Sam Smiths, Theakstons, Websters Yorkshire, Woodfordes Wherry, and a guest beer on handpump, and a good choice of malt whiskies. Kind staff serve bar snacks such as sandwiches or wholemeal hoagies (from £1.50), home-made soup (£1.85), ploughman's (£5.25), burgers (from £3.25), local herb sausage (£4.25), daily specials such as stilton and walnut filo parcels with an orange, thyme and onion chutney (£3.75), moules marinières (£3.95), mixed vegetable and peanut stir-fry (£5.25), chicken in a cheese and mushroom sauce (£5.75), and baked fillet of sea bream with a deep-fried leek and black olive butter sauce (£7.95), puddings such as chocolate and almond torte, toffee apple tart or tiramisu (from £2.20); Sunday roast beef (£5.25), and children's helpings of most meals. *(Recommended by John Fahy, Nigel Clifton, P A Devitt, Roger and Fiona Todd, Frank Gadbois, Joyce McKimm, Ian and Christina Allen, George Atkinson, R D Greaves, Simon Penny, Charles Bardswell)*

Free house ~ Lease: Barry Walker~ Real ale ~ Meals and snacks (12-3, 7-10) ~ Restaurant ~ (01842) 878233 ~ Children welcome ~ Open 11-11; 12-10.30 Sun ~ Bedrooms: £32.50B/£49.50B

NORWICH TG2308 Map 5
Adam & Eve ♀

Bishopgate; follow Palace Street from Tombland N of the cathedral

It's a real pleasure to find a place like this tucked away in the centre of a bustling city. This is Norwich's oldest pub and is thought to date back to at least 1249 – though the striking Dutch gables were added in the 14th and 15th c. The little old-fashioned characterful bars quickly fill at lunchtime with a good mixed crowd of people, and there are antique high-backed settles (one handsomely carved), cushioned benches built into partly panelled walls, and tiled or parquet floors; the snug room is no smoking. Enjoyable, good value food includes sandwiches, granary baps or filled french bread (from £2.25), cheese and ale soup with a pastry top (£2.95), ploughman's (from £3.55), shepherd's pie or vegetable bake (£4.05), chilli (£4.15), fish pie or ham and egg (£4.30), pork in cider and rosemary (£4.35), game pie (£4.40), daily specials, and puddings like home-made spicy bread and butter pudding (from £2); good Sunday roasts. Well kept Adnams Best, Marstons Pedigree, John Smiths, Theakstons Old Peculier, Wadworths 6X, and weekly guest beers on handpump, a wide range of malt whiskies, about a dozen decent wines by the glass or bottle, and Addlestone's cider. An outside terrace has seats and the pub is prettily decked out in summer with tubs and hanging baskets. *(Recommended by John Wooll, Robert and Anne Lees, A Albert, JDM, KM, Mr and Mrs N Chesher, Tina and David Woods-Taylor, Tim Barrow, Sue Demont, Jim Cowell, Wayne Brindle, Simon Penny, Ian Phillips, Paul Boot)*

Courage ~ Lease: Colin Burgess ~ Real ale ~ Meals and snacks (12-7; till 2.30 Sun) ~ (01603) 667423 ~ Children welcome ~ Open 11-11; 12-10.30 Sun

Fat Cat ◖

49 West End Street (A1074 W of centre, but inside ring road)

This vivid re-creation of a traditional alehouse is a magnet for beer lovers, with a splendid range of around 25 changing well kept ales such as Adnams Best, Extra and Regatta, Elgoods Golden Newt, Hop Back Summer Lightning and Thunderstorm, Kelham Island Pale Rider, Moorhouses Pendle Witches Brew, Woodfordes Great Eastern Ale, Nelsons Revenge, and Wherry, and so forth. About half are on handpump, while the rest are tapped from the cask in a still room behind the bar – big windows reveal all. They also keep two draught Belgian beers (a wheat and a fruit), draught lagers from Germany and the Czech Republic, bottled Belgian beers, eight country wines, and local cider. The no-nonsense furnishings include plain scrubbed pine tables and simple solid seats, and there's a good lively bustling atmosphere – no music or machines. Not unexpectedly, customers are predominantly male; bar food consists of a dozen or so rolls at lunchtime (60p). There are tables outside. No children. *(Recommended by Jim Cowell, D Rumney, SR, PM, Tim Barrow, Sue Demont, David Twitchett, Ian Phillips)*

Free house ~ Licensee Colin Keatley ~ Real ale ~ Snacks ~ (01603) 624364 ~ Open 12-11(10.30 Sun)

REEDHAM TG4101 Map 5
Ferry

B1140 Beccles—Acle; the ferry here holds only two cars but goes back and forth continuously till 10pm, taking only a minute or so to cross – fare £2 per car, 25p pedestrians

Plenty of well spaced tables on the terrace of this marvellously placed pub look out over the River Yare and the passing boats or graceful swans, and indeed, many people do arrive by boat – either on the interesting working chain ferry or on a holiday hire boat. There are very good moorings (and showers for boaters). Inside, the long front bar has big picture windows, comfortable banquettes and some robust rustic tables carved from slabs of tree-trunk; the secluded back bar has antique rifles, copper and brass, and a fine log fire. Generous helpings of enjoyable food include home-made soup (£2.60), a light hot chicken mousse wrapped with fresh leeks with a smoked bacon and cheese sauce (£3.25), hot pitta bread filled with chicken tikka (£4.50), home-made lasagne (£5.50), vine leaves stuffed with savoury rice with a fresh basil and tomato sauce (£5.95), local pheasant supreme in a creamy mushroom and fresh tarragon sauce (£6.75), fresh salmon with a dill beurre blanc sauce (£7.50), steaks (from £9.95), and puddings; good fresh vegetables. The restaurant and family room are no smoking. Well kept Adnams Best and Broadside, Woodfordes Wherry and Great Eastern Ale on handpump, quite a few malt whiskies, country wines, and good cheerful staff; piped music. They're well geared up for families, with arrangements for baby food, and changing facilities. The woodturner's shop next door is worth a look. *(Recommended by Anthony Barnes, M Buchanan, Tina and David Woods-Taylor, J E Hilditch, MDN, Philip and Susan Philcox, Geoff and Linda Dibble)*

Free house ~ Licensee David Archer ~ Real ale ~ Meals and snacks ~ Restaurant ~ (01493) 700429 ~ Children in restaurant and family room ~ Open 11-3, 6.30(6 Sat)-11; 11-2, 7-11 in winter; 12-10.30 Sun

RINGSTEAD TF7040 Map 8
Gin Trap

Village signposted off A149 near Hunstanton; OS Sheet 132 map reference 707403

This attractive white painted pub is full of interesting things to look at. Copper kettles, carpenters' tools, cartwheels, and bottles hang from the beams in the lower part of the well kept friendly bar, there are toasting forks above the woodburning stove, a couple of gin traps ingeniously converted to electric candle-effect wall lights, and captain's chairs and cast-iron-framed tables on the green-and-white patterned motif carpet. A small no-smoking dining room has quite a few chamber-pots suspended from the ceiling, and high-backed pine settles; you can book a table in here. Well kept Adnams Best and Broadside, Woodfordes Nog, and Gin Trap Bitter brewed by Woodfordes for the pub on handpump. Enjoyable bar food includes lunchtime sandwiches (£1.75) and ploughman's (from £3), as well as nut cutlet or local sausages (£4), home-made steak and kidney pie or lasagne (£5.25), steaks (from £8.35)), daily specials, puddings such as chocolate crunch (£2.50), and children's meals (from £1.95). A handsome spreading chestnut tree shelters the car park, and the back garden has seats on the grass or small paved area and pretty flowering tubs. The pub is close to the Peddar's Way; hikers and walkers are welcome, but not their muddy boots. There's an art gallery next door, and boules in the back car park. *(Recommended by J M Wooll, Mrs J Burrows, R Vincent, A F Gifford, Anthony Barnes, David Carr, Gordon Theaker, M J Morgan, D and J Tapper, John Beeken, Chris Mawson, Peter and Pat Frogley, Eric Locker, V G and P A Nutt)*

Free house ~ Brian and Margaret Harmes ~ Real ale ~ Meals and snacks (not winter Sun evenings) ~ (01485) 525264 ~ Children in eating area of bar only ~ Occasional piano player or Morris dancers ~ Open 11.30-2.30, 6.30(7 winter weekdays)-11; 12-2.30, 7-10.30 Sun

SCULTHORPE TF8930 Map 8
Sculthorpe Mill

Pub signed off A148 W of Fakenham, opposite village

This converted watermill is in a quiet and pretty spot, with a little millstream emerging from the bridge just in front, and plenty of tables outside – including one virtually out on an island among the mallards. The three small genteel rooms of the bar have soberly attractive furnishings, with good well polished tables, sensible chairs for diners (food is the main thing here), black beams and joists, and generous open fires in winter. The reception desk on the left of the bar and the neatly uniformed staff add a touch of dignity. Quickly served bar food includes sandwiches (from £2.75), ploughman's (£4.35), filled french bread (£4.70), beef stroganoff (£7.95) and a popular fish pie (£8.75), and specials such as devilled whitebait or smoked trout (£3.55), fresh crab salad (£5.45), steak and kidney pie (£6.95) and stir-fried monkfish or grilled turkey (£7.20). Adnams Best, Courage Directors, Greene King IPA, John Smiths and a guest beer on handpump; decent wines; piped music. We would like to hear from readers who have stayed here. *(Recommended by Ian Phillips, R C Vincent, M A Mees, Helen and Ian Cookson; more reports please)*

Free house ~ Licensees Ken McGranthin and Catherine Cameron ~ Real ale ~ Meals and snacks ~ Restaurant ~ (01328) 856161 ~ Children welcome ~ Open 11-11; 11-3, 6-11 in winter ~ Bedrooms: £40B/£60B

SNETTISHAM TF6834 Map 8
Rose & Crown ♀

Village signposted from A149 King's Lynn—Hunstanton Rd, just N of Sandringham

Some careful redecoration and refurbishment has taken place at this pretty white cottage. The Back Bar now has a dark wooden floor, the landlord's sporting trophies, old rackets and real tennis rackets, golf clubs and fishing rods, cushioned seats, and a big log fire. The no-smoking Small Bar has been painted a dark (but not gloomy) green, has a fine collection of prints of local interest, including Queen Victoria leaning from her window at Sandringhm to acknowledge the gentlemen of the Snettisham hunt, and a newspaper rack; this room is popular with eaters. The Old Dining Room is now a glowing dark red with some lovely old pews and other new, though old-looking, furniture on the wooden floor, shelves with old bottles and books, and old prints and watercolours; they plan to put in a working fire. The upgraded (and pretty) lavatories have been commented on, too. Eight more bedrooms are planned (the present three having been considerably smartened up) and they rent out two cottages in the village as well. The old-fashioned beamed front bar still has lots of carpentry and farm tools, cushioned black settles on the red tiled floor, and a great pile of logs by the fire in the vast fireplace (which has a gleaming black japanned side oven). They now produce two menus a year – supplemented by a daily specials board – and use local produce, fresh daily delivered fish, and fresh bread. Nothing except chips, scampi and some prawns is frozen, and they work hard to remain a pub serving good food (there is no separate restaurant menu) with a friendly relaxed atmosphere. The menu includes home-made soup (£2.40), lunchtime freshly baked filled french bread (from £3.25; grilled 4oz steak with fried onion rings £5.25), home-made smoked trout pâté (£3.85), fresh Cromer crab (£4.25; main course £5.95), ploughman's or home-made fishcakes with a fresh tomato and basil sauce (£4.95), fresh vegetable stir fry with egg noodles (£5.50), lasagne (£5.95), fresh cod in home-made batter (£6.50), beef in Guinness pie (£7.25), chicken on wild mushrooms in a madeira cream sauce (£8.75), sirloin steak (£10.75), puddings, and children's menu (from £2.95). Five real ales on handpump kept under light blanket pressure include Adnams Best, Attleborough Wolf, Bass, Greene King Abbot and Woodfordes Wherry. Lots of wines by the glass, freshly squeezed orange juice, and farm cider. The colourful garden is particularly attractive, with picnic tables among the flowering shrubs, and two spectacular willow trees; summer barbecues. The adjoining adventure playground has forts, a walkway, climbing net, slide, swings and cages of guinea pigs, chipmunks and budgerigars. We would like to hear from readers about the changes, please. *(Recommended by John Wooll, R C Vincent, Mr and Mrs C Fraser, Mike and Wena Stevenson, Robert and Anne Lees, Kay and Neville Rolfe, Edward Froggatt, Helen Crookston, MDN)*

Free house ~ Licensee Anthony Goodrich ~ Real ale ~ Meals and snacks ~ Restaurant ~ (01485) 541382 ~ Children in Garden Room and elsewhere if not too busy ~ Blues every second Thurs ~ Open 11-11; 12-10.30 Sun ~ Bedrooms: £35B/£55B

STIFFKEY TF9743 Map 8
Red Lion
A149 Wells—Blakeney

Although this friendly old pub has changed hands, Jo Wishart is still the manageress. And apart from redecorating the outside of the building, very little will change. There's a very traditional atmosphere, with stairs going up and down between its three fairly spartan interestingly shadowy bars. The oldest parts have a few beams, aged flooring tiles or bare floorboards, open fires, a mix of pews, small settles, built-in wooden wall seats and a couple of stripped high-backed settles, a nice old long deal table among quite a few others, and oil-type or lantern wall lamps. Bar food continues to offer fresh local fish, Blakeney whitebait or soft herring roes (£3.95), and Stiffkey mussels and Cromer crab (£5.95); roast beef and shoulder of lamb on Sundays (£6.50). Well kept Adnams Best, Greene King Abbot, Woodfordes Wherry, and a guest beer on handpump or tapped from the cask, Adnams wines, and Stowford Press cider. A games room, detached from the main building, has darts, backgammon, chess, draughts, Scrabble, cribbage and dominoes. The back restaurant leads into a conservatory, and there are wooden seats and tables out on a back gravel terrace, and on grass further up beyond. There's a pretty stream with ducks and swans across the road, and some pleasant walks from this unspoilt village. *(Recommended by John Wooll, R Suddaby, Frank Davidson, John Bowdler, Charles Bardswell, Dennis and Barbara Cook, Mark Hydes, Anthony Barnes, David Gregory, P and M Pumfrey, Paul Hilditch, Philip and Susan Philcox, Helen and Ian Cookson, BHP, M Morgan, Jack and Philip Paxton, Mrs Pat Crabb)*

Free house ~ Licensee Matthew Rees ~ Real ale ~ Meals and snacks (not mid-winter Sun evenings) ~ Restaurant ~ (01328) 830552 ~ Children welcome ~ Live music every other Fri evening ~ Open 11-3, 6-11; 12-3, 7-10.30 Sun

STOW BARDOLPH TF6205 Map 5
Hare Arms ♀
Just off A10 N of Downham Market

You can be quite sure of a friendly welcome in this bustling and happy country pub – both from the licensees who have been here for over 20 years, and from the chatty locals, too. The welcoming bar is decorated with old advertising signs and fresh flowers, and has plenty of tables around its central servery, and a good log fire; maybe two friendly ginger cats and a sort of tabby. This bar opens into a spacious heated and well planted no-smoking conservatory, and that in turn opens into a pretty garden with picnic tables under cocktail parasols and wandering peacocks, turkeys and chickens. Reliably good food includes sandwiches (from £1.60), filled baked potatoes (from £3.25), ploughman's (from £4.75), home-made mushroom stroganoff (£5.95), gammon and pineapple (£7.45), steaks (from £11.50), daily specials such as chicken breast filled with prawns in a lemon tarragon sauce (£6.25), sea bream with roasted red pepper sauce, rolled smoked haddock filled with spinach in a mornay sauce or steak, Guinness and oyster pie (all £6.95), children's menu (from £2.75); roast Sunday lunch. Well kept Greene King IPA, Abbot, Rayments and their seasonal ales on handpump, a good range of wines, and quite a few malt whiskies; maybe cockles and whelks on the bar counter; fruit machine. *(Recommended by Quentin Williamson, Brian and Jill Bond, Jenny and Michael Back, John Wooll, J F Knutton, M A and C R Starling, Basil Minson,*

Paul and Maggie Baker, Ken and Jenny Simmonds, Stephen and Julie Brown, C H and P Stride, Andrew and Jo Litten, John Fahy, M Morgan, Charles Bardswell, Paul Boot)

Greene King ~ Tenants Trish and David McManus ~ Real ale ~ Meals and snacks (till 10pm) ~ Restaurant ~ (01366) 382229 ~ Children in conservatory and on Sundays in Old Coach House ~ Open 11-2.30, 6-11; 12-2.30, 7-10.30 Sun; cl 25-26 Dec

SWANTON MORLEY TG0117 Map 8
Darbys 🍺

B1147 NE of Dereham

There's a good, relaxed country atmosphere and a fine mix of customers of all ages in this cosy beamed pub. The bar has photographs on the left-hand end wall of the pub conversion from two derelict farm cottages, a good log fire (with the original bread oven alongside), tractor seats with folded sacks lining the long, attractive serving counter, fresh flowers on the pine tables, and lots of gin-traps and farming memorabilia. A fine range of perfectly kept real ales might include Adnams Best and Broadside, Badger Tanglefoot, Scotts Blues & Bloater, Woodfordes Wherry and three weekly changing guest beers on handpump. As well as interesting daily specials such as cream of carrot and rice or celery with almonds and butter bean soups (£1.95), good smoked haddock and shellfish lasagne, nice mushroom cheesy bake, ratatouille niçoise with spinach tagliatelle and mozzarella cheese (£5.50), home-baked ham salad (£5.60), and lamb casserole (£6.25); there might be filled french bread (from £3.30), filled baked potatoes (from £3.45), ploughman's (£3.75), vegetable curry (£4.85), tagliatelle salmon (£5.50), tasty steak and kidney pudding (£7.50), steaks (from £8.75), and puddings like lemon and lime crunch flan and summer pudding (£2.50); the restaurant is no smoking. The staff stay friendly and helpful even when they're busy, and there are two dogs, a labrador and a border collie; darts, dominoes, cribbage, piped music, children's room with toy box (and a glassed-over well), and a really good play area out in the garden; they hope to hold cook-your-own barbecues in summer. The bedrooms are in carefully converted farm buildings, and there's plenty to do if you're staying – the family also own the adjoining 720-acre estate, and can arrange clay pigeon shooting, golf, fishing, nature trails, and craft instruction. *(Recommended by Ron and Sheila Corbett, Jenny and Michael Back, John Wooll, David Gregory, Mike and Sue Davis, John Fahy, Eric Locker, Bill and Sheila McLardy, D and J Tapper, R C Vincent, B N F and M Parkin, Anthony Barnes, Philip and Susan Philcox)*

Free house ~ Licensee John Carrick ~ Real ale ~ Meals and snacks (till 9.45) ~ Restaurant ~ (01362) 637647 ~ Children welcome ~ Open 11-2.30, 6-11; 11-11 Sat; 12-3, 7-10.30 Sun; closed evening 25 Dec ~ Bedrooms: £22(£25B)/£35(£43B)

THORNHAM TF7343 Map 8
Lifeboat

Turn off A149 by Kings Head, then take first left turn

Popular with families, this rambling old white-painted stone pub faces half a mile of coastal sea flats – plenty of surrounding walks. The main bar, dimly lit with antique paraffin lamps, has low settles, window seats, pews, and carved oak tables on the rugs on the tiled floor, great oak beams hung with traps and yokes, and masses of guns, swords, black metal mattocks, reed-slashers and other antique farm tools; there are five open fires and no noisy games machines or piped music, though they still play the ancient game of 'pennies', outlawed in the late 1700s. Bar food includes home-made soup (£2.75), chicken liver pâté (£3.95), huge open sandwiches (from £4.25), smoked chicken and mango salad (£4.25; main course £7.50), ploughman's (£4.75), oriental vegetable stir fry (£6.75), pure beef burger topped with bacon and cheese (£6.95), salmon and dill fishcakes on a watercress sauce (£7.25), and steak (£10.25); children's menu (from £2.95). Adnams, Greene King IPA and Abbot, Woodfordes Wherry, and guest beers on handpump. Up some steps from the smart new conservatory is a sunny terrace with picnic tables, and further back is a children's playground with fort and slide. *(Recommended by P and M Pumfrey, M Rutherford, John Wooll, Michael Switzer, John Bowdler, Pat and Clive Sherriff, Eric Locker, Mrs J Burrows, Sam Samuells, Lynda Payton, A*

Austin, Sue Holland, Dave Webster, Quentin Williamson, Ken and Jenny Simmonds, Helen Crookston, Dr and Mrs S Jones, David Austin, Jack and Philip Paxton,)

Free house ~ Licensees Charles and Angie Coker ~ Real ale ~ Meals and snacks (till 10pm) ~ Restaurant ~ (01485) 512236 ~ Children welcome ~ Open 12-11; 12-10.30 Sun ~ Bedrooms: £55B/£65B

TITCHWELL TF7543 Map 8
Manor Hotel 🛏

A149 E of Hunstanton

This comfortable hotel is ideal for birdwatchers as it overlooks Titchwell RSPB reserve – and for golfers, with the championship golf courses moments away; lots of good walks and footpaths nearby, too. From the end bar there are wonderful views over the salt marshes to the sea from the seats by the picture windows. The tranquil lounge has magazines, an open fire, and a good naturalists' record of the wildlife in the reserve. The pretty no-smoking restaurant is to have a conservatory added which will open onto the sheltered neatly kept walled gardens. Bar food includes home-made soup (£3), sandwiches (£3.50), Cromer crab salad (£5.50), 6 local oysters (£6), leek and mushroom stroganoff (£7), medallions of monkfish with citrus fruits and dry vermouth (£10.50), bass with asparagus sauce (£11.50), grilled fillet of salmon and king scallops glazed with hollandaise (£14), and puddings (£3); children's dishes (£5.95); the eating area of the bar is no smoking. Greene King IPA and Abbot on handpump. *(Recommended by Brian and Jill Bond, Charles Bardswell, Deborah and Miles Protter, John Bowdler, Edward Froggatt, David Carr, M J Morgan, PGP, Anthony Barnes)*

Free house ~ Licensees Ian and Margaret Snaith ~ Real ale ~ Meals and snacks ~ Restaurant ~ (01485) 210221 ~ Children welcome ~ Open 12-2.30, 6.30-11(10.30 Sun) ~ Bedrooms: £45B/£90B

TIVETSHALL ST MARY TM1686 Map 5
Old Ram 🍷

Ipswich Rd; A140 15 miles S of Norwich

Particularly popular at lunchtime, this is a reliable family dining pub. Served by friendly staff, the wide choice of food includes some good daily specials such as mushroom stroganoff (£7.95), calf liver and black pudding topped with bacon and fried onions (£8.95), a big skate wing with black butter (£9.95), red snapper fillets with sautéed scallops with a chilli pepper sauce (£10.95), and duck breast on a fresh orange and grand marnier sauce (£11.95); from the menu there might be filled rolls (from £2.25), filled baked potatoes (from £2.75), meaty or vegetable lasagne or chicken curry (£6.95), roast rack of pork ribs (£8.95), and steaks (from £10.50). They also do a two-course meal of salmon or cod and a pudding (£11.95). Well kept Adnams, Boddingtons, Ruddles County, and Woodfordes Wherry on handpump, decent house wines, and freshly squeezed orange juice; unobtrusive fruit machine and piped music. The spacious main room, ringed by cosier side areas, has standing-timber dividers, stripped beams and brick floors, a longcase clock, antique craftsmen's tools on the ceiling, and a huge log fire in the brick hearth; other rooms ramble off, and there are pretty lamps and fresh flowers. An attractive, no-smoking dining room has an open woodburning stove and big sentimental engravings, and leads to another comfortable no-smoking dining room and gallery, with Victorian copper and brassware. Seats on the sheltered flower-filled terrace and lawn behind. No dogs. *(Recommended by Brian Horner, Brenda Arthur, Ian and Nita Cooper, John Wooll, Bill and Sheila McLardy, J E Rycroft, Beryl and Bill Farmer, David Carr, Paul Boot, SR, PM)*

Free house ~ Licensee John Trafford ~ Real ale ~ Meals and snacks (from 7.30 for breakfast – non-residents welcome – till 10pm) ~ Restaurant ~ (01379) 676794 ~ Children in eating area of bar, under 7s must leave by 8pm ~ Live entertainment several times a year ~ Open 11-11; 12-10.30 Sun; closed 25-26 Dec ~ Bedrooms: £49B/£68B

WARHAM TF9441 Map 8

Three Horseshoes 🛏 🍺

Warham All Saints; village signposted from A149 Wells next the Sea—Blakeney, and from B1105 S of Wells

The new extension here with its indoor lavatories has been well received by readers, who feel it has not spoilt the marvellously unspoilt traditional atmosphere in any way at all. It's a super country local, unpretentious and friendly, and the three rooms have gas lighting, stripped deal or mahogany tables (one marked for shove-ha'penny) on the stone floor, a sturdy red leatherette settle built around the yellowing beige walls, and a log fire; an antique American Mills one-arm bandit is still in working order (it takes 5p pieces; there's a 1960s one that takes 1p pieces), there's a big longcase clock with a clear piping strike, and a twister on the ceiling (you give it a twist and according to where it ends up you pay for the next round). Reasonably priced and generously served, the enjoyable bar food includes lunchtime snacks like sandwiches and filled rolls (from £2), filled baked potatoes (from £2.80), and ploughman's (from £3.60), as well as Norfolk potted herrings (£3), baked mushrooms in a stilton cream sauce (£3.20), beef in beer pie (£6.30), fish or good game pie (£6.50), and puddings like rhubarb crumble; good vegetables. The dining room is no smoking. Notably well kept Greene King IPA and Abbot on handpump, and Woodfordes Mardlers Mild, Nelsons Revenge, Wherry or Great Eastern Ale tapped from the cask, good home-made lemonade, local cider, and country wines. Darts, cribbage, shove-ha'penny, dominoes, and one of the outbuildings houses a wind-up gramophone museum – opened on request. There are rustic tables out on the side grass. *(Recommended by John Wooll, Mr and Mrs Dennis Cook, David and Anne Culley, Jeff Davies, Derek and Sylvia Stephenson, Anthony Longden, Robert and Anne Lees, Mrs M Sloper, Mrs J Hale, Dennis and Barbara Cook, Stephen Harvey, P and M Pumfrey, Dr B and Mrs P B Baker, Chris and David Stephenson, John Beeken, Ian Phillips, E Robinson, MDN, Philip and Susan Philcox, Christopher Harper, Ken and Jenny Simmonds, Howard Clutterbuck, Miss D J Hobbs, Jenny and Michael Back)*

Free house ~ Licensee Iain Salmon ~ Real ale ~ Meals and snacks (not 25-26 Dec) ~ Restaurant ~ (01328) 710547 ~ Children in eating area of bar ~ Open 11.30-2.30, 6-11; 12-3, 6-10.30 Sun ~ Bedrooms: £22/£44(£48B)

WELLS NEXT THE SEA TF9143 Map 8

Crown

The Buttlands

By the time this book is published, the bars and restaurant in this black and white Georgian-faced inn will have been refurbished. The pubby front bar has bowed beams showing that it's a fair bit older than the frontage suggests, and a relaxed atmosphere, and the two quieter back rooms have some interesting pictures on the wall over the roaring log fire, including several big Nelson prints and maps showing the town in the 18th and 19th centuries. Waitress-served bar food includes sandwiches (from £1.60), soup (£2.25), ploughman's (£4.50), vegetable curry (£4.75), three-egg omelettes (£4.95), seafood tagliatelle (£5.50), steak and kidney pie or grilled trout (£5.75) lamb chops (£6.75), rump steak (£10.50), and daily specials like brioche bun with beef in beer (£5.75), herby haddock goujons with sour cream dip (£5.95), and salmon and mushroom pasta (£6.25); children's dishes. Adnams, Bass and Marstons Pedigree on handpump; piped music. A neat conservatory has small modern settles around the tables. The central square of quiet Georgian houses is most attractive, and archers used to practise on the tranquil village green opposite. *(Recommended by Ian Phillips, R Suddaby, Sue Holland, Dave Webster, Charles Bardswell, George Atkinson, Roy Bromell, Jo and Den Reeve, F H Collier)*

Free house ~ Licensee Wilfred Foyers ~ Real ale ~ Meals and snacks ~ Restaurant ~ (01328) 710209 ~ Children in eating area of bar ~ Open 11-2.30, 6-11 ~ Bedrooms: £45(£55B)/£58(£68B)

If we know a pub does summer barbecues, we say so.

WINTERTON ON SEA TG4919 Map 8
Fishermans Return 🍺 🍴

From B1159 turn into village at church on bend, then turn right into The Lane

After 22 years as tenants, Mr and Mrs Findlay bought the freehold of this traditional brick and flint pub, and hope to start a microbrewery. The white-painted panelled lounge bar has neat brass-studded red leatherette seats, a winter log fire, and a friendly atmosphere, while the panelled public bar has low ceilings and a glossily varnished nautical air. Tasty home-made bar food includes daily specials such as spicy aubergine soup with coriander chutney (£3), pheasant and rabbit terrine with port jelly (£3.75), spinach stuffed cannelloni on a ratatouille base or oyster and button mushrooms in stilton sauce on tagliatelle (£4.50), chicken marengo (£5.75), baked lamb in rhubarb and ginger sauce (£6.50), and medley of poached salmon and plaice in watercress sauce (£7.50); also, toasties (from £1.50), filled baked potatoes (from £3), burgers (from £4.50), omelettes (from £4.50), steaks (from £9.50); children's dishes (£2.50). Well kept Adnams Best, Scotts Blues and Bloater, Strong Mild, Theakstons, and guest beers on handpump, decent wines, around 30 malt whiskies, and James White cider; darts, dominoes, cribbage, pool, fruit machine, video game, and juke box. Seats in front by a quiet lane have nice views, as do the sheltered garden and terrace, which opens out from the back bar. There's a pets corner and pond with ornamental chickens and bantams. The characterful bedrooms, up the steep curving stairs, have low doors and uneven floors; no-smoking garden room. The pub is not far from the sandy beach, with good birdwatching – even from the doorstep of the bar. *(Recommended by Robert and Anne Lees, JDM, KM, Derek and Sylvia Stephenson, David and Anne Culley, I P G Derwent, David Carr, Philip and Susan Philcox, Simon Penny)*

Free house ~ Licensees John and Kate Findlay ~ Real ale ~ Meals and snacks ~ (01493) 393305 ~ Children in small dining room in winter, in family room in summer ~ Open 11-2.30, 6(6.30 in winter)-11; 11-11 Sat; 12-10.30 Sun ~ Bedrooms: £30/£45

WOODBASTWICK TG3315 Map 8
Fur & Feather 🍴

Off B1140 E of Norwich

The style and atmosphere here is not what you'd expect of a brewery tap as it's set out more like dining pub – though it's the range of fine beers which is the primary draw. Set next door to the Woodfordes Brewery, they keep the full range of ales tapped from the cask: Broadsman, Great Eastern Ale, Wherry, Mardlers Mild, Baldric, Norfolk Nog (a strong dark ale, good for keeping out the winter cold), very strong Head Cracker, and Nelsons Revenge; you can take some home with you. Set in a particularly lovely estate village, this row of thatched cottage buildings was carefully converted into a comfortably, roomy pub in 1992 – olde-worlde without being overdone. Tasty bar food includes sandwiches (from £2.50), filled baked potatoes (from £3.25), ploughman's (£5.25), burgers (£5.50), ratatouille and bean pie, crispy chicken breast or lasagne (£5.95), yorkshire pudding filled with beef in ale or ham and mushroom tagliatelle or gammon and pineapple (all £6.75), and steaks (from £9.95); helpful, pleasant staff. The restaurant and part of the bar are no smoking. The staff stay friendly and very efficient even when busy; piped music and cards. There are tables out in the garden. *(Recommended by Brian Horner, Chris and Shirley Machin, Jenny and Michael Back, John Baker, D and J Tapper, Tony Dickinson, David and Julie Glover, J E Rycroft, Jack and Philip Paxton, Arthur Gunn, David Toulson)*

Woodfordes ~ Tenants John and Jean Marjoram ~ Real ale ~ Meals and snacks ~ Restaurant (Tues-Sat evenings) ~ (01603) 720003 ~ Children in restaurant ~ Open 11-3, 6-11; 12-2.30, 6-11 winter weekdays; 12-3, 7-10.30 Sun

---

If we don't specify bar meal times for a main entry, these are normally 12-2 and 7-9; we do show times if they are markedly different.

Lucky Dip

Besides the fully inspected pubs, you might like to try these Lucky Dips recommended to us and described by readers (if you do, please send us reports):

Aldborough [TG1834], *Old Red Lion*: Worth knowing for good food at sensible prices; pretty position on huge village green (*Mrs M Sloper, Mrs J Hale, BB*)

Attleborough [off A11; TM0495], *Griffin*: Medieval-looking town pub, well kept Greene King Abbot, good choice of Anglo-Indian food in clean and friendly restaurant area (*Steve Jennings*); [London Rd (off A11)], *White Lodge*: Good value food in attractive low thatched and beamed cottage, two roaring log fires, Boddingtons, Flowers IPA, Greene King IPA and Morlands Old Speckled Hen (*Ian Phillips, Brian Horner, Brenda Arthur*)

Aylmerton [Holt Rd (A148); TG1840], *Roman Camp*: Recently transformed, with comfortable bar, sitting room and conservatory, well kept Adnams and other beers, interesting tasty food, tables in garden behind, smiling service even when busy; bedrooms added since (*Judy Wayman, Bob Arnett*)

☆ **Aylsham** [Norwich Rd (bypass); TG1926], *Greens*: Wide choice of good value home cooking inc good puddings in spacious modern barn conversion, cheery attentive service, pleasant lawns (*Simon Penny, Sheila and Robert Robinson, J and P Daggett*)

Bacton [B1159 towards Walcott; TG3433], *Poachers Pocket*: On sea wall, very welcoming, well kept beers inc Theakstons Bitter, good bar food inc huge helping of cod (*Tom Claxton*)

Beeston [TF9015], *Ploughshare*: Fairly recently renovated, pleasant big sunny bar with old tables, benches, woodburner in big fireplace, magazines to read, small no-smoking area, separate restaurant, pool room; fairly wide choice of food inc good choice of puddings; Greene King IPA, Abbot, Rayments and guest beers, decent house wines (*John Wooll*)

☆ **Binham** [B1388 SW of Blakeney; TF9839], *Chequers*: Long beamed bar with coal fires each end, one in inglenook, sturdy plush seats, ales such as Adnams, Bass, Greene King Abbot, Wolf BB and Woodfordes Wherry, good value promptly served food inc imaginative dishes (Sun lunch very popular), no-smoking dining area, picnic tables on grass behind; open all day, interesting village with huge priory church; bedrooms (*Philip and Susan Philcox, Robert and Anne Lees, Mrs Pat Crabb, John Beeken, BB*)

Blakeney [TG0243], *Manor*: Attractive tiled house in own grounds, opp wildfowl reserve and sea inlet, waitress-served bar food in big refined but cosy hotel bar, sunny seats outside; bedrooms (*Charles Bardswell*)

☆ **Brancaster Staithe** [A149 Hunstanton—Wells; TF7743], *Jolly Sailors*: Good freshly cooked specials and good range of home-made puddings in simple but stylish and rather upmarket old-fashioned pub, popular with yachtsmen and the local gentry; well kept Bass and Greene King, good wines, provision for children, log fire, attractive restaurant, sheltered tables in nice garden with enclosed play area, open all Sun in summer (*M Morgan, Charles Bardswell, R Suddaby, Howard and Margaret Buchanan, R D Greaves, LYM*)

☆ **Briston** [B1354, Aylsham end of village; TG0532], *John H Stracey*: Welcoming, clean and well run country dining pub, wide choice of good value quickly served food inc fresh fish Tues, well kept Greene King Abbot, decent house wines, comfortable seats, log fire, long-serving landlord, dog and cat; popular restaurant; good value bedrooms with good breakfasts – nice for people who like being part of family (*Mr and Mrs J Hall, John Wooll*)

Burnham Overy Staithe [A149; TF8442], *Hero*: Pleasant service, good beer and service, carefully presented food, friendly atmosphere, interesting bygones (*BHP, Janet and Peter Race*)

Caister on Sea [TG5211], *Ship*: Good old-fashioned inn, good range of enjoyable food and of well kept beers; very pretty hanging baskets (*John Kirk*)

Cantley [TG3805], *Cock*: Wide choice of good value food in friendly pub with Woodfordes Wherry and guest beers, conservatory, garden; dogs and children welcome (*Denis and Margaret Kilner*)

☆ **Castle Acre** [Stocks Green; village signed off A1065 N of Swaffham; TF8115], *Ostrich*: Mixed reports on this interesting and ungentrified pub prettily placed overlooking a tree-lined green, with some ancient beams and masonry, huge fireplace, well kept Greene King ales; at best the food's very enjoyable and good value (with plenty of vegetarian dishes), and service individual and welcoming; dominoes, cribbage, fruit machine, piped music, family room, picnic tables in sheltered garden; jazz 2nd and 3rd Weds of month, folk last Weds, attractive village with castle and monastery remains (*Brigid Purcell, John Benjafield, Sue Rowland, John Beeken, Ann and Mike Bolton, Charles Bardswell, Nigel Clifton, Stephen Barney, LYM*)

Castle Rising [TF6624], *Black Horse*: Comfortable and spotless Beefeater family dining pub in pleasant unspoilt village, usual reliable food, mainly Whitbreads-related ales, friendly unhurried service; children welcome, own menu and play packs; no dogs, pleasant tables out under cocktail parasols, play area (*John Wooll, David Carr, M J Morgan, R C Vincent, JCW*)

☆ **Cawston** [Eastgate, S of village – on B1149 from Norwich turn left towards Haveringland at crossroads ½ mile before the B1145

Cawston turn; TG1323], *Ratcatchers*:
Bustling pub-restaurant very popular for good
freshly prepared food from sandwiches with
own-baked bread to steaks, with good
vegetarian choice; prices reflect the
restaurant atmosphere (and people there just
for a drink wouldn't feel welcome) but are
good value; well kept Adnams Extra, Bass,
Hancocks HB and a guest, good range of
wines and country wines, several malt
whiskies; L-shaped beamed bar with open
fire, quieter no-smoking candlelit dining room
(not Sun evening); darts, cribbage, dominoes,
piped music; children welcome; service
normally good but can be rushed and is not
unfailingly accommodating *(Bill and Sheila
McLardy, Anthony Barnes, C J Darwent, Ann
and Mike Bolton, I P G Derwent, J F
Knutton, Helen and Ian Cookson, Bill and
Brenda Lemon, Mrs J Huntly, LYM)*

✩ Cley next the Sea [Holt Rd, off A149 W of
Sheringham; TG0443], *George & Dragon*:
Edwardian pub by salt-marsh birdwatching
country, cosy locals' bar, comfortable lounge
and dining area, St George artefacts, wide
choice of generous bar food inc good
Cumbrian speciality pan haggerty and good
vegetarian choice, well kept Greene King IPA,
Abbot and a seasonal ale; sizeable garden
over road, with boules pitch; bedrooms *(John
Beeken, Mr and Mrs C H Phillips, Stephen
Pine, Alfred Lawrence, David and Anne
Culley, LYM)*

✩ Cley next the Sea [Holt Rd, Newgate Green,
nr church], *Three Swallows*: Friendly
unostentatious village local, banquettes
around long high leathered tables, roaring
fire, steps up to second simpler bar, decent
generous quickly served home-cooked food
from sandwiches to fresh fish, well kept
Greene King IPA and Tetleys, good wines;
dogs welcome, wandering tabbies; on
attractive village green, barbecues in fine big
garden with croquet, aviary, goat pen and
lovely view of church; bedrooms simple but
clean and comfortable, handy for the salt
marshes *(Helen and Ian Cookson, Paul
Hilditch, Mike Turner, M A Mees, PGP)*

✩ Cockley Cley [TF7904], *Twenty
Churchwardens*: Welcoming small village pub
in converted former school, well kept
Adnams, courteous landlord, friendly helpful
waitresses, limited but good bar food, beams,
darts alcove; plenty of worthwhile places to
visit nearby *(Patrick Godfrey, John Fahy)*

✩ Coltishall [Church St (B1354); TG2719], *Red
Lion*: Friendly modernised family pub, away
from water but pleasant setting; decent
straightforward generous food inc good
puddings, up to a dozen mainly Whitbreads-
related ales inc Weasel brewed for them by
Woodfordes, several attractive split-level
rooms, restaurant; tables out under cocktail
parasols, good play area; bedrooms *(David
and Julie Glover)*

Coltishall [Church St (B1354)], *Kings Head*:
Refurbished pub with well kept John Smiths,
Marstons Pedigree and a cheap house beer,

decent wines, tasty good value imaginative
food, personable landlord, moorings nearby
*(A J Thomas, R Stewart, Christopher
Harper)*; [The Common], *Rising Sun*: Useful
big Chef & Brewer with moorings on pretty
bend of River Bure; Courage-related ales,
food from sandwiches up, waterside and
other outside tables, family room, friendly
service even when busy; piped music *(SR, PM,
LYM)*

Colton [TG1009], *Ugly Bug*: Good home-
made food inc vegetarian in friendly,
comfortable and attractive family-run lakeside
barn conversion, separate dining area, well
kept ales inc Adnams Old, sensible choice of
wines, good atmosphere and service; children
in conservatory, big garden, fishing; two
comfortable bedrooms *(Anthony Barnes)*

✩ Cromer [Promenade; TG2142], *Bath House*:
Busy local in splendid seafront position
(exciting in winter with high seas), lots of
dark panelling, well kept Greene King Abbot
and guest beer, cheery service, standard bar
food inc massive sandwiches, dining room;
plenty of tables out on prom, good bedrooms
*(F H Collier, Sue Holland, Dave Webster,
JDM, KM)*

Crostwick [B1150 Norwich—Coltishall;
TG2515], *White Horse*: Dining pub with long
menu of good value generous bar food inc
home-made pies, friendly service, Courage
Directors, Marstons Pedigree and other ales
(Mark Whitmore)

✩ Denver Sluice [signed via B1507 off A1122
Downham Mkt bypass; TF6101], *Jenyns
Arms*: Extensive and well laid out roadhouse-
style pub in fine spot by the massive hydraulic
sluices which control the Great Ouse, tables
out by the waterside with strutting peacocks,
ales such as Adnams, Boddingtons, Flowers
Original, Fullers London Pride, Greene King
IPA and Websters Yorkshire, generous usual
food from sandwiches to steaks inc
vegetarian; big light and airy games area,
piped music; handy for Welney wildfowl
reserve *(Charles Bardswell, John and
Elizabeth Cox, BB)*

✩ Dereham [Swaffham Rd; TF9913], *George*:
Good cheap home-cooked bar lunches, good
carvery, Scottish Courage and other ales,
carefully attentive landlord; bedrooms good
(Bill and Sheila McLardy, Frank Davidson)

Dereham [High St], *Bull*: Very substantial
standard pub food, Greene King ales,
reasonably priced house wines, cheerful
service, central open fire *(Frank Davidson)*;
[London Rd], *Fox & Hounds*: Good
imaginative bar meals, good value *(V L
Parker)*

✩ Dersingham [Manor Rd; B1440 towards
Sandringham; TF6830], *Feathers*: Solid
Jacobean sandstone inn with relaxed
modernised dark-panelled bars opening on to
attractive garden with elaborate play area;
well kept Adnams, Bass and a quickly
changing guest beer, log fires, generous bar
food from sandwiches up, restaurant (not Sun
evening); good range of pub games in third

bar, children welcome, can get very busy in season; some live music in barn; comfortable well furnished bedrooms *(K H Frostick, F H Collier, John Wooll, Edward Froggatt, David Carr, J H Bell, John Fahy, Sheila and Robert Robinson, LYM)*

Docking [High St; TF7637], *Pilgrims Reach*: Small bar (can be busy), quiet restaurant, good generous food inc interesting soups, good-humoured landlady, well kept Adnams Bitter and Broadside; tables on attractive sheltered back terrace, children's room *(Mrs J Burrows, M J Morgan)*

Downham Market [Bridge St; TF6103], *Crown*: 17th-c coaching inn with log fire in small homely oak-panelled bar, well kept changing real ales, good value bar meals (can be eaten in restaurant), friendly staff; owned by Old English Pub Co; comfortable bedrooms, big breakfasts *(R C Vincent)*

☆ **East Ruston** [Oak St; back rd Horning—Happisburgh, N of Stalham; TG3427], *Butchers Arms*: Big helpings of well presented food inc bargain lunchtime specials in well run comfortable village pub with well kept Bass and other ales, lots of golf talk, restaurant, attractive garden, pretty hanging baskets *(Pat and Clive Sherriff)*

☆ **Edgefield** [TG0934], *Three Pigs*: Unpretentious pub with 18th-c smuggling connections, taken over as this book comes out by the former landlady of the nearby Hare & Hounds at Hempstead, which she made so friendly and individual – should be well worth knowing, expect good straightforward food, decent wines and well kept ales such as Bass, Adnams, Greene King Abbot, M&B Mild, Stones and Woodfordes Wherry; attractive and secluded site for a few caravan tourers at the back *(Reports please)*

Elsing [TG0516], *Mermaid*: Welcoming local, bright clean lounge bar, good food inc Sun lunch, well kept ales, nice garden *(David Gregory)*

Foulden [TL7698], *White Hart*: Friendly old pub with library for lone drinkers, toys and books for children, separate snug, reasonably priced meals, Celtic ales from nearby small brewery *(Rita Scarratt)*

Framingham Pigot [Loddon Rd (A146); TG2703], *Old Feathers*: Comfortable atmospheric well laid-out interior, friendly staff, comfortable airy conservatory restaurant, good value food inc good well priced Sun lunch *(Albert and Margaret Horton)*

☆ **Garboldisham** [The Street; TM0081], *Fox*: Popular food inc fresh tasty unusual sandwiches and full Adnams range kept well in sympathetically updated old pub with original beams, old pews, massive woodburner in deep brick hearth, friendly helpful staff; daily papers *(Ian and Liz Phillips)*

Geldeston [TM3991], *Wherry*: Good food, well kept Adnams; garden *(Denis and Margaret Kilner)*

Gissing [Lower St; TM1485], *Crown*: Open-plan village pub with lots of beams, popular lunchtime esp with older people for simple good value food from sandwiches and ploughman's up; faultless service, well kept Adnams, Greene King IPA and ten or so guests inc locals like Wolf from Attleborough *(John Baker, Tim Barrow, Sue Demont)*

Gooderstone [The Street; TF7601], *Swan*: Old village pub doubling as PO, reasonably priced food, well kept local Celtic and Elgoods, sun lounge, huge garden with play area; opp historic church, handy for nearby water gardens *(Rita Scarratt)*

☆ **Great Cressingham** [Water End; just off A1064 Swaffham—Brandon – OS Sheet 144 map ref 849016; TF8401], *Windmill*: Roomy family pub with three beamed bars, cosy nooks and crannies, huge log fireplace, lots of farm tools, conservatory, games room; good value standard food, quick service, well kept Adnams, Batemans, Bass, Sam Smiths and guest beers; well kept big garden, dogs allowed *(Charles Bardswell, Frank Davidson)*

☆ **Great Ellingham** [Church St; pub signed off B1077, which is off A11 SW of Norwich; TM0196], *Crown*: Neatly kept open-plan bar well divided into quiet alcoves, comfortable plush and other seats, soft lighting, relaxed atmosphere, decent food inc good fresh fish and seafood, home-made bread and pickles, bargain lunches, three small attractive dining rooms (one for families), well kept Adnams, John Smiths, Woodfordes Wherry and local Wolf; no dogs *(Bill and Sheila McLardy, P M Lapsley, BB)*

☆ nr **Great Yarmouth** [St Olaves; A143 towards Beccles, where it crosses R Waveney; TM4599], *Bell*: Busy riverside pub doing well under hospitable current licensees, attractive Tudor brickwork and heavy timbering but extensively modernised, with good varied bar food, well kept Whitbreads-related ales from long bar counter, decent wines, games and juke box on public side, restaurant where children allowed; garden with good play area and barbecues *(John Brockington, LYM)*

Hainford [Station Rd; TG2218], *Chequers*: Friendly thatched cottage in charming setting, wide range of well prepared food, real ales such as Adnams, Hook Norton Old Hookey and Morlands Old Speckled Hen, big airy bar area and rooms off, pleasant staff, well laid-out gardens with play area; children welcome *(Mr and Mrs M A Steane)*

Happisburgh [by church; TG3830], *Hill House*: Heavy-beamed village pub with plush seats, woodburner in big inglenook, open fire other end, bar billiards in games area, well kept changing ales such as Marstons Pedigree and Shepherd Neame Spitfire, welcoming service, wide choice of popular generous food inc good value sandwiches and original dishes, dining area (children allowed here); tables outside front and back; bedrooms, pleasant setting *(PGP, K Flack, David Carr, BB)*; *Pebbles*: Friendly landlord, food inc good Sun roast; heavily refurbished *(David and Anne Culley)*

Harpley [off A148 Fakenham—Kings Lynn; TF7825], *Rose & Crown*: Good home-made food inc fresh veg, unusual vegetarian dishes and good children's meals in small comfortable lounge, small choice of well kept ales, decent wine, friendly hard-working landlord; high chairs provided; lovely garden, quietly attractive village *(E Taylor, John Wooll)*

☆ **Hempstead** [signed from A148 in Holt, pub towards Baconsthorpe; TG1137], *Hare & Hounds*: Unspoilt and relaxed country pub with tiled floor, big woodburner, mix of old-fashioned furnishings and lots of pine, informal garden with pond, rockery and play area; has been very popular for several well kept ales, decent house wine and good straightforward food, but the landlady is moving to the nearby Three Pigs at Edgefield *(News please)*

☆ **Hethersett** [Old Norwich Rd; TG1505], *Kings Head*: Cheerful and homely traditional pub with good value generous lunchtime bar food, half a dozen well kept changing ales, comfortable carpeted lounge, obliging staff, old chairs and tables, big log-burning stove in inglenook, traditional games in cosy public bar, attractive and spacious back lawn, good play area *(Ian Phillips, Charles Bardswell, O C Winterbottom, LYM)*

☆ **Hevingham** [B1149 N of Norwich; TG1921], *Marsham Arms*: Roomy modern-feeling roadside pub with wide range of good generous straightforward food inc fresh seafood, self-serve salads and children's helpings, well kept ales inc Adnams and Fullers London Pride, country wines, friendly helpful staff; double family room on right, tables in garden behind; well appointed roomy chalet bedrooms behind, good wheelchair access *(Sue Rowland, Paul Mallett, Mr and Mrs Rutland, Mr and Mrs R Thurston, Cliff Blakemore, BB)*

☆ **Hilborough** [A1065 S of Swaffham; TF8100], *Swan*: Welcoming early 18th-c pub with good simple home cooking done to order (so may be a wait), well kept Adnams, Greene King Abbot and guest beers, pleasant helpful staff, plenty of old-fashioned pub and board games, small back restaurant; picnic tables on pleasant sheltered lawn *(Charles Bardswell, Norman S Smith, BB)*

☆ **Holkham** [A149 nr Holkham Hall; TF8943], *Victoria*: Quiet and simply furnished brick-and-flint inn with communicating bar rooms, interesting pictures, well kept Ansells, Greene King IPA and Tetleys, decent house wine, good range of family food from sandwiches and bar dishes to smarter restaurant food, good service; dominoes, cribbage, piped music; children allowed in restaurant, tables outside; bedrooms, handy for coastal nature reserves, open all day Sat *(M J Brooks, Charles Bardswell, John Wooll, John Beeken, Michael Switzer, George Atkinson, LYM)*

Holme next the Sea [Kirkgate St; TF7043], *White Horse*: Good value straightforward generous food, welcoming licensees and locals, big garden; cl Mon lunchtime *(John Wooll, David Carr)*

☆ **Holt** [6 Market Pl; TG0738], *Feathers*: Interesting bar used by locals, comfortably extended around panelled area with open fire, attractive entrance/reception area with antiques, friendly efficient staff, good value generous food, well kept ales inc Bass and Greene King Abbot, decent wines; bedrooms spacious and comfortable *(David and Ruth Hollands, Sue Holland, Dave Webster, Addie and Irene Henry, Stephen Pine, Alfred Lawrence)*

Hunstanton [part of Marine Hotel, St Edmunds Terr; TF6842], *Marine Bar*: Small bar packed with tables, prompt welcoming service, wide range of good value quick food all day, Stones and Worthington, lots of china and 50s advertisements; tables out on lower terrace; bedrooms *(Jenny and Michael Back)*

Ingham [B1151 E of Stalham; TG3826], *Swan*: Extensive olde-worlde refurbishment of low-beamed thatched inn with interesting corners in rambling rooms on two levels, scrubbed tables and fishing boat photographs, friendly landlord, good food, five well kept ales, family room by small enclosed garden; bedrooms in detached block *(Sue and Bob Ward, Brenda Crossley)*

☆ **Itteringham** [TG1430], *Walpole Arms*: Good welcoming service even when busy in delightfully old-fashioned village pub on River Bure, lively atmosphere, big helpings of well presented good food, well kept local beers; children welcome *(R M Broadway, Malcolm Taylor, Anthony Barnes, A Larter, Philip and Susan Philcox)*

Kenninghall [B1113 S of Norwich; TM0485], *Red Lion*: Well restored; good food *(Geoffrey and Ro Baber)*

Kings Lynn [Tuesday Mkt Pl; TF6220], *Maydens Heade*: Centrally placed Scottish Courage pub, cosmetically refurbished, popular with all ages at lunchtime and a younger set in the evening; tasty bar food, separate good value carvery restaurant *(R C Vincent)*; [Gayton Rd, Gaywood], *Wildfowler*: Useful Big Steak pub, smart but comfortable and relaxed even when busy, popular food, well kept Tetleys-related beers, good choice of wines in big glasses, friendly staff *(R C Vincent, John Wooll)*

☆ **Letheringsett** [A148 just W of Holt; TG0538], *Kings Head*: Set well back from the road like a private house, with plenty of tables on spacious lawn, informally furnished bar (not smart) with sepia prints of Norfolk life, friendly staff, well kept Adnams, Greene King IPA and Abbot and Woodfordes Wherry, usual food from sandwiches to steaks inc children's, log fire, small lounge, games room with darts, pool, shove ha'penny, dominoes, cribbage, fruit machines; piped music, occasional live, children and dogs welcome, open all day *(Philip and Susan Philcox, P Gillbe, John Beeken, M A Mees, Bill and Sheila McLardy, Charles Bardswell, LYM)*

Little Plumstead [B1140; TG3112], *Brick*

Kilns: Very good choice of vegetarian, vegan and ordinary food inc good fish and nicely cooked veg; Scottish Courage ales *(Dean Burgess)*

Lyng [The Street; TG0617], *Fox & Hounds*: Friendly local on River Wensum, good food esp local game and seafood and puddings, Adnams and Woodfordes Wherry, big comfortable lounge with open fire and bar billiards, public bar with pool and loud juke box, restaurant with no-smoking area; interesting pottery opp *(Mike and Sue Davis)*

☆ Neatishead [Irstead Rd; TG3420], *Barton Angler*: Good reasonably priced straightforward food, well kept Greene King IPA, comfortable cosy bar, friendly staff, well furnished no-smoking restaurant, decent piped music, lovely quiet gardens; good bedrooms, two with four-posters – a nice place to stay, boat hire possible *(Tony Dickinson, Clive Gilbert)*

Newton [A1065 4 miles N of Swaffham; TF8315], *George & Dragon*: Distinctive recently redecorated roadside pub with some imaginative reasonably priced bar food, obliging staff, good choice of beers, back restaurant *(Keith Day)*

☆ North Elmham [B1110/B1145 N of E Dereham; TF9820], *Kings Head*: Welcoming old-fashioned inn, neat and tidy, with good value home-cooked food in log-fire lounge or lovely small dining room; friendly efficient service even when busy, Scottish Courage ales and Greene King IPA, unusual hat collection and coaching prints, no-smoking room, restaurant; garden with play area; bedrooms, pleasant walks *(R C Vincent, John Beeken, E G Drain)*

North Tuddenham [off A47; TG0414], *Lodge*: Wide choice of good value food *(FD)*

☆ Norwich [149 Newmarket St], *Unthank Arms*: Friendly and relaxed Victorian local, spaciously refurbished, with well kept mainly Whitbreads-related ales, decent wines, good interesting inexpensive home-cooked food, open fires, candlelit upstairs dining room, friendly service; garden behind *(Paula and Adrian Le Roux, Brian Horner, Brenda Arthur, Bob Arnett, Judy Wayman)*

☆ Norwich [Wensum St, S side of Fye Bridge], *Ribs of Beef*: Warm and welcoming, well kept ales such as Adnams, Boddingtons Mild, Fullers London Pride and Woodfordes Wherry, farm cider; deep leather settees and small tables upstairs, attractive smaller downstairs room with river view and some local river paintings, cheap reliable standard food from filled baps up (served till 5 Sat/Sun), quick friendly service; can be studenty evenings, but without deafening music *(Ian Phillips, John Wooll, SR, PM, Tony and Wendy Hobden)*

Norwich [Stafford St], *Alexandra*: Good range of food and beer, real fire *(Jim Cowell)*; [Hall Rd, off inner ring rd nr A11], *Billy Bluelight*: Friendly real-ale local with well kept Woodfordes and guest beers, cheapish food inc doorstep sandwiches *(Richard Houghton)*; [Thorpe Rd], *Coach & Horses*: Busy unpretentious local with scrubbed tables on bare boards in big rambling open-plan bar, cheap cheerful food, good range of beers inc four from their own on-site Chalk Hill Brewery, regular live music *(John Wooll, Geoff and Linda Dibble)*; [Prince of Wales Rd, on bridge by stn], *Compleat Angler*: Chef & Brewer right on the bridge, with pleasant conservatory overlooking river (not very special here), riverside terrace; good range of beers, no evening food *(Jim Cowell, John Wooll)*; [Timber Hill], *Gardeners Arms*: Small attractive rooms converted from some of the last original shops and houses in old part of town, neatly themed inc convincing kitchen, more room in glassed-over former yard, real ales inc Murderer (recalling pub's former name), good value food from breakfast on, no smoking and air-conditioned areas, friendly staff, families welcome *(Ian Phillips, John Wooll)*; [Heigham St], *Gibraltar Gardens*: Genuinely old timbered riverside pub, vast hall separated by central fireplace, well kept Scottish Courage ales, cheap food from sandwiches up; children welcome, good garden *(Ian Phillips)*; [36 Yarmouth Rd (A47), Thorpe St Andrew], *Kings Head*: Wide range of Whitbreads-related and other ales, fairly priced bar food, nice atmosphere, friendly helpful staff, restaurant; riverside garden, free moorings *(Ian Phillips)*; [Prince of Wales Rd], *Nelson*: Hotel with quite pubby bar, clean, bright and friendly, with good reasonably priced bar snacks, big wine glasses, free parking; bedrooms *(Frank Davidson)*; [Yarmouth Rd, Thorpe St Andrew], *Red Lion*: Unsmart but cosy, good value food inc seafood and bargain roasts, well kept beers, good coffee, efficient service, entertaining Glaswegian landlord; live jazz and blues *(David and Anne Culley)*; [St Andrews St], *St Andrews*: Simply furnished big panelled room with friendly service, tasty basic food inc wide range of sandwiches (get there early for a good place at lunch), good choice of well kept ales, pleasant conservatory (now no smoking) leading to tables in small back yard *(Brian Horner, Brenda Arthur)*; [St Andrews Hill, next to Cinema City], *Take Five*: Not a pub (in the evenings you can only get in through Cinema City for which it serves as the cafeteria, and you can't go just for a drink), but very pleasant relaxed atmosphere, and has real ales inc one brewed for them, also farm cider; good choice of wines, good value very health-and-trend-conscious food, relaxed atmosphere, changing local art, piped classical music, tables in nice old courtyard *(John Wooll, Tim Barrow, Sue Demont)*; [78 St Benedicts], *Ten Bells*: Originally tiny pub knocked through to next door, done up with telephone boxes and station signs; Greene King beers, pleasant staff *(Tim Barrow, Sue Demont)*; [Trafford Rd, off A11/A140 Ipswich rd], *Trafford Arms*: Large estate-type pub with well kept beers and interesting snacks *(Richard Houghton)*; [St Martin, nr

Palace Plain], *Wig & Pen*: Big partly modernised old beamed bar opp cathedral close, lawyer and judge prints, roaring stove with horsebrasses on overmantle, filling cheap bar food, real ales inc guests, good value wine, quick service *(John Wooll)*

Old Hunstanton [part of L'Estrange Arms Hotel, Golf Course Rd; TF6842], *Ancient Mariner*: Attractively furnished old bar, comfortable and interesting, with lots of dark wood, bare bricks and flagstones, several little areas inc upstairs gallery, good value usual food, up to half a dozen well kept ales inc Adnams and Broadside, Bass and Charrington IPA, decent wines, open fires, papers and magazines, friendly staff; bedrooms *(John Wooll)*

Pulham Market [TM1986], *Crown*: Very wide choice of good home-cooked food inc popular Sun lunch in restaurant (must book) *(Bill Shorten)*

Reedham [17 The Havaker; TG4101], *Railway*: Friendly and comfortable, with good range of real ales, dozens of whiskies, log fire, good bar and restaurant food, games room with darts, pool etc *(Bryan Tye, Anthony Barnes)*

☆ **Reepham** [Market Sq; TG0922], *Old Brewery House*: Rambling Georgian inn with big sundial over two-columned porch, imaginative well prepared fresh food inc good fish in roomy eating areas, well kept Adnams and changing guest ales in small cosy inner bar, friendly service, restaurant; comfortable attractive bedrooms with use of sports club *(Mr and Mrs M A Steane, J Barber, W W Burke, Mr and Mrs T Lyons, David and Anne Culley)*

☆ **Salthouse** [A149 Blakeney—Sheringham; TG0743], *Dun Cow*: Warmly welcoming old country local looking over salt marshes, good bar food, well kept Greene King and other ales, straightfoward decor with stripped beams and cob walls, maybe figs and apples from the big attractive walled garden; children welcome, play area, pool in outbuilding, good walks and birdwatching nearby (also seafood/samphire shack) *(Peter and Pat Frogley, Capt David, MN, DN)*

☆ **Scole** [off A140 just N of A143; TM1579], *Scole Inn*: Stately old coaching inn of outstanding architectural interest, with a real sense of history, antique settles and other old-fashioned features in lounge and bare-boards public bar; bar food from snacks up, no-smoking restaurant, well kept Adnams Best and Worthington on handpump or tapped from the cask; cribbage, dominoes, piped music; children welcome, open all day, comfortable bedrooms *(D E Twitchett, Eric and Jackie Robinson, LYM; more reports on current regime please)*

☆ **Sedgeford** [B1454, off A149 Kings Lynn—Hunstanton; TF7136], *King William IV*: Relaxed and friendly local, with good value food inc Sun roast with good veg, warm woodburner, fast service, well kept Bass and Worthington, restaurant; children allowed in

lounge if eating, some live music and quiz nights *(John Wooll, David Carr)*

Sheringham [promenade; TG1543], *Two Lifeboats*: Lovely sea view from comfortable lounge and terrace tables, big helpings of usual bar food inc fresh fish (no-smoking dining area), well kept Greene King ales, friendly service; bedrooms *(George Atkinson, Sue Holland, Dave Webster)*; [Wyndham St], *Wyndham Arms*: Comfortable lounge bar with big no-smoking area, Norfolk ales inc Wolf and Woodfordes Wherry, friendly service, good fresh straightforward home-cooked food inc fine veg, public bar with pool and piped music, occasional mini beer festivals; children's room, tables outside *(Stephen Pine, Alfred Lawrence)*

☆ **Skeyton** [off A140 N of Aylsham; TG2524], *Goat*: Friendly extended thatched low-beamed pub with good value food in bar and restaurant (best to book Sat evening), well kept Adnams, Marstons Pedigree and Ruddles County, log-effect gas fire, enthusiastic staff; pleasant terrace and garden *(David and Anne Culley, Harry Seddon, Christopher Harper, David and Lesley Elliott)*

Smallburgh [A149; TG3225], *Crown*: 15th-c thatched and beamed village inn with friendly landlord, well kept Greene King Abbot and other ales, limited fresh home-made bar food, popular restaurant; tables outside; bedrooms *(Clive Gilbert)*

South Creake [B1355 Burnham Mkt—Fakenham; TF8535], *Ostrich*: New owners doing imaginative fresh bar food inc local fish, pine tables in long narrow bar and lounge, well kept local beers; plans for back barn restaurant, also mini beer festivals *(Dr B and Mrs P B Baker)*

South Wootton [Grimston Rd (A148/A149), part of Knights Hill Hotel; TF6422], *Farmers Arms*: Olde-worlde conversion of barn and stables, Courage-related ales with a guest such as Marstons Pedigree, wide choice of tasty, reasonably priced food, friendly service; children welcome, open all day; comfortable motel bedrooms, health club *(M J Morgan, John Wooll)*

Sporle [TF8411], *Squirrels Drey*: Open fire in comfortable lounge, restaurant, above average food under new landlord, good puddings *(Nigel Clifton)*

☆ **Stanhoe** [B1155 towards Burnham Mkt; TF8036], *Crown*: Good friendly atmosphere in small bright country local, popular good value home cooking, well kept Elgoods Cambridge, decent wine and coffee, convivial licensees, central log fire, one beam studded with hundreds of coins; well behaved children allowed; tables on side lawn, lots of fancy fowl (and chicks) outside; caravan site, s/c cottage available *(Roger Williams, John Wooll, BB)*

☆ **Surlingham** [village signed off A146 just SE of A47 Norwich ring rd, then Coldham Hall signed; TG3206], *Coldham Hall*: Well kept ales such as Batemans XB, Shepherd Neame Spitfire and Woodfordes Wherry, comfortable high-backed settles, friendly service, woodburner, pool in games area, broads-view dining area, sensible dress code, well reproduced piped music (also juke box), wide range of food; picnic tables by big well kept waterside lawn with shrubs and weeping willows; children in family room *(John Brockington, W W Burke, BB)*

☆ Surlingham [from village head N; pub on bumpy track into which both village roads fork], *Ferry House*: Lively and enjoyable riverside pub (though no view from the bar), comfortably modernised, friendly and unpretentious, by rowing-boat ferry over Yare; well kept Adnams and Scottish Courage ales, central woodburner, traditional games, sensibly priced standard food, comfortable restaurant; children welcome, with own menu; winter evening opening may be restricted, very busy with boats and visitors in summer – free mooring; handy for RSPB reserve *(MDN, John Brockington, LYM)*

Sutton Staithe [village signposted from A149 S of Stalham; TG3823], *Sutton Staithe*: In a particularly unspoilt part of the broads, with cosy alcoves, built-in seats, flagstones, oak beams, an antique settle among more modern furnishings, well kept Adnams and other ales tapped from the cask, usual food inc children's, good puddings and all-day filled long rolls, friendly helpful service, restaurant; children welcome, flower-filled courtyard and grassy areas; good nearby moorings, comfortable bedrooms *(Jenny and Brian Seller, LYM)*

Swanton Abbot [off B1150 S of N Walsham; TG2625], *Jolly Farmers*: Welcoming partly modernised country local, lots of bric-a-brac in three linked dim-lit rooms, well kept Greene King IPA and Abbot and a guest such as Lowestoft Blues and Bloaters, food inc huge cheap steak sandwich, easy chairs, parrot, pool table; open all day *(Jenny and Michael Back)*

Tasburgh [A140; TM1996], *Countryman*: Welcoming main-road pub with reasonably priced food, willing service, well kept Adnams and two other ales, decent wine *(Frank Davidson)*

☆ Thornham [Church St/A149; TF7343], *Kings Head*: Pretty old pub with lots of hanging baskets, low-beamed bars with banquettes in well lit bays, decent food inc vegetarian and fresh fish, Greene King IPA and Abbot, Marstons Pedigree and Tetleys, good service, open fire, no-smoking area; dogs allowed; well spaced tables on back lawn with barbecues, three homely and comfortable bedrooms *(A E Horton, MS, KM, JM, Mrs J Burrows)*

Thorpe Market [North Walsham Rd; A149 N Walsham—Cromer; TG2335], *Green Farm*: 16th-c farmhouse with big pine-furnished lounge, good value original food inc vegetarian in bar and smart restaurant, friendly service, real ales; children welcome, attractive bedrooms *(David and Ruth Hollands)*

Titchwell [Main St; TF7543], *Briarfields*: Hotel not pub, but attractive and comfortable, with good value meals inc vegetarian, good beer and wine in back bar, terrace overlooking salt marshes, suntrap courtyard with pond; well appointed bedrooms *(John Wooll, Chris Rounthwaite)*; [A149], *Three Horseshoes*: Good range of generous bar food, well kept Adnams and Woodfordes Wherry and friendly service in refurbished bar with rough walls, exposed wood, beams and struts, log fires; family room, restaurant, play area in garden overlooking RSPB reserve; peaceful pleasantly furnished bedrooms, handy for beach *(M A Mees)*

Upper Sheringham [B1157, off A148 Cromer—Holt or A149 just W of Sheringham; TG1441], *Red Lion*: Two small no-frills bars with stripped high-backed settles and country-kitchen chairs, red tiles and bare boards, no-smoking snug, open fire; generally good if not cheap food (can be a wait), well kept Adnams Best, Greene King Abbot and Woodfordes, dozens of malt whiskies, good wine choice, newspapers to read, dominoes and cribbage; children very welcome, cats around, basic outside gents'; bedrooms, cl winter Sun evenings *(J F Knutton, Ken and Jenny Simmonds, Malcolm Taylor, Moira and John Cole, Philip and Susan Philcox, Colin Barnes, Peter and Pat Frogley, Stephen Pine, Alfred Lawrence, Anthony Barnes, LYM)*

Walcott [Stalham Rd; nr church; B1159 S of village; TG3632], *Lighthouse*: Friendly and busy, with wide range of good generous food freshly cooked to order inc interesting vegetarian dishes, four changing real ales, helpful attentive service; children in no-smoking dining room and function room, tables outside, good walks nearby *(David Culley, Richard S Albrow, J and P Daggett, Jim Cowell)*

Wells next the Sea [Freeman St; TF9143], *Ark Royal*: Worth a visit for the large intricate model of the *Ark Royal* in the bar; Ruddles County, Theakstons, Woodfordes, piped nostalgic pop music, usual food from sandwiches up, restaurant *(A H Denman, IP)*; [Buttlands], *Globe*: Cheap and cheerful, with well kept Greene King ales *(Sue Holland, Dave Webster)*; [Stn Rd], *Lifeboat*: Unpretentious local with TVs, friendly landlady, food inc local fish and good meals for children (who are welcome), well kept Fullers London Pride and Woodfordes Wherry and Mardlers Mild, decent wine; pleasant garden *(Neil Gordon-Lee, Dr B and Mrs P B Baker, Sue Holland, Dave Webster)*

☆ West Beckham [Bodham Rd, just E; TG1339], *Wheatsheaf*: Homely and welcoming beamed bar with cottagey doors and banquettes, feature log fire and a coal one, good range of reasonably priced food with fresh veg inc lots of Fri fish and popular Sun lunch, deft service, well kept ales such as Bass and Woodfordes Wherry and Nelsons Revenge, decent choice of wine in generous measures, children's room, garden, quiz night; bedrooms clean, comfortable and cheap, with good breakfasts *(John Wooll, R C Morgan, Frank Davidson, Malcolm Taylor)*

☆ **West Rudham** [A148 Fakenham—Kings Lynn; TF8127], *Dukes Head*: 17th-c, with three attractively homely rooms, short choice of generous fresh home-made food from sandwiches up inc interesting fish dishes, well kept Adnams, Woodfordes Wherry and a guest such as Shepherd Neame Spitfire, decent wines, friendly service, newspapers and plenty of books *(Dennis Parberry, John Wooll, Dr N and Mrs Chamberlain, R C Vincent, Derek and Syvlia Stephenson)*

Weybourne [TG1042], *Maltings*: Cosy, comfortable old building with good fresh fish and fresh vegetarian dishes *(Tom and Ruth Rees)*

Whinburgh [B1135 Dereham—Wymondham; TG0008], *Mustard Pot*: Long low-beamed bar with open fire each end, well cooked usual food, Woodefordes Wherry and guest ales *(John Wooll)*

☆ **Wiveton** [B1156 Blakeney—Holt; TG0342], *Bell*: Big open-plan local with lots of Jaguar and other motoring mementoes (even an engine in the fireplace), dozens of model planes, usual food with interesting specials, well kept Morlands Old Speckled Hen, Wolf BB and Woodfordes Wherry, daily papers, piped music (may be loud); more automania in carpeted no-smoking conservatory, picnic tables on lawn; dogs welcome; bedrooms *(Mr and Mrs M A Steane, Jenny and Michael Back, Charles Bardswell, Frank Davidson, Helen and Ian Cookson, John Wooll, BB)*

☆ **Wreningham** [TM1598], *Bird in Hand*: Tastefully refurbished dining pub with good varied reasonably priced food inc unusual vegetarian dishes and well presented Sun lunch; well kept Whitbreads-related and Woodfordes ales, good friendly service, cosy Victorian-style panelled dining area, local bygones and Lotus car photographs *(Christine Seager)*

Wroxham [Rackheath; A1151 towards Norwich; TG2814], *Green Man*: Notable for its beautifully kept bowling green, but well kept and comfortable inside too – easy chairs, plush banquettes and other seats in open-plan bar, log fires, interesting WWII memorabilia (nearby air base), good popular food, Boddingtons and Ind Coope Burton, piped music; children allowed in eating area *(Wendy, Liz and Ian Phillips, LYM)*

Wymondham [Market Pl; TG1101], *Cross Keys*: Attractive old pub with friendly staff and locals, relaxed atmosphere, well kept Sam Smiths, usual food from sandwiches up; piped music; bedrooms simple but clean and reasonably priced *(Comus Elliott)*

Yaxham [TG0110], *Yaxham Mill*: Spotless and comfortable newly converted dining pub with good value food (small restaurant surcharge) inc intelligently cooked veg, good service, short good value wine list; mainly older lunchtime customers with a few businessmen *(Frank Davidson)*

Children welcome means the pubs says it lets children inside without any special restriction. If it allows them in, but to restricted areas such as an eating area or family room, we specify this. Places with separate restaurants usually let children use them, hotels usually let them into public areas such as lounges. Some pubs impose an evening time limit – let us know if you find this.

Northamptonshire

*New main entries for this edition of the Guide are the George & Dragon at
Chacombe, transformed over the last couple of years by its current landlord,
the cheerfully villagey Eastcote Arms at Eastcote, and the welcoming old
Kings Arms at Farthingstone (enjoyable food). The best places for food here
are the Red Lion at East Haddon and the Falcon at Fotheringhay; it's the Red
Lion which we choose as Northamptonshire Dining Pub of the Year. Other
pubs here currently doing particularly well are the Windmill at Badby (good
combination of pub and hotel), the Brampton Halt at Chapel Brampton (nice
spot for an outing), and the attractive and distinctive Star at Sulgrave. The
Lucky Dip section at the end of the chapter seems exceptionally strong now,
and we'd very much welcome readers' views on which are the most likely
candidates for main entrydom: based on our own inspections, we'd suggest the
Navigation at Cosgrove, Boat at Stoke Bruerne, Narrow Boat at Weedon and
Shoulder of Mutton at Welford. There are several interesting new places in
Northampton. Drinks prices in the county are around the national average –
perhaps a little higher, and definitely tending to rise more quickly than
elsewhere. We found the Falcon at Fotheringhay and very welcoming Bulls
Head at Clipston cheaper than most – and the Bulls Head has a fabulous
collection of malt whiskies.*

ASHBY ST LEDGERS SP5768 Map 4
Olde Coach House ⇐ ♀ ◖

4 miles from M1, junction 18; A5 S to Kilsby, then A361 S towards Daventry; village is
signposted left. Alternatively 8 miles from M1 junction 16, then A45 W to Weedon, A5 N to
sign for village.

There's a wonderfully traditional feel at this handsome creeper-covered stone inn
which is well placed in an attractive village full of thatched stone houses – the nearby
manor house was owned by one of the gunpowder plotters. The several comfortable,
rambling little rooms have high-backed winged settles on polished black and red tiles,
old kitchen tables, harness on a few standing timbers, hunting pictures (often of the
Pytchley, which sometimes meets outside), Thelwell prints, and a big winter log fire. A
front room has darts, pool, video game, trivia, TV (very popular for sport) and piped
music. Well kept Everards Old Original, Flowers Original, Jennings Cumberland (a
beer named for the pub) and four guests on handpump, with lots more during their
Spring beer festivals; also over a dozen wines by the glass, farm cider, fresh orange
juice, quite a few malt whiskies, and an unusual choice of non-alcoholic drinks. Bar
food includes filled rolls (from £1.95), home-made soup (£2.25), chicken liver and
cognac pâté with green peppercorns (£3.50), burgers (from £6), brie and broccoli
pancake (£6.25), turkey masala (£6.45), pasta provençale (£6.50), lemon chicken
(£8.25), salmon (£10.25), steaks (from £10.50) and half a dozen daily specials like
button mushrooms in tomato and basil with herb rice (£5.95), leg of lamb roasted in
fruit beer (£8.25) and mixed grill of shellfish and seafood (£10.50), and puddings;
children's menu (from £2.50), and a good Sunday lunch (from £5.95). Between 6 and
7pm on Fridays and Saturdays accompanied children eat free. The dining rooms are
no -smoking. Although most people enjoy eating here very much there are still one or

two mixed reports about food and service. There are seats among fruit trees and under a fairy-lit arbour (maybe summer barbecues), and a marvellous activity centre for children; disabled entrance and baby-changing facilities, too. They have a very full diary of events throughout the year, with everything from Indian food festivals to firework displays and bank holiday pig roasts. *(Recommended by Jo and Gary Charlton, David Carr, Susan and John Douglas, Mike and Wena Stevenson, Andy Cunningham, Yvonne Hannaford, Barbara Wensworth, Angus Lyon, Mrs P V Burdett, Eddy and Emma Gibson, Mayur Shah, Wayne Brindle, Vicky and David Sarti, Eric and Jackie Robinson, Mike Whitehouse, AW, BW, Mr and Mrs B Langrish, James Waller, Stephen and Julie Brown, Bruce Bird)*

Free house ~ Licensees Brian and Philippa McCabe ~ Real ale ~ Meals and snacks ~ Restaurant ~ (01788) 890349 ~ Children welcome ~ Open 12-2.30, 6-11; 12-11 Sat; 12-4, 7-10.30 Sun ~ Bedrooms: £48B/£60B

BADBY SP5559 Map 4
Windmill 🛏 ♟

Village signposted off A361 Daventry—Banbury

The front part of this attractive old thatched inn has a wonderful old-fashioned thriving pubby charm, which is carefully blended with efficient management and modern hotel facilities for staying guests. The two friendly beamed and flagstoned bars are popular with locals and businessmen and have cricketing pictures and appropriately simple country furnishings in good solid wood; there's an enormous inglenook fireplace in one area and a cosy and comfortable lounge. Good promptly served wholesome bar food includes home-made soup (£1.95), sandwiches (from £1.95, steak £3.95), stilton mushrooms or pork liver, bacon and brandy pâté (£3.50), ploughman's (£4.25), lasagne (£5.50), pasta with stir-fried vegetables (£6.25), curry of the day (£6.50), chicken and ham pie or venison burgers (£6.95), salmon with dill mayonnaise (£8.50), leg of lamb steak (£8.95), roast duck breast with orange and port sauce (£10.25), steaks (from £9.25), puddings (£2.95), and children's meals (£2.50). There's a pleasant restaurant and marquee in summer. Well kept Bass, Boddingtons, Flowers Original, Highgate Dark Mild, Wadworths 6X and a couple of guests on handpump, and obliging service from the courteous licensees. Dominoes, video game, piped music. Lots of tables in front overlook the village green. *(Recommended by D Wall, Roy Bromell, George Atkinson, Mr and Mrs Andrew Barsby and friends, Brenda and Rob Fincham, John Bowdler, Mrs K V and Miss J Weeks, Barry and Anne, C H and P Stride, M L Hughes, James Grant)*

Free house ~ Licensees John Freestone and Carol Sutton ~ Real ale ~ Meals and snacks ~ Restaurant ~ (01327) 702363 ~ Children in eating area of bar till 8.30 ~ Live jazz one Fri a month, nostalgic dance trio one Sat a month ~ Open 11.30-3, 5.30-11; all day Sat and Sun in summer ~ Bedrooms: £42B/£55B

CHACOMBE SP4943 Map 4
George & Dragon

2½ miles from M40 junction 11: A361 towards Daventry, then village signposted on right; Silver Street

Just what we always hope to find near a motorway, but hardly ever do: a genuine relaxing village pub, with good food, service that can cope with people who need to get back on the road fairly quickly yet doesn't hurry those who have more time to spare, and a really welcoming atmosphere. There are comfortable seats, beams, flagstones, and logs burning in a massive fireplace, and Marstons Pedigree, Morlands Old Speckled Hen, Theakstons XB and Best and a guest on handpump; fruit wines. Carefully cooked bar food includes mushroom and asparagus pancake (£7.25), baked breast of chicken in red wine and mushrooms (£8.95) and crispy duck pancake with honey and ginger or baked red snapper with pepper relish and chilli sauce (£9.75); afternoon teas and snacks; no-smoking area in restaurant; very friendly attentive staff; darts and dominoes. *(Recommended by David Regan, John and Shirley Dyson, James Nunns)*

Free house ~ Licensee Ray Bennett ~ Real ale ~ Meals and snacks (all day) ~ Restaurant ~ (01295) 711500 ~ Open 12-11(10.30 Sun); Bedrooms: £35B/£50B

CHAPEL BRAMPTON SP7266 Map 4
Brampton Halt
Pitsford Road; off A50 N of Northampton

Recently converted, this attractive Victorian station master's house which stands alone
by the little Northampton & Lamport Railway makes part of a terrific day out for the
family. There are train rides at the weekends with additional bank holiday and Santa
specials, and there's a 14-mile walk and cycle-way along an adjacent converted old
track through pretty countryside. During the week you may see enthusiasts working
on the rolling stock. Inside, one low-ceilinged area with a woodburning stove has
wash drawings of steam trains; by the bar counter, a high-raftered dining area has
some stuffed fish, dagging shears and other agricultural bygones; there's Victorian-
style floral wallpaper throughout, with matching swagged curtains, and furnishings
are sturdily comfortable. There are a few tables in a small sun lounge. Good value
food includes bacon sandwiches (£2.50), ham, egg and chips (£4.50), jumbo cod
(£5.25) and one or two additional evening dishes like steak pie, chicken, leek and
tarragon pie or brie and broccoli pithivier (£5.50) and fillet steak (£8.50). Well kept
Adnams, Bass, Everards Old Original and Fullers London Pride on handpump;
friendly service; possibly piped music. There may be a playful alsatian called Max out
in the neatly kept garden. *(Recommended by George Atkinson, Ian Phillips, Stephen and Julie
Brown, David and Mary Webb, K H Frostick, Gill and Keith Croxton)*

*Free house ~ Licensee Roger Thom ~ Real ale ~ Meals and snacks (not Sun evening) ~
Restaurant ~ (01604) 842676 ~ Well behaved children welcome ~ Open 12-3, 5(7
Sun)-11*

CLIPSTON SP7181 Map 4
Bulls Head 🍺
B4036 S of Market Harborough

The atmosphere at this lovely village inn is notably welcoming – they greet you as
soon as you walk in, and everyone immediately feels comfortable. The black beams
glisten with countless coins, carrying on an odd tradition started by US airmen based
nearby in World War II – they used to wedge the money waiting for their next drink
in cracks and crannies of the ancient woodwork. The bar is cosily divided into three
snug areas leading down from the servery, with comfortable seats, sturdy small settles
and stools upholstered in red plush, a grandmother clock, some harness and tools, and
a log fire. Well kept Batemans, Greene King IPA, Ruddles County, Worthington and
Wychwood Dogs Bollocks on handpump, and an incredible choice of about 480 malt
whiskies. The long back games bar, lively in the evenings, has darts, pool, table
skittles, dominoes, cribbage, fruit machine, video game, juke box, and piped music.
Good bar food includes sandwiches and other light snacks, and daily specials such as
cumberland sausage (£4.65), Drunken Bull pie, dijon chicken or local trout poached in
white wine (£4.95), home-baked gammon and egg (£5.95), and T-bone steak topped
with stilton (£9.95); one room is no smoking. There may be a couple of friendly dogs.
Slightly saucy pin-ups decorate the gents', and indeed the ladies'. Outside, a terrace has
a few white tables under cocktail parasols. *(Recommended by Eric Locker, Joy and Peter
Heatherley, Stephen Brown, George Atkinson, Sheila Keene, Sue Grossey, Ted George)*

*Free house ~ Licensees Colin and Jenny Smith ~ Real ale ~ Meals and snacks (not Sun
evening or all day Mon) ~ (01858) 525268 ~ Children in eating area and games room
~ Occasional live entertainment ~ Open 11.30-2.30, 6.30-11; 12-3, 7-10.30 Sun; cl
Mon lunchtime ~ Bedrooms;£29.50B/£35.50B*

If you report on a pub that's not a main entry, please tell us any lunchtimes or
evenings when it doesn't serve bar food.

CRICK SP5872 Map 4

Red Lion 🍺

A mile from M1 junction 18; A428

A very handy refuge from the M1, this comfortable thatched pub has a pleasant low-ceilinged bar with stripped stonework, a notably relaxed chatty atmosphere, and two roaring log fires (filled in summer with big, bright copper dishes and brassware); it's quietest and snuggest in the inner part of the bar. Four well kept changing beers might include Morlands Old Speckled Hen, Ruddles Best, Wadworths 6X and Websters Yorkshire on handpump. No noisy games machines or piped music. Lunchtime snacks include sandwiches, ploughman's, and steak and kidney pie or a roast (£4.10), and in the evening they do things like chicken kiev, gammon, roast duck, trout and different steaks (between £5.50 and £9); no hot food Sunday lunchtimes. In summer, you can eat on a Perspex-roofed sheltered terrace in the old coach yard, with lots of pretty hanging baskets. There are a few picnic tables under cocktail parasols on grass by the car park. *(Recommended by Bob and Maggie Atherton, James Nunns, Ted George)*

Free house ~ Lease: Tom and Mary Marks ~ Real ale ~ Meals and snacks (not Sun evenings; lunchtime service stops 1.45) ~ (01788) 822342 ~ Children over 14 in snug lunchtime only ~ Open 11.30-2.30, 6.30-11; 12-3, 7-10.30 Sun

EAST HADDON SP6668 Map 4

Red Lion 🛏 🍺

High St; village signposted off A428 (turn right in village) and off A50 N of Northampton

Northamptonshire Dining Pub of the Year

Readers all speak very highly of this rather smart substantially-built golden stone hotel, most visiting for the very good bar food from a well balanced daily changing menu: soups (£3), sandwiches (from £3.50), ploughman's or pâté (£6.95), Irish rarebit or fried brie with cumberland sauce (£7.95), lamb moussaka, steak and kidney pie, cod fillet with lobster and white wine sauce, stilton quiche or lamb and basil rissoles with tomato sauce (£8.95) and puddings like coffee and walnut cheesecake, bread and butter pudding or chocolate roulade (£3.50); it's worth booking for their three-course set Sunday lunch and there's a more elaborate menu in the pretty restaurant; good breakfasts. The well appointed neat lounge bar has oak panelled settles, library chairs, soft modern dining chairs, and a mix of oak, mahogany and cast-iron-framed tables; also, white-painted panelling, recessed china cabinets, old prints and pewter, and little kegs, brass pots, swords and so forth hung sparingly on a couple of beams. The small public bar has sturdy old-fashioned red leather seats. Very well kept Adnams Broadside, Badger Tanglefoot, Charles Wells Eagle and Bombardier, Morlands Old Speckled Hen on handpump, and decent wines; attentive, friendly service; piped music. The walled side garden is attractive, with lilac, fruit trees, roses and neat little flowerbeds; it leads back to the bigger lawn, which has well spaced picnic tables. There are more tables under cocktail parasols on a small side terrace, and a big copper beech shades the gravel car park. *(Recommended by Geoffrey and Penny Hughes, J and P Maloney, L Eadon, Kim and Sara Tidy, Maysie Thompson, John Bowdler, James Waller, F C Johnston, Vicky and David Sarti)*

Charles Wells ~ Tenants Mr and Mrs Ian Kennedy ~ Real ale ~ Meals and snacks ~ Restaurant ~ (01604) 770223 ~ Children in eating area of bar and restaurant, must be over 14 in evenings ~ Open 11(12 Sun)-2.30, 6-11; cl Sun evening ~ Bedrooms;£50B/£65B

EASTCOTE SP6753 Map 4

Eastcote Arms £

Gayton Rd; village signposted from A5 3 miles N of Towcester

The welcoming licensee at this unspoilt and welcoming village pub describes it as a rugby supporters' pub, but there's also a good cheerful villagey atmosphere. There are lots of rugby prints above the dark brown wooden dado in the bar as well as traditional furnishings with two winter log fires, cottagey curtains, fresh flowers; dominoes, cribbage, and unobtrusive piped music. Simple good value bar food (check serving times below) such as sandwiches (from £1.50), soup (£1.50), ploughman's (from £3) and daily specials like macaroni cheese (£4.25), steak and ale pie or fish pie (£5.25) or cajun chicken (£5.95); no-smoking area in dining room. Well kept Bass, Fullers London Pride, Jennings Bitter and a guest on handpump. There are picnic tables and other tables in an attractive back garden, with roses, geraniums and so forth around the neat lawn. *(Recommended by Bruce Bird, Richard and Maria Gillespie, John Baker, CMW, JJW, Tom Evans)*

Free house ~ Licensee John Hadley ~ Real ale ~ Meals and snacks (not Mon-Thurs or Sun evening) ~ (01327) 830731 ~ Children in eating area of bar and in restaurant ~ Open 12-2.30, 6-11; 12-3, 7-10.30 Sun; cl Mon lunchtime except bank holidays

FARTHINGSTONE SP6155 Map 4
Kings Arms

Off A5 SE of Daventry; village signposted from Litchborough on former B4525 (now declassified)

This handsome well weathered 18th-c stone building has friendly licensees who are putting some emphasis on a wide choice of good imaginative food, all freshly prepared. It might include very good toasties, soup (£1.90), vegetable and stilton tart (£2.90), hot game pâté (£3.75), filled yorkshire pudding (£4.50), steak and kidney pie (£5.25), mediterranean cod bake (£5.95), fillet of salmon with parsley sauce (£6.20), venison with bacon and prunes (£6.65), breast of barbary duck with redcurrant and raspberry sauce (£7.25), with several vegetarian specials like spicy tomato and bean potato-topped pie (£5.15). There's a huge log fire in the unassuming flagstoned bar, with comfortably homely sofas and armchairs near the entrance; whisky-water jugs hang from oak beams, and there are lots of pictures and decorative plates on the walls. An attractive dining area (no-smoking area and booking is recommended at weekends) is up a few steps, and a games room at the far end of the bar has darts, dominoes, cribbage, table skittles and board games. Well kept Hook Norton Best, Tetleys and guest beers such as Adnams and Jennings Best on handpump, decent wines, good informal service. There are tables in a neatly kept sheltered garden; interesting outside gents'. It's a pretty village, with good walks nearby (including the Knightley Way). *(Recommended by Robert Thorne, Pete Baker, George Atkinson, D I Williams)*

Free house ~ Licensees Paul and Denise Egerton ~ Real ale ~ Meals and snacks (till 1.45; not Sun evening) ~ (01327) 361604 ~ Children welcome in eating area of bar, restaurant and games rooms ~ Open 12-2.30(3 Sat), 6.30-11; cl Mon, Tues lunchtime; 12-3, 7-10.30 Sun

FOTHERINGHAY TL0593 Map 5
Falcon ★

Village signposted off A605 on Peterborough side of Oundle

It can get very busy at this stylish but relaxed old country pub – with some customers even content to eat standing at the bar – but service remains calmly efficient and friendly throughout. In summer the terrace is a particulary nice place for an al fresco meal. The comfortable lounge has cushioned slatback armchairs and bucket chairs, antique engravings on its cream walls, winter log fires in stone fireplaces at each end, lovely dried flower arrangements, and a hum of quiet conversation; the landlord prefers to keep the simpler public bar for the locals. The pleasant conservatory is popular for Sunday lunch. Reasonably priced, good waitress-served bar food in satisfying helpings changes daily and might include french onion soup or pâté or beefsteak tomato with mozzarella cheese and basil dressing (£3), quail's eggs with smoked salmon (£4.60), baboti or spinach and mushroom lasagne (£5.10), rabbit in cider with apples and walnuts (£6.50), roast duckling with apple and rosemary stuffing or baked thick pork chop stuffed with celery and mushrooms (£7.60), calf liver with onions and tomato (£8.50), beef bourgignon or wild boar in nutmeg and orange sauce (£8.90); puddings (£2.60); the dining room is no smoking. Well kept

Adnams Southwold, Bass, Elgoods Cambridge, Greene King IPA, Nethergate IPA, and Ruddles County on handpump, fresh orange juice, and wines of the month; darts, shove-ha'penny, cribbage and dominoes. Behind is a well liked neat garden with seats under the chestnut tree. The vast church behind is worth a visit, Richard III was born in the village, and the site of Fotheringhay Castle is nearby (where Mary Queen of Scots was executed in 1587). *(Recommended by David and Mary Webb, Jenny and Michael Back, Maysie Thompson, Tony Dickinson, P and D Carpenter, Quentin Williamson, Sue Holland, David Webster, Peter Burton, Edward Froggatt, Mike and Penny Sanders, J A Letham, Brian and Jill Bond, John Bowdler, A Cowell, M J Morgan, Ted George, Tom Saul, George Atkinson)*

Free house ~ Licensee Alan Stewart ~ Real ale ~ Meals and snacks (till 9.45; sandwiches only Mon lunchtime, not Mon evening, or 25-30 Dec) ~ Restaurant ~ (01832) 226254 ~ Children welcome ~ Open 10-3, 6-11; 12-3, 7-10.30 Sun

GREAT BRINGTON SP6664 Map 4
Fox & Hounds ★

Signposted off A428 NW of Northampton, near Althorp Hall; can also be reached via Little Brington, off A45 (heading W from M1 junction 16 it's the first right turn, signed The Bringtons)

The bar at this carefully restored golden stone thatched village inn has a delightfully relaxed informal feel, with lots of old beams and saggy joists, an attractive mix of country tables and chairs on its broad flagstones and bare boards, plenty of snug alcoves, some stripped pine shutters and panelling, two fine log fires, and an eclectic medley of bric-a-brac and country pictures; well reproduced piped music. A good range of real ales includes Fullers London Pride, Judges Magistrates, Theakstons Best, XB and Old Peculier and half a dozen or more interesting changing guest beers, usually including a Mild; country wines. Unfortunately the new licensees couldn't find the time to give us up-to-date prices for the food they're now doing, but things readers have recently enjoyed here (with prices the readers have told us of) include a huge cheddar ploughman's (£5.50), crispy garlic chicken (£6.95), and big steaks; they also do sandwiches. A cellarish games room down steps has pool. A coach entry goes through to an attractive paved courtyard with sheltered tables, and there are more, with a play area, in the side garden. *(Recommended by Stephen, Julie and Hayley Brown, Andrew Shore, Bob and Maggie Atherton, Simon Walker, D Etheridge, Joy and Peter Heatherley, Stephen and Brenda Head, Neville Kenyon)*

Free house ~ Licensee Chris Murray ~ Real ale ~ Meals and snacks (not Mon, Tues and Sun evenings) ~ Well behaved children in eating area of bar ~ (01604) 770651 ~ Live jazz, blues and country Tues and Sun ~ Open 12-3, 5.30-11; 12-11 Sat; 12-10.30 Sun

HARRINGWORTH SP9298 Map 4
White Swan ⇐

Seaton Road; village SE of Uppingham, signposted from A6003, A47 and A43

In a pretty village with a famous 82-arch railway viaduct, this stone-built Tudor inn still shows signs of its coaching days in the blocked-in traces of its carriage-entry arch. Inside, the refurbished central bar area has good solid tables, an open fire, and old village photographs (in which many of the present buildings are clearly recognisable). There are comfortable settles in the roomy and welcoming lounge/eating area, which is decorated with a collection of carpenter's planes and other tools; a quieter no-smoking dining room has a number of old rolling pins on the walls. The menu changes every day, but might include soup (£2.50), spinach and feta goujons (£3.95), steak and kidney pie (£5.75), tagliatelle carbonara (£5.95), scampi, liver fried with wine and herbs (£6.25), chicken breast stuffed with onion and mushrooms grilled with stilton (£6.95), rump steak (£7.95) and duck breast with orange sauce (£9.50); puddings (£2.50). Well kept Greene King IPA and Abbot and a guest beer such as Marstons Pedigree or Theakstons XB on handpump; spotless housekeeping, and excellent service from friendly staff happy to chat about local beauty-spots. Darts, dominoes, shove-ha'penny and piped music; tables outside on a little terrace. *(Recommended by Anthony*

Barnes, PGP, Stephen Brown, Steve, Julie and Hayley Brown, Joan and Michel Hooper-Immins)

Free house ~ Licensees Christine Sykes and Miguel Moreno ~ Real ale ~ Meals and snacks (till 10) ~ Restaurant ~ (01572) 747543 ~ Children in eating area of bar and restaurant ~ Open 11.30-2.30, 6.30-11; 12-3, 7-10.30 Sun; cl evening 25, 26 Dec and 1 Jan ~ Bedrooms: £38.50B/£52B

OUNDLE TL0487 Map 5
Mill

Barnwell Rd out of town; or follow Barnwell Country Park signs off A605 bypass

Set beside a pretty pond, this splendid old mill is popular with diners enjoying the wide choice of well served and carefully prepared (but not cheap) meals: soup (£2.95), snails baked with garlic and herbs (£4.35), several pizzas (from £5.25), burgers (from £5.55), steak and kidney pie (£7.95), nachos (£8.55) and fajitas (from £9.95) and roast duck with orange and grand marnier sauce (£12.95). Stairs outside take you up to the most popular part, the Trattoria, which has stalls around tables with more banquettes in bays, stripped masonry and beams, and a millstone feature; its small windows look down over the lower millpond and the River Nene. A ground floor bar has red leatherette button-back built-in wall banquettes against its stripped-stone walls; on the way in a big glass floor panel shows the stream race below the building. Two-thirds of the bar is no smoking. Courage Directors on handpump; the beamed partly no-smoking top-floor restaurant houses the corn hoist; bar billiards, piped music. There are picnic tables under cocktail parasols among willow trees by the pond, with more on the side grass, and some white cast-iron tables on a flagstoned terrace. *(Recommended by Howard and Margaret Buchanan, David and Mary Webb, P J and S E Robbins)*

Free house ~ Licensees Noel and Linda Tulley ~ Real ale ~ Meals and snacks ~ Restaurant ~ (01832) 272621 ~ Children in eating area of bar ~ Open 11-3, 6.30-11; 12-4, 6.30-10.30 Sun

Ship £ 🍴
West St

The two sons of the previous licensee have taken over this cheerful well worn and unpretentious local, which has always been popular for its genuinely welcoming lively atmosphere. The heavily beamed lounge bar is made up of three rooms that lead off the central corridor on the left: up by the street there's a mix of leather and other seats including a very flowery piano stool (and its piano), with sturdy tables and a log fire in a stone inglenook, and down one end a panelled snug has button-back leather seats built in around it. Well kept Bass, Hop Back Summer Lightning, Tetleys and Wadworths 6X on handpump, a good range of malt whiskies, cappuccino and espressos. Very good value bar food might include stilton soup (£2), smoked salmon or chicken liver pâté (£3.50), seafood pie (£5) and lunchtime specials (£3.50-£4.50). Smiling, efficient service. Dominoes, maybe free Sunday nuts and crisps on the bar. The tiled-floor public side has darts, pinball, fruit machine, juke box and piped music. A series of small sheltered terraces strung out behind has wooden tables and chairs, lit at night. Several of the bedrooms are in a new extension. The pub can get busy with a lively young crowd, especially at lunchtimes or Saturday evenings. *(Recommended by David and Mary Webb, Quentin Williamson, Sue Holland, David Webster, A L and J D Turnbull, J Curtis, G Hughes)*

Free house ~ Licensees Andrew and Robert Langridge ~ Real ale ~ Meals and snacks (till 10) ~ (01832) 273918 ~ Children welcome ~ Disco Sat evening, live music in winter ~ Open 11-11; 12-10.30 Sun; may close in the afternoon in winter; cl 25 Dec evening ~ Bedrooms: £25(£30B)/£40(£50B)

Planning a day in the country? We list pubs in really attractive scenery at the back of the book.

SULGRAVE SP5545 Map 4
Star 🛏️

E of Banbury, signposted off B4525; Manor Road

The pleasantly neat bar at this very hospitable creeper-covered stonebuilt inn is divided by a timbered and leaded-light screen. The part by the big inglenook fireplace (with a paper skeleton on its side bench) has polished flagstones, the other part a red carpet, and furnishings are mainly small pews, cushioned window seats and wall benches, kitchen chairs and cast-iron-framed tables. Lots of things to look at include front pages of newspapers from notable days (Kennedy's assassination, say), collections of this and that, and some rather jokey stuffed animals. The staff are welcoming and friendly, as are one or two very regular locals. Generous helpings of seasonal dishes from the changing blackboard menu might include very good double-decker sandwiches, soup, Orkney rollmops, filo wrapped tiger prawns, smoked halibut, houmous with pitta bread or guacamole (£3.50-£4.50), main courses like ploughman's (£4.95), black eye bean and tomato goulash, watercress and goat's cheese tart, cod and chips or spinach and ricotta wholemeal tart (£6.95) or grilled smoked chicken breast (£7.95) and puddings like bread and butter pudding, treacle tart or tipsy trifle (£2.75). Well kept Hook Norton Best and Old Hookey and a monthly changing guest beer like Fullers London Pride on handpump. No-smoking back restaurant; piped music. There are some tables outside. Some of the comfortable bedrooms have good views. Note they don't allow children inside. The pub is on the road to George Washington's ancestral home. *(Recommended by Ian Phillips, Mr and Mrs C Moncrieffe, Stephen Brown, Mr and Mrs R Jones, Eric Locker, Rona Murdoch, E and M Corrin, Colin Sansom, Paul Moore, Lynda Payton, Sam Samuells, John Baker, Mrs J Box)*

Hook Norton ~ Tenant Andrew Willerton ~ Real ale ~ Meals and snacks ~ Restaurant ~ (01295) 760389 ~ Open 11-2.30, 6-11; 12-3, 7-11 Sun; 12-6 Sun in winter; cl 25 Dec ~ Bedrooms: £30S/£60S

WADENHOE TL0083 Map 5
Kings Head 🛏️

Church Street; village signposted (in small print) off A605 S of Oundle

A rough but extensive swathe of grass with picnic tables among willows and aspens slopes down from the back of this very lovely part-thatched stone-built old pub to boat moorings on the River Nene. There's a very nice atmosphere and friendly service from the young licensees in the partly stripped-stone main bar which has pleasant old worn quarry-tiles, solid pale pine furniture with a couple of cushioned wall seats, and a leather-upholstered chair by the woodburning stove in the fine inglenook. The bareboards public bar has similar furnishings and another fire, with steps down to a games room with darts, dominoes, cribbage, hood skittles and board games, and there's yet more of the pale pine furniture in an attractive little beamed no-smoking dining room. In the summer lunchtime bar food is limited to soup (£2.25), sandwiches (£2.50 – £1 extra with soup), filled baguettes (£3), welsh rarebit (£3.50) and ploughman's (£5), but in the evening and at lunchtime in winter there's a sensible choice of imaginative well cooked dishes that might include onion tart (£3.50), chicken liver pâté with onion marmalade (£3.75), home-pickled salmon with cucumber relish (£4.75), pasta (£5), steak and kidney casserole with herb dumplings (£7.25), fried gnocchi with roast mediterranean vegetables on a tomato sauce (£8) and baked salmon on a fresh herb cream sauce (£9.75); they do good Sunday roasts. Well kept Adnams Bitter and Broadside, and Marstons Pedigree on handpump, several freshly squeezed juices and an extensive wine list; magazines to read, no piped music. Readers tell us this is a lovely place to stay. *(Recommended by Stephen, Julie and Hayley Brown, John Coulter, Tim Hall, Oliver Crispin, Mrs J C Crispin, George Atkinson)*

Free house ~ Licensees Catherine and Alasdair Belton ~ Real ale ~ Meals and snacks (not Sun or Mon evening) ~ Restaurant ~ (01832) 720024 ~ Children in eating area of bar ~ Open 12-3, 6-11(10.30 Sun); cl Mon lunchtime; cl Sun evening in winter ~ Bedrooms: £30S/£50S

Lucky Dip

Besides the fully inspected pubs, you might like to try these Lucky Dips recommended to us and described by readers (if you do, please send us reports):

☆ Abthorpe [Silver St; signed from A43 at 1st roundabout S of A5; SP6446], *New Inn*: Surprised we don't get more reports on this distinctive country local, partly thatched, with its rambling take-us-as-you-find-us dim-lit bars, stripped stone, inglenook log fire, attractively priced home cooking (not Sun/Mon), well kept Hook Norton Best, Old Hookey and Double Stout, good choice of malt whiskies, friendly service, lots of old family photographs etc; big garden with goldfish pool and aviary, quiet village *(Martin and Penny Fletcher, Dr and Mrs B Baker, BB)*

Apethorpe [Kings Cliffe Rd; TL0295], *Kings Head*: Roomy stonebuilt pub in attractive conservation village, comfortable lounge with real fire, ales such as Fullers London Pride, Marstons Bitter and Pedigree and Wadworths 6X, obliging landlord, bar food (not Mon), arch to big dining area with separate menu (inc Mon), cosy bar with pool; children welcome, picnic tables in small enclosed garden *(George Atkinson, L Eadon)*

Arthingworth [just above A14 by A508 junction; SP7581], *Bulls Head*: : Refurbished pub, with good value food in bar and restaurant esp Sun lunch, jovial landlord, well kept ales; open all day summer *(John Liddell, Bryan and Betty Southwell)*

☆ Ashton [the one NE of Oundle, signed from A427/A605 island; TL0588], *Chequered Skipper*: As we went to press rebuilding (after the 1996 fire) was still not finished, but most had been done inc rethatching, and reopening was planned for later in the summer of 1997; has been a nice pub in an attractive village – under the new landlord expect well kept ales such as Adnams and Marstons Pedigree, generous food, friendly staff and a welcome for children *(News please)*

Barnwell [off A605 S of Oundle – 2nd left off village rd; TL0484], *Montagu Arms*: Attractive and unspoilt pub in lovely village setting, warm, cosy, welcoming and old-fashioned; four well kept ales such as Brains SA, Hook Norton Old Hookey and Wadworths 6X, good choice of bar food; garden has potential *(PGP, Quentin Williamson)*

☆ Blakesley [High St (Woodend rd); SP6250], *Bartholomew Arms*: Cosy beamed pub with lots of dark panelling in bar and two lounge areas (children welcome in one), stuffed birds and bric-a-brac, good food, friendly service, well kept Marstons Pedigree and Tetleys, lovely sheltered back garden with summer house; next to interesting little art gallery *(Ken and Jenny Simmonds, Martin and Penny Fletcher, George Atkinson)*

Braunston [Dark Lane, Little Braunston, just N of canal tunnel; SP5466], *Admiral Nelson*: Popular 18th-c ex-farmhouse by Grand Union Canal Lock 3 and hump bridge, with pleasant waterside garden and towpath walks; well kept Batemans and Scottish Courage ales, friendly staff, good quick bar food inc children's, restaurant *(David and Karen Berry)*; [London Rd (A45); SP5366], *Mill House*: Next to canal, smart interior, friendly quick service, good food inc early evening bargains for two; bedrooms *(David and Karen Berry)*

Bulwick [Main St; just off A43 Kettering—Duddington; SP9694], *Queens Head*: Long bar with small fire each end, wheelback chairs, plush stools, wall seats, a few beams; well kept Bass, Ruddles County and Worthington, good bar food (must book for Sun roasts); can be smoky *(Michel Hooper-Immins, Eric Locker, K H Frostick, Stephen G Brown, BB)*

Burton Latimer [Bake House Lane, off Church St; SP9075], *Olde Victoria*: Spacious mix of genuine and contrived old-world inc ornate gas lamps and lots of china, with nice atmosphere, real ales such as Marstons Pedigree, Morlands Old Speckled Hen, John Smiths and Wadworths 6X, food from baked potatoes up (sandwiches come at a price with salad and chips), friendly staff; quiet piped music, machines, back restaurant with cover charge; garden and terrace with picnic tables under cocktail parasols *(George Atkinson, Mr and Mrs P Finlay, John Waller)*

☆ Castle Ashby [SP8659], *Falcon*: Stone walls and hop-hung dark beams in 16th-c cellar bar down tricky steps from smart hotel in attractive preserved village, Adnams Extra, welcoming landlord, good food, open fire; restaurant overlooking pretty garden; bedrooms beautifully decorated, good breakfast *(Margaret and Nigel Dennis, George Atkinson)*

Chapel Brampton [SP7266], *Spencer Arms*: Very big recently refurbished Chef & Brewer family dining pub, lots of tables; real ales maybe inc Theakstons Old Peculier *(Patrick Tailyour)*

☆ Collingtree [High St; 1¼ miles from M1 junction 15; SP7555], *Wooden Walls of Old England*: Tidy thatched pub with stripped stonework, low black beams, model galleon and some other nautical memorabilia, well kept Mansfield ales, friendly staff, well priced standard food, open fire; table skittles and fruit machine in one bar; children welcome, lots of picnic tables, swings and tuck shop in back garden *(CMW, JJW, George Atkinson, BB)*

Corby [Tower Hill Rd; off A6003, W edge; SP8988], *Knights Lodge*: Attractive early 17th-c pub, long bar with areas off, lots of stonework and beams, fire each end, copper, brass and bric-a-brac; good value food, Everards and three guest ales, machines, piped music; restaurant upstairs; children welcome *(CMW, JJW)*

☆ Cosgrove [Thrupp Wharf, towards

Castlethorpe; SP7942], *Navigation*: Lovely canalside setting, well kept ales inc Wadworths 6X and local Frog Island Shoemaker, usual food inc god toasties, cheerful open-plan bar up steps with chesterfield and armchairs around open fire, lots of canal prints and memorabilia, character landlord, helpful obliging staff; summer jazz, children welcome, lots of tables out by water (a long way round from front entrance), moorings; can be very busy weekends and school hols *(George Atkinson, Lynda Payton, Sam Samuells, Kevin O'Rourke, John Baker, BB)*

Daventry [Brook St; SP5762], *Dun Cow*: Interesting former coaching inn, log fire and lots of old local photographs in down-to-earth cosy character bar (no piped music), roomier more peaceful rare Elizabethan gallery bar, cheap lunchtime food (not Sun) inc home-made steak and kidney pie, back family eating room, attentive service, well kept Bass, Davenports and a guest such as Elgoods *(Patrick Tailyour, Pete Baker)*

Evenley [The Green; SP5834], *Red Lion*: Small friendly local with strong cricket connections, opp attractive village green; some flagstones, Banks's and Marstons Pedigree, decent choice of wines, reasonably priced food inc good sandwiches and Sun lunch *(K H Frostick)*

Finedon [Bell Hill; SP9272], *Bell*: Attractive 19th-c stone pub with several linked rooms, woodburner, some old beams, nautical-theme back dining room; good value lunches inc Sun roast, four real ales on handpump and two tapped from the cask; piped music, darts, fruit machine; tables out in front *(CMW, JJW)*

Gayton [20 High St; SP7054], *Eykyn Arms*: Cheerful and friendly stonebuilt pub keeping much of its original style; plush lounge full of naval memorabilia, roomy bar with lots of village prints and photographs, well kept Charles Wells ales, usual food inc sandwiches, useful covered terrace and toys for children *(John C Baker)*

Geddington [Bridge St; just off A43 Kettering—Corby; SP8983], *Star*: Good if not cheap food inc good value Fri fish, well kept beers, attractive bar, restaurant, tables outside – pleasant setting not far from picturesque packhorse bridge, handy for Broughton House *(J and P Maloney, David and Mary Webb)*

Great Everdon [SP5857], *Plough*: Friendly and spotless pub dating from 16th c, two coal fires, pictures and jugs in lounge/dining area, well kept Banks's Bitter and Morrells Varsity, wide choice of low-priced appetising food, games room, juke box; spacious garden with hens and barbecue, good walks nearby *(CMW, JJW)*

Great Oxendon [Harborough Rd (A508); SP7383], *George*: Civilised L-shaped bar/lounge, pleasant no-smoking conservatory overlooking big garden and terrace, pleasant staff, Adnams and Bass, food inc good assorted cheese ploughman's, restaurant;

bedrooms *(George Atkinson)*

Hardingstone [61 High St; SP7657], *Crown*: Two-bar pub with good value simple lunchtime food, Thurs supper bargains, friendly service, Scottish Courage beers, games room; maybe piped music; children and dogs welcome, picnic tables in sizeable garden with play area, dovecot and pets corner *(JJW, CMW)*; [9 High St], *Sun*: Stripped stone, tankards and jugs hanging from beams, friendly atmosphere, big helpings of good value basic food (not Sun evening or Mon) inc bargain OAP lunch Thurs, Everards Tiger and other real ales, quiet piped music, gas fire, games room, docile st bernard called Henry, tables outside *(CMW, JJW)*

Hargreave [Church St; TL0370], *Nags Head*: Olde-worlde village pub, originally three thatched 16-c cottages, well cooked meals (not Sun evening), newly refurbished no-smoking dining room, two changing real ales *(E Robinson)*

Harlestone [A428; SP7064], *Fox & Hounds*: Comfortable old beamed pub with two rooms off central bar, nice wooden furniture, stripped masonry, lots of brasses, usual moderately priced lunchtime food inc good snacks, friendly service and country atmosphere, Scottish Courage ales and Tetleys; piped pop music, machines, TV; tables in garden with covered eating area, attractive village nr Althorp House, pleasant walks *(Gill and Keith Croxton, JJW, CMW)*

☆ **Harrington** [High St, off A508 S of Mkt Harboro; SP7779], *Tollemache Arms*: Newish licensees doing good home-cooked fresh food in civilised beamed Tudor pub, Charles Wells ales, open fires, small back garden; children welcome, clean and attractive bedrooms, quiet stonebuilt village *(K H Frostick)*

Hartwell [3 Park Rd; off A508 or B526 S of Northampton; SP7850], *Rose & Crown*: Popular old pub with Bass, Tetleys and a guest beer, real fires, games room, no-smoking dining area, views; fruit machine, maybe piped radio *(CMW, JJW)*

☆ **Hellidon** [off A425 W of Daventry; SP5158], *Red Lion*: Clean, cosy and comfortable, good value food inc good Weds OAP lunch in bars and restaurant, well kept Bass and Worthington, two farm ciders; welcoming landlord and above-average service, roaring log fire, friendly labradors, games room; bedrooms, beautiful setting by village green, tables outside, pleasant walks nearby *(George Atkinson, John Brightley)*

☆ **Holcot** [Main St; SP7969], *White Swan*: Attractive partly thatched two-bar village inn with Fullers London Pride, Greene King IPA, Morlands Old Speckled Hen, Tetleys and Websters from thatched servery, good reasonably priced food (not Sun-Weds evening) inc good value Sun lunch, helpful staff, games room with skittles, pool and darts; children welcome; bedrooms *(Michael and Jenny Back, Eric Locker)*

Kettering [1 Sheep St, Market Pl; SP8778], *Cherry Tree*: Welcoming local with good reasonably priced home-cooked food all day (not after 6 Tues, afternoon break Sun) inc two-person bargains, friendly staff, gas fire, well kept Charles Wells, no piped music, unobtrusive fruit machines *(Keith and Janet Morris, Jeff Weston)*

Litchborough [just off former B4525 Banbury—Northampton; SP6353], *Old Red Lion*: Attractive sandstone village local opp church and little green, well kept Banks's and Benskins Best, reasonably priced food from sandwiches up, great deep inglenook with winter fires, incongruous chrome bar stools *(Ian Phillips)*

☆ **Little Brington** [4½ miles from M1 junction 16, first right off A45 to Daventry; also signed from A428; SP6663], *Saracens Head*: Another change of licensee but still a good choice of well kept ales inc Frog Island (but served through sparkler now) and wide choice of good generous reasonably priced food; recently extended no-smoking restaurant area, roomy lounge with alcoves, lots of pictures, books and odds and ends, even a red telephone box, log fire, games bar; piped pop music; tables in neat back garden, handy for Althorp House and Holdenby House *(K H Frostick, Bruce Bird, George Atkinson, Simon Walker, BB)*

☆ **Little Harrowden** [Main St; SP8771], *Lamb*: Good fresh reasonably priced home-cooked food (not Sun evening) inc game and vegetarian dishes in spotlessly refurbished 17th-c pub, cosy three-level lounge with log fire, brasses on beams, intimate no-smoking dining area, well kept Charles Wells Eagle and Bombardier and guests such as Frog Island and Youngs Winter Warmer served through sparkler, decent coffee, friendly attentive staff, quiet piped music; public bar, games room with darts and hood skittles; children welcome; garden, delightful village *(David Etheridge, John C Baker, L Eadon, K H Frostick, CMW, JJW, John Waller)*

☆ **Marston Trussell** [Main St; SP6985], *Sun*: More hotel than pub, with comfortable good value bedrooms, but well worth knowing for wide choice of beautifully presented home-made food in bar and restaurant, well kept Bass, decent house wines, unusual malt whiskies, helpful uniformed staff *(Bruce Cooper, Jim Farmer)*

Mears Ashby [Wilby Rd; SP8466], *Griffins Head*: Quiet pleasantly refurbished country pub with three rooms off central bar, bucolic views, good friendly service, generous food from good sandwiches to good value Sun roasts, attractive pictures, well kept ales such as Black Sheep, Charles Wells Eagle, Frog Island and Wadworths 6X; skittles, piped music, seats out in small garden *(Bruce Bird, George Atkinson)*

☆ **Milton Malsor** [Towcester Rd (old A43); SP7355], *Greyhound*: Biggish partly 15th-c beamed pub given new lease of life by olde-worlde refurbishment complete with old paintings and china, pewter-filled dresser etc; very wide choice of good food from soup and

doorstep sandwiches up, John Smiths, Theakstons Best and XB, good choice of wines, candlelit tables, good service from pleasant attentive staff, good log fire, piped classical music; open all day, substantial front lawn with duck pond *(George Atkinson, Mrs S Parsons, K Campbell, Dave Braisted)*

Naseby [Church St; B4036 Mkt Harboro—Daventry; SP6878], *Fitzgerald Arms*: 18th-c pub with emphasis on reasonably priced food in the lounge side with its big dining area, also locals' side with ferret-and-rabbit chat and games area for pool and table skittles; Bass, pleasant garden with noisy cockerel, nr source of River Avon and Naseby Battle Museum; cl Mon lunchtime *(Ian Phillips, George Atkinson)*

☆ **Nassington** [2 Fotheringhay Rd; TL0696], *Black Horse*: Civilised 17th-c beamed and panelled dining pub in nice village, wide choice of food from sandwiches to interesting main dishes, with children's helpings; splendid big stone fireplace, panelling, easy chairs and small settees in two rooms linked by bar servery, well kept Scottish Courage ales, good varied wine list; attractive garden, open all day summer weekends *(Quentin Williamson, A Cowell, Gordon Theaker, Mary and David Webb, L Eadon, J and M Back, Maysie Thompson, LYM; more reports on current regime please)*

Nether Heyford [Middle Lane; off A45 W of M1 junction 16; SP6558], *Olde Sun*: Friendly old stone pub packed with brassware, railway memorabilia and other bric-a-brac; three beamed bars, rugs on parquet, red tiles or flagstones, big open fire, homely restaurant, good standard bar food, real ales inc Banks's, Marstons Pedigree and Ruddles Best and County; picnic tables in yard with dovecote, flowers and shrubs among old farm equipment *(Sam Samuells, Lynda Payton, John Saul)*

Newton Bromswold [Church Lane; E of Rushden; SP9965], *Swan*: Very friendly new licensees in village local with largeish mock-Tudor lounge, food inc good lunchtime sandwiches, well kept Greene King ales, real fire, games room with darts and hood skittles, big pleasant garden full of birds (and feeders) *(George Atkinson)*

☆ **Northampton** [Wellingborough Rd], *Abington Park*: Large open-plan Victorian pub visibly brewing its own good beers, several bars, good range of lunchtime bar food, friendly helpful staff, restaurant, family room; piped pop music, games machines; picnic tables outside, handy for cricket ground *(Bruce Bird, Stephen Brown)*

Northampton [Fish St], *Beamhouse*: Newish pub in former DSS office (originally 1900 building for hanging undyed leather for local shoe trade); one big bar with carpet on polished boards, comfortable chairs and banquettes, good value late breakfast and lunchtime food (not Sun), Mansfield ales, newspapers, piped pop, games machines; disabled access *(JJW, CMW)*; [11 Fish St],

Fish: Nice bustling atmosphere, good value weekday lunches (service can slow when busy), very good range of real ales, farm cider, bare boards, newspapers, games machines, disabled access; bedrooms *(JJW, CMW)*; [Drapery], *Hogshead*: New old-style pub with assorted old furniture, shoe industry memorabilia, newspapers, good value food, at least seven real ales on handpump and four guests tapped from the cask, Weston's Old Rosie cider; TV, Monopoly machine, can be smoky, service can be a bit slow; open all day *(CMW, JJW)*; [121 Bridge St], *Malt Shovel*: Long bar recently refurbished in pine and stripped brick, with local memorabilia, good value home-cooked food, good changing choice of real ales, farm cider, occasional beer festivals, daily papers, darts; piped music, service can slow when busy; picnic tables on small back terrace *(CMW, JJW)*; [Mkt Sq], *Moon on the Square*: Recently opened comfortable Wetherspoons pub, standard interior with shelves of books, partly no-smoking raised eating area, food all day inc some unusual dishes, six real ales, no piped music; good disabled access inc stairlift to restaurant conservatory area *(CMW, JJW, Daryl J Davey)*

Norton [off A5 N of Weedon; SP6063], *White Horse*: Old village pub settling down under friendly newish licensees, well kept Charles Wells ales and a guest such as Adnams Broadside, attentive service, cheap good food, beamed lounge with dining annexe, public bar with pool and skittles; seats out in front and small back garden *(George Atkinson)*

☆ **Old** [Walgrave Rd; N of Northampton between A43 and A508; SP7873], *White Horse*: Wide choice of good sensibly priced food inc some interesting snacks, cosy lounge with welcoming log fire, lots of pictures and plates, cheerful service, well kept Banks's and Marstons Pedigree, decent wines, restaurant; ample seating *(George Atkinson, Robert and Sally Thorne)*

Oundle [52 Benefield Rd; A427 towards Corby; TL0388], *Black Horse*: Small roadside local expanding into plush new restaurant area with its popular good value straightforward food; well kept Bass, John Smiths, a beer brewed for the pub and maybe a changing guest beer, lots of up-to-date paperbacks to borrow, simple plush bar, attentive service, quiet piped music, big games room; picnic tables in garden behind, Sat karaoke *(Jenny and Michael Back, C W McKerrow, BB)*

Polebrook [just SE of Oundle; TL0687], *Kings Arms*: Welcoming young licensees, good friendly atmosphere, good choice of food inc really good value sandwiches, real ales such as Boddingtons, Greene King IPA and Marstons Pedigree; big partly divided open-plan lounge *(PGP)*

☆ **Pytchley** [Isham Rd; SP8574], *Overstone Arms*: Interesting changing food in long countrified dining room packed every evening, often with big parties; good range of weekday lunchtime food in small bar too, well kept Scottish Courage beers with a guest such as Batemans XB, pleasant attentive service, children allowed if eating; big orchard garden, weekend barbecue/salad bar in smaller enclosed one, attractive countryside *(George Atkinson, Roger Byrne)*

Ravensthorpe [Church Lane; SP6670], *Chequers*: Wide range of bar food inc good well priced Sun lunch (worth booking this), well kept cheap Sam Smiths OB and other northern ales, lots of bric-a-brac in spotless L-shaped bar with jugs and mugs on beams, friendly locals, good service, restaurant (Weds-Sat); TV, fruit machine, piped music, monthly quiz night; quiet garden with play area *(George Atkinson, Ted George, Bruce Bird, CMW, JJW)*

Rothwell [Sun Hill (A6); SP8181], *Rowell Charter*: Welcoming ancient pub with two open fires, good choice of home-cooked food, unusual range of consistently well kept beers such as Hartleys XB *(Patrick Tailyour, Stephen Brown)*

Rushton [SP8482], *Thornhill Arms*: Recently refurbished, in lovely setting opp village green cricket ground; decent low-priced food, well kept ales inc Ruddles *(Stephen Brown)*

☆ **Sibbertoft** [SP6782], *Red Lion*: Cosy and civilised beamed bar with big tables and comfortably cushioned wall seats, huge range of good generous food inc vegetarian, well kept Bass and Tetleys, decent wines, good service, piano, magazines *(Robert and Sally Thorne, Dorsan Baker)*

Southwick [TL0192], *Shuckburgh Arms*: Reopened 1996 after renovation, friendly staff, substantial tasty well priced food *(David and Mary Webb)*

☆ **Staverton** [Daventry Rd (A425); SP5361], *Countryman*: Friendly service and atmosphere, well kept Theakstons XB from thatched servery, good imaginatively presented food from club sandwiches to Angus beef and unusual specials like bison and kangaroo; booking advisable *(Michael Lenihan, David Shillitoe)*

☆ **Stoke Bruerne** [3½ miles from M1 junction 15 – A508 towards Stony Stratford then signed on right; SP7450], *Boat*: Ideal canal location by beautifully restored lock opp British Waterways Museum and shop; little character flagstoned bar by canal, more ordinary back lounge without the views (children allowed in this bit), tables by towpath; well kept ales such as Marstons Best and Pedigree, Sam Smiths OB, Theakstons XB, Wadworths 6X and guests, skittle alley; bar snacks, no-smoking restaurant (not Mon lunchtime) and all-day tearooms, pub open all day summer Sats, canal boat trips *(Lynda Payton, Sam Samuells, Bruce Peckett, George Atkinson, James Nunns, LYM)*

☆ **Stoke Doyle** [S of Oundle; TL0286], *Shuckborough Arms*: Good food inc vegetarian in peaceful welcoming L-shaped panelled bar or dining room, well kept ales inc guests, log fires, comfortable chesterfields, hospitable landlord, no music or fruit machines, games room with hood skittles; picnic tables in garden with play area; bedrooms good, with own bathrooms *(George Atkinson, L Eadon)*

☆ **Sudborough** [High St (off A6116); SP9682], *Vane Arms*: Cheery take-us-as-you-find us thatched pub notable for its fine choice of well kept ales mostly from interesting small breweries and often strong, also Belgian fruit beers, farm cider, country wines; stripped stonework, good inglenook fires, games in public bar, food (not Sun evening, Mon lunch) from sandwiches to steaks inc lots of Mexican dishes; piped music, and Nelson the dog gets around; lounge, dining area and upstairs restaurant (not Sun evening) all no smoking; children in eating area, bedrooms; cl Mon lunchtime *(Stephen and Julie Brown, L Eadon, John Fahy, Joan and Michel Hooper-Immins, David and Shelia, PGP, Julian Holland, LYM)*

Syresham [off A43 Brackley—Towcester; SP6241], *Kings Head*: Recently refurbished as family dining pub, with toys, high chairs, baby-changing, felxibility over food; friendly newish licensees, dark beams, brasses, pictures, real fire, well kept Banks's and other ales, separate bar with games and juke box; tables in garden, children welcome *(J Warren, DC)*

☆ **Thornby** [Welford Rd – A50 Northampton—Leicester, handy for A14; SP6775], *Red Lion*: Friendly bar with lots of decorative china, pews and some leather armchairs, amiable dogs, log fire, good home-made bar food from sandwiches to steaks inc Sun roasts and children's helpings, well kept Greene King IPA, Marstons Pedigree Robinsons Best and Thwaites, good range of traditional games; piped music; open all day weekends, children welcome; nice, but due for some renovation *(John Fahy, M J Morgan, George Atkinson, LYM)*

☆ **Thorpe Mandeville** [former B4525; SP5344], *Three Conies*: Cosy and attractive, with brasses, low beams, some stripped stone, gin-trap over inglenook fireplace, horse-racing photographs and conversation, furnishings to suit the old building; good reasonably priced food, well kept Hook Norton and Old Hookey, good choice of wines and spirits, friendly efficient service, games room, appealing restaurant; children welcome, lots of seats in big garden *(Ted George, David Carr, LYM)*

Upper Boddington [Warwick Rd; SP4753], *Plough*: Really old-fashioned village pub with few concessions to the 1990s, fine chatty landlord of the old school, walls covered with news cuttings of various ages, lovely Dolls Parlour, Bass and Marstons Pedigree under light blanket pressure, coffee, limited choice of enjoyable food inc nice open sandwiches, skittles and darts; decor scarcely in first flush of youth, but a very welcoming place – nice sitting outside in summer *(George Atkinson)*

Walgrave [Zion Hill; off A43 Northampton—Kettering; SP8072], *Royal Oak*: Old ironstone building, bar and dining lounge split into smaller areas, well kept Batemans XXXB, Morrells Oxford and Wadworths 6X, good coffee, wide choice of good food inc vegetarian, friendly landlord, efficient service; piped music, pictures for sale; children welcome, tables outside *(Michelle Matel, Bruce Bird)*

☆ **Weedon** [Stowe Hill; A5 S; SP6458], *Narrow Boat*: Warm and welcoming well worn-in main bar, plain decor with canal prints and big aquarium, high-raftered ex-kitchen family dining room, good range of bar food inc some dishes from the Cantonese/Indonesian restaurant (spacious and airy, with canal and country views – booking advised Sat), well kept Charles Wells ales with a guest such as Adnams; fruit machine, skittles and quiet piped music, very busy in summer; spacious terrace, big garden by canal, barbecues; bedrooms in motel extension, narrowboat hire next door *(Lynda Payton, Sam Samuells, Simon Stafford, JJW, CMW, LYM)*

☆ **Weedon** [junction A5/A45], *Globe*: Usefully placed attractive country hotel with comfortable atmosphere, reliable fresh bar food inc vegetarian and take-aways, small helpings for children or OAPs, quick friendly service, Marstons Bitter and Pedigree, Websters Yorkshire and usually a northern guest beer, log fire, restaurant; picnic tables outside; bedrooms *(George Atkinson)*

☆ **Welford** [High St (A50); SP6480], *Shoulder of Mutton*: Friendly and spotless low-ceilinged pub nr canal marina, partly divided by standing timbers and arches, plenty of tables and wheelback chairs, copper and brass, sensibly priced straightforward food inc children's, Batemans XB and Ruddles Best, good house wines and coffee, eager service; piped music; skittle room, exemplary lavatories, good back garden with play area; cl Thurs *(Frank Davidson, Roger and Pauline Pearce, C H and P Stride, BB)*

Weston [High St; the one N of Brackley; SP5846], *Crown*: Pleasant 17th-c flagstoned village pub, log fires, sporting trophies, four well kept ales such as Elgoods Golden Newt, good coffee, unpretentious furnishings and unusual long room (former skittle alley) with cubicle seating, bar food; handy for NT Canons Ashby and Sulgrave *(Tom Evans)*

Wicken [Deanshanger Rd; SP7439], *Wicken Arms*: Pine furniture, ancient beams and fine new back dining conservatory, relaxed atmosphere, friendly efficient service, enjoyable bar food from filled warm french bread to Sun lunch, well kept real ales inc Jennings Cumberland and Ushers Best; piped music, children welcome, picnic tables in garden; bedrooms *(George Atkinson)*

Wollaston [London Rd, off A509 S of Wellingborough; SP9163], *Nags Head*: Lots of pictures and photographs in lounge, Camerons, Marstons Pedigree and Morrells Graduate and Varsity, huge choice of food cooked to order in bar and restaurant, high chairs, quiet piped music, swing in small garden *(CMW, JJW)*

Woodnewton [Main St; TL0394], *White Swan*: Friendly country local with several well kept changing ales such as Black Sheep and Oakham JHB, some emphasis on good value if not particularly cheap food inc good steak and kidney pudding, lots of veg, Sun lunch; local radio, gas fire, attentive cheerful service *(George Atkinson)*

Yardley Gobion [30 High St (off A508); SP7644], *Coffee Pot*: Roomy and pleasant, real fires, Scottish Courage ales, friendly local licensees, good freshly cooked standard food, children in eating area, tables outside; pool, live music most weekends *(Mr and Mrs D S Price)*

Yardley Hastings [off A428 Bedford—Northampton; SP8656], *Rose & Crown*: Relaxed and spacious pub in pretty village, beams, stripped stonework and flagstones, lots of nooks and crannies for a quiet drink, good value food from excellent sausage baps to generous carvery, vegetarian and children's dishes, comfortable family area; Thurs OAP reduction, Tues bargain roast and puddings; Ind Coope Burton with a guest such as Greene King Abbot, friendly licensees *(Penny and Ron Westwood, T G Saul, George Atkinson)*

☆ **Yelvertoft** [49 High St; SP5975], *Knightley Arms*: Simple clean lounge divided by log fire, teapots, brasses, copper and pictures, solid wooden furnishings, small neat dining area, good value freshly cooked food inc children's, well kept Bass, Marstons Pedigree and Websters Yorkshire, good coffee, hood skittles, two dogs; darts, TV and machines one end; garden, occasional barbecues *(CMW, JJW, Lynda Payton, Sam Samuells)*

Northumbria
(Durham & Northumberland)

This area stands out for a really warm welcome in most of its pubs. Ones which have been showing up particularly well in readers' reports over the last few months include the eccentric Allenheads Inn up at Allenheads (warm-hearted licensees, comfortable new bedrooms), the carefully run Saddle at Alnmouth (tasty food – a new main entry), the Percy Arms at Chatton (a well run village inn), the Fox & Hounds at Cotherstone (good all round), the unspoilt Dipton Mill Inn at Diptonmill (good local ales and wholesome food), the pretty thatched Black Bull at Etal (back in these pages after a long absence, under a friendly new landlady), the relaxing Feathers at Hedley on the Hill (now doing food on weekday evenings too), and the Masons Arms at Rennington (comfortable, friendly, good value). The very well run Rose & Crown at Romaldkirk stands out for so successfully combining pub, restaurant and hotel – and it gains our award as Northumbria Dining Pub of the Year. The Manor House at Carterway Heads has also been doing extremely well; it's just changed hands, but they're keeping the same chef and menu – the food has been the main thing here. Pub food is generally good value here, and is often particularly cheap in the big towns. Drinks prices too are well below the national average; the Manor House at Carterway Heads came out cheapest in our survey. In the Lucky Dip section at the end of the chapter, we'd highlight the High Force at High Force (the waterfall it's named after), George at Piercebridge, Waterford Arms at Seaton Sluice, Dun Cow at Sedgefield, Hadrian at Wall and Bay Horse at West Woodburn (almost all inspected and approved by us); there's a good choice in Durham, and a very good ever-widening choice in Newcastle.

This chapter includes Tyneside and Teesside pubs, which we've labelled Tyne & Wear and Cleveland, respectively.

ALLENDALE (Northumberland) NY8355 Map 10
Kings Head 🛏
Market Place (B6295)
New licensees have taken over this old coaching inn and plan to redecorate the bars. The spacious bar/lounge has a big log fire, straightforward pub furnishings, and Theakstons Best, XB and Old Peculier and four or five guest ales such as Butterknowle Bitter, Courage Directors, Durham Sunstroke and Old Hundred, Greene King Abbot, Jennings Cumberland, Marstons Pedigree, and Timothy Taylors Landlord on handpump, kept well in a temperature-controlled cellar; 75 malt whiskies. Bar food now includes sandwiches, beef in ale or jester chicken (£4.95), fried wild salmon (£5.95), chicken fillets with leeks and stilton in a port sauce, and puddings (£1.95). Darts and piped pop music. There are good walks in the area, and the road through the valley is a fine scenic drive. *(Recommended by JJW, CMW, Steve and Marianne Webb-Phillips, Eric Larkham, Christopher Warner, David and Margaret Bloomfield, Craig and Gillian Brown; more reports on the new regime, please)*

Free house ~ Licensees Margaret and Alan Taylor ~ Real ale ~ Meals and snacks ~ Children welcome ~ (01434) 683681 ~ Live music Fri evening ~ Open 11-11; 12-10.30 Sun ~ Bedrooms: £23B/£45B

ALLENHEADS (Northumberland) NY8545 Map 10
Allenheads Inn 🛏

Just off B6295

In the few years they've been here, the extremely cheerful, entertaining and eccentric licensees have packed every available space with all sorts of really crazy (but clean and enthusiastically well cared for) bric-a-brac in a series of loosely themed rooms: stuffed animals, mangles, old radios, typewriters and sewing machines, long-silenced musical instruments, a ship's engine-room telegraph, brass and copper bygones, even nostalgic old tins and postcards; the naval room is no smoking. The games room (with darts, pool, cribbage and antique juke box) has perhaps the most effervescent collection, and the car club discs and number plates on the panelling are a symptom of the fact that members of a classic car club try to persuade their vehicles to wend their way up here every other Tuesday. They do huge helpings of good straightforward cheap food such as soup (£1.50), sandwiches (from £1.50), lasagne or sweet and sour chicken (£4.50), steak or chicken pies (£5), and puddings (from £1.50); there is a Harley Davidson on one big table in the dining room; roast Sunday lunch (£4.25). Alongside well kept Ind Coope Burton and Tetleys, four or five guests might include Calders, Flowers Original, Hodges Best or Original, Mansfield Red Admiral or Youngs on handpump, decent coffee, real fire, piped music, friendly alsatian, very warm-hearted service. There are tables outside, flanked by more machinery – the sorts of machinery that wouldn't fit inside, including a vintage Rolls-Royce parked in front; it's on the Sustrans C2C cycle route. *(Recommended by Pat and John Denby, Margaret Whitaker, Mr and Mrs J Beard, David and Margaret Bloomfield, Margaret and Roy Randle)*

Free house ~ Licensees Peter and Linda Stenson ~ Real ale ~ Meals and snacks ~ Restaurant (bookings only) ~ (01434) 685200 ~ Children in the games room ~ Open 11-3, 7-11; 12-4, 7-10.30 Sun; cl Tues lunchtime in winter ~ Bedrooms: £21.50B/£43B

ALNMOUTH (Northumberland) NU2511 Map 10
Saddle 🛏

Northumberland Street (B1338)

Clean, friendy and unpretentious, this well run pub turns out to be bigger than you'd expect from outside, rambling through several areas including a roomy dining space. It's attractively decorated, with local landscapes and other pictures for sale on the walls; the conservatory is no smoking. A wide choice of generous well cooked keen-priced food includes home-made soup (£1.25), sandwiches (from £1.50), ploughman's (from £3.95), steak and kidney pie, lamb and leek casserole, broccoli and cauliflower bake in a blue cheese sauce or fresh cod or haddock (all £5.25), hot haddock smokie pie with cheese (£5.50), sirloin steak (£8.50), crocodile steak (£13.50), excellent Craster kippers, good puddings such as their Lindisfarne cocktail (ice cream with honey and mead) or spotted dick (£1.50), and an outstanding cheeseboard; fresh vegetables. Half-a-dozen well kept real ales on handpump (some occasionally under a light carbon dioxide blanket) such as Belhaven 90/-, Border Brewery Special Bitter, Jennings Cumberland, Marstons Owd Rodger, Morlands Old Speckled Hen, Northumberland Castles Bitter, and Wychwood Dogs Bollocks; they hold an annual beer festival in August with 30 ales, live bands, barbecues, and bouncy castles. Decent wines, friendly helpful staff (and a frequent ghost); darts, winter pool, cribbage, dominoes, fruit machine, and unobtrusive piped music. Breakfasts are good (usually with those kippers again). There are picnic tables in the back garden, overlooking the estuary. This seaside village has attractive beaches, good coastal walks, and plenty for summer visitors. *(Recommended by John Oddey, Diana Crawford, Eric Larkham, Jack and Heather Coyle, Nigel and Amanda Thorp, June and Tony Baldwin, Guy Consterdine)*

Free house ~ Licensee John Orde ~ Real ale ~ Meals and snacks ~ Restaurant ~ (01665) 830216 ~ Children welcome away from bar ~ Folk/country & western music Weds evening ~ Open 11-11; 12-10.30 Sun ~ Bedrooms: £34.50B/£69B

BAMBURGH (Northumberland) NU1835 Map 10
Lord Crewe Arms 🛏

Overlooked by the impressive Norman castle and opposite the cricket pitch, this old hotel is a comfortable place to stay with plenty to do nearby. Just opposite is a good beach of tidal sand, and there are plenty of bracing walks. The back cocktail bar, with comfortably upholstered banquettes, windsor armchairs and the like around cast-iron traditional pub tables, has a bar counter studded with thousands of pre-decimal polished copper coins, and its beams are festooned with swordfish swords, armadillo skins, miners' lamps, lobster pots, fishing nets and lots more; there's a winter log fire. A more modern side bar has hunting murals; dominoes and piped music. Lunchtime bar food includes home-made soup (£1.95), sandwiches (from £2.10), basket meals (£3.75), ploughman's (£4.25), local deep-fried haddock fillet (£4.95), local kippers (£5.25), steak in ale pie (£5.95), and puddings like home-made fruit crumble (£2.95), with evening dishes such as warm squid salad with chilli and orange dressing (£3.95), fillet of pork with cranberry jus and deep-fried sweet potatoes (£9.25), roast duck breast with cranberry sauce (£9.75), and sirloin steak (£10.75); the restaurant is no smoking. Bass and Stones on handpump kept under light blanket pressure, and some malt whiskies; friendly helpful staff. The castle is still lived in, and has a splendid collection of arms and armour. *(Recommended by Geoffrey and Brenda Wilson, Avril Hanson, John and June Gale, Chris Rounthwaite, Martin Hickes, Annette and Steven Marsden, P J Hanson; more reports please)*

Free house ~ Licensee Malcolm Eden ~ Real ale ~ Meals and snacks ~ Evening restaurant ~ (01668) 214243 ~ Children in eating area of bar and in restaurant ~ Open 11.30-3, 6-11; maybe all day in high season; 12-3, 6-10.30 Sun; hotel is closed end Oct-week before Easter ~ Bedrooms: £37(£49B)/£52(£74B)

BLANCHLAND (Northumberland) NY9750 Map 10
Lord Crewe Arms

In a very special village, this stone stronghold of an inn was built originally in 1235 as part of the guest-house of a Premonstratensian monastery and remained largely untouched for centuries; part of the cloister still stands in the neatly terraced gardens. The barrel-vaulted crypt bar has plush bar stools, built-in wall benches, ancient flagstones, and stone and brick walls that are eight feet thick in some places. Vaux Samson on handpump; darts, dominoes and cribbage. Upstairs, the quietly welcoming Derwent Room has low beams, old settles, and sepia photographs on its walls, and the Hilyard Room has a massive 13th-c fireplace once used as a hiding place by the Jacobite Tom Forster (part of the family who had owned the building before it was sold to the formidable Lord Crewe, Bishop of Durham). Lunchtime bar food includes soup (£1.85), filled rolls (mostly £2.90), ploughman's (from £4.40), salmon fishcakes or vegetarian sausages (£4.95), and wild boar and pheasant pie (£4.50); in the evening, there might be baked salmon steak (£8.25), provençale nut wellington (£8.50), or sirloin steak (£9); puddings (£2.50). There's a pleasant enclosed garden. *(Recommended by Martin Hickes, Steve and Marianne Webb-Phillips, Paul and Ursula Randall, Richard Fallon, George and Chris Miller, Avril Hanson, Val Stevenson, Rob Holmes, Liz and John Soden, Wayne Brindle, Joyce McKimm, P J Hanson)*

Free house ~ Licensees A S Todd, Peter Gingell, Ian Press ~ Real ale ~ Meals and snacks ~ Restaurant ~ (01434) 675251 ~ Children welcome ~ Open 11-3, 6-11; closed winter Tues and Weds mornings; 12-3, 7-10.30 Sun ~ Bedrooms: £80B/£110B

Please let us know what you think of a pub's bedrooms. No stamp needed: *The Good Pub Guide*, FREEPOST TN1569, Wadhurst, E Sussex TN5 7BR.

CARTERWAY HEADS (Northumberland) NZ0552 Map 10

Manor House ⏹ ♀ ◗

A68 just N of B6278, near Derwent Reservoir

As we went to press, the licensees here changed. They plan to alter very little, and luckily for us, have kept on the same chef. From a changing menu, the popular food might include sandwiches, soup such as creamy mushroom (£1.95), chicken liver pâté with onion marmalade (£2.65), cumberland sausage with mash and mustard sauce (£4.45), sautéed Italian vegetables in puff pastry with pesto (£5.35), sweet and sour tiger prawns (£5.50), spiced pork casserole with cumin and tomatoes (£6.50), baked salmon fillet on spinach with crayfish butter (£8.95), roast venison steak with sun-dried tomatoes and red wine, sirloin steak (£9.65), and puddings like chocolate and plum brûlée, lemon and honey syllabub of sticky toffee pudding (£2.85); part of the restaurant is no smoking. Well kept Courage Directors and Theakstons Best with guest beers like Greene King Abbot or local Mordue Five Bridge Bitter on handpump, Westons and Bulmers Original ciders, around 20 malt whiskies, and decent wines. The comfortable lounge bar has picture windows with fine southerly views over moorland pastures, and a woodburning stove. The beamed locals' bar is furnished with pine tables, chairs and stools, old oak pews, and a mahogany bar. Darts, dominoes and maybe piped music. Rustic tables out on a small side terrace and lawn. *(Recommended by Joy and Peter Heatherley, Richard Dolphin, Eric Larkham, M J Morgan, Mrs M Hughes, T M Dobby, Roger Bellingham, Chris Rounthwaite, Dave Braisted, Graham and Karen Oddey, M Hughes, M Fryer, Wayne Brindle, Tony Hall; more reports on the new regime, please)*

Free house ~ Licensees Chris and Moira Brown ~ Real ale ~ Meals and snacks ~ Restaurant ~ (01207) 255268 ~ Children in eating area of bar and restaurant ~ Open 11-3, 6-11; 12-3, 7-10.30 Sun ~ Bedrooms: £22/£38.50

CHATTON (Northumberland) NU0628 Map 10

Percy Arms 🛏

B6348 E of Wooller

This friendly stone local is very popular with locals and visitors alike. The attractively lit and neatly kept bar has green stripy upholstered wooden wall seats, cushioned farmhouse chairs and stools, horse bits and brasses on beams, maps and country pictures on the walls, and through a stone arch, a similar room with a woodburning stove. The panelled dining room with its pretty plates on a delft shelf is most attractive. Tasty bar food at lunchtime includes good filled french bread (£2.65), home-made soup (£2.75), sweet pickled herring salad (£3.40), ploughman's (£3.95), filled baked potatoes (from £4.35), a vegetarian dish of the day or steak and kidney pie (£5.25), and fresh local cod (£5.35), with evening dishes like fresh trout stuffed with prawns (£8.75), gammon with brown sugar and crushed pineapple (£7.95), half a roast duckling with cranberry and orange sauce (£10.45), and Aberdeen Angus steaks (from £10.45); puddings (from £1.95); good breakfasts. Well kept Theakstons XB on handpump, a wine of the month plus blackboard specials, and a fine choice of about two dozen malt whiskies; unobtrusive piped music; public bar with darts, pool, dominoes, cribbage, fruit machine, video game, and juke box. There are picnic tables on its small front lawn above the village road, and a holiday cottage is available; large comfortable bedrooms. No dogs in public areas. Residents have the use of 12 miles of private fishing, where there may be salmon, sea trout or stocked rainbow trout. *(Recommended by T J Smith, June and Tony Baldwin, Chris Rounthwaite, J H and S A Harrop, Steve and Marianne Webb-Phillips, Dr and Mrs J H Hills, Michael Wadsworth, R C Wiles, M J Morgan, Neil Townend, Avril Hanson, N E Bushby, W Atkins, David and Mary Webb, P J Hanson, John Allsopp)*

Free house ~ Licensees Pam and Kenny Topham ~ Real ale ~ Meals and snacks (12-1.30, 6.30-9.30) ~ Restaurant ~ (01668) 215244 ~ Children welcome ~ Open 11-3, 6-11; 12-3, 7-10.30 Sun ~ Bedrooms: £25B/£50B

It's against the law for bar staff to smoke while handling food or drink.

COTHERSTONE (Durham) NZ0119 Map 10
Fox & Hounds 🍺

B6277 – incidentally a good quiet route to Scotland, through interesting scenery

Readers enjoy staying at this simple white-painted old country pub. It's prettily placed overlooking a picturesque village green, and there are good nearby walks. The beamed bar has various alcoves and recesses, with comfortable furnishings such as thickly cushioned wall seats, local photographs and country pictures on the walls, and a winter open fire. Home-made bar food – served in the L-shaped lounge – includes sandwiches, soup (£1.95), omelette (£4.95), brunch (£5.25), yorkshire pudding filled with lamb liver and onion gravy or braised beef in Guinness or gammon and egg (£5.95), cauliflower and potato balti (£6.95), grilled lamb cutlets (£8.95), and puddings like good lemon sponge or fruit crumble with custard (£2.95); you can also eat from the more adventurous (and pricy) restaurant menu in the bar; one of the restaurants is no smoking. Well kept Hambleton Bitter, Stud, White Boar, and Bull on handpump, a fair choice of malt whiskies, and a useful wine list; helpful, friendly staff. *(Recommended by DAV, Kim Maidment, Philip Vernon, Mr and Mrs D Wilson, Mr Crichton, Ian and Karen Hargreaves, Phil Putwain, Anthony Barnes, Richard Dolphin, M J Morgan, Ian S Morley, David Gittins, Basil Minson, Margaret and Roy Randle)*

Free house ~ Licensees Michael and May Carlisle ~ Real ale ~ Meals and snacks ~ Restaurant ~ (01833) 650241 ~ Children welcome ~ Open 11-3, 6-11; 12-3, 7-11 Sun ~ Bedrooms: £37.50B/£50B

CRASTER (Northumberland) NU2620 Map 10
Jolly Fisherman £

Off B1339 NE of Alnwick

From the big picture windows or the little garden of this unpretentious local, there are lovely views over the harbour and out to sea. Workers from the harbour or the kippering shed opposite are regulars in the relaxed and atmospheric original bar (liking especially the snug by the entrance), but strangers will quickly be welcomed into the swing of things. Simple but popular snacks (available all the time the pub is open) include stottie pizza (£1.50), sandwiches or toasties (from £1.60), home-made soup (£1.75; the crabmeat with whisky and cream is really delicious, £2.25), home-made local kipper pâté (£2.25), and maybe a hot dish of the day. Well kept Wards Thorne Best Bitter on handpump, and a range of malt whiskies; friendly service. Darts, pool, shove-ha'penny, dominoes, cribbage, fruit machine, trivia and juke box. The pub can get crowded on sunny days, but unlike places in similar settings never begins to feel like a tourist attraction. There's a splendid clifftop walk to Dunstanburgh Castle close by. *(Recommended by A W and K J Randle, R T and J C Moggridge, Denis and Margaret Kilner, Richard Dolphin, Jack and Philip Paxton, Roger Wain-Heapy, Pauline and Bleddyn Davies, Jenny and Brian Seller, John and June Gale, Darren Salter, Mr and Mrs J M Lefeaux, Annette and Stephen Marsden, David Austin, GSB)*

Vaux ~ Lease: W P Silk ~ Real ale ~ Snacks (all day) ~ (01665) 576461 ~ Children in eating area of bar only ~ Open 11-11; 11-3, 6-11 in winter; 12-10.30 Sun; 12-3, 7-10.30 winter Sun

DIPTONMILL (Northumberland) NY9361 Map 10
Dipton Mill 🍺

Off B6306 S of Hexham at Slaley, Blanchland and Dye House, Whitley Chapel signposts and HGV route sign

The friendly, helpful landlord in this little country local is a partner in the Hexhamshire Brewery, hence the good choice of their well kept beers: Hexhamshire Shire Bitter, Devil's Water and Whapweasel; they also keep Theakstons Best, too. The snug little bar has dark ply panelling, red furnishings and open fires. Good wholesome bar food includes sandwiches, soup such as carrot and celery (£1.60), ploughman's (£3.25), smoked salmon flan (£4), steak and kidney pie (£4.50), bacon chop in cider sauce (£4.75), chicken breast in sherry sauce (£5), and puddings like lime cheesecake or syrup sponge (£1.60); home-made cakes and coffee (£1.60). Darts, bar billiards, shove-ha'penny and dominoes. You can sit on the sunken crazy-paved terrace by the restored mill stream, or by the garden's pretty plantings and aviaries. It's in a very peaceful wooded valley and there are easy-walking footpaths nearby. *(Recommended by Eric Larkham, Joy and Peter Heatherley, M J Morgan, Mr Miller, L Dixon, Chris Rounthwaite, Ian Wilson, Robin and Gloria Underwood)*

Free house ~ Licensee Geoffrey Brooker ~ Real ale ~ Meals and snacks (12-2.30, 6.30-8.30) ~ Children in simple games room ~ Open 12-2.30, 6-11; 12-4.30, 7-10.30 Sun; closed 25 Dec

ETAL (Northumberland) NT9339 Map 10
Black Bull
Off B6354, SW from Berwick

This is the only thatched pub in Northumberland. It's a white-painted cottage with a spacious open-plan lounge bar, windsor chairs around the tables on its carpet, glossily varnished beams, a stone fireplace at each end (they are not allowed to have real fires because of the thatched roof), and a friendly, relaxed atmosphere. Enjoyable food includes soup (£1.95), filled rolls (from £1.95), ploughman's (£4.95), pasta with ham and mushrooms in a creamy sauce, cashew paella, yorkshire puddings filled with a roast, Northumberland sausage, steak and kidney pie or lasagne (all £5.95), gammon and egg (£7.50), a huge seafood platter with crab, smoked salmon, herring, mussels, calamari and so forth (£9.50), 12oz steaks (from £10.95), and puddings such as lemon brûlée or hot chocolate pudding with rum and honey sauce (£3); there are plans to open a restaurant. Well kept Lorrimers Scotch and Wards Thorne on handpump, and good prompt service; darts, dominoes, and quiet piped music. There are a few picnic tables in front. A three-mile light railway runs between Heatherslaw (where there's a working watermill from which you can buy flour ground on the premises) and the bare ruins of Etal Castle on the banks of the River Till at the far end of this particularly picturesque village. *(Recommended by Roger Wain-Heapy, K M Thorpe, A W and K J Randle, Eric Larkham, Jenny and Brian Seller, Chris Rounthwaite, R T and J C Moggridge)*

Vaux ~ Licensee Fiona Anderson ~ Real ale ~ Meals and snacks (12-3, 7-9) ~ Children welcome ~ Open 11-11; 12-10.30 Sun; best to phone in winter to check opening hours – not decided as we went to press; closed 25 Dec

GREAT WHITTINGTON (Northumberland) NZ0171 Map 10
Queens Head 🍺
Village signposted off A68 and B6018 just N of Corbridge

Behind its simple stone exterior, the two beamed rooms of this friendly pub are comfortably furnished and neatly decorated. There are some handsome carved oak settles among other more modern furnishings, a mural over the fireplace near the bar counter, old prints and a collection of keys, and log fires. Good bar food includes sandwiches, ploughman's, mushrooms filled with pâté and coated with a dill crumb (£3.95), avocado and smoked bacon salad (£4.25), breast of chicken with sweet peppers and grapes, and local guinea fowl roasted with a port and apricot sauce (£9.95); the restaurant is no smoking. Although there is quite an emphasis on food, readers feel that the pubby atmosphere has not been lost, and it is still liked by locals. Well kept Queens Head (brewed for them by the local Hadrian Brewery), Courage Directors, Durham Magus, and Hambleton Bitter and Stud on handpump, 30 malt whiskies, and decent wines; friendly attentive service, unobtrusive piped music. There are six picnic tables on the small front lawn, and the surrounding partly wooded countryside is pretty. *(Recommended by Eric Larkham, Ian Phillips, John Honnor, John Oddey, Dr Peter Smart, Paul and Ursula Randall, R Shepherd)*

Free house ~ Ian Scott ~ Real ale ~ Meals and snacks ~ Restaurant ~ (01434) 672267 ~ Children in eating area of bar ~ Open 12-3, 6-11; 12-3, 7-10.30 Sun; closed evening 25 Dec nr HALTWHISTLE (Northumberland) NY7164 Map 10

Milecastle ◀

Military Rd; B6318 NE – OS Sheet 86 map reference 715660

Alone on the remote moorland road running alongside Hadrian's Wall, this extended 17th-c pub is a welcome refuge on a cold winter's night. It's well liked for its food which might include lunchtime sandwiches (from £2.40) and ploughman's (£4.25), home-made soup (£1.90), smoked duck breast on an apricot coulis (£3.95), vegetable curry (£4.95), tasty venison sausage (£5.75), pies such as wild boar and duckling, rabbit and wild mushroom, steak and kidney or turkey, ham and chestnut (from £5.95), gammon and egg (£6.95), sirloin steak (£8.95), and daily specials like smoked cumberland sausage (£6.50) or chicken breast in port and basil sauce (£6.95); home-made puddings (from £2.50). The local meat is well hung and the fresh local vegetables good. Well kept Butterknowle Bitter, Four Seasons (a local brew), Hexhamshire Bitter and Devils Water, and Tetleys on handpump, a fair collection of malt whiskies, and a good wine list. The snug small rooms of the beamed bar, decorated mainly with brasses, horsey and local landscape prints and attractive dried flowers, do get very busy in season (or when the local farmers crowd in); there's a lunchtime overflow into the small comfortable restaurant. Good friendly chatty service; a splendid coal fire, with a welcome for walkers (but no rucksacks allowed). No games or music. There are some white plastic seats and tables outside in a sheltered walled garden with a dovecote. *(Recommended by L Dixon, Chris Rounthwaite, D J and P M Taylor, Joy and Peter Heatherley, Ian and Deborah Carrington, Stephe, Julie and Hayley Brown)*

Free house ~ Licensees Ralph and Margaret Payne ~ Real ale ~ Meals and snacks ~ Restaurant ~ (01434) 320682 ~ Children over 5 welcome if eating ~ Open 12-3, 6.30-11

HALTWHISTLE (Northumberland) NY6860 Map 10

Wallace Arms

Rowfoot, Featherstone Park – OS Sheet 86 map reference 683607

The licensee of this rambling thick-walled former farmhouse is quite a character, and both he and his staff offer a genuinely warm welcome to all. There are five interlinked rooms with simple furnishings and unpretentious decorations. The small beamed main bar has dark oak woodwork, some stripped stone, comfortable seats, and a good log fire; the side games room has another fire (also darts, pool, Scrabble and chess), and there's a third in the middle of the big no-smoking dining room (a former barn), which has its own interesting menu. At lunchtime good value bar food includes soup (£1.95), sandwiches (from £2.50), filled baked potatoes (£2.95), vegetarian quiche (£4.50), cumberland sausage (£4.75), Whitby haddies (crumbed haddock pieces, £5.50), puddings (£2.50), and children's menu (£2); in the evening there might be vegetable pasta bake (£5), beef in ale pie (£5.95), gammon and egg (£6.95), and sirloin steak (£8.95). Good Sunday roasts and vegetarian choices. Well kept local Hexhamshire Shire Bitter and Whapweasel on handpump, and several malt whiskies; quizzes every second Wednesday. Access for disabled people is fairly easy. Picnic tables outside on both sides of the quiet lane have lovely fell views, and you can walk straight from the pub (one good walk, with fine views, is along the former Alston railway line); there's a play area at the back and quoits. *(Recommended by A W and K J Randle, Eric Larkham, Leonard Dixon, Christopher Warner, John Oddey)*

Free house ~ Licensees John and Mary Stenhouse ~ Real ale ~ Meals and snacks (not Mon or Tues lunchtime or Sun evening) ~ Restaurant ~ (01434) 321872 ~ Children in snug and games room ~ Open 4-11 Mon/Tues; 12-2.30, 4-11 Wed/Thurs; 12-11 Fri/Sat; 12-4, 7-10.30 Sun

---

The ◀ symbol shows pubs which keep their beer unusually well or have a particularly good range.

HEDLEY ON THE HILL (Northumberland) NZ0859 Map 10
Feathers

Village signposted from New Ridley, which is signposted from B6309 N of Consett; OS Sheet 88 map reference 078592

Due to constant enquiries, the thoughtful and friendly landlady of this little stone local has agreed to do food on weekday evenings (not Monday); the menu will be similar to the previous weekend only one, but slightly shorter. It's an enjoyable pub to visit with loyal and enthusiastic locals mixing happily with the visitors. The three well kept turkey-carpeted traditional bars have beams, woodburning stoves, stripped stonework, solid brown leatherette settles, country pictures, and a relaxed and welcoming atmosphere. Well kept Boddingtons and three guest beers such as Butterknowle First Gold, Hexhamshire Devils Water or Mordue Workie Ticket and Radgie Gadgie on handpump; they hold a mini beer festival around Easter with ten real ales on at any one time, which ends with a barrel race on Easter Monday; around 30 malt whiskies. The changing range of good imaginative food includes soups such as cream of carrot, leek and lentil (£1.95), ploughman's, cumberland sausage or feta tart with caramelised red onion in cheese pastry (£3.95), courgette, aubergine and tomato moussaka (£4.25), steak and kidney in ale (£5), lamb casserole with port and orange (£5.95), daily specials such as lentil and vegetable hotpot with a herby scone, spicy minced turkey pancake or cheese and spinach pancake (all £3.95), and venison in redcurrant jelly, port and orange (£6.95), with puddings like plum and sour cream tart topped with brown sugar and cinnamon, ginger and mango pavlova or sticky toffee pudding (£1.95). Darts, shove-ha'penny, table skittles, cribbage, and dominoes. *(Recommended by Joy and Peter Heatherley, L M Anderson, John Fazakerley, Joan Bunting, GSB, Peter and Patricia Burton)*

Free house ~ Licensee Marina Atkinson ~ Real ale ~ Meals and snacks (not weekday lunchtime; not Mon eves) ~ (01661) 843607 ~ Children in eating area of bar and in family room until 9pm ~ Open 6-11 weekdays; 12-3, 6-11 Sat; 12-3, 7-10.30 Sun; closed weekday lunchtimes

MATFEN (Northumberland) NZ0372 Map 10
Black Bull

Village signposted off B6318 NE of Corbridge

This creeper-covered long stone inn is set by the green of an attractive 18th-c estate village, and in summer there's a profusion of hanging baskets, shrubs and bedding plants; plenty of seats on an outside terrace. The spacious turkey-carpeted main bar has windsor chairs around copper-topped tables, and steeplechasing pictures, and there's a side room with red plush button-back built-in wall banquettes, and attractive 1940s photographs. Well presented bar food includes sandwiches, duck liver pâté with cumberland sauce (£3.75), fillet of haddock (£5), home-made steak, mushroom and ale pie (£5.25), large filled yorkshire pudding (£5.40), sirloin steak (£11.95), and daily specials like hot beef sandwich (£3.75), mussels in parsley sauce (£4.50), chicken marengo (£5), and paella (£5.30); good, fresh vegetables; you can order from the very good seasonally changing restaurant menu – the restaurant is no smoking at lunchtime. Obliging staff serve well kept Theakstons Black Bull, Morlands Old Speckled Hen, and guest beers on handpump; 20 malt whiskies. Log fires, sensibly placed darts, pool, dominoes, and juke box. No dogs. *(Recommended by Ian Phillips, J S and J Reed, T Dobby, Simon Barriskell, Tina Rossiter, Chris Rounthwaite, Mr Miller, Mrs M Armini, John Allsopp, Stephen, Julie and Hayley Brown)*

Free house ~ Licensees Colin and Michele Scott ~ Real ale ~ Meals and snacks ~ Restaurant ~ (01661) 886330 ~ Children in eating area of bar ~ Open 11-11; 11-3, 6-11 in winter; 12-10.30 Sun ~ Bedrooms: £32.50B/£55B

If you see cars parked in the lane outside a country pub have left their lights on at night, leave yours on too: it's a sign that the police check up there.

NEW YORK (Tyne & Wear) NZ3370 Map 10
Shiremoor House Farm ★

Middle Engine Lane/Norham Road; from A1 going N from Tyne Tunnel, right into A1058 then next left signposted New York, then left at end of speed limit (pub signed); or at W end of New York A191 bypass turn S into Norham Road, then first right (pub signed)

At lunchtime, this smartly relaxed place is popular with businessmen and families, and there's a good bustling atmosphere. There's a charming mix of interesting and extremely comfortable furniture, a big kelim on the broad flagstones, warmly colourful farmhouse paintwork on the bar counter and several other tables, conical rafters of the former ging-gang, a few farm tools, and good rustic pictures such as mid-West prints, big crisp black and white photographs of country people and modern Greek bull sketches. Gentle lighting in several well divided spacious areas cleverly picks up the surface modelling of the pale stone and beam ends. Well kept Stones, Theakstons Best, Timothy Taylors Landlord, and a guest like Cains Formidable on handpump, and decent wines by the glass. No music or games machines; Monday evening quiz. A separate bar serves the equally attractive rather smart restaurant. Bar food include sandwiches, vegetarian stir fry (£3.75), steak and kidney pie (£4.35), scampi (£4.45), daily specials, and children's helpings. The granary extension is good for families with high chairs, and bottles or baby food are warmed on request. There are picnic tables on neat grass at the edge of the flagstoned farm courtyard, by tubs and a manger filled with flowers; no-smoking area. *(Recommended by Gregg Davies, Eric Larkham, Peter Lewis, Joy and Peter Heatherley, Richard Dolphin, E A Thwaite, GSB)*

Free house ~ Licensee Bill Kerridge ~ Real ale ~ Meals and snacks (12-9) ~ Restaurant ~ (0191) 257 6302 ~ Children in eating areas of bar and in restaurant ~ Open 11-11; 12-10.30 Sun

NEWCASTLE UPON TYNE (Tyne & Wear) NZ2266 Map 10
Crown Posada ▰ £

31 The Side; off Dean Street, between and below the two high central bridges (A6125 and A6127)

A few minutes' stroll from the castle, this is the city's second oldest pub. The golden crown adds grandeur to an already imposing carved stone facade – as do the pre-Raphaelite stained-glass windows, and inside there's lots of architectural charm such as an elaborate coffered ceiling and stained glass in the counter screens, and decorations like a line of gilt mirrors each with a tulip lamp on a curly brass mount which match the great ceiling candelabra, and Victorian flowered wallpaper above the brown dado; below this are fat heating pipes – a popular footrest when the east wind brings the rain off the North Sea. It's a very long and narrow room, making quite a bottleneck by the serving counter, and beyond that, a long soft green built-in leather wall seat is flanked by narrow tables. Well kept Bass, Boddingtons, Butterknowle Conciliation, Jennings, Theakstons Best and a guest on handpump; lunchtime sandwiches and toasties (£1). Friendly barmen, chatty customers; fruit machine. Best to visit during the week when regulars sit reading the papers put out in the front snug; at the weekend it's usually packed. No children. *(Recommended by Eric Larkham, Denis and Margaret Kilner, E A Thwaite, Val Stevenson, Rob Holmes, N Meachen)*

Free house ~ Licensee Malcolm McPherson ~ Real ale ~ Lunchtime snacks ~ (0191) 232 1269 ~ Open 11-11; 12-3, 7-10.30 Sun

NEWTON ON THE MOOR (Northumberland) NU1605 Map 10
Cook & Barker Arms ⇌

Village signposted from A1 Alnwick—Felton

The unfussy, long beamed bar in this busy pub has stripped, partly panelled walls, brocade-seated settles around oak-topped tables, framed banknotes and paintings by local artists on the walls, brasses, a highly polished oak servery, and a coal fire at one end with a coal-effect gas fire at the other; another room has tables, chairs, an old settle, and darts (popular with locals), and the games room has scrubbed pine furniture and french windows leading onto the terrace. Popular bar food includes sandwiches, roast pepper terrine or stilton and pear pâté (£3.95), steak in ale pie or baked goat's cheese with avocado (£4.95), and monkfish and scallops with a chive butter sauce (£9.85); the lounge is no smoking. Well kept Courage Directors, Ruddles County, and Theakstons Best on handpump, quite a few malt whiskies, and a comprehensive wine list. In recent months, service has not always been as helpful as we remember it; we hope this phase will quickly be over. *(Recommended by D Knott, Bruce Jamieson, R A Underwood, A Twyford, A J Morton, Lucy James, Simon Morton, Roger Bellingham, John Oddey, J H and S A Harrop, Neil Townend, Nigel and Amanda Thorp, R H Rowley; more reports please)*

Free house ~ Licensee Phil Farmer ~ Real ale ~ Meals and snacks (12-2, 6-8) ~ Restaurant ~ (01665) 575234 ~ Children in eating area of bar and in restaurant ~ Open 11-3, 6-11; 12-3, 6-10.30 Sun ~ Bedrooms: £35B/£65B

RENNINGTON (Northumberland) NU2119 Map 10
Masons Arms 🛏

Stamford Cott; B1340 NE of Alnwick

Readers have enjoyed staying in this well run old coaching inn over the years, so we have decided to give them a Stay Award. The comfortable, spotlessly clean bedrooms are in an adjacent stable block, and breakfasts are good. The good value, generously served bar food is what draws most people here though, and with prices unchanged since last year, there might be lunchtime sandwiches, home-made soup (£1.95), home-made chicken liver and brandy pâté (£3.75), fried haddock (£4.95), vegetable bake or lentil and mushroom cannelloni (£5.65), game casserole (£6.55), gammon steak or chicken chasseur (£6.25), steaks (from £9.95), and several daily specials; good Sunday lunch, and children's meals. Courage Directors, Northumberland Best Bitter, and Ruddles Best on handpump, served by friendly, helpful staff; piped music. The comfortably modernised beamed lounge bar has wheelback and mate's chairs around solid wooden tables on the patterned carpet, plush bar stools, lots of brass, pictures and photographs on the walls, and a relaxed atmosphere; the dining rooms have pine panelling and wrought-iron wall lights. Shove-ha'penny and dominoes. There are sturdy rustic tables on the little front terrace, surrounded by lavender. *(Recommended by June and Tony Baldwin, T Loft, A W and K J Randle, J H and S A Harrop, John Cockell, Sarah and Peter Gooderham, Peter Bennett, Ian and Deborah Carrington, Martin Hickes)*

Free house ~ Licensees Frank and Dee Sloan ~ Real ale ~ Meals and snacks ~ Restaurant ~ (01665) 577275 ~ Children in restaurant (must be over 5 in evening) ~ Open 12-2, 6.30-11; 12-2.30, 7-10.30 Sun ~ Bedrooms: /£48B

ROMALDKIRK (Durham) NY9922 Map 10
Rose & Crown 🍴 🛏

Just off B6277

Northumbria Dining Pub of the Year

Cleverly here, they've managed to combine the best of a good hotel and fine restaurant with the better aspects of a pleasant country pub. The beamed traditional bar (to be redecorated soon) has old-fashioned seats facing the log fire, a Jacobean oak settle, cream walls decorated with lots of gin-traps, some old farm tools and black and white pictures of Romaldkirk at the turn of the century, as well as a grandfather clock, and lots of brass and copper. The smart refurbished Crown Room, where bar food is served, has more brass and copper, original etchings of game shooting scenes and farm implements. The hall is hung with wine maps and other interesting prints; no-smoking oak-panelled restaurant. After considerable kitchen upgrading, the particularly good bar food includes interesting daily specials such as split pea and smoked ham soup (£3.75), warm east coast crab tart (£4.25), hot crisp confit of duck leg with puy lentils (£6.50), fricassee of hare with smoked bacon and creamed polenta (£7.50), calf liver with green peppercorns (£8.50), lemon sole with button mushrooms, crème fraîche and chives (£9.95), and puddings like sherry and toasted almond trifle, sticky toffee pudding or baked chocolate cheesecake; from the lunchtime menu there might be brown baps (from £2.95), scrambled eggs with smoked salmon (£4.75), ploughman's with proper cheeses and three home-made pickles (£5.25), and steak, kidney and mushroom pie (£7.50), with evening extras such as pork fillet with mushrooms, cream and fresh pasta (£8.95), chargrilled chicken breast with a fresh tomato sauce, basil, and parmesan (£8.95), and steaks (from £10.50); children's dishes (from £1.75), and good three-course Sunday lunch (£12.50). Well kept Marstons Pedigree and Theakstons Best on handpump, and about eight wines by the glass; good, friendly service. Tables outside look out over the village green, still with its original stocks and water pump. The village is close to the superb Bowes Museum and the High Force waterfall, and has an interesting old church. *(Recommended by Joy and Peter Heatherley, M J Morgan, Richard Fallon, Mr and Mrs D Powell, David and Ruth Hollands, Paul and Ursula Randall, Sue and Geoff Price, June and Tony Baldwin, Ian S Morley, E A Thwaite, Dr T H M Mackenzie, R T and J C Moggridge, T and G Alderman, Margaret and Roy Randle)*

Free house ~ Licensees Christopher and Alison Davy ~ Real ale ~ Meals and snacks (12-1.30, 7-9) ~ Restaurant (not Sun evening) ~ (01833) 650213 ~ Children welcome ~ Open 11-3, 5.30-11; 12-3, 7-10.30 Sun; closed 25/26 Dec ~ Bedrooms: £58B/£80B

SEAHOUSES (Northumberland) NU2232 Map 10
Olde Ship ★ 🛏 🍺

B1340 coast road

Although this relaxed atmospheric pub is very popular with visitors, it remains very much a fisherman's local. The welcoming bar is a treasure-trove of seafaring memorabilia: shiny brass fittings, sea pictures and model ships (including a fine one of the North Sunderland lifeboat and a model of Seahouses' lifeboat *The Grace Darling*), as well as ship's instruments and equipment, and a knotted anchor made by local fishermen; all the items are genuine. Even the floor of the saloon bar, with its open fire, is scrubbed ship's decking. The one clear window (the others have stained-glass sea pictures) looks out across the harbour to the Farne Islands, and as dusk falls you can watch the Longstones lighthouse shine across the fading evening sky; there's another low-beamed snug bar. One room is no smoking. There are plans to add a conservatory. Bar food include soup (£1.50), sandwiches (£2), roast beef and yorkshire pudding, steak and kidney pie or cod bake (all £5). A good choice of real ales takes in Bass, Marstons Pedigree, Morlands Old Speckled Hen, Ruddles Best, Theakstons Best, and a beer named after the pub and guest beers in summer; several malt whiskies; dominoes and piped music. Pews surround barrel tables in the back courtyard, and a battlemented side terrace with a sun lounge looks out on the harbour. An anemometer is connected to the top of the chimney. You can book boat trips to the Farne Islands Bird Sanctuary at the harbour, and there are bracing coastal walks, particularly to Bamburgh, Grace Darling's birthplace. The pub is not really suitable for children. *(Recommended by Judith Hirst, John Honnor, Richard Fallon, Guy Consterdine, Eric Larkham, John Cockell, A Twyford, Archie and Thelma Jack, Martin Hickes, David Atkinson, G Alderman, Ian S Morley, James Nunns, June and Tony Baldwin, J E Rycroft, David Austin)*

Free house ~ Licensees Alan and Jean Glen ~ Real ale ~ Meals and snacks (12-2, 7-8.30) ~ Restaurant ~ (01665) 720200 ~ Open 11-3, 6-11; 12-3, 7.30-10.30 Sun ~ Bedrooms: £36.50B/£73B

STANNERSBURN (Northumberland) NY7286 Map 10
Pheasant 🛏

Kielder Water road signposted off B6320 in Bellingham

This unpretentious inn was the post house for the back road over the hills. It's in a peaceful valley with picnic tables in the streamside garden, a pony paddock behind, and quiet forests all around. Inside, the traditional and comfortable lounge is partly stripped stone and partly panelled, and the separate public bar, similar but simpler, opens into a games room with darts, pool, and dominoes. A good mix of visitors and locals in the evening. The dining room is no smoking. Bar food includes sandwiches, steak pie or lasagne (£5.95), lamb with a redcurrant and rosemary sauce (£8.50), chicken breast with asparagus sauce or lemon sole with prawn sauce (£8.75), and monkfish with parsley butter (£9.50). Well kept Ind Coope Burton and Tetleys Bitter on handpump, and lots of malt whiskies. Darts and pool. *(Recommended by D Knott, Tim and Sue Halstead, Paul and Ursula Randall, Graham and Karen Oddey, John Poulter, Humphrey and Angela Crum Ewing, Chris Rounthwaite, David and Margaret Bloomfield)*

Free house ~ Licensees Walter and Irene Kershaw ~ Real ale ~ Meals and snacks ~ Restaurant ~ (01434) 240382 ~ Children welcome ~ Open 11-3, 5.30-11; 12-2, 6.30-11 Mon-Sat in winter; 12-3, 7-10.30 Sun; closed Mon in Jan/Feb ~ Bedrooms: £35B/£56B

WARENFORD (Northumberland) NU1429 Map 10
Warenford Lodge
Just off A1 Alnwick—Belford, on village loop road

There's no pub sign, so it's easy to drive straight past this small stone house. The bar is actually quite old but looks modern, with cushioned wooden seats around pine tables, some stripped stone walls, and a warm fire in the big stone fireplace; steps lead up to an extension which now has comfortable dining tables and chairs, and a big woodburning stove. Interesting home-made bar food includes home-made soup (£2.25), cold honey roast duckling breast (£3.90), saffron risotto with pecorino cheese (£4.70), pork and apple crumble (£4.95), lovely Lindisfarne oysters with a crispy topping of seaweed, hatcho miso and breadcrumbs (£5.60), local cod in beer batter (£6.50), rabbit with Ilchester sage cheese and white wine (£8.50), Northumberland fish soup (£8.70), sirloin steak (£11.90), and puddings like steamed marmalade pudding with drambuie cream (£2.05). A decent selection of wines and malt whiskies, and a good choice of teas. *(Recommended by John Cockell, Jenny and Brian Seller; more reports please)*

Free house ~ Licensee Raymond Matthewman ~ Meals and snacks (not lunchtimes, except weekends when lunchtime service stops 1.30, or all day Mon) ~ Evening restaurant ~ (01668) 213453 ~ Children in restaurant only ~ Open 7-11 (closed weekday lunchtimes and all day Mon except bank holidays), plus 12-2 Sat and Sun

---

Lucky Dip

Besides the fully inspected pubs, you might like to try these Lucky Dips recommended to us and described by readers (if you do, please send us reports):

Acomb N'land [NY9366], *Sun*: Improved cosy village local, very welcoming husband and wife team, good beer, good standard bar food *(John Oddey)*

☆ **Allendale** N'land [Mkt Pl, B6295; NY8355], *Golden Lion*: Friendly old pub with Flowers and Websters Yorkshire, country wines, wide choice of good value food (not Mon) inc vegetarian, partly no-smoking dining area with more room upstairs, two real fires, pictures, old bottles, willow-pattern plates; games area with pool and darts, piped music; children welcome; bedrooms *(Eric Larkham)*

Alnmouth N'land [NU2511], *Schooner*: Georgian coaching inn with one busy bar, another quieter with red plush seats, interesting local and nautical pictures, bar food, changing real ale, cheerful service, pleasant conservatory, candlelit Italian restaurant *(Eric Larkham, June and Tony Baldwin)*

Anick N'land [signed NE of A69/A695 Hexham junction; NY9665], *Rat*: Quaint little pub, friendly and nicely refurbished, with well kept Scottish Courage ales, lovely north Tyne views, good service, food from hot counter; children welcome, pretty garden with well planted boots *(Chris Rounthwaite, Eric Larkham)*

☆ **Barrasford** N'land [NY9274], *Barrasford Arms*: Friendly country local with blazing fires in compact bar, lounge across hall, usual food in big high-ceilinged dining room, cheery regulars, children's room; lovely sandstone building with wonderful views, good value bedrooms handy for Hadrian's Wall, good breakfast (but early-morning quarry traffic passes) *(Annette and Stephen Marsden, PC, HC)*

☆ **Beamish** Dur [NZ2254], *Shepherd & Shepherdess*: Very useful for its position nr outstanding open-air heritage museum; good range of quick fairly priced straightforward food, standard layout with tables around walls, but comfortable, with good service, well kept Vaux Samson and Wards Sheffield

Best, decent wines, coal fires; can get crowded, piped music; children welcome, tables and play area with fibreglass monsters out among trees; has been open all day *(John and June Gale, D W and J W Wilson, John Fazakerley, LYM)*

Beamish [Front St, No Place; off A693 signed No Place and Cooperative Villas, S of museum], *Beamish Mary*: Friendly down-to-earth 1960s pub, quiet lunchtime, with Durham NUM banner in games room, very assorted furnishings and bric-a-brac in bar with Aga; huge choice of good value basic bar food and Sun lunch, well kept Jennings, Theakstons, a beer brewed for them by Big Lamp and several guest beers, annual beer festival; piped music, two dogs, children allowed until evening; live music in converted stables concert room (Weds, Fri, Sat); bedrooms *(Matthew Mardling, CMW, JJW)*

Belford N'land [Market Pl; village signed off A1 S of Berwick; NU1134], *Blue Bell*: Good service and welcoming atmosphere in family stable bar (the Belford Tavern) with wide choice of sensibly priced straightforward food inc children's and cut-price OAPs' helpings, Theakstons, darts, pool and piped music; separate hotel lounge, pleasantly old-fashioned restaurant; children in eating areas, bedrooms *(M Morgan, R T and J C Moggridge, LYM)*

☆ **Belsay** N'land [NZ1079], *Highlander*: Good range of food in recently refurbished comfortable side bar and open-plan dining area, nice plain wood tables, reasonable prices, good welcoming service, well kept Scottish Courage ales, good log fires *(John, Graham and Karen Oddey)*

☆ **Berwick upon Tweed** N'land [Dock View Rd, Spittal (Tweedmouth); NT9952], *Rob Roy*: Local fish a speciality, not cheap but very fresh, in quiet and cosy seaview pub, fishing-theme traditional bar with roaring fire and polished wood floor, friendly landlord; keg beers but decent wines and good fresh coffee; bedrooms *(John and June Gale)*

Berwick upon Tweed [Bridge St], *Barrels*: Bistro style, old school desks, reasonably priced interesting short menu, wide choice of well kept ales inc local Border Rampart, pleasant staff, good juke box *(Jenny and Brian Seller, A Keys)*

Billy Row Dur [Old White Lea, off A689; NZ1638], *Dun Cow*: Unspoilt pub in same family for 100 years, cosy old-fashioned front room with warming range, comfortable wall settles, photographs of long-gone and more recent local football teams; bar in back room serving well kept Butterknowle, very friendly landlord and locals; folk music last Fri of month *(Jack and Philip Paxton)*

Bowes Dur [NY9914], *Ancient Unicorn*: Substantial stone inn with spacious open-plan plush bar cum pool room, white walls, dark wood, sparing decoration, good honest bar food from sandwiches up, several Scottish Courage ales, friendly licensees, *Nicholas Nickleby* connection; clean and comfortable bedrooms in well converted stables block around big courtyard *(LYM)*

Cambois N'land [Cambium Manor, Wansbeck Close; NZ3184], *Buccaneer*: Large hospitable nautical-theme pub in good position with sea views, warm welcome, well kept beer *(Ian David Smart)*

Castle Eden Dur [B1281 S of Peterlee; NZ4338], *Castle Eden*: Useful pub serving local Whitbreads Castle Eden, decent reasonably priced meals; can get very busy, TV room *(Alan Eames)*

☆ **Catton** N'land [B6295 N of Allendale; NY8358], *Crown*: Bargain home-cooked lunches in friendly and cosy traditional pub with other good value food till 10 inc children's and lots of sandwiches, newish dining area, roaring log fire, four ales such as Butterknowle and Theakstons, good teas and coffee, jovial landlord, pool, darts, piped music; small garden; well behaved children and dogs welcome *(JJW, CMW, John Oddey, Jack and Heather Coyle)*

☆ **Corbridge** N'land [Middle St; NY9964], *Black Bull*: Roomy low-ceilinged pub with wide range of well kept Whitbreads-related and guest ales, reasonably priced wines, good house wines, good choice of generous food inc interesting dishes, traditional settles on stone floor, mix of comfortable chairs, roaring fire, efficient staff, friendly civilised atmosphere; open all day *(Eric Larkham, L Dixon, John Prescott)*

Corbridge [Newcastle Rd], *Angel*: Small hotel with welcoming neat staff and good value bar food in plushly comfortable lounge; locals' back bar, restaurant, Scottish Courage ales; bedrooms *(E Locker, LYM)*; [Watling St/St Helens St, just N of centre], *Wheatsheaf*: Open-plan pub with comfortable banquettes, wide choice of food in pleasantly decorated dining lounge and big conservatory, well kept Darleys Thorne and Vaux Waggledance, good choice of wines and malt whiskies, friendly licensees; pub games, piped music, children welcome, some picnic tables outside; bedrooms *(Stephen and Julie Brown, SB, TR, Martin Hickes, LYM)*

Cornforth Dur [Metal Bridge, off B6291 N; NZ3134], *Poachers Pocket*: Comfortable and welcoming family pub with good value food, bric-a-brac in main bar, overhead model railway in big friendly family room, upstairs bistro, Bass and interesting guest ales, prompt obliging service; garden with big play area and rides on miniature railway; BR intercity trains run by *(Verity Kemp, Richard Mills)*

Cramlington N'land [Village Sq; NZ2676], *Blagdon Arms*: Extended village pub broken into small intimate areas, real ales; no food Sun evening *(Eric Larkham)*; [Northumbrian Rd; NZ2675], *Brockwell Seam*: Out of centre, comfortable lounge, pool table in bar, bar food (till 8, not Sun), open all day *(Eric Larkham)*; [Middle Farm Buildings; NZ2673], *Plough*: Stylishly converted stone farm building, lunchtime bar food, real ales; open all day Fri-Sun *(Eric Larkham)*

Durham [Saddler St], *Brewer & Firkin*: Closest pub to castle and cathedral, decent food, six well kept ales, alluring atmosphere, interesting memorabilia *(Gwen and Steve Walker, Eric Larkham, Wayne Brindle, Lesley Sones)*; [Hawthorn Terr], *Colpitts*: Basic bar, lounge and pool room, Sam Smiths OB, open fire, fruit machine, sandwiches *(Eric Larkham)*; [Darlington Rd, S of Nevilles Cross on A167], *Duke of Wellington*: Busy but spacious Victorian-style local useful for wide range of hearty good value food inc vegetarian and Sun lunch – tables in bar a bit low for eating, but there is a restaurant; well kept Bass, Worthington and a guest such as Adnams, attentive service; children welcome *(Richard Dolphin, P A Legon, John Allsopp, M Borthwick, Gwen and Steve Walker)*; [37 Old Elvet], *Dun Cow*: Unsmart but enjoyable traditional town pub in pretty black and white timbered cottage, cosy front bar, cheap snacks, well kept Whitbreads Castle Eden; children welcome *(Eric Larkham, Gwen and Steve Walker, LYM)*; [New Elvet], *Half Moon*: Well kept Bass, Worthington and an interesting guest beer, good service, some basic snacks even on Sun; comfortable unpretentious lower bar, bare-boards top one *(John Fazakerley, Eric Larkham, Gwen and Steve Walker)*; [Market Sq], *Market*: Two-level pub done out as 1900s tavern, very popular with younger people; simple wooden furniture, sepia prints, bare boards, Scottish Courage and guest ales, well listed foreign bottled beers (one on draught), good value straightforward food *(John Fazakerley, Gwen and Steve Walker, Eric Larkham)*; [Darlington Rd (A167)], *Nevilles Cross*: City pub with friendly bar mixing locals and academics; bargain bedrooms with hearty fried breakfasts, but lots of stairs *(Alan Eames)*; [86 Hallgarth St – A177 nr Dunelm House], *Victoria*: Attractive and unassuming Victorian local with well kept Scottish Courage and guest ales, lots of whiskies, coal fires in bar and back room; has been open all day; bedrooms *(Anon)*

Eachwick N'land [extension of B6324 NW of Newcastle; NZ1271], *Plough*: Large, well furnished and clean, with lots of pictures of landlady's racehorse; good choice of sensibly priced generous food inc roast of the day, good value house wine *(Cynthia Waller)*
☆ **Egglescliffe** Clvd [NZ4214], *Pot & Glass*: Three warmly welcoming panelled rooms with some slabby tree-trunk tabletops, stools and settles, well kept Bass and Tetleys, decent wine, friendly staff and locals, good value food; darts, no music; tables on terrace, lovely setting behind church *(Mike and Karen England)*
☆ **Eglingham** N'land [B6346 Alnwick—Wooler; NU1019], *Tankerville Arms*: Comfortable village dining pub improved under new management, some stripped stonework, coal fire each end, well kept ales, enjoyable if not cheap food (vegetarians could do with more choice), decent choice of wines and malt

whiskies, friendly service; children welcome, restaurant, tables in garden *(N Bushby, W Atkins, GSB, Tim and Sue Halstead, Chris Rounthwaite, LYM)*
Elwick Clvd [¼ mile off A19 W of Hartlepool; NZ4532], *McOrville*: Warm and cosy, friendly service, good generous straightforward food (bookings only Sun lunchtime) *(Miss P Woodward)*
Falstone N'land [NY7287], *Blackcock*: Pleasant friendly local with open fires, good value food esp baked potatoes and yorkshire puddings, well kept ales inc Boddingtons, Whitbreads Castle Eden and their own cheap Blackcock; children allowed in pool room, quiet juke box; bedrooms, handy for Kielder Water *(Denis and Margaret Kilner, Rita and Keith Pollard)*
☆ **Framwellgate Moor** Dur [Front St; NZ2745], *Tap & Spile*: Fine range of rapidly changing well kept beers, decent food at low prices, daily papers, tourist guides, free Sun nibbles; child-friendly, one room with board games, another with pool and fruit machine *(Richard R Dolphin, Eric Larkham, Gwen and Steve Walker, P A Legon)*
Gateshead T&W [Eighton Banks; NZ2758], *Lambton Arms*: Comfortable, with good range of reasonably priced food all day, Whitbreads-related and guest beers, good coffee; quiz nights Mon and Thurs *(Denis and Margaret Kilner)*; [South Shore Rd; NZ2663], *Schooner*: By the Keelmans riverside walk, surrounded by trees and shrubs, with big outdoor seating area (could do with more tables); well kept real ale, good lunchtime bar food, restaurant *(Eric Larkham)*
Great Stainton Dur [NZ3422], *Kings Arms*: Friendly atmosphere, wide range of good generous food inc real chips, well kept Whitbreads-related and guest beers, good service, spotless and comfortable; restaurant; lovely spot *(Peter Guy, M and G Brown)*
Greenhead N'land [NY6666], *Greenhead Inn*: On Pennine Way nr Youth Hostel, good food and good choice of beers *(Steve Jennings)*
☆ **Greta Bridge** Dur [hotel signed off A66 W of Scotch Corner; NZ0813], *Morritt Arms*: Interesting and prettily placed old hotel, not cheap but enjoyable, with unusual Pickwickian mural in sturdily traditional civilised bar, well kept ales such as Butterknowle Conciliation, Stones, Tetleys, Theakstons Best and Timothy Taylors Landlord, friendly staff; attractive garden with play area, restaurant; comfortable bedrooms *(Anthony Barnes, John and Joan Nash, Philip Cooper, James Nunns, LYM)*
Haltwhistle N'land [Castle Hill; NY7164], *Spotted Cow*: Friendly local with wide choice of good value food inc vegetarian, dining area, games area; open all day Sat, seats out in front *(D J and P M Taylor)*
Hartburn N'land [E of village, B6343 W of Morpeth; NZ1286], *Dyke Neuk*: Newly transformed into decent pub with restaurant; friendly landlord, reasonable food, Theakstons. Wide choice of reasonably priced

carefully cooked food, friendly landlord, Theakstons; restaurant *(J S and J Reed)*

☆ **Haydon Bridge** N'land [NY8464], *General Havelock*: Civilised and individually furnished dining pub with limited choice of lunchtime bar food (not Sun), open fires, horse racing pictures, Tyne-view stripped stone restaurant (evenings exc Sun, and Sun lunch) with good interesting if rather pricy full meals; well kept Tetleys, good wines by the glass, children and dogs allowed; tables on terrace, cl Mon/Tues, also early Jan and Sept, also week after Easter *(Chris Rounthwaite, Larry Franks, LYM)*

Hexham N'land [E end of main st; NY9363], *Coach & Horses*: Log fire, good freshly cooked pub food, Ind Coope Burton, Tetleys and Theakstons; unpretentious and friendly *(David and Margaret Bloomfield)*; [Priestpopple, E end of main st], *County*: Reliably good straightforward lunches from good sandwiches up in comfortably worn in hotel lounge with lots of game bird prints, good friendly waitresses, proper coffee, keg beer; bedrooms *(John Fazakerley)*; [Battle Hill/Eastgate], *Tap & Spile*: Two bars, eight real ales (1/3 pint nips available), country wines, cheap but limited weekday lunchtime food; no dogs *(JJW, CMW, Eric Larkham)* nr **Hexham** N'land [East Wallhouses; Military Rd (B6318)], *Robin Hood*: Three real ales, blazing real fires, promising food from friendly new owners; piped music *(John Oddey)*

☆ **High Force** Dur [B6277 about 4 miles NW of Middleton; NY8728], *High Force*: Beautifully placed high-moors hotel, named for England's highest waterfall nearby and doubling as mountain rescue post; now brewing its own good value Teesdale Bitter and Forest, also Theakstons and good choice of bar food (and of malt whiskies), good service, friendly atmosphere, quiz night Fri; children allowed, comfortable bedrooms *(Kevin Thorpe, Mike and Sue Walton, Maurice Thompson, Roxanne Chamberlain, LYM)*

Holwick Dur [back rd up Teesdale from Middleton; NY9027], *Strathmore Arms*: Quiet and cosy unspoilt country pub in beautiful scenery just off Pennine Way, good reasonably priced standard food, well kept Scottish Courage and a guest ale, friendly staff and locals, log fire, lovely dog called Bisto, games, books etc; bedrooms, camp site *(Liz and John Soden, Maurice Thompson, Hugh Becker)*

☆ **Holy Island** N'land [Marygate; NU1343], *Ship*: Cosy bar with eating area off, beamery, bare boards, panelling, maritime/fishing memorabilia; good value food inc vegetarian and local seafood, quick chatty service, well kept ales at least in summer such as Border Blessed, Holy Island and Sacred Kingdom, good choice of whiskies; children welcome, nice setting; three comfortable Victorian-decor bedrooms, may close for a while Jan/Feb *(Tony Dickinson, Brian and Jenny Seller, I Polsik, N Haslewood, Denis and Margaret Kilner, Kurt and Kiki Angelrath)*

Horncliffe N'land [NT9350], *Fishers Arms*: Small cosy one-bar pub with fishing nets on ceiling, big aquarium dividing off informal small eating area, good range of reasonably priced home-cooked food inc decidedly unusual dishes, pleasant efficient service *(Tessa Dickinson)*

Ireshopeburn Dur [NY8639], *Ranch*: Converted school, one end a real country pub with short choice of good pub food inc properly cooked veg *(Mr Miller)*

Lanchester Dur [NZ1647], *Queens Head*: Good generous often interesting food (sandwiches on request), well kept Vaux beers, decent wines and friendly and attentive Swedish landlady in village pub with smallish locals' bar and plushly comfortable dining room *(John Fazakerley)*

Langley on Tyne N'land [A686 S, junction B6305; NY8160], *Carts Bog*: Isolated early 18th-c pub on edge of moors, big log fire, black-beamed bar with local photographs and horse tack, welcoming licensees, well filled rolls and good freshly cooked hot dishes, comfortable settles and chairs, well kept Scottish Courage ales; some live music, no juke box, tables and barbecue outside, quoits team *(Dave Cave, Jean Southwell, BB)*

Langley Park Dur [Firs Terrace; NZ2145], *Centurion*: Well cooked reasonably priced fresh food, good atmosphere, well kept Vaux ales *(Janet Lee)*

Longbenton T&W [Front St; NZ2768], *Benton Ale House*: Recently refurbished, warm and comfortable, with four Camerons and other ales and up to four guests, lined glasses, friendly staff, hot lunches, pool, fruit machine, juke box, TV; open all day *(Eric Larkham)*

Longframlington N'land [NU1301], *Granby*: Comfortably modernised family-run two-room bar very popular for very wide choice of generous food inc good vegetarian dishes, Worthington real ale, good collection of malt whiskies, decent wines, restaurant; bedrooms in main building good, with big breakfasts *(Mike and Di Saxly, LYM)*

Lowick N'land [B6353, off A1 S of Berwick; NU0139], *Black Bull*: Busy country pub with comfortable main bar, small back bar, decent food inc vegetarian in back dining room, well kept Scottish Courage ales, pleasant service; three attractive bedrooms, on edge of small pretty village *(David and Mary Webb, R T and J C Moggridge)*

Marsden T&W [Sea Rd; passage to lift in A183 car park, just before Marsden from Whitburn; NZ4164], *Grotto*: Uniquely built into seaside cliff caverns, with 10p lift (or dozens of steps) down to two floors – upper pink plush, lower brown varnish; Vaux Samson real ales, food in bar and restaurant, good sea views *(Rob and Linda Davis)*

Mickley N'land [Mount Pleasant; off A695 Prudhoe—Stocksfield; NZ0761], *Blue Bell*: Cosy little pub very popular locally for good home-cooked food prepared to order; Courage Directors and Marstons Pedigree, friendly staff *(John Oddey)*

☆ **Middleton in Teesdale** Dur [Mkt Pl;
NY9526], *Teesdale*: Pleasantly worn in hotel
bar with good service, good choice of food
from tapas bar and other bar food inc
vegetarian, well kept Tetleys, log fire; tables
outside, comfortable bedrooms *(David and
Ruth Hollands, M J Morgan)*

Morpeth N'land [High Church; NZ2086],
Sun: Welcoming bustle in stonebuilt local,
Scottish Courage ales, shelves stacked with
books, comfortable chairs and settles; good
value standard food, pool *(John Oddey, Eric
Larkham)*; [Manchester St], *Tap & Spile*: Up
to ten well kept ales and farm cider in cosy
and easy-going two-room pub with limited
choice of good value food made by excellent
landlady, fair prices, stripped pine furniture,
interesting old photographs, folk music Sun
afternoons, dominoes, cards, darts etc, fruit
machine; unobtrusive piped music, children
welcome, open all day *(Ian and Nita Cooper,
Eric Larkham)*

Netherton N'land [NW of Rothbury;
NT9807], *Star*: Remote local, spartan but
clean, well kept Whitbreads Castle Eden
tapped from the cask, friendly staff and
regulars; no food *(Jack and Philip Paxton)*

Newburn T&W [Grange Rd, by Tyne
Riverside Country Park; NZ1665], *Keelman*:
Recently opened by Big Lamp in same
building as their new brewery; former 19th-c
pumping station, with high ceiling, lofty
windows, their full range of beers at attractive
prices, limited but good waitress-served bar
food inc children's dishes; brewery open to
visitors; fruit machine, piped pop music,
tables outside *(L Dixon, Eric Larkham)*

☆ **Newcastle upon Tyne** [32 The Close,
Quayside], *Cooperage*: One of city's oldest
buildings, all bare stone and wooden beams;
now a Bass managed house, though still with
a good range of other ales such as Ind Coope
Burton, Marstons Owd Rodger, Stones,
Timothy Taylors Landlord and Tetleys, with
Addlestone's cider and a good choice of cheap
food; as we went to press was still unchanged
as a genuine and enjoyable pub, but was
about to close for what looked like a lengthy
refurbishment; pool, juke box, machines;
restaurant, night club *(Eric Larkham, M
Phillips, Denis and Margaret Kilner, LYM;
news please)*

☆ **Newcastle upon Tyne** [33 Shields Rd, Byker;
NZ2664], *Tap & Spile*: Good choice of
interesting well kept ales and two farm ciders
in well run traditional pub with games in
front bar, quieter solidly furnished back
room, decent lunchtime bar food inc
sandwiches; open all day *(Eric Larkham, E A
Thwaite, Jim and Maggie Cowell, LYM)*

Newcastle upon Tyne [High Bridge East],
Bacchus: Two beautifully fitted rooms with
lovely old mirrors, panelling and elbow-height
tables (but a refurbishment looming), well
kept Stones, Tetleys, Theakstons XB,
Youngers IPA and two guest beers, cheap hot
lunches (not Sun); piped music, machines;

cosy and comfortable when not too busy,
open all day (cl Sun afternoon) *(Eric
Larkham, E A Thwaite, Val Stevenson, Rob
Holmes)*; [Broad Chare, by river], *Baltic
Tavern*: Spacious and comfortably converted
warehouse, lots of stripped brick and
flagstones or bare boards (as well as plusher
carpeted parts) in warren of separate areas,
good value bar food, well kept Whitbreads
and guest beers, farm cider; open all day (cl
Sun) *(Val Stevenson, Rob Holmes, Eric
Larkham)*; [Percy St, Haymarket], *Bar Oz*:
Australian-theme bar with appropriate bric-a-
brac – giant marlin, crocodiles, sailfish,
kangaroos etc; good range of Oz beers (esp
from ice-cream fridges under the bar), cheap
spirits, food all day; big screen sports TV,
weekend DJs *(Russell Allen)*; [11 Groat Mkt],
Blackie Boy: Wonderful old-fashioned
atmosphere, narrow bar gets very crowded
(but room to move in front entrance), good
range of cheap lunchtime food, Theakstons
beers, TV, fruit machine; open all day *(Eric
Larkham)*; [125 Westgate Rd], *Bodega*:
Beautifully refurbished partly divided
Edwardian drinking hall, bare boards,
colourful walls and ceiling, two magnificent
stained-glass domes; good low-priced home-
made lunchtime food inc interesting
vegetarian, six well kept mainly local beers
tapped from the cask, friendly staff; open all ·
day, juke box may be loudish, machines, TV,
Tues quiz night, busy evenings (and if
Newcastle Utd at home or on TV); next to
Tyne Theatre *(Eric Larkham, GSB)*; [Castle
Garth, next to high level bridge], *Bridge*:
Newly refurbished, big high-ceilinged room
divided into several areas leaving plenty of
space by the bar with its unusual pull-down
slatted snob screens, six well kept ales,
welcoming staff, magnificent fireplace,
sensibly priced hot and cold lunches; piped
music, fruit machines, some live music
upstairs; tables on flagstoned terrace with
views of river, bridges and section of old town
wall; open all day *(Eric Larkham, LYM)*;
[Chillingham Rd, Heaton; NZ2765],
Chillingham Arms: Two big rooms, fine
woodwork and furnishings, six well kept ales,
occasional mini beer festivals, good cheap
lunchtime food inc Sun; pool tables in room
off, juke box, TV, machines; children in
lounge (cl afternoon – rest open all day) *(Eric
Larkham)*; [Brandling; NZ2565],
Collingwood Arms: Long and narrow,
popular with students, Scottish Courage and
interesting guest beers, juke box, TV,
machines; opens noon *(Eric Larkham)*; [High
Bridge West], *Duke of Wellington*: Often
crowded L-shaped Victorian-style pub with
lots of photographs, good choice of well kept
ales inc guests, popular hearty good value
food inc vegetarian; juke box, machines,
restaurant, children welcome, open all day (cl
Sun afternoon) *(Eric Larkham, Denis and
Margaret Kilner, Peter Todd, Graham and
Karen Oddey)*; [118 Grey St, Eldon Sq], *FMs*:
Trendy and interesting, the UK's first pub

with working radio station broadcasting live, may see stars like Cher, Sting etc; three linked floors, pleasant outside drinking areas; open for breakfast from 8am; video banks previewing forthcoming broadcasts, Tetleys, Marstons Pedigree, food all day *(Russell Allen)*; [60 Grey St], *Fitzgeralds*: Stunning beautifully refurbished Victorian pub on fringe of Bigg Market, all red mahogany and polished brass, real ales inc interesting guests, good value lunchtime food; can get very busy, piped music, machines; cl Sun am *(Eric Larkham)*; [City Rd, nr Milk Mkt, opp Keelmans Hosp], *Fog & Firkin*: Striking Victorian-style decor in big open-plan two-level pub overlooking quayside, bare boards, nautical decorations, real ales brewed for the pub (by Fly & Firkin brewpub), friendly service even when busy, basic good value food inc vegetarian; facilities for the disabled *(Ian and Nita Cooper, Eric Larkham)*; [St Lawrence Rd, Byker – off A186 Walker Rd into what looks like industrial estate; NZ2765], *Free Trade*: Awesome Tyne views from rough and ready but friendly pub with good choice of ales usually inc full local Mordue range, lunchtime sandwiches, interesting juke box, no machines; open all day, tables outside *(Eric Larkham)*; [High St, Gosforth; NZ2467], *Gosforth*: Newly refurbished with bare boards and flagstones, four real ales and regularly changing guests, TV, juke box, machines; open all day *(Eric Larkham)*; [Neville St, opp Central Stn], *Gotham Town*: Huge refurbishment, four well kept ales (though UV lights don't flatter them), interesting food 11-7, TVs, juke box, fruit machine; drinks priced according to time of day, can get very full and loud *(Eric Larkham)*; [103 Percy St], *Hotspur*: Light and airy Victorian pub, big front windows and decorated mirrors, Scottish Courage and up to three guest beers, farm cider, lots of bottled Belgian beers, good value wine; machines, TV; open all day, sandwiches and hot snacks till 9 *(Eric Larkham, John Wooll)*; [St Marys Pl E], *Luckies*: Two-room pub with hot and cold lunches inc vegetarian, several TVs, occasional DJ, tables outside; open all day *(Eric Larkham)*; [72 Pilgrim St], *Market Lane*: Two-room local, good friendly staff, hot and cold food, juke box, machines, pinball; open all day Mon-Sat *(Eric Larkham)*; [57 St Andrews St], *Newcastle Arms*: Open-plan pub on fringe of China Town, good range of real ales with occasional mini beer festivals, lunchtime sandwiches etc, pin table, juke box, fruit machine, video game; open all day (cl Sun afternoon), can get very busy *(Eric Larkham)*; [Fawdon Cl, Fawdon; NZ2269], *Northumbrian Piper*: Shipping magnate's former home converted to pub about 30 years ago, varied furnishings in each room, very popular lunchtime for consistently good food – businessmen weekdays, families weekends; helpful welcoming staff, Scottish Courage and/or Marstons ales, spacious grounds *(John Oddey)*; [Cloth Mkt, down alley past

Pumphreys], *Old George*: Former coaching inn with splendid panelling, beams and attractive fireplace; well kept Bass and Stones, good lunches *(Eric Larkham)*; [35 The Close], *Quayside*: Friendly Beefeater in converted old warehouse by Tyne, tables outside *(E A Thwaite, Eric Larkham)*; [Stepney Bank; NZ2664], *Ship*: Traditional local popular with craft and music workers from nearby arts centre, Whitbreads-related beers, lunchtime sandwiches, pin table, pool, juke box, fruit machine, TV; seats outside, open all day; next to Byker city farm *(Eric Larkham)*; [7 Strawberry Pl], *Strawberry*: Pleasant dark decor with a touch of style, busy and friendly, with ten well kept Scottish Courage and other ales, farm cider, continental bottled beers, bar food inc good pies, open fires, bar billiards, old juke box, pictures of old Newcastle, SkyTV for sports; open all day *(Russell Allen, Ian Jolly, Eric Larkham)*; [Nun St/Grainger St], *Tap & Spile*: Victorian pub with old local pictures, nine real ales and Weston's Old Rosie farm cider, moderate choice of cheap basic lunchtime pub food; piped music, TV, fruit machine, some live music downstairs; open all day (cl Sun afternoon) *(Eric Larkham)*; [Westgate Rd], *Tilleys*: Popular with people from the Tyne Theatre next door; mirrored snug lounge, generous lunchtime cheeses and pâtés with chunks of crusty bread; full Jennings range kept well, occasional guest beers, juke box, machines, open all day (evening only, Sun) *(Eric Larkham)*; [52 Clayton St W], *Tut 'n' Shive*: A bit bizarre, with no two pieces of carpet matching, doors fixed to ceiling etc; well kept Whitbreads and guest ales, lunchtime sandwiches, juke box, machines, TV; open all day, live music upstairs most nights *(Eric Larkham)*; [1 Maling St], *Tyne*: Single-room pub below Glasshouse Bridge at confluence of Ouseburn and Tyne, four real ales, lunchtime sandwiches, Sun lunchtime barbecues on terrace, good free juke box; open all day, sports TV, can get very full – but good-natured crowd *(Eric Larkham)*

☆ **Newton by the Sea** N'land [The Square, Low Newton; NU2426], *Ship*: Good genuine local quaintly tucked into top corner of courtyard of old cottages facing beach and sea, friendly licensees and atmosphere, good reasonably priced crab sandwiches and ploughman's, coffee, tea, maybe real ale in summer, pool table, ices served outside in summer; very busy on a hot day, children welcome, tables out on green *(Peter Todd, John Cockell, Leonard Dixon, Ian Wilson, Denis and Margaret Kilner)*

North Bitchburn Dur [NZ1733], *Red Lion*: 17th-c beams, log fires, enthusiastic landlord and staff, good food, well kept beers, thriving atmosphere *(M J Morgan)*

☆ **North Shields** T&W [1 Camden St; NZ3468], *Magnesia Bank*: Big brightly lit bar in well run Victorian pub overlooking Tyne, half a dozen well kept ales such as Butterknowle Conciliation, Mordue Workie Ticket and

Timothy Taylors Landlord, vast choice of cheerful food (not Sun evening), pleasant atmosphere, open fire, quiet piped pop music, TV, fruit machines, tables outside; children welcome, open all day, live music Thurs and Sun *(L Dixon, Eric Larkham, CMW, JJW, Andy and Jill Kassube, Ben Anderson)*

North Shields [New Quay], *Chain Locker*: Close to pedestrian ferry, simple nautical-theme Victorian pub under new regime, half a dozen well kept ales inc unusual local ones, farm cider, open fire; food (not Sun evening) from lunchtime sandwiches up; piped music (may be loud), fruit machine; children welcome, open all day Thurs-Sun, Fri folk night *(Eric Larkham, LYM)*; [184 Tynemouth Rd], *Tap & Spile*: Wide changing range of ales in simply furnished open-plan pub with public and lounge ends, decent lunchtime sandwiches, friendly staff and regulars, fruit machines, some live music, open all day *(Eric Larkham)*; [103 Hudson St], *Wooden Doll*: Dozens of paintings by local artists, high view of Shields Fish Quay and outer harbour, informal mix of furnishings in bare-boards bar, ales such as Ind Coope Burton, Tetleys and Timothy Taylors Landlord, helpful staff, largely no-smoking eating area; children welcome till 8, live music Sat, open all day Sat *(Eric Larkham, E A Thwaite, R Warner, LYM)*

Ovington N'land [off A69 E of Corbridge; NZ0764], *Ship*: Italian licensee, reasonably priced pasta and pizzas, Sun roast, friendly locals, restaurant, clean and quiet *(L Dixon)*

Penshaw T&W [nr Monument; NZ3253], *Grey Horse*: Welcoming, with cheap food (just snacks and toasties on the bar on Sun), well kept Tetleys; no juke box *(Denis and Margaret Kilner)*

Piercebridge Dur [B6275 just S of village, over bridge – so actually in N Yorks; NZ2116], *George*: Three bars with five open fires between them, comfortably worn-in solid furnishings, wide choice of generous bar food from sandwiches to good steaks inc vegetarian dishes, river-view restaurant, Scottish Courage ales, decent wines, the famous clock that stopped short never to go again, fine waterside garden; so rambling as not to suit disabled people; children in eating areas, piped music; open all day, good value bedrooms *(Dr P D Smart, Paul and Janet Waring, John Poulter, D Kay, Lynne Gittins, Basil Minson, Beryl and Bill Farmer, WAH, LYM)*

Ponteland N'land [Street Houses (A696 SE); NZ1871], *Badger*: New conversion of 18th-c house, lots of interesting rooms and alcoves, flagstones, carpet or bare wood, timbered ceilings, stripped stone, brick and timbering, lots of charm, real fires, three Bass-related ales, welcoming efficient service, good food *(John Oddey)*

Ponteland [Main St], *Seven Stars*: Unremarkable stone building on Main St, nostalgic interior works well, huge range of mainly Scottish Courage beers inc nice strong Belgian one, very lively feel, good service, good value food *(Graham and Karen Oddey)*

Rennington N'land [NU2119], *Horseshoes*: Clean and comfortable flagstoned pub with good helpings of reasonably priced freshly cooked straightforward food, friendly service, tables outside; attractive village well placed for coast *(S E Paulley)*

Ridsdale N'land [A68 S of Otterburn; NY9184], *Gun*: Long lounge/eating area, big picture window with lovely view, real fire, well kept Whitbreads Castle Eden, usual food (reasonable prices) inc good Sun roast, bargain malt whisky doubles, helpful staff, gun memorabilia; juke box in separate bar; bedrooms *(L Dixon)*

☆ **Romaldkirk** Dur [NY9922], *Kirk*: Cosy and very friendly little two-room pub, well worn but clean, with wide choice of interesting good value food (not Tues), well kept ales such as Black Sheep and Butterknowle, good coffee, 18th-c stonework, good log fire, darts, piped popular classics; picnic tables out by green of attractive moorland village; doubles as PO *(Roxanne Chamberlain, M J Morgan)*

Rookhope Dur [off A689 W of Stanhope; NY9443], *Rookhope*: Basic friendly local with bar, lounge/games room, small restaurant; good Sun roast, cheap bar food, two real ales, sports TV, seats outside; nearby alpine bunkers nursery *(L Dixon)*

Rothbury N'land [NU0602], *Newcastle*: Recently refurbished comfortable lounge with separate dining area, Tetleys and other real ales, friendly service, good popular food; comfortable bedrooms, imposing spot at end of green – handy for Cragside (NT) *(Bob and Marg Griffiths, Dave Braisted)*; *Queens Head*: Friendly waiter service in bar, food inc good granary bread sandwiches; bedrooms *(R T and J C Moggridge)*

☆ **Saltburn by the Sea** Clvd [A174 towards Whitby; NZ6722], *Ship*: Beautiful setting among beached fishing boats, sea views from tasteful nautical-style black-beamed bars and big plainer summer dining lounge; good range of bar food, quick friendly service, evening restaurant (not Sun), children's room and menu, seats outside; busy at holiday times, smuggling exhibition next door *(WAH, Basil Minson, Val Stevenson, Rob Holmes, K and E Leist, LYM)*

☆ **Seaton Sluice** Dur [A193 N of Whitley Bay; NZ3477], *Waterford Arms*: Comfortable dining pub with wide choice of very generously served fresh fish and seafood (all day summer Suns, not winter Sun evenings), partly no-smoking restaurant, Wards Sheffield Best and Thorne, Vaux Samson and Waggledance, children welcome; piped music; recently refurbished good value simple bedrooms *(Richard Dolphin, John Oddey, Ian and Nita Cooper, Eric Larkham, Neil Townend, Graham and Karen Oddey, David Honeyman, LYM)*

☆ **Sedgefield** Dur [Front St; NZ3629], *Dun Cow*: Large village inn, friendly and attractive, with wide choice of good if not cheap food inc game and fresh Whitby fish in two bars and restaurant, welcoming service, ales such as Courage Directors, Hambleton Stallion, Tetleys and Theakstons, good range of whiskies, pleasantly upmarket feel; children welcome; good bedrooms sharing bathrooms *(Richard Dolphin, Peter Compton)*

Shincliffe Dur [A177, Durham end; NZ2941], *Rose Tree*: Clean and comfortable local by River Wear, with friendly helpful staff, wide range of good value substantial food, well kept Vaux and Wards ales with a guest such as Greene King Abbot; tables outside *(Lesley Sones, Mrs K Burvill)*

Slaley N'land [Main St; NY9757], *Rose & Crown*: Good choice of food from sandwiches to restaurant meals inc good value Sun lunch, Butterknowle Conciliation, Jennings, Theakstons Best and a beer brewed for the pub, good choice of malt whiskies, welcoming service, dark-beamed lounge with lots of hanging mugs and jugs, public bar with fruit machine, juke box, darts; bedrooms attractive and well equipped *(Alan Thwaite, L Dixon)*

South Shields T&W [137 Commercial Rd; B1301/B1302; NZ3766], *Dolly Peel*: Well kept Courage Directors, Timothy Taylors Landlord, Youngers No 3, guest ales and lots of malt whiskies in friendly and busy local named after legendary fishwife; two rooms with old photographs, nautical and railway mementos, good variety of filled rolls, free Sun bar nibbles, bar billiards, local radio or piped pop; children welcome, open all day (cl Sun afternoon) *(Eric Larkham)*

Stamfordham N'land [off B6309; NZ0872], *Bay Horse*: Long cheery and comfortable beamed bar with harness on walls, mainly Whitbreads-related ales, wide range of decent bar food, good coffee, friendly service; at end of green in attractive village *(John Oddey, Tony Dickinson)*

Tanfield Lea Dur [NZ1954], *Peacock*: Friendly pub with short choice of mainly home-cooked food inc good salads, welcoming staff and regulars *(Pat Woodward)*

☆ **Tynemouth** T&W [Tynemouth Rd (A193); ½ mile W of Tynemouth Metro stn; NZ3468], *Tynemouth Lodge*: Particularly well kept ales and farm ciders, cheap lunchtime filled rolls and coal fire in genuine-feeling friendly and quiet little Victorian-style pub – no juke box or machines, no dogs or children; open all day, can be packed *(Eric Larkham, LYM)*

Tynemouth [29 Front St], *Fitzpatricks*: Well refurbished in mahogany, red leather and cast iron, cosy open-plan rooms on split levels, good mix of low and tall tables, settles, armchairs and so forth; six well kept ales, huge helpings of usual bar food, friendly helpful staff; machines, TV, live music Tues, open all day *(Eric Larkham)*; [Front St], *Salutation*: Single long bar in handsome former coaching inn's big split-level lounge, lots of mahogany and brass rails, comfortable settles along some walls, six beautifully kept Whitbreads-related ales, friendly staff, good range of standard food *(John Oddey, Eric Larkham)*

☆ **Wall** N'land [NY9269], *Hadrian*: Solidly cushioned two-room beamed lounge with wide choice of well presented good bar food inc fresh fish and local cheeses, well kept Vaux Samson and Wards Thorne, good house wine, interesting reconstructions of Romano-British life, no-smoking area, woodburner, smart efficient staff, unobtrusive piped music, games in public bar, no-smoking Victorian dining room; children welcome, neat garden; bedrooms – back ones quieter, with good views *(Phil and Heidi Cook, Lise Kerslake, Guy Consterdine, LYM)*

Warden N'land [½ mile N of A69; NY9267], *Boatside*: Dining pub recently smartly refurbished and extended, good range of good food, attentive service, real ale; perhaps needs time to develop atmosphere *(Chris Rounthwaite, John Oddey)*

Wark N'land [NY8677], *Battlesteads*: Greatly refurbished, with very welcoming Dutch landlady, Stones and Theakstons, good food; bedrooms *(John Oddey)*

☆ **Warkworth** N'land [23 Castle St; NU2506], *Hermitage*: Interesting decor, with old range for heating, well kept Jennings ales, generous food from sandwiches to good fresh fish reasonably priced, good cheerful service, small plush upstairs restaurant *(Brian and Jenny Seller, John Oddey, Eric Larkham, Verity Kemp, Richard Mills, BB)*

Warkworth [3 Dial Pl], *Masons Arms*: Welcoming thriving local, slick service, good value generous starters and main dishes, well kept Youngers Scotch and No 3; attractive back flagstoned courtyard *(Tony Dickinson, Verity Kemp, Richard Mills)*

Washington T&W [The Green; NZ3156], *Washington Arms*: Attractive pub nr Washington Old Hall, good value generous lunchtime food, nice atmosphere, framed cigarette cards, discreet piped music; can get very busy evenings – young in back bar, others in front *(Denis and Margaret Kilner)*

Weldon Bridge N'land [signed just off B6344 nr A397 junction; NZ1399], *Anglers Arms*: Welcoming pub in splendid location, well kept Boddingtons, rather austere decor featuring fish, generous bar food inc good steak and kidney pie; restaurant booked well ahead; bedrooms *(Andrew and Kerstin Lewis, P D R Milner)*

West Boldon T&W [Rectory Bank; just off A184; NZ3561], *Black Horse*: Friendly dining pub with good range of tasty food inc Sun lunch, big bookable evening restaurant, Whitbreads-related ales with a local guest such as Mordues Radgie Gadgie, friendly attentive staff; parking can be a problem *(Maurice Thompson)*

☆ **West Woodburn** N'land [A68; NY8987], *Bay Horse*: Welcoming service in open-plan bar with red plush banquettes and other seats, open fire, well kept Theakstons XB, good bar food inc vegetarian, children's and Sun roasts; airy dining room, games room, children welcome, riverside garden, play area; cl Mon/Tues lunchtime in winter; comfortable well equipped bedrooms, excellent breakfast *(Revd Richard and Revd Kathleen Allen, SS, Kay Neville-Rolfe, LYM)*

Whalton N'land [NZ1382], *Beresford Arms*: Tudoresque decor in dining pub particularly popular with older people for genuine home cooking at reasonable prices; friendly helpful staff, well kept Vaux Lorimers Scotch and Wards, pretty village *(H E and E A Simpson, Chris Rounthwaite)*

Whitley Bay T&W [2 South Parade; NZ3572], *Fitzgeralds*: Big main room with raised dining area, smaller more intimate snug, well kept beer, good food; can get very busy in the evenings with live music Weds, DJ Thurs-Sat; open all day *(Eric Larkham)*; [278 Whitley Rd], *Tap & Spile*: Lots of different areas in big open-plan pub with good atmosphere, changing choice of well kept beers, farm cider, good staff; children welcome, open all day *(Eric Larkham)*

Whittonstall N'land [B6309 N of Consett; NZ0857], *Anchor*: Attractively refurbished stonebuilt beamed village pub, comfortable banquettes in L-shaped lounge and dining area, well kept Scottish Courage ales, huge choice of good generous food from sandwiches through interesting hot dishes to popular Sun lunch, efficient friendly service, pleasant dining room, piped music; pool, darts and fruit machine in public bar; nice countryside *(Bob and Marg Griffiths, Jack and Heather Coyle, CMW, JJW, Mrs C Sawyer)*

Wolsingham Dur [NZ0737], *Mill Race*: New landlord (and name change), well presented popular bar lunches inc vegetarian, good service, dining room; bedrooms *(Jack and Heather Coyle)*

Wooler N'land [B6351 N; NT9928], *Tankerville Arms*: Pleasant hotel bar in tastefully modernised old building, good choice of food inc some local products, Border Farne Islands, Marstons Pedigree and Theakstons Best, good service; bedrooms *(Jenny and Brian Seller)*

Wylam N'land [Station Rd; NZ1265], *Boathouse*: Eight well kept ales inc Timothy Taylors Landlord, good choice of malt whiskies, good cheap generous food *(L Dixon, Stephen and Julie Brown, Eric Larkham)*

Looking for a pub with a really special garden, or in lovely countryside, or with an outstanding view, or right by the water? They are listed separately, at the back of the book.

Nottinghamshire

In the last few years our Nottinghamshire list of main entries has changed out of all recognition, and this year there are another two newcomers: the friendly and very well run Robin Hood at Elkesley (an excellent break from the A1), and the Three Horseshoes up in Walkeringham (very good food). The most enjoyable meals here are to be had at the Martins Arms at Colston Bassett – our choice as Nottinghamshire Dining Pub of the Year. Another place for a good meal out is the bustling yet relaxing French Horn at Upton. And the Victoria in Beeston has good imaginative cooking, too; quite a surprise in a pub whose obvious strength is its fine choice of real ales. Nottingham has an excellent choice of pubs, both among the main entries and in the Lucky Dip section at the end of the chapter; the interesting Olde Trip to Jerusalem here has come out of a refurbishment with even more to see, and the cheery and lively Lincolnshire Poacher is quite a favourite. Three pubs (all inspected and approved) that stand out among the Lucky Dips are Tom Browns at Gunthorpe, the Bramley Apple in Southwell and Cross Keys at Upton. Drinks prices are well below the national average here, with the local Hardys & Hansons brewing fine ales at relatively low prices; the cheapest pub we found was Fellows Morton & Clayton in Nottingham, brewing its own beers.

BEESTON SK5338 Map 7
Victoria 🍺
Dovecote Lane, backing on to railway station

Around 10 well kept changing real ales on handpump in this carefully converted railway hotel might include Batemans XB, Bramcote Hemlock, Everards Tiger, Marstons Pedigree, a guest Mild, a guest Porter or Stout, and up to five other guest beers; also, two traditional ciders, 105 malt whiskies, 20 Irish whiskeys, and half-a-dozen wines by the glass. The three downstairs rooms in their original long narrow layout have simple solid traditional furnishings, unfussy decor, stained-glass windows, stripped woodwork and floorboards (woodblock in some rooms), newspapers to read, and a good chatty atmosphere. The lounge and bar back on to the station, and picnic tables in a pleasant area outside look over on to the station platform – the trains pass within feet. The no-smoking area on the left is where they serve the good, interesting food: roasted artichoke and fennel salad (£5.25), tasty poacher's pie, chargrilled Welsh lamb with garlic and rosemary (£7.25), seared monkfish wrapped in pancetta (£8.95), and trio of game birds in madeira and redcurrant jus (£9.50). Puddings like delicious apple crumble, hot banana pudding or jam roly-poly; cribbage. *(Recommended by Roger and Jenny Huggins, Mike and Wena Stevenson, Dr David Webster, Sue Holland, Simon Walker, Derek Martin, R M Taylor, Andy and Jill Kassube, Paul Barnett, D Eberlin, Jack and Philip Paxton, TBB, Elizabeth and Anthony Watts, Chris Raisin, R and A Cooper)*

Free house ~ Licensee Neil Kelso ~ Real ale ~ Meals and snacks (12-9 Sun-Wed; 12-10 Thurs-Sat) ~ Restaurant ~ (0115) 925 4049 ~ Children in eating area ~ Jazz every 2nd Sunday ~ Open 11-11; 12-10.30 Sun

COLSTON BASSETT SK7033 Map 7

Martins Arms

Signposted off A46 E of Nottingham

Nottinghamshire Dining Pub of the Year

Smart uniformed staff serve the very good food at this civilised place. It isn't cheap, but is carefully prepared to order from fresh, daily-delivered produce: home-made soup (£2.95), sandwiches (from £2.95; baked ham, grain mustard, brie and watercress on warm ciabatta £3.95), confit of duck with sherry vinegar dressing (£6.95), warm vegetarian tartlette or ploughman's (£7.95), hot marinated chicken with warm ratatouille (£9.95), roast loin of wild rabbit with tarragon dumplings or seared salmon with tapenade and tomato fondue (£11.95), loin of lamb (£12.95), daily specials, and puddings such as caramelised thick lemon tart or tarte tatin of pears (from £4.50). Their gourmet or wine tasting evenings are proving popular; afternoon teas on bank holidays and maybe during the summer months. The well laid out restaurant is decorous and smart, with well spaced tables. A good choice of real ales on handpump might include Adnams Bitter, Bass, Batemans XB (and a beer brewed by Batemans for them, Martins Arms Beer), Black Sheep Bitter, Greene King Abbott, Marstons Best, Morlands Old Speckled Hen, and changing guests; a good range of malt whiskies and cognacs, and an interesting wine list. There are two open fires in one of the comfortable, attractively decorated bars, and a proper snug; cribbage, dominoes, and croquet. The pub is run by the same people as the Crown at Old Dalby, a main entry in the Leicestershire chapter; sizeable garden; no children. *(Recommended by Chris Raisin, David Atkinson, Peter and Jenny Quine, M Buchanan, Brian and Jill Bond, June and Malcolm Farmer, Roy Bromell, Keith Wright, MT, Jack and Philip Paxton, SS, Norman Smith, A and R Cooper, Gareth Morgan, Keith Archer)*

Free house ~ Licensees Lynne Strafford Bryan and Salvatore Inguanta ~ Real ale ~ Meals and snacks (till 10pm; not Sun evenings) ~ Restaurant (not Sun evening) ~ (01949) 81361 ~ Open 12-3, 6-11; 12-3, 7-10.30 Sun ~ Bedrooms: £35B/£60B

DRAKEHOLES SK7090 Map 7

Griff Inn

Village signposted from A631 in Everton, between Bawtry and Gainsborough

In summer, customers head for the neat landscaped gardens here with their pretty view down over the Idle Valley and canal basin. The handsome 18th-c brick inn was originally built to serve the Chesterfield canal which now passes under the road through a long tunnel – a map in the lounge shows its route. Inside, the civilised and carefully colour-coordinated main lounge bar has small plush seats around its tables, and little landscape prints on silky-papered walls; one bar is no smoking. Under the new licensee, bar food now includes soup (£1.90), sandwiches (from £2.75; nice open bacon and brie or chicken with avocado), filled baked potatoes (from £3.25), battered haddock (£4.95), steak and kidney pie (£5.20), mixed grill (£7.95), and daily specials (from £5.50). As well as the no-smoking restaurant, there's a more airy brasserie-style summer restaurant and a cosy cocktail bar. Ruddles Best and a weekly changing guest on handpump; video game, piped music. *(Recommended by Eric Grigor, Pat and Tony Martin, Peter Hartnell, David Carr, Alan and Charlotte Sykes, Mrs Cynthia Archer; more reports on the new regime, please)*

Free house (Inns & Taverns) ~ Licensee Stephen Fox ~ Meals and snacks (till 10) ~ Restaurant ~ (01777) 817206 ~ Children in eating area of bar only ~ Open 11-3, 5-11; 11-11 Sat; 11-3, 6-11 winter Sat; 12-10.30 Sun; 12-3, 7-10.30 winter Sun ~ Bedrooms: £30B/£45B

Anyone claiming to arrange or prevent inclusion of a pub in the *Guide* is a fraud. Pubs are included only if recommended by genuine readers and if our own anonymous inspection confirms that they are suitable.

ELKESLEY SK6975 Map 7

Robin Hood

High Street; village well signposted just off A1 Newark—Blyth

Nice to find a proper pub so handy for the A1 – and what's more, a place that does good value food. Certainly, most of our readers who have come here have been in search of just such a refuge from the trunk road – but one of our most regular reporters actually flies in for lunch, to Gamston airfield just on the other side of the A1 (and the landlord usually finds the time to drive him back to the airfield afterwards). The roomy and comfortably furnished carpeted family dining lounge has pictures, some copper pans and so forth – even a small collection of handcuffs. There's also a plain but neatly kept public bar, with pool and games machines; and a garden moderately well screened from the A1 has picnic tables and a play area. The food comes in big helpings and includes good hot filled rolls (from £1.70) such as sausage (good local pork and sage ones), home-made soup (£2.40), home-made chicken liver pâté or winter moules marinières (£3.60), a daily vegetarian dish (from £4.50), sautéed liver with onion, garlic and parsley (£5), chicken breast or gammon and eggs (£5.50), steaks (from £6.50), daily specials, and home-made puddings such as chocolate truffle cake or tiramisu (£2.50); a good choice of fresh fish might run from basic cod in batter (£4.95) to baby halibut or stir-fried monkfish (from £6.70). Service is friendly and efficient; well kept Boddingtons and a guest such as Flowers Original or Marstons Pedigree on handpump; piped music. *(Recommended by Christopher Turner, Andy and Jill Kassube, Arnold and Maureen East, Eddy and Emma Gibson, Jason Warren)*

Whitbreads ~ Lease: Allen Draper ~ Real ale ~ Meals and snacks (not Sun evening) ~ Restaurant ~ (01777) 838259 ~ Children welcome ~ Open 11-3, 6-11; 11-11 Sat; 12-3, 7-10.30 Sun; closed evening 25 Dec

KIMBERLEY SK5044 Map 7

Nelson & Railway 🍺

2 miles from M1 junction 26; Kimberley signposted from exit roundabout, pub in Sation Rd, on right from centre

Originally this two-roomed Victorian pub was known as the Lord Nelson Railway Hotel. The beamed bar and lounge have an attractive mix of Edwardian-looking furniture, interesting brewery prints and railway signs on the walls, and a relaxed atmosphere – though it can get busy. As the brewery is directly opposite, the Hardys & Hansons Bitter, Classic, Mild and seasonal ales here are particularly well kept; several malt whiskies. Good value straightforward bar food includes soup (£1.20), sandwiches (from £1.30; hot rolls from £1.60), cottage pie (£2.75), filled baked potatoes (from £2.75), tomato and vegetable tagliatelle or steak and kidney pie (£4.25), chicken curry (£4.85), gammon and egg (£4.95), sirloin steak (£5.95), puddings (£1.85), and children's meals (£1.65); Sunday lunch (£3.95 adults, £2.95 children); darts, alley skittles, dominoes, cribbage, fruit machine, and juke box. There are tables and swings out in a good-sized cottagey garden. *(Recommended by Alan Morton, Andy and Jill Kassube, K Fell, M L and G Clarke, K Frostick, Jeanne and George Barnwell, Alan Hopkin, I P G Derwent, Jack and Philip Paxton, Roy Bromell)*

Hardys & Hansons ~ Tenants Harry and Pat Burton ~ Real ale ~ Meals and snacks (12-2.30, 5.30-9) ~ (0115) 938 2177 ~ Children in eating area of bar ~ Open 10.30-3, 5-11 Mon-Weds; 10.30-11 Thurs-Sat; 12-10.30 Sun ~ Bedrooms: £19/£33

LAXTON SK7267 Map 7

Dovecote

Signposted off A6075 E of Ollerton

The Laxton Historical Visitor Centre is part of this cosy red brick house – though it's in a separate building – and is open every day. The pub is next to three huge uniquely surviving medieval open fields, and as part of this ancient farming system the grass is auctioned for haymaking in the third week of June, and anyone who lives in the parish is entitled to a bid – as well as to a drink. The central room has brocaded button-back built-in corner seats, stools and chairs, and a coal-effect gas fire, and opens through a small bay, which was the original entry, into another similar room. Around the other side a simpler room with some entertaining Lawson Wood 1930s tourist cartoons leads through to a pool room with darts, juke box, fruit machine, cribbage and dominoes. Simple but tasty bar food in generous helpings includes sandwiches (from £1.65), home-made soup (£1.85), chilli (£4.40), cottage pie (£4.50), home-made steak and kidney pie or lasagne (£4.60), mushroom stroganoff (£4.65), lemon chicken (£5.10), seafood au gratin (£5.40), steaks (from £7.15), and children's meals (£2.20); pleasant service. Well kept Boddingtons, Mansfield Riding, and three or four guests such as Everards Tiger, Fullers London Pride, Morlands Old Speckled Hen, and Charles Wells Bombardier on handpump or electric pump; helpful service. There are white tables and chairs on a small front terrace by a sloping garden with a disused white dovecote, and a children's play area; also, a site for seven caravans with lavatories and showers. *(Recommended by John Fahy, Angela Copeland, CMW, JJW, John Prescott, Garry Fairclough, R F Wright)*

Free house ~ Licensees Stephen and Betty Shepherd ~ Real ale ~ Meals and snacks ~ (01777) 871586 ~ Children welcome ~ Open 11.30-3, 6.30-11; 12-3, 7-10.30 Sun

NORMANTON ON TRENT SK7969 Map 7
Square & Compass
Signposted off B1164 S of Tuxford

Busy in the evenings and at weekends, this low-beamed village pub is old-fashioned and friendly, and run by a pleasant landlord who is keen on shooting, so game features on the menu quite often. The bar has an attractive grandfather clock, and is divided by an enormous woodburning stove in a central brick fireplace. There are several more or less separate snug areas, alcoves and bays, mainly with green plush furnishings, farming photographs, a flowery red carpet, red curtains and roughcast shiny cream walls; piped music. Good value bar food includes soup (£1.10), sandwiches (from £1.15), burgers (from £1.50), home-made pâté (£2.25), steak and kidney pie (£4.10), mushroom and nut fettucine (£4.25), chicken kiev (£4.50), 8oz sirloin steak (£7.75), with a couple of blackboard specials like rabbit pie or gingered beef (£4.25), puddings (from £1.40), and children's meals (from £1.60); Sunday roast. Well kept Adnams Bitter, Springhead Bitter, and Theakstons Best on handpump. The public side has pool, table skittles, cribbage, dominoes, and piped music. Outside, there are seats and a well equipped children's play area, and you can camp here. *(Recommended by Angela Copeland, Mary and David Webb, Ian Phillips, Derek and Sylvia Stephenson, Thomas Nott, R C Wiles, Tony Gayfer, Helen and Ian Cookson)*

Free house ~ Licensee Janet Lancaster ~ Real ale ~ Meals and snacks ~ Restaurant ~ (01636) 821439 ~ Children welcome ~ Open 12-3, 6-11, 12-11 Sat; 12-4, 7-10.30 Sun ~ Bedroom: £20S/£40S

NOTTINGHAM SK5640 Map 7
Fellows Morton & Clayton
54 Canal Street (part of inner ring road)

Buzzing with businessmen and lawyers at lunchtime, this carefully converted old canal building brews its own beer. From a big window in the quarry-tiled glassed-in area at the back you can see the little brewery: Samuel Fellows and Matthew Claytons. They also have Boddingtons, Burtonwood Top Hat, Timothy Taylors Landlord, Wadworths 6X and Whitbreads Castle Eden on handpump. The softly lit bar has dark blue plush seats built into alcoves, wooden tables, some seats up two or three steps in a side gallery, and bric-a-brac on the shelf just below the glossy dark green high ceiling; a sympathetic extension provides extra seating. Good value lunchtime bar food includes filled rolls (from £1.20), home-made soup (£1.75), burgers (from £1.75), pasta bows in rich cheese and tomato sauce with broccoli or chicken curry (£4.25), home-made lasagne (£4.50), home-made steak and kidney pie (£4.95), battered haddock (£5.25), and rump steak (£5.95); prompt, friendly service. Well reproduced nostalgic pop music, trivia, fruit machine and daily newspapers on a rack. Outside there's a terrace with seats and tables. In the evening the pub is popular with a younger crowd. The canal museum is nearby, and Nottingham station is just a short walk away. *(Recommended by SLC, M Rutherford, Norma and Keith Bloomfield, Andy and Jill Kassube, Roger Huggins, Alan Hopkin, R M Taylor, Stephen and Julie Brown, Jack and Philip Paxton)*

Own brew (Whitbreads) ~ Lease: Les Howard ~ Real ale ~ Lunchtime meals and snacks ~ Restaurant ~ (0115) 950 6795 ~ Children in restaurant ~ Open 11-11; 12-10.30 Sun

Lincolnshire Poacher 🍺

Mansfield Rd; up hill from Victoria Centre

Very much enjoyed by readers, this bustling and cheerful pub keeps a fine range of real ales. A splendid arrangement with Batemans allows them to serve Bass, Marstons Pedigree and four guest ales alongside perfectly kept Batemans XB, XXXB, Salem Porter, Valiant, and Victory Ale on handpump; also good ciders, and over 70 malt whiskies and 10 Irish ones. The traditional big wood-floored front bar has wall settles and plain wooden tables, and is decorated with breweriana; it opens on to a plain but lively room on the left, from where a corridor takes you down to the chatty panelled back snug – newspapers to read; cribbage, dominoes, cards, piped Irish music. Good daily specials might include hummus and pitta bread with olives and salad (£3.75), lasagne (£3.95), vegetable pie (£4.50), Lincolnshire sausages and mash (£4.50), and chicken stuffed with boursin cheese (£5.50); Sunday roast (from £4.95); no chips, and efficient, pleasant service. It can get busy in the evenings when it's popular with a younger crowd. A conservatory overlooks tables on a large terrace behind.
(Recommended by David Atkinson, Roger and Jenny Huggins, Andy and Jill Kassube, Irene and Geoffrey Lindley, Dr and Mrs J H Hills, Mr and Mrs J T V Harris, R M Taylor, Derek and Sylvia Stephenson, Simon Walker, M Rutherford, Chris Raisin, Alan Hopkin, Graham Fogelman, Mr and Mrs Blackbourn, Jack and Philip Paxton)

Batemans/Tynemill ~ Lease: Paul Montgomery and Amelia Bedford ~ Real ale ~ Meals and snacks (12-8 Mon-Fri; 12-3 Sat and Sun – not Sat or Sun evenings) ~ (0115) 9411584 ~ Children welcome in conservatory till 8pm ~ Open 11-11; 12-10.30 Sun

Olde Trip to Jerusalem ★

Brewhouse Yard; from inner ring road follow The North, A6005 Long Eaton signpost until you are in Castle Boulevard then almost at once turn right into Castle Road; pub is up on the left

Despite some extensive renovation, this unusual pub seems to have emerged superficially unchanged. They have found two more caves (now open to the public), and have created a parlour/snug from what was the manager's office. The unique upstairs cavern bar – thought to have served as cellarage for an early medieval brewhouse which stood here – is cut into the sandstone rock below the castle, its panelled walls soaring narrowly into the dark chasm above; unfortunately, this part is often closed at lunchtime. The friendly downstairs bar is also mainly carved from the rock, with leatherette-cushioned settles built into the dark panelling, barrel tables on tiles or flagstones, and more low-ceilinged rock alcoves. Well kept real ales include Hardys & Hansons Kimberley Best, Best Mild and their cellarman's cask (brewed every two months or so), and Marstons Pedigree on handpump. Home-made bar food includes cobs and sandwiches (from £1.85), filled baked potatoes (from £1.99), giant yorkshire pudding filled with roast beef, pork, lamb or sausages or leek, cheese and onion hotpot (£4.49), steak and kidney pudding (£4.79), liver and bacon (£5.49), pork and apple cider bake (£6.49), and puddings (from £1.99). Cribbage, chess, fruit machine, ring-the-bull; seats outside. No children. *(Recommended by Rona Murdoch, Timothy Smith, R M Taylor, Sue Holland, Dave Webster, Chris Raisin, Mr and Mrs J T Harris, M Rutherford, SLC, Stephen and Julie Brown, Vicky and David Sarti, N Gilbourne)*

Hardys & Hansons ~ Manager Patrick Dare ~ Real ale ~ Lunchtime meals and snacks (till 4pm; not Sun) ~ (0115) 9473171 ~ Open 11-11; 12-10.30 Sun

UPTON SK7354 Map 7
French Horn
A612

Most of the tables in this busy, friendly dining pub are laid for eating – and you may need to book, even on a weekday lunchtime. Served by friendly, efficient staff, there might be sandwiches (from £2.25), soup (£1.95), mushrooms stuffed with stilton in a port and redcurrant sauce (£2.95), steak pie (£4.95), and good specials like grilled sardines with a lemon and herb stuffing (£5.25), brie and broccoli crêpes with a spicy tomato sauce (£5.75), medley of salmon, sea trout and shark in a white wine and cream sauce (£6.95), poached salmon in a cream and dill sauce or beef bourguignon (£7.25), grilled loin of lamb filled with mustard sauce and a redcurrant jus (£7.95), and puddings like home-made chocolate truffle torte or lemon meringue pie (£2.95). Usefully they also do a range of sandwiches and hot snacks all afternoon. The neat and comfortable open-plan bar has a nicely relaxed feel, with cushioned captain's chairs, wall banquettes around glossy tables, and watercolours by local artists on the walls. Well kept Vaux Waggle Dance, Wards Best, Thorne Best, Darleys Mild, and a guest like Shepherd Neame Spitfire on handpump, and several wines by the glass; piped music. The big sloping back paddock, with picnic tables, looks over farmland. *(Recommended by Alan Wilcock, Christine Davidson, Andy and Jill Kassube, J F Knutton, Lawrence Bacon, Luke Worthington, David and Ruth Hollands, David and Lynne Cure, Paul Barnett, Norma and Keith Bloomfield, Angela Copeland, Anthony Barnes, Jack Morley, Alan Hopkin, A F and J Gifford, Brian and Jill Bond, Sarah and Peter Gooderham)*

Wards ~ Tenant Joyce Carter ~ Real ale ~ Meals and snacks (12-2, 6-9.45; light snacks 2-6) ~ Restaurant ~ (01636) 812394 ~ Children welcome ~ Open 11-11; 12-10.30 Sun

WALKERINGHAM SK7792 Map 7
Three Horseshoes
High Street; just off A161, off A631 W of Gainsborough

These northern fringes of the county, dominated by the River Trent, where the broad drainage channels of these flatlands seem to run straighter than the roads, have a touch of foreign-ness that half-prepares you for this distinctive pub. We could certainly see what readers meant when they had told us it reminded them of a French logis: pretty flowers and hanging baskets outside (using 9,000 plants – quite amazing) combine attractively with the slight austerity of the simple old-fashioned decor inside – not to mention the menu and blackboard of dishes of the day to greet you in the hall. The bar, with well kept Bass, Stones, Worthington Best and a guest beer on handpump, is warmly welcoming, and the dining room is again gently reminiscent of many a small hotel in remote parts of France. Of the two brothers who run it, John keeps the bar, while Ray is responsible for the often inventive cooking: a wide choice that might include lunchtime sandwiches (from £1.25), home-made soup (£1.40), ploughman's (from £2.75), tortellini in a tomato, pepper and cream sauce (£5.25), steak and kidney pie with herb pastry (a proper pie, not a lid of pastry £5.50), cheese, leek, mushroom and nut pie (£5.75), roast breast of lamb with a special stuffing or gammon and pineapple (£5.95), chicken with a creamy leek and stilton sauce or with fresh spices in a tomato and cream sauce, bass in a dill, mustard, wine and cream sauce or medallions of pork in a peppercorn, mustard, wine and cream sauce (all £7.50), steaks (from £8.75), seasonal game dishes, and puddings such as strawberry cocotte in a caramelised cointreau cream (£2.25); vegetables are fresh and lightly cooked. Darts, dominoes, fruit machine, video game, and piped music. There are seats on a lawned area. *(Recommended by M Godfrey, J and M Hall)*

Free house ~ Licensees Ray and John Turner ~ Real ale ~ Meals and snacks (not Sun evening, not Mon) ~ Restaurant ~ (01427) 890959 ~ Children welcome ~ Open 11-3, 7-11; 12-3, 7-10.30 Sun; closed evening 25 Dec

---

Pubs staying open all afternoon are listed at the back of the book.

WELLOW SK6766 Map 7

Olde Red Lion

Eakring Road; pub visible from A616 E of Ollerton

On the walls of the bar in this 16th-c pub are the original deeds – it was rented for one peppercorn per annum. Throughout the other comfortably furnished series of friendly low-beamed rooms are photographs on the panelled walls tracing the building's development. Of four well kept real ales, one is always from the local Maypole brewery (usually Lions Pride, brewed specially for the pub), alongside three changing guest beers on handpump. Reasonably priced bar food includes sandwiches, home-made soup (£1.20), vegetarian dishes (from £3.95), home-made steak and kidney pie (£4.75), grills (from £4.75), garlic chicken breast (£5.95), and children's meals (£1.95). The dining area is no smoking. Dominoes, table skittles. An L-shaped strip of grass above the car park has picnic tables under cocktail parasols, and on the green in front of the pub is a tremendously tall brightly spiral-painted maypole which confirms that May Day celebrations are still a lively part of this conservation village's life.
(Recommended by Sue and Geoff Price, Wayne Brindle, Roger Bellingham, John Fahy, Christopher Turner, R Davies, V Leach, Andrew and Jo Litten, Keith and Margaret Kettell, A and R Cooper)

Free house ~ Licensee Richard Henshaw ~ Real ale ~ Meals and snacks (till 10pm) ~ Restaurant ~ (01623) 861000 ~ Children in eating area of bar ~ Open 11.30-3(4 Sat), 5.30-11; 12-4, 6-10.30 Sun

Lucky Dip

Besides the fully inspected pubs, you might like to try these Lucky Dips recommended to us and described by readers (if you do, please send us reports):

☆ **Barnby in the Willows** [Front St – off A17 E of Newark; SK8652], *Willow Tree*: Tastefully extended 17th-c village local with original features in open-plan L-shaped bar, friendly chatty licensees, good reasonably priced food in bar and restaurant, well kept Batemans and guest beers; children welcome, games room; bedrooms *(Chris and Gill Green, Alan Bowker)*

Bleasby [SK7149], *Hazleford Ferry*: Attractively refurbished riverside pub with welcoming licensees, popular food in bar and restaurant, well kept beers, pleasant dining room and conservatory; comfortable bedrooms *(Jackie Moffat)*

Carlton on Trent [Ossington Rd; signed just off A1 N of Newark; SK7964], *Great Northern*: Large busy local next to railway line, comfortable and welcoming, with lots of railway memorabilia, toys in large family room; Mansfield Riding, local Springhead and guest ales, decent food inc good fish and chips, small dining area, good service; play area in garden *(A M Pring, Chris Westmoreland)*

☆ **Caunton** [Main St; off A616 Newark—Ollerton; SK7460], *Caunton Beck*: Newish pub with low beams, distressed paintwork, pine furnishings; taken over early 1997 by the people who have made the Wig & Mitre in Lincoln such a successful main entry, with food up to their usual standard, good choice of real ales, good house wines *(David and Ruth Hollands)*

Caunton [Main St], *Plough*: Clean and friendly L-shaped bar, well kept Marstons

Pedigree and guest beers, fairly priced honest generous food in dining area, good roast, friendly attentive landlady; lovely garden *(Keith Wells)*

Cotgrave [off A46 SE of Nottingham; SK6435], *Manvers Arms*: Assorted comfortable furniture in various areas, brick and beams, pictures, bric-a-brac up high, friendly service; wide choice of good cheap lunchtime food inc vegetarian, well kept Shipstones, quiet piped music; well behaved children welcome, small attractive garden with picnic tables; open all day *(JJW, CMW)*

☆ **East Bridgford** [Kneeton Rd, off A6075; can also be reached from A46; SK6943], *Reindeer*: Popular unpretentious village local with beamed dining bar, well kept Ruddles Best and County and Charles Wells Bombardier, good generous food cooked to order (so may be a wait), separate restaurant, log-effect gas fires; children welcome *(Derek and Sylvia Stephenson, Elizabeth and Anthony Watts, BB)*

Edingley [Main St; off A617 Newark—Mansfield at Kirklington; SK6656], *Old Reindeer*: Early 18th c, with amusing collection of chamber-pots in tap room, darts and TV; comfortable lounge with sofa leading into dining area, quite a wide choice of food, Mansfield ales, back lobby leading to garden with picnic tables and paddock with duck pond and animals *(CMW, JJW)*

Gotham [Nottingham Rd; SK5330], *Star*: Neat games-oriented pub, comfortable and well run, with good value food *(Dr and Mrs A K Clarke)*

✩ Gunthorpe [Trentside, off A6097 E of Nottingham; SK6844], *Tom Browns*: Modern brick bar over road from River Trent (pleasant walks), wok cooking in glass booth, decent bar food (not Sun) too, six Scottish Courage and interesting guest beers, good choice of wines, easy-going atmosphere, log fire; well reproduced pop music (may be loud evening), fruit machine, no dogs; restaurant, Sun carvery, seats outside *(JJW, CMW, David and Shelia, BB)*

Gunthorpe [Trentside], *Unicorn*: Picturesque riverside setting, well furnished hotel but with well kept Mansfield Old Baily and Theakstons Old Peculier and wide range of good value food in bar and smart panelled restaurant; busy with summer river trade; bedrooms *(P A Legon, Clive Gilbert)*

Hoveringham [Main St; SK6946], *Reindeer*: Open fires in bar and lounge, lots of beams, some antiques; friendly and unpretentious, with popular bar food, well kept Marstons Pedigree *(Chris Raisin, Graham Doyle)*

Kirkby in Ashfield [opp former Bentinck Mine; SK5056], *Countryman*: Upgraded former miners' local, traditional atmosphere, attractive bas relief murals of shooting scenes, mining memorabilia, Theakstons and guest beers, generous bar food *(Peter and Audrey Dowsett)*

Linby [Main St; SK5351], *Horse & Groom*: Theakstons XB, bar food (restricted Tues to good choice of hot and cold filled rolls); in attractive village nr Newstead Abbey *(David Atkinson)*

Lowdham [1 Southwell Rd; SK6646], *Magna Charta*: Attractive Hardys & Hansons pub with good range of food, plenty of tables, garden, lots of busy young staff; special children's lavatory *(Jenny and Michael Back)*

✩ Maplebeck [signed from A616/A617; SK7160], *Beehive*: Snug little unspoiled beamed country tavern unchanged by (local) new owners, traditional furnishings, open fire, free antique juke box, well kept Mansfield Riding and Old Baily, tables on small terrace with flower tubs and grassy bank running down to small stream – very peaceful; play area with swings; may be cl Mon lunchtime *(JJW, CMW, Chris Raisin, Graham Doyle, BB)*

✩ Morton [back rd SE of Southwell; SK7251], *Full Moon*: Comfortable L-shaped lounge in welcoming 16th-c local, good value freshly cooked generous food (may be a wait) inc lots of puddings; well kept Theakstons and guest beers, enthusiastic landlord, children welcome, pool and TV in separate games room, no piped music or dogs; big garden with terrace, picnic tables, play area; delightfully out-of-the-way hamlet *(Jack Morley, JJW, CMW, Irene and Geoffrey Lindley)*

Newark [19 Kirkgate; SK8054], *Old Kings Arms*: Distinguished old building with pleasantly refurbished and extended vaulted-ceiling bar, very generous cheap straightforward food, well kept Marstons,

upstairs partly no-smoking eating area *(David and Shelia, David Carr, Geoffrey Lindley, LYM)*

✩ Nottingham [18 Angel Row; off Market Sq], *Bell*: Quaint low-beamed 15th-c pub enjoyed by all ages, Boddingtons, Jennings Mild, Marstons Pedigree, Theakstons XB, Ruddles County and a guest like Black Sheep Special kept well in extraordinarily deep sandstone cellar, three bustling timbered and panelled bars (very crowded and maybe smoky late evening), ancient stairs to attractive calmer raftered room with nice window seats used as lunchtime family restaurant – good value simple well presented lunchtime food; good value wines, friendly hard-working staff; trad jazz Sun lunchtime (rolls only then), Mon and Tues evenings; open all day weekdays *(R M Taylor, Norma and Keith Bloomfield, Geoffrey and Irene Lindley, Elizabeth and Anthony Watts, M Rutherford, SLC, LYM)*

✩ Nottingham [40 Broad St; corner of Lower Parliament St, on inner ring rd], *New Market*: Austerely neo-classical facade, well kept Scottish Courage ales, interesting array of gins from magnificent engraved bottles, comfortable back bar with carved fittings, open fire in snug, occasional Victorian or Edwardian themed entertainment, efficient staff, good value food inc some interesting dishes *(Russell and Carolynne Allen, M Rutherford, LYM)*

Nottingham [nr Theatre Royal], *Applejacks*: Good value plain food esp bread and cheese, cider and perry brewed for the pub, guests such as Addlestone's, Weston's and Thatcher's, some beers *(Pat and Tony Martin)*; [2 Canal St], *Canal*: This attractive pub has been demolished to make way for a new development *(Anon)*; [Lincoln St, Old Basford; SK5442], *Fox & Crown*: Pleasantly refurbished open-plan local with back microbrewery producing its own Fiddlers Bitter, Mild, Finest and Porter; freshly prepared reasonably priced meals in dining area, helpful staff *(Alan Bowker, Richard Houghton)*; [Wellington Circus], *Limelight*: Lively long bar and restaurant attached to Playhouse theatre, nine constantly changing well kept ales, good choice of reasonably priced food, urbane atmosphere, theatre pictures, occasional modern jazz, seats outside; same group as Lincolnshire Poacher *(Derek and Sylvia Stephenson, M Rutherford, R M Taylor, SLC)*; [Lower Mosley St, New Basford; SK5541], *Lion*: Recently refurbished in contemporary open-plan spartan style, with very wide range of real ales, good choice of good home-cooked food and sandwiches; frequent jazz nights *(Alan Bowker, Colin Sims)*; [Alfreton Rd], *Red Lion*: A dozen interesting well kept ales, good reasonably priced food with Tues supper bargain, traditional atmosphere, Sun breakfast with papers; open all day, Mon quiz night *(D J Atkinson)*; [St Nicholas St, Castlegate], *Royal Children*: Three basic but comfortable bars with lots of panelling and old pictures, busy but relaxed, good choice of well kept beers, good bar meals *(M Rutherford)*; [Maid Marion Way], *Salutation*: Ancient back part with beams, flagstones and cosy corners, plusher modern front, cheap cheerful food, up to a dozen or more changing ales, sensible prices and good atmosphere *(N Gilbourne, SLC, Roger and Jenny Huggins, M Rutherford, BB)*; [1 Ilkeston Rd (A52 towards Derby)], *Sir John Borlase Warren*: Traditional local with several connecting rooms, lots of old prints, interesting Victorian decorations and fittings, well kept Greenalls Original, Shipstones, Tetleys, also guests tapped from the cask; cheap lunchtime bar food, no-smoking eating area, tables in back garden with barbecues; children welcome (not Fri/Sat evenings) *(Alan Hopkin, Chris Raisin, Graham Doyle, LYM)*; [Gordon Sq, West Bridgford; SK5837], *Test Match*: Art deco, with revolving door, high ceiling and sweeping staircase (to the lounge and lavatories); unspoilt, with big cricketing prints, some signed bats *(Chris Raisin, Graham Doyle)*

Nuthall [Nottingham Rd (B600, away from city), off A610 nr M1 junction 26; SK5144], *Three Ponds*: Friendly and tastefully refurbished Hardys & Hansons roadhouse with wide range of good value food inc OAP bargains, well kept Best, Best Mild and Classic, good coffee, good staff; piped music may obtrude; big back garden with play area *(Kev Jackson, Mike and Penny Sanders)*

Ollerton [Market Pl (off A614); SK6667], *Hop Pole*: Old coaching inn, pretty village setting, good value bar food and carvery, two sittings for Sun lunch, good friendly service, singing chef; good disabled access; comfortable bedrooms *(B A Grocott)*

Orston [Church St; SK7741], *Durham Ox*: Cosy and welcoming split-level open-plan local, tasty rolls, well kept ales, interesting collection of whisky bottles, local photographs, tables outside (and hitching rails for horses) *(R M Taylor)*

Plumtree [just off A606 S of Nottingham; SK6132], *Griffin*: Civilised and tastefully refurbished, popular generous food in airy conservatory, well kept Hardys & Hansons *(Chris Raisin)*

☆ Retford [off West Carr Rd, Ordsall; follow Leisure Centre signs from A620 then just after industrial estate sign keep eyes skinned for pub sign on left; SK6980], *Market*: Exceptional choice of well kept ales, comfortable plush banquettes, good value genuine home cooking inc great fresh haddock, cheerful service *(David Carr, Pat and Tony Martin, Virginia Jones, LYM)*

Skegby [Forest Rd; SK5060], *Forest*: Comfortable and popular, with wonderful collection of plates naming every mine in Notts; friendly staff, Home and Mansfield ales, quick efficient service; filled baps, quiet piped music *(Peter and Audrey Dowsett)*

☆ Southwell [Church St (A612); SK6953], *Bramley Apple*: Friendly prompt service,

generous good value food inc two-sitting Sun carvery, fresh fish and vegetarian, very crisp veg, well kept Mansfield and guest ales, attractively worked Bramley apple theme, eating area screened off by stained glass, TV zone; bedrooms *(Norma and Keith Bloomfield, Miss E Evans, Chris Raisin, Graham Doyle, G P Kernan, Rona Murdoch, BB)*

☆ Staunton in the Vale [Main St; SK8043], *Staunton Arms*: Warm and welcoming country pub, good value food (limited Mon/Tues) with imaginative French touches in cosy bar and raised restaurant area, well kept Bass, Fullers London Pride and Marstons Pedigree, no juke box or machines, rolling Vale of Belvoir views *(Ian McLachlan, M J Morgan, David and Ruth Hollands)*

Sutton in Ashfield [bypass (A38); SK5059], *Snipe*: Roomy well furnished family pub, good choice of reasonably priced food inc OAP discounts some days, quick service, Mansfield ales, good coffee; unobtrusive piped music; play areas inside and out *(Peter and Audrey Dowsett)*

Teversal [Fackley Rd (B6014); SK4861], *Carnarvon Arms*: Village pub with modern comfort inc ship room with porthole windows and leaning cabin walls, family room; bar meals (free chip butties some nights), Mansfield ales, friendly service; can be noisy with quiz nights or karaoke *(Peter and Audrey Dowsett)*; [Carnarvon St/Skegby Rd], *Teversal Grange*: Friendly upgraded village local with big restaurant and entertainment stage, popular family room with snooker table, bar food, Mansfield and other ales such as Morlands Old Speckled Hen *(Peter and Audrey Dowsett, Robert Marshall)*

Toton [Nottingham Rd; SK5034], *Manor*: Good value Tom Cobleigh dining pub with tasty food, friendly efficient service, big no-smoking area, Boddingtons, Flowers IPA, Ruddles County, Worthington and guest ales, several cheap wines by bottle; handy for Attenborough Nature Reserve – good birdwatching, fine walks *(Mike and Penny Sanders)*

☆ Upton [Main St (A612); SK7354], *Cross Keys*: Rambling heavy-beamed bar with good welcoming service, lots of alcoves, central log fire, masses to look at from sporting cartoons and local watercolours to decorative plates and metalwork, interesting medley of furnishings; well kept Batemans XXXB, Boddingtons, Brakspears, Marstons Pedigree and local Springhead, decent wines, popular fairly priced food; friendly dog, unobtrusive piped music, folk evenings; children in back extension with carved pews or dovecote restaurant *(Keith Wells, Derek and Sylvia Stephenson, David Carr, June and Malcolm Farmer, LYM)*

Warsop [Peafield Lane, off A6075 NE of Mansfield; SK5665], *Redbrick House*: Comfortable and friendly bar in former farm building surrounded by forest and farmland, good range of ales, good value creative food in bar and restaurant inc bargain meals for two, good service *(B A Grocott)*

☆ **Watnall Chaworth** [3 miles from M1 junction 26: A610 towards Nottingham, left on to B600, then keep right; SK5046], *Queens Head*: Tastefully extended old pub with wide range of good value food, well kept Home Bitter and Mild, Theakstons XB and Old Peculier, efficient friendly service; snug bar and dining area, beams and stripped pine, coal fires; fruit machine, piped music; picnic tables in spacious garden with big play area; open all day Fri/Sat *(N Gilbourne, Mike and Penny Sanders)*

☆ **West Leake** [off A6006; SK5226], *Star*: Traditional beamed and quarry-tiled country bar with a good deal of character, hunting trophies, wall settles, comfortable partly panelled lounge with good log fire, short choice of good value simple weekday lunchtime food, well kept Bass and Marstons Pedigree; children in eating area *(Chris Raisin, LYM)*

Wilford [Main Rd; just off A52 S of Nottingham; SK5637], *Ferryboat*: Clean traditional pub with low ceilings and bare boards, two snugs, dining lounge with lofted roof and imposing fireplace; decent food, well kept sensibly priced ales, tidy back terrace, garden with play area, view over river to Nottingham Castle *(Peter and Jenny Quine)*

Worksop [112 Bridge St; SK5879], *Lion*: 16th-c coaching inn extended behind, obliging service, reasonably priced bar food, enjoyable restaurant; good value bedrooms *(Gordon Neighbour)*

Wysall [off A60 at Costock, or A6006 at Wymeswold; SK6027], *Plough*: Lively and attractive 17th-c beamed country local, well kept Bass and guest ales, very welcoming staff, nice mix of furnishings, soft lighting, lovely log fire, dog and cat wandering about, french doors to terrace and good compact garden with barbecues Fri night, Sun afternoon; no cooked lunches Sun *(A and R Cooper, R M Taylor, Chris Raisin)*

If a service charge is mentioned prominently on a menu or accommodation terms, you must pay it if service was satisfactory. If service is really bad you are legally entitled to refuse to pay some or all of the service charge as compensation for not getting the service you might reasonably have expected.

Oxfordshire

A lot of changes here this year: new licensees in the Red Lion at Adderbury, the Romany at Bampton (still doing very cheap food), the Crown at Church Enstone (very friendly, refurbished throughout), the Pear Tree in Hook Norton, and the handsome old Shaven Crown at Shipton under Wychwood; the Falkland Arms at Great Tew has been given up by the Milligans and is now a Wadworths pub, under management, but still well worth a visit as a striking piece of old England. The pretty new night-lit terrace at the Chequers at Burcot has been popular this last summer; the Clanfield Tavern at Clanfield no longer lets bedrooms, but its refurbishments are good (kitchen on view, conservatory); and the Trout at Tadpole Bridge has a bit more space for diners, and more peace for drinkers, after relocating the kitchen and cellar. Among new entries, the Milligans are back in the Guide, this time at the Reindeer in Banbury – a stunning building; the charming Red Lion at Chalgrove, owned by the church for at least 350 years, has very good food; the flagstoned White Horse at Duns Tew is an attractive country retreat; the Kings Arms in Oxford is good on any terms as a town pub, but splendid as a slice of Oxford life; and, after an absence, the civilised and relaxed Kings Head at Wootton comes back into these pages under a newish landlord on such sparkling form that it earns our award as Oxfordshire Dining Pub of the Year. Other pubs doing specially well here this year include the very well run Five Bells at Broadwell, the civilised old Lamb in Burford (a special favourite), the chatty and enjoyable Half Moon at Cuxham, the lovely medieval White Hart at Fyfield, the charmingly set Bell at Shenington (good food), the classic traditional Red Lion at Steeple Aston (super wine list), and the bustling Crown at Toot Baldon (huge helpings of homely food). Some pubs to mention particularly in the Lucky Dip section at the end of the chapter are the Lamb at Buckland, Bell at Charlbury (and for food the very restauranty Bull there), Hand & Shears at Church Hanborough (another foody place), Vine at Cumnor, renamed Deddington Arms at Deddington, Trout at Godstow (a classic), Old Swan at Minster Lovell, Lamb at Satwell, Crooked Billet at Stoke Row (another very restauranty place), Six Bells at Warborough (first-class new licensees) and North Arms at Wroxton; we have inspected and can firmly vouch for most of these. Oxford itself has a fine choice of good pubs. Drinks prices in the county's pubs tend to be higher than the national average, with those supplied by the big national chains (or tied to Brakspears of Henley) charging most; pubs supplied by Hook Norton were generally much cheaper than average – especially the Romany at Bampton and Bell at Shenington.

The Post Office makes it virtually impossible for people to come to grips with British geography, by using a system of post towns which are often across the county boundary from the places they serve. So the postal address of a pub often puts it in the wrong county. We use the correct county – the one the pub is actually in. Lots of pubs which the Post Office alleges are in Oxfordshire are actually in Berkshire, Buckinghamshire, Gloucestershire or the Midlands.

ADDERBURY SP4635 Map 4
Red Lion ♀ 🛏

A4260 S of Banbury; not far from M40 junction 11

Originally called The Crown, this smartly civilised inn was prudently renamed when the Roundheads occupied the village. The right-hand bar has a lovely big inglenook, high stripped beams, prints, and comfortable chairs, and the left-hand bar is more for eating, with cosy floral tablecloths, and leads through to the comfortable and prettily decorated residents' lounge. On one of the terracotta walls is a list of all the landlords since 1690, along with various quotations and pithy sayings. The attractive back dining room is no smoking. Under the new licensee, the good – if not cheap – bar food includes home-made soup (£2.50), filled french bread (from £3.75), stilton and port pâté (£4.25), filled baked potatoes (from £4.25), various pasta dishes (from £6.95), home-made pie of the day (£8.95), chicken fillet in a wild mushroom sauce (£10.50), seafood mornay (£10.95), duck breast in orange and port sauce (£11.95), fillet steak (£13.95), daily specials, and puddings (£3.25). Well kept Hook Norton Best, Marstons Pedigree, and Websters Yorkshire on handpump, and several wines by the glass. Tables out on the well kept garden terrace. *(Recommended by Gordon, S Williamson, Piotr Chodzko-Zajko, Maysie Thompson, Dave Braisted, Mrs J Oakes, M L and G Clarke; more reports on the new regime, please)*

Free house ~ Licensees Alan and Linda Clarke ~ Real ale ~ Meals and snacks (till 10pm) ~ Restaurant ~ (01295) 810269 ~ Children in eating area of bar ~ Open 11-11; 11-3, 6-11 winter; 12-3, 7-10.30 Sun ~ Bedrooms: £47.50B/£65B

ARDINGTON SU4388 Map 2
Boars Head 🍴 ♀

Village signposted off A417 Didcot—Wantage, 2 miles E of Wantage

As well as running a very successful and civilised dining pub, the enthusiastic Basterfields have also started up their own business producing top quality oils and dressings which they use in the imaginative dishes produced here: sweet pepper sauce, orange and honey dressing, bitter chocolate sauce and so forth. From constantly changing blackboards, the food might include filled ciabatta bread and toasted bagels (from £2.80), home-made soup (£3), glazed artichoke and cherry tomato tart (£4.95), ploughman's (£5), Chinese chicken and prawn noodles (£10.95), salmon and mushroom hotpot (£11), chump of lamb with basil and tomato (£13.95), and puddings like roast banana with butterscotch sauce and banana ice cream with a honey tuille or rhubarb and lemon tart (£4). Fullers London Pride, Mansfield Riding, and Morlands Original on handpump kept under light blanket pressure, a good wine list, fresh fruit juices, and draught cider; caring, friendly service. The three simply furnished but smart interconnecting rooms have low beams and timbers, a few notices and pictures on the pale warm apricot walls above the dado, fresh flowers, and a pleasant light-coloured wood block floor. One room is primarily for eating, with pine settles and well spaced big pine tables, the others have smaller country tables and chairs – still with room for drinkers. Shove-ha'penny, dominoes, cribbage, trivia, and piped music. In a peaceful and attractive village, the pub is part of the Ardington estate; good walks nearby. *(Recommended by Gordon, R V G Brown, Julia Cohen, R Watkins, Richard Judd, MLC, GC, Sue Demont, Tim Barrow; more reports please)*

Free house ~ Licensees Duncan and Elizabeth Basterfield ~ Real ale ~ Meals and snacks (not Sun evening, not Mon) ~ Restaurant ~ (01235) 833254 ~ Well behaved children welcome ~ Open 11.30-2.30, 6-11; 12-3, 7-10.30 Sun; closed Mon

BAMPTON SP3013 Map 4
Romany £ 🍴

Bridge St; off A4095 SW of Witney

You'd be very hard pushed to find a decent meal cheaper than one of the dishes served in this unassuming 17th-c local – particularly in this area – and the beer is 26p cheaper that the county average, too. The comfortable bars have plush cushioned windsor chairs and stools around wooden tables, foreign currency notes from all over the world, plates and prints on the partly stripped stone walls, and a winter open fire. Under the new licensee, the menu includes club sandwiches or filled croissants (from £2.25), home-made soup (£1.25), home-made pâté (£1.75), filled baked potatoes (from £2.50), lasagne or spaghetti carbonara (£3.25), pork in cider casserole or chicken curry (£3.95), mixed grill (£6.50), daily specials, and a Monday curry night (including a pudding, £3.50), and a Tuesday pie night (including a pudding, £4.95); best to book for their popular 3-course Sunday lunch. The restaurant is no smoking. Well kept Archers Village, Donnington SBA, Hook Norton Best, Wadworths 6X, and a guest beer handpumped from the Saxon cellars below the bar; cribbage, dominoes, fruit machine, and piped music. The big garden has picnic tables, Aunt Sally, and a children's play area with tree house, see-saw, and mushroom slide and house. *(Recommended by Tom McLean, Mrs Kay Neville-Rolfe, Derek and Sylvia Stephenson, Gordon, Keith Macaulay, Marjorie and David Lamb; more reports on the new regime, please)*

Free house ~ Licensees Robert and Tessa Smith ~ Real ale ~ Meals and snacks (11.30-2.30, 6-9.30) ~ Restaurant ~ (01993) 850237 ~ Well behaved children welcome ~ Open 11-11; 12-4, 7-11 Sun ~ Bedrooms: £21B/£30B

BANBURY SP4540 Map 4
Reindeer £
47 Parsons Street, off Market Place

John and Hazel Milligan, who made the Falkland Arms at Great Tew one of Britain's best-loved traditional country pubs before its sale to Wadworths, have put the same commitment into this interesting old place. When it reopened after careful restoration a few years ago, Mr Milligan said that he hoped to attract Banbury's more seasoned drinkers, and the bar certainly has all the ingredients that lubricated the Falkland Arms atmosphere so richly – well kept Hook Norton Best, Old, Mild, and Generation and a monthly changing guest ale on handpump, country wines, 30 Irish whiskeys, good coffee, even snuffs and clay pipes for the more adventurous. Restoration seems to have consisted largely in stripping out the mediocre modern 'olde' trappings that we remember from a previous visit in 1981, and letting the building's genuine antiquity speak for itself. Outside are massive stone-mullioned windows into the cellars, handsome curved steps, and formidable Tudor gates; the long front room has heavy 16th-c beams, very broad polished oak floorboards scattered with rugs, a magnificent carved overmantel for one of the two roaring log fires, and traditional solid furnishings. Ask to be shown the Globe Room: this beautifully proportioned room, where Cromwell held court before the Battle of Edgehill, has since our previous visit had its original gloriously carved 17th-c panelling restored to it, after a remarkable odyssey which involved exile first in an Islington warehouse and then in what used to be the Banbury council chambers. Lunchtime bar food includes doorstep or hot sandwiches (from £1.80), home-made chicken liver pâté (£2.80), bubble and squeak with ham, egg and baked beans (£3), filled baked potatoes (from £3), ploughman's (from £3.20), shepherd's pie (£3.30), steak in ale pie (£4.50), and daily specials such as courgette and red pepper soup (£1.80), mushrooms in stilton and garlic sauce or pasta dishes like tagliatelle with smoked salmon (from £3), fish such as grilled red snapper or trout with mustard sauce (from £3.50), orange and ginger chicken or lamb chops with redcurrant sauce (£3.80), and cod and prawn crumble (£3.80); they do a Thursday OAP special. A smaller back room up steps is no smoking at lunchtime. Efficient cheerful service; unobtrusive piped music. The grey fluffy cat is called Cromwell and the tabby, Oliver. Small back courtyard with picnic tables under parasols, and Aunt Sally, and pretty flowering baskets in front; no under-21s (but see below). *(Recommended by Charles Gysin, George Atkinson, Kevin and Penny McDonald, Ted George)*

Hook Norton ~ Tenants John and Hazel Milligan ~ Real ale ~ Lunchtime meals and snacks ~ (01295) 264031 ~ Children in Globe Room lunchtime only if eating ~ Open 11-11; closed Sun and 25 Dec

Pubs with attractive or unusually big gardens are listed at the back of the book.

BARFORD ST MICHAEL SP4332 Map 4
George

Lower Street, at N end of village: coming from Bloxham, take first right turn

This 300-year-old golden stone pub has a thatched roof, mullioned windows, and a good chatty local atmosphere. The three rambling modernised rooms have open fires, cushioned rustic seats and captain's chairs around the dark wood tables, and quite a few company and regimental ties hanging from the beams, most donated by customers. Over the fireplace there's a big painting of the Battle of Agincourt, using many of the locals as the soldiers, and assorted mugs and tankards, horsebrasses, and an old organ. Bar food includes sandwiches, lamb balti or chicken kiev (£5.30), breaded trout with almonds (£6.30), vegetarian dishes, and fresh pizzas (which they will deliver). Well kept Adnams Broadside, Fullers London Pride, and Morlands Original and Old Speckled Hen on handpump, and lots of country wines. Darts, pool, shove-ha'penny, table skittles, cribbage, dominoes, fruit machine, video game, and piped music. The pleasant garden has picnic tables, a giant chess set, boules, an adventure playground, and views over fields. Just up the road is a caravan/camp site with trout fishing. *(Recommended by CMW, JJW, Gordon, Daren Haines, Brian and Anna Marsden, Simon Collett-Jones)*

Free house ~ Licensees Spencer and Theresa Richards ~ Real ale ~ Meals and snacks (not Mon) ~ Restaurant ~ (01869) 338226 ~ Children welcome ~ Blues Mon evenings ~ Open 12-2.30, 6-11; 12-11 summer Sat; 12-3, 7-10.30 Sun

BARNARD GATE SP4010 Map 4
Boot

Village signposted off A40 E of Witney

True to its name, this friendly dining pub has quite a collection of celebrities' boots displayed on the walls. The decor is pleasant and civilised, with good solid country tables and chairs on bare boards, and stout standing timbers and stub walls with latticed glass breaking up the main area; there's a huge log fire. Served by very willing staff, the good food might include soup (£2.25), grilled king prawns with dip and garlic bread (£4.25), pasta with shredded chicken, bacon, shallots, mushrooms, cream and chilli (£7.80), minute steak with pepper sauce (£8), steak and kidney pudding (£8.30), casserole of beans and pulses (£8.65), thai chilli chicken curry (£9.20), scottish salmon with a basil cream sauce (£10.80), Aberdeen Angus steak (£14), daily specials (mostly under £8), and puddings like sticky toffee pudding (£3.75); part of the restaurant is no smoking. Well kept Hook Norton Best and Morlands Old Speckled Hen on handpump, and decent wines. There are tables out in front of the stone-tiled stone pub, which despite being so handy for the A40 is out of earshot. *(Recommended by TRS, John and Hazel Waller, D G Hayman, A J Carter, M Sargent)*

Free house ~ George Dailey ~ Real ale ~ Meals and snacks (till 10pm) ~ Restaurant ~ (01865) 881231 ~ Children welcome ~ Piano Mon, Weds, Fri evenings ~ Open 11-11; 12-10.30 Sun; closed 25 Dec

BINFIELD HEATH SU7478 Map 2
Bottle & Glass ★

Village signposted off A4155 at Shiplake; in village centre fork right immediately after Post Office (signposted Harpsden) and keep on for half mile

Parts of this very pretty thatched and black and white timbered pub are 15th c and it was probably three little farm cottages before its conversion 287 years ago. The neatly kept bar has attractive flagstones, low beams, a roaring log fire in the big fireplace, and scrubbed, ancient tables, a bench built into black squared panelling, and spindleback chairs. The smaller, relaxed side room, similarly decorated, has a window with diamond-scratched family records of earlier landlords. Written up on blackboards, the range of promptly served bar food might include lunchtime sandwiches, large mussels (£4.95), smoked salmon salad (£6.75), large gammon and egg or beef Oxford (£7.25), half a guinea fowl (£8.50), 10oz steak (£9.75), and noisettes of lamb (£10.50); friendly staff. Brakspears Bitter, and seasonal Old or Special on handpump, and quite a few malt whiskies. The lovely big garden has old-fashioned wooden seats and tables under little thatched roofs (and an open-sided shed like a rustic pavilion). No children or dogs. *(Recommended by Sandra Kench, Steven Norman, TBB; more reports please)*

Brakspears ~ Tenants Mike and Anne Robinson ~ Real ale ~ Meals and snacks (12-1.45, 7-9.30; not Sun evening) ~ (01491) 575755 ~ Open 11-3, 6-11; 12-3, 7-10.30 Sun

BIX SU7285 Map 2
Fox
On A4130 Henley—Wallingford

During the week, this friendly creeper-clad country pub is a fine place to come for a peaceful drink in a relaxed, pubby atmosphere – it does get busier at weekends. The cosy L-shaped lounge bar has panelling, beams, armchairs and settles making the most of the big log fires, and gleaming brasses. There's another log fire and some settles in the connecting wood-floored farmers' bar, with darts, dominoes and a fruit machine. Promptly served bar food includes sandwiches, filled baked potatoes (from £3.25), ratatouille (£4.55), ham and two eggs (£4.95), ham and mushroom tagliatelle or cheese and broccoli pasta bake (£5.50), popular game dishes, evening rump steak (£6.95), and Sunday roast (£5.95). Well kept Brakspears Bitter and seasonal Old or Special on handpump, picnic tables in the good-sized garden behind. The friendly dog is called Henry, and there's a much-used hitching rail for horses outside. No children. *(Recommended by Chris Glasson, Gordon Prince, Bill Ingham, TBB, Joan Olivier, A C Morrison, Eric Locker, Dr G W Barnett)*

Brakspears ~ Tenants Richard and Sue Willson ~ Real ale ~ Meals and snacks (not Mon evening) ~ (01491) 574134 ~ Open 11-3, 7-11; 12-3, 7-10.30 Sun; closed 25 Dec

BLEWBURY SU5385 Map 2
Red Lion
Take the lane with the tree in the middle; off the A417

This is a restful village pub with a steadily ticking station clock and no noisy games machines or music to disturb the relaxing atmosphere. The engaging beamed bar has upholstered wall benches and armed seats on its scrubbed quarry tiles, cupboards and miniature cabinets filled with ornaments, and foreign banknotes on the beams; in winter you can roast chestnuts over the big open fire. Good bar food includes filled french bread, good triple decker turkey sandwich (£3), ratatouille with pasta (£5.75), smoked salmon and scrambled egg (£6.50), and rack of lamb with a herb and garlic crust, pork with cider and apple sauce, and chicken breast with tarragon and cream (£6.50-£7.50); the restaurant is no smoking. Well kept Boddingtons and Brakspears Bitter, Old Ale and Special on handpump, decent wines, and good range of non-alcoholic drinks; attentive service. The extended garden has a terrace with quite a few seats and tables. *(Recommended by TBB, Mary Walters, Tim Brierly, Gordon; more reports please)*

Brakspears ~ Tenant Roger Smith ~ Real ale ~ Meals and snacks ~ Restaurant (weekends) ~ (01235) 850403 ~ Children in restaurant ~ Open 11-2.30(3 Sat), 6-11; 12-3, 7-10.30 Sun ~ Bedrooms: £25/£35

BLOXHAM SP4235 Map 4
Elephant & Castle £
Humber Street; off A361, fairly hndy for M40 junction 11

The relaxed and elegantly simple public bar here has a striking 17th-c stone fireplace and a strip wood floor, and the comfortable lounge is divided into two by a very thick wall, and has a good winter log fire in its massive fireplace, too; sensibly placed darts, dominoes, cribbage, fruit machine, and trivia, and they have been using the same hardy shove-ha'penny board for over a century now. Good value straightforward lunchtime bar food (they tell us prices have not increased since last year) includes soup, decent sandwiches, sausage, eggs and beans (£3), and steak and kidney pie, lasagne, or haddock (£3.50). Well kept Hook Norton Best (cheaper than the county average), Old Hookey, Generation, summer Haymaker, Twelve Days, and Double Stout, and guest beers on handpump; quite a few malt whiskies. The flower-filled extended yard has Aunt Sally in summer and maybe weekend barbecues. *(Recommended by David Carr, Ted George, Gordon, Alan and Paul McCully, Tom Evans)*

Hook Norton ~ Tenants Chas and Simon Finch ~ Real ale ~ Lunchtime meals and snacks (not Sun) ~ Restaurant (not Sun) ~ (01295) 720383 ~ Children in eating area of bar and in restaurant ~ Open 10-3, 6(5 Sat)-11; 12-10.30 Sun

BROADWELL SP2503 Map 4
Five Bells

Village signposted off A361 N of Lechlade, and off B4020 S of Carterton

Run by a welcoming and considerate licensee, this former coaching inn is much liked by readers at the moment. The neatly kept series of well furnished rooms have a pleasant mix of flagstones and carpeting, low beams, antique pistols, plates and rural pictures on the walls, and big warming log fires. The sizeable dining room to the right of the lounge, and the small conservatory (both no smoking), overlook the spacious, attractive garden – where they play Aunt Sally, and grow some of the vegetables used in the kitchen. A wide choice of reliably enjoyable bar food includes sandwiches, soup (£2.25), stilton mushrooms (£3.50), vegetable pasta bake (£5.25), salmon and prawn gratin or steak and kidney pie (£5.50), honey-glazed lamb steak (£5.95), pheasant in red wine or grilled swordfish (£6.50), steaks (from £8.95), and puddings like fruit crumbles or pavlovas; good vegetables in separate tureens. Well kept Hook Norton Best, Wadworths 6X, and a guest such as Oakhill Bitter on handpump, and decent house wine. The public bar has darts; piped music. Wheelchair access. *(Recommended by Ted George, Marjorie and David Lamb, Joan Olivier, Kay Neville-Rolfe, HNJ, PEJ, G W A Pearce, D P Bailey, Peter and Audrey Dowsett)*

Free house ~ Licensees Trevor and Ann Cooper ~ Real ale ~ Meals and snacks (not Mon) ~ Restaurant (not Mon) ~ (01367) 860076 ~ Children in eating areas – must be over 7 on Sat evening ~ Open 11.30-2.30, 6.30-11; 12-3, 7-10.30 Sun; closed Mon except bank hol lunchtimes ~ Chalet bedrooms: /£45B

BURCOT SU5695 Map 4
Chequers

A415 Dorchester—Abingdon

This year, a terrace with seats, pretty plants, and night lighting has been added to this attractive black and white thatched pub; they've also created a vegetable patch at the lower end of the garden to grow their own salad and herb produce. The mass of pots, mixed bedding plants, trailing plants and hanging baskets looks lovely, and there are tables and chairs among roses and fruit trees on the neatly kept roadside lawn. Inside, the smartly comfortable and surprisingly spacious lounge has beams, an open fire, and a very relaxed and friendly atmosphere; the Weekses have now been here for 20 years and plan some celebrations this year. Well kept Brakspears, Ruddles County, and Ushers Best on handpump, with some good whiskies, unusual liqueurs, and a large collection of miniatures in dispay cabinets. Home-made bar food – using fresh local supplies – includes filled french bread (£2.25), home-made soup (£2.25), chicken and apricot pie or steak and kidney pudding (£5.50), gammon steak (£7.50), sirloin steak (£8.50), and puddings such as Mary's disaster cake or syrup pudding (£2.25); they bake their own bread daily; traditional Sunday roast. They have their own decent little no-smoking art gallery. *(Recommended by B and K Hypher, Jenny and Brian Seller; more reports please)*

Free house ~ Lease: Mary and Michael Weeks ~ Real ale ~ Meals and snacks (not Sun evening) ~ (01865) 407771 ~ Children in eating area of bar and in gallery ~ Grand piano Sat evenings ~ Open 11-2.30, 6-11; 12-3, 7-10.30 Sun

BURFORD SP2512 Map 4

Lamb ★★ ⑪ 🛏 ♀ ◀

Sheep Street; A40 W of Oxford

The unchanging character and atmosphere of this civilised 500-year-old Cotswold inn appeals a great deal to people – indeed, to many, it's an old favourite. The spacious beamed main lounge has distinguished old seats including a chintzy high winged settle, ancient cushioned wooden armchairs, and seats built into its stone-mullioned windows, bunches of flowers on polished oak and elm tables, oriental rugs on the wide flagstones and polished oak floorboards, and a winter log fire under its fine mantelpiece. Also, a writing desk and grandfather clock, and attractive pictures, shelves of plates and other antique decorations. The public bar has high-backed settles and old chairs on flagstones in front of its fire. There may be nibbles on the bar counter, as well as good bar lunches such as sandwiches or filled french bread (from £2.50; bacon and avocado £3.95), home-made soups like lentil and ham (£2.95), ploughman's (£4.75), terrine of salmon, sole and monkfish with a ginger and chilli yoghurt dressing (£4.95), tagliatelle with mushrooms and provençal vegetables (£5.95), grilled fresh sardines with a tomato and tarragon sauce (£6.25), coq au vin or steak and asparagus pie (£7.50), and puddings like white chocolate and Baileys torte, gooseberry crumble or sherry trifle (£2.50). Note they don't do bar meals Sunday lunchtimes (three courses with a bucks fizz to start, £17.50); the restful formal restaurant is no smoking. Well kept Hook Norton Best and Wadworths IPA, 6X and winter Old Timer are dispensed from an antique handpump beer engine in a glassed-in cubicle; good wines. A pretty terrace leads down to small neatly-kept lawns surrounded by flowers, flowering shrubs and small trees, and the garden itself can be really sunny, enclosed as it is by the warm stone of the surrounding buildings. *(Recommended by Rona Murdoch, John and Chris Simpson, Paul Williams, Alan and Paula McCully, Pam Adsley, Rob Whittle, Liz Bell, Paul McPherson, John and Hazel Waller, James Nunns,   Basil Minson, Brian Wainwright, Lynn Sharpless, Bob Eardley, Dave Irving, James Nunns, Andrew and Ruth Triggs, Malcolm Taylor, David Carr, Eric and Jackie Robinson, Dr I Maine, M J Dowdy)*

Free house ~ Licensee Richard de Wolf ~ Real ale ~ Lunchtime bar meals and snacks (not Sun) ~ Evening restaurant ~ (01993) 823155 ~ Children welcome ~ Open 11-2.30, 6-11; 12-3, 7-10.30 Sun; closed 25-26 Dec ~ Bedrooms: £57.50B/£90B

Mermaid

High St

The handsome Tudor-style frontage of this busy pub juts out onto the broad pavement of this famously picturesque sloping Cotswold street. Inside, the attractive long and narrow bar has beams, polished flagstones, brocaded seats in bays around the single row of tables down one side, and pretty dried flowers. The inner end, with a figurehead over the fireplace and toby jugs hanging from the beams, is panelled, the rest has stripped stonework; there's also a no-smoking dining conservatory and upstairs restaurant. Bar food is usefully served all day and might include soup (£3), filled french bread (from £3.50), filled baked potatoes or omelettes (£4.95), fish of the day (from £4.95), filled yorkshire puddings (£5.65), chicken curry (£5.95), steak and kidney pie (£6.95), a roast of the day (from £6.95), daily specials, children's menu, puddings, and afternoon cream teas. Well kept Morlands Original, Old Masters, and Old Speckled Hen on handpump; fruit machine, piped music. There are picnic tables under cocktail parasols. *(Recommended by Liz Bell, Mr and Mrs N Spink, KM, JM, Andrew and Ruth Triggs, Dr S Willavoys, Brian Wainwright, R D Greaves, Alan and Paula McCully, Simon Collett-Jones, David Carr, Pat and Roger Fereday, R and A Cooper)*

Morlands ~ Lease: John Titcombe ~ Real ale ~ Meals and snacks (noon-9.45pm) ~ Restaurant ~ (01993) 822193 ~ Children in restaurant ~ Parking may be difficult ~ Open 10.30-11; 12-10.30 Sun; closed evening 25 Dec

CHALGROVE SU6396 Map 4
Red Lion

High St (B480 Watlington—Stadhampton)

Opposite the village cross, and behind the little stream that runs right along the pretty partly thatched main street, this delightful pub has been owned by the local church ever since it first appeared in written records in 1637, and probably a good deal longer: some of the timbers date back to the 11th c. Though the style and atmosphere of the place are very traditional (it's clearly still a centre of the community), there's a smartly contemporary twist to the decor. All the walls are painted a crisp white contrasting sharply with the simple dark furnishings, the windows have neatly chequered green curtains and fresh flowers, and there's an old woodburner and a log fire. Across from the fireplace is a painting of the landlady's aunt, and there are a few carefully collected prints and period cartoons; piped music, darts in the tiled public bar. Imaginative and very well presented bar food might include baked spinach and goat's cheese tartlet with cumberland sauce (£3.95), crostini of duck breast with wild mushrooms and dressed leaves (£4.95), medallions of pork with caramelised coarse grain mustard and a madeira sauce (£7.95), chicken filled with stilton and prawns in a white wine sauce (£8.95), excellent grilled lemon sole and salmon plait with roasted vegetables, red peppers and a touch of balsamic vinegar (£10.95), and home-made puddings (£3.25); potatoes usually come in a separate side dish. The helpful landlord will generally open a bottle of wine and buy back the remainder if you don't finish it. Well kept Brakspears, Fullers London Pride and two or three guests like Marlow Bottom Mutiny or Ringwood Fortyniner on handpump; attentive individual service. The back dining room (sometimes used for functions) is no smoking. There's a good big garden behind with a variety of well spaced furnishings (including a park bench) and play equipment, and more tables in front, attractively floodlit at night. The church has some notable medieval wall paintings. *(Recommended by Marjorie and David Lamb, Joan Olivier, R J Chenery)*

Free house ~ Licensees Jonathan and Maggi Hewitt ~ Real ale ~ meals and snacks (not Sun evening) ~ Restaurant (not Sun evening) ~ (01865) 890625 ~ Well behaved children welcome ~ Open 12-3, 5.30(6 Fri and Sat)-11

CHECKENDON SU6684 Map 2
Black Horse

Village signposted off A4074 Reading—Wallingford; coming from that direction, go straight through village towards Stoke Row, then turn left (the second left turn after the village church); OS Sheet 175 map reference 666841

For many decades this utterly unpretentious, homely country local has been kept by the same family. It's in fine walking country, and the field opposite is a site for gymkhanas, so at times, the pub does get busy. The room with the bar counter has some tent pegs ranged above the fireplace, a reminder that they used to be made here; a homely side room has some splendidly unfashionable 1950s-look armchairs, and beyond that there's a third room; dominoes, cards. Well kept Brakspears and a few local guests like Old Luxters Barn Ale, Rebellion and West Berkshire Good Old Boy are tapped from casks in a back still room (the ladies' is back beyond that). They'll usually do fresh filled rolls (from £1.20), and keep pickled eggs. There are seats out on a verandah. Connoisseurs of antiquated lavatories will enjoy the gents'. No children. *(Recommended by Pete Baker, Dr D E Granger, David Warrellow, Jenny and Roger Huggins, Dick Brown, Gordon)*

Free House ~ Licensees Margaret and Martin Morgan ~ Real ale ~ Snacks ~ (01491) 680418 ~ Open 12-2(3.30 Sat), 7-11; 12-3.30, 7-10.30 Sun; cl evening 25 Dec

---

You are now allowed 20 minutes after 'time, please' to finish your drink – half-an-hour if you bought it in conjunction with a meal.

nr CHINNOR SU 7698 Map 4
Sir Charles Napier 🍴 ♀

Spriggs Alley; from B4009 follow Bledlow Ridge sign from Chinnor; then, up beech wood hill, fork right (signposted Radnage and Sprigg Alley) then on right; OS Sheet 165 ref 763983

Although this decidedly civilised place is almost classed as a restaurant, it does have the relaxed approach of a pub, and at quiet moments during the week you'll generally feel quite welcome coming for just a drink, particularly in the cosy and simply furnished little front bar. At other times you may find the whole place is virtually dedicated to the stylish back restaurant, and there's little point coming at weekends unless you want to eat. This is definitely somewhere to come for a treat, and a typical day's bar menu might include baked mussels with basil pesto (£5.50), toasted cheese and red pepper tart (£5.75), baked black pudding with poached egg and sauté potatoes (£6), grilled scallops with sorrel and bacon (£7.80), chargrilled calf liver with porcini and polenta (£11.50), crispy Gressingham duck with soy, lime, ginger and papaya salsa (£12.75), chargrilled tuna with confit of fennel, tomatoes, basil and coriander (£13), roast saddle of lamb with cumin, coriander and dauphinois potatoes (£13.50), puddings (£5.50), and English cheeses (£6.50); service is not included. Two-course set lunch (£13.50), and Sunday lunch is distinctly fashionable – in summer it's served in the crazy-paved back courtyard with rustic tables by an arbour of vines, honeysuckle and wisteria (lit at night by candles in terracotta lamps). An excellent range of drinks takes in well kept Wadworths 6X tapped from the cask, champagne on draught, an enormous list of exceptionally well chosen wines by the bottle (and a good few half-bottles), freshly squeezed juice, Russian vodkas and quite a few malt whiskies. Piped music is well reproduced by the huge loudspeakers, there's a good winter log fire, a smartly relaxed feel and friendly staff. The croquet lawn and paddocks by the beech woods drop steeply away to the Chilterns, and there's a boules court out here too. *(Recommended by Karen Eliot, Graham and Karen Oddey, KC; more reports please)*

Free house ~ Licensee Julie Griffiths ~ Real ale ~ Lunchtime bar meals (not Sun) ~ Restaurant ~ (01494) 483011 ~ Children welcome lunchtimes, but must be over 7 in evenings ~ Open 12-2, 6.30-11; 12-2 Sun; closed Sun evening and all day Mon

CHURCH ENSTONE SP3724 Map 4
Crown 🛏

From A44 take B4030 turn-off at Enstone

Friendly new licensees have taken over this cottagey Cotswold stone inn and have refurbished throughout. The comfortable beamed bar has open fires, gleaming brasses, windsor chairs, and local prints on the bare stone walls, and Boddingtons, Flowers Original, and Hook Norton Old Hookey on handpump from the horseshoe-shaped bar; several malt whiskies and a good wine list with nine by the glass. Good, freshly prepared bar food is served throughout the two bars and conservatory, and includes home-made soup (£2.95), tagliatelle with tomato, basil, pine nuts and parmesan (£3.95), thai green vegetable curry (£4.95), moussaka (£5.95), steak, kidney and mushroom pie (£6.95), stuffed chicken breast with oyster mushrooms (£8.95), red snapper niçoise (£9.50), steaks (from £9.75), and puddings like treacle tart, crème brûlée or sticky toffee pudding (£2.95). Cribbage, dominoes, and piped music. There are some white metal tables and chairs on the front terrace. Lots of nearby walks and the medieval church nearby is worth a visit. *(Recommended by Eddie Edwards, Mike and Wena Stevenson, Marjorie and David Lamb, P and J Shapley, Sir Nigel Foulkes, Tony Dickinson, Ted George, Pam Adsley, Margaret Dyke, Tim Brierly, Lynn Sharpless, Bob Eardley, Gordon Smith; more reports on the new regime, please)*

Free house ~ Licensees Stephen Marnham and Keith Maby ~ Real ale ~ Meals and snacks (not 25 Dec) ~ Restaurant ~ (01608) 677262 ~ Children in conservatory and upper bar area ~ Open 12-3, 7-11(10.30 Sun) ~ Bedrooms: £30(£32B)/£42(£45B)

CLANFIELD SP2802 Map 4
Clanfield Tavern ♀

A4095 5 miles S of Witney

The refurbishments here have now been completed – with great success. A new no-smoking conservatory now links the pub to a barn and there's a courtyard with a fountain just outside it; there's a new bar lounge, striking new lavatories with zebra stripes (disabled facilities, too), new kitchens (on view), and an enlarged car park. Despite this, comments from readers imply that locals and drinkers are still very much welcomed, though of course many people do come to enjoy the imaginative food. This is cooked to order (so any special dietary needs can be easily catered for) and totally home-made: cauliflower and stilton soup (£2.95), feta cheese parcels on creamed spinach with chive yoghurt (£3.95), trio of provençal vegetables on a sour tomato coulis (£7.25), marinated fillet of pork with apricot sauce (£8.95), breast of guinea fowl filled with chicken and pistachio mousse on a masala cream sauce (£10.25), fresh fillet of halibut with king prawns in white wine, garlic and rosemary (£10.95), and puddings such as steamed chocolate rum and raisin pudding with home-made white chocolate ice cream or lemon tart with plum compote (£3.25). Several flagstoned, heavy-beamed and stone-walled small rooms lead off the busy main bar, furnished with a good mix of seats, brass platters, hunting prints, and a handsome open stone fireplace crowned with a 17th-c plasterwork panel. Well kept Boddingtons, Flowers IPA, Hook Norton Best, and Marstons Pedigree on handpump, quite a few bin end wines, and several malt whiskies. It's pretty in summer, with tiny windows peeping from the heavy stone-slabbed roof and tables on a flower-bordered small lawn that look across to the village green and pond. Please note, they no longer do bedrooms. *(Recommended by TRS, Kay Neville-Rolfe, Liz Bell, John and Hazel Waller, Peter and Audrey Dowsett, Maureen Hobbs, Gordon, Pat and Derek Westcott, David Rule, M A and C R Starling, . Mike and Heather Watson, D C T and E A Frewer, Mr and Mrs Christopher Ball, Mrs Mary Walters, John Waller, Malcolm Taylor)*

Free house ~ Licensee Keith Gill ~ Real ale ~ Meals and snacks (11.30-2.30, 6-10) ~ Cottagey restaurant ~ (01367) 810223 ~ Children welcome ~ Open 11.30-2.30(3 Sat), 6-11

CLIFTON SP4831 Map 4
Duke of Cumberlands Head ♀ 🛏

B4031 Deddington—Aynho

By the time this Guide is published, the planned alterations upstairs and to the restaurant will have been completed. It's a stylish but relaxed place with a spacious, simply furnished lounge with a lovely log fireplace and well kept Adnams Southwold, Hampshire King Alfreds, Hook Norton Best, and Warden Brewery CHB on handpump, a good wine list, and 25 or so malt whiskies. Enjoyable bar food includes sandwiches, soup (£2.75), goat's cheese salad with egg and olives (£3.50), local sausages (£6), steak and stout pie, deep-fried fresh cod or haddock, vegetable lasagne or lamb and aubergine casserole (£6.50), beef curry (£7), and puddings such as honey and ginger cheesecake, cherry and almond tart or sticky toffee pudding (£3.25); children's helpings are half price; decent breakfasts. There are tables out in the garden, and the canal is a short walk away. *(Recommended by Dave Braisted, Sir Nigel Foulkes, Joan Olivier, Simon Collett-Jones, John Bowdler, Catherine and Andrew Brian, Georgina Cole, Mike Forrester, Mr and Mrs H D Spottiswoode, Richard Gibbs)*

Free house ~ Licensee Nick Huntington ~ Real ale ~ Meals and snacks (not Sun evening, not winter Mon) ~ Restaurant (not Sun evening, not winter Mon) ~ (01869) 338534 ~ Children in eating area of bar until 9pm ~ Open 12-3, 7-11(10.30 Sun); closed Mon Nov-Apr ~ Bedrooms: £25S/£45S

It's very helpful if you let us know up-to-date food prices when you report on pubs.

CLIFTON HAMPDEN SU5495 Map 4
Plough ♀ ⇔

On A415 at junction with Long Wittenham turn-off

Three more bedrooms with four-poster beds have been added in the converted building across the courtyard from this enjoyable inn. It is one of the few pubs we know of that is totally no smoking, which makes it popular with quite a few of our readers. The opened-up bar area has beams and panelling, black and red floor tiles, antique furniture, attractive pictures, and a friendly, relaxed atmosphere. It is very much a place people come to for a meal, with lunchtime dishes such as home-made soup (£2.75), sandwiches (from £3), ploughman's (£5.25), and fusilli pasta with sweet peppers and parmesan (£5.75), as well as daily specials like smoked chicken salad and steak in ale pie; two-course Sunday lunch (£10.95); the restaurant has an engaging portrait of the charming licensee and a much more comprehensive menu. Well kept Courage Best, Ruddles County, and Websters Yorkshire on handpump, plenty of good wines, and a dozen malt whiskies; no games or piped music. Some tables and seats outside. (*Recommended by Dr and Mrs Mervyn Jaswon, Mrs I Folkard-Evans, Hazel and Michael Duncombe, Mike and Mary Carter, Joyce McKimm, Hanns P Golez, Gordon, TBB, D C and E A Frewer, Mrs J Gubbins, Mrs S Wright, Chris Wehaton, David Carr, Dr G W Barnett*)

Courage ~ Lease: Yuksel Bektas ~ Real ale ~ Meals and snacks (served all day) ~ Restaurant ~ (01865) 407811 ~ Children welcome ~ Open 11-11 ~ Bedrooms: £49.50B/£69.50B

CROPREDY SP4646 Map 4
Red Lion

Off A423 4 miles N of Banbury

A handsome old church stands opposite this peaceful and friendly old thatched pub; the raised churchyard has some of the graves in which are casualties of the Civil War battle that took place nearby. The simply furnished and old-fashioned bar has ancient low beams, high-backed settles, seats in one of the inglenooks, quite a lot of brass, plates and pictures on the walls, and winter open fires; the two rooms on the right are more for eating. Popular home-made bar food includes sandwiches, barbecued spare ribs (£6.50), chicken breast malibu (£6.95), and quite a few Mexican dishes such as nachos (£3.95), taco salads (£5.95), sizzling chicken fajitas (£7.50), and steak fajitas (£7.95), all served with home-made fresh salsa, soured cream and guacamole; puddings like ginger pudding or bread and butter pudding, and Sunday roasts. Well kept Courage Directors, Ruddles Best, John Smiths, and Theakstons Best on handpump; darts, pool, cribbage, dominoes, fruit machine, and piped music. Seats in the small back garden. This is a lovely village, and the pub is a short walk from a pretty lock and the Oxford Canal. (*Recommended by Ted George, Peter and Anne Hollindale, Sheila and John French, George Atkinson, Mr and Mrs R Maggs, Rona Murdoch, Alan and Paula McCully, Mrs J Box*)

Courage ~ Lease: John Dando ~ Real ale ~ Meals and snacks ~ (01295) 750224 ~ Children in restaurant only ~ Parking may be difficult in summer ~ Open 12-3, 6-11; 12-3, 6-10.30 Sun

CUDDESDON SP5903 Map 4
Bat & Ball

S of Wheatley; if coming from M40 junction 7 via Gt Milton, turn towards Little Milton past church, then look out for signpost

Every inch of wall-space here is covered with cricketing programmes, photographs, porcelain models in well-lit cases, score books, cigarette cards, pads, gloves and hats, and signed bats, bails and balls. The immaculately kept L-shaped bar has beams and low ceilings, comfortable furnishings, a partly flagstoned floor, and a relaxed, friendly atmosphere. Popular bar food includes home-made soup (£2.75), lunchtime filled french sticks (from £2.75; minute steak with apricot chutney £3.75), lots of dishes at £5.75 such as brie and tomato tartlets, grilled fillet of cod, hot smoked chicken and ginger salad, honey and sage sausage with onion gravy and mash, lasagne, and honey-glazed gammon steak, and daily specials; puddings like chocolate pudding with hot chocolate sauce or bread and butter pudding (£3). The restaurant is no smoking. Well kept Flowers IPA, Wadworths 6X, and guest beers on handpump. A very pleasant terrace at the back has seats, Aunt Sally, and good views over the Oxfordshire plain. *(Recommended by Giles Francis, G V Price, Caroline Raphael; more reports please)*

Free house ~ Licensee David Sykes ~ Real ale ~ Meals and snacks ~ Restaurant ~ (01865) 874379 ~ Children in eating area of bar ~ Open 12-3, 5-11; 12-3, 6-10.30 Sun ~ Bedrooms: £40S/£45S

CUMNOR SP4603 Map 4
Bear & Ragged Staff

19 Appleton Road; village signposted from A420: follow one-way system into village, bear left into High St then left again into Appleton Road signposted Eaton, Appleton

The comfortably rambling, softly lit bar in this smart old place has roaring log fires, easy chairs, sofas and more orthodox cushioned seats, and wall banquettes, and a relaxed but decidely civilised atmosphere; one part has polished black flagstones, another a turkey carpet; the dining area of the bar is no smoking. Very good food includes lunchtime sandwiches, griddled Cornish scallops with potato chowder (£7.95), pastry puff of Angus beef with onion confit (£13.95), fillet of sea bass with crab fishcakes (£14.50), and a plate of lemon puddings (£4.95). Well kept Morrells Oxford Bitter, Graduate, and Varsity, and a changing guest beer on handpump, plus up to 10 wines by the glass from a good wine list. Service is pleasant and obliging. The building is named for the three-foot model of a Warwick heraldic bear which guards the large open fire. *(Recommended by D C amd E A Frewer, TRS, Dr and Mrs A Whiteway, Mr and Mrs R Maggs, Roger Crisp, Tim Barrow, Sue Demont, Joan Olivier, Chris and Martin Taylor, Nigel and Amanda Thorp, Gordon, John and Joan Nash, David Carr, Prof A N Black, John Waller, Neville Kenyon, Ewan McCall, Roger Huggins, Dave Irving, Tom McLean)*

Morrells ~ Tenants Bruce and Kay Buchan ~ Real ale ~ Meals and snacks (till 10pm) ~ Restaurant ~ (01865) 862329 ~ Children in eating area of bar and in restaurant ~ Big band jazz every 2nd Tues evening 8pm ~ Open 11.30-3, 5.30-11; 12-3, 7-10.30 Sun; closed several days between Christmas and New Year

CUXHAM SU4588 Map 2
Half Moon

4 miles from M40, junction 6; S on B4009, then right on to B480 at Watlington

Spotlessly kept, this thatched and rather cottagey village pub is warmly welcoming and friendly and enjoyed by readers. The comfortable low-beamed bars have country-style furnishings, an inglenook fireplace with winter log fires or summer flower displays, and a few clues to one of the chatty landlord's interests – vintage motorcycles. Good bar food includes home-made soup (£2.50; the onion is delicious), filled french bread (from £2.75; not Sunday lunchtime), filled baked potatoes (from £3.50; not Sunday lunchtime), ploughman's, garlic mushrooms (£3.95), beefburger (£4.75), chilli potato wedges with melted mozzarella (£5.95), steak and kidney pudding or garlic and herb chicken (£6.95), rump steak (£8.50), rack of barbecued ribs or stincotto (knuckle of ham with brown sugar; £9.95), and daily specials; children's menu (£2.75). Well kept Brakspears Bitter, plus a guest such as Special, Old or Mild, Boddingtons Bitter or Theakstons on handpump; darts, shove-ha'penny, table skittles, cribbage, and dominoes. There are seats sheltered by an oak tree on the back lawn, as well as a climbing frame and maybe summer barbecues. Across the road, a stream runs through this quiet village. *(Recommended by Martin and Karen Wake, TBB, Maggie Washington, Helen Hazzard, James Waller, Marjorie and David Lamb)*

Brakspears ~ Tenants Simon and Loraine Daniels ~ Real ale ~ Meals and snacks (till 10pm Fri/Sat; not Sun evening) ~ (01491) 614110 ~ Children in family room ~ Open 12-2.30(3 Sat), 6-11; 12-3, 7-10.30 Sun (may open longer at peak times)

DORCHESTER SU5794 Map 4
George ♀ 🛏

High St; village signposted just off A4074 Maidenhead—Oxford

This lovely old coaching inn was originally built as a brewhouse for the Norman abbey that still stands opposite. There's lots of old-fashioned charm in the civilised beamed bar with its roaring winter log fire, comfortable seats and fine old furniture (including cushioned settles and leather chairs), fresh flowers on the tables, and copies of *Country Life*. Good bar food includes home-made soup (£2.95), seafood terrine with a cucumber and sweet pepper relish (£3.95), macaroni cheese (small £4.10; large £5.50), potato, leek and broccoli bake (£5.50), steak and kidney pie (£6.25), game casserole (£6.95), bacon and brie chicken (£7.50), and sirloin steak (£9.50); roast Sunday lunch (no bar food then). Well kept Brakspears Bitter and Greene King IPA on handpump, good wine by the glass from a quite exceptional wine list, and a range of malt whiskies. Pleasant and welcoming service; piped music. *(Recommended by Mike and Heather Watson, Sheila and John French, David Carr, TBB, Chris and Martin Taylor; more reports please)*

Free house ~ Licensee Brian Griffin ~ Real ale ~ Meals and snacks ~ Restaurant ~ (01865) 340404 ~ Children in restaurant ~ Open 11-11; 12-10.30 Sun ~ Bedrooms: £57.50B/£75B

DUNS TEW SP4528 Map 4
White Horse 🛏

Off A4260 N of Kidlington

It was a beautifully sunny summer evening when we slipped into this 16th-c beamed inn on our anonymous inspection, but very few of the enthusiastically gossiping locals felt moved to abandon the warmly inviting bar for the tables squeezed on to the little terrace behind. As the light started to fade the landlady began lighting candles in the smart little side restaurant (though as yet there was no sign of diners); the softly flickering lights blending in well with the orange glow from the lamps on the oak-panelled walls. The main part of the bar has simple wooden tables and chairs around rugs on the flagstoned floor, a pile of newspapers to read, and a big inglenook fireplace up by a side room used as an overflow for eating. Towards the terrace the low ceiling gives way to a carefully added raftered area. Chalked up above two flowery patterned sofas, the range of good bar food might include toasted open sandwiches (£2.95), ploughman's (£4.95), sausage and mash (£5.25), lamb kidneys or sweet pepper and pine kernel terrine with a spiced plum chutney (£5.95), steak and kidney pie (£6.25), ballotine of chicken and mushroom with a ginger, lime and soy dressing (£6.75), fresh fish from Brixham, and delicious puddings; Sunday lunch (£6.95), and occasional themed menu nights. Courage Best, Hook Norton and Theakstons Best on handpump, good coffee, and around 15 malt whiskies; service is friendly and efficient. Cribbage, darts, cards. The bedrooms are in a sympathetically converted stable block behind; they organise special golfing breaks. The country lanes around here are very pleasant. *(Recommended by Martin Jones, Joan Olivier, George Atkinson, Martin and Karen Wake)*

Free house ~ Licensees Annette and John Marsh ~ Real ale ~ Meals and snacks ~ Restaurant ~ (01869) 340272 ~ Children in side room ~ Open 11-11; 12-3.30, 7-10.30 Sun; closed bank hol afternoons ~ Bedrooms: £55B/£65 with four poster)

EXLADE STREET SU6582 Map 2
Highwayman ♀ 📖 🛏

Signposted just off A4074 Reading—Wallingford

The surrounding wooded countryside here is lovely, and the attractive garden has tables and fine views. Inside, this rambling old inn is a friendly place with helpful staff and popular food. The two beamed rooms of the bar have quite an unusual layout, with an interesting variety of seats around old tables and even recessed into a central sunken inglenook; an airy conservatory dining room has more seats (mainly for eating) and overlooks the garden. Well presented bar food includes sandwiches, garlic mushrooms, steak, Guinness and mushroom pie or seafood pancake (£7.95), fishcakes (£11.50), chilli prawns (£13.95), fillet steak (£14.95), and weekly changing specials. Well kept Brakspears, Fullers London Pride, and Gibbs Mew Bishops Tipple on handpump, several malt whiskies, and decent wines; piped music. The friendly mongrel is called Gurty and the black and white spaniel, Saigon. *(Recommended by Margaret Dyke, Maureen Hobbs, Gordon, Nick Holmes)*

Free house ~ Licensees Carole and Roger Shippey ~ Real ale ~ Meals and snacks (12-2.30, 6-10.30; all day weekends) ~ Restaurant ~ (01491) 682020 ~ Children in eating area of bar ~ Open 11-3, 5.45-11; 11-11 Sat and Sun; closed evening 25 Dec ~ Bedrooms: £50S/£60S

FINSTOCK SP3616 Map 4
Plough ♀ ⇆
The Bottom; just off B4022 N of Witney

Brothers Keith and Nigel Ewers are most obliging and good natured licensees and make you genuinely welcome in this neatly kept thatched pub. The long, low beamed rambling bar is comfortable and relaxed and nicely split up by partitions and alcoves, with an armchair by the open log-burning stove in the massive stone inglenook, tiles up at the end by the servery (elsewhere is carpeted), and walls decorated with rosettes the licensees have won at Crufts and other doggy-related paraphernalia. Their llasl apso is called Jumbo, and other dogs are welcome in the garden (on a lead) and in the public bar. Bar food includes sandwiches, and specials such as lamb cutlet with a red onion compote (£7.45), boneless breast of chicken stuffed with stilton and cream cheese (£8.25), Bressingham duck glazed with port and morello cherries (£8.95), and haunch of venison with a blackcurrant sauce (£9.95). A comfortable low-beamed stripped-stone dining room is on the right. Adnams Best and Broadside, Archers Gold, Greene King Abbot, Hook Norton Best, Merivales Twister, Morlands Old Speckled Hen, Ringwood Fortyniner, and Wychwood Dogs Bollocks tapped from the cask or on handpump (under light blanket pressure); summer fruit cocktails, farm cider (when they can get it), and a decent choice of wines and malt whiskies. A separate games area has darts, bar billiards, cribbage, and dominoes. There are tables (and Aunt Sally) in the good, sizeable garden and several rare specimen roses (heavily scented). Good surrounding walks. *(Recommended by Nigel Clifton, Wayne Brindle, Liz Bell, Gill and Keith Croxton, John and Shirley Dyson, Mike and Mary Carter, W W Burke, H T Flaherty, Paul Barnett, Susan and John Douglas, Mr and Mrs Garrett, Robin and Laura Hillman, Tim Brierly, Graham and Karen Oddey)*

Free house ~ Licensees Keith and Nigel Ewers ~ Real ale ~ Meals and snacks ~ Restaurant ~ (01993) 868333 ~ Children welcome ~ Open 12-2.30, 6-11; 12-11 Sat (and summer Fri); 12-10.30 Sun ~ One bedroom: £40B/£50B

FYFIELD SU4298 Map 4
White Hart
In village, off A420 8 miles SW of Oxford

Owned since the Reformation by St John's College, Oxford, this humble-looking building was originally constructed as a chantry house. Inside, it's quite a surprise to find an impressive medieval building with soaring eaves, huge stone-flanked window embrasures, and an attractive carpeted upper gallery making up the main room – a grand hall rather than a traditional bar. A low-ceilinged side bar has an inglenook fireplace with a huge black urn hanging over the grate, and a framed history of the pub on the wall. The priests' room and barrel-vaulted cellar are dining areas – most of which are no smoking. Well kept Boddingtons, Hook Norton Best, Theakstons Old Peculier, Wadworths 6X, and guest beers on handpump or tapped from the cask, Westons cider, and country wines. Good, promptly served bar food includes lunchtime sandwiches, home-made soup (£2.75), home-made chicken liver pâté (£3.50), fried sardines (£3.95; main course £6.50), spicy cashew nut and vegetable stir-fry or steak sandwich (£6.25), steak, mushroom and Guinness pie (£6.50), chicken korma (£6.95), poached trout with mushroom and dill sauce (£8.25), steaks (from £9.50), half a roast duck with black cherry and orange sauce (£9.95), daily specials, and home-made puddings (£2.95); friendly, attentive service. Darts, shove-ha'penny, dominoes, cribbage, and piped music. A heavy wooden door leads out to the rambling, sheltered and flowery back lawn, which has a children's playground. *(Recommended by D and D Savidge, Ted George, W H Bruton, Roger Byrne, Wayne Brindle, Tony Dickinson, Adrian and Jane Tierney-Jones, C Moncreiffe, Andy Petersen, Nigel Norman)*

Free house ~ Licensees John and Sherry Howard ~ Real ale ~ Meals and snacks (till 10pm) ~ Restaurant ~ (01865) 390585 ~ Children in eating area of bar ~ Open 11-3, 6-11; 12-3, 7-10.30 Sun; closed 25-26 Dec

GREAT TEW SP3929 Map 4
Falkland Arms

Off B4022 about 5 miles E of Chipping Norton

This lovely inn is set in a charming village of untouched golden-stone thatched cottages. The partly panelled bar has high-backed settles and a diversity of stools around plain stripped tables on flagstones and bare boards, one, two and three handled mugs hanging from the beam-and-board ceiling, dim converted oil lamps, shutters for the stone-mullioned latticed windows, and a fine inglenook fireplace. At the bar counter, decorated with antique Doulton jugs, mugs and tobacco jars, there are lots of different snuffs, tankards, a model of the pub, and handkerchiefs; the dining room is no smoking. Well kept Adnams Broadside, Badger Best and Tanglefoot, Hook Norton Best, and Wadworths 6X and IPA on handpump, 60 malt whiskies, 22 country wines, and Westons farm ciders; dominoes. Bar food includes sandwiches (from £2.50), ploughman's, and meals like beef in ale pie, lamb and raisin casserole, and roasted shoulder of lamb (£4.95-£6.95). There are tables outside in front of the pub, with picnic tables under umbrellas in the garden behind – where there's a dovecot. Until its sale to Wadworths in early 1997, this was one of the best loved pubs in the country. *(Recommended by Chris Raisin, Graham Doyle, Jo and Gary Charlton, Peter Baggott, Liz Bell, Ted George, Mr and Mrs R Maggs, Paul Barnett, Kerry Law, Hilary Soms, Denis Harbord, D P Brown, Mr and Mrs P Goldman, John Read, John Bowdler, Monica Shelley, Laura Darlington, Lynn Sharpless, Bob Eardley)*

Wadworths ~ Manager Stephen Tickner ~ Real ale ~ Meals and snacks (not Sun evening) ~ Restaurant ~ (01608) 683653 ~ Children in eating area of bar and in restaurant; family room at lunchtime ~ Folk music Sun evening ~ Open 11.30-11; 11.30-2.30, 6-11 in winter; 11-11 Sat; 12-10.30 Sun ~ Bedrooms: £40B/£50B

nr HOOK NORTON SP3533 Map 4
Gate Hangs High ♀

Banbury Rd; a mile N of village towards Sibford, at Banbury—Rollright crossroads

The flowering tubs and wall baskets around the picnic tables in front of this tucked away pub are quite spectacular, and at the back, the broad lawn with holly and apple trees, has swings for children to play on and fine views. Inside, there's a warm welcome from the friendly licensee, and quite an emphasis on the popular, weekly changing food: sandwiches, home-made lentil and celery soup (£2.25), pâté (£2.95), sweet and sour vegetables (£5.95), home-cooked honey baked ham with egg (£6.50), beef in red wine (£6.75), fresh smoked haddock cooked in lemon butter or ham and mushrooms in a creamy garlic sauce on fresh tagliatelle (£6.95), and home-made puddings (£2.95). The bar has joists in the long, low ceiling, a brick bar counter, stools and assorted chairs on the carpet, and a gleaming copper hood over the hearth in the inglenook fireplace. Well kept Hook Norton Best, Old Hooky, Haymaker, and Twelve Days on handpump, a good wine list, and a range of malt whiskies; dominoes. Five miles south-west of the pub are the Bronze Age Rollright Stones – said to be a king and his army who were turned to stone by a witch. *(Recommended by Marjorie and David Lamb, E A George, Chris Raisin, Graham Doyle, Sir Nigel Foulkes, John Bowdler, Alan and Paula McCully, Margaret and Roy Randle, Rona Murdoch)*

Hook Norton ~ Tenant Stuart Rust ~ Real ale ~ Meals and snacks (not Sun evening) ~ Restaurant (not Sun evening) ~ (01608) 737387 ~ Children in eating area of bar and in restaurant ~ Open 11.30-3, 6.30-11; 12-3, 7-10.30 Sun; closed 25 Dec

HOOK NORTON SP3533 Map 4
Pear Tree ◥

Village signposted off A361 SW of Banbury

As we went to press, the friendly licensees were about to move from this much enjoyed and largely unspoilt village pub. But as this is the brewery tap for Hook Norton (the brewery is barely 100 yards down the lane), we are hoping that the incoming tenants will be just as popular. The knocked together bar area has country-kitchen furniture, including long tables as if for communal eating, a well stocked magazine rack, open fires, and a friendly and relaxed atmosphere; maybe locals drifting in with their dogs. Well kept Hook Norton Best, Old Hookey, and Mild along with the seasonal Haymaker or Twelve Days; a respectable wine list, and quite a few malt and Irish whiskies. Bar food has included home-made soups, sandwiches, cheesy topped ratatouille, lamb liver in marsala wine, stir fries or fish pie, rack of lamb with bubble and squeak patties, and puddings like banoffi pie or lemon cheesecake. Shove-ha'penny, cribbage, dominoes, trivia. The attractive, sizeable garden has plenty of seats, and Aunt Sally. We include bedroom prices below, but the new tenant may decide not to do them – best to check. *(Recommended by John Bowdler, Ray Blake, Chris Raisin, Graham Doyle, Margaret and Roy Randle, Alan and Paula McCully, Robert Gomme, M Benjamin; more reports on the new regime, please)*

Hook Norton ~ Real ale ~ Meals and snacks ~ (01608) 737482 ~ Open 12-2.30(3 Sat), 6-11; 12-10.30 Sun ~ Bedroom: £20S/£35S

KELMSCOT SU2499 Map 4
Plough ⟷

NW of Faringdon, off A417 or A4095

At one time, this rather pretty little inn was called the Manor Inn which was most confusing, as this peaceful hamlet by the upper Thames does include an altogether more famous building of that name, William Morris's summer home. The Thames (where there are moorings) is only a few minutes' walk away, and the attractive garden has seats amongst the unusual flowers. Inside, the small traditional front bar has ancient flagstones and stripped stone walls, and a relaxed chatty atmosphere, and there's also a larger cheerfully carpeted lounge bar with interesting prints on the walls; dogs are allowed in the public bar (where there is satellite TV for sport). The licensee is happy to offer advice on local walks. A wide choice of home-cooked food includes sandwiches (from £1.80; toasties from £2.05, filled french bread from £3.10), soup (£2.50), filled baked potatoes (from £2.80), ploughman's (from £3.90), ham and egg (£4.75), filled pancakes (from £5.95), beef and Guinness pie (£6.50), cajun chicken (£6.95), lamb kidneys in madeira (£7.25), steaks (from £8.95), daily specials, and home-made puddings like chocolate sponge with chocolate sauce, fruit fool or apple flapjack crumble (from £2.50). On Sunday they only serve snacks and a roast. Well kept Morlands Original and Old Speckled Hen, and a guest such as Fullers London Pride on handpump; darts, bar billiards, shove-ha'penny, cribbage, dominoes, and piped music. *(Recommended by Jenny and Roger Huggins, J and P Maloney, Ted George, Peter Neate, DI, Mr and Mrs Peter Smith)*

Free house ~ Licensees Trevor and Anne Pardoe ~ Real ale ~ Meals and snacks ~ Restaurant ~ (01367) 253543 ~ Children welcome ~ Singer or duo Sat evening ~ Open 11-11; 12-3, 7-10.30 Sun ~ Bedrooms: £30B/£45B – no accomm 24-30 Dec

---

By law pubs must show a price list of their drinks. Let us know if you are inconvenienced by any breach of this law.

LEWKNOR SU7198 Map 4
Olde Leathern Bottel

Under a mile from M40 junction 6; just off B4009 towards Watlington

As this spotlessly kept pub is so handy for the M40, it can get busy at lunchtime – best to arrive early. There's always a warm welcome from the attentive licensee, and a relaxed, cheerful atmosphere in the two rooms of the bar which have open fires, heavy beams in the low ceilings, rustic furnishings, and an understated decor of old beer taps and the like; the no-smoking family room is separated only by standing timbers, so you don't feel cut off from the rest of the pub. Good, popular and generously served bar food (they tell us prices are the same as last year) includes lunchtime sandwiches and snacks as well as pâté (£3.95), vegetable or chicken curries (£4.50), home-made steak and kidney pie (£4.95), gammon and egg or barbecued spare ribs (£5.95), steaks (from £7.95), daily specials, and puddings like treacle tart or cheesecake (£2); quick, obliging service. Well kept Brakspears Bitter, SB and winter Old on handpump. There are tables on the sizeable lawn alongside the car park; this is a pretty village. *(Recommended by Hazel and Michael Duncombe, Phyl and Jack Street, Mr and Mrs C Moncreiffe, Neville Kenyon, Mr C Crichton, TBB, D Voller, Jane Bailey, GWB, Mrs Hilarie Taylor, Dr and Mrs Baker)*

Brakspears ~ Tenants Mike and Lesley Fletcher ~ Real ale ~ Meals and snacks ~ (01844) 351482 ~ Children welcome ~ Open 11-2.30(3 Sat), 6-11; 12-3, 7-10.30 Sun

MAIDENSGROVE SU7288 Map 2
Five Horseshoes ⊕ ♀

W of village, which is signposted from B480 and B481; OS Sheet 175, map reference 711890

Although this busy pub places great emphasis on its popular food, there's a separate bar for walkers where boots are welcome – plenty of surrounding walks in the Chiltern beechwoods. The sheltered back garden has a rockery, some interesting water features, and fine views down over the woods; they have an outside bar where summer barbecues are held. The rambling bar is furnished with mostly modern wheelback chairs around stripped wooden tables (though there are some attractive older seats and a big baluster-leg table), and has a good log fire in winter; the low ceiling in the main area is covered in bank notes from all over the world, mainly donated by customers. There's also a dining conservatory (booking is pretty much essential in here at weekends). Good bar food includes soup (£2.95; well liked stilton soup £3.50), ploughman's (£4.25), home-made chicken liver pâté (£4.95), warm salads such as goat's cheese grilled with pine kernels and served with seared sweet peppers or seared king scallops with bacon (from £5.50), mixed hors-d'ouevres (£5.95 per person), filled baked potatoes (from £5.95), pancakes filled with smoked chicken and mushroom or spicy thai vegetables (£6.50), steak and kidney pie (£7.50), mixed game crumble (£8.95), chargrilled salmon with lemon butter (£8.95), grilled lamb cutlets with blackcurrant and kirsch sauce or fresh halibut with a herb and turmeric crust (£9.95), and steaks (from £13.50). Well kept Brakspears Bitter, Special and seasonal ales on handpump, and a dozen wines by the glass. *(Recommended by R Morgan, David Burgner, Graham and Karen Oddey, John Dickson, Dr G W Barnett, June S Bray, Gill and Andy Plumb, M Sargent, D Hayman)*

Brakspears ~ Tenant Graham Cromack ~ Real ale ~ Meals and snacks ~ Conservatory restaurant ~ (01491) 641282 ~ Children welcome if over 8 ~ Open 11.30-2.30, 6-11; 12-3, 7-10.30 Sun; closed 25 Dec

MURCOTT SP5815 Map 4
Nut Tree ♀

Off B4027 NE of Oxford, via Islip and Charlton on Otmoor

Roundhead soldiers used this low-thatched old house extensively when Cromwell had his headquarters at nearby Boarstall. Nowadays, it's more civilised, and the welcoming beamed lounge has a long polished bar with brasses, antiques and pictures all round, fresh flowers on its tables (set for food), and a winter log fire; there's also a small back conservatory-style extension. Good bar food includes soup (£2.50), sandwiches (from £2.75), ploughman's or ham and egg (£4.75), vegetarian lasagne (£5.50), fresh cod or haddock (£6.50), calf liver and bacon (£8.95), rack of lamb (£9.50), steaks (from £10.20), duck breast with madeira sauce (£10.50), daily specials, and puddings or good cheeses. Well kept Hook Norton Best and Morrells Oxford, and guests like Bass, Brakspears, Morrells Varsity, Wadworths 6X, and Wychwood Hobgoblin on handpump, a fair number of malt whiskies, a decent range of wines, and farm cider. Darts, shove-ha'penny, cribbage, dominoes, and frequent Sunday quiz nights. The pub is particularly pretty in summer with its colourful hanging baskets, ducks on a front pond, trim lawns, and usually plenty of animals such as donkeys, peacocks and rabbits; also Aunt Sally, and an unusual collection of ten gargoyles, each loosely modelled on one of the local characters, and carved into a magnificently grotesque form from a different wood. Nine of them hang in the walnut tree and one from a pillar overlooking the well. The pub is handy for walks through the boggy Otmoor wilderness. *(Recommended by Marjorie and David Lamb, D and J McMillan, Ted George, Gordon, Carolyn and Michael Hedoin, A Preston, M Sargent, Derek and Sylvia Stephenson, Lucy James, Dean Foden)*

Free house ~ Licensee Gordon Evans ~ Real ale ~ Meals and snacks (not Sun) ~ (01865) 331253 ~ Children in conservatory (not Sun evenings) ~ Open 11-3, 6.30-11; 12-3, 7-10.30 Sun

OXFORD SP5016 Map 4
Kings Arms

40 Holywell St

Owned by Wadham College, and leased to Youngs for the last few years, this bustling place – dating from the 16th c – is still run by the son of the previous long-term tenants. The stripped pine dado, green walls, bar counter and gantry, and an extra back room with a sofa and more tables date from the Youngs takeover, as does the opening between the 'Office' and the tiny room behind it, which used to be the snuggest of all, but for the most part the layout and atmosphere are much as they've always been. There's a big rather bare main room, with a no-smoking coffee room just inside the Parks Road entrance, and several cosy and comfortably worn-in side and back rooms, each with a different character and customers. It's often very busy and is popular with students, but civilised, with amiable service; they still keep a dictionary for the crossword buffs in the Dons Bar, with its elderly furnishings and tiled floor; bar billiards, cribbage, dominoes, fruit machine, and trivia. There's a mix of old prints and photographs of customers, and sympathetic lighting. Well kept Youngs Bitter, Ram Rod, and Special and a guest such as Wadworths 6X on handpump or tapped from the cask, a good choice of wines with 22 by the glass, 20 malt whiskies, and decent bar food such as sandwiches, home-made soup (£1.95), six types of greasy spoon dishes (£3.95), and home-made chicken in stout pie (£4.95); daily papers, tables out on the pavement. *(Recommended by Christopher Gallop, Gordon, James Nunns, John and Hazel Waller, J and P Maloney, Dick Brown, Pat and Roger Fereday, David Carr, Hugh MacLean)*

Youngs ~ Manager David Kyffin ~ Real ale ~ Meals and snacks (11-3, 5.30-9.30) ~ (01865) 242369 ~ Children welcome ~ Open 10.30am-11pm; 12-10.30 Sun

Turf Tavern

Bath Place; via St Helen's Passage, between Holywell Street and New College Lane

Several readers have known this pub since their undergraduate days and say it has not changed since. Certainly it can be dominated by students, but the two little rooms still have a snug feel, dark beams, and low ceilings, and are much as Hardy described them when Jude the Obscure discovered that Arabella the barmaid was the wife who'd left him years before; there's also a bar in one of the courtyards. A changing range of real ales might include Archers Golden, Boddingtons, Flowers Original, Morlands Old Speckled Hen, Wadworths 6X and five other rotating guest beers on handpump or tapped from the cask; also, a few country wines and a couple of farm ciders; trivia.

Straightforward bar food includes doorstep sandwiches (from £2.75), filled baked potatoes (from £2.90), basket meals (£3.95), a vegetarian dish (£4.75), and steak in ale pie (£4.95); the top food area is no smoking. This is a pretty place – especially in summer, when there are tables in the three attractive walled-in flagstoned or gravelled courtyards around the old-fashioned building; in winter you can huddle around the braziers in the courtyard. (Recommended by A C Morrison, Mark Percy, Lesley Mayoh, Rona Murdoch, Gordon, Tony Scott, Tony Dickinson, Dr and Mrs A Whiteway, Hazel and Michael Duncombe, D Voller, Simon Penny, Ian and Villy White, Chris and Martin Taylor, LM, John Hill, Simon Ludlow, Nigel and Amanda Thorp, Pat and Roger Fereday, D C and E A Frewer, Hanns P Golez, Sue Demont, Tim Barrow)

Whitbreads ~ Manager Trevor Walter ~ Real ale ~ Meals and snacks (noon-8pm) ~ (01865) 243235 ~ Children in eating area of bar ~ No nearby parking ~ Open 11-11; 12-10.30 Sun

RAMSDEN SP3515 Map 4
Royal Oak ♀ ⏺

Village signposted off B4022 Witney—Charlbury

Set opposite the church, this bustling and unpretentious village inn is popular for its enjoyable food. Served by helpful staff, this might include lunchtime sandwiches, ploughman's (£3.95), oyster mushroom and herb omelette (£4.50) or pork and sage sausage with onion gravy (£5.95), as well as home-made soup (£2.75), chicken liver and cointreau pâté (£3.25), lasagne or chicken tikka masala (£5.75), home-made burgers (from £5.75), spare ribs (£7.50), game casserole (£7.95), steaks (from £9.25), a vegetarian dish, daily specials, and puddings; on Thursday evenings they offer a steak, pudding and glass of wine special (£10.95); roast Sunday lunch (no snacks then). The traditional beamed bar is simply furnished and decorated but comfortable, and has a cheery winter log fire and well kept Adnams Broadside, Archers Golden and Bitter, Hook Norton Best, and Morrells Graduate on handpump; enjoyable house wines. The evening dining room is no smoking. The cosy bedrooms are in separate cottages. (Recommended by M S Catling, Roger Crisp, Mike and Mary Carter, John Waller, Deborah Jackson, John C Baker)

Free house ~ Licensee Jon Oldham ~ Real ale ~ Meals and snacks (till 10pm) ~ Restaurant ~ (01993) 868213 ~ Children in eating area of bar and in restaurant ~ Open 11.30-2.30, 6.30-11; 12-3, 7-10.30 Sun ~ Bedrooms: £30B/£45B

ROKE SU6293 Map 2
Home Sweet Home

Village signposted off B4009 Benson—Watlington

Big log fires warm the two smallish rooms of the bar in this rather smart thatched place. There are heavy stripped beams, leather armed chairs on the bare boards, a great high-backed settle with a hefty slab of a rustic table in front of it, a few horsey or game pictures such as a nice Thorburn print of snipe on the stone walls, and a good country atmosphere. On the right, a carpeted room with low settees and armchairs and an attractive corner glass cupboard, leads through to the restaurant. Good bar food includes sandwiches, fresh salmon fishcakes with parsley sauce, baked tomato with potted shrimps or warm crab and saffron tart (£6.95), calf liver with crispy bacon (£7.95), and chicken with gorgonzola, spring onion and sun-dried tomato stuffing or smoked haddock with welsh rarebit (£8.95); friendly service. Well kept Brakspears Bitter and Eldridge Pope Royal Oak on handpump, and a good choice of malt whiskies. The low-walled front garden is ideal for eating on a sunny day; there are lots of flowers around the tables out by the well. (Recommended by John and Hazel Waller, Marjorie and David Lamb, Margaret Dyke, John Waller, June S Bray)

Free house ~ Licensees Jill Madle, Peter and Irene Mountford ~ Real ale ~ Meals and snacks ~ Restaurant ~ (01491) 838249 ~ Well behaved children welcome ~ Open 11-3, 6-11; 12-3, 7-10.30 Sun; closed evening 25 Dec

SHENINGTON SP3742 Map 4
Bell ♀

Village signposted from A422 W of Banbury

This is a tranquil and picturesque village and the 300-year-old pub is part of a row of golden Hornton stone cottages; tables at the front look across to the green. The heavy-beamed and carpeted lounge has cushioned wall and window seats, vases of flowers on the tables, and old maps and documents on the cream walls; the wall in the flagstoned area on the left is stripped to stone and decorated with heavy-horse harness, and the right side opens into a neat little pine-panelled room (popular with locals) with decorated plates; darts, cribbage, dominoes, coal fire. Enjoyable bar food includes sandwiches, nice mushrooms on toast, courgette and tomato lasagne (£5.75), lamb and lime casserole or chicken in cider and cumin (£7.25), seasonal pheasant in redcurrant jelly and red wine sauce (£8.95), and tasty giant prawns in garlic. Well kept Bass and Hook Norton Best on handpump, and a good choice of wines; friendly service. There's a west highland terrier, Lucy and a labrador, Daisy. The tables at the front look across to the green. *(Recommended by Maysie Thompson, R Watkins, J H Kane, John Bowdler, Sir Nigel Foulkes, Mr and Mrs C Moncreiffe, Sharon Hancock, Suzanne and John Jones, Mr and Mrs Vancourt Carlyle-Lyon, John Read, Tony Ingham, Gordon Tong, Joan Olivier, D C T and E A Frewer, Nigel Clifton, I D Irving)*

Free house ~ Licensee Jennifer Dixon ~ Real ale ~ Meals and snacks (till 10) ~ (01295) 670274 ~ Children welcome ~ Open 12(11.30 Sat)-3, 6.30-11; 12-4, 7-10.30 Sun ~ Bedrooms: £15/£40B

SHIPTON UNDER WYCHWOOD SP2717 Map 4
Lamb ⊕ ♀ ⇔

Just off A361 to Burford

The beamed bar in this civilised old place has a fine oak-panelled settle, a nice mix of solid old farmhouse-style and captain's chairs on the wood-block floor, polished tables, cushioned bar stools, solid oak bar counter, pictures on old partly bared stone walls, and maybe newspapers on rods to read. Well liked bar food includes home-made soup (£2.95), home-made duck and orange pâté (£3.90), sandwiches (from £3.50), grilled goat's cheese with bacon (£3.95), vegetable stroganoff (£7.50), excellent seafood tart (£8.95), popular cotswold pie (£8.50), chicken supreme (£8.95), fresh fish from Cornwall like lemon sole, plaice, crab and lobster (from £8.50), fillet of pork with calvados (£8.95), lovely duck in orange (£11.95), and puddings such as lemon tart, fruit crumbles and bread and butter pudding (£3.75); enjoyable Sunday lunch, and good breakfasts. The restaurant is no smoking. Well kept Hook Norton Best, Wadworths 6X, and Wychwood Best on handpump, several malt whiskies, carefully chosen wines, and champagne by the glass. In summer, you can sit at tables among the roses at the back. *(Recommended by T L Rees, Liz Bell, Scott Antel, M A and C R Starling, Pam Adsley, Mrs Jean Dundas, Michael Kirby, Maysie Thompson, H T Flaherty, John Bowdler, George and Jean Dundas, BHP, M S Catling; also in Good Hotel Guide)*

Old English Pub Co ~ Managers Michael and Jenny Eastick ~ Real ale ~ Meals and snacks (till 10pm) ~ Restaurant (not Sun evening) ~ (01993) 830465 ~ Children in eating area and restaurant ~ Open 11-3, 6-11; 12-2.30, 7-10.30 Sun ~ Bedrooms: £58B/£68B

Shaven Crown ⇔

Parts of this grand old place are said to have been used as a hunting lodge by Elizabeth I. There's a magnificent double-collar braced hall roof, lofty beams and a sweeping double stairway down the stone wall, and the beamed bar has a relief of the 1146 Battle of Evesham, as well as seats forming little stalls around the tables and upholstered benches built into the walls. Under the new licensees, bar food now includes sandwiches, soup (£2.65), smoked salmon mousse with oatcakes (£3.50), ploughman's (£4), Mexican spiced pork or Scottish salmon fishcakes with a rich tomato sauce (£5.25), venison sausages braised in red wine (£5.75), Gloucester Spot pork chop (£6.90), sirloin steak (£8.95), and puddings such as chocolate mousse or bread and butter pudding (£2.50); children's helpings, and Sunday lunch. Well kept Hook Norton Best and two guests such as Morlands Old Speckled Hen and Tetleys on handpump, and farm cider; shove-ha'penny and cribbage. Originally, this was a hospice for the monastery of Bruern in the 14th c, and in the medieval courtyard garden behind, little has changed since the days when it was used as an exercise yard by monks. A tranquil place on a sunny day, it has old-fashioned seats out on the stone cobbles and crazy paving, with a view of the lily pool and roses. The pub has its own bowling green. *(Recommended by Pam Adsley, John Bowdler, Dr S P Willavoys, George Atkinson, Marjorie and David Lamb, Colin and Sarah Pugh, A J Carter, David Campbell, Vicki McLean, Andrew and Ruth Triggs, Alan and Paula McCully, Dr S Willavoys, Joyce McKimm)*

Free house ~ Licensees Robert and Jane Burpitt ~ Real ale ~ Meals and snacks (not 25 Dec) ~ Restaurant ~ (01993) 830330 ~ Children welcome ~ Open 12-2.30, 5-11; 11.30-11 Sat; 12-10.30 Sun ~ Bedrooms: £35(£53B)/£72B

SOUTH STOKE SU5983 Map 2
Perch & Pike 🍴 ♈

Off B4009 2 miles N of Goring

Run by friendly licensees, this attractive flint pub is well liked for its interesting food. From the lunchtime menu there might be sandwiches (from £2.95), ploughman's or sliced avocado and bacon on cheesebread (£4.95), and salads like chargrilled chicken or rare roast beef (from £6.25); also, home-made soup (£3.25), fried black pudding on warm apple, broad beans and mint (£5.50), chargrilled fillets of red mullet with a tapenade crust or roasted artichoke and goat's cheese tart with sun-dried tomatoes and olives (£5.95), pork, cranberry and orange sausages with a cider and onion gravy (£8.95), filo pastry filled with stir-fried vegetables, lemon grass and coconut milk (£9.50), lamb cutlets with white wine and bacon gravy (£10.75), Aberdeen Angus steaks (from £11.95), and fried fillet of salmon on mustard and creamed cabbage (£12.75). Diners have linen table napkins in old napkins rings and bone-handled cutlery gleaned from antique markets. Well kept Brakspears Bitter and Special on handpump, and 12 wines by the glass served from the old oak bar counter. The relaxing bar has quite a light and spacious feel, as well as open fires, comfortable seats, and a nice assortment of tables. The window boxes are pretty, and there are seats out on the large flower-bordered lawn. The Thames is just a field away. *(Recommended by Herbert and Susan Verity, Sarah Bemrose, Nicholas Holmes; more reports please)*

Brakspears ~ Tenants Michael and Jill Robinson ~ Real ale ~ Meals and snacks (not Sun evening) ~ Restaurant ~ (01491) 872415 ~ Children in eating area of bar only ~ Open 12-2.30, 6-11; 12-3, 7-10.30 Sun; closed 25 Dec

STANTON ST JOHN SP5709 Map 4
Star

Pub signposted off B4027; village is signposted off A40 heading E of Oxford (heading W, you have to go to the Oxford ring-road roundabout and take unclassified road singposted to Stanton St John, Forest Hill etc); bear right at church in village centre

On a level with the car park here is a busy and well refurbished extension with rugs on flagstones, pairs of bookshelves on each side of an attractive inglenook fireplace, old-fashioned dining chairs, an interesting mix of dark oak and elm tables, shelves of good pewter, terracotta-coloured walls with a portrait in oils, and a stuffed ermine; down a flight of stairs are little low-beamed rooms – one has ancient brick flooring tiles and the other quite close-set tables. Tasty bar food includes sandwiches (£1.85; toasties £2.10), home-made soup (£2), ploughman's (£3.85), home-made quiche (£5.40), lemon chicken (£6.75), gammon and pineapple (£6.95), fresh salmon steak (£7.45), sirloin steak (£8.25), daily specials such as broccoli and mushroom quiche (£5.65), and beef in Guinness or cheesy tuna bake (£5.75), and a dozen puddings (£2.65); children's menu (from £1.95). Well kept Wadworths IPA, Farmers Glory, 6X and winter Old Timer, and a weekly guest beer on handpump, and country wines. Behind the bars is a display of brewery ties, beer bottles and so forth; shove-ha'penny, dominoes, cribbage, and piped music. The family room is no smoking. The walled garden has picnic tables among the rockeries, and swings and a sandpit. There are annual classic car rallies, and the pub gets busy then. *(Recommended by Joan Olivier, Maureen Hobbs, Robert Gomme, TBB, Chris Wheaton, Marjorie and David Lamb)*

Wadworths ~ Tenants Nigel and Suzanne Tucker ~ Real ale ~ Meals and snacks (till 10pm) ~ (01865) 351277 ~ Children in two family rooms ~ Folk music first Sun of month ~ 11-2.30, 6.30-11; 12-2.30, 7-10.30 Sun

Talk House ♀ ⇐

Wheatley Road (B4027 just outside village)

Although most of the tables in this capacious and splendidly realised series of linked areas are for dining, there is plenty of room for people who just want a drink and a chat: flagstoned and tiled floors, stripped 17th-c stonework, lots of oak beams, simple but solid rustic furnishings, and attractive pictures and other individual and often light-hearted decorations. It's at its best when it's busy (on a Saturday night, particularly, and it does need a lot of people to fill it), with a cheery bustle, and deft service by well trained good-humoured staff. At lunchtime, bar food includes sandwiches, filled baked potatoes and salads (from £3.50-£4.95) and a buffet with soup, pâté, cheeses, and curries (£7.95). In the evening there might be herring fillets marinated in madeira or chicken satay with hot peanut dip (£4.95), chicken piri piri for two people (£6.95 each), ham off the bone with two eggs (£7.95), chicken breast stuffed with blue stilton, breadcrumbed and fried (£8.95), half a shoulder of English lamb with honey, rosemary and garlic (£10.95), sirloin steak or half a Gressingham duck with orange sauce (£11.95), a vegetarian, pasta and fresh fish of the day dish, and puddings. Well kept Morlands Original, Old Speckled Hen, Tanners Jack and their seasonal ales, and Wychwood Best on handpump, good house wines, and several malt whiskies. The sheltered courtyard has tables around an impressive fountain. *(Recommended by David Oakes, Peter and Audrey Dowsett, M Sargent, Graham and Karen Oddey)*

Free house ~ Licensee Johnny Chick ~ Real ale ~ Meals and snacks (till 10pm; all day Sun) ~ Restaurant ~ (01865) 351648 ~ Children welcome ~ Jazz band Sun lunchtime ~ Open 11-3, 5.30-11; 11-11 Sun ~ Bedrooms: £45.50B/£59.50B

STEEPLE ASTON SP4725 Map 4
Red Lion ♀

Off A4260 12 miles N of Oxford

Happily, little changes in this civilised little village pub, and jovial Mr Mead, who has now been here for 25 years, continues to warmly welcome all his customers. He is also very keen on his wines – the cellar contains over 100 different bottles. The comfortable partly panelled bar has beams, an antique settle and other good furnishings, and under the window a collection of interesting language and philosophy books that crossword fans find compelling. Enjoyable lunchtime bar food might include tasty stockpot soup (£2.30), sandwiches (£2.30, the rare beef is good), smoked pork in a large roll with tomato and shallot (£3.25), excellent ploughman's with nicely ripe stilton (£3.90), home-made pâté (£4), goulash with ham and smoked sausage (£4.80), fresh salmon salad or whole fresh baby crab (£5.50), smoked salmon platter (£5.80), and puddings (from £1.95); the evening restaurant is more elaborate with a good three-course meal (£19.50). Well kept (and reasonably priced) Badger Tanglefoot, Hook Norton Best and Wadworths 6X on handpump, and a choice of sixty or so malt whiskies. The suntrap front terrace with its lovely flowers is a marvellous place to relax in summer. *(Recommended by D C T and E A Frewer, Gordon, Peter Baggott, Mr and Mrs C Moncreiffe, Maysie Thompson, Martin and Karen Wake, James Nunns, J and D Tapper, Mr and Mrs B Pullee, Jan and Colin Roe, M Sargent, Andrew and Jo Litten)*

Free house ~ Licensee Colin Mead ~ Real ale ~ Lunchtime bar meals and snacks (not Sun) ~ Evening restaurant (not Sun) ~ (01869) 340225 ~ Children in restaurant ~ Open 11-3, 6-11; 12-3, 7-10.30 Sun

TADPOLE BRIDGE SP3300 Map 4
Trout

Back road Bampton—Buckland, 4 miles NE of Faringdon

A new kitchen and cellar have been built at the back of this busy but friendly Thames-side pub, so the licensees have moved the bar to create more dining space. The small L-shaped original bar with plenty of seats on the flagstones, is dedicated only to enjoying the Archers Village, Fullers London Pride, Gibbs Mew Salisbury, and Morlands Original on handpump, and darts, dominoes and cribbage; there's a small but comprehensive wine list. Bar food includes lunchtime sandwiches, snacks, and daily specials, and evening dishes such as soup (£2.25), mussels in a cream and white wine sauce (£3.25), deep-fried brie with a ginger and apricot sauce (£3.75), warm chicken and bacon salad (£4.25), ham and egg (£5), knuckle of ham with cabbage (£7.65), roast cod on creamed leeks (£7.95), poached darne of salmon with hollandaise sauce (£8.25), sirloin steak (£9.45), and fillet of beef on a crouton with a chasseur sauce (£11.25); piped music. The garden (with Aunt Sally) is pretty in summer with small fruit trees, attractive hanging baskets, and flower troughs, and you can fish on a two-mile stretch of the river (the pub sells day tickets); moorings for boaters, too. *(Recommended by Daren Haines, David Carr, Peter Holman, Joan Olivier, Val Stevenson, Rob Holmes, Gordon, Marjorie and David Lamb, Dr G W Barnett)*

Free house ~ Licensee Christopher Green ~ Real ale ~ Meals and snacks ~ (01367) 870382 ~ Children in eating area of bar ~ Open 11.30-3, 6-11; 12-3, 7-10.30 Sun

TOOT BALDON SP5600 Map 4
Crown

Village signed from A4074 at Nuneham Courtenay, and B480

Warm and welcoming, this friendly, bustling pub is popular for its memorably generous helpings of enjoyable homely food. As well as sandwiches and ploughman's, there might be gammon and pineapple (£5.95), a prawn and mushroom dish (£7), chicken supreme or salmon (£8), rack of lamb (£8.50), and mixed grill (£8.95); they use home-grown herbs and other produce whenever possible. Best to book, especially at weekends. The simple beamed bar has a log fire, solid furnishings on the tiled floor, and a pleasant atmosphere. Well kept Adnams Broadside and Mansfield Bitter on handpump; darts, shove-ha'penny, and dominoes. Aunt Sally, summer barbecues, and tables on the terrace. *(Recommended by Mr and Mrs W Welsh, Kendall Davis, D C and E A Frewer, Canon M A Bourdeaux, G T Hughes, Ian and Villy White, M Sargent)*

Free house ~ Licensees Liz and Neil Kennedy ~ Real ale ~ Meals and snacks (not Sun or Mon evenings) ~ (01865) 343240 ~ Well behaved children in eating area of bar ~ Open 11-3, 6.30-11; 12-3, 7-10.30 Sun

WATLINGTON SU6894 Map 4
Chequers

3 miles from M40, junction 6; Take B4009 towards Watlington, and on outskirts of village turn right into residential rd Love Lane which leads to pub

Although this cheerful pub is hidden away from the main streets, there are plenty of customers. The relaxed rambling bar has a low panelled oak settle and character chairs such as a big spiral-legged carving chair around a few good antique oak tables, a low oak beamed ceiling darkened to a deep ochre by the candles which they still use, and red and black shiny tiles in one corner with rugs and red carpeting elsewhere; steps on the right lead down to an area with more tables. A conservatory with very low hanging vines looks out over the garden. Popular bar food includes toasties (£2.50), ploughman's (£4), filled baked potatoes (£4.80), aubergine and lentil moussaka (£5.50), seafood pie (£5.70), steak and kidney pie or chicken curry (£6.70), balti chicken (£7.60), calf liver and bacon (£9.60), steaks (from £9.60). Well kept Brakspears Bitter, Special, and OBJ and seasonal ales on handpump, a decent little wine list, and friendly staff. The cheese shop in Watlington itself is recommended. The garden is notably pretty – quite refreshing after the bustle of the main street – with picnic tables under apple and pear trees, and sweet peas, roses, geraniums, begonias, and rabbits. No children. *(Recommended by Gordon, Hazel and Michael Duncombe, Bill Ingham, P J Keen, Simon Collett-Jones, TBB)*

Brakspears ~ Tenants John and Anna Valentine ~ Real ale ~ Meals and snacks (not Sun evening) ~ (01491) 612874 ~ Open 11.30-2.30, 6-11; 12-3, 7-10.30 Sun

WESTCOTT BARTON SP4325 Map 4
Fox

Enstone Road; B4030 off A44 NW of Woodstock

Now that so many menus include lasagne and canelloni under the heading of traditional English dishes, it's easy to forget what genuine Italian pasta tastes like – so the wide choice of authentic meals at this lovely stonebuilt village pub is really quite refreshing. That they're named in Italian is no affectation; for the landlord and his brother, who shares the cooking, it's the native language. The various pastas come with sauces such as mushroom and salmon or broccoli, courgette and tomato (all around £4.95), and they do other dishes like diced chicken in a mushroom, pepper, onion and tomato sauce (£5.95); also ploughman's (£3.25), chicken and mushroom pie (£4.95), a Sunday roast, and children's meals. Hops hang from the low beams in the deceptively small and very relaxed bar, above snug little window seats, high-backed settles and pews around tables on flagstones, and the odd trap or horsebrass on the stone walls; open fires, juke box. A narrow corridor leads to a tucked-away back room with a faded tapestry and an old coach wheel, and an elegant restaurant. Well kept Hook Norton and two changing guests like Hampshire 1066 or Theakstons XB on handpump; espresso and cappuccino. There are a few tables out in front, and more in the very pleasant garden behind, overlooking a verdant sheep-filled field. There's a wooden play fort out here for children, and quite a few trees. Watch your head as you go inside – the porch is very low. *(Recommended by David Campbell, Vicki McLean, D C T and E Frewer)*

Free house ~ Licensee Vito Logozzi ~ Real ale ~ Meals and snacks ~ Restaurant (not Sun evening) ~ (01869) 340338 ~ Children welcome ~ Occasional live music ~ Open 12-3, 5-11

WOODSTOCK SP4416 Map 4
Feathers 🍴 🛏

Market St

Although this is a charming and civilised Cotswold stone hotel with prices to match, the old-fashioned garden bar at the back is well liked by readers. It's old-fashioned and quietly relaxed with oils and watercolours on its walls, stuffed fish and birds (a marvellous live parrot, too), and a central open fire, and opens on to a splendid sunny courtyard with attractive tables and chairs among geraniums and trees. Service is excellent. Good, imaginative food from a short but thoughtful menu might include soup (£3.65), chicken liver parfait with toasted brioche (£3.95), smoked mussel fritter with lime pickle (£4.50), grilled smoked salmon with tomato and basil (£5.75 small, £8.65 large), British cheeses with chutney and walnut bread (£7.25), pastry leaves with mediterranean vegetables (£7.30), chargrilled lamb with pulses and red wine (£7.50), confit of duck with soya and ginger (£7.95), fillet of salmon with noodles, chilli and coriander (£8.35), and puddings such as banana pudding with banana custard, toasted brioche with almond cream and raspberries, and hot chocolate cheesecake (£4.15); salad and vegetables £2.35 extra. The restaurant is no smoking. Well kept (rather pricy) Wadworths 6X on handpump, a good choice of malt whiskies, home-made lemonade, and freshly squeezed orange juice. Get there early for a table. *(Recommended by C Gilbert, Paul Barnett, M J Dowdy, Nigel Norman, Hugh MacLean, S Dominey, Adam and Elizabeth Duff; also in Good Hotel Guide)*

Free house ~ Licensees Tom Lewis, Andrew Leeman, Howard Malin ~ Real ale ~ Meals and snacks (not Sat or Sun evenings) ~ Restaurant ~ (01993) 812291 ~ Children welcome ~ Open 11-2.30, 6-11; 12-2.30, 7-10.30 Sun; closed evening 25 Dec ~ Bedrooms: £88B/£105B

WOOTTON SP4320 Map 4
Kings Head 🍷

Chapel Hill; off B4027 N of Woodstock

Oxfordshire Dining Pub of the Year

The enthusiastic and friendly licensee in this pretty 17th-c Cotswold stone house extends a warm welcome to all his customers – visitors or regulars. The civilised and relaxing beamed lounge bar has a nice mix of old oak settles and chairs around wooden tables, comfortable armchairs and chintzy sofas, an open log fire, and old prints and ceramics on the pale pink walls. The spacious formal restaurant leads off here. Particularly good, enjoyable food (which can be eaten either in the bar, restaurant or garden) changes frequently and might include sandwiches (not Saturday evening or Sunday lunchtime), home-made soup (£2.95), warm goat's cheese with tomato chutney or avocado stilton bake (£3.95), warm salad niçoise with fresh tuna (£4.50), grilled fresh sardines or moules marinières (£5.50), chicken breast in a creamy tarragon sauce (£7.50), fillet of salmon on a julienne of vegetables (£9.95), noisettes of lamb with a redcurrant and burgundy sauce (£12.50), monkfish roasted with garlic and black pepper and served with a beurre blanc (£13.50), and home-made puddings (from £3.25). Well kept Morlands Original and Old Speckled Hen on handpump, and decent wines, including glasses served in 'normal' or 'friendly' sizes. *(Recommended by Heather Couper, M Hasslacher, Sir Nigel Foulkes, J Oakes, C Barrett, Mr and Mrs Peter Smith, B Haywood, Alan Tye, Pam Adlsey)*

Free house ~ Licensees Tony and Amanda Fay ~ Real ale ~ Meals and snacks (till 10pm) ~ Restaurant ~ (01993) 811340 ~ Well behaved children welcome ~ Open 11-3, 6-11; 12-3, 7-10.30 Sun ~ Bedrooms: £54B/£65B

WYTHAM SP4708 Map 4
White Hart

Village signposted from A34 ring road W of Oxford

Very well run, this picturesque creeper-covered pub is charmingly placed in an unspoilt village with houses owned and preserved by Oxford University. The partly panelled, flagstoned bar has high-backed black settles built almost the whole way round the cream walls, a shelf of blue and white plates, and a winter log fire with a fine relief of a heart on the iron fireback; there's a small no-smoking area, and trivia. Well kept ABC Best, Ind Coope Burton, Tetleys, and a guest beer on handpump, and a good choice of malt whiskies; helpful, knowledgeable bar staff. Bar food from the food servery includes cheese or pâté with bread (from £2.70), filled baked potatoes or help-yourself salads (around £3.60), steaks (from £8), fresh fish like plaice, trout or salmon, swordfish and tuna (from £8.20), daily pasta and vegetarian specials, and puddings (£2.90); maybe barbecues in the lovely walled rose garden. The pub's name is said to have come from a badge granted to the troops of Richard II after the Battle of Radcot Bridge in 1390. *(Recommended by M Sargent, David Carr, Gordon, Andrew Rogers, Amanda Milsom, Alan and Paula McCully, Hazel and Michael Duncombe, J I Davies, Wayne Brindle, Tony and Joan Walker, Tim Brierly, Pat and Roger Fereday, Joan Olivier)*

Allied Domecq ~ Managers Donald and Louise Tran ~ Real ale ~ Meals and snacks ~ (01865) 244372 ~ Children in eating area of bar ~ Open 11.30-11; 11.30-2.30, 6-11 in winter; 12-10.30 Sun

---

> If you stay overnight in an inn or hotel, they are allowed to serve you an alcoholic drink at any hour of the day or night.

Lucky Dip

Besides the fully inspected pubs, you might like to try these Lucky Dips recommended to us and described by readers (if you do, please send us reports):

☆ **Abingdon** [St Helens Wharf; SU4997], *Old Anchor*: Well kept Morlands in little front bar looking across Thames, flagstoned back bar with shoulder-height serving hatch, roomy lounge, panelled dining room overlooking neat almshouse gardens; warm fire, some comfortable leather armchairs, decent food inc children's, friendly service; charming spot *(TBB, Mrs I Folkard-Evans)*

Abingdon [Town Bridge], *Mill House*: Former Nags Head, built into medieval bridge over Thames; new river-view restaurant extension below, original pub part rebuilt, with four real ales; handy for boaters *(Quentin Williamson)*

Adderbury [just off A4260; SP4635], *Bell*: Homely and welcoming beamed village local with chiming grandfather clock, sofa by huge log fire, generous good fresh food, well kept Hook Norton inc seasonal ales; second bar with character old settles, candlelit back restaurant *(Pete Baker)*

☆ **Alvescot** [B4020 Carterton—Clanfield – OS Sheet 163 map ref 273045; SP2604], *Plough*: Partly 17th-c beamed village pub with good range of good value food inc vegetarian and Sun lunch (must book), quick welcoming service, well kept Boddingtons and Wadworths 6X, decent wines, good coffee, end dining area, old maps, log fire (but cool and pleasant on hot days), quiet piped music; separate public bar *(G Pearce, Peter and Audrey Dowsett, Marjorie and David Lamb, Kay Neville-Rolfe)*

Ardley [B430 (old A43) just SW of M40 junction 10; SP5427], *Fox & Hounds*: Keen young new licensees, beamed lounge/dining area opened up, snug small bar, two attractive inglenooks, food inc good value Sun lunch and old-fashioned puddings, Banks's and Morlands ales, decent house wines, pictures and old glassware; quiet piped music, Sun evening singalong *(D and E Frewer)*

Ashbury [B4507/B4000; SU2685], *Rose & Crown*: Comfortable open-plan beamed pub nr Ridgeway with highly polished woodwork, settees, pews and oak tables and chairs, traditional pictures, good range of usual food, sensible prices, well kept Arkells, friendly helpful staff, neat lavatories; bedrooms *(HNJ, PEJ, Peter Neate)*

☆ **Asthall** [off A40 at W end of Witney bypass, then 1st left; SP2811], *Maytime*: Genteel dining pub with very wide choice of good value well served meals inc plenty for vegetarians, some bar snacks, slightly raised plush dining lounge neatly set with tables, more airy conservatory restaurant (children allowed behind screen), Morrells and Wadworths 6X, decent wines, prompt service, interesting pictures, small locals' bar; piped music; in tiny hamlet, nice views of Asthall Manor and watermeadows from garden, big car park; quiet comfortable bedrooms around

striking courtyard, attractive walks *(Ian and Villy White, Pam Adsley, Marjorie and David Lamb, Jean and George Dundas, David Surridge, BB)*

Banbury [Parsons Lane; SP4540], *Wine Vaults*: Basic pub with bare boards and plain seating; exceptional range of well kept beers and good range of bottled beers; very cheap basic wholesome food *(Ted George)*

☆ **Beckley** [High St; signed off B4027; SP5611], *Abingdon Arms*: Busy food pub with interesting dishes (not Sun evening), well kept Hook Norton Best and Wadworths 6X, good range of wines, comfortably modernised simple lounge with interesting old photographs, smaller public bar with a couple of antique carved settles, bar billiards, dominoes, cribbage, shove-ha'penny; floodlit terrace, extensive pretty garden dropping away into orchard; good walks, no children, generally taciturn service *(Martin and Karen Wake, Prof A N Black, George Atkinson, D C T and E A Frewer, Adam and Elizabeth Duff, Hugh Quick, B J P Edwards, TBB, LYM)*

Begbroke [A44 Oxford—Woodstock; SP4613], *Royal Sun*: Spotless much refurbished open-plan stripped-stone pub with emphasis on prompt reasonably priced food; well kept Tetleys-related and guest ales, piped music and machines, tables on terrace and in small garden *(Dr and Mrs A K Clarke)*

Benson [SU6191], *Three Horseshoes*: Busy village pub, wide choice of generous fair-priced good fresh food changing daily in bar and neat dining room, good welcoming service, well kept Brakspears and changing guests; big rather informal garden *(Mrs I Folkard-Evans)*

Bletchingdon [Station Rd; B4027 N of Oxford; SP5017], *Blacks Head*: Friendly local overlooking village green, good value food, well kept ABC, Flowers IPA, Ind Coope Burton and Marstons Pedigree, big woodburner, darts, cards and dominoes in public bar, pool room, garden with Aunt Sally; informal singalong Thurs *(Ian and Liz Phillips, Pete Baker)*

Boars Hill [between A34 and B4017; SP4802], *Fox*: Attractive relaxed timbered pub in pretty countryside, dark wood tables and chairs in several 18th-c feel rambling rooms on different levels, good value food inc vegetarian and children's, Tetleys-related and other changing ales, decent wine, huge log fireplaces, family area, no piped music; restaurant, pleasant raised verandah, big garden with play area *(D C T and E A Frewer, Paul Robinshaw, Tim Brierly)*

Brightwell [signed off A4130 2 miles W of Wallingford; SU5790], *Red Lion*: Small basic unspoilt pub in peaceful village, warmly welcoming traditional landlord, comfortable lounge, rather spartan public bar with bar billiards in end games area, log fires, good value standard food (not Sun), up to seven well kept ales (Pete Baker)

☆ Brightwell Baldwin [signed off B480 Chalgrove—Watlington and B4009 Benson—Watlington; SU6595], Lord Nelson: Civilised turkey-carpet pub with dining chairs around country-kitchen tables, most laid for the food, Courage Best, Ruddles Best and Charles Wells Bombardier, decent house wines, no-smoking restaurant, simple decor with some maritime pictures; piped music, well behaved children allowed; front verandah, back terrace and attractive garden; now owned by Old English Pub Co (James Waller, Joan Olivier, LYM)

Britwell Salome [B4009 Watlington—Benson; SU6793], Red Lion: Friendly, with huge range of reasonably priced freshly prepared food (so may be a slight delay at busy times), Brakspears PA and Marstons Pedigree, separate back restaurant area (Marjorie and David Lamb, J and B Cressey)

☆ Buckland [off A420 E of Faringdon; SU3497], Lamb: Plushly refurbished and extended 18th-c stone-built dining pub very popular for good if not cheap food (not Mon) in front bar and restaurant, half-helpings at half price, smart helpful service, Morlands Original and a guest ale, decent wines; comfortable bedrooms, tiny village, lovely walking country (Dr and Mrs R H Wilkinson, Angus Lyon, J Tross, A C Morrison)

Bucknell [handy for M40 junction 10; SP5525], Trigger Pond: Neat stone-built pub opp the pond, well kept changing ales such as Adnams, Badger Best and Tanglefoot and Hook Norton Best, bar food, attentive staff; piped music; pleasant terrace and garden (Marjorie and David Lamb, George Atkinson)

☆ Burford [High St (A361); SP2512], Bull: Comfortable sofas in interestingly restored long narrow beamed and panelled hotel bar, Scottish Courage and a guest ale, woodburner, good choice of wines by the glass, wide choice of bar food inc lunchtime buffet, restaurant; piped music; children welcome, open all day; comfortable bedrooms (David Carr, Mr and Mrs N Spink, Andrew and Ruth Triggs, David Regan, LYM)

Burford [14 Witney St], Angel: Partly 14th c, long, narrow and attractive if austere, with heavy beams, panelling and flagstones, rather pricy food (not Sun evening) in bar and no-smoking dining room, big log fire, well kept Morlands Original and Marstons Pedigree; piped music, no children, open all day; clean comfortable bedrooms; the previous very friendly landlady is now to be found at the Fish in Bray – see Berks main entries (Mark Percy, Lesley Mayoh, Liz Bell, Charles Faragher, Miss Sarah Corlett, LYM); [Witney St], Royal Oak: Stripped stone, wide range of good simple food inc treacle tart as it used to be, well kept Wadworths ales, bar billiards, friendly staff; bedrooms (David Carr, Sally Shaw, Mr and Mrs N Spink)

☆ Caulcott [Lower Heyford Rd (B4030);

SP5024], Horse & Groom: Welcoming part-thatched creeper-covered 16th-c pub, cosy little unspoilt L-shaped bar, good log fire in stone fireplace, beams and brasses, dining end with good choice of straightforward home cooking by landlord inc good fish, Charles Wells Bombardier, Hook Norton Old Hookey and local Notley ale, happy hour 6-7, friendly landlady; outside lavatories, garden with picnic tables under cocktail parasols, no car park but lay-by opp (D C T and E A Frewer, M Sargent, Gwen and Peter Andrews, Marjorie and David Lamb, D and J McMillan, Chris Halek)

☆ Chadlington [Mill End; off A361 S of Chipping Norton, and B4437 W of Charlbury; SP3222], Tite: Comfortable and welcoming rambling local with settles, wooden chairs, prints, well kept changing ales, decent wines, good log fire in huge fireplace, good choice of sensibly priced food, rack of guidebooks; children welcome; lovely views, suntrap garden and terrace, pretty Cotswold village, good walks nearby (Tim Brierly, Pam Adsley, Derek and Sylvia Stephenson)

☆ Charlbury [Church St (B4437); SP3519], Bell: Small and attractive civilised bar, warm and friendly, with flagstones, stripped stonework, huge open fire, short choice of good interesting bar lunches (not Sun) from sandwiches up, well kept Hook Norton and Wadworths real ales, wide choice of malt whiskies, decent if pricy restaurant; children in eating area; comfortable bedrooms, good breakfasts (Alan and Paula McCully, Gordon, LYM)

☆ Charlbury [Sheep St], Bull: Very good bistro-style atmosphere and surroundings, restaurant on left and freshly furnished dining bar on right, good range of well presented very good food in generous helpings – not really a place for just a drink; cl Mon (John and Judy Fennell, BB)

Charlbury [Mkt St], Rose & Crown: Good range of beers inc guests, real pubby feel; open on Sun (Eddie Edwards)

Charney Bassett [SU3794], Chequers: Popular two-room village-green local with freshly prepared food (not Mon), well kept Fullers London Pride, Morlands and Theakstons XB; some singalongs, pool, piped music; children welcome (PB)

Checkendon [SU6682], Four Horseshoes: Attractive partly thatched local, good pub food, friendly landlord, music-free stripped-floor dining lounge (where children allowed), local public bar with pool table and piped music; well kept Brakspears, good simple wine list; big garden with picnic tables, super hanging baskets (G V Price)

Chesterton [SP5621], Red Cow: Nicely updated village local with two log fires, small dining area, well kept Morlands, subdued Victorian decor; interesting inn sign (Dr and Mrs A K Clarke)

☆ Chipping Norton [Goddards Lane; SP3127], Chequers: Three nicely old-fashioned beamed rooms, plenty of character, well kept Fullers ales inc Chiswick, straightforward lunchtime food, popular French-run evening restaurant, friendly staff, lively atmosphere; tables in courtyard *(P M Dodd, D Irving, E McCall, R Huggins, T McLean, M Benjamin)*

Chipping Norton [High St], *Blue Boar*: Spacious well worn-in stone-built pub divided by arches and pillars, wide choice of food from separate servery, John Smiths, Ruddles County and Wadworths 6X, cheap coffee, cheery staff; juke box or piped music, fruit machines, TV, piano, separate beamed back restaurant, long flagstoned conservatory *(George Atkinson, G V Price)*; [High St], *Crown & Cushion*: Handsome 16th-c hotel with attractive homely and pubby bar, some stripped stone and flagstones, well kept ales, bar food, flower-decked conservatory, tables in sheltered garden with suntrap terrace; children welcome, good bedrooms *(D Irving, E McCall, R Huggins, T McLean, LYM)*; [High St], *Fox*: Clean, tidy and quiet, with prompt friendly service, well kept Hook Norton Best, rambling lounge, open fire, upstairs dining room (can be used for sensibly priced lunchtime bar food); soft piped music, fruit machines; children welcome; well equipped good value bedrooms *(Simon Collett-Jones, David Carr, BB)*

☆ **Christmas Common** [signed from B480/B481; SU7193], *Fox & Hounds*: Unspoilt Chilterns cottage, cosy beamed bar with wall benches, bow-window seats, floor tiles and big inglenook log fire, locals' side bar with traditional games, good home-made soup, well kept Brakspears Bitter, Special and winter Old tapped from the cask in a back still room, tables outside, friendly staff; on a short lease – what are Brakspears' plans for this timeless place? *(Pete Baker, Derek Harvey-Piper, LYM)*

☆ **Church Hanborough** [opp church; signed off A4095 at Long Hanborough, or off A40 at Eynsham roundabout; SP4212], *Hand & Shears*: Attractively refurbished as dining place, long gleaming bar, steps down into spacious back eating area, another small dining room, wide choice of good brasserie-style food from simple bar dishes to fish and grills inc good thai curries, friendly efficient staff, Adnams Broadside, Fullers London Pride and Morlands Original, decent wines, open fires, good atmosphere, soft piped music *(John Waller, Kate Clear, Mr and Mrs R Maggs, BB)*

☆ **Clifton Hampden** [towards Long Wittenham, S of A415; SU5495], *Barley Mow*: Friendly thatched Chef & Brewer a short stroll from the Thames, very low ancient beams, oak-panelled family room, usual food, Scottish Courage ales, piped music, restaurant, tables in well tended garden; bedrooms *(David Carr, Joan Olivier, Edward, LYM)*

☆ **Coleshill** [B4019 Faringdon—Highworth; SU2393], *Radnor Arms*: Atmospheric high-raftered bar dominated by huge forge chimney, two coal-effect gas fires, lots of

smith's tools, two other cosy bars; Flowers tapped from the cask, good choice of reasonably priced food cooked to order, friendly quick service, small garden behind; piped music; charming preserved village (NT), lots of good walks *(Peter and Audrey Dowsett, HNJ, PEJ)*

Combe [off A4095 at Long Hanborough; SP4115], *Cock*: Spick and span pub facing green in charming village, friendly landlord, Morrells beers, evening food *(Peter and Audrey Dowsett)*

Cothill [SU4699], *Merry Miller*: Large popular pub/restaurant contrived from 17th-c granary, stripped stone and flagstones, friendly efficient staff, wide choice of sensibly priced food inc good sandwiches and children's dishes, no-smoking restaurant with wide-ranging menu inc vegetarian, good choice of wines and of well kept beers; disabled access *(Susan Trevaldwyn, JO, Stephen Rudge)*

☆ **Crawley** [SP3412], *Lamb*: 17th-c stone-built village pub on several levels with very welcoming new young landlord and Irish wife, unspoilt old beamed bar with log fire in big fireplace, good choice of food inc tasty soup, well kept Adnams Broadside and Hook Norton Best, decent wines, small family area, restaurant; piped Irish music; lots of tables in pleasant garden *(Tim Brierly, Peter and Audrey Dowsett)*

☆ **Cumnor** [Abingdon Rd; SP4603], *Vine*: Busy extended 18th-c pub with remarkably wide choice of enjoyable food esp starters (which would do as light lunch), original fireplace, carpeted back dining area, no-smoking area in conservatory, friendly well organised service, three well kept guest ales, good range of malt whiskies and wines, picnic tables in attractive back garden *(Mrs Linda Jordan, D and E Frewer, W B Baker, Adam and Elizabeth Duff, Mr and Mrs H W Clayton)*

Curbridge [Bampton Rd (A4095); SP3308], *Lord Kitchener*: Good food cooked to order (so may be a wait), old local photographs, big log fire, end dining area, well kept Morrells Bitter and Varsity, friendly efficient service; piped music may be loud; garden with play area *(Marjorie and David Lamb, Peggy and Bill Linfield)*

☆ **Deddington** [Horse Fair, off A4260/B4031; SP4631], *Deddington Arms*: 16th-c former Kings Arms, smartened up outside, with more emphasis on good imaginative food inside; nooks and crannies, black beams and timbers, mullioned windows, attractive settles and other comfortable country furnishings, fine log fire, well kept real ales, good choice of wines by the glass, friendly staff, children in eating area, spacious restaurant, small end games area; comfortable bedrooms *(Graham and Karen Oddey, Cyril Aydon, Rev John Cooper, J Oakes, Tim Brierly, LYM)*

☆ **Denchworth** [SU3791], *Fox*: Picturesque old thatched pub with two good log fires in low-ceilinged comfortable connecting areas, good range of good value food from sandwiches up, efficient service even when busy, Morlands Original and Revival Mild, quiet piped music, carvery in small beamed restaurant; peaceful garden, isolated ancient village (HNJ, PEJ, Marjorie and David Lamb)

☆ **Dorchester** [High St; SU5794], *Fleur de Lys*: Small 16th-c village pub opp abbey, two-level comfortably traditional interior, wide choice of good value home cooking, all fresh (not Mon; no sandwiches), Mansfield and Morlands Old Speckled Hen and Old Masters, friendly helpful service; unobtrusive piped music (Simon Collett-Jones, David Carr)

☆ **Drayton** [A422 W of Banbury; SP4241], *Roebuck*: Comfortable 16th-c creeper-covered pub with fresh imaginative food in cosy bar and evening restaurant, welcoming staff, well kept ales inc Boddingtons, Fullers London Pride and Hook Norton Best, solid fuel stove (F M Bunbury)

☆ **East Hendred** [Orchard Lane; SU4588], *Plough*: Enjoyable straightforward food in beamed village pub's attractive and airy main bar, Morlands ales with a guest such as Charles Wells Bombardier, quick friendly service, farm tools; occasional folk nights, attractive recently extended garden with good play area; pleasant village (Dick Brown, A G Drake, Andrew Bunting, BB)

☆ **East Hendred** [Chapel Sq], *Wheatsheaf*: Attractive 16th-c timbered village pub evidently settling down after landlord changes, high-backed settles and stools around tables on quarry tiles by inglenook fireplace, broad steps up to booth tables, well served home-cooked bar food, well kept Morlands Original and Old Speckled Hen, good house wines; children welcome, darts, dominoes, cribbage and Aunt Sally teams, piped music; open all day, colourful back garden (RCW, Steve Goodchild, LYM)

☆ **Eaton** [SP4403], *Eight Bells*: Low-beamed small-roomed Tudor pub with friendly staff, good value food inc enjoyable baked potatoes, well kept Morlands, open fires, horse tack and brasses, welcoming landlord, dining room (children allowed here) off cosy lounge; no dogs, tables in garden, tethering rail for horses (Joan Olivier, Gordon, Dr and Mrs A K Clarke, E McCall, R Huggins, T McLean, D Irving)

Emmington [Sydenham Rd; SP7302], *Inn at Emmington*: Family-run free house at foot of Chilterns, recently refurbished by hardworking new owners, interesting menu; bedrooms (David Regan)

Enslow [Enslow Bridge; off A4095 about 1½ miles SW of Kirtlington; SP4818], *Rock of Gibraltar*: Good value Beefeater in beautiful setting, tall building with modern dining extension overlooking canal, upper conservatory with even better view, beams, stripped stone, bright narrowboat paintwork, Scottish Courage ales; piped pop music; pretty garden (Ian Phillips)

Ewelme [off B4009 about 5 miles SW of M40 junction 6; SU6491], *Shepherds Hut*:

Unpretentious extended local, cheery welcoming staff, good value pub food, quick service, well kept Morlands Bitter and Old Masters, decent coffee, pot plants, darts, small restaurant; piped pop music, fruit machine; children welcome, tables and swing in small pleasant side garden (Margaret Dyke, Nick Holmes, M C Heath)

Faringdon [Market Pl; SU2895], *Bell*: Relaxing well worn in bar with red leather settles, inglenook fireplace with 17th-c carved oak chimney-piece, interesting mural in inner bar, well kept Wadworths 6X, straightforward bar food, friendly and helpful new management, restaurant; piped music; children welcome, tables out among flowers in attractive cobbled back coachyard; bedrooms (Gordon, LYM); [Market Pl], *Crown*: Civilised old inn, flagstones, panelling, woodburner, two bars and tiny side snug, popular reasonably priced well presented food, efficient friendly staff, well kept real ales; children welcome; good big bedrooms, lovely summer courtyard; the very long delay in sorting out one reader's double-debited Switch payment prevents a higher rating (Gordon, Sophie Prendergast, Peter and Audrey Dowsett, LYM)

☆ **Fernham** [B4508, off A420 SW of Oxford; SU2992], *Woodman*: Heavily beamed atmospheric 17th-c country pub, previously very popular for its combination of extreme candlelit rusticity with mildly upmarket feel – bolstered by very high beer prices; now charging less for the well kept ales tapped from the cask, and aiming higher in the food stakes (good choice, running up to kangaroo), but it may take a bit of time for the change of style to settle in properly; great log fire, children welcome (Mr and Mrs B J Cox, Michael Kirby, LYM; more reports please)

☆ **Fifield** [Stow Rd (A424); SP2318], *Merrymouth*: Isolated rambling old pub with relaxed atmosphere, flagstones, lots of stripped stone, bay windows, farm tools on low beams, open fires, Donnington and perhaps other ales, unobtrusive piped music, food in bar and restaurant; tables on terrace and in back garden; children allowed one end; bedrooms (John Waller, LYM)

Filkins [signed off A361 Lechlade—Burford; SP2304], *Five Alls*: Old-fashioned Cotswold stone pub with two unpretentious lounges, good value food from ploughman's up, Flowers Original, Hook Norton Best and Old Hookey, decent house wine, log fires, sizeable restaurant, coffee lounge; cl Mon (Andrew and Ruth Triggs, Mr and Mrs Cresswell); [A361], *Lamb*: Generous food all home-cooked (limited Sun), well kept Morlands and John Smiths, decent house wines in two-bar stonebuilt local, part Elizabethan, warm, friendly and comfortable; no piped music, big garden, pleasant bedrooms; cl Mon (Peter and Audrey Dowsett, K Frostick)

☆ **Freeland** [Witney Rd; A4095 SW of Long Hanborough; SP4112], *Shepherds Hall*: Large comfortable bar with open fire and gleaming copper, long-serving welcoming and caring licensees, good varied food – nothing too expensive; well kept Flowers IPA and Wadworths 6X, discreet piped pop music, back games room with two pool tables, garden with play area; comfortable bedrooms *(Trevor Moore, Peter and Audrey Dowsett, K Neville-Rolfe)*

Frilford [Frilford Heath; SU4497], *Dog House*: Pleasant dining room, good generous food *(Miss M Oakeley)*

Fringford [off A421 N of Bicester; SP6028], *Butchers Arms*: Remote but friendly and bustling village pub, well kept Tetleys, freshly cooked usual food inc Sun roast, darts and TV in L-shaped bar, fruit machine and piped music in lounge, amiable scotch terrier; quiz night Mon; seats (and rather spartan lavatories) outside *(Margaret Dyke, CMW, JJW)*

☆ **Fulbrook** [SP2513], *Masons Arms*: Welcoming and chatty village pub with good value home cooking using local produce, nice open fire, well kept Hook Norton, Wadworths 6X and a guest beer, interesting malt whiskies, good service, bar billiards, locals with dogs; children very welcome *(Bob Tivey)*

Garsington [The Green; SP5702], *Three Horseshoes*: Largish village pub with usual bygone-ish decorations, mainly Morrells beers, extensive bar menu, cheerful service; busy at lunchtime with E Oxford business people *(Anon)*

☆ **Godstow** [SP4809], *Trout*: Creeper-covered medieval pub, much extended and commercialised as big tourist draw, but nicely done, with fires in three huge hearths, beams and shiny ancient flagstones, furnishings to suit, attractive pictures, roomy recently expanded dining area, back extension with Inspector Morse memorabilia and children's area; food inc big pies, Bass and Fullers London Pride, winter mulled wine – at its best midweek out of season, but no denying the summer charm of its lovely terrace by a stream full of greedily plump perch, with peacocks in the grounds *(Mr and Mrs S Talling, Mr and Mrs R Maggs, D Maplethorpe, B Helliwell, Tim Brierly, E McCall, R Huggins, T McLean, D Irving, Mark Percy, Lesley Mayoh, Gordon, M Rutherford, David Carr, LYM)*

Goring [Manor Rd; SU6080], *John Barleycorn*: Endearing low-beamed traditional village local in pretty Thames village, prints in cosy little lounge bar, good choice of well priced food in adjoining eating area, well kept Brakspears, pool in end room, friendly helpful service; bedrooms clean and simple *(Mrs I Folkard-Evans, Gordon, Ron Leigh)*

Goring [Station Rd], *Catherine Wheel*: Good value food in roomy bar and restaurant, well kept Brakspears, friendly licensee, good log fire; notable door to gents' *(M Holdsworth, Mrs I Folkard-Evans, TRS, Gordon)*

☆ **Hailey** [Whiteoak Green, B4022 Witney—

Charlbury; SP3414], *Bird in Hand*: Large friendly modern country inn with wide range of interesting generous food in lounge or attractive restaurant, helpful attentive service, well kept Boddingtons, Courage Directors and Marstons Pedigree, lots of wood, well chosen pictures and subdued lighting (inc candles on tables), nice views, a welcome for walkers; comfortable cottage-style bedrooms *(Mrs B Sugarman, Mimi and Alastair McNeil, Dick Brown, Allan Mooney)*

Hailey [B4022 a mile N of Witney; SP3512], *Lamb & Flag*: Friendly welcome, good range of low-priced food, prompt service, well kept Morlands Original and Old Speckled Hen *(Marjorie and David Lamb)*

☆ **Hailey** [entirely different village from previous entry – leave Wallingford on A4130, turn left to Hailey 2 miles on; SU6485], *King William IV*: The long-standing tenant of this attractive 16th-c Brakspears pub, in charming peaceful countryside, tells us he's retiring – and disposing of the amazing collection of rural bygones which has helped make the pub so memorable; beams and bare brickwork, big log fire, sturdy furnishings on the tiled floor, but we have no idea yet what the food will be like under the new regime *(LYM)*

Henley [Friday St; SU7882], *Anchor*: Cosy and relaxing informally run local almost right on the Thames, homely country furniture and bric-a-brac in softly lit parlourish beamed front bar, huge helpings of reasonably priced food, well kept Brakspears, friendly and obliging landlady; darts, bar billiards, piano and TV in room on right, back dining room; charming back terrace *(GWB)*; [Northfield End], *Old White Horse*: Friendly and comfortable beamed pub in nice spot by Thames, tasteful furnishings, good value varied food, well kept Boddingtons and Brakspears; pleasant tables in courtyard, new licensees planning bedrooms *(Mr and Mrs D Goodger)*; [5 Market Pl], *Three Tuns*: Heavy beams and panelling, two rooms opened together around old-fashioned central servery with well kept Brakspears, straightforward generous home-cooked food all day, floodlit back terrace and separate games bar with pinball, juke box and fruit machine; no children *(David Carr, LYM)*

☆ **Highmoor** [B481 N of Reading, off A423 Henley—Oxford; SU6984], *Dog & Duck*: Cosy and cottagey low-beamed country pub with chintzy curtains, floral cushions, lots of pictures; relaxing bar on left, dining room on right, log fire in each, smaller dining room behind, good food inc good vegetarian dishes, friendly landlord, well kept Brakspears Bitter, Old and Special; tables in garden *(Vicky Cashell)*

☆ **Hook Norton** [SP3533], *Sun*: Attractively enlarged old village local with two bars, no-smoking restaurant, huge choice of good food from sandwiches to wild boar steaks, well kept Hook Norton ales inc Mild from the nearby brewery, decent wines, reasonable drinks prices, nice bar staff, darts; wheelchair access and disabled facilities, comfortable bedrooms *(Deryck and Margaret Watkinson, Margaret and Roy Randle, Chris Raisin, Graham Doyle)*

Horton Cum Studley [Old Green; SP5812], *Kings Arms*: Heavy beams, stripped stone or dark red paintwork, unusual central fireplace with vented stonework, sofa and rattan-style chairs; good value food, well kept beers, good friendly service; bedrooms *(Pat and Derek Westcott)*

Iffley [Church Rd; SP5203], *Prince of Wales*: Good range of well kept ales inc Smiles, Wadworths and regular beer festivals, nice decor, interesting pictures and memorabilia, relaxed atmosphere, good service, generous food; seats outside *(Jenny and Brian Seller)*

Islip [B4027; SP5214], *Swan*: Old stonebuilt pub, much renovated with wooden floors, tables and chairs in long L-shaped bar; good choice of home-made food inc Sun lunch, three Morrells ales; dogs welcome, picnic tables out in front, opp river *(CMW, JJW, BB)*

Kingston Lisle [SU3287], *Blowing Stone*: No reports on this since closure autumn 1996 (said at time to be temporary) when previous landlord moved to Crown at Broad Hinton (Wilts), but has been popular pub in attractive village, handy for Ridgeway walks, with small relaxing refurbished lounge bar, tiny snug, elegant roomy dining conservatory, good generous food from sandwiches to Sun lunch, decent wine, good range of changing ales; roomy public bar with pool and piped music, pretty bedrooms *(JO, GWAP; news please)*

Langford [SP2402], *Bell*: Unassuming village pub with two big log fires, usual food, Wadworths 6X; no piped music *(Peter and Audrey Dowsett)*

Little Coxwell [A420 just SW of Faringdon; SU2793], *Plough*: Friendly roadside pub with log fires, good choice of reasonably priced food, well kept real ales, quiet piped music, back restaurant, family room; swings in big garden *(Peter and Audrey Dowsett)*

☆ **Little Milton** [3 miles from M40, junction 7: A329 towards Wallingford; SP6100], *Lamb*: Pretty 17th-c thatched pub with beams, stripped stone, low windows, soft lighting, lots of tables for food (all day Sun) from sandwiches to good specials and steaks, well kept Bass, Benskins and Ind Coope Burton; children in eating area (lots of food choice for them), peaceful and attractive garden with swings, pleasant countryside *(Mr and Mrs R Maggs, John Waller, LYM)*

Littleworth [A420 NE of Faringdon; SU3197], *Fox & Hounds*: Straightforward pub with good value simple food, well kept Hook Norton and Morlands, friendly service, good log fire, small no-smoking restaurant; quiet piped music, games in public bar; garden with swings and apple trees, small caravan site *(JJW, CMW)*

☆ **Long Wittenham** [Fieldside, off A415 SE of Abingdon; SU5493], *Machine Man*: Good choice of genuine food freshly made to order, wide range of ales inc Eldridge Pope Royal

Oak and Wadworths, decent wines, friendly unpretentious local atmosphere, good service, darts; bedrooms *(Marjorie and David Lamb, D and J McMillan)*

☆ **Long Wittenham**, *Plough*: Good value food in friendly low-beamed refurbished lounge with lots of brass, games in public bar, inglenook log fires, Ushers ales, pool and children's room; Thames moorings at bottom of long spacious garden; bedrooms *(A Kilpatrick, Hazel and Michael Duncombe, Margaret Dyke, Paul Pownall)*

☆ **Longworth** [off A420 Oxford—Faringdon; SU3899], *Blue Boar*: Cosy thatched country local with plenty of character, two good log fires and unusual decor (skis on beams etc); good value food inc unusual dishes and speciality evenings, well kept Bass and Morrells Best, piped music, friendly quick service *(Gordon, Michael and Hazel Duncombe, Marjorie and David Lamb)*

Lower Assendon [B480; SU7484], *Golden Ball*: Attractive 16th-c beamed pub popular for food; log fire, well kept Brakspears, decent house wines, garden behind *(Gordon, GWB, James Nunns)*

☆ **Marston** [Mill Lane, Old Marston; SP5209], *Victoria Arms*: Attractive grounds by River Cherwell inc spacious terrace, good play area, punt moorings and hire; full Wadworths range and guest beers, generous good value food (not Sun evening in winter) from chunky sandwiches up inc children's dishes, lots of tables in civilised main room and smaller ones off, real fires; soft piped music, children and dogs allowed; lavatory for disabled; beware vicious sleeping policemen *(David Campbell, Vicki McLean, Joan Olivier, BB)*

Middleton Stoney [B430/B4030; SP5323], *Jersey Arms*: Small 19th-c stonebuilt hotel, low and rambling, with cosy traditional oak-beamed bar, log fire in small comfortable panelled lounge, upmarket feel, good food in bar and restaurant, Tetleys, Theakstons Best and Wadworths 6X, good coffee, friendly helpful staff; piped music, popular for business lunches; garden; bedrooms comfortable *(D and E Frewer, George Aktinson)*

Milton Hill [A4130, junction A34 nr Didcot Power Stn; SU4790], *Packhorse*: Completely refurbished by Morlands, with friendly attentive mini-skirted waitresses in no-smoking restaurant, piping hot food, children welcome, disabled access (perhaps best from front); big garden – no dogs allowed – with floodlit terrace *(Joan Olivier)*

☆ **Minster Lovell** [just N of B4047 Witney—Burford; SP3111], *Old Swan*: Interesting and attractive old inn, rather upmarket but relaxing and comfortable, very popular lunchtime for good if not cheap snacks and light meals (no sandwiches), Marstons ales, log fire, friendly obliging service, deep armchairs, rugs on flagstones, restaurant, tables in lovely garden; bedrooms *(Joan Olivier, A C Morrison, David Carr, Gordon, Gordon Tong, LYM)*

Minster Lovell [B4047], *White Hart*: Welcoming 17th-c former coaching inn, big pleasant lounge, well kept changing ales, wide choice of reasonably priced bar food from sandwiches up, good log fire, big separate restaurant; piped music *(Anthony Lock, Peter and Audrey Dowsett, Dave Braisted)*

Mollington [just off A423 N of Banbury; SP4447], *Green Man*: Lots of brasses, corn dollies, old photographs, low beams (one so low as to need head-padding), friendly attentive landlord, basic menu *(Ted George)*

Moreton [SP6904], *Royal Oak*: Free house with country views from big terrace, well kept ales, good wine list, great atmosphere; live entertainment *(Douglas Harrison)*

☆ **Moulsford** [Ferry Lane, off A329 N of Streatley; SU5983], *Beetle & Wedge*: Good though far from cheap leisurely meals (more vegetarian choice would be appreciated), chatty Boathouse bar/restaurant by the Thames with well kept Adnams Best, Badger Tanglefoot and Wadworths 6X, good wines, pleasant waterside garden; well behaved children welcome, charming comfortable bedrooms *(Fhiona Skaife, Dayl Gallacher, Douglas Frewer, Mr and Mrs P Smith, LYM)*

☆ **Newbridge** [A415 7 miles S of Witney; SP4001], *Maybush*: New licensees doing good food at attractive prices in low-beamed unpretentious local in lovely Thamesside setting; well kept Morlands Original and Old Speckled Hen, no piped music; children welcome, moorings, pretty and neatly kept waterside garden with terrace *(Mrs L M Jordan, Lynda Payton, Sam Samuells, LYM)*

☆ **Newbridge**, *Rose Revived*: Big pub well worth knowing for its lovely lawn by the upper Thames, across the road from our other entry here, prettily lit at night (good overnight mooring free); inside knocked through as busy Morlands dining pub – usual food all day inc Sun carvery, prompt polite service, helpful landlord, real ales, piped music, fruit machines; children welcome, comfortable bedrooms with good breakfast *(Colin and Meg Hamilton, Miss M Oakeley, Peter and Audrey Dowsett, James Nunns, Meg and Colin Hamilton, LYM)*

☆ **North Hinksey** [off A34 southbound just S of A420 interchange; SP4805], *Fishes*: Comfortable Victorian-style open-plan lounge and conservatory, friendly new French licensees doing enjoyable reasonably priced food esp fish, well kept Morrells, decent house wines, pleasant conservatory; soft piped music; big streamside garden with play area and two Aunt Sally pitches *(Dick Brown, Joan Olivier)*

☆ **North Newington** [High St, just W of Banbury; SP4139], *Roebuck*: Open fires and piped classical music in attractive bistro-style dining bar, touch of the Orient in very wide range of good value interesting home-made food, themed dinners, individual furnishings, well kept Morlands, good wines and country wines, lovely briards, welcoming attentive service; open fire in traditional public bar,

children very welcome, good garden with play area and animals; in quiet village nr Broughton Castle *(Mrs Tudor Hughes, John Bowdler, D and E Frewer)*

Northmoor [B4449 SE of Stanton Harcourt; SP4202], *Red Lion*: Small 15th-c stonebuilt village local, heavily beamed bar and small dining room off, welcoming log fire, wide range of home-cooked bar food inc Fri fish and chips and good value Sun lunch, well kept Morlands Original, friendly staff, garden; no dogs *(Margaret Dyke, Marjorie and David Lamb, Joan Olivier, James Nunns)*

☆ **Nuffield** [A423/B481; SU6687], *Crown*: New tenants, food from sandwiches up inc daily fresh fish, country furniture and inglenook log fire in redecorated beamed lounge bar, well kept Brakspears Bitter, Special, Hop Demon and a seasonal ale; children in small family room, tables outside front and back, good walks *(J and B Cressey, Joan Olivier, LYM)*

☆ **Oxford** [Broad St], *White Horse*: Busy and cheerfully studenty, sandwiched between bits of Blackwells bookshop; single small narrow bar with snug one-table raised back alcove, mellow oak beams and timbers, ochre ceiling, beautiful view of the Clarendon building and Sheldonian, good lunchtime food (the few tables reserved for this), well kept Tetleys-related ales and Wadworths 6X, Addlestone's cider, friendly licensees *(Tim and Ann Newell, Gordon, James Nunns, Alan and Paula McCully, BB)*

☆ **Oxford** [North Parade Ave], *Rose & Crown*: Particularly well kept Tetleys-related ales in friendly and unspoilt old local in appealing narrow street; character landlord, limited but popular and well priced bar lunches inc Sun roasts, decent wine, prompt service; reference books for crossword buffs, no piped music or machines, jazz piano Tues; traditional small rooms, pleasant back yard with motorised awning and huge gas heater – children not allowed here or inside unless with friends of landlord *(Margaret Dyke, Roger Crisp, Gordon, John and Hazel Waller, BB)*

☆ **Oxford** [Alfred St], *Bear*: Four friendly little low-ceilinged and partly panelled rooms, not over-smart and often packed with students; massive collection of vintage ties, simple food most days inc sandwiches (kitchen may be closed Weds), good range of well kept Tetleys-related and other ales from centenarian handpumps on rare pewter bar counter, no games machines, tables outside; open all day summer *(David Carr, J and P Maloney, Sue Demont, Tim Barrow, Gordon, LYM)*

☆ **Oxford** [St Giles], *Eagle & Child*: Busy rather touristy pub (tiny mid-bars full of actors' and Tolkien/C S Lewis memorabilia), but students too; nice panelled front snugs, tasteful modern back extension with no-smoking conservatory, well kept Tetleys-related ales and Wadworths 6X, plentiful quickly served food, piped classical music, newspapers *(Keith and Janet Morris, Christopher Glasson, Tim and Ann Newell, Gordon, David Carr, BB)*

Oxford [Hollybush Row], *Albion*: Basic local with well kept Morrells, back pool room, friendly landlord *(Richard Lewis)*; [17 Victor St, Jericho], *Bookbinders Arms*: Friendly and unpretentious little local, darts, cards and serious shove ha'penny, light snacks and some hot dishes inc good value mild chicken curry, well kept Morrells *(Pete Baker)*; [St Thomas St], *Brewer & Gate*: Spacious, with bare boards, lots of prints, log fire, friendly staff and locals, bar food, full Morrells range kept well, also brewery shop; tables outside *(Richard Lewis)*; [Summertown], *Dewdrop*: Friendly service, reasonably priced spicy Indian dishes and traditional food, generous helpings, well kept Theakstons and Wadworths 6X, cheerful young customers *(R T and J C Moggridge)*; [38 Abingdon Rd], *Folly Bridge*: Friendly open-plan Wadworths pub (though its old-fashioned 1950s style is more reminiscent of a Firkin), with five real ales (more 1st Thurs in month), jolly atmosphere, straightforward food; landlord can suggest nearby B&Bs; children welcome if eating, short walk from Thames *(G Coates, Dr and Mrs A K Clarke)*; [St Giles/Banbury Rd], *Lamb & Flag*: Well kept Scottish Courage ales, good food, friendly service; can be packed with students, back rooms with exposed stonework and panelled ceilings have more atmosphere *(Pat & Roger Fereday, John and Hazel Waller, BB)*; [Binsey Lane – narrow lane on right leaving city on A420, just before Self Operated Storage], *Perch*: Lovely thatched pub in pleasant setting with big garden off riverside meadow; big and busy, with low ceilings, flagstones, stripped stone, high-backed settles as well as more modern seats, log fires, no-smoking eating area (children allowed), Tetleys-related ales and Wadworths 6X, decent wine, well meaning service; machines, piped music; good play area, barbecues, landing stage, attractive waterside walks *(Tim Brierly, BB)*; [Woodstock Rd, opp Radcliffe Infirmary], *Royal Oak*: Maze of little rooms meandering around central bar, low beams, celebrity pictures in front bar, lunchtime food bar with good soup and doorsteps of bread, simple main dishes, several real ales, daily papers, open fire, games room with darts, pool etc, small back terrace; well used by doctors and nurses, open all day *(John and Wendy Trentham, Gordon)*; [Friars Entry, St Michael St], *Three Goats Heads*: Two good-sized friendly and attractive bars, relaxed downstairs, more formal up; well kept cheap Sam Smiths, good choice of quick generous food, dark wood and booths *(Hugh MacLean, David Carr)*; [George St], *Yates's Wine Lodge*: Recently opened, usual Yates's pattern; good range of beers, good cheap food, plenty of room on two levels, lots of woodwork, civilised feel *(Dick Brown)*

☆ **Pishill** [B480 Nettlebed—Watlington; SU7389], *Crown*: Ancient pub in pretty country setting, home-cooked bar food (not Sun or Mon evenings) from sandwiches to steaks, tastefully redecorated candlelit bar with black beams, standing timbers and three blazing log fires, well kept Brakspears, Flowers Original and a guest beer, picnic tables on attractive side lawn, nice surroundings; bedrooms in separate cottage; children allowed Sun lunchtime in restaurant *(Susan and John Douglas, Gordon, LYM)*

Play Hatch [just off A4155; SU7476], *Crown*: Spacious rambling 16th-c pub with two bars and several rooms inc big no-smoking conservatory, well kept Brakspears PA, SB and Old tapped from casks, decent wines, good food and service *(Gordon)*

☆ **Pyrton** [handy for M40 junction 6; off B4009 towards Wallingford; SU6896], *Plough*: Clean and cosy 17th-c thatched pub with good generous fresh food inc vegetarian, fine choice of winter casseroles and well priced puddings, well kept Adnams, Brakspears and Fullers ESB, prompt friendly service, spotless old-fashioned stripped-stone beamed main bar with big woodburner, evening dining area; maybe piped local radio, cl Mon evening, picnic tables outside *(GWB, James Waller, John Barker, P J Keen)*

Ramsden [Whiteoak Green; B4022 N of Witney; SP3414], *Bird in Hand*: Greatly extended old Cotswold stone pub, smart and clean, with well kept beer, friendly service; very popular for food *(Gordon)*

Rotherfield Peppard [Gallowstree Rd; SU7181], *Greyhound*: Picture-book cottagey pub in lovely country setting, spotless attractive beamed bar with walking stick collection, friendly service, good choice of beers; wide choice of good home-made food, pine-furnished barn restaurant; charming front garden with terrace, arbour and boules *(Susan and John Douglas, Maysie Thompson)*

☆ **Satwell** [just off B481, 2 miles S of Nettlebed; follow Shepherds Green signpost; SU7083], *Lamb*: Cosy and attractive 16th-c low-beamed cottage, very small (so can get cramped), with tiled floors, pine furniture, friendly licensees, huge log fireplace, filled baguettes, ploughman's and wide range of good hot food, well kept Brakspears, traditional games, small carpeted family room, tables outside *(W W Burke, Martin and Karen Wake, BB)*

☆ **Shilton** [off B4020 S of Burford; SP2608], *Rose & Crown*: Mellow 17th-c low-beamed stonebuilt village local with wide choice of good home-made food from sandwiches up, friendly attentive staff, well kept Morlands Old Masters and Old Speckled Hen, woodburner, soft piped music, darts in beamed and tiled public bar, restaurant; pretty village *(Joan Olivier, Peter and Audrey Dowsett, Marjorie and David Lamb, G W A Pearce)*

Shiplake [SU7678], *Plowden Arms*: Neat and friendly open-plan local, good range of home-made food inc good value Sun lunch, well kept Boddingtons and Brakspears, children's room; handy for Thames walk *(P J Caunt)*

Shrivenham [High St; SU2488], *Prince of*

Wales: Ancient stone pub with spotless low-beamed lounge, wholesome plain food, small dining area, cheerful thoughtful landlord, Wadworths ales, brasses and pictures, big L-shaped public bar with fruit machine *(HNJ, PEJ)*

☆ Sibford Gower [signed off B4035 Banbury—Shipston on Stour; SP3537], *Wykham Arms*: Cordial new licensees in pretty thatched cottage, comfortable open-plan low-beamed stripped-stone lounge, table made from glass-topped well, inglenook tap room, attractive partly no-smoking restaurant; wide choice of food from sandwiches up inc lots of vegetarian and fish, well kept Banks's, Hook Norton and a guest ale, good coffee, decent wines, dominoes, children welcome; country views from big well planted garden, lovely manor house opp; cl Mon lunchtime *(Martin Jones, Mrs Tudor Hughes, LYM)*

☆ Souldern [Fox Lane (off B4100); SP5131], *Fox*: Charming beamed stone pub, cosy, spotless and comfortable; good interesting food from ploughman's to good value Sun lunch, well kept Hook Norton and other real ales, decent wines, friendly landlord, separate dining room, nice village location; comfortable bedrooms, good breakfasts *(Margaret Dyke, Tim Brierly, Andy and Jill Kassube)*

South Hinksey [Manor Rd; SP5004], *General Elliott*: Totally unpretentious village pub, off the beaten track; lovely garden, two Aunt Sally pitches *(Dr and Mrs A K Clarke)*

South Leigh [3 miles S of A40 Witney—Eynsham; SP3908], *Mason Arms*: Very restauranty now, and the style may not appeal to everyone, with high prices (even £1 cover charge for bar snacks!), limited beers (Ind Coope Burton) and management that's not exactly self-effacing; but pleasant layout, with two big log fires, pictures on dusky red walls, candlelight and flagstones, sturdy antique furnishings, nice table linen in the main dining room; no children in bar, tables outside, cl Mon *(Dr and Mrs A Whiteway, W B Baker, Alan and Susan Dominey, LYM)*

☆ South Moreton [High St, just W of Wallingford; SU5588], *Crown*: Above-average fresh home-made food inc some interesting dishes in opened-out family country pub, particularly well kept Wadworths and guest ales tapped from the cask, good friendly service; children allowed, discount scheme for OAPs, Mon quiz night, small garden *(John Baker, Tony Merrill)*

☆ Sparsholt [SU3487], *Star*: Good home-cooked food cooked to order (so may be a short wait) in comfortable and relaxed old racing-country local, log fire, attractive pictures, attentive staff, Morlands Original, Worthington BB and a guest such as Brains SA, daily papers, subdued piped music, back garden; pretty village *(Marjorie and David Lamb)*

☆ Standlake [High St, off A415 SE of Witney; SP3902], *Bell*: Unusual plush restaurant/bar area and separate lounge bar, consistently good well presented food inc wide choice of

doorstep sandwiches, interesting hot dishes – no bar lunches Sun/Mon, evening food in restaurant, also Sun lunch; well kept Morlands and a guest such as Everards Tiger, good value wine, friendly licensees *(Simon Miles, DWJ, Craig and Gillian Brown)*

☆ Stanton Harcourt [B4449 S of Eynsham; SP4105], *Harcourt Arms*: More restaurant than pub, good meals in three welcoming, attractive, simply furnished and pleasantly informal dining areas with Spy cartoons and huge fireplaces; good choice of wines; piped music; children welcome *(Mr and Mrs H W Clayton, LYM)*

☆ Steventon [The Causeway – central westward turn off main rd; village signed off A34; SU4691], *North Star*: A special favourite for lovers of the unspoilt, tiled passage leading to main bar with built-in settles forming snug, steam-engine pictures, interesting local horsebrasses and other brassware; open fire in parlourish lounge, simple dining room; Morlands Mild, Bitter and Best tapped from casks in a side tap room, cheap weekday lunchtime bar food, cribbage; tables on grass by side grass *(Gordon, PB, LYM)*

☆ Steventon, *Cherry Tree*: New licensees doing particularly good choice of good well priced food in spacious and relaxing interconnecting rooms, dark green walls, two or three old settles among more modern furnishings, interesting bric-a-brac; well kept Wadworths Farmers Glory and 6X and three guest beers, efficient friendly service, log-effect gas fires; unobtrusive piped music in public bar, tables on newly extended terrace *(Dick Brown, Bruce Bird)*

Steventon [Milton Hill; SU4790], *Packhorse*: In area renowned for cherries, pretty at blossom-time; two dining areas, one non smoking, food inc good Sun lunch, tables outside *(Joan Olivier)*

☆ Stoke Lyne [off B4100; SP5628], *Peyton Arms*: Unspoilt tiny snug, bigger public bar with good range of traditional games (no juke box or machines), welcoming service, well kept Hook Norton tapped from the cask, limited cold lunchtime snacks, pleasant garden with Aunt Sally *(Pete Baker, Andy and Jill Kassube)*

☆ Stoke Row [Newlands Lane, off B491 N of Reading – OS Sheet 175 map ref 684844; SU6884], *Crooked Billet*: Opened-up beamed country pub/restaurant with wide choice of very good interesting meals inc full vegetarian menu, relaxed homely atmosphere – like a French country restaurant; well kept Brakspears tapped from the cask, decent wines, good log fires, children welcome; big garden, by Chilterns beech woods *(James Nunns, Paul McPherson, C Baxter, LYM)*

Stoke Talmage [signed off A40 at Tetsworth; SU6799], *Red Lion*: Unspoilt country tavern, basic, friendly and welcoming, with cards and dominoes in parlour-like lounge, well kept Butcombe and Morlands, great character landlord; pleasant garden *(PB)*

☆ Stonor [B480 N of Henley; SU7388], *Stonor*

Arms: Elegantly refurbished upmarket village inn with comfortable flagstoned bar, log fires, very good individual food inc sophisticated dishes at appropriate prices (canapes with drinks, petits fours with good coffee), welcoming young staff, Luxters real ale, daily papers and magazines, lovely conservatory and garden; good bedrooms *(Tim Brierly, Mrs E Macdonald)*

Stratton Audley [off A421 NE of Bicester; SP6026], *Red Lion*: Welcoming village local with log fire, stripped stone and beams, suitably old varnished wooden furniture, enjoyable food, good choice of beers; small garden, pretty village *(Tim Brierly, David Regan)*

Swalcliffe [Bakers Lane; just off B4035; SP3737], *Stags Head*: Country local little changed under its new owners, hub of village life, lots of jugs hanging from ceiling, nice garden dropping in terraces down the hillside, Fullers Chiswick, good food, very friendly chatty landlord *(George Atkinson)*

☆ **Swinbrook** [back rd a mile N of A40, 2 miles E of Burford; SP2811], *Swan*: New tenants welcoming children and dogs to this dim-lit little beamed and flagstoned 16th-c country pub, antique settles, sporting prints and woodburner in friendly flagstoned tap room and back bar, carpeted dining room; enjoyable food (all day weekends), traditional games, Morlands Original and Wadworths 6X, farm ciders, no piped music; seats outside, nice surroundings *(Ted George, Daren Haines, Peter and Audrey Dowsett, LYM)*

☆ **Sydenham** [off A40 NW of High Wycombe, and B4445 SE of Thame; SP7201], *Crown*: Relaxed rambling low-beamed village local, a little lamp in each small window, unusual choice of good interesting food, Morrells Best and Varsity with a guest such as Adnams, good choice of wines by the glass, friendly staff (and Max the pub labrador), children welcome, dominoes and darts; quiz nights, treasure hunts, maybe piped radio, can be smoky; picturesque village, views of lovely church *(M and S Rollinson, C and T Stone, Paul Kitchener, Jenny and Michael Back)*

☆ **Tackley** [off A4260 N of Kidlington; SP4720], *Gardiners Arms*: Comfortable spick and span lounge bar with beams, brasses and coal-effect gas fire in inglenook, well presented good value food from sandwiches up inc good vegetarian choice, charming Dickensian landlord, well kept Morrells ales, good coffee; separate public bar with darts and piped pop music, bookable skittle alley, picnic tables on sunny terrace; handy for Rousham House *(Ian Phillips, George Atkinson)*

Tetsworth [A40; SP6801], *Lion on the Green*: Wide choice of good bar food and good Sun lunch, well kept Boddingtons and Brakspears, friendly service, real fire, no dogs; bedrooms *(Dave Braisted, Sandria Parker)*

Thame [21 Cornmarket; SP7005], *Abingdon Arms*: Friendly family atmosphere, generous food inc home-made fresh pasta and speciality doorstep sandwiches, helpful staff, well kept Bass, Brakspears, Fullers London Pride, good choice of bottled beers, small no-smoking front lounge and no-smoking bar, simple bright main bar with bare boards and oriental rugs, three real fires; piped music, busier and noisier evenings; open all day, tables in nice back garden with swings *(P Worth)*; *Bird Cage*: Quaint black and white beamed and timbered pub, bare boards, some carpet, homely chairs, lots of bric-a-brac, open fires; short reasonably priced bar lunch menu, well kept ales, good bar food, piped music, friendly staff *(Ted George, LYM)*; [26 High St], *Rising Sun*: Flagstones and bare boards in three linked rooms, new licensees doing generous food inc good range of sandwiches, well kept Brakspears with guests such as Boddingtons and Theakstons, real fire, pleasant atmosphere *(Tim and Ann Newell, Douglas Harrison)*; [44 Lower High St], *Six Bells*: Comfortable and bustling, with some 16th-c ship's timbers, simply furnished dining lounge with rugs on bare boards, cosy beamed snug with darts, well kept Fullers ales, food with emphasis on steaks, bargains some nights; back terrace with barbecue *(Andy and Jill Kassube)*; [9 Upper High St], *Swan*: Nice surroundings inc comfortable chairs and sofas, antiques and old books which can be read, mounted boar's head; well kept beers inc Brakspears *(Andy and Jill Kassube)*

☆ **Thrupp** [off A4260 just N of Kidlington; SP4815], *Boat*: Relaxing and friendly little 16th-c stone-built local in lovely canalside surroundings, good value genuine home cooking, quick service, well kept Morrells, local paintings for sale, no piped music; restaurant, tables in garden *(Tim Barrow, Sue Demont, Colin and Meg Hamilton)*

Thrupp [Banbury Rd], *Jolly Boatman*: Extended pub with enjoyable cheap food, Morrells beers, eating area and conservatory overlooking canal; children allowed *(Hugh Spottiswoode)*

Upton [A417 Harwell—Blewbury; SU5186], *George & Dragon*: Reopened after refurbishment, good food prepared to order (so can be a wait), small end dining area, Morlands Old Speckled Hen and Original, welcoming service *(Marjorie and David Lamb)*

Wallingford [St Leonards Ln; SU6089], *Little House Around the Corner by the Brook*: Welcoming and comfortable smallish tasteful bar with pews, good well presented home-made food inc imaginative children's dishes, changing real ales, raised dining area with antique furniture, fresh flowers, candles; piped music; next to church in beautiful spot by brook *(GWB, David Dimock)*

Wantage [Mill St (A417 W of square); SU4087], *Lamb*: Low beams, timbers and soft lighting, attractive and comfortable furnishings, unpretentious atmosphere, well kept Morlands, generous reasonably priced usual bar food, friendly quick service; good play area *(E Locker, Rona Murdoch, LYM)*

☆ **Warborough** [The Green South; just E of A329, 4 miles N of Wallingford; SU5993], *Six Bells*: Low-ceilinged thatched pub facing cricket green, with country furnishings, big fireplace, antique photographs and pictures; taken over 1997 by the Salters who had made the Three Horseshoes in Witney such an enjoyable main entry during their tenancy – expect worthwhile food, well kept Brakspears, decent wines and a warmly welcoming atmosphere; tables in back orchard *(LYM)*

Watchfield [SU2590], *Kings Head*: Friendly cottagey pub, considerate staff cope well when busy, good reasonably priced food, Ushers beers, garden, walkers welcome *(Dick Brown)*

Wendlebury [a mile from M40 junction 9; signposted from A41 Bicester—Oxford; SP5619], *Red Lion*: Wide choice of good value food in friendly and spacious low-beamed stone-built pub with parquet floor, open fire, Badger and Worthington ales, games room, juke box and fruit machine, restaurant; big garden with play area, grotesque wooden statuary, waterfowl, peacocks and rabbits; service can slow on busy evenings *(Lynda Payton, Sam Samuells, D and J McMillan)*

☆ **West Hanney** [off A338 N of Wantage; SU4092], *Plough*: Pretty thatched pub with attractive timbered upper storey, original timbers and uneven low ceilings, homely and welcoming panelled lounge with open fire in stone fireplace, unusual plates, brasses and exotic butterflies, very friendly landlord, good value simple freshly made food, Tetleys-related ales, interesting whiskies, darts in public bar; back garden with aviaries; children welcome *(Marjorie and David Lamb, Margaret Dyke, Paul McPherson)*

☆ **West Hendred** [Reading Rd, off A417; SU4489], *Hare*: Civilised local, homely and welcoming, very popular for generous good value food served till late evening; decent wine, Morlands ale, two bars – one eating, one drinking *(Hugh Spottiswoode)*

☆ **Weston on the Green** [B430 nr M40 junction 9; SP5318], *Ben Jonson*: Thatched pub with comfortable dark wood settles in welcoming beamed lounge bar, snug with roaring winter fire, wide choice of good value generous food, well kept Bass and Flowers IPA, good house wine, daily papers, discreet pool room; usually open all day, children very welcome; big sheltered garden with occasional barbecues *(RTM, JCM)*

☆ **Weston on the Green** [B430, a mile from M40 junction 9], *Chequers*: Extended thatched pub with interesting bric-a-brac in long comfortably refurbished raftered bar, view of Thai cook producing good value food, well kept Fullers, farm cider, cheerful service; tables under cocktail parasols in attractive garden with animals *(George Atkinson, Pete Yearsley)*

☆ **Whitchurch** [High St, just over toll bridge from Pangbourne; SU6377], *Greyhound*: Pretty cottage with neat relaxed low-beamed L-shaped bar, bric-a-brac inc signed miniature cricket bats, good value fresh no-chips food, well kept Flowers and Wadworths 6X, polite service, no music or machines; dogs on leads allowed, pleasant garden; nr Thames in attractive village, good walks *(GWB)*

☆ **Witney** [78 Corn St; SP3510], *Three Horseshoes*: New licensees summer 1997, too late for us to gauge its status, but it's an attractive stonebuilt pub, with heavy beams, flagstones, log fires, simple well polished old furniture, and has had enjoyable food and well kept Morlands and other ales; the Salters who made it a very popular main entry can now be found at the Six Bells at Warborough *(LYM)*

☆ **Witney** [Church Green], *Angel*: Friendly well used extended 17th-c local, roaring log fires, limited cheap food, Wychwood ales, pool room, coffee bar; piped music *(Peter and Audrey Dowsett, W W Burke, John and Hazel Waller)*; [Wood Green], *Three Pigeons*: Two quiet cosy beamed bars, stripped stone, big log fire, reasonably priced lunchtime snacks, Courage Best, quiet piped music; children allowed in restaurant *(Peter and Audrey Dowsett)*

☆ **Wolvercote** [signed off A40/A44 roundabout N of Oxford; SP5009], *Plough*: Convivial new licensees in refurbished pub with armchairs and Victorian-style carpeted bays in main lounge, flagstoned dining room opening off, traditional snug, good-sized public bar with pool and machines; good varied food esp soups and fresh seafood, well kept Morrells, decent wines; children welcome, tables outside looking over rough meadow to canal and woods *(Tim Brierly)*

☆ **Woodstock** [Park St; SP4416], *Bear*: Handsome old inn with relaxing heavy-beamed bar on right, cosy alcoves, tasteful medley of well worn antique oak, mahogany and leather furniture, tartan curtains, chintz cushions, paintings, sporting trophies, log fire, well kept Morrells and Worthington, good fresh sandwiches, bar lunches, afternoon tea, helpful service; not cheap; restaurant; good bedrooms *(Rebecca and Chris Stanners, Gordon, Dave Irving, Ewan McCall, Roger Huggins, Tom McLean, Liz Bell, BB)*

Woodstock [59 Oxford St (A44)], *Queens Own*: Small friendly local recently refurbished in old-world style – bare boards, stripped stone, beamery, antique settles, elderly tables, hops on beams, candles; well kept Hook Norton and several guest ales, country wines, wide range of homely food inc Italian (less in evening), daily papers, discreet piped music; small back courtyard, lively Mon quiz night *(E A and D C T Frewer)*; [22 Market St], *Star*: Warm and friendly, with welcoming obliging owners, decent food from sandwiches up; bedrooms clean and spacious, good breakfast *(M R Johnson, GO, KO)*

☆ **Woolstone** [off B4507 W of Wantage;

SU2987], *White Horse*: Plushly refurbished partly thatched 16th-c pub, two big open fires in spacious beamed and part-panelled room with air of highly polished well cared-for antiquity, quickly served food inc several vegetarian dishes, Arkells BBB and Wadworths 6X served through sparkler, decent wines, good coffee; children allowed in eating area, sheltered garden; four charming good value bedrooms, secluded interesting village, handy for White Horse *(HNJ, PEJ, Peter and Audrey Dowsett, J and P Maloney)*

☆ **Wootton** [Glympton Rd (B4027) N of Woodstock; SP4320], *Killingworth Castle*: Striking three-storey 17th-c inn, with good local atmosphere, friendly new landlady, good value food in long narrow main bar with candles and log fire, well kept ales, bar billiards and other games in smaller room, pleasant garden; bedrooms cosy and comfortable *(S Boorne, Mr and Mrs Garrett, Gordon)*

☆ **Wroxton** [Church St; off A422 at hotel – pub at back of village; SP4142], *North Arms*: Pretty thatched stone pub with good bar food, well kept Morrells, cheerful service, log fire, eclectic furnishings, lots of beer mugs; character restaurant (not Mon); piped music, darts, dominoes, fruit machine; attractive quiet garden, lovely village *(Rona Murdoch, H D Spottiswoode, LYM)*

Please keep sending us reports. We rely on readers for news of new discoveries, and particularly for news of changes – however slight – at the fully described pubs. No stamp needed: *The Good Pub Guide*, FREEPOST TN1569, Wadhurst, E Sussex TN5 7BR.

Shropshire

This is a fine area for enjoyable pubs, typically with good if not gourmet food, well kept interesting beers, nice licensees – and all this often in buildings of real character. These traits are exemplified by the good clutch of new entries here: the bustling and lively Three Tuns in Bishops Castle, reopened under new owners and brewing its own good value ales in a remarkable Victorian brewhouse; the immaculately cottagey old Burlton Inn at Burlton, the striking and civilised new Cholmondeley Riverside at Cressage (very good food – an extremely nice discovery), the carefully refurbished Old Three Pigeons at Nesscliffe (also very popular for food), and the Armoury in Shrewsbury, a splendid conversion of a waterside warehouse – this too has very good food. It's an existing main entry, the welcoming Unicorn in Ludlow, which gains our award as Shropshire Dining Pub of the Year; and another pub doing outstandingly well here this year is the ancient Horseshoe in its beautiful riverside position at Llanyblodwel. In the Lucky Dip section at the end of the chapter, current front-runners include the Bear in Bridgnorth, Black Lion in Ellesmere, Lion at Hampton Loade (when it's open), New Inn at Ironbridge (actually part of the museum) and Stiperstones at Stiperstones; there's a good choice in Shrewsbury. Drinks prices here are generally lower than the national average, with the Lion of Morfe at Upper Farmcote particularly cheap (very good value lunches here, too); the Three Tuns in Bishops Castle, recently refurbished Red Lion at Llanfair Waterdine and extremely welcoming Wenlock Edge Inn on Wenlock Edge also have attractive drinks prices.

BISHOPS CASTLE SO3289 Map 6
Three Tuns 🍺
Salop Street

Since 1642, beer has been brewed here. It's now produced in the many-storeyed Victorian brewhouse across the yard. Each stage of the brewing process descends from floor to floor within the unique tower layout (it's a Grade 1 listed building) and there are brewery tours by appointment. Well kept Three Tuns XXX Bitter, Mild, Old Scrooge (winter), Steamer, summer Special on handpump, with bottled Clerics Cure; they do home brew kits and carry-out kegs, sales by the barrel or cases of Clerics Cure – phone Steve Dunn the brewer on (01588) 638023. They hold an annual beer festival in July with Morris dancers in the yard; decent wine list. There's a bustling, lively atmosphere in the simply furnished beamed rooms, with low backed settles, heavy walnut tables, newspapers to read, and a good mix of customers. Good home-made bar food includes fish soup or game terrine with home-made chutney (£3), grilled goat's cheese salad (£4.50), roasted cod with a basil and tomato topping, three bean casserole or sausages and mash with onion gravy (all £6), steak, kidney and ale pie (£6.50), and lots of game in season. Darts, dominoes, backgammon and cards – no piped music. There's a small garden and terrace. *(Recommended by Hazel and Michael Duncombe, Gary Roberts, Andrew Rogers, Amanda Milsom, P and M Rudlin, Pat and Tony Martin)*

Own brew ~ Licensee Elaine Fraser ~ Real ale ~ Meals and snacks ~ Restaurant ~ (01588) 638797 ~ Children in eating area of bar ~ Jazz, classical, folk music in upstairs room ~ Open 11-11; 12-10.30 Sun

BRIDGES SO3996 Map 6
Horseshoe £

Near Ratlinghope, below the W flank of the Long Mynd

The son of the former landlord has taken over this attractive old pub, charmingly set by the little River Onny. He is a real-ale enthusiast, has expanded the menu, and plans to open a beer garden to the side of the building. The comfortable bar has interesting windows, a good log fire, and Adnams Southwold and Extra, Shepherd Neame Spitfire and two guest beers on handpump; good choice of bottled beers, too. A small dining room leads off the bar. Lunchtime bar food now includes sandwiches and filled rolls (from £1.50), home-made soup (£1.60; toasties £1.95), ploughman's (from £2.50), home-made vegetable lasagne (£2.80) and chilli con carne (£3.10), good ham salad (£3.25), and home-made puddings. Darts and dominoes. There are tables outside, and the pub's very handy for walks on the Long Mynd itself and on Stiperstones – despite its isolation, it can get very busy in summer. *(Recommended by David Sadler, Gwen and Peter Andrews, Patrick Freeman, Kerry Law, Simon Smith, David and Julie Glover, Nigel Woolliscroft, Dave Braisted, Robin and Molly Taylor)*

Free House ~ Licensee Simon Muller ~ Real ale ~ Lunchtime meals and snacks ~ (01588) 650260 ~ Children in dining room ~ Open 12-2.30(3 Sat), 6-11; 12-3, 7-11 Sun; closed Mon lunchtime (and Tues-Thurs lunchtimes, too, in winter)

BROCKTON SO5894 Map 4
Feathers 🍽

B4378

In a quiet rural spot, this stylish stone-built pub is popular for its very good changing food, and for its relaxed, friendly atmosphere. Relying on seasonal produce, the menu might include soup (£2.45), garlic bread topped with chopped bacon, peppers and melted cheddar (£2.95), Greek salad or chicken liver pâté (£3.65), pasta with spinach, tomato, and pumpkin seeds with mozzarella (£6.95), chilli garlic chicken (£7.95), fresh fillet of fish with a lemon and chive crust and a lemon butter sauce (£8.95), teriyaki duck (£9.75), and puddings; good Sunday lunch, and efficient and friendly waitress service. The charming beamed rooms have stencilling on the terracotta or yellow colour wash walls, comfortable seats, and a rather restauranty feel. The restaurant itself is no smoking, and they have a policy not to sell cigarettes. Well kept Banks Bitter and Morrells Varsity. A new conservatory was added last summer. *(Recommended by Patrick Freeman, The Harrowes, Paul and Maggie Baker; more reports please)*

Free house ~ Licensee Martin Hayward ~ Real ale ~ Meals and snacks (6.30-9.30) ~ (01746) 785202 ~ Children welcome ~ Open 6.30-11 (closed lunchtimes during the week); 12-2.30, 6.30(7 Sun)-11 Sat; closed Mon

BURLTON SJ4626 Map 6
Burlton Inn

A528 Shrewsbury—Ellesmere, near junction with B4397

A couple of horses drew up outside this immaculate old local as we left it, fitting in nicely with the relaxed mood our inspection had induced. The very friendly licensees made their last pub a popular Oxfordshire main entry, and the amount of energy they've put into this new venture suggests they haven't lost their touch. Mr Bean and his son spent two months after their arrival last summer completely refurbishing the bar, moving round beams and fireplaces, and redecorating the walls and ceiling in a welcoming shade of pink to give it a lighter, fresher feel. Everything in the three cottagey connecting rooms seems meticulously arranged and cared for, from the flower displays in the brick fireplace or beside the neatly curtained windows, to the piles of *Country Living* and interior design magazines left seemingly casually in the corner. There are a few racing prints, spurs and brasses on the walls, and open fires in winter. As well as sandwiches (from £1.75), ploughman's (£3.75), and steak and kidney pie (£5.95), the tasty and thoughtfully presented bar food might include their popular bacon chop (£6.50), and changing specials such as vegan avocado with raspberry vinaigrette (£6.50), poached salmon stuffed with cream cheese, grapes and tarragon (served cold, £8.95), and fresh fish from Brixham. Well kept Banks's, Camerons Strongarm and two changing guests like Ridleys Rumpus and Morrells Graduate on handpump; obliging, helpful service. It's often rather peaceful at lunchtimes, though it gets much busier with cheery regulars in the evening; dogs welcome. There are tables on a small lawn behind, with more on a strip of grass beyond the car park; there's a climbing frame here too. They have plans to develop a more unified garden area. The pub sign is a reminder of the days when this was known as the Cross Keys. *(Recommended by Mr and Mrs F Carroll, Peter Astbury)*

Free house ~ Licensees Gerry and Ann Bean ~ Real ale ~ Meals and snacks (limited menu Mon lunch) ~ (01930) 270284 ~ Open 11-3, 6-11; 12-3, 7-10.30 Sun

CARDINGTON SO5095 Map 4
Royal Oak £

Village signposted off B4371 Church Stretton—Much Wenlock, pub behind church; also reached via narrow lanes from A49

New licensees have taken over this wisteria-covered white stone inn but don't plan any major changes, and early reports from readers are good. The friendly, rambling, low-beamed bar has a vast inglenook fireplace with a roaring winter log fire, cauldron, black kettle and pewter jugs, old standing timbers of a knocked-through wall, hops draped along the bar gantry, and gold plush, red leatherette and tapestry seats solidly capped in elm. Home-made bar food includes macaroni cheese (£2.80), cauliflower cheese (£3), cottage pie or fidget pie (£3.80), meat or vegetable lasagne (£4.50) and fish and chips (£5.30). Bass, Hobsons, Woods Shropshire Lad and guest beers on handpump kept under light blanket pressure; dominoes and cribbage in the main bar, and there's a no-smoking area. Tables in the rose-filled front courtyard have lovely views over hilly fields, and a mile or so away – from the track past Willstone (ask for directions at the pub) – you can walk up Caer Caradoc Hill which looks over scenic countryside. *(Recommended by KC, Tim Barrow, Sue Demont, SLC, Pat and Clive Sherriff, Edward Froggatt, DAV, MDN)*

Free house ~ Licensees David and Christine Baugh ~ Real ale ~ Meals and snacks (not Mon except bank holidays) ~ Children welcome during mealtimes ~ (01694) 771266 ~ Open 12-2.30, 6-11; 11-11 summer Sat; 12-10.30 summer Sun; closed Mon except bank holidays ~ One bedrooms: /£40B

CRESSAGE SJ5904 Map 6
Cholmondeley Riverside 🍴 🍷

Off A458 SE of Shrewsbury, slightly before Cressage itself if coming from Shrewsbury

Overlooking a ridiculously pretty stretch of the Severn, this converted white hotel is under the same management as the Cholmondeley Arms near Bickley Moss (see Cheshire chapter), and in the few months since opening has already started drawing the same kind of praise that its more established cousin has been attracting for years. Devotees of the Cheshire pub will find things here organised in much the same way, which means a decided emphasis on the good and rather unusual food. As well as home-made baguettes (£3.50) and soups such as carrot and orange, you might find fresh lobster bisque (£4.25), salmon marinated in lime, pink peppercorns and ginger (£4.50), baked tomatoes stuffed with peppers, spring onion, basil and rice (£7.50), beef cooked with Shropshire blue cheese (£7.75), rack of lamb with rosemary, mint and red wine sauce or king prawns in garlic, ginger and coriander (£8.95), and puddings such as hot fudge bananas (£3.50); booking is recommended at weekends. Totally refurbished before the grand opening in March 1997, the civilised and rather roomy bar has a variety of church pews, cushioned settles and oak tables dotted around the central servery, with a mix of country prints, plates and tapestries on the walls; also a fox's head, and a couple of stuffed birds. Marstons Best and Pedigree on handpump, along with a couple of weekly changing guests; there's an excellent choice of interesting wines, and they do tea and coffee. French windows lead out into the perfectly positioned garden, where the tables are much the best spot to enjoy your meal on a sunny day; in less amenable conditions you can have the same idyllic view down to the water from the big new conservatory. Coarse fishing on the river costs £4 a day, though is free if you're staying – we've not yet had reports from people who have stayed here, but expect good news. From the outside the pub still looks very much like the more formal hotel it once was, and is set back slightly from the road, with plenty of space for parking in front. *(Recommended by W C M Jones, Liz and Andrew Camp)*

Free house ~ Licensees John Radford, John Patrick Wrigley ~ Real ale ~ Meals and snacks ~ (01952) 510900 ~ Well behaved children welcome ~ Open 11-3, 6-11; 12-3, 7-10.30 Sun; closed 25 Dec ~ Bedrooms: £45B/£60B(£80 for the room with the four poster)

LLANFAIR WATERDINE SO2476 Map 6
Red Lion ⇌

Village signposted from B4355 approaching eastwards; turn left after crossing bridge

The bedrooms in this old inn have been extensively refurbished this year, over 120 new trees and shrubs have been planted around the cark park and along the banks of the River Teme, and the garden borders have all been re-planted, too. Inside, the traditional rambling lounge bar has heavy beams, cosy alcoves, easy chairs, some long, low settles and little polished wooden seats on its turkey carpet, and a woodburning stove. Perhaps even nicer is the small black-beamed tap room, with plain wooden chairs on its flagstoned floor, and table skittles, dominoes, cribbage, shove-ha'penny, sensibly placed darts, and piped music. Bar food includes soup (£2.10), lunchtime sandwiches (£2.30), ploughman's (£4.95), vegetable curry (£5.40), pasta dish of the day (£5.50), chicken piri piri (£6.50), sirloin steak (£8.90), and daily specials like wild mushroom strudel or goujons of plaice on pasta with a tomato and cream sauce (£6.95), glazed gammon steak with fresh nectarines (£7.20), and lamb en croûte (£7.95). The no-smoking back restaurant has views down to the River Teme, the border of England and Wales. Marstons Pedigree, Tetleys and a guest like Wye Valley Dorothy Goodbody or Supreme on handpump, kept under light blanket pressure, and a good wine list; quoits. The area is renowned for beautiful walks (a good stretch of Offa's Dyke is nearby) and designated an area of outstanding natural beauty. *(Recommended by Wendy Arnold, P Barrett, Mike and Maggie Betton)*

Free house ~ Licensees Chris and Judy Stevenson ~ Real ale ~ Meals and snacks (not Sun evening, not Tues lunch) ~ Restaurant ~ (01547) 528214 ~ Children in eating area of bar ~ Open 12-2, 7-11(10.30 Sun); closed Tues lunchtime ~ Bedrooms: £40B/£45B

LLANYBLODWEL SJ2423 Map 6
Horseshoe

Village and pub signposted from B4936

Handy for Lake Vyrnwy and Bala, this delightfully quaint black and white timbered Tudor inn is in a lovely spot by the River Tanat; there are plenty of outside seats and a mile of fly-fishing (free for residents, day tickets otherwise). The simple low-beamed front bar has an old black range in the inglenook fireplace, traditional black built-in settles alongside more modern chairs around oak tables on a reclaimed maple floor, and lots of brass and china. In the rambling rooms leading off you'll find darts, pool, dominoes, fruit machine, and piped music. Tasty bar food (they tell us prices have not increased since last year) includes lunchtime baguettes (from £2.50), soup (£2.25), king prawns pan-fried in garlic butter (£4.95), mediterranean bean casserole (£5.50), steak and kidney pie (£5.95), grilled fresh fish of the day with lemon and dill butter (£6.50), game casserole (£6.95), and roast poussin with sherry and brandy sauce, grilled lemon sole or chicken breast in a mushroom, cream and white wine sauce (£8.95), with puddings (£3.25), and children's meals £2.75). The dining room is oak panelled. Marstons Best and Pedigree, and a range of malt whiskies. *(Recommended by K N Hay, Roger Byrne, George Atkinson, Sue and Bob Ward, David and Judy Walmsley, Basil Minson, Nigel and Lindsay Chapman, JKW, John and Joan Nash, Gill and Maurice McMahon, David and Fiona Pemberton, Jeff Davies)*

Free house ~ Lease: Dennis and Jessica Plant ~ Real ale ~ Meals and snacks (not Sun evening, not Mon) ~ Restaurant ~ (01691) 828969 ~ Children in eating area of bar at landlord's discretion ~ Open 11.30-3, 6.30-11; 12-3, 7-10.30 Sun; closed winter Mon ~ Bedrooms: /£40 – no children

LONGVILLE SO5494 Map 4
Longville Arms 🛏️

B4371 Church Stretton—Much Wenlock

Two more bedrooms in the converted stables have been added to this popular inn this year, and once again, readers' comments on staying here have been warmly enthusiastic; you may be lucky and find home-made biscuits – but you will certainly have a marvellous breakfast and a friendly welcome from the attentive licensees. Of the two spacious bars, the left one is simpler with sturdy elm or cast-iron-framed tables, newly covered banquettes, and a woodburning stove at each end. The right-hand lounge has dark plush wall banquettes and cushioned chairs, with some nice old tables. There's a wide range of good-value homely bar food, including sandwiches, soup (£1.75), deep fried camembert with home-made chutney (£3.75), a vegetarian dish (£4.65), fresh grilled trout with almonds (£6.20), cajun chicken (£6.60), sirloin steak (£8.50), and daily specials; children's meals (from £2.25), and excellent puddings. Well kept Bass and Worthington BB on handpump, with maybe a guest in summer, and several malt and Irish whiskies. There are picnic tables under cocktail parasols in a neat terraced side garden, with a good play area. The pub is well placed near to an excellent range of local attractions. They accept no credit cards. *(Recommended by Charles Faragher, Miss Sarah Corlett, the Harrowes, Jeff Davies, John Cumberland, Edward Froggatt, Judi Wayman, Bob Arnett, Mr and Mrs A R Corfield, Maureen Hobbs, D O Evans, Nigel Woolliscroft)*

Free house ~ Licensee Patrick Egan ~ Real ale ~ Meals and snacks (not Tues) ~ (01694) 771206 ~ Children welcome ~ Occasional live music ~ Open 12-2.30, 7-11(10.30 Sun); closed Tues ~ Bedrooms: £20S/£35(£40S)

LUDLOW SO5175 Map 6
Unicorn 🍴 🛏️

Lower Corve St, off Shrewsbury Rd
Shropshire Dining Pub of the Year

There's a genuinely warm atmosphere and welcome in this very much enjoyed 17th-c inn, built in a row of black and white houses along the banks of the River Corve. The single large beamed and partly panelled bar has a bustling atmosphere and a good mix of friendly locals and visitors, and a huge log fire in a big stone fireplace. There's also a timbered, candlelit restaurant (where they prefer you not to smoke). Good, tasty, properly home-made bar food (you can also eat the restaurant food in the bar might include lovely soup, sandwiches, black pudding with cider and mustard sauce or ham in parsley sauce (£5.25), an authentic Greek salad, steak and kidney pie (£5.95), devilled kidneys (£6.95), bacon-wrapped chicken in creamy mushroom sauce (£8.95), and rack of lamb in mulberry sauce (£10.25), and a splendid choice of home-made puddings like chocolate, toffee and rum gateau or sticky gingerbread; good breakfasts, and a good value Sunday lunch. Service is attentive, cheerful and willing. Well kept Bass and Worthington BB on handpump; cribbage, dominoes. Beyond the car park is a terrace with tables sheltering pleasantly among willow trees by the modest river. The warm and comfortable timbered rooms are a good size. *(Recommended by Andrew Shore, Norman and Sarah Keeping, Alan and Barbara Mence, Paul Robinshaw, Theo, Anne and Jane Gaskin, Gwen and Peter Andrews, D Voller, Wayne Brindle, Michael Butler, Andrew Shore, Steve*

Gilbert, Helen Cox, Lynda Payton, Sam Samuells, Neville Kenyon, Ray and Wendy Bryn Davies, Sue and Bob Ward)

Free house ~ Licensees Alan and Elisabeth Ditchburn ~ Real ale ~ Meals and snacks ~ Restaurant ~ (01584) 873555 ~ Well behaved children welcome ~ Open 12-2.30, 6-11; 12-3, 7-10.30 Sun; closed 25 Dec ~ Bedrooms: £15(£20B)/£30(£40B)

MUCH WENLOCK SJ6200 Map 4
George & Dragon ◀
High St

Over one thousand water jugs hang from the beams in this unpretentious town local. Other collections in the cosily atmospheric rooms range from old brewery and cigarette advertisements, through to bottle labels and beer trays, and George-and-the-Dragon pictures. There are a few antique settles as well as conventional furnishings, a couple of attractive Victorian fireplaces (with coal-effect gas fires), and an old till on the bar. At the back, the quieter snug old-fashioned rooms have black beams and timbering, little decorative plaster panels, tiled floors, a stained-glass smoke room sign, a big mural as well as lots of smaller pictures (painted by local artists), and a little stove in a fat fireplace. Quickly served enjoyable food includes sandwiches (from £2), home-made soup (£2.35), filled baked potatoes (from £3.50), ploughman's with home-made chutney (from £3.75), home-made duck pâté with orange and apricot chutney (£3.85), spinach and cheese stuffed pancakes (£5), home-baked ham salad with cumberland sauce (£5.25), good thai chicken (£5.75), pepper crusted fillet of salmon with lime and coriander dressing (£6.25), sirloin steak with peppercorn sauce (£8.75), and daily specials like home-made rabbit pie (£6.75), breast of duck with spiced apricot sauce (£8.95) or roast rack of lamb with plum sauce (£9.25); evening prices are slightly higher. Well kept Hook Norton Best and three often unusual guest beers like Hobsons Town Crier, Sarah Hughes Dark Ruby, and Wye Valley Supreme on handpump; piped music, usually jazz, and often from a vintage wireless; cribbage and dominoes. *(Recommended by D Voller, Pat and Tony Martin, DFL, Mike and Wendy Proctor, Mike and Maggie Betton, M Joyner, PM, AM, Paul Boot, Simon Groves)*

Free house ~ Licensee Eve Nolan ~ Real ale ~ Meals and snacks (not Sun evening) ~ Evening restaurant (not Sun evening) ~(01952) 727312 ~ Well behaved children welcome ~ Open 11-2.30(3 Sat), 6-11; 12-3, 7-10.30 Sun

Talbot ⇔
High Street

There are several neatly kept areas in this partly 14th-c civilised inn with comfortable green plush button-back wall banquettes around highly-polished tables, low ceilings, and two big log fires (one in an inglenook); the walls are decorated with prints of fish and brewery paraphernalia. Lunchtime bar food includes sandwiches (from £2.50), home-made soup (£2.95), ploughman's (£3.75), filled baked potatoes (from £3.75), omelettes (from £5.95), chicken supreme (£7.50), grilled lamb chops with mint and garlic butter or poached salmon in white wine sauce (£7.95), sirloin steak (£10.95), daily specials, and home-made puddings like fruit crumble or treacle tart (£3.25); Sunday roast lunch (£9.45). The restaurant is no smoking. Well kept changing ales might include Courage Directors, John Smiths, and Theakstons on handpump, and several malt whiskies. Through the coach entry, there are white seats and tables in an attractive sheltered yard. *(Recommended by M Joyner, Geoff and Angela Jaques, Janet and Peter Race, Edward Froggatt, SLC, Mike and Wendy Poctor, Basil Minson, M Joyner, Mr and Mrs K Giles, N Evans)*

Free house ~ Licensees Sean and Cheryl Brennan ~ Real ale ~ Meals and snacks ~ Restaurant ~ (01952) 727077 ~ Well behaved children in eating area of bar and in restaurant ~ Open 10-3, 6-11; 10-3, 7-10.30 Sun ~ Bedrooms: £45B/£90B

If we know a pub has an outdoor play area for children, we mention it.

MUNSLOW SO5287 Map 2
Crown ◀

B4368 Much Wenlock—Craven Arms

Behind the Georgian facade here is a Tudor interior with oak beams, nooks and crannies. The warm and friendly split-level lounge bar has a pleasantly old-fashioned mix of furnishings on its broad flagstones, a collection of old bottles, country pictures, a bread oven by its good log fire, seats in a traditional snug with its own fire, maybe Sarge the cat or Tosh the friendly dog; the eating area has tables around a central oven chimney, stripped stone walls, more beams and flagstones. From their own microbrewery, they produce Munslow Boys Pale Ale, Munslow Ale, and sometimes a third brew named after one of the locals; they also keep Banks's Mild and Marstons Pedigree on handpump. A wide choice of generous home-made food served with al dente vegetables includes home-made soup (£2.25), spicy chicken wings (£2.95), ploughman's (£3.50), ratatouille au gratin (£5.50), lasagne or chicken in gravy (£5.95), steaks (from £7.50), and salmon fillet (£7.95), with evening dishes like mushrooms in garlic butter with grilled soft cheese (£3.50), pork dijon (£8.50), and plaice with prawns and a lobster and cream sauce (£9.25), weekend specials, Sunday roast, and children's meals (from £2.25). Relaxed and friendly family service; games room with darts, shove-ha'penny, table skittles, and dominoes. Tables outside. *(Recommended by Edward Froggatt, Richard Lewis; more reports please)*

Own brew ~ Licensee Vic Pocock ~ Real ale ~ Meals and snacks ~ Restaurant ~ (01584) 841205 ~ Children welcome ~ Open 12-2.30, 7-11; 12-3, 7-10.30 Sun

NESSCLIFFE SJ3819 Map 6
Old Three Pigeons

A5 Shrewsbury—Oswestry

People come from quite some distance to eat at this busy recently refurbished dining pub, said to date back in part to the 14th c. The licensees hang and butcher their own meat, cater for plenty of other places in the area, and every morning collect the eggs fresh from the hen coop in the garden. Fresh fish features heavily on the huge chalkboard menu, with plaice (£6.95), baked red snapper (£9.95), monkfish, brill (£11.95), and Welsh bass (£13.95) among the more popular choices on our summer visit; they also do ploughman's, home-made sausages, a good value Sunday lunch, and dishes such as lamb, pork crumble, and guinea fowl on a bed of red cabbage (£11.95). There may be a wait at busy times. The long low building looks quite big from the outside; the restaurant takes up much of the space, leaving two traditional bar areas separated by a brick pillar mostly covered by the food blackboard. These have brown cushioned sofas along the walls, a mix of plain wooden chairs and tables, log fires, and quite a few brasses on the walls or hanging from the ceiling. There's a food servery under the window, though it's generally used only for functions; the juke box by here isn't always switched on. Well kept Morlands Summer Glory, Theakstons XB and a guest such as Youngers IPA on handpump, with a decent choice of wines (including quite a few bin-ends); friendly service. They plan to extend the decent-sized back garden over the next few months, and by spring hope to have added a lake, caravan site, and even a couple of llamas and other animals; quite a few tables out here. In the meantime don't be alarmed if you come across a Russian tank or similar piece of military hardware – they own quite a few, and often lend them to museums or shows. A couple of readers felt the rear of the pub around the car park could look a bit unkempt, but all seemed tidy enough on our visit. It's handy for Kynaston Cave, and some good cliff walks. *(Recommended by K Frostick, J S M Sheldon, M Joyner, Sue and Bob Ward, SLC, John Cumberland, Edward Froggatt)*

Free house ~ Licensee Dylan Brooks ~ Real ale ~ Meals and snacks ~ Restaurant ~ (01743) 741279 ~ Children welcome ~ Open 11.30-3, 6.30-11; 12-4, 7-10.30 Sun; in winter closed Sun eves and all day Mon

NORTON SJ7200 Map 4

Hundred House 🍽 ⌭ 🛏

A442 Telford—Bridgnorth

This popular and carefully thought out inn is very much a family business. The bar is divided into several spick and span separate areas, with old quarry tiles at either end and modern hexagonal ones in the main central part – which has high beams strung with hop-bunches and dried flowers. Steps lead up past a little balustrade to a partly panelled eating area where stripped brickwork looks older than that elsewhere. Handsome fireplaces have log fires or working Coalbrookdale ranges (one has a great Jacobean arch with fine old black cooking pots), and around sewing-machine tables are a variety of interesting chairs and settles with some long colourful patchwork leather cushions. From the brasserie menu, food includes home-made soup, chicken liver pâté with pumpkin and orange (£3.95), coriander cured salmon with lime, peanuts and beansprouts (£4.95), lasagne (£6.50), steak and kidney pie with stout (£6.95), open beef sandwich with pickled vegetables, garlic mayonnaise, onions and rocket (£7.50), pork chop with caponata and polenta (£7.95), three onion risotto with goat's cheese and tempura onion (£8.50), daily fish dishes, sirloin steak (£12.50), and puddings; there is a surcharge on this menu if you eat from it in the restaurant. Well kept Brains Dark Mild, Everards Tiger on handpump, along with Ailrics Old, and Heritage Bitter (light and refreshing, not too bitter) brewed for them by a small brewery; also an extensive wine list with house wines by the carafe, half carafe, and big or small glass, and lots of malt whiskies; shove-ha'penny, cribbage. The gardens are very pretty and filled with unusual roses, trees, and herbaceous plants, and there's a big working herb garden; seats outside. *(Recommended by Andrew and Ruth Triggs, SLC, Ian Morley, Michael Begley, Edward Froggatt, Yvonne and Peter Griffiths, John Knighton, Robert Sheard, Mrs I Tooze, Basil Minson, Carolyn Reynier, RP, BP, Peter and Patricia Burton)*

Free house ~ Licensees Henry, Sylvia, Stuart and David Phillips ~ Real ale ~ Meals and snacks (till 10pm) ~ (01952) 730353 ~ Children in eating area of bar ~ Open 10.30-3.30, 6-11; 12-3.30, 7-10.30 Sun ~ Bedrooms: £65B/£79B

PULVERBATCH SJ4202 Map 6

White Horse

From A49 at N end of Dorrington follow Pulverbatch/Church Pulverbatch signposts, and turn left at eventual T-junction (which is sometimes signposted Church Pulverbatch); OS Sheet 126 map reference 424023

The several rambling areas in this bustling and welcoming country pub have black beams and heavy timbering, as well as unusual fabric-covered high-backed settles and brocaded banquettes on the turkey carpet, sturdy elm or cast-iron-framed tables, and an open coalburning range with gleaming copper kettles. There's a collection of antique insurance plaques, big brass sets of scales and willow-pattern plates, and pewter mugs hang over the serving counter, and there's even a good Thorburn print of a grouse among the other country pictures. Good bar food includes sandwiches (from £1.50; hot roast beef and melted cheese on french bread £2.20), cullen skink (heavily creamed smoked fish soup £1.75), filled baked potatoes (from £1.95), burgers (from £2.75), omelettes (from £3.50), fresh fish of the day in breadcrumbs or batter (£4.50), gammon and egg (£4.95), hot vegetarian platter (£5.50), prawn curry (£5.75), anytime breakfast (£5.95), steaks (from £7.25), and home-made puddings like cherry pie or pecan and treacle pie (£3.25); children's dishes (from £1.50). Well kept Boddingtons, Flowers Original and Marstons Pedigree on handpump, several decent wines by the glass, and 115 malt whiskies; friendly efficient service. The quarry-tiled front loggia with its sturdy old green leatherette seat is a nice touch. The entrance is around the back of the pub. *(Recommended by B Johnson, A Walsh, Basil Minson, RP, BP, A J S Bellamy, Nigel and Lindsay Chapman, Steve and Angela Maycock, Roy Bromell; more reports please)*

Whitbreads ~ Lease: Hamish and Margaret MacGregor ~ Real ale ~ Meals and snacks (till 10pm) ~ (01743) 718247 ~ Children welcome ~ Open 11.30-3, 7-11(10.30 Sun)

SHREWSBURY SJ5210 Map 6
Armoury ♀

Victoria Quay, Victoria Avenue

Hardly an inch of wall space is wasted at this enormous recently converted warehouse, just along the riverside from Welsh Bridge. Like the other members of the small Pubs Ltd chain (such as the Grosvenor Arms at Aldford, described in our Cheshire chapter), it's lined with old prints, documents and other neatly framed ephemera, and glass cabinets show off collections of explosives and shells as well as corks and bottle openers. One entire wall is covered with copiously filled bookshelves, so that if you visit during a rare quiet moment it can look a little like a cross between a library and a museum. What catches your eye as you come in is the long bar counter – and in particular the hugely varied range of drinks behind it; in addition to well kept Boddingtons, Timothy Taylors Landlord and two or three changing guests such as Ushers Summer Madness and Woods Shropshire Lad, there's a good wine list that includes around 25 by the glass, around 70 malt whiskies, a dozen different gins, similarly eclectic rums and vodkas, a wide choice of brandies, and some unusual liqueurs. Big arched windows overlooking the river help keep the single cavernous room light and airy, and there's quite a mix of good heavy wooden tables, chairs and high-backed settles, interspersed by the occasional green-painted standing timber; colonial fans whirr away on the ceiling. Tables at one end of the room are laid out for eating, while at the other is a grand stone fireplace. Good bistro-style food – well in the running for one of our Awards – includes soup or sandwiches (£2.95), ploughman's (£3.95), filo-wrapped tiger prawns (£4.75), baked aubergine filled with vegetable ratatouille and topped with a cheese and herb crust (£7.25), thai chicken in coconut milk, lemon grass, ginger, green chilli and lime sauce (£8.25), baked cod on tomatoes topped with rarebit (£9.25), and duck breast in five spice jus with spring onion, mange tout and noodles (£11.45). A convent stood on this site until the Dissolution, then in 1922 the current building was moved here brick from its original position; it had its rather smart conversion to a pub in 1995. The place can get busy in the evenings, particularly at weekends. You can paddle boats along the Severn outside, escorted past rows of weeping willows by swans and gently quacking ducks. *(Recommended by Dr H V Hughes, SLC)*

Free house ~ Managers Barbie Dixon-Bate and Eugene Millea ~ Real ale ~ Meals and snacks ~ (01743) 340525 ~ Open 11-3, 5-11 Mon-Fri, all day weekends

UPPER FARMCOTE SO7792 Map 4
Lion of Morfe £ ◖

Follow Claverley 2½ signpost off A458 Bridgnorth—Stourbridge

If you want to enjoy the good value food at lunchtime in this pleasant country pub, you must arrive very early; often the daily specials are disappearing fast by midday. The smartly comfortable brown-carpeted lounge bar has pink plush button-back built-in wall banquettes in curving bays, and a good log fire; it opens into the no-smoking modern feeling conservatory, with cushioned cane chairs around glass tables on its red-tiled floor. There's a traditional public bar with wood-backed wall seats on red tiles and a game trophy over the coal fire, and a carpeted pool room with a big black kitchen range, and darts and dominoes. Especially well liked by a value-conscious older set, the lunch menu includes home-made soup (£1.45), home-made pâté (£2.25), filled baked potatoes (from £2.75), ploughman's (£3.15), steak and kidney pie or cottage pie (£3.25), lasagne, a vegetarian dish or chicken and mushrooms in a savoury sauce (£3.45), daily specials, and puddings (£1.85); in the evening they do dishes like tuna pasta bake (£4.25), hake fillet on a tomato base topped with mozzarella and cheddar (£4.95), spare ribs (£5.95) or sirloin steak (£6.95). Well kept and priced Bass, Banks's Bitter and Mild, and a guest beer on electric pump or handpump. The garden has picnic tables under cocktail parasols on a terrace, a lawn spreading out into an orchard with a floodlit boules pitch, and nice views. *(Recommended by Theo, Anne and Jane Gaskin, Edward Froggatt, Stephen Brown, DAV, G Coates, Anthony Hoyle, Basil Minson, Barbara and Denis Melling)*

Free house ~ Licensees Bill and Dinah Evans ~ Real ale ~ Meals and snacks (not Sat or Sun evening) ~ (01746) 710678 ~ Children in eating area of bar and in conservatory ~ Folk club monthly, and jazz nights ~ Open 11.30-2.30(4 Sat), 7-11; 12-4, 7-10.30 Sun

WENLOCK EDGE SO5796 Map 4
Wenlock Edge Inn ★ 🛏

Hilltop; B4371 Much Wenlock—Church Stretton, OS Sheet 137 map reference 570962

What makes this place so special is the genuinely warm welcome from the friendly landlord and his family, and the way visitors are immediately involved in the bar room chat. The cosy feel is perhaps at its best on the second Monday in the month – story telling night, when the right hand bar is packed with locals telling tales, some true and others somewhat taller. In the right hand bar is a big woodburning stove in an inglenook, as well as a shelf of high plates, and it leads into a little dining room. The room on the left has pews that came from a Methodist chapel in Liverpool, a fine oak bar counter, and an open fire. Some of their most popular dishes from the blackboards include starters like celeriac and tomato or celery, apple and lovage soup, fresh marinated Orkney herrings or spicy prawns (£2.50-£3.80), leek and lentil layer (£5.90), pies such as beef and vegetable or venison or smoked chicken and asparagus quiche (from £6), salmon baked with peppers or fresh fillet with a sauce (from £6.25), roast pork with prune and apricot stuffing (£6.50), and organically reared beef steaks (from £7); good breakfasts. The dining room is no smoking. Well kept local Hobsons Best and Town Crier, Ruddles Best and an occasional guest on handpump, interesting whiskies, decent wines by both glass and bottle, draught Merrydown cider, and no music – unless you count the deep-throated chimes of Big Bertha the fusee clock. Water comes from their own 190 foot well. There are some tables on a front terrace and the side grass, and they are constructing a herb garden to fit in with the wildlife pond. The building is in a fine position just by the Ippikins Rock viewpoint and there are lots of walks through the National Trust land that runs along the Edge. *(Recommended by Gwen and Peter Andrews, Pat and Clive Sherriff, Michael Begley, Edward Froggatt, SLC, Mr and Mrs Corelis, Mike and Wena Stevenson, Ian Morley, Liz Bell, Geoff and Angela Jaques, M Joyner, Luke Worthington, Fiona Jarman, Mr and Mrs Lawson, Joy and Peter Heatherley, Mark Percy, Lesley Mayoh, Tim Barrow, Sue Demont, DAV, Mike and Wendy Proctor, R and S Bentley, John and Phyllis Maloney, Paul and Maggie Baker, Phyl and Jack Street, Michael Butler, John Mark Noone, MDN, JKW; also in Good Hotel Guide)*

Free house ~ Licensee Stephen Waring ~ Real ale ~ Meals (not Mon except for residents in evening) ~ Restaurant ~ (01746) 785678 ~ Children in eating area of bar and restaurant; must be over 5 in lounge bar ~ Open 11.30-2.30, 6.30-11; 12-2.30, 7-10.30 Sun; closed Mon lunchtime except bank holidays; closed 24-26 Dec ~ Bedrooms: £45S/£70S

WHITCHURCH SJ5345 Map 7
Willey Moor Lock

Actually just over the Cheshire border, the pub is signposted off A49 just under two miles N of Whitchurch

On a sunny day, this lock keeper's cottage is particularly nice to visit as you can sit and watch the activities on the Llangollen Canal. Inside, several neatly decorated low-beamed rooms have brick-based brocaded wall seats, stools and small chairs around dimpled copper and other tables, low ceilings, a large teapot collection and a decorative longcase clock, and two winter log fires. Well kept Theakstons Best and four guest beers such as Exmoor Gold, Hanbys Cascade, Morrells Varsity, and North Yorkshire Dizzy Dick and Flying Herbert on handpump, and quite a few malt whiskies; friendly landlady and staff. Generous helpings of bar food such as sandwiches (lunchtime only, £1.75), filled baked potatoes (£2.95), chicken curry or vegetable chilli (£4.50), home-made steak pie or lasagne (£5), gammon and egg (£7), steaks (from £7), and puddings like spotted dick (£1.70); children's menu (from £2). Fruit machine, piped music, and several dogs and cats. There are tables under cocktail parasols on a terrace, and a children's play area with swings and slides in the garden.

(*Recommended by Wayne Brindle, SLC, Basil Minson, Richard Lewis*)

*Free house ~ Licensee Mrs Elsie Gilkes ~ Real ale ~ Meals and snacks ~ (01948)
663274 ~ Children in eating areas away from bar area ~ Open 12-2.30(2 in winter),
6-11; 12-2.30, 7-10.30 Sun; closed 25 Dec*

Lucky Dip

Besides the fully inspected pubs, you might like to try these Lucky Dips recommended to us
and described by readers (if you do, please send us reports):

☆ All Stretton [Shrewsbury Rd (B4370);
SO4695], *Yew Tree*: Comfortable beamed
bars, good bar food, well kept Bass and
Worthington BB, quick helpful service, quiet
piped music, dining room; children welcome,
small village handy for Long Mynd (*Robin
Morton, DC, J S Green*)
Alveley [A442; SO7684], *Squirrel*: Cottagey
beamed and panelled pub recently well
refurbished, raised log fire, tasteful lighting,
furniture and carpets, friendly licensees and
locals; good unusual food, well kept Banks's
Bitter and Mild (*Ron and Isobel Kearton,
Dave Braisted*)
Ash [Ash Magna; SJ5739], *White Lion*:
Village pub with good choice of real ales inc
guest beers such as Woods Woodcutter,
Czech lager, lots of brewery memorabilia,
good atmosphere, friendly service, blazing log
fires, sandwiches and snacks (*SLC*)
Bicton [Bicton Heath; A458 just W of
Shrewsbury; SJ4513], *Grapes*: Big Steak pub,
useful food all day, Tetleys and Marstons
Pedigree; big playroom (*SLC*)
☆ Bishops Castle [The Square; SO3289], *Castle*:
Cosy and friendly local atmosphere in
unspoilt panelled 17th-c coaching inn, very
welcoming landlady cooks tasty cheap
generous food, good sandwiches, well kept
ales such as Bass, Hobsons, Woods
Shropshire Lad and Worthington; tables in
front and in big back garden; good value old-
fashioned bedrooms, good breakfast, nice
views (*Hazel and Michael Duncombe, Mr
Kennedy, Andrew Rogers, Amanda Milsom*)
Bishops Castle [Church St], *Boars Head*:
Comfortable stripped-stone bar with well
made wall benches around pleasant tables, big
open fires, welcoming young staff, well kept
Courage Directors and John Smiths, good
varied food from imaginative sandwiches up;
good roomy high-raftered bedrooms in
converted barn (*D T Deas, K N Hay*)
Boningale [A464 NW of W'hampton;
SJ8102], *Horns*: Three friendly bars with
changing ales such as Bass, Blackbeard
Stairway to Heaven, Hook Norton and Old
Hookey, wholesome nicely presented food inc
good quickly served Sun lunch, panelled
dining room (*Ian and Elizabeth Rispin,
Edward Froggatt*)
☆ Bridgnorth [just past Northgate; SO7293],
Bear: Busy two-room timbered town pub with
good fresh unusual lunchtime food (not Sun)
inc sandwiches and good fish, good value
gourmet night Thurs, friendly efficient service,

well priced changing ales such as Bathams,
Boddingtons, Holdens and Timothy Taylors
Landlord, good choice of bottled beers,
decent wines, old photographs and posters;
tables in sheltered enclosed garden; bedrooms
(*W E and E Thomas, SLC, M Joyner, Tony
Goff, Judy Van Der Sande, Richard and Jean
Phillips, Derek and Sylvia Stephenson, NWN*)
☆ Bridgnorth [Stn; A458 towards Stourbridge],
Railwaymans Arms: Good interesting real ales
in converted waiting-room at Severn Valley
steam railway terminus, bustling on summer
days; simple summer snacks, coal fire, station
nameplates, superb mirror over fireplace,
seats out on platform; children welcome
(*Nigel Woolliscroft, Barnie, PM, AM, SLC,
LYM*)
Bridgnorth [Old Ludlow Rd; B4364, a mile
out], *Punch Bowl*: Unpretentious beamed and
panelled 17th-c country pub, good generous
food inc fresh veg and good carvery,
Marstons Pedigree, superb views; piped music
(*A Jeffreys, Edward Froggatt*)
Broseley [Avenue Rd; SJ6802], *Foresters
Arms*: Attractive stripped-stone beamed
lounge bar, good choice of food partly
reflecting new licensees' Australian
connections, well kept Enville ales; juke box,
public bar with TV, restaurant; seats outside
with summer barbecues (*Barnie*)
Burwarton [B4364 Bridgnorth—Ludlow;
SO6285], *Boyne Arms*: Unassuming country
local, inside imposing Georgian building,
generous good value home-made food,
changing well kept ales such as Bass, Ind
Coope Burton and Woods, cheery
atmosphere; tables in garden, bedrooms (*RP,
BP, Edward Froggatt, Jim and Pam
Townsley*)
Claverley [SO7993], *Plough*: Welcoming and
relaxed, with good food esp daily specials,
Tetleys-related ales with a guest such as
Shepherd Neame Spitfire, helpful staff,
interesting pictures made from watch parts;
separate bistro (*Paul and Sue Merrick,
Barbara and Denis Melling*); [Upper Ludstone
(B4176, just S of A454); SO8095],
Woodman: Small, clean and friendly, with
wide choice of good food, welcoming
landlord, well kept Banks's and occasional
guest beer, attractive prices; garden (*Rev J
Greatbatch*)
☆ Cleobury Mortimer [Church St; SO6775],
Kings Arms: 16th-c inn with lively local
atmosphere in open-plan bar, friendly
attentive staff, well kept Hobsons Best, Wye

Valley HPA and interesting guest ales, good value food inc serious vegetarian choice, Sun roast and good sandwiches, dining room; children welcome; bedrooms well appointed (but thin walls, and the floorboards of the front ones are the bar ceiling); good breakfast *(M Lavery, G Coates, Derek and Sylvia Stephenson, Michael Kirby)*

☆ Clun [High St; SO3081], *Sun*: Friendly Tudor pub, timbers and beams, some sturdy antique furnishings, enormous open fire in flagstoned public bar, good food, well kept ales inc Banks's Bitter and Mild, Marstons Pedigree and Woods Special; children allowed in eating area, tables on sheltered back terrace; lovely village *(Edward Froggatt, Dagmar Junghanns, Colin Keane, LYM)*

☆ Clun [Market Sq], *White Horse*: Well laid out and neatly kept beamed L-shaped bar with inglenook and woodburner, well kept Bass, Worthington and a guest such as Wye Valley, farm cider, good coffee, decent standard food, friendly efficient service, pool table; children welcome, tables in front and small back garden; bedrooms *(P J Sibbett, RP, BP, David Sadler)*

Coalbrookdale [Wellington Rd; SJ6704], *Coalbrookdale*: Seven changing well kept ales, good value often imaginative food, affable landlord, real fires, good mix of people, no loud music; dogs allowed *(Alan O'Riordan, Barnie)*; [10 Wellington Rd], *Grove*: Large pub next to Museum of Iron, good menu, fast friendly service, Marstons, Morlands Old Speckled Hen and lots of guest beers; light and airy twin bars, one with sofas, friendly helpful landlord *(G Coates)*

☆ Coalport [off A442 S of Telford at Coalport/Broseley sign; SJ7002], *Woodbridge*: Lovely setting with rustic benches on steepish Severnside lawns giving great view of world's second-oldest iron bridge, softly lit beamed and bow-windowed bar with lots of copper and brass, Victorian prints, good open fire, tables on side terrace with barbecue; good food inc fresh fish, no-smoking restaurant, well kept Scottish Courage ales, good service, piped music not too loud, children in eating areas; coarse fishing; open all day Sat, bedrooms *(C Moncreiffe, Dave Braisted, LYM)*

Coalport [Salthouse Rd, Jackfield; nr Mawes Craft Centre, over footbridge by chinaworks museum; SJ6903], *Boat*: Cosy waterside pub, quarry-tiled bar redecorated by hard-working newish licensees, coal fire in lovely range, food inc good roast pork sandwiches and good value Sun lunch, well kept Banks's Bitter and Mild, darts; summer barbecues on tree-shaded lawn, in delightful part of Severn Gorge *(Basil Minson, BB)*; [Salthouse Rd], *Half Moon*: Refurbished pub by Severn nr Maws Craft Centre, seven or eight real ales, decent malt whiskies, bar food inc very popular Sun lunch, nice atmosphere *(Basil Minson)*; *Shakespeare*: Simple friendly cream-washed pub by pretty Severn gorge park, handy for china museum, with good value

quickly served home-made food; keg beers *(Keith and Janet Morris, BB)*

Coton [Tilstock Rd; B5476 Wem—Whitchurch; SJ5234], *Bull & Dog*: Black and white open-plan Greenalls pub with screened-off dining area, good value food, pleasant service; piped music *(Sue and Bob Ward, SLC)*

Ellerdine Heath [off A442 at garden centre; SJ6122], *Royal Oak*: Happy atmosphere (maybe lots of children), four or more well priced real ales, interesting cheap food inc bargain Sat night specials *(Sue and Bob Ward)*

☆ Ellesmere [Scotland St (A495); SJ4035], *Black Lion*: Clean, comfortable and attractively refurbished with bare boards, ornaments, prints, high-backed settles etc, wide range of good well prepared food all day inc OAP bargains and children's dishes (they offer money back if you're not satisfied), friendly staff, well kept Marstons Bitter and Pedigree, dining area *(Keith and Janet Morris, Dorothee and Dennis Glover, SLC, W L G Watkins, Miss S Watkin, P Taylor, S W Armstrong)*

Gledrid [B5070, handy loop through Chirk off new A5; SJ2937], *Poachers Pocket*: Pretty pub in chain of 20 or so country-style family pubs named thus; seats out by flower tubs overlooking canal, several small rooms with bare boards, lots of stuffed and artificial animals, comical hunting prints and memorabilia; reasonably priced food inc good value special, real chips, Sun lunch, good choice of beers *(Miss S Watkin, P Taylor)*

Goldstone [Goldstone Wharf; off A529 S of Mkt Drayton, at Hinstock; keep on towards Cheswardine; SJ7128], *Wharf*: Good food in two simply decorated bars and grill room; Bass, quick service, pool one end, canalside garden; pleasant walks *(Barbara and Denis Melling, SLC)*

☆ Hampton Loade [off A442 S of Bridgnorth; SO7586], *Lion*: Fine ancient tucked-away stripped-stone inn with good unusual food, friendly efficient service, well kept Hook Norton Best and Simpkiss, country wines, good day-ticket fishing on River Severn, dining room; very busy in summer or when Severn Valley Rly has weekend steam spectaculars, quiet otherwise; children welcome if eating lunchtime (or if booked to dine evening); cl Mon, winter weekday lunchtimes, maybe some other times *(Nigel Woolliscroft, Edward Froggatt, Sue and Bob Ward)*

☆ Harley [A458 NW of Much Wenlock; SJ5901], *Plume of Feathers*: Spacious and popular beamed pub with big open fire, reasonably priced food inc interesting specials, well kept Scottish Courage and guest ales, good welcoming service even when busy, darts, piped music (Sun evening live); dining room, tables outside; bedrooms with own baths *(Janet and Peter Race, SLC, J H Bell, RP, BP)*

Harmer Hill [SJ4822], *Bridgewater Arms*:

Brewers Fayre pub with big dining area, decent food and refreshingly interested staff; play area *(Pat and Robert Watt, SLC)*; *Red Castle*: Greenalls pub with Bass and Tetleys, good value food, pool table, juke box, TV *(SLC)*

☆ **Hodnet** [Drayton Rd (A53); SJ6128], *Bear*: Welcoming 16th-c pub with good range of reasonably priced food inc imaginative dishes, well kept Scottish Courage ales, friendly obliging service, sofas and easy chairs in foyer, sizeable refurbished bar popular with locals, restaurant with small no-smoking area and corner alcove with glass-tile floor over unusual sunken garden in former bear pit; six good value comfortable bedrooms, opp Hodnet Hall gardens *(Olive and Ray Hebson, Keith and Janet Morris, Edward Froggatt)*

Hope [Drury Lane, Hopesgate; just off A488 3 miles S of Minsterley; SJ3401], *Stables*: Cosy rambling small-roomed local with Shipstones, Tetleys and guest beers, generous straightforward food, roaring log fire, welcoming landlord, friendly dog; fine views from newly done back garden; has been cl winter Mon/Tues lunchtime *(PM, Warren Marsh, SLC, C Parsons, LYM)*

☆ **Hopton Wafers** [A4117; SO6476], *Crown*: Friendly and attractive old creeper-covered inn with tables out on terraces and in garden running down to stream, warmly decorated beamed bar with big inglenook fire and woodburner, nice mix of individually chosen tables and chairs, good choice of well prepared food, well kept Whitbreads-related ales, good house wines, restaurant with no-smoking area; provision for children, comfortable and pretty timbered bedrooms *(Wayne Brindle, Paul and Maggie Baker, Gwen and Peter Andrews, Alan and Barbara Mence, Mrs U Hofheinz, LYM)*

☆ **Ironbridge** [Blists Hill Open Air Museum – follow brown museum sign from M54 exit 4, or A442; SJ6704], *New Inn*: Rebuilt Victorian pub in this good heritage museum's re-created working Victorian community (shares its opening hours); informative landlord, friendly staff in period dress, well kept Banks's ales, pewter measure of mother's ruin for 2½d (money from nearby bank), good pasties, gas lighting, traditional games, good generous home cooking in upstairs tearoom; back yard with hens, pigeon coop, maybe children in costume playing hopscotch and skipping; children welcome *(Steve and Angela Maycock, David and Fiona Pemberton, Sue and Mike Todd, LYM)*

☆ **Ironbridge** [Buildwas Rd], *Meadow*: Popular and welcoming Severnside dining pub done up with old-fashioned beamery, cigarette cards, tasteful prints and brasses; wide choice of good value generous freshly prepared food in lounge and downstairs restaurant, quick service, well kept Scottish Courage ales and Marstons Pedigree, decent wines; pretty waterside garden *(Denis and Barbara Melling, M Joyner, Sue and Mike Todd, SLC)*

Ironbridge [Waterloo St], *Olde Robin Hood*: Friendly, comfortable and attractive, five connecting rooms with various alcoves, lots of gleaming brass and old clocks; well kept Bass-related and guest beers, pleasant landlord, good value standard food inc sandwiches; seats out in front, handy for museums complex; good value lunchtime, nice riverside setting by bridge *(M Joyner, SLC)*

Knockin [Main St; B4396 NW of Shrewsbury; SJ3422], *Bradford Arms*: Popular and busy, with good fresh standard food from huge ploughman's to Sun lunch, well kept Bass-related and guest ales, friendly service, reasonably priced restaurant; maybe piped Radio 2 *(R H Martyn, SLC)*

Knowbury [SO5775], *Penny Black*: Reopened after closure, simple but comfortable, with good value bar food inc good Sun carvery, well kept Scottish Courage and interesting guest beers, farm ciders, decent wines, enthusiastic staff, small restaurant; big garden *(TP)*

☆ **Little Stretton** [Ludlow Rd; village well signed off A49; SO4392], *Green Dragon*: Well kept Tetleys, Wadworths 6X, Woods and quickly changing guest beers, reasonably priced straightforward food, pleasant service, cheap house wine, malt whiskies, children in eating area and restaurant; tables outside, handy for Cardingmill Valley (NT) and Long Mynd *(Paul Robinshaw, John and Joan Wyatt, Nigel Woolliscroft, LYM)*

Little Stretton [Ludlow Rd], *Ragleth*: Neatly kept bay-windowed lounge, walkers welcome in brick-and-tile-floored bar with huge inglenook, very wide range of reasonably priced home-made food from sandwiches to steaks, quick service, well kept ales such as Theakstons, Marstons Pedigree, Woods Parish, farm cider, tables on lawn by tulip tree; children welcome, restaurant *(M Joyner, W Burke, LYM)*

Little Wenlock [SJ6507], *Huntsman*: Quiet village pub with bar, lounge and restaurant, horse paintings, ornamental central fireplace, Tetleys and interesting guest beers; well behaved children welcome, some tables outside; handy for Wrekin walks *(M Joyner, SLC)*

Loppington [B4397; SJ4729], *Dickin Arms*: Cosy traditional two-bar country pub with heavy beams, open fire, well kept Bass, Wadworths and Youngers, good food inc fresh veg and good value Sun lunch, good staff, dining room; babies and dogs welcome; pretty village *(Mr and Mrs F Carroll, RP, BP, Lorna and Howard Lambert)*

Ludlow [Bull Ring/Corve St; SO5175], *Feathers*: Superb timbered building, striking inside with Jacobean panelling and carving, fine period furnishings; sadly you'll probably be diverted to a fairly ordinary side bar for the good sandwiches and other decent bar food, or a casual drink – well kept Flowers Original and Wadworths 6X; pleasant service, restaurant, good parking; comfortable bedrooms, not cheap *(J C Simpson, Edward Froggatt, Michael Butler, LYM)*; [King St],

Olde Bull Ring: Striking timbered building, good food in bar and restaurant, pleasant friendly service, real ales *(Alan and Barbara Mence)*; [Broadgate/Lower Bridge St – bottom of Broad St], *Wheatsheaf*: Nicely furnished traditional 17th-c beamed pub spectacularly built into medieval town gate, Bass, M&B Brew XI and Ruddles County, choice of farm ciders, wide range of food, good friendly service, restaurant; attractive bedrooms, warm and comfortable *(David Peakall, W Burke, Michael Butler)*

Madeley [Coalport Rd; SJ6904], *All Nations*: Spartan but friendly one-bar pub brewing its own distinctive well priced pale ale since the 1930s; good value lunchtime sandwiches, handy for Blists Hill *(PB)*

Morville [A458 Bridgnorth—Shrewsbury; SO6794], *Acton Arms*: Good new tenants, enjoyable home-made food in dining lounge, well kept Banks's and sensibly priced wines, big attractive garden *(Robert Whittle)*

Myddle [A528 7 miles N of Shrewsbury; SJ4724], *Red Lion*: Comfortably old-fashioned two-bar Banks's country pub with coal fire, Marstons Pedigree, friendly staff, good home cooking, dining area; piped music; pleasant small village *(SLC)*

☆ **Newcastle** [B4368 Clun—Newtown; SO2582], *Crown*: Good value usual food in quite spacious lounge bar with log fire and piped music, lively locals' bar with darts, pool and so forth in games room, well kept Tetleys, decent wines, friendly efficient service, friendly great dane called Bruno; tables outside; charming well equipped bedrooms, attractive walks *(Peter and Sarah Gooderham, LYM)*

Northwood [SJ4634], *Horse & Jockey*: Quiet and friendly low-beamed country pub with simple decor, wide choice of good value food inc good children's dishes, well kept beer, good service, lots of horse and jockey memorabilia; children and dogs welcome, play area *(Mr and Mrs F Carroll)*

Norton in Hales [SJ7039], *Hinds Head*: Three rooms, open fire, prints and plates, pleasant staff, good range of decent food, Bass, Worthington and Hancocks HB; piped music *(SLC)*

☆ **Queens Head** [just off A5 SE of Oswestry, towards Nesscliffe; SJ3427], *Queens Head*: Emphasis on good value food from speciality sandwiches to full meals, keen polite young staff, well kept Theakstons and guest beers, two dining areas with roaring coal fires, conservatory; seats out by newly restored Montgomery Canal, country walks *(Pete Yearsley, Jeff Davies, Basil Minson)*

Rodington [SJ5914], *Bulls Head*: Generous food in village pub with well kept Burtonwood *(M Joyner)*

☆ **Ryton** [the one nr Dorrington, S of Shrewsbury; SJ4904], *Fox*: Smart country pub, very friendly and relaxed, with comfortable lounge bar and dining area, golfing prints, good range of tasty food, Bass and a guest such as Crown Buckley Rev

James, friendly landlord; hill views *(SLC)*

☆ **Shrewsbury** [Abbey Foregate], *M A D O'Rourkes Dun Cow Pie Shop*: Zany but homely decor, good range of good value food, friendly staff, welcoming atmosphere, lots of jugs hanging from ceiling and enjoyably silly meat-pie and pig's-head memorabilia on walls, well kept Tetleys-related ales and Lumphammer, sharply trained attentive staff; attractive timber-framed building with enormous model cow on porch which looks pure O'Rourke but long predates his 'Little' chain *(Addie and Irene Henry, John Honnor, SLC, Sue and Bob Ward, BB)*

☆ **Shrewsbury** [New St/Quarry Park; leaving centre via Welsh Bridge/A488 turn into Port Hill Rd], *Boathouse*: Comfortably modernised pub in lovely position opp park by Severn, river views from long lounge bar, tables out on sheltered terrace and rose lawn; one of Whitbreads' Hogshead chain, with good changing choice of well kept real ales, friendly helpful staff, good range of standard food; children welcome, summer barbecues, popular with young people evening; open all day *(Malcolm and Pat Rudlin, SLC, M Joyner, Sue and Bob Ward, LYM)*

Shrewsbury [Castle Gates], *Albion*: Popular friendly local opp railway stn, pub games and games machines, friendly staff, lunchtime food, well kept Burtonwood *(Richard Lewis)*; [16 Castle Gates], *Castle Vaults*: Friendly old timbered local popular for wide choice of well kept changing esoteric ales in proper lined glasses, good choice of wines and malt whiskies, good chatty landlord; generous helpings of good food in adjoining Mexican restaurant, little roof garden with spiral staircase up towards castle; bedrooms good *(Richard and Anne Lewis, SLC, Andy and Jill Kassube)*; [Swan Hill/Cross Hill], *Coach & Horses*: Unspoilt Victorian pub with pine-panelled bar, two lounge areas, back restaurant with carvery, well kept Bass and two interesting guest beers, good home-made lunchtime food, attentive service; pretty flower boxes outside *(Richard Lewis, SLC)*; [Dogpole], *Cromwells*: Pub with wine bar and restaurant, Scottish Courage beers with several unusual guest beers, good value imaginative food, raised garden and terrace behind; piped music; open all day Sat *(SLC)*; [48 St Michaels St (A49 1/2 mile N of stn)], *Dolphin*: Early Victorian gas-lit tavern with five different well kept ales changing each week; can be smoky, but cosy and interesting, with friendly staff (and abyssinian blue cat); no food (apart from crisps etc), music or machines, no lagers or g&ts *(Richard Lewis)*; [Wyle Cop], *Lion*: Grand largely 18th-c coaching inn with cosy oak-panelled bar and sedate series of high-ceilinged rooms opening off, civilised if not swift service, Scottish Courage ales, reasonably priced bar lunches, tea or coffee and cakes other times; children welcome, bedrooms comfortable *(George Atkinson, LYM)*; [49 Wyle Cop], *Lion & Pheasant*: Beamed bar with good bar food, well kept ales inc

Marstons Pedigree, big log fire; bedrooms simple but well priced, newly decorated *(Andy and Jill Kassube)*; [Church St], *Loggerheads*: Bought and recently refurbished in old style by Banks's, one room with scrubbed-top tables and high-backed settles, other rooms with lots of prints, real fire, food all day Mon-Sat till 6, friendly staff and locals, well kept ales *(Richard Lewis)*; [Smithfield Rd], *Proud Salopian*: Welcoming open-plan local with good choice of well kept mainstream changing ales, lunchtime food inc sandwiches, friendly landlord, darts, pool; wide screen TV, juke box, machines, can get smoky; open all day *(Richard Lewis)*; [4 Fish St], *Three Fishes*: Extensively refurbished heavy-beamed timbered pub, no smoking throughout, with six well kept changing ales, lots of prints and bric-a-brac, friendly quick service; open all day; kitchen closed May 1997 – was to reopen in summer as we went to press – has had good value lunchtime food inc vegetarian *(Richard Lewis, SLC, Keith and Janet Morris)*; [High St], *Wheatsheaf*: Comfortable open-plan beamed lounge, bar food, well kept Banks's; games machine, TV, juke box; open all day Mon-Sat *(Richard Lewis)*; [Wenlock Rd (car park London Rd)], *White Horse*: Big refurbished steak house with usual prints and decor, Ansells, Tetleys *(SLC)*; [St Marys Pl], *Yorkshire House*: Attractive panelling, very low beams and brasses (the best kept in a leaded-light wall cupboard), sloping floor – said to be haunted; well kept Tetleys and Worthington Best, friendly staff; juke box; open all day Mon-Sat *(Richard Lewis)*

☆ Stiperstones [village signed off A488 S of Minsterley – OS Sheet 126 map ref 364005; SO3600], *Stiperstones*: Very good value simple food served all day, inc vegetarian and their famous local whinberry pie, in welcoming little modernised lounge bar with comfortable leatherette wall banquettes, lots of brassware on ply-panelled walls, well kept Flowers IPA and Woods Parish, good service, interesting landlord, darts in plainer public bar, maybe unobtrusive piped music; restaurant, tables outside; clean basic cheap bedrooms, good breakfast; good walking *(Nigel and Lindsay Chapman, Edward Froggatt, Nigel Woolliscroft, Jeanne Cross, Paul Silvestri, BB)*

Telford [Station Hill, St Georges; SJ7010], *Albion*: Woody partitioned bar with pews and traditional tables, kitchen range one end, usual bar food, reasonably priced Marstons ales, terrace and play area; two comfortable well equipped bedrooms, limited disabled access *(G Coates)*; [Shawbirch; SJ6413], *Apley Arms*: Harvester restaurant, good food, Bass *(SLC)*; [Long Lane (A442)], *Bucks Head*: Hotel bar with well kept Banks's, Davenports and Tetleys, good quick food inc good value Sun lunch, family eating area and restaurant; piped music, fruit machine, pool; play area outside; bedrooms *(M Joyner, SLC)*; [Market St, Oakengates; SJ7011], *Crown*: Seven or more ever-changing real ales, frequent beer festivals, knowledgeable staff, friendly locals, comfortable seating round edge of three spartan rooms with standing room in centre, pool table in public bar, tables outside, no food; close to BR station *(G Coates, Richard Lewis)*

☆ Tilley [just S of Wem; SJ5128], *Raven*: Well kept dining pub in pretty 18th-c black and white building, bright, clean and attractive, with good service, separate restaurant (booking advised), Fullers London Pride and Marstons Pedigree, log-effect gas fire, prints and bric-a-brac; nice terrace, beautiful village *(Sue and Bob Ward, Mr and Mrs F Carroll, SLC, Dr and Mrs C D E Morris)*

☆ Tong [A41 just N of M54 junction 3, just beyond village; SJ7907], *Bell*: Good value food inc children's and Sun lunch in friendly and efficient Milestone Tavern dining pub, well kept reasonably priced Banks's and Marstons Pedigree, olde-worlde stripped brickwork, big family room, dining room, unobtrusive piped music, no dogs; pleasant back conservatory, big garden, attractive countryside nr Weston Park *(Paul and Sue Merrick, Edward Froggatt, D and D Savidge, M Joyner)*

Uckington [B5061 E of Atcham; SJ5810], *Horseshoes*: Good family atmosphere in big Brewers Fayre dining pub with Whitbreads-related ales, children's eating area and play area *(M Joyner, SLC)*

☆ Upton Magna [Pelham Rd (off B5062 or B5064 E of Shrewsbury; SJ5512], *Corbet Arms*: Wide choice of good value food cooked to order, well kept Banks's ales and short but decent choice of wines in big L-shaped lounge bar with armchairs by log fire; darts and juke box in smaller public bar, good service; handy for Attingham Park (NT), busy at weekends *(Margaret and Peter Brierley, M Joyner)*

Wentnor [SO3893], *Crown*: Welcoming new management in popular 16th-c dining pub at foot of Long Mynd, good value food, well kept Hobsons, Morlands Old Speckled Hen, Wadworth 6X and Woods Shropshire Lad, decent wines, big log fire, lots of bric-a-brac; tables outside; four good bedrooms, fine views *(Paul Robinshaw, R W Sheppard, SLC)*

☆ Whitchurch [St Marys St; SJ5341], *Old Town Hall Vaults*: Good value promptly served home-cooked lunchtime food in attractive and civilised 18th-c pub, well kept Marstons Pedigree and Best, cheerful service; piped light classics – birthplace of Sir Edward German *(SLC)*

Whittington [A495, just off A5; SJ3331], *Olde Boot*: Panelled lounge with copper-topped tables and lots of brass, well kept Robinsons Best, Hatters Mild and a guest such as Hartleys XB, good value food inc popular Sun roast and OAP specials Mon and Tues night, friendly staff, small restaurant area, TV and games in popular friendly bar; bedrooms, attractive spot opp 13th-c castle *(SLC, Richard Lewis)*

☆ Wistanstow [N of Craven Arms, nr junction A49/A489; SO4385], *Plough*: High rafters, bright lighting, modern feel, good home-cooked food inc interesting dishes, pleasant atmosphere, well kept Woods Parish, Shropshire Lad, Special, Wonderful and a seasonal beer from the small brewery just behind, farm ciders, good choice of wines by the glass; games area, children welcome lunchtime, tables outside *(Andrew Rogers, Amanda Milsom, Basil Minson, LYM)*

Woofferton [A456/B4362 S of Ludlow; SO5269], *Salwey Arms*: Has been popular for wide choice of good food and well kept Bass and Tetleys, but licensees moved in summer 1997 *(Anon)*

☆ **Woore** [London Rd (A51); SJ7342], *Falcon*: Huge choice of generous good value food in bars and comfortable dining room inc good fresh fish, good friendly service, well kept Ansells Mild and Marstons Bitter and Pedigree, interesting prints; dining room more comfortable for eating than bars; nr Bridgemere garden centre *(Alan and Heather Jacques, Sue Holland, Dave Webster, J Lowe, Liz and Peter Elsey)*

Yorton [SJ5023], *Railway*: Same family for 60 years, unchanging atmosphere, simple bar and big lounge, real fire, well kept Wadworths 6X, Woods Parish and Shropshire Lad, pub games – no piped music or machines, no food *(Richard Lewis)*

Ideas for a country day out? We list pubs in really attractive scenery at the back of the book – and there are separate lists for waterside pubs, ones with really good gardens, and ones with lovely views.

Somerset

Visitors to Somerset are spoilt for choice among pubs, and their many reports to us show the warmest appreciation: buildings full of character and interest (often remarkably unspoilt), friendly people, good food, an unusual variety of local beers (and ciders), and some lovely scenery. Pubs that are on particularly good form these days include the charming Globe at Appley, the cosy Old Green Tree in Bath, the civilised George in Castle Cary (a new entry, nice place to stay in), the prettily set Wheatsheaf at Combe Hay (now has bedrooms), the New Inn at Dowlish Wake, the very foody Fitzhead Inn at Fitzhead (excellent wines), the Kingsdon Inn at Kingsdon (but it's been up for sale), the Rising Sun at Knapp (super fish), the Devonshire Arms at Long Sutton (another new entry, genuinely welcoming to all, yet with gently upmarket touches), the Royal Oak at Luxborough (changes all for the better at this Exmoor-edge favourite), the chatty old Talbot at Mells (gains a Place to Stay Award this year), the Halfway House at Pitney (great choice of real ales), the engagingly laid out Sparkford Inn at Sparkford (yet another newcomer), the Rose & Crown at Stoke St Gregory (good all round), and the rather genteel thatched Royal Oak at Winsford; new people at the Royal Oak at Withypool are settling in very well. All these in their different ways can be recommended for food, but among the many pubs here which have been giving special pleasure for enjoyable meals out, our choice as Somerset Dining Pub of the Year is the Fitzhead Inn at Fitzhead. Our pick of the entries in the Lucky Dip section at the end of the chapter would include the Lamb in Axbridge, Crystal Palace in Bath (where there's a very wide choice), Bell at Buckland Dinham, Old Mill at Haselbury Plucknett, Royal Oak at Over Stratton, Montague at Shepton Montague, Greyhound at Staple Fitzpaine, Masons Arms in Taunton, City Arms in Wells and Burcott Inn near Wookey; as we have not yet had the opportunity of inspecting many of these, we'd be particularly grateful for readers' views on which are most likely to be main entry candidates. There's a wide choice of interesting pubs in Bristol. Drinks prices in Somerset are close to the national average, with pubs tied to smaller breweries such as Smiles of Bristol or Palmers down in Bridport (Dorset) generally rather cheaper; the cheapest place we found for drinks was the New Inn at Blagdon, tied to Wadworths the Wiltshire brewery.

APPLEY ST0621 Map 1
Globe 🍽️

Hamlet signposted from the network of back roads between A 361 and A38, W of B3187 and W of Milverton and Wellington; OS sheet 181, map ref 072215

A good mix of customers comes to this friendly old place to enjoy consistently good food served by charming, friendly staff. The simple beamed front room is relaxed and chatty, with benches and a built-in settle, bare wood tables on the brick floor, and pictures of magpies. As well as the restaurant, there's a further room with easy chairs and other more traditional ones; alley skittles. Generously served, the bar food might include sandwiches, home-made soup (£2.25), mushrooms in cream, garlic and horseradish (£3.95), a light cold egg pancake filled with prawns, celery and pineapple in marie rose sauce (£4.75), chilli con carne (£4.95), home-made steak and kidney pie in stout or savoury vegetable crumble (£5.95), fresh salmon with chive, white wine and cream sauce (£7.95), steaks (from £7.95), lovely breast of local chicken stuffed with pine nuts, bacon, raisins and apricots and served with a madeira sauce (£8.95), puddings, children's dishes (£3.25), and popular Sunday roast (£5.25). The restaurant is no smoking. A stone-flagged entry corridor leads to a serving hatch from where Cotleigh Tawny and Barn Owl, and Teignworthy Reel Ale are served on handpump, and they keep Lanes farmhouse cider. Seats, climbing frame and swings outside in the garden; the path opposite leads eventually to the River Tone. (Recommended by DJW, Douglas Miller, B J Cox, S G N Bennett, Patrick Renouf, Adrian and Jane Tierney-Jones, Michael and Lynne Steane, Robin Priest, David Gittins)

Free house ~ Licensees A W and E J Burt, R and J Morris ~ Real ale ~ Meals and snacks (till 10pm) ~ Restaurant (not Sun evening) ~ (01823) 672327 ~ Children welcome ~ Open 11-3, 6.30-11; 12-3, 7-10.30 Sun; closed Mon lunchtime, except bank holidays

ASHCOTT ST4337 Map 1
Ashcott Inn
A39 about 6 miles W of Glastonbury

This pleasant old pub has an attractive bar with stripped stone walls and beams, some interesting old-fashioned seats among more conventional ones, a mix of oak and elm and other tables, and a log-effect gas fire in its sturdy chimney. Tasty bar food includes sandwiches, home-made soup (£2.20), leeks topped with stilton and breadcrumbs (£3.50), cider baked ham with two eggs (£5.20), beef in ale pie or oriental stir fry (£5.95), steaks (from £6.95), grilled plaice (£7.25), and chicken ricotta (£9.95); the restaurant is no smoking. Butcombe Bitter and guest beers on handpump kept under light blanket pressure; cribbage, dominoes, shove-ha'penny, fruit machine, alley skittles, and piped music. Seats on the terrace, and a pretty walled garden; this year, there are two new children's adventure play areas. (Recommended by Dr and Mrs A K Clarke, Alan and Paula McCully, Jean and Richard Phillips, Donald Godden, Jack and Gemima Valiant, Mr and Mrs Beck, A Preston, Julie and Tony Baldwin, V H and J M Vanstone)

Heavitree (who no longer brew) ~ Managers Jon and Helen Endacott ~ Real ale ~ Meals and snacks ~ Restaurant ~ (01458) 210282 ~ Well behaved children in eating area of bar and in restaurant ~ Open 11-11; 12-10.30 Sun

nr ASHILL ST3217 Map 1
Square & Compass
Windmill Hill; turn left off A358 when see Stewley Cross Garage on a side road

Bustling and friendly, this pleasantly remote local has picnic tables outside on the grass, a good children's play area with badminton and volleyball, and sweeping views over rolling pastures. There's a touring caravan site. Inside, there are upholstered window seats in the cosy little bar, other comfortable seats (with extra room for eating), and an open fire in winter. Bar food includes sandwiches, mixed salami platter (£4.50), mozzarella and cherry tomato quiche (£4.95), chicken breast topped with mozzarella and pesto (£6.50), seafood paella or tagliatelle with a smoked salmon and cream sauce (£6.80), pork with three mustard stroganoff (£7.50), and rump steak with a pepper and brandy sauce (£9.75). Well kept Exmoor Ale, Greene King Abbot, Marstons Pedigree, Morlands Old Speckled Hen, and guest beers on handpump; darts, shove-ha'penny, cribbage, dominoes and piped music. (Recommended by Derek and Iris Martin, Lynn Sharpless, Bob Eardley, Mr and Mrs Beck, Geoff and Linda Dibble, David Crafts, Howard Clutterbuck, D Godden, Helen and Keith Bowers and friends, Revd A Nunnerley)

Free house ~ Simon and Ginny Reeves ~ Real ale ~ Meals and snacks ~ (01823) 480467 ~ Children in eating area of bar and in restaurant ~ Occasional folk evenings ~ Open 12-2.30, 6.30-11; 12-3, 7-10.30 Sun

BATH ST7565 Map 2
Old Green Tree ◀

12 Green St

A genuinely unspoilt pub with a cheerful, bustling atmosphere, well kept changing local beers, enjoyable food, and efficient, helpful staff. The three oak-panelled little rooms include a comfortable lounge on the left as you go in, its walls decorated with wartime aircraft pictures, and a no-smoking back bar. The big skylight lightens things up attractively. Good home-made lunchtime bar food includes soup such as bacon and parsnip (£3), filled baps (£3.30), good ploughman's (from £3.30), spaghetti with a rich tomato and parmesan sauce (£4.50), interesting salads (£4.80), thai chicken curry or popular bangers and mash with tomato and onion or apple, cream, mustard and cider sauces (all £4.80), seafood platter (£6), and daily specials such as faggots with onion beer gravy and mash, pesto pasta or beef rogan josh. There are usually five well kept beers on handpump such as Butcombe Wilmot's Premium Ale, Oakhill Black Magic, RCH Pitchfork, Uley Hogshead, and Wickwar Brand Oak Bitter, lots of malt whiskies, a nice little wine list with helpful notes and 12 wines by the glass, and a perry on draught. The gents', though good, are down steep steps. *(Recommended by Dr and Mrs A K Clarke, Dave Irving, Ewan McCall, Roger Huggins, Simon and Amanda Southwell, Mike Pugh, Giles Francis, John Hayter, David Peakall, Roger Wain-Heapy, Pat and John Millward, Richard Lewis, John and Lynn Busenbark, J and P Maloney, N J Lawless, Gordon, Veronica M Brown)*

Free house ~ Licensees Sarah Le Feure and Nick Luke ~ Real ale ~ Lunchtime meals and snacks (not Sun) ~ (01225) 448259 ~ Children in eating area of bar at lunchtime if over 12 ~ Open 11-11; 7-10.30 Sun – closed Sun lunchtime

BECKINGTON ST8051 Map 2
Woolpack ♀ ⇌

Off A36 Bath—Warminster

Now owned by the Old English Pub Company, this friendly old inn has an attractive no-smoking lounge with antique furnishings and pictures, a lively flagstoned public bar with stripped pine tables and a good log fire, and a cosy candlelit no-smoking dining room. Under the new licensee, the good, if pricy, food includes lunchtime sandwiches (not Sunday), starters (that can be had as a main course, too) like home-made soup (£3.50), stilton and goat's cheese soufflé with pesto sauce (£5.50), terrine of duck and pistachio nuts with cumberland sauce (£5.95), and warm salad of king prawns and cashews tossed in sweet soy sauce (£6.95), and main courses such as breast of chicken with grain mustard and tarragon sauce and linguine pasta (£10.95), confit of barbary duck with braised red cabbage and rich game jus (£11.95), best end of local lamb with port, redcurrant and wild mushrooms (£12.95), and daily specials; vegetables are £1.95 extra. Well kept Courage Directors, Greene King IPA, and guest beers on handpump, several malt whiskies, and a decent wine list; cheerful helpful service. *(Recommended by John and Lynn Busenbark, Sandria Parker, Andrew Shaw, Paul and Ursula Randall, Pat and John Millward, Dr and Mrs A K Clarke; also in Good Hotel Guide; more reports on the new regime, please)*

Free house ~ Licensee Andrew Morgan ~ Real ale ~ Meals and snacks (till 10pm) ~ Restaurant ~ (01373) 831244 ~ Children welcome until 9pm ~ Open 11-3, 6-11; 12-3, 7-10.30 Sun ~ Bedrooms: £54.50B/£64.50B

BLAGDON ST5059 Map 2
New Inn

Church Street, off A368

From the picnic tables at the back of this old-fashioned pub there are fine views looking down over fields to wood-fringed Blagdon Lake, and to the low hills beyond. Inside, the two characterful rooms have ancient beams decorated with gleaming horsebrasses and a few tankards, some comfortable antique settles – one with its armrests carved as dogs as well as little plush armchairs, mate's chairs and so forth, and big logs burning in both stone inglenook fireplaces; a new no-smoking area has been opened up. Bar food includes home-made soup (£1.95), sandwiches (from £1.95; open ones from £3.50), yorkshire pudding filled with sausage and onion gravy (£3.50), filled baked potatoes (from £3.75), ploughman's (£3.95), home-made steak and kidney pie or vegetable chilli (£4.95), lasagne (£5.50), lamb tagine (£6.25), chicken en croûte (£7.25), steaks (from £9.50), daily specials, and puddings (from £2.25). Well kept Butcombe Bitter, Wadworths IPA and 6X, and a guest beer on handpump, and several malt whiskies; darts, table skittles, cribbage, dominoes, trivia, and piped music. *(Recommended by Philip and Jude Simmons, Mark and Heather Williamson, David Warrellow, Gwen and Peter Andrews, F J Willy, Meg and Colin Hamilton, Jenny and Roger Huggins)*

Wadworths ~ Manager John Chester ~ Real ale ~ Meals and snacks (till 10pm) ~ (01761) 462475 ~ Children in no-smoking area ~ Open 11.30-2.30, 7-11; 12-3, 7-10.30 Sun

BRADLEY GREEN ST2538 Map 1
Malt Shovel

Pub signposted from A39 W of Bridgwater, near Cannington; though Bradley Green is shown on road maps, if you're booking the postal address is Blackmoor Lane, Cannington, BRIDGWATER, Somerset TA5 2NE; note that there is another different Malt Shovel on this main road, three miles nearer Bridgwater

Friendly staff welcome you into the neatly kept straightforward main bar here. There are window seats, some functional modern elm country chairs and sturdy modern winged high-backed settles around wooden tables, various boating photographs, and a black kettle standing on a giant fossil by the woodburning stove. There's also a tiny snug with white walls and black beams, a solid oak bar counter with a natural stone front, and red tiled floor. Decent bar food includes lunchtime sandwiches (£1.55, crusty rolls £1.95) and ploughman's (from £3.10), as well as pasta and spinach mornay (£3.55), lamb and potato provençale (£3.85), filled baked potatoes (£4.10; you can choose any three fillings out of 12), salads (from £4.40), smoked haddock cheesy bake (£3.85), home-made steak and kidney pie (£4.65), grilled gammon and egg (£4.90), home-made fish pie (£5.75), steaks (from £8.50), daily specials, and children's menu (from £1.95). Well kept Butcombe Bitter, Morlands Old Speckled Hen, John Smiths, and a guest beer on handpump, farm ciders, and a fair choice of wines by the glass; sizeable skittle alley, dominoes, cribbage, and piped music. The family room opens on to the garden, where there are picnic tables and a fishpond. No dogs inside. West of the pub, Blackmore Farm is a striking medieval building. *(Recommended by Nick Lawless, K H Frostick, Maysie Thompson, Eddie Edwards, Roger and Jenny Huggins, Jo and Gary Charlton, Stephen and Julie Brown, D Alexander, M and A Sandy, Brian and Barbara Matthews, Ian Phillips, Richard Gibbs)*

Free house ~ Licensees Robert and Frances Beverley, Philip and Sally Monger ~ Real ale ~ Meals (not winter Sun evening) and lunchtime snacks ~ Restaurant (not winter Sun evenings) ~ (01278) 653432 ~ Children in family room and in restaurant ~ Open 11.30-2.30(3 Sat), 6.30(7 winter)-11; 12-3, 7-10.30 Sun; closed Sun evening Nov-Feb ~ Bedrooms: £26.50B/£38B

BRISTOL ST5872 Map 2
Highbury Vaults £

St Michaels Hill, Cotham; main road out to Cotham from inner ring dual carriageway

The attractive back terrace here has tables built into a partly covered flowery arbour that is heated on winter evenings; this effectively doubles the size of the pub. The bustling little front bar with the corridor beside it, leads through to a long series of little rooms – wooden floors, green and cream paintwork, and old-fashioned furniture and prints, including lots of period Royal Family engravings and lithographs in the front room. It's one of the handful of pubs tied to the local Smiles brewery, so has all their beers on handpump at attractive prices, as well changing guests such as Brains SA, Crown Buckley Reverend James, and Fullers London Pride. Incredibly cheap bar food includes filled rolls, and hot dishes such as chilli con carne, vegetable coconut curry, pork in ginger wine, beef in beer or fresh pasta (all £2.90). Bar billiards, dominoes, and cribbage. In early Georgian times this was a lock-up where condemned men ate their last meal, and some of the bars can still be seen on the windows. *(Recommended by Simon and Amanda Southwell, Pat and John Millward, Mrs H Murphy, Barry and Anne, JJB)*

Smiles ~ Manager Bradd Francis ~ Real ale ~ Meals and snacks (12-2, 5.30-8.30; not Sat or Sun evenings) ~ (0117) 973 3203 ~ Children welcome until 9pm ~ Open 12-11; 12-10.30 Sun

CASTLE CARY ST6332 Map 2
George 🛏

Market Place; just off A371 Shepton Mallet—Wincanton

The massive black elm mantelbeam over the log fire in this thatched coaching inn's beamed front bar is said to be over 1,000 years old. This is a cosy room, with beams, bow window seat, a cushioned high-backed settle by the fire, and just six or seven tables – they fill quickly at lunchtime, when there's a very civilised and relaxed atmosphere (despite the piped pop music). An inner no-smoking bar, separated by a glazed partition from the inn's central reception area, has a couple of big landscapes, some pictures made from butterfly wings, and a similarly decorous but busy feel. Good value food includes sandwiches (from £1.90), soup (£2.50), honey-roast ham with egg (£4), ploughman's (£4.25), local goat's cheese with salad, walnuts and walnut dressing on warm toast (£4.50), steak, kidney and mushroom pie with ale (£6.25), sweet and sour pork (£6.75), risotto with wild mushrooms or vegetarian moussaka (£6.95), salmon and cod fishcakes (£7.25), excellent chargrilled liver and bacon (£7.50), sirloin steak (£12.50), and home-made puddings (from £2.50). The restaurant is also no smoking. Well kept Butcombe and Wilmots on handpump, decent house wines, a fair range of malt whiskies and other spirits; pleasant staff. Cribbage and piped music. *(Recommended by John Knighton, Pamela Goodwyn, Janet Pickles)*

Free house ~ Licensees Sue and Greg Sparkes ~ Real ale ~ Meals and snacks ~ Restaurant ~ (01963) 350761 ~ Children welcome ~ Open 10.30-3, 6-11; 12-3, 7-10.30 Sun ~ Bedrooms: £45B/£75B

CATCOTT ST3939 Map 1
King William

Village signposted off A39 Street—Bridgwater

This neatly kept cottagey pub has a spacious bar with one or two rugs on the stone floors, traditional furnishings such as kitchen and other assorted chairs, brown-painted built-in and other settles, window seats, and Victorian fashion plates and other old prints; big stone fireplaces. Decent bar food includes sandwiches (from £1.50), home-made soup (£1.80), ploughman's (from £2.90), mushroom stroganoff (£4.45), steak and kidney pie or curry (£4.60), smoked haddock in cider sauce (£4.75), trout with almonds (£6.75), steaks (from £7.65), duckling with orange and Grand Marnier sauce (£10.45), daily specials, and puddings. Well kept Palmers Bridport, IPA, and 200 on handpump, and a good range of malt whiskies; darts, cribbage, dominoes, and piped music. A large extension at the back includes a skittle-alley and a glass-topped well. *(Recommended by Stephen Brown, Dave Irving, Roger Huggins, Tom McLean, Ewan McCall, M Carr, Tom Evans, S H Godsell)*

Palmers ~ Tenant Phillip Rowland ~ Real ale ~ Meals and snacks ~ Restaurant ~ (01278) 722374 ~ Children in eating area of bar until 9pm ~ Open 11.30-2.30, 6-11; 12-2.30, 7-10.30 Sun

---

Places with gardens or terraces usually let children sit there – we note in the text the very few exceptions that don't.

CHURCHILL ST4560 Map 1
Crown 🍺
Skinners Lane; in village, turn off A368 at Nelson Arms

Both visitors and regulars are made welcome in this unchanging country cottage. The small and local stone-floored and cross-beamed room on the right has a wooden window seat, an unusually sturdy settle, and built-in wall benches; the left-hand room has a slate floor, and some steps past the big log fire in a big stone fireplace lead to more sitting space. Well kept Bass, Cotleigh Batch Bitter (brewed by Cotleigh for them), Palmers IPA, Smiles Golden Brew, and guest beers such as Greene King Abbot or Palmers Tally Ho! all tapped from casks at the back, and country wines. Good value bar food includes home-made soups (from £2.20), rare beef sandwich (£2.50), a good ploughman's, chilli con carne or faggots (£3.95), and various casseroles (from £4.95); some of the meat comes from their own farm. They can be busy at weekends, especially in summer. There are garden tables on the front and a smallish but pretty back lawn with hill views; the Mendip Morris Men come in summer. Good walks nearby. (Recommended by Barry and Anne, Mike and Mary Carter, David Warrellow, Amanda and Simon Southwell, A R and B E Sayer, Barry and Anne, S H Godsell)

Free house ~ Licensee Tim Rogers ~ Real ale ~ Lunchtime meals and snacks ~ (01934) 852995 ~ Children in eating area of bar ~ Live entertainment on first Sun of month ~ Open 11.30-3, 5.30-11; 12-10.30 Sun

CLAPTON IN GORDANO ST4773 Map 2
Black Horse
4 miles from M5 junction 19; A369 towards Portishead, then B3124 towards Clevedon; in N Weston opp school turn left signposted Clapton, then in village take second right, maybe signed Clevedon, Clapton Wick

In the evening in particular, this unchanging country pub has a good bustling atmosphere. The partly flagstoned and partly red-tiled main room has amusing cartoons and photographs of the pub, winged settles and built-in wall benches around narrow, dark wooden tables, pleasant window seats, and a big log fire with stirrups and bits on the mantelbeam. A window in an inner snug is still barred from the days when this room was the petty-sessions gaol; high-backed settles – one a marvellous carved and canopied creature, another with an art nouveau copper insert reading East, West, Hame's Best – lots of mugs hanging from its black beams, and plenty of little prints and photographs. There's also a simply furnished room just off the bar (where children can go), with high-backed corner settles and a gas fire; darts, dominoes, cribbage, and piped music. Bar food includes filled french bread, ploughman's (£3.60), and hot dishes like chilli con carne or lasagne (£4.50). Well kept Courage Best and Georges Bitter Ale, Smiles Best, and Wickwar Olde Merryford Ale on handpump or tapped from the cask, and Thatchers farm cider. The little flagstoned front garden is exceptionally pretty in summer with a mass of flowers in tubs, hanging baskets and flowerbeds; there are some old rustic tables and benches, with more to one side of the car park and in the secluded children's play area with its sturdy wooden climber, slide, rope ladder and rope swing. Paths from here lead up Naish Hill or along to Cadbury Camp. (Recommended by Adrian and Jane Tierney-Jones, Pamela Goodwyn, David Warrellow, Brian and Bett Cox, Mr and Mrs W Welsh, Comus Elliott, Ian and Gayle Woodhead, Tom Evans)

Scottish Courage ~ Tenants Nicholas Evans and Alfonso Garcia ~ Real ale ~ Lunchtime meals and snacks (not Sun) ~ (01275) 842105 ~ Children in separate bar area ~ Live music Mon evenings ~ Open 11-3, 6-11; 11-11 Sat; 12-3, 7-11 Sun

COMBE HAY ST7354 Map 2
Wheatsheaf
Village signposted from A367 or B3110 S of Bath

Three ensuite bedrooms have been added to this well liked friendly country pub. It's in a pretty setting on the edge of a steep wooded valley (good nearby walks), and has three dovecotes built into the walls, and tables on the spacious terraced lawn looking down to the church and ancient manor stables. The pleasantly old-fashioned rooms have low ceilings, brown-painted settles, pews and rustic tables, a very high-backed winged settle facing one big log fire, old sporting and other prints, and earthenware jugs on the shelf of the little shuttered windows. Reliably good, popular bar food includes home-made soup (£2.75), ploughman's (from £4.50), game terrine (£4.75), quiche (£5.50), hot baked ham (£5.75), seasonal pheasant or venison, fresh trout (£8.75), daily specials like chicken livers (£5.25), pasta in a creamy mushroom and courgette sauce (£5.95), shredded crispy duck in an orange and pineapple sauce (£6.25), sautéed tiger prawns (£7.95), and tasty puddings like strawberry and melon fruit salad with hazelnut sauce(£2.95). Well kept Courage Best and a guest like Butcombe Bitter or Marstons Pedigree tapped from the cask, several malt whiskies, and decent wines; shove-ha'penny and cribbage. *(Recommended by Mark and Heather Williamson, Andrew Chantrill, J P Anderson, Dr and Mrs A K Clarke, Howard Clutterbuck, J C Simpson, Susan and Nigel Wilson, A Thistlethwaite, Mrs B Sugarman, C A Foulkes, Howard Clutterbuck)*

Free house ~ Licensee Mike Taylor ~ Real ale ~ Meals and snacks ~ Restaurant ~ (01225) 833504 ~ Children allowed away from bar ~ Open 11-2.30, 6(6.30 in winter)-10.30(11 Sat); 12-2.30, 7-10.30 Sun; closed 25-26 Dec ~ Bedrooms: £39B/£68B

COMPTON MARTIN ST5457 Map 2
Ring o' Bells
A368 Bath—Weston

Even when this cheerful country pub is really busy, the licensee and his staff cope with quiet efficiency. The snugly traditional front part of the bar has rugs on the flagstones, inglenook seats right by the log fire, and a warmly cosy atmosphere; up a step is a spacious carpeted back part with largely stripped stone walls and pine tables. Popular bar food includes sandwiches (from £1.35; toasties from £2.15), soup (£1.75), filled baked potatoes (from £2.75), omelettes (from £3), ploughman's (from £3.35), grilled ham and eggs (small £3.50, large £4.40), lasagne or mushroom, broccoli and almond tagliatelle (£4.60), beef in ale (£5.25), generous mixed grill (£9.20), daily specials like chicken fricassee, raspberry lamb, salmon carbonara or duck pancakes, and children's meals (or helpings; from £1.10). Well kept Butcombe Bitter, Wadworths 6X and guest beers such as Butcombe Wilmots Premium Ale on handpump, and local cider. The public bar has darts and shove-ha'penny, and a spacious, no-smoking family room has a rocking horse, table skittles and fruit machine. The large garden has swings, a slide, and a climbing frame. The pub is not far from Blagdon Lake and Chew Valley Lake, and is overlooked by the Mendip Hills. *(Recommended by David Warrellow, JCW, C Sinclair, Gwen and Peter Andrews, A E Brace, Barry and Anne, Hugh MacLean, Tom Evans, Jenny and Roger Huggins, Don Kellaway, Angie Coles)*

Free house ~ Licensee Roger Owen ~ Real ale ~ Meals and snacks (till 10pm Fri/Sat) ~ Children in family room ~ (01761) 221284 ~ Open 11.30-3, 6-11; 12-3, 7-10.30 Sun

CRANMORE ST6643 Map 2
Strode Arms ★ ⏺ ♀
West Cranmore; signposted with pub off A361 Frome—Shepton Mallet

Through the stone-mullioned windows of this neatly kept early 15th-c former farmhouse you can see the village duckpond – it's an attractive setting. Much emphasis inside is, not surprisingly, on the good, popular, generously served food, but those wanting a quiet drink are made just as welcome. The same menu is used in both the bar and restaurant: sandwiches, soup (£2.75), very good egg mayonnaise with prawns, capers, smoked trout, anchovy and asparagus tips (£3.95), scallops and bacon (£5.50), tasty home-made steak and kidney pie or pancake filled with spinach and baked with a cheese sauce (£6.75), gammon and egg or fresh salmon fishcakes (£7.50), honey roast duckling with an orange sauce (£8.50), steaks (from £9.25), daily specials such as Greek meatballs with spicy tomato sauce, delicious veal rosti with stilton sauce or vegetarian strudel, and puddings like fresh orange and chocolate mousse or sticky toffee pudding (from £2.50); Sunday roasts; friendly service. There are charming country furnishings, a grandfather clock on the flagstones, fresh flowers and pot plants, remarkable old locomotive engineering drawings and big black and white steam train murals in a central lobby, good bird prints, newspapers to read, and lovely log fires in handsome fireplaces. Well kept Flowers IPA, Fullers London Pride, and Marstons Pedigree on handpump, an interesting choice of decent wines by the glass and lots more by the bottle, and quite a few liqueurs and ports. There's a front terrace with some benches and a back garden. On the first Tuesday of each month, there's a vintage car meeting, and the pub is handy for the East Somerset Light Railway. *(Recommended by A L and J D Turnbull, Dr B Hamilton, M G Hart, Evelyn and Derek Walter, P H Roberts, Luke Worthington, Mrs H Murphy, Mr and Mrs J McCurdy, Tom Evans, John and Lynn Busenbark, Jerry and Alison Oakes, Dr and Mrs A H Young, GSB, MRSM, Andrew Shore, Paul and Lynn Benny, David Shillitoe, Jane and Adrian Tierney-Jones, Revd A Nunnerley, Mr and Mrs M J Matthews)*

Free house ~ Licensees Rodney and Dora Phelps ~ Real ale ~ Meals and snacks (till 10pm Fri/Sat) ~ Cottagey restaurant ~ (01749) 880450 ~ Children in restaurant ~ Open 11.30-2.30, 6.30-11; 12-3, 7-10.30 Sun; closed Sun evening Oct-March

DOWLISH WAKE ST3713 Map 1
New Inn 🍴

Village signposted from Kingstone – which is signposted from old A303 on E side of Ilminster, and from A3037 just S of Ilminster; keep on past church – pub at far end of village

Readers continue to enjoy this neatly kept village pub, mainly popular for its good food. The bar has dark beams liberally strung with hop bines, old-fashioned furnishings that include a mixture of chairs, high-backed settles, and attractive sturdy tables, and a woodburning stove in the stone inglenook fireplace. Competitively priced, bar food includes soup (£1.75), sandwiches (from £1.75), filled baked potatoes (from £3), soft roes on toast, ploughman's or spicy sausage in a big yorkshire pudding with gravy, onions and peas (£3.25), omelettes (from £3.25), ham and two eggs (£3.75), chicken tikka masala, nut and lentil roast or liver and bacon (£4.75), steaks (from £7.75), and children's menu. Well kept Butcombe Bitter and two guests such as Theakstons Old Peculier and Wadworths 6X on handpump, a decent choice of whiskies, and Perry's cider. This comes from just down the road, and the thatched 16th-c stone cider mill is well worth a visit for its collection of wooden bygones and its liberal free tastings (you can buy the half-dozen different ciders in old-fashioned earthenware flagons as well as more modern containers; it's closed on Sunday afternoons). In a separate area they have darts, shove-ha'penny, dominoes, cribbage, bar billiards, table skittles as well as alley skittles and a fruit machine; maybe piped music. The family room is no smoking. In front of the stone pub there's a rustic bench, tubs of flowers and a sprawl of clematis; the pleasant back garden has flowerbeds and a children's climbing frame. *(Recommended by Howard Clutterbuck, Ian and Villy White, Theo, Anne and Jane Gaskin, John Franklin, Ted George, Douglas Allen, Mr and Mrs Leslie Edie, Jo and Gary Charlton, Galen Strawson, Derek and Iris Martin, A Preston, Andy Petersen, Revd A Nunnerley, James Nunns)*

Free house ~ Licensees Therese Boosey and David Smith ~ Real ale ~ Meals and snacks (not winter Sun evening) ~ (01460) 52413 ~ Children in family room ~ Open 11-3, 6-11; 12-3, 7-10.30 Sun

DUNSTER SS9943 Map 1
Luttrell Arms 🛏

A396

A new licensee has taken over this 15th-c Gothic hall and has redecorated the bar and restaurants and added some new furniture. The comfortable back bar is the place to head for, with high beams hung with bottles, clogs and horseshoes, a stag's head and rifles on the walls above old settles and more modern furniture, and winter log fires (though one tends to smoke in the wrong weather conditions). Ancient black timber uprights glazed with fine hand-floated glass, full of ripples and irregularities, separate the room from a small galleried and flagstoned courtyard. At lunchtime, bar food includes home-made soup (£2.25), sandwiches (from £3.30; filled french bread from £3.65), filled baked potatoes (from £3.30), smoked ham with two eggs (£4.55), vegetable curry (£5.25), beef stew in ale with dumplings (£5.30), and cod in beer batter (£5.65), with evening dishes like a roast of the day (£6.35) and steaks (from £8.50); both restaurants are no smoking. Well kept Bass and Exmoor Gold on handpump, farm cider, and jugs of pimms and sangria. In the gardens there are cannon emplacements dug out by Blake in the Civil War when – with Praise God Barebones and his pikemen – he was beseiging the castle for six months. The town, on the edge of Exmoor National Park, is pretty and full of interest. *(Recommended by Steve Goodchild, Evelyn and Derek Walter, Peter and Liz Wilkins, Kevin and Katharine Cripps, Chris Ball, J and P Maloney, Geoff and Linda Dibble, David and Ruth Hollands, David Carr, Richard Gibbs)*

Free house ~ Licensee David Dolling ~ Real ale ~ Meals and snacks ~ Restaurant ~ (01643) 821555 ~ Children in restaurant only ~ Open 11-11; 12-10.30 Sun ~ Bedrooms: £84.50B/£114B

EAST LYNG ST3328 Map 1
Rose & Crown
A361 about 4 miles W of Othery

Although the name of the licensee is different, Mr Mason has actually just bought out his partner of ten years and is now the sole owner; the staff and the entire business remain quite unchanged. It's an enjoyable, traditional pub and the open-plan beamed lounge bar has a winter log fire (or a big embroidered fire screen) in a stone fireplace, a corner cabinet of glass, china and silver, a court cabinet, a bow window seat by an oak drop-leaf table, copies of *Country Life*, and impressive large dried flower arrangements. Generous helpings of good bar food include sandwiches (from £1.70), soup (£2), ploughman's (from £3.35), home-cooked ham and egg (£3.75), omelettes (from £4.40), cashew and mixed nut paella or spicy chick pea and vegetable hotpot (£5.25), trout (£6), steaks (from £9.50), lovely roast duckling with orange sauce (£11.25), and puddings like home-made treacle tart or sherry trifle (£2.65); pleasant waitress service. Well kept Butcombe Bitter and Wilmots Premium Ale, and Eldridge Pope Royal Oak on handpump; skittle alley and piped music. The back garden (largely hedged off from the car park) is prettily planted and there are picnic tables. *(Recommended by Richard Dolphin, B J Harding, Meg and Colin Hamilton, Dave and Doreen Irving)*

Free house ~ Licensee Derek Mason ~ Real ale ~ Meals and snacks (till 10pm) ~ Restaurant ~ (01823) 698235 ~ Children in restaurant ~ Open 11-2.30, 6.30-11; 12-3, 7-10.30 Sun ~ Bedrooms: £26B/£42B

EAST WOODLANDS ST7944 Map 2
Horse & Groom 🍽 ♀ ◧
Signed off Frome bypass off A361/B3092 junction

Run by charming licensees, this little civilised pub has picnic tables in the nice front garden by five severely pollarded limes and attractive troughs and mini wheelbarrows filled with flowers; more seats behind the big no-smoking dining conservatory. The comfortable little lounge has a relaxed atmosphere (no games or piped music), an easy chair and settee around a coffee table, two small solid dining tables with chairs, and a big stone hearth with a small raised grate. The pleasant bar on the left with its stripped pine pews and settles on dark flagstones has Batemans XB, Butcombe Bitter, Greene King IPA, and Wadworths 6X tapped from the cask; good wines by the glass. Very well presented food (they tell us prices have not changed since last year) includes filled home-made french bread (from £1.60), ploughman's (from £2.95), lovely liver, bacon and onion (£4.95), asparagus and pesto pasta (£4.80), home-cooked ham with parsley sauce (£4.90), smoked haddock topped with mozzarella (£6), and delicious cod with mussels and prawns (£6); five or six interesting vegetables are served separately on a side plate, and super puddings; helpful service. Shove-ha'penny, cribbage and dominoes. The village is very quiet. *(Recommended by Mrs C Jimenenz, John and Lynn Busenbark, M Hart)*

Free house ~ Licensee Timothy Gould ~ Real ale ~ Meals and snacks (not Sun evening, not Mon) ~ Restaurant (not Sun evening, not Mon) ~ (01373) 462802 ~ Children in small lounge bar ~ Open 11.30-2.30(3 Sat), 6.30-11; 12-3, 7-10.30 Sun

EXEBRIDGE SS9224 Map 1
Anchor 🛏️
B3222 S of Dulverton

Ideal as a base for Exmoor, this popular place has a sheltered garden overlooking the River Exe with plenty of well spaced tables, and a play area for children. It's delightfully set beside the handsome three-arched bridge, and the licensees have fishing rights (brown trout and salmon) and can organise lots of other local sports; many surrounding walks. Inside, the main front bar has individually chosen tables and seats such as a big winged settle and a nice old library chair among more orthodox furnishings, some carpet on its floor tiles, Cecil Aldin hunting prints and Exmoor pictures above the stripped wooden dado, some hunting trophies, and a warm woodburning stove; piped music. Bar food includes good sandwiches (from £1.65; open baps from £2.50, bacon, sausage and fried egg £3.50), home-made soup (£1.95), filled baked potatoes (from £3.50), ploughman's (from £3.95), four-egg omelette (from £3.95), lasagne (£5.95), broccoli and cream cheese bake (£6.50), chicken breast filled with avocado and wrapped with bacon in a stilton sauce (£9.95), Scotch rump steak (£9.50), and children's dishes (£2.35). There's a back games bar with darts, pool, shove-ha'penny, cribbage, dominoes, and trivia divided by a flexiwall from a no-smoking lounge bar with button-back leather chesterfields, modern oak tables and chairs, and french windows to the garden. Well kept Courage Directors, Morlands Old Speckled Hen, Ushers Best, and Wadworths 6X on handpump; alley skittles. The inn is mentioned in R D Blackmore's *Lorna Doone*. *(Recommended by Janet Pickles, Tom Evans, K Flack, Mike Gorton, Ben and Sheila Walker, John and Christine Vittoe, Tina and David Woods-Taylor, Cheryl and Keith Roe, H F C Barclay)*

Free house ~ Licensees John and Judy Phripp ~ Real ale ~ Meals and snacks (till 10pm) ~ Restaurant ~ (01398) 323433 ~ Children welcome ~ Open 11-3, 6-11; 12-11 Sat and Sun; 12-3, 7-11 winter Sat and Sun ~ Bedrooms: £37B/£70B

FAULKLAND ST7354 Map 2
Tuckers Grave £
A366 E of village

For some people, this marvellously atmospheric and warmly friendly, basic cider house is one of their all-time favourite pubs. It has for many years, claimed the title of the smallest pub in the *Guide*, with a flagstoned entry that opens into a teeny unspoilt room with casks of well kept Bass and Butcombe Bitter on tap and Cheddar Valley cider in an alcove on the left. Two old cream-painted high-backed settles face each other across a single table on the right, and a side room has dominoes and shove-ha'penny. There's a skittle alley and tables and chairs on the back lawn, as well as winter fires and maybe newspapers to read. Food is limited to sandwiches and ploughman's at lunchtime. *(Recommended by Pete Baker, Roger Huggins, Tom McLean, Dave Irving, Ewan McCall, John Poulter, Gordon)*

Free house ~ Licensees Ivan and Glenda Swift ~ Real ale ~ Lunchtime snacks (not Sun) ~ (01373) 834230 ~ Children welcome ~ Open 11-3, 6-11; 12-3, 7-10.30 Sun

---

> If we know a pub does sandwiches we always say so – if they're not mentioned, you'll have to assume you can't get one.

FITZHEAD ST1128 Map 1
Fitzhead Inn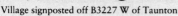
Village signposted off B3227 W of Taunton
Somerset Dining Pub of the Year

Run by friendly and enthusiastic licensees, this bustling village pub is very popular –
though they take care to avoid packing too many people in: once the variously sized
polished tables in the main bar are full, they'd rather turn people away than face
overcrowding. Very well presented, the food varies day by day, and is consistently
good – not a large choice, but an imaginative one, which might at lunchtime include
sandwiches (from £1.30), ploughman's (from £4.25), liver and onions (£4.95), and
spinach pasta with salmon or pigeon breasts with a redcurrant and cherry sauce
(£6.50); in the evening, dishes are more elaborate, such as fried chicken livers or
chargrilled squid (£3.25), seafood gratin (£3.50), fillet steak with stilton and bacon
(£11.95), lobster and crab thermidor (£12.95), and scallops wrapped in bacon
(£13.50). Well kept Cotleigh Tawny and guests like Black Sheep Special, Dartmoor
Best, Exmoor Ale, and Moles Best Bitter on handpump. There's a particularly good
choice of 200 wines, and the knowledgeable landlord will happily open many of them
for just a glass; fine choice of malt whiskies, too. A pleasant relaxed atmosphere,
genial attentive service, unobjectionable piped music, and tables out in the garden.
*(Recommended by Adrian and Jane Tierney-Jones, Sarah Comins, Graham Stanton, Geoff and
Linda Dibble, Paul and Wendy Bachelor, John Barker, John and Pat Smyth, Ken and Janet
Bracey; more reports please)*

*Free house ~ Licensee Patrick Groves ~ Real ale ~ Meals and snacks (till 10pm) ~
(01823) 400667 ~ Children welcome ~ Open 12-3, 7-11(10.30 Sun)*

HINTON ST GEORGE ST4212 Map 1
Lord Poulett ♀
Village signposted off A30 W of Crewkerne; and off Merriott road (declassified – former
A356, off B3165) N of Crewkerne; take care – there is another pub of the same name a mile
or so away, at a roundabout on the former A30

A new licensee has taken over this pleasant dining pub, set in a quiet, largely
retirement village. The rooms have been redecorated and the bar has been opened up
into the larger dining room. It has big black beams, stripped masonry, cushioned
captain's chairs, lots of old settles, and nice old tables, and a log fire in the imposing
stone fireplace; two cosy smaller rooms opening off – one with a big disused inglenook
fireplace. Bar food now includes home-made soup (£2), sandwiches (from £2),
ploughman's (£3.95), home-made steak and kidney pie (£5.95), vegetable pie (£6.25),
cod gratin or chicken casserole (£6.95), steaks (from £9.75), and puddings (from
£2.25). Well kept Butcombe Bitter and Wadworths 6X tapped from the cask, and a
compact wine list; cribbage, dominoes, and piped music, and a skittle alley with darts.
The prettily planted back garden has some seats. *(Recommended by S Godsell, Theo, Anne
and Jane Gaskin, Derek and Iris Martin, Galen Strawson; more reports on the new regime, please)*

*Free house ~ Licensee Basil Lazenby ~ Real ale ~ Meals and snacks ~ (01460) 73149 ~
Children in family room ~ Open 11.30-2.30, 6.30-11*

HUISH EPISCOPI ST4326 Map 1
Rose & Crown
A372 E of Langport

The friendly landlady tells us that she can remember their cider selling at 3d a pint, ale
for 4d a pint, and clay bubble pipes for a halfpenny – her family have run this
marvellously unspoilt old cider house for well over 130 years. It is known locally as
'Eli's' after Mrs Pittard's father who held the licence for 55 years (having taken over
from his father-in-law – who also ran the place for 55 years). The atmosphere and
character are determinedly unpretentious and welcoming, and there's no bar as such –
to get a drink, you just walk into the central flagstoned still room and choose from the

casks of well kept Bass, Boddingtons, and two local guests, or the wide choice of Somerset farm ciders (and local cider brandy) and country wines which stand on ranks of shelves all around (prices are very low); this servery is the only thoroughfare between the casual little front parlours with their unusual pointed-arch windows and genuinely friendly locals. Food is home-made, simple and cheap: generously filled sandwiches (from £1.60), a good choice of soups (£2), good filled baked potatoes (from £2.30), ploughman's (from £3), steak in ale pie, stilton, celery and walnut pie or spinach and mushroom lasagne (all £4.50), and pork, apple and cider casserole or lamb hotpot (£4.75); good helpful service. Shove-ha'penny, dominoes and cribbage, and a much more orthodox big back extension family room has darts, pool, fruit machine, trivia, and juke box; skittle alley and popular quiz nights. There are tables in a garden outside, and a second enclosed garden with a children's play area. George the dog will welcome a bitch but can't abide other dogs, though Bonny the welsh collie is not so fussy. A beer and music festival is held in the adjoining field every September, and on some summer weekends you might find the pub's cricket team playing out here (who always welcome a challenge); good nearby walks. *(Recommended by Jack and Gemima Valiant, Pete Baker, Hilarie Dobbie, Stephen Brown, Dave Irving, Roger Huggins, Tom McLean, Ewan McCall, Guy Thornington)*

Free house ~ Licensee Eileen Pittard ~ Real ale ~ Snacks (mainly 12-2.30, 5.30-8 but maybe all day on summer weekends) ~ (01458) 250494 ~ Children welcome ~ Open 11.30-2.30, 5.30-11; all day Fri/Sat; 12-10.30 Sun

KELSTON ST7067 Map 2
Old Crown ◗
Bitton Road; A431 W of Bath

This traditional old place is just how a village pub should be – plenty of atmosphere, a friendly welcome, enjoyable food, and good beer. The four small rooms are genuinely preserved and have beams strung with hops, interesting carved settles and cask tables on polished flagstones (attractively candlelit in the evenings), logs burning in an ancient open range (there's another smaller, open range and a Victorian open fireplace – both with coal-effect gas fires), and lovely tableau photographs. Well kept Bass, Butcombe Bitter, Smiles Best, and Wadworths 6X on handpump, and several malt whiskies; shove-ha'penny and dominoes. Enjoyable lunchtime bar food (with prices unchanged since last year) includes home-made soup (£1.85), ploughman's (from £3.65), cottage pie (£4.70), ham and leek pie (£4.90), a daily vegetarian dish, beef and Guinness casserole (£5.90), steaks (from £8.95) and puddings like fruit crumble or sticky toffee pudding (£2.80); helpful service. Picnic tables under apple trees in the neat, sheltered back garden look out towards distant hills; you'd hardly believe you were just four miles from Bath's city centre. The car park is over quite a fast road. No children. *(Recommended by Simon and Amanda Southwell, Pat and John Millward, Peter Neate, Don Kellaway, Angie Coles, Barry and Anne)*

Free house ~ Licensee Michael Steele ~ Real ale ~ Lunchtime meals and snacks (not Sun) ~ Restaurant (not Sun) ~ (01225) 423032 ~ Open 11.30-2.30(3 Sat), 5-11; 12-3, 7-10.30 Sun; closed evening 25 Dec, all day 26 Dec

KINGSDON ST5126 Map 2
Kingsdon Inn
At Podimore roundabout junction of A303, A372 and A37 take A372, then turn right onto B3151, and right again opposite village post office

An inviting atmosphere, a friendly, chatty licensee, and really good food are what readers enjoy about this pretty little thatched cottage. On the right are some very nice old stripped pine tables with attractive cushioned farmhouse chairs, more seats in what was a small inglenook fireplace, a few low sagging beams, and an open woodburning stove with colourful dried and artificial fruits and flowers on the over-mantel; down three steps through balustrading to a light, airy room with peach-coloured cushions on stripped pine built-in wall seats, curtains matching the scatter cushions, more stripped pine tables, and a big leaf and flower arrangement in the stone fireplace (open fire in winter). Another similarly decorated room has more tables and another fireplace. From a sensibly short menu and served by efficient, helpful staff, lunchtime bar food includes cream of asparagus soup (£1.90), ploughman's (£3.60), soused herring fillets with dill sauce (£3.90), tomato, onion and basil quiche (£4.20), grilled gammon with a grain mustard sauce, lamb liver, bacon and onions or baked haddock and prawn mornay (all £4.90), and tasty braised oxtail in Guinness (£5.20), with evening dishes like mushrooms topped with garlic, cheese and crispy bacon (£3.60), king prawns with lime and ginger sauce (£4.60), delicious wild rabbit in a dijon mustard sauce (£8.90), cod, sole and salmon with a shrimp sauce or tenderloin of pork with apricots and almonds (£9.80), guinea fowl breast with calvados, cream and apple (£10.20), and nice steaks (from £10.20); puddings like chocolate and brandy roulade, rhubarb and date crumble or raspberry and apple tart (£2.40). Well kept Butcombe Bitter, Fullers London Pride, Morlands Old Speckled Hen, Oakhill Best, and Smiles Best on handpump, and local cider; table skittles, darts, shove-ha'penny, cribbage, and quiet piped music, and they have rugby, cricket and golf teams. Picnic sets and umbrellas on the grass. As we went to press, we heard that the pub was up for sale. *(Recommended by Janet Pickles, Stephen Brown, Steve and Maggie Willey, Ian Jones, Galen Strawson, Steve Goodchild, Mrs J Silversides, Barry Brown, Mark and Heather Williamson, Gethin Lewis, Evelyn and Derek Walter, Sandria Parker, Mary Woods, John and Elspeth Howell, R T Walters, Max Johnson, Mr and Mrs S A Lea, MRSM)*

Free house ~ Licensee Duncan Gordon ~ Real ale ~ Meals and snacks (not Sun evening) ~ (01935) 840543 ~ Children in eating area of bar; must be over 6 in evenings ~ Open 11-3, 6-11; 12-3, 7-10.30 Sun

KNAPP ST3025 Map 1
Rising Sun ♀

Lower Knapp – OS Sheet 182 map reference 304257; off A38/A358/A378 E of Taunton

Fresh from Brixham and St Mawes, the fish and seafood used in the dozen or so different fish dishes here continue to please readers: starters like moules marinières (£3.25 or £4.90), smoked herring mousse (£4.50), good smoked eel (£5), and crab and prawn gratin (£4.75), and enjoyable main courses such as grilled lemon sole with a wine and herb sauce or scallops and mushrooms with a vermouth, dijon mustard and cream sauce (£11), brill topped with a salmon mousse and cucumber with a white wine sauce (£11.50), crevettes with cajun spices, cream and brandy (£11.75), and john dory with sun-dried tomatoes, anchovies and capers (£13). There is also soup (£2.60), lunchtime ploughman's (from £3.50), lunchtime open sandwiches (from £3.60), and lunchtime ham and egg (£4.50), nut roast with provençale sauce (£6.50), and steaks (from £11.50). On Sunday lunchtimes, there are nibbles on the bar. The big single room has two inglenook fireplaces (one with an old bread oven and range), well moulded beams, woodwork, and some stonework in its massive rather tilting walls, and a relaxed atmosphere. Well kept Bass, Boddingtons and Exmoor Ale on handpump, farm ciders, and a decent wine list. The staff (and dogs – Pepi the poodle and Pompey, who weighs in at nine stone) are very welcoming. The terrace outside this lovely 15th-c Somerset longhouse is a suntrap in summer. *(Recommended by Theo, Anne and Jane Gaskin, Davie Warrellow, Mike Pugh, Simon Pyle, Mr and Mrs D Wilson, Keith Waters, Mr and Mrs C Roberts, D I Smith, Gethin Lewis, Tom Evans, E H and R F Warner)*

Free house ~ Licensee Tony Atkinson ~ Real ale ~ Meals and snacks ~ Restaurant ~ (01823) 490436 ~ Children welcome ~ Open 11.30-2.30, 6.30-11; 12-3, 7-10.30 Sun ~ Bedrooms: £25/£36

LANGLEY MARSH ST0729 Map 1
Three Horseshoes ★ ◗

Village signposted off B3227 from Wiveliscombe

The hard-working, friendly licensees continue to make improvements to this nice little country pub. The no-smoking dining area now has antique settles and tables and benches, and the games room can now accommodate more family customers. The back bar has low modern settles and polished wooden tables, dark red wallpaper, planes hanging from the ceiling, banknotes papering the wall behind the bar counter, a piano, and a local stone fireplace. Well kept Bass, Otter Best, Palmers IPA, Ringwood Best, Wadworths 6X, and Youngs Bitter tapped from the cask, and Perry's farm cider; polite staff. Genuinely home-made food (with prices unchanged since last year) includes filled rolls, soup (£1.50), pizzas (£3 or £3.95; can take away as well), butterbean bourguignon (£3.95), courgette and mushroom bake (£4.50), lamb in pernod or good steak and kidney pie (£4.95), pigeon breasts in cider and cream (£5.10), enjoyable fish pie (£5.25), popular steaks (from £7.95), daily fresh fish dishes like mussels in wine and cream, john dory or lemon sole (£7.95), and skate wings or smoked trout fillet (£8.95), and lovely puddings such as apple-filled pancake or lemon mousse (£2.10); no chips or fried food and some vegetables come from the garden. The lively front room has sensibly placed darts, shove-ha'penny, table skittles, dominoes, and cribbage; separate skittle alley, and piped music. It is small, so they can get crowded. The pub's elderly alsatian is called Guinness and the other is called Ruddles. You can sit on rustic seats on the verandah or in the sloping back garden, with a fully equipped children's play area and a view of farmland. In fine weather there are usually vintage cars outside. *(Recommended by Patrick Freeman, Adrian and Jane Tierney-Jones, Wayne Wheeler, V Kavanagh, Anthony Barnes, Mr and Mrs J Brown, J and P Maloney, Tina and David Woods-Taylor)*

Free house ~ Licensee John Hopkins ~ Real ale ~ Meals and snacks ~ (01984) 623763 ~ Well behaved children allowed away from bar ~ Folk and music quiz alternate Sun evenings, and Morris dancing sessions ~ Open 12-2.30(3 Sat/Sun), 7-11(10.30 Sun)

LITTON ST5954 Map 2
Kings Arms
B3144; off A39 Bath—Wells

Reached down a flight of steps from the car park, this partly 15th-c pub has tiered, neatly kept gardens with picnic tables, excellent heavy wooden play equipment including a commando climbing net, and slides and baby swings; the River Chew runs through the bottom of the garden. From a big entrance hall with polished flagstones, the bars lead off to the left with low heavy beams and more flagstones; a nice bit on the right beyond the huge fireplace has a big old-fashioned settle and a mix of other settles and wheelback chairs; a full suit of armour stands in one alcove and the rooms are divided up into areas by standing timbers. Good bar food includes sandwiches (from £2.60), garlic mushrooms (£3.25), lots of platters and salads (from £3.75; marinated pork ribs with sour cream and barbecue sauces £7.25), daily vegetarian and pasta dishes, battered cod (£4.75), good lamb cutlets (£6.95), chicken and broccoli bake (£7.25), chicken tikka (£7.50), king prawns in garlic butter (£9.95), and steaks; children's colouring sheet menu with crayons. Well kept Bass, Courage Best, and Wadworths 6X on handpump. *(Recommended by Derek Patey, Philip and Jude Simmons, John Abbott, Andrew Shore, Meg and Colin Hamilton, Roger and Lin Lawrence)*

Free house ~ Licensee Neil Sinclair ~ Real ale ~ Meals and snacks (12-2.30, 6.30-10; not 25 Dec) ~ (01761) 241301 ~ Children in two separate rooms ~ Open 11-2.30, 6-11; 12-3, 6-10.30 Sun; closed evenings 26 Dec and 1 Jan

LONG SUTTON ST4625 Map 1
Devonshire Arms 🍽
B3165 Somerton—Martock, just off A372 E of Langport

Looking down the village green, this solid stone inn looks quite imposing, with its mullioned windows and tall gables. Inside, the cosily old-fashioned front bar is separated from the rather smart restaurant area on the left by not much more than a sideboard – which makes for a very friendly and relaxed atmosphere. The built-in green plush corner seat is the prime spot, and there's a charming decor – deep green ceiling, lighter green walls, good sporting and country prints, fresh flowers and plants. There's also a flagstoned back bar, with horse tack, shelves of china, seats with lots of scatter cushions, and darts. Bar food changes daily, but might include hot crab terrine with a crab bisque, salmon mousse (£4.25), honey-baked ham with egg (£4.25), avocado bake with three cheeses or pasta bake (£4.50), garlic chilli prawns (£5.25), steak and mushroom pie (£5.50), salmon salad with pink peppercorn and dill mayonnaise (£5.75), moules marinières or chicken breast with tarragon (£5.95) and scallops and bacon with dill and cream sauce (£6.45); they also do soup and sandwiches (from £3.50), tagliatelle with fresh tomato sauce (£3.95), coconut prawns (£5.25), and steaks (from £8.50). Well kept Flowers IPA and Wadworths 6X on handpump, decent wines, a good collection of malt whiskies, excellent coffee; friendly effective service. *(Recommended by Mr and Mrs S A Lea, Stephen and Julie Brown, Roger Wain-Heapy, Mrs D Bromley-Martin, Mrs J Watts)*

Free house ~ Licensees David and Pam Naish ~ Real ale ~ Meals and snacks ~ Restaurant ~ (01458) 241271 ~ Children in eating area of bar ~ Open 12-2.30, 6-11 ~ Bedrooms: £40.45B/£50.85B

LUXBOROUGH SS9837 Map 1
Royal Oak ★ ⇌ ◗

Kingsbridge; S of Dunster on minor rds into Brendon Hills – OS Sheet 181 map reference 983378

Kevan Draper, helped by his mother Rose, has invested a great deal of time and care into the thoughtful refurbishment of this delightful, welcoming inn. The new bedrooms have been very well received by readers, breakfasts are first class, and if you are staying, their Land-Rover wildlife safaris are much enjoyed. They have bought the cottage next door and opened up a new dining room, and reopened the Post Office and shop. There's an easy-going, friendly atmosphere in the three attractive bar rooms, with flagstones in the front public bar, beams and inglenooks, a real medley of furniture, and good log fires. Well kept real ales such as Butcombe Bitter, Cotleigh Tawny, Exmoor Gold, Flowers IPA, and guest beers on handpump or tapped from the cask, and farm cider, several malt whiskies, and a decent wine list. Good bar food includes memorable home-made soup (£2.15), sandwiches (from £2.45), filled baked potatoes (from £3.90), home-made port and stilton pâté (£4.35), various ploughman's (from £4.40), lamb curry (£5.45), spinach and nut lasagne (£6.20), good venison burgers with home-made cumberland sauce, beef in ale pie (£5.75), and evening dishes such as fresh local trout pâté (£4.65), fresh fish such as squid, scallops, brill, bass, shark or tuna (from around £9), venison casserole in a rich three berry sauce (£9), and steaks (from £10.90); puddings like banana and sticky toffee pudding or lemon cheesecake (£2.70), and children's meals (£2.90). Pool, dominoes, cribbage, and shove-ha'penny, no machines or music. Tables outside and lots of surrounding walks. *(Recommended by Adrian and Jane Tierney-Jones, Sue and Bob Ward, George and Jeanne Barnwell, Victoria Herriott, Simon Watkins, Steve Goodchild, M Fynes-Clinton, Jo and Gary Charlton, Dagmar Junghanns, Colin Keane, J D Cloud, K Flack, Chris Tasker, Brian Barnes, Anne Wine, Paul Barnett, Nigel Woolliscroft, Anthony Barnes, Sue Demont, Tim Barrow, Julian Thomas, Rosalyn Guard, Richard Gibbs, Pete and Rose Flower, John and Elspeth Howell, Jonathan Williams, Ian Williams, Linda Mar, Maureen and Jeff Dobbelaar, Paul McKeever, C A Hall, David Gittins, Geoff and Linda Dibble)*

Free house ~ Licensees Kevan and Rose Draper ~ Real ale ~ Meals and snacks (till 10pm) ~ Restaurant ~ (01984) 640319 ~ Children in eating area of bar only ~ Folk music Fri evening ~ Open 11-3, 6-11; 12-2.30, 7-11 Sun ~ Bedrooms: £22.50(£25.50B)/£35(£45B)

MELLS ST7249 Map 2
Talbot ◗ ⇌

W of Frome; off A362 W of Buckland Dinham, or A361 via Nunney and Whatley

Mr Elliott is a cheerful and resourceful licensee, and this unspoilt and friendly old coaching inn is an enjoyable place to stay. An attractive room leads off the informally planted cobbled courtyard (where there are cane chairs around tables), and has stripped pews, mate's and wheelback chairs, fresh flowers and candles in bottles on the mix of tables, and sporting and riding pictures on the walls, which are partly stripped above a broad panelled dado, and partly rough terracotta-colour. A small corridor leads to a nice little room with an open fire. Good food at lunchtime includes home-made soup (£2.25), creamy garlic mushrooms on toast (£3.75), smoked salmon and scrambld egg or seafood crêpes (£4.50), hot cheese and ratatouille flan (£6.50), lamb and apricot or steak and kidney pies (from £7.50), chicken stuffed with mushrooms (£8.50), good barbecued spare ribs (£8.75), steaks (from £8.95), daily specials such as quail, pheasant, monkfish or bass, and children's helpings; two-course Sunday roast (£6.95), and nice breakfasts. Well kept Bass, Butcombe Bitter, and a changing weekly guest beer tapped from the cask, and good wines; well chosen staff. The two-roomed public bar has an appealing room nearest the road with big stripped shutters, a high dark green ceiling, a mix of chairs and a tall box settle, candles in bottles on the stubby pine tables, and a rough wooden floor; the locals' room has sports trophies, darts, cribbage, dominoes, and simple furnishings; skittle alley. They hold an Irish music weekend during the second week of September and a Daffodil Weekend with 350 members of the English Civil War over the Easter weekend. The village was purchased by the Horner family of the 'Little Jack Horner' nursery rhyme and the direct descendants still live in the manor house next door. The inn is surrounded by lovely countryside and good walks. *(Recommended by Ellen McPherson, Paul McPherson, Susan and Nigel Wilson, John and Lynn Busenbark, BHP, Robert Huddleston, Pat and John Millward, Andy Wilson, Veronica M Brown)*

Free house ~ Lease: Roger Elliott~ Real ale ~ Meals and snacks ~ Restaurant ~ (01373) 812254 ~ Children welcome ~ Open 12-2.30(3 Sat), 6-11; 12-3, 7-10.30 Sun ~ Bedrooms: £29B/£46B

MONKSILVER ST0737 Map 1
Notley Arms ★ ⑪
B3188

Deservedly popular, this bustling pub remains well liked for its friendly atmosphere and reliably good food. The characterful beamed and L-shaped bar has small settles and kitchen chairs around the plain country wooden and candlelit tables, original paintings on the black-timbered white walls, fresh flowers, a couple of woodburning stoves, and maybe a pair of cats. Continually changing, the bar food might include home-made soup (£2.25), sandwiches (from £2.50), very good ploughman's (from £3.25), home-made tagliatelle with ham, mushrooms, cream and parmesan cheese (£3.95), honey and mustard glazed chicken with roasted vegetables (£4.95), wild mushroom strudel with a sherry and cream sauce (£5.50), smoked haddock fishcakes with piquant crème friâche sauce (£5.75), fresh salmon and asparagus bouchée (£5.95), lamb curry with spinach and tomato (£6.25), and puddings such as pear and almond tart or treacle tart (from £2.35). Well kept Exmoor Ale, Morlands Old Speckled Hen, Ushers Best, and Wadworths 6X on handpump, and country wines; dominoes and trivia, and alley skittles. Families are well looked after, with colouring books and toys in the bright no-smoking little family room. There are more toys outside in the immaculate garden, running down to a swift clear stream. *(Recommended by W H and E Thomas, Paul Barnett, IHR, Mike and Mary Carter, Maureen and Jeff Dobbelaar, Tom Evans, Graham Stanton, Tina and David Woods-Taylor, Richard Gibbs)*

Scottish Courage ~ Lease: Alistair and Sarah Cade ~ Real ale ~ Meals and snacks (see below) ~ (01984) 656217 ~ Children in eating area of bar and in own room ~ Open 11.30-2.30, 6.30-11; 12-2.30, 7-10.30 Sun; closed last week Jan, first week Feb

NORTH CURRY ST3225 Map 1
Bird in Hand ◀
Queens Square; off A378 (or A358) E of Taunton

A boules court has been developed in the back garden of this traditional village local, and there's now a play area for children. The bar has pews, settles, and old yew tables (candlelit at night) and benches on the flagstones, original beams and timbers, and inglenook fireplaces, and a proper public bar has bar billiards, and shove-ha'penny. Well presented home-made food includes pasta with mushrooms, spinach, peppers and crème friâche (£5.25), a good green thai lamb curry, beef rogan josh or chicken tikka masala (all £5.75), faggots in a rich wine gravy or poacher's pie (£5.85), pork with apple, calvados and cream (£7.25), steaks (from £7.95), and puddings (£2.75). There's a separate restaurant area with a conservatory. Every other Sunday, they offer jazz with the three-course Sunday lunch (£6.50). Well kept Badger Tanglefoot, Branscombe Vale Branoc, Hambleton Stallion, Otter Ale, and Teignworthy Reel Ale on handpump or tapped from the cask, a short but wide-ranging choice of wines, Rich's farm cider, and good waitress service; skittle alley and piped music. They hold a jazz festival in October and a beer festival over the May (Whit) bank holiday. *(Recommended by Janet Pickles, John Barker, Adrian and Jane Tierney-Jones, Stephen Brown, Mary Doxford)*

Free house ~ Licensee Jeremy Hook ~ Real ale ~ Meals and snacks (not Sun or Mon evenings in winter) ~ Restaurant ~ (01823) 490248 ~ Children welcome ~ Live music alternate Fri evenings ~ Open 12-3(4 Sat), 7-11(10.30 Sun); closed Monday lunchtime Nov-April

NORTON ST PHILIP ST7755 Map 2
George ★
A366

For nearly 600 years, this exceptional building has been a pub. There's an external Norman stone stair-turret, a fine half-timbered and galleried back courtyard, massive stone walls and high mullioned windows. Furnishings are simple: square-panelled wooden settles, plain old tables, wide bare floorboards, and lofty beams hung with hops. A long, stout bar serves well kept Bass, and Wadworths IPA, 6X and seasonal beers on handpump; warmly welcoming licensee and staff. A panelled lounge is furnished with antique settles and tables; it's all perhaps even more atmospheric in winter when the fires are lit. Good, popular bar food places most emphasis on daily specials such as tasty turkey parcel, sausage platter (£8.95), game casserole or huge whole plaice (£9.95), venison with a redcurrant glaze (£10.50), and tiger prawn curry (£10.95); nice puddings like white and dark chocolate terrine, and Sunday roast. Darts, pool and dominoes. The Duke of Monmouth stayed here before the Battle of Sedgemoor, and after their defeat his men were imprisoned in what's now the Dungeon cellar bar. When a sympathetic customer held the courtyard gate open for them as they were led out to their execution, he was bundled along with them and executed too. A stroll over the meadow behind the pub leads to an attractive churchyard around the medieval church whose bells struck Pepys (here on 12 June 1668) as 'mighty tuneable'. *(Recommended by Jack and Gemima Valiant, Dave Irving, Ewan McCall, Roger Huggins, Tom McLean, Philip and Jude Simmons, Nigel Wilson, M Rutherford, Susan and Nigel Wilson, Simon and Amanda Southwell, Gordon, Andrew Shore, John and Lynn Busenbark, Mark and Heather Williamson, Tim and Ann Newell, James Nunns, Helen Pickering, James Owen, Mr and Mrs C Moncrieffe, Mrs Cynthia Archer)*

Wadworths ~ Tenants Andrew and Juliette Grubb ~ Real ale ~ Meals and snacks (not evenings 25-26 Dec) ~ Lunchtime restaurant ~ (01373) 834224 ~ Children welcome ~ Open 11-3, 5.30(5 Sat)-11; 12-3, 7-11 Sun

PITNEY ST4428 Map 1
Halfway House ◖
Just off B3153 W of Somerton

Between six and ten well kept real ales are tapped from the cask in this friendly old-fashioned pub, with regulars such as Butcombe Bitter, Cotleigh Tawny, Hop Back Summer Lightning, and Teignworthy Reel Ale, and changing guests from small local breweries. They also keep Czech Pilsners and other European beers, with a good interesting bottled range, as well as local farm cider and quite a few malt whiskies. It's a friendly and cosy place, with plenty of space in the three rooms (all have good log fires), and the homely feel is underlined by a profusion of books, maps and newspapers; cribbage, dominoes, trivia and chess. Good simple food includes sandwiches (from £1.75), filled baked potatoes (from £1.95), soup (£2.25), and a fine ploughman's with home-made pickle (from £3.50). In the evening they do about half a dozen home-made curries to complement their real ales (from £4.95). There are tables outside. *(Recommended by Adrian and Jane Tierney-Jones, Ian and Nita Cooper, R Brie, Stephen Brown, Chris Dower, Keith Darke, Andy Jones, Robert Colledge, John Carter)*

Free house ~ Licensees Julian and Judy Litchfield ~ Real ale ~ Meals and snacks (not Sun) ~ (01458) 252513 ~ Well behaved children welcome ~ Open 11.30-2.30(3 Sat), 5.30-11; 12-3, 7-10.30 Sun

RUDGE ST8251 Map 2
Full Moon 🍴 🛏 🍺
Off A36 Bath—Warminster

This is a charming pub with a lot of character in the differently shaped rooms, and a gently upmarket but friendly atmosphere. The two rooms on the right have low white ceilings with a few black beams, a built-in settle by the bar, wheelbacks and slatback chairs around mainly cast-iron-framed tables, a woodburning stove in a big stone fireplace with riding boots on the mantelbeam, and big shutters by the red velvet-cushioned window seats. Other rooms are similarly furnished except the smallish flagstoned dining room with stripped pine tables and high traditional settles; there's also a small plush restaurant and a big back carpeted extension alongside the skittle alley; shove-ha'penny. Generous helpings of good bar food include soup (£2.25), filled french bread (£3.50), garlic and mushroom tart topped with cheese (£3.95), ploughman's (from £4.25), scallops with bacon, cream and white wine, fresh fish in their own beer batter with chips or mushroom and vegetable stroganoff (all £4.95), curry (£5.25), seafood medley, ham and eggs or chicken with pineapple in a light korma sauce (all £5.50), popular mixed grill (£9.50), and home-made puddings (£2.95); they do a weekday lunchtime two-course meal for two people (£7.50), and Sunday lunchtime roast carvery (£5.95; two sittings). Well kept Bass, Butcombe Bitter, Fullers London Pride, and Wadworths 6X on handpump, local ciders, and several malt whiskies. The village green opposite the pub was nearing completion as we went to press, and there are wonderful views across the valley to Salisbury Plain and Westbury White Horse. *(Recommended by John and Lynn Busenbark, M G Hart, Pat and John Millward, Howard James)*

Free house ~ Licensees Patrick and Christine Gifford ~ Real ale ~ Meals and snacks ~ Restaurant (not Sun evening) ~ (01373) 830936 ~ Children welcome ~ Open 12-11; 12-3, 7-11 in winter ~ Bedrooms: £35B/£50B

SOUTH STOKE ST7461 Map 2
Pack Horse £ ·
Village signposted opposite the Cross Keys off B3110, leaving Bath southwards – just before end of speed limit

A popular place after a Sunday walk (and the two-course lunch is very good value at £3.25), this friendly and unpretentious country local is enjoyed by families and young and older people alike. The entrance alleyway that runs through the middle is still a public right of way to the church, and used to be the route along which the dead were carried to the cemetery. It stops along the way at a central space by the serving bar with its well kept Courage Best, and Ushers Best and Founders on handpump. The ancient main room has a good local atmosphere, a log fire in the handsome stone inglenook, antique oak settles (two well carved), leatherette dining chairs and cushioned captain's chairs on the quarry-tiled floor, some Royalty pictures, a chiming wall-clock, a heavy black beam-and-plank ceiling, and rough black shutters for the stone-mullioned windows (put up in World War I); the cupboard in the fireplace used to be where they kept drunks until they sobered up. There's another room down to the left (with less atmosphere). Cheap bar food includes filled rolls (from 90p), good pasties or sausage plait (£1.40), daily specials (from £2), a Wednesday special of roast lunch and pudding (£2.85), ploughman's (£2.90), and two course Sunday lunch (£3.25); friendly staff. Rather fine shove-ha'penny slates are set into two of the tables, and there's dominoes, a fruit machine, piped music, and Sky TV. The spacious back garden, with swings, looks out over the stolid old church and the wooded valley.

(Recommended by Luke Worthington, Tom McLean, Ewan McCall, Mrs H Murphy, Virginia Jones)

Ushers ~ Lease: Colin Williams ~ Real ale ~ Snacks ~ Restaurant ~ (01225) 832060 ~ Children in eating area of bar ~ Open 11-4, 6-11; 11-11 Sat; 12-10.30 Sun

SPARKFORD ST6026 Map 2
Sparkford Inn
High Street; just off A303 bypass W of Wincanton

An excellent layout and decor here: a rambling series of softly lit rather low-beamed rooms, with a nice mix of old tables in varying sizes, good dining chairs, a colour scheme leaning towards plummy browns and dusky pinks, and plenty of worthwhile prints and other things to look at – including an intricate old-fashioned scrapbook screen. Decent good value food comes from a separate servery, and at lunchtime includes sandwiches (from £1.85; roast meat of the day £2.85), ploughman's (£3.95), a roast of the day (£5.75), and daily specials such as home-made cream of mushroom soup (£2), poached fresh salmon with white wine and pink peppercorn sauce (£6.75), baked duck's breast with drambuie sauce (£7), steaks (from £7.95), and home-made puddings; evening extras such as smoked salmon (£4.25), home-cooked ham and egg (£4.65), cauliflower and broccoli in stilton sauce (£4.95), beef in ale (£5.15), lemon chicken (£5.75), and leg of lamb steak (£7.25). Well kept Bass and Worthington Best with four guests such as Butcombe Bitter, Fullers London Pride, Morlands Old Speckled Hen, and Wadworths Old Timer or Farmers Glory on handpump; country wines and local cider; pleasant service. Basil the parrot may put in an appearance. There's a proper public bar with darts, well lit pool table, darts, shove-ha'penny, table skittles, dominoes, old-fashioned juke box, piano and TV; indoor playroom; line dancing alternate Thursdays. Tables outside, with a good play area; pretty tubs of flowers and so forth. We have not yet heard from readers who have stayed in the bedrooms here. *(Recommended by Iain Robertson, Stephen, Julie and Hayley Brown, John Barker, Mrs Rushton)*

Free house ~ Licensees Nigel and Sue Tucker ~ Real ale ~ Meals and snacks (till 10pm) ~ (01963) 440218 ~ Children in eating area of bar and in restaurant ~ Country & western music in fuction room 2nd Sat of month ~ Open 11-3, 6.30-11; 12-3, 7-10.30 Sun; closed evening 25 Dec ~ Bedrooms: £28B/£35B

STANTON WICK ST6162 Map 2
Carpenters Arms 🛏 ♟
Village signposted off A368, just W of junction with A37 S of Bristol

A popular place, particularly for lunch, this is efficiently run by a helpful, friendly licensee. The Coopers Parlour on the right has one or two beams, red-cushioned wall pews around heavy tables, fresh flowers, and swagged-back curtains and houseplants in the windows; on the angle between here and the bar area there's a fat woodburning stove in an opened-through corner fireplace. The bar has wood-backed built-in wall seats and some red fabric-cushioned stools, stripped stone walls, and a big log fire. Diners are encouraged to step down into a snug inner room (lightened by mirrors in arched 'windows'), or to go round to the sturdy tables angling off on the right; most of these tables get booked at weekends. Good bar food includes home-made soup (£2.50), filled french bread (from £2.95; steak, onion and mushroom £5.75), deep-fried brie on home-made tomato and cucumber chutney (£3.95), ploughman's (£4.25), mussels with white wine, garlic and cream or pasta with tuna, black olives and tomato sauce (£4.25 regular, £6.25 large), omelettes or crab cakes with a chive butter sauce (£5.75), lamb liver and bacon with onions and gravy (£6.95), fish pie (£7.45), and steaks (from £9.75); good breakfasts. Well kept Bass, Butcombe Bitter, Wadworths 6X, and Worthington Best on handpump, a decent wine list, and quite a few malt whiskies; cribbage, dominoes, fruit machine, piped music, and big satellite TV screen. There are picnic tables on the front terrace and pretty flower-filled flowerbeds. *(Recommended by Comus Elliott, Theo, Anne and Jane Gaskin, Robert Gomme, Dick Mattick, DP, DC, David Gittins, Don Kellaway, Angie Coles, A R and B E Sayer)*

Free house ~ Licensee Nigel Pushman ~ Real ale ~ Meals and snacks (till 10pm) ~ Restaurant ~ (01761) 490202 ~ Children welcome (though no facilities for them) ~ Pianist twice a week ~ Open 11-11; 12-10.30 Sun ~ Bedrooms: £52.50B/£69.50B

STOGUMBER ST0937 Map 1
White Horse 🛏

From A358 Taunton—Williton, village signposted on left at Crowcombe

A pleasant place to stay and with comfortable bedrooms, this agreeable pub is set in a quiet conservation village. The neatly kept long bar room has old-fashioned built-in settles, other settles and cushioned captain's chairs around the heavy rustic tables on the patterned carpet, a warm winter coal fire, and piped classical music. Good, reasonably priced food includes sandwiches (from £1.10), home-made vegetable or turkey soup (£1.70), salmon mousse (£2.60), ploughman's (£3.20), omelettes (£3.20), ham and egg (£3.30), seafood lasagne (£4.10), liver and bacon casserole (£4.60), steak and kidney pudding (£5.80), trout with almonds (£6.90), steaks (from £8.80), and puddings like treacle tart, apple crumble or home-made pineapple ice cream (from £1.50); best to book for Sunday lunch, and breakfasts are good; prompt service. Well kept Cotleigh Tawny, Otter Ale and a guest such as Brakspears on handpump, and farm cider in summer. A side room has sensibly placed darts and a fruit machine; shove-ha'penny, dominoes, cribbage, and video game – as well as a separate skittle alley. The garden is quiet except for rooks and sheep in the surrounding low hills. *(Recommended by K H Frostick, Mike and Mary Carter, Brian and Bett Cox, H O Dickinson, Mark Hydes, Eddie Edwards, Iain Robertson, J and P Maloney, John A Barker, James Nunns)*

Free house ~ Licensee Peter Williamson ~ Real ale ~ Meals and snacks (11-2, 6-10) ~ (01984) 656277 ~ Children in dining room ~ Open 11-2.30, 6-11; 12-3, 7-10.30 Sun ~ Bedrooms: /£35B

STOKE ST GREGORY ST3527 Map 1
Rose & Crown 🍽 🍷 🛏

Woodhill; follow North Curry signpost off A378 by junction with A358 – keep on to Stoke, bearing right in centre and right again past church

Warmly welcoming and hard-working licensees run this busy country cottage. The neatly kept bar is decorated in a cosy and pleasantly romanticised stable theme: dark wooden loose-box partitions for some of the interestingly angled nooks and alcoves, lots of brasses and bits on the low beams and joists, stripped stonework, and appropriate pictures including a highland pony carrying a stag; many of the wildlife paintings on the walls are the work of the landlady, and there's an 18th-c glass-covered well in one corner. Mrs Browning's two sons are responsible for the good, honest cooking – using fresh local produce, fresh fish from Brixham, and their own eggs: sandwiches in home-made granary bread (from £1.50), soup (£1.75), local ham and egg (£4), omelettes (£4.25), grilled kidneys and bacon (£5.50), scrumpy chicken (£5.95), mushroom, tomato and bean bake or vegetable stroganoff (£6), skate wings (£6.50), steaks (from £8), dover sole (£12.50), and puddings (£2.50); prices are higher in the evening; good breakfasts, three-course evening menu (£12; lots of choice), and a good three-course Sunday lunch (£7.95). Obliging service, even when busy. One small dining area is no smoking. Well kept Eldridge Pope Hardy and Royal Oak, Exmoor Ale, and a guest beer on handpump, and decent wines; unobtrusive piped classical music, dominoes, and skittle alley. Under cocktail parasols by an apple tree on the sheltered front terrace are some picnic tables; summer barbecues and a pets corner for children. In summer, residents have use of a heated swimming pool. The pub is in an interesting Somerset Levels village with willow beds still supplying the two basket works. *(Recommended by DMT, Bett and Brian Cox, P P and J Salmon, N C Hinton, Jo and Gary Charlton, M G Hart, Wayne Wheeler, Richard Dolphin, Theo, Anne and Jane Gaskin, J J M Davies Webb, Mr and Mrs Perris, Jay Sally, Dan Taylor, S I Collins, Jane Warren, George Atkinson, Dr and Mrs Brian Hamilton, Vera and John Race, Debbie Tunstall, Mark Sullivan, Jane and Adrian Tierney-Jones, John and June Hayward)*

Free house ~ Licensees Ron and Irene Browning ~ Real ale ~ Meals and snacks (till 10pm) ~ Restaurant ~ (01823) 490296 ~ Children welcome ~ Open 11-3, 6.30-11; 12-3, 7-10.30 Sun ~ Bedrooms: £25/£38; s/c cottage

STOKE ST MARY ST2622 Map 1
Half Moon

2¾ miles from M5 junction 25; A358 towards Ilminster, then first right, then right at T-junction and follow the signs. Westbound turn left at sign

Handy for the M5, this much-modernised village pub has five neat open-plan main areas with a roomy, relaxed feel to each of them and quite a bit of character to the furnishings and decor. Quite a lot of emphasis is placed on the bar food: sandwiches, home-made soup (£2.25), grilled sardines (£3.50), ham and egg (£4.75), home-made lasagne (£4.95), mushroom stroganoff (£5.25), a daily curry (£5.50), liver and bacon (£6.25), home-made steak and kidney pie (£6.50), baked smoked haddock with cream, cheese and chives (£6.95), chicken paprika (£7.75), roast duckling with an orange and cointreau sauce (£9.25), and steaks (from £10.50); home-made chips and bread, and seasonal vegetables and herbs from their garden. One restaurant is no smoking. Well kept Bass, Butcombe Bitter, Flowers IPA, Fullers London Pride, and Wadworths 6X on handpump, and quite a few malt whiskies. Picnic tables on a well kept lawn and more tables on a small gravel terrace. *(Recommended by Derek and Iris Martin, F J Robinson, Richard Dolphin, Comus Elliott, Alan Newman, Cliff Blakemore, John and Wendy Trentham, Geoff and Linda Dibble, Mr and Mrs C Roberts, Prof A N Black, Sue and Bob Ward, Ian and Nita Cooper)*

Whitbreads ~ Tenant Clive Parsons ~ Real ale ~ Meals and snacks ~ Two restaurants ~ (01823) 442271 ~ Children welcome ~ Open 11-3, 6-11; 12-3, 7-10.30 Sun

WAMBROOK ST2907 Map 1
Cotley 🍴 🛏

Village signposted off A30 W of Chard; *don't* follow the small signs to Cotley itself

Tucked away down country lanes and surrounded by lovely walks, this bustling country pub is always warmly welcoming – no matter how busy it is. There is a smart but unpretentious local atmosphere and the simple flagstoned entrance bar opens on one side into a small plush bar, with beyond that a two-room no-smoking dining area; several open fires. An extension is often used for painting sessions, and the results (complete with price-tags in case you see something you like) can be seen around the walls of the various rooms. Most enjoyable food includes home-made soup (£2.50), sandwiches and rolls (from £2.50), sausage and chips (£3.20), filled baked potatoes (from £3.50), mushroom fritters with garlic mayonnaise (£3.75), ploughman's (from £3.95), omelettes (from £4.95), ham and egg (£6.20), lamb kidneys in port and cream (£6.50), steaks (from £6.75), chicken in a ginger and pumpkin sauce (£7.25), salmon steak with white wine and tarragon (£7.95), three lamb chops with creamy mint sauce (£8.50), and a mixed grill (£10.25). The restaurant is no smoking. Flowers Original and Otter Ale on handpump kept under light blanket pressure, and a good choice of wines; pool and piped music. Out in the garden below are some picnic tables, with a play area and goldfish pool. *(Recommended by Paul and Madeleine Morey, Mr and Mrs J B Bishop, Chris Raisin, John Barker, Peter Toms, Clem Stephens, M E Wellington, K R Harris, D Alexander)*

Free house ~ Licensee David Livingstone ~ Real ale ~ Meals and snacks (till 10) ~ Restaurant ~ (01460) 62348 ~ Children welcome ~ Open 12-3, 7-11.30; 12-3, 7-10.30 Sun ~ Bedrooms: £25.85B/£37.60B

If you see cars parked in the lane outside a country pub have left their lights on at night, leave yours on too: it's a sign that the police check up there.

WEST HUNTSPILL ST3044 Map 1

Crossways 🥤

2¾ miles from M5 junction 23 (A38 towards Highbridge); 4 miles from M5 junction 22 (A38 beyond Highbridge)

This hospitable dining pub – run by efficient, friendly licensees – is a very worthwhile lunchtime stop from the motorway. The main part of the bar has dining-room chairs, a mixture of settles, and seats built into one converted brick fireplace, with good winter log fires in the others. At one end there's more of a dining room, attractively decorated with old farm machinery engravings, Albert and Chic cartoons (chiefly about restaurants), and 1920ish hunting prints – on Friday and Saturday evenings this area becomes a no-smoking bistro. The other end has an area with big winged settles making booths, and there's a family room with bamboo-back seats around neat tables. Enjoyable bar food includes generous sandwiches (from £1.60; sirloin steak £4), home-made soup (£2.20), garlic mushrooms (£3), ploughman's (£3.20), curried nut roast (£4.50), local faggots or steak and kidney pie (£4.80), gammon and egg (£6.50), steaks (from £8.50), daily specials such as stilton and walnut pâté (£3), grilled fresh sardines (£3.50), tuna pasta bake or cashew nut moussaka (£4.50), liver and bacon casserole (£4.80), rabbit in mustard and chives (£5.20), whole grilled lemon sole (£7), home-made puddings (£2.20), and children's meals (£2); good breakfasts. Well kept Butcombe Wilmots Premium Ale, Flowers IPA, Eldridge Pope Royal Oak, Exmoor Stag, Oakhill Yeoman Strong, Smiles Best, and Whitbreads Best on handpump, Rich's farm cider, and a decent wine list. Fruit machine and skittle alley. There are picnic tables among fruit trees in quite a big garden. If you're staying, the back rooms are quieter. *(Recommended by SHG, John and Elisabeth Cox, P H Roberts, C M Raybould, L W King, Comus Elliott, JCW, Chris and Shirley Machin, DJW, B J Harding, D Allsop, Nigel Clifton, Dave Irving, Roger Huggins, Tom McLean, E McCall, E J Mutter, Andrew and Ruth Triggs, M and A Sandy, Ian Phillips, Tom Evans, Mr and Mrs D S Price, Sue and Bob Ward, Ian Williams, Linda Mar, Jenny and Michael Back)*

Free house ~ Licensees Michael Ronca and Tony Eyles ~ Real ale ~ Meals and snacks (till 10pm Fri/Sat) ~ Restaurant (Fri/Sat evenings only) ~ (01278) 783756 ~ Children welcome away from main bar ~ Open 10.30-3, 5.30(6 Sat)-11; 12-3, 7-10.30 Sun; closed 25 Dec ~ Bedrooms: £24B/£34B

WINSFORD SS9034 Map 1

Royal Oak 🥤 ♀

In Exmoor National Park, village signposted from A396 about 10 miles S of Dunster

Set beneath peaceful rolling fields and hills, this beautiful thatched inn has an attractively furnished and cosy lounge bar with a cushioned big bay-window seat from which you can look across the road towards the village green and foot and packhorse bridges over the River Winn; it's a lovely spot. There are tartan-cushioned bar stools by the panelled counter (above which hang horsebrasses and pewter tankards), the same cushions on the armed windsor chairs set around little wooden tables, and a splendid iron fireback in the big stone hearth (with a log fire in winter). Another similarly old-fashioned bar offers more eating space with built-in wood-panelled seats creating booths, fresh flowers, and country prints; there are several pretty and comfortable lounges. Bar food includes good home-made soup (£2.50), sandwiches (from £2.75; filled french bread from £4.75), home-made terrine (£3.95), ploughman's or mushroom, nut and pasta bake (£4.75), home-made Exmoor lamb pasty (£4.95), chicken and leek pie or steak and kidney pudding (£7.65), and Aberdeen Angus sirloin steak (£10.95); evening extras such as seafood pancake (£3.95), Exbridge trout with a prawn and parsley butter (£8.25), medallions of pork tenderloin with shallots, black peppercorns, brandy and cream (£8.50), and puddings like sherry trifle (£2.50). Well kept Flowers IPA and Original on handpump with a guest beer such as Shepherd Neame Spitfire or Wadworths 6X tapped from the cask; friendly staff. They do a useful guide to Exmoor National Park identifying places to visit and there are good nearby walks – up Winsford Hill for magnificent views, or over to Exford. *(Recommended by David and Jane Russell, Jim Winzer, Peter and Audrey Dowsett, Paul Barnett,*

V Kavanagh, Maurice and Joan George, Nigel Woolliscroft, John and Christine Vittoe)

Free house ~ Licensee Charles Steven ~ Real ale ~ Meals and snacks ~ Restaurant ~ (01643) 851455 ~ Children in eating area of bar ~ Open 11-2.30, 6-11; 12-3, 7-10.30 Sun ~ Bedrooms: £85B/£97.50B

WITHYPOOL SS8435 Map 1
Royal Oak 🛏 ♉

Village signposted off B3233

New licensees have taken over this bustling and friendly country village inn – early reports from readers are good. They've added more paintings, ornaments, stuffed fish and old wooden barrels to the smartly cosy beamed lounge bar – which also has a stag's head and several fox masks on its walls, comfortably cushioned wall seating and slat-backed chairs, and a fine log fire in a raised stone fireplace; another quite spacious bar is similarly decorated. Good bar food includes home-made soup (£1.95), sandwiches (from £2), ploughman's (from £3.80), filled baked potatoes (from £3.90), two big venison and bacon sausages with two free range eggs (£6.25), steaks (from £10, though they also do a 4oz minute one for £6.50), half crispy duck (£10.65), and daily specials such as fish chowder (£2), lightly breadcrumbed fried prawn balls with garlic mayonnaise (£3), soft roes on toast (£3.50), stilton and broccoli quiche (£5), and fresh fish such as skate, plaice, trout, salmon, cod (which they batter themselves), prawns, lemon sole, and so forth (from £6.50). Well kept Flowers IPA and Wadworths 6X on handpump, several malt whiskies, and a fair number of cognacs and armagnacs. It can get very busy (especially on Sunday lunchtimes), and is popular with the local hunting and shooting types; shove-ha'penny, cribbage and dominoes. There are wooden benches on the terrace, and just up the road, some grand views from Winsford Hill, with tracks leading up among the ponies into the heather past Withypool Hill. The River Barle runs through the village itself, with pretty bridleways following it through a wooded combe further upstream. This is another pub with a *Lorna Doone* connection; R D Blackmore stayed here while writing the book. *(Recommended by Brian and Bett Cox, Mark Hydes, Paul Barnett, Neil and Anita Christopher, David and Jane Russell, R C Watkins, Mr and Mrs Bemis, Jill Grain, Maurice and Joan George, V Kavanagh, Kate and Kevin Gamm, Richard Gibbs; more reports on the new regime, please)*

Free house ~ Licensees Richard and Jo-Anne Howard ~ Real ale ~ Meals and snacks ~ Restaurant ~ (01643) 831506 ~ Children in eating area of bar and in restaurant if over 8 ~ Open 11(11.30 in winter)-3, 6-11; 12-3, 7-10.30 Sun ~ Bedrooms: £33B/£76B

Bedroom prices normally include full English breakfast, VAT and any inclusive service charge that we know of. Prices before the '/' are for single rooms, after for two people in double or twin (B includes a private bath, S a private shower). If there is no '/', the prices are only for twin or double rooms (as far as we know there are no singles).

Lucky Dip

Besides the fully inspected pubs, you might like to try these Lucky Dips recommended to us and described by readers (if you do, please send us reports):

Ashcott [70 Bath Rd; ST4337], *Pipers*: Nice atmosphere, good range of food in eating area, Scottish Courage ales, prompt welcoming service, roomy comfort, log fire, pleasant roadside garden *(Alan Williams)*

☆ **Axbridge** [The Square; quite handy for M5; ST4255], *Lamb*: Welcoming old inn in attractive square, dark beams, rambling odd corners, good reasonably priced generous food inc good vegetarian choice and lots of puddings, well kept ales such as Bass, Butcombe and Wadworths 6X, Thatcher's farm cider, huge log fire, pub games inc table skittles, pretty little garden, skittle alley; children in eating area; *old-world spacious bedrooms, huge breakfast (Alan and Paula McCully, Mrs D M Graham, John and Elisabeth Cox, LYM)*

☆ **Backwell** [Farleigh Rd; A370 W of Bristol; ST4968], *George*: Former coaching inn with well priced bar food, wide choice in restaurant inc delicious puddings and Sun lunch, well kept Ushers, good choice of wines; children welcome *(Alan and Paula McCully)*

Banwell [Main Rd; ST3959], *Whistling Duck*: Modern well done two-bar rural-theme pub, cheerful staff, well kept real ale, fair choice of good generous food *(DWAJ)*

Barrington [ST3818], *Royal Oak*: Welcoming old stone pub opp church in pretty village, handy for Barrington Court, with small welcoming lounge, chatty locals' bar and skittle alley, good choice of well kept beers, big helpings of food, friendly licensees *(Richard Houghton)*

☆ **Barrow Gurney** [Barrow St (B3130, linking A370/A38 SW of Bristol; ST5367], *Princes Motto*: Very welcoming cosy unpretentious local, well kept Bass and other ales such as Boddingtons, Smiles Best and Wadworths 6X; snug traditional tap room, long room up behind, cheap wholesome lunchtime snacks, pleasant new garden *(Alan and Paula McCully, Amanda and Simon Southwell, LYM)*

☆ **Batcombe** [off A359 Bruton—Frome, or A361 at Cranmore; ST6838], *Batcombe Inn*: Well furnished low-beamed 14th-c pub behind church in pretty village, wide choice of good attractively presented home-made food inc vegetarian, well kept Butcombe, Flowers Original and Marstons Pedigree, big log fire and woodburning stoves, copper and brass, games room, comfortable minstrel's gallery; busy with families weekends (playroom, children's videos Sun), tables in fine walled garden with terrace and play area; two bedrooms with own bathrooms *(R H Martyn, John Barker, Gwen and Peter Andrews, K H Frostick)*

☆ **Bath** [Abbey Green], *Crystal Palace*: Cheerfully busy modernised bar, sheltered courtyard with lovely hanging baskets, heated conservatory; good value freshly prepared straightforward food (not Sun evening) inc lunchtime snacks, speedy friendly service, well kept ales, log fire; fruit machines, video game, pinball, piped music *(M and A Sandy, Susan and Nigel Wilson, Gordon, Richard Lewis, Neil Calver, Vann and Terry Prime, DI, EMcC, RH, TMcL, Mrs P J Pearce, Barry and Anne, GSB, Andrew Hodges, LYM)*

☆ **Bath** [23 The Vineyards; the Paragon, junction with Guinea Lane], *Star*: Genuinely friendly feel in small interconnecting rooms separated by glass and panelling, staunchly basic and old-fashioned; particularly well kept Bass, Butcombe and Wadworths 6X in jugs from the cask, enthusiastic landlord, low prices, card-playing locals in snug, dim lighting (famously bricked-in windows), no piped music *(J and P Maloney, Dr and Mrs A K Clarke, David Knibb, PB, BB)*

☆ **Bath** [Mill Lane, Bathampton (off A36 towards Warminster or A4 towards Chippenham)], *George I*: Attractive creeper-covered canalside pub, well run and friendly, with wide choice of well presented good food inc fish and vegetarian, good log fires, well kept Bass and Courage Directors; dining room by towpath, no-smoking family room, tables on quiet safe spacious back terrace with garden bar (traffic noise at front); can get crowded, esp weekends *(Rob and Linda Davis, Gordon, Dr and Mrs A K Clarke, Paul and Ursula Randall)*

☆ **Bath** [Midford Rd; ST7461], *Cross Keys*: Well refurbished dining lounge with end restaurant (best to book), good food cooked to order from home-made burgers and sausages through popular pies to duck with cherry sauce, daunting choice of puddings, Courage Directors, Ushers Bitter and Founders, friendly service, locals' public bar; big garden with aviary *(Meg and Colin Hamilton, Andy and Jill Kassube, Neil Calver)*

Bath [Belvedere, Lansdown Rd], *Beehive*: Basic unspoilt cider house with several farm ciders, Moles and Georges ales, and perfect cheddar *(J Pettifer)*; [Walcot St], *Bell*: Musicians' pub, with well kept Butcombe, Wadworths 6X and guest beers, good cheap rolls, friendly efficient service; frequent free music *(Dr and Mrs A K Clarke, Michael Richards)*; [17 Northumberland Pl, off High St by W H Smith], *Coeur de Lion*: Tiny single-room pub in charming flower-filled flagstoned pedestrian alley, cosy little bar, well kept mainly Whitbreads-related ales, lunchtime filled rolls in summer – perhaps Bath's prettiest pub, especially in summer *(Richard Lewis, LYM)*; [1 Lansdown Rd], *Farm House*: Pleasant setting on hill overlooking Bath, good choice of food and well kept beer, jazz some evenings *(JJB, J Pettifer)*; [2 South Parade], *Georges*: A hotel, but comfortable panelled bar well used by local regulars, with Flowers IPA and Original, good bar food from sandwiches to steaks inc special roast with free glass of wine, friendly service, tables on big front terrace; Greek Cypriot restaurant downstairs; bedrooms *(Richard Lewis)*; [North Parade], *Huntsman*: Popular 18th-c pub claiming oldest stone shop front in Bath, long comfortable lounge, panelled side room, efficient friendly staff, wide choice of food inc well filled sandwiches, well kept Eldridge Pope beers; terrace *(Richard Lewis)*; [2 Saracen St], *Pig & Fiddle*: Small busy pub with good unusual choice of real ales from island bar, friendly service, two big open fires, clocks set to different time zones, very relaxed daytime, lively at night, good piped music, seats on big front terrace; home-cooked food here and in upper restaurant area, takeaways too *(Ben Hanna, Susan and Nigel Wilson, DI, EMcC, RH, TMcL)*; [27 Daniel St], *Pulteney Arms*: Small basic town pub with good atmosphere, well kept Ushers and Wadworths 6X, good chip baps and other bar food, good choice of juke box music, pavement tables; popular with Rugby players *(Roger Wain-Heapy, Dr and Mrs A K Clarke)*; [Upper Borough Walls], *Sam Weller*: Well kept Bass and Wadworths 6X, good food cooked to order inc all-day breakfast, friendly young staff, lively mixed clientele *(Dr and Mrs A K Clarke)*; [42 Broad St], *Saracens Head*: Beamed coaching inn with 19th-c prints inc mid-Victorian *Punch* title pages; well kept Scottish Courage ales, good well presented food at sensible prices inc generous Sat cold table, quick service; children in dining area *(Tony Dickinson, Hugh MacLean, Andrew Hodges, Dr and Mrs A K Clarke)*

Bathford [2 Bathford Hill, signed off A363; ST7966], *Crown*: Spacious and attractively laid out, several distinct but linked areas inc no-smoking garden room, good log fire, wide choice of home-cooked food (not that cheap), well kept Worthington Best and other ales, decent wines; families welcome, tables on terrace, nice garden *(Susan and Nigel Wilson, LYM)*

Bicknoller [ST1139], *Bicknoller*: Good value varied food *(G V Stanton, G W Stevenson)*

Bishops Wood [off A303/B3170 S of Taunton; ST2512], *Candlelight*: Roomy yet cosy, wide choice of good food from sandwiches up, fresh veg, pleasant dining room, genial owners, spotless housekeeping, local real ales, no-smoking areas *(Mr and Mrs K W Johnson)*

Blagdon [ST5059], *Queen Adelaide*: Quiet clean one-bar pub in lovely spot overlooking Blagdon Lake, plenty of tables, open fire, food inc good homely soup, substantial filled baguettes *(DJW)*

Blagdon Hill [4 miles S of Taunton; ST2217], *Lamb & Flag*: Cosy clean and welcoming, newly refurbished but keeping country style, beams, settles etc; good food, Otter ales, log fire *(Mrs M N Brown)*

Bradford on Tone [ST1722], *White Horse*: Stonebuilt local in quiet village, pleasant decor, varied reasonably priced good food (worth the wait) in bar; new bedrooms not ready yet *(Shirley Pielou, Joan and Michel Hooper-Immins)*

☆ **Brendon Hills** [junction B3190/B3224; ST0434], *Raleghs Cross*: Isolated upland inn, views to Wales on clear days, good walking country; huge comfortably modernised bar with rows of banquettes, refurbished back restaurant beyond new windowed wall, plenty of tables outside with play area, wide choice of popular generous food (some tables no smoking), carvery Fri-Sun evenings and Weds lunch, well kept Exmoor and Flowers Original; children in restaurant and family room; open all day summer; bedrooms *(Phil and Heidi Cook, LYM)*

☆ **Brent Knoll** [2 miles from M5 junction 22; right on to A38, then first left; ST3350], *Red Cow*: Sensibly short choice of good well priced food inc proper veg and beautifully served Sun lunch in warmly welcoming spotless dining lounge where children allowed, with well spaced tables, quick pleasant staff, well kept Whitbreads-related ales, skittle alley, pleasant sheltered gardens *(D A Walker, BB)*

☆ **Bristol** [Upper Maudlin St/Colston St], *Brewery Tap*: Small and chatty, but get there early for a seat; tap for Smiles brewery with their beers kept well and sensibly priced, also interesting Continental bottled ones; interesting unpretentious decor, good atmosphere even when packed, log fire in no-smoking room; food inc filled rolls and vegetarian, drinks 11-8, cl Sun *(Barry and Anne, Amanda and Simon Southwell, David Warrellow, Steve Willey)*

Bristol [31 Corn St], *31 Corn St*: Lively and very spacious pub in former bank, well served Courage beers *(Dr and Mrs A K Clarke)*; [off Boyce's Ave, Clifton; ST5773], *Albion*: Friendly and unpretentiously old-fashioned pub with unusual flagstoned courtyard off cobbled alley, well kept Courage ales, simple snacks *(Dr and Mrs A K Clarke, LYM)*; [Alma Vale Rd, Clifton], *Alma Vale*: Cheerful town pub, friendly service, no music, good value food, Courage *(Jim and Will Norman)*; [Merchant St], *Almshouse*: Two-level converted almshouse, elegantly refurbished as part of galleried shopping centre *(Dr and Mrs A K Clarke)*; [Alfred Pl, Kingsdown; ST5873], *Bell*: Small welcoming panelled bar with good atmosphere and service, good home-made food, well kept Ushers and a guest beer, decent wines, reasonable prices, traditional furnishings *(J Cobban, Pat and John Millward)*; [Park St], *Berkeley*: Lively student pub, cheap drinks *(Kaya Evans)*; [207 Cheltenham Rd, Bishopston; ST5874], *Cat & Wheel*: Genuine local, well kept Moles, emphasis on games *(Dr and Mrs A K Clarke)*; [43 Corn St], *Commercial Rooms*: Vast Wetherspoons establishment, lofty ceiling, snug cubicles along one side, comfortable quieter no-smoking back room; reasonable prices, good real ales, food all day; very busy weekend evenings *(Andy Jones, Comus Elliott)*; [Sion Pl, off Portland St], *Coronation Tap*: Friendly bustling old-fashioned low-ceilinged tavern with fat casks of interesting farm ciders, Courage Best and Directors, simple lunchtime food *(Richard Gibbs, LYM)*; [15 Cotham Rd S], *Cotham Porter Stores*: Lively little cider pub, well kept keenly priced Courage real ales, cheap snacks; benches facing each other along narrow panelled bar, sensibly placed darts, dominoes, cribbage *(Comus Elliott, LYM)*; [Lower Clifton Hill], *Eldon House*: Recently decorated, new licensee, Ushers ales, huge helpings of reasonably priced good food *(P B Godfrey)*; [Fulford Rd, Hartcliffe; ST5867], *Fulford House*: Vibrant active estate pub, well kept ales, skittle alley *(Dr and Mrs A K Clarke)*; [38 Jacobs Wells Rd, Clifton], *Hope & Anchor*: Brews its own Lucifer ales, also well kept guest beers; bare boards, good varied home-made food, summer evening barbecues in picturesque garden, occasional live music *(Dr and Mrs A K Clarke)*; [Little Paul St, Kingsdown], *Kings Arms*: Large comfortable open-plan pub with well kept Bass *(Dr and Mrs A K Clarke)*; [80 Victoria St], *Kings Head*: Old and well refurbished, keeping original features, lots of polished brass and wood, well kept Courage Best, interesting gas pressure gauge behind bar; friendly atmosphere, tram car saloon *(Mr and Mrs P Byatt, Gordon Tong)*; [32 Park St], *Le Chateau*: Now run by Smiles, with their ales kept well; Victorian feel, lots of pictures, open fires, conservatory, good home-made lunchtime food (many tables reserved Sat), more limited evening *(Simon and Amanda Southwell)*; [124 Park Rd, Stapleton; ST6176], *Masons Arms*: Unspoilt and traditional, good range of real ales inc some local ones, spectacular views from good terrace *(Dr and Mrs A K Clarke)*; [17 King St], *Naval Volunteer*: Well done re-creation of traditional city pub, locals' front snug, long bar buzzing with conversation, nice dark wood decor, good range of changing ales, limited but good food inc popular pizzas, prompt friendly service *(David Warrellow)*; [45 King St], *Old Duke*: Duke Ellington, that is – inside, the ochre walls and ceiling are festooned with jazz posters, besides one or two instruments, and the side stage has good bands most nights, and at Sun lunchtime; usual pub furnishings, simple food, Scottish Courage ales; in attractive cobbled area between docks and Bristol Old Vic, gets packed evenings *(Andy Jones, Dr and Mrs A K Clarke, Dr and Mrs B D Smith)*; [Westbury Lane, Coombe Dingle; ST5577], *Progress*: Huge two-bar pub on outskirts, big garden, well kept Courage *(Dr and Mrs A K Clarke)*; [2 Princess Victoria St, Clifton], *Quadrant*: Well run, with well kept beer inc Bass *(P B Godfrey)*; [15 Upper Maudlin St], *Sea Horse*: Spartan two-bar studenty pub, very limited lunchtime food, Smiles and other ales *(Simon*

and Amanda Southwell); [Lower Park Row], *Ship*: Low-ceilinged long narrow bar with nautical memorabilia, dimly lit back balcony, spiral stairs down to lower area with pool table, small lounge, several well kept ales such as Smiles and Wadworths 6X, reasonably priced food; small sunny terrace, well reproduced piped music esp evening, open all day *(B R Shiner)*; [Frenchay Common; ST4077], *White Lion*: Fairly roomy, with friendly staff, quickish food service, decent food inc good value OAP lunch; looking on to common *(D G Clarke)*;

Brompton Regis [SS9531], *George*: Pleasantly refurbished 17th-c ex-farmhouse, food inc authentic curries and good steaks, three real ales maybe inc bargain 12 Bore, organic wines, woodburners, skittle alley, quick friendly service; Exmoor views from garden by churchyard, dogs welcome, no juke box or machines *(Chris Tasker, Graham and Jill Wood)*

Bruton [High St; ST6834], *Castle*: Good value food, changing well kept ales and welcoming landlady in unpretentious chatty town local, small darkish bars, striking mural of part of town in skittle alley, tables in sheltered back garden; children in eating area and skittle alley *(John Barker, LYM)*

☆ **Buckland Dinham** [A362 Radstock—Frome; ST7551], *Bell*: Rambling old-fashioned 16th-c stone-built local in small Mendip village, attractive decor showing some flair, adventurous choice of good food (they'll also do picnic hampers), big dining area, half a dozen or more well kept ales, welcoming character landlord, hard-working staff, log fires, frequent theme nights *(Susan and Nigel Wilson, K R Harris, W Marsh, Chris and Tricia Hubbard)*

Burnham on Sea [High St; ST3049], *Somerset & Dorset*: Good range of real ales, sensible reasonably priced menu, daily roasts with fresh veg, carvery, good no-smoking area for children *(K R Harris)*

Burtle [ST3942], *Tom Mogg*: Modernised country pub with emphasis on food inc generous Sun lunch, well kept ales such as Butcombe and John Smiths, terrace and garden; open all day *(D Irving, R Huggins, T McLean, E McCall)*

Cannington [High St (A39); ST2539], *Kings Head*: Wide choice of good food, decent beers and wines; bedrooms *(K H Frostick)*

Catsgore [A372 E of Langport; ST5025], *Lime Kiln*: Comfortable roadside pub with real ales and reasonably priced food *(Ann and Colin Hunt)*

Chard [East St; ST3208], *Happy Return*: Unpretentious outside, charming in, with warm welcome, pleasant ambience, good reasonably priced food *(D H Braggins)*; [Hornsbury Hill (A358 N); ST3310], *Hornsbury Mill*: Restaurant with rooms rather than pub, but also does snacks in comfortable bar; tidy dress; bedrooms *(Howard Clutterbuck)*

☆ **Charlton Musgrove** [B3081, 5 miles SE of

Bruton; ST7229], *Smithy*: Spaciously open-plan 18th-c pub, sparkling clean, with stripped stone, heavy beams, log fires, good range of cheap home-cooked food inc Sun lunch and good vegetarian choice, well kept Butcombe, Fullers London Pride and Wadworths 6X, good welcoming service; arch to small restaurant overlooking charming garden full of cottagey flower tubs and hanging baskets; skittle alley and pool table *(Brian Chambers, John Barker)*

☆ Chilcompton [Broadway; ST6452], *Somerset Wagon*: Cosy, friendly and atmospheric, with well kept Wadworths IPA and other ales, wide range of consistently good food from generous filled rolls up; lots of settles, log fire, books, stuffed animals and militaria *(G and M Stewart, Susan and Nigel Wilson, M G Hart)*

Chilcompton [Frys Well (B3139)], *Redan*: Friendly simple local with wide choice of good value home cooking inc vegetarian and foreign-theme monthly banquets, no-smoking eating area, well kept Courage Best and Theakstons Best, farm cider, decent wines, friendly staff, skittle alley; quiz nights, maybe piped jazz *(Susan and Nigel Wilson)*

Churchingford [Honiton Rd; ST2112], *York*: Unspoilt and attractive, wide choice of good food, three real ales, woodburner, good welcoming service; bedrooms with own bathrooms *(D A C T Hancock)*

☆ Clevedon [Elton Rd; ST4071], *Little Harp*: Busy promenade pub open all day for enjoyable low-priced food inc vegetarian and doorstep sandwiches, views towards Exmoor and the Welsh hills from terrace and conservatory, pleasant no-smoking family area with mezzanine floor, well kept Marstons inc seasonal ales, methodical service *(Tom Evans, Alan and Paula McCully, JCW, Mike and Mary Carter, M Joyner)*

☆ Clevedon [15 The Beach], *Moon & Sixpence*: Substantial seafront Victorian family dining pub with good choice of generous food (superb puddings free to OAPs), efficient friendly service, balconied mezzanine floor with good pier and sea views to Brecon Beacons, well kept Marstons Pedigree *(Alan and Paula McCully, Tom Evans)*

Clutton Hill [King Lane, off A39 Bristol—Wells; ST6360], *Hunters Rest*: Carefully extended stonebuilt pub with wide choice of bar food from interestingly filled rolls to steaks, several real ales, family room, no-smoking area, log fires, restaurant, big garden with play area, weekend miniature railway and view to Mendips; facilities for disabled *(Meg and Colin Hamilton)*

☆ Combe Florey [off A358 Taunton—Williton, just N of main village turn-off; ST1531], *Farmers Arms*: Neatly rebuilt bustling dining pub, picturesquely thatched and beamed, popular food, plenty of tables outside, good log fire *(Mrs Pamela Curtis, Howard Clutterbuck, BB)*

Combe St Nicholas [2½ miles N of Chard; ST3011], *Green Dragon*: Recently pleasantly refurbished, good value food, welcoming service, well kept ales, decent wines, open fire; well behaved children allowed; open all day Sat, bedrooms *(Howard Clutterbuck)*

Compton Dundon [B3151 S of Street; ST4933], *Castlebrook*: Small friendly two-bar village local with super flagstone floors, cheap unpretentious food inc good Sun roasts, obliging landlord, well kept Bass and Courage Best, skittle alley, tables on lawn behind; can be crowded, caravan campsite behind *(John Barker, M Knowles, Richard Burton, Mr and Mrs T A Bryan)*

☆ Congresbury [St Pauls Causeway; ST4363], *Old Inn*: Unpretentious tucked-away family local, with well kept Bass, Smiles and other ales tapped from the cask, tasty cheap food, friendly landlord, some no-smoking tables, open fire, ancient stove, low beams with hops; tables in back garden *(Philip and Jude Simmons, J Matthews)*

Congresbury [Brinsea Rd (B3133)], *Plough*: Welcoming unspoilt flagstoned local with three seating areas off main bar, two fires, old prints, farm tools and sporting memorabilia; lunchtime filled rolls, well kept Bass, Butcombe, Worthington BB and guest beers, darts, table skittles, shove ha'penny and cards, jack russells called Pepper and Mustard, hair cuts 1st Sat of month; small garden with boules, aviary and occasional barbecues *(Alan and Paula McCully, Mike and Mary Cartern)*; [A370], *Ship & Castle*: Well kept Marstons ales at very sane prices, tasty food inc good pasta and vast mixed grill, attentive service *(Tom Evans)*; [Wrington Rd], *White Hart & Inwood*: Welcoming modernised pub with conservatory extension, good food inc vegetarian, terrace with Mendip views, big play area, aviary *(Mr and Mrs C Barker)*

☆ Corfe [B3170; ST2319], *White Hart*: Good food inc vegetarian all cooked to order (worth the wait), priced in snack size or full meal size, also sandwiches and ploughman's; comfortable and well appointed, with attractive small no-smoking dining room, friendly licensees, good choice of real ales; children welcome *(Jane Warren, Howard Clutterbuck, Shirley Pielou, John Barker)*

Corton Denham [OS Sheet 183 map ref 634225; ST6322], *Queens Arms*: Welcoming and attractive old stonebuilt village inn, good fresh reasonably priced food, real ales, comfortable smallish main bar with woodburner, fresh flowers and brasses; nr Cadbury Castle, clean comfortable homely bedrooms with good views *(G D Payne, R C H Dakin)*

Cossington [Middle Rd; ST3540], *Red Tile*: Small welcoming local, with well kept Butcombe, Exmoor, Smiles and other ales, fine choice of ports, good generous food inc daily fresh Brixham fish, speciality steaks and wicked puddings, cosy fire; children and dogs welcome, well kept garden with big adventure play area *(Adrian and Jane Tierney-Jones, John Barker)*

☆ **Croscombe** [A371 Wells—Shepton Mallet; ST5844], *Bull Terrier*: Cosy and clean, with beams, flagstones, parquet and carpet, flame-effect fires, three communicating rooms with a no-smoking family room, generous food from sandwiches to steaks (not winter Sun evening), well kept Butcombe Bitter, Smiles, a beer brewed for the pub and a guest such as Adnams, farm cider, friendly service and border collie called Penny, traditional games; cl Mon in winter *(Mr and Mrs R Fowler, Philip Orbell, Bruce Bird, MT, DT, LYM)*

☆ **Doulting** [Chelynch, off A361; ST6443], *Poachers Pocket*: Popular modernised black-beamed bar with log fire in stripped-stone end wall, gundog pictures, generous straightforward food from sandwiches up, Butcombe, Oakhill, Wadworths 6X and a guest beer, local farm cider, pub games, children in eating area, back garden with country views *(Mark and Heather Williamson, LYM)*

☆ nr **Doulting** [Doulting Beacon; E of A37 on Mendip ridge, just S of A367 junction; ST6445], *Waggon & Horses*: Well run civilised 18th-c pub with enjoyable food, real ale, good house wines, friendly staff, horse-loving Colombian landlord; good Mendip view from olde-worlde entrance, neat but homely interconnecting rooms, prints and log fires, large beamed upper gallery (classical or jazz concerts some Sundays), small restaurant, skittle alley/art gallery, free range eggs; attractive walled garden with play area and rare poultry *(Brennig Jones, Alan and Lilian Meecham, Mrs D M Graham)*

☆ **Dulverton** [2 Bank Sq; SS9127], *Lion*: Good generous food inc good value soup and specials in comfortable and homely old-fashioned country-town hotel with well kept Exmoor and Ushers, decent wine and coffee, helpful service; children allowed in room off, pleasant setting *(W H and E Thomas, John and Elspeth Howell)*

Dunster [High St; SS9943], *Dunster Castle*: Good bar snacks and reasonably priced drinks in well appointed hotel – handy to have good parking in this congested beauty spot; bedrooms with own bathrooms *(W H and E Thomas)*

East Harptree [off B3114; ST5655], *Waldegrave Arms*: Traditional 17th-c pub, warm welcome, well presented good food inc popular Sun lunch; lovely garden, children and well behaved dogs welcome *(Mrs M Thompson)*

☆ **Easton in Gordano** [Martcombe Rd; A369 a mile from M5 junction 19; ST5276], *Rudgleigh*: Bustling roadside pub, attractive in summer with tables in big garden with willows, tamarisks and play area (but Tannoy food announcements); small nicely laid-out lounge with lots of commemorative mugs, other china, old guns, well kept Scottish Courage and Smiles ale, quick friendly service, wide range of prompt generous food; rather bleak little family room; open all day weekdays *(R W A Suddaby, John and Vivienne Rice, B J Harding, Bronwen and Steve Wrigley, Andrew Hodges, LYM)*

☆ **Edington Burtle** [Catcott Rd; ST4043], *Olde Burtle*: Good reasonably priced food inc fresh fish, local veg and good Sun lunch in character bar, much refurbished lounge and comfortable restaurant, lovely log fire, well kept Fullers London Pride, Wadworths 6X and an interesting guest beer *(P H Roberts, Tom Evans)*

☆ **Exford** [B3224; SS8538], *White Horse*: Exmoor hotel with rustic-style open-plan Dalesman bar, hunting prints and trophies, pine tables and settles, very wide choice of food from filled baguettes to venison pie etc, generous Sun carvery, ales such as Bass, Cotleigh Tawny, Exmoor and Worthington, log fire, pleasant safe garden by River Exe; children in eating area, dogs allowed; open all day summer, lovely village setting; bedrooms comfortable, stabling available *(Shirley Pielou, Richard Gibbs, LYM)*

☆ **Exford** [The Green], *Crown*: Country hotel's bar popular with farmers and smart local couples, generous food from good ploughman's to beautifully presented main dishes with lots of veg, well kept Wadworths 6X, decent wines, log fire, welcoming service, attractive streamside garden; bedrooms *(Mary Woods, Nigel Harrison, Patrick Renouf)*

Failand [B3128 Bristol—Portishead; ST5171], *Failand Inn*: Attractive beamed country pub, popular for good straightforward food (get there early for a comfortable seat); well kept Bass, Courage and Wadworths 6X, friendly staff *(Tom Evans, David Warrellow, Alan and Paula McCully)*

☆ **Farleigh Hungerford** [A366 Trowbridge—Norton St Philip; ST8057], *Hungerford Arms*: Friendly well furnished pub with good views, decent food in main bar, more airy room off, and popular lower-level restaurant, well kept Scottish Courage ales; landlord never forgets a face *(Ted George, W F C Phillips)*

☆ **Freshford** [signed off B3108; ST7960], *Inn at Freshford*: Excellent new landlord likely to be the making of this neat comfortably modernised beamed pub, partly no smoking; well kept Ruddles County and Ushers, open fire, huge choice of food from sandwiches up, restaurant (not Sun evening); children welcome, piped music; pretty gardens, nice spot by River Frome, walks to Kennet & Avon Canal *(Andrew Shore, LYM)*

☆ **Glastonbury** [Northload St; ST5039], *Who'd A Thought It*: Interesting bric-a-brac and memorabilia, well kept ales such as Bass, Eldridge Pope Blackdown Porter and Thomas Hardy and Palmers, decent wines, stripped brickwork, flagstones and polished pine, coal fires, pleasant staff, entertaining decorations in lavatories, popular varied food, no-smoking restaurant; bedrooms cosy and comfortable, good breakfasts *(Jo Rees, Jo and Gary Charlton, M J How)*

Glastonbury [27 Benedict St], *Mitre*: Good value food inc fresh fish and veg, home-made pies and big puddings, well kept Ushers

Founders and other ales *(Annette and Stephen Marsden, Jack and Gemima Valiant)*; [4 Chilkwell St (A361, SE of centre)], *Riflemans Arms*: Chatty popular local with real ales such as Flowers IPA, Eldridge Pope Royal Oak and Palmers, farm cider, good games room, play area and sunny terrace *(Veronica M Brown, Jack and Gemima Valiant, LYM)*

☆ **Hallatrow** [Wells Rd; ST6357], *Old Station*: Formidable collection of bric-a-brac from ancient typewriters to beeping car coming through wall, model train running around ceiling, wide changing choice of food, well kept Bass and other ales, good staff; garden behind with recently opened railway carriage restaurant; bedrooms *(Alan and Paula McCully)*

Halse [off B3227 Taunton—Bampton; ST1427], *New Inn*: Enjoyable generous home cooking, good range of beers, friendly family service, woodburner in big inglenook; bedrooms clean and homely, with good breakfasts, lovely village *(J Howse)*

Hardway [rd to Alfreds Tower, off B3081 Bruton—Wincanton at Redlynch; pub named on OS Sheet 183 map ref 721342; ST7234], *Bull*: Pretty and welcoming country dining pub, popular locally esp with older people weekday lunchtimes, warm comfortable bar, character dining rooms, log fire, Butcombe and Wadworths 6X, farm cider; piped music; sell paintings and meringues; tables and barbecue in rose garden over road *(A Madden)*

☆ *nr* **Haselbury Plucknett** [off A30 E of Crewkerne, towards Merriott; ST4611], *Old Mill*: Very modernised country dining pub in quiet spot, big picture windows looking over duck pond, good enjoyable food and well spaced tables in comfortable light and airy dining lounge, snug low-ceilinged bar on right, tables out on informal lawn by pretty stream; cl Sun; inspected and approved as main entry for this edition, with very good landlord, but up for sale summer 1997 *(Howard Clutterbuck, Galen Strawson, Penny Elphick, BB)*

☆ **Hatch Beauchamp** [old village rd, not bypass; ST3220], *Hatch*: Wide choice of good honest food, welcoming licensees, lots of copper and brass in carpeted lounge bar with attractive bow-window seats, well kept west country ales, farm ciders; games room across yard; good value bedrooms *(John Barker, BB)*

Hillfarance [ST1624], *Anchor*: Welcoming modernised pub with lots of flower tubs outside, good food inc children's in attractive bar and two good eating areas, good value evening carvery, well kept Adnams and Exmoor, family room with wendy house, speedy friendly service, garden with play area; bedrooms, caravan site, holiday apartments *(Bett and Brian Cox, Shirley Pielou, Richard Dolphin)*

Hinton Blewett [signed off A37 in Clutton; ST5957], *Ring o' Bells*: Charming low-beamed stone-built country local with good value home cooking (not Sun evening), well kept Wadworths and guest ales, log fire, pleasant view from tables in sheltered front yard; children welcome *(Hugh MacLean, LYM)*

Hinton Charterhouse [B3110 about 4 miles S of Bath; ST7758], *Rose & Crown*: Attractive panelled bar with well kept Bass, Butcombe and Smiles tapped from casks, good choice of food in bar and restaurant, friendly staff *(Meg and Colin Hamilton, D Irving, E McCall, R Huggins, T McLean)*

☆ **Holton** [off A303 W of Wincanton; ST6827], *Old Inn*: Charming rustic 16th-c pub, unassuming and friendly, with beams, ancient flagstones, log fire, hundreds of key fobs, attractive bric-a-brac, big open woodburner, plump cat; pleasant service, Butcombe, Wilmots and Wadworths 6X, food in bar and restaurant (must book Sun lunch); walking sticks for sale, tables outside, sheltered garden up steps *(James Nunns, Dr and Mrs S Jones, BB)*

Holywell Lake [off A38; ST1020], *Holywell*: Good value food inc wide range of puddings, several local real ales, fast friendly service, quiet relaxed atmosphere (no music); cl lunchtime Mon-Weds *(I F Milne, Peter Woolls)*

Horsington [signed off A357 S of Wincanton; ST7023], *Half Moon*: Pleasant knocked-through bars with beams and stripped stone, oak floors, inglenook log fires; good value home-made food, well kept ales, decent wines, quick service, evening restaurant; big back garden with play area, good value bedrooms in chalets *(Brian Chambers, BB)*

☆ **Howley** [ST2609], *Howley Tavern*: Spacious bar with good atmosphere, wide choice of imaginative bar food inc vegetarian and popular Sun lunch, Bass, Flowers Original and changing guest beers, decent wines, attractive old-world restaurant; bedrooms *(John Barker, Howard Clutterbuck)*

Ilchester [The Square; ST5222], *Ilchester Arms*: Hotel well refurbished by new owner, good food all freshly cooked in bar and restaurant, friendly service; keg beer; comfortable bedrooms *(C H Beaumont)*

Ilminster [B3168 W; ST3614], *Lord Nelson*: Quiet, pleasant and friendly, good value bar food, good service, well kept beer; bedrooms *(Howard Clutterbuck, M J How)*

Kenn [B3133 Yatton—Clevedon; ST4169], *Drum & Monkey*: Village local in shades of pink and red, brasses and copper-topped tables, open fires, simple good value bar food, well kept Ushers ales *(Alan and Paula McCully)*

Keynsham [A4175; ST6568], *Lock Keeper*: Smiles pub in lovely spot by Avon with lock, marina and weir, big garden; their beers well kept, decent food *(Tony Dickinson)*

☆ **Kilve** [A39 E of Williton; ST1442], *Hood Arms*: Woodburner in bar, cosy little plush lounge, no-smoking restaurant, wide choice of popular bar food (no sandwiches), friendly service, Cotleigh Tawny, Exmoor and Flowers Original; skittle alley, tables on sheltered back terrace by garden; nice bedrooms – back are quietest *(Maysie Thompson, Dorothy and Leslie Pilson, V Kavanagh, Mr and Mrs D T Deas, David and Brenda Begg, K H Frostick, Jo and Gary Charlton, LYM)*

Kingsbury Episcopi [ST4321], *Wyndham Arms*: Unspoilt welcoming flagstoned country pub with roaring open fires, pleasant staff, good range of reasonably priced food inc good big steaks and impressive choice of puddings, well kept Bass and Fullers London Pride; tables in garden *(A Preston, John Barker, Stephen Brown)*

Langford Budville [off B3187 NW of Wellington; ST1022], *Martlet*: Old pub sensitively done up, warm atmosphere, good range of food inc unusual hot filled rolls, well kept beer *(John Barker, Bett and Brian Cox)*

Leigh upon Mendip [ST6847], *Bell*: Friendly service, good value home-made pies, Bass, Butcombe and Wadworths 6X; garden *(Nigel and Susan Wilson)*

☆ **Midford** [Bath Rd; ST7560], *Hope & Anchor*: Cosy and clean, with welcoming service, particularly good interesting food in bar and flagstoned restaurant end, well kept Bass, Butcombe and Smiles, good Spanish wines, good friendly service, log fire; tables outside, pretty walks along River Frome *(Roger Wain-Heapy, Pat and John Millward, Lyn and Geoff Hallchurch)*

Minehead [Blue Anchor Bay; end of B3191, off A39 E; ST0343], *Blue Anchor*: Well run split-level hotel bars, clifftop spot giving bay views, friendly atmosphere, good range of food, beers inc Eldridge Pope, pleasant staff, big garden; children welcome, piped music; bedrooms clean, pretty and comfortable, site for touring caravans *(Gwyneth and Salvo Spadaro-Dutturi)*

☆ **Misterton** [Middle St (A356); ST4508], *White Swan*: Small cottagey pub, welcoming, comfortable and well kept, with good choice of bar and restaurant food cooked by landlady, good range of beers, no-smoking rooms, framed tapestries, collection of old wireless sets; attractive garden behind, skittle alley *(Mr and Mrs K W Johnson, Howard Clutterbuck)*

☆ **Montacute** [The Borough, off A3088 W of Yeovil; ST4916], *Phelips Arms*: Roomy and airy pub, comfortably unpretentious, with varied good freshly cooked fair-priced food inc sandwiches and interesting specials, friendly efficient service, well kept Palmers; skittle alley, tables in appealing garden, delightful village, handy for Montacute House; bedrooms *(Galen Strawson, Dr S Willavoys, Mr and Mrs J Russell, Stephen Brown)*

Montacute, *Kings Arms*: More hotel than pub now, with blazing log fires, stripped 16th-c hamstone walls, mix of chintz, grey-gold plush and oak, good food (not Sun evening) from filled baguettes up, no-smoking restaurants, decent wines; service could sometimes be more gracious; children welcome, bedrooms *(Derek and Iris Martin,*

Stephen Brown, Dr and Mrs B Smith, D B Jenkin, LYM)

Moorlinch [Pit Hill Lane, signed off A39; ST3936], *Ring of Bells*: Friendly atmosphere, good hearty food, well kept ales such as Berrow, Bridgwater, Oakhill and Smiles; cosy attractive lounge with log fire; cl Mon-Thurs lunchtime in winter *(Jane and Adrian Tierney-Jones, John Barker)*

Nether Stowey [Lime St; ST1939], *Ancient Mariner*: Friendly atmosphere and varied good food inc some home-grown veg *(Mr and Mrs B Tizard)*; *Rose & Crown*: Good basic local with farm cider and good choice of real ales *(Veronica Brown)*

Nettlebridge [A367 SW of Radstock; ST6548], *Nettlebridge Inn*: Large modern bar, popular for good value lunchtime food; good range of Oakhill beers *(Nigel Wilson)*

☆ **North Brewham** [off A359 NE of Bruton; ST7236], *Old Red Lion*: Welcoming traditional flagstoned low-beamed former farmhouse with good home cooking inc fish and vegetarian, comfortable dining room, well kept Butcombe, Fullers and Greene King ales, good coffee, open fire, friendly efficient service; handy for King Alfred's monument; bedrooms *(Mrs Y Thorner, Mavis and Robert Harford)*

North Cadbury [ST6327], *Catash*: Happy local family atmosphere, wide choice of food, well kept Eldridge Pope ale, decent wines, attractive garden; bedrooms *(Stephen, Julie and Hayley Brown)*

North Petherton [High St, nr M5 junction 24; ST2932], *Walnut Tree*: Welcoming hotel, comfortable bar with good food in eating area, good range of beers, restaurant; bedrooms spacious and well equipped, substantial breakfasts *(Andrew and Ruth Triggs, Rex Miller)*

Norton St Philip [ST7755], *Fleur de Lys*: Friendly village local, well kept Bass, Oakhill, Wadworths 6X and Worthington, good value food, skittle alley *(Susan and Nigel Wilson)*

☆ **Over Stratton** [S of A303 via South Petherton roundabout; ST4315], *Royal Oak*: Attractive and welcoming dining pub, flagstones, prettily stencilled beams, scrubbed pine kitchen tables, pews, settles etc, log fires and rustic decor; wide choice of food, no-smoking restaurant, well kept Badger ales; open all day Aug, tables outside with barbecues and good play areas for toddlers and older children; signs as we went to press that things were settling down well again after a management change earlier in 1997 *(Mrs H Murphy, Rob Chandler, Guy Consterdine, LYM)*

☆ **Panborough** [B3139 Wedmore—Wells; ST4745], *Panborough Inn*: Spacious 17th-c village inn with attentive friendly service, wide range of consistently good generous food inc vegetarian and splendid puddings; several clean, comfortable and attractive rooms, inglenook, beams, brass and copper, real ales, unobtrusive piped music; skittle alley, small restaurant, tables in front terraced garden; bedrooms comfortable *(Mr and Mrs*

Beck, J H Kane, K R Harris)

Pitminster [off B3170 S of Taunton (or reached direct); ST2119], *Queens Arms*: Peaceful village pub, cosy and unspoilt, with smiling service, log fire, seven well kept ales, interesting wines, good bar food from fine crab sandwiches up, wonderful fish restaurant in pleasant dining room; no music, dogs allowed, bedrooms with own bathrooms *(Howard Clutterbuck, John Barker, D A C T Hancock)*

Porlock [High St (A39); SS8846], *Ship*: Picturesque thatched huge-chimneyed partly 13th-c pub, basic low-beamed locals' front bar with flagstones, inglenooks each end, hunting prints, back lounge, well kept Bass, Cotleigh, Courage Best and a local guest beer such as Bosuns Tackle, good country wines, easy-going service, bar food, pub games and pool table, garden; children welcome in eating area; bedrooms *(Mr and Mrs R Maggs, Simon Collett-Jones, Dorothy and Leslie Pilson, Jonathan Williams, LYM)*

Porlock Weir [end of B3225, off A39 in Porlock; SS8547], *Ship*: Prettily restored old inn included for its wonderful setting by peaceful harbour, with tables in terraced rose garden and good walks (but no views to speak of from bars); friendly service, usual bar food and well kept ales such as Bass and Exmoor in straightforward Mariners Bar with family room; roaring fire, unusual space-age gents', attractive bedrooms *(Sue and Bob Ward, David Carr, Mr and Mrs T Crawford, M C and S Jeanes, Jenny and Michael Back, LYM)*

Portishead [High St; ST4777], *Poacher*: Wide range of good reasonably priced freshly cooked food with real veg – get there early as many things sell out by 1ish, though they'll do the good trout much later; well kept Butcombe and Wickwar BOB, friendly amusing service; cl Sun pm *(Tom Evans, K R Harris, John Millward)*

Priddy [from Wells on A39 pass hill with TV mast on left, then next left; ST5450], *Hunters Lodge*: Welcoming and unassuming walkers' and potholers' inn in same family for generations, well kept local Oakhill ales tapped from casks behind the bar, simple good food inc bread and local cheese, low prices, log fire, flagstones; tables in garden; bedrooms *(Veronica M Brown, Martin Grass, BB)*

Priddy [off B3135; ST5250], *New Inn*: Bustling low-beamed pub, modernised but still traditional, with good log fire, spacious conservatory, good value food inc interesting dishes, well kept Bass, Eldridge Pope Hardy and Wadworths 6X, good local cider and house wines, good welcoming service, skittle alley; motorcyclists made welcome; bedrooms comfortable and homely, on quiet village green *(David Warrellow, Jean and Richard Phillips)*

Puriton [Puriton Hill, just off M5 junction 23; ST3241], *Puriton*: Friendly character pub with good value food; busy lunchtime, good

service *(J F M West, Dr West)*

Radstock [62 Frome Rd; ST6954], *Fromeway*: Pleasant modern bar and restaurant, good generous food (meat from own butcher's shop), no-smoking restaurant, quick friendly service, well kept Butcombe and Wadworths 6X; bedrooms clean, bright and reasonably priced *(Mrs J Clark, Susan and Nigel Wilson)*

Rickford [off A368 (trickily from W); ST4859], *Plume of Feathers*: Unspoilt and cottagey, relaxed atmosphere, good choice of well cooked food, friendly service, Ushers ales, log fire; seats outside *(David Warrellow)*

☆ **Rowberrow** [about ½ mile from A38 at Churchill; ST4558], *Swan*: Good bar food from fine sandwiches up amd quick courteous service in olde-worlde pub with comic hunting prints and grandfather clock, well kept Bass and Wadworths 6X; good walking country *(Alan and Paula McCully, MRSM, D A Walker)*

Rumwell [A38 Taunton—Wellington, just past Stonegallows; ST1923], *Rumwell*: Welcoming and comfortable, with old beams, lots of tables in several areas, very wide choice of well presented good value food, friendly efficient service, children's room; immaculate lavatories *(Shirley Pielou, F J Willy)*

Saltford [High St; ST6867], *Bird in Hand*: Lively local, comfortable and friendly, with lots of bird pictures, reasonably priced well cooked food, conservatory dining area, small family area; live entertainment; handy for Bristol—Bath railway path *(Gordon Tong)*

Shepton Mallet [63 Charlton Rd; ST6445], *Thatched Cottage*: A bit hotelish and plush, but quite cosy and comfortable, with good varied reasonably priced food in bar and restaurant, Bass and Theakstons Best; bedrooms with own baths *(Meg and Colin Hamilton, James Nunns)*

☆ **Shepton Montague** [off A359 Bruton—Castle Cary; ST6731], *Montague*: Welcoming old-fashioned deep-country pub, with very good interesting food (generous bar nibbles too), well kept Butcombe, Greene King IPA and Marstons Pedigree, decent wines, sensible prices, log fire in attractive fireplace, small elegant candlelit dining rooms (one no smoking), no machines or music, pretty terrace, brilliant views; three attractive bedrooms with own bathrooms; has been closed lunchtime *(Alan and Barbara Moss, Mr and Mrs A Allom, Mrs C Jimenez, M Ward)*

Simonsbath [SS7739], *Exmoor Forest*: Exmoor inn with several bar rooms inc games room, straightforward furnishings, log fires, lots of whiskies, well kept real ales, food from ploughman's up; bedrooms – nine miles of good trout fishing for residents *(Brian and Jill Bond, LYM)*

Somerton [Mkt Pl; ST4828], *Globe*: Chatty two-bar local with log fire, wide choice of good bar food, well kept Bass and Oakhill, good choice of wine, friendly staff, dining conservatory, back billiard room; no music, skittle alley, tables in garden *(Janet Pickles, John and Elspeth Howell, John Barker)*; [Church Sq], *White Hart*: Attractive 18th-c stonebuilt pub with welcoming service, daily papers, good value food, Ushers ales, three bars and games room *(John and Elspeth Howell)*

South Petherton [Silver St; ST4317], *Wheatsheaf*: Newish licensees, good food, well kept beer, friendly atmosphere *(Jeremy and Duncan Webb)*

☆ **Staple Fitzpaine** [off A358 or B3170 S of Taunton; ST2618], *Greyhound*: Relaxing sophisticated atmosphere in interesting rambling country pub with antique layout, flagstones and inglenooks; enthusiastic landlord, warm welcome, well kept changing ales, good food *(Richard Dolphin, LYM)*

☆ **Stoke sub Hamdon** [West St, off A303/A3088 W of Yeovil; ST4717], *Fleur de Lis*: Golden stone inn dating from 14th c, spacious rambling part-flagstoned bar with homely mix of furnishings, wide changing choice of food inc vegetarian here and in simple dining room, well kept Eldridge Pope and other beers and local ciders, open fires, friendly landlady; good value bedrooms, pretty village *(Mrs M Walters, Stephen Brown, BB)*
Stoke sub Hamdon [Ham Hill], *Prince of Wales*: Superb views, recently refurbished, several real ales, decent menu from fresh ingredients; busy in summer *(Stephen Brown)*
Street [opp Clarkes museum; ST4836], *Bear*: Refurbished as comfortable dining pub, good staff, Eldridge Pope, Greenalls, Smiles and Tetleys, usual food; well equipped bedrooms, buffet breakfast *(N E Bushby, W Atkins)*

☆ **Taunton** [Magdalene St], *Masons Arms*: Fine friendly town pub, often very busy, with good range of well kept ales inc Exmoor, good reasonably priced quick food (not Sun but served late other evenings) inc succulent sizzler steaks and interesting soups, no chips, comfortably basic furnishings, no music or pool tables; good bedrooms *(Howard Clutterbuck, Andrew Brockbank, Veronica Brown, Julian Pyrke, Barry Nowlan, Jane and Adrian Tierney-Jones, Ian Phillips, Peter Skinner)*
Taunton [Deane Gate; Hankridge Way, nr Sainsbury; very handy for M5 junction 25], *Hankridge Arms*: Old-style new pub in modern shopping complex, well appointed, with good atmosphere and service, good choice of reasonably priced generous food in bar and restaurant, Badger ales *(Mr and Mrs W B Walker, John Barker, Steve and Maggie Willey)*; [Shuttern], *Pen & Quill*: Friendly, warm and cosy, with good value food inc good choice of puddings *(Veronica M Brown, John A Barker)*; [Middleway, Wilton – across Vivary Park from centre], *Vivary Arms*: Pretty pub with good range of home-made fresh lunchtime bar food esp good soup and fish, in snug plush lounge and small dining room; prompt friendly service, no music; bedrooms with own bathrooms in Georgian house next door *(Shirley Pielou)*

Tickenham [B3130 Clevedon—Nailsea; ST4571], *Star*: Dining pub with good range of food (can be a wait), log fire, big family room, no-smoking conservatory, Bass, Morlands Old Speckled Hen and John Smiths, decent wines, friendly landlord, piped music, high chairs; garden with good play area *(Tom Evans, TJS)*

Tintinhull [Church St; ST4919], *Lamb*: Quiet village pub with wide range of food inc good value Sun lunch (must book for restaurant); well kept Wadworths 6X, welcoming service, nice garden; handy for Tintinhull Manor (NT) *(K R Harris, J Bidgood)*

☆ **Triscombe** [signed off A358 NW of Taunton; ST1535], *Blue Ball*: Snug little unspoilt thatched pub tucked into Quantocks, tables out in colourful garden with peaceful hill views, neat beamed bar with sporting prints, no-smoking conservatory (children allowed), well kept Butcombe, Cotleigh Barn Owl, Exmoor and Otter, Sheppy's farm cider, quickly served food (not Sun evening) inc unusual dishes, traditional games, skittle alley; piped music; bedroom suite in annexe; cl Sun evening in winter *(H F C Barclay, John and Maureen Fletcher, Mr and Mrs Perris, Jane and Adrian Tierney-Jones, DJW, DMT, John Brightley, LYM)*

☆ **Trudoxhill** [off A361 Frome—Wells; ST7443], *White Hart*: Beams, stripped stone, friendly atmosphere, mainly table seating with a couple of easy chairs by one of the two log fires; main attraction the fine range of Ash Vine ales brewed here (you can usually visit the brewery), also Thatcher's farm cider and country wines; wide choice of bar food, children in eating area, restaurant, picnic tables in flower-filled sheltered side garden *(Jerry and Alison Oakes, SGNB, Ted George, S G N Bennett, M G Hart, James Nunns, John and Lynn Busenbark, LYM)*
Trull [Church Rd; ST2122], *Winchester Arms*: Welcoming lively small local, good varied food, well kept Butcombe, obliging service, cosy atmosphere, small dining room; bedrooms *(Derek Patey, John Barker, Shirley Pielou)*
Wadeford [ST3110], *Haymaker*: Friendly and pleasant pub, good generous food, Whitbreads-related ales, separate games room; bedrooms *(T Cooper)*
Walton [ST4636], *Pike & Musket*: Nicely presented food from ploughman's to kangaroo, friendly service; prettily placed *(David and Brenda Begg)*
Waterrow [A361 Wiveliscombe—Bampton; ST0425], *Rock*: Character pub with well kept ales inc Cotleigh Tawny and Exmoor Gold, wide choice of good home-made food, attractive prices, log fire in smallish bar exposing the rock it's built on, couple of steps up to lunchtime dining room doubling as evening restaurant, friendly helpful service; good well equipped bedrooms, charming setting in small valley village *(Cliff Blakemore)*

☆ **Wellow** [signed off A367 SW of Bath;

ST7458], *Fox & Badger*: Friendly flagstoned bar with snug alcoves, small winged settles, flowers on the tables, three log fires, well kept Boddingtons, Butcombe, Wadworths 6X and a changing bargain beer, Thatcher's farm cider, well priced food, games and piped music in cosy public bar, restaurant, courtyard with barbecues; children in eating areas, open all day Thurs/Fri – can get very busy *(Barry and Anne, D Irving, E McCall, Jenny and Roger Huggins, T McLean, Neil Calver, Wayne Wheeler, LYM)*

Wells [High St, nr St Cuthberts; ST5545], *City Arms*: Good choice of good value food inc well prepared sandwiches and unusual dishes in big comfortable L-shaped rambling bar and upstairs restaurant of interestingly converted largely early 18th-c building – some parts even older (said to have been a Tudor jail); well kept Bass, Butcombe and Fullers London Pride, decent wines, welcoming prompt service, interesting bric-a-brac, attractive cobbled courtyard with well planted flower tubs etc; piped music *(Chris Ball, Peter and Audrey Dowsett, Tony and Wendy Hobden, Bruce Bird, F C Johnston, N E Bushby, W Atkins, M Wellington, John and Lynn Busenbark)*

Wells [St Thomas St], *Fountain*: Good vaue generous original food in pleasantly pubby downstairs bar with roaring log fire and popular upstairs restaurant – worth booking weekends, good Sun lunch; friendly quick staff, well kept Scottish Courage ales, farm cider, good choice of wines, piped music; right by cathedral; children welcome *(Veronica M Brown, D I Smith, D and B Taylor)*

West Bagborough [off A358 NW of Taunton; ST1633], *Rising Sun*: Welcoming local in tiny village below Quantocks, family service, short choice of fresh generous home-cooked food, well kept Exmoor and Oakhill, wide choice of wines, unobtrusive piped music, darts, table skittles, big log fires; bedrooms comfortable, with own bathrooms *(Graham Stanton, Veronica Brown)*

West Camel [ST5724], *Walnut*: Smartly upmarket inside, popular for lunch, with good service, several real ales; bedrooms *(John Barker)*

West Horrington [Haydon – B3139 NE; ST5948], *Slab House*: Remote and windswept pub, bright in summer and cosy in winter, with roaring fire, pleasant decor, food from sandwiches to imaginative dishes in bar and small restaurant area, quick friendly service, well kept ales; play area *(Joyce and Peter Andre, Hilary Aslett)*

West Pennard [A361 E of Glastonbury; ST5438], *Lion*: Welcoming new management, good quickly served food in three neat dining areas opening off small flagstoned and black-beamed core with log fire in big stone inglenook, second log fire in stripped-stone family area, well kept Ushers Best and Founders; tables on big forecourt, bedrooms comfortable and well equipped, in neatly converted side barn *(J Holland, Peter and Audrey Dowsett, BB)*

West Pennard, *Apple Tree*: Well renovated food pub, flagstones, exposed brickwork, beams, good woodburner, comfortable seats, thatch above main bar, second bar and two eating areas; well kept Bass, Cotleigh and Worthington BB, good coffee, pleasant staff; can get crowded lunchtime; tables on terrace *(E H and R F Warner)*

Weston in Gordano [B3124 Portishead—Clevedon; ST4474], *White Hart*: Useful highly organised food stop, clean and tidy, with early evening bargains, well kept Marstons Pedigree; open all day *(TE)*

Weston super Mare [Knightstone Parade; ST3261], *Pavilion*: Stylish new place, looks like its name, rather 'end of the pier' inside but fun, with dusky pinks and blues for Edwardian look, old local photographs, period framed posters; well kept Whitbreads-related ales, good bar food, helpful service, Beefeater restaurant; lots of tables on sea-facing terrace *(Alan and Paula McCully, Susan and John Douglas)*; [St Georges – just off M5, junction 21; ST3762], *Woolpack*: Lively olde-worlde local with well kept Courage, Fullers and up to three changing guest ales, pleasant window seats and library-theme area, good well priced bar food inc home-made pies, small but attractive restaurant *(Alan and Paula McCully, Andy and Jill Kassube)*

Westport [B3168 Ilminster—Curry Rivel; ST3819], *Old Barn Owl*: Cheery modern-style stripped-stone family pub with wide choice of well presented moderately priced food, well kept Boddingtons and Wadworths 6X; bedrooms, handy for Somerset Levels *(Keith Plested)*

☆ Wheddon Cross [A396/B3224, S of Minehead; SS9238], *Rest & Be Thankful*: Wide range of generous home-cooked food inc children's, friendly staff, comfortably modern two-room bar with buffet bar and no-smoking restaurant, well kept Morlands Old Speckled Hen, Ruddles, Theakstons XB and Ushers Best, two good log fires, huge jug collection, aquarium and piped music; communicating games area, skittle alley, public lavatory for the disabled; bedrooms *(Carol and Brian Perrin, Phil and Heidi Cook, John and Elspeth Howell, Pete and Rosie Flower, LYM)*

☆ Widcombe [Culmhead – OS Sheet 193 map ref 222160; ST2216], *Holman Clavel*: Simple but comfortable old-fashioned deep-country pub dating from 14th c and named after its massive holly chimney-beam, good cheap home-cooked food, welcoming hard-working landlord, well kept Cotleigh and Flowers Original, nice atmosphere; dogs welcome, handy for Blackdown Hills *(John Barker, BB)*

Wincanton [South St; ST7028], *Nog*: Cheerful welcoming local, generous reasonably priced food, farm cider *(Brian Chambers)*

Winsley [B3108 W of Bradford-on-Avon (pub

just over Wilts border); ST7961], *Seven Stars*: Big stripped-stone open-plan bar doing well under current licensees, good food, Ushers ales, helpful staff, lots of old tables and chairs, snug alcoves, log-effect gas fires; picnic tables out on terrace, attractive village *(Meg and Colin Hamilton)*

Wiveliscombe [10 North St; ST0827], *Bear*: Friendly, with home-cooked food, well kept local beers; has local beer festival with music and Morris dancers *(Adrian and Jane Tierney-Jones)*

☆ **Wookey** [Wookey Rd, Burcott; B3139 W of Wells; ST5145], *Burcott Inn*: Friendly and popular, with enthusiastic landlord, comfortable lounge, interesting smaller room, prints of old advertisements etc, scrubbed wood tables, log fire, well kept Cotleigh Tawny, Cottage Southern and a changing guest beer, decent wine, good bar food inc interesting specials and doorstep sandwiches, attentive service, cottagey back restaurant; children welcome, pleasant walled garden; handy for the caves, can be busy weekends *(Bruce Bird, Andy and Jill Kassube, P H Roberts)*

Woolverton [A36 N of village; ST7954], *Red Lion*: Roomy beamed pub, panelling, flagstones and rugs on parquet, smart Regency chairs and chandeliers, well kept Bass and Wadworths 6X, wide choice of decent wines by the glass, straightforward food inc popular filled baked potatoes, friendly service; open all day *(John and Wendy Trentham, LYM)*

Worth [B3139 Wells—Wedmore; ST5545], *Pheasant*: Cheerful L-shaped bar with several real ales, decent house wines, good home cooking up to ostrich steak, smiling service; skittle alley; garden *(Gwen and Peter Andrews)*

Wrantage [A378 E of M5 junction 25; ST3022], *Canal*: Small welcoming three-roomed pub with well kept Cotleigh Tawny and others, farm cider, log fires, quickly served food in bar and dining room, helpful staff; darts, skittle alley, garden with play area *(John Barker)*

Yarlington [ST6529], *Stags Head*: Friendly and obliging landlord, good food in simple bar and fine restaurant, well kept beer, nice garden; now has two bedrooms *(John Knighton)*

Yeovil [Silver St; ST5516], *Pall*: Genial newish licensees in popular but trouble-free local, wide choice of food, well kept Badger, varied live entertainment; down-to-earth but sociable regulars *(Andy Hynes)*

Most pubs in the *Guide* sell draught cider. We mention it specifically only if they have unusual farm-produced 'scrumpy' or specialise in it. Do please let us know about any uncommon draught cider you find in a pub.

Staffordshire

After finding several good new main entries here last year, this year we have drawn something of a blank – though several Lucky Dip entries at the end of the chapter show real promise; these, all inspected and enjoyed by us, are the Crown in Abbots Bromley, Boat at Cheddleton, Swan at Fradley, and Worston Mill at Little Bridgeford. The Manifold at Hulme End and Crown at Yoxall have also made good starts under new landlords; the Black Lion at Butterton is a firm old favourite, though as we went to press we knew too little about the new people there to be sure of its standing; and there's a good choice of enjoyable pubs in Lichfield. Back among the main entries proper, the comfortably civilised Moat House at Acton Trussell is doing particularly well these days, and some gentle tidying-up has made the Yew Tree at Cauldon with its wonderful collections (and remarkably low prices) even more worth visiting. It's hard to beat weekday lunch at the Izaak Walton at Cresswell for value, though the French landlord of the Swan With Two Necks at Longdon is doing imaginative specials (and huge helpings of fresh fish); other places for good food here are the quaint Holly Bush at Salt (a wide and imaginative choice) and the Greyhound at Warslow (good home cooking – visitors feel like locals), with some interesting Belgian dishes at the unusual Wellington in Uttoxeter (its priest/landlord conducts Orthodox divine liturgy here on Sundays). Drinks, like pub food, tend to be cheaper than the national average in Staffordshire; besides the Yew Tree, the Rising Sun at Shraleybrook is exceptionally cheap, brewing its own ales on the premises. The Burton Bridge Inn in Burton on Trent is another pub here brewing its own – right under the noses of the industry giants, as Burton is of course the capital of British brewing, housing Bass, Carlsberg Tetleys' Ind Coope brewery, and Marstons. The county also has some interesting much smaller breweries such as Enville (using honey from its own bees in some of its ales), Lichfield and Titanic.

ACTON TRUSSELL SJ9318 Map 7
Moat House

Village signposted from A449 just S of Stafford; the right turn off A449 is only 2 miles (heading N) from M6 junction 13 – go through the village to find the pub on the W side, by the canal

Attractively set in six acres of lovely landscaped grounds next to the duck-populated Staffordshire & Worcestershire canal, with mooring facilities for narrowboats, and picnic tables in front by the water, this big and fairly smart 14th-c timbered pub is very efficiently run by welcoming staff and licensees. The family have a 400-acre farm which supplies some produce for the very good well presented bar food which includes filled baguettes (from £2.50) as well as daily specials like roast leg of lamb (£5.50), plaice fillet or poached haddock fillet with white wine, prawn, chive and sun-dried tomato sauce (£5.95), vol au vent filled with chicken, smoked bacon and asparagus and herb cream sauce (£6.50), chicken curry (£6.75) and entrecote steak and chasseur sauce (£10.50). It can get quite busy in the charmingly civilised oak-beamed bar which has a big open fireplace and comfortable armchairs as well as well kept Banks's Bitter and Marstons Pedigree with two guests such as Morrells Graduate and Varsity and Morlands Old Speckled Hen on handpump, a good wine list with about ten by the glass, and a decent range of spirits; no-smoking restaurant. Fruit machine, piped music; some readers have found it a bit noisy outside with motorway noise.

(Recommended by S J and C C Davidson, S Watkin, P Taylor, Karen Eliot, Basil Minson, Mike and Maggie Betton, David Hoult, DC, Thomas and Audrey Nott, Kate and Robert Hodkinson, George Atkinson, Peter and Jenny Quine, Suzanne and Steve Griffiths, Mike and Maggie Betton, Dick Brown, Margaret and Roy Randle, Addie and Irene Henry, Chris Raisin, Dorothee and Dennis Glover, Iain Robertson, C H and P Stride, Carole and Philip Bacon, John and Chris Simpson, Carl Travis, Bronwen and Steve Wrigley)

Free house ~ Licensee John Lewis ~ Real ale ~ Meals and snacks (not Sat evening or Sun) ~ Restaurant ~ (01785) 712217 ~ Children welcome in eating area of bar and restaurant ~ Open 11-3, 5.30-11; 11-11 Sat in summer; 12-10.30 Sun; cl 26 Dec

ALSTONEFIELD SK1355 Map 7
George
Village signposted from A515 Ashbourne—Buxton

Charmingly placed in the middle of a quiet farming hamlet, this delightfully simple 16th-c stone inn is prettily positioned by the village green. Locals, campers and hikers gather by the warm fire in the unchanging straightforward low-beamed bar – although muddy boots and dogs may not be welcome. There's a collection of old photographs and pictures of the Peak District, and pewter tankards hanging by the copper-topped bar counter. A spacious family room has plenty of tables and wheelback chairs. Generous helpings of good straightforward bar food from a printed menu – you order at the kitchen door – include: sandwiches (£1.85), soup (£1.95), ploughman's (from £3.85), meat and potato pie (£4.95), smoked trout or Spanish quiche (£5.30), lasagne or chicken (£5.50) and a couple of daily specials like asparagus flan or onion tart (£5.50). Well kept Burtonwood Bitter, Forshaws and a Burtonwood guest on handpump; dominoes, cribbage and maybe piped radio. The big sheltered stableyard behind the pub has a pretty rockery with picnic tables, and there are some stone seats beneath the attractive inn sign at the front. You can arrange with the landlord to camp on the croft. *(Recommended by John Waller, Erick Locker, Victoria Herriott, Hugh and Sarah McShane, Paul Robinshaw, Graham and Karen Oddey, John and Christine Lowe, John and June Freeman, Peter Marshall, J E Rycroft, Nigel Woolliscroft, Pat and Roger Fereday)*

Burtonwood ~ Tenants Richard and Sue Grandjean ~ Real ale ~ Meals and snacks (till 10pm)~ (01335) 310205 ~ Children in eating area ~ Open 11-3, 6.30(7 in winter)-11; 11-11 Sat; 12-10.30 Sun; cl 25 Dec

Watts Russell Arms
Hopedale

Gloriously set down a quiet lane outside the village in a deep valley of the Peak District National Park close to Dovedale and the Manifold, this friendly 18th-c shuttered house is popular with walkers, and busy at weekends. The cheerful beamed bar has brocaded wall banquettes and wheelback chairs and carvers, an open fire below a copper hood, a collection of blue and white china jugs hanging from the ceiling, bric-a-brac around the roughcast walls, and an interesting bar counter made from copper-bound oak barrels. Bar food includes soup (£1.75), filled baps (from £1.75, hot bacon and tomato £3), filled baked potatoes (from £3), English breakfast or ploughman's (£4.50), vegetable lasagne or chilli (£4.75), scampi (£5.25), gammon (£6.25) and three or four daily specials like smoked cod in cheese and mushroom sauce (£4.95) and chicken balti (£5.95); children's meals (£2.75). Well kept Mansfield Best and Old Baily and a guest like Morlands Old Speckled Hen on handpump, and about a dozen malts; darts, dominoes and piped music. Outside there are picnic tables on the sheltered tiered little terrace, and garden; no-smoking area. *(Recommended by Sue and Geoff Price, George Atkinson, Monica Shelley, Laura Darlington, Mike and Wendy Proctor, Joy and Peter Heatherley, Peter Marshall)*

Free house ~ Licensees Frank and Sara Lipp ~ Real ale ~ Meals and snacks (not winter Sun evenings) ~ (01335) 310271 ~ Children welcome ~ Open 12-2, 7-11(10.30 Sun); cl Mon lunchtime Dec-Easter

BURTON ON TRENT SK2423 Map 7
Burton Bridge Inn £ 🍺

24 Bridge St (A50)

You can go round the brewery in the long old-fashioned yard at the back of this unpretentious and friendly local on Tuesdays if you book in advance. It's here that they brew the beautifully kept Burton Bridge Bitter, XL, Porter and seasonal ales which are served on handpump in the simple little front bar, which also has wooden pews, plain walls hung with notices and awards and brewery memorabilia; even when it's quiet people tend to spill out into the corridor. Basic but good bar snacks such as good filled cobs (from 90p, hot roast pork or beef £1.80), and giant filled yorkshire puddings with ratatouille, faggots and mushy peas, a roast of the day or sausages (from £1.95-£3.10). The panelled upstairs dining room is open at lunchtime only; there's also a skittle alley, (booked well in advance), with gas lighting and open fires; country wines; about a dozen malt whiskies; dominoes. *Recommended by Richard Lewis, Penny and Martin Fletcher, BB)*

Own brew ~ Tenant Kevin McDonald ~ Real ale ~ Lunchtime meals and snacks (not Sun) ~ (01283) 536596 ~ Children in eating area of bar and dining room at lunchtimes ~ Open 11.30-2.15, 5.30-11; 12-2, 7-10.30 Sun; cl bank holidays till 7pm

CAULDON SK0749 Map 7
Yew Tree ★ ★ £

Village signposted from A523 and A52 about 8 miles W of Ashbourne; OS Sheet 119 map reference 075493

Most readers are enchanted by the unique profusion of fascinating, mostly Victorian treasures that the eccentrically characterful landlord Alan East has lovingly crowded into the dimly lit rooms of this apparently plain roadside local. The most impressive pieces are perhaps the working Polyphons and Symphonions – 19th-c developments of the musical box, often taller than a person, each with quite a repertoire of tunes and elaborate sound-effects; go with plenty of 2p pieces to work them. But there are also two pairs of Queen Victoria's stockings, ancient guns and pistols, several penny-farthings, an old sit-and-stride boneshaker, a rocking horse, swordfish blades, and even a fine marquetry cabinet crammed with notable early Staffordshire pottery. Soggily sprung sofas mingle with 18th-c settles and a four-person oak church choir seat with carved heads which came from St Mary's church in Stafford; above the bar is an odd iron dog-carrier (don't ask how it works!) As well as all this there's an expanding set of fine tuneful longcase clocks in the gallery just above the entrance, a collection of six pianolas (one of which is played most nights), with an excellent repertoire of piano rolls, a working vintage valve radio set, a crank-handle telephone, a sinuous medieval wind instrument made of leather, and a Jacobean four-poster which was once owned by Josiah Wedgwood and still has the original wig hook on the headboard. Remarkably cheap simple snacks like hot pork pies (65p), meat and potato pies, chicken and mushroom or steak pies (75p), hot big filled baps and sandwiches (from 80p), and quiche or smoked mackerel (£2.50). Beers include very reasonably priced Bass, Burton Bridge and M & B Mild on handpump or tapped from the cask, and there are some interesting malt whiskies such as overproof Glenfarclas; spirits prices are very low here, too. Darts, shove-ha'penny, table skittles (taken very seriously here), dominoes and cribbage. Hiding behind a big yew tree, the pub is difficult to spot – unless a veteran bus is parked outside. Dovedale and the Manifold Valley are not far away. *(Recommended by Simon Walker, John and Christine Lowe, Chris Raisin, Sue Holland, Dave Webster, Jerry and Alison Oakes, Graham and Karen Oddey, Victoria Herriott, Mike and Sue Walton, Mr and Mrs P Byatt, D and D Savidge, Mike and Wendy Proctor, David Carr, Vicky and David Sarti, Ian and Gayle Woodhead, Ann and Colin Hunt)*

Free house ~ Licensee Alan East ~ Real ale ~ Snacks (11-3, 6-9.30 but generally something to eat any time they're open) ~ (01538) 308348 ~ Children in Polyphon room ~ Occasional live folk ~ Open 10-3, 6-11; 10-3, 7-10.30 Sun

CRESSWELL SJ9837 Map 7
Izaak Walton

Village signposted from Draycott in the Moors, on former A50 Stoke—Uttoxeter

What makes this smart dining pub a particularly good value place for a meal is the £2 lunchtime and early evening discount on their menu prices – till seven, not Saturday and not in December. Nicely presented bar food is notably good and includes soup (£2.50), steak and kidney pie or lasagne (£4.95), chicken and broccoli bake (£5.75), poached salmon (£7.50), mixed grill (£8.45), a choice of seven vegetarian dishes including broccoli and hazelnut bake (£6.50), and daily specials like lamb and apricot curry (£5.95), grilled red snapper (£7.95) and game casserole or shoulder of lamb (£8.95). All eating areas are no smoking. The neatly kept light and airy bar is prettily decorated with little country pictures, dried flowers on walls and beams, pastel flowery curtains, a little settee in one window, lots of uniform solid country-kitchen chairs and tables in polished pale wood, going nicely with the fawn carpet, and gentle lighting at night. Well kept Marstons Pedigree and Best on handpump, and wines of the month on a blackboard; piped music; relaxed friendly service. There's a surcharge of 2% on credit cards. *(Recommended by F C Johnston, Paul and Maggie Baker, John and Annette Derbyshire, Simon Morton, Becky and Karen, Andy Petersen, Comus Elliott, Dr R F Fletcher, M A Robinson)*

Free house ~ Licensees Anne and Graham Yates ~ Real ale ~ Meals and snacks (till 10; all day Sun) ~ Restaurant ~ (01782) 392265 ~ Well behaved children welcome ~ Open 12-3, 6(6.30 Sat)-11; 12-10.30 Sun; cl 25, 26 Dec

LONGDON SK0714 Map 7
Swan With Two Necks

Brook Road; just off A51 Rugeley—Stafford

The long quarry-tiled bar at this atmospheric neatly kept pub is divided into three room areas, with low beams (very low at one end), a restrained decor, five cosy warm coal fires, and houseplants in the windows; there's a two-room carpeted restaurant. The pub fills quickly, people drawn mainly by the good food – a straightforward menu with more interesting daily specials, but all cooked freshly and really well by the French licensee. Fish in particular is outstanding: lunchtime sandwiches (from £1.50), soup (£1.60), lunchtime ploughman's (£4.10), seafood platter (£5), ham salad (£5.10), smoked salmon (£6.50), and daily specials such as very good beef, ale and venison casserole (£4.80), roast tenderloin of pork à l'orange, seasonal poacher's casserole or wild trout, haddock and prawn thermidor (£5), and a very tasty big fresh cod (£5.50). Particularly well kept Ansells, Ind Coope Burton, a third beer from the brewer and three changing guests such as Fullers London Pride and Otter ale; decent wines, friendly helpful service; piped music. The garden, with an outdoor summer servery, has picnic tables and swings, and the village is attractive. *(Recommended by S M Bradbury, Colin Fisher, Alan and Judith Gifford, Martin Jones, Eric Locker)*

Carlsberg Tetleys ~ Lease: Jacques Rogue ~ Real ale ~ Meals and snacks ~ Restaurant ~ (01543) 490251 ~ Children over 10 welcome in restaurant ~ Open 12-2.30(3 Sat), 7-11; 12-3, 7-10.30 Sun

---

Children welcome means the pub says it lets children inside without any special restriction. If it allows them in, but to restricted areas such as an eating area or family room, we specify this. Some pubs may impose an evening time limit.

ONECOTE SK0555 Map 7
Jervis Arms ◧
B5053, off A523 Leek—Ashbourne

The gardens at this cheery bustling 17th-c pub run down to the banks of the River Hamps (the licensee does warn that this isn't safe for children), with picnic tables under cocktail parasols on the ashtree-sheltered lawn, a little shrubby rockery, slides and swings, play trees, and a footbridge leading to the car park. Without detracting from its character, families are particularly welcome – as well as the various amusements in the garden, there are two family rooms (one no smoking) with high chairs, as well as a mother and baby room. The irregularly shaped cosy main bar has white planks above shiny black beams, window seats, wheelback chairs, two or three unusually low plush chairs, little hunting prints on the walls, and toby jugs and decorative plates on the high mantelpiece of its big stone fireplace. A similar but simpler inner room has a fruit machine. Very well kept Fiddlers (new small Nottinghamshire brewer) Best and Finest, Marstons Pedigree, Theakstons XB and Best and Worthington on hand or electric pump, a fair range of malt whiskies, and Scrumpy Jack cider. Generous helpings of good bar food include soup (£1.20), filled rolls (£1.60), filled baked potatoes (from £3.75), scampi (£3.95), ploughman's (from £4.25), lasagne or home-made pies (£4.50), several vegetarian dishes like lasagne or leek and mushroom crumble (£4.95) and 12oz sirloin (£8.25), and puddings including a selection of hot sponges or banana split (£1.95); usual children's meals (from £1.25); winter two-course special (£3.95). Very friendly landlord and staff. Darts, fruit machine, and piped music. A spacious barn behind the pub has been converted to self-catering accommodation. *(Reports on the new regime please)*

Free house ~ Licensees Ann and Chas Foster ~ Real ale ~ Meals and snacks (all day Sat in summer and Sun) ~ (01538) 304206 ~ Children welcome in family room ~ Open 12-3, 7-11; 12-11 summer Sats; 12-10.30 Sun ~ Self-catering barn (with two bedrooms, sleeps five): £25 a night for the whole unit

SALT SJ9527 Map 7
Holly Bush
Village signposted off A51 S of Stone (and A518 NE of Stafford)

The original part of this pretty thatched white-painted house dates back to the 14th c, and has a heavy beamed and planked ceiling (some of the beams attractively carved), a salt cupboard built in by the coal fire, and some nice old-fashioned touches – the antique pair of clothes brushes hanging by the door, attractive sporting prints and watercolours, the ancient pair of riding boots on the mantelpiece. Around the standing-room serving section several cosy areas spread off, including a modern back extension which tones in well; there are comfortable settees as well as more orthodox seats. Very well prepared tasty good value food, prepared as much as possible from fresh local produce, includes lunchtime sandwiches (from £1.55) and filled baked potatoes (from £2.35), as well as soup (£1.65), prawn cocktail (£3.10), fried cod, gammon steak (£5.20), steak and ale pie or Greek lamb (£5.45), mixed grill (£5.95), chicken piri piri (£6.20), with particularly good dishes of the day such as pork, leek and stilton or pork, ginger and apple sausages or rabbit casserole with herb dumplings (£5.95), red sea bream chargrilled with lime and oregano sauce, grilled fillet of salmon with lemongrass and pink peppercorn sauce, steak, kidney and oyster pudding or lamb liver with onions in a rich meat sauce (£6.95), grilled lamb steak with orange and brandy glaze (£7.50) and rack of lamb with fresh rosemary (£7.85); puddings (£2.25); Sunday roasts. Well kept Bass, Burtonwood Bitter and Forshaws on handpump, pleasant attentive staff, maybe piped nostalgic pop music; darts, shove-ha'penny, cribbage, backgammon, jenga, fruit machine. The big back lawn, where they may have traditional jazz and a hog roast in summer, has rustic picnic tables, a rope swing and a busy dovecot; this is an attractive village. *(Recommended by S J and C C Davidson, Peter and Jenny Quine, Dorothee and Dennis Glover, Gordon Tong, Chris Raisin)*

Free house ~ Licensee Geoffrey Holland ~ Real ale ~ Meals and snacks (all day Sunday) ~ (01889) 508234 ~ Children in eating area of bar till 8.30pm ~ Open 12-2.30, 6-11; 12-11 Sat; 12-10.30 Sun

SHRALEYBROOK SJ7850 Map 7
Rising Sun ◖

3 miles from M6 junction 16; from A500 towards Stoke take first right turn signposted
Alsager, Audley; in Audley turn right on the road still shown on many maps as a A52, but now
in fact a B, signposted Balterley, Nantwich; pub then signposted on left (at the T-junction
look out for the Watneys Red Barrel)

Making up part of an impressive range of drinks served at this easy-going pub are the
appropriately named Rising, Setting and Porter, which are produced in the brew house
behind the pub, and are well kept alongside four guests like Batemans XXXB, Burton
Bridge Festival, Fullers London Pride, Greene King Abbot. There are also over 120
malts, 12 cognacs and 100 liqueurs; and foreign beers from Belgium, Germany, Spain,
and India. Simple but generous bar food includes omelettes (from £3.80), pizzas (from
£4), cheeseburger (£4), beef casserole or 17 vegetarian pot meals (£7), and seafood
platter or lasagne (£7.50); friendly service. The well worn, casual bar has shiny black
panelling and beams and timbers in the ochre walls, red leatherette seats tucked into
the timberwork and cosy alcoves, brasses and some netting, dim lighting, curtains
made from beer towels sewn together, and a warm open fire. Dominoes, fruit machine
and piped music; camping in two paddocks. *(Recommended by Andy and Jill Kassube, Dr A
C Williams, Dr F M Ellard, Richard Houghton, Sue Holland, Dave Webster, Richard Lewis,
Wayne Brindle, Esther and John Sprinkle, Mike and Wendy Proctor)*

*Own brew ~ Licensee Mrs Gillian Holland ~ Real ale ~ Meals and snacks (till 10pm)
~ Restaurant ~ (01782) 720600 ~ Children welcome ~ Folk music second and fourth
Thurs in month ~ Open 12-3.30, 6.30-11; 12-11(10.30 Sun) Fri, Sat and bank
holidays*

TUTBURY SK2028 Map 7
Olde Dog & Partridge ⊨

A444 N of Burton on Trent

The carvery restaurant at this civilised 15th-c dining pub is particularly popular, with
roast of the day at £7.50 and prime sirloin of beef with big yorkshire pudding £8.50.
A pianist plays every evening in the big, softly lit partly no-smoking carvery, and you
need to arrive early to be sure of a table, especially in one of the snugger corners.
There's a separate short bar menu including soup (£1.50), cheddar platter (£2.95),
pork and crackling or beef bap (from £2.95) and venison sausage (£3.35); puddings
are from the cold counter in the carvery (from £2.35). The stylish but pleasantly
pubby bar has two warm turkey-carpeted rooms, one with red plush banquettes,
brocaded stools, sporting pictures, stags' heads and a sizeable tapestry, the other with
a plush-cushioned oak settle, an attractive built-in window seat, brocaded stools and a
couple of Cecil Aldin hunting prints. Well kept Marstons Pedigree and a guest beer
from the oak bar counter, freshly squeezed fruit juices and decent wines; friendly
efficient service; piped music. The half timbered frontage is prettily hung with hanging
baskets and the neat garden has white cast-iron seats and tables under cocktail
parasols, with stone steps between its lawns, bedding plants, roses and trees. The pub
is near Tutbury Castle, where Mary Queen of Scots was imprisoned on the orders of
Elizabeth I. The quiet bedrooms are in a separate building across the drive.
*(Recommended by D Green, Peter and Audrey Dowsett, Martin Bromfield, Bernadette Garner,
Peter and Patricia Burton, O K Smyth, John and Doreen Crowder, William Cissna)*

*Free house ~ Licensees Andrea and Michael Mortimer ~ Real ale ~ Meals and snacks
(not Sun lunchtime) ~ Carvery ~ (01283) 813030 ~ Children welcome ~ Pianist
evenings and Sunday lunch ~ Open 11-3, 6-11; 11.45-11 Sun; cl 25, 26 Dec and 1 Jan
evenings ~ Bedrooms: £55B/£72B*

Anyone claiming to arrange or prevent inclusion of a pub in the *Guide* is a
fraud. Pubs are included only if recommended by genuine readers and if our
own anonymous inspection confirms that they are suitable.

UTTOXETER SK0933 Map 7
Wellington ♀ ◧

High St, opposite cinema

It's probably unique to find the Orthodox Divine Liturgy served in a function room above a pub on Sunday, but this is no ordinary pub. The superficialities are interesting enough, especially the fine collection of antique Waterloo prints in the left-hand room, and the pair of six-pounder cannon. Then there's the *Church Times* (Dr Miln, the landlord, complete with beard and pince-nez, doubles as an Orthodox Priest) and a Belgian newspaper (Dr Miln's family hails from Bruges) alongside the rack of local and other papers. In the yard behind, with its row of flower-planted lavatory bowls (the Waterloos), there's a Welsh Mountain Grey (called Copenhagen, after the Iron Duke's mount), a Shetland called Marengo, Marshal Blucher the ferret and Marshal Ney, a fine cockerel that heads a court of ladies who provide eggs for breakfast. Bar furnishings are simple and traditional, with coal fires; unobtrusive piped music (not always on) varies from Classic FM through 1960s country & western to Welsh male voice choirs. The handsome greyhound Josephine keeps a gentle eye on things from her protected seat, whilst General Picton, the house feline, is fond of a place by the fire; dominoes, cribbage, shove-ha'penny, board games and boules. Preserving a 17th-c tradition, this is still the home of the Uttoxeter Lunar Society. There are a dozen or so Belgian beers alongside the very well kept Bass on handpump. Bar food includes baguettes (90p), faggots and chips (£3), veal goulash (£4.50), mussels and chips (£5) and steak and chips (£6). The house wines are good. *(Recommended by Peter Marshall, Dave Irving, Sue Holland, Dave Webster; more reports please)*

Inn Business Ltd ~ Tenant Revd Dr Peter Miln ~ Real ale ~ Meals and snacks (11.30-2, 7-10; not Sun lunch) ~ Restaurant ~ (01889) 562616 ~ Well behaved children welcome ~ Open 10.30-11; 12-10.30 Sun ~ Bedrooms: £16/£32

WARSLOW SK0858 Map 7
Greyhound ⇔

B5053 S of Buxton

Visitors are made to feel like locals at this plain but cheerily welcoming slated stone pub which is handy for the Manifold Valley, Alton Towers and Dovedale. The cosy long beamed bar has cushioned oak antique settles (some quite elegant), a log fire, houseplants in the windows, and quietly restrained landscapes on the cream walls. The pool room has darts, dominoes, cribbage, and fruit machine; piped classical music at lunchtimes. Big helpings of good home-made bar food include sandwiches (from £1.80), filled baked potatoes (from £3.25), ploughman's (from £4.50), with blackboard specials like soup (£1.90), butterfly prawns with garlic dip or prawn cocktail (£3), chicken in leek and stilton sauce, venison casserole, pork and peaches in peppercorn sauce, game pie, pork and mushrooms in wholegrain mustard sauce, smoked haddock and prawn mornay and vegetable provençal (£5.50-£6.50). Beware as they do end food service promptly according to the times below – no leeway if you're a few minutes late. Well kept Marstons Pedigree and a guest beer such as Everards Tiger or Timothy Taylors Landlord on handpump. There are picnic tables under ash trees in the side garden, with rustic seats out in front. The simple bedrooms are comfortable and clean, and breakfasts good. The licensees also run the Devonshire Arms in Hartington. *(Recommended by Paul and Maggie Baker, Anthony Barnes, David Carr, Derek and Sylvia Stephenson, Dennis Stevens, Mike and Wendy Proctor, James Waller, Eric Locker)*

Free house ~ Licensees David and Dale Mullarkey ~ Real ale ~ Meals and snacks ~ (01298) 84249 ~ Children welcome ~ Live bands Sat night ~ Open 12-2.30(3 Sat), 7-11; 12-3, 7-10.30 Sun; cl Mon and Tues lunchtime (not bank holidays) Oct-May ~ Bedrooms: £16.50/£33

WETTON SK1055 Map 7

Olde Royal Oak 🍺

One reader tells us that this welcoming old family-run pub hasn't changed since he last drank there 53 years ago – although we're not sure that it was famous back then for their toe wrestling championships (held on the first Saturday in June) which have recently begun receiving world wide publicity: it seems regulars are keen on the sport. As a tribute to the importance of this event Black Bull (in nearby Fenny Bentley) brews a beer for them which you can taste all year, called Anklecracker. There's also well kept Ruddles County and Rutland, Theakstons XB and a weekly guest beer on handpump, about 18 malt whiskies, Addlestone's cider and two wines of the month. There's a good mix of locals and visitors, and a timelessly relaxed atmosphere in the older part of the building which has black beams – hung with golf clubs – supporting the white ceiling boards, small dining chairs sitting around rustic tables, a piano surrounded by old sheet music covers, an oak corner cupboard, and a log fire in the stone fireplace; this room extends into a more modern-feeling area with another fire which in turn leads to a carpeted sun lounge looking out on to the small garden. Hearty bar food includes sandwiches (from £1.45), home-made mince and onion pie (£4.95), local trout (£5.45), plaice filled with prawns and mushrooms (£5.85) and fresh gammon (£6.25). Darts, dominoes, cribbage, shove-ha'penny and piped music. Places like Wetton Mill and the Manifold Valley are nearby, and behind the pub is a croft suitable for caravans and tents. *(Recommended by Paul Robinshaw, Paul Barnett, David Carr, Mike and Wendy Proctor, Janet and Peter Race, Mike Gorton, Ron Gentry, Jack and Philip Paxton, Gill and Maurice McMahon, Chris and Angela Wells, Richard Houghton)*

Free house ~ Licensee George Burgess ~ Real ale ~ Meals and snacks ~ (01335) 310287 ~ Children welcome in family room ~ Open 12(11.30 Sat)-3, 6.30-11; 12-3, 6.30-10.30 Sun; 12-2, 7-11 in winter ~ Bedrooms: /£35S

Lucky Dip

Besides the fully inspected pubs, you might like to try these Lucky Dips recommended to us and described by readers (if you do, please send us reports):

☆ **Abbots Bromley** [Mkt Pl; SK0724], *Crown*: Welcoming much modernised lounge and bright public bar with games, food freshly cooked to order inc vegetarian and fish, well kept Banks's Mild and Fullers London Pride, entertaining licensees, good service; big mural of the pretty village's famous ancient Horn Dance (first Mon after first Sun in Sept); children welcome, good value clean bedrooms *(Kate and Robert Hodkinson, William Cissna, Richard Lambert, Eric Locker, DC, B R Dunn, LYM)*
Abbots Bromley [High St], *Coach & Horses*: Comfortable Tudor village pub with good helpings of well prepared food, veg extra, in refurbished beamed bar and restaurant, well kept Bass and related beers, friendly young staff, pleasant garden; good value bedrooms *(J Curtis, G Hughes, SLC);* [Bagot St], *Royal Oak*: Wide choice of good imaginative food in clean, comfortable and attractive dining lounge (worth booking), well kept Marstons and a guest ale, good wine, efficient friendly service, open fire, interesting restaurant *(Tricia and Geoff Alderman)*

☆ **Alrewas** [High St (off A38); SK1715], *George & Dragon*: Three friendly low-beamed linked rooms with consistently well kept Marstons Pedigree, good value generous bar food (not Sun) inc children's dishes, efficient staff,

attractive paintings; piped music; pleasant partly covered garden with good play area, children welcome in eating area; opens at 5 weekdays *(Graham Richardson, LYM)*
Alton [SK0742], *Talbot*: Welcoming stone-built pub, small and cosy, with well kept beer, good choice of varied food *(Mike and Wendy Proctor)*
Appleby Parva [A444; under a mile from M42 junction 11; SK3109], *Appleby*: Well run hotelish family pub, good value food in restaurant and spacious lounge (coach parties sometimes); motel bedrooms, six suited to disabled; handy for Twycross Zoo, open all day *(Graham Richardson, SB)*
Audley [Bignall End; SJ7951], *Plough*: Particularly well kept Banks's, Marstons Pedigree and interesting guest beers from customers' wish list, good range of food (not Sun evening) in dining area off lounge, lots of flowers outside; can get smoky, parking not always easy *(Richard Lewis, Andy and Jill Kassube, Sue Holland, Dave Webster);* [Nantwich Rd], *Potters Lodge*: Comfortable friendly family pub, well kept Whitbreads-related ales inc a seasonal special, wide choice of generous food inc children's, no-smoking areas; play area, open all day *(Richard Lewis, Sue Holland, Dave Webster)*
Balterley [Newcastle Rd (A531); SJ7650],

Broughton Arms: Busy Greenalls pub, clean and airy, with comfortable low-ceilinged lounge, nice decor, prints, real fire; wide choice of generous well served bar food, back restaurant, friendly staff, well kept Tetleys-related ales *(Richard Lewis)*

Brocton [A34 Stafford—Cannock; SJ9619], *Seven Stars*: Big Steak pub with big indoor children's play area, well kept Ansells and Burtonwood, good service, reliable food up to 24oz steaks *(John and Chris Simpson)*

Burslem [off Leek Rd; SJ8749], *Vine*: Big comfortable local with back bar, well kept Scottish Courage and other ales such as Joules Old Priory, friendly staff *(Richard Lewis)*

Burton on Trent [51 Derby St; SK2423], *Alfred*: Tied to local small Burton Bridge brewery, wide range of their ales kept well; bare boards, pleasant seating, raised side lounge/eating area, back pool room, friendly landlord, good menu, lots of country wines; cheap bedrooms *(Richard Lewis)*; [Cross St], *Coopers Tavern*: Fine example of traditional counterless back tap room with notably well kept Bass, Hardys & Hansons Classic, Best and Mild and Marstons Pedigree straight from imposing row of casks, barrel tables, cheap nourishing lunchtime hot filled cobs, pie and chips etc (not Sun), comfortable front lounge with piano and coal fire, very friendly staff *(Richard Lewis, LYM)*; [63 Uxbridge St], *Oddfellows Arms*: Small basic friendly local with bottled beer collection, emphasis games, well kept Marstons Pedigree *(Richard Lewis)*; [Station St], *Roebuck*: Comfortable tap for Ind Coope brewery with lots of well kept Tetleys-related ales and interesting changing guests, good value food, friendly staff, prints and artefacts; piped music, open all day weekdays; decent bedrooms *(Richard Lewis)*; [Anglesey Rd], *Thomas Sykes*: In former stables and waggon shed of ex-Everards brewery (latterly Heritage Brewery Museum), two high-ceilinged rooms with stable fittings and breweriana, wood benches, cobbled floors, well kept changing beers inc Marstons Pedigree and Owd Rodger, fine pumpclip collection, good cheap basic food *(Richard Lewis)*

☆ **Butterton** [signed off B5053; SK0756], *Black Lion*: Charming homely and atmospheric low-beamed 18th-c stone inn in Peak District conservation village, fine old traditional furnishings, log fire, kitchen range in inner room, seven real ales, reasonably priced standard food, pleasant bistro; well lit pool room, darts, trivia etc, piped music (may be loud), TV; new licensees still settling in at this fine pub as we go to press; comfortable bedrooms; cl Weds lunchtime *(DA, Joan and Tony Walker, LYM; more reports please)*

Cauldon Lowe [Waterhouses; A52 Stoke—Ashbourne; SK0748], *Cross*: Unsmart but attractive and friendly, with well kept beers and decent food inc vegetarian, reasonable prices, scenic setting *(Mike and Wendy Proctor)*

☆ **Cheddleton** [Basford Bridge Lane, off A520; SJ9651], *Boat*: Cheerful local with neat long bar, low plank ceilings, particularly well kept Marstons and other ales, good value simple food, interesting pictures, attractive fireplace in airy extension; handy for flint mill, railway museum and country park; children welcome, fairy-lit tables outside overlooking canal *(Mike and Wendy Proctor, John Beeken, Bill Sykes, LYM)*

☆ **Consall** [Consallforge; best approach from Nature Pk, off A522 – OS Sheet 118 map ref 000491; SJ9748], *Black Lion*: Country tavern tucked away in rustic old-fashioned canalside settlement; smartened up but still traditional, with good generous cheap food, good coal fire, well kept Marstons Bitter and Pedigree, Titanic and other guest beers such as Morlands Old Speckled Hen, friendly landlady, traditional games, piped music; children (but not muddy boots) welcome; busy weekends, good walking area *(Bill Sykes, Mike and Wendy Proctor, LYM)*

☆ **Dovedale** [Thorpe—Ilam rd; Ilam signed off A52, Thorpe off A515, NW of Ashbourne; SK1452], *Izaak Walton*: Relaxing and informal low-beamed bar in sizeable hotel, some distinctive antique oak settles and chairs, good log fire in massive central stone chimney; Ind Coope Burton and two other ales, ample nicely presented food in bar and restaurant, morning coffee and afternoon tea; very tranquil spot – seats on spacious well kept lawn by sheep pastures, superb views; bedrooms comfortable *(Mike and Wendy Proctor, B and M Parkin, LYM)*

☆ **Eccleshall** [Castle St; SJ8329], *St George*: Good generous home-cooked food in hotel's comfortably pubby beamed bar with old prints and open fire, or attractive bistro; good wines, interesting guest beers and, brewed here by friendly landlord, several good Slaters ales; comfortable individually decorated bedrooms *(Sue Holland, Dave Webster, John Scarisbrick)*

☆ **nr Endon** [Denford, some way E, off A53 SW of Leek; SJ9553], *Holly Bush*: Friendly staff, wide range of well kept ale, good value food from sandwiches up; nice rural position on Caldon Canal, very busy in summer *(Mike and Wendy Proctor, Sue Holland, Dave Webster)*

Enville [A458 W of Stourbridge; SO8286], *Cat*: Mainly 17th c, with four friendly bar areas, cheerful fire, very wide choice of ales inc local Enville, mulled wine, decent food with unusual specials, popular upstairs restaurant; has been cl Sun, popular with walkers – on Staffordshire Way *(Martin and Karen Wake, C Smith)*

☆ **Etruria** [Hanley rd (off A53 opp Festival site); SJ8647], *Plough*: Small busy two-room pub, nice atmosphere and decor, coal fire, five well kept Robinsons beers inc Old Tom and Fredericks, friendly licensees, wide choice of food served till late esp steaks and hot sandwiches, will do anything on request; busy lunchtime and weekends *(Sue Holland, Dave Webster, Richard Lewis, Mike and Wendy Proctor)*

☆ **Fradley** [Fradley Park signed off A38 Burton—Lichfield, OS Sheet 128 map ref 140140; SK1414], *Swan*: Cheery pub in picturesque canalside spot, very popular summer weekends; wide choice of quickly served food from sandwiches to Sun lunch inc vegetarian, friendly service, well kept Tetleys-related ales inc Mild, traditional public bar, quieter plusher lounge and lower vaulted back bar (where children allowed), lots of malt whiskies, real fire, cribbage, dominoes, piped music; waterside tables, good canal walks *(Mrs P J Pearce, Chris Raisin, D A Goult, Colin Fisher, S P Watkin, P A Taylor, LYM)*

Fradley [Ryknield St (A38); *Fradley Arms*: Greenalls Millers Kitchen family dining pub, with sizeable indoor playroom as well as play area outside, but nice pubby feel, good service and very civilised range of food; comfortable modern bedrooms *(E G Parish)*

☆ **Hanley** [65 Lichfield St; SJ8747], *Coachmakers Arms*: Unpretentious unchanging friendly town local, three small rooms and drinking corridor, well kept Bass and Worthington, popular darts, cards and dominoes, skittles *(Pete Baker, Sue Holland, Dave Webster)*

Hartshill [296 Hartshill Rd (A52); SJ8545], *Jolly Potters*: Unspoilt local, well kept Bass and M&B Mild, simple snacks, four little rooms off drinking corridor *(Sue Holland, Dave Webster, Nigel Woolliscroft)*

Haughton [Newport Rd (A518); SJ8620], *Shropshire*: Tastefully modernised, part of lounge showing barn rafters, friendly efficient service, wide range of enjoyable food, well kept Ind Coope Burton, relaxed atmosphere, pleasant garden *(Paul and Maggie Baker)*

☆ **Hednesford** [Mount St; SJ9913], *West Cannock*: Wide choice of well kept reasonably priced beers and good value food in cosy Victorian-style pub, good friendly service; tables outside *(John and Chris Simpson)*

Hill Chorlton [Stone Rd (A51); SJ7939], *Slaters*: Comfortable beamed bar, good standard bar food from sandwiches up inc vegetarian and Sun roasts, well kept Ansells Mild, Boddingtons and Marstons Pedigree, decent wines, upstairs restaurant, children's room; tables out in attractive garden, animals in barn; bedrooms *(Miss S Watkin, P Taylor)*

☆ **Hollington** [the one between Alton and Uttoxeter; SK0538], *Raddle*: Quiet extended country pub with good generous bar food inc vegetarian and children's, well kept Bass, Boddingtons, Ind Coope Burton and Whitbreads, neatly modernised rambling bar pleasantly decorated with horsebrasses etc, sizeable upstairs family room with own servery, helpful young staff; sweeping views from garden with big play area *(William D Cissna, BB)*

Hopwas [Hints Rd; SK1704], *Tame Otter*: Former Chequers, reopened end 1995 after rustic refurbishment, three fires, easy chairs, settles, dining chairs, nooks and alcoves, old photographs and canalia, friendly service,

reasonably priced food all day, good choice of wines, malt whiskies and real ales *(S P Watkin, P A Taylor, BB)*

☆ **Huddlesford** [off A38 2 miles E of Lichfield; SK1509], *Plough*: Extended and refurbished Greenalls dining pub with wide choice of good value generous food from sandwiches to seafood and Sun roasts in four eating areas, well kept Bass, Greenalls Original and guest beers tapped from the cask, good range of wines, attentive young staff, games area; attractive hanging baskets, tables out by canal *(Colin Fisher, David R Shillitoe, Mark Sutcliffe, Dorothee and Dennis Glover)*

☆ **Hulme End** [SK1059], *Manifold*: Welcoming 18th-c country pub nr river, doing well after refurbishment by new landlord – formerly at main entry Watts Russell Arms at Alstonefield; spacious lounge bar with open fire, well kept real ales, generous popular food inc Sun lunch, separate dining room; children and cyclists welcome; new bedrooms in converted stone smithy in secluded back courtyard, disabled facilities *(Paul Robinshaw, Dennis Stevens, BB)*

Ipstones [B5053, signed from A52 and A523; SK0249], *Red Lion*: Pleasant and comfortable, roaring coal fire, low ceilings, lots of brass, valley view, friendly helpful service, well kept Marstons Pedigree and Theakstons Best, generous food from sandwiches up, end games area; tables outside; bedrooms, generous breakfast *(Esther and John Sprinkle, Richard Lewis, LYM)*; *Marquis of Granby*: Small friendly local, basic but cosy, well kept Bass and rare Bass Mild, snacks *(Richard Lewis)*

Keele [A525 W of Newcastle-under-Lyme; SJ8045], *Sneyd Arms*: Solid 19th-c stone building, formerly local court; Tetleys-related ales, wide choice of lunchtime food inc fish, friendly staff, good landlord; cribbage, pool, popular with students and conference delegates *(Richard Lewis, Sue Holland, Dave Webster)*

Knighton [B5415 Woore—Mkt Drayton; SJ7240], *White Lion*: Good food with French influence beautifully presented in cosy dining area, conservatory and (not Mon or Sun evening) restaurant; also big bar with well kept Marstons and guests, large adventure playground *(SLC, Gail Kendall, Kent Miller)*

☆ **Leek** [St Edward St; SJ9856], *Swan*: Comfortable old three-room pub with good reasonably priced lunchtime food, pleasant helpful staff, no-smoking lounge, well kept Bass and guest ales, occasional beer festivals, lots of malt whiskies, choice of coffees; now has downstairs wine bar; folk club, seats in courtyard *(John Scarisbrick, Mike and Wendy Proctor, Sue Holland, Dave Webster, Richard Houghton)*

Leek [St Edward St], *Den Engel*: Over 40 Belgian beers, bottled and draught, in former bank with foreign-bar feel, waitress service (good food all day); also Ash Vine Hell for Leather, Batemans Draymans Tipple *(Richard Lewis)*; [Sheep Market], *Market*: Bare boards, prints on painted walls, comfortable seating, good cheap food, well kept Marstons Coopers, Best and Pedigree; open all day *(Richard Lewis)*; [Blackshaw Moor (A53 NNE)], *Three Horseshoes*: Large well appointed pub, lots of nooks and crannies, good atmosphere, open fire, no-smoking area, children's area, restaurant, young friendly staff, generous food inc self-service veg, good puddings, good range of real ales *(B and M Parkin)*; [off St Edward St], *Valiant*: Comfortable Marstons local, also well kept Bass and Timothy Taylors Landlord, friendly staff *(Richard Lewis)*; [St Edward St], *Wilkes Head*: Basic friendly two-room local with well kept Whim and interesting guest ales, good choice of whiskies, pub games; children welcome, tables outside *(Richard Lewis, Sue Holland, Dave Webster)*

☆ Lichfield [Tamworth St; SK1109], *Pig & Truffle*: Nicely decorated panelled dining pub, friendly and enthusiastic landlady, good value well thought out menu, well kept ales, good coffee, seats in sunny back yard; piped music; no food Fri-Sun evenings when more a younger person's preserve *(Paul and Ursula Randall, S P Watkin, P A Taylor)*

☆ Lichfield [Market St], *Scales*: Cosy traditional oak-panelled bar with wooden flooring, screens, gas lights, sepia photographs of old Lichfield; welcoming service, reasonably priced food, well kept Bass, related ales and interesting guest beers, daily papers, darts; piped music, machines; suntrap back courtyard *(Richard Lewis, CMW, JJW, LYM)* Lichfield [Christ Church Lane (off A461 W)], *Carpenters Arms*: Banks's local with low-cost real ale, picnic tables in quiet new garden with lawn and high-rise rabbit hutches, also a couple of dogs; bar food inc bacon sandwiches, darts; sweets and soft drinks for children *(T G Thomas)*; [14 Queen St], *Queens Head*: Marstons alehouse-theme pub with their own and well kept guest beers, bare boards and comfortable old wooden furniture, short but interesting range of well-cooked daily specials and vast choice of unusual cheeses with sour-dough bread or muffins, huge helpings (doggy bags provided) at very reasonable prices; friendly staff *(Dr and Mrs M Beale, Miss S Watkin, P Taylor, Richard Lewis)*

☆ Little Bridgeford [nr M6 junction 14; right off A5013 at Little Bridgeford; SJ8727], *Worston Mill*: Popular family dining pub, spacious and welcoming, in attractively converted 1814 watermill, wheel and gear still preserved; lots of oak and leather, well kept Marstons Pedigree and other ales, good value wine, wide choice of reasonably priced good food from sandwiches up, polite efficient staff, conservatory, children well cared for inside and out – attractive garden with adventure playground and nature trail (lakes, islands etc) *(Richard Lewis, S J and C C Davidson, LYM)*

☆ Newcastle under Lyme [High St; SJ8445], *Golden Lion*: Good value simple home

cooking weekdays in comfortably modernised but old-fashioned unpretentious pub with well kept Bass; handy for open market, haven for rugby players Fri/Sat *(Sue Holland, Dave Webster, Tony Kemp, Rachel Weston)*

☆ Penkhull [Manor Court St; SJ8644], *Greyhound*: Relaxed traditional two-room pub in hilltop 'village', particularly good value filling snacks, well kept Marstons Pedigree and Tetleys; children in eating area, picnic tables on back terrace *(Sue Holland, Dave Webster, LYM)* Penkridge [Market St; SJ9214], *Horse & Jockey*: Friendly licensees, good service, changing guest beer, food lunchtime and evening *(John and Chris Simpson)* Ranton [SJ8422], *Hand & Cleaver*: Tastefully extended recently redecorated country pub with lots of exposed timber, quiet atmosphere, food in bar and restaurant, several real ales *(Paul and Maggie Baker)*

☆ Rolleston on Dove [Church Rd; SK2427], *Spread Eagle*: Attractive old village pub with good range of well kept Bass-related ales, good value food all day, small restaurant with fresh fish, popular Sunday carvery; pleasant garden, nice village *(Stephen and Jane Asbury, C Campling)* Rugeley [A51/A513 NW; SK0220], *Wolseley Arms*: Large and busy, good atmosphere, decent beer, good straightforward food, handy for canal *(Kate and Robert Hodkinson)* Shebden [signed off A519 N of Newport; SJ7626], *Wharf*: No-nonsense family pub, wide choice of good value simple food and of guest beers, welcoming landlord, bar billiards, games machines; children welcome, big garden and playground, nr canal; cl winter lunchtimes *(John and Shirley Dyson, Nigel Woolliscroft)* Shenstone [A5127 S of Lichfield; SK1004], *Black Bull*: Roomily refurbished Bass pub with flagstones, bare bricks, panelling, old pine tables and mixed chairs, good value food inc fish and chips, good welcoming food service even when busy, well kept Bass, M&B Brew XI and Highgate Dark; children welcome *(Basil Minson, Irene and Geoffrey Lindley)*

☆ Stafford [turn right at main entrance to station, 100 yards down], *Stafford Arms*: Busy but friendly and relaxing real-ale pub with full Titanic range well kept and interesting changing small-brewery guests, farm cider, cheap simple food (all day weekdays; not Sun evening or Sat), chatty staff, wide range of customers (no under-21s – exc babies); Titanic memorabilia, bar billiards, juke box, skittle alley; barbecues and live bands during summer beer festivals; open all day, can be very busy *(Richard Lewis, G Coates)* Stafford [Eastgate St], *Forester & Firkin*: Typical bare floorboards, lots of barrels, print and brewery artefacts, beer mats on walls; friendly staff, well kept beer, music evenings *(Richard Lewis)*; [Eastgate St], *Lord Nelson*: Big bustling local with well kept ales such as cheap Flowers IPA, Mitchells, Newcastle Exhibition, Theakstons Best, XB and Old Peculier and Youngers No 3 and IPA, farm ciders, open fires, friendly staff, limited food; open all day weekdays *(Richard Lewis, S J and C C Davidson)*; [Mill St], *Nags Head*: Friendly town local, well kept Bass, Highgate Old, Worthington Best and a guest such as Vaux Waggle Dance, popular lunchtime for good choice of food inc vegetarian and cheap steaks; late evening loud juke box for young people *(Richard Lewis)*; [Bridge St], *Picture House*: Splendid Wetherspoons conversion of Grade II listed former cinema, good choice of well kept ales inc interesting ones and a farm cider, lots of comfortable seating, no-smoking areas, good choice of food all day, friendly efficient staff *(Richard Lewis)*; [Peel Terr, just off B5066], *Tap & Spile*: Constantly changing real ales, country wines, friendly new landlord, bare boards and bricks with lots of prints; pool, traditional games *(S J and C C Davidson)*

Stanley Moor [Stanley Rd; off A53 Stoke—Leek; SJ9351], *Rose & Crown*: Nice decor, esp at Christmas; good value home-cooked lunchtime food, well kept Marstons ales *(Mr and Mrs C Woodings)*

Stoke on Trent [259 King St, Fenton; SJ8944], *Malt 'n' Hops*: Comfortable, with nice atmosphere, good choice of real ales *(Richard Houghton)*; [Hill St], *Staff of Life*: Character Bass city local, welcoming even when packed, unchanging layout of three rooms and small drinking corridor; well kept ales *(SH, DW, PB)*; [Shelton], *Tap & Spile*: Lots of wood but comfortable, good choice of changing well kept beers, perry, wide choice of good value food, friendly staff and locals, enough artefacts for a pub museum *(Richard Lewis, NW, SH, DW)*

☆ **Swynnerton** [signed off A51 Stone—Nantwich; SJ8535], *Fitzherbert Arms*: Good interesting food inc ostrich and kangaroo in traditional friendly country pub, log fires, well kept Bass, separate dining area; lovely village setting *(Peter Astbury, S J and C C Davidson)*

Tamworth [Lichfield St; SK2004], *Boot*: Roomy and pleasantly decorated Marstons pub, plenty of tables in various areas, lots of prints, friendly staff, well kept Pedigree and Stout, food, wheelchair access; juke box; open all day *(Richard Lewis)*; [George St], *Bow Street Runner*: Recently refurbished part of hotel, tasteful decor with smoked wood-effect wallpaper, lots of comfortable seating, pleasant mix of carpets and bare boards, plenty of decoration; well kept Mansfield Bitter and Old Baily, food, friendly staff, happy hour reductions; bedrooms *(Richard Lewis)*; [Cliff (A51 S)], *Malt House*: Marstons Tavern Table chain food pub; good value, quick service, dining areas off bar, no-smoking room, Marstons Pedigree; piped music; small garden and play area; bedrooms *(CMW, JJW)*; [Lichfield St], *Three Tuns*: Busy but relaxing, with well

kept Bass, M&B Mild and Brew XI and Ruddles County, cosy lounge, friendly staff and locals, separate bar with pool, darts, TV etc *(Richard Lewis)*; [Albert Rd/Victoria Rd, nr stn], *Tweeddale Arms*: Traditional and homely with very well kept Bass, M&B Mild and Brew XI, comfortable lounge, friendly staff, limited food, fruit machine, juke box *(Richard Lewis)*; [Aldergate], *White Lion*: Large and imposing, with well kept Banks's Bitter and Mild and Marstons Pedigree, darts in long lounge, pool room, friendly staff, lunchtime food; open all day Fri/Sat *(Richard Lewis)*

☆ **Tatenhill** [off A38 W of Burton via A5121, then signed; SK2021], *Horseshoe*: Pleasant garden view from back family area, tiled-floor civilised bar, snug side area with woodburner, cosy partly no-smoking two-level restaurant; good value bar food (all day Sat) from sandwiches to steaks inc vegetarian and children's, well kept Marstons Pedigree and Owd Rodger, quick polite service; good play area *(Michael and Hazel Lyons, Dennis and Dorothee Glover, Andy and Jill Kassube, LYM)*

Teanford [Cheadle Rd; SK0040], *Ship*: Small local with good food, all home-made *(Mrs F M Orchard)*

Tutbury [Burton Rd; SK2028], *Cross Keys*: Well kept Ind Coope Burton, Morlands Old Speckled Hen and Tetleys, good reasonably priced bar food, not so cheap restaurant; popular with brewery staff *(K Lorriman)*

Upper Hulme [SK0161], *Rock*: Most people here to eat – good changing choice, low prices *(Mr and Mrs C Woodings)*

Waterfall [SK0851], *Red Lion*: Friendly old stone pub in quiet Peak village, good log fires in both adjoining rooms, separate restaurant; good value food from home-made pork pies to three-course meals, well kept Bass, friendly local licensees, horsebrasses; children welcome, good walking country *(C Randall, Christopher Joseph)*

☆ **Weston** [The Green, off A518; SJ9726], *Woolpack*: Well modernised, open-plan but separate areas with cosy corners, reasonably priced good fresh food, extended dining room, well kept Marstons and guest ales, smart pleasant staff, antique furniture inc high-backed settle, polished brass, secluded well tended garden *(Peter and Jenny Quine, S J and C C Davidson)*

☆ **Whitmore** [3 miles from M6 junction 15 – A53 towards Mkt Drayton; SJ8141], *Mainwaring Arms*: Popular old place of great character, rambling interconnected oak-beamed rooms, stone walls, four open fires, antique settles among more modern seats; well kept Bass, Boddingtons, Marstons Pedigree, wide range of foreign bottled beers and ciders, friendly service, seats outside, children in eating area, no piped music; open all day Fri/Sat, picturesque village *(Richard Gibbs, LYM)*

Whittington [the one nr Lichfield; SK1608], *Dog*: Extensively refurbished, with good bar food, warm welcome, well kept beers *(Paul Robinshaw)*

☆ **Wombourne** [High St, just off A449; SO8792], *Vine*: Tastefully modernised and extended Vintage Inn, popular good value bar food all day, inventive more expensive meals, huge helpings; well kept Bass and a guest such as Morlands Old Speckled Hen, unobtrusive piped music *(Paul and Sue Merrick, G Kernan)*

Wombourne [by Staffs & Worcs Canal], *Round Oak*: Welcoming, with good staff, simple well cooked food, well kept ale *(Anne Heaton)*

☆ **Wrinehill** [Den Lane; pub signed just off A531 Newcastle—Nantwich; SJ7547], *Crown*: Well kept Marstons Pedigree and Head Brewers Choice, Banks's Mild and guests such as Timothy Taylors Landlord, wide choice of good generous food inc vegetarian, in busy but cosy neatly refurbished beamed pub with friendly staff, plush seats but olde-worlde feel, interesting pictures, two log fires, well reproduced pop music; children allowed lunchtime, early evening; cl weekday lunchtimes exc bank hols; lovely floral displays in summer *(Richard Lewis, LYM)*

☆ **Yoxall** [Main St; SK1319], *Crown*: Excellent landlord, relaxed atmosphere, limited choice of good value fresh tasty food, well kept Marstons Pedigree, decent wines, quick friendly service, cosy refurbished lounge with log-effect gas fire, separate raised dining room; children welcome lunchtime *(Addie and Irene Henry, Michael and Hazel Lyons)*

Yoxall, *Golden Cup*: Refurbished and revitalised Victorian village pub doing well under new management, good bar food, well kept Marstons ales *(Norma and Keith Bloomfield)*

Real ale may be served from handpumps, electric pumps (not just the on-off switches used for keg beer) or – common in Scotland – tall taps called founts (pronounced 'fonts') where a separate pump pushes the beer up under air pressure. The landlord can adjust the force of the flow – a tight spigot gives the good creamy head that Yorkshire lads like.

Suffolk

Pubs currently doing really well in this favoured county include the Froize at Chillesford (excellent fresh fish, very good drinks, nice atmosphere – not cheap, but our choice as Suffolk Dining Pub of the Year), the welcoming and atmospheric Ship at Dunwich, the Crown at Great Glemham (good food, nice quiet place to stay), the Beehive at Horringer (a very popular dining pub), the Angel in Lavenham (outstanding all round), the Star at Lidgate (gains a Food Award this year), the Brewers Arms at Rattlesden (back in these pages after a break – the newish licensees settling into this dining pub very well now), the old-fashioned Plough at Rede (emphasis on game and fish), the Angel at Stoke by Nayland (excellent all round, imaginative food), and (another newcomer) the attractively renovated and reopened De La Pole Arms at Wingfield, tied to St Peters, a new small Suffolk brewery. Beers from another small brewery here, Scotts of Lowestoft, seem to be increasingly widely available, joining those from Adnams, Mauldons, Nethergate and Tolly, and their big brother Greene King. Despite such a strong array of local and regional brewers, drinks prices here are if anything slightly higher than the national average. There are some fine pubs to be found among the Lucky Dip entries at the end of the chapter; on their current form, we'd pick out the Bull at Cavendish, Swan at Clare, Kings Head at East Bergholt, Eels Foot at Eastbridge, Crown in Framlingham, Old Chequers at Friston, Kings Arms at Haughley, Black Tiles at Martlesham, and both Westleton entries (we have inspected and approved most of these). There's a good choice in Long Melford, an excellent one in Southwold, Adnams' home town, and for a very promising newcomer we'd point to the Cock at Polstead.

ALDEBURGH TM4656 Map 5
Cross Keys 🍺
Crabbe Street

New licensees have re-upholstered the furnishings, and added antique settles, lots of Victorian prints and copper and brass artefacts to the two communicating rooms – divided by a sturdy central chimney with woodburning stoves on either side – at this attractive old pub. There's a friendly, unchanging atmosphere and a good mix of customers from musicians to lifeboat crew and holidaymakers. Several readers have found it a bit too smoky, and although they do welcome children (see below) it doesn't have the most comfortable family accommodation. Very well kept Adnams Bitter, Broadside and Old Ale and Dark Mild in the summer on handpump. Plans are to extend the kitchen and increase the range of simple but good bar food – as we went to press the menu included soup (£2.50), tasty open sandwiches (from £3), kidney turbago (£6), pork in cider, lamb in apricot sauce or fish pie (£6.25), chicken curry (£6.50), excellent marinated hock of pork (£8.20) and seafood platter (£12.50); fruit machine. A courtyard at the back opens directly on to the promenade and shingle beach, and there are wooden seats and tables out here to take in the view; the hanging baskets are colourful in summer; they are planning to add three bedrooms with sea views by Easter. *(Recommended by PGP, P and M Pumfrey, Thomas Nott, Gwen and Peter Andrews, Geoffrey and Brenda Wilson, N S Smith, John Waller, June and Perry Dann)*

Adnams ~ Tenant Michael Clement ~ Real ale ~ Meals and snacks ~ (01728) 452637 ~ Children in eating area of bar during food serving hours ~ Open 11-3, 5.30-11; 12-3, 7-10.30 Sun; 11-11, 12-10.30 Sun in July/Aug

BARDWELL TL9473 Map 5

Six Bells ♀

Village signposted off A143 NE of Bury; keep straight through village, then fork right into Daveys Lane off top green

At the end of a track running off the green, this quietly placed and neatly kept 16th-c pub is a well run and peaceful retreat with good flexible caring service. The cosy bar has a comfortable mix of easy chairs and settees alongside other seats under its low heavy beams; its timbered walls have an attractive collection of decorative china, black and white etchings and old fashion plates, and the big fireplace has a coal-effect fire. The dining room to one side has been refurbished to serve as an additional bar with a coal-effect gas fire, exposed stone walls and mixed armchairs, pine carvers and pine tables. The bigger restaurant on the other side has a no-smoking conservatory beyond. A wide range of carefully cooked food includes soup (£2.55), lunchtime ploughman's (£3.50), Suffolk sausages with mustard, red wine and onion gravy and crusty bread (£3.95), salmon rosti spiced with ginger, chilli and coriander (£4.25), black pudding layered with potato pancakes, apple and caramelised onions and spicy dressing (£4.50), steak and kidney casserole with herb dumplings (£6.50), pork escalope with sausagemeat and apricot stuffing baked in puff pastry (£7.95), grilled chicken breast on cous cous with cucumber and mint salsa (£9.95), and puddings like filo basket filled with lemon mousse and orange sauce and fresh strawberry cream brûlée (£3.50); three course Sunday lunch (£9.95). Polite service; Adnams and Theakstons Best on handpump and a guest in the summer. As well as several malt whiskies they have five wines by the glass and about 40 by the bottle or half bottle; mulled wine in winter; maybe unobtrusive piped classical music; board games. There are picnic tables under cocktail parasols on a small front gravel terrace, and plastic tables on the back lawn, with a small wendy house and lots of young trees. Cottagey bedrooms in the converted barn and stables (which were used in a few episodes of *Dad's Army*) have country views. *(Recommended by Margaret and Nigel Dennis, Gwen and Peter Andrews, Ian Phillips, Pamela Goodwyn, Charles and Pauline Stride, M J Morgan, A H N Reade)*

Free house ~ Licensees Carol and Richard Salmon ~ Real ale ~ Meals and snacks ~ Restaurant ~ (01359) 250820 ~ Children welcome ~ Open 12-2, 6.30-10.30(11 Fri/Sat); 12-2.30, 6.30-10 Sun; cl 25-26 Dec ~ Bedrooms: £40S/£55S

BILDESTON TL9949 Map 5

Crown 🛏

104 High St (B1115 SW of Stowmarket)

The entertaining histories of the several ghosts at this handsome black and white timbered 15th-c inn are displayed on the cream walls. The pleasantly comfortable bar also has dark beams, dark wood tables with armchairs and wall banquettes upholstered to match the floral curtains, latticed windows, an inglenook fireplace (and a smaller more modern one with dried flowers). A good choice of well liked bar food includes sandwiches (from £1.95; three-tier ones from £3.95; toasties from £2.25), filled baked potatoes (from £2.50), ploughman's (£3.95), omelettes or roast leg of cajun-spiced chicken (from £4.95), spinach tagliatelle with tomato sauce (£5.25), home-made burger (£5.75), steaks (from £10.95), and daily specials such as cod in beer batter (£4.95), vegetable stroganoff, thai chicken or honey spiced lamb (£5.95), steak and kidney pie (£6.95) and lamb with apricots and cumin (£7.95). Well kept Adnams and Nethergate Bitter and a weekly changing guest like Ringwood Fortyniner or Wolf Granny Wouldn't Like It tapped straight from the cask; several malt whiskies, James White cider and fresh fruit juices. Darts, bar billiards, shove-ha'penny, table skittles, cribbage, dominoes, fruit machine, and piped music. *(Recommended by Patrick Trafford, Wayne Brindle, Mrs P Pearce, Charles and Penny Stride, Eric and Jackie Robinson)*

*Free house ~ Licensees Dinah and Ted Henderson ~ Real ale ~ Meals and snacks ~
Restaurant ~ (01449) 740510 ~ Well behaved children in eating area of bar ~ Open
11-2.30, 6-11; 12-3, 7-10.30 Sun; cl 25 Dec evening ~ Bedrooms:
£25(£35B)/£35(£55B)*

BLYFORD TM4277 Map 5
Queens Head
B1123

The beams at this beautifully thatched village pub really are low so be careful not to
bang your head. The unpretentious bustling and attractively furnished low-beamed
bar has some antique settles, pine and oak benches built into its cream walls, heavy
wooden tables and stools, and a huge fireplace filled with antique lamps and other
interesting implements. They still use water from the original well. Huge helpings of
popular country style food include lunchtime sandwiches, home-made soups such as
cheese and broccoli (£2.75), spinach and ricotta cannelloni (£5.65), fresh large
Lowestoft cod in batter (£6.95), very good steak and kidney pie (£7.10), whole roast
pheasant with brandy and burgundy sauce (£7.95), a whole leg of greek-style lamb
(£9.95), half a roast duck in a mango, peach and brandy sauce (£10.50) and Sunday
roast (£6.55); the restaurant is no smoking. Well kept Adnams Bitter, Mild, and
Broadside on handpump or tapped from the cask. There are seats on the grass outside,
and a good play area for children. The small village church is opposite, and another
church a mile south at Wenhaston has a fascinating 15th-c wall-painting.
*(Recommended by Gwen and Peter Andrews, David and Anne Culley, Robert Turnham, Mr and
Mrs Charles Gysin, P and M Pumfrey, J F Knutton, June and Perry Dann, Chris and Kate Lyons,
Sheila Keene, Beryl and Bill Farmer, Judy Booth, J E Hilditch, Malcolm Taylor, W W Burke,
Bernard and Becky Robinson)*

*Adnams ~ Tenant Tony Matthews ~ Real ale ~ Meals and snacks ~ Restaurant ~
(01502) 478404 ~ Children in restaurant only ~ Open 11-3, 6.30-11; 12-3, 7-10.30
Sun ~ Bedrooms: /£50*

BRANDESTON TM2460 Map 5
Queens Head
Towards Earl Soham

The simply decorated open-plan bar at this busy country local is divided into separate
bays by the stubs of surviving walls, and has some panelling, brown leather banquettes
and old pews. Good news is that the family room has been brightened up with fresh
paint; shove-ha'penny, cribbage, dominoes, and faint piped music. Good value bar
food includes sandwiches (from £1.50; hoagies from £2), soup (£2), ploughman's
(from £4.25), chilli or home-baked gammon and egg (£4.50), nut and mushroom
pancake (£4.25), home-made sausage and onion pie or lasagne (£4.95), steak, ale and
mushroom pie or all-day breakfast (£5.25), scampi (£5.50), and weekend evening
extras like warm stilton and bacon salad (£3.75) and plaice fillets stuffed with prawns
and mushrooms with lemon sauce (£7.25), and puddings (£2.50). Well kept Adnams
Bitter on handpump with Broadside, Mild and seasonal ales kept under light blanket
pressure; helpful staff. The big rolling garden – delightful in summer – has plenty of
tables on the neatly kept grass among large flowerbeds; also, a play tree, climbing
frame, and slide. The inn has a caravan and camping club site at the back. You can
visit the nearby cider farm. *(Recommended by I R Bell, J F Knutton, Pamela Goodwyn, Jenny
and Brian Seller, Howard Clutterbuck, Mrs P Goodwyn, Bill and Sheila McLardy, John Saul)*

*Adnams ~ Tenant Anthony Smith ~ Real ale ~ Meals and snacks (not Sun evenings) ~
(01728) 685307 ~ Children in family room ~ Jazz 3rd Mon in month ~ Open 11.30-
2.30, 6-11; 12-2.30, 7.10.30 Sun; cl 25 Dec, 26 Dec evening ~ Bedrooms: £17/£34*

Real ale to us means beer which has matured naturally in its cask – not
pressurised or filtered.

BUTLEY TM3651 Map 5
Oyster
B1084 E of Woodbridge

The licensee at this cheerful little country pub is including more game and unusual meats like kangaroo in his menu to provide an alternative to the many pubs in the area that are concentrating on fresh fish. Dishes might include chicken liver pâté (£3.25), New Zealand mussels or hot and spicy nibbles (£3.95), ploughman's (from £3.60), cumberland sausage (£4.95), steak and kidney or game pie (£5.95), lamb kleftiko (£7.95), venison with pepper sauce (£8.95) and lobster or seafood platter (£12.95); children's helpings (£2.95), puddings (£2.25), and Sunday roast (£4.95). The low ceilinged, relaxed and airy bar has a pair of good coal fires in fine Victorian fireplaces, a medley of stripped pine tables, stripped pews, high-backed settles and more orthodox seats, and a spinning dial hanging below one of the very heavy beams, for deciding who'll buy the next round – the Adnams Bitter, Mild, Broadside and their seasonal beer on handpump is well kept. Friendly staff; darts. The back garden has picnic tables and solid wooden tables and chairs, with budgerigars and rabbits in an aviary. *(Recommended by Derek Hayman, Pamela Goodwyn)*

Adnams ~ Licensee Mr Hanlon ~ Real ale ~ Meals and snacks (not Sun evening) ~ (01394) 450790 ~ Children welcome ~ Folk music Sun evening ~ Open 11.30-11; 11.30-3, 7-11 in winter; 12-3, 7-10.30 Sun; cl 25 Dec

nr CHELMONDISTON TM2037 Map 5
Butt & Oyster
Pin Mill – signposted from B1456 SE of Ipswich

Named for the flounders and oysters which used to be caught here, this simple old bargeman's pub is marvellously placed by the River Orwell. There are fine views from plenty of benches outside, of boats going and up and down the water, and across the water to the wooded slopes beyond. The same views can also be had from the bay window inside, where there's quite a nautical theme to match the surroundings. The half-panelled timeless little smoke room is pleasantly worn and unfussy, with model sailing ships around the walls and high-backed and other old-fashioned settles on the tiled floor; spare a glance for the most unusual carving of a man with a woman over the mantelpiece. Good bar food includes lunchtime sandwiches (from £1.25), ploughman's (£2.85), ravioli (£3.65), tiger prawns in garlic butter (£5.65), honey-roast half duck (£6.95), daily specials like tuna and mushroom crumble, seafood provençale or normandy pork (£4.50-£5), and popular hot and cold buffet on weekend lunchtimes. Tolly Cobbolds Bitter, Original, Shooter, and Mild, and occasional guest beers on handpump or tapped from the cask, and decent wines; shove-ha'penny, cribbage, and dominoes. A good time to visit the pub would be when the annual Thames Barge race is held (end June/beginning July). *(Recommended by Julian, Pamela Goodwyn, Derek and Sylvia Stephenson, David Peakall, Thomas Nott, C H and P Stride, Mrs P Goodwyn, John Prescott, Paul Kitchener, Paul Mason, PM, AM, Dave Braisted, June and Perry Dann, John Fahy, Mr and Mrs E Head, Jack and Philip Paxton, Stuart Earle)*

Pubmaster ~ Tenants Dick and Brenda Mainwaring ~ Real ale ~ Meals and snacks ~ (01473) 780764 ~ Children welcome except in main bar ~ Open 11-11; 12-10.30 Sun; 11-3, 7-11 Mon-Fri in winter

CHILLESFORD TM3852 Map 5
Froize 🍴 🍷 🍺
B1084 E of Woodbridge
Suffolk Dining Pub of the Year

There's an astonishingly wide choice of beautifully prepared fresh fish from Lowestoft on the menu and specials board at this particularly well run restaurary pub, which is exactly the place for a relaxed and civilised leisurely meal. Just a few examples from the menu and changing specials board are starters like dressed Cromer crab or seared squid with plum tomatoes on herb salad (£5.25), crab and coriander cake with spring onion and crème fraîche or home-made fresh potted brown shrimps (£5.95), fresh lobster cocktail (£7.65) and main courses, grilled or fried skate with brown butter and capers (£6.95), pancake filled with scallops in orange, chive and Cinzano sauce, baked baby pike with lemon and tarragon or fried fillets of red gurnard (£9.45), king prawn curry (£9.75), halibut fillet with oregano and citrus sauce or brill boulangière (£10.25) and seafood ragoût (£13.45). There are several non fish dishes like thai vegetable omelette or vegetable curry (£6.45), duck breast with plum and brandy sauce (£9.45), loin of lamb stuffed with black pudding or fillet steak (£11.95). Helpings are very generous, and there's a good choice of puddings including schoolboy treats. Licensee Alistair Shaw is in charge of the kitchen (popping out, apron and all, to see that everything's going well), while Joy Shaw runs the comfortable open-plan dining lounge (with gentle good humour, and help from the latest in a long succession of courteous young men from one particular village in the Loire valley). A no-smoking restaurant was being built as we went to press. They show a continued interest in locally brewed beers and offer three (out of four) beers brewed for them by Mauldons: Naughty Novice, Nun Chaser, Nun Trembler and Nun's Revenge, as well as three other local beers such as Adnams Best, Greene King IPA and a seasonal guest like Old Chimney's Ale-Bop; a good range of wines by the glass; dominoes, shove-ha'penny, cribbage and fruit machine. The bar has beams, a turkey carpet, a mix of mate's chairs and red-cushioned stripped pews around the dark tables, and a couple of housekeeper's chairs by the open stove in the big arched brick fireplace. This has a huge stuffed pike over it, and the big room is full of interesting things to look at. There are tables outside on a terrace and a play area; disabled loos, baby changing facilities. *(Recommended by H T Conroy, Michael Hyde, Mr and Mrs A Albert, Charles and Pauline Stride, Richard Smith, Pamela Goodwyn, Derek and Sylvia Stephenson, Reg and Kate Wheaton, Roy Oughton, Mrs P Goodwyn, Martin Warwick)*

Free house ~ Licensees Alistair and Joy Shaw ~ Real ale ~ Meals and snacks (not Mon) ~ (01394) 450282 ~ Children in eating areas ~ Live entertainment winter Sun evenings ~ Open 11-3(4 Sat), 6(6.30 in winter)-11; 12-4, 6-10.30 Sun; cl Mon except bank holidays ~ Bedrooms: £20(£30B)/£40(£45B)

COTTON TM0766 Map 5
Trowel & Hammer ♀

Mill Rd; take B1113 N of Stowmarket, then turn right into Blacksmiths Lane just N of Bacton

The large spreading lounge at this friendly partly thatched and tiled white pub has wheelbacks and one or two older chairs and settles around a variety of tables, lots of dark beamery and timber baulks, a mix of chairs and tables, fresh flowers, a big log fire, and at the back an ornate woodburning stove. The reasonably priced daily-changing bar menu might include creamy mushroom soup (£1.95), moules marinières or warm mozzarella salad (£3.75), fresh dressed crab (£5.25), steak and kidney pie (£5.75), goat's cheese vol au vent with walnuts or spinach and mushroom lasagne (£5.75), fillet of pork satay (£6.75), fried chicken breast with white wine sauce (£6.95) and lamb cutlets with redcurrant and mint sauce (£7.25). Well kept Adnams, Greene King IPA and Abbot, and maybe Nethergate Bitter and a local guest on handpump, and an interesting wine list; pool, fruit machine, and piped music. A pretty back garden has lots of roses and hollyhocks, neat climbers on trellises, picnic tables and a fine swimming pool. *(Recommended by Paul and Maggie Baker, Simon Morton, Ian and Nita Cooper, Gwen and Peter Andrews, C H and P Stride, Janet Pickles, A Albert, Bill and Sheila McLardy, Paul and Maggie Baker, Ray Watson)*

Free house ~ Licensees Julie Huff and Simon Piers-Hall ~ Real ale ~ Meals and snacks (12-2, 6.30-10) ~ Restaurant ~ (01449) 781234 ~ Children in eating area of bar ~ Open 11.30-3, 5.30-11; 11.30-11 Sat; 12-10.30 Sun

---

Pubs with outstanding views are listed at the back of the book.

DENNINGTON TM2867 Map 5
Queens Head
A1120

Readers all comment on the warmly friendly atmosphere and really welcoming greeting at this Tudor pub, which has the added bonus of being one of Suffolk's most attractive pub buildings. Locals gather for the well kept Bass, Adnams Bitter and Broadside and a guest such as Morlands Old Speckled Hen on handpump from the brick bar counters in the main L-shaped room, which has carefully stripped wall timbers and beams – the great bressumer beam over the fireplace is handsomely carved – and new comfortable padded wall seats on the partly carpeted and partly tiled floor. The arched rafters of the steeply roofed part on the right give the impression that this part could be a little chapel. Good bar food includes sandwiches (from £1.75) ploughman's (from £4.25), as well as soup (£2.25), tiger prawns in filo pastry and garlic dip (£3.55), vegetable curry (£4.25), fish pie (£4.65), chicken curry (£4.95), braised sausages in red wine (£5.50), steak and mushroom pie or layered sausage pie (£5.95), chicken and creamy asparagus sauce or salmon and prawn au gratin (£6.75), steaks (from £8.95), lots of puddings like apricot sponge pudding with butterscotch, pistachio and apricot sauce or treacle tart (£2.60); Sunday roast (£5.75); with some dishes, vegetables and chips are extra; they serve very good breakfasts (£4.95), too, from 9am; piped classical music. The side lawn, attractively planted with flowers, is sheltered by some noble lime trees, and has picnic tables; this backs onto Dennington Park where there are swings and so forth for children. *(Recommended by Gwen and Peter Andrews, I R Bell, Pamela Goodwyn, Eric Locker, David and Laraine Webster, Miss M Joynson, Caroline and Martin Page)*

Free house ~ Licensee Ray Bumstead ~ Real ale ~ Meals and snacks ~ Restaurant ~ (01728) 638241 ~ Children in family area, no under 7s on Sat evening ~ Open 11.30-- 2.30, 5.30(6 Sat)-11; 12-3, 6.30-10.30 Sun; cl 25, 26 Dec

DUNWICH TM4770 Map 5
Ship ★ ⏩ ◗

The wonderfully cosy bar at this delightful old brick pub – just a stone's throw from the sea – was once the haunt of smugglers and seafarers. It's traditionally furnished with benches, pews, captain's chairs and wooden tables on its tiled floor, a wood-burning stove (left open in cold weather) and lots of old fishing nets and paintings on the walls; darts, dominoes and cribbage. There's a good bustling atmosphere, especially at lunchtime, but the friendly, helpful staff and licensees manage to cheerfully cope with the crowds and make everyone feel personally welcome. Said to be the best for miles around, it's the fresh fish (whatever's been caught, straight from the boats on the beach) with home-made chips that readers love (£4.95 lunchtime, from £7.95 in the evening), but at lunchtime there are also simple dishes like home-made soup (£1.75), cottage pie (£3.55), ploughman's (from £3.95), macaroni cheese (£4.10); and in the evening several more dishes like fishcakes with salsa dipi (£3.95), seafood cocktail (£4.65), spinach and mushroom lasagne (£6.75), goat's cheese and tomato salad (£6.95), steak and mushroom vol au vent or seafood pancakes (£7.95) and home-made puddings (£2.95); no-smoking area in dining room. Very well kept Adnams Bitter, Broadside (in summer) and Old (in winter), and Greene King Abbot on handpump at the handsomely panelled bar counter. There's a conservatory and attractive, sunny back terrace, and a well kept garden with an enormous fig tree. Dunwich today is such a charming little place it's hard to imagine that centuries ago it was one of England's major centres. Since then fairly rapid coastal erosion has put most of the village under the sea, and there are those who claim that on still nights you can sometimes hear the old church bells tolling under the water. The pub is handy for the RSPB reserve at Minsmere. *(Recommended by Neil Calver, Eric Locker, Derek Hayman, Pat and John Millward, Gwen and Peter Andrews, Derek and Sylvia Stephenson, Fiona Duncan, Klaus and Elizabeth Leist, Helen Crookston, Peter Woolls, Colin and Joyce Laffan, P and M Pumfrey, Margaret and Nigel Dennis, June and Perry Dann, Joy and Peter Heatherley, Graham and Liz Bell, John Fahy, John Waller, Bill and Sheila McLardy, MN, DN, Jowanna Lewis, D Hayman, Nigel Wikeley, James Nunns, Tom McLean, Mrs P Goodwyn, Paul Mason, Chris and Kate Lyons, Ian Phillips)*

Free house ~ Licensees Stephen and Ann Marshlain ~ Real ale ~ Meals and snacks ~ Evening restaurant ~ (01728) 648219 ~ Children welcome away from bar ~ Open 11-3(3.30 Sat), 6-11; 12-2.30, 7-11 Sun; cl evening 25 Dec ~ Bedrooms: £35B/£50B

EARL SOHAM TM2363 Map 5
Victoria ◖

A1120 Stowmarket—Yoxford

You can visit the microbrewery which produces the Victoria Bitter, a mild called Gannet, and a stronger ale called Albert that are all well kept and served on handpump at this warmly friendly unpretentious pub. The relaxed bar has kitchen chairs and pews, plank-topped trestle sewing-machine tables and other simple country tables with candles, tiled or board floors, stripped panelling, an interesting range of pictures of Queen Victoria and her reign, and open fires. Enjoyable quickly served bar food includes good soup (£1.75), sandwiches (from £1.75), beef in beer, chicken and peach curry, beef or vegetable lasagne and pizzas (£4.50-£4.95); hot pudding and custard (£2.25); decent wine. Darts, shove-ha'penny, cribbage and dominoes; seats out in front and on a raised back lawn. The pub is close to a wild fritillary meadow at Framlingham and a working windmill at Saxtead. *(Recommended by Pat and Tony Martin, Jack and Philip Paxton, M R Hyde, D and J Tapper, Graham and Liz Bell, Paul Mason, Simon Cottrell, Nick and Hilary Jackson, John C Baker, PM, AM, N S Smith)*

Own brew ~ Licensees Clare and John Bjornson ~ Real ale ~ Meals and snacks ~ (01728) 685758 ~ Impromptu folk music Tues evenings ~ Open 12-2.30(3 Sat), 5.30-11; 12-3, 7-10.30 Sun

ERWARTON TM2134 Map 5
Queens Head ♀ ◖

Village signposted off B1456 Ipswich—Shotley Gate; pub beyond the attractive church and the manor with its unusual gate (like an upturned salt-cellar)

The comfortably furnished bar at this friendly restful pub has bowed 16th-c black oak beams in the shiny low yellowing ceiling, a cosy coal fire and several sea paintings. The same good value menu is served in both the bar and more modern restaurant and includes sandwiches, good soups like broccoli and stilton or apple, celery and tomato (£1.95), prawn cocktail or ploughman's (£3.75), moussaka, beef and ale casserole or chicken breast in peach and almond sauce (£5.50), steak and kidney pudding (£6.50), breaded plaice stuffed with prawn, chardonnay and mushroom sauce (£6.95), daily specials like stuffed loin of pork, Mexican lamb, sweet and sour quorn and seasonal game; puddings such as blueberry and lime cheesecake or treacle and nut tart (£2.50). Very well kept Adnams Bitter and Broadside and Tally Ho in winter, Greene King IPA, and Morlands Old Speckled Hen on handpump; a decent wine list with several half bottles, and a wide choice of malt whiskies. Darts, bar billiards, shove-ha'penny, cribbage, dominoes, and piped music. There are fine views over fields to ships on the Stour and the distant Parkeston Quay from seats on the terrace. The gents' have a fascinating collection of navigational maps. Handy for Erwarton Hall with its peculiar gatehouse. *(Recommended by Pamela Goodwyn, A Albert, Peter Woolls, Mike and Mary Carter, Colin Savill)*

Free house ~ Licensees Mr B K Buckle and Mrs Julia Crisp ~ Real ale ~ Meals and snacks ~ Restaurant ~ (01473) 787550 ~ Children in restaurant ~ Open 11-3, 6.30(6 Sat)-11; 12-3, 7-10.30 Sun; cl 25 Dec

---

Cribbage is a card game using a block of wood with holes for matchsticks or special pins to score with; regulars in cribbage pubs are usually happy to teach strangers how to play.

FRAMSDEN TM1959 Map 5
Dobermann 🖛 🍺

The Street; pub signposted off B1077 just S of its junction with A1120 Stowmarket—Earl Soham

There's a very friendly atmosphere at this charmingly restored pretty thatched pub. The two spotlessly kept bar areas have very low, pale stripped beams, a big comfy sofa, a couple of chintz wing armchairs, and a mix of other chairs, and plush-seated stools and winged settles around polished rustic tables; there's a wonderful twin-facing fireplace, photographs of show rosettes won by the owner's dogs on the white walls, and a friendly tabby, Tinker. Well Adnams Bitter and Broadside and guests such as Bass, Mauldons or Morrells on handpump; efficient service. Shove-ha'penny, table skittles, cribbage, dominoes, and piped radio. Good bar food includes sandwiches (from £1.45), home-made soup or deep-fried squid (£2.95), home-made chicken liver pâté or brown shrimps (£3.45), huge ploughman's (from £4.95), spicy nut loaf with tomato sauce (£5.75), chilli or mixed grill (£6.95), scampi (£7.45), steak and mushroom pie (£7.75), venison pie (£8.95), steaks (from £9.95) and dover sole (£13.50). They play boules outside, where there are picnic tables by trees and a fairy-lit trellis, and lots of pretty hanging baskets and colourful window boxes. No children. *(Recommended by Jenny and Brian Seller, David and Doreen Gregory, David and Laraine Webster, Sarah and Ian Shannon, Mrs P Goodwyn, John Waller, Jill Bickerton)*

Free house ~ Licensee Susan Frankland ~ Real ale ~ Meals and snacks ~ (01473) 890461 ~ Open 12-3, 7-11(10.30 Sun) ~ Classical guitar or clarinet player alternate Sats ~ Bedroom: £25S/£35S

GREAT GLEMHAM TM3361 Map 5
Crown 🖛 🍷 🍺

Between A12 Wickham Mkt—Saxmundham, B1119 Saxmundham—Framlingham

Readers particularly enjoy staying at this neatly kept, quietly set pub – the landlady's breakfasts are quite something, and bar food is very good too. The open-plan beamed lounge has two enormous fireplaces with logs blazing in winter, one or two big casks, brass ornaments or musical instruments, wooden pews and captain's chairs around stripped and waxed kitchen tables, and a chatty atmosphere. Local photographs and paintings decorate the white walls, and there are plenty of fresh flowers and pot plants, with more in a side eating room. Well kept Adnams Bitter, Broadside and Old in winter, and Bass from old brass handpumps; good choice of malt whiskies and decent wines. From a changing menu, the good food might include filled rolls, french onion soup (£2.50), baked aubergine with cream and garlic, grilled mackerel fillet with garlic butter (£3.25), cannelloni (£5.25), steak and kidney pie (£6.50), grilled halibut fillet with red pepper coulis (£6.75), duck with onion and garlic mayonnaise or grilled lamb steak with red wine and orange sauce (£7.50), steaks (from £8.95), and puddings such as whiskey and honey syllabub or spotted dick (£3.25). The restaurant is no smoking. Shove-ha'penny, dominoes, and cribbage. There's a tidy, flower-fringed lawn, raised above the corner of the quiet village lane by a retaining wall, and some seats and tables under cocktail parasols. *(Recommended by David and Doreen Gregory, John Le Sage, Nigel Wilkinson, J Burley, Simon Cottrell, Jenny and Brian Seller, Eric Locker, R T and J L Moggridge, Pamela Goodwyn, Pete Yearsley, Mr and Mrs Charles Gysin, Quentin Williamson, Jill Bickerton, June and Perry Dann, Mark Baynham, Miss Ward, Comus Elliott, Paul Kitchener)*

Free house ~ Licensee Roger Mason ~ Real ale ~ Meals and snacks ~ Restaurant ~ (01728) 663693 ~ Children in restaurant ~ Open 12-2.30, 7-11; 12-3.30, 7-10.30 Sun; cl Mon except bank holidays ~ Bedrooms: £20B/£38B

HARTEST TL8352 Map 5
Crown
B1066 S of Bury St Edmunds

This comfortably modernised, attractive pink-washed dining pub is prettily set by the village green and church. Reliable, reasonably priced home cooking includes good sandwiches (from £1.75), soup (£2), ploughman's or chicken liver pâté (£3.50), battered chicken fillets (£3.75), ricotta and spinach cannelloni, dressed Cromer crab, hake or plaice fillet (£6.50), dover sole (£12.50) and daily specials; they do a Wednesday lunchtime home-made pie plus pudding and coffee, and a Friday lunchtime fresh fish and pudding menu with coffee, both £6. There's plenty of space for its many regular dark wood tables, and besides two no-smoking dining areas there's a family conservatory. Well kept Greene King IPA, Abbot and seasonal ales on handpump, decent house wines, quick and friendly black-tie staff, a chatty local atmosphere, and quiet piped music. The big back lawn has picnic tables among shrubs and trees, and there are more under cocktail parasols in a sheltered side courtyard, by a plastic play treehouse. *(Recommended by Gwen and Peter Andrews, Nicholas Stuart Holmes, E A George, Pam Adsley, J F M West, B N F and M Parkin)*

Greene King ~ Tenants Paul and Karen Beer ~ Real ale ~ Meals and snacks ~ Restaurant ~ (01284) 830250 ~ Children welcome ~ Open 11-2.30, 6-11; 12-2.30, 7-10.30 Sun

HORRINGER TL8261 Map 5
Beehive 🍴 ♀
A143

The little rambling rooms at this very well run place make a delightful setting for a particularly well cooked imaginative meal. As well as nibbles such as olive and tomato bread, a dish of olives or savoury dip with corn chips (from £1.55), bar food includes soup (£2.95), chicken liver and chunky bramley apple pâté (£4.25), ploughman's or steak sandwich (£4.95), warm tomato tart (£5.95), omelette filled with prawns and double cream lobster sauce (£6.50), mild thai-style chicken curry (£8.95), and daily specials such as smoked haddock and ricotta pancake (£6.95), wild mushroom torcetti pasta with chicken and tarragon sauce or chicken livers sautéed with red wine (£7.95) and fried red mullet with ginger and rosemary (£8.95), and about eight puddings such as chocolate and prune soufflé with crème fraîche and baked blueberry cheesecake (£3.25). There are some very low beams in some of the furthest and snuggest alcoves, as well as carefully chosen dining and country kitchen chairs with tartan cushions on the coir or flagstones, one or two wall settles around solid tables, picture-lights over lots of 19th-c prints, stripped panelling or brickwork, and a woodburning stove. This is a notably well run place with extremely helpful and friendly staff and quickly served, excellent food. Well kept Greene King IPA and Abbot on handpump and decent changing wines with half-a-dozen by the glass. Their dog Muffin is very good at making friends, though other dogs aren't really welcome. The gents' has a frieze depicting villagers fleeing from stinging bees. A most attractively planted back terrace has picnic tables, with more seats on a raised lawn. The licensees have now reopened a fine old pub just over the Cambs border, the Queens Head at Kirtling; initial reports from readers suggest that this is a real find, which we look forward to inspecting. *(Recommended by Gwen and Peter Andrews, Maysie Thompson, P and M Pumfrey, John Fahy, Pamela Goodwyn, Janet Pickles, Simon Cottrell, Helen Crookston, R C Wiles, David Regan)*

Greene King ~ Tenant Gary Kingshott ~ Real ale ~ Meals and snacks ~ (01284) 735260 ~ Children welcome ~ Open 11.30-2.30, 7-11; 12-2.30, 7-10.30 Sun

---

Please let us know what you think of a pub's bedrooms. No stamp needed:
The Good Pub Guide, FREEPOST TN1569, Wadhurst, E Sussex TN5 7BR.

HOXNE TM1777 Map 5
Swan

Off B1118; village signposted off A140 S of Diss

The front bar at this carefully restored late 15th-c house has a peaceful and relaxed atmosphere, two solid oak counters, heavy oak floors, and a deep-set inglenook fireplace, with an armchair on either side and a long bench in front of it; you can still see the ancient timber and mortar of the walls. A fire in the back bar divides the bar area and snug, and the dining room has an original wooden fireplace. Bar food under the new licensee includes sandwiches (from £1.95), ploughman's (from £4), avocado mousse (£4.25), stilton and mushroom in puff pastry (£5.95), tuna steak with salmon and chive butter (£7.95) and daily specials like fisherman's, lamb and mint or steak and kidney pie (£5.95), lamb balti or game pie (£6.95) and lamb steak with redcurrant gravy or duck breast with oyster sauce (£8.95). If you're sitting outside and waiting for your food order, keep your eye on the roof; rather than use a Tannoy, they briefly sound a school bell and then prop scoreboard type numbers up there when your meal is ready; no-smoking restaurant. Well kept Adnams Bitter and three guests like Courage Directors, Greene King Abbot and Nethergate on handpump or tapped from the cask, and decent wines; dominoes, piped music. There is an extensive lawn behind used for croquet, and hand-made elm furniture sheltered by a willow and other trees and a shrub-covered wall. Nearby is the site of King Edmund the Martyr's execution; the tree to which he was tied for it is now reputed to form part of a screen in the neighbouring church. *(Recommended by PM, AM, Frank Davidson, Ian Phillips, Pat and Tony Martin, J E Rycroft, Anthony Barnes, P H Roberts, Gwen and Peter Andrews, Wayne Brindle, Dr Ronald Church, Pamela Goodwyn)*

Free house ~ Licensee Mike Griffiths ~ Real ale ~ Meals and snacks (not Sun evening) ~ Restaurant ~ (01379) 668275 ~ Children welcome ~ Open 12-2.30, 6.30-11; 12-11 summer Sat; 12-10.30 summer Sun

HUNDON TL7348 Map 5
Plough 🛏

Brockley Green – nearly 2 miles SW of village, towards Kedington

Nicely positioned on top of one of the few hills in the area, and with good views, this extended and modernised pub has been run by the same friendly family for three generations. The neat carpeted bar has low side settles with Liberty-print cushions, pine kitchen chairs and sturdy low tables on the patterned carpet, lots of horsebrasses on the beams, and striking gladiatorial designs for Covent Garden by Leslie Hurry, who lived nearby; there's still a double row of worn old oak timbers to mark what must once have been the corridor between its two rooms. Decent bar food includes lunchtime sandwiches (from £1.95) and ploughman's (£3.75) as well as soup (£2.95), snails in garlic butter or seafood cocktail (£4.75), quiche (£5.95), beef in Guinness pie (£6.75), game pie (£7.50), rack of lamb with mustard and herb crust or fried chicken breast with crème fraîche and peppercorns (£8.95) chicken with barbecue sauce (£7.95), seafood platter (£10.95) and lemon sole with crabmeat and prawns in herbed butter (£11.25). Well kept Adnams, Greene King IPA and a guest beer on handpump, quite a few wines, and freshly squeezed orange juice; piped music. Parts of the bar and restaurant are no smoking. It's also a certified location for the Caravan Club, with a sheltered site to the rear for tourers. Behind are five acres of landscaped gardens, part of which are to become a wildlife sanctuary and trout lake. There's also a terrace with a pergola and ornamental pool, croquet, boules, and fine views over miles of East Anglian countryside; the pub's two friendly retrievers may be out here, too. *(Recommended by Ron and Sheila Corbett, Gwen and Peter Andrews, F C Johnston, John and Karen Gibson, Heather Martin, Quentin Williamson)*

Free house ~ Licensee David Rowlinson ~ Real ale ~ Meals and snacks ~ Restaurant ~ (01440) 786789 ~ Children welcome ~ Open 11(12 in winter)-2.30, 5.30-11; 12-3, 7-10.30 Sun ~ Bedrooms: £40B/£60B

ICKLINGHAM TL7772 Map 5

Red Lion ⊕

A1101, Mildenhall—Bury St Edmunds

The beamed open-plan bar at this attractive thatched pub has a calmly civilised dining atmosphere, as well as turkey rugs on the polished wood floor, candlelit tables, a nice mixture of wooden chairs, two big fireplaces, daily newspapers, and piped classical music. Very popular bar food in generous helpings includes soup (£2.55), pâté (£3.25), Newmarket sausages (£4.95), lamb liver with bacon and onion gravy (£6.75), steak and ale pie (£7.25), warm fillet of chicken and crispy pasta salad (£8.95), prawns in garlic butter (£9.95) and daily specials like wild mushrooms in cream and herb sauce in puff pastry (£4.95), lamb liver and kidneys with bordelaise sauce (£10.50), chicken breast with diced peppers and herb cream cheese with mushrooms and muscadet (£10.75), roast monkfish fillet in puff pastry on prawn sauce (£11.95), roast duck breast with cherry brandy sauce (£12.50), venison steak with red wine, shallot and mushroom sauce (£12.55). Well kept Greene King IPA and Abbot and occasional guest beers on handpump, lots of country wines and elderflower and citrus pressé, and mulled wine in winter. Picnic tables on a raised back terrace face the fields including an acre of the pub's running down to the River Lark, with Cavenham Heath nature reserve beyond. In front (the pub is well set back from the road) old-fashioned white seats overlook the car park and a flower lawn. Handy for West Stow Country Park and the Anglo-Saxon Village. *(Recommended by R Suddaby, J F M and M West, Scott Rumery, Gwen and Peter Andrews, Ian Phillips, Mrs P Goodwyn, Stephen Barney, K Neville-Rolfe, J F M West, Frank Gadbois, John and Chris Simpson, K H Frostick, Nigel Pawsey, James Macrae, Philip and Susan Philcox)*

Greene King ~ Lease: Jonathan Gates ~ Meals and snacks (till 10 Mon-Sat) ~ Restaurant ~ (01638) 717802 ~ Children welcome ~ Open 12-3, 6-11; 12-3, 7-10.30 Sun

IXWORTH TL9370 Map 5

Pykkerel

Village signposted just off A143 Bury St Edmunds—Diss

A reader describes how nice it is to sit in one of the neatly kept little rooms at this characterful dining pub with a tasty pint in his hand and reading the newspaper to his heart's content – they provide all the daily papers. Leading off the central servery, they have moulded Elizabethan oak beams, attractive brickwork, big fireplaces, antique tables and chairs, and persian rugs on the gleaming floors; there's a similarly furnished dining area, and a small back sun lounge facing a sway-backed Elizabethan timbered barn across the old coach yard. Much emphasis is placed on the good popular bar food which includes stilton and potato brûlée (£4.45), smoked salmon roulade (£5.75), crumbled chicken breast in red onion, courgette and tomato salsa topped with bearnaise butter sauce (£10.75), fillet of pork with sage and onion stuffing on sautéed mushroom and garlic with red currant sauce (£11.45), beef stroganoff (£11.95) and roast loin of lamb (£12). Well kept Greene King IPA on handpump and country wines. *(Recommended by J F M West, Frank Davidson, Ian Phillips, Simon Penny, Donald Rice, M Borthwick)*

Greene King ~ Tenants Ian Hubbert and J Gates ~ Real ale ~ Meals and snacks (till 10) ~ Restaurant ~ (01359) 230398 ~ Children welcome ~ Open 12-2.30, 6-11; 12-2.30, 7-10.30 Sun

LAVENHAM TL9149 Map 5

Angel ★ ⊕ 🛏 ♀ 🍷

Market Pl

We're very pleased to report that this civilised and carefully renovated Tudor inn, which was our *Pub of the Year* in last year's edition of the Guide, is still doing terribly well, and is as popular as ever with readers. Much of this is down to the complete commitment of the licensees to their customers' enjoyment, the relaxed and buoyantly pubby atmosphere means that people just dropping in for a quick drink feel as welcome as those turning up for the particularly good food. The long bar area, facing on to the charming former market square, is light and airy, with plenty of polished dark tables. There's a big inglenook log fire under a heavy mantelbeam, and some attractive 16th-c ceiling plasterwork (even more elaborate pargeting in the residents' sitting room upstairs). Round towards the back on the right of the central servery is a no-smoking family dining area with heavy stripped pine country furnishings. Changing twice a day, the carefully cooked food may include carrot and coriander soup (£2.50), smoked salmon and asparagus pâté (£3.95), ploughman's (£4.50), and warm salad of scallops and bacon (£4.50), and main courses like steak and ale pie (£6.25), vegetable stuffed field mushrooms (£6.75), hare braised in red wine and mushrooms or lamb in paprika and cream (£8.25), chicken breast with sherry and tarragon (£8.50), grilled venison steak with apples and blackberry (£9.95), and puddings such as sticky toffee pudding, blueberry cream brûleé or rhubarb and orange crumble (£3.25). Well kept Adnams Bitter, Greene King IPA, Mauldons White Adder and Nethergate Bitter on handpump, quite a few malt whiskies, and several decent wines by the glass or part bottle (you get charged for what you drink). They have shelves of books, a good range of board games, and hold a quiz on Sundays (all are welcome); dominoes, cribbage, trivia and board games; piped music. The big ginger cat is called Dilly. There are picnic tables out in front, and white plastic tables under cocktail parasols in a sizeable sheltered back garden; it's worth asking if they've time to show you the interesting Tudor cellar. *(Recommended by Gwen and Peter Andrews, Tony Hall, Melanie Jackson, J F Knutton, Alan Parsons, Fiona and John Richards, Pamela Goodwyn, Dr I Crichton, Maysie Thompson, Joy and Peter Heatherley, Lynn Sharpless, Bob Eardley, Simon Morton, Tina and David Woods-Taylor, Wayne Brindle, John Baker, John Saul, Simon Walker, Mike and Heather Watson, Margaret and Nigel Dennis, Bill and Steph Brownson, Graham and Liz Bell, Jamie and Ruth Lyons, IK, I P G Derwent, John Baker, Trent and Tina Conyers, J E Hilditch, Eric and Jackie Robinson, Susan May, Frank Gadbois, Sarah and Ian Shannon, C McFeeters, Prof R Orledge, W W Burke, John Evans, Heather Martin, Heather and Trevor Shaw)*

Free house ~ Licensees Roy and Anne Whitworth, John Barry ~ Real ale ~ Meals and snacks ~ Restaurant ~ (01787) 247388 ~ Children in eating area of bar and in restaurant ~ Classical piano Fri evenings and some lunchtimes (played by the landlord) ~ Open 11-11; 12-10.30 Sun; cl 25, 26 Dec ~ Bedrooms: £39.50B/£65B

Swan ★ ✏

Set in what is probably England's most charming village, this stately timbered Elizabethan inn is one of the striking buildings that gives this once-prosperous wool town its appeal. It's quite smart, but ideal for an atmospheric afternoon tea or for those who need that extra bit of luxury as it does have all the trimmings of a well equipped hotel (and not a cheap one). It incorporates several lovely half-timbered buildings, including an Elizabethan house and the former Wool Hall. The peaceful little tiled-floor bar, buried in its heart, has leather chairs and memorabilia of the days when this was the local for the US 48th Bomber Group in the Second World War (many Americans still come to re-visit old haunts); the set of handbells used to be employed by the local church bellringers for practice. From here it's an easy overflow into the drift of armchairs and settees that spreads engagingly through a network of beamed and timbered alcoves and more open areas. Overlooking the well kept and sheltered courtyard garden is an airy Garden Bar. Well kept Bass, Greene King IPA and Stones on handpump or tapped from the cask; darts, cribbage, dominoes and piped music. Fairly limited and not particularly cheap bar food includes home-made soup (£2.95), sandwiches (from £3.50), British cheeses and biscuits (£4.95), honey-baked ham and roast turkey salad (£7.95), a vegetarian dish, and one or two daily hot dishs such as steamed salmon with citrus dressing, fillet of chicken with mushroom and tarragon sauce and fillet steak with peppercorn sauce (all £9.95), and home-made puddings (£3.50); also, morning coffee and good afternoon tea. There is also a lavishly timbered no-smoking restaurant with a minstrel's gallery. *(Recommended by K and J Brooks, J F M West, D E Twitchett, Pam Adsley, Maysie Thompson, Tina and David Woods-Taylor, Graham and Liz Bell, John Fahy, W W Burke, Janet Pickles)*

Free house ~ Licensee Elizabeth Combridge ~ Real ale ~ Meals and snacks ~ Restaurant ~ (01787) 247477 ~ Children welcome ~ Open 11-2.30, 6-11; 12-2.30, 7-10.30 Sun ~ Bedrooms: £84.95B/£139.80B

LAXFIELD TM2972 Map 5
Kings Head 🍺

Behind church, off road toward Banyards Green

Readers enjoy the marvellously old-fashioned pubby front room at this genuinely traditional thatched Tudor pub, and on Tuesday lunchtimes you can really cast yourself back into the past when a live band plays old country songs. It's delightfully furnished with a high-backed built-in settle on the tiled floor and an open fire: a couple of other rooms have pews, old seats, scrubbed deal tables, and some interesting wall prints. Decent bar food includes parsnip and apple soup (£2.10), parfait of chicken livers with cranberry relish (£3.60), tagliatelle with roast pepper and pesto sauce or local pork and apple sausages with pickle (£4.95), salad of jellied bacon and parsley (£5.50), Norfolk dumpling filled with pork and thyme (£5.75), 8oz steak (£8.50), and puddings like sticky toffee pudding or rice pudding with toasted almonds (£2.95). Well kept Adnams Bitter, Broadside, Extra and winter Old and Tally Ho, and Greene King IPA on handpump, and good James White cider; shove ha'penny and dominoes. Going out past the casks in the back serving room, you find benches and a trestle table in a small yard. From the yard, a honeysuckle arch leads into a sheltered little garden and the pub's own well kept and secluded bowling, badminton and croquet green. *(Recommended by Klaus and Elizabeth Leist, Gwen and Peter Andrews, Ian and Nita Cooper, M R Hyde, Anthony Barnes, P and M Pumfrey, Richard Balls, David and Doreen Gregory, June and Perry Dann, Sarah and Ian Shannon, H Turner, Jack and Philip Paxton)*

Free house ~ Managers Adrian and Sylvia Read ~ Real ale ~ Meals and snacks ~ (01986) 798395 ~ Children in family room ~ Old country songs with squeeze box lunchtime, Irish band alternate Fri evenings ~ Open 11-3, 6-11; 12-3, 7-10.30 Sun; cl 25 Dec evening

LEVINGTON TM2339 Map 5
Ship

Gun Hill; village signposted from A45, then follow Stratton Hall sign

It's worth arriving early at this charmingly traditional inn – popular with ramblers, birdwatchers and users of the nearby local marina – as it does get full, and favourite bar meals can run out. Generous helpings of tasty home-made bar food might include lamb and vegetable casserole, meatballs with spicy tomato sauce, leek, cheese and potato pie or tortellini with ricotta cheese (£5.95) and braised peppered steak or chicken with asparagus sauce (£6.25) and puddings like banana cream pie or lemon meringue pie (£2.75). The rooms have quite a nautical theme with lots of ship prints and photos of sailing barges, beams and benches built into the walls, and in the middle room a marine compass set under the serving counter, which also has a fishing net slung over it. There are also a number of comfortably upholstered small settles, some of them grouped round tables as booths, and a big black round stove. The no-smoking dining room has more nautical bric-a-brac, beams taken from an old barn, and flagstones; another dining area is also no smoking. Up to eight real ales include well kept Boddingtons, Greene King IPA, Ind Coope Burton and Tetleys with guests like Flowers IPA on handpump or tapped from the cask; country wines. Service is friendly and professional. Cribbage, dominoes. If you look carefully enough, there's a distant sea view from the benches in front. In summer, the hanging baskets are magnificent. No dogs or children. *(Recommended by Ian Phillips, Neil Calver, Paula Williams, Charles and Pauline Stride, Mrs P J Pearce, C H and P Stride, Malcolm Taylor, Prof M J Salmon, Ian and Nita Cooper)*

Pubmaster ~ Tenants William and Shirley Waite ~ Real ale ~ Meals and snacks (not Sun/Mon/Tues evenings) ~ Restaurant ~ (01473) 659573 ~ Folk music first Tues of month ~ Open 11.30-3, 6-11; 12-3, 7-10.30 Sun

LIDGATE TL7257 Map 5
Star 🍴 ♀

B1063 SE of Newmarket

There's a gloriously relaxed feel in the characterful rooms of this pretty little pub with its chatty Spanish landlady, who has made a delightfully continental mark on the place. The small main room has lots of English pubby character, with handsomely moulded heavy beams, a good big log fire, candles in iron candelabra on good polished oak or stripped pine tables, bar billiards, dominoes, darts and ring the bull, and just some antique Catalan plates over the bar to give a hint of the Mediterranean. The easy-going atmosphere, and the changing menu with crisp and positive seasonings in some dishes speak more openly of the South. There might be mediterranean fish soup or hot garlicky little prawns (£4.50), a beautifully dressed Catalan salad or a massive Spanish omelette (£4.50) scallops in bacon and garlic (£4.50), herby roast chicken (£7.50), monkfish marinière, herby fresh scallops, paella, lasagne, lamb steaks in blackcurrant or wild boar or venison in port (£8.50). Helpings are big, vegetables are well cooked with good dry continental-style chips, and the sorbets and home-made cheesecake are good. Greene King IPA, Abbot, and a seasonal beer on handpump, enjoyable house wines, maybe good unobtrusive piped music; darts, bar billiards, dominoes, and ring-the-bull. Besides a second similar room on the right, there's a cosy simple dining room on the left. There are tables out by the quiet front lane and in a pretty little rustic back garden. *(Recommended by David Regan, N S Smith, Gwen and Peter Andrews, Ian and Nita Cooper, Mrs P Goodwyn, P and D Carpenter, J F M West)*

Greene King ~ Tenant Maria Teresa Axon ~ Real ale ~ Meals and snacks (not Sun evening) ~ Restaurant ~ (01638) 500275 ~ Children welcome ~ Open 11-3, 5 (6 Sat)-11; 12-3, 7-11 Sun

ORFORD TM4250 Map 5
Jolly Sailor

There are lovely views from the back of this unspoilt old smugglers' inn across marshes and saltings, as it's right by a busy little quay on the River Ore, opposite Orford Ness and close to marshy Havergate Island, where avocets breed. Inside, there are several snugly traditional rooms served from counters and hatches in an old-fashioned central cubicle, and an uncommon spiral staircase in the corner of the flagstoned main bar – which also has 13 brass door knockers and other brassware, local photographs, and a good solid fuel stove; a small room is popular with the dominoes and shove-ha'penny players, and has draughts, chess and cribbage too. The chatty easy-going barman serves well kept Adnams Bitter, Broadside and Mild and a seasonal beer on handpump and straightforward bar food such as fish and chips, home-cooked ham and egg, and daily roasts (all £4.50). The dining room is no smoking. One or two picnic tables on grass by the car park. No children. *(Recommended by Susan May, Gwen and Peter Andrews, David and Doreen Gregory, Ian Phillips, Joy and Peter Heatherley, R E and P Pearce, Tom McLean, David Heath, Nick and Hilary Jackson, W W Burke)*

Adnams ~ Tenant Philip M Attwood ~ Real ale ~ Bar meals (not Tues-Thurs evenings 1 Oct-Easter; not 25-26 Dec) ~ (01394) 450243 ~ Open 11.30-2.30, 7-11; 12-2.30, 7-10.30 Sun; cl 25 Dec evening ~ Bedrooms: /£35

RAMSHOLT TM3141 Map 5
Ramsholt Arms

Village signposted from B1083; then take turning after the one to Ramsholt Church

The engine bar at this beautifully placed old ferryman's cottage – quite isolated by an old barge quay – has a big picture window with wonderful views of the River Deben which winds past here to the sea. There's also some neatly nautical woodwork, tide tables and charts, and simple dark oak brocaded seats on the plain carpet. The uncarpeted riverside bar has comfortable banquettes and chairs and a good winter log fire. Well kept Adnams Bitter, Brakspears Bitter, Flowers Original and Theakstons

Best on handpump, several malt whiskies and wines by the glass. Readers report highly about the very tasty bar food which might include fresh oyster and herring platter or fresh salmon and bacon kebab (£4.50), local asparagus with samon and hollandaise (£4.75), fresh battered cod (£5.95), pot-roast partridge (£8.50) and grilled lemon sole (£8.95). The restaurant is no smoking. There is a riverside terrace bar which is open every afternoon from 14 May to 28 August, excluding Sundays. We'd be very interested to hear from readers about the newly refurbished bedrooms. *(Recommended by Ian Phillips, Pamela Goodwyn, Simon Cottrell, David Peakall, Dr and Mrs P J S Crawshaw, PM, AM, Mrs P Goodwyn)*

Free house ~ Licensees Michael and Kirsten Bartholomew ~ Real ale ~ Meals and snacks (not Sun evening in winter) ~ Restaurant ~ (01394) 411229 ~ Children welcome ~ Steep longish walk down from car park ~ Open 11-3, 6-11; 12-4, 7-10.30 Sun ~ Bedrooms: £35/£70

RATTLESDEN TL9758 Map 5
Brewers Arms

Signposted on minor roads W of Stowmarket, off B1115 via Buxhall or off A45 via Woolpit

The welcoming new licensees at this 16th-c pub are concentrating on developing the food side of the business, and readers' reports suggest that things are going very well. The reasonably priced imaginative menu changes constantly but might include tomato and basil salad with parmesan (£3.25), chicken liver, courgette and red pepper pâté (£3.25), lemon prawns (£3.95) and main courses like roast vegetables in tomato ragoût with pasta (£6), fried pork with mandarin orange sauce (£7.25), chicken breast with tarragon cream sauce (£7.50), stuffed noisettes of lamb with mint and port wine sauce (£9.25), monkfish wrapped in smoked ham with cream sauce (£9.50), and puddings like toffee and banana sponge, lemon mousse gateau and hot caramelised pineapple with brandy (£3.25). Very welcoming and friendly service, and well kept Greene King Abbot and IPA on handpump, and decent wines. The small but lively public bar on the right has pool, and on the left, the pleasantly simple beamed lounge bar has horsebrasses, and individually chosen pictures and bric-a-brac on the walls; piped music. It winds back through standing timbers to the main eating area, which is partly flint-walled, has a magnificent old bread oven and new more comfortable seating. French windows open on to a garden edged with bourbon roses, with a boules pitch. *(Recommended by Evelyn and Derek Walter, Pamela Goodwyn, Ian and Nita Cooper, Mrs B Gallagher, Mrs R Talbot)*

Greene King ~ Lease: Jeffrey Chamberlain ~ Real ale ~ Meals and snacks (not Sun evening) ~ (01449) 736377 ~ Children in restaurant and till 8pm in bar ~ Open 12-2.30(3 Sat), 6.30-11; 12-3, 7-10.30 Sun; cl Mon

REDE TL8055 Map 5
Plough 🍴 ♀

Village signposted off A143 Bury St Edmunds—Haverhill

You can be sure of a delicious well prepared meal, and a wonderfully warm personal welcome at this peacefully set, partly thatched pub. There's quite an emphasis on game and always lots of fresh fish: wild rabbit braised in cider with bacon, mushrooms and herbs, moroccan-style chicken with apple, ginger and sultana stuffing and fruit and nut sauce or pheasant braised with apples and cider (£7.95), venison shanks in red wine and mushroom sauce or chicken with kumquats and orange sauce (£8.95) and good steaks; helpful service and decent wines. The simple and traditional cosy bar has copper measures and pewter tankards hanging from low black beams, decorative plates on a delft shelf and surrounding the solid fuel stove in its brick fireplace, and red plush button-back built-in wall banquettes; fruit machine, piped pop music. On a sunny summer's day, the sheltered cottagey garden behind with little dovecote, aviary and pheasants strutting on the lawn is a lovely place to enjoy a drink; picnic tables in front. *(Recommended by David Regan, R E and P Pearce, J F M West, Mr and Mrs N Chesher, Gwen and Peter Andrews, Brian and Jill Bond, SS)*

Greene King ~ Lease: Brian Desborough ~ Meals and snacks (not Sun evening) ~ Evening restaurant ~ (01284) 789208 ~ Children in eating area of bar and restaurant ~ Open 11.30-3, 6.30-11; 12-3, 7-10.30 Sun

SNAPE TM3959 Map 5
Crown 🍴 🍷 🛏
B1069

This unspoilt smugglers' inn is very close to Snape Maltings and is popular with concert-goers. The atmosphere is relaxed and warmly friendly, and there are some striking horseshoe-shaped high-backed settles around the big brick inglenook, spindleback and country kitchen chairs, nice old tables, old brick floors, and lots of beams in the various small side rooms. Served by helpful, smiling staff, the well presented and particularly good food might include spinach and parmesan roulade or toasted goat's cheese and pesto (£4.25), griddled baby squid on salad with lemon and chilli dressing or ploughman's (£4.50), crayfish tails with mango and orange salad with soy dressing (£4.95) pork tenderloin with prune and apple stuffing and cider sauce (£7.95), confit of honeyed duck on creamy herb polenta (£9.50), salmon fillet on thai broth with chinese noodles and mooli salad (£8.95), rack of lamb with dijon herb crust, red wine and redcurrant gravy (£10.50) and king scallops with deep-fried spinach and chilli sauce (£11.50), and home-made puddings like lemon tart, sticky toffee pudding and chocolate and prune tart (£3.50); Sunday roast is usually topside of beef (£6.95). Well kept Adnams Bitter and Broadside and a seasonal beer on handpump, and a good thoughtful wine list with a dozen by the glass (including champagne). There are tables and umbrellas in the pretty roadside garden. No children. Timbered bedrooms are well equipped and comfortable. *(Recommended by Phil and Heidi Cook, Joy and Peter Heatherley, Gordon Neighbour, Anthony Barnes, Evelyn Sanderson, Mrs P Goodwyn, Nick and Hilary Jackson, Dr Andrew Schuman, Anna Brewer)*

Adnams ~ Tenant Paul Maylott ~ Real ale ~ Meals and snacks ~ Restaurant ~ (01728) 688324 ~ Open 12-3, 6-11; 12-3, 7-10.30 Sun; cl 25 Dec, evening 26 Dec ~ Bedrooms: £35B/£50B

Golden Key ★
Priory Lane

The licensees at this quietly elegant and rather civilised inn are Adnams' most longstanding tenants – they've been here for twenty years now. They serve the full range of Adnams beers on handpump including the seasonal ones, as well as a good wine list, and about a dozen malt whiskies. The low-beamed stylish lounge has an old-fashioned settle curving around a couple of venerable stripped tables on the tiled floor, a winter open fire, and at the other end, some stripped modern settles around heavy Habitat-style wooden tables on a turkey carpet, and a solid fuel stove in the big fireplace. The cream walls are hung with pencil sketches of customers, a Henry Wilkinson spaniel and so forth; a brick-floored side room has sofas and more tables. There's quite an emphasis on the popular bar food which might include grilled sardines (£4.25), smoked haddock quiche (£6.25), steak, mushroom and Guinness pie (£6.95), fresh cod fillet with cream parsley sauce (£8.25), bass fillet with lemon and prawn butter (£10.95) and fresh vegetables and good home-made puddings. There are plenty of white tables and chairs on a terrace at the back near the small sheltered and flower-filled garden. *(Recommended by Joy and Peter Heatherley, Lynn Sharpless, Bob Eardley, Michael Hyde, Mike and Mary Carter, Gwen and Peter Andrews, Peter Woolls, D J Hayman, Nigel Wilkinson, M R Hyde, Ian Phillips, Phil and Heidi Cook, D Hayman, Nicola Coburn, PM, AM, Derek Patey, DH)*

Adnams ~ Tenants Max and Susie Kissick-Jones ~ Real ale ~ Meals and snacks ~ (01728) 688510 ~ Children allowed in dining room only ~ Open 11-3, 6-11; 12-3, 7-10.30 Sun ~ Bedrooms: £45B/£55B

Plough & Sail ⊛ ♀

Snape Maltings Riverside Centre

When the original malting business finally ground to a halt in 1965 the buildings were purchased by George Gooderham, a local farmer and relative of the present licensee. Over the years they were developed into the Riverside Centre – with famous concert hall, art gallery, craft shop, and a house and garden shop and so forth. The buff-coloured pub itself is a long narrow building with the bar facing you as you walk through the door; beyond this on the right is a raised airy eating room with attractive pine furniture and – to one side – a settle in front of the open fire; beyond this is the busy little restaurant. To the left of the bar and down some steps is a quarry-tiled room with dark traditional furniture. The atmosphere is relaxed and friendly, and one room is no smoking. Generous helpings of delicious food include sandwiches (from £2.25), a choice of three soups (£3.25), smoked local sprats (£3.95), Aldeburgh cod topped with cheddar (£6.95), pork tenderloin with port and stilton sauce (£7.25), loin of lamb stuffed with apricots (£8.25), local dover sole (£9.95) and about a dozen puddings (£3.25); Sunday carvery (£6.95). Well kept Adnams ales on handpump, and a fine wine list with a few by the glass; darts. The big enclosed back terrace has lots of picnic tables and a giant chess set. *(Recommended by Pamela Goodwyn, Ian Phillips, June and Perry Dann, A Albert, John C Baker, MN, DN, Susan May, Ray Watson, Alan Jarvis)*

Free house ~ Licensees G J C and G E Gooderham ~ Real ale ~ Meals and snacks ~ Restaurant~ (01728) 688413 ~ Children in eating area of bar ~ Open 11-3, 5.30-11; 12-3, 7-10.30 Sun

SOUTHWOLD TM5076 Map 5

Crown ★ ⊛ ⇤ ♀ ◗

High Street

This smart old hotel is among the most popular places listed in the Guide. It's very well run and earns praise for almost every aspect – as a friendly welcoming place for a drink (perfectly kept beer and an excellent wine list), for its very well prepared imaginative meals, and for its very comfortable accommodation. The elegant beamed main bar has a stripped curved high-backed settle and other dark varnished settles, kitchen chairs and some bar stools, pretty, fresh flowers on the mix of kitchen pine tables, newspapers to read, a carefully restored and rather fine carved wooden fireplace, and a relaxed atmosphere; the small no-smoking restaurant with its white cloths and pale cane chairs leads off. The smaller back oak-panelled locals' bar has more of a traditional pubby atmosphere, red leatherette wall benches and a red carpet; the little parlour on the left is also no smoking. There's a particularly carefully chosen wine list (they have the full Adnams range, well over 300), with a monthly changing choice of 20 interesting varieties by the glass or bottle kept perfectly on a cruover machine; you can get any of them from the cash and carry by the mixed dozen round the corner. Adnams brewery is nearby, and the Crown is understandably their flagship – perfectly kept Adnams Bitter, Broadside and Mild on handpump; also a good choice of malt whiskies, tea, coffee and herbal infusions. The very good, creative bar food changes every day, but might typically include cream of aubergine and mushroom soup (£2.95), grilled venison sausages with yellow pease pudding, roast loin of pork, apple and thyme mash with red wine sauce, salmon and basil fishcake with watercress salad, braised beef steak with sun-dried tomato mash and herb sauce and steamed salmon fillet with crayfish tails and tarragon butter (£8) and puddings such as poached pear stuffed with goat's cheese and marshmallow mousse, apple crumble, iced rhubarb parfait and home-made meringue with fresh fruit and chantilly cream (£3.25). Shove-ha'penny, dominoes and cribbage. There are some tables in a sunny sheltered corner outside. *(Recommended by P and M Pumfrey, Gwen and Peter Andrews, Dr F M Halle, K and J Brooks, Mr and Mrs C H Phillips, Joy and Peter Heatherley, David and Doreen Gregory, J F Knutton, Robert Gomme, Wayne Brindle, Richard Balls, Dr B and Mrs P B Baker, Pat and John Millward, Richard Siebert, Evelyn and Derek Walter, Sarah and Ian Shannon, J E Hilditch, Eric and Jackie Robinson, J F M West, Jamie and Ruth Lyons, W W Burke, John Waller, Frank Gadbois, Alan Jarvis, Dr P J S Crawshaw, Roger Danes, James Macrae, Pat and Roger Fereday, Mavis and John Wright, Graham and Liz Bell, D Hayman; also in Good Hotel Guide)*

Adnams ~ Manager Anne Simpson ~ Real ale ~ Meals and snacks (till 9.45) ~ Restaurant ~ (01502) 722275 ~ Children in eating area of bar ~ Open 10.30-3, 6-11; 12-3, 6(7 in winter)-10.30 Sun; cl first week Jan ~ Bedrooms: £40B/£63B

STOKE BY NAYLAND TL9836 Map 5
Angel ⓜ ⇔ ♀

B1068 Sudbury—East Bergholt; also signposted via Nayland off A134 Colchester—Sudbury

You do need to arrive early as this elegant dining pub fills up very quickly with visitors keen to enjoy the attractively presented, delicious food. There might be home-made soup (£2.55), fishcakes with remoulade sauce or mushroom and pistachio pâté (£3.95), steamed mussels in white wine (£4.50), liver and bacon with madeira sauce (£6.25), vegetable filo parcels with fresh tomato coulis or steak and kidney pudding (£6.75), roast loin of pork with crackling, apple mousse and braised red cabbage (£6.95), chicken and king prawn brochette with yoghurt and mint dip (£8.50), griddled fresh wing of skate (£8.95), honey glazed roast rack of new season's lamb (£9.95), and puddings like steamed apple pudding with vanilla sauce or dark chocolate ganache gateau (£3.45). The comfortable main bar area has handsome Elizabethan beams, some stripped brickwork and timbers, a mixture of furnishings including wing armchairs, mahogany dining chairs, and pale library chairs, local watercolours and older prints, attractive table lamps, and a huge log fire. Round the corner is a little tiled-floor stand-and-chat bar – with well kept Adnams, Greene King IPA and Abbot and a guest beer on handpump, and a thoughtful wine list. One no-smoking room has a low sofa and wing armchairs around its woodburning stove, and Victorian paintings on the dark green walls. There are cast-iron seats and tables on a sheltered terrace. No children. *(Recommended by Peter Baggott, Pamela Goodwyn, J F Knutton, Pat and John Millward, Ian Phillips, D E Twitchett, Mr and Mrs J R Morris, John Evans, MDN, Malcolm Taylor, Paul and Maggie Baker, Eric and Jackie Robinson, DAV, Gwen and Peter Andrews, Graham and Liz Bell, M R Hyde, Carolyn and Michael Hedoin, John Prescott)*

Free house ~ Licensee Peter Smith ~ Real ale ~ Meals and snacks ~ Restaurant ~ (01206) 263245 ~ Open 11-2.30, 6-11; 12-3, 7-10.30 Sun ~ Bedrooms: £45B/£59B

THORNHAM MAGNA TM1070 Map 5
Four Horseshoes ⇔

Off A140 S of Diss; follow Finningham 3¼ signpost, by White Horse pub

Said to date back to the 12th c, this spacious handsome thatched pub has a lot of charm and character, and because it rambles round so much, a good deal of space. The extensive bar is well divided into alcoves and distinct areas, with very low and heavy black beams, some tall windsor chairs as well as the golden plush banquettes and stools on its spread of fitted turkey carpet, country pictures and farm tools on the black-timbered white walls, and logs burning in big fireplaces; the area with the inside well is no smoking. The new licensee does have plans to change the range of bar food but it won't be dissimilar to the range as we went to press: sandwiches (from £2.25), vegetarian lasagne or battered cod fillet (£5.25), a large mixed grill (£7.95) and daily specials such as meatballs (£4.95), gammon in madeira sauce (£5.95) and rib eye steak, ploughman's or cold poached salmon with prawn salad (£6.95); puddings (from £2.95); two-course meal for OAPs (£4.95, not weekends). The restaurant is no smoking. Well kept Adnams Bitter, Courage Best, Shepherd Neame Spitfire, and Theakstons Best and XB on handpump, some malt whiskies and country wines, and piped music. In summer, you can sit at the picnic tables beside the flowerbeds on a sheltered lawn. Thornham Walks nearby consists of nearly 12 miles of permissive footpaths on the beautiful and privately owned Thornham Estate and there is a half mile hard-surfaced path through the parkland, woodland and farmland which is suitable for wheelchairs and pushchairs as well as those with walking difficulties. The thatched church at Thornham Parva is famous for its ancient wall paintings. *(Recommended by M and M Carter; more reports please)*

Free house ~ Licensees Peter and Pam Morris ~ Real ale ~ Meals and snacks ~ Restaurant ~ (01379) 678777 ~ Children in eating area of bar ~ Open 12-3, 6.45(6.30 Sat)-11 ~ Bedrooms: £35B/£50B

TOSTOCK TL9563 Map 5
Gardeners Arms 🍺

Village signposted from A14 (former A45) and A1088

Popular with locals of all ages, there's a warm old-fashioned welcome for all customers at this charmingly unspoilt pub. The smart lounge bar has a pleasantly bustling villagey atmosphere, as well as low heavy black beams, and lots of carving chairs around the black tables, and in the lively tiled-floor public bar there's darts, pool, shove-ha'penny, dominoes, cribbage, juke box, and a fruit machine. The Greene King Abbot and IPA and seasonal beers on handpump are particularly well kept. Enjoyable quickly served bar food from a fairly limited range includes sandwiches (from £1.40), ploughman's (from £3.50), scampi (£5.25) and daily specials like lamb balti (£5.75), spiced beef with cashews or hot chicken salad with sun-dried tomatoes (£6.25), thai king prawn green curry (£7.50) and duck breast with ginger sauce and stir fry (£9.50). The picnic tables among the roses and other flowers on the sheltered lawn are a lovely place to sit. *(Recommended by Pamela Goodwyn, Charles Bardswell, Pat and Tony Martin, Ron Nightingale, Gordon and Clare Phillips, Neville Kenyon, John Saul, J E Hilditch, David and Mary Webb, Phillip Fox)*

Greene King ~ Tenant Reg Ransome ~ Meals and snacks (not Mon or Tues evenings or Sun lunchtime) ~ (01359) 270460 ~ Children in eating area of bar ~ Open 11.30(11 Sat)-2.30, 7-11; 12-3, 7-10.30 Sun

WANGFORD TM4679 Map 5
Angel 🛏

High St; village signposted just off A12 at junction of B1126 to Southwold

There's a pleasant feeling of relaxed solidity in the carefully restored airy bar at this handsome Georgian-faced 17th-c village inn, which attracts locals and visitors. Good, well spaced, simple but substantial furniture includes some sturdy elm tables, cushioned winged wall benches, and a splendid old bar counter. It's all kept spick and span. As well as half a dozen daily specials like steak and kidney pie (£4.75), chicken and mushroom lasagne (£5.25) or half a barbecue chicken (£5.95), the fairly straightforward bar food includes sandwiches (from £1.50), prawn cocktail (£3.50), hot baguettes (£3.25), ploughman's (£4.75), scampi (£5.25), several vegetarian dishes like quorn and leek bake (£5.50), mixed grill (£8.25), puddings (£1.95) and children's menu (£2.95); 3-course Sunday lunch (£4.95). The restaurant is no smoking. Well kept Adnams, John Smiths, Morlands Old Speckled Hen, Theakstons Best and Youngs Special on handpump, decent house wines from the Adnams list, good generous coffee; pleasant staff, but maybe piped pop music (local radio on our inspection visit); trivia. The garden behind has picnic tables under cocktail parasols. *(Recommended by D H Tarling, Gwen and Peter Andrews, June and Perry Dann, Nick Holmes, Michael Johnson)*

Free house ~ Licensee Richard Pearson ~ Real ale ~ Meals and snacks (all day till 9.45) ~ Restaurant ~ (01502) 578636 ~ Children welcome ~ Open 11-11; 12-10.30 Sun ~ Bedrooms: £40B/£49B

WINGFIELD TM2277 Map 5
De La Pole Arms 🍺

Between B1118 SE of Diss and B1116 S of Harleston

Closed for a few years, this village pub has been reopened after being carefully restored as a properly old-fashioned country tavern. It's been done well, with interesting bric-a-brac, comfortable traditional seating, and no distraction by juke boxes, machines or flashing lights. Despite the deliberate simplicity – and the fact that locals are clearly delighted to have it open again, as somewhere to drop in for a chat and a drink – there's a pleasantly civilised feel. Good bar food, with some emphasis on local fish and seafood, includes filled baguettes like smoked chicken and bacon or brie and sun-dried tomato (£4.50), fish platter (£6.75), haddock and prawn in fish sauce in a yorkshire pudding (£6.95), fresh dressed Cromer crab (£7.50), fried cod fillet on tomato, basil and courgette sauce with crème fraîche (£7.95), and home-made puddings like sticky toffee pudding, lemon sponge and cappuccino mousse (from £2.95). The well kept St Peters Best, Strong, Extra and Wheat Beer on handpump and under light blanket pressure come from a newish small brewery at South Elmham, some 11 or 12 miles to the NE. Service is prompt and welcoming; cribbage, dominoes and piped music. *(Recommended by Mrs P Goodwyn, D S Marshall, Tom Gondris)*

St Peters ~ Manager Tom Harvey ~ Real ale ~ Meals and snacks ~ Restaurant ~ (01379) 384545 ~ Open 11-3, 6-11; 12-3, 7-10.30 Sun

---

Lucky Dip

Besides the fully inspected pubs, you might like to try these Lucky Dips recommended to us and described by readers (if you do, please send us reports):

Aldeburgh [Market Pl, opp Moot Hall; TM4656], *Mill*: Friendly, with locals' bar, cosy no-smoking eating area, sea view; good food cooked to order inc local fish; good service, well kept Adnams ales, sensible prices; can get rather full in summer *(June and Perry Dann, Norman Smith)*; [Seafront], *White Lion*: Well kept Adnams, good value lunchtime bar food inc fresh local fish, cheerful service, pine furniture in spacious heavily beamed restaurant, afternoon teas *(Margaret and Nigel Dennis)*

Barham [Old Norwich Rd; TM1451], *Sorrel Horse*: Attractive pink-washed pantiled country pub, nicely refurbished bar with lots of beams, lounge and two dining areas off, particularly well kept Tolly ales inc Cobbolds IPA, decent bar food inc interesting specials, prompt friendly service; good garden with big play area and barbecue, timber stables opp; well placed for walks *(John Baker, Brian and Jenny Seller)*

Barrow [39 Bury Rd; off A45 W of Bury; TL7663], *Weeping Willow*: Gleaming tables, beautifully presented fresh food (not Mon) inc interesting home-made breads, good curries, huge salads, vegetarian dishes, bargain Sun lunch; friendly helpful landlord *(June and Roy Cozens)*

Beccles [New Market; TM4290], *Kings Head*: Hospitable central hotel, handy for coffee or afternoon tea; Tudor behind 18th-c front, two welcoming busy bars, real ales such as Adnams Bitter and Old, Bass, Greene King IPA, reasonably priced food with fresh veg (two for one evening bargains), Sun carvery 12-5; bedrooms *(Ian Phillips, June and Perry Dann)*

Beyton [The Green; TL9362], *White Horse*: Well kept Greene King Abbot, enjoyable food *(David and Margaret Bloomfield)*

Blundeston [from B1074 follow Church Lane, right into Short Lane, then left; TM5197], *Plough*: Smartly modernised old country pub which was the home of Barkis the carrier in *David Copperfield*; good bar food, Adnams;

handy for Jacobean Somerleyton Hall *(Anthony Barnes, LYM)*

Blythburgh [A12; TM4575], *White Hart*: Useful open-plan family dining pub with fine ancient beams, woodwork and staircase, big open fires, well kept Adnams Bitter, Old and Broadside, decent wines; children in eating area and restaurant, open all day Fri/Sat; spacious lawns looking down on tidal marshes, magnificent church over road *(Colin and Joyce Laffan, Nigel Wilkinson, Klaus and Elizabeth Leist, LYM)*

☆ **Bramfield** [A144; TM4073], *Queens Head*: Pleasantly refurbished high-beamed lounge bar, good friendly service, good fresh food, big log fire, well kept Adnams Bitter, Old and Broadside, piped music; darts in public bar; restaurant *(June and Perry Dann, Rosemary Woodburn, Pamela Goodwyn)*

Brandon [by level crossing, A1065 N – so pub actually in Norfolk; TL7886], *Great Eastern*: Unpretentious small town pub with basic well prepared reasonably priced food, particularly well kept beer esp Woodfordes Great Eastern brewed for them *(John Baker)*

Brome [TM1376], *Brome Grange*: Helpful staff, well kept Adnams, good bar food, restaurant; good spacious bedrooms, in courtyard *(Cliff Blakemore)*

Bulmer Tye [TL8438], *Fox*: More restaurant than pub, but has small bar; good service, nice atmosphere, pleasant lunch stop inc carvery *(David Regan)*

Bungay [Broad St; TM3491], *Green Dragon*: Unpretentious local brewing its own fine well priced ales, food inc good filled baked potatoes and curry nights, liberal attitude towards children; piped music may be loud, very popular with young people – side room quieter; Sun quiz night *(John Baker, Les Myford, Ian Phillips)*

☆ **Bury St Edmunds** [Whiting St; TL8564], *Masons Arms*: Particularly good value home-made food from really good snacks up, three well kept Greene King ales and prompt friendly service in busy but comfortable and relaxing dining lounge with lots of oak timbering, separate bar, terrace tables; more of a local evenings *(FWG, PGP, Mrs P J Pearce)*

Bury St Edmunds [Angel Hill], *Angel*: Thriving long-established country-town hotel with popular food in Regency restaurant and terrace rooms, faultless friendly service, well kept Adnams in rather plush bar, cellar grill room; bedrooms comfortable *(J F M West, John Baker, A Albert)*; [Mount Rd; minor rd towards Thurston, parallel to A143; TL8967], *Flying Fortress*: Much enlarged former farmhouse HQ of USAF support group, on edge of Rougham ex-airfield – the original for the film *Twelve O'Clock High*, with WWII bomber models and evocative black and white pictures; comfortable modern lounge area, well kept Adnams and other ales from long bar, wide range of food cooked here (not cheap) inc carvery (big echoic restaurant area), friendly staff, take-away wines, tables outside, old fire-engine for children to play on *(John Baker, Michael Hyde, FWG)*; [Traverse, Abbeygate St], *Nutshell*: Quaint and attractive corner pub, perhaps the country's smallest inside, with particularly well kept Greene King IPA and Abbot, friendly landlord, lots of odd bric-a-brac – an interesting tourist attraction; cl Sun and Holy Days *(PGP, Comus Elliott, Robert Gomme)*; [39 Churchgate St], *Queens Head*: Much modernised 18th-c coaching inn with Dutch tiles in high-ceilinged panelled Victorian bar, well kept Adnams Bitter and Broadside, Nethergate and maybe a guest ale, usual food inc Sun, low prices, quick friendly service, restaurant; busy with professionals and OAPs lunchtime, young people Fri/Sat evening; open all day all week, nr abbey ruins *(David Lamb, Tony and Wendy Hobden, Quentin Williamson, John C Baker)*; [88 St Johns St], *Wolf*: Former pizza parlour converted to Wetherspoons replica of Victorian town pub, with cheerful efficient service, faultless housekeeping, well kept beer – can be on the cold side (they'll remove the sparklers if you ask); food above average, prices below *(John C Baker)*

Carlton Colville [A146 W of Lowestoft; TM5189], *Crown*: Smart and friendly, very handy for East Anglian Transport Museum; good cheap lunches, three real ales inc John Smiths *(Quentin Williamson)*

☆ **Cavendish** [High St (A1092); TL8046], *Bull*: Cheerful and attractive 16th-c beamed pub with emphasis on wide range of good value food (not Mon) from good sandwiches up; good service, well kept Adnams, decent house wines, nice fireplaces; bar, dining area, garden with barbecue; fruit machines, darts and pool tucked away, no piped music; children welcome, reasonably priced bedrooms *(Richard and Valerie Wright, Gwen and Peter Andrews, Oliver Richardson, Nick Holmes)*

Chelsworth [B1115, off A1141 NW of Hadleigh; TL9848], *Peacock*: Attractive old building, run as dining pub by Old English

Pub Co chain, but small bar by entrance kept for drinkers (well kept Adnams and Greene King IPA); lots of Tudor brickwork and exposed beams, big inglenook log fire, fairly intimate pubby decor, well spaced comfortable tables, wide choice of robustly presented rather upmarket food, nice small garden; open all day Sat; bedrooms – the two at the back are quieter; pretty village *(Pamela Goodwyn, MDN, LYM)*

☆ **Chevington** [TL7860], *Greyhound*: Particularly good authentic Indian dishes cooked from scratch as well as usual food; pub modernised in 1970s, big woodburner, interesting memorabilia, well kept Greene King IPA and Abbot, enthusiastic service, restaurant; garden with good play area *(John Baker)*

☆ **Clare** [High St (A1092 W of Sudbury); TL7645], *Swan*: Much modernised early 17th-c village local, lots of copper and brass and huge log fire, public bar with WWII memorabilia (dogs allowed here), friendly landlord, good straightforward home-made food from huge bargain huffers, lovely flower tubs out behind; very special village, lovely church *(Heather Martin, J A Howl, Nick Holmes, BB)*

Clare [Market Hill], *Bell*: Large timbered inn with rambling lounge bar, splendidly carved black beams, old panelling and woodwork around the open fire, side rooms (one with lots of canal and other prints), well kept Nethergate ales, decent wines, food inc children's dishes in dining conservatory opening on to terrace; darts, pool, fruit machine; bedrooms off back courtyard, open all day, interesting village *(PM, AM, Pam Adsley, Pat and Tony Martin, M A and C R Starling, Gwen and Peter Andrews, LYM)*

Cockfield [Stows Hill; A1141 towards Lavenham; TL9054], *Three Horseshoes*: Attractive olde-worlde village pub dating from 14th c, cosy and friendly, with well kept Greene King ales, good reasonably priced generous food *(J West)*

Cratfield [TM3175], *Cratfield Poacher*: Well kept Adnams and Greene King IPA and Abbot, stuffed animals, bottle collection, super character landlord *(Michael Gibbs)*

Darsham [just off A12; TM4169], *Fox*: Well prepared reasonably priced bar food, friendly licensees, restaurant *(June and Perry Dann)*

☆ **East Bergholt** [Burnt Oak, towards Flatford Mill; TM0734], *Kings Head*: Well kept attractive beamed lounge with comfortable sofas, interesting decorations, quick pleasant service, good value home-made bar food from fresh-filled baguettes up, well kept Tolly, decent wines and coffee, piped classical music (juke box in plain public bar); lots of room in pretty garden, flower-decked haywain, baskets and tubs of flowers in front *(E A George, Pamela Goodwyn, Mike and Heather Watson)*

☆ **Eastbridge** [off B1122 N of Leiston; TM4566], *Eels Foot*: Light and clean new look in friendly country pub with wide choice of generous cheap food (neat new back dining area welcoming children), well kept Adnams and other ales, a welcome for walkers, darts in side area; more tables outside, pretty village handy for Minsmere bird reserve and heathland walks; open all day in summer for coffee and cream teas *(June and Perry Dann, Pamela Goodwyn, Gwen and Peter Andrews, Chris and Kate Lyons, Amanda, Paul and Rebecca Longley, Tim and Linda Collins, EJL, LYM)*

☆ Easton [N of Wickham Mkt, Earl Soham rd; TM2858], *White Horse*: Quaint and neatly kept pink-washed two-bar country local with open fires, well kept Adnams, food in bar and homely dining room, welcoming staff, children in eating area, garden with good play area *(Pamela Goodwyn, Graham and Liz Bell, LYM)*

Felixstowe Ferry [TM3337], *Ferry Boat*: 17th-c pub tucked away between golf links and dunes nr harbour and Martello tower, extended and much modernised as family pub; decent choice of food, busy on summer weekends – can be very quiet other times *(James Nunns, LYM)*; *Victoria*: Helpful licensees in child-friendly riverside pub, good food emphasising local seafood, competitively priced Adnams and guest beers, sailing charts in gents' *(Keith Sale, Pamela Goodwyn)*

Felsham [TL9457], *Six Bells*: Open-plan rural local with well kept Greene King ale, food inc good proper home-made pies and filled baked potatoes; friendly landlord, bar billiards, children welcome *(J R Hughes-Lewis)*

☆ Framlingham [Market Hill; TM2863], *Crown*: Traditional small inn with old-fashioned heavy-beamed public bar opening into hall and comfortable character lounge with armchairs by log fire, good bar and restaurant food (not cheap), Adnams and Banks's, lively atmosphere on Sat market day, help-yourself morning coffee; comfortable period bedrooms *(Ian Phillips, John Evans, N S Smith, LYM)*

Framlingham [Castle Approach; – OS Sheet 156 map ref 286637], *Framlingham Castle*: Friendly old small pub with Whitbreads and other ales, wide range of good bar food from toasties to steaks; children welcome *(Anon)*

Fressingfield [TM2677], *Fox & Goose*: 16th-c inn by churchyard and duckpond, beautiful timbering, good upmarket pub food inc good fishcakes and tangy lemon tart *(J F M West)*

☆ Friston [B1121; just off A1094 Aldeburgh—Snape; TM4160], *Old Chequers*: Crisply painted welcoming country dining pub with simple but stylish country pine furnishings, airy decor, good interesting food with help-yourself lunchtime veg, well kept Adnams, good value wines; splendidly redone car park *(Norman Smith, Joy and Peter Heatherley, Simon Watkins, Keith Archer, LYM)*

Gislingham [High St; TM0771], *Six Bells*: Real village pub, tastefully refurbished, friendly staff, good cheap food, particularly well kept ales brewed specially by Old Chimneys of Market Weston *(John Baker)*

Great Barton [A143 NW of Bury; TL8967], *Bunbury Arms*: Much extended 19th-c pub, cheerful, light and roomy open-plan L-shaped bar, staider dining area, well kept Greene King ales, interesting well prepared home-made food from good sandwiches up, darts at public end; play area *(W H and E Thomas, John Baker, Andrew and Ruth Triggs, Richard Balls)*

☆ Great Wenham [The Row, off A12 via Capel St Mary; TM0738], *Queens Head*: Country pub, relaxed and cheerful even though the licensees have quads; creative Indian food (not Mon evening) among other dishes, comfortably traditional pubby atmosphere, well kept Adnams Bitter and Broadside, Greene King Abbot and a guest beer, good value wines; families welcome in cosy snug *(John Baker, Richard Balls)*

Great Wratting [School Rd; TL6848], *Red Lion*: Welcoming immaculate pub in lovely setting, huge neat colourful garden behind with dovecotes and goldfish pond, good home cooking, well kept Adnams; bedrooms *(Richard Balls)*

Grundisburgh [TM2250], *Dog*: Good bar food inc bargain OAP Mon lunches in well run carefully extended elegant period pub, good range of well kept beers *(Pamela Goodwyn)*

Halesworth [The Thoroughfare; TM3877], *Angel*: Well run 16th-c coaching inn with traditional bar food, well kept ales, decent wines, good Italian restaurant; seven well equipped bedrooms, interesting interior courtyard with 18th-c clock and vines trained round the walls *(R J Sinfield, Nick and Carolyn Carter)*

Halesworth *White Hart*: Welcoming well restored open-plan local with well kept beer and good home-cooked food with local veg *(D S Marshall, June and Perry Dann)*

☆ Haughley [off A45/B1113 N of Stowmarket; TM0262], *Kings Arms*: Wide choice of good value home-made bar food inc good Greek dishes (landlady's mother comes from Cyprus), airy beamed dining lounge with lots of shiny dark tables, restaurant area on left, busy public bar with games, log fire, well kept Greene King IPA, Abbot and Rayments, friendly service; piped music; tables and play house on back lawn *(Mrs P Goodwyn, Simon Morton, David Frostick, Norman Smith, BB)*

☆ Haughley [Station Rd – towards Old Newton by level crossing], *Railway*: Pleasantly refurbished 19th-c country local with no frills, enjoyable food esp ratatouille, particularly well kept Greene King ales with a couple of good guest beers, sometimes tapped from casks in the cellar, log fire, welcoming locals; children in neat back room *(John Baker, Richard Balls, BB)*

☆ Hawkedon [Rede Rd, between A143 and B1066; TL7952], *Queens Head*: Sympathetically refurbished 17th-c inn, cheerful atmosphere, good sensibly priced home-made food inc unusual dishes, well kept Mauldons, Woodfordes and interesting guest beers *(FWG, John Baker)*

☆ **Holbrook** [Ipswich Rd; TM1636], *Compasses*: Good value food inc interesting dishes in bar and restaurant, welcoming staff, log fire, well kept ales inc Flowers and Tolly, garden with play area *(Pamela Goodwyn)*

Homersfield [TM2885], *Black Swan*: Friendly efficient staff, good food, competitive prices *(J Garrard)*

Hulver Street [TM4687], *Hulvergate Lodge*: Large pub in pleasant countryside, good food in bar or restaurant, big terrace and garden with weekend barbecues *(June and Perry Dann)*

Huntingfield [TM3374], *Huntingfield Arms*: Neat pub overlooking green, light wood tables and chairs, pleasant combination of beams and stripped brickwork, good range of attractively presented bar food inc good fresh fish, well kept Adnams, friendly service, restaurant, games area with pool beyond woodburner *(Pamela Goodwyn, June and Perry Dann)*

☆ **Icklingham** [A1101 NW of Bury; TL7772], *Old Plough*: Attractively decorated country pub with well kept Adnams, Greene King IPA and a couple of guests such as Wadworths 6X, good range of cheap home-made food, lots of cricketing memorabilia and books, subdued piped music; big garden with play area *(FWG, Scott Rumery)*

☆ **Ipswich** [Cliff Rd, by Tolly's Cliff Brewery; TM1744], *Brewery Tap*: Ground floor of early 19th-c building nestling under vast brewery, across rd from docks; a pleasant oasis in a difficult town, with decent food (not Sun/Mon evenings) from big scotch eggs and filled baps up, well kept Tolly ales (and cases of bottled beers), traditional pub games, children's room, brewery tours twice a day; piped music may obtrude; open all day *(M R Hyde, Neil Calver, Ian Phillips, Pete Yearsley, LYM)*

Ipswich [Spring Rd], *Fat Cat*: Cheerful spotless town pub, carefully renovated and opened up, with a museum of old advertisements; efficient service, good choice of well kept beer (some tapped from the cask) *(John Baker)*; [Henley Rd/Anglesea Rd], *Greyhound*: Comfortable Victorian-style decor, well kept Adnams and guest ales, good home cooking inc plenty for vegetarians, reasonable prices; children welcome *(Gordon and Clare Phillips, Rosemary Shipsey, Mary Williamson)*; [Tower St], *Old Rep*: Converted from former theatre, keeping main structure, with balcony sweeping round, impressive stairway, theatrical memorabilia; good reasonably priced food 12-7.30, Greene King ales; open all day, can get very busy *(Neil Calver)*

Kentford [Bury Rd; TL7066], *Cock*: Comfortable, friendly and innovative, cosy lounge bar with fire, open airy restaurant, good fresh British and Scandinavian food (Swedish landlady), fair prices, well kept Greene King beers; neat garden *(Mrs A Garnett)*

Kersey [signed off A1141 N of Hadleigh; TL9944], *Bell*: Quaint flower-decked Tudor building in picturesque village, low-beamed public side with tiled floor and log fire divided from lounge by brick and timber screen, wide choice of bar food, well kept ales, decent house wines, restaurant, sheltered back terrace with fairy-lit side canopy; open all day (afternoon teas), children allowed, small caravan site *(Alan Parsons, LYM)*

☆ **Kettleburgh** [Easton Rd; TM2660], *Chequers*: Good food inc fresh fish and local quail, reasonable prices, Thurs evening bargains, well kept Whitbreads-related and other ales, decent wines; unrenovated lively bar with open fire, cosy panelled dining room, attentive courteous service *(John and Sara Wheatley, Dr P J S Crawshaw, Pamela Goodwyn, Jenny and Brian Seller)*

Lavenham [High St; TL9149], *Greyhound*: Unspoilt narrow lounge, 14th-c beams, simpler public bar with polished tables and matching settles, and back dining area; good basic food, well kept Greene King IPA and Abbot, friendly staff; busy at weekends *(R T and J C Moggridge)*

Leavenheath [A134 Sudbury—Colchester, nr junction with B1068; TL9537], *Hare & Hounds*: Friendly and attractive, with plenty of tables, good choice of reasonably priced food from sandwiches up, Greene King ales, decent wines, discreet piped popular classical music; tables outside, safe play area *(Christopher Day)*

☆ **Lindsey** [Rose Green; off A1141 NW of Hadleigh; TL9744], *White Rose*: Pleasantly refurbished thatched and timbered country dining pub reopened after fire repairs, wide choice of generous upmarket food inc vegetarian and small helpings for children, well kept Adnams and Greene King, good wines, welcoming service, good log fire *(Mrs P Goodwyn, MDN, Jeremy and Louise Kemp)*

Little Bealings [Sandy Lane; TM2347], *Admirals Head*: Careful modern copy of beamed Georgian pub, good choice of food in restaurant and bar, well kept Adnams, Boddingtons, Scotts Golden and Theakstons; comfortable and friendly *(Ian Phillips)*

Little Glemham [The Street (A12); TM3458], *Lion*: Well kept Adnams, wide choice of attractively priced food, garden with animals and aviary *(Anon)*

Little Waldingfield [TL9245], *Swan*: Popular local with helpful landlady, good value food from hot rolls up, comfortable dining room, bar with pool, Flowers IPA and Original and Mauldons; tables outside *(Jenny and Michael Back)*

☆ **Long Melford** [A134; TL8645], *Bull*: Medieval former manorial great hall, old-fashioned timbered front lounge with beautifully carved beams, log fire in huge fireplace, antique furnishings, daily papers; more spacious back bar with sporting prints; good range of bar food from sandwiches to fresh fish, no-smoking restaurant, well kept Adnams Best, Greene King IPA and

Nethergate; children welcome, tables in courtyard, open all day Sat/Sun; comfortable if pricy bedrooms *(J Warren, Pam Adsley, Margaret and Nigel Dennis, LYM; more reports on new management please)*

Long Melford, Crown: Generous food cooked to order, served in cosy bar or comfortable restaurant; friendly attentive service, well kept Bass, Greene King and Hancocks, good open fire; well equipped bedrooms, huge breakfast *(Pam Adsley, LYM); Scutchers Arms:* Good food and service, pleasant bar with good choice of drinks *(Nicholas Holmes)*

Lowestoft [Pakefield St; TM5490], *Jolly Sailors:* Overlooking the sea, well kept and friendly, with good value straightforward food inc Sun carvery; restaurant *(Albert and Margaret Horton)*

☆ **Market Weston** [Bury Rd (B1111); TL9877], *Mill:* Pleasantly brightened up old pub with civilised atmosphere, well kept Adnams, Greene King IPA and an Old Chimneys beer from the village brewery, reasonably priced original food, cheerful staff *(John C Baker, FWG)*

☆ **Martlesham** [off A12 Woodbridge—Ipswich; TM2547], *Black Tiles:* Spotless and spacious family pub with pleasantly decorated bistro-style garden-room restaurant (children allowed here), big woodburner in characterful old bar, wide choice of good inexpensive generous quick home-made food, quick service from smart helpful staff, well kept Adnams Bitter and Broadside and a guest beer, tables in garden; open all day *(Norman S Smith, Nick Pickering, LYM)*

☆ **Melton** [Wilford Bridge (A1153 E of Woodbridge); TM2950], *Wilford Bridge:* Light and roomy, with good value food inc local fish in bar and restaurant, steak nights Mon/Tues, takeaways, prompt friendly service, decent wines; nearby river walks *(Malcolm Taylor)*

Mildenhall [Main St; TL7174], *Bell:* Well kept Courage Best and Directors in old inn's spacious beamed bar, open fires, friendly obliging service, good value generous food; darts, juke box; comfortable bedrooms *(FWG, Sue Rowland, Paul Mallett)*

Nayland [B1087, just off A134 Sudbury—Colchester; TL9734], *White Hart:* Smart restaur4ury pub in carefully renovated 16th-c building behind 17th-c coaching frontage, now with strong emphasis on upmarket country food, much liked by retired folk and businessmen; big comfortable settee by blazing log fire in cosy back bar, Adnams Southwold and Greene King IPA in straight glasses, good value wines; bedrooms *(Gwen and Peter Andrews)*

Newbourne [TM2643], *Fox:* 17th-c pub with straightforward home cooking using fresh local produce, well kept Tolly tapped from the cask, cosy unspoilt oak-beamed drinking area around log fire, separate family room, plans for extension; pretty hanging baskets, lots of tables out in front, musical evenings *(Pamela Goodwyn)*

Norton [Ixworth Rd (A1088); TL9565], *Dog:* Cheerful old pink-washed local with pretty hanging baskets, good value basic food in functional eating areas, relatively unspoilt lounge bar, Greene King ales, handsome weimaraner *(Ian Phillips, MDN)*

☆ **Polstead** [The Green, off A1071 or B1068 E of Sudbury; TL9938], *Cock:* Fine choice of good interesting home-made food using local ingredients and showing real flair, now doing their own smoking too; low beams, woodburner, well kept ales such as Butcombe, Fullers London Pride, Everards Tiger, Greene King IPA and Mauldons Suffolk Punch, good choice of wines, charming enthusiastic landlord *(Mrs S Wenlock)*

Reydon [Wangford Rd; TM4978], *Cricketers:* Relaxed local atmosphere, good choice of good food inc plenty of fish and vegetarian, Adnams beers and wines, light and airy bar, tables in garden; comfortable bedrooms, bath across landing *(Mr and Mrs E Gorton, Dererk and Sylvia Stephenson)*

Rickinghall [A143 Diss—Bury St Edmunds; TM0475], *Hamblyn House:* Tastefully refurbished 16th-c inn with big beamed and timbered lounge, comfortable and relaxing, roaring log fires, good traditional food in restaurant, local St Peters ales kept well, warm welcome; attractive bedrooms *(John Baker, Mrs Eileen Chandler)*

☆ **Risby** [slip rd off A14; TL7966], *White Horse:* Obliging new owners doing wide choice of food in bar and restaurant (given notice, will cook anything); log fire, beams, brickwork and panelling, mats on flagstones, attractive and interesting decor and furnishings *(W H and E Thomas, LYM)*

☆ **Rumburgh** [NW of Halesworth; TM3481], *Buck:* Pretty and popular rambling country local, several rooms inc restaurant, good value food inc generous Sun roasts and fresh veg, lots of character, well kept ales such as Adnams Extra, friendly atmosphere, games in end room; quiet back lawn *(June and Perry Dann)*

☆ **Saxtead Green** [B1119; TM2665], *Old Mill House:* Nicely placed across green from working windmill, attractively refurbished with neat country look, brick servery, wooden tables and chairs, pretty curtains, good reasonably priced home-made food inc lunchtime carvery, rotating well kept guest ales, pleasant service; sizeable garden, pretty back terrace, good new play area *(Pete Yearsley, Mrs P Goodwyn, Graham and Liz Bell, Mr and Mrs Newby, LYM)*

South Cove [B1127 Southwold—Wrentham; TM4981], *Five Bells:* Wide choice of good value food inc home-made puddings and weekday OAP bargains in nice old country pub *(June and Perry Dann)*

☆ **Southwold** [7 East Green; TM5076], *Sole Bay:* Homely and welcoming little Victorian local moments from sea, opp brewery (and the Sole Bay lighthouse); particularly good value simple lunchtime food (not Sun in winter) esp local smoked sprats, well kept full

Adnams range, chatty landlord, friendly locals and dog (other dogs allowed), lots of polished seafaring memorabilia, unobtrusive piped music, conservatory with cockatoos, tables on side terrace *(John Walker, Pat and John Millward, Gwen and Peter Andrews, R T and J C Moggridge, Paul Mason, Dave Cave, Jean Southwell, PGP, Richard Balls, Geoff and Linda Dibble, BB)*

☆ **Southwold** [42 East St], *Lord Nelson*: Bustling cheerful little local nr seafront, very smoothly run, with low ceilings, panelling and tiled floor, with random old furniture and lamps in nice nooks and crannies, particularly well kept Adnams Mild, Bitter, Extra, Broadside and Old, good basic lunchtime food, attentive service, sheltered back garden; open all day, children welcome *(A J Thomas, Eric Locker, John Waller, Adrian and Jane Tierney-Jones, PGP, Tom McLean, Richard Balls, BB)*

Southwold [Blackshore Quay; from A1095, right at Kings Head – pass golf course and water tower], *Harbour*: Popular basic harbour local, tiny low-beamed front bar, upper back bar with lots of nautical bric-a-brac – even ship-to-shore telephone and wind speed indicator; simple but imaginative food (not Sun evening; just fish and chips in newspaper Fri evening/Sat lunch), well kept Adnams Bitter and Broadside, coal fires, solid old furnishings, friendly service (though can slow at busy times), darts, table skittles, tables outside with play area, ducks and animals – can be a bit untidy out here *(Richard Balls, LYM)*; [High St], *Kings Head*: Spacious dining pub with lots of maroon and pink plush, very wide choice of decent food esp fish with good fresh veg, well kept Adnams, good house wines, friendly staff; comfortable family/games room with well lit pool table; jazz Sun night, decent bedrooms in house across road *(Dr B and Mrs P Baker, Ian Blackwell, Richard Balls, BB)*; [Market Pl], *Swan*: Very much a hotel, but most like its relaxed comfortable back bar, chintzy and airy front lounge, well kept Adnams and Broadside with the full range of their bottled beers, decent wines and malt whiskies; good bedrooms inc garden rooms where (by arrangement) dogs can stay too *(Robert Turnham, John Waller, Richard Balls, LYM)*

Spexhall [Stone St; TM3780], *Huntsman & Hounds*: Unpretentious exterior hiding old beams and character, warm welcome, cosy village atmosphere, good freshly made food inc fresh veg; low prices *(June and Perry Dann)*

Sproughton [Old Hadleigh Rd; TM1244], *Beagle*: Plushly comfortable 1920s timber-framed pub, beamery and inglenooks, five open fires, decent food all day inc interesting puddings, ales inc Bass and Fullers London Pride, good choice of wines by glass, back conservatory *(Mike and Maggie Betton)*

Stanton [TL5673], *Rose & Crown*: Tidy pub open all day, with wide range of well priced food up to ostrich, kangaroo and wild boar,

scottie and west highland white pictures, parrot; smart conservatory restaurant, booking advised; children welcome *(Glenn and Lesley Cowlam, Clive Gilbert)*

☆ **Stradishall** [A143; TL7452], *Cherry Tree*: Two small traditional beamed bars, good home cooking inc vegetarian, pleasant atmosphere, open fires, Greene King beers under light pressure; friendly ducks and pond in huge rustic garden (dogs allowed here); outside gents' *(John and Karen Gibson, BB)*

☆ **Sudbury** [Church Walk; TL8741], *Waggon & Horses*: Comfortable welcoming local with interesting decor, well presented food even Sun afternoon, well kept Greene King ales, bar billiards, log fire; pleasant walled garden with picnic tables *(Ian Phillips)*

Sudbury [Friars St], *Angel*: Attractive town pub between church and theatre, good value food esp curries, new no-smoking restaurant, Greene King ales and farm cider, quick pleasant service; pool, piped music *(Keith and Janet Morris)*

Swilland [High Rd; TM1852], *Moon & Mushroom*: Friendly landlord, food (not Sun/Mon) inc home-cooked casseroles with lots of fresh veg in dining room, real ales inc Adnams, Scotts and Woodfordes *(Norma and Keith Bloomfield)*

Thorington Street [B1068 Higham—Stoke by Nayland; TM0035], *Rose*: Partly Tudor, with good home-made food inc good value Sun lunch and delicious puddings, well kept Adnams, decent house wines, friendly service, big garden with view of Box valley; bedrooms *(Mrs M A Burton, Jeremy and Louise Kemp)*

☆ **Walberswick** [B1387, off A12 S of Lowestoft; TM4974], *Bell*: Timeless rambling place with ancient flooring bricks, flagstones and beams, curved high-backed settles, big open fire and woodburner – can be crowded and noisy, but that's usually at a time of year when you can escape to the sizeable flower-filled lawn; bar food from interesting sandwiches to local fish and stir fries, no-smoking restaurant, family room, well kept Adnams Bitter, Broadside and Extra, darts, shove-ha'penny, and fruit machine; bedrooms with views, nr beach; open all day summer Sats, some folk nights *(June and Perry Dann, Mike Pickup, Wayne Brindle, Pamela Goodwyn, LYM)*

Walberswick, *Anchor*: Airy and comfortably modern well furnished hotel bar, reasonably priced food inc good range of seafood, well kept Adnams tapped from the cask, decent wines, cheerful service, cosy log fires; bedrooms *(W Brewster, John Waller, D and J Tapper, P Burrows-Smith)*

Waldringfield [nr Woodbridge; TM2844], *Maybush*: Atmospheric riverside pub renovated by new owners, sailing memorabilia inc Giles cartoons *(Richard May)*

☆ **Wenhaston** [off A12, or B1123 E of Halesworth; TM4276], *Star*: Unpretentious country pub with limited choice of good reasonably priced lunchtime home cooking (not Sat or maybe Mon – landlady's day off), well kept Adnams, pleasant views; suntrap lounge, games in public bar, tables on sizeable lawn *(Keith Archer, June and Perry Dann, LYM)*

☆ **Westleton** [B1125 Blythburgh—Leiston; TM4469], *Crown*: Upmarket extended beamed country inn with country chairs, attractive stripped tables, good local photographs and farm tools in smallish decorous bar area, six interesting real ales, lots of malt whiskies, good wines, farm cider, log fires, pleasant if not always speedy service, piped classical music; wide range of home-made food inc good vegetarian choice in big dining area opening off on left (children allowed) and in roomy no-smoking dining conservatory, pretty garden with aviary and floodlit terrace, beautiful setting, good walks nearby; 19 bedrooms, comfortable if not large, with good breakfasts *(John Fahy, David and Anne Culley, Paul Mason, June and Perry Dann, M J Morgan, Paul Kitchener, Margaret and Nigel Dennis, Sarah and Ian Shannon, Colin and Joyce Laffan, Jamie and Ruth Lyons, J F Knutton, Pamela Goodwyn, Richard Balls, David and Anne Culley, Mr and Mrs J Brown, LYM)*

☆ **Westleton** [Darsham Rd, off B1125 Blythburgh—Leiston], *White Horse*: Less smart and cheaper than the Crown, friendly village pub with good generous straightforward food (not winter Tues) in unassuming high-ceilinged bar and attractive no-smoking Victorian back dining room; agreeably busy decor, well kept Adnams Bitter and Broadside and seasonal ales, quiet piped music, friendly service; picnic tables in cottagey back garden with climbing frame, and out by village duckpond); handy for Fisks clematis nursery, children in eating area, bedrooms *(John and Barbara Spencer, Alan Jarvis, MDN, M A Mees, Paul Mason, LYM)*

Wherstead [Bourne Hill; junction A137/B1456 N, just S of Ipswich; TM1641], *Oyster Reach*: Very old pub renamed (was Ostrich) and extensively reworked as Beefeater, with light relaxing decor, reasonable value food all day, good breezy service; bedrooms in attached Travel Inn *(Thomas Nott)*

Wissett [TM3679], *Plough*: New licensees doing good reasonably priced food inc bargain lunches Mon-Thurs, good value Sun lunch, well kept Adnams; live music some Sats, buskers some Weds *(June and Perry Dann)*

Witnesham [TM1851], *Barley Mow*: New tenant in pleasant old pub with home-made food in separate dining room, well kept Greene King *(Norma and Keith Bloomfield)*

Woodbridge [opp quay; TM2749], *Anchor*: Good value food inc sandwiches, baked potatoes and well priced fresh local fish, Greene King IPA and Abbot *(Pat and Tony Martin)*; [The Thoroughfare], *Crown*: Small bar, friendly service, good food in dining room; bedrooms in converted old stables *(M Lavery)*; [Market Hill], *Kings Head*: Interesting mix of customers in spacious bar with blazing inglenook log fire, full Adnams range kept well, good generous food inc lots of fish, no loud music *(Pat and Tony Martin)*

Yaxley [A140 Ipswich—Norwich; TM1274], *Bull*: Plusher decor and good food under current landlord; well kept Adnams *(John C Baker)*

Post Office address codings confusingly give the impression that some pubs are in Suffolk when they're really in Norfolk or Cambridgeshire (which is where we list them).

Surrey

By no means a cheap county for pub-lovers, Surrey compensates by having a surprising number of interesting and friendly pubs of considerable character, often tucked away in beautiful spots – the sort that local insiders know about, but the rest of us might easily drive straight past without knowing what we've missed. Three good examples are new entries this year: the Villagers up a narrow lane at Blackheath near Chilworth, the Sun on the green at Dunsfold, and the Three Horseshoes at Thursley – only just off the hectic A3, yet it could be in another entirely more peaceful world. Two other pubs here that have been giving special pleasure recently are the Woolpack at Elstead (get there early to enjoy its good food), and the King William IV on its hillside at Mickleham (much enjoyed all round, and earning one of our Beer Awards this year). This time round the contest for our dining pub award is really between these two, and by a short head it is the King William IV which gains the title of Surrey Dining Pub of the Year – but be warned, it is on a steep hill, and access isn't ideal for the less mobile. Other places for an enjoyable meal out include the Plough at Blackbrook (lovely garden, good wines), the smart and stylish Withies at Compton, the Sir Douglas Haig at Effingham (a reliable lunch place), the simple but very civilised Fox & Hounds at Englefield Green, the beautifully placed White Horse at Hascombe, the Plough at Leigh (fills up quickly at lunchtime – excellent choice of wines by the glass), and the Fox & Hounds at South Godstone. The Plough at Coldharbour now brews its own beer (and stocks a fine range from elsewhere); the Ram at Farncombe is a must for cider lovers, with a tremendous range (nice in other ways too, with an attractive garden). In the Lucky Dip section at the end of the chapter, up-and-coming pubs include the Jolly Farmer in Bramley, Queens Head at East Clandon, Bell at Outwood, Hurtwood at Peaslake, White Horse at Shere, Volunteer at Sutton and Barley Mow at Tandridge. We have inspected almost all of these, and vouch for their quality – as we do for the virtues we describe for the Drummond Arms at Albury, Cricketers near Cobham and Onslow Arms at West Clandon. As we've said, this county's pubs are not easy on the pocket, with beer costing around 20p a pint more than the national average. In general pubs supplied by the region's smaller breweries tended to be a bit cheaper than those supplied by the big nationals – particularly those tied to small breweries such as Morlands or Youngs; some King & Barnes pubs also have attractive prices.

BETCHWORTH TQ2049 Map 3
Dolphin

The Street; 2½ miles W of Reigate on A25 turn left into Buckland, then take the second left

Enjoyed by a wide mix of customers, this friendly village local is the sort of place that people go back to time and again. The homely front room is furnished with kitchen chairs and plain tables on the 400-year-old scrubbed flagstones, and the carpeted back saloon bar is black-panelled with robust old-fashioned elm or oak tables; nostalgic touches include three coal fires and a well chiming longcase clock. Well priced Youngs Bitter, Special, Ram Rod and seasonal brews on handpump, and a cruover machine guarantees that most wines can be served by the glass; efficient service. Bar food includes soup (£1.95), ploughman's (from £3.35), sausage and egg (£3.25), filled baked potatoes (from £3.95), meat or vegetable lasagne (£4.95), gammon steak (£5.95), daily specials, and puddings like spotted dick or apple pie (£1.95). Darts, dominoes, cribbage, and fruit machine. There are some seats in the small laurel-shaded front courtyard and picnic tables on a lawn by the car park, opposite the church and on the back garden terrace. Get there early, the pub fills up fast, sometimes with a lively younger crowd. No children inside. *(Recommended by Andy and Jill Kassube, Rick Cottrell, Hilton Lord, G W Stevenson, Don Mather, DWAJ, Pat Booker, P J Caunt, Dorsan Baker)*

Youngs ~ Manager: George and Rose Campbell ~ Real ale ~ Meals and snacks (12-2.30, 7-10) ~ (01737) 842288 ~ Open 11-3, 5.30-11; 11-11 summer Sat; 12-10.30 summer Sun; closed 25 Dec evening)

BLACKBROOK TQ1846 Map 3
Plough ♀

On byroad E of A24, parallel to it, between Dorking and Newdigate, just N of the turn E to Leigh

Once again, Mr and Mrs Squire have won awards for the carefully planted and secluded back garden and marvellous hanging baskets and window boxes of this civilised white-fronted pub. There are a good few tables, and children can play in the prettily painted Swiss playhouse furnished with tiny tables and chairs. Fresh flowers sit on the tables and sills of the large linen curtained windows in the partly no-smoking saloon bar, and down some steps, the public bar has brass-topped treadle tables, a formidable collection of ties as well as old saws on the ceiling, and bottles and flat-irons; piped music. Good bar food includes daily specials such as stilton and onion soup (£2.65), mixed mushrooms in garlic cream sauce (£3.45), pork, apple and cider pie (£5.95), poached chicken with lemon and tarragon sauce (£7.45), swordfish grilled with sultanas, olives and almonds (£8.95), and puddings such as pear and ginger crumble or hot chocolate fudge pudding (£2.75); also, filled baked potatoes (from £3.45), basket meals (from £3.75), ploughman's (£3.95), toasted bagels (from £3.95), ham and pineapple (£4.75), fillet of plaice with chips (£4.95), ratatouille niçoise (£5.45), prawn curry with naan bread, mango chutney, and cucumber and yoghurt raita (£5.95), and steaks (from £9.95). Well kept King & Barnes Sussex, Broadwood, Festive, and seasonal beers on handpump, quite a few good wines by the glass, and several malt whiskies and port. Tess the blind black labrador puts in an appearance after 10pm. The countryside around here is a particularly good area for colourful spring and summer walks through the oak woods. They usually have an atmospheric carol concert the Sunday before Christmas. No children inside. *(Recommended by Colin Draper, Don Mather, Derek and Maggie Washington, TOH, G P Kernan, James Nunns, Margaret and Nigel Dennis, R V G Brown, Ron Gentry, Helen Morton, John Evans)*

King & Barnes ~ Tenants: Chris and Robin Squire ~ Real ale ~ Meals and snacks (not Mon evening) ~ (01306) 886603 ~ Open 11-2.30(3 Sat), 6-11; 12-3, 7-10.30 Sun; closed 25/26 Dec and 1 Jan

CHARLESHILL SU8944 Map 2
Donkey

Near Tilford, on B3001 Milford—Farnham; as soon as you see pub sign, turn left

For three generations, the same family has run this nicely old-fashioned cottage. The bright saloon has lots of polished stirrups, lamps and watering cans on the walls and prettily cushioned built-in wall benches and wheelback chairs, while the lounge has a lovely old high-backed settle and a couple of unusual three-legged chairs, as well as highly polished horsebrasses, a longcase clock, some powder pouches, and swords on the walls and beams. Reasonably priced home-made bar food includes sandwiches and toasted sandwiches (from £2), filled baked potatoes (from £2.40), five home-made daily specials like cauliflower and macaroni bake, lasagne, good haddock pie, nice

Welsh lamb pie, and cottage pie (all £5.25), and puddings such as gooseberry cheesecake or honey and hazelnut tart. A no-smoking conservatory with blond wheelback chairs and stripped tables, fairy lights and some plants, has sliding doors into the garden. During the week the pub is a popular lunchtime stop for the ladies of the county. Well kept and priced Morlands IPA and Old Speckled Hen, and Charles Wells Bombardier on handpump, maybe under light blanket pressure, and country wines; shove-ha'penny, dominoes and cribbage, and perhaps quiet piped music. The garden is very attractive, with bright flowerbeds, white garden furniture, a tiny pond, and a big fairy-lit fir tree. There's a children's play area out here too. *(Recommended by David Shillitoe, J S M Sheldon, Tony and Wendy Hobden, Derek Harvey-Piper, Pat and Tony Martin, Andy and Gill Plumb, M L and G Clarke, B and K Hypher)*

Morlands ~ Lease: Peter and Shirley Britcher ~ Real ale ~ Meals and snacks (not Sun evening) ~ (01252) 702124 ~ Children in conservatory ~ Open 11-2.30, 6-11; cl 25, 26 Dec evening

CHILWORTH TQ0346 Map 3
Villagers

Blackheath; off A248 SE of Guildford, by station, over level crossing – at Blackheath turn left

Almost alone on a quiet lane through mixed woodland, this has tables on a sheltered back terrace bright with begonias, with steps up past roses to a good-sized lawn, and a short path through the trees to a cricket green. A small flagstoned room with a big fireplace by the entrance suits walkers, and beyond this the main beamed and carpeted bar rambles around among standing timbers, with a mix of furniture including cushioned pews and more orthodox chairs; a neat dining room is partly separate from this by a largely knocked-through wall. Besides excellent sandwiches (from £3), filled baked potatoes (from £4) and ploughman's (from £4.75), a short choice of good home-made food might include soused fresh anchovy with a tomato and basil salad (£6.25), courgette and dill pasta bake, honey-roast chicken or aubergines stuffed with spicy mint lamb (£6.50), steak and kidney pie or pudding or barnsley chop with cranberry sauce (£6.75), seafood in a creamy wine sauce (£7.25), and puddings such as hot chocolate fudgecake or bread and butter pudding (£3); well kept Courage Best and Directors, Marstons Pedigree, and Morlands Old Speckled Hen on handpump (they may not all be on), decent house wines, pleasant young staff, unobtrusive laid-back piped music. There are good walks all around – the table-mats show some. We have not yet heard from readers staying in the newly decorated bedrooms – but it's a nice quiet spot. *(Recommended by Ian and Liz Phillips, G W Stevenson, Herbie, Mrs W D Morrison, Stephen and Judy Parish)*

Free house ~ Licensee Emma Rowe ~ Real ale ~ Meals and snacks ~ Restaurant ~ (01483) 893152 ~ Well behaved children welcome ~ Open 11-3, 6-11; 12-10.30 Sun; 12-3, 7-10.30 winter Sun ~ Bedrooms: £30/£40

COLDHARBOUR TQ1543 Map 3
Plough ◀

Village signposted in the network of small roads around Abinger and Leith Hill, off A24 and A29

As well as a fine range of seven or eight real ales on handpump, such as Adnams Broadside, Badger Best and Tanglefoot, Hogs Back Hop Garden Gold, Ringwood Old Thumper, Wadworths 6X and a guest beer, the friendly licensees now brew two of their own beers – Crooked Furrow and Tollywhacker; they also keep country wines and Biddenden farm cider on handpump. The two bars have a relaxed atmosphere, a good mix of customers, stripped light beams and timbering in the warm-coloured dark ochre walls, with quite unusual little chairs around the tables in the snug red-carpeted room on the left, and little decorative plates on the walls and a big open fire in the one on the right – which leads through to the no-smoking restaurant (currently being refurbished). Enjoyable home-made bar food includes starters such as cream of fresh tomato and basil soup, duck liver pâté or garlic mushrooms in a bacon and stilton sauce (from £3.25), ploughman's (from £4.25), filled baked potatoes (from £4.95), main courses like broccoli and stilton quiche, rabbit and smoky bacon pie, a fresh fish dish, navarin of lamb or steaks and game (£5.95-£10.95), and puddings like pecan, pumpkin and rum pie or cranberry and almond tart (from £3.25). The games bar on the left has darts, pool, and there is piped music. Outside there are picnic tables by the tubs of flowers in front and in the the terraced garden with fish pond and waterlilies. Good walks all around. *(Recommended by Brian and Jenny Seller, Tim Barrow, Sue Demont, Mr and Mrs J Otten, Derek Harvey-Piper, Tom Hall, Piotr Chodzko-Zajko, James Nunns, Mr and Mrs D Carter, Simon Skinner, J Sheldon, Wayne Brindle)*

Free house ~ Licensees Richard and Anna Abrehart ~ Real ale ~ Meals and snacks ~ Restaurant ~ (01306) 711793 ~ Children in eating area of bar if eating ~ Open 11.30-3, 6.30-11; 11.30-11 summer Sat, 11.30-4, 6.30-11 winter Sat; 12-10.30 Sun ~ Bedrooms: /£50S

COMPTON SU9546 Map 2
Harrow

B3000

Fairly close to the North Downs Way, this busy village pub has a brightly lit main bar with interesting racing pictures below the ancient ceiling – mostly portraits of horses, jockey caricatures and signed race-finish photographs. Opening off here are more little beamed rooms with latched rustic doors, and nice touches such as brass horse-head coat hooks, photographs of the area, and a bas relief in wood of the pub sign; piped music. Bar food is pricy and includes sandwiches (from £3.50), toasties from £4.25), soup (£4.25), ploughman's (from £5.50), baked potatoes (from £5.75), creamy mixed mushroom pasta (£7), honey-roast ham and eggs (£7.25), cod in batter (£7.75), duck breast with a chinese-style honey and soy sauce (£10), steaks (from £11.50), and puddings such as fruit crumble (£3.50); breakfast is available to non-residents. You may need to book on Friday and Saturday evenings. Well kept Greene King IPA, Ind Coope Burton, Harveys Best Bitter, and Tetleys on handpump. There are some seats outside by the car park, looking out to gentle slopes of pasture. In the pretty village the art nouveau Watts Chapel and Gallery are interesting, and the church itself is attractive; Loseley House is nearby too. *(Recommended by J S M Sheldon, Lady M H Moir, Derek Harvey-Piper, Ian Phillips, Ed Birch, Derek and Margaret Underwood, G W Jensen, Hilarie Taylor, Margaret and Nigel Parker)*

Allied Domecq ~ Lease: Roger and Susan Seaman ~ Real ale ~ Meals and snacks (12-3, 6-10; breakfast from 8; not Sun evening) ~ Restaurant (not Sun evening) ~ (01483) 810379 ~ Children welcome ~ Open 11-3, 5.30(6 Sat)-11; 12-4 Sun, closed Sun evening ~ Bedrooms: £30B/£37.50B

Withies

Withies Lane; pub signposted from B3000

Smart yet atmospheric, this fine 16th-c dining pub is mainly somewhere to come for a meal – though there's still a genuinely pubby small low-beamed bar with a massive inglenook fireplace and a roaring log fire, some attractive 17th-c carved panels between the windows, and a splendidly art nouveau settle among the old sewing machine tables. A short and straightforward choice of bar food includes soup (£2.50), sandwiches (from £3.25), a choice of pâté (£3.50), good ploughman's (from £3.75), cumberland sausages (£4.25), filled baked potatoes (from £4) and seafood platter (£6.50); the restaurant has more elaborate food and is popular with business people during the week. Well kept Bass, Friary Meux, and King & Barnes Sussex on handpump. The immaculate garden, overhung with weeping willows, has tables under an arbour of creeper-hung trellises, more on a crazy-paved terrace and yet more under old apple trees. The neat lawn in front of the steeply tiled white house is bordered by masses of flowers. *Recommended by John Evans, Martin and Karen Wake, Miss A Drake, Tom Mann, Derek Harvey-Piper, B Lake, Mark Stevens, Gill and Andy Plumb, Hilarie Taylor, Barbara Wensworth, Mrs P F Raymond-Cox)*

Free house ~ Licensees Brian and Hugh Thomas ~ Real ale ~ Meals and snacks (till 10pm; not Sun evening) ~ Restaurant (not Sun evening) ~ (01483) 421158 ~ Children welcome ~ Open 11-3, 6-11; closed Sun evening

DUNSFOLD TQ0035 Map 3
Sun

Off B2130 S of Godalming

Set by a quiet village green, this elegant brick-fronted 18th-c pub has symmetrical arched double porches and neat twin bottle-glass bow windows – pleasant in summer to sit outside at one of the tables. Inside, there's a friendly old-fashioned atmosphere, scrubbed pine furniture, log fires, and Friary Meux Best, King & Barnes Sussex, and Marstons Pedigree on handpump – along with country wines and a decent wine list. Quickly served in generous helpings, the good popular home-made bar food includes sandwiches (from £1.90), home-made soup (£2.75), ploughman's (from £4.50), venison sausages in red wine (£5.95), rabbit casserole (£6.50), steak and kidney pie (£6.75), tandoori chicken (£6.95), steaks (from £10.50), fresh fish dishes, and puddings like hot pecan and white chocolate slice or blackberry and apple pie (£2.95); cottagey restaurant. Darts, table skittles, cribbage, dominoes, and trivia. (*Recommended by Paul Williams, David Clifton, Mrs W D Morrison, June and Malcolm Farmer*)

Vanguard (Carlsberg-Tetleys) ~ Lease: Mrs Judith Dunne ~ Real ale ~ Meals and snacks (till 10pm) ~ Restaurant ~ (01483) 200242 ~ Children in eating area of bar ~ Occasional live music Sun ~ Open 11-3, 6-11; 12-4, 7-10.30 Sun

EFFINGHAM TQ1253 Map 3
Sir Douglas Haig

The Street; off A246 W of Leatherhead

Large and open-plan, this busy pub has an open fire at each end of the long room, small settles, banquettes and kitchen chairs in the dining area, a replica of the tail section of a World War I aeroplane in the rafters, lots of obscure agricultural implements dotted around, and a mix of seats including armchairs on the wood-stained floor at the drinking end. It's a reliable place for a good value lunch: sandwiches (from £1.90), good filled french bread (£2.25), daily specials like good liver and bacon, leek and potato pie, sausage, bacon and bean pot, tomato and basil quiche or chicken in a red and green pepper sauce (from £4.50), gammon and egg (£4.95), steak, mushroom and ale pie (£5.50), a range of steaks (from £5.95 for 5oz steak – £10.95 for T-bone), and a popular mixed grill (£11.95); Sunday roast (£5.95), and a good choice of coffees. Well kept Fullers London Pride, Gales Best and HSB, and changing guest such as Hampshire Glory on handpump, and quick, friendly service. There's a back lawn and an attractive terraced area with seats and tables; fruit machine, juke box (only in the late evening), and a TV in the corner of the lounge. No children. (*Recommended by DWAJ, George Atkinson, Mrs D W Cook, T Pascall, Mike Gilbert, G W Jensen, J Sheldon, John Pettit*)

Free house ~ Licensee Laurie Smart ~ Real ale ~ Meals and snacks ~ (01372) 456886 ~ Open 11-3, 5-11; 11-11 Sat; 12-3.30, 7-10.30 Sun ~ Bedrooms: £50B/£60B

ELSTEAD SU9143 Map 2
Woolpack 🍴

The Green; B3001 Milford—Farnham

It's best to arrive at this bustling, friendly pub early to be sure of a table – particularly on weekend evenings or Sunday lunchtime. The generous helpings of interesting food is the main draw, though there's a relaxed and informal atmosphere and well kept real ales, too. The long airy main bar has fireplaces at each end, window seats and spindleback chairs around plain wooden tables, and a fair amount of wool industry memorabilia, such as the weaving shuttles and cones of wool that hang above the high-backed settles. Leading off here is a big room decorated with lots of country prints, a weaving loom, scales, and brass measuring jugs; the fireplace with its wooden pillars lace frill is unusual. Changing regularly, the much enjoyed food includes home-made soup (£2.50), baked goat's cheese with mango and chives (£4.50), turkey strips in orange, mustard and almond breadcrumbs with an orange and cranberry sauce (£4.75), chicken casseroled in whisky, stilton and almonds or pork green thai curry with lime leaves and coriander (£6.95), large home-made pies like tasty cod and prawn or steak and kidney (£7.10), venison steak in sloe gin, tarragon and cream or salmon steak in pernod and fennel cream sauce (£8.95), and home-made puddings like sticky toffee pudding; Sunday lunch is popular. Well kept Greene King Abbot and guests such as Greene King IPA, Harveys PA or Youngs Bitter tapped from the cask, and a decent wine list. Dominoes, cribbage, and fruit machine. A family room leads to the garden with picnic tables and a children's play area. *(Recommended by David Peakall, Piotre Chodzko-Zajko, Margaret and Nigel Dennis, Mr and Mrs T Bryan, Ian Jones, Mike Fitzgerald, Liz and Ian Phillips, Andrew Lee, Colin McKerrow, P Gillbe, Mr and Mrs T A Bond, R Crail, Chris Elford, G and M Stewart, Lady M H Moir, Helen Hazzard, TOH, Graham and Karen Oddey, Peter Burton, M L and G Clarke, JEB, Derek and Margaret Underwood, G W Jensen, Bob and Maggie Atherton, Ed Birch, E D Bailey)*

Ind Coope (Carlsberg-Tetleys) ~ Lease: J A Macready and S A Askew ~ Real ale ~ Meals and snacks ~ Restaurant ~ (01252) 703106 ~ Children in family room, restaurant (if well behaved) or two other rooms ~ Open 11-2.30, 6-11; 12-3, 7-10.30 Sun; closed evening 25 Dec, all day 26 Dec

ENGLEFIELD GREEN SU9772 Map 2
Fox & Hounds

Bishopsgate Road; off A328 N of Egham

On the edge of Windsor Park and a very short stroll from the main gate to the Savile Garden, this smart 17th-c pub is well liked for its well prepared food. It's a simple but civilised place with good sturdy wooden tables and chairs, prints in sets of four, a good log fire in the big fireplace, and some stuffed animals and fading red gingham curtains. The bar has sandwiches (from £2.25), a good choice of baguettes (Saturday and Sunday only, from £2.50), soup (£3.75), and pâté (£5.95). More substantial – and expensive – dishes can be found in the attractive back dining room, candlelit at night, with a blackboard menu brought to your table and more choice on further wall boards: lots of starters (from £5), home-made steak and kidney pudding (£10), fresh fish like salmon with a dill and mayonnaise sauce (£10.50) or lemon sole (£14.75), half a shoulder of English lamb (£10.75), calf liver with bacon and onion (£11), and half a roast duckling with orange sauce (£12.50); they do a three-course Sunday lunch (£16.50); friendly service. Well kept Courage Best and Directors, John Smiths and a guest such as Greene King IPA on handpump. There are picnic tables on the neat and pretty front lawn, and more on a back terrace. The licensees also run the Thatched Tavern at Cheapside in Berkshire. *(Recommended by Mrs M L Carter, Jerry Hughes, Ian Phillips, A and A Moncreiffe, Tony and Wendy Hobden, Martin and Karen Wake, Linda Hayden, Peter Stadoon, Susan and John Douglas)*

Courage ~ Licensees Robert King and Jonathan Michael Mee ~ Real ale ~ Meals and snacks ~ Restaurant ~ (01784) 433098 ~ Well behaved children welcome ~ Jazz Mon evening ~ Open 11-3, 6-11; closed 25 Dec

FARNCOMBE SU9844 Map 3
Ram

Catteshall Lane; behind Catteshall industrial estate on outskirts of Godalming beyond Sainsbury's; after Farncombe boathouse take second left, then first right, followed by first left

30 different ciders, both cask and keg, are the speciality of this 16th-c cider house. They do also keep Fullers London Pride and a guest such as Batemans XB, Brakspears Bitter, Fullers ESB or Shepherd Neame Spitfire on handpump, and quite a few country wines as well. Bar food might include filled rolls and sandwiches, game pâté (£3), rabbit pie (£3.70), roast pheasant (£4.95), wild boar (£5.50), and puddings like treacle tart (£2.70); obliging service from friendly staff. The three simple small rooms have

coal-effect fires in old brick hearths, heavy-beams, and wooden tables and pews; there's a talking parrot in the public bar (which can be smoky), and maybe a huge german shepherd, Yum-Yum; darts and shove-ha'penny. The pub gets very popular with a younger set later in the evening. It's especially appealing in summer, when the big back garden proves very popular with families; a softly rippling stream runs through the middle, and there are a good few picnic tables and tables and chairs beside the trees on the grass, and on a covered patio. Throughout the year, they hold various celebrations – St George's Day, May Day, Guy Fawkes, and so forth; there's a small play area, as well as a big carved wooden ram. *(Recommended by Susan and John Douglas, Wayne Brindle)*

Free house ~ Licensees Harry Ardeshir and Carolyn Eley ~ Real ale ~ Meals and snacks ~ (01483) 421093 ~ Children welcome ~ Folk music Mon and Weds evenings ~ Open 11-11; 12-10.30 Sun

FRIDAY STREET TQ1245 Map 3
Stephan Langton
Village signed off B2126, or from A25 Westcott—Guildford

Surrounded by good walks, with Leith Hill particularly rewarding, this busy country local is in a beautiful peaceful spot. The comfortable bar and parlour-like lounge have prints of various historic figures and events, as well as a couple of old-fashioned musical instruments, a stuffed bird in a case, fresh flowers, and pictures of the licensee's dogs; these don't generally appear in the bar until late evening, though other dogs are welcome. There are some handsome vases in front of the fireplace, which has a seat fashioned from a beer barrel amongst the mix of furnishings around it. The popular bar food (cooked by the landlord) is listed above here: soup (£2.45), filled rolls (from £2.50), ploughman's (from £4), sausages or vegetable quiche (£4.95), calamari (£5.25), omelettes, curry or a roast of the day (£5.75), game casserole (£6.50), steak (£9.50), daily specials, and children's meals (from £2.95); two-course Sunday lunch (£7.50). Well kept Fullers London Pride, Harveys BB, Hogs Back APB, and a guest beer on handpump. Prompt and efficient service. Plenty of tables in a front courtyard, with more on a back terrace. The village is so unspoilt they prefer you to leave your car in a free car park just outside, but if you don't fancy the lovely stroll there are a few spaces in front of the pub itself. *(Recommended by Ian Phillips, Derek Harvey-Piper, Ian Jones, Steve Goodchild, Tina and David Woods-Taylor, Dick Brown, J Sheldon)*

Free house ~ Licensees Jan and Maria Walaszkowski ~ Real ale ~ Meals and snacks (not Sun or Mon evenings) ~ Restaurant ~ (01306) 730775 ~ Children welcome ~ Open 11-3, 6-11; 11-11 Sat; 12-10.30 Sun

HASCOMBE TQ0039 Map 3
White Horse
B2130 S of Godalming

The simple but characterful rooms of this rose-draped inn have a bustling, friendly atmosphere, and the cosy inner beamed area has a woodburning stove and quiet small-windowed alcoves that look out onto the garden; there's also a conservatory with light bentwood chairs and peach coloured decor. Generous helpings of good, popular bar food might typically include huge sandwiches (£2.95), home-made soup (£2.50), ploughman's (from £4.40), vegetable au gratin (£6.50), home-made pies (£7.50), lamb and mint kebabs (£7.95), swordfish steaks or salmon fishcakes (£8.25), chicken curry or roast pheasant (£8.70), steaks (from £10.45), and puddings like treacle and walnut tart or chocolate truffle cake (£3.75); best to get there early for a table at lunchtime, especially at weekends. Quick cheerful service. Well kept Badger Best, King & Barnes Sussex and Wadworths 6X on handpump; quite a few wines. Darts, shove-ha'penny, dominoes, and fruit machine. There are quite a few tables on the spacious sloping back lawn, with more on a little terrace by the front porch. The village is pretty, and the National Trust's Winkworth Arboretum, with its walks among beautiful trees and shrubs, is nearby.

(Recommended by Lady M H Moir, Ian Phillips, Chris and Kate Lyons, Mr and Mrs D Ross, James Nunns, Susan and John Douglas, G W Stevenson)

Allied Domecq ~ Lease: Susan Barnett ~ Real ale ~ Meals and snacks (12-2.30, 7-10) ~ Restaurant ~ (01483) 208258 ~ Children in eating area of bar and restaurant ~ Open 11-3, 5.30-11; 11-11 Sat; 12-10.30 Sun

LEIGH TQ2246 Map 3
Plough

3 miles S of A25 Dorking—Reigate, signposted from Betchworth (which itself is signposted off the main road); also signposted from South Park area of Reigate; on village green

Not long after midday, many of the seats in this pretty and welcoming tiled and weatherboarded cottage are already full, mainly with people keen to enjoy the nicely presented food. This might include a choice of dips with poppadums, tiger prawns in filo pastry or potato skins (from £1.50), home-made soup (£2.50), welsh rarebit (£2.95), filled baked potatoes (from £3.95), ploughman's or creamy garlic mushrooms topped with cheese (£4.25), honey-roast ham and egg (£4.95), breaded plaice (£5.25), vegetable lasagne (£5.75), steaks (from £9.50), daily specials, and puddings (£2.95). Well kept King & Barnes Bitter, Broadwood, Festive and seasonal ales on handpump, most kept under light blanket pressure, and a decent wine list (all bottles are available by the glass as well). On the right is a very low beamed cosy white walled and timbered dining lounge and on the left, the more local pubby bar has a good bow-window seat and an extensive choice of games that takes in darts, shove-ha'penny, dominoes, table skittles, cribbage, trivia, a fruit machine and video game, Jenga, backgammon, chess and Scrabble; piped music. There are picnic tables under cocktail parasols in a pretty side garden, fairy lights in the evening, and pretty hanging baskets. Parking nearby is limited. Attractively set overlooking the village green, the pub is handy for Gatwick airport. The licensees also run the Gate at Ifield in West Sussex. *(Recommended by C P Scott-Malden, DWAJ, Chris and Shirley Machin, Derek Harvey-Piper, Mike and Heather Watson, David Peakall, G W Stevenson, Brian and Jenny Seller, B and M Kendall, Bob and Maggie Atherton)*

King & Barnes ~ Tenant Sarah Broomfield ~ Meals and snacks (till 10pm) ~ Restaurant ~ (01306) 611348 ~ Children in restaurant only ~ Open 11-11; 12-10.30 Sun

MICKLEHAM TQ1753 Map 3
King William IV 🍴 🍺

Byttom Hill; short but narrow steep track up hill just off A24 Leatherhead—Dorking by partly green-painted restaurant – public car park down here is best place to park; OS Sheet 187 map reference 173538

Surrey Dining Pub of the Year

It's quite a climb up to this bustling and friendly pub, cut into the hillside, and there are panoramic views back down again from the snug plank-panelled front bar. The lovely terraced garden is neatly filled with sweet peas, climbing roses and honeysuckle and plenty of tables (some in an open-sided wooden shelter); a path leads straight up through woods where it's nice to walk after lunch – quite a few walkers do come here. The more spacious back bar is quite brightly lit with kitchen-type chairs around its cast-iron-framed tables, log fires, fresh flowers on all the tables, and a serviceable grandfather clock. As well as good daily specials such as brie and leeks in filo pastry (£6.50), steak, kidney and mushroom pie (£6.95), summer cold poached salmon with a strawberry and avocado salad (£7.95), and tandoori chicken (£8.50), the much enjoyed food includes weekday sandwiches, spinach and aubergine lasagne (£5.40), lamb hotpot or sausages like pork and leek, lamb and apricot or mustard and honey (£5.75), thai vegetable curry (£6), cajun chicken salad (£6.30), seafood casserole (£8.25), breast of chicken with stilton and bacon (£9.35), sirloin steak with wild mushroom sauce (£10.15), and puddings like hot chocolate fudge cake or caramel apple tart (£2.75); the choice is more limited on Sundays and bank holidays. Well kept Adnams, Badger Best, Hogs Back TEA, and guests like Hogs Back Hop Garden Gold or Ringwood Fortyniner on handpump; quick and friendly service. Dominoes, and light piped music. *(Recommended by Alan Griffiths, Derek Harvey-Piper, Brian and Jenny Seller, Peter and Gwen Andrews, Mrs D W Cook, Lady M H Moir, Ian Jones, Simon Penny, R T and J C Moggridge, Mr and Mrs G Turner, Mr and Mrs B Hobden, James Nunns, Jean Minner, Ron Gentry, J S Sheldon, Patricia and Anthony Daley, Mr and Mrs J A Phipps, Peter and Wendy Arnold, John Pettit, Tom Hall, Stephen and Sophie Mazzier, Margaret and Nigel Parker,)*

Free house ~ Licensees C D and J E Grist ~ Real ale ~ Meals and snacks (not Mon evening) ~ (01372) 372590 ~ Very limited space for children – best to phone ~ Open 11-3, 6-11; 12-3, 7-10.30 Sun; closed 25 Dec

OUTWOOD TQ3245 Map 3
Dog & Duck

From A23 in Salfords S of Redhill take Station turning – eventually after you cross the M23 the pub's on your left at the T-junction; coming from the village centre, head towards Coopers Hill and Prince of Wales Road

The comfortable, rambling bar in this friendly country cottage has a good log fire, comfortable settles, oak armchairs and more ordinary seats, ochre walls, stripped dark beams, rugs on the quarry tiles, and daily newspapers to read; there's another huge fireplace in the eating area which leads off the bar. As well as sandwiches (from £1.50), bar food under the new manager includes home-made soup (£2.25), ploughman's (£3.95), burgers (from £4.45), ham and egg (£4.95), locally made sausages with onion gravy (£5.25), steak, mushroom and ale pie or poached smoked haddock with a poached egg (£5.65), cajun chicken breast (£6.25), sirloin steak (£9.95), and puddings (£2.75); they do smaller appetite dishes, a children's menu (£2.45), and Sunday roast lunch. Badger Best, IPA, and Tanglefoot, and Gribble Reg's Tipple on handpump, kept under light blanket pressure; darts, shove-ha'penny, dominoes, cribbage, fruit machine, trivia, and board games; unobtrusive piped music. There are three cats, Stan and Stella, who are rarely seen, and more sociable Trevor, who may try and sit on your knee. Picnic tables under cocktail parasols on the grass outside look over a safely fenced-off duck pond to the meadows. It's a nice walk to the village, with its old windmill, if you have an hour spare for the round trip. *(Recommended by Paul and Pam Penrose, Mayur Shah, Andy and Jill Kassube, M Owton, Niki and Terry Pursey, Jenny and Brian Seller, Alan Wright, Peter and Wendy Arnold, John and Elspeth Howell, G Simpson)*

Badger ~ Manager Michael Nicholson ~ Real ale ~ Meals and snacks (12-10pm) ~ (01342) 842964 ~ Children in eating area of bar only ~ Open 11-11; 12-10.30 Sun

PIRBRIGHT SU9455 Map 2
Royal Oak 🍺

Aldershot Rd; A324S of village

Up to nine changing real ales are served on handpump in this neatly kept old cottage. They have served over 100 beers over the last year and hold regular festivals: Boddingtons, Crown Buckley Merlins Oak, Flowers IPA and Original, Gales Hampshire Glory, Youngs Bitter and Special, Whitbread Fuggles, Wychwood Owzat on handpump; they also have around 15 wines by the glass and bottle. This year a bar extension has been added which overlooks the back garden and is joined onto the existing dining area. A rambling series of snug side alcoves have heavy beams and timbers, ancient stripped brickwork, and gleaming brasses set around the three real fires, and furnishings include wheelback chairs, tapestried wall seats, and little dark church-like pews around the trim tables; one area is no smoking. No noisy games machines or piped music. Bar food includes lunchtime filled french bread and baked potatoes as well as soup (£1.95), duck and port pâté (£2.55), ploughman's (£4.85), liver, ale and onions or vegetable korma (£5.25), steak in ale pie (£5.95), lemon chicken (£6.25), salmon with a butter and tarragon sauce (£6.95), sirloin steak (£8.95), and daily specials such as fried chicken livers with chestnuts (£3.25), mustard and mango gammon (£4.50), and fidget pie (£5.95). Children may be allowed to sit at limited tables in the dining area to eat with their parents. The front gardens are very colourful and look particularly attractive on fine evenings when the fairy lights are switched on. The big back garden is popular too, and less affected by noise from passing traffic; there may be barbecues and spit-roasts out here in summer. Good walks lead off in all directions, and the licensees are usually happy to let walkers leave their cars in the car park – if they ask first. *(Recommended by KC, P A Legon, George Atkinson, Guy Consterdine, Wayne Brindle)*

Whitbreads ~ Manager John Lay ~ Real ale ~ Meals and snacks (all day Sat and Sun) ~ (01483) 232466 ~ Open 11-11; 12-10.30 Sun

REIGATE HEATH TQ2349 Map 3
Skimmington Castle

3 miles from M25 junction 8: through Reigate take A25 Dorking (West), then on edge of Reigate turn left past Black Horse into Flanchford Road; after ¼ mile turn left into Bonny's Road (unmade, very bumpy track); after crossing golf course fork right up hill

Well liked by ramblers, this old cottage has a bright main front bar leading off a small central serving counter with dark simple panelling. There's a miscellany of chairs and tables, shiny brown vertical panelling, a brown plank ceiling, and ABC Bitter, Ansells Bitter, Flowers Original, and Ind Coope Burton on handpump. The cosy back rooms are partly panelled too, with old-fashioned settles and windsor chairs; one has a big brick fireplace with its bread-oven still beside it – the chimney is said to have been used as a highwayman's look-out. A small room down steps at the back has shove-ha'penny and dominoes; piped music. Bar food includes sandwiches (from £2.50), ploughman's and baked potatoes (from £3.95), vegetable canelloni or minted lamb pie (£5.95), chicken tikka (£6.50), fresh lemon sole with caper and parsley butter (£7.95), sirloin steak (£8.50), and puddings (£2.50). There are nice views from the crazy-paved front terrace and tables on the grass by lilac bushes, with more tables at the back overlooking the meadows and the hillocks. There's a hitching rail outside for horses. The pub was changing hands just as we went to press. The new licensees have two other pubs and are putting in managers charged with keeping up the pub's traditional appeal – obviously a challenging task. No children. *(Recommended by Ian Phillips, Paul and Pam Penrose, J L Torond, Rob Burnside, DWAJ, James Nunns; more reports on the new regime, please)*

Pubmaster ~ Licensee Tony Pugh ~ Real ale ~ Meals and snacks ~ (01737) 243100 ~ Open 11-2.30(3 Sat), 5.30-11; they may open longer on summer weekends

SOUTH GODSTONE TQ3648 Map 3
Fox & Hounds

Tilburstow Hill Rd; just outside village, turn off A22 into Harts Lane, pub is at the end; handy for M25 junction 6

In a pleasant spot on Tilburstow Ridge, this old-fashioned and pretty inn is not huge, but does have lots of little nooks and crannies to sit in. The cosy low-beamed bar has some fine high-backed old settles amongst more modern ones, cushioned wall-benches and a window seat around the few low tables, racing prints on the walls, prettily arranged dried hops, and a big kettle on the woodburning stove; there are a couple more seats and tables around the tiny bar counter, up a step and beyond some standing timbers; piped classical music. Popular home-made bar food might include soup (£3.75), open sandwiches (from £4.40), ploughman's (£5), prawn, samphire and pasta gratin (£6.50), daily specials like lamb and mint sausages with bubble and squeak (£6.25) or steak, mushroom and ale pie (£7.60), and well liked fresh fish dishes such as wing of skate with black butter (£7.30); the chips are very highly praised. You can reserve tables in the restaurant, which is the only part of the pub where food is served in the evening. Greene King IPA and Abbot on handpump; the very extensive restaurant wine list is usually also available in the bar. Friendly licensees and staff. There are a good few picnic tables out in the garden. *(Recommended by Mayur Shah, J S M Sheldon, Paul and Pam Penrose, Margaret and Nigel Dennis, Jenny and Brian Seller, TBB, Jonathan Nettleton, BHP, Dr and Mrs S Pleasance)*

Greene King ~ Tenants David and Lorraine McKie ~ Real ale ~ Lunchtime bar meals and snacks ~ Restaurant ~ (01342) 893474 ~ Children in eating area of bar lunchtimes only ~ Open 11-3, 7-11; 12-3, 7-10.30 Sun

THURSLEY SU9039 Map 2
Three Horseshoes
Just off A3 SW of Godalming

Hard-working and friendly licensees run this rather civilised tile-hung partly 16th-c pub. The dark, cosy bar has beams, log fires, fine old country furniture, including lovingly polished elm tables, and some Brockbank cartoons (he lived here). Well kept Gales Butser and HSB on handpump; maybe piped classical music. Good home-made bar food includes sandwiches (from £3.50; toasties £4; rare beef french bread £5), ploughman's (£4), salmon gratin or crab-filled mushrooms (£4.95), cheesy aubergines (£5.25), chicken and ham bake or beef in ale pie (£5.95), devilled pork (£6.95), curries (£7.50), and puddings such as lemon cheesecake, bread and butter pudding or tiramisu (£3); they try to keep smokers separate in the restaurant. There are plenty of tables in the two acres of back garden, and pleasant views over the green. The village church is worth a visit. *(Recommended by Martin and Karen Wake, Mr and Mrs C Simons, David Peakall, Guy Consterdine, Robert Crail, C Perry)*

Free house ~ Licensees Ann and Steve Denman ~ Real ale ~ Meals and snacks (not Sun or Mon evenings) ~ Restaurant ~ (01252) 703268 ~ Children over 5 in restaurant lunchtime only ~ Open 12-3, 6-11; 12-4, 7-10.30 Sun; closed winter Sun evening

WALLISWOOD TQ1138 Map 3
Scarlett Arms
Village signposted from Ewhurst—Rowhook back road; or follow Oakwoodhill signpost from A29 S of Ockley, then follow Walliswood signpost into Walliswood Green Road

A new licensee had just taken over this unspoilt little country pub as we went to press – happily he plans no major changes. The original small-roomed layout has been carefully preserved, and the three neatly kept communicating rooms have low black oak beams, deeply polished flagstones, simple but perfectly comfortable benches, high bar stools with backrests, trestle tables, country prints, and two roaring winter log fires. As well as daily specials, the good value bar food includes filled rolls (from £2.25), ploughman's (£3.95), mushroom stroganoff (£4.95), cod, trout or plaice (from £4.95), lasagne (£5.25), steak, port and stilton or steak and kidney pies (from £5.25), a daily roast (£5.75), steaks (from £7.95), and puddings (from £2.10). Well kept King & Barnes Sussex, Broadwood, Festive and Mild on handpump. Darts, bar billiards, cribbage, table skittles, dominoes and a fruit machine in a small room at the end. There are old-fashioned seats and tables with umbrellas in the pretty well tended garden. No children. *(Recommended by Alan and Brenda Williams, DWAJ, Derek Harvey-Piper, J S M Sheldon, Klaus and Elizabeth Leist, G R Sunderland, G W Jensen, James Nunns, Bob and Maggie Atherton; more reports on the new regime, please)*

King & Barnes ~ Tenant Jess Mannino ~ Real ale ~ Meals ~ (01306) 627243 ~ Open 11-2.30, 5.30-11; 12-3, 7-10.30 Sun

WARLINGHAM TQ3658 Map 3
White Lion
B269

On the outskirts of London, this unspoilt old pub has at its heart, a fine Tudor fireplace enclosed by high-backed settles, and there's a friendly warren of dark-panelled rooms with nooks and crannies, wood-block floors, very low beams, and deeply aged plasterwork. A side room decorated with amusing early 19th-c cartoons has darts, cribbage, and fruit machine. Bar food is served in the bigger, brighter room at the end of the building, from a range including lunchtime sandwiches (from £1.80), filled baked potatoes (from £2.95), ploughman's (from £3.25), home-cooked ham

(£4.25), rump steak (£4.95), home-made daily specials, puddings (£1.95), and children's menu; quick service. Well kept (and well priced) Bass, Fullers London Pride, Hancocks HB, and guests like Gales Anniversary or Morlands Old Speckled Hen on handpump. Piped music in the eating area, which is no smoking at lunchtimes. The well kept back lawn, with its rockery, is surrounded by a herbaceous border; there may be outside service here in summer. *(Recommended by Paul Hilditch, Christopher Wright, A Kilpatrick, Ian Phillips, Niki and Terry Pursey)*

Bass ~ Manager Charlie Evans ~ Real ale ~ Meals and snacks (not Sun evening) ~ (01883) 624106 ~ Children in eating area of bar until 8pm ~ Open 11-11; 12-10.30 Sun

---

Lucky Dip

Besides the fully inspected pubs, you might like to try these Lucky Dips recommended to us and described by readers (if you do, please send us reports):

Abinger Common [Abinger signed off A25 W of Dorking – then right to Abinger Hammer; TQ1145], *Abinger Hatch*: Still well liked for lovely setting nr pretty church and duck pond in clearing of rolling woods, with tables in nice garden; character bar with lots of potential – heavy beams, flagstones, basic furnishings, log fires *(Ian Phillips, Susan and John Douglas, J Sheldon, Gill and Andy Plumb, LYM)*

Abinger Hammer [Dorking rd; TQ0947], *Abinger Arms*: Quaint pub, bare public bar with larger dining room off, good variety of reasonably priced food, well kept Flowers and Fullers London Pride *(R B Crail)*

Addlestone [New Haw Rd (A318 S); TQ0562], *White Hart*: Cheerful local with attractive garden by Wey Navigation, good value simple food, well kept ales inc Hogs Back TEA tapped from the cask, quick service, darts, bar billiards, juke box *(Jenny and Brian Seller, John Crowley, BB)*

☆ **Albury** [off A248 SE of Guildford; TQ0547], *Drummond Arms*: Comfortable and civilised panelled alcovey bar, conservatory overlooking pretty streamside back garden with fountain and covered terrace, accommodating new licensees, food from sandwiches up, maybe summer Sunday spitroasts, well kept Courage Best and Directors, King & Barnes Broadwood, Festive and Sussex, and Youngs; piped music; good bedrooms, attractive village, popular with walkers *(John and Lynn Busenbark, LYM)*

☆ **Albury Heath** [Little London, off A25 Guildford—Dorking—OS Sheet 187 map ref 065468; TQ0646], *William IV*: Bustling take-us-as-you-find-us country pub in good walking area, old-fashioned character low-beamed flagstoned bar with big log fire, simple cafe-style dining area, close-packed tables in upstairs restaurant; home-made food from sandwiches up, monthly seafood nights and spitroasts, well kept ales such as Boddingtons, Fullers London Pride, Greene King Abbot, Whitbreads Castle Eden and local Hogs Back; shove-ha'penny and cards, tables outside; children welcome *(R Lake, G W Jensen, Don Mather, MLC, GC, G R*

Sunderland, Ian Phillips, LYM)

Ash Vale [Lynchford Rd; by North Camp Stn; SU8853], *Old Ford*: Simple pub with good range of real ales inc Hogs Back, usual food *(Dr M Owton)*

☆ **Banstead** [High St, off A217; TQ2559], *Woolpack*: Busy open-plan dining pub completely refurbished under new management, very cheap food (helpings not among the largest but adequate; no sandwiches now), well kept Scottish Courage ales with a guest such as Shepherd Neame Bishops Finger, good no-smoking area; open all day *(DWAJ, Don Mather)*

Banstead [Park Rd], *Mint*: Recently comfortably opened up, generous food (not Sun evening) from sandwiches up inc vegetarian (may be a wait when busy), garden with play area *(DWAJ)*

Betchworth [TQ2049], *Red Lion*: Good generous food inc unusual dishes, good service and well kept ales in friendly old pub with smallish fairy-lit bar, not too much music; plenty of tables in rose-trellised garden with play area, squash court *(Mrs W D Morrison)*

Blackbrook [TQ1846], *Royal Oak*: Pleasant low-beamed country pub with nice outside seating area, bar food, Wadworths 6X and Youngs Special *(Jenny and Brian Seller)*

Blackheath [TQ0346], *Cricketers*: Well kept beer, good food *(Mr and Mrs J B Bishop)*

☆ **Bletchingley** [Outwood Lane; TQ3250], *Prince Albert*: Good food esp fish in recently extended attractive pub doing well under welcoming new licensees; several nooks and corners, well kept beer, smallish restaurant, tables on terrace and in small pretty garden *(Sheila and John French, Philip Cooper)*

Box Hill [TQ1751], *Boxhills*: Hardly an ancient timbered inn, but fine setting, good efficient service, Charles Wells Bombardier and other real ales, tables outside; on North Downs long distance walk *(Jenny and Brian Seller)*

☆ **Bramley** [High St (A281 S of Guildford); TQ0044], *Jolly Farmer*: Cheerful and lively, very popular now for wide choice of good generous freshly prepared food, Theakstons

Old Peculier and Pilgrim Talisman served by sparkler, welcoming service, two log fires, beer-mat and banknote collections, big restaurant; bedrooms *(DWAJ, B A Hayward, Jonathan Greenwood, BB)*

Brockham [Brockham Green; TQ1949], *Royal Oak*: Friendly refurbished pub with Adnams, Gales HSB, Greene King Abbot, Harveys Best, Wadworths 6X and Youngs, good food, good garden with play area, nice spot on green; children and dogs welcome *(James Nunns)*

Brook [A286 N of Haslemere; SU9337], *Dog & Pheasant*: Busy low-beamed roadside pub in attractive spot opp cricket green nr Witley Common, friendly service, good range of well kept ales, good choice of reasonably priced food, shove-ha'penny, walking-stick collection; children welcome, small pretty garden *(Andrew W Lee)*

Burrowhill [B383 N of Chobham; SU9763], *Four Horseshoes*: Friendly cottagey pub overlooking village pump, varied good value food all day in bar and expanded restaurant section, Scottish Courage ales, friendly atmosphere, snug bar for families; lots of picnic tables (some under ancient yew), pleasant common views *(Ian Phillips)*

☆ Byfleet [104 High Rd; TQ0661], *Plough*: Medley of furnishings in friendly local with good value straightforward food, well kept Courage and guest ales, lots of farm tools, brass and copper, log fire, dominoes; prices low for Surrey; picnic tables in pleasant back garden *(Richard Houghton, Ian Phillips)*

Charlton [142 Charlton Rd, off B376 Laleham—Shepperton; TQ0869], *Harrow*: Comfortable carefully updated 17th-c thatched pub, short choice of generous interesting no-frills food (tables can be booked), good friendly service even when crowded, well kept Fullers London Pride and Morlands Old Speckled Hen *(James Nunns)*

☆ Chertsey [Ruxbury Rd, St Anns Hill (nr Lyne); TQ0267], *Golden Grove*: Busy local with lots of stripped wood, cheap straightforward home-made food from sandwiches up (not Sat-Mon evenings) in pine-tabled eating area, well kept Adnams and Tetleys-related ales, cheerful service, coal-effect gas fire; piped music, fruit and games machines; big garden with friendly dogs and goat, play area, wooded pond – nice spot by woods *(Ian Phillips, Clem Stephens)*

☆ Chertsey [London St (B375)], *Crown*: Friendly and relaxed Youngs pub with button-back banquettes in attractively renovated high-ceilinged bar, well kept ales, good choice of reasonably priced food on right, good service; neatly placed darts, discreet fruit machines; separate garden bar with conservatory, tables in courtyard and garden with pond; children welcome; smart 30-bedroom annexe *(Simon Collett-Jones, Ian Phillips, R B Crail)*

Chertsey [Bridge Rd; TQ0566], *Boathouse*: Comfortable Galleon Inn family chain pub, good spot upstream of Chertsey bridge; friendly staff, reasonably priced food, Adnams, Nethergate, Theakstons and Wadworth 6X; bedrooms *(Ian Phillips)*

☆ Chiddingfold [A283; SU9635], *Crown*: Picturesque old inn in attractive surroundings, handsome hotel bar with fine carving, massive beams, big inglenook log fire, tapestried panelled restaurant, simpler side bar, mulled wine, ales such as Badger Tanglefoot and Wadworths 6X, tables out on verandah; children allowed; has been open all day; bedrooms *(Martin and Karen Wake, Steve Goodchild, LYM)*

Chilworth [Dorking Rd; TQ0247], *Percy Arms*: Roomy nicely refurbished well lit bar, good choice of food, well kept Greene King ales and good service; pretty views of vale of Chilworth from garden behind, pleasant walks *(Gordon Prince)*

☆ Chipstead [Outwood Lane (B2032); TQ2757], *Ramblers Rest*: Recently converted pub in collection of partly 14th-c buildings, extensive range of different drinking areas with different atmospheres, panelling and low ceilings, wide range of well kept mainly Whitbreads-related ales, good generous well presented bar food, family restaurant; big pleasant garden behind, decent walks nearby; pervasive piped music; open all day inc Sun, no dogs *(Jenny and Brian Seller, Marianne and Lionel Kreeger, David Peakall)*

Chipstead [3 miles from M25, junction 8; A217 towards Banstead, right at second roundabout], *Well House*: Cottagey and comfortable partly 14th-c pub with lots of atmosphere, simple lunchtime food (not Sun) from sandwiches up, welcoming staff, log fires in all three rooms, well kept Fullers ales; dogs allowed; attractive garden with well reputed to be mentioned in Doomsday Book (collect your own food if you eat out here), delightful setting *(DWAJ, Ian Phillips, Jenny and Brian Seller, LYM)*

Chobham [Windsor Rd; SU9761], *Cricketers*: Refurbished by new licensees, good choice of good food, small side dining area *(Guy Charrison)*

Churt [SU8538], *Crossways*: Small take-us-as-you-find-us village pub with usual food, listed for its good choice of up to seven or eight changing well kept ales at reasonable prices, such as local Hogs Back TEA and Woldham Golden Summer *(Mike Fitzgerald)*

☆ Cobham [Downside Common, not far from M25 junction 10; TQ1058], *Cricketers*: Lovely setting opp green, very low beams, bowed timbers, warm log fire, dimly lit rustic back bar, tables out in charming neat garden – lots of atmosphere, but often packed; well kept Scottish Courage ales, masterly pimms (drinks not cheap), friendly service, bar food from sandwiches up; restaurant very popular for weekend lunch, children in Stable Bar, dogs welcome *(Derek Harvey-Piper, G W Jensen, Margaret and Nigel Dennis, John and Joan Calvert, Lady M H Moir, Thomas Nott, G W and I L Edwards, Clem Stephens, Ron Gentry, J Sheldon, Simon Penny, LYM)*

☆ **Cobham** [Plough Lane; TQ1059], *Plough*: Cheerful black-shuttered local with comfortably modernised low-beamed lounge bar, well kept Scottish Courage ales, helpful staff, pine-panelled snug with darts, lunchtime food; piped pop music may be rather loud some evenings; seats outside *(B L Sullivan, G W Stevenson, LYM)*

☆ **Cox Green** [Baynards Station Yard; Baynards Lane (W off B2128 just N of Rudgwick); TQ0734], *Thurlow Arms*: Full of bric-a-brac inc some relating to former railway here, now Downs Link Path – busy summer weekends, when cyclists may turn up by the score; well kept own-brew and Badger ales, good value food in extensive dining area, public bar with pool, darts and juke box *(Peter Bourdon, Mike Fitzgerald)*

☆ **Dorking** [45 West St; TQ1649], *Kings Arms*: 16th-c half-timbered pub in antiques area, part-panelled low-beamed lounge divided from bar by timbers, nice lived-in old furniture, warm relaxed atmosphere, good choice of home-cooked usual food, friendly service, Batemans XB, Eldridge Pope Royal Oak, King & Barnes, Ringwood, Tetleys and Wadworths 6X, attractive old-fashioned back dining area; piped music; open all day *(James Nunns, John Beeken, Tony and Wendy Hobden)*

Dorking [High St], *Surrey Yeoman*: Newly refurbished local, well kept Bass, Brakspears, King & Barnes *(James Nunns)*

Dormansland [TQ4042], *Old House At Home*: Nice country local with wide choice of popular bar food, good Sun lunch (booking recommended), Shepherd Neame Bitter, Spitfire and Bishops Finger *(Andy and Jill Kassube)*; [Plough Rd, off B2028 NE], *Plough*: Traditional old pub in quiet village, log fires, original features, well kept Whitbreads-related ales, popular food in large dining area, friendly helpful staff, restaurant; busy weekday lunchtime *(Margaret and Nigel Dennis, J R Tunnadine)*

☆ **East Clandon** [TQ0651], *Queens Head*: Small rambling connecting rooms, big inglenook log fire, fine old elm bar counter, bookcases, pictures, copperware; staff and customers seem much happier now it's shrugged off its short Big Steak phase; good sensibly priced food under friendly new manager, well kept ales, no lunchtime piped music; tables in quiet garden, handy for two NT properties *(John Evans, KC, J S M Sheldon, T A Bizat, LYM)*

☆ **Effingham** [Orestan Lane; TQ1253], *Plough*: Characteristic commuter-belt Youngs local with consistently well kept ales, honest home cooking (fresh veg and potatoes may be extra) inc enjoyable Sun lunch, two coal-effect gas fires, beamery, panelling, old plates and brassware in long lounge, no-smoking extension; popular with older people – no dogs, children or sleeveless T-shirts inside, no music or machines, attractive garden with play area; convenient for Polesdon Lacey (NT) *(Alan Kilpatrick, G W Stevenson, Alan and Brenda Williams, P Gillbe, John Pettit)*

Egham [38 High St; TQ0171], *Crown*: Busy simply furnished local with good promptly served basic food, changing ales such as Adnams, Fullers and Gales, restful walled back garden with noisy aviary and pretty pond *(Ian Phillips)*

Elstead [Elstead Mill; SU9143], *Nellie Deans*: Lovely setting, good service; shame about the piped music *(WDM)*

Englefield Green [Northcroft Rd; SU9970], *Barley Mow*: Lots of farming paraphernalia in well place pub overlooking green, reasonably priced food, back dining area with no-smoking section, Scottish Courage ales with a guest such as Marstons Pedigree, darts; pleasant garden *(Tony and Wendy Hobden, Ian Phillips)*; [Wick Lane, Bishopgate], *Sun*: Welcoming atmosphere, well kept Scottish Courage and other ales, decent wines, good choice of food inc lots of sandwiches, reasonable prices, daily papers, roaring log fire; biscuit and water for dogs, handy for Savile Garden and Windsor Park *(Ian Phillips)*

Epsom [opp racecourse; TQ2160], *Tattenham Corner*: Big reliable Beefeater, prompt friendly service, good range of usual food all day, mainly Whitbreads-related ales; play fort and barbecues in garden *(R C Vincent)*

☆ **Esher** [West End La; off A244 towards Hersham, by Princess Alice Hospice; TQ1464], *Prince of Wales*: Now a Chef & Brewer, impressively refurbished and well equipped as traditional pub, with good choice of very generous well prepared food, at least four well kept Scottish Courage ales, good wine choice, well laid out eating area, quick friendly staff; big garden, nr green and pond *(R B Crail)*

Esher [Alma Rd/Chestnut Ave], *Marneys*: Good varied food in friendly village atmosphere, family dining area, quick service, Scottish Courage ales, decent wines; tables outside, quiet lane on golf course with duck pond *(Margaret Parker)*

Ewell [Kingston Rd; TQ2262], *Queen Adelaide*: Refurbished mainly as carvery restaurant, decent straightforward food in smallish bar, welcoming service *(DWAJ)*; [1 London Rd], *Spring*: Comfortable and popular Edwardian-style pub with friendly efficient service, good value bar food inc vegetarian, real ales such as Fullers London Pride and Worthington, restaurant; TV and machines not obtrusive; garden with barbecues *(Sue and Mike Todd)*

Ewhurst [Pitch Hill; a mile N of village on Shere rd; TQ0940], *Windmill*: Spacious series of hillside lawns give beautiful views, as does conservatory restaurant; smart modern bar behind, good interesting food in bar and restaurant, half a dozen well kept ales inc Hogs Back, welcoming atmosphere; occasional live music; lovely walking country *(Ian and Liz Phillips, LYM)*

☆ **Farleigh** [Farleigh Common; TQ3659], *Harrow*: Stripped-flint former barn refurbished in rustic style with country bric-a-brac, even an owl high in the rafters; good lunchtime food from good sandwiches up, raised no-smoking area, well kept Bass and Charrington IPA, cheerful efficient staff; separate locals' bar, tables on big lawn with pasture behind; no dogs, popular with younger people evening *(Jenny and Brian Seller, Christopher Wright, Niki and Terry Pursey)*

Farnham [SU8446], *Bull:* Good food and atmosphere, good licensee, reasonable prices *(Victor Harris)*; [Tilford Rd, Lower Bourne], *Spotted Cow:* Welcoming rural local with wide choice of good food inc lots of fish, well kept Adnams, Courage and Hogs Back TEA, decent wine, attentive friendly service, reasonable prices; play area in big garden *(Vann and Terry Prime, John and Vivienne Rice)*

☆ **Felbridge** [Woodcock Hill – A22 N; TQ3639], *Woodcock:* Busy little flagstoned bar opening on to richly furnished room a bit like a film props department, spiral stairs up to another opulent room, candlelit and almost boudoirish, nice small Victorian dining room off; also big seafood restaurant; well kept Harveys, Ringwood Old Thumper, Charles Wells Bombardier, piped music (can be loud and late), relaxed atmosphere – service can be very leisurely; children in eating area, open all day, some tables outside *(R C Watkins, BHP, A C Morrison, LYM)*

☆ **Forest Green** [nr B2126/B2127 junction; TQ1240], *Parrot:* Quaint rambling country pub, pleasant and comfortable, with pervasive parrot motif, well kept Courage Directors, Fullers London Pride, Hogs Back TEA, John Smiths and Wadworths 6X, good often interesting food (many tables reserved, giving it something of a restaurant feel in the evening), good cheerful service even when crowded; children welcome, open all day; plenty of space outside by cricket pitch, good walks nearby *(James Nunns, LYM)*

Frensham [SU8341], *Holly Bush:* Bright pub nr Frensham Ponds, Charles Wells Bombardier and Morlands, good value generous food inc toasted sandwiches (service can slow when busy), friendly landlord *(Jenny and Brian Seller)*

Frimley Green [205 Frimley Green Rd; SU8856], *Old Wheatsheaf:* Busy Morlands pub with good hands-on landlord, friendly staff; good value food *(R Crail)*

☆ **Godalming** [Ockford Rd, junction Portsmouth Rd (A3100) and Shackstead Lane; SU9743], *Inn on the Lake:* Cosy and comfortable family bar with well presented reasonably priced bar food inc vegetarian, well kept Whitbreads-related and guest real ales, decent wines, log fire and friendly staff; elegant restaurant with indoor fishpond and grand piano, good choice of wines; tables out in lovely garden overlooking lake, summer barbecues; rather steep car park; bedrooms *(G C Hackemer)*

Godstone [handy for M25 junction 6; TQ3551], *White Hart:* Pleasant Beefeater

with proper bar, abundant ancient beams, two enormous log fires, friendly service, well prepared food; pleasant views across green with pond *(Ian Phillips, LYM)*

☆ **Gomshall** [Station Rd (A25); TQ0847], *Compasses:* Plain bar (open all day) and much bigger comfortable no-smoking dining area (lunchtime and evening) with good value well presented food; well kept Gibbs Mew Salisbury, Deacon and Bishops Tipple with a guest such as Bass, good value wines, quick friendly service; spacious neatly kept lawn by roadside stream with weeping willows; walkers welcome *(Tony Scott, John Pettit, Andrew Worby, James Nunns, R B Crail, BB)*

Guildford [Shalford Rd, Millbrook; across car park from Yvonne Arnaud Theatre, beyond boat yard; SU9949], *Jolly Farmer:* Decent food all day from upstairs counter in big two-level pub by River Wey, extensive terrace and moorings, lots of picnic tables, pleasant conservatory, Flowers and Marstons Pedigree, friendly young staff; some live music summer *(Tony Scott, Mark Percy, Wayne Brindle)*; [Old Portsmouth Rd], *Olde Ship:* Well kept Morlands, fairly priced food inc good pizzas, decent wines, obliging service; no music *(Roy Shutz, P A Legon)*; [Millmead], *White House:* Refurbished riverside pub with well kept Fullers, pretty setting, pleasant helpful staff, hot and cold food, small upstairs no-smoking bar; for over-25s *(Dr M Owton, Tony Scott, Derek Patey)*

Hale [104 Upper Hale Rd; SU8448], *Ball & Wicket:* Friendly and comfortable, brewing its own ales *(Richard Houghton)*

Holmbury St Mary [TQ1144], *Royal Oak:* Well run 17th-c beamed coaching inn in pleasant spot by green and church, warm and cheery, log fire, fresh food *(John Yardley, Mark Percy)*

Horley [Brighton Rd (A23); TQ2842], *Air Balloon:* Big Steak pub with exceptionally speedy friendly service even when busy, good value food, good adjoining children's indoor play barn, small outdoor play area; handy for Gatwick *(R C Vincent, George Atkinson)*; [Church Rd], *Olde Six Bells:* Interesting building – part of heavy-beamed open-plan bar was probably a medieval chapel, and some masonry may date from 9th c; local atmosphere, reasonably priced food, Bass ales and a guest such as Fullers London Pride, upstairs raftered dining room, conservatory, tables out by bend in River Mole; open all day weekdays *(Tony Scott, Ian Phillips, LYM)*

Horsell [123 High St; SU9959], *Red Lion:* Good reasonably priced in comfortably renovated pub with pleasant terrace, well kept Fullers London Pride, decent wines, friendly staff, picture-filled converted barn where children allowed, tables outside; good walks nearby *(Ian Phillips, Jason Shipp, Chris and Martin Taylor)*

Horsell Common [Chertsey Rd; The Anthonys; A320 Woking—Ottershaw; SU9959], *Bleak House:* Welcoming and cheerful, with decent food, Tetleys-related ales, comfortable seats, picnic tables and barbecues on back lawn; good walks to the sandpits which inspired H G Wells's *War of the Worlds (Ian Phillips, Chris and Martin Taylor)*

Hurtmore [just off A3 nr Godalming by Hurtmore/Shackleford turn-off; SU9545], *Squirrels*: Comfortable, fresh and airy, with upmarket hotelish feel, sofas, country-kitchen furniture, partly no-smoking restaurant and conservatory, children's playroom, books for adults and children, friendly service, well kept Ruddles County, decent wines, facilities for disabled people; pleasant garden, good bedrooms *(G R Sunderland, Wayne Brindle, SRB, LYM)*

☆ **Irons Bottom** [Sidlow Bridge, off A217; TQ2546], *Three Horseshoes*: Friendly country local, rather sophisticated feel, with new landlord doing well – he's a careful cook using good ingredients, and the menu reflects his time abroad; excellently kept Fullers London Pride and interesting guest ales, quiz or darts night Tues, summer barbecues *(Mike and Heather Watson, Don Mather)*

Kingswood [Waterhouse Lane; TQ2455], *Kingswood Arms*: Big and busy, with wide variety of reasonably priced popular food, cheerful quick service (announcements when orders are ready), Scottish Courage ales, conservatory dining extension; spacious rolling garden with play area *(P Gillbe, TOH, Niki and Terry Pursey)*

☆ **Laleham** [B376, off A308 W of M3 junction 1; TQ0568], *Three Horseshoes*: Popular and plushly modernised, but dating from 13th c, with flagstones, heavy beams, interesting history, lots of tables in enjoyable garden, and easy stroll to Thamesside lawns; generous usual bar food (not cheap), well kept Fullers London Pride and Websters Yorkshire, decent wines, efficient service, piped music, restaurant; children in no-smoking conservatory, open all day *(Ron and Sheila Corbett, Ian Phillips, Derek Harvey-Piper, Clive Gilbert, Stephen Barney, Clem Stephens, LYM)*

Laleham [The Broadway], *Feathers*: Friendly old cottage, surprisingly roomy inside, with bar in single-storey front extension, traditional decor, lots of hanging pewter mugs, beamed dining lounge with reasonably priced generous home-made food, well kept Scottish Courage ales with a guest such as Adnams, Brakspears or Marlow Rebellion; piped music; tables outside *(Richard Houghton, T I M Cusk)*

Leatherhead [5 North St; TQ1656], *Penny Black*: Busy Whitbreads Hogshead in converted post office, big partitioned beamed bar, framed stamp collections on brick walls, bare boards, lots of tables and chairs, solid fuel stove, wide choice of Whitbreads and guest ales, straightforward reasonably priced cheerfully served bar food; some seats outside, live entertainment some evenings *(John Pettit, J S M Sheldon)*

☆ **Leigh** [S of A25 Dorking—Reigate; TQ2246],

Seven Stars: Pretty country local with pine furniture in airy and spacious flagstoned bar, friendly efficient staff, wide choice of good food, sensible prices, Youngs ales, woodburner in inglenook; flower-filled garden, maybe summer Sun barbecues *(John and Shirley Dyson, James Nunns, Mr and Mrs N B Dyson, John H L Davis, BB)*

Limpsfield Chart [TQ4251], *Carpenters Arms*: Tidy much modernised pub in delightful setting by common, lovely walks, easy reach of Chartwell; good straightforward food, Tetleys-related ales, prompt friendly service *(Dave Braisted, A Kilpatrick)*

Lower Kingswood [Brighton Rd; A217, 1½ miles from M25 junction 8; TQ2453], *Fox on the Hill*: Spacious refurbished bar, popular lunchtime for well presented straightforward good value food; friendly attentive staff; bedrooms *(DWAJ)*; [Buckland Rd, just off A217], *Mint Arms*: Family-run, with decent bar food all day inc Sun, wider restaurant choice, friendly service, wide choice of ales such as Courage Best, Fullers London Pride, Gales HSB, King & Barnes, Theakstons Old Peculier, Wadworths 6X, and Youngs, lots of brasses and copper, pool and darts in games area, big garden with play area *(DWAJ)*

Martyrs Green [Old Lane, handy for M25 junction 10 – off A3 S-bound, but return N of junction; TQ0957], *Black Swan*: Extensively enlarged, open all day, bustling cheery family place by day (the sort where menu might be headed 'yum yum tummy fillers'), with simple furnishings, well worn back bar, fine range of a dozen or more well kept ales, log fires, restaurant; can get crowded with young people evenings, piped pop music may be loud then, maybe karaoke or live entertainment; plenty of tables in big woodside garden with play area and maybe summer barbecue and bouncy castle; handy for RHS Wisley Garden *(CD, D B Close, Steve Felstead, Herbie, G W Stevenson)*

☆ **Mickleham** [Old London Rd; TQ1753], *Running Horses*: Current landlord doing particularly well in refurbished 16th-c beamed village pub well placed nr Box Hill, interesting choice of well presented food, well kept Tetleys-related ales, cheerful service even when swamped by impatient walkers, two lovely open fires, comfortable and attractive dining extension/conservatory; nice view from pretty courtyard garden *(John Pettit, G W Stevenson, Chris and Martin Taylor, G S and E M Dorey, R Worthing)*

Mogador [from M25 up A217 past 2nd roundabout, signed off; edge Banstead Hth; TQ2452], *Sportsman*: Interesting and welcoming low-ceilinged local, quietly placed on Walton Heath, a magnet for walkers and riders; well kept ales, popular food, darts, bar billiards; dogs welcome if not wet or muddy; tables out on common, on back lawn, and some under cover – shame about the loudspeaker food announcements *(Lady M H Moir, Vicki Berry, Alex Roberts)*

Newchapel [Wire Mill Lane; off A22 just S of

B2028 by Mormon Temple; TQ3641],
Wiremill: Spacious pub in beautiful lakeside
spot, good choice of well kept beer, good
varied food, good service even when crowded,
piped music; tables outside *(Mr and Mrs A
Marsh)*

Newdigate [TQ2042], *Six Bells*: Popular local
with good range of well kept ales, decent
food, friendly service, plenty of tables in
pleasant garden *(Jenny and Brian Seller, J R
Tunnadine, G W Stevenson)*

Normandy [Guildford Rd E (A323) – OS
Sheet 186 map ref 935518; SU9351], *Duke of
Normandy*: Well kept Greene King IPA,
Abbot and a seasonal ale, reasonably priced
food, good service *(R B Crail)*

☆ **Ockley** [Stane St (A29); TQ1439], *Cricketers
Arms*: Pretty 15th-c stonebuilt village local
with Horsham slab roof, flagstones, low
beams, inglenook log fires, shiny pine
furniture, good simple generous bar food inc
good value Sun roast, well kept ales such as
Fullers London Pride and Ringwood Best,
country wines, friendly staff, quiet piped
music, darts area, small attractive dining
room with cricketing memorabilia; seats in
back garden with duck pond and play area
*(Tony and Wendy Hobden, Tony Scott,
LYM)*

Ockley [Stane St (A29)], *Kings Arms*: 17th-c
beamed country inn brightened up under new
landlord, inglenook log fire, imaginative fresh
food, good service, small restaurant; discreetly
placed picnic tables in pleasant well kept back
garden; bedrooms *(Margaret and Nigel
Parker)*; *Old School House*: Fine school house
attractively converted to bar and restaurant,
good value generous food esp fresh fish,
friendly service, well kept King & Barnes,
good wines, wonderful log fire *(Tony Scott,
TOH)*

☆ **nr Ockley** [Oakwoodhill – signed off A29 S;
TQ1337], *Punch Bowl*: Friendly, welcoming
and cosy country pub with huge inglenook
log fire, polished flagstones, lots of beams,
well kept Badger Best and Tanglefoot and
Wadworths 6X, wide choice of decent bar
food, lots of traditional games, juke box;
children allowed in dining area, tables outside
with flower tubs and maybe weekend
barbecues; has been open all day *(DWAJ, J
Sheldon, LYM)*

☆ **Ottershaw** [222 Brox Rd (off A320 N of
Woking); TQ0263], *Castle*: Comfortable and
friendly local, lots of farm tools etc, stripped
brick and beamery, good home-cooked food
(popular for business lunches), well kept
changing ales such as Adnams, Eldridge Pope,
Fullers London Pride, Marstons Pedigree,
Tetleys and Youngs Special, Addlestone's
cider, log fire, no-smoking dining area; garden
with tables in pleasant creeper-hung arbour
(Ian Phillips, James Nunns)

☆ **Outwood** [off A23 S of Redhill; TQ3245],
Bell: Attractive extended 17th-c country
dining pub, wide choice of food (roasts only,
Sun) in olde-worlde beamed bar or sparser
restaurant area, quick friendly service, indoor

barbecues, summer cream teas, good choice of
well kept ales inc Pilgrims, log fires, children
welcome, has been open all day; pretty garden
with country views, handy for windmill *(E G
Parish, Margaret and Nigel Dennis, Klaus and
Elizabeth Leist, Jenny and Brian Seller, LYM)*

Oxshott [Leatherhead Rd (A244); TQ1460],
Bear: Busy yet relaxed Youngs pub with well
kept beer, big conservatory dining room,
friendly courteous staff, usual pub food with
fresh veg, good log fire, teddy bear collection,
occasional barbecues in small garden *(Ian
Phillips, James and Lynne House, Mike and
Heather Watson)*

☆ **Oxted** [52 High St, Old Oxted; off A25 not
far from M25 junction 6; TQ3951], *George*:
Neat and tidy, with chatty atmosphere,
attractive prints, pleasant restaurant area; has
been very popular for good generous food all
day from sandwiches to seafood and steaks,
but no reports on this since takeover by
Badger; now has their Best and Tanglefoot,
Adnams Best, Fullers London Pride, Harveys
and Youngs; children welcome over 10 *(LYM;
news please)*

Oxted [High St, Old Oxted], *Old Bell*:
Country Carvery beamed and panelled
pub/restaurant with welcoming staff and
reasonably priced food inc all-day Sun
carvery, with good wheelchair access,
disabled facilities and a welcome for children;
bar has fruit machines and maybe very mixed
customers; garden *(A H Denman, Deryck and
Margaret Watkinson)*

☆ **Peaslake** [off A25 S of Gomshall; TQ0845],
Hurtwood: Delightfully placed small prewar
country hotel, friendly bar popular with
locals, good freshly made bar food (worth the
wait), well kept ales inc local Hogs Back,
reasonable prices, attentive staff; sizeable
popular restaurant, comfortable bedrooms
*(Derek and Margaret Underwood, R B Crail,
BB)*

Puttenham [Seale Lane; SU9347], *Good
Intent*: Friendly and atmospheric country
local, good range of attractively presented
reasonably priced food, constantly changing
range of ales, Inch's farm cider, roaring log
fire; dogs allowed, no children *(G W
Stevenson)*; [Hook Lane, just off A31
Farnham—Guildford], *Jolly Farmer*: Well
presented food, welcoming efficient young
staff, several comfortably refurbished rooms,
well kept ales, children welcome; picnic tables
outside *(G C Hackemer, LYM)*

☆ **Pyrford Lock** [Lock Lane; 3 miles from M25
junction 10 – S on A3, then take Wisley slip
rd and go on past RHS Garden; TQ0458],
Anchor: Busy modern pub starred for its
position by bridge and locks on River Wey
Navigation; big terrace, canteenish
conservatory, picture-window bar, upstairs
room with narrow-boat memorabilia; Scottish
Courage ales, usual food inc vegetarian and
children's (may be queues and Tannoy
announcements), juke box, sports TV,
machines etc; open all day in summer
(Vincent Wingate, Clive Gilbert, GA, Chris

and Martin Taylor, Ian Phillips, Ron Gentry, Derek Harvey-Piper, LYM)

Redhill [44 Hatchlands Rd; A25 towards Reigate; TQ2650], *Hatch*: U-shaped Edwardian bar with blue decor, mirrors and lamps, pictures, fire, eight real ales, some rare, fine range of lagers and bottled beers, country wines, adjoining restaurant *(Tony Scott)*; [11 Church Rd, St Johns; TQ2749], *Plough*: Small welcoming old-fashioned pub said to date from 13th c, low beams, waggon wheels, brass and bric-a-brac, flame-effect fires, little snug for two, well kept Tetleys-related and guest ales, reasonably priced home-made food inc vegetarian, friendly efficient staff; back garden with terrace *(David and Carole Chapman, Tony Scott)*

Reigate [99 Reigate Hill Rd; ½ mile from M25; TQ2550], *Yew Tree*: Comfortable panelled pub, decent straightforward food, well kept Scottish Courage ales *(Tony Scott)*

Ripley [High St; TQ0556], *Anchor*: Old-fashioned cool dark low-beamed connecting rooms in Tudor inn with all-you-can-eat salad bar, Flowers and Theakstons, games in public bar, tables in coachyard *(Ian Phillips, J Sheldon, BB)*; [High St], *Ship*: Comfortable 16th-c two-bar local with low beams, flagstones, cosy nooks, log fire in vast inglenook; well kept Scottish Courage beers, sensible food, small raised games area with bar billiards, window-seats and stools rather than chairs; small high-walled terrace *(J Sheldon, Martin and Karen Wake)*; [High St], *Talbot*: Old-world low-beamed inn with two adjoining bars – Nelson connections, some atmosphere, pleasant service, well kept ales inc Friary Meux and Treason, restaurant; piped music; bedrooms *(James Nunns)*

Rowledge [Cherry Tree Rd (off A325 just S of Farnham); SU8243], *Cherry Tree*: Cheerfully done-up two-bar 16th-c Morlands pub (also has Bass), good fresh food inc seafood and fine puddings, interesting landlady, restaurant area, big well kept garden with play area; juke box; very popular, handy for Birdworld and Alice Holt Forest *(G C Hackemer, G and M Stewart)*

Sendmarsh [Marsh Rd; TQ0455], *Saddlers Arms*: Friendly low-beamed local with good value straightforward food inc vegetarian and Sun lunch, well kept Tetleys-related ales, toby jugs, brassware etc, quiet piped music, machines in separate bar; tables outside *(G W and I L Edwards, DWAJ, Ian Phillips)*

Shackleford [Pepperharrow Lane; SU9345], *Cyder House*: Doing well under new licensees, very wide choice of good food, friendly atmosphere, well kept ales inc Piston Broke and Old Shackle brewed here, farm ciders, log fires, families welcome; utilitarian furnishings, piped pop music; picnic tables on back lawn, nice village setting *(Mr and Mrs A Duke)*

☆ **Shamley Green** [B2128 S of Guildford; TQ0343], *Red Lion*: Attractively furnished dining pub under new tenant, rows of books, local cricketing photographs, enjoyable if pricy food from sandwiches to steaks inc children's helpings, well kept Ansells, Greene King Abbot and Flowers, good choice of wines; open all day, children welcome, sturdy tables outside; bedrooms *(LYM)*

☆ **Shepperton** [Church Sq (off B375); TQ0867], *Kings Head*: Immaculate old pub in quiet and attractive square, coal fire in inglenook, neat panelling, oak beams, highly polished floors and furnishings, various discreet little rooms, big conservatory extension; good value unpretentious bar food (not Sun), well kept Scottish Courage ales, attentive service, sheltered back terrace; children welcome, open all day Sat *(James Nunns, Ian Phillips, Jenny and Brian Seller, LYM)*

☆ **Shepperton** [Shepperton Lock, Ferry Lane, off B375], *Thames Court*: Rambling old place gutted and refurbished to give galleried central atrium with separate attractive panelled areas up and down stairs, two good log fires, tremendous range of food inc interesting dishes, well kept Bass and Fullers London Pride, daily papers, friendly staff; children welcome, attractive riverside tree-shaded terrace with big gas radiant heaters *(Ian Phillips, R B Crail, Margaret and Nigel Dennis)*

☆ **Shepperton** [Russell Rd], *Red Lion*: Roomy and welcoming old wisteria-covered local across rd from Thames, plenty of tables on terrace among fine displays of shrubs and flowers, more on lawn over road (traffic noise) with lovely river views and well run moorings; wide choice of food in spacious bar and restaurant, well kept Scottish Courage ales with guests such as Fullers London Pride, interesting prints, red-cushioned seating, restaurant *(Mayur Shah, D P and J A Sweeney)*

Shepperton [Church Sq], *Anchor*: Roomy refurbished olde-worlde panelled front bar with interesting food, panelling, good service, well kept Eldridge Pope and other ales, maybe jazz in back bar; seats in front (no garden), short walk to river; bedrooms *(152 Laleham Rd)*, *Bull*: Small local, unassuming but comfortable and well kept, with good simple generous food at sensible prices inc bookable Sun lunch (food area themed as teddy bears' picnic), friendly helpful staff, tables outside; live music some nights *(W L G Watkins, Margaret and Nigel Dennis)*

☆ **Shere** [village signed off A25 3 miles E of Guildford; TQ0747], *White Horse*: Striking half-timbered medieval pub under new management, efficiently served good food, King & Barnes and Theakstons, uneven floors, massive beams, oak wall seats, two log fires, one in a huge inglenook, Tudor stonework; tables outside, children in eating area, open all day Sun – beautiful village *(Ian Phillips, Hazel and Michael Duncombe, LYM)*

Shipley Bridge [Antlands Lane, Burstow – OS Sheet 187 map ref 307405; TQ3040], *Shipley Bridge*: Popular carvery with reasonably priced food and good service, big dining area *(A H Denman, Tony Scott)*

Shottermill [Liphook Rd; S of Haslemere; SU8732], *Mill*: 17th-c, with good generous food, good choice of wines and beers, service quick and friendly even when busy; small restaurant, pleasant garden with play area *(David Lupton, Andrew W Lee)*

☆ **Staines** [The Hythe; S bank, over Staines Bridge; TQ0471], *Swan*: Two pleasantly refurbished bars and dining area, splendid Thameside setting, good choice of food, cheerful service, Fullers ales, tables on riverside verandah, conservatory, soft piped music; can be very busy Sun lunchtime and summer evenings; moorings, comfortable bedrooms *(Sandra Kench, Steven Norman, Simon Collett-Jones, Ron and Sheila Corbett, LYM)*

Staines [124 Church St], *Bells*: Well kept Scottish Courage ales, good prompt food from sandwiches up, friendly staff, cosy traditional furnishings and central fireplace, darts, cribbage, fruit machine, quiet juke box; plenty of seats in big garden *(Ian Phillips)*; [Leacroft], *Old Red Lion*: Clean, warm and welcoming pub with good value food, quick service, ales inc Courage Best and Fullers London Pride; seats outside, pretty spot by village green *(Ian Phillips)*; [Moor Lane], *Swan on the Moor*: Worth knowing for good range of real ales, cosy fire, decent food; piped music can be loud *(Guy Charrison)*; [1 Penton Rd], *Wheatsheaf & Pigeon*: Welcoming 1920s local with well kept Scottish Courage ales, good fresh food esp fish in largish bar/lounge and small dining area – evenings may be booked weeks ahead *(Ian Phillips)*

Stoke Dabernon [Station Rd; off A245; TQ1259], *Plough*: Comfortably modernised and homely local, with reasonably priced good sensible bar food in airy conservatory, well kept Scottish Courage ales and Wadworths 6X, big window seats, coal fire, helpful staff, sizeable garden *(James Nunns, BB)*

Sunbury [64 Thames St; TQ1068], *Magpie*: Pleasantly refurbished, with good views from upper bar, lower real ale bar opening on to nice small terrace by river and boat club, well kept Arkells Kingsdown, Bass, Boddingtons and Gibbs Mew Bitter and Bishops Tipple, decent wine, reasonably priced food; bedrooms *(Bob and Maggie Atherton, Philip Watson, James Nunns)*

☆ **Sutton** [via Raikes Lane, just off B2126 1½ miles S of Abinger Hammer; TQ1046], *Volunteer*: Attractive good-sized terraced lawns in lovely quiet setting, three low-ceilinged linked traditional rooms with antique military prints, well kept Ansells, Marstons Pedigree, Morlands Old Speckled Hen and Youngs Special, decent wines, well chosen piped music; courteous and obliging new licensees doing good reasonably priced food esp fish; restaurant, comfortable bedrooms, handy for Leith Hill walks *(J S M Sheldon, Norman and Angela Harries, R B Crail, BB)*

Tadworth [Dorking Rd (B2032) – OS Sheet 187 map ref 237546; TQ2354], *Blue Anchor*: Cosily refurbished, with log fires, subdued decorations, homely feel; varied good value generous food, well kept Bass, Fullers London Pride and Worthington, decent wine; piped music may obtrude *(Keith Ward, TOH, GT)*

☆ **Tandridge** [off A25 W of Oxted; TQ3750], *Barley Mow*: Pretty whitewashed pub with window-boxes and shutters, spacious refurbished bar, pleasant restaurant area, helpful welcoming staff, fairly priced home-made food, Badger ales tapped from the cask, log fires; no music or machines, big garden; interesting church nearby, good walks to Oxted or Godstone; well equipped small bedrooms, good breakfast *(Margaret and Nigel Dennis, Jenny and Brian Seller, Paul and Pam Penrose, Mike Pugh, Derek and Maggie Washington)*

☆ **Tandridge** [Tandridge Lane, off A25 W of Oxted], *Brickmakers Arms*: Good atmosphere in popular and pretty country dining pub, dating from 15th c but much extended and modernised, with good range of freshly made food inc some German dishes and lots of fish, well kept Whitbreads-related ales, decent wines inc local ones, restaurant with good log fires, prompt friendly service *(Gordon Smith, R and S Bentley)*

Tatsfield [Westmore Green; TQ4156], *Old Ship*: Big bar with lots of interesting pictures and bric-a-brac, Bass, Charrington IPA and Worthington, good value varied food inc Sun lunch in restaurant with log fire, prompt friendly service; opp village duck pond, with play area in big garden *(Paul McKeever, Paul and Pam Penrose)*

Thames Ditton [Hampton Court Way, Weston Green; TQ1566], *Greyhound*: Food-oriented Wayside Inn, with Whitbreads-related and guest ales, helpful staff, pleasant atmosphere, big pine tables in airy rooms *(D P and J A Sweeney, Christopher Wright)*

Thorpe [Ten Acre Lane; TQ0268], *Red Lion*: Handy for Thorpe Park, with friendly atmosphere and staff, beamed bar, Theakstons XB, log fire, reasonably priced food, back terrace and orchard garden; pool, darts and fruit machines *(George Atkinson, Ian Phillips)*; [Sandhills Ln, Thorpe Green], *Rose & Crown*: Good outdoor children's area with play things and big black rabbits, Scottish Courage ales, friendly efficient staff, wide range of food inc good value steak baguettes *(Ian Phillips)*

☆ **Tilford** [The Green, off B3001 SE of Farnham; SU8743], *Barley Mow*: Good food esp vegetarian (but strict numbered service rota may mean long inter-course gap if you don't order all at once), well kept Scottish Courage ales, good log fire in big inglenook, comfortable traditional seats around scrubbed tables, interesting prints; small back eating area, weekend afternoon teas; darts, table skittles, no children; pretty setting between river and geese-cropped cricket green nr ancient oak, with waterside garden – village does get busy in summer though *(Margaret and Nigel Parker, G R Sunderland, G and M Stewart)*

Virginia Water [Callow Hill; SU9969], *Rose & Olive Branch*: Comfortable Morlands pub with guest beer such as Theakstons, good range of reasonably priced home-made food inc good pies and huge mixed grill (busy Fri night, best to book then), decent wines, friendly helpful service, matchbox collection, quiet piped music; children allowed lunchtime, big garden *(John Athersuch, John Ince)*

Walton on Thames [50 Manor Rd, off A3050; TQ1066], *Swan*: Three-bar riverside Youngs pub, lots of interconnecting rooms, huge neatly kept garden leading down to Thames, good reasonably priced food in bar and attractive restaurant, well kept ales, weekend barbecues; moorings, riverside walks *(R B Crail, Ed Birch)*

☆ **Walton on the Hill** [Walton St], *Fox & Hounds*: Decent food esp puddings in chatty bar and pleasant adjoining restaurant (must book), well kept Bass, Fullers London Pride and two other ales, brisk service, nice surroundings; open all day Sun *(J S M Sheldon, LYM)*

☆ **Warlingham** [Limpsfield Rd; TQ3857], *Botley Hill Farmhouse*: Converted 16th-c farmhouse, more restaurant than pub, but attractively presented fresh bar food too, and well kept if not cheap ales such as Boddingtons, Flowers, Greene King, Pilgrims and Shepherd Neame Spitfire; friendly polite service, children welcome, with attractions for them; cream teas, wonderful North Downs views, good walking country; very busy weekends, with entertainments inc comedians *(G Simpson, Paul Randall, Mrs J Blanks)*

☆ **West Clandon** [The Street (A247); TQ0452], *Onslow Arms*: Partly 17th-c rambling country pub, pricy but good and convivial; comfortable seating in nooks and corners, heavy beams, flagstones, inglenook log fires, soft lighting, lots of brass and copper, thick carpets, efficient staff; eight well kept ales, decent wines, nicely presented sandwiches, carvery-style hot-lamp bar food servery (not Sun evening), stylish partly no-smoking restaurant (popular Sun lunches), great well lit garden; children welcome, open all day *(Susan and John Douglas, Ronald Buckler, B and M Parkin, Nigel Fox, Ian Phillips, Mike and Heather Watson, Wayne Brindle, M L and G Clarke, LYM)*

☆ **West Clandon** [The Street], *Bulls Head*: Friendly and comfortably modernised 16th-c country local, small lantern-lit bar with open fire and some stripped brick, old local prints, raised rather canteenish back inglenook dining area very popular esp with older people lunchtime for good value enjoyable straightforward food (same food evenings), bookable Sun lunch, genial landlord, efficient service, Courage Best and Marstons Pedigree, good coffee, games room with darts and pool; lots of tables and good play area in garden,

convenient for Clandon Park, good walking country *(DWAJ, Mr and Mrs D J Ross, KC, R Lake, John Pettit, G W and I L Edwards, G W Jensen)*

☆ **West Horsley** [The Street, off A246 E of Guildford; TQ0753], *Barley Mow*: Modest village local with flagstones, beams, extraordinary collection of pig ornaments, well kept ales inc Greene King, decent wines and spirits, good value lunchtime food, comfortable little dining room, cheerful staff *(R B Crail, John Evans)*

West Horsley, *King William IV*: Comfortable and relaxing, very low beams but plenty of space, well kept Courage Directors and Best and Harveys, log fire, friendly service, good disabled access, food inc children's *(John Evans)*

Weybridge [Thames St; TQ0764], *Farnell Arms*: This popular pub has closed, to make way for housing *(Anon)*; [Princes Rd], *Jolly Farmer*: Warm and cosy small local opp picturesque cricket ground, interesting reasonably priced food, well kept and priced Fullers London Pride; lovely garden with terrace, tented extension and barbecue *(Ian Phillips, Simon Penny, Maurice Southon)*; [83 Thames St], *Old Crown*: Friendly old-fashioned three-bar pub, warm and comfortable, very popular lunchtime for reasonably priced generous straightforward food esp fish (served evening too); Scottish Courage and other ales, friendly rugby-fan landlord, no music or machines; children welcome, suntrap streamside garden *(DWAJ, R B Crail, J Sheldon, P Gillbe)*; [Oatlands Dr], *Pickled Newt*: Well refurbished in usual Magic Pub Co style, with Bass, Boddingtons, Greene King Abbot and Websters, friendly service, generous cheap food; piped music, live Thurs *(Alec and Marie Lewery, Graham and Lynn Mason, James Nunns)*; [Bridge Rd/Quadrant], *Queens Head*: Good architectural mix of old and new, comfortingly welcoming and opulent, with local sporting connections, decent food, tables out in front, lots of hanging baskets; popular evenings with young people – Thurs is 70s and 80s music, Sun disco *(Fraser Lobb, Graham and Lynn Mason)*

☆ **Windlesham** [Chertsey Rd (B386 E of Bagshot); SU9264], *Brickmakers Arms*: Popular well run dining pub with good interesting freshly made food esp ciabatta sandwiches and fish, not cheap but good value, cheerful busy bar, well kept Scottish Courage and other ales, wide choice of wines, splendid service, daily papers; well behaved children allowed in restaurant, attractive garden with boules and barbecues, lovely hanging baskets *(Guy Consterdine, Malcolm Phillips, Jerry Hughes, Margaret and Nigel Dennis)*

☆ **Witley** [Petworth Rd (A283); SU9439], *White Hart*: Tudor beams, good oak furniture, log fire in cosy panelled inglenook snug where George Eliot drank; well kept Marstons Pedigree and Shepherd Neame Spitfire, very wide choice of good value food in bar and restaurant from new kitchen, friendly licensees, public bar with usual games; piped music; seats outside, lots of pretty hanging baskets etc, play area *(Mrs J Beale, James Nunns, LYM)*

Worcester Park [Cheam Common Rd; TQ2266], *Old Crown*: Good value generous food inc sandwiches and vegetarian in comfortably refurbished beamed pub with Scottish Courage ales, friendly staff, restaurant; well kept garden with play area *(DWAJ, Jason Reynolds)*

Wotton [A25 Dorking—Guildford; TQ1247], *Wotton Hatch*: Extensively refurbished around traditional tiled-floor core with good log fire, as comfortable family dining pub, lots of room with plenty of seating, conservatory, garden with play area and impressive views; good if inflexible range of enjoyable food, well kept Bass, Hancocks HB and guest beers, decent wines *(Mrs W D Morrison, Mr and Mrs Carey, Dick Brown, LYM)*

Wrecclesham [Sandrock Hill Rd; SU8245], *Sandrock*: Good range of well kept changing ales mostly from smaller breweries, often Midlands ones, in simply converted local with friendly knowledgeable staff; real fire, games room and garden, no food or piped music *(G C Hackemer)*

Post Office address codings confusingly give the impression that some pubs are in Surrey when they're really in Hampshire or London (which is where we list them). And there's further confusion from the way the Post Office still talks about Middlesex – which disappeared in 1974 local government reorganisation.

Sussex

New entries here include the friendly and unassuming Black Horse in the attractive village of Amberley (currently in very good hands), the Woodmans Arms at Hammerpot (relaxing escape from the A27 near Angmering), the Blacksmiths Arms at Offham (reliable food in this spotless pub), the Badgers just south of Petworth (good food and wine in a very civilised dining pub), the Ypres Castle in Rye (good views from the garden of this properly pubby place – with a fine choice of wines by the glass), the Salehurst Halt at Salehurst (we've been delighted to find this pub within striking distance of our editorial office) and the Sloop tucked away down its country lane at Scaynes Hill. Other pubs on fine form here these days are the unspoilt Fountain at Ashurst, the charming Cricketers Arms at Berwick (good food), the bustling Blackboys Inn at Blackboys (big garden), the homely Ash Tree at Brownbread Street (good beer, enjoyable food), the George & Dragon at Burpham (good food, and gains one of our Beer Awards this year), the Black Horse at Byworth (simple but smart, with a great garden), the Old House At Home at Chidham (good all round), the Blacksmiths Arms at Donnington (couldn't be more welcoming, with good straightforward food), both Elsted pubs (very hard to choose between these two gems – the village to move to), the Griffin at Fletching (excellent all round), the friendly and relaxed Queens Head at Icklesham, the rather hippy junk-filled Snowdrop in Lewes (much loved if you're into that scene), the handsome Middle House in Mayfield, the very well run Golden Galleon at Seaford (gains a Food Award this year – often packed, despite its size), the Horse Guards at Tillington and the Dorset Arms at Withyham. Most of these in their different ways have decent food – or better. For a really enjoyable meal out, though, our final choice would boil down to either the Elsted Inn at Elsted (real efforts to use the best local produce wisely, and a nice relaxed local atmosphere) or the Griffin at Fletching (interesting food, great wines by the glass); though it can be on the pricy side, the extra sense of occasion just tips the balance to our award of Sussex Dining Pub of the Year to the Griffin at Fletching. We must mention some pubs in the Lucky Dip section, too, most inspected and approved by us: the Gardeners Arms at Ardingly (not yet inspected, but clearly a reliable place for lunch), Swan in Arundel, Old Vine at Cousleywood, Cock at Ringmer, Best Beech near Wadhurst and Lamb at West Wittering. We also like the Shepherd & Dog at Fulking and Star at Normans Bay. That nice old pub the Gun on Gun Hill had new licensees too late for us to form a view, and the Peacock at Shortbridge, reopened after fire damage repairs, looks promising; there's a good interesting choice in Brighton. This is an expensive county for both food and drinks, with beer typically costing about 15p a pint more than the national average; the cheapest places we found for beer, all clearly undercutting the national average, were the Golden Galleon at Seaford (brewing its own), the Bull at Ticehurst (a beer brewed for the pub), the Old House At Home at Chidham (Burts Nipper, from the Isle of Wight just across Southampton Water) and the Queens Head at Icklesham (the local Harveys).

Yet again, this underlines the message for seeking real value in beer – think small (small brewery, that is), and think local.

ALCISTON TQ5005 Map 3
Rose Cottage
Village signposted off A27 Polegate—Lewes

This is a genuinely old-fashioned little cottage with a welcoming licensee who works hard at keeping his pub as traditional as possible. The interesting food remains quite a draw, particularly as they use fresh, local ingredients wherever possible – organic vegetables grown a quarter of a mile up the road, eggs from their own chickens, pheasants shot by landlord, and good daily fresh fish. Daily specials are very popular, and might include thai-style tiger prawns with a hot soy dip or cheesy topped garlicky mussels (£3.65; main course £6.95), rabbit and bacon or beef in ale pies (£5.50), a vegetarian dish or barbecued spare ribs (£6.25), chargrilled leg of lamb steak with cream of tarragon sauce (£7.25), and venison braised in port and Guinness (from the landlord's brother-in-law, £7.95); from the menu there might be home-made soup, sausages and chips (£4.25), lunchtime ploughman's (£4.50), honey-roast ham with poached egg (£4.65), gammon steak (£4.85), and steaks (from £9.50). Sunday roasts (£6.95). Well kept Harveys Best and a monthly guest beer on handpump, decent wines including a 'country' of the month and five by the glass, Merrydown cider, and summer kir and pimms. Small and cosy, the relaxed and friendly bar soon fills up, so get there early for one of the half-dozen tables with their cushioned pews – under quite a forest of harness, traps, a thatcher's blade and lots of other black ironware, with more bric-a-brac on the shelves above the dark pine dado or in the etched glass windows. In the mornings you may also find Jasper, the talking parrot (it can get a little smoky for him in the evenings). There's a lunchtime overflow into the no-smoking restaurant area; log fires, darts, maybe piped classical music. There are some seats under cover outside, and a small paddock in the garden has ducks and chickens. The house martins and swallows have returned again to nest above the porch, seemingly unperturbed by the people going in and out beneath them. A once-common Sussex tradition now lives on only at this pub, when every Good Friday lunchtime you can still see locals long-rope skipping to make the crops grow faster. *(Recommended by Mike and Heather Watson, P Rome, A Cowell, Wayne Brindle, John Beeken, Sue Demont, Tim Barrow, R and S Bentley, Hugh MacLean, JEB, R Walden, M Holdsworth, Colin Laffan, Mr and Mrs B Pullee)*

Free house ~ Licensee Ian Lewis ~ Real ale ~ Meals and snacks (till 10pm) ~ Evening restaurant ~ (01323) 870377 ~ Children welcome – must be over 6 in evenings ~ Open 11.30-3, 6.30-11; 12-3, 7-10.30 Sun; closed 25/26 Dec ~ Self-catering flat

ALFRISTON TQ5103 Map 3
Star 🏠

Built in the 15th c by Battle Abbey as a guest house for pilgrims, this smart old place has a facade decorated with fine medieval carvings, and the striking red lion on the corner – known as Old Bill – was probably the figurehead from a wrecked Dutch ship. The front part is welcoming and full of atmosphere, and in the bustling heavy-beamed bar is a sanctuary post – holding it gave the full protection of the Church; in 1516 one man rode a stolen horse from Lydd in Kent to take advantage of the offer – and avoided the death penalty. Elegant furnishings include a heavy Stuart refectory table with a big bowl of flowers, antique windsor armchairs worn to a fine polish and a handsome longcase clock; the fireplace with its big log fire is Tudor. Under the new manager, the simple bar menu includes sandwiches (from £3), home-made soup (£2.95), filled baked potato (from £3.80), ploughman's (from £4.80), and daily specials. There's also a no-smoking lounge. Bass on handpump, a good range of wines by the glass and malt whiskies; good, helpful service. The comfortable bedrooms are in an up-to-date part at the back. *(Recommended by Sue and Steve Griffiths, Ian Phillips, Janet and Colin Roe, Steve Goodchild)*

Free house ~ Manager James Leeming ~ Real ale ~ Meals and snacks (snacks only Sun) ~ Restaurant ~ (01323) 870495 ~ Children in eating area of bar ~ Open 11-2.30, 6-11; 12-3, 7-10.30 Sun ~ Bedrooms: £81.75B/£111B

AMBERLEY TQ0212 Map 3
Black Horse

Off B2139

Reached up a flight of steps, this very pretty village pub has high-backed settles on the flagstones, beams over the serving counter festooned with sheep and cow bells, traps and shepherds' tools, and walls decorated with lots of old local prints and engravings; there are plenty of pictures too in the similar but more comfortable saloon bar. There's a log fire at either end of the main bar and one in the lounge. Good, well presented bar food includes sandwiches (from £2.25), winter soup (£2.75), ploughman's with a choice of nine different cheeses (£4.50), popular steak and kidney pie (£5.50), fresh fillet of plaice (£5.90), and daily specials such as home-made vegetable lasagne (£6.75), smoked salmon cornet stuffed with prawns (£7.25), fresh crab (£8.50), and pheasant with apple and calvados; on Tuesday they offer a three-course lunch for £5; the restaurant is no smoking. Well kept Friary Meux and Ind Coope Burton with a guest beer on handpump; friendly, welcoming staff. Darts, and fruit machine, and piped music; two big dogs and a sleepy cat. There are seats in the garden. The attractive village is close to the River Arun, with a castle, and the pub is handy for the South Downs Way and Amberley Industrial Museum. *(Recommended by Mrs P Boxford, John Beeken, Tony Scott, Mrs P M Jolins, N E Bushby, W Atkins)*

Pubmaster ~ Tenants Mr and Mrs C Acterson ~ Real ale ~ Meals and snacks ~ Restaurant ~ (01798) 831700 ~ Children welcome ~ Open 11-3, 6-11; 11-2.30, 6.30-11 winter; 12-3, 7-10.30 Sun

ASHURST TQ1716 Map 3
Fountain

B2135 N of Steyning

The charmingly rustic tap room on the right in this 16th-c country local is the place to head for: scrubbed old flagstones, a couple of high-backed wooden cottage armchairs by the log fire in its brick inglenook, two antique polished trestle tables and, depending on the season, between three and seven well kept real ales on handpump or tapped from the cask. The range might include Adnams Broadside, Courage Best and Directors, Fullers London Pride, John Smiths, and Ushers Chadwicks Finest. A bigger carpeted room with its orginal beams and woodburning stove is where most of the popular bar food is served: fresh cod (£5.95), steak and kidney pudding or rogan josh (£6.95), poached salmon in brioche pastry (£8.45), and Sunday roasts (£6.45). Best to book in the evenings; pleasant service. A gravel terrace has picnic tables by an attractive duckpond, and there are swings and a see-saw in the pretty enclosed garden with fruit trees and roses. Shove-ha'penny, dominoes, and skittle alley. *(Recommended by Colin Draper, Pat and Tony Martin, John Beeken, R J Walden, David Holloway, Gwen and Peter Andrews, James Nunns, Ron Gentry, Alan Jarvis)*

Free house ~ Licensee Maurice Caine ~ Real ale ~ Meals and snacks (not Sun evening) ~ Restaurant (not Sun evening) ~ (01403) 710219 ~ Children over 10 in restaurant until 8pm ~ Open 11-2.30, 6-11; 12-2.30, 7-10.30 Sun; closed evenings 25/26 Dec

BARCOMBE TQ4114 Map 3
Anchor

From village follow Newick, Piltdown sign, then turn right at Boast Lane leading to Anchor Lane, marked with a No Through Rd sign, then first left (by post box)

At the end of a long single-track lane, this cheerful little pub is in a quiet setting by the River Ouse. The neatly kept waterside lawns and fairy-lit terrace have plenty of picnic tables and white metal seats and tables, and you can hire boats on an unspoilt three-mile stretch of the river as it winds through the meadows (£3.20 an hour per adult, half price for children under 14, free if under 4) – reckon on about two hours if you're going all the way to the fish ladder Falls near Sutton Hall and back. A riverside kiosk serves cream teas and cold drinks, and there are barbecues most summer weekends. In winter the approach road can flood and cut the pub off – they leave out a boat or two then. Inside, there are two tiny bars decorated with a good few motor racing trophies won by the landlord's late father, along with some car models, and other racing and RAF memorabilia – it's the HQ for the Jaguar Owner's Club. There's an intimate candlelit restaurant. Bar food includes filled french bread or baked potatoes (from £4.25), local sausage and egg (£4.75), daily specials such as spaghetti with a bacon and mushroom sauce (£4.95), field mushrooms with stilton, apple and walnuts (£5.50), beef, mushroom and Guinness pie or roast leg of chicken with an orange and mustard sauce (£6.95), poached salmon (£7.95), mixed grill (£9.50), and puddings such as spotted dick (£2.75). Well kept Badger Best, IPA and Tanglefoot, and Harveys Best on handpump, and a decent wine list including some local English ones. Good friendly service; dominoes, shut-the-box, Scrabble, chess and draughts. The family room has toys and children's videos. The pub has been run by the same family for the last 30 years. *(Recommended by Anthony Byers, John Beeken, Jenny and Brian Seller, Comus Elliott, M Martin, Dr S Savvas, Eddie Edwards)*

Free house ~ Licensees Graham and Jaci Bovet-White ~ Real ale ~ Meals and snacks (not 25 Dec; 12-3, 6-9.30) ~ Restaurant ~ (01273) 400414 ~ Children in restaurant, family room, and conservatory ~ Open 11-11; 12-10.30 Sun; closed 25 Dec, evening 1 Jan ~ Bedrooms: £30/£52(£65B)

BERWICK TQ5105 Map 3
Cricketers Arms
Lower Rd, S of A27

Overlooking the downs, this delightful and unspoilt old flint cottage has three little similarly furnished rooms with simple benches against the half-panelled walls, a happy mix of old country tables and chairs, burgundy velvet curtains on poles, a few bar stools, and some country prints; quarry tiles on the floors (nice worn ones in the middle room), two log fires in little brick fireplaces, a huge black supporting beam in each of the low ochre ceilings, and (in the end room) some attractive cricketing pastels; a relaxed and friendly atmosphere and helpful, friendly staff – even when really busy. Good bar food includes home-made soup (£2.75), ploughman's (from £3.75), filled baked potatoes (from £3.75), nice scampi (£4.50), ham and egg (£4.25), tasty rump steak (from £6.50), daily specials such as steak and kidney pudding or thai prawns in garlic and vegetable bolognese, and puddings like enjoyable home-made treacle tart or bread and butter pudding (£2.50). Well kept Harveys Best, PA and seasonal ales tapped from the cask, and decent wine; darts, dominoes, cribbage, shove-ha'penny, and an old Sussex game called toad-in-the-hole. The old-fashioned garden is very pretty with mature flowering shrubs and plants, lots of picnic tables in front of and behind the building, and little brick paths – idyllic on a sunny summer's day. The wall paintings in the nearby church done by the Bloomsbury group during WWII are worth a look. *(Recommended by Tony Scott, Rex Martyn, Stephen Harvey, A Cowell, John Beeken, Paul and Heather Bettesworth, Tony Scott, Sue Demont, Tim Barrow, Mavis and John Wright, Mrs R D Knight)*

Harveys ~ Tenant Peter Brown ~ Real ale ~ Meals and snacks ~ (01323) 870469 ~ Children in eating area of bar only ~ Open 11-3, 6-11; 11-11 summer Sat; 12-10.30 summer Sun

nr BILLINGSHURST TQ0830 Map 3
Blue Ship 🍺
The Haven; hamlet signposted off A29 just N of junction with A264, then follow signpost left towards Garlands and Okehurst

Genuinely unspoilt and peaceful, this friendly little country pub has a cosy beamed and brick-floored front bar with a blazing fire in the inglenook fireplace and hatch service; a corridor leads to a couple of similar little rooms. Well kept King & Barnes Broadwood, Sussex and seasonal beers tapped from the cask. A games room has darts, bar billiards, shove-ha'penny, cribbage and dominoes. It can get crowded with a pleasant mix of customers, particularly at weekends; there may be a couple of playful cats. Straightforward but enjoyable bar food includes sandwiches (from £1.90), ham and vegetable soup (£2.50), ploughman's (from £3.70), macaroni cheese (£4.30), cottage pie (£4.50), and steak and kidney pie or scampi (£5.90). It's very nice in summer, when you can relax at the tree-shaded side tables or by the tangle of honeysuckle around the front door, and there's a play area for children. *(Recommended by Lady M H Moir, Guy Consterdine, Mr and Mrs C G Fraser, LM, Richard J Raeon, Karen Barnes, Paul Kitchener)*

King & Barnes ~ Tenant J R Davie ~ Real ale ~ Meals and snacks (not Sun or Mon evenings) ~ (01403) 822709 ~ Children in two rooms without bar ~ Open 11-3, 6-11; closed evening 25 Dec

BLACKBOYS TQ5220 Map 3
Blackboys

B2192, S edge of village

This bustling 14th-c weatherboarded house has a string of old-fashioned and unpretentious little rooms with dark oak beams, bare boards or parquet, masses of bric-a-brac and antique prints, and a good inglenook log fire. Good waitress-served food includes soup (£2.50), ploughman's with good home-smoked ham (from £3.50), fish curry or chilli con carne (£5.50), tagliatelle carbonara (£6.50), seafood pancakes with scallops, prawns and mussels or steak and kidney pie (£5.95), steaks (from £7.95), summer crab salad or half lobster salad (£8.50), daily specials like calamari (£5.50), chargrilled sea bream (£7.95), cajun chicken (£8.50), and Spanish lamb (£8.95), and winter game dishes; friendly, efficient staff even when busy. Well kept Harveys Best, Pale Ale, Mild and seasonal brews on handpump; welcoming service, and darts, chess, shove-ha'penny, dominoes, cribbage, fruit machine, video game, and a novel version of ring-the-bull – ring-the-stag's-nose. Outside, there's masses of space, with rustic tables in the back orchard, some seats overlooking the pretty front pond, a play area with a challenging wooden castle and quite a few animals, and a barn with a big well equipped playroom; good Woodland Trust walks opposite the pub. *(Recommended by Ros Barber, David Miles, Kevin Thorpe, Colin Laffan, Margaret and Nigel Dennis, Bruce Bird, R and S Bentley, Dr S Savvas, M Martin, Mr Grant)*

Harveys ~ Tenant Nicola Russell ~ Real ale ~ Meals and snacks (till 10pm; not Sun evening) ~ Restaurant ~ (01825) 890283 ~ Children in eating area and restaurant ~ Occasional Morris dancers and singers ~ Open 11-3, 6-11; 12-3, 7-11 Sun

BROWNBREAD STREET TQ6715 Map 3
Ash Tree ◀

Village signposted off the old coach road between the Swan E of Dallington on B2096 Battle—Heathfield and the B2204 W of Battle, nr Ashburnham

There's a good homely atmosphere in the cosy beamed bars of this tucked away country local – as well as nice old settles and chairs, candles at night, stripped brickwork, and three inglenook fireplaces. Bar food is well liked, and changing dishes might include sandwiches, chestnut and red wine pâté (£2.60), cottage pie (£3.95), home-made prawn and cucumber mousse (£3.95), pasta dishes (from £4.50), crab salad (£5.75), steak and kidney pie (£5.25), half a roast guinea fowl (£6.50), rump steak (£8.50), and half a duckling in orange and brandy sauce (£8.95); on Sundays there's a choice of roasts (from £5.75). They may only do full meals at some of their busiest times. Very well kept Harveys Best and a guest such as Fullers London Pride on handpump; cheerful, friendly service, and darts, bar billiards, dominoes, fruit machine, and piped music in the simple games room on the left. The black labrador cross is a little shy and keeps out of the way – the elderly ginger cat isn't quite so reticent. There's a pretty garden with picnic tables. *(Recommended by Mike Fitzgerald, R J Walden, Mr and Mrs Jonathan Russell, D and J Tapper, Mr and Mrs R D Knight, Ken Frostick, D*

H and M C Watkinson, Dave Braisted, R and S Bentley, Dr S Savvas, M Martin, Colin Laffan, Pam and Tim Moorey)

Free house ~ Licensees Malcolm and Jennifer Baker ~ Real ale ~ Meals and snacks (not Mon) ~ Restaurant ~ (01424) 892104 ~ Children in restaurant only ~ Open 12-3, 7-11; 12-4, 7-10.30 Sun; closed Mon

BURPHAM TQ0308 Map 3
George & Dragon ◀

Warningcamp turn off A27 a mile E of Arundel, then keep on up

Just a short walk away from this popular pub, set in a remote hill village of thatch and flint, there are splendid views down to Arundel Castle and the river; there are plenty of pretty surrounding walks and quite a few ramblers drop in for a pint of the well kept Arundel ASB, Harveys Best, Cotleigh Tawny, Hop Back Summer Lightning, Timothy Taylors Landlord, and Woodfordes Wherry on handpump. The spacious and civilised open-plan bar is immaculately kept, with good strong wooden furnishings, and a warm welcome from the friendly licensees. It's the daily specials that really stand out: moules marinières (£4.80), tasty local crab and avocado (£4.95), lamb, mint and apricot pie (£5.60), duck and black cherry pie (£6.50), monkfish fillet with saffron sauce (£6.95), turkey escalope in asparagus sauce (£7.25), lovely duck with rhubarb and cointreau or simply grilled local brill, and puddings such as white chocolate mousse, lovely mango cheesecake, pineapple upside-down cake or sticky toffee pudding (£2.95); also, sandwiches (from £2.50), club sandwiches (£4.50), soup (£2.70), ploughman's (£3.60), filled baked potatoes (from £3.60), poached chicken breast with creamy dijon mustard sauce (£7.25), and gammon steak. Many of the tables get booked up in advance; lots of whiskies. The nearby partly Norman church has some unusual decoration. *(Recommended by Margaret and Nigel Dennis, Mark Matthewman, R T and J C Moggridge, Jo and Gary Charlton, Derek and Maggie Washington, Bebba Smithers, Ian Jones, Pamela Goodwyn, Lawrence Pearse, B and M Kendall, Tony Scott, J Reay, Pam and Tim Moorey, Mrs P Boxford, Winifrede Morrison, David Holloway)*

Belchers Pubs ~ Tenants James Rose and Kate Holle ~ Real ale ~ Meals and snacks (not winter Sun evening) ~ Restaurant (not winter Sun) ~ (01903) 883131 ~ Well behaved children allowed in eating area of bar ~ Occasional jazz/cajun music ~ Open 11-2.30, 6-11; 12-3, 7-10.30 Sun; closed Sun evenings Nov until Easter

BURWASH TQ6724 Map 3
Bell

A265 E of Heathfield

In a pretty village, this pleasant local has a relaxed pubby L-shaped bar to the right of the main door: built-in pews and a mix of seats, all sorts of ironwork, bells and barometers on its ochre Anaglypta ceiling and dark terracotta walls, and a good winter log fire. Well kept Arundel ASB, Batemans XB, Harveys Best and seasonal brews, and Wadworths Easter Ale on handpump, a range of malt whiskies, and some new world wines. Darts, bar billiards, shove-ha'penny, ring-the-bull and toad-in-the-hole, table skittles, cribbage, dominoes, and unobtrusive piped music. Bar food includes sandwiches and ploughman's, chicken chasseur (£5.50), and Scottish salmon fillet with tarragon butter, garlic and herb prawns, fresh crab and prawn platter or rogan josh (all £5.95). Seats in front of the flower-covered mainly 17th-c building look across the busy road to the church. Car park at the back. *(Recommended by T Pascall, A and A Dale, Graham and Lynn Mason, Dr S Savvas, M Martin, R A and J A Buckler)*

Beards (who no longer brew) ~ Lease: Colin and Gillian Barrett ~ Real ale ~ Meals and snacks (not Sun evening) ~ Restaurant (not Sun evening) ~ (01435) 882304 ~ Children welcome till 9.30 ~ Open 11(12 winter)-3, 6-11; 11-11 Sat; 12-10.30 Sun ~ Bedrooms: £20/£40

We say if we know a pub has piped music.

BYWORTH SU9820 Map 2
Black Horse
Signposted from A283

Though perhaps the outside of this old pub is rather unprepossessing, once inside, there's a warm welcome and relaxed, informal atmosphere. The bar is simply furnished yet smart, with pews and scrubbed wooden tables on the bare floorboards, and open fires; the back dining room has lots of nooks and crannies and a tented curtain to keep out the draughts. Bar food includes sandwiches, ploughman's (from £3.25), daily specials, puddings, and Sunday roasts. Well kept Flowers Original, Fullers London Pride, Youngs Ordinary and maybe a guest or two on handpump, and good wines; they hold an annual beer festival. Darts, shove-ha'penny, cribbage, and dominoes. It can be busy at weekends, especially in summer when people come to enjoy the lovely gardens – top tables on a steep series of grassy terraces, sheltered by banks of flowering shrubs, look across a drowsy valley to swelling woodland, and a small stream runs along under an old willow by the more spacious lawn at the bottom; dogs are welcome on a lead. *(Recommended by Keith Ward, Susan and John Douglas, Graham and Karen Oddey, John and Sherry Moate, Peter Wade, Hugh MacLean, Keith Ward, MCG)*

Free house ~ Licensees Michael Courage, Rob Wilson, Teri Figg ~ Real ale ~ Meals and snacks (not evening 24 Dec) ~ Restaurant ~ (01798) 342424 ~ Children in restaurant only ~ Occasional live music ~ Open 11-2.30, 6-11; 12-3.30, 7-10.30 Sun; closed evenings 25/26 Dec

CHIDDINGLY TQ5414 Map 3
Six Bells ★ £
Village signed off A22 Uckfield—Hailsham

A really wide mix of customers blends happily together at this idiosyncratic country pub, and the friendly landlord loves to chat and will certainly remember your face the next time you visit. The characterful beamed rooms have solid old wood furnishings including some pews and antique seats, log fires, lots of fusty artefacts and interesting bric-a-brac, and plenty of local pictures and posters. A sensitive extension provides some much needed family space; darts, dominoes and cribbage. The atmosphere is quite lively when they have live music evenings. A big draw is the remarkably low-priced bar food, straightforward but tasty, with dishes such as french onion soup (90p), a choice of grilled french breads (from £1.20), meat or vegetarian lasagne (£1.85), steak and kidney pie (£2.40), filled baked potatoes (from £2.70), ploughman's (from £3), cheesy vegetable bake (£3.20), chicken curry (£3.60), garlic prawns (£4), and salmon and broccoli bake (£4.75); vegetables are an extra 60p. Well kept Courage Best and Directors and Harveys Best on handpump or tapped from the cask. Outside at the back, there are some tables beyond a big raised goldfish pond, and a boules pitch; the church opposite has an interesting Jeffrey monument. Vintage and Kit car meetings outside the pub once a month. This is a pleasant area for walks. *(Recommended by Mr and Mrs R D Knight, Quentin Williamson, K M Thorpe, Wayne Brindle, LM, David Lamb, Dr S Savvas, M Martin)*

Free house ~ Licensee Paul Newman ~ Real ale ~ Meals and snacks (till 10.30pm) ~ (01825) 872227 ~ Children in family room ~ Jazz, blues and other live music in the barn Tues, Fri, Sat and Sun evenings (from 9), and jazz Sun lunch ~ Open 11-3, 6-11; 12-3, 7-10.30 Sun

CHIDHAM SU7903 Map 2
Old House At Home
Cot Lane; turn off A27 at the Barleycorn pub

Doing very well at the moment, this charming pub is down a quiet country lane and part of a cluster of farm buildings. The homely bar has timbering and low beams, windsor chairs around the tables, long seats against the walls, and a welcoming log fire. Food is good and popular and from an extensive range (they tell us prices have not changed since last year) including sandwiches (from £1.75), soup (£2.50), filled baked potatoes (from £3.25), ploughman's (from £3.50), salads (from £4.50), quite a few vegetarian dishes such as mushroom curry (£5.50), pies such as steak and kidney, rabbit or lamb and apricot (£5.75), grilled trout with almonds (£6.25), steaks (from £9.75), and a good range of daily specials; booking is recommended for summer evenings. Well kept real ales such as Badger Best, Ringwood Best and Old Thumper, Old House (Burts Nipper), and a weekly changing guest beer on handpump, as well as a good selection of country wines and several malt whiskies; cheery service; there's a large friendly german shepherd. It's quite handy for good walks by Chichester harbour, and in summer has a couple of picnic tables on its terrace, with many more in the garden behind. (*Recommended by Tim Abel, Ann and Colin Hunt, Mrs D Bromley-Martin, Janet and John Pamment, Gladys Howden, Jo and Gary Charlton, Victoria Herriott, R J Bland, N E Bushby, W E Atkins, Edward Froggatt, R J Walden, N P Smith, Dennis Stevens, Lynn Sharpless, Bob Eardley, Hugh MacLean, John Fahy, John Sanders*)

Free house ~ Licensees Mike Young and Terry Brewer ~ Real ale ~ Meals and snacks (not 25 Dec, not evening 26 Dec) ~ (01243) 572477 ~ Children in eating area of bar ~ Open 11.30(12 Sat)-3, 6-11.30; 12-3, 7-10.30 Sun; closed evening 25 Dec

COWBEECH TQ6114 Map 3
Merrie Harriers
Village signposted from A271

Particularly popular, both locally and with those further afield, this white-clapboarded village pub was once a farmhouse. The friendly bar is beamed and panelled, and has a traditional high-backed settle by the brick inglenook, as well as other tables and chairs, and darts. A wide range of lunchtime bar food (very popular with the older set) includes sandwiches (from £2.25; filled rolls from £2.75), home-made soup (£2.65), ploughman's (from £4.50), vegetarian dishes (£5.50), home-made steak and kidney pie (£7.25), various fresh local fish (£8.95), a two-course special (£5.95), and home-made puddings like apple pie or summer pudding (£2.95); in the evening they add dishes such as mixed grill or steaks, and do a good Sunday roast. The restaurant is no smoking. Well kept Flowers IPA and Harveys Best on handpump, good choice of wines; charming, professional service. The brick-walled and oak-ceilinged back restaurant is no smoking. Rustic seats in the terraced garden. (*Recommended by Colin Laffan, J H Bell, Bob Arnett, Judy Wayman, Mr and Mrs J A Phipps, Dr S Savvas, M Martin*)

Free house ~ Licensees J H and C P Conroy ~ Real ale ~ Meals and lunchtime snacks ~ Restaurant ~ (01323) 833108 ~ Children in eating area of bar at lunchtime ~ Open 11-3, 6-11; 12-3, 7-10.30 Sun

CUCKFIELD TQ3025 Map 3
White Harte £ 🍺
South Street; off A272 W of Haywards Heath

Cheery and friendly, this pretty partly medieval tile-hung pub is well liked for its good value lunchtime specials, promptly served by pleasant staff. The comfortable partly carpeted lounge has a few local photographs, padded seats on a slightly raised area, some fairly modern light oak tables and copper-topped tables, and a brick bar counter – and there's an appealing traditional feel, with beams, polished floorboards, some parquet and ancient brick flooring tiles, standing timbers, and small windows looking out on to the road. Furnishings in the public bar are sturdy and comfortable with a roaring log fire in the inglenook, and sensibly placed darts. The straightforward meals include regular dishes like ploughman's (from £3.20), salads, and scampi, but most people tend to go for the five or so very good value home-cooked specials: pies like chicken and mushroom, fish, or steak and kidney, turkey breast in mushroom sauce, smoked haddock bake, or stilton and celery quiche (all £3.90). These often go by around 1.30 (and the tables may be snapped up even earlier), so it pays to arrive early. Well kept King & Barnes Bitter and Broadwood and a guest beer on handpump; fruit machine, shove-ha'penny. The village is attractive. (*Recommended by DWAJ, Mr and Mrs A Budden, David Holloway*)

King & Barnes ~ Tenant Ted Murphy ~ Real ale ~ Lunchtime meals and snacks (not Sun) ~ (01444) 413454 ~ Well behaved children in eating are of bar at lunchtime ~ Open 11-3, 6-11; 12-3, 7-10.30 Sun

DONNINGTON SU8502 Map 2
Blacksmiths Arms

Left off A27 on to A286 signed Selsey, almost immediate left on to B2201

You can be sure of a genuinely warm welcome from the character landlord in this homely little white roadside cottage – you will be greeted with a handshake, introduced to the barmaid, and may even have your coats taken. The small down-to-earth rooms are crammed with bric-a-brac: low ceilings are densely hung with hundreds of jugs, pots and kettles (each scrupulously cleaned by the landlord every week), the walls crowded with Victorian prints, and there's a grandfather clock and an interesting old cigarette vending machine on the sill of one of the pretty little windows. Solid and comfortable furnishings on the patterned carpet include several 1950s sofas; shove-ha'penny, dominoes, fruit machine. Well kept Bass, Badger Best, Fullers London Pride, Ringwood Best and Wadworths 6X on handpump or tapped from the cask, sometimes kept under light blanket pressure. Enjoyable bar food includes sandwiches or crusty rolls (from £1.75), soup (£1.80), filled baked potatoes (from £3.60), pizzas (from £3.85), ploughman's (£3.95), a vegetarian dish of the day or home-made lasagne (£6.95), home-made steak and kidney pie (£7.25), Selsey crab salad (£8.95), puddings (from £2.80), and quite a choice of children's meals (from £1.75). The big garden has a well fenced play area where the grass is virtually obscured by ride-on-toys (some of them have seen better days), and there's also a plastic tree house, swings, and trampolines. *(Recommended by Janet and Colin Roe, David Peakall, Ann and Colin Hunt, Edward Froggatt, Mary Woods, RTM, JCM, Alec and Marie Lewery)*

Free house ~ Fergus and Gill Gibney ~ Real ale ~ Meals and snacks (till 10pm, not winter Sun evenings) ~ Restaurant (not winter Sun evening) ~ (01243) 783999 ~ Children welcome ~ Open 11-2.30, 6-11; 12-3, 7-10.30 Sun; closed evenings 25/26 Dec

DUNCTON SU9617 Map 3
Cricketers

Set back from A285 N

Set back from the road, this pretty little white house has a jovial landlord and friendly staff who make both visitors and regulars feel very welcome. The bar has a few standing timbers giving the room an open-plan feel, there's an inglenook fireplace at one end with a large summer dried flower arrangement and some brass pots and warming pans on either side of the grate, local photographs on the mantelpiece, half-a-dozen bar stools and a mix of country tables and chairs, and green-cushioned settles; wildlife pictures, a cartoon of the licensee and his wife, and a relaxed, cheerful atmosphere. Down a couple of steps a similarly furnished room is set for eating and is decorated with farming implements, pictures, and cricketer cigarette cards; doors from here lead out into a charming back garden (enlarged this year) with a proper barbecue (summer Sunday lunchtime barbecues), picnic tables, and an attractive little creeper-covered seating area. Good, popular bar food includes soup (£2.50), jumbo filled rolls (£2.75), garlic mushrooms (£3.95), beef bourguignon (£5.95), ploughman's (£4.50), steak and kidney pie (£6.25), cod in batter (£6.95), chicken breast on ratatouille (£7.25), grilled whole lemon sole (£7.95), local trout or crispy duck with noodles and stir-fried vegetables (£8.95), and best end of lamb with redcurrants and rosemary (£9.95). Well kept Archers Golden, Friary Meux Bitter, Ind Coope Burton, Youngs, and guest beers on handpump, lots of malt whiskies, decent wines; cribbage. There's a separate skittle alley at the front to one side of the building, lovely flowering baskets and tubs, and a rope swing for children. *(Recommended by Bruce Bird, Tony and Wendy Hobden, MCG, Peter Lewis, Michael Grigg; more reports please)*

Free house ~ Licensee Philip Edgington ~ Real ale ~ Meals and snacks (not Sun or Mon winter evenings) ~ Restaurant ~ (01798) 342473 ~ Well behaved children in restaurant only ~ Open 11-2.30, 6-11; closed winter Sun evenings

EARTHAM SU9409 Map 2
George

Signposted off A285 Chichester—Petworth; also from Fontwell off A27 and Slindon off A29

Handy for Goodwood, this bustling and friendly country pub is in a pretty part of the county. It's popular for the well-presented bar food which might include french bread open sandwiches (from £2.50), filled baked potatoes (from £3.50), several vegetarian dishes such as a good mushroom stroganoff, warm salad of avocado and mushrooms with a poppy seed dressing or vegetable crumble with a topping of oats, fruit, nuts and cheese (£5.20), interesting pies such as lamb and orange, rabbit and juniper berries or steak in ale (£5.95), steaks (from £6.95 for a 6oz rump), various daily changing fresh fish dishes (from £7.95), breast of duck in caramelised orange marmalade or rack of lamb (£9.95), and puddings (from £2.50); it's worth booking at busy periods. Well kept Gales Best, Butser, HSB, and maybe a guest on handpump, and courteous staff. The cosy lounge is pleasantly comfortable without being fussily overdecorated, and there's a pubbier public bar; both have a relaxed atmosphere even at the busiest times. Darts, cribbage, fruit machine, and piped music. The restaurant is no smoking. *(Recommended by JDM, KM, R J Walden, Elizabeth and Klaus Leist, Edward Froggatt, B and M Parkin, John and Barbara Howdle, Iain Robertson, DWAJ, Bruce Bird, Christopher Warner)*

George Gale ~ Manager James Crossley ~ Real ale ~ Meals and snacks ~ Restaurant ~ (01243) 814340 ~ Children welcome in eating area of bar and restaurant ~ Open 11-3, 5-11; 11-11 summer Sat; 12-10.30 summer Sun; closed evenings 25 Dec, 1 Jan

EAST DEAN TV5597 Map 3
Tiger ♀

Pub (with village centre) signposted – not vividly – from A259 Eastbourne—Seaford

The delightful cottage-lined green makes a perfect setting for this long low white tiled pub with its window boxes, clematis and roses, big bright painting of a tiger on a branch, and rustic seats and tables on the brick front terrace; the green itself can act as an overflow when the pub is busy – which it often is. Inside, the smallish rooms have low beams hung with pewter and china, traditional furnishings including polished rustic tables and distinctive antique settles, and old prints and so forth. Well kept Flowers Original, Greene King Abbot and Harveys Best on handpump; also a fair choice of wines with several interesting vintage bin-ends, 4 good wines by the glass, and some good clarets. A short but good choice of home-made bar meals, listed on a blackboard, might include local sausage ploughman's (£4.25), warm chicken liver salad with apple and bacon (£4.75), macaroni cheese topped with melted stilton and tomato (£4.95), fillet of local fish and chips (£5.25), and local game stew with horseradish dumplings (£5.95); their meat comes from the very good local butcher who wins awards for his sausages. The upstairs family room is no smoking. Morris dancers visit every bank holiday. The lane leads on down to a fine stretch of coast culminating in Beachy Head, and there are plenty of good walks. *(Recommended by John Voos, Charles Bardswell, Brian and Anna Marsden, John Beeken, Comus Elliott, Isabel de Alayo Rimmer, S Pyle, E G Parish)*

Free house ~ Licensee Nicholas Denyer ~ Real ale ~ Meals and snacks ~ (01323) 423209 ~ Children in separate family room ~ Open 11-3, 6-11; all day (inc Sun) July/Aug

---

The 🍴 rosette distinguishes pubs where the food is of exceptional quality.

ELSTED SU8119 Map 2
Elsted Inn ★ ⑪ ◖

Elsted Marsh; from Midhurst left off A272 Petersfield Rd at Elsted and Harting sign; from Petersfield left off B2146 Nursted Rd at South Harting, keep on past Elsted itself

It would be easy to drive past this plain Victorian roadside pub, built originally to serve the railway when there was a station next door (this explains the old railway photographs in the bars). The two bars are unpretentious and unmodernised (and redecorated this year) with simple country furniture on wooden floors, original shutters, Victorian stuffed birds, three open log fires, and no piped music or noisy games machines; darts, shove-ha'penny, dominoes, cribbage, backgammon, and cards; the small restaurant (candlelit at night) has new patchwork curtains, an old oak dresser, and restored old polished tables and chairs. They use the best ingredients for their good cooking: local game, Jersey cream from a local farm, hand-made bread from the National Trust bakery at Slindon, free range eggs, free range chicken and duck, winter mutton from the landlady's aunt's sheep, and local vegetables and fruit. The menu sometimes changes twice a day and might include sandwiches (from £2.20), macaroni cheese (£4.50), filled baked potatoes or ploughman's (£4.95), good mussels baked with garlic and cheese (£5.50), good local sausages, vegetarian bean korma or roast rib of beef (£7), salmon fishcakes (£7.75), local rabbit in mustard sauce or bacon pudding (£7.95), lemon sole grilled with wine and butter (£8.25), and puddings such as home-made ice creams like honey and ginger or banana and chocolate (£2.25) as well as popular treacle tart or plum crumble (£3); two-course weekday lunch (£6.50), and they usually have a Wednesday themed evening. As there isn't much space, they now reluctantly advise booking for meals. Well kept Ballards Trotton, Best, Wassail and Wild, Bunces Old Smokey, Fullers London Pride, and a guest beer on handpump; friendly, helpful staff; two big friendly dogs, Sam and Truffle who welcome guests. The lovely enclosed garden has a big terrace, plenty of wooden garden furniture, a wooden playhouse for children, and a good view of the South Downs; floodlit boules pitch, and well used barbecue. *(Recommended by Ian Jones, N E Bushby, W E Atkins, Edward Froggatt, Paul Williams, Julie Peters, Colin Blinkhorn, Mark Matthewman, Tony Gayfer, Martin and Karen Wake, John Evans, Peter Wade, Howard Allen, Ann and Colin Hunt, R and S Bentley, Wendy Arnold, Dr S Savvas, M Martin)*

Free house ~ Licensees Tweazle Jones and Barry Horton ~ Real ale ~ Meals and snacks ~ Restaurant ~ (01730) 813662 ~ Children in restaurant until 8pm ~ Folk music first Sun evening of the month ~ Open 11.30-3, 5.30(6 Sat)-11; 12-3, 7-11 Sun; closed evening 25 Dec ~ Bedrooms should be available by the time this book is published

Three Horseshoes ★ ◖

Village signposted from B2141 Chichester—Petersfield; also reached easily from A272 about 2 miles W of Midhurst, turning left heading W

There's a happy, relaxed atmosphere in this enjoyable 16th-c pub, and a lovely garden, too, with free-roaming bantams and marvellous views over the South Downs. The snug little rooms are full of rustic charm, with ancient beams and flooring, enormous log fires, antique furnishings, attractive prints and photographs, and night-time candlelight. Good home-made food, in big helpings, includes soups (£3.50), avocado with stilton and mushroom sauce topped with bacon (£5.50), generous ploughman's with a good choice of cheeses (£5), steak, kidney and ale pie (£8.50), chicken breast with a fresh asparagus, shallot and madeira sauce or braised lamb with apples and apricots in a tomato chutney sauce (£8.95), game in season, puddings like delicious treacle tart (you can take it away) or raspberry and hazelnut meringue (£3.50). Well kept changing ales racked on a stillage behind the bar counter might include Ballards Best, Cheriton Pots and Diggers Gold, Hampshire King Alfreds and Hop Back Summer Lightning, and Ringwood Fortyniner; also farmhouse ciders and summer pimms. Service is friendly and obliging, even when the pub gets busy – as it often does in summer, especially at weekends. Darts, dominoes and cribbage. *(Recommended by Mr and Mrs C Neve, N E Bushby, W E Atkins, John Evans, John and Joan Calvert, Lynn Sharpless,*

Bob Eardley, J S Evans, Jo and Gary Charlton, Christopher Warner, Judith Reay, Stephen
Goodchild, Howard West, Mr and Mrs D E Powell, Wendy Arnold, Peter and Lynn Brueton,
Peter Wade, Ann and Colin Hunt)

*Free house ~ Licensees Andrew and Sue Beavis ~ Real ale ~ Meals and snacks (not
winter Sun evenings) ~ Restaurant ~ (01730) 825746 ~ Well behaved children in
eating area and restaurant ~ Open 11-2.30(3 Sat), 6-11; closed Sun night from
October to Easter*

FAIRWARP TQ4626 Map 3
Foresters Arms

Set back from B2026, N of northern Maresfield roundabout exit from A22

Near to the Vanguard Way and Weald Way at the south end of Ashdown Forest, this
bustling pub is prettily set on a small green among oak trees. Inside, it's homely and
welcoming, with a comfortable lounge bar, a public bar with a big aquarium, and well
kept King & Barnes Bitter, Festive, Mild, Old and Broadwood on handpump, decent
wines, and farm cider. Popular, carefully prepared food (well liked by the older set at
lunchtime) inlcudes sandwiches (from £3.50), ploughman's (£3.95), home-made pies
(from £5.50), lamb fillet in mustard sauce (£7.50), steaks (from £10) and daily specials
like home-made curries (£5.95), steak and Guinness pie (£6.50), and chicken breast
wrapped in bacon in a creamy stilton sauce (£8.25); good popular Sunday lunch, and
efficient service. Darts, pool, cribbage, dominoes, fruit machine, video game, trivia,
and piped music. There are some tables outside. *(Recommended by Pat and Tony Martin,
Mr and Mrs R D Knight, Colin Laffan, Sue and Steve Griffiths)*

*King & Barnes ~ Tenants Mel and Lloyd West ~ Real ale ~ Meals and snacks ~
Restaurant ~ (01825) 712808 ~ Children welcome ~ Open 11-3, 6-11; 12-3, 7-10.30
Sun ~ Bedrooms: £20/£30*

FIRLE TQ4607 Map 3
Ram

Signposted off A27 Lewes—Polegate

The bustling bars in this family run village pub are still mainly unspoilt, with winter
log fires, comfortable seating, soft lighting, and a nice, friendly feel; the snug is no
smoking. Well kept Harveys Best, Cotleigh Barn Owl, and Otter Bitter on handpump,
and decent wines. Darts, shove-ha'penny, dominoes, cribbage and toad-in-the-hole.
The gents' has a chalk board for graffiti, and there are tables in a spacious walled
garden behind. They have a fine ginger cat called Orange, and two comical geese. Well
presented, if pricy, bar food might include home-made leek and mushroom soup
(£2.50), smoked trout pâté or tortillas with a fresh tomato and chilli salsa with melted
cheese (£2.95), ploughman's with good local cheeses or lovely ham (from £5.15),
mushroom and broccoli tart (£7.15), sausage and bacon roly poly (£7.35), fish pie
(£8.50), chicken and apricot pie (£9.95), and puddings like chocolate roly-poly
(£3.25). Nearby Firle Place is worth visiting for its collections and furnishings, and the
pub is handy for Glyndebourne and for exploring a particularly fine stretch of the
South Downs. *(Recommended by K M Thorpe, Tony and Wendy Hobden, Wayne Brindle, Jo
and Gary Charlton, Bruce Bird, Sue Demont, Tim Barrow, John Beeken, Tim Barrow, Ian Jones)*

*Free house ~ Licensees Michael and Keith Wooller and Margaret Sharp ~ Real ale ~
Meals and lunchtime snacks ~ (01273) 858222 ~ Children in eating area of bar only ~
Folk music second Mon and first Weds of month ~ Open 11.30-3, 7-11; 12-3, 7-10.30
Sun; closed evening 25 Dec ~ Bedrooms: /£50(£65S)*

Real ale to us means beer which has matured naturally in its cask – not
pressurised or filtered.

FLETCHING TQ4223 Map 3

Griffin ★ (🍴) 🛏 ♀

Village signposted off A272 W of Uckfield

Sussex Dining Pub of the Year

On an impeccably kept main street just down from the Norman church, this civilised old country inn has blazing log fires in the quaintly panelled bar rooms, beams, old photographs and hunting prints, straightforward furniture including some captain's chairs, china on a delft shelf, a small bare-boarded serving area off to one side, and a relaxed, friendly atmosphere. A separate public bar has darts, pool, fruit machine, juke box, chess and backgammon. The very good innovative bar food is quite a draw, and might include sweet tomato and rocket soup with crème fraîche or hot ciabatta sandwich with salami, mozzarella and olives (£3.95), small thai-spiced salmon fishcakes with dill mayonnaise (£4.95), local sausage, mash and onion gravy (£5.50), penne with roast aubergines, pesto and goat's cheese (£5.95), stuffed pancakes with minced spiced lamb (£6.50), local rabbit with cider, bacon and red onions or steak in ale pie (£7.50), fish pie with squid, mussels, cod and red mullet (£7.95), chargrilled rib-eye steak (£8.50), and puddings such as rhubarb crumble, sticky toffee pudding or tarte tatin (£3.95); enjoyable breakfasts. Well kept Harveys Best and Hogs Back TEA plus Badger Tanglefoot, Courage Directors, and a guest beer on handpump, a good wine list with ten wines (including champagne) by the glass; pleasant friendly service. There are tables in the beautifully arranged back garden with lovely rolling Sussex views, with more on a sheltered gravel terrace (used for dining). By the time this book is published, they hope to have developed the barn to give them a couple of extra bedrooms (several of the existing ones have four-poster beds) and to create an attractive room for private parties. The pub is in a pretty spot just on the edge of Sheffield Park. *(Recommended by A E Brace, Liz Bell, R D Knight, Margaret and Nigel Dennis, Peter Glenser, Charlie Ballantyne, Brian and Anna Marsden, Pat and Tony Martin, Kate and Robert Hodkinson, Sebastian Leach, Wayne Brindle, Betsy Brown, Nigel Flook, Bob and Maggie Atherton, Tina and David Woods-Taylor, Hugh MacLean, James Nunns, Margaret and Nigel Dennis, C Barrett, HD, Eric and Jackie Robinson, David Holloway, Derrick and Shirley Thomas, Brenda and Derek Savage, Dr S Savvas, M Martin)*

Free house ~ Licensees James and Nigel Pullan and John Gatti ~ Real ale ~ Meals and snacks (till 10 Fri, Sat) ~ Restaurant (not Sun evening) ~ (01825) 722890 ~ Children welcome ~ Piano/sax jazz Fri/Sat evenings and Sun lunchtime ~ Open 11.30-3, 6-11; 12-3, 7-10.30 Sun; closed 25 Dec ~ Bedrooms: /£55B

HAMMERPOT TQ0605 Map 3

Woodmans Arms

Pub visible and well signposted on N (eastbound) side of A27 just under 4 miles E of A284 Arundel; heading westbound, go past pub until you can turn on to eastbound carriageway – after leaving the pub you can rejoin the westbound one almost immediately

A delightful and relaxing escape from the trunk road, this thatched flint pub dates from the 16th c, with such low beams that several are strung with fairy lights as a warning. The brick-floored entrance area has a chatty atmosphere, its seats including one cosy armchair by the inglenook's big log fire, with lots of brass, and genuine old photographs of regulars. On the right a carpeted dining area with candles on the tables has wheelback chairs around its tables, and cheerfully cottagey decorations; on the left is a small no-smoking room with a few more tables; the local flavour is at its best on occasional special evenings such as their annual home-made sloe gin competition. Despite road noise, the garden is a delight, with tables and picnic tables on a terrace, under a fairy-lit arbour and on small lawns among lots of roses and tubs of bright annuals. Good well presented home-made food in generous helpings includes sandwiches (from £2.45), ploughman's (£5.25), bacon and onion roly poly, celery and mushroom stroganoff or chicken casserole (all £5.50), curries (£5.90), light-crusted steak and kidney pie (£5.95), weekend fresh fish such as whole plaice (£5.95), dressed local crab (£6.95), poached salmon in dill sauce (£7.95), evening duck breast with port and cumberland sauce (£8.95), steaks (from £8.95), and puddings like apple pie or rhubarb crumble (£2.95). Well kept Gales Best, HSB and a changing beer such as Force 8 or Hampshire Glory on handpump; country wines, decent conventional wines; good friendly service; cribbage, dominoes and maybe some piped music. The yellow labrador is called Tikka. They have a free map of a circular walk from the pub – best to phone ahead if you are a sizeable party of walkers. *(Recommended by Colin Draper, Bruce Bird, Ann and Colin Hunt, Tony and Wendy Hobden, Mimi and Alastair McNeil, P R White)*

Gales ~ Tenants Malcolm and Anne Green ~ Real ale ~ Meals and snacks (not Sun evening) ~ Restaurant ~ (01903) 871240 ~ Well behaved children welcome ~ Folk club every 2nd Sun evening ~ Open 11-3, 6-11; 12-3, 7-10.30 Sun

HARTFIELD TQ4735 Map 3
Anchor 🍺
Church Street

Another bar has been created in what was the old kitchens here, with old beams and a flagstone floor, a dining area with good tables and chairs, and huge logs burning in an old inglenook fireplace. The original bar which rambles informally around the central servery has heavy beams, old advertisements and little country pictures on the walls above the brown-painted dado, houseplants in the brown-curtained small-paned windows, and a woodburner. Well kept Flowers Original, Fremlins, Harveys Best, Marstons Pedigee and Wadworths 6X on handpump. Good bar food includes sandwiches (from £1.50), home-made soup (£2.25), filled baked potatoes (from £3.25), ploughman's (from £3.50), home-made quail pâté, local sausages, omelettes or ratatouille tarts (all £4), home-cooked ham and egg (£4.50), prawn and crab curry (£5.75), gammon steak with parsley butter (£6.50), lamb kebab with yoghurt and mint (£8.50), sirloin steak (£10.50), daily specials, and puddings (from £2.50); children's meals (£2.50); quick friendly service. Darts in a separate lower room; shove-ha'penny, cribbage, dominoes, and piped music. The front verandah soon gets busy on a warm summer evening. It's only been a pub since the last century, but dates back much further, with spells as a farmhouse and women's workhouse. There's a play area in the popular garden. *(Recommended by Colin and Joyce Laffan, LM, R and S Bentley, David Peakall, Nigel Wikeley; more reports please)*

Free house ~ Licensee Ken Thompson ~ Real ale ~ Meals and snacks (till 10pm) ~ Restaurant ~ (01892) 770424 ~ Children welcome ~ Open 11-11; 12-10.30 Sun; closed evening 25 Dec ~ Bedrooms: £30S/£40S

nr HEATHFIELD TQ5920 Map 3
Star
Old Heathfield – head East out of Heathfield itself on A265, then fork right on to B2096; turn right at signpost to Heathfield Church then keep bearing right; pub on left immediately after church

Tucked away below the handsome Early English church tower, this 14th-c inn has some well worn steps leading into the L-shaped beamed bar with its panelling, built-in wooden wall settles, four or five tables, seats in the inglenook fireplace with its warming log fire, and relaxed, chatty atmosphere; a doorway leads into a similarly furnished smaller room. A wide range of bar food chalked up on a board includes ploughman's (£4.75), fresh mussels or cold meats with bubble and squeak (£5.95), good local cod with chips, fresh crab (£7.95), half a free range duckling (£11.95), fresh lobster (£15), and winter game dishes; efficient, friendly service. Well kept Harveys Best and Greene King IPA and guests such as Bass, Greene King Abbot, Hop Back Summer Lightning, and Youngs Special on handpump, some malt whiskies and farm cider; bar billiards, shove-ha'penny, cribbage, dominoes and piped music. The prettily planted sloping garden with its rustic furniture has year-round table service, and views of rolling oak-lined sheep pastures Turner thought it fine enough to paint. *(Recommended by Wayne Brindle, Margaret and Nigel Dennis, K M Thorpe, J S M Sheldon, Steve Goodchild, Dr S Savvas, M Martin, Keith Ward)*

Free house ~ Lease: Mike and Sue Chappell ~ Real ale ~ Meals and snacks (until 10pm; not evening 25 Dec) ~ Restaurant ~ (01435) 863570 ~ Children in eating area of bar ~ Jazz some Suns ~ Open 11.30-3, 5.30-11; 12-3, 7-10.30 Sun

HORSHAM TQ1730 Map 3
Black Jug
31 North St

With no piped music or noisy machines, this town pub has a good relaxed chatty atmosphere. Big windows light the airy open-plan turn-of-the-century-style room which runs around a large central bar, with a nice collection of heavy dark wood sizeable tables, and comfortable chairs on a stripped wood floor. Above dark wood panelling, the cream walls are crammed with interesting old prints and photographs, and the ceiling is a warm terracotta. A spacious dark wood conservatory has similar furniture and lots of hanging baskets; dominoes and cribbage. Alongside Courage Directors, Marstons Pedigree, John Smiths, Wadworths 6X and a guest like Boddingtons, all well kept on handpump, they serve decent bin ends, two dozen malt whiskies, and nine chilled vodkas from Poland and Russia. The changing bar menu, densely written on a blackboard, is very popular so you may need to book on weekend evenings: sandwiches, tomato and bacon soup (£2.95), pheasant and bacon pâté (£3.95), celery and stilton quiche (£4.25), lasagne (£5.95), steak in Guinness pie (£7.95), chicken breasts marinated in lemon, chilli and garlic with an oriental salad (£8.75), salmon wrapped in smoked bacon on savoy cabbage with hollandaise sauce (£9.25), grilled tuna loin on tagliatelle with a mediterranean sauce (£9.75), and rack of lamb with sun-dried tomato sauce (£12.25). There are quite a few tables sheltered under a pagoda outside on a back terrace. No children. *(Recommended by Pat and Tony Martin, Tony Scott, Simon Hurst, Anne Painter-Ellacott, Richard Lewis, Mr and Mrs David Lee, Derek and Margaret Underwood, Peter Carne)*

Courage ~ Managers Neil Stickland and Christopher Holland ~ Real ale ~ Meals and snacks (till 10pm) ~ Conservatory restaurant ~ (01403) 253526 ~ Open 11-11; 12-3, 7-10.30 Sun; cl evening 25 Dec, all day 26 Dec

ICKLESHAM TQ8816 Map 3
Queens Head ♀ ◀
Small sign partly obscured by plants off A259

One reader tells us that in 25 years of visits to this comfortably relaxed old pub, he has never been disappointed. It's run very personally by the friendly licensees who make both visitors and locals welcome. The open plan areas work round a very big serving counter, which stands under a vaulted beamed roof, and this year they have converted what was a storage area into a dining room, though it is just as often used as an overspill seating area for the rest of the pub. The high beamed walls and ceiling of the easy-going bar are covered with lots of farming implements and animal traps, with well used pub tables and old pews on the brown patterned carpet. Two other areas (one no smoking) are popular with diners – the bar food is very reasonably priced – and have big inglenook fireplaces. The generously served food is listed on a blackboard on a lofty exposed brick chimney, and includes sandwiches (from £1.95; steak in french bread £4.25), home-made soup (£2.50), soft herring roes on toast (£3.95), ploughman's (£4.10), ham and egg (£4.75), steak and kidney pie (£6.25), steaks (from £9.50), and home-made daily specials that include game pies, vegetarian dishes, fresh fish and seafood, curries, and casseroles (£5-£7). Four very well kept changing real ales might be Cotleigh Tawny, Courage Directors, Fullers London Pride, Greene King Abbot, Harveys Best, Ringwood Old Thumper or Rother Valley Level Best; a good choice of wines by the glass, Biddenden cider, and sparkling elderflower cordial. There are broad views over the vast gently sloping plain of the Brede valley from wooden picnic tables in the little garden, and a children's play area; boules. Good walks. *(Recommended by Kevin Thorpe, E G Parish, George Bingham, Bruce Bird)*

Free House ~ Licensee Ian Mitchell ~ Real Ale ~ Meals and snacks (12-2.45, 6.30-9.45; not 25/26 Dec) ~ (01424) 814552 ~ Well supervised children welcome till 9pm ~ Open 11-11; 12-5, 7-10.30 Sun; closed evening 25 Dec

KINGSTON NEAR LEWES TQ3908 Map 3

Juggs ◗

The Street; Kingston signed off A27 by roundabout W of Lewes, and off Lewes—Newhaven road; look out for the pub's sign – may be hidden by hawthorn in summer

An interesting mix of furnishings in the rambling beamed bar of this 15th-c tile-hung cottage ranges from an attractive little carved box settle, Jacobean-style dining chairs and brocaded seats and other settles to the more neatly orthodox tables and chairs of the small no-smoking dining area under the low-pitched eaves on the right. The cream or stripped brick walls are hung with flower pictures, battle prints, a patriotic assembly of postcards of the Lloyd George era, posters, and some harness and brass. Popular bar food includes home-made vegetable soup (£3.50), open sandwiches (from £3.50), ploughman's or sausages (£3.95), haddock and chips (£4.50), vegetable savoury (£5.75), pitta bread with chicken tikka (£5.95), home-made steak and kidney pudding (£8.75), steaks (from £10.50), daily specials, and home-made puddings (£2.95). On Sunday lunchtime food is limited to a cold buffet. One of the family rooms is no smoking. Service remains speedy and efficient (aided by a rather effective electronic bleeper system to let you know when meals are ready) even when the pub is very busy. Well kept Harveys Best, King & Barnes Festive, and a guest on handpump, and a wider choice than usual of non-alcoholic drinks. Log fires, dominoes, shove-ha'penny. There are a good many close-set rustic teak tables on the sunny brick terrace; a neatly hedged inner yard has more tables under cocktail parasols, and there are two or three out on grass by a timber climber and commando net. Covered with roses in summer, the pub was named for the fish-carriers who passed through on their way between Newhaven and Lewes. *(Recommended by Tony Hobden, Martin and Karen Wake, Bruce Bird, Tim Locke, Mavis and John Wright, K Flack, Steve Goodchild)*

Free house ~ Licensees Andrew and Peta Browne ~ Real ale ~ Meals (not Sun lunchtime) and snacks ~ Restaurant (not Sun lunchtime) ~ (01273) 472523 ~ Children in two family rooms ~ Open 11-11 summer weekdays; 11-3, 6-11 in winter weekdays and Sat; 12-10.30 summer Sun; closed evenings 25/26 Dec, 1 Jan

KIRDFORD TQ0126 Map 3

Half Moon

Opposite church; off A272 Petworth—Billingshurst

Since the licensees have had links with Billingsgate for 130 years, it's not surprising that the main reason to visit this interesting old pub is the good fresh fish. Carefully chosen by the licensees, there might be such rarities as tile fish, porgy, parrot fish, soft shell crabs, Morton Bay bugs, scabbard fish, razor shells, mahi mahi, and baramundi. But as fresh fish is seasonal, there may be times when the range isn't as big as you might hope. They also do less exotic fish like swordfish, bass, lobster, tiger prawns and snapper, and more ordinary dishes like sandwiches, ploughman's and steak and kidney pie: thai mussels (£3.95), mackerel with gooseberry sauce (£5.95), scabbard fish with chilli and garlic (£9.70), and red snapper fillet with ginger and spring onions (£10.20). Well kept Arundel Best, Boddingtons, Flowers Original, Fullers London Pride and Wadworths 6X on handpump. The simple partly quarry-tiled bars are kept ship-shape and very clean, and there's a beamed eating area with an open fire; darts, pool, fruit machine and jazz or classical radio. The restaurant is partly no smoking. There's a back garden with swings, barbecue area, tables, and big boules pitch, and more tables in front facing the pretty village's church. *(Recommended by Mike Fitzgerald, Andrew W Lee, John Beeken, Kim Maidment, Philip Vernon, Guy Consterdine, Dr S Savvas, M Martin, Mavis and John Wright, Vann and Terry Prime, R Walden, Mrs R D Knight)*

Waterside pubs are listed at the back of the book.

Whitbreads ~ Lease: Anne Moran ~ Real ale ~ Meals and snacks (not Sun evening or winter Mons) ~ Restaurant ~ (01403) 820223 ~ Children welcome ~ Open 11-3, 6.30(6 Sats)-11; winter evening opening 7; 12-3, 7-10.30 Sun; closed evening 25 Dec ~ Bedrooms: £20/£42(£50B)

LEWES TQ4110 Map 3
Snowdrop

South Street; off Cliffe High Street, opp S end of Malling Street just S of A26 roundabout

Reading the description of this positively laid-back pub might put some people off, but it's much enjoyed by quite a cross-section of our readers of all ages. The interior is unusual to say the least with a glorious profusion of cast-iron tables, bric-a-brac and outlandish paraphernalia that no doubt owes much to the next-door antique shop. Unfolding the rather dreamlike maritime theme, downstairs there are three ships' figureheads dotted around walls covered with rough sawn woodplank; and upstairs are a huge star chart painted on a dark blue ceiling, and a sunset sea mural with waves in relief. The pub is quiet at lunchtime but a young people's preserve, and lively to match, in the evenings, when the loudish juke box plays anything from Bob Dylan or Ella Fitzgerald to Indian chants. They serve no red meat, and the good value light hearted menu includes sandwiches, burritos or large home-made pizzas (from £2, margherita pizza £4.75), paella (£6.50), fresh fish, and lots of well priced vegan and vegetarian dishes like delicious hearty home-made tomato soup, hummus in pitta bread (£2.50), and cheesy tuna and pasta bake (£4.50); free range chicken is the Sunday roast, and they do children's helpings. Five (occasionally up to seven) well kept real ales such as Gales HSB, Harveys Best, Hop Back Summer Lightning, Ringwood Old Thumper and Shepherd Neame Spitfire on handpump, good coffee, friendly licensees and staff; pool and juke box. There are a few tables in the garden. *(Recommended by Comus Elliott, Jan Wilson, Tony Scott, M and M Carter, Pat and Tony Martin, Sue Demont, Tim Barrow, Ann and Colin Hunt)*

Free house ~ Licensees Tim and Sue May ~ Real ale ~ Meals and snacks 12-3(2.30 Sun), 6(7 Sun)-9 ~ (01273) 471018 ~ Children in eating area of bar only ~ Live jazz Mon evening and other live music some weekends ~ Open 11-11; 12-10.30 Sun

LODSWORTH SU9223 Map 2
Halfway Bridge ★ 🍽 ♀ 🍷

Just before village, on A272 Midhurst—Petworth

With a decidedly upmarket feel, the three or four comfortable rooms in this civilised family-run pub have good oak chairs and an individual mix of tables (many of them set for dining), and use attractive fabrics for the wood-railed curtains and pew cushions. Down some steps the charming no-smoking country dining room has a dresser and longcase clock. Log fires include one in a well polished kitchen range and paintings by a local artist line the walls. But it's the well presented often interesting food that draws most comments from readers: soup (£3.50), lunchtime sandwiches like BLT or smoked chicken and avocado served with salad and sautéed potatoes (£4.50 or £5.95), crabcakes with tomato salsa (£4.95), smoked haddock with bubble and squeak and a poached egg (£5.95), steak, kidney, mushroom and Guinness pudding (£7.50), baked aubergine with wild mushrooms (£7.95), roast half shoulder of lamb or grilled salmon with a coriander and dijon mustard sauce (£9.50), honey roast duck breast with a red wine and ginger sauce (£13.50), 8oz fillet steak (£14.20), and puddings such as rhubarb and ginger crumble or apple and almond tart (£3.50); popular Sunday roasts; polite service. A good range of well kept beers includes Cheriton Pots Ale, Fullers London Pride, Gales HSB, and guests from breweries such as Brewery on Sea, Hampshire Brewery, Harveys, Hogs Back or Pilgrim, farm ciders, and a thoughtful little wine list with a changing choice by the glass. Dominoes, shove-ha'penny, cribbage, backgammon, and other games like Scrabble, Jenga, bagatelle, and mah jong. At the back there are attractive blue wood tables and chairs on a terrace with a pergola. *(Recommended by Paula Williams, Julie Peters, Colin Blinkhorn, Martin and Jane Wright, G C Hackemer, Edward Froggatt, Mr and Mrs G Turner, Margaret and*

Nigel Dennis, Simon Small, Lady M H Moir, Steve Goodchild, J A Blanks, Tony and Wendy Hobden, Andrew Shore, Linda and Brian Davis, Dennis Stevens, John Evans, Ann and Colin Hunt, Peter Wade, John Fahy, R A Buckler)

Free house ~ Licensees Sheila, Edric, Simon and James Hawkins ~ Real ale ~ Meals and snacks (till 10pm) ~ Restaurant ~ (01798) 861281 ~ Children over 10 in restaurant ~ Jazz Sun evenings ~ Open 11-3, 6-11; 12-3, 7-10.30 Sun; closed winter Sun evenings, 25 Dec and evening 26 Dec

LOWER BEEDING TQ2225 Map 3
Crabtree 🍴 ♀

Brighton Rd; A281 S of village, towards Cowfold

The cosy beamed bars in this busy dining pub have an air of civilised simplicity, and there's plenty of character in the back no-smoking restaurant (the only place where they do food in the evening). It's the food which most people come to enjoy, which at its best is very good indeed and might include sandwiches (from £1.95) and ploughman's (from £4), both using walnut bread, vegetable soup with fresh herbs and a cheese crouton (£3.25), marinated herrings and anchovies with onions and chives in a sour cream and tomato dressing (£4.65), duck livers on a salad of salsify, green beans and oranges with balsamic vinegar (£5.10), spring vegetable risotto with chervil, saffron and fresh parmesan (£8), calf liver and bacon with celeriac and garlic mash and caramelised red onions or pork kebab with tabbouleh, fresh coriander and a spicy satay sauce (£9.50), and puddings like chocolate truffle cake or rhubarb compote with creamed rice (£3.50); they do a set two-course lunch for £10.50. Well kept King and Barnes Sussex, Festive and seasonal brews on handpump, and good wines, including a wine of the month. Cribbage, dominoes and piped music. A pleasant back garden has seats, and there may be summer barbecues. The pub is very handy for Leonardslee Gardens, which are closed in winter. *(Recommended by Derek Harvey-Piper, R J Walden, TOH, R Walden, Mr and Mrs G Turner, Mavis and John Wright, Graham Tayar, David Shillitoe, M Holdsworth, Michael and Alison Leyland, John Beeken, Dr S Savvas, M Martin; more reports please)*

King & Barnes ~ Tenants Jeremy Ashpool and Xanthe Woraker ~ Real ale ~ Lunchtime bar meals and snacks ~ Restaurant ~ (01403) 891257 ~ Well behaved children in eating area of bar and in restaurant ~ Live music monthly Sun evening ~ Open 11-3, 6-11; 12-3, 7-10.30 Sun; closed 25 Dec

LURGASHALL SU9327 Map 2
Noahs Ark

Village signposted from A283 N of Petworth; OS Sheet 186 map reference 936272

Smarter after a new roof, tarmacked car park and new lavatories, this 16th-c local is in a pretty setting overlooking the village green; tables on the grass in front are ideal for watching the cricket matches out there in summer. The two neatly furnished bars have fresh flowers or warm log fires (one in a capacious inglenook), depending on the season, as well as darts, pool, shove-ha'penny, table skittles, dominoes, and cribbage. Well kept Greene King Abbot, IPA and Rayments on handpump. Bar food includes sandwiches (from £3.30, toasties such as bacon and mushroom £3.95), ploughman's (from £4.50), tuna and pasta bake or tomato and vegetable tagliatelle (£5.75), steak and kidney pudding (£6.15), lamb cutlets (£7.50), calf liver and bacon (£7.95), smoked salmon salad (£8.75), and fillet steak (£12.50). The summer flowering baskets are splendid. *(Recommended by Mr and Mrs Carey, Mrs D W Cook, Derek Harvey-Piper, John Evans, James Nunns, R J Bland, John Fahy, R Lake)*

Greene King ~ Lease: Kathleen G Kennedy ~ Real ale ~ Meals and snacks (not Sun evening) ~ Restaurant ~ (01428) 707346 ~ Children welcome ~ Open theatre annually, dances in garden in summer, in function room in winter ~ Open 11.30-3, 6-11; 12-3, 7-10.30 Sun; winter weekday opening is half-an-hour later

MAYFIELD TQ5827 Map 3

Middle House 🏠

High St; village signposted off A267 S of Tunbridge Wells

Most unusually for a pub, this fine 16th-c black and white timbered inn is Grade I listed. It's doing very well at the moment and seems to be busy whatever day of the week it is. Comfortable and chatty, the largely original L-shaped beamed main bar is dominated by a massive fireplace surrounded by menu boards at one end, has straightforward pub furniture, fresh flowers, and well kept Greene King Abbot, Harveys Best, and a guest like Badger Tanglefoot, Fullers ESB, Hook Norton Old Hookey or Morlands Old Speckled Hen on handpump; local cider and decent wine list. There's a cosy group of comfortable russet chesterfields in the tranquil lounge area set around a log fire in an ornately carved fireplace (disputedly by Grinling Gibbons). Generous helpings of good bar food include large open sandwiches (£5.25), quite a few ploughman's (from £5.50), cheese fondue served with garlic bread (£5.95), roasted Italian vegetables served warm with balsamic vinegar and olive oil dressing (£6.95), salads with half a chargrilled chicken or cornets of ham filled with cream cheese and chives (from £6.95), chargrilled rib-eye steak (£9.95), and daily specials like aubergine stuffed with spinach, wild mushrooms and a provençale sauce (from £6.50), steak in ale pie (£6.95), a huge toad in the hole or pasta with smoked turkey and ham in a sage cream sauce (£7.50), daily fresh fish like red snapper with ginger wine and spring onions or chargrilled swordfish with lime and grain mustard (from £9.95), wild boar steak on a parsnip rosti with claret sauce (£10.50), and puddings such as poached pears with shortbread and caramel sauce, french lemon tart or crêpe suzette (£3.95). They do a three-course Sunday lunch for £14.95, and Wednesday jazz evening menu £13.95; enjoyable breakfasts; friendly service. One of the restaurants has some handsome panelling (and is no smoking), and another room was once a chapel; shove-ha'penny, cribbage, and piped music. Afternoon tea is served in the fairly formal terraced back garden which has picnic tables, white plastic sets with cocktail parasols, lovely views, and a slide and a log house for children; bedrooms are attractive and comfortable. *(Recommended by Serena Hebeler, Robert Gibb, Mr and Mrs G J Cotton, Margaret and Nigel Dennis, Wayne Brindle, David Gittins, K A C Jeffery, Mrs Sandison, Simon Gardner, Paul Casbourne, Miss A M Phillips)*

Free house ~ Licensee Monica Blundell ~ Real ale ~ Meals and snacks ~ Two restaurants (not Sun evening) ~ (01435) 872146 ~ Children welcome ~ Live jazz Weds ~ Open 11-11; 12-10.30 Sun ~ Bedrooms: £35(£45B)/£45(£55B)

Rose & Crown

Fletching Street; off A267 at NE end of village

Especially pretty in summer when the tubs and flowering baskets are at their best, this charming weatherboarded old inn has several bars that wander round the tiny central servery. The two cosy little front rooms are the most atmospheric: low beams, benches built in to the partly panelled walls, an attractive bow window seat, low ceiling boards with coins embedded in the glossy ochre paint, and log fire in the big inglenook fireplace. Under the new licensee, lunchtime bar food includes toasties (from £2.50), filled french bread (from £3.25), filled baked potatoes (from £3.60), ploughman's (from £4.25), stew and dumplings (£4.95), cottage pie (£5.20), minted lamb chops (£6.75), and home-baked honey ham with egg or venison sausages with mash and cumberland gravy (£6.95); also, home-made soup (£2.50), thai-style prawns (£3.95), aubergine and tomato au gratin (£6.25), home-made steak in ale pie (£6.75), filled giant yorkshire pudding or chicken and spinach curry (£7.95), steaks (from £9.95), and daily specials such as pasta carbonara (£2.50), chicken and lobster sausage (£3.85), lamb and apricot pie (£6.75), halibut with ginger, peppers and orange (£8.95), and breast of duck with a peppercorn sauce (£9.25). Well kept Greene King Abbot, Harveys Best, and Morlands Old Speckled Hen on handpump; shove-ha'penny and piped music. The bedrooms are very pretty and comfortable although there may be a little noise from the restaurant below. There are some rustic tables in front. *(Recommended by Wayne Brindle, Eddie Edwards, Brenda and Derek Savage, Mavis and John Wright, Claude and Bonnie Bemis, John Rhodes, Margaret and Nigel Dennis; more reports on the new regime, please)*

Free house ~ Licensee K D Scandrett-Whitlam ~ Real ale ~ Meals and snacks ~ Restaurant ~ (01435) 872200 ~ Children welcome ~ Open 11-3, 5-11; 11-11 Sat; 12-3.30, 7-10.30 Sun ~ Bedrooms: £38B/£48B

MIDHURST SU8821 Map 2
Spread Eagle 🛏
South St

Under the new licensee there are quite a few changes to this smart old place. A new conservatory has been added, a new terrace created, and a health spa added to the hotel side. Most of the building dates from the 17th c, but some of the original 1430 parts still remain. Best of all is is the spacious massively beamed and timbered lounge, with its dramatic fireplace, imposing leaded-light windows looking out on the most attractive part of this old town, and handsome yet quite unpretentious old armchairs and settees spread among the rugs on the broad-boarded creaking oak floor. There's apparently a secret room six feet up one chimney. The light lunchtime menu can be eaten anywhere and changes constantly – as we went to press they had chilled gazpacho with focaccia bread (£4.25), Hebridean scallop and bacon salad (£4.50 smaller size, £9.95 main course), citrus-marinated chicken breast (£4.65 smaller size, £8.45 main course), vegetarian pasta with plum tomatoes and olives (£4.80 smaller size, £7.75 main course), fresh cod with home-made chips (£8.25), and puddings such as summer pudding with clotted cream or elderflower sorbet (from £4.50). The highly regarded restaurant is no smoking. Well kept (but not cheap) Fullers London Pride on handpump, a good choice of malt whiskies, and an extensive wine list. The inn was described by Hilaire Belloc in *The Four Men* as 'the oldest and most revered of all the prime inns of this world'. *(Recommended by J S M Sheldon, Edward Froggatt, Graham and Karen Oddey; more reports please)*

Free house ~ Licensee Ian Fleming ~ Real ale ~ Lunchtime meals and snacks ~ Restaurant ~ (01730) 816911 ~ Well behaved children welcome ~ Open 11-2.30, 6-11; 12-3, 7-10.30 Sun; closed evenings 25 Dec and 1 Jan ~ Bedrooms: £80B/£100B

NUTHURST TQ1926 Map 3
Black Horse 🍺
Village signposted from A281 SE of Horsham

Both the front terrace and the back woodland streamside garden here are pretty and much liked by walkers from the lovely surrounding countryside. Inside, it's old-fashioned and friendly, and the main bar has big Horsham flagstones in front of the inglenook fireplace, interesting pictures on the walls, and magazines to read. At one end it opens out into other carpeted areas including a dining room. Well kept Greene King Abbot, Morlands Old Speckled Hen, Edridge Pope Hardy, and Wadworths 6X on handpump, and they hold beer festivals with a dozen or so real ales around bank holidays; country wines, Addlestones cider, and wines of the week. Bar food includes soups or potato wedges (from £2.75), ploughman's, filled baked potatoes, a pie, curry or casserole of the day (£3.95-£6.25), and puddings (£2.95); children's menu. The restaurant is no smoking; cribbage, Jenga, and piped music. *(Recommended by Louise Lyons, Peter Elliot, R J Walden, Dr Jim Mackay, Eamonn and Natasha Skyrme, Susan and John Douglas, Andrew and Jo Litten, LM, Bruce Bird, Michael Grigg)*

Free house ~ Licensees Karen Jones and Julian Clayton ~ Real ale ~ Meals and snacks (11.30-2.30, 6-9.30; not 25 Dec) ~ Restaurant (not Sun evening) ~ (01403) 891272 ~ Children welcome ~ Open 11-3, 6-11; 12-4, 7-10.30 Sun

---

If you enjoy your visit to a pub, please tell the publican. They work extraordinarily long hours, and when people show their appreciation it makes it all seem worth while.

OFFHAM TQ4012
Blacksmiths Arms
A275 N of Lewes; on left

The quiet hum of contented conversation fills the peacefully civilised open-plan rooms of this useful dining pub. The spotlessly kept bar, with dark wood tables and chairs on deep red carpet, runs around a gleaming central counter from a huge inglenook fireplace with logs stacked at one side, to the airy dining area. Nice old prints of London, some Spy prints and several old sporting prints decorate the walls above shiny black wainscoting. Most people are attracted by the generous helpings of very fairly priced and carefully prepared food which includes bar meals such as creamed curried tomato soup (£2.55), ploughman's (from £3.95), home-made seafood sausage with carrot leaf sauce, home-made game pâté with cumberland sauce, chicken liver with bacon skewer and ginger pickle or sausage, egg and chips (£4.25), smoked salmon with fresh lime and pink peppercorns (£4.50), chicken, prawn or vegetable curry (from £5.25), breaded plaice fillet (£5.95), scampi (£6.25), chicken and bacon pie (£6.50), steak and Guinness pie (£6.95), fried pork fillet with fennel and carraway sauce (£7.50), poached salmon steak in muscadet wine (£8.50), roast duck breast with Chinese spices (£8.50), puddings like home-made fruit pie and custard, fresh lime mousse and marinated kiwi and almond pear and chocolate tart with amaretto ice cream and dark chocolate sauce (all £3.50), as well as a couple of daily specials like Sussex smokie with cheese topping (£3.75), grilled pork chop with cajun sauce (£7.25), skate with breaded mustard crust (£7.75) and grilled lemon sole with prawn and crabmeat butter (£8.25); careful efficient service. Well kept real ales include Harveys Best and Old when it's available on handpump. French windows open onto a tiny little brick and paved terrace with a couple of flowering tubs and picnic tables with umbrellas and the car park; beware of the dangerous bend when leaving the car park; spotless disabled lavatories. *Recommended by Dave Wilcock, Brian Carter, P Keen; more reports please*

Free House ~ Licensee Jean Large ~ Real ale ~ Meals and snacks ~ (01273) 472971 ~ Children over five in restaurant ~ Open 11-3, 6.30-11; 12-3, 7-10.30 Sun; cl 25 Dec

OVING SU9005 Map 2
Gribble ◀

Between A27 and A259 just E of Chichester, then should be signposted just off village road; OS Sheet 197 map reference 900050

Under the new managers of this charming rose-covered thatched cottage, readers will be in safe hands – they have just come from Somerset where they successfully ran another of our main entries, the Royal Oak in Over Stratton. The friendly bar has lots of heavy beams and timbering, and old country-kitchen furnishings and pews. On the left, there's a family/dining room with pews which provides one of the biggest no-smoking areas we've so far found in a Sussex pub. But the pub has been best known for its own-brew beers – Gribble Ale, Reg's Tipple, Black Adder II, Pigs Ear and Ewe Brew; they also have Badger Best on handpump, 20 country wines, and farm cider. Home-made bar food now includes garlic mushrooms (£2.95), granary bread sandwiches (from £2.95), squid with garlic mayonnaise (£3.25), ploughman's (£4.50), home-made burgers, ratatouille (£4.95), beef in ale pie (£5.45), seafood tagliatelle (£5.95), shark steak with lemon and black peppercorn butter (£6.95), chicken filled with Austrian smoked cheese and asparagus (£7.95), wild boar steak with redcurrant sauce (£10.25), six daily specials, and puddings. Shove-ha'penny, dominoes, cribbage, a fruit machine and a separate skittle alley. There are seats in the pretty garden and a covered seating area. *(Recommended by A E Green, J Brisset, Ann and Colin Hunt, Lawrence Pearse, Mrs D Bromley-Martin, Bruce Jamieson, David Holloway, Sally Cooke, Brian Dodsworth, John Beeken; more reports on the new regime, please)*

Own brew (Badger) ~ Managers Brian and Lyn Elderfield ~ Real ale ~ Meals and snacks ~ (01243) 786893 ~ Children in big family room and eating area of the bar ~ Open 11-3, 5-11; 11-11 Sat during July/Aug; 12-10.30 Sun during July/Aug

PETWORTH SU9719 Map 2
Badgers ♀

Coultershaw Bridge; just off A285 1½ miles S

We hesitated about including this stylish dining pub, because most evenings it's already fully booked even without the extra attention a main entry in this *Guide* tends to bring. Moreover, the owners have a policy of complete non-co-operation with guidebooks such as ours (even threatening to sue us if we included them!) which means that we have not been able to check factual details with them. But the sheer quality demands attention. There is a small chatty drinking area by the entrance, with a couple of tables (and an attractive antique oak monk's chair) and some bar stools. All the rest of the space around the island bar servery is devoted to dining tables – well spaced, and an attractive mix of chairs and of tables, from old mahogany to waxed stripped pine. White walls, the deep maroon colour of the high ceiling, charming wrought-iron lamps, winter log fires, stripped shutters for the big Victorian windows, and a modicum of carefully chosen decorations including a few houseplants and dried flower arrangements induce a feeling of contented relaxation in the several linked areas; this is underlined by informal yet punctilious service. Besides the good if not cheap restaurant menu, two tested examples give an idea of the imaginative changing choice of attractively presented bar dishes: pasta with prawns, scallops, sun-dried tomatoes and basil (£8.95), and thai-style seafood (£9.95). (And please do record for us the price and details of any other dishes you particulary enjoy here, so that we can expand our examples in future editions.) Well kept Badger Best, Hop Back Summer Lightning and Theakstons Best on handpump, with a good range of well chosen house wines and a fine list by the bottle; maybe faint piped music (the dominant sound is quiet conversation). A terrace by a waterlily pool has stylish metal garden furniture under parasols, and some solid old-fashioned wooden seats. No motorcyclists. *(Recommended by Mrs D M Gray, Martin and Karen Wake, Peter Siddon)*

Free house ~ Real ale ~ Meals and snacks ~ Restaurant ~ (01798) 342651 ~ Children over 5 may be allowed away from bar

PLAYDEN TQ9121 Map 3
Peace & Plenty

A268/B2082

The cosy bar in this cottagey dining pub has a woodburning stove in a big inglenook at one end with comfortable armchairs either side, a good mix of tables, deep pink walls and shelves nicely crowded with lots of little pictures, china and lamps, a big bay window with a long comfortable cushioned seat, and a relaxed atmosphere; gentle classical piped radio. There are two similarly cosy cottagey dining areas. Enjoyable bar food might include soup, bangers and mash (£6.50), lamb or chicken pies (£6.95), steak and kidney pudding (£7.95), lamb liver and bacon (£8.25), fresh salmon fishcakes or fillet of chicken wrapped in bacon with a cheese centre (£8.95), puddings, and children's dishes; attentive service. Well kept Greene King IPA, Abbot and Rayments on handpump from a small counter. The bar staff say they are happy to keep an eye on children in their own friendly little room which has a comfy sofa for watching TV and lots of toys scattered on the floor; cards, trivial pursuit, and mind trap on each table. There are seats in the pretty flowery garden though there is traffic noise. *(Recommended by Lin and Roger Lawrence, Tony McLaughlin, Joy and Graham Eaton, Simon Evans; more reports please)*

Free house ~ Licensee Yvonne Thomas ~ Real ale ~ Meals and snacks (11-9.30) ~ Restaurant ~ (01797) 280342 ~ Children welcome ~ Open 11-11; 12-10.30; cl 25/26 Dec

---

People named as recommenders after the main entries have told us that the pub should be included. But they have not written the report – we have, after anonymous on-the-spot inspection.

nr PUNNETTS TOWN TQ6220 Map 3
Three Cups
B2096 towards Battle

New licensees have taken over this unspoilt traditional local. The peaceful and friendly long low-beamed bar has attractive panelling, comfortable seats including some in big bay windows overlooking a small green, and a log fire in the big fireplace under a black mantelbeam dated 1696. A partly no-smoking back dining room leads out to a small covered terrace with seats in the garden beyond. Bar food is totally home-made and includes sandwiches (from £2), soup (£2.50), ploughman's (from £3.75), ham and egg or sausages (£3.80), cauliflower cheese (£4.50), meaty or vegetarian lasagne (£4.75), fresh cod and chips (£5), steak in ale pie (£5.25), chicken in a mushroom and sherry sauce (£6), local cod (£7), sirloin steak (£8.50), and puddings such as fruit crumble or banoffi pie (£2.50). Well kept Beards Best and Harveys Best and two guests like Fullers London Pride and Hook Norton Old Hookey on handpump, and Scrumpy Jack cider. Darts, shove-ha'penny, cribbage and quiet piped music. The two dogs are called Lettie and Monty, and the fluffy ginger cat, Hattie. Good walks lead off from here, on either side of this high ridge of the Weald. *(Recommended by Dave Braisted, K M Thorpe, Mr and Mrs R D Knight; more reports on the new regime, please)*

Beards ~ Tenants Barbara and Colin Wood ~ Real ale ~ Meals and snacks ~ (01435) 830252 ~ Children in dining room ~ Occasional solo singer or duo weekends ~ Open 11-2.30(3 Sat), 6.30-11; 12-3, 7-10.30 Sun; closed evening 25 Dec

RYE TQ9220 Map 3
Mermaid 🛏

Mermaid St

It's worth coming to this ancient place to enjoy the building itself. The black and white timbered facade is beautiful with its distinctive inn sign hanging over the steeply cobbled street, and has barely altered since the hotel was built in the 15th and 16th centuries. Fine panelling, antique woodwork and rare frescoes fill the civilised rooms, and there are some unusual intricately carved antique seats, one in the form of a goat, as well as an enormous fireplace. The cellars that hold the well kept Marstons Pedigree and Morlands Old Speckled Hen date back seven centuries; good wine list. Bar food includes soup (£3), filled french bread (from £3.50), moules marinières or cheese ploughman's (£5), mild turkey curry (£5.50), cod and prawn gratin (£6.50), Scotish entrecote steak (£10.50), and puddings like apple pie (£2.50). Piped music, chess and cards. There are seats on a small back terrace. *(Recommended by Mr and Mrs D Ross, Paula Williams, T Pascall, Dorothee and Dennis Glover, David and Margaret Bloomfield, Betsy Brown, Nigel Flook, Kevin Thorpe, Paul Hilditch, Jacquie and Jim Jones, Hanns P Golez, R T and J C Moggridge, Chris and Martin Taylor)*

Free house ~ Licensees Robert Pinwill and Mrs J Blincow ~ Real ale ~ Meals and snacks (11-6 in summer) ~ Restaurant ~ (01797) 223065 ~ Well behaved children welcome ~ Open 11-11; 12-10.30 Sun ~ Bedrooms: £45(£62B)/£90(£128B)

Ypres Castle 🍴 ♀
Gun Garden, off A259

Quite a contrast with our other main entry here, this is a proper straightforward pub, in a fine setting up near the 13th-c Ypres Tower, with a steep flight of stone steps between the two. Ypres, pub and tower, is pronounced WWI-style, as Wipers. The style of the pub is fairly spartan, with basic furnishings, local events posters and so forth. What transforms it is the friendly atmosphere, which seems particularly warm and embracing on a blustery winter's night; and the three friendly labradors do their bit to help. In summer, there's the big bonus of a sizeable lawn; picnic tables out here have a fine view out over the River Rother winding its way through the shore marshes. What's on the menu depends on what the landlord's found in the markets – not just the fresh local fish and seafood, but the products of his weekly trips to London. Besides good value filled baguettes, it might include soup (£2.25), ploughman's (from

£4.20), roast fillet of cod (£7.70), moules marinières (£7.95), excellent scallops in garlic butter (£8.95), and daily specials such as tagliatelle in spicy tomato, pepper and mushroom sauce (£5.50), spinach and ricotta cheese crêpes (£6.60), roast duck in morello cherry and brandy sauce (£8.40), rack of local lamb with mint and redcurrant glaze (£9.60), and prime Scotch steak (£11.60); good fresh vegetables. Well kept changing ales such as Hook Norton, Youngs Special, and a guest such as Fullers London Pride or Harveys Best and Mild on handpump, good value wine (especially by the bottle) with 20 by the glass; maybe old yachting magazines to leaf through. Darts, shove-ha'penny, cribbage, and piped music. *(Recommended by Betsy Brown, Nigel Flook, R T and J C Moggridge, T Pascall, E P Gray)*

Free house ~ Licensee R J Pearce ~ Real ale ~ Meals and snacks ~ (01797) 223248 ~ Blues Sun evening ~ Children in family room ~ Open 12-11; 12-10.30 Sun; closed evening 25 Dec

SALEHURST TQ7424 Map 3
Salehurst Halt ♀

Village signposted from Robertsbridge bypass on A21 Tunbridge Wells—Battle Rd

This is a warmly friendly and quietly set little village local in a converted station building by the dismantled railway line and close to the attractive 14th-c church. The L-shaped bar has good plain wooden tables and chairs on flagstones at one end, an attractively cushioned window seat, beams, a little open brick fireplace, a time punch clock and olde worlde pictures; lots of hops on a big beam divide this from the beamed carpeted area with its mix of tables, wheelback and farmhouse chairs, and a half wall leads to a dining area with a grandfather clock. Nice home-made food includes at lunchtime, filled baked potatoes (£3.90), burgers made with minced top rump with a choice of cheese, bacon or barbecue sauces (very popular, £5.50), home-baked ham with egg (£5.90), lasagne or chilli (£5.90), and steaks (£6.95), with evening dishes such as pâté or snails, spicy vegetable parcel or beef in ale pie (£7.50), beef stroganoff or seafood pie (£8.45), supper specials like beef curry, vegetable pie or a fish dish (£6.90), and puddings such as fruit crumbles, fudgecake or bread and butter pudding (£2.75). There are fresh flowers on the bar, well kept Harveys Best on handpump, good wines, and a relaxed and chatty atmosphere; piped music. The little garden with its terraces and picnic tables is pleasant, and the window boxes and tubs are very pretty. *(Recommended by Paula Williams, Hugh MacLean, TBB)*

Free house ~ Licensee Jane Steed ~ Real ale ~ Meals and snacks (not Mon or Tues) ~ (01580) 880620 ~ Well behaved children may be allowed ~ Open 12-3, 7-11(10.30 Sun); closed Mon/Tues

nr SCAYNES HILL TQ3623 Map 3
Sloop

Freshfield Lock; at top of Scaynes Hill by petrol station turn N off A272 into Church Rd, keep on for 1½ miles and then follow Freshfield signpost

In a lovely spot beside what used to be the Ouse canal, this tucked-away country pub has a sheltered garden with lots of tables to enjoy the sunshine and birdsong. The Bluebell Line steam railway is nearby, and the pub is quite handy for Sheffield Park. Inside, the long saloon bar is going back to its roots with a mix of pine furniture and some comfortable old seats, and there are benches in the old-fashioned brick porch. Good home-made bar food includes filled french sticks (from £2.95), ploughman's (from £3.95), steak and kidney pie (£6.95), salmon fillet (£9.95), and daily specials such as venison terrine (£4.25), asparagus and parma ham with balsamic vinegar and thyme (£4.95), venison casserole (£7.95), lemon sole meunière (£9.95), marinated medallions of pork fillet in a spicy thai sauce (£11.95), and lobster thermidor (£14.95). Well kept Harveys Best and a guest beer such as Hook Norton Old Hookey on handpump, and a decent wine list; piped music. The basic but airy public bar has also been cleaned up, and has a stripped woodwork and bare boards – a small games room leading off with sensibly placed darts and bar billiards. *(Recommended by Simon and Sally Small, Mr and Mrs R D Knight)*

Beards ~ Tenant Ian Philpots ~ Real ale ~ Meals and snacks (not Sun evening) ~
(01444) 831219 ~ Children welcome ~ Open 11-3, 6-11; 12-3, 7-10.30 Sun; closed
evening 25 Dec

nr SEAFORD TV4899 Map 3

Golden Galleon 🍴 ♀ ◀

Exceat Bridge; A259 Seaford—Eastbourne, near Cuckmere

After a walk along the river to the sea or inland to Friston Forest and the downs, this
very popular pub is a fine place for a drink or lunch; in good weather you can sit at
tables in the sloping garden with views towards the Cuckmere estuary and Seven
Sisters Country Park. There's a summer marquee, a conservatory and river room, and
the high trussed and pitched rafters in the main bar area create quite an airy feel;
there's a relaxed, bustling atmosphere, and service is friendly and efficient even at
really busy times; two thirds of the premises are no smoking. A fine choice of real ales
includes up to six from their own little microbrewery. Brewed by the landlord's brother,
these might include Cuckmere Haven Best, Guv'nor, Golden Peace, Gentleman's Gold
and an old-fashioned cask conditioned stout, Saxon King; they also keep other ales like
Harveys Armada, and Greene King Abbot and IPA, on handpump or tapped from the
cask; farm cider, good wines by the glass, a decent selection of malts, continental
brandies, Italian liqueurs, and cappuccino or espresso coffee. But it's really the excellent
food that draws most people here: a good choice of starters and small snacks such as
home-made soups (£2.45), bruschetta romana (a chunk of garlic bread topped with
warm plum tomatoes, garlic, onion, finely chopped celery, and fennel £2.75), tuna fish
and butter beans with capers, onion, garlic and parsley with olive oil (£3.25), Italian
rarebit (toasted bread with melting cheddar, mozzarella and parma ham £3.75), insalata
di frutti di mare (Italian seafood salad £3.95) or whole king prawns in garlic butter with
aioli dip (£5.25), plus ploughman's (from £3.95), lunchtime baked potatoes (from
£4.50), very good fresh local fish of the day (£5.95), chicken in tomato, fresh ginger and
garlic sauce (£7.25), loin of pork with a choice of five sauces (£8.75), Scottish steaks
(from £8.95), quite a few Thai and Indian curries and pasta dishes, and they now have
their own smokery; children's menu. *(Recommended by Tony Scott, P Rome, LM, Frank
Gadbois, E G Parish, Sue Demont, Tim Barrow)*

*Own brew ~ Licensee Stefano Diella ~ Real ale ~ Meals and snacks
(ploughman's/salads all day; no food winter Sun evenings) ~ (01323) 892247 ~
Children welcome ~ Open 11-11(10.30 winter weekdays); 12-10.30 Sun; closed
winter Sun evening*

nr TICEHURST TQ6830 Map 3

Bull ◀

Three Legged Cross; coming into Ticehurst from N on B2099, just before Ticehurst village
sign, turn left beside corner house called Tollgate (Maynards Pick Your Own may be
signposted here)

This is a popular place at any time of the year. In summer the charming garden is a
lovely place to sit at tables beside an ornamental fish pond looking back at the rose
and clematis-covered building; outside bar and barbecue, and at weekends they
usually have a bouncy castle for children. In winter, the original part of this peaceful
old pub (a 14th-c Wealden hall) with its huge log fire, is where most people head for.
A series of small flagstoned, brick-floored or oak parquet rooms run together, with
heavy oak tables and seats of some character; it's well liked by locals in the evening,
when the friendly very low beamed rooms soon fill up. Well kept Harveys Best and
Knots of May, Morlands Old Speckled Hen, locally brewed Rother Valley Level Best
and a changing guest on handpump; friendly service. Bar food might include soup,
filled french bread (from £2.45), fresh plaice (£4.75), broccoli en croûte (£5.25), lamb
liver and bacon (£5.50), steak and mushroom pie (£6.50), half shoulder of lamb
(£7.25), and sirloin steak (£7.50); the evening menu is fuller; Sunday buffet (£5.25).
There's an unusual round pool table, as well as darts, bar billiards, table skittles,
dominoes, cribbage and piped music, and a couple of boules pitches. Tucked away in

little country lanes, the pub is handy for visiting the lovely gardens of Pashley Manor. *(Recommended by B and M Parkin, James and Lynne House, Paula Williams, C and M Starling, Mavis and John Wright, Sue Lee)*

Free house ~ Licensee Mrs E M Wilson-Moir ~ Real ale ~ Meals and snacks (not Sun or Mon evenings) ~ Restaurant ~ (01580) 200586 ~ Children welcome ~ Live entertainment Sun evenings ~ Open 11-3, 6-11; 12-3, 7-10.30 Sun

TILLINGTON SU9621 Map 2
Horse Guards Ⓨ 🛏 ♀
Village signposted from A272 Midhurst—Petworth

The renowned warm welcome and the much enjoyed food are what draw so many people to this neatly kept 300-year-old inn. It's in a pretty setting perched high over the lane and there's a lovely view beyond the village to the Rother Valley from the seat in the big black-panelled bow window of the cosy beamed front bar – which also has some good country furniture and a log fire. A wide choice of food includes sandwiches (from £2.50), ploughman's (£4.75), good caesar salad (from £4.50), chicken curry or mushroom stroganoff (£5.95), and seafood pie (£6.95) from the light bar menu, as well as lunchtime dishes like avocado, quail egg and rocket salad with a rocquefort dressing (£4.50), cod and spinach florentine with thermidor sauce (£5.50), flavoured sausages with a white onion sauce and duchesse potatoes (£5.95), steak and kidney pie or mixed seafood tagliatelle in a provençale sauce (£6.95), sirloin steak (£11.75), daily specials such as asparagus, smoked haddock and salmon soup (£3.25), courgette and cheddar mousse (£4.75), roast rib of beef with yorkshire pudding (£7.45), casserole of lamb with honey and garlic (£7.50), and skate wing with nut brown butter and capers (£9.95), with evening extras such as grilled sardines with lemon butter (£3.95), a trio of peppers stuffed with curried rice and cashew nuts in a creamy curry sauce (£5.95), seafood kebabs on a bed of soy spiced leaf salad (£10.50), and half a roast duck with apple and blackberries (£11.95); lovely home-made puddings (£3.50). Most ingredients come from local producers, and fresh fish is delivered five times a week. The good wine list usually has a dozen by the glass; well kept Badger Best and King & Barnes Best on handpump, good coffee. Darts, cribbage, and piped music. There's a terrace outside, and more tables and chairs in a sheltered garden behind. The church opposite is 800 years old. *(Recommended by Sue Stevens, Clive Gilbert, Margaret and Nigel Dennis, Betsy Brown, Nigel Flook, K M Thorpe, Patrick Hall, Susan and John Douglas, Peter Lewis, Diane Edmond, Ann and Colin Hunt, J O Jonkler)*

Free house ~ Licensees Aidan and Lesley Nugent ~ Real ale ~ Meals and snacks (till 10pm) ~ Restaurant ~ (01798) 342332 ~ Children in eating area of bar; must be over 8 in evening ~ Open 11-3, 6-11; 12-3, 7-10.30 Sun ~ Bedrooms: /£60B

WEST ASHLING SU8107 Map 2
Richmond Arms 🍺
Mill Lane; from B2146 in village follow Hambrook signpost

The good range of real ales in this out-of-the-way and friendly village pub is eye-catching: Boddingtons, Brakspears, Greene King Abbot, King & Barnes Sussex, Marstons Pedigree, Morlands Old Speckled Hen, Timothy Taylors Landlord, and Wadworths 6X on handpump; also farm ciders, country wines, Belgian fruit beers and continental bottled beers. The main bar is dominated by the central servery, and has a 1930s feel with its long wall benches, library chairs, black tables and open fire (maybe with a couple of black cats in front of it); it can get smoky. Bar food includes sandwiches, ploughman's, home-made steak and mushroom pie (£6.10), Texas brunch – a 6oz rump steak on garlic bread, with two fried eggs on top (£7.60), and several fish and vegetarian dishes; roast Sunday lunch. Service is obliging even when the pub is busy, as it often is, especially at weekends. Darts, shove-ha'penny, dominoes, and cribbage; the skittle alley doubles as a function and family room, and is used at weekends for eating. There's a pergola, and some picnic tables by the car park. *(Recommended by Bruce Bird, Ann and Colin Hunt, Phyl and Jack Street, D and J Tapper, Jo and Gary Charlton, Edward Froggatt)*

Free house ~ Licensee Bob Garbutt ~ Real ale ~ Meals and snacks (till 10pm) ~ Restaurant ~ (01243) 575730 ~ Children welcome ~ Open 11-2.30(3 Sat), 5.30-11; 12-10.30 Sun; closed Sun evening and all day Mon in winter

WINEHAM TQ2320 Map 3
Royal Oak

Village signposted from A272 and B2116

The layout and style of this unchanging and old-fashioned place are commendably traditional, and it has been run by the same family now for over 50 years. There are logs burning in an enormous inglenook fireplace, ancient corkscrews decorating the very low beams above the serving counter, racing plates, tools and a coach horn on the walls, and simple furnishings. Well kept beers tapped from the cask in a still room on the way to a little snug include Flowers Original, Harveys Best, and Marstons Pedigree; darts, shove-ha'penny, dominoes, cribbage. The limited range of bar snacks includes fresh-cut or toasted sandwiches (from £1.50, roast beef £2 or lovely smoked salmon £2.80), home-made soup in winter (£1.75) and ploughman's (£3.25). It gets very busy at weekends and on summer evenings; courteous service. The charming frontage has a lawn with wooden tables by a well. On a clear day sharp-eyed male readers may be able to catch a glimpse of Chanctonbury Ring from the window in the gents'. *(Recommended by R and S Bentley, Greta and Christopher Wells; more reports please)*

Inn Business ~ Tenant Tim Peacock ~ Real ale ~ Snacks (available during opening hours) ~ (01444) 881252 ~ Children in family room ~ Open 11-2.30, 5.30(6 Sat)-11; 12-3, 7-10.30 Sun; closed evenings 25 Dec and 1 Jan

WITHYHAM TQ4935 Map 3
Dorset Arms

B2110

It's rather unusual that you have to go up a short flight of outside steps to enter this 16th-c inn. Once inside, the L-shaped bar has sturdy tables and simple country seats on the wide oak floorboards, a good log fire in the stone Tudor fireplace, and a traditional welcoming atmosphere. Good, enjoyable bar food includes sandwiches (from £1.95), soup (£2.25), ploughman's (from £3.75), filled baked potatoes (£3.75), ham, egg and chips (£4.95), fresh baked trout (£6.50), and daily specials such as cheese topped ratatouille bake with garlic bread (£4.75), smoked ham and pasta bake with herbs or smoked salmon flan (£4.95), stir-fried king prawns in a thai sauce (£5.50), baked half shoulder of lamb with red wine gravy (£6.50), and puddings like white chocolate cheesecake with Baileys, deep lemon tart or sticky toffee pudding (£2.85); seats go quickly, so it's best to book, especially in the pretty restaurant. Well kept Harveys Best, Pale Ale, Mild and seasonal beers on handpump, and a reasonable wine list including some local ones. Darts, dominoes, shove ha'penny, cribbage, fruit machine, cards and piped music. There are white tables on a brick terrace raised well above the small green. The countryside around here is nice, and the nearby church has a memorial to Vita Sackville-West. *Recommended by A Cowell, Ron Gentry, R D Knight, Tony Scott, Colin and Joyce Laffan, Tom Wild)*

Harveys ~ Tenants John and Sue Pryor ~ Real ale ~ Meals and snacks (not Mon evening) ~ Restaurant (not Sun evening) ~ (01892) 770278 ~ Children in restaurant ~ Open 11.30(11 Sat)-3, 5.30(6 Sat)-11; 12-3, 7-10.30 Sun

---

Bedroom prices normally include full English breakfast, VAT and any inclusive service charge that we know of. Prices before the '/' are for single rooms, after for two people in double or twin (B includes a private bath, S a private shower). If there is no '/', the prices are only for twin or double rooms (as far as we know there are no singles).

Lucky Dip

Besides the fully inspected pubs, you might like to try these Lucky Dips recommended to us and described by readers (if you do, please send us reports):

Alfold Bars W Sus [B2133 N of Loxwood; TQ0333], *Sir Roger Tichbourne*: Old-fashioned welcoming beamed country pub with good relaxed atmosphere, friendly licensees, well kept King & Barnes, reasonably priced bar food, garden with views and play area *(Phil and Sally Gorton)*

Alfriston E Sus [High St; TQ5103], *George*: 14th-c timbered inn, roomy heavy-beamed bar with huge fireplace, intimate candlelit dining area, home-made bar food inc good fish, fresh veg; efficient service, well kept Harveys; comfortable attractive bedrooms *(Mr and Mrs A Albert)*

☆ **Amberley** [Houghton Bridge, B2139; TQ0211], *Bridge*: Attractive, busy open-plan dining pub with pretty riverside terrace garden, wide range of good value generous food, well kept Flowers Original, decent wines, country wines, friendly staff, interesting pictures, unobtrusive piped music; provision for children; bedrooms *(Maureen and Jeff Dobbelaar, Mrs P Elkin)*

☆ **Amberley** [Rackham Rd, just off B1239], *Sportsman*: 17th c, three small unpretentious rooms, conservatory and garden, lovely views from balcony, good value genuine home cooking inc sandwiches, fresh salads, vegetarian and Sun roasts, decent wines and country wines, well kept Harveys, friendly welcome – even for dogs *(S Needham, Tony and Wendy Hobden)*

Angmering W Sus [off main st opp Lamb, then 3rd left into cul de sac; TQ0704], *Spotted Cow*: Well kept Harveys, King & Barnes and several other ales, efficient good value lunch system from sandwiches up (very popular weekdays with older people), friendly service, smuggling history; restaurant, roomy garden, good play area; lovely walk to Highdown hill fort *(Bruce Bird, Tony and Wendy Hobden, R T and J C Moggridge, Mrs P J Pearce)*

☆ **Ardingly** W Sus [B2028 2 miles N; TQ3429], *Gardeners Arms*: Immaculately refurbished olde-worlde dining pub very popular for consistently good if not cheap fresh home-made food, big inglenook log fire, service pleasant and cheerful even when crowded, well kept Boddingtons, Harveys and Theakstons, good house wines, morning coffee and tea, maybe soft piped music, no children; well spaced tables out among small trees, handy for Borde Hill and Wakehurst Place *(Elizabeth and Klaus Leist, Fred Chamberlain, Gordon Smith, John Pettit, Lady M H Moir, Tony and Wendy Hobden, Tony Scott, Eamonn and Natasha Skyrme)*

Ardingly [Street Lane], *Ardingly*: Spacious and comfortable, with wide choice of good quick generous food, good veg and roasts, good new landlord, decent wines, attractive restaurant; bedrooms reasonably priced *(Margaret and Nigel Dennis, Mr and Mrs P A King, D and J Tapper)*; [Street Lane], *Oak*: Beamed 14th-c dining pub, quick helpful service, Scottish Courage and guest ales, lots of brass and lace curtains, magnificent old fireplace; bright comfortable restaurant, pleasant tables outside *(Ron Gentry, M A Mees)*

☆ **Arlington** E Sus [off A22 nr Hailsham, or A27 W of Polegate; TQ5407], *Yew Tree*: Neatly modernised two-bar village local, reliable generous home cooking inc children's, well kept Courage Directors, Harveys Best and Morlands Old Speckled Hen, log fires, efficient cheery service, subdued piped music, darts; dining area with french windows to good big garden and play area, by paddock with farm animals *(John Beeken, Keith Ward, Dr S Savvas, M Martin, Mrs Allerston)*

☆ **Arlington** [Caneheath, E of village], *Old Oak*: 17th-c, with big cosy L-shaped beamed bar, dining room, popular reasonably priced food (not Mon), well kept Badger, Harveys and usually a guest beer tapped from the cask, pleasant staff, log fires, peaceful garden; children allowed, handy for Bluebell Walk *(Dr S Savvas, M Martin)*

☆ **Arundel** W Sus [High St; TQ0107], *Swan*: Spotlessly refurbished, with unusual beaten brass former inn-sign now in open-plan L-shaped bar, good choice of food inc vegetarian, full range of good Arundel beers with a guest such as Fullers London Pride, all well kept, friendly young staff; restaurant, good bedrooms *(Clive Gilbert, Tony and Wendy Hobden, John and Chris Simpson, Chris and Anne Fluck, LYM)*

Arundel [Mill Rd; keep on and don't give up!], *Black Rabbit*: Big touristy pub, plenty of provision for families, best on a quiet day – lovely spot, with lots of riverside tables looking across to bird-reserve watermeadows and Castle; Badger Best and Tanglefoot and guest ales, restaurant, open all day in summer, doubling as tea shop then; summer boat trips here *(A Pring, David Holloway, Lady M H Moir, R Silberrad, Miss A G Drake, Pamela Goodwyn, D Maplethorpe, B Helliwell, Tony and Wendy Hobden, Tony Scott, LYM)*; [London Rd, by cathedral], *St Marys Gate*: Quiet comfortable open-plan bar with friendly staff and locals, alcoves, lots of horse-racing caricatures, generous good value home-made food, well kept Badger Best and Tanglefoot and guest beer, restaurant, no-smoking area; unobtrusive piped music; bedrooms quiet and good value *(Bruce Bird, Norman and Sarah Keeping)*

Balcombe W Sus [London Rd (B2036/B2110); TQ3130], *Cowdray Arms*: Roomy country pub, popular for good choice of well prepared lunchtime meals, attentive welcoming service, Harveys ales, occasional beer festivals; garden with play area *(DWAJ, A Kilpatrick, Tony Scott)*

Balls Cross W Sus [signed off A283 N of Petworth; SU9826], *Stag*: Small flagstoned 15th-c pub with inglenook, good value food (not Sun eve) inc reasonably priced Sun lunch, well kept King & Barnes, lots of prints of horses and dogs in pleasant restaurant, efficient staff, no piped music; seats in garden *(Bruce Bird)*

Barcombe E Sus [Barcombe Mills; off A26 N of Lewes – OS Sheet 198 map ref 429149; TQ4214], *Anglers Rest*: Homely welcoming Victorian brick pub in quiet spot nr River Ouse, changing ales such as Ash Vine Challenger, Brewery on Sea Raindance, Burtonwood Tom Thumper, Gales HSB and Harveys; extensive imaginative menu (no sandwiches) inc good puddings, big collection of miniatures and prints of surrounding area; large sheltered garden with verandah, play house; good walks *(John Beeken)*

☆ **Barnham** W Sus [Yapton Rd; SU9604], *Murrell Arms*: Genuine old pub with lots of pictures, old maps and local bric-a-brac, three friendly bars, particularly well kept Gales tapped from the cask, good simple cheap food esp cheese or bacon doorsteps; games inc ring-the-bull, occasional live music *(Mark Gregory, R T and J C Moggridge)*

Battle E Sus [Mount St; TQ7416], *Olde Kings Head*: Friendly well kept Tudor pub with decor in keeping, good log fire in one darkly atmospheric narrow room, other side lighter, games room, chatty staff, well cooked simple food, well kept Harveys and guest ale; children welcome; low-priced bedrooms *(George Atkinson, R C Tanton)*

Bexhill E Sus [Little Common Rd, Little Common; A259 towards Polegate; TQ7107], *Denbigh*: Attractive and friendly small bar and dining area, good choice of real ales, good generous well priced food, pretty floral decorations *(Christopher Turner, A R Milton)*; [Turkey Rd], *Rose & Crown*: Unpretentious suburban local with good range of decent food inc Sun lunch, old-fashioned rather domestic atmosphere, well kept Harveys Best *(Stephen Harvey, Alec and Marie Lewery)*

Billingshurst W Sus [High St; A29; TQ0925], *Olde Six Bells*: Picturesque partly 14th-c flagstoned and timbered pub with well kept King & Barnes, cheery service, inglenook fireplace, pretty roadside garden *(TOH, LYM)*

☆ **Binsted** W Sus [Binsted Lane, off A27 about 2 miles W of Arundel; SU9806], *Black Horse*: 17th-c, with ochre walls and open fire in big bar, seven or eight well kept ales, darts and pool one end, welcoming young licensee, wide range of restaurant food, shorter bar choice inc well presented freshly cooked specials; idyllic garden with country views; bedrooms *(Colin Draper, JDM, KM)*

Bodle Street Green E Sus [off A271 at Windmill Hill; TQ6514], *White Horse*: Simply modernised country pub popular with older people midweek for good value generous lunches, friendly service, well kept

Harveys and Shepherd Neame Spitfire, decent wines and malt whiskies, open fires, bar billiards, darts, cheery piped music; some tables outside *(Mr and Mrs Beams and friends, Janet and Colin Roe, BB)*

Bolney W Sus [The Street; TQ2623], *Eight Bells*: Friendly, clean and comfortable, with Harveys and Flowers Original, attentive staff, promptly served food, local paintings, open fires *(Colin and Joyce Laffan, Tony and Wendy Hobden)*

Bosham W Sus [High St; SU8003], *Anchor Bleu*: Lovely sea and boat views from low-beamed waterside pub, in attractive village; Scottish Courage beers, log-effect gas fire, seats outside; very popular with tourists *(MCG, John Sanders, LYM)*

Bramber W Sus [TQ1710], *Bramber Castle*: Good spot, pleasant and roomy old-fashioned quiet lounge, wide choice of reasonably priced food, good service, pretty back garden *(Andrew Rogers, Amanda Milsom, Hugh MacLean)*

☆ **Brighton** E Sus [15 Black Lion St; TQ3105], *Cricketers*: Bustling down-to-earth town pub with ageing Victorian furnishings and lots of bric-a-brac – even a stuffed bear; usual well priced lunchtime bar food inc vegetarian and fresh veg, well kept Courage Directors, Morlands Old Speckled Hen and Wadworths 6X tapped from the cask, friendly staff, upstairs restaurant (where children allowed), covered courtyard bar; open all day, can get smoky, piped music may be loud *(Ann and Colin Hunt, M L and G Clarke, Klaus and Elizabeth Leist, Tony and Wendy Hobden, Val Stevenson, Eddy Street, Jenny and Roger Huggins, F Chamberlain, Tim Barrow, Sue Demont, LYM)*

☆ **Brighton** [10 New Rd, off North St], *Colonnade*: Small but beautifully kept, with velvet, shining brass, gleaming mirrors, theatrical posters and lots of signed photographs, good friendly service even when very busy, some snacks esp salt beef sandwiches (free seafood nibbles Sun lunchtime instead), Boddingtons, Flowers and Harveys (early-evening weekday happy hour), good choice of house wines, tiny front terrace; next to Theatre Royal, they take interval orders *(F Chamberlain, Ian Phillips, Val Stevenson, Tim Barrow, Sue Demont)*

☆ **Brighton** [105 Southover St, Kemp Town], *Greys*: Buoyant atmosphere in very small basic single-room corner local with two or three rough and ready tables for eating – must book, strongly recommended for limited choice of good food lunchtime and Tues-Thurs evening, Belgian chef with some adventurous original recipes; very friendly landlord, well kept ale, well chosen and reproduced piped music, live music Sun lunchtime *(Graham Parker, R J Walden, BB)*

Brighton [County Oak Ave, Hollingbury], *County Oak*: Cheap food, Whitbreads-related ales, children welcome *(Alec and Marie Lewery)*; [Union St, The Lanes], *Font & Firkin*: Sometimes wildly busy but worth the effort, clever church refurbishment (still has pulpit and bell pulls, alongside Sunday comedians and other live entertainment; mezzanine floor, good loud music, pleasant service, good choice of well kept ales inc some brewed here, decent food inc good value Sun roasts *(Mr and Mrs Carey, Pat and Tony Martin, Betsy Brown, Nigel Flook)*; [Market St, Lanes], *Pump House*: Friendly, lively and relaxed, light and airy with nice view out, but cosy and nicely decorated, with very mixed age groups, good choice of wines *(Tony Hobden, Betsy Brown, Nigel Flook)*; [32 Russell Sq], *Regency*: Ornately refurbished, with friendly landlord and locals, well kept Bass, Fullers London Pride, Harveys, Greene King Abbot, Morlands Old Speckled Hen and a guest ale, quickly served fresh sandwiches and other lunchtime food, piped jazz or classical music *(Arnold Day)*; [50 Southover St], *Sir Charles Napier*: Warmly welcoming cosy and busy Gales pub with well kept guest ales, friendly staff and locals, maybe Morris dancing outside *(Jan Wilson)*; [Guildford Rd], *Sussex Yeoman*: Friendly town pub with eight or so real ales, several dozen different sausages inc six vegetarian *(Adrian and Gilly Heft, David Dale)*

Bucks Green W Sus [A281 Horsham—Guildford; TQ0732], *Fox*: Ancient open-plan pub with wide choice of good bar food, well kept King & Barnes (full range), inglenook, friendly staff, wide choice of good value food, play area *(Peter Bourdon)*

Burwash E Sus [Ham Lane – inn sign on A265; TQ6724], *Rose & Crown*: Timbered and low-beamed local tucked away down lane in pretty village, wide choice of ales such as Adnams, Fullers and Greene King, good log fire, friendly new licensees, good value varied food (not Sun eve) inc children's, restaurant; tables on quiet terrace; cosy good value bedrooms *(Brian Wilkinson, Beverley Daniels, Richard Carey, Gaetana Vella, BB)*

Burwash Weald E Sus [A265 two miles W of Burwash; TQ6624], *Wheel*: Good home cooking all day in well run open-plan pub with big log fire, well kept Harveys and other ales, friendly and obliging service, back games area; tables out in front and in back garden, along with goats and chickens *(Mr and Mrs R D Knight, BB)*

☆ **Bury** W Sus [off A29 Pulborough—Arundel – OS Sheet 197 map ref 014132; TQ0113], *Black Dog & Duck*: Ancient unpretentious black and white country pub tucked away among thatched cottages, tiny beamed front snug with open fire, walkers welcome in flagstoned traditional locals' bar with bar billiards and lots of games, good simple fresh food, particularly well kept King & Barnes, welcoming staff; restaurant, small pleasant garden with play area; good walking country *(JEB, LM)*

Bury [A29], *White Horse*: Pleasant service, well kept Badger Best, good specials; restaurant, tables in garden *(R T and J C Moggridge)*

Chailey E Sus [A275 9 miles N of Lewes; TQ3919], *Five Bells*: Well run, with good mix of locals, visitors and families, interesting changing choice of home-made food all day inc vegetarian, big log fire, Whitbreads-related ales, good service; picnic tables in big garden with play area *(JEB, Steve Goodchild, A H Denman)*

Chalvington E Sus [signed off A27 and A22, then Golden Cross rd; TQ5209], *Yew Tree*: Isolated proper country pub, low beams, stripped bricks and flagstones, inglenook fireplace, simple good bar food (not Sun lunchtime), well kept Harveys and Fremlins; can be packed weekends; attractive little walled terrace, extensive grounds inc own cricket pitch *(Mavis and John Wright, Guy Vowles, BB)*

Chelwood Gate E Sus [A275; TQ4129], *Red Lion*: Good quickly served bar food, well kept ales, green plush furnishings, small coal fire, dining room; delightful big sheltered garden with well spaced tables; children welcome *(Mavis and John Wright, BB)*

Chichester W Sus [North St; SU8605], *George & Dragon*: Quick pleasant staff, wholesome plentiful food from sandwiches up, Wadworths 6X and decent house wine, uncluttered bar, conservatory, tables on quiet back terrace; piped music may be loud *(Keith and Janet Morris, BHP)*; [Little London], *Jacksons Cellar*: Interesting conversion of three curved cellars, well kept Ballards Best, Cheriton Pots, Hop Back Summer Lightning and a guest ale tapped from the cask, also Belgian beers; good food often cooked with beer, piped music; cl Sun, live music nights *(Bruce Bird)*; [Whyke Rd], *Mainline*: Good food, warm quiet surroundings *(David Gould)*; [65 North St], *Old Cross*: A Chef & Brewer, but keeping restrained traditional atmosphere *(Dr and Mrs A K Clarke)*; [Priory St, opp park], *Park*: Pleasant L-shaped bar with decent food from sandwiches up, Gales and a guest beer *(Tony and Wendy Hobden)*

Chilgrove W Sus [just off B2141 Petersfield—Chichester; SU8214], *White Horse*: More smart restaurant than pub, lunches cheaper than evening, good food in bar too; remarkable list of outstanding wines, idyllic downland setting with small flower-filled terrace and big pretty garden *(MCG, Mrs D Bromley-Martin, Ann and Colin Hunt)*

☆ **nr Chilgrove** [Hooksway, signed off B2141 down steep track; SU8116], *Royal Oak*: Smartly simple country tavern in very peaceful spot, beams, brick floors, country-kitchen furnishings, huge log fires; home-made standard food inc vegetarian, well kept Gibbs Mew ales, friendly service, games, attractive seats outside; provision for children, has been cl winter Mons, good walks *(Ann and Colin Hunt, Hugh MacLean, Jill Geser, LYM)*

☆ **Cocking** W Sus [A286 S of Midhurst; SU8717], *Blue Bell*: Neatly kept unspoilt country local, well presented home-made food from ample filled baked potatoes and ploughman's to Sun roasts inc fresh veg and children's helpings, roaring log fire, friendly landlord, well kept Boddingtons and other ales; bedrooms; just off South Downs Way *(Mrs Nora Kingbourn, Nick Birch)*

Coldwaltham W Sus [pub signed down lane about 2 miles S of Pulborough – OS Sheet 197 map ref 027167; TQ0216], *Labouring Man*: Clean, friendly and comfortable, with great atmosphere, good value food, ales inc Eldridge Pope Royal Oak, Fullers London Pride, Wadworths 6X and a guest; children welcome *(Mrs L Phillips)*

Colemans Hatch E Sus [signed off B2026; or off B2110 opp church; TQ4533], *Hatch*: Simple traditional Ashdown Forest pub attractively refurbished by new landlord, increased range of food, Harveys ales *(Colin Laffan, BB)*

☆ **Compton** W Sus [B2146 S of Petersfield; SU7714], *Coach & Horses*: Spotless 15th-c former coaching inn, good atmosphere, enjoyable food, well kept ales such as Ballards Best, Fullers ESB, Hampshire Best and Porky, King & Barnes and Theakstons Old Peculier, plush beamed lounge, bigger walkers' bar, smart restaurant, friendly Flemish landlady, attentive staff; tables out in front, small secluded back garden, handy for Uppark *(Phyl and Jack Street, Michael Grigg, Ann and Colin Hunt)*

Copsale W Sus [Copsale Rd; signed off A24; TQ1725], *Bridge House*: Welcoming modern local by Downs Link footpath, usual food, King & Barnes beers, dining room, jazz Weds, garden with play area; busy weekends *(Alan and Brenda Williams)*

☆ **Cousleywood** E Sus [TQ6533], *Old Vine*: Attractive tastefully redecorated dining pub with lots of old timbers and beams, wide range of generously served modestly priced decent food (jazz suppers Mon), good house wines, four well kept ales; rustic pretty restaurant on right, rather more pubby brick-floored area with woodburner by bar, a few tables out behind *(Colin and Joyce Laffan, Tina and David Woods-Taylor, F Barwell, Mr and Mrs J Ayres, Stephen Goodchild, R and S Bentley, BB)*

Crawley W Sus [High St; TQ2636], *Old Punch Bowl*: Greene King pub in former bank, friendly staff, reasonably priced food all day, no-smoking room; very popular lunchtimes and weekend evenings, cl Sun lunchtime *(Alec and Marie Lewery)*

Crawley Down W Sus [Turners Hill Rd; A264/A2028; TQ3437], *Dukes Head*: Beefeater dining pub with Beards and Youngs ales, reasonably priced food, good friendly staff; children truly welcomed *(Andy and Jill Kassube)*

Cuckfield W Sus [Broad St; TQ3025], *Wheatsheaf*: Friendly and busy, with ten well kept ales, home cooking, tables outside; children welcome, bedrooms *(Sally Smith, David Holloway)*

Dallington E Sus [Woods Corner (B2096 E); TQ6619], *Swan*: Country local with good log fires in both traditional front bars, inglenook

fireplace, far views from plain but comfortable no-smoking back eating room, well kept Harveys, Flowers IPA and Wadworths 6X, decent food, pleasant staff; tables in back garden with boules; bedrooms *(Sussannah Anderson, BB)*

☆ **Danehill** E Sus [School Lane, Chelwood Common; off A275; TQ4128], *Coach & Horses*: Consistently good home-cooked food inc vegetarian in cottagey local with two small bars and roomy ex-stables dining extension, well kept Harveys, Greene King and guest beers, decent house wine, friendly service, good atmosphere, pews in bar, two big dogs; big neatly kept garden *(Ron Gentry, Susan and John Douglas, G G Lawrence, Mr and Mrs R D Knight)*

Dell Quay W Sus [SU8302], *Crown & Anchor*: Modernised 15th-c pub on site of Roman quay, yacht-harbour views from garden and comfortable bow-windowed lounge bar, panelled public bar with unspoilt fireplace, Courage Best, Marstons Pedigree and Wadworths 6X; good choice of popular food esp fish in bar and restaurant *(Miss A Drake, BB)*

Ditchling E Sus [B2112/B2116; TQ3215], *Bull*: Beamed 14th-c inn with attractive antique furnishings in civilised main bar, old pictures, inglenook fireplace, usual bar food inc vegetarian dishes, well kept Whitbreads-related ales, good choice of malt whiskies, comfortable family room, no-smoking restaurant, fairly good wheelchair access; picnic tables in good-sized pretty garden and on suntrap terrace, comfortable bedrooms, charming old village just below downs *(J Sheldon, Jane Bailey, Eddie Edwards, R Walden, M L and G Clarke, Peter Burton, LYM)*

Donnington W Sus [Selsey Rd (B2201); SU8502], *Selsey Tram*: Friendly Brewers Fayre pub with decent food, big children's area inside and out – slides, swings, race track, bouncy castle *(Alec and Marie Lewery, David Gould)*

☆ **Easebourne** W Sus [off A272 just NE of Midhurst; SU8922], *Olde White Horse*: Cosy local with promptly served generous home-made food inc fresh veg, good friendly service, Greene King IPA and Abbot, small log fire, traditional games in tap room, tables on back lawn and in courtyard *(R A Buckler, G C Hackemer, LYM)*

East Chiltington E Sus [Chapel Lane; 2 m N of B2116; TQ3715], *Jolly Sportsman*: Friendly local with well kept Courage Best and King & Barnes, John Smiths and Wadworths 6X, fresh well presented food, pool room; lovely garden with rustic furniture, play area and South Downs views; nice spot next to small nursery run by landlord's father-in-law, good walks *(LM, Ron Gentry)*

East Dean W Sus [formerly Star & Garter; signed off A286 and A285 N of Chichester – OS Sheet 197 map ref 904129; SU9012], *Hurdlemakers*: 1997

East Dean W Sus [signed off A286 and A285 N of Chichester; SU9012], *Hurdlemakers*: Charmingly placed by peaceful green of quiet village, with rustic seats and swing in pretty walled garden; good value food inc vegetarian, friendly efficient staff, well kept Ballards Wassail, Wadworths 6X and a guest beer, pleasant atmosphere and staff; piped music, playful cat; handy for South Downs Way (and Goodwood), children welcome *(Bruce Bird, P Gillbe, Ann and Colin Hunt, LYM)*

East Hoathly E Sus [TQ5216], *Kings Head*: Good reasonably priced food, well kept ales, well run bar, good wines; former coach house, oak beams, log fires *(Mr and Mrs M J C Pilbeam)*

East Lavant W Sus [Pook Lane; signed off A286 N of Chichester; SU8608], *Royal Oak*: Simple furnishings, rugs on bare boards and flooring tiles, two open fires and a woodburner, attractively planted gardens, Gales real ales, country wines, short choice of food (not cheap, and may take a while), children welcome if eating; new licensees *(John H L Davies, JDM, KM, Martin and Karen Wake, Bruce Bird, LYM)*

East Preston W Sus [TQ0702], *Sea View*: Not far from beach, with tables for eating in garden; bedrooms comfortable, good breakfast *(Pamela Goodwyn)*

☆ **Eastbourne** E Sus [The Goffs, Old Town; TV6199], *Lamb*: Two main heavily beamed traditional bars off pretty Tudor pub's central servery, spotless antique furnishings, good inglenook log fire, well kept Harveys ales, friendly polite service, well organised food bar, upstairs dining room (Sun lunch), no music or machines; dogs seem welcome, children allowed in very modernised side room; by ornate church away from seafront; popular with students evenings *(Beryl and Bill Farmer, Tony Scott)*

Eastbourne [Beachy Head; TV5895], *Beachy Head*: Typical Brewers Fayre in excellent position, nice bars, well kept beer, decent food inc restaurant with lunchtime carvery; handy for walks *(A Pring)*; [14 South St], *Dolphin*: Well refurbished, warm and welcoming, with log fires, well kept Harveys, wide choice of good value food from well presented sandwiches to Sun lunch, good mix of old tables in restaurant with grand piano; pool, piped music *(B R Shiner)*; [Grange Rd], *New Inn*: Pleasant helpful staff, good value food inc different snacks, Bass, Courage Directors, Harveys, John Smiths and a guest such as Tolly; restaurant *(E Robinson)*; [Cornfield Terr], *Port Hole*: Very friendly small pub with newish Dutch landlord, comfortable wooden seats and tables, imaginative home-made food, well kept beer, upstairs dining room open some days *(David Clifton)*; [Langney Rd], *Windsor*: Stylish local with Greene King Abbot, Belgian guest beers (and landlord), good food inc good value Sun lunch, long garden behind *(B R Shiner)*

Ewhurst Green E Sus [TQ7925], *White Dog*:

Extensive and attractive partly 17th-c pub/restaurant in fine spot above Bodiam Castle with tables in big garden making the most of the view, interesting choice of reasonably priced food (not Mon; may be a longish wait at busy times), well kept Fullers London Pride and Harveys, decent wines, cheerful service; bedrooms *(D Bardrick, Brian and Anna Marsden, P J Howell, Roger Crowther, LYM)*

Falmer E Sus [Middle St; TQ3508], *Swan*: Attractive pub in traditional flint village, three bars, several well kept ales inc Palmers Best and 200, usual food *(Tony and Wendy Hobden)*

Faygate W Sus [TQ2134], *Cherry Tree*: Lovely old place, pity about the dual carriageway nearby; obliging landlord, King & Barnes real ales, nice atmosphere, reasonable food *(Comus Elliott, Tony Scott)*; [Faygate Lane, off A264 nr stn], *Holmbush*: Old, quiet and friendly, spotlessly clean; reasonably priced food, quiet piped music *(A Budden)*

Felpham W Sus [A259; SZ9599], *Southdowns*: Friendly and efficient service, cheerful atmosphere, usual food running up to steaks, Tetleys-related ales *(R T and J C Moggridge)*

☆ **Fernhurst** W Sus [The Green, off A286 beyond church; SU9028], *Red Lion*: Heavy-beamed old pub tucked quietly away by green nr church, good reasonably priced food inc interesting specials, attractive layout and furnishings, friendly if not always speedy service, well kept King & Barnes and other ales, good wines, no-smoking area, good relaxed atmosphere; children welcome, pretty garden *(C D Harvey-Piper, J Sheldon, Hugh MacLean, BB)*

Fernhurst [A286 towards Midhurst], *Kings Arms*: Attractive 17th-c pub in pleasant setting with good enterprising choice of food in addition to plain things like steaks and sandwiches; very civilised service, five real ales, imported Guinness *(Mrs J Blanks, R Wills)*

Ferring W Sus [TQ0902], *Bull*: Old, attractively beamed, with nooks and corners, barn-style dining room off; warm relaxed atmosphere, attentive staff, well kept Theakstons Best and XB as well as local ales *(Colin Draper)*

Fishbourne W Sus [99 Fishbourne Rd; just off A27 Chichester—Emsworth; SU8404], *Bulls Head*: Full Gales range kept well, interesting guest beers, friendly landlord and locals, good choice of bar food (not Sun evening), log fires, no-smoking area, children's area, skittle alley, boules pitch, restaurant *(Bruce Bird)*

Fletching E Sus [High St; TQ4223], *Rose & Crown*: Welcoming 16th-c pub with good fresh home-made food in bar and small restaurant, attentive service, real ales, beams, inglenooks and log fires, tables in pretty garden *(Derek and Maggie Washington)*

Forest Row E Sus [TQ4235], *Brambletye*: Long bar at side of hotel with drinks one end, good value partly self-service food buffet the other, well kept Courage Directors and Harveys, friendly staff, open fire; restaurant; children welcome, seats in colourful courtyard with fountain and service *(LM)*

Framfield E Sus [The Street; B2012 E of Uckfield; TQ5020], *Hare & Hounds*: Unpretentious but comfortable and pleasant, with good home-cooked food, good range of real ales, helpful and friendly landlord and staff; no music *(Mrs R D Knight)*

Frant E Sus [High St, off A267 S of Tunbridge Wells; TQ5835], *George*: Quietly placed off green by ancient church and cottages, welcoming and busy, with well kept ales such as Adnams Extra and Harveys, log fire in bar leading to comfortable dining area, good food and service, darts in public bar *(Colin Laffan, Gordon Tong, Paula Williams)*

Frant [A267], *Abergavenny Arms*: Cosy main-road pub dating from 15th c, reasonably priced popular wholesome food (can be a wait at peak times), up to a dozen changing well kept ales tapped from casks in unusual climate-controlled glass-fronted chamber, friendly helpful staff; log fire, bar billiards, children welcome; piped music *(Gwen and Peter Andrews, Simon Gardner)*

Fulking W Sus [off A281 Brighton—Henfield via Poynings; TQ2411], *Shepherd & Dog*: Charming partly panelled country pub with antique or stoutly rustic furnishings around log fire, attractive bow windows, bar food from sandwiches to steaks, well kept Harveys Best, Flowers Original, and changing guest beers, good downs views from pretty streamside garden with upper play lawn; open all day Sat; has long been a popular main entry, but couldn't be bothered to return our fact checking sheet despite reminders, and tends to be too busy even to answer the telephone; this, and the service problems some readers have faced, suggest that its present management arrangements are not reliably up to the limelight which a main entry tends to bring *(Hanns P Golez, Gareth and Toni Edwards, Michael and Alison Leyland, Colin Draper, LM, John Beeken, Iain Robertson, Gordon Prince, David Holloway, Dr S Savvas, M Martin, Helen Morton, LYM)*

Graffham W Sus [off A272 or A285 SW of Petworth; SU9217], *White Horse*: New licensees doing good food in spotless and friendly family pub with good South Downs views from conservatory, small dining room, terrace and big garden; very good range of well kept ales, walkers welcome *(Mr and Mrs Vancourt Carlyle-Lyon, F H Stokes)*

Graffham, *Foresters Arms*: Smallish traditional two-bar pub, peaceful midweek lunchtime, with good reasonably priced food, well kept Gales HSB, big log fire, no music; walkers welcome, may be crowded weekends; pretty restaurant (can be fully booked) *(Martin and Karen Wake, R D Knight)*

Gun Hill E Sus [off A22 NW of Hailsham, or off A267; TQ5614], *Gun*: Big country inn, several interestingly furnished rambling

rooms, several log fires (and an Aga which they've done some of the cooking on), lovely garden with big play area, right on Wealden Way; has been a hit with readers, with good food, well kept Adnams Extra, Flowers Original, Harveys Best and Larkins and a very good choice of other drinks, and above all for very thoughtful cheerful service, with children allowed in two no-smoking rooms, but licensees leaving as we go to press in summer 1997, with no news of their successors' plans (though bedrooms unlikely to be available now) *(LYM; news please)*

☆ **Halnaker** W Sus [A285 Chichester-Petworth; SU9008], *Anglesey Arms*: Welcoming service and quickly cooked genuine food with occasional interesting Spanish specialities in bar with traditional games (can be a bit smoky), well kept King & Barnes and Tetleys-related ales, good wines (again inc direct Spanish imports); simple but smart candlelit dining room with stripped pine and flagstones (children allowed), tables in garden *(Hugh MacLean, Rex Martyn, John H L Davies, Clive Gilbert, DC, LYM)*

Hartfield E Sus [Gallipot St; B2110 towards Forest Row; TQ4634], *Gallipot*: Comfortable L-shaped bar with no frills, a couple of well kept ales, wide range of worthwhile home-cooked food (may be a wait), no music or machines, log fire, obliging service, restaurant; on edge of attractively set village, good walks nearby *(Colin Laffan, Eamonn and Natasha Skyrme)*

☆ **Hastings** E Sus [14 High St, Old Town; TQ8109], *First In Last Out*: Open-plan room attractively divided by settles, pews forming booths, posts and open raised log fire, good reasonably priced beers brewed here, guest ales, farm cider, friendly landlord, chatty atmosphere, no games or juke box; interesting simple lunchtime food, free Sun cockles, central log fire *(P R Morley)*

☆ **Hermitage** W Sus [36 Main Rd (A259); SU7505], *Sussex Brewery*: Cosy atmosphere and good log fires in small friendly pub done out with bare bricks, boards, flagstones and sawdust; well kept Archers Golden, Badger Best, Tanglefoot and Hard Tackle, Charles Wells Bombardier, Wadworths 6X and an ale brewed for them, good value simple food from sandwiches up inc masses of speciality sausages, neat back restaurant up a few steps, no machines or piped music, small garden; can get very busy and a bit smoky, open all day Sat *(Tim Abel, D H T Dimock)*

Herstmonceux E Sus [Gardner St; TQ6312], *Brewers Arms*: Welcoming licensees, generous well priced food; well kept real ales inc Beards and Harveys; theme nights *(John and Karen Kendall)*

Heyshott W Sus [off A286 S of Midhurst; SU8918], *Unicorn*: Prettily placed small country local with cheerful service, well kept beer, generous bar food, friendly service, restaurant, garden with barbecue; children allowed, reasonable disabled access *(J S Evans)*

☆ **Holtye** E Sus [Holtye Common; A264 East Grinstead—Tunbridge Wells; TQ4539], *White Horse*: Unpretentiously refurbished ancient village pub with friendly and helpful young staff, good value if not cheap food, well kept ales inc Brakspears, popular carvery restaurant with illuminated aquarium set into floor; good facilities for the disabled, marvellous view from back lawn; bedrooms *(Klaus and Elizabeth Leist, Mrs R D Knight)*

☆ **Hooe** E Sus [A259 E of Pevensey; TQ6809], *Lamb*: Prettily placed dining pub, extensively refurbished with lots of stripped brick and flintwork, one snug area around huge log fire and lots of other seats, very wide choice of generous popular food from well filled sandwiches up, well kept Harveys, quick friendly service *(Mrs S Wilkinson)*

Horam E Sus [A267 S; TQ5818], *May Garland*: Fairy-lit main-road local with lots of tables laid for eating, reasonably priced home-made food; garden *(Mr and Mrs R D Knight)*

Horsham W Sus [Guildford Rd, Bishopric; TQ1730], *Kings Arms*: Comfortable pub with villagey atmosphere, popular with workers from nearby King & Barnes brewery – their beers, good food *(Richard Lewis, Tony Scott)*; [Carfax], *Olde Kings Head*: Large open fire in rambling old hotel's bar, well prepared usual bar food, coffee shop (not Sun), restaurant; bedrooms *(Margaret and Nigel Dennis)*; [29 Carfax], *Stout House*: Small friendly unpretentious local with well kept King & Barnes Festive, Sussex and Broadwood, good lunchtime rolls, friendly licensees and regulars; cl Tues evening *(Richard Lewis, Bill Smith, Tony Scott)*

nr Horsham [Langhurst/Gt Benhams; back rd N, E of A24 between Warnham and Rusper], *Royal Oak*: Quietly placed handsome little country pub on Sussex Border Path, cosy main bar with two small rooms off, old photographs, cushioned stone benches out on suntrap walled terrace and tables under trees, well kept King & Barnes Sussex, Festive and Broadwood and Marstons Pedigree, interesting wines, decent food (not Sun) from ploughman's up; children welcome, swings, climbing frame and play tunnel *(Christopher Gallop)*

☆ **Houghton** W Sus [B2139; TQ0111], *George & Dragon*: Fine old timbered pub with civilised rambling heavy-beamed bar, nice comfortable mix of furnishings inc some antiques, decent straightforward food inc good puddings, well kept Courage Directors, Tetleys, a beer brewed locally for the pub and a guest ale, log fire, good friendly staff, no-smoking room, charming garden with pretty views; children (and maybe dogs) welcome; handy for South Downs Way *(G R Sunderland, B Johnson, A Walsh, R M Macnaughton, D M Sayers, John Beeken, Giles Francis, LYM)*

Hunston W Sus [B2145 Chichester—Sidlesham; SU8501], *Spotted Cow*: Small but attractive, doing well under new licensees, comfortable sofas, well kept Gales IPA and Butser, reasonably priced lunches from sandwiches up, more elaborate evening restaurant meals; skittles, big garden; handy for towpath walkers *(N E Bushby, Miss W E Atkins)*

☆ **Ifield** W Sus [Rusper Rd; TQ2437], *Gate*: Low-beamed country pub managed and even laid out much like the Plough at Leigh (see Surrey main entries); same tenants, similar nicely presented generous food, welcoming service, well kept King & Barnes; restaurant, tables in little tree-shaded side garden *(DWAJ)*; [Ifield Green]

Ifield, *Royal Oak*: Friendly 18th-c inn, recently refurbished, small public bar, larger low-beamed bar and comfortable lounge with country pictures, good value food, Bass; pleasant garden *(David and Carole Chapman)*

Isfield E Sus [Rose Hill (A26); TQ4516], *Halfway House*: Beams, fine fireplaces, well polished fittings, well kept Harveys Bitter and Old, good home cooking, good service, lovely cottage garden *(Tony Scott, Adrian and Gilly Heft)*

Johns Cross E Sus [A21/A2100 Battle Rd; TQ7421], *Johns Cross*: Popular roadside retreat, cosy and warm, with wide choice of well kept ales and of generous food all day, in bar and tiny dining room; decent wines, friendly licensees and regulars, pool and darts in public bar *(Comus Elliott, A M Pring)*

Keymer W Sus [Keymer Rd; TQ3115], *Greyhound*: Old refurbished village pub, generous home-made food with lots of veg, Boddingtons, Harveys and Theakstons, ceiling hung with lots of jugs, no-smoking restaurant area *(Alec Lewery)*

Kingsfold W Sus [A24 Dorking—Horsham, nr A29 junction; TQ1636], *Dog & Duck*: Cosy and friendly old country pub, well kept King & Barnes and other ales, good value nicely presented food (not after 2 lunchtime) inc popular lunches, open fires, good welcoming service *(Jayne and Douglas McLuckie)*

Lavant W Sus [Lavant Rd (A286); SU8508], *Earl of March*: Spacious village pub with friendly enthusiastic staff, well kept ales such as Ballards Best, Ringwood Old Thumper, Woodfordes Wherry and guests, Weston's Old Rosie cider, generous home-cooked food inc vegetarian, naval memorabilia, bric-a-brac and prints, games and puzzles; good views from garden, good local walks *(Bruce Bird)*

☆ **Lewes** E Sus [Castle Ditch Lane/Mount Pl; TQ4110], *Lewes Arms*: Charming unpretentious street-corner local below castle mound, cosy front lounge and two larger rooms (one with pool), particularly well kept Harveys, newspapers and tatty old books, no music – great place for conversation; comically small garden, so people migrate to pavement and street; simple but unusual lunchtime food, friendly service *(Richard Gibbs, Janet and Colin Roe, Tim Locke, Sue Demont, Tim Barrow)*

Lewes [22 Malling St], *Dorset Arms*: Generous bar food inc good sandwiches and fresh fish Fri lunchtime in popular much refurbished pub, clean and airy, with well kept Harveys, well equipped family room, restaurant, outside terraces; comfortable bedrooms *(Fred Chamberlain)*; [179 High St], *Rainbow*: Comfortable softly lit lounge with new landlord's paintings, food inc good stews, well kept Flowers and Wadworths 6X, friendly service, centre table with flowers, papers and magazines *(David Clifton)*; [8 Station St], *Royal Oak*: Popular local with helpful landlord, well kept beers, relaxing atmosphere *(Richard Houghton)*

☆ **Lickfold** W Sus [NE of Midhurst, between A286 and A283; SU9226], *Lickfold Inn*: Handsome old place, Tudor beams, ancient flooring bricks, enormous log fireplace, interestingly laid out garden; reopened early summer 1997 after refurbishment for new owners *(LYM; reports please)*

☆ **Littlehampton** W Sus [Wharf Rd; westwards towards Chichester, opp rly stn; TQ0202], *Arun View*: Clean and comfortable 18th-c inn right on harbour with river directly below windows, Whitbreads-related ales, wide choice of reasonably priced decent bar food, restaurant strong on fish (wise to book), flower-filled terrace; summer barbecues evenings and weekends; bedrooms *(Christopher Gallop, Clare and Roy Head)*

Littleworth W Sus [pub sign on B2135; village signed off A272 southbound, W of Cowfold; TQ1920], *Windmill*: Small spotless King & Barnes local with log fires in compact but cosy beamed lounge and memorably rustic public bar; good bar food (not Sun eve), well kept ales, friendly staff; windmill and other bric-a-brac, darts, dominoes, cards and bar billiards; children welcome *(Pete Baker, Bruce Bird, Mrs L Phillips)*

Lodsworth W Sus [off A272 Midhurst—Petworth; SU9223], *Hollist Arms*: Two small cosy and friendly bars, big cheerful dining room, good value home-made food, well kept Ballards and Arundel guest beer, two log fires, darts, shove ha'penny etc; whole lamb barbecues *(Howard West, Mrs L Phillips, Paula Williams)*

☆ **Loxwood** W Sus [B2133; TQ0431], *Onslow Arms*: Well refurbished, with lively young staff, well kept full King & Barnes range, good house wines, big helpings of good value simple food, picnic tables in garden sloping to river and nearby canal under restoration *(Stephen Goodchild, Alan and Brenda Williams)*

Maplehurst W Sus [TQ1924], *White Horse*: Quiet friendly family-run beamed country local with at least six real ales inc Harveys, King & Barnes and far-flung guest beers, good value basic food, efficient staff; pub cat, no music or machines; sun lounge no smoking at lunchtimes; children welcome, garden *(Bruce Bird)*

Maresfield E Sus [Piltdown; A272 Newick Rd; TQ4422], *Piltdown Man*: Reopened after refurbishment by new builder/landlord (after being closed for three years); quite nice settles,

big log fire, tables rather small for the usual food, Harveys and Wadworths 6X, children's area, some mementoes of the famous local hoax – the skull inn sign is worth seeing *(K M Thorpe)*

Milland W Sus [SU8328], *Rising Sun*: Gales pub with well kept ales, wide range of reasonably priced food (can get smaller helpings), two loudly welcoming parrots; garden with imaginative play area and animals *(Marjorie and David Lamb)*

☆ **Newick** E Sus [A272 Uckfield—Haywards Heath; TQ4121], *Bull*: Welcoming, comfortable and peaceful for a midweek lunch, lots of beams and character, good value food esp fresh Newhaven fish quickly served in sizeable eating area, well kept mainly Scottish Courage ales, inglenook fire each end; no music *(Mrs R D Knight, R and M Draper, Colin Laffan, BB)*

☆ **Normans Bay** E Sus [signed off A259 E of Pevensey, or off B2182 W out of Bexhill; TQ6806], *Star*: Spaciously extended and modernised comfortable dining lounge, often very busy indeed, with massive choice of very generous fairly priced food inc local fish and fine changing range of ales such as Adnams, Batemans, Charles Wells Bombardier, Harveys Best, Hopback Summer Lightning, Marstons Owd Roger and Morlands Old Speckled Hen, also lots of continental bottled beers, good country wines, plenty of ciders etc; piped music, games in children's room, friendly efficient staff, garden with good play area; open all day, jazz Tues, good walks inland away from the caravan sites *(David Lamb, Mr Taylor, Dr S Savvas, M Martin, Colin Laffan, R Walden, E G Parish, Sue and Steve Griffiths, Hanns P Golez, John Beeken, Miriam King, Jenny and Michael Back, Tim and Pam Moorey, M P Evans, A Pring, LYM)*

Nutbourne W Sus [the one nr Pulborough; TQ0718], *Rising Sun*: Simple old clean pub with friendly service, Badger and other ales, generous good value food; children and dogs allowed, some live music; tables on small back terrace under apple tree *(John Davis)*

Pagham W Sus [Nyetimber Lane; SZ8897], *Lion*: Cosy 15th-c pub, two bars, wooden seating, uneven flooring, low beams, well kept beers, food in bar and small restaurant, big terrace *(June and Malcolm Farmer)*

Pease Pottage W Sus [by M23 junction 11; TQ2533], *James King*: Welcoming and genuine, with good log fire, decent bar food, friendly willing service, well kept ale *(J S Rutter, Tony Scott, BB)*

☆ **Pett** E Sus [off A259 Hastings—Winchelsea; TQ8714], *Two Sawyers*: Friendly old country pub with character main bar, small public bar, back snug, small oak-beamed back restaurant where children allowed; well kept ales from neighbouring Olde Forge microbrewery and others, log fires, welcoming staff, good choice of food; tables in big relaxing garden with swings and boules pitch; bedrooms *(M P Evans, K M Thorpe)*

☆ **Petworth** [A283 towards Pulborough;

SU9721], *Welldiggers*: Picturesquely cluttered low-ceilinged stripped stone bar, long tables in stylishly simple dining room, good if not cheap food esp fish, friendly landlord, well kept Ballards and Youngs, decent wines, no music or machines; plenty of tables on attractive lawns and terraces, lovely views *(G C Hackemer, Patrick Hall, Kate Wilcox, Margaret and Nigel Dennis, BB)*

Plumpton E Sus [Ditchling Rd (B2116); TQ3613], *Half Moon*: Picturesque, long bar with prompt friendly service, good log fire and interesting painting of over 100 regulars, Ballards, Courage Directors and Ruddles, good ploughman's and other bar food inc some home-made dishes; games room, well behaved children welcome, cosy evening restaurant, rustic seats in big garden with downs view, play house and two retired tractors; good walks *(John Beeken, Alec Lewery)*

Poundgate E Sus [A26 Crowborough—Uckfield – OS Sheet 199 map ref 493289; TQ4928], *Crow & Gate*: Well refurbished, with pleasantly busy beamed bar, popular back dining extension, wide choice of food inc bargain carvery, good value family Sun lunches, well kept Flowers Original and Ruddles County, efficient service, restaurant; children welcome, tables outside, play area *(Colin and Joyce Laffan)*

☆ Ringmer E Sus [Old Uckfield Rd; blocked-off rd off A26 N of village turn-off; TQ4412], *Cock*: Heavily beamed country pub with welcoming landlord, good inglenook log fire, piped music, modernised no-smoking lounge, restaurant, well kept Greene King Abbot and Harveys Best and Mild, good well priced food, good service; children allowed in overflow eating area; piped music; seats out on terrace and in attractive sloping fairy-lit garden *(Colin Laffan, John Beeken, LYM)*

☆ nr Ringmer [outside village; A26 Lewes—Uckfield, S of Isfield turnoff], *Stewards Enquiry*: Good varied food inc good vegetarian and reasonably priced Sun roasts in tastefully refurbished olde-worlde beamed pub; good service, well kept Harveys, children welcome; some outside tables, play area *(Colin Laffan)*

☆ Ripe E Sus [signed off A22 Uckfield—Hailsham, or off A27 Lewes—Polegate via Chalvington; TQ5010], *Lamb*: Interestingly furnished snug little rooms around central servery, attractive antique prints and pictures, nostalgic song-sheet covers, Victorian pin-ups in gents'; good generous home-made food inc children's and Weds bargain lunch, well kept Scottish Courage ales and a guest such as Harveys, several open fires, friendly service; pub games ancient and modern, pleasant sheltered back garden with play area and barbecues *(K M Thorpe, LYM)*

Robertsbridge E Sus [High St, off A21 N of Hastings; TQ7323], *Seven Stars*: Characterful inn said to date from 11th c, very wide range of beers, good value generous food, welcoming service; restaurant area, garden

(Nigel Pritchard)

☆ Rogate W Sus [A272; SU8023], *Wyndham Arms*: Small welcoming village local with well kept Ballards, King & Barnes and Ringwood ales tapped from the cask, good home-cooked food using local ingredients, helpful staff; dogs and well behaved children welcome *(Mrs L C Robertson, KC, J O Jonkler, Keith Stevens, M B Griffith)*

Rotherfield E Sus [TQ5529], *Crown*: Pleasant inn in pretty village, friendly service, good home cooking, well kept Harveys and Youngs; bedrooms *(Dagmar Junghanns, Colin Keane)*

☆ Rowhook W Sus [off A29 NW of Horsham; TQ1234], *Chequers*: Unpretentious 16th-c beamed and flagstoned front bar with inglenook fire, step up to low-ceilinged lounge, good choice of bar food inc children's, well kept Boddingtons, Flowers Original, Fullers London Pride and Whitbreads Fuggles, traditional games, restaurant; piped music, live Sun lunchtime; tables out on terraces and in pretty garden with good play area *(Sally Cooke, J Sheldon, LYM)*

☆ Rushlake Green E Sus [signed off B2096; TQ6218], *Horse & Groom*: Very welcoming country pub overlooking quiet village green, beams and timbers, big log fire, good choice of enjoyable food, well kept Harveys, tables on front lawn *(JC, John and Karen Kendall, S N Robieson, LYM)*

☆ Rusper W Sus [signed from A24 and A264 N and NE of Horsham; TQ2037], *Plough*: Padded very low beams, panelling and big inglenook, good value food, attractive dining area, good range of well kept ales, lovely log fire, bar billiards and darts in raftered room upstairs; fountain in back garden, pretty front terrace, occasional live music; children welcome *(Tony Scott, DWAJ, LYM)*

Rye [The Strand; TG9220], *Grist Mill*: Flagstones, beams, real oil lamps, decent reasonably priced food in big helpings, piped blues music; open 10am-midnight *(Jane Keeton)*; *Hope Anchor*: Agreeable hotel with good value food inc sandwiches and fresh fish, roomy and tasteful dining room, attentive landlady, well kept Harveys and other ales; bedrooms *(Stephen Harvey, Gordon Tong)*; [The Mint], *Olde Standard*: Cosy dark atmosphere in small interesting pub with lots of beers inc local Pett, open fires, some bar food; open all day *(K M Thorpe)*; [East St], *Union*: Nice old pub with lots of Civil War memorabilia, wide choice of good food, decent beer *(K M Thorpe)*

Seaford E Sus [20 Church St; TV4899], *Old Plough*: Comfortably refurbished 17th-c inn with good value well prepared food in bars and restaurant, friendly staff, real ales *(June Phillips)*

Sedlescombe E Sus [TQ7718], *Queens Head*: Clean, comfortable and relaxing country local opp village green, big inglenook log fire, Doulton toby jugs, hunting prints, limited good value bar food, well kept Whitbreads-related ales, decent coffee, friendly landlord; restaurant, attractive garden *(Comus Elliott, Michael Grigg)*

Selham W Sus [S of A272 E of Midhurst; SU9320], *Three Moles*: Former railway station below downs converted to very welcoming cheerful one-room country local, well kept King & Barnes, no food exc crisps, no music, peaceful informal garden *(R J Bland, Derek Harvey-Piper)*

☆ **Shoreham by Sea** W Sus [Upper Shoreham Rd, Old Shoreham; TQ2105], *Red Lion*: Dim-lit low-beamed 16th-c pub with series of alcoves, well kept Scottish Courage ales, King & Barnes, Wadworths 6X and several interesting guest beers, occasional beer festivals, decent wines, farm cider, log fire in unusual fireplace, no-smoking dining room, pretty sheltered garden; piped music may obtrude; river walks, good South Downs views *(Bruce Bird, David Holloway, R H Martyn, John Beeken)*

Shoreham by Sea [signed off A27, A259], *Airport Bar*: Not a pub, but this small bar in 1930s art deco airport building has three real ales brewed for it by local Brewery on Sea; relaxed atmosphere, good value basic bar food, tables on terrace, uninterrupted views all round, small airport museum *(John Beeken)*; [88 High St], *Lazy Toad*: Good range of real ales tapped from cooled casks, all well kept, changing choice such as Badger Best, Fullers London Pride, Shepherd Neame and Wadworths 6X; enthusiastic welcoming landlord with sense of humour, good lunchtime food inc speciality sausages, local prints and photographs – and toad collection *(Bruce Bird)*

☆ **Shortbridge** E Sus [Piltdown; TQ4521], *Peacock*: Attractive old pub rebuilt and reopened after fire damage, attractive cosy beamed bar with timbered walls, big inglenook, very generously served nicely presented bar food served piping hot, friendly landlord, several real ales; restaurant, children welcome, sizeable garden *(Mrs G M Deane, Colin Laffan, Linda Forde, BB)*

☆ **Sidlesham** W Sus [Mill Lane, off B2145 S of Chichester; SZ8598], *Crab & Lobster*: Old country local very much enjoyed by those in tune with its uncompromising individuality, log fire in chatty traditional bar, no-smoking plusher side dining lounge, charming back garden looking over to the bird-reserve of silted Pagham Harbour; limited choice of good meals (not Sun evening) inc summer seafood platters, well kept Archers Village and Gales Best and BBB, decent wines, country wines, traditional games; dogs welcome, no music or machines *(P R White, Phyl and Jack Street, John Beeken, LYM)*

Singleton W Sus [A286; SU8713], *Horse & Groom*: Friendly staff, well kept ales inc Ballards Best and Cheriton Pots, generous promptly served reasonably priced home-made food, quiet piped classical music, no-smoking restaurant, garden; open all day Sun *(Bruce Bird)*

☆ **Slindon** W Sus [Slindon Common; A29 towards Bognor; SU9708], *Spur*: Smallish attractive 17th-c pub, good choice of reasonably priced food changing daily inc vegetarian, two big log fires, well kept Scottish Courage beers, friendly staff and dogs; children welcome, games room with darts and pool, sizeable restaurant, pleasant garden *(Miss D Hobbs, John Davis)*

Slindon, *Newburgh Arms*: Good food, well kept real ales *(Richard Dolphin)*

☆ **South Harting** W Sus [B2146; SU7819], *White Hart*: Attractive unspoilt pub with good generous home cooking (may be a wait) inc vegetarian and sandwiches, lots of polished wood, hundreds of keys, big log fire in cosy snug, cheerful long-serving licensees, well kept Tetleys-related ales, good coffee, restaurant, separate public bar; well behaved dogs allowed, children welcome (toys in games room); good garden behind for them too, with spectacular downs views *(MCG, Ann and Colin Hunt, N E Bushby, W Atkins)*

South Harting W Sus, *Ship*: Very wide choice of good value food in informal unspoilt 17th-c local with Palmers and Eldridge Pope ales, good coffee, unobtrusive piped classical music, dominoes, maybe chestnuts to roast by public bar's log fire; nice setting in pretty village *(N E Bushby, W Atkins, N McSwiggan, MCG)*

Staplefield W Sus [Warninglid Rd; TQ2728], *Victory*: Unpretentious whitewashed pub, dovecote in roof, picnic tables and play area in garden overlooking cricket green; well kept Courage Directors, King & Barnes and Wadworths 6X, decent wines, vast choice of good value food, welcoming licensees, log fire, games area, decorative plates and horse-brasses; popular, get there early *(John Beeken, John Kimber, Tony Scott, R Walden)*

☆ **Stedham** W Sus [School Lane (off A272); SU8522], *Hamilton Arms*: Proper English local run by friendly Thai family, village shop in car park, basic pub food but also interesting Thai bar snacks and popular restaurant (cl Mon); pretty hanging baskets, seats out by quiet lane, good walks nearby *(KC, Ann and Colin Hunt)*

☆ **Steyning** W Sus [41 High St; TQ1711], *Chequer*: Timber-framed Tudor pub with labyrinthine bars, friendly staff, good range of well kept Whitbreads-related beers, wide choice of generous food from good snacks up, friendly efficient service *(Niki and Terry Pursey, Guy Consterdine)*

☆ **Stopham** W Sus [off A283 E of village, W of Pulborough; TQ0218], *White Hart*: Friendly old beamed pub with open fire in one of its three snug rooms, good freshly made bar food (not winter Sun evening), candlelit no-smoking restaurant specialising in unusual fresh fish, well kept Flowers Original and Whitbreads Strong Country; children welcome, play area over rd, with grass walks by pretty junction of Arun and Rother rivers *(R Walden, PGP, John Beeken, Dr S Savvas, M Martin, Hanns P Golez, R H Martyn, Alan Jarvis, Derek*

Harvey-Piper, Colin Draper, LYM)

Storrington W Sus [Main St; TQ0814], *Anchor*: Large friendly family-run beamed pub with wide choice of good value food, spacious dining area, good atmosphere, well kept Whitbreads-related and guest ales, unobtrusive piped music, games room *(M Carey, Miss A Groocock, K Frostick)*

☆ **Stoughton** W Sus [signed off B2146 Petersfield—Emsworth; SU8011], *Hare & Hounds*: Much modernised pub below downs with reliably good home-cooked food in airy pine-clad bar, big open fires, half a dozen changing well kept ales such as Adnams Broadside and Gibbs Mew Bishops Tipple, friendly staff, restaurant, back darts room, tables on pretty terrace; nr Saxon church, good walks nearby; children in eating area and restaurant *(Ann and Colin Hunt, LYM)*

Tangmere W Sus [Arundel Rd (A27); SU9006], *Olde Cottage*: Homely and popular, with friendly staff, well presented good food (not Sun evening), well kept Brakspears *(Clive Gilbert)*

Trotton W Sus [A272 W of Midhurst; SU8323], *Keepers Arms*: Helpful newish licensees doing good value food in beamed and timbered L-shaped bar and dining area, well kept Morlands Old Speckled Hen and Wadworths 6X, log fire, relaxed piped music; country views from latticed windows and terrace *(Ann and Colin Hunt, BB)*

☆ **Wadhurst** E Sus [Mayfield Lane (B2100 W); TQ6131], *Best Beech*: Well run dining pub, pleasant dim-lit bar on left with wall seats, quiet but individual decor and coal fire, eating area with lots of pictures and china on right, well done fresh bar food (not Sun/Mon evenings) from sandwiches to juicy steaks, well kept Harveys and other ales, decent wines, quick service; back restaurant, good value bedrooms *(Jill Bickerton, BB)*

Wadhurst E Sus [St James Sq (B2099); TQ6431], *Greyhound*: Neatly kept village pub with wide choice of usual bar food and set Sun lunch in neat restaurant or pleasant beamed bar with big inglenook log fire, real ales such as Bass, Fullers, Harveys, Ruddles County and Tetleys, good service, no piped music; tables in well kept back garden; bedrooms *(James and Lynne House, S Barrow, BB)*

Walderton W Sus [Stoughton rd, just off B2146 Chichester—Petersfield; SU7810], *Barley Mow*: Pretty village pub with fish pond in attractive back garden; flagstoned bar where dogs allowed, comfortable lounge, two log fires, generous food inc good value ploughman's and Sun lunch, well kept Gales ales and country wines, cheerful staff, popular skittle alley; children welcome, good walks, handy for Stansted House *(MCG, PS, JS)*

Warnham W Sus [Friday St; TQ1533], *Greets*: 15th-c beamed pub, uneven flagstones and inglenook log fire, lots of nooks and corners, well kept Whitbreads-related ales, decent wines, friendly attentive staff, wide choice of good though not cheap straightforward home cooking (not Sun evening – and worth getting there early as some things run out); convivial locals' side bar, tables in garden *(Audrey and Peter Reeves, F H Keens, Joy Crowley)*

☆ **Washington** W Sus [just off A24 Horsham—Worthing; TQ1212], *Franklands Arms*: Well kept, roomy and welcoming, with wide choice of food all day (lots of fried food), well kept Flowers Original and King & Barnes, decent house wines, prompt service; big bar, smaller dining area, games area with pool and darts; tables in neat garden, quiet spot yet busy weekends *(R H Martyn)*

☆ **West Chiltington** W Sus [Church St; TQ0918], *Elephant & Castle*: Friendly and lively pub behind ancient church, good range of reasonably priced freshly cooked food, well kept King & Barnes ales, helpful service, no music; children welcome, good garden with ducks and chickens *(Bruce Bird, Tony and Wendy Hobden)*

☆ **West Chiltington** W Sus [Smock Alley, off B2139 S; TQ0916], *Five Bells*: Consistently good reasonably priced fresh food, well kept King & Barnes and other ales from small breweries, annual beer festival, enthusiastic landlord, big sun lounge, pleasant garden *(Bruce Bird, Brian Charman)*

☆ **West Hoathly** W Sus [signed off A22 and B2028 S of E Grinstead; TQ3632], *Cat*: Ancient pub delightfully placed in pretty hilltop village, with fine views; heavy beams and timbers, lots of character, spotless tables with candles and flowers, good if not cheap food (may be a wait), well kept Beards and Fullers London Pride, good coffee, decent wine, big log fire *(Susan and John Douglas, Tony Scott, Mr and Mrs R Mann, Heather Martin, LYM)*

West Itchenor W Sus [SU8001], *Ship*: Large pub in good spot nr Chichester Harbour, cheery welcome and service, well kept Scottish Courage ales, good range of food in bar and restaurant, spotless parquet floor and panelling, children in eating area, tables out under cocktail parasols; said to be able to get supplies for yachtsmen (nearest shop is two miles away) *(Ann and Colin Hunt, Pete Yearsley)*

☆ **West Wittering** W Sus [Chichester Rd; B2179/A286 towards Birdham; SU7900], *Lamb*: Immaculate 18th-c country pub, several rooms neatly knocked through with tidy new furnishings, rugs on tiles, well kept ales such as Ballards, Bunces Benchmark, Harveys Old, Hop Back Summer Lightning and Ringwood Fortyniner, decent wines, interesting reasonably priced food from separate servery, big log fire, prompt friendly service; tables out in front and in small sheltered back garden – good for children, with outside salad bar on fine days; busy in summer *(John and Wendy Trentham, P R White, Bruce Bird, Mrs S Fortescue, Ann and Colin Hunt, N E Bushby, W E Atkins, BB)*

Westbourne W Sus [Silverlock Pl; SU7507], *Cricketers*: Simple open-plan village local with well kept Gales and a guest beer, friendly licensees, darts one end, piped 60s music (not too loud), occasional live music; garden with chipmunks and canaries *(Ann and Colin Hunt)*; [North St], *Good Intent*: Friendly two-bar local with well kept Tetleys-related ales, good value simple food, real fires, darts, juke box, monthly live music; barbecues *(Colin and Ann Hunt)*

Westfield E Sus [TQ8115], *Plough*: Attractive newly refurbished pub with good atmosphere, coal fires, wooden floors, interesting decor, hanging baskets; quite a wide choice of generous home-cooked food, nicely presented and good value, with well kept Shepherd Neame Bitter and Spitfire; children welcome, with good facilities *(R C Tanton)*

☆ **Wilmington** E Sus [just off A27; TQ5404], *Giants Rest*: Unpretentious, with pine furniture and basic seating in small chatty rooms; good choice of imaginative sensibly priced home-made food inc devastating puddings, well kept ales such as Adnams, Harveys and Timothy Taylors, farm ciders, friendly service; very popular lunchtimes; picnic tables outside *(Paul and Beverley Edwards, Ian Coldrick, E G Parish, Thomas and Audrey Nott, M Martin, Dr S Savvas)*

☆ **Winchelsea** E Sus [German St; TQ9017], *New Inn*: Variety of solid comfortable furnishings in well decorated bustling rambling beamed rooms, some emphasis on food inc good fresh fish (sandwiches too), well kept changing ales such as Everards Tiger, Harveys, Wadworths 6X and one brewed for them by Adnams, decent wines and malt whiskies, friendly though not always speedy service; separate public bar with darts, children in eating area, pretty bedrooms (some sharing bathrooms), delightful setting *(Michael Sargeant, Bob and Maggie Atherton, Hanns P Golez, B J Harding, George Atkinson, A Bradbury, Mr and Mrs J Jackson, LYM)*

☆ **Wisborough Green** W Sus [A272 W of Billingshurst; TQ0526], *Three Crowns*: Big clean and polished open-plan bar stretching into dining room, stripped bricks and beams, good reasonably priced food inc big ploughman's and popular Sun lunch, well kept ales such as Greene King Abbot, quick attentive service, sizeable back garden *(Christopher Warner, Colin Laffan)*

Woodmancote W Sus [the one nr Emsworth; SU7707], *Woodmancote Arms*: Simple village local with reasonably priced bar food, well kept Gibbs Mew; restaurant, play area *(Ann and Colin Hunt)*

☆ **Worthing** W Sus [High St, W Tarring; TQ1303], *Vine*: Welcoming unpretentious local, small, cosy and comfortable, with six well kept ales inc Ballards Best, Hop Back Summer Lightning, Village Bitter brewed for the pub and guests, October beer festival, good home-made lunchtime food; can get smoky when crowded, occasional live music; attractive garden *(Bruce Bird, Richard Houghton, B and M Kendall)*

Worthing [20 Chapel Rd], *Fathom & Firkin*: Typical own brew Firkin, pleasant atmosphere, good service, visitors made welcome *(Richard Houghton)*; [Portland Rd, just N of Marks & Spencer], *Hare & Hounds*: Friendly bustling busy extended pub with well kept Whitbreads-related ales, good choice of reasonably priced straightforward food, wide range of customers, pleasant staff; no car park but three multi-storeys nearby *(Tony and Wendy Hobden, Peter Sweet, Chris and Anne Fluck)*; [Warwick St], *Hogshead*: Long narrow beamed bar with lots of banquettes, unusual decorations, around a dozen well kept ales, mostly Whitbread-related but some unusual ones too, also farm ciders; an unpretentious place, good for serious drinking (the food is plain, though tasty enough); well behaved children allowed *(Michael Sandy, M Carey, Miss A Groocock)*; [Old Brighton Rd – A259 nr Beach House Park], *Royal Oak*: Good helpings of bar food (may be a wait), pleasant staff, nice atmosphere, picnic tables on sunny front terrace *(Chris and Anne Fluck, Tony and Wendy Hobden)*; [High St], *Swan*: Big open-plan pub with good value basic pub food, Bass and related ales; handy for hospital *(Tony and Wendy Hobden)*; [Richmond Rd], *Wheatsheaf*: Popular open-plan pub, nicely furnished front lounge with open fire, plainer back bar, well kept Bass and Charrington IPA, good choice of decent food, welcoming atmosphere; quiz night *(Chris and Anne Fluck, Michael Sandy)*

Yapton W Sus [Maypole Lane; signed off B2132 Arundel rd – OS Sheet 197 map ref 977042; SU9703], *Maypole*: Friendly staff, customers and cats, two log fires in lounge, generous good value home cooking (not Sun or Tues evenings), well kept Courage Best, Ringwood Best and guests from small breweries, beer festivals Easter and August bank hol; seats ourside, skittle alley *(Bruce Bird)*

Warwickshire

All the main entries here seem to be showing really well currently, but those which have been earning the warmest reports in recent months are the Bear at Berkswell (a new main entry – the best Chef & Brewer we have found recently), the Fox & Hounds at Great Wolford (improved food from a new French chef at this charming old place), the Howard Arms at Ilmington (an excellent dining pub, of considerable character), the Navigation at Lapworth (a warm-hearted canalside local), the Fleur de Lys at Lowsonford (another canalside pub, successfully combining a sunny-day pubby garden with a flourishing dining side), and the Green Dragon at Sambourne (this consistently good place now has bedrooms). Against a background of generally good value food throughout the county, the Howard Arms at Ilmington stands out as Warwickshire Dining Pub of the Year. You have to look among the Lucky Dip entries at the end of the chapter for the wide if not compelling choice of decent pubs in Birmingham (we include the West Midlands conurbations in this chapter); other pubs to note there, all of them inspected by us, are the Dun Cow at Dunchurch, Castle on Edge Hill, George at Lower Brailes (new landlord settling in very promisingly) and Manor House in West Bromwich. Drinks prices here are lower than the national average – especially in those pubs supplied by the area's smaller breweries, which we found averaged 20p a pint cheaper for beer than those here which are supplied by the big national breweries. Cheapest of all was the delightfully unspoilt Case is Altered at Five Ways (a free house selling Sam Smiths from Yorkshire), followed by the quaint Crooked House in Himley (a Banks's pub); the Red Lion at Little Compton (tied to Donnington) and the Vine in Brierley Hill (the tap for Bathams brewery) are also very pocket-friendly.

ALDERMINSTER SP2348 Map 4
Bell ⑪ ♀

A3400 Oxford—Stratford

The tremendously welcoming energy of the licensees at this fairly smart dining pub is apparent in the extensive programme of parties, food festivals, classical and light music evenings which they host throughout the year. They've also built a very good reputation for their monthly changing imaginative menu, with dishes produced as much as possible from fresh ingredients. There might be tomato, celery and apple soup with croutons (£2.95), pot of mixed mushrooms and cubes of cheese under pastry lid (£4.95), fresh scallops in a cream and chardonnay sauce au gratin (£5.95), fresh pasta with wild mushroom, cheese and fresh basil sauce (£6.25), babotie (£7.50), pork chop in mustard and ale sauce with noodles or grilled lamb liver and smoked bacon with orange and green peppercorn sauce (£8.50), minted lamb casserole or moroccan chicken with apricots, garlic and cous cous (£8.95), as well as several fresh fish dishes like grilled lemon sole with smoked salmon butter (£9.95) and grilled fish kebab with cream and wine sauce (£11.50). The communicating areas of the neatly kept spacious bar have plenty of stripped slatback chairs around wooden tables on the flagstones and wooden floors, little vases of flowers, small landscape prints and swan's-neck brass-and-globe lamps on the cream walls, and a solid-fuel stove in a stripped brick inglenook; apart from the small entrance bar the whole pub is no smoking. Well kept changing beers might include Marstons Pedigree, Shepherd Neame Spitfire, Smiles Golden Best and Wadworths 6X on handpump, a good range of wines by the glass, freshly squeezed juice and a cocktail of the month. Civilised and friendly waitress service, and readers with children have felt particularly welcome here – they have high chairs but no children's menu. A conservatory and terrace overlook the garden and Stour Valley. *(Recommended by Peter Lloyd, J H Kane, Dorothee and Dennis Glover, Brian Skelcher, Theo, Anne and Jane Gaskin, John Bowdler, Hugh Spottiswoode, Maysie Thompson, Lawrence Bacon, David Shillitoe, Sharon Hancock, C and M Starling, Roy Bromell, Henry Paulinski, Paul and Janet Waring)*

Free house ~ Licensees Keith and Vanessa Brewer ~ Real ale ~ Meals and snacks ~ (01789) 450414 ~ Children welcome ~ Open 12-3, 7-11; cl 24-26 Dec and 1-2 Jan evenings

BERKSWELL SP2479 Map 4
Bear

Spencers Lane; village signposted off A452 W of Coventry

This picturesque 16th-c timbered pub has had its ups and downs, but in its latest guise it's a splendid example of how well the Chef & Brewer formula can work, at its best – given a substantial degree of staff commitment, and in this case the recent injection of £½ million spent on a very sympathetic programme of refurbishment. It now has a thoroughly traditional relaxed atmosphere, with comfortably snug low-beamed areas, alcoves, nooks and crannies, panelling, low beams, a longcase clock, bric-a-brac and prints, and in one place the heavy timbers showing the slope of the cats'-slide eaves. Furnishings now match the old-fashioned style, and there are roaring log fires in winter. The wide choice of good value food is cooked to order, running from well served doorstep sandwiches (from £2.45), filled ciabattas (from £3.75), ploughman's (£3.95), peppered mushrooms (£5.35), steak and kidney pie (£5.75) and mediterranean swordfish (£7.15) and about half a dozen daily specials like wild boar and venison pie (£10.50) and sea bass (£13.95), and puddings like crème brûlée and lemon mousse (£2.95). Well kept Theakstons Best and up to three guests like Old Peculier, and two that are new to us – Batemans Mystic Brew and Courage Rocketeer; decent house wines and unusually for this chain quite a few by the glass; unobtrusive piped classical music. There are tables behind on a tree-sheltered back lawn; the cannon in front of the building is a veteran of the Crimean War, and the village church is well worth a visit. *(Recommended by Brian Skelcher, Roy Bromell)*

Scottish Courage ~ Manager Mrs Robinson ~ Real ale ~ Meals and snacks (till 10pm) ~ Restaurant ~ (01676) 533202 ~ Children welcome if eating ~ Open 10am-11pm; Sun 12-10.30; cl 25 Dec evening and 26 Dec

BRIERLEY HILL SO9187 Map 4
Vine £ 🍺

Delph Rd; B4172 between A461 and A4100, near A4100

What some would descibe as the archetypal English pub, this warmly welcoming place is full of local characters, serves really good value food and is also the tap for the next-door Batham brewery – so the Bitter and Mild, and Delph Strong in winter, are well kept and also very reasonably priced. It's a popular place so it can get crowded in the warmly welcoming front bar which has wall benches and simple leatherette-topped oak stools; the extended and refurbished snug on the left has solidly built red plush seats, and the back bar has brass chandeliers as well as darts, cribbage, dominoes, fruit machine and trivia. Good fresh lunchtime snacks include samosas (60p), really tasty sandwiches (£1), ploughman's, curry or marvellous-value salads from a cold table (£2) and faggots and peas or steak and kidney pie (£2.30). The pub is known in the Black Country as the Bull & Bladder, from the good stained glass bull's heads and very approximate bunches of grapes in the front bow windows. *(Recommended by Andy and Jill Kassube, Chris Raisin, Graham Doyle, Pat and Tony Martin, Mike Begley, W L G Watkins)*

Bathams ~ Manager Melvyn Wood ~ Real ale ~ Lunchtime snacks (Mon-Fri only) ~ (01384) 78293 ~ Children welcome in children's room ~ Blues Sun evening ~ Open 12-11; 12-4, 7-10.30 Sun

COVENTRY SP3379 Map 4
Old Windmill £

Spon Street

Still known locally as Ma Brown's after a former landlady, this attractive and unpretentious place also has a good local reputation as the friendliest pub in Coventry. Unlike the rest of the buildings in the street – a collection of transplanted survivors from the blitz – this timber-framed 15th-c pub is on its original site. One of the rambling series of tiny cosy old rooms is little more than the stub of a corridor, another has carved oak seats on flagstones and a woodburner in a fine ancient inglenook fireplace, and another has carpet and more conventionally comfortable seats. There are exposed beams in the uneven ceilings, and a back room preserves some of the equipment which was used in the days when Ma Brown brewed here. Well kept Courage Directors, John Smiths, Marstons Pedigree, Morlands Old Speckled Hen, Websters and then a couple of guests like Crown Buckley Reverend James and Oakhill Best, all kept under light blanket pressure. Bulmer's cider; dominoes, fruit machine, juke box. Food passed out straight from the kitchen door: filled batches (from £1.10) and all day breakfast, battered cod, cottage pie, steak pie, faggots and mushy peas, gammon, salads, lasagne and several other dishes (all £3.25); no-smoking dining area. The pub is popular with students, extremely busy on Friday and Saturday evenings, and handy for the Belgrave Theatre. *(Recommended by John Brightley, Stephen and Julie Brown; more reports please)*

Courage ~ Lease: Lynne Ingram ~ Real ale ~ Lunchtime meals and snacks (not Sun) ~ (01203) 252183 ~ Children in eating area ~ Open 11-3, 6-11; 11-11 Sat; 12-3, 7-10.30 Sun; cl 25 Dec

FARNBOROUGH SP4349 Map 4
Butchers Arms

Off A423 N of Banbury

There's a nice choice of carefully renovated rooms at this pleasantly welcoming village pub, which is nicely set well back from the road on the side of a hill. The pleasant main lounge bar has lots of oak furniture and fittings, flagstone floors and some carpet, piped Classic FM, and well kept Bass, Hook Norton and a weekly guest like Wardens Best on handpump; decent wine list, too. There's a prettily countrified dining extension with big timbers, and a front public bar with darts. Bar food includes sandwiches (from £1.85), soup (£2.35), good filled baguettes (£2.85), toasted bread filled with ham and cheese and topped with a fried egg (£3.85), home-made pâté (£3.85), lots of ploughman's (£4.65), omelettes, ratatouille lasagne or lamb curry (£4.85), steak and kidney pie (£5.85), seafood gratin (£9.85), children's dishes (from £1.85), and home-made puddings like banoffi pie, treacle tart or fruit crumble (£2.85); Sunday roast (£6.85); friendly staff. It's handy for Farnborough Hall. *(Recommended by Dr John Bassett, John Bowdler, Jill Bickerton; more reports please)*

Free house ~ Licensee Kathryn Robinson ~ Real ale ~ Meals and snacks (till 10) ~ Restaurant ~ (01295) 690615 ~ Children welcome away from bar ~ Live music Fri evenings ~ Open 12-3, 7-11; 12-3, 7-10.30 Sun

FIVE WAYS SP2270 Map 4
Case is Altered ◼

Follow Rowington signposts at junction roundabout off A4177/A4141 N of Warwick

Year after year, virtually nothing changes at this delightful white cottage which has been licensed to sell beer for over three centuries. There's no food, no children or dogs, and no noisy games machines or piped music – but you can be sure of a delightfully warm welcome from the landlady, cheery staff and regulars. The small, unspoilt simple main bar is decorated with a fine old poster showing the Lucas Blackwell & Arkwright brewery (now flats) and a clock with its hours spelling out Thornleys Ale, another defunct brewery; there are just a few sturdy old-fashioned tables, with a couple of stout leather-covered settles facing each other over the spotless tiles. From this room you reach the homely lounge (usually open only weekend evenings and Sunday lunchtime) through a door lit up on either side. A door at the back of the building leads into a modest little room, usually empty on weekday lunchtimes, with a rug on its tiled floor and an antique bar billiards table protected by an ancient leather cover (it takes pre-decimal sixpences). Well kept Ansells Mild and Traditional, Flowers Original, well priced Sam Smiths OB and a guest like Warwickshire Kings Champion served by rare beer engine pumps mounted on the casks that are stilled behind the counter. Behind a wrought-iron gate is a little brick-paved courtyard with a stone table under a chestnut tree. *(Recommended by Ted George, Brian Skelcher, Pete Baker, Stephen Brown, Andy and Jill Kassube, Jenny and Roger Huggins)*

Free house ~ Licensee Gwen Jones ~ Real ale ~ (01926) 484206 ~ Open 11.30-2.30, 6-11; 12-2, 7-10.30 Sun (cl evening 25 Dec)

GREAT WOLFORD SP2434 Map 4
Fox & Hounds ★ ◗

Village signposted on right on A3400 3 miles S of Shipston on Stour

The new French chef at this inviting 16th-c stone pub has introduced a range of very well prepared imaginative specials that change twice a day. There might be fresh sardines stuffed with onions and basil with provençal sauce (£2.95), smoked salmon terrine (£3.25), pork fillet wrapped in bacon and spinach with light green peppercorn sauce (£8.95), lamb kleftico (£9.50) and grilled red snapper with provençal butter, capers and lemon (£10.50) and puddings like banana and rum parfait with dark chocolate sauce or lime bavarois with apricot coulis (£2.95), as well as more usual menu items such as soup (£2.50), sandwiches (from £3), prawn cocktail (£3.95), ploughman's (from £4.95) and scampi (£6.95). Locals still gather for a drink in the very welcoming, cosy low-beamed old-fashioned bar which has a nice collection of chairs and candlelit old tables on spotless flagstones, as well as a window seat with delightful views, old hunting prints on the walls, and a roaring log fire in the inglenook fireplace with its fine old bread oven. A small tap room serves a terrific choice of eight weekly changing beers like Black Sheep, Butcombe, Fullers London Pride, Hook Norton Best, Morlands Old Speckled Hen, Shepherd Neame Spitfire and Wadworths 6X on handpump, and about 185 malt whiskies. There's a well on the terrace outside. *(Recommended by John Bowdler, Simon Walker, Martin Jones, K H Frostick, Dr J R Hilton, Mrs J Crawford, Alan and Paula McCully, Dr and Mrs M Beale, Angus Lyon)*

Free house ~ Licensees Graham and Anne Seddon ~ Meals and snacks ~ (01608) 674220 ~ Children in eating area of bar ~ Open 12-3, 7-11(10.30 Sun) ~ Bedrooms: £35S (breakfast not served)

HIMLEY SO8889 Map 4
Crooked House ★

Pub signposted from B4176 Gornalwood—Himley, OS Sheet 139 map reference 896908; readers have got so used to thinking of the pub as being near Kingswinford in the Midlands (though Himley is actually in Staffs) that we still include it in this chapter – the pub itself is virtually smack on the county boundary

You lose all sense of balance as you walk into this remotely set wonky old house that sits on a maze of old mine shafts, and has shifted considerably over the years. The adjustments they've made to the doors and windows throw your perceptions into confusion – on one table a bottle on its side actually rolls 'upwards' against the apparent direction of the slope, and for a 10p donation you can get a big ball-bearing from the bar to roll 'uphill' along a wainscot. There's a friendly atmosphere in the characterful old rooms, and at the back is a large, level and more modern extension with local antiques. Very reasonably priced Banks's Bitter and Marstons Pedigree on hand or electric pump; dominoes, fruit machine and piped music. Good value bar food in generous helpings includes smokies (£3.25) and steak and kidney pie (£3.85). The conservatory is no smoking at food times, and there's a spacious outside terrace; It can get very busy in summer with coach trips; one reader found they'd closed early one weekday afternoon in winter. *(Recommended by Jeanne Cross, Paul Silvestri, Mark Hughes; more reports please)*

Banks's ~ Manager Gary Ensor ~ Real ale ~ Meals and snacks (not Sun evening) ~ (01384) 238583 ~ Children welcome in conservatory during food times ~ Open 11-11; 12-10.30 Sun; 11.30-2.30, 6.30-11 winter weekdays; 12-3, 7-10.30 winter Sun

ILMINGTON SP2143 Map 4
Howard Arms 🍽 ♀

Village signposted with Wimpstone off A34 S of Stratford
Warwickshire Dining Pub of the Year

The imaginative well prepared bar food at this attractive golden-stone inn is popular with a fairly smart crowd. It can get busy, but the welcoming and efficient young staff cope well. The menu changes constantly but there may be soup (£2.50), chicken liver parfait (£3.50), butterfly prawns with garlic dip (£3.95), lamb and rosemary, steak and kidney pie or spiced chicken balti (£6), oxtail stew with herb dumplings or grilled goat's cheese salad (£6.50), fresh poached salmon with chive and vermouth, seafood thermidor or filo parcel of wild mushrooms with creamy sherry sauce (£7.95), poached supreme of chicken with dill cream sauce or salad with barbecued king prawns (£8.50) and noisettes of venison with prunes and brandy (£9); small helpings of some dishes for children. There's a cosy atmosphere in the friendly heavy-beamed bar (possibly full of shooting gents on Saturday) which has rugs on lovely polished flagstones, comfortable seats, highly polished brass, and open fires, a couple of tables in a big inglenook, screened from the door by an old-fashioned built-in settle). A snug area off here is no smoking. Well kept Everards Tiger, Marstons Pedigree and an interesting guest like Fiddlers Elbow or Wychwood on handpump and under light blanket pressure, decent wines of the month, and excellent freshly pressed apple juice; friendly, polite service, and nice labrador; shove-ha'penny and Aunt Sally on Thursday evenings; piped music. The garden is lovely in summer with fruit trees sheltering the lawn, a colourful herbaceous border and well spaced picnic tables, with more tables on a neat gravel terrace behind. It's nicely set beside the village green, and there are lovely walks on the nearby hills (as well as strolls around the village outskirts). *(Recommended by Roy Bromell, Dorothee and Dennis Glover, Nigel and Sue Foster, Martin and Karen Wake, Maysie Thompson, J and P Maloney, Neil Porter, Simon Walker, Cyril Brown, G R Braithwaite, Alan and Barbara Mence, John Bowdler, Martin Jones, E V Walder, Pat and Roger Fereday, Pam Adsley, Peter Lloyd, Martin Jones, Henry Paulinski, George Atkinson)*

Free house ~ Licensee Alan Thompson ~ Real ale ~ Meals and snacks (not winter Sun evenings) ~ Restaurant (not winter Sun evenings) ~ (01608) 682226 ~ Well behaved children welcome ~ Open 11-2.30, 6-11; 12-3, 7-10.30 Sun ~ Bedrooms: £35B/£55B

LAPWORTH SP1670 Map 4
Navigation

Old Warwick Rd (B4439 Warwick—Hockley Heath)

A new extension – nicely done with rugs on oak floors, cast-iron tables and bentwood chairs – at the back of this simple bustling local has delightful views over the sheltered flower-edged lawn, and on down to the busy canal behind. In summer canal-users and locals sit on a back terrace where they have barbecues, jazz, Morris dancers or even travelling theatre companies, and outside hatch service, and it's all prettily lit at night. The bustling friendly flagstoned bar is decorated with some brightly painted canal ware and cases of stuffed fish, and has high-backed winged settles, seats built around its window bay and a coal fire in its high-mantled inglenook. Another quieter room has tables on its board-and-carpet floor. Service stays cheery and efficient when it's busy. Generously served bar food includes lunchtime sandwiches (from £2.25), chicken or prawn balti (from £6), beef, Guinness and mushroom pie (£6.50), 16oz cod in beer batter (£6.50), steaks (from £7.95), grilled duck breast with plum sauce (£8.95), and traditional puddings made by the licensee's mother (£2.50). Very well kept Bass, Highgate Dark Mild, M&B Brew XI, and two guests like Batemans XXXB and Warwickshire Kings Champion on handpump, and a guest farm cider; fruit machine, dominoes, shut-the-box, shove-ha'penny. *(Recommended by Mr and Mrs C Moncreiffe, Brian and Anna Marsden, Lynn and Peter Brueton, Mike Gorton, Andy and Jill Kassube, John Franklin, Andrew Scarr, Joan and Tony Walker, M Joyner, Iona Thomson, RTM, JCM, Rona Murdoch)*

M&B (Bass) ~ Lease: Andrew Kimber ~ Real ale ~ Meals and snacks ~ (01564) 783337 ~ Children welcome in eating area until 9 ~ Occasional jazz evenings, Morris dancing and canal theatre in summer ~ Open 11-3, 5.30-11; 11-11 Sat; 12-10.30 Sun; cl 25, 26 Dec evenings

LITTLE COMPTON SP2630 Map 4
Red Lion ♀

Off A44 Moreton in Marsh—Chipping Norton

Conveniently positioned for exploring the Cotswolds, this pretty 16th-c stone inn is well liked for its reasonably priced tasty food, friendly welcome and good service. The simple but civilised and comfortable low-beamed lounge has snug alcoves and a couple of little tables by the log fire. Bar food includes soup (£2.25), chicken liver pâté (£3.25), filled baguettes (from £2.95), ploughman's (£3.95), filled baked potatoes (from £3.50), ham and egg (£4.95), breaded scampi, tagliatelle niçoise or lasagne (£5.95), seafood pie (£6.75) and daily specials like spicy chicken wings with garlic mayonnaise and chilli dip (£3.25), fried brie with cumberland sauce (£3.50), crêpes filled with salmon, white fish and prawns in white wine, cream and basil sauce (£6.50), venison casserole with sherry, chestnuts and dried apricots (£6.95), pheasant in apple and brandy sauce or marinated lamb steaks in honey, soy sauce, ginger and garlic (£7.95), roast rack of lamb with glazed mint sauce (£8.95) and roast duck with Grand Marnier and orange sauce (£10.50), and very tasty puddings; smaller helpings for children. Booking is recommended on Saturday evenings especially; no-smoking restaurant. The plainer public bar has another log fire, and darts, pool, dominoes, cribbage, fruit machine and juke box. Well kept Donnington BB and SBA on handpump and an extensive wine list; good service; piped music. The bedrooms are good value. No dogs – even in garden (where there's a children's play area with climbing frame), and Aunt Sally. *(Recommended by Sheila and John French, BHP, Iona Thomson, John Franklin, Barry and Anne, H O Dickinson, Sharon Hancock, Andrew and Ruth Triggs)*

Donnington ~ Tenant David Smith ~ Real ale ~ Meals and snacks ~ Restaurant ~ (01608) 674397 ~ Children welcome in eating area of bar ~ Occasional folk music ~ Open 11(12 in winter)-2.30(3 Sat), 6-11; 12-3, 7-10.30 Sun ~ Bedrooms: £24/£36 (no under 8s)

LOWSONFORD SP1868 Map 4
Fleur de Lys ♀

Village signposted off B4439 Hockley Heath—Warwick; can be reached too from B4095 via Preston Bagot

One of the best canalside pubs, this holds a successful balance between the lovely setting which acts as quite a crowd puller on sunny days – with people gathering at picnic tables on the grass among tall weeping willows by the Stratford-upon-Avon Canal – and the civilised village dining atmosphere inside. The big comfortable spreading bar has lots of low black beams in the butter-coloured ceiling, brocade-cushioned mate's, wheelback and dining chairs around the well spaced tables, and rugs on the flagstones and antique tiles. Down steps on the right is a log fire and a couple of long settles; newspapers, magazines and unobtrusive piped music. Bar food includes soup (£1.95), stilton mushrooms (£2.95), soup and sandwich (£3.95), bangers and mash (£4.45), ploughman's or plaice and chips (£4.85) steak and ale pie or salads like hot chicken and bacon (£5.95), chicken breast in lemon and ginger sauce

(£6.25), salmon in butter and tarragon sauce (£6.95), rack of lamb (£8.45), 8oz sirloin steak (£8.95), and puddings (from £2.25); there may be delays on hot days when busy; no-smoking dining area. Well kept Flowers Original, Wadworths 6X and a guest on handpump, and decent wines including good New World ones (lots by the glass). Although there are no family facilities inside, there's a good play area outside. *(Recommended by Chris Walling, Brian Skelcher, D P Brown, John Franklin, C A Hall, Roy Bromell, M L and G Clarke, Karen Eliot, Mike Begley, Nigel Clifton, Stephen, Julie and Hayley Brown, Aland and Paula McCully)*

Whitbreads ~ Manager David Tye ~ Real ale ~ Meals and snacks ~ (01564) 782431 ~ Children welcome in eating area of bar ~ Open 11-11; 12-10.30 Sun; cl 25 Dec evening

MONKS KIRBY SP4683 Map 4
Bell 🍴 ♀

Just off B4027 (former A427) W of Pailton; Bell Lane

As well as the quite astonishing range of hugely tempting Spanish dishes on their menu, they're now offering a list of even more tapas on a blackboard at this timbered old pub. Our inspection meal consisted of a splendid selection of these delicious garlic-drenched tapas, all served in little frying pans, such as grilled sardines, prawns in white wine, garlic and chilli, Spanish salami cooked in garlic and white wine, squid fried in butter or cooked modizo-style, king prawns in garlic and chilli, and scallops cooked with white wine, tomato, lemon juice and breadcrumbs (from £3.75-£4.75). There are plenty of Spanish dishes among the main courses as well: vegetable paella (£6.25), rabbit in garlic, white wine and tomato sauce (£6.75), grilled loin of pork with garlic, white wine, lemon and parsley (£8.25), paellas (from £7.75), tuna in an iron pan cooked with tomatoes, white wine and prawns or honey-roasted saddle of lamb with red wine sauce (£9.95), salmon with chorizo in a white wine sauce (£10.75), steak flamed with port and topped with pâté and mixed sea grill (£11.75). There's a comfortably informal southern European atmosphere in the dusky flagstoned bars where locals chat with the friendly licensee from Santiago de Compostella; no-smoking dining area. As well as well kept Boddingtons and Flowers Original on handpump there's a very good wine list, ports for sale by the bottle and a healthy range of brandies and malt whiskies. The plain little back terrace has rough-and-ready rustic woodwork, geese and chickens and a pretty little view across a stream to a buttercup meadow. Fairly loud piped music. *(Recommended by Stephen Brown, D P Brown, Susan and John Douglas, Heather Roberts, Michael Begley, Ted George, Luke Worthington, Roy Bromell, Mike Begley, Stephen, Julie and Hayley Brown)*

Free house ~ Licensees Paco and Belinda Maures ~ Real ale ~ Meals and snacks (during opening hours) ~ (01788) 832352 ~ Children welcome ~ 12-2.30, 7-10.30; cl Mon lunchtime; cl 26 Dec, 1 Jan

NETHERTON SO9387 Map 4
Little Dry Dock

Windmill End, Bumble Hole; you really need an A-Z street map to find it or OS Sheet 139 map reference 953881

Readers love the characterfully friendly atmosphere at this tiny but lively and eccentric, red, white and blue painted canalside pub. An entire narrow-boat is squeezed into the right-hand bar and used as the servery (its engine is in the room on the left), and there's also a huge model boat in one front transom-style window, winches and barge rudders flanking the door, marine windows, and lots of brightly coloured bargees' water pots, lanterns, jugs and lifebuoys; fruit machine and piped music. They have their own Little Lumphammer ale brewed for them by Carlsberg Tetleys as well as Ind Coope Burton, Marstons Pedigree and Morlands Old Speckled Hen well kept on hand or electric pump, and fruit wines; friendly service. Very generous helpings of simple good value bar food include soup (£1.75), black pudding thermidor (£2.10), faggots and peas (£4.45), home-cooked ham with parsley sauce or chilli (£4.50), lasagne (£4.65), scampi, fish or minted lamb pie (£4.95), gammon and egg (£5.20), steak and kidney in Guinness pie (£5.25), rump steak (£6.25) and mixed grill (£6.95), and traditional puddings (from £1.75). There are pleasant towpath walks nearby. *(Recommended by Mike and Wendy Proctor, Lucy James, Dean Foden, Peter and Jenny Quine, Anthony Marriott, Howard West, Pat and John Millward)*

Carlsberg Tetleys ~ Tenant Frank Pearson ~ Real ale ~ Meals and snacks (till 10pm) ~ (01384) 235369 ~ Children welcome ~ Irish folk music Mon evenings ~ Open 11-3, 6(5.30 Sat)-11; 12-3, 6-10.30 Sun

NEWBOLD ON STOUR SP2446 Map 4
White Hart

A34 Shipston on Stour—Stratford

Readers enjoy the wide range of tasty, reasonably priced food served in good sized helpings at this welcoming 15th-c pub: soup (£2.25), home-made chicken liver pâté or garlic mushrooms in cream and white wine (£3.95), home-baked ham and eggs (£5.95), or grilled fresh local trout with almonds (£6.85) chicken breast poached in cider with rosemary and fresh cream (£7.25), steaks (from £7.65), and daily specials like fried lamb kidneys with garlic, sherry and cream or seafood pie (£5.95) fishcakes with parsley sauce (£6.50), lamb braised in cream and asparagus sauce (£6.85), knuckle of lamb braised in wine with garlic and herbs (£6.95), grilled chicken breast topped with ham and smoked cheese (£7.25) and puddings like treacle tart and chocolate and brandy trifle (£2.50). It's best to book weekend evenings and for the two-course Sunday lunch (£8.95). The atmospheric airy beamed main bar – partly divided by stub walls and the chimney – has modern high-backed winged settles, seats set into big bay windows, a fair amount of brass, and a gun hanging over the log fire in one big stone fireplace. The roomy back public bar has pool, dominoes, fruit machine and juke box; very well kept Bass and M&B Brew XI on handpump. There are picnic tables under cocktail parasols and boules in front of the pub, with its well tended hanging baskets, and giant draughts at the back. *(Recommended by Colin Fisher, Dave Braisted, John Bowdler, Derek Allpass, Peter Lloyd, Michael Butler; more reports please)*

M&B (Bass) ~ Lease: Mr and Mrs J C Cruttwell ~ Real ale ~ Meals and snacks (not Sun evening) ~ Restaurant ~ (01789) 450205 ~ Children welcome ~ Open 11-2.30, 6-11; 11-11 Sat

SAMBOURNE SP0561 Map 4
Green Dragon

A435 N of Alcester, then left fork onto A448 just before Studley; village signposted on left soon after

Good standards are steadily maintained at this pretty cottage which is peacefullly placed by a historic village green. There's a warm welcome for every customer at lunchtime when it quickly fills up with people coming for the impressive range of very good bar food: nice sandwiches (from £1.95), home-made soup (£2.50), home-made pâté (£2.95), sausage and mash, home-made steak pie and very good curry (all £5.50), five interesting vegetarian dishes like roasted peppers stuffed with tomato and mozarella with oregano and white wine sauce (£5.95), steaks (from £9.25), roast duckling with port and redcurrant sauce (£10.50), fried salmon and monkfish with white wine sauce (£10.95), and beef wellington (£14.50) and several daily specials like salmon fishcake or steak and kidney pudding (£5.95) and fresh dressed crab (£6.95); puddings (£2.50), and children's menu (from £2.50). The cheery modernised beamed communicating rooms have little armed seats and more upright ones, some small settles, and open fires; piped music. Well kept Bass, Hobsons, and M & B Brew XI on handpump; cheerful, attentive service. It's very pretty in summer with its climbing roses around the shuttered and timbered facade, and picnic tables and teak seats among flowering cherries on a side courtyard, by the car park. We'd be very interested to hear from readers about the new bedrooms. *(Recommended by John Franklin, Ian Phillips, B Adams, Mike Gorton, Kay Neville-Rolfe, Tom Gondris, Michael Begley, J H Kane, Alan and Paula McCully)*

M & B (Bass) ~ Lease: Phil and Pat Burke ~ Real ale ~ Meals and snacks (till 10; not Sun) ~ Restaurant (not Sun) ~ (01527) 892465 ~ Children welcome in eating area of bar ~ Open 11-3, 6(5.30 Fri)-11; 12-3, 7-10.30 Sun; cl 25 Dec evening ~ Bedrooms: £48B/£60B

SHUSTOKE SP2290 Map 4
Griffin ◨

5 miles from M6, junction 4; A446 towards Tamworth, then right on to B4114 and go straight through Coleshill; pub is at Furnace End, a mile E of village

Very little changes from year to year at this popular unpretentious village local. One of its main features is the ten or so real ales served by the cheery licensee. One or two will always be from their own microbrewery which produces very tasty Church End, Choir Boy, Cuthberts, Old Pal, Vicar's Ruin or perhaps Pew's Porter. These are served alongside interesting guests such as Bathams, Exmoor Gold, Holdens, Otter Bright, Theakstons Mild and Old Peculier, Timothy Taylors Landlord, all from a servery under a very low, thick beam; country wine, mulled wine and hot punch also. The simple friendly pub attracts a good crowd even mid week, and the low-beamed L-shaped bar has an old-fashioned settle and cushioned cafe seats (some quite closely packed), sturdily elm-topped sewing trestles, lots of old jugs on the beams, beer mats on the ceiling, and log fires in both stone fireplaces (one's a big inglenook); the conservatory is popular with families. Lunchtime bar food is quickly served even when it's busy (you may need to arrive early for a table) and includes sandwiches (from £1.65), steak cob (£2.45), steak pie, curry of the day or chilli (£4.65), cod (£6), 8oz sirloin steak (£7) and a few blackboard specials. There are old-fashioned seats and tables on the back grass, a children's play area, and a large terrace with plants in raised beds. *(Recommended by Kerry Law, Simon Smith, Peter and Gwyneth Eastwood, Mark Fennell, Lady M H Moir, Dorothee and Dennis Glover, Graham Richardson, E McCall, R Huggins, T McLean, D Irving)*

Own brew ~ Licensee Michael Pugh ~ Real ale ~ Lunchtime meals and snacks (not Sun) ~ (01675) 481205 ~ Children welcome in conservatory ~ Open 12-3, 7(6 Thurs and Fri)-11; cl evenings 25/26 Dec

STRATFORD UPON AVON SP2055 Map 4
Slug & Lettuce ♀

38 Guild Street, corner of Union Street

It's probably best to visit this lively bustling town pub at lunchtime or for an early evening meal before a theatre visit, as it can get very crowded with a younger set later on. The nicely furnished open plan bar has old pine kitchen tables and chairs on rugs and flagstones, a few period prints on stripped squared panelling, a newspaper rack, and a solid-fuel fire; cribbage, piped music, and a few no-smoking tables at one end although the whole place can get quite smoky. Bar food is very popular and includes dishes like home-made soup (£2.55), hot creamy garlic mushrooms (£4.55), baked chicken pieces with mild mustard and mushroom sauce, pasta of the day, cumberland sausages in creamy dijonnaise sauce and sautéed chicken livers in creamy spinach and wholegrain mustard sauce (£5.95), lamb cutlets with herb and honey crust and plum and port glaze, fried lamb liver with bacon and port and onion sauce or chicken breast stuffed with avocado and garlic (£9.95) and duck breast topped with orange and green pepper sauce (£10.95); helpful staff. Well kept beers such as Ansells, Ind Coope Burton, Tetleys and a guest beer on handpump, and decent wine. There's a small flagstoned back terrace, floodlit at night, with lots of flower boxes and sturdy teak tables under cocktail parasols, with more up steps. *(Recommended by J and P Maloney, James Morrell, Ted George, Kathleen Newton, M Holdsworth, Derek and Margaret Underwood)*

Allied Domecq ~ Manager Andy Cooper ~ Real ale ~ Meals and snacks (12-2, 5.30-9) ~ (01789) 299700 ~ Children welcome ~ Open 11-3, 5.30-11; 11-11 Thurs-Sat; 12-10.30 Sun

TEMPLE GRAFTON SP1255 Map 4
Blue Boar ♀
Off A422 W of Stratford; a mile E, towards Binton

One reader told us he thought this old-fashioned country dining pub was the only place to get a proper steak and kidney pie. Popular and consistently good lunchtime bar food includes devilled roes (£3.45), filled baked potatoes (from £3.65), ploughman's (from £3.95), thai spiced crab cake (£4.95), cheese and leek potato bake (£4.25), mushroom stroganoff (£5.75) and half a dozen daily specials like home-made venison sausages (£4.75), thai spiced chicken (£8.25), lamb kidneys au poivre (£5.95), and fresh fish like kingclip (£9.75) and tilapia (£11.95). There are a few more things on offer in the evening (when dishes are quite a bit more pricy) such as poached salmon steak with asparagus, oyster mushroom cream sauce (£9.25), fried chicken breast with pesto, mushrooms and cream (£9.75) and rack of lamb with red wine and rosemary gravy (£10.95), pork cutlet stuffed with black pudding with an apple and cider sauce (£11.25), and home-made puddings. Well kept Courage Directors, Hook Norton Best, Marstons Pedigree, Morlands Old Speckled Hen and Theakstons XB on handpump, and nearly 40 different wines with several by the glass. There are several good log fires in the comfortable atmospheric beamed rooms, with cast-iron-framed tables and built-in wall and bow-window seats, and cribbage, dominoes and sensibly placed darts in a flagstoned side room stripped back to golden Binton stone. The comfortable stripped-stone restaurant, with its own log fire and a glass-covered old well, is very popular, with excellent service and a small no-smoking section. It's set in a lovely position with picnic tables overlooking the rolling countryside of the Vale of Evesham. (*Recommended by John Bowdler, Roy Bromell, R Davies, Brian Skelcher, Dr and Mrs M Beale, Sharon Hancock, Genie and Brian Smart, Mike Gorton, John and Christine Vittoe*)

Free house ~ Licensee John Senan Brew ~ Real ale ~ Meals and snacks (till 10) ~ Restaurant ~ (01789) 750010 ~ Children welcome ~ Open 11.30-2.30, 6-11.30; 11.30am-12pm summer Sat; 12-10.30 summer Sun ~ Bedrooms: £39.50B/£59.50B

TIPTON SO9592 Map 4
M A D O'Rourkes Pie Factory
Hurst Lane, Dudley Rd towards Wednesbury (junction A457/A4037) – look for the Irish flag

The strangely eccentric theme which has been put together with real loving care at this buoyantly cheerful place means it's very far removed from any other ordinary theme pub. It's a stylish pastiche of a 1940s butcher's, with all sorts of meat-processing equipment from the relatively straightforward butcher's blocks to the bewilderingly esoteric (part of the fun is trying to guess what it's all for), not to mention strings of model hams, sausages and so forth hanging from the ceiling and sawdust on the floor. Labels for pigs' heads mounted on the walls tell you about the dogs and abbots that are alleged to go into their recipes. In fact the food's good solid value with black pudding thermidor (£2.10), the gargantuan Desperate Dan cow pie complete with pastry horns or fish pie (£5.75), vegetable pie or minted lamb pie (£5.45), mixed grill (£7.45), about four daily specials like cheese and onion pie, faggots and peas or sausage and beer pie (all £4.75), chicken tikka masala (£4.95), and puddings such as spotted dick or gateaux (from £2.25); children's dishes (£2.50). A simpler menu is available all afternoon, with baguettes or filled baked potatoes (from £2.50) and salads (from £4.75); Sunday roast (£4.95). They have their own variable but generally good Lumphammer ale brewed for them by Carlsberg Tetleys, as well as Ansells Mild, Greene King Abbot, Marstons Pedigree and Tetleys on electric pump; fruit machine, juke box and piped music. Though it's roomy, with more space upstairs, it can get very busy (packed on Friday and Saturday evenings), especially if there's a party from a Black Country coach tour wandering around. *Recommended by Chris Raisin, Graham Doyle, Daren Haines, Stephen Brown, James Nunns, Mike Begley, Ian Phillips)*

Carslberg Tetleys ~ Manager Peter Towler ~ Real ale ~ Meals and snacks (till 9.45, snacks all day) ~ 0121 557 1402 ~ Children welcome ~ Irish folk Tues-Thurs ~ Open 11-11; 12-10.30 Sun

WARMINGTON SP4147 Map 4
Plough £

Village just off B4100 N of Banbury

This attractive early 17th-c pub was quite new when Charles I marched through here towards Edge Hill with 18,000 men in October 1642; some of those men are buried in the village churchyard. There's a nicely relaxed unambitious local atmosphere in the warmly cosy bar which has old photographs of the village and locals, an old high-backed winged settle, cushioned wall seats and lots of comfortable Deco small armed chairs and library chairs, and good winter log fires. Well kept Hook Norton Best and Marstons Pedigree on handpump, and several malt whiskies; darts, dominoes, cribbage and piped pop music. Simple but very generously served meals include cottage pie or chilli (£3.95), flavoursome home-baked ham, egg and chips (£4.95) and ploughman's (£4.50), and a popular Sunday lunch. It's very well placed in a delightful village a few yards up a quiet lane from a broad sloping green with duck pond and ducks, and it looks especially pretty in the autumn, when the creeper over the front of the building turns a striking crimson colour. *(Recommended by Sheila and John French, John Bowdler, Ted George, Brian and Anna Marsden, Andrew and Jo Litten, Susan and John Douglas, Alan and Paula McCully)*

Free house ~ Licensee Denise Willson ~ Real ale ~ Meals and snacks (till 8.30pm; not Sun or bank hol Mon evening) ~ (01295) 690666 ~ Children in eating area ~ Open 12-3, 6-11; 12-3, 7-10.30 Sun; cl evening 25 Dec

WOOTTON WAWEN SP1563 Map 4
Bulls Head ⑩

Stratford Road; A34 N of Stratford

There's usually a daily choice of about seven, often unusual, fresh fish dishes such as squid, marlin, strawberry grouper, tilapia or john dory, all priced according to the day's market (that tends to mean double figures) at this smart black and white Elizabethan timbered dining pub (booking is advised). Other dishes include soup (£2.95), roast pepper and goat's cheese tart (£4.70), smoked haddock chowder (£4.95), roast red and yellow peppers filled with mushroom and parmesan risotto (£7), grilled spiced lamb kebabs with yoghurt, mint and coriander dressing and couscous (£7.25), roast pork loin on dijon mash with madeira flavoured gravy (£8.25), fried calf liver with smoky bacon (£10.50), seared duck breast with honey and Chinese five spice (£10.75), seafood platter for two (£35), and puddings such as banana and toffee pancakes with clotted cream, sticky ginger cake with stem ginger and chocolate and Grand Marnier mousse (from £3.25), and farmhouse cheeses (£4.95). The attractive low-ceilinged L-shaped lounge has massive timber uprights, fairly smart decorations and furnishings that go well with the building, and rugs setting off the good flagstones; there's also a rather austere tap room with pews and a sawdusted floor, and a handsome restaurant. There are fresh flowers, and service by the notably friendly enthusiastic young staff is quick. Well kept Fullers London Pride, Marstons Bitter and Pedigree, Morlands Old Speckled Hen and Wadworths 6X on handpump, and several wines by the glass; dominoes, shove-ha'penny. There are tables out in the garden, with some in a vigorous young vine arbour. It's handy for walks by the Stratford Canal. *(Recommended by Mr and Mrs B J Cox, Mr and Mrs M J Bastin, Liz Bell, Rydon Bend, Kim Maidment, Philip Vernon, Paul and Maggie Baker, Neville Kenyon, Mike and Wendy Proctor, Paul Leather, Julian Kirwan-Taylor, Gethin Lewis, Sue Holland, Dave Webster, Alan and Paula McCully, Fhiona Skaife, Dayl Gallacher, S Palmer)*

Free house ~ Licensee John Willmott ~ Real ale ~ Meals and snacks (till 10) ~ Restaurant ~ (01564) 792511 ~ Children welcome ~ Open 12-3, 6-11; 12-3, 7-10.30 Sun

Lucky Dip

Besides the fully inspected pubs, you might like to try these Lucky Dips recommended to us and described by readers (if you do, please send us reports):

Alcester [34 High St; SP0857], *Three Tuns*: Unspoilt single Jacobean room, flagstones, low ceilings, whited wattle and daub walls, plain furniture, own-brew beer not unlike Bathams, other well kept ales such as Crouch Vale and Burton Bridge, friendly service, cheery customers, no food; occasional jazz *(G Coates, Rona Murdoch)*

Amblecote W Mid [196 Collis St; SO8985], *Robin Hood*: Cosy and informal open-plan local, changing well kept ales inc Bathams, the unique honeyed Enville and a Mild, farm ciders, good value food in dining area, friendly staff, children allowed till 8.30 if eating; comfortable bedrooms *(Andrew Rogers, Amanda Milsom)*

Ansty [B4065 NE of Coventry; SP3983], *Rose & Castle*: Popular low-beamed pub with particularly good friendly service, wide choice of good value food, well kept Bass, Holt Plant & Deakins and other ales inc a rotating guest beer, some canal-bank decoration; not big, fills up quickly; children welcome, lovely canalside garden with play area *(Andy and Jill Kassube, Brian Attmore, Lawrence Sale, Thomas and Audrey Nott)*

☆ **Ardens Grafton** [towards Wixford – OS Sheet 150 map ref 114538; SP1153], *Golden Cross*: Pleasant L-shaped room lined with cases of teddy bears and dolls, also Shakespearean murals, photographic magazines (local society meets here); good generous bar food, well kept Badger Tanglefoot, Bass, Tetleys and up to three guests, very welcoming efficient service, unobtrusive piped music, fruit machine, restaurant with antique doll collection; seats outside, nice views *(Dave Braisted, Andy and Jill Kassube, Dr and Mrs M Beale, Alan and Barbara Mence)*

Armscote [off A3400 Stratford—Shipston; SP2444], *Armscote Inn*: Spotlessly clean free house in picturesque Cotswold stone village, warm atmosphere, good presented food, friendly service, well kept beers inc Hook Norton Best and a guest *(J H Kane)*

Aston Cantlow [SP1359], *Kings Head*: Pretty village local not far from Mary Arden's Wilmcote, lots of timbers and low beams, flagstones, inglenook, cheery log fire, well used old furniture inc settles, grandfather clock; good prompt straightforward food (not Sun or Mon evenings) from sandwiches to steaks, well kept Whitbreads-related ales, friendly landlord and cat *(Mary Walters, LYM)*

Barford [A429, handy for M40; SP2760], *Joseph Arch*: Well kept Flowers and Theakstons and good reasonably priced generous food in pub named for founder of agricultural workers' union *(Dave Braisted, Neville Kenyon)*

Barston W Mid [from M42 junction 5, A4141 towards Warwick, first left, then signed; SP2078], *Bulls Head*: Attractive partly Tudor village local, oak-beamed bar with log fires and Buddy Holly memorabilia, comfortable lounge with pictures and plates, dining room, friendly relaxed service, good value basic food, well kept Bass, M&B Brew XI and Tetleys, secluded garden, hay barn behind *(Joan and Tony Walker, Brian Skelcher, PB)*; [Barston Lane], *Malt Shovel*: Friendly old-fashioned local, good value food in converted barn restaurant, lunchtime bar snacks, well kept Bass, wide range of wines, no gaming machines, great landlady, pleasant garden *(Liz and John Soden, Paul Whitehead)*

Baxterley [SP2797], *Rose*: Large warm pub with family area, huge choice of good food, well kept Bass and other beers; pleasant garden by village duckpond *(Andrew Ward)*

Bidford on Avon [High St; SP1051], *Frog & Bulrush*: Riverside pub with good range of unusual bar food from interestingly filled fresh-baked baguettes to substantial main dishes, Bass and other well kept ales, carefully chosen house wines; tables outside *(John and Moira Cole)*

Birmingham [308 Bradford St, Digbeth], *Anchor*: Perfectly preserved three-room Edwardian pub, carefully restored art nouveau glass, long high-ceilinged bar with basic seating, well kept Ansells Mild, Everards Tiger and Tetleys, interesting quickly changing guest beers, beer festivals; well priced food all day inc huge chip butties, friendly staff, back games room with pool, TV, juke box; tables outside *(Richard Lewis, SLC, G Coates)*; [Hurst St/Bromsgrove St], *Australian Bar*: Banks's, Boddingtons, Davenports, juke box and fruit machines (can be noisy), bar food *(SLC)*; [144 High St, Aston (A34) – easily reached from M6 junction 6], *Bartons Arms*: Magnificent specimen of Edwardian pub architecture, with inventive series of richly decorated rooms from the palatial to the snug; well kept M&B ales, limited food; piped music can be a bit loud; open all day *(Chris Raisin, Graham Doyle, LYM)*; [Factory Rd, Hockley], *Black Eagle*: Character old pub with good varied low-priced home-cooked food, good friendly service, well kept beers *(E A Moore)*; [Broad St], *Brasshouse*: Comfortably refurbished former bank, so popular they have doormen and queues after 9; good food inc baltis and gourmet nights, helpful friendly staff, well kept Marstons Pedigree and Tetleys; nightly DJs exc Mon *(Richard Lewis, David Marshall)*; [1 Price St, Aston, off A34], *Bulls Head*: Unspoilt side-street local with displays of guns, bullets etc, open all day, breakfast from 7am, cheap sizzler food, real ales *(Steve Jennings, Dave Braisted)*; [182 Corporation St], *Crown*: Open all day, with food all day, well kept Bass, good atmosphere, bars upstairs and down, SkyTV, Sun quiz night *(SLC)*; [Bennetts Hill], *Factotum & Firkin*:

Friendly and lively big hall with balcony, side bar, bare boards, lots of artefacts, red telephone box, friendly staff; usual food, well kept beers, theme nights, stage for live music *(Richard Lewis)*; [76 Franchise St, Perry Barr], *Fellow & Firkin*: Studenty pub with well kept ales and generous food *(Steve Jennings)*; [Corporation St, outer end], *Fibber McGees*: Large Irish theme pub with bare boards, high ceilings, memorabilia, pleasant welcome, bar food, Marstons Pedigree *(SLC)*; [236 Broad St], *Figure of Eight*: Large open-plan Wetherspoons pub with raised side area, nicely decorated and furnished, no-smoking areas, lots of old books, friendly efficient staff, good choice of food all day, no music, good range of Scottish Courage and other well kept beers, sensible prices *(Richard Lewis)*; [Cambrian Wharf, Kingston Row – central canal area], *Flapper & Firkin*: Popular bare-boards two-floor canalside pub behind Symphony Hall, typical Firkin features, lots of wood, own brew and guest ales, reasonably priced food, friendly staff; piped music may be loud, TV, some live entertainment, skittles Weds, tables outside *(SLC, Richard Lewis)*; [Margaret St/Cornwall St, basement of BMI], *Keys*: Ten well kept interesting real ales, an American Boston Beer on tap, nicely refurbished restaurant separated from bar and games area, friendly staff, good food esp baltis; calls itself a club, but more like a pub, open all day till 10 (not Sun) *(Richard Lewis)*; [157 Barford St, Digbeth], *Lamp*: Two small well furnished rooms, cosy and intimate, lunchtime food, well kept ales such as Batemans Mild, Boddingtons, Stanway Stanney and Wadworths 6X; open 12-11 (cl Sun afternoon) *(Richard Lewis, SLC)*; [King Edwards Rd, Brindley Pl], *Malt House*: Handsome and spacious Greenalls conversion in main new canal development, lots of wood, some balcony tables, decent range of food, live music some nights, well kept ales; service mostly if not universally good; handy for National Indoor Arena, Convention Centre and Symphony Hall, bouncers after 7 *(Rona Murdoch, Paul and Ursula Randall, Martin Reynolds)*; [Palisades, New St – off Stephenson St], *Newt & Cucumber*: Large two-bar pub with lots of comfortable seating, cosy intimate areas, bric-a-brac, friendly staff, extensive well priced menu, no-smoking areas, well kept Bass and related ales with changing guest beers, cut prices 5-7.30; popular with young people evenings *(Richard Lewis, Mr and Mrs J Brown, Ruth Bott, SLC)*; [Curzon St, just off the middle ring], *O'Neills Ale House*: Irish theme pub, bare wood and black and white tiles, high ceilings, a couple of snugs, Bass and Worthington, bar meals, piped music, back garden *(SLC)*; [1 Lichfield Rd, Aston], *O'Reillys*: Irish pub with food inc cheap Sun lunch, SkyTV, Ansells Bitter and Mild, Marstons Pedigree; handy for Aston Villa FC *(SLC)*; [176 Edmund St], *Old Contemptibles*: Spacious and comfortable Edwardian pub with lofty ceiling and lots of woodwork, a bit spoilt by sales posters and loud piped music; well kept Bass, M&B Brew XI, Highgate Dark Mild and changing guest beers, friendly staff, food lunchtime and early evening (not Sat eve or Sun); open all day, cl Sun *(Richard Lewis, SLC, BB)*; [Hurst St], *Old Fox*: Lots of original Victorian features, central bar with high-ceilinged drinking and seating areas, good choice of ever-changing real ales and good value lunchtime food; friendly staff *(Richard Lewis)*; [Alcester Rd, Kings Heath], *Pavilions*: Tastefully converted big Victorian pub, good range of beers inc Banks's, Marstons and Morrells, straightforward food *(J Barnwell)*; [84 Cambridge St, behind Symphony Hall], *Prince of Wales*: Good traditional stand-alone local (part of demolished terrace), bare boards, hatch service to snug, hatch-served snug, two quiet and comfortable back parlours – one of them frozen in 1900 – ochre walls, bare boards, lively friendly atmosphere, well kept Ansells Bitter and Mild, Ind Coope Burton, Marstons Pedigree and Tetleys; wide choice of good cheap food; piped Irish music, can get packed *(SLC, Richard Lewis, Douglas Smart)*; [Temple St], *Shakespeare*: Refurbished but keeping several Victorian features, friendly staff, well kept Bass, Fullers London Pride and Worthington Best, decent food *(Richard Lewis)*; [115 Corporation St], *Square Peg*: Massive busy Wetherspoons (ground floor of former department store), nicely decorated with pictures of Birmingham's past, long bar, various areas inc no smoking, prompt friendly service, good choice of well kept beers at attractive prices, farm cider, decent wines, no music, food all day *(Richard Lewis, Rob Howe, SLC)*; [Brindley Wharf/Gas St], *Tap & Spile*: Well converted three-level canalside building, lots of reclaimed woodwork, exposed brick, separate areas, comfortable seating, prints and posters, nice fireplace, decent food, friendly efficient staff; well kept expensive beers *(Richard Lewis)*; [Bennetts Hill], *Wellington*: Old-style well worn high-ceilinged pub, roomy and comfortable; lots of prints, friendly staff, wide choice of cheap food from sandwiches up, lunchtime dining area, well kept Scottish Courage and guest ales such as Greene King Abbot and Timothy Taylors Landlord; piped music, back garden *(SLC, Richard Lewis)*; [Edmund St], *White Swan*: Roomy and comfortable two-bar pub with alcove tables, food from sandwiches to sizzler dishes, back dining area, well kept Bass and M&B Brew XI, decent wine, friendly staff; games machine, TV, piped music; open all day *(Richard Lewis, John Wooll)*; [276 Bradford St, Digbeth], *White Swan*: Unfussy but clean and comfortable friendly local with serving hatch to Victorian-tiled corridor, big bar, fire in small back lounge, charming staff, lovely fresh rolls, well kept Ansells Bitter and Mild and Tetleys *(Douglas Smart, SLC)*

Brierley Hill W Mid [Merry Hill; SO9187], *Brewers Wharf*: Smart converted warehouse by shopping centre, usual food, reasonably priced wines; children in restaurant *(Andy and Jill Kassube)*

☆ **Brinklow** [Fosse Way; A427, fairly handy for M6 junction 2; SP4379], *Raven*: 15th-c beams and open fire in dark-panelled lounge, more basic bar with alcoves and plants, collection of mugs and frog curios, well kept Marstons, good friendly service, almost too wide a choice of usual food inc vegetarian – popular and good value; piped local radio; tables on lawn with various pets; said to be haunted *(Dorothy and Leslie Pilson, Andy and Jill Kassube)*

Broom [High St; SP0853], *Broom Tavern*: Attractive timber-framed pub, comfortable and relaxing, popular reasonably priced food, good choice of beers inc Wadworths 6X, good value house wine, efficient welcoming staff *(S Needham, Desmond Dezelsky)*

Bubbenhall [Lower End; off A445 S of Coventry; SP3672], *Malt Shovel*: Attractive inside and out, small bar and larger L-shaped lounge rather geared to food (reasonably priced), beams, brass and copper, comfortable banquettes, quiet piped music, fresh flowers, play area with basketball net, Ansells, Bass, Tetleys and Marstons Pedigree, kindly staff; delightful village *(Roy Bromell)*

Burton Green [Cromwell Lane, SW of Coventry; SP2675], *Peeping Tom*: Modernised pub with young friendly licensees, short but good value range of meals *(Roy Bromell)*

Church Lawford [Green Lane; SP4576], *Old Smithy*: Much extended thatched and beamed 16th-c dining pub with dark woodwork in L-shaped lounge on various levels, good range of food cooked to order from separate servery, up to nine well kept ales, good service; games room, conservatory; no dogs, children welcome, garden with slide *(CMW, JJW, Stu)*

☆ **Churchover** [handy for M6 junction 1, off A426; SP5180], *Haywaggon*: Carefully modernised old pub with good range of rather upmarket food with Italian leanings, esp seafood – Italian landlord; two snug eating areas, friendly atmosphere, must book Sun lunch; on edge of quiet village, beautiful views over Swift valley *(John Brightley, BB)*

☆ **Claverdon** [B4095 towards Warwick; SP1964], *Red Lion*: Tasteful dining pub with rooms partly opened together, hop-hung beams, good if not cheap food, well kept Whitbreads-related ales and Marstons Pedigree, log fire, good friendly and attentive service, no-smoking back dining area, country views from sheltered back terrace and gardens; piped music *(George Atkinson, John Bowdler, BB)*

Claverdon [Henley Rd], *Crown*: Pleasant and friendly, with good choice of generous good value food esp specials, fish and roasts; Ansells *(Alan and Barbara Mence)*

Coleshill [Station Rd; SP1989], *Wheatsheaf*: Spotless M&B Harvester with interesting exterior, traditional interior loaded with farm

tools, relaxing friendly atmosphere, good staff, wide choice of usual food inc vegetarian, well kept beer, pleasant garden *(Dave Braisted, Ian Phillips)*

Coventry W Mid [Lord St; SP3379], *Nursery*: Informal local, basic furnishings and not a winner for decor, but popular for its well kept ales inc changing guest beers and two annual beer festivals *(Mark Fennell)*

Deppers Bridge [4 miles N of M40 junction 12; B4451; SP4059], *Great Western*: Roomy and airy family food pub (all day Sun), model train often clattering round overhead, interesting train photographs, Ansells and Holt Plant & Deakins Entire from new-fangled dispensers (unless they run out), decent wines, friendly staff; play area, tables on terrace *(Mrs B Sugarman)*

☆ **Dorridge** W Mid [177 Four Ashes Rd; SP1775], *Drum & Monkey*: Comfortable and spacious Greenalls Millers Kitchen dining pub doing really well under present hard-working landlady, wide choice of reliable good value food all day (£2 discounts for Lottery losers Mon-Thurs), well kept Tetleys-related ales, no-smoking dining area; big garden with play area *(Jack Barnwell)*

Dudley W Mid [Black Country Museum; SO9390], *Bottle & Glass*: Splendid reconstruction of old Black Country alehouse in extensive open-air working Black Country Museum (well worth a visit for its re-created assortment of shops, cinema, fairground, school, barge wharf and tram system); friendly staff in period clothes, two roaring fires, Holt Plant & Deakins Entire, good filled rolls, children welcome in two separate rooms off passage *(Andy Jones, LYM)*; [King St], *Old Vic*: Friendly service, good value rolls *(Dave Braisted)*; [George Rd, Woodsetton; SO9293], *Park*: Well kept cheap ales from next-door Holdens Brewery, welcoming staff, good low-priced lunchtime food inc hot beef, pork and chicken sandwiches, very busy then; happy hour 4-7pm *(Colin Fisher, Dave Braisted)*

☆ **Dunchurch** [handy for M45 junction 1; SP4871], *Dun Cow*: Beautifully refurbished old coaching inn with handsome central courtyard, heavy beams, fires blazing in inglenooks, panelling, pleasant traditional pubby decor and furnishings, separate no-smoking room, changing good value bar food from separate servery, good range of Bass beers, decent house wines; bedrooms *(Ian Irving, George Atkinson, Anthea Robinson, Patrick Tailyour, LYM)*

Dunchurch [Daventry Rd], *Green Man*: Straightforward small friendly beamed village pub, big back garden, generous good value food, Courage Directors, Marstons Pedigree, Theakstons XB and a guest beer, restaurant, good service; bedrooms *(Anthea Robinson)*

☆ **Eathorpe** [car park off Fosse Way (B4455); SP3868], *Plough*: Big helpings of good food inc some bargain meals in long neat and clean split-level lounge/dining area with matching walls, carpets and table linen, huge piranha in tank by bar, good friendly chatty service; good cappuccino *(Roy Bromell)*

☆ **Edge Hill** [off A422 or B4086 NW of Banbury; SP3747], *Castle*: Extraordinary well renovated 18th-c battlemented folly perched on steep hill, with well kept Hook Norton Best and Old Hookey, Stowford Press cider, charming landlord, quick friendly service, roaring log fire in interesting main bar with armoury and battle paintings, pool in separate room, good ploughman's, other straightforward food, drawbridge to turreted lavatories; children welcome; thoughtfully placed play house in pretty garden, terrace with fabulous views through trees; bedrooms *(Susan and John Douglas, Ted George, Mike Gorton, Angus Lyon, LYM)*

☆ **Ettington** [A422 Banbury—Stratford; SP2749], *Chequers*: Quickly served cheap usual food (not Mon evening) inc OAP lunches Tues and Thurs and reasonably priced Sun roasts, bright neat dining lounge with sporting prints, roomy conservatory, changing ales such as Bass, Hook Norton Best and M&B Brew XI, good service, basic front public bar with games and piped music, pool room; tables in good-sized back garden with Aunt Sally; children over 5 if eating *(Mrs Spottiswoode, Nigel and Sue Foster, John Bowdler, Cyril Brown, M Joyner, K H Frostick, LYM)*

Frankton [about 1¼ miles S of B4453 Leamington Spa—Rugby; SP4270], *Friendly*: Friendly old low-ceilinged village pub with good value food, wooden settles, coal fire, well kept Ansells *(Pat and Robert Watt)*

Gaydon [Church Lane; just off M40 junction 12, across B4100 nr church; SP3654], *Malt Shovel*: Unusual panelled bar with big stained-glass window at one raised end, relaxing atmosphere, good value standard food, Flowers IPA, filter coffee, welcoming service *(Ian Phillips, Thomas and Audrey Nott)*

Grandborough [off A45 E of Dunchurch; SP4966], *Shoulder of Mutton*: Well refurbished creeper-covered pub with attractive pine furnishings in beamed and panelled lounge, friendly staff, no music, well priced ample food, Marstons Pedigree and Whitbreads-related ales; garden with play area *(George Atkinson, Ted George)*

Halesowen W Mid [21 Stourbridge Rd; SO9683], *Waggon & Horses*: Fairly basic, with very welcoming locals, friendly service, well kept Bathams, a house beer and eight or so interesting changing ales from small independent brewers; no food *(Dr and Mrs A K Clarke, Richard Houghton, Robert Catley)*

☆ **Hampton in Arden** W Mid [1½ miles from M42 junction 6 via village slip rd from exit roundabout; SP2081], *White Lion*: Unpretentious inn with unfussy beamed lounge, real fire, nautical decor inc navigation lights, welcoming staff, quick cheap food (not Sun) from sandwiches to steaks inc children's dishes, well kept Bass, M&B Brew XI and John Smiths, decent wine, public bar with

cribbage and dominoes, refurbished back dining room; children allowed; bedrooms, attractive village, handy for NEC *(John and Christine Lowe, LYM)*

Hampton in Arden [High St], *White Swan*: Welcoming old coaching inn with interesting guest beer, bar food; bedrooms *(Richard Houghton)*

☆ **Hampton Lucy** [E of Stratford; SP2557], *Boars Head*: Friendly beamed local, traditional decor, log fire, lots of brasses, well kept ales inc Theakstons and Youngers, prompt friendly service, well presented straightforward food; small enclosed garden, pretty village nr Charlcote House *(George Atkinson, Brian Skelcher)*

Harborough Magna [Main St; SP4779], *Old Lion*: Well run spotless Marstons Tavern Table, reasonable prices, well kept ales inc guests, quick cheerful service, restaurant popular for business lunches *(Patrick Tailyour, Bob Blenkinsop)*

Harbury [Crown St, just off B4452 S of A425 Leamington Spa—Southam; SP3759], *Crown*: Good atmosphere in attractive old stonebuilt pub, comfortable carpeted bar, friendly licensees, good value food inc sandwiches, well kept Charles Wells Bombardier, Freeminer, Theakstons and a changing guest beer, TV in larger room; children welcome, picnic tables on back terrace *(Mike Gorton)*; [Mill St], *Shakespeare*: Friendly service and reliable individually cooked food (not Sun evening) in popular dining pub with linked beamed rooms, stripped stonework, well kept Whitbreads-related ales with guests such as Fullers London Pride and Timothy Taylors Landlord, inglenook log fire, horsebrasses, bright and airy garden room, separate pool room; children welcome; tables in back garden with aviaries *(Jenny and Michael Back, Mrs B Sugarman)*

Hawkesbury W Mid [close to M6 junction 3, exit past Novotel northwards on Longford Rd (B4113), 1st right into Black Horse Rd, cross canal and into Sutton Stop; SP3684], *Greyhound*: Cosy pub brimming with bric-a-brac, good interesting pies and other generous food, proper chips, well kept Bass and Banks's Mild, happy staff, coal-fired stove, unusual tiny snug; booking essential for the Pie Parlour – lots of canalia and quite private olde-worlde atmosphere; tables on attractive terrace with safe play area by junction of Coventry and N Oxford Canals; children welcome *(Lynda Payton, Sam Samuells)*

Henley in Arden [A34; SP1466], *Bird in Hand*: Wide choice of good value food inc bargain two-course lunches, friendly attentive service; pretty conservation town with good churches *(W H and E Thomas)*; *Black Swan*: Good value well kept pub, simple furnishings, friendly staff, good range of food *(Liz and John Soden)*; [High St], *Blue Bell*: Impressive timber-framed building with fine gateway to former coachyard; modern furnishings in beamed lounge, well kept Flowers and Hook Norton, restaurant, back bar, some tables outside *(SLC)*; [High St], *White Swan*: Large low-beamed rambling lounge bar, cosy seats in bay windows, half a dozen real ales, wide choice of good value food from hot filled baguettes to steaks, restaurant; piped music; bedrooms *(Dorsan Baker, SLC)*

☆ **Hockley Heath** W Mid [Stratford Rd (A34 Birmingham—Henley-in-Arden); SP1573], *Wharf*: Friendly modernised Chef & Brewer, quick good value generous food from hot meat rolls to carvery, Scottish Courage ales, plenty of seats; darts, TV, games machines, piped pop music; children welcome; attractive garden with adventure playground by Stratford Canal, interesting towpath walks *(I Blackwell, Alan and Barbara Mence)*

Ilmington [SP2143], *Red Lion*: Unspoilt stone pub, two small bars, flagstones, traditional furnishings, well kept Hook Norton ales, basic food, friendly service; lots of walkers Sun lunchtime; delightful secluded garden *(Bob Scott, J and P Maloney)*

☆ **Kenilworth** [High St; opposite A429 Coventry Rd at junction with A452; SP2871], *Virgins & Castle*: Several dim-lit old-fashioned rooms off inner servery, simply furnished small snugs by entrance corridor, flagstones, heavy beams, some booth seating, coal fire, upstairs games bar, restaurant; cheap bar food (not Sun/Mon evenings) from sandwiches up, well kept Bass, Davenports, Greenalls Original and guest beers; frequent live music, open all day, children in eating area, tables in sheltered garden *(Mark Fennell, JH, RH, Alan and Paula McCully, Stephen and Julie Brown, LYM)*

☆ **Kenilworth** [High St], *Clarendon House*: Comfortable traditional hotel, welcoming and civilised, with partly panelled bar, antique maps, prints, copper, china and armour, well kept Flowers IPA and Original and Hook Norton Best and Old Hookey, decent wines, good value simple bar food, interesting restaurant specials, friendly helpful staff; bedrooms good value *(Joan and Tony Walker)*

Kenilworth [Castle Green], *Queen & Castle*: Busy Beefeater opp castle, quick well cooked food inc OAP discount card, friendly staff, well kept Whitbreads-related ales, quaint corners, beams and pictures; piped pop music, games machines; extensive lawns, good play area *(G R Braithwaite)*

Kingswinford W Mid [55 High St; SO8888], *Court House*: Friendly, with well kept Banks's Mild, Bass, Bathams, Worthington and four changing guest beers, good range of food in bistro-style conservatory, tables out on terrace; bedrooms *(Jon Izzard, DAV)*; [Greensforge; out W of A449 by Staffs & Worcs Canal, over Staffs border; SO8688], *Navigation*: Comfortable lounge bar, separate public bar, reasonably priced generous food inc sandwiches, Banks's Mild, Bass and Tetleys; small garden, pleasant setting with boats working through the lock, nice walks *(Dr A Drummond)*

Knowle W Mid [about 1½ miles S off A4177;

SP1876], *Black Boy*: Much extended M&B canalside pub, good value food, friendly staff *(Dave Braisted)*

Langley W Mid [Station Rd, Oldbury; SO9788], *Brewery*: This previously delightful pub, loved by many readers for its cottagey individuality, has been stripped bare as just another Firkin chain pub, renamed Finings & Firkin; much lamented *(RIP)*

Lapworth [Old Warwick Rd (B4439); SP1670], *Boot*: Busy canalside pub with two small bars, good atmosphere, tasty well presented food, well kept beers, decent wines, reasonable prices, friendly service; refurbished restaurant upstairs, pleasant walks *(Phil and Julia Wigley, Geoffrey and Penny Hughes, Barrie and Jayne Baker, P R Ferris)*

Leamington Spa [Clarendon Ave; SP3165], *White Horse*: Cheerful old coaching inn with good varied lunch menu in long rambling bar, cheap specials, good choice of beers, quick welcoming service *(JCW)*; [Park St/Satchwell Walk], *Wig & Pen*: Large open-plan pub with good atmosphere, dining areas, some upstairs, no-smoking areas, usual food 12-8, weekday early evening bargain suppers, quick service; some piped music, happy hours *(M Joyner)*

Leek Wootton [Warwick Rd; SP2868], *Anchor*: Busy and welcoming, with bookable dining lounge and smaller bar, good choice of tasty food (all day Sat, not Sun), friendly efficient service, particularly well kept Bass and a guest ale, popular with older people, picnic tables in pleasant garden behind *(Thomas and Audrey Nott)*

☆ **Long Itchington** [Church Rd; SP4165], *Harvester*: Unpretentious welcoming two-bar pub, neat and tidy, with efficiently served good value straightforward food inc very good steaks, three well kept Hook Norton and a guest ale, cosy relaxed restaurant *(Roger Mullis, Ted George)*

☆ **Lower Brailes** [B4035 Shipston on Stour—Banbury; SP3039], *George*: Pleasant old inn in lovely village setting, generous well presented food with fresh veg, well kept Hook Norton, good quietly welcoming service, roomy flagstoned front bar with big sripped pine tables and woodburner in inglenook, panelled oak-beamed back bar, smart country-style flagstoned restaurant; provision for children, newly renovated bedrooms, sizeable neatly kept sheltered garden *(John Bowdler, LYM)*

☆ **Lower Quinton** [off A46 Stratford—Broadway; SP1847], *College Arms*: Wide range of good fresh food, well kept Whitbreads-related ales, welcoming efficient service, spacious open-plan lounge with stripped stone and heavy beams, unusual highly polished tables inc one in former fireplace, leather seats, partly carpeted parquet floor, bric-a-brac; piped music, games in public bar; on green of pretty village *(Martin Jones, JO, George Atkinson)*

Meer End W Mid [A4147 Warwick—Brownhills; SP2474], *Tipperary*: Low ceilings, open fire, enormous goldfish in piano-aquarium, friendly courteous staff, good service even when busy, good value varied food inc super traditional puddings, children welcome with own menu, Greenalls ales with a weekly guest; picnic tables in garden *(Tricia and Geoff Alderman, Michael and Hazel Lyons, LYM)*

Meriden W Mid [Main Rd; SP2482], *Bulls Head*: Very wide choice of good value generous home-made food all day in big busy Vintage Inn dating from 15th c, three log fires, lots of nooks and crannies, good prompt service; well kept Adnams Broadside and Bass, ancient staircase to restaurant *(M Joyner, Mrs C Ashton)*

Middleton [Church Lane; SP1798], *Green Man*: Pleasantly refurbished as Vintage Inn dining pub, decent food all day inc fine vegetarian dishes (may be a wait when busy), well kept Bass and guest beer, plenty of atmosphere *(Andrew Cameron, John and Hazel Williams)*

Monks Kirby [SP4683], *Denbigh Arms*: Good pubby atmosphere, big helpings of good food *(Patrick Tailyour)*

Napton [High St; SP4661], *Crown*: Enthusiastic new landlord and well trained chef giving short choice of good freshly cooked bar food, also sandwiches; well kept Banks's and other ales, evening restaurant (not Mon) *(Kate and Harry Taylor)*; [Folly Lane, off A425 towards Priors Hardwick], *Folly*: Beamed canalside pub in lovely spot by Napton locks, three bars on different levels, attractive mix of furnishings inc huge farmhouse table in homely front bar, generous food inc good home-made pies, well kept Scottish Courage ales, two big log fires, back games room; good big garden with play area, wishing well and fine views (also all-day summer shop and small agricultural museum); very busy weekends, but winter hours may be curtailed *(Sam Samuells, Lynda Payton)*; [Napton Bottom Lock, A425 towards Leamington], *Napton Bridge*: Big busy unpretentious canal pub with magazines in pleasant lounge, simpler bar, well kept Greenalls, good food inc a vegetarian dish, open fire, friendly service; piped music, no dogs, children welcome *(Rona Murdoch)*

New Invention W Mid [Lichfield Rd; SJ9601], *Broadway*: Recently refurbished, welcoming and clean, with no-smoking area, good reasonably priced food; children's ball park *(M Carter)*

Norton Lindsey [SP2263], *New Inn*: Clean and comfortable modern village pub, generous food cooked by landlady *(D Green)*

Old Hill W Mid [132 Waterfall Lane; SO9685], *Waterfall*: Friendly down-to-earth local open all day, well kept Bathams, Everards and Hook Norton and three or four interesting guest beers, farm cider, cheap plain food from good filled rolls to Sun lunch, tankards and jugs hanging from boarded ceiling; piped music, children welcome, play area *(Dave Braisted, Wayne Wheeler)*

☆ **Oldbury** W Mid [Church St, nr Savacentre;

SO9888], *Waggon & Horses*: Impressive Edwardian tiles and copper ceiling in busy town pub with well kept changing ales such as Bathams Best, Enville, Everards Tiger, Morlands Old Speckled Hen and Woods Special, wide choice of generous food inc lots of puddings in bar and bookable upstairs bistro, decent wines, friendly staff, simple furnishings inc high-backed settles and big tables, open fire, Black Country memorabilia, tie collection *(Andy Petersen, Richard Lewis)*

Pathlow [A3400 N of Stratford; SP1857], *Dun Cow*: Low beams, flagstones, roaring fires in inglenooks, properly cooked food; good cellar *(D D'Vigne)*

Pelsall W Mid [Norton Rd; SK0204], *Royal Oak*: Cosy old pub by humpy canal bridge, welcoming new licensees, well kept Ansells and Ind Coope Burton, daily changing food, good dining room *(Cliff Blakemore)*

Rugby [Lawford Rd; SP5075], *Half Moon*: Small unpretentious local with well kept Ansells, Ind Coope Burton and an interesting guest beer, friendly old dog, lots of pictures and plates, amazing candlestick collection, open fire, friendly staff, interesting piped music; no food but Sun bar nibbles *(CLS, RMB)*; [Sheep St], *Three Horseshoes*: Friendly Swiss-run hotel with good relaxed atmosphere in comfortable olde-worlde lounge, very well kept ales such as Boddingtons, Flowers Original and local Judges, decent coffee, usual food from sandwiches and good soup up, popular eating area; piped classical radio; bedrooms *(Richard Lewis, George Atkinson)*

Salford Priors [Evesham Rd; SP0751], *Bell*: Small comfortable easy-going pub with good English food at low prices in restaurant, bar with darts, pool and TV, friendly down-to-earth licensees *(Mrs M Spedding)*

☆ **Shipston on Stour** [Station Rd (off A3400); SP2540], *Black Horse*: Ancient thatched and beamed pub with good value home cooking inc Mon-Thurs bargain meals, well kept Scottish Courage ales, properly pubby atmosphere, friendly staff and locals, inglenook log fire, small dining room, back garden with terrace and barbecue, newfoundland dog and a couple of cats *(Peter Lloyd, Alan and Paula McCully)*

☆ **Shipston on Stour** [High St], *White Bear*: Massive settles and cheerful atmosphere in traditional front bar, back bistro-style restaurant, good value freshly home-made food inc good vegetarian choice and nicely filled baguettes, well kept Bass and Marstons Pedigree, friendly staff, tables in small back yard and benches on street; bedrooms simple but clean, with huge breakfast *(Tony Hughes, Mr and Mrs C Roberts, LYM)*

Shipston on Stour [Sheep St], *White Horse*: Well kept Bass, Hook Norton Best and M&B Brew XI, landlord part of local colour, pleasant staff, lovely alsatian *(Neil Porter)*

Shirley W Mid [Tanworth Lane; SP1177], *Cheswick Green*: Extensively refurbished spacious pub, family dining area, indoor children's play area (not intrusive), Bass and

Hancocks HB, good range of wines by the glass, wide choice of food, big garden *(J Barnwell)*

Snitterfield [Smiths Lane/School Rd; off A46 N of Stratford; SP2159], *Fox Hunter*: Attractive and comfortable, with banquettes and hunting pictures in L-shaped bar/lounge, wide range of well presented and reasonably priced standard food inc Sun roasts, Bass and M&B Brew XI; piped music (turned down on request), fruit machine, children allowed; tables outside *(JJW, CMW, Dorothy and Leslie Pilson)*

☆ **Southam** [A423, towards Coventry; SP4161], *Old Mint*: Impressive 14th-c pub smartly refurbished by new owners, two character heavy-beamed rooms, well kept Bass, Fullers London Pride, Hook Norton Best, Shepherd Neame Spitfire, Wadworths 6X and a guest, good reasonably priced bar food, friendly service, log fire; small garden *(Rydon Bend, Richard Houghton, LYM)*

Stonnall W Mid [Main St, off A452; SK0703], *Old Swann*: Recently extended with big new dining area, welcoming staff, wide choice of good home-made lunchtime food inc fine sandwiches and bargain OAP meals (booking advised Sun), cold Bass, M&B Brew XI and Worthington *(Cliff Blakemore, John Barnwell)*; [Main St], *Royal Oak*: Popular refurbished local, four Scottish Courage ales and a guest such as Morlands Old Speckled Hen, farm cider, attentive landlord, varied food esp fish in bar and evening restaurant, also Sun lunch *(Colin Fisher, Cliff Blakemore)*

Stourbridge, W Mid [Brook Rd, Old Swinford, nr stn; SO9283], *Seven Stars*: Large Victorian pub with impressive wooden carved bar, decorative ceramic tiles, good generous food inc all-day cold snacks, well kept Bathams, Theakstons and a guest beer; comfortably bustling atmosphere, nice staff *(Kerry Law, Simon Smith)*

☆ **Stratford upon Avon** [Southern Way; SP0255], *Black Swan*: Great atmosphere, mildly sophisticated, in neat 16th-c pub nr Memorial Theatre – still attracts actors, lots of signed RSC photographs; wide choice of plainly served bar food at moderate prices, Flowers and other Whitbreads-related ales, quick service, open fire, bustling public bar (little lounge seating for drinkers), children allowed in small dining area; attractive little terrace looking over riverside public gardens – which tend to act as summer overflow; known as the Dirty Duck *(Michael Butler, Brian Skelcher, Peter and Audrey Dowsett, SLC, LYM)*

☆ **Stratford upon Avon** [High St, nr Town Hall], *Garrick*: Fine ancient building, with bare boards, lots of beams and timbers, stripped stone, lively evening theatrical character, cosy front bar, busier back one, central open fire, well kept Whitbreads-related ales with guests such as Fullers London Pride, sensibly priced bar food inc good puddings (popular with office workers lunchtime), friendly service, thoughtfully chosen piped music; children

allowed away from bar *(Michael Butler, Alan and Barbara Mence, Angus Lyon, SLC, LYM)*

Stratford upon Avon [Waterside], *Arden*: Hotel not pub, but closest bar to Memorial Theatre, Courage Best and Directors, good baguettes and other bar food, smart evening bouncer; very popular, get there early; bedrooms good, not cheap *(Sue Holland, Dave Webster)*; [Arden St/Greenhill St, nr stn], *Froth & Elbow*: Spacious Whitbreads pub, flagstones, bare boards and beams, well kept Flowers, Wadworths 6X and other ales, reasonably priced bar food, welcoming staff, TV; small terrace *(Nigel and Sue Foster, SLC)*; [Bridgefoot], *Pen & Parchment*: L-shaped split-level lounge and snug refurbished with Shakespeare story, big open fire, decent food, Whitbreads-related beers; tables in garden, good views, pretty hanging baskets *(Mrs P Teasdale)*; [Ely St], *Queens Head*: Authentic local (the only one here?) with decent cheap food inc unusual snacks and Sun lunch, well kept M&B Brew XI and guest beers, welcoming open fire, cheerful long-serving staff; no piped music *(R and D Carpenter, SLC)*; [Warwick Rd, opp Midland Red bus depot], *Red Lion*: Large friendly Brewers Fayre pub by canal, reasonably priced standard food, good range of real ales, modern pub games; children welcome, play area *(Tony Scott)*; [Church St], *Windmill*: Cosy old pub beyond the attractive church, mix of seating and flooring, wide choice of reasonably priced food inc vegetarian, well kept Whitbreads-related and interesting guest ales; shame about the fruit machine *(Sue Holland, Dave Webster, SLC)*

Streetly W Mid [Chester Rd; SP0898], *Hardwick Arms*: Bright youngish Scottish landlord, well kept Bass-related beers, good bar food, friendly attentive staff *(Colin Fisher)*

Stretton on Dunsmore [Brookside, off A45 via B4455; SP4172], *Oak & Black Dog*: Friendly village local, pleasant long room with end dining area, lots of beams and china, fire, tasty good value lunchtime food, good cheerful chatty service, evening restaurant area, real ales inc unusual guest beers; children welcome, garden *(George Atkinson, Pete Harris)*; *Shoulder of Mutton*: Another friendly local with coal fire in snug Victorian panelled public bar, well kept M&B Mild and Brew XI, relaxed welcoming landlord, cards and dominoes, pictures of old Coventry, spotless furniture; spacious 1950s lounge with fancy tiled floor, grand piano and two darts boards; cl Mon-Thurs lunchtime, erratic opening Sat lunchtime *(Ted George, PB)*

Stretton on Fosse [just off A429; SP2238], *Plough*: Pleasant beamed 17th-c inn, small bar with darts, larger lounge, Theakstons XB, good value usual bar food, friendly attentive staff *(George Atkinson, Dr and Mrs A K Clarke)*

Studley [SP0763], *Boot*: Beefeater with good value bar food, Boddingtons and Morlands Old Speckled Hen, restaurant; piped pop music, fruit machines, play area, quiz nights

(Andrew and Ruth Triggs)

☆ **Ufton** [White Hart Lane; just off A425 Daventry—Leamington, towards Bascote; SP3761], *White Hart*: Friendly old hilltop pub with big lounge/dining area, good choice of usual food, well kept Greenalls and Wadworths 6X, quick friendly service; hatch service to garden with boules and fine views (Tannoy food announcements out here) *(J H Bell, Julie Brown)*

Warmington [Warwick Rd; B4100 towards Shotteswell; SP4147], *Wobbly Wheel*: Greenalls Millers Kitchen family dining pub, with decent food, friendly efficient staff, attractive lounge, sizeable indoor playroom as well as play area outside; bedrooms clean and smart if not full of character *(R Vincent)*

☆ **Warwick** [11 Market Pl; SP2865], *Tilted Wig*: Roomy and airy Georgian town pub divided into three neat areas, some stripped stone, scattered rugs on bare boards, country-kitchen furniture, good views over square; well kept Tetleys-related and interesting guest ales, good range of wines, wide choice of good value home-made food (not Sun evening), lively bustle, quick friendly service; tables in garden, live jazz and folk Sun evening, open all day Fri/Sat and summer *(George Atkinson, M Joyner)*

☆ **Warwick** [11 Church St], *Zetland Arms*: Pleasant town pub with limited choice of cheap bar food (not weekend evenings), well kept Davenports, friendly quick service, functional bar, comfortable lounge; small conservatory, interestingly planted sheltered garden; children may be allowed; bedrooms, sharing bathroom *(Owen Warnock, SLC, LYM)*

Warwick [27 Crompton St, nr racecourse], *Old Fourpenny Shop*: Friendly and comfortable split-level M&B pub with five well kept changing guests, lunchtime bar food, cheerful service, restaurant, no piped music; bedrooms *(Ian and Nita Cooper, SLC)*; [30 Market Pl], *Rose & Crown*: Recently refurbished, cosy and clean, with snug bar; good range of food and beer *(Patrick Tailyour)*; [Guy's Cliffe, A429 just N], *Saxon Mill*: Converted mill with long history, wheel turning slowly behind glass, mill race under glass floor-panel, tables in lovely setting by broad green wooded river, delightful views; inside is straightforward Harvester family eating pub, with OAP discount card, beams and flagstones, well kept Scottish Courage ales, summer weekend barbecues, good play area; open all day *(G R Braithwaite, LYM)*; [West St], *Tudor House*: Attractive and popular old coaching inn, lots of black timber, parquet floor, suits of armour; good promptly served food inc ploughman's and yorkshire puddings, decent wine, reasonable prices; piped music *(James Nunns, Peter Neate)*; [West St, towards Stratford], *Wheatsheaf*: Well kept Tetleys-related and guest ales, wide range of good value food from sandwiches to steaks, attractive bric-a-brac, good staff; pool, fruit

machine, two friendly cats; bedrooms, handy for castle; *(Mr and Mrs R C Watson, SLC)*

☆ **Welford on Avon** [High St (Binton Rd); SP1452], *Bell*: Dim-lit dark-timbered low-beamed lounge, open fires, good value food inc vegetarian, friendly keen staff, well kept Whitbreads-related ales, dining conservatory (children allowed here), flagstoned public bar with darts, pool and so forth; piped music; tables in pretty garden and back courtyard; attractive riverside village *(Chris Baldwin, Karen Arnett, LYM)*; [Binton Bridges; SP1455], *Four Alls*: Efficiently run busy friendly Wayside Inn by river, wide choice of generous food inc OAP specials, no-smoking eating area, nice garden *(Philip and Trisha Ferris)*

Wellesbourne [SP2755], *Kings Head*: High-ceilinged lounge bar, lively public bar, well kept real ales, interesting decor, tables in garden facing church; bedrooms – handy for Stratford but cheaper *(Dr and Mrs A K Clarke, M Joyner, LYM)*

☆ **West Bromwich** W Mid [Hall Green Rd, 2 miles from M6, junction 9; SP0091], *Manor House*: Remarkable genuinely medieval building in unexpected spot (ie modern housing estate), with moat and gatehouse; flagstoned no-smoking 13th-c great hall with massive oak trusses and beams, interesting snug upper rooms; a whole lot of mock-medieval paraphernalia, even knight on neighing horse, and apart from the building itself – which really is worth a visit – is best thought of as a jolly family dining pub, with fair-priced meals and well kept Banks's Bitter and Mild; fruit machines, piped music may be loud; children welcome, open all day Sun *(Mike Begley, Chris Raisin, Graham Doyle, John and Elizabeth Cox, Joy and Peter Heatherley, Roy Bromell, LYM)*

☆ **Whitnash** [Tachbrook Rd; SP3263], *Heathcote*: Well refurbished by Greenalls as country alehouse, lots of beams and woodwork, roaring fire, plenty of comfortable seating inc armchairs, big tables, rustic fittings and memorabilia; eight interesting well kept quickly changing guest ales tapped from the cask behind the central bar, six more on handpump; darts, pub games, SkyTV, food all day *(Richard Lewis)*

☆ **Willey** [just off A5, N of A427 junction; SP4984], *Sarah Mansfield*: Hospitable and welcoming, back to its old name (after a few years as the Old Watling), revamped and extended, with small bar area, lots of dining tables in two comfortable rooms mainly given over to eating, Laura Ashleyesque curtains, polished flagstones, stripped masonry, cosy corners, open fires; ambitious range of food from sandwiches up, pleasant young staff, well kept ales inc Adnams Broadside and a guest such as Exmoor Gold *(George Atkinson, PT)*

Willoughby [Main St; just off A45 E of Dunchurch; SP5267], *Rose*: Friendly small partly thatched beamed pub with good value lunchtime food from toasties to fish and Sun carvery, OAP lunches Tues and Thurs, low panelled bar, evening restaurant, Scottish Courage ales, cheerful staff, games room, garden with play area; cl Mon and Weds lunchtimes *(George Atkinson, Dave Braisted)*

Wilmcote [The Green; SP1657], *Mary Arden*: Former Swan House, taken over by Old English Pub Co, bigger tables, comfortable chairs, glass-topped well in smart 18th-c beamed lounge, darts in main bar, Scottish Courage ales, bar food; comfortable bedrooms, front terrace overlooking Mary Arden's cottage, tables in back garden *(Joan and Michel Hooper-Immins, AM, BM)*; [Aston Cantlow Rd], *Masons Arms*: Friendly local, neat and snug, with good generous lunches – can eat in restaurant for same price as bar; well kept Whitbreads-related ales *(Alan and Barbara Mence)*

☆ **Withybrook** [B4112 NE of Coventry, not far from M6, junction 2; SP4384], *Pheasant*: Comfortable timbered dining pub, big and busy, with lots of dark tables, plush-cushioned chairs, open fire, generous bar food inc good value specials, generally friendly efficient service, Scottish Courage ales under light blanket carbon dioxide blanket; piped music (can be obtrusive); children welcome, tables under lanterns on brookside terrace *(Virginia Jones, H Paulinski, Bronwen and Steve Wrigley, Howard and Margaret Buchanan, Michael Butler, Roy Bromell, Thomas Nott, Janet Pickles, John Franklin, David Peakall, Michael Begley, LYM)*

☆ **Wixford** [SP0954], *Three Horseshoes*: Roomy and nicely furnished, with consistently good generous food, interesting choice (esp weekends, when it can get crowded), charming landlord and staff, good range of well kept mainly Whitbreads-related ales *(Peter Lloyd, W and E Thomas)*

☆ **Wolverhampton** W Mid [Sun St, behind old low-level stn; SO9198], *Great Western*: Three-bar pub with particularly well kept Bathams and Holdens, very promptly served good cheap food inc local specialities, lots of railway memorabilia, friendly staff; SkyTV; open all day, roomy back conservatory, tables in yard with good barbecues *(Richard Lewis, Addie and Irene Henry, DAV)*

Wolverhampton [Penn Wood Lane, Penn Common (off A449, actually just over Staffs border); SO9094], *Barley Mow*: Tiny 17th-c

free house tucked away in rural setting beyond a housing estate, sensibly limited range of good home-made food using meat from local butcher, huge helpings, friendly welcome, unusual real ales and cider, reasonable prices; children's play area *(A P Jeffreys, Wendy Proctor)*; [9 Princess St], *Feline & Firkin*: Large lively split-level bare-boards pub with lots of brewery memorabilia, big tables, friendly staff, good value food, well kept ales from sister pub in Stafford, back pool table, machines, games; back terrace tables, open all day, very busy weekends *(Richard Lewis)*; [53 Lichfield St], *Moon Under Water*: Popular and roomy Wetherspoons pub in former Co-op, nicely decorated, with several areas inc comfortable snugs, panelling and prints, friendly staff, good value food, several well kept Scottish Courage and other ales, relaxing atmosphere *(Richard Lewis)*; [Riches St], *Newhampton*: Friendly local with real fires, well kept Scottish Courage and guest beers, farm cider, pool room, bar billiards, folk music upstairs some Sats; garden with barbecue and good crown green bowling green *(Ian and Elizabeth Rispin)*; [Princess St], *Tap & Spile*: Several lounge areas, lots of wood, bare boards, eight mainly unusual well kept changing ales and a farm cider from central bar with interesting glasswork, good cheap food, friendly new manager, daily papers, pub games and games machine; open all day, can be very busy *(Richard Lewis)*

Wolvey Heath [SP4390], *Axe & Compass*: Good value food from sandwiches up, well kept Bass, Hook Norton Best, M&B Brew XI, several guest beers and decent wines, genial landlord, good friendly service, restaurant; piped music *(Michael Jeanes, Genie and Brian Smart)*

Wootton W Mid [High St; SP7656], *Yeomen of England*: Country Carvery with good value food (all day Sun) inc children's and OAP lunches, Scottish Courage ales; SkyTV, pool, games machine, juke box; garden with play area and picnic tables *(CMW, JJW)*

Wootton Wawen [A34; SP1563], *Navigation*: Pleasant spacious dining pub by Stratford Canal, Whitbreads-related ales, good value food inc children's, restaurant; TV and pool, piped music; garden with play area, open all day *(D Stokes, SLC)*

The letters and figures after the name of each town are its Ordnance Survey map reference. *How to use the Guide* at the beginning of the book explains how it helps you find a pub, in road atlases or large-scale maps as well as in our own maps.

Wiltshire

We have really enjoyed checking out the six pubs which we greet as new main entries here this year: the civilised Beckford Arms at Fonthill Gifford, the enterprisingly run Angel at Heytesbury, the friendly old Sun in Marlborough, the thatched Victoria & Albert at Netherhampton with its fine clutch of real ales, the entirely no-smoking New Inn in Salisbury (another ancient place, despite its name), and the stylish old Seven Stars just outside Woodborough. All these in their different ways have decent food – we'd rate the Seven Stars as one of the best places in the county for a really enjoyable meal out. Other top dining pubs here are the Three Crowns at Brinkworth, the White Hart at Ford and the George & Dragon at Rowde; this last has been doing so very well throughout the year that, for the second year running, we name the George & Dragon at Rowde as Wiltshire Dining Pub of the Year. The ancient George in Lacock is another pub that is doing particularly well these days, and other pubs currently on good form are the Compasses at Chicksgrove, the Owl at Little Cheverell, the Raven at Poulshot, the Haunch of Venison in Salisbury and the Barge at Seend. The Lucky Dip section at the end of the chapter confirms how well Salisbury is provided with good pubs. Other front-runners in that section are the Crown at Alvediston, Waggon & Horses at Beckhampton, Crown at Bishops Cannings, Jolly Tar at Hannington and Radnor Arms at Nunton; we're also still fond of the Red Lion at Axford (though its food isn't cheap) and the distinctive old Benett Arms at Semley. Drinks prices generally in the county are close to the national average, but do vary very widely from pub to pub; the cheapest places we found were the George and Red Lion in Lacock and Raven at Poulshot, all tied to Wadworths of Devizes.

BARFORD ST MARTIN SU0531 Map 2
Barford
Junction A30/B3089

The various well cared for chatty interlinking rooms and bars at this atmospheric old-fashioned pub all have dark wooden tables and red-cushioned chairs. Generally busier in the evenings than at lunchtime, the front bar also has some interesting squared oak panelling, and a big log fire in winter. Reliable food includes soup (£2.25), big sandwiches (from £2.50), cottage pie or lasagne (£4.95), falafel with hummous (£5.25), ham and two eggs (£4.95), broccoli and mushroom casserole (£5.25), steak and kidney pie (£6.50), 8oz sirloin (£8.95), children's dishes (£3), and puddings (£2.50); their Friday evening Israeli barbecues (all year round, from 7pm) are well liked; friendly attentive service. Well kept Badger Best and Tanglefoot on handpump, quite a few country wines, and lots of Israeli wines; darts and piped music. Part of the restaurant is no smoking; disabled access and lavatories. There are tables on an outside terrace, and more in a back garden. (Recommended by Steve Goodchild, George and Jeanne Barnwell, Phyl and Jack Street, R Walden, Stephen Harvey, Mayur Shah, Sheila Edwards, Stephen and Julie Brown)

Badger ~ Tenant Ido Davids ~ Real ale ~ Meals and snacks ~ Restaurant ~ (01722) 742242 ~ Children welcome ~ Open 11.30-11; 11.30-3, 7-11 winter; 12-3, 7-10.30 Sun ~ Bedrooms: £28B/£40B

BERWICK ST JOHN ST9323 Map 2
Talbot
Village signposted from A30 E of Shaftesbury

The single long heavy-beamed bar at this charming village pub is simply furnished, with cushioned solid wall and window seats, spindleback chairs, a high-backed built-in settle at one end, and tables that are candlelit in the evenings. There's a huge inglenook fireplace with a good iron fireback and bread ovens, and nicely shaped heavy black beams and cross-beams with bevelled corners. Carefully prepared bar food includes garlic mushrooms (£4.50), sliced smoked trout with mustard and dill sauce (£4.50), lasagne (£6.95), steak and kidney pie (£7.95), pasta with stilton and walnut cream sauce (£5.50), fresh lemon sole (£9.50), fresh rainbow trout (£7.95), chicken tikka masala (£8.50), and home-made puddings like treacle tart, bread and butter pudding and local organic ice cream (£3.50). Adnams Best and Broadside, Bass, and Wadworths 6X on handpump, farm cider, fresh juices and good wines; cribbage and dominoes. There are some tables on the back lawn. The licensees (who are particulary helpful) did warn us that they are considering selling some time in the next year. (Recommended by DP, Joy and Peter Heatherley)

Free house ~ Licensees Roy and Wendy Rigby ~ Real ale ~ Meals and snacks (not Sun) ~ Restaurant ~ (01747) 828222 ~ Children in eating area of bar; no under 10s in evening ~ Open 11.30-2.30, 7(6.30 Sat)-11; 12-2.30 Sun, cl Sun evening

BOX ST8369 Map 2
Quarrymans Arms
Box Hill; coming from Bath on A4 turn right into Bargates 50 yds before railway bridge, then at T-junction turn left up Quarry Hill, turning left again near the top at grassy triangle; from Corsham, turn left after Rudloe Park Hotel into Beech Rd, then third left onto Barnetts Hill, and finally right at the top of the hill

A good combination of well cooked traditional pub favourites and several more beautifully prepared imaginative dishes means there's something for everyone on the changing menu at this popular tucked away pub. A typical day's menu might include stilton and asparagus pancake (£3.50), fried sardines (£5.25), spicy beef and vegetable puff pastry parcels with home-made pear chutney (£4.25), bangers and mash or ploughman's (£5.25), fish and chips (£5.50), warm salad of marinated mackerel fillets with poached egg and blackcurrant vinaigrette (£5.75), warm salad of chicken and bacon or smoked haddock fishcakes with lime hollandaise (£6.50), steak and kidney pie (£6.75), pork loin stuffed with sage and thyme on redcurrant jus (£8.75), rack of lamb with port, thyme and redcurrant sauce or roasted monkfish with orange sauce (£9.95), steamed bass with mustard and tarragon sauce (£11.50). Service is helpful and friendly, though can be rather slow. Well kept Bath Gem, Butcombe, Wadworths 6X and Wickwar Brand Oak on handpump or tapped from the cask, good wines, 40 malt whiskies, and ten or so vintage cognacs. Darts, shove-ha'penny, cribbage, dominoes, fruit machine, video game, piped music, boules. Despite the emphasis on food, the much-modernised bar is still the kind of place you can come to for just a drink – interesting quarry photographs and memorabilia cover the walls, and the pub's great hilltop position gives dramatic views over the valley. There are picnic tables out on an attractive terrace, and it's ideally situated for cavers, potholers and walkers, even running interesting guided trips down the local Bath stone mine. (Recommended by Susan and Nigel Wilson, Comus Elliott, Lyn and Geoff Hallchurch, Brian and Anna Marsden, Meg and Colin Hamilton, Robert Huddleston, John and Wendy Trentham, Dr and Mrs A H Young, Miss A Board, M G Hart)

Free house ~ Licensees John and Ginny Arundel ~ Real ale ~ Meals and snacks (12-3, 6.30-10.30) ~ Restaurant ~ (01225) 743569 ~ Children welcome ~ Open 11-11; 12-10.30 Sun ~ Bedrooms: £20/£30

nr BRADFORD ON AVON ST8060 Map 2

Cross Guns

Avoncliff; pub is across footbridge from Avoncliff Station (road signposted Turleigh turning left off A363 heading uphill N from river in Bradford centre, and keep bearing left), and can also be reached down very steep and eventually unmade road signposted Avoncliff – keep straight on rather than turning left into village centre – from Westwood (which is signposted from B3109 and from A366, W of Trowbridge); OS Sheet 173 map reference 805600

It's not surprising that this interestingly placed country pub with its splendid views, its atmospheric pubby bar, and its very good reasonably priced home cooking is so popular. Generously served food might include sandwiches (from £1.70), pâté (£2.50), very good stilton or cheddar ploughman's (from £3.20), steak and kidney pie (£4.95), steaks (from £5.80), various fish dishes such as trout (£4.90) or lemon sole (£6.25), and duck in orange sauce (£5.95), with delicious puddings (from £1.95). Well kept Courage Best and Directors, Millworkers (brewed for the pub), Moles, Smiles, Ushers Best and a guest beer on handpump, about 100 malt whiskies and two dozen country wines; good service. There's a nice old-fashioned feel to the bar, with its core of 17th-c low rush-seated chairs around plain sturdy oak tables (most of which are set for diners, and many of them reserved), stone walls, and a large ancient fireplace with a smoking chamber behind it; piped music. There may be a system of Tannoy announcements for meal orders from outside tables. Walkers are welcome, but not their muddy boots. The pub gets very busy, especially at weekends and summer lunchtimes, so if you want to eat it's probably best to book. The views from the terraced and floodlit gardens take in the wide river Avon, with its maze of bridges, aqueducts (the Kennet & Avon Canal) and tracks that wind through this quite narrow gorge. *(Recommended by Susan and Nigel Wilson, Charles and Pauline Stride, Peter and Rosie Flower, Andrew Shore, Dr and Mrs A H Young, Stephen G Brown, Peter and Audrey Dowsett, Gordon)*

Free house ~ Licensees Dave and Gwen Sawyer ~ Real ale ~ Meals and snacks (till 10.15) ~ (01225) 862335 ~ Children in eating area ~ Open 10.20-3.30, 6-11; 10.30-11.30 Sat and Sun

BRINKWORTH SU0184 Map 2

Three Crowns 🍽 ♀

The Street; B4042 Wootton Bassett—Malmesbury

It's worth getting here early as they don't take bookings, and it does get very busy. If you have to wait for a table your time will be happily filled reading through the imaginative changing menu which covers an entire wall – they do take orders before you sit down. It's not cheap, but there is a corresponding leap in quality. There might be steak and kidney pie (£8.95), apple and stilton filo parcel with tomato and basil sauce and yoghurt (£9.45), seafood or lamb and mint pie (£9.95), half a smoked chicken with a rich mustard sauce (£12.95), roast duck with mushroom and madeira sauce or baked blue marlin with prawns and capers (£13.45), fried venison with spring onions, smoked bacon and juniper berries soaked in port (£14.45), filo basket with strips of crocodile with stem ginger and of ostrich with sun-dried tomato, oyster mushrooms and capers (£15.95), all served with half a dozen fresh vegetables; the fancier dishes tend to be flamed in fruit wines. Puddings include crème brûlée, bread and butter pudding, strawberry shortbread and chocolate and orange truffle torte (from £3.75). Particularly nice is the way that this has remained very much a pub, despite its appeal to diners. As most people choose to eat in the elegant no-smoking conservatory, the rambling bar is busy with drinkers too, with well kept Archers Village, Bass, Boddingtons, Wadworths 6X and Whitbreads Castle Eden on handpump (and there are ten wines by the glass, and mulled wine in winter). There's a good traditional feel in all its little enclaves, as well as big landscape prints and other pictures on the walls, some horsebrasses on the dark beams, a dresser with a collection of old bottles, tables of stripped deal (and a couple made from gigantic forge bellows), big tapestry-upholstered pews and blond chairs, and log fires; sensibly placed darts, shove-ha'penny, dominoes, cribbage, chess, fruit machine, piped music. This year there's a new terrace with pond, fountain, and big outdoor heaters. The garden stretches around the side and back, with well spaced tables, and looks over a side lane to the village church, and out over rolling prosperous farmland. *(Recommended by Brian and Bett Cox, Laura Bradley, Andrew Shore, T L Rees, Dr D G Twyman, Tracy Lewis, B J Cox, David Saunders, Marion Nott, Neville Kenyon, Andy Petersen, Pat Crabb, Philip Orbell, Lynn Sharpless, Bob Eardley, Steve and Angela Maycock, Dave Irving, Ewan McCall, Tom McLean, Roger Huggins, M L and G Clarke, Mr and Mrs T F Marshall, Cherry Ann Knott)*

Whitbreads ~ Lease: Anthony Windle ~ Real ale ~ Meals and lunchtime snacks ~ (01666) 510366 ~ Children in eating area of bar until 9pm ~ Open 10-3, 6-11; 11-11 Sat, 12-10.30 Sun; cl 25 Dec

CHICKSGROVE ST9629 Map 2
Compasses 🏠 ♀

From A30 5½ miles W of B3089 junction, take lane on N side signposted Sutton Mandeville, Sutton Row, then first left fork (small signs point the way to the pub, in Lower Chicksgrove; look out for the car park); OS Sheet 184 map ref 974294

This photogenic old thatched house is prettily placed in a delightful hamlet. The bar has old bottles and jugs hanging from the beams above the roughly timbered bar counter, farm tools, traps and brasses on the partly stripped stone walls, and high-backed wooden settles forming snug booths around tables on the mainly flagstone floor. It's also very pleasant sitting out in the quiet garden or the flagstoned farm courtyard. All home-made, the food might include sandwiches, soup or pâté (£2.95), mussels with bacon, garlic and cream (£3.75), steak and Guinness pie (£5.95), salmon in tarragon sauce (£6.95), venison (£8.95), sirloin steak (£9.95), and good puddings like lemon flan (£2.75). Well kept Adnams, Bass, Tisbury Peter Austin and Wadworths 6X on handpump; welcoming hard-working licensees. Darts, shove-ha'penny, table skittles, cribbage, dominoes, and shut-the-box. *(Recommended by Howard and Margaret Buchanan, Mark Percy, Lesley Mayoh, Hugh Chevallier, John and Lynn Busenbark, Nigel and Elizabeth Holmes, David Surridge, Stephen and Julie Brown, David and Brenda Tew, David Shillitoe)*

Free house ~ Licensees Tony and Sarah Lethbridge ~ Real ale ~ Meals and snacks ~ (01722) 714318 ~ Children welcome ~ Open 11-3, 6.30-11; 12-3, 7-10.30 Sun; cl Mon ~ Bedrooms: £35B/£45B

CORSHAM ST8670 Map 2
Two Pigs 🍺

A4, Pickwick

For that group of our readers who like their music blue and don't like to see children in pubs, this old-fashioned and quirky drinking house is a splendid example of what's fast becoming a dying breed: under-21s aren't allowed, the emphasis is firmly on drinking, the only piped music is the blues (with live blues Mon evenings), and they don't serve any food whatsoever. They keep an inspired range of beers, mostly from smaller independent breweries. Alongside Pigswill (from local Bunces Brewery) four changing guest beers might be Cottage Goldrush, Hop Back Summer Lightning, RCH Pitchfork and Woods Shropshire Lad; also a range of country wines. The very narrow long bar has stone floors, wood-clad walls and long dark wood tables and benches; a profuse and zany decor includes enamel advertising signs, pig-theme ornaments, and old radios, a bicycle and a canoe. The country atmosphere is lively and chatty, the landlord entertaining, the staff friendly, and there's a good mix of customers. A covered yard outside is called the Sty. Beware of their opening times – the pub is closed every lunchtime, except on Sunday. *(Recommended by Dr and Mrs A K Clarke, Susan and Nigel Wilson, LM; more reports please)*

Free house ~ Licensees Dickie and Ann Doyle ~ Real ale ~ (01249) 712515 ~ Live blues Mon evenings ~ Open 7pm-11pm; 12-2.30, 7-10.30 Sun

DEVIZES SU0061 Map 2

Bear ☞ ◀

Market Place

The big main bar is a focal point for visitors to the town and locals alike, with its roaring winter log fires, black winged wall settles and muted red button-back cloth-upholstered bucket armchairs around oak tripod tables. Today as for 300 years, this imposing old coaching inn is very much the centre of the town. The traditionally styled Lawrence room (named after Thomas Lawrence the portrait painter, whose father once ran the inn), separated from the main bar by some steps and an old-fashioned glazed screen, has dark oak-panelled walls, a parquet floor, shining copper pans on the mantelpiece above the big open fireplace, and plates around the walls; part of this room is no smoking. Straightforward bar food includes sandwiches (from £1.95), home-made soup (£1.95), filled baked potatoes (from £2.95), ploughman's (from £3.25), omelettes (from £3.50), ham, egg and chips (£3.45) and game, Italian or spicy garlic sausages (from £3.95) and home-made puddings (£2.25); there are buffet meals in the Lawrence room – you can eat these in the bar too. On Saturday nights they have a good value set menu. Well kept Wadworths 6X and a guest beer, wines by the glass and freshly squeezed juices are served on handpump from an old-fashioned bar counter with shiny black woodwork and small panes of glass, along with freshly squeezed juices, decent wines, and a good choice of malt whiskies; especially friendly and helpful service. Wadworths beers are brewed in the town, and from the brewery you can get them in splendid old-fashioned half-gallon earthenware jars. *(Recommended by Gwen and Peter Andrews, John and Tony Walker, M Clifford, Jane Warren, A R and B E Sayer, Gordon, Philip Orbell)*

Wadworths ~ Tenant W K Dickenson ~ Real ale ~ Meals and snacks (not Sun lunch) ~ Restaurant ~ (01380) 722444 ~ Children welcome in eating area of bar ~ Open 11-11(10.30 Sun); cl 25, 26 Dec ~ Bedrooms: £50B/£75B

EBBESBOURNE WAKE ST9824 Map 2

Horseshoe ☞ ◀

On A354 S of Salisbury, right at signpost at Coombe Bissett; village is around 8 miles further on

Even if the very welcoming landlord's friend doesn't turn up on his penny farthing during your Sunday lunchtime visit to this charming old country pub, as readers all agree, a visit here is a perfect diversion. The pub is delightfully set – the pretty little garden has seats that look out over the steep sleepy valley of the River Ebble, and a paddock at the bottom with three goats; there's also couple of entertaining dogs. There are fresh flowers from the garden on the tables in the beautifully kept bar, which also has lanterns, farm tools and other bric-a-brac crowded along its beams, and an open fire. Simple but well cooked home-made bar food is served by kind efficient staff, and might include sandwiches (£2.95), fresh trout pâté (£4.95), a very good ploughman's, locally made faggots (£5.95), fresh battered cod or liver and bacon (£6.25), pies such as steak and kidney or venison (£6.95), duck with gooseberry sauce (£11.95), and excellent home-made puddings; good breakfasts, and three-course Sunday lunch (£8.95). Well kept Adnams Broadside, Ringwood Best and Wadworths 6X tapped from the row of casks behind the bar, farm cider, country wines, and several malt whiskies; friendly service. Booking is advisable for the small no-smoking restaurant, especially at weekends. The barn opposite is used as a pool room, with darts and a fruit machine. *(Recommended by Jerry and Alison Oakes, Hugh Chevallier, Dr D G Twyman, R J Walden, Angus Lyon, John David, John and Lynn Busenbark, Mike and Heather Watson, Michael and Hazel Lyons, Tom Hall, Mayur Shah, Percy and Cathy Paine, James Nason)*

Free house ~ Licensees Anthony and Patricia Bath ~ Real ale ~ Meals and snacks (not Mon evening or Sun) ~ Restaurant ~ (01722) 780474 ~ Children in restaurant ~ Open 11.30-3, 6.30-11; cl evening 25 Dec ~ Bedrooms: £25B/£40B

FONTHILL GIFFORD ST9232 Map 2
Beckford Arms 🛏
Off B3089 W of Wilton at Fonthill Bishop

There's a good sedately relaxed atmosphere in this high-ceilinged Edwardian lounge bar, with a deeply comfortable leather chesterfield and armchair as well as the more upright blond chairs on its pink carpet, and a big log fire. It leads into a light and airy back room with similar furnishings but a high pitched plank ceiling, and picture windows on to a terrace; tables on this, and up in the garden sloping away among shrubs and a weeping elm. A separate simple public bar has darts, pool, TV and juke box. A wide range of moderately priced food includes good sandwiches (from £2), ploughman's (£4.95), steak and kidney pie (£5.25) and pork casserole, herbs, tomato and apple (£6.25) and daily specials like poached breast of chicken glazed with blue cheese and bacon sauce or mildly spiced lamb steaks on stir fry (£5.95), game pie (£6.95) and sea bass (£10.95). There's a pretty Laura Ashleyesque dining room. Well kept Courage Best, Wadworths 6X and a guest like Hampshire Lionheart, good value wines, local country wines, good friendly service, piped music. The inn is on the edge of a fine parkland estate, with a lake and sweeping vistas. *(Recommended by Stephen Goodchild, Colin Fisher, Michael and Hazel Lyons, Martin and Jane Wright, N Phillips, Alan and Paula McCully)*

Free house ~ Licensee Steve Clem ~ Real ale ~ Meals and snacks ~ Restaurant ~ (01747) 870385 ~ Children in Garden room and restaurant ~ Open 11-3, 6-11; 12-3, 7-10.30 Sun; cl 25 Dec evening ~ Bedrooms: £34.50S/£54.50S

FORD ST8374 Map 2
White Hart ★ 🍽 🛏 ♟ 🍺
A420 Chippenham—Bristol; follow Colerne sign at E side of village to find pub

It's a fine combination of things that makes this stone country inn so popular with so many of our readers: the splendid food (you will need to book), the atmospheric bar, the friendly licensees, and the range of well kept beers. And in summer there's the bonus of its terrace by a stone bridge and trout stream. Served in generous helpings, the weekly-changing food might include sandwiches (from £2.50), soups such as leek and potato or chicken and vegetable (from £1.95), ploughman's (from £4.25), a couple of well priced specials such as broccoli and blue cheese crumble (£4.50) or beef stroganoff (£4.75), and delicious more elaborate meals like tagliatelle with spinach, sun-dried tomatoes, pesto and pecarino cheese, supreme of chicken with pesto, tomato and olive oil dressing or onion tart with grilled goat's cheese and roasted peppers on a watercress sauce (£8.95), roast pork tenderloin with caramelised apples, marinaded sultanas and a cider sauce (£9.50), wild boar sausages with mustard and tarragon sauce (£9.95), supreme of salmon with herb crust, black olive tapenade and smoked garlic juices and yellow pepper coulis (£10.95), duck breast with sweet and sour red onion confit, honey and balsamic dressing (£13.25), and excellent puddings like crème brûlée and a very popular hot toffee pudding (£3.50). Service is commendably flexible, helpful and very friendly. There are heavy black beams supporting the white-painted boards of the ceiling, tub armchairs around polished wooden tables, small pictures and a few advertising mirrors on the walls, and an ancient fireplace (inscribed 1553). Despite the number of people who come to eat, it's still a good place for just for a drink; beside fine wines, they keep farm ciders, a dozen malt whiskies, and well kept Badger Tanglefoot, Bass, Boddingtons, Fullers London Pride and ESB, Hook Norton, Marstons Pedigree and Owd Roger, Shepherd Neame Spitfire and Theakstons Old Peculier on handpump or tapped from the cask. Piped music. It's a particularly nice place to stay, with a secluded swimming pool for residents. *(Recommended by Susan and Nigel Wilson, D G Clarke, Dr and Mrs I H Maine, Pat and Roger Fereday, Mr and Mrs Mark Hancock, KC, Luke Worthington, Andrew Shore, Eddy Street, Derek Clarke, Dagmar Junghanns, Colin Keane, Val and Rob Farrant, Kerry Law, Kay McGeehan, Denise Harbord, Pat and John Millward, Mrs M Mills, Yvonne and Peter Griffiths, Paul and Nicky Clements, Barry and Anne, Rob Holt, Dr and Mrs A K Clarke, Lyn and Geoff Hallchurch, Susan and Nigel Wilson, Suzanne and John Jones, Steve Willey, BJP Edwards, Viv Middlebrook, G U Briggs, John and Wendy*

Trentham, C H and P Stride, Mr and Mrs J Liversidge, Stephen and Julie Brown, Eric and Jackie Robinson, GSB, RJH, Simon Collett-Jones, Dr and Mrs A H Young, Ian and Villy White, Dr and Mrs M Beale, Susan and John Douglas, A R and B E Sayer, Don Kellaway, Angie Coles, PM, AM, Paul Boot, Brian and Anna Marsden, Ian Phillips)

Free house ~ Licensees Chris and Jenny Phillips ~ Real ale ~ Meals and snacks (till 10) ~ Restaurant ~ (01249) 782213 ~ Children in restaurant ~ Open 11-3, 5-11; cl 25 Dec evening ~ Bedrooms: £45B/£65B

HEYTESBURY ST9242 Map 2
Angel 🛏 🍺

High St; just off A36 E of Warminster

The cosy and homely lounge on the right, with well used overstuffed armchairs and sofas, flower and Japanese prints and a good fire, opens into a charming back dining room, simple but smart – blue carpet, blue-cushioned chairs, lots more flower prints on the white-painted brick walls. On the left is a long beamed bar with quite a vibrant atmosphere, a woodburner, some attractive prints and old photographs on the terracotta-coloured walls, and straightforward tables and chairs. A wide choice of consistently good food includes cream of watercress soup (£3.25), tomato and spinach tart (£5.25), wild boar and apple sausages (£6.25), salmon fishcakes with dill mayonnaise (£5.75), whole dressed crab (£7.25), rack of lamb (£9.75) and duck breast (£10.50); the french bread is made with authentic flour flown in from France. Well kept Marstons Pedigree, Ringwood Best and Timothy Taylors Landlord and a guest on handpump, decent wines, good coffee, hot nuts, cheerful young staff, maybe piped Phil Collins; cribbage. The dining room opens on to an attractive secluded courtyard garden. *(Recommended by DP, Gwen and Peter Andrews, Mrs C Jimenez, Pat and Robert Watt, B Kilcullen, Simon and Alison Rudd-Clarke)*

Free house ~ Licensees Philip Roose-Francis, Sue and Tim Smith ~ Real ale ~ Meals and snacks ~ Restaurant ~ (01985) 840330 ~ Supervised children welcome ~ Open 11.30-3, 6.30-11; 12-3, 7-10.30 Sun ~ Bedrooms: £37.50B/£49B

HINDON ST9132 Map 2
Lamb

B3089 Wilton—Mere

Dating back in part to the 13th c, this prettily set, solidly built old inn is open all day – useful for this good secondary route to the West Country. It has a roomy long bar split into several areas, with the two lower sections perhaps the nicest. There's a long polished table with wall benches and chairs, a big inglenook fireplace, and at one end a window seat with a big waxed circular table, spindleback chairs with tapestried cushions, a high-backed settle, brass jugs on the mantelpiece above the small fireplace, and a big kitchen clock; up some steps, a third, bigger, area has lots of tables and chairs. Bar food includes leek and broccoli soup (£2.50), ploughman's (£3.95), stilton and vegetable lasagne (£5.25), pigeon and venison pie (£5.95), pork fillet with cider and mustard (£6.50), grilled trout or plaice or seafood and leek au gratin and a fish of the day (£6.95), and a well liked good value Sunday roast; the restaurant is no smoking. They usually do cream teas throughout the afternoon. The three real ales vary but might include local or unusual brews such as Ash Vine, Butcombe or Lionheart Ironside, alongside more familiar ales like Fullers London Pride and Wadworths 6X on handpump. They serve just under a dozen wines by the glass, and a range of whiskies includes all the malts from the Isle of Islay. Service can slow down when they get busy, but remains helpful and friendly. There are picnic tables across the road. No dogs. The licensees tell us that they have plans to improve the lavatories. *(Recommended by John Evans, Mrs Valerie Thomas, Alan and Paula McCully, Mrs M Rolfe, Elven Money, Susan and Nigel Wilson, Ann and Colin Hunt, James Nunns, R C Watkins, Gwen and Peter Andrews, Pam and Tim Moorey, John and Vivienne Rice, Colin Laffan, Mr and Mrs G Turner, John and Christine Vittoe, D H and B R Tew, Anthony Barnes, Paul Randall, Ian Phillips, Mrs J A Blanks, Gordon, Peter and Audrey Dowsett, F C Johnston, A R Hands, W Matthews)*

Free house ~ Licensee John Croft and Cora Scott ~ Real ale ~ Meals and snacks (till 10pm) ~ Restaurant ~ (01747) 820573 ~ Children welcome ~ Open 11-11; 12-10.30 Sun ~ Bedrooms: £43B/£65B

KILMINGTON ST7736 Map 2
Red Lion 🛏

Pub on B3092 Mere—Frome, 2½ miles S of Maiden Bradley; 3 miles from A303 Mere turnoff

Stourhead Gardens are only a mile away from this unpretentious 400-year-old local, which used to keep a pair of horses to help the stage coach up the steep part of the Roman road behind the pub. The comfortably cosy bar is nicely individual, with a curved high-backed settle and red leatherette wall and window seats on the flagstones, photographs on the beams, and a couple of big fireplaces (one with a fine old iron fireback) with log fires in winter. A newer no-smoking eating area has a large window and is decorated with brasses, a large leather horse collar, and hanging plates. Good value usefully simple lunchtime bar meals include home-made soup (£1.50), filled baked potatoes (from £2.40), toasted sandwiches (from £2.50), ploughman's (from £3.25), steak and kidney or lamb and apricot pie (£3.75), meat or vegetable lasagne (£4.65), and a daily special such as very good home-cooked ham. Butcombe and Wadworths 6X on handpump along with a weekly changing guest (most likely local), under light blanket pressure; also farm cider, elderflower pressé, citrus pressé and monthly changing wines. Sensibly placed darts, dominoes, shove-ha'penny and cribbage. Picnic tables in the big garden, and maybe Kim, the labrador. It's popular with walkers – you can buy the locally made walking sticks, and a gate leads on to the lane which leads to White Sheet Hill, where there is riding, hang gliding and radio-controlled gliders. *(Recommended by Mike Gorton, Mrs C Jimenez, Mr and Mrs D Ross, Guy Consterdine, Stephen Goodchild, Hugh MacLean, David Surridge)*

Free house ~ Licensee Chris Gibbs ~ Real ale ~ Lunchtime meals and snacks ~ (01985) 844263 ~ Children in eating area of bar till 9pm ~ Open 11.30-2.30, 6.30-11; 12-3, 7-11 Sun ~ Bedrooms: £25/£30

LACOCK ST9168 Map 2
George

Readers like the consistency of standards at this ancient inn, which has been licensed continuously since the 17th c, and under the same licensee now for over a decade. One of the talking points has long been the three-foot treadwheel set into the outer breast of the magnificent central fireplace: this used to turn a spit for roasting worked by a specially bred dog. Often very busy indeed, the comfortably welcoming bar has a low beamed ceiling, upright timbers in the place of knocked-through walls making cosy corners, candles on tables even at lunchtime, armchairs and windsor chairs, seats in the stone-mullioned windows and flagstones just by the bar. The well kept Wadworths IPA, 6X, and seasonal ale, under light blanket pressure, are very reasonably priced. There's a decent choice of wines by the bottle. Good helpings of good value bar food might include sandwiches, home-made soup (£2.10), pork and beef sausages, ham and mushroom tagliatelle, broccoli and cream cheese bake (£4.75), lasagne (£5.75), game casserole in red wine (£5.95), breaded stuffed lemon sole with crab and seafood sauce or scampi (£6.50), chicken breast stuffed with stilton in leek sauce or salmon steak with a lightly garlic-flavoured sauce (£7.25), and puddings like chocolate fudge cake or lemon meringue pie (£2.95); prompt and friendly service; no-smoking barn restaurant. Darts, shove-ha'penny, cribbage and piped music. There are picnic tables with umbrellas in the back garden, as well as a play area with swings, and a bench in front that looks over the main street. It's a nice area for walking. The bedrooms (very highly praised by readers) are up at the landlord's farmhouse, and free transport to and from the pub is provided. *(Recommended by Ian Phillips, Janet Pickles, Brian and Bett Cox, Derek Stafford, Joan and Michael Hooper-Immins, Peter and Audrey Dowsett, Andrew Shore, Clare and Chris Tooley, Terry Griffiths, Susan and Nigel Wilson, Brian and Anna Marsden, Pat and Roger Fereday, JCW, John and Lynn Busenbark, John and Christine Vittoe, Philip Orbell, Nigel Norman, Tom McLean, Roger Huggins, Dave Irving, Ewan McCall, Tim Dobby, Dave Braisted, M Clifford, Romey Heaton, Peter Neate)*

Wadworths ~ Tenants John and Judy Glass ~ Real ale ~ Meals and snacks ~ Restaurant ~ (01249) 730263 ~ Children welcome ~ Open 10-11(10.30 Sun) ~ Bedrooms (see above): £25B/£35B

Red Lion

High Street; village signposted off A350 S of Chippenham

This tall brick Georgian inn is fairly plain from the outside but nicely spacious inside. The popular long bar is divided into separate areas by cart shafts, yokes and other old farm implements, and old-fashioned furnishings including a mix of tables and comfortable chairs, turkey rugs on the partly flagstoned floor, and a fine old log fire at one end. Plates, paintings, and tools cover the walls, and stuffed birds, animals and branding irons hang from the ceiling. Bar food includes soup (£2.25), sandwiches (from £2.85), pâté (£3.10), ploughman's (from £5.50), scampi (£6.75) salmon steak with white wine and cream sauce (£8.95), 8oz rump steak (£9.50), puddings (£2.50), and daily specials; one side of the dining area is no smoking. Well kept and priced Badger Tanglefoot, Wadworths IPA, 6X and Farmers Glory on handpump, and several malt whiskies; darts, shove ha'penny, dominoes, fruit machine, and piped music. It can get busy, and towards the latter half of the evening especially is popular with younger people. Close to Lacock Abbey and the Fox Talbot Museum. *(Recommended by Peter and Audrey Dowsett, Dr and Mrs B Smith, Tom Evans, June and Tony Baldwin, Ian Phillips, Mark Matthewman)*

Wadworths ~ Managers Peter and Ann Oldacre ~ Real ale ~ Meals and snacks ~ (01249) 730456 ~ Children away from bar area ~ Open 11.30-11; 11.30-3, 6-11 in winter; 12-10.30 Sun ~ Bedrooms: £55B/£75B

LIMPLEY STOKE ST7861 Map 2
Hop Pole

Coming S from Bath on A36, 1300 yds after traffic-light junction with B3108 get ready for sharp left turn down Woods Hill as houses start – pub at bottom; if you miss the turn, take next left signposted Limpley Stoke then follow Lower Stoke signs; OS Sheet 172 map reference 781610

Dating back to 1350, the picture-book cream stone exterior of this monks' wine lodge has its name deeply incised in the front wall. Welcoming and atmospheric, the homely dark-panelled room on the right has red velvet cushions for the settles in its alcoves, some slat-back and captain's chairs on its turkey carpet, lantern lighting, and a log fire. The spacious left-hand bar (with an arch to a cream-walled inner room) also has dark panelling, and a log-effect gas fire. Well cooked and presented bar food (you may need to book) includes filled baps (from £1.90), soup (£2.25), trout pâté (£2.95), ploughman's (£3.75), mushrooms in stilton and basil cream sauce (£3.85), a daily pie including steak and ale pie (£4.95), sweet and sour cauliflower and scampi (£5.45), whole local trout (£5.95), duck breast with orange sauce (£6.95), stir fry chicken with smoked trout in mustard and wine sauce (£7.95), daily specials, local game like guinea fowl and pheasant in season, and Sunday roast (£4.95); friendly, courteous service. Part of the restaurant is no smoking. Bass, Butcombe, Courage Best and a changing guest on handpump, with a range of malt whiskies; darts, shove ha'penny, cribbage, dominoes, trivia and piped music. There's an attractive garden behind with a pond and boules, and it's only a few minutes' walk to the Kennet & Avon canal. *(Recommended by Meg and Colin Hamilton, Janet Pickles, Howard Clutterbuck, Chris Foulkes)*

Free house ~ Licensee Robert Williams ~ Real ale ~ Meals and snacks ~ Restaurant ~ (01225) 723134 ~ Children in restaurant at the landlord's discretion ~ Open 11-3, 6-11; 12-3, 7-10.30 Sun

---

We mention bottled beers and spirits only if there is something unusual about them – imported Belgian real ales, say, or dozens of malt whiskies; so do please let us know about them in your reports.

LITTLE BEDWYN SU2966 Map 2
Harrow ♀
Village signposted off A4 W of Hungerford

The three rooms at this friendly village local have quite a relaxed chatty feel, as well as a massive ship's wheel on the left, a mixture of country chairs and simple wooden tables on the well waxed boards (one table in the bow window), a bright mural of scenes from the village, and a big woodburning stove. The two inner rooms have locally done watercolours and photographs for sale, and there might be newspapers and local guides to read. Well kept Bunces Benchmark, Butts Barbel and Hook Norton Best on handpump, and lots of changing New World wines by the glass. There are seats out in the small, pretty garden. Well presented tasty imaginative meals might include soup (£2.95), bacon and brie baguette (£4.25), smoked salmon lasagne with caviar (£4.95), poached artichoke and fricassee of wild mushrooms (£4.75), tuna salad (£5.25), beef, Guinness and mushroom pudding (£6.25), stuffed aubergine with cracked wheat, rosemary and home-made tomato chutney (£7.50) and fillet of lamb with sweetbreads (£11.95), and puddings like lemon torte (£3.20); the restaurant is no smoking. The managers run another canalside pub, the Pelican at Froxfield. *(Recommended by Luke Worthington, Charles and Pauline Stride, C Baxter, Rex and Mary Hepburn, Dr M J Harte, David Rule, Sam Samuells, Lynda Payton, Phyl and Jack Street)*

Free house ~ Licensees Claude Munro and Mita Bhatt ~ Real ale ~ Meals and snacks (not Sun eve or Mon lunch except bank hols) ~ Restaurant ~ (01672) 870871 ~ Children welcome ~ Open 11-2.30, 5.30(6 Sat)-11; 12-2.30, 7-10.30 Sun ~ Bedrooms: £25B/£50B

LITTLE CHEVERELL ST9853 Map 2
Owl ◖
Low Rd; just off B3098 Westbury—Upavon, W of A360

A new pergola with climbers and hanging baskets across the front of this delightfully cosy little local provides a lovely new area of tranquil seating. This is a delightful spot, where at times the only sound might be the cooing woodpigeons in the lovely tall ash- and willow-lined garden behind, with its rustic picnic tables on a long lawn that runs down over two levels to a brook; there are plastic tables and chairs on a terrace above here. Very comfortable and relaxing, the peaceful and neatly traditional bar seems a lot bigger than it really is, thanks to plenty of chairs, stools, high-backed settles and tables; a piano separates the main area from a snugger room at the back. There are fresh flowers on the tables, local papers and guides to read, a gently ticking clock, two or three stuffed owls behind the bar, a few agricultural tools on the walls, and noticeboards advertising local events and activities. A couple of well kept real ales on handpump might be from Ash Vine, Bunces, Butts, Hambleton, Oakhill or Wadworths; a blackboard lists forthcoming brews, and there's usually a beer festival the last weekend in April and in early September. They also have country wines, maybe farm cider and jugs of pimms in summer; friendly smiling service. Good value bar food includes soup (£1.95), pâté (£2.50), ploughman's (from £3.50), scampi (£5), smoked local trout (£5.95), and about eight daily specials on a blackboard above the fireplace, which might include home-made bratwurst sausages with potato salad (£3.95), curries and chilli (£4.50), home-made pies (£4.95), barnsley lamb chop (£6.25) or lamb en croûte (£6.95). Vegetables are nicely cooked and presented, puddings might include lemon meringue pie (from £1.60), and they do children's helpings as well as specific dishes for them; you'll probably need to book for well priced Sunday lunch (£3.75). On Wednesday nights they do a mixed grill (£5.95), and a two-course bargain midweek lunch (£3.95). Dogs are welcome (they have their own, and a cat). *(Recommended by Colin and Joyce Laffan, Gwen and Peter Andrews, John Hayter, Lyn and Geoff Hallchurch)*

Free house ~ Licensee Mike Hardham ~ Real ale ~ Meals and snacks (till 10; not Mon) ~ (01380) 812263 ~ Well behaved children welcome ~ Open 12-2.30, 7-11; 12-3, 7-10.30 Sun; cl Mon

LOWER CHUTE SU3153 Map 2
Hatchet

The Chutes well signposted via Appleshaw off A342, 2½ miles W of Andover

This unchanging 16th-c thatched cottage with its eyebrow-like curving eaves over the windows really does draw gasps of admiration when people first see it – very pretty indeed. There are especially low beams over a pleasant mix of captain's chairs and cushioned wheelbacks set around oak tables, and the huge fireplace, with a big log fire, has a splendid 17th-c fireback. Good bar food includes sandwiches (from £2.25, steak £4.95), home-made soup (£2.50), ploughman's (£3.95), giant filled yorkshire pudding (£4.45), moules marinières, chilli, half a roast chicken or mushroom stroganoff (£4.95), boeuf bourguignon (£5.25), steak and stout pie (£5.45), tiger prawns in filo pastry (£6.95), and tasty puddings. The five real ales, kept well on handpump and served by a friendly barmaid, will probably be Adnams, Greene King Abbot, Marstons Pedigree, Timothy Taylors Landlord and possibly a summer wheat beer; they have a range of country wines. Darts, shove-ha'penny, dominoes, cribbage, and piped music. There are seats out on a terrace by the front car park, or on the side grass, and a children's sandpit. *(Recommended by Dr S Willavoys, Peter Neate, Stephen, Julie and Hayley Brown, G W A Pearce, Gordon, Lynn Sharpless, Bob Eardley)*

Free house ~ Licensee Jeremy McKay ~ Real ale ~ Meals and snacks (till 9.45) ~ Restaurant ~ (01264) 730229 ~ Children welcome in eating area of bar and restaurant ~ Open 11.30-3, 6-11; 12-3.30, 7-10.30 Sun ~ Self-contained flat: (£35)

LOWER WOODFORD SU1235 Map 2
Wheatsheaf

Leaving Salisbury northwards on A360, The Woodfords signposted first right after end of speed limit; then bear left

The new licensees at this nicely refurbished old pub are well known to us through their successful years at two previous main entries in the Guide, and readers' reports suggest that they've already settled in well here. At the heart of the bar there's an unusual indoor pond with goldfish: to get from one part of the pub to the other you have to cross a miniature footbridge. There's a welcoming and rather cosy feel to the place, and though many of the tables are busy with people eating, the front bar is still used mainly by drinkers. The very wide choice of food includes home-made soups like spinach and broccoli (£1.95), sandwiches (from £2.45), ploughman's (£4.25), filled baked potatoes (from £4.55), country vegetable pie (£5.95), prawn korma (£5.95), mushroom and nut fettucine (£5.95), chicken, ham and mushroom pasta bake (£5.95), steak and kidney pie (£6.15), breaded plaice (£5.25), or grilled chicken breast with garlic and herb butter (£7.25), steaks (from £9.45), and children's meals (from £1.95), daily specials like baked potatoes filled with salmon marinated in dill and honey (£4.95), beef curry (£5.25), haddock goujons (£5.95) and game pie (£6.15), and puddings like apple pie or raspberry meringue nest (from £2.75); part of the dining room is no smoking. Well kept Badger Best and Tanglefoot and a related guest like Gribble Black Adder on handpump, promptly served by helpful, friendly staff; dominoes and cribbage. Good disabled access, and baby-changing facilities. The big walled garden has picnic tables, a climber and swings, and is surrounded by tall trees. *(Recommended by Mr and Mrs Peter Smith, Gordon, Stephen, Julie and Hayley Brown, Colin and Alma Gent, Dr D G Twyman, Phyl and Jack Street, Don and Shirley Parrish, Joy and Peter Heatherley)*

Badger ~ Managers Ron and Ann May ~ Real ale ~ Meals and snacks (till 10pm) ~ (01722) 782203 ~ Children welcome ~ Open 11-2.30(3 Sat), 6.30-11; 12-3, 7-10.30 Sun

---

Bedroom prices are for high summer. Even then you may get reductions for more than one night, or (outside tourist areas) weekends. Winter special rates are common, and many inns cut bedroom prices if you have a full evening meal.

MARLBOROUGH SU1869 Map 2
Sun

High Street

You don't need the annual visit by the town crier in full regalia as an excuse to visit this interesting 15th-c pub – it now has plenty of attractions of its own. It's brought back into these pages, after an absence of some years, by a very friendly and helpful new landlord. The attractively furnished and dimly lit bar, with heavy sloping beams and wonky floors, has brasses and harness hanging above the log fire, benches built into the black panelling, an antique high backed settle, and newspapers. Where possible the reasonably priced bar food is made from local produce, and might include chicken liver pâté or fish soup (£2.50), pies or very tasty fresh battered haddock (£5.95) or sizzling chicken in black bean sauce (£6.50); no-smoking dining area. Well kept Bass and Courage Directors on electric pump, and several reasonably priced wines. You can sit outside in a small sheltered back courtyard. Although bedrooms are fairly simple they are enjoyably placed, one in a garret with a nostalgic view of the high street. The pub itself is nicely placed adjacent to the church of St Peter where Cardinal Wolsey was inducted as a priest. *(Recommended by David Griffiths; more reports please)*

Scottish Courage ~ Licensee Peter Brown ~ Real ale ~ Meals and snacks ~ Restaurant ~ (01672) 512081 ~ Children in eating area of bar and restaurant till 9pm ~ Open 11-11; 12-10.30 Sun ~ Bedrooms: £25(£30B)/£35(£40B)

NETHERHAMPTON SU1029 Map 2
Victoria & Albert 🏠

Just off A3094 W of Salisbury

This thatched cottage opposite the church has a charmingly timeless feel inside, with ancient polished floor tiles, black beams and joists, nicely cushioned old-fashioned wall settles and some attractive small armed chairs, a good mix of individual tables (with little bunches of flowers), and pleasant decorations. The newish licensees keep a fine range of ales on handpump, often local, such as Bunces Sign of Spring and Pigswill, Cheriton Pots and Diggers Gold, and Ringwood Fortyniner, True Glory and Old Thumper; maybe piped radio. Properly cooked food, served quickly and generously, includes fresh fish (from £5.95), steak, mushroom and ale casserole or chicken breast in stilton and mushroom sauce (£6.95). There's hatch service for the sizeable garden behind, with well spaced picnic tables, a fountain and a big weeping willow. Handy for Wilton House (and Nadder Valley walks). *(Recommended by Sally Sharp, Phyl and Jack Street, N Thompson, J Sanderson, Peter and Penelope Gurowich)*

Free house ~ Licensees Sarah and Nigel Allen ~ Real ale ~ Meals and snacks ~ (01722) 743174 ~ Children in eating area and snug ~ Open 11-3, 5.30-11; 11-11 Fri, Sat; 12-10.30 Sun; cl from 2.30 winter afternoons

PITTON SU2131 Map 2
Silver Plough ♀

Village signposted from A30 E of Salisbury

Since taking over this civilised dining pub, Badger have kept its foody emphasis, and, besides sandwiches (from £2.45) and ploughman's (£4.25), the changing menus might include pasta with smoked seafood, dill and horseradish (£4.85), yorkshire pudding filled with cumberland sausage (£5.45), roast aubergine filled with ratatouille with herby cheese crust and couscous (£5.25), moules marinières (£5.95), steak (£8.25), and daily specials like smoked sea trout on sliced avocado with grain mustard and poppy seed dressing (£3.75), fried duck breast with cherry and orange sauce, grilled chicken breast with wild mushroom sauce or grilled whiting fillet on salad leaves with caper and lemon dressing (all £8.95). Old jugs, glass rolling pins and other assorted curios hang from the beams in the main bar, which has paintings, prints and comfortable oak settles. Well kept Badger Best and Tanglefoot, John Smiths and Wadworths 6X on handpump, ten wines by the glass and some well priced and carefully chosen bottles. There's a skittle alley next to the snug bar; cribbage, dominoes and piped music. There are picnic tables and other tables under cocktail parasols on a quiet lawn, with an old pear tree. *(Recommended by J Brisset, Douglas and Jean Troup, Brian and Jill Bond, Richard and Rosemary Hoare, Roger and Valerie Tarren, M V and J Melling, Stephen Goodchild, H L Davis)*

Badger ~ Manager Adrian Clifton ~ Real ale ~ Meals and snacks ~ Restaurant (not Sun evening) ~ (01722) 712266 ~ Children in eating area till 9pm ~ Open 11-3, 6-11; 12-3, 7-10.30 Sun; cl 25 Dec evening

POTTERNE ST9958 Map 2
George & Dragon 🛏 🍺
A360 beside Worton turn-off

Originally built for the Bishop of Salisbury, this pub is the kind of place where visitors instantly feel at home. There's a convivial atmosphere in the traditional bar, which has old bench seating and country-style tables, banknotes from around the world, and pictures of customers by a local cartoonist. You can still see the fireplace and old beams of the original hall. Bar food includes soup (£2.25), filled baked potatoes (from £3.25), omelettes (from £3.45), macaroni cheese or pork and leek sausages (£3.95), filled yorkshire puddings (from £4.25), steak and kidney pie (£4.95), salmon steak (£5.95), daily specials, and puddings like toffee apple cheesecake (£2.50). The dining room is no smoking. Well kept and nicely priced Wadworths IPA, 6X and seasonal beers on handpump. A separate room has pool, darts, shove-ha'penny, cribbage, dominoes, and a fruit machine, and through a hatch beyond here is a unique indoor .22 shooting gallery (available for use by groups, though they need notice to arrange marshals and insurance); there's a full skittle alley in the old stables. At the back of the pub is a small museum of hand-held agricultural implements. There's a pleasant garden and a suntrap yard with a grapevine. *(Recommended by David Warrellow, John Hayter; more reports please)*

Wadworths ~ Tenants David and Jenny Wood ~ Real ale ~ Meals and snacks (not Mon lunchtime or all day Tues) ~ (01380) 722139 ~ Well behaved children in eating area of bar ~ Open 12-2.30, 7-11(10.30 Sun); cl Mon lunchtime ~ Bedrooms:£25/£35

POULSHOT ST9559 Map 2
Raven 🍺
Village signposted off A361 Devizes—Seend

The great popularity of this splendidly tucked-away pub hasn't detracted in any way from its natural rural friendliness, thriving chatty atmosphere and smiling helpful service. Neat enough from the outside, especially in contrast to the long rather shaggy nearby village green, it's spick and span inside. The two cosy and intimate rooms of the black-beamed bar are well furnished with sturdy tables and chairs and comfortable banquettes, and there's an attractive no-smoking dining room. The landlord keeps personal charge of the kitchen, and his good value menu includes sandwiches (from £2.25), cream of vegetable soup (£2.30), ploughman's (from £2.95), corned beef hotpot or scampi (£5.95), grilled lamb steaks with red wine and cranberry sauce (£7.05), poached salmon with tarragon and dill sauce (£7.20), pork stroganoff (£7.95) and 10oz rump steak (£8.95); good fresh vegetables. Particularly well kept Wadworths IPA, 6X and seasonal brews tapped straight from the cask; piped music. The gents' are outside. *(Recommended by Colin and Joyce Laffan, Simon Collett-Jones, Gwen and Peter Andrews, A Sharp, John Hayter, M Hart)*

Wadworths ~ Tenants Susan and Philip Henshaw ~ Real ale ~ Meals and snacks ~ Restaurant ~ (01380) 828271 ~ Children in restaurant ~ Open 11-2.30, 6.30-11; 12-3, 7-10.30 Sun; cl evening 25, 26 Dec

---

Children – if the details at the end of an entry don't mention them, you should assume that the pub does not allow them inside.

RAMSBURY SU2771 Map 2
Bell ◗

Village signposted off B4192 (still shown as A419 on many maps) NW of Hungerford, or from A4 W of Hungerford

This comfortably civilised pub, nicely placed in a smart but picturesque village, keeps a good range of drinks including well kept Hook Norton Best, Shepherd Neame Spitfire, Wadworths 6X and IPA and a guest on handpump, about 50 bin ends, and around 20 malt whiskies. Victorian stained-glass panels in one of the two sunny bay windows look out on to the quiet village street, and a big chimneybreast with a woodburning stove divides the smartly relaxed and chatty bar areas, nicely furnished with fresh flowers on their polished tables; evening piped music. Well presented and cheerfully served good bar meals might include lunchtime sandwiches (from £1.75) and ploughman's (£4.75), as well as soup (£2.45), king prawns in filo pastry with sweet and sour dip (£4.25), cumberland sausage or red onion and cheese tarte tartin (£5.95), fresh salmon fishcakes or battered cod (£6.95), stir-fried chicken with oyster sauce, mushrooms, baby corn and penne (£7.95), red mullet fillets on sweet potato cake with tomato and basil sauce or venison pie (£8.50), and mixed grill (£9.95); children's meals (from £1.95). Tables can be reserved in the restaurant, though the same meals can be had in the bar; one section is no smoking. There are picnic tables on the raised lawn. Roads lead from this quiet village into the downland on all sides. *(Recommended by Tom Evans, Tim Brierly, R J Walden, David Warrellow)*

Free house ~ Licensee Graham Dawes ~ Real ale ~ Meals and snacks (not winter Sun evenings) ~ Restaurant ~ (01672) 520230 ~ Children in restaurant and room between bar and restaurant ~ Open 12-2.30(3 Sat) 6.30-11; 12-3, 7-10.30 Sun; cl winter Sun evenings

ROWDE ST9762 Map 2
George & Dragon 🍴

A342 Devizes—Chippenham
Wiltshire Dining Pub of the Year

The licensees at this warmly welcoming old pub seem to be celebrating the recent purchase of their succesful business from the brewery with outstanding efforts to please their customers. You will need to book to try the exceptionally good cooking, as it is very popular now, although in spite of the emphasis on food, it has kept admirably to its roots: you'll be just as welcome if all you want is a pie and a beer. Ingredients are fresh, well chosen, and used to good effect, with fresh Cornish fish as a special highlight. The deftly inspired seasonally changing menu might include provençale fish soup with rouille, gruyère and croutons, mushroom caviar on toasted brioche or scallop mousseline with spiced lentil sauce (£4.50), smoked chicken salad with mango and dill mayonnaise or crab pancakes (£6), salmon fishcakes with hollandaise sauce or lamb sweetbreads with piquant tomato salsa (£8), skate with capers and black butter (£8.50), fresh squid with lemon, garlic and parsley or roast marinated lamb (£12), monkfish with chive and muscat sauce (£14), tiger prawns tossed in butter (£15), red mullet fillet with orange and anchovy (£16), whole Cornish lobster (£23), and excellent puddings such as chocolate torte with coffee bean sauce, sticky toffee pudding or crème brûlée served with a jug of help-yourself cream (£4). Several dishes come in two sizes, and there's a good value two or three-course set lunch; no-smoking dining room. The bar has some interesting furnishings, plenty of dark wood, and a log fire (with a fine collection of brass keys by it), while the bare-floored dining room has quite plain tables and chairs. Well kept local ales include Bunces Pigswill, Butcombe, Hop Back GFB and Wadworths 6X on handpump, and they have a local farm cider and continental beers and lagers; friendly and efficient service; shove ha'penny, cribbage, dominoes and trivia. *(Recommended by Gwen and Peter Andrews, Dr D G Twyman, F and A Parmenter, Dagmar Junghanns, Colin Keane, John and Barbara Howdle, Pat and John Millward, John Hayter, Lyn and Geoff Hallchurch, Chris Ball, Mr and Mrs M Clifford, A V Neal, Dr and Mrs A H Young)*

Free house ~ Licensees Tim and Helen Withers ~ Real ale ~ Meals and snacks (till 10; not Sun or Mon) ~ Restaurant ~ (01380) 723053 ~ Children welcome ~ Open 12-3, 7-11(10.30 Sun); cl Mon lunchtime

SALISBURY SU1429 Map 2
Haunch of Venison ★

1 Minster Street, opposite Market Cross

There's something about this marvellously atmospheric old building that lures visitors into a long and lingering visit. Built some 650 years ago as the church house for St Thomas's, just behind, it has massive beams in the ochre ceiling, stout red-cushioned oak benches built into its timbered walls, genuinely old pictures, a black and white tiled floor, and an open fire; a tiny snug opens off the entrance lobby. A quiet and cosy upper panelled room has a small paned window looking down on to the main bar, antique leather-seat settles, a nice carved oak chair nearly three centuries old, and a splendid fireplace that dates back to the building's early years; behind glass in a small wall slit is the smoke-preserved mummified hand of an unfortunate 18th-c card player. Well kept Courage Best and Directors on handpump from a unique pewter bar counter, with a rare set of antique taps for gravity-fed spirits and liqueurs; about 100 malt whiskies, decent wines (including a wine of the week), and a range of brandies; chess. A fairly short and basic but useful range of very English lunchtime bar food – with quite a few venison dishes – includes sandwiches (from £2.25), filled ciabatta (from £2.95), ploughman's (from £3.95), spicy Dorset crab cakes or recommended venison pie (£4.50) and steak and kidney pudding, coronation chicken or yorkshire pudding filled with strips of venison (£4.95). The pub can get a little smoky. *(Recommended by Gordon, Howard England, David Peakall, Jerry and Alison Oakes, Stephen Brown, Mr and Mrs Carey, M Joyner, Tim Barrow, Sue Demont, Dr and Mrs J Hills, Frank Gadbois, Stephen and Julie Brown, Barry and Anne, Rupert Willcocks, Hanns P Golez, Lynn Sharpless, Bob Eardley, David Carr, Dr and Mrs A H Young)*

Courage ~ Tenants Antony and Victoria Leroy ~ Real ale ~ Lunchtime meals and snacks (not Sat) ~ Restaurant ~ (01722) 322024 ~ Children in restaurant and one side room ~ Nearby parking may be difficult ~ Open 11-11; 12-3.30, 7-10.30 Sun; cl evening 25 Dec

New Inn

New Street

For many readers, the outstanding appeal of this place is that it's one of the very small but now slowly growing number of pubs which are no smoking throughout. But it's also very attractive in its own right. There are ancient heavy beams, horsebrasses, timbered walls, an inglenook fire in the largest room, and a panelled dining room, with quiet cosy alcoves, and a relaxing unpretentious atmosphere. A good range of well presented home-made food served throughout the pub includes sandwiches (from £2.95), ploughman's (from £4.50), lamb and leek casserole or pies such as beef and mushroom (£6.75), changing dishes of the day such as pheasant casserole or plaice stuffed with tomatoes (£7.95), honey duck with chestnut stuffing (£9.95), good vegetarian dishes such as spinach and mushroom lasagne or broccoli and cauliflower bake, and good sturdy puddings (£2.95); friendly helpful licensees and staff, well kept Badger Best and Tanglefoot and Charles Wells Eagle, decent house wines; maybe piped Radio 2. Tables out in the sizeable pleasant walled garden look up to the nearby cathedral. The back bedrooms are quieter; no cooked breakfast. *(Recommended by John and Christine Vittoe, Rona Murdoch, Tim Barrow, Sue Demont, N B Thompson, Mark Percy, Lesley Mayoh)*

Badger ~ Tenants John and M G Spicer ~ Real ale ~ Meals and snacks (01722) 327679 ~ Children away from main bar ~ Open 11-3, 6-11; 11-11 Sat, 11-4, 7-10.30 Sun ~ Bedrooms: £35B/£45B

The 🍴 rosette distinguishes pubs where the food is of exceptional quality.

SEEND ST9361 Map 2
Barge

Seend Cleeve; signposted off A361 Devizes—Trowbridge, between Seend village and signpost to Seend Head

In summer the picnic tables among old street-lamps in the neat waterside gardens are an understandably popular place to pass the time watching the barges and other boats on the Kennet & Avon Canal – there are moorings by the humpy bridge. The unusual barge-theme decor in the friendly and relaxed bar is perhaps at its best in the intricately painted Victorian flowers which cover the ceilings and run in a waist-high band above the deep green lower walls. A distinctive mix of attractive seats includes milk churns and the occasional small oak settle among the rugs on the parquet floor, while the walls have big sentimental engravings. The watery theme continues with a well stocked aquarium, and there's also a pretty Victorian fireplace, big bunches of dried flowers, and red velvet curtains for the big windows. As well as a help-yourself salad counter (from £5.95), a good range of bar food served in big good value helpings by cheery uniformed staff includes soup (£2.25), sandwiches (from £2.25), ploughman's (£4.50), filled yorkshire puddings or mixed bean chilli in taco shell (£5.95), tasty steak and kidney or chicken, ham and mushroom pie (£6.50), battered cod (£6.75), curries (£6.85), roast salmon with gooseberry and horseradish sauce (£8.25), as well as daily specials like fresh tortellini with four-cheese sauce (£5.25), ratatouille in crispy potato skins (£5.95), tuna steak (£7.95), rack of pork ribs (£8.75), and duck breast with redcurrant sauce (£11.95). In the evening food comes with fresh vegetables, with a couple of extra more restauranty dishes; the restaurant extension is no smoking. They recommend booking for meals, especially at weekends. Well kept Wadworths IPA and 6X, and a fortnightly changing guest beer like Badger Tanglefoot on handpump; mulled wine in winter. Good service; trivia. Barbecues outside on summer Sundays. At the busiest times you may have to queue to get in the car park. *(Recommended by Luke Worthington, G W A Pearce, Charles and Pauline Stride, Derek Clarke, John and Vivienne Rice, Phyl and Jack Street, Meg and Colin Hamilton, Peter Neate, Peter and Audrey Dowsett, Nigel and Lindsay Chapman)*

Wadworths ~ Tenant Christopher Moorley Long ~ Real ale ~ Meals and snacks (till 10 Fri, Sat) ~ Restaurant ~ (01380) 828230 ~ Children welcome ~ Open 11-2.30(3 Sat), 6-11; 12-3, 7-10.30 Sun

SHERSTON ST8585 Map 2
Rattlebone

Church St; B4040 Malmesbury—Chipping Sodbury

Recently taken over by a small Bristol brewery, this cheery bustling old 16th-c pub has several rambling rooms with nooks and crannies, pink walls, pews and settles, country kitchen chairs around a mix of tables, big dried flower arrangements, lots of jugs and bottles hanging from the low beams, and plenty of little cuttings and printed anecdotes. In the public bar there's a hexagonal pool table, darts, table football, Connect Four, shove ha'penny, fruit machine, cribbage, dominoes and juke box; also table and alley skittles. Bar food is still good under the new manager: filled rolls (from £2.50), ploughman's (from £3.50), soup (£2.25), smoked salmon and yoghurt mousse (£3.75), prawn fritters with garlic mayonnaise and crusty bread (£3.95), grilled goat's cheese with nut dressing (£4.25), chilli with tortilla chips (£4.50), breaded plaice (£4.75), vegetable crêpes (£6.25), mushroom and nut stroganoff or steak and kidney pie (£6.50), salmon fillet with water chestnuts, dry vermouth and cream (£8.75), pork tenderloin with stilton and cream sauce topped with toasted cashew nuts (£9.25), lamb escalopes with raspberry and mint coulis (£9.50), and puddings like fruit crumble or pecan nut and treacle pie (from £2.50); three-course Sunday roast and coffee (£8.95). They hope to have more of their well liked fish specials this year. Part of the dining area is no smoking. Well kept Bass, Greene King Abbot, Smiles Best and Golden and a guest on handpump, over 50 malt whiskies, 20 rums, fruit wines, decent wines, and quick obliging service. The smallish garden is pretty, with flowerbeds, a gravel terrace, and picnic tables under umbrellas. There are four boules pitches.

(Recommended by Tom McLean, Ewan McCall, Roger Huggins, Dave Irving, Andrew Shore, Pat and John Millward, Janet Pickles, JCW, Nick and Meriel Cox, M G Hart, John and Elizabeth Cox, Desmond and Pat Morris, Margaret and Douglas Tucker, Charles and Pauline Stride, MRSM, S H Godsell, KC, Peter and Audrey Dowsett, Mr and Mrs Claude Bernis, Peter Neate, John and Annette Derbyshire)

Smiles ~ Manager David Baker ~ Real ale ~ Meals and snacks (till 9.45) ~ (01666) 840871 ~ Children in eating area ~ Open 11-3, 5.30-11; 11-11 Sat; 12-10.30 Sun

WILCOT Map 2 SU1360
Golden Swan 🍺

Village signposted off A345 N of Pewsey, and in Pewsey itself (forking right past hospital)

Prettily set in a quiet thatched village, this steeply gabled old thatched inn is very pretty, with tables out on its neat flower-edged front lawn, and more in the attractive back garden. Its two main rooms are unpretentiously welcoming. The larger, with a dining area at one end, has lots of decorative jugs and mugs hanging from its beams, comfortable chairs, a collection of brass shell cases and other brassware on the mantelpiece, and attractive pen and wash drawings of local scenes; there's an aquarium at the dining end. A third room has a fruit machine, sensibly placed darts and bar billiards. A short choice of good value home-made bar food includes faggots, peas and chips (£4) and lasagne, cod or plaice (£4.50); Sunday roast (£4.50); no-smoking dining room. Well kept Wadworths IPA and 6X and in winter perhaps Old Timer on handpump, maybe unobtrusive piped music, a friendly golden retriever and a prize-winning cat. Bedrooms are simple but big and airy and good value, and there's a field for camping. The restored Kennet & Avon canal is a couple of minutes' walk away. *(Recommended by Ann and Colin Hunt, Angus Lyon, Gordon, D G Clarke, Phyl and Jack Street, Ron Shelton)*

Wadworths ~ Tenants Terry and June Weeks ~ Real ale ~ Meals and snacks (not Sun evening or Mon) ~ (01672) 562289 ~ Children welcome ~ Open 12-3.30, 6-11(10.30 Sun) ~ Bedrooms: £17.50/£35

WOODBOROUGH SU1159 Map 2
Seven Stars 🍴 🍷

Off A345 S of Marlborough: from Pewsey follow Woodborough signposts, then in Woodborough bear left following Bottlesford signposts; OS Sheet 173, map reference 113591

A find, this, with a winning combination of relaxed but civilised pub atmosphere and traditional furnishings with really good Anglo-French country cooking. At first all seems straightforward: polished bricks by the bar counter, well kept Badger IPA, Bunces Best and Wadworths 6X on handpump, hunting prints, attractively moulded panelling, a hot coal fire in the old range at one end, a big log fire at the other, a pleasant mix of antique settles, country kitchen chairs, pew, wheelback chairs, cast-iron-framed tables, cosy nooks here and there; there are house plants, a couple of pub dogs and a black cat. It's when you notice the strings of onions and shallots by one fireplace, and then the profusion of retired wine bottles on delft shelves – and perhaps the gingham tablecloths and decidedly non-standard art up steps in the attractive back dining area – that you realise all is not quite what it seems. So ask for the menu: changing daily, it might include soup (£2.45), sandwiches (from £2.95), ploughman's (£4.25), lasagne or chilli (£5.25), cassoulet (£7.25), jugged hare (£9.75), pork fillet with cream and apples (£8.95), monkfish provençale (£8.75) and half a lobster thermidor (£14.75). At our inspection meal, mallard done with orange and local rabbit cooked in the Normandy style with cider and cream came with beautiful waxy french potatoes (they get regular supplies direct from France) and excellent leaf-wrapped cabbage patties. If there is a criticism, it would be that this is not really a place for a quick snack, even at lunchtime – think more in terms of a leisured meal. The wine list is exemplary, with about a dozen including plenty of French by the glass in the £1.70ish range, and interesting bin ends. There's an attractive restaurant with handsome Victorian pictures; maybe intelligent piped music. Seven acres of riverside gardens. *(Recommended by Peter Brimacombe, Nick and David Clifton, Ian Harding, Neville Burrell)*

Free house ~ Licensees Philippe Cheminade and Kate Lister ~ Real ale ~ Meals and snacks ~ Restaurant ~ (01672) 851325 ~ Jazz/blues Fri night ~ Children welcome away from main bar ~ Open 11.30-3; 6-11; 12-3 Sun; cl Sun evening, Mon

WOOTTON RIVERS SU1963 Map 2
Royal Oak ♀

Village signposted from A346 Marlborough—Salisbury, from A345 Marlborough—Pewsey, and B3087 E of Pewsey

It's advisable to book for an evening meal (when some customers may be quite smartly dressed), as this 16th-c thatched pub is so popular locally for its very extensive range of bar food. As well as lunchtime sandwiches (from £2.25) and ploughman's (from £5), the choice might include soup (£2.25), Cornish crab soup (£3.50), baked goat's cheese on sweet pepper salad with anchovies (£4.50), spicy fried breaded prawns (£4.75), filled ciabatta (£5), scampi (£7.75), grilled salmon or grilled chicken breast with cajun spices (£8.50), seafood salad (£10.50), several steaks (from £11.50), and daily specials like chilli (£5), steak and Guinness pie (£7) and grilled lamb cutlets with port and redcurrant sauce (£9.50); puddings include sherry trifle, hot chocolate fudge cake and stem ginger with cream (from £3). The friendly L-shaped dining lounge has slat-back chairs, armchairs and some rustic settles around good tripod tables, a low ceiling with partly stripped beams, partly glossy white planks, and a woodburning stove. The timbered bar is comfortably furnished, and has a small area with darts, pool, cribbage, dominoes, chess, fruit machine, trivia and juke box. Well kept Wadworths 6X tapped from the cask and a guest ale like Ushers seasonal beer on handpump, interesting whiskies, and a good wine list (running up to some very distinguished vintage ones). There are tables under cocktail parasols in the back gravelled yard. The thatched and timbered village is worth exploring, particularly the 13th-c church. The family also run the True Heart at Bishopstone, and the Pheasant at Shefford Woodlands. *(Recommended by Charles and Pauline Stride, TRS, Mr and Mrs Tew, Luke Worthington, Brian and Bett Cox, Julie Peters, Colin Blinkhorn, C Baxter, Michael and Alison Leyland, Phyl and Jack Street, Stephen Barney, A R and B E Sayer, D and D Savidge, Cherry Ann Knott, Mrs S Miller)*

Free house ~ Licensees John and Rosa Jones ~ Real ale ~ Meals and snacks ~ Restaurant ~ (01672) 810322 ~ Children welcome ~ Open 11-3, 6(7 winter)-11; 11-11 Sat; cl 25 Dec and evening 26 Dec ~ Bedrooms (in adjoining house): £27.50(£35B)/£40(£45B)

Lucky Dip

Besides the fully inspected pubs, you might like to try these Lucky Dips recommended to us and described by readers (if you do, please send us reports):

☆ **Aldbourne** [The Green (off B4192); SU2675], *Blue Boar*: Ancient huge Tudor public bar, friendly and relaxed, with homely feel and boar's head; extensive more modern lounge/dining area, busy at lunchtime, with good choice of food from generous sandwiches up, fresh veg; nice furnishings, well kept Archers Village, Wadworths IPA and 6X, friendly attentive staff; children allowed, neatly kept small back country garden; nr church on pretty village green *(HNJ, PEJ, Gordon, Mr and Mrs P Smith)*

☆ **Aldbourne**, *Crown*: Unpretentious village pub with oak bar furnishings in two-part beamed lounge, unusual huge log fireplace linking to public bar, well presented generous food, small nicely laid out dining room; friendly quick service, pleasant atmosphere, well kept Ushers, interesting bric-a-brac, quiet piped music; tables under cocktail parasols in neat courtyard *(HNJ, PEJ)*

☆ **Alvediston** [Ebble Valley SW of Salisbury; ST9723], *Crown*: Welcoming thatched low-beamed country inn carefully extended behind without spoiling the comfortable and attractive rather upmarket main bar, generous helpings of good food in bar and restaurant, well kept Courage, Ringwood and Wadworths, good prices, friendly efficient service, pretty garden, peaceful location; very good newly decorated bedrooms *(Bryan and Jean Warland, LYM)*

Amesbury [High St; SU1541], *George*: Rambling coaching inn with unusually extensive surviving coach yard; well kept Gibbs Mew Salisbury, well priced bar food and friendly helpful staff; piped music, pool in public bar; bedrooms *(Gordon, LYM)*; [High St], *New Inn*: Simple decor, comfortable and welcoming, with good food from sandwiches up, well kept ales, big curving bar with restaurant area *(Phyl and Jack Street, R Boyd)*

Ashton Keynes [High Rd; SU0494], *White Hart*: Smart and friendly village local with well priced homely cooking, well kept Whitbreads-related ales, good log fire, efficient service; piped music; garden, delightful village *(A and M Matheson, Mrs K Neville-Rolfe, Keith Astin)*

Atworth [Bath Rd (A365); ST8666], *White Hart*: Traditional furnishings, friendly welcome, interesting reasonably priced food inc good puddings; bedrooms *(Lyn and Geoff Hallchurch)*

☆ **Avebury** [A361; SU0969], *Red Lion*: Much-modernised thatched pub in the heart of the stone circles; pleasant original core, friendly staff, unpubby restaurant extension, well kept Whitbreads-related ales *(Veronica Brown, LYM)*

☆ **Axford** [off A4 E of Marlborough, back rd Mildenhall—Ramsbury; SU2370], *Red Lion*: Beams, pine panelling, clean decor and picture windows for fine valley view, with good though not cheap food (strong emphasis on fish, nice puddings trolley) in bustling solidly furnished bar and plush no-smoking restaurant; smiley if not always speedy service, well kept changing ales such as Boddingtons, Hook Norton Best, Shepherd Neame Spitfire and Wadworths 6X, some good value wines, pub games; children welcome, picnic tables in sunny sheltered garden; bedrooms *(Mr and Mrs Cresswell, D Clarke, M V and J Melling, Alan Griffiths, Lynda Payton, Sam Samuells, M L and G Clarke, Philip Orbell, LYM)*

☆ **Beckhampton** [A4 Marlborough—Calne; SU0868], *Waggon & Horses*: Friendly stone-and-thatch pub handy for Avebury and open all day, full range of Wadworths ales and a guest beer kept well, good coffee, old-fashioned unassuming atmosphere, understated Dickens connections, wide choice of popular good value bar food inc children's helpings, teas, family room, pub games and machines, CD juke box, pleasant garden with good play area; parking over road, no dogs; bedrooms *(PM, AM, Lyn and Geoff Hallchurch, TRS, LYM)*

☆ **Biddestone** [The Green; ST8773], *White Horse*: Busy traditional and relaxing rather than smart (outside lavatories), small cosy carpeted rooms, wide choice of cheap well cooked food and filled rolls, well kept Courage ales, quick friendly service; children welcome, shove-ha'penny, darts and table skittles; overlooks duckpond in picturesque village, tables in good garden with play area, aviary and chipmunks; bedrooms *(Robert Huddleston, Mr and Mrs J Brown, Barry Regan)*

☆ **Bishops Cannings** [off A361 NE of Devizes; SU0364], *Crown*: Carefully refurbished unassuming village local with welcoming licensees, good generous food, fair prices, well kept Wadworths IPA and 6X, decent wines, enjoyable atmosphere; dogs welcome, next to handsome old church in pretty village, walk to Kennet & Avon Canal *(Marjorie and David Lamb, June and Tony Baldwin, F J and A Parmenter, John and Chris Simpson, C Stokoe, Colin and Joyce Laffan, Lyn and Geoff Hallchurch)*

Box [off A4 E of junction with A365 – sharp narrow turn; ST8268], *Chequers*: Friendly and attractive, with well kept Courage Best, Flowers IPA and Wadworths 6X, ancient stonework, log fires, oak parquet and traditional furnishings *(Brian and Anna Marsden, LYM)*

☆ **Bradford on Avon** [Silver St; ST8261], *Bunch of Grapes*: Atmospheric wine-bar style decor though definitely a pub, with several well kept ales inc Oakhill and Smiles as well as good range of wines and malt whiskies; on two levels in picturesque steep street, good choice of reasonably priced food, willing newish licensees *(Susan and Nigel Wilson, Meg and Colin Hamilton, M E Wellington)*

Bradford on Avon [17 Frome Rd], *Barge*: Good food, friendly staff and local atmosphere, nicely set canalside garden, relaxing views, good value bedrooms *(Sian Hamilton)*; [Masons Hill], *Dandy Lion*: Busy old-world pub doing well under hard-working new licensees, good lunchtime food, real ales inc Bass and Wadworths 6X, friendly staff, upstairs evening restaurant specialising in steaks *(Susan and Nigel Wilson)*; [Silver St], *Sprat & Carrot*: Busy and lively, big open fire, popular dining area, six real ales inc Greene King Abbot, Smiles and Theakstons Best *(Susan and Nigel Wilson)*

Bratton [B3098 E of Westbury; ST9052], *Duke*: Warmly welcoming and civilised, well refurbished, with comfortable lounge bar, public bar and nice small dining room, wide choice of good generous home-made food inc good sandwiches, welcoming service, Moles Best (tied to them) and Ushers, amiable labrador; ancient whalebone arch to garden; bedrooms *(Colin Laffan, Lyn and Geoff Hallchurch, Mr and Mrs Peter Smith)*

☆ **Broad Chalke** [North St; Ebble Valley SW of Salisbury; SU0325], *Queens Head*: Heavy beams, inglenook with woodburner, padded settles and chairs, some stripped brickwork, wide range of home-made food from sandwiches up, welcoming service, well kept ales inc Fullers London Pride and Ringwood Best, decent wines and country wines, good coffee; maybe piped music; wheelchair access from back car park, tables in pretty courtyard; comfortable well equipped bedrooms in newish separate block *(John Davis, Nigel and Elizabeth Holmes, Angus Lyon, Christopher Warner)*

☆ **Broad Hinton** [High St; off A4361 about 5 miles S of Swindon; SU1076], *Crown*: Light and airy open-plan bar, plush and roomy eating area, good home-cooked food esp salads and puddings, friendly uniformed waitresses, well kept Arkells BB, BBB, Kingsdown and Mild, no-smoking area, interesting bric-a-brac, unobtrusive piped music; unusual gilded inn sign, attractive spacious garden with fishpond and play area; bedrooms *(June and Tony Baldwin, Jenny and Michael Back, Martin Freeman, CMW, JJW)*

Brokerswood [ST8352], *Kicking Donkey*: Charles Wells Bombardier, Hook Norton Old Hookey, Smiles, Wadworths 6X and a beer brewed for the pub, welcoming service, several bars and various nooks, log fires; delightful lawn, lovely rural setting *(Colin and Joyce Laffan)*

Broughton Gifford [ST8763], *Bell on the Common*: Friendly and popular old stone-built Wadworths pub with traditional furnishings, generous good value straightforward food in bars and pleasant restaurant, big coal fire, copper bar counter with handpumps on back wall, darts, pool etc, children welcome; garden, bowls club

next door *(Ian Phillips)*

Callow Hill [B4042 Swindon—Malmesbury; SU0384], *Suffolk Arms*: Pleasant atmosphere, decent if not cheap food, well kept local Archers beer *(Comus Elliott)*

☆ nr **Castle Combe** [The Gibb; B4039 Acton Turville—Chippenham, nr Nettleton – OS Sheet 173 map ref 838791; ST8379], *Salutation*: Good choice of attractively served good food inc vegetarian and Aberdeen Angus steaks in comfortable lounge bar and raftered thatched and timbered restaurant, friendly landlord and staff, welcoming and pubby locals' bar, Whitbreads-related ales, decent wines *(Desmond and Pat Morris, R Murmann, Ken Hull, Vanessa Mudge)*

Charlton [B4040 toward Cricklade; ST9588], *Horse & Groom*: Good well presented food in civilised and relaxing refurbished pub with good log fire, well kept Archers and Wadworths, farm cider, decent wines; restaurant (good value Sun lunch), tables outside; has been cl Mon *(D G King, LYM)*

Cherhill [A4 E of Calne; SU0370], *Black Horse*: Popular beamed dining pub under same management as Cross Guns nr Bradford on Avon (see main entries), linked areas crowded with tables for wide range of good value generous food, prompt service, no-smoking area, huge fireplace, four Ushers ales, children welcome; two evening sittings *(Colin and Joyce Laffan, Tony Beaulah)*

☆ **Chilmark** [B3089 Salisbury—Hindon; ST9632], *Black Dog*: Well kept Marstons, Tisbury and Wadworths 6X, good value food and good local atmosphere in comfortably modernised 15th-c pub with armchairs by lounge log fire, fossil ammonites in the stone of another bar, games in third bar *(R T and J C Moggridge, LYM)*

Chippenham [Malmesbury Rd; ST9173], *Cepen Arms*: Big brash modern Brewers Fayre, just the ticket for grandchildren (and grandparents, come to that); good friendly service, well kept Whitbreads-related beer, fast food, play areas indoors and out *(Peter Neate, Mr and Mrs G Snowball)*

Chiseldon [A345 Marlborough rd; just S of M4 junction 15; SU1879], *Plough*: Good atmosphere, friendly efficient service, well kept Arkells BBB, wide choice of good value food, good wine list *(R T and J C Moggridge, David Leonard)*

Cholderton [A338 Tidworth—Salisbury; SU2242], *Crown*: Cosy and welcoming thatched low-beamed cottage, L-shaped bar with bar billiards one end, wide choice of reasonably priced food the other, Gibbs Mew ales, brewing cartoons, friendly fat black and white cat; seats outside *(G Coates)*

☆ **Christian Malford** [B4069 Lyneham—Chippenham, 3½ miles from M4 junction 17; ST9678], *Mermaid*: Long bar pleasantly divided into areas, good food inc some interesting dishes, well kept Bass, Courage Best, Wadworths 6X and Worthington BB, decent whiskies and wines, some attractive pictures, bar billiards, darts, fruit machine, piped music (live Thurs), tables in garden; bedrooms *(John and Wendy Trentham, BB)*

Clyffe Pypard [SU0777], *Goddard Arms*: Fine 16th-c pub among lovely thatched cottages, good food from traditional home cooking to thai meals, well kept Greene King Abbot, Flowers IPA, Marstons Pedigree and Wadworths 6X; local art shows *(Keith Wills)*

Collingbourne Ducis [SU2453], *Blue Lion*: Comfortable and popular, with wide choice of reasonably priced food, several real ales, decent wines, no piped music, quick friendly service, big log fires; back garden, pretty village *(Peter and Audrey Dowsett)*

☆ **Coombe Bissett** [Blandford Rd (A354); SU1026], *Fox & Goose*: Tasty reasonably priced food (interesting vegetarian, fine puddings) and Wadworths 6X and other ales in thriving spacious neatly kept open-plan pub by delightful village green; welcoming staff, rustic refectory-style tables, coal fires, old prints, hanging chamber-pots; can be very busy weekends, piped music (classical at lunchtime), children catered for, evening restaurant; picnic tables on terrace and in garden with play area, good access for wheelchairs *(Kate Murley, E A George, Ian Phillips, Jerry and Alison Oakes)*

Corsham [High St; ST8670], *Methuen Arms*: Cosy old-world inn, formerly a priory; good food in bar and pricier restaurant, Gibbs Mew Wiltshire, good local atmosphere; tables in attractive courtyard with outside staircase and dovecot in wall; skittle alley; bedrooms comfortable *(Meg and Colin Hamilton, Peter Neate)*

Corsley Heath [A362 Frome—Warminster; ST8245], *Royal Oak*: Very popular lunchtime for generous reasonably priced food inc vegetarian, very friendly service, Wadworths ales, pleasant seating in two small bars, back children's room, big garden, restaurant; handy for Longleat *(DWAJ)*

Corton [off A36 Warminster—Wilton; ST9340], *Dove*: Welcoming and attractive country local pub with generous food, daily papers, its own-brewed Wylye Valley beer and well kept local guest beers; bedrooms *(R T and J C Moggridge, Lyn and Geoff Hallchurch, LYM)*

Crudwell [A429 N of Malmesbury; ST9592], *Plough*: Quiet lounge, bar with darts and juke box, pool room, dining area with comfortable well padded seats and more in elevated part; wide range of reasonably priced food, well kept ales such as Bass, Boddingtons, local Foxley, Morlands Old Speckled Hen and Wadworths 6X, quick service, maybe open fires, pleasant side garden *(R Huggins, T McLean, D Irving, T McCall, Ian Phillips, JKW, Geoffrey and Penny Hughes)*; *Wheatsheaf*: Pleasant decor and furniture (used to be a bistro wine bar, and it shows), decent food from doorstep sandwiches up, good house wines *(Peter Neate)*

Dauntsey [Dauntsey Lock; B4069 – handy for M4 junctions 16 and 17; ST9782], *Peterborough Arms*: Welcoming landlord, good value generous food, good changing range of real ales, pool, skittle alley; children welcome, sizeable garden with play area – nice spot by old Wilts & Berks Canal *(Patrick Godfrey)*

☆ **Devizes** [Long St; SU0061], *Elm Tree*: Welcoming heavy-beamed local with wide choice of good food, well kept Wadworths, decent house wines, no-smoking area; piped music; restaurant, clean and tidy bedrooms *(Jason Reynolds, John and Chris Simpson)*

Devizes [New Park St], *Castle*: Tastefully refurbished, with friendly helpful staff, well kept Wadworths ales, interesting freshly prepared good value specials, unobtrusive piped soul music; open all day, bedrooms *(Dagmar Junghanns, John and Chris Simpson)*

☆ **Donhead St Andrew** [off A30 E of Shaftesbury, just E of Ludwell; ST9124], *Forester*: Small old country pub with inglenook fireplace, friendly staff and locals, well kept Hop Back Thunderstorm, Ringwood Best and Smiles, generous interesting bar food, good sandwiches; quiet piped classical music, live music weekends *(Bruce Bird)*

☆ **East Knoyle** [The Green, off A350 S of A303; ST8830], *Fox & Hounds*: Lovely out-of-the-way setting, superb views from manicured green opp, good choice of freshly made food, very reasonable prices, comfortable seats and pleasant layout, six well kept ales such as Shepherd Neame Bishops Finger, farm cider, enviable range of malt whiskies, friendly efficient landlord, smart courteous young staff *(R H Martyn, Pat and Robert Watt, Phyl and Jack Street)*

East Knoyle, *Seymour Arms*: Pretty 17th-c pub, clean and comfortable, good food, eating area on left, china display, quotations on beams, well kept Wadworths ales; tables in garden with play area; bedrooms good value *(John and Joan Nash)*

Easton Royal [SU2060], *Bruce Arms*: Fine old unspoilt pub, nicely basic, with scrubbed pine tables, brick floor, well kept Wadworths 6X and Whitbreads Strong Country, Pewsey organic cider; cheese rolls *(R Swift)*

☆ **Farleigh Wick** [A363 Bath—Bradford; ST8064], *Fox & Hounds*: Good fresh food served quickly by friendly helpful staff in welcoming low-beamed rambling bar, highly polished old oak tables and chairs, gently rural decorations; attractive garden; can get packed weekends *(Susan and Nigel Wilson, Meg and Colin Hamilton, Lyn and Geoff Hallchurch, MRSM)*

Farley [SU2229], *Hook & Glove*: Small chatty bar, emphasis on larger restaurant with good value good food, careful housekeeping, efficient careful service; fine wooded countryside, good walking *(Phyl and Jack Street)*

Fonthill Bishop [ST9333], *Kings Arms*: Comfortable open-plan bar with interesting decor and bric-a-brac, quiet side room, interesting reasonably priced food in huge club sandwich and good warm bacon salad, entertaining staff; children welcome *(Lyn and Geoff Hallchurch)*

Froxfield [A4; SU2968], *Pelican*: Nice relaxed atmosphere, good welcome and service, some emphasis on tasty good value food *(Christopher Ball, Clare and Chris Tooley)*

Great Bedwyn [SU2764], *Three Tuns*: Friendly village pub, freshly cooked good value food inc bargain local steak, Wadworths 6X *(Margaret Dyke)*

☆ **Great Cheverell** [off B3098 Westbury—Mkt Lavington; ST9754], *Bell*: Spaciously extended well run dining pub in same hands as Cross Guns nr Bradford on Avon (see main entries), very popular for hearty good value food inc duck and kangaroo on big plates with lots of trimmings, at low prices; comfortable chairs and settles, cosy little alcoves, well kept Scottish Courage ales and Wadworths 6X, upstairs dining room, friendly attentive service, attractive village *(Colin Laffan, H R Holloway)*

Great Durnford [SU1338], *Black Horse*: Attractive open-plan pub divided by standing timbers, good value food inc imaginative dishes under present experienced landlord, good log fires, restaurant *(Jerry and Alison Oakes)*

☆ **Great Hinton** [3½ miles E of Trowbridge, signed off A361 opp Lamb at Semington; ST9059], *Linnet*: Pleasantly refurbished village local with good value home-made food from sandwiches up inc vegetarian, children's and good Sun lunch, well kept Wadworths IPA and 6X, decent house wines, friendly efficient service, three dining areas off bar, walking-sticks for sale, unobtrusive piped music; children welcome, picnic tables on new front terrace, pretty village *(Colin and Joyce Laffan, BB)*

☆ **Great Wishford** [off A36 NW of Salisbury; SU0735], *Royal Oak*: Very wide choice of food in pleasant old pub in pretty village, beams, panelling, bare boards and carpets, brass ornaments, log fires, well kept Courage Best, Flowers Original and Wylye, good choice of whiskies, friendly landlord, big family dining area, public bar with pool alcove, restaurant; maybe quiet piped jazz *(James Nunns, Gwen and Peter Andrews, LYM)*

☆ **Hannington** [off B4019 W of Highworth; SU1793], *Jolly Tar*: Wide choice of good value honest food, well kept Arkells BB, BBB and Kingsdown, decent wines, welcoming ex-sailor landlord, big log fire in relaxing lounge bar, ships' crests on beams, stripped stone and flock wallpaper; games bar, skittle alley, upstairs grill room; maybe piped music; good robust play area in big garden, tables out in front too; pretty village *(Peter and Audrey Dowsett, G W A Pearce, R Huggins, T McLean, D Irving, E McCall, TRS, BB)*

☆ **Highworth** [Market Pl; SU2092], *Saracens Head*: Comfortable and relaxed rambling bar, several distinct interesting areas around great central chimney block, friendly service, wide choice of good value straightforward bar food (limited Sun) inc vegetarian and children's, well kept Arkells BB and BBB; piped music (may be loud), public bar with TV; children in eating area, tables in sheltered courtyard, open all day weekdays; comfortable bedrooms *(Peter and Audrey Dowsett, Karen Hazeldon, TBB, LYM)*

Hindon [High St; ST9132], *Grosvenor Arms*: Recently decorated olde-worlde bar, open fires, decent food inc speciality fish and chips served in elegantly arranged paper boat, well kept Bass, good house wines; bedrooms *(Alan and Paula McCully)*

Holt [ST8662], *Old Ham Tree*: Impressive frontage, basic locals' bar, comfortable beamed restaurant/lounge, friendly welcome, wide-ranging generous bar food, reasonable prices, well kept Badger Tanglefoot, Bass, Wadworths 6X and guest beer; handy for the lovely gardens of The Courts (NT) *(Ian and Nita Cooper)*

Honeystreet [SU1061], *Barge*: Unspoilt canalside pub in nice setting (good downland walks) with well kept ales, pleasant pictures, good food from sandwiches to fresh trout, log fires; garden, bedrooms *(T G Brierly)*

Horningsham [by entrance to Longleat House; ST8141], *Bath Arms*: Civilised old inn, cosy and well appointed, with Smiles ales and a guest such as Crown Buckleys Revd James, food from sandwiches up, attractive gardens; bedrooms well equipped, clean and comfortable, pretty village *(John and Lynn Busenbark)*

Horton [SU0463], *Bridge*: Spacious pub by Kennet & Avon canal, partitioned into four well furnished areas with carpets or flagstones, dark wood and warm colours, good atmosphere, good value generous food, Badger Tanglefoot, Wadworths 6X, prompt friendly service; disabled lavatories *(F J and A Parmenter, June and Tony Baldwin)*

Kington Langley [Days Lane; handy for M4 junction 17; ST9277], *Hit or Miss*: Clean cricket-theme bar with no-smoking area, darts and pool in room off, busy restaurant with good log fire; well kept Courage and a guest ale, decent generous food; attractive village *(D King)*; *Plough*: Spacious and comfortable, welcoming landlord, good food, well kept Archers and Butcombe, big back conservatory *(Janet Pickles, D Irving, E McCall, R Huggins, T McLean)*

Kington St Michael [handy for M4 junction 17; ST9077], *Jolly Huntsman*: Roomy, with scrubbed tables and old-fashioned settees, well kept changing ales inc Marstons Head Brewers Choice (friendly landlord interested in them), good value fresh-cooked food; maybe sports on TV; two cheap bedrooms *(Jeff Davies, G V Price)*

☆ **Lacock** [Bowden Hill, Bewley Common – back rd to Sandy Lane, OS Sheet 173 map ref 935679; ST9367], *Rising Sun*: Lovely spot with pretty garden and great views, mix of old chairs and basic kitchen tables on stone floors, stuffed animals and birds, country pictures, open fires, friendly landlord and locals, good range of Moles ales, good value food (no hot dishes Mon lunchtime) from sandwiches up, provision for children *(Dagmar Junghanns, Colin Keane, Herbert and Susan Verity, Brian and Anna Marsden, LYM)*

☆ Landford [Hamptworth; village signed down B3079 off A36, then right towards Redlynch; SU2519], *Cuckoo*: Unpretentious thatched cottage with friendly chatty local atmosphere, good range of well kept ales from smaller breweries, cheap filled rolls, pies and pasties, impromptu folk music Fri and maybe Sat and Sun; children in small room off bar; tables outside, big play area and bantams *(Gordon, LYM)*

Liddington [Bell Lane; a mile from M4 junction 15, via A419; SU2081], *Village Inn*: Comfortable traditional decor in split-level bar, popular lunchtime esp with older people for wide choice of good value freshly prepared food (may be a wait), Arkells ales, friendly homely service, log fire, new conservatory, no piped music; bedrooms simple but clean *(J Bliss, JJW, CMW, Mr and Mrs P Smith)*

☆ Luckington [High St; off B4040 SW of Malmesbury; ST8383], *Old Royal Ship*: Traditional 17th-c roadside country pub with long partly divided bar and dining area, good range of rather sophisticated food inc some bargains, several well kept ales, farm cider, decent wines (two glass sizes), good coffee, darts, maybe piped pop music; attractive garden with boules, play area with big wooden fort, bedrooms *(Anne Morris, Peter and Audrey Dowsett, BB)*

☆ Malmesbury [62 High St; ST9287], *Smoking Dog*: Cosy beamed and stripped stone local, rather upmarket weekends, with big stripped pine tables, changing well kept ales from casks behind bar, farm ciders, decent wines, good coffee, log fires, daily papers, board games, reference books, soft piped music; back bistro, garden; open all day, friendly *(Peter Neate, TBB, Peter Neate, T McLean, E McCall, R Huggins, D Irving, Mark Percy, Lesley Mayoh)*

Malmesbury [29 High St], *Kings Arms*: Popular 16th-c town pub with two bars, good choice of well presented home-made food inc seafood and good value specials and lots of puddings, Whitbreads-related ales, good courtyard garden, jazz last Sat of month; recently refurbished bedrooms *(D Irving, R Huggins, T McLean, E McCall, JF)*; [B4014 towards Tetbury], *Suffolk Arms*: Knocked-through bar and big no-smoking panelled dining room, well kept Wadworths IPA and 6X and a changing guest beer, log fire, usual food well prepared; children welcome *(Mark Percy, Lesley Mayoh, LYM)*; [Market Cross], *Whole Hog*: Friendly unsmart town-centre bar with several machines, piggy theme, papers to read, well kept ales such as Archers, Eldridge Pope Royal Oak, Ridleys ESX and one called Pigs Swill; generous cheapish food,

restaurant (not Sun evening) *(Robert Gomme, Paul and Sue Merrick)*

☆ Marlborough [1 High St], *Bear*: Large Victorian inn with impressive central log fire, well kept Arkells ales, generous often interesting food inc good fish in old-fashioned side bar, small front lunchtime tapas bar (evening restaurant), medieval-style banqueting hall for special occasions, skittle alley *(Lyn and Geoff Hallchurch, Lynda Payton, Sam Samuells)*

Marlborough [High St], *Green Dragon*: Bustling well run town pub with full Wadworths range kept well, good value lunchtime bar food (plenty of eating areas), big coal-effect gas fire, stripped brickwork, lots of blue and white plates, leatherette wall banquettes, pine furniture, steps down to back games room, skittle alley, back terrace; bedrooms, pretty little breakfast room *(Brian Wilkinson, Beverley Daniels, Lynda Payton, Sam Samuells)*

☆ Marston Meysey [off A419 Swindon—Cirencester; SU1297], *Old Spotted Cow*: Big well laid out open-plan Cotswold stone pub, good value generous food, well kept Flowers IPA, Wadworths 6X and guest beers, welcoming landlord, comfortable chairs, huge log fire in raised stone fireplace, plants and pictures; bar billiards, darts, board and children's games, fruit machine, piped music; open all day weekends, spacious garden with picnic tables on terrace and lots of play equipment *(FWG, JJW, CMW, D Irving, E McCall, R Huggins, T Mclean, Dr and Mrs A K Clarke)*

Melksham [ST9063], *Bear*: Lively locals' bar with musical instruments and Irish bric-a-brac, plusher lounge, back room with juke box more popular with younger people; well kept Wadworths *(Tom McLean, Roger Huggins)*

Mere [Castle St; ST8132], *Old Ship*: Interesting 16th-c building with log fires, cosy hotel bar, spacious separate more pubby bar across coach entry divided into cosy areas by standing timbers, bar food, well kept ales, pub games and piped music, good value timber-walled restaurant; children allowed in eating area; good value bedrooms *(James Nunns, J S M Sheldon, LYM)*

☆ Newton Tony [off A338 Swindon—Salisbury; SU2140], *Malet Arms*: Very popular nicely placed local opp footbridge over chalk stream, enjoyable food in cosy bar and restaurant, well kept Badger, Bass, Butcombe and Hampshire King Alfred, pleasant mix of customers, efficient friendly staff *(Phyl and Jack Street, Jacquie and Jim Jones, Tom McLean, Jerry and Alison Oakes)*

☆ North Newnton [A345 Upavon—Pewsey; SU1257], *Woodbridge*: Open all day for enormous hop-wrong choice of generous good value food inc imaginative vegetarian dishes, also afternoon teas; well kept Wadworths ales, good wines and coffee, good friendly service, log fire, newspapers and magazines; big garden with boules, fishing available; nice bedrooms, small camping/caravan site *(C Baxter, June and Tony Baldwin, Gordon)*

☆ Norton [4 miles from M4 junction 17, off A429; ST8884], *Vine Tree*: New licensees making changes at this attractively set 18th-c pub, three smallish linked rooms with lots of stripped pine, more tables now inc extra space for families, food inc attractively priced vegetarian dishes, Archers Best, Arkells 3B and a beer brewed for the pub, friendly if not always speedy service, picnic tables under cocktail parasols in garden with new heated area, fountain and play area; open all day Sun in summer *(Rona Murdoch, Sheila and John French, LYM)*

☆ Nunton [off A338 S of Salisbury; SU1526], *Radnor Arms*: Good interesting food esp fish and local game in lovely ivy-clad village pub with friendly helpful staff, inexpensive beers; three pleasantly decorated linked rooms inc cheerfully busy yet relaxing bar and staider restaurant; log fires, very friendly labrador, attractive garden popular with children *(Jerry and Alison Oakes, Mark Barker, Tony Shepherd, Dr David Tomlinson)*

Oaksey [ST9893], *Wheatsheaf*: Honest village local with dining end, well kept Whitbreads PA, games room with pool and darts *(D Irving, E McCall, R Huggins, T McLean)*

☆ Odstock [off A338 S of Salisbury; SU1426], *Yew Tree*: Pretty old thatched country dining pub, very busy weekends, with immense choice of wholesome food, not cheap but good value, good range of real ales, welcoming unpretentious atmosphere, efficient service; good walks *(Phyl and Jack Street, D R Blake)*

Ogbourne St George [A345 Marlboro—Swindon; SU1974], *Old Crown*: Well kept ales, good food from thick crusty bread sandwiches to restaurant meals, pleasant decor and pictures, one table a glass-covered well; small village off Ridgeway path *(Lynda Payton, Sam Samuells, TB)*

Ramsbury [Crowood Lane/Whittonditch Rd; SU2771], *Crown & Anchor*: Friendly beamed village pub, well presented food, well kept Bass, Tetleys and usually a guest beer, open fires, pool in public bar; no piped music, children welcome, improved garden with terrace *(Mr and Mrs Peter Smith, John Scott)*

Redlynch [N of B3080; SU2021], *Kings Head*: Comfortable cottagey 16th-c pub doing well under current regime, with wide choice of good generous food, helpful attentive service *(Bill and June Howard)*

Rowde [ST9762], *Cross Keys*: Good range of well priced meals, friendly service *(Brian and Anna Marsden)*

☆ Salisbury [St John St; SU1429], *Kings Arms*: Creaky old Tudor inn, darkly panelled and heavily beamed, with friendly staff, comfortable furnishings, Whitbreads-related ales, good choice of wines, good value generous food in bar and restaurant; comfortable bedrooms *(Gordon, N Thompson, David Carr, LYM)*

☆ Salisbury [Castle St], *Avon Brewery*: Old-fashioned city bar, long, narrow, busy and friendly, with dark mahogany, frosted and engraved curved windows, friezes and attractive pictures, two open fires; competitively priced food (not Sun evening), well kept Eldridge Pope ales, decent wines, maybe classical piped music; long sheltered garden running down to river; open all day *(Tim Barrow, Sue Demont, LYM)*

☆ Salisbury [Town Path, W Harnham; SU1328], *Old Mill*: Former mill in lovely setting, with floodlit garden by millpond, cathedral view famous from Constable's paintings – it's a stroll across the meadows; simple but comfortable beamed bars, over 500 china and other ducks, well kept Boddingtons, Flowers Original, Hop Back GFB and Summer Lightning and a guest beer, decent malt whiskies and wines, friendly staff, bar food, restaurant; children welcome, bedrooms *(Tim Barrow, Sue Demont, Paul McPherson, John and Christine Vittoe, Barry and Anne, Dr and Mrs A H Young, Neil and Angela Huxter, LYM)*

☆ Salisbury [Milford St], *Red Lion*: Mix of old-fashioned seats and modern banquettes in two-roomed nicely local-feeling panelled bar opening into other spacious and interesting areas, medieval restaurant, well kept Bass, Ushers, Wadworth 6X and a strong guest beer, lunchtime bar food, loggia courtyard seats; children in eating areas; bedrooms comfortable *(N B Thompson, G Pearce, Jerry and Alison Oakes, LYM)*

Salisbury [Gigant St], *Anchor*: Tap for Gibbs Mew brewery, with their Salisbury, Lake, Deacon and Overlord, simple food, good prices, low beams, wooden chairs, lots of posters, darts and pool one end, relaxed friendly atmosphere *(G Coates)*; [Castle St], *George & Dragon*: Friendly local, with good value generous home cooking *(P and B Bruce)*; [Milford St], *Oddfellows Arms*: Small pleasant unchanging local, friendly and chatty; bar food *(Gordon)*; *Old Ale House*: Tasteful refurbishment, lots of guest ales *(Dr and Mrs A K Clarke, Jerry and Alison Oakes)*

Sandy Lane [A342 Devizes—Chippenham; ST9668], *George*: Neat stonebuilt pub with pleasant atmosphere, new landlord doing wide choice of food inc unusual dishes, well kept Wadworths, decent wines, pleasant efficient service, interesting decor, bons mots chalked on beams; car park on dodgy bend *(M Wellington, Peter Neate, LYM)*

☆ Seend [Bell Hill (A361); ST9461], *Bell*: Attractively refurbished four-room pub with cosy lounge, friendly efficient but unfussy service, well kept Wadworths IPA and 6X, good value food from sandwiches to steaks (not Mon evening), good views from tasteful upstairs restaurant, no music *(Gwen and Peter Andrews, J S Green, Dennis Heatley, Dennis Johnson, Pat and Tony Martin, Lyn and Geoff Hallchurch)*

☆ Semington [The Strand; A361 Devizes—

Trowbridge, nr Keevil; ST9259], *Lamb*: Very popular indeed under its previous regime as a smartish no-smoking dining pub, this series of rooms winding off the serving counter has been redecorated by its new owners to give a pubbier feel, and bar food has also gone in this direction, with more usual dishes inc more snacky things; Butcombe, Ringwood Best and Shepherd Neame Spitfire, decent wines, woodburner and log fire, children in eating area, tables out in colourful walled garden; can be smoky now, cl Sun evening *(John and Lynn Busenbark, Lyn and Geoff Hallchurch, LYM)*

Semington [A350 2 miles S of Melksham], *Somerset Arms*: 16th-c coaching inn with heavy-beamed long bar, real and flame-effect fires, high-backed settles, plenty of tables, lots of prints and brassware, niches with stuffed woodpeckers and the like, some farm tools, generous interesting if not always cheap food inc OAP bargains, friendly efficient service, real ales, good coffee; piped music; garden behind *(Mrs S Peregrine, Lyn and Geoff Hallchurch)*

☆ **Semley** [off A350 N of Shaftesbury; ST8926], *Benett Arms*: Character village inn across green from church, in lovely countryside, two cosy rooms with nicely worn-in mix of furnishings and log fire, good relaxed atmosphere, well kept Gibbs Mew Bishops Tipple, Deacon and Salisbury Best, decent wines and good range of other drinks, traditional games, no music; bar food usually enjoyable, landlord usually friendly and helpful; children and well behaved dogs allowed, restaurant, pleasant seats outside, bedrooms *(James Nunns, P Reeves, Roger and Jenny Huggins, Stephen Goodchild, M G Hart, Marjorie and David Lamb, David Surridge, Peter Burton, Bruce Bird, LYM)*

☆ **Sherston** [Easton, B4040 Malmesbury— Chipping Sodbury; ST8585], *Carpenters Arms*: Cosy beamed pub with extraordinarily wide choice of food inc children's and lots of fresh fish, Whitbreads-related ales tapped from the cask, shiny tables on carpeted floors, log fire, friendly efficient staff, dining area; TV in locals' bar; tables in pleasant garden *(Paul and Sue Merrick, Margaret and Douglas Tucker, John and Elizabeth Cox)*

South Marston [SU1987], *Carpenters Arms*: Olde-worlde farmhouse-style pub, spaciously extended, with good value generous food, well kept Arkells and Marstons, friendly landlord and staff; animals in big back garden *(Jeff Davies, T McLean, R Huggins, D Irving, E McCall)*

South Wraxhall [off B3109 N of Bradford on Avon; ST8364], *Longs Arms*: Remote but busy and cosily refurbished country local with welcoming landlord, well kept Wadworths, interesting good value menu *(Lyn and Geoff Hallchurch)*

☆ **Stapleford** [Warminster Rd (A36); SU0637], *Pelican*: Long bar with big dining area, well kept ales inc Bunces, Wadworths and changing rarities such as Otter, bargain prices

by the jug, wide choice of freshly prepared food inc good value monster mixed grill – book Sat night or get there early; big riverside garden with climbing tree man and swings, pleasant despite nearby road *(Howard and Margaret Buchanan, Jerry and Alison Oakes)*

Staverton [B3105 Trowbridge—Bradford on Avon; ST8560], *Old Bear*: Wide choice of good food in stone pub's long bar divided into sections, Bass, Marstons Pedigree, Ushers Best, Wadworths 6X, big fireplace, friendly helpful staff; booking recommended Sun lunchtime *(Meg and Colin Hamilton, James Nunns)*

Steeple Langford [off A36 E of A303 junction; SU0339], *Rainbows End*: Well appointed, with good view from conservatory, good varied home-made food, friendly welcome, well kept beers *(Pat and Robert Watt)*

☆ **Stibb Green** [SU2262], *Three Horseshoes*: Friendly and spotless old-world pub with inglenook log fire in small beamed front bar, second smaller bar, wide range of good food, well kept Wadworths ales, country wines, farm cider, lively landlord *(Tony Hobden, TRS)*

☆ **Stourton** [Church Lawn; follow Stourhead signpost off B3092, N of junction with A303 just W of Mere; ST7734], *Spread Eagle*: NT pub in lovely setting at head of Stourhead lake (though views from pub itself not special), cool and spacious civilised back dining room popular mainly with older people; standard food till 3, and evening, Ash Vine, Bass and Wadworths 6X, friendly waitress service (can slow when busy), open fire in parlour bar, tables in back courtyard; bedrooms *(Alan and Paula McCully, G W A Pearce, Wendy Arnold, David Lamb, LYM)*

Sutton Benger [ST9478], *Wellesley Arms*: Interesting changing food (and real chips) in large Cotswold stone country pub with rural atmosphere, range of beers, separate dining room *(K R Harris)*

Swindon [Redcliffe St, Rodbourne; SU1385], *Famous Ale House*: Busy low-ceilinged pub with Bass, Smiles, Wadworths and up to eight guest beers; popular lunchtime with local office workers for well priced simple food such as big sandwiches and home-made pizzas (not weekends); ales, pool, darts, unobtrusive piped music; busy weekends or karaoke nights *(Andy and Jill Kassube)*; [Emlyn Sq], *Glue Pot*: Bare boards, good atmosphere, weekday lunchtime food, Archers Village, Black Jack and Golden; in Brunel's Railway Village *(Andy and Jill Kassube)*; [Kingsdown Rd, Upper Stratton; SU1687], *Kingsdown*: Opp Arkells Brewery, pleasantly refurbished, with energetic helpful staff, good food (even on the day the kitchen caught fire they rustled up sandwiches) *(Neville Kenyon, J A Harvey)*

Tilshead [A360 Salisbury—Devizes; SU0348], *Rose & Crown*: Well cared for, with welcoming attentive family service, well kept beer, good value simple wholesome food inc some unusual dishes *(Colin Laffan, D G King)*

Upper Minety [SU0191], *New Inn*: Quite unspoilt, with authentic rather spartan public and lounge bars; no juke box or machines, log fire, simple bar food, well kept Wadworths and occasional guest ale *(Nigel Wilson)*

Upper Woodford [SU1237], *Bridge*: Roomy pub in delightful setting, friendly staff, well presented food inc good vegetarian choice, ploughman's with lots of bread (handy for ducks in riverside garden across road), well kept Gibbs Mew ales *(Rosemary Shipsey, Mark Percy, Lesley Mayoh)*

Wanborough [Callas Hill; 2 miles from M4 junction 15, former B4507 towards Bishopstone; SU2083], *Black Horse*: Arkells country local with lovely downland views, beams and tiled floor, informal elevated garden with play area; has been much enjoyed, but no reports since welcoming very long-serving tenant left early summer 1997 *(News please)*; [High St, Lower Wanboro], *Harrow*: Pretty thatched pub reopened after 1996 refurbishment, two-level beamed main bar with big stone fireplace and bay window alcoves, Brakspears, Hook Norton Old Hookey, Morlands Old Speckled Hen, promising bar food, simple stripped stone dining room; tables on small terrace *(Lynda Payton, Sam Samuells, Brian Clegg)*; [High St, Lower Wanboro], *Plough*: Long low thatched stone pub, three old-world rooms with huge centrepiece log fire in one, another more or less for evening dining; well kept ales inc Archers Village, Bass and Wadworths 6X, good interesting home-made food (not Sun), bar billiards; open all day Sat *(Andy and Jill Kassube, Lynda Payton, Sam Samuells, Cherry Ann Knott)*; [Foxhill; from A419 through Wanborough turn right, 1½ miles towards Baydon; SU2381], *Shepherds Rest*: Remote but friendly Ridgeway pub with recently refurbished long lounge and dining extension, good value well presented food, well kept Whitbreads-related ales, cheerful landlord, welcoming service, lots of pictures, pool in small public bar; play area in attractive garden; children and walkers welcome, very busy in summer, camping *(HNJ, PEJ, Brian Clegg)*

Westbury [Market Pl; ST8751], *Westbury*: Pleasant bar, good service; bedrooms *(R C Watkins)*

☆ **Winterbourne Bassett** [off A4361 S of Swindon; SU0975], *White Horse*: Carefully restored and nicely decorated atmospheric old bar, new dining conservatory, well kept Wadworths, good reasonably priced bar food inc several fish dishes, cheerful friendly service *(June and Tony Baldwin)*

Wootton Bassett [Swindon Rd; A420 just off M4 junction 16; SU1082], *Sally Pusseys*: Named for former landlady; good choice of unpretentious food at sensible prices, busy main bar, lower restaurant; mainly dining, but well kept Arkells *(RL, Alan Vere)*

Wylye [just off A303/A36 junction; SU0037], *Bell*: Nicely set in peaceful village, black beams, timbering, stripped masonry, three log fires, sturdy rustic furnishings, Eldridge Pope, Wadworths 6X and a guest beer, good range of country wines, no-smoking area, side eating area, pleasant service; children welcome, fine downland walks; handy for Stonehenge *(Colin Laffan, Phyl and Jack Street, Jim Reid, MRSM, Hugh MacLean, John and Vivienne Rice, Gordon, D J and P M Taylor, Howard Clutterbuck, James Macrae, LYM)*

Stars after the name of a pub show exceptional character and appeal. They don't mean extra comfort. And they are nothing to do with food quality, for which there's a separate knife-and-fork rosette. Even quite a basic pub can win stars, if it's individual enough.

Yorkshire

Yorkshire stands out for value, with good generous food at sensible prices in most of the pubs we list; at some, the food is outstanding, at prices that won't break the bank. Drinks too are good value, with beer prices nearly 20p a pint less than the national average, and prices holding steadier here than almost anywhere else, especially in pubs getting their beers from the smaller local and more distant breweries. New entries here are the interesting old Bingley Arms in Bardsey (good food and wines, and a nice place to stay), the ancient Black Bull in Boroughbridge (a fine refuge from the A1), the attractively furnished and very welcoming Cross Keys at East Marton, the Blacksmiths Arms prettily placed at Lastingham, the smart Windmill at Linton (doing very well under new licensees, interesting food), the Dawnay Arms with its riverside gardens at Newton on Ouse (again, new people doing good home-made food), the Three Tuns at Osmotherley (nice mix of simple pub and smart restaurant, with good food in both – and a pleasant place to stay), the New Barracks in Sheffield (excellent choice of real ales, and good honest food), and the splendidly placed old Duke of York in Whitby. Other pubs doing really well at the moment here include the friendly old Ship at Aldborough (charming new licensee), the Crab & Lobster at Asenby (excellent food – and now it has good bedrooms too), the George & Dragon at Aysgarth (this dining pub appeals particularly to older readers), the Three Hares at Bilbrough (imaginative food), the bustling Red Lion at Burnsall (great walks here), the very well run Foresters Arms at Carlton, the Blue Lion at East Witton (lovely food, good atmosphere), the outstanding Angel at Hetton, the George & Dragon at Kirkbymoorside (a fine all-rounder), the civilised Black Bull at Moulton, the Kings Arms at Redmire, the Milburn Arms at Rosedale Abbey (gains one of our Food Awards this year), the civilised and very individually run Sawley Arms at Sawley (very close to a Food Award), the atmospheric and friendly Golden Lion in Settle, the beautifully set Fox & Hounds in Starbotton, the Old Hall at Threshfield (good interesting food, friendly landlord), the Wombwell Arms at Wass (good all round, nice licensees), and the interesting Olde Starre in York. For a really enjoyable meal out, places which stand out are the Crab & Lobster, the Three Hares at Bilbrough, the Malt Shovel at Brearton, the Foresters Arms, the Blue Lion, the Angel, the George & Dragon, the Milburn Arms, the Three Acres in Shelley, the Wombwell Arms, and the Sportsmans Arms at Wath. With such strong contenders it's a close-run thing, but our final choice as Yorkshire Dining Pub of the Year is the Blue Lion at East Witton. Yorkshire is so very well provided with outstanding pubs that a higher proportion than usual of the Lucky Dip entries at the end of the chapter are really worth visiting – certainly too many to mention individually here. As always, let the stars be your guide (and to get more down to earth, we have deliberately included directions to more of the Yorkshire Dip entries this year).

ALDBOROUGH (N Yorks) SE4166 Map 7
Ship 🛏

Village signposted from B6265 just S of Boroughbridge, close to A1

Seats in the heavily beamed bar of this attractive and neatly kept old pub look through latticed windows to the ancient village church across the lane. There are some old-fashioned seats around heavy cast-iron tables, sentimental engravings on the walls, and a coal fire in the stone inglenook fireplace. Good bar food includes home-made soup (£1.60), well filled sandwiches (from £1.95; open ones from £3.75), garlic mushrooms (£2.95), ploughman's (£4.50), giant yorkshire pudding with roast beef (£4.90), home-made steak and kidney pie, lasagne or home-made chicken curry (all £5.25), battered cod (£5.95), steaks (from £7.25), and daily specials such as various pasta dishes (from £5.50), seafood pancakes (£5.95), calf liver and bacon or bacon chop (£6.95), chicken with coriander (£7.95), and puddings (from £2.75); good breakfasts and friendly brisk service. Well kept John Smiths, Tetleys Bitter, and Theakstons Best on handpump, and quite a few malt whiskies; shove-ha'penny, dominoes, and piped music. There are seats on the front terrace or on the spacious lawn behind. The Roman town with its museum and Roman pavements is nearby. *(Recommended by Martin Hickes, A J L Gayfer, Michael Butler, T M Dobby, Mr and Dr J Harrop, Tony Gayfer, Janet and Peter Race, Tony Kemp, Rachel Weston, Martin Hickes, Peter and Patricia Burton)*

Free house ~ Licensee Duncan Finch ~ Real ale ~ Meals and snacks (not Sun evening) ~ Restaurant (not Sun evening) ~ (01423) 322749 ~ Children in eating area of bar ~ Open 12-2.30, 5.30-11; 12-11 summer Sat; 12-3, 5.30-11 winter Sat; 12-3, 7-10.30 Sun ~ Bedrooms: £31S/£43S

APPLETREEWICK (N Yorks) SE0560 Map 7
Craven Arms ♀ 🍴

Village signposted off B6160 Burnsall—Bolton Abbey

The small cosy rooms in this creeper-covered country pub have roaring fires (one in an ancient iron range), attractive settles and carved chairs among more usual seats, beams covered with banknotes, harness, copper kettles and so forth, and a warm atmosphere; the landlord is quite a character. Generous bar food includes home-made soup (£1.90), sandwiches (from £1.95), potted shrimps (£3), ploughman's (£3.90), cumberland sausage and onion sauce (£4.90), home-made steak and kidney pie (£5.20), ham and eggs (£6.05), steaks (from £8.70); quick table service in the charming small dining room. Well kept Black Sheep Bitter and Riggwelter, Tetleys Bitter, and Theakstons Best, Old Peculier, and XB on handpump, decent, keenly priced wines, and several malt whiskies; darts, cribbage, and dominoes – no music. The view from the picnic tables in front of the building is splendid and looks south over the green Wharfedale valley to a pine-topped ridge; there are more seats in the back garden. The pub is popular with walkers. *(Recommended by M Buchanan, P R White, Paul and Madeleine Morey, John Fazakerley, Judith Hirst, Gwen and Peter Andrews, Andrew and Ruth Triggs, Prof and Mrs S Barnett, WAH, Martin Hickes, Geoffrey and Irene Lindley, M Joyner, Jim and Maggie Cowell, David Sadler, J E Rycroft)*

Free house ~ Licensees Jim and Linda Nicholson ~ Real ale ~ Meals and snacks (not Tues evening) ~ (01756) 720270 ~ Children welcome ~ Open 11.30-3, 6.30-11; 12-3, 7-10.30 Sun

ASENBY (N Yorks) SE3975 Map 7
Crab & Lobster ★ 🍲 ♀ 🛏

Village signposted off A168 – handy for A1

A couple of our readers are happy to drive the 300 miles from London to enjoy the exemplary food in this very popular thatched dining pub. But this isn't just a straightforward dining pub – there's a lot of character in the rambling, cosily cluttered L-shaped bar: an interesting jumble of seats from antique high-backed and other settles through settees and wing armchairs heaped with cushions to tall and rather theatrical corner seats and even a very superannuated dentist's chair; the tables are almost as much of a mix, and the walls and available surfaces are quite a jungle of bric-a-brac, with standard and table lamps and candles keeping even the lighting pleasantly informal. The much enjoyed food might include goat's cheese crostini with hazelnut mustard salad (£4.50), lunchtime fish club sandwich (£5), garlic and lemon baked scallops (£5.50), duck foie gras and prune terrine (£6), fish pie with gruyère potato crust (£9), thai chicken with coconut cream risotto (£9.50), crispy duck confit with sweet apples and black pudding (£11), calf liver, crispy bacon, bubble and squeak (£11.50), roast halibut and crab wellington with shellfish cream (£12), and delicious puddings such as raspberry and milky bar crème brûlée, cinnamon pear tart tatin or fruit terrine with sorbets (£4.25); the little chocolate truffles with the coffee are divine; three course set lunch £14.50, and there are usually nibbles on the bar counter. Black Sheep, John Smiths, Theakstons Best, and Timothy Taylors Landlord on handpump, and good wines by the glass, with interesting bottles; well reproduced piped music. This year they have extended the garden by 100 metres and created a mediterranean-style terrace in front of the pub for outside eating; wood-stove barbecues every Friday evening and Sunday lunchtime with entertainment during the spring and summer, weather permitting. A permanent marquee is attached to the no-smoking restaurant. They have integrated a country house surrounding the pub and opened up ensuite rooms – three acres of mature gardens, tennis court and 180 metre golf hole with full practice facilities. *(Recommended by Susan and John Douglas, Tony Hall, Melanie Jackson, Pat Bruce, Walker and Debra Lapthorne, Stephen and Brenda Head, T Halstead, John and Chris Simpson, Ian Morley, David and Fiona Pemberton, Peter Marshall, Martin Hickes, J O Jonkler, Jason Caulkin, Walter and Susan Rinaldi-Butcher, Allan Worsley, T Large, Miss V Smith, Peter Bell, Mr and Mrs Chapman, David Stafford, Mr and Mrs C Cole)*

Free house ~ Licensees David and Jackie Barnard ~ Real ale ~ Meals and snacks (not Sun evening) ~ Restaurant (not Sun evening) ~ (01845) 577286 ~ Children welcome ~ Regular jazz/blues evenings ~ Open 11.30-3, 6-11; 12-3 Sun (closed Sun evening) ~ Bedrooms: £45B/£65B

ASKRIGG (N Yorks) SD9591 Map 10
Kings Arms ♀ 🛏

Village signposted from A684 Leyburn—Sedbergh in Bainbridge

Built originally in 1760 to house a famous racing stables and converted in 1810 to a coaching inn, this bustling inn is in a lovely village surrounded by fine countryside. There are three atmospheric, old-fashioned bars with lots of mementoes and photographs of the filming of James Herriot's *All Creatures Great and Small* – the inn itself, in the series, was the Drovers Arms. The very high-ceilinged central room has an attractive medley of furnishings that includes a fine sturdy old oak settle, nineteenth-c fashion plates, a stag's head, hunting prints, and a huge stone fireplace; a curving wall with a high window shows people bustling up and down the stairs and there's a kitchen hatch in the panelling. The small low-beamed and oak panelled front bar has period furnishings, some side snugs, and a lovely green marble fireplace. A simply furnished flagstoned back bar has yet another fire, and a fruit machine, and juke box. Darts, shove-ha'penny, dominoes, and cribbage. Enjoyable food can be eaten in the bars or the no-smoking, waitress-served Silks Grill Room: lunchtime sandwiches, home-made soup (£2.50), prawn and smoked salmon terrine (£3.95), spaghetti provençale (£4.95), panacalty (grated potato with bacon and onions topped with poached eggs and melted cheese, £5.50), peat bog pie (shepherd's pie topped with black pudding and oatmeal, £6.25), steak in ale pie, halibut steak with spinach in a cream and vermouth sauce or cantonese chicken (all £6.50), honey-roasted local lamb ribs (£7.95), supreme of duck with kumquats and crème de cassis (£8.25), traditional home-made puddings (£2.95), and children's dishes (from £1.95); good breakfasts. The Club Room is also no smoking. Well kept Dent Bitter, Theakstons XB, Websters Yorkshire Bitter, Youngers No 3, and a summer guest on handpump, quite a few malt whiskies, and a very good wine list (including interesting champagnes); pleasant, helpful staff. The two-level courtyard has lots of tables and chairs. Both Wordsworth and Turner stayed here. *(Recommended by R H Rowley, B Edgeley, Gwen and Peter Andrews, Andrew and Ruth Triggs, Marianne Lantree, Steve Webb, Paul Boot, Peter and Patricia Burton, R White)*

Free house ~ Licensees Raymond and Elizabeth Hopwood ~ Real ale ~ Meals and snacks ~ Restaurants ~ (01969) 650258 ~ Children welcome ~ Live entertainment monthly Fri evening ~ Open 11-3(5 Sat), 6.30-11; 12-3, 7-10.30 Sun ~ Bedrooms: £50B/£79B

AYSGARTH (N Yorks) SE0088 Map 10
George & Dragon

This 17th-c coaching inn is set at the heart of the Pennines and surrounded by the lovely scenery of Upper Wensleydale. The small, cosy and attractive bar has built-in cushioned wooden wall seats and plush stools around a few pubby tables, tankards, jugs, and copper pots hanging from the thick beams, portraits of locals by the landlord on the panelled walls, a warm open fire with a dark wooden mantelpiece, and high bar stools by the decorative wooden bar; well kept Black Sheep Bitter, John Smiths, and Theakstons Best on handpump. There's also a polished hotel lounge with antique china, and a grandfather clock; friendly obliging service, and a welcome for children and dogs. A lot of emphasis is placed on the food which can be eaten in the bar or two other attractive dining areas. At lunchtime this might include home-made soup or sandwiches (£2.50), home-made chicken liver pâté (£3.95), ploughman's or three-egg omelettes (£5.95), cumberland sausage (£6.25), leek, cheese and potato pie (£6.50), fresh battered haddock (£6.95), gammon with two eggs (£7.95), and venison casserole (£8.75); a larger choice in the evening takes in king prawns in garlic (£5.95), lemon chicken (£8.50), duckling and orange sauce (£9.75), baked halibut (£10.95), and steaks (from £10.95); puddings, and children's menu (£3.50). Piped music, and a grey and white cat called Smokey. Outside on the gravelled beer garden are some picnic tables and tubs of pretty flowers. *(Recommended by Ray and Liz Monk, Charles and Pauline Stride, David and Judy Walmsley, Clare Wilson, Hazel and Michael Duncombe, Pat and Clive Sherriff, Angus Lyon, Ian Morley)*

Free house ~ Licensees Nigel and Joan Fawcett ~ Real ale ~ Meals and snacks (12-2, 6-9) ~ (01969) 663358 ~ Children welcome ~ Open 11-3(4 Sat), 6-11; 12-4, 6-10.30 Sun ~ Bedrooms: £25B/£50B

BARDSEY SE3643 (W Yorks) Map 7
Bingley Arms ♀ 🛏

Church Lane, off A58 Leeds—Wetherby

With much more character than most pubs of this size, this ancient place has some claim to look for its origins before the Norman Conquest, though even the oldest parts of the present building measure their age in centuries rather than millennia. The large lounge area, with a huge fireplace, is divided into several more intimate areas including a no-smoking part, and there are all sorts of interesting features – most picturesque of all is the upstairs brasserie. There's a smaller public bar; darts, dominoes, fruit machine, and piped music. Bought from the brewery only a couple of years or so ago, the inn seems to have come into its own now, with a really friendly atmosphere and speedy pleasant service. A very wide range of good value bar food includes sandwiches (from £2.50; soup and a sandwich £3.95), bangers and mash (£3.95), lasagne (£4.50), cod and salmon fishcake or steak and kidney pudding (£4.95), thai spiced chicken breast chargrilled on a coriander, cucumber and red onion salad (£5.95), and daily specials such as wild mushroom ragout, scallops in parma ham or calf liver with pancetta and onion timbale. Well kept Black Sheep Bitter and Tetleys Bitter and Mild on handpump, good wines. There are tables out in a charming quiet terraced garden, and barbecues out here run to inventive herby vegetarian dishes as well as the usual meats. *(Recommended by Martin Hickes, Sue Blackburn, Drs A and A C Jackson, Andy and Jill Kassube)*

Free house ~ Licensees Jim and Jan Wood ~ Real ale ~ Meals and snacks (12-2.30, 5.30-10) ~ Restaurant ~ (01937) 572462 ~ Well behaved children welcome ~ Open 12-3, 5.30-11; 12-11 Sat/Sun

BECKHOLE (N Yorks) NZ8202 Map 10
Birch Hall

Quite unique and unchanging, this pub-cum-village shop has two rooms with the shop selling postcards, sweeties and ice creams in between, and hatch service to both sides. Furnishings are simple – built-in cushioned wall seats and wooden tables and chairs on the floor (flagstones in one room, composition in the other), and well kept ales such as Black Sheep Bitter, Theakstons Best and XB, and local guest beers on handpump. Bar snacks such as butties (£1.80), locally-made pies (£1.20), and home-made scones and cakes including their lovely beer cake (from 60p); friendly, welcoming staff. Outside, an ancient mural hangs on the pub wall, there are benches out in front, and steep steps up to a charming little steeply terraced side garden with a nice view. This is a lovely spot and close to the steam railway. *(Recommended by R Borthwick, S Clegg, E A Thwaite, Eddie Edwards; more reports please)*

Free house ~ Licensee Colin Jackson ~ Real ale ~ Snacks (available throughout opening hours) ~ (01947) 896245 ~ Children in small family room ~ Parking is difficult, so park in the nearest car park ~ Open 11-11; 11-3, 7.30-11 in winter; 12-10.30 summer Sun; closed winter Mon evenings

BEVERLEY (E Yorks) TA0340 Map 8
White Horse ('Nellies')

Hengate, close to the imposing Church of St Mary's; runs off North Bar Within

Although a new manager has taken over here, nothing has changed to spoil the carefully preserved Victorian feel. The basic but very atmospheric little rooms are huddled together around the central bar, with brown leatherette seats (high-backed settles in one little snug) and basic wooden chairs and benches on bare floorboards, antique cartoons and sentimental engravings on the nicotine-stained walls, a gaslit pulley-controlled chandelier, a deeply reverberating chiming clock, and open fires – one with an attractively tiled old fireplace. Well kept and very cheap Sam Smiths OBB on handpump. Cheap, simple food includes toasties (from £1.75), filled baked potatoes (from £1.95), and roast beef with yorkshire pudding, big deep-fried haddock or home-made steak pie (£3.95). A separate games room has dominoes, pinball, fruit machine, juke box, and two pool tables – these and the no-smoking room behind the bar are the only modern touches. Those whose tastes are for comfortable modern pubs may find it a little spartan, anyone else will quickly feel at home. *(Recommended by Paul and Pam Penrose, Pete Baker, Stephen, Julie and Hayley Brown, Rona Murdoch)*

Sam Smiths ~ Manager John Etherington ~ Real ale ~ Lunchtime meals and snacks (not Mon) ~ (01482) 861973 ~ Children welcome except in bar ~ Folk night Mon, jazz night Weds, poetry and music night 1st Thurs of month – all poets/musicians welcome ~ Open 11-11; 12-10.30 Sun; closed 25 Dec

BILBROUGH SE5346 Map 7
Three Hares 🍴 ♀ 🍺

Off A64 York—Tadcaster

The enjoyable and imaginative food remains the main draw to this smartly refurbished dining pub. Using top quality local produce and served in the lounge bar, this might include lunchtime sandwiches (not Sunday), home-made soups, deep-fried vegetables in a crisp yeast batter with a sweet and sour sauce (£3.50), ciabatta bread topped with roasted vegetables, mozzarella, cheddar and basil oil (£4.25), fresh crab cake with a lemon grass and coriander dressing (£4.50), mushroom korma (£6.50), Whitby fish pie with herb crumble topping, confit of duck leg with cassoulet of beans, chorizo sausage and tomato or home-made pork, herb and chilli sausages on bubble and squeak with a shallot gravy (all £6.95), pasta with smoked cod, asparagus tips, crème fraîche and a light curry sauce (£7.25), stir fry of chicken and king prawns in black bean sauce with crispy egg noodles (£8.25), sirloin steak (£9.95), and home-made puddings such as chilled raspberry délice with deep-fried mango, steamed dark chocolate sponge with white chocolate chips or bread and butter pudding (£3.25); they sell the recipes over the counter for charity. Two well kept real ales on handpump such as Black Sheep Bitter, Jennings Cumberland, John Smiths Bitter or Timothy Taylors Landlord, and a good, interesting and sensibly priced wine list (Mr Whitehead's wholesale wine business is thriving) with eleven by the glass. The old village smithy forms part of the no-smoking restaurant and the old forge and implement hooks are still visible; the prettily papered walls of the traditional bar are hung with pictures of the village (taken in 1904 and showing that little has changed since then), and there's plenty of polished copper and brass. The churchyard close to the pub is where Sir Thomas Fairfax, famous for his part in the Civil War, lies buried. *(Recommended by Janet Pickles, William Cunliffe, Pat Martin, M Buchanan, H Bramwell, Joy and Peter Heatherley, R Grace, J V Dadswell, Martin Bromfield, Bernadette Garner, Jason Caulkin, Gill and Andy Plumb, Syd and Wyn Donald, David and Fiona Pemberton, Neville Kenyon, Eric and Shirley Broadhead, Pat and Tony Martin, Carole and Philip Bacon, Keith and Margaret Kettell)*

Free house ~ Lease: Peter and Sheila Whitehead ~ Real ale ~ Meals and snacks (not Mon) ~ Restaurant (not Sun evening or Mon) ~ (01937) 832128 ~ Well behaved children in eating area of bar and those over 10 in restaurant but must be gone by 8pm ~ Open 12-2.30, 7(6.30 Fri/Sat)-11; 12-3, 7-10 Sun; closed Mon (except bank hols), and evenings 26 Dec and 1 Jan

BLAKEY RIDGE (N Yorks) SE6799 Map 10

Lion 🍺 🍽

From A171 Guisborough—Whitby follow Castleton, Hutton le Hole signposts; from A170 Kirkby Moorside—Pickering follow Keldholm, Hutton le Hole, Castleton signposts; OS Sheet 100 map reference 679996

A good mix of customers from walkers, passing motorists, coach parties, and campers (the pub provides camping) come to this isolated 16th-c inn to enjoy the generous helpings of good value food. The views from here are stunning and this isolated place is said to be the fourth highest in England (1325 ft up). The cosy and characterful beamed and rambling bars have a bustling, friendly atmosphere, warm open fires, a few big high-backed rustic settles around cast-iron-framed tables, lots of small dining chairs on the turkey carpet, a nice leather settee, and stripped stone walls hung with some old engravings and photographs of the pub under snow (it can easily get cut off in winter). As well as lunchtime sandwiches (£2.25) and ploughman's (£4.45), the bar food includes giant yorkshire pudding and gravy (£1.95), breaded haddock (£5.25), home-cooked ham and egg, home-made steak and mushroom pie or home-made vegetable lasagne (all £5.75), chicken tikka (£5.95), pork fillet (£6.75), steaks (from £8.95), and puddings such as apple pie or spotted dick and custard (£2.25); good breakfasts, and quick service even when busy – which it usually is. One of the restaurants is no smoking. Well kept Courage Directors, Morlands Old Speckled Hen, John Smiths, Tetleys Bitter, and Theakstons Best, Old Peculier, and XB on handpump; dominoes, fruit machine and piped music. *(Recommended by Joan and Andrew Life, Piotr Chodzko-Zajko, Brian Seller, Paul Barnett, Andy and Jill Kassube, Geoffrey and Irene Lindley, Stephen, Julie and Hayley Brown, Richard Fallon, Eddie Edwards, Addie and Irene Henry, Martin Jones, Mr and Mrs R P Begg, R N Hutton)*

Free house ~ Licensee Barry Crossland ~ Real ale ~ Meals and snacks (11-10) ~ Restaurant ~ (01751) 417320 ~ Children welcome ~ Open 10.30am-11pm; 12-10.30 Sun ~ Bedrooms: £16.50(£26.50B)/£45(£53B)

BOROUGHBRIDGE SE3967 (N Yorks) Map 7
Black Bull

St James Square (B6265, just off A1(M))

This attractive village is a quiet respite from the A1, and this lovely old inn has been looking after people travelling between Scotland and England for many centuries (it's said to date from the 13th, and its ancient low beams are certainly very venerable). The main bar area, with a big stone fireplace and brown leather seats, is served through an old-fashioned hatch, and there's a cosy and attractive snug with traditional wall settles. The well presented food is totally home made (bread rolls, pasta, sorbets, ice creams) and is served in the bar and extended dining room: soup (£1.95), sandwiches (from £2.50), chicken with brie and pasta or canelloni (£4.95), beef in ale with bacon and mushrooms (£5.25), breast of chicken stuffed with cheese and sage on a bed of leek and mushroom cream sauce or oriental stir-fried vegetables with mild thai spices, ground peanuts and chinese noodles (£5.95), duck leg salad with chargrilled vegetables (£6.75), smoked haddock with a mushroom and gruyère sauce (£8.50), chargrilled salmon with a choice of sauces (£9), steaks (from £10.50), fishy daily specials such as fillet of red bream roasted with tomato and crushed pesto, potato and pancetta (£8.25) or roast fillet of monkfish with spinach and parmesan risotto and tomato and basil sauce (£10.55), and puddings such as very popular tart tatin with home-made vanilla ice cream or wonderful chocolate mousse (£3.25). Well kept Black Sheep Bitter and Special and John Smiths on handpump, enjoyable wines (with ten by the glass), proper coffee – and they do afternoon teas (not on Sunday). Service is friendly and attentive; the fat ginger cat is called Sprocket. Cribbage, dominoes, chess and Captain's Lady; classical piped music in the restaurant. The comfortable bedrooms are in a more modern wing; good breakfasts. *(Recommended by Miss J Hirst, Eric and Shirley Broadhead, James Nunns, Andy and Jill Kassube, Michael Butler)*

Free house ~ Licensees Margaret Chrystal, Terry McKenne ~ Real ale ~ Meals and snacks (all day Sat; no food 1 Jan) ~ Restaurant ~ (01432) 322413 ~ Children welcome ~ Open 11-11; 12-10.30 Sun; closed evening 25 Dec ~ Bedrooms: £35B/£45B

nr BRADFIELD (S Yorks) SK2692 Map 7
Strines Inn

Strines signposted from A616 at head of Underbank Reservoir, W of Stocksbridge; or on A57 heading E of junction with A6013 (Ladybower Reservoir) take first left turn (signposted with Bradfield) then bear left

One couple visiting this handsome 13th-c stone-built inn while it was snowing outside, very much wished they were staying – as well as four-poster beds, two of the ensuite rooms have open log fires; breakfast can be served in your room. The main bar has a warmly welcoming and relaxed atmosphere, black beams liberally decked with copper kettles and so forth, quite a menagerie of stuffed animals, homely red-plush-cushioned traditional wooden wall benches and small chairs, and a coal fire in the rather grand stone fireplace; there's a good mixture of customers. A room off on the right has another coal fire, hunting photographs and prints, and lots of brass and china, and on the left, a similarly furnished room is no smoking. Genuinely home-made bar food includes sandwiches (hot roast pork or beef cut straight from the joint £2.25 and £2.80), soup (£1.95), filled baked potatoes or omelettes (from £3), garlic mushrooms (£3.95), ploughman's (£4.95), carrot, tomato, cheese and herb bake or giant yorkshire pudding filled with a roast of the day (£4.75), a pie of the day (£5.95), gammon with egg (£6.95), grilled trout (£6.95), big mixed grill (£8.25), daily specials, puddings, and Sunday roast lunch (£5.95; children £3). Well kept Boddingtons, Marstons Pedigree, Morlands Old Speckled Hen, Wards Thorne, and Whitbreads Castle Eden on handpump, a dozen malt whiskies, and particularly good coffee; good service, and piped music. The inn is surrounded by superb scenery on the edge of the High Peak National Park and there are fine views from the outside picnic tables; swings and some rescued animals – Gideon the old donkey, pigs, goats, geese, hens, sheep and a rabbit called Budweiser; well behaved dogs welcome. *(Recommended by John and Joan Nash, Mr and Mrs D Hack, Dave and Karen Turner, Geoffrey and Irene Lindley, Eric Locker, A J Hilton)*

Free house ~ Licensee Jeremy Stanish ~ Real ale ~ Meals and snacks ~ (0114) 2851247 ~ Well behaved children welcome away from main bar and until 9pm ~ Open 11-11; 10.30-3, 7-11 winter weekdays; 12-10.30 Sun ~ Bedrooms: £35B/£45B

BRANDESBURTON (E Yorks) TA1247 Map 8
Dacre Arms

Village signposted from A165 N of Beverley and Hornsea turn-offs

An inn has stood here since the 16th c and for some time it was one of the most important posting stations in the East Riding. The rambling rough-plastered modernised bar is vividly furnished with plenty of tables, and has a roomily comfortable feel; well kept Tetleys, Theakstons Old Peculier and summer guest beers tapped from the cask. A wide choice of bar food includes sandwiches (not Sunday), home-made tomato and basil soup (£1.65), filled baked potatoes (from £2.75), steak and kidney casserole (snack size £3.30, king size £4.75), chicken curry (snack size £3.55, king size £4.85), filled yorkshire puddings (from £4.35), Spanish omelette (£4.95), steaks (from £9.65), house specials like steak in ale pie (£5.35), southern fried chicken (£5.65), fresh fillet of salmon (£6.65), and green king prawn curry (£7.45), and puddings (from £2.10); Sunday roast lunch £4.50. Fruit machine and video game. *(Recommended by Stephen, Julie and Hayley Brown, I Maw, C A Hall; more reports please)*

Free house ~ Lease: Jason and Liza Good ~ Real ale ~ Meals and snacks (12-2, 6-10 Mon-Thurs; 12-2, 5.30-10.30 Fri/Sat; 12-10 Sun) ~ Restaurant ~ (01964) 542392 ~ Children welcome ~ Open 11.30-2.30, 6(5.30 Fri)-11; 11.30-11 Sat; 12-10.30 Sun; closed 25 Dec

BREARTON (N Yorks) SE3261 Map 7
Malt Shovel ⑪ ♀

Village signposted off A61 N of Harrogate

Run by particularly friendly, helpful licensees, this much liked 16th-c village inn now has special heaters so you can eat outside on the small terrace on all but the coldest of days. Mr Mitchell told us that some customers took just a little persuasion to eat outside in overcoat weather, but once they had tried, they loved it. Several heavily-beamed rooms radiate from the attractive linenfold oak bar counter with plush-cushioned seats and a mix of tables, an ancient oak partition wall, tankards and horsebrasses, both real and gas fires, and lively hunting prints. The very good food might include sandwiches (from £2.25), garlic mushroom bake (£4.75), nut roast with pesto sauce or rabbit and mushroom pie in port (£4.95), smoked goat's cheese and roast red pepper tart (£5.25), honey-baked ham with grain mustard and honey sauce (£5.30), cajun fresh haddock, a good haggis, or steak in ale pie (all £5.50), lamb shanks braised in white wine with garlic and mint (£5.65), Whitby sole with a caper and lemon butter sauce (£6.75), chargrilled loin of venison with a red wine and wild mushroom sauce (£9.50), and puddings such as banana cheesecake with toffee sauce, fresh fruit brûlée or treacle tart (£2.25). Well kept Black Sheep Bitter, Daleside Nightjar, Theakstons Best, and many guest beers from small local breweries on handpump, 25 malt whiskies, and small but interesting and reasonably priced wine list (they will serve any wine by the glass) with a wine of the week; they serve their house coffee (and a guest coffee) in cafetières. Darts, shove-ha'penny, cribbage, and dominoes. There are more tables on the grass. *(Recommended by M Buchanan, Andrew and Ruth Triggs, Janet Edwards, Rita Horridge, Janet and Peter Race, Marian and Andrew Ruston, Syd and Wyn Donald, Walter and Susan Rinaldi-Butcher, Mr and Mrs Chapman, M Heys, Derek and Sylvia Stephenson, David Watson, Paul Boot)*

Free house ~ Licensees Les and Charlotte Mitchell ~ Real ale ~ Meals and snacks (not Sun evening, not Mon) ~ (01423) 862929 ~ Children welcome ~ Open 12-2.30, 6.45-11(10.30 Sun); closed Mon

BUCKDEN (N Yorks) SD9278 Map 7
Buck ♀

B6160

Of the many fine pubs in and around Wharfedale, this attractive creeper-covered stone inn is perhaps the most usefully placed for the hill walks; seats on the terrace enjoy good surrounding moorland views. Inside, the modernised and extended open-plan bar has upholstered built-in wall banquettes and square stools around shiny dark brown tables on its carpet – though there are still flagstones in the snug original area by the serving counter – local pictures, hunting prints, willow-pattern plates on a delft shelf, and the mounted head of a roebuck on bare stone wall above the log fire. Helpful uniformed staff quickly serve the popular bar food which includes sandwiches, home-made soup (£2.45), home-made tart of fresh Whitby crab with aioli dressing or tagliatelle of wild mushrooms, smoked bacon and avocado (£4.25), baked provençale vegetable terrine topped with brie, served with a mustard seed sauce (£6.95), corn fed chicken breast wrapped in smoked bacon and braised in fiery red pepper and onion mustard seed compote (£8.50), pigeon breasts on root vegetable mash with a bacon and shallot jus (£8.95), highland venison steak with a port and redcurrant sauce or chargrilled sirloin steak with wild mushroom, peppercorn and shallot sauce (£12.75), and home-made puddings like sticky toffee pudding, a trio of Swiss chocolate terrines, and caramelised lemon tart (from £3.25); the dining area and restaurant are no smoking. Well kept Morlands Old Speckled Hen and Theakstons Best, Old Peculier, Black Bull and XB on handpump, a fair choice of malt whiskies, and decent wines; piped music and fruit machine (which some readers feel is a shame). *(Recommended by Andrew and Ruth Triggs, P Rome, Ann and Colin Hunt, Sue Blackburn, Vann Prime, Wm Van Laaten, Geoffrey and Brenda Wilson, Walter and Susan Rinaldi-Butcher, R N Hutton, E George, Chris Wheaton, Dr P Jackson, I Maw, F J Robinson, M Morgan, J E Rycroft, K Frostick)*

Free house ~ Licensee Nigel Hayton ~ Real ale ~ Meals and snacks ~ Evening restaurant ~ (01756) 760228 ~ Children welcome away from bar ~ Open 11-11; 12-10.30 Sun ~ Bedrooms: £34B/£68B

BURNSALL (N Yorks) SE0361 Map 7
Red Lion ♀ ⇌

B6160 S of Grassington, on Ilkley road; OS Sheet 98, map reference 033613

This year, the terrace behind this popular old ferryman's inn has been extended – it's lit by old gas lamps and there are fine views of the River Wharfe; you can also see the river from more seats on the front cobbles and from most of the bedrooms. Lots of fine surrounding walks, and fishing permits for 7 miles of river. Inside, the bustling main bar has sturdy seats built in to the attractively panelled walls (decorated with pictures of the local fell races), windsor armchairs, oak benches, rugs on the floor, and steps up past a solid fuel stove to a back area with sensibly placed darts (dominoes players are active up here, too). The carpeted, no-smoking front lounge bar, served from the same copper-topped counter through an old-fashioned small-paned glass partition, has a log fire. Enjoyable bar food includes home-made soup (£2.75), lunchtime sandwiches (from £3.50; open sandwiches £5.50), good Cumbrian air-dried ham cured in molasses and served with their own chutney or a light terrine of local game layered with pheasant, pigeon and duck (£4.25), spinach, mushrooms, shallots and feta cheese baked in a filo triangle (£6.50), ploughman's with home-made chutneys and relishes (£6.95), steak and kidney in ale pie (£7.25), fillet of fresh cod with a lemon, parsley and sun-dried tomato crust (£7.95), braised shoulder of Herdwick lamb stuffed with garlic, rosemary, wild mushrooms and lemon (£9.50), Aberdeen Angus sirloin steak (£10.50), and daily specials such as local rabbit or Aberdeen Angus pot roast or medallions of monkfish with a creamy lime and lemon sauce (£8.95); half helpings for children. The restaurant is no smoking. Well kept Black Sheep Bitter, Tetleys Bitter, Theakstons Best, and guest beers on handpump, several malt whiskies, and a very good wine list with an interesting choice by the glass. *(Recommended by D Stokes, B M and P Kendall, Mr and Mrs D J Ross, M Buchanan, Gill and*

Keith Croxton, Bob and Maggie Atherton, David and Judy Walmsley, Simon Watkins, Prof and Mrs S Barnett, Pat and Clive Sherriff, Paul and Madeleine Morey, Ann and Colin Hunt, Norma Hardy, Ian and Christina Allen, Tim Davidson, Jim Bedford)

Free house ~ Licensee Elizabeth Grayshon ~ Real ale ~ Meals and snacks (12-2.30, 6-9.30) ~ Restaurant ~ (01756) 720204 ~ Children welcome ~ Open 11(11.30 Sat)-11.30; 12-10.30 Sun ~ Bedrooms: £45B/£74B

BYLAND ABBEY (N Yorks) SE5579 Map 7
Abbey Inn

The Abbey has a brown tourist-attraction signpost off the A170 Thirsk—Helmsley

Friendly new licensees had just taken over here as we went to press but had kept on the chef – so the good, popular food will, hopefully, continue to draw people to this busy dining pub. The rambling, characterful rooms have big fireplaces, oak and stripped deal tables, settees, carved oak seats, and Jacobean-style dining chairs on the polished boards and flagstones, various stuffed birds, cooking implements, little etchings, willow-pattern plates and china cabinets, and some discreet stripping back of plaster to show the ex-abbey masonry; the big back room has lots of rustic bygones; piped music. Served by neat and friendly waitresses, bar food at lunchtime might include sandwiches (from £2.95), home-made chicken liver or hazelnut, mushroom and lentil pâté (£4.95), a platter of beef, ham and pâté with salad (£5.95), vegetarian lasagne or trout fillet breton (£6.75), poached haddock with cheese sauce (£7.50), and lamb and mint pie (£8), with evening dishes like herring hors d'oeuvre (£4.20), turkey terrine with cranberry sauce (£4.25), chicken breast tandoori (£8.50), pork steak with sweet mustard and herb sauce (£8.75), and salmon and leek bake (£9.75), with puddings such as chocolate marble cheesecake, summer pudding or bread and butter pudding (£3); three-course roast Sunday lunch (£12; children £6). Well kept Black Sheep Bitter and Theakstons Best on handpump, and an interesting wine list. The grey tabby cat is called Milly and the black one, Woody. There's lots of room outside in the garden. The setting, opposite the abbey ruins, is lovely. *(Recommended by R F Grieve, Syd and Syn Donald, John Fahy, Mr and Dr J Harrop, Paul Barnett, Richard Fallon, Geoffrey and Brenda Wilson, Paul and Ursula Randall, David and Fiona Pemberton, Peter and Patricia Burton, Mr and Mrs W B Draper, Chris Mawson, Geoffrey and Irene Lindley; more reports on the new regime, please)*

Free house ~ Licensees Jane and Martin Nordli ~ Real ale ~ Meals and snacks (not Sun evening, not Mon) ~ (01347) 868204 ~ Children welcome ~ Open 11-2.30, 6.30-11; 12-2 Sun; closed Sun evening, all day Mon and 25 Dec

CARLTON (N Yorks) SE0684 Map 10
Foresters Arms 🍴 ♀ 🛏

Off A684 W of Leyburn, just past Wensley; or take Coverdale hill road from Kettlewell, off B6160

This is as successful a pub as it is a restaurant, and once again, praise for this comfortable ex-coaching inn has been very warm this year. Staff are friendly, there's a good, relaxed atmosphere, open log fires, low beamed ceilings, well kept real ales, and most enjoyable food from an extensive and imaginative menu. As well as lots of fish dishes such as moules marinières (£4.50), baked crab and asparagus gateau (£5.25), chargrilled tuna with garlic vinaigrette (£8.50), fillet of salmon in filo pastry with a rosemary cream (£8.95), mediterranean prawn salad with soy and lime vinaigrette (£9.95), and fillet of lemon sole with crab mousse and tarragon butter sauce (£12.95), there might be roast pepper and tomato soup (£2.95), wild boar sausage (£3.95), boneless quail piped with a pâté of pork and pistachio nuts with a red wine jelly (£4.75), leek and blue cheese strudel with chargrilled vegetables (£8.95), calf liver and bacon with onion marmalade (£9.50), chicken breast layered with king prawns, pesto and sun-dried tomatoes (£9.75), rib of beef with mustard sauce (£10.25), and puddings such as baked chocolate tart with armagnac ice-cream, hot baked raspberry soufflé or steamed syrup sponge with a vanilla sauce (from £3.50); a choice of good cheeses with a glass of port (£6.50). Well kept Black Sheep Bitter, John Smiths, Tetleys

Bitter, Theakstons Best, and Websters Yorkshire on handpump, a good restauranty wine list, 40 malt whiskies, freshly squeezed orange juice, and fresh fruit coulis with sparkling mineral water. The restaurant is partly no smoking. Darts, dominoes, and piped music. There are some picnic tables among tubs of flowers. *(Recommended by A J Morton, David and Judy Walmsley, Mr and Mrs M Thompson, W James, A C Chapman, Gwen and Peter Andrews, B and M and P Kendall, Jill Hallpike, Carl Upsall, Mrs S M Halliday, E A Thwaite, Walter and Susan Rimaldi-Butcher, Andrew and Ruth Triggs, Jess Parrish, David and Fiona Pemberton)*

Free house ~ Lease: Barrie Higginbotham ~ Real ale ~ Meals and snacks (not Sun evening, not Mon) ~ Restaurant (not Sun evening, not Mon) ~ (01969) 640272 ~ Children in eating area of bar and must be over 12 in restaurant ~ Open 12-3, 6.30-11; 12-3, 7-10.30 Sun; closed Mon lunchtime and 3 weeks Jan ~ Bedrooms: £35S/£60S

CARTHORPE (N Yorks) SE3184 Map 10
Fox & Hounds ★ ⊕
Village signposted from A1 N of Ripon, via B6285

The food in this neatly kept and friendly extended village pub is really good and enjoyable without being over fancy. As well as daily specials such as chicken and asparagus soup (£2.45), curried vegetable pancake (£3.95), queen scallop and prawn mornay (£4.95), steak and kidney pie (£6.95), salmon fillet with ginger and spring onions (£8.95), and roast breast of duckling with honey and cloves (£10.95), the menu includes duck liver pâté in port jelly (£3.95), whole fresh dressed Whitby crab (£4.95), baby chicken cooked in ale (£7.95), rolled lemon sole fillets filled with fresh salmon and prawns in a white wine sauce (£8.95), steaks or rack of English lamb (£9.95), and puddings such as pear, apricot and raspberry pie, sticky toffee pudding with pecan toffee sauce or strawberry shortcake with fruit coulis (£3.25). There is some theatrical memorabilia in the corridors, and the cosy L-shaped bar has quite a few mistily evocative Victorian photographs of Whitby, a couple of nice seats by the larger of its two log fires, plush button-back built-in wall banquettes and chairs, plates on stripped beams, and some limed panelling; piped light classical music. An attractive high-raftered no-smoking restaurant leads off with lots of neatly black-painted farm and smithy tools. Well kept John Smiths Bitter on handpump, and decent wines with bin-ends listed on a blackboard. *(Recommended by F J Robinson, Geoffrey and Brenda Wilson, David and Julie Hart, Fiona and David Pemberton, Ian Morley)*

Free house ~ Licensee Howard Fitzgerald ~ Meals and snacks (not Mon) ~ Restaurant (not Mon) ~ (01845) 567433 ~ Children welcome until 8pm ~ Open 12-2.30, 7-11(10.30 Sun); closed Mon and first week of the year

COXWOLD (N Yorks) SE5377 Map 7
Fauconberg Arms ★ ♀
The furniture in the two cosy knocked-together rooms of the lounge bar in this old stone inn has been carefully chosen by the friendly licensees – most of it is either Mouseman or the work of some of the other local craftsmen – or cushioned antique oak settles and windsor high-backed chairs and oak tables; there's a marvellous winter log fire in an unusual arched stone fireplace, and gleaming brass. For those wanting an informal drink and chat, there's also an old-fashioned back locals' bar. Good bar food includes home-made soup (£2.10), enjoyable sandwiches (from £2.60), chicken liver and ham terrine with home-made fruit chutney and a tomato and apple salad (£3.35), roast breast of chicken poached in a creamy sauce of buttered mushrooms and leeks, asparagus and cashew nut filo pastry plait with a port, red onion and honey glaze, steak in ale pie or stuffed aubergine with red lentils, cumin and apricots (all £5.95), trout fillets in almond breadcrumbs with a sauce of crème fraîche, parsley and apricot brandy (£6.35), sirloin steak (£9.25), puddings such as grand marnier white chocolate mousse with whipped cream, white chocolate fingers and maple syrup or seasonal fruit pie (£2.95), and children's menu (£2.50); they do a take-away menu (not winter Monday evenings). Well kept Morlands Old Speckled Hen, John Smiths, Tetleys

Bitter, and Theakstons Best on handpump, and an extensive wine list with most available by the glass. Darts, dominoes, fruit machine, and piped music. The bedrooms should have all have been upgraded by the time this book is published. The inn is named after Lord Fauconberg, who married Oliver Cromwell's daughter Mary. *(Recommended by K and J Brooks, David Cooke, Syd and Wyn Donald, Peter and Ruth Burnstone, Howard England, P R White, Martin Harlow, Mr and Mrs R P Begg, Bill and Sheila McLardy, Dr and Mrs A H Young, R L Gorick, Janet Pickles, Iain Bennett, Fiona Haycock, Martin Hickes)*

Free house ~ Tenants Robin and Nicky Jaques ~ Meals and snacks (not Mon evening in winter) ~ Restaurant (not winter Mon evening) ~ (01347) 868214 ~ Children welcome ~ Open 11-3, 6.30(6 Sat)-11; winter evening opening 7pm; 12-3, 7-10.30 Sun ~ Bedrooms: £24(£30S)/£40(£55S)

CRAY (N Yorks) SD9379 Map 7
White Lion 🍺

B6160, Upper Wharfedale N of Kettlewell

Surrounding this former drovers' hostelry is some superb countryside which you can enjoy from picnic tables above the very quiet steep lane or on the great flat limestone slabs in the shallow stream which tumbles down opposite. Inside, the simply furnished bar has a traditional atmosphere, seats around tables on the flagstone floor, shelves of china, iron tools and so forth, a high dark beam-and-plank ceiling, and a warming open fire; there's also a no-smoking family snug. Bar food includes sandwiches, home-made soup (£2), cumberland sausage (£5.95), meaty or vegetarian lasagne (£6.25), gammon with two eggs (£7.50), evening steaks (from £10.50), and daily specials such as yorkshire pudding filled with savoury mince (£4.50), home-made steak and mushroom pie or chicken curry (£6.95), home-made madeira pork with paprika (£7.50), home-made venison casserole (£8.75), and puddings like toffee crunch cheesecake or hot chocolate fudge cake (£2.20). Well kept Moorhouses Pendle Witches Brew, Tetleys Bitter, and a guest beer on handpump; dominoes and ring-the-bull. *(Recommended by David and Judy Walmsley, Ann and Colin Hunt, David Varney, Vann Prime, Wm Van Laaten, Andy and Jill Kassube, Geoffrey and Brenda Wilson)*

Free house ~ Licensees Frank and Barbara Hardy ~ Real ale ~ Meals and snacks ~ (01756) 760262 ~ Children in dining room ~ Limited parking ~ Open 11-11; 11-3, 7-11 winter weekdays; 11-10.30 summer Sun ~ Bedrooms: £27.50(£30S)/£40(£50S)

CROPTON (N Yorks) SE7588 Map 10
New Inn 🍺

Village signposted off A170 W of Pickering

A local artist has designed historical posters all around the no-smoking downstairs conservatory in this neatly kept and comfortably modernised village inn, and the Cropton Brewery shop is quite a feature with take-home packs of bottle-conditioned beers and stout. Their ales consist of Two Pints, King Billy, Monkmans Slaughter, Uncle Sams, Backwoods and Scoresby Stout (brewery trips are encouraged), with a guest like Tetleys Bitter on handpump; country wines and Lindisfarne Mead. The airy lounge bar has Victorian church panels, terracotta and dark blue plush seats, lots of brass, and a small open fire. Substantial helpings of bar food include lunchtime sandwiches (not Sunday), steak and mushroom in ale pie (£5.95), a chicken dish (£6.50), pork steak normandie (£7.55), their speciality whole leg of lamb (£7.95), and steaks; friendly staff. The elegant small no-smoking restaurant is furnished with genuine Victorian and early Edwardian furniture. Darts, dominoes, fruit machine, piped music, and pool room. There's a neat terrace and garden with pond. Comfortable, good value bedrooms. *(Recommended by Andy and Jill Kassube, Christopher Turner, J and P Maloney, Andrew Hazeldine, Merilyn and Geoffrey Burt, Dave Braisted, R N Hutton, Nigel Hopkins, Basil Minson, David Heath)*

Own brew ~ Licensee Michael Lee ~ Real ale ~ Meals and snacks ~ Restaurant ~ (01751) 417330 ~ Children in conservatory and restaurant ~ Open 11-11; 11-2.30, 7-11 in winter; 12-10.30 Sun ~ Bedrooms: £27B/£54B

DACRE BANKS (N Yorks) SE1962 Map 7
Royal Oak

Run by friendly licensees, this peaceful old stone pub is set in a village just above the River Nidd and with beautiful views; there are seats outside and a boules piste. Inside, it's open-plan and the two comfortable lounge areas have interesting old photographs and poems with a drinking theme on the walls, an open fire in the front part, and well kept Black Sheep Bitter, John Smiths, Theakstons, and a beer named after the pub on handpump; good house wine. A wide choice of good chip-free, home-made food includes soup (£2.15), sandwiches (from £2.25), garlic mushrooms (£2.75), ploughman's (£4.45), mushroom stroganoff (£4.75), lamb hotpot (£4.95), cider-baked ham or rabbit, ham, mushroom and onion pie (£5.25), braised oxtail (£5.95), coq au vin (£6.25), grilled halibut steak with prawns (£7.95), daily specials, and traditional puddings like bread and butter or sticky toffee pudding; smaller helpings for children. Darts, pool, cribbage, dominoes, and piped music. *(Recommended by Andrew and Ruth Triggs, E A George, P R White, Klaus D Baetz)*

Free house ~ Licensee Lee Chadwick ~ Real ale ~ Meals and snacks (not Sun evening) ~ Restaurant ~ (01423) 780200 ~ Children in eating area of bar and in games room; they do not cater for infants ~ Open 12-2(3 Sat), 7-11; closed 25 Dec

EAST MARTON SD9051 (N Yorks) Map 7
Cross Keys

Marton Bridge; A59 Gisburn—Skipton

Roomy and comfortably old-fashioned, this old stone building is set back behind a small green near the Leeds & Liverpool Canal – drawing quite a few customers from that, and from the nearby Pennine Way. Antique high-backed settles, oak cupboards, china and pictures combine with the mugs and brasses on the heavy black beams, and the log fire in the big fireplace, to give a feeling of contentment, but there's always plenty of life and bustle here, with service quick, cheerful and helpful even at the busiest times. A good range of generous food at tempting prices includes fine salads, as well as home-made soup (£2.30), filled french bread (from £3.50), home-made steak and kidney pie or vegetable curry (£5.80), chicken burritos (£6.50), salmon steak in a cream, white wine and prawn sauce (£6.95), gammon and egg (£6.95), steaks (from £8.50), and puddings such as sticky toffee pudding (from £2.25); roast Sunday lunch (£5.95). Well kept Flowers Original, Tetleys Bitter, and Theakstons Best and XB on handpump, decent wines with clear tasting notes; darts, cribbage, dominoes, fruit machine, and piped music. The main children's area is by the counter where food orders are taken, and there are tables outside. *(Recommended by Sue and Mike Todd, Ann and Colin Hunt, Gill and Keith Croxton, JF, Brian Ellis)*

Free house ~ Licensee Bob White ~ Real ale ~ Meals and snacks (12-8 in summer; 12-2, 7-9 in winter) ~ Evening restaurant ~ (01282) 843485 ~ Children welcome ~ Open 11.30-11; 11.30-3, 6-11 in winter; 12-10.30 Sun

EAST WITTON (N Yorks) SE1586 Map 10
Blue Lion 🍸 ⇌

A6108 Leyburn—Ripon

Yorkshire Dining Pub of the Year

This incredibly popular and rather stylish place clearly has the Royal seal of approval – Prince Charles dined here two nights running while shooting with the Duke of Northumberland. Most people do come here for a civilised meal but there is still some pubby atmosphere, and it does pay to get there early as you can't book a table in the busy bar (though you can, of course, in the restaurant), and there may be quite a wait. The big squarish bar has high-backed antique settles and old windsor chairs and round tables on the turkey rugs and flagstones, ham-hooks in the high ceiling decorated with dried wheat, teazles and so forth, a delft shelf filled with appropriate bric-a-brac, several prints, sporting caricatures and other pictures on the walls, a log fire, and daily papers; the friendly black labrador is called Ben. Particularly good and very popular, the bar food might include sandwiches, home-made soup (£2.95), baked filo pastry filled with wensleydale cheese, cranberries and onions with a cumberland sauce (£3.25), antipasti of cold meats, pickles and chutneys (£4.95), warm terrine of game and foie gras with a rich game jus served with toasted hazelnut brioche (£5.75), tagliatelle tossed with red peppers, garlic, mushrooms and basil (£6.75), smoked haddock, saffron and risotto fishcakes with a smoked salmon and lemon butter sauce (£8.75), confit of lamb shoulder baked in filo pastry with a pearl barley, tomato and onion gravy (£9.25), chargrilled venison steak with a compote of blueberries and shallots with a sherry vinegar sauce or calf liver with an olive mash and a grilled bacon and red onion sauce (£10.25), sirloin steak (£10.95), thai-style seafood choice of clams, scallops, langoustine and squid (£13.95), and puddings such as prune and armagnac parfait with a sauternes bavarois, tarte tatin of apples with ginger ice cream or chocolate nemises with crème chantilly (from £3.25); good breakfasts; no snacks on Sunday lunchtime. Well kept Black Sheep Bitter and Riggwelter, John Smiths, and Theakstons Best on handpump, and decent wines. Picnic tables on the gravel outside look beyond the stone houses on the far side of the village green to Witton Fell, and there's a big pretty back garden. *(Recommended by John Oddey, Mike and Maggie Betton, Angela Copeland, John and Vivienne Rice, Walter and Susan Rinaldi-Butcher, David and Judy Walmsley, Susan and John Douglas, Richard Dolphin, Paul McPherson, Dr and Mrs I H Maine, Tim Halstead, Jill Hallpike, Carl Upsall, Simon and Amanda Southwell, M Morgan, Paul Boot, Anthony Barnes)*

Free house ~ Lease: Paul Klein ~ Real ale ~ Meals and snacks ~ Restaurant (closed Sun evening) ~ (01969) 624273 ~ Children welcome ~ Open 11-11; 12-10.30 Sun ~ Bedrooms: £49B/£80B

EGTON BRIDGE (N Yorks) NZ8105 Map 10
Horse Shoe 🛏

Village signposted from A171 W of Whitby; via Grosmont from A169 S of Whitby

Friendly new licensees have taken over this charmingly placed inn. The bar has high-backed built-in winged settles, wall seats and spindleback chairs around the modern oak tables, a big stuffed trout (caught near here in 1913), a fine old print of a storm off Ramsgate and other pictures on the walls, and a warm log fire. Bar food now includes lunchtime sandwiches, baked green-lipped mussels with pernod butter (£3.85), garlic king prawns (£4.25), roasted vegetable moussaka (£6.25), bacon chops with peach sauce (£7.45), salmon and cod in a pastry lattice (£8.50), and lamb shank with a herby garlic sauce (£10.50). Well kept Tetleys Bitter, Theakstons Best and Old Peculier and two guest beers on handpump; darts, dominoes, and piped music. Perhaps the best way to reach this beautifully placed pub is to park by the Roman Catholic church, walk through the village and cross the River Esk by stepping stones. There are some comfortable seats on a quiet terrace and lawn beside a little stream with ducks and geese. Not to be confused with a similarly named pub up at Egton. *(Recommended by Ian Piper, Tom Thomas, M Rutherford, Stephen, Julie and Hayley Brown, Ian Irving, RB, SC, Jim and Maggie Cowell, Val Stevenson, Rob Holmes, Phil and Heidi Cook, R N Hutton)*

Free house ~ Licensees Tim and Suzanne Boulton ~ Real ale ~ Meals and snacks (not 25 Dec) ~ Restaurant ~ (01947) 85245 ~ Children in eating area of bar only ~ Open 11-11; 11.30-3, 6.30-11 in winter; 12-10.30 Sun ~ Bedrooms: £26(£30B)/£38(£46B)

FLAMBOROUGH (E Yorks) TA2270 Map 8
Seabirds ♀

Junction of B1255 and B1229

There's a cheerful, welcoming atmosphere and a good mix of customers in this straightforward village pub. The public bar has quite a shipping theme, and leading off here the comfortable lounge has a whole case of stuffed seabirds along one wall, as well as pictures and paintings of the local landscape, and a woodburning stove. The daily fresh fish specials are well liked, and other dishes include sandwiches, soup (£1.60), prawns in garlic butter (£3.75), yorkshire pudding filled with savoury mince or cumberland sausage (£4.25), home-made steak and mushroom pie (£4.70), broccoli and cream cheese tagliatelle (£5.50), salmon steak mornay (£6.95), evening steaks (from £10.25), and half-a-dozen daily specials such as chicken breast filled with pâté in a brandy and mushroom sauce, sausage and onion pie, poacher's pie or roast barbary duck on a bed of celeriac mash with marmalade sauce. Well kept Boddingtons, John Smiths, and a weekly changing guest on handpump, good reasonably priced wine list, and a wide range of whiskies and liqueurs. Friendly, hardworking staff; darts, dominoes, fruit machine, and piped music. There are seats in the garden. *(Recommended by William Cunliffe, Joan and Andrew Life, Stephen and Brenda Head, Susan and Nigel Wilson, David and Fiona Pemberton)*

Free house ~ Licensee Jean Riding ~ Real ale ~ Meals and snacks (not Sun or Mon evenings in winter) ~ Restaurant ~ (01262) 850242 ~ Children welcome ~ Open 11-3, 7(6.30 Sat)-11; 12-3, 7-10.30 Sun; closed Mon evening in winter

GOOSE EYE (W Yorks) SE0340 Map 7
Turkey

High back road Haworth—Sutton-in-Craven, and signposted from back roads W of Keighley; OS Sheet 104, map ref 028406

Refurbished this year, the various cosy and snug alcoves in this tucked away pub have brocaded upholstery and walls covered with pictures of surrounding areas, and the restaurant is no smoking. Generous helpings of decent bar food include egg and tuna mayonnaise (£2.50), sandwiches such as hot beef (£2.75), cheese and onion quiche (£4.60), fillet of breaded haddock (£4.90), good steaks (from £7.20), daily specials like filled yorkshire puddings (£3.80), and puddings (from £2.10); Sunday roast beef (£5.80). Well kept Goose Eye Bitter and Bronte, Ind Coope Burton, Tetleys and up to four guest beers on handpump, and 26 malt whiskies; piped music. A separate games area has pool, dominoes, cribbage, fruit machine, and video game. *(Recommended by M Buchanan, Piotre Chodzko-Zajko, Andy and Jill Kassube, Richard Fallon, WAH, PM, AM)*

Free house ~ Licensees Harry and Monica Brisland ~ Real ale ~ Meals and snacks (not Mon) ~ Restaurant ~ (01535) 681339 ~ Children welcome until 9pm ~ Open 12-3, 5.30-11; 12-4, 7-11 Sat; 12-3, 7-10.30 Sun; closed Mon lunchtime

HARDEN (W Yorks) SE0838 Map 7
Malt Shovel

Follow Wilsden signpost from B6429

Some refurbishment has taken place in this handsome dark stone building this year, but readers are quick to tell us that no character has been lost. The three spotlessly clean rooms (one is no smoking at lunchtime) have kettles, brass funnels and the like hanging from the black beams, horsebrasses on leather harness, blue plush seats built into the walls, and stone-mullioned windows; one room has oak panelling, a beamed ceiling, and an open fire. Good value bar food (they tell us prices have not changed since last year) includes hot beef sandwiches, giant yorkshire pudding with sausages or beef and gravy (£3.50), home-made steak pie or chilli (£4.50), omelettes (from £4.50), and fresh haddock (£4.95). Well kept Tetleys on handpump, and efficient service; dominoes and piped music. This is a lovely spot by a bridge over Harden Beck, and the big garden is open to the public. *(Recommended by Jane Aldworth, John Keeler, Mr and Mrs R Maggs, J E Rycroft, A Preston)*

Carlsberg Tetleys ~ Managers Keith and Lynne Bolton ~ Real ale ~ Lunchtime meals and snacks (not Sun) ~ (01535) 272357 ~ Children welcome until 8pm ~ Open 12-11; 12-3, 5-11 winter weekdays; 12-10.30 Sun; 12-3, 7-10.30 winter Sun

---

Looking for a pub with a really special garden, or in lovely countryside, or with an outstanding view, or right by the water? They are listed separately, at the back of the book.

HEATH (W Yorks) SE3519 Map 7
Kings Arms

Village signposted from A655 Wakefield—Normanton – or, more directly, turn off to the left opposite Horse & Groom

This old-fashioned pub is in a fine setting with seats along the front of the building facing the village green, picnic tables on a side lawn, and a nice walled flower-filled garden. Inside, the original bar has a fire burning in the old black range (with a long row of smoothing irons on the mantelpiece), plain elm stools and oak settles built into the walls, and dark panelling. A more comfortable extension has carefully preserved the original style, down to good wood-pegged oak panelling (two embossed with royal arms), and a high shelf of plates; there are also two other small flagstoned rooms, and the conservatory opens onto the garden. The restaurant is partly no smoking. Good value bar food includes home-made soup (£1.75), sandwiches (from £1.65; hot sausage and onion £1.85), ploughman's or omelettes (£4.50), home-made lasagne or beef in ale pie, gammon and egg or battered haddock (all £4.75), puddings (£1.95), and children's meals (£2.50). As well as cheap Clarks Bitter and Festival, they also serve guests like Tetleys Bitter and Timothy Taylors Landlord on handpump. *(Recommended by Dr A J and Mrs P G Newton, Tim Halstead, Derek and Sylvia Stephenson, JJW, CMW, Michael Butler, Ian Phillips, Mike and Maggie Betton, Wayne Brindle)*

Clarks ~ Managers Terry and Barbara Ogden ~ Real ale ~ Meals and snacks ~ Restaurant ~ (01924) 377527 ~ Children welcome ~ Open 11.30-3(4 Sat), 5.30-11; 12-10.30 Sun; closed winter Sun afternoons

HECKMONDWIKE (W Yorks) SE2223 Map 7
Old Hall

New North Road; B6117 between A62 and A638; OS Sheet 104, map reference 214244

A friendly new manager has taken over this interesting 15th-c building, once the home of the Nonconformist scientist Joseph Priestley. There are lots of old beams and timbers, latticed mullioned windows with worn stone surrounds, brick or stripped old stone walls hung with pictures of Richard III, Henry VII, Catherine Parr, and Joseph Priestley, and comfortable furnishings. Snug low-ceilinged alcoves lead off the central part with its high ornate plaster ceiling, and an upper gallery room, under the pitched roof, looks down on the main area through timbering 'windows'. Home-made bar food now includes rolls (from £1.95), vegetable lasagne or a pie of the day (£3.95), chicken with cashew nuts, beef curry or chilli con carne (£4.25), good beer-battered haddock (£4.95), gammon and egg (£5.35), steaks (from £5.95), winter casseroles and liver and bacon, and puddings such as home-made fruit crumbles or pies (£1.95). Well kept (and cheap) Sam Smiths OB on handpump; fruit machine, piped music, and sports or music quizzes on Tuesday night and a general knowledge one on Thursday evening. *(Recommended by Michael Butler, Tom Thomas, Andy and Jill Kassube, DC, Ian Phillips, Peter Marshall, David and Linda Barraclough, JJW, CMW)*

Sam Smiths ~ Manager Robert Green ~ Real ale ~ Meals and snacks (all day Sun) ~ (01924) 404774 ~ Children welcome ~ Open 11-3, 6-11; 11-11 Sat; 12-10.30 Sun

HELMSLEY (N Yorks) SE6184 Map 10
Feathers ♀

Market Square

Though the main inn (with its own comfortable lounge bar, Mouseman furniture and relaxed atmosphere) is a handsomely solid three-storey stone building, the friendly adjoining pub part is much lower and a good deal older: heavy medieval beams and dark panelling, unusual cast-iron-framed tables topped by weighty slabs of oak and walnut, a venerable wall carving of a dragonfaced bird in a grape vine, and a big log fire in the stone inglenook fireplace. Bar food includes sandwiches (from £2.95; filled french bread £4.50), soup (£2), home-made salmon pâté (£3.50), vegetarian nut cutlets (£4.95), home-made lasagne (£5.75), Scarborough haddock in batter (£6.50), home-made steak pie (£6.75), deep-fried battered prawns in sweet and sour sauce

(£7.25), gammon and egg (£7.50), and steaks (from £8.50). Well kept Batemans XXXB, Black Sheep Bitter, Morlands Old Speckled Hen, John Smiths, Theakstons Best and Old Peculier, and Youngers Scotch on handpump, and a large choice of wines chalked on a blackboard; friendly service, darts and dominoes. There's an attractive back garden with seats and tables. Rievaulx Abbey (well worth an hour's visit) is close by. The pub does get very busy on Friday (market day) and Sunday lunchtime. *(Recommended by Richard Fallon, Michael Switzer, Janet Pickles, Paul Barnett, J and P Maloney, Toby Carlson, Andrew and Joan Life)*

Free house ~ Licensees Lance and Andrew Feather ~ Real ale ~ Meals and snacks ~ Restaurant ~ (01439) 770275 ~ Children welcome ~ Open 11-11; 12-10.30 Sun; closed 25 Dec ~ Bedrooms: £35B/£60B

HETTON (N Yorks) SD9558 Map 7
Angel ★ ⑪ ♀

Just off B6265 Skipton—Grassington

Even before opening time there is usually a queue outside this friendly, particularly well run dining pub, and people drive from miles around for a special meal out. Served by hard-working uniformed staff, there might be home-made cream of cauliflower and red pepper soup (£2.95; lovely rustic fish soup with aioli £4.50), crostini with three styles of fish topping (£3.95), terrine of ham shank and foie gras (£5.75), open sandwich of smoked salmon, cream cheese, smoked bacon and home-made chutney (£5.50), risotto of fresh basil, spinach and sun-dried tomatoes (£5.95), pasta with mussels, spicy Italian sausage, garlic, tomato and red peppers (£6.50), chargrilled breast of locally shot wood pigeon (£7.80), shoulder of lamb slowly braised in its own juices with garlic jus, pesto oil, olive mash and red wine (£9.50), confit of duck with braised normandy red cabbage and orange and thyme sauce (£10.50), calf liver on a parsnip purée with crispy pancetta and roast shallots (£10.95), daily specials such as moules marinières, grilled duo of red sea bream and grey mullet or seared yellow fin of tuna with soya, sesame and ginger vinaigrette, and puddings such as mango mousse, sticky toffee pudding with hot butterscotch sauce or lemon and raspberry sponge pudding (from £3.75). Well kept Black Sheep Bitter and Special, and Tetleys on handpump, 250 wines (with 25 by the glass, including champagne), and a good range of malt whiskies. The four timbered and panelled rambling rooms have lots of cosy alcoves, comfortable country-kitchen chairs or button-back green plush seats, Ronald Searle wine snob cartoons and older engravings and photographs, log fires, a solid fuel stove, and in the main bar, a Victorian farmhouse range in the big stone fireplace; the snug is no smoking. Sturdy wooden benches and tables are built on to the cobbles outside. *(Recommended by Dr and Mrs I H Maine, Philip and Ann Falkner, Stephen and Brenda Head, Gwen and Peter Andrews, Ann and Colin Hunt, Ron Gentry, David and Judy Walmsley, Tom Thomas, John Honnor, RJH, Allen Ferns, Jane Taylor, David Dutton, Julie and Steve Anderston, S P Watkin, P A Taylor, Prof and Mrs S Barnett, Fred and Christine Bell, Mrs D P Dick, M Holdsworth, Ian and Christina Allen, Patrick Milner, Jim and Maggie Cowell, Paul Boot, J E Rycroft, Kenneth and Muriel Holden, WAH, Prof and Mrs S Barnett, Chris and Martin Taylor)*

Free house ~ Licensees Denis Watkins and John Topham ~ Real ale ~ Meals and snacks (till 10pm) ~ Restaurant ~ (01756) 730263 ~ Well behaved children welcome ~ Open 12-2.30, 6-11(10.30 Sun)

HUBBERHOLME (N Yorks) SD9178 Map 7
George

Village signposted from Buckden; about 1 mile NW

The two neat and cosy rooms in this unspoilt old inn have genuine character: heavy beams supporting the dark ceiling-boards, walls stripped back to bare stone and hung with antique plates and photographs, seats (with covers to match the curtains) around shiny copper-topped tables on the flagstones, and an open stove in the big fireplace. Good bar food includes sandwiches, home-made chicken liver pâté (£2.75), mussels in garlic and cream (£3.20), cumberland sausage with egg (£5.25), pasta with tomatoes, peppers, mushrooms and a creamy cheese topping (£5.95), 10oz gammon steak with two eggs (£6.75), lamb and apricot pie or chicken penang (£6.95), peppered steak with a brandy, cream and crushed peppercorn sauce (£11.95), and puddings such as sticky toffee pudding with a fudge and cream sauce or rum and raisin cheesecake on a ginger biscuit base (£2.50). Very well kept Theakstons Black Bull and XB, and Youngers Scotch on handpump, over 20 malt whiskies, and decent wines. Dominoes, and a game they call 'pot the pudding'. There are seats and tables overlooking the moors and River Wharfe – where they have fishing rights. The pub is near the ancient church where J B Priestley's ashes are scattered (this was his favourite pub).

(Recommended by Tom Thomas, B M and P Kendall, Gwen and Peter Andrews, David and Judy Walmsley, Paul and Madeleine Morey, Andrew and Ruth Triggs, K Frostick, Brenda and Derek Savage, Paul McPherson, T Dobby, John Allsopp)

Free house ~ Licensees Jerry Lanchbury and Fiona Shelton ~ Real ale ~ Meals and snacks ~ Restaurant ~ (01756) 760223 ~ Children in eating area of bar ~ Open 11.30-3, 6.30-11; 11.30(12 Sun)-4, 6-11 Sat ~ Bedrooms: £25/£38(£47B)

HULL (E Yorks) TA0927 Map 8

Minerva ◀

From A63 Castle Street/Garrison Road, turn into Queen Street towards piers at central traffic lights; some weekday metered parking here; pub is in pedestrianised Nelson Street, at far end

You can watch the harbour activity from this picturesque Georgian pub as it is set at the heart of the attractively restored waterfront and bustling marina. Another attraction is their own-brew beers – Pilots Pride and occasional other brews such as Midnight Owl (available between December and February) and a Special Ale for their beer Festival in August or September; also, Tetleys Bitter and a couple of guest beers on handpump. You can visit the brewery (best to phone beforehand). The several rooms ramble all the way round a central servery, and are filled with comfortable seats, quite a few interesting photographs and pictures of old Hull (with two attractive wash drawings by Roger Davis) and a big chart of the Humber; the lounge is no smoking during mealtimes. A tiny snug has room for just three people, and a back room (which looks out to the marina basin) houses a profusion of varnished woodwork. Good sized helpings of straightforward bar food such as soup (£1.45), hot or cold filled baguettes (from £2.25), filled baked potatoes (from £2.15), ploughman's (from £3.95), home-made steak in ale pie (£4.25), home-made curry (£4.25), popular huge battered haddock (£4.70), and rump steak (£6.45), daily specials (several are vegetarian), and puddings (from £1.80); Sunday roast. Darts, dominoes, cribbage, fruit machine, and piped music. *(Recommended by Richard Fallon, Chris Westmoreland, M Walker)*

Own brew (Allied Domecq) ~ Managers Eamon and Kathy Scott ~ Real ale ~ Meals and snacks (not Fri/Sat/Sun evenings) ~ (01482) 326909 ~ Children in eating area of bar at mealtimes only ~ Open 11-11; 12-10.30 summer Sun; closed 25 Dec

Olde White Harte ★ £

Off 25 Silver Street, a continuation of Whitefriargate (see previous entry); pub is up narrow passage beside the jewellers' Barnby and Rust, and should not be confused with the much more modern White Hart nearby

It's on quiet weekday evenings that you get the best chance to appreciate this ancient tavern's fine features. In the downstairs bar attractive stained-glass windows look out above the bow window seat, carved heavy beams support black ceiling boards, and two brocaded Jacobean-style chairs sit in the big brick inglenook with its frieze of delft tiles. The curved copper-topped counter serves well kept Courage Directors, Theakstons Old Peculier and XB and Youngers IPA and No 3 on handpump. The second bar is very similar; dominoes, cribbage, shove ha'penny, table skittles, fruit machine, and trivia. Simple, traditional bar food includes sandwiches (from £1.25), ploughman's (from £1.95), chilli con carne (£2.65), fish pie (£2.75), a daily roast (£3.45), and puddings (from £1.65); they open 10am for morning coffee. Seats in the courtyard outside. It was in the heavily panelled room up the oak staircase that in 1642 the town's governor Sir John Hotham made the fateful decision to lock the nearby gate against Charles I, depriving him of Hull's arsenal; it didn't do him much good, as in the Civil War that followed, Hotham, like the king, was executed by the parliamentarians. *(Recommended by William Cunliffe, Richard Fallon, M Walker, Chris Westmoreland)*

Youngers (S & N) ~ Manager Phillip Asquith ~ Real ale ~ Snacks and lunchtime meals ~ Lunchtime restaurant ~ (01482) 326363 ~ Children in restaurant ~ No nearby parking ~ Open 11-11; 12-10.30 Sun

KIRKBYMOORSIDE SE6987 Map 7
George & Dragon 🍴 🍸 🛏
Market place

Very much liked by readers, this particularly well run and civilised 17th-c coaching inn has a friendly and properly pubby front bar. There are fresh flowers and daily newspapers, walls entertainingly covered with lots of photographs, prints, shields and memorabilia connected with cricket and rugby (the landlord's own interest), panelling stripped back to its original pitch pine, brass-studded solid dark red leatherette chairs set around polished wooden tables, horsebrasses hung along the beams, and a blazing log fire; no games machines, pool or juke boxes, and the piped music is either classical or jazz, and not obtrusive. The very good bar food might include sandwiches, home-made soups (at least one vegetarian, £2.50), smooth chicken liver pâté with cumberland sauce (£3.50), black pudding with apple, onion and crispy bacon or seafood hotpot (£4.95), home-made steak and mushroom pie or gammon with two eggs (£7.90), rabbit casserole with dijon mustard sauce or chicken breast in Guinness (£8.90), fillet of pork in calvados with thyme (£9.90), several vegetarian dishes, fresh fish such as salmon fishcakes with dill sauce (£6.95) or salmon fillet in white wine (£8.90), and good puddings; enjoyable breakfasts, and they offer children's helpings. The attractive no-smoking restaurant was the old brewhouse until the early part of this century. Well kept Black Sheep Bitter, Theakstons XB, and Timothy Taylors Landlord on handpump, a fine wine list with 10 by the glass, and over 30 malt whiskies; dominoes, and shove-ha'penny. There are seats under umbrellas in the back courtyard and a surprisingly peaceful walled garden for residents to use. The bedrooms are in a converted cornmill and old vicarage at the back of the pub. Wednesday is Market Day. This is a nice place to stay. *(Recommended by John and Joan Wyatt, David Heath, T G Brierly, Mr and Dr J Harrop, Mrs P Hare, Bruce Jamieson, Michael Switzer, Richard Fallon, C Beadle, Joan and Andrew Life, R Gardiner, David and Ruth Hollands, Andrew Low, Paul and Ursula Randall, Alan Griffiths, Allan Worsley, Michael and Janice Gwilliam)*

Free house ~ Licensees Stephen and Frances Colling ~ Real ale ~ Meals and snacks ~ Restaurant ~ (01751) 433334 ~ Well behaved children welcome ~ Open 10.30-3, 6-11; 12-3, 7-10.30 Sun ~ Bedrooms: £49B/£78B

KIRKHAM (N Yorks) SE7466 Map 7
Stone Trough
Kirkham Abbey

With fine nearby walks and a good outside seating area with lovely valley views, this attractively situated inn is handy for Kirkham Abbey and Castle Howard. Inside, the several beamed and cosy rooms are neatly kept and attractive, with warm log fires, a friendly atmosphere, and well kept Jennings Cumberland, Tetleys, Theakstons Old Peculier, and Timothy Taylors Landlord on handpump; farm cider. Good bar food includes home-made vegetable soup (£2.75), spinach and tomato pasta, salmon, halibut and dill fishcakes, ploughman's or fresh Whitby haddock (all £5.95), steaks (from £6.25), and breast of chicken stuffed with cream cheese and asparagus (£6.95). The no-smoking farmhouse restaurant has a fire in an old-fashioned kitchen range. Darts, pool, shove-ha'penny, cribbage, dominoes, fruit machine, video game, and piped music. *(Recommended by Christopher Turner, Philip and Ann Falkner, Andrew and Joan Life, David Heath, Ian Irving)*

*Free house ~ Licensee Holly Dane ~ Real ale ~ Meals and snacks (not winter Mon
lunchtime) ~ Restaurant ~ (01653) 618713 ~ Well behaved children welcome ~ Open
12-2.30, 6-11; 12-3.30, 6-10.30 Sun; closed winter Mon lunchtime*

LASTINGHAM (N Yorks) SE7391 Map 10
Blacksmiths Arms ◀

Off A170 W of Pickering at Wrelton, forking off Rosedale rd N of Cropton; or via Appleton
or via Hutton le Hole

Set opposite the ancient church with its Norman crypt, this little village pub has a
comfortable, oak beamed bar with a good winter fire, an attractive cooking range
with swinging pot-yards, some sparkling brass, and cushioned windsor chairs and
traditional built-in wooden wall seats. Well kept Black Sheep Bitter, Hambleton Stud,
and Websters Yorkshire on handpump, and quite a few malt whiskies. Enjoyable bar
food includes open rolls (from £1.95), Whitby scampi or savoury flans and quiches
(£4.75), home-made turkey and ham pie (£5.50), pork steak in cider and apple sauce
(£5.95), grilled Yorkshire ham (£6.25), vegetarian dishes, and home-made puddings.
A traditionally furnished, no-smoking dining area opens off the main bar and serves
Sunday roasts (£5.50) and evening meals; a decent range of malt whiskies. There is a
pool and games room as well as darts and dominoes. The surrounding countryside is
lovely and there are tracks through Cropton Forest. *(Recommended by Richard Fallon,
Mrs P Hare, Tom Thomas, Chris and Sue Bax)*

*Free house ~ Licensees Mike and Janet Frank ~ Real ale ~ Meals and snacks ~
Restaurant ~ (01751) 417247 ~ Well behaved children welcome ~ Open 11.30-3,
6.30-11; 12-3, 7-11 Sun ~ Bedrooms: /£33(£40B)*

LEDSHAM (W Yorks) SE4529 Map 7
Chequers

Claypit Lane; a mile W of A1, some 4 miles N of junction M62

As we went to press, the friendly licensees of this bustling village pub told us that they
were hoping to start brewing their own real ale – they also keep John Smiths,
Theakstons Best, and Youngers No 3 and Scotch. The old-fashioned little central
panelled-in servery has several small, individually decorated rooms leading off, with
low beams, lots of cosy alcoves, a number of toby jugs, and log fires. Good, well liked
straightforward bar food includes home-made soup (£2.20), sandwiches (from £2.95),
ploughman's (£4.55), scrambled eggs and smoked salmon (£4.95), lasagne (£5.25),
vegetable pasta bake (£5.75), generous grilled gammon and two eggs (£6.95), daily
specials such as cumberland sausage (£4.95), stilton and celery quiche (£5.25), home-
made steak and mushroom pie (£5.85), chicken with white wine, cream and asparagus
(£6.25), and puddings (£2.55). A sheltered two-level terrace behind the house has
tables among roses (a sanctuary from a bad stretch of the A1). No children.
*(Recommended by John Fahy, IHR, T Loft, Carolyn Reynier, Miss S Watkin, P Taylor, Mike and
Maggie Betton, M W Turner, Thomas Nott, Sue and Bob Ward, I P G Derwent, David Atkinson)*

*Free house ~ Licensee Chris Wraith ~ Real ale ~ Meals and snacks (not Sun) ~
Restaurant (not Sun) ~ (01977) 683135 ~ Open 11-3, 5.30-11; 11-11 Sat; closed Sun*

LEEDS (W Yorks) SE3033 Map 7
Whitelocks ★ £

Turks Head Yard; alley off Briggate, opposite Debenhams and Littlewoods; park in shoppers'
car park and walk

There are few city centre pubs that remain as unchanging as this marvellously
preserved and atmospheric place. And although it might be best to get here outside
peak times as it does get packed, the friendly staff are quick and efficient. The long
and narrow old-fashioned bar has polychrome tiles on the bar counter, stained-glass
windows and grand advertising mirrors, and red button back plush banquettes and
heavy copper-topped cast-iron tables squeezed down one side. Good, reasonably

priced lunchtime bar food includes cornish pasties (95p), sandwiches (from £1.35), chilli or good meat and potato pie (£2.35), and jam roly poly or fruit pie (£1.35). Well kept Theakstons Best, Youngers IPA, Scotch and No 3, and a guest beer on handpump. At the end of the long narrow yard another bar is done up in Dickensian style. No children. *(Recommended by Steve Willey, Bob and Maggie Atherton, Peter Plumridge, Andy and Jill Kassube, Martin Hickes, Graham and Karen Oddey, Chris Westmoreland, Reg Nelson, Thomas Nott, David Carr, Christopher Turner, George Atkinson)*

Youngers (S & N) ~ Manager Brian Cottingham ~ Real ale ~ Meals and snacks (12-8; not Sun evening) ~ Restaurant (not Sun evening) ~ (0113) 245 3950 ~ Open 11-11; 12-10.30 Sun

LEVISHAM (N Yorks) SE8391 Map 10
Horseshoe
Pub and village signposted from A169 N of Pickering

In a fine spot above the unspoilt village, this is a neatly kept, traditional pub with a warm welcome for both locals and visitors. There are brocaded seats, a log fire in the stone fireplace, bar billiards, and well kept Malton Double Chance (summer only), Tetleys Bitter, and Theakstons Best, XB and Old Peculier on handpump, and quite a few malt whiskies. Good bar food includes home-made soup (£2), sandwiches (from £2.85; the steak one is good, £5.15), egg mayonnaise using free range eggs (£3.10), ploughman's (£5.10), fresh Whitby haddock (£6.10), prawn thermidor, steak and kidney pie or beef curry (all £6.15), gammon and egg (£6.20), cajun chicken (£7.15), steaks (from £10.40), daily specials, vegetarian dishes, children's menu (£3.45), and puddings (£2.75); the dining room is no smoking. On warm days, the picnic tables on the attractive village green are a fine place to enjoy a drink. Three to five times a day in spring and autumn, and seven times in summer, two steam trains of the North Yorks Moors Railway stop at this village (it is a bit of an uphill walk to the pub). *(Recommended by Colin Savill, Dr Morley, T M Dobby, Mrs P Hare, Piotre Chodzko-Zajko, M Buchanan, R N Hutton, Gill and Andy Plumb, Nigel Hopkins, Eddie Edwards, Andrew and Ruth Triggs, C A Hall)*

Free house ~ Licensees Brian and Helen Robshaw ~ Real ale ~ Meals and snacks (not 25 Dec) ~ (01751) 460240 ~ Children welcome ~ Open 11-3, 6.30-11; 12-2.30, 7-10.30 in winter; 12-3, 6.30-10.30 Sun; closed Mon during Jan/Feb ~ Bedrooms: £24/£48(£48B)

LEYBURN (N Yorks) SE1191 Map 10
Sandpiper
Market Place – bottom end

Though only a pub for about 30 years, this pretty little stone cottage is said to be the oldest building in Leyburn, dating back to 1640 – it's been refurbished this year but has kept its character. There's a friendly welcome from the licensees, and the bar has a couple of black beams in the low ceiling, a stuffed pheasant in a stripped-stone alcove, antlers, and just seven tables – even including the back room up three steps, where you'll find attractive Dales photographs, toby jugs on a delft shelf, and a collection of curious teapots. Down by the nice linenfold panelled bar counter there are stuffed sandpipers, more photographs and a woodburning stove in the stone fireplace. There's also a spic-and-span dining area on the left; dominoes. Traditional bar food at lunchtime includes home-made soup (£1.95), sandwiches (from £1.95; toasties £2.25), filled baked potatoes (£2.95), ploughman's or cumberland sausage (£4.25), chicken curry or meaty or vegetarian lasagne (£5.25), and daily specials like chicken casserole, sweet and sour chicken, steak and kidney pie or fresh fish pie (all £5.25), with evening dishes such as garlic mushrooms (£3.50), gammon with peaches and cheese (£9.50), and steaks (from £9.50); puddings (£2.75). Well kept Black Sheep Riggwelster and Dent Bitter on handpump, around 100 malt whiskies, and a decent wine list. The friendly english pointer is called Sadie. There are lovely hanging baskets, white cast-iron tables among the honeysuckle, climbing roses, cotoneaster and so forth on the front terrace, with more tables in the back garden. *(Recommended by John Fazakerley,*

Andrew and Ruth Triggs, Ann and Colin Hunt, Ian and Villy White, Mr and Mrs Greenhalgh, J E Rycroft, M J Morgan, Wayne Brindle)

Free house ~ Licensees Peter and Beryl Swan ~ Real ale ~ Meals and snacks (not 25 Dec) ~ Evening restaurant ~ (01969) 622206 ~ Well behaved children may be allowed ~ Open 11-2.30, 6.30-11; closed 25 Dec ~ Bedrooms: £25B/£40B

LINTHWAITE (W Yorks) SE1014 Map 7
Sair 🍺

Hoyle Ing, off A62; 3½ miles after Huddersfield look out for two water storage tanks (painted with a shepherd scene) on your right – the street is on your left, burrowing very steeply up between works buildings; OS Sheet 110 map reference 101143

Tidied up this year, the four rooms in this unspoilt and old-fashioned pub all have a roaring log fire and a warm welcome. But it remains the fine range of own-brewed ales that most people come to enjoy, and if Mr Crabtree is not too busy, he is glad to show visitors the brewhouse: pleasant and well balanced Linfit Bitter, Mild, Special, Swift, Ginger Beer, Old Eli, Leadboiler, Autumn Gold, and the redoubtable Enochs Hammer; there's even stout (English Guineas), a porter (Janet St), and occasional Xmas Ale, Springbok Bier, and Smokehouse Ale. Thatchers farm cider and a few malt whiskies. The rooms are furnished with pews or smaller chairs on the rough flagstones or carpet, bottle collections, and beermats tacked to beams; one room is no smoking. The room on the right has shove-ha'penny, dominoes, Jenga, chess, and juke box; piano players welcome. There's a striking view down the Colne Valley – through which the Huddersfield Narrow Canal winds its way; in the 3½ miles from Linthwaite to the highest and longest tunnel in Britain, are 25 working locks and some lovely countryside. No food. *(Recommended by Andrew and Ruth Triggs, Judith Hirst, John Flumridge, Miss J Hirst, H K Dyson, Joan and Michel Hooper-Immins, Robert Ross, RWD)*

Own brew ~ Licensee Ron Crabtree ~ Real ale ~ (01484) 842370 ~ Children in three rooms away from the bar ~ Open 7-11 only on weekdays; 12-11 Sat; 12-10.30 Sun

LINTON W Yorks SE3947 Map 7
Windmill

Leaving Wetherby W on A661, fork left just before Hospital and bear left; also signposted from A659, leaving Collingham towards Harewood

Friendly new licensees – a father and son, together with their wives – have taken over this old stone village pub. The carefully restored small beamed rooms are spotlessly kept and have walls stripped back to bare stone, polished antique oak settles around copper-topped cast-iron tables, pots hanging from the oak beams, a high shelf of plates, and log fires. Enjoyable food includes good sandwiches (lunchtime only), fresh battered haddock (£5.95), sea bream breton (£7.50), aromatic duck salad (£7.95), popular paella (£14 for two people), medallions of fillet steak in a pâté, marsala wine and cream sauce, and puddings such as home-made tiramisu, rice pudding or fruit pie (£2.50). Well kept John Smiths, Theakstons Best and three weekly guest beers on handpump. The two black labradors are called Jet and Satchmo. The pear tree outside was planted with seeds brought back from the Napoleanic War and there is a secret passage between the pub and the church next door. *(Recommended by Rupert and Mary Jane Flint, Michael Butler, Mr and Mrs Curry, M Phillips)*

Scottish Courage ~ Tenants Geoff Stoker and Daron Stoker ~ Real ale ~ Meals and snacks (12-2, 5.30-9; half-an-hour later on evening weekends ~ (01937) 582209 ~ Children welcome until 8.30pm ~ Open 11.30-3, 5-11 Mon-Thurs; 11-11 Frit/Sat; 12-10.30 Sun

LINTON IN CRAVEN (N Yorks) SD9962 Map 7

Fountaine

On B6265 Skipton—Grassington, forking right

The setting here is very pretty and there are seats outside looking over the village green to the narrow stream that runs through this delightful hamlet. The little rooms are furnished with stools, benches and other seats, and they have well kept Black Sheep Bitter and Riggwelter, John Smiths, and Theakstons Best, Black Bull and Old Peculier on handpump; decent malt whiskies and farm cider. Bar food includes home-made soup (£2.75), home-made game and fruit terrine (£3.50), open sandwich platters (from £4.85), vegetable risotto (£5.50), bacon chops with fried egg (£6.45), supreme of chicken in lemon, prawn and chardonnay sauce (£6.75), and specials such as fresh Whitby haddock (£6.45), home-made steak and kidney pie (£6.50), roast sirloin of beef with thyme and mushroom sauce, mini leg of lamb roasted on the bone or swordfish brochette with lime and ginger dressing (£7.50); one small eating area is no smoking; friendly service. The pub is named after the local lad who made his pile in the Great Plague – contracting in London to bury the bodies. *(Recommended by P R White, Ann and Bob Westbrook, David and Judy Walmsley, Andrew and Ruth Triggs, Julie and Steve Anderton, Vann and Terry Prime, S P Watkin, P A Taylor, John Fazakerley, A N Ellis, Gwen and Peter Andrews, E A George, Derek and Sylvia Stephenson, Ian and Christina Allen, Martin Hickes, Angus Lyon, Mr and Mrs C Roberts)*

Free house ~ Licensee Colin Nauman ~ Real ale ~ Meals and snacks (not Sun or Mon evenings) ~ (01756) 752210 ~ Children in eating area of bar ~ Open 11.30-11; 12-10.30 Sun

LITTON (N Yorks) SD9074 Map 7

Queens Arms

From B6160 N of Grassington, after Kilnsey take second left fork; can also be reached off B6479 at Stainforth N of Settle, via Halton Gill

Mr Thompson is a friendly landlord who obviously loves his job and is just as welcoming to visitors as he is to his regulars. The inn is in a fine spot at the head of Litton Dale, and has an attractive two-level garden with stunning views over the fells; there are fine surrounding walks, too – a track behind the inn leads over Ackerley Moor to Buckden and the quiet lane through the valley leads on to Pen-y-ghent. Inside, the main bar on the right has a good coal fire, stripped rough stone walls, a brown beam-and-plank ceiling, stools around cast-iron-framed tables on the stone and concrete floor, a seat built into the stone-mullioned window, and signed cricket bats. On the left, the red-carpeted room has another coal fire and more of a family atmosphere with varnished pine for its built-in wall seats, and for the ceiling and walls themselves. Decent bar food includes sandwiches (from £2.45; hot or cold crusty rolls from £3), filled baked potatoes (from £2.80), ploughman's (£3.80), meaty or vegetable lasagne (£4.10), home-made pies such as rabbit or steak, kidney and Guinness (from £5.30), gammon and egg (£6.25), vegetarian dishes, daily specials, a larger evening menu, and children's meals (from £2.20). Well kept Theakstons Best and Youngers Scotch on handpump; darts, dominoes, shove-ha'penny, and cribbage. *(Recommended by Paul and Madeleine Morey, Neil and Angela Huxter, Gwen and Peter Andrews, David and Judy Walmsley)*

Free house ~ Licensees Tanya and Neil Thompson ~ Real ale ~ Meals and snacks (not Mon except bank hols) ~ (01756) 770208 ~ Children in family room ~ Open 12-3, 7-11; 11.30-3, 6.30-11.30 Sat; 12-3, 7-10.30 Sun; closed Mon (except bank hols); closed 4th-end Jan ~ Bedrooms: £21.50(£21.50B)/£32(£39B)

People named as recommenders after the main entries have told us that the pub should be included. But they have not written the report – we have, after anonymous on-the-spot inspection.

LOW CATTON (E Yorks) SE7053 Map 7
Gold Cup

Village signposted with High Catton off A166 in Stamford Bridge or A1079 at Kexby Bridge

The three communicating rooms of the lounge in this comfortable white-rendered house have a friendly atmosphere, open fires at each end, plush wall seats and stools around good solid tables, flowery curtains, some decorative plates and brasswork on the walls, and a very relaxed atmosphere. Generous helpings of good, well liked food might include soup (£1.95), lunchtime sandwiches (from £1.85; not Sun), crusty rolls (from £2.95), and ploughman's (£4), steak and mushroom pie (£4.95), and good fisherman's pie or spicy cajun chicken (£5.25); the no-smoking restaurant has pleasant views of the surrounding fields. Well kept John Smiths and Tetleys Bitter on handpump. The back games bar is comfortable, with a well lit pool table, darts, dominoes, fruit machine, and well reproduced music. There may be fat geese in the back paddock. *(Recommended by Roger Bellingham, Beryl and Bill Farmer, Sheila and Robert Robinson; more reports please)*

Free house ~ Licensees Ray and Pat Hales ~ Real ale ~ Meals and snacks (all day weekends) ~ Restaurant ~ (01759) 371354 ~ Children welcome ~ Open 12-2.30, 6-11; 12-11 Sat; 12-10.30 Sun; closed Mon lunch (except bank hols); closed evening 25 Dec

MASHAM (N Yorks) SE2381 Map 10
Kings Head 🏠

Market Square

From the two opened-up rooms of the neatly kept and spacious lounge bar, you can watch the world go by from the front windows overlooking the market square of this lovely village – market day is Wednesday. One room is carpeted and one has a wooden floor, and there are green plush seats around wooden tables, a big War Department issue clock over the imposing slate and marble fireplace, and a high shelf of Staffordshire and other figurines. Good value bar food includes sandwiches (not Sunday), home-made soup (£1.30), eggs with a spicy mango and curried mayonnaise (£1.95), lamb liver and bacon or three cheese and broccoli bake (£4.95), chicken breast wrapped in bacon with a sherry cream sauce, Whitby cod or rack of lamb (£5.95), steaks (from £6.95), roasts of the day and daily specials, and puddings (£1.95); nice breakfasts. Well kept Theakstons Best, XB, Old Peculier, Black Bull and seasonal ales on handpump; fruit machine, dominoes, piped music. The handsome inn's hanging baskets and window boxes are most attractive, and there are picnic tables under cocktail parasols in a partly fairy-lit coachyard. *(Recommended by Rachel Sayer, Andrew and Ruth Triggs, James Nunns, R N Hutton, Roberto Villa, Ian Phillips, David and Fiona Pemberton, R T and J C Moggridge, John and Chris Simpson, David and Judith Hart, Mrs B Sugarman)*

S & N ~ Manager Paul Mounter ~ Real ale ~ Meals and snacks ~ Restaurant ~ (01765) 689295 ~ Well behaved children welcome until 9.30pm ~ Open 11-11; 12-10.30 Sun ~ Bedrooms: £39B/£58B

White Bear 🍺

Signposted off A6108 opposite turn into town centre

The Theakstons old stone headquarters buildings are part of this pub and the brewery is on the other side of town; tours can be arranged at the Theakstons Brewery Visitor Centre (01765 89057, extension 4317, Weds-Sun); morning visits are best. Not surprisingly, the Theakstons Best, XB, Old Peculier, and guest such as Black Bull on handpump are very well kept, and the traditionally furnished public bar is packed with bric-a-brac such as copper brewing implements, harness, pottery, foreign banknotes, and stuffed animals – including a huge polar bear behind the bar. A much bigger, more comfortable lounge has a turkey carpet. Under the new licensees, bar food includes soup (£1.50), sandwiches (from £2.25), and daily specials like vegetable pasta bake (£4.25), plaice goujons with a white wine and butter sauce (£4.95), and Old

Peculier casserole with sage dumplings (£6.95). Dominoes, cribbage, fruit machine and CD juke box. In summer there are seats out in the yard. Please note, they no longer do bedrooms. *(Recommended by Vann Prime, Wm Van Laaten, Andrew and Ruth Triggs, Beryl and Bill Farmer, R T and J C Moggridge, Neil and Angela Huxter, Simon and Amanda Southwell, R N Hutton, J E Rycroft, Val Stevenson, Rob Holmes)*

Scottish & Newcastle ~ Tenant John Thompson ~ Real ale ~ Meals and snacks (limited Mon lunchtime; not Sat/Sun/Mon evenings) ~ (01765) 689319 ~ Children welcome until 8.30pm ~ Open 11-11; 12-10.30 Sun

MELTHAM (W Yorks) SE0910 Map 7
Will's o' Nat's ♀
Blackmoorfoot Road; off B6107; a couple of miles out of village to north west

Very well run by friendly licensees, this bustling pub alone in a fine spot up on the moors is well liked for its reliably good food, well kept real ales, and a relaxed friendly atmosphere. From a wide choice, bar food might include soup such as carrot and apple (£1.25), lots of sandwiches (from £1.50; bacon and black pudding £2; steak with onions £4.50), yorkshire pudding with onion gravy (£1.95), ploughman's (from £3.25), deep-fried fresh haddock, nut roast with tomato sauce, steak and kidney pie or moussaka (all £4.10), wild boar sausage with onion sauce (£4.20), roast pork with apple sauce and stuffing (£4.60), fresh salmon with parsley butter (£5.35), steaks (from £7.45), puddings like hot chocolate pudding or treacle and orange tart (from £2.15), and children's dishes (from £1.85); cheeses are traditionally made and are farmhouse or from a small dairy (£2.55). Well kept Old Mill Bitter and Tetleys Bitter and Mild on handpump, a good little wine list, and around 30 malt whiskies. By the bar there are comfortably cushioned heavy wooden wall seats around old cast-iron-framed tables, and the cream walls have lots of interesting old local photographs and a large attractive pen and wash drawing of many local landmarks, with the pub as its centrepiece. A slightly raised dining extension at one end, with plenty of well spaced tables, has the best of the views. Dominoes, fruit machine and piped music (not obtrusive). The pub is situated on both the Colne Valley and Kirklees circular walks and close to Blackmoorfoot reservoir (birdwatching). The name of the pub means 'belonging to, or run by, William, son of Nathaniel'. *(Recommended by H K Dyson, Neil Townend, Mike and Wendy Proctor, Bronwen and Steve Wrigley, Syd and Wyn Donald, Andrew and Ruth Triggs, CW, JW, H Dyson, M C and B Forman, Dave Braisted, Drs A C and A Jackson)*

Carlsberg Tetleys ~ Lease: Kim Schofield ~ Real ale ~ Meals and snacks (11.30-2, 6-9.30 – 6.30-10 Sat) ~ (01484) 850078 ~ Well behaved children welcome ~ Open 11.30-3, 6(6.30 Sat)-11; 12-3, 7-10.30 Sun; closed evenings 25/26 Dec

MIDDLEHAM (N Yorks) SE1288 Map 10
Black Swan
Market Pl

This 17th-c stone inn is an enjoyable place to visit. The immaculately kept heavy-beamed bar has a good cheerful local feel – as well as high-backed settles built in by the big stone fireplace, racing memorabilia on the stripped stone walls, horsebrasses and pewter mugs, and well kept John Smiths Bitter and Theakstons Best, Old Peculier, and XB on handpump or tapped from the cask; lots of malt whiskies and decent little wine list. Reasonably priced bar food includes lunchtime snacks such as sandwiches (from £1.85), filled baked potatoes (from £1.95), and ploughman's (from £3.50), as well as home-made soup (£1.70), egg mayonnaise (£1.95), battered haddock (£4.75), vegetable lasagne or home-cooked ham or beef (£4.95), lasagne or chicken with a creamy spicy, coconut sauce (£5.25), and evening gammon with pineapple (£7.50), and steaks (from £10.25); children's dishes (from £2.95), and substantial breakfasts. Dominoes and piped music. There are tables on the cobbles outside and in the sheltered back garden. Good walking country. *(Recommended by Ann and Colin Hunt, Alan Morton, John and Lianne Smith, R F Orpwood, Chris Reeve)*

Free house ~ Licensees George and Susan Munday ~ Real ale ~ Meals and snacks (not evening 25 Dec) ~ Restaurant ~ (01969) 622221 ~ Children in eating area of bar until 9pm ~ Open 11-4, 6-11; 12-3.30, 6.30-10.30 Sun; closed evening 25 Dec ~ Bedrooms: £26B/£46B

MOULTON (N Yorks) NZ2404 Map 10

Black Bull 🍴

Just E of A1, 1 mile S of Scotch Corner

A most civilised place for an enjoyable meal out, this is somewhere with a lot of character and is much loved by its regular customers. The bar has a huge winter log fire, fresh flowers, an antique panelled oak settle and an old elm housekeeper's chair, built-in red-cushioned black settles and pews around the cast-iron tables (one has a heavily beaten-copper top), silver-plate Turkish coffee pots and so forth over the red velvet curtained windows, and copper cooking utensils hanging from black beams. A nice side dark-panelled seafood bar has some high seats at the marble-topped counter. Excellent lunchtime bar snacks include lovely smoked salmon: sandwiches (£3.25), pâté (£4.95), and smoked salmon plate (£5.25); they also do a very good home-made soup served in lovely little tureens (£2.50), fresh plump salmon sandwiches (£3.25), black pudding and pork sausage with caramelised apple (£4.25), tartlet of leek, gruyère and walnut or welsh rarebit and bacon (£4.75), pasta with queen scallops, chilli and garlic (£4.95), curried fish mornay (£5.25), and puddings (£2.50); you must search out someone to take your order – the bar staff just do drinks. In the evening (when people do tend to dress up), you can also eat in the polished brick-tiled conservatory with bentwood cane chairs or in the Brighton Belle dining car – though they also do a three-course Sunday lunch. Good wine, and a fine choice of sherries. There are some seats under trees in the central court. *(Recommended by John and Chris Simpson, Roger Bellingham, David Shillitoe, Cynthia Waller, SS, Beryl and Bill Farmer, Susan and John Douglas, R J Robinson)*

Free house ~ Licensees Mrs A Pagendam and Miss S Pagendam ~ Lunchtime bar meals and snacks (not Sun) ~ Restaurant (not Sun evening) ~ (01325) 377289 ~ Children in eating area of bar if over 7 ~ Open 12-2.30, 6-10.30(11 Sat); closed Sun evening and 24-29 Dec

MUKER (N Yorks) SD9198 Map 10

Farmers Arms

B6270 W of Reeth

Popular with walkers, this unpretentious and remote Dales pub has plenty of nearby rewarding walks, and there are interesting drives up over Buttertubs Pass or to the north, to Tan Hill and beyond. The cosy bar has a warm open fire and is simply furnished with stools and settles around copper-topped tables. Straightforward bar food includes lunchtime baps and toasties (from £1.95), filled baked potatoes (£2.95), home-made steak pie, vegetable lasagne or potato, cheese and leek bake (£4.75), gammon or half a roast chicken (£5.75), steaks (from £7.75), children's dishes (from £2.65) and puddings. Butterknowle Bitter, John Smiths Bitter, and Theakstons Best, XB and Old Peculier on handpump; darts and dominoes. They have a self-catering studio flat to rent. *(Recommended by Ray and Liz Monk, Hazel and Michael Duncombe, R T and J C Moggridge; more reports please)*

Free house ~ Licensees Chris and Marjorie Bellwood ~ Real ale ~ Meals and snacks ~ (01748) 886297 ~ Children welcome ~ Open 11-3, 6.30-11; 11-11 Sat; 12-10.30 Sun; winter evening opening 7

Children welcome means the pubs says it lets children inside without any special restriction; readers have found that some may impose an evening time limit – please tell us if you find this.

NEWTON ON OUSE (N Yorks) SE5160 Map 7
Dawnay Arms

Village signposted off A19 N of York

One of the draws to this black-shuttered 18th-c inn is the neat, sloping lawn that runs down to the River Ouse where there are moorings for three or four cruisers; plenty of seats on the terrace. Inside, on the right of the entrance is a comfortable, spacious room with a good deal of beamery and timbering and plush wall settles and chairs around wooden or dimpled copper tables. To the left is another airy room with plush button-back wall banquettes built into bays and a good log fire in the stone fireplace; lots of brass and copper. Good bar food now includes sandwiches and ploughman's, soup (£2.25), home-made pâté (£2.95), cheesy mushrooms (£3.25), courgette provençal or home-made lasagne (£4.95), beef bourguignon (£5.95), chicken mornay (£6.50), pigeon breasts in red wine sauce (£6.95), fillet of salmon (£8.95), monkfish and bacon (£9.95), sirloin steak (£10.95), daily specials such as local smoked trout or steak, mushroom and ale pie (£5.95), and puddings (£2.50); the restaurant is no smoking. Well kept Boddingtons, Morlands Old Speckled Hen and Tetleys on handpump, and 40 malt whiskies; darts, pool, fruit machine, and unobtrusive piped music. Benningbrough Hall (National Trust) is five minutes' walk away. Please note, the pub no longer does accommodation. *(Recommended by Piotr Chodzko-Zajko, Janet and Peter Race, Joan and Andrew Life, Andrew and Ruth Triggs, John Knighton; more reports on the new regime, please)*

Free house ~ Licensees Alan and Richard Longley ~ Real ale ~ Meals and snacks ~ Restaurant ~ (01347) 848345 ~ Children welcome ~ Open 12-3, 6-11; 12-3, 7-10.30 Sun

NUNNINGTON (N Yorks) SE6779 Map 7
Royal Oak 🍽

Church Street; at back of village, which is signposted from A170 and B1257

This spotlessly kept and attractive little dining pub remains as popular as ever for its consistently good food. Served by friendly and efficient staff – and with prices unchanged since last year – there might be sandwiches (from £2.25), good home-made vegetable soup (£2.50), spicy mushrooms or stilton pâté (£3.75), egg mayonnaise with prawns (£4.50), ploughman's or lasagne (£6.50), black-eyed bean casserole, chicken in an orange and tarragon sauce or ham and mushroom tagliatelle (£7.50), enjoyable fisherman's pot or steak and kidney casserole (£7.95), sirloin steak (£10.95), daily specials such as leek and pine kernel pasta (£7.50), rack of lamb (£8.95), and fillet steak au poivre (£13.95), and lovely puddings like home-made apple pie or chocolate fudge cake (£2.50). Well kept Tetleys and Theakstons Best and Old Peculier on handpump. The bar has carefully chosen furniture such as kitchen and country dining chairs or a long pew around the sturdy tables on the turkey carpet, and a lectern in one corner; the high black beams are strung with earthenware flagons, copper jugs and lots of antique keys, one of the walls is stripped back to the bare stone to display a fine collection of antique farm tools, and there are open fires. Handy for a visit to Nunnington Hall (National Trust). *(Recommended by Rita Horridge, R Gardiner, Mr and Mrs W B Draper, R White)*

Free house ~ Licensee Anthony Simpson ~ Real ale ~ Meals and snacks (not Mon) ~ (01439) 748271 ~ Children in restaurant only, if over 8 ~ Open 12-2.30, 6.30-11; closed Mon

OSMOTHERLEY SE4499 (N Yorks) Map 10
Three Tuns 🛏

South End, off A19 N of Thirsk

The main food emphasis here is on the roomy, crisply stylish and comfortable back restaurant, with particular emphasis on fish – on evenings when the restaurant is very busy you may have to wait for bar food. This gives a clue to much of the pub's charm: as far as the front part is concerned, it has stayed very much an unassuming pub, hardly knocked-about at all – popular with walkers, and with visitors to this lovely village centred around Mount Grace Priory. It has a modest stone facade (with an old-fashioned wooden seat out by the door), and inside on the left are a simple small square bar and tap room, which fill quite quickly at weekends. Bar food includes good sandwiches and toasties (from £2.65), ploughman's with interesting cheeses from small producers and really good bread (£5.25), grilled fresh sardines (£5.95), smoked salmon with scrambled eggs (£6.50), gammon and two eggs (£6.95), roast breast of barbary duck stuffed with pâté and herbs and a madeira sauce (£9.75), steaks (from £12.25), and daily specials such as cream of lemon sole and lobster soup (£2.95), black pudding with a rich tomato and coriander sauce (£3.25), mini rack of local pork with a fresh apricot and sage sauce (£9.50), baron of local lamb with fresh strawberry and mint sauce (£13.50), and whole bass grilled with parsely butter (£14.95). Well kept Theakstons Best, XB and Old Peculier and Youngers Scotch, smart courteous and efficient service, attractive coal fire, exemplary lavatories. Tables out in the pleasant back garden have lovely views. The bedrooms are well equipped and comfortable. *(Recommended by R T and J C Moggridge, RB, Michael Butler)*

Free house ~ Licensee Hugh Dyson ~ Real ale ~ Meals and snacks (not Sun evening) ~ Restaurant ~ (01609) 883301 ~ Children welcome ~ Open 11.45-3.30, 6.45-11; 12-3.30, 7-10.30 Sun ~ Bedrooms: £47.50B/£60B

PICKHILL (N Yorks) SE3584 Map 10

Nags Head 🍴 ♈

Take the Masham turn-off from A1 both N and S, and village signposted off B6267 in Ainderby Quernhow

For over 27 years, the friendly Boynton brothers have run this very popular inn – which manages to be a pub, hotel and restaurant all rolled into one. The busy tap room on the left has beams hung with jugs, coach horns, ale-yards and so forth, and masses of ties hanging as a frieze from a rail around the red ceiling. The smarter lounge bar has deep green plush banquettes on the matching carpet, and pictures for sale on its neat cream walls, and another comfortable beamed room (mainly for restaurant users) has red plush button-back built-in wall banquettes around dark tables, and an open fire. Much enjoyed food includes soup (£2.50), kipper and pink peppercorn terrine or timbale of Italian vegetables with goat's cheese (£3.95), corned beef hash or very hot mixed bean chilli (£4.95), smoked haddock and prawn kedgeree (£5.25), brochette of thai-style king prawns or vegetarian moussaka (£5.50), chicken korma (£6.80), steak and vegetable pie (£7.95), grilled duck breast with plum sauce (£9.95), sirloin steak au poivre (£10.95), venison fillet with port and juniper berry sauce (£12.95), and puddings such as almond crème brûlée, lime and mascarpone cheesecake or individual summer pudding (£2.95); service can slow down under pressure; the restaurant is no smoking. Well kept Hambleton Bitter, Tetleys Bitter, and Theakstons Black Bull and Old Peculier on handpump, a good choice of malt whiskies, and good value wines (several by the glass). One table's inset with a chessboard, and they also have cribbage, darts, dominoes, shove-ha'penny, and faint piped music. *(Recommended by D W and J W Wilson, Paul and Ursula Randall, Sarah and Peter Gooderham, Andrew and Ruth Triggs, Andy and Jill Kassube, Sue and Geoff Price, Dave Braisted, Giles Francis, Nigel Wilson, Helen and Andy, Stephen and Brenda Head, Alan Morton, Esther and John Sprinkle, John and Chris Simpson, Ian Morley, Eddie Edwards, David Stafford, David Heath)*

Free house ~ Licensees Raymond and Edward Boynton ~ Real ale ~ Meals and snacks (till 10pm) ~ Restaurant (closed Sun evening) ~ (01845) 567391 ~ Well behaved children welcome but small ones must be gone by 7pm ~ Open 11-11; 12-10.30 Sun ~ Bedrooms: £36B/£50B

If you have to cancel a reservation for a bedroom or restaurant, please telephone or write to warn them. A small place – and its customers – will suffer if you don't.

POOL (W Yorks) SE2445 Map 7
White Hart
Just off A658 S of Harrogate, A659 E of Otley

The four rooms in this friendly pub have a restrained country decor, a pleasant medley of assorted old farmhouse furniture on the mix of stone flooring and carpet, and a quiet and comfortable atmosphere; there are two log fires, and a no-smoking area. Bar food (with prices unchanged since last year) includes lunchtime sandwiches (not Sunday), soup (£1.95), savoury bacon and cheddar melt (£2.50), gammon and egg (£4.95), lemon chicken or beef and ale pie (£5.25), seafood salad (£5.95), rump steak (£6.95), daily specials such as liver and bacon (£4.75), broccoli and brie pastry with sherry, cream and tomato sauce (£5.50) or grilled double chicken breast in a creamy french mustard sauce (£6.15), and puddings like treacle tart or spotted dick (from £1.95); roast Sunday beef (£5.95). Well kept Bass, Stones, and Worthington Best on handpump, and 11 wines by the glass. Fruit machine, dominoes, and piped music. There are tables outside, with a play area well away from the road. This part of lower Wharfedale is a pleasant walking area. *(Recommended by Lynne Gittins; more reports please)*

Bass ~ Manager Felix Moakler ~ Real ale ~ Meals and snacks (11-9.30) ~ (0113) 284 3011 ~ Open 11-11; 12-10.30 Sun; closed evening 25 Dec

RAMSGILL (N Yorks) SE1271 Map 7
Yorke Arms 🛏
Take Nidderdale rd off B6265 in Pateley Bridge; or exhilarating but narrow moorland drive off A6108 at N edge of Masham, via Fearby and Lofthouse

Set in a peaceful dale and surrounded by fells, this is a very enjoyable small country hotel. The bars have two or three heavy carved Jacobean oak chairs, a big oak dresser laden with polished pewter and other antiques, and open log fires. Under the friendly new licensees (who took over just as we went to press), we would expect the food to be very good indeed: home-made soup (£2.50), a warm salad of black pudding, apple and poached egg (£4.50), thai-spiced fishcakes or a plate of cheese (£4.95), smoked salmon on a toasted bap with chive cream cheese, tomatoes and capers (£5.50), turnover of butternut squash, leek and thyme (£6.30), lemon sole with prawn and butter sauce (£6.50), chargrilled salmon with horseradish, wilted greens and orange (£7.50), venison steak with olive oil mash and grilled vegetables or caesar salad with fresh chargrilled tuna (£8.20), sirloin steak (£11.95), and puddings such as sticky toffee pudding or summer fruit shortbread. Theakstons XB on handpump. They prefer smart dress in the no-smoking restaurant in the evening. The inn's public rooms are open throughout the day for tea and coffee. You can walk up the magnificent if strenuous moorland road to Masham, or perhaps on the right-of-way track that leads along the hill behind the reservoir, also a bird sanctuary. *(Recommended by Janet and Peter Race, David and Judy Walmsley, John Plumridge, Greta and Christopher Wells; more reports on the new regime, please)*

Free house ~ Licensees Bill and Frances Atkins ~ Real ale ~ Meals and snacks (no bar food Sun evening) ~ Restaurant ~ (01423) 755243 ~ Children welcome ~ Open 11-11; 12-10.30 Sun ~ Bedrooms: £40B/£70B

REDMIRE (N Yorks) SE0591 Map 10
Kings Arms ◨
Wensley—Askrigg back road: a good alternative to the A684 through Wensleydale

This is a charming and genuinely friendly little pub tucked away in an attractive small village. The simply furnished bar has been refurbished this year and the wall settles and wall seats are now cloth-covered and set around cast-iron tables, and there's a fine oak armchair (its back carved like a mop of hair) and a woodburning stove. Enjoyable bar food includes sandwiches, good soup (£2.25), home-made lasagne (£5.95), vegetarian dishes (from £5.95), very good steak and kidney pie or marvellous local fish and chips (£6.95), wild boar pie (£7.95), venison pie (£7.95), steaks, a huge mixed grill, and Sunday roast; the restaurant is no smoking. Well kept Redmire Brew (brewed for the pub by Hambleton Ales), as well as Black Sheep Special, Richardson Brothers Four Seasons, John Smiths, and Theakstons Black Bull and Lightfoot on handpump, over 50 malt whiskies, and decent wines. The rather sweet staffordshire bull terrier is called Kim. Darts, pool, dominoes, and cribbage; quoits. From the tables and chairs in the pretty garden here there's a superb view across Wensleydale; fishing nearby. Handy for Castle Bolton where Mary Queen of Scots was imprisoned. *(Recommended by Michele and Clive Platman, B Edgeley, Marion Tasker, Vann and Terry Prime, Darren Staniforth, Jane Evans, David Hilton, M Morgan, Chris Reeve)*

Free house ~ Licensee Roger Stevens ~ Meals and snacks ~ Restaurant ~ (01969) 622316 ~ Children in eating area of bar until 9.30pm ~ Open 11-3, 6-11; 12-3, 7-10.30 Sun ~ Two bedrooms: £18B/£36B

RIPPONDEN (W Yorks) SE0419 Map 7
Old Bridge ♀

Priest Lane; from A58, best approach is Elland Road (opposite Golden Lion), park opposite the church in pub's car park and walk back over ancient hump-backed bridge

Set by the medieval pack horse bridge over the little River Ryburn, this rather civilised 14th-c pub has been run by Mr Beaumont since 1963. The three communicating rooms are each on a slightly different level and have oak settles built into the window recesses of the thick stone walls, antique oak tables, rush-seated chairs, a few well-chosen pictures and prints, a big woodburning stove, and a relaxed atmosphere; fresh flowers in summer. Bar food includes a popular weekday lunchtime cold meat buffet which always has a joint of rare beef, as well as spiced ham, quiche, scotch eggs and so on (£7.50 with a bowl of soup and coffee); also, sandwiches, starters such as salmon, lemon and dill pâté, garlic mushrooms or deep-fried camembert (£2-£3.50), main courses like chicken, broccoli and stilton pie, salmon and leek pasta bake, smoked haddock and spinach pancakes and meat and potato pie (£4.25-£4.95), and puddings (£2.25). Well kept Black Sheep Special, Ryburn Best, Timothy Taylors Best and Golden Mild, and a weekly guest beer on handpump, 30 malt whiskies, a good choice of foreign bottled beers, and interesting wines with half-a-dozen by the glass. The popular restaurant is over the bridge. *(Recommended by P H Roberts, M L and G Clarke, Greta and Christopher Wells; more reports please)*

Free house ~ Licensee Ian Beaumont, Manager Timothy Walker ~ Real ale ~ Meals and snacks (no bar meals Sat or Sun evening) ~ Restaurant ~ (01422) 822595 ~ Children in eating area of bar until 7pm ~ Open 12-3, 5.30-11; 12-11 Sat; 12-10.30 Sun

ROBIN HOODS BAY (N Yorks) NZ9505 Map 10
Laurel ◀

Village signposted off A171 S of Whitby

At the bottom of a row of fishermen's cottages at the heart of one of the prettiest and most unspoilt fishing villages on the North East coast, sits this charming little pub. The friendly beamed main bar bustles with locals and visitors, and is decorated with old local photographs, Victorian prints and brasses, and lager bottles from all over the world; there's a roaring open fire. Bar food consists of lunchtime sandwiches (from £1.50) and winter soup. Well kept John Smiths and Theakstons Old Peculier with guests like Marstons Pedigree, Ruddles Best, and Theakstons Black Bull and Old Peculier on handpump; darts, shove-ha'penny, dominoes, cribbage, trivia, and piped music. In summer, the hanging baskets and window boxes are lovely. They have a self-contained apartment for two people. *(Recommended by Richard Fallon, Stephen and Brenda Head, Rita Horridge, John Fahy, Paul Barnett, Stephen, Julie and Hayley Brown, Mike and Wendy Proctor, Fiona and David Pemberton, R N Hutton, Gill and Andy Plumb, Mrs Kathy Newens, James Nunns)*

Scottish Courage ~ Lease: Brian Catling ~ Real ale ~ Lunchtime snacks ~ (01947) 880400 ~ Children in snug ~ Open 12-11; 12-10.30 Sun

ROSEDALE ABBEY (N Yorks) SE7395 Map 10

Milburn Arms 🍺 ♀ 🛏

The easiest road to the village is through Cropton from Wrelton, off the A170 W of Pickering

The steep moorland surrounding this 18th-c inn is very fine and in warm weather, the terrace and garden have plenty of seats on which to relax. Inside, the kind and chatty landlord will make you feel welcome, and there's a good atmosphere and log fire in the neatly kept L-shaped and beamed main bar. Much enjoyed by readers and served by smartly dressed waitresses, the good bar food includes home-made soup (£2.25), good lunchtime sandwiches (from £2.75), grilled brie parcels with red onion marmalade (£3.95), Whitby crab cocktail (£4.25), sautéed chicken livers with balsamic vinegar on seasonal leaves (£4.50), lasagne (£4.75), home-made steak and Guinness pie (£6.50), fresh crab salad (£6.95), pork and apple casserole topped with black pudding (£7.25), breast of chicken filled with spinach with a smoked bacon and tomato sauce or vegetable and nut en croûte with a parsley and garlic sauce (£7.50), half roast pheasant with roasted shallots and yorkshire sauce (£7.95), grilled whole lemon sole with lemon and garden herb butter (£8.95), sirloin steak (£10.50), daily specials such as grilled queenie scallops with blue wensleydale cheese, steak in ale pie or roast lamb shank with a rosemary and garlic jus, and home-made puddings (£2.50); huge breakfasts. The restaurant is no smoking. Well kept Bass, Black Sheep Special and Riggwelter, and Stones on handpump; 20 malt whiskies and eight good house wines by the glass. Darts, shove-ha'penny, cribbage, dominoes, fruit machine, and piped music. *(Recommended by Stephen, Julie and Hayley Brown, J and P Maloney, Chris and Sue Bax, Mrs G M Roberts, Geoffrey and Irene Lindley, David Heath, Sue and Bob Ward, Val Stevenson, Rob Holmes, Alison Turner, Barry and Anne)*

Free house ~ Licensee Terry Bentley ~ Real ale ~ Meals and snacks ~ Restaurant ~ (01751) 417312 ~ Well behaved children in eating area of bar till 9pm ~ Open 11-3(4 Sat), 6-11; 12-3, 6.30-10.30 Sun; winter opening half-an-hour later; bedrooms and restaurant closed last two weeks Jan ~ Bedrooms: /£74B

SAWLEY (N Yorks) SE2568 Map 7

Sawley Arms ♀

Village signposted off B6265 W of Ripon

It would be hard to find more beautiful and varied flower displays than the ones in the tubs, baskets and lovely gardens here – not surprisingly, they have won the Yorkshire in Bloom competition four times now. Inside, Mrs Hawes puts as much enthusiasm into the running of this rather smart place. The series of small turkey-carpeted rooms have log fires and comfortable furniture ranging from small softly cushioned armed dining chairs and comfortable settees, to the wing armchairs down a couple of steps in a side snug; there may be daily papers and magazines to read, and two small rooms (and the restaurant) are no smoking. Good bar food includes lunchtime sandwiches, interesting soups such as leek and coconut or cauliflower and orange (£2.40; special seafood £3.50), salmon mousse or stilton, port and celery pâté (£4.25), scampi terrine with fresh tomato sauce (£4.75), good spicy chicken pancakes, steak pie (£5.95), plaice mornay (£6.95), roast duckling (£12.50), and puddings such as lovely bread and butter pudding (£3.50); good, friendly service. Good house wines and quiet piped music. The pub is handy for Fountains Abbey (the most extensive of the great monastic remains – floodlit on late summer Friday and Saturday evenings, with a live choir on the Saturday). *(Recommended by R L Gorick, Brian Wainwright, Peter and Ruth Burnstone, Mr and Mrs R Maggs, P R White, John Honnor, Janet and Peter Race, Gwen and Peter Andrews, Geoffrey and Brenda Wilson, M A Butler, Donald and Mollie Armitage, Andrew and Ruth Triggs)*

Free house ~ Licensee Mrs June Hawes ~ Meals and snacks (not Sun or Mon evenings) ~ Restaurant ~ (01765) 620642 ~ Well behaved children allowed if over 9 ~ Open 11.30-3, 6.30-10.30; 12-3, 7.30-10.30 Sun; closed Mon evenings except bank hols

SETTLE (N Yorks) SD8264 Map 7

Golden Lion

A65

Doing well at the moment, this rather grand looking coaching inn has a surprisingly splendid staircase sweeping down into the spacious high-beamed hall bar here. There's an enormous fireplace, comfortable settles and plush seats, brass, prints and Chinese plates on dark panelling, and a cheerful atmosphere. Enjoyable bar food includes sandwiches (from £2.50; hot roast sirloin of beef £3.50; prawns, banana and pineapple £4.25), filled baked potatoes (from £3.20), omelette of the day (£4.75), mushroom provençale with pasta (£5.45), and daily specials such as vegetable stir fry (£5), cajun-style chicken (£7.25), and baby leg of lamb in redcurrant gravy (£9.75); potatoes are £1.25 extra and vegetables £1.95 extra. Well kept Thwaites Bitter and Craftsman and a monthly guest beer on handpump, wines by the glass, bottle, litre or half-litre, and country wines; friendly helpful staff. The lively public bar has pool, fruit machine, and piped music; the labrador-cross is called Monty, and the black and white cat, Luke. *(Recommended by J H and S A Harrop, B M and P Kendall, Ann and Colin Hunt, Judith Hirst, Andrew and Ruth Triggs, Chris and Martin Taylor, Mr and Mrs C Roberts, K and F Giles)*

Thwaites ~ Tenant Philip Longrigg ~ Real ale ~ Meals and snacks (till 10pm) ~ Restaurant ~ (01729) 822203 ~ Children welcome ~ Occasional live entertainment Fri evening ~ Open 11-11; 12-10.30 Sun ~ Bedrooms: £22.50(£28.50B)/£45(£54B)

SHEFFIELD (S Yorks) SK3687 Map 7

Fat Cat £ ◀

23 Alma St

It's the ten real ales that draw people to this friendly city pub. As well as their own-brewed (and cheap) Kelham Island Bitter (named after the nearby Industrial Museum), they also serve well kept Marstons Pedigree, Timothy Taylors Landlord, and seven interesting guest beers on handpump (usually including another beer from Kelham island), and keep Belgian bottled beers (and a Belgian draught beer), country wines, and farm cider. Good bar food (they tell us prices and examples have not changed since last year) includes sandwiches, soup (£1.30), vegetable cobbler, ploughman's, Mexican mince, leek and butter bean casserole, and pork and pepper casserole (all £2.50), and puddings such as apple and rhubarb crumble or jam roly poly (80p); Sunday lunch. The two small downstairs rooms have coal fires and simple wooden tables and cushioned seats around the walls, and a few advertising mirrors; the one on the left is no smoking; cribbage and dominoes. Steep steps take you up to another similarly simple room (which may be booked for functions) with some attractive prints of old Sheffield; there are picnic tables in a fairylit back courtyard. *(Recommended by Christopher Turner, Richard Fallon, Andy and Jill Kassube, David Carr, R N Hutton, Terry Barlow, Mike and Wendy Proctor, JJW, CMW, David and Fiona Pemberton)*

Own brew ~ Licensee Stephen Fearn ~ Real ale ~ Lunchtime meals and snacks (not 1 Jan) ~ (0114) 249 4801 ~ Children in upstairs at lunchtime and early evening if not booked ~ Open 12-3, 5.30-11; 12-3, 7-10.30 Sun; closed 25-26 Dec

New Barracks

601 Penistone Road, Hillsborough (A61 N of centre)

This big pub, formerly called the Hillsborough Barracks, has been pleasantly refurbished by a partnership involving people from the Kelham Island Brewery and the Lincolnshire Poacher in Nottingham – anyone who knows either that pub or the Fat Cat here in this city will have some idea of what to expect. The comfortable front lounge has red leather banquettes, old pine floors, a gas fire, and collections of decorative plates and of bottles, and there are two smaller rooms behind, one with TV and darts – the family room is no smoking. They keep eight or nine ales in fine condition (serving from no less than 17 handpumps), and the choice might include regulars such as Barnsley Bitter, Hardington Moonshine, John Smiths Magnet, and

Stones, with guests such as Durham Sunstroke, Iceni Gold, Phoenix Double Dagger, Rooster's Yankee, and Ushers Founders on handpump; they do plan to start brewing their own beer; darts, cribbage, dominoes, and piped music. The good value simple food is all freshly made (so there may be a short wait for it). It includes sandwiches (from £1.20), home-made soup (£1.85), a huge satisfying ploughman's (from £3.25), potato ragoût or cheese and carrot bake (£3.75), sausage and tomato casserole or beef in ale (£3.95), steaks (£5.95), puddings such as peach crumble or cinnamon and carrot bake (£1.75), and a good value Sunday lunch. Service is friendly and competent; daily papers and magazines to read; maybe quiet piped radio. There are tables out behind. Local parking is not easy. *(Recommended by CMW, JJW, Jack and Philip Paxton, Terry Barlow, Alan Paulley, Adam Dawson)*

Free house ~ Licensee Mr Birkett ~ Real ale ~ Meals and snacks (12-2, 5-7.30; no food Sun evening) ~ (0114) 234 9148 ~ Children welcome ~ Folk music Tues evening, live bands Sat evening ~ Open 12-11 Mon-Thurs; 11.30-11 Fri/Sat; 12-10.30 Sun; they may close winter afternoons

SHELLEY (W Yorks) SE2112 Map 7
Three Acres 🍺 ♀ 🛏

Roydhouse; B6116 and turn left just before Pennine Garden Centre; straight on for about 3 miles

This is not a place for jeans and a quick pint – though there are still some tables where you could sit without eating. But somehow that would defeat the object of visiting this civilised former coaching inn as it is the very good food that is so much enjoyed by readers. The roomy lounge bar has an urbane and relaxed atmosphere, tankards hanging from the main beam, button-back leather sofas, old prints and so forth, and maybe a pianist playing light music. Good bar food includes a fine range of interesting sandwiches such as hot home-made cumberland sausage, fried onion and mild mustard mayonnaise, ox tongue with tomato and piccalilli or smoked breast of fresh chicken with asparagus and mayonnaise (all £2.95), toasted ciabatta with roasted tomatoes, aubergines, mozzarella, basil and spinach salad (£3.25), and an open club sandwich with smoked chicken breast, bacon, lettuce and tomato and topped with a free range poached egg (£5.50); also, home-made soup or yorkshire pudding with caramelised onion gravy (£2.95), home-made terrine or pâté (£4.95), a roast of the day, deep-fried Whitby cod, steak, lamb kidney and mushroom pie or crispy Japanese chicken with stir fry greens and chilli sauce (all £7.95), and calf liver, cumberland sausage and home-smoked bacon with sage and mustard butter and lyonnaise potatoes or seared tranche of fresh salmon on a potato and herb cake with crème fraîche and sauce gribiche (£8.95), with lovely puddings such as warm liquid centre chocolate banana bread pudding with mascarpone, sauternes custard with poached apricots in vanilla syrup and tuiles biscuits and scrunchy brown bread ice cream with hot toffee sauce (£3.95); they have a seafood bar with anything from Irish oysters (from £5.95) to a big fruits de mer platter (£25). Well kept changing ales such as Adnams Extra, Holt, Plant and Deakin Deakin's Golden Drop, Mansfield Bitter and Riding, Morlands Old Speckled Hen, and Timothy Taylors Landlord on handpump, and a good choice of malt whiskies. The choice of wines, admittedly not cheap, is exceptional, and service is good and friendly even when busy. There are fine views across to Emley Moor, occasionally livened up by the local hunt passing. *(Recommended by Derek and Sylvia Stephenson, Chris Platts, Andy and Jill Kassube, Michael Butler, D and D Savidge, A Preston, Neil Townend, Susan Scanlan)*

Free house ~ Licensees Neil Truelove, Brian Orme ~ Real ale ~ Meals and snacks ~ Restaurant ~ (01484) 602606 ~ Children in eating area of bar ~ Open 12-3, 7-11(10.30 Sun); closed Sat lunchtime and 25 Dec ~ Bedrooms: £47.50B/£60B

Places with gardens or terraces usually let children sit there – we note in the text the very few exceptions that don't.

STARBOTTON (N Yorks) SD9574 Map 7
Fox & Hounds 🍽 🛏

B6160 Upper Wharfedale rd N of Kettlewell; OS Sheet 98, map reference 953749

Walkers are fond of this old-fashioned and notably well run inn, and seats in a sheltered corner enjoy the view over the hills all around this little hamlet. The popularity of the food means that there can be quite a rush for tables at opening times, especially at weekends: carrot and orange soup (£2.25), double baked cheese soufflé (£3), stilton, sun-dried tomatoes and sweet roast pecan salad (£3.75), chick pea and vegetable curry (£5.25), mexican-style pork in a hot chilli sauce or steak and mushroom pie (£6.25), chicken, ham and mushroom crumble (£6.75), and puddings such as sticky toffee pudding, chocolate pudding with white chocolate sauce or apricot and almond tart with maple syrup ice cream (£2.25); at lunchtime there are also filled french sticks (from £2.75) and ploughman's and yorkshire pudding filled with mince or ratatouille (£4.75), and in the evening, extra dishes like baked salmon with a herb crust and creamy dill sauce (£8.25) or peppered venison steak with a port, lemon and redcurrant sauce (£9.95). The dining area is no smoking. The bar has traditional solid furniture on the flagstones, a collection of plates on the walls, whisky jugs hanging from the high beams supporting ceiling boards, a big stone fireplace (with an enormous fire in winter), and a warmly welcoming atmosphere. Well kept Theakstons Best and Black Bull, and Timothy Taylors Landlord on handpump, and quite a few malt whiskies. Dominoes, cribbage, and well reproduced, unobtrusivte piped music. *(Recommended by J E Rycroft, Ian and Christina allen, Neil and Angela Huxter, Chris Wheaton, John Allsopp, I Maw, David and Judy Walmsley, John Honnor, Wayne Wheeler, John and Chris Simpson)*

Free house ~ Licensees James and Hilary McFadyen ~ Real ale ~ Meals and snacks (see below) ~ (01756) 760269 ~ Children in eating area of bar ~ Open 11.30-3, 6.30-11; 12-3, 7-11 Sun; closed Mon evening and all day Mon Oct-March ~ Bedrooms: £30S/£50S

STUTTON (N Yorks) SE4841 Map 7
Hare & Hounds

There's a friendly welcome and cosy low-ceilinged rooms unusually done out in 1960s style in this stone-built pub. And as well as Sam Smiths OB on handpump, decent wine, and good, helpful service, there's a wide choice of very popular, good food set out on a huge blackboard in the lounge bar. With prices unchanged since last year, there might be home-made soup (£1.65), home-made pâté or deep-fried brie with raspberry sauce (£3.50), lunchtime haddock or home-made steak and mushroom pie (£4.95), roast lamb (£5.50), breast of chicken in a cheese and ham sauce (£5.95), and evening extras such as barnsley chops (£9.25), and fillet steak in a stilton and cream sauce (£13.50). Occasional piped music. In summer, the lovely long sloping garden is quite a draw for families, and there are toys out here for children. It does tend to get crowded at weekends. *(Recommended by Tim Halstead, Andy and Jill Kassube, Janet Pickles, JJW,CMW, Chris Westmoreland, Gill and Andy Plumb, K R Fell)*

Sam Smiths ~ Tenant Mike Chiswick ~ Real ale ~ Meals and snacks (11.30-2, 6.30-9.30; not Sun or Mon evenings) ~ Restaurant ~ (01937) 833164 ~ Children in eating area of bar and in restaurant ~ Open 11.30-3.30, 6.30-11

SUTTON UPON DERWENT (E Yorks) SE7047 Map 7
St Vincent Arms 🍽

B1228 SE of York

As well as having a good reputation as a place to eat, this cosy old family-run pub keeps a fine range of around ten real ales on handpump: Adnams Extra, Camerons Strongarm, Fullers London Pride, ESB, and Chiswick, John Smiths, Timothy Taylors Landlord, Charles Wells Bombardier, and two others; also a range of malt whiskies, and very reasonably priced spirits. Good friendly service. Well liked bar food includes sandwiches (from £1.55), home-made soup (£1.90), filled baked potatoes (from

£1.95), salmon fishcakes with a lemon and dill sauce (£3.50), ploughman's (from £3.50), good fillet of haddock in their own batter (£5.20), steak and kidney pie (£6.50), stir fry of the day (£8.50), steaks (from £10.40), and puddings like home-made treacle tart or apple pie (£2.20). One eating area is no smoking. The parlour-like, panelled front bar has traditional high-backed settles, a cushioned bow-window seat, windsor chairs and a coal fire; another lounge and separate dining room open off. No games or music. An attractive garden has tables and seats, and there are pleasant walks along the nearby River Derwent. The pub is named after the admiral who was granted the village and lands by the nation as thanks for his successful commands – and for coping with Nelson's infatuation with Lady Hamilton. *(Recommended by John Burley, Paul and Pam Penrose, Geoffrey and Brenda Wilson)*

Free house ~ Licensee Phil Hopwood ~ Real ale ~ Meals and snacks ~ Restaurant ~ (01904) 608349 ~ Children welcome (must be well behaved in restaurant) ~ Open 12-3, 6-11; 12-3, 7-10.30 Sun; closed evening 25 Dec

TERRINGTON (N Yorks) SE6571 Map 7
Bay Horse

W of Malton; off B1257 at Hovingham (towards York, eventually sigposted left) or Slingsby (towards Castle Howard, then right); can also be reached off A64 via Castle Howard, or via Welburn and Ganthorpe

Set in an unspoilt village, this charming country pub has a cosy lounge bar with a friendly, relaxed atmosphere, country prints, china on delft shelves, magazines to read, and a good log fire, and a traditional public bar has darts, dominoes, shove-ha'penny and table skittles. There's a dining area handsomely furnished in oak, and a back family conservatory has a collection of old farm tools on the walls. Well presented bar food includes lunchtime sandwiches, baps or crusty bread (from £1.85), filled baked potatoes (£2.25), and ploughman's (£4.95), as well as home-made soup (£1.75), Scarborough smokie browned with cream and parmesan (£3.25), terrine of duck with lime pickle (£3.50), leek, apple, stilton and walnut strudel in a wild mushroom sauce (£5.45), lamb hotpot or home-made steak and kidney pie (£5.75), grilled Ampleforth trout (£5.95), pork marinated in orange, wine and herbs and cooked with smoked sausage and button onions (£6.95), steaks (from £9.85), and puddings such as banana yoghurt cheesecake or home-made coffee, cream and brandy trifle (£2.45); children's dishes (from 90p), and on Tuesday lunchtimes, they only serve soup and sandwiches. Well kept Courage Best, Theakstons Best, and Youngers Scotch on handpump, and 68 blended and malt whiskies. There are tables out in a small but attractively planted garden. *(Recommended by Peter and Ruth Burnstone, Philip and Ann Falkner, Arthur and Margaret Dickinson, Mr and Mrs R P Begg)*

Free house ~ Licensees Robert and Jill Snowdon ~ Real ale ~ Meals and snacks (not Sun or Tues evenings) ~ (01653) 648416 ~ Restaurant ~ Children welcome ~ Open 12-3, 6.30-11; 12-3, 7-10.30 Sun

THORNTON WATLASS (N Yorks) SE2486 Map 10
Buck 🍺 🛏 ◼

Village signposted off B6268 Bedale—Masham

Very much the heart of the local community, this very friendly country pub borders the village cricket green – indeed one wall of the pub is actually the boundary; they also play quoits in summer, have popular musical entertainment every Saturday and Sunday evenings, and jazz every third Sunday lunchtime. The sheltered garden has an equipped children's play area and there are summer barbecues – both quite a draw for families. If you wish to stay, they offer golfing, racing, and fishing breaks and there are plenty of good surrounding walks. The pleasantly traditional right-hand bar has upholstered old-fashioned wall settles on the carpet, a fine mahogany bar counter, a high shelf packed with ancient bottles, several mounted fox masks and brushes (the Bedale hunt meets in the village), a brick fireplace, and a relaxed atmosphere; piped music. Good, popular food at lunchtime might include light dishes such as mushroom rarebit with wensleydale cheese, Theakstons Ale, and a rasher of bacon or locally smoked kipper and scrambled egg (£3.95), as well as soups, home-made lasagne or steak and kidney pie (£5.95), much liked fresh Whitby cod (£6.25), mediterranean lamb pasta, crumbed chicken breast or popular pork chop casseroled in sage, mushrooms and apple (all £6.25), and evening rump steak (£6.25); home-made ppuddings such as mint chocolate cheesecake, banoffi pie or double chocolate mousse (£2.45), and traditional Sunday roast (£5.50). Well kept Black Sheep Bitter, John Smiths, Tetleys, Theakstons Best, and a local guest beer on handpump, and around 30 malt whiskies. The beamed and panelled no-smoking dining room is hung with large prints of old Thornton Watlass cricket teams. A bigger plainer bar has darts, pool, and dominoes. *(Recommended by Andrew and Ruth Triggs, RB, Joan and Andrew Life, Derek and Sylvia Stephenson, David and Judy Walmsley, Elizabeth and Alex Rocke, Chris and Andy Crow, David and Fiona Pemberton, Angus Lyson, Anthony Barnes, R N Hutton, E A Thwaite, Ian Phillips)*

Free house ~ Licensees Michael and Margaret Fox ~ Real ale ~ Meals and snacks (not 25 Dec) ~ Restaurant ~ (01677) 422461 ~ Well behaved children welcome ~ Live music Sat/Sun evenings, jazz every 3rd Sun lunchtime ~ Open 11-3, 6-11; 11-11 Sat; 12-10.30 Sun; closed evening 25 Dec ~ Bedrooms: £30(£34S)/£44(£52S)

THRESHFIELD (N Yorks) SD9763 Map 7
Old Hall 🍴🍷 ◧

B6265, just on the Skipton side of its junction with B6160 near Grassington

Run by an extremely pleasant landlord, this friendly pub is much liked for its good, interesting food. Using fresh local ingredients, there might be baked ciabatta with tomatoes, olives, chorizo sausage and mozzarella (£3.75), moules in a thai coconut and lemon grass sauce (£3.95), smoked haddock and spinach pancakes with a cheese sauce (£4.25), fresh queen scallops poached in a garlic, coriander and lime sauce, served in a pastry case (£4.75), wild boar and Black Sheep ale sausages on garlic mash with caramelised shallots (£6.25), individual lamb joints with a port and redcurrant sauce (£9.45), fried pheasant breasts with chicory and an apple and calvados sauce (£9.95), fillet steak with a wild mushroom sauce (£12.50), and puddings such as iced tiramisu parfait, home-made stout cake with lots of chocolate sauce or mille feuille of shortbread biscuits with strawberries and a fruit coulis (£2.50). The three communicating rooms have a high beam-and-plank ceiling hung with lots of chamber-pots, unfussy decorations such as old Cadburys advertisements and decorative plates on a high delft shelf, simple, cushioned pews built into the white walls, a tall well blacked kitchen range, and a good, bustling atmosphere with a mix of locals and visitors. Well kept Timothy Taylors Bitter, Landlord, Golden Best and Dark Mild on handpump, and up to 60 malt whiskies. Darts, dominoes, and piped music. A neat, partly gravelled side garden has young shrubs and a big sycamore, some seats, and an aviary with cockatiels and zebra finches. This is, of course, a fine base for Dales walking; there are two cottages behind the inn for hire. *(Recommended by Martin Hickes, Lynne Gittins, Andrew and Ruth Triggs, Vann and Terry Prime, Pat and Clive Sherriff, Ann and Colin Hunt, J E Rycroft, James Todd)*

Free house ~ Licensees Ian and Amanda Taylor ~ Real ale ~ Meals and snacks (not Sun evening Oct-May; not Mon) ~ Restaurant ~ (01756) 752441 ~ Children in eating area of bar ~ Open 11-3, 6-11; 12-3, 6-10.30 Sun; closed Mon lunchtime

WASS (N Yorks) SE5679 Map 7
Wombwell Arms 🍴 🍷 🛏

Back road W of Ampleforth; or follow brown tourist-attraction sign for Byland Abbey off A170 Thirsk—Helmsley

As well as the good interesting food and beers from local breweries, what people enjoy so much here is the warm welcome from the chatty and helpful licensees. The little central bar is spotlessly kept and cosy, and the three low-beamed dining areas are comfortable and inviting and take in a former 18th-c granary. At lunchtime, bar food might include curried parsnip, apple and celery soup (£2.25), sandwiches (from £2.25), ploughman's with home-made pickles (£3.95), goat's cheese on a pine nut salad (£4.75), smoked haddock with a welsh rarebit topping or pasta with various sauces (£5.75), and lamb in a mint, rosemary and red wine sauce (£6.95); in the evening, there is grilled sardines with a spicy tomato salsa (£3.25), smoked venison with onion marmalade (£3.95), aubergine and tomato layered with mozzarella and parmesan (£5.95), Whitby cod with a garlic and herb crust (£7.75), local rabbit in a red wine, bacon, shallot and mushroom sauce (£7.85), stilton chicken (£7.95), king prawns in garlic butter (£8.75), and strips of beef fillet with red onions, cream, mushrooms and grain mustard (£8.95). Well kept Black Sheep Bitter, Timothy Taylors Landlord, and a guest such as Butterknowle Bitter or Banner Bitter, Daleside Legover, Dales Delight or Nightjar, Highwood Tom Wood Best Bitter, and Tetleys Autumn Ale on handpump, decent malt whiskies, and around 8 wines by the glass. *(Recommended by John Fahy, Simon Collett-Jones, John Honnor, R J Robinson, Chris and Shirley Machin, Paul and Ursula Randall, Paul Barnett, Chris and Elaine Lyon, Mr and Mrs R P Begg, Paul Boot, R Borthwick, S Clegg, Greta and Christopher Wells, Barry and Anne, Allan Worsley)*

Free house ~ Licensees Alan and Lynda Evans ~ Real ale ~ Meals and snacks ~ (01347) 868280 ~ Children in eating area of bar (no under-5s evening) ~ Open 12-2.30, 7-11; 12-3, 7-10.30 Sun; closed Sun evening and all day Mon in winter and 10 days in Jan ~ Bedrooms: £27.50B/£49B

WATH IN NIDDERDALE (N Yorks) SE1467 Map 7
Sportsmans Arms 🍽️ ♀ 🛏️

Nidderdale rd off B6265 in Pateley Bridge; village and pub signposted over hump bridge on right after a couple of miles

Strictly speaking, this 17th-c mellow sandstone building is more of a restaurant with bedrooms than a pub, but it does have a welcoming bar where locals do drop in for just a drink. It remains the marvellous food, however, that most people come here to enjoy. Using the best local produce – game from the moors, fish delivered daily from Whitby and the East Coast and Nidderdale lamb, pork and beef – the carefully presented and prepared food might include cream of leek and celeriac soup (£3), black pudding with caramelised apples and white wine sauce (£4.25), fresh Whitby dressed crab mayonnaise (£4.50), salmon and bacon tagliatelle (£4.80), Scottish salmon grilled with a sesame crust and served with a tomato and basil sauce (£7.20), lovely baked Scarborough woof in a parsley and garlic crust (£7.40), breast of Pateley chicken on a bed of leeks and garlic mushrooms or loin of pork with a seed mustard and mushroom sauce (£7.50), monkfish sautéed in a ginger and chive butter (£8.50), roast best end of lamb on a bed of spinach served with natural jus (£9.20), and puddings such as tart au citron, sticky toffee pudding or rich chocolate pots with chocolate ice cream (from £3); various lunchtime sandwiches and rolls. The restaurant is no smoking. There's a very sensible and extensive wine list, a good choice of malt whiskies, several Russian vodkas, and attentive service; open fires, dominoes. Benches and tables outside. *(Recommended by Brian Wainwright, Janet and Peter Race, Walker and Debra Lapthorne, Tony Hall, Melanie Jackson)*

Free house ~ Licensee Ray Carter ~ Meals and snacks (not 25 Dec) ~ Evening restaurant ~ (01423) 711306 ~ Children welcome ~ Open 12-2.30, 6.30-11 ~ Bedrooms: £35(£39S)/£55(£60S)

WHITBY NZ9011 (N Yorks) Map 10
Duke of York

Church Street, Harbour East Side

A good place to fortify yourself before trying the famous nearby 199 Steps, this bustling and welcoming pub has a splendid outlook over the harbour entrance and the western cliff from its comfortable beamed lounge bar. Decorations include quite a bit of fishing memorabilia, but it's the wide choice of good value fresh local fish on the menu itself which appeals most: there might be fresh crab sandwiches (£2.50), large fillet of fresh cod (£4.95), and fresh crab salad (£5.50), as well as sandwiches (from £1.95), ploughman's (£4.25), leek and stilton bake (£4.50), steak and mushroom pie (£4.75), chicken tikka masala or lamb balti (£4.95), puddings (£1.95), and children's meals (from £2.25). Well kept Black Sheep Bitter, Courage Directors John Smiths Magnet, and Ruddles Best on handpump, decent wines, and quick pleasant service even when busy; piped music, fruit machine. Sweep the cat is generally friendly. We have not yet heard from readers who have tried the bedrooms here. *(Recommended by Sue and Bob Ward, Beryl and Bill Farmer, M Rutherford, Denis and Margaret Kilner, JJW, CMW, David and Ruth Hollands, Chris Mawson, Janet Pickles, M Borthwick)*

Free house ~ Licensee Lawrence Bradley ~ Real ale ~ Meals and snacks (12-9) ~ (01947) 600324 ~ Children in family room ~ Open 11-11; 12-10.30 Sun; closed 25 Dec ~ Bedrooms: /£25(£39B)

WIDDOP (W Yorks) SD9333 Map 7
Pack Horse

The Ridge; from A646 on W side of Hebden Bridge, turn off at Heptonstall signpost (as it's a sharp turn, coming out of Hebden Bridge road signs direct you around a turning circle), then follow Slack and Widdop signposts; can also be reached from Nelson and Colne, on high, pretty road; OS Sheet 103, map ref 952317

A haven for walkers in this bleak moorland, this is a pleasant and friendly traditional pub. The bar has window seats cut into the partly panelled stripped stone walls that take in the moorland view, sturdy furnishings, and warm winter fires. Generous helpings of good bar food include sandwiches, tasty soup, cottage hotpot, ploughman's, home-made steak and kidney pie, steaks, and specials such as vegetarian dishes, chicken jambalaya (£4.95), haddock mornay (£5.95), rack of lamb (£8.95), and summer crab. Well kept Theakstons XB, Thwaites Bitter, Youngers IPA, and a guest beer on handpump, around 130 single malt whiskies, and some Irish ones as well, and New World wines; efficient service. There are seats outside. *(Recommended by D Stokes, Rev John Hibberd, Dave Braisted, Karen Eliot, PGP, RTM, JCM)*

Free house ~ Licensee Andrew Hollinrake ~ Real ale ~ Meals and snacks (see below) ~ (01422) 842803 ~ Children welcome until 8pm ~ Open 12-3, 7-11; closed weekday lunchtimes and Mon Oct-Easter ~ Bedrooms: £28B/£40B

WORMALD GREEN (N Yorks) SE3065 Map 7
Cragg Lodge £

A61 Ripon—Harrogate, about half way

Nearly 1,000 malt whiskies – probably the widest choice in the world – are kept in this comfortably modernised dining pub, including two dozen Macallans going back to 1937. They have 16 price bands, between £1.15 and £6.50, depending on rarity – with a 17th 'by negotiation' for their unique 1919 Campbelltown. Also, well kept Tetleys Bitter and Theakstons Best, XB and Old Peculier on handpump, several distinguished brandies, and mature vintage port by the glass. The big open-plan bar is laid out for eating and has Mouseman furniture as well as little upholstered chairs around dark rustic tables, horsebrasses and pewter tankards hanging from side beams, a dark joist-and-plank ceiling, and a coal fire. Good value bar food at lunchtime is popular with older people and includes home-made soup (£1.50), sandwiches (from £1.55), ploughman's (£2.80), home-cooked ham in cherry sauce or chicken and vegetable pie (£3.50), fresh battered cod or nut cutlets (£3.90), poached salmon in white wine and mushroom sauce (£4.50), puddings such as sherry trifle or sticky toffee pudding (£1.90), and children's meals (from £1.50); in the evenings, there's a larger, more elaborate menu, with a roast of the day (£4.80), quite a few fish dishes such as fresh cod mornay (£5.50), and halibut bretonne or salmon and plaice in a white wine and grape sauce (£6.80), and steaks (from £8.50); enjoyable daily specials. The restaurant is partly no smoking. Shove-ha'penny, cribbage, dominoes and piped music. There are picnic tables under cocktail parasols on the side terrace, with more in a sizeable garden and pretty hanging baskets in summer. *(Recommended by Piotr Chodzko-Zajko, L Dixon; more reports please)*

Free house ~ Licensee Garfield Parvin ~ Real ale ~ Meals and snacks ~ Restaurant (not Sun evening) ~ (01765) 677214 ~ Children in eating area of bar and in restaurant ~ Open 11.30-2.30, 6-11; 12-3, 7-10.30 Sun ~ Bedrooms: £30B/£50B

YORK (N Yorks) SE5951 Map 7

Black Swan

Peaseholme Green; inner ring road, E side of centre; the inn has a good car park

The timbered and jettied facade of this surprisingly unspoilt but very popular pub, and the original lead-latticed windows in the twin gables, are very fine indeed. The busy black-beamed back bar (liked by locals) has wooden settles along the walls, some cushioned stools, and a throne-like cushioned seat in the vast brick inglenook, where there's a coal fire in a grate with a spit and some copper cooking utensils. The cosy panelled front bar, with its little serving hatch, is similarly furnished but smaller and more restful. The crooked-floored hall that runs along the side of both bars has a fine period staircase (leading up to a room fully panelled in oak, with an antique tiled fireplace); there is provision for non smokers. Good bar food includes sandwiches, filled french sticks (£3.50), generously filled giant home-made yorkshire puddings (from £2.25), and home-made steak pie, lasagne or vegetable curry (all £4.10). Well kept Bass, Black Sheep Bitter, Fullers London Price, Stones, and Timothy Taylors Landlord on handpump, and several country wines; dominoes, fruit machine, trivia, and piped music. If the car park is full, it's worth knowing that there's a big public one next door. *(Recommended by Eric Larkham, Paul and Ursula Randall, Sue and Geoff Price, Chris Westmoreland, M Walker)*

Bass ~ Manager Pat O'Connell ~ Meals and snacks (not Fri evening) ~ (01904) 625236 ~ Children in separate room ~ Jazz Mon, folk Thurs evenings ~ Open 11-11; 12-10.30 Sun ~ Bedrooms: /£50B

Olde Starre

Stonegate; pedestrians-only street in centre, far from car parks

Parts of this old building date back to 900 and the cellar was used as a hospital in the Civil War – it's also the city's oldest licensed pub (1644). The main bar has original panelling, green plush wall seats, a large servery running the length of the room, and a large leaded window with red plush curtains at the far end. Several other little rooms lead off the porch-like square hall – one with its own food servery, one with panelling and some prints, and a third with cream wallpaper and dado; the tap room is no smoking. Well kept John Smiths, Theakstons Best, XB and Old Peculier, and Youngers No 3 on handpump, and decent whiskies – most spirits are served in double measures for a single's price; helpful, friendly and knowledgeable staff. Piped music, fruit machine, video game, and CD juke box. Good bar food includes sandwiches, filled yorkshire pudding, steak and kidney pie or lamb liver, sausage and onion (£4.25), tipsy beef or Irish stew (£4.50), and cumberland sausage (£4.65). *(Recommended by Andrew and Ruth Triggs, Howard England, Eric Larkham, SLC, Esther and John Sprinkle, Mark Walker, Gill and Andy Plumb, A and R Cooper, M Borthwick)*

Scottish Courage ~ Managers Bill and Susan Embleton ~ Real ale ~ Meals and snacks (11.30-3, 5.30-8) ~ (01904) 623063 ~ Children welcome away from bar area ~ Open 11-11; 12-10.30 Sun

Spread Eagle 🏮

98 Walmgate

A good range of well kept real ales is kept on handpump in this bustling pub, well liked by younger customers. As well as Mansfield Riding, Bitter and Old Bailey on handpump, they have guests such as Batemans XXXB, Brains SA, Marstons Pedigree, Morlands Old Speckled Hen, Shepherd Neame Spitfire, and York Stonewall and Yorkshire Terrier on handpump; malt whiskies and a few country wines. The main bar is a dark vault with two smaller, cosier rooms leading off – lots of old enamel advertisements and prints on the walls, and a relaxed atmosphere. Large helpings of good value bar food might include home-made soup (£1.80), sandwiches (from £1.95; hot beef in a warm french stick with lots of gravy and onion £2.95), filled baked potatoes (from £2.15), omelettes (£3.95), lasagne (£4.15), curries (from £3.95), very hot chilli or a daily roast (£4.95), and daily specials such as chicken and mushroom pie (£4.95), mixed vegetable crumble (£6.45), salmon and broccoli bake (£6.75), and pork stilton or chicken breast stuffed with mango in a cheese sauce (£6.95). Fruit machine, juke box, and piped music. *(Recommended by Eric Larkham, Thomas Nott, Esther and John Sprinkle, Dr A C and Dr A Jackson, P R Morley)*

Mansfield Brewery ~ Manager Mike Dandy ~ Real ale ~ Meals and snacks (11-10pm) ~ Restaurant ~ (01904) 635868 ~ Children welcome ~ Live Blues Sun lunchtime ~ Open 11-11; 12-10.30 Sun

Tap & Spile £ 🍺

Monkgate

It's the marvellous choice of ten well kept real ales on handpump that attracts people to this traditionally furnished pub: Tap & Spile Premium, Old Mill Bitter and Theakstons Old Peculier, and seven constantly changing guests on handpump; ciders, perrys, and 20 country wines. The big split-level bar has bare boards, green leatherette wall settles right around a big bay window, with a smaller upper area with frosted glass and panelling; darts, shove-ha'penny, dominoes, fruit machine, video game, and piped music. Under the new manager, straightforward bar food includes home-made soup (£1.50), sandwiches (from £1.60; chip butty £1.80), filled baked potatoes (from £1.80), filled giant yorkshire puddings (from £2.25), omelette (£3), home-made beef or vegetable chilli (£3.25), 8oz rump steak (£4.50), and daily specials. There are a few picnic tables outside. *(Recommended by Piotr Chodzko-Zajko, PM, AM, Andy Cunningham, Yvonne Hannaford, Thomas Nott, Eric Larkham, Carol and Philip Bacon)*

Pubmaster ~ Manager Andy Mackay ~ Real ale ~ Lunchtime meals and snacks ~ (01904) 656158 ~ Well behaved children welcome ~ Singalong every 2nd Sun ~ Open 11.30-11; 12-10.30 Sun

---

Lucky Dip

Besides the fully inspected pubs, you might like to try these Lucky Dips recommended to us and described by readers (if you do, please send us reports):

Aberford W Yor [Old North Rd; best to use A642 exit off A1; SE4337], *Swan*: Vast choice of good value generous food from sandwiches to carvery and display of puddings, in attractively refurbished popular dining place, lots of black timber, prints, pistols, cutlasses, stuffed animals and hunting trophies, cosy layout, well kept Boddingtons, Flowers, Tetleys and Timothy Taylors, generous glasses of wine, friendly uniformed staff, more upmarket upstairs evening restaurant; children welcome, comfortable bedrooms *(Mark Gillis, Neil and Anita Christopher, Michael Butler, H Bramwell, Eddy and Emma Gibson)*

Aberford [Old North Rd], *Arabian Horse*: Relaxed down-to-earth beamed local with comfortable lounge area, friendly efficient staff, good value food, good fire, well kept Theakstons Best and Old Peculier; open all day Sat *(Mark Gillis, Jenny and Brian Seller, Martin Hickes)*

Allerthorpe E Yor [off A1079 nr Pocklington; SE7847], *Plough*: Clean and airy pub taken over this year by new chain started by ex-Tetleys directors, two-room lounge bar with snug alcoves, hunting prints, WWII RAF and RCAF photographs, open fires, wide choice of good value food, well kept Tetleys and Theakstons XB and Old Peculier, restaurant, games extension with pool, juke box etc; pleasant garden, handy for Burnby Hall

(Roger Bellingham, LYM)

Ampleforth N Yor [Main St; SE5878], *White Swan*: Extensive modern lounge/dining bar in small attractive village, wide choice of generous food from good big filled buns to popular Sun lunch, front country bar with several real ales inc a guest beer, lots of malt whiskies, darts and a couple of fruit machines; decent wines, good friendly service; back terrace *(Denis and Margaret Kilner)*

Appleton Roebuck N Yor [SE5542], *Shoulder of Mutton*: Cheerful and attractive pub bar overlooking village green, queues at opening time each night for the wide choice of good value food inc cheap steaks, Sam Smiths OB and Museum, quick service; can be crowded with caravanners summer; bedrooms *(H Bramwell, Beryl and Bill Farmer)*

☆ **Appletreewick** N Yor [SE0560], *New Inn*: Welcoming stonebuilt pub with good value simple food inc good sandwiches, well kept John Smiths, Theakstons Best and Daleside, willing service, interesting photographs, pub games, family room, no music; in fine spot, lovely views, garden, good walking; bedrooms *(Gwen and Peter Andrews, Judith Hirst)*

☆ **Arncliffe** N Yor [off B6160; SD9473], *Falcon*: Classic old-fashioned haven for walkers, ideal setting on moorland village green, no frills, Youngers tapped from cask to stoneware jugs in central hatch-style servery, generous plain lunchtime bar snacks, open fire in small bar with elderly furnishings and humorous sporting prints, airy back sunroom (children allowed here lunchtime) looking on to garden; run by same family for generations – they take time to get to know; cl winter Thurs evenings; bedrooms (not all year), good breakfasts and evening meals – real value *(Neil and Angela Huxter)*

Askrigg N Yor [SD9591], *Crown*: Unassuming and beautifully kept, several separate areas off the main bar with blazing fires inc old-fashioned range, reasonably priced generous food, Black Sheep and Theakstons XB and Old Peculier, Seabrooks crisps, helpful courteous staff; walkers welcome *(Jim and Pam Townsley, W H E Thomas)*

☆ **Askwith** W Yor [3 miles E of Ilkley; SD1648], *Black Horse*: Biggish family pub doing well as part of chain, in lovely spot with good views from terrace; good choice of well cooked food (best to book Sun lunch), well kept ales inc Theakstons Best and XB, pleasant helpful staff, open fire *(Lynne Gittins)*

Aston S Yor [The Warren; B6067 ½ mile from M1 junction 31; SK4685], *Blue Bell*: Refurbished pub with decent generous food, Stones and Worthington; bedrooms *(G P Kernan)*

Austwick N Yor [A65 Settle—Ingleton; SD7668], *Cross Streets*: Substantial good value meals in bar and restaurant; Tetleys *(J A Swanson); Game Cock*: Newish management revitalising this prettily placed pub below the Three Peaks, pleasant atmosphere in simple old-fashioned beamed back bar, sensibly priced simple bar food, well kept Thwaites, good fire, smarter no-smoking restaurant, seats outside with good play area; clean bedrooms *(T M Dobby, Gwen and Peter Andrews, LYM)*

Bainbridge N Yor [A684 Leyburn—Sedbergh; SD9390], *Rose & Crown*: Ancient inn overlooking moorland village green, old-fashioned beamed and panelled front bar with big log fire, busy less charismatic back extension popular with families (pool, juke box etc), John Smiths Magnet and Websters Yorkshire, simple bar food, restaurant; children welcome, open all day, bedrooms *(Michele and Clive Platman, LYM)*

Bawtry S Yor [Gainsborough Rd; SK6593], *Ship*: Good value bar food *(E Robinson)*

☆ **Beverley** E Yor [North Bar Within (A164); TA0340], *Beverley Arms*: Spacious traditional oak-panelled bar in comfortable and well run long-established hotel with two bars, well kept ales, easy-going friendly atmosphere, choice of several decent places to eat inc interesting former coachyard (now enclosed) with formidable bank of the ranges that were used for cooking; good bedrooms, some with Minster view *(H Bramwell, LYM)*

Beverley [Molescroft (A164/B1248 NW)], *Molescroft*: Comfortable Mansfield pub with Mild and Bitter from central bar, food inc Sun roast, piped music, TV, games machines *(JJW, CMW)*; [North Bar Without (A164)], *Rose &*

Crown: Prompt cheerful service even when busy, decent piping hot food inc good speciality giant haddock, well kept Wards; bedrooms *(I Maw, Malcolm Baxter)*

Bingley W Yor [Ireland Bridge; B6429 just W of junction with A650 – OS Sheet 104 map ref 105395; SE1039], *Brown Cow*: Genuine and unpretentious, open-plan but snugly divided, with easy chairs, toby jugs, lots of pictures, panelling; bar food from sandwiches to steaks, no-smoking restaurant, well kept Timothy Taylors Bitter, Best, Landlord and winter Ram Tam; maybe piped music; children welcome, tables on sheltered terrace, pleasant spot; jazz Mon *(Steve Harvey, Chris Westmoreland, LYM)*; [Gilstead Lane, Gilstead], *Glen*: Open all day, with good choice of reasonably priced food from good sandwiches to steaks, well kept Tetleys Mild, Bitter and a guest ale, pleasant staff, railway memorabilia; garden with play area, rural setting *(JER, Pat and Tony Martin)*

Birstall W Yor [Church Lane, off Bradford—Dewsbury rd at church – OS Sheet 104 map ref 218262; SE2126], *Black Bull*: Old building opp ancient Norman church, low beams, lots of panelling, former upstairs courtroom, Whitbreads-related ales, well priced home-made food (new landlord still doing the bargain early meals), old local photographs; recent small extension *(Michael Butler)*

Bishop Burton E Yor [Main St; A1079 Beverley—York; SE9939], *Altisidora*: Good value Landlords Table family food pub open all day, comfortable alcoves inc raised no-smoking area off low-beamed modernised lounge, three Mansfield ales and Deakins White Rabbit; quiz night; nr pretty pond in lovely village green *(CMW, JJW, LYM)*

Bishopdale N Yor [B6160 nr W Burton; SD9885], *Street Head*: 17th-c coaching inn with Websters ales, separate games room, bar meals; bedrooms *(Ann and Colin Hunt)*

☆ **Bolton Percy** N Yor [off A659 in Tadcaster; SE5341], *Crown*: Basic unpretentious country local, well kept Sam Smiths, generous simple food (not Mon or Tues), low prices, friendly dogs, tables on sizeable terrace with ageing pens of ornamental pheasants, summer evening barbecues, quiet setting nr interesting 15th-c church and medieval gatehouse; children welcome *(Janet Pickles, Tim Halstead, LYM)*

Bradfield S Yor [High Bradfield – OS Sheet 110 map ref 268927; SK2692], *Old Horns*: Friendly old stonebuilt pub with comfortably refurbished divided L-shaped bar, lots of pictures, no-smoking area, good choice of reasonably priced food, efficient friendly staff, ales such as Boddingtons, Courage Directors, John Smiths Magnet and Stones; quiet piped music, children welcome, picnic tables and play area outside, hill village with stunning views, interesting church, good walks *(Alan and Heather Jacques, JJW, CMW)*

☆ **Bradford** W Yor [Preston St (off B6145); SE1633], *Fighting Cock*: Busy bare-floor basic alehouse with particularly well kept Timothy Taylors Landlord and lots of changing ales such as Black Sheep, Exmoor Gold, Sam Smiths and Theakstons, also farm ciders, foreign bottled beers, doorstep sandwiches and other snacks, coal fires; low prices *(Reg Nelson, Mike Lee, Susan and Nigel Wilson)*

Bradford W Yor [Grattan Rd/Barry St], *Castle*: Plain town local owned by group of small independent brewers, distinguished by its good collection of cheap well kept unusual ales such as Goose Eye Bitter and Wharfedale, Griffin Lions, Merry Marker, Riding Bitter and Mild, Ryburn, Timothy Taylors Golden Pale; basic cheap food, well reproduced piped music (maybe some live) *(Susan and Nigel Wilson, Pat and Tony Martin, BB)*

Bramhope W Yor [SE2543], *Fox & Hounds*: Popular civilised two-roomed pub with well kept Tetleys Mild and Bitter, lunchtime food, open fire; children welcome, has been open all day *(Martin Hickes, JER, David Watson)*

Brighouse W Yor [Brookfoot; A6025 towards Elland; SE1323], *Red Rooster*: Homely traditional alehouse, newish licensees keeping up its great turnover of country-wide interesting well kept real ales, no food, no machines, brewery memorabilia, open fire, separate areas inc one with books to read or buy *(Shaun Daniel, Tony Hobden)*

Brompton N Yor [just off A64 W of Scarborough; SE9582], *Cayley Arms*: Quiet uncluttered pub in pretty village, welcoming landlady, friendly efficient staff, good food freshly cooked to order, well kept ales inc Theakstons, reasonable prices *(A Burt)*

Brompton N Yor [the one off A684 just N of Northallerton; SE3896], *Village Inn*: Pleasant surroundings, consistently good value bar meals *(Joseph Watson)*

☞ **Broughton** N Yor [just off A59 W of Skipton; SD9351], *Bull*: Smartly modernised old-fashioned pub popular for good food inc children's meals in bar and restaurant; cosy and comfortable, pleasant busy atmosphere, polished brass and china, friendly service, well kept Black Sheep and Tetleys *(Ann and Colin Hunt, JER, LYM)*

☞ **Burnt Yates** N Yor [B6165, 6 miles N of Harrogate; SE2561], *Bay Horse*: Friendly 18th-c dining pub with log fires, low beams, brasses; wide range of bar food inc
- outstanding steaks, well kept Theakstons, courteous staff, pleasant restaurant, traditional atmosphere (shame about the piped music); bedrooms in modest extension *(Howard and Margaret Buchanan)*

☞ **Burton Leonard** N Yor [off A61 Ripon—Harrogate; SE3364], *Hare & Hounds*: Good generous reasonably priced food inc fresh veg and good chips in cheerful spotless beamed bar and spacious restaurant, well kept Black Sheep, Tetleys and Theakstons, decent wines, quality service, paintings, copper and brass on walls, big fairy-lit beech branch over ceiling, cosy coffee lounge, no games or juke box *(D V Clements, David Watson)*

☞ **Cadeby** S Yor [off A1(M) via A630, then Sprotbrough turn; SE5100], *Cadeby Inn*: Biggish, with open fire, gleaming brasses and lots of house plants in back lounge, quieter front sitting room, no-smoking snug, separate games area; generous food from good hot beef sandwich to carvery, well kept Courage Directors, John Smiths and Magnet, Sam Smiths OB and Tetleys, over 200 malt whiskies, good service even when busy, seats out in front; children in eating area, open all day Sat *(Peter Marshall, L Dixon, Lawrence Pearse, LYM)*

Calder Grove W Yor [Broadley Cut Rd; just off M1 junction 39; A636 signposted Denby Dale, then 1st right; SE3017], *Navigation*: Useful motorway break – cheery waterside local full of canalia, with well kept Tetleys and Timothy Taylors Landlord, low prices, good simple food, tables outside *(P M Lane, LYM)*

Camblesforth N Yor [Selby Rd; SE6426], *Black Dog*: Clean and friendly refurbished pub, new licensees doing good value home-made food in pretty restaurant off lounge bar, well kept Ind Coope Burton and Tetleys *(Mr and Mrs B Twiddy)*

☆ **Carlton** N Yor [just off A172 SW of Stokesley; NZ5004], *Blackwell Ox*: Three linked rooms and big central bar, lots of dark wood, open fires, cigarette card collection, well kept Bass, Courage and Theakstons; Thai landlady, good reasonably priced bar food inc lots of Thai dishes as well as more traditional ones inc excellent home-made duck and pork pie; garden with big play area; bedrooms, picturesque village location, handy for coast-to-coast and Cleveland Way walkers *(Val Stevenson, Rob Holmes, T Dobby)*

Catterick N Yor [Catterick Bridge; SE2497], *Bridge House*: Smart former manor house overlooking race course, good value bar food inc interesting dishes, Theakstons Best; bedrooms – one said to be haunted *(Brian Seller)*

☆ **Cawood** N Yor [King St (B1222 NW of Selby); SE5737], *Ferry*: Unspoilt but neatly kept 16th-c inn, smallish comfortable rooms, massive inglenook, stripped brickwork, bare boards, well kept reasonably priced Mansfield Riding and two or more guest beers tapped from the cask, good reasonably priced food from refitted kitchen, tables out on flagstone terrace and grass by River Ouse swing bridge *(Chris Westmoreland, TN, Simon Orme)*

☆ **Chapel le Dale** N Yor [B6655 Ingleton—Hawes, 3 miles N of Ingleton; SD7477], *Old Hill*: Basic stripped-stone flagstone-floor moorland bar with potholing pictures and Settle railway memorabilia, roaring log fire in cosy back parlour, well kept Dent and Theakstons Bitter, XB and Old Peculier, generous simple home-made food in separate room inc good beef sandwiches and pies, plenty of vegetarian; juke box; children welcome; bedrooms basic but good, with good breakfast – wonderful isolated spot, camping possible *(R H Rowley, LYM)*

Chapeltown S Yor [Smithy Wood Rd; off

Cowley Hill at M1 junction 35; SK3596],
Travellers: Friendly two-bar pub with no-
smoking dining room/conservatory, well kept
Banks's Bitter in lined glasses – good measure,
decent food (not Sun/Mon evenings); piped
music, high chairs for children; garden with
play area *(CMW, JJW)*

Cherry Burton E Yor [34 Main St; off B1248
NW of Beverley; SE9942], *Bay Horse*: 17th-c
modernised Mansfield pub, roomy lounge
with restaurant and games area, wide choice
of good value freshly prepared food (can be a
wait) inc children's, Deakins as guest beer;
piped music, TV, fruit machines, various
evening entertainments *(CMW, JJW)*

Church Fenton N Yor [Main St; SE5136],
White Horse: Recently refurbished, friendly
staff, very big helpings of good wholesome
food, good service, well kept John Smiths,
conservatory, small garden *(G J McGrath)*

Clapham N Yor [off A65 N of Settle;
SD7569], *New Inn*: Riverside pub in lovely
village, small comfortable panelled lounge,
Dent, John Smiths, Tetleys and Youngers No
3, public bar with games room, popular food
in bar and restaurant, friendly service; handy
for walks; bedrooms *(Paul McPherson, Ann
and Colin Hunt)*

☆ **Clifton** W Yor [Towngate/Coalpit Lane; off
Brighouse rd from M62 junction 25; SE1622],
Black Horse: Comfortably smart dining pub,
enormous choice of good generous traditional
food in popular restaurant; cosy oak-beamed
bars, at least four well kept Whitbreads-
related beers, friendly service, open fire;
bedrooms comfortable; *(Mrs P Tullie, Andy
and Jill Kassube, RJH, Michael Butler)*

Cloughton, N Yor [A171 Scarboro—Whitby;
TA0195], *Falcon*: Stone-built pub dating from
18th c, on edge of Staintondale moor, views
to sea; big open-plan bar with welcoming real
fire, friendly licensee and staff, huge helpings
of good value food, well kept Theakstons,
restaurant; good bedrooms with own
bathrooms *(Mark Lancaster)*; [N of village],
Hayburn Wyke: In nice spot nr NT Hayburn
Wyke and Cleveland Way coastal path, lots of
tables outside; very black and white L-shaped
bar, restaurant and eating area beyond, well
kept Scottish Courage beers, John Smiths,
Theakstons Best and Youngers, friendly
informal service, well behaved children
welcome; bedrooms *(Mike and Wendy
Proctor, Dave Braisted, M Borthwick)*

☆ **Cloughton Newlands** N Yor [A171;
TA0196], *Bryherstones*: Several
interconnecting rooms, well kept Youngers,
over 50 whiskies, decent generous food,
plenty of atmosphere, welcoming locals and
new management; pool room, quieter room
upstairs; children welcome, delightful
surroundings *(M Borthwick, Mike and
Wendy Proctor)*

☆ **Coley** W Yor [a mile N of Hipperholme; Lane
Ends, Denholme Gate Rd (A644 Brighouse—
Keighley); SE1226], *Brown Horse*: Clean and
busy, with particularly good interesting
sensibly priced home cooking, prompt quietly

welcoming service by smart staff, well kept
Scottish Courage ales, decent house wines,
open fires in three bustling rooms, golfing
memorabilia, pictures, delft shelf of china and
bottles, no-smoking restaurant *(Geoffrey and
Brenda Wilson, Jonathan Harrison)*

Colton N Yor [off A64 York—Tadcaster;
SE5444], *Old Sun*: Attractive 17th-c beamed
pub with low doorways, old settles and
banquettes, sparkling brasses, good value
food (not Mon), Bass, John Smiths and
Stones, decent wines, log fires, welcoming
staff; picnic tables outside *(CMW, JJW, Mike
Temple)*

☆ **Cracoe** N Yor [B6265 Skipton—Grassington;
SD9760], *Devonshire Arms*: Solidly
comfortable low-beamed pub with nicely
divided old-fashioned bar and snug no-
smoking dining area; has been very popular
esp for food, with very good licensees, but
recently taken over by Jennings, with their
beers and new management; pretty garden,
children welcome, bedrooms *(Mike and
Wendy Proctor, LYM; more reports please)*

☆ **Crayke** N Yor [off B1363 at Brandsby,
towards Easingwold; SE5670], *Durham Ox*:
Relaxed old-fashioned flagstoned lounge bar
with antique settles and other venerable
furnishings, interestingly carved panelling, log
fire in imposing inglenook, bustling public
area with darts and fruit machine, decent
food (not Sun evening) from sandwiches up,
well kept Banks's, Camerons and Marstons
Pedigree; restaurant, children welcome,
bedrooms *(Chris and Sue Bax, Malcolm and
Nancy Watson-Steward, Philip and Ann
Falkner, T Halstead, LYM)*

Dalton N Yor [NZ1108], *Travellers Rest*:
Good moderately priced French food in old
stone pub with pleasant, warm atmosphere,
friendly service; quiet hamlet *(Mrs S
Wilkinson)*

☆ **Danby** N Yor [off A171 E of Guisborough;
NZ7109], *Duke of Wellington*: Roomy and
popular, with wide choice of good value well
cooked food inc vegetarian, friendly efficient
service, well kept ales such as Camerons Ruby
and Ruddles Best, good coffee; bedrooms very
well appointed *(Val Stevenson, Rob Holmes,
A N Ellis)*

Darley Head N Yor [B6451; SE1959],
Wellington: Tastefully extended old pub, big
room with open fire, plenty of seating, two
smaller rooms, good bar food, sweeping views
from restaurant, well kept real ales; bedrooms
well furnished *(Janet and Peter Race)*

Deighton N Yor [A19 N of Escrick; SE6344],
White Swan: Two comfortable rooms,
separate restaurant, wide choice of food inc
vegetarian, several wines by the glass *(Janet
Pickles)*

Dewsbury W Yor [2 Walker Cottages,
Chidswell Lane, Shaw Cross, just off A653;
SE2623], *Huntsman*: Cosy converted cottages
alongside urban-fringe farm, friendly locals,
lots of brasses and bric-a-brac, well kept Bass-
related ales; no food evening or Sun/Mon
lunchtime, busy evenings *(Michael Butler)*;

[Westtown], *Sir Geoffrey Boycott OBE*: Limited lunchtime sandwiches, food comes into its own evenings, with good pies, pasta and home-made pizzas, well kept Scottish Courage ales and beers from smaller local breweries, at least two farm ciders *(Andy and Jill Kassube)*; *Squash Club*: Good blend of music inc heavy metal, indie, britpop, hip-hop, techno, skate punk and comedy songs, even Abba; warm friendly atmosphere for a good night out *(Shaun Robinson)*; [Station, Wellington Rd], *West Riding Refreshment Rooms*: Attractively converted station building, good food inc interesting vegetarian dishes from nutritionist licensee, popular curry night, three Batemans ales and up to four changing real ales; occasional beer festivals *(Andy and Jill Kassube, H Cooper)*

Dore S Yor [Hathersage Rd; A625 SW of Sheffield; SK3082], *Dore Moor*: Just out of city on edge of Peak Park, well restored for family dining with lots of stripped pine, good value ample food, good range of beers inc Stones and guests; helpful service *(David Carr)*

Downholme N Yor [off A6108 Leyburn—Richmond; SE1198], *Bolton Arms*: Roomy two-bar village local with lots of pictures, old advertisements and Royal Scots Greys memorabilia; real food cooked to order and nicely presented, well kept Theakstons, restaurant upstairs *(Pat and Clive Sherriff)*

Driffield E Yor [Great Kelk (A166); TA0258], *Chestnut Horse*: Good evening atmosphere, pleasant staff, flowers on tables, no music, well presented food inc fish of the day; locals playing dominoes *(Margaret Watson)*

Dungworth S Yor [B6076 W of Sheffield; SK2889], *Royal*: Village local with food inc good value Sun lunch, well kept ales Bass, John Smiths Magnet and guest beers such as Abbeydale Absolution *(Andy and Jill Kassube)*

Durkar W Yor [nr M1 junction 39; SE3117], *Navigation*: Attractive canalside pub, family room and garden; usual range of bar food, reasonably priced, well kept beers inc Tetleys, Timothy Taylors Landlord and guests such as Theakstons Mild *(Andy and Jill Kassube)*

East Layton N Yor [A66 not far from Scotch Corner; NZ1609], *Fox Hall*: Warm and welcoming, with wide choice of freshly prepared food and good obliging service in panelled bar with cosy booths, sporting prints, more open back part with big south-facing window, well kept Theakstons Best (more ales in summer), good range of malt whiskies and wines; games room, juke box, piped music; tables on back terrace; evening restaurant, Sun lunches; children and well behaved dogs welcome; bedrooms comfortable, good breakfasts *(Steve and Maggie Willey)*

Eastby N Yor [Barden Rd; back rd NE of Skipton past Embsay; SE0254], *Masons Arms*: Doing well under present landlord, well kept Scottish Courage ales, enjoyable food *(Geoffrey and Brenda Wilson)*

Edenthorpe S Yor [Thorne Rd (A18); SE6206], *Beverley*: 18th-c former farmhouse, comfortable T-shaped bar and good value carvery dining area (popular Sun), pictures and photographs, three real ales inc Black Heart, cheap house wine, lunchtime and early evening bargains, children welcome; fruit machine in alcove, piped music, TV; 14 bedrooms *(CMW, JJW)*

Elland W Yor [Park Rd, next to canal; quite handy for M62 junction 24; SE1121], *Barge & Barrel*: Friendly old-fashioned pub with huge helpings of cheap food, wide changing range of good beers, family room (with air hockey), piped radio; seats by industrial canal *(Tony Hobden)*; [Park Rd; opp crematorium], *Colliers Arms*: Good value lunchtime food inc hot beef sandwiches, friendly service, well kept Sam Smiths, back conservatory and seats by canal *(Pat and Tony Martin)*

☆ Ellerton E Yor [signed off B1228 – OS Sheet 105 map ref 705398; SE7039], *Boot & Shoe*: Low-beamed 16th-c cottage, comfortable and friendly, with good generous reasonably priced food from sandwiches to busy Sun lunches, interesting puddings, well kept Old Mill and John Smiths; children welcome, friendly obliging service *(Janet Pickles, Derek and Sylvia Stephenson, Mrs P J Pearce, LYM)*

☆ Elslack N Yor [off A56 Earby—Skipton; SD9249], *Tempest Arms*: Useful road stop, with wide interesting choice in restaurant and bar esp fish and puddings, good helpful service, comfortable chintzy seats as well as all the tables, well kept Black Sheep and Jennings ales, decent wine, choice of teas and coffees; children in room off bar if eating, good bedrooms *(PGP, Prof D Elliott, Prof and Mrs S Barnett, Dr and Mrs I H Maine, Gwen and Peter Andrews, Walter and Susan Rinaldi-Butcher, C Beadle, N Stansfield, LYM)*

☆ Embsay N Yor [Elm Tree Sq; SE0053], *Elm Tree*: Civilised well refurbished open-plan beamed village pub with good honest hearty home-made food inc good-sized children's helpings, friendly helpful service, old-fashioned prints, log-effect gas fire; half a dozen interesting well kept changing ales, no-smoking dining room, games area; busy weekends esp evenings; comfortable bedrooms; handy for steam railway *(JER, Allen Ferns, M Joyner, M S Catling, Andy and Jill Kassube)*

☆ Escrick N Yor [E of A19 York—Selby; SE6442], *Black Bull*: Warm cosy unpretentious village pub doing well under new ownership (see Plough, Allerthorpe, above), well spaced tables in bar, good imaginative if not cheap freshly prepared food in good-sized comfortable and relaxed dining area, small helpings for children and OAPs, well kept beer, decent wines, happy hour 5-7 weekdays, good friendly service; very popular weekends; bedrooms *(Ann and Peter Shaw, Roger Bellingham, Janet Pickles, P Morley)*

Fairburn N Yor [just off A1; SE4727], *Bay Horse*: Spacious and comfortable, with good generous cheap food inc good value roasts, pleasant staff, wildfowl lake views from terrace; keg beer *(Neil and Anita Christopher)*

☆ **Farndale East** N Yor [Church Houses; next to Farndale Nature Reserve; SE6697], *Feversham Arms*: Friendly pub in lovely daffodil valley (very busy then), two unspoilt but bright smallish rooms with flagstone floors and real fires, well kept Tetleys, good value home-cooked food, open fire, smart beamed and stripped-stone restaurant, friendly service; very popular weekends; walkers with wet boots and dogs not welcome; nice small garden, good bedrooms, big breakfast *(A M Pring, Maurice Thompson, Dr Wallis Taylor)*

Fearby N Yor [SE1980], *Black Swan*: Low, long two-bar beamed stonebuilt pub with massive collection of chamber-pots, stuffed foxes, parrots and other birds, nice pictures, Black Sheep, John Smiths and Theakstons Best, valley view, helpful service *(Jenny and Michael Back)*

☆ **Ferrensby** N Yor [A6055 N of Knaresboro; SE3761], *General Tarleton*: A new offshoot of the Angel at Hetton (see main entries), with similar choice of good food and pricing, exceptional choice of wines by the glass, real ales, big open fire, cosy corner seating, new conservatory; reasonably priced good bedrooms *(Miss G Hume)*

Filey N Yor [Sea Front; TA1281], *Coble Landing Bar*: Magnificent sea view, good food, well kept beer, entertaining landlord *(R Barker)*

Follifoot N Yor [Main St; SE3452], *Lascelles Arms*: Interesting reasonably priced food, very friendly atmosphere, good open fires, small and cosy lounge area, well kept Sam Smiths OB, decent wines *(JER, B Speight)*

Fridaythorpe E Yor [A166; SE8759], *Manor House*: Useful extended pub with big dining area, wide choice of generous reasonably priced food inc good vegetarian dishes, good friendly service, no piped music *(M Watson)*

Galphay N Yor [off B6265 W of Ripon; SE2573], *Galphay Inn*: Cosy dining pub with good food inc speciality roasts and very hospitable helpful service, one side pine-panelled with matching solid tables and settles, adjoining larger more open area with pictures; Boddingtons and Theakstons, decent house wine, log fire; cl Mon evening and weekday lunchtimes *(Mr and Mrs M Thompson)*

Ganton N Yor [A64 Malton—Scarborough; SE9977], *Greyhound*: Clean and comfortable, with good reasonably priced home-cooked food inc fresh fish, steaks and vegetarian dishes, fresh veg, well kept beer, friendly staff; well placed for the championship golf course *(Colin Savill)*

☆ **Gargrave** N Yor [Church St/Marton Rd; SD9354], *Masons Arms*: Friendly and busy well run local, attractive and homely, well kept Whitbreads-related ales, generous quick bar food inc vegetarian and good sandwiches, copper-canopied log-effect gas fire dividing two open-plan areas; tables in garden,

bowling green behind; children if well behaved; on Pennine Way, between river and church *(WAH, Ann and Colin Hunt, A Preston, P M Lane)*

Gargrave [A65 W], *Anchor*: Big Brewers Fayre family eatery catering well for children and worth knowing for all-day food service (from 7.30 b'fast) and superb play area, with canalside tables; welcoming competent service, Whitbreads-related ales, good wheelchair access; piped music; economically run bedrooms in modern wing *(F R Fell, WAH, Ann and Colin Hunt, LYM)*

☆ **Gillamoor** N Yor [off A170 at Kirkbymoorside; SE6890], *Royal Oak*: Well run traditional village inn, clean and comfortable, with roomy old L-shaped beamed and panelled bar, generous genuinely home-made food, well kept beer, reasonable prices, efficient friendly service, no music; comfortable bedrooms, good breakfast, handy for Barnsdale Moor *(T M Dobby, Bridget Batchelor)*

☆ **Goathland** N Yor [opp church, off A169; NZ8301], *Mallyan Spout*: Ivy-clad stone hotel, popular from its use by TV's *Heartbeat* series cast, with three spacious lounges (one no smoking), traditional relaxed bar, good open fires, fine views, Malton PA and Double Chance, good malt whiskies and wines; children in eating area, usually open all day, handy for Mallyan Spout waterfall; comfortable bedrooms *(Derek and Sylvia Stephenson, Andrew Hazeldine, Phil and Heidi Cook, Stephen, Julie and Hayley Brown, E A Thwaite, R N Hutton, LYM)*

Golcar W Yor [74 High St; off A62 (or A640) up W of Huddersfield; SE0816], *Scapehouse*: Roomy and friendly, with built-in settles, wooden tables and stools, interesting pews in end alcove, real fire, separate dining room; friendly staff, enjoyable food, Morlands Old Speckled Hen and Theakstons Best and Old Peculier *(Judith Hirst)*

☆ **Grange Moor** W Yor [A642 Huddersfield—Wakefield; SE2215], *Kaye Arms*: Civilised and busy family-run dining pub, a place for an enjoyable meal out (people tend to dress accordingly), with good choice of interesting proper food, efficient service, exceptional value house wines, no real ale but hundreds of malt whiskies, no-smoking room; children allowed lunchtime, handy for Yorkshire Mining Museum; cl Mon lunchtime *(Geoffrey and Brenda Wilson, Neil Townend, Michael Butler, R Borthwick, S Clegg, LYM)*

☆ **Grassington** N Yor [Garrs Lane; SE0064], *Black Horse*: Comfortable and cheerful open-plan modern bar, very busy in summer, with well kept Black Sheep Bitter and Special, Tetleys and Theakstons Best and Old Peculier, open fires, generous straightforward home-cooked bar food inc children's and vegetarian, darts in back room, sheltered terrace, small attractive restaurant; bedrooms comfortable, well equipped and good value *(Dave and Karen Turner, Judith Hirst, Ron Gentry, M Joyner, BB)*

Grassington [The Square], *Devonshire*: Busy and comfortable hotel, good window seats overlooking sloping village square, interesting pictures and ornaments, open fires, good range of well presented food inc good Sun lunch in big well furnished dining room, good family room, attentive landlord, full range of Theakstons ales kept well, tables outside; maybe faint piped music; well appointed good value bedrooms, good breakfasts *(JER, Judith Hirst, Mr and Mrs C Roberts, Gwen and Peter Andrews, Ann and Colin Hunt, BB)*

Grassington [20 Main St], *Foresters Arms*: Unpretentious and friendly old coaching inn with good choice of real ales inc Tetleys Mild and Bitter, Theakstons Best and Old Peculier and guest beers, bar food lunchtime and evening, pleasant atmosphere, no music; reasonably priced bedrooms *(Mr and Mrs M Thompson, Prof and Mrs S Barnett)*

Great Ayton N Yor [Low Green; NZ5611], *Buck*: Cosy rambling low-ceilinged pub across road from local riverside beauty spot, changing well kept Whitbreads-related ales, June beer festival, popular generous food inc vegetarian; a few tables outside *(Dorsan Baker)*

Great Barugh N Yor [off A169 Malton—Pickering; SE7479], *Golden Lion*: Interesting and welcoming country pub, good home-made food esp steak pie, well kept John Smiths and Tetleys, helpful staff, separate dining room (must book lunchtime), tables in garden; children allowed in daytime *(Mr and Mrs D Lawson)*

Great Heck N Yor [Main St, by boat basin not far from M62 jtn 34; SE5921], *Bay Horse*: Pleasant and friendly, small aquarium between drinking and dining areas, bay horse painting, plates and warming pans, jugs hanging from beams, five real ales, good value standard bar food; open all day Fri/Sat, maybe piped music; walks by Aire & Calder Canal *(CMW, JJW)*

Great Ouseburn N Yor [SE4562], *Crown*: Lots of effort has gone into the interesting decor of this smartly updated dining pub; wide choice of good often elaborate food, good range of beers *(C A Hall, TH)*

Grenoside S Yor [Skew Hill Lane, 3 miles from M1 junction 35 – OS Sheet 110 map ref 328935; SK3293], *Cow & Calf*: Neatly converted recently refurbished farmhouse, three friendly connected rooms, one no smoking, high-backed settles, stripped stone, brass and copper hanging from beams, plates and pictures, good value hearty home-made bar food (not Sun evening) inc sandwiches, children's and badminton suppers Fri, well kept Sam Smiths OB, tea and coffee; piped music, music quiz nights; family room in block across walled former farmyard with picnic tables; splendid views over Sheffield, disabled access, open all day Sat *(CMW, JJW, Michael Butler, David Carr, LYM)*

Grenoside S Yor [Main St; SK3394], *Old Harrow*: Open-plan, with comfortable banquettes, plates, pictures and old photographs, adjoining flagstoned former tap room, good value basic lunchtime food, Boddingtons, Stones and Whitbreads Castle Eden; fruit machine, TV, darts, maybe loud piped music; small garden with picnic tables; children and dogs allowed *(JJW, CMW, David Carr)*

☆ **Grewelthorpe** N Yor [back rd NW of Ripon; SE2376], *Crown*: Popular local with well kept Black Sheep and Theakstons, good generous straightforward food inc fresh fish, reasonable prices, whistling landlord *(Drs A C and A Jackson)*

☆ **Grinton** N Yor [B6270 W of Richmond; SE0598], *Bridge*: Welcoming and attractive riverside inn in lovely spot opp charming church, two bars, very friendly service, good range of good value simple well prepared food inc good steaks, well kept Black Sheep Special, John Smiths Magnet and Theakstons, decent wines; attractive tables outside, front and back; bedrooms with own bathrooms; open all day *(F M Bunbury, Anthony Barnes)*

☆ **Halifax** W Yor [Paris Gates, Boys Lane – OS Sheet 104 map ref 097241; SE0924], *Shears*: Hidden down steep cobbled lanes among tall mill buildings, dark unspoilt interior, welcoming landlord, well kept Marstons Pedigree, Timothy Taylors Landlord and unusual guest beers; very popular lunchtime for good cheap food from hot-filled sandwiches to home-made pies, curries, casseroles etc; sporting prints, local sports photographs, collection of pump clips and foreign bottles; seats out above the Hebble Brook *(Ian and Gayle Woodhead, Stephen Chippendale)*

Halifax [Bradford Old Rd; off A647 at Ploughcroft, right at ski slope sign, up steep cobbles; SE0926], *Sportsman*: Fine Calderdale views from prominent hilltop which this friendly and comfortable 17th-c pub shares with dry ski slope and squash court; good choice of bar food inc cheap lunches and good value carvery, well kept Timothy Taylors Landlord, Tetleys and a beer brewed for the pub, family extension *(Pat and Tony Martin)*

Harewood W Yor [diagonally opp Harewood House; SE3245], *Harewood Arms*: Busy former coaching inn opp Harewood House, three attractive, comfortable and spacious lounge bars with wide choice of good food from sandwiches up, friendly prompt service, well kept ales inc Sam Smiths OB, decent house wines; coffee and afternoon tea *(Janet Pickles)*

Harome N Yor [2 miles S of A170, nr Helmsley; SE6582], *Star*: Attractive and ancient thatched pub reopened 1996 after refurbishment by new owners, now more restaurant than pub, with good if not cheap food, attractive layout and furnishings, well kept Theakstons *(J and P Maloney, LYM)*

☆ **Harrogate** N Yor [Crimple Lane; off A661 towards Wetherby; SE3353], *Travellers Rest*: Country pub in pleasant valley setting, beamed locals' bar, shiny woodwork in main bar with cosy corners, conservatory, two real fires, friendly service; good freshly but quickly prepared cheap food inc fish and Sun roasts, well kept Theakstons Best and XB and Youngers Scotch; children welcome, side play area, open all day *(Andrew and Ruth Triggs)*

Harrogate [Montpellier Gdns], *Drum & Monkey*: Not a pub but well worth knowing for enjoyable downstairs fish bar with splendid seafood, eat at long bar or pub-style tables, good French wines; busy, noisy and friendly *(Rita Horridge, H Bramwell)*; [Whinney Lane, Pannel Ash, off B6162 W], *Squinting Cat*: Rambling big-brewery chain pub with dark oak panelling, beams, brasses and copper, stone-walled barn-like restaurant extension, well priced usual bar food from sandwiches to steaks inc popular Sun lunch, well kept Tetleys and guest beers, good range of New World wines, pleasant young staff, tables outside; piped music; open all day, handy for Harlow Carr gardens *(H Bramwell, Andrew Hodges, LYM)*

☆ **Hartoft End** N Yor [Pickering—Rosedale Abbey rd; SE7593], *Blacksmiths Arms*: Immaculate and civilised 16th-c wayside inn by moors, originally a farmhouse and gradually extended, lots of original stonework, brasses, cosy nooks and crannies, relaxing atmosphere, good bar food inc good fish and fresh veg, well kept beer, friendly staff, attractive restaurant with cane furnishings; bedrooms *(Colin Savill)*

Hartshead W Yor [SE1822], *New Inn*: Country pub with good food, well kept ales such as Boddingtons, Morlands Old Speckled Hen, Moorhouses Pendle Witches Brew and guest beers *(Andy and Jill Kassube)*

☆ **Hatfield Woodhouse** S Yor [Bearswood Green, a mile from M18 junction 5 via A18/A614 towards Bawtry; SE6808], *Green Tree*: Attractively furnished series of linked panelled areas popular for good value food all day running up to steaks and Sun carvery, with well kept Jennings Snecklifter, Shepherd Neame Bitter and Wards Thorne Best, no-smoking restaurant, provision for children, tables in garden; piped music; bedrooms *(Michael Butler, Derek and Sylvia Stephenson, FMH, David and Fiona Pemberton, Andrew and Joan Life, LYM)*

Hawes N Yor [High St; SD8789], *White Hart*: Friendly, warm and cosy, busy around bar (esp on Tues market day), quieter on left, wide choice of reasonably priced food in bar and restaurant, welcoming service; bedrooms good value *(Mrs D P Dick)*

☆ **Hawnby** N Yor [SE5489], *Hawnby Inn*: Good choice of well cooked generous food in spotless and very friendly inn, lovely location in village surrounded by picturesque countryside, a magnet for walkers; well kept Vaux beers, helpful service, owl theme; tables in garden with country views; well equipped bedrooms *(Addie and Irene Henry, T G Brierly)*

Haworth W Yor [West Lane; SE0337], *Old White Lion*: Very good value home-made

food, well kept Websters and Wilsons, good popular restaurant (booked up Sat), friendly staff; warm and comfortable, with plush banquettes and timber-effect decor; children welcome, spotless comfortable bedrooms, very handy for museum *(Arnold Day, Mike and Maggie Betton)*

Hebden Bridge W Yor [Billy Lane, Wadsworth; SD9927], *Hare & Hounds*: Warm welcome, friendly staff, well kept Timothy Taylors ales, wide range of bar food (not Mon evening or winter Tues evening); some seats outside – lovely hillside scenery with plenty of good walks; handy for Automobile Museum *(Bruce Bird)*; [Bridge Gate], *White Lion*: Solid stone-built inn pleasantly refurbished with comfortable bar and country-furnished bare-boards dining lounge, good choice of reasonably priced generous food all day, well kept Whitbreads-related ales, pleasant atmosphere; bedrooms comfortable *(Andy and Jill Kassube)*; *White Swan*: Good range of reasonably priced plain home cooking, daily roast, fresh veg, filled Yorkshire puddings; Black Sheep and Tetleys; gets busy *(Annette and Stephen Marsden)*

Helmsley N Yor [Market Sq; SE6184], *Crown*: Simple but pleasantly furnished beamed front bar opening into bigger unpretentious central dining bar, wide choice of food inc enjoyable teas, range of well kept beers, roaring fires, tables in sheltered garden behind with conservatory area; bedrooms pleasant *(Janet Pickles, BB)*; [Market Pl], *Royal Oak*: Welcoming, comfortable and popular, with three well decorated rooms, antiques, good food inc superb roasts and filled yorkshire puddings, well kept Camerons; bedrooms good *(Ian and Margaret Borthwick, K and E Leist)*

Helperby N Yor [SE4470], *Farmers*: Friendly unspoilt local with pine country furniture, good value food, small restaurant, Theakstons Best, XB and Old Peculier, comfortable games room with fruit machine and darts, tables in garden; bedrooms *(Janet Pickles)*

High Hoyland S Yor [Bank End Lane; SE2710], *Cherry Tree*: Clean and attractive stone-built village pub, low beams, brasses, cigarette card collections, friendly staff, good range of beers inc John Smiths and Tetleys, open fire, small popular restaurant (best to book, esp Sun lunch); lovely views over Cannon Hall Country Park from front *(Michael Butler)*

☆ **Holme** W Yor [A6024 SW of Holmfirth; SE1006], *Fleece*: Cosy pleasant L-shaped bar, lots of lifeboat memorabilia, well kept Tetleys, Theakstons and Youngers, good coffee, popular fresh pub food inc special offers, very welcoming landlord, efficient staff, real fire; conservatory with nice flowers, pool/darts room, quiet piped music; attractive village setting below Holme Moss TV mast, great walks *(JER, Philip and Ann Falkner, Martin Hickes, Gwen and Peter Andrews)*

Holme on Spalding Moor E Yor [Old Rd; SE8038], *Olde Red Lion*: Well run village pub, clean and comfortable, good food with fish emphasis in old-world panelled L-shaped lounge bar and dining room, friendly staff, eclectic range of wines, sunny terrace with koi carp; comfortable bedrooms in chalets behind *(H Bramwell, Rona Murdoch)*

Hopperton N Yor [A59 Harrogate—York; SE4256], *Masons Arms*: Good food esp steaks, relaxed atmosphere, well kept Bass; evenings only; jazz first and third Sun of month *(Les Brown)*

Horbury W Yor [Quarry Hill; SE3018], *Quarry*: Recently bought by Marstons whose beers now dominate, old photographs of stone quarry on stripped stone walls, relaxed affluent atmosphere, popular well priced food; bedrooms in attached cottage *(Michael Butler)*

Horsehouse N Yor [Coverdale rd Middleham—Kettlewell; SE0481], *Thwaite Arms*: Friendly little family pub popular for good simple food – only a few tables in pretty homely dining room, so worth booking; fine Sun roast, well kept Theakstons and John Smiths, farm cider, charming friendly landlord, chatty local farmers evening, open fire in cosy snug, bigger plainer locals' bar; early 19th-c former farm building in village with beautiful little church, lots of paths to nearby villages and moors; children welcome; two bedrooms *(Paul and Madeleine Morey)*

Horton in Ribblesdale N Yor [SD8172], *Crown*: Clean and pleasant low-ceilinged bar with dark woodwork, brasses and good fire, good interesting food inc vegetarian, well kept Theakstons, friendly helpful service; bedrooms *(John Hobbs, Dagmar Junghanns, Colin Keane)*

Hoyland S Yor [Milton Rd; SE3700], *Furnace*: Really friendly up-dated pub with good bar food; overlooks the old furnace pond in the village where *Kes* was filmed *(Dr and Mrs A K Clarke)*

Hoyland Common S Yor [nr M1 junction 36; SE3500], *Hare & Hounds*: Useful road stop with good very cheap food, lively atmosphere, well kept John Smiths, good value house wine, friendly helpful staff *(CLS, RMB)*

Huby N Yor [Main St; the one nr Easingwold; SE5665], *New Inn*: Traditional four-bar beamed pub with Victorian range, brasses, old photographs of local RAF base, racing memorabilia, good value bar and restaurant food, well kept Scottish Courage ales, lots of malt whiskies, helpful staff; quiet piped music, domino and darts teams *(Brian and Angela Walker)*

Huddersfield W Yor [Crosland Moor, off A62 W; SE1115], *Sands House*: New landlady in this popular dining pub, with Boddingtons, Courage Directors, Ruddles County and Wilsons, food served all day (sounds decent, but no reports since her arrival); children in eating area, downstairs dining room, lots of woodwork, contemporary clocks and watches, piped music; garden with play area *(LYM; news please)*

Huddersfield [Queen St], *Court House*: Former county court building, bright and airy, with gas lamps, reasonably priced food 12-4, quick service, a dozen real ales inc four brewed on the premises – the top of the brew copper, surrounded by glass, sticks up through the floor of the high-ceilinged public bar *(Joan and Michel Hooper-Immins)*; [Station Building], *Head of Steam*: Railway memorabilia, model trains and cars for sale; pies, sandwiches and Sun roasts, Clarks ale and changing guest beers *(Pat and Tony Martin)*; [New Hey Rd, Fixby; handy for M62 junction 24, by A643; SE1119], *Nags Head*: Long, olde-worlde bar with comfortable seating, reliable reasonably priced bar food, carvery in converted barn; well kept Scottish Courage ales *(Joyce and Gordon Westerman)*; [40 Chapel Hill, just off ring rd opp public car park], *Rat & Ratchet*: Bare-boards two-room local brewing its own Experimental Ale alongside well kept ales inc Marstons Pedigree, Smiles, Timothy Taylors Landlord and Best and lots of changing guest beers; two more comfortable rooms up steps, basic well cooked cheap bar food inc Weds curry night *(John Plumridge, A Preston, Judith Hirst, Tony Hobden)*; [Colne Bridge (B6118 just off A62 NE); SE1720], *Royal & Ancient*: Spacious, comfortable and popular, with log fires, good interesting bar food, Marstons ales, welcoming service, golfing theme in bar, Bette Davis memorabilia, school magazine photographs and football programmes in extended dining area *(Michael Butler)*

☆ **Huggate** E Yor [off A166 or B1246 W of Driffield; SE8855], *Wolds*: Attractively refurbished small 16th-c pub, mildly upmarket, popular for good inventive food, reasonable prices, friendly staff, well kept real ale, benches out in front and pleasant garden behind with delightful views, popular restaurant; cl Mon; two bedrooms – lovely village, good easy walks *(H Bramwell, Paul and Ursula Randall)*

☆ **Hull** E Yor [Land of Green Ginger, Old Town; TA0927], *George*: Handsomely preserved traditional long Victorian bar, open all day; lots of oak, mahogany and copper, good choice of cheap, generous and tasty freshly cooked lunchtime food inc good fish, well kept Bass, Bass Mild and Stones, good service; quiet piped music, fruit machines, can get very busy – get there early; handy for the fine Docks Museum; children allowed in plush upstairs dining room *(JJW, CMW, Thomas Nott, Chris Westmoreland, LYM)*

Hull [Beverley Rd/Pearson Ave], *Chesters*: Big modern bar and conservatory with two pool tables, fruit machines, TV, mix of locals and students, good value basic bar meals, three Mansfield ales; quiz night Sun and Weds, open all day Sat; picnic tables outside *(CMW, JJW)*; [Humber Dock St], *Last Word*: Continental-style cafe in former docks warehouse, food 10am-10pm every day, lots of bottled beers; children welcome *(Rona*

Murdoch); [150 High St], *Olde Black Boy*:
Tap & Spile in Old Town conservation area,
little black-panelled low-ceilinged front smoke
room, lofty 18th-c back vaults bar, good
value upstairs dining room with very friendly
if not speedy service, eight real ales, about 20
country wines, interesting Wilberforce-related
posters etc, old jugs and bottles, quiet piped
local radio, darts, piano *(JJW, CMW, Chris
Westmoreland, BB)*

☆ **Hunton** N Yor [off A684 Leyburn—Bedale;
SE1992], *New Inn*: Small friendly country
local with wide changing choice of freshly
cooked food (not Tues) inc good vegetarian
choice, big helpings of fresh veg, good salads
and puddings; helpful efficient service, well
kept local beer, decent wines, no piped music
*(Mr and Mrs D Pearce, K Bowers, Mr and
Mrs J Thompson)*

Hutton Rudby N Yor [NZ4706], *Bay Horse*:
Pleasant and roomy, with good well presented
food in bar and restaurant from wide choice
of filled baguettes to big Sun lunch, children's
dishes, tables in garden, pretty village *(Clare
Wilson, Shirley Pielou)*

Ilkley W Yor [Stockeld Rd/Stourton Rd (off
A65 Leeds—Skipton); SE1147], *Ilkley Moor
Vaults*: Friendly flagstone-floored drinkers'
pub with tastefully furnished lounge and
public bars, well kept Tetleys and North
Yorks Flying Heart and toffee-flavoured
Jawbreaker, good reasonably priced basic
lunches, good atmosphere and service even
when packed; games room upstairs, pleasant
seats outside; aka The Taps *(Dr and Mrs B
Baker)*

☆ **Ingbirchworth** S Yor [Welthorne Lane; off
A629 Shepley—Penistone; SE2205], *Fountain*:
Neat and spacious red plush turkey-carpeted
lounge, cosy front bar, comfortable family
room, open fires; generous bar food inc exotic
salads and superb puddings, well kept Tetleys
and Marstons Pedigree, well reproduced pop
music, friendly service, tables in sizeable
garden overlooking reservoir *(Andy Mathers,
BB)*

Ingleby Cross N Yor [NZ4501], *Blue Bell*:
Cosy country local near stunning scenery,
friendly and helpful ex-jockey landlord and
staff, well kept John Smiths Magnet and
Theakstons Best, wide choice of good value
often interesting bar food from sandwiches to
steaks; simple but good bedrooms in
converted barn, camping facilities (and cricket
ground) next door, handy for coast-to-coast
walk *(Rita and Keith Pollard, Brian Seller)*

Ingleton N Yor [SD6973], *Wheatsheaf*:
Friendly pub with long bar serving well kept
Black Sheep Best and Riggwelter and
Theakstons Mild, good value food prepared
to order from fresh ingredients, big garden;
walkers and children welcome, handy for
Ingleborough *(Pete Adams)*

Kelfield N Yor [off B1222 S of York;
SE5938], *Grey Horse*: Pleasant new licensees
and surroundings, well kept beer *(John
Burley)*

☆ **Kettlesing**, N Yor [signed off A59 W of

Harrogate; SE2256], *Queens Head*: Friendly
recently renovated dining pub with nicely
presented good value food, popular weekday
lunchtimes with older people, lots of quite
close-set tables, well kept Theakstons Best
and XB, Youngers Scotch, good house wines,
quick service, unobtrusive piped music,
attractive and interesting decorations;
children welcome *(Marian and Andrew
Ruston, JER, Martin Hickes, BB)*

☆ **Kirby Hill** N Yor [off A66 NW of Scotch
Corner, via Ravensworth; NZ1406], *Shoulder
of Mutton*: Unassuming village inn with green
plush wall settles, stone arch to public bar,
open fires, good bar food from lunchtime
sandwiches to steaks, vegetarian dishes, Black
Sheep Bitter and Riggwelter, John Smiths and
Websters Yorkshire, quite a few malt
whiskies, restaurant; darts, dominoes,
cribbage, piped music; children in eating area,
fine views from picnic tables in yard behind;
good value bedrooms, cl Mon lunchtime
*(Wayne Brindle, R H Rowley, Andrew and
Joan Life, A N Ellis, J H and Dr S A Harrop,
Graham Morecroft, LYM)*

Kirkby Malzeard N Yor [NW of Fountains
Abbey; SE2172], *Henry Jenkins*: Village pub
with decent food from good sandwiches up in
small comfortable lounge bar with beams and
brasses; John Smiths, Theakstons and their
own Henry Jenkins Light Bitter – the man it's
named for is said to have lived in the village
from 1500 to 1670! *(Anon)*

☆ **Kirkby Overblow** N Yor [off A61 S of
Harrogate; SE3249], *Shoulder of Mutton*:
Very popular esp with older people for wide
choice of good nicely presented food using
fresh local produce inc good veg, several
interesting dishes, upstairs seafood restaurant;
friendly service, five well kept Theakstons
ales, good wines, upstairs seafood restaurant,
children welcome, tables in lovely garden with
play area by meadows *(Arthur and Margaret
Dickinson, Sean Guinness, Michael Butler,
Lawrence Pearse, BB)*

Kirkby Overblow, *Star & Garter*: Cosy
welcoming local with generous good value
bar food from asparagus through fine
yorkshire puddings to wild boar and
pheasant, dining room for evening meals; well
kept Camerons and Everards *(Mr and Mrs E J
W Rogers, Andy and Jill Kassube)*

☆ **Knaresborough** N Yor [19 Market Pl;
SE3557], *Blind Jacks*: Former 18th-c shop
done out a few years ago as charming multi-
floor traditional tavern, with simple but
attractive furnishings, brewery posters etc; as
we go to press they no longer do the food
which readers have been so enthusiastic
about, but have well kept Black Sheep,
Hambleton White Boar and Nightmare Stout
and Timothy Taylors Landlord with changing
guest beers, farm cider and foreign bottled
beers; well behaved children allowed away
from bar, open all day, cl Mon till 5.30
(LYM)

Knaresborough [by Beech Avenue, at Low
Bridge end of riverside Long Walk], *Mother*

Shipton: Beams, panelling, antique furnishings inc 16th-c oak table, good low-priced food inc good sandwiches, efficient service, several well kept Scottish Courage ales with a guest such as Morlands Old Speckled Hen; pity about the piped music; big terrace overlooking river *(James Nunns)*; [High Bridge, Harrogate Rd], *Yorkshire Lass*: Big unassuming pub-restaurant in fine riverside position, popular with groups visitng Mother Shipton's Cave; lively decoration, friendly Scottish landlord, good value generous food, comfortable dining room, five well kept Scottish Courage and guest ales, several dozen malt whiskies, daily papers; live jazz/blues some nights; good bedrooms and breakfast, picturesque views from terrace *(C Maclean, A Marsh, Dr A J and Mrs P G Newton)*

Langsett S Yor [A616 nr Penistone; SE2100], *Waggon & Horses*: Comfortable main-road moors pub, welcoming helpful staff, blazing log fire, stripped stone and woodwork, good home cooking inc good value Sun lunch, well kept Bass and Stones, magazines to read, friendly small dog *(CMW, JJW, James Waller)*

☆ **Langthwaite** N Yor [just off Reeth—Brough rd; NZ0003], *Red Lion*: Unspoilt, individual and relaxing, in charming dales village, with local books and maps for sale, basic cheap nourishing lunchtime food, Black Sheep, Theakstons XB and Youngers Scotch, country wines, tea and coffee; well behaved children allowed lunchtime in very low-ceilinged (and sometimes smoky) side snug, quietly friendly service; good walks all around, inc organised circular ones from the pub *(Richard R Dolphin, Maurice Thompson, Anthony Barnes, LYM)*

Langthwaite [Arkengarthdale, outside village – aka the CB Inn; NY9902], *Charles Bathurst*: Clean and spartan newly renovated interior, roaring fire in warm welcoming bar, friendly helpful landlord, well kept Theakstons, good fresh home-made food using local ingredients, frequently changing menu; bedrooms, attractive spot with wonderful views *(W James, Jennifer Oswald-Sealy)*

Leavening N Yor [SE7963], *Jolly Farmers*: Well kept Tetleys-related ales and Timothy Taylors landlord, good bar food with lots of fresh veg in separate dining room, friendly licensees; good bedrooms *(Christopher Turner)*

☆ **Leeds** [Gt George St, just behind Town Hall; SE3033], *Victoria*: Well preserved ornate Victorian pub with grand etched mirrors, impressive globe lamps extending from the ornately solid bar, smaller rooms off; well kept Tetleys inc Mild, friendly smart bar staff, reasonably priced food in luncheon room with end serving hatch *(M Walker, Reg Nelson, Chris Westmoreland)*

☆ **Leeds** [Hunslet Rd], *Adelphi*: Well restored handsome Edwardian tiling, woodwork and glass, several rooms, impressive stairway; particularly well kept Tetleys (virtually the brewery tap); prompt friendly service, good

spread of cheap food at lunchtime, crowded but convivial then; live jazz Sat *(PGP, Graham and Karen Oddey)*

Leeds [Johnston St, Woodhouse], *Chemic*: Welcoming two-room local with attractive decor, good choice of well kept beer, good atmosphere, food inc good toasted sandwiches; no intrusive piped music *(Dr and Mrs A K Clarke)*; [Mabgate, nr E end of inner ring rd], *City of Mabgate*: Cosy and friendly unspoilt backstreet pub, good choice of well kept ales without going silly, good weekday lunchtime bar snacks, interesting old photographs and beer-mat collection, plainer back room with pool and TV (no juke box), tables on small terrace; attractive tiled exterior, handy for the Playhouse *(Barrie Pepper, Reg Nelson)*; [25 Cookridge St], *Courtyard*: Very modern brasserie/pub, inside seating minimalist and none too comfortable, courtyard balcony; good food, reasonably efficient service, beers inc well kept Timothy Taylors *(Ian Phillips, Julian Jackson)*; [Merrion St, by Merrion Shopping Centre], *Edwards*: Big airy wine bar/pub, well presented home-made food, decent big glass of wine, friendly efficient service *(John Wooll)*; [Gt George St], *Felon & Firkin*: Own Fuzz, Felon, Bobbys and Dogbolter, big sandwiches, ploughman's, chilli, steaks etc; nr law courts *(Andy and Jill Kassube)*; [68 Otley Rd, Headingley], *O'Hagans*: Well done and friendly Irish theme pub *(Dr and Mrs A K Clarke)*; [Kirkgate], *Palace*: Up to twelve particularly well kept Tetleys-related and other ales, polished wood, simple good value food from sandwiches up *(Andy and Jill Kassube)*; [Mill St, nr stn], *Prince of Wales*: Warmly welcoming newly refurbished pub with consistently well kept ales such as Black Sheep Special and Riggwelter, John Smiths Best and Magnet, good range of guest beers *(Andy and Jill Kassube)*; [98 Otley Rd, Headingley], *Three Horseshoes*: Handsome and friendly sporting pub with lots of hanging baskets, good choice of typical bar food inc good vegetarian specials, well kept beer, lots of sporting photographs and so forth; busy evenings *(Dr and Mrs A K Clarke)*

☆ **Leyburn** N Yor [Market Pl; SE1191], *Golden Lion*: Relaxing bay-windowed two-room panelled bar, light and airy, with log-effect gas fire in eating area, good value generous straightforward bar food esp puddings, evening restaurant; good beer brewed to their own recipe in Harrogate as well as Theakstons Best and Youngers No 3, decent coffee, friendly efficient service, tables out in front; open all day, dogs allowed; bedrooms good value *(M J Morgan, Ian and Villy White, Simon and Amanda Southwell, Andrew and Ruth Triggs, BB)*

Linthwaite W Yor [Manchester Rd; SE1014], *Royal Oak*: Good local, roaring log fire, attentive landlord, particularly well kept Whitbreads-related and unusual local guest beers *(John Plumridge)*

Liversedge W Yor [Roberttown Lane;

SE1922], *Geordie Pride*: Well decorated local with good helpings of well priced bar food, Scottish Courage ales, decorative china and big prints, pleasant restaurant; bedrooms good value, in opp annexe; good breakfasts *(Andy and Jill Kassube)*

Long Preston N Yor [A65 Settle—Skipton; SD8358], *Maypole*: Clean and friendly dining pub with spacious beamed dining room and comfortable lounge with copper-topped tables, stag's head, open fire; big helpings of good value food inc home-made pies and Sun lunch, well kept Timothy Taylors Landlord and Whitbreads-related real ales, helpful service; bedrooms *(Malcolm and Lynne Jessop)*

Low Row N Yor [B6270 Reeth—Muker; SD9897], *Punch Bowl*: Useful youth-hostelish family bar, open all day in summer, with Theakstons Best, XB and Old Peculier and guests, rows of malt whiskies, wide choice of good value food, log fire, games room; fine Swaledale views; popular tea room 10-5.30 with home-made cakes, small shop, bicycle and cave lamp hire, folk music Fri; good basic bedrooms, also bunkhouse, big breakfast *(Judith Hirst)*

☆ **Lund** E Yor [off B1248 N of Beverley; SE9748], *Wellington*: Smartly refurbished village pub with open fire in comfortable main lounge bar, interesting fireplace in small locals' bar, cosy separate dining room with intimate anteroom (worth booking), limited choice of reliably good food, smiling attentive service, well kept ales inc John Smiths, Batemans, Timothy Taylors Landlord, good wines; lovely village on edge of Wolds *(D Hancock, H Bramwell, Ian Morley, N H White)*

☆ **Malham** N Yor [off A65 NW of Skipton; SD8963], *Lister Arms*: Friendly easy-going open-plan lounge, busy weekends, relaxed attitude to children, very generous food, well kept changing ales such as Black Sheep, Ind Coope Burton and Wadworths 6X, even Liefmans fruit beers in summer, lots of malt whiskies, well worn-in furnishings and fittings, roaring fire, restaurant famous for steaks, games area with pool and maybe loudish piped music; seats outside the substantial stone inn overlooking green, more in back garden – nice spot by river, ideal for walkers; bedrooms *(Paul McPherson, Rita and Keith Pollard, Prof and Mrs S Barnett, Marianne Lantree, Steve Webb, Neil Calver)*
Malham, *Buck*: Big village pub, wide range of generous home-made food, Black Sheep and Theakstons Best, log fires, comfortable lounge and big bar welcoming walkers, separate candlelit dining room, picnic tables in small garden; decent well equipped bedrooms, many good walks from the door *(Marianne Lantree, Steve Webb, Ron Gentry, Neil Calver, Cyril Brown)*
Malton N Yor [Commercial St, Norton; SE7972], *Cornucopia*: Well run dining pub with interesting choice of good food in big helpings well served by friendly staff; owner is a racing man *(Mr and Mrs Garrett)*

Marsden W Yor [Peel St; SE0612], *New Inn*: Spacious and friendly modern pub in *Last of the Summer Wine* country, newish landlady, good choice of well kept beer, occasional live music, karaoke and discos, tables in garden, attractive countryside nearby; good-sized bedrooms, hearty breakfast *(Anon)*; [2 Peel St, next to Co-op], *Riverhead*: Basic own-brew pub opened on a shoestring in converted grocer's by the former brewer at the Sair in Linthwaite, particularly good beers and stouts named after local reservoirs (the higher the reservoir, the higher the strength), farm cider, friendly chatty service and frank advice about the beers, nice stop after a walk by canal or on the hills; brewhouse viewed through window in bar, unobtrusive piped music, maybe sandwiches *(John Plumridge, Stephen and Brenda Head, R J Bland, Joan and Michel Hooper-Immins)*; *Swan*: Well kept frequently changing beer and good bar food inc good value Sun lunches *(R J Bland)*

Masham N Yor [SE2381], *Black Sheep Brewery*: Modern bistro-style drinking area in the visitor centre – not a pub, but likely to appeal to *Good Pub Guide* readers, together with a brewery visit; some worthwhile beery tourist trinkets *(Vann Prime, Wm Van Laaten)*

Micklebring S Yor [Greaves Sike Lane; A631/B6376 N of Maltby; SK5295], *Plough*: Large mainly dining pub with high views over Rotherham, reasonably priced food inc Sun roast and children's meals, polite obliging service, well kept John Smiths Magnet and Marstons Pedigree, log fire; piped music, TV; a few picnic tables outside *(CMW, JJW)*

Middleham N Yor [Mkt Pl; SE1288], *Richard III*: Big bustling friendly local, horsey pictures, quick service, open fire in front bar, side pool area, back bar with tables for reasonable range of well presented food inc good cheap sandwiches; well kept Tetleys, Theakstons and John Smiths; good bedrooms *(PGP, K H Frostick)*

Middlesmoor N Yor [up at the top of the Nidderdale rd from Pateley Bridge; SE0874], *Crown*: Friendly little inn with coal fires in small cosy rooms, homely dining room, beautiful view over stone-built hamlet high in upper Nidderdale, particularly well kept Theakstons Black Bull, tables outside; cheap bedrooms *(Tony and Jenny Hainsworth, Mr and Mrs M Thompson)*

Middleton Tyas N Yor [just E of A1 Scotch Corner roundabout; NZ2306], *Shoulder of Mutton*: Unpretentious exterior, warren of small rooms and different-level nooks inside, dark woodwork; well kept Vaux beers, wide choice of popular bar food, cheap pot of coffee, agreeable service *(Mrs K Burvill)*

☆ nr **Midgley** W Yor [signed from Hebden Br, with evening/Sun bus to pub; coming from Halifax on A646 turn right just before Hebden Bridge town centre on to A6033 towards Keighley, take first right up steep Birchcliffe Rd and keep on to the top – OS Sheet 104 map ref 007272; SE0027], *Mount*

Skip: Spectacular views of Pennines and mill-town valleys, welcoming staff, well kept Tetleys and Timothy Taylors Bitter, Landlord and Golden Best, good log fire, lots of prints and old photographs, china and brasses, generous cheap food inc vegetarian, Sun lunches and two sizes for children; games area, unobtrusive piped music, restaurant, benches outside – right by Calderdale Way footpath; children allowed (not late); open all day Sat, cl Mon lunchtime Oct-Easter, Tues lunchtime Jan-Easter *(Tony Hobden, Bruce Bird, LYM)*

☆ **Midhopestones** S Yor [off A616 W of Stocksbridge; SK2399], *Midhopestones Arms*: Cosy and friendly character 17th-c pub, flagstones, stripped stone and pine, three small rooms, woodburner, pictures, assorted chairs, tables and settles; eight well kept ales inc Scottish Courage ones, Barnsley, Timothy Taylors Landlord and Wards, friendly staff, log fires, good value home cooking (not Sun evening, restricted Mon/Tues lunch) esp Sun lunch, breakfasts too; piped music; restaurant, seats outside; children welcome *(Peter Marshall)*

Mirfield W Yor [212 Huddersfield Rd; A644; SE2019], *Railway*: Welcoming two-bar pub with well priced Bass, Stones, Worthington and guest beers, wide variety of good value food from double-decker sandwiches to tasty evening dishes; a few tables out in front *(PGP, P M Lane)*

Mixenden W Yor [Mill Lane; SE0528], *Hebble Brook*: Reopened under new owners, five changing guest beers from small breweries, also beers from Belgium or Holland, good value lunchtime food, curry and steak nights, open fires; attractive brookside setting *(Jonathan Harrison, Bonzai)*

Mytholmroyd W Yor [New Rd, nr stn; SE0126], *Shoulder of Mutton*: Simple uncomplicated menu, well cooked, esp fish – remarkably low prices, but big helpings (no food Tues evening), also children's helpings; well kept Black Sheep, Boddingtons and guest beers, toby jugs, small no-dining area for locals *(Andy and Jill Kassube, Tony Hobden)*

North Cave E Yor [Main St (B1230); SE8932], *White Hart*: Reasonably priced food inc big beef sandwiches with chips, large bar with dining tables, games room, smaller red plush lounge *(Jenny and Michael Back)*

☆ **North Dalton** E Yor [B1246 Driffield—Pocklington; SE9352], *Star*: Good choice of decent bar food from soup and generous open sandwiches up in comfortably refurbished lounge bar with welcoming coal fire, obliging young staff, well kept changing real ales, character restaurant; a striking sight, one wall rising straight from sizeable pond; charming well equipped good value bedrooms *(A V Bradbury, Julie Peters, Colin Blinkhorn, BB)*

Northallerton N Yor [formerly Three Standards; SE3794], *Tap & Spile*: Wide range of well kept ales, constantly changing, in big comfortable flagstoned bar, tables on back terrace *(R J Bland)*

Nun Monkton N Yor [off A59 York—Harrogate; SE5058], *Alice Hawthorn*: Modernised down-to-earth beamed village local with lots of brass etc, big brick inglenook fireplace, Tetleys and other ales, freshly prepared basic food, keen darts players; on broad village green with pond and lovely avenue to church and Rivers Nidd and Ouse *(T Halstead, BB)*

☆ **Oakworth** W Yor [Harehills Lane, Oldfield; 2 miles towards Colne; SE0038], *Grouse*: Comfortable, interesting and spotless old pub packed with bric-a-brac, gleaming copper and china, lots of prints, cartoons and caricatures, dried flowers, attractively individual furnishings; limited choice of well presented good home-made lunchtime bar food (not Mon), charming evening restaurant, well kept Timothy Taylors, good range of spirits, entertaining landlord, good service, good Pennine views *(Arthur and Margaret Dickinson, WAH, Bruce Bird)*

Old Denaby S Yor [Denaby Lane; SK4899], *Manor Farm*: Wide choice of good home-made food in converted farmhouse with interesting Laura Ashleyesque decor; children welcome, open all day, garden with play area *(Colin and Helen Kitching)*

☆ **Oldstead** N Yor [off A170 Thirsk—Helmsley; SE5380], *Black Swan*: Unpretentious spotless inn in beautiful surroundings with pretty valley views from two big bay windows and picnic tables outside, reasonably priced good food, well kept Theakstons, friendly landlord; children welcome, bedrooms in comfortable modern back extension *(Mr and Mrs R Horton, BB)*

Osmotherley N Yor [The Green, off A19 N of Thirsk; SE4499], *Golden Lion*: Helpful new landlord, decent straightforward food, well kept John Smiths Magnet and Theakstons XB, fresh flowers, tables out overlooking village green; 44-mile Lyke Wake Walk starts here *(R F Grieve, R J Bland)*

☆ **Ossett** W Yor [Low Mill Rd/Healey Lane – OS Sheet 104 map ref 271191; SE2719], *Brewers Pride*: Warmly friendly basic local, wide range of well kept changing ales mainly from small independent brewers, cosy front room and bar both with open fires, basic but interesting decor, small games room, tasty reasonably priced weekday lunchtime food, generous Sun nibbles, big back garden with local entertainment summer weekends; quiz night Mon, country & western Thurs, open all day Fri/Sat *(M A Butler, H Cooper, Richard Houghton)*

Ossett [Manor Rd], *Victoria*: Locally popular for wide-ranging reasonably priced food inc Sun carvery, even kangaroo steaks, well kept Tetleys and changing guest beers; cl Mon-Thurs lunchtime *(Michael Butler)*

☆ **Oswaldkirk** N Yor [signed off B1363/B1257 S of Helmsley; SE6279], *Malt Shovel*: Former small 17th-c manor house, heavy beams and flagstones, fine staircase, simple traditional furnishings, huge log fires, two cosy bars (one may be crowded with well heeled locals), family room, interestingly decorated dining room, unusual garden *(S E Paulley, Darren Salter, LYM)*

☆ **Otley** W Yor [Newall with Clifton; B6451 towards Blubberhouses, a mile N – just over N Yorks boundary; SE2047], *Spite*: Only a shortage of reports from readers keeps this good beamed pub out of the main entries this year; popular and welcoming, with wildfowl prints, walking stick collection, traditional furnishings, good log fire, good value honest food (not Sun or Mon evenings) in bar and restaurant, well kept Black Sheep and Websters with guest beers; children in eating area, open all day Sat, tables out in neat well lit rose garden *(F J Robinson, David and Helen Wilkins, LYM)*

Otley [18 Bondgate], *Bowling Green*: Full of bizarre artefacts, with lots of interesting things to look at; welcoming *(Dr and Mrs A K Clarke)*

Outwood W Yor [605 Leeds Rd; just N of Wakefield; SE3324], *Kirklands*: Large hotel with four Old Mill ales in spacious and comfortable bars, good helpings of reasonably priced food, friendly attentive staff; children welcome, lots of locals weekends; comfortable well equipped bedrooms *(G Coates)*

Oxenhope W Yor [B6141; SE0335], *Bay Horse*: Spick and span village local with polished brass and copper plates, Tetleys, unspoilt back games room; good value food, some tables out in front *(Ann and Colin Hunt)*; [nr Leeming, off B6141 towards Denholme], *Dog & Gun*: Well kept Timothy Taylors Landlord and Best in roomy bar with beamery, copper, brasses and delft shelves of plates and jugs, open fire each end, padded settles and stools, a couple of smaller rooms; warm welcome, good varied bar food from sandwiches up inc lots of fish, attractive bistro-style restaurant, nice views *(Mr and Mrs Newby, WAH)*; [Denholme Rd, Lower Town], *Lamb*: Clean, tidy, light and modern-feeling, with several well kept ales, friendly welcome, good cheap home-made food inc Sun lunch, open fires in small bar and second room; good views *(Jonathan Harrison)*

Patrick Brompton N Yor [A684 Bedale—Leyburn; SE2291], *Green Tree*: Friendly old stone local, well kept Black Sheep, Hambleton and Theakstons beers, open fire, wide choice of good value food (not Sun), pleasant service; public bar, separate dining lounge with waitress service *(Dorsan Baker)*

☆ **Penistone** S Yor [Mortimer Rd; outskirts, towards Stocksbridge; SE2402], *Cubley Hall*: This interesting place deserves a main entry, but this year it's kept out by an absence of reports from readers – a former grand Edwardian country house, panelling, elaborate plasterwork, mosaic tiling, plush furnishings, roomy new conservatory, distant views beyond the neat formal gardens (with a good play house and adventure playground), wide choice of good neatly served food served all day from sandwiches up, well kept Ind Coope Burton, Tetleys Bitter and Imperial

and guest beers, decent wines, restaurant; piped music, children in restaurant and conservatory; comfortable bedrooms *(LYM)*

Penistone [Hazlehead, Crow Edge; junction A616/A628, well W; SE1901], *Flouch*: Bar for drinkers, rest of pub good big Chinese restaurant, relatively cheap for its quality; may have to book *(Brian Wainwright)*

☆ **Pickering** N Yor [Market Pl; SE7983], *White Swan*: Attractive stone coaching inn with two small panelled bars, good interesting well priced bar food inc lunchtime sandwiches and good vegetarian choice, well kept Black Sheep and Malton ales, open fires, friendly helpful staff, busy but comfortable family room, good restaurant with interesting wines esp St Emilion clarets; bedrooms comfortable, good breakfast *(Eric Larkham, Ian Irving, Stephen and Brenda Head)*

Pickering [18 Birdgate], *Black Swan*: Attractive hotel keeping pubby atmosphere in bar – juke box in lively top end, quieter plush middle area, bric-a-brac on ceilings, well furnished back dining part; good service, good value tasty food, well kept Scottish Courage ales; bedrooms *(Eric Larkham)*

Pocklington E Yor [5 Market Pl; SE8049], *Feathers*: Roomy open-plan lounge with banquettes (busy Tues market day), well kept Theakstons Best and Youngers Scotch, helpful landlady, usual bar food; children welcome, timbered restaurant, no-smoking conservatory, quiz and jazz nights, comfortable motel-style bedrooms *(CT, Eric and Shirley Broadhead, LYM)*

Preston E Yor [Main St; TA1930], *Cock & Bell*: Useful welcoming family pub, busy and friendly; lounge, small pool room, restaurant, good value usual food esp curries, obliging landlord, seven well kept ales, plastic tables and chairs out on terrace, big garden with adventure playground *(JJW, CMW, Paul and Ursula Randall)*

Pudsey W Yor [Bankhouse Lane; SE2132], *Bankhouse*: Cosy Tudor-style pub charmingly decorated with brass fittings, warm lighting and comfortable chairs; Scottish Courage ales, bar food, popular restaurant (book Sats), tables out on terrace *(Martin Hickes)*

Rawdon W Yor [Town St; SE2139], *Emmott Arms*: Well priced Sam Smiths OB, good choice of bar food inc sandwiches, burgers, pizzas, lasagne and tagliatelle; restaurant *(Andy and Jill Kassube, Walter and Susan Rinaldi-Butcher)*

☆ **Reeth** N Yor [Market Pl (B6270); SE0499], *Kings Arms*: Popular dining pub by green, with oak beams, pine pews around walls, huge log fire in lovely 18th-c stone inglenook, warm plum carpet, quieter room behind; good reasonably priced food, friendly efficient service, well kept full Theakstons range, John Smiths Bitter and Magnet; children very welcome, caged parrot, maybe sports TV; bedrooms *(A Jeffreys, Brian Seller, JN)*

Reeth [B6270], *Black Bull*: Friendly if not entirely conventional local in fine spot at foot of broad sloping green, traditional dark beamed and flagstoned L-shaped front bar, well kept John Smiths and Theakstons inc Old Peculier tapped from the cask, reasonably priced usual bar food, open fires, helpful staff, children welcome; piped music in pool room; comfortable bedrooms, good breakfast *(James Nunns, A Jeffreys, Brian Seller, JT, DD, LYM)*

Ribblehead N Yor [B6255 Ingleton—Hawes; SD7880], *Station*: Interesting walkers' pub, very isolated, by Ribblehead Viaduct – ideal for railway enthusiasts, with appropriate decor in bar; good log fire in woodburner, well kept beer, big helpings of bar food, dining room; open all day in season; comfortable bedrooms, good breakfast *(R Vincent)*

Richmond N Yor [Finkle St; NZ1801], *Black Lion*: Bustling local atmosphere in well used coaching inn with well kept Camerons and guest ales, friendly staff, several separate rooms inc no-smoking lounge, dark traditional decor, briskly served no-frills food; bedrooms reasonably priced *(GSB, Hazel and Michael Duncombe, R T and J C Moggridge, Mr and Mrs M Thompson)*

Richmond N Yor [Hudswell Lane; NZ1601], *Holly Hill*: Friendly pub with jovial landlord and helpful staff, imaginative range of good food, decent bars, separate lively bar and games area *(P R Morley)*

☆ **Ripley** N Yor [off A61 Harrogate—Ripon; SE2861], *Boars Head*: Beautiful old hotel (not long since converted from private house) with long flagstoned bar, neat and well run, with tables in series of stalls, good value interesting and unusual well cooked bar food, also lunchtime sandwiches, well kept Theakstons Best, XB and Black Bull, smart friendly service, plenty of tables in charming garden; good restaurant; charming bedrooms, next to castle in pretty village *(Walker and Debra Lapthorne)*

Rishworth W Yor [Oldham Rd (A672); opp Booth Wood reservoir, nr M62 junction 22 – OS Sheet 110 map ref 026164; SE0216], *Turnpike*: Very clean pub with fine view of Booth Wood reservoir and surrounding moorland, well cooked and presented food, very reasonable prices, big bar area, small dining room, large restaurant, polite friendly staff, well kept Marstons Pedigree and Tetleys *(Michael Butler, N Revell)*; *Royal*: Well kept Ruddles County and other beers, alert and friendly landlord, big helpings of good low-priced food esp haddock; can be packed *(Herbert and Susan Verity)*

☆ **Robin Hoods Bay** N Yor [King St, Bay Town; NZ9505], *Olde Dolphin*: Roomy 18th-c inn stepped up above sea front in attractive little town; unpretentious furnishings, friendly service, convivial atmosphere, good range of well kept Scottish Courage ales, good open fire, good value bar food inc local seafood, popular back games room; dogs welcome in bar if well behaved, piped music, can get smoky and crowded weekends, long walk back up to village car park; Fri folk club,

bedrooms basic but cheap *(Mike and Wendy Proctor, Hazel and Michael Duncombe, Nigel Hopkins)*

☆ **Rosedale Abbey** N Yor [300 yds up Rosedale Chimney; SE7395], *White Horse*: Cosy and comfortable farm-based country inn in lovely spot above the village, local feel in character bar with lots of stuffed animals and birds, well kept Tetleys and Theakstons, quite a few wines and good choice of malt whiskies, friendly service, good generous reasonably priced home-made bar food esp range of pies, restaurant, grand views from terrace (and from bedrooms); children allowed if eating, open all day Sat; attractive bedrooms – a nice place to stay, good walks *(Mike and Grete Turner, Nigel Hopkins, LYM)*

☆ **Saxton** N Yor [by church in village, off A162 in Tadcaster; 2½ miles from A1 via B1217; SE4736], *Greyhound*: Unchanging delectable local in attractive quiet village, Victorian fireplace in chatty tap room (children allowed here), traditional snug, corridor to games toom, well kept cheap Sam Smiths OB tapped from the cask, lunchtime sandwiches, a couple of picnic tables in side yard; open all day weekends *(Chris Westmoreland, David Watson, LYM)*

☆ **Saxton** [Headwell Lane], *Plough*: Smart dining pub, small bar with lunchtime snacks and blazing coke fire, good choice of very good food (not Sun evening) inc beautifully presented puddings in adjacent dining room, friendly staff, well kept Theakstons and Youngers No 3, good choice of house wines, good coffee; seats outside, cl Mon *(K Rangeley, K and G Yapp)*

Scammonden Reservoir W Yor [A672; SE0215], *Brown Cow*: Dramatic views over M62, reservoir and moors in old-fashioned pub with long bar, reasonably priced food and interesting changing guest beers; busy evenings and weekends *(H K Dyson)*

☆ **Scawton** N Yor [SE5584], *Hare*: Low and pretty, much modernised, with a couple of cosy settees, simple wall settles, little wheelback armchairs, air force memorabilia; friendly service, well kept Black Sheep, Theakstons Best and XB, sensibly priced generous food inc good vegetarian range, two friendly dogs, eating area, pool room; tables in big back garden with caged geese, nice inn-signs; children welcome, handy for Rievaulx *(Darren Salter, Geoffrey and Brenda Wilson, BB)*

Seamer N Yor [the one NW of Stokesley; NZ4910], *Kings Head*: Small bar, three cosy lounges with beautiful well stoked coal fires in each, lots of horse tack *(Steve Pearson)*

Sedbusk N Yor [SD8891], *Stone House*: A hotel, but with a pleasant bar where people do drop in for a drink; Jeeves said to have originated here; bedrooms *(Paul S McPherson)*

Selby N Yor [Mkt Pl; SE6132], *Cricketers Arms*: Popular pub handy for abbey, friendly and chatty; long bar with alcove banquettes, lots of cricketing memorabilia, generous good value home-made lunchtime food (not Sun), Sam Smiths OB; games machines, juke box, piped music, quiz nights Sun and Mon; disabled access, open all day exc Tues and Weds *(JJW, CMW)*

Settle N Yor [Market Pl; SD8264], *Royal Oak*: Market-town inn under new management, roomy partly divided open-plan panelled bar, comfortable seats around brass-topped tables, well kept Whitbreads-related ales with Timothy Taylors Landlord as a guest beer, bar food all day, restaurant; children welcome, bedrooms *(Tom Thomas, Judith Hirst, Mike and Maggie Betton, LYM)*

Sheffield S Yor [1 Mkt Pl], *Bankers Draft*: Wetherspoons conversion of a former Midland Bank, roomy and well kept, with standard food all day, good range of sensibly priced real ales, no-smoking area *(David Carr)*; [1 Mosborough Moor], *British Oak*: Greenalls pub recently refurbished with old oak beams and pine panels complete with woodworm holes from nearby pit; areas off bar, different levels, three real ales, generous decent food, two dining areas (one no smoking), lots of bric-a-brac, old photographs; TV, fruit machine, piped music *(CMW, JJW)*; [537 Attercliffe Common (A6178)], *Carbrook Hall*: Dating from 1620, surviving part of even older building, popular with ghost-hunters; no-smoking dining room (children welcome here) with armour, helmets and Civil War artefacts, pool room with old bread ovens, Oak Room with panelling, beautiful carved fireplace and Italianate plaster ceiling (games machines, piped music etc); good value lunchtime bar food and Sun roasts, John Smiths Magnet and Stones, attractive small garden with dovecote and play area; open all day Fri *(CMW, JJW, David Carr)*; [1 Henry St], *Cask & Cutler*: Well refurbished small two-room pub with five particularly well kept changing ales from small breweries (and plans to brew its own), food till 6.30, lots of posters, friendly landlord, coal fire, no juke box; annual beer festival; rather bleak area *(Andy and Jill Kassube, Jack and Philip Paxton)*; [Trippett Lane], *Dog & Partridge*: Irish-style pub with good busy atmosphere, lots of students *(David Carr)*; [Division St/Westfield Terr], *Frog & Parrot*: Bare boards, lofty ceiling, huge windows, comfortable banquettes up a few steps, lively studenty cafe-bar atmosphere in evenings, interesting beers brewed on the premises – one fearsomely strong *(David Carr, LYM)*; [94 Crookes], *Noahs Ark*: Six mainly Whitbreads-related ales and huge range of generous good value food (not Sun evening) all freshly prepared (so may be a wait) inc early evening bargains in friendly pub, open all day (not Sun); disabled lavatory; pool, piped music *(JJW, CMW)*; [Crookes/Lydgate Lane], *Old Grindstone*: Busy Victorian pub recently refurbished to give more tables inc raised no-smoking area, good value food inc choice of Sun roasts, Timothy Taylors Landlord, Vaux Waggle

Dance and Wards, teapot collection, obliging service, friendly black cat, games area with two pool tables and SkyTV etc, piped music; open all day all week, jazz Mon *(JJW, CMW, D and D Savidge)*; [145 Duke St], *Red Lion*: Welcoming and utterly traditional, central bar serving four separate rooms each with original ornate fireplace and coal fire, attractive panelling and etched glass; cosy and comfortable, well kept Burtonwood, no food *(Pete Baker)*; [Tofts Lane, just off Rivelin Valley Rd], *Rivelin*: Popular pub with reasonably priced food and well kept Bass and Tetleys, pelmets with plates and horsebrasses, ideal for walkers *(John Davis)*; [Victoria Quays, off B6073 N of centre], *Sheaf Quay*: Fine old building in canal basin development nicely altered by Tom Cobleigh, relaxed atmosphere, good value cheerful bar food *(David Carr)*; [Shirecliffe Rd, Shirecliffe], *Timbertop*: Fine estate pub, friendly, with well kept beer, stunning views; interesting Swiss chalet construction *(Dr and Mrs A K Clarke)*

☆ **Shelf** W Yor [Stone Chair; A644 Brighouse–Queensbury; SE1029], *Duke of York*: Popular and welcoming 17th-c beamed dining pub, vast array of antique brass and copper, almost equally vast menu inc daily Scottish fish and seafood, even ostrich and kangaroo; well kept ales inc Timothy Taylors and Whitbreads, open fires; booking advised evenings *(M R Rimmer, Geoffrey and Brenda Wilson)*

Shepley W Yor [44 Marsh Lane; links A629 and A635, from village centre by Black Bull; SE2010], *Farmers Boy*: Converted beamed cottages with Bass-related beers, interesting food, simple country furnishings and woodwork, flower pictures, pleasant homely atmosphere, back barn restaurant; very popular with youngish locals *(Michael Butler, P R Morley)*

Sheriff Hutton N Yor [The Square; SE6566], *Highwayman*: Cosy old coaching inn overlooking castle; log fires, snug bars, oak beams in lounge and dining room, decent range of beers, big garden; 12th-c church *(Philip and Ann Falkner)*

Shiptonthorpe E Yor [A1079 Mkt Weighton—York; SE8543], *Crown*: Warm and comfortable, good welcoming service, good food inc Sun lunch, well kept Stones Best, decent house wine *(Roger A Bellingham)*

Sicklinghall N Yor [Main St; signed off A661 in Wetherby; SE3648], *Scotts Arms*: This old favourite, long a main entry, closed for three months in summer 1997 for refurbishment as a Scottish Courage Chef & Brewer; it reopened under new management too late for us to reassess it for this edition *(LYM; news please)*

☆ **Sinnington** N Yor [off A170 W of Pickering; SE7586], *Fox & Hounds*: Two clean and welcoming bar areas, nice paintings and old artefacts, cosy fires, good choice of home-cooked food inc interesting veg, well kept Bass and Camerons, dining area, separate pool room; attractive village with pretty stream and lots of grass; cosy well equipped bedrooms *(Elizabeth and Anthony Watts, M J Morgan)*

Skelton N Yor [Shipton Rd; A19 just N of York ring rd; SE5756], *Tom Cobleighs Riverside Farm*: Big designer-built chain pub with friendly helpful staff, decent food, good coffee, well kept beers inc interesting guest such as Yorkshire Terrier *(Roger Bellingham)*

☆ **Skerne** E Yor [Wansford Rd (off B1249 SE of Driffield); TA0455], *Eagle*: Quaint and unspoilt village local with two simple rooms either side of hall, coal fire, well kept Camerons from rare Victorian cash-register beer engine in kitchen-style servery, chatty locals, friendly landlord brings drinks to your table; no food, open 7-11 Mon-Fri, 12-2 weekends *(PB)*

☆ **Skipton** N Yor [Canal St; from Water St (A65) turn into Coach St, then left after canal bridge; SD9852], *Royal Shepherd*: Busy old-fashioned local in pretty spot by canal, well kept Whitbreads-related ales and guests such as Cains, decent wine, friendly service, unusual sensibly priced whiskies, open fires, low-priced standard quick food, ageing banquettes, photographs of Yorks CCC in its golden days, white cat called William; big bar, snug and dining room, tables outside, games and juke box; children welcome in side room *(Mr and Mrs C Roberts, L Dixon, Prof and Mrs S Barnett)*

Skipwith N Yor [signed off A163 NE of Selby; SE6638], *Drovers Arms*: Two-room pub with good log fires, very friendly landlord, good food inc sandwiches and daily-changing specials, guest beers, choice of wines by glass; separate dining room, children welcome *(Janet Pickles)*

Sneaton N Yor [Beacon Way; NZ8908], *Wilson Arms*: Good value generous food from sandwiches up inc good Sun menu, Barnsley, Black Sheep and Theakstons, friendly atmosphere, good open fires, pleasant dining room; bedrooms *(M Borthwick, Mike and Wendy Proctor)*

South Kilvington N Yor [SE4384], *Old Oak Tree*: Good food inc good reasonably priced vegetarian range, landlord does the cooking and will adapt to dietary requirements; all freshly prepared so may be a short wait; well kept beers, relaxed friendly and informal atmosphere, big back conservatory restaurant, secluded side restaurant *(Ian and Michelle Juden)*

Spofforth N Yor [A661 Harrogate—Wetherby; SE3650], *Railway*: Welcoming licensees, good freshly prepared food and well kept Sam Smiths; ordinary bar, simple unfussy lounge, garden and play area *(Graham and Helen Brown)*

☆ **Sprotbrough** S Yor [Lower Sprotbrough; 2¾ miles from M18 junction 2; SE5302], *Boat*: Interesting roomy stonebuilt ex-farmhouse with lovely courtyard in charming quiet spot by River Don, three individually furnished areas, big stone fireplaces, latticed windows, dark brown beams, good value bar food inc

generous hot dishes (no sandwiches), well kept Scottish Courage beers, farm cider, helpful staff; piped music, fruit machine, no dogs; big sheltered prettily lit courtyard, river walks; restaurant (Tues-Sat evening, Sun lunch); open all day summer Sats *(Mike and Grete Turner, Alan and Charlotte Sykes)*

☆ **Staithes** N Yor [off A174 Whitby—Loftus; NZ7818], *Cod & Lobster*: Basic pub in superb waterside setting in unspoilt fishing village under sandstone cliff, well kept beers inc Camerons Best and Red Dragon, good crab sandwiches, friendly service and locals, lovely views from seats outside; quite a steep walk up to top car park *(Mike and Wendy Proctor, Judith Hirst, LJ, Dr and Mrs A H Young, Andrew Hazeldine, LYM)*

Staithes N Yor [High St; NZ7818], *Black Lion*: Small comfortable hotel bar with real fire, good choice of real ale, friendly staff; unspoilt fishing village *(Judith Hirst)*; *Royal George*: Small friendly old inn nr harbour, with locals' bar on right, three plusher interconnected rooms, straightforward food, well kept Camerons Bitter and Strongarm, children welcome; piped music, darts; good value bedrooms *(Andrew Hazeldine, Mike and Wendy Proctor)*

Stamford Bridge E Yor [A166 W of town; SE7155], *Three Cups*: Spacious friendly recently refurbished family dining pub with popular food all day, Bass and Tetleys, decent wines; children welcome, good play area behind; bedrooms *(Roger Bellingham, LYM)*

Stannington S Yor [Uppergate Rd; SK3088], *Crown & Glove*: On edge of the Sheffield lake district, friendly and popular for good value lunches; Wards Bitter, no music *(Peter Marshall)*

Stokesley N Yor [1 West End; NZ5209], *White Swan*: Five well kept ales inc two or three changing interesting guest beers in well worn-in but clean, comfortable and tidy split-level panelled bar, several pates and tremendous choice of cheeses, hat display, welcoming staff, friendly ridgeback called Bix and little black dog called Titch; midweek live blues and jazz *(Val Stevenson, Rob Holmes, Tim Abel, Pete Boydell, Jim Cornish, Andy and Jill Kassube)*

☆ **Sutton on the Forest** N Yor [B1363 N of York; SE5965], *Rose & Crown*: Picturesque and comfortable two-room dining pub, relaxed and informal cross between typical pub and bistro, with good fresh generous food inc imaginative dishes and good steaks, Theakstons ales, interesting wines, smart customers, welcoming licensees; charming wide-street village *(H Bramwell, Mrs H Walker)*

☆ **Sutton under Whitestonecliffe** N Yor [A170 E of Thirsk; SE4983], *Whitestonecliffe*: Beamed 17th-c roadside pub with wide range of good value traditional generous bar meals (can be eaten in small bookable restaurant) inc fresh fish and veg and good puddings, open fires in relaxing and comfortable front lounge with good solid modern oak settles, back pool/family room with comfortable settees, juke box and fruit machine, pleasant tap room with traditional games; well kept John Smiths, Tetleys and Theakstons Best, decent wines, very friendly service; children welcome; back bedroom wing; *(Andrew and Ruth Triggs, Brian and Peggy Mansfield, Ann Bolton)*

☆ **Tadcaster** N Yor [1 Bridge St; SE4843], *Angel & White Horse*: Tap for Sam Smiths brewery, cheap well kept OB and Museum, friendly staff, big helpings of good simple lunchtime food (not Sat) from separate counter; big often under-used bar with alcoves at one end, fine oak panelling and solid furnishings; restaurant (children allowed there); piped music; the dappled grey dray horses are kept across the coachyard, and brewery tours can be arranged – tel (01937) 832225; open all day Sat *(Chris Westmoreland, Gill and Andy Plumb, LYM)*

☆ **Tan Hill** N Yor [Arkengarthdale (Reeth—Brough) rd, at junction with Keld/W Stonesdale rd; NY8906], *Tan Hill Inn*: Simple furnishings, flagstones, big open fires and a cheery atmosphere in Britain's highest pub, on the Pennine Way, nearly five miles from the nearest neighbour; well kept Theakstons Best, XB and Old Peculier (in winter the cellar does chill down – for warmth you might prefer coffee or whisky with hot water), inexpensive hearty food from sandwiches up, some good old photographs; children welcome, open all day at least in summer; bedrooms, inc some in newish extension; often snowbound, with no mains electricity (juke box powered by generator); Swaledale sheep show last Thurs in May *(Nigel Woolliscroft, M Morgan, LYM)*

☆ **Thoralby** N Yor [SE0086], *George*: Lively little Dales village local, down to earth and welcoming, with limited but generous good value food, Black Sheep, John Smiths and Websters, great landlady, darts, dominoes; three good value spotless bedrooms, huge breakfast *(Tim Dobby, Ray and Liz Monk)*

Thorganby N Yor [SE6942], *Jefferson Arms*: Taken over recently by two Irish brothers, thriving relaxed atmosphere and good food in bar and restaurant, well kept Boddingtons; bedrooms *(Eric Dix)*

Thorner W Yor [Thorner Lane, off A64; SE3840], *Beehive*: Friendly landlord, good cheap wholesome food, Tetleys; very busy Sun and hols; *(Phil and Anne Smithson)*

Thornhill, W Yor [Combs Hill, off A6117 S of Dewsbury; SE2519], *Alma*: Relaxed local, comfortable and friendly, good choice of reasonably priced food, flagstones by counter, carpeting elsewhere, attractive pine furniture and pink banquettes in partitioned bays, cigarette card collections, well kept Bass, Stones, Theakstons and Worthington BB; small restaurant *(Michael Butler)*

☆ **Thornton** W Yor [Hill Top Rd, off B6145 W of Bradford; SE0933], *Ring o' Bells*: Spotless 19th-c moortop dining pub noted for its success in pub catering competitions, wide

choice of well presented good home cooking inc fresh fish, meat and poultry specialities, superb steaks, bargain early suppers, pleasant bar, popular air-conditioned no-smoking restaurant; good range of Scottish Courage and other ales, very welcoming service, wide views towards Shipley and Bingley *(K H Frostick, Geoffrey and Brenda Wilson, Andy and Jill Kassube, Sheila and Brian Wilson)*

☆ **Thornton in Lonsdale** N Yor [just NW of Ingleton; SD6976], *Marton Arms*: Quiet country pub with good relaxed atmosphere, plain pine furniture, up to a dozen or more well kept ales, farm cider, lots of malt whiskies, good value food inc home-made pizzas, enormous gammon and daily specials, real fire, efficient friendly service even when busy; children, walkers and cavers welcome, attractive Dales setting opp church where Conan Doyle was married; newly decorated bedrooms in annexe, good breakfast *(Alan Morton, Andy and Jill Kassube, Stuart Steels, Vann Prime, Wm Van Laaten, Arthur and Margaret Dickinson)*

Thorpe Salvin S Yor [Church St; SK5281], *Parish Oven*: Spacious beamed pub with old cooking range in no-smoking dining room, good value bar food inc children's and Sun roast, John Smiths and Theakstons, TV and pool in bar, amusements in children's room (children's parties can be arranged); garden with picnic tables and play area, karaoke Fri *(CMW, JJW)*

Tickton E Yor [Hull Bridge, off A1035; TA0642], *Crown & Anchor*: Busy friendly Mansfield pub with good food choice inc vegetarian and children's, play area and picnic tables in riverside garden, riverside walks *(CMW, JJW)*

☆ **Upper Poppleton** N Yor [A59 York—Harrogate; SE5554], *Red Lion*: Consistently good value well presented food inc good vegetarian in dark and cosy olde-worlde bars and dining areas, quiet and sparkling clean – popular with older people and businessmen; good service, pleasant garden; bedroom extension *(F J Robinson)*

☆ **Wakefield** W Yor [77 Westgate End; SE3321], *Tap & Spile*: Traditional gas-lit flagstoned pub with attractive Victorian-style layout and fittings, a real ale brewed for them by Youngs and several interesting well kept guest beers, cheap bar snacks; open all day, no children *(Roger A Bellingham, Michael Butler, LYM)*

Wakefield [Newmillerdam (A61 S); SE3315], *Dam*: By reservoir dam, attractive walking country – so busy in summer; neatly kept L-shaped stripped-stone bar with usual furnishings, adjoining popular Toby carvery/restaurant, well kept Stones and Worthington, pleasant coffee lounge, prompt service, generous usual food *(Michael Butler, Thomas Nott)*; [Kirkhamgate], *Star*: Varied good reasonably priced food in comfortable long bar of terrace restaurant, friendly staff, fish pool; fenced play area *(Alan Nicholson, Jan Strattan)*

☆ **Walkington** E Yor [B1230; SE9937], *Ferguson Fawsitt Arms*: Mock-Tudor bars in 1950s style, with good choice of properly cooked good value food and good puddings from airy no-smoking flagstone-floored self-service food bar, very popular lunchtime with older people; friendly cheerful service, decent wine; tables out on terrace, games bar with pool table; delightful village *(H Bramwell, K and J Brooks, LYM)*

Walsden W Yor [A6033 S of Todmorden; SD9322], *Bird i' th' Hand*: Small roadside pub very popular for wide choice of good home-made food *(Tony Hobden)*; [by Rochdale Canal], *Cross Keys*: Good range of well kept ales such as Black Sheep, Buchanans and Tetleys, good value genuine home cooking *(Tony Hobden)*

Weaverthorpe N Yor [SE9771], *Star*: Comfortable little inn in relaxing village setting, good straightforward food, well kept ales, exceptionally welcoming staff; nice bedrooms, good breakfast; cl weekday lunchtimes *(Bob Ellis, Colin Savill)*

Wentbridge W Yor [Great North Rd (off A1); SE4817], *Blue Bell*: Several communicating rooms, beams, stripped stone, farm tools and other bric-a-brac, solid wooden tables, chairs and settles; wide choice of good quick generous food inc Sun evening, friendly efficient service, well kept Tetleys and Timothy Taylors Landlord; piped music can be rather intrusive; family room, good view from garden *(N Christopher)*

☆ **Wentworth** [3 miles from M1 junction 36; B6090, signed off A6135; SK3898], *Rockingham Arms*: Warmly welcoming country inn with comfortable traditional furnishings, hunting pictures, open fires, stripped stone, rooms off inc a dining room and family room, good choice of reasonably priced food (not Sun evening) from sandwiches to inventive specials, several well kept Scottish Courage ales, cheerful service; piped music; tables in attractive garden with own well kept bowling green; has been open all day; bedrooms *(Andy and Jill Kassube, LYM)*

Wentworth [B6090], *George & Dragon*: Friendly rambling split-level bar, reasonably priced well cooked honest food, well kept Timothy Taylors Landlord, assorted old-fashioned furnishings, ornate stove in lounge, back small games room, restaurant; high chairs provided; benches in front courtyard *(G P Kernan, LYM)*

☆ **West Burton** N Yor [off B6160 Bishopdale—Wharfedale; SE0186], *Fox & Hounds*: Clean and cosy unpretentious local on long green of idyllic Dales village, simple generous inexpensive fresh food inc children's, well kept Black Sheep and Theakstons ales, chatty budgerigar, residents' dining room, children welcome; nearby caravan park; good modern bedrooms, lovely walks and waterfalls nearby *(Marianne Lantree, Steve Webb)*

West Witton N Yor [SE0688], *Fox & Hounds*: Doing well under nice new local

couple *(Peter Swan)*; [A684 W of Leyburn], *Wensleydale Heifer*: Comfortable genteel dining pub with low-ceilinged small interconnecting areas in front lounge, big attractive bistro, separate restaurant, good food inc interesting dishes and seafood (generous though not cheap), good log fire, attractive prints, pleasant decor; small bar with decent wines, Black Sheep, John Smiths and Theakstons Best; back bedrooms quietest, good breakfast *(Malcolm Phillips, M J Morgan, Dr P Jackson, Gwen and Peter Andrews)*

Westow N Yor [SE7565], *Blacksmiths Arms*: Good local with warm country atmosphere, decent food, John Smiths and Tetleys *(CT)*

Whashton N Yor [N of Richmond; NZ1506], *Hack & Spade*: Immaculate, with wide choice of good food in bar or restaurant, first-class service, well kept Theakstons Best and Mild, good coffee and house wine *(Rita and Keith Pollard)*

Whitby N Yor [Flowergate; NZ9011], *Elsinore*: Clean and well kept, popular with locals and visitors, lifeboat and other boating memorabilia, particularly well kept Camerons, lunchtime food *(Hazel and Michael Duncombe)*; [New Quay Rd], *Tap & Spile*: Well decorated bare-boards pub, no-smoking area, good value bar food inc good local fish and chips noon-7, up to eight well kept ales, country wines, farm ciders, traditional games; open all day *(JJW, CMW, Hazel and Michael Duncombe, Rita Horridge)*

☆ **Wigglesworth** N Yor [B6478, off A65 S of Settle; SD8157], *Plough*: Little rooms off bar, some spartan yet cosy, others smart and plush, inc no-smoking panelled dining room and snug; ample popular bar food inc huge sandwiches, good specials and children's dishes, conservatory restaurant (minimum price limit) with panoramic Dales views, well kept Boddingtons and Tetleys, decent wines and coffee, good friendly service; attractive garden, pleasant bedrooms *(Mr and Mrs J Harrop, LYM)*

☆ **Wighill** N Yor [off A659 in Tadcaster, or off A1 Wetherby bypass via Thorpe Arch trading estate; SE4746], *White Swan*: Unspoilt village pub firmly finding its feet again in summer 1997 after unexpected management changes, several rooms with individual decor and open fires, well kept Tetleys, Theakstons Best and a guest beer, attentive service, small but interesting choice of good food inc delicious puddings (not Mon evenings), lots of tables out on terrace and in garden; children in restaurant or family room *(Marian and Andrew Ruston, Peter and Anne Hollindale, LYM)*

Wilberfoss E Yor [off A1079 E of York; SE7351], *Oddfellows Arms*: Friendly helpful staff, good generous food inc vegetarian in tasteful beamed dining extension, good Sun carvery, Bass and Stones, good house wine, interesting pictures, delft shelf *(Canon E R Cook)*

Worsborough S Yor [signed off A61, N of
M1 junction; SE3402], *Edmunds Arms*:
Sizeable two-bar stone-built pub opp church,
comfortable banquettes, good value food (not
Mon eve) inc Sun lunch, Sam Smiths OB;
piped music, provision for children; picnic
tables and slide in garden *(CMW, JJW)*

☆ **York** [High Petergate], *Hole in the Wall*:
Good atmosphere in rambling open-plan pub
handy for Minster, beams, stripped
brickwork, turkey carpeting, plush seats, well
kept Mansfield beers, good coffee, cheap
simple food noon-8 inc generous Sun lunch,
friendly prompt service; juke box, piped
music not too loud; open all day *(Esther and
John Sprinkle, Andy Cunningham, Yvonne
Hannaford, M Walker, LYM)*

☆ **York** [18 Goodramgate], *Royal Oak*: Cosy
black-beamed 16th-c pub with good value
generous imaginative food (limited Sun
evening) served 11.30-7.30, speedy service
from cheerful bustling young staff, well kept
Ind Coope Burton, Tetleys, Whitbreads Castle
Eden, wines and country wines, good coffee;
prints, swords and old guns, no-smoking
family room; handy for Minster, can get
crowded *(Chris Westmoreland, Joan and
Andrew Life, Scott Rumery, BB)*

☆ **York** [Tanners Moat/Wellington Row, below
Lendal Bridge], *Maltings*: Rough-and-ready
small pub with vast range of well kept
changing beers from small breweries, good
choice of continental ones, farm ciders, decent
well priced generous lunchtime food,
welcoming service, interesting salvaged
fittings like suburban front door for ladies',
plenty of atmosphere, friendly staff, daily
papers in gents'; open all day, handy for Rail
Museum, some live entertainment *(Tony Hall,
SLC, Eric Larkham, Tony and Wendy
Hobden, Howard England)*

☆ **York** [26 High Petergate], *York Arms*: Snug
little basic panelled bar, big modern no-
smoking lounge, cosier partly panelled room
full of old bric-a-brac, prints, brown-
cushioned wall settles, dimpled copper tables
and an open fire; quick friendly service, well
kept Sam Smiths OB and Museum, good
value simple food lunchtime and early
evening, no music; by Minster, open all day
(M Walker, BB)

☆ **York**, [7 Stonegate], *Punch Bowl*: Attractive
Hogarthian local with small dim-lit rooms off
corridor, helpful service, good generous
lunchtime food, well kept Bass, Stones,
Worthington Best and a guest such as
Timothy Taylors Landlord; piped music may
obtrude; open all day all week, some live
music and quiz nights, good value bedrooms
(Mark Walker, Chris Westmoreland)

York [53 Fossgate], *Blue Bell*: Two small
friendly Edwardian panelled rooms off
drinking corridor, coal fires, several well kept
Vaux ales with a guest such as Badger
Tanglefoot, fresh lunchtime sandwiches and

pickled eggs, lively atmosphere, chatty locals;
open all day (not Sun) *(SLC, PB, Chris
Westmoreland, Eric Larkham, M Walker)*;
[Monkgate, far end by roundabout], *Brigadier
Gerard*: Elegant Georgian exterior,
comfortable and friendly in, memorabilia of
the great racehorse, good solid Yorkshire
food *(H Bramwell, Eric Larkham)*; [Fulford
Rd (A19 S)], *Gimcrack*: Clean and bright,
with sweeping stairway to palatial inner area
with high ceilings and marble columns,
friendly staff, food from traditional dishes to
shark, inc vegetarian and early evening
bargains, guest beers such as Yorkshire
Terrier and Ruddles County; disabled access
not good *(G Coates)*; [9 Church St], *Golden
Lion*: Big open-plan T J Bernards pub recently
given Edwardian refurbishment, dark with
plenty of lamps; friendly efficient staff, good
value generous lunchtime bar, Scottish
Courage ales with good range of guest beers
such as Black Sheep, Ridleys Rumpus and
ESX; fruit machine, piped music *(Mark
Walker, SLC)*; [St Helens Sq], *Harkers*: Bar
rather than pub, with rather upmarket decor
and service, good new world wines from the
long serving counter, food inc all-day
breakfast, bangers and mash and fish and
chips alongside lamb, steaks etc *(H
Bramwell)*; [Kings Staithe], *Kings Arms*: Fine
riverside position with lots of picnic tables out
on cobbled waterside terrace; bowed black
beams and flagstones inside, straightforward
furnishings, good lunchtime food from
sandwiches up; CD juke box can be loud, keg
beers; open all day *(Esther and John Sprinkle,
Scott Rumery, Mark Walker, LYM)*; [13
Grape Lane], *Kites Rest*: Above-average food
in upstairs dining room *(Paul McPherson)*; [6
Fishergate], *Masons Arms*: Unchanged 1930s
pub, good range of beers, interesting food
(Eric Larkham); [Goodramgate], *Old White
Swan*: Victorian, Georgian and Tudor themed
bars, delightful covered courtyard, bar food,
Bass and Worthington, friendly staff; juke
box, piped music, games machines, popular
with younger people at night *(Mark Walker,
Eric Larkham)*; [North St, opp Viking Hotel],
Tap & Spile: Three smallish rooms, well kept
reasonably priced changing local and other
beers, good simple wholesome food; relaxed
and friendly *(Chris Westmoreland, Eric
Larkham, Thomas Nott)*; [Goodramgate],
Snickleway: Snug little old-world pub, lots of
antiques, copper and brass, good coal fires,
cosy nooks and crannies, good simple
wholesome lunchtime snacks (not Sun) inc
good value sandwiches, unobtrusive piped
music, prompt service, well kept John Smiths
(Mark Walker, Giles Bird); [12 Coppergate],
Three Tuns: Smallish single room, subdued
lighting, prints, bar meals, well kept
Mansfield beers and occasional Deakins
guest; TV, fruit machines, piped music; open
all day *(SLC)*

London
Scotland
Wales
Channel Islands

London

London pubs charge much more for drinks than the national average – nearly 20p a pint more. To drink economically, go for beers produced by London's own good value brewers, Fullers and Youngs, or by one of the other smaller breweries. Our price survey showed that in London pubs these undercut the big national breweries by nearly that full 20p a pint. By contrast, London pub food is relatively low-priced – cheaper than in most other parts of the country. To be frank, this has in the past been more a reflection of its quality than anything else. Pubs in London have been slower than elsewhere to catch on to the great revolution in pub food quality which this Guide has charted over recent years. At last, though, London pubs are catching up. Some can even be thought of primarily as places for an enjoyable meal out: the Eagle (EC1, Central), the Chapel (NW1, North), the Fire Station (SE1, South), the Ladbroke Arms (W11, West) and a new entry in this edition the Anglesea Arms (W6, West) are prime examples. Of these, it's the Anglesea Arms, Wingate St, W6 which gains our accolade of London Dining Pub of the Year; all the readers who have reported on it have described the food as either 'fabulous' or 'fantastic', and even our own dourer vocabulary stretched as far as 'excellent'. Further good news is that what might be thought of as classic London pubs are now doing food that's well worth knowing about – places like the other Anglesea Arms (SW7, West), the Churchill Arms (W8, West) or another new entry the Flask (NW3, North). On the subject of new entries, others to mention are the sumptuous Lord Moon of the Mall (SW1, Central), the stylishly modern Moon Under Water (Charing Cross Rd, Central – it stretches off far into Soho), the cosy Jerusalem Tavern (EC1, Central – a clever recreation of an 18th-c coffee house, with fine beers from a new Suffolk brewery), the ancient Bulls Head by the Thames (W4, West), the unspoilt rural-seeming White Swan a bit further upstream (Twickenham, West), and for its rollicking sense of fun as well as its dockland river views the touristy but genuinely old Prospect of Whitby (E1, East). Now that we have moved our offices down to Sussex, Central London pubs which we ourselves feel deprived of on a day-to-day basis include the Cittie of Yorke (WC1), Grenadier (SW1), Nags Head (SW1), Olde Mitre (EC1 – a favourite for atmosphere and service, and such good value sandwiches), and Princess Louise (WC1).

CENTRAL LONDON

Covering W1, W2, WC1, WC2, SW1, SW3, EC1, EC2, EC3 and EC4 postal districts

Parking throughout this area is metered throughout the day, and generally in short supply then; we mention difficulty only if evening parking is a problem too. Throughout the chapter we list the nearest Underground or BR stations to each pub; where two are listed it means the walk is the same from either

Albert (Westminster) Map 13

52 Victoria Street, SW1; ⊖ St James's Park

Over the years civil servants, MPs and even royalty have all added to the wonderfully diverse mix of customers filling this splendid Victorian pub, one of the great sights of this part of London. Handsome, colourful and harmonious, it's rather dwarfed by the faceless cliffs of dark modern glass around it, but still towers above them in architectural merit. The ground floor is a huge open-plan bar, with good solid comfortable furniture, gleaming mahogany, original gas lamps, and a surprisingly airy feel thanks to great expanses of heavily cut and etched windows along three sides. Despite the space, it can be packed on weekday lunchtimes and immediately after work. Service from the big island counter is generally swift and friendly (particularly obliging to overseas visitors), with well kept Courage Best and Directors, John Smiths, and Theakstons Best and Old Peculier on handpump. The separate food servery is good value, with sandwiches (from £1.40), salads (from £3.50) and five home-cooked hot dishes such as cottage pie, steak pie, quiche or lasagne (all £4.25). The upstairs restaurant does an eat-as-much-as-you-like carvery, better than average (all day inc Sunday, £13.95). The handsome staircase that leads up to it is lined with portraits of former prime ministers, and it's likely that several of those pictured would have enjoyed a drink here at some stage – it's not far to Westminster, and they even sound the Division Bell. Piped music, fruit machine. *(Recommended by Ian Phillips, Mark Baynham, Rachael Ward, Tony Scott, Alan and Paula McCully, Gordon, C Walker, Robert Lester, John and Wendy Trentham, Wayne Brindle)*

Scottish Courage ~ Managers Roger and Gill Wood ~ Real ale ~ Meals and snacks (11-10.30; 12-10 Sun) ~ Restaurant ~ (0171) 222 5577 ~ Children in eating area and restaurant (except lunchtimes Mon and Fri) ~ Open 11-11; 12-10.30 Sun; cl 25/26 Dec

Argyll Arms 🍷 (Oxford Circus) Map 13

18 Argyll St W1; ⊖ Oxford Circus, opp tube side exit

It's clear from the speed people move around Oxford Circus that they can't wait to get away, and while this unexpectedly traditional Victorian pub is no less bustling than its increasingly dispiriting surroundings, it's one of the few places in the vicinity that could cause you to make a return visit. Easy to spot by the profusion of plants and flowers that festoon its frontage, it's much as it was when built in the 1860s, especially in the most atmospheric and unusual part, the three cubicle rooms at the front. All oddly angular, they're made by wooden partitions with distinctive frosted and engraved glass, with hops trailing above. A good range of changing beers typically includes Banks, Brakspears, Hook Norton Best, Smiles Best, Timothy Taylors Landlord on handpump, along with one or two more unusual guests; also Addlestone's cider, malt whiskies, and freshly squeezed orange juice. A long mirrored corridor leads to the spacious back room, with the food counter in one corner; this area is no smoking at lunchtime. Chalked up on a blackboard (which may also have topical cartoons), the choice of meals includes good and unusual sandwiches like generously filled stilton and grape (£2.50), salt beef (£3.25), or roast chicken, bacon and melted cheese (£3.65), and main courses such as salads or a pie of the day. Prompt, efficient staff; two fruit machines, piped music. The quieter upstairs bar, which overlooks the busy pedestrianised street (and the Palladium theatre if you can see through the foliage outside the window), is divided into several snugs with comfortable plush easy chairs; swan's neck lamps, and lots of small theatrical prints along the top of the walls. The gents' has a copy of the day's *Times* or *Financial Times* on the wall. Though the pub gets crowded, there's space for drinking outside. *(Recommended by John Fazakerley, TBB, Tony Scott, Mark Baynham, Rachael Ward, Ian Phillips, Wayne Brindle, Hanns P Golez, Christopher Gallop, Bob and Maggie Atherton, Thomas Thomas, John and Anne Peacock, David Carr, Richard Lewis)*

Nicholsons (Allied; run as free house) ~ Managers Mike and Sue Tayara ~ Real ale ~ Meals (12-7.30) and snacks (till 9.30) ~ Restaurant~ 0171-734 6117 ~ Children in eating area ~ Open 11-11; 12-9 Sun

Black Friar ◀ (City) Map 13

174 Queen Victoria Street, EC4; ◕ Blackfriars

The inner back room at this unique pub has some of the best fine Edwardian bronze and marble art-nouveau decor to be found anywhere – big bas-relief friezes of jolly monks set into richly coloured Florentine marble walls, an opulent marble-pillared inglenook fireplace, a low vaulted mosaic ceiling, gleaming mirrors, seats built into rich golden marble recesses, and tongue-in-cheek verbal embellishments such as Silence is Golden and Finery is Foolish. The whole place is much bigger inside than seems possible from the delightfully odd exterior, and that's quite a good thing – they do get very busy, particularly after work; lots of people spill out onto the wide forecourt in front, near the approach to Blackfriars Bridge. See if you can spot the opium smoking-hints modelled into the fireplace of the front room. Lunchtime bar food includes filled rolls (£2.50), baked potatoes or ploughman's (£2.95), and a daily hot dish like chicken curry (£3.95); service is obliging and helpful. Well kept Adnams, Brakspears, Marstons Pedigree and Tetleys on handpump; fruit machine. If you're coming by Tube, choose your exit carefully – it's all too easy to emerge from the network of passageways and find yourself on the other side of the street or marooned on a traffic island. *(Recommended by Chris Westmoreland, Eric and Jackie Robinson, Christopher Gallop, David Carr, Mark Baynham, Rachael Ward, Karen and Graham Oddey)*

Nicholsons (Allied) ~ Manager Mr Becker ~ Real ale ~ Lunchtime meals (11.30-2.30) ~ 0171-236 5650 ~ Open 11.30-10(11 Thurs/Fri); closed weekends and bank holidays

Cittie of Yorke ◀ (Holborn) Map 13

22 High Holborn, WC1; find it by looking out for its big black and gold clock; ◕ Chancery Lane

Looking rather like a vast baronial hall, the main back room of this unique pub takes your breath away when seen for the first time. The extraordinarily extended bar counter (reputedly the longest in Britain) stretches off into the distance, vast thousand-gallon wine vats rest above the gantry, and big bulbous lights hang from the soaring high raftered roof. It does get packed at lunchtime and in the early evening, particularly with lawyers and judges, but it's at busy times like these when the pub seems most magnificent. Most people tend to congregate in the middle, so you should still be able to bag one of the intimate, old-fashioned and ornately carved cubicles that run along both sides. The triangular Waterloo fireplace, with grates on all three sides and a figure of Peace among laurels, used to stand in the Grays Inn Common Room until barristers stopped dining there; we used to think this was unique, but a reader tells us there's a similar one in the Oxford Union. Appealingly priced Sam Smiths OB on handpump and some unusually flavoured vodkas such as chocolate orange or pear and ginger; smartly dressed staff, fruit machine, video game and piped music. A smaller, comfortable wood-panelled room has lots of little prints of York and attractive brass lights, while the ceiling of the entrance hall has medieval-style painted panels and plaster York roses. There's a lunchtime food counter in the main hall with more in the downstairs cellar bar: the choice typically includes filled baps, ploughman's and salads, various pies (£4.25) and half a dozen daily specials (£6). A pub has stood on this site since 1430, though the current building owes more to the 1695 coffee house erected here behind a garden; it was reconstructed in Victorian times using 17th-c materials and parts. *(Recommended by Christopher Gallop, Ian Phillips, Mike Gorton, Alan and Paula McCully, R J Bland, Jill Bickerton, Mark Baynham, Rachael Ward, Tony Scott, Ted George, Val Stevenson, Rob Holmes, Eric and Jackie Robinson, John Fahy, Chris Westmoreland, Mick Hitchman, Jens Arne Grebstad, E A Thwaite, David Carr)*

Sam Smiths ~ Manager Stuart Browning ~ Real ale ~ Meals and snacks (12-10) ~ 0171-242 7670 ~ Children in eating area ~ Open 11.30-11; closed all day Sun

---

Waterside pubs are listed at the back of the book.

Dog & Duck (Soho) Map 13

18 Bateman St, on corner with Frith Street, W1; ✜ Tottenham Court Rd/Leicester Square

Trendy bars and ever-changing restaurants surround this delightful little Soho landmark, a pint-sized corner house likely to outlast them all. On the floor by the door is a mosaic of a dog, tongue out in hot pursuit of a duck, and the same theme is embossed on some of the shiny tiles that frame the heavy old advertising mirrors. The little bar counter is rather unusual, and serves well kept Tetleys, Timothy Taylors Landlord, and a couple of guests on handpump; they do doorstep sandwiches (from £1.80). The chatty main bar really is tiny, though at times manages to squeeze in a wonderfully varied mix of people; there are some high stools by the ledge along the back wall, and further seats in a roomier area at one end, as well as in a snug upstairs bar overlooking the street. There's a fire in winter, and newspapers to read. In good weather especially there tend to be plenty of people spilling onto the bustling street outside. No machines or piped music – though if you fancy a few tunes Ronnie Scott's Jazz Club is near by. *(Recommended by Gerry Christie, Steve Harvey, David Carr, Maggie and Bob Atherton; more reports please)*

Nicholsons (Allied) ~ Manageress Mrs Gene Bell ~ Real ale ~ Snacks (not weekends) ~ 0171-437 4447 ~ Open 12-11; closed Sat and Sun lunchtimes, opening 6 Sat evening (7 Sun)

Eagle 🍴 ♇ (City) Map 13

159 Farringdon Rd, EC1; opposite Bowling Green Lane car park; ✜ Farringdon/Old Street

Remember those not so long gone days when London pubs serving good food were as hard to find as the proverbial streets paved with gold? The Eagle changed all that, and its highly distinctive Mediterranean-style meals are still some of the best of their type, despite the number of welcome imitators that have sprung up all over the city. If anything, it's almost a little too successful, as we often hear from readers who've waited in vain for one of the seemingly random assortment of tables to become available. Even then dishes from the blackboard menu can run out or change fairly early, so it really is worth getting here as early as you possibly can if you're hoping to eat, especially at lunchtime. Made with the finest quality ingredients, typical dishes might include aubergine and yoghurt soup with roast piquillo peppers (£4), Gypsy baked eggs and tomatoes with chorizo, pancetta and garlic (£6.50), grilled Italian sausages with chickpeas and and choricero chillies (£7.50), grilled black bream with romesco sauce and rocket (£8), leg of free-range pork roasted with fennel seed and garlic (£8.50) and Portuguese fish stew with saffron, potato and green peppers (£10); they also do Spanish and goat's milk cheeses (£5), and Portuguese custard tarts (90p). Note they don't take credit cards – though the food is out of the ordinary, the atmosphere is still lively, noisily chatty and pubby (especially in the evenings, when dress veers strongly towards back-to-front baseball caps and the like), so it's not the kind of place you'd go to for a smart night out or a quiet dinner. The open kitchen forms part of the bar, and furnishings in the single room are simple but stylish – school chairs, a couple of sofas on bare boards, and modern paintings on the walls (there's an art gallery upstairs, with direct access from the bar). There's quite a mix of customers, but at times there's quite a proliferation of media folk (*The Guardian* is based just up the road). Well kept Boddingtons, Marstons Pedigree and Wadworths 6X on handpump, decent wines including a dozen by the glass, good coffee, and properly made cocktails; piped music. *(Recommended by Nick Rose, R J Bland, Rachael Ward, Mark Baynham, Sebastian Leach, James Macrae, Maggie and Bob Atherton, Dave Braisted)*

Free house ~ Licensees Michael Belben and David Eyre ~ Real ale ~ Meals 12.30-2.30(3.30 Sat), 6.30-10.30 ~ 0171-837 1353 ~ Children welcome ~ Open 12-11; closed Sun, bank holidays, Easter, and 2 weeks at Christmas

---

If we know a pub does summer barbecues, we say so.

Grapes (Mayfair) Map 13

Shepherd Market, W1; ● Green Park

Bang in the middle of civilised Shepherd Market, this traditional and friendly pub always has a busily chatty atmosphere, and on sunny evenings you'll generally find the square outside packed with smart-suited drinkers. The dimly lit bar is cheery and old-fashioned, with plenty of stuffed birds and fish in glass display cases, and a snug little alcove at the back. Bar food might include sandwiches (from £2.75), seafood platter or half roast chicken (£4.55), and ploughman's (£5.25). A good range of six or seven well kept (though fairly pricy) beers on handpump usually takes in Boddingtons, Flowers IPA and Original, Fullers London Pride, Greene King Abbot, Marstons Pedigree, and Wadworths 6X; fruit machine. What was the restaurant is now a private members' club, though membership is free and they say applications to join are welcome. *(Recommended by Mark Baynham, Rachael Ward, Peter Todd, Wayne Brindle, Thomas Nott, Tim Barrow, Sue Demont, Eric and Jackie Robinson)*

Free house ~ Licensees Gill and Eric Lewis ~ Real ale ~ Lunchtime meals and snacks ~ 0171-629 4989 ~ Children over 10 in eating area of bar ~ Open 11-11; 12-10.30 Sun; closed 25 Dec

Grenadier (Belgravia) Map 13

Wilton Row, SW1; the turning off Wilton Crescent looks prohibitive, but the barrier and watchman are there to keep out cars; walk straight past – the pub is just around the corner; ● Knightsbridge

Patriotically painted in red, white and blue, this snugly characterful pub is a real favourite with readers; one has been coming here for over 30 years. Famous for its bloody marys and well documented poltergeist (it's reckoned to be the capital's most haunted pub), it was used for a while as the mess for the officers of the Duke of Wellington, whose portrait hangs above the fireplace, alongside neat prints of Guardsmen through the ages. The bar is tiny (some might say cramped), but you should be able to plonk yourself on one of the stools or wooden benches, as despite the charms of this engaging little pub it rarely gets crowded. Friendly staff serve well kept Courage Best, Theakstons Best and two regularly changing guests from handpumps at the rare pewter-topped bar counter – or can shake you a splendid bloody mary from the long-kept-secret recipe. Bar food runs from bowls of chips and nachos (very popular with after work drinkers), through hot steak sandwiches (£4) and burgers (£5); shortly before we went to press they started doing a Sunday roast (£11.95). The intimate back restaurant is quite pricy, but good for a romantic dinner. There's a single bench outside in the peaceful mews, from where on a sunny summer evening it's lovely watching the slowly darkening sky, idly dreaming you might one day be able to afford one of the smart little houses opposite. *(Recommended by Stephen and Brenda Head, Tom McLean, Roger Huggins, Dave Irving, Ewan McCall, Gordon, Thomas, Suzanne and Therese Schulz, M J Dowdy, Ian Phillips, Richard Gibbs, David Carr, P Williamson, Ted George, Scott and Patti Frazier, Steve Harvey, Peter Plumridge)*

S & N ~ Managers Paul and Alexandra Gibb ~ Real ale ~ Meals and snacks (12-2.30, 6-10) ~ Restaurant ~ 0171-235 3074 ~ Children in restaurant ~ Open 12-11(10.30 Sun); closed 25 Dec

Jerusalem Tavern 🍺 (City) Map 13

55 Britton St, EC1; ● Farringdon

This carefully restored old coffee house is one of only four pubs belonging to the newish small Suffolk-based St Peters Brewery. It's a vivid recreation of an 18th-c tavern, and the architect has clearly done his homework; darkly atmospheric and characterful, it seems so genuinely old that you'd never guess the work was done little more than a year ago. There's been a pub of this name around here for quite some time, though the current building was developed around 1720, originally as a merchant's house, then becoming a clock and watchmaker's. It still has the shop front added in 1810, immediately behind which is a light little room with a couple of wooden tables and benches, a stack of *Country Life* magazines, and some remarkable old tiles on the walls at either side. This leads into the tiny dimly lit bar, from where the rather tasty St Peters Best, Extra, Fruit Beer, Golden Ale, Mild, Strong and Wheat beers are tapped from casks behind the little counter. There are a couple of unpretentious tables on the bare boards, with another up some stairs on a discreetly precarious balcony. The atmosphere is relaxed and quietly chatty, with quite a few of the customers on our inspection visit happy to stow their coats and bags on bannisters slightly away from their own tables. A plainer back room has a few more tables, as well as a fireplace and a stuffed fox in a case. Blackboards list the simple but well liked food: soup (£3), unusual sandwiches such as salami and red onion (£3.95), locally made sausages such as venison and red wine or lamb and mint (£4.25), spaghetti bolognese or vegetable kiev (£4.95), and carrot cake (£3); they open at 9 am for breakfasts and coffee. A couple of tables outside overlook the quiet street. St Peters has another pub at Wingfield (see Suffolk main entries), with others at Brome and Rickinghall there, and more planned for London. *(Recommended by Simon Allen, John Murphy, Sue Demont, Tim Barrow)*

St Peters ~ Manager Mike Robinson ~ Real ale ~ Meals and snacks (9am-9.15pm) ~ 0171-490 4281 ~ Children welcome in front bar ~ Open 9am-11pm Mon-Fri, 9-3 Sat; closed Sun

Lamb ★ ◖ (Bloomsbury) Map 13

94 Lamb's Conduit Street, WC1; ✚ Holborn

Quite a few of our London readers tell us that wherever their evening starts they always seem to end up at this old favourite, and indeed this year we were intriguingly assured by one couple that they find its delights undimmed 'even after a row'. It's famous for its cut-glass swivelling 'snob-screens' all the way around the U-shaped bar counter, but sepia photographs of 1890s actresses on the ochre panelled walls and traditional cast-iron-framed tables with neat brass rails around the rim very much add to the overall effect. Decimal currency doesn't quite fit in, and when you come out you almost expect the streets to be dark and foggy and illuminated by gas lamps. Consistently well kept Youngs Bitter, Special and seasonal brews on handpump, and around 40 different malt whiskies; prompt friendly service, and a good mix of customers. They now do bar food pretty much right through the day, with sandwiches and ploughman's, steak and ale pie (£3.95), vegetable cannelloni, lamb kebabs (£4.50) and a couple of daily specials such as chicken and sweetcorn in cider pie or stuffed lambs' hearts in three-mustard sauce (£3.95); on Sunday lunchtimes the choice is limited to their popular Sunday roast (£4.95). There are slatted wooden seats in a little courtyard beyond the quiet room down a couple of steps at the back; dominoes, cribbage, backgammon. No machines or music. A snug room at the back on the right is no smoking. It can get very crowded, especially in the evenings. *(Recommended by Mark Baynham, Rachael Ward, Nigel Williamson, Ian Phillips, Stephen and Jean Curtis, Richard Lewis, Alice Ridgway, David Carr, Roger and Pauline Pearce, Paul Byatt, Gordon)*

Youngs ~ Manager Richard Whyte ~ Real ale ~ Meals and snacks (not betwuen 3.30 and 7 Sun; limited choice Sun lunch) ~ 0171-405 0713 ~ Children in eating area till 7pm ~ Open 11-11; 12-10.30 Sun; closed evening 25 Dec

Lamb & Flag ◖ (Covent Garden) Map 13

33 Rose Street, WC2; off Garrick Street; ✚ Leicester Square

Much the nicest pub around Covent Garden, this hasn't really changed since Dickens described the Middle Temple lawyers who frequented it when he was working in nearby Catherine Street. It's a well liked place for Londoners to meet after work, and even in winter you'll find plenty of people drinking and chatting in the little alleyways outside. The busy low-ceilinged back bar has high-backed black settles and an open fire, and in Regency days was known as the Bucket of Blood from the bare-knuckle prize-fights held here. It fills up quite quickly, though you might be able to find a seat in the upstairs Dryden Room. There may be darts in the tiny plain front bar. Well kept Courage Best and Directors, John Smiths and Theakstons XB on handpump, and a good few malt whiskies. Lunchtime bar food includes a choice of several well kept cheeses and pâtés, served with hot bread or french bread, as well as doorstep sandwiches (£3.50), ploughman's (£3.50), and, upstairs, hot dishes like shepherd's pie or bangers and mash (£3.95). It was outside here on a December evening in 1679 that Dryden was nearly killed by a hired gang of thugs; despite several advertisements in newspapers he never found out for sure who was behind the dastardly deed, though the most likely culprit was Charles II's mistress the Duchess of Portsmouth, who suspected him of writing scurrilous verses about her. They still celebrate Dryden Night each year. *(Recommended by Alan and Paula McCully, RWD, Sue Demont, Tim Barrow, Mark Baynham, Rachael Ward, Gordon, P A Legon, David Carr, Mick Hitchman, Val Stevenson, Rob Holmes, RWD, Bob and Maggie Atherton)*

Courage ~ Lease: Terry Archer and Adrian Zimmerman ~ Real ale ~ Lunchtime meals (till 2.30) and snacks (12-4.30); limited Sun ~ (0171) 497 9504 ~ Live jazz Sunday evening ~ Children welcome ~ Open 11-11; 12-10.30 Sun; closed 25 Dec, 1 Jan

Lord Moon of The Mall (Trafalgar Square) Map 13

16 Whitehall, SW1; ⊖ Charing Cross

The back doors of this former bank are now used only in an emergency, but were apparently built as a secret entrance for account holders living in Buckingham Palace (Edward VII had an account here from the age of three). Opening in 1872, it was originally a wing of the rather exclusive Corks, Biddulph and Co, then was a branch of slightly less select Barclays before its conversion by Wetherspoons in 1992. The impressive main room has a very high ceiling and quite an elegant feel to it, with smart old prints and a huge painting that seems to show a well-to-do 18th-c gentlemen; in fact it's Tim Martin, the founder of the Wetherspoons chain, who's also immortalised as a statue elsewhere in the bar. Big arched windows look out over Whitehall, and there are quite a few seats and tables around the walls. Once through an arch the style is more recognisably Wetherspoons, but slightly classier than usual, with a couple of neatly tiled areas and nicely lit bookshelves opposite the long bar; black and white photographs of nearby sights are accompanied by brief historical notes. The three games machines don't quite fit in. The area at the end by the doors is no smoking. Attractively priced Courage Directors, Fullers London Pride, Theakstons Best and a couple of quickly changing guests such as Charles Wells Bombardier or Smiles on handpump. Bar food, from the standard Wetherspoons menu, is good value and reliable, ranging from soup (£2.10), filled baguettes (from £2.25) and baked potatoes (£2.95) to vegetarian pasta (£4.45), chicken, ham and leek pie (£4.95), salmon in a prawn, tomato, white wine and herb sauce (£5.95), and a couple of daily specials such as spicy bean casserole; Sunday roasts (£4.95). The terms of the licence rule out fried food. Many of central London's highlights are within easy walking distance, making this an ideal pitstop for sightseers and visitors; as you come out of the pub you'll see Nelson's Column immediately to the left, and Big Ben a walk of ten minutes or so to the right. *(Recommended by David Chamberlain, Meg and Colin Hamilton, Sue Demont, Tim Barrow, Helen Pickering, James Owen)*

Free house ~ Manager Diane English ~ Real ale ~ Meals and snacks (till 10) ~ 0171-839 7701 ~ Open 11-11. 12-10.30 Sun

Moon Under Water (Soho) Map 13

Charing Cross Rd, WC2; ⊖ Tottenham Court Rd/Leicester Square

A breathtaking conversion of the old Marquee club, this fiercely modern Wetherspoons pub has been open for only a few months, but has quickly established itself as one of the most popular pubs in this busy part of town. Perhaps the most remarkable thing about it – apart from its size – is the intriguing mix of customers it attracts, from Soho trendies and students to tourists and the local after-work crowd; scarcely a place for a quiet drink, but for people-watching it's hard to beat. The carefully designed main area is what used to be the Marquee's auditorium, now transformed into a cavernous white-painted room stretching far off into the distance, with seats and tables lining the walls, and a few more with high stools dotted about along the way. It effortlessly absorbs the hordes that pour in on Friday and Saturday evenings, and even when it's at its busiest you shouldn't have any problem traversing the room, or have to wait very long to be served at the bar. Good value drinks and food are the same as at other Wetherspoons pubs (see previous entry), and the small seating area upstairs (perfect for looking down on the crowds below) is no smoking. The former stage is the area with the most seats, and like the rest of the pub is now music-free; from here a narrower room leads past another bar and ends up at a back door that opens on to Greek St (quite a surprise, as the complete lack of windows inside means you don't quite realise how far you've gone). Essentially this is a very traditional pub that just happens to have a rather innovative design, so it's worth a look just to see how well the two can be combined; if you find it's not quite your style, at the very least it's a handy shortcut to Soho. In common with other pubs in the area, on particularly busy evenings there might be someone on the main door.

Free house ~ Manager Tadgh O'Shea ~ Real ale ~ Meals and snacks ~ 0171-287 6039 ~ Open 11-11; 12-10.30 Sun

Museum Tavern ◗ (Bloomsbury) Map 13

Museum Street, WC1; ◗ Holborn or Tottenham Court Rd

J B Priestley claimed that the only thing necessary to make him more of a British Museum man was a room with fewer exhibits, an easy chair, and encouragement to smoke, so one hopes that he was a regular visitor to this old-fashioned little pub across the road, which seems to meet most of his requirements. Its proximity to the museum perhaps accounts for the civilised air you might find in quiet moments (late afternoon, say), and certainly explains why lunchtime tables can be hard to come by, but unlike most other pubs in the area it generally stays pleasantly uncrowded in the evenings. Karl Marx is fondly supposed to have had the odd glass here, and it's tempting to think that the chap at the next table scribbling furiously into a notebook is working on a similarly seminal set of ideas. The single room is simply furnished and decorated, with high-backed benches around traditional cast-iron pub tables, and old advertising mirrors between the wooden pillars behind the bar. There's a good range of well kept beers on handpump, usually taking in Courage Best and Directors, Theakstons Best, XB and Old Peculier, and a couple of guests such as Waggledance, but even for this area they're not cheap: this is rapidly becoming one of the most expensive pubs in central London. They also have several wines by the glass, a choice of malt whiskies, and tea, coffee, cappuccino and hot chocolate. Available all day from a servery at the end of the room, bar food might include cold pasties, pie or quiche with salads, ploughman's and hot dishes like steak and ale pie (all £5.99). They now do cooked breakfasts (£4.99) most mornings from 9.30. It gets a little smoky when busy; fruit machine. There are a couple of tables outside under the gas lamps and 'Egyptian' inn sign. *(Recommended by Mike Gorton, Sue Demont, Tim Barrow, Gordon, Jens Arne Grebstad, Steve Harvey, Mick Hitchman, Hanns P Golez, Hugh MacLean, David Carr)*

Scottish Courage ~ Manager Lachlan Mackay ~ Real ale ~ Meals (11-10) ~ 0171-242 8987 ~ Children in eating area ~ Open 11-11; 12-10.30 Sun; closed 25/26 Dec, 1 Jan

Nags Head ◗ (Belgravia) Map 13

53 Kinnerton St, SW1; ◗ Knightsbridge

As unspoilt a pub as you'll ever come across in central London, this snug little gem is the kind of place where they greet you when you come in and say goodbye as you leave – not exactly the norm in this neck of the woods. Hidden away in an attractive and peaceful mews, it's one of those pubs that claims to be the capital's smallest, though despite being so handy for Harrods it really doesn't feel like London at all; you could be forgiven for thinking you'd been transported to an old-fashioned local somewhere in a sleepy country village, right down to the friendly regulars chatting around the unusual sunken bar counter. Cosy, homely and warmly traditional, it's rarely busy, even at weekends, and the atmosphere is always relaxed and welcoming. The small, panelled and low-ceilinged front area has a wood-effect gas fire in an old cooking range (seats by here are generally snapped up pretty quickly), and a narrow passage leads down steps to an even smaller back bar with stools and a mix of comfortable seats. There's a 1930s What-the-butler-saw machine and a one-armed bandit that takes old pennies, as well as rather individual piped music, generally jazz, folk or show tunes. The well kept Adnams and Tetleys are pulled on attractive 19th-c china, pewter and brass handpumps. Decent food includes sandwiches (from £3), ploughman's or plenty of salads (from £4.25), real-ale sausage, mash and beans, chilli, or sweet and sour pork (all £4.65) and specials like roasts or cod mornay; there's a £1 service charge added to all dishes in the evenings. There are a few seats and a couple of tables outside. *(Recommended by Pete Baker, M J Dowdy, Bob and Maggie Atherton, C Smith, James Nunns, B J Harding, Gordon, Peter Plumridge, Dave Irving, Roger Huggins, Ewan McCall, Tom McLean, Steve Harvey, Hanns P Golez, Virginia Jones, Hugh MacLean, Wayne Brindle, David Carr)*

Free house ~ Licensee Kevin Moran ~ Real ale ~ Meals and snacks (12-9.30) ~ 0171-235 1135 ~ Children in eating area ~ Open 11-11; 12-10.30 Sun

Old Bank of England ♀ (City) Map 13

194 Fleet St, EC4; ⊖ Temple

Easy to spot in winter by the Olympic-style torches blazing outside, this splendidly converted rather austere Italianate building was until the mid-1970s a subsidiary branch of the Bank of England built to service the nearby Law Courts; it was then a building society until transformed into a pub by Fullers in 1995. The opulent bar never fails to impress first and even second-time visitors: three gleaming chandeliers hang from the exquisitely plastered ceiling high above the unusually tall island bar counter, and the green walls are liberally dotted with old prints, framed bank notes and the like. Though the room is quite spacious, screens between some of the varied seats and tables create a surprisingly intimate feel, and there are several cosier areas at the end, with more seats in a galleried section upstairs. The mural that covers most of the end wall looks like an 18th-c depiction of justice, but in fact was commissioned specially for the pub and features members of the Fuller, Smith and Turner families. Fullers Chiswick, ESB and London Pride on handpump (the first of these very nicely priced for the area), along with a monthly changing guest like Marstons Pedigree, freshly squeezed orange juice, and around 20 wines by the glass. Bar food includes sandwiches (from £2.85), ploughman's (£3.95), sausages and mash (£4.95), a vegetarian dish, specials like poached salmon, and several pies like chicken and bacon or lamb and rosemary (£5.35); they do cream teas in the afternoon. Efficient service from smartly uniformed staff. The entrance is up a flight of stone steps. Note they don't allow children. Pies have a long if rather dubious pedigree in this area; it was in the tunnels and vaults below the Old Bank and the surrounding buildings that Sweeney Todd butchered the clients destined to provide the fillings in his mistress Mrs Lovett's nearby pie shop. *(Recommended by Tony Scott, Simon Walker, Richard Gibbs, Mark Brock, Chris Westmoreland)*

Fullers ~ Manager Peter Biddle ~ Real ale ~ Meals and snacks (12-8) ~ Restaurant ~ 0171-430 2255 ~ Open 11-11; closed all day weekends and bank holidays

Old Coffee House (Soho) Map 13

49 Beak Street, W1; ⊖ Oxford Circus

Useful to know about for a decent well priced lunch, this friendly little pub was one of the first in London to pile itself high with bric-a-brac – not the boring bought-in bits that seem to come with the fixtures in so many places these days, but an intriguing jumble of nostalgic ephemera that all but fills the busy downstairs bar. The best time to see it properly is on a quiet lunchtime (it's generally so popular in the evenings you won't get an unbroken view), when you might find yourself sitting beside or under a stuffed pike or fox, a great brass bowl or bucket, or maybe one of the ancient musical instruments (brass and string sections both well represented). On the walls are a good collection of Great War recruiting posters, golden discs, death-of-Nelson prints, theatre and cinema handbills, old banknotes and so forth – and there's even a nude in one corner (this is Soho, after all). Upstairs, the food room has as many prints and pictures as a Victorian study. Bar food isn't especially unusual, but is good value, and there's a wider choice than you'll find in most other pubs in the area, including filled baked potatoes (from £2.25), burgers (£3), various platters (£4), quite a few hot dishes like chicken, ham and leek pie, macaroni cheese, chilli, lasagne, tuna and pasta bake, or winter stews and casseroles (all £4), and puddings like treacle sponge or rhubarb and custard flan (£1.75). Well kept Courage Best and Directors and Marstons Pedigree on handpump; helpful service, fruit machine, piped music. *(Recommended by Jill Bickerton, Virginia Jones, David Carr, Wayne Brindle, Ian Phillips)*

Courage ~ Lease: Barry Hawkins ~ Real ale ~ Lunchtime meals and snacks (12-3; evenings and Sun toasted sandwiches only) ~ (0171) 437 2197 ~ Children in upstairs food room 12-3pm ~ Open 11-11; 12-3, 7-10.30 Sun

Olde Cheshire Cheese (City) Map 13

Wine Office Court; off 145 Fleet Street, EC4; ⊖ Blackfriars

Though this 17th-c former chop house is one of London's most famous old pubs, it's remarkably untouristy. Over the years Congreve, Pope, Voltaire, Thackeray, Dickens, Conan Doyle, Yeats and perhaps Dr Johnson have visited its unpretentious little rooms, a couple of them probably coming across the famous parrot that for over 40 years entertained princes, ambassadors, and other distinguished guests. When she died in 1926 the news was broadcast on the BBC and obituary notices appeared in 200 newspapers all over the world; she's still around today, stuffed and silent. Up and down stairs, the profusion of little bars and rooms have bare wooden benches built in to the walls, sawdust on bare boards, and on the ground floor high beams, crackly old black varnish, Victorian paintings on the dark brown walls, and a big open fire in winter. Surprisingly untouristy, it's been extended in a similar style towards Fleet St. Lunchtime bar food includes sandwiches, filled jacket potatoes (£2.95), and ploughman's (£3.95), and several weekly changing hot dishes such as steak, ale and vegetable pie, chicken korma, or vegetarian quiche (around £4.25). Well kept (and, as usual for this brewery, well priced) Sam Smiths OB on handpump, friendly service. Some of the Cellar bar is no smoking at lunchtimes. *(Recommended by Richard Fallon, Gordon, Tony Scott, Graham and Karen Oddey, RWD, Chris Westmoreland, Mark Baynham, Rachael Ward, David Carr)*

Sam Smiths ~ Licensee Gordon Garrity ~ Real ale ~ Lunchtime meals and snacks (not weekends) ~ Two evening restaurants (not Sun) ~ 0171-353 6170 ~ Children in eating area of bar and restaurant ~ Open 11.30-11; 12-5 Sun; closed Sun evening and bank holidays

Olde Mitre £ (City) Map 13

Ely Place, EC1; there's also an entrance beside 8 Hatton Garden; ⊖ Chancery Lane

Another of London's most special pubs, this quaint little place is so hidden away you're always surprised to find so many other visitors enjoying its charms. In addition to the character and history, what draws people back is the exceptional service and welcome; the landlord clearly loves his job, and works hard to pass that enjoyment on to his customers. On the edge of the City, the carefully rebuilt tavern carries the name of an earlier inn built here in 1547 to serve the people working in the nearby palace of the Bishops of Ely. The dark panelled small rooms have antique settles and – particularly in the back room, where there are more seats – old local pictures and so forth. An upstairs room, mainly used for functions, may double as an overflow at peak periods; on weekdays, the pub is good-naturedly packed between 12.30 and 2.15, with an interesting mix of customers. It fills up again in the early evening, but by around nine becomes a good deal more tranquil. Popular bar snacks include really good value sandwiches such as ham, salmon and cucumber or egg mayonnaise (£1, including toasted), as well as pork pies or scotch eggs (75p). Well kept Friary Meux, Ind Coope Burton and Tetleys on handpump; notably chatty staff; darts. There are some seats with pot plants and jasmine in the narrow yard between the pub and St Ethelreda's church. The iron gates that guard Ely Place are a reminder of the days when the law in this distrit was administered by the Bishops of Ely; even today it's still technically part of Cambridgeshire. *(Recommended by Gordon, Tony Scott, Rachael Ward, Mark Baynham, Tim Heywood, Sophie Wilne, R J Bland, Mayur Shah, John Fazakerley, Chris Westmoreland, David Carr, Christopher Gallop)*

Allied ~ Manager Don O'Sullivan ~ Real ale ~ Snacks (11-10) ~ 0171-405 4751 ~ Open 11-11; closed weekends and bank holidays

Orange Brewery ◖ (Pimlico) Map 13

37 Pimlico Road, SW1; ⊖ Sloane Square

Every week this lively and friendly pub produces over 500 gallons of their popular ales – SW1, a stronger SW2, a seasonal Porter, and Victoria lager. They may also have a couple of guest beers, and some bottled Trappist beers. Bar food is often built around the beers too, with dishes such as sausages with beer and onion gravy (£3.25) or beef and beer pie flavoured with their SW2; they also do sandwiches (£2.30), ploughman's, and fish and chips (£5.25). Refurbishments in recent years have perhaps left the pub's appearance slightly less distinctive, but above the simple wooden chairs, tables and panelling you'll still find examples of vintage brewing equipment and related bric-a-brac, and there's a nicely tiled fireplace; fruit machine, piped music. A viewing area looks down into the brewery, and you can book tours for a closer look. Some readers feel it's like a posh version of a Firkin pub, and it's after-work appeal is such that there may be times when it's hard to find anywhere to sit; a few seats outside face a little concreted-over green beyond the quite busy street. *(Recommended by Stephen Holman, Gordon, Eddy and Emma Gibson, Dr S P Willavoys, Susan and John Douglas, David Carr, Val Stevenson, Rob Holmes, Frank W Gadbois, Richard Lewis, Mark Baynham, Rachael Ward, Tom McLean, Ewan McCall, Dave Irving, Roger Huggins)*

Own brew (though tied to S & N) ~ Manager Billy Glass ~ Real ale ~ Meals and snacks (12-11; limited choice Sun) ~ 0171-730 5984 ~ Children welcome ~ Open 11-11; 12-10.30 Sun

Princess Louise ◖ (Holborn) Map 13

208 High Holborn, WC1; ⊖ Holborn

The range of well kept real ales is one of the things that draws the crowds to this old-fashioned gin-palace, but it's the vibrant atmosphere and relaxed and cheery bustle that's made it such a favourite with so many readers. Many comment on the way it's managed to keep its genuine period appeal intact; even the gents' has its own preservation order. The elaborate decor includes etched and gilt mirrors, brightly coloured and fruity-shaped tiles, and slender Portland stone columns soaring towards the lofty and deeply moulded crimson and gold plaster ceiling. Quieter corners have comfortable green plush seats and banquettes. The long main bar usually offers around 10 regularly changing beers including Adnams, Brakspears PA, Gales HSB, Greene King IPA and Abbot, Youngs, a beer named for them by Bass, and maybe a couple of more unusual guests; also several wines by the glass – including champagne. Neat, quick staff. They do good big sandwiches (from £1.95) just about all day. Fruit machine. On weekday lunchtimes the quieter upstairs bar has very good authentic Thai meals (quite a draw in themselves). Though it does get crowded during the week, it's usually quieter later on in the evening, or on a Saturday lunchtime. *(Recommended by Michael Sandy, Gordon, Simon Penny, Eric and Jackie Robinson, David Carr, James Macrae, Wayne Brindle, Chris Westmoreland, Steve Harvey, E A Thwaite)*

Free house ~ Licensee David Tracey ~ Real ale ~ Snacks and weekday lunchtime meals ~ 0171-405 8816 ~ Open 11-11; 12-3, 6-11 Sat; closed Sun and 25/26 Dec

Red Lion ◖ (Mayfair) Map 13

Waverton Street, W1; ⊖ Green Park

In one of Mayfair's quietest and prettiest corners, this civilised place has something of the atmosphere of a smart country pub; only the presence of so many suited workers reminds you of its true location. The main L-shaped bar has small winged settles on the partly carpeted scrubbed floorboards, and London prints below the high shelf of china on its dark-panelled walls. A good range of well kept beers includes Courage Best and Directors, Fullers London Pride, Greene King Abbot, and Theakstons Best on handpump, and they do rather good bloody marys (though we've yet to hear from anyone who's braved the Very Spicy option); also a choice of malt whiskies. Bar food, served from a corner at the front, includes sandwiches (from £2.50), cumberland sausage (£4.75), cod and chips or half rack of ribs with barbecue sauce (£6.95) and a couple of daily specials (£5). Unusually for this area, they serve food morning and evening seven days a week. It can get crowded at lunchtime, and immediately after work. The gents' has a copy of the day's *Financial Times* at eye level. *(Recommended by Gordon, Christopher Wright, Mike and Karen England, Mark Walker, P R Morley, Hugh MacLean)*

S & N ~ Manager Greg Peck ~ Real ale ~ Meals and snacks ~ Restaurant ~ 0171-499 1307 ~ Children welcome ~ Open 11.30-11 weekdays; 11-3, 6-11 Sat; 12-3, 7-11 Sun; closed 25 Dec, 1 Jan

Seven Stars £ (City) Map 13

53 Carey St, WC2; ❷ Holborn (just as handy from Temple or Chancery Lane, but the walk through Lincoln's Inn Fields can be rather pleasant)

Though this tranquil little gem faces the back of the Law Courts, it attracts a far wider range of customers than the barristers and legal folk you might expect. We're not using the word little lightly – it's hard to tell whether it's mild temperatures that lead people to stand in the peaceful street outside, or the lack of space inside. The door, underneath a profusion of hanging baskets, is helpfully marked General Counter, as though you couldn't see that the simple counter is pretty much all there is in the tiny old-fashioned bar beyond. Lots of caricatures of barristers and other legal-themed prints on the walls, and quite a collection of toby jugs, some in a display case, the rest mixed up with the drinks behind the bar. Friendly chatty licensees, Courage Best and Directors on handpump, several malt whiskies, and very good value bar snacks such as sandwiches (£1.50), pork pies and sausages, with maybe a couple of hot dishes like lamb curry, goulash or cottage pie (£2.95); you'll probably have to eat standing up – the solitary table and stools are on the left as you go in. A cosy room on the right appears bigger than it is because of its similar lack of furnishings; there are shelves round the walls for drinks or leaning against. Stairs up to the lavatories are very steep – a sign warns that you climb them at your own risk. *(Recommended by Tony Hobden, Gordon, Thomas Nott, Richard Davies, Chris Westmoreland)*

Courage ~ Lease: Geoff and Majella Turner ~ Real ale ~ Snacks (all day) ~ 0171-242 8521 ~ Open 11-10 weekdays only, may close earlier if not busy; closed weekends except Sat of Lord Mayor's Show

Star ◖ (Belgravia) Map 13

Belgrave Mews West – behind the German Embassy, off Belgrave Sq; ❷ Knightsbridge

London cabbies can give the impression they've seen and done it all, so when a pair of readers arriving at this warmly traditional place by taxi heard their driver enthusing about the flowering tubs and hanging baskets outside, they knew it was high praise indeed. Though it can get busy at lunchtime and on some evenings, it's another of those places that seems distinctly un-London, and there's a pleasantly quiet and restful local feel outside peak times. As another correspondent memorably put it, it's the sort of pub you might see in an old black and white film. Service is obliging and helpful; they're quite happy being flexible with the menu or providing something slightly different if they can. The small entry room, which also has the food servery, has stools by the counter and tall windows; an arch leads to a side room with swagged curtains, lots of dark mahogany, stripped mahogany chairs and tables, heavy upholstered settles, globe lighting and raj fans. The back room has button-back built-in wall seats, and there's a cosy room upstairs. Good value bar food might include sandwiches (from £1.80), ploughman's or sausage, chips and beans (£3.50), beef in beer (£3.80) and evening dishes such as gammon and egg or barbecue chicken (£5), and very well liked steaks (£6.50); they do sandwiches on Saturdays, but otherwise there's no food at weekends. Very well kept Fullers Chiswick, ESB and London Pride – the first at a particularly nice price for this part of town. *(Recommended by Bob and Maggie Atherton, Mr and Mrs Jon Corelis, Gordon, M J Dowdy, Mark Baynham, Rachael Ward, E A Thwaite, Jasper Sabey, Wayne Brindle, John Fazakerley, M L and G Clarke, Virginia Jones)*

Fullers ~ Managers Bruce and Kathleen Taylor ~ Real ale ~ Meals and snacks (not Sat or Sun) ~ 0171-235 3019 ~ Children in eating area of bar ~ Open 11.30-3, 6.30-11 Sat; 12-3, 7-10.30 Sun; closed 25/26 Dec

Westminster Arms 🔳 (Westminster) Map 13

Storey's Gate, SW1; ⊖ Westminster

After work this busy Westminster local is usually full of staff and researchers from the Houses of Parliament just across Parliament Square. Many are drawn by the range of real ales, with the choice typically including Bass, Boddingtons, Brakspears PA, Gales IPA, Greene King Abbot, Theakstons Best, Wadworths 6X, Westminster Best brewed for them by Charringtons, and a monthly changing guest; they also do decent wines. Furnishings in the plain main bar are simple and old-fashioned, with proper tables on the wooden floors and a good deal of panelling; there's not a lot of room, and it can get crowded, so come early for a seat. Pleasant, courteous service. Most of the bar food is served in the downstairs wine bar, with some of the tables in cosy booths; typical dishes include filled rolls (from £2.50), salads and ploughman's, lasagne or steak and kidney pie (£5), and fish and chips or scampi (£5.50). Piped music in this area, and in the more formal upstairs restaurant, but not generally in the main bar; fruit machine. There are a couple of tables and seats by the street outside. *(Recommended by James Nunns, Sue Demont, Tim Barrow, Gordon, Dr and Mrs A H Young, Hanns P Golez, Jan and Colin Roe)*

Free house ~ Licensees Gerry and Marie Dolan ~ Real ale ~ Meals and snacks (all day weekdays, till 8 Sat, till 6 Sun) ~ Restaurant (not Sun) ~ 0171-222 8520 ~ Children in restaurant lunchtimes only ~ Open 11-11(8 Sat); 12-10 Sun (6 in winter); closed 25/26 Dec

NORTH LONDON

Parking is not a special problem in this area, unless we say so

Chapel ♀ (Marylebone) Map 13

48 Chapel St, NW1; ⊖ Edgware Rd

We had a letter this year from someone lucky enough to live next to this attractively refurbished and very cosmopolitan pub; as he says, the food would put quite a few restaurants to shame. It's particularly relaxed and civilised at lunchtimes, especially in summer, when tables on the sheltered terrace outside can be busy with chic, suited creative folk enjoying a break. Light and spacious, the cream-painted main room is dominated by the open kitchen, which produces unusual soups such as lemon and courgette, and generously served dishes like smoked salmon and artichoke roulade or goat's cheese tomato galette with basil dressing (£4.50), chargrilled beef or lamb steak (£7.50), baked seabass fillets with spinach and saffron butter sauce (£9), and puddings including an excellent tarte tatin. Prompt and efficient service from helpful staff, who may bring warm walnut bread to your table while you're waiting. Furnishings are smart but simple; there are plenty of wooden tables around the bar, with more in a side room with a big fireplace. One of these has newspapers to read, and the pictures on the walls are all for sale; soft piped music. At lunchtime most people come to eat (it fills up quite quickly then, though you can book), but in the evening trade is usually more evenly split between diners and drinkers. Fullers London Pride and Greene King Abbot on handpump, a good range of interesting wines (up to half by the glass), well liked cappuccino and espresso, and a choice of teas such as peppermint or strawberry and vanilla. The Chapel is among the best of several recent conversions rather reminiscent of the Eagle (see above), and is in similarly incongruous surroundings. *(Recommended by Nick Rose, Sebastian Leach, Charlie Ballantyne, Sue Demont, Tim Barrow, Paris Hills-Wright, Kim Inglis, C Leach)*

Bass ~ Lease: Lakis Hondrogiannis ~ Real ale ~ Meals ~ 0171-402 9220 ~ Children welcome ~ Open 12-11; 12-4, 7-10.30 Sun

Flask ♀ (Hampstead) Map 12

14 Flask Walk, NW3; ⊖ Hampstead

Just round the corner from the Tube, but miles away in spirit, this civilised old local is a popular haunt of Hampstead artists and actors, much as it has been for the last 300 years. The snuggest and most individual part is the cosy lounge at the front, with plush green seats and banquettes curving round the panelled walls, a unique Victorian screen dividing it from the public bar, an attractive fireplace, and a very laid-back and rather villagey atmosphere. A comfortable orange-lit room with period prints and a few further tables leads into a much more recent but rather smart dining conservatory, which with its plants, prominent wine bottles and neat table linen feels a bit like a wine bar. A couple of white iron tables are squeezed into a tiny back yard. Unusual and good value daily changing bar food might include sandwiches, fresh fish and home-made chips (£3.50), pasta with asparagus and aioli (£3.70), mushroom and leek risotto with pine nūts (£3.50), fillet of beef in black bean sauce (£3.90), and cajun chicken fillet (£4.50). Well kept Youngs Bitter, Special and seasonal brews on handpump, around 20 wines by the glass, and decent coffees; a big german shepherd dog occasionally puts in an appearance. A plainer public bar (which you can only get into from the street) has leatherette seating, lots of space for darts, fruit machine, trivia, and Sky TV, and cribbage and backgammon. A notice board has the latest news of their darts and cricket teams. There are a few tables outside in the alley. The pub's name is a reminder of the days when it was a distributor of the mineral water from Hampstead's springs. *(Recommended by Mr and Mrs Jon Corelis, Pete Baker, Gordon)*

Youngs ~ Manager J T Orr ~ Real ale ~ Meals and snacks (12-3, 6-9; not evenings Sun or Mon) ~ 0171-435 4580 ~ Children in eating area till 9pm ~ Open 11-11; 12-10.30 Sun

Holly Bush (Hampstead) Map 12

Holly Mount, NW3; ⊖ Hampstead

A cheery old local where readers immediately feel at home even if they only have time for half a pint, this friendly pub has quite a range of evening entertainments: jazz on Sundays, a guitarist on Wednesdays, folk on Thursdays, and their very popular informal poetry reading on Tuesdays. In the last year they've had a wider range of guest beers than before, with brews like Batemans XB joining the regular Benskins, Ind Coope Burton and Tetleys on handpump. Real Edwardian gas lamps light the atmospheric front bar, there's a dark sagging ceiling, brown and cream panelled walls (decorated with old advertisements and a few hanging plates), open fires, and cosy bays formed by partly glazed partitions. Slightly more intimate, the back room, named after the painter George Romney, has an embossed red ceiling, panelled and etched glass alcoves, and ochre-painted brick walls covered with small prints and plates. During the week bar food includes toasted sandwiches (from £1.90), filled baguettes (from £2.25), a choice of ploughman's (£3.25), and a daily special like pasta or shepherd's pie (around £4.50), with maybe home-made scouse at winter weekends (the cheery licensees are from Liverpool), and traditional Sunday roasts (£5); though they don't do meals in the evening, it's the kind of place where they'll happily rustle up a pizza or something like that. Darts, shove-ha'penny, cribbage, dominoes, fruit machine, and video game. The walk up to the pub from the tube station is delightful, along some of Hampstead's most villagey streets and past several of its more enviable properties; London seems so far away you'd hardly think you were so close to Hampstead High Street. *(Recommended by Tom McLean, Mr and Mrs Jon Corelis, Gordon, Hugh MacLean, Mick Hitchman, Mark Baynham, Rachael Ward, Christopher Wright)*

*Taylor-Walker (Allied) ~ Manager Peter Dures ~ Real ale ~ Snacks and lunchtime
meals ~ 0171-435 2892 ~ Children in coffee bar till 9 ~ Live entertainment four
evenings a week ~ Nearby parking sometimes quite a squeeze ~ Open 12-3, 5.30-11;
12-11 Sat; 12-10.30 Sun; closed evening 25 Dec*

Olde White Bear (Hampstead) Map 12

Well Road, NW3; ⊖ Hampstead

Quite a few readers go out of their way to visit this villagey and almost clubby neo-
Victorian pub; in part that's because the beer prices are a refreshing change from the
London norm, but it's mainly thanks to the way they pull off the rare trick of making
all sorts of different types of people feel at home. Next to the smart mother fussing
over her student daughter you might find a builder with holes in his jumper and
cement-encrusted boots, what could be the local bank manager, or maybe an elderly
gentleman carefully rolling his cigarettes from a rusty old tin. Friendly and traditional,
the dimly-lit main room has lots of Victorian prints and cartoons on the walls, as well
as wooden stools, cushioned captain's chairs, a couple of big tasselled armed chairs, a
flowery sofa, handsome fireplace and an ornate Edwardian sideboard. A similarly-lit
small central room has Lloyd Loom furniture, dried flower arrangements and signed
photographs of actors and playwrights. In the brighter end room there are elaborate
cushioned machine tapestried pews, and dark brown paisley curtains. The very good
range of beers on handpump usually includes Adnams, Greene King Abbot, Morlands
Old Speckled Hen, Tetleys, Wadworths 6X and Youngs, with the cheapest of these
priced at £1.40 a pint as we went to press, practically a giveaway in this part of the
world. They also have 18 or so malt whiskies, and maybe winter mulled wine. Good
bar food includes filled baguettes or baked potatoes (£2.25), lasagne or ploughman's
(£3.95), cajun chicken (£4.95), sirloin steak (£5.95), and in summer the popular Greek
platter – a huge salad with olives, dips, pitta bread and feta cheese (£4.95); Sunday
roast (£4.50). Darts, cribbage, shove ha'penny, dominoes, fruit machine, piped music.
Note they don't allow children inside, and parking may be a problem – it's mostly
residents' permits only nearby. *(Recommended by Tom McLean, Gordon, Ian Phillips, R
Sheard)*

*Allied ~ Lease: Peter and Peggy Reynolds ~ Real ale ~ Lunchtime meals and snacks
(12-3) ~ 0171-435 3758 ~ Open 11-11; 12-10.30 Sun*

Spaniards Inn 🍷 (Hampstead) Map 12

Spaniards Lane, NW3; ⊖ Hampstead, but some distance away; or from Golders Green
station take 220 bus

Jutting out into the road like King Canute holding back the tide of traffic, this
comfortable and authentically old-fashioned former toll-house is named after the
Spanish ambassador to the court of James I, who is said to have lived here. The low-
ceilinged oak-panelled rooms of the attractive main bar have open fires, genuinely
antique winged settles, candle-shaped lamps in pink shades, and snug little alcoves.
Behind is a very nice sheltered garden, with slatted wooden tables and chairs on a
crazy-paved terrace opening on to a flagstoned walk around a small lawn, with roses,
a side arbour of wisteria and clematis, and an aviary. Daily changing bar food might
include stilton ploughman's (£3.95), home-made quiche or asparagus and leek
fricassee (£5.25), lamb moussaka (£5.75), beef and Guinness pie (£5.95), and evening
steaks (£8.95); the food bar is no smoking. A quieter upstairs bar may be open at busy
times. Well kept Bass, Fullers London Pride, Hancocks BB and a guest like Adnams
Extra on handpump; piped classical music, fruit machine, trivia. Some readers feel the
staff can be a little too keen to whisk away plates and glasses. The pub is very handy
for Kenwood, and indeed during the 1780 Gordon Riots the then landlord helped save
the house from possible disaster, cunningly giving so much free drink to the mob on its
way to burn it down that by the time the Horse Guards arrived the rioters were lying
drunk and incapable on the floor. Dogs welcome. *(Recommended by Richard Fallon, Mr
and Mrs Jon Corelis, Gordon, Michael and Hazel Lyons, Ian Phillips, JSMS)*

Charringtons (Bass) ~ Manager D E Roper ~ Real ale ~ Meals and snacks (12-9.30) ~ 0181-455 3276 ~ Children in eating area of bar, upstairs room, and various small snug areas ~ Open 11-11; 12-10.30 Sun

Waterside   (King's Cross) Map 13

82 York Way, N1; ⊖ King's Cross

With an unexpectedly calm outside terrace overlooking the Battlebridge Basin, this friendly little oasis is all the more rewarding considering the fact that King's Cross isn't exactly what you'd call an appealing area for visitors. The building really isn't very old but it's done out in firmly traditional style, with stripped brickwork, latticed windows, genuinely old stripped timbers in white plaster, lots of dimly lit alcoves (one is no smoking), spinning wheels, milkmaid's yokes, and horsebrasses and so on, with plenty of rustic tables and wooden benches. Some of the woodwork was salvaged from a disused mill. Boddingtons, Flowers IPA, Marstons Pedigree and Youngs Special on handpump; pool, pinball, fruit machine, and sometimes loudish juke box. The menu is these days a standard Berni one, with things like sandwiches, soup (£1.35), steak and mushroom pudding (£4.25), vegetable curry (£4.85), barbecue chicken (£5.25), and lots of steaks (from £4.95). There may be barbecues on the terrace on sunny days. No dogs inside. *(Recommended by David Carr, Chris Westmoreland, Graham Tayar, Steve Harvey; more reports please)*

Whitbreads ~ Manager John Keyes ~ Real ale ~ Meals and snacks (12-2.30, 5-8.30) ~ (0171) 837 7118 ~ Children in no-smoking part of eating area till 7pm ~ Open 11-11; 12-10.30 Sun; may be closed 25/26 Dec

SOUTH LONDON

Parking is bad on weekday lunchtimes at the inner city pubs here (SE1), but is usually OK everywhere in the evenings – you may again have a bit of a walk if a good band is on at the Bulls Head in Barnes, or at the Windmill on Clapham Common if it's a fine evening

Alma ♀ (Wandsworth) Map 12

499 York Road, SW18; ⇌ Wandsworth Town

Comfortable and unexpectedly civilised, this stylish local has something of the feel of a french cafe-bar, with an air of chattily relaxed bonhomie. There's a mix of chairs around cast-iron-framed tables, a couple of sofas, lots of ochre and terracotta paintwork, gilded mosaics of the Battle of the Alma, an ornate mahogany chimney-piece and fireplace, bevelled mirrors in a pillared mahogany room divider, and pinball and a fruit machine. The popular but less pubby dining room has a fine turn-of-the-century frieze of swirly nymphs; there's waitress service in here, and you can book a particular table. Even when it's very full with smart young people – which it often is in the evenings – service is careful and efficient. Youngs Bitter, Special and seasonal brews on handpump from the island bar counter, decent house wines (with several by the glass), freshly squeezed orange juice, good coffee, tea or hot chocolate, newspapers out for customers. Unusual and tasty, the good value bar food typically includes sandwiches (from £2), soup (£2.50), croque monsieur (£2.60), mussels with garlic, parsley, cream and Scrumpy Jack cider (£3.20), vegetable cous-cous (£4.50), eggs benedict (£4.95), salmon and cod duo with rocket mash (£6.95), specials like chicken breast with a creamy ginger, coriander and cashew nut sauce, daily fresh fish, and steak (£9.25); the menu may be limited on Sunday lunchtimes. If you're after a quiet drink don't come when there's a rugby match on the television, unless you want a running commentary from the well heeled and voiced young locals. Cribbage, pinball, dominoes, fruit machine. Charge up their 'smart-card' with cash and you can pay with a discount either here or at the management's other pubs, which include the Ship at Wandsworth (see below). Travelling by rail into Waterloo you can see the pub rising above the neighbouring rooftops as you rattle through Wandsworth Town. *(Recommended by Richard Fallon, James Macrae, Richard Gibbs; more reports please)*

Youngs ~ Tenant Charles Gotto ~ Real ale ~ Meals and snacks (12-11) ~ Restaurant ~
0181-870 2537 ~ Children welcome ~ Open 11-11; 12-10.30 Sun; closed 25/26 Dec

Anchor (South Bank) Map 13

34 Park St, Bankside, SE1; Southwark Bridge end; ⊖ London Bridge

A warren of dimly lit little rooms and passageways, this atmospheric riverside spot has
a hard to beat view of the Thames and the City from its busy front terrace. The
current building dates back to about 1750, when it was built to replace an earlier
tavern, possibly the one that Pepys came to during the Great Fire of 1666. 'All over
the Thames with one's face in the wind, you were almost burned with a shower of fire
drops,' he wrote. 'When we could endure no more upon the water, we to a little alehouse on the Bankside and there staid till it was dark almost, and saw the fire grow.'
Inside are creaky boards and beams, black panelling, old-fashioned high-backed
settles, and sturdy leatherette chairs. Even when it's invaded by tourists it's usually
possible to retreat to one of the smaller rooms. Bass, Flowers Original, Greenalls
Original and four rapidly changing guest beers such as Harringtons or Greene Kings
on handpump or tapped from the cask; they also do jugs of pimms and sangria.
Cribbage, dominoes, three fruit machines, and fairly loud piped music. Bar food
includes sandwiches (from £2.95) and salads, winter soup, and five daily changing hot
dishes like steak and kidney pie, vegetable lasagne, or fish and chips (all around
£4.50); they do a Sunday roast in the restaurant. The pub can get smoky, and service
can slow down at busy periods. Tom Cruise enjoys a pint at the Anchor at the end of
the film version of *Mission: Impossible*. Sword dancers were strutting their stuff
outside on our last visit, though thanks in part to the rather aggressive heckling from a
ferocious little dog they didn't stay long. There's an increasing number of satisfying
places to visit nearby; the Clink round the corner is good for history buffs.
(Recommended by Mark Baynham, Rachael Ward, Ian Phillips, Jens Arne Grebstad, GWB, Tim
Barrow, Sue Demont)

Greenalls ~ Licensees Barry and Jane Jackson ~ Real ale ~ Meals and snacks (12-9) ~
Restaurant ~ 0171-407 1577 ~ Children in eating areas and restaurant till 8.30 ~
Open 11-11; 12-10.30 Sun; cl 25 Dec

Bulls Head ♀ £ (Barnes) Map 12

373 Lonsdale Road, SW13; ⇌ Barnes Bridge

The Thameside setting of this imposing pub would be a draw in itself, but what really
draws the crowds is the top-class modern jazz groups that perform every night. You
can hear the music quite clearly from the lounge bar (and on peaceful Sunday
afternoons from the villagey little street as you approach), but for the full effect and
genuine jazz club atmosphere it is worth paying the admission to the well equipped
music room. Back in the bustling bar alcoves open off the main area around the island
servery, which has Youngs Bitter, Special and seasonal beers on handpump, over 80
malt whiskies, and a good range of decent wines. Around the walls are large photos of
the various jazz musicians and bands who have played here; dominoes, cribbage,
Scrabble, chess, cards, and fruit machine in the public bar. All the food is home-made,
including the bread, pasta, sausages and ice cream, and they do things like soup
(£1.80), sandwiches, and pasta, pies, or a popular carvery of home-roasted joints (all
around £3.95); service is efficient and very friendly. Bands play 8.30-11 every night
plus 2-4.30 Sundays, and depending on who's playing prices generally range from
£3.50 to around £6. *(Recommended by Lynda Payton, Sam Samuells, John H L Davis; more*
reports please)

Youngs ~ Tenant Dan Fleming ~ Real ale ~ Meals and snacks ~ Evening restaurant
(not Sun evening, though they do Sun lunch) ~ 0181-876 5241 ~ Children welcome ~
Jazz or blues every night, and Sun afternoon ~ Nearby parking may be difficult ~
Open 11-11; 12-10.30 Sun

Crown & Greyhound (Dulwich) Map 12

73 Dulwich Village, SE21; ⇌ North Dulwich

Readers like the way this grand place caters so well for children, offering Lego and toys as well as children's meals, and never making families feel like second-class citizens. They have baby changing facilities, and an ice-cream stall in the very pleasant big two-level back terrace, which also has a good many picnic tables under a chestnut tree. Inside is imposing and astonishingly spacious – it gets very busy in the evenings but there's enough room to absorb everyone without any difficulty. The most ornate room is on the right, with its elaborate ochre ceiling plasterwork, fancy former gas lamps, Hogarth prints, fine carved and panelled settles and so forth. It opens into the former billiards room, where kitchen tables on a stripped board floor are set for the good bar food. Changing every day (the friendly landlady likes to try out new recipes and ideas), the lunchtime choice might include enormous doorstep sandwiches and toasties, ploughman's, and a range of specials like chicken, leek and mushroom crumble, steak and mushroom pie, vegetable moussaka, smoked haddock and spinach cannelloni, or prawn pilaff (all £5.25). Best to arrive early for their popular Sunday carvery, they don't take bookings. A central snug leads on the other side to the saloon – brown ragged walls, upholstered and panelled settles, a coal-effect gas fire in the tiled period fireplace, and Victorian prints. Well kept Ind Coope Burton and Youngs on handpump, along with a monthly changing guest like Adnams or Greene King Abbot; they have a wine of the month too. Dominoes, fruit machines, trivia, and piped music. Known locally as the Dog, the pub has long-established links with poetry groups (they still have well regarded readings today), and is handy for walks through the park. *(Recommended by Bob and Maggie Atherton, Sue Demont, Tim Barrow, Christopher Gallop)*

Allied ~ Managers Barney and Sandra Maguire ~ Real ale ~ Meals and snacks (12-2.30, 6-10; not Sun evening) ~ Restaurant (not Sun evening) ~ 0181-693 2466 ~ Children in restaurant and no-smoking family room ~ Open 11-11; 12-10.30 Sun; closed evening 25 Dec

Cutty Sark (Greenwich) Map 12

Ballast Quay, off Lassell St, SE10; ⇌ Maze Hill, from London Bridge, or from the river front walk past the Yacht in Crane St and Trinity Hospital

They like to claim that the view of the Thames from this attractive late 16th-c white-painted house is better than at any other pub in London, and it's certainly well in the running. Tables on a waterside terrace across the narrow cobbled lane from the pub are perhaps the nicest place to take it in, but you'll see more from inside through the big upper bow window, itself striking for the way it jetties out over the pavement. Under the new management there have been some changes to the decor, but the atmospheric bar still conjures up images of the kind of London we imagine Dickens once knew, with flagstones, rough brick walls, wooden settles, barrel tables, open fires, low lighting and narrow openings to tiny side snugs. Well kept Bass, Fullers London Pride and three fortnightly changing guests on handpump, a good choice of malt whiskies, and a decent wine list. An elaborate central staircase leads up to an upstairs area; fruit machine, trivia, juke box. Served in a roomy eating area, the popular range of promptly arriving food includes soup (£1.95), filled baguettes (from £2.99), salads (from £3.50), all-day breakfast (£3.95), steak and ale pie (£4.95), lentil crumble or thai vegetable stir-fry (£5), a decent choice of children's meals (£2.50) and daily specials. The pub can be very busy with young people on Friday and Saturday evenings. *(Recommended by Mrs P J Pearce, John Fahy, David Carr, Robert Gomme, RWD, GWB)*

Free house ~ Managers Octavia Gleedwood and David Jackson ~ Real ale ~ Meals and snacks (12-9; 12-7 Sat) ~ 0181-858 3146 ~ Children upstairs till 9pm ~ Various live music Weds eve, quiz night Thurs eve ~ Open 11-11; 12-10.30 Sun

---

Please let us know of any pubs where the wine is particularly good.

Fire Station (Waterloo) Map 13

150 Waterloo Rd, SE1; ✪ Waterloo

A remarkable conversion of the former LCC central fire station, this bustling place is perhaps best known for the imaginative food served from the open kitchen in the back dining room, but the two vibrantly chatty rooms at the front are very popular with people who only want a drink. It's hardly your typical local, but does a number of traditionally pubby things far better than anywhere else nearby, and certainly seems to be the favoured choice for the area's after work drinkers. The decor is something like a cross between a warehouse and a schoolroom, with plenty of wooden pews, chairs and long tables (a few spilling out onto the street outside), some mirrors and rather incongruous pieces of dressers, and brightly red-painted doors, shelves and modern hanging lightshades; the determinedly contemporary art around the walls is for sale, and there's a table with newspapers to read. Well kept Adnams Best, Brakspears, Youngs, and a beer brewed for them by Hancocks on handpump, as well as a number of bottled beers, and a good choice of wines (several by the glass); helpful service. They serve a short range of bar meals between 12.30 and 6, which might include filled baguettes (the hot steak one is £5.25), roasted mediterranean vegetables with pesto (£3.95), mussels and chips (£5.95), half a dozen Irish oysters (£6.50), and maybe a selection of British cheeses, but it's worth paying the extra to eat from the main menu. Changing every lunchtime and evening, this has things like chargrilled smoked cod with parsley mash and tomato and chilli salsa (£9.75), guinea fowl with risotto verde and courgette flowers (£9.95), and puddings such as peach and almond tart with custard sauce (£3.50); they don't take bookings, so there may be a slight wait at busy times. Piped modern jazz and other music fits well into the good-natured hubbub. Those with quieter tastes might find weeknights here a little too hectic – it's quieter at lunchtimes and during the day. *(Recommended by Mark Baynham, Rachael Ward, Sebastian Leach, Paul Hilditch, Stephen Holman, Sue Demont, Tim Barrow, Dr and Mrs A K Clarke)*

Free house ~ Manager Peter Nottage ~ Real ale ~ Snacks (12-30-6.30) and meals ~ Restaurant ~ 0171-401 3267 ~ Children welcome away from bar ~ Open 11-11; 12-5 Sun; closed bank holidays

George ★ 🍺 (Southwark) Map 13

Off 77 Borough High Street, SE1; ✪ Borough or London Bridge

Noted as one of London's 'fair inns for the receipt of travellers' as early as 1598, this splendid-looking 17th-c coaching inn is such a London landmark that it's easy to forget it's still a proper working pub. Rebuilt on its original plan after the great Southwark fire in 1676, it was owned for a while by Guys Hospital next door, and then by the Great Northern Railway Company, under whose stewardship it was 'mercilessly reduced' as E V Lucas put it, when the other wings of the building were demolished. Now preserved by the National Trust, the remaining part is a unique survival, the tiers of open galleries looking down over a cobbled courtyard with plenty of picnic tables, and maybe Morris men in summer. It's just as unspoilt inside, the row of simple ground-floor rooms and bars all containing square-latticed windows, black beams, bare floorboards, some panelling, plain oak or elm tables and old-fashioned built-in settles, along with a 1797 'Act of Parliament' clock, dimpled glass lantern-lamps and so forth. The snuggest refuge is the simple room nearest the street, where there's an ancient beer engine that looks like a cash register. They use this during their regular beer festivals (generally the third week of each month), when they might have around ten unusual real ales available; the ordinary range includes Boddingtons, Flowers Original, Whitbread Castle Eden and a couple of beers brewed for them, Bishops Restoration and St George. Also farm cider, country wines, and mulled wine in winter; bar billiards, darts and trivia. Lunchtime bar food might include club sandwiches (£3), ploughman's (from £4), broccoli lasagne (£4), and chilli or home-made steak and mushroom pie (£4.50). A splendid central staircase goes up to a series of dining rooms and to a gaslit balcony. One room is no smoking. Unless you know where you're going (or you're in one of the many tourist groups that flock here during the day in summer) you may well miss it, as apart from the great gates there's little to indicate that such a gem still exists behind the less auspicious looking buildings on the busy high street. *(Recommended by*

Paul Hilditch, Ian Phillips, Janice Smith, David Carr, William G Hall Jr, Tim Barrow, Sue Demont, Simon Penny, RWD, Mark Baynham, Rachael Ward)

Whitbreads ~ Manager John Hall ~ Real ale ~ Meals and snacks ~ Restaurant (not Sun; often used for groups only – check first) ~ 0171-407 2056 ~ Children in restaurant ~ Nearby daytime parking difficult ~ Folk night first Mon of month (except bank holidays); occasional Morris dancers in summer ~ Open 11-11; 12-10.30 Sun; closed 25/26 Dec, 1 Jan

Horniman (Southwark) Map 13

Hays Galleria, Battlebridge Lane, SE13; ⊖ London Bridge

Wonderful views of the Thames, HMS *Belfast* and Tower Bridge from the picnic tables outside this elaborate pub, like the surrounding area much busier during the day than it is beyond early evening. The spacious and gleaming bar is rather like a cross between a French bistro and a Victorian local – and something else besides. The area by the sweeping bar counter is a few steps down from the door, with squared black, red and white flooring tiles and lots of polished wood. Steps lead up from here to various comfortable carpeted areas, with the tables well spread so as to allow for a feeling of roomy relaxation at quiet times but give space for people standing in groups when it's busy. There's a set of clocks made for tea merchant Frederick Horniman's office showing the time in various places around the world. Bar food includes filling triple-decker sandwiches (from £3.50), ploughman's (£4.50), and daily changing hot dishes like steak and mushroom pie or a couple of vegetarian meals (£5). Well kept Adnams Extra, Fullers London Pride, Morlands Old Speckled Hen, Timothy Taylor Landlord and maybe a couple of other guests on handpump. A tea bar serves tea, coffee, chocolate and other hot drinks, and danish pastries and so forth; a hundred-foot frieze shows the travels of the tea. Fruit machine, trivia, unobtrusive piped music. The pub is at the end of the visually exciting Hays Galleria development, several storeys high, with a soaring glass curved roof, and supported by elegant thin cast-iron columns; various shops and boutiques open off. *(Recommended by Mark Baynham, Rachael Ward, Wayne Brindle, Bob and Maggie Atherton, Niki and Terry Pursey; more reports please)*

Nicholsons (Allied) ~ Manager David Matthews ~ Real ale ~ Lunchtime meals and snacks ~ 0171-401 6811 ~ Children in eating area of bar till 6pm ~ Occasional live entertainment ~ Open 10am-11pm (till 4 weekends); closed 25 Dec, and some evenings Christmas week

Market Porter (Southwark) Map 13

9 Stoney Street, SE1; ⊖ London Bridge

An old tradition has been revived at this busy and pubby place since our last edition, as they're once again open between 6.30 and 8.30 am for market workers and porters (and anyone else who's passing) to enjoy a drink at the start of the day. It's particularly well liked for its range of well kept beers, one of the most varied in London, with up to eight ales on handpump usually including a combination of Bunces Pig Swill, Courage Best and Directors, Fullers London Pride, Gales HSB, Harveys Sussex, Thirsty Willey and Youngs Bitter. The main part of the atmospheric long U-shaped bar has rough wooden ceiling beams with beer barrels balanced on them, a heavy wooden bar counter with a beamed gantry, cushioned bar stools, an open fire with stuffed animals in glass cabinets on the mantelpiece, several mounted stags' heads, and 20s-style wall lamps. Sensibly priced simple bar food includes good sandwiches (from £1.95), ploughman's (from £3.75), vegetarian dishes like ratatouille suet pudding, burgers or all-day breakfast (£3.95), steaks (from £5.75), and changing daily specials; Sunday lunch. Obliging service; darts, shove-ha'penny, cribbage, dominoes, fruit machine, video game, pinball, and piped music. A small partly panelled room has leaded glass windows and a couple of tables. Part of the restaurant is no smoking. The company that own the pub – which can get a little full and smoky – have similar establishments in Reigate and nearby Stamford St. *(Recommended by Dr and Mrs A K Clarke, Mark Baynham, Rachael Ward, RWD, David Carr, Thomas Nott)*

Free house ~ Licensee Greg Parker ~ Real ale ~ Lunchtime meals and snacks ~ Restaurant (not Sun evening) ~ 0171-407 2495 ~ Children in restaurant and eating area of bar ~ Open 11-11; 12-10.30 Sun

Phoenix & Firkin ★ (Denmark Hill) Map 12

5 Windsor Walk, SE5; ⇌ Denmark Hill

Lively, loud, and crowded with young people in the evenings, this vibrant place is an interesting conversion of a palatial Victorian railway hall, but the atmosphere, rather than the architecture, is what draws so many varied people in. A model railway train runs back and forth above the bar, and there are paintings of steam trains, old-fashioned station name signs, a huge double-faced station clock (originally from Llandudno Junction in Wales), solid wooden furniture on the stripped wooden floor, old seaside posters, Bovril advertisements, and plants. At one end there's a similarly-furnished gallery, reached by a spiral staircase, and at the other arches lead into a food room; chess, dominoes, Twister, fruit machine, video game, pinball, and juke box. Their own Phoenix, Rail and Dogbolter on handpump (you can buy own-brew kits), and maybe one or two guest beers. Straightforward food includes big filled baps (usually available all day), a good cold buffet with pork pies, salads, quiche and so forth, and daily hot dishes like beef or vegetable chilli (£3.95), beef and Dogbolter pie (£4.50), and daily specials (from £3.95); they do a Sunday roast (£4.95). One of the Firkin flagships, the pub can get smoky at times, and though the piped music can be loud later in the day, it's much quieter at lunchtimes. There are a couple of long benches outside, and the steps which follow the slope of the road are a popular place to sit. As we went to press they told us comedy nights are planned. *(Recommended by Richard Fallon, RWD, Nigel Wikeley; more reports please)*

Own Brew ~ Managers Lisa Dovey and Mark Fogg ~ Real ale ~ Meals and snacks (12-3, 6-9; not Sun evening) ~ 0171-701 8282 ~ Children welcome till 8.30 ~ Tues quiz nights ~ Open 11-11; 12-10.30 Sun

Ship ♀ (Wandsworth) Map 12

41 Jews Row, SW18; ⇌ Wandsworth Town

With a Thames barge moored alongside, the extensive two-level riverside terrace of this smartly bustling place really comes into its own in summer, when it has picnic tables, pretty hanging baskets and brightly coloured flowerbeds, small trees, and its own bar. Inside, only a small part of the original ceiling is left in the main bar – the rest is in a light and airy conservatory style; wooden tables, a medley of stools, and old church chairs on the wooden floorboards, and a relaxed, chatty atmosphere. One part has a Victorian fireplace, a huge clock surrounded by barge prints, and part of a milking machine on a table, and there's a rather battered harmonium, old-fashioned bagatelle, and jugs of flowers around the window sills. The basic public bar has plain wooden furniture, a black kitchen range in the fireplace and darts, pinball and a juke box. Youngs Bitter, Special and Winter Warmer on handpump, freshly squeezed orange juice, a wide choice of wines (a dozen by the glass) and good choice of teas and coffees. The sensibly short range of very good and unusual bar food (made with mostly free-range produce) might include sandwiches, celery, onion and caraway soup (£3), home-made fishcakes with tartar sauce and mixed leaf salad (£4.50), chargrilled burgers (£5.50), caesar salad (£6.50), crispy duck with a tangy orange sauce (£7), and sauté chicken with cream cheese and asparagus sauce (£8); there's an al fresco restaurant on the terrace. Service is friendly and helpful. The pub's annual firework display draws huge crowds of young people, and they also celebrate the last night of the Proms. Barbecues and spit roasts every weekend in summer, when the adjacent car park can get full pretty quickly. *(Recommended by Richard Fallon, RWD, Michael Lamb, Richard Gibbs, James Macrae; more reports please)*

Youngs ~ Licensees Charles Gotto, Desmond Madden, R Green ~ Real ale ~ Meals and snacks (12-3, 7-10.30; all day Sun) ~ Restaurant ~ 0181-870 9667 ~ Open 11-11; 12-10.30 Sun

White Cross ♀ (Richmond) Map 12

Water Lane; ⊖/⇌ Richmond

Almost all the tables at this perfectly set riverside pub seem well placed for delightful Thames views, and though the scene is most obviously pretty on a sunny day, a recent visit found that even in wet weather it has a wonderfully evocative and almost wistful charm. In front is a paved garden that in summer takes on the flavour of a civilised and cosmopolitan seaside resort; the tables and seats out here are sheltered by a big fairy-lit tree which not so long ago was identified by a couple of gardeners from nearby Kew as a rare Greek Whitebeam. There's an outside bar at this time of year, when the pub can get busy. Inside, the two chatty main rooms still have something of the feel of the hotel this once was, as well as comfortable long red banquettes curving round the tables in the deep bay windows, local prints and photographs, and a good mix of variously aged customers; the old-fashioned wooden island servery is on the right. Two of the three log fires have mirrors above them – unusually, the third is underneath a window. Upstairs a big bright and airy room has lots more tables and a number of plates on a shelf running round the walls; there are a couple of tables squeezed onto a little balcony. From a servery at the foot of the stairs, good bar food – all home-made – might include tasty soups like cream of garlic or celery and almond (£2.25), sandwiches (from £2.50), ploughman's, salads (from £5.25, with home-cooked meats), and several daily changing hot dishes like Kenyan sweet potato, cheese and onion bake (£5.75), turkey and ham pie (£5.95), venison sausages in red wine and celery sauce or roast cod with garlic and saffron (£6.25), and puddings such as banana and kiwi crumble (£2.75). Youngs Bitter, Special and seasonal beers on handpump, and a good range of 22 or so carefully chosen wines by the glass, including three or four wines of the month. No music or machines – the only games are backgammon and chess (they have a Tues chess night). Boats leave from immediately outside to Kingston or Hampton Court. Bonzo the flat coat retriever loves fetching sticks that customers throw for him, even if this means taking a dip in the river. Make sure when leaving your car outside that you know the tide times – it's not unknown for the water to rise right up the steps into the bar, completely covering anything that gets in its way. *(Recommended by David Peakall, David and Nina Pugsley, Nigel Williamson, Jenny and Roger Huggins, Martin and Karen Wake, Tony Scott, Peter Marshall, A M M Hodges, Donald Boydell, Val Stevenson, Rob Holmes, Helen Pickering, James Owem, M L and G Clarke)*

Youngs ~ Managers Quentin and Denise Thwaites ~ Real ale ~ Lunchtime meals and snacks (12-6) ~ 0181-940 6844 ~ Children in big upstairs room (high chairs and changing facilities) ~ Very occasional live music – perhaps a harpist on the balcony or jazz in the garden ~ Open 11-11; 12-10.30 Sun; closed afternoon/evening 25 Dec

Windmill ♀ (Clapham) Map 12

Clapham Common South Side, SW4; ⊖ Clapham Common/Clapham South

A particularly nice place to stay, this bustling Victorian inn was about to have something of a face-lift as we went to press. The comfortable and smartly civilised main bar is set to lose its centrepiece illuminated aquarium, but in its place they hope to expose a spiral staircase. Though at times in summer the pub seems to serve all the visitors to neighbouring Clapham Common, it's such a spacious place that however lively it gets you should be able to find a quiet corner. There are plenty of prints and pictures on the walls above colourfully upholstered L-shaped banquettes, while the no-smoking conservatory is well known for its monthly opera nights, when the genre's rising stars perform various solos and arias; they also have good jazz in here, all nicely segregated from the main bar. Bar food such as sandwiches and baguettes (from £1.60), soup (£1.95), ploughman's (from £3.95), vegetable kiev (£4.75), chicken satay (£4.95), beef stroganoff (£5.95), daily specials, and chargrilled sirloin steak (£8.95); service is friendly and cheerful. Youngs Bitter, Special and seasonal beers on handpump, a good choice of wines by the glass and plenty more by the bottle; fruit machine and video game. There's a barbecue area in the secluded front courtyard with tubs of shrubs. A painting in the Tate by J P Herring has the Windmill in the background, shown behind local turn-of-the-century characters returning from the Derby Day festivities. A good deal of time and effort has been spent upgrading the accommodation side over the last few years. *(Recommended by Ian Phillips, Tim Barrow, Sue Demont, Val Stevenson, Rob Holmes, James Macrae; more reports please)*

Youngs ~ Managers James and Rachel Watt ~ Real ale ~ Meals and snacks (12-2.30, 7-10) ~ Restaurant (not Sun evening) ~ 0181-673 4578 ~ Children in no-smoking conservatory ~ Live opera first Mon evening of month, jazz second Thurs ~ Open 11-11; 12-10.30 Sun ~ Bedrooms: £84B/£95B, around £20 less at weekends

WEST LONDON

During weekday or Saturday daytime you may not be able to find a meter very close to the Chelsea Anglesea Arms or the Windsor Castle, and parking very near in the evening may sometimes be tricky with both of these, but there shouldn't otherwise be problems in this area

Anglesea Arms (Chelsea) Map 13

15 Selwood Terrace, SW7; ⊖ South Kensington

This old favourite is now run by the same people who look after another of our London main entries, the Ladbroke Arms. That's good news for anyone passing around lunchtime; the extended menu bears more than a passing resemblance to the one at its Holland Park cousin, which over the last few years has firmly established itself as one of the capital's best pubs for food. It would be nice if the Anglesea proves able to do the same, but it's even nicer that the new management is hoping to do so without spoiling the pub's chatty atmosphere or genuinely old-fashioned appearance. Despite the surrounding affluence the pub has always been notably friendly and unpretentious, managing to feel both smart and cosy at the same time. The bar has central elbow tables, leather chesterfields, faded turkey carpets on the bare wood-strip floor, wood panelling, and big windows with attractive swagged curtains; at one end several booths with partly glazed screens have cushioned pews and spindleback chairs, and down some steps there's a small carpeted room with captain's chairs, high stools and a Victorian fireplace. The traditional mood is heightened by some heavy portraits, prints of London, a big station clock, bits of brass and pottery, and large brass chandeliers. On busy evenings customers spill out onto the terrace and pavement. Well kept Adnams, Boddingtons, Brakspears SB, Eldridge Pope Royal Oak, Fullers London Pride, Harveys, and Marstons Pedigree on handpump, and several malt and Irish whiskies. Bar meals might include soup (£2.75), filled baguettes (from £3.50), grilled black pudding (£3.50), cumberland sausage or skillet of garlic mushrooms and melted cheese (£4.50), and salads such as smoked salmon and smoked halibut or tomato, avocado and mozzarella with basil dressing (£5.50); Sunday roasts in winter. As we went to press they told us they hoped to open all day soon. The pub is very popular with well heeled young people, but is well liked by locals too; perhaps that's because many of the locals *are* well heeled young people. *(Recommended by D E Twitchett, Lynda Payton, Sam Samuells, Mark Baynham, Rachael Ward, Tim Barrow, Sue Demont)*

Free House ~ Licensee Scott Craig ~ Real ale ~ Lunchtime meals and snacks ~ 0171-373 7960 ~ Children welcome till 7pm ~ Daytime parking metered ~ Open 11-3, 5.30(7 Sun)-11; closed 25/26 Dec

Anglesea Arms ♀ 🍴 (Hammersmith) Map 12

35 Wingate St, W6; ⊖ Ravenscourt Park
London Dining Pub of the Year

This busy place is one of the most obviously successful of London's new breed of gastro-pubs, a feat all the more remarkable given its rather out of the way location. A number of smart locals come here just for a drink, but it's the food that encourages most people to seek it out. Changing every lunchtime and evening, the inventive menu might include several starters like fish broth (£3.25) or girolle and cepe risotto with parmesan, truffle oil and chives (£5.50), and half a dozen or so main courses such as warm chicken liver salad with chorizo, green beans and cherry vinegar (£7.50), grilled mullet with chargrilled vegetables, hummus and red basil (£8.75), or rare rump of beef with watercress and bearnaise (£9.50); they have some unusual farmhouse cheeses. The eating area leads off the bar but feels quite separate, with skylights creating a brighter feel, closely packed tables, and a big modern mural along one wall; directly opposite you can see into the kitchen, with several chefs busily working on the meals. You can't book, so best to get there early for a table. It feels a lot more restauranty than, say, the Eagle, and they clearly have their own way of doing things; though the meal on our last visit was excellent, the service was a little inflexible, and efficient rather than friendly. The bar is quite plainly decorated ('In a designer way,' they insist), but is rather welcoming in winter when the roaring fire casts long flickering shadows on the dark panelling. Neatly stacked piles of wood guard either side of the fireplace (which has a stopped clock above it), and there are some well worn green leatherette chairs and stools. Courage Best and Directors and Theakstons XB on handpump, and a good range of carefully chosen wines listed above the bar. Several tables outside overlook the quiet street. *(Recommended by Bob and Maggie Atherton, Sophie and Mike Harrowes, J Flitney)*

Courage ~ Tenants Dan and Fiona Evans ~ Real ale ~ Meals and snacks ~ 0181-749 1291 ~ Open 11-11; 12-10.30 Sun

Bulls Head (Chiswick) Map 12

Strand-on-the-Green, W4

Strand-on-the-Green is a delight for those who like their pubs old-fashioned and riverside, and it can be difficult choosing between this well worn place and its even older neighbour the City Barge. The original building on this site, then an inn, served as Cromwell's HQ several times during the Civil War, and it was here that Moll Cutpurse overheard Cromwell talking to Fairfax about the troops' pay money coming by horse from Hounslow, and got her gang to capture the moneybags; they were later recovered at Turnham Green. The pleasant little rooms ramble through black-panelled alcoves and up and down steps, and the traditional furnishings include benches built into the simple panelling and so forth. Small windows look past attractively planted hanging flower baskets to the river just beyond the narrow towpath. Well kept Courage Directors, Greene King IPA, Theakstons XB and Old Peculier and Wadworths 6X on handpump. Bar food includes sandwiches, herb and brie crêpes (£5.25), spinach and ricotta cheese cannelloni (£5.50), chicken tikka or roast chicken (£5.99), rack of lamb (£6.99) and 14oz T-bone steak (£9.99). A games room at the back has darts, fruit machine and trivia. The pub isn't too crowded even on fine evenings, though it can get busy at weekends, especially when they have a raft race on the river. *(Recommended by Gordon, Eddy and Emma Gibson, Chris Shaw)*

Scottish Courage ~ Manager Kate Dale ~ Real ale ~ Meals and snacks (12-10) ~ 0181-994 1204 ~ Children in eating area of bar ~ Open 11-11(10.30 Sun)

Churchill Arms 🍺 (Kensington) Map 12

119 Kensington Church St, W8; ⊖ Notting Hill Gate/Kensington High St

The friendly and chatty Irish landlord tells us that for several years this bustling place has been Fullers' most profitable pub. The pub's atmosphere and popularity are largely down to him, as he works hard and enthusiastically to give visitors an individual welcome. One of his hobbies is collecting butterflies, so you'll see a variety of prints and books on the subject dotted around the bar. There are also lamps, miners' lights, horse tack, bedpans and brasses hanging from the ceiling, a couple of interesting carved figures and statuettes behind the central bar counter, prints of American presidents, and lots of Churchill memorabilia. It feels very much like a busy village local, with lots of effort put into organising special events, particularly around Halloween or the week leading up to Churchill's birthday (November 30th), decorating the place with balloons, candles and appropriate oddities, serving special drinks and generally just creating a lively carefree atmosphere. St Patrick's Day and Christmas are also marked with gusto. The spacious and rather smart plant-filled dining conservatory may be used for hatching butterflies, but is better known for its big choice of really excellent thai food: chicken and cashew nuts (£4.95) or thai noodles, roast duck curry or beef curry (£5.25). They also do things like lunchtime sandwiches (from £1.95), ploughman's (£2.75), home-made steak and kidney pie (£2.95), and Sunday lunch (£4.75). Well kept Fullers ESB, London Pride, and very nicely priced Chiswick on handpump; cheerful service. The pub can get rather smoky. Shove-ha'penny, fruit machine, and unobtrusive piped music; they have their own cricket and football teams. *(Recommended by David Peakall, GM, Paul Hilditch, Frank Ashbee, Thomas Thomas, LM; Maggie and Bob Atherton, Neville Vickers)*

Fullers ~ Manager Gerry O'Brien ~ Real ale ~ Meals and snacks (12-2.30, 6-9.30; not Sun evening) ~ Restaurant (not Sun evening) ~ 0171-727 4242 ~ Children welcome ~ Open 11-11; 12-10.30 Sun; closed evening 25 Dec

Dove (Hammersmith) Map 12

19 Upper Mall, W6; ⊖ Ravenscourt Park

The nicest of the clutch of pubs punctuating this stretch of the river, this old-fashioned Thameside house has a very pleasant tiny back terrace, where the main flagstoned area, down some steps, has a few highly prized teak tables and white metal and teak chairs looking over the low river wall to the Thames reach just above Hammersmith Bridge. If you're able to bag a spot out here in the evenings, you'll often see rowing crews practising their strokes. By the entrance from the quiet alley, the main bar has black wood panelling, red leatherette cushioned built-in wall settles and stools around dimpled copper tables, old framed advertisements, and photographs of the pub; well kept Fullers London Pride and ESB on handpump. Up some steps, a room with small settles and solid wooden furniture has a big glass food cabinet, offering sandwiches, filled baked potatoes (£3.50), salads (£3.95), cottage pie (£4.50), steak and kidney pie or smoked haddock pasta (£4.95), and lots of changing daily specials; they also do a range of thai meals, particularly in the evening (from £5.50). No games machines or piped music. Perhaps the best time to visit is at lunchtime when it's not quite so crowded. We've had several poor reports about both the food and service in the last year, and though some readers feel an element of complacency has crept in, most agree that the building's general appeal remains unchanged. A plaque marks the level of the highest-ever tide in 1928. *(Recommended by Richard Fallon, Gordon, Tony Scott, Kayo Emoto, Wayne Brindle, Stephen and Julie Brown, Gill and Andy Plumb, SK, Peter Marshall, M L and G Clarke)*

Fullers ~ Tenant Brian Lovrey ~ Real ale ~ Meals and snacks (12-2.30, 6-10) ~ 0181-748 5405 ~ Open 11-11; 12-10.30 Sun

Ferret & Firkin (Fulham) Map 12

Lots Road, SW10; ⊖ Fulham Broadway, but some distance away

Like the other Firkin pubs this unusually curved corner house has a very jolly and infectiously cheerful feel in the evenings, but at lunchtimes it can have quite a different atmosphere, and on occasions is almost deserted then. Popular with a good mix of mostly young, easy-going customers, the bar is determinedly basic, with traditional furnishings well made from good wood on the unsealed bare floorboards, slowly circulating colonial-style ceiling fans, a log-effect gas fire, tall airy windows, and plenty of standing room in front of the long curved bar counter. Several readers have described it as a sort of anglicised Wild-West saloon. Well kept beers brewed in the cellar downstairs include the notoriously strong Dogbolter, Balloonastic, and Ferret; with 24 hours' notice you may be able to collect a bulk supply. A food counter serves heftily filled giant meat-and-salad rolls (from £2.50, usually available all day) and one or two hot dishes like chilli con carne, steak and kidney pie or casseroles (£3.95); Sunday roast (£4.95). Good – and popular – juke box, as well as chess, backgammon, table football, and video game. It's handy for Chelsea Harbour, which, to continue the Western analogies, at times feels rather like a ghost town. *(Recommended by Gordon, Sue Demont, Tim Barrow, David Carr, Steve Felstead)*

Own brew ~ Manager Graeme Macdonald ~ Real ale ~ Meals and snacks (12-7) ~ 0171-352 6645 ~ Daytime parking is metered and may be difficult ~ Live music Sat evenings, occasional theatre nights and other live music ~ Children welcome till 9pm ~ Open 12-11(10.30 Sun)

Ladbroke Arms 🍴 (Holland Park) Map 12

54 Ladbroke Rd, W11; ⊖ Holland Park

Though this stylish pub is close to Holland Park and Notting Hill, it's not the kind of place crowds will stumble across by chance – it's sufficiently out of the way to ensure that you have to know it's there. That so many people not only know of it but keep coming back is due mainly to the excellent meals, among the best we know in any pub in London. Chalked up on a couple of blackboards on the right hand side of the central servery, the imaginative range of home-made dishes might typically include grilled goat's cheese with mango chutney (£5.75), pasta with pesto and sun-dried tomatoes (£5.95), pancakes stuffed with mixed mushrooms (£6.95), very popular home-made salmon fishcakes with hollandaise sauce or chicken breast stuffed with avocado and garlic (£7.95), escalope of turkey filled with mozzarella and bacon on a bed of noodles (£8.95), 8oz rump steak in a pink peppercorn sauce (£10.75), and freshly delivered fish such as baked cod with coriander; friendly staff bring french bread to the table, and even the mustards and other accompaniments are better quality than average. It comes as quite a bonus that the pub itself would still be worth a stop even if the only food was a curled-up sandwich or packet of roasted peanuts. There's a warm red hue to some parts of the neatly kept bar (especially up in a slightly raised area with a fireplace), as well as simple wooden tables and chairs, comfortable red-cushioned wall-seats, several colonial-style fans on the ceiling, some striking moulding on the dado, colourful flowers on the bar, newspapers and *Country Life* back numbers to read, and a broad mix of customers and age-groups; soft piped jazz blends in with the smartly chatty atmosphere. The landlord deals in art so the interesting prints can change on each visit. The well kept beers are rotated from a range that takes in Courage Directors, Eldridge Pope Royal Oak, Theakstons XB, and maybe a guest like Morrells Graduate; also a dozen malt whiskies. Lots of picnic tables in front, overlooking the quiet green. A sympathetic refurbishment is planned towards the end of 1997. *(Recommended by Mark Baynham, Rachael Ward, Ian Phillips, Sebastian Leach, Bob and Maggie Atherton, Dr and Mrs A K Clarke, C Leach, Tim Haigh, Wayne Brindle)*

Courage ~ Lease: Ian McKenzie ~ Real ale ~ Meals and snacks (12-2.30, 7-10; all day weekends) ~ 0171-727 6648 ~ Children welcome ~ Open 11-3, 5.30-11; 11-11 Fri and Sat; 12-10.30 Sun; closed 25 Dec

White Horse 🍷 🍺 (Fulham) Map 12

1 Parsons Green, SW6; ⊖ Parsons Green

The eclectic range of drinks and the smiling service particularly stand out at this chatty and meticulously run pub. It's usually busy, but there are enough helpful staff behind the solid panelled central servery to ensure you'll rarely have to wait to be served. One reader appreciated the fact that at least one of the staff on his visit was fluent in French. Particularly well kept and often unusual beers might include Adnams Extra, Bass, Harveys Sussex, Highgate Mild and a guest on handpump, with some helpful tasting notes; they also have 15 Trappist beers, dozen malt whiskies, and good, interesting and not overpriced wines. Well liked weekday lunches might include sandwiches, soup (£2.75), steamed mussels (£4), grilled baby calamari with balsamic vinegar (£4.50), baked aubergine, mozzarella and sun-dried tomatoes in tomato and garlic sauce (£7), roast duck on bok choi with an orange sauce (£7.95), and 8oz rib-eyed steak (£9.25). In winter they do a very good Sunday lunch in the old billiard room upstairs. The spacious and tastefully refurbished U-shaped bar has big leather chesterfields and huge windows with slatted wooden blinds; to one side is a plainer area with leatherette wall banquettes on the wood plank floor, and a tiled Victorian fireplace. Several of the high-backed pews on the right hand side may be reserved for eating. Dominoes, cribbage, chess, cards, fruit machine. It's a favourite with smart young people, so earning the pub its well known soubriquet 'the Sloaney Pony'; many locals never refer to it at all by its proper name. On summer evenings the front terrace overlooking the green has something of a continental feel, with crowds of people drinking al fresco at the white cast-iron tables and chairs; there may be imaginative Sunday barbecues out here in summer. They have monthly beer festivals (often spotlighting regional breweries) – the best known is for strong old ale held on the last

Saturday in November; lively celebrations too on American Independence Day or Thanksgiving. It's odd we don't hear more from readers about this place, to our minds one of the best pubs in London. *(Recommended by S Williamson, Derek Harvey-Piper, Richard Houghton; more reports please)*

Bass ~ Managers Mark Dorber, Rupert Reeves ~ Real ale ~ Meals and snacks (12-3.30, 6-10.30) ~ 0171-736 2115 ~ Children in eating area ~ Monthly jazz nights ~ Open 11-11; closed 25-28 Dec

White Swan (Twickenham) Map 12

Riverside; ⇌ Twickenham

This picturesque and delightfully unspoilt 17th-c riverside house is built on a platform well above ground level, with steep steps leading up to the door and a sheltered terrace, full of tubs and baskets of flowers. Even the cellar is raised above ground, as insurance against the flood tides which wash right up to the house. Across the peaceful almost rural lane is a little riverside lawn, where tables look across a quiet stretch of the Thames to country meadows on its far bank past the top of Eel Pie Island. Reassuringly traditional, the friendly bar has bare boards, big rustic tables and a mixture of other simple wooden furnishings, and blazing winter fires. The photographs on the walls are of regulars and staff as children, while a back room reflects the landlord's devotion to rugby, with lots of ties, shorts, balls and pictures. Readers particularly like the weekday lunchtime buffet, which in summer might include everything from cheese and ham to trout and smoked salmon; other bar food includes sandwiches (from £2), soup (£2), and winter lancashire hotpot or calf liver (£5). Well kept Courage Best, Marstons Pedigree, Theakstons XB, Wadworths 6X and Websters on handpump, and around 10 wines by the glass; backgammon, cribbage, piped blues or jazz. They have an annual raft race on the river the last Saturday in July, and there's an equally enthusiastic Burns Night celebration. The pub can get busy at weekends and some evenings. It's a short stroll to the imposing Palladian Marble Hill House in its grand Thameside park (built for a mistress of George II). *(Recommended by J Gibbs, Susan and John Douglas, John Tindale)*

Courage ~ Real ale ~ Managers Steve Roy and Kirsten Faul ~ Meals and snacks (not weekend evenings) ~ 0181-892 2166 ~ Children welcome away from bar ~ Folk duo fortnightly in winter ~ Open 11-11 (11-3, 5.30-11 Mon-Thurs in winter); 12-10.30 Sun

Windsor Castle (Holland Park/Kensington) Map 12

114 Campden Hill Road, W8; ⊖ Holland Park/Notting Hill Gate

Many London pubs promising a garden in truth have little more than a cramped and concreted yard, so the big tree-shaded area at the back of this unusual old place is a real draw in summer. There are lots of sturdy teak seats and tables on flagstones (on sunny days you'll have to move fast to bag one), as well as a brick garden bar, and quite a secluded feel thanks to the high ivy-covered sheltering walls. The series of unspoilt and small rooms inside all have to be entered through separate doors, so it can be quite a challenge finding the people you've arranged to meet – more often than not they'll be hidden behind the high backs of the sturdy built-in elm benches. Time-smoked ceilings and soft lighting characterise the bar, and a cosy pre-war-style dining room opens off. Good bar food typically includes sandwiches (from £2.25), seafood chowder (£2.95), salads such as riccotta and aubergine (from £3.25), vegetable cous-cous (£4.75), salmon fishcakes or moules marinières (£4.95), half a dozen oysters (£5), and steak and kidney pudding, game pie or rabbit pie (all £5.95). They currently specialise in sausages made by the landlord's brother, with some unusual varieties like duck and pork or leek and black pepper. Bass, Fullers London Pride and a guest on handpump, along with decent house wines, various malt whiskies, and maybe mulled wine in winter; a round of drinks can turn out rather expensive. No fruit machines or piped music. Usually fairly quiet at lunchtime (when one room is no smoking), the pub can be packed some evenings, often with smart young people. As so much about the place really stands out, it's a shame it can be let down by inconsistent and sometimes uninterested service; some of the mostly young staff are polite, friendly and helpful, but others might leave you waiting alone at the bar for quite some time. *(Recommended by Jacqueline Orme, Susan and John Douglas, Gordon, Giles Francis, Wayne Brindle, JO, Sue Demont, Tim Barrow)*

Bass ~ Manager Matthew O'Keefe ~ Real ale ~ Meals and snacks (12-11) ~ (0171) 727 8491 ~ Children in eating area of bar ~ Daytime parking metered ~ Open 12-11; 12-10.30 Sun

EAST LONDON

Grapes (Limehouse) Map 12

76 Narrow Street, E14; ❷ Shadwell (some distance away) or Westferry on the Docklands Light Railway; the Limehouse link has made it hard to find by car – turn off Commercial Rd at signs for Rotherhithe tunnel, Tunnel Approach slip-road on left leads to Branch Rd then Narrow St

One of London's most characterful riverside pubs, this 16th-c tavern has the added appeal of being nicely off the tourist track. It was used by Charles Dickens as the basis of his 'Six Jolly Fellowship Porters' in *Our Mutual Friend*: 'It had not a straight floor and hardly a straight line, but it had outlasted and would yet outlast many a better-trimmed building, many a sprucer public house.' Not much has changed since, though as far as we know watermen no longer row out drunks from here, drown them, and sell the salvaged bodies to the anatomists as they did in Dickens' day. It was a favourite with Rex Whistler who came here to paint the river (the results are really quite special). The back part is the oldest, with the recently refurbished back balcony a fine place for a sheltered waterside drink; steps lead down to the foreshore. The partly-panelled bar has lots of prints, mainly of actors, some elaborately etched windows, and newspapers to read. Friary Meux, Ind Coope Burton, Tetleys and a guest beer on handpump, and a choice of malt whiskies. Bar food such as soup (£2.50), prawn or crab mayonnaise (£2.95), ploughman's (£3.95), moules marinières or a pint of prawns (£4.25), bangers and mash with a thick onion gravy (£4.75), daily fresh fish like plaice or cod or home-made salmon fishcakes with caper sauce (£5.25), and a Sunday roast (no other meals then). Though several readers have noted how hard the bar staff work, a couple feel that service could be a little faster. Booking is recommended for the upstairs fish restaurant, which has fine views of the river. Shove ha'penny, table skittles, cribbage, dominoes, backgammon, maybe piped classical or jazz; no under 14s. *(Recommended by Bob and Maggie Atherton, David Carr, Tim Heywood, Sophie Wilne, John Fahy, R J Bland)*

Allied ~ Manager Barbara Haigh ~ Real ale ~ Meals and snacks (not Sun evening) ~ Restaurant (closed Sun) ~ 0171-987 4396 ~ Open 12-3, 5.30-11; 7-11 Sat (closed lunchtime)

Prospect of Whitby (Wapping) Map 12

57 Wapping Wall, E1; ❷ Wapping

Some of the best known figures in English history have called at this entertaining old pub over the centuries. Turner came here for weeks at a time to study its glorious Thames views, Pepys and Dickens were both frequent visitors, and in the 17th c the notorious Hanging Judge Jeffreys was able to combine two of his interests while sitting outside at the back – enjoying a drink while looking down over the grisly goings on in Execution Dock. With plenty more stories like these it's no wonder they do rather play on the pub's pedigree, and it's an established favourite for evening coach tours (it's usually quieter at lunchtimes). The tourists that flock in lap up the colourful tales of Merrie Olde London, and only the most unromantic of visitors could fail to be carried along by the fun. Plenty of beams, bare boards, panelling and flagstones in the L-shaped bar (where the long pewter counter is over 400 years old), while tables in the waterside courtyard look out towards Docklands. Well kept Courage Directors, Theakstons XB and Youngs Special on handpump, and quite a few malt whiskies;

basic bar meals such as roasts and salads (mostly just under the £5 mark), with a fuller menu in the upstairs restaurant. One area of the bar is no smoking. Built in 1520, the pub was for a couple of centuries known as the Devil's Tavern thanks to its popularity with river thieves and smugglers. *(Recommended by James Nunns, David Carr, Sue Demont, Tim Barrow, Tony Scott, Darren Thake)*

Scottish Courage ~ Managers Christopher and Anne Reeves ~ Real ale ~ Meals and snacks ~ Restaurant ~ 0171-481 1095 ~ Children in eating areas ~ Modern jazz first Weds evening of month ~ Open 11.30-3, 5.30-11; 11.30-11 Sat; 12-10.30 Sun

Town of Ramsgate (Wapping) Map 12

62 Wapping High St, E1; ⊖ Wapping

Unspoilt despite its proximity to the City, and rarely crowded, this old pub has an evocative old-London setting, overlooking King Edward's Stairs (also known as Wapping Old Stairs), where the Ramsgate fishermen used to sell their catches. Inside, an enormous fine etched mirror shows Ramsgate harbour as it used to be. The softly lit panelled bar is a fine combination of comfort and good housekeeping on the one hand with plenty of interest on the other: it has masses of bric-a-brac from old pots, pans, pewter and decorative plates to the collection of walking canes criss-crossing the ceiling. There's a fine assortment of old Limehouse prints. Bar food includes sandwiches (from £1.95, steak £3.95), filled baked potatoes (£2.75), pizzas (from £3.75), ploughman's (£3.95) and cumberland sausage and mash (£4.95), with three or four daily specials like sweet and sour chicken (£4.95); well kept Bass and Fullers London Pride under light blanket pressure; friendly service; cribbage, trivia, unobtrusive piped music; good sociable mix of customers. At the back, a floodlit flagstoned terrace and wooden platform (with pots of flowers and summer barbecues) peeps out past the stairs and the high wall of Olivers Warehouse to the Thames. *(Recommended by Marjorie and David Lamb, Sue Demont, Tim Barrow)*

Charringtons (Bass) ~ Manager Julie Allix ~ Real ale ~ Meals and snacks (11.30-3, 6.30-10; 12-4, 6.30-9 Sun)~ (0171) 488 2685 ~ Children welcome ~ Open 11.30-11; 12-10.30 Sun

---

Real ale may be served from handpumps, electric pumps (not just the on-off switches used for keg beer) or – common in Scotland – tall taps called founts (pronounced 'fonts') where a separate pump pushes the beer up under air pressure. The landlord can adjust the force of the flow – a tight spigot gives the good creamy head that Yorkshire lads like.

Lucky Dip

Besides the fully inspected pubs, you might like to try these Lucky Dips recommended to us and described by readers (if you do, please send us reports). We have split them into the main areas used for the full reports – Central, North, and so on. Within each area the Lucky Dips are listed by postal district, ending with Greater London suburbs on the edge of that area.

CENTRAL LONDON
EC1

[102 Clerkenwell Rd], *Burgundy Bens*: Well done Davys bar with tables outside and well kept real ale, usual Davys food and wines *(Dr and Mrs A K Clarke)*

[1 Middle St], *Hand & Shears*: Traditional Smithfield pub dating from 16th c, three rooms around central servery, hubbub of lively conversation, Scottish Courage ales, quick friendly service, interesting bric-a-brac, reasonably priced too; open all day but cl weekends *(R J Bland, LYM)*

[33 Seward St], *Leopard*: Solid traditional pub with good food using only fresh produce esp fish and steaks (attractive prices), well kept ales such as Gibbs Mew Bishops Tipple; conservatory, picnic tables on big terrace *(Bridget Burgess)*

[St John St], *Peasant*: Good interesting food in upstairs restaurant with striking furnishings in purple upholstery and beige wood, subtle spot-lighting gently dimmed as evening wears on; genuine pub atmosphere downstairs, with some cheaper dishes from the same menu *(Sue Demont, Tim Barrow)*

[166 Goswell Rd], *Pheasant & Firkin*: Down-to-earth concentration on good beer (own cheap light Pluckers, also good value Pheasant and powerful Dogbolter brewed here), and basic food at very reasonable prices; bare boards, good cheery service, congenial company from all walks of life, daily papers, good cheap CD juke box *(PGP, Sue Demont, Tim Barrow, LYM)*

[Rising Sun Ct, Cloth Fair], *Rising Sun*: Neatly tucked away antiquated pub with well kept Sam Smiths beers, good choice of food, friendly atmosphere; open weekends *(Mark Baynham, Rachael Ward, TH, SW)*

[56 Chiswell St], *St Pauls*: Extended corner pub with around a dozen mainly Whitbreads-related ales, country-style decor; packed at lunchtime for good value food *(Ian Phillips)*

EC2

[Andrews House, Fore St/Wood St], *Crowders Well*: Nice view over water from neatly kept Greene King pub with well kept ale, American landlord *(Dr and Mrs A K Clarke, Stuart Balfore)*

[36 Wilson St], *Fleetwood*: Successful modern pub with well kept beer, cheerful helpful staff; well decorated in modern style *(Dr and Mrs A K Clarke)*

[Bishopsgate/L'pool St Stn], *Hamilton Hall*: A Wetherspoons flagship, stunning Victorian baroque decor, plaster nudes and fruit mouldings, chandeliers, mirrors, upper mezzanine, good-sized no-smoking section, comfortable groups of seats, reliable food all day from well filled baguettes up brought to your table, well kept low-priced Scottish Courage and guest beers; fruit machine, video game but no piped music; open all day, can get very crowded early evening *(Thomas Nott, Heather Martin, AB, John Fahy, Sue Demont, Tim Barrow, Tony Scott, D P Brown, LYM)*

[12 New St; off Liverpool St], *Magpie*: Classic little corner pub, cosy and friendly, with good atmosphere, well kept ales, friendly chatty staff; can get smoky if packed early evening *(Rachael Ward, Mark Baynham)*

[High Walk, Moorgate], *Plough*: Friendly atmosphere, good food, good choice of beers *(D P Hutchinson)*

[8 Artillery Lane], *Williams*: Friendly tucked-away City pub with good choice of Whitbreads-related beers, wide choice of good food *(Mark Baynham, Rachael Ward)*

EC3

[Fenchurch St], *Elephant*: Full range of Youngs ales, kept well, with lunchtime food and busy basement *(Ian Phillips)*

[10 Grand Ave; Leadenhall Mkt], *Lamb*: Old-fashioned stand-up bar with plenty of ledges and shelves, spiral stairs to mezzanine with lots of tables, light and airy top-floor no-smoking carpeted lounge bar overlooking market's central crossing, with plenty of seats and corner servery strong on cooked meats inc hot sandwiches; well kept Youngs; also smoky basement bar with shiny wall tiling and own entrance *(Richard Nemeth, Christopher Gallop, Tony Scott)*

[8 Lombard St], *Red Lion*: Jolly and busy Nicholsons pub, with decent food and well kept ales *(Dr and Mrs A K Clarke)*

[11 Talbot Ct], *Ship*: Well kept real ales esp Adnams in well done Nicholsons pub *(Dr and Mrs A K Clarke)*

[Ship Tavern Passage], *Swan*: Busy businessmen's pub with tiny flagstoned bar, upstairs room, unspoilt Victorian decor, good friendly service, generous lunchtime sandwiches, particularly well kept Fullers; no music or machines in main bar *(Steve Willey)*

EC4

[9 Queen St], *Golden Fleece*: Well run Greene King pub, welcoming atmosphere, well kept beer, pub games *(Dr and Mrs A K Clarke, Hazel Potter)*

☆ [Fleet St, nr Ludgate Circus], *Old Bell*: Unusually cosy for a City pub, flagstoned front bar with trap door to cellar, stained-glass window, nice window seat; back bar with cast-iron tables and three-legged triangular stools on sloping bare boards; particularly well kept beer; rebuilt by Wren as commissariat for his workers on former church behind *(Mark Baynham, Rachael Ward)*

☆ [Ludgate Circus], *Old King Lud*: 10 to 15
changing reasonably priced real ales in busy
beams-and-sawdust-style pub, no music,
knowledgeable and helpful staff; yesterday's
sports page from *The Times* framed in the
gents' *(Mark Baynham, Rachael Ward, Tony
Scott)*

☆ [99 Fleet St], *Punch*: Warm, comfortable,
softly lit Victorian pub, not too smart, fine
mirrors, dozens of *Punch* cartoons, ornate
plaster ceiling with unusual domed skylight,
good bar food, Tetleys-related and other ales
such as Marstons and Wadworths *(Tony
Scott)*

[103 Cannon St], *Vino Veritas*: Good busy
wine bar/pub with well kept Theakstons and
accent on food *(Dr and Mrs A K Clarke)*

[28 Tudor St, off Fleet St], *White Swan*:
Scottish Courage ales, framed copies of
Illustrated London News (Dave Braisted)

SW1

☆ [Eaton Terr], *Antelope*: Stylish rather superior
panelled local, well kept Tetleys-related and
guest ales, good house wines, decent food –
quiet and relaxed upstairs weekday
lunchtimes, can get crowded evenings; open
all day, children in eating area *(David Carr,
LYM)*

[6 Bennett St], *Blue Post*: Good service,
atmosphere, food, upstairs restaurant; handy
for Piccadilly *(Anon)*

☆ [62 Petty France], *Buckingham Arms*:
Congenial Youngs local close to Passport
Office and Buckingham Palace, lots of mirrors
and woodwork, unusual long side corridor
fitted out with elbow ledge for drinkers, well
kept ales, decent simple lunchtime food,
reasonable prices, service friendly and
efficient even when busy *(Rachael Ward,
Mark Baynham, Derek and Sylvia
Stephenson, LYM)*

[Piccadilly], *Cafe Royal*: Daniels Bar here is a
useful place to meet; friendly efficient waiter
drinks service, no pressure to use restaurant,
free nibbles, and not as expensive
as you might have thought; piped music may
be on the loud side *(Liz and Ian Phillips)*

[25 Wilfred St], *Colonies*: Friendly and
comfortable open-plan split-level pub,
lunchtime food, John Smiths and Theakstons
Best, African theme *(Robert Lester)*

[Churton St], *Constitution*: Comfortable,
fairly roomy, with welcoming staff,
reasonably priced food in bar and upstairs
dining room; piped music *(Stephen Holman)*

☆ [29 Passmore St/Graham Terr], *Fox &
Hounds*: Quaint and homely little local, no
spirits licence – just well kept ales such as
Adnams, Bass and Greene King at sensible
prices, also wines, sherries, vermouths etc;
narrow bar with wall benches, hunting prints,
old sepia photographs of pubs and customers,
some toby jugs and a piano – so near a
wooden partition that it would be practically
impossible to hit the bass notes; coal-effect
gas fire; can be very busy Fri night, maybe
quieter Sat *(Gordon, C F Fry)*

☆ [14 Little Chester St, just off Belgrave Sq],
Grouse & Claret: Smart, well run and
discreetly old-fashioned, but welcoming, with
attractive solid furnishings, well kept ales
such as Boddingtons, Brakspears, Greene
King IPA, Wadworths 6X and Youngs
Special, games area, decent bar food;
basement wine bar with three-course lunches,
swish upstairs restaurant; children in eating
area, open all day weekdays, cl Sun evening
and bank hols *(E A Thwaite, LYM)*

[Dean Bradley St], *Marquis of Granby*: Big
open-plan pub, well kept Bass and guest
beers, lunchtime food, very busy then and
early evenings, with some interestingly
indiscreet conversations to be overheard; open
all day, cl weekends *(Sue Demont, Tim
Barrow)*

☆ [58 Millbank], *Morpeth Arms*: Roomy
Victorian Youngs pub handy for the Tate, old
books and prints, photographs, earthenware
jars and bottles; busy lunchtimes, quieter
evenings – well kept ales, good choice of
wines, food, helpful staff; seats outside (a lot
of traffic) *(Tony Scott, John Fazakerley, Eddy
and Emma Gibson, BB)*

[14 Lower Belgrave St], *Plumbers Arms*:
Small, tastefully refurbished to keep old
charm, well kept John Smiths, good bar food
inc fish and chips, choice of puddings *(M H
Pritchard)*

☆ [23 Crown Passage; behind St James's St, off
Pall Mall], *Red Lion*: Small cosy local, one of
West End's oldest, tucked down narrow
pedestrian alley nr Christie's; friendly relaxed
atmosphere, panelling and leaded lights,
decent lunchtime food, unobtrusive piped
music, real ales such as Fullers and Ruddles
*(Hugh MacLean, B J Harding, John Fahy,
BB)*

☆ [D of York St], *Red Lion*: Busy little pub
notable for dazzling mirrors, crystal
chandeliers and cut and etched windows,
splendid mahogany, ornamental plaster
ceiling – architecturally, central London's
most perfect small Victorian pub; good value
sandwiches, snacks and hot dishes, well kept
Eldridge Pope Hardy Country and Tetleys
(Hugh MacLean, Ian Phillips, LYM)

☆ [Victoria Stn], *Wetherspoons*: Warm,
comfortable and individual, a calm haven
above the station's bustle, with very cheap
ever-changing real ales, wide choice of
reasonably priced decent food all day, prompt
friendly service, good furnishings and
housekeeping – and heaven for people-
watchers, with glass walls and tables outside
overlooking the main concourse *(Simon
Penny, Paul McKeever, Eddy and Emma
Gibson, Anthony Barnes, Mrs D Carpenter,
Sue Demont, Tim Barrow)*

SW3

☆ [87 Flood St], *Coopers Arms*: Relaxed
atmosphere, interesting style with country
furnishings and lots of stuffed creatures, good
food (not Sat/Sun evenings) inc some
inventive hot dishes and attractive show of

cheeses and cold pies on chunky deal table; well kept Youngs Bitter and Special, good choice of wines by the glass; under same management as Alma and Ship in South London (see main entries) *(Richard Gibbs, David Carr, LYM)*

[Old Church St], *Front Page*: Civilised local with good interesting bistro food, heavy wooden furnishings, huge windows and big ceiling fans for airy feel, good wines, well kept Boddingtons, Ruddles County and Websters Yorkshire; open all day *(James Macrae, David Carr, Richard Gibbs, LYM)*

[Brompton Rd], *Hour Glass*: Very small, traditional and quiet, with good food; handy for V&A and other nearby museums; does food on days when many other nearby pubs don't *(Mr and Mrs Jon Corelis)*

[50 Cheyne Walk], *Kings Head & Eight Bells*: Attractive location by gardens across (busy) road from Thames, some tables outside; recently carefully refurbished so as not to lose traditional local feel, clean, comfortable and friendly, with well kept ales such as Adnams, Boddingtons, Brakspears, Flowers, Greene King Abbot, Morlands Old Speckled Hen, Youngs and a seasonal brew, good staff; well behaved dogs allowed *(Gordon, Tim Barrow, Sue Demont, BB)*

[Christchurch Terr], *Surprise in Chelsea*: Unpretentious local with well kept Bass and related ales, decent food, friendly service, and anyone from the local bookie to a family party straight from Buckingham Palace investiture; often surprisingly quiet evenings, cosy and warm; not overly done up considering location, attractive stained-glass lanterns, mural around top of bar; well behaved dogs welcome *(David Dimock, Tim Barrow, Sue Demont, BB)*

W1

[Kingly St], *Clachan*: Wide changing range of ales in comfortable well kept pub with ornate plaster ceiling supported by two large fluted and decorated pillars, smaller drinking alcove up three or four steps; can get very busy *(Sue Demont, Tim Barrow)*

[62 Wigmore St], *Cock & Lion*: Comfortable and well kept, handy for Wigmore Hall, with relaxed rather continental atmosphere, good service, bar meals from hot sandwiches to beef and Theakstons pie etc, good salads; restaurant upstairs *(F Chamberlain)*

[43 Weymouth Mews], *Dover Castle*: Quiet and cosy, some panelling and old prints, snug back area, Sam Smiths OB and Museum at decidely rural prices *(Paul Mason, DK)*

[Praed St/Norfolk Pl], *Fountains Abbey*: Popular local for St Marys Hospital staff, well kept Courage, Theakstons Best, XB and Old Peculier and two or more interesting guest beers, friendly helpful staff, surprising range of no-fuss cheap food; can get busy after 6 *(Mark Baynham, Rachael Ward)*

[55 Great Portland St], *George*: Solid old-fashioned BBC local where your Editor once shook hands with a man who'd shaken hands with a man who shook hands with Napoleon; lots of mahogany and engraved mirrors, friendly atmosphere, well kept Greene King ales, straightforward food; open all day, cl 6 Sat *(David Carr, Ian Phillips, LYM)*

☆ [42 Glasshouse St], *Glassblower*: Handy tourist refuge from Regents St, unfussy furnishings, gaslight, busy bar and more relaxing upstairs lounge, good choice of simple food all day, Scottish Courage ales, a good few malt whiskies; fruit machine, video game, trivia, juke box; children in eating area, open all day *(Bob and Maggie Atherton, Steve Harvey, Mick Hitchman, Ian Phillips, Hanns P Golez, LYM)*

[2 Shepherd Mkt], *Kings Arms*: Lively and busy, minimalist bare wood and rough concrete decor, dim upper gallery, friendly young staff, Greene King Abbot, Sam Smiths and Theakstons, standard bar food inc filled baguettes; piped music can be a little loud; summer pavement overflow *(Mark Baynham, Rachael Ward, BB)*

[Wardour St], *Moon & Sixpence*: Wetherspoons pub in former bank, original big arched windows giving very light feel in rather spacious main bar, big eating area, sensible food all day, very well priced Youngs and other well kept ales, pile of board games, no music – just chat *(Michael Sandy, Sue Demont, Tim Barrow)*

☆ [23 Rathbone St, corner Newman Passage], *Newman Arms*: Friendly and informal, with well kept Fullers and Youngs in small panelled bar, good value home-made pies upstairs *(Simon Penny, Ian Phillips)*

[Goodge St], *Northumberland Arms*: Small but cosy, well furnished, with lots of wood, good choice of well kept changing ales, bar food, newspapers and magazines; attractive exterior – tiles and hanging baskets *(Richard Lewis)*

☆ [88 Marylebone Lane], *O'Conor Don*: Genuinely Irish without being in your face about it, hassle-free waitress drinks service (so you don't have to wait for your Guinness to settle), generous helpings of good straightforward food, no piped music; attractive formal upstairs dining room – Galway oysters flown in daily; good Irish folk music Sat *(Jim and Liz Meier, Richard Gibbs, BB)*

[Kingly St], *Red Lion*: Friendly, solidly modernised without being spoilt, with well kept Sam Smiths OB and Museum at sensible prices, reasonably priced food upstairs; video juke box *(Mark Walker, BB)*

[50 Hertford St], *Shepherds Tavern*: Useful stop, with Courage Directors, Morlands Old Speckled Hen, Theakstons Best, reasonably priced simple bar food inc sandwiches, good shepherd's pie upstairs; piped music *(George and Chris Miller, MB, RW)*

[Langham Pl; take express lift in far corner of hotel lobby], *St Georges*: Undoubtedly one of the finest views in London from the Summit Bar's floor-to-ceiling picture windows looking out over the city to the west (the gents', facing the other way, also has a splendid view); well spaced settees, low gilt and marble tables, properly mixed cocktails (not cheap) and good sandwiches and other bar food; bedrooms *(TBB, LYM)*

W2

[Bathurst St, opp Royal Lancaster Hotel], *Archery*: Well kept Badger and other ales and good helpings of decent food in homely early Georgian three-room pub with pots and hanging baskets of dried flowers and herbs in pleasant front rooms, darts etc in back room, horses stabled in yard behind; tables outside *(Stephen and Jean Curtis, Sue Holland, Dave Webster)*

[15 Chilworth St], *Fettler & Firkin*: Vibrant and interesting mix of people, typical Firkin decor with emphasis on nearby station, well kept ales brewed here, reasonably priced food; piped music not excessive, can get lively evenings *(Mark Baynham, Rachael Ward)*

[Sale Pl], *Royal Exchange*: Small and pleasant, with good inexpensive food, friendly service, nice ambiance with sporting theme, ales such as Boddingtons, Brakspears and Flowers IPA, quiet piped music *(Ian Phillips)*

[10a Strathearn Pl], *Victoria*: Unusual corner local, lots of Victorian royal and other memorabilia, interesting little military paintings, two cast-iron fireplaces, mahogany panelling, friendly managers, Fullers ales, well priced generous food, picnic tables on pavement; upstairs (not always open) replica of Gaiety Theatre bar, all gilt and red plush *(Ian Phillips, LYM)*

WC1

[Red Lion St], *Dolphin*: Whitbreads-related beers and warm friendly atmosphere; handy for music at Conway Hall *(Comus Elliott)*

☆ [38 Red Lion St], *Enterprise*: Lively no-frills pub with great decor of tiled walls, big mirrors, bare boards; good choice of Bass-related and guest ales, wide range of good value food, friendly staff, small back garden; gets busy evening *(Geoff Coe, David Blackledge, Rachael Ward, Mark Baynham)*

WC2

☆ [29 St Martins Lane], *Chandos*: Open all day from 9 (for breakfast), very busy downstairs bare-boards bar, quieter more comfortable upstairs Opera Room with alcoves, low wooden tables, panelling, leather sofas, opera memorabilia, orange, red and yellow leaded windows; generally enjoyable food from sandwiches to Sunday roasts, well kept Sam Smiths Mild, Stout and Museum, air conditioning, cheerful service; children upstairs till 6, darts, pinball, fruit machines, video game, trivia and piped music; note the automaton on the roof (working 10-2 and 4-9) *(Susan and Nigel Wilson, Steve Harvey, Tony and Wendy Hobden, John C Baker, Mick Hitchman, Gordon, John Fahy, C Smith, Gordon Prince, Hanns P Golez, Mayur Shah, Eddy and Emma Gibson, Helen Pickering, James Owen, D J and P M Taylor, LYM)*

[42 Wellington St], *Coach & Horses*: Small Irish pub with imported Dublin Guinness from old-fashioned copper-topped bar, food inc good lunchtime hot roast beef baps, careful professional service, well kept Courage Best; can get crowded *(Simon Walker)*

☆ [31 Endell St], *Cross Keys*: Festooned with hanging baskets and window boxes, friendly and cosy, with masses of of photographs, posters, brasses and bric-a-brac, good comfortable feel; basic lunchtime food, fruit machine, small upstairs bar, tables outside *(Gordon)*

[Betterton St/Drury Lane], *Hogshead*: Done up in olde-worlde tavern style, comfortable upstairs, with good range of well kept Whitbreads-related and other ales, basic cheap food, pleasant bustling atmosphere *(Simon Walker, Tim Barrow, Sue Demont)*

[39 Bow St], *Marquess of Anglesey*: Transformed by recent light and airy refurbishment, quiet and roomy, with good bar food at sensible prices, consistently well kept Youngs, seating upstairs, good service even when busy (they try to serve quickly if you're going to the theatre) *(Simon Walker, L Dixon, Hanns P Golez, Frank Ashbee)*

[28 Leicester Sq], *Moon Under Water*: Typical Wetherspoons pub conversion beside Odeon, Courage Directors, Theakstons XB, Wadworths 6X and Youngers Scotch, generous good value food all day *(Andrew Hodges, Robert Lester)*

☆ [90 St Martins Lane], *Salisbury*: Floridly Victorian, sweeps of red velvet, huge sparkling mirrors and cut glass, glossy brass and mahogany; decent food inc salad bar (even doing Sun lunches over Christmas/New Year), well kept Tetleys-related ales, decent house wines, no-smoking back room, friendly service; shame about the piped music and games machines *(John Fazakerley, John Fahy, Hanns P Golez, Mark Baynham, Rachael Ward, BB)*

NORTH LONDON

N1

☆ [10 Thornhill Rd], *Albion*: Recently refurbished but still unspoilt, with low ceilings, snug nooks and crannies inc cosy back hideaway, some old photographs of the pub, horsebrasses and tack recalling its coaching days, open fires, some gas lighting, good range of real ales, food, very friendly landlord; now has flower-decked front courtyard as well as the big back terrace with vine canopy; interesting Victorian gents' *(Mary Creagh, Roberto Villa, Mary Wright, BB)*

☆ [4 Compton Ave, off Canonbury Rd], *Compton Arms*: A surprise for London, simple, unspoilt and cottagey, with no video games or juke box, neighbourhood customers, friendly but not obtrusive service, cheap limited food (all day weekends, not Tues eve)

inc good cheese choice and speciality sausages, well kept Greene King IPA, Abbot, Rayments and a seasonal ale, lots of wines by the glass, shady courtyard seating; children welcome, open all day *(Mary Olden, Eric and Jackie Robinson, David Carr, JEB, LYM)*
[Upper St], *Hogshead*: Good format, with many real ales and seven Belgian beers *(James Nunns)*
[87 Noel Rd], *Island Queen*: Good freshly made and often unusual food in amiable character pub with well kept Bass and Worthington BB, good value wines, upstairs restaurant, welcoming atmosphere, good juke box, big mirrors with appliqué jungle vegetation; handy for Camden Passage antiques area; children welcome; can get rather smoky; sadly the life-size caricature figures which have been such a feature here were missing as we went to press – perhaps they'll reappear after remodelling? *(Tim Barrow, Sue Demont, Ian Phillips, LYM)*
[115 Upper St], *Kings Head*: Wide choice of real ales, good spot opp antiques area, live music Sat; popular bistro, good theatre in back room (but hard seats there) *(Ian Phillips, James Nunns)*
[54 Pentonville Rd], *Pint Pot*: Friendly split-level bar which demands sure footing, good range of beers, some interesting Victorian fittings *(Dr and Mrs A K Clarke)*

N4
[Stroud Green Rd], *White Lion of Mortimer*: One of the first Wetherspoons pubs, good value for all-day food and drink, with good choice of both incl well kept ales, country wines and farm cider, pleasantly solid furnishings, restful back conservatory; part no-smoking *(David Carr, Mick Hitchman, LYM)*

N6
[77 Highgate West Hill], *Flask*: Comfortable Georgian pub, largely modernised but still has intriguing up-and-down layout, sash-windowed bar hatch, panelling and high-backed carved settle tucked away in snug lower area (this original core open only weekends and summer); usual food all day inc salad bar, good barman, Tetleys-related and Youngs ales, coal fire; very busy Sat lunchtime, well behaved children allowed, tables out in attractive front courtyard with big gas heater-lamps *(Graham Tayar, Ian Phillips, Mick Hitchman, Gordon, Gavin May, Gordon Neighbour, LYM)*
[1 North Hill], *Gate House*: Wetherspoons pub with consistently good food, well kept beers at low prices, no-smoking area; tables in back yard *(Gordon Tong)*

N12
[283 Ballards Lane], *Moss Hall*: Good range of hot food; one of Fullers' few N London pubs *(Gordon Neighbour)*
[749 High Rd], *Tally Ho*: Imposing landmark pub comfortably renovated, with old local

photographs, Courage Best and Directors, Greene King Abbot and Theakstons XB, sensible prices, useful food all day; one of the relatively few Wetherspoons pubs to allow children, if eating *(Robert Lester, Gordon Tong)*

N16
[Allen Rd], *Shakespeare*: Friendly bare-boards local with theatrical element – classical figures dancing on walls, central Victorian bar with Flowers, Ind Coope Burton, Timothy Taylors Landlord, continental draught beers, wide choice of bottled beers; good juke box, lots of young people, small garden; can park bike inside *(Tim Cole, Mick Hitchman)*

N20
☆ [Totteridge Village], *Orange Tree*: Spacious pub by duckpond, plush decor, separate comfortable restaurant, friendly service, usual food but reliable, inc generous carvery with self-service veg; pleasant surroundings – still a village feel *(A C Morrison, LYM)*

NW1
[313 Royal College St], *Black Horse*: Small friendly Irish pub, pool table, darts, reasonable prices *(TAB)*
[65 Gloucester Ave], *Engineer*: Mix of foodies and drinkers in big open-plan bar, individual atmospheric candlelit rooms upstairs, ornate and baroque; good interesting food, good wine list, Greene King IPA; lively and popular – may need to book upstairs *(Sue Demont, Tim Barrow)*
[120 Euston Rd], *Friar & Firkin*: Large brewpub with its own half-dozen well kept ales inc a Mild, Addlestone's cider, good choice of bar food, friendly staff; usual Firkin decor, bare boards, lots of prints and brewery memorabilia, various casks dotted around, central back bar; open all day, happy hour, quiz nights, live music *(Richard Lewis)*
[Arlington Rd], *Good Mixer*: Friendly staff, good atmosphere, good drinks, fair prices *(Anon)*
[1 Eversholt St], *Head of Steam*: Large bar up stairs from bus terminus and overlooking it, fun for train/rail buffs with lots of memorabilia, also Corgi collection, interesting model trains and buses and magazines for sale; interesting well kept ales (also take-away), most from little-known small breweries, Biddenham farm cider and lots of bottled beers; TV, bar billiards, downstairs restaurant; open all day *(George Atkinson, Richard Houghton, Richard Lewis, Simon Walker, BB)*
[Gloucester Ave], *Pembroke Castle*: Split-level pub with good mix of customers, well kept ales, daily papers – relaxing on Sun lunchtime *(Sue Demont, Tim Barrow)*
[65 Kentish Town Rd], *Quinns*: Subtly understated Irish pub with wide range of bottled beers and a continental draught beer as well as Fullers London Pride, Greene King IPA and other ales, helpful staff, friendly

atmosphere, attractive food, comfortable seats; small terrace *(David Dansky, Dr and Mrs A K Clarke)*

[222 Marylebone Rd], *Regent Hotel*: Cellars Bar is opulent and expensive, with the feel of a gentlemen's club – and outstanding free bar snacks; bedrooms *(Dr and Mrs A K Clarke)*

[2 Mornington Terr], *Victoria*: Well kept ales in curved bar with photographs and other memorabilia; pleasant atmosphere, though piped music can be a little obtrusive *(Sue Demont, Tim Barrow)*

[Regents Park Rd], *Victoria*: Smart, almost opulent, one-bar local by Primrose Hill *(Mr and Mrs S Groves)*

NW3

[2 Haverstock Hill], *Enterprise*: Has now become yet another Irish-theme pub, but a good one, with friendly service and well kept beer *(Dr and Mrs A K Clarke)*

☆ [32 Downshire Hill], *Freemasons Arms*: Big pub with spacious but busy garden right by Hampstead Heath, good arrangements for serving food and drink outside; several comfortable rooms inside, well spaced variously sized tables, leather chesterfield in front of log fire; usual bar food inc Sun roast beef (no-smoking eating area, at lunchtime), Bass and Charrington IPA; children allowed in dining room, dogs in bar, open all day summer *(Mr and Mrs Jon Corelis, LYM)*

[154 Haverstock Hill], *Haverstock Arms*: Lively, with good mix of customers inc actors and musicians, good weekday food, endearing long-serving Irish tenant; sports TV, good free Eddie Condon-style jazz Sun evening *(GT, ANM)*

☆ [North End Way], *Old Bull & Bush*: Attractively decorated in Victorian style, comfortable sofa and easy chairs, nooks and crannies, side library bar with lots of bookshelves and pictures and mementoes of Florrie Ford who made the song about the pub famous; friendly landlord, efficient staff, good food bar inc good Sun specials, decent wines and mulled wine, good provision for families *(Gordon, BB)*

NW7

[Ridgeway, Mill Hill], *Adam & Eve*: Welcoming open-plan pub aiming at country feel; good lunches *(Dr and Mrs A K Clarke)*

[211 Holders Hill Rd], *Mill*: Large busy 1960s pub with heart, well kept beer, good range of facilities *(Dr and Mrs A K Clarke)*

NW8

[21 Loudoun Rd], *Blenheim Arms*: Large modern L-shaped bar/restaurant, lots of paintings, polished floorboards, young friendly service, modern European cooking *(Bob and Maggie Atherton)*

☆ [24 Aberdeen Pl], *Crockers*: Magnificent original Victorian interior, full of showy marble, decorated plaster and opulent woodwork; relaxing and comfortable, with well kept Bass and wide range of other

sensibly priced ales, friendly service, decent food inc vegetarian and good Sun roasts, tables outside *(John Fahy, Sue Demont, Tim Barrow, Stephen and Julie Brown, Tony Scott, LYM)*

NW10

[50 Old Oak Lane], *Fishermans Arms*: Friendly pre-war pub with accent on sport; their Fishermans Bitter is extraordinarily cheap *(Dr and Mrs A K Clarke)*

BARNET

[Barnet Rd (A411); nr Hendon Wood Lane], *Gate at Arkley*: Good friendly service, wide choice of food from good value lunchtime baguettes up, some wines by the glass, small no-smoking conservatory as well as main eating area, attractive sheltered garden with aviary and piggery *(A C Morrison, BB)*

[148 High St], *Moon Under Water*: Wetherspoons pub with fine choice of low-priced ales inc regular guest beers, no-smoking area, no music, good value food, mock-Victorian decor, conservatory feel in back area, picnic tables in back garden; usually pleasantly relaxed, busy with young people some nights *(Gordon Tong)*

ENFIELD

[Enfield Rd (A110)], *Jolly Farmer*: Big modern McMullens family pub with welcoming atmosphere, plenty of dining space, well kept ales, enormous choice of food from sandwiches up, very efficient staff *(Gwen and Peter Andrews, Gordon Neighbour)*

[White Webbs Lane; A10 from M25 junction 25, right at 1st lights, right at l-hand bend], *King & Tinker*: Country pub opp riding stables, not over-modernised, busy and friendly, with good choice of well kept ales, good lunches inc huge filled rolls, authentic character, interesting old local photographs, well kept Tetleys-related and guest ales, decent wines, welcoming staff; can be rather smoky; attractive garden with fenced play area, occasional Morris men *(Joy and Peter Heatherley, Mrs P J Pearce)*

SOUTH LONDON
SE1

[Waterloo Stn], *Coopers*: Grand staircase down to spacious Victorian-style bar with sepia decor, pastel carpet, prints, brass and light washed wood; lively and noisy, nine wines by the glass, interesting changing real ales *(Richard Dolphin)*

☆ [Bankside], *Founders Arms*: Sparkling view of Thames and St Pauls from spacious glass-walled plush-seat modern bar and big waterside terrace; well kept Youngs Bitter and Special, reasonable food, pleasant service, genuine feel *(Annette and Stephen Marsden, David Carr, LYM)*

☆ [5 Mepham St – a bit hidden by Jubilee Line works], *Hole in the Wall*: No-frills drinkers' pub in railway arch virtually underneath

Waterloo Stn – rumbles and shakes when trains go over; not a place for gastronomes or comfort-lovers but well worth knowing for its dozen well kept changing ales and nearly as many lagers, also good malts and Irish whiskeys; loudish juke box, pinball and games machines; basic food all day (afternoon closure weekends) *(Mark Baynham, Rachael Ward, RWD, LM, Richard Fallon, LYM)*

[24 Southwark St], *Hop Cellars*: Balls Bros wine bar serving a real ale – worth seeing the old Hop Exchange building above it with its remarkable galleried inner court *(Dr and Mrs A K Clarke)*

[89 Upper Ground], *Mulberry Bush*: Attractively done sympathetically lit newish Youngs pub, open-plan with slightly raised balustraded area and back conservatory, decent wines, good service, well priced bar food, spiral stairs to bistro with wider choice inc steak and salmon; handy for the South Bank complex *(Gill and Andy Plumb, Frank Ashbee)*

[30 Webber St], *Stage Door*: Behind Old Vic, open and bright, with theatre posters, friendly staff, simple well priced bar food, well kept Scottish Courage ales *(Stephen Holman)*

SE3

[Tranquil Vale], *O'Neils*: New Irish theme pub, friendly staff, good bar food all day till early evening *(M Gibbs)*

SE5

[149 Denmark Hill], *Fox on the Hill*: Large and civilised, with good garden, plenty of real ales (up to 30 on occasion), wines by the glass, friendly service; one of the relatively few Wetherspoons pubs to allow children, if eating *(AMP)*

SE6

[Bromley Rd/Southend Ln], *Tigers Head*: Pleasant Wetherspoons pub festooned with flowers in hanging baskets, tubs and window-boxes, picnic tables on attractive front terrace, small lawn with conifers; comfortable and roomy inside, with decent inexpensive bar meals, impressive choice of ales (one very cheap), pleasant service, no music or machines *(EGP)*

SE10

[13 Greenwich Mkt; Blackheath Rd], *Coach & Horses*: Busy pub, friendly and efficient, with particularly well kept Adnams *(Dr and Mrs A K Clarke)*

[River Way, Blackwall Lane], *Pilot*: Busy, with brisk friendly service, well kept Bass, Courage Best and Youngs Special, wide range of sandwiches, baked potatoes and hot dishes at very reasonable prices; handy for Millennium site *(Tony Gayfer)*

[Park Row], *Trafalgar*: Attractive 18th-c building with splendid river view, fine panelled rooms, friendly efficient staff, good atmosphere, usual food, good house wines; handy for Maritime Museum, may have live

jazz weekends *(RWD, Peter Neate, J Williams)*

[Crane St], *Yacht*: Friendly, clean and civilised, with good river view from spacious upper room, light wood panelling, portholes, yacht pictures, cosy banquettes, reasonable food *(David Carr)*

SE16

☆ [Bermondsey Wall East], *Angel*: Superb Thames views to Tower Bridge and the City upstream, and the Pool of London downstream, esp from balcony supported above water by great timber piles; straightforward bar food, Scottish Courage and other ales, upstairs restaurant where children allowed *(David Carr, LYM)*

[117 Rotherhithe St], *Mayflower*: Friendly and cosy riverside local with black beams, high-backed settles and open fire, good views from upstairs and atmospheric wooden jetty, well kept Bass and Greene King IPA, Abbot and Rayments, decent bar food (not Sun night), friendly staff; children welcome, open all day; in unusual street with beautiful church *(K Flack, David Carr, Nigel and Amanda Thorp, LYM)*

SE19

[14 Cawnpore St], *Railway Bell*: Good backstreet local, clean and sparkling, with wide range of Youngs ales *(Comus Elliott)*

SE20

[164 High St, Penge], *Moon & Stars*: Wetherspoons pub in former cinema, nice little alcoves, food all day inc good filled baked potatoes and maybe bargain meals for two, very low-priced beer, immaculate lavatories, life-size image of Dorothy from *Wizard of Oz* hanging from high ceiling; sheltered back terrace *(A M Pring)*

SE22

☆ [Barry Rd, Peckham Rye], *Clock House*: Friendly and popular local, two rooms with dark woodwork, carpets, plenty of ornaments inc lots of clocks and measuring instruments; some seating outside, lots of colourful flower baskets, tubs and window boxes; well kept Youngs, nice mixed crowd esp evenings and Sun lunchtime, no music, decent home cooking *(Andy Thwaites, Christopher Gallop, Jenny and Brian Seller)*

SE23

☆ [Dartmouth Rd, Forest Hl], *Bird in Hand*: Civilised Wetherspoons pub, attractive glass-topped panelled recesses, marble-topped tables in no-smoking food area, spotless throughout; very pleasant staff, good moderately priced food all day, four real ales *(EGP)*

SE24

[31 Hinton Rd], *Lord Stanley*: Friendly local with good range of real ales, good pub food, interesting environment *(Dr and Mrs A K Clarke)*

SE26

☆ [39 Sydenham Hill], *Dulwich Wood House*:
Welcoming Youngs pub in Victorian lodge
gatehouse complete with turret, well kept
ales, food popular at lunchtime with local
retired people, lots of tables in big pleasant
back garden with barbecues *(EGP)*

SW2

[2 Streatham Hill, on South Circular], *Crown
& Sceptre*: Ornate and substantial
Wetherspoons pub, good traditional decor,
sensible-sized areas inc no smoking, well kept
reasonably priced ales inc some unusual ones,
good value well organised food, good service
(Sue Demont, Tim Barrow)

[New Park Rd], *Sultan*: Unpretentious
backstreet local with well kept Scottish
Courage ales, friendly service, secluded and
peaceful fairy-lit back garden *(Sue Demont,
Tim Barrow)*

SW4

[Clapham Park Rd], *Bellevue*: Refurbished as
trendy dining bar, with no real ales but good
range of wines, comfortable sofas, armchairs,
daily papers etc; innovative well priced food
can be good, good atmosphere; piped music
can be a little loud *(Sue Demont, Tim
Barrow, BB)*

[Clapham Manor St], *Bread & Roses*:
Interesting variant on the new wave of
London food pubs, in that it's owned by the
Workers Beer Co, with its own Workers Ale
brewed for it, and various leftish cultural
events; good wine list inc unusual Italians and
Chileans; customers generally 20-somethings,
piped music can be rather loud *(Sue Demont,
Tim Barrow)*

[The Pavement], *Rose & Crown*: Lively and
friendly, with wide choice of ales inc guests,
attractive rambling interior with alcoves; can
get a bit noisy and smoky *(Sue Demont, Tim
Barrow)*

SW8

[169 South Lambeth Rd], *Rebatos*:
Consistently good authentic food in front
tapas bar and pink-lit mirrored back
restaurant – which has great atmosphere, and
frequent evening live music; lots of Spanish
customers, real Spanish feel, always full and
never short of atmosphere *(Susan and John
Douglas, Sue Demont, Tim Barrow, BB)*

SW11

[115 Battersea High St], *Castle*: Friendly, airy
and spacious Youngs pub with real log fire,
restaurant area, back conservatory, pleasant
walled garden, daily papers on upright piano,
kitchen tables, country furnishings, good wine
choice, reasonably priced food inc good Sun
roast *(HC, Richard Gibbs)*

[St Johns Hill], *Falcon*: Lots of glass and
mirrors, comfortable back lounge, more
spartan front bar, good welcoming staff,
honest basic lunchtime food till 3, good range
of well kept ales inc annual beer festival, cheap

tea or coffee *(Sue Demont, Tim Barrow)*

[Battersea Rise], *La Bouffe*: More a bar than
a pub but lots of fun, good bar food and
French-style restaurant, friendly atmosphere,
seats out in front; open all day till about
midnight *(Rachel Milne)*

☆ [opp Battersea Pk BR stn], *Masons Arms*:
Trendy young people's local doubling as
stylish food pub with short but interesting
choice of well prepared food (esp Italian)
from open-plan kitchen, good range of wines,
light modern decor – battered wooden tables,
spotlights, some armchairs and sofas behind;
only limited beer, service may suffer from
language problems (you may get lemon tart
instead of tortellini), and there may be very
loud piped throbbing hardcore dance music
*(Sue Demont, Tim Barrow, Richard Gibbs,
BB)*

☆ [60 Battersea High St], *Woodman*: Busy,
friendly and individual young people's local,
with little panelled front bar, long main room,
log-effect gas fires, lots of enamel advertising
signs; tied to Badger, with their beers and
those from their own-brew pub at Oving in
Sussex, also several guests such as Wadworths
6X, at fair prices, cappuccino coffee; food inc
Sun breakfast from 9.30, bar billiards, darts
and games machines at one end, picnic tables
on partly covered back terrace with barbecue;
good with children *(Tim Barrow, Sue
Demont, BB)*

SW12

[97 Nightingale Lane], *Nightingale*:
Welcoming, comfortable and civilised local,
good bar food, well kept Youngs, sensible
prices, very friendly staff, timeless cream and
brown decor with gallery of sponsored guide-
dog pictures on one wall, attractive back
family conservatory; children in useful small
family area *(Sue Demont, Tim Barrow, BB)*

SW13

☆ [7 Church Rd], *Sun*: Several spacious
traditionally renovated areas around central
servery, pleasant atmosphere, six Tetleys-
related and guest ales, usual home-cooked
food, benches and tables over road overlooking
duckpond; very popular in summer *(Sue
Demont, Tim Barrow, Richard Harvie)*

SW14

[42 Christ Church Rd], *Plough*: Relaxing pub
dating from 17th c, real ales, home-made
food, pleasant well mannered staff, tables out
on terrace; four comfortable bedrooms *(Neil
Egan)*

SW15

☆ [8 Lower Richmond Rd], *Dukes Head*:
Classic Youngs pub, spacious and grand yet
friendly, in great spot by Thames, well kept
ales, 20 wines by the glass; main bar light and
airy with big ceiling fans, very civilised feel,
tables by window with great Thames view,
smaller more basic locals' bar, good fresh
lunchtime food; plastic glasses for outside,

service can slow right down on sunny days *(Tony Scott, BB)*

☆ [14 Putney High St], *Slug & Lettuce*: Bright, spacious, smart and tasteful, with mix of Shaker-style decor and comfortable sofas, good food esp risottos, home-baked bread, real ales and wide range of premium bottled beers, proper coffee, freshly squeezed fruit drinks, chatty staff, piped classical music lunchtime, quiet pop evenings; others recommended in this useful chain in Warwick Way (SW1), Islington Green (N1), Alma Lane (SW18), Water Lane (Richmond) and Fulham Rd (SW6) *(BB)*

SW16

[498 Streatham High Rd], *Pied Bull*: Large open-plan bar with well kept Youngs, reasonably priced food, a couple of sofas and piano *(Dr and Mrs A K Clarke)*

SW18

[East Hill], *Beehive*: Welcoming unspoilt Fullers local, small and neat; efficient service, well kept ales, good mix of customers, unobtrusive piped music; very popular evenings esp weekend *(LM, Sue Demont, Tim Barrow, BB)*
[68 Wandsworth High St], *Brewery Tap*: Fine Victorian tap for Youngs Brewery, with their full range kept very well, lots of comfortable seating, relevant prints and artefacts, good choice of food inc lots of specials, good friendly staff; piped music; open all day *(Richard Lewis, Dr and Mrs A K Clarke)*
[345 Trinity Rd], *County Arms*: Character three-room Youngs local, younger in front, wider mix in back, from grannies with dogs to families; back grand piano for customers – Scott Joplin to Mozart; well kept beer, good value food from fresh filled rolls to cheap Sun lunch, traditional decor, relaxed feel, summer spills out on to nearby grass *(DK, BB)*

SW19

[Wimbledon Common], *Crooked Billet*: Olde-worlde Youngs pub by common, lovely spot for summer drinking, open all day; well kept beer, good bar food, pleasant helpful service, restaurant in 16th-c barn behind *(Tony Scott, Colin McKerrow)*
[Camp Rd], *Fox & Grapes*: By common, pleasant on summer evenings when you can sit out on the grass; open all day, traditional furnishings, Scottish Courage ales with a guest such as Wadworths 6X, usual bar food; piped music, big screen sports TV; children welcome till 7 *(Gregor Macdonald, LYM)*
☆ [6 Crooked Billet], *Hand in Hand*: Very well kept Youngs, good straightforward food inc home-made pizzas and burgers, relaxed and cheerful U-shaped bar serving several small areas, some tiled, others carpeted, log fire; rather spartan no-smoking family annexe with bar billiards, darts etc; tables out in courtyard with vine and hanging baskets, benches out by common; can be very crowded with young people esp summer evenings

(Tony Scott, A M Stephenson, BB)
[The Ridgeway], *Swan*: Helpful new Yorkshire licensees, good choice of decent wines, reasonable choice of good food *(Colin McKerrow)*

BECKENHAM

[Chancery Lane], *Jolly Woodman*: Cosy little local, very friendly, cheap beer; seats out in cosy garden and tiny street *(A Homes)*

BIGGIN HILL

Fox & Hounds: Main-rd Big Steak pub, open all day, with jelly bean and nut machines, decent coffee, efficient young staff, picnic tables under cocktail parasols in big side garden, play area; can get busy weekends *(AMP)*

BROMLEY

[Bromley Common], *Crown*: Useful Beefeater family dining pub with separate dining room *(A M Pring)*

CARSHALTON

[17 West St], *Racehorse*: Popular and busy, with generous food, friendly atmosphere, welcome absence of false airs and graces, well kept Gales and other ales *(Jenny and Brian Seller)*

CHEAM

Bell: Clean and pleasantly refurbished, with good value enjoyable home-made food from doorstep sandwiches up, well kept Bass. Clean and pleasantly refurbished, with good value enjoyable food from generous sandwiches up, Fullers ales *(DWAJ, Tony and Wendy Hobden)*
[17 Park Rd], *Olde Red Lion*: Small low-ceilinged 16th-c pub, recently refurbished without being spoilt, nicely presented food (not Sun evening) from sandwiches up, ales such as Fullers London Pride, Hancocks HB, Morlands Old Speckled Hen and Worthington Best, island bar, tables out on terrace *(DWAJ)*

CHELSFIELD

Five Bells: Little changed over the years, with old photographs of this Miss Read village, food inc good toasties, Scottish Courage ales with a guest such as Tolly Original *(Dave Braisted)*

CHISLEHURST

[outskirts, on rly stn side of town], *Imperial Arms*: Welcoming, with full range of usual pub food at sensible prices, well kept Scottish Courage ales *(Tony Hobden)*
☆ [High St], *Queens Head*: Charming comfortable and friendly local by attractive pond on green, pleasantly modernised inside keeping its quiet separate public bar (can be busy evenings), food inc superb value ploughman's, well kept ales inc Adnams and more unusual ones, good service; tables in garden *(Jenny and Brian Seller, R Boyd)*
[Old Perry St], *Sydney Arms*: Good value bar

food, Scottish Courage ales, efficient service, friendly atmosphere, big conservatory and pleasant garden – good for children; almost opp entrance to Scadbury Park – lovely country walks *(B J Harding)*

COULSDON
[Old Coulsdon; Coulsdon Rd (B2030) on edge of Common], *Fox*: Busy partly 18th-c family dining pub with good big enclosed play garden inc summer bouncy castle and ball pool, maybe a magician; good value usual food done to order, generous helpings, well kept real ale, decent wine, considerate service, log fires, interesting displays; handy for North Downs walks, no dogs *(D F T Gurner, Christopher Gallop)*

CROYDON
[17 George St], *George*: All the usual Wetherspoons features, with their standard menu, several real ales, no-smoking area, no music *(Tony and Wendy Hobden)*
[22 Longley Rd], *Princess Royal*: Like a small country pub, with discerning landlord, well kept Greene King IPA, Abbot and Rayments, good food throughout opening hours *(Iain Gordon)*
[Shirley Hills Rd], *Sandrock*: Clean and wholesome, with well kept Bass and Charrington, good food inc good value granary bread sandwiches, good friendly service; nice spot next to Shirley Hills, on the newly opened London Loop trail *(Jenny and Brian Seller, Christopher Wright)*
[Sheldon St/Wandle Rd], *Standard*: Welcoming, with well kept Fullers London Pride, ESB, Porter, Cream and seasonal ales, good Sun bar snacks *(Alex Gorton)*

CUDHAM
☆ [Cudham Lane], *Blacksmiths Arms*: Decent generous reasonably priced food inc interesting soups, good ploughman's, well kept Courage, Fullers London Pride and Morlands Old Speckled Hen, good coffee, quick friendly service; nearly always busy yet plenty of tables, with cheerful cottagey atmosphere, soft lighting, blazing log fires, low ceiling; big garden, pretty window boxes, handy for good walks *(Jenny and Brian Seller, B J Harding, R Boyd)*

DOWNE
[High St], *Queens Head*: Quaint and civilised refurbished village pub, open all day, with friendly helpful service, good value food, well kept ales inc Burts, comfortable seating, log fire (can be smoky sometimes), well equipped children's room; small back courtyard with aviary *(A M Pring, R Boyd, E G Parish)*

KEW
[Pond Corner], *Greyhound*: Light and bright continental cafe-style interior behind half-timbered exterior; Adnams Broadside, Courage Best, Marstons Pedigree, piped music *(James Nunns)*

KINGSTON
[2 Bishops Hall; off Thames St – down alley behind W H Smiths], *Bishop out of Residence*: Riverside Youngs pub with pleasant Thames views, big bar and eating area, wide range of good value quick food, young efficient staff, well kept ales, decent house wines, customers of all ages; tables out on balcony *(John Wooll)*
[Hawkes Rd], *Bricklayers Arms*: Doing well under hard-working licensees, particularly well kept ales *(Gary Roberts)*
[Elm St; off Richmond Pk], *Wych Elm*: Good recently decorated Fullers local with food inc decent sandwiches and rolls, well kept Chiswick, London Pride and ESB, reasonable prices, good service, Spanish landlord, no blarey music, attractive little back garden; quiz nights, SkyTV in public bar *(D E Hall, M Tews)*

LEAVES GREEN
[main rd], *Kings Arms*: Attractive oldish two-bar pub with low beams and log fire, airy conservatory, wide range of good value lunchtime food (not Sun) from sandwiches up, friendly staff, jovial landlord, Courage-related ales; tables in garden, by end of Biggin Hill aeroplane runway *(A M Pring)*

MALDEN RUSHETT
☆ [Chessington Rd; A243 just N of M25 junction 9], *Star*: Busy dining pub with well cooked reasonably priced generous food inc vegetarian, jovial long-serving ex-sea captain landlord, helpful quick friendly service, well kept King & Barnes and Scottish Courage ales, decent wines, maybe a splendid locally made elderflower champagne, big log fire; handy for Chessington World of Leisure, quickly fills at lunchtime *(Paul and Ursula Randall, DWAJ, John Sanders, J S M Sheldon, TBB)*

NEW MALDEN
☆ [Thetford Rd], *Woodys*: Plethora of sporting memorabilia on every wall and rafter (originally a sports pavilion), medley of furnishings, hearty good value food from separate servery with kitchen behind inc good chunky well filled sandwiches, well kept Whitbreads-related and other real ales; big-screen sports TV, tables out on lawn *(Paul and Ursula Randall)*

ORPINGTON
[Pinewood Dr; towards Sevenoaks], *Buff*: Well kept main-road local, with long-serving management, handy stop for a drink and lunchtime food; lively evenings, with games room and theme nights (also good pub footbal team) *(AMP, Joseph Molloy)*

PETTS WOOD
[Station Sq], *Daylight*: Former Toby Inn recently upgraded by Bass, usual chain menu but well done, cheery management, provision for children, tables outside

(Bridget Burgess, R Boyd)
Sovereign of the Seas: Good Wetherspoons pub, wide choice of beers, very friendly atmosphere; gets crowded – lots of young people but no trouble *(A M Pring, Paul McKeever, R Boyd)*

PURLEY
[8 Russell Hill Rd], *Foxley Hatch*: Smart modern Wetherspoons pub converted from bathroom centre, warmly friendly local atmosphere, Scottish Courage and other well kept ales, decent food all day, low prices, good staff, no music; no-smoking area *(Alan Kilpatrick)*

RICHMOND
☆ [45 Kew Rd], *Orange Tree*: Interesting main bar with fine plasterwork, big coaching and Dickens prints, fine set of 1920s paintings; open all day, with theatre club upstairs, well kept Youngs, friendly service, good food all day (not Sun evening) in civilised and spacious cellar bar; pleasant tables outside *(Malcolm Welchman, Tony Scott, LYM)*
[28 The Green], *Princes Head*: Large friendly open-plan pub nr theatre, good traditional areas off big island bar, good lunchtime food cooked to order, Fullers Chiswick and London Pride, open fire, seats outside – fine spot *(J and P Maloney)*
☆ [Petersham Rd], *Rose of York*: Comfortable seats inc leather chesterfields, Turner prints on stripped pine panelling, old photographs, attractive layout inc no-smoking area; good choice of reasonably priced Sam Smiths ales, pleasant helpful service; high chairs, bar billiards, fruit machines, TV, piped pop music; lighting perhaps a bit bright; bedrooms *(GWB, Tony Scott)*
[14 Worple Way, off Sheen Rd], *White Horse*: Fullers pub converted to dining spot, good imaginative Mediterranean-influenced British food at very reasonable prices, menu changing daily and intelligent use of local suppliers *(Peter Burton)*
☆ [25 Old Palace Lane], *White Swan*: Pleasant setting for charming respite from busy Richmond, barbecues, easy welcoming feel in dark-beamed open-plan bar, well kept Scottish Courage beers, good coal fires, good freshly cooked bar food; children allowed in conservatory, pretty paved garden *(Comus Elliott, Graham Tayar, David Carr, Sara Jessop, Mrs D W Cook, LYM)*

SURBITON
☆ [1 Surbiton Hill], *Waggon & Horses*: Roomy traditional local, extensive reasonably priced lunchtime menu inc winter Sun lunches, well kept Youngs, central panelled saloon, galleried upper lounge leading to attractive grapevine courtyard with popular summer weekend barbecues, separate small lounge by small character public bar with TV; efficient staff inc friendly long-serving licensees and full-time potboy, no piped music or juke box *(J K Ives, Clive Ashcroft, Peter Hartnell)*

WEST LONDON
SW5
[209 Earls Court Rd], *Blackbird*: Big comfortable pub, dark panelling, plenty of nooks and corners, decent lunchtime food esp home-made pies and freshly carved roasts in barm cakes, full range of Fullers ales kept well, up-to-date atmosphere (music can be loud) *(Alex Malmaeus, Paul Mason)*

SW10
☆ [Burnaby St], *Chelsea Ram*: Youngs pub comfortably spruced up, with some emphasis on good food changing daily, inc vegetarian, pasta, fish and Smithfield meat; well kept Youngs, interesting wines inc good choice by the glass, outstanding bloody mary, good pimms; lively mix of customers, friendly service, lovely fire, pleasant golden walls, shutters, books, pine tables, no music, quiet back part *(Pippa Scott, Sue Demont, BB)*
[190 Fulham Rd], *Kings Arms*: Well preserved Victorian Finch's pub, good range of real ales *(Dr and Mrs A K Clarke)*
☆ [6 Camera Pl], *Sporting Page*: Unusual civilised and upmarket local off Kings Rd, genuinely good interesting food, well kept Scottish Courage and a guest ale, decent house wines, one or two seats outside *(David Carr, LYM)*

W4
☆ [72 Strand on the Green], *Bell & Crown*: Big busy pub with lovely river-view terrace, very friendly feel, local paintings and photographs, simple good value food inc sandwiches and lunchtime hot dishes, well kept Fullers, log fire, no piped music or machines; good towpath walks *(Tim Barrow, Sue Demont, Eddy and Emma Gibson, Tony Scott)*
☆ [27 Strand on the Green], *City Barge*: Small panelled riverside bars in picturesque partly 15th-c pub (this original part reserved for diners lunchtime), also airy newer back part done out with maritime signs and bird prints; usual bar food (not Sun), well kept Courage Directors and Wadworths 6X, back conservatory, winter fires, some tables on towpath – lovely spot to watch sun set over Kew Bridge *(Richard Gibbs, Eddy and Emma Gibson, Christopher Round, Christopher Wright, LYM)*
[aka Fox & Hounds; 110 Chiswick Lane S, by Gt West Rd at Fullers Brewery], *Mawson Arms*: Fullers brewery tap recently refurbished, with lots of seating, bare boards, nice minimalist decor, settee at one end, papers to read, decent food, well kept ESB, London Pride and IPA, also full range of their bottled beers; personable landlady and helpful friendly staff; open all day *(Richard Lewis, Michel Hooper-Immins)*

W6
☆ [2 South Black Lion Lane], *Black Lion*: Chef & Brewer with cosy and welcoming local atmosphere, helpful staff, food reasonably priced and quite imaginative, served evenings

too; big log-effect gas fire separating off area with pool tables, machines etc *(Helen Pickering, James Owen, BB)*

[40 Hammersmith Broadway], *Edwards*: One of a small new chain (others in Shepherds Bush and Ealing), converting previously ordinary pubs into smartly comfortable and stylish places, reminiscent of the spruced-up Slug & Lettuces *(BB)*

W8

[Hammersmith Rd], *Albion*: Popular corner local with particularly well kept Courage Best and Directors and Youngs Bitter and Special, friendly staff, comfortable lounge, Rugby Union theme *(Richard Lewis)*

☆ [1 Allen St, off Kensington High St], *Britannia*: Peaceful local little changed since the 60s, good value fresh home-cooked lunches, well kept Youngs, helpful long-serving landlady, no music; attractive indoor back 'garden', friendly dog and cat *(Ian Phillips, BHP)*

W9

☆ [93 Warrington Cres], *Warrington*: Comfortable Victorian pub with luscious mirrors, arches and alcoves (said once to have been a brothel – hence the murals); well kept full Fullers range with a guest such as Brakspears, good pub food, small coal fire, imposing staircase up to Thai restaurant; good tables on big back terrace, nr Little Venice *(Ian Phillips)*

W12

[1 Wood Lane], *Albertine*: Masses of wine by the glass inc good value champagne, good food, though a little cramped for eating unless you get a side table – can get packed, with good buzzy atmosphere *(Bob and Maggie Atherton)*

W14

[24 Blythe Rd, Olympia], *Frigate & Firkin*: Typical bare-boards style with lots of prints and artefacts, friendly chatty atmosphere, enthusiastic staff, well kept beers brewed here maybe inc an unusual chilli one; live entertainment *(Richard Lewis)*

[247 Warwick Rd], *Radnor Arms*: Classic pub architecture, interesting windows, plenty of character, London's first Everards outlet – usually a guest beer too; friendly staff who are real-ale enthusiasts, good choice of whiskies, pub games; open all day, no food Sun *(Richard Lewis)*

[160 Warwick Rd], *Warwick Arms*: Open-plan, but otherwise a fine example of an early 19th-c London pub, with lots of old woodwork; comfortable atmosphere, friendly regulars (some playing darts or bridge), service fast, friendly and courteous, Fullers beers in top condition from elegant Wedgwood handpumps, limited tasty food (not Sun evening), sensible prices, no piped music; open all day, tables outside, handy for Earls Court and Olympia *(Bruce Bird)*

EASTCOTE

[High Rd], *Case is Altered*: Attractive old pub in quiet setting, well kept Allied ales, pleasant garden; no food *(Mark Hydes)*

HAMPTON

☆ [70 High St], *White Hart*: Well kept Boddingtons, Flowers, Greene King Abbot and five changing guest ales, helpful knowledgeable staff, usual decent lunchtime food, warm log fire and quiet relaxed atmosphere; subdued lighting, good staff, small front terrace *(Roy Shutz, Dr M Owton)*

HAMPTON COURT

☆ [Hampton Court Rd, next to Lion Gate], *Kings Arms*: Newly refurbished and opened up, with more space for food (but loss of the old-fashioned bar games which readers had liked so much); pleasant black-panelled middle bar, stripped-brick lounge with bric-a-brac, brighter lighting and newly opened fireplace, new food servery, well kept Badger and guest ales, upstairs restaurant; unobtrusive piped music, children welcome; open all day, picnic tables on roadside cobbles *(Susan and John Douglas, LYM)*

HAMPTON WICK

[Kingston Bridge], *White Hart*: Comfortable and friendly Fullers pub with good Thai food *(Ian Phillips)*

HEATHROW AIRPORT

[Terminal 4], *Moon Under Water*: Wetherspoons pub, with a branch on the public side and another in Departures; welcome refuge from the airport hotels (and this busy and most modern Heathrow terminal), with good range of real ales, good value food *(Arnold Day)*

NORWOOD GREEN

☆ [Tentelow Lane (A4127)], *Plough*: Attractive old-fashioned low-beamed decor, cheerful villagey feel, well kept Fullers ales inc Chiswick, welcoming service, cosy family room, even a bowling green dating to 14th c; decent lunchtime food, flame-effect gas fire; can get crowded weekends; occasional barbecues in lovely garden with play area, open all day, lavatories for the disabled *(Tom Evans, Ian Phillips)*

SIPSON

[Sipson Rd; entrance next to Post House], *Plough*: Tucked behind Heathrow hotels and almost in shadow of M4, but very welcoming, clean and quiet, with six well kept Scottish Courage and other ales, good food lunchtime and evening *(Arnold Day)*

TWICKENHAM

[London Rd], *Cabbage Patch*: Bar with raised central fire, comfortable seating in quieter areas, attractively priced food, games room *(Anon)*

☆ [9 Church St], *Eel Pie*: Busy and

unpretentious, open all day (not Mon afternoon) and wide range of Badger and other ales; usual bar food (lunchtime not Sun) and all-day sandwiches (not Sun), lots of rugby player caricatures, bar billiards, pinball and other pub games, some seats outside; open all day (but cl at 8 on big rugby days – when it can be very busy), children allowed till 6; nice street *(Steve Felstead, M L and G Clarke, MS, LYM)*

☆ [Cross Deep], *Popes Grotto*: Roomy and relaxing suburban pub, helpful staff, good value lunchtime bar food from sandwiches to Sun roasts, well kept Youngs, good range of other drinks, no music, games in small public bar; tables in own garden, and attractive public garden over rd sloping down to Thames (cl at night); children in eating area *(M L and G Clarke, LYM)*

[Winchester Rd, St Margarets; behind A316 roundabout], *Turks Head*: Friendly local with well kept Fullers, home-cooked food changing daily; manic on rugby days; stand-up comics Mon/Sat in hall behind *(Terry and Jayne Harmes)*

UXBRIDGE

☆ [Villiers St; off Clevedon Rd opp Brunel University], *Load of Hay*: Popular small local with wide choice of good value freshly made generous food, friendly staff, well kept Scottish Courage and genuine guest beers, thoughtful choice of teas, impressive fireplace in no-smoking back lounge-area part used by diners, more public-bar atmosphere nearer serving bar, another separate bar, local paintings; dogs welcome, back garden *(R J Ward)*

EAST LONDON
[Wapping High St], *Captain Kidd*: Thames views from enormous rooms of newish nautical-theme pub in renovated docklands warehouse, good choice of hot and cold food all day inc several puddings, Sam Smiths keg beers, obliging bow-tied staff, chunky tables on roomy terrace *(David Carr, Tony Scott)*

[St Katharines Way], *Dickens Inn*: Splendid position above smart docklands marina, well kept Scottish Courage ales, interesting baulks-and-timbers interior, several floors; popular with overseas visitors *(John Fazakerley, Paul A Green, LYM)*

☆ [9 Exmouth St], *Hollands*: Well worth penetrating the surrounding estates for this unspoilt Victorian gem, friendly and entirely genuine, with lots of original fittings inc bar snob-screens and fine mirrors, interesting bric-a-brac, Youngs ales, simple bar food, darts; open all day *(Prof J R Leigh, David Carr, Eric and Jackie Robinson, LYM)*

E4
[420 Hale End Rd], *County Arms*: Big, busy mock-Tudor pub built 1908 by Douglas Scott for the Herts & Essex Public House Trust (forerunner of Trust Houses) - good solid materials; friendly atmosphere, Scottish

Courage ales, pool and other pub games, quiz nights *(Robert Lester)*

[95 Forest Side], *Queen Elizabeth*: Beamed main bar with Scottish Courage ales, good friendly atmosphere, restaurant, children's room, pool room; piped music in the lavatories *(Robert Lester)*

E6
[419 Barking Rd], *Millers Well*: Typical Wetherspoons pub opp Town Hall, local pictures, good friendly atmosphere and staff, food all day, some interesting real ales *(Robert Lester)*

E7
[178 Forest Lane; off Woodgrange Rd], *Fox & Hounds*: Friendly open-plan pub with local prints and West Ham photographs, customers play piano Sun night, Ruddles County, darts, pool – giant wooden spoon nr pool table *(Robert Lester)*

[212 Upton Lane], *Old Spotted Dog*: Good front bar, plush back bar, Henry VIII associations *(Dr and Mrs A K Clarke)*

E10
[640 High Rd (A112)], *Three Blackbirds*: Large three-bar pub with Scottish Courage ales, good friendly atmosphere, two pool tables, live music Fri *(Robert Lester)*

E11
☆ [36 High St, nr Wanstead tube stn], *Clutterbucks*: Long narrow bar with lots of panelling, friendly service, well kept Tetleys and a house beer, cheap lunchtime food, board games, lovely old black and white photographs; one of Jack the Ripper's victims said to have been murdered in a next-door yard *(Mark Baynham, Rachael Ward)*

[692 High Rd (A11)], *Crown*: Recently refurbished under new owners, with open-plan bar, upstairs pool room doubling as function room; keg beer *(Robert Lester)*

[31 Wanstead High St], *Cuckfield*: Tastefully refurbished open-plan pub divided by partitions, with Bass and Hancocks HB, real fire, good friendly atmosphere, conservatory; smart dress, no under-21s *(Robert Lester)*

[57 Lambourne Rd; nr A112], *Two Brewers*: Timber, panelling and brasses in smart and comfortable open-plan local with Whitbreads-related ales, tables on terrace, restaurant; handy for Hainault Forest *(Robert Lester)*

E14
☆ [44 Narrow St], *Barley Mow*: Spacious if breezy terrace overlooking Limehouse Basin, mouth of Regents Canal and two Thames reaches; clean and comfortable pump-house conversion, lots of sepia Whitby photographs, food, Tetleys-related ales, conservatory *(David Carr)*

[Hertsmere Rd, West India Dock Gate], *Dockmasters House*: Well restored Georgian house with good cellar pub, good ground floor restaurant *(Ian Phillips)*

E17

[112 Wood St], *Dukes Head*: Open-plan bar with Scottish Courage ale, darts, pool and Fri live music; tables in garden *(Robert Lester)*

[47 Shernhall St], *Lord Brooke*: Recently refurbished three-bar pub with very friendly new landlord and staff, well kept Charrington IPA, lunchtime snacks and meals, lots of darts teams, shove-ha'penny, tables on terrace *(Robert Lester)*

[185 Wood St], *Pig & Whistle*: Open-plan but cosy and atmospheric, with food all times, real ales such as Border Exhibition, Courage Directors and Marstons Pedigree, tables in garden *(Robert Lester)*

[55 Hoe St], *Rose & Crown*: Pleasant two-bar pub, two pool tables, darts, three tables upstairs; live music Fri *(Robert Lester)*

☆ [off Whipps Cross Rd], *Sir Alfred Hitchcock*: More atmosphere than usual round here, rather countrified, with well kept ales such as Boddingtons, Flowers, Fullers ESB, enthusiastic Irish landlord, big open fires, Chinese bar meals and restaurant, reasonable prices; TV in bar; dogs welcome, sunny terrace; bedrooms *(Mark Baynham, Rachael Ward, Neil and Jenny Spink)*

ILFORD

[902 Eastern Ave, Newbury Park], *Avenue*: Good friendly atmosphere, Courage Best, plush lounge, darts and pool in public bar *(Robert Lester)*

[229 Ilford High Rd; nr A118], *General Havelock*: Friendly refurbished local, lots of panelling, Tetleys; handy for Magum's nightclub *(Robert Lester)*

[104 Ley St], *Red Cow*: Smart and comfortable, with good friendly atmosphere, Tetleys; pool in public bar *(Robert Lester)*

[16 Ilford Hill; nr A406], *Rose & Crown*: Recently refurbished open-plan split-level pub, much brighter, with good atmosphere and particularly well kept ales such as Adnams and Eldridge Pope Hardy Country (maybe Tetleys on sparkler) *(Robert Lester)*

[225 Clayhall Ave], *Unicorn*: Large dining pub with waitress drinks service in plushly refurbished roomy saloon, books and bric-a-brac, good beer choice inc Flowers Original; good atmosphere in public bar with pool and two darts boards, quiz night Mon, karaoke Weds *(Robert Lester)*

WOODFORD

[The Broadway (A1168)], *Sir Winston Churchill*: Fullers London Pride and Scottish Courage ales and enjoyable food in big modern pub, recently tastefully refurbished *(Robert Lester)*

Children welcome means the pub says it lets children inside without any special restriction. If it allows them in, but to restricted areas such as an eating area or family room, we specify this. Some pubs may impose an evening time limit.

Scotland

Edinburgh and Glasgow have some excellent town pubs, with a good choice in the main entries and many more in the Lucky Dip section at the end of the chapter. A new find in Glasgow this year is the Counting House, a sumptuous conversion of a former bank. Outside these cities, many of the places that do duty as pubs in Scotland are in fact hotels, and this does tend to make them different from what people used to English pubs might expect – either more hotelish in style and atmosphere, or very much a locals' bar tacked on to a bigger place, without the equivalent of a lounge bar. Even so, there are plenty of good places to be discovered, throughout the country and often in marvellous positions. Pubs and inns currently doing particularly well here include the Village Inn at Arrochar (entirely new to the Guide, a most enjoyable find), the unspoilt and unchanging Fishermans Tavern in Broughty Ferry, the civilised yet homely Riverside at Canonbie (good food and wines), the showy Guildford Arms in Edinburgh (under a fine new landlord), the very well run Babbity Bowster in Glasgow, the Queens Head in Kelso (new to the main entries – a thoroughly well run old coaching inn), the remote Kilberry Inn at Kilberry (delicious food and a nice place to stay – it's our choice as Scotland's Dining Pub of the Year), the civilised Lade Inn at Kilmahog (another new entry, good food and wine), the bustling Oban Inn in Oban (another good new manager), the recently refurbished Killiecrankie Hotel just outside Pitlochy, the Plockton Hotel in the idyllic waterside village of Plockton, the Skeabost House Hotel on Skye (marvellous lunchtime buffet), the Wheatsheaf at Swinton (excellent food), the Tushielaw Inn at Tushielaw in the Ettrick Valley (good all round), the arty bustling Ceilidh Place in Ullapool, and the Ailean Chraggan at Weem. We have divided the Lucky Dip section at the end of the chapter into the various regions, so as to help narrow the choice by areas. Following a poll of readers we will be sticking to these regions, at least for the time being, as more familiar and more useful than the new unitary authority districts being phased in instead (we are adopting the same approach in Wales). Places to look out for particularly in this section include the Tibbie Shiels at St Marys Loch (Borders), Inverarnan Drovers Inn at Inverarnan (Central), Murray Arms in Gatehouse of Fleet and Black Bull in Moffat (Dumfries & Galloway), Cambo Arms at Kingsbarns, Grange outside St Andrews and Cabin at St Monance (Fife), Crooked Inn at Crook of Alves and Towie at Turriff (Grampian), Royal in Cromarty, Clachaig at Glencoe, Glenelg Inn at Glenelg, Kylesku Hotel at Kylesku and Creag Nan Darach at Plockton (Highland), Cramond Inn in Cramond and Drovers in East Linton (Lothian), Ship in Broughty Ferry and Nivingston House at Cleish (Tayside), and on the islands Sligachan Hotel and Stein Inn on Skye and Pollachar Hotel on South Uist. Drinks prices in Scottish pubs are rather higher than the national average, with pubs taking the trouble to bring in beer from good value distant breweries (such as the Riverside at Canonbie) generally the best value; the new Counting House in Glasgow stood out as particularly cheap.

ABERDEEN (Grampian) NJ9305 Map 11
Prince of Wales £ ◀

7 St Nicholas Lane

Standing in the narrow cobbled lane outside this individual old tavern, it would be easy to forget that this the very heart of the city's shopping centre, with Union Street almost literally overhead. A bustlingly cosy, unspoilt flagstoned area has the city's longest bar counter and is furnished with pews and other wooden furniture in screened booths, while a smarter main lounge has a fruit machine. A minor refurbishment is planned. Popular and generous home-made lunchtime food includes filled french bread (£2.70), filled baked potatoes (£3), macaroni cheese (£3.30), steak pie or lamb stew (£3.50), chicken curry (£3.95), and fresh breaded haddock (£4). A fine range of particularly well kept beers includes Bass, Caledonian 80/-, Orkney Dark Island, Theakstons Old Peculier, Youngers No 3, and guest ales on handpump or tall fount air pressure. No children. *(Recommended by Andrew Rogers, Amanda Milsom, Tom McLean, Esther and John Sprinkle, Graham Reeve, Angus Lyon, George Atkinson, Mark Walker, Chris Raisin)*

Free house ~ Licensee Peter Birnie ~ Real ale ~ Lunchtime meals and snacks (not Sun) ~ (01224) 640597 ~ No nearby parking ~ Open 11-midnight; 12.30-11 Sun

APPLECROSS (Highland) NG7144 Map 11
Applecross Inn ⓜ

Off A896 S of Shieldaig

The exhilarating drive over the 'pass of the cattle' (one of the highest in Britain), on a fine evening and to then find this friendly compact inn, takes some beating. The simple bar is quite comfortable, and favoured by the cheerful locals, and the good, popular food includes sandwiches (from £1.50), home-made vegetable soup (£1.75), nice venison or cheese burgers (£2.15), garlic mushrooms (£2.50), fresh deep-fried cod or haddock (£4.95), squat lobster curry or half-a-dozen local oysters (£5.95), queen scallops in a cream wine and mushroom sauce or dressed local crab salad (£7.50), sirloin steak (£9.95), and puddings like home-baked apple crumble (£2.50); you must book for the no-smoking restaurant; marvellous breakfasts. Darts, pool, dominoes, and juke box (unless there are musicians in the pub); a good choice of around 50 malt whiskies, and efficient service. There is a nice garden by the shore with tables. Bedrooms are small and simple but adequate, all with a sea view. Mountain bikes for hire. *(Recommended by Andrew Hazeldine, E Locker, David and Judy Walmsley, D G Clarke, Mark and Diane Grist, Vicky and David Sarti)*

Free house ~ Licensee Judith Fish ~ Meals and snacks (12-9 in summer; 12-2, 7-9 in winter) ~ Restaurant ~ (01520) 744262 ~ Children welcome until 8pm ~ Open 11-11(midnight Fri, 11.30 Sat); 12.30-11 Sun; cl 3-5 Mon-Thur from Nov to Mar; closed 1 Jan ~ Bedrooms: £22.50/£45

ARDFERN (Strathclyde) NM8004 Map 11
Galley of Lorne

B8002; village and inn signposted off A816 Lochgilphead—Oban

Ideally placed across from Loch Craignish, and popular with locals and boating people, this enjoyable inn has marvellous views from seats on the sheltered terrace over the sea and yacht anchorage. The same views can be enjoyed from the cosy main bar, which also has a log fire and is decorated with old Highland dress prints and other pictures, big navigation lamps by the bar counter, and an unfussy assortment of furniture, including little winged settles and upholstered window seats on its lino tiles. Good bar food includes home-made soup (£1.85; soup and a sandwich £3.75), haggis with whisky and cream (£3.25), lunchtime open sandwiches (from £3.50), ploughman's or burgers (from £4.75), moules marinières (£4.95; large £8.95), vegetable korma (£5.25), home-made steak pie (£5.95), fresh battered sole fillets (£7.85), daily specials like deep-fried brie with redcurrant jelly (£2.95), wild boar braised in beer (£8.75) or Loch Craignish langoustines, and puddings such as home-made sticky ginger pudding with toffee sauce (from £2.50); children's menu (from £1); spacious restaurant. Quite a few malt whiskies; darts, pool, dominoes, fruit machine. *(Recommended by John and Sheila French, Richard Gibbs, Vicky and David Sarti, A F Ford)*

Free house ~ Licensee Susana Garland ~ Meals and snacks ~ Restaurant ~ (01852) 500284 ~ Children in eating area of bar ~ Occasional folk music ~ Open 11-2.30, 5-11.30; 11am-11.30pm Sat; 12-11 Sun; closed 25 Dec ~ Bedrooms: £37.50B/£65B

ARDUAINE (Strathclyde) NM7910 Map 11
Loch Melfort Hotel 🛏

On A816 S of Oban and overlooking Asknish Bay

It's just a short stroll from this comfortable cream-washed Edwardian hotel through grass and wild flowers to the rocky foreshore, where the licensees keep their own lobster pots and nets, and from the wooden seats on the front terrace, there's a magnificent view over the wilderness of the loch and its islands. The airy and modern bar has a pair of powerful marine glasses which you can use to search for birds and seals on the islets and on the coasts of the bigger islands beyond. The creamy walls are papered with nautical charts, there are wheelback chairs around wooden tables, a panelled bar counter, a wooden planked ceiling, and a log-effect gas fire. An extensive bar food menu might include home-made soup or sandwiches (£2.50), large filled baguettes (£3.95), Aberdeen Angus burger (£4.75), ploughman's (£4.95), tagliatelle provençale (£5.50), Ormsary venison sausages with caramelised onions (£5.95) half-a-dozen Ardencaple oysters (£6.50), local langoustines with herb or garlic butter (£9.50), their own cured gravadlax with dill and sweet mustard sauce (£8.95), Aberdeen Angus steaks (from £11.50), half a local lobster (from £12.00), and daily specials like chicken liver parfait with peppercorn dressing and salad (£5.95), freshly dressed local crab (£7.95), and local split langoustines grilled with herb or garlic butter (£9.50); home-made puddings (from £2.25), and children's menu (£3.50). The main restaurant is no smoking; good wine list and selection of malt whiskies. Passing yachtsmen are welcome to use the mooring and drying facilities, and hot showers. From late April to early June the walks through the neighbouring Arduaine woodland gardens are lovely. The comfortable bedrooms have sea views. *(Recommended by John and Barbara Burns, Stephen Holman, Julie and Steve Anderton, Mark and Diane Grist, J E Rycroft; also in Good Hotel Guide)*

Free house ~ Licensees Philip and Rosalind Lewis ~ Meals and snacks ~ Restaurant ~ (01852) 200233 ~ Children welcome ~ Open 10am-11pm; cl 5 Jan-28 Feb ~ Bedrooms: £64B/£99B

ARDVASAR (Isle of Skye) NG6203 Map 11
Ardvasar Hotel 🛏

A851 at S of island; just past Armadale pier where the summer car ferries from Mallaig dock

A good mix of visitors and locals enjoy this friendly and comfortably modernised white stone inn. The simple public bar has stripped pews and kitchen chairs, and the cocktail bar is furnished with plush wall seats and stools around dimpled copper coffee tables on the patterned carpet, and Highland dress prints on the cream hessian-and-wood walls. In a room off the comfortable hotel lounge there are armchairs around the attractive coal-effect gas fire; darts, dominoes, cribbage, pool, pinball, juke box, fruit machine, and background music. Particularly good home-made bar food includes country-style lamb and vegetable broth (£2.50), basket meals (from £3.50), lentil and cheese bake with provençale sauce (£6.30), roast prime rib of Scottish beef with bordelaise sauce (£6.80), roast marinaded local pheasant breast with venison served with apple and calvados sauce (£12.90), large baked scallops with grapes, cheese, mustard and wine sauce (£13.90). The cold menu includes roast gigot of Skye lamb with minted orange salad (£6.50) and fresh dressed local crab with mixed salad (£8.00). Puddings include warm apricot and marmalade almond flan with cream (£2.20), blueberry cheesecake with cream (£2.60) and banana meringue ice-cream sundae with hot chocolate sauce (£2.90). Well kept St Andrews ale and a weekly guest beer tapped from the cask, and lots of malt whiskies. The views across the Sound of

Sleat – an area often referred to as the Island's garden – and to the dramatic mountains of Knoydart are very fine. Handy for the Clan Donald centre. *(Recommended by Stephen Holman, Andrew and Kerstin Lewis, Walter and Susan Rinaldi-Butcher; more reports please)*

Free house ~ Licensees Bill and Gretta Fowler ~ Real ale ~ Bar meals and snacks (12-2, 5-7 and 8.30-9.30) ~ Restaurant ~ (01471) 844223 ~ Children welcome until 8 ~ Live entertainment in winter ~ Open 12(12.30 Sun)-11; closed all day Mon; Jan/Feb open 5-11 only ~ Bedrooms: £40B/£70B

ARROCHAR (Strathclyde) NN2904 Map 11
Village Inn

A814, just off A83 W of Loch Lomond

Though it's not an old building, this warm and cheerful place has recently been refurbished in a style that gives it some character, and a pleasantly old-world atmosphere. The comfortable bar has a good open fire, with steps up to what for readers is the real heart of the place – a larger informal dining area, with lots of bare wood, and lovely views (over the shore road) of the head of Loch Long, and the hills around The Cobbler, the main peak opposite. Good straightforward home-made food includes large filled rolls (£2.50), ploughman's (£3.95), stilton and broccoli quiche (£4.05), haggis, neeps and tatties (£4.80), grilled trout with almonds (£5.40), venison pie (£7.50), rack of lamb (£8.95), excellent fresh fish such as herring in oatmeal and succulent steamed mussels, daily specials such as roast duck breast on peach sauce with a citrus fruit dressing (£10.25) or half lobster with cheese and monkfish sauce (£12.75), and puddings such as fresh plum pudding, Drambuie parfait with fruits of the forest or sticky toffee pudding (from £2.50); children's menu (£2.65). Service is efficient but unobtrusive, and the sociable landlord makes a point of circulating – ready for a chat if customers want it. Well kept Maclays 70/-, 80/- and Wallace IPA and a guest such as Heather Fraoch Ale on handpump, and 42 malt whiskies; piped music. *(Recommended by Dr Jim Mackay, Simon and Karen Lemieux, James Paterson, Mr and Mrs Scott-Gall)*

Free house ~ Licensee J A Paterson ~ Real ale ~ Meals and snacks (11-10) ~ Restaurant ~ (01301) 702279 ~ Children welcome until 8pm ~ Folk music Sun lunchtime ~ Open 11am-12pm; 11am-1am Sat ~ Bedrooms: £35B/£50B

BRIG O TURK (Central) NN5306 Map 11
Byre

A821 Callander—Trossachs

This is a lovely setting on the edge of a network of forest and lochside tracks in the Queen Elizabeth Forest Park – lots of walking, cycling, and fishing. Inside this carefully converted friendly 18th-c place, the cosy, spotless beamed bar has prints and old photographs of the area, some decorative plates, stuffed wildlife, comfortable brass-studded black dining chairs, an open fire, and rugs on the stone and composition floor. Using fresh local produce, bar food includes home-made soup (£2.10), sandwiches (from £2.75), haggis, neeps and tatties (£2.95), filled baked potatoes (£3.25), mushroom stroganoff (£4.95), deep fried haddock or wild game casserole (£5.95), chicken, bacon and haggis with a whisky and grain mustard sauce (£6.50), and puddings (£2.95). The no-smoking à la carte restaurant is popular in the evenings so it is best to book (there is no bar food on Saturday evening, though you can eat from the restaurant menu in the bar). Well kept Maclays 70/-, Wallace IPA and guests on handpump, and 20 malt whiskies; traditional Scottish piped music. There are tables under parasols outside. *(Recommended by H L Dennis, Bill and Brenda Lemon, Susan and John Douglas, Mr and Mrs J R Morris, RWD)*

Free house ~ Licensees Liz and Eugene Maxwell ~ Real ale ~ Meals and snacks ~ Restaurant ~ (01877) 376292 ~ Children welcome ~ Open 12-11; 12.30-11 Sun; closed 3-6 winter afternoons

BROUGHTY FERRY (Tayside) NO4630 Map 11
Fishermans Tavern £ ⇌ ■

12 Fort St; turning off shore road

Happily, little changes at this unspoilt, bustling town pub, and they still have an impressive range of well kept real ales such as Belhaven Sandy Hunters and St Andrews Ale, Boddingtons Bitter, and Maclays 80/-, and three guest ales changing daily on handpump or tall fount air pressure; there's also a good choice of malt whiskies, some local country wines, and bottled wheat beer. The little brown carpeted snug on the right with its nautical tables, light pink soft fabric seating, basket-weave wall panels and beige lamps is the more lively bar, and on the left is a secluded lounge area. The carpeted back bar (popular with diners) has a Victorian fireplace; dominoes and fruit machine, and an open coal fire. Lunchtime bar food includes filled rolls or home-made steak and gravy pie (£1.10), prawns in ginger and garlic breadcrumb coating (£2.25), filled jacket potatoes (£3.10), hot Mexican flour tortilla with spicy chicken, chilli and tomato filling (£3.25); enjoyable breakfasts. The nearby seafront gives a good view of the two long, low Tay bridges. Disabled lavatories. The breakfast room is no smoking. The landlord also runs the Speedwell Bar in Dundee.
(Recommended by Tom McLean, Roger Huggins, L G Milligan, Eric Locker, Susan and John Douglas, Dave Braisted, Audrey Jackson)

Free house ~ Licensee Jonathan Stewart ~ Real ale ~ Lunchtime meals 12-2.30 and snacks all day (Jul/Aug no food exc high teas for guests; snacks only Sun) ~ Restaurant ~ (01382) 775941 ~ Children welcome ~ Open 11am-midnight(1am Sat) ~ Bedrooms: £19/£38

CANONBIE (Dumfries and Galloway) NY3976 Map 9
Riverside ⑩ ⇌ ♀

Village signposted from A7

Civilised and welcoming, this little inn remains most popular for its lovely food and wine. The comfortable communicating rooms of the bar have a mix of chintzy furnishings and dining chairs, pictures on the walls for sale, some stuffed wildlife, and a relaxing atmosphere; half of the bar and the dining room are no smoking. Tables are usually laid for dining and the varied bar menu, on two blackboards, might include soups such as smoked ham and lentil, mushroom and mustard or broccoli and pea, with home-made breads like tomato and courgette or Guinness and treacle loaf (£2.20); starters such as potted guinea fowl with mushrooms or smoked mackerel and peppercorns (£4.95), and six Loch Fyne oysters (£5.95), with main courses such as beef hash (£6.55), enormous haddock fillet in beer batter (£6.95), roast chunky cod with cheese and red onion crust (£7.55), fried lemon sole (£7.95), guinea fowl with lemon and rosemary (£8.25), thick barnsley chop (£8.95), rib-eye steak (£10.95), and fine puddings such as hot rhubarb and ginger crumble or toffee apple bake, and cold orange mousse or dark chocolate profiteroles (£2.95). Traditional three course Sunday lunch (£11.95). They have always used top quality ingredients and suppliers – Aberdeen Angus beef, free-range chicken and pork, local roe deer, free-range eggs, organic breads and unpasteurised cheeses, fresh fish three times a week and fresh, seasonal vegetables. Well kept Yates Bitter and various guests every couple of weeks on handpump, a good range of properly kept and served wines, and quite a few malt whiskies. In summer – when it can get very busy – there are tables under the trees on the front grass. Over the quiet road, a public playground runs down to the Border Esk (the inn can arrange fishing permits), and there are lovely walks in the area.
(Recommended by Joy and Peter Heatherley, Alan Lillie, V W Prime, Wm Van Laaten, Mr and Mrs G Dundas, John and Beryl Knight, John and Barbara Burns, Luke Worthington, Christine and Malcolm Ingram, SS, John and Phyllis Maloney, G McGrath, Mrs G Bishop, Peter Bell, J M Potter; also in Good Hotel Guide)

Free house ~ Licensee Robert Phillips ~ Real ale ~ Meals and snacks ~ Children welcome ~ Restaurant (cl Sun) ~ (013873) 71512/71295 ~ Open 11-2.30, 6.30-11(midnight Sat); 12-2.30, 6.30-11 Sun; closed 2 weeks in Feb and Nov, 25/26 Dec and 1/2 Jan ~ Bedrooms: £55B/£75B

CARBOST (Isle of Skye) NG3732 Map 11
Old Inn

This is the Carbost on the B8009, in the W of the central part of the island

Before a trip around the Talisker distillery (only 100 yards away), this simple stone house is a useful place to come. From the terrace, there are fine views of Loch Harport and the harsh craggy peaks of the Cuillin Hills – and the place is popular with walkers and climbers. The three simple areas of the main bare-board bar are knocked through into one, and furnished with red leatherette settles, benches and seats, amusing cartoons on the part-whitewashed and part-stripped stone walls, and a peat fire; darts, pool, cribbage, dominoes, and piped traditional music. A small selection of sustaining bar meals includes spicy tomato soup (£1.60), sandwiches, sausage hotpot (£5.25), battered cod (£5.50), fresh salmon salad (£6.50), sirloin steak (£9.50). Several malt whiskies – including Talisker. Children's play area. Non-residents can come for the breakfasts if they book the night before, and the bedrooms in a separate annexe have sea views. *(Recommended by Julie and Steve Anderton, A P Jeffreys, John and Joan Nash, Mrs Olive Oxley, Tim Heywood, Sophie Wilne, R J Bland)*

Free house ~ Licensee Deirdre Cooper ~ Meals and snacks (12-2, 6-10) ~ (01478) 640205 ~ Children welcome ~ Occasional live music ~ Open 11am-midnight(11.30 Sat); 11-2.30, 5-11 in winter; 12.30-11 Sun ~ Bedrooms: £24B/£48B

CAWDOR (Highland) NH8450 Map 11
Cawdor Tavern

Just off B9090 in Cawdor village; follow signs for post office and village centre

The outside of this little Highland village pub is modern, so it's a surprise to find inside a substantial lounge with surprisingly eclectic and stately furnishings. A refurbishment is planned which will not affect either the beautiful oak panelling – gifted to the tavern by a former Lord Cawdor and salvaged from the nearby castle – or the chimney breast. The public bar on the right has elaborate wrought-iron wall lamps, chandeliers laced with bric-a-brac and an imposing pillared serving counter, and the lounge has green plush button-back built-in wall banquettes and bucket chairs, a delft shelf with toby jugs and decorative plates (chiefly game), small tapestries, attractive sporting pictures, and a log fire. Good bar food includes sandwiches, fresh mussels steamed with garlic, shallots, cream and white wine (£3.15), home-made salmon fishcakes (£3.25), smoked seafood platter (£4.25), venison sausages with creamed potatoes and onion gravy (£5.25), steamed sole fillets with white wine and chive sauce (£7.25), chicken breast filled with haggis in a Drambuie cream sauce (£8.95), puddings like lemon soufflé (from £2.95); the restaurant is partly no smoking. Darts, pool, cribbage, dominoes, board games, cards, fruit machine, video games, juke box, piped music. There are tables on the front terrace, with tubs of flowers, roses, and creepers climbing the supports of a big awning. *(Recommended by Richard Dolphin, J G Kirby, Joan and Tony Walker; more reports please)*

Free house ~ Licensee Norman Sinclair ~ Meals and snacks (12-2, 5.30-9) ~ Restaurant ~ (01667) 404777 ~ Children welcome away from public bar ~ Frequent Scottish folk music ~ Open 11-11 (12.30am Fri and Sat); 11-3, 5-11 winter weekday afternoons; 12.30-11 Sun; closed 25 Dec

CLACHAN SEIL (Highland) NM7718 Map 11
Tigh an Truish

This island is linked by a bridge via B844, off A816 S of Oban

Near a lovely anchorage and set next to the attractive old bridge which joins Seil Island to the mainland, this is a traditional 18th-c local. The unpretentious and informal L-shaped bar has pine-clad walls and ceiling, some fixed wall benches along with the wheelback and other chairs, tartan curtains for the bay windows overlooking the inlet, prints and oil paintings, and a woodburning stove in one room, with open fires in the others. Tasty bar food includes home-made soup (£1.70), sweet pickled herring (£2.75), home-made nut burgers (£3.75), lasagne (£4.95), seafood pie (£5.50), locally caught prawns with garlic mayonnaise (£6.95), and puddings such as chocolate pudding or treacle tart (from £1.60). Well kept McEwans 80/- and Youngers No 3, and regular summer guest beers on handpump, and a good choice of malt whiskies; darts and dominoes. There are some seats in the small garden, and they have their own filling station just opposite. (*Recommended by Paul and Ursula Randall, Julie and Steve Anderton, Jean and George Dundas, Neil Townend, Mark and Diane Grist, GSB, Andrew and Kerstin Lewis, Roberto Villa, Mrs Olive Oxley*)

Free house ~ Licensee Miranda Brunner ~ Real ale ~ Meals and snacks 12-2.15, 6-8.30 ~ Restaurant ~ (01852) 300242 ~ Children in restaurant ~ Occasional live music ~ Open 11(12.30 Sun)-11.30; 11-2.30, 5-11.30 winter Mon-Thurs ~ Self-catering twin/double flats: £40B

CREEBRIDGE (Dumfries and Galloway) NX4165 Map 9
Creebridge House 🛏
Minnigaff, just E of Newton Stewart

Set in three acres of gardens and woodland, this sizeable country house is a fine place to stay with lots to do nearby – fishing, walking, pony-trekking, and complimentary golf at the local golf course. There are tables under cocktail parasols out on the front terrace looking across a pleasantly planted lawn, and croquet. The welcoming and neatly kept carpeted bar has that great rarity for Scotland, a bar billiards table – as well as Black Sheep, Orkney Dark Island and Theakstons on handpump, and about 40 malt whiskies. Enjoyable bar food includes home-made soup (£2.10), lunchtime sandwiches (from £2.75; baguettes from £3.75), home-made chicken liver pâté (£3.60), Creebridge curry, home-made lasagne or gammon and egg (£5.95), lamb shank (£7.95), local salmon with creamed leek and asparagus (£9.50), and good steaks (from £10.95); daily specials, excellent fresh fish on Fridays, and Sunday lunchtime carvery in the comfortable restaurant. Meats are local and well hung, presentation is careful with good attention to detail. Fruit machine, comfortably pubby furniture, and maybe unobtrusive piped music. The garden restaurant is no smoking. (*Recommended by Julian Holland, Neil Townend; also in Good Hotel Guide; more reports please*)

Free house ~ Licensees Susan and Chris Walker ~ Real ale ~ Meals and snacks ~ Restaurant ~ (01671) 402121 ~ Children welcome ~ Open 12-2.30, 6-11.30(midnight Sat), 12-2, 6-11 Sun ~ Bedrooms: £48B/£82B

CRINAN (Strathclyde) NR7894 Map 11
Crinan Hotel 🍴 🛏
A816 NE from Lochgilphead, then left on to B841, which terminates at the village

For over 27 years Mr and Mrs Ryan have run this beautifully positioned large hotel. It has marvellous views of the busy entrance basin of the Crinan Canal with its fishing boats and yachts wandering out towards the Hebrides – picture windows in the two stylish upstairs bars make the most of this view. The simpler wooden-floored public bar (opening onto a side terrace) has a cosy stove and kilims on the seats, and the cocktail bar (no smoking during lunch) has a nautical theme with wooden floors, oak and walnut panelling, antique tables and chairs, and sailing pictures and classic yachts framed in walnut on a paper background of rust and green paisley, matching the tartan upholstery. The Gallery bar is done in pale terracotta and creams and has a central bar with stools, Lloyd Loom tables and chairs, and lots of plants. Popular bar food (lunchtime only) includes home-made soup (£3.25), smoked haddock (£5.75), local mussels or cold ham salad (£8.95), pastry boats filled with fresh seafood (£9.50), locally seafood wild salmon (£10.50), seafood stew (£13.50), and a pudding of the day such as lemon tart or chocolate roulade (£3.75); Scottish farmhouse cheddar (from a 75lb cheese) with oatcakes (£3.75); you can get sandwiches and so forth from their coffee shop. There's a good wine list, and about 20 malt whiskies and freshly squeezed orange juice. The restaurants are very formal. (*Recommended by D P Brown; more reports please; also in Good Hotel Guide*)

Free house ~ Licensee Nicholas Ryan ~ Lunchtime meals (12-2.30) ~ Restaurants ~ (01546) 830261 ~ Children in eating area of bar ~ Open 11(12 Sun)-11; 11-2.30, 5-11 winter ~ Bedrooms: £105B/£210B – these prices also include dinner

EDINBURGH (Lothian) NT2574 Map 11

The two main areas here for finding good pubs, both main entries and Lucky Dips, are around Rose St (just behind Princes St in the New Town) and along or just off the top part of the Royal Mile in the Old Town. In both areas parking can be difficult at lunchtime, but is not such a problem in the evenings.

Athletic Arms ◗ £

Angle Park Terr; on corner of Kilmarnock Rd (A71)

At its busiest when football or rugby matches are being played at Tynecastle or Murrayfield (when they may have a team of up to 15 red-jacketed barmen serving), this thoroughly unpretentious, old-fashioned, plain pub is also known as the Diggers, thanks to its earlier popularity with workers from the nearby cemetery. It's the official home of McEwans 80/-, so you'll find it exceptionally well kept, and dispensed from a gleaming row of eleven tall air-pressure fonts which also serve guests like Courage Best, Exmoor Gold, Hopback Summer Lightning, and Orkney Raven; several malt whiskies. Opening off the central isle and servery there are some cubicles partitioned in glossy grey wood with photographs of Hearts and Scotland football teams – a side room is crowded with keen dominoes players; fruit machine, cribbage and darts; predominantly young customers. Good value pies (from 80p), stovies (£1.20) and burgers (£1.35) are served all day. No children. *(Recommended by Keith Torrie, David Carr; more reports please)*

Scottish Courage ~ Manager Scott Martin ~ Real ale ~ Snacks all day ~ (0131) 337 3822 ~ Folk music some evenings ~ Open 11-midnight; 12.30-6 Sun

Bannermans Bar ◗ £

212 Cowgate

Before this became a pub, it was used to store oysters. It's set in the heart of the city and has a unique warren of simple crypt-like flagstoned rooms with barrel-vaulted ceilings, bare stone walls and bright strip lighting, wood panelling and pillars at the front, and theatrical posters and handbills in the rooms leading off. A huge mixture of purely functional furnishings includes old settles, pews and settees around barrels, red-painted tables and a long mahogany table. A no-smoking back area, with tables and waitress service, is open when they're busy. It's popular with students, and one of the best times to visit is during the Festival when there's even more atmosphere. Well kept Caledonian 80/- and Caledonian Deuchars IPA, Theakstons Best, Youngers No 3, and regular guests from smaller Scottish breweries on handpump, with plenty of malt whiskies and Belgian fruit beers. Good value, popular food includes toasties (from £1), particularly good soup (from £1.40), stuffed peppers (£3.20), french bread filled with things like brie and black grape or salami, radicchio and avocado (£3.45), mushroom tortellini pasta or crêpes stuffed with smoked fish and parsley cream (£3.85), and puddings (from £1.65); budget lunch (soup and bread plus a hot main course £2.85), and popular weekend breakfasts (11-3.45; from £3.25). Dominoes, cribbage, trivia, cards and board games. *(Recommended by Terry Barlow, Jenny and Roger Huggins, Peter Todd, Peter Marshall, Ian Williams, Linda Mar, David Carr)*

Free house ~ Licensee Kevin Doyle ~ Real ale ~ Lunchtime meals and snacks, evening snacks ~ (0131) 556 3254 ~ Children welcome until 7pm ~ Live music Tues/Weds/Thurs/Sun evenings ~ Open 11-1am; 11am (licensed from 12.30)-midnight Sun

---

Tipping is not normal for bar meals, and not usually expected.

Bow Bar ★ £ ◧

80 West Bow

This traditional drinking pub is conveniently located just below the Castle. Around a dozen very well kept real ales are served from impressive tall founts made by Aitkens, Mackie & Carnegie, Gaskell & Chambers, and McGlashan, dating from the 1920s: Caledonian 80/- and Deuchars IPA, Courage Directors, Dent Aviator, Exmoor Gold, Village Brewer White Boar, and guest beers. The grand carved mahogany gantry has an impressive array of malts (over 140) including lots of Macallan variants and cask strength whiskies; the pub is an exclusive supplier of Scottish Still Spirit, with a good collection of vodkas (nine) and gins (eight), and, particularly, rums (24). The spartan rectangular bar has a fine collection of appropriate enamel advertising signs and handsome antique trade mirrors, sturdy leatherette wall seats and heavy narrow tables on its lino floor, cafe-style bar seats, an umbrella stand by the period gas fire, a (silent) prewar radio, a big pendulum clock, and a working barograph. Look out for the antiqued photograph of the bar staff in old-fashioned clothes (and moustaches). Simple, cheap bar snacks – steak and mince pies or submarine sandwiches (£1.00), steak pies (£1.20); no games or music – just relaxed chat, and the clink of glasses. *(Recommended by Andy and Jill Kassube, M Walker, Vicky and David Sarti, Wayne Brindle, David Carr, Andy Schweizer, Bjorn Vondras; more reports please)*

Free house ~ Licensee Grant Cairncross ~ Real ale ~ Lunchtime snacks 12-4 (not Sun) ~ (0131) 226 7667 ~ Open 11am-11.30pm; 12.30-11 Sun; closed 25/26 Dec, 1/2 Jan

Cafe Royal Circle Bar

West Register St

Built last century as a flagship for the latest in Victorian gas and plumbing fittings, the interesting cafe rooms here have a series of highly detailed Doulton tilework portraits (although sadly they are partly obscured by the fruit machines) of historical innovators Watt, Faraday, Stephenson, Caxton, Benjamin Franklin and Robert Peel (famous here as the introducer of calico printing). The gantry over the big island bar counter is similar to the one that was here originally, the floor and stairway are laid with marble, there are leather-covered seats, and chandeliers hang from the fine ceilings. Well kept McEwans 80/-, Morlands Old Speckled Hen, Theakstons Best, and a weekly guest beer on handpump (some kept under light blanket pressure); about 25 malt whiskies. The bar has a lunchtime carvery with hot roast beef, pork and lamb sandwiches and rolls carved to order (£1.50-£2.20). Good choice of daily newspapers, video game. *(Recommended by Roger Huggins, Eric Larkham, Mark Walker, David Carr, Wayne Brindle)*

Scottish Courage ~ Manageress Maureen Diponio ~ Real ale ~ Lunchtime snacks (not Sun) ~ Restaurant ~ (0131) 556 1884 ~ Children in restaurant ~ Open 11-11(midnight Thurs; till 1am Fri/Sat); 12.30-11 Sun

Guildford Arms ◧

West Register St

A most enjoyable Victorian city pub with a friendly, bustling atmosphere and a good mix of customers. The main bar has lots of mahogany, glorious colourfully painted plasterwork and ceilings, big original advertising mirrors, and heavy swagged velvet curtains at the arched windows. The snug little upstairs gallery restaurant gives a dress-circle view of the main bar (notice the lovely old mirror decorated with two tigers on the way up), and under this gallery a little cavern of arched alcoves leads off the bar. A fine choice of real ales on handpump, six of which are usually Scottish, might include Bass, Belhaven 60/-, Caledonian Deuchars IPA and 80/-, Harviestoun 70/- and Ptarmigan, Orkney Dark Island, and around four guest ales (three English) on handpump. During the Edinburgh Festival they may hold a beer and folk festival. Good choice of malt whiskies; fruit machine, lunchtime piped jazz and classical music. Bar food includes chargrilled steak burger (£4.75), home-made steak pie (£4.85), breaded haddock (£4.95); daily specials all under £5. It is very popular, but even at its busiest you shouldn't have to wait to be served. No children. *(Recommended by Andy and Jill Kassube, Eric Larkham, Roger Huggins, P Rome, Mark Walker, Wayne Brindle, John Fazakerley, David Carr, Ian Williams, Linda Mar, Neil Townend)*

Free house ~ Licensee David Stewart ~ Real ale ~ Lunchtime meals and snacks ~ (0131) 556 4312 ~ Open 11-11(midnight Thurs/Fri/Sat); 12.30-11 Sun

Kays Bar £

39 Jamaica St West; off India St

John Kay was the original owner selling whisky and wine; wine barrels were hoisted up to the first floor and dispensed through pipes attached to nipples which can still be seen around the light rose. The cosy little bar is bigger than the exterior suggests and has casks, vats and old wine and spirits merchant notices, gas-type lamps, well worn red plush wall banquettes and stools around cast-iron tables, and red pillars supporting a red ceiling. A quiet panelled back room leads off, with a narrow plank-panelled pitched ceiling; very warm open coal fire in winter. A good range of constantly changing and interesting real ales might include well kept Belhaven 80/-, Boddingtons, Exe Valley Devon Glory, Exmoor Ale, McEwans 80/-, Theakstons Best and XB, Tomintoul Wild Cat, and Youngers No 3 on handpump; up to 70 malts, between eight and 40 years old and 10 blended whiskies. Simple lunchtime bar food (with prices unchanged for a second year) includes soup (95p), haggis, neaps and tatties, chilli or steak pie (£2.60), filled baked potatoes (£2.75) and chicken balti, lasagne or mince and tatties (£3); dominoes and cribbage. *(Recommended by John Cockell, Roger Huggins, David Carr; more reports please)*

Scottish Courage ~ Tenant David Mackenzie ~ Real ale ~ Lunchtime meals and snacks (12-2.30) ~ (0131) 225 1858 ~ Children in back room until 5pm (must be quiet) ~ Open 11am-11.45pm; 12.30-11 Sun

Starbank ♀ ◀

67 Laverockbank Road, off Starbank Road; on main road Granton—Leith

The picture windows in the neat and airy bar of this comfortably elegant pub give marvellous views over the Firth of Forth. It's also an excellent place for a wide range of rotating beers, with around ten well kept real ales on handpump: Belhaven 80/-, St Andrews Ale and Sandy Hunters Traditional Ale, Boddingtons, Broughton Special Bitter, Courage Directors, Marstons Pedigree, Timothy Taylors Landlord. A good choice of wines too, with usually around 12 by the glass, and 25 malt whiskies. Well presented good bar food (with prices unchanged since last year) includes home-made soup (£1.20), madeira herring salad (£2.50), a daily vegetarian dish (£4.25), lasagne or chilli con carne (£4.50), ploughman's (£4.75), baked haddock mornay (£5.25), mixed seafood salad or roast lamb (£5.50), poached salmon with lemon and herb butter (£6.50); puddings (£2.50). Service is helpful and friendly, the conservatory restaurant is no smoking, and there are no noisy games machines or piped music; sheltered back terrace. *(Recommended by Angus Lyon, David Carr, Dave Braisted, Neil Townend; more reports please)*

Free house ~ Licensee Valerie West ~ Real ale ~ Meals and snacks (12-9 Sat/Sun) ~ Restaurant ~ (0131) 552 4141 ~ Children welcome till 8pm ~ Very occasional jazz ~ Open 11-11(12 Sat); 12.30-11 Sun

ELIE (Fife) NO4900 Map 11
Ship

Harbour

New this year is the acquisition of the next door guest house; if you stay here, you receive concessions on the good food and wine on offer in this welcoming harbourside pub. The villagey, unspoilt beamed bar with friendly locals and staff has a lively nautical feel, as well as coal fires and winged high-backed and button-back leather seats against the partly panelled walls that are studded with old maps; there's a simple carpeted back room. Good bar food includes dishes such as soup (£1.50), garlic mushrooms (£3.80), fresh local haddock and chips (£5.60), vegetable curry (£5.70), chilli pork (£5.75), lentil and mushroom lasagne (£5.90), steak casserole or cider soaked roast ham (£6.20), Scottish steaks from (£11.95), and puddings (from £3); children's dishes (£3.25), and roast Sunday lunch (£7.95; children £3.95). Well kept Belhaven Best and 80/-, and Theakstons Best on handpump; darts, dominoes, captain's mistress, cribbage and shut-the-box. In summer, the pub really comes into its own – the gardens sit prettily above the beach which at low tide is mostly sand, and on summer Sundays provides a pitch for the pub's (successful) cricket team. There are views across the water to the grassy headland which swings round the bay, to the pier and the old stone fish granary on the left, and to the little town on the right – or you can look more closely through a telescope positioned on the balcony of the restaurant; barbecues. *(Recommended by Eric Locker, E A Thwaite, R M Macnaughton)*

Free house ~ Licensees Richard and Jill Philip ~ Real ale ~ Meals ~ Restaurant ~ (01333) 330246 ~ Children welcome (not in front bar) ~ Open 11-midnight(1am Sat); 12.30-11 Sun; closed 25 Dec ~ Bedrooms: £30B/£50B

FORT AUGUSTUS (Highland) NH3709 Map 11
Lock

This is a real pub (rather than a hotel bar) full of locals and characters and with a welcoming and amusing landlord. It's a homely and comfortable place, with a gently faded decor and some stripped stone, and is set at the foot of Loch Ness, and right by the first lock of the flight of five that start the Caledonian Canal's climb to Loch Oich. The atmosphere is lively and cheerful – crowded in summer, when it can be packed in the evenings with a good mix of locals and boating people (it can get a bit smoky then). Good value plain substantial food, with good helpings of chips, includes a pint of mussels (£4.50), seafood chowder or fresh Mallaig haddock (£4.95), terrine of wild salmon mousseline (£5.25), seafood stew (£5.95), game casserole (£6.50), grilled sea trout (£7.95), salmon steak in filo pastry (£10.50), venison (£11.25), and daily specials; quite a bit of the space is set aside for people eating – one part is no smoking. Mr MacLennen has his own fishmonger's shop next door, so the fish dishes are very fresh indeed. McEwans 80/- and guests like Orkney Raven or Tomintoul Stag every week, kept under light blanket pressure, a fine choice of about 100 malt whiskies (in generous measures), and big open fire; there's often unobtrusive piped traditional Scottish music. The upstairs restaurant is no smoking. *(Recommended by P R and S A White, Sue and Bob Ward)*

Free house ~ James MacLennen ~ Real ale ~ Meals and snacks (12-10) ~ Evening restaurant ~ (01320) 366302 ~ Children in eating area of bar and in restaurant ~ Folk music Mon and Weds evenings ~ Open 11am-midnight(11.45 Sat); 11-11 Nov-beg Mar; 12.30-11 Sun

GIFFORD (Lothian) NT5368 Map 11
Tweeddale Arms ⇐

High St

Set in a quiet Borders village, this civilised old inn manages to be a good pub as well as a good hotel and restaurant. The comfortably relaxed lounge bar has cushioned wall seats, chairs and bar chairs, dried flowers in baskets, big Impressionist prints on the apricot coloured walls, and a big curtain that divides off the eating area. The tranquil hotel lounge has antique tables and paintings, chinoiserie chairs and chintzy easy chairs, an oriental rug on one wall, a splendid corner sofa and magazines on a table. Sandwiches are available all day except Sundays, and the lunchtime bar food includes soup (£1.30), a bowl of mussel and onion stew (£3.50), deep-fried battered haddock or leek, basil, broccoli and cauliflower bake (£5.25), poached supreme of salmon with mustard sauce or cold meat platter (£5.50), sautéed supreme of chicken, red chillies, ginger and garlic in a cream sauce or steak and kidney in ale casserole (£5.75), noisettes of lamb with a whole grain mustard sauce or cold salmon and cucumber salad (£6.00), Aberdeen Angus steak (£8.50), and puddings (£2.35). In the evening you may be able to order dishes in the bar from the restaurant. Belhaven 70/-,

Greenmantle, and guest beers such as Borders SOB, Broughton Black Douglas, and Morlands Old Speckled Hen on handpump kept under light blanket pressure, quite a few malt whiskies, and charming, efficient and friendly service; dominoes, fruit machine, cribbage, and piped music. The inn looks across the peaceful green to the 300-year-old avenue of lime trees leading to the former home of the Marquesses of Tweeddale. *(Recommened by Paul and Ursula Randall, John and Joan Wyatt, P W Taylor, Ian Phillips)*

Free house ~ Licensee Mrs W Crook ~ Real ale ~ Meals and snacks ~ Restaurant ~ (01620) 810240 ~ Children welcome ~ Open 11-11(midnight Sat/Sun) ~ Bedrooms: £42.75B/£65B

GLASGOW (Strathclyde) NS5865 Map 11
Babbity Bowster 🏮 ♀

16-18 Blackfriars St

A good mix of customers gathers at this lively but stylish 18th-c town house – more like a continental cafe than a traditional pub. The simply decorated light interior has fine tall windows, well lit photographs and big pen-and-wash drawings in modern frames of Glasgow and its people and musicians, dark grey stools and wall seats around dark grey tables on the stripped wooden boards, and an open peat fire. The bar opens on to a small terrace which has tables under cocktail parasols, and boules. They serve breakfast from 8am-10.30 (till 12.30 Sunday) when you can have a bacon roll (£1.45), Loch Fyne kipper (£1.95), Arbroath smokie (£2.50), and a cooked breakfast (£3.65); all day food includes four home-made soups in three sizes (from £1.50-£3.95), croque monsieur (£2.95), stovies (from £4.50), haggis, tatties and neeps (£3.75; they also do a vegetarian version), pork, garlic and bean casserole or ratatouille (£4.75), west coast mussels (£5.25), and daily specials. There are more elaborate meals in the airy upstairs restaurant. Well kept Maclays 70/- and 80/-, and changing guest beers on air pressure tall fount, a remarkably sound collection of wines, malt whiskies, freshly squeezed orange juice and good tea and coffee. Enthusiastic service is consistently efficient and friendly, taking its example from the energetic landlord. Piped Celtic music and dominoes. Car park. *(Recommended by Andy and Jill Kassube, Stephen Holman, Richard Lewis, Ian Phillips, R Morgan, Mr and Mrs B Langrish, David and Michelle James, Val Stevenson, Rob Holmes; also in Good Hotel Guide)*

Free house ~ Licensee Fraser Laurie ~ Real ale ~ Meals and snacks (12-11) ~ Restaurant ~ 0141 5525055 ~ Children welcome ~ Acoustic music at weekends ~ Open 11(11.30 Sun)-midnight; closed 25 Dec and 1 Jan ~ Bedrooms: £45B/£65B

Bon Accord 🍺 £

153 North St

Attractively done up in the style of a Victorian kitchen, this busy friendly and basic traditional pub keeps a fine range of real ales served from tall founts: Marstons Pedigree, McEwans 80/-, Theakstons Best and Old Peculier, Youngers No 3, and several guest beers on handpump; a decent choice of malt whiskies; nine wines by the glass. Tasty well priced bar food includes filled baked potatoes (£2.25-£2.55), traditional pies (£2.95-£3.75), ploughman's lunch or sausage and mash (£3.45), cod and prawn crumble or broccoli and cheese pasta bake (£3.75), and puddings (£1.15). Dominoes, cribbage, chess and draughts; quiz night is Wednesdays and everyone is welcome. No children. *(Recommended by Ian Jolly, Chris and Sue Bax, Paul Kerr)*

Scottish Courage ~ Manageress Anne Kerr ~ Real ale ~ Meals and snacks (all day) ~ Restaurant ~ (0141) 248 4427 ~ Daytime parking restricted ~ Open 11am-11.45pm; 12.30-11 Sun

---

It's very helpful if you let us know up-to-date food prices when you report on pubs.

Counting House ◀■

24 George Square

A new pillar of the city's financial district, sharing its imposing square with the Chamber of Commerce and firms like Ernst & Young, this grand new Wetherspoons pub was formerly a premier branch of the Royal Bank of Scotland. The conversion has been gloriously done, and once through the stately doors one's first impressions are dominated by the sheer scale of the place. It's a perfect antidote for those who get a slight feeling of claustrophobia in some other Glasgow pubs. A lofty richly decorated coffered ceiling culminates in a great central dome, with nubile caryatids doing a fine supporting job in the corners. There's the sort of decorative glasswork that nowadays seems more appropriate to a landmark pub than to a bank, and plenty of interesting prints and decorative signs on the walls. It's all kept spotless (you can practically set your watch by the rounds of the polisher, who wipes each table several times an hour), and plenty of well spaced solidly comfortable seating in several attractive carpeted areas includes a good no-smoking area. The central island servery has a particularly good range of well kept ales on handpump, such as Caledonian Deuchars, Courage Directors, Tomintoul Black Gold, Theakstsons Best, and two guests such as Hop Back Summer Lightning or Stillmans 80/- and Wild Cat, with a good choice of bottled beers and malt whiskies, and 12 wines by the glass. Sound efficiently served food includes burgers (from £2.95), chicken, ham and leek pie or chicken balti (£4.75), evening steaks (£6.95), daily specials such as cornish pasty (£2.95), chicken goujons (£3.75) or vegetable lasagne (£4.25), and puddings such as chocolate cake or cheesecake (£1.95). Fruit machine, video game. *(Recommended by Ian Baillie, Richard Lewis)*

Free house ~ Licensees Philip and Andrea Annett ~ Real ale ~ Meals and snacks (11-10; 12.30-9.30 Sun) ~ (0141) 248 9568 ~ Open 11am-12pm; 12.30-12 Sun

Horseshoe £

17-19 Drury Street

There's a great deal of fine Victoriana in this friendly pub – lots of old photographs of Glasgow and its people, antique magazine colour plates, pictorial tile inserts of decorous ladies, glistening mahogany and darkly varnished panelled dado, a mosaic tiled floor, a lustrous pink and maroon ceiling, standing height lean-on tables, and curly brass and glass wall lamps; the bar has authentic old-fashioned brass water taps and pillared snob-screens. The horseshoe motif spreads through the place from the opposite promontories of the bar itself to the horseshoe wall clock and horseshoe-shaped fireplaces (most blocked by mirrors now). Bass and Broughton Greenmantle on handpump, and a large selection of malts; fruit machine, video machine, trivia and piped music. Amazingly cheap food is served in the upstairs bar which is less special with seating in rows, though popular with young people: from a choice of 12 main courses, there's a 3-course lunch (£2.40); the resyaurant is no smoking. Not far from Central station. *(Recommended by Richard Lewis, Ian Williams, Linda Mar, Val Stevenson, Rob Holmes)*

Bass ~ Manager David Smith ~ Real ale ~ Meals and snacks (12-7.30) ~ 0141 221 3051 ~ Children in restaurant until 7.30pm ~ Open 11am-midnight; 12.30-midnight Sun

GLENDEVON (Tayside) NN9904 Map 11
Tormaukin ⇌ ♇

A823

Originally a drovers' inn, this smallish, remote hotel has plenty of good walks over the nearby Ochils or along the River Devon – plus over 100 golf courses (including St Andrews) within an hour's drive. It's a comfortable and neatly kept place, and the softly lit bar has plush seats against stripped stone and partly panelled walls, ceiling joists, and maybe gentle piped music; log fires. Good bar food includes soup (£1.95), smooth chicken liver and herb pâté (£3.60), chinese-style pork spare ribs (£4.65), fresh east coast haddock (£6.25), local venison sausages (£6.45), steaks (from £8.95), grilled barnsley chop with redcurrant and red wine sauce (£8.25). Vegetarian and salad dishes include herby crêpes filled with creamy mushrooms and roasted garlic or cajun spiced corn and pepper gumbo (£6.95), duck terrine with orange salad or coronation chicken (£6.95). Puddings like summer fruit crumble with custard or sticky date and walnut pudding (£3.25), and children's menu (from £2.65); good breakfasts. Three well kept real ales on handpump such as Harviestoun 80/-, Ptarmigan 85/-, Montrose or Schiehallion, and Ind Coope Burton on handpump, a decent wine list, and quite a few malt whiskies. Some of the bedrooms are in a converted stable block. Loch and river fishing can be arranged. *(Recommended by Julian Holland, SR, PM, Sue Rowland, Mrs G Bishop, Ian Wilson)*

Free house ~ Licensee Marianne Worthy ~ Real ale ~ Meals and snacks (12-2, 5.30-9.30; all day Sun) ~ (01259) 781252 ~ Restaurant ~ Children welcome ~ Live music winter most Fri evenings ~ Open 11-11; 12-11 Sun; closed two weeks mid Jan ~ Bedrooms: £51B/£72B

INNERLEITHEN (Borders) NT3336 Map 9
Traquair Arms 🛏

Traquair Rd (B709, just off A72 Peebles—Galashiels; follow signs for Traquair House)

This is a hospitable and pleasantly modernised inn with welcoming licensees, and the simple little bar is popular locally, and has a warm open fire, a relaxed atmosphere, and well kept Greenmantle and (from Traquair House) Traquair Bear on handpump; several malt whiskies and draught cider. Enjoyable bar food served by friendly staff includes home-made soup (£1.50), filled baked potatoes (from £2.15), omelettes (from £3.50), ploughman's (£5.20), baked chicken with peaches, spinach and cheese filo pie, border lamb hotpot or venison sausage casserole (all £5.30), steak in ale pie (£5.50), finnan savoury (£5.55), lamb cutlets (£7.65), steaks (from £11.50), and puddings (from £2.50). A pleasant and spacious no-smoking dining room has an open fire and high chairs for children if needed. No music or machines. *(Recommended by Andy and Jill Kassube, Mark Walker, Wayne Brindle, Dr D A Spencer, J M Potter, M J Morgan)*

Free house ~ Licensee Hugh Anderson ~ Real ale ~ Meals and snacks (12-9) ~ Restaurant ~ (01896) 830229 ~ Children welcome ~ Open 11am-midnight ~ Bedrooms: £42B/£64B

ISLE ORNSAY (Isle of Skye) NG6912 Map 11
Tigh Osda Eilean Iarmain 🛏 ♀

Signposted off A851 Broadford—Armadale

This is a lovely little inn with a civilised but friendly and relaxed atmosphere and set in fine position overlooking the sea in a picturesque part of Skye. Gaelic is truly the first language of the charming staff, many of whom have worked here for some years; even the menus are bilingual. The big and cheerfully busy bar has a swooping stable-stall-like wooden divider that gives a two-room feel: good tongue-and-groove panelling on the walls and ceiling, leatherette wall seats, brass lamps, a brass-mounted ceiling fan, and a huge mirror over the open fire. There are about 34 local brands of blended and vatted malt whisky (including their own blend, Te Bheag, and a splendid vatted malt, Poit Dhubh Green Label, bottled for them but available elsewhere), and an excellent wine list; darts, dominoes, cribbage, and piped music. Bar food includes home-made soup (£1.75), lunchtime sandwiches (from £1.50), filled baked potatoes (from £1.95), mussels in white wine (£3.50), venison casserole or fresh Mallaig haddock (£5.95), wild salmon (£7.50), puddings (£1.75), and children's menu (£3.50). The pretty, no-smoking dining room has a lovely sea view past the little island of Ornsay itself and the lighthouse on Sionnach (you can walk over the sands at low tide). Some of the bedrooms are in a cottage opposite. The most popular room has a canopied bed from Armadale Castle. *(Recommended by Paul and Ursula Randall, R and S Bentley, Scott J Macdonald, Jackie Moffat, Andrew and Kerstin Lewis, Mark and Diane Grist, Walter and Susan Rinaldi-Butcher, John and Joan Nash, Lucy James; also in Good Hotel Guide)*

Free house ~ Licensee Sir Iain Noble ~ Meals and snacks (12-2.30, 6.30-9.30) ~ Restaurant ~ (01471) 833332 ~ Children welcome (but only till 8.30 in the bar) ~

Live music mostly Thurs evenings ~ Open 12-12(11.30 Sat); 12-2.30, 6.30-12 Sun ~
Bedrooms: £67.50B/£90B

ISLE OF WHITHORN (Dumfries and Galloway) NX4736 Map 9

Steam Packet 🏠 £

From the big picture windows of this comfortably modernised inn you can look out
on to a picturesque natural working harbour with its bustle of yachts and inshore
fishing boats. Inside, the cheery low-ceilinged bar is split into two: on the right, plush
button-back banquettes and boat pictures, and on the left, green leatherette stools
around cast-iron-framed tables on big stone tiles, and a woodburning stove in the bare
stone wall. Bar food can be served in the lower-beamed dining room, which has a big
model steam packet boat on the white walls, excellent colour wildlife photographs,
rugs on its wooden floor, and a solid fuel stove, and there's also a small eating area off
the lounge bar. The food includes soup (95p), filled rolls (from £1.15), venison pâté
(£2.10), stuffed cheese and garlic mushrooms (£2.25), tagliatelle niçoise or mushroom
stroganoff (£4.25), stuffed haddock or vegetable lasagne (£4.50), vegetable balti
(£4.75), scampi (£5.25), cutlet of salmon and broccoli (£5.50), steaks (from £11.50).
Daily specials may include home-made steak pie (£3.50), grilled brill or plaice or fried
langoustines (£8.50); decent children's menu. Well kept Theakstons XB on handpump,
and guest beers like Caledonian Deuchars IPA and Orkney Raven; two dozen malt
whiskies; pool, dominoes and piped music. White tables and chairs in the garden.
Every 1½ to 4 hours there are boat trips from the harbour; the remains of St Ninian's
Kirk are on a headland behind the village. *(Recommended by Francis and Deirdre Gevers,*
Vann and Terry Prime, Margaret Mason, Dave Thompson, Chris Wheaton; more reports please)

Free house ~ Licensee John Scoular ~ Real ale ~ Meals and snacks (not 25 Dec) ~
Restaurant ~ (01988) 500334 ~ Children welcome away from public bar ~
Occasional folk music ~ Open 11-11(midnight Sat); 11-2.30, 5.45-11 in winter; 12-11
Sun ~ Bedrooms: £22.50B/£45B

KELSO (Borders) NT7334 Map 10

Queens Head 🏠 🍷

Bridge Street (A699)

This 18th-c Georgian coaching inn has a very pleasant atmosphere in the roomy and
attractive back lounge, with its comfortable mix of modern and traditional, Tables fill
quickly at lunchtime for the wide choice of good generous food, which might include
sandwiches (from £1.95), ploughman's (£3.25), haddock in breadcrumbs (£4.55),
steak pie (£4.65), daily specials such as duck stir fry or a pasta dish (from £4), evening
dishes like chargrilled cajun salmon (£6.95), medallions of pork loin (£7.75) and
sizzling mixed grill (£12.25), and puddings (£2.50); service is by courteous waitresses,
with very helpful and efficient licensees. There's also a small simpler traditional
streetside front bar, with a lively local atmosphere; pool. Well kept Courage Directors,
Morlands Old Speckled Hen, Marstons Pedigree, and Whitbreads Castle Eden on
handpump; dominoes, fruit machine, video game, and piped music; they can arrange
golf, fishing and horse riding. *(Recommended by Nigel Woolliscroft, Michael Wadsworth, R T*
and J C Moggridge, James Nunns)

Free house ~ Licensee Ian Flannigan ~ Real ale ~ Meals and snacks (12-2, 6-9) ~
Restaurant ~ (01573) 224636 ~ Children welcome ~ Open 11-2.30, 4.45-11; 11am-
12pm Sat; 11-11 Sun ~ Bedrooms: £35B/£50B

If a service charge is mentioned prominently on a menu or accommodation
terms, you must pay it if service was satisfactory. If service is really bad you
are legally entitled to refuse to pay some or all of the service charge as
compensation for not getting the service you might reasonably have expected.

KILBERRY (Strathclyde) NR7164 Map 11

Kilberry Inn 🍴 🛏

B8024

Scotland's Dining Pub of the Year

Run by particularly attentive, welcoming and hard-working licensees, this well kept little former post office is doing very well at the moment. It's a lovely place to stay with neat, cosy bedrooms, and most enjoyable food using local produce brought in by taxi. This might include home-made malted granary garlic bread (£1.95), cream of broccoli soup with home-made bread (£2.75), port and stilton pâté (£4.50), country sausage pie (£7.50), freshly baked stilton and walnut pie (£7.95), baked rump steak cooked in red wine and topped with stilton (£13.95); puddings such as freshly baked apple and raspberry pie, banana shortcake or lemon meringue pie (£3.95); lovely home-made syrups, marmalades (a different one for breakfast each day), pickles and chutneys for sale. They appreciate booking if you want an evening meal. The small relaxed dining bar is tastefully and simply furnished but warmly welcoming, with a good log fire. No real ale, but a good range of bottled beers and plenty of malt whiskies; the family room is no smoking. The pub is on a delightful slow winding and hilly circular drive over Knapdale, from the A83 S of Lochgilphead, with breathtaking views over the rich coastal pastures to the sea and the island of Gigha beyond. *(Recommended by John and Barbara Burns, Dr D G Twyman, Derek and Maggie Washington, Vicky and David Sarti, Dr and Mrs J J Brown, J E Rycroft, Dr and Mrs P Martin)*

Free house ~ Licensee John Leadbeater ~ Meals and snacks ~ (01880) 770223 ~ Well behaved children in family room ~ Open 11-2, 5-10; closed Sun, closed mid-Oct-Easter ~ Bedrooms: £36.50S/£63B

KILMAHOG (Central) NN6108 Map 11

Lade Inn ♀

A84 just NW of Callander, by A821 junction

In the beautiful richly wooded surroundings of the Pass of Leny, with high hills all around and the Trossachs not far off, this feels like a proper pub (as opposed to the hotel bars which are so much more the rule around here). It's clean and well run, with a wide range of good interesting freshly made bar food – no frozen things at all, not even peas: lunchtime sandwiches (from £3.75) and baked potatoes (from £4.75), as well as steak pie (£5.99), venison casserole (£6.99), vegetarian dishes like vegetable pancakes (£5.99) or mushroom and cheese pasta (£6.99), sirloin steak (£12.95), daily specials such as poached salmon with garlic dill butter (£8.75), rabbit casserole (£8.95), rack of lamb (£13.95), and venison steak (£14.50), with puddings like treacle sponge, crannachan (a rich mousse with whisky) or bread and butter pudding (£2.99); they do small helpings for children, and even the fish fingers are home-made. Besides well kept Broughton Greenmantle or Black Douglas, Heather Fraoch Ale, Morlands Old Speckled Hen, and Orkney Red MacGregor on handpump, they'll let you have just a glass of any of their wines (which are strong on New World ones); cheerful informal service, dogs allowed. The main carpeted dining bar has blond wood chairs around pine tables, with beams, some panelling, stripped stone and Highland prints; a no-smoking room opens on to the terrace and attractive garden, where they have three ponds stocked with fish, and hold summer evening barbecues; piped Scottish music. *(Recommended by Jeremy Brittain-Long, Dr John Bassett, H L Dennis)*

Free house ~ Licensee Paul Roebuck ~ Real ale ~ Meals and snacks (12-2.30, 5.30-9.15) ~ (01877) 330152 ~ Children at mealtimes only ~ Ceilidh Sat evenings ~ Open 12-11; 12-3.30, 5.30-11 in winter; 12-12 Sat/Sun

---

Please tell us if the decor, atmosphere, food or drink at a pub is different from our description. We rely on readers' reports to keep us up to date. No stamp needed: *The Good Pub Guide*, FREEPOST TN1569, Wadhurst, E Sussex TN5 7BR.

KIPPEN (Central) NS6594 Map 11
Cross Keys Hotel 🏠

Main Street; village signposted off A811 W of Stirling

In an historic village, this little family-run 18th-c inn is warmly welcoming. The relaxed and straightforward lounge has a good log fire, there's a coal fire in the attractive family dining room, and a separate public bar. Good value food using fresh local produce includes home-made soup (£1.60), home-made bramble and port liver pâté (£2.75), omelettes (from £3.00), haddie pancakes (£4.25), ploughman's (£4.50), venison burgers with brown onion gravy (£4.95), steak pie (£6.15), poached salmon with a lemon and dill sauce (£6.50), Aberdeen Angus sirloin steak (£11.75), and puddings like home-made bread and butter pudding (£2.50) and apple pie (£2.60); smaller helpings for children. Well kept Broughton Greenmantle on handpump, and quite a few malt whiskies; pool, dominoes, shove-ha'penny, fruit machine, and juke box. The garden has tables and a children's play area. *(Recommended by Carolyn and Michael Hedoin, GSB, Paul and Sue Merrick; more reports please)*

Free house ~ Licensees Angus and Sandra Watt ~ Real ale ~ Meals (12-2, 5.30-9.30) ~ Restaurant ~ (01786) 870293 ~ Children in restaurant ~ Open 12-2.30, 5.30-11(midnight Sat); 12.30-11 Sun; closed evening 25 Dec, 1 Jan ~ Bedrooms: £19.50/£39

KIRKTON OF GLENISLA (Tayside) NO2160 Map 11
Glenisla Hotel 🏠

B951 N of Kirriemuir and Alyth

Quite the centre of local life, this friendly 17th-c former posting inn is set in one of the prettiest of the Angus Glens. The simple but cosy carpeted pubby bar has beams and ceiling joists, a roaring log fire, wooden tables and chairs, decent prints, and a rather jolly thriving atmosphere. The lounge is comfortable and sunny, and the elegant high-ceilinged dining room has rugs on the wooden floor, pretty curtains, candles and fresh flowers, and crisp cream tablecloths. Good, carefully prepared bar food from the daily menu includes soup (£1.95), Orkney herrings in dill (£3.15), ploughman's (£4.95), home-baked ham with free-range eggs (£5.55), goujons of deep-fried chicken in breadcrumbs or barnsley pork chop with apple sauce (£5.90), seafood kebabs (£7.95), and evening dishes like fresh salmon marinated in juniper berries and spices (£4.25), haggis with black pudding and a nip (£4.35), rainbow trout coated with herbs (£10.15), rack of spring lamb basted with rosemary (£11.75), steaks cut to order and priced by weight (eg £10.80 for 8oz), and puddings from the blackboard. Boddingtons, McEwans 70/- and 80/-, and Theakstons Best on handpump, a fair range of island malt whiskies, and caring and attentive service. A refurbished stable block has darts, pool, cribbage, and a TV and video for children. The bedrooms are attractively individual, and the hotel has fishing and clay pigeon shooting. No smoking in dining room. *(Recommended by Mrs R Scholes, Dr M J S Scorer; more reports please)*

Free house ~ Licensees Simon and Lyndy Blake ~ Real ale ~ Meals and snacks ~ Restaurant ~ (01575) 582223 ~ Children welcome ~ Occasional Gaelic and ceilidh bands ~ Open 11-11; 11-2.30, 6-11 Oct-June; 11-11 Sun; closed 24-26 Dec ~ Bedrooms: £40B/£75B

LINLITHGOW (Lothian) NS9976 Map 11
Four Marys 🍺

65 High St; 2 miles from M9 junction 3 (and little further from junction 4) – town signposted

Mary Queen of Scots was born at nearby Linlithgow Palace, and this atmospheric and friendly pub is named after her ladies-in-waiting. The comfortable and friendly, L-shaped bar has masses of mementoes of the ill-fated queen, such as pictures and written records, a piece of bed curtain said to be hers, part of a 16th-c cloth and swansdown vest of the type she'd be likely to have worn, and a facsimile of her death-mask. Seats are mostly green velvet and mahogany dining chairs around stripped period and antique tables, there are a couple of attractive antique corner cupboards, and an elaborate Victorian dresser serves as a bar gantry, housing several dozen malt whiskies (they stock around 100 altogether). The walls are mainly stripped stone, including some remarkable masonry in the inner area. A very good choice of around eight constantly changing, very reasonably priced well kept real ales includes Belhaven 70/- and 80/-, Boddingtons, Broughton Ghillie, Butterknowle Conciliation, Caledonian Deuchars IPA, Harviestoun Schiehallion, Orkney Dark Island, and Theakstons Best on handpump; friendly and helpful staff. Good waitress-served bar food includes soup (£1.45), toasties or sandwiches (from £1.50), filled baked potatoes (£2.50), pie of the day (from 4.50), beef goulash or chicken basque (£4.50), fresh fillet haddock in breadcrumbs or batter (£4.95); a range of puddings (from £1.95). When the building was an apothecary's shop, David Waldie experimented in it with chloroform – its first use as an anaesthetic. Parking is difficult. *(Recommended by Ian Phillips, David Carr, T and G Alderman, Vann and Terry Prime)*

Belhaven ~ Manageress Mrs E Forrest ~ Real ale ~ Meals and snacks (12-2.30, 5.30-8.45; not Sun evening) ~ (01506) 842171 ~ Children in eating area of bar ~ Open 11-11(11.45 Sat); 12.30-11 Sun

LYBSTER (Highland) ND2436 Map 11
Portland Arms 🛏

A9 S of Wick

Built as a staging post on the early 19th-c Parliamentary Road, this staunch old granite hotel is our most northerly main entry. The knocked-through open-plan bar is comfortable and attractively furnished, and there's also a small but cosy panelled cocktail bar. Good bar food includes soup (£1.85), chicken liver pâté (£3.95), liver and bacon, smoked haddock tagliatelle, baked fillet of sole or generous fresh salmon salad (£5.95), cajun chicken or prawn salad (£6.95), steaks (from £11.95), and puddings (£2.95); friendly and obliging staff. They keep 40 or more malt whiskies (beers are keg). They can arrange fishing and so forth, and the inn is a good base for the area with its spectacular cliffs and stacks. *(Recommended by Richard Dolphin, Dr G Craig, Alan Wilcock, Christine Davidson)*

Free house ~ Licensee Gerald Henderson ~ Meals and snacks ~ Restaurant ~ (01593) 721208 ~ Children welcome ~ Open 11-11; 12-11 Sun ~ Bedrooms: £45B/£65B

MELROSE (Borders) NT5434 Map 9
Burts Hotel 🍽 🛏

A6091

To enjoy the popular lunchtime food, it's best to get to this rather smart and comfortable old hotel early. Served by helpful, cheerful staff there might be vegetable soup (£1.80), smoked cajun-style salmon with lemon and thyme dressing or prawns, bacon and mushrooms sautéed in garlic butter (£3.95), warm salad of wild mushrooms and black pudding garnished with a duck egg (£5.50), sautéed cantonese-style chicken served on a nest of linguini pasta or traditional quiche lorraine (£5.85), smoked haddock and ham crêpes (£6.25). The supper menu may include parfait of wild local game with marinated berries (£3.95), deep-fried brie with cumberland sauce (£4.25), wild mushroom and pepper stroganoff (£5.95), breast of chicken stuffed with goat's cheese wrapped in filo pastry or gateau of pork centred with black pudding and bramley apples (£7.95), and puddings like iced blueberry parfait served with a berry cluster or double chocolate fudge cake (£3.65); extremely good breakfasts. The comfortable and friendly L-shaped lounge bar has lots of cushioned wall seats and windsor armchairs on its turkey carpet, and Scottish prints on the walls; the Tweed Room and the restaurant are no smoking. Belhaven 80/- and Sandy Hunters, and Marstons Pedigree on handpump, 50 malt whiskies, and a good wine list; dominoes. There's a well tended garden (with tables in summer). Melrose with its striking ruined abbey is probably the most villagey of the Border towns; an alternative if distant way to view the abbey ruins is from the top of the tower at Smailholm. *(Recommended by R T and J C Moggridge, Sharon Hancock, R M Macnaughton, R H Sawyer, Mark Walker, Chris Rounthwaite, Wayne Brindle)*

Free house ~ Licensee Graham Henderson ~ Real ale ~ Meals and snacks ~ Restaurant ~ (01896) 822285 ~ Children welcome (must have left bar by 8pm) ~ Open 11-2.00, 5-11; 12-2, 6-11 Sun; closed 26 Dec ~ Bedrooms: £48B/£82B

MOUNTBENGER (Borders) NT3125 Map 9
Gordon Arms

Junction A708/B709

A welcoming sight amidst splendid empty moorlands, this welcoming and remotely set little inn has a warmly welcoming and comfortable public bar with an interesting set of period photographs of the neighbourhood (one dated 1865), some well illustrated poems, and a warm winter fire. Well kept Broughton Greenmantle, Jennings Oatmeal Stout, and various summer guest beers on handpump, 56 malt whiskies, and a fair wine list. Bar food includes sandwiches (lunchtime only), vegetarian dishes, and home-made steak pie (£5.50), roast beef and yorkshire pudding (£5.95), braised steak (£6.50) and lamb chops (£7.50); children's dishes and summer high teas in the dining room. Pool, dominoes, and trivia. The resident family of bearded collies are called Jura, Misty and Morah. In addition to the hotel bedrooms, there's a bunkhouse which provides cheap accommodation for hill walkers, cyclists and fishermen, all of whom should find this area particularly appealing; they also offer lots of outdoor activity holidays, too. *(Recommended by Dr A C Williams, Dr F M Ellard, Wayne Brindle; more reports please)*

Free house ~ Licensee Harry Mitchell ~ Real ale ~ Meals and snacks ~ Restaurant ~ (01750) 82232 ~ Children in eating area of bar ~ Accordion and fiddle club third Weds every month ~ Open 11-11(midnight Sat); 12.30-11 Sun; closed Tues end Oct-Easter ~ Bedrooms: £26/£42

OBAN (Strathclyde) NM8630 Map 11
Oban Inn

North Pier, between Stafford St and Oban

Bustling and traditional, this late 18th-c harbourside inn offers a friendly welcome from both locals and the efficient, hard-working staff. The beamed downstairs bar has small stools, pews and black-winged modern settles on its uneven slate floor, blow-ups of old Oban postcards on the cream walls, and unusual brass-shaded wall lamps. The smarter, partly panelled upstairs bar has button-back banquettes around cast-iron-framed tables, a coffered woodwork ceiling, and little backlit arched false windows with heraldic roundels in aged stained glass; the children's area is no smoking. Well kept McEwans 70/- and 80/-, and a large selection of whiskies. Good value straightforward lunchtime bar food includes garlic mushrooms (£2.65), lasagne or huge haddock in beer batter (£3.95), steak and kidney pie (£4.25), cauliflower and coconut korma (£4.90), gammon and egg (£4.75), sizzling platters such as all day breakfast (£1.49) or 8oz steak (£2.99), and puddings; shove-ha'penny, table skittles, dominoes, fruit machine, video game, juke box, and piped music. *(Recommended by David Warrellow, P R and S A White, Dr A C Williams, Dr F M Ellard, Paul Hilditch, Hazel and Michael Duncombe, Julie and Steve Anderton, Mrs Olive Oxley)*

Scottish Courage ~ Manager David Weir ~ Real ale ~ Meals and snacks (11-9) ~ (01631) 562484 ~ Children in eating area of bar till 7pm ~ Singer most weekends, folk groups Sun ~ Open 11-12.45; 12.30-12.45 Sun

nr PITLOCHRY (Tayside) NN9162 Map 11
Killiecrankie Hotel 🍷 🛏

Killiecrankie signposted from A9 N of Pitlochry

Very much enjoyed by our readers, this smart but relaxed country hotel is well run by warmly welcoming licensees. It is splendidly set in lovely peaceful grounds with dramatic views of the mountain pass, a putting course, a croquet lawn – and sometimes roe deer and red squirrels. The attractively furnished bar (refurbished this year) has some panelling, upholstered seating and mahogany tables and chairs, as well as stuffed animals and some rather fine wildlife paintings; in the airy conservatory extension (which overlooks the pretty garden) there are light beech tables and upholstered chairs, with discreetly placed plants and flowers. Unfailingly good food is served by friendly staff and might include soup (£2.25), smoked salmon pâté (£3.50), sweet cured herrings (£4.25), ploughman's (£5.75), deep-fried fresh haddock in beer batter or popular cumberland sausage with hot onion chutney (£6.95), steak burger (£7.25), oak-smoked chicken breast with minted mango and papaya compote (£8.95), and daily specials; puddings like pecan, whisky and maple flan or banoffi pie (£3.50). The restaurant is no smoking. Decent wines and lots of malt whiskies, coffee and a choice of teas. *(Recommended by Sue and Bob Ward, Bill and Brenda Lemon, Dr D G Twyman, Joan and Tony Walker, Susan and John Douglas, James Nunns, A P Jeffreys, June and Perry Dann, Mr and Mrs W M Graham, Lucy James, T and G Alderman)*

Free house ~ Licensees Colin and Carole Anderson ~ Meals and snacks ~ Evening restaurant ~ (01796) 473220 ~ Children in eating area of bar ~ Open 11-2.30, 5.30-11; 12-2.30, 6.30-11 Sun; closed one week mid Dec, all Jan/Feb ~ Bedrooms: £52.50B/£105B

PLOCKTON (Highland) NG8033 Map 11
Plockton Hotel

Village signposted from A87 near Kyle of Lochalsh

Even out of season, this friendly little hotel remains very popular – best to book well in advance for either an evening meal or for a bedroom. It's set in a row of elegant but pretty houses with a delightful outlook across the palm tree and colourful flowering shrub-lined shore, and across the sheltered anchorage to the rugged mountainous surrounds of Loch Carron. The comfortably furnished, bustling lounge bar has window seats looking out to the boats on the water, as well as antiqued dark red leather seating around neat Regency-style tables on a tartan carpet, three model ships set into the woodwork, and partly panelled stone walls. The separate public bar has pool, darts, shove-ha'penny, dominoes, and piped music. Very popular bar food includes home-made soup (£1.65), sandwiches (from £1.95), filled baked potatoes (from £2.50), home-made chicken liver and whisky pâté (£3.25), a vegetarian dish of the day (£4.95), poached smoked fillet of haddock (£5.50), prawns fresh from the bay (starter £5.95, main course £11.75), local scallops (£9.75), monkfish and prawn provençal in garlicky sauce (£9.85), and steaks (from £11.50); usual children's menu (from £1.95); good breakfasts; small no-smoking restaurant. Tennents 70/- and 80/- on tall fount air pressure, a good collection of malt whiskies, and a short wine list. This Scottish National Trust village is lovely. *(Recommended by Dr D G Twyman, Stephen Holman, Eric Locker, David and Judy Walmsley, Joan and Tony Walker, Lynn and Peter Brueton, Dr and Mrs S Jones, Mrs Olive Oxley, Mark and Diane Grist)*

Free house ~ Licensee Tom Pearson ~ Real ale ~ Meals and snacks ~ Restaurant ~ (01599) 544274 ~ Children welcome (away from public bar) ~ Occasional ceilidh band ~ Open 11am-midnight(11.30 Sat); 12.30-11 Sun (July/Aug); closed Sun 2.30-6.30 rest of year ~ Bedrooms: £27.50B/£55B

PORTPATRICK (Dumfries and Galloway) NX0154 Map 9
Crown ★ 🛏

Whether you are a local or visitor, you can be sure of a friendly welcome in this bustling and atmospheric harbourside inn. The rambling old-fashioned bar has lots of little nooks, crannies and alcoves, and interesting furnishings such as a carved settle with barking dogs as its arms, an antique wicker-backed armchair, a stag's head over the coal fire, and shelves of old bottles above the bar counter. The partly panelled butter-coloured walls are decorated with old mirrors with landscapes painted in their side panels. With quite an emphasis on seafood, the popular bar food might include home-made soup (£2), open sandwich (from £2.50), herring in oatmeal or dressed local crab (£4.35), mussels with a cream and chive sauce (£4.85), delicious grilled scallops wrapped in bacon (£5.15), chicken and mushroom pancake (£7.90), grilled lamb cutlets (£8.75), fillet of plaice with anchovy butter (£9.60), steaks (from £11.55), whole grilled jumbo prawns (£12.15), and local lobster (from £20), huge seafood platter (£25), and puddings (£2.80); good breakfasts. Carefully chosen wine list, and over 250 malt whiskies; maybe piped music. An airy and very attractively decorated early 20th-c, half no-smoking dining room opens through a quiet no-smoking conservatory area into a sheltered back garden, and you can sit outside on seats served by a hatch in the front lobby and make the most of the evening sun. *(Recommended by Paul and Nicky Clements, Richard Holloway, Patrick Osborne, Carolyn and Michael Hedoin, Carolyn Reynier)*

Free house ~ Licensee Bernard Wilson ~ Meals and snacks (till 10) ~ Restaurant ~ (01776) 810261 ~ Children welcome ~ Open 11am-11.30pm; 12-11 Sun ~ Bedrooms: £48B/£72B

SHERIFFMUIR (Central) NN8202 Map 11
Sheriffmuir Inn

Signposted off A9 just S of Blackford; and off A9 at Dunblane roundabout, just N of end of M9; also signposted from Bridge of Allan; OS Sheet 57 map reference 827022

Despite the comparative isolation of this early 18th-c drovers' inn – it's set in the middle of lonely moorlands with wonderful views – there are generally plenty of people eating, all pleased they had made the journey. The welcoming L-shaped bar is basic but comfortable with pink plush stools and button-back built-in wall banquettes on a smart pink patterned carpet, polished tables, olde-worlde coaching prints on its white walls, and a woodburning stove in a stone fireplace. Well kept Arrols 80/-, Marstons Pedigree and always two guests on handpump, kept under light blanket pressure, and a good choice of whiskies; friendly, neatly uniformed staff, and piped music. Promptly-served lunchtime bar food includes home-made soup (£1.75), chicken curry (£6.25), steak pie (£6.50), and scampi (£6.95). There are tables and a children's play area outside. *(Recommended by Mark and Heather Williamson; more reports please)*

Free house ~ Licensee Roger Lee ~ Real ale ~ Lunchtime meals and snacks ~ Restaurant ~ (01786) 823285 ~ Children welcome ~ Open 11.30-2.30, 5.30-11; 11.30-11 Sat; 12-11 Sun; closed Mon Oct-Mar

SHIELDAIG (Highland) NG8154 Map 11
Tigh an Eilean 🏠

Village signposted just off A896 Lochcarron—Gairloch

Many of our Scottish entries are in fine countryside with lovely views, but the setting of this friendly hotel stands out as one of the best. It looks over the Shieldaig Island – a sanctuary for a stand of ancient Caledonian pines – to Loch Torridon and then out to the sea beyond. It's a usefully comfortable place to stay with easy chairs, books and a well stocked help-yourself bar in the neat and prettily decorated two-room lounge, and an attractively modern comfortable dining room specialising in good value local shellfish, fish and game. Quickly served, simple, well priced bar food includes home-made soup (£1.10), sandwiches (£1.50), local scallops in batter or fresh crab cocktail (£3.75), roast lamb, roast beef or chicken in red wine (£5.75), fresh monkfish in batter (£6.25), and puddings like apple crumble or crème caramel (£2.00); Tennents 80/- on air pressure. The smallish bar, which is popular with locals, is very simple with red brocaded button-back banquettes in little bays, picture windows looking out to sea and three picnic tables outside in a sheltered front courtyard. Winter darts, juke box. They have private fishing, and the National Trust Torridon estate and the Beinn Eighe nature reserve aren't too far away. *(Recommended by D G Clarke, Dr D G Twyman, Mrs Olive Oxley, Lucy James, Mark and Diane Grist; also in Good Hotel Guide)*

Free house ~ Licensee Mrs Elizabeth Stewart ~ Meals and snacks (12-2.15, 6-8.30) ~ Restaurant ~ (01520) 755251 ~ Children in eating area of bar until 8pm ~ Open 11-11; 11-2.30, 5-11 in winter; 12.30-2.30 Sun – closed Sun evening; closed all day winter Sun ~ Bedrooms: £43.50B/£95.50B

SKEABOST (Isle of Skye) NG4148 Map 11

Skeabost House Hotel ★ 🛏

A850 NW of Portree, 1½ miles past junction with A856

One of the great draws to this civilised and friendly family-run hotel is the marvellous lunchtime buffet with a very wide choice of cold meats and fresh salmon (£7.95), and served in the spacious and airy conservatory; also, home-made soup (£2), good filled baked potatoes (from £2.95), baguettes (from £2.99), haggis with oatcakes (£3.90), savoury mushroom quiche (£6.20), breaded fillet of haddock (£6.45), home-made chilli con carne with rice (£6.85), home-made lasagne (£7.20), and Scottish sirloin steak (£13.90); children's dishes (from £2.50). There's a main dining room, too; all the eating areas are no smoking. The bustling high-ceilinged bar has a pine counter and red brocade seats on its thick red carpet, and a fine panelled billiards room leads off the stately hall; there's a wholly separate public bar with darts, pool, fruit machine, trivia, juke box, piped music (and even its own car park). A fine choice of over 100 single malt whiskies, including their own and some very rare ones. Twelve acres of secluded woodland and gardens surround the hotel, with glorious views over Loch Snizort (said to have some of the best salmon fishing on the island). *(Recommended by E Locker, Walter and Susan Rinaldi-Butcher, David and Judy Walmsley, Joan and Tony Walker, Jane Taylor, David Dutton)*

Free house ~ Licensee Iain McNab ~ Meals and snacks (12-1.30, 6.30-9.30) ~ Restaurant ~ (01470) 532202 ~ Children in eating area of bar ~ Accordion/fiddle in public bar Sat evening ~ Open 11.30-2.30, 5-midnight(11 Sat); 12.30-6.30 Sun; cl end Nov-beg Mar ~ Bedrooms: £46B/£98B

nr STONEHAVEN (Grampian) NO8493 Map 11

Lairhillock ♀

Netherley; 6 miles N of Stonehaven, 6 miles S of Aberdeen, take the Durris turn-off from the A90 (old A92)

Smart but friendly and relaxed, this extended country pub is well liked for its food. In the bar, this might include soup (£2.15), cullen skink (£3.25), a changing terrine or pâté (£3.95), filled baguettes (£4.25), seafood pancakes (£4.95), lunchtime ploughman's (£5.15), wholemeal broccoli and stilton quiche, lasagne or curry of the day (£6.95), grilled venison (£8.80), salmon fillet (£8.95), Aberdeen Angus steaks (from £12.25), several vegetarian dishes, and home-made puddings (from £2.95); Sunday buffet lunch. The cheerful beamed bar has panelled wall benches, a mixture of old seats, dark woodwork, harness and brass lamps on the walls, a good open fire, and countryside views from the bay window. The spacious separate lounge has an unusual central fire; the traditional atmosphere is always welcoming, even at its busiest. Well kept Boddingtons, Courage Directors, Flowers IPA, McEwans 80/-, and changing guest beers on handpump, over 50 malt whiskies, and an extensive wine list; friendly efficient staff; darts, cribbage, dominoes, shove-ha'penny, trivia, and piped music. The restaurant in a converted raftered barn behind is cosy, with another log fire. Panoramic southerly views from the conservatory. *(Recommended by Isabel McIntyre, Chris Raisin, Neil Townend, Mark Walker; more reports please)*

Free house ~ Licensee Frank Budd ~ Real ale ~ Meals and snacks (12-2, 6-9.30 (10 Fri/Sat) ~ Restaurant ~ (01569) 730001 ~ Children in restaurant/conservatory ~ Pianist in restaurant/singing and accordion Fri ~ Open 12-2.30, 5-11(midnight Sat); 12-2.30, 6-11 Sun

STRACHUR (Strathclyde) NN0901 Map 11

Creggans 🛏

A815 N of village

From this decidedly smart little hotel you can walk for hours through beautiful countryside – it's close to the spot where Mary Queen of Scots landed in 1563. The cosy and attractively tweedy cocktail bar (partly no-smoking) has wooden ceilings, signed showbusiness photographs, and panoramic views overlooking the loch to the hills on the far side; there are more seats in a no-smoking conservatory. The public bar, lively with locals, has a central stove, a pool room, fruit machine, dominoes, juke box, satellite TV, and piped music. There's a good selection of malt whiskies, including their own vatted malt, a thoughtful wine list, and a cappuccino bar and gift shop with home-baked produce. Popular, good value bar food includes Loch Fyne oysters (£1.10 each), toasties or home-made soup (£2.35), home-made game pâté (£3.95), half pint of fresh Oban prawns (£4.25), curry of the day (£5.95), Loch Fyne mussels or venison casserole (£6.25), Scotch sirloin steak (£10.95), and puddings (£3.25); no-smoking restaurant. In front are some white tables. *(Recommended by John and Beryl Knight, Lucy James; more reports please)*

Free house ~ Licensee Sir Charles MacLean ~ Meals and snacks ~ Restaurant ~ (01369) 860279 ~ Children welcome ~ Monthly live entertainment summer ~ Open 11am-midnight; 11-1am Sat/Sun ~ Bedrooms: £55B/£90B

SWINTON (Borders) NT8448 Map 10
Wheatsheaf 🍴 🛏️
A6112 N of Coldstream

Just a few miles from the River Tweed is this popular and very well run place in a pretty village surrounded by rolling countryside. The bedrooms are simple but comfortable (they have added a superior one this year), the welcome from the friendly licensees is genuinely warm, and the food excellent. At lunchtime, this might include sandwiches, soup such as cream of leek and asparagus (£2.20), marinated herring fillets in a mustard sauce (£3.60), fresh quail salad in thai dressing (£3.95), spinach and basil pancake (£5.40), liver and bacon (£6.25), roast leg of Border lamb with redcurrant sauce (£6.90), grilled fillet of salmon with prawns (£7.95), peppered sirloin steak in cream and brandy sauce (£12.90); evening dishes like roast parsnip and coriander soup (£2.85), filo pastry tartlet with Paris brown mushrooms and spinach (£4.35), breast of wood pigeon on black pudding with puy lentils in a madeira sauce (£4.60), seared fillet of salmon on stir-fried green vegetables with a fresh herb and lemon butter sauce (£10.70), sautéed tiger prawns and roasted monkfish tails with lime and stem ginger (£13.45), two medaillons of scotch beef fillet with a red wine and tarragon sauce (£14.90), local seafood every day, and delicious puddings. Booking is advisable, particularly from Thursday to Saturday evening. Well kept Boddingtons, Broughtons IPA and Greenmantle on handpump, a decent range of malt whiskies and brandies, good choice of wines, and cocktails. The friendly service and careful decor all indicate tremendous attention to detail. The hall and stairs have been redecorated and the main area has an attractive long oak settle and some green-cushioned window seats, as well as the wheelback chairs around the tables, a stuffed pheasant and partridge over the log fire, and sporting prints and plates on the bottle-green wall covering; a small lower-ceilinged part by the counter has pubbier furnishings, and small agricultural prints on the walls – especially sheep. At the side is a separate locals' bar; no smoking in front conservatory with a vaulted pine ceiling and walls of local stone; dominoes. The garden has a play area for children. *(Recommended by Christine and Malcolm Ingram, A J Morton, Chris Rounthwaite; also in Good Hotel Guide; more reports please)*

Free house ~ Licensees Alan and Julie Reid ~ Real ale ~ Meals and snacks (12-2, 6-9.30) ~ Restaurant ~ (01890) 860257 ~ Children welcome ~ Open 11.30-2.30, 6-11; 12.30-2.30, 6.30-10.30 Sun; cl Mon to non-residents, Sun evening Dec-March; cl last two weeks Feb and last week Oct, 25 Dec ~ Bedrooms: £32(£44S)/£52(£68S)

TAYVALLICH (Strathclyde) NR7386 Map 11
Tayvallich Inn 🍴
B8025, off A816 1 mile S of Kilmartin; or take B841 turn-off from A816 two miles N of Lochgilphead

As the sheltered yacht achorage and bay of Loch Sween are just across the lane from the simply furnished cafe/bar, there should be good fresh seafood caught by local fishermen on the menu. In the bar, the menu might include home-made soup (£1.80), moules marinières (£3.50), fillet of haddock or stir-fried vegetables (£4.50), baked goat's cheese and roasted peppers (£4.90), beef curry (£5.10), cajun chicken (£5.50), half-a-dozen Loch Sween oysters or locally smoked salmon (£7), fried scallops (£10.50), sirloin steak (£11.00), delicious seafood platter (£15.50), and home-made puddings (from £3); half helpings for children; decent wines and Islay malt whiskies. Service is friendly and helpful and people with children are very much at home here. The small bar has cigarette cards and local nautical charts on the cream walls, exposed ceiling joists, and pale pine upright chairs, benches and tables on its quarry-tiled floor, and extends into a no-smoking (during meal times) dining conservatory; sliding glass doors open on to the terrace with picnic tables and lovely views, and there's a garden, too. *(Recommended by John and Barbara Burns, Neil Townend, Vicky and David Sarti, A F Ford, R Macnaughton; more reports please)*

Free house ~ Licensee John Grafton ~ Meals and snacks ~ Restaurant ~ (01546) 870282 ~ Children welcome ~ Open 11-11(1am Fri/Sat); 11-2.30, 6-11 in winter; 11am-midnight Sun; closed Mon Nov-Mar

THORNHILL (Central) NS6699 Map 9
Lion & Unicorn

A873

The constantly changing and much enjoyed food plays quite a big part in drawing customers to this pleasant, friendly inn. At lunchtime, this might include soup such as carrot and coriander (£1.75), mushrooms stuffed with cream cheese in a garlic and chive butter (£3.50), haggis in puff pastry with Drambuie cream sauce (£4), filled baguettes (from £4), ostrich burger (£4.50), herring fried in oatmeal (£5.75), steak, mushroom and Guinness pie (£5.95), wild mushroom stroganoff (£7.50) or duck with tagliatelle verdi (£7.50), Aberdeen Angus steaks (from £12), puddings like banoffi pots, strawberry parfait or bread and butter pudding (from £2.50), and children's helpings (from £3). Well kept Broughtons IPA, Merlin's, and Greenmantle, and Marstons Pedigree on handpump, with a fine range of malt whiskies, and a good choice of wines. The open-plan front room has a warm fire, beams and stone walls, and comfortable seats on the wooden floors. The beamed public bar with stone walls and floors has darts, pool, cribbage, and dominoes. The no-smoking restaurant is in the original part of the building which dates from 1635 and contains the original massive fireplace (six feet high and five feet wide). In summer it's pleasant to sit in the garden where they have a children's play area and summer Sunday barbecued spit-roasted whole pig, lamb or venison (weather permitting), and watch the bowling on the pub's own bowling green – it can be used by non-residents. *(Recommended by Mrs J Kemp, Dr A C Williams, Dr F M Ellard, Susan and John Douglas, Mrs B Oliver, Roger Bellingham, Ian and Deborah Carrington, Esther and John Sprinkle, Lawrence Bacon, Paul and Sue Merrick)*

Free house ~ Licensees Walter and Ariane MacAulay ~ Real ales ~ Meals and snacks (12-10pm) ~ Restaurant ~ (01786) 850204 ~ Children welcome ~ Open 11-12(1am Sat); 12.30-midnight Sun ~ Bedrooms: £40/£60

TUSHIELAW (Borders) NT3018 Map 9
Tushielaw Inn 🍺

Ettrick Valley, B709/B7009 Lockerbie—Selkirk

Remote as it is, this friendly and traditional country hotel remains popular with both locals and visitors. There are pretty views over Ettrick Water, and it's a good base for walkers or for touring, with its own fishing on Clearburn Loch up the B711. The unpretentious but comfortable little bar has decent house wines, a good few malts, an open fire, and opens on to a terrace with tables for those who are lucky with the weather; darts, shove-ha'penny, cribbage, dominoes, and piped music. Welcoming owners, and a good range of home-cooked food (they tell us prices have not changed since last year) such as home-made soup (£2.25), lunchtime filled baguettes (£3.50) and ploughman's (from £3.95), marinated Orkney herring fillets or mushrooms stuffed with stilton (£3.25), cheese and haggis fritters with home-made cumberland sauce (£3.50), vegetarian lasagne or deep-fried haddock fillets (£4.95), home-made steak and stout pie (£5.25), grilled Aberdeen Angus steak (£9.50), daily specials such as creamy smoked haddock crumble (£2.95) or good roast rack of lamb with a cranberry and orange sauce (£9.50), and home-made puddings (£2.95); Sunday roast. The restaurant is no smoking; over 30 malt whiskies. *(Recommended by Sue and Bob Ward, Peter and Anne Cornall, A N Ellis, Rita Lionel Twiss, Chris Rounthwaite, M J Morgan, Wayne Brindle)*

Free house ~ Licensees Steve and Jessica Osbourne ~ Meals and snacks ~ Restaurant ~ (01750) 62205 ~ Children in eating area of bar and in restaurant ~ Open 12(12.30 Sun)-2.30, 7-11; cl Mon-Fri afternoons and Mon-Weds evenings in winter ~ Bedrooms: £25B/£38B

ULLAPOOL (Highland) NH1294 Map 11
Ceilidh Place
West Argyle St

From tables on a terrace in front of this pretty, rose-draped white house, you can look over the other houses to the distant hills beyond the natural harbour. There's usually quite a lot going on inside, and the atmosphere is rather like that of a stylish arty cafe-bar, but with a distinctly Celtic character. There's an art gallery and regular jazz, folk, ceilidh and classical music, a bookshop, and a coffee shop. Furnishings include bentwood chairs and one or two cushioned wall benches among the rugs on its varnished concrete floor, spotlighting from the dark planked ceiling, attractive modern prints and a big sampler on the textured white walls, magazines to read, venetian blinds, houseplants, and mainly young upmarket customers; woodburning stove, dominoes, and piped music. The side food bar – you queue for service at lunchtime – does good food from fresh ingredients such as salads (from £1.95), home-made soups and breads (£2), baked potato and venison mince (£3.95); there's always a good choice for vegetarians. Decent wines by the glass, an interesting range of high-proof malt whiskies, and a choice of cognac and armagnac that's unmatched around here. There's an attractive no-smoking conservatory dining room with a menu that includes the award-winning Cockburn's haggis glazed with whisky and cream (£3.95), pine nut and pepper terrine with orange and redcurrant sauce (£5.95), venison (£10.50), and quite a few fish dishes. The bedrooms are comfortable and pleasantly decorated. *(Recommended by J G Kirby, Andrew Hazeldine, Stephen Holman, Roberto Villa, K Archard, R S Reid; also in Good Hotel Guide)*

Free house ~ Mrs Jean Urquhart ~ Meals and snacks 11-10(6 winter) ~ Evening restaurant ~ (01854) 612103 ~ Children welcome ~ Regular traditional and folk music (not Sun) ~ Open 11-11; 12.30-11 Sun ~ Bedrooms: £40(£55B)/£80(£110B)

Ferry Boat
Shore St

The simple two-roomed pubby bar in this friendly, traditional pub has brocade-cushioned seats around plain wooden tables, quarry tiles by the corner serving counter and patterned carpet elsewhere, big windows with nice views, a stained-glass door hanging from the ceiling and a fruit machine. And from a choice of two or more, the range of well kept, changing real ales on tall founts might include Boddingtons, Broughton Greenmantle, Fullers London Pride, Jennings, Orkney ales, various Shepherd Neame ales, Red Cuillin and Black Cuillin, and Wadworths 6X. The quieter inner room has a coal fire, a delft shelf of copper measures and willow-pattern plates. Straightforward, tasty bar lunches include home-made tomato, bacon and garlic soup (£2.10), sandwiches (from £1.90), filled baked potatoes (£3.95), ploughman's (£3.95), chilli bean casserole (£5.45), goujons of plaice with lime mayonnaise or deep-fried chicken with garlic butter (£6.45), puddings (from £1.95); the restaurant is no smoking. In summer you can sit on the wall across the road and take in the fine views to the tall hills beyond the attractive fishing port with its bustle of yachts, ferry boats, fishing boats and tour boats for the Summer Isles. *(Recommended by Andrew Hazeldine, K Archard, R S Reid, Mike and Penny Sanders, John Abbott)*

Free house ~ Licensee Richard Smith ~ Real ale ~ Lunchtime meals and snacks ~ Evening restaurant ~ (01854) 612366 ~ Children in eating area of bar and restaurant ~ folk music Thurs evening ~ Open 11-11; 12.30-11 Sun ~ Bedrooms: £31B/£58B

Morefield Motel ⓌⓁ

North Rd

For lovers of fresh fish and seafood, this is the place to come to – the owners (themselves ex-fishermen and divers) have a ship-to-shore radio in the office which they use to corner the best of the day's catch before the boats have even come off the sea; there's also a rotating display fridge in the lounge filled with alternative displays of fresh seafood, and a lobster tank in the cellar from which customers can take their pick. Depending on availability, the generous helpings of food might include soup of the day (£2.50), oak-roasted smoked salmon (£5.75), a basket of prawns (£6.25), crisp battered haddock (£6.95), moules marinières (£8.95), seafood thermidor (£8.75), locally caught scallops with bacon (£9.50), a marvellous seafood platter (£16.75), and daily specials such as fresh dressed local brown crab (£7.25), bass with fresh ginger (£8.95), and giant langoustines with garlic or herb butter (£9.95); non-fishy dishes also feature, such as chicken done in various ways (from £7.25), fillet steak with haggis and Drambuie sauce (£14.50), and various vegeterian choices. You can also eat in the smarter Mariners restaurant which has a slightly more elaborate menu; enjoyable breakfasts. In winter the diners tend to yield to local people playing darts or pool, though there's bargain food, including a very cheap three-course meal. Well kept Boddingtons, Orkney Dark Island, and weekly changing guests on handpump, and over 100 malt whiskies, some nearly 30 years old; decent wines and friendly tartan-skirted waitresses. The L-shaped lounge is mostly no smoking and the restaurant is totally no smoking, and there are tables on the terrace; this year they've put in a conservatory. All the bedrooms have been extensively refurbished and remain popular with hill-walking parties. *(Recommended by Alastair C Fraser, Neil and Angela Huxter, Jackie Moffat, Carolyn and Michael Hedoin)*

Free house ~ Licensee David Smyrl ~ Real Ale ~ Meals and snacks (12-2, 5.30-9.30) ~ Restaurant ~ (01854) 612161 ~ Children welcome (but not in restaurant under 12) ~ Occasional live music winter Fri ~ Open 11-2.30, 5-11; 12.30-2.30, 6-11 Sun; closed winter Sun lunchtime; closed 25/26 Dec, 1/2 Jan ~ Bedrooms: £35B/£45B

WEEM (Tayside) NN8449 Map 11
Ailean Chraggan 🛏

B846

This is an enjoyable place to stay – small and friendly and set in two acres with a lovely view across the flat ground between the hotel and the Tay to the mountains beyond, sweeping up to Ben Lawers (the highest in this part of Scotland); there are two outside terraces. The good food remains a big draw for customers. From a changing menu, there might be soup (£1.95), asparagus tart, warm stilton and walnut roulade or home-made chicken liver pâté (£3.35), fresh salmon fillet with herb butter sauce, venison casseroled in red wine and redcurrant jelly or creamy garlic chicken breast (£7.50), sirloin steak (£10.50), lovely Loch Etive whole prawn platter (£12.50), and puddings such as chocolate and hazelnut tart or banana and white chocolate cheesecake (£3.25). The menu is the same in the restaurant; a very good wine list, lots of malt whiskies, and separate children's menu. The modern lounge has long plump plum-coloured banquettes, and Bruce Bairnsfather First World War cartoons on the red and gold Regency striped wallpaper. Winter darts and dominoes. *(Recommended by Dr D G Twyman, Sue and Jim Sargeant, Ann Bolton, Paul and Ursula Randall, Susan and John Douglas, Neil Townend)*

Free house ~ Licensee Alastair Gillespie ~ Meals and snacks ~ Restaurant ~ (01887) 820346 ~ Children welcome ~ Open 11-11; 11-3, 5-11 winter weekdays; closed 25/26 Dec, 1/2 Jan ~ Bedrooms: £35B/£70B

WESTRUTHER (Borders) NT6450 Map 10
Old Thistle

B6456 – off A697 just SE of the A6089 Kelso fork

In the evenings, local farmers, fishermen, gamekeepers and shepherds all come down from the hills to this unpretentious, friendly local. A tiny, quaint bar on the right has some furnishings that look as if they date back to the inn's 1721 foundation – the elaborately carved chimney piece, an oak corner cupboard, the little bottom-polished seat by the coal fire; some fine local horsebrasses. A simple back room with whisky-water jugs on its black beams has darts, pool, dominoes, fruit machine and video game, and doors from here lead out onto the terrace; there's a small, plain room with one or two tables on the left. On the food front, what really stands out is the quality of the evening steaks fine local Aberdeen Angus, hung and cooked to perfection (8oz sirloin £9, 8oz fillet £11, 20oz T-bone £14); the weekend lunchtime menu is very simple and includes soup, sandwiches, jumbo sausage (£3), cheeseburger (£3.50), haddock (£4.90) and lasagne (£6.50). A more conventionally comfortable two-roomed lounge has flowery brocaded seats, neat tables and a small coal fire, leading into the restaurant; the bedrooms have all been recently redecorated. *(Recommended by John and Margaret Priestley, Syd and Syn Donald; more reports please)*

Free house ~ Licensee David Silk ~ Meals and snacks (5-9 Mon-Fri, 12.30-9 Sat, Sun) ~ Restaurant ~ (01578) 740275 ~ Children welcome ~ Open 5-11.30 (closed weekay lunchtimes); 12.30-11.30(11 Sun) ~ Bedrooms: £22.50B/£45B

Lucky Dip

Besides the fully inspected pubs, you might like to try these Lucky Dips recommended to us and described by readers (if you do, please send us reports):

BORDERS

☆ Allanton [B6347 S of Chirnside; NT8755], *Allanton*: Unassuming but very welcoming, in stone village terrace; cheerful L-shaped bar, separate dining room, Buchan Gold, Belhaven 80/- and St Andrews real ales, interesting wine list, particularly good food with above-average range of puddings; open all day weekends; bedrooms *(Peter and Anne Cornall)*

Auchencraw [NT8661], *Craw*: Pleasant roadside pub in small village doing well under welcoming new management, beamed main bar with horse tack etc, open fire, new back extension restaurant, imaginative food here and in bar using local produce esp fish and steaks, well kept Belhaven and Greenmantle, decent wines *(Simon Heafield)*

Coldingham [A1107; NT9066], *Anchor*: Small two-bar village pub, local sea memorabilia, McEwans, decent menu; handy for St Abbs *(K M Thorpe)*

☆ Kelso [7 Beaumont St; NT7334], *Cobbles*: Small two-room dining pub with wall banquettes, some panelling, warm log and coal fires, good value food inc good home-made soups and puddings; real ales such as Boddingtons, Caledonian 70/- and McEwans 80/-, decent wines and malt whiskies; piped music; disabled lavatory *(M J Morgan, John Pickup, Mrs Jane Hansell)*

Kirk Yetholm [NT8328], *Border*: Welcome end to 256-mile Pennine Way walk, consistently well cooked generous food, well kept Belhaven Sandy Hunter, pleasant service, very friendly locals *(R T and J C Moggridge)*

Melrose [High St; NT5434], *Kings Arms*: Late 18th-c, with old chairs, interesting ornaments and cosy log fire in welcoming beamed bar, well kept Tetleys-related and other ales, good choice of malt whiskies, good varied reasonably priced largely home-made food inc fine Aberdeen Angus steaks and good children's menu; can get busy Sat; bedrooms *(Mike and Penny Sanders, Hazel and Michael Duncombe)*

☆ Oxton [A697 Edinburgh—Newcastle, by junction with A68; NT5053], *Carfraemill*: Attractive oak-beamed bar with log fire in substantial red sandstone hotel, good value food, good service, two real ales, separate games room, restaurant; big comfortable bedrooms *(R C Davey, BB)*

☆ St Boswells [A68 just S of Newtown St Boswells; NT5931], *Buccleuch Arms*: Restful Georgian-style no-smoking pink plush bar with light oak panelling in well established sandstone inn, wide choice of imaginative well prepared bar food (not Sun), sandwiches all day, restaurant, tables in garden behind; children welcome; bedrooms *(Gordon Smith, Susan and John Douglas)*

☆ St Marys Loch [A708 SW of Selkirk; NT2422], *Tibbie Shiels*: Down-to-earth inn, quite firmly run, in fine quiet setting by a beautiful loch, handy for Southern Upland Way and Grey Mares Tail waterfall – quite a few caravans and tents in summer; stone back bar, no-smoking lounge bar, straightforward waitress-served lunchtime bar food, well kept Belhaven 80/- and Greenmantle, several dozen malt whiskies, traditional games; children welcome, restaurant, open all day (cl Mon/Tues Nov-Mar); bedrooms *(Sharon Hancock, Carolyn and Michael Hedoin, Peter and Anne Cornall, M J Morgan, Sheila and John French, Mike and Penny Sanders, Andy and Jill Kassube, LYM)*

☆ Tweedsmuir [A701 a mile N of village; NT0924], *Crook*: Informal new management, unusual mix of 17th c (as in simple flagstoned back bar) with 1930s art deco (airy lounge, classic lavatories); log fires, decent bar food, well kept Greenmantle, good choice of malt whiskies, restaurant, traditional games, tables outside, play area, garden over road; craft centre behind, children welcome, open all day, bedrooms, Tweed trout fishing *(Mrs A Storm, LYM; more reports on new regime please)*

CENTRAL

Dollar [NS9796], *Kings Seat*: Friendly family-run pub with comfortable lounge, good home-made food inc vegetarian, Harviestoun and Orkney Dark Island ales *(Julian Holland)*

Drymen [The Square; NS4788], *Clachan*: Small cottagey pub, licensed since 1734, friendly and welcoming; original fireplace with side salt larder, tables made from former bar tops, former Wee Free pews along one wall; decent food in tartan-carpeted lounge, well kept Belhaven, hard-working friendly licensee; piped music; on square of attractive village *(Richard and Chris Worsley, PR, UR)*

☆ Inverarnan [A82 N of Loch Lomond; NN3118], *Inverarnan Drovers Inn*: Unique, with sporting trophies, other stuffed animals, armour, deerskins slung over the settles, haphazard decaying fabric and furnishings, Hogarthian candle-light, peat or log fires, some very stray customers and animals, kilted landlord; readers with a taste for the unusual like it a lot, probably much closer to what inns were really like 200 years ago than the usual anaemic imitations – though it does now have central heating; Scots music, great collection of malt whiskies, well kept McEwans 80/-, farm cider, well behaved children allowed, open all day; creaky ageing bedrooms, late breakfast *(Nigel Woolliscroft, Mr and Mrs I Keenleyside, John and Joan Nash, Paul and Ursula Randall, David Warrellow, LYM)*

☆ Killearn [Main St (A875); NS5285], *Old Mill*: Open fire, rustic cushioned built-in settles and wheelback chairs around neat dark tables, good bar food, friendly service, tables in garde; simple bedrooms, open all day summer, fine views of Campsie Fells from behind *(Mrs J Kemp, LYM)*

Stirling [Baker St; NS7993], *Hogs Head*: Traditionally done out by Whitbreads with stripped wood and mock gaslamps, eight real ales on handpump, more tapped from the cask, usual lunchtime food; open all day *(Julian Holland)*; [St Marys Wynd], *Settle*: Early 18th-c, restored to show beams, stonework, great arched fireplace and barrel-vaulted upper room; bar games, Belhaven 70/-

and 80/- and Maclays, friendly staff; piped music, open all day *(Mark and Diane Grist, BB)*; [St Marys Wynd], *Whistlebinkies*: Interesting late 16th-c pub, originally part of castle stables – lots of low ceilings and stairs; warm welcome, several real ales, reasonably priced standard food served beautifully hot; very handy for castle *(H L Dennis)*

☆ nr Stirling [Easter Cornton Rd, Causewayhead; off A9 N], *Birds & the Bees*: Convivial and interestingly furnished dim-lit ex-byre, Caledonian 80/-, Tennents Special and 80/-, guests such as Alloa 80/-, Harviestoun, Marstons Pedigree, good range of food, helpful staff; decor includes milk churns, iron sculptures and re-fleeced sheep; live bands most weekends, open all day till 1am – very popular with young people, reliably well run; children welcome *(Julian Holland, LYM)*

DUMFRIES AND GALLOWAY

Annan [High St; NY1966], *Blue Bell*: Welcoming local with Scots pictures, maps and ornaments on panelled walls, games area on different level, well kept Belhaven, St Andrews, Theakstons and a guest beer *(PB)*

☆ Auchencairn [about 2½ miles off A711; NX8249], *Balcary Bay*: A hotel (and a good one), but also has honest reasonably priced food from soup and open sandwiches up (inc huge child's helpings) in civilised but friendly bar, good service even when busy; lovely spot for eating outside, terrace and gardens in peaceful seaside surroundings, idyllic views over Solway Firth; keg beers; comfortable bedrooms, cl Oct-Mar *(David and Margaret Bloomfield, Humphry and Angela Crum Ewing)*

Dumfries [back street; NX9776], *Tam o' Shanter*: Backstreet pub, nothing special fom outside, that's like stepping back in time – poky smoky back bar with old pumps on thick wooden counter, bare boards, basic old chairs and tables, frosted windows, old men playing cards, basic food, changing beers such as Orkney Dark Island (served tepid as it should be) *(Kevin Thorpe)*

☆ Gatehouse of Fleet [B727 NW of Kirkcudbright; NX5956], *Murray Arms*: Pleasantly casual inn with wide choice of food all day inc good buffet with seafood, meats, lots of salads, cheeses and puddings, well kept ale such as Theakstons XB, lots of malt whiskies, decent wines, interesting layout of mainly old-fashioned comfortable seating areas inc one with soft easy chairs, friendly staff, games in quite separate public bar, rather upmarket restaurant; children welcome; comfortable well kept bedrooms *(Richard Holloway, LYM)*

Kingholm Quay [signed off B725 Dumfries—Glencaple; NX9773], *Swan*: Small friendly dining pub on River Nith overlooking old fishing jetty, Theakstons and Youngers, wide choice of good value food inc daily roast, good puddings, also high teas; two well kept bars and restaurant, children welcome, tables in garden; bedrooms *(Mrs M McGurk)*

☆ **Moffat** [1 Churchgate; NT0905], *Black Bull*: Quick friendly service, generous hearty food, friendly public bar with railway memorabilia and good open fire (may be only bar open out of season), plush softly lit cocktail bar, simply furnished tiled-floor dining room, side games bar with juke box; children welcome, open all day; bedrooms comfortable and good value *(Wayne Brindle, Stephen Holman, Alan Wilcock, Christine Davidson, E Locker, LYM)*

☆ **Moffat** [High St], *Moffat House*: Well run extended Adam-style hotel with good value reliable food in spacious old-fashioned plush lounge, relaxed and quiet; prompt helpful service, real ale all year; comfortable bedrooms with good breakfast *(Paul and Sue Merrick, Nick and Meriel Cox, Chris Rounthwaite, Neil Townend)*

Moffat [High St], *Buccleuch Arms*: Georgian coaching inn with pleasant bar, good reasonably priced evening meals in informal upstairs restaurant, friendly accommodating owners and attentive welcoming staff, interesting wines; modern bedrooms *(Joan and Tony Walker)*; [High St], *Balmoral*: Well kept ale, good simple food, quick cheerful service, comfortable peaceful bar *(Hazel and Michael Duncombe)*

☆ **Moniaive** [High St (A702); NX7790], *George*: 17th-c inn with interesting no-frills old-fashioned flagstoned bar of considerable character; friendly staff and locals, simple bedrooms *(Mark and Diane Grist, Ian and Villy White, LYM)*

New Abbey [NX9666], *Criffel*: Welcoming and lively, popular with locals, bar food inc good fresh fish and vegetarian dishes; bedrooms, nice village with attractive ruined abbey *(Richard Holloway)*

FIFE

Anstruther [High St, W end; NO5704], *Dreel*: Cosy and friendly ancient building in attractive spot with garden overlooking Dreel Burn, small bar, back pool room, open fire and stripped stone in atmospheric dining room, good helpings of traditional bar food; popular with locals *(Ian and Villy White)*

Auchtermuchty [NO2311], *Forest Hills*: Comfortable 18th-c old-world village inn used for recent version of *Dr Finlay's Casebook*, food in bar and restaurant; bedrooms *(Gordon Neighbour)*

Carrick [A919 NW of St Andrews; NO4423], *St Michaels*: Attractive red-walled bar newly and tastefully refurbished in pine, more rustic public bar (good for families), two dining areas, good value well presented bar food all day, helpful friendly staff, attractive back terrace and big garden; open all day, bedrooms *(Susan and John Douglas)*

☆ **Ceres** [Main St (B939 W of St Andrews); NO4011], *Meldrums*: Pleasant spacious bars and clean and attractive beamed dining lounge with good choice of well prepared and presented reasonably priced bar lunches,

prompt friendly service even when busy; bedrooms *(Eric Locker, E A Thwaite)*

☆ **Crail** [4 High St; NO6108], *Golf*: Welcoming service, small unpretentious beamed bar, restrained plush lounge, old-fashioned dining room, well kept Scottish Courage ales, good range of malt whiskies, good service, coal fire, above-average food inc good fresh local fish, quaint fishing-village atmosphere; simple comfortable bedrooms, good breakfast *(Mr and Mrs J Harrop)*

☆ **Falkland** [Mill Wynd; NO2507], *Stag*: Charming late 17th-c single-storey stone-built pub very prettily set on small green of this historic village, a few steps from Falkland Palace (NTS); helpful service, Calders 80/- and Timothy Taylors, food (not Tues) inc wide range of pizzas, also take-aways; fruit machine, bar billiards, back extension dining room with framed posters; unobtrusive piped pop music, children welcome *(Susan and John Douglas)*

☆ **Kingsbarns** [A917 St Andrews—Crail; NO5912], *Cambo Arms*: Doing well now under local farming family, real fires in comfortable armchair lounge and small simple front bar, real ales such as Belhaven 80/-, Brains Dark and St Andrews, homely books and pictures, good food all home-cooked to order using much local produce in bar and (not every evening) tiny restaurant – steaks from own beef herd; well equipped bedrooms in former back stables/outbuildings *(Paul and Ursula Randall)*

☆ **North Queensferry** [A90; NT1380], *Queensferry Lodge*: Useful motorway break with good views of Forth bridges and the Firth from light and airy modern hotel lounge, tastefully decorated with lots of wood and plants; McEwans real ale, good value bar food inc good buffet 12-2.30, 5-10; bedrooms good *(Neil Townend)*

Pitscottie [B939/B940; nr Cupar; NO4113], *Pitscottie*: More eating house than pub, spick and span with light wood tables on bright carpet, prompt service by smart waitresses, good value food inc children's dishes, good coffee, reasonably priced wines; high chairs available *(Jean and George Dundas)*

St Andrews [40 The Scores; NO5116], *Ma Bells*: By golf course, open all day, with big lively basement cafe/bistro bar brimming with students during term-time, well kept Deuchars IPA, Theakstons XB and guest beers (unless they run out), lots of interesting bottled beers and malt whiskies, popular food, friendly service; no-smoking raised back area, bar mirrors, old enamel signs; well reproduced piped music, pleasant seafront views from outside *(Paul and Ursula Randall)*

☆ *nr* **St Andrews** [Grange Rd (off A917) a mile S; NO5114], *Grange*: More restaurant than pub (Have you booked? I'm sure we can squeeze you in), good choice of carefully cooked enjoyable food in spotless small beamed and flagstoned bar too, friendly service, good range of malt whiskies, decent wines (but keg beers), furniture in keeping with the age of the building, attractive setting; cl Mon/Tues Nov-Mar *(John Honnor)*

☆ **St Monance** [16 West End; SO5202], *Cabin*: Well run restaurant/dining pub, good if not cheap fresh food virtually all day inc local seafood, well kept Belhaven 80/- and St Andrews, coffee all day, cheerful well groomed staff, old fishing photographs in lounge, local salts in simple public bar, elegant back restaurant with fine views over harbour and Firth of Forth; small sheltered terrace with same view *(Paul and Ursula Randall, Eric Locker)*

Tayport [Dalglish St; NO4528], *Bell Rock*: Traditional pubby local, really friendly and cheerful, with well kept Scottish Courage ales, home-made food, masses of photographs – local railways, RAF, submarines, tankers *(Paul and Ursula Randall)*

Wormit [NO4026], *Sandford*: Elegant and comfortable yet friendly bar of golfing hotel, cushioned window seat overlooks pretty garden as does the terrace, limited choice of reliable bar food, friendly waitresses in Highland dress; bedrooms good *(Susan and John Douglas)*

GRAMPIAN

☆ **Aberdeen** [Bon Accord St; NJ9305], *Ferryhill House*: Four well kept Scottish Courage ales and well over 100 malt whiskies in well run small hotel's comfortable communicating spacious and airy bar areas, friendly staff, generous lunchtime bar food, wide choice in restaurant; lots of well spaced tables on neat sheltered lawns; open all day, children allowed in restaurant; bedrooms comfortable *(Graham Reeve, LYM)*

Aberdeen [504 Union St], *Cocky Hunters*: Busy lively bare-boards pub, lots of alcoves, dark panelling and bric-a-brac, well kept ales inc Boddingtons and Caledonian 80/-, neat friendly staff, usual lunchtime food (not Sun), big-screen sports TV, piped music, machines, live rock band Fri, disco dancing nights *(Graham Reeve, Mark Walker, Tom McLean)*; [Holburn St], *Granary*: Nice atmosphere, good food, friendly staff, wide choice of drinks at affordable prices *(Anon)*; [55 Castle St], *Tilted Wig*: Long open-plan bar with thriving atmosphere, well kept Tetleys-related and other ales such as Caledonian Deuchars and Marstons Pedigree, reasonably priced usual food 11-9, friendly staff; fruit machine, juke box or piped music, TV *(Mark Walker, Reg Nelson, Graham Reeve)*

Ballater [NO3695], *Prince of Wales*: A shining beacon for walkers, little local with assorted bric-a-brac, plenty of atmosphere, particularly well kept St Andrews beer *(Reg Nelson)*

☆ **Braemar** [A93; NO1491], *Fife Arms*: Well refurbished big Victorian hotel, comfortable sofas and tartan cushions, reasonably priced reliable pub food, particularly friendly helpful staff, huge log fire; children and dogs welcome, piped music; on the coach routes, used by school ski trips, appropriate entertainment; bedrooms warm and comfortable with mountain views, pleasant strolls in village *(Esther and John Sprinkle, Susan and John Douglas, George Atkinson)*

☆ **Crook of Alves** [Burghead Rd, just off A96 Elgin—Forres; NJ1362], *Crooked Inn*: Generous enjoyable food (all day Sun) inc vegetarian and good Sun roasts in bustling beamed village inn with built-in high-backed brocaded settles, lots of prints and bric-a-brac, open fires, some stripped stone, well kept Theakstons Best, decent wines, friendly service, chess; children in eating area, piped music; cl lunchtime Mon-Thurs, cl Mon in Oct, Nov and Jan *(LYM)*

☆ **Findhorn** [NJ0464], *Crown & Anchor*: Useful family pub with food all day inc imaginative and children's dishes (model train takes orders to kitchen), up to six changing real ales, big fireplace in lively public bar, separate lounge, friendly individual staff; bedrooms comfortable, good boating in Findhorn Bay (boats for residents) *(Andrew Rogers, Amanda Milsom, LYM)*

Fochabers [NJ3458], *Gordon Arms*: Comfortable traditional small hotel with decent fresh food from sandwiches up in quietly decorated bars and restaurant, well kept McEwans 80/-, good choice of whiskies, good coffee; can arrange stalking and fishing for residents; bedrooms *(R Macnaughton, LYM)*

Fraserburgh [Smiddyhill Rd; NJ9966], *Findlays Uptown*: Good choice of food in conservatory and dining room, superb Aberdeen Angus steaks, fresh local fish *(Ian and Sandra Thornton)*

☆ **Stonehaven** [Shorehead; NO8786], *Marine*: Welcoming basic harbourside pub with good cheap food, five real ales inc McEwans 80/- and guests, coffee and tea, polite service, upstairs lounge and restaurant, superb view – in summer people drink out on the harbour wall; lively downstairs, piped music, TV, dogs allowed; juke box, games machines and pool table in room past bar; open all day; bedrooms *(Chris Raisin, Mark Walker)*

☆ **Turriff** [Auchterless; A947, 5 miles S; NJ7250], *Towie*: Only a shortage of reader reports keeps this comfortable and warmly welcoming dining pub out of the main entries this year – good interesting home-made food (all day Sun), reasonable prices, elegant no-smoking dining room, helpful service, well kept Theakstons Best and a weekly changing guest beer, decent wines, lots of malt whiskies; children welcome, darts, pool, shove-ha'penny, cribbage, dominoes, trivia, and piped music; handy for Fyvie Castle (NTS) and Delgatie Castle, open all day w/e *(Neil Townend, LYM)*

HIGHLAND

Aviemore [Coylumbridge Rd; NH8912], *Olde Bridge*: Well kept friendly and attractive inn, small but busy, with good bar food inc four-course meals (with whisky for the haggis), changing real ales such as Caledonian and Lairds, Tues ceilidh; pleasant surroundings *(James Nunns)*

☆ **Badachro** [B8056 by Loch Gairloch; NG7773], *Badachro Inn*: Welcoming pub in splendid setting by sheltered harbour, helpful landlord, nice atmosphere – locals and yachtsmen (two moorings, shower available); decent basic food esp stovies in simple public bar, more comfortable than usual, friendly and relaxing; good log fire, children welcome; Nov-Mar open only Weds and Fri evenings, Sat lunch and evening; nice garden and tables on terrace over loch; homely bedrooms *(Mrs Olive Oxley, D G Clarke)*

Ballachulish [Oban Rd (A828); NN0858], *Ballachulish Hotel*: Biggish hotel's pleasant lounge bar with beautiful loch view, very friendly staff, good bar food inc sandwiches, vegetarian and children's, wide range of malt whiskies, McEwans 80/- and Theakstons ales; basic public bar; comfortable bedrooms, cl most of Jan *(Neil Townend, Jean and George Dundas)*

Banavie [off A830 N of Fort William; NN1177], *Moorings*: Mainly hotel with dining room catering to local businessmen, but also good basement bar attractively panelled with wood from old Edinburgh Bank, interesting nautical bric-a-brac (caters for yachtsmen passing through nearby Caledonian Canal lock flight); McEwans 70/-, dozens of vintage wines, good bar food from separate kitchen, charming local waitresses; bedrooms *(CLS, RMB)*

Beauly [The Square; NH5246], *Priory*: Hotel not pub, but useful for food all day in welcoming eating area, pleasant helpful staff, good coffee; separate restaurant *(Bill and Brenda Lemon, Neil Townend)*

Bettyhill [NC7062], *Bettyhill Hotel*: Old north coast hotel, clean and reasonably priced; good choice of snacks in lounge, separate restaurant, owners eager to please; bedrooms *(Gordon Neighbour)*

☆ **Carrbridge** [nr junction A9/A95 S of Inverness; NH9022], *Dalrachney Lodge*: Consistently good food and friendly staff in pleasantly relaxed traditional shooting-lodge-type hotel with simple bar, comfortable lounge with books and log fire in ornate inglenook, decent malt whiskies, McEwans 70/-, old-fashioned dining room; very busy with locals weekends; children welcome, bedrooms, most with mountain and river views; open all year *(Mark and Diane Grist, David Dolman, Neil Townend)*

☆ **Cromarty** [Marine Terr; NH7867], *Royal*: Very friendly small old-fashioned harbourside hotel, good value food, beautiful view across Cromarty Firth to Ben Wyvis; bedrooms – very popular in summer *(I S Thomson, Paul and Ursula Randall, Mark and Diane Grist)*

☆ **Dores** [B852 SW of Inverness; NH5934], *Dores Inn*: Good value well prepared food inc good seafood, well kept beer and friendly staff in attractive traditional country inn; stripped stone, low ceilings, basic public bar, more comfortable lounge with open fire; beautiful views over Loch Ness, front garden and tables out behind *(Lynn and Peter Brueton)*

Dornoch [Castle St; NH8089], *Eagle*: Well refurbished, with good reasonably priced generous food presented well, pleasant atmosphere, good choice of well kept beers; open all day, restaurant; six bedrooms *(Bill and Sheila McCardy)*; [Church Rd], *Mallin House*: Good well priced food inc tasty local fish and superb langoustine in welcoming lounge or restaurant, well kept Theakstons Best and other S&N beers, good range of malt whiskies, friendly service, interesting collections of whisky-water jugs and golf balls; comfortable bedrooms *(Mick Hitchman, Mike and Penny Sanders)*

Dunnet [A836; ND2171], *Northern Sands*: Our most northerly mainland entry, and an oasis for these parts, on lovely bay nr Dunnet Head – on clear day you can see from Duncansby Head to Cape Wrath; comfortable bar and lounge with moderately priced mainly Italian food and pleasant atmosphere; bedrooms *(Dr D G Twyman)*

Fort William [66 High St; NN1174], *Grog & Gruel*: Done out in traditional alehouse style, half a dozen well kept real ales, helpful staff, upstairs restaurant with wide range of home-made usual modern pub food inc pizzas, pasta, Mexican and vegetarian, starters available as bar snacks downstairs; children welcome; in pedestrian part *(Andy Hazeldine, Hazel and Michael Duncombe, John Abbott)*

Gairloch [just off A832 near bridge; NG8077], *Old Inn*: Usefully placed over rd from small harbour, nr splendid beach; dimpled copper tables and so forth in two small rooms of comfortable lounge, a good few malts, up to eight real ales inc several English ones in summer, popular bar food, games in public bar; piped music may be loud, and does catch the tourist coaches; picnic tables out by stream, open all day; bedrooms *(Andy Hazeldine, Neil and Angela Huxter, BB)*

☆ **Glencoe** [old Glencoe rd, behind NTS Visitor Centre; NN1256], *Clachaig*: Spectacular setting, surrounded by soaring mountains, inn doubling as mountain rescue post and cheerfully crowded with outdoors people in season, with walkers' bar (two woodburners and pool), pine-panelled snug, big modern-feeling lounge bar; good simple snacks all day, wider evening choice, lots of malt whiskies, well kept ales such as Arrols 80/-, Maclays 80/-, Marstons Pedigree, Theakstons Old Peculier, Tetleys and Youngers No 3; children in no-smoking restaurant; frequent live music; simple bedrooms, good breakfast *(John and Beryl Knight, Mark and Diane Grist, John and Joan Nash, David Trump, LYM)*

☆ **Glenelg** [unmarked rd from Shiel Bridge (A87) towards Skye; NG8119], *Glenelg Inn*: Overlooking Skye across own beach and sea loch; big bright traditional bar with blazing fire even in summer, plain solid furnishings, pool table, piped music, homely pictures; good simple fresh food (residents only, Sun), lots of whiskies, decent wine list, fine set menu inc excellent fish in nice restaurant, young enthusiastic kilted landlord, tables on terrace; steep narrow road to inn has spectacular views of Loch Duich – there's a short summer ferry crossing from Skye, too; luxurious bedrooms, superb views *(Dr A Kelly)*

Invergarry [NH3001], *Invergarry Inn*: Good friendly service and good food inc wide vegetarian choice, two guest beers; juke box, lively pool room; bedrooms *(Lynn and Peter Brueton)*; [93 Academy St], *Blackfriars*: Big open-plan town local with exceptional choice of beer *(J V Dadswell, Esther and John Sprinkle)*; [10 Bridge St], *Gellions*: Darkish long room with well kept ale and friendly staff *(Andrew Hazeldine)*; [11 Island Bank Rd (B862 S, opp Ness Islands)], *Haydens*: Good home-cooked food inc fresh produce and in-house patisserie, courteous, efficient and helpful service, pleasant rather elegant two-level dining area with comfortable seats and unusual indoor fountain, decent bar, well kept real ales; open from noon *(Paul and Ursula Randall)*

☆ Kingussie [High St; NH7501], *Royal*: Big comfortable lounge with wide choice of good well served cheap food from fresh sandwiches and filled baguettes up, several well kept mainly Tetleys-related ales with a guest such as Bass or Orkney Dark Island, friendly helpful staff, no-smoking area; open all day, bedrooms *(E Locker, M Thompson)*

☆ Kylesku [A894, S side of former ferry crossing; NC2234], *Kylesku Hotel*: Useful for this remote NW coast (but in winter open only weekends, just for drinks), rather spartan but pleasant and busy local bar (unusual in facing the glorious view, with seals often in sight), friendly helpful service, short choice of reasonably priced wonderfully fresh local seafood, also sandwiches and soup; open all day in summer, comfortable seaview restaurant, well refurbished peaceful bedrooms, good breakfast; boatman does good loch trips *(P W Taylor, J and S French)*

Lochinver [NC0923], *Inver Lodge*: Largish modern plush hotel in lovely spot on hill overlooking harbour and sea; good bar lunches esp local fish and venison, very friendly service, well furnished bar area; bedrooms *(June and Tony Baldwin)*

Melvich [A836; NC8765], *Melvich Hotel*: Good food inc fresh wild salmon in civilised lounge bar or restaurant, relaxed atmosphere, friendly staff, peat or log fire; lovely spot, beautiful sea and coast views; bedrooms *(Dr D G Twyman)*

☆ Plockton [Innes St, off A87 or A890 NE of Kyle of Lochalsh; NG8033], *Creag Nan Darach*: Fresh substantial well cooked food with real chips and veg done just right, well kept McEwans 80/- and Theakstons, good range of malt whiskies, pleasant efficient

service, congenial bustling atmosphere even in winter; some live traditional music, comfortable bedrooms *(Dr and Mrs S Jones, D Stokes, Neil Townend)*

☆ Spean Bridge [A82 7 miles N; NN2491], *Letterfinlay Lodge*: Well established hotel, extensive comfortably modern main bar with popular lunchtime buffet and usual games, small smart cocktail bar, no-smoking restaurant; real ales at least in summer, good malt whiskies, friendly service, children and dogs welcome, pleasant lochside grounds, own boats for fishing; clean and comfortable bedrooms, good breakfasts; gents' have good showers and hairdryers – handy for Caledonian Canal sailors *(Sue and Bob Ward, LYM)*

Tomdoun [NH1501], *Tomdoun Hotel*: 19th-c country house in middle of nowhere, good views, fishing, walking etc; basic bar with some fine whiskies, good food esp fish; bedrooms large and reasonably priced, front ones with view *(Andrew Hazeldine)*

Tongue [A836; NC5957], *Ben Loyal*: Lovely views up to Ben Loyal and out over Kyle of Tongue, good value bar meals (stop 2 prompt), Tennents 80/-, fresh local (even home-grown) food in restaurant; traditional live music in lounge bar in summer; comfortable good value bedrooms *(Dr D G Twyman)*

LOTHIAN

Bathgate [Livery St; NS9768], *Livery Lounge*: Popular and cheery, good reasonably priced food, Belhaven and Tennents, blazing coal fire, comfortable stable-theme decor *(Ian Phillips)*

☆ Cramond [Cramond Glebe Rd (off A90 W of Edinburgh); NT1876], *Cramond Inn*: Softly lit little rooms with comfortable brown-and-brass decor, traditional English-style pub furnishing but Scottish bric-a-brac, good coal and log fires, prompt friendly service, Sam Smiths OB, emphasis on good generous well priced salads, grills etc; very popular with retired couples at lunchtime; in picturesque waterside village *(M Walker, Ian and Villy White, Victor Brilliant, LYM)*

☆ Dirleton [B1345 W of N Berwick; NT5184], *Open Arms*: Small comfortable hotel with welcoming new owners, not a place for just a drink, but good for bar food inc generous snacks and well presented hot dishes with good fresh veg; lovely little sitting room with good open fire, fine position facing castle; good bedrooms *(P Rome, Chris Rounthwaite)*

☆ East Linton [5 Bridge St (off A1 Haddington—Dunbar); NT5977], *Drovers*: Small dining pub dating from 18th c, cleanly refurbished in an attractive style that gives it something of a wine-bar atmosphere; inventive well presented bistro-style food inc fresh local fish and well cooked veg, interesting changing well kept ales, friendly helpful service, upstairs restaurant *(O K Smyth, Andy and Jill Kassube, F J and A Parmenter)*

☆ **Edinburgh** [8 Leven St], *Bennets*: Elaborate Victorian bar with wonderfully ornate original glass, mirrors, arcades, panelling and tiles, well kept McEwans 80/- and other ales from tall founts, lots of rare malt whiskies, bar snacks and simple lunchtime hot dishes, children allowed in eating area lunchtime; open all day, cl Sun lunchtime *(Ian Phillips, Andy and Jill Kassube, David Carr)*

☆ **Edinburgh** [3 Rose St, by S St Davids St], *Abbotsford*: Traditional part-panelled dining bar with polished Victorian island servery, long wooden tables and leatherette benches, handsome ornate high ceiling, well kept ales such as Batemans XB, Boddingtons, Caledonian Deuchars IPA, Courage Directors, McEwans 70/- and 80/-, dozens of whiskies, good reasonably priced mealtime food, efficient neat service; children in eating area, open all day, cl Sun *(David Carr, Amanda and Simon Southwell, Mark Walker, LYM)*

☆ **Edinburgh** [55 Rose St], *Rose Street Brewery*: Malt-extract beer brewed on the premises, mild-flavoured though quite potent Auld Reekie 80/- and stronger sticky 90/-; tiny brewery can be seen from upstairs lounge (cl at quiet times); back-to-basics downstairs bar open all day, with well reproduced pop music from its CD juke box, machines; usual bar food, good service, tea and coffee, live music some evenings *(Sue and Mike Todd, Eric Larkham, David Carr, Susan and Nigel Wilson, Stephen and Jean Curtis, Andy and Jill Kassube, Esther and John Sprinkle, Mark Walker, BB)*

☆ **Edinburgh** [Rose St, corner of Hanover St], *Milnes*: Large bar with another downstairs, dark wood, bare floorboards, cask tables and old-fashioned decor; lots of Scottish Courage real ales with a guest or two such as Burton Bridge and Marstons Pedigree, good range of snacks and hot food (not Sun evening) inc various pies charged by size; very busy but cheerful quick aproned staff; mixed customers, lively atmosphere *(Eric Larkham, Esther and John Sprinkle)*

☆ **Edinburgh** [The Causeway, out below Arthurs Seat at Duddingston; beware that on Sun you can't reach it via the Holyrood Pk ring rd], *Sheep Heid*: Old-fashioned rather upmarket ex-coaching inn in lovely spot beyond Holyroodhouse, relaxed pubby atmosphere, interesting pictures and fine rounded bar counter in main room, well kept Caledonian 80/-, Bass and Worthington BB, newspapers, children allowed; piped music; restaurant, pretty garden with summer barbecues, skittle alley; open all day, can get crowded *(Richard Holloway, LYM)*

☆ **Edinburgh** [Lindsay Rd, Newhaven], *Peacock*: Good straightforward food esp fresh seafood in neat plushly comfortable pub with conservatory-style back room leading to garden, well kept McEwans 80/-; very popular, best to book evenings and Sun lunchtime; children welcome, open all day *(David Carr, Ian and Villy White, LYM)*

Edinburgh [1 Princes St], *Balmoral*: Certainly no pub, but this corner lobby of the landmark former North British Hotel is a relaxing refuge in its comfortable clubby armchairy way (despite the piped music); welcoming staff, canapés with the expensive cocktails, good hot rolls filled with daily roast (not cheap either); also good value champagne by the glass in the Palm Court, and very good teas; bedrooms *(Bob and Maggie Atherton, Peter Todd, Mark Walker, Stephen and Jean Curtis)*; [18-20 Grassmarket], *Beehive*: Civilised comfortable lounge with good range of well kept ales, fun atmosphere (esp after a rugby match), good value food noon-6pm, upstairs restaurant *(Laura Wendt, Scot Mario, LYM)*; [Raeburn Pl, Stockbridge], *Bests*: Recently refurbished bar with very broad mix of customers, good range of well kept beers such as Ind Coope Burton, Marstons Pedigree, Orkney Dark Island and Timothy Taylors Landlord, good wines *(Gregg Davies)*; [Broughton St], *Cask & Barrel*: Spacious bar with wide choice of well kept real ales at reasonable prices, good selection of continental bottled beers, good value bar food esp stovies Mon-Fri, good Thai lunch Fri, pleasant staff *(William Angold, Vann and Terry Prime)*; [435 Lawnmarket], *Deacon Brodies*: Entertainingly commemorating the notorious highwayman town councillor who was eventually hanged on the scaffold he'd designed; limited decent food inc some unusual home-made dishes, Arrols 80/-, comfortable leather-chair upstairs lounge; piper outside can be a little wearing after a while *(David Carr, Peter Todd, Stephen and Jean Curtis)*; [159 Rose St], *Dirty Dicks*: Pleasant ambience, decent bar food *(Ian and Villy White, Eric Larkham)*; [Royal Mile, last pub on right before Castle], *Ensign Ewart*: Charming old-world pub handy for Castle, lots of interesting memorabilia relating to Ewart and Waterloo, Alloa, Caledonian Deuchars and 80/-, Orkney Dark Island, wide range of whiskies, usual food lunchtime and some summer evenings, friendly efficient staff; juke box, fruit machine, piped Scottish music, folk music Thurs/Sun; no children, open all day *(Peter Todd, Mark Walker)*; [30 Wrights Houses], *Olde Golf Tavern*: Dating from 1456 though does not seem old, overlooking Bruntisfield Links (where golf first played here – it's still a sort of unofficial clubhouse for this free public golf course); good atmosphere, consistently good food all day, McEwans 80/-, Theakstons Best and two other real ales, leather chesterfields, old golf prints, newspapers, moderate prices, prompt friendly service, upstairs restaurant; fruit and quiz machines, piped music *(Ian Phillips, Mark Walker, BB)*; [1 High St], *Royal Archer*: Friendly bar/bistro with masses of prints and other bric-a-brac, good all-day bar snacks inc cheap Scotch broth *(Dave Braisted, David Carr)*; [118 Biggar Rd (A702), Hill End; NT2467], *Steading*: Popular modern pub, several cottages knocked together at foot of dry ski slope, a dozen Scottish and English real ales inc Timothy Taylors Landlord, very varied good value generous food 10am-10pm in bar, restaurant and conservatory – dining pub atmosphere evening; friendly staff *(Mr and Mrs T Bryan, B A Hayward, Norma Hardy)*; [W Register St], *Tiles*: Exquisite tiling from floor to ceiling, good reasonably priced fresh food, prompt obliging service *(Susan Wood, Eric Larkham)*

Haddington [Waterside; NT5174], *Waterside*: Bistro-style riverside pub, locally very popular, often crowded; snug main bar, separate lounge and restaurant, friendly staff, wide range of fresh food, real ales such as Caledonian Deuchars, Courage Directors and Marstons Pedigree, good house wines; tables outside in summer *(M S Saxby, Anna Bisset)*

North Middleton [off A7 S of Gorebridge; NT3659], *Middleton*: Welcoming atmosphere, wide choice of good sensibly priced food, good range of drinks inc Belhaven, concerned management; tables in garden *(Ian and Sandra Thornton)*

Pathhead [Ford; A68 just N, nr Oxenford Castle; NT3964], *Stair Arms*: Large main-road pub with good varied unusual bar food inc small helpings for children; well equipped playroom inside, good big play area outside *(Christine and Malcolm Ingram)*

☆ **Queensferry** [South Queensferry (B924, just off A90); NT1278], *Hawes*: Featured famously in *Kidnapped*, now comfortably modernised, with fine views of the Forth bridges, friendly staff, well kept Arrols 80/-, Ind Coope Burton and guest beers such as Caledonian 80/- from tall founts, usual food from efficient servery, games in small public bar, no-smoking family room, restaurant, children welcome; tables on back lawn with play area; bedrooms *(David Carr, Ian Baillie, LYM)*

☆ **Ratho** [Baird Rd; signed off A8, A71, B7030 W of Edinburgh; NT1370], *Bridge*: Very welcoming extended 18th-c pub enjoyed by all ages, food all day inc vegetarian, good children's dishes and tactful range of food for those with smaller appetites, choice between quick Pop Inn menu and more expensive things, well kept Belhaven 80/- and Summer Ale, pleasant helpful and chatty staff; garden by partly restored Union Canal, good well stocked play area, own canal boats (doing trips for the disabled, among others); open all day from noon, very busy in summer *(Roger Bellingham, Ian and Villy White, Dr A C Williams, Dr F M Ellard)*

STRATHCLYDE

Ayr [Burns Statue Sq; NS3321], *O'Briens*: Irish bar with wooden floors, bric-a-brac and coal fire, good mix of customers, friendly service, simple food 12-5; popular folk nights Weds, Fri and Sun *(Julian Holland)*

Balloch [Balloch Rd; just N of A811; NS3881], *Balloch*: Pleasantly pubby big bar broken up by pillars, helpful young staff, four particularly well kept ales such as Caledonian Deuchars, Ind Coope Burton and Timothy Taylors Landlord, good value food all day inc good haggis; many small tables, scattering of fish tackle, restaurant area; bedrooms, nice spot by River Leven's exit from Loch Lomond *(Joy and Peter Heatherley, Ian Baillie)*

Campbeltown [Kilkerran Rd; NS1950], *Ardshiel*: Amazing range of malt whiskies inc malt of the month, good choice of reasonably priced food; bedrooms *(Ian and Sandra Thornton)*

Dunure [just off A719 SW of Ayr; NS2515], *Anchorage*: Small place attractively set by harbourside ruined castle; specialises in well cooked reasonably priced pub lunches, splendid sauces, vegetarian dishes; busy restaurant, friendly service; pleasant detour, not far from Culzean Castle *(Christine and Malcolm Ingram)*

☆ **Glasgow** [154 Hope St], *Cask & Still*: Comfortable and welcoming, with bare boards and panelling, big carpets, good lounge seating, reasonably priced food all day (menu limited evenings) with well kept Caledonian Deuchars, Merman XXX and 80/-, McEwans 80/-, Theakstons Best and Youngers No3 (taster samples available), lots of unusual bottled beers, shelves and shelves of malt whiskies, Bulmer's cider, friendly helpful staff, interesting prints, good piped music *(Richard Lewis, Ian Phillips)*

☆ **Glasgow** [12 Ashton Lane], *Ubiquitous Chip*: Thriving atmosphere, minimal decoration apart from some stained glass, real ale, wide choice of malt whiskies, good wines by the glass, good daily changing home-cooked lunchtime food in upstairs cafe dining area inc vegetarian dishes, not too expensive, peat fire; wider choice in downstairs restaurant opening on to courtyard, with outstanding wines; often packed with university staff and students *(Monica Shelley, Stephen Holman)*

☆ **Glasgow** [83 Hutcheson St], *Rab Ha's*: Same family as Babbity Bowster – see main entries; civilised dark-panelled bar in sensitively converted Georgian town house, well cooked seafood in bar and basement restaurant, informal atmosphere, candlelight, friendly young staff, newspapers for customers, well kept McEwans 80/-; intermittent robust live music but otherwise relatively quiet; bedrooms elegant and immaculate; bedrooms *(Ian Phillips)*

Glasgow [Byres Rd], *Aragon*: Very pubby, an institution for students, pleasant decor, lots of well kept Scottish Courage and guest beers – occasional mini beer festivals; quite small and friendly, pleasant and unintimidating *(Ian Baillie)*; [780 Pollokshaws Rd], *Athena*: Modern single-bar Greek cafe with Belhaven 80/-, up to five guest beers and good bottled range esp German, restaurant with the food you'd expect inc a good range of puddings; can be very busy evenings, cl Sun *(Andy and Jill Kassube)*; [6 North Ct, St Vincent Pl], *Auctioneers*: Lots of wood in bare-boards high-ceilinged lounge area, interesting bar, side room with big wooden dresser, antiques, prints, sofas and big fireplace, back bar too;

good choice of food and of real ales, plenty of wines and whiskies; friendly helpful staff *(Richard Lewis)*; [Duke St, Parkhead; NS6263], *Black Bull*: Good food, well kept beer, fun atmosphere, nicely decorated *(Derek O'Brian)*; [36 Bell St], *Blackfriars*: Rapidly changing range of interesting well kept Tetleys-related and other beers, Belgian beer on tap, continental bottled beers, Addlestone's cider, friendly and efficient service; bare-boards room with round tables and chairs, then lounge area, with snack food servery; walls and ceilings covered with local arts and music posters, open all day, live music, comedy shows *(Andy and Jill Kassube, Richard Lewis, SLC)*; [1055 Sauchiehall St], *Brewery Tap*: Lively two-room pub handy for galleries and museums, cosy dark decor, up to eight well kept and interesting British real ales, also Belgian beers all served in the appropriate glass, at the right temperature, plenty of malt whiskies, bottled beers, Inch's cider; good value lunchtime food, friendly efficient service even when busy with students; open all day, frequent live music *(Richard Lewis, Andy and Jill Kassube)*; [St Enoch Sq], *Fat Boabs*: Busy modern saloon with bare boards, lots of seating, decent food, friendly staff, well kept beers *(Richard Lewis)*; [1397 Argyle St, by Kelvin Hall arena, opp art galleries], *Hogshead*: Wide choice of Whitbreads-related and other well kept changing ales on handpump or tapped from cask, appropriate artefacts, simple bar lunches, good comfortable atmosphere, friendly service, well reproduced piped blues music, games machines, quiz nights, beer festivals; opp art galleries, open all day, can get busy – popular with students *(Andy and Jill Kassube, Angus Lyon, Richard Lewis)*; [Jamaica St], *MacSorleys*: Popular roomy pub by Glasgow station arches, back side bar with food counter (good choice and prices), upstairs lounge/eating area, friendly staff *(Richard Lewis)*; [12 Brunswick St], *Mitre*: Classic unspoilt small Victorian pub with horseshoe bar and coffin gantry, three or four real ales such as Belhaven, Orkney Dark Island, St Andrews and one brewed for the pub, also unusual Belgian and other bottled beers; friendly sports-loving staff, wholesome cheap food, upstairs restaurant; open all day, cl Sun *(Paul MacDonald, Richard Lewis, SLC)*; [112 Stockwell St], *Scotia*: Friendly welcome to newcomers, low ceiling, panelling, lots of cosy seating around island bar, service friendly even when very busy; well kept Belhaven Sandy Hunters, Caledonian Deuchars IPA, Greenmantle, Maclays 80/- and Broadsword on tall fount, daytime food; popular for folk music, also promotes poetry and writers' groups; open all day *(Richard Lewis, Alf Sludden)*; [148 Holland St], *State*: Good well priced lunchtime food from sandwiches to casseroles, pleasant attentive service, good range of beers such as Belhaven, Orkney Dark Island, St Andrews, ever-changing guest ales

(Andy and Jill Kassube); [Airport; NS4766], *Tap & Spile*: Sometimes seems packed to the gills with home-sick Englishmen – well done in the style of a traditional pub, bright yet peaceful and comfortable, with plenty of seats, well kept Arrols 80/- and guest beers such as Ind Coope Burton and Greenmantle, decent malt whiskies, good snacks inc fresh sandwiches, no-smoking area *(Monica Shelley)*; [Byres Rd], *Tennents*: Big lively high-ceilinged pub with well kept Caledonian 70/- or 80/-, Greenmantle, Theakstons Best and lots of interesting changing guest ales, also plenty of good malt whiskies, decent house wine; cheerful atmosphere, usual bar food *(Monica Shelley)*; [141 Dumbarton Rd], *Three Judges*: Eight well kept ales changing day by day, Addlestone's cider, friendly licensees, staff and locals, plenty of seating in long back bar, massive pump clip collection; open all day *(Richard Lewis)*; [159 Bridgegate], *Victoria*: Well worn long narrow bar with basic wooden decor, very warm and friendly, plenty of old panelling, lots of cultural event posters, well kept Caledonian Deuchars, Maclays 70/-, 80/-, Kanes Amber and Wallace on tall fount, lounge on left popular with folk musicians, back bar with wonderful historic bottled beer collection; open all day, cheap food till 6, friendly staff and locals *(Richard Lewis)*

☆ **Houston** [Main St (B790 E of Bridge of Weir); NS4166], *Fox & Hounds*: Village pub with quick friendly service, good atmosphere (busy evening, quieter daytime), several interesting well kept ales such as Heather Fraoch, Isle of Skye Red Cuillin, Moorhouses Premier and Tomintoul Wildcat, clean plush hunting-theme lounge, comfortable seats by fire, wide range of food from sandwiches up, restaurant upstairs, no-smoking areas, piped music; separate livelier bar with video game and pool; open all day, children welcome *(B A Hayward, LYM)*

☆ **Inveraray** [Main St E; NN0908], *George*: Pleasant old-fashioned pub, very popular locally, interesting old Highland feel to friendly low-beamed public bar with real fires, stone walls and fine flagstones; good value pub food served noon to 9pm, friendly helpful staff, Tennents 80/- and occasional guest beers, good choice of whiskies, reasonably priced wines, bar games; children welcome; bedrooms reasonably priced, quieter at the back *(Chris Bax, LYM)*

☆ **Kilchrenan** [B845 7 miles S of Taynuilt; NN0322], *Taychreggan*: Friendly airy hotel bar in beautiful setting, easy chairs and banquettes around low glass-topped tables, stuffed birds and fish and good local photographs; wide range of reasonably priced and well served lunchtime bar food inc local fish, well kept beers inc Aitkens (bar service stops 2), polite efficient staff, Sun lunch in no-smoking dining room, unusual lochside garden (good fishing), pretty inner courtyard, children welcome; cl Nov-March, comfortable bedrooms *(John Knighton, LYM)*

Kilmarnock [Glencairn Sq; NS4238], *Hunting Lodge*: Good value changing food, friendly staff *(David Little)*

Largs [NS2058], *George*: Friendly, pictures of paddle steamers, popular food *(Dave Braisted)*

Lochwinnoch [Lares Rd; NS3558], *Mossend*: Reliable Brewers Fayre family dining pub with efficiently served food, four well kept changing ales from the Whitbreads portfolio, periodic beer festivals; playground, good walking area *(Joy and Peter Heatherley)*

Milngavie [Main St; NS5574], *Talbot Arms*: Completely refurbished, pleasant simple decor, wide choice of rasonably priced lunchtime food from substantial sandwiches up, five real ales such as Alloa Talbot 80/-; handy for start or finish of West Highland Way; TVs in bar *(Ian Baillie)*

Oban [Cologin, Lerags; off A816 S – follow Ardoran Marine sign; NM8526], *Barn*: Friendly converted barn in lovely quiet countryside nr sea, donkeys, rabbits and hens all around, wide choice of good changing chip-free home-made food esp Fri seafood, Calders and Tetleys ales, wooden tables and settles, Scottish accordion Tues, ceilidh Thurs and folk group Sun; part of chalet holiday complex *(Mrs Olive Oxley, June and Perry Dann)*

Old Kilpatrick [159 Dumbarton Rd; NS4673], *Ettrick*: Warmly welcoming and comfortable, good value bar food from cheap pies and toasties to steaks and fish, real ales such as Bass, Caledonian Deuchars, Orkney Dark Island, weekend live music; in picturesque Clyde village *(Andy and Jill Kassube)*

Uplawmoor [Neilston Rd; A736 SW of Neilston; NS4355], *Uplawmoor*: Comfortable atmosphere, warm welcome, good well priced food, particularly well kept ales such as Bass and Caledonian 80/-; tables out on terrace; bedrooms good value *(Andy and Jill Kassube)*

TAYSIDE

Abernethy [NO1816], *Crees*: Has been gradually refurbished; real fire in main bar, usually three well kept real ales, good whiskies, basic food; monthly folk music *(Catherine Lloyd)*

Blair Atholl [NN8765], *Atholl Arms*: Good food – and the singing gets better as the beers go down; bedrooms *(Martin Savage, Norrie H)*

Blairgowrie [NO1745], *Cargills*: Varied food, pleasantly served *(Jean Dundas)*

Bridge of Cally [NO1451], *Bridge of Cally*: Good atmosphere and charming welcoming service in straightforward comfortable bar, sensible choice of good value food inc sandwiches and ploughman's using superb home-made bread, Orkney Dark Island real ale; bedrooms, attractive area *(R M Macnaughton)*

☆ **Broughty Ferry** [Shore Terr/Fishers St; NO4630], *Ship*: Small local by lifeboat station, friendly and busy, handsomely refurbished in burgundy and dark wood,

stately model sailing ship and other mainly local nautical items, bar food, keg beer; good more formal generous imaginative meals in pretty nautical-theme upstairs dining room with fantastic Tay view, attractive prices, friendly staff *(Susan and John Douglas, Roderick Stewart, L G Milligan)*

☆ **Cleish** [near M90 junction 5; follow B9097 W till village signpost; NT0998], *Nivingston House*: Sadly too few reports this year to keep its place in the main entries, but this hospitable country hotel is highly recommended by us as a relaxing place, for just a drink, for a meal, or for a stay; well presented interesting reasonably priced bar lunches and good more formal evening meals, log fire, separate no-smoking lounge, Alloa Calders tapped from the cask, dozens of malt whiskies, decent wines, snooker; children in eating area, good bedrooms, handsome gardens *(LYM)*

☆ **Crieff** [N, signed off A85, A822; open Mar-Dec Mon-Fri till 5.30, also Apr-Oct Sat till 4; NN8562], *Glenturret Distillery*: Not a pub, but good adjunct to one of the best whisky-distillery tours; good value whiskies in big plain bar/dining area with tasty sandwiches, good generous Highland soups, stews, pies, salmon and venison, and knock-out Glenturret ice cream, from self-service food counter *(Susan and John Douglas, Mark and Diane Grist)*

☆ **Dundee** [Brook St; NO4030], *Royal Oak*: Friendly and unusual, with sombre dark green decor and all tables laid for surprising range of interesting reasonably priced food esp curries; well kept Ind Coope Burton, Eldridge Pope Royal Oak and some Scottish ales *(Neil Townend, Susan and John Douglas, Gordon D H Bruce)*

Dundee [Westport], *Globe*: Friendly staff and atmosphere, guest beers, interesting cocktails *(James Steven)*; [Rep Theatre, Tay Sq], *Het Theatercafe*: Not a pub, but comfortable cafe/bar/restaurant with good food esp soups, good coffee, daily papers, friendly service; cl Sun *(Joanna Reid)*; [Commercial St], *Mercantile*: Family-owned, good atmosphere, Victorian decor, wide choice of Scottish real ales, good reasonably priced food till 8, restaurant upstairs *(Peter Leyland, Susan and John Douglas)*

Eassie [A94 Coupar Angus—Forfar; NO3547], *Castleton House*: More hotel than pub, but worth knowing for nicely presented well cooked interesting food served all day in attractive green tabled conservatory extending into garden, very affable staff; bedrooms *(Jean Dundas)*

☆ **Errol** [The Cross (B958 E of Perth); NO2523], *Old Smiddy*: Good food inc fresh local ingredients and interesting recipes, well kept Belhaven 80/-, lots of country wines, attractive heavy-beamed bar with assorted old country furniture, farm and smithy tools inc massive bellows; open all day Sun, cl Mon/Tues lunchtime *(Susan and John Douglas)*

Glamis [NO3846], *Strathmore Arms*: Reopened after closure for some years, now has enjoyable food inc interesting dishes *(Jean and George Dundas)*

Kenmore [A827 W of Aberfeldy; NN7745], *Kenmore Hotel*: Civilised and quietly old-fashioned small hotel beautifully set in pretty 18th-c village by Loch Tay, long landscape poem composed here written in Burns' own handwriting on residents' lounge chimneybreast, clean, friendly and smart back bar, lively separate barn bar, lovely views from back terrace; good bar food, helpful staff, children welcome, restaurant, Tay fishing, fine walks; comfortable bedrooms *(Susan and John Douglas, Nick and Meriel Cox, LYM)*

Kinloch Rannoch [NN6658], *Bunrannoch House*: Hotel not pub, but like other hotels in these parts does duty as one; delicious food inc particularly good breakfast; bedrooms *(Bob Ellis)*

Kinnesswood [A911 Glenrothes—Milnathort; NO1703], *Lomond*: Well appointed and friendly small inn with lovely sunset views over Loch Leven, good value bar and restaurant food strong on fresh local produce, delicious puddings, well kept Belhaven, Jennings and guest beers, helpful landlord, log fire; bedrooms comfortable *(Andy and Jill Kassube, Margaret and Nigel Dennis)*

Kinross [49 The Muirs; NO1102], *Muirs*: Carefully refurbished, with rare original Edwardian bar fittings and mirrors in small plain standing bar, second panelled bar with small pot still, lounge and supper room with banquettes; good traditional Scottish food and up to eight ales such as Belhaven, Caledonian, Greenmantle and Orkney Dark Island, superb choice of malt whiskies, interesting bottled beers, lavatory for the disabled; charming bedrooms *(Andy and Jill Kassube, Ian and Sandra Thornton)*

Loch Tummel [B8019 4 miles E of Tummel Bridge; NN8460], *Loch Tummel*: Fine quiet spot between wooded mountains and loch; long plain white-painted bar, lovely loch views, big woodburning stove, separate games bar, good bar food, friendly service, simple upstairs restaurant; children in eating area, open all day; bedrooms comfortable, with good breakfasts *(Diane Devine, LYM)*

Meikleour [A984 W of Coupar Angus; NO1539], *Meikleour*: Two lounges, one with stripped stone, flagstones and armour, another more chintzy, both with open fires (shame about the fruit machines); helpful friendly service, good bar food inc fine range of open sandwiches and lunchtime snacks, well kept Maclays 70/-, back public bar; pretty building, charming garden with tall pines and distant Highland view; nr famous 250-yr-old beech hedge over 30 m (100 ft) high *(Susan and John Douglas)*

Montrose [131 High St; NO7157], *Corner House*: Popular with locals, comfortable lounge bar, reasonably priced food all day *(Ian and Villy White)*

Pitlochry [11 Kirkmichael Rd, Moulin; NE of centre; NN9459], *Moulin*: Good reasonably priced food in pleasant old-world traditional pubby bar and restaurant, prompt friendly service, log fires, well kept Boddingtons and, all brewed in the inn's own microbrewery, Light, Braveheart, Ale of Athol and Old Remedial; brewery tours 12-5 (evening by arrangement); spacious well kept bedrooms, good walks *(June and Perry Dann, Ruth Holloway, Andrew Hazeldine)*

St Fillans [NN6924], *Achray House*: Stunning lochside position, good friendly service, good varied reasonably priced food esp puddings, extensive wine list; bedrooms *(Ian and Sandra Thornton)*

Wester Balgedie [A911/B919 nr Milnathort; NO1604], *Balgedie Toll*: Beamed bar with good food, friendly helpful service, Ind Coope Burton and Tetleys, coal fire; motorcyclists welcome *(David Logan)*

THE ISLANDS
Arran
Catacol [NR9049], *Catacol Bay*: Friendly and welcoming, totally unpretentious, in wonderful setting overlooking bar, good beer and good home-cooked food, tables outside; comfortable bedrooms, share bathroom *(Lynn Pearson)*

Gigha
Gigha [NR6450], *Gigha Hotel*: Well kept, nicely furnished and clean, in lovely spot overlooking the Sound and Kintyre; pine-decor public bar, sofas in drawing-room bar, tables in garden, good friendly service, afternoon teas; bedrooms *(Derek and Maggie Washington)*

Mull
Fionnphort [NM3023], *Keel Row*: Wonderful seaside atmosphere, roaring fire, good beer and food, great view over Iona from the restaurant; children welcome *(Richard May)*

Orkney
Kirkwall [harbour; HY4511], *Queens*: Good bar food esp fish dishes, restaurant; good value bedrooms *(Gordon Neighbour)*

Stromness [Victoria St; HY2509], *Stromness*: McEwans and Orkney Dark Island ales, good choice of reasonably priced snacks and meals, upstairs dining room; bedrooms *(Gordon Neighbour)*

Skye
Broadford [A87, first main settlement after bridge; NG6423], *Broadford*: Comfortable modern furnishings in lounge bar of inn in well placed village, good juke box in public bar (lively Sat night), homely staff, good choice of beers; restaurant; bedrooms *(Steve Jennings, BB)*

☆ **Sligachan** [A850 Broadford—Portree, junction with A863; NG4830], *Sligachan Hotel*: Remote inn with almost a monopoly on the Cuillins, capacious and comfortable, with well laid-out huge modern pine-clad bar (children's play area, games room, red telephone ox) separating the original basic climbers' and walkers' bar from the plusher more sedate hotel side; well kept McEwans 80/- and two ales brewed on Skye, dozens of malt whiskies on optic, quickly served bar food inc particularly fresh seafood, fine log fire, good meals in hotel restaurant, good home-made cakes and coffee; very lively some nights, with summer live entertainment and big campsite opp; bedrooms good value, cl winter *(John and Joan Nash, Mark and Diane Grist, RJB, BB)*

☆ **Stein** [NG2556], *Stein Inn*: Down-to-earth small inn delightfully set above quiet sea inlet, with peat fire in flagstoned and stripped-stone public bar, really welcoming licensees and locals, good malt whiskies, bar food (in winter only for people staying); bedrooms thoroughly renovated *(Jens and Birgitte Hoiberg, LYM)*

Uig [NG3963], *Uig*: Newly refurbished hotel in lovely spot overlooking sea, friendly caring licensees, well trained staff, tartan chairs and fire in lounge, good food esp steak and moss green pudding with whisky marmalade cream sauce; modern bedrooms in new annexe with good views *(Jean Panepinto, Bill Cote, BB)*

South Uist

Loch Carnan [signed off A865 S of Creagorry; NF8044], *Orasay*: Wide choice of home-made food inc good local seafood and puddings in modern lounge (drinks only if you're eating), open all day; bedrooms with own bathrooms *(Jack and Heather Coyle)*

☆ **Pollachar** [S end of B888; NF7414], *Pollachar Hotel*: Recently comfortably modernised and extended 17th-c inn in glorious setting on seashore with dolphins, porpoises and seals; big public bar, new residents' bar, separate dining room, good bar meals; very helpful friendly staff and locals (all Gaelic speaking), fantastic views to Eriskay and Barra; 12 well renovated bedrooms with own bathrooms, good breakfast *(Mrs Olive Oxley, Nigel Woolliscroft)*

Children welcome means the pubs says it lets children inside without any special restriction. If it allows them in, but to restricted areas such as an eating area or family room, we specify this. Places with separate restaurants usually let children use them, hotels usually let them into public areas such as lounges. Some pubs impose an evening time limit – let us know if you find this.

Wales

Pubs and inns on top form here these days are the Penhelig Arms in Aberdovey (the food is showing benefits from the new kitchen, and we give it one of our Stay Awards this year), the Sailors Return in Beaumaris (a new entry, often full of happy diners), the attractively placed St Govans at Bosherston, the Bear in Crickhowell (first-class all round – its family bar refurbished this year), the Nantyffin Cider Mill just outside Crickhowell (finding interesting new sources of supply for the ingredients of its very good food), the Walnut Tree at Llandewi Skirrid with its glorious food, the Queens Head near Llandudno Junction (imaginative food here too), the Leyland Arms at Llanelidan (a gem), the ancient Green at Llangedwyn (a new main entry, good all round), the cheerful Coach & Horses at Llangynidr (another newcomer), the Ferry Inn at Pembroke Ferry (really good fresh fish), the Clytha Arms near Raglan (excellent all round), the Ship in its fine position on Red Wharf Bay on Anglesey, the Carpenters Arms at Shirenewton (this new main entry has an interesting warren of rooms), the Halfway House at Talycoed (another new entry – a pretty 17th-c cottage with good food) and the beautifully decorated Groes at Ty'n y Groes (a Stay Award for its new mountain-view bedrooms – and this year a Star for its all-round quality). Not for the first time, the Walnut Tree at Llandewi Skirrid gains our award as Wales Dining Pub of the Year. Quite a lot of the Lucky Dip entries at the end of the chapter deserve a close look: the Sun at Rhewl (Clwyd), Druidstone at Broad Haven, Brunant Arms at Caio, and Golden Grove and Paxton at Llanarthne (Dyfed), the Bear in Cowbridge and Green Dragon at Llancadle (S Glamorgan), Greyhound at Oldwalls and King Arthur at Reynoldston (W Glamorgan), Abbey Hotel at Llanthony, Hostry at Llantilio Crosseny, Red Hart at Llanvapley, Fountain at Trelleck Grange and Nags Head in Usk (Gwent), both Capel Curig entries, Llew Cock at Dinas Mawddwy, Harp and Llandwrog, George III at Penmaenpool, Ship in Porthmadog, Tal y Cafn at Tal y Cafn, Golden Fleece at Tremadog and Lion at Tudweiliog (Gwynedd), and Blue Boar among other pubs in Hay on Wye, Dragons Head at Llangenny, Glansevern Arms near Llangurig, White Lion in Machynlleth and Harp at Old Radnor (Powys). Drinks in Welsh pubs are a shade lower than the national average.

Post Office address codings confusingly give the impression that some pubs are in Gwent or Powys, Wales when they're really in Gloucestershire or Shropshire (which is where we list them).

ABERDOVEY (Gwynedd) SN6296 Map 6

Penhelig Arms 🍴 ♀ 🛏

Opp Penhelig railway station

With a new Stay Award this year, and some of its refurbished bedrooms overlooking the sea, this mainly 18th-c hotel is doing particularly well at the moment. Refurbishments to the kitchen have led to an improved bar menu, service is cheerfully welcoming, and there's a lively local atmosphere in the bar. With some emphasis on really fresh seafood which is delivered daily, the menu includes sandwiches (from £1.95), soup (£1.95), filled baguettes (£4.50), terrine of chicken and lemon (£3.75), fresh dressed local crab (£4.95), savoury bread pudding with layers of cheese and ham (£5.50), coq au vin (£6.75), grilled plaice (£6.95), and several additional evening dishes like lamb in spicy pepper and tomato sauce or lasagne (£6.50), or roast fillet of cod on mashed potato (£6.95), seared fillets of salmon and monkfish with hollandaise (£7.50), red mullet, haddock and whiting baked in a spicy tomato and white wine sauce (£7.95), and puddings like gooseberry fool or sticky toffee pudding (£2.75); children's helpings. Three-course Sunday lunch (£12.50) or dinner (£18.50) in the no-smoking restaurant. The excellent wine list has over 40 half bottles, two dozen malt whiskies, fruit or peppermint teas, and coffee. The small original beamed bar has a cosy feel, and winter fires, changing real ales such as Bass, Tetleys and Tapsters Choice on handpump, and about two dozen malt whiskies; dominoes. In summer you can eat out by the harbour wall while you take in the lovely views across the Dyfi estuary. *(Recommended by Basil Minson, Amanda and Simon Southwell, Peter Lewis, Yvonne and Peter Griffiths, Mike and Wena Stevenson, Dr M Owton, Jacquie and Jim Jones, Sue and Bob Ward, D W Jones-Williams, E Holland)*

Free house ~ Licensees Robert and Sally Hughes ~ Real ale ~ Meals and snacks ~ Restaurant ~ (01654) 767215 ~ Children in eating area of bar and restaurant ~ Open 12-4(3 winter), 6(7 winter)-10.30 Sun; open all day bank hols; cl 25 Dec ~ Bedrooms: £39B/£68B

ABERGORLECH (Dyfed) SN5833 Map 6

Black Lion

B4310 (a pretty road roughly NE of Carmarthen)

Many of the locals at this friendly old-fashioned black and white pub speak Welsh, which adds to the atmosphere of the plain but comfortable stripped-stone bar. It's traditionally furnished with plain oak tables and chairs, high-backed black settles facing each other across the flagstones by the log-effect gas fire, horsebrasses on the black beams, and some sporting prints; a restaurant extension has light oak woodwork. It's delightfully placed in the beautiful Cothi Valley with the Brechfa Forest around; picnic tables, wooden seats and benches across the quiet road luxuriate in the views. The garden slopes down towards the River Cothi where there's a Roman triple-arched bridge; the licensee has fishing rights and the river is good for trout, salmon and sea trout. Bar food includes ginger and garlic prawns (£3.50), mussels (£3.75), leek and mushroom crumble (£4.95), pork escalopes with lemon and pepper (£5.25), trout stuffed with prawns and asparagus (£7.50), roast duck with orange sauce (£9.50), and children's meals; in summer there may be afternoon teas with a selection of home-made cakes, and Saturday barbecues. Well kept Buckleys and Worthingtons Best on handpump, and Addlestone's cider; good friendly service; sensibly placed darts, cribbage, dominoes, trivia, and unobtrusive piped music. Remy the jack russell loves to chew up beer mats. Lots of good walks nearby. *(Recommended by Jenny and Brian Seller, Miss J Reay, Jack and Gemima Valiant, Richard Siebert)*

Free house ~ Licensee Mrs Brenda Entwistle ~ Real ale ~ Meals and snacks (not Mon except bank hols) ~ Restaurant ~ (01558) 685271 ~ Children welcome ~ Open 11.30-3.30, 7-11; 12-3.30, 7-10.30 Sun

---

It's against the law for bar staff to smoke while handling food or drink.

nr ABERYSTWYTH (Dyfed) SN6777 Map 6

Halfway Inn

Pisgah (not the Pisgah near Cardigan); A4120 towards Devil's Bridge, 5¼ miles E of junction with A487

Full of genuine old-fashioned charm, the friendly atmospheric beamed and flagstoned bar at this enchanting old place has stripped deal tables and settles, bare stone walls, and a dining room/restaurant area where tables can be reserved. Darts, pool, dominoes, alley skittles and piped music (classical at lunchtimes, popular folk and country in the evenings); and Felinfoel Double Dragon, Flowers Original, Hancocks HB and weekly guests on handpump, possibly five draught ciders, and a few malt whiskies. Under the new licensee, generously served bar food includes soup (£1.30), filled baked potatoes (from £1.75), sandwiches (from £2.25), ploughman's (£5), breaded scampi with lemon mayonnaise (£5.75), chicken, mushroom and ham pie (£6.95), chargrilled steaks (from £8.95), home-made puddings, and children's meals (from £2.75). With its panoramic views down over the wooded hills and pastures of the Rheidol Valley from picnic tables under cocktail parasols it's not surprising that it does get busy in summer. There's a very simple play area, free overnight camping for customers, a new nursery, and a baling rail for pony-trekkers. *(Recommended by David Peakall; more reports please)*

Free house ~ Licensee David Roberts ~ Real ale ~ Meals and snacks ~ Restaurant ~ (01970) 880631 ~ Children in eating area of bar ~ Occasional live music Fri ~ Open 12-2.30, 6.30-11(10.30 Sun); 7-11 only in winter ~ Bedroom: £19S/£38S

BEAUMARIS (Anglesey) SH6076 Map 6

Olde Bulls Head ★ ♀

Castle Street

Two of this smartly cosy old inn's earlier visitors, Samuel Johnson and Charles Dickens, wouldn't look out of place here today. The quaintly old-fashioned rambling bar is full of reminders of its long and interesting past: a rare 17th-c brass water clock, a bloodthirsty crew of cutlasses, even the town's oak ducking stool. There's also lots of copper and china jugs, snug alcoves, low beams, low-seated settles, leather-cushioned window seats and a good open fire. The entrance to the pretty courtyard is closed by the biggest simple hinged door in Britain. Very good daily changing lunchtime bar food might include sandwiches (from £1.80), home-made split pea, vegetable and ham broth (£2), good ploughman's with Welsh cheeses (£3.60), cold poached salmon with mayonnaise, grilled cumberland sausage or baked cod fillet with cheese and leeks (£4.95), bresaola salad with parma ham and olives or rabbit and mushroom casserole (£5.50), and puddings such as lemon tart or chocolate mousse with strawberries (£2). There is also a smart no-smoking restaurant. Very well kept Bass, Worthington Best and a guest on handpump, a good comprehensive list of over 180 wines (with plenty of half bottles), and freshly squeezed orange juice; cheerful, friendly service; chess and cards. The charming bedrooms (with lots of nice little extras) are named after characters in Dickens's novels. *(Recommended by David Peakall, Chris and Shirley Machin, Dr D G Twyman, Dr W M Owton, WAH, KB, DH, the Goldsons; also in Good Hotel Guide)*

Free house ~ Licensee David Robertson ~ Real ale ~ Meals and snacks (not evenings or Sun lunch) ~ Restaurant ~ (01248) 810329 ~ Children welcome till 8pm ~ Open 11-11; 12-10.30 Sun; cl evening 25 Dec ~ Bedrooms: £47B/£77B

Sailors Return

Church Street

Quite a contrast to our other entry here, this bright and cheerful place, more or less open-plan, is nowadays often packed with happy diners, especially in the evenings (lunchtimes tend to be quieter); all the tables in the dining area on the left can be booked. The food, done well, with fresh vegetables and a sensibly limited choice of daily specials, might include casserole of venison with pickled walnuts, steak with caramelised red onions and a balsamic glaze, or navarin of welsh lamb; the bread and butter pudding is irresistible. Furnishings include comfortable banquettes, and they've used quite rich colours in refurbishing a pub which previously only rarely attracted readers, but now has suddenly come close to the top of their list; it's very popular with all ages. There's a quaint collection of car-shaped china teapots, and maps of Cheshire among the old prints and naval memorabilia betray the landlord's origins. Bar food includes sandwiches (from £1.95, smoked salmon and cream cheese £3.50), Japanese prawns with seafood dip (£2.95), garlic mushrooms (£3.50), pork sausage and eggs (£4.25), omelettes (from £4.50), roast chicken breast with sage and onion stuffing and gravy (£5.50) and a daily special like poached salmon fillet with creamy seafood sauce (£6.25). Welcoming swift service; well kept Boddingtons, Flowers IPA, Morlands Old Speckled Hen, Welsh Bitter and a guest like Tetleys on handpump. Helpful friendly service (you get the feeling the landlord really enjoys his calling); maybe unobtrusive piped music. *(Recommended by Joy and Peter Heatherley, Mark Percy, Lesley Mayoh, Diana Smart, E Evans, Peter and Anne Hollindale, J D and J A Taylor)*

Free house ~ Licensee Peter Ogan ~ Real ale ~ Meals and snacks ~ (01248) 811314 ~ Children welcome during meal times ~ Open 11.30-3, 6-11; 12-3, 7-10.30 Sun; cl 25 Dec

BETWS-Y-COED (Gwynedd) SH7956 Map 6

Ty Gwyn 🛏

A5 just S of bridge to village

The terms of the licence at this cottagey coaching inn do mean that you must eat or stay overnight if you want a drink but it is well placed for the area's multitude of attractions, while still managing to maintain a nice personally welcoming atmosphere. The beamed lounge bar has an ancient cooking range worked in well at one end, and rugs and comfortable chintz easy chairs on its oak parquet floor. The interesting clutter of unusual old prints and bric-a-brac reflects the fact that the owners run an antique shop next door. Generously served tasty meals from the changing menu might include good soup (£2.25), potted shrimps with toast or hickory smoked chicken wings (£3.25), mushroom and nut fettucine (£5.50), fresh fillet of cod in real ale butter or breast of chicken with lemon and garlic (£5.95), fillet of plaice with parsley and cheddar sauce or grilled lamb chop (£7.95) fresh Conwy salmon with a dill and Dubonnet sauce (£8.25), local pheasant in a beaujolais and wild mushroom sauce (£9.25), and marinated fresh seafood kebab with lobster and brandy sauce (£9.95); children's menu (from £2.50) – highchair and toys available. Theakstons Best on handpump, maybe two friendly cats; piped music. *(Recommended by Gordon Theaker, Liz Bell, Dr Jim Mackay, B M and P Kendall, Joy and Peter Heatherley, Eric Locker, Basil Minson, Mr and Mrs C Cole, KC, J C T Tan)*

Free house ~ Licensees Jim and Shelagh Ratcliffe ~ Real ale ~ Meals and snacks ~ Restaurant ~ (01690) 710383 ~ Children welcome ~ Open 12-2, 7-9.30(8.30 winter); cl winter lunchtimes ~ Bedrooms: £19(£27B)/£35(£54B)

BODFARI (Clwyd) SJ0970 Map 6

Dinorben Arms ★ ♀

From A541 in village, follow Tremeirchion 3 signpost

The incredible range of about 300 malt whiskies (including the full Macallan range and a good few from the Islay distilleries) earned this friendly black and white inn our *Whisky Pub of the Year* award last year. They also have plenty of good wines (with several classed growth clarets), vintage ports and cognacs, and quite a few unusual coffee liqueurs. The good value lunchtime smorgasbord is a big draw here. You help yourself and eat as much as you like from a changing range of hot soups, main courses and puddings (£8.50). It's advisable to book. Other snacks include home-made steak and kidney pie or chicken, ham and mushroom pie (£4.45), scampi (£4.85), lasagne (£5.50), grilled salmon (£5.95), seafood mornay (£6.50), sirloin steak or Welsh lamb chops (£7.95). One child can eat free if both parents are dining (except on Saturday nights). A no-smoking area in the upstairs Badger Suite has a carvery on Friday and

Saturday (£12.95) and a good help-yourself farmhouse buffet on Wednesday and Thursday (£8.95). As well as a glassed-over well, the three warmly welcoming neat flagstoned rooms which open off the heart of this carefully extended building have plenty of character, with beams hung with tankards and flagons, high shelves of china, old-fashioned settles and other seats, and three open fires; there's also a light and airy garden room. They have an impressive range of drinks, as well as Tetleys and two guests such as Aylesbury Best and Charles Wells Bombardier on handpump. There are lots of tables outside on the prettily landscaped and planted brick-floored terraces, with attractive sheltered corners and charming views, and there's a grassy play area which – like the car park – is neatly sculpted into the slope of the hills. *(Recommended by KC, Mr and Mrs Irving, John Fazakerley, Liz Bell, Marjorie and Ken Hardcastle, Mr and Mrs A Craig, Bill and Irene Morley, Mr and Mrs E J W Rogers, J E Hilditch)*

Free house ~ Licensee David Rowlands ~ Real ale ~ Meals and snacks (12-3, 6-10.30; Sun lunchtime smorgasbord only, till 4.30pm) ~ Restaurant ~ (01745) 710309 ~ Children welcome ~ Open 12-3, 6-10.30; 12-11 Sun

BOSHERTON (Dyfed) SR9694 Map 6
St Govans
Village signed from B4319 S of Pembroke

The south wall of the bar of this comfortably modernised inn is decorated with murals of local beauty spots painted by a local artist, W S Heaton. It's a lovely area: quite close by there's a many-fingered inlet from the sea, now quite land-locked and full of water-lilies in summer, while some way down the road terrific cliffs plunge to the sea. Not surprisingly it's very popular with walkers and climbers comparing climbs and there are lots of very good climbing photographs. Stone pillars support the black and white timbered ceiling of the spacious bar which has a woodburning stove in a large stone fireplace, plenty of button-back red leatherette wall banquettes and armed chairs around dimpled copper tables, and stags' antlers; darts, pool, cribbage, dominoes, fruit machine, trivia, juke box, chess, ludo and backgammon. A small but useful choice of mostly home-made bar food might include cawl with roll or bean soup (£2.50), steak and kidney pie (£4.35), several curries (£4.95), grilled cajun chicken breast (£5.95) and fresh local trout or gammon (£6.50). About a quarter of the pub is no smoking. Well kept real ales include Bass, Fullers London Pride, Hancocks HB, Wadworths 6X, Worthington Best and a guest in the summer months on handpump, about ten malt whiskies. There are a few picnic tables on the small front terrace. *(Recommended by Jean and Richard Phillips, Mr and Mrs S Thomas)*

Free house ~ Licensee Sheila Rosemary Webster ~ Real ale ~ Meals and snacks ~ (01646) 661311 ~ Children welcome till 9pm ~ Open 11-11; 12-3, 7-11 in winter; 12-10.30 Sun; cl 25 Dec evening ~ Bedrooms: £17.50S/£35S

CAERPHILLY (Mid Glam) ST1484 Map 6
Courthouse
Cardiff Road; one-way system heading N, snugged in by National Westminster Bank – best to park before you get to it

Much of the original age and character of this ancient 14th-c longhouse survives in its stone walls and roof and the raftered gallery. The long bar has pews, comfortable cloth-upholstered chairs and window seats, rugs on ancient flagstones, shutters and curtains on thick wooden rails for the small windows and a formidably large stone fireplace. There are splendid views of the adjacent castle and its peaceful lake from tables out on the grassy terrace behind (Tannoy system for food), and from the light and airy modern cafe/bar at the back. Bar food includes filled baked potatoes (£2.25), steak baguette (£3.95), chicken or beef curry (£4.45), chicken breast with mustard and honey sauce (or white wine and mushroom), or a selection of pies including beef and burgundy, chicken and mushroom or steak and ale (£4.95), breaded plaice (£5.45), poached salmon or seafood basket (£5.95), beef wellington (£7.95), weekly specials (£2.95), several vegetarian dishes, and children's meals (from £1.40). Part of the restaurant is no smoking. Well kept Burtonwoods Top Hat, Courage Best, Federation

Buchanans Original and Wye Valley Classic on handpump, good coffee; cribbage, draughts, fruit machine; some readers have found the piped pop music (even outside) a bit loud. *(Recommended by Ian Phillips, S P Bobeldijk, David and Nina Pugsley, Jacquie and Jim Jones, Comus Elliott, M and A Sandy)*

Scottish Courage ~ Lease: James Jenkins ~ Real ale ~ Meals and snacks (Mon, Fri and Sat 9.30-5.30, Tues-Thurs 9.30-9.30, Sun 12-3) ~ Restaurant ~ (01222) 888120 ~ Children welcome in restaurant and cafe ~ Open 11-11, 12-10 Sun; cl 25 Dec

CAREW (Dyfed) SN0403 Map 6
Carew Inn
A4075 just off A477

Seats in a pretty little flowery front garden at this popular and unchanging inn look down to the river where a tidal watermill is open for afternoon summer visits, it's also opposite the imposing ruins of Carew Castle. There's a notably friendly welcome in the very characterful snug little panelled public bar and comfortable lounge, as well as old-fashioned settles and scrubbed pine furniture, and interesting prints and china hanging from the beams. The no-smoking upstairs dining room has an elegant china cabinet, a mirror over the tiled fireplace and sturdy chairs around the well spaced tables. Generously served, reasonably priced bar food includes sandwiches (from £1.95), ploughman's (£3.50), mussels provençale (£3.95), spaghetti bolognese or chilli (£4.50), chicken, leek and mushroom pie (£5.95), seafood pie (£6.50) and 10oz sirloin steak (£9.95); with daily specials such as half a pint of prawns (£2.25), home-made salmon fishcakes or chicken liver pâté (£3.50), salmon steak with chive sauce or cod fillet with anchovy and fennel crust (£6.95), pork tenderloin with madeira sauce (£7.95) puddings (from £1.95) and usual children's meals (from £2.25). The local mackerel and sea bass can be caught and served within two hours. Well kept Crown Buckley Reverend James and Worthington Best; sensibly placed darts, dominoes, cribbage, piped music. Dogs in the public bar only. The back garden has a wheelchair ramp and is safely enclosed, with a sandpit, climbing frame, slide and other toys, as well as a remarkable 9th-c Celtic cross. *(Recommended by Mike and Mary Cartern, Michael Sargent, Jack and Philip Paxton, Ian Phillips, Jack and Jemima Valiant, Charles and Pauline Stride, T L Rees, Tony Pounder, Brian and Anna Marsden, Joan and Michel Hooper-Immins, Sarah Bradbury, Allan Worsley, Mrs S Wright, Nick and Meriel Cox, M D Davies, J G Quick)*

Free house ~ Licensees Mandy and Rob Hinchliffe ~ Real ale ~ Meals and snacks ~ Restaurant ~ (01646) 651267 ~ Children in eating area of bar ~ Live music Thurs evening and summer Sun evenings ~ Open 11-11; 12-2.30, 4.30-11 winter weekdays; 12-10.30 Sun; 12-3, 7-10.30 winter Sun ~ Bedrooms: £15/£25

CILGERRAN (Dyfed) SN1943 Map 6
Pendre
Village signposted from A478

This unspoilt traditional pub – one of the oldest in West Wales – has massive stripped 14th-c medieval stone walls above a panelled dado, with armchairs and settles on a beautifully polished slate floor. Good bar food includes home-made soup (£1.95), ham and chips (£2.95), ploughman's (£3.95), tortellini or lasagne (£4.50), filled yorkshire pudding (£5), and daily specials like game pie (from £4.50). Bass and Worthington BB and a guest like Everards Tiger on handpump and lots of malt whiskies; personal service from the licensee and staff. The public bar has darts and pool. There are seats outside, with an enclosed play area. The other end of the town leads down to the River Teifi, with a romantic ruined castle on a crag nearby, where coracle races are held on the Saturday before the August bank holiday. There's a good local wildlife park nearby, and this is a good area for fishing. *(Recommended by Peter Lewis; more reports please)*

Free house ~ Licensee Bob Lowe ~ Real ale ~ Meals and snacks (12-9) ~ Restaurant ~ (01239) 614223 ~ Children welcome ~ Open 11.30am-12pm; 12-3, 7-11 Sun; cl 3-6 winter

COLWYN BAY (Clwyd) SH8578 Map 6
Mountain View £

Mochdre; take service-road into village off link road to A470, S from roundabout at start of new A55 dual carriageway to Conwy; OS Sheet 116 map reference 825785

A big picture of the Aberglaslyn Pass hangs near the entrance of this neatly kept plush pub, with several others of Conwy Castle hung throughout the spreading carpeted areas which are divided by arched walls. There are quite a few houseplants (and bright window boxes in the large windows). Under the new licensee big helpings of promptly served good value bar food from a fairly extensive menu include soup (£1.95), filled baguettes (from £2), filled baked potatoes (from £2.75), sausage and mash (£3.50), cauliflower cheese (£3.95), broccoli and cream cheese bake (£4.95), seafood platter, lamb in red wine, cranberry and pepper sauce, trout in almonds, devilled lamb, chicken curry, or a choice of stir frys (£5.95), shoulder of lamb (£6.50), baked pork fillet topped with onions, mushrooms, mozzarella, Austrian smoked and cheddar cheese on cream sauce (£6.95), steaks (from £8.95), and lunchtime specials. Well kept real ales include Burtonwood Bitter, Buccaneer, James Forshaws and Top Hat on handpump, as well as just under two dozen malt whiskies; darts, pool, dominoes, fruit machine, table football, juke box, trivia. Unobtrusive piped music but some readers have found the Thursday night karaoke obtrusive. The raised seating area is no smoking. *(Recommended by KC, S P Watkin, P A Taylor, Roger Byrne, Mr and Mrs Hobden; more reports please)*

Burtonwood ~ Tenant Malcolm Gray ~ Real ale ~ Meals and snacks ~ (01492) 544724 ~ Children in eating area of bar ~ Karaoke Thurs night ~ Open 11.30-3.30, 6-11; 11.30-11 Sat/Sun; 12-4, 7-10.30 winter Sun; cl 25 Dec evening

CRESSWELL QUAY (Dyfed) SN0406 Map 6
Cresselly Arms

Village signposted from A4075

There are seats outside this marvellously traditional old Welsh-speaking creeper-covered local facing the tidal creek of the Cresswell River – if the tides are right you can get here by boat. There's a relaxed and jaunty feel in the two simple comfortably unchanging communicating rooms, which have red and black flooring tiles, built-in wall benches, kitchen chairs and plain tables, an open fire in one room, a working Aga in the other, and a high beam-and-plank ceiling hung with lots of pictorial china. A third red-carpeted room is more conventionally furnished, with red-cushioned mate's chairs around neat tables. Well kept Worthington BB is tapped straight from the cask into glass jugs by the landlord, whose presence is a key ingredient of the atmosphere; fruit machine and winter darts. *(Recommended by Pete Baker, Jack and Philip Paxton, Ian Phillips, Peter and Michele Rayment)*

Free house ~ Licensees Maurice and Janet Cole ~ Real ale ~ (01646) 651210 ~ Children welcome in back room ~ Open 12-3, 5-11; 11-11 Sat; 12-3, 7-10.30 Sun

CRICKHOWELL (Powys) SO2118 Map 6
Bear ★ ⊕ ⇌ ⬤

Brecon Road; A40

Consistently high standards on all counts make this civilised old coaching inn a real favourite with readers – it's a particularly nice place to stay, eat and drink. Beautifully presented bar meals might include welsh rarebit with grilled bacon (£3.95), ratatouille or filo tartlet of creamy cheese and leeks (£4.25), chicken, potato and garlic casserole (£6.95), fresh salmon cutlet with lemon barley and sorrel (£7.50), hock of braised Welsh lamb with silver birch wine and herbs (£8.50); very good puddings like bread and butter with banana pudding with rum and brown bread ice cream or lemon and cream pie (all £3.25). The refurbished family bar is partly no smoking. Well kept Bass, John Smiths, Ruddles Best and County on handpump; malt whiskies, vintage and late-bottled ports, and unusual wines (with about ten by the glass) and liqueurs, with some hops tucked in among the bottles. The heavily beamed lounge has lots of little plush-seated bentwood armchairs and handsome cushioned antique settles, and a window seat looking down on the market square. Up by the great roaring log fire, a big sofa and leather easy chairs are spread among the rugs on the oak parquet floor; antiques include a fine oak dresser filled with pewter and brass, a longcase clock and interesting prints. It can get terribly busy, but service remains welcoming and friendly; piped music. The back bedrooms – particularly in the quieter new block – are the most highly recommended, though there are three more bedrooms in the pretty cottage at the end of the garden. Lovely window boxes, and you can eat in the garden in summer; disabled lavatories. *(Recommended by Chris Philip, Gordon Theaker, Mrs M Mills, David and Nina Pugsley, Liz Bell, Adrian and Jane Tierney-Jones, Wayne Brindle, Adrian Levine, D and L Berry, B M and P Kendall, John and Joan Nash, A R and B E Sayer, Phil Putwain, Verity Combes, PM, AM, Gavin May, Mrs P Goodwyn)*

Free house ~ Licensee Mrs Judy Hindmarsh ~ Real ale ~ Meals and snacks (till 10pm) ~ Restaurant ~ (01873) 810408 ~ Children in family bar ~ Open 10.30-3, 6-11; 12-3, 7-10.30 Sun ~ Bedrooms: £42B/£56B

nr CRICKHOWELL (Powys) SO2118 Map 6
Nantyffin Cider Mill 🍴 ♀
1½ miles NW, by junction A40/A479

Relying wherever possible on local and organic meat and vegetables – with quite a lot coming from a relative's nearby farm – the beautifully presented food from a changing range of meals at this handsome pink-washed inn is easily of restaurant standard, and might include starters such as home-made soup (£2.60), warm crispy chicken or chinese-style braised belly pork (£4.50), and main courses such as fresh salmon and spinach fishcakes (£7.95), vegetarian provençal tart, chicken with smoked bacon and mushroom stuffing or Glamorgan sausages (£8.95), with daily specials like griddled squid with dried tomatoes or crab tartlet with gruyère cheese (£4.95), pot roast spring lamb (£9.95), roast monkfish with tomato chilli salsa and pesto or tandoori baked hake (£10.50), and puddings like pecan pie or white chocolate cheesecake (£3.30); children's meals or smaller helpings. The look of the place is smartly traditional – almost brasserie style, with a woodburner in a fine broad fireplace, warm grey stonework, cheerful bunches of fresh and dried flowers, and good solid comfortable tables and chairs. The bar at one end of the main open-plan area has a large rotating choice of real ales including Batemans, Brains SA, London Pride and Marstons Pedigree on handpump, with draught ciders, good wines (several by the glass or half bottle), and popular home-made lemonade and fruit cocktails in summer. A raftered barn with a big cider press has been converted into quite a striking restaurant. The building faces an attractive stretch of the River Usk, and has charming views from the tables out on the lawn above its neat car park. A ramp makes disabled access easy. *(Recommended by Mike Pugh, Margaret and Nigel Dennis, Liz Bell, David Gregory, B M and P Kendall, Gordon Theaker, Nick and Meriel Cox, David and Nina Pugsley, D and L Berry, George and Brenda Jones, N H E Lewis, Chris Philip, M D Davies, Mrs P Goodwyn, A R and B E Sayer, Caroline Raphael, Ian Williams, Linda Mar)*

Free house ~ Licensees Glyn Bridgeman, Sean Gerrard ~ Real ale ~ Meals and snacks (till 10pm) ~ Restaurant ~ (01873) 810775 ~ Children welcome ~ Open 12-3, 6-11; 12-4, 7-10 Sun; cl Mon and first two weeks in Jan

EAST ABERTHAW (South Glamorgan) ST0367 Map 6
Blue Anchor ★ ◀
B4265

The warren of snug, low-beamed rooms in this thatched and creeper-covered pub dates back to 1380. Nooks and crannies wander through massive stone walls and tiny doorways, and there are open fires everywhere, including one in an inglenook with antique oak seats built into its stripped stonework. Other seats and tables are worked into a series of chatty little alcoves, and the more open front bar still has an ancient lime-ash floor; darts, dominoes, fruit machine and video game. Bar food includes sandwiches (from £1.75), soup (£2.25), filled baked potatoes (from £2.75), roast pork, tagliatelle, battered hake or chicken, ham and mushroom pie (£4.75), steak (£7.50), a good selection of specials, puddings (£2.10), and children's meals (£2.25). Evening dishes such as tenderloin of pork stuffed with rabbit and apple (£11.50), or fried medaillons of welsh beef fillet with a shallot and madeira sauce (£12.95); they do a three-course roast lunch (£9.45) on Sundays, for which it's best to book. Carefully kept Boddingtons, Buckleys Best, Flowers IPA, marstons Pedigree, Theakstons Old Peculier, along with a guest beer that changes three times weekly. Rustic seats shelter peacefully among tubs and troughs of flowers outside, with more stone tables on a newer terrace. From here a path leads to the shingly flats of the estuary. The pub can get packed in the evenings and on summer weekends, and it's a shame the front seats are right beside the car park; readers have suggested that the lavatories could do with some attention. *(Recommended by D and N Pugsley, D and L Berry, R Michael Richards, Daren Haines, John and Joan Nash, Jason Aspinall, E Holland, A R and B E Sayer, Jonathan Davies)*

Free house ~ Licensee Jeremy Coleman ~ Real ale ~ Meals and snacks (12-2, 6-8 Mon to Fri) ~ Evening restaurant ~ (01446) 750329 ~ Children welcome till 8pm (later if eating) ~ Open 11-11; 12-10.30 Sun

ERBISTOCK (Clwyd) SJ3542 Map 6
Boat

Village signposted from A539 W of Overton, then pub signposted

Given the enchanting setting virtually alone by a country church, looking out over the sleepy River Dee, with ducks, grebes and maybe a heron on the water, and more birds singing in the steep woodland opposite, it's not surprising that this 16th-c dining pub gets very busy in summer. Old-fashioned seats by tables under cocktail parasols on a gravel terrace are surrounded by flowers and charming informal up-and-down lawns, with hanging baskets adorning the pub itself, and in early summer what amounts to a curtain of flowers on the low sandstone cliff behind it. Inside the character of the place is almost that of a restaurant, and drinkers (most of them going on to eat) really have just the one small bar with oak tripod tables on crazy-paved flagstones, spindleback chairs, and a fire in an open-grate kitchen range. Tasty lunchtime bar food includes sandwiches (from £2.75), soup (£2.95), ploughman's (£3.95), fried liver, kidneys and bacon in red wine, steak and kidney pie, cumberland sausage ring or cold poached salmon with lemon mayonnaise (£5.95), lamb chops with redcurrant sauce (£6.50) and fried chicken and green pepper with oyster sauce (£6.95). The comfortable beamed no-smoking dining room, with plush seats around antique oak tables, has small windows overlooking the river. Another new licensee to this pub has maintained two well kept real ales which include Marstons Pedigree and a regularly changing guest like Hook Norton or Smiles Mayfly, alongside a good range of malt whiskies; piped music. *(Recommended by John S McCullogh, Phil and Dilys Unsworth, Gail Kendall, Kent Miller)*

Free house ~ Licensee Terry Whalley ~ Lunchtime meals and snacks ~ Restaurant ~ (01978) 780143 ~ Children welcome in restaurant ~ Open 12-3, 6.30-11; 12-11.30(10.30 Sun) Sat; cl Sat afternoon in winter

GRESFORD (Clwyd) SJ3555 Map 6
Pant-yr-Ochain ♀

Off A483 on N edge of Wrexham: at roundabout take A5156 (A534) towards Nantwich, then first left towards the Flash

Standing in its own beautiful grounds with a small lake and some lovely trees, this roomy old country house has been stylishly decorated, with a wide range of interesting prints and bric-a-brac on its walls and on shelves, and a good mix of individually chosen country furnishings including comfortable seats for chatting as well as more upright ones for eating. There are good open fires, and the big dining area is set out as a library, with books floor to ceiling. Consistently good, interesting food from a menu that changes about every three months might include home-made soup (£2.95), chicken, pork and brandy pâté or ploughman's (£4.95), steak, red wine and smoked bacon pie (£7.95), roasted aubergines stuffed with tomato and vegetable ratatouille or grilled plaice (£8.75), chicken with cashew nut and ginger sauce or malaysian fruit curry (£8.95), roast fillet of salmon on a bed of stir-fried vegetables (£9.25), and braised half shoulder of lamb with redcurrant, port and rosemary sauce (£10.75). They have a good range of decent wines, strong on up-front New World ones, as well as Boddingtons, Flowers Original, Plassey Bitter, Timothy Taylor Landlord and a changing guest, and a good collection of malt whiskies. Service is polite and efficient. This is in the same small family of pubs as the Grosvenor Arms at Aldford (see Cheshire main entries), and not dissimilar in style and gently upmarket atmosphere; one room is no smoking. *(Recommended by Andrew and Anna Schuman, Mark Jones, P H Boot)*

Free house ~ Licensee Duncan Lochead ~ Real ale ~ Meals and snacks (12-2, 6-9.30) ~ (01978) 853525 ~ Children welcome at lunchtime ~ Open 12-3, 5.30-11; 12-11 Sat; 12-10.30 Sun

HALKYN (Clwyd) SJ2172 Map 6
Britannia
Pentre Rd, off A55 for Rhosesmor

Pleasantly well run, this cosy place which dates back in part to the 15th c (extensions blend well) is a handy lunchtime stop if you're driving along the North Wales coast. Great views from the newly decorated partly no-smoking dining conservatory and terrace stretch to Liverpool and the Wirral, and you may even be able to pick out Blackpool tower and Beeston Castle; it's best to book if you want a window table. The cosy unspoilt lounge bar has some very heavy beams, with horsebrasses, harness, jugs, plates and other bric-a-brac; there's also a games room with darts, pool, dominoes, fruit machine and board games. Very good value reliable bar food in generous helpings includes home-made soup (£1.15), sandwiches served on Rhes-y-Cae bread (from £2.40), spicy mexican appetisers (£2.85), minted lamb and barley casserole, steak and kidney pie, or pork in a spicy tomato sauce (£4.95), grilled lamb steak with honey and rosemary sauce (£5.95), steak of the day and daily specials, puddings (from £1.75). Lees Bitter, GB Mild and Moonraker on handpump, a dozen or so malt whiskies, and a choice of coffees. Attractions for the children include Jacob, a 26-year-old donkey, tame goats, and Fleur the gloucester old spot pig. *(Recommended by Phil Putwain, KC, David Hoult; more reports please)*

J W Lees ~ Tenant Keith Pollitt ~ Real ale ~ Meals and snacks (12-2.30, 6.30-9.30) ~ Restaurant ~ (01352) 780272 ~ Supervised children welcome ~ Various entertainment throughout year ~ Open 11-11; 12-10.30 Sun

HAY ON WYE (Powys) SO2342 Map 6
Old Black Lion ♀ 🛏
26 Lion St

If you plan to stay at this lovely old hotel we do recommend that you book well in advance as it's very popular. It sits on the town wall and was once the gatehouse to this civilised little medieval town, now internationally famous for the plethora of secondhand and antiquarian bookshops that line its steep twisting streets. The smartly civilised and attractive bar has low beams, some black panelling, old pine tables, an oak and mahogany bar counter and two old timber and glass screens; it's candlelit at night. A wide choice of thoughtful and very carefullly prepared bar meals includes sandwiches (from £2.95), home-made soup (£2.95), ploughman's (from £4.75), filled baked potatoes (£4.95), quite a few vegetarian dishes such as herby tagliatelle (£5.95) or vegetable goulash (£6.95), tempura battered plaice (£7.45), seafood crumble (£7.55), braised lamb with Indian spices (£7.65), spicy peppered venison (£7.95), salads (from £7.95), large selection of steaks (from £9.85), a good selection of specials like deep fried spicy crab cakes with curried apple chutney, chick pea falafel with avocado salsa, vegetable cassoulet with herb crust, chicken supreme on fennel and madeira butter beans and fresh Loch Fyne oysters and langoustine at the weekend, and puddings (from £3.30); Sunday 3-course lunch, and special breakfasts for fishermen (with Loch Fyne kippers). The cottagey restaurant, also candlelit, is no smoking. Well kept Wadworths 6X, Wye Valley Bitter and their own Black Lion (made for them by the Wye Valley brewery) on handpump – as well as an extensive, good value wine list, several malt whiskies, and decent coffee. Service is good but this is a firmly run place and they do like to shut the bar at closing time in the evening so don't expect to stay up all night if you're staying. A sheltered back terrace has some tables. The inn has trout and salmon fishing rights on the Wye, and can arrange pony trekking and golf. *(Recommended by Nicholas Holmes, J A Riemer, Jack and Gemima Valiant, Dorothee and Dennis Glover, Barry and Anne, Sue Demont, Tim Barrow, Gill and Maurice McMahon, RJH, KB, DH, Revd A Nunnerley, BB, Barry Watling, Gwen and Peter Andrews, W C M Jones)*

Free house ~ Licensees John and Joan Collins ~ Real ale ~ Meals and snacks ~ Restaurant ~ (01497) 820841 ~ Children over 5 in eating area of bar ~ Open 11-11; 12-3, 7-10.30 Sun ~ Bedrooms: £23B/£49.90B

KENFIG (Mid Glamorgan) SS8383 Map 6
Prince of Wales £ 🍺

2¼ miles from M4 junction 37; A4229 towards Porthcawl, then right at roundabout leaving Cornelly, signposted Maudlam and Kenfig

Unspoilt and unpretentious, this old local houses the alderman's mace, a relic from the days when this scatter of houses among windswept dunes was an important medieval port. More surprisingly, the local Sunday school meets here. With its walls stripped back to the stone, the friendly relaxed main bar has heavy settles and red leatherette seats around a double row of close-set cast-iron-framed tables, a warming open fire, and small storm windows. A very good range of well kept real ales might include Bass, Brains SA, Marstons Pedigree, Morlands Old Speckled Hen, Wadworths 6X and guests, all tapped from the cask; a good selection of malt whiskies. Quickly served very simple home-made bar food includes large filled rolls or sandwiches (from £1.20 – the home-roasted meat is well done), home-made steak pie, chicken and mushroom pie and roast of the day (£4.95), and fresh fish specials. In summer all the vegetables and potatoes come from the garden, and the eggs are from their own hens. Dominoes, cribbage and card games. There's a national nature reserve just across the road, and plenty of rewarding walks nearby. *(Recommended by Mr and Mrs T A Bryan, David and Nina Pugsley, Gordon Theaker, Ian Phillips, Brian and Anna Marsden, Steve Thomas, Mr and Mrs G Turner, John and Joan Nash, John and Pat Smyth, David Holloway, F A Owens)*

Free house ~ Licensee Jeremy Evans ~ Real ale ~ Meals and snacks (till 10pm) ~ Restaurant ~ (01656) 740356 ~ Children welcome ~ Open 11.30-4, 6-11; cl evening 25 Dec

LITTLE HAVEN (Dyfed) SM8512 Map 6
Swan

Little Haven is one of the prettiest coastal villages in west Wales, and this welcoming pub is right on the coast path, with lovely views across the broad and sandy hill-sheltered cove from seats in its bay window, or from the sea wall outside (just the right height for sitting on). The two communicating rooms have quite a cosily intimate feel, as well as comfortable high-backed settles and windsor chairs, a winter open fire, and old prints on walls that are partly stripped back to the original stonework. Cooked by the genial landlord (who's now been here over a decade), the compact choice of well liked lunchtime bar food includes home-made soup (£2.50), traditional Welsh lamb and vegetable soup (£3.25 – with cheese on the side £3.50), ploughman's (from £3.95), crab bake or sardines grilled with spinach, egg and mozzarella (£4.95), chicken or beef curry (£5.25), locally smoked salmon or fresh local crab (£6.95), lobster in season, and home-made puddings (£2.25). Well kept Wadworths 6X and Worthington BB on handpump from the heavily panelled bar counter, and a good range of wines and whiskies; pleasant, efficient service; no children, dogs or dirty boots. *(Recommended by Malcolm and Helen Baxter, Hilarie Dobbie, Mr and Mrs M J Bastin, Jack and Gemima Valiant, IHR, Christopher Turner, Drs R and M Woodford, E J Wilde, Dr G W Barnett, W H Cooke, Richard Siebert)*

James Williams (Narberth) ~ Tenants Glyn and Beryl Davies ~ Real ale ~ Lunchtime meals and snacks ~ Restaurant ~ (01437) 781256 ~ Open 11-3, 6(7 winter)-11; 12-3, 7-10.30 Sun; cl Dec 25 evening

LLANBEDR-Y-CENNIN (Gwynedd) SH7669 Map 6
Olde Bull
Village signposted from B5106

There are good views of the Conway valley from this delightful little 16th-c drovers' inn which is perched on the side of a steep hill, and from plenty of seats in the particularly lovely garden with its big wild area with waterfall and orchard, a fishpond and hanging baskets round the terrace. Inside, the knocked-through rooms are full of massive low beams (some salvaged from a wrecked Spanish Armada ship), elaborately carved antique settles, a close crowd of cheerfully striped stools, brassware, photographs, Prussian spiked helmets, and good open fires (one in an inglenook); there might be some subdued classical music or opera in the background. Well kept Lees Bitter and Mild on handpump from wooden barrels, and several malt whiskies; friendly service. Generous helpings of bar food under the new licensees might include country vegetable soup (£1.50), large open sandwiches with fresh salads (from £3.50), vegetarian bean bourguignon or curries (£4.50), steaks (from £7.95), a selection of fresh fish including shark, sea bass and fisherman's pie; a children's menu (£2.50). The pub is popular with walkers and does a large breakfast (£4.99). Darts, dominoes and cribbage. Lavatories are outside. *(Recommended by Roger Byrne, Liz Bell, S P Watkin, P A Taylor, Barbara Wensworth)*

Lees ~ Tenants John and Debbie Turnbull ~ Real ale ~ Meals and snacks ~ Restaurant ~ (01492) 660508 ~ Children welcome ~ Open 12-3, 7(6.30 Sat)-11; cl Mon lunchtimes in winter

nr LLANBERIS (Gwynedd) SH6655 Map 6
Pen-y-Gwryd 🏠
Nant Gwynant; at junction of A498 and A4086, ie across mountains from Llanberis – OS Sheet 115 map reference 660558

You will need to book early if you want to stay at this magnificently set old climbers' pub, isolated high in the mountains of Snowdonia. Although bedrooms are clean and sensible rather than luxurious, residents have their own charmingly furnished, panelled sitting room and a sauna out among the trees. There's a wonderfully friendly atmosphere in the homely log cabin bar with its rugged slate floor – it doubles as a mountain rescue post. A smaller room has a collection of illustrious boots from famous climbs, and a cosy panelled smoke room more climbing mementoes and equipment. Like many other mountaineers, the team that first climbed Everest in 1953 used the inn as a training base, leaving their fading signatures scrawled on the ceiling. A snug little room with built-in wall benches and sturdy country chairs lets you contemplate the majestic surrounding mountain countryside – like precipitous Moelsiabod beyond the lake opposite. There's a hatch where you order lunchtime bar meals: good value robust helpings of home-made food such as soup (£1.80), ploughman's using home-baked french bread, quiche lorraine or pâté (£3.50), with casseroles in winter. In the evening residents sit down together for the hearty and promptly served dinner (check on the time when you book); the dining room is no smoking. As well as Bass and mulled wine in winter, they serve sherry from their own solera in Puerto Santa Maria; friendly, obliging service; table tennis, darts, pool, table skittles and shove-ha'penny. *(Recommended by Mark Percy, Lesley Mayoh, DC, Martin Pritchard, Jacquie and Jim Jones, Martin Howard Pritchard, Mr and Mrs C Cole, Mr and Mrs B Langrish; also in Good Hotel Guide)*

Free house ~ Licensee Jane Pullee ~ Real ale ~ Lunchtime meals and snacks ~ Evening restaurant ~ (01286) 870211 ~ Well behaved children welcome, except in residents' bar ~ Open 11-11(10.30 Sun); cl Nov-Dec, open weekends only Jan-Feb ~ Bedrooms: £20(£25B)/£40(£50B)

LLANDEWI SKIRRID (Gwent) SO3416 Map 6
Walnut Tree ★ 🍽 ♀

B4521

Wales Dining Pub of the Year

Although this is a restaurant of national renown – with prices to match – the atmosphere is wonderfully relaxed, with a very much hands-on approach by the licensees, who are quite happy if people just pop in for a glass of attractively priced good wine. The excellent imaginative food combines strong southern European leanings with an almost fanatical pursuit of top-class fresh and often recherché ingredients. It includes carefully prepared soups such as asparagus and tarragon (£4.35), crispy crab pancakes (£6), bruschetta with seafood (£7.45), home-made Italian sausages with butter beans (£7.65), half-a-dozen oysters (£9.70), black and white fettucine with smoked salmon and dill (£9.90), vegetarian platter (£10.95), panache of skate and scallops with balsamic dressing (£11.75), lamb sweetbreads with wild mushrooms, parma ham and marsala (£13.20), escalope of salmon with rhubarb and ginger (£14.15), pigeon with lentils, sausage and bacon (£14.30), roast monkfish with scallops, prawns and laverbread sauce (£16.50) and seafood platter (£26.35); vegetables are £3 extra. Puddings are delicious – just try that Toulouse chestnut pudding (£6.10); no credit cards, and £1 cover charge. The attractive choice of wines is particularly strong in Italian ones (they import their own), and the house wines by the glass are good value. The small white-walled bar has traditional wall seats and small chairs around gilt cast-iron-framed pub tables, with a good log fire, and Taruschio cookbooks for sale on the bar counter, alongside a big vase of flowers. It opens into an airy and relaxed dining lounge with more close-set tables and ladderback chairs. There are a few white cast-iron tables outside in front.
(Recommended by Michael Coshall, A E Brace, David Peakall, Gordon Theaker, Candida Leaver, Pamela and Merlyn Horswell, Stan and Hazel Allen, Nick and Meriel Cox, Liz Bell, Gwen and Peter Andrews, Verity Combes, Pat and John Millward, David Peel)

Free house ~ Licensees Ann and Franco Taruschio ~ Meals and snacks (12-3, 7-10.15, not Sun or Mon) ~ Restaurant (not Sun or Mon) ~ (01873) 852797 ~ Children welcome ~ Open 12-4, 7-12; cl Sun and Mon

LLANDRINDOD WELLS (Powys) SO0561 Map 6
Llanerch £ 🍺

Waterloo Road; from centre, head for station

There are peaceful mountain views looking over the Ithon Valley from tables on the back terrace of this individual 16th-c town local. This leads on to a garden (with boules), and a front play area and orchard give it all the feeling of a country pub. There is a really cheerful local atmosphere in the busy squarish beamed main bar, with old-fashioned settles snugly divided by partly glazed partitions, and a big stone fireplace that's richly decorated with copper and glass; there are more orthodox button-back banquettes in communicating lounges (one of which is no smoking at lunchtimes and early evenings). Popular lunchtime dishes include sandwiches (£1.95), omelettes (from £2.95), vegetable pancake rolls, fisherman's pie, lasagne, or gammon casserole (£3.50), salads or steak, kidney and mushroom pie (£4.95), mixed grill (£7.95), and children's meals (from £1.75), and evening extras like baked ginger chicken (£5.95) or beef julienne (£6.50). Well kept Hancocks HB and two regularly changing guests on handpump; there may be up to 20 real ales during their late August Victorian Festival. Service is prompt and generally friendly; fruit machine, video game, trivia and piped music, while a separate pool room has darts and dominoes. *(Recommended by Joan and Michel Hooper-Immins)*

Free house ~ Licensee John Leach ~ Real ale ~ Meals and snacks ~ Restaurant ~ (01597) 822086 ~ Children welcome ~ Live music Sat night ~ Open 11.30-2.30, 6- 11; 11.30-11 Sat; 11.30-3.30, 6-11 winter Sat; 12-3, 6-10.30 Sun ~ Bedrooms: £27.50B/£45B nr LLANDUDNO JUNCTION (Gwynedd) SH8180 Map 6

Queens Head 🍺 ♀

Glanwydden; heading towards Llandudno on B5115 from Colwyn Bay, turn left into
Llanrhos Road at roundabout as you enter the Penrhyn Bay speed limit; Glanwydden is
signposted as the first left turn off this

The carefully prepared and generously served imaginative home-made food at this
modest-looking village pub is very popular, so you do need to get here early for a
table. The weekly changing menu might include soup such as fresh pea and mint
(£2.15), open rolls (from £3.50), home-made pâtés or deep-fried brie (£4.25), baked
black pudding with puréed apple and brandy (£4.50), lasagne (£5.75), local mussels in
garlic butter and topped with smoked local cheese or salmon and pasta bake (£6.50),
salads (from £6.95), seafood platter (£9.95), and daily specials like steak and
mushroom pie (£6.95), grilled lamb cutlets with fresh plum and rosemary sauce or
braised beef in a rich burgundy and mushroom sauce (£8.50). The evening menu has
extra dishes like steamed breast of chicken filled with prawn mousse coated with a
chive butter sauce (£8.50), or roast duck with blackcherry and brandy sauce (£10.50).
Delicious puddings include bread and butter pudding, treacle tart and chocolate nut
fudge pie (£2.75). Fresh local produce is firmly in evidence, and even the mints with
the coffee might be home-made. Well kept Benskins, Ind Coope Burton, Tetleys and
guests on hand or electric pump, decent wines, several malts, and good coffee (maybe
served with a bowl of whipped cream). The spacious and comfortably modern lounge
bar has brown plush wall banquettes and windsor chairs around neat black tables and
is partly divided by a white wall of broad arches and wrought-iron screens; there's also
a little public bar. There are some tables out by the car park. No dogs. *(Recommended
by KC, Basil Minson, Neville Kenyon, Mike and Wena Stevenson, Joy and Peter Heatherley,
Abigail Dombey, Kate Naish, S P Watkin, P A Taylor, Brian and Lis Whitford, Liz Bell, Paul
Hilditch, Mike and Wendy Proctor, Jane and Adrian Tierney-Jones, AW, BW, J E Hilditch)*

*Ansells (Carlsberg Tetley) ~ Lease: Robert and Sally Cureton ~ Real ale ~ Meals and
snacks ~ (01492) 546570 ~ Children over 7 in garden ~ Open 11-3, 6-11; 12-2, 6-11
Sun; cl 25 Dec*

LLANELIDAN (Clwyd) SJ1150 Map 6

Leyland Arms

Village signposted from A494, S of Ruthin; pub is on B5429 just E of village; OS Sheet 116,
map reference 110505

Originally the dairy of the old village inn – the much grander building in front which
you see first as you approach – this unusual and very relaxing pub is part of a cluster
of prettily set former farm buildings by a country church, separated by a stretch of
quiet fields from the village itself. Though the food is a powerful draw, this isn't just a
dining pub; the atmosphere gains a lot from local people dropping in for a drink. It's
been sensitively refurbished in an attractive country style, with little bunches of flowers
on dark wood tables, and mugs hanging from the beams of the smaller room by the
servery. There is pool, darts, dominoes, a fruit machine and juke box in the games
room. Very good food might include lunchtime sandwiches (from £2.65),
ploughman's (from £4.25), chicken balti or vegetarian mushroom bake (£6.95), steak
and kidney pie or dimsum (£7.50), and venison steak in juniper berry sauce (£10.95).
The menu is a bit more elaborate in the evening with perhaps wild boar steak in
burgundy sauce, lamb cutlets in redcurrant jelly or chicken in wild mushroom, cream
and brandy (£8.95), sirloin in pepper or stilton sauce or salmon in Pernod and bay
leaves (£9.25). Their home-baked soda bread is delicious, and the midweek lunches
(three courses for £8.50, decent choice) are a bargain; no-smoking dining room.
Welcoming licensee, good friendly service, good coffee and well kept Bass and
Worthington on handpump. There are tables out in the charming garden, with a dozy
background of bird and animal noises. *(Recommended by Phil Putwain, KC, John and Anne
Heaton)*

Free house ~ Licensee Elizabeth Meikle ~ Real ale ~ Meals and snacks (not Mon except bank hols; till 10 Fri and Sat) ~ (01824) 750502 ~ Children welcome till 9pm ~ Open 12-2.30, 7-11; 12-11 Sat; 12-10.30 Sun; possibly not all day winter weekends; cl 25 Dec evening

LLANFERRES (Clwyd) SJ1961 Map 7

Druid 🍺

A494 Mold—Ruthin

Tables sheltered in a corner by a low wall with rock-plant pockets outside this extended 17th-c inn make the most of the view looking down over the road to the Alyn valley and the Craig Harris mountains beyond, as does the broad bay window in the civilised and sympathetically refurbished smallish plush lounge. You can also see the hills from the bigger welcoming beamed back bar, also carpeted (with quarry tiles by the log fire), with its two handsome antique oak settles as well as a pleasant mix of more modern furnishings. The attractive dining area, two rooms newly opened together, is relatively smoke-free, and service is very obliging. The interesting range of very good bar food includes tomato and coriander or chicken and lemon grass soup (£2.20), delicious granary baps filled with mozzarella and mushrooms, chicken fillet and lemon mayonnaise or pepperoni and mozzarella (£3.45), stilton-stuffed mushrooms, mussels and mozzarella cheese in a creamy pesto sauce or steak and mushroom pie with good pastry (£5.95), cajun-style hake steak with tiger prawns or chicken curry (£8.95), fillet steak (£11.50), and good vegetarian dishes such as baked mushrooms and sweet peppers with mozzarella (from £5.95); vegetables are fresh and generous. Well kept Burtonwood Best and Golden Bough on handpump, decent malt whiskies and wine list; games area with darts and pool, also dominoes, bagatelle, Jenga and other board games; maybe unobtrusive piped music. *(Recommended by KC, Robert Woodward, Ian Jones, Andrew Shore, Peter and Jan Humphreys)*

Burtonwood ~ Tenant James Dolan ~ Real ale ~ Meals and snacks (12-3, 6-10; all day Sat, Sun and bank hols) ~ Restaurant ~ (01352) 810225 ~ Children welcome ~ Traditional piano sing-along first Sat of month ~ Open 12-3, 5.30-11; 12-11 Sat and bank hols; 12-10.30 Sun ~ Bedrooms: £22.50/£36.50

LLANFIHANGEL CRUCORNEY (Gwent) SO3321 Map 6

Skirrid

Village signposted off A465 nr Abergavenny

Between 1110 and the 17th c, nearly 200 people were hanged here; you can still see the rope scorch marks on the beam above the foot of the stairs which served as the traditional scaffold in the days when this unusual place was the area's courthouse. The inn still has some medieval windows, oak beams made from ships' timbers, and panelling in the dining room that's said to be from a British man o' war. The high-ceilinged bar has settles and wooden tables on its flagstones, walls stripped back to show ancient stonework, and a big open fire with winter roast chestnuts in the stone hearth. Good bar food in substantial helpings includes sandwiches, home-made soup, Welsh cheeses with bread and home-made pickles (£5.25), vegetarian loaf (£5.95), roast beef (£6.25), venison sausages with warm home-made redcurrant and port jelly or lamb liver in sherry gravy with bacon (£6.95), and local lamb chops glazed with an apple and mint jelly (£8.50). Well kept Ushers Best, Founders and seasonal brews on handpump, a range of malt whiskies; darts, pool and piped music. A crazy-paved back terrace has white seats and tables, and there are more rustic ones on a small sloping back lawn. *(Recommended by JKW, Dr A Drummond, Neil and Anita Christopher, R A and E B Sayer, S H Godsell, Gavin May, M G Hart, Barry and Anne, Gwyneth and Salvo Spadaro-Dutturi)*

Ushers ~ Lease: Heather Gant ~ Real ale ~ Meals and snacks (not Sun evenings) ~ Restaurant ~ (01873) 890258 ~ Children welcome ~ Occasional folk singer ~ Open 11-11(10.30 Sun); 11-3, 6-11 winter ~ Bedrooms: £60B

LLANFRYNACH (Powys) SO0725 Map 6
White Swan ◖

Village signposted from B4558, just off A40 E of Brecon bypass

Popular with walkers, this pretty black and white village pub has an enjoyably tranquil atmosphere. The rambling lounge bar is relaxed and friendly with its series of softly lit alcoves, plenty of well spaced tables on the flagstones, partly stripped stone walls, a roaring log fire and maybe piped classical music. A secluded terrace behind with plenty of stone and other tables is attractively divided into sections by roses and climbing shrubs, and overlooks peaceful paddocks. Very good bar food includes french onion soup (£2.60), ploughman's (from £4.75), lasagne, ratatouille, or macaroni and broccoli cheese (£4.75), fisherman's pie (£6.75), hot chicken curry (£7), Welsh-style grilled trout with bacon (£9.50), lamb chops marinated in garlic and herbs (£8.75), well hung steaks (from £11.50), puddings such as sherry trifle (£2.25), children's dishes (£3.90), and maybe weekend specials; nicely cooked vegetables. Service is courteous and efficient; well kept Brains Bitter and Flowers IPA on handpump. The churchyard is across the very quiet village lane. *(Recommended by David and Nina Pugsley, KC, Margaret and Nigel Dennis, Michael Rowe, GWB, Dr G W Barnett, Liz and Peter Elsey)*

Free house ~ Licensees David and Susan Bell ~ Real ale ~ Meals and snacks ~ (01874) 665276 ~ Children welcome ~ Open 12-3(2.30 Sun), 7-11; cl Mon (except bank hols), and last three weeks of Jan

LLANGATTOCK (Powys) SO2117 Map 6
Vine Tree

A4077; village signposted from Crickhowell

The front part of the bar at this friendly well run dining pub has soft seats, some stripped stone masonry, and brass ornaments around its open fireplace. The back is set aside as a dining area with windsor chairs, scrubbed deal tables, and decorative plates and Highland cattle engravings on the walls; most of the tables are set out for eating. Fresh fish comes twice a week from Cornwall, and they use local meat and vegetables in the wide range of carefully prepared dishes such as stockpot soup (£1.75), prawn cocktail or smoked venison with cranberry sauce (£4.30), roast chicken (£4.95), half a dozen vegetarian dishes like lasagne or curry (all £5.75), home-made steak and kidney pie (£6.10), chicken curry (£7.35), rabbit in a wine, celery and almond sauce (£7.60), pork stuffed with apricots in a tangy orange sauce (£8.35), lamb kidneys in sherry sauce (£8.60), pheasant in cream, grape and white wine sauce (£9.30), very tasty monkfish in white wine, Pernod and leek sauce (£9.40), and steaks (from £10.40). Well kept Boddingtons, Fremlins and Wadworths 6X on handpump and air pressure. Tables under cocktail parasols give a view of the splendid medieval stone bridge over the River Usk, and a short stroll takes you to our Crickhowell main entry, the Bear. *(Recommended by Margaret and Nigel Dennis, George and Brenda Jones, Paul Robinshaw, Daren Haines, Pamela and Merlyn Horswell, B M and P Kendall, Andrew Shore, A R and B E Sayer)*

Free house ~ Licensee I S Lennox ~ Real ale ~ Meals and snacks ~ Restaurant ~ (01873) 810514 ~ Children welcome ~ Open 12-2.30, 6(7 Sun)-11

LLANGEDWYN (Clwyd) SJ1924 Map 6
Green

B4396 SW of Oswestry

Just inside Wales in a lovely spot in the Tanat Valley, this ancient place is very well run as a dining pub. Kept spotless inside, it has a nice layout, with various snug alcoves, nooks and crannies, a good mix of furnishings including oak settles and attractively patterned fabrics, and a blazing log fire in winter; there's a pleasant evening restaurant upstairs. In summer this road is well used as a scenic run from the Midlands to the coast, so the pub sees a lot of business then but that's when its attractive garden over the road comes into its own, with lots of picnic tables down towards the river. An impressive range of good home-made food includes sandwiches (from £1.40), ploughman's (£3.85), chicken curry, steak and kidney, chicken and mushroom or cottage pie (£4.90), scampi (£5.25), fresh local trout (£5.45) and several home-made daily specials like shepherd's pie (£5.45), game pie (£6.45), fresh salmon steak with tarragon sauce (£6.95) and sirloin steak (£7.95), as well as tasty puddings like syrup pudding, trifle and meringue (from £2.50). Well kept Boddingtons and about five guests like Brains SA, Eldridge Pope Hardy Country, Flowers Original, Morlands Old Speckled Hen and Woods Special on handpump, a good choice of malt whiskies and wines, friendly quick service; darts, dominoes and piped music; the restaurant is no smoking. The pub has some fishing available to customers, a permit for the day is £5. *(Recommended by Paddy Moindrot, KB, DH, S E Paulley, Pearl Williams)*

Free house ~ Licensee Mrs R G Greenham ~ Real ale ~ Meals and snacks (till 10 Mon-Fri) ~ Restaurant ~ (01691) 828234 ~ Children welcome ~ Open 11-3.30, 6(7 winter)-11; 12-3.30, 6(7 winter)-10.30 Sun; cl 25 Dec eve

LLANGYNIDR (Powys) SO1519 Map 6
Coach & Horses 🍺

B4558

Lots of space inside and (over the road) plenty of tables on a well fenced lawn running down to a lock on the narrow Monmouth and Brecon Canal (with moorings) make this well run pub popular. What marks it out as special for many readers is the way the friendly landlord gets such a jovial atmosphere going. The spacious turkey-carpeted lounge has small armchairs and comfortable banquettes against the stripped stone walls, and in winter a big open fire. An efficient food counter serves sandwiches (from £2.25), filled baguettes (from £2.50), ploughman's (£3.50), steak and kidney pie (£5.95), several chicken curries (from £6.50), 10oz rump (£8.95) and roast duck with game or orange sauce (£10.95) as well as lots of fresh fish on the specials board such as salmon and asparagus bake (£4.25), skate with caper butter (£8.75), cod and prawn mornay (£8.95), poached Wye salmon (£9.95), grilled halibut (£10.95); no-smoking area in restaurant. Well kept Bass, Hancocks HB and a guest like Morlands Old Speckled Hen on handpump; pool, fruit machine, video game and piped music. Canal walks. *Recommended by LM, Gordon Theaker, Mrs P Goodwyn, Roger and Fiona Todd)*

Free house ~ Licensee Derek Latham ~ Real ale ~ Meals and snacks (till 10pm) ~ (01874) 730245 ~ Well behaved children welcome ~ Open 11-11; 12-10.30 Sun ~ Bedrooms: £25B/£30(£45B)

LLANGYNWYD (Mid Glamorgan) SS8588 Map 6
Old House

From A4063 S of Maesteg follow signpost Llan ¾ at Maesteg end of village; pub behind church

A new inn sign in Welsh with a painting of the Mari Lwyd itself refers to the ancient Mari Lwyd tradition which takes place here at Christmas: villagers parade around a horse's skull on a stick decorated with ribbons, calling at each house and singing impromptu verses about the occupants. This lovely thatched pub which dates back to 1147 has been much modernised, but there are still comfortably traditional touches in the two cosy rooms of its busy bar, which have high-backed black built-in settles, lots of china and brass around the huge fireplace, shelves of bric-a-brac, and decorative jugs hanging from the beams; piped music. They've built up quite a reputation for well cooked fresh fish – the landlord goes to the local fish market regularly – and for their reasonably priced bar food such as generously served soup (£1.90), sausages (£2.95), omelettes (£3.75), salads (from £4.45), aubergine lasagne (£4.50), home-made steak and kidney pie (£4.60), beef or chicken curry (£4.70), trout and almonds (£6.90), poached salmon (£8.50), steaks (from £11.15), puddings (£2), daily specials, and children's meals (from £1.25). Well kept Bass, Brains SA, Flowers Original and IPA, Morlands Old Speckled Hen and Worthington on handpump; over 150 whiskies and a choice of wines by the glass. An attractive conservatory extension (half no smoking) leads on to the garden with good views, play area, and a soft ice-cream machine for children. *(Recommended by John and Joan Nash, Ian Phillips, George and Brenda Jones, David and Nina Pugsley, Michael and Alison Sandy, Nigel Clifton, David Holloway)*

Whitbreads ~ Lease Richard and Paula David ~ Real ale ~ Meals and snacks (11-2.30, 5-10) ~ Restaurant ~ (01656) 733310 ~ Children in eating area of bar and restaurant ~ Open 11-11(10.30 Sun)

LLANNEFYDD (Clwyd) SH9871 Map 6
Hawk & Buckle

Village well signposted from surrounding main roads; one of the least taxing routes is from Henllan at junction of B5382 and B5429 NW of Denbigh

The long knocked-through black-beamed lounge bar at this welcoming little hotel perched over 200m up in the hills has comfortable modern upholstered settles around its walls and facing each other across the open fire, and a neat red carpet in the centre of its tiled floor. The lively locals' side bar has darts, pool and piped music. In very clear weather you can see as far as the Lancashire coast, possibly even Blackpool Tower 40 miles away, from most of the modern comfortable and well equipped bedrooms. Bar food is well above average, with a choice of home-made dishes like toasted sandwiches (from £1.85), soup (£1.95), ploughman's (£3.95), steak and kidney pie or various vegetarian dishes like mushroom and nut fettuccine (£5.65), chicken madras, lasagne or turkey and ham pie (£5.95), lemon sole (£7.95) and sirloin steak (from £8.95); good Spanish house wines; the dining room is no smoking. Friendly licensees, two cats and a friendly labrador. There's an attractive mosaic mural on the way through into the back bedroom extension. *(Recommended by Paul Hilditch, S P Watkin, P A Taylor, KC, Margaret Dyke, D W Jones-Williams; more reports please)*

Free house ~ Licensees Bob and Barbara Pearson ~ Meals and snacks ~ Restaurant ~ (01745) 540249 ~ Children in eating area of bar till 8pm ~ Open 12-2, 7-11(10.30 Sun); cl Mon lunchtimes; cl winter lunchtime Mon, Tues, Thurs, Fri ~ Bedrooms: £38B/£50B

LLANYNYS (Clwyd) SJ1063 Map 7
Cerrigllwydion Arms

Village signposted from A525 by Drovers Arms just out of Ruthin, and by garage in Pentre further towards Denbigh

This wonderfully remote and lovely old place looks quite small from the outside but once you're inside it actually rambles about delightfully. Its maze of atmospheric little rooms is filled with dark oak beams, a good mix of seats, old stonework, interesting brasses, and a collection of teapots. Well kept Bass and Tetleys on handpump, and a good choice of malt whiskies, liqueurs and wines; darts, dominoes and unobtrusive piped music. Besides sandwiches and standard bar snacks, food includes home-made soup (£1.75), and changing dishes of the day such as baked pork chops in apple and cider sauce (£6.20), duck in port and brandy sauce (£8.45), roasted lamb in mint and redcurrant sauce (£8.60), and a big mixed grill (£10.25); the restaurant is no smoking. Dogs welcome. Across the quiet lane is a neat garden with teak tables among fruit trees looking across the fields to wooded hills. The adjacent 6th-c church has a medieval wall painting of St Christopher which was discovered under layers of whitewash in the 60s. *(Recommended by D W Jones-Williams, KC, Paul Hilditch, Sue and Bob Ward, B Eastwood, J and B Gibson)*

Free house ~ Licensee Brian Pearson ~ Real ale ~ Meals and snacks (not Mon evening) ~ Restaurant ~ (01745) 890247 ~ Children in restaurant ~ Open 12-3, 7-11(10.30 Sun); cl Mon lunchtime

---

Ideas for a country day out? We list pubs in really attractive scenery at the back of the book – and there are separate lists for waterside pubs, ones with really good gardens, and ones with lovely views.

LLWYNDAFYDD (Ceredigion) SN3755 Map 6
Crown ✇

Coming S from New Quay on A486, both the first two right turns eventually lead to the village; the side roads N from A487 between junctions with B4321 and A486 also come within signpost distance; OS Sheet 145 map reference 371555

The pretty tree-sheltered garden at this attractive white-painted 18th-c pub has won several awards with its delightfully placed picnic tables on a terrace above a small pond among shrubs and flowers, as well as a good play area for children. The friendly, partly stripped-stone bar has red plush button-back banquettes around its copper-topped tables, and a big woodburning stove; piped music. Reliably good home-made bar food includes decent lunchtime sandwiches (from £1.70), as well as soup (£2.30), garlic mushrooms (£2.95), pizzas (from £5.45), vegetarian lasagne or steak and kidney pie (£5.65), salads (from £5.95), local trout (£5.95), steaks (from £7.55), and daily specials such as lamb pie or chicken, stilton and broccoli pie (£5.95), and fresh salmon with roast pepper butter or fresh plaice with watercress, orange and aioli (£6.25); children's meals (from £2); the choice may be limited at Sunday lunchtime, when they do a roast. Very well kept Flowers IPA and Original, Boddingtons, Imperial IPA and guests on handpump, a range of wines, and good choice of malt whiskies. The side lane leads down to a cove with caves by National Trust cliffs. *(Recommended by David and Michelle James, Mr and Mrs G Turner, Mrs S Wright, Christopher Gallop, W H Cooke, RJH)*

Free house ~ Licensee Keith Soar ~ Real ale ~ Meals and snacks ~ Restaurant ~ (01545) 560396 ~ Children in eating area of bar ~ Open 12-3, 6-11(10.30 Sun); cl Sun evenings Nov-Mar

LLYSWEN (Powys) SO1337 Map 6
Griffin ★ ⇌ ♀

A470, village centre

This attractive ivy-covered inn is a lovely place to stay: it's run with real enthusiasm by its welcoming licensees. A good range of very good hearty country cooking relies firmly on local produce, some from their own gardens. Most days after Easter they serve brown trout and salmon, caught by the family or by customers in the River Wye just over the road, and they're well known for very good seasonal game such as pheasant or jugged hare. In the evenings you may find a range of tapas, and they do regular wine tasting nights. Excellent lunchtime meals might include delicious home-made soups such as carrot and sweetcorn (£2.95), pâté, terrine or ploughman's (£4.95), warm duck breast salad (£5.25), seafood pie (£5.95), hot smoked salmon (£6.75). In the evening the menu is more elaborate, with dishes such as roast lamb with rosemary and redcurrant sauce (£9.90), lemon sole with garlic sauce (£10.50), sirloin steak with chargrilled vegetables (£11.50). Crown Buckley Reverend James and Tomas Watkin (a local beer) on handpump, and a good varied wine list with several half bottles. The Fishermen's Bar is popular with chatty locals; it's decorated with old fishing tackle and has a big stone fireplace with a good log fire, and large windsor armchairs and padded stools around tables; at lunchtime there's extra seating in the no-smoking dining room for bar meals. Quoits, and a huge mastiff, Amber; other dogs are allowed. You can shoot or fish here – they have a full-time ghillie and keeper. Service is friendly and helpful, though can slow down at busy times. *(Recommended by Wayne Brindle, Jason Caulkin, TRS, Miss E Evans, Gwen and Peter Andrews, R Morgan, Bill and Steph Brownson)*

Free house ~ Licensees Richard and Di Stockton ~ Real ale ~ Meals and snacks (not Sun) ~ Restaurant ~ (01874) 754241 ~ Children welcome ~ Open 12-3, 7-11 ~ Bedrooms: £40B/£70B

All main entries have been inspected anonymously by the Editor or Deputy Editor. We accept no payment for inclusion, no advertising, and no sponsorship from the drinks industry – or from anyone else.

MAENTWROG (Gwynedd) SH6741 Map 6

Grapes ★ ⌑ ♀

A496; village signposted from A470

From the good-sized sheltered verandah of this warmly welcoming and lively pub you can see trains on the Ffestiniog Railway puffing through the wood beyond the pleasant back terrace and walled garden (there's a fountain on the lawn). It's well geared for families, but at the same time is quite a favourite with locals: you'll often hear Welsh spoken among the visitors, here for the reliable bar food. Home-made, wholesome, and served in hearty helpings, it includes lunchtime sandwiches (not Sun, from £1.75), soup (£1.95), deep-fried potato wedges with dips or filled baked potatoes (£3.50), burgers or salads (from £5.25), several vegetarian dishes like broccoli and walnut bake or spicy vegetable tortillas served with salsa and sour cream (£5.75), pork ribs, steak and mushroom pie or lasagne (£6), curries (£6.75), lamb chops with a creamy leek and stilton sauce (£7.75), and good specials tending to concentrate on fresh fish. Quick friendly service even at the busiest times, with well kept Bass and a local guest on handpump, good house wines, over 30 malt whiskies, and good coffee. All three bars are attractively filled with lots of stripped pitch-pine pews, settles, pillars and carvings, mostly salvaged from chapels. Good log fires – there's one in the great hearth of the restaurant where there may be spit-roasts. An interesting juke box in the public bar, where there's also an intriguing collection of brass blowlamps. The dining room is no smoking; disabled lavatories. *(Recommended by Paul Barnett, Mike Pugh, Roger Byrne, Tim Barrow, Sue Demont, John Baker, Mark Percy, Lesley Mayoh, John Scarisbrick, Jack and Gemima Valiant, Howard James, the Goldsons, J C T Tan, J E Hilditch, E Holland, MRSM, Caroline Raphael, Dr M I Crichton, KB, DH, J A Pickup)*

Free house ~ Licensees Brian and Gill Tarbox ~ Real ale ~ Meals and snacks (12-9.30 Sat, Sun) ~ (01766) 590365 ~ Children in eating area and verandah ~ Open 11-11; 12-10.30 Sun ~ Bedrooms: £25B/£50B

MONTGOMERY (Powys) SO2296 Map 6

Dragon ◧ ⌑

The Square

You can order a meal at this 17th-c timbered hotel, have a free swim in their pool and your food will be ready when you come out. Bar food is a big draw here and might include sandwiches and toasties (from £2.20), filled baked potatoes (from £3.10), ploughman's (from £3.95), grilled chicken breast marinated in lemon and lime, grilled plaice fillet, filled yorkshire pudding or mushroom stroganoff (£6.95), steaks (from £8.15), mixed grill (£9.15), and children's meals (£2.95); three-course Sunday lunch (£8.50, more in restaurant). Many of the beams and much of the masonry here are reputed to have come from a nearby castle after it was destroyed by Cromwell. The carpeted lounge bar has a window seat looking down to the market square and the peaceful old town hall, tapestried stools and wall benches around dimpled copper tables, game bird, old England prints, and willow-pattern plates on a high shelf, up by the colonial ceiling fan. Efficient service, well kept Woods Special Bitter and one or two guests on handpump, and good coffee; chess, draughts, and jigsaws in winter, and maybe unobtrusive piped music. *(Recommended by Walter and Susan Rinaldi-Butcher, Alan and Barbara Mence, Mike and Wendy Proctor, Gwen and Peter Andrews)*

Free house ~ Licensees Mark and Sue Michaels ~ Real ale ~ Meals and snacks ~ Restaurant (lunchtime bookings essential) ~ (01686) 668359 ~ Children in eating area of bar and restaurant till 9.30 ~ Live jazz most Wed evenings ~ Open 11-11; 12-10.30 Sun ~ Bedrooms: £42B/£72B

The letters and figures after the name of each town are its Ordnance Survey map reference. *How to use the Guide* at the beginning of the book explains how it helps you find a pub, in road atlases or large-scale maps as well as in our own maps.

PEMBROKE FERRY (Dyfed) SM9603 Map 6

Ferry Inn

Nestled below A477 toll bridge, N of Pembroke

There are tables out on the waterside terrace at this former sailors' haunt, and the fish they serve is so marvellously fresh it tastes as if it's just flopped straight out of the water. In fact the choice and price depend on market supplies, but it's always incredibly good value and simply cooked so as not to mask the delicacy of its freshness. Prices will be in the region of: moules marinières (£3.95), plaice (£4.25) cod (£4.50), fresh crab, brill or turbot (from £5.95), lobster (from £8.95), as well as dover sole, crayfish, sea bass, halibut or salmon. Other meals could include vegetable kiev or chilli con carne (£3.50), garlic tiger prawns (£3.95), schnitzel with a creamy mushroom sauce (£5.25) and steak (£8.25). Booking is virtually essential for Sunday lunch. The bar has a buoyantly pubby atmosphere, nautical decor to suit its past, and good views over the water. Well kept Bass and Hancocks HB on handpump, and a decent choice of malt whiskies. Efficient service, fruit machine, unobtrusive piped music. *(Recommended by Charles and Pauline Stride, Graham Lynch-Watson, Michael Sargent, Mike and Karen England, Drs R and M Woodford, Christopher Turner, W H Cooke)*

Free house ~ Licensee David Henderson ~ Real ale ~ Meals and snacks (till 10) ~ Restaurant ~ (01646) 684927 ~ Children in restaurant ~ Open 11.30-2.45, 6.30 (7 Mon)-11; 12-2.45, 7-11 Sun; cl 25/26 Dec

PONTYPOOL (Gwent) ST2998 Map 6

Open Hearth ◀

The Wern, Griffithstown; Griffithstown signposted off A4051 S – opposite British Steel main entrance turn up hill, then first right

A splendid range of up to nine changing real ales – much better than you'll find anywhere else in the area – at this well run welcoming local might include Archers Best and Golden, Boddingtons, Burton Bridge, Butcombe, Crown Buckley Best and Reverend James, Greene King Abbot and Hancocks HB on handpump, as well as a good choice of wines and malt whiskies. It's usually busy with people coming for the reliably tasty, good value bar food: soup (£2.15), filled baked potatoes (from £2.85), various curries (from £4.50), vegetable stir fry (£4.75), scampi or cod (£5.50), steak and ale pie (£5.45), pork glazed in a fresh ginger and orange sweet caramel (£6.95), lamb chops served on tarragon and Pernod-scented potato (£8.95), sirloin steak cooked in a Mexican sauce (£9). They do their best to suit you if you want something not on the menu, and the downstairs no-smoking restaurant is something of a local landmark; decent coffee, cheap tea, very friendly and efficient service. You can watch the comings and goings on a stretch of the Monmouthshire & Brecon Canal from seats outside. The comfortably modernised smallish lounge bar has a turkey carpet and big stone fireplace, and a back bar has leatherette seating. Cribbage, dominoes, and piped music; boules in summer. There are picnic tables, swings, and shrubs in the garden. *(Recommended by Mike Pugh, Pamela and Merlyn Horswell, Gwyneth and Salvo Spadaro-Dutturi, PM, AM, Howard James)*

Free house ~ Licensee Gwyn Philips ~ Real ale ~ Meals and snacks (till 10) ~ Restaurant ~ (01495) 763752 ~ Children in eating area and restaurant ~ Open 11.30-3.30, 6-11; 11.30-11.30 Sat; 12-4, 7-10.30 Sun

PRESTEIGNE (Powys) SO3265 Map 6

Radnorshire Arms ⇔

High Street; B4355 N of centre

The old-fashioned charm and atmosphere at this rambling, timbered place never seem to change. Renovations have revealed secret passages and priest's holes, with one priest's diary showing he was walled up here for two years. Discreet modern furnishings blend with venerable dark oak panelling, latticed windows and elegantly moulded black oak beams, decorated with horsebrasses. Reasonably priced bar food might include good sandwiches (from £1.30), home-made soup (£1.95), filled baguettes (from £3.65), whole breaded plaice (£5.25), chicken kiev or grilled lamb cutlets (£5.95), grilled rump steak (£6.50), and puddings (£2.95); children's helpings (from £2.25), as well as dishes of the day such as breast of chicken with mushrooms and tarragon (£5.95) and poached salmon with lobster and prawn sauce (£6.25). Well kept real ales include a brew from Banks's on handpump, with English wines by the glass, several malt whiskies, and welcoming attentive service; separate no-smoking restaurant, morning coffee, afternoon tea. There are some well spaced tables on the sheltered flower-bordered lawn, which used to be a bowling green. *(Recommended by Graham and Karen Oddey, Basil Minson; more reports please)*

Free house ~ Manager Aidan Treacy ~ Real ale ~ Meals and snacks ~ Restaurant ~ (01544) 267406 ~ Children welcome ~ Open 11-11; 12-10.30 Sun ~ Bedrooms: £50B/£80B

nr RAGLAN (Gwent) SO3608 Map 6
Clytha Arms 🍺 🛏 🍺

Clytha, off Abergavenny road – former A40, now declassified

Looking more like a small country house in its well cared for extensive grounds (they're a mass of colour in spring), this fine old country inn impresses readers with its easy gracious comfort, excellent food and fine range of beers. The changing choice of fresh food is well prepared and presented, and might include sandwiches (from £1.85), ploughman's (£4.95), faggots and peas with beer and onion gravy (£3.95), black pudding with apple and mustard sauce or leek and laverbread rissoles (£4.25), wild boar sausage with potato pancakes (£4.65), salmon burger with tarragon and mayonnaise, wild mushroom ragoût with pasta or smoked haddock with piperade (£5.50), thai green chicken curry (£6.25) or mixed shellfish grill (£7.95), and delicious home-made puddings (£3.30); good value three-course Sunday lunch in the no-smoking restaurant. A well stocked bar serves well kept Bass, Banks, Brains Bitter and three guests such as Badger Tanglefoot, Felinfoel Double Dragon and Nethergate Old Growler all on handpump as well as Weston's farm ciders and freshly squeezed orange juice. You will find locals in the tastefully refurbished bar, which has a good traditional atmosphere, with solidly comfortable furnishings and a couple of log fires, and charmingly helpful staff and licensees who are interested in your visit; darts, shove ha'penny, boules, table skittles, cribbage, draughts and chess. *(Recommended by Wayne Brindle, Dennis Heatley, Michael Coshall, David Gittins, Barry and Anne, Malcolm Taylor, Gwyneth and Salvo Spadaro-Dutturi, Peter and Audrey Dowsett, David Luke, KB, DH, F J Willy, IHR, A R and B E Sayer, Nigel Clifton)*

Free house ~ Licensees Andrew and Beverley Canning ~ Real ale ~ Meals and snacks (not Sun evening) ~ Restaurant ~ (01873) 840206 ~ Children welcome ~ Open 12-3, 6-11; 12-11 Sat; 12-4, 7-10.30 Sun; cl Mon lunchtime Sept-Apr except bank hols ~ Bedrooms: £45B/£50B

RED WHARF BAY (Anglesey) SH5281 Map 6
Ship 🍺

Village signposted off B5025 N of Pentraeth

Superb fresh sea views from tables on the front terrace of this very popular family-run 16th-c house look down over ten square miles of treacherous tidal cockle-sands, with low wooded hills sloping down to the broad bay. Inside is old-fashioned and interesting, with big friendly rooms on each side of the busy stone-built bar counter, both with long cushioned varnished pews built around the walls, glossily varnished cast-iron-framed tables, and quite a restrained decor including toby jugs, local photographs, attractive antique foxhunting cartoons and coal fires. Enterprising and well presented daily changing bar food might typically include cream of celery and bacon soup (£2.40), chicken liver pâté (£4.20), mussels (£4.40), grilled fresh salmon (£6.20), peppered beef with ginger (£6.70), braised meatballs (£6.80), baked shoulder of lamb with garlic and rosemary (£9.10), and puddings like rhubarb and ginger crumble or crème brûlée (£2.70). There may be delays at busy times (it can be quite crowded on Sundays, when food service stops promptly at 2, and you do need to arrive early for a table), but service is always friendly and smiling; the cheery licensee has been here now for over 20 years. The dining room and cellar room are no smoking. Well kept Benskins, Burtons, Tetleys Mild, Bitter and Imperial and changing guests are drawn by handpump with a sparkler; a wider choice of wines than usual for the area, and about 30 malt whiskies. Pool, darts and dominoes in the back room, and a family room; piped music. There are rustic tables and picnic tables by an ash tree on grass by the side. *(Recommended by S P Watkin, P A Taylor, Mark Percy, Lesley Mayoh, G S and E M Dorey, Chris and Shirley Machin, Alan and Paula McCully, Joy and Peter Heatherley, WAH, Margaret and Roy Randle)*

Free house ~ Licensee Andrew Kenneally ~ Real ale ~ Meals and snacks ~ (01248) 853568 ~ Restaurant ~ Children welcome in eating area of bar ~ Open 11-11; 12-10.30 Sun

ROSEBUSH (Dyfed) SN0630 Map 6
New Inn ♀ ◖

B4329 Haverfordwest—Cardigan, NW of village

With an unassuming exterior, this welcoming outpost on the edge of the unspoilt Preseli Hills has been most attractively restored in tune with its origins as a 17th-c drovers' inn, and later a combined farm and coaching inn. Three cosy rooms have interesting stripped stonework, simple antique oak country furniture on handsome slate flagstones or red and black diamond Victorian tiles, and a couple of coal fires – one in a quite cavernous fireplace. All this gives a cosy and cottagey feel, and the atmosphere is quiet and relaxed. There is a small garden room. Good wide-ranging bar food using carefully chosen local ingredients might include soup (£2.50), cawl with cheese (£3.50), garlic mushrooms or a pint of prawns (£3.85), gratin of cockles, bacon and laverbread (£4.25/£5.25), warm salad of goat's cheese (£4.60/£5.60), seafood lasagne (£6), outstanding thai red curry pork or mushroom stroganoff (£6.75), as well as puddings such as bread and butter pudding (£2.75), and good local cheeses. As the food is freshly prepared there may be a wait. Up to six rotating well kept real ales might include Crown Buckley Best and Reverend James, Felinfoel Double Dragon, Fullers London Pride and Morrells Graduate on handpump; well chosen wines by the bottle or glass, Weston's farm cider and friendly staff. There are tables outside, and plenty of good walks nearby. *(Recommended by Nick and Meriel Cox, Mr and Mrs M J Bastin, Jack and Gemima Valiant, Richard Siebert, R Michael Richards, Mr and Mrs J R Morris, John and Pat Smyth, Robert and Sarah Connor)*

Free house ~ Licensee Diana Richards ~ Real ale ~ Meals and snacks (12-2.30, 6-9.30) ~ Restaurant ~ (01437) 532542 ~ Children welcome ~ Live music Mon ~ Open 11-11; 12-3, 6-11 Sun; 11-3, 6-11 winter weekdays

ST HILARY (S Glamorgan) ST0173 Map 6
Bush

Village signposted from A48 E of Cowbridge

The comfortable and snugly cosy low-beamed lounge bar at this genuinely old-fashioned 16th-c thatched pub has walls stripped to the old stone, and windsor chairs around copper-topped tables on the carpet, while the public bar has old settles and pews on aged flagstones; darts, cribbage, dominoes and subdued piped music. Good bar food, using fresh ingredients, includes sandwiches (from £1.75), home-made soup (£2.20), laverbread and bacon (£2.50), welsh rarebit (£3.20), spinach and cheese crêpe (£3.35), ploughman's (£3.75), liver with onion gravy or lasagne (£4.25), salads (from £4.25), steak and ale pie (£4.95), gammon (£5.50), mixed grill (£6.95), and good daily specials; the restaurant menu is available in the bar in the evenings, with meals like trout fried in sherry (£8.95) or breast of duck in orange (£10.95); they will do smaller helpings for children. Well kept Bass, Hancocks Best and Morlands Old Speckled Hen on handpump, with a range of malt whiskies and a farm cider; efficient service. There are tables and chairs in front, and more in the back garden. *(Recommended by David and Nina Pugsley, R B Mowbray, D and L Berry, C A Hall, Miss E Evans, Mrs S Wright, David Holloway, the Sandy family)*

Bass ~ Lease Sylvia Murphy ~ Real ale ~ Meals and snacks (not Sun evenings) ~ Restaurant ~ (01446) 772745 ~ Children welcome ~ Open 11-11; 12-10.30 Sun ~ Bedrooms: £20/£30

SHIRENEWTON (Gwent) ST4894 Map 6

Carpenters Arms ◀

B4235 Chepstow—Usk

Once inside past the eye-catching array of hanging baskets, it's well worth wandering around this hive of small interconnecting rooms before you settle: there's plenty to see, from chamber-pots and a blacksmith's bellows hanging from the planked ceiling of one lower room, which has an attractive Victorian tiled fireplace, through an interesting case of sugar-tongs, to a collection of chromolithographs of antique Royal occasions under another room's pitched ceiling (more chamber-pots here, too). Furnishings run the gamut too, from one very high-backed ancient settle to pews, kitchen chairs, a nice elm table, several sewing-machine trestle tables and so forth. Food includes cumberland sausage or faggots and peas (£4.25), paella (£4.95), chicken supreme in leek and stilton sauce (£5.25), home-made steak and mushroom pie or beef bourguignon (£5.95) lamb korma (£6.50) and salads (£6.55); Sunday lunch is good value. Well kept Boddingtons, Flowers IPA, Fullers London Pride, Marstons Pedigree and Owd Rodger, and a guest such as Youngs Special on handpump; a good collection of malt whiskies; cheerful service, maybe loudish piped pop music. *(Recommended by Emma Kingdon, A R and B E Sayer, Peter Hesketh)*

Free house ~ Licensee James Bennett ~ Real ale ~ Meals and snacks ~ (01291) 641231 ~ Children in family area ~ Open 11-2.30(3 Sat), 6-11; 12-3, 7-10.30 Sun

STACKPOLE (Dyfed) SR9896 Map 6

Armstrong Arms ⑪

Village signposted off B4319 S of Pembroke

Tucked away on the Stackpole estate this delightful rather Swiss-looking inn is very popular for its freshly cooked and efficiently served (cheerful black-and-white uniformed waitresses) bar food. From an imaginative changing range, at lunchtime there might be home-made soup (£2.95), cawl with Welsh cheddar or welsh rarebit with tomato and crispy bacon (£3.95), club sandwich (£4.45), beef tomatoes stuffed with savoury rice (£4.75), poached egg salad with black pudding, smoked bacon and sautéed potatoes (£4.95), chicken tikka masala (£5.25), with more elaborate evening dishes such as poached fillet of salmon with a lemon and lime hollandaise (£7.95), pork schnitzel with a caper sauce, sirloin steak or rack of lamb with a cranberry, redcurrant, port and orange sauce (£8.95); vegetables are delicious, with a choice of potatoes. Tasty puddings include crème brûlée, pear and almond tart or chocolate and rum torte with a raspberry coulis (£3); coffee is good and unlimited. A traditional lunch only is served on Sundays (£6.95). Well kept Charles Wells Bombardier and guests such as Caledonian IPA, Fullers London Pride or Marstons Pedigree on hand and electric pump, and about two dozen malt whiskies. One spacious area has darts and pool, but the major part of the pub, L-shaped on four different levels, is given over to diners, with neat light oak furnishings, and glossy beams and low ceilings to match. There are tables out in the attractive gardens, with colourful flowerbeds and mature trees around the car park; no credit cards or dogs. *(Recommended by Graham Lynch-Watson, Michael Sargent, Mr and Mrs M J Bastin, Brian and Anna Marsden, Nick and Meriel Cox, T L Rees, W H Cooke, Drs R and M Woodford, Christopher Turner, Mr and Mrs Blackbourn, Sarah Bradbury, Mrs M Boulson, Ian and Lynn Brown, Rob Holt, M E Wellington, Heather Wellington)*

Free house ~ Licensees Senga and Peter Waddilove ~ Real ale ~ Meals and snacks ~ Restaurant ~ (01646) 672324 ~ Children in restaurant till 9.30; no prams or pushchairs ~ Open 11.30-3, 6-11; 12-3, 7-10.30 Sun; cl Sun evenings Nov-Mar

TALYBONT-ON-USK (Powys) SO1122 Map 6
Star £ 🍷
B4558

This no-frills little canalside pub keeps an incredible range of changing real ales that might include Boddingtons, Felinfoel Double Dragon, Freeminer, Marstons Pedigree and Old Peculier and Wye Valley, as well as farm cider on handpump too. Several plainly furnished pubby rooms – unashamedly stronger on character than on creature comforts – radiate from the central servery, including a brightly lit games area with pool, fruit machine and juke box; roaring winter fires, one in a splendid stone fireplace. Cheerily served hearty bar food includes soup (£2), ploughman's (£3), faggots, peas and chips (£4), chilli, lasagne, chicken curry or pork goulash (£4.50), lamb liver casserole (£5.25), carbonnade of beef (£6.50), sirloin with savoury sauce (£8.95), and vegetarian dishes such as vegiburger, chilli or spinach and leek pasta bake (from £3.50); children's meals (£2). You can sit outside at picnic tables in the sizeable tree-ringed garden or walk along the tow path, and the village, with both the Usk and the Monmouth & Brecon Canal running through, is surrounded by the Brecon Beacons national park. *(Recommended by Jack and Philip Paxton, John and Joan Nash, Charles and Pauline Stride, John Abbott, A P Jeffreys, Ian Mabberley, Gwyneth and Salvo Spadaro-Dutturi, BH)*

Free house ~ Licensee Mrs Joan Coakham ~ Real ale ~ Meals and snacks (till 9.30) ~ (01874) 676635 ~ Children welcome till 9pm ~ Live blues/rock Wed evenings ~ Open 11-3, 6-11; 11-11 Sat; 12-10.30 Sun ~ Bedrooms: £25B/£40B

TALYCOED (Gwent) SO4115 Map 6
Halfway House
B4233 Monmouth—Abergavenny; though its postal address is Llantilio Crossenny, the inn is actually in Talycoed, a mile or two E

A huge wisteria surrounds the handsome ancient door of this pretty 17th-c cottage: inside, a step up on the left takes you into a cosy little no-smoking dining room with burgundy furnishings and carpet, sporting and other prints, and black kettles around its hearth. The main bar is also snug and cosy: soft lighting, bare boards, polished brasses around a nice old stone fireplace, wall settles, a few red plush bar stools, and a back area with a couple of antique high-backed settles and enormous foresters' saws. Lovers of picturesque old inns will recognise many old friends in their collection of Wills cigarette cards. Carefully presented bar food includes sandwiches (£1.60), a good ham ploughman's (£3.50) and hot dishes, using much local produce, such as steak and stout pie (£5.95), lamb pepper pot (£6.20), salmon en croûte (£6.70) and duck in orange sauce (£8.45); welcoming service; no-smoking area in dining room. Well kept Bass and Felinfoel Bitter and Double Dragon on handpump; darts, maybe quiet piped radio. All is neat and clean, including the outside gents'. There are picnic tables out on a front terrace with a big barbecue, and in a neatly kept garden; the cricket field behind has two or three caravans – and a team that prospers. *(Recommended by Salvo and Gwyneth Spadaro-Dutturi, Malcolm Taylor, Gethin Lewis, Paul and Heather Bettesworth)*

Free house ~ Licensees Mr and Mrs L M Stagg ~ Real ale ~ Meals and snacks (not Sun eve) ~ (01600) 780269 ~ Open 12-3.30, 6-11(7-10.30 Sun) ~ Bedrooms: £20/£35

TY'N Y GROES (Gwynedd) SH7672 Map 6
Groes ★ 🍴 🛏
B5106 N of village

Going from strength to strength, this charmingly situated neat old pub is marvellously run, with great attention to detail, by the attentive family who have put so much energy into it. The new bedrooms, some with terraces or balconies, have magnificent views over the mountains or scenic reaches of the Conwy River (also from the no-smoking airy verdant conservatory, and seats on the flower decked roadside), receive glowing reports from readers. The excellent range of traditional country cooking is also much praised. There might be sandwiches (from £2.95), soup and a sandwich or smoked haddock and bacon fishcakes (£5.50), lasagne or scampi (£5.95), pie of the day or garlic mushrooms with stilton (£6.50), daily specials such as lancashire hotpot with home-made red pickled cabbage or roast gammon on a wild damson sauce (£5.95), game casserole with herb dumplings or roast of the day (£6.95), local lamb with a caper, honey and garlic marinade (£7.25), seafood platter (£8.50) and a good selection of fresh fish; lots of tasty puddings like banoffi pie, treacle tart or lemon and apple pudding (£2.75), and tempting home-made ice creams like lemon curd or caramelised pears with maple syrup (£2). The homely series of rambling, low-beamed and thick-walled rooms are beautifully decorated with antique settles and an old sofa, old clocks, portraits, hats and tins hanging from the walls and fresh flowers. A fine antique fireback is built into one wall, perhaps originally from the formidable fireplace which houses a collection of stone cats as well as winter log fires. Well kept Banks's and Marstons Pedigree on handpump, a good few malt whiskies, and a fruity pimms in summer; cribbage, dominoes and light classical piped music at lunchtimes (nostalgic light music at other times). It can get busy, but this shouldn't cause any problems with the efficient friendly service. There are seats in the pretty back garden with its flower-filled hayricks. *(Recommended by Pearl Williams, Gordon Theaker, Roger Byrne, Joy and Peter Heatherley, Liz Bell, Dr Phil Putwain, R H Sawyer, Paul Hilditch, D L Evans, Eric Locker, AW, BW, Barbara Wensworth, E Holland, J E Hilditch, Gethin Lewis)*

Free house ~ Licensees Dawn, Tony and Justin Humphreys ~ Real ale ~ Meals and snacks ~ Restaurant ~ (01492) 650545 ~ Well behaved children in eating area of bar till 8pm (no pushchairs); in restaurant if over 10 ~ Open 12-3, 6.30-11(10.30 Sun) ~ Bedrooms: £55B/£70B

USK (Gwent) SO3801 Map 6
Royal 🏷

New Market Street (off A472 by Usk bridge)

This characterful and unspoilt Georgian country-town pub was once owned by John Trelawney and frequented by Mary Shelley, and even today there's a good mix of people filling up the two simple open-plan rooms – still furnished with some original pieces – of the homely old-fashioned bar. Many come for the tasty bar meals, served in big helpings from a range that might include deep-fried breaded plaice or half a roast chicken (£6.25), cold home-baked ham or mushroom, cashew nut and tagliatelle pie (£6.75), lasagne verdi or beef and beer pie (£6.95), grilled lamb chops or breast of chicken in a cream, tarragon and white wine sauce (£7.95) and lovely tender steaks (from £9.50); they do a popular Sunday lunch (£6.75) (when the ordinary menu isn't available). Service can slow down at busy times. The left-hand room is the nicer, with a cream-tiled kitchen range flush with the pale ochre back wall, a comfortable mix of tables and chairs, a rug on neat slate flagstones, plates and old pictures on the walls, china cabinets, a tall longcase clock, and open fires. Particularly well kept Bass, Felinfoel Double Dragon, Hancocks HB and a guest such as Adnams Broadside on handpump, and an extensive wine list. *(Recommended by Pamela and Merlyn Horswell, Gwyneth and Salvo Spadaro-Dutturi, Jenny and Brian Seller, George and Brenda Jones, H L Dennis, A R and B E Sayer, Ian Williams, Linda Mar)*

Free house ~ Licensee Anthony Lyons ~ Real ale ~ Meals and snacks (not Sun evening and Mon lunchtime) ~ (01291) 672931 ~ Well behaved children welcome ~ Jazz every other Sun ~ Open 12-3, 7-11; cl Mon lunchtime

---

Bedroom prices are for high summer. Even then you may get reductions for more than one night, or (outside tourist areas) weekends. Winter special rates are common, and many inns cut bedroom prices if you have a full evening meal.

Lucky Dip

Besides the fully inspected pubs, you might like to try these Lucky Dips recommended to us and described by readers (if you do, please send us reports):

ANGLESEY

Beaumaris [Castle St; SH6076], *Liverpool Arms*: Friendly staff in refurbished pub with banquettes in alcoves, nautical memorabilia, decent food with lots of chips, Brains ale; piped music may obtrude; bedrooms, nice spot nr seafront *(Mark Percy, Lesley Mayoh, P H Sawyer)*

Cemaes Bay [High St; SH3793], *Stag*: Popular straightforward village local, small, warm and cosy; good value bar food, well kept Burtonwood, real fire; lounge, bar and pool room *(Alan and Paula McCully)*; [High St], *Vigour*: Smoke room, bar, lounge and commercial rooms off covered passage, good value food, well kept Worthington Best *(Alan and Paula McCully)*

Dulas [A5025 N of Moelfre; SH4687], *Pilot Boat*: Warm, friendly, clean and comfortable with big dining area, good food all cooked to order, sensible prices *(Mr and Mrs T Pitwell)*

Llanfair Pg [SH5372], *Tafarn Ty Gwyn*: Friendly hotel with home-made food cooked to order, good prices; clean and comfortable; bedrooms *(Mr and Mrs T Pitwell)*

☆ **Marianglas** [B5110; SH5084], *Parciau Arms*: Useful pub with comfortable built-in banquettes and other seating, old coaching prints, interesting bric-a-brac inc lots of gleaming brass, decent bar food inc sandwiches, OAP discounts and children's dishes, airy family dining room, well kept ales such as Bass, Ind Coope Burton and Marstons Pedigree, good range of other drinks, cheerful service, pub games; terrace and good-sized garden with excellent play area, open all day *(Alan and Paula McCully, WAH, LYM)*

☆ **Menai Bridge** [St Georges Pier, by Straits; SH5572], *Liverpool Arms*: Unpretentious old-fashioned four-roomed local with cheerful relaxed atmosphere, low beams, interesting mostly maritime photographs and prints, panelled dining room, conservatory catching evening sun, one or two tables on terrace; good value bar food, well kept Greenalls Special and Best, welcoming landlord, good service; no music *(N Gilbourne, T G Thomas)*

Menai Bridge [N side of roundabout just S of Britannia Bridge], *Jodies*: Three dining rooms and a bar, with thousands of banknotes from all over the world; pleasant atmosphere, good food (cheaper at lunchtime), Boddingtons *(Mark Percy, Lesley Mayoh)*

CLWYD

Betws yn Rhos [SH9174], *Wheatsheaf*: Well furnished old-fashioned two-bar 17th-c inn with friendly service, well kept beers, wide choice of reasonably priced food inc bargain suppers for two, good log fires; good value bedrooms, lovely village *(S P Watkin, P A Taylor)*

☆ **Burton Green** [Llyndir Lane, off B5445 W of Rossett; SJ3558], *Golden Grove*: Friendly relaxed timbered pub dating from 13th c, partly knocked-through rooms with open fires, comfortable settees and settles, plates, horsebrasses, figures carved in the beams; Marstons Best and Pedigree, restaurant, children welcome, piped music; big streamside garden with play area, open all day w/e in summer; has been popular all round, with good home-made food, but no reports yet on new landlady *(LYM)*

☆ **Bylchau** [A543 3 miles S; SH9863], *Sportsmans Arms*: Wide views from highest pub in Wales, reliable straightforward food with all fresh veg and vegetarian dishes, well kept Lees Traditional and Best Dark Mild, drinks cheaper than usual; Welsh-speaking locals, cheerful and welcoming prompt service, good log fire, old-fashioned high-backed settles among more modern seats, darts and pool, no piped music, harmonium and Welsh singing Sat evening; children allowed in eating area, cl Mon/Tues lunchtimes in winter (and maybe other lunchtimes then) *(NAK, LYM)*

Carrog [off A5 Llangollen—Corwen; SJ1144], *Grouse*: Friendly and unpretentious, with welcoming new landlord, splendid River Dee view from bay window and tables on terrace with pretty walled garden; two small rooms and a pool room, good value usual food, Lees bitter; piped music; bedrooms *(George Atkinson, Ray and Liz Monk)*

Chirk [Chirk Bank; B5070 S (just over Shrops border); SJ3038], *Bridge*: Plain old local below Llangollen Canal nr aqueduct, well kept Banks's Mild and Bitter and Marstons Pedigree (summer), water-jugs on beams, back eating area, children welcome *(Keith and Janet Morris, Ian and Nita Cooper)*

☆ **Cilcain** [signed from A494 W of Mold; SJ1765], *White Horse*: Homely country local with several rooms, low joists, mahogany and oak settles, inglenook fire, quarry-tiled back bar allowing dogs, reasonably priced home-made food inc interesting dishes and lots of puddings, three well kept changing ales such as Marstons Pedigree, Morlands Old Speckled Hen or Timothy Taylors Landlord, pub games; no children inside, picnic tables outside; delightful little village *(Iain Robertson, E Holland, Anthony Hoyle, LYM)*

Denbigh [Old Ruthin Rd; SJ0666], *Brookhouse Mill*: Friendly pub/restaurant in lovely setting by River Ystrad, well kept beer, good choice of other drinks, decent food in bar and restaurant; play area outside *(S P Watkin, P A Taylor)*

Graianrhyd [B5430; signed off A494 and A5104; SJ2156], *Rose & Crown*: Small two-room local in remote part of Clwydian Hills,

roaring fire, good choice of home-cooked food inc swordfish steak and heaped mixed grill, well kept Whitbreads-related ales, efficient service, interesting decor; may be open all day in summer *(Ray and Liz Monk)*
Graig Fechan [signed off B5429 S of Ruthin; SJ1554], *Three Pigeons*: Extended two-bar 17th-c inn with fine views, friendly staff, good food in bar or dining room, well kept Bass, Brains SA, Crown Buckley Best and Ushers Founders tapped from the cask; children allowed if eating; big garden with barbecue, small camping/caravan site *(Richard Lewis, Graham and Lynn Mason)*
Gwytherin [B5384 W of Denbigh – OS Sheet 116 map ref 876615; SH8761], *Lion*: Well run small pub with roaring log fire, well kept beer, wide choice of good food, attractive restaurant with another log fire, very welcoming licensees; bedrooms *(Jerry and Alison Oakes, D W Jones-Williams)*
Lixwm [B5121 S of Holywell; SJ1671], *Crown*: Well kept village pub, changing guest beers, good home cooking esp roast Sun lunch; colourful front flower tubs and baskets *(Mr and Mrs D Jackson)*
☆ **Llanarmon Dc** [end of B4500 W of Chirk; SJ1633], *West Arms*: Warm welcome and roaring log fires in extended 16th-c beamed and timbered inn, good base for walking; picturesque upmarket lounge bar full of antique settles, sofas, even an elaborately carved confessional stall, well kept Boddingtons, good range of wines and malt whiskies, more sofas in old-fashioned entrance hall, comfortable back bar too; good bar food inc fresh fish; pretty lawn running down to River Ceiriog (fishing for residents), children welcome; bedrooms comfortable *(Peter Lewis, LYM)*
Llanarmon yn Ial [B5431 NW of Wrexham; SJ1956], *Raven*: Friendly 18th-c country local with well kept Burtonwood Bitter and Dark Mild, good value food, pleasant seats outside – attractive village, unspoilt countryside; bedrooms *(Ray and Liz Monk, LYM)*
Llanasa [SJ1082], *Red Lion*: Tucked away in the hills above Prestatyn, well kept beer, good bar food, lovely atmosphere, welcoming licensees and log fire; good service even when busy *(S P Watkin, P A Taylor, T Dobby)*
Llandrillo [SJ0337], *Tyddyn Llan*: A hotel, but people do drop in for a drink; pleasant atmosphere, decent food; bedrooms *(Paul S McPherson)*
Llangollen [S of bridge; SJ2142], *Royal*: Ex-Forte hotel, small quiet bar, roomy elegant lounge overlooking River Dee, armchairs and sofas, daily papers, helpful friendly staff, attractively priced food inc vegetarian, Courage Directors, Marstons Pedigree, good coffee and tea; bedrooms *(Annette and Stephen Marsden)*; [Mill St; A539 E of bridge (N end)], *Sarah Ponsonby*: Large pub next to canal museum on quieter side of the Dee, good value varied food, well kept Theakstons, pleasant garden overlooking

park *(S W Armstrong)*
nr **Llangollen** [A542 1½ miles W; SJ2142], *Abbey Grange*: More hotel than pub, but welcoming, with good service, moderately priced food in family bar (all day, at least in summer) and evening restaurant, good Sun lunch, Banks's ales with two or three guests, picnic tables outside, shire horses in the grounds; beautiful spot with superb views nr Valle Crucis Abbey; comfortable bedrooms *(Mrs E Everard, Ray and Liz Monk)*; [Horseshoe Pass (A542 N)], *Britannia*: Included for position, with lovely Dee Valley views from picturesque though much extended pub, two quiet bars and brightly cheerful dining areas (one no smoking), Whitbreads-related ales; well kept garden; good value attractive bedrooms *(RP, BP, Alan and Barbara Mence)*
Llanrhaeadr [just off A525 Ruthin—Denbigh; SJ0863], *Kings Head*: Good value food, well kept beer, pleasant atmosphere; nice village – good Jesse window in church; bedrooms *(Ray and Liz Monk)*
Llansilin [B4580 W of Oswestry; SJ2128], *Wynnstay*: Pleasant unpretentious village pub, well kept Marstons Pedigree, good value food, welcoming newish landlords, friendly locals; bedrooms comfortable *(Dr B and Mrs P B Baker)*
☆ **Maeshafn** [off A494 SW of Mold; SJ2061], *Miners Arms*: Small friendly local, happy relaxing atmosphere, Theakstons Bitter, Old Peculier and XB, good value home-made food in bar and dining room, theatre and jazz memorabilia *(Adam Robertson, Ray and Liz Monk)*
Mold [A541 Denbigh rd nr Bailey Hill; SJ2464], *Bryn Awel*: Good choice of satisfying food inc vegetarian, good service, pleasant atmosphere *(KC)*
nr **Mold** [Loggerheads; A494, 3 miles towards Ruthin; SJ1962], *We Three Loggerheads*: Comfortable two-level bar, games area, friendly service, decent usual food, unobtrusive piped music; open all day in summer; picnic tables out on side terrace overlooking river *(Miss S Watkin, P Taylor, KC, LYM)*
Pandy [SJ1936], *Woolpack*: Former 16th-c mill, much altered but water still running through cellar bar; Boddingtons and another Whitbreads-related guest beer, interesting food in two-level bar or restaurant, settees and easy chairs, daily papers, terrace, fishing available – beautiful peaceful valley; comfortable bedrooms *(Dr B and Mrs R B Baker, Bob Savage)*
☆ **Rhewl** [the one off A5 W of Llangollen; SJ1744], *Sun*: Unpretentious little cottage in lovely peaceful spot, good walking country just off Horseshoe Pass, relaxing views from terrace and small pretty garden; simple good value food from sandwiches to good Sun lunch, well kept Felinfoel Double Dragon, Worthington BB and a guest beer, old-fashioned hatch service to back room, dark little lounge, portakabin games room –

children allowed here and in eating area *(KB, DH, KC, D Maplethorpe, B Helliwell, Ray and Liz Monk, Joan and Michel Hooper-Immins, LYM)*

Ruthin [SJ1258], *Eagles Nest*: Good wide-ranging bar food, good value restaurant meals, efficient staff *(Mrs E Everard)*; [Rhos St], *Olde Anchor*: Pretty, lots of flower baskets, good bar food and restaurant, friendly chef/landlord, well kept Bass and Worthington; bedrooms good value, attractive country town *(Margaret and Nigel Dennis)*

St George [off A55 nr Abergele; SH9576], *Kinmel Arms*: Clean and comfortable pub/restaurant with interesting freshly cooked food often using unusual local ingredients (plenty of time needed, as everything cooked for you); good range of real ales with weekly guest; bedrooms, attractive village *(Don Mills, J E Hilditch)*

☆ **Tremeirchion** [off B5429 up lane towards church; SJ0873], *Salusbury Arms*: Lovely log fires in beamed pub with some 14th-c panelling, comfortable attractive furnishings, well kept Marstons Bitter and Pedigree and three guest beers, well equipped games room, restaurant; children welcome, pretty garden with under-cover barbecue, open all day summer *(Paul Boot, Richard Lewis, LYM)*

☆ **Trofarth** [B5113 S of Colwyn Bay; SH8470], *Holland Arms*: Good value generous food inc lunchtime bargains in old-fashioned 17th-c former coaching inn, warm cosy atmosphere, prompt friendly service, Ansells Mild and Tetleys, farm tools in one room, stuffed owls in the other, raised dining area open when busy; some tables outside with valley and mountains views; handy for Bodnant *(Roger Byrne)*

DYFED

Aberystwyth [SN6777], *Lord Beeching*: Popular railway-theme pub with thriving atmosphere, good value well prepared food, good range of beers *(Albert and Margaret Horton)*; [Mill St], *Mill*: Friendly local open all day, several well kept Tetleys-related ales, simple lunchtime cold snacks, pool table, friendly staff and locals inc rugby players *(Joan and Michel Hooper-Immins, Jack and Gemima Valiant)*

Alltwalis [A485 about 7 miles N of Carmarthen; SN4431], *Masons Arms*: Clean, attractively furnished, with welcoming newish landlord, nicely arranged tables, enjoyable food from snacks and basket meals to duck with orange sauce, good coffee, helpful staff, pleasant piped music; open all day *(Mrs M Brown)*

Amroth [SN1607], *Amroth Arms*: Food inc good value Sun lunch *(M and M Carter)*

Bancyfelin [off A40 W of Carmarthen; SN3217], *Fox*: Popular for its good bar food *(R B Mowbray)*

Bow Street [A487 N of Aberystwyth; SN6285], *Black Lion*: Good mainly home-made food inc children's, early-evening start,

efficient service, Worthington *(Mr and Mrs S Davies)*

☆ **nr Broad Haven** [N of village on coast rd, bear L for about 1½ miles then follow sign L to Druidstone Haven – inn a sharp left turn after another ½ mile; OS Sheet 157 map ref 862168, marked as Druidston Villa], *Druidstone*: Very unusual and for people it suits a favourite place to stay in; its club licence means you can't go for just a drink and have to book to eat there (the food is inventively individual home cooking, with fresh ingredients and a leaning towards the organic; restaurant cl Sun evening); a lived-in informal country house alone in a grand spot above the sea, with terrific views, spacious homely bedrooms, erratic plumbing, cellar bar with a strong 1960s folk-club feel, well kept Worthington BB tapped from the cask, good wines, country wines and other drinks, ceilidhs and folk jamborees, chummy dogs (dogs welcomed), all sorts of sporting activities from boules to sand-yachting; cl Nov and Jan; bedrooms *(Dr G W Barnett, J Giles Quick, LYM)*

☆ **Caio** [off A482 Llanwrda—Lampeter; SN6739], *Brunant Arms*: Unspoilt chatty village local popular for well kept Hereford and other ales; good layout of pews etc, good value tasty changing food (best to book for small eating area), welcoming efficient staff, interesting egg cup collection, pool table, quiz nights; bedrooms good value, good walks *(Howard James, Jack and Gemima Valiant, M E Wellington, M E Hughes)*

Cardigan [Pendre; SN1846], *Commercial*: Low black beams, well kept Felinfoel Bitter and Double Dragon and Bitter, lots of ship pictures, nets and nautical objects on walls, friendly landlord and locals, tables outside behind; no food *(Joan and Michel Hooper-Immins)*

☆ **Cwm Gwaun** [Pontfaen; Cwm Gwaun and Pontfaen signed off B4313 E of Fishguard; SN0035], *Dyffryn Arms*: Very basic and idiosyncratic Welsh-speaking country tavern known locally as Bessie's, run by same family since 1840; plain deal furniture, well kept Bass and Ind Coope Burton served by jug through a hatch, good sandwiches if you're lucky, Great War prints, draughts-boards inlaid into tables, very relaxed atmosphere; pretty countryside *(Jack and Philip Paxton, Andy Jones, LYM)*

Cwmann [A482 SE of Lampeter; SN5847], *Ram*: Lively atmosphere, good value tasty food, welcoming staff *(Jack and Gemima Valiant)*

Cwmbach [Llanelli—Trimsaran rd; SN4802], *Farriers Arms*: Recently reopened country pub with high wooden settles in stripped stone bar, big informal garden with play area reached by bridge over trout stream, popular barbecue area, woodland setting; well kept real ales, decent wines *(Steve Thomas)*

Cwmduad [SN3731], *Tafarn yr Afon Duad*: Unpretentious roadside pub, small lounge and dining area, back games area with pool, well kept Worthingtons Best, hospitable service and atmosphere, simple but appealing home-made food, all well and heartily presented; spotless bedrooms, homely and comfortable *(Bill Hyett)*

Cynghordy [A483 NE of Llandovery; SN8040], *Glanbrane Arms*: Good mix of locals and visitors, huge woodburner in bar, good generous low-priced food in lounge bar and dining room, Worthington Best and a guest beer which might be local T Watkin ESB *(Howard James)*

Dale [SM8006], *Griffin*: Clean but no-frills old building, lively and friendly, with good range of seafood, Worthington and a couple of local beers, good view of boats in estuary, can sit out on sea wall; children allowed when eating *(Keith Archer, Mr and Mrs T A Bryan)*

✩ **Dreenhill** [Dale Rd (B4327); SM9214], *Denant Mill*: Welcoming 16th-c converted watermill with great atmosphere, well kept changing ales, inexpensive wines, decent coffee, good informal stripped-stone restaurant with often exotic freshly cooked food inc authentic Goan dishes; remote setting down narrow lane, big safe garden with ducks on millpond, extensive wood behind *(Andy Jones, Ken and Jenny Simmonds, Jack and Gemima Valiant)*

Fishguard [The Square, Upper Town – OS Sheet 157 map ref 958370; SM9537], *Royal Oak*: Busy but well organised, with low-beamed long narrow front bar, woodburner and pictures commemorating defeat here of second-last attempted French invasion, steps down to big picture-window dining extension, decent food, well kept Bass, Hancocks HB and Worthington *(Peter Lewis, Phil and Heidi Cook)*

Goodwick [Goodwick Sq; SM9438], *Rose & Crown*: Good crab salad and sandwiches in basic friendly pub with big back sea-view dining room *(Simon Watkins)*

Haverfordwest [Old Quay, Quay St; from A40 E, keep left after crossing river, then first left; SM9515], *Bristol Trader*: In lovely waterside setting, much modernised but still darkly old-fashioned, with friendly service, cheap generous home-made lunchtime food, good choice of well kept ales, decent malt whiskies, CD juke box; children allowed if well behaved, tables out overlooking water; open all day Fri, Sat *(Steve Thomas, LYM)*

Lamphey [SN0100], *Dial*: Good varied home-made food, Bass, Hancocks HB and guest beer, good value house wine, big public bar, family room, games room and eating area, friendly attentive staff *(T L Rees)*

✩ **Little Haven** [off B4341 W of Haverfordwest; SM8512], *Castle*: New management doing well in pub well placed by green looking over sandy bay, good food inc fresh local fish, well kept Worthington BB, quick friendly service, beams and stripped stone, big oak tables, castle prints, restaurant, outside seating; children welcome *(Tony Pounder, David and Nina Pugsley)*

✩ **Llanarthne** [B4300 E of Carmarthen; SN5320], *Golden Grove Arms*: Interestingly laid-out inn with roomy lounge, open fire, well kept ales inc local Crown Buckley BB and Rev James, huge choice of food inc some sophisticated dishes, very pleasant prompt service, children's play area; many Welsh-speaking customers, Tues folk night; bedrooms *(Anne Morris, Tom Evans, R B Mowbray, LYM)*

✩ **Llanarthne** [B4300], *Paxton*: Enthusiast new licensees have introduced an element of control (and more reliable opening hours) without losing the wackily unrestrained decor of the back bar; dim lighting, cosy friendly atmosphere, two cats, lots of bric-a-brac, more sober restaurant, helpful service, wide choice of generous bar food, well kept Crown Buckley, farm cider, decent malt whiskies; folk, jazz and blues nights; opp wood leading to Paxtons Tower (NT); open all day w/e *(Jack and Gemima Valiant, Howard James, Lynda Payton, Sam Samuells, PB)*

Llanddarog [SN5016], *Butchers Arms*: Good generous home cooking from sandwiches up inc quite sophisticated daily specials, well kept Felinfoel Double Dragon and other ales tapped from the cask, tiny low-beamed central bar with woodburner, brasses and old photographs, two mainly dining areas off, friendly helpful staff; tables outside *(R B Mowbray)*; [just off A48], *White Hart*: Beautiful ancient stone-built thatched pub with heavy beams, lovely carved settles, Welsh tapestries and so forth; good popular food, restaurant area *(Miss J Reay, R B Mowbray)*

Llandeilo [Salem; unclassified rd N, off B4302; SN6226], *Angel*: Attractive open-plan food pub, busy and well run, with good home cooking, restaurant area, Felinfoel Double Dragon; tables outside, children's play area, lovely country setting; bedrooms *(Jack and Gemima Valiant, Mrs Wyn Churchill)*; *Castle*: Newly renovated, brewing its own very good value T Watkin beers, with other guest beers; big bar, several tidy rooms, good basic food, tables in spacious yard *(Jack and Gemima Valiant)*

Llandovery [Kings Rd; SN7634], *Castle*: Refurbished hotel next to castle ruins, with popular new bar, good straightforward food (not Sun evening), good friendly service; comfortable bedrooms, good walking *(Jenny and Brian Seller)*

✩ **Llandybie** [6 Llandeilo Rd; SN6115], *Red Lion*: Wide choice of generous fresh food inc good fish and Sun lunch in attractive inn's tastefully modernised, spacious and comfortable bar and restaurant; several well kept Whitbreads-related ales, local pictures for sale; bedrooms *(J A and R E Collins, Howard James, Jack and Gemima Valiant, R B Mowbray)*

Llangadog [Queens Sq; this is the Llangadog up towards Llandovery; SN7028], *Carpenters Arms*: Straightforward local with darts in bar, slightly plusher largeish lounge, pool room, good value snacks inc nice toasties, fair-priced T Watkin BB (from Castle in Llandeilo) and Worthington BB *(Jack and Gemima Valiant)*

Llangain [B4312 S of Carmarthen; SN3816], *Yr Derwyn*: Comfortable country pub next to golf course, decent bar food *(R B Mowbray)*

Llechryd [SN2144], *Carpenters Arms*: Village pub with huge range of reasonably priced bar food, well kept Hancocks HB *(D L Evans)*

Lydstep [SS0898], *Lydstep Inn*: Comfortable and appealing bar and clean, tidy family room; good home-made food, friendly service, well kept Tetleys and Worthington *(Brian and Anna Marsden, Mr and Mrs Blackbourn)*

Manorbier [SS0697], *Castle*: Friendly, special little place useful for coast path, open all day in summer, with idyllic tree-sheltered garden – home-made furniture, cottage flowers; old-fashioned atmospheric lounge, games room with pool, Scottish Courage and other ales, good home-made food inc sandwiches, vegetarian, seafood and children's; shame about all the minatory notices, and service hiccoughs *(Wendy, Liz and Ian Phillips)*

Mathry [Brynamlwg; off A487 Fishguard—St Davids; SM8732], *Farmers Arms*: Happy atmosphere and good food esp fresh local fish and seafood, fair prices, well kept Bass, Crown Buckley and Worthington; tables in small walled garden, safe for children, and has been open all day in summer: in winter much more of a village pub *(Mike Pugh)*

Meidrim [off B4298/A299, W of village; SN2820], *Maenllwyd*: Old-fashioned unspoilt pub with lounge like 1940s parlour, games room with darts and cards, no bar counter – well kept Crown Buckley from back room, friendly landlord; cl lunchtime and Sun *(Jack and Philip Paxton, Pete Baker)*

☆ **Narberth** [High St; SN1114], *Angel*: Newish landlord goes far and wide to track down interesting guest beers, food a cut above the usual, with very reasonable prices inc good value Sun lunch; very welcoming, with quick polite service *(Mike Pugh, R Swift)*

☆ **Nevern** [B4582; SN0840], *Trewern Arms*: Extended inn in lovely setting nr notable church and medieval bridge over River Nyfer, stripped-stone slate-floored bar, rafters hung with rural bric-a-brac, high-backed settles, plush banquettes, usually several well kept Whitbreads-related ales, usual bar food from sandwiches to steaks inc children's, separate lounge, restaurant, tables in pretty garden; loudish games room, lunchtime service can stop too promptly; comfortable bedrooms, big breakfast *(Jack and Gemima Valiant, Bill Hyett, J Giles Quick, LYM)*

Newport [East St; SN0539], *Llwyngwair Arms*: Friendly straightforward local with good food inc genuine Indian dishes (takeaways too), well kept Worthington and a cheap house beer, coal-effect fire, landlord as big as ever despite a sponsored slim, lots of rugby and rowing mementoes; copes well with the busy holiday season *(Michael*

Richards, Dr and Mrs S A Jones, J Lloyd Jones, Mr and Mrs T Savage)

Pembroke Dock [Diamond St; SM9603], *Station*: Converted railway station full of memorabilia; well kept real ales and live music *(Jack and Philip Paxton)*

Penally [Strawberry Lane; SS1199], *Cross*: Stunning views of Caldy Island from terrace, reasonable choice of food, friendly staff, Bass or Worthington BB *(Ian Phillips)*

☆ **Pont ar Gothi** [A40 6 miles E of Carmarthen; SN5021], *Cresselly Arms*: Cosy low-beamed restaurant overlooking river, step up to tiled bar area with fishing memorabilia and copper-topped tables around the edges, another step to relaxing lounge area with woodburner and TV; good value bar food, well kept Whitbreads-related ales, welcoming service, riverside walks *(Derek and Margaret Underwood, R B Mowbray, Howard James, Jack and Gemima Valiant, R M Richards)*

Pont ar Gothi, *Salutation*: Friendly traditional pub with promptly served plentiful bar food inc fish, game and good value Sun lunch, good veg, well kept Felinfoel Double Dragon, log fire, big settles in small flagstone-floored rooms, restaurant; bedrooms *(Jack and Gemima Valiant, Joan and Michel Hooper-Immins)*

Pontrhydygroes [SN7472], *Miners Arms*: Interesting mix of customers, decent bar food, well kept ales such as Hancocks HB and John Smiths; music nights *(Rob Thorley, Julia Turner)*

☆ **Porthgain** [off A487 at Croes-goch; SM8132], *Sloop*: Largely unspoilt pub in interesting village, close to old harbour; friendly relaxing local atmosphere, dark bare stone, alcoves, comfortably worn old furniture, nautical and wreck memorabilia, newer family/eating extension; well kept Felinfoel Double Dragon and Worthington, good value food (all day in summer) inc nice full crab sandwiches, lots of polite young staff, afternoon teas, tables outside *(Simon Watkins, Joan and Michel Hooper-Immins, Steve Thomas)*

Pwll [Bassett Terr; A484 W of Llanelli; SN4801], *Tafarn y Sospan*: A local favourite with welcoming Welsh atmosphere, wide range of bar and restaurant food, good choice of beers *(Steve Thomas)*

Rhosmaen [SN6424], *Plough*: Good value generous fresh bar food inc good puddings in lounge with picture-window views, well kept Bass, tiled front bar, separate less cheap popular restaurant; long-serving friendly licensees *(Jack and Gemima Valiant, LYM)*

Rosebush [SN0729], *Tafarn Sinc*: Good interesting atmosphere, good beer; reconditioned railway halt with life-size dummy passengers in big garden *(Jack and Gemima Valiant)*

☆ **Saundersfoot** [Wogan Terr; SN1304], *Royal Oak*: Friendly unspoilt local, well kept Bass, Boddingtons and Flowers Original, many dozen malt whiskies, no music or machines, two rooms used for tasty food esp fresh fish (booking advised in season), tables outside *(Rob Holt, Steve Turner)*

☆ **Solva** [Lower Solva; SM8024], *Cambrian Arms*: Attractive and interesting dining pub with pleasant atmosphere, popular bar food inc authentic pasta and huge mixed grill, decent Italian wines, well kept Tetleys-related ales, log fires; no dogs or children *(Dr G W Barnett, IHR, Dr D G Twyman, Simon Watkins)*

St Clears [SN2716], *Butchers Arms*: Cosy pub with new landlord, log fire with oven for roasting potatoes and chestnuts; Felinfoel beer *(P Manning)*

St Davids [Goat St; SM7525], *Farmers Arms*: Cheeful and busy genuine pub, good food and atmosphere, well kept Worthington BB, cathedral view from tables in tidy back garden *(N Gilbourne, Simon Watkins)*; [centre], *Old Cross*: Good basic food inc delicious ploughman's with local cheese, sensible prices, polite service, genteel atmosphere, good position – get there before the tourist coaches arrive; pleasant garden, bedrooms *(IHR, Heather Martin, Miss E Evans)*

St Dogmaels [SN1645], *Ferry*: Old stone building with modern additions overlooking Teifi estuary, friendly character bar, pine tables, nice clutter of bric-a-brac inc many old advertising signs; Ansells and guest beers, generous bar food inc ploughman's with Welsh cheese, sandwiches inc devilled crab, restaurant, children welcome, tables out on terrace *(N P Smith, Mr and Mrs J R Morris, LYM)*

Talybont [SN6589], *Black Lion*: Substantial stone village inn with comfortably modernised back lounge, games in and off front public bar, decent bar food inc vegetarian, friendly staff, Bass, restaurant; seats in sheltered back garden; bedrooms *(Jack and Gemima Valiant, BB)*

Tenby [Upper Frog St; SN1300], *Five Arches*: Simple but clean, with some character, and some interesting specials inc local fish *(Michael Sargent)*; [Quay Hill], *Plantagenet House*: Unusual nicely renovated medieval building with marvellous old chimney, three floors with stripped stonework, tile and board floors, interesting food inc fine soups, fresh local crab and fish, Welsh cheeses; friendly service, Flowers Original and Wadworths 6X; fine Victorian lavatories; open all day in season, but cl lunchtime out of season, and local licensees have now ganged up to block its drinks licence – so alcohol only with food *(J A and R E Collins, Gordon Theaker, Lynda Payton, Sam Samuells)*

Trapp [now often spelled Trap; SN6518], *Cennen Arms*: Attractive small country pub by bridge, good choice of simple well cooked food, proper sandwiches, well priced Hancocks HB or Worthington BB, local pictures; picnic tables in small garden, pretty hanging baskets; nr Careg Cennen castle, good walks and lovely countryside *(Anne Morris, Jeff and Rhoda Collins)*

☆ **Wolfs Castle** [A40 Haverfordwest— Fishguard; SM9526], *Wolfe*: Wide choice of good popular home-made food (not Sun or Mon evenings in winter) in comfortable dining lounge, garden room and conservatory, well kept Flowers IPA and Original, decent wines, welcoming staff, attractively laid-out garden; simpler public bar with darts, restaurant; children welcome; bedrooms *(Peter Churchill, Ken and Jenny Simmonds)*

GLAMORGAN – MID

Caerphilly [Van Rd; ST1586], *Goodrich*: Big recently refurbished pub, darts, pool and machines in popular locals; bar, efficient service, good value food inc Sun lunch *(Emma Kingdon)*; [Groeswen, NW of town – OS Sheet 171 map ref 128869], *White Cross*: Two-bar stonebuilt pub with good atmosphere, well kept Theakstons and guest beers, good wholesome cheap food; dining room, games area, children welcome; weekend evening barbecues, play area *(S P Bobeldijk)*

☆ **nr Caerphilly** [Watford; Tongwynlais exit from M4 junction 32, then right just after church; ST1484], *Black Cock*: Big helpings of good value food from cheap snacks up in neat blue-plush bar with open fire in pretty tiled fireplace, and interesting brass-tabled public bar where children allowed; well kept Bass, happy atmosphere, friendly staff, sizeable terraced garden among trees with play area and barbecue, restaurant extension; up in the hills, just below Caerphilly Common *(Mrs B Sugarman, BB)*

☆ **Llangeinor** [nr Blackmill; SS9187], *Llangeinor Arms*: Comfortable partly 15th-c beamed pub with terrific views from front conservatory (children allowed here), left-hand lounge with old Welsh china and bygones, coal fire, friendly helpful staff, generous good value food, well kept Crown Buckley Rev James and Smiles Best, evening restaurant *(John and Joan Nash, LYM)*

Nant Ddu [Cwm Taf, A470 Merthyr Tydfil—Brecon; SO0015], *Nant Ddu Lodge*: Hotel doubling as restaurant and pub, very popular, with wide range of imaginative reasonably priced food; bright well equipped bedrooms, good walking country *(C Philip)*

Pontneddfechan [SN9007], *Angel*: Welcoming 16th-c inn handy for the waterfalls, well kept Bass and Boddingtons, nicely furnished flagstoned hikers' bar, tables laid for good value food in light and airy main bar; tables on terrace; bedrooms, good walks *(Salvo and Gwyneth Spadaro-Dutturi, John and Joan Nash)*

Pontsticil [above A465 N of Merthyr Tydfil; SO0511], *Butchers Arms*: Reasonably priced genuine home cooking inc local game and home-cured gammon, Boddingtons and Flowers IPA, raised dining area and hidden-away pool and games room, rugby match programmes on beams, welcoming service;

no dogs (there's a pub one); tables outside with stunning views inc mountain railway *(Gwen and Peter Andrews)*

Thornhill [A469 towards Caerphilly – OS Sheet 171 map ref 144846; ST1484], *Travellers Rest*: Carefully enlarged attractive old thatched pub with wide choice of food inc vegetarian, good veg, Hancocks HB, sensibly priced wine, good service even when busy, daily papers and magazines, huge fireplace in atmospheric low-ceilinged bar on right; other bars more modernised; tables out on grass; good walks with great views *(R Michael Richards)*

GLAMORGAN – SOUTH

Cardiff [10 Quay St], *City Arms*: Great atmosphere, warm welcome, Brains Bitter, Dark and SA kept to perfection, limited range of rolls – good sandwich shop virtually opp; perfect for Arms Park *(Andy and Jill Kassube)*; [St Marys St, nr Howells], *Cottage*: Popular for well kept Brains SA, Bitter and Dark Mild and good value home-cooked lunches, long bar with narrow frontage and back eating area, lots of polished wood and glass, good cheerful service, relaxed friendly atmosphere (even Fri/Sat when it's crowded; quiet other evenings), decent choice of wines; open all day *(Nicola Sheehy, Andy and Jill Kassube, Jack and Gemima Valiant)*; [Bute St], *Eli Jenkins*: Traditional-style ale house in regenerated docks area, well kept Hancocks HB, good range of reasonably priced bar food, good baguettes *(Alan Kilpatrick)*; [Merthyr Rd, Whitchurch; ST1580], *Plough*: Friendly three-bar local, skittle alley, well kept Brains, good value standard food; busy at lunchtime *(Rob Holt)*; [Schooner Way; follow Atlantic Wharf signs behind County Hall], *Wharf*: Big Victorian-look pub in pleasant largely residential setting by old dock, paddle-steamer prints and authentic nautical memorabilia downstairs, small lounge bar, maybe restaurant upstairs, family room tucked out like station platform, Brains and changing guest ales, lunchtime bar food; piped music can be noisy, local bands weekends, sometimes Thurs *(Joan and Michel Hooper-Immins, Jack and Gemima Valiant, Peter Neate)*

Colwinston [SS9475], *Sycamore*: Comfortable, with well kept ale *(David and Nina Pugsley)*

☆ **Cowbridge** [High St, signed off A48; SS9974], *Bear*: Neatly kept old coaching inn with Brains Bitter and SA, Hancocks HB, Worthington BB and a guest beer, decent house wines, friendly young bar staff, flagstones, panelling and big log fire in beamed bar on left, pool and pin table in back games area, quieter room with plush armchairs on right, log-effect gas fires, busy lunchtime for usual bar food from sandwiches up; children welcome; bedrooms quiet and comfortable, good breakfast *(Ian Williams, Linda Mar, David and Nina Pugsley, Mr and Mrs I Buckmaster, Pamela*

and Merlyn Horswell, LYM)

☆ **Craig Penllyn** [SS9777], *Barley Mow*: Welcoming, with good value food and well kept varied real ales; bedrooms comfortable *(David and Nina Pugsley)*

Dinas Powis [ST1571], *Cross Keys*: Well presented good cheap food, good atmosphere, no-smoking room *(David and Nina Pugsley)*; [Station Rd], *Star*: Well kept Brains and good choice of food inc fish in spacious well run four-room village pub, stripped stonework and attractive panelling, heavy Elizabethan beams, two open fires, plainer no-smoking room, juke box elsewhere; friendly licensees, cheerful locals, decent wines by the glass; best to book Sun lunch *(S Thomas, Jack and Gemima Valiant, LYM)*

Lisvane [Cherry Tree Cl, towards Thornhill; ST1883], *Old Cottage*: Old-style pub on edge of new housing estate, Tetleys-related ales, good range of bar and restaurant food; open all day; handy for Cefn Onn Park, lovely walks any time of year *(I J and N K Buckmaster)*

Llancadle [signed off B4265 Barry—Llantwit just E of St Athan; ST0368], *Green Dragon*: Attractively rebuilt after fire, traditional bar on left with hunting and other country prints, copper, china and harness, well kept Bass, Hancocks HB and an interesting guest beer, · friendly uniformed staff, maybe piped pop music; good value generous food, comfortably relaxed dining lounge on right with nice pictures; picnic tables on covered back terrace *(R B Mowbray, BB)*

☆ **Llancarfan** [signed off A4226; can also be reached from A48 from Bonvilston or B4265 via Llancadle; ST0570], *Fox & Hounds*: Prettily set dining pub by interesting church, streamside tables out behind; neat comfortably modernised open-plan bar rambling through arches, traditional settles and plush banquettes, coal fire, weekly changing real ale, bar food inc interesting dishes, candlelit bistro; children welcome; darts, fruit machine, unobtrusive piped music; open all day w/e, but may not always open some lunchtimes out of season *(R M Richards, David and Nina Pugsley, LYM)*

Llandaff [Cardiff Rd; A4119; ST1578], *Maltsters Arms*: Local atmosphere and lively chatty bustle in cheerful spaciously refurbished downstairs bar, more comfort upstairs, well kept Bass and Brains ales, good quick lunchtime food, reasonable prices; busy later with students and BBC people *(Miss E Evans, Pamela and Merlyn Horswell, BB)*

☆ **Monknash** [Marcross, Broughton sign off B4265 St Brides Major—Llantwit Major, then left at end of Water St; SS9270], *Plough & Harrow*: Unspoilt isolated country pub, welcoming and very basic – flagstones, old-fashioned stripped settles, logs burning in cavernous fireplace with huge side bread oven, simple choice of good value food inc vegetarian, up to six ales such as Bass, Hancocks HB, Worthington and maybe some from the Whitbreads family tapped from the cask, daily papers, children welcome; pool, juke box and fruit machine in room on left, unrestored gents'; picnic tables on grass outside the white cottage *(RMR, BB)*

Penllyn [village signposted from A48 Cowbridge—Bridgend; SS9776], *Red Fox*: Good choice of real ales, bargain pub lunches, obliging service, evening restaurant *(David and Nina Pugsley, BB)*

☆ **Sigingstone** [off B4270 S of Cowbridge; SS9771], *Victoria*: Friendly and spotless neo-Victorian country pub/restaurant with quickly served good value food inc nice veg, good upstairs restaurant, well kept Bass (though not the sort of place to go to for just a drink), pleasant surroundings, good service *(James Young, David and Nina Pugsley)*

GLAMORGAN – WEST

Bishopston [opp Joiners Arms; SS5789], *Valley*: Much enlarged, but keeps old style with wood partitions, beams and stencilled rough plasterwork; Hancocks HB and Worthington, good value sizzling menu, friendly helpful staff; children welcome *(the Sandy family)*

Gowerton [2 Mount St; by traffic lights junction B4296/B4295; SS5896], *Welcome to Gower*: Friendly and comfortable, with long plush bar with lots of banquettes, big panelled dining room, helpful staff, good value bar food inc children's and good range of pizzas, Crown Buckley Best, Rev James and Black Prince *(Michael Sandy)*

☆ **Kittle** [18 Pennard Rd; SS5789], *Beaufort Arms*: Attractive old pub below ancient chestnut tree, plenty of character in carefully renovated saloon with low beams and dark walls, comfortably cushioned settles, shortish choice of good food esp fresh fish, also sandwiches, quick friendly service, well kept Crown Buckley Best and Rev James with a summer guest beer, small family area, TV in public bar, restaurant *(Michael Sandy)*

Llanmadoc [the Gower, nr Whiteford Burrows – NT; SS4393], *Britannia*: Lovely setting with fine estuary views from good gardens and terrace with good play area, donkeys, ducks, geese and aviary; low beams, flagstones, well kept Courage Navigator and Marstons Pedigree, big helpings of usual decent food (styrofoam trays to keep it warm outside), friendly service, old-fashioned lounge bar up steps, games bar; piped music, cl lunchtime Tues/Weds, open all day Fri/Sat *(Michael and Alison Sandy)*

☆ **Oldwalls** [SS4891], *Greyhound*: Good value food inc unusual starters, local fish and ploughman's with choice of Welsh cheeses in busy but spacious and comfortable beamed and dark-panelled lounge bar, half a dozen well kept ales, some tapped from the cask, inc Bass and Hancocks HB, good coffee inc decaf, decent wine, roaring coal or log fires, friendly service; back bar with display cases; restaurant popular at weekends, folk club Sun; big tree-shaded garden with play area

and good views *(Richard Startup, Jason Caulkin, R B Mowbray)*

Parkmill [A4118; SS5589], *Gower*: Roomy beamed pub in nice wooded area, long plush lounge, no-smoking eating area up steps, walkers' bar with pool and boot store, good quick service, good range of bar food inc vegetarian and children's, Bass and Hancocks HB; quiet piped music; picnic tables on big terrace with play area, open all day in summer *(Michael Sandy, R B Mowbray)*

Penclawdd [Berthlwyd; B4295 towards Gowerton; SS5495], *Berthlwyd*: Fine estuary views from plush fairly modern open-plan pub with Bass, Worthington and Felinfoel Double Dragon, settles in restaurant end, helpful staff, seats on hillside lawn by road *(Michael Sandy)*

Penllergaer [handy for M4 junction 47; SS6199], *New Inn*: Roomy extended pub with good value food *(R B Mowbray)*

Pontardawe [SN7204], *Pontardawe*: Small lively riverside pub owned by syndicate of locals; changing well kept beers, regular live music *(Jack and Gemima Valiant)*

☆ **Reynoldston** [Higher Green; SS4789], *King Arthur*: Prettily set overlooking green and common, in good walking country (discounts for YHA members), spacious stripped-stone bar with big log fire, rugs on floorboards, prints, warming pans, interesting displays eg bullets, delft shelf; pine tables in light airy restaurant, back games bar; popular food inc children's and lots of fresh fish, well kept Bass, Worthington and Felinfoel Double Dragon, cheerful staff, quiet piped music; back garden with adventure play area, seats out on common in front; bedrooms *(Michael Sandy, Dorothy and Leslie Pilson)*

Swansea [86 Kingsway; SS6593], *Potters Wheel*: Extremely long Wetherspoons pub broken up by seats and pillars, more tables on raised area; wide range of bar food all day, reasonably priced beers *(Michael Sandy)*; [Vivian Rd, Sketty (A4118/A4216); SS6292], *Vivian Arms*: Popular local with banquettes in big comfortable lounge, friendly service, good value weekday bar lunches cooked by landlady inc some interesting specials, Brains ales; tables out on gravel terrace *(Michael Sandy)*

Three Crosses [NW end; SS5694], *Poundffald*: Friendly 17th-c timbered local with lots of beams, old tables, horse tack, armchair lounge bar, separate dining room, Ansells Mild, Tetleys and Worthington, extensive cheap menu; cheerful efficient staff, quiz nights, tables on side terrace, small pretty garden *(Michael Sandy)*

West Cross [A4067 Mumbles—Swansea; SS6089], *West Cross*: Great view over Mumbles Bay, comfortably refurbished with steps up to glassed back extension and garden below by pedestrian/cycle way around Bay; good choice of usual pub food inc fine fish and chips, decent range of beers *(R B Mowbray)*

GWENT

☆ **Abergavenny** [Mkt St; SO3014], *Greyhound*:
Warm hospitable dining pub (not a place for
just a drink), interesting food at sensible
prices, Boddingtons, decent wines, good
service, comfortable friendly surroundings;
good evening meals – more restauranty then
*(Mrs Linda Bonnell, Pamela and Merlyn
Horswell)*

Abergavenny [Flannel St], *Hen & Chickens*:
Small well worn traditional local just bought
by Brains but with Bass too, basic wholesome
cheap lunchtime food (not Sun; shame about
all the young smokers), friendly staff, popular
darts, cards and dominoes *(Pete Baker)*;
[Raglan Rd, Hardwick (B4598, 2 miles E)],
Horse & Jockey: Good range of well
presented reasonably priced food inc popular
salad bar in well furnished and attractive
three-room pub, nice family room, well kept
Bass and well stocked bar, good staff; big
(Pamela and Merlyn Horswell); [Castle St],
Kings Arms: Popular and welcoming, small
but one part is no smoking; good choice of
good value generous food esp salads *(Shirley
Pielou)*; [B4598, 3 miles E], *Lamb & Flag*:
Generous good value food in big relaxed
lounge bar or two dining rooms, well kept
Brains Bitter and SA, good service; children
welcome, high chairs; open all day in
summer, country views – tables outside with
play area; comfortable bedrooms *(Joan and
Michel Hooper-Immins)*; [Brecon Rd (A40
halfway to Crickhowell)], *Llanwenarth
Arms*: Beautifully placed 16th-c riverside inn
with views of hills, good restaurant, several
real ales, conservatory; 18 well equipped
bedrooms *(Margaret and Nigel Dennis,
Pamela and Merlyn Horswell)*

Caerleon [Llanhennock, N; ST3592],
Wheatsheaf: Ancient-seeming pub with
country views, cosy and friendly bar and
snug, good collection of small plates and
mugs, three well kept beers inc Bass, good
value food (not weekend evenings or Sun
lunchtime); children welcome, tables in
garden with ducks, cat and play hut *(A R and
B E Sayer, Christopher Gallop, Emma
Kingdon, Ian Williams, Linda Mar)*

○ **Clydach** [Old Black Rock Rd, signed off
A465; SO2213], *Rock & Fountain*: Good
generous fresh food inc vegetarian, unusual
bar with integral rock 'waterfall' in big plush
dining area, lovely mountainside spot, very
welcoming owners, well kept Bass, Brains
and Theakstons; dogs and children welcome,
good value clean bedrooms, good traditional
breakfast *(John and Elisabeth Cox, Gwyneth
and Salvo Spadaro-Dutturi, BB)*

Clydach, *Drum & Monkey*: Old pub in
scenic spot, cheerful helpful staff, good rather
upmarket reasonably priced food in pretty
bar and restaurant, real ale *(A R and B E
Sayer, Margaret and Nigel Dennis)*

Grosmont [SO4024], *Angel*: Simple friendly
17th-c village pub on attractive steep single
street, seats out by ancient market hall, not
far from castle and 13th-c church; welcoming

atmosphere, well kept Crown Buckley *(Neil
and Anita Christopher, BB)*

Llandenny [SO4104], *Raglan Arms*:
Renovated village pub, real fire, Italian chef
doing good food inc unusual dishes, pasta
and steaks, three well kept real ales,
conservatory restaurant *(Colin Mansell)*

Llanfihangel Crucorney [Pandy; A465 N of
Llanfihangel; SO3321], *Pandy*: Keen
interested new licensees, interesting beers,
straightforward food *(Pamela and Merlyn
Horswell)*

☆ **Llantarnam** [Newport Rd (A4042 N of M4
junction 26); ST3093], *Greenhouse*:
Welcoming and roomy, lots of dark wood,
big civilised good value dining room (children
welcome, anything from good sandwiches to
kangaroo), well kept Scottish Courage ales,
beautiful big tree-sheltered garden with
terrace and play area *(the Sandy family,
George and Brenda Jones)*

☆ **Llanthony** [off A465, back rd Llanvihangel-
Crucorney—Hay; SO2928], *Abbey Hotel*:
Enchanting peaceful setting in border hills,
lawns among Norman abbey's graceful ruins;
basic dim-lit vaulted flagstoned crypt bar,
well kept Bass, Flowers Original, Ruddles
County and Wadworths 6X, farm cider in
summer, simple lunchtime bar food, no
children; occasional live music, open all day
Sat (and Sun in summer); in winter cl Sun
evening and weekdays exc Fri evening;
bedrooms *(R C Hopton, Jack and Gemima
Valiant, Wayne Brindle, LYM)*

☆ **Llantilio Crosseny** [signed off B4233
Monmouth—Abergavenny; SO3915],
Hostry: Flagstones and grey carpet, bowed
Tudor beams, traditional pubby bar
furnishings, some stripped stonework, guns
above one fireplace, Rolls-Royce cigar cards,
neat dining room, good home cooking inc
wide vegetarian choice and good value Sun
lunch, well kept ales such as Wye Valley,
table skittles; children welcome; bedrooms
comfortable – very quiet village *(A R and E B
Sayer, Warren Marsh, Karen Burgess, Dylan
Hawkings, BB)*

☆ **Llantrisant** [off A449; ST3997], *Greyhound*:
Good hill views from largeish busy country
pub, attractive and prettily set, with well
presented reasonably priced reliable home-
cooked bar food inc vegetarian, spacious
open-plan rooms, friendly service; gardens
attractive even in winter, good bedrooms in
small attached motel *(B Adams, George and
Brenda Jones, Malcolm Taylor, A R and B E
Sayer)*

☆ **Llanvapley** [B4223 Abergavenny—
Monmouth; SO3714], *Red Hart*: Friendly
country local, neat and clean, with good log
fire, well kept Bass, Hancocks HB and guest
beers such as Smiles Best and Wye Valley,
stripped stone walls with copper and china
plates, sizeable plush dining room, separate
pool room, chatty landlord; picnic tables on
sloping back lawn and terrace, nice spot by
cricket pitch in interesting village with Saxon
church *(Alan Baird, A R and B E Sayer, BB)*

Mamhilad [¼ mile N; SO3004], *Horseshoe*: Pleasant roomy bar with well kept Brains and Felinfoel, lots of malt whiskies, friendly landlord, good fresh ploughman's and well cooked main dishes, good service; lovely views, particularly from tables by car park over road; play area *(Warren Marsh)*

☆ **Monmouth** [Agincourt Sq; SO5113], *Punch House*: 17th-c market-town pub with relaxed and chatty open-plan beamed bar, red leatherette settles, old bound *Punch* volumes (even the dog is called Punch), big fireplace, no-smoking area; generous straightforward food inc four roasts, prompt friendly service, well kept Bass, Hancocks HB, Wadworths 6X and Worthington Best, decent wines; restaurant, tables out on cobbles overlooking square; children in eating area, occasional live entertainment, open all day (exc Sun afternoon) *(Joan and Michel Hooper-Immins, Pamela and Merlyn Horswell, Colin Laffan, Daren Haines, LYM)*

☆ **Monmouth** [Lydart; B4293 towards Trelleck; SO5009], *Gockett*: Cavernously extended country pub with hops in rafters of light and airy room on left, houseplants, sliding doors to pleasant garden, no-smoking dining room with low beams, some stripped stone, coaching prints and log fire, enjoyable generous efficiently served food inc interesting dishes, Bass and Eldridge Pope Hardy Country; children welcome; bedrooms with own bathrooms, good breakfast *(Rev A Nunnerley, R T and J C Moggridge, LM, BB)*

Nantyderry [between A4042 and B4598 (former A471), N of Pontypool and Usk – OS Sheet 161 map ref 332061; SO3306], *Foxhunter*: Comfortable and busy country pub with wide range of good food inc vegetarian in bar and restaurant, well kept Bass and other ales, reasonable prices, quick service, spotless housekeeping; good garden with fountain, lawn and swing *(M E Tennick, Pamela and Merlyn Horswell)*

Newbridge on Usk [ST3894], *New Bridge*: Character comfortably worn-in pub with good reasonably priced food, friendly staff, restaurant *(Malcolm Taylor)*

Parkhouse [SO5003], *Parkhouse*: Good traditional steak place with huge choice of mustards, old-fashioned homely pub in beautiful location with lovely views; very child-friendly, good ploughman's too *(Sarah Evans)*

Shirenewton [village signed off B4235 just W of Chepstow; ST4893], *Tredegar Arms*: Comfortable sofa and chairs in tastefully chintzy lounge bar with big bay window, good choice of food (booking advised w/e), well kept changing guest beers, good choice of malt whiskies, cheerful staff, interesting sugar-tongs collection; games in public bar, seats outside; children in eating area; good value bedrooms *(Emma Kingdon, LYM)*

Skenfrith [SO4520], *Bell*: Basic village local in beautiful setting by bridge over River Monnow, good value standard bar food, pleasant garden, games room with pool and darts, big old fireplace with flame-effect fire *(Neil and Anita Christopher)*

The Narth [off B4293 Trelleck—Monmouth; SO5206], *Trekkers*: Unusual and welcoming, esp for children, like a log cabin high in valley, lots of wood with central fireplace, helpful licensee, good generous food inc fun ice creams, good range of well kept ales inc Felinfoel, facilities for the disabled; dogs, long back garden, skittle alley *(LM, Margaret and Nigel Dennis)*

Tintern [Devauden Rd; off A446 Chepstow-Monmouth about ¼ mile W of main village; SO5301], *Cherry Tree*: Quaint unspoilt country pub in quiet spot by tiny stream, steps up to simple front room, well kept Hancocks HB and farm cider, cards and dominoes, bar billiards in second room, charming garden; children welcome *(Pete Baker, Paul and Heather Bettesworth)*; [A466], *Moon & Sixpence*: Good value food and well kept ale in attractively furnished small pub, friendly service, natural spring feeding indoor goldfish pool, pleasantly soft piped music; tiny windows, but nice view over River Wye *(Dennis Heatley, Mike and Mary Carter)*

Trelleck [B4293 6 miles S of Monmouth; SO5005], *Lion*: Clean and comfortable country pub, welcoming newish licensees (now open lunchtimes too), unpretentious lounge bar, wide choice of good food inc good value Sun lunch, three well kept ales, good service *(Mrs B Sugarman, Paul and Heather Bettesworth)*

☆ **Trelleck Grange** [minor rd St Arvans—Trelleck; SO4902], *Fountain*: Tucked away on a back road through quiet countryside, unassuming inn with well kept Boddingtons and Wadworths 6X in cheerful dark-beamed bar, roomy and comfortable dining room, popular food from good fresh sandwiches to good value Sun lunch and Fri fish night; service friendly if not always swift, maybe nostalgic piped pop music, darts, decent malt whiskies and wines; children allowed away from bar, small sheltered garden with summer kids' bar; bedrooms *(Pat and John Millward, LM, BB)*

☆ **Usk** [The Square; SO3801], *Nags Head*: Relaxed beamed main bar with lots of brassware, old saws and other rustic artefacts, tables set for food (drinkers tend to head for the back bar), welcoming family service, well kept Brains and Crown Buckley, wide choice of generous food inc home-made pies, Usk salmon and game in season *(LM, Dr and Mrs A K Clarke, David and Nina Pugsley, Malcolm Taylor, A E Brace, June and Peter Gregory, Mike Pugh)*

Usk [The Square], *Castle*: Useful for food all day, with generous helpings and Whitbreads-related ales *(Anne Morris, Mike Pugh)*; [Bridge St], *Cross Keys*: Small, friendly little pub dating from 14th c, oak beams, log fire, well presented food, good range of drinks *(A E Brace)*; [1 Chepstow Rd], *Greyhound*: Neat, tidy and very welcoming, well kept changing ales such as Hardington, Smiles and Wye Valley, generous tasty food at fair prices; a place women feel comfortable in *(Mike Pugh)*

GWYNEDD

Aberdovey [SN6296], *Britannia*: Great harbour and distant mountain views from upstairs bar with balcony; good value generous food, friendly bustle, well kept Bass, good service, children in side room *(Mark Percy, Lesley Mayoh)*

Barmouth [Church St; SH6116], *Last*: Welcoming 15th-c harbourside local behind modern facade; low beams, flagstones, nautical bric-a-brac, little waterfall down back bar's natural rock wall, wide choice of good cheap bar lunches inc vegetarian, well kept Marstons Pedigree, friendly service; roadside tables overlooking harbour and bay *(Joan and Michel Hooper-Immins)*

Barmouth [St Annes Pl], *Tal-y-Don*: Welcoming comfortably worn two-bar Burtonwood pub, well kept Bitter and Mild served through sparkler, good simple bar food, good service, restaurant inc speciality steaks; open all day in summer; bedrooms good value *(John Baker)*

Beddgelert [A498 N of Porthmadog; SH5948], *Prince Llewelyn*: Plush hotel bar with log fire and raised dining area, simpler summer bar, good atmosphere, quick helpful service, wide choice of good value generous bar food, well kept Robinsons, rustic seats on verandah overlooking village stream and hills – great walking country; busy at peak holiday times, children allowed at quiet times; bedrooms pleasant, with good breakfast *(R Morgan, Howard James, BB)*

Beddgelert, *Tanronen*: Recently refurbished comfortable hotel bar, with decent food, attentive staff, Robinsons; good bedrooms overlooking river across road, or fields and mountains behind *(Gordon Theaker, BB)*

Betws y Coed [A5; SH7956], *Royal Oak*: Much more hotel than pub, but good interesting food esp local fish in civilised grill room, more upmarket restaurant and big side stables bar with pool, juke box and TV one end, no-smoking eating area the other; reasonable prices, Whitbreads-related ales, friendly staff; lots of tables out in courtyard, open all day; bedrooms *(E G Parish, Jack and Gemima Valiant, G S and E M Dorey, Roger Byrne)*

Betws y Coed [A5 next to BP garage and Little Chef], *Waterloo*: Wide choice of well served generous food, even mountain mutton sometimes; pleasant efficient service, spotless housekeeping, no piped music, no smokers; bedrooms *(KC)*

Bontddu [SH6719], *Half Way*: Good fresh food esp fish, beautifully served *(D W Jones-Williams)*

Bontnewydd [A487 S of Caernarfon; SH4860], *Newborough Arms*: Welcoming comfortable local with increasing emphasis on food (curries tipped), well kept

Burtonwood and other ales, fair range of decent food, dining room; juke box; enclosed back garden, bedrooms *(M Mason, D Thompson, E Evans)*

☆ **Capel Curig** [A5 W of Betws y Coed; SH7258], *Bryn Tyrch*: Walkers' and climbers' pub in lovely setting, hearty food with great vegetarian emphasis, well kept ales such as Marstons Pedigree and Whitbreads Castle Eden, organic country wines, cheery young staff, cosy pleasantly informal beamed bar with old pews and faded leather easy chairs, good atmosphere, big restaurant; basic good value bedrooms most with mountain views, huge brakfast *(Neville and Sarah Hargreaves, S P Watkin, P A Taylor, HJ, M Mason, D Thompson)*

☆ **Capel Curig**, *Cobdens*: Civilised yet relaxed and friendly, with good varied satisfying food inc home-made bread and interesting vegetarian dishes, sensible prices, well kept local Cambrian and Scottish Courage beers, good pleasant service, fine easy mix of locals, visitors, children, babies, friendly old english sheepdog and border collie cross; so close to mountain that back bar has bare rockface, lovely river scene across road, good walks all around; bedrooms *(Mike Pugh, N Gilbourne, Jack and Gemima Valiant)*

☆ **Capel Garmon** [signed from A470 just outside Betwys y Coed, towards Llanrwst; SH8255], *White Horse*: Dark-beamed inn dating from 16th c, comfortable and homely, with log fires, well kept Bass, Stones and Worthington BB, wide choice of food, good amiable service even when very busy, prettily refurbished cottage restaurant, games in public bar; bedrooms small and simple but comfortable (quietest in new part), fine countryside with magnificent views *(KC)*

☆ **Dinas Mawddwy** [just off A470; SH8615], *Llew Coch*: Genuine country local with charming timbered front bar dripping with sparkling brasses, well kept Bass, quick friendly service, cheap cheerful food inc trout or salmon from River Dovey just behind; plainer inner family room lively with video games, pool and Sat evening live music, lounge extension (open at busy times), good wheelchair access, tables out on quiet lane; surrounded by steep fir forests, good walks *(KB, DH, Howard James, Richard Lewis)*

Ganllwyd [SH7224], *Tyn-y-Groes*: Friendly old inn owned by NT in lovely Snowdonia setting, fine forest views, old-fashioned furnishings in partly panelled lounge, well kept Felinfoel and Whitbreads-related ales, quite a few malt whiskies, good choice of reasonably priced food, no-smoking restaurant, public bar with games; may not open till 7 evenings; comfortable well equipped bedrooms, salmon and seatrout fishing, good walks *(Amanda and Simon Southwell, LYM)*

Llanbedr [A496; SH5827], *Victoria*: Riverside pub geared to lots of summer visitors, big refurbished lounge (has kept old-fashioned inglenook), useful choice of decent food from counter in dining area, well kept Robinsons Best from electric pump; attractive garden with big adventure slide; children welcome – even a nappies bin in ladies', bedrooms *(Dr M I Crichton, MHI, LYM)*

Llanbedrog [SH3332], *Glyn-y-Weddw*: Friendly and pleasant, with good choice of attractively presented food, good quick service, tables on terrace, garden *(Joan Hilditch)*

Llanbedrog [Bryn-y-Gro, B4413; SH3332], *Ship*: Extended refurbished pub with thriving atmosphere, well kept Burtonwood, lively simple front family lounge, good range of popular straightforward food; good outside seating area *(Thomas, Suzanne and Therese Schulz, LYM)*

Llandudno [Conway Rd; SH7881], *Links*: Friendly family service, wide choice of food inc bargain w/e carvery and children's dishes (high chairs available), well kept Lees, lounge, middle bar and roomy suntrap conservatory; outdoor play area, quiz nights, disabled facilities; bedrooms *(Richard Lewis)*

☆ **Llandwrog** [aka Ty'n Llan; ½ mile W of A499 S of Caernarfon; SH4456], *Harp*: Attractive pub in pretty village, friendly and welcoming, with happy staff, good value food inc Sun roast, well kept Whitbreads-related real ales, comfortable straightforward furnishings; good bedrooms *(M A Cameron, Mr and Mrs R Head, Douglas and Jean Troup)*

Llanuwchllyn [aka The Eagles; SH8731], *Eryrod*: Good food, well kept beer, reasonable prices, very friendly atmosphere, panoramic view of mountains with Lake Bala in distance *(Mr and Mrs J O Hicks)*

☆ **Penmaenpool** [A493 W of Dolgellau; SH6918], *George III*: Attractive inn with cheery 17th-c beamed and flagstoned bottom bar and civilised partly panelled upstairs bar opening into cosy and chintzy inglenook lounge; lovely views over Mawddach estuary, sheltered terrace, good walks; good interesting though unpretentious food in bar and restaurant, courteous hard-working staff, Scottish Courage ales under light CO_2 blanket, good choice of wines by the glass, children in eating area, open all day; good bedrooms inc some in interesting conversion of former station on disused line *(Miss E Evans, Philip Campness, Rosie Davies, Peter and Sarah Gooderham, Patrick Freeman, Sharon Hancock, LYM)*

☆ **Porth Dinllaen** [beach car park signed from Morfa Nefyn, then a good 15-min walk – which is part of the attraction; SH2741], *Ty Coch*: Right on curving beach, far from the roads, with stunning view along coast to mountains; pub itself full of attractive salvage and RNLI memorabilia; keg beer, decent coffee, usual food; may be closed much of winter, but open all day summer – on a hot still day this is an idyllic spot *(DC, LYM)*

☆ **Porthmadog** [aka Y Llong; Lombard St, behind playing fields in centre, nr harbour; SH5639], *Ship*: Cosy and relaxed backstreet local with wide choice of mostly fresh generous nicely cooked bar food inc Chinese, popular upstairs evening Cantonese restaurant, well kept ales such as Cambrian and Tetleys, beer festival early Oct; huge open fireplace in lounge (mainly eating in here), masses of ship prints, long comfortable public bar, Welsh-speaking regulars; children may be allowed in small back room with video games/fruit machines, beyond pool room *(Peter and Anne Hollindale, Tony Hobden, J C T Tan)*

Rhyd Ddu [A4085 N of Beddgelert; SH5753], *Cwellyn Arms*: More eatery than pub, popular with Snowdon walkers for good generous sensibly priced food inc vegetarian – anything from bar snacks to ostrich, emu, kangaroo, buffalo, crocodile or alligator; lots of real ales inc Bass, Worthington, Shepherd Neame Spitfire, flagstones, log fire in huge ancient fireplace, small games bar with pool, darts and TV; children and walkers welcome, fine Snowdon views from garden tables with barbecue, babbling stream just over wall, big adventure playground; open all day Sun at least in summer *(Howard James, Mark Percy, Lesley Mayoh)*

Rhydymain [A494 2 miles NE; SH7922], *Hywel Dda*: Isolated stone roadside inn with good views over mountains opp, comfortable front lounge, bigger back dining room (with DJ equipment), Websters ale, side room with pool table, small roadside garden *(Brian and Anna Marsden)*

☆ **Tal y Cafn** [A470 Conway—Llanrwst; SH7972], *Tal y Cafn*: Handy for Bodnant Gardens, cheerful and comfortable lounge bar with big inglenook, good value satisfying food inc vegetarian, Greenalls beer, children welcome, seats in spacious garden; pleasant surroundings *(KC, Roger Byrne, LYM)*

Talyllyn [SH7209], *Ty'n y Cornel*: Pleasant gloriously placed fishing inn with big lounge looking out over the lake, helpful service, good reasonably priced bar food, restaurant; decent bedrooms with own bathrooms *(W H and E Thomas, D W Jones-Williams)*

☆ **Tremadog** [off A487 just N of Porthmadog; SH5640], *Golden Fleece*: Busy stonebuilt inn on attractive square, friendly attentive staff, good value generous bar food inc vegetarian, well kept Bass, Mild and Marstons Pedigree, decent wines, cosy partly partitioned rambling beamed lounge with open fire, nice little snug, separate bistro (children allowed here and in small family room), games room, intriguing cellar bar, tables in sheltered inner courtyard; cl Sun *(E H and R F Warner, Tony Hobden, LYM)*

☆ **Tudweiliog** [Nefyn Rd; B4417, Lleyn Peninsula; SH2437], *Lion*: Cheerful village inn with wide choice of decent food inc well prepared vegetarian dishes and good puddings in bar and no-smoking family dining conservatory (small helpings for children); fast helpful service, well kept Boddingtons, Marstons Pedigree, Ruddles Best and Theakstons Best and Mild, lots of whiskies, games and juke box in lively public bar; pleasant garden, good value bedrooms *(Jack and Gemima Valiant, Mr and Mrs D J Brooks, Keith and Maureen Barnes, the Goldsons, LYM)*

POWYS

☆ **Abermule** [off A483 NE of Newtown; SO1594], *Abermule Inn*: Fine country inn now open all day under new but experienced licensees, good home cooking, well kept real ales inc a guest beer, garden with play area *(Paddy Moindrot)*

Berriew [SJ1801], *Lion*: Black and white timber-framed country inn in interesting attractive village, good home-cooked food in bar and restaurant, Bass and Worthington with guest beers such as Greene King and Shepherd Neame, decent house wines, fairly smart atmosphere, friendly attentive service, separate public bar; good bedrooms *(Peter Gooderham, John and Joan Wyatt)*

Bleddfa [A488 Knighton—Penybont; SO2168], *Hundred House*: Welcoming country local with comfortable and attractively furnished stripped-stone lounge bar, big inglenook log fire, enjoyable food, well kept Flowers Original and Worthington Best, big separate bar and games room – walkers welcome; tables in garden with barbecue, lovely countryside; bedrooms simple but comfortable, good breakfast *(G R Sunderland, Dorsan Baker, Graham and Karen Oddey)*

Bwlch [A40; SO1522], *New Inn*: Friendly, with welcoming fire in flagstoned bar, ales such as Crown Buckley Black Prince and Fullers London Pride; good walks *(John and Joan Nash)*

Caersws [SO0392], *Merton Arms*: Decent food, obliging service, garden with well spaced tables and play area; children welcome *(Dr W Wynne Willson)*

☆ **Carno** [A470 Newtown—Machynlleth; SN9697], *Aleppo Merchant*: Plushly modernised stripped stone bar, small lounge with open fire, unusual tapestries, no-smoking area, games in public bar, decent food from sandwiches to steaks, well kept Boddingtons, occasional guest beer, restaurant (well behaved children allowed here), tables in garden; piped music; good value comfortable bedrooms *(K Andrews, Mr and Mrs G M Pierce, Gerald Fleit, LYM)*

☆ **Crickhowell** [New Rd; SO2118], *Bridge End*: Chatty and darkly attractive roomy local in good spot by many-arched bridge over weir of river Usk, straightforward food, well kept Bass and Worthington BB; open all day *(Barry and Anne, David and Nina Pugsley)*

☆ **Derwenlas** [A487 Machynlleth—Aberystwyth; SN7299], *Black Lion*: Quaint but smart 16th-c country pub, huge log fire in low-beamed cottagey bar divided by oak posts and cartwheels, good home-cooked food inc vegetarian in dining area, well kept Boddingtons, decent wines, attentive service, unobtrusive piped music; garden up behind

with adventure playground and steps up into woods *(Peter and Sarah Gooderham, J A Collins)*

Dylife [off B4518 Llanidloes—Llanbrynmair – OS Sheet 135 map ref 863941; SN8694], *Star*: Cheerful pub, small, warm and cosy, in remote former 18th-c lead-mining village on mountain road; prompt friendly flexible service, wide choice of well priced food inc vegetarian; pool, darts *(Mrs F J Somervell)*

Four Crosses [SJ2718], *Golden Lion*: Good service, friendly welcome, Brains SA, lots of decorative crosses; good bedrooms with own bathrooms *(Roger Davey)*

Garthmyl [SO1999], *Nags Head*: Attractive brick house, simple inside, with generous usual food done well (even properly cured home-cooked ham for the sandwiches), helpful service, well kept Worthington BB, open fire in woodburner; handy for Montgomery Canal, good towpath walks *(Jack and Gemma Valiant)*

☆ **Gladestry** [B4594 W of Kington; SO2355], *Royal Oak*: Relaxing unpretentious beamed and flagstoned village pub handy for Offa's Dyke Path, friendly landlord, interesting locals, well kept Bass and Hancocks HB, low-priced claret, inexpensive simple home cooking; refurbished lounge, separate bar, children allowed, picnic tables in lovely secluded garden behind, safe for children; lunch opening 12-2; cheap well refurbished bedrooms, good breakfast *(David Gittins, Drs Sarah and Peter Gooderham, KB, DH, Geoffrey Lindley)*

☆ **Hay on Wye** [Castle St/Oxford Rd; SO2342], *Blue Boar*: Ancient stone building nr castle, beams and flagstones, chintzy sofas around central log fire, three lemon-painted linked rooms with floral fabrics and mix of chairs and settles around set tables, good value generous home-made lunchtime bar food from long buffet counter, also cakes and scones, thai evening meals (authentic but not cheap), lots of bric-a-brac, informal friendly atmosphere and service, well kept ales such as Bass, Boddingtons and Wadworths 6X, decent wines, good coffees and teas *(S Watkin, P Taylor, Nigel Woolliscroft, Gwyneth and Salvo Spadaro-Dutturi, Ian Williams, Linda Mar, Annette and Stephen Marsden, KB, DH, Sue Demont, Tim Barrow)*

☆ **Hay on Wye** [Bull Ring], *Kilvert Court*: Small well furnished hotel bar popular with young people, flagstones and candles, friendly staff, well kept Boddingtons and Whitbreads Castle Eden, decent house wines, good range of food in bar and restaurant; live music some Thurs, quiz Sun; outside tables overlooking small town square; bedrooms immaculate and well equipped *(Ian Williams, Linda Mar, Jack and Gemima Valiant, Sarah and Peter Gooderham)*

Hay on Wye [Broad St], *Three Tuns*: Charming old-fashioned pub with tiny quarry-tiled bar in one of Hay's oldest buildings, landlady knowledgeable about local history, wall benches, well kept ales tapped from the cask, Edwardian bar fittings, lots of bric-a-brac; no food *(Pat Eckley, KB, DH, Jack and Philip Paxton)*; [Lion St], *Wheatsheaf*: Beams strung with hops, nooks and crannies filled with bygones, log fire, attractively priced good home-made food, cheerful friendly staff *(Tracy Dawson, Dr and Mrs R Booth)*

Hundred House [SO1154], *Hundred House*: Attractive, clean and interesting pub full of curios, well kept Bass and Hancocks HB with interesting guest beers, good wine list, decent food, welcoming staff, small dining room, big garden with play area; children welcome *(Graham and Karen Oddey)*

Knighton [SO2972], *Horse & Jockey*: Good food and service, well kept John Smiths and Tetleys, friendly atmosphere, brasserie meals all day on Sun, tables in pleasant courtyard *(Gill and Maurice McMahon, Dave Braisted)*

Libanus [A470 SW of Brecon; SN9925], *Bull*: Popular local with well kept Hancocks HB, good value plain food, very friendly staff *(Dr G W Barnett, G W A Pearce)*

Llanbedr [nr Crickhowell; SO2420], *Red Lion*: Quaint old pub with log fires, well kept ales such as Felinfoel Double Dragon, attractive food, friendly licensees; tiny village in good walking country *(Gwyneth and Salvo Spadaro-Dutturi)*

Llanfihangel nant Melan [A44/A481; SO1858], *Fforest*: 16th-c pub with friendly and cosy lounge bar, beams and stripped stone, welcoming service, good value home cooking, good changing real ales; big restaurant in former cow byre; decent bedrooms *(Peter and Sarah Gooderham, Dr Peter Castaldi)*; [A44], *Red Lion*: Warm and friendly stripped-stone 16th-c inn, homely and old-fashioned, with eating area beyond standing timbers, good individual cooking at sensible prices, well kept Hook Norton, reasonably priced wines; comfortable simple chalet bedrooms *(Paul Catcheside)*

Llanfyllin [High St (A490); SJ1419], *Cain Valley*: Old coaching inn with welcoming helpful staff, decent food inc fresh veg and well kept beers in hotelish panelled lounge bar, good restaurant; handsome Jacobean staircase to comfortable bedrooms, good breakfast *(Martin Jones, KB, DH)*

☆ **Llangenny** [SO2417], *Dragons Head*: Charmingly set pub doing well under new owners, two-room bar with low beams, big log fire, pews, housekeeper's chairs and a high-backed settle among other seats, two charming restaurant areas, wide choice of good value home-made food, well kept real ales; tables in riverside garden *(John and Margaret Harvey, LYM)*

Llangorse [SO1327], *Castle*: Smallish stone pub with cosy and comfortable flagstoned main bar, side room set out more for eating; wide choice of good food to suit hungry walkers, well kept Brains SA and Dark, Crown Buckley and T Watkin real ales *(John Nash)*

☆ **Llangurig** [Pant Mawr; A44 Aberystwyth rd, 4½ miles W; SN8482], *Glansevern Arms*: Very civilised, by main road but quite alone up in the mountains – a fine place to stay, with big warm clean bedrooms; cushioned antique settles and log fire in high-beamed bar (used by locals too), well kept Bass and Worthington Dark Mild, decent malt whiskies and wines, lunchtime sandwiches and hot soup (not Sun) with maybe cold wild salmon in season; good value seven-course dinners (not Sun evening; must book, and courses served to fairly strict timing), comfortable residents' lounge *(G Nagle, Heather Martin, LYM)*

Llanwddyn [SJ0219], *Lake Vyrnwy*: Comfortable old-feeling well done newish pub extension alongside smart late 19th-c country hotel in remote beautiful spot, lake view from big-windowed blue-carpeted lounge and balcony, well kept Brains, wide range of food worth the wait at busy times, friendly staff, darts, quiet piped music; bedrooms *(Gwen and Peter Andrews)*

☆ **Llanwrtyd Wells** [The Square; SN8746], *Neuadd Arms*: Attractively rustic bar with bench seats and open fire, second carpeted corner bar with proper chairs and occasional live music, well kept ales inc Boddington, Felinfoel Double Dragon and Hancocks HB, very friendly staff, food inc vegetarian; beer festival Nov, various other events, attractive little town, good walking area, mountain bike hire; bedrooms pleasant and well equipped *(G Coates, Joan and Michel Hooper-Immins)*

☆ **Machynlleth** [Heol Pentrerhedyn; A489, nr junction with A487; SH7501], *White Lion*: Welcoming mix of locals and visitors in roomy rather hotelish bar with dark oak and copper-topped tables, dark pink plush seats, well kept Banks's Bitter and Mild and Marstons Pedigree, big log fire, wide range of food inc good vegetarian and children's choices, side dining area, service brisk and cheerful even on busy Weds market day; best to book for 3-course Sun lunch; pretty views from picnic tables in attractive back garden, some tables out by road too; neatly modernised stripped pine bedrooms *(Howard James, J B and C N Ennion, Mervyn and Zilpha Reed, M Joyner, PG)*

Middletown [A458 Welshpool—Shrewsbury; SJ3012], *Breidden*: Bright and spacious, with good value food inc good toasties and vegetarian choice, Whitbreads-related ales with an interesting guest beer such as Wood Hopping Mad; SkyTV sports can obtrude *(Joan and Michel Hooper-Immins)*

Montgomery [SO2296], *Crown*: Simple friendly local with just a couple of tables in lounge, really obliging service, food inc outstanding low-priced Sun lunch *(Basil Minson)*

☆ **Old Radnor** [SO2559], *Harp*: Superb peaceful hilltop position, with lovely views and good walks nearby (despite the quarries), fine inglenook and elderly seats in slate-floored lounge, stripped-stone public bar with a smaller log fire and old-fashioned settles, limited but generous bar food (not Mon), real ales inc Woods, decent wines, character dining room with antique curved settle and other high-backed seats, friendly service, three sleepy amiable cats; seats outside with play area, pleasant bedrooms, good breakfast *(Lynn Sharpless, Bob Eardley, Drs Sarah and Peter Gooderham, Graham and Karen Oddey, David Gittins, Chris and Tricia Hubbard, Peter and Lynn Brueton, G R Sunderland, LYM)*

Welshpool [High St; SJ2207], *Pheasant*: Town-centre pub, wide choice of changing real ales, reasonably priced bar food; open all day, small back terrace *(Paddy Moindrot)*; [Church St/Severn St], *Royal Oak*: Pleasant beamed and timbered bar with well spaced tables, good value food, well kept Boddingtons, Tetleys, Worthington and a Woods special brew, good value bar food, open fire, partly panelled restaurant; bedrooms *(Keith and Janet Morris)*

If a service charge is mentioned prominently on a menu or accommodation terms, you must pay it if service was satisfactory. If service is really bad you are legally entitled to refuse to pay some or all of the service charge as compensation for not getting the service you might reasonably have expected.

Channel Islands

On Guernsey, the two outstanding pubs are the Hougue du Pommier in Castel (with a new conservatory this year) and the Fleur du Jardin at Kings Mills (public bar redone this year; it has particularly good food); both are civilised places, in keeping with the island's restrained and relaxed appeal. Other really worthwhile places here (see Lucky Dip section at the end of the chapter) are the upgraded Happy Landings at Forest, Auberge Divette in St Martin and Ship & Crown in St Peter Port. Note that pubs on Guernsey close on Sundays. On Jersey, there's a much wider and generally pubbier choice. For an enjoyable evening meal out, the Rozel Bay Inn at Rozel stands out, with imaginative well presented food including fresh fish – it's our choice as Channel Islands Dining Pub of the Year. The Chambers in St Helier, open till very late, is a great place, with unusually cheap food. The Tipsy Toad Town House there has lost its microbrewery this year (in favour of more restaurant space); its beers – the cheapest we found on the island – now come from its very friendly companion pub, the Star & Tipsy Toad out at St Peter. Other places we particularly like outside St Helier are the Old Court House across the bay at St Aubin, and the quaint Old Smugglers down on Ouaisne Bay in St Brelade (good service even when really busy). Good family places are the Old Portelet in St Brelade, and Les Fontaines up in St John. In the Lucky Dip section, the Dolphin at Gorey and the Prince of Wales in St Helier stand out; as do the Georgian House at St Anne on Alderney, and the Dixcart Hotel on Sark. Although drinks prices are rising a bit more quickly than on the mainland, drinks are still comparatively very cheap out here – averaging 35p a pint less for beer than the typical mainland price.

CASTEL (Guernsey) Map 1
Hougue du Pommier 🛏️

Route de Hougue du Pommier, off Route de Carteret; just inland from Cobo Bay and Grandes Rocques

The oak-beamed bar at this calmly civilised and well equipped hotel is quite roomy, with leatherette armed chairs around wood tables, old game and sporting prints, guns, sporting trophies and so forth. The nicest seats are perhaps those in the snug area by the big stone fireplace with its attendant bellows and copper fire-irons. Pool, darts, dominoes, cribbage and maybe unobtrusive piped music; part of the bar is no-smoking. Good bar food is efficiently served by friendly staff and includes sandwiches (from £2.20), soup (£2.20), filled baguettes (from £2.80), cottage pie (£4.80), steak and kidney pie, mushroom stroganoff or smoked salmon and sour cream quiche (£4.80), pork and apple cobbler, scampi (£5.40) and fillet steak (£9.20); seven wines by the glass or bottle. A new conservatory with cane furniture overlooks fruit trees shading tables on the neatly trimmed lawn. There are more by the swimming pool in the sheltered walled garden, and in a shady flower-filled courtyard. Leisure facilities include a pitch-and-putt golf course and a putting green (for visitors as well as residents), and for residents there's free temporary membership to the Guernsey Indoor Green Bowling association (the stadium is next door and rated as one of the best in Europe); daily courtesy bus into town. No dogs.
(Recommended by R Davies, Bob and Maggie Atherton, Steve and Carolyn Harvey)

*Free house ~ Licensee Stephen Bone ~ Meals and snacks ~ Restaurant ~ (01481)
56531 ~ Children welcome ~ Singer/guitarist Fri evening ~ Open 11-2, 6-11.45; 12-
2.30 only Sun ~ Bedrooms: £44B/£88B*

GREVE DE LECQ (Jersey) OS583552 Map 1

Moulin de Lecq

This serenely placed black-shuttered old mill is a very proper pub with plenty of local
custom and a warm and pleasant atmosphere. Well kept Ann Street Ann's Treat and
Old Jersey and Guernsey Bitter on handpump. There's a good log fire, toasting you as
you come down the four steps into the cosy bar, as well as plush-cushioned black
wooden seats against the white-painted walls; piped music. Good generously served
bar food might include ploughman's (£3.50), steak and kidney pie (£4.95), rabbit
casserole in winter and summer barbecued tuna, shark and kebabs (all £5.25) and
king prawns in garlic (£6.95); Sunday roast in winter (£4.95). Most people eat in the
former granary upstairs. Service is welcoming and helpful. The massive restored
waterwheel still turns outside, with its formidable gears meshing in their stone housing
behind the bar. The terrace has picnic tables under cocktail parasols, and there's a
good children's adventure playground. The road past here leads down to pleasant
walks on one of the only north-coast beaches. *(Recommended by Sue Rowland, John Evans,
Steve and Carolyn Harvey, BB)*

*Ann Street ~ Manager Shaun Lynch ~ Real ale ~ Meals and snacks (12-2.15, 6-8.30,
not Sun eve) ~ (01534) 482818 ~ Children welcome ~ Open 11-11 (inc Sun)*

KINGS MILLS (Guernsey) Map 1

Fleur du Jardin 🍴 ⏱ 🛏

Kings Mills Rd

This old-fashioned inn with its own two acres of beautiful gardens is in one of the
prettiest spots on the island in a delightful conservation village. Picnic tables are
surrounded by flowering cherries, shrubs, colourful borders, bright hanging baskets,
and unusual flower barrels cut lengthwise rather than across. The cosy and sensitively
refurbished rooms have low-beamed ceilings and thick granite walls, a good log fire in
the friendly public bar which is still popular with locals, and individual country
furnishings in the lounge bar on the hotel side. As well as sandwiches (from £1.95, hot
chargrilled steak £4.95), soup (£3.75), crab cocktail (£4.95), steak, kidney and ale pie,
lasagne or chicken curry (£4.75), mushroom stroganoff (£4.95), lamb cutlets with
roast garlic and thyme sauce (£7.50) and sirloin steak with teriyaki sauce (£9.50) from
the menu there are several imaginative daily specials like whiting fillet on white wine
sauce (£7.25), duck breast with raspberry vinegar jus (£8.75), scallops and turbot on
creamed leeks (£11.25), and puddings like lemon parfait with raspberry coulis and
tiramisu with amaretto sauce (from £3.50). Well kept Guernsey Sunbeam and their
winter or summer ale on handpump, and maybe other guest beers, decent wines by the
glass or bottle; friendly efficient service; unobtrusive piped music. Part of the
restaurant is no smoking. *(Recommended by David and Jane Russell, R Davies, Bob and
Maggie Atherton, D J Underhill, Steve and Carolyn Harvey, J S Rutter, H K Dyson)*

*Free house ~ Licensee Keith Read ~ Real ale ~ Meals and snacks ~ Restaurant ~
(01481) 57996 ~ Children welcome ~ Open 11-3, 5-11.45; 12-3, 7-10.30 Sun ~
Bedrooms: £38.50B/£77B*

ROZEL (Jersey) Map 1

Rozel Bay Inn 🍴

Channel Islands Dining Pub of the Year

Booking is recommended at this idyllic little pub which has quickly built up a very
good reputation for the landlady's splendid cooking. Beautifully presented dishes
include sandwiches (from £1.35), tomato soup with smoked bacon (£1.75), rillettes of
duck with caramelised oranges (£2.75), ploughman's (£3.75), baked cod fillet with
bacon, thyme and red wine or chicken breast with buttered spinach and wild

mushrooms (£5.95). In the evening there are several more dishes like grilled pork cutlet with caramelised apples and madeira sauce (£9.95), salmon with chargrilled peppers and sun-dried tomato pesto (£10.95) as well as fresh catches of the day on the blackboard; three course Sunday lunch (£12). The pub is set on the edge of a sleepy little fishing village, just out of sight of the sea and the delightful harbour. Snug and cosy, the small dark-beamed back bar has an open fire, old prints and local pictures on its cream walls, dark plush wall seats and stools around tables. Leading off is a carpeted area with flowers on big solid square tables; darts, cribbage, dominoes and juke box in the games room. Well kept Bass on handpump. Award winning flower displays flank tables under cocktail parasols by the quiet lane, and there are more tables in the attractive steeply terraced hillside gardens behind. *(Recommended by Mr and Mrs D G Parry, Steve and Carolyn Harvey, Mrs D Benham)*

Randalls ~ Tenant Mrs Eve Bouchet ~ Real ale ~ Meals and snacks (not Sun evening or Mon) ~ (01534) 863438 ~ Children welcome till 9pm ~ Open 10(11 Sun)-11.30

ST AUBIN (Jersey) OS 607486 Map 1
Old Court House Inn 🛏

The conservatory at this charming 15th-c inn overlooks the tranquil harbour, with views stretching past St Aubin's fort right across the bay to St Helier. The front part of the building used to be the home of a wealthy merchant, whose cellars stored privateers' plunder alongside more legitimate cargo, while the restaurant still shows signs of its time as a courtroom. The three main bars are rather individual: upstairs the Mizzen Mast bar is elegantly (and cleverly) crafted as the aft cabin of a galleon, while the Westward bar is constructed from the actual gig of a schooner, with the ceiling made from old ship beams. The atmospheric main basement bar has cushioned pale wooden seats built against its stripped granite walls, low black beams and joists in a white ceiling, a turkey carpet and an open fire; it can get crowded and smoky at times. A dimly lantern-lit inner room has an illuminated rather brackish-looking deep well, and beyond that is a spacious cellar room open in summer. Reasonably priced bar food includes open sandwiches (from £2.60), ploughman's (from £3.75), pizzas (£3.95), lasagne (£4.75), moules marinières (£4.95), grilled prawns (£6.95), plaice (£8.95), dover sole (£13.95) and a huge seafood platter for two with a whole crab and lobster, and oysters, moules, whelks, winkles and gambas (£60); children's meals. Plenty more fresh fish in the restaurant. Well kept Marstons Pedigree and a guest like Morlands Old Speckled Hen or Wadworths 6X on handpump; cribbage, dominoes, Scrabble, chess, shut the box, piped music, and darts in winter. The bedrooms, individually decorated and furnished, are small but comfortable, and you might get one on the harbour front. *(Recommended by K G and J Archer, Steve and Carolyn Harvey)*

Free house ~ Licensee Jonty Sharp ~ Meals and snacks (not Sun evening) ~ Restaurant ~ (01534) 46433 ~ Children welcome till 9pm ~ Open 11am-11.30pm ~ Bedrooms: £40B/£80B

ST BRELADE (Jersey) OS 603472 Map 1
Old Portelet Inn

Portelet Bay

This characterful 17th-c clifftop farmhouse has been extensively redeveloped to be appealing to families and beach visitors. There's a sheltered cove right below which is reached by a long flight of steps with glorious views across Portelet (Jersey's most southerly bay) on the way down. The atmospheric low ceilinged, beamed downstairs bar has a stone bar counter on bare oak boards and quarry tiles, a huge open fire, gas lamps, old pictures, etched glass panels from France and a nice mixture of old wooden chairs. It opens into the big timber ceilinged family dining area, with standing timbers and plenty of highchairs. Outside there are picnic tables on the partly covered flower-bower terrace by a wishing well, with more in a sizeable landscaped garden with lots of scented stocks and other flowers (the piped music may follow you out here). Reliable bar food includes sandwiches (from £1.40), ploughman's (from £3.95), tuna and pasta bake, cannelloni or lasagne (£4.20), steak and mushroom pie, moules marinières or scampi (£4.95) poached salmon (£6.25) and daily specials; children's meals (including baby food), and Sunday cream teas. Friendly neatly dressed staff are quick and well drilled. Well kept Boddingtons and a guest like Marstons Pedigree under light blanket pressure, and reasonably priced house wine; plenty of board games in the wooden-floored loft bar. No-smoking areas, disabled and baby changing facilities, and a superior supervised children's play area (entrance £1); pool, dominoes, cribbage and board games. *(Recommended by Steve and Carolyn Harvey, John Evans, Sue Rowland)*

Randalls ~ Manageress Tina Lister ~ Real ale ~ Meals and snacks (12-2.10, 6-8.55) ~ (01534) 41899 ~ Children in family dining room ~ Live music most nights in summer, Fri night in winter ~ Open 10(11 Sun)-11

Old Smugglers

Ouaisne Bay; OS map reference 595476

Even on the days when this popular extended pub is really busy, the staff still remain calmly helpful and food is quickly served. It's in a pretty position overlooking Ouaisne Bay and Common, and was originally a pair of old fishermen's cottages. There's a genuinely relaxed, pubby atmosphere, as well as thick walls and black beams, open fires, and cosy black built-in settles. Two well kept real ales might include Bass and Ringwood Best on handpump; sensibly placed darts as well as cribbage. Bar food includes home-made soup (£1.60; local seafood chowder £2.20, filled baked potatoes (from £3.50), ploughman's (£3.35), burgers (from £3.95), steak and mushroom pie (£4.50), cod in beer batter (£5.20), ragoût of seafood with a herb and lemon sauce or chicken satay (£5.95), king prawns in various sauces like black bean (£7.50), and daily specials like thai beef or local lobster; children's menu (with a couple of puzzles). A room in the restaurant is no smoking. Close by are some attractive public gardens. *(Recommended by Sue Rowland, John Evans, Steve and Carolyn Harvey)*

Free house ~ Licensee Nigel Godfrey ~ Real ale ~ Meals and snacks (till 8 Sun evening) ~ Restaurant ~ (01534) 41510 ~ Children welcome till 9pm ~ Open 11am-11.30pm

ST HELIER (Jersey) Map 1

Admiral £

St James St

There are plenty of interesting bits and pieces at this big atmospheric candlelit pub. As well as dark wood panelling, attractive solid country furniture, and heavy beams – some of which are inscribed with famous quotations – there are old telephones, a clocking-in machine, copper milk churn, enamel advertising signs (many more in the small back courtyard which also has lots of old pub signs), and nice touches such as the daily papers to read and an old penny 'What the Butler Saw' machine. Bar food includes soup (£1.90), filled baked potatoes (from £2.75), half a spit-roast chicken (£3.95), scampi and salads (from £4), steak and onion pie (£4.25) and half a dozen daily specials; four course Sunday lunch (£7.95). Well kept Boddingtons on handpump; efficient, friendly staff; dominoes, cribbage and chess. There are plastic tables outside on a flagged terrace – quite a suntrap in summer. The pub is busier in the evenings, when it is well liked by a younger set. *(Recommended by Sue Rowland, Steve and Carolyn Harvey)*

Randells ~ Manager Joanna Dyke ~ Real ale ~ Meals and snacks (12-2, 6-8; not Fri or Sun evening or all day Sat) ~ (01534) 30095 ~ Children welcome till 8 ~ Open 11am-11.30pm; cl 25 Dec evening

Chambers £

Mulcaster Street

Well designed around a law-courts theme, this impressive place is partly divided into separate room areas with heavy beams (decorated with apt quotations), lots of imposing paintings, prints and mirrors, and a careful mixture of heavy dark wood furniture with more individual antique and ornate mahogany pieces, a clubby-feeling library room, and an oak-panelled room with deep leather armchairs and daily papers. Candlelit tables stand on bare boards and stone floors, and there are a couple of huge cut-glass chandeliers and gentle wall lamps. The massively long bar counter dispenses well kept Courage Directors, Marstons Pedigree and Theakstons XB and Old Peculier on hand or electric pump, decent wines. It's popular at lunchtime with local office workers attracted by the generous helpings of good value food, and with a lively spread of rather younger customers in the evenings – especially late on, with its hotel licence letting it stay open later than most competitors. But even at its loudest it always stays civilised, with a no-trainers rule after 7pm, and security staff at the door. Very reasonably priced bar food includes filled baked potatoes (from £2.50), salads (from £3.50), and daily specials like cream of onion and cheese soup (£1.95), chicken liver pâté (£2.15), lasagne, chilli, pepper, ham and cheese quiche or braised pork and honey sausages with onion gravy (£3.70), stir-fried beef in black bean sauce (£3.90) and roast leg of pork with honey and pepper sauce (£4.30). The neatly uniformed waistcoated staff are well drilled and hard-working. There is a separate gallery dining room up a few steps at the back. A few old penny slot machines cock a gentle snook at fruit-machine culture, and there are log-effect gas fires. *(Recommended by Steve and Carolyn Harvey)*

Randalls ~ Manager Stephen Jones ~ Real ale ~ Meals and snacks (12-2.30, 5.30-9.30) ~ Restaurant ~ (01534) 35405 ~ Supervised children welcome till 8pm ~ Live entertainment every evening ~ Open 11am-1am

Tipsy Toad Town House 🏴
New Street

The on-site microbrewery with its gleaming copperwork that used to fill the glass-windowed central room at this attractive 1930s corner building has been removed to make room for additional restaurant seating. The beers that were brewed here are now all brewed at its sister pub, the Star & Tipsy Toad in St Peter. The pub is on two floors, and as well as creating a new restaurant downstairs, they plan improvements to the downstairs traditional bar (old photographs, solid furnishings, some attractive panelling and stained glass, heavy brass doors between its two main parts) to allow in more light; there's wheelchair access and loos. There will be a new bar menu by the time this book reaches the shops, but as we went to press, bar food included lunchtime filled baguettltes (from £1.85), sausages and mash or warm salads such as chicken liver or bacon lardons (£4.95), haggis, neeps and tatties (£5.95), stir-fried king prawns (£7.50), very popular fajitas with salsa, guacamole and cream dips (from £7.75), chargrilled steaks (from £8.95), lots of fresh fish and daily specials on the blackboard and children's meals (from £2). Alongside two or three guests like Bass and Shepherd Neame Spitfire, one of their own-brew beers – Horny Toad, Jimmys, and well-priced Tipsy Toad – is always priced at just 99p. The house wines are sound, and the whole place is immaculate, running like clockwork; it can get busy in the evenings. Upstairs has at least as much space again as downstairs, very well planned with a lot of attention to detail, rather more toadery and a garden room; one area is no smoking; baby changing facilities and high chairs. *(Recommended by Stephen Holman, Stephen and John Curtis, Steve and Carolyn Harvey, John Evans)*

Own brew ~ Manager Liz Mitchell ~ Real ale ~ Meals and snacks (12.30-2.30, 6.30-10; not Mon evening or Sun) ~ Restaurant ~ (01534) 615000 ~ Children welcome till 9pm ~ Live jazz Sun morning ~ Open 11-11; 11-2.30, 7.30-11 Sun; cl 25 Dec

ST JOHN (Jersey) OS 620564 Map 1
Les Fontaines
Le Grand Mourier, Route du Nord

The place to head for here is the distinctive public bar – and particularly the unusual inglenook by the large 14th-c stone fireplace. There are very heavy beams in the low dark ochre ceiling, stripped irregular red granite walls, old-fashioned red leatherette cushioned settles and solid black tables on the quarry-tiled floor, and for decoration antique prints and Staffordshire china figurines and dogs; look out for the old smoking chains and oven by the granite columns of the fireplace. This part of the building is easy to miss; either look for the worn and unmarked door at the side of the building, or as you go down the main entry lobby towards the bigger main bar slip through the tiny narrow door on your right. The main bar is clean and carpeted, with plenty of wheelback chairs around neat dark tables, and a spiral staircase leading up to a wooden gallery under the high pine-raftered plank ceiling. For families a particularly popular feature is the supervised play area for children, Pirate Pete's (entry £1), though children are also made welcome in the other rooms of the bar. A wide range of changing bar food includes soup (£1.50), sandwiches (from £1.50), large cod and chips (£4.75), steak and mushroom pie (£4.75), and about 20 daily specials like melon and prawn salad (£5.60), rack of lamb (£6.20) and half a lobster (£6.50); children's meals (£2). One large area is no smoking; dominoes, cribbage, cards and piped music. Well kept Wadworths 6X on handpump. This pub is attractively set on the northernmost tip of the island, where the 300-feet high granite cliffs face the distant French coast, and there are good coastal walks nearby. *(Recommended by Steve and Carolyn Harvey; more reports please)*

Randalls ~ Manager Georgina Berresford ~ Real ale ~ Meals and snacks (12-2.30, 5.30-9.30) ~ (01534) 862707 ~ Children welcome ~ Open 10am-11pm

ST LAWRENCE (Jersey) Map 1
British Union
Main Rd

Children are welcome in the plainly furnished games room with pool, video games, cribbage and dominoes and juke box at this roadside pub, and there is even a child-sized cat flap leading out to a small enclosed terrace with a playhouse. The lounge bar is decorated in a cottagey style with pretty wallpaper, beams and panelling, *Punch*-style cartoons, and royal prints, and a large ceiling fan; leading off here is an interconnecting no-smoking snug, largely set out for diners, with a woodburning stove, and toy cupboard full of well loved toys, books and games. The quieter little bar has cigarette card collections, gun cartridges, and brass beer spigots on the walls, and darts. Good bar food includes soup (£1.95), filled baked potatoes (from £3.20), ploughman's (£3.75), several vegetarian dishes like vegetable lasagne (£4.25), moules (£4.95), scampi (£5.75), duck breast with orange sauce (£5.95), rack of lamb with red wine and rosemary sauce (£6.95), sirloin steak (£8.50), a couple of daily specials like cumberland sausage (£3.95) and scallops wrapped in bacon and grilled with garlic butter (£7.85). Well kept Ann Street Sunbeam on handpump; efficient, thoughtful service; piped music. *(More reports please)*

Ann Street ~ Manager Yvonne Ruellan ~ Real ale ~ Meals and snacks (12-2, 6-8.30, not Sun evening) ~ (01534) 861070 ~ Children welcome ~ Live entertainment Sun evenings ~ Open 10am(11 Sun)-11.30pm; cl 25 Dec

MARTIN (Jersey) Map 1
Royal
Grande Route de Faldouet (B30)

Nicely set by the church in an attractive and untouristy village, this big family pub has a snug straightforward public bar, a cosy and comfortable lounge recently extended with a sizeable partly no-smoking eating area, and a little children's room off that with toys and video games (children in pushchairs are not allowed in the bar area). You can have lunchtime bar food at no extra charge in the attractive upstairs restaurant, which has interesting old pine tables and fittings, country-kitchen chairs, and attractive antique prints and bric-a-brac. The wide choice of bar food includes soup (£1.75), filled baked potatoes (from £4), half a roast chicken, chicken curry, lasagne or pie of the day (£5), grilled trout or local plaice (£6.50) and 8oz sirloin (£8), and daily specials. Sunday lunch here is popular – as are the set-price restaurant meals (best to book). Helpings are generous. Boddingtons and Marstons Pedigree under light blanket pressure; service is quick and friendly; open fire. There are tables out on a large terrace, with a small enclosed play area; pool, darts, bar billiards, cribbage, pinball, dominoes, video game, fruit machines, piped music. *(Recommended by Steve and Carolyn Harvey, Mary Reed, Rowly Pitcher)*

Randalls ~ Tenant: John Alan Barker ~ Real ale ~ Meals and snacks (12-2, 6-8; not Sun) ~ (01534) 856289 ~ Children welcome in eating area of bar) ~ Open 9.30am-11.30pm; Sun 11am-11.30pm Sun

ST PETER (Jersey) OS 595519 Map 1
Star & Tipsy Toad ◀

In village centre

There are tours of the on-site microbrewery every day at this busy friendly own-brew pub, and at other times you can see the workings through a window in the pub. As well as their own brews, Horny Toad, Jimmys, and Tipsy Toad (99p) on handpump they have one guest – probably Bass. There's a particularly friendly welcome in the sensitively refurbished cottagey bar which has plenty of panelling, exposed stone walls, tiled and wood-panelled floors. A small games room has darts, pool, alley skittles, cribbage, pinball, video game, and piped music, and there's a good family conservatory, and children's playground and terraces. Tasty bar food includes home-made soup (£1.60), lunchtime filled rolls (from £1.95), home-made pâté (£2.30), lunchtime ploughman's (£3.50), burgers (from £3.95), fresh cod in their own beer batter (£4.75), broccoli and cream cheese bake (£4.95), cajun spiced butterfly chicken breast (£4.95), steak and ale pie (£5.80) and steaks (from £5.95), specials like coq au vin on a bed of tagliatelli (£5.75), and children's meals (£2). Friendly staff; wheelchair access and disabled lavatories. They often have a well-regarded World Music Festival. See also the Tipsy Toad Town House in St Helier. *(Recommended by S J Barber, Stephen and Jean Curtis, John Evans, Steve and Carolyn Harvey)*

Own brew ~ Manager John Dryhurst ~ Real ale ~ Meals and snacks (12-2.15, 6-8.15; 12.30-3 only Sun; not winter Mon evenings) ~ (01534) 485556 ~ Children welcome ~ Live bands Fri, Sat evenings in summer, Sat only in winter ~ Open 9am(11 Sun)-11pm

---

Lucky Dip

Besides the fully inspected pubs, you might like to try these Lucky Dips recommended to us and described by readers (if you do, please send us reports):

ALDERNEY
☆ **Newtown**, *Harbour Lights*: Varied good bar food esp fresh local fish and seafood at (for mainlanders) ridiculously low prices, in welcoming, clean and well run hotel/pub in a quieter part of this quiet island; pleasant garden; caters particularly for families with children; well kept Guernsey Bitter, terrace; bedrooms; *(Michael Inskip)*
☆ **St Anne** [Victoria St], *Georgian House*: Enjoyable interesting food at reasonable prices in small hotel bar, relaxing and civilised, with very accommodating owners and charming staff, Ringwood Best and Old Thumper, restaurant; nice back garden with barbecue and summer food servery; comfortable bedrooms *(Keith Taylor, Michael Inskip)*

GUERNSEY
☆ **Forest** [Le Bourg], *Happy Landings*: Unusual bistro-style pub doing well under new licensee, lovely floral displays, individual atmosphere and surroundings, very friendly

local staff, wide choice of good imaginative low-cost food, huge helpings, well kept beer; may have to order food at bar and wait there drinking until food ready before going through to candlelit dining room *(H Gridley, J Tensini, David and Jane Russell)*
☆ **St Martin** [Jerbourg, nr SE tip of island], *Auberge Divette*: Glorious view of coast and Herm from fairy-lit garden high above sea; unpretentious picture-window saloon and lounge both with button-back banquettes, sensibly placed darts and bar billiards in back public bar; well kept Guernsey Bitter and Mild, basic food inc children's (may be a wait); spectacular cliff walk to St Peter Port *(H K Dyson, Norma and Keith Bloomfield, LYM)*
☆ **St Martin** [La Fosse], *Bella Luce*: Former 12th-c manor with lovely gardens, more hotel than pub, but has a super small and cosy bar with old-world pubby traditional atmosphere, good service, decent wines and reasonably priced food in bar and restaurant; keg beer; comfortable bedrooms *(Steve and Carolyn*

Harvey, Rudy Jacobs, J S Rutter)

St Martin [Saints Bay Rd], *La Barbarie*: Hotel serving bar lunches inc good three-decker sandwiches; bedrooms *(R Davies)*; [La Fosse], *Les Douvres*: Real pub atmosphere in civilised if busy Tudor-style bar with generous well prepared food, friendly efficient staff, well kept Theakstons; lots of beautiful walks nearby; bedrooms *(Rudy Jacobs)*

☆ **St Peter Port** [North Esplanade], *Ship & Crown*: Lively town pub very popular with yachting people and smarter locals, sharing building with Royal Guernsey Yacht Club; good harbour view from bay windows, interesting photographs (esp concerning WWII German occupation, also boats and ships), good value food from sandwiches to steak, well kept Guernsey Bitter, welcoming service *(Bob and Maggie Atherton, Judith Hirst, H K Dyson, Norma and Keith Bloomfield, LYM)*

St Peter Port [Le Charroterie], *Drunken Duck*: Well kept Gales, King & Barnes, Ringwood and Theakstons, popular bar lunches, pleasant young Irish landlord, bar billiards; live music inc Irish folk, little nearby parking *(Bob and Maggie Atherton, Howard England, Stephen Holman)*; [Lower Pollet], *Thomas De La Rue*: Well renovated, nautical bric-a-brac, good furnishings, locally popular food, well kept Guernsey real ales; music gets louder after 8 *(Stephen Holman)*

St Peters [Rue de Longfrie; SO8439], *Longfrie*: Well run family food pub based on 16th-c farmhouse well placed for the south of the island, good quick service even when busy, several well kept Guernsey ales, wide choice of straightforward food, indoor play area, pleasant garden; bedrooms *(Steve and Carolyn Harvey, David and Jane Russell, Norma and Keith Bloomfield, R Davies)*

St Sampsons [Rte du Braye], *Chandlers*: Something of a rarity in Guernsey as it concentrates on well kept real ale, inc Randalls Patois *(David and Jane Russell)*

HERM

Ship: Excellent local seafood, attractive wines and friendly service; charming surroundings, distant sea view if you choose your viewpoint carefully; bedrooms *(Judith Hirst)*

JERSEY

☆ **Gorey** [The Harbour; map ref 714503], *Dolphin*: Basic fishing theme (nets etc), unpretentious pubby atmosphere, good fish and seafood inc scallops, big prawns, grilled sardines, seafood platter; restaurant, children in eating area; very busy indeed Sun lunchtime; piped music, Iberian waiters; comfortable bedrooms *(Ian and Villy White, LYM)*

☆ **St Helier** [Hilgrove St], *Prince of Wales*: Tranquil and dim-lit old listed building, shining clean, next to St Helier market (worth a visit), calm walled back garden,

Boddingtons, Theakstons Best and Mild, sound choice of food, daily papers, lots of old framed newspaper front pages, photographs and prints esp of Royalty *(Steve and Carolyn Harvey)*

☆ **St Helier** [Mulcaster St], *Lamplighter*: Reassuringly unchanging atmosphere in gas-lit pub with admirable facade, heavy timbers, rough panelling and scrubbed pine tables; good value simple lunchtime food inc children's, well kept Bass, Boddingtons, Marstons Pedigree, Theakstons Old Peculier and a guest beer; open 14 hours a day *(Steve and Carolyn Harvey, LYM)*

St Helier [Halkett St], *Dog & Sausage*: Comfortable and neatly refurbished town pub in pedestrianised shopping area, snug small rooms, dark green decor, fans, old photographs, and Victorian/train theme; piped music not too intrusive, tables outside *(Sue Rowland, BB)*

St Ouens Bay [S end, at end of Five Mile Rd – map ref 562488], *La Pulente*: Across road from the island's longest beach; small and simple, popular with older local people for lunch, with sandwiches, ploughman's, filled baked potatoes (fillings may include scallops and fish), scampi, salads; more main dishes in evening, inc steaks; well kept Bass and Fullers London Pride; green leatherette armchairs in smallish sea-view lounge, sailing ship prints, leatherette-topped tables; fairy-lit side terrace *(Ian and Villy White, BB)*

SARK

La Moinerie: Attractive stone house with woodburner in small low-ceilinged lounge bar, mix of eating-height tables with appropriate chairs and lower tables with settees and easy chairs, good reasonably priced bar food, swift efficient service, Guernsey Captains Bitter, restaurant with open fire; tables out on good-sized sloping lawn; pleasant bedrooms, peaceful spot *(Steve and Carolyn Harvey) Bel Air*: First tourist stop (where the tractors climb to from the jetty): big woodburning stove in comfortable Boat Bar with plank ceiling, easy chairs and settees, model ship, boat-shaped counter; old boat pictures in simpler Pirate Bar; snacks, darts, piped pop music, tables on terrace outside this pretty cottage *(Steve and Carolyn Harvey, John Evans, BB); Dixcart*: Granite hotel, originally 16th-c farm, in extensive grounds sloping to sheltered cove; comfortable public bar with log fire, stripped vertical panelling and nautical touches, decent children's room off, reasonably priced bar food, picnic tables out in front yard; bedrooms comfortable and pleasantly decorated *(Steve and Carolyn Harvey); Petit Champ*: Not exactly a pub, but a hotel serving good pub lunches inc fresh lobster and crab and splendid stilton ploughman's; beautiful setting, keg Guernsey Bitter; bedrooms *(Patrick Renouf)*

Overseas Lucky Dip

We're always interested to hear of good bars and pubs overseas – preferably really good examples of bars that visitors would find memorable, rather than transplanted 'British pubs'. We start with ones in the British Isles (but over the water), then work alphabetically through other countries. A star marks places we can be confident would deserve a main entry.

IRELAND

Bandon, *Half Door*: Good friendly two-bar pub, lots of wood, open fire, piped music and darts, food 11-9, TV in back bar; popular with young people for loud live country, western and traditional music with lots of audience participation Thurs, Fri and Sat evenings *(CMW, JJW)*

☆ **Belfast** [Gt Victoria St; opp Europa Hotel], *Crown*: Bustling 19th-c gin palace with pillared entrance, opulent tiles outside and in, elaborately coloured windows, almost church-like ceiling, handsome mirrors, individual snug booths with little doors and bells for waiter service, gas lighting, mosaic floor – wonderful atmosphere, very wide range of customers (maybe inc performers in full fig from Opera House opp); good lunchtime meals inc oysters, Hilden real ale, open all day; National Trust *(Mark and Diane Grist)*

Blarney, *Christys*: Busy, friendly and hospitable, very popular with tourists – handy for Blarney Castle and the Stone; snacks and a few meals, tea and coffee with real milk; Guinness and Smithwicks *(CMW, JJW)*

Bunratty [in Castle Folk Park – daytime entry fee], *McNamaras*: Converted old house with piano and lots of bric-a-brac, good lunchtime snacks inc cheap sandwiches, wider choice evening (when entry's free – but park and castle are worth the daytime visit); Guinness and Smithwicks, children until 7pm *(CMW, JJW)*

Bushmills, *Bushmills*: Genteel atmosphere in old tastefully renovated inn, perfect place for Guinness; good food, bedrooms *(Dave Braisted)*

Carne, *Lobster Pot*: Good seafood in bar and restaurant *(Gordon Tong)*

Dublin [Crown Alley, Temple Bar], *Bad Ass Cafe*: Trendy pizza, burger and pasta place, good value and fun; cold beers *(Chris Raisin)*; [Merrion Row; aka Big Jacks], *Baggot*: Jack Charlton's pub, comfortably refurbished, with varied live music and impromptu sing-alongs *(Chris Raisin)*; [Harry St; off Grafton St], *Bruxelles*: Cosy and friendly Victorian bar with dark panelling, mirrors and outstanding Guinness *(Chris Raisin)*; [Merrion Row; by the Shelburne just below St Stephens Green],

Doheny & Nesbitt: Very old and original former grocer's, with Victorian bar fittings, pub mirrors, signs and posters; good Guinness *(Chris Raisin)*; [East Essex St; Temple Bar], *Fitzsimons*: Touristy, but worth it for the free traditional music and set dancing, good Guinness and friendly staff; lots of varnished wood, polished floor and bar counter, good bar food *(Chris Raisin)*; [Capel St], *J F Handell*: Gently refurbished bar with nice fireplace, fine solid wall settles, shelf of bric-a-brac; good Guinness *(Chris Raisin)*; [Merrion St], *James Toner*: Quite original smallish Victorian bar, booths down one side; good Guinness *(Chris Raisin)*; [14 Mary St; off O'Connell St], *John M Keating*: Small town bar often very busy on market days – two or three floors, staff will gladly find you room; good Guinness *(Chris Raisin)*; [Dame St], *Mercantile*: Popular split-level pub, interesting interior with stair to gallery over bar; maybe fairly loud modern music, can get very crowded with young people *(Chris Raisin)*; [Lower Baggot St/Merrion Row; off St Stephens Green], *O'Donoghues*: Small traditional bar popular with musicians – maybe an impromptu riot of Celtic tunes played on anything from spoons to banjo or pipes; gets packed but long-armed owner ensures quick service; mirrors, posters and snob screens in Victorian main bar, fine Guinness, great atmosphere; plainer back bar has live music too; open all day *(Chris Raisin, Martin Ellis and friends)*; [Suffolk St], *O'Neills*: Large early Victorian pub, lots of dark panelling, several rooms off big bar, very popular lunchtime hot food bar, super thick sandwiches, good Guinness *(Chris Raisin, Martin Ellis and friends)*; [17 Anglesea St; Temple Bar], *Old Dubliner*: Very popular and friendly, well kept and served Guinness, traditional interior, snob screens, wall settles, round cast-iron-framed tables *(Chris Raisin)*; [Anglesea St, Temple Bar], *Oliver St John Gogarty*: Popular, with bric-a-brac inc bicycle above bar, live music upstairs; good Guinness *(Chris Raisin)*; [21 Fleet St, Temple Bar], *Palace*: Splendid original Victorian bar with snob screens, rooms through etched glass doors, tiny snug, good Guinness *(Chris*

Raisin); [Capel St], *Slatterys*: Good Guinness in well known traditional music pub with central bar *(Chris Raisin, Martin Ellis)*; [Temple Bar], *Temple Bar*: Rambling multi-levelled, multi-roomed pub, rather bohemian, usually crowded; good Guinness; tables out in big yard *(L Dixon)*

Dundrum, *Bucks Head*: Popular dining pub, spacious conservatory eating area and bar, generous helpings of good imaginative food, friendly helpful service *(Margaret and Nigel Dennis)*

Galway [Spanish Arch], *Hooker Jimmys*: Great seafood, in part of town known as the Fishmarket, formerly the main quays of Galway *(Gordon Tong)*; [West St], *Quays*: Stunning large converted chapel with multiple levels and a marvellous atmosphere; upstairs bars, crypt restaurant, bar food on the main level; good Guinness *(Mr and Mrs Carey)*

Glencullen [about 4 miles NW of Enniskerry], *Johnnie Foxs*: Primarily a dining pub, with wide choice of food, not cheap but good, inc fine seafood and excellent bread; very friendly service, good buzzy atmosphere, good value wine, interesting decor with antique settles, scrubbed tables, beams, stripped stone and a forest of bric-a-brac, traditional music and Irish dancing till midnight (must book) *(Bob and Maggie Atherton)*

Killala [N of Ballina], *Anchor*: Very popular, with good seafood at reasonable prices inc huge crab sandwiches; good Guinness, two petrol pumps outside *(L Dixon)*

Killarney [Main St], *O'Mearas*: Friendly singing bar with good Guinness, good bar food, good value upstairs restaurant *(Mr and Mrs Carey)*

Kilmore Quay, *Silver Fox*: Good seafood *(Gordon Tong)*

Lisdoonvarna, *Royal Spa*: Friendly and chatty atmosphere, good Irish music every night, darts and TV, fair choice of good value basic food, good Guinness and Smithwicks; children welcome, bedrooms *(CMW, JJW)*

Malin Head, *Crossroads*: Dark bar decorated with ship photographs and naval charts; Smithwicks *(Dave Braisted)*

Portaferry, *Portaferry*: More hotel than pub, but wide range of good food all day; beautiful waterfront setting overlooking mouth of Strangford Lough, with ferry boat chugging across – very pretty at night; good bedrooms *(Margaret and Nigel Dennis)*

Redcross, *Jim Cullens*: No name, no sign, no refurbishment, no food and no fridge for cold drinks, but loads of character and a real local, live music inc Irish music *(Giles Francis)*

Shedding, *Sheddings*: Typical Northern Irish pub, in the middle of nowhere; basic bar menu with wholesome helpings, Bass *(Dave Braisted)*

Tramore, *Seahorse*: Busy, lively little pub with upstairs dining overspill, TV, piped music; good Guinness and Smithwicks ales, tea and coffee all day; children welcome *(CMW, JJW)*

Wexford [George St], *Whites*: Delightfully peaceful and genteel big 18th-c hotel, good food in panelled bar, highly personable barman; bedrooms *(Joan and Michel Hooper-Immins)*

ISLE OF MAN

Glenmaye, Isle of Man [just off A27 3 miles S of Peel – OS Sheet 95 map ref 236798; SC2480], *Waterfall*: Named for the waterfall nearby; very popular, with good service, reasonably priced usual food, Cains, Tetleys and sometimes Okells ale *(Derek and Sylvia Stephenson, Stephen Holman)*

☆ **Laxey** [Tram Station – OS Sheet 95 map ref 433846; SC4484], *Mines Tavern*: Beamed pub in lovely woodland clearing where Manx electric railway and Snaefell mountain railway connect, just below the Lady Isabella wheel (largest working water wheel in the world); splendid old tram photographs, advertisements and other memorabilia in one bar with counter salvaged from former tram, other bar dedicated to mining; fresh sandwiches and reasonably priced home cooking, well kept Bushys, Okells and Tetleys ales; piped music, darts, fruit machines (public bar not lounge); lovely sitting outside to watch Victorian trams *(Derek and Sylvia Stephenson, Peter and Patricia Burton)*

AUSTRALIA

Atherton Tablelands [Malanda; N Queensland], *Malanda Pub*: Large wooden turn-of-century pub catering for local country people, with good food inc wonderful help-yourself Fri/Sat buffet of 20 different veg *(Mrs Anne Grubb)*

Cairns [6 Grove St; Queensland], *Cock & Bull*: Pleasant seating indoors and in garden, good reasonably priced generous food (must intend to dine to get a drink), wide range of bottled and draught beers inc unusual Australian ones as well as imports; can be a bit of a wait for food at busy times *(Michael Begley)*

Darwin [Esplanade; Northern Territory], *Hotel Darwin*: Time-warp colonial feel in Green Room (all British Racing Green), with cane furniture, lots of Air Force and other WWII memorabilia, ceiling fans; long room open on two sides, echoes of old-fashioned male pub, local and major southern brews – their Darwin stubby is stubby-shaped but holds about 2½ litres *(Jane Kingsbury)*

Robe [S Australia], *Caledonian*: Like an English pub inside and out – even the inside walls are ivy-covered; log fires, candles on tables, locals drinking at the bar, wonderful food, friendly staff, tables in yard and on grass overlooking beach; bedrooms, also two-storey garden flats *(Jane Kingsbury)*

☆ **Sydney** [Argyle Pl, The Rocks], *Lord Nelson*: Solid stone, with beams and bare floorboards – the city's oldest pub; brews its own Nelsons Revenge, Three Sheets, Trafalgar and Victory, and has tastings first Weds of month (not Jan); good choice of other Australian beers, great easy-going service, interesting reasonably priced home-made food, nautical theme, upmarket atmosphere, pine furniture; open all day, gets touristy; delightful bedrooms *(Neville and Sarah Hargreaves)*

BELGIUM
☆ **Brussels** [R Montagne aux Herbes Potageres], *Mort Subite*: A local institution, producing its own good traditional Gueuze, sweet Faro and fruit ales; long Belle Epoque room divided by two rows of pillars into nave with two rows of small tables and side aisles with single row, mirrors on all sides, leather seats, swift uniformed waiters and waitresses scurrying from busy bar on right; good snacks such as omelettes and croques monsieur *(Ian Phillips, Joan and Michel Hooper-Immins)*

CANADA
North Uxbridge [37 Main St; Ontario], *Hobby Horse Arms*: Beautifully appointed bar with big oak beams in mid 19th-c timbered farmhouse, no piped music, very friendly licensees, well kept Elora (real ale brewed in Canada with Kentish hops), 80 or more malt whiskies, keg UK and Irish beers, good reasonably priced food *(D Tapper)*

CZECH REPUBLIC
Prague [Kremencova 11], *U Fleku*: Brewing its own strong flavoursome black ale since 1843 (some say 1499) – usually served with a short; huge, with benches and big refectory tables in courtyard after courtyard, dark beams, very popular and atmospheric; good basic food – sausages, pork, goulash with dumplings; open early morning to late night, with early evening piano and drums, later brass band; very popular with tourists at weekends *(M A and C R Starling, Ian Phillips)*

FALKLAND ISLANDS
Port Stanley [Snake Hill], *Globe*: Comfortable local where servicemen and locals alike meet and socialise, very friendly youngish atmosphere, blazing peat fire; bottled and canned beers only *(Chris Burt)*; *Upland Goose*: Good choice of decent food in pleasant quiet hotel bar, adjoining public bar called the Ship; bottled and canned beers only; friendly staff; bedrooms comfortable *(Chris Burt)*; *Victory*: Comfortable, with particularly enjoyable atmosphere; bottled and canned beers only *(Chris Burt)*

FRANCE
Paris [rue de Dunkerque, opp Gare du Nord], *Rendez-vous des Belges*: Long and narrow, busy with locals and (mainly Belgian) travellers, good beers esp draught Straffe de Bruges, slick quick service, good French fast food inc delicious sandwiches, painstaking housekeeping *(John C Baker)*
Val d Isere [off 3rd floor of Hotel Val D'Isere], *L'Aventure*: Done out as Norman Rockwell 1950s apartment complete with bath, bunk beds, washtub etc, movies on black and white TV; pleasant curiosity,

English-run, drinks not too expensive, but music very loud after 10.30 at night; upstairs low-light cafe/restaurant *(Ian Phillips)*

GERMANY
Bamberg [Dominikaner Str], *Schlenkerla*: Tap for delicious smoky Rauchbier from tiny 17th-c Heller brewery, inc wondrous strong Bock version; two marvellous rooms, one stone-vaulted, the other heavy-beamed, reasonably priced typical German pub food *(Stephen Pine, Alfred Lawrence)*
Nuremberg, *Heilig-Geist-Spital*: Wonderful 16th-c building restored after WWII, on arches out over river, its upper floors still an old people's home; very German-feeling restaurant, wide range of wines, local beers inc malty Alt Franken Dunkel served in wonderful tall handled glasses *(Stephen Pine, Alfred Lawrence)*; [Johannesstr 26], *Shamrock*: Friendly Irish pub with good service, darts, Sat disco, maybe Irish bands *(TAB)*; *Zum Kettensteg*: Clean and simple half-timbered stube in lovely spot on riverbank, by early 19th-c footbridge (Germany's first suspension bridge), below towering arch of medieval city wall *(Stephen Pine, Alfred Lawrence)*

ITALY
Como [L Lario Trieste], *Bar Al Molo*: Marvellous view of lake and mountains, friendly efficient staff, good rich fruity Birra Rossa *(John C Baker)*

MAJORCA
☆ **Cala D'or** [carrer Den Rito 12], *Fowlers*: Exquisitely furnished (remaining stock of owner's former antique shop), lots of marble busts, wonderful paintings, oriental rugs, objets, extravagant flower arrangements, candles everywhere, glossy magazines, colourful lanterns; good choice of drinks inc remarkable range of Spanish brandies, coffee in antique silver and Wedgwood bone china (with Bendicks mint), well reproduced opera or jazz (if landlady not playing light classics or musical comedy on the corner grand piano); terrace with pretty balcony overlooking marina *(Susan and John Douglas)*

NEW ZEALAND
Auckland, *Loaded Hog*: Lively pub with good friendly atmosphere, attached to local brewery – good Red Dog Bitter; good food such as barbecued lamb and smoked chicken salad *(DAV)*; [Customs St E], *Rose & Crown*: Good value food such as quiche or steak and kidney pie; beware big surcharge for half-pints instead of pints *(DAV)*
Christchurch [opp Victoria Park], *Oxford on the Avon*: Busy bar and cafeteria, huge range of very popular plain food inc outstanding value and quality lamb from carvery, good range of nicely served local beers, decent wine by the glass, quite a pub-like atmosphere; food all day from good value breakfasts on

(bar opens later), tables out by the river with evening gas heaters *(A Albert, DAV)*

Golden Bay [South Island], *Mussel Inn*: Brews its own good Strong Ox beer and Golden Goose lager, popular food inc home-made pies, fish, vegetarian and steaks, plenty of woodwork inside, barbecue out; cl Easter-Oct *(F J Willy)*

Rotorua [Tutanekai/Haupapa St; North Island], *Pig & Whistle*: Former 40s police station with appropriate murals and memorabilia, high ceilings, tall windows, three beers brewed upstairs, food such as chowder, pumpkin soup, BELT club sandwich with fries *(DAV)*

Wellington, *Loaded Hog*: Good food such as seafood fettucine, own Red Dog Bitter, young customers but strict dress code – no sand-shoes (ie trainers) *(DAV)*

PERU

Cuzco [Plaza de Armas], *Cross Keys*: Very sociable upstairs pub with very popular pizzas, a good place to meet people *(BB)*

SOUTH AFRICA

Knysna [Western Province], *Crabs Creek Tavern*: Very pleasant pub by lagoon, low beams, lots of atmosphere, particularly good value seafood in bar and restaurant, good local Mitchells beers (which are rather unusual for SA); popular with tourists and locals *(Norma and Keith Bloomfield)*

SPAIN

Madrid [Puerta Cerrada 13], *La Fontaniles*: Fine tiled panels outside showing the seasons, good combination inside of traditional taberna atmosphere with Irish and Scottish beers and lagers; nr good restaurants, not far from Plaza Mayor *(Ian and Liz Phillips)*

THAILAND

Koh Samui [Bophut Beach], *Happy Elephant*: Thai bar/restaurant with local beer, wonderful choice of cocktails and fresh fruit juices, fresh local fish displayed on ice each evening – they barbecue your choice with a Thai marinade, and soups and curries are also good; magical evening atmosphere on beach, and unlike other bars here there's freedom from piped pop music *(Jane Kingsbury)*

USA

Boston [Massachussetts], *Back Bay*: Brewpub doing decent lunches and excellent Burton-style Bitter Brewpub producing good choice of beers in both English and European styles (their Burton-style Bitter is excellent), inc a seasonal ale – you can see the back brewery through a glass partition; upstairs restaurant and second bar, good food in generous helpings – esp the soups *(Amanda and Simon Southwell)*

Breckenridge [Lincoln St; Colorado], *Briar Rose*: Close in atmosphere to a genuine British pub, with good range of bottled beers and good collection of malt whiskies, very welcoming service, good restaurant (not cheap, but two-for-price-of-one bargains early evening); enjoyably homely atmosphere on Sun evening, with live entertainment *(John and Joan Nash)*

Chicago [Clark St/Oakdale St; Illinois], *Duke of Perth*: Outstanding fish and chips Weds and Fri – all you can eat; British pub decor, lots of Imperial antiques and photographs, Fullers, McEwans and Youngs; landlord used to be an Edinburgh policeman – his helmet now graces a 17th-c stag trophy *(Malcolm Armstrong)*; [1800 N Clybourn], *Goose Island Brewing Co*: Large microbrewery with fine own-brewed ales, British-style or European, changing seasonally, also imports inc Bass; very good value generous food, good atmosphere, former loft warehouse with stripped bricks and heavy beams, pre-Prohibition photographs and enamel advertisements *(Malcolm Armstrong)*

Flagstaff [Arizona], *Flagstaff Brewing Co*: Busy and friendly, tables outside overlooking Route 66 and the railroad, a couple of own-brewed beers and wide range of others from the area, popular with students as well as visitors; small but cheery university town not far from the Grand Canyon *(BB)*

Grants Pass [Oregon], *Wild River Brewery*: Wide range of beers brewed here inc at least one real ale, great pizzas, pasta and burgers drawing family crowds *(Stephen R Holman)*

Larkspur [Larkspur Landing; mall next to Larkspur/San Francisco ferry terminal; California], *Marin Brewery*: Welcoming microbrewery, big and slick and a bit yuppy, with good, interesting and even eccentric beers; good restaurant with standbys like ploughman's, bangers and mash, fabulous burgers, two dartboards, young friendly staff; worthwhile 50-min ferry trip past Alcatraz and San Quentin, footbridge from ferry – the mall is lovely *(Stephen R Holman)*

Los Angeles [Citrus Ave, Covina; California], *Rude Dogs*: Great food till 6, two pool tables, two dart boards, ping-pong, happy hour 2-7; live music Thurs thru Sat *(Tracey)*

Muir Beach [from Highway 101 take Stinson Beach/Highway 1 exit; California], *Pelican*: A very authentic-seeming re-creation of a Tudor country inn, great place to stay for strenuous hikes through Muir Woods or up the mountain; beautiful beach/mountain location, more English than England itself, with inglenook, Bass and Courage, bangers and mash etc; olde-worlde bedrooms *(Betsy Brown, Nigel Flook)*

Nashville [Market St; Tennessee], *Market Street Brewery*: Long narrow lively bar in touristy part of downtown, windows on to microbrewery with good range of cold beers inc Wheat, Blackberry Wheat, Vanilla Creme, Golden, Coal Porter (made with chocolate) and lauded Oktoberfest *(BB)*

New Orleans [S Carrolton Ave; Louisiana], *Cooter Browns*: 50 beers on tap, with many dozen more from around the world by the bottle; huge choice of food inc good bar snacks *(Sidd Hingoraney)*

Portsmouth [174 Fleet St; New Hampshire], *Coat of Arms*: Friendly British pub with regionally brewed real ale on handpump, lots of imported keg and bottled beers, good food from bar snacks to restaurant meals inc Sun roast beef; good welcoming service, now run by the son of its UK founder *(Peter and Sylvia Donahue)*

Prestcott [Arizona], *Prestcott Brewing Co*: Looks a bit too like a cafe, not as characterful or as busy as many, but produces a good range of really good beers; service very friendly *(BB)*

Raleigh [Martin St; N Carolina], *Greenshields*: Brews its own good Nut Brown and IPA, good food and outdoor tables, smoking and no-smoking sections *(Andy Ketcham)*

San Diego [Gaslamp Quarter; California], *Bitter End*: Nicely decorated, like a neo-Victorian gin palace with some contemporary twists; wide range of local beers, very popular with smarter after-work crowd *(BB)*

San Francisco [11th St, nr Folsom; California], *21 Tank Brewery*: No-frills brewpub with at least five beers on tap, great bar food, lots of fun *(Stephen R Holman)*

San Francisco [California], *Suppenkuche*: The best place here for German food, like a German country inn, with big shared tables and casual atmosphere; about eight German beers on tap *(Joel Dobris)*

Please keep sending us reports. We rely on readers for news of new discoveries, and particularly for news of changes – however slight – at the fully described pubs. No stamp needed: *The Good Pub Guide*, FREEPOST TN1569, Wadhurst, E Sussex TN5 7BR.

Special Interest Lists

PUBS WITH GOOD GARDENS

The pubs listed here have bigger or more beautiful gardens, grounds or terraces than are usual for their areas. Note that in a town or city this might be very much more modest than the sort of garden that would deserve a listing in the countryside.

Bedfordshire
Bolnhurst, Olde Plough
Riseley, Fox & Hounds

Berkshire
Aldworth, Bell
Hamstead Marshall, White Hart
Holyport, Belgian Arms
West Ilsley, Harrow

Buckinghamshire
Amersham, Queens Head
Bledlow, Lions of Bledlow
Bolter End, Peacock
Fawley, Walnut Tree
Ford, Dinton Hermit
Hambleden, Stag & Huntsman
Little Horwood, Shoulder of Mutton
Northend, White Hart
Skirmett, Old Crown
Waddesdon, Five Arrows
West Wycombe, George & Dragon

Cambridgeshire
Fowlmere, Chequers
Great Chishill, Pheasant
Heydon, King William IV
Horningsea, Plough & Fleece
Madingley, Three Horseshoes
Swavesey, Trinity Foot
Wansford, Haycock

Cheshire
Aldford, Grosvenor Arms
Brereton Green, Bears Head
Lower Peover, Bells of Peover
Macclesfield, Sutton Hall
Swettenham, Swettenham Arms
Weston, White Lion

Cornwall
Helford, Shipwrights Arms
Philleigh, Roseland
St Agnes, Turks Head
St Kew, St Kew
St Mawgan, Falcon
Tresco, New Inn

Cumbria
Bassenthwaite, Pheasant
Bouth, White Hart
Cockermouth, Trout
Eskdale Green, Bower House

Derbyshire
Birch Vale, Waltzing Weasel
Buxton, Bull i'th' Thorn
Grindleford, Maynard Arms
Melbourne, John Thompson
Woolley Moor, White Horse

Devon
Avonwick, Avon
Berrynarbor, Olde Globe
Broadhembury, Drewe Arms
Clyst Hydon, Five Bells
Cornworthy, Hunters Lodge
Dartington, Cott
Exeter, Imperial
Exminster, Turf
Haytor Vale, Rock
Lower Ashton, Manor
Lydford, Castle

Sidford, Blue Ball
South Zeal, Oxenham Arms
Torbryan, Old Church House
Weston, Otter

Dorset
Christchurch, Fishermans Haunt
Corfe Castle, Fox
Farnham, Museum
Kingston, Scott Arms
Nettlecombe, Marquis of Lorne
Osmington Mills, Smugglers
Plush, Brace of Pheasants
Shave Cross, Shave Cross
Tarrant Monkton, Langton Arms
West Bexington, Manor

Essex
Castle Hedingham, Bell
Chappel, Swan
Coggeshall, Compasses
Great Yeldham, White Hart
Hastingwood, Rainbow & Dove
Littlebury, Queens Head
Mill Green, Viper
Peldon, Rose
Stock, Hoop
Toot Hill, Green Man
Wendens Ambo, Bell
Woodham Walter, Cats

Gloucestershire
Amberley, Black Horse
Ampney Crucis, Crown of Crucis
Bibury, Catherine Wheel
Blaisdon, Red Hart
Coleford, Dog & Muffler
Ewen, Wild Duck
Great Rissington, Lamb
Greet, Harvest Home
Gretton, Royal Oak
Guiting Power, Farmers Arms

Kilkenny, Kilkeney
Kineton, Halfway House
Kingscote, Hunters Hall
Minchinhampton, Old
  Lodge
North Nibley, New Inn
Oddington, Horse &
  Groom
Old Sodbury, Dog
Redbrook, Boat
Sapperton, Daneway
Withington, Mill

Hampshire
Alresford, Globe
Battramsley, Hobler
Bramdean, Fox
Ovington, Bush
Owslebury, Ship
Petersfield, White Horse
Steep, Harrow
Tichborne, Tichborne
  Arms

Hereford & Worcester
Aymestrey, Riverside
Bretforton, Fleece
Much Marcle, Slip
  Tavern
Sellack, Lough Pool
Ullingswick, Three
  Crowns
Woolhope, Butchers
  Arms

Hertfordshire
Ayot St Lawrence,
  Brocket Arms
Great Offley, Green Man
Tewin, Plume of Feathers
Walkern, White Lion

Isle of Wight
Chale, Clarendon (Wight
  Mouse)
Shorwell, Crown

Kent
Biddenden, Three
  Chimneys
Bough Beech, Wheatsheaf
Boyden Gate, Gate
Chiddingstone, Castle
Dargate, Dove
Fordcombe, Chafford
  Arms
Groombridge, Crown
Newnham, George
Penshurst, Bottle House
Ringlestone, Ringlestone

Selling, Rose & Crown
Smarden, Bell
Toys Hill, Fox &
  Hounds
Ulcombe, Pepper Box

**Lancashire (inc Greater
  Manchester,
  Merseyside)**
Darwen, Old Rosins
Newton, Parkers Arms
Whitewell, Inn at
  Whitewell

Leicestershire & Rutland
Braunston, Old Plough
Exton, Fox & Hounds
Medbourne, Nevill Arms
Old Dalby, Crown

Lincolnshire
Newton, Red Lion
Stamford, George of
  Stamford

Norfolk
Great Bircham, Kings
  Head
Reedham, Ferry
Sculthorpe, Sculthorpe
  Mill
Stow Bardolph, Hare
  Arms
Titchwell, Manor
Woodbastwick, Fur &
  Feather

Northamptonshire
Ashby St Ledgers, Olde
  Coach House
East Haddon, Red Lion
Eastcote, Eastcote Arms
Wadenhoe, Kings Head

**Northumberland,
  Durham, Tyneside &
  Teeside**
Blanchland, Lord Crewe
  Arms
Diptonmill, Dipton Mill

Nottinghamshire
Colston Bassett, Martins
  Arms
Drakeholes, Griff
Kimberley, Nelson &
  Railway
Upton, French Horn

Oxfordshire
Binfield Heath, Bottle &
  Glass
Broadwell, Five Bells
Burford, Lamb
Chalgrove, Red Lion
Chinnor, Sir Charles
  Napier
Clifton, Duke of
  Cumberlands Head
Finstock, Plough
Fyfield, White Hart
Hook Norton, Gate
  Hangs High
Hook Norton, Pear Tree
Kelmscot, Plough
Maidensgrove, Five
  Horseshoes
Shipton under
  Wychwood, Shaven
  Crown
South Stoke, Perch &
  Pike
Stanton St John, Star
Tadpole Bridge, Trout
Watlington, Chequers
Westcott Barton, Fox
Woodstock, Feathers

Shropshire
Bishops Castle, Three
  Tuns
Cressage, Cholmondeley
  Riverside
Norton, Hundred House
Upper Farmcote, Lion of
  Morfe

Somerset
Ashcott, Ashcott
Bristol, Highbury Vaults
Combe Hay, Wheatsheaf
Compton Martin, Ring o'
  Bells
Dunster, Luttrell Arms
Exebridge, Anchor
Litton, Kings Arms
Monksilver, Notley Arms
South Stoke, Pack Horse
West Huntspill,
  Crossways

Staffordshire
Acton Trussell, Moat
  House
Onecote, Jervis Arms
Salt, Holly Bush
Tutbury, Olde Dog &
  Partridge

Suffolk
Bildeston, Crown
Brandeston, Queens
  Head
Dennington, Queens
  Head
Hoxne, Swan
Lavenham, Angel
Lavenham, Swan
Laxfield, Kings Head
Rede, Plough

Surrey
Charleshill, Donkey
Chilworth, Villagers
Coldharbour, Plough
Compton, Withies
Farncombe, Ram
Hascombe, White Horse
Mickleham, King William
  IV
Outwood, Dog & Duck
Pirbright, Royal Oak
Warlingham, White
  Lion

Sussex
Amberley, Black Horse
Ashurst, Fountain
Barcombe, Anchor
Berwick, Cricketers Arms
Blackboys, Blackboys
Byworth, Black Horse
Eartham, George
Elsted, Three Horseshoes
Firle, Ram
Fletching, Griffin
Hammerpot, Woodmans
  Arms
Heathfield, Star
Kirdford, Half Moon
Oving, Gribble
Scaynes Hill, Sloop
Seaford, Golden Galleon
Wineham, Royal Oak

Warwickshire
Farnborough, Butchers
  Arms
Ilmington, Howard Arms
Lowsonford, Fleur de Lys
Stratford upon Avon,
  Slug & Lettuce

Wiltshire
Bradford on Avon, Cross
  Guns
Brinkworth, Three
  Crowns
Chicksgrove, Compasses

Ebbesbourne Wake,
  Horseshoe
Lacock, George
Little Cheverell, Owl
Lower Woodford,
  Wheatsheaf
Netherhampton, Victoria
  & Albert
Salisbury, New Inn
Seend, Barge
Wilcot, Golden Swan
Woodborough, Seven
  Stars

Yorkshire
East Witton, Blue Lion
Egton Bridge, Horse Shoe
Heath, Kings Arms
Osmotherley, Three Tuns
Stutton, Hare & Hounds
Sutton upon Derwent, St
  Vincent Arms
Threshfield, Old Hall

London, Central
London W1, Red Lion

London, North
London N1, Waterside
London NW3, Spaniards

London, South
London SE21, Crown &
  Greyhound
London SW18, Ship

London, West
London W6, Dove
London W8, Windsor
  Castle
Twickenham, White Swan

London, East
London E1, Prospect of
  Whitby

Scotland
Ardfern, Galley of Lorne
Arduaine, Loch Melfort
Creebridge, Creebridge
  House
Edinburgh, Starbank
Gifford, Tweeddale Arms
Kilmahog, Lade
Pitlochry, Killiecrankie
Skeabost, Skeabost
  House
Strachur, Creggans
Thornhill, Lion &
  Unicorn

Wales
Aberystwyth, Halfway
Bodfari, Dinorben Arms
Caerphilly, Courthouse
Crickhowell, Bear
Crickhowell, Nantyffin
  Cider Mill
Llandrindod Wells,
  Llanerch
Llanelidan, Leyland Arms
Llanfrynach, White Swan
Llangedwyn, Green
Llangynidr, Coach &
  Horses
Llwyndafydd, Crown
Presteigne, Radnorshire
  Arms
St Hilary, Bush
Stackpole, Armstrong
  Arms
Tyn y Groes, Groes

Channel Islands
Castel, Hougue du
  Pommier
Kings Mills, Fleur du
  Jardin
Rozel, Rozel Bay

WATERSIDE PUBS
The pubs listed here are
right beside the sea, a
sizeable river, canal, lake
or loch that contributes
significantly to their
attraction.

Bedfordshire
Odell, Bell

Berkshire
Great Shefford, Swan

Cambridgeshire
Cambridge, Anchor
Holywell, Old Ferry Boat
Sutton Gault, Anchor
Wansford, Haycock

Cheshire
Chester, Old Harkers
  Arms
Wrenbury, Dusty Miller

Cornwall
Cremyll, Edgcumbe Arms
Falmouth, Chain Locker
Falmouth, Quayside
Helford, Shipwrights
  Arms

Mousehole, Ship
Mylor Bridge, Pandora
Polkerris, Rashleigh
Polruan, Lugger
Porthallow, Five
  Pilchards
Porthleven, Ship
St Agnes, Turks Head
Trebarwith, Port William
Tresco, New Inn

Cumbria
Cockermouth, Trout
Ulverston, Bay Horse

Derbyshire
Shardlow, Old Crown

Devon
Avonwick, Avon
Brendon, Rockford
Dartmouth, Royal Castle
Exeter, Double Locks
Exminster, Turf
Lynmouth, Rising Sun
Plymouth, China House
Topsham, Passage House
Torcross, Start Bay
Tuckenhay, Maltsters
  Arms
Weston, Otter

Dorset
Chideock, Anchor
Lyme Regis, Pilot Boat

Essex
Chappel, Swan
Leigh on Sea, Crooked
  Billet

Gloucestershire
Ashleworth Quay, Boat
Great Barrington, Fox
Redbrook, Boat
Withington, Mill

Hampshire
Alresford, Globe
Bursledon, Jolly Sailor
Langstone, Royal Oak
Ovington, Bush
Portsmouth, Still & West
Wherwell, Mayfly

Hereford & Worcester
Aymestrey, Riverside
Knightwick, Talbot
Michaelchurch Escley,
  Bridge

Wyre Piddle, Anchor

Hertfordshire
Berkhamsted, Boat

Isle of Wight
Cowes, Folly
Seaview, Seaview
Shanklin, Fishermans
  Cottage
Ventnor, Spyglass

Kent
Faversham, Albion
Oare, Shipwrights Arms
Whitstable, Pearsons
  Crab & Oyster House

**Lancashire (inc Greater
  Manchester,
  Merseyside)**
Bilsborrow, Owd Nells
Garstang, Th'Owd
  Tithebarn
Manchester, Dukes 92
Manchester, Mark Addy
Whitewell, Inn at
  Whitewell

Lincolnshire
Brandy Wharf, Cider
  Centre

Norfolk
Reedham, Ferry
Sculthorpe, Sculthorpe
  Mill

Northamptonshire
Oundle, Mill
Wadenhoe, Kings Head

Oxfordshire
Tadpole Bridge, Trout

Shropshire
Cressage, Cholmondeley
  Riverside
Llanyblodwel, Horseshoe
Ludlow, Unicorn
Shrewsbury, Armoury
Whitchurch, Willey
  Moor Lock

Somerset
Exebridge, Anchor

Staffordshire
Acton Trussell, Moat
  House

Onecote, Jervis Arms

Suffolk
Aldeburgh, Cross Keys
Chelmondiston, Butt &
  Oyster
Ramsholt, Ramsholt
  Arms

Sussex
Barcombe, Anchor

Warwickshire
Lapworth, Navigation
Lowsonford, Fleur de Lys
Netherton, Little Dry
  Dock

Wiltshire
Bradford on Avon, Cross
  Guns
Seend, Barge

Yorkshire
Hull, Minerva
Newton on Ouse,
  Dawnay Arms
Whitby, Duke of York

London, North
London N1, Waterside

London, South
London SE1, Anchor
London SE1, Horniman
London SE10, Cutty Sark
London SW13, Bulls
  Head
London SW18, Ship

London, West
London W4, Bulls Head
London W6, Dove
Twickenham, White
  Swan

London, East
London E1, Prospect of
  Whitby
London E1, Town of
  Ramsgate
London E14, Grapes

Scotland
Ardfern, Galley of Lorne
Arduaine, Loch Melfort
Carbost, Old Inn
Clachan Seil, Tigh an
  Truish
Crinan, Crinan

Edinburgh, Starbank
Elie, Ship
Fort Augustus, Lock
Isle Ornsay, Tigh Osda
  Eilean Iarmain
Isle of Whithorn, Steam
  Packet
Plockton, Plockton
Portpatrick, Crown
Shieldaig, Tigh an Eilean
Skeabost, Skeabost
  House
St Mary's Loch, Tibbie
  Shiels
Strachur, Creggans
Tayvallich, Tayvallich
Ullapool, Ferry Boat

Wales
Aberdovey, Penhelig
  Arms
Abergorlech, Black Lion
Cresswell Quay, Cresselly
  Arms
Erbistock, Boat
Little Haven, Swan
Llangedwyn, Green
Llangynidr, Coach &
  Horses
Pembroke Ferry, Ferry
Pontypool, Open Hearth
Red Wharf Bay, Ship

Channel Islands
St Aubin, Old Court
  House

**PUBS IN ATTRACTIVE
SURROUNDINGS**
These pubs are in
unusually attractive or
interesting places – lovely
countryside, charming
villages, occasionally
notable town
surroundings. Waterside
pubs are listed again here
only if their other
surroundings are special,
too.

Berkshire
Aldworth, Bell
Frilsham, Pot Kiln
Waltham St Lawrence,
  Bell

Buckinghamshire
Bledlow, Lions of
  Bledlow

Brill, Pheasant
Frieth, Prince Albert
Hambleden, Stag &
  Huntsman
Ibstone, Fox
Little Hampden, Rising
  Sun
Northend, White Hart
Turville, Bull & Butcher

Cheshire
Barthomley, White Lion
Langley, Leathers Smithy
Lower Peover, Bells of
  Peover
Marbury, Swan
Swettenham, Swettenham
  Arms

Cornwall
Boscastle, Cobweb
Chapel Amble, Maltsters
  Arms
Helston, Halzephron
Porthallow, Five
  Pilchards
Ruan Lanihorne, Kings
  Head
St Agnes, Turks Head
St Breward, Old Inn
St Kew, St Kew
St Mawgan, Falcon
Tresco, New Inn

Cumbria
Askham, Punch Bowl
Bassenthwaite, Pheasant
Boot, Burnmoor
Bouth, White Hart
Braithwaite, Coledale
Broughton in Furness,
  Blacksmiths Arms
Cartmel, Cavendish Arms
Chapel Stile,
  Wainwrights
Coniston, Black Bull
Crosthwaite, Punch Bowl
Dent, Sun
Dockray, Royal
Elterwater, Britannia
Garrigill, George &
  Dragon
Grasmere, Travellers Rest
Hawkshead, Drunken
  Duck
Hawkshead, Kings Arms
Ings, Watermill
Lanercost, Abbey Bridge
Langdale, Old Dungeon
  Ghyll

Little Langdale, Three
  Shires
Loweswater, Kirkstile
Melmerby, Shepherds
Scales, White Horse
Seathwaite, Newfield
Troutbeck, Mortal Man
Troutbeck, Queens Head
Ulverston, Bay Horse

Derbyshire
Ashford in the Water,
  Ashford
Brassington, Olde Gate
Froggatt Edge, Chequers
Hardwick Hall,
  Hardwick
Hayfield, Lantern Pike
Holmesfield, Robin
  Hood
Kirk Ireton, Barley Mow
Ladybower Reservoir,
  Yorkshire Bridge
Little Hucklow, Old Bulls
  Head
Monsal Head, Monsal
  Head
Woolley Moor, White
  Horse

Devon
Blackawton, Normandy
  Arms
Branscombe, Fountain
  Head
Brendon, Rockford
Broadclyst, Red Lion
Chagford, Ring o' Bells
Dunsford, Royal Oak
Exminster, Turf
Haytor Vale, Rock
Holbeton, Mildmay
  Colours
Horndon, Elephants Nest
Horsebridge, Royal
Iddesleigh, Duke of York
Knowstone, Masons
  Arms
Lower Ashton, Manor
Lustleigh, Cleave
Lydford, Castle
Lynmouth, Rising Sun
Meavy, Royal Oak
Peter Tavy, Peter Tavy
Postbridge, Warren
  House
Rattery, Church House
Stokenham, Tradesmans
  Arms
Widecombe, Rugglestone

Wonson, Northmore Arms

Dorset
Abbotsbury, Ilchester Arms
Askerswell, Spyway
Burton Bradstock, Three Horseshoes
Corfe Castle, Fox
Corscombe, Fox
East Chaldon, Sailors Return
Farnham, Museum
Kingston, Scott Arms
Loders, Loders Arms
Milton Abbas, Hambro Arms
Osmington Mills, Smugglers
Plush, Brace of Pheasants
Worth Matravers, Square & Compass

Essex
Fuller Street, Square & Compasses
Leigh on Sea, Crooked Billet
Little Dunmow, Flitch of Bacon
Mill Green, Viper
North Fambridge, Ferryboat

Gloucestershire
Amberley, Black Horse
Ashleworth Quay, Boat
Bibury, Catherine Wheel
Bisley, Bear
Bledington, Kings Head
Brockweir, Brockweir
Chedworth, Seven Tuns
Chipping Campden, Eight Bells
Cold Aston, Plough
Coleford, Dog & Muffler
Coln St Aldwyns, New Inn
Great Rissington, Lamb
Guiting Power, Farmers Arms
Minchinhampton, Old Lodge
Nailsworth, Weighbridge
Newland, Ostrich
North Nibley, New Inn
Sapperton, Daneway
St Briavels, George
Stanton, Mount

Hampshire
Alresford, Globe
Crawley, Fox & Hounds
East Tytherley, Star
Hawkley, Hawkley
Micheldever, Dever Arms
Ovington, Bush
Petersfield, White Horse
Soberton, White Lion
Tichborne, Tichborne Arms

Hereford & Worcester
Aymestrey, Riverside
Hanley Castle, Three Kings
Kidderminster, King & Castle
Knightwick, Talbot
Michaelchurch Escley, Bridge
Much Marcle, Slip Tavern
Pensax, Bell
Ruckhall, Ancient Camp
Sellack, Lough Pool
Walterstone, Carpenters Arms
Weobley, Olde Salutation
Woolhope, Butchers Arms

Hertfordshire
Ashwell, Bushel & Strike
Sarratt, Cock
Westmill, Sword in Hand

Isle of Wight
Chale, Clarendon (Wight Mouse)

Kent
Boughton Aluph, Flying Horse
Brookland, Woolpack
Chiddingstone, Castle
Groombridge, Crown
Hever, Henry VIII
Lamberhurst, Brown Trout
Newnham, George
Selling, Rose & Crown
Toys Hill, Fox & Hounds

Lancashire (inc Greater Manchester, Merseyside)
Blackstone Edge, White House

Downham, Assheton Arms
Fence, Forest
Newton, Parkers Arms
Whitewell, Inn at Whitewell

Leicestershire & Rutland
Exton, Fox & Hounds
Glooston, Old Barn
Hallaton, Bewicke Arms

Lincolnshire
Aswarby, Tally Ho

Norfolk
Blakeney, White Horse
Blickling, Buckinghamshire Arms
Burnham Market, Hoste Arms
Great Bircham, Kings Head
Heydon, Earle Arms
Horsey, Nelson Head
Thornham, Lifeboat
Woodbastwick, Fur & Feather

Northamptonshire
Chapel Brampton, Brampton Halt
Harringworth, White Swan

Northumberland, Durham, Tyneside & Teeside
Allenheads, Allenheads
Bamburgh, Lord Crewe Arms
Blanchland, Lord Crewe Arms
Craster, Jolly Fisherman
Diptonmill, Dipton Mill
Great Whittington, Queens Head
Haltwhistle, Milecastle
Haltwhistle, Wallace Arms
Matfen, Black Bull
Romaldkirk, Rose & Crown
Stannersburn, Pheasant

Nottinghamshire
Laxton, Dovecote

Oxfordshire
Ardington, Boars Head

Burford, Mermaid
Chalgrove, Red Lion
Checkendon, Black Horse
Chinnor, Sir Charles Napier
Cropredy, Red Lion
Great Tew, Falkland Arms
Kelmscot, Plough
Maidensgrove, Five Horseshoes
Oxford, Kings Arms
Oxford, Turf Tavern
Shenington, Bell
Shipton under Wychwood, Shaven Crown

Shropshire
Bridges, Horseshoe
Cardington, Royal Oak
Llanfair Waterdine, Red Lion
Wenlock Edge, Wenlock Edge

Somerset
Appley, Globe
Blagdon, New Inn
Combe Hay, Wheatsheaf
Cranmore, Strode Arms
Luxborough, Royal Oak
Stogumber, White Horse
Wambrook, Cotley
Winsford, Royal Oak

Staffordshire
Alstonefield, George

Suffolk
Dennington, Queens Head
Dunwich, Ship
Lavenham, Angel
Levington, Ship
Ramsholt, Ramsholt Arms
Snape, Plough & Sail

Surrey
Blackbrook, Plough
Chilworth, Villagers
Dunsfold, Sun
Englefield Green, Fox & Hounds
Friday Street, Stephan Langton
Mickleham, King William IV

Reigate Heath, Skimmington Castle

Sussex
Amberley, Black Horse
Barcombe, Anchor
Billingshurst, Blue Ship
Brownbread Street, Ash Tree
Burpham, George & Dragon
Burwash, Bell
Eartham, George
East Dean, Tiger
Fletching, Griffin
Heathfield, Star
Kirdford, Half Moon
Lurgashall, Noahs Ark
Mayfield, Middle House
Seaford, Golden Galleon
Wineham, Royal Oak

Warwickshire
Himley, Crooked House
Warmington, Plough

Wiltshire
Bradford on Avon, Cross Guns
Ebbesbourne Wake, Horseshoe
Wootton Rivers, Royal Oak

Yorkshire
Appletreewick, Craven Arms
Askrigg, Kings Arms
Beck Hole, Birch Hall
Blakey Ridge, Lion
Bradfield, Strines
Buckden, Buck
Burnsall, Red Lion
Byland Abbey, Abbey
Cray, White Lion
East Witton, Blue Lion
Heath, Kings Arms
Hubberholme, George
Lastingham, Blacksmiths Arms
Levisham, Horseshoe
Linton in Craven, Fountaine
Litton, Queens Arms
Masham, Kings Head
Meltham, Will's o' Nat's
Middleham, Black Swan
Muker, Farmers Arms
Ramsgill, Yorke Arms
Robin Hoods Bay, Laurel

Rosedale Abbey, Milburn Arms
Shelley, Three Acres
Starbotton, Fox & Hounds
Terrington, Bay Horse
Thornton Watlass, Buck
Wath-in-Nidderdale, Sportsmans Arms
Widdop, Pack Horse

London, Central
London EC1, Olde Mitre

London, North
London NW3, Spaniards

London, South
London SE1, Horniman
London SE21, Crown & Greyhound
London SW4, Windmill

Scotland
Applecross, Applecross
Arduaine, Loch Melfort
Brig o Turk, Byre
Clachan Seil, Tigh an Truish
Crinan, Crinan
Kilberry, Kilberry
Kilmahog, Lade
Mountbenger, Gordon Arms
Pitlochry, Killiecrankie
Sheriffmuir, Sheriffmuir
St Mary's Loch, Tibbie Shiels
Strachur, Creggans
Tushielaw, Tushielaw

Wales
Abergorlech, Black Lion
Aberystwyth, Halfway
Bosherston, St Govans
Caerphilly, Courthouse
Carew, Carew
Crickhowell, Nantyffin Cider Mill
Erbistock, Boat
Kenfig, Prince of Wales
Llanbedr-y-Cennin, Olde Bull
Llanberis, Pen-y-Gwryd
Llanelidan, Leyland Arms
Llangedwyn, Green
Maentwrog, Grapes
Red Wharf Bay, Ship

Channel Islands
St Brelade, Old Portelet
St Brelade, Old Smugglers
St John, Les Fontaines

PUBS WITH GOOD VIEWS

These pubs are listed for their particularly good views, either from inside or from a garden or terrace. Waterside pubs are listed again here only if their view is exceptional in its own right – not just a straightforward sea view, for example.

Berkshire
Chieveley, Blue Boar

Buckinghamshire
Brill, Pheasant

Cheshire
Higher Burwardsley, Pheasant
Langley, Hanging Gate
Langley, Leathers Smithy
Overton, Ring o' Bells

Cornwall
Cremyll, Edgcumbe Arms
Polruan, Lugger
Ruan Lanihorne, Kings Head
St Agnes, Turks Head

Cumbria
Braithwaite, Coledale
Cartmel Fell, Masons Arms
Hawkshead, Drunken Duck
Langdale, Old Dungeon Ghyll
Loweswater, Kirkstile
Troutbeck, Queens Head
Ulverston, Bay Horse

Derbyshire
Monsal Head, Monsal Head

Devon
Postbridge, Warren House

Dorset
Kingston, Scott Arms
West Bexington, Manor
Worth Matravers, Square & Compass

Gloucestershire
Amberley, Black Horse
Cranham, Black Horse
Edge, Edgemoor
Gretton, Royal Oak
Kilkenny, Kilkeney
Sheepscombe, Butchers Arms
Stanton, Mount

Hampshire
Beauworth, Milbury's
Owslebury, Ship

Hereford & Worcester
Pensax, Bell
Ruckhall, Ancient Camp
Wyre Piddle, Anchor

Hertfordshire
Great Offley, Green Man

Isle of Wight
Ventnor, Spyglass

Kent
Penshurst, Spotted Dog
Ulcombe, Pepper Box

Lancashire (inc Greater Manchester, Merseyside)
Blackstone Edge, White House
Darwen, Old Rosins

Leicestershire & Rutland
Knipton, Red House

Northumberland, Durham, Tyneside & Teeside
Haltwhistle, Wallace Arms
Seahouses, Olde Ship

Shropshire
Cressage, Cholmondeley Riverside

Somerset
Blagdon, New Inn

Suffolk
Erwarton, Queens Head
Hundon, Plough
Levington, Ship

Sussex
Byworth, Black Horse
Elsted, Three Horseshoes
Fletching, Griffin
Icklesham, Queens Head
Rye, Ypres Castle

Wiltshire
Box, Quarrymans Arms

Yorkshire
Appletreewick, Craven Arms
Blakey Ridge, Lion
Bradfield, Strines
Kirkham, Stone Trough
Litton, Queens Arms
Meltham, Will's o' Nat's
Shelley, Three Acres
Whitby, Duke of York

Scotland
Applecross, Applecross
Ardvasar, Ardvasar
Arrochar, Village Inn
Crinan, Crinan
Edinburgh, Starbank
Isle Ornsay, Tigh Osda Eilean Iarmain
Kilberry, Kilberry
Pitlochry, Killiecrankie
Sheriffmuir, Sheriffmuir
Shieldaig, Tigh an Eilean
St Mary's Loch, Tibbie Shiels
Strachur, Creggans
Tushielaw, Tushielaw
Ullapool, Ferry Boat
Weem, Ailean Chraggan

Wales
Aberdovey, Penhelig Arms
Aberystwyth, Halfway
Bodfari, Dinorben Arms
Caerphilly, Courthouse
Halkyn, Britannia
Llanbedr-y-Cennin, Olde Bull
Llanberis, Pen-y-Gwryd
Llanferres, Druid
Llangynwyd, Old House
Llannefydd, Hawk & Buckle
Tyn y Groes, Groes

Channel Islands
St Aubin, Old Court House

PUBS IN INTERESTING BUILDINGS

Pubs and inns are listed here for the particular interest of their building – something really out of the ordinary to look at, or occasionally a building that has an outstandingly interesting historical background.

Berkshire
Cookham, Bel & the Dragon

Buckinghamshire
Forty Green, Royal Standard of England

Derbyshire
Buxton, Bull i' th' Thorn

Devon
Dartmouth, Cherub
Harberton, Church House
Rattery, Church House
Sourton, Highwayman
South Zeal, Oxenham Arms

Hampshire
Beauworth, Milbury's

Hereford & Worcester
Bretforton, Fleece

Lancashire (inc Greater Manchester, Merseyside)
Garstang, Th'Owd Tithebarn
Liverpool, Philharmonic Dining Rooms

Lincolnshire
Stamford, George of Stamford

Northumberland, Durham, Tyneside & Teeside
Blanchland, Lord Crewe Arms

Nottinghamshire
Nottingham, Olde Trip to Jerusalem

Oxfordshire
Banbury, Reindeer
Fyfield, White Hart

Somerset
Norton St Philip, George

Suffolk
Lavenham, Swan

Sussex
Alfriston, Star
Rye, Mermaid

Warwickshire
Himley, Crooked House

Wiltshire
Salisbury, Haunch of Venison

Yorkshire
Hull, Olde White Harte

London, Central
London EC4, Black Friar
London WC1, Cittie of Yorke

London, South
London SE1, George
London SE5, Phoenix & Firkin

Scotland
Edinburgh, Cafe Royal
Edinburgh, Guildford Arms
Glasgow, Horseshoe

Wales
Llanfihangel Crucorney, Skirrid

PUBS THAT BREW THEIR OWN BEER

The pubs listed here brew their own brew on the premises; many others not listed have beers brewed for them specially, sometimes to an individual recipe (but by a separate brewer). We mention these in the text.

Cornwall
Helston, Blue Anchor

Cumbria
Cartmel Fell, Masons Arms
Coniston, Black Bull
Dent, Sun

Derbyshire
Derby, Brunswick
Melbourne, John Thompson

Devon
Ashburton, London
Hatherleigh, Tally Ho
Holbeton, Mildmay Colours
Horsebridge, Royal
Newton St Cyres, Beer Engine

Hereford & Worcester
Aymestrey, Riverside

Hertfordshire
Barley, Fox & Hounds

Lancashire (inc Greater Manchester, Merseyside)
Manchester, Lass o' Gowrie

Lincolnshire
Snaith, Brewers Arms

Norfolk
Woodbastwick, Fur & Feather

Nottinghamshire
Nottingham, Fellows Morton & Clayton

Shropshire
Bishops Castle, Three Tuns
Munslow, Crown

Staffordshire
Burton on Trent, Burton Bridge
Shraleybrook, Rising Sun

Suffolk
Earl Soham, Victoria

Warwickshire
Brierley Hill, Vine

Yorkshire
Cropton, New Inn
Hull, Minerva
Linthwaite, Sair
Sheffield, Fat Cat

London, Central
London SW1, Orange
  Brewery

London, South
London SE5, Phoenix &
  Firkin

London, West
London SW10, Ferret &
  Firkin

**OPEN ALL DAY (AT
LEAST IN SUMMER)**
We list here all the pubs
that have told us they
plan to stay open all day,
even if it's only on a
Saturday. We've included
the few pubs which close
just for half an hour to an
hour, and the many
more, chiefly in holiday
areas, which open all day
only in summer. The
individual entries for the
pubs themselves show the
actual details. A few pubs
in England and Wales,
allowed to stay open only
in the last two or three
years, are still changing
their opening hours – let
us know if you find
anything different.

Bedfordshire
Odell, Bell

Berkshire
East Ilsley, Crown &
  Horns
Hare Hatch, Queen
  Victoria
West Ilsley, Harrow

Buckinghamshire
Brill, Pheasant

Cheddington, Old Swan
Easington, Mole &
  Chicken
Great Missenden, George
Long Crendon, Angel
Northend, White Hart
West Wycombe, George
  & Dragon
Wheeler End, Chequers
Wooburn Common,
  Chequers

Cambridgeshire
Cambridge, Anchor
Cambridge, Eagle
Etton, Golden Pheasant
Godmanchester, Black
  Bull
Holywell, Old Ferry Boat
Huntingdon, Old Bridge
Wansford, Haycock

Cheshire
Aldford, Grosvenor Arms
Barthomley, White Lion
Broxton, Egerton Arms
Chester, Old Harkers
  Arms
Higher Burwardsley,
  Pheasant
Langley, Leathers Smithy
Macclesfield, Sutton Hall
Plumley, Smoker
Tarporley, Rising Sun
Wettenhall, Boot &
  Slipper
Whitegate, Plough
Wrenbury, Dusty Miller

Cornwall
Boscastle, Cobweb
Cremyll, Edgcumbe Arms
Edmonton, Quarryman
Falmouth, Chain Locker
Falmouth, Quayside
Helston, Blue Anchor
Lostwithiel, Royal Oak
Mousehole, Ship
Mylor Bridge, Pandora
Pelynt, Jubilee
Polruan, Lugger
Port Isaac, Golden Lion
Porthleven, Ship
St Agnes, Railway
St Agnes, Turks Head
St Just in Penwith, Star
St Mawes, Victory
St Teath, White Hart
Trebarwith, Port William
Treen, Logan Rock

Tresco, New Inn
Truro, Old Ale House

Cumbria
Ambleside, Golden Rule
Bowland Bridge, Hare &
  Hounds
Bowness on Windermere,
  Hole in t' Wall
Braithwaite, Coledale
Brampton, New Inn
Cartmel, Cavendish Arms
Cartmel Fell, Masons
  Arms
Chapel Stile,
  Wainwrights
Dent, Sun
Dockray, Royal
Elterwater, Britannia
Eskdale Green, Bower
  House
Grasmere, Travellers Rest
Hawkshead, Kings Arms
Hawkshead, Queens
  Head
Heversham, Blue Bell
Kirkby Lonsdale, Snooty
  Fox
Kirkby Lonsdale, Sun
Langdale, Old Dungeon
  Ghyll
Little Langdale, Three
  Shires
Loweswater, Kirkstile
Melmerby, Shepherds
Seathwaite, Newfield
Sedbergh, Dalesman
Tirril, Queens Head
Troutbeck, Queens Head
Ulverston, Bay Horse

Derbyshire
Ashbourne, Smiths
  Tavern
Ashford in the Water,
  Ashford
Beeley, Devonshire Arms
Buxworth, Navigation
Derby, Alexandra
Derby, Brunswick
Derby, Olde Dolphin
Froggatt Edge, Chequers
Grindleford, Maynard
  Arms
Hardwick Hall,
  Hardwick
Hayfield, Lantern Pike
Holmesfield, Robin Hood
Ladybower Reservoir,
  Yorkshire Bridge

Monsal Head, Monsal Head
Wardlow, Three Stags Heads
Whittington Moor, Derby Tup

Devon
Abbotskerswell, Court Farm
Ashburton, London
Axmouth, Harbour
Bishops Tawton, Chichester Arms
Branscombe, Masons Arms
Brendon, Rockford
Budleigh Salterton, Salterton Arms
Chagford, Ring o' Bells
Cockwood, Anchor
Dartmouth, Cherub
Dartmouth, Royal Castle
Exeter, Double Locks
Exeter, Imperial
Exeter, White Hart
Exminster, Turf
Iddesleigh, Duke of York
Lustleigh, Cleave
Newton St Cyres, Beer Engine
Plymouth, China House
Postbridge, Warren House
Rackenford, Stag
Ringmore, Journeys End
Stoke Gabriel, Church House
Topsham, Passage House
Torcross, Start Bay
Torrington, Black Horse
Ugborough, Anchor
Wonson, Northmore Arms
Woodland, Rising Sun

Dorset
Abbotsbury, Ilchester Arms
Bridport, George
Chideock, Anchor
Christchurch, Fishermans Haunt
Corfe Castle, Greyhound
Dorchester, Kings Arms
Kingston, Scott Arms
Loders, Loders Arms
Lyme Regis, Pilot Boat
Osmington Mills, Smugglers

Tarrant Monkton, Langton Arms
West Bexington, Manor
Worth Matravers, Square & Compass

Essex
Coggeshall, Compasses
Dedham, Marlborough Head
Leigh on Sea, Crooked Billet
Littlebury, Queens Head
Navestock, Plough
Peldon, Rose
Saffron Walden, Eight Bells
Stock, Hoop
Stow Maries, Prince of Wales

Gloucestershire
Amberley, Black Horse
Ampney Crucis, Crown of Crucis
Bibury, Catherine Wheel
Bisley, Bear
Blockley, Crown
Broad Campden, Bakers Arms
Brockweir, Brockweir
Clearwell, Wyndham Arms
Coleford, Dog & Muffler
Coln St Aldwyns, New Inn
Ewen, Wild Duck
Ford, Plough
Great Barrington, Fox
Kingscote, Hunters Hall
Littleton upon Severn, White Hart
Oddington, Horse & Groom
Old Sodbury, Dog
Redbrook, Boat
Sheepscombe, Butchers Arms
South Cerney, Eliot Arms
Stanton, Mount
Stow on the Wold, Coach & Horses
Tetbury, Gumstool

Hampshire
Bentworth, Sun
Boldre, Red Lion
Bursledon, Jolly Sailor
Froyle, Hen & Chicken
Langstone, Royal Oak

Locks Heath, Jolly Farmer
Owslebury, Ship
Pilley, Fleur de Lys
Portsmouth, Still & West
Rotherwick, Coach & Horses
Soberton, White Lion
Sopley, Woolpack
Southsea, Wine Vaults
Sway, Hare & Hounds
Titchfield, Fishermans Rest
Well, Chequers
Wherwell, Mayfly
Winchester, Wykeham Arms

Hereford & Worcester
Bewdley, Little Pack Horse
Defford, Monkey House
Kidderminster, King & Castle
Knightwick, Talbot
Ledbury, Feathers
Longdon, Hunters
Lugwardine, Crown & Anchor
Michaelchurch Escley, Bridge
Ombersley, Kings Arms
Pensax, Bell
Walterstone, Carpenters Arms
Weobley, Olde Salutation

Hertfordshire
Ashwell, Bushel & Strike
Ashwell, Three Tuns
Ayot St Lawrence, Brocket Arms
Berkhamsted, Boat
Flaunden, Bricklayers Arms
Great Offley, Green Man
Knebworth, Lytton Arms
Sarratt, Cock
St Albans, Garibaldi
Wadesmill, Sow & Pigs
Walkern, White Lion
Watton at Stone, George & Dragon

Isle of Wight
Arreton, White Lion
Chale, Clarendon (Wight Mouse)
Cowes, Folly
Shorwell, Crown

Ventnor, Spyglass
Yarmouth, Wheatsheaf

Kent
Barfrestone, Yew Tree
Bough Beech, Wheatsheaf
Boughton Aluph, Flying
  Horse
Chiddingstone, Castle
Groombridge, Crown
Ightham Common,
  Harrow
Lamberhurst, Brown
  Trout
Langton Green, Hare
Luddesdown, Cock
Oare, Shipwrights Arms
Ringlestone, Ringlestone
Speldhurst, George &
  Dragon
Tunbridge Wells, Sankeys
Whitstable, Pearsons
  Crab & Oyster House

**Lancashire (inc Greater
  Manchester,
  Merseyside)**
Bilsborrow, Owd Nells
Bispham Green, Eagle &
  Child
Chipping, Dog &
  Partridge
Croston, Black Horse
Darwen, Old Rosins
Garstang, Th'Owd
  Tithebarn
Liverpool, Philharmonic
  Dining Rooms
Lytham, Taps
Manchester, Dukes 92
Manchester, Lass o'
  Gowrie
Manchester, Marble Arch
Manchester, Mark Addy
Manchester, Royal Oak
Newton, Parkers Arms
Raby, Wheatsheaf
Ribchester, White Bull
Stalybridge, Station
  Buffet
Yealand Conyers, New
  Inn

Leicestershire & Rutland
Braunston, Blue Ball
Empingham, White
  Horse
Glaston, Monckton Arms
Loughborough, Swan in
  the Rushes

Redmile, Peacock
Somerby, Old Brewery

Lincolnshire
Coleby, Bell
Grantham, Beehive
Lincoln, Wig & Mitre
Stamford, George of
  Stamford

Norfolk
Bawburgh, Kings Head
Blakeney, Kings Arms
Burnham Market, Hoste
  Arms
Hunworth, Hunny Bell
Kings Lynn, Tudor Rose
Larling, Angel
Mundford, Crown
Norwich, Adam & Eve
Norwich, Fat Cat
Reedham, Ferry
Sculthorpe, Sculthorpe
  Mill
Snettisham, Rose &
  Crown
Swanton Morley, Darbys
Thornham, Lifeboat
Tivetshall St Mary, Old
  Ram
Winterton-on-Sea,
  Fishermans Return

Northamptonshire
Ashby St Ledgers, Olde
  Coach House
Badby, Windmill
Chacombe, George &
  Dragon
Great Brington, Fox &
  Hounds
Oundle, Ship

**Northumberland,
  Durham, Tyneside &
  Teeside**
Allendale, Kings Head
Alnmouth, Saddle
Bamburgh, Lord Crewe
  Arms
Craster, Jolly Fisherman
Haltwhistle, Wallace
  Arms
Matfen, Black Bull
New York, Shiremoor
  House Farm
Newcastle upon Tyne,
  Crown Posada

Nottinghamshire
Beeston, Victoria
Drakeholes, Griff
Kimberley, Nelson &
  Railway
Normanton on Trent,
  Square & Compass
Nottingham, Fellows
  Morton & Clayton
Nottingham, Lincolnshire
  Poacher
Nottingham, Olde Trip
  to Jerusalem

Oxfordshire
Adderbury, Red Lion
Bampton, Romany
Banbury, Reindeer
Barford St Michael,
  George
Barnard Gate, Boot
Bloxham, Elephant &
  Castle
Burford, Mermaid
Clifton Hampden, Plough
Dorchester, George
Duns Tew, White Horse
Exlade Street,
  Highwayman
Finstock, Plough
Great Tew, Falkland
  Arms
Hook Norton, Pear Tree
Kelmscot, Plough
Oxford, Kings Arms
Oxford, Turf Tavern
Shipton under
  Wychwood, Shaven
  Crown
Stanton St John, Talk
  House
Wytham, White Hart

Shropshire
Bishops Castle, Three
  Tuns
Cardington, Royal Oak
Shrewsbury, Armoury

Somerset
Ashcott, Ashcott
Bath, Old Green Tree
Bristol, Highbury Vaults
Churchill, Crown
Clapton in Gordano,
  Black Horse
Dunster, Luttrell Arms
Exebridge, Anchor
Huish Episcopi, Rose &
  Crown

Rudge, Full Moon
South Stoke, Pack Horse
Stanton Wick, Carpenters
  Arms

Staffordshire
Acton Trussell, Moat
  House
Alstonefield, George
Cresswell, Izaak Walton
Onecote, Jervis Arms
Salt, Holly Bush
Shraleybrook, Rising Sun
Tutbury, Olde Dog &
  Partridge
Uttoxeter, Wellington

Suffolk
Aldeburgh, Cross Keys
Butley, Oyster
Chelmondiston, Butt &
  Oyster
Chillesford, Froize
Cotton, Trowel &
  Hammer
Lavenham, Angel
Wangford, Angel

Surrey
Chilworth, Villagers
Coldharbour, Plough
Effingham, Sir Douglas
  Haig
Farncombe, Ram
Friday Street, Stephan
  Langton
Hascombe, White Horse
Leigh, Plough
Outwood, Dog & Duck
Pirbright, Royal Oak
Reigate Heath,
  Skimmington Castle
Warlingham, White Lion

Sussex
Barcombe, Anchor
Burwash, Bell
Eartham, George
East Dean, Tiger
Fletching, Griffin
Hartfield, Anchor
Horsham, Black Jug
Icklesham, Queens Head
Kingston near Lewes,
  Juggs
Lewes, Snowdrop
Mayfield, Middle House
Mayfield, Rose & Crown
Midhurst, Spread Eagle
Oving, Gribble

Playden, Peace & Plenty
Rye, Mermaid
Rye, Ypres Castle
Seaford, Golden Galleon
West Ashling, Richmond
  Arms

Warwickshire
Berkswell, Bear
Brierley Hill, Vine
Coventry, Old Windmill
Himley, Crooked House
Lapworth, Navigation
Lowsonford, Fleur de Lys
Newbold on Stour, White
  Hart
Stratford upon Avon,
  Slug & Lettuce
Temple Grafton, Blue
  Boar
Tipton, M A D
  O'Rourkes Pie Factory

Wiltshire
Barford St Martin,
  Barford
Box, Quarrymans Arms
Bradford on Avon, Cross
  Guns
Brinkworth, Three
  Crowns
Devizes, Bear
Hindon, Lamb
Lacock, George
Lacock, Red Lion
Marlborough, Sun
Netherhampton, Victoria
  & Albert
Salisbury, Haunch of
  Venison
Salisbury, New Inn
Sherston, Rattlebone
Wootton Rivers, Royal
  Oak

Yorkshire
Aldborough, Ship
Bardsey, Bingley Arms
Beck Hole, Birch Hall
Beverley, White Horse
Blakey Ridge, Lion
Boroughbridge, Black
  Bull
Bradfield, Strines
Brandesburton, Dacre
  Arms
Buckden, Buck
Burnsall, Red Lion
Cray, White Lion
Cropton, New Inn

East Marton, Cross Keys
East Witton, Blue Lion
Egton Bridge, Horse Shoe
Harden, Malt Shovel
Heath, Kings Arms
Heckmondwike, Old
  Hall
Helmsley, Feathers
Hull, Minerva
Hull, Olde White Harte
Ledsham, Chequers
Leeds, Whitelocks
Linthwaite, Sair
Linton, Windmill
Linton in Craven,
  Fountaine
Low Catton, Gold Cup
Masham, Kings Head
Masham, White Bear
Muker, Farmers Arms
Pickhill, Nags Head
Pool, White Hart
Ramsgill, Yorke Arms
Ripponden, Old Bridge
Robin Hoods Bay, Laurel
Settle, Golden Lion
Sheffield, New Barracks
Thornton Watlass, Buck
Whitby, Duke of York
York, Black Swan
York, Olde Starre
York, Spread Eagle
York, Tap & Spile

London, Central
London EC1, Eagle
London EC1, Olde Mitre
London EC4, Black Friar
London EC4, Old Bank
  of England
London EC4, Olde
  Cheshire Cheese
London SW1, Albert
London SW1, Grenadier
London SW1, Nags Head
London SW1, Orange
  Brewery
London SW1, Star
London SW1,
  Westminster Arms
London W1, Argyll Arms
London W1, Dog &
  Duck
London W1, Grapes
London W1, Old Coffee
  House
London W1, Red Lion
London WC1, Cittie of
  Yorke
London WC1, Lamb

London WC1, Museum Tavern
London WC1, Princess Louise
London WC2, Lamb & Flag
London WC2, Seven Stars

London, North
London N1, Waterside
London NW1, Chapel
London NW3, Flask
London NW3, Olde White Bear
London NW3, Spaniards

London, South
London SE1, Anchor
London SE1, Fire Station
London SE1, George
London SE1, Horniman
London SE1, Market Porter
London SE5, Phoenix & Firkin
London SE10, Cutty Sark
London SE21, Crown & Greyhound
London SW4, Windmill
London SW13, Bulls Head
London SW18, Alma
London SW18, Ship
Richmond, White Cross

London, West
London SW6, White Horse
London SW10, Ferret & Firkin
London W4, Bulls Head
London W6, Dove
London W8, Windsor Castle
London W11, Ladbroke Arms

London, East
London E1, Prospect of Whitby
London E1, Town of Ramsgate

Scotland
Aberdeen, Prince of Wales
Applecross, Applecross
Ardfern, Galley of Lorne
Arduaine, Loch Melfort

Ardvasar, Ardvasar
Arrochar, Village Inn
Brig o Turk, Byre
Broughty Ferry, Fishermans Tavern
Carbost, Old Inn
Cawdor, Cawdor Tavern
Clachan Seil, Tigh an Truish
Crinan, Crinan
Edinburgh, Abbotsford
Edinburgh, Bannermans Bar
Edinburgh, Bow Bar
Edinburgh, Cafe Royal
Edinburgh, Guildford Arms
Edinburgh, Kays Bar
Edinburgh, Starbank
Elie, Ship
Fort Augustus, Lock
Gifford, Tweeddale Arms
Glasgow, Babbity Bowster
Glasgow, Bon Accord
Glasgow, Counting House
Glasgow, Horseshoe
Glendevon, Tormaukin
Innerleithen, Traquair Arms
Isle Ornsay, Tigh Osda Eilean Iarmain
Isle of Whithorn, Steam Packet
Kilmahog, Lade
Kippen, Cross Keys
Kirkton of Glenisla, Glenisla
Linlithgow, Four Marys
Lybster, Portland Arms
Mountbenger, Gordon Arms
Oban, Oban
Plockton, Plockton
Portpatrick, Crown
Sheriffmuir, Sheriffmuir
Shieldaig, Tigh an Eilean
St Mary's Loch, Tibbie Shiels
Strachur, Creggans
Tayvallich, Tayvallich
Thornhill, Lion & Unicorn
Ullapool, Ceilidh Place
Ullapool, Ferry Boat
Weem, Ailean Chraggan
Westruther, Old Thistle

Wales
Beaumaris, Olde Bulls Head
Bodfari, Dinorben Arms
Bosherston, St Govans
Caerphilly, Courthouse
Carew, Carew
Cilgerran, Pendre
Colwyn Bay, Mountain View
East Aberthaw, Blue Anchor
Erbistock, Boat
Gresford, Pant-yr-Ochain
Halkyn, Britannia
Hay on Wye, Old Black Lion
Llanberis, Pen-y-Gwryd
Llandrindod Wells, Llanerch
Llanelidan, Leyland Arms
Llanferres, Druid
Llanfihangel Crucorney, Skirrid
Llangynidr, Coach & Horses
Llangynwyd, Old House
Maentwrog, Grapes
Montgomery, Dragon
Pontypool, Open Hearth
Presteigne, Radnorshire Arms
Raglan, Clytha Arms
Red Wharf Bay, Ship
Rosebush, New Inn
St Hilary, Bush
Talybont-on-Usk, Star

Channel Islands
Greve de Lecq, Moulin de Lecq
Rozel, Rozel Bay
St Aubin, Old Court House
St Brelade, Old Portelet
St Brelade, Old Smugglers
St Helier, Admiral
St Helier, Chambers
St Helier, Tipsy Toad Town House
St John, Les Fontaines
St Lawrence, British Union
St Martin, Royal
St Peter, Star & Tipsy Toad

NO-SMOKING AREAS

We list here all the pubs that have told us they set aside at least some part of the pub as a no-smoking area. Look at the individual entries for the pubs themselves to see just what they do: provision is much more generous in some pubs than in others.

Bedfordshire
Houghton Conquest, Knife & Cleaver
Keysoe, Chequers

Berkshire
Binfield, Stag & Hounds
Bray, Fish
Cookham, Bel & the Dragon
East Ilsley, Crown & Horns
Frilsham, Pot Kiln
Hamstead Marshall, White Hart
Hare Hatch, Queen Victoria
Waltham St Lawrence, Bell
West Ilsley, Harrow
Yattendon, Royal Oak

Buckinghamshire
Amersham, Queens Head
Bledlow, Lions of Bledlow
Bolter End, Peacock
Cheddington, Old Swan
Fawley, Walnut Tree
Forty Green, Royal Standard of England
Great Missenden, George
Hambleden, Stag & Huntsman
Ibstone, Fox
Little Hampden, Rising Sun
Long Crendon, Angel
Prestwood, Polecat
Skirmett, Old Crown
Waddesdon, Five Arrows
West Wycombe, George & Dragon

Cambridgeshire
Barnack, Millstone
Bythorn, White Hart
Cambridge, Anchor
Cambridge, Eagle
Cambridge, Free Press
Cambridge, Live & Let Live
Elsworth, George & Dragon
Etton, Golden Pheasant
Fowlmere, Chequers
Gorefield, Woodmans Cottage
Heydon, King William IV
Hinxton, Red Lion
Holywell, Old Ferry Boat
Horningsea, Plough & Fleece
Keyston, Pheasant
Newton, Queens Head
Peterborough, Charters
Stilton, Bell
Sutton Gault, Anchor
Swavesey, Trinity Foot
Wansford, Haycock
Woodditton, Three Blackbirds

Cheshire
Broxton, Egerton Arms
Higher Burwardsley, Pheasant
Langley, Hanging Gate
Langley, Leathers Smithy
Marbury, Swan
Peover Heath, Dog
Plumley, Smoker
Pott Shrigley, Cheshire Hunt
Swettenham, Swettenham Arms
Weston, White Lion
Wrenbury, Dusty Miller

Cornwall
Boscastle, Cobweb
Chapel Amble, Maltsters Arms
Constantine, Trengilly Wartha
Edmonton, Quarryman
Helston, Halzephron
Lanlivery, Crown
Ludgvan, White Hart
Mithian, Miners Arms
Mylor Bridge, Pandora
Polruan, Lugger
Ruan Lanihorne, Kings Head
Scorrier, Fox & Hounds
St Agnes, Turks Head
St Breward, Old Inn
St Mawgan, Falcon
St Teath, White Hart
Treburley, Springer Spaniel
Tresco, New Inn

Cumbria
Appleby, Royal Oak
Bassenthwaite, Pheasant
Beetham, Wheatsheaf
Braithwaite, Coledale
Cartmel, Cavendish Arms
Chapel Stile, Wainwrights
Cockermouth, Trout
Crosthwaite, Punch Bowl
Dent, Sun
Dockray, Royal
Elterwater, Britannia
Eskdale Green, Bower House
Garrigill, George & Dragon
Grasmere, Travellers Rest
Hawkshead, Drunken Duck
Hawkshead, Kings Arms
Hawkshead, Queens Head
Heversham, Blue Bell
Ings, Watermill
Kirkby Lonsdale, Snooty Fox
Lanercost, Abbey Bridge
Levens, Hare & Hounds
Little Langdale, Three Shires
Melmerby, Shepherds
Scales, White Horse
Seathwaite, Newfield
Sedbergh, Dalesman
Tirril, Queens Head
Troutbeck, Mortal Man
Troutbeck, Queens Head
Ulverston, Bay Horse
Yanwath, Gate

Derbyshire
Ashford in the Water, Ashford
Beeley, Devonshire Arms
Birchover, Druid
Brassington, Olde Gate
Derby, Brunswick
Derby, Olde Dolphin
Fenny Bentley, Coach & Horses
Froggatt Edge, Chequers
Grindleford, Maynard Arms

Hardwick Hall, Hardwick
Hayfield, Lantern Pike
Kirk Ireton, Barley Mow
Ladybower Reservoir, Yorkshire Bridge
Melbourne, John Thompson
Monsal Head, Monsal Head
Wardlow, Three Stags Heads
Whittington Moor, Derby Tup
Woolley Moor, White Horse

Devon
Ashprington, Durant Arms
Axmouth, Harbour
Berrynarbor, Olde Globe
Bishops Tawton, Chichester Arms
Branscombe, Fountain Head
Branscombe, Masons Arms
Churchstow, Church House
Cockwood, Anchor
Dartington, Cott
Dartmouth, Royal Castle
Doddiscombsleigh, Nobody
Drewsteignton, Drewe Arms
Dunsford, Royal Oak
Exeter, Imperial
Exeter, White Hart
Exminster, Turf
Harberton, Church House
Hatherleigh, Tally Ho
Haytor Vale, Rock
Holbeton, Mildmay Colours
Horsebridge, Royal
Kingsteignton, Old Rydon
Knowstone, Masons Arms
Lustleigh, Cleave
Lydford, Castle
Lynmouth, Rising Sun
Miltoncombe, Who'd Have Thought It
Peter Tavy, Peter Tavy
Plymouth, China House
Ringmore, Journeys End

Sidford, Blue Ball
Sourton, Highwayman
South Zeal, Oxenham Arms
Staverton, Sea Trout
Tipton St John, Golden Lion
Topsham, Passage House
Torcross, Start Bay
Trusham, Cridford
Woodland, Rising Sun

Dorset
Abbotsbury, Ilchester Arms
Askerswell, Spyway
Bishops Caundle, White Hart
Bridport, George
Burton Bradstock, Three Horseshoes
Chideock, Anchor
Christchurch, Fishermans Haunt
Church Knowle, New Inn
Cranborne, Fleur-de-Lys
East Chaldon, Sailors Return
East Knighton, Countryman
Kingston, Scott Arms
Lyme Regis, Pilot Boat
Marnhull, Blackmore Vale
Nettlecombe, Marquis of Lorne
Osmington Mills, Smugglers
Plush, Brace of Pheasants
Shave Cross, Shave Cross
Tarrant Monkton, Langton Arms
West Bexington, Manor

Essex
Castle Hedingham, Bell
Chappel, Swan
Clavering, Cricketers
Fyfield, Black Bull
Great Yeldham, White Hart
Horndon-on-the-Hill, Bell
Lamarsh, Lion
Littlebury, Queens Head
Peldon, Rose
Saffron Walden, Eight Bells
Toot Hill, Green Man
Wendens Ambo, Bell

Gloucestershire
Almondsbury, Bowl
Amberley, Black Horse
Ampney Crucis, Crown of Crucis
Aust, Boars Head
Awre, Red Hart
Barnsley, Village Pub
Bisley, Bear
Blaisdon, Red Hart
Bledington, Kings Head
Brimpsfield, Golden Heart
Clearwell, Wyndham Arms
Cold Aston, Plough
Coln St Aldwyns, New Inn
Edge, Edgemoor
Great Rissington, Lamb
Greet, Harvest Home
Gretton, Royal Oak
Hyde, Ragged Cot
Kilkenny, Kilkeney
Kineton, Halfway House
Kingscote, Hunters Hall
Little Washbourne, Hobnails
Littleton upon Severn, White Hart
Meysey Hampton, Masons Arms
Minchinhampton, Old Lodge
Oakridge Lynch, Butchers Arms
Old Sodbury, Dog
Oldbury on Severn, Anchor
Sapperton, Daneway
Sheepscombe, Butchers Arms
South Cerney, Eliot Arms
St Briavels, George
Stanton, Mount
Withington, Mill

Hampshire
Alresford, Globe
Boldre, Red Lion
Bramdean, Fox
Bursledon, Jolly Sailor
Chalton, Red Lion
Droxford, White Horse
East Tytherley, Star
Froyle, Hen & Chicken
Ibsley, Old Beams
Langstone, Royal Oak
Locks Heath, Jolly Farmer

Micheldever, Dever Arms
Pilley, Fleur de Lys
Portsmouth, Still & West
Rockbourne, Rose &
  Thistle
Soberton, White Lion
Sparsholt, Plough
Sway, Hare & Hounds
Titchfield, Fishermans
  Rest
Winchester, Wykeham
  Arms

Hereford & Worcester
Bransford, Bear &
  Ragged Staff
Bredon, Fox & Hounds
Bretforton, Fleece
Kempsey, Walter de
  Cantelupe
Lugwardine, Crown &
  Anchor
Ombersley, Crown &
  Sandys Arms
Ruckhall, Ancient Camp
Sellack, Lough Pool
Stockton Cross, Stockton
  Cross
Upton Bishop, Moody
  Cow
Weobley, Olde Salutation
Winforton, Sun
Woolhope, Crown

Hertfordshire
Ashwell, Bushel & Strike
Ayot St Lawrence,
  Brocket Arms
Barley, Fox & Hounds
Burnham Green, White
  Horse
Knebworth, Lytton Arms
Rushden, Moon & Stars
St Albans, Garibaldi
St Albans, Rose &
  Crown
Walkern, White Lion
Watton at Stone, George
  & Dragon
Westmill, Sword in Hand

Isle of Wight
Arreton, White Lion
Bonchurch, Bonchurch
Chale, Clarendon (Wight
  Mouse)
Cowes, Folly
Shorwell, Crown
Ventnor, Spyglass
Yarmouth, Wheatsheaf

Kent
Boyden Gate, Gate
Groombridge, Crown
Oare, Shipwrights Arms
Smarden, Bell
Tunbridge Wells, Sankeys
Ulcombe, Pepper Box

**Lancashire (inc Greater
  Manchester,
  Merseyside)**
Balderstone, Myerscough
Bilsborrow, Owd Nells
Bispham Green, Eagle &
  Child
Chipping, Dog &
  Partridge
Croston, Black Horse
Darwen, Old Rosins
Downham, Assheton
  Arms
Fence, Forest
Goosnargh, Bushells
  Arms
Liverpool, Philharmonic
  Dining Rooms
Mellor, Oddfellows Arms
Newton, Parkers Arms
Ribchester, White Bull
Yealand Conyers, New
  Inn

Leicestershire & Rutland
Braunston, Blue Ball
Braunston, Old Plough
East Langton, Bell
Empingham, White
  Horse
Glooston, Old Barn
Hose, Rose & Crown
Knipton, Red House
Lyddington, Old White
  Hart
Old Dalby, Crown
Redmile, Peacock
Sibson, Cock
Somerby, Old Brewery
Thorpe Langton, Bakers
  Arms

Lincolnshire
Allington, Welby Arms
Coleby, Bell
Donington on Bain, Black
  Horse
Dyke, Wishing Well
Gedney Dyke, Chequers
Newton, Red Lion
Snaith, Brewers Arms

Norfolk
Bawburgh, Kings Head
Blakeney, Kings Arms
Blakeney, White Horse
Burnham Market, Hoste
  Arms
Burnham Thorpe, Lord
  Nelson
Colkirk, Crown
Fakenham, Wensum
  Lodge
Great Bircham, Kings
  Head
Heydon, Earle Arms
Kings Lynn, Tudor Rose
Norwich, Adam & Eve
Reedham, Ferry
Ringstead, Gin Trap
Snettisham, Rose &
  Crown
Stow Bardolph, Hare
  Arms
Swanton Morley, Darbys
Titchwell, Manor
Tivetshall St Mary, Old
  Ram
Warham, Three
  Horseshoes
Winterton on Sea,
  Fishermans Return
Woodbastwick, Fur &
  Feather

Northamptonshire
Ashby St Ledgers, Olde
  Coach House
Chacombe, George &
  Dragon
Clipston, Bulls Head
Eastcote, Eastcote Arms
Farthingstone, Kings Arms
Fotheringhay, Falcon
Harringworth, White
  Swan
Oundle, Mill
Sulgrave, Star
Wadenhoe, Kings Head

**Northumberland,
  Durham, Tyneside &
  Teeside**
Allenheads, Allenheads
Bamburgh, Lord Crewe
  Arms
Carterway Heads, Manor
  House
Cotherstone, Fox &
  Hounds
Great Whittington,
  Queens Head

Haltwhistle, Wallace Arms
Matfen, Black Bull
Newton on the Moor, Cook & Barker Arms
Romaldkirk, Rose & Crown
Seahouses, Olde Ship
Stannersburn, Pheasant

Nottinghamshire
Beeston, Victoria
Drakeholes, Griff
Wellow, Olde Red Lion

Oxfordshire
Adderbury, Red Lion
Bampton, Romany
Banbury, Reindeer
Barnard Gate, Boot
Blewbury, Red Lion
Broadwell, Five Bells
Burcot, Chequers
Burford, Lamb
Burford, Mermaid
Chalgrove, Red Lion
Chinnor, Sir Charles Napier
Church Enstone, Crown
Clanfield, Clanfield Tavern
Clifton Hampden, Plough
Cuddesdon, Bat & Ball
Cumnor, Bear & Ragged Staff
Fyfield, White Hart
Great Tew, Falkland Arms
Lewknor, Olde Leathern Bottel
Oxford, Kings Arms
Oxford, Turf Tavern
Ramsden, Royal Oak
Roke, Home Sweet Home
Shipton under Wychwood, Lamb
Stanton St John, Star
Woodstock, Feathers
Wytham, White Hart

Shropshire
Bridges, Horseshoe
Brockton, Feathers
Cardington, Royal Oak
Llanfair Waterdine, Red Lion
Ludlow, Unicorn
Much Wenlock, Talbot
Upper Farmcote, Lion of Morfe

Wenlock Edge, Wenlock Edge

Somerset
Appley, Globe
Ashcott, Ashcott
Bath, Old Green Tree
Beckington, Woolpack
Blagdon, New Inn
Castle Cary, George
Compton Martin, Ring o' Bells
Dowlish Wake, New Inn
Dunster, Luttrell Arms
Exebridge, Anchor
Hinton St George, Lord Poulett
Knapp, Rising Sun
Langley Marsh, Three Horseshoes
Monksilver, Notley Arms
Norton St Philip, George
Sparkford, Sparkford
Stoke St Gregory, Rose & Crown
Stoke St Mary, Half Moon
Wambrook, Cotley
West Huntspill, Crossways

Staffordshire
Acton Trussell, Moat House
Alstonefield, George
Alstonefield, Watts Russell Arms
Cresswell, Izaak Walton
Onecote, Jervis Arms
Tutbury, Olde Dog & Partridge

Suffolk
Bardwell, Six Bells
Blyford, Queens Head
Dunwich, Ship
Great Glemham, Crown
Hartest, Crown
Hundon, Plough
Lavenham, Angel
Lavenham, Swan
Levington, Ship
Orford, Jolly Sailor
Ramsholt, Ramsholt Arms
Snape, Plough & Sail
Southwold, Crown
Stoke by Nayland, Angel
Thornham Magna, Four Horseshoes

Wangford, Angel

Surrey
Blackbrook, Plough
Charleshill, Donkey
Coldharbour, Plough
Friday Street, Stephan Langton
Pirbright, Royal Oak
Thursley, Three Horseshoes
Warlingham, White Lion

Sussex
Alfriston, Star
Amberley, Black Horse
Barcombe, Anchor
Byworth, Black Horse
Cowbeech, Merrie Harriers
Eartham, George
East Dean, Tiger
Firle, Ram
Hammerpot, Woodmans Arms
Icklesham, Queens Head
Kingston near Lewes, Juggs
Kirdford, Half Moon
Lodsworth, Halfway Bridge
Lower Beeding, Crabtree
Lurgashall, Noahs Ark
Mayfield, Middle House
Midhurst, Spread Eagle
Nuthurst, Black Horse
Oving, Gribble
Punnetts Town, Three Cups
Rye, Ypres Castle
Seaford, Golden Galleon

Warwickshire
Alderminster, Bell
Coventry, Old Windmill
Himley, Crooked House
Ilmington, Howard Arms
Little Compton, Red Lion
Lowsonford, Fleur de Lys
Monks Kirby, Bell
Temple Grafton, Blue Boar

Wiltshire
Barford St Martin, Barford
Box, Quarrymans Arms
Brinkworth, Three Crowns
Devizes, Bear

Ebbesbourne Wake, Horseshoe
Hindon, Lamb
Kilmington, Red Lion
Lacock, George
Lacock, Red Lion
Limpley Stoke, Hop Pole
Little Bedwyn, Harrow
Lower Woodford, Wheatsheaf
Marlborough, Sun
Netherhampton, Victoria & Albert
Potterne, George & Dragon
Poulshot, Raven
Ramsbury, Bell
Rowde, George & Dragon
Salisbury, New Inn
Seend, Barge
Sherston, Rattlebone
Wilcot, Golden Swan

Yorkshire
Asenby, Crab & Lobster
Askrigg, Kings Arms
Beverley, White Horse
Bilbrough, Three Hares
Blakey Ridge, Lion
Bradfield, Strines
Buckden, Buck
Burnsall, Red Lion
Carlton, Foresters Arms
Carthorpe, Fox & Hounds
Cray, White Lion
Cropton, New Inn
Dacre Banks, Royal Oak
Goose Eye, Turkey
Harden, Malt Shovel
Hetton, Angel
Hull, Minerva
Kirkbymoorside, George & Dragon
Kirkham, Stone Trough
Lastingham, Blacksmiths Arms
Levisham, Horseshoe
Linthwaite, Sair
Linton in Craven, Fountaine
Low Catton, Gold Cup
Meltham, Will's o' Nat's
Newton on Ouse, Dawnay Arms
Pickhill, Nags Head
Pool, White Hart
Ramsgill, Yorke Arms
Redmire, Kings Arms

Rosedale Abbey, Milburn Arms
Sawley, Sawley Arms
Sheffield, Fat Cat
Sheffield, New Barracks
Starbotton, Fox & Hounds
Sutton upon Derwent, St Vincent Arms
Thornton Watlass, Buck
Wath-in-Nidderdale, Sportsmans Arms
Wormald Green, Cragg Lodge
York, Black Swan
York, Olde Starre

London, Central
London EC4, Olde Cheshire Cheese
London SW1, Lord Moon of the Mall
London W1, Argyll Arms
London WC1, Lamb

London, North
London N1, Waterside
London NW3, Spaniards

London, South
London SE1, George
London SE1, Market Porter
London SE21, Crown & Greyhound

London, West
London W8, Windsor Castle

London, East
London E1, Prospect of Whitby

Scotland
Applecross, Applecross
Arduaine, Loch Melfort
Brig o Turk, Byre
Canonbie, Riverside
Cawdor, Cawdor Tavern
Creebridge, Creebridge House
Edinburgh, Starbank
Fort Augustus, Lock
Glasgow, Horseshoe
Innerleithen, Traquair Arms
Isle Ornsay, Tigh Osda Eilean Iarmain
Kilberry, Kilberry

Kirkton of Glenisla, Glenisla
Melrose, Burts
Oban, Oban
Pitlochry, Killiecrankie
Plockton, Plockton
Portpatrick, Crown
Skeabost, Skeabost House
St Mary's Loch, Tibbie Shiels
Strachur, Creggans
Swinton, Wheatsheaf
Tayvallich, Tayvallich
Thornhill, Lion & Unicorn
Tushielaw, Tushielaw
Ullapool, Ceilidh Place
Ullapool, Ferry Boat
Ullapool, Morefield Motel

Wales
Aberdovey, Penhelig Arms
Beaumaris, Olde Bulls Head
Bodfari, Dinorben Arms
Bosherston, St Govans
Caerphilly, Courthouse
Carew, Carew
Colwyn Bay, Mountain View
Crickhowell, Bear
Erbistock, Boat
Gresford, Pant-yr-Ochain
Hay on Wye, Old Black Lion
Llanberis, Pen-y-Gwryd
Llandrindod Wells, Llanerch
Llanelidan, Leyland Arms
Llangedwyn, Green
Llangynidr, Coach & Horses
Llangynwyd, Old House
Llannefydd, Hawk & Buckle
Llanynys, Cerrigllwydion Arms
Llyswen, Griffin
Maentwrog, Grapes
Pontypool, Open Hearth
Presteigne, Radnorshire Arms
Raglan, Clytha Arms
Red Wharf Bay, Ship
Rosebush, New Inn
Talycoed, Halfway House
Tyn y Groes, Groes

Channel Islands
Castel, Hougue du
Pommier
Kings Mills, Fleur du
Jardin
St Brelade, Old Portelet
St Brelade, Old Smugglers
St Helier, Tipsy Toad
Town House
St John, Les Fontaines
St Lawrence, British
Union
St Martin, Royal

PUBS CLOSE TO MOTORWAY JUNCTIONS

The number at the start
of each line is the number
of the junction. Detailed
directions are given in the
main entry for each pub.
In this section, to help
you find the pubs quickly
before you're past the
junction, we give in
abbreviated form the
name of the chapter
where you'll find them
in the text.

M1
18: Crick (Northants) 1
mile; Ashby St Ledgers
(Northants) 4 miles
24: Kegworth (Leics)
under a mile; Shardlow
(Derbys) 2½ miles
26: Kimberley (Notts) 2
miles
29: Hardwick Hall
(Derbys) 4 miles

M3
5: Mattingley (Hants) 3
miles; Rotherwick
(Hants) 4 miles
7: Dummer (Hants) ½
mile

M4
8: Bray (Berks) 1¾ miles
9: Holyport (Berks) 1½
miles
12: Stanford Dingley
(Berks) 4 miles
13: Chieveley (Berks) 3½
miles
14: Great Shefford
(Berks) 2 miles

18: Old Sodbury (Gloucs)
2 miles
21: Aust (Gloucs) ½ mile;
Littleton upon Severn
(Gloucs) 3½ miles
37: Kenfig (Wales) 2¼
miles

M5
7: Kempsey (Herefs &
Worcs) 3¾ miles
9: Bredon (Herefs &
Worcs) 4½ miles
16: Almondsbury
(Gloucs) 1¼ miles
19: Clapton in Gordano
(Somerset) 4 miles
23: West Huntspill
(Somerset) 2¾ miles
25: Stoke St Mary
(Somerset) 2¾ miles
28: Broadhembury
(Devon) 5 miles
30: Topsham (Devon) 2
miles; Woodbury
Salterton (Devon) 3½
miles; Exeter (Devon) 4
miles

M6
13: Acton Trussell (Staffs)
2 miles
16: Barthomley
(Cheshire) 1 mile;
Shraleybrook (Staffs) 3
miles; Weston
(Cheshire) 3½ miles
17: Brereton Green
(Cheshire) 2 miles
19: Plumley (Cheshire)
2½ miles
29: Brindle (Lancs etc) 3
miles
31: Balderstone (Lancs
etc) 2 miles
32: Goosnargh (Lancs
etc) 4 miles
35: Yealand Conyers
(Lancs etc) 3 miles
40: Yanwath (Cumbria)
2¼ miles; Stainton
(Cumbria) 3 miles;
Tirril (Cumbria) 3½
miles; Askham
(Cumbria) 4½ miles

M9
3: Linlithgow (Scotland)
2 miles

M11
7: Hastingwood (Essex)
¼ mile
10: Hinxton (Cambs) 2
miles

M25
8: Reigate Heath (Surrey)
3 miles; Betchworth
(Surrey) 4 miles
18: Chenies (Bucks) 2
miles; Flaunden (Herts)
4 miles

M27
1: Cadnam (Hants) ½
mile
8: Bursledon (Hants) 2
miles
9: Locks Heath (Hants)
2½ miles

M40
2: Beaconsfield (Bucks) 2
miles; Wooburn
Common (Bucks) 2
miles; Forty Green
(Bucks) 3½ miles
5: Ibstone (Bucks) 1 mile;
Bolter End (Bucks) 4
miles
6: Lewknor (Oxon) ½
mile; Watlington
(Oxon) 3 miles;
Cuxham (Oxon) 4
miles
11: Chacombe
(Northants) 2½ miles

M50
3: Upton Bishop (Herefs
& Worcs) 2 miles

M56
12: Overton (Cheshire) 2
miles

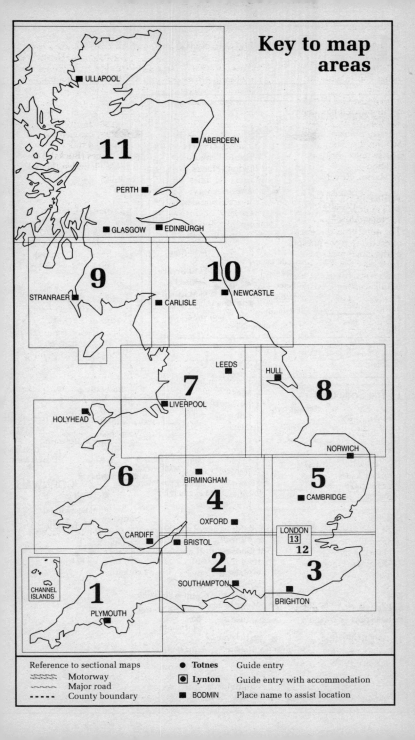

Key to map areas

ULLAPOOL

11

ABERDEEN

PERTH

GLASGOW EDINBURGH

9

10

STRANRAER CARLISLE NEWCASTLE

LEEDS HULL

7 **8**

HOLYHEAD LIVERPOOL

NORWICH

6 **5**

BIRMINGHAM

4 CAMBRIDGE

OXFORD

CARDIFF LONDON
13
12

BRISTOL

2

CHANNEL
ISLANDS

SOUTHAMPTON **3**

1 BRIGHTON

PLYMOUTH

Reference to sectional maps	● **Totnes**	Guide entry
Motorway	◉ **Lynton**	Guide entry with accommodation
Major road	■ BODMIN	Place name to assist location
----- County boundary		

1

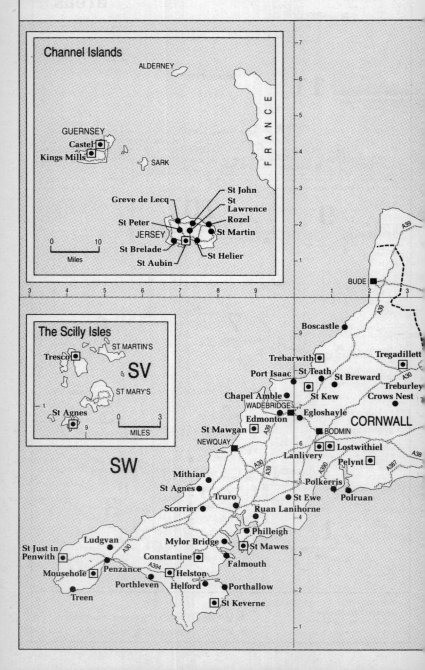

Channel Islands

ALDERNEY

GUERNSEY
Castel
Kings Mills

SARK

FRANCE

St John
Greve de Lecq
St
Lawrence
St Peter
Rozel
JERSEY
St Martin
St Brelade
St Helier
St Aubin

0   10
Miles

The Scilly Isles

ST MARTIN'S
Tresco
SV
ST MARY'S
St Agnes

0   3
MILES

SW

BUDE

Boscastle

Trebarwith
Tregadillett
Port Isaac
St Teath
St Breward
St Kew
Treburley
Chapel Amble
Crows Nest
WADEBRIDGE
Egloshayle
Edmonton
CORNWALL
St Mawgan
BODMIN
NEWQUAY
Lostwithiel
Lanlivery
Pelynt
Mithian
Polkerris
St Agnes
St Ewe
Polruan
Scorrier
Truro
Ruan Lanihorne
Phalleigh
St Just in Penwith
Ludgvan
Mylor Bridge
St Mawes
Constantine
Mousehole
Penzance
Falmouth
Helston
Porthleven
Helford
Porthallow
Treen
St Keverne

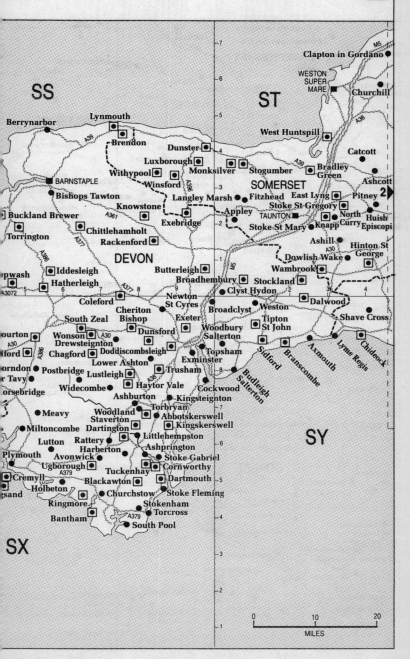

1

SS

ST

SY

SX

Clapton in Gordano
WESTON SUPER MARE
Churchill
West Huntspill
Catcott
Bradley Green
Ashcott
SOMERSET
Pitney
Fitzhead
East Lyng
North Curry
Huish Episcopi
Stoke St Gregory
Knapp
TAUNTON
Stoke St Mary
Ashill
Hinton St George
Dowlish Wake
Wambrook
Stockland
Dalwood
Shave Cross
Weston
Chideock
Axmouth
Lyme Regis
Branscombe
Sidford
Budleigh Salterton
Tipton St John
Clyst Hydon
Broadhembury
Butterleigh
Newton St Cyres
Broadclyst
Exeter
Woodbury Salterton
Topsham
Exminster
Cockwood
Coleford
Cheriton Bishop
Dunsford
South Zeal
Wonson
Drewsteignton
Chagford
Doddiscombsleigh
Lower Ashton
Trusham
Lustleigh
Haytor Vale
Widecombe
Postbridge
Ashburton
Kingsteignton
Torbryan
Kingskerswell
Abbotskerswell
Woodland
Staverton
Dartington
Littlehempston
Meavy
Rattery
Ashprington
Miltoncombe
Lutton
Harberton
Stoke Gabriel
Avonwick
Cornworthy
Ugborough
Tuckenhay
Dartmouth
Plymouth
Blackawton
Stoke Fleming
Cremyll
Churchstow
Holbeton
Stokenham
Ringmore
Torcross
Bantham
South Pool
Berrynarbor
Lynmouth
Brendon
Dunster
Luxborough
Monksilver
Stogumber
Withypool
Winsford
Langley Marsh
Appley
BARNSTAPLE
Bishops Tawton
Knowstone
Exebridge
Buckland Brewer
Chittlehamholt
Rackenford
Torrington
DEVON
pwash
Iddesleigh
Hatherleigh
Coleford
bourton
ford
orndon
r Tavy
orsebridge

0   10   20
MILES

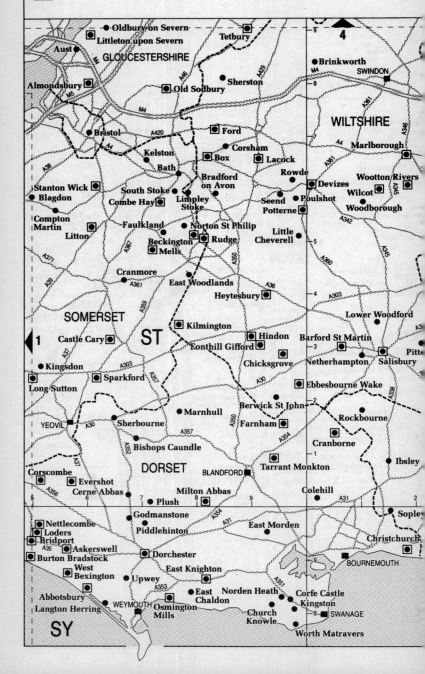

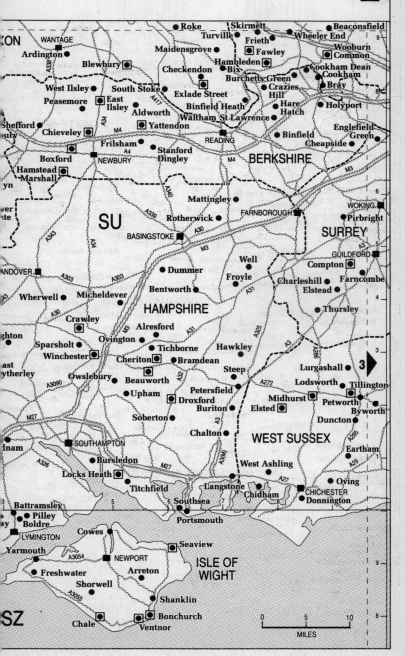

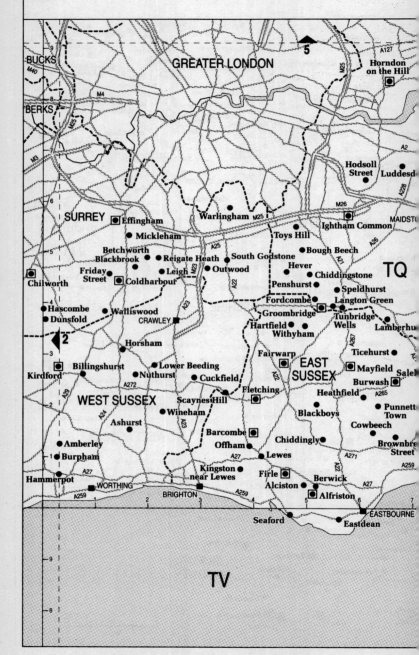

3

BUCKS
M40

BERKS

GREATER LONDON

5

A127

Horndon
on the Hill

M25

M4

M25

M40

A2

Hodsoll
Street

Luddesd

A228

SURREY

Effingham

Mickleham

Warlingham

M25

M26

Ightham Common

MAIDSTO

Toys Hill

Bough Beech

A26

Betchworth
Blackbrook

Reigate Heath

South Godstone

Hever

Chiddingstone

TQ

Friday
Street

Leigh

Outwood

Penshurst

Speldhurst

Chilworth

Coldharbour

M23

A22

Fordcombe

Langton Green

Hascombe

Dunsfold

Walliswood

CRAWLEY

Groombridge

Hartfield

Withyham

Tunbridge
Wells

Lamberhu

2

Horsham

Fairwarp

EAST
SUSSEX

Ticehurst

A267

Billingshurst

Lower Beeding

Mayfield

Sale

Kirdford

Nuthurst

Cuckfield

Fletching

Burwash

A24

A272

Heathfield

A265

WEST SUSSEX

Scaynes Hill

Wineham

Blackboys

Punnett
Town

Ashurst

Barcombe

Chiddingly

Cowbeech

Brownbre
Street

Amberley

Offham

Burpham

Lewes

A271

A259

A27

A271

Hammerpot

WORTHING

Kingston
near Lewes

Firle

Berwick

A27

BRIGHTON

A259

Alciston

Alfriston

EASTBOURNE

Seaford

Eastdean

TV

3

ESSEX

A127

SOUTHEND-ON-SEA

Leigh
on Sea

SHEERNESS

MARGATE

Whitstable   A299

RAMSGATE

A2

Oare   Dargate   Boyden Gate

M2   Faversham

Newnham   CANTERBURY   A251

Selling   A2

Ringlestone

A20   KENT

A28   Barfrestone

TR

A256

A2   A258

Icombe   M20   Boughton Aluph

A274   A229

Pluckley   ASHFORD

Smarden   M20

Biddenden   A260   DOVER

A28   A20

M20   FOLKESTONE

A2070   Sandgate

A259

Brookland   3

A259

Playden   Rye   2

Ickesham   A259

HASTINGS   1

8   9   1   2   3   4   5

9

8

0   5   10

MILES

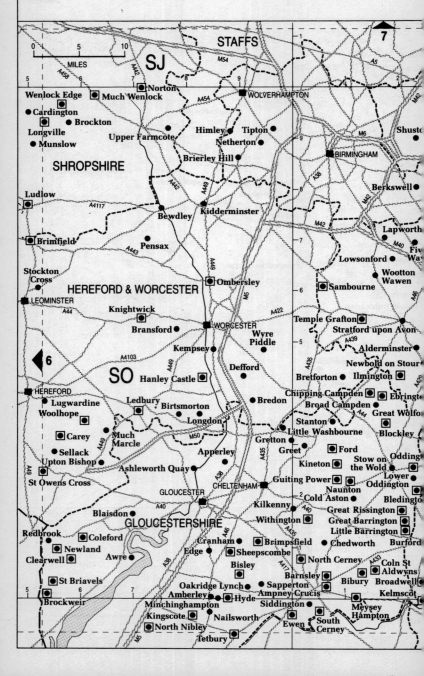

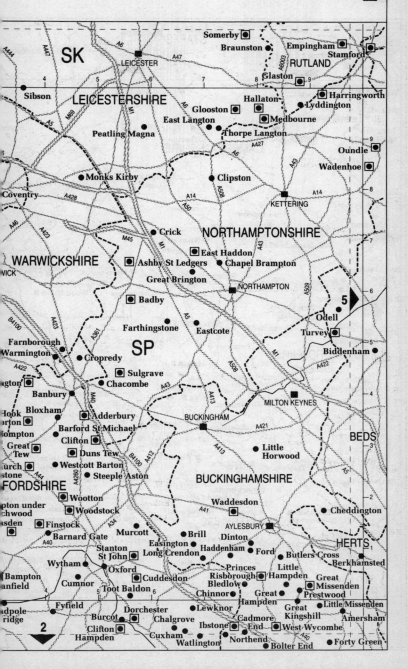

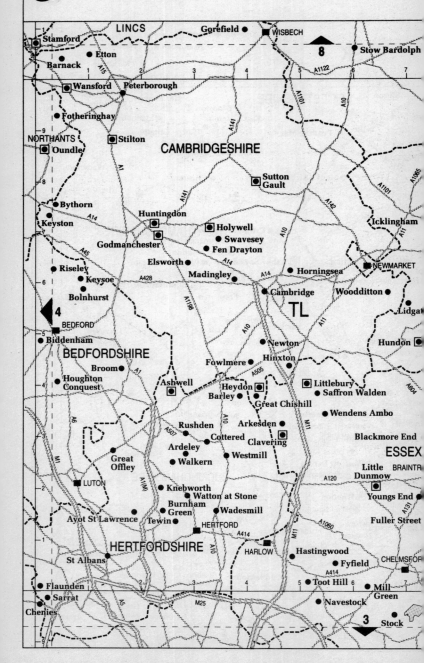

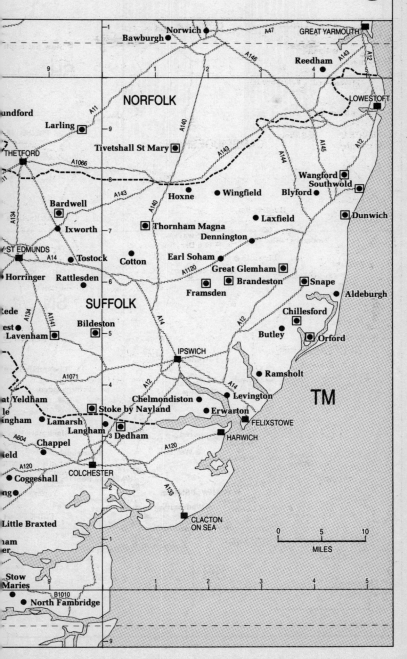

Norwich

Bawburgh

GREAT YARMOUTH

A47

A146

Reedham

A143

A12

LOWESTOFT

NORFOLK

A11

Larling

A140

Tivetshall St Mary

A143

A145

A12

THETFORD

A1066

A143

A144

Wangford
Southwold

Bardwell

A140

Hoxne

Wingfield

Blyford

A134

Ixworth

Thornham Magna

Laxfield

Dunwich

ST EDMUNDS

A14

Tostock

Cotton

Dennington

Earl Soham

A1120

Great Glemham

Snape

Horringer

Rattlesden

Framsden

Brandeston

Aldeburgh

SUFFOLK

A14

Chillesford

Rede

A1141

Bildeston

A12

Butley

Orford

est

Lavenham

IPSWICH

A1071

A12

Ramsholt

at Yeldham

A14

Levington

TM

le
ingham

Lamarsh

Stoke by Nayland

Chelmondiston

Erwarton

A604

Langham

Dedham

FELIXSTOWE

Chappel

A120

HARWICH

ield

A120

COLCHESTER

A133

Coggeshall

ng

Little Braxted

CLACTON
ON SEA

ham
er

0   5   10

MILES

Stow
Maries

B1010

North Fambridge

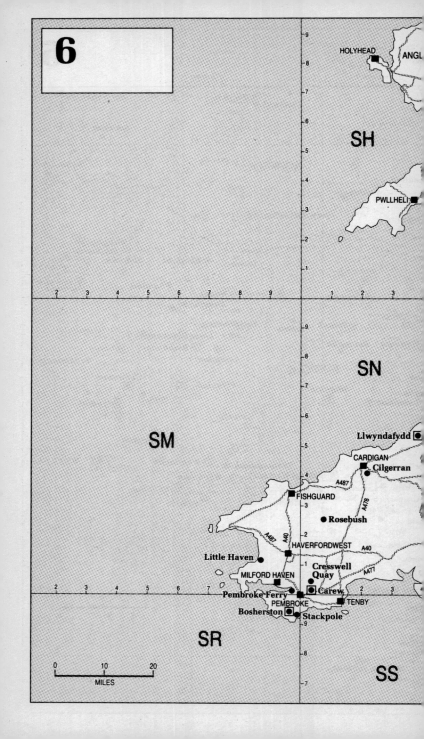

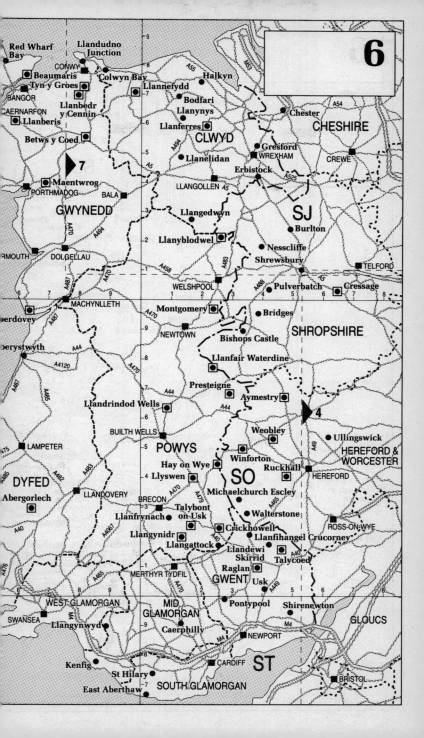

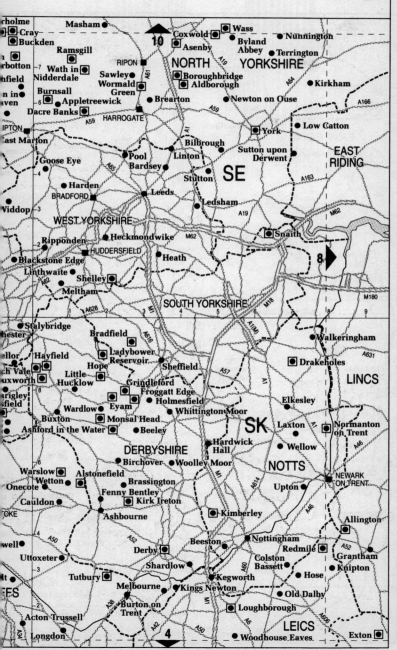

10

holme
Cray
Buckden
Ramsgill
Wath in
Nidderdale
rbotton
field
n in
aven
Burnsill
Appletreewick
Dacre Banks
East Marton
Goose Eye
Harden
BRADFORD
Viddop
Ripponden
Blackstone Edge
Linthwaite
Shelley
Meltham

Masham
Coxwold
Asenby
RIPON
Sawley
Wormald
Green
Brearton
HARROGATE
Pool
Bardsey
Leeds
WEST YORKSHIRE
Heckmondwike
HUDDERSFIELD
Heath
SOUTH YORKSHIRE

Wass
Byland
Abbey
Nunnington
Terrington
NORTH
YORKSHIRE
Boroughbridge
Aldborough
Newton on Ouse
Kirkham
York
Billbrough
Linton
Sutton upon
Derwent
Stutton
SE
Ledsham
Snaith
Low Catton
EAST
RIDING

8

Stalybridge
hester
ellor
Hayfield
h Vale
uxworth
rigley
field
Wardlow
Buxton
Ashford in the Water
Warslow
Wetton
Onecote
Cauldon
OKE
well
Uttoxeter
Tutbury
Melbourne
Burton on
Trent
Acton Trussell
Longdon
FS

Bradfield
Ladybower
Reservoir
Hope
Little
Hucklow
Grindleford
Froggatt Edge
Eyam
Monsal Head
Beeley
DERBYSHIRE
Birchover
Alstonefield
Brassington
Fenny Bentley
Kirk Ireton
Ashbourne
Derby
Shardlow
Kings Newton
Kegworth
Woodhouse Eaves

Sheffield
Holmesfield
Whittington Moor
Hardwick
Hall
Woolley Moor
Walkeringham
Drakeholes
Elkesley
Laxton
Wellow
SK
Kimberley
Beeston
Colston
Bassett
Loughborough
LINCS
Normanton
on Trent
NOTTS
NEWARK
ON TRENT
Upton
Allington
Nottingham
Redmile
Grantham
Hose
Knipton
Old Dalby
LEICS
Exton

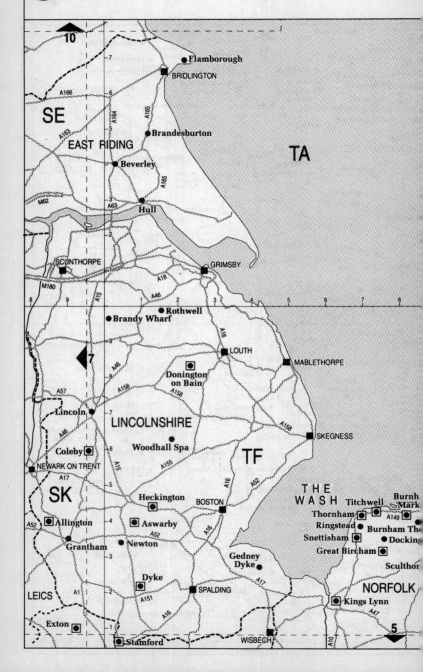

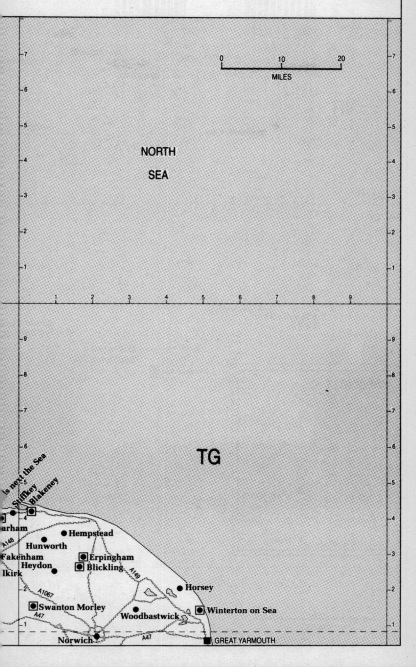

8

0   10   20
MILES

NORTH

SEA

TG

7

6

5

4

3

2

1

1   2   3   4   5   6   7   8   9

9

8

7

6

5

4

3

2

1

ls next the Sea
Stiffkey
Blakeney
arham
Hempstead
Hunworth
Fakenham
Heydon
Erpingham
Blickling
lkirk
A149
Horsey
A1067
Swanton Morley
Woodbastwick
Winterton on Sea
A47
Norwich
A47
GREAT YARMOUTH
A148

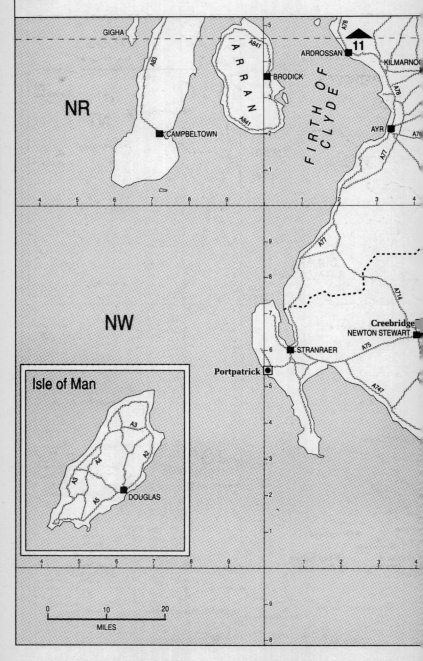

9

GIGHA

ARRAN

A841

BRODICK

A83

NR

CAMPBELTOWN

FIRTH OF CLYDE

11

ARDROSSAN

KILMARNO

A78

A78

AYR

A77

A70

A77

NW

A77

A714

Creebridge
NEWTON STEWART

STRANRAER

A75

Portpatrick

A747

Isle of Man

A3

A2

A4

A3

A5

DOUGLAS

---

0   10   20

MILES

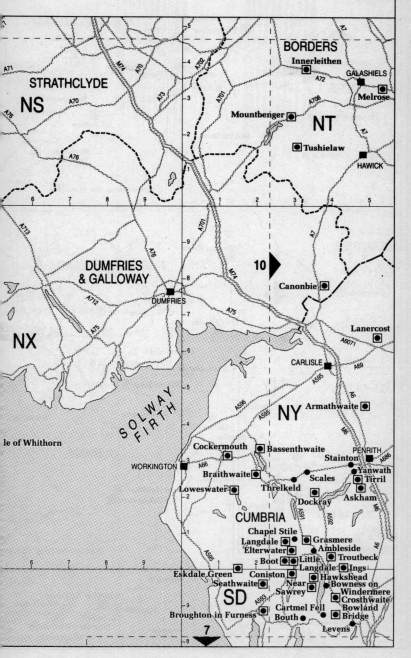

BORDERS

STRATHCLYDE

NS

A71
A76
M74
A70
A703
A73
A702
A701
A706

Innerleithen
GALASHIELS
Melrose
Mountbenger
NT
Tushielaw
HAWICK
A72
A7

DUMFRIES & GALLOWAY

A713
A76
A712
A75
A701
M74
A75

NX

DUMFRIES

10

Canonbie

Lanercost
A6071

CARLISLE
A595
A69
A6

NY

Armathwaite

A596
A595
M6

SOLWAY FIRTH

le of Whithorn

Cockermouth
Bassenthwaite
Stainton
PENRITH
Yanwath
Tirril
Askham
A66
WORKINGTON
Braithwaite
Scales
Threlkeld
Loweswater
Dockray
A66
A592
A6
M6
A696

CUMBRIA

Chapel Stile
Langdale
Grasmere
Elterwater
Ambleside
Boot
Little
Troutbeck
Langdale
Ings
Eskdale Green
Coniston
Hawkshead
Seathwaite
Near
Bowness on
Sawrey
Windermere
Crosthwaite
Bowland
Cartmel Fell
Bridge
SD
Bouth
Broughton in Furness
Levens
A595
A593
A591

7

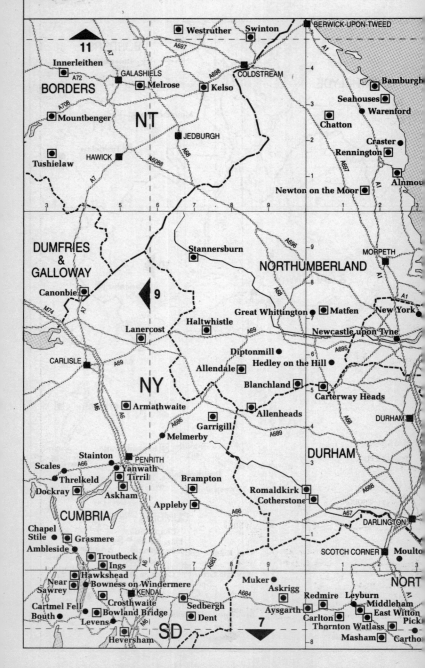

Map Labels

BORDERS
- Innerleithen (A72)
- GALASHIELS
- Melrose
- Mountbenger (A708)
- NT
- HAWICK
- Tushielaw
- A7
- JEDBURGH (A68)

- Westruther
- Swinton
- BERWICK-UPON-TWEED
- A1
- COLDSTREAM (A698)
- Kelso
- A697
- A6088

DUMFRIES & GALLOWAY
- Canonbie
- M74
- A7

- Bamburgh
- Seahouses
- Warenford
- Chatton
- Craster
- Rennington
- Alnmou(th)
- Newton on the Moor
- A697

- Stannersburn
- A696
- MORPETH
- A1

NORTHUMBERLAND
- Haltwhistle
- Lanercost
- CARLISLE
- A69
- Great Whittington
- Matfen
- New York
- Newcastle upon Tyne
- A68
- A695

NY
- Armathwaite
- A6
- A66
- Diptonmill
- Hedley on the Hill
- Allendale
- Blanchland
- Carterway Heads
- Allenheads
- Garrigill
- Melmerby
- A689
- DURHAM

- Stainton
- A66
- Scales
- Threlkeld
- Dockray
- PENRITH
- Yanwath
- Tirril
- Askham
- Brampton
- Appleby
- Romaldkirk
- Cotherstone
- A67
- DARLINGTON
- A688

DURHAM

CUMBRIA
- Chapel Stile
- Grasmere
- Ambleside
- Troutbeck
- Ings
- Near Sawrey
- Hawkshead
- Bowness on Windermere
- KENDAL
- Cartmel Fell
- Bouth
- Crosthwaite
- Bowland Bridge
- Levens
- Heversham

SD
- Muker
- Askrigg
- A684
- Sedbergh
- Dent

- SCOTCH CORNER
- Moulto(n)
- NOR(TH)
- Redmire
- Leyburn
- Middleham
- East Witton
- Pick(...)
- Aysgarth
- Carlton
- Thornton Watlass
- Masham
- Cartho(...)

- 7
- 9
- 11

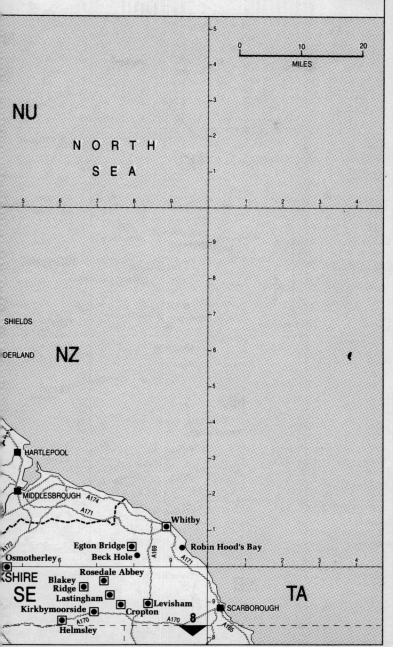

NU

N O R T H

S E A

0   10   20

MILES

5   6   7   8   9   1   2   3   4

9

8

7

SHIELDS

DERLAND   NZ   6

5

4

HARTLEPOOL   3

MIDDLESBROUGH A174   2

A171

A171

Whitby   1

Egton Bridge   Robin Hood's Bay
Beck Hole
Osmotherley 6   9   1   2   3   4
Rosedale Abbey
Blakey   TA
Ridge
Lastingham   9
Kirkbymoorside   Levisham   SCARBOROUGH
Cropton   SE
A170   8
Helmsley   A170   A165
8

KSHIRE   SE

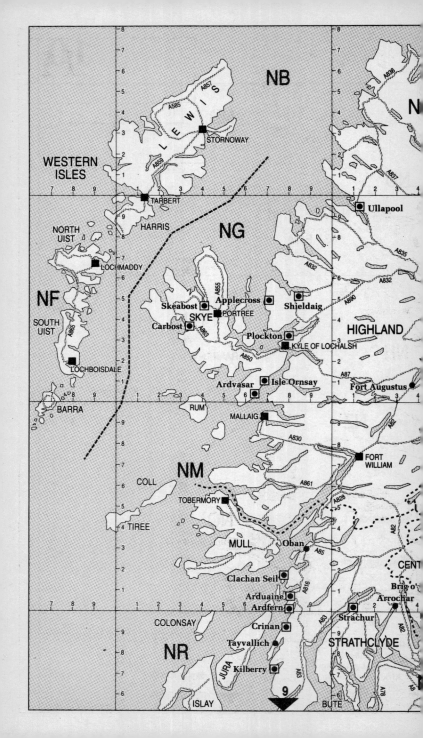

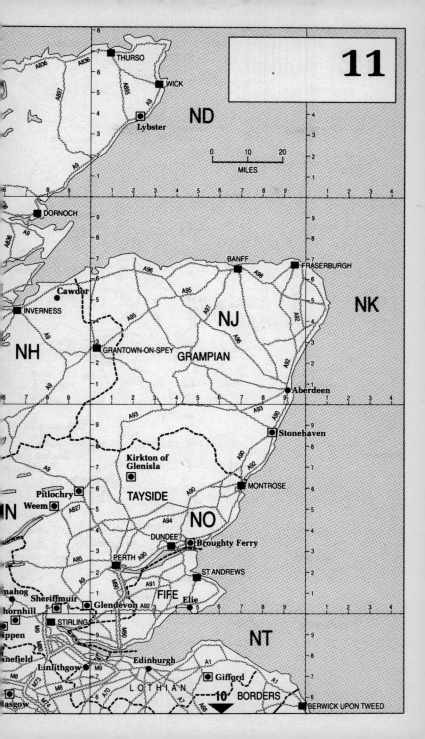

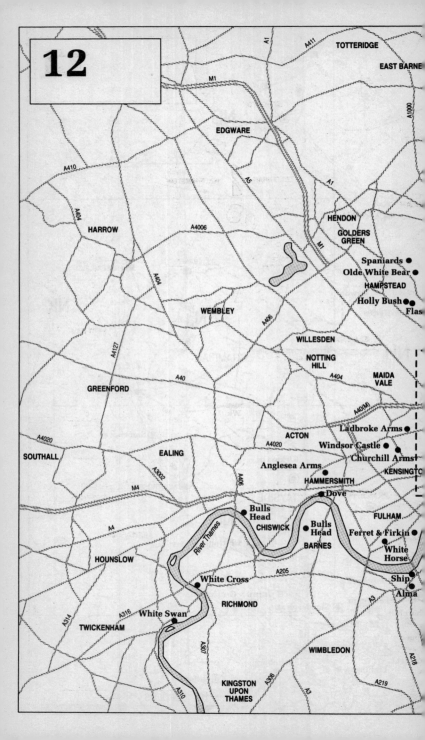

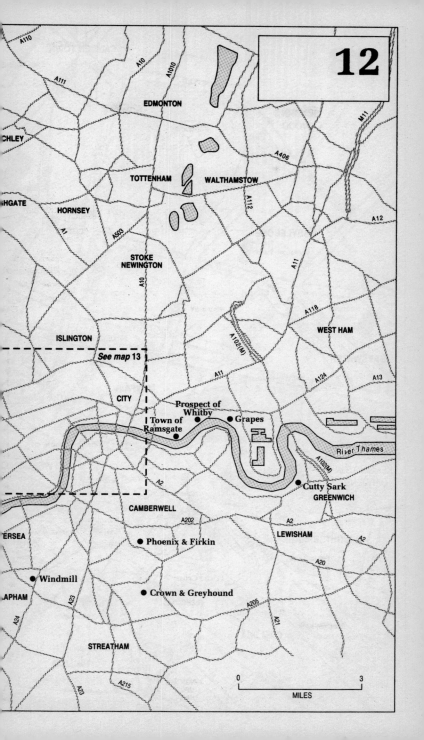

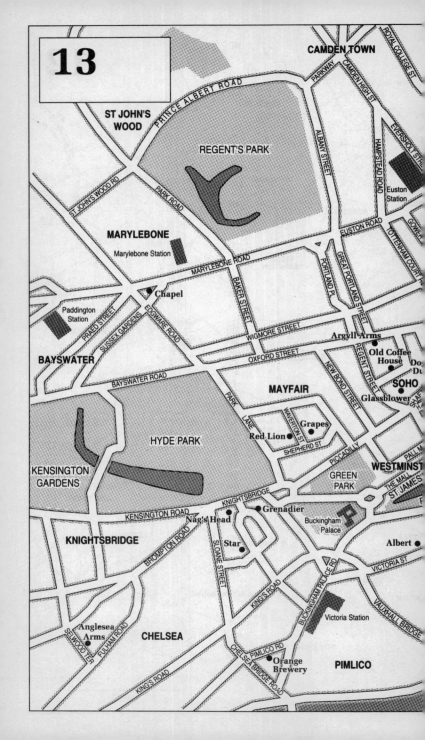

13

CAMDEN TOWN

ROYAL COLLEGE ST

ST JOHN'S WOOD

PRINCE ALBERT ROAD

PARKWAY

CAMDEN HIGH ST

EVERSHOLT ST

REGENT'S PARK

ALBANY STREET

HAMPSTEAD ROAD

ST JOHN'S WOOD RD

PARK ROAD

EUSTON ROAD

Euston Station

GOWER ST

TOTTENHAM COURT RD

MARYLEBONE

Marylebone Station

MARYLEBONE ROAD

BAKER STREET

GREAT PORTLAND STREET

PORTLAND PL

● Chapel

Paddington Station

PRAED STREET

SUSSEX GARDENS

EDGWARE ROAD

WIGMORE STREET

Argyll Arms ●

Old Coffee House ●

Do
Du

BAYSWATER

OXFORD STREET

REGENT STREET

SOHO

BAYSWATER ROAD

MAYFAIR

NEW BOND STREET

Glassblower ●

HYDE PARK

PARK LANE

WAVERTON ST

● Grapes

Red Lion ●

SHEPHERD ST

PICCADILLY

WESTMINST

KENSINGTON GARDENS

GREEN PARK

PALL M

THE MALL

ST JAMES'

KENSINGTON ROAD

KNIGHTSBRIDGE

● Grenadier

Nag's Head ●

Buckingham Palace

BROMPTON ROAD

KNIGHTSBRIDGE

SLOANE STREET

Star ●

Albert ●

VICTORIA ST

KING'S ROAD

BUCKINGHAM PALACE RD

VICTORIA STREET

Victoria Station

VAUXHALL BRIDGE

Anglesea Arms ●

SELWOOD TER

FULHAM ROAD

CHELSEA

CHELSEA BRIDGE ROAD

CHELSEA PIMLICO RD

Orange Brewery ●

PIMLICO

KING'S ROAD

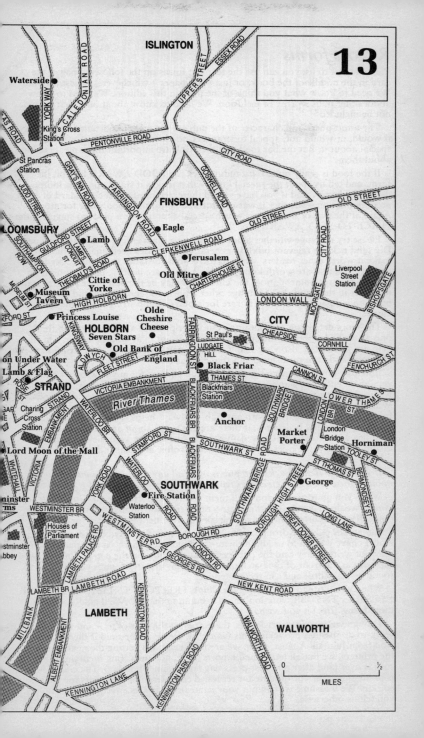

Report forms

Please report to us: you can use the tear-out forms on the following pages, the card in the middle of the book, or just plain paper – whichever's easiest for you. We need to know what you think of the pubs in this edition. We need to know about other pubs worthy of inclusion. We need to know about ones that should not be included.

The atmosphere and character of the pub are the most important features why it would, or would not, appeal to strangers, so please try and describe what is special about it. But the bar food and the drink are important too – please tell us about them.

If the food is really quite outstanding, tick the FOOD AWARD box on the form, and tell us about the special quality that makes it stand out – the more detail, the better. And if you have stayed there, tell us about the standard of accommodation – whether it was comfortable, pleasant, good value for money. Again, if the pub or inn place is worth special attention as a place to stay, tick the PLACE-TO-STAY AWARD box.

Please try to gauge whether a pub should be a main entry, or is best as a Lucky Dip (and tick the relevant box). In general, main entries need qualities that would make it worth other readers' while to travel some distance to them; Lucky Dips are the pubs that are worth knowing about if you are nearby. But if a pub is an entirely new recommendation, the Lucky Dip may be the best place for it to start its career in the *Guide* to encourage other readers to report on it, and gradually build up a dossier on it; it's very rare for a pub to jump straight into the main entries.

The more detail you can put into your description of a Lucky Dip pub that's only scantily decribed in the current edition (or not in at all), the better. This'll help not just us but also your fellow-readers gauge its appeal. A description of its character and even furnishings is a tremendous boon.

It helps enormously if you can give the full address for any new pub – one not yet a main entry, or without a full address in the Lucky Dip sections. In a town, we need the street name; in the country, if it's hard to find, we need directions. Without this, there's little chance of our being able to include the pub. Better still for us is the postcode. And with any pub, it always helps to let us know about **prices** of food (and bedrooms, if there are any), and about any lunchtimes or evenings when food is **not** served. We'd also like to have your views on drinks quality – beer, wine, cider and so forth, even coffee and tea; and do let us know if it has bedrooms.

If you know that a Lucky Dip pub is open all day (or even late into the afternoon), please tell us – preferably saying which days.

When you go to a pub, don't tell them you're a reporter for the *Good Pub Guide*; we do make clear that all inspections are anonymous, and if you declare yourself as a reporter you risk getting special treatment – for better or for worse!

Sometimes pubs are dropped from the main entries simply because very few readers have written to us about them – and of course there's a risk that people may not write if they find the pub exactly as described in the entry. You can use the form at the front of the batch of report forms just to list pubs you've been to, found as described, and can recommend.

When you write to *The Good Pub Guide*, FREEPOST TN1569, WADHURST, East Sussex TN5 7BR, you don't need a stamp in the UK. We'll gladly send you more forms (free) if you wish.

Though we try to answer letters, there are just the four of us – and with other work to do, besides producing this *Guide*. So please understand if there's a delay. And from June till August, when we are fully extended getting the next edition to the printers, we put all letters and reports aside, not answering them until the rush is over (and after our post-press-day late summer holiday). The end of May is pretty much the cut-off date for reasoned consideration of reports for the next edition. We'll assume we can put your name or initials as a recommender unless you tell us otherwise.

I have been to the following pubs in *The Good Pub Guide 1998* in the last few months, found them as described, and confirm that they deserve continued inclusion:

Continued overleaf
PLEASE GIVE YOUR NAME AND ADDRESS ON THE BACK OF THIS FORM

Pubs visited continued...

Your own name and address *(block capitals please)*

Please return to
The Good Pub Guide,
FREEPOST TN1569,
WADHURST,
East Sussex
TN5 7BR

REPORT ON *(pub's name)*

....

Pub's address

....

☐ **YES MAIN ENTRY** ☐ **YES** *Lucky Dip* ☐ **NO don't include**
*Please tick one of these boxes to show your verdict, and give reasons and
descriptive comments, prices etc*

☐ Deserves FOOD award ☐ Deserves PLACE-TO-STAY award 98:1

PLEASE GIVE YOUR NAME AND ADDRESS ON THE BACK OF THIS FORM

....✂

REPORT ON *(pub's name)*

....

Pub's address

....

☐ **YES MAIN ENTRY** ☐ **YES** *Lucky Dip* ☐ **NO don't include**
*Please tick one of these boxes to show your verdict, and give reasons and
descriptive comments, prices etc*

☐ Deserves FOOD award ☐ Deserves PLACE-TO-STAY award 98:2

PLEASE GIVE YOUR NAME AND ADDRESS ON THE BACK OF THIS FORM

Your own name and address *(block capitals please)*

DO NOT USE THIS SIDE OF THE PAGE FOR WRITING ABOUT PUBS

✂ ....

Your own name and address *(block capitals please)*

DO NOT USE THIS SIDE OF THE PAGE FOR WRITING ABOUT PUBS

If you would like to order a copy of *The Good Guide to Britain 1998* (£14.99), *The Good Gardens Guide 1998* (£14.99), *The Good Hotel Guide 1998 Great Britain & Ireland* (£12.99) or *The Good Hotel Guide 1988 Europe* (£14.99), direct from Ebury Press (p&p free), please call our credit-card hotline on **01621 819596**, or send a cheque/postal order made payable to Ebury Press to **TBS Direct, Church Road, Tiptree, Colchester, Essex CO5 0SR**

REPORT ON *(pub's name)*

....

Pub's address

....

☐ **YES MAIN ENTRY** ☐ **YES** *Lucky Dip* ☐ **NO don't include**
Please tick one of these boxes to show your verdict, and give reasons and descriptive comments, prices etc

☐ Deserves FOOD award ☐ Deserves PLACE-TO-STAY award 98:3

PLEASE GIVE YOUR NAME AND ADDRESS ON THE BACK OF THIS FORM

....✂

REPORT ON *(pub's name)*

....

Pub's address

....

☐ **YES MAIN ENTRY** ☐ **YES** *Lucky Dip* ☐ **NO don't include**
Please tick one of these boxes to show your verdict, and give reasons and descriptive comments, prices etc

☐ Deserves FOOD award ☐ Deserves PLACE-TO-STAY award 98:4

PLEASE GIVE YOUR NAME AND ADDRESS ON THE BACK OF THIS FORM

Your own name and address *(block capitals please)*

DO NOT USE THIS SIDE OF THE PAGE FOR WRITING ABOUT PUBS

✂ ....

Your own name and address *(block capitals please)*

DO NOT USE THIS SIDE OF THE PAGE FOR WRITING ABOUT PUBS

If you would like to order a copy of *The Good Guide to Britain 1998* (£14.99), *The Good Gardens Guide 1998* (£14.99), *The Good Hotel Guide 1998 Great Britain & Ireland* (£12.99) or *The Good Hotel Guide 1988 Europe* (£14.99), direct from Ebury Press (p&p free), please call our credit-card hotline on **01621 819596**, or send a cheque/postal order made payable to Ebury Press to **TBS Direct, Church Road, Tiptree, Colchester, Essex CO5 0SR**

EPORT ON   *(pub's name)*

....

ub's address

□ **YES MAIN ENTRY**   □ **YES** *Lucky Dip*   □ **NO don't include**
lease tick one of these boxes to show your verdict, and give reasons and
escriptive comments, prices etc

□ Deserves FOOD award   □ Deserves PLACE-TO-STAY award   98:5

LEASE GIVE YOUR NAME AND ADDRESS ON THE BACK OF THIS FORM

--- ✂ ---

EPORT ON   *(pub's name)*

....

ub's address

□ **YES MAIN ENTRY**   □ **YES** *Lucky Dip*   □ **NO don't include**
lease tick one of these boxes to show your verdict, and give reasons and
escriptive comments, prices etc

□ Deserves FOOD award   □ Deserves PLACE-TO-STAY award   98:6

LEASE GIVE YOUR NAME AND ADDRESS ON THE BACK OF THIS FORM

Your own name and address *(block capitals please)*

DO NOT USE THIS SIDE OF THE PAGE FOR WRITING ABOUT PUBS

✄ ···

Your own name and address *(block capitals please)*

DO NOT USE THIS SIDE OF THE PAGE FOR WRITING ABOUT PUBS

If you would like to order a copy of *The Good Guide to Britain 1998* (£14.99), *T
Good Gardens Guide 1998* (£14.99), *The Good Hotel Guide 1998 Great Britain
Ireland* (£12.99) or *The Good Hotel Guide 1988 Europe* (£14.99), direct from
Ebury Press (p&p free), please call our credit-card hotline on **01621 819596,**
or send a cheque/postal order made payable to Ebury Press to
TBS Direct, Church Road, Tiptree, Colchester, Essex CO5 0SR

REPORT ON *(pub's name)*

Pub's address

☐ **YES MAIN ENTRY** ☐ **YES** *Lucky Dip* ☐ **NO don't include**
Please tick one of these boxes to show your verdict, and give reasons and descriptive comments, prices etc

☐ Deserves FOOD award ☐ Deserves PLACE-TO-STAY award 98:7

PLEASE GIVE YOUR NAME AND ADDRESS ON THE BACK OF THIS FORM

✂ ....

REPORT ON *(pub's name)*

Pub's address

☐ **YES MAIN ENTRY** ☐ **YES** *Lucky Dip* ☐ **NO don't include**
Please tick one of these boxes to show your verdict, and give reasons and descriptive comments, prices etc

☐ Deserves FOOD award ☐ Deserves PLACE-TO-STAY award 98:8

PLEASE GIVE YOUR NAME AND ADDRESS ON THE BACK OF THIS FORM

Your own name and address *(block capitals please)*

DO NOT USE THIS SIDE OF THE PAGE FOR WRITING ABOUT PUBS

✂️ ....

Your own name and address *(block capitals please)*

DO NOT USE THIS SIDE OF THE PAGE FOR WRITING ABOUT PUBS

REPORT ON *(pub's name)*

....

Pub's address

☐ **YES Main Entry**   ☐ **YES** *Lucky Dip*   ☐ **NO don't include**
*Please tick one of these boxes to show your verdict, and give reasons and
descriptive comments, prices etc*

☐ Deserves Food award   ☐ Deserves Place-to-stay award   98:9

PLEASE GIVE YOUR NAME AND ADDRESS ON THE BACK OF THIS FORM

....✄

REPORT ON *(pub's name)*

....

Pub's address

☐ **YES Main Entry**   ☐ **YES** *Lucky Dip*   ☐ **NO don't include**
*Please tick one of these boxes to show your verdict, and give reasons and
descriptive comments, prices etc*

☐ Deserves Food award   ☐ Deserves Place-to-stay award   98:10

PLEASE GIVE YOUR NAME AND ADDRESS ON THE BACK OF THIS FORM

Your own name and address *(block capitals please)*

DO NOT USE THIS SIDE OF THE PAGE FOR WRITING ABOUT PUBS

✂ ··

Your own name and address *(block capitals please)*

DO NOT USE THIS SIDE OF THE PAGE FOR WRITING ABOUT PUBS

If you would like to order a copy of *The Good Guide to Britain 1998* (£14.99), *The Good Gardens Guide 1998* (£14.99), *The Good Hotel Guide 1998 Great Britain & Ireland* (£12.99) or *The Good Hotel Guide 1988 Europe* (£14.99), direct from Ebury Press (p&p free), please call our credit-card hotline on **01621 819596**, or send a cheque/postal order made payable to Ebury Press to **TBS Direct, Church Road, Tiptree, Colchester, Essex CO5 0SR**

REPORT ON *(pub's name)*

....

Pub's address

....

☐ **YES Main Entry**   ☐ **YES** *Lucky Dip*   ☐ **NO don't include**
Please tick one of these boxes to show your verdict, and give reasons and descriptive comments, prices etc

☐ Deserves Food award   ☐ Deserves Place-to-stay award   98:11

PLEASE GIVE YOUR NAME AND ADDRESS ON THE BACK OF THIS FORM

REPORT ON *(pub's name)*

....

Pub's address

....

☐ **YES Main Entry**   ☐ **YES** *Lucky Dip*   ☐ **NO don't include**
Please tick one of these boxes to show your verdict, and give reasons and descriptive comments, prices etc

☐ Deserves Food award   ☐ Deserves Place-to-stay award   98:12

PLEASE GIVE YOUR NAME AND ADDRESS ON THE BACK OF THIS FORM

Your own name and address *(block capitals please)*

DO NOT USE THIS SIDE OF THE PAGE FOR WRITING ABOUT PUBS

✂ ....

Your own name and address *(block capitals please)*

DO NOT USE THIS SIDE OF THE PAGE FOR WRITING ABOUT PUBS

If you would like to order a copy of *The Good Guide to Britain 1998* (£14.99), *The Good Gardens Guide 1998* (£14.99), *The Good Hotel Guide 1998 Great Britain & Ireland* (£12.99) or *The Good Hotel Guide 1988 Europe* (£14.99), direct from Ebury Press (p&p free), please call our credit-card hotline on **01621 819596**, or send a cheque/postal order made payable to Ebury Press to **TBS Direct, Church Road, Tiptree, Colchester, Essex CO5 0SR**

REPORT ON   *(pub's name)*

....

Pub's address

....

☐ **YES MAIN ENTRY**   ☐ **YES** *Lucky Dip*   ☐ **NO don't include**
*Please tick one of these boxes to show your verdict, and give reasons and
descriptive comments, prices etc*

☐ Deserves FOOD award   ☐ Deserves PLACE-TO-STAY award   98:13

PLEASE GIVE YOUR NAME AND ADDRESS ON THE BACK OF THIS FORM

....✂

REPORT ON   *(pub's name)*

....

Pub's address

....

☐ **YES MAIN ENTRY**   ☐ **YES** *Lucky Dip*   ☐ **NO don't include**
*Please tick one of these boxes to show your verdict, and give reasons and
descriptive comments, prices etc*

☐ Deserves FOOD award   ☐ Deserves PLACE-TO-STAY award   98:14

PLEASE GIVE YOUR NAME AND ADDRESS ON THE BACK OF THIS FORM

Your own name and address *(block capitals please)*

DO NOT USE THIS SIDE OF THE PAGE FOR WRITING ABOUT PUBS

✄ ....

Your own name and address *(block capitals please)*

DO NOT USE THIS SIDE OF THE PAGE FOR WRITING ABOUT PUBS

REPORT ON   *(pub's name)*

....

Pub's address

....

☐ **YES Main Entry**   ☐ **YES** *Lucky Dip*   ☐ **NO don't include**
*Please tick one of these boxes to show your verdict, and give reasons and
descriptive comments, prices etc*

☐ Deserves **Food** award   ☐ Deserves **Place-to-stay** award   98:15

PLEASE GIVE YOUR NAME AND ADDRESS ON THE BACK OF THIS FORM

....✂

REPORT ON   *(pub's name)*

....

Pub's address

....

☐ **YES Main Entry**   ☐ **YES** *Lucky Dip*   ☐ **NO don't include**
*Please tick one of these boxes to show your verdict, and give reasons and
descriptive comments, prices etc*

☐ Deserves **Food** award   ☐ Deserves **Place-to-stay** award   98:16

PLEASE GIVE YOUR NAME AND ADDRESS ON THE BACK OF THIS FORM

Your own name and address *(block capitals please)*

DO NOT USE THIS SIDE OF THE PAGE FOR WRITING ABOUT PUBS

✂ ....

Your own name and address *(block capitals please)*

DO NOT USE THIS SIDE OF THE PAGE FOR WRITING ABOUT PUBS

If you would like to order a copy of *The Good Guide to Britain 1998* (£14.99), *The Good Gardens Guide 1998* (£14.99), *The Good Hotel Guide 1998 Great Britain & Ireland* (£12.99) or *The Good Hotel Guide 1988 Europe* (£14.99), direct from Ebury Press (p&p free), please call our credit-card hotline on **01621 819596**, or send a cheque/postal order made payable to Ebury Press to **TBS Direct, Church Road, Tiptree, Colchester, Essex CO5 0SR**

REPORT ON *(pub's name)*

....

Pub's address

....

☐ **YES MAIN ENTRY**   ☐ **YES** *Lucky Dip*   ☐ **NO don't include**
Please tick one of these boxes to show your verdict, and give reasons and descriptive comments, prices etc

☐ Deserves FOOD award   ☐ Deserves PLACE-TO-STAY award   98:17

PLEASE GIVE YOUR NAME AND ADDRESS ON THE BACK OF THIS FORM

✂ -

REPORT ON *(pub's name)*

....

Pub's address

....

☐ **YES MAIN ENTRY**   ☐ **YES** *Lucky Dip*   ☐ **NO don't include**
Please tick one of these boxes to show your verdict, and give reasons and descriptive comments, prices etc

☐ Deserves FOOD award   ☐ Deserves PLACE-TO-STAY award   98:18

PLEASE GIVE YOUR NAME AND ADDRESS ON THE BACK OF THIS FORM

Your own name and address *(block capitals please)*

DO NOT USE THIS SIDE OF THE PAGE FOR WRITING ABOUT PUBS

✂ ....

Your own name and address *(block capitals please)*

DO NOT USE THIS SIDE OF THE PAGE FOR WRITING ABOUT PUBS

If you would like to order a copy of *The Good Guide to Britain 1998* (£14.99), *The Good Gardens Guide 1998* (£14.99), *The Good Hotel Guide 1998 Great Britain & Ireland* (£12.99) or *The Good Hotel Guide 1988 Europe* (£14.99), direct from Ebury Press (p&p free), please call our credit-card hotline on **01621 819596**, or send a cheque/postal order made payable to Ebury Press to **TBS Direct, Church Road, Tiptree, Colchester, Essex CO5 0SR**